WHO'S WHO IN SCOTLAND
1st EDITION 1986

Who's Who in Scotland

1st EDITION 1986

Carrick Publishing

02 0146655

Published by Carrick Publishing
28 Miller Road, Ayr KA7 2AY
0292 266679

Printed in Great Britain by
Billing & Sons Ltd., Worcester

Typeset from BBC disk by Pennart, 6 North Charlotte Street, Edinburgh

PREFACE

The last work of contemporary Scottish biography was published in 1938. It is not clear why the (London) publisher never attempted a second edition, nor why the idea was not taken up by another publisher. Almost fifty years on, the appearance of Who's Who in Scotland fills an extraordinary gap in Scottish bibliography.

This first edition contains about 5,000 biographies of people from all walks of Scottish life, including politics and public service, law, religion and education, business and finance, science and medicine, the arts and sport. It should be emphasised that the title of the book means what it says, and that prominent Scots living outwith Scotland are not included.

Entries are arranged in alphabetical order, according to surname. Each entry contains full name, present occupation, date and place of birth, followed by details of family, education and career, publications, recreations and address. The following abbreviations are commonly used: b. (born); m. (married); s. (son); d. (daughter).

Great care has been taken to ensure that information given is accurate, but during the period of a year in which the book has been in preparation, it is inevitable that some circumstances will have changed. The publishers cannot accept liability for errors arising out of information supplied to them for publication.

We intend to publish a second edition of Who's Who in Scotland in 1988, and preparatory work will begin in the autumn of 1986.

BRITISH INSTITUTE OF MANAGEMENT
Scotland and Northern Ireland Region

The BRITISH INSTITUTE OF MANAGEMENT is the largest professional management institute in the world.

We currently have over 75,000 individual members and around 6,500 organisations in the U.K. which subscribe to the Institute and benefit from our many services.

If you would like to hear more, then contact
JOHN LAMBERT, the Regional Director, or
BILL WALKER, the Regional Manager, at

15 Woodside Terrace, Glasgow G3 7XH
Telephone: 041-333 0707

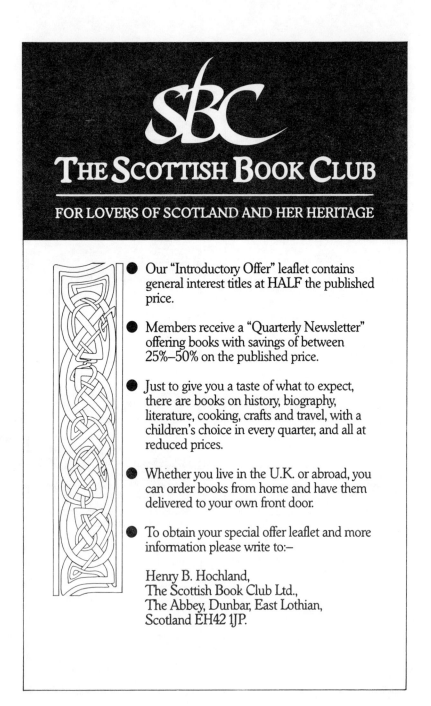

A

Abbott, Mollie Pearson, CBE (1984), DPE. Member, Court, Heriot-Watt University; b. 4.2.28, Peebles. Educ. Edinburgh Ladies' College; Dunfermline College of Physical Education. Assistant Teacher of Physical Education, Norton Park Junior Secondary School, Edinburgh; Visiting Teacher, Blackhall Primary School, Edinburgh; Sole Teacher, Broughton Senior Secondary School, Edinburgh; Temporary Lecturer, Moray House College of Education, Edinburgh, 1952-56; Sole Lecturer, then Senior Lecturer, Ripon Training College, 1956-62; Principal Lecturer, Aberdeen College of Education, 1962-63; HM Inspector of Schools, 1964-70; Principal, Dunfermline College of Physical Education, 1970-83. Past Chairman: Association of Higher Academic Staff in Colleges of Education in Scotland, Scottish Central Committee on Physical Education, Scottish Joint Consultative Committee on Physical Education; former Member: General Teaching Council for Scotland, National Committee for the In-Service Training of Teachers, Scottish Arts Council, Scottish Council of Physical Education, Scottish Sports Council. Recreations: golf; reading; skiing; swimming; walking; wind-surfing; listening to music. Address: (h.) 131 Craigleith Road, Edinburgh, EH4 2EH; T.-031-332 2327.

Abbott, Walter Hugh Alexander, MA, MIPM. Chief Careers Adviser, Stirling University, since 1969; b. 2.3.28, Darjeeling, India; m., Anne Judith Scott; 1 s.; 1 d. Educ. Trinity Academy, Edinburgh; Edinburgh University. Diploma, Social Studies. Personnel Trainee, Metropolitan-Vickers Electrical Co. Ltd., 1951-52; MV Electrical Co. Ltd. (latterly named GEC/AEI Power Engineering Co. Ltd.): Recruitment Assistant, Education Department, 1952-56, Senior Assistant, Overseas Recruitment, 1956-58, Senior Assistant, Recruitment and Selection, 1958-61, Head of Recruitment and Non-Engineering Training, 1961-69. Member and former Secretary, Central Scotland Marriage Guidance Council; Selector, Voluntary Service Overseas; serves on various committees of St. Mary's Episcopal Church, Dunblane. Recreations: music (member of three choirs); gardening; reading; theatre; sport. Address: (h.) 51 Argyle Way, Dunblane, FK15 9DX; T.-0786 822937.

Aberdeen and Temair, Marchioness of (Beatrice Mary June Gordon), MBE (1971), DL, FRCM, FRSE, DStJ, Hon. LLD (Aberdeen). Musical Director and Conductor, Haddo House Choral Society, since 1945; Chairman, Scottish Children's League, since 1969; Chairman, local Advisory Committee, Aberdeen International Festival of Music and the Performing Arts, since 1980; Governor, Gordonstoun School, since 1971. Address: (h.) Haddo House, Aberdeen, AB4 OER.

Abernethy, Barclay Chivas, MB, ChB, FRCS, FRCSEdin. Consultant Surgeon, Fife Area Health Board, since 1966; Honorary Senior Lecturer, St. Andrews, Edinburgh and Manchester Universities; b. 18.1.28, Aberdeen; m., Isobel Ellen; 1 s.; 2 d. Educ. Robert Gordon's College, Aberdeen; Aberdeen University; Middlesex Hospital, London. Initial medical appointments: Aberdeen Royal Infirmary, Woodend Hospital, Aberdeen, and Northampton General Hospital; Surgical Registrar, Middlesex Hospital, London, 1957-60; Senior Surgical Registrar, East Fife Hospitals, Fife Area Health Board. President, Kirkcaldy Rotary Club. Recreations: curling (Past President, Markinch Curling Club); gardening; fishing. Address: (h.) The Brackens, 10 Abbots Walk, Kirkcaldy, KY2 5NL; T.-0592 261085.

Abramovich, David Reuben, MB, BS, DGO, PhD, FRCOG. Reader in Obstetrics and Gynaecology, Aberdeen University, since 1984; Honorary Consultant, Grampian Health Board, since 1972; b. 25.10.36, Sydney, Australia; m., Flora; 1 s.; 1 d. Educ. Canterbury Boys' High School; Sydney University. Royal Prince Alfred Hospital, Sydney: House Officer, 1960-61, Registrar in Obstetrics and Gynaecology, 1962-64; Liverpool University: Lecturer in Obstetrics and Gynaecology, 1965, Research Fellow, 1966-70; Senior Lecturer in Obstetrics and Gynaecology, Aberdeen University, 1972-84. Recreation: tennis. Address: (h.) 1 Beaconhill View, Milltimber, Aberdeen; T.-0224 868571.

Adam, Caroline, MA (Hons). Senior Producer/ Presenter, BBC Radio Tweed, since 1983; b. 17.4.51, Edinburgh. Educ. George Watson's Ladies College, Edinburgh; Edinburgh University; Brunel University. BBC Radio Scotland: Producer, Current Affairs (daily and weekly output), 1978-82, Acting Senior Producer, Current Affairs (responsible for Afternoon Report), 1982. Recreations: people; the countryside; all arts; most sports. Address: (b.) BBC Radio Tweed, Municipal Buildings, High Street, Selkirk, TD7 4BU.

Adams, Allen. MP (Labour), Paisley North, since 1983 (Paisley, 1979-83); b. 1946. Educ. Camphill High School, Paisley; Reid-Kerr Technical College, Paisley. Computer Analyst.

Adams, Andrew Stewart, FIH, MBIM, DPA. Director of Housing, Midlothian District Council, since 1982; b. 2.3.47, Glasgow. Educ. Whitehill Senior Secondary School, Glasgow; Glasgow College of Building and Printing; Bell College, Hamilton. Glasgow Corporation: General Division Clerk, 1964-67, various posts, Housing Department, 1967-72; Housing Accounts and Computer Liaison Officer, Paisley Corporation, 1972-75; Principal Management Assistant, Hamilton District Council, 1975-77; Principal Administrative Officer, Motherwell District Council, 1977-82. Recreations: golfing; gardening. Address: (b.) 1 White Hart Street, Dalkeith, Midlothian, EH22 1DE; T.-031-663 2881.

Adams, David Anstey, MA. Principal, Aberdeen College of Education, since 1983; b. 2.3.42, Wakefield, Yorkshire; m., Margaret Ishbel; 1 s.; 1 d. Educ. Harris Academy, Dundee; St. Andrews University. Teacher of English and History, High School of Dundee; Principal Teacher of English, Arbroath Academy; Assistant Director of Education: Angus County Council, Tayside

Regional Council. Member: Scottish Examination Board, Committee of Principals of Colleges of Education in Scotland; Chairman: Advisory Committee on Guidance, Advisory Committee on Special Educational Needs (Non-Recorded Children), Advisory Committee on Admission to Scottish Colleges of Education. Recreations: fishing; shooting. Address: (b.) Aberdeen College of Education, Hilton Place, Aberdeen, AB9 1FA; T.-0224 42341.

Adams, Frederick George, MB, ChB, FRCR. Consultant Radiologist, Western Infirmary, Glasgow, since 1971; b. 24.9.38, Aberdeen; m., Allison; 1 s.; 2 d. Educ. Aberdeen Grammar School; Aberdeen University. Chairman, Medical Practitioners' Union (Glasgow), since 1984. Publications: numerous papers on radiology and nuclear medicine. Recreations: contract bridge; swimming. Address: (h.) 54 Terregles Avenue, Glasgow, G41 4LX; T.-041-423 2447.

Adams, Gordon Cassie, MBE. Member, Aberdeen District Council, since 1974; b. 4.2.24, Aberdeen; m., Jean Murray; 2 d. Commissioned Officer, Reconnaisance Corps, 1942-47. Technical Advisor: Government of Pakistan, 1962-68, University of Minas Gerais, Brazil, 1968-70. JP, 1974-84; Parliamentary candidate, Aberdeen North, 1979; former Secretary, Scotland in Europe Movement, 1979; Leader, Conservative Group, Aberdeen City Council, 1976-84; Member, Aberdeen Local Health Council, 1975-79. Recreations: Indian/African history; music; writing; reading. Address: (h.) 11c Kings Gate, Aberdeen; T.-Aberdeen 645834.

Adams, James Gordon Leitch, MA, PhD. Director of Development, Scottish Tourist Board, since 1983; b. 17.10.40, Glasgow; m., Rowan; 1 s.; 1 d. Educ. Dundee High School; St Andrews University; Queen's University, Canada; McGill University. Economist: Canadian Federal Government, 1966-70, Highlands and Islands Development Board, 1970-75; Lecturer, Glasgow University, 1975-82; British Council Visiting Lecturer in India, 1981. Recreations: mountaineering; golf. Address: (h.) 5 Corrennie Drive, Edinburgh; T.-031-447 8073.

Adams, Robert William, OBE, FCMA, FCCA, JDipMA. Writer; Director, John Cairney & Co. Ltd., since 1983; Member, Committee of Management, Hanover Housing Association, since 1982; b. 27.9.22, Glasgow; m., Mary Ann Ritchie; 2 s.; 1 d. Educ. Shawlands Academy, Glasgow. H.C. Stewart & Co., CA, Glasgow; Lieutenant, Parachute Regiment; South of Scotland Electricity Board; James Colledge (Cocoa) Ltd., West Africa; Highland Home Industries Ltd.; Managing Director, A.H. McIntosh & Co. Ltd., until 1982. Treasurer, British Furniture Manufacturers Federation; Director, British Furniture Manufacturers Exhibitions Ltd., since 1979; Member, Glenrothes Development Corporation, 1976-84; former Member: Scottish Sports Council; Council, Institute of Cost and Management Accountants; Scottish Sports Council; former Convenor, Scottish Athletic Coaching Committee. Recreations: tennis; badminton; golf. Address: (h.) Whitehall, Shore Road, Aberdour, Fife; T.-0383 860269.

Adamson, Donald MacFarlane Reid, MB, ChB. Surgeon; Unit Medical Officer, Dunoon and District General Hospital, since 1984; Police Surgeon, Strathclyde, since 1972; b. 22.10.27, Ayr; 1 s.; 1 d. Educ. Ayr Academy; Glasgow University. House Officer, Ballochmyle Hospital; Senior House Officer, Stockton and Thornaby Hospital; Registrar, then Associate Specialist, Dunoon and District General Hospital. Recreations: golf; walking. Address: (h.) Linden Lea, Royal Crescent, Dunoon; T.-Dunoon 4053.

Adamson, Iain Thomas Arthur Carpenter, BSc, MSc, AM, PhD. Senior Lecturer in Mathematical Sciences, Dundee University, since 1965; b. 17.6.28, Dundee; m., Robin Andison; 1 d. Educ. Morgan Academy, Dundee; St. Andrews University; Princeton University. Assistant in Instruction, Princeton University, 1950-52; Lecturer: Queen's University of Belfast, 1952-59, Queen's College, Dundee (St. Andrews University), 1960-65; visiting appointments, University of Western Australia, 1965-66, 1972-73, 1978. President, Edinburgh Mathematical Society, 1983-84; Session Clerk: Dundee Meadowside Church, 1975-81, Meadowside St. Paul's Church, 1982-84; licensed as Auxiliary Minister, Church of Scotland, 1985. Books: Introduction to Field Theory; Rings, Modules and Algebras; Elementary Rings and Modules; Elementary Mathematical Analysis. Recreation: reading. Address: (h.) 3 Chalmers Street, Dundee; T.-0382 42280.

Adamson, Rev. John Jagger. Minister, Burghead Free Church of Scotland, since 1969; b. 15.8.22, Fenwick; m., Margaret MacGruer MacQueen; 1 s.; 1 d. Educ. Govan High School; King's College, Aberdeen University; Free Church College, Edinburgh. Administration, civil engineering contractor, 1937-59; student, 1959-64; Minister, Farr Free Church of Scotland, 1964-69. Secretary, local branch, Sailors Orphans Society; Editor, Fellowship, magazine of Moray Coast Evangelical Fellowship. Recreations: reading; tapestry. Address: Free Church Manse, Burghead, Moray; T.-835463.

Adamson, Rev. Sidney, MA, BD. Minister, St. Michael's, Inveresk, Musselburgh, 1959-85; b. 3.8.11, Arbroath; m., Margaret T. Sharpe, JP; 1 s. Educ. Dumbarton Academy; Glasgow University and Trinity College. War service with Army, in India. Minister: St. Ninian's, Sanquhar, 1937-47, Trinity Church, Renfrew, 1947-54, High Kirk of Rothesay, 1954-59. Founder President, Renfrew branch, British Legion; former Industrial Chaplain, Babcock and Wilcox Ltd. Books: Two Centuries of Service (history of Sanquhar congregation); St. Michael's Kirk at Inveresk (parish history). Recreations: freelance journalism; swimming. Address: 48 Hailes Gardens, Colinton, Edinburgh, EH13 0JH; T.-031-441 2471.

Adamson, William Christie, MBE, FCIS, FIB. Honorary Sheriff, Tayside, Fife and Central, at Perth, since 1970; b. 10.7.18, Perth; m., Elizabeth Ann Johnston. Educ. Perth Academy. Joined Trustee Savings Bank, 1933; War Service, Black Watch, 1939-46; General Manager: Perth TSB, 1962-75, TSB of Tayside and Central Scotland, 1975-82; Director, TSB Pension Trust Ltd.,

1976-82. Chairman, Appeals Committee, UN Association Educational Trust for Scotland; Member, Executive, Perth and Kinross Group, National Trust for Scotland; Session Clerk, St. Paul's Church, Perth. Address: (h.) Tomliadh, 10A Mansfield Road, Scone, Perth, PH2 6SA; T.-0738 51612.

Adler-Bell, Marianne. Dress Designer, since 1939; Member, Board of Directors, Citizens' Theatre, Glasgow, since 1973; b. 17.1.15, Berlin, Germany; m., John Bell (deceased); 1 s. Educ. Staatliche Augusta Schule, Berlin; Art School, Berlin. Vice-Chairman, Citizens' Theatre Society; Committee Member: New Glasgow Music Society, Glasgow Art Gallery. Awarded Bundesverdienstkreuz (similar in Germany to OBE) for work in furthering Scottish-German relations. Recreations: opera; gardening. Address (h.) 348 Knightswood Road, Glasgow, G13 2BT; T.-041-959 1696.

Agnew of Lochnaw, Sir Crispin Hamlyn. 11th Baronet (created 1629); Chief of the Agnews; Advocate, since 1982; Unicorn Pursuivant of Arms, since 1981; b. 13.5.44, Edinburgh; m., Susan Rachel Strang Steel; 1 d. Educ. Uppingham School; Royal Military Academy, Sandhurst. Commissioned Royal Highland Fusiliers, 1964, as 2nd Lieutenant; Major, 1977; Retired, 1981. Member: Royal Navy Expedition to East Greenland, 1966; Joint Services Expedition to Elephant Island, Antarctica, 1970-71; Army Nuptse Himal Expedition, 1975; Army Everest Expedition, 1976; Leader: Army East Greenland Expedition, 1968; Joint Services Expedition to Chilean Patagonia, 1972-73; Army Api Himal Expedition, 1980. Publications: articles in various newspapers and journals. Recreations: mountaineering; offshore sailing. Address: 6 Palmerston Road, Edinburgh, EH9 1TN; T.-031-667 4970.

Agnew, Ian, MA (Hons) (Cantab). Rector, Perth High School, since 1975; b. 10.5.32, Newcastle-upon-Tyne; m., Gladys Agnes Heatherill; 1 d. Educ. King's College School, London; Pembroke College, Cambridge. Assistant Teacher of Modern Languages, Melville College, Edinburgh, 1958-63; Assistant Teacher of Modern Languages, then Principal Teacher of Russian, George Heriot's School, Edinburgh, 1964-70; Housemaster, Craigmount Secondary School, Edinburgh, 1970-73; Deputy, Liberton High School, Edinburgh, 1973-75. Chairman, Tayside Regional Working Party on Religious Education, since 1977; Minute Secretary, Headteachers Association of Scotland, 1979-81; Committee Member, SCCORE; President: Perthshire Musical Festival, since 1978, Perth Chamber Music Society, since 1982; Secretary, Rotary Club of Perth St. John's; Past Chairman: Barnton and Cramond Conservative Association and West Edinburgh Conservative and Unionist Association; Elder, St. Andrew's Parish Church, Perth. Recreations: music (opera); reading; tennis; gardening. Address: (h.) Northwold, Heughfield Road, Bridge of Earn, Perthshire, PH2 9BH; T.-0738 81 2273.

Agnew, Peter Frank, CA. Chief Executive, Lanarkshire Industrial Field Executive, since 1983; b. 31.5.43, Glasgow; m., Patricia Morton; 1 s.; 1 d. Educ. Eastwood School; Glasgow University. IBM; Gilbert-Ash (Scotland) Ltd.; British Steel Corporation; BSC (Industry) Ltd. Recreation: golf. Address: (b.) Old Town Hall, Motherwell, ML1 3HU; T.-Motherwell 66622.

Agnew, Stanley Clarke, CB, BSc, FEng, FICE, FIWES, FIPHE, Hon. FIWPC. Chief Engineer, Scottish Development Department, since 1976; b. 18.5.26, Belfast; m., Isbell Evelyn Parker Davidson; 2 d. Educ. Royal Belfast Academical Institution; Queen's University, Belfast. Fifteen years' varied experience with civil engineering contractors, local authorities and consulting engineers; joined Scottish Development Department as an engineering inspector, 1962; appointed Deputy Chief Engineer, 1968. Recreations: golf; gardening; photography. Address: (h.) Duncraig, 52 Blinkbonny Road, Edinburgh, EH4 3HX; T.-031-332 4072.

Ah-See, Antoine Kim-Nen, MB, ChB, CHM, FRCSEdin. Senior Lecturer in Surgery, Aberdeen University, since 1977; b. 1.6.38, Quatre-Bornes, Mauritius; m., Catherine Ross Matheson; 1 s.; 2 d. Educ. St. Andrews School, Mauritius; Aberdeen University. Pre-registration House Officer, Aberdeen Royal Infirmary, 1966-67; Senior House Officer, Queen Mary's Hospital, Sidcup, Kent, 1967-68; Surgical Registrar, Aberdeen Royal Infirmary, 1969-70; Research Fellow, Uppsala, Department of Experimental Medicine, Pharmacia, 1970-71; Lecturer in Surgery, Aberdeen University, 1972-76; Research Fellow, Institute of Naval Medicine (Hyperbaric), Gosport, 1976-77. Recreations: travel; antiquities. Address: (h.) St. Ronan's House, Peterculter, Aberdeen; T.-732290.

Ailsa, The Marquess of, (Archibald David Kennedy), OBE; b. 3.12.25, Witham, Essex; m., Mary Burn; 2 s.; 1 d. Educ. Nautical College, Pangbourne. Commissioned Scots Guards, 1944; served with Royal Northumberland Fusiliers in Korea; commissioned 4/5th Bn., Royal Scots Fusiliers TA (commanded, 1966-68); commanded 3rd Bn., Royal Highland Fusiliers T&AVR; Honorary Colonel, Ayr and Renfrew Bn., Army Cadet Force. Recreation: sailing. Address: (h.) Blanefield, Kirkoswald, Ayrshire; T.-065 56 646.

Airlie, 13th Earl of, (David George Coke Patrick Ogilvy), PC, GCVO, DL. Lord Chamberlain of Her Majesty's Household; Ensign, Queen's Body-guard for Scotland (Royal Company of Archers), since 1975; Deputy Chairman, General Accident Fire & Life Assurance Corporation Ltd., since 1975; Director, Royal Bank of Scotland, since 1980; Trustee, Nuffield Hospitals, since 1985; b. 17.5.26, London; m., Virginia Fortune Ryan; 3 s.; 3 d. Educ. Eton College. Lieutenant, Scots Guards, 1944; serving 2nd Bn., Germany, 1945; Captain, ADC to High Commissioner and C-in-C Austria, 1947-48; Malaya, 1948-49; resigned commission, 1950; Chairman, Ashdown Investment Trust Ltd., 1968-82; Director, J. Henry Schroder Wagg & Co. Ltd., 1961-84 (Chairman, 1973-77); Chairman, Schroders plc, 1977-84; Scottish and Newcastle Breweries plc, until 1983. Treasurer, Scout Association; Deputy Lieutenant, Angus. Address: (h.) Cortachy Castle, Kirriemuir, Angus; T.-Cortachy 231.

Aitchison, Rev. James, MA, BD. Minister, Broomhill Church, Glasgow, since 1963; b. 26.5.20, Kilmarnock; m., Catherine Auld Gilmour; 2 d. Educ. Kilmarnock Academy; Glasgow University and Trinity College. Minister: Renton, 1947-52, St. Stephen's Comely Bank, Edinburgh, 1952-63. Capped 69 times for Scotland as cricketer. Recreations: cricket; badminton (University blue). Address: 27 St. Kilda Drive, Glasgow, G14; T.-041-959 3204.

Aitchison, Thomas Milne, MBE, BL, NP, SSC. Sole Partner, Aitchison & Co., Solicitors, Whitburn, West Lothian, since 1984; b. 28.5.30, Longridge, West Lothian; m., Flora Jane Stewart Paris; 3 s. Educ. Bathgate Academy; Edinburgh University. 1st Legal Assistant, Lanark County Council, 1962-67; Depute County Clerk (Senior), Ross and Cromarty County Council, 1967-75; Chief Executive, Ross and Cromarty District Council, 1974-78; Partner, P.H. Young & Co., Solicitors, Whitburn, 1983. Recreations: sailing; skiing; photography. Address: (h.) 12 Merlin Park, Dollar, Clackmannanshire; T.-Dollar 3156.

Aitken, Adam Jack, MA, DLitt. Editor, A Dictionary of the Older Scottish Tongue, since 1956; Editorial Consultant and Pronunciation Editor, Concise Scots Dictionary, since 1975; University Fellow, Edinburgh University; b. 19.6.21, Edinburgh; m., Norma Ward Manson; 3 s.; 1 d. Educ. Lasswade Secondary School; Edinburgh University. Assistant Lecturer in English Language, Edinburgh University, 1947-48; Research Fellow, Universities of Glasgow, Aberdeen and Edinburgh, 1948-54; Lecturer, Universities of Glasgow and Edinburgh, 1954-64 (Assistant Editor and Editor, Dictionary of the Older Scottish Tongue); Edinburgh University: Honorary Senior Lecturer, 1965-71, Senior Lecturer (part-time) in English Language, 1971-75, Reader (part-time) in English Language, 1975-79; Chairman, Language Committee, Association for Scottish Literary Studies, 1971-76; Chairman, Universities' Forum for Research on the Languages of Scotland, 1978-81; Biennial Sir Israel Gollancz Prize of British Academy, 1981; Honorary Professor, Edinburgh University, since 1984. Publications: Edinburgh Studies in English and Scots, 1971; The Computer and Literary Studies, 1973; Lowland Scots, 1973; Bards and Makars, 1977; Languages of Scotland, 1979. Address: (b.) Dictionary of the Older Scottish Tongue, 27 George Square, Edinburgh, EH8 9LD; T.-031-667 1011, Ext. 6678.

Aitken, George Pattullo Hogg, TD, BL. Assistant Secretary, Scottish Home and Health Department, since 1975; b. 19.2.30, Dundee; m., Agnes Gray; 5 d. Educ. Morgan Academy; Edinburgh University. Senior Examiner, Estate Duty Office, Edinburgh, 1958-69; Principal: Scottish Home and Health Department, 1969-72, Scottish Courts Administration, 1972-75. Kirk organist. Address: (b) St Andrews House, Edinburgh; T.-031-556 8501.

Aitken, Professor Robert Cairns Brown, MB, ChB, DPM, MD, FRCPEdin, FRCPsych. Professor of Rehabilitation Studies, Edinburgh University, since 1974; Honorary Consultant in Rehabilitation Medicine, Lothian Health Board, since 1974; b. 20.12.33, Dunoon; m., Audrey May Lunn; 1 s.; 1 d. Educ. Dunoon Grammar School; Cargilfield School, Edinburgh; Sedbergh School, Yorkshire; Glasgow University. Institute of Aviation Medicine, RAF, 1959-62; Orpington and Maudsley Hospitals, 1962-66; Senior Lecturer/Consultant Psychiatrist, Royal Infirmary and Royal Edinburgh Hospitals, 1967-74. President, International College of Psychosomatic Medicine, since 1985; Chairman, Napier College Council, since 1983; Member, Council for Professions Supplementary to Medicine, since 1983; Editor, Journal of Psychosomatic Research, 1979-85; occasional WHO consultant; Foundation Secretary, then President, Society for Research in Rehabilitation, 1981-83. Publications: papers on measurement of mood; flying phobia; management of disability. Recreations: people, places and pleasures of Edinburgh, Scotland and beyond. Address: (h) 11 Succoth Place, Edinburgh, EH12 6BJ; T.-031-337 1550.

Aitken, Robin Elliot Guild, MB, ChB, MSc, MFCM. Senior Medical Officer, Scottish Home and Health Department; b. 7.11.39, Edinburgh; m., Gillian Ann Odell (deceased); 1 s.; 1 d. Educ. Robert Gordon's College, Aberdeen; Aberdeen University. Medical Officer, 23 Parachute Field Ambulance, 1965-68; Regimental Medical Officer, 1st Bn., Black Watch, 1968-69; Army Health Specialist, 1969-72; retired as Major, 1972; Community Medicine Specialist, Grampian Health Board, 1972-79. Commanding Officer, 252 Field Ambulance (TA) as Lieutenant Colonel, 1977-79; Regimental Medical Officer (Lieutenant Colonel), 2nd 52nd Lowland Volunteers (TA), 1980-83; Elder, Colinton Parish Church. Recreations: running; mountaineering; skiing; cycling; fishing; shooting. Address: (h.) Carnferg, 31 Dreghorn Loan, Colinton, Edinburgh, EH13 ODF; T.-031-441 6116.

Aitken, William Duff, MM (FG). Director, William Aitken Highland Exports Ltd., since 1973; Member, Board of Directors, Eden Court Theatre, since 1984; Member, Inverness District Council; b. 12.3.27, Newton Mearns; m., Eva Alexandra Kjellsson; 2 d. Educ. Merchant Taylors'; Liverpool Nautical College. Seafaring, 1943-53; tanning industry, 1953-72. Recreations: philately; swimming; RNXS. Address: (h) Thistles, 19 Swanston Avenue, Inverness, IV3 6QW; T.-0462 230068.

Aitken, William Mackie, ACII. Member, Glasgow District Council, since 1976; b. 15.4.47, Glasgow. Educ. Allan Glen's School, Glasgow. Chairman, Scottish Young Conservatives, 1975-77; Convener, Glasgow Licensing Committee, 1977-79; Vice-Convener, Manpower Committee, 1977-79; Leader of the Opposition, 1980-84; Bailie of the City of Glasgow, 1980-84. Recreations: football; walking; reading. Address: (h.) 36 Dudley Drive, Glasgow, G12 9JA; T.-041-357 1284.

Aitken, William Russell, MA, PhD, FLA. Bibliographer; b. 7.2.13, Calderbank, Lanarkshire; m., Betsy Mary Murison; 1 d. Educ. Dunfermline High School; Edinburgh University. Assistant Librarian, Scottish Central Library, 1936-40;

war service, RAF, 1941-46; County Librarian: Clackmannanshire, 1946-49, Perth and Kinross, 1949-58, Ayr, 1958-62; Lecturer, then Senior Lecturer, latterly Reader, Department of Librarianship, University of Strathclyde, 1962-78. President, Scottish Library Association, 1965; Editor, Library Review, 1964-76. Books: A History of the Public Library Movement in Scotland, 1971; William Soutar's Poems in Scots and English (Editor), 1961, 1975; The Complete Poems of Hugh MacDiarmid (Editor, with Michael Grieve), 1978, 1985; Scottish Literature in English and Scots (a bibliographical guide), 1982. Address: (h.) 6 Tannahill Terrace, Dunblane, FK15 OAX; T.-Dunblane 823650.

Aitkenhead, John M., MA (Hons), MEd, JP. Headmaster and Founder, Kilquhanity House International School for Boys and Girls, since 1940; b. 21.5.10, Glasgow; m., Morag MacKinnon; 2 s.; 2 d. Educ. Ardrossan Academy; Glasgow University. Worked in Scottish education system until 1940; conscientious objector during World War II; established school inspired by work and writing of A.S. Neill; ardent Scottish nationalist. Recreations: singing; poetry; dancing; Gaelic; gardening. Address: Kilquhanity, Castle Douglas, Kirkcudbrightshire; T.-055 665 242.

Akhtar, Anwar Jahil, BSc, MB, ChB, FRCPEdin. Consultant Physician, Royal Victoria Hospital, Edinburgh, since 1972; Senior Lecturer, Edinburgh University, since 1972; b. 25.7.36, Lahore, Pakistan; m., Valerie Joan Penman; 1 s.; 2 d. Educ. Edinburgh University. MRC Research Fellow, Respiratory Diseases Unit, City Hospital, Edinburgh; Senior Registrar, Professorial Unit, Stobhill Hospital, Glasgow. Recreations: music; dogs; restoring pianos. Address: (b.) Royal Victoria Hospital, Edinburgh; T.-031-332 2566.

Alcock, Professor Leslie, MA, FSA, FRSE, FRHistS. Professor of Archaeology, Glasgow University, since 1973; b. 24.4.25, Manchester; m., Elizabeth A. Blair; 1 s.; 1 d. Educ. Manchester Grammar School; Brasenose College, Oxford. 7th Gurkha Rifles, 1943-47; Archaeological Survey of Pakistan, 1950-52; Lecturer, Reader, Professor of Archaeology, University College, Cardiff, 1953-73; Member, Board of Trustees, National Museum of Antiquities of Scotland, 1973-85; Member, Ancient Monuments Board, Scotland, since 1974; Commissioner, Royal Commission on Ancient Monuments of Scotland, since 1977; President, Cambrian Archaeological Association, 1982-83; President, Society of Antiquaries of Scotland, since 1984. Publication: Arthur's Britain, 1971. Recreations: mountain and coastal scenery; music. Address: (b.) Glasgow University, Glasgow, G12 8QQ; T.-041-339 8855.

Alcock, Stephen Robert, MB, ChB, PhD. Senior Lecturer in Bacteriology, Glasgow University, since 1981; Honorary Consultant in Bacteriology, Greater Glasgow Health Board, since 1981; b. 24.6.45, Sutton Coldfield; m., Jean Margaret Diack; 1 s.; 1 d. Educ. Aberdeen Academy; Bearsden Academy; Aberdeen University. House Officer appointments, Aberdeen Royal Infirmary, 1970; Lecturer, Aberdeen University,

1970-81; consultancy work with diving industry, 1974-81, and Sultanate of Oman, since 1984. Recreations: angling; books. Address (h.) 2 Midlothian Drive, Shawlands, Glasgow; T.-041-645 1521.

Alexander of Ballochmyle, Sir Claud Haggart-, 3rd Bt, JP, BA, MInstMC. Vice Lord-Lieutenant, Ayr and Arran, since 1983; b. 6.1.27; m.; 2 s.; 2 d. Educ. Sherborne; Corpus Christi College, Cambridge. Address: (h.) Kingencleugh House, Mauchline, Ayrshire, KA5 5JL.

Alexander, David Alan, MA (Hons), PhD, ABPS. Senior Lecturer, Medical School, Aberdeen University, since 1980 (Director of Course for the Diploma in Psychotherapy, since 1983); b. 28.8.43, Ellon, Aberdeenshire; m., Anita Alexander. Educ. George Watson's College, Edinburgh; Morgan Academy, Dundee; St. Andrews University; Dundee University. Holder of MRC scholarship; Senior Clinical Psychologist, Grampian Health Board; Lecturer in Mental Health, Aberdeen University; Senior Lecturer in Mental Health, Aberdeen University and External Examiner, University of West Indies. Recreations: badminton; squash; climbing; riding. Address: (b.) Department of Mental Health, Medical School, Foresterhill, Aberdeen; T.-Aberdeen 681818.

Alexander, David Crichton, CB. Commandant, Scottish Police College, since 1979; b. 28.11.26, Aberdour; m., Diana Joyce (Jane) Fisher; 1 s.; 1 step-s.; 2 d. Educ. Edinburgh Academy; Staff College, Camberley; Royal College of Defence Studies. Royal Marines, 1944-77 (2nd Lieutenant to Major-General, including Equerry and Acting Treasurer to Duke of Edinburgh); Director-General, English Speaking Union, 1977-79. Governor, Corps of Commissionaires; Member, Civil Service Final Selection Board; Director, Edinburgh Academy; Freeman, City of London; Liveryman, Painter Stainers' Company. Recreations: fishing; golf; gardening. Address: (b.) Tulliallan Castle, Kincardine, Alloa, FK10 4BE; T.-0259 30333.

Alexander, David Richard Watson, CBE (1972), MA. Member, Lothian Regional Council, since 1982 (Chairman, Planning and Development Committee); b. 12.8.18, Montrose; m., Mrs M.A.E. James; 1 s., 1 d. by pr. m.; 3 step-s. Educ. Montrose Academy; Edinburgh University. Served World War II, latterly with rank of Lieutenant Colonel, in Hong Kong, India, Ceylon and Malaya; awarded MBE (Military) for gallant and distinguished service with SOE behind the Japanese lines in Malaya. Colonial Administrative Service: appointed Administrative Officer, Somaliland, 1948; seconded to Cyrenaica (Libya) for service with War Office, then Foreign Office Administration of African Territories, finally with Government of Cyrenaica; transferred to Hong Kong, 1953; appointments including Commissioner, Essential Services Corps and Chief Staff Officer, Civil Aid Services; Director of Social Welfare; Commissioner of Labour; Chairman, Urban Council, Director of Urban Services and Chairman, Housing Authority; Member, Legislative Council; retired, 1975. Member:

Planning Committee, COSLA; Development Consultative Committee, Scottish Development Agency; Consultative Committee, Lothian Region Development Authority. Address: (h.) 2 Crarae Avenue, Edinburgh, EH4 3JD.

Alexander, David Stevenson, MA (Hons), MLitt. Rector, Bannerman High School, Baillieston, since 1983; b. 3.2.43, Glasgow; m., Una Stewart; 2 s. Educ. Uddingston Grammar School; Glasgow University; Jordanhill College of Education. Assistant Head Teacher, Bannerman High School, 1973-77; Deputy Head Teacher, Whitehill Secondary School, 1977-78; Head Teacher, Barrhead High School, 1978-83. Address: (b.) Bannerman High School, Glasgow Road, Baillieston, Glasgow; T.-041-771 7301.

Alexander, Rev. Douglas Niven, MA, BD. Minister, Erskine Parish Church, Bishopton, since 1970; Vice-Convener, Church of Scotland Board of Communication, since 1982; Convener, Church of Scotland Committee on Broadcasting, since 1985; b. 8.4.35, Eaglesham; m., Dr. Joyce O. Garven; 1 s.; 2 d. Educ. Hutchesons' Boys' Grammar School, Glasgow; Glasgow University (President, SRC, 1958); Union Theological Seminary, New York. Assistant Minister, St. Ninian's Church, Greenock, 1961-62; Warden, Iona Community House, Glasgow, 1963-70. Secretary, Scottish Union of Students, 1958; Assessor to Lord Rector, Glasgow University, 1969-71; Chaplain to Erskine Hospital, since 1970; Moderator, Paisley Presbytery, 1984. Recreation: researching ways of salmon poachers! Address: The Manse, Newton Road, Bishopton, Renfrewshire, PA7 5JP; T.-0505 862161.

Alexander, Rev. Eric J., MA, BD. Minister, St. George's-Tron Parish Church, Glasgow, since 1977; b. 9.5.32, Glasgow; m., Margaret D. Connell; 1 s.; 1 d. Educ. Allan Glen's School, Glasgow; Glasgow University. Publication: The Search for God, 1962. Address: (h.) 12 Dargarvel Avenue, Glasgow, G41.

Alexander, John Huston, BLitt, MA, DPhil Oxon. Senior Lecturer in English, Aberdeen University, since 1984; Assistant Editor, Scottish Literary Journal, since 1980; b. 5.4.41, Coleraine, Northern Ireland; m., Flora Ross; 2 s.; 2 d. Educ. Campbell College, Belfast; St. Edmund Hall, Oxford. Sessional Lecturer in English, University of Saskatchewan, Canada, 1966-67; Lecturer in English, Aberdeen University, 1968-84. Editor, The Scott Newsletter, since 1982. Publications: Two Studies in Romantic Reviewing, 1976; The Lay of the Last Minstrel: Three Essays, 1978; The Reception of Scott's Poetry By His Correspondents: 1796-1817, 1979; 'Marmion': Studies in Interpretation and Composition, 1981; Scott and his Influence (Editor, with David Hewitt), 1983. Recreation: music. Address: (h.) 45A Queen's Road, Aberdeen, AB1 6YN; T.-0224 317424.

Alexander, Sir Kenneth John Wilson, BSc (Econ), LLD, DUniv, FRSE, CBIM. Principal and Vice-Chancellor, Stirling University, since 1981; b. 14.3.22, Edinburgh; m., Angela-May; 1 s.; 4 d. Educ. George Heriot's School, Edinburgh; School of Economics, Dundee; London School of Economics. Taught at Universities of Leeds, Sheffield and Aberdeen; Professor of Economics, Strathclyde University, 1963-80. Member, Advisory Committee on University of the Air, 1965; Chairman: Committee on Adult Education in Scotland, 1970-73, Social Science Research Council, 1975-76; President, Section F, British Association, 1974; Chairman, Highlands and Islands Development Board, 1976-80; Economic Consultant to the Secretary of State for Scotland, since 1968; Member, Scottish Development Agency, since 1975; Chairman, Council for Applied Science in Scotland, 1980-85; Member, Council, British Institute of Management, since 1980; Governor, Technical Change Centre, since 1981; Director, Scottish Television Ltd., since 1981; Member, Council for Tertiary Education in Scotland, 1981-82; Deputy Chairman, Scottish Council (Development and Industry), since 1982; Honorary President: The Highland Fund, since 1983; Scottish National Dictionary Association Ltd., since 1983; Deputy Chairman, Scottish Theatre Company, since 1983; President, Town and Country Planning (Scottish Section), 1982. Publications: The Economist in Business, 1967; Fairfields, a study of industrial change (with C.L. Jenkins), 1971; The Political Economy of Change (Editor), 1976. Recreation: Scottish antiquarianism. Address: (b.) Stirling University, Stirling, FK9 4LA; T.-0786 73171.

Alexander, Peter Robert, DipArch. Head of Design, Scottish Television, since 1958; b. 10.4.28, Alsager, Cheshire; m., Maureen; 3 s.; 1 d. Educ. Taunton School; University College, London. Design Assistant, BBC London, 1955-58. Address: (h.) 394 Kilmarnock Road, Glasgow, G43 2DJ.

Alexander, Robert George, OBE, FCBSI. Honorary Sheriff, Paisley, since 1974; b. 9.11.14, Portsmouth; m., Mary Matilda Faith Taylor; 1 s.; 1 d. Educ. Kinross Elementary School; Dollar Academy; Edinburgh University. Qualified as Solicitor, 1937; Legal Assistant, R.S. Young & Son, Kinross, until 1939; War Service (Territorial) with Argyll and Sutherland Highlanders (Colour Sergeant), 1939-42; commissioned 10/7 Rajput Regiment, 1942; appointed Deputy Assistant Judge Advocate General, HQ Central Command, India, with rank of Major, 1944; Legal Assistant, R.S. Young & Son and Shiell & Small, Dundee, 1946; Branch Manager/Divisional Manager, Dunfermline Building Society, 1948; Assistant Secretary/Manager and Secretary/General Manager and Director, Paisley Building Society, 1958-78; retired, 1978. General Commissioner of Income Tax, 1972-75; Member, Renfrewshire Valuation Appeal Committee, 1972-75; Member of Council, Building Societies Association, 1970-75; President: Scottish Building Societies Association, 1973-74, Paisley Chamber of Commerce, 1970-71; Scottish Chairman, National House-Building Council, 1975-81 (Honorary Vice-President, since 1982); Member of Council, National Trust for Scotland, 1971-76; Elder, Church of Scotland, since 1955; Treasurer, Durisdeer Church, since 1980. Recreations: golf; gardening. Address: (h.) Hope Cottage, Durisdeer, Thornhill, Dumfriesshire, DG3 5BJ; T.-084 85 285.

Alexander, Samuel, BL. Honorary Sheriff, Sheriffdom of Dumbarton, since 1983; b. Glasgow; m., Isabella Kerr Ligertwood; 2 s. Educ. Govan High School; Glasgow University. Senior Partner, Keyden Strang & Co., Solicitors, Glasgow. Recreations: golf; reading. Address: (h.) 1 Hillneuk Avenue, Bearsden, Glasgow, G61; T.-041-942 4674.

Ali, Nasir, MB, BS, DPM, MRCPsych. Consultant Psychiatrist, since 1973; Honorary Senior Lecturer, Aberdeen University, since 1982; b. 21.8.39, Lucknow, India; m., D. Rosemary; 1 s.; 1 d. Address: (h.) 4 Muirfield Gardens, Inverness, IV2 4HF; T.-Inverness 222033.

Allan, Andrew D.C., MA (Hons). Head Teacher, Mainholm Academy, Ayr, since 1974; b. 16.4.31, Irvine; m., Margaret; 2 d. Educ. Irvine Royal Academy; Glasgow University; Jordanhill College of Education. National Service, RAEC, 1954-56; Mathematics Teacher, Kilmarnock Academy, 1956-58; Principal Teacher of Mathematics: Dalry High School, 1958-62, John Neilson Institution, 1962-65, Kilmarnock Academy, 1965-71; Assistant Head Teacher, Kilmarnock Academy, 1970-72; Depute Head Teacher, Ardrossan Academy, 1972-74. Elder, Church of Scotland, since 1956; Vice-President, Alloway Rotary Club, 1985-86. Recreations: golf; walking; travelling. Address: (h.) 46 Taybank Drive, Ayr; T.-Alloway 41067.

Allan, Arthur Lang, BL. Member, Argyll and Bute District Council, since 1984; Clerk, Mid Argyll General Commissioners of Income Tax, since 1968; Solicitor in private practice, since 1949; b. 25.10.25, Dunoon; m., Katharine Morag McDonnell; 1 s.; 2 d. Educ. Dunoon Grammar School; Glasgow University. Royal Navy, 1943-46. Chairman, National Insurance Tribunal, since 1981; Dean, Faculty of Procurators of Greenock, 1983-85; Dean, Dunoon Faculty of Procurators, 1985. Address: (h.) 14 Mary Street, Dunoon; T.-0369 3033.

Allan, David Smith, BSc (Hons), DipEd. Headmaster, Preston Lodge High School, Prestonpans, since 1970; b. 17.1.35, Prestonpans; m., Alexandra; 2 s.; 1 d. Educ. Preston Lodge School, Prestonpans; Edinburgh University. Teacher, George Heriot's School, Edinburgh, 1958-63; Principal Teacher of Science, Preston Lodge High School, Prestonpans, 1963-70. Hon. President, Preston Lodge FP Club; President, Lothian Headteachers Association. Recreations: rugby committee work; golf. Address: (b.) Preston Lodge High School, Prestonpans, East Lothian; T.-Prestonpans 811170.

Allan, George Alexander, MA (Hons). Headmaster, Robert Gordon's College, Aberdeen, since 1978; b. 3.2.36, Edinburgh; m., Anne Violet Veevers; 2 s. Educ. Daniel Stewart's College, Edinburgh; Edinburgh University. Teacher of Classics, Glasgow Academy, 1958-60; Daniel Stewart's College: Teacher of Classics, 1960-63, Head of Classics, 1963-73 (appointed Housemaster, 1967); Deputy Headmaster, Robert Gordon's College, 1973-77. Secretary, Headmasters' Conference (Scottish Division), since

1980 (Member, National Committee, 1982 and 1983); Governor, Welbeck College, since 1980; Member, ISIS Scotland Committee, since 1983. Recreations: gardening; golf; music. Address: 24 Woodend Road, Aberdeen, AB2 6YH; T.-0224 321733.

Allan, John Balfour, MA, LLB. Divisional Solicitor, Office of Solicitor to Secretary of State for Scotland, since 1982; b. 11.10.33, Linlithgow Bridge. Educ. George Watson's College, Edinburgh; Edinburgh University. Legal Assistant, Auld & Macdonald, WS, 1958-60; Office of Solicitor to Secretary of State for Scotland: Legal Assistant, 1961-66, Senior Legal Assistant, 1967-71, Divisional Solicitor, 1971-72; Secretary, Scottish Law Commission, 1972-79; Deputy Solicitor to Secretary of State for Scotland, 1979-82. Recreation: men's hockey. Address: (h.) 10 Craigleith Hill Gardens, Edinburgh, EH4 2JJ; T.-031-332 6420.

Allan, John Douglas, BL, DMS, FBIM. Procurator Fiscal for Edinburgh and Regional Procurator Fiscal for Lothians and Borders, since 1983; b. 2.10.41, Edinburgh; m., Helen E.J. Aiton; 1 s.; 1 d. Educ. George Watson's College, Edinburgh; Edinburgh University. Solicitor in private practice, Edinburgh, 1963-67; Procurator Fiscal Depute, Edinburgh, 1967-71; Solicitor, Crown Office, Edinburgh, 1971-76; Assistant Procurator Fiscal, then Senior Assistant Procurator Fiscal, Glasgow, 1976-79; Solicitor, Crown Office, Edinburgh, 1979-83. Part-time Lecturer in Law, Napier College, Edinburgh, 1963-66; Holder, Scout "Medal of Merit"; Session Clerk, Greenbank Parish Church of Scotland. Recreations: Scouts; youth leadership; walking; Church. Address: (b.) 3 Queensferry Street, Edinburgh, EH2 4RB; T.-031-226 4962.

Allan, Robert. Chief Executive, Scottish Fishermen's Federation, since 1982; b. 14.11.33, Peterhead; m., Moira W. Morrison; 2 d. Educ. Aberdeen Grammar School. Audit Assistant, R.C. Kelman & Shirreffs, CA, Aberdeen, 1949-62; Assistant Secretary, latterly Secretary, Aberdeen Fishing Vessel Owners' Association Ltd. and Scottish Trawlers' Federation, 1962-71; Chief Executive, Aberdeen Fishing Vessel Owners' Association Ltd. and Aberdeen Fish Producers' Organisation Ltd., 1971-82. Recreation: keen follower of the fortunes of Aberdeen FC. Address: (h.) 40 Parkhill Circle, Dyce, Aberdeen, AB2 OFN; T.-0224 724366.

Allanbridge, Lord (William Ian Stewart), QC. Senator of the College of Justice in Scotland, since 1977; b. 8.11.25; m.; 1 s.; 1 d. Educ. Loretto; Glasgow University; Edinburgh University. Sub-Lt., RNVR, 1944-46; called to the Bar, 1951; Advocate-Depute, 1959-64; Home Advocate-Depute, 1970-72; Solicitor-General for Scotland, 1972-74; Temporary Sheriff Principal, Dumfries and Galloway, 1974.

Allardyce, John Grahame, MA; b. 4.10.17, Dublin; m., Euphemia Mary Wilson; 2 s.; 2 d. Educ. Cheltenham College; Royal Military Academy, Woolwich; Christ's College, Cambridge. Commissioned Royal Engineers, 1937;

War Service in France, North Africa, Sicily, Italy; mentioned in Despatches (twice); US Bronze Star Medal; later in 52 (Lowland) Division/District, Gibraltar and Malaya and with NATO; retired from Army, 1966, as Lt. Col.; Technical Director, International Standards Organization, Geneva, 1967-79. Fellow, Institute of Linguists; Secretary, Nairn Amenities Protection Society and Civic Trust. Address: (h.) Caskieben, Moss-side, Nairn.

Allen, Professor Derek Henry, BSc, PhD, CEng, FIChemE, FBIM, FRSA. Professor of Management Science and Director, Technological Economics Research Unit, Stirling University, since 1978; b. 6.2.33, Exeter; m., Mary Valerie Stabler; 3 d. Educ. Brockenhurst High School; Birmingham University. Research and Development Engineer, British Gas Council, 1957-59; Refinery Engineer, Refinery Operations Coordinator, Esso Petroleum Company, 1959-63; Research Fellow, Lecturer, Senior Lecturer and Reader in Chemical Engineering and Engineering Management, Nottingham University, 1963-78. Recreations: hill-walking; choir and music; gardening; DIY. Address: (b.) University of Stirling, Stirling, FK9 4LA; T.-0786 73171.

Allen, Professor John Walter, MA, FSAS, FRSE. Professor of Solid State Physics, St. Andrews University, since 1980; b. 7.3.28, Birmingham. Educ. King Edward's High School, Birmingham; Sidney Sussex College, Cambridge. RAF, 1949-51; Staff Scientist, Ericsson Telephones Ltd., 1951-56; Services Electronics Research Laboratory, 1956-68; Visiting Associate Professor, Stanford University, 1964-66; joined Department of Physics, St. Andrews University, 1968. Recreations: archaeology; country dancing. Address: (b.) Department of Physics, St. Andrews University, North Haugh, St. Andrews, Fife, KY16 9SS; T.-0334 76161.

Allison, Joseph Philip Sloan, MA (Cantab), CertEd. Headmaster, St. Mary's Music School, Edinburgh, since 1979; b. 6.2.44, Leeds; m., Caroline Margaret Paton; 2 s.; 1 d. Educ. Rugby; Churchill College, Cambridge; Moray House College of Education. Jardine Matheson & Co. Ltd., Hong Kong, 1967-70; Assistant Master, then Assistant Head, Belhaven Hill, Dunbar, 1970-77; Deputy Head, St. Mary's Music School, 1977-79. Recreations: sailing; bird-watching; hill-walking. Address: (h.) 4 Raeburn Street, Edinburgh, EH4 1HY; T.-031-332 9768.

Allison, Marjorie Elisabeth Marion, BSc, MD, FRCP. Senior Lecturer in Medicine, Glasgow University, since 1977; Honorary Consultant Nephrologist, Glasgow Royal Infirmary, since 1977; b. 7.9.40, Glasgow. Educ. Hamilton Academy; Glasgow University. Clinical training in nephrology, Glasgow Royal Infirmary, 1966-69; Research Fellow in Kidney Pathophysiology, University of North Carolina, 1969-72, 1979-81. Publications: contributed chapters on acute kidney failure to textbooks. Recreations: gardening; cooking; medical antiquities. Address: (b.) Renal Unit, Glasgow Royal Infirmary, Glasgow; T.-041-552 3535, Ext. 5292.

Allison, Robert H., MB, ChB, FFARCSI. Consultant Anaesthetist, Dundee Teaching Hospitals, since 1980; b. 10.2.48, Perth; m., Lizbeth Bain; 1 s.; 2 d. Educ. Perth Academy; St. Andrews University. House Surgeon, Maryfield Hospital, Dundee, 1972; House Physician, Bridge of Earn Hospital, Perth, 1973; Registrar in Anaesthesia, Dundee Teaching Hospitals, 1973-77; Senior Registrar in Anaesthesia, Western Infirmary, Glasgow, 1977-80. Recreation: golf (St Andrews University blue, 1969). Address: (h.) 4 Ericht Road, Wormit, Newport-on-Tay, Fife; T.-0382 541415.

Allsop, Rev. Thomas Douglas, MA, BD. Minister, Beechgrove Church, Aberdeen, since 1977; b. 2.3.34, Kilmaurs; m., Marion Morrison Urie; 2 s.; 1 d. Educ. Kilmarnock Academy; Glasgow University and Trinity College. Assistant Minister, St. Marnock's, Kilmarnock; Minister: Kirriemuir South (after a union called Kirriemuir St. Andrew's), 1959-65; Minister, Knightswood St. Margaret's, Glasgow, 1965-77. Founder Chairman, Kirriemuir Round Table; Moderator, Dumbarton Presbytery, 1975; Burgess, City of Aberdeen. Recreations: photography; golf; musical appreciation. Address: 156 Hamilton Place, Aberdeen, AB2 4BB; T.-0224 642615.

Alty, Professor James Lenton, BSc, PhD, FBCS. Professor of Computer Science, Strathclyde University, since 1982; Executive Director, Turing Institute, Glasgow, since 1984; b. 21.8.39, Haslingden; m., Mary Eleanor; 2 s.; 2 d. Educ. King Edward VII School, Lytham; Liverpool University. Liverpool University: Oliver Lodge Fellow (Nuclear Physics), 1964, Leverhulme Fellow (Metallurgy), 1966; Systems Engineer, Senior Systems Engineer, Account Executive, IBM (UK) Ltd., 1968-72; Director, Computer Laboratory, Liverpool University, 1972-82. Publications: Computing Skills and the User Interface (with M.J. Coombs); Expert Systems - Concepts and Examples (with M.J. Coombs). Recreations: musical composition; mountain climbing. Address: (b.) Computer Science Department, Strathclyde University, Richmond Street, Glasgow; T.-041-552 4400.

Ancram, Michael Andrew Foster Jude, MA, LLB, MP. Minister for Home Affairs and the Environment, Scottish Office, since 1983; MP (Conservative) for Edinburgh South, since 1979; b. London; m., Lady Jane Fitzalan-Howard; 2 d. Educ. Ampleforth; Christ Church, Oxford; Edinburgh University. Advocate, Scottish Bar, 1970; MP, Berwickshire and East Lothian, February to September, 1974; Chairman, Conservative Party in Scotland, 1980-83. Recreations: skiing; folk singing; photography. Address: (h.) 6 Ainslie Place, Edinburgh; T.-031-226 3147.

Anderson, Alexander George, BSc, FIHT, FCIOB, FRSA, FFB. Chairman, Aberdeen Construction Group P.L.C., since 1981; b. 29.7.24, Aberdeen; m., Patricia; 1 s.; 1 d. Educ. Aberdeen Grammar School; Aberdeen University. Chairman, W.J. Anderson Ltd. and Aberdeen Concrete Co. Ltd., 1962; Director, Aberdeen Construction Group and various subsidiaries, 1969-72; Divisional Director, Civil Engineering Division, Aberdeen Construction Group P.L.C., 1972-81. Recreations: amateur radio; philately.

Anderson, Rev. Andrew Fraser, MA, BD. Minister, Greenside Parish Church, since 1981; b. 2.9.44, Aberdeen; m., Hazel Neary; 2 s. Educ. Harrow School; Magdalen College, Oxford; Edinburgh University. Industrial management, Dickinson Robinson Group Ltd., 1967-77. Recreations: music; gardening. Address: (h.) 80 Pilrig Street, Edinburgh, EH6 5AS; T.-031-554 3277.

Anderson, David, MBE, JP. Member, Grampian Regional Council, since 1974 (Leader, Liberal Group, since 1982); b. 17.1.16, St Andrews; m., Jessie Watt Taylor; 2 s.; 1 d. Educ. Madras College, St Andrews. Employed in forestry, various estates in Fife, until 1939; Sergeant, Royal Corps of Signals, 1939-46; various posts in Forestry Commission, 1946-81, latterly as Chief Forester in charge, Huntly Forest; Member, Aberdeen County Council, 1961-74; Chairman, Education Committee, 1973-74. Chairman, Rhynie Branch, Royal British Legion. Recreation: bowling. Address: (h.) Burmah, 6 Watson Avenue, Huntly, Aberdeenshire, AB5 5BF; T.-Huntly 2878.

Anderson, David Colville, VRD, QC, BA Oxon, LLB; b. 8.9.16, Cupar; m., Juliet Hill Watson; 2 s.; 1 d. Educ. Glenalmond College; Pembroke College, Oxford; Edinburgh University. RNVR, 1935-61; served World War II in destroyers; mentioned in Despatches, 1942; special operation, Norway, 1945; King Haakon VII Freedom Medal; Lieutenant Commander, 1947. Advocate, 1946; Lecturer in Scots Law, Edinburgh University, 1947-60; Standing Junior Counsel, Ministry of Works, 1954-55, and War Office, 1955-57; QC, 1957; Solicitor-General for Scotland, 1960-64; MP (Conservative) for Dumfries, 1963-64; Honorary Sheriff, 1965-72; Chairman, Industrial Appeal Tribunals, 1970-72; Chief Reporter for Public Inquiries and Under-Secretary, Scottish Office, 1972-74; Commissioner, Northern Lighthouses, 1960-64. Subject of play, The Case of David Anderson QC, by John Hale. Recreations: travel; hillwalking; golf. Address: (h.) 8 Arboretum Road, Edinburgh, EH3 5PD; T.-031-552 3003.

Anderson, David Rae, MA (Hons), LLB, LLM, WS, NP. Solicitor, since 1961 (Senior Partner in private practice); part-time Legal Chairman, Industrial Tribunals, since 1971; Honorary Sheriff, since 1981; b. 27.1.36, Stonehaven; m., Jean Strachan. Educ. Mackie Academy, Stonehaven; Aberdeen University; Edinburgh University; Australian National University, Canberra. Barrister and Solicitor of Supreme Court of Victoria, Australia, 1962; Legal Officer, Attorney-General's Department, Canberra, 1962-65; part-time research student, Law Faculty, Australian National University, Canberra, and part-time Lecturer in Legal History, 1962-65; returned to Scotland, 1965, in private legal practice, Edinburgh, 1965-67, Alloa and Central Scotland, since 1967; Interim Town Clerk, Burgh of Alva, 1973; former part-time Reporter to Secretary of State for Scotland for public enquiries; Member, Council, Law Society of Scotland. Elder, Church of Scotland; President, Rotary club; former Parliamentary candidate, 1970 and 1971; formerly served, RNVR. Recreations: climbing and hill-walking; reading, especially historical

biography and English literature; music; interested in current affairs, architecture, stately homes and travel. Address: (h.) 3 Smithfield Loan, Alloa, FK10 1NJ; T.-0259 213096; (b.) 8 Shillinghill, Alloa, FK10 1JT; T.-0259 723201.

Anderson, David William, CBE (1976), OBE (1972), ADC (1981). Chief Executive, Cumbernauld Development Corporation, since 1985; b. 4.1.29, Wooler; m., Eileen Dorothy; 1 s.; 2 d. Educ. St. Cuthbert's Grammar School; Royal Military Academy, Sandhurst; Staff College, Camberley. Army service: private soldier to Brigadier, 1946-82; Chief Executive, North East Fife District Council, 1982-85. Recreations: golf; gardening; walking dogs. Address: (b.) Cumbernauld Development Corporation, Cumbernauld House, Cumbernauld.

Anderson, Don S.H., IPFA, FRVA. Director of Finance and Management Services, Clydesdale District Council, since 1983; b. 9.1.43, Forfar; m., Irene R.; 3 d. Educ. Mackie Academy, Stonehaven. Trainee Accountant, Clackmannan County Council, 1961-66; Accountancy Assistant, Airdrie Town Council, 1966-69; Accountant, Kilmarnock Town Council, 1969-75; Finance Manager, Clydesdale District Council, 1975-83. Recreations: golf; swimming. Address: (b.) District Offices, South Vennel, Lanark, ML11 7JT; T.-0555 61331, Ext. 134.

Anderson, Douglas M.W., DSc, PhD, CChem, FRSC, FRSE. Reader in Chemistry, Edinburgh University, since 1954; b. 10.11.25, Edinburgh; m., Margaret Joan Laing; 1 s.; 3 d. Educ. Montrose Academy; Edinburgh University. War Service, RAF, 1943-46 (Radar duties). Secretary and General Scientific Adviser, International Natural Gums Association for Research Ltd.; adviser and consultant to industry; Editor, two series of monographs on aspects of analytical chemistry. Recreations: music; angling; philately; all kinds of DIY. Address: (b.) Chemistry Department, The University, Edinburgh, EH9 3JJ; T.-031-667 1081, Ext. 3446.

Anderson, George, BSc, PhD. Deputy Director, Macaulay Institute for Soil Research, since 1980 (Head of Department of Soil Organic Chemistry, since 1974); b. 20.3.25, Peebles; m., Jeanette Lilian Rayment; 2 s.; 1 d. Educ. Peebles High School; Edinburgh University. Assistant, lecturing and research, Chemistry Department, Edinburgh and East of Scotland College of Agriculture, 1949-52; Research Scientist, Department of Soil Fertility, Macaulay Institute, 1952-73; Honorary Research Associate, Aberdeen University, since 1974. Recreations: walking; photography; tennis. Address: (h.) 5 Cairn Road, Bieldside, Aberdeen; T.-0224 868005.

Anderson, George Alexander Barrie, SDA. Farmer, since 1962; Chairman, Scottish Farm and Food Group, since 1984; Vice President, National Farmers' Union for Scotland, since 1981; b. 4.11.42, Aberdeen; m., Gillian Campbell; 4 s. Educ. Fettes College; North of Scotland College of Agriculture, Aberdeen. Member, Council, British Simmental Cattle Society, 1970-79; Director, Royal Highland & Agricultural Society,

1976-82; Director, North Eastern Farmers Ltd., since 1977; NFU for Scotland: President, Aberdeen Area, 1978-79, Livestock Convener, 1978-84; Member, Governing Body, Animal Diseases Research Association, since 1981. Recreations: no time for any. Address: Kair, Fordoun, by Laurencekirk, Kincardineshire; T.-05612 406.

Anderson, Gordon Alexander, CA, FCMA. Partner, Arthur Young, Chartered Accountants, and predecessor firms, since 1958; Vice President, Institute of Chartered Accountants of Scotland, since 1984; b. 9.8.31, Glasgow; m., Eireme Cochrane Howie Douglas; 2 s.; 1 d. Educ. High School of Glasgow. Apprentice CA, Moores Carson & Watson, Glasgow, 1949-54; qualified CA, 1955; National Service, Royal Navy, 1955-57 (Sub Lieutenant); Partner, Moores Carson & Watson, 1958 (firm name changed to McClelland Moores, 1958, Arthur Young McClelland Moores, 1968, Arthur Young, 1985). Member, Scottish Milk Marketing Board, 1979-85; Member of Council, Institute of Chartered Accountants of Scotland, 1980-84. Recreations: golf; gardening; rugby football (as spectator). Address: (h.) Ardwell, 41 Manse Road, Bearsden, Glasgow, G61 3PN; T.-041-942 2803.

Anderson, Rev. Professor Hugh, MA, BD, PhD, DD. Professor of New Testament Language, Literature and Theology, Edinburgh University, since 1966; b. 18.5.20, Galston, Ayrshire; m., Jean Goldie Torbit; 1 s.; 1 s. (deceased); 1 d. Educ. Kilmarnock Academy; Glasgow University. Chaplaincy work, Egypt and Palestine, 1945-46; Lecturer in Old Testament, Glasgow University, 1946-51; Minister, Trinity Church, Pollokshields, Glasgow, 1951-57; Professor of Biblical Criticism, Duke University, North Carolina, 1957-66; special appointments including A.B. Bruce Lecturer in New Testament, Glasgow University, 1954-57; Katharine McBride Visiting Professor, Bryn Mawr College, Pennsylvania, 1972-73; Kenan Distinguished Visiting Professor, Meredith College, North Carolina, 1982-83; Pendergrass Visiting Professor, Florida Southern College, 1985-86. Awarded Schweitzer Medal from North Carolina History and Science Foundation. Publications: Psalms 1-45; Historians of Israel; The New Testament in Historical and Contemporary Perspective (Editor with W. Barclay); Jesus and Christian Origins; Jesus; The Gospel of Mark: Commentary; 3 and 4 Maccabees (Commentary). Recreations: golf; gardening; music. Address: (h.) 5 Comiston Springs Avenue, Edinburgh, EH10 6NT.

Anderson, James Alexander, BL, NP. Solicitor, since 1948; Member, Glasgow and North Argyll Legal Aid Committee, since 1960; Honorary Sheriff at Oban, since 1980; b. 17.5.21, Glasgow; m., Jean Jeffrey Brown; 2 s.; 1 d. Educ. Elgin Academy; Edinburgh University. Army, 1942-46 (Staff Captain, RA); joined Anderson Banks & Co., Solicitors, Oban, 1950 (Senior Partner); Local Representative, Legal Aid Committee, 1960-79; Dean of Faculty, Oban Procurators, 1975-78. Treasurer and Convener, Business Committee, Lorn & Mull Presbytery;

Treasurer, Oban and District Christian Aid Committee. Recreations: writing; gardening; golf; pool. Address: (b.) 4/6 Stevenson Street, Oban, Argyll; T.-0631 63158.

Anderson, James Frazer Gillan, CBE, JP, DL. Convener, Central Regional Council, since 1974; b. 25.3.29, Maddiston, by Falkirk; m., May Harley; 1 s.; 1 d. Educ. Maddiston School; Graeme High School, Falkirk. Convener, Stirling County Council, 1971-75; Member: Health and Safety Commission, 1974-80; Montgomery Committee, 1982-84; Scottish Economic Committee, since 1983. Treasurer, Maddiston Old Folks Association. Recreations: gardening; walking; reading. Address: (b.) Viewforth, Stirling; T.-Stirling 73111.

Anderson, James Killoch, OBE, MB, ChB, FFCM, FCR, JP. Unit Medical Officer, Glasgow Royal Infirmary and Royal Maternity Hospital, Glasgow; b. 3.2.23, Johnstone; m., Irene Webster Wilson; 1 s.; 2 d. Educ. High School of Glasgow; Glasgow University. Deputy Medical Superintendent, Glasgow Royal Infirmary and Associated Hospitals, 1954; appointed Medical Superintendent, 1957; District Medical Officer, Eastern District, Greater Glasgow Health Board, 1974; Unit Medical Officer, Unit East 1, Greater Glasgow Health Board, 1984. Corps Commandant and Council Member, St. Andrew's Ambulance Association, 1957-82; Member of Committee, Scottish Ambulance Service, 1957-74; Director, North Parish, Washing Green Society, Glasgow, since 1957; Member, Scottish Technical Education Council, since 1974; Member, Science Development Team, 16-18s Action Plan, Scottish Education Department. Recreations: gardening; golf. Address: (h.) 15 Kenilworth Avenue, Helensburgh, G84 7JR; T.-0436 3739.

Anderson, James Masson, OBE, DL, JP, CDA. Farmer, since 1934; Honorary Sheriff, since 1977; b. 21.3.17, Elgin; m., Phyllis Adam Taylor; 1 s.; 1 d. Educ. Elgin Academy; North of Scotland College of Agriculture. Military Service, 1939-46: Seaforth Highlanders and Dogra Regiment (Indian Army). Member, Moray County Council and Joint County Council for Moray and Nairn, 1961-74; Chairman, Moray District Council, 1974-84. Recreations: reading; walking; gardening; bridge. Address: (h.) 6 Fleurs Road, Elgin, Moray, IV30 1TA; T.-0343 7807.

Anderson, John, MA (Hons). Rector, High School of Stirling, since 1982; Vice-Chairman, General Teaching Council for Scotland, since 1982; b. 20.11.37, Oyne, Aberdeenshire; m., Christina M. Murray; 2 d. Educ. Banchory Academy; Aberdeen University. Assistant Teacher, Robert Gordon's College, Aberdeen, 1961-65; Principal Teacher of Geography, Buckie High School, 1965-70; Rector, Speyside High School, 1970-82. Council Member, SCOTVEC. Recreations: golf; fishing. Address: (b.) High School of Stirling, Ogilvie Road, Torbrex, Stirling; T.-Stirling 72451.

Anderson, John Charles Lindsay, VRD (and clasp), OStJ, MA (Oxon), LLB. Solicitor; Senior Partner, J.L. Anderson & Co.; Arable and

Fruit Farmer; Quarrymaster, Fife Redstone and Brackmont Quarries; b. 8.9.08, Cupar; m., Elsie Margaret Begg; 1 s.; 2 d. Educ. St. Salvators, St. Andrews; Glenalmond College; Pembroke College, Oxford; Edinburgh University. Solicitor, since 1931; Member, St. Andrews Town Council, 1938-51 (Honorary Treasurer, 1945-51); Parliamentary candidate (Conservative), West Stirling, 1945; joined RNVR as Sub Lt., 1930; served World War II, Northern Patrol, Convoys, Gunnery Specialist; Captain, RNR, 1954; commanded HMS Unicorn, Tay Division RNVR/RNR, 1954-59; RNR ADC to The Queen, 1959-60; Founder Governor, Unicorn Preservation Society, since 1968; Member, Business Committee, Edinburgh University General Council, since 1982; Member, Council, Law Society of Scotland, since 1983; President, Royal Caledonian Curling Club, 1978-79; Chairman, Kirkcaldy Ice Rink, since 1978; Honorary President, St. Andrews Branch, Royal British Legion. Recreations: curling; shooting; golf; tennis. Address: (h.) Pittormie, Dairsie, Fife, KY15 4SW; T.-0334 870233.

Anderson, John MacKenzie, MB, ChB, DPath, FRCPath. Consultant Histopathologist, Dundee Hospitals, since 1975; Honorary Senior Lecturer in Pathology, Dundee University, since 1975; b. 13.8.35, Dundee; m., Mary Ursula Nolan; 2 s.; 2 d. Educ. Dollar Academy; St. Andrews University. Medical Officer, RAMC, 1960-63; Assistant Pathologist, Glasgow Royal Infirmary, 1959-60 and 1963-65; Maudsley Hospital, London, 1965-67; Consultant Pathologist, Greenock Hospitals, 1967-69; Stobhill Hospital, Glasgow, 1969-70; Royal Hospital for Sick Children, Edinburgh, 1970-75. Recreations: golf; gardening; and other cultural activities. Address: (b.) Department of Pathology, Ninewells Hospital, Dundee; T.-Dundee 60111, Ext. 2667.

Anderson, Joseph Aitken, BA (Hons), CSD, MBIM. Managing Director, North of Scotland Milk Marketing Board, since 1982; Director, Company of Scottish Cheesemakers, since 1983; b. 1.7.36, Prestonpans; m., Sheila Armstrong; 2 s. Educ. Preston Lodge; Open University. Managing Secretary: Carluke Co-operative Society, 1962-65, East Fife Co-operative Society, 1965-71; Depute Chief Executive, Central and East Fife Co-operative Society, 1971-79; Executive Officer and Secretary, Fife Regional Co-operative Society, 1979-82. Member, United Kingdom Dairy Association Council; Chairman, NE Branch, Society of Dairy Technology. Recreations: golf; fly fishing; photography. Address: (b.) 29 Ardconnel Terrace, Inverness; T.-0463 232611.

Anderson, Kathleen Janette, BSc, PhD, CBiol, FIBiol, CChem, FRSC. Depute Principal, Napier College, Edinburgh, since 1983; b. 22.5.27, Glasgow; m., Mark Elliot Muir Anderson; 1 s.; 1 d. Educ. Queens Park School, Glasgow; Glasgow University. Lecturer, West of Scotland Agricultural College, Glasgow, 1948-54; Johnson and Florence Stoney Research Fellow, University of Sydney, Australia, 1952-53; Commonwealth Travelling Research Fellow, Australia and New Zealand, 1953; Sir James Knott Research Fellow,

Durham University, 1955-57; King's College, Durham University: Lecturer in Biochemistry, 1958-59, Lecturer in Microbiology, 1962-63, Lecturer (part-time) in Landscape Horticulture, 1963-65, Lecturer (part-time), Extra-Mural Department, 1959-65; Lecturer (part-time), Department of Extra-Mural Studies, Edinburgh University, 1965-68; Napier College, Edinburgh: Senior Lecturer, Department of Biological Sciences, 1968-69, Head of Department, Biological Sciences, 1969-83. Crown Trustee, National Library for Scotland, since 1981; Deacon, Church of Scotland, 1974-78, Elder, since 1978; CNAA Environmental Sciences Board, since 1978; Chairman: Joint Committee for Biology, SCOTEC, since 1979, Biology Board D1, SCOTEC, since 1980; Institute of Biology: Chairman, Scottish Branch, 1977-79, Member of Council, 1977-80, Fellowship Committee, 1980-83, Environment Division, 1982-86; Founder Chairman, Heads of Biology in Tertiary Education, 1975-77; Heads of Biology in Polytechnics, 1974-83; Nurse Education Committee, Royal Edinburgh Hospital, 1974-77; Council Member, SCOTVEC, since 1984. Publications: Discover Lothian Beaches; Holyrood Park Teachers Handbook; Safety in Biological Laboratories. Recreations: primary Sunday School leader; knitting; gardening; foreign travel. Address: (b.) Napier College, Colinton Road, Edinburgh, EH10 5DT; T.-031-447 7070.

Anderson, Kenneth D., MA. Rector, Grove Academy, Broughty Ferry, since 1981; b. 13.11.31, Glasgow; m., Heather; 1 s. Educ. Glasgow Academy; University College, Oxford. Teacher of Classics, Dunfermline High School, 1955-62; Principal Teacher of Classics: Beath High School, 1962-64, Robert Gordon's College, Aberdeen, 1964-72; Assistant Head Teacher, Portobello High School, Edinburgh, 1972-75; Deputy Rector, Perth Grammar School, 1975-81. Recreations: choral singing; Church work. Address: (b.) Grove Academy, Camperdown Street, Broughty Ferry, Dundee; T.-0382 730284.

Anderson, Professor Malcolm, MA, DPhil Oxon. Professor of Politics, University of Edinburgh, since 1979; b. 13.5.34, Knutsford; 2 s.; 1 d. Educ. Altrincham Grammar School; University College, Oxford. Lecturer in Government, Manchester University, 1960-63; Research Fellow, Institut National des Sciences Politiques, 1964-65; Senior Lecturer, then Professor, Warwick University, 1965-79; Visiting Fellow, Institute of Higher Studies, Vienna, 1977-78; temporary teaching posts in North America. Chairman, University Association for Contemporary European Studies. Publications: Government in France, 1970; Conservative Politics in France, 1974; Frontier Regions in Western Europe, 1983. Recreations: walking; reading; photography. Address: (h.) 72 Dundas Street, Edinburgh, EH3 6QZ; T.-031-556 2113.

Anderson, Moira, OBE. Singer; b. Kirkintilloch; m., Dr. Stuart Macdonald. Educ. Ayr Academy; Royal Scottish Academy of Music, Glasgow. Began with Kirkintilloch Junior Choir, aged six; made first radio broadcast for BBC in Scotland, aged eight; was Teacher of Music in Ayr before becoming professional singer; made first professional broadcast, White Heather Club, 1960; has toured overseas, had her own radio and TV series; has introduced Stars on Sunday, ITV; appeared in summer shows, cabaret, pantomime and numerous other stage shows; several Royal Variety performances.

Anderson, Noel Barber, JP, BSc, MICE, CEng, DipTP. Buildings Officer, Edinburgh University, since 1971; b. 25.12.25, Edinburgh; m., Vera Gair Sutherland; 1 s.; 3 d. Educ. George Watson's Boys College; Edinburgh University. Engineering Assistant, Partridge Earp and Partners; South of Scotland Electricity Board; Lothian River Purification Board; Cumbernauld Development Corporation; Assistant Buildings Officer, Edinburgh University. Member, Board of Management, Edinvar Housing Association. Recreations: hill-walking; pottering. Address: (b.) University of Edinburgh, Old College, South Bridge, Edinburgh; T.-031-667 1011, Ext. 4345.

Anderson, Peter David, MA, PhD, FSA Scot. Conservation Officer, Scottish Record Office, since 1985; b. 10.3.47, Greenock; m., Jean Johnstone Smith; 1 s.; 1 d. Educ. Hutchesons' Grammar School, Glasgow; St. Andrews University; Edinburgh University. Assistant Teacher of History, Cranhill Secondary School, Glasgow, 1972-73; Research Assistant, Scottish Record Office, 1974-80; Registrar, National Register of Archives (Scotland), 1980-83; Secretary, NRA(S), 1984-85. Honorary Secretary, Scottish Oral History Group, since 1984. Publication: Robert Stewart, Earl of Orkney, Lord of Shetland, 1533-93, 1982. Recreations: drawing and painting; drama. Address: 76 Burghmuir Court, Linlithgow, EH49 7LR; T.-Linlithgow 844663.

Anderson, Robert David, MA, DPhil. Reader in History, Edinburgh University, since 1985; b. 11.7.42, Cardiff. Educ. Taunton School, Somerset; Queen's and St. Antony's Colleges, Oxford. Assistant Lecturer, Glasgow University, 1967-69; Lecturer, then Senior Lecturer, Edinburgh University, 1969-85. Publications: Education in France 1848-1870, 1975; France 1870-1914: Politics and Society, 1977; Education and Opportunity in Victorian Scotland, 1983 (winner, Scottish Arts Council Literary Award, 1984). Address: (b.) Department of History, Edinburgh University, Edinburgh; T.-031-667 1011.

Anderson, Robert Geoffrey William, BSc, MA, DPhil, FRSC. Director, National Museums of Scotland, since 1985 (Director, Royal Scottish Museum, 1984-85); b. 2.5.44; m.; 2 s. Educ. Woodhouse School, London; St. John's College, Oxford. Assistant Keeper: Royal Scottish Museum, 1970-75, Science Museum, 1975-78; Deputy Keeper, Wellcome Museum of History of Medicine and Secretary, Advisory Council, Science Museum, 1978-80; Keeper, Department of Chemistry, Science Museum, 1980-84.

Anderson, Professor William, BSc, PhD, FPS. Professor of Pharmacy, Strathclyde University, since 1970; b. 22.11.27, Edinburgh; m., Anne C. Inglis; 2 s. Educ. Boroughmuir School; Strathclyde University. Head of pharmaceutical

research and development in drug industry; Professor of Pharmaceutical Technology, later Pharmacy. Recreations: wood-working; gardening; golf; Christian literature. Address: (h.) 24 Rosemount Place, Gourock, Renfrewshire.

Anderson, William. Editor, The Sunday Post, since 1967; b. 10.2.34, Motherwell; m., Margaret Cross McClelland; 3 s. Educ. Dalziel High School; Glasgow University. Journalist since first producing school newspapers, with interruptions as cook steward, male nurse, medical student and Army officer. Recreations: fishing; sailing; cooking. Address: (b.) Courier Building, Meadowside, Dundee; T.-0382 23131.

Anderson, William Archibald, MC, TD, JP, MA. Member, Shetland Islands Council, since 1982; b. 22.12.19, Edinburgh; m., Patricia Smith (daughter of late Ex-Provost James A. Smith); 2 s. Educ. Daniel Stewart's College; Aberdeen University. Served with Black Watch (RHR), 1939-46. Woollen manufacturer, 1946-52; schoolmaster, 1952-82. Recreations: gardening; golf. Address: (h.) The Sea Chest, East Voe, Scalloway, Shetland; T.-Scalloway 326.

Anderson, William Beveridge, OBE, MA, FEIS. Chairman of Governing Body, Aberdeen College of Education, since 1983; b. 29.1.23, Dunfermline; m., Mary Lowson Stewart; 1 s.; 1 d. Educ. Bell Baxter High School, Cupar; St. Andrews University. Rector: Kingussie High School, 1964-68, Inverness High School, 1968-83; Governor, Aberdeen College of Education, since 1971; Member, SJNC (FE), since 1982; Life Member, Educational Institute of Scotland. Recreations: music; fishing; walking. Address: 21 Cairnhill Gardens, St Andrews, Fife, KY16 8QY.

Anderson, Professor Sir (William) Ferguson, KT (1974), OBE, MB, MD, FRCPG, FRCPE, FRCP, FRCPI, FRCP (C), KStJ. Vice-President, Age Concern (Scotland); Vice-President, Abbeyfield Society; Chairman, Scottish Retirement Council; Honorary President, Crossroads (Scotland) Care Attendant Schemes; b. 8.4.14; m.; 1 s.; 2 d. Educ. Merchiston Castle School; Glasgow Academy; Glasgow University. David Cargill Professor of Geriatric Medicine, Glasgow University, 1965-79; President, British Medical Association, 1977-78; St. Mungo Prize, Glasgow, 1968.

Anderson, William Lilburn, JP, BSc. Head Teacher, Aith Junior High School, Shetland, since 1966; b. 10.3.31, Glasgow; 4 d. Educ. Hillhead High School; Glasgow University. Regional Secretary (Shetland), EIS; Second Coxswain, Aith Lifeboat, RNLI. Recreation: building. Address: (h.) Schoolhouse, Aith, Bixter, Shetland, ZE2 9NB; T.-0595 81414.

Andrew, Douglas Graham, MA (Cantab), LLB. Partner, Morton Fraser & Milligan, WS, since 1956; b. 19.5.26, Elgin; m., Gratian Elizabeth Salvesen; 2 s. Educ. Uppingham; Emmanuel College, Cambridge; Edinburgh University. Writer to the Signet. Recreations: bird-watching; wildlife conservation. Address: (h.) Muirfield Gate, Gullane, East Lothian; T.-0620 843307.

Andrew, William, MA. Writer; b. 31.8.31, Glasgow. Educ. Shawlands Academy, Glasgow; Glasgow University. Taught English in London and Glasgow; turned to full-time writing, 1979; plays for stage, radio and television, including Project Flora, The Best Baby, Behind the Circle; numerous episodes of Take The High Road, STV; several short stories. Council Member, Scottish Society of Playwrights, 1975-83. Recreations: local history; cats. Address: (h.) 24 Queen's Drive, Glasgow, G42; T.-041-423 8033.

Angus, David George, MA (Hons), DipEd. Freelance Writer and Lecturer; b. 20.4.25, Brora; m., Florence Jean Manson. Educ. Inverness Royal Academy; Lanark Grammar School; Edinburgh University. Assistant Teacher of English, Beath High School, 1951-59; freelance Writer, Edinburgh, 1959-61; Special Assistant Teacher of English, Alloa Academy, 1961-71; Extramural Lecturer in Scottish Literature, Stirling University, ten years; has published verse in Scots, English and French; contributed prose in Scots to Lallans magazine and in English to Scots Magazine and The Scotsman; Historian, Edinburgh Wax Museum; former Council Member and Vice-Chairman, Saltire Society; founder Member and former Secretary, Scots Language Society. Publication: Roses and Thorns - Scottish Teenage Verse (Editor). Recreations: historical, literary and genealogical research. Address: (h.) 122 Henderson Street, Bridge of Allan, Stirling, FK9 4HF; T.-832306.

Annan, Hugh Ross, BL. Procurator Fiscal, Linlithgow, since 1976; b. 27.12.34, Perth; m., Sheila McNicol; 2 s. Educ. Bell-Baxter School, Cupar; St. Andrews University. Solicitor, 1959; Procurator Fiscal, Cupar, February-October, 1976. Recreations: reading; astronomy. Address: (h.) 14 Deacons Court, Linlithgow, West Lothian; T.-Linlithgow 844684.

Annand, James King, MA. Writer; b. 2.2.08, Edinburgh; m., Beatrice Violet Lindsay; 4 d. Educ. Broughton Secondary School, Edinburgh; Edinburgh University. Assistant Teacher, James Clark School, Edinburgh, 1932-49 (War Service, Royal Navy, 1941-46); Lecturer in Current Affairs, Regent Road Day Release Centre, 1949-53; Principal Teacher of History, James Clark School, 1953-58; Headmaster, Whithorn Junior Secondary School, 1959-62; Principal Teacher of History, Firrhill Secondary School, Edinburgh, 1962-71. Founder Member and holder of various offices, Scottish Youth Hostels Association, since 1931; Council Member: Saltire Society, 1951-54, Historical Association of Scotland, 1954-58; founder Member, Scots Language Society, 1972 (Honorary Vice-President, since 1983); Councillor, Royal Burgh of Whithorn, 1960-62; Editor: The Rebel Student, 1929, Lines Review, 1958-59, Lallans, 1973-83. Awarded Burns Chronicle Poetry Prize, 1955; Scottish Arts Council Special Award for contribution to Scottish poetry, 1979. Publications: Sing it Aince for Pleisure, 1965; Two Voices, 1968; Twice for Joy, 1973; Poems and Translations, 1975; Songs from Carmina Burana, 1978; Thrice to Show Ye, 1979; Dod and Davie, 1985; Early Lyrics by Hugh MacDiarmid (Editor), 1968;

A Scots Handsel (Editor), 1980. Recreations: mountaineering; natural history; photography; book-binding. Address: (h.) 10 House o Hill Row, Edinburgh, EH4 2AW; T.-031-332 6905.

Annand, Louise Gibson, MBE, MA (Hons), AMA. Artist; Member, Royal Fine Art Commission for Scotland, since 1979; b. 27.5.15, Uddingston; m., Alistair Matheson (deceased). Educ. Hamilton Academy; Glasgow University. Teacher, primary and secondary schools, Glasgow, 1939-49; Assistant, Schools Museum Service, 1949-70; Museums Education Officer, 1970-80. Past Chairman: Scottish Educational Film Association (Glasgow Production Group); Glasgow Lady Artists Club Trust; National Vice-Chairman, Scottish Educational Media Association, 1979-84; President: Society of Scottish Women Artists, 1963-66 and 1980-85; Glasgow Society of Women Artists, 1977-79; Visiting Lecturer in Scottish Art, Regina University, 1982; Chairman, J.D. Fergusson Foundation, since 1982 (Trustee, since 1983); Member, Business Committee, General Council, University of Glasgow, since 1981; exhibited widely since 1945; produced numerous 16mm films, including the first on Charles Rennie Mackintosh, 1966. Recreations: mountaineering (Ladies Scottish Climbing Club). Address: (h.) 22 Kingsborough Gardens, Glasgow, G12 9NJ; T.-041-339 8956.

Annandale and Hartfell, Earl of, (Patrick Andrew Wentworth Hope Johnstone of Annandale and of That Ilk). Farmer; Chief, Clan Johnstone; Baron of the Barony of the Lands of the Earldom of Annandale and Hartfell, and of the Lordship of Johnstone; Hereditary Steward, Stewartry of Annandale; Hereditary Keeper, Keys of Lochmaben Castle; Member, Dumfries and Galloway Regional Council, since 1975; b. 19.4.41, Auldgirth, Dumfriesshire; m., Susan Josephine; 1 s.; 1 d. Educ. Stowe School; Royal Agricultural College, Cirencester. Member: Dumfriesshire County Council, 1970-75, Scottish Valuation Advisory Council, 1982, Solway River Purification Board, 1973; Underwriter, Lloyds, London, 1976. Address: (b.) Annandale Estates Office, St. Anns, Lockerbie, Dumfriesshire; T.-Johnstone Bridge 317.

Anstruther, Sir Ralph (Hugo), 7th Bt, KCVO, MC, DL, BA. Equerry to the Queen Mother, since 1959; b. 13.6.21. Educ. Eton; Magdalene College, Cambridge. Member, Queen's Bodyguard for Scotland (Royal Company of Archers); DL, Fife, 1960; DL, Caithness-shire, 1965. Address: Balcaskie, Pittenweem, Fife; Watten, Caithness.

Arbuthnott, David Carnegie, FIB (Scot), MIPM. General Manager (Staff), Royal Bank of Scotland, since 1977; b. 27.3.26, Aberdeen; m., Nora Pirie Duguid; 1 d. Educ. Robert Gordon's College, Aberdeen. Entered service of Commercial Bank of Scotland Ltd., 1941; War Service, Fleet Air Arm; Royal Bank: Assistant Staff Manager, 1966, Staff Manager, 1970. Council Member, Institute of Bankers in Scotland; Member, CBI Scotland Employment Committee. Recreations: golf; gardening. Address: (h.) 88 Whitehouse Road, Cramond, Edinburgh; T.-031-336 5239.

Arbuthnott, 16th Viscount of (John Campbell Arbuthnott), DSC, FRSE, FRSA, KStJ, MA. Lord Lieutenant, Grampian Region (Kincardineshire), since 1977; Chairman, Scottish Widows' Fund and Life Assurance Society, since 1984; b. 26.10.24; m.; 1 s.; 1 d. Educ. Fettes College; Gonville and Caius College, Cambridge. Member, Countryside Commission for Scotland, 1967-71; Chairman, Red Deer Commission, 1969-75; Member, Aberdeen University Court, since 1978; President, Scottish Landowners Federation, 1974-79; President, Royal Zoological Society of Scotland, since 1976; President, Scottish Agricultural Organisation Society, 1980-83; Deputy Chairman, Nature Conservancy Council, since 1980. Address: (h.) Arbuthnott House, by Laurencekirk, Kincardineshire.

Arbuthnott, The Hon. William David, MBE. Regimental Secretary, The Black Watch, since 1978; b. 5.11.27, Colchester; m., Sonja Mary Thomson; 1 s.; 2 d. Educ. Fettes. Army Officer, The Black Watch, since 1948. Recreations: gardening; reading; civil engineering. Address: (h.) The Old Manse, Trochry, by Dunkeld, PH8 ODY; T.-Trochry 205.

Argyll, 12th Duke of, (Ian Campbell). Chief of Clan Campbell; Hereditary Master of the Royal Household, Scotland; Hereditary High Sheriff of the County of Argyll; Admiral of the Western Coast and Isles; Keeper of the Great Seal of Scotland and of the Castles of Dunstaffnage, Dunoon, and Carrick and Tarbert; b. 28.8.37; m., Iona Mary Colquhoun; 1 s.; 1 d. Educ. Le Rosey, Switzerland; Glenalmond; McGill University, Montreal. Member, Queen's Bodyguard for Scotland (Royal Company of Archers). Address: Inveraray Castle, Inveraray, Argyll.

Armour, Archibald, MA (Hons), FEIS. Head Teacher, Camphill High School, Paisley, 1975-85; b. 3.6.20, Paisley; m., Margaret B.L. Hebditch; 1 s.; 1 d. Educ. Camphill Senior Secondary School, Paisley; Glasgow University. Teacher, Camphill Senior Secondary School, 1950-54; Principal Teacher of English: Abercorn Junior Secondary School, Paisley, 1954-61, Renfrew High School, 1961-68 (Depute Head, 1965-68); Head Teacher, Mount School (later Cowdenknowes High School), Greenock, 1968-75. President, Educational Institute of Scotland, 1976-77 (Vice-President, 1971-72). Recreations: golf; gardening; bridge; Burns Suppers. Address: (h.) Marvin, 9 Douglas Avenue, Elderslie, Johnstone, PA5 9ND; T.-Johnstone 20884.

Armour, Professor James, PhD, Dr hc Utrecht, MRCVS. Professor of Veterinary Parasitology (Personal Chair), Glasgow University, since 1976; b. 17.9.29, Basra, Iraq; m., Irene Morris; 2 s.; 2 d. Educ. Marr College, Troon; Glasgow University. Colonial veterinary service, Nigeria, 1953-60; Research Scientist, Wellcome Ltd., 1960-63; Glasgow University: Research Fellow, 1963-67, Lecturer/Senior Lecturer, 1967-73, Reader, 1973-76; Dean Elect, Faculty of Veterinary Medicine. Member, Government Committee on Animal Medicines; Chairman, Editorial Board, In Practice (veterinary journal). Publications:

joint author of textbook on veterinary parasitology; edited two books; 150 scientific articles. Recreation: golf. Address: (h.) 10 Willockston Road, Troon, Ayrshire; T.-0292 314068.

Armour, John Campbell (Ian), TD. Organising Secretary, Glasgow and West of Scotland Blood Transfusion Service, since 1983; b. 29.9.48, Glasgow; m., Margaret Catherine Leitch; 2 d. Educ. Bearsden Academy. Retail travel industry, 1964-74; sales and marketing appointments in travel industry, 1974-82. Member, Executive Council, Scottish National Blood Transfusion Association. Recreations: railway history; bowling; music. Address: (b.) 80 St. Vincent Street, Glasgow, G2 5UA; T.-041-226 4111.

Armour, Mary Nicol Neill, DA, RSA, RSW, RGI, LLD Glasgow (1980). Artist; b. 27.3.02, Blantyre; m., William Armour. Educ. Hamilton Academy; Glasgow School of Art. Elected ARSA, 1941; RSW, 1956; RSA, 1958; RGI, 1977; Honorary President: Glasgow School of Art, 1982; Royal Glasgow Institute of the Fine Arts, 1983; Vice President, Paisley Art Institute, 1983. Guthrie Award, RSA, 1937; Cargill Prize, RGI, 1972. Recreations: gardening; dressmaking. Address: 2 Gateside Place, Kilbarchan, PA10 2LY; T.-Kilbarchan 2873.

Armson, Rev. Canon John Moss, MA, PhD. Principal, Edinburgh Theological College, since 1982; Canon, St. Mary's Cathedral, Edinburgh, since 1982; Pantonian Professor of Theology, since 1982; b. 21.12.39, Coalville, Leicestershire. Educ. Wyggeston Grammar School; Selwyn College, Cambridge; St. Andrews University. Chaplain and Fellow, Downing College, Cambridge, 1969-73; Vice-Principal, Westcott House, Cambridge, 1973-82. Recreation: pottering in the garden. Addres: The Theological College, Rosebery Crescent, Edinburgh, EH12 5JT; T.-031-337 3838.

Armstrong, Andrew, MB, ChB, FRCPEdin, MRCPGlas. Consultant Physician, Dumfries and Galloway Royal Infirmary, since 1968 (Postgraduate Tutor, since 1981); Honorary Clinical Lecturer, Aberdeen University, since 1968; b. 3.12.29, Edinburgh; m., Dr. Norah Evelyn Stewart; 2 s.; 1 d. Educ. Edinburgh University. Recreations: mountaineering; skiing; curling. Address: (h.) Deil's Dike, Lochmaben, Dumfriesshire; T.-Lochmaben 514.

Armstrong, Edward Calvert, MBE, FSA Scot. Member, Dumfries and Galloway Regional Council, since 1982; b. 20.11.16, Langholm. Educ. Langholm Academy. Joined staff of Stevenson & Johnstone, WS, Langholm, 1935; appointed Depute Town Clerk, Langholm, 1939; undistinguished service, RAF, 1940-46; appointed Town Clerk/Town Chamberlain etc., Langholm, 1946; on reorganisation, became Local Government Officer for Eskdale, 1975-81. Honorary President, Langholm Operatic Society; Founder President, Langholm Rotary and Probus Clubs; Chairman, local committee, Earl Haig Fund. Recreations: reading; photography; music. Address: (h.) 2 Charlotte Street, Langholm, DG13 ODZ; T.-0541 80810.

Armstrong, John Frederick Cunningham.
Managing Director, Mallinson-Denny (Scotland)
Ltd., since 1981; Executive Director, Mallinson-
Denny Group Ltd., since 1985; Member, Forth
Valley Health Board, since 1983; b. 29.12.39,
Glasgow; m., Evelyn Myra Armstrong McKell; 2
s.; 1 d. Educ. Merchiston Castle School. Engin-
eering apprenticeship, Albion Motors, Glasgow,
1958-63; Technical Sales Department, Albion
Motors, 1963-64; Assistant Export Sales Manager
(Far East and Africa), Leyland Motors, 1964-
66; Export Sales Manager, Gloster-Saro Ltd.,
1966-70; Assistant Regional Manager - Africa,
British Leyland, 1970-73; Managing Director,
Leyland Ghana Ltd., 1973-75; Assistant
Managing Director, Leyland East Africa Ltd.,
1975-76; Managing Director, Leyland Kenya
Ltd., Leyland East Africa Ltd., Leyland Albion
Uganda Ltd., and Leyland Albion Tanzania
Ltd., 1976-81. Recreations: golf; fishing; skiing;
curling. Address: (h.) Glenairthrey, 12 Upper
Glen Road, Bridge of Allan, Stirling, FK9 4PX;
T.-0786 832862.

Armstrong, Rev. William Sinclair, MA, BD.
Minister, Penninghame St. John's, Newton
Stewart, since 1971; b. 7.3.24, Coventry; m.,
Jessie Clowes Hazle Kerr; 3 d. Educ. Dalziel
High School, Motherwell; Glasgow University;
Edinburgh University. Member, British Section,
Palestine Police Force, 1943-46; Minister: Parish
of Rothes, 1951-55, Trinity Church, Renfrew,
1955-66, St. Marnock's Parish Church, Kilmar-
nock, 1966-71. Publication: Trinity Church,
Renfrew, 1862-1962. Recreations: reading; the-
atre; music; gardening; curling. Address: The
Manse, Newton Stewart, Wigtownshire, DG8
6HH; T.-0671 2259.

Arnold, James Edward, BA, CertEd. Manager,
New Lanark Conservation Trust, since 1974;
b. 16.3.45, Glasgow; m., Rose. Educ. Caludon
Castle Comprehensive School; York University;
London University. Recreations: New Lanark
and life. Address: (b.) The Counting House,
New Lanark, Lanark; T.-0555 61345.

Arnott, Rev. Andrew David Keltie, MA, BD.
Minister, Netherlee Church, Glasgow, since 1977;
b. 22.7.45, Dunfermline; m., Rosemary Jane
Batchelor; 2 s.; 1 d. Educ. George Watson's
College, Edinburgh; St. Andrews University;
Edinburgh University. Assistant Minister, St.
Ninian's Church, Greenock, 1970-71; Minister,
Stobhill Church, Gorebridge, 1971-75, and re-
named Gorebridge Church, 1975-77. Recreation:
fishing. Address: 532 Clarkston Road, Glasgow,
G44 3RT; T.-041-637 2884.

Arnott, James Mackay, TD, BL. Solicitor;
Partner, MacRobert Son & Hutchison, Glasgow
and Paisley, since 1964; b. 22.3.35, Blackford,
Perthshire; m., Jean Barbara Allan; 3 s. Educ.
Merchiston Castle School, Edinburgh; Edinburgh
University. National Service, RAF, 1957-60;
TA, 1961-77. Council Member, Law Society of
Scotland, since 1983 (Convenor, Law Reform
Committee). Recreation: cricket. Address: (b.)
91 West George Street, Glasgow, G2 1PA;
T.-041-204 2888; 27 Walker Street, Edinburgh,
EH3 7HX; T.-031-226 2552.

Aronson, Sheriff Hazel Josephine, LLB. Sheriff
of Lothian and Borders at Edinburgh, since 1983;
b. 12.1.46, Glasgow; m., John A. Cosgrove; 1
s.; 1 d. Educ. Glasgow High School for Girls;
Glasgow University. Advocate at Scottish Bar,
1968-79; Sheriff of Glasgow and Strathkelvin at
Glasgow, 1979-83. Recreations: reading; walking;
opera; foreign travel. Address: (h.) 14 Gordon
Terrace, Edinburgh, EH16 7QR; T.-031-667
8955.

Arthur, David S.C., MA (Hons), DipEd.
Principal, Lomond School, Helensburgh, since
1977; b. 23.2.30, Kenya; m., Mary Frost; 3 d.
Educ. Loretto School, Musselburgh; Edinburgh
University; Moray House College of Education.
Assistant Teacher: Larchfield, 1954-56, Melville
College, 1957-62; Senior History Master, Robert
Gordon's College, 1962-68; Depute Rector, High
School of Stirling, 1968-70; Rector, Greenfaulds
High School, 1970-76. Chairman: Samaritans
(Scotland), 1960-68, Samaritans Inc., 1972-76.
Publication: Someone To Turn To. Recreations:
gardening; hill-walking; photography; tennis.
Address: (h.) Underwood, Sutherland Crescent,
Helensburgh, Dunbartonshire; T.-0436 2476.

Arthur, Peter Drummond, BSc, PhD, CEng,
MICE, MIStructE. Senior Lecturer in Civil
Engineering, Glasgow University, since 1965; b.
4.7.27, Glasgow; m., Jean Brown Robb; 1 s.; 2 d.
Educ. Queen's Park Senior Secondary School;
Glasgow University. Babtie Shaw & Morton, civil
engineers, 1947-51; Assistant, Glasgow Univer-
sity, 1951-52; Lecturer: St. Andrews University,
1952-58, Glasgow University, 1958-64; Visiting
Professor, University of Madras, 1964-66; Senior
Lecturer, Glasgow University, 1966-81; Reader,
University of Malawi, 1981-83. Past Chairman,
The Concrete Society - Scotland. Publication:
Ultimate Strength Design for Structural Con-
crete (Co-author). Address: (b.) Department
of Civil Engineering, The University, Glasgow,
G12 8QQ; T.-041-339 8855.

Ashley-Miller, Michael, MA, BM, BCh,
D(Obst)RCOG, DPH, FFCM. Senior Principal
Medical Officer, Scottish Home and Health De-
partment, since 1983; b. 1.12.30, London; m.,
Yvonne Marcell; 3 d. Educ. Charterhouse; Ox-
ford University; Kings College Hospital. Kings
College Hospital, 1956-57; Dulwich Hospital,
1957-58; RAF, 1958-61; Isle of Wight County
Council, 1961-64; Medical Research Council,
1964-74; entered Scottish Home and Health
Department, 1974; Director, Chief Scientist
Office, 1977. Recreations: tennis; golf; walking;
collecting miniatures. Address: (h.) 22 Belgrave
Crescent, Edinburgh, EH4; T.-031-332 9203.

Ashmall, Harry Alfred, MA, MLitt, FBIM. Rector, Morrison's Academy, since 1979; presenter
of religious programmes on radio and television, since 1976; b. 22.2.39, Stirling; m., Edna
Reid; 2 d. Educ. Kilsyth Academy; Glasgow
University. Teacher and Careers Master, High
School of Glasgow, 1961-66; Principal Teacher of
History and Modern Studies, Lochend Secondary School; Principal Teacher of History, High
School of Glasgow; Rector, Forfar Academy,
1971-79. Member, Executive and Central Committees, World Council of Churches; various

national committees, Church of Scotland; Elder and Lay Reader; Member: Scottish Council for Research in Education; Schools Broadcasting Council. Publications: The High School of Glasgow: a history, 1976; Belief yet Betrayal, 1971; Preparing a Staff Manual, 1977; Pupils and their courses, 1981. Recreations: reading; skiing; golf. Address: (b.) Morrison's Academy, Crieff, PH7 3AN; T.-0764 3885.

Athanas, Christopher Nicholas, MA, LLB. Partner, Dundas & Wilson, Solicitors, Edinburgh, since 1969; b. 26.8.41, Aden; m., Sheena Anne Stewart; 1 s.; 2 d. Educ. Fettes College, Edinburgh; Aberdeen University. Law Apprentice, then Legal Assistant, Paull & Williamsons, Advocates, Aberdeen, 1964-68; Legal Assistant, Dundas & Wilson, Solicitors, Edinburgh, 1968-69. Member, Society of Writers to the Signet; Invited Member, Edinburgh Registrars Group; former Director, Edinburgh Junior Chamber of Commerce. Recreations: art; angling; golf; philately; walking. Address: (b.) Dundas & Wilson, 25 Charlotte Square, Edinburgh; T.-031-225 1234.

Atholl, The Duke of, ((George) Iain Murray), MA. Chairman, Westminster Press Ltd.; Chairman, RNLI, since 1979; Vice-President, National Trust for Scotland, since 1975; Honorary President, Scottish Wildlife Trust, since 1974; b. 19.6.31, London. Educ. Eton; Christ Church, Oxford. Past Convener, Scottish Landowners Federation; Member, Committee on the Preparation of Legislation; Member, Red Deer Commission, 1969-83. Recreations: golf; bridge; shooting; stalking. Address: (h.) Blair Castle, Blair Atholl, Perthshire; T.-Blair Atholl 212.

Atkinson Brian, MM, MNI. Harbour Master, Aberdeen, since 1970; b. 31.7.32, Kingston-upon-Hull; m., Nancy; 2 s.; 2 d. Educ. Hymers College. Ship management, Merchant Navy officer, 1951-62; port management, since 1963. Honorary Secretary and Launching Authority, Aberdeen Branch, RNLI. Recreations: curling; shooting; gardening; DIY; boat construction. Address: (h.) Granuaille, 24 North Deeside Road, Peterculter, Aberdeen, AB1 OQP; T.-Aberdeen 733134.

Attridge, Professor Derek, BA (Hons), MA, PhD. Professor (and Chairman of Department) of English Studies, Strathclyde University, since 1984; b. 6.5.45, Dundee, Natal, South Africa. Educ. Maritzburg College; University of Natal; Cambridge University. Research Lecturer, Christ Church, Oxford, 1971-73; Department of English, Southampton University: Lecturer, 1973-83, Senior Lecturer, 1983-84; Visiting Professor: University of Illinois, 1980, Rutgers University, New Jersey, 1984. Publications: Well-Weighed Syllables: Elizabethan Verse in Classical Metres, 1974; The Rhythms of English Poetry, 1982; Post-Structuralist Joyce: Essays from the French (Co-Editor), 1984. Address: (b.) Department of English Studies, Strathclyde University, Livingstone Tower, 26 Richmond Street, Glasgow, G1 1XH; T.-041-552 4400.

Atwell, Sir John (William), Kt (1976), CBE (1970), FEng, FIMechE, FRSE, Hon. LLD (Strathclyde). President, Royal Society of

Edinburgh, since 1982; b. 2411.11; m. Educ. Hyndland Secondary School, Glasgow; Royal Technical College, Glasgow; Cambridge University. Director: Anderson Strathclyde Ltd., 1975-78, Govan Shipbuilders Ltd., 1975-79. Chairman, Court, Strathclyde University, 1975-80; Member, Executive Committee, Scottish Council (Development and Industry), 1972-77; Council Member, Scottish Business School, 1972-80; President, IMechE, 1973-74.

Auchinachie, Henry Williamson, ACIS, AIB (Scot). Chairman, Finance Committee, Grampian Regional Council, since 1978; farmer; b. Keith, Banffshire; m., Edith Russell Taylor; 1 s.; 4 d. Educ. Keith Grammar School; Metropolitan College (Correspondence). Cadet Officer, Mercantile Marine; bank official (branches, Inspection and Legal Departments, finally bank manager). Former JP; former Member: Banchory Town Council; Kincardine County Council; Aberdeen County Council; Deer District Council; Treasurer, Lonmay Parish Church, 29 years; Secretary/Treasurer, Lonmay Public Hall, 30 years; Life Member: British Show Jumping Association; Fraserburgh Burns Club; Co-Founder, Banchory Festival of Scottish Music. Recreations: music; horses. Address: (h.) Mill of Crimond, Fraserburgh, Aberdeenshire, AB4 4XQ; T.-0346 32216.

Auld, Margaret Gibson, SRN, SCM, FRCN, MTD, CertNA (Edin), MPhil, CBIM. Chief Nursing Officer, Scottish Home and Health Department, since 1977; b. 11.7.32, Cardiff. Educ. Glasgow; Cardiff High School for Girls; Edinburgh University. Trained, Radcliffe Infirmary, Oxford, 1950-53; midwifery, St. David's Hospital, Cardiff, 1953-54; Queen's Park Hospital, Blackburn, 1953-54; Staff Midwife, then Sister, Cardiff Maternity Hospital, 1955-56; Sister, Queen Mary Hospital, Dunedin, NZ, 1959-60; Departmental Sister, Cardiff Maternity Hospital, 1962-66; Simpson Memorial Maternity Pavilion: Assistant Matron, 1966-68, Matron, 1968-73; Acting Chief Regional Nursing Officer, South-Eastern Regional Hospital Board, 1973; Chief Area Nursing Officer, Borders Health Board, 1973-76. Member: Briggs Committee on nursing; General Nursing Council for Scotland; Central Midwives Board for Scotland; Common Services Agency. Recreations: reading; music. Address: (h.) Staddlestones, Bellwood Road, Milton Bridge, Penicuik, Midlothian, EH26 ONL; T.-Penicuik 72858.

Austin, Richard Keith, WS. Solicitor; Partner, Steedman Ramage & Co., WS, since 1976; b. 29.1.48, Edinburgh; m., Morag Gillespie Webster; 2 s.; 1 d. Educ. Royal High School, Edinburgh; Edinburgh University; LLB; Diploma, History of Art. Elder, Barclay Church, Edinburgh; Curator, Signet Library, Edinburgh. Recreations: music; looking (at pictures and buildings, mainly). Address: (b.) 6 Alva Street, Edinburgh; T.-031-226 3781.

Avonside, Rt. Hon. Lord (Ian Hamilton Shearer), PC, QC, MA, LLB. Senator of the College of Justice in Scotland, since 1964; b. 6.11.14; m.; 1 s.; 1 d. by pr. m. Educ. Dunfermline High School; Glasgow University; Edinburgh

University. Admitted, Faculty of Advocates, 1938; RA, 1939-45 (Major); QC (Scotland), 1952; Sheriff of Renfrew and Argyll, 1960-62; Lord Advocate, 1962-64; Chairman, Lands Valuation Court, since 1975; Chairman, National Health Service Tribunal, Scotland, 1954-62; Chairman, Scottish Valuation Advisory Council, 1965-68.

Axup, William Bernard Noel, CEng, FIMarE. Dockyard Director, Yarrow Shipbuilders Ltd., since 1985; b. 22.6.31, Bubwith, Yorkshire; m., Isabell. Educ. Vale of Leven Academy; Royal Technical College, Glasgow. Apprentice draughtsman, 1948-53; engineer, Merchant Navy, 1953-58; divisional manager, shipbuilding, 1958-71; Yarrow Shipbuilders Ltd.: General Manager Production, 1971-78, Production Director, 1978-79, Deputy Managing Director (Production), 1979-85. Recreations: golf; fishing. Address: (b.) Yarrow Shipbuilders Ltd., South Street, Scotstoun, Glasgow, G14 OXN; T.-041-959 1207, Ext. 4002.

B

Bailey, Colin John, BA (Hons), PhD. Art Historian; Head, Department of Humanities and Complementary Studies, Edinburgh College of Art, since 1982 (Dean of Art and Design, since 1984); b. 22.5.46, Hastings. Educ. Hastings Grammar School; Leicester University; Nottingham University. Assistant Keeper of British Art, Walker Art Gallery, Liverpool; Librarian, Barber Institute of Fine Arts, Birmingham University; part-time Lecturer in Art History, Department of Extra-Mural Studies, Birmingham University. British Academy Scholar, 1984. Publications: Edward Lear and Knowsley; German Nineteenth-Century Drawings from the Ashmolean Museum; edition of Johann David Passavant's Tour of a German Artist in England. Recreations: hillwalking; snooker; foreign travel. Address: (h.) Church Cottage, West Byres, Ormiston, East Lothian.

Bailey, Jonathan Gordon, BSocSc (Hons), AAPSW, FBIM. Director of Social Work, Highland Regional Council, since 1974; b. 23.5.40, Woking; m., Marion; 2 d. Educ. Ryde School; Sandown Grammar School; Birmingham University; Southampton University. Probation Officer, Sheffield, 1963-66; Senior Child Care Officer, Sheffield, 1966-68; Assistant Children's Officer, Sheffield, 1968-70; Depute Director of Social Work, Moray and Nairn, 1970-72; Director of Social Work, Banffshire, 1972-74. Secretary, Association of Directors of Social Work, 1981-84. Recreations: choral singing; gardening; sailing. Address: (b.) Regional Buildings, Glenurquhart Road, Inverness; T.-0463 234121, Ext. 320.

Baillie, Professor John, MA, CA. Johnstone-Smith Professor of Accountancy, Glasgow University, since 1983; Partner, HMG Thomson McLintock & Co., since 1978; b. 7.10.44; m., Annette Alexander; 1 s.; 1 d. Educ. Whitehill School. Member, various technical and professional affairs committees, Institute of Chartered Accountants of Scotland. Recreations: keeping fit; reading; music; golf. Address: (h.) The Glen, Glencairn Road, Kilmacolm, Renfrewshire; T.-Kilmacolm 3254.

Baillie, Robert Martin. Senior Lecturer in History of Fine Art, Glasgow University; b. 4.3.20, Edinburgh; m., Patricia Ireland; 2 s.; 1 d. Educ. Royal High School, Edinburgh; Edinburgh College of Art. Teacher of Drawing, Edinburgh College of Art, 1947-50; Lecturer in Painting, Leeds College of Art, 1950-53; Lecturer in History of Art, Glasgow University, 1954; Art Critic, The Glasgow Herald, 1969-79. Regular exhibitor of paintings, Royal Scottish Academy, Royal Glasgow Institute. Recreations: reading; walking. Address: (h.) 2 North Park Villas, Summerlea Road, Thornliebank, Glasgow, G46 8PB; T.-041-638 3890.

Baillie, William James Laidlaw, RSA, PRSW. Painter; Treasurer, Royal Scottish Academy, since 1980; Senior Lecturer in Drawing and Painting, Edinburgh College of Art, since 1968; b. 19.4.23; m.; 1 s.; 2 d. Educ. Dunfermline High School; Edinburgh College of Art.

Bain, Robert Garden. Farmer; Director, R.G. Bain Ltd., since 1959; Council Member, National Farmers' Union of Scotland; b. 22.2.34, Aberdeen; m., Elizabeth Ann (Lann); 2 s. Educ. Kirkwall Grammar School; Aberdeen Grammar School; Gordonstoun School. Accountancy until 1959. Elder, Church of Scotland; Chairman, local Community Council. Recreations: coin and stamp collecting. Address: Hall of Tankerness, Orkney; T.-0856 86 275.

Bain, Professor William Herbert, MD, FRCS. Titular Professor in Cardiac Surgery, Glasgow University, since 1981; Consultant Cardio-Thoracic Surgeon, since 1962; b. 20.11.27, Kilmacolm; m., Helen Craigie; 1 d. Educ. Glasgow High School; Glasgow University. Graduated MB, ChB; House Officer posts, Glasgow, 1950-51; McIntyre Research Scholar, 1952-53; Registrar in General Surgery, Glasgow Royal Infirmary, 1954-58; Lecturer in Experimental Surgery, Honorary Senior Registrar, 1958-62; Andrews Fellow, University of Chicago, 1961; Senior Lecturer/Reader in Surgery, Glasgow, 1962-81; Consultant Surgeon, Royal Infirmary, Western Infirmary, Stobhill Hospital. Examiner for Glasgow and Edinburgh Royal Colleges; Member, British Standards Institute. Publications: Blood Flow Through Tissues and Organs, 1968; Essentials of Cardiovascular Surgery, 1974; Intensive Care, 1980. Recreations: sailing; fishing. Address: (h.) 8 Grange Road, Bearsden, Glasgow, G61 3PL; T.-041-942 3846.

Baird, Alister, MREHis, MInstWM, DPA. Director of Environmental Health, Hamilton District Council, since 1974; b. 11.12.38, Glasgow; m., Margaret Lynne; 2 s. Educ. Eastbank Academy, Glasgow. Student, Glasgow Corporation, 1957-61; Assistant Sanitary Inspector,

Airdrie Town Council, 1961-63; Fife County Council: Assistant Sanitary Inspector, 1963-64, Senior Assistant, 1964-65; Depute Director of Environmental Health, East Kilbride Town Council, 1965-74. Chairman, Scottish Centre, Institute of Waste Management; Secretary, Scottish Society of Directors of Environmental Health; Officer Advisor, COSLA. Recreations: music; hockey; golf. Address: (b.) 207-209 Quarry Street, Hamilton; T.-Hamilton 282323.

Baird, Basil John. Farmer, since 1962; Member, Eastwood District Council, since 1980; Council Member, National Farmers' Union of Scotland, since 1981; b. 26.6.36, Eaglesham; m., Jessie Parker Wilson; 2 s.; 2 d. Educ. Allan Glen's School, Glasgow; West of Scotland College of Agriculture. National Service, RAOC, 1955-57. Director: Glasgow Agricultural Society; East Kilbride Show Society; Elder, Church of Scotland, since 1965; elected to Eaglesham Community Council, 1976. Recreation: curling. Address: Windhill Farm, Eaglesham, Glasgow; T.-041-644 2704.

Baird, Professor David Tennent, BA (Cantab), MB, ChB, DSc, FRCP Edin, FRCOG. Professor of Obstetrics and Gynaecology, Edinburgh University, since 1977; Consultant Obstetrician and Gynaecologist, Simpson Memorial Maternity Pavilion, Edinburgh Royal Infirmary, since 1970; b. 13.3.35, Glasgow; m., Frances Lightveld; 2 s. Educ. Aberdeen Grammar School; Aberdeen University; Trinity College, Cambridge; Edinburgh University. After clinical training in endocrinology as well as obstetrics, spent three years (1965-68) as an MRC travelling Research Fellow at Worcester Foundation for Experimental Biology, Shrewsbury, Mass., USA, conducting research on reproductive endocrinology; Deputy Director, MRC Unit of Reproductive Biology, Edinburgh, 1972-77; served on a number of national and international committees. Publications: four books on reproduction. Recreations: ski mountaineering; music; sport. Address: (b.) Department of Obstetrics and Gynaecology, Edinburgh University, Centre for Reproductive Biology, 37 Chalmers Street, Edinburgh, EH3 9EW; T.-031-229 2575.

Baird, Isabel Duncan. General Secretary, United Free Church of Scotland, since 1981; b. 15.9.34, Aberdeen; m., Ronald C.F. Baird; 1 s. Educ. Rosemount Secondary School; Central School (commercial course). Shorthand typist, 1950; private secretary, 1953; private secretary to General Secretary, United Free Church of Scotland, 1971-81. Boys' Brigade officer, 1968-77. Recreations: reading; knitting; Boys' Brigade; local/national Church. Address: (b.) 11 Newton Place, Glasgow, G3 7PR; T.-041-332 3435.

Baird, Lt.-Col. Niall Caldecott, (Rt.), OBE. Managing Director, Lossie Holiday Homes, since 1975; b. 14.10.17, London; m., Susan Davidson (m. dissolved); 4 s. Educ. Stowe School; Royal Military College, Sandhurst. Commissioned, Queen's Own Cameron Highlanders, 1937; served in Burma, World War II; Parachute Regiment, 1947-51; commanded 1st Bn., Queen's Own Cameron Highlanders, 1959-61, and 1st Bn.,

Queen's Own Highlanders, 1961-62; mentioned in Despatches (twice); entered commerce upon retirement, 1963; set up self-catering company, Elgin, 1975. Member, Queen's Bodyguard in Scotland (Royal Company of Archers). Recreations: golf; gardening. Address: Palmers Cross, Elgin, Moray, IV30 1YF; T.-Elgin 7240.

Baird, William Bramwell, LLB (Hons), LLM, ACII. General Secretary, The Salvation Army, Scotland, since 1984; b. 20.11.27, Glasgow; m., Rita Gravett; 1 s.; 1 d. Educ. Kilmarnock Academy; London University. Salvation Army: served in corps, business and social work, 1949-66, Finance Officer, Pakistan, 1966-69, Secretary, The Mothers' Hospital, 1970-73, Personnel Officer, Social Services, 1973-74, Legal Officer, International Headquarters, 1974-82, Chief Secretary, Social Services, 1982-84. Recreation: music. Address: (h.) 74 Roffey Park Road, Old Hall, Paisley; T.-041-882 3572.

Baird, Rev. William Gordon Glen, DPA, ACII. Minister, Inverkeithing St. John's and North Queensferry Churches, since 1977; b. 7.1.28, Glasgow; m., Morag Thorburn Crichton; 1 s.; 1 d. Educ. William Hulme's Grammar School, Manchester; Glasgow University; Glasgow and West of Scotland Commercial College; Edinburgh University. Inland Revenue, 1944-46; Royal Navy, 1946-48; Ministry of National Insurance, 1948-66; Senior Executive Officer, HM Treasury (O & M Division), Scottish Branch, 1967-68; Training Officer for Scotland, Department of Health and Social Security, 1969-72; student, University of Edinburgh, 1972-74; Assistant Minister, St. Ninian's Church, Corstorphine, Edinburgh, 1974-75. Recreations: gardening; railways; the solitude of the Western Isles. Address: St. Johns Manse, 34 Hill Street, Inverkeithing, Fife; T.-0383 412422.

Baker, Archibald James, BSc, PhD. Assistant Director of Chemical Laboratories, Glasgow University, since 1981 (Senior Lecturer in Chemistry, since 1972); b. 3.6.34, Inverkip; m., Joyce R. Thomson; 4 s. Educ. Greenock Academy; Glasgow University. Glaxo Fellow, Glasgow University, 1961-63; Lecturer in Chemistry, 1963-72. Recreations: golf; target shooting. Address: (h.) Bellary, Monkton, Prestwick; T.-0292 78135.

Baker, Barbara Dagmar. Member, Borders Regional Council, since 1982; b. 18.8.25, Edinburgh; m., Ernest Frederick Baker; 2 s.; 1 d. Educ. St. George's School for Girls; Edinburgh College of Domestic Science. Diploma, Institutional Management. Decoding, WRNS, Bletchley Park; managing director, shipping and export; Regional Organiser, WRNS. Recreations: small flock, Oxford sheep; walking dogs; looking after eight grandchildren. Address: (h.) Lugate, Stow, Galashiels; T.-05783 243.

Baker, Professor Michael John, TD, BA, BSc (Econ), DipM, CertITP (Harvard), DBA (Harvard), FInstM, FCAM. Professor of Marketing, Strathclyde University, since 1971 (Deputy Principal, since 1984); Vice Chairman, Institute of Marketing, since 1983; b. 5.11.35, Debden; m., Sheila; 1 s.; 2 d. Educ. Worksop

College; Bede, Gosforth and Harvey Grammar Schools; Durham University; London University; Harvard University. Royal Artillery, 1957 (2nd Lt.); Richard Thomas & Baldwins (Sales) Ltd., 1958-64; Lecturer: Medway College of Technology, 1964-66, Hull College of Technology, 1966-68; FME Fellow, Harvard Business School, 1968-71; Member, Vice-Chairman and Chairman, SCOTBEC, 1973-85; Member, SSRC Management Committee, 1976-80; Dean, Strathclyde Business School, 1978-84; Chairman, Marketing Education Group, since 1974; Member, SHERT, since 1983; Member, Chief Scientist's Committee, since 1985; Governor, CAM. Publications: Marketing New Industrial Products, 1975; Market Development, 1983; Marketing Strategy and Management, 1985; Marketing, 4th edition, 1985. Recreations: sailing; gardening; travel; DIY. Address: (b.) Strathclyde University, 173 Cathedral Street, Glasgow, G4 ORQ; T.-041-552 4400.

Baker, Thomas Neville, BMet, PhD, DMet, FIM, FInstP, CEng. Reader in Metallurgy, Strathclyde University, since 1983; b. 11.1.34, Southport; m., Eileen May Allison. Educ. King George V School, Southport; Sheffield University. Research Metallurgist, Nelson Research Laboratories, English Electric Co., Stafford, 1958-60; Scientist, Project Leader, Tube Investments Research Laboratories, Hinxton Hall, Cambridge, 1961-64; Department of Metallurgy, Strathclyde University: SRC Research Fellow, 1965, Lecturer, 1966, Senior Lecturer, 1976. Recreations: music; literature; gardening. Address: (b.) Department of Metallurgy, Strathclyde University, Colville Building, 48 N. Portland Street, Glasgow; T.-041-552 4400.

Baldwin, Olaf A.C., BL. Solicitor, since 1950; Notary Public; b. 4.1.27, Edinburgh; m., Sheila MacDonald; 1 s.; 1 d. Educ. Dumfries Academy; Edinburgh University. War Service commission, Indian Army; served with 3rd Gurkha Rifles; demobbed T. Captain; enrolled Solicitor, 1950; Qualified Assistant, Partner, then Senior Partner, Whitelaw, Edgar & Baldwin, Dumfries; appointed Honorary Sheriff, Dumfries, 1976; Dean of Faculty of Procurators of Dumfriesshire, 1983-85. Recreations: sailing; skiing. Address: (h.) Castledykes, Glencaple Road, Dumfries; T.-Dumfries 52023.

Balekjian, Wahe Hagop, Dr (Law), Dr (pol sc), PhD. Head of Department and Senior Lecturer in European Law, Glasgow University, since 1976; Visiting Titular Professor, University of Salzburg, Austria, since 1981; Titular Professor, European Faculty, Land Use Planning, Strasbourg, since 1982; b. 2.10.24, Cairo; m., Eva Birgitta. Educ. College of Arts and Sciences, Cairo; Vienna University; Manchester University. Diploma, Hague Academy of International Law. Lecturer, Vienna University, 1957-73; Simon Research Fellow, Manchester University, 1963-65; Head of Department, European Studies, National Institute of Higher Education, Limerick, 1973-76. Publications: Legal Aspects of Foreign Investment in the EEC, 1967 (awarded Prize of European Communities, 1967); The

Status of Unrecognised States in International Law (published in German, 1971). Recreations: hill-walking; piano playing; languages. Address: (b.) Department of European Law, The University, Glasgow, G12 8QQ; T.-041-339 8855, Ext. 7539.

Balfour, Rt. Hon. Christopher Patrick (5th Baron Kinross), LLB, WS. Solicitor, since 1975; b. 1.10.49, Edinburgh; m., Susan Jane Pitman; 2 s. Educ. Belhaven Hill Preparatory School; Eton College; Edinburgh University. Honorary Treasurer: British Digestive Foundation Appeal for Scotland; James IV Association of Surgeons. Recreations: pistol, rifle and shotgun shooting; deer stalking. Address: (b.) 16 Charlotte Square, Edinburgh; T.-031-225 8585.

Balfour, 4th Earl of, (Gerald Arthur James Balfour), JP; b. 23.12.25; m. Educ. Eton; HMS Conway. Member, East Lothian County Council, 1960-75. Address: (h.) The Tower, Whittingehame, Haddington.

Balfour, Ian Leslie Shaw, MA, LLB, BD, PhD, SSC, NP. Solicitor (Partner, Balfour & Manson), since 1955; b. 16.6.32, Edinburgh; m., Joyce Margaret Ross Pryde; 3 s.; 1 d. Educ. Edinburgh Academy; Edinburgh University. Qualified as Solicitor, 1955; commissioned, RASC, 1955-57; Partner, Balfour & Manson, since 1959; Secretary, Oliver & Son Ltd., since 1959; Fiscal to Law Society of Scotland, since 1981. Baptist Union of Scotland: President, 1976-77, Law Agent, since 1964, Secretary, Charlotte Baptist Chapel, Edinburgh, since 1980, Secretary, Scottish Bapist College, since 1983; Secretary, Elba Housing Society Ltd., since 1969; Director, Edinburgh Medical Missionary Society. Recreations: hill-walking; home computing; lay preaching. Address: (b.) 58 Frederick Street, Edinburgh; T.-031-225 8291.

Balfour, John Charles, OBE, MC, JP, DL, BA. Chairman, Fife Area Health Board, since 1983; b. 28.7.19; m.; 3 s. Educ. Eton; Trinity College, Cambridge. Royal Artillery, 1939-45 (Major); Member, Queen's Bodyguard for Scotland (Royal Company of Archers),since 1949; Chairman, Fife County Children's Panel, 1970-75, Fife Region Children's Panel, 1975-77; Chairman, Scottish Association of Youth Clubs, 1968-79.

Balfour, Peter Edward Gerald, CBE. Chairman, Scottish Council (Development and Industry), 1978-85; Director, Royal Bank of Scotland, since 1972; Chairman, Edinburgh American Assets Trust and First Charlotte Assets Trust; b. 9.7.21, Woking; m., 1, Grizelda Ogilvy, 2, Diana Wainman; 3 s.; 2 d. Educ. Eton College. Served Scots Guards, 1940-54; joined William McEwan & Co., brewers, 1954; appointed Director, 1958; Director, Scottish Brewers, 1959; Scottish and Newcastle Breweries, 1961 (Chairman and Managing Director, 1970-83); Director and Vice Chairman, RBS Group, 1978; Chairman, National Commercial and Glyn's, 1983; Director, British Assets Trust and Charterhouse Japhet. Recreations: farming; forestry. Address: (h.) Scadlaw House, Humbie, East Lothian; T.-087 533 252.

Balfour of Burleigh, Lord, (Robert Bruce), CEng, FIEE. Director, Bank of Scotland, since 1968; Director, Scottish Investment Trust, since 1971; Director, Tarmac plc, since 1981; Chairman, Federation of Scottish Bank Employers, since 1977; b. 6.1.27; m.; 2 d. RN, 1945-48. Chairman, Scottish Arts Council, 1971-80; Chairman, NBL Scotland, since 1982; Member, British Rail Scotland Regional Board, since 1982; Forestry Commissioner, 1971-74.

Balfour, Robert Melville. Deputy Director, Scottish Conservative Party, since 1980; b. 16.10.34, Hemel Hempstead; m., Margaretta Rose Ferguson; 1 s.; 1 d. Educ. Kingswood School, Bath; Gwydyr Forester Training School, Betwys-y-Coed. National Service, RAF Police, 1952-54; certificated forester, Forestry Commission Research Station, specialising in entomology, 1958-62; sub-postmaster and general store owner, Kilmun, Argyll, 1962-68; Conservative Party agent: Newcastle-upon-Tyne East, 1968-71, West Aberdeenshire, 1971-75, Argyll, 1975-79. Elder, Dean Parish Church, Edinburgh; Past Chairman: Kilmun District Community Council; Kilmun Hall and Recreation Association. Recreations: walking; carpet bowling; philately; wine-making; reading; music; fishing. Address: (h.) 118 East Claremont Street, Edinburgh, EH7 4JZ; T.-031-556 6776.

Balfour, William Harold St. Clair. Solicitor; b. 29.8.34, Edinburgh; m., Patricia Waite (m. dissolved); 1 s.; 2 d. Educ. Hillfield, Ontario; Edinburgh Academy; Edinburgh University. Partner, Balfour & Manson, Solicitors; Clerk to Admission of Notaries Public; Seminar Leader, Edinburgh University; Director and trustee of various bodies. Chairman: Basic Space Dance Theatre; Garvald Trustees; Central Edinburgh New Town Residents Association; Friends of Talbot Rice Art Gallery. Recreations: sailing; walking. Address: (b.) 58 Frederick Street, Edinburgh, EH2 1LS; T.-031-225 8291.

Balharrie, Brigadier John Charles, MBE, MC, CStJ, TD, DL. Deputy Lieutenant, Dunbartonshire; President, Scottish International Gathering Trust; b. 21.12.19, Glasgow; m., Sara Jean Ferguson. Educ. Glasgow Academy. Commissioned, 1938; active service, Middle East and NW Europe, 1939-45, Palestine, Cyprus and Aden, 1945-59; commanded Royal Scots Greys, 1962-64; Chief Staff Officer, 52nd Lowland Division, 1964-67; Commander, Lowland Area, Edinburgh Castle, 1969-73; retired as Brigadier, 1974, and served as Secretary, Lowland TAVR Association, 1974-84. Honorary Colonel, Glasgow and Lanarkshire Bn., Army Cadet Force; President: Glasgow Area HQ Branch, Royal British Legion Scotland, City of Glasgow Joint Council, Naval, Army and Air Force Associations; Chairman: Glasgow Branch, St. John Association of Scotland (and Member of Chapter, Order of St. John in Scotland), Glasgow Branch, Forces Help Society and Lord Roberts Workshops, Glasgow Branch, Royal Scots Dragoon Guards Association, 52nd Lowland Division Officers Club; Vice-Convenor, Chaplains Committee, Church of Scotland. Recreations:

country pursuits; reading. Address: (h.) Blairquhosh House, Blanefield, Stirlingshire, G63 9AJ; T.-Blanefield 70232.

Ball, Derek William, MB, MRCPsych. Composer; b. 30.12.49, Letterkenny, Ireland; m., Marie Knox; 1 d. Educ. Kings Hospital, Dublin; Royal Irish Academy of Music; Trinity College, Dublin. Studied composition under the late Dr. Archie Potter; founder Member, Association of Young Irish Composers; writes chamber and orchestral music; numerous performances in Dublin, and at festivals in Paris and Bordeaux. Works as a consultant psychiatrist, with a special interest in rehabilitation, in the Northern District of Glasgow. Address: (h.) 1 Moidart Gardens, Kirkintilloch, G66 3ST.

Ball, Geoffrey A., FCA. Group Managing Director, City of Aberdeen Land Association plc, since 1974; Member, Scottish Arts Council; b. 4.8.43, Bristol; m., Mary Elizabeth; 3 s.; 1 d. Educ. Cotham Grammar School, Bristol. Former Managing Director, Greencoat Properties Ltd.; non-executive Director: Abaco Investments p.l.c.; Scottish Mortgage & Trust p.l.c.; Edinburgh Venture Enterprise Trust Ltd.; Stenhouse Western Ltd. Member, Independent Schools Careers Organisation. Recreations: golf; music. Address: (b.) 42 Colinton Road, Edinburgh, EH10 5BT; T.-031-346 0194.

Ball, Professor John Macleod, BA (Cantab), DPhil. Professor of Applied Analysis, Department of Mathematics, Heriot-Watt University, Edinburgh, since 1982; Senior Fellow, Science and Engineering Research Council, 1980-85; b. 19.5.48, Farnham, Surrey. Educ. Mill Hill School; St. John's College, Cambridge. SERC postdoctoral research fellowship, 1972-74, at Department of Mathematics, Heriot-Watt University, and Lefschetz Center for Dynamical Systems, Brown University, Providence, Rhode Island, USA; Heriot-Watt University: Lecturer in Mathematics, 1974-78, Reader in Mathematics, 1978-82. Elected Fellow, Royal Society of Edinburgh, 1980; Whittaker Prize, Edinburgh Mathematical Society, 1981; Junior Whitehead Prize, London Mathematical Society, 1982; Member, editorial boards, Archive for Rational Mechanics and Analysis; Proceedings of Royal Society of Edinburgh (A); Annales de l'Institut Henri Poincare (Analyse Non Lineaire). Recreations: music; travel. Address: (h.) 11 Gloucester Place, Edinburgh, EH3 6EE.

Ballinger, Brian Richard, MA, BM, BCh, FRCPEd, FRCPsych, DPM. Consultant Psychiatrist, Dundee Psychiatric Service, since 1971; Honorary Senior Lecturer, Dundee University, since 1971; b. 1.6.37, Newport, Gwent; m., Dr. C. Barbara Ballinger; 2 s. Educ. Manchester Grammar School; University College, Oxford; St. Mary's Hospital Medical School, London. Postgraduate training in London, Oxford, Sheffield and Dundee; special interest in psychiatry of old age; Chairman, Division of Psychiatry, Dundee Psychiatric Service, since 1981. Recreations: painting; music; travel. Address: (b.) Royal Dundee Liff Hospital, Dundee; T.-0382 580441.

Bamert, Matthias. Principal Guest Conductor, Scottish National Orchestra, since 1985; Director, Musica Nova, since 1985; b. 5.7.42, Ersigen, Switzerland; m., Susan; 1 s.; 1 d. Assistant to George Szell in Cleveland; Assistant to Leopold Stokowski at American Symphony Orchestra; worked under Pierre Boulez, then Lorin Maazel, in Cleveland; Music Director, Swiss Radio Orchestra, 1978-84; made debut with SNO, 1983; recent engagements with Scottish Chamber, Halle, Bournemouth Symphony, CBSO and BBC Scottish Symphony Orchestras. Address: (b.) Scottish National Orchestra, 3 La Belle Place, Glasgow, G3 7LH; T.-041-332 7244.

Bancroft, John Henry Jefferies, MA, MD, MRCP, FRCPsych. Clinical Consultant, MRC Reproductive Biology Unit, since 1976; Honorary Senior Lecturer, Department of Psychiatry, Edinburgh University, since 1976; b. 18.6.36, Peterborough; m., Judy Greenwood; 2 s.; 1 d. Educ. Bedford School; Caius College, Cambridge. Clinical Reader, Department of Psychiatry, Oxford, 1969-76. President, International Academy of Sex Research, 1976-77; Chairman: British Association for Behavioural Psychotherapy, 1983-84; Marital Sex Therapy Advisory Board, National Marriage Guidance Council; Member, Scientific Advisory Board, Kinsey Institute for Research in Sex and Gender Reproduction. Publications: Deviant Sexual Behaviour, 1974; Human Sexuality and its Problems, 1983. Recreations: music; sailing. Address: (h.) 26 Calton Hill, Edinburgh, EH1 3BJ; T.-031-556 5098.

Band, Thomas Mollison. Director, Historic Buildings and Monuments, Scottish Development Department, since 1984; b. 28.3.34, Aberdeen; m., Jean McKenzie Brien; 1 s.; 2 d. Educ. Perth Academy. Principal, Tariff Division, Board of Trade, London, 1969-73; Director (Location of Industry), Department of Industry, Glasgow, 1973-76; Assistant Secretary (Industrial Policy), Scottish Economic Planning Department, 1976-78; Assistant Secretary (Housing), Scottish Development Department, 1978-82; Assistant Secretary (Finance), Scottish Office, 1982-84. Recreations: gardening; skiing; beating. Address: (h.) Heathfield, Pitcairngreen, Perthshire; T.-073 883 403.

Banks, Philip, MA, MEd. HM Inspector of Schools, since 1983; b. 17.1.46, Stockton-on-Tees; m., Inger Haagensen-Banks; 1 s.; 1 d. Educ. St. Chad's College, Wolverhampton; Trinity Hall, Cambridge; Edinburgh University. Teacher, Ipswich Academy and Edinburgh Academy, 1969-73; Principal Teacher of English, Queen Anne High School, Dunfermline, 1973-81; Development Officer, Scottish Education Department, 1981-83. Recreations: reading; squash; walking. Address: (b.) Greyfriars House, Gallowgate, Aberdeen; T.-0224 642544.

Banks, William McKerrell, BSc, MSc, PhD, CEng, MIMechE. Senior Lecturer, Department of Mechanics of Materials, University of Strathclyde, since 1982; b. 28.3.43, Dreghorn, Ayrshire; m., Martha Ruthven Hair; 3 s. Educ. Irvine Royal Academy; Strathclyde University. Senior Research Engineer, Weir Pumps Ltd.;

joined Strathclyde University, 1970. Recreations: reading; family; active interest in local church. Address: (h.) 19 Dunure Drive, Hamilton, ML3 9EY; T.-0698 823730.

Bannerman, Eric William, CA, ATII. Partner, Carson & Trotter, CA, since 1963; Council Member, Institute of Chartered Accountants of Scotland, 1980-85; b. 21.10.32, Dumfries; m., Jean McKillop Jones; 1 d. Educ. Strathallan School. Past Chairman: Dumfries and Galloway Association of Scottish Chartered Accountants; South West Scotland Area Committee, Institute of Chartered Accountants of Scotland; Honorary President, Dumfries Rugby Football Club; Past President, Dumfries Burns Club; Past Treasurer: Maxwelltown West Church; Dumfries Guild of Players. Recreations: gardening; golf; reading. Address: (h.) Steilston House, Dumfries, DG2 OJJ; T.-0387 720697.

Bannerman, James Pirie, OBE, JP, FPS, FPSI. Member, Strathclyde Regional Council, since 1982 (Leader, Alliance Group); b. 24.5.35, Glasgow; m., Marjorie Seddon; 1 s.; 1 d. Educ. Glasgow Academy; Strathclyde University. President, Pharmaceutical Society of Great Britain, 1974-76; Member, Medicines Commission, since 1978; Director, A.G. Bannerman Ltd. Recreations: golf; marathon running; wind-surfing. Address: (h.) 5 Boclair Crescent, Bearsden, Glasgow, G61; T.-041-942 5200.

Barbenel, Joseph Cyril, BDS, BSc, MSc, PhD, LDS RCS(Eng), CPhys, MInstP. Reader, Bioengineering Unit, Strathclyde University, since 1982 (Head, Tissue Mechanics Division, since 1970); b. 2.1.37, London; m., Lesley Mary Hyde Jowett; 2 s.; 1 d. Educ. Hackney Downs Grammar School, London; London Hospital Medical College; Queen's College, Dundee (St. Andrews University); Strathclyde University. Dental House Surgeon, London Hospital, 1960; National Service, RADC, 1960-61 (Lieutenant, 1960, Captain, 1961); general dental practice, London, 1963; student, 1963-67; Lecturer, Department of Dental Prosthetics, Dental School, Dundee, 1967-69; Senior Lecturer, Strathclyde University, 1970-82. Member of Council and Professional Committee, Biological Engineering Society; Member of Committee, and Secretary for Standardisation, International Society for Bioengineering and the Skin; Member, Steering Committee, Forum on Clinical Haemorheology; Council Member, Society for Tissue Viability. Recreations: music; theatre. Address: (b.) University of Strathclyde, Bioengineering Unit, 106 Rottenrow, Glasgow, G4 ONW; T.-041-552 4400.

Barber, Professor James Hill, MB, ChB, MD, FRCGP, FRCPSG, DRCOG. Norie Miller Professor of General Practice, Glasgow University, since 1974; Principal, Greater Glasgow Health Board, since 1972; Honorary Consultant, Medicine, Royal and Western Infirmaries, Glasgow, since 1972; b. 28.5.33, Dunfermline; m., Helen Keir; 4 s.; 3 d. Educ. Edinburgh Academy; University of Edinburgh. Medical Branch, RAF, 1958-63; General Practitioner: Callander, 1964-66, Livingston, 1966-72; Senior Lecturer, General Practice, Glasgow University, 1972-74.

Publications: General Practice Medicine, 1975 and 1985; Towards Team Care, 1980. Recreations: sailing; model fishing-boat construction; photography. Address: (b.) Woodside Health Centre, Barr Street, Glasgow; T.-041-332 9977.

Barber, Rev. Peter Horne, MA, BD. General Secretary, Baptist Union of Scotland, since 1980; b. 25.8.30, Edinburgh; m., Isobel; 1 s.; 2 d. Educ. Boroughmuir Secondary School, Edinburgh; Edinburgh University and New College. Minister: East Kilbride Baptist Church, 1955-73; Upton Vale Baptist Church, Torquay, 1973-80. Centenary President, Baptist Union of Scotland, 1969-70. Recreations: golf; swimming; music. Address: 12 Attow Road, Glasgow, G43 1BZ; T.-041-632 5649.

Barclay, Kenneth Forsyth, BL, NP. Divisional Solicitor, Scottish Office; b. 1.2.38, Glasgow; m., Jean Broom Curwen; 1 s.; 1 d. Educ. Woodside Senior Secondary School, Glasgow; Glasgow University. Solicitor in private practice, 1960-71; Principal Solicitor, Cumbernauld Development Corporation, 1971-73; joined Office of Solicitor to Secretary of State for Scotland, 1973; Legal Secretary, Royal Commission on Legal Services in Scotland, 1976-80. Recreations: golf; walking; tennis; badminton; reading. Address: (b.) New St. Andrews House, Edinburgh; T.-031-556 8400.

Barker, John R., MA (Cantab), FLA. University Librarian, Dundee University, since 1962; b. 23.5.24, Liverpool; m., Dr. Ruth M. Barker; 1 s.; 1 d. Educ. Liverpool Collegiate School; Cambridge University. Diploma in Librarianship, University College, London. Assistant Librarian, Liverpool University; Sub-Librarian, Bristol University. Recreations: music; hill-walking. Address: (b.) University Library, Dundee, DD1 4HN; T.-0382 23181.

Barlow, Professor (Arthur) John, PhD, DIC, BSc, ACGI, MIEE, CEng. Titular Professor, Electronics and Electrical Engineering Department, Glasgow University; b. 17.3.34, Nottinghamshire; m., Alma Marshall; 1 s.; 1 d. Educ. Nottingham High School; Imperial College. Turner and Newall Research Fellow, Imperial College, 1958-61; Glasgow University: Lecturer, 1961-66, Senior Lecturer, 1966-68, Reader, 1968-75. Address: (h.) 5 Auchencruive, Milngavie, Glasgow, G62 6EE.

Barnes, John Clive, MA. Senior Lecturer and Head of Department of Italian, Aberdeen University, since 1979; b. 27.4.46, Croydon; m., Judith Mary Clarke; 2 s. Educ. Batley Grammar School; Wyggeston Boys' School, Leicester; Oriel College, Oxford. Hull University: Assistant Lecturer, Italian, 1969-72, Lecturer, Italian, 1972-79. Recreation: music. Address: (b.) Department of Italian, King's College, Aberdeen, AB9 2UB; T.-0224 40241, Ext. 5105.

Barnes, John Conquest, BSc, PhD, CChem, FRSC. Senior Lecturer, Department of Chemistry, Dundee University, since 1980; b. 6.11.35, London; m., Hazel Anne Sampson; 2 d. Educ. Bournemouth School; University College of Wales, Aberystwyth. Research Associate,

Massachusetts Institute of Technology, 1960-61; NATO postdoctoral Fellow, Inorganic Chemistry Laboratory, Oxford, 1961-63; Lecturer, Queen's College, Dundee/Dundee University, 1963-80. Member, Vestry, St Andrews Episcopal Church, 1972-83. Recreations: travel; photography. Address: (b.) Chemistry Department, The University, Dundee, DD1 4HN; T.-0382 23181.

Barnes, Robin Adam Boyd, MA (Hons), MEd. Director of Education, Shetland Islands Council, since 1975; b. 3.4.27, Glasgow; m., Cecilia; 3 d. Educ. Glasgow Academy; Glasgow University. Royal Navy, 1945-48; Teacher of English, Larkhall Academy, Lanarkshire, 1953-54; Special Assistant Teacher of English, Kelvinside Academy, Glasgow, 1954-64; Assistant Director of Education, Edinburgh, 1964-72; Director of Education, Zetland County Council, 1972-75. Education Officer, RNR Glasgow, 1958-64; Member, East of Scotland Schools/Industry Liaison Working Party with SED, 1966-68; Secretary, Edinburgh Primary Schools Working Party, 1968-72; President, Isleburgh Drama Group, Lerwick, since 1982. Recreations: performing music (piano); walking; gardening. Address: (b.) Education Office, 1 Harbour Street, Lerwick, Shetland, ZE1 OLS; T.-0595 3535, Ext. 254.

Barnes, William Jonathan Peter, BSc, PhD. Senior Lecturer in Zoology, Glasgow University, since 1983; b. 9.12.40, Heathend, England; m., Kristeen Margaret; 1 s.; 1 d. Educ. Leighton Park School; St. Andrews University. Glasgow University: Assistant Lecturer in Zoology, 1966-69, Lecturer, 1969-83; research fellowship from Alexander Von Humboldt Stiftung to work at University of Konstanz, West Germany, 1974-75; Organiser, International Symposium on Feedback and Motor Control, Glasgow, 1984; Committee Member, Neurobiology Group, Society for Experimental Biology; Symposium Committee Member, Scottish Electrophysiological Society; Committee Member, Clyde Area branch, Scottish Wildlife Trust; Executive Committee Member, Glasgow Urban Wildlife Group; Chairman, Park Terrace Association. Recreations: hill-walking; cricket. Address: (h.) 8 Kirklee Road, Glasgow, G12; T.-041-334 5780.

Barnetson, Ross St. Clair, MD, FRCP. Consultant Dermatologist, Edinburgh Royal Infirmary, since 1981; part-time Senior Lecturer, Edinburgh University, since 1981; b. 10.10.39, Edinburgh; m., Sheila Ann Corson; 2 d. Educ. Loretto School, Musselburgh; Edinburgh University. House Physician and House Surgeon, Edinburgh Royal Infirmary; service, RAMC, hospitals in Cyprus, West Malaysia and Singapore; Registrar in Dermatology, Edinburgh Royal Infirmary; Clinical Research Physician, MRC Leprosy Project, Addis Ababa, Ethiopia; Lecturer in Dermatology, Edinburgh University. Member, Medical Advisory Board, LEPRA. Recreations: sailing; skiing; tennis; opera. Address: (h.) 32 Queens Crescent, Edinburgh, EH9 2BA; T.-031-667 5173.

Barr, Professor Allan David Stephen, BSc, PhD, CEng, FIMechE, FRSE. Jackson Professor of Engineering, Aberdeen University, since 1985; b. 11.9.30, Glasgow; m., Eileen Patricia

Redmond. Educ. Daniel Stewart's College, Edinburgh; Edinburgh University. Student apprentice, Bristol Aeroplane Company; Lecturer, Department of Engineering, Edinburgh University; Visiting Associate Professor, Department of Theoretical and Applied Mechanics, Cornell University, USA; Senior Lecturer, then Reader, Department of Mechanical Engineering, Edinburgh University; Professor and Head, Department of Mechanical Engineering, Dundee University. Recreations: fly fishing; oil painting. Address: (b.) Department of Engineering, Kings College, University of Aberdeen, AB9 2UE.

Barr, David, DPE. Director of Physical Education, Dundee University, since 1968; b. 7.3.34, Motherwell; 1 s.; 1 d. Educ. Dalziel High School, Motherwell; Scottish School of Physical Education, Jordanhill College of Education, Glasgow. Physical Fitness Officer, RAF, 1957-60; Games Master, Glyn Grammar School, Ewell, Surrey, 1960-63; Assistant Director of Physical Education, Aberdeen University, 1963-66; Director of Physical Recreation, Bradford University, 1966-68. National water polo coach, Great Britain, 1961-65; director of water polo, Scotland, 1972-75; Team manager/coach, water polo, GB at World Student Games, Budapest, 1965, Turin, 1970, Moscow, 1973. Publications: A Guide to Water Polo, 1964; Play Better Water Polo, 1970; Water Polo, 1980. Recreations: golf; gardening. Address: (b.) Department of Physical Education, The University, Dundee DD1 4HN; T.-Dundee 23181, Ext. 4117.

Barr, Rev. David, MA, BD. Hospital Chaplain, Glasgow Royal Infirmary and Canniesburn Hospital, 1962-84; b. 14.6.14, Airdrie. Educ. Airdrie Academy; Glasgow University and Trinity College. Student Assistant, New Monkland Parish Church, 1935-37; Minister, Kirkintilloch South Church, 1938-42; part-time Hospital Chaplain, Broomhill and Lanfine Hospitals; Minister, St. Mary's, Partick, 1942-62; part-time Hospital Chaplain, Glasgow Western Infirmary, 1960-62. Moderator, Glasgow Presbytery, 1969-70; Chairman, National Association of Whole-Time Hospital Chaplains for England, Scotland and Wales, 1978-82. Recreations: motoring; reading; topography; ecclesiology; medicine. Address: (h.) 17 Victoria Park Gardens South, Broomhill, Glasgow, G11 7BX; T.-041-339 5364.

Barr, David George Dryburgh, MB, ChB, FRCPEd, DCH. Consultant Paediatrician, Lothian Health Board, since 1971; part-time Senior Lecturer, Department of Child Life and Health, Edinburgh University, since 1977; b. 14.2.36, Edinburgh; m., Anna Blair; 2 s.; 1 d. Educ. Daniel Stewart's College, Edinburgh; Edinburgh University. Senior Registrar, Royal Hospital for Sick Children, Edinburgh, 1965-69; Research Fellow, Children's hospital, Zurich, Switzerland, 1969-70; Consultant Paediatrician, Edinburgh Northern and West Fife Hospitals, 1971-77; Consultant Paediatrician, Royal Hospital for Sick Children and Simpson Memorial Maternity Pavilion, since 1977; seconded to Ministry of Health and University of Riyadh, Saudi Arabia, 1980-83. Address: (b.) Royal Hospital for Sick Children, Sciennes Road, Edinburgh; T.-031-667 1991.

Barr, Gavin Hamilton, DFC, MA, EdB. Principal, Cardonald College, since 1969; b. 6.9.21, Ardrossan; m., Mary Margaret Conway; 1 s.; 1 d. Educ. Greenock Academy; Glasgow University. RAF, 1941-46; schools, 1950-56; further education, 1956-69. Past President, Govan Rotary Club. Recreations: reading; bird-watching. Address: (h.) 140 Finnart Street, Greenock; T.-0475 21329.

Barr, Rev. George Kidd, DA, ARIBA, BD. Minister, Viewpark Parish Church, Uddingston, since 1967; b. 26.6.28, Motherwell; b. Muriel Margaret Harvey; 3 d. Educ. Greenock Academy; Kingussie Secondary School; Glasgow School of Architecture; Glasgow University. Scots Guards, 1946-48; architectural practice, 1955-64; County Architect, Zetland County Council, 1960-64; graduated in divinity, 1967. Address: Viewpark Manse, 14 Holmbrae Road, Uddingston, Glasgow, G71 6AP; T.-Uddingston 813113.

Barr, Ian. Chairman, Scottish Postal Board, since 1984; Chairman, Post Office National Arts Committee (UK), since 1976; b. 6.4.27, Edinburgh; m., Gertrud Karla Odefey; 2 d. Educ. Boroughmuir High School. Post Office: Assistant Postal Controller (North Western Region, England), 1955; Inspector of Postal Services, 1957; Assistant Controller (Planning), 1962 (both in Post Office HQ, London); Principal, 1966; Assistant Secretary, 1971; Regional Director (Eastern Region, England), 1976; Post Office Headquarters Director of Buildings, Mechanisation and Transport, 1978; Director, Post Office Estates Executive, 1981-84; Member, Civil Service Selection Board, 1966-71; Member, Scottish Council, CBI, since 1984; Chairman, Conference Europeeune des Postes et des Telecommunications (Batiments), since 1982; Member, British Materials Handling Board, 1978-81. Recreations: composing serial music; writing esoteric poetry; reading epistemology; practising solipsism. Address: (b.) West Port House, Edinburgh, EH3 9HS.

Barr, Rev. John Gourlay Crichton. Deputy Secretary, Law Society of Scotland, since 1978; non-stipendiary Priest, Scottish Episcopal Church, since 1985; b. 10.5.23, Berwick-upon-Tweed; m., Mary Wanklyn Branford; 2 s. Educ. Struan School, Berwick; George Watson's College, Edinburgh; Edinburgh University. Royal Navy, 1942-46; mentioned in Despatches, Normandy, 1944; admitted Solicitor, 1947; Partner: Robertson Dempster & Co., Perth, 1953-74, Cundie, Mackenzie & Co., Perth, 1974-78. Former Member of Board, Royal Lyceum Theatre and Perth Repertory Theatre (Chairman, 1972-78); Scottish Episcopal Church: Lay Reader, Diocese of St Andrews, 1958-78, Diocesan Registrar, 1974-78; involved in team ministry, St. Mark's Episcopal Church, Portobello, since 1981; Past Chairman: Laity Committee, Scottish Churches Council; Perth Council of Churches; Council Member, Law Society of Scotland, 1968-77; Unionist candidate, West Stirlingshire, 1964; Lieutenant, RNVR, 1965-66. Recreations: theatre; bird-watching; creative writing. Address: (h.) 3 Hamilton Terrace, Edinburgh, EH15 1NB; T.-031-669 3300.

Barr, Sheriff Kenneth Glen, MA, LLB. Sheriff, South Strathclyde, Dumfries and Galloway, at Dumfries, since 1976; b. 20.1.41; m. Educ. Ardrossan Academy; Royal High School; Edinburgh University.

Barratt, Michael, MA (Hons). Headmaster, Rannoch School, since 1982; b. 31.12.40, Edinburgh; m., Valerie Anne Dixon; 1 s.; 1 d. Educ. George Watson's College, Edinburgh; Merchiston Castle School; St. Andrews University; St. Edmund Hall, Oxford. Assistant Master, Epsom College, Surrey, 1964-73; Housemaster, Strathallan School, Perth, 1973-82. Recreations: golf; gardening; mountaineering; theatre. Address: Headmaster's House, Rannoch School, Rannoch, Perth, PH17 2QQ; T.-088 22 332.

Barratt, Oliver William, SDA. Secretary, Cockburn Association (Edinburgh Civic Trust), since 1971; Secretary, Cockburn Conservation Trust, since 1978; b. 7.7.41, Belfast. Educ. Radley College; East of Scotland College of Agriculture. National Committee, Scottish Association for Public Transport; Trustee, Scottish Historic Buildings Trust and Lothian Building Preservation Trust. Recreations: the hills; travel; most of the arts. Address: (h.) 1 London Street, Edinburgh, EH3 6LZ; T.-031-556 5107.

Barrie, Alistair T., BSc (Hons), DipTP, MRTPI. Chief Planning Officer, City of Dundee District Council, since 1974; b. 19.2.38, Dundee; m., Elizabeth; 2 s.; 1 d. Educ. Harris Academy, Dundee; University of St Andrews; Heriot-Watt University. Former Honorary Secretary and Treasurer (Past Chairman), Scottish Society of Directors of Planning. Recreation: athletics. Address: (b.) City of Dundee District Council, 21 City Square, Dundee, DD1 3BS; T.-0382 23141, Ext. 4400.

Barrie, Derek Andrew, MA, DipEd, JP. Chairman, North East Fife District Council, since 1984 (Member, since 1977); Principal Teacher of History, Buckhaven High School, since 1974; b. 3.8.42, Guardbridge, Fife; m., Lesley Brown. Educ. Bell-Baxter High School, Cupar; St. Andrews University; Dundee University. Member, Cupar Town Council, 1971-74; Chairman, North East Fife District Sports Council, 1977-79; Member, St Andrews Links Trust, 1984; Liberal candidate, East Fife, General Election, 1966; President, Midlands Rugby Union Referees Society, 1979-81. Recreations: rugby refereeing; golf; gardening; cooking. Address: (h.) 13 Lindsay Gardens, St Andrews, Fife; T.-0334 75502.

Barron, John Mackay, BSc. Headmaster, Melrose Grammar School, since 1965; Member, Ettrick and Lauderdale District Council, since 1980; b. 30.9.22, Fraserburgh; m., Evelyn Sheena Adams; 1 s.; 2 d. Educ. Inverurie Academy; Aberdeen University. Royal Corps of Signals, Far East, 1944-47. Teacher of Mathematics and Science, Insch Junior Secondary School, 1950-56; Headmaster: Craigievar School, Aberdeenshire, 1957-62, Rayne North School, Aberdeenshire, 1962-65; Member, Melrose Town Council, 1971-75; Chairman: Melrose Liberal Association,

since 1969; Melrose Festival Committee, 1979-84; Melrose branch, Rheumatism and Arthritis Council; Member, Eildon Housing Association; Clerk, Melrose Parish Church Congregational Board. Recreations: soccer; cricket; golf. Address: (h.) Schoolhouse, Huntly Road, Melrose, Roxburghshire, TD6 9SB; T.-Melrose 2103.

Barron, Professor Laurence David, DPhil, BSc, MInstP. Professor of Chemistry, University of Glasgow, since 1984; b. 12.2.44, Southampton; m., Sharon Aviva Wolf; 1 s.; 1 d. Educ. King Edward VI Grammar School, Southampton; Northern Polytechnic, London; Lincoln College, Oxford. Post-doctoral research, Cambridge University, 1969-75; Ramsay Memorial Fellow, 1974-75; University of Glasgow: Lecturer in Chemistry, 1975-80, Reader, 1980-84. Corday-Morgan Medal, Chemical Society, 1977; G.M.J. Schmidt Memorial Lecturer, Weizmann Institute of Science, 1984. Publication: Molecular Light Scattering and Optical Activity, 1982. Recreations: walking; music; radio-controlled model aircraft. Address: (b.) Chemistry Department, The University, Glasgow, G12 8QQ; T.-041-339 8855.

Barrow, Professor Geoffrey Wallis Steuart, MA (Hons), BLitt, DLitt, FBA, FRSE, FSA, FSA Scot, FRHistS. Sir William Fraser Professor of Scottish History and Palaeography, Edinburgh University, since 1979; b. 28.11.24, Headingley, Leeds; m., Heather Elizabeth Agnes Lownie; 1 s.; 1 d. Educ. St. Edward's School, Oxford; Inverness Royal Academy; St. Andrews University; Pembroke College, Oxford. Royal Navy and RNVR (Sub-Lieutenant), 1943-46; Lecturer in History, University College, London, 1950-61; Professor of Medieval History, Newcastle-upon-Tyne University, 1961-74; Professor of Scottish History, St. Andrews University, 1974-79. Member, Royal Commission on Historical Manuscripts, since 1984; Royal Historical Society: Council Member, 1963-74, Joint Literary Director, 1964-74, Vice President, since 1983; Past Chairman of Council, Scottish History Society (President, 1973-77). Publications: Feudal Britain, 1956; Acts of Malcolm IV, 1960; Robert Bruce, 1965 and 1982; Acts of William I, 1971; The Kingdom of the Scots, 1973; The Scottish Tradition (Editor), 1974; The Anglo-Norman Era in Scottish History, 1980; Kingship and Unity: Scotland 1000-1306, 1981. Recreations: hillwalking; visiting graveyards; travel. Address: (h.) 12A Lauder Road, Edinburgh, EH9 2EL; T.-031-668 2173.

Barry, Rt. Rev. Mgr. John Charles McDonald, MA (Cantab), DCL. Parish Priest, St. Mark's RC Church, Edinburgh, since 1977; b. 26.9.17, Edinburgh. Educ. Abbey School, Fort Augustus; Trinity College, Cambridge; University of Fribourg, Switzerland; Oscott College, Birmingham; Gregorian University, Rome. Ordained priest, 1944; appointed Curate, St. Patrick's, Kilsyth; sent to Rome to study canon law, 1946; appointed to St. Cuthbert's, Edinburgh, 1949; transferred to St. Anthony's, Polmont, 1950; St. Andrew's College, Drygrange: Lecturer, 1953, Rector, 1960. Editor, Canon Law Abstracts, Canon Law Society of Great Britain, 1959-84;

Consultor to the Pontifical Commission for the Revision of Canon Law, 1966-78. Recreations: golf; walking. Address: St. Mark's, Oxgangs Avenue, Edinburgh, EH13 9HX; T.-031-441 3915.

Barry, (Donald Angus) Philip, CBE (1980), OBE (1969). HM Chief Inspector of Prisons for Scotland, 1981-85; b. 16.9.20, Edinburgh; m., Margaret Orr; 5 s.; 1 d. Educ. Abbey School, Fort Augustus. HM Forces, 1939-46 (Captain, Gordon Highlanders, 57 Division, North Africa, Sicily); Director, John Barry Ltd., 1946-80 (Managing Director, from 1963); Secretary of State appointment to Visiting Committee, Edinburgh Prison Borstal Section, 1947-50; Vice Chairman, Visiting Committee, Dumfries Borstal, 1950-63; Polmont Borstal, 1963-68 (Chairman, 1965-68); Member, Kilbrandon Committee on Scottish marriage law, 1965; Member, Parole Board for Scotland, 1969-80 (Chairman, 1974-80); Honorary Vice Consul for Spain, 1975-80. Address: (b.) St. Andrew's House, Edinburgh.

Bartlett, Professor Christopher John, BA, PhD, FRHistS. Professor of International History, Dundee University, since 1978 (Head of Modern History Department, since 1983); Member, Scottish Examination Board, since 1984; b. 12.10.31, Bournemouth; m., Shirley Maureen Briggs; 2 s. Educ. Queen Elizabeth's Grammar School, Wimborne; University College, Exeter; London School of Economics. Assistant Lecturer, Edinburgh University, 1957-59; Lecturer, University of the West Indies, Jamaica, 1959-62; Lecturer, Queen's College, Dundee, 1962-68; Reader, Dundee University, 1968-78. Publications: Great Britain and Sea Power 1815-53; Castlereagh; The Long Retreat; The Rise and Fall of the Pax Americana; A History of Postwar Britain 1945-74; The Global Conflict 1880-1970. Address: (b.) Department of History, The University, Dundee.

Bartlett, Keith, MB, BCH, FRCR, DMRT, FRCP. Consultant Radiotherapist, Aberdeen Royal Infirmary, since 1979; b. 10.6.44, Tredegar, Monmouthshire; m., Lilian M. Banthes; 1 s.; 2 d. Educ. Pontllanfraith Grammar School; Welsh National School of Medicine, Cardiff. Four years in Canadian hospitals, latterly (1977-78) as Consultant; returned to UK, 1978; pioneered use of RF hyperthermia in cancer in Scotland, 1983. Recreations: music; renovating old cars; electronics. Address: (h.) 58 Victoria Street, Dyce, Aberdeen, AB2 OEE; T.-0224 722221.

Barty, James Webster, OBE (1981), MA, LLB. Retired Solicitor; Honorary President, Scottish Law Agents Society, since 1984; b. 9.3.12, Dunblane; m., Elisabeth Beryl Roebuck; 1 s.; 2 d. Educ. Hurst Grange School, Stirling; Fettes College, Edinburgh; St. Andrews University; Edinburgh University. Qualifed as Solicitor, 1935; Partner, Tho. & J.W. Barty, Dunblane, 1937-84; Scottish Law Agents Society: Secretary, 1940-82, President, 1982-84; Honorary Sheriff, since 1970. Clerk, Dunblane Cathedral Kirk Session, 1949-69; Council Member, Friends of Dunblane Cathedral, 1940-84 (Vice-Chairman, 1974-84). Recreations: life-long interest in sport

(rugby, tennis, cricket, badminton) and in all arts, including theatre, opera, ballet, literature and painting. Address: (h.) Easterton, Argaty, Doune, Perthshire; T.-0786 841 372.

Basson, John Vincent, MB, ChB, BSc (Hons), MPhil, MRCPsych. Consultant Forensic Psychiatrist, Royal Edinburgh Hospital; b. 23.11.45, Manchester. Educ. De La Salle College, Salford; Edinburgh University. Fellowship in Community Psychiatry, 1976-78; Member, Secretary of State's Committee on Difficult Prisoners, 1979-82; Scottish Member, Council, SACRO; Chairman, Edinburgh Cyrenian Trust. Recreations: gardening; keep fit; golf; travel. Address: (b.) Royal Edinburgh Hospital, Mackinnon House, Morningside Place, Edinburgh; T.-031-447 2011.

Bastable, Arthur Cyprian, OBE, BSc, CEng, FIEE, FIBM. General Manager, Ferranti plc, Dundee, since 1958; Director, Ferranti Astron Ltd., since 1983; Director, Ferranti Industrial Electronics Ltd., since 1984; Deputy Chairman, Dundee Port Authority, since 1981 (Member, since 1967, Convener, Corporate Planning Committee, since 1975); b. 9.5.23, Kobe, Japan; m., Joan Cardwell; 1 s.; 1 d. Educ. St. Georges School, Harpenden; Manchester University. Joined Ferranti, 1950; President, Dundee & Tayside Chamber of Commerce, 1970-71 (Convener, Overseas Trade and Development, since 1973); Member, Tayside Development Authority, 1972-75; Vice-Chairman, Board of Governors, Dundee College of Technology, 1975-77; Member, Scottish Council, CBI, 1980; Member, Dundee Project Steering Committee, since 1983. Recreations: sailing; skiing; ornithology. Address: (h.) Hunters Moon, 14 Lorne Street, Monifieth, Dundee, DD5 4DU.

Batchelor, Derek William, LLB (Hons). Procurator Fiscal, Jedburgh, since 1983; b. 26.1.49, Perth; m., Lorna Elizabeth Mary Gibson; 3 s.; 1 d. Educ. Perth Academy; Edinburgh University. Procurator Fiscal Depute, Stirling, 1976-78; seconded, Scottish Law Commission, 1978-79; Senior Legal Assistant, Crown Office, 1979-83; Secretary, Stewart Committee on Alternatives to Prosecution, 1980-83; Consultant, Council of Europe Select Committee on Criminal Procedure, since 1982. International Coach and Convener of Coaching, Scottish Men's Hockey Association. Recreations: hockey and other sports; photography; music; reading. Address: (h.) Oatlands House, Parsonage Road, Galashiels; T.-Galashiels 2159.

Batchelor, Sir Ivor (Ralph Campbell), Kt (1981), CBE, FRCPEdin, FRCPsych, DPM, FRSE. Member, Scottish Hospital Endowments Research Trust, since 1984; Emeritus Professor of Psychiatry, Dundee University; b. 29.11.16; m.; 1 s.; 3 d. Educ. Edinburgh Academy; Edinburgh University. Squadron Leader, RAFVR, 1941-46. Professor of Psychiatry, Dundee University, 1967-82; Chairman, Committee on Staffing Mental Deficiency Hospitals, 1967-70; MRC: Chairman, Clinical Research Board, 1973-74; Neuro-Sciences Board, 1974-75; Member, Royal Commission on the National Health Service, 1976-79.

Batt, Leslie, BSc, MSc, PhD, DSc, CChem. Senior Lecturer in Physical Chemistry, Aberdeen University, since 1962; b. 25.4.35, Greenford, England; m., Patricia Mary Mitchell; 2 s.; 1 d. Educ. Ealing Grammar School; University of Wales (Swansea); Birmingham University; Cambridge University. Research Associate, University of Southern California; NATO Research Fellow, Cambridge University. Fellow, Royal Society of Chemistry. Recreations: sailing; squash; cross-country skiing. Address: (b.) Department of Chemistry, Aberdeen University, Aberdeen, AB9 2UE; T.-0224 40241.

Baxby, Keith, BSc, MB, BS, FRCS. Consultant Urological Surgeon, Tayside Health Board, since 1977; Honorary Senior Lecturer, Dundee University, since 1977; b. 17.4.44, Sheffield. Educ. King Edward VII School, Sheffield; Durham University. House Officer, Royal Victoria Infirmary, Newcastle-upon-Tyne, 1968-69; Surgical Registrar, Newcastle University Hospitals, 1969-73; Northern Counties Kidney Fund Research Fellow, 1973-74; Senior Urological Registrar, Newcastle General Hospital, 1974-77; Visiting Professor of Urology, Louisiana State University, 1981; WHO Fellow in Clinical Urodynamics, 1984. Recreation: deer stalking. Address: (b.) Department of Urology, Royal Infirmary, Dundee; T.-0382 23125.

Baxter, Professor James Thomson, MA, PhD, CBiol, FIBiol, MRCVS, FRSH. William Dick Professor of Veterinary Medicine, Edinburgh University, since 1970 (Dean, Faculty of Veterinary Medicine, since 1984); b. 6.2.25, Edinburgh; m., Muriel Elizabeth Knox; 2 s.; 1 d. Educ. Trinity Academy, Edinburgh; Royal (Dick) Veterinary College, Edinburgh. Royal Navy, 1944-46; general veterinary practice, 1950-52; Veterinary Officer, then Veterinary Research Officer, Ministry of Agriculture, Northern Ireland, 1952-60; Lecturer, Loughry Agricultural College, 1955-60; Assistant Lecturer in Veterinary Science, Queen's University, Belfast, 1958-60; Professor in Clinical Veterinary Practices, Dublin University, 1960-70; Director, School of Veterinary Medicine, Dublin University, 1963-70; Fellow, Trinity College, Dublin, 1965-70; Visiting Professor, Al-Fateh University, Tripoli, Libya, 1984, 1985. Chairman, North of Ireland Veterinary Officers' Association, 1958; Council Member, Irish Grassland and Animal Production Society, 1961-70 (President, 1963-64); Chairman, Association of Veterinary Teachers and Research Workers (Ireland), 1965; Council Member, Royal College of Veterinary Surgeons, 1962-70, 1978-82, since 1984; Joint Editor-in-Chief, Veterinary Science Communications (now Veterinary Research Communications), since 1976. Address: (b.) Royal (Dick) School of Veterinary Studies, Veterinary Field Station, Easter Bush, Roslin, Midlothian, EH25 9RG; T.-031-445 2001.

Bayley, Professor Peter Charles, MA (Oxon). Berry Professor of English (Head of English Department), St. Andrews University, since 1978; b. 25.1.21, Gloucester; m., 1 s.; 2 d. Educ. Crypt School, Gloucester; University College, Oxford. War Service, Royal Artillery, 1941-44; Intelligence Corps, India, 1944-45; Junior Research Fellow, University College, Oxford, 1947-49; Fellow, 1949-72 ; Master, Collingwood College, Durham University, 1972-78; Visiting Professor, Yale University, 1970; Distinguished Brown Visiting Professor, University of the South, Tennessee, 1978. Publications: Edmund Spenser, Prince of Poets, 1971; Minor Poems of John Milton (commentary and notes), 1982; An ABC of Shakespeare, 1985; Spenser's The Faerie Queene, Books I and II (Editor); A Casebook on The Faerie Queene; Loves and Deaths. Address: (b.) Department of English, St. Andrews University, St. Andrews, Fife; T.-St. Andrews 76161.

Bayliss, Anthony Paul, MB, ChB, FRCR, DMRD. Consultant Radiologist, Aberdeen Royal Infirmary, since 1975; b. 7.2.44, Oldham; m., Margaret Anne; 3 s. Educ. Oldham Hulme Grammar School; St. Andrews University. Medical Intern., Mount Sinai Hospital, Minneapolis, 1969-70; House Officer, Ballochmyle Hospital, Ayrshire, 1970-71; Trainee Radiologist, Western Infirmary, Glasgow, 1971-75. Recreation: golf. Address: (h.) 1 Marchbank Road, Bieldside, Aberdeen; T.-Aberdeen 861229.

Bealey, Professor Frank William, BSc (Econ) (Hons). Professor of Politics, Aberdeen University, since 1964; b. 31.8.22, Bilston, Staffordshire; m., Sheila Hurst; 1 s.; 2 d. Educ. King Edward VI Grammar School, Stourbridge; London School of Economics. Extra-Mural Lecturer, Manchester University, 1951-52; Lecturer, Keele University, 1952-64; Temporary Lecturer, Birmingham University, 1958-59. Treasurer and founder Member, Society for the Study of Labour History, 1960-63; Convener, Committee for Social Sciences, Aberdeen University, 1970-74; Fellow, Royal Historical Society, 1971; Editorial Board, Political Studies, 1975-83; Visiting Fellow, Yale University, 1980. Publications: Labour and Politics 1900-1906 (Co-author); Consituency Politics (Co-author); The Social and Political Thought of the British Labour Party; The Post Office Engineering Union; The Politics of Independence (Co-author). Recreations: reading poetry; darts; eating and drinking; watching football and cricket. Address: (h.) 355 Clifton Road, Aberdeen, AB2 2DT; T.-Aberdeen 44689.

Beastall, Graham Hedley, BSc, PhD, MRCPath. Top Grade Biochemist (Endocrinology), Glasgow Royal Infirmary, since 1981; Honorary Lecturer, Glasgow University, since 1983; b. 11.12.47, Liverpool; m., Judith; 2 s. Educ. Liverpool Institute High School for Boys; Liverpool University. Lecturer in Biochemistry, Liverpool University, 1971-72; Lecturer in Steroid Biochemistry, Glasgow University, 1972-76; Senior Biochemist (Endocrinology), then Principal Biochemist (Endocrinology), Glasgow Royal Infirmary, 1976-81. Secretary, Caledonian Society for Endocrinology, since 1984; Area Commissioner, Greater Glasgow Scout Council. Recreations: Scouting; gardening; sport. Address: (b.) Department of Clinical Biochemistry, Royal Infirmary, Glasgow, G4 OSF; T.-041-552 3535, Ext. 4444.

Beat, Janet Eveline, BMus, MA. Composer; Lecturer, Royal Scottish Academy of Music and Drama, since 1972; b. 17.12.37, Streetly.

Educ. High School for Girls, Sutton Coldfield; Birmingham University. Freelance Orchestral Player, 1960s; Lecturer: Madeley College of Education, 1965-67, Worcester College of Education, 1967-71; founder Member, and former Council Member, Scottish Society of Composers; writes musical criticism for The Scotsman; G.D. Cunningham Award, 1962; her compositions include The Gossamer Web, a dance drama for soprano, piano, percussion and tape, commissioned for Edinburgh Festival Fringe, 1975, and Dancing on Moonbeams, an electronic fantasy, 1980 (released on gramophone record); her works have received performances throughout Scotland, as well as in Switzerland, Poland, North America, South America, Greece and Japan. Recreations: travel; reading; photography. Address: (h.) 5 Letham Drive, Glasgow, G43 2SL; T.-041-637 1952.

Beattie, Alastair, MA, LLB. Chief Executive, Caithness District Council, since 1974; b. 11.10.37, Aberdeen; m., Rosaline; 2 s.; 1 d. Educ. Robert Gordon's College, Aberdeen; Aberdeen University. Legal/Principal Legal Assistant, Dumfries County Council, 1961-67; Caithness County Council: Depute County Clerk, 1967-74, Chief Executive, 1974. Recreations: squash; bridge. Address: (b.) Council Offices, Market Square, Wick, Caithness; T.-0955 3761.

Beattie, Alastair George, MSc, FRMetS. Principal, Scottish Office, since 1981; Assessor of Public Undertakings (Scotland), 1982-85; Secretary, Scottish Valuation Advisory Council, 1981-85; b. 5.3.52, Liverpool; m., Margaret Helen Neilson. Educ. Robert Gordon's College, Aberdeen; Edinburgh University; Alberta University. Joined Scottish Office, 1975; Private Secretary to Permanent Under Secretary of State, 1978-80. Honorary Treasurer, Scottish Genealogy Society, since 1981; Rotary Foundation Graduate Fellow, 1974-75. Publications: Pre-1855 Gravestone Inscriptions in Kilmarnock and Loudoun District (Co-author), 1985; Pre-1855 Gravestone Inscriptions in Upper Deeside (Co-author), 1985. Recreations: hill-walking; golf; genealogy; travel; gardening; music (listening). Address: (h.) 14 Inverleith Gardens, Edinburgh, EH3 5PS; T.-031-552 1222.

Beattie, Henry Thomson, OBE (1974). Member, Perth and Kinross District Council, since 1980 (Convenor of Architectural Services, 1982-85; Leader, Conservative Group, since 1985); b. 14.6.20, Glasgow; m., Harriet Hall Hughes; 2 s. Educ. Hutchesons' Grammar School, Glasgow. Pilot, RAF, 1944-45; joined Rivers Steam Navigation Co., 1946; Controlling Agent, Assam, 1954-64 (Director, Assam Sillimanite Co. Ltd., 1956-64); General Manager, Assam Railways & Trading Co. Ltd., 1965-73; Chairman, Hocte Timber Co. Ltd., 1965-73; Housemaster, Morrison's Academy, Crieff (retired, 1985). Appointed MBE, 1963, for services to British people during Chinese incursion into India; Chairman, Assam branch, UK Citizens Association, 1968-72; Chairman, Crieff Community Council, 1975-78. Recreations: fencing; golf. Address: The Cottage, Rectory Road, Crieff, PH7 3DZ; T.-Crieff 2295.

Beattie, Rev. Walter Gordon, MA, BD. Minister, Arbroath Abbey Church, since 1977; b. 25.4.32, Aberdeen; m., Catherine Fiona Matheson; 1 s.; 2 d. Educ. Robert Gordon's College, Aberdeen; Aberdeen University. Assistant Minister, St. Machar's Cathedral, Aberdeen, 1956-57; Minister: Sorbie Parish, Wigtownshire, 1957-62; Fraserburgh West Church, 1962-77. Hospital and school Chaplain. Recreations: reading; gardening; walking. Address: Abbey Church Manse, 51 Cliffburn Road, Arbroath, Angus, DD11 5BA; T.-Arbroath 72196.

Beaumont, Phillip Barrington, BEcon (Hons), MEcon, PhD. Senior Lecturer, Department of Social and Economic Research, Glasgow University, since 1983; b. 13.10.49, Melbourne, Australia; m., Patricia Mary Ann McKinlay. Educ. Camberwell High School, Melbourne; Monash University, Melbourne; Glasgow University. Research Fellow, then Lecturer, Glasgow University, 1976-83; Visiting Professor, Massachusetts Institute of Technology, Boston, 1983. Publications: Bargaining in the Public Sector, 1978; Safety at Work and the Trade Unions, 1981; Job Satisfaction in Public Administration, 1983. Recreations: tennis; badminton; shooting; fishing. Address: (b.) The University, Glasgow, G12 8QG; T.-041-339 8855.

Bechhofer, Frank, MA. Reader in Sociology, Edinburgh University, since 1971 (Director, Research Centre for Social Sciences, since 1984); b. 10.10.35, Nurnberg, Germany; m., Jean Barbara Conochie; 1 s.; 1 d. Educ. Nottingham High School; Queens' College, Cambridge. Junior Research Officer, Department of Applied Economics, Cambridge University, 1962-65; Lecturer in Sociology, Edinburgh University, 1965-71. Address: (b.) Research Centre for Social Sciences, 56 George Square, Edinburgh, EH8 9JU; T.-031-667 1011, Ext. 6322.

Beck, Professor John Swanson, BSc, MD, FRCPGlas, FRCPEdin, FRCPath, FRSE. Professor of Pathology, Dundee University, since 1971; Honorary Consultant Pathologist, Tayside Health Board, since 1971; b. 22.8.28, Glasgow; m., Marion Tudhope Paterson; 1 s.; 1 d. Educ. Glasgow Academy; Glasgow University. House Officer, Western Infirmary and Royal Hospital for Sick Children, Glasgow, 1953-54; Trainee Pathologist, Western Infirmary and Glasgow University, 1954-63; Clinical Research Fellow, National Institute for Medical Research, London, 1960-61; Senior Lecturer in Pathology, Aberdeen University, 1963-71. Chairman, Biomedical Research Committee, Chief Scientist Organisation, Scottish Home and Health Department, since 1983 (Member, Chief Scientist Committee, since 1983); Chairman, Breast Tumour Panel, Medical Research Council, since 1979; Member, Tayside Health Board, since 1983; former Member, Cell Biology and Disorders Board, Medical Research Council; former Assistant Editor, Journal of Pathology. Recreation: DIY. Address: (b.) Department of Pathology, Ninewells Hospital and Medical School, PO Box 120, Dundee, DD1 9SY; T.-0382 60111, Ext. 2169.

Beckett, Rev. David Mackay, BA, BD. Minister, Greyfriars Tolbooth and Highland Kirk, Edinburgh, since 1983; b. 22.3.37, Glasgow; m.,

Rosalie Frances Neal; 2 s. Educ. Glenalmond; Trinity Hall, Cambridge; St. Andrews University. Assistant Minister, Dundee Parish Church (St. Mary's), 1963-66; Minister, Clark Memorial Church, Largs, 1966-83. Convener, Committee on Public Worship and Aids to Devotion, General Assembly, 1978-82; Secretary, Scottish Bible Society; Vice-President, Church Service Society. Publication: The Lord's Supper, 1984. Address: (h.) 12 Tantallon Place, Edinburgh, EH9 1NZ; T.-031-667 8671.

Beckett, Geoffrey James, BSc, PhD. Senior Lecturer in Clinical Chemistry, Edinburgh University, since 1984; b. 22.11.50, Manchester; m., Catriona; 2 s. Educ. Moston Brook High School, Manchester; Manchester University (UMIST); Edinburgh University. Postdoctoral Research Fellow, 1975-76; NHS biochemist, 1976-79; Lecturer, Edinburgh University, 1979-84. Recreations: gardening; DIY. Address: (b.) Department of Clinical Chemistry, Royal Infirmary, Edinburgh; T.-031-229 2477, Ext. 2940.

Bedborough, William F., MA (Hons), DipEdTech. Rector, Forfar Academy, since 1979; b. 6.11.42, Glasgow; m., Sheena J. McLullich; 1 s.; 1 d. Educ. Hutchesons' Boys' Grammar School, Glasgow; Glasgow University. Assistant Teacher (History), Hutchesons' Boys Grammar School, 1965-68; Special Assistant Teacher (History), Hamilton Academy, 1968-69; Principal Teacher (History), Bellshill Academy, 1969-72; Assistant Rector, Arbroath Academy, 1972-75; Depute Rector, Galashiels Academy, 1975-79. Recreations: sailing; golf; squash; Forfar Rotary Club; Strathmore Speakers Club. Address: (b.) Forfar Academy, Taylor Street, Forfar; T.-0307 64545.

Bedi, Tarlochan Singh, MB, BS, MRCPsych, DPM. Consultant Psychiatrist, Southern General Hospital, Glasgow, since 1980; b. 11.6.40, Jullandar, India; m., Dr. Taj Ratani; 1 s. Educ. Eastleigh Secondary School, Nairobi; Poona University, India. House Officer, Aga Khan Hospital, Nairobi, 1965; Senior House Officer, Glenside Hospital, Bristol, 1966; Registrar, Coney Hill Hospital, Gloucester, 1967-70; Senior Registrar, Gartnaval Royal Hospital, Glasgow, 1970-72; Consultant Psychiatrist, Woodilee Hospital, Lenzie, 1972-80. President: Indian Graduates Society; Indian Social and Cultural Association; Member, Executive Committee, Scottish Asian Action Committee; Member: Crime Prevention Panel, Bearsden and Milngavie; Media Sub-Committee, Strathclyde Community Relations Council. Recreations: badminton; photography. Address: (h.) 156 Prestonfield, Milngavie; T.-041-445 2466.

Beeley, Josie Ann, BSc, MSc, PhD. Senior Lecturer in Oral Biochemistry, Glasgow University Dental School, since 1978; b. 30.1.39, Crewe; m., John G. Beeley; 1 s. Educ. Sir John Deane's Grammar School, Northwich, Cheshire; Manchester University. Assistant Lecturer in Biochemistry, Sheffield University, 1964-65; Research Associate, University of Washington, Seattle, 1965-67; Glasgow University: Assistant Lecturer in Biochemistry, 1967-68; Lecturer in

Oral Biochemistry, 1968-78. Awarded ORCA-Rolex Prize by European Organisation for Caries Research, 1975. Recreations: tennis; swimming; photography; genealogy. Address: (b.) Oral Biochemistry Unit, Glasgow University Dental School, 378 Sauchiehall Street, Glasgow, G2 3JZ; T.-041-332 7020, Ext. 205.

Beeston, Michael Harding, ARMCM, GRSM. Viola Player, Edinburgh Quartet, since 1971; b. 11.5.48, Blackpool; m., Janet Bond; 1 s.; 2 d. Educ. Royal Manchester College of Music. Sub-Principal Viola, BBC Scottish Symphony Orchestra; Principal Viola, Scottish Chamber Orchestra; present teaching appointments: Royal Scottish Academy of Music, St. Mary's Music School, Edinburgh, Broughton High Special Music Unit, Edinburgh; frequent appearances as soloist in concertos/recitals; occasional adjudicator. Recreations: travel; food; photography. Address: (h.) 119 Craigleith Road, Edinburgh, EH4 2EH; T.-031-332 8691.

Begg, Hugh MacKemmie, MA, PhD, DipTP, MRTPI, MBIM, MCIT, MInstPet. Director, Department of Town and Regional Planning, Duncan of Jordanstone College of Art, Dundee, since 1981; Dean, Faculty of Environmental Studies, Dundee University, since 1983; b. 25.10.41, Glasgow; m., Jane Elizabeth Harrison; 2 d. Educ. High School of Glasgow; St. Andrews University; University of British Columbia. Lecturer in Political Economy, St. Andrews University; Research Fellow, Tayside Study; Lecturer in Economics, Dundee University; Assistant Director of Planning, Tayside Regional Council; Visiting Professor, Technical University of Nova Scotia. Recreations: local history; reading; rugby. Address: (h.) 4 Esplanade, Broughty Ferry, Dundee; T.-0382 79642.

Begg, Norman Roderick Darroch, MA, LLB. Deputy Secretary, Aberdeen University; b. 23.12.41, London; m., Anne Fleck; 1 d. Educ. Aberdeen Grammar School; Aberdeen University. Administrative Assistant, East Anglia University, 1964-66; Aberdeen University, since 1966: Administrative Assistant; Assistant Secretary; Registry Officer; Clerk to Senatus. Member, Children's Panel, Grampian Region, since 1984; Past Chairman, Aberdeen Studio Theatre Group; Director, Edinburgh Festival Fringe Society, 1980-83. Recreation: amateur drama. Address: (h.) 10 The Chanonry, Old Aberdeen; T.-0224 41101.

Begg, Robert William, CBE (1977), MA, FRSA, CA. Partner, Mann Judd Gordon, Chartered Accountants, Glasgow, since 1951; Chairman of Trustees, National Galleries of Scotland, since 1980; b. 19.2.22; m., Sheena Margaret Boyd; 2 s. Educ. Greenock Academy, Glasgow University. Royal Navy, 1942-46 (Lt., RNVR) (Despatches); Honorary Treasurer, Royal Philosophical Society of Glasgow, 1952-62; Honorary Treasurer, Royal Glasgow Institute of Fine Arts, since 1975; Member, Board of Governors, Glasgow School of Art, 1975-77 (Chairman, 1970-76); Council Member, National Trust for Scotland, since 1984. Recreation: painting. Address: (h.) 3 Colquhoun Drive, Bearsden, Glasgow, G61 4NQ; T.-041-942 2436.

Beggs, Rev. Rebecca McCrae, DTST, LCST. Minister of Religion; b. 23.4.20, Ardrossan. Educ. Ardrossan Academy; Glasgow School of Speech Therapy; New College, Edinburgh. Speech Therapist, Ayrshire; Regional Speech Therapist, Western Regional Hospital Board; Lecturer in Speech Pathology: Glasgow School of Speech Therapy, Jordanhill College of Education; Deputy Director, Dublin College of Speech Therapy; Consultant Adviser on Speech Therapy Training, Iran (WIIO); Associate Minister, Pollokshields Church of Scotland; Co-Editor, Pollokshields Gazette; Minister, St. Bride's, Callander (retired). Recreations: walking; painting; writing. Address: (h.) 7A Savile Terrace, Edinburgh, EH9 3AD; T.-031-667 9045.

Belch, Alexander Ross, CBE (1972), LLD Strathclyde (1978), BSc, FRSE, FRINA, CBIM, CEng. Company Director; Chairman, Irvine Development Corporation; b. 13.12.20, London; m., Janette Finnie Murdoch; 4 d. Educ. Morrison's Academy, Crieff; Glasgow University. Lithgows Ltd.: Director and General Manager, 1954, Managing Director, 1964; Managing Director, Scott Lithgow Group, 1969-80; part-time Member, Organising Committee for British Shipbuilders, and Member, Board, British Shipbuilders, 1976-79; Shiprepair Adviser, Gibraltar Government, 1982-83; Deputy Chairman, Jebsens Drilling plc; Chairman: Jebsens Travel Ltd.; Gleddoch Hotels Ltd.; a Director: Jebsens (UK) Ltd.; Gault Armstrong and Kemble (Holdings) Ltd.; Lithgows Ltd.; YARD Ltd. (subsidiary of Yarrow & Company); J.H. Carruthers & Co. Ltd.; Kongsberg Ltd.; Data-Ship (UK) Ltd.; President, Shipbuilders and Repairers National Association, 1974-76; former Member, Scottish Regional Board, British Railways. Chairman: Mining Machinery Economic Development Committee; Trustees of the Scottish Maritime Museum; Member, Board of Governors, Morrison's Academy, Crieff. Address: A.R. Belch Associates Ltd., 9 Clairmont Gardens, Glasgow, G3 7LS; T.-041-332 8651.

Bell, Albert Elliot, MA, MB, ChB, MFCM. Community Medicine Specialist, Fife Health Board, since 1985; Senior Medical Officer, Scottish Home and Health Department, 1974-85; b. 26.11.24, Edinburgh; m., Dr. Fiona McCully; 3 s. Educ. Glasgow University. Industry; RAF, 1944-47; Deputy Medical Superintendent, Glasgow Royal Infirmary Group, 1962-63; Assistant Dean, Faculty of Medicine, Glasgow, 1963-70; joined SHHD, 1970. Recreation: golf. Address: (h.) 6B Juniper Park Road, Edinburgh; T.-031-453 3692.

Bell, Alexander Gilmour, BL. Chief Reporter for Public Inquiries, Scottish Office, since 1979; b. 11.3.33; m.; 4 s. Educ. Hutchesons' Grammar School, Glasgow; Glasgow University. Solicitor, 1954; joined Scottish Office as Legal Officer, 1967; appointed Deputy Chief Reporter, 1973.

Bell, Sheriff Andrew Montgomery, BL. Sheriff of Glasgow and Strathkelvin, at Glasgow, since 1984; b. 21.2.40, Edinburgh; m., Ann Margaret Robinson; 1 s.; 1 d. Educ. Royal High School, Edinburgh; Edinburgh University. Solicitor,

1961-74; called to Bar, 1975; Sheriff of South Strathclyde, Dumfries and Galloway, at Hamilton, 1979-84. Address: (h.) 5 York Road, Edinburgh, EH5 3EJ; T.-031-552 3859.

Bell, Sheriff Archibald Angus, QC (Scot), MA, LLB. Sheriff of Glasgow and Strathkelvin, at Glasgow, since 1973; b. 13.4.23; m.; 2 s. Educ. The Leys School, Cambridge; St. Andrews University; Glasgow University. Royal Navy, 1941-45 (Sub Lt., RNVR); admitted, Faculty of Advocates, 1949; Reporter, Court of Session Cases, 1952-55. President, Scottish Cricket Union, 1975.

Bell, Colin John, MA (Hons). Broadcaster; Journalist; Author; b. 1.4.38, London; m., Caroline Rose Bell; 1 s.; 3 d. Educ. St. Paul's School; King's College, Cambridge. Journalist, The Scotsman, 1960-62 and 1975-78; Journalist/Contributor, London Life, Sunday Times, Sunday Telegraph, Daily Mirror, Sunday Mail, etc.; Lecturer, Morley College, 1965-68; College Supervisor, King's College, Cambridge, 1968-75; Parliamentary candidate (SNP), West Edinburgh, 1979; European Parliamentary candidate (SNP), North East Scotland, 1979; Vice-Chairman, SNP, 1978-84; Campaign Director, Euro Election, 1984. Publications: City Fathers, 1969; Boswell's Johnson, 1971; Scotch Whisky, 1985; Radical Alternative (Contributor), 1978; The Times Reports (Series) (Editor). Recreations: jazz; Scottish history. Address: (h.) Cockburnhill, Balerno, Midlothian.

Bell, Donald Atkinson, BSc, PhD, CEng, MIEE. Director, National Engineering Laboratory, since 1983; b. 28.5.41, Belfast; m., Joyce Louisa Godber; 2 s. Educ. Royal Belfast Academical Institution; Queen's University, Belfast; Southampton University. National Physical Laboratory, Teddington, 1966-77; Electronics Applications Division, Department of Industry, 1978-82. Address: (b.) National Engineering Laboratory, East Kilbride; T.-03552 20222.

Bell, George Armour, JP, BSc, MB, ChB. Member, Lanarkshire Health Board; b. 8.7.20, Bellshill; m., Elizabeth Davidson Porteous; 2 s. Educ. Bellshill Academy; Glasgow University. War Service, 609 Squadron, RAF; retired General Practitioner, Bellshill; Chairman, Crime Prevention Panel, Bellshill and District; Red Cross Detachment Medical Officer, Bellshill; Member, Management Committee, Citizens Advice Bureau; Chairman, Lanarkshire Branch, Tenovus Scotland; Founder Chairman, Community Council for Mossend; Honorary Medical Officer, Bellshill Bn.; Boys Brigade; President, Bellshill Branch, Arthritis Care. Address: (h.) Chudleigh, 449 Main Street, Bellshill, Lanarkshire, ML4 1DB; T.-749084.

Bell, George Scott, AIB, AIB (Scot). Honorary Sheriff, Tayside, Central and Fife, at Dunfermline, since 1976; General Commissioner of Income Tax, Dunfermline District, since 1976; b. 27.6.14, Johnstone; m., 1, Agnes Ewing Stark (deceased); 2, Violet Woolcock; 1 d. Educ. Madras College, St. Andrews. Began career with British Linen Bank, St. Andrews, 1931; as Member, RAFVR, called up for active service,

1939; mentioned in Despatches, 1946; British Linen Bank: Assistant Trustee Manager, 1952, Manager, Linlithgow, 1957, Manager, Dunfermline, 1963 (merged with Bank of Scotland, 1971); part-time Lecturer in banking subjects, Heriot-Watt College, Edinburgh, three years; Examiner, Institute of Bankers in Scotland, 10 years; retired from Bank, 1974. Elder, Church of Scotland, since 1957; at various times Treasurer, St. Michael's Church, Linlithgow, and St. Margaret's Church, Dunfermline. Recreations: golf; bowls. Address: (h.) Kilrymont, 16 Over Haven, Limekilns, Dunfermline, Fife, KY11 3JH; T.-0383 872484.

Bell, G. Susan, ACIS. Director, Scotland Direct Limited, since 1973; Partner, The Scottish Gourmet, since 1975; Board Member, Scottish Tourist Board, since 1983; b. 31.8.46; m., Arthur J.A. Bell; 2 s.; 2 d. Educ. College of Commerce, Glasgow. Investment Analyst, Edinburgh, 1970-74; Conservative Parliamentary candidate: Motherwell, 1970, Caithness & Sutherland, February 1974; Chairman: Conservative Candidates Association, 1971-74, Clydesdale Constituency, 1980-83, South of Scotland Euro Constituency, 1983-84; Member, Council, National Trust for Scotland. Recreations: garden; riding; reading. Address: (h.) Culter House, Coulter, Biggar; T.-0899 20064.

Bell, Professor Henry B., BSc, PhD, FIM, CEng. Professor of Metallurgy, Strathclyde University, since 1974; b. 3.7.22, Greenock; m., Barbara M. Smith; 1 d. Educ. Greenock High School; Royal College of Science and Technology. Assistant Metallurgist, Scotts Shipbuilding and Engineering Company; Research Assistant, Lecturer, Reader, Metallurgy Department, Strathclyde University; Visiting Professor, Concepcion University, Witwatersrand University, Toronto University; Distinguished Visiting Scientist, National Research Council, Halifax. Kroll Medallist, Metals Society; President, Scottish Association for Metals, since 1984; Member, Editorial Panel, Ironmaking and Steelmaking. Recreation: gardening. Address: (b.) Metallurgy Department, Strathclyde University, North Portland Street, Glasgow, G1 1XN; T.-041-552 4400.

Bell, Jeanne Elisabeth, BSc, MD, MRCPath. Senior Lecturer in Pathology, Edinburgh University, since 1984; Honorary Consultant in Neuropathology, Western General Hospital, Edinburgh, since 1984; b. 10.8.42, England; m., Dr. Denis Rutovitz; 1 s. Educ. Newcastle-upon-Tyne University. Lecturer, Department of Anatomy, Newcastle-upon-Tyne, 1967-70; part-time Scientific Officer, MRC Clinical and Population Cytogenetics Unit, Edinburgh, 1975-79; Senior Registrar in Paediatric Pathology, Royal Hospital for Sick Children, Edinburgh, 1979-84. Address: (b.) Neuropathology Laboratory, Western General Hospital, Crewe Road, Edinburgh, EH4 2XU; T.-031-332 2525.

Bell, John Alexander, BEd, JP. Secretary for Scotland, Professional Association of Teachers, since 1983; Member, Kirkcaldy District Council, since 1984; b. 19.4.46, Glasgow; m., Catherine Roy Rankine. Educ. St. Augustine's School,

Glasgow; Glasgow University; Jordanhill College of Education. Principal Teacher of Modern Studies, Glenrothes High School, 1975-83; Member, Scottish Joint Negotiating Committee (School Education), since 1983. Recreations: running; walking; reading; music. Address: (h.) 17 Cardean Way, Balgeddie, Glenrothes, Fife; T.-0592 742550.

Bell, Neil, MusB, GRSM, ARMCM, ARCO, CertEd. Director of Music, Broughton High School, Edinburgh, and Director, Lothian Specialist Music Scheme, since 1980; b. 17.10.43, York; m., Gillian Gray; 1 s. Educ. Nunthorpe Grammar School, York; Manchester University; Royal Manchester College of Music. Assistant Music Master, Cheadle Hulme School, 1967; Head of Music, West Bridgford School, Nottingham, 1971; joined teaching staff, South Nottinghamshire School of Music, becoming Vice Principal, then Principal; professional Singer, formerly with BBC Northern Singers, now John Currie Singers. Recreations: the arts; gardening; hill-walking. Address: (b.) Broughton High School, Carrington Road, Edinburgh, EH4 1EG; T.-031-332 7805.

Bell, Robin, MA (Hons), MSc (Hons). Writer; b. 4.1.45, Dundee; m., Suzette; 2 d. Educ. Morrison's Academy, Crieff; St. Andrews University; Perugia University, Italy; Union College, New York; Columbia University, New York. Director of Information, City University of New York, Regional Opportunity Program; Professor, John Jay College of Criminal Justice, City University of New York; Member, US Office of Education Task Force in Educational Technology; Audio-Visual Editor, Oxford University Press; Editor, Guidebook series to Ancient Monuments of Scotland; Secretary, Scottish Association for the Speaking of Verse; Journalist and Broadcaster; Scottish Radio and Television Industries Award for Best Radio Feature, 1985; Sony Award, Best British Radio Documentary, 1985. Publications: (poetry): The Invisible Mirror; Culdee, Culdee; Sawing Logs; Strathinver: A Portrait Album 1945-53; Collected Poems of James Graham, Marquis of Montrose (Editor). Recreations: books; walking. Address: (h.) 38 Dovecot Road, Edinburgh, EH12 7LE; T.-031-334 5241.

Bell, Sheriff Stewart Edward, QC (Scot), MA (Cantab), LLB. Sheriff Principal of Grampian, Highland and Islands, since 1983; b. 4.8.19; m., Isla Spencer (deceased); 3 d. Educ. Kelvinside Academy, Glasgow; Trinity Hall, Cambridge; Glasgow University. Commissioned, Loyal Regiment, 1939; served, 2nd Bn., Singapore and Malaya; wounded; POW, Singapore and Korea, 1942-45; Advocate, 1948; Sheriff of Lanarkshire, at Glasgow, then of Glasgow and Strathkelvin, 1961-82.

Bell, William Wallace, MA, BSc, MSc, PhD, AFIMA. Senior Lecturer in Engineering, Aberdeen University, since 1974; b. 29.1.36, Dumfries; m., Nancy Cairns; 1 s.; 1 d. Educ. Dumfries Academy; Edinburgh University. Lecturer in Mathematics, Heriot-Watt College, Edinburgh, 1962-63; Aberdeen University: Lecturer in Natural Philosophy, 1963-68, Lecturer in Engineering Mathematics, 1968-74. Publications: Special Functions for Scientists and Engineers; Matrices for Scientists and Engineers. Recreations: music; gardening. Address: (b.) Department of Engineering, The University, Aberdeen; T.-0224 40241.

Beloff, Halla, BSc, PhD, FBPS. Senior Lecturer, Department of Psychology, Edinburgh University, since 1963; b. 11.5.30; m., John Beloff; 1 s.; 1 d. Educ. South Hampstead High School; London University; Illinois University; Queen's University, Belfast. Former Editor, British Journal of Social and Clinical Psychology; former Member, Psychology Committee, Social Science Research Council; President, British Psychological Society, 1983-84. Occasional broadcaster, BBC Radio Scotland. Publications: Psychology Survey 5 (Co-Editor), 1984; Camera Culture, 1985. Recreations: following the arts and not being shocked by the new; needlework. Address: (h.) 6 Blacket Place, Edinburgh, EH9 1RL; T.-031-667 3200.

Belton, Neville Richard, BSc, PhD, CChem, MRSC. Senior Lecturer, Department of Child Life and Health, Edinburgh University, since 1975; Honorary Biochemist, Lothian Health Board; b. 5.10.37, Nottingham; m., Elisabeth Foster Inglis; 1 s.; 1 d. Educ. Nottingham High School; Birmingham University. Research Associate, Children's Memorial Hospital, Chicago, 1963-67; Lecturer in Pharmacology and Associate in Pediatrics, Northwestern University, Chicago, 1964-67; Lecturer, Department of Child Life and Health, Edinburgh University, 1967-75. Member, DHSS Working Party on the Composition of Infant Foods, 1974-80. Recreations: travel; sport (squash, tennis, hockey); music. Address: (h.) 10 Cammo Brae, Edinburgh, EH4 8ET; T.-031-339 5920.

Beltrami, Joseph, BL, NP. Solicitor (Beltrami & Co.); b. 15.5.32, Rutherglen; m., Brigid D.; 3 s. Educ. St. Aloysius College, Glasgow; Glasgow University. Intelligence Corps, 1954-56 (Sgt.); qualified as Solicitor, 1956; specialised in criminal law; has instructed in more than 500 murder cases; closely associated with two cases of Royal Pardon. Chairman, soccer testimonials: Jim Johnstone and Bobby Lennox, 1976; Danny McGrain, 1980. Publications: The Defender, 1980; Glasgow - A Celebration (Contributor), 1984. Recreations: bowls; soccer; snooker; writing; boxing. Address: (h.) 5 St. Andrew's Avenue, Bothwell, Lanarkshire; T.-Bothwell 852374.

Benington, (Charles) Kenneth, BSc, PhD, CEng, MIMechE. Managing Director, Brown Brothers & Co. Ltd., since 1981; Technical Director, Vickers Marine Engineering Division, since 1981; b. 1.4.31, Belfast; m., Margaret Malcolm; 1 s.; 1 d. Educ. Dalriada Grammar School, Ballymoney; Queen's University, Belfast; Heriot-Watt University. Graduate apprentice and design engineer, Associated Electrical Industries Ltd., 1953-60; Assistant Chief Engineer, Trials, British Ship Research Association, 1960-63; Lecturer, Heriot-Watt University, 1963-72; Senior Engineer, Marine Industries Centre, Newcastle University, 1972-74; Brown Brothers & Co. Ltd.:

Systems Manager, 1974-75; Technical Manager, 1975-77; Technical Director, 1977-80; Assistant Manager and Technical Director, 1980-81. Member, Executive Committee, Scottish Engineering Employers' Association, since 1984. Address: (b.) Brown Brothers & Co. Ltd., Broughton Road, Edinburgh, EH7 4LF; T.-031-556 2440.

Bennet, Donald John, BSc, MS, PhD, CEng, MIMechE. Senior Lecturer, Department of Thermodynamics, Strathclyde University, since 1975; Author; b. 6.11.28, London; m., Eileen Anne Lowry; 2 s. Educ. Melville College, Edinburgh; Heriot-Watt College, Edinburgh. RAF, 1952-55; Instructor, Outward Bound Trust, 1955-56; Lecturer: Royal Technical College, Glasgow, 1956-61; University of British Columbia, Canada, 1961-62; Lecturer, Strathclyde University, 1963-75. Member, Countryside Commission for Scotland, since 1982; Chairman, Scottish branch, Combined Heat and Power Association, 1982-85; Honorary Secretary, Scottish Mountaineering Club, 1967-80. Publications: Elements of Nuclear Power, 1971; The Staunings Alps, 1971; The Southern Highlands, 1971; Scottish Mountain Climbs, 1980; The Western Highlands, 1982. Recreations: photography; mountaineering; skiing. Address: (h.) 4 Morven Road, Bearsden, Glasgow, G61 3BU; T.-041-941 1387.

Bennett, Bruce, MB, ChB (Hons), MD (Hons), MRCP, FRCP, MRCPath. Reader in Medicine, Aberdeen University; b. 5.7.38, Gorakhpur, India; m., Dr. G. Adey Bennett. Educ. Brechin High School; Aberdeen University. Aberdeen University: Ashley Mackintosh Research Fellow, 1964; MRC Junior Research Fellow, 1965; Lecturer in Medicine, 1967; Eli Lilly Travelling Research Fellow, then Visiting Research Fellow, Case Western Reserve University, Cleveland, Ohio, 1970-72; Wellcome Senior Research Fellow, Aberdeen University, 1973; appointed Senior Lecturer, 1978. Address: (b.) Department of Medicine, Phase II, Aberdeen Royal Infirmary, Foresterhill, Aberdeen; T.-0224 681818, Ext. 3348.

Bennett, Rev. David Keith Patterson, BA. Minister, Findochty and Portknockie, since 1974; b. 26.9.31, Duns; 1 s.; 1 d. Educ. Berwickshire High School; Christ's College, Aberdeen; Glasgow University; Open University. Master builder, 1948-64 (National Service, 1st KOSB, 1953-55); Lay Missionary, Kilmeny, Isle of Islay, 1966-71. Moderator, Moray Presbytery, 1984-85. Recreation: chess. Address: The Manse, 20 Netherton Terrace, Findochty, Buckie, Banffshire, AB5 2QD; T.-0542 32545.

Bennett, Roderick, BSc, PhD, CChem, MRIC, MIBiol, MIHEc. Head of School of Home Economics, Robert Gordon's Institute of Technology, since 1972; b. 14.9.37, Sheffield; m., Morag Hamilton. Educ. Sheffield University. Recreations: sailing; squash. Address: Robert Gordon's Institute of Technology, Schoolhill, Aberdeen, AB9 1FR; T.-Aberdeen 633611.

Bennett, Ronald Alistair, QC (Scot), MA, LLB. Vice-President for Scotland, Value Added Tax Tribunals, since 1977; b. 11.12.22; m., Margret

Magnusson; 3 s.; 3 d. Educ. Edinburgh Academy; Edinburgh University; Balliol College, Oxford. Lt., 79th (Scottish Horse) Medium Regiment, RA, 1943-45; Captain, attached RAOC, India and Japan, 1945-46; called to Scottish Bar, 1947; Standing Counsel to Ministry of Labour and National Service, 1957-59; Sheriff-Principal: Roxburgh, Berwick and Selkirk, 1971-74, South Strathclyde, Dumfries and Galloway, 1981-82, North Strathclyde, 1982-83; Chairman, Medical Appeal Tribunals (Scotland), since 1971; Chairman, Agricultural Wages Board for Scotland, since 1973; Chairman, Local Government Boundary Commission for Scotland, since 1974; Chairman, Industrial Tribunals (Scotland), since 1977. Address: (h.) Laxamyri, 46 Cammo Road, Barnton, Edinburgh, EH4 8AP.

Bennie, Ernest Harry, MB, ChB, MRCPsych. Consultant Psychiatrist, Leverndale Hospital, since 1970; Honorary Clinical Lecturer, Glasgow University; b. 12.11.38, Glasgow; m., Norma Bennie; 2 s.; 1 d. Educ. Queens Park Senior Secondary School, Glasgow; Glasgow University. General medical career, three years; began psychiatric specialty, Duke Street Hospital, Glasgow, 1965. Recreations: yachting; sailing. Address: (b.) Leverndale Hospital, 510 Crookston Road, Glasgow, G53 7TU; T.-041-882 6255.

Bennie, Thomas, FIB (Scot). Joint General Manager, Bank of Scotland, since 1984; b. 7.11.32, Falkirk; m., Jean M. Bennie; 2 s.; 2 d. Educ. Falkirk High School. British Linen Bank (later merged with Bank of Scotland): entered, 1949; appointed Assistant Superintendent of Branches, 1969; Assistant General Manager, Bank of Scotland Finance Co. Ltd., 1973; Deputy Chief Executive and Assistant Director, British Linen Bank Ltd. (subsidiary of Bank of Scotland), 1977; appointed Director, British Linen Bank Ltd., 1978; Divisional General Manager, Bank of Scotland International Division, 1980-84. Recreations: fishing; golf; bowls; gardening. Address: (b.) Bank of Scotland, The Mound, Edinburgh, EH1 1YZ; T.-031-442 7777.

Bentham, Professor Richard Walker, BA, LLB, Barrister. Professor of Petroleum and Mineral Law and Director of the Centre for Petroleum and Mineral Law Studies, Dundee University, since 1983; b. 26.6.30, Holywood, Co. Down; m., Stella Winifred Matthews; 1 d. Educ. Campbell College, Belfast; Trinity College, Dublin. Lecturer in Law: Tasmania University, Hobart, 1955-5; Sydney University, New South Wales, 1957-61; Legal Department, British Petroleum Co., 1961-83 (Deputy Legal Adviser to the Company, 1979-83). Council Member: British branch, International Law Association; International Bar Association (Section on energy and natural resources law). Recreations: cricket; military history and military modelling. Address: (h.) West Bryans, 87 Dundee Road, West Ferry, Dundee; T.-0382 77100.

Berry, David Richard, MA, MSc, PhD, MiBiol. Reader, Department of Bioscience and Biotechnology, Strathclyde University, since 1985; b. 1.3.41, Huddersfield; m., Elisabeth Ann; 1 s.; 1 d. Educ. Holme Valley Grammar School; St. Peter's College, Oxford. Scientific Officer,

Glaxo Ltd., Ulverston, 1962-64; graduate student, 1964-70; Lecturer, then Senior Lecturer, Strathclyde University, 1970-84. Address: (b.) Department of Bioscience and Biotechnology, Strathclyde University, George Street, Glasgow; T.-041-552 4400.

Berry, John, CBE (1968), DL (Fife) (1969), BA (Cantab), MA (Cantab), PhD (St. Andrews) Hon. LLD Dundee (1970), FRSE. Adviser and Consultant on environmental and wildlife conservation; b. 5.8.07, Edinburgh; m., Hon. Bride Fremantle; 2 s.; 1 d. Educ. Ardvreck School, Crieff; Eton College; Trinity College, Cambridge. Salmon Research Officer, Fishery Board for Scotland, 1930-31; Biological Research Station, University College, Southampton: Research Officer, 1932-36; Director, 1936-39; Chief Press Censor for Scotland, 1940-44; Biologist and Information Officer, North of Scotland Hydro-Electric Board, 1944-49; Director of Nature Conservation in Scotland, 1949-67; consultancy work since 1968. Honorary Life Member, Swiss League for Protection of Nature, 1946; founder Member (1948) and first President (1954), International Union for Conservation of Natural Resources Commission on Ecology; Member, Executive Board, International Waterfowl Research Bureau, 1963-72; Honorary Corresponding Member, Danish Natural History Society, since 1957; Vice-President and Honorary Life Fellow, Royal Zoological Society of Scotland, since 1959; Honorary Life Fellow: Wildfowl Trust, 1983; Glasgow Natural History Society, 1951; Member, Dundee University Court, 1970-78. Recreations: natural history (especially water birds and fish); music. Address: (h.) Tayfield, Newport-on-Tay, Fife, DD6 8HA; T.-0382 543118.

Berry, William, MA, LLB, WS, NP. Partner, Murray Beith & Murray, WS, Edinburgh, since 1967; Director: Scottish Life Assurance Co.; Scottish American Investment Co. Plc; Fleming Universal Investment Trust Plc; and other companies; b. 26.9.39, Newport-on-Tay; m., Elizabeth Margery; 2 s. Educ. Ardvreck, Crieff; Eton College; St. Andrews University; Edinburgh University. Interests in farming, forestry, etc. Member, Council/Board: Edinburgh Festival Society; New Town Concerts Society Ltd.; Thistle Foundation; New Club, Edinburgh; performer in three records of Scottish country dance music. Recreations: music; shooting; forestry. Address: (b.) 39 Castle Street, Edinburgh, EH2 3BH; T.-031-225 1200.

Bertram, Robert David Darney, MA, LLB (Hons), ATII. Member, Scottish Law Commission, since 1978; Partner, Dundas & Wilson, WS, Edinburgh, since 1969; non-executive Director, The Weir Group PLC, since 1983; part-time Member, VAT Tribunal, since 1985; b. 6.10.41, Accrington; m., Patricia Joan Laithwaite; 2 s. Educ. Edinburgh Academy; Oxford University; Edinburgh University. Recreation: collecting. Address: (b.) 25 Charlotte Square, Edinburgh; T.-031-225 1234.

Besson, John Alexander Owen, BSc, MB, ChB, DPM, MRCPsych. Wellcome Senior Lecturer in Mental Health, Aberdeen University, since

1981; Honorary Consultant Psychiatrist, since 1981; b. 29.6.44, New Amsterdam, Guyana; m., Margaret Jean Adair. Educ. Edinburgh University. Consultant Psychiatrist, Lothian Health Board, 1977-80. Address: (b.) Department of Mental Health, Royal Cornhill Hospital, Aberdeen; T.-Aberdeen 639828.

Best, John R., BA. Scottish Organiser, Social Democratic Party, since 1982; b. 15.8.28, Beckenham. Educ. Dulwich College; Magdalene College, Cambridge. Address: (b.) 5 Royal Exchange Square, Glasgow, G1 2AF; T.-041-221 8871.

Best, Professor Jonathan James Kerle, MB, ChB, MSc, FRCPEdin, FRCR. Professor and Head of Department of Medical Radiology, Edinburgh University, since 1979; Honorary Consultant Radiologist, Lothian Health Board, since 1979; b. 29.11.42, Bristol; m., Elizabeth Margaret Frances McLean; 2 s.; 1 d. Educ. Kelly College; Edinburgh University; London University. Senior Registrar, Radiology, Hammersmith Hospital; Tutor in Radiology, Royal Post-Graduate Medical School; Senior Lecturer, Diagnostic Radiology, Manchester University; Honorary Consultant Radiologist, South Manchester District (Teaching). Address: (h.) 5 Merchiston Avenue, Edinburgh, EH10 4PJ; T.-031-229 6791.

Bethell, Denis Edwin, MA, PhD. Senior Lecturer in Chemistry, Dundee University; b. 19.9.25, Bebington, Cheshire; m., Janet M.W. Brown; 1 s.; 2 d. Educ. Birkenhead School; Queens' College, Cambridge. Dean of Students, Faculty of Science, Dundee University, 1974-84. Recreations: mountaineering; music; photography; travelling by train. Address: (b.) Dundee University, Dundee, DD1 4HN; T.-0382 23181.

Bethell, John, BSc (Hons). Chief Executive, Scottish Seed Potato Development Council, since 1982; Secretary: Aspel Ltd., since 1983; V.T. Growers Ltd., since 1984; b. 30.4.39, Nuneaton; m., Gillian Stewart Robertson McCartney; 1 s.; 3 d. Educ. Hutchesons' Boys Grammar School; Glasgow University. Geologist, Government of Sierra Leone; District Manager, Texaco Africa Ltd.; Managing Director: Argus of Ayr Ltd.; Argoventure Ltd. Assistant Secretary, Edinburgh Rotary Club, until 1982. Recreations: mountaineering; skin-diving; shellfish farming. Address: (h.) Riselaw House, Edinburgh; T.-031-228 6768.

Bevan-Baker, John Stewart, FRCO. Composer and freelance Musician; b. 3.5.26, Staines, Middlesex; m., June Mary Findlay; 1 s.; 4 d. Educ. Blundells School, Tiverton; Royal College of Music, London. Bevin boy, 1944-46; City Carillonneur, Aberdeen, 1958-63; Music Teacher in London, Aberdeen, Highlands of Scotland, and Glasgow. Recreations: gardening; reading; conservation. Address: (h.) 12 Academy Street, Fortrose, Ross-shire, IV10 8TW; T.-0381 20936.

Beveridge, George William, MB, ChB, FRCPE. Consultant Dermatologist, Edinburgh Royal Infirmary, since 1965; Honorary Senior Lecturer, Edinburgh University, since 1965; b. 23.2.32, Edinburgh; m., Janette Millar; 2 s.; 2 d. Educ.

Dollar Academy; Edinburgh University. President, Scottish Dermatological Society, 1982-85; Elder, Church of Scotland. Recreations: golf; gardening. Address: (h.) 6 Avon Road, Edinburgh, EH4 6JZ; T.-031-336 3680.

Beveridge, Professor Gordon Smith Grieve, BSc, ARCST, PhD, FEng, FIChemE, FRSE. Professor and Head of Department of Chemical and Process Engineering, Strathclyde University, since 1971; President and Vice-Chancellor-designate, Queen's University of Belfast; President, Institution of Chemical Engineers, 1984-85; Vice-Chairman, Engineering Council, since 1984; b. 28.11.33, St. Andrews; m., Geertruida Bruyn; 2 s.; 1 d. Educ. Inverness Royal Academy; Glasgow University; Edinburgh University. Assistant Lecturer, Edinburgh University, 1956-60; postdoctoral Harkness Fellow of Commonwealth Fund of New York, Minnesota University, 1960-62; Visiting Professor, Texas University, 1962; Lecturer, Edinburgh University and Heriot-Watt University, 1962-67; Senior Lecturer/Reader, Heriot-Watt University, 1967-71. Chairman: Process Engineering Committee, SERC; Advisory Council, ESDU International Ltd. Recreations: hill-walking; family golf. Address: (b.) Department of Chemical and Process Engineering, Strathclyde University, Glasgow, G1 1XJ; T.-041-552 4400.

Beveridge, Kathleen Mary, MA, DipEd. Organising Secretary, Church of Scotland Woman's Guild, 1977-85; b. 15.11.20, Edinburgh; m., Ian S. Beveridge; 3 d. Educ. George Watson's Ladies' College, Edinburgh; Edinburgh University. School teacher, 1943-49. Recreations: reading; crossword puzzles; walking; country life. Address: (b.) Woman's Guild Office, Church of Scotland, 121 George Street, Edinburgh; T.-031-225 5722.

Bewick, James Thomas, MA. Rector, Morgan Academy, Dundee, since 1970; b. 2.5.25, Glasgow; m., Jane C.B. Brash; 1 s.; 1 d. Educ. Albert Road Academy, Glasgow; Glasgow University. Teacher of English, Wishaw High School, 1950-54; Principal Teacher of English, Gordon Schools, Huntly, 1954-61; Aberdeen Academy: Principal Teacher of English, 1961-68; Depute Rector, 1968-70. Member: Central Committee on English, 1966-71; Scottish Examination Board, 1981-84; Board of Governors, Dundee College of Education; College Council, Dundee College of Commerce. Recreations: reading; pursuing an interest in the arts; gardening; travelling, particularly in France. Address: (h.) 6 Bingham Terrace, Dundee, DD4 7HH; T.-Dundee 455509.

Bewsher, Peter Dixon, MB, ChB, MD, FRCPE. Reader in Therapeutics, Aberdeen University, since 1977; Honorary Consultant Physician, Grampian Health Board, since 1969; b. 6.4.34, Cockermouth; m., Marlyn Crichton; 2 s.; 1 d. Educ. Cockermouth Grammar School; St. Andrews University. Medical Registrar, Aberdeen Hospitals; Research Associate, Indiana University; Lecturer, then Senior Lecturer in Therapeutics, Aberdeen University. Recreations: music; golf; hill-walking. Address: (h.) 83 Abbotshall Drive, Cults, Aberdeen, AB1 9JJ; T.-Abrdeen 868078.

Biggart, Thomas Norman, CBE (1983), WS, MA, LLB. Partner, Biggart Baillie & Gifford, WS, Solicitors, Glasgow and Edinburgh, since 1959; Director, Clydesdale Bank, since 1985; b. 24.1.30; m., Eileen Jean Anne Gemmell; 1 s.; 1 d. Educ. Morrison's Academy, Crieff; Glasgow University. Royal Navy, 1954-56 (Sub-Lt., RNVR). Law Society of Scotland: Council Member, since 1977; Vice-President, 1981-82; President, 1982-83; President, Business Archives Council, Scotland, since 1977; Member, Executive, Scottish Council (Development and Industry), since 1984; Member, Scottish Tertiary Education Advisory Council, since 1984; OStJ, 1968. Recreations: golf; hill-walking. Address: (h.) Gailes, Kilmacolm, Renfrewshire, PA13 4LZ; T.-Kilmacolm 2645.

Binns, John Kenneth, MB, ChB, FRCPEdin, FRCPsych. Physician Superintendent, Leverndale Hospital, Glasgow, since 1969 (Consultant Psychiatrist, since 1964); Honorary Clinical Lecturer, Glasgow University, since 1964; b. 25.6.28, Halifax; m., Sylvia Sharp; 1 s.; 1 d. Educ. Rishworth School, West Yorkshire; Edinburgh University. Fulbright Scholar and Rotating Intern., Erie, Pa., 1951-52; Medical Officer, RAMC, 11th Hussars, 1952-54; psychiatric training, Royal Edinburgh Hospital, 1956-64. Member of numerous professional committees at various times. Publication: Psychiatry in Medical Practice (Contributor). Recreations: gardening; photography. Address: (h.) 1 Balvie Avenue, Giffnock, Glasgow, G46 6NE.

Birks, Professor Peter Brian Herrenden, MA (Oxon), LLM (Lond). Professor of Civil Law, Edinburgh University, since 1981; b. 3.10.41, Hassocks, Sussex; m., Jacqueline Susan Stimpson; 1 s.; 2 d. Educ. Chislehurst and Sidcup Grammar School, Kent; Trinity College, Oxford. Teaching Fellow, Northwestern University, Chicago, 1965; Lecturer, University College, London, 1966-71; Fellow, Brasenose College, Oxford, 1971-81. Recreations: Roman Law; legal history; opera; general reading. Address: (h.) 12/3 Forrest Hill, Edinburgh; T.-031-225 2429.

Birnie, Rev. Charles John, MA. Minister of Aberdour linked with Tyrie, since 1982; b. 19.7.25, Kininmonth, Lonmay; m., Isabel Moir; 2 s.; 1 d. Educ. Peterhead Academy; Kings College, Aberdeen; Christs College, Aberdeen. Higher Diploma in Religious Education. Teacher of English, Bowmore, Islay, 1950-53; Head Teacher: Watten Primary School, Caithness, 1953-59; Melness Junior Secondary School, Sutherland, 1959-61; English-teaching posts in Banffshire, 1961-67; Minister, Annbank, Ayrshire, 1969-82. Publication: Makar's Quair anthology (Editor), 1968. Recreations: composition of original bothy ballads; collecting Scottish anecdotes; writing scripts featuring vocabulary and rural life of Buchan; country concerts. Address: The Manse, Tyrie, Fraserburgh, AB4 4DN; T.-Memsie 325.

Birse, Rev. George Stewart, BD, CA. Minister, Bourock Parish Church, Barrhead, since 1980; b. 13.4.48, Broughty Ferry; m., Sandra Elisabeth Borthwick; 3 d. Educ. Dunfermline High School; Edinburgh University. Area Internal Auditor/ Area Financial Accountant, Ayrshire and Arran Health Board; Principal Internal Auditor, Lothian Regional Council. Address: 14 Maxton Avenue, Barrhead, Glasgow, G78 1DY; T.-041-881 1462.

Birss, Rev. Alan David, MA (Hons), BD (Hons). Minister, Inverkeithing Parish Church of St. Peter, since 1982; b. 5.6.53, Ellon; m., Carol Margaret Pearson. Educ. Glenrothes High School; St. Andrews University; Edinburgh University. Assistant Minister, Dundee Parish Church (St. Mary's), 1978-80. Member: Executive Committee, Edinburgh Cripple Aid Society; Council, Church Service Society; Council, Scottish Church Society. Address: St. Peter's Manse, 14 Chapel Place, Inverkeithing, Fife, KY11 1NQ; T.-0383 412626.

Bishop, Alan Henry, MA (Hons). Principal Establishment Officer, Scottish Office, since 1984; b. 12.9.29, Edinburgh; m., Marjorie Anne Conlan; 1 s.; 1 d. Educ. George Heriot's School, Edinburgh; Edinburgh University. Private Secretary to Parliamentary Under Secretaries of State for Scotland, 1958-59; Principal, Department of Agriculture and Fisheries for Scotland, 1959; First Secretary, Food and Agriculture, Copenhagen and The Hague, 1963-66; Assistant Secretary: Commission on the Constitution, 1969-73, Devolution Division, Scottish Office, 1973-76, Health Building and Liaison Divisions, SHHD, 1976-80; Assistant Under-Secretary of State, Scottish Office, London, 1980-84. President, Scottish Bridge Union, 1979-80. Recreation: contract bridge. Address: (h.) 10 Wester Coates Avenue, Edinburgh, EH12 5LS; T.-031-337 2163.

Bisset, Rev. Peter Thomas, MA, BD. Evangelist, Church of Scotland, since 1974; Warden, St. Ninian's Training Centre, Crieff, since 1974; b. 16.6.27, Motherwell; m., Margaret Russell; 1 s.; 2 d. Educ. Rutherglen Academy; Glasgow University. Minister: Livingstone Church, Stevenston, 1953-60, Rutherford Church, Glasgow, 1960-68, High Church, Bathgate, 1968-74. Publications: Ten Growing Churches (Contributor); Prospects for Scotland (Contributor). Recreations: music; walking. Address: St. Ninian's, Comrie Road, Crieff, Perthshire, PH7 4BG; T.-0764 3766/7.

Bisset, Raymond George, JP, BSc. Headmaster, Kintore Primary School, since 1977; Member, Gordon District Council, since 1974 (Convenor, Environmental and Miscellaneous Committee, since 1984); b. 16.8.42, Ellon, Aberdeenshire; m. Heather McQueen Smith. Educ. Inverurie Academy; Aberdeen University. Science Teacher, Insch School, 1965-74; Head Teacher: Keithhall Primary School, 1975-77. Past Chairman, Inverurie and District Round Table, 1971-72; President, Inverurie Angling Association, 1972-74; founder Chairman, North East of Scotland Anglers Federation, 1973. Recreations: angling; hill-walking; golf; reading. Address: (h.) Keithhall Schoolhouse, Inverurie, Aberdeenshire, AB5 OLX; T.-Inverurie 21015.

Bissett, Norman, MA (Aberdeen), MPhil (Yale), MA (Lancaster). Representative, The British Council, Scotland, since 1984; b. 19.7.38,

Burntisland, Fife; m., Faith Lillian Svajian; 3 s. Educ. Aberdeen Academy; Aberdeen University; Aberdeen College of Education; Yale; Lancaster University. British Council Lecturer, Beirut, 1965-66; Head of English Department, Faculty of Political Science, Ankara University, 1969-71; Director, Anglo-Uruguayan Cultural Institute, Montevideo, 1971-75; Director of Studies, British Institute, Barcelona, 1975-79; English Language Officer, The British Council, Egypt, 1980-84. Recreations: books; art; music; hill-walking. Address: (b.) The British Council, 3-4 Bruntsfield Crescent, Edinburgh, EH10 4HD; T.-031-447 4716.

Bjarnason, Rev. Sven (Sveinbjorn Sesselius). Minister, Cairns Parish Church, Cowdenbeath, since 1976; b. 19.8.41, Reykjavik, Iceland; m., Catherine MacDonald; 1 s.; 1 d. Educ. primary and secondary schools in Iceland; University of Iceland; Edinburgh University. Emergency and disaster planning, Ministry of Justice and Church Affairs, Iceland, 1965-73 (Temporary Governor, Icelandic State Prison); ordained Minister, Icelandic Evangelical Lutheran Church, 1973; Associate Minister, Walls, Shetland, 1975; ordained as Minister, Church of Scotland, 1976; Chairman, Way to Life Crusade, Central Fife, 1985. Recreations: angling; photography. Address: Cairns Manse, 11 Foulford Road, Cowdenbeath; T.-0383 511267.

Black, Antony, MA (Cantab), PhD (Cantab). Senior Lecturer in Political Science, Dundee University, since 1980; author; b. 23.6.36, Leeds; m., Sarah Kieme; 3 s.; 1 d. Educ. Shrewsbury School; King's College, Cambridge. Assistant Lecturer, Department of Political Science, Queen's College, Dundee, 1963-66; Lecturer, Department of Political Science, Dundee University, 1967-80; Visiting Associate Professor, School of Government and Public Administration, The American University, Washington, DC, 1975-76. Publications: Monarchy and Community: political ideas in the later conciliar movement (1430-50); Council and Commune: the Council of Basle and the 15th-century heritage; Guilds and civil society in European political thought from the 12th century to the present. Recreation: hill-walking. Address: (b.) Department of Political Science, Dundee University, Dundee; T.-Dundee 23181, Ext. 4592.

Black, Hugh Blair, MA (Hons). Head Teacher, Greenock High School, 1968-85; Minister, Struthers Memorial Church, Greenock, since 1956; b. 22.7.22, Kilmacolm; m., Isobel B.M. Wright; 3 d. Educ. Greenock High School; Glasgow University; Jordanhill College of Education. History Teacher, latterly Principal Teacher of History, Port Glasgow High School, 1951-64; Head Teacher, Mount School, Greenock, 1964-68. Chairman, Central Committee on Social Subjects, seven years; Chairman, Social Subjects Centre, Jordanhill, seven years. Address: (h.) 27 Denholm Street, Greenock; T.-Greenock 87432.

Black, Rev. James Graham, BD. Minister, Hamilton Burnbank linked with Hamilton North, since 1978; b. 10.2.52, Motherwell; m., Isobel Ann Taylor Hamilton; 1 d. Educ. Dalziel High School, Motherwell; Glasgow University. Assistant Clerk, Hamilton Presbytery. Recreation: music. Address: 9 South Park Road, Hamilton; T.-Hamilton 424609.

Black, Professor Robert, LLB (Hons), LLM. Professor of Scots Law, Edinburgh University, since 1981; Deputy General Editor, The Laws of Scotland: Stair Memorial Encyclopaedia, since 1981; Temporary Sheriff, since 1981; b. 12.6.47, Lockerbie. Educ. Lockerbie Academy; Dumfries Academy; Edinburgh University; McGill University, Montreal. Advocate, 1972; Lecturer in Scots Law, Edinburgh University, 1972-75; Senior Legal Officer, Scottish Law Commission, 1975-78; practised at Scottish bar, 1978-81. Publications: An Introduction to Written Pleading, 1982; Civil Jurisdiction: The New Rules, 1983. Recreations: beer and books, not necessarily in that order. Address: (h.) 6/4 Glenogle Road, Edinburgh, EH3 5HW; T.-031-557 3571.

Blackie, John Walter Graham, BA (Cantab), LLB. Lecturer in Scots Law, Edinburgh University, since 1975; Director, Blackie & Son Ltd., publishers, since 1970; Advocate, since 1974; b. 2.10.46, Glasgow; m., Jane Ashman. Educ. Uppingham School; Peterhouse, Cambridge; Harvard; Merton College, Oxford; Edinburgh University. Open Exhibitioner, Peterhouse, Cambridge, 1965-68; St. Andrews Society of New York Scholar, Harvard, 1968-69; practised at Scottish bar, 1974-75. Recreation: music. Address: (h.) The Old Coach House, 23A Russell Place, Edinburgh, EH5 3HW; T.-031-552 3103.

Blacklaws, Allan Farquharson, OBE, CBIM, CIPM. Chairman, Scottish National Camps Association, since 1978; Human Resource Consultant, since 1983; b. 24.7.24, Glasgow; m., Sylvia Noble; 3 d. Educ. Whitehill School, Glasgow; University College, Swansea. Personnel Director, Scottish & Newcastle Breweries p.l.c., 1962-83; original Member, National Industrial Relations Court; Member: Employment Appeal Tribunal; ACAS Panel of Arbitrators. Recreation: bowls. Address: (h.) Craigmore House, 25 Craigmillar Park, Edinburgh, EH16 5PE; T.-031-667 3765.

Blacklock, Lt. Col. Michael David. Director of Marketing Services, National Trust for Scotland, since 1984; b. 30.4.28, London; m., Patricia Mary Ann Johnston; 1 s.; 1 d. Educ. Charterhouse; Royal Military Academy, Sandhurst. Regular Army Officer, Royal Scots Greys, 1948-72 (Instructor, Staff College, Camberley, 1967-68, Commanding Officer, Royal Scots Greys, 1969-71, Defence Fellowship, Edinburgh University, 1972); Development Secretary, National Trust for Scotland, 1973. Recreations: shooting; fishing. Address: (h.) Stable House, Maxton, St. Boswells, Roxburghshire; T.-0835 23024.

Blackwood, Edward, MRSH, ARSH, AMIBCO. Director of Technical Services, Banff and Buchan District Council, since 1975; b. 3.4.34, Johnstone; m., Anna; 3 s.; 1 d. Educ. Camphill Senior

Secondary School, Paisley. Assistant Burgh Surveyor, Johnstone, 1957-59; Burgh Surveyor and Sanitary Inspector, Banff, 1959-75. Committee Member, Scottish Association of Chief Building Control Officers. Recreation: golf. Address: (b.) Town House, Low Street, Banff; T.-026 12 2521.

Blackwood, Robert Whyte. Honorary Sheriff-Substitute, North Strathclyde, since 1961; b. 14.5.07, Kilmarnock; m., Mary Hately Dinwoodie (deceased); 2 d. Educ. Kilmarnock Academy; Merchiston Castle School, Edinburgh; Leeds University. RAF, 1941-46; Member, Kilmarnock Town Council, 1947-51; Additional Commissioner for Income Tax, Cunninghame Sub-Division, Ayrshire, 1950-57; General Commissioner for Income Tax, Ayrshire Sub-Area of Strathclyde, 1957-82 (Chairman of Commissioners, 1974-82); Member, Advisory Committee, Kilmarnock, Trustee Savings Bank of Glasgow, 1950-75 (Chairman, 1961-65); Member, Valuation Appeals Committee, Ayrshire Sub-Area of Strathclyde, 1965-80; Director, Ayrshire Mission to the Deaf, 1966-81 (Chairman, 1974-80). Recreations: golf; fishing. Address: (h.) 3 Howard Street, Kilmarnock, KA1 2BP; T.-Kilmarnock 42834.

Blair, Sir Alastair Campbell, KCVO, TD, WS, JP, BA, LLB. Captain, Queen's Bodyguard for Scotland (Royal Company of Archers), since 1982; b. 16.1.08; m.; 4 s. Educ. Cargilfield; Charterhouse; Clare College, Cambridge; Edinburgh University. RA (TA), 1939; served World War II (mentioned in Despatches); Secretary, Queen's Bodyguard for Scotland (Royal Company of Archers), 1946-59; Purse Bearer to Lord High Commissioner to General Assembly of Church of Scotland, 1961-69; retired Partner, Dundas & Wilson.

Blair, Alastair William, MB, ChB, FRCPE, DCH. Consultant Paediatrician, Fife Area Health Board, since 1970; Honorary Senior Lecturer: Department of Biochemistry and Microbiology, St. Andrews University, since 1975; Department of Child Life and Health, Edinburgh University, since 1979; b. 11.8.36, Preston; m., Irene Elizabeth McFee; 2 s. Educ. Harris Academy, Dundee; St. Andrews University. House Officer/Senior House Officer: Arbroath Infirmary; Maryfield Hospital, Dundee; Kings Cross Hospital, Dundee; Hospital for Sick Children, Great Ormond Street, London; Lecturer in Child Health, St. Andrews University; Registrar in Medical Paediatrics, Hospital for Sick Children, Great Ormond Street, London; Lecturer in Child Health, Aberdeen University; Wellcome-Swedish Research Fellow, Karolinska Children's Hospital, Stockholm; Senior Registrar in Paediatrics, Southmead Hospital, Bristol. Publication: Prenatal Paediatrics: a handbook for obstetricians and paediatricians (Co-author and Editor), 1971. Recreations: private aviation; camping; restoring old property. Address: (h.) Bellcraig Farm, by Leslie, Fife, KY6 3JE; T.-0592 741754.

Blair, David Wilson, MD, ChM, FRCSE. General Surgeon (Consultant), since 1963; b. 16.2.23, Dundee; m., Hilda C.; 1 s.; 2 d. Educ.

Morgan Academy, Dundee; St. Andrews University. Recreations: golf; hill-walking; painting. Address: (h.) East Mount, 354A North Deeside Road, Cults, Aberdeen; T.-0224 868023.

Blair, James Eric, BL. Solicitor, since 1948; Honorary Sheriff, since 1980; b. 18.3.23, Airdrie. Educ. Glasgow Academy; Glasgow University. Chairman, Airdrie Legal Aid Committee; Member, Executive Committee, Abbeyfield Airdrie Society. Recreation: golf. Address: (h.) Dunedin, Forrest Street, Airdrie.

Blair, John, BA (Cantab), CA, TD. Vice President, St. Andrews Ambulance Association; retired Chartered Accountant; b. 24.10.04, Edinburgh; m., Anna Fullarton Mackintosh; 1 s.; 1 d. Educ. Edinburgh Academy; Charterhouse; Clare College, Cambridge. Commissioned TA, 1938; served throughout World War II, Royal Artillery (demobilised in substantive rank of Major); in practice as CA in Glasgow, 1934-68. Council Member, St. Andrews Ambulance Association, 39 years; former Member, Central Committee, Scottish Ambulance Service; Honorary Treasurer, Royal Glasgow Institute of Fine Arts, 21 years; former Governor, Glasgow School of Art; Past Chairman, City of Glasgow Society of Social Service; former Honorary Treasurer, Glasgow Old Peoples Welfare Committee; former Director, Merchants House of Glasgow. Recreations: golf; gardening. Address: (h.) 15A Lampson Road, Killearn, Glasgow, G63 9PD.

Blair, John Samuel Greene, OBE (Mil), TD, OStJ, BA, ChM, FRCSEdin, FICS, D(Obst)RCOG. Consultant Surgeon, Perth Royal Infirmary, since 1966; Honorary Senior Lecturer in Surgery, Dundee University, since 1967; Honorary Senior Lecturer in Anatomy, St. Andrews University, since 1985; b. 31.12.28, Wormit, Fife; m., Ailsa Jean Bowes; 2 s.; 1 d. Educ. Dundee High School; St. Andrews University. National Service, RAMC, 1952-55; Tutor, Department of Anatomy, St. Salvator's College, St. Andrews, 1955; surgical and research training, Manchester, Dundee, Cambridge, London, 1957-65; Member, Court of Examiners, Royal College of Surgeons of Edinburgh, 1965; postgraduate Clinical Tutor, Perth, 1966-74; first North American Travelling Fellow, St. Andrews/Dundee Universities, 1971; TA Advisor to various Army Medical Ministry of Defence Departments, 1973-79; Secretary, Tayside Area Medical Advisory Committee, 1974-83; Member, Education Advisory Committee, Association of Surgeons, 1984; Secretary, Perth and Kinross Division, British Medical Association, 1982. Honorary Colonel (TA), RAMC; Elder, Church of Scotland. Publications: books on medical history and anatomy. Recreations: golf; history; travel; bridge. Address: (h.) 143 Glasgow Road, Perth; T.-Perth 23739.

Blair, Rev. Thomas James Loudon, MA, BD. Minister, Galston Parish Church, since 1980; Clerk, Irvine and Kilmarnock Presbytery, since 1985; b. 24.7.40, Glasgow; m., Patricia Anne Bell; 1 s.; 2 d. Educ. Hutchesons' Grammar School, Glasgow; Glasgow University. Minister: Campsie Trinity and Milton of Campsie, 1965-71;

Wallacetown Parish Church, Dundee, 1971-80; Mid Craigie Parish Church, Dundee (temporarily linked with Wallacetown), 1975-80. Recreations: golf; reading. Address: The Manse, Galston, Ayrshire; T.-Galston 820246.

Blair-Cunynghame, Sir James (Ogilvy), Kt (1976), OBE, FBIM, CIPM, FIB, MA. Deputy Chairman, Provincial Insurance plc, since 1979; b 28.2.13. Educ. Sedbergh School; King's College, Cambridge. Served World War II, RA and Intelligence, Mediterranean and Europe; Lt.-Col., 1944. Chairman, Royal Bank of Scotland Group plc, 1968-78; Chairman, Royal Bank of Scotland plc, 1971-76; Chairman, Williams & Glyn's Bank plc, 1976-78; Member, Queen's Bodyguard for Scotland (Royal Company of Archers); Hon. LLD, St. Andrews, 1965; Hon. DSc (SocSci), Edinburgh, 1969; Hon. FRCSEd, 1978.

Blair-Kerr, Sir Alastair, KB (1973), MA, LLB. President of the Court of Appeal for Bermuda, since 1979; President of the Court of Appeal for the Bahamas, 1978-81; Member, Gibraltar Court of Appeal, since 1983; b. 1.12.11, Killin, Perthshire; m., Esther Margaret Fowler Wright; 1 s.; 1 d. Educ. McLaren High School, Callander; Edinburgh University. Solicitor, 1939; Advocate, Scots bar, 1951; Advocate and Solicitor, Singapore, 1939-41; Straits Settlements Volunteer Force, 1941-42; escaped from Singapore, 1942; Indian Army: Staff Capt., "A" Bombay District HQ, 1942-43; DAAG 107 Line of Communication area HQ, Poona, 1943-44; British Army: GS02, War Office, 1944-45; SO1 Judicial, BMA Malaya, 1945-46; Colonial Legal Service (HM Overseas Service), Hong Kong: Magistrate, 1946-48; Crown Counsel, 1949; President, Tenancy Tribunal, 1950; Crown Counsel, 1951-53; Senior Crown Counsel, 1953-59; District Judge, 1959-61; Puisne Judge, Supreme Court, 1961-71; Senior Puisne Judge, Supreme Court, 1971-73; Acting Chief Justice of Hong Kong; President, various commissions of inquiry. Recreations: music; walking. Address: Gairn, Kinbuck, Dunblane, Perthshire, FK15 ONQ; T.-0786 823377.

Blake, Professor Christopher, FRSE, MA, PhD. Bonar Professor of Applied Economics, Dundee University, since 1974; b. 28.4.26; m.; 2 s.; 2 d. Educ. Dollar Academy; St. Andrews University. Royal Navy, 1944-47; teaching posts, 1951-53; Assistant, Edinburgh University, 1953-55; Stewarts & Lloyds Ltd., 1955-60; Lecturer, then Senior Lecturer, St. Andrews University, 1960-67; Senior Lecturer, then Professor of Economics, Dundee University, 1967-74; Director, Alliance Trust plc, since 1974; Director, William Low & Co. plc, since 1980; Member, Council for Applied Science in Scotland, since 1978; Deputy Chairman, Clothing Industry Wages Council, since 1981. Recreation: golf. Address: (h.) Westlea, Wardlaw Gardens, St. Andrews, Fife, KY16 9DW.

Blakey, Rev. Ronald Stanton, MA, BD, MTh. Assistant Secretary, Department of Education, Church of Scotland, since 1981; b. 3.7.38, Glasgow; m., Kathleen Dunbar; 1 s. Educ. Hutchesons' Boys' Grammar School, Glasgow; Glasgow University. Minister: St. Mark's, Kirkconnel,

1963-67; Bellshill West, 1967-72; Jedburgh Old Parish with Edgerston and Ancrum, 1972-81. Member, Roxburgh District Council, 1974-80 (Chairman of Council, 1977-80); Religious Adviser, Border Television, 1973-81; Member, Borders Region Children's Panel, 1974-80; JP, 1974-80. Publication: The Man in the Manse, 1978. Recreation: collecting antiquarian books on Scotland. Address. (h.) Flat 3, 21 Stuart Crescent, Edinburgh, EH12 8XR.

Blanche, John Jamieson, CA. Chairman: Teacher (Distillers) Ltd., since 1985; William Teacher & Sons Ltd., since 1985; United Rum Merchants Ltd., since 1985; Director, Showerings, Vine Products & Whiteways Ltd., since 1979; b. 10.7.29, Paisley; m., Fiona; 1 s.; 1 d. Educ. Glasgow Academy; Strathallan School. Hardie, Caldwell, Ker & Hardie, CA, Glasgow, 1954-56; Sales Manager, J.J. Blanche & Co. Ltd., 1956-60; Divisional Manager, Victoria Wine Co. Ltd., 1960-69; Financial Director, William Grant & Sons (Standfast) Ltd., 1967-85; Chairman and Managing Director, Stewart & Son of Dundee, 1969-79; Managing Director, William Teacher & Sons Ltd., 1979-85. Director, Clyde Port Authority; Governor, Strathallan School; Council Member, Scotch Whisky Association; Scottish Council Member, CBI; President, Junior Chamber Scotland, 1967. Recreations: golf; camping; hill-walking; gardening. Address: (b.) 14 St. Enoch Square, Glasgow, G1 4BZ; T.-041-204 2633.

Bland, Richard, MA. Senior Lecturer in Sociology, Stirling University, since 1982; b. 6.10.44, Glasgow; m., Rosemary E. Fitch; 2 s.; 1 d. Educ. George Watson's College, Edinburgh; Edinburgh University. Research Associate, Edinburgh University, 1969-72; Lecturer in Sociology, Stirling University, 1972-82; SSRC Senior Computing Fellow, 1978-79. Address: (b.) Department of Sociology, Stirling University, Stirling, FK9 4LA; T.-Stirling 73171.

Blight, David Philip, BSc, MSc, PhD, CEng, FIMechE, FIAgrE, FSA Scot. Director, Scottish Institute of Agricultural Engineering, since 1977; b. 25.3.30, Truro; m., Catherine Montgomery; 2 d. Educ. St. Austell County Grammar School; Reading University; Durham University; King's College, Newcastle-upon-Tyne. Research Assistant, King's College, Newcastle-upon-Tyne, 1953-55; Scottish station, National Institute of Agricultural Engineering: Scientific Officer/Senior Scientific Officer, 1955-66; Head of Cultivations and Farm Transport section, 1966-71; Head of Agricultural Department, Scottish Institute of Agricultural Engineering, 1971-77. Recreations: genealogy; history of technology; photography. Address: (b.) Scottish Institute of Agricultural Engineering, Bush Estate, Penicuik, Midlothian, EH26 OPH; T.-031-445 2147.

Bluck, Brian John, BSc, PhD, DSc, FGS, FRSE. Reader in Geology, Glasgow University, since 1981; b. 29.8.35, Bridgend, South Wales; m.; 1 s.; 1 d. Educ. Bridgend County Grammar School; University College, Swansea. Research Scholar, Illinois University, 1962; Research Fellow, NATO, 1963; Glasgow University:

Assistant; Lecturer; Senior Lecturer. Keith Medal, Royal Society, Edinburgh; Lyell Award, Geological Society, London. Recreations: hill-walking; theatre; music. Address: Department of Geology, The University, Glasgow, G12 8QQ.

Blyth, Professor Thomas Scott, BSc, DSc (St. Andrews), D-es-Sc (Paris), FRSE, FIMA. Professor of Pure Mathematics, St. Andrews University, since 1977; b. 3.7.38, Newburgh, Fife; m., Jane Ellen Christine Pairman; 1 d. Educ. Bell-Baxter High School, Cupar; St. Andrews University. NATO Research Scholar, Sorbonne, 1960-63; St. Andrews University: Lecturer in Mathematics, 1963-72, Senior Lecturer, 1972-73, Reader, 1973-76; Visiting Lecturer, University of Western Australia, 1966; Visiting Professor, University of Western Ontario, 1968-69. Past President, Edinburgh Mathematical Society; Executive Editor, Proceedings A, Royal Society of Edinburgh. Publications: Residuation Theory (Co-author), 1972; Set Theory and Abstract Algebra, 1975; Module theory, 1977; Algebra Through Practice, Books 1 to 6 (Co-author), 1984-85. Address: (h.) Wheaton Cottage, 4 Main Street, Strathkinness, Fife, KY16 9RU; T.-0334 85661.

Blyth, William, MA, LLB, BCom, SSC, NP. Director of Administration, City of Edinburgh District Council, since 1980; b. 3.8.37, Kirkcaldy; m., Anna Cecilia; 2 s.; 1 d. Educ. George Heriot's School, Edinburgh; Edinburgh University. Edinburgh Corporation: Head of Conveyancing and Contracts, 1971; Senior Depute Director of Administration, 1974. Recreation: gardening. Address: City Chambers, High Street, Edinburgh; T.-031-225 2424.

Boag, Archibald, BSc. Rector, Lossiemouth High School, since 1973; b. 1.7.31, Ardnadam, Dunoon; m., Fiona Wilson Mackenzie; 2 s. Educ. Dunoon Grammar School; Glasgow University; Jordanhill College of Education. National Service, 2nd Lt., Royal Artillery, 1955-57; Teacher of Mathematics and Science, Dunoon Grammar School, 1957-61; Principal Teacher of Mathematics, Bankhead Academy, Bucksburn, 1961-73. Publication: Mathematics for General Education (Chairman of Joint Authors). Recreations: bridge; bowling; sailing. Address: (h.) Torfness, James Street, Lossiemouth, Moray, IV31 6QZ; T.-034 381 2544.

Boag, Hugh Alexander, MA, DipEd, MLitt. Senior Lecturer in German, Strathclyde University, since 1972; b. 10.12.30, Glasgow; m., 1, Alexandrina Milligan (deceased); 1 s.; 1 d.; 2, Patricia Smith. Educ. Woodside School; Glasgow University; Jordanhill College of Education. Flt. Lt., RAF, 1955-58 (Air Ministry Examiner for Scotland and Northern Ireland); school teacher, Glasgow Corporation, 1958-62; Lecturer in Modern Languages, Scottish College of Commerce, 1962-64; Lecturer in German, Strathclyde University, 1964-72. Past Chairman, Hyndland Residents' Association; Chairman, St. Andrew Society of Glasgow, since 1980. Recreations: swimming; hill-walking. Address: (h.) 16 Kirklee Road, Glasgow, G12 OST.

Boal, William Wyld Mather, DiplArch, ARIBA, ARIAS, FSA Scot. Superintending Architect, Historic Buildings and Monuments, Scottish Development Department, 1980-85; b. 25.9.24, Harrogate. Educ. Harrogate Grammar School; Leeds School of Architecture. War service, Royal Navy, 1943-47 (Ordinary Seaman to Lt., RNVR); Architectural Assistant, Harrogate Borough Architect's Department, 1951-53; entered Government service as Architectural Assistant, 1953. Vice President, Edinburgh Civil Service Hockey Club. Recreations: hockey; tennis; skiing; walking. Address: (h.) Rowan Cottage, West Linton, Peeblesshire, EH46 7ER; T.-West Linton 60286.

Boe, Norman W., LLB (Hons). Divisional Solicitor, Office of Solicitor to Secretary of State for Scotland, since 1982; b. 30.8.43, Glasgow; m., Margaret; 1 s.; 1 d. Educ. George Heriot's School, Edinburgh; Edinburgh University. Legal apprenticeship, Lindsays WS, 1965-67; Legal Assistant, Menzies & White, WS, 1967-70; Office of Solicitor, Scottish Office: Legal Assistant, 1970, then Senior Legal Assistant. Recreations: golf; dog-walking; holidaying. Address: (b.) New St. Andrew's House, Edinburgh; T.-031-556 8400, Ext. 5435.

Bold, Alan. Writer; b. 20.4.43, Edinburgh; m., Alice Howell; 1 d. Educ. Broughton Secondary School; Edinburgh University. Full-time writer and visual artist since 1966; has published numerous books of poetry including: To Find the New; The State of the Nation; a selection in Penguin Modern Poets 15; In This Corner: Selected Poems 1963-83; collaborated on A Celtic Quintet and Haven; Editor, numerous anthologies, including: The Penguin Book of Socialist Verse; The Martial Muse; Cambridge Book of English Verse 1939-75; Making Love; The Bawdy Beautiful; Mounts of Venus; Drink To Me Only; The Poetry of Motion; books of criticism including: Thom Gunn & Ted Hughes; George Mackay Brown; The Ballad; Modern Scottish Literature; MacDiarmid: The Terrible Crystal; Editor: The Thistle Rises: a MacDiarmid Miscellany; The Letters of Hugh MacDiarmid; has exhibited illuminated poems in a variety of venues; regular contributor to The Scotsman and occasionally to the New Statesman, Times Literary Supplement, Glasgow Herald and Tribune. Recreations: walking; playing alto saxophone; watching films. Address: (h.) Balbirnie Burns East Cottage, near Markinch, Glenrothes, Fife, KY7 6NE; T.-0592 757216.

Bolton, Professor Arthur Bolton, MScTech, PhD, FEng, FIStructE, FICE. Head, Department of Civil Engineering, Heriot-Watt University, since 1965; b. 14.9.21, Blackburn; m., Alice; 1 s. Educ. Blackburn Grammar School; Manchester University. Assistant Lecturer and Lecturer in Structural Engineering, Manchester University, 1949-53; Lecturer and Senior Lecturer in Civil Engineering, Liverpool University, 1953-65. IStructE: Chairman, Education and Examinations Committee, Past Chairman, Scottish Branch; Past Chairman, Edinburgh and East of Scotland Association of Civil Engineers; Council Member, CET; Trustee, AUT. Recreation: amateur radio. Address: (b.) Department of Civil Engineering, Heriot-Watt University, Edinburgh, EH14 4AS; T.-031-449 5111.

Bolton, Lyndon, Manager: Alliance Trust PLC, Dundee, since 1972; Second Alliance Trust PLC; b. 24.1.37, London; m., Rosemary Jane Toler Mordaunt; 2 s. Educ. Wellington College; Royal Military Academy, Sandhurst. National Service, Royal Artillery, 1955-57; Deloitte Plender Griffiths & Co., London, 1957-63; Alliance Trust, Dundee, since 1964; Trustee, Trustee Savings Bank, since 1967; Board Member, TSB Group, since 1979; Board Member, TSB Scotland, since 1983; Director: UDT Group, since 1982; General Accident Fire and Life Assurance Corporation PLC, since 1982. Governor, Dundee College of Education, since 1980. Recreations: golf; fishing; painting. Address: (h.) Arrat's Mill, Brechin, Angus, DD9 7PR; T.-Bridge of Dun 220.

Bonallack, Michael Francis, OBE. Secretary, Royal and Ancient Golf Club of St. Andrews, since 1983; b. 31.12.34; m., Angela Ward; 1 s.; 3 d. British Amateur Champion, 1961-65-68-69-70; Captain, Walker Cup Team, 1971; Chairman, Golf Foundation, 1977-83; President, English Golf Union, 1982.

Bond, Professor Michael R., MD, PhD, FRCSEdin, FRCPsych, FRCPSGlas, DPM. Professor of Psychological Medicine, Glasgow University, since 1973; b. 15.4.36, Balderton, Nottinghamshire; m., Jane; 1 s.; 1 d. Educ. Magnus Grammar School, Newark; Sheffield University. Member: Court, Glasgow University; sub-committees, University Grants Committee; Research Consultant, NIH, Washington, DC; Councillor, International Association for the Study of Pain. Recreations: reading; music; painting. Address: (b.) 6 Whittinghame Gardens, Great Western Road, Glasgow; T.-041-334 9826.

Bone, Thomas R., MA, MEd, PhD, FCCEA. Principal, Jordanhill College of Education, since 1972; Chairman, Scottish Council for Educational Technology, since 1981; Vice-Chairman, Scottish Tertiary Education Advisory Council, since 1984; b. 2.1.35, Port Glasgow; m., Elizabeth Stewart; 1 s.; 1 d. Educ. Port Glasgow High School; Greenock High School; Glasgow University; Jordanhill College. Teacher of English, Paisley Grammar School, 1957-62; Lecturer in Education, Jordanhill College, 1962-63; Lecturer in Education, Glasgow University, 1963-67; Head of Education Department, Jordanhill College, 1967-71. Member: General Teaching Council for Scotland, since 1974; Dunning Committee, 1975-77; Vice-Chairman, Scottish Examination Board, 1977-84; Chairman: Schools Committee, IBA, since 1981; Standing Conference on Studies in Education, 1982-84; Council for National Academic Awards Board for Organisation and Management, since 1983. Publication: School Inspection in Scotland, 1968. Recreation: golf. Address: (b.) Jordanhill College of Education, Southbrae Drive, Glasgow, G13 1PP; T.-041-959 1232.

Boney, Professor Arthur Donald, BSc, PhD, DSc, CBiol, FIBiol, FRSE, FLS. Emeritus Professor of Botany, Glasgow University, since 1984; b. 31.5.25, Plymouth; m., Rosemary Mavis Hocking; 2 s. Educ. Plympton Grammar School, Devon; Plymouth College of Technology; University College, Exeter. Assistant Master, Tamar Secondary School, Plymouth, 1948-50; Lecturer, Plymouth College of Technology, 1950-63; Lecturer, then Senior Lecturer, Department of Botany, University College of Wales, Aberystwyth, 1963-69; Senior Lecturer, then Reader, then Professor, Department of Botany, Glasgow University, 1969-84. British Phycological Society: Council Member at various times; Honorary Secretary, 1971-75, Vice-President, 1976-78; President, 1978-80; Member, Committee of Management, University Marine Biological Station, Millport, 1970-75; Council Member, Scottish Marine Biological Association, 1980-82, 1983-85. Recreations: walking; reading. Address: (h.) 15 Falkland Street, Glasgow, G12 9PY; T.-041-339 3333.

Bonney, Norman Leonard, BSc (Econ), MA, PhD. Member, Aberdeen City Council, since 1974 (Convenor, Town Planning Committee, since 1981); Lecturer, Aberdeen University, since 1971; m., 4.3.44, Great Yarmouth; 1 s.; 2 d. Educ. Great Yarmouth Grammar School; London School of Economics; Chicago University. Research Scientist, Institute of Juvenile Research, Chicago, 1968-71. Member: Executive Committee, Scottish Council (Development and Industry), 1974-84; Planning Committee, COSLA, since 1981; Management Committee, Planning Exchange, since 1981; Chairman, Aberdeen Association for Social Studies, since 1983; Member, Executive Committee, Scottish branch, British Sociological Association. Recreations: walking; swimming; tennis. Address: (b.) Department of Sociology, Edward Wright Building, Aberdeen University, Aberdeen; T.-0224 40241, Ext. 5239.

Bonomy, John, MA, LLB. Chief Executive and Director of Administration, Motherwell District Council, since 1983; b. 25.4.38, Motherwell; m., Isabella Margaret; 3 s. Educ. Dalziel High School, Motherwell; Glasgow University. Depute Town Clerk: Arbroath, 1966; Motherwell and Wishaw, 1966-74; Director of Administration, Motherwell, 1974-83. Recreations: golf; reading. Address: (b.) Civic Centre, Motherwell; T.-Motherwell 66166.

Bor, Sam. Violinist, Conductor and Teacher; b. 10.9.12, Hastings, Sussex; m., 1, Rosemary Kerrich (deceased); 1 s.; 2 d.; 2, Dorothie Sawtell; 1 s.; 2 d. Educ. King Edward VI Grammar School, Birmingham; Birmingham School of Music. Founder Member, BBC Symphony Orchestra, London, 1930; Royal Artillery, 1940-45; Sub-Leader, BBC Symphony Orchestra, London, 1945; Leader, London Chamber Orchestra, 1947-48; Leader and Assistant Conductor, Adelaide Symphony Orchestra, 1949-59; Scottish National Orchestra: Leader and Assistant Conductor, 1959-73; Musical Associate, 1973-74; staff: Royal Scottish Academy of Music, since 1974; Douglas Academy Music School, since 1979; Musical Director, Strathclyde Schools Symphony Orchestra, since 1979. Recreations: reading; walking; watching intelligent television. Address: (h.) The Loaning, Crawfordjohn, Biggar, ML12 5SW; T.-Crawfordjohn 237.

Borley, Lester. Director, National Trust for Scotland, since 1983; b. 7.4.31; m.; 3 d. Educ. Dover Grammar School; London University. Chief Executive, Scottish Tourist Board, 1970-75; Chief Executive, English Tourist Board, 1975-83.

Borthwick, Professor Edward Kerr, MA (Aberdeen), MA, PhD (Cantab). Professor of Greek, Edinburgh University, since 1980; b. 9.6.25, Aberdeen; m., Betty Jean Orton; 2 s.; 1 d. Educ. Aberdeen Grammar School; Aberdeen University; Christ's College, Cambridge. Croom Robertson Fellow, Aberdeen University, 1948-51; Lecturer in Classics, Leeds University, 1951-55; Edinburgh University: Lecturer in Greek, 1955-67, Senior Lecturer, 1967-70, Reader, 1970-80. Recreations: music; tennis; golf. Address: (h.) 9 Corrennie Drive, Edinburgh, EH10 6EQ; T.-031-447 2369.

Borthwick of Borthwick, Lt.-Col. John Henry Stuart, TD (1943), DL, JP; The Borthwick of Borthwick; 23rd Lord Borthwick; Baron of Heriotmuir, Borthwick and Locherwart; Chairman: Heriotmuir Properties Ltd., since 1965; Heriotmuir Exporters Ltd., since 1972; Partner, Crookston Farms, since 1971; Director, Ronald Morrison & Co. Ltd., since 1972; b. 13.9.05, Borthwick; m., Margaret Frances Cormack (deceased); 2 s. Educ. Fettes College, Edinburgh; King's College, Newcastle-upon-Tyne. Diploma in Agriculture. Formerly RATA, re-employed 1939; served NW Europe, Allied Military Government Staff (Junior Staff College, SO 2), 1944; CCG (CO 1, Lt.-Col.), 1946; Department of Agriculture for Scotland, 1948-50; farming own farms, 1950-71; National Farmers Union of Scotland: Midlothian branch Committee, 1963; Mid and West Lothian Area Committee, 1967-73 (President, 1970-72); Council Member, 1968-72; Member: Lothians Area Committee, NFU Mutual Insurance Society, 1969; Chairman, Monitoring Committee, Scottish Tartans, 1976; Scottish Southern Regional Committee, Wool Marketing Board, 1966; Chairman, Area Committee, South of Scotland Electricity Board Consultative Council, 1972-76; Member, Midlothian County Council, 1937; Member: Local Appeal Tribunal (Edinburgh and the Lothians), 1963-75; Midlothian Valuation Appeal Committee, 1966; Member: Standing Council of Scottish Chiefs; The Committee of the Baronage of Scotland; Member Corresponding, Istituto Italiano di Genealogie e Araldica, Rome and Madrid, 1964; Honorary Member: Council of Scottish Clans Association, USA, 1975; Royal Military Institute of Canada, 1976; Kt of Justice and Honour, GCLJ (Grand Croix, 1975); CL (Commander of the Rose of Lippe), 1971; NN, 1982. Recreations: shooting; travel; history. Address: Crookston, Heriot, Midlothian, EH38 5YS; T.-Heriot 232.

Borthwick, Rev. Stewart Webster, ThM, ThD, FPHS. Minister, Abbotsford Parish Church, Clydebank, since 1956; b. 24.6.11, Edinburgh; m., Christina Huntly; 2 s. Educ. Bonnington Road Senior Secondary School, Leith; Glasgow University; American Bible School, Florida and Chicago. Detective Constable, CID, Glasgow, 1933; left police to study for the ministry, 1947; first charge, Kirkintilloch, 1951. Chaplain, Singer,

Clydebank, 15 years. Recreations: swimming (Western Baths, Glasgow); painting (oil and water colour). Address: 35 Montrose Street, Clydebank, G81 2PA.; T.-041-952 5151.

Botter, Very Rev. Constant J., SCJ. Parish Priest, St. John Ogilvie's, Irvine, since 1982; b. 10.11.32, Padang, Sumatra, Indonesia. Educ. Sacred Heart College; St. Joseph's College, Malpas, Cheshire. Teacher, Sacred Heart College, Woodcote Hall, Newport; Vocation Director; Hospital Chaplain; Youth Director; Parish Priest. Recreation: swimming. Address: St. John Ogilvie's, Bourtreehill, Irvine, KA11 1JX; T.-0294 212587.

Bouchier, Professor Ian Arthur Dennis, MB, ChB, MD, FRCP, FRCPEdin, FRSE. Professor of Medicine, Dundee University, since 1973; b. 7.9.32, Cape Town, South Africa; m., Patricia Norma Henshilwood; 2 s. Educ. Ronde Bosch Boys High School; Cape Town University. Instructor in Medicine, School of Medicine, Boston University, 1964; London University: Senior Lecturer in Medicine, 1965; Reader in Medicine, 1970. Member: Court, Dundee University; Chief Scientist Committee, Scotland; Medical Research Council; Secretary General, World Organization of Gastroenterology; Dean, Faculty of Medicine and Dentistry, Dundee University. Publications: Clinical Skills (2nd edition), 1982; Gastroenterology (3rd edition), 1982; Textbook of Gastroenterology, 1984. Recreations: music; history of whaling; cooking. Address: (b.) Department of Medicine, Ninewells Hospital and Medical School, Dundee, DD1 9SY; T.-0382 60111.

Boulton, Frank Ernest, BSc, MB, BS, MD, FRCPath. Deputy Director, Edinburgh Regional Blood Transfusion Service, since 1981; b. 26.5.41, Ashford, Middlesex; m., Elizabeth Ruth Westcott; 3 s. by pr. m. Educ. Godalming County Grammar School; St. Thomas's Hospital Medical School, London University. Senior Lecturer, The London Hospital Medical School, 1973-75; Senior Lecturer and Consultant Haematologist, Royal Liverpool Hospital and Liverpool University, 1975-80. Chairman, Edinburgh branch, Medical Campaign Against Nuclear Weapons. Recreations: music (amateur trombone player); literature. Address: (b.) Edinburgh Blood Transfusion Service, Edinburgh Royal Infirmary, Edinburgh; T.-031-229 2585.

Bovey, Keith S., BL. Solicitor, since 1951; Chairperson, Scottish CND; b. 31.7.27, Renfrew; m., Helen Cameron; 1 s.; 1 d. Educ. Paisley Grammar School; Glasgow University. Army, 1944-48. Elected Member of National Council, Scottish National Party. Publication: Misuse of Drugs, A Handbook for Lawyers. Address: (b.) 313 Byres Road, Glasgow, G12 8UH; T.-041-339 8474.

Bowden, Peter, BSc, PhD, DIC. Senior Lecturer in Geochemistry, St. Andrews University, since 1980; b. 26.3.36, Birch Vale, Derbyshire; m., Mary Dodd; 1 s.; 2 d. Educ. New Mills Grammar School; King's College, Durham; Imperial College, London. Geochemist, Geological Survey, Tanzania, 1961, specialising in search for gemstones, gold and diamond deposits; Senior Scientific Officer, Overseas Division, Institute of Geological Sciences, London, 1966; Lecturer in Geochemistry, St. Andrews University, 1967; Professeur associe Universite Paris, 1978-79. Chairman, Organising Committee, 13th Colloquium of African Geology, St. Andrews, 1985. Recreations: skiing; hill-walking; cricket; tennis. Address: (h.) 17 Irvine Crescent, St. Andrews, Fife, KY16 8LG; T.-0334 77401.

Bowen, Sheriff Edward Farquharson, TD, LLB. Sheriff of Tayside, Central and Fife, at Dundee, since 1983; b. 1.5.45, Edinburgh; m., Patricia Margaret Brown; 2 s.; 1 d. Educ. Melville College, Edinburgh; Edinburgh University. Admitted Solicitor, 1968; Advocate, 1970; Standing Junior Counsel, Scottish Education Department, 1976; Advocate Depute, 1979-83. Served RAOC TA/TAVR, 1964-80. Recreation: golf (Member, Honourable Company of Edinburgh Golfers and Panmure GC). Address: (h.) Westgate, 12 Glamis Drive, Dundee.

Bowen, Stanley, CBE (1972). Honorary Sheriff, Lothian and Borders, since 1975; b. 4.8.10, Carnoustie; m., Mary Shepherd Greig; 2 s.; 1 d. Educ. Barry School, Angus; Grove Academy, Dundee; University College, Dundee. Qualified as Solicitor in Scotland, 1932; entered Procurator Fiscal service, 1933; Depute Procurator Fiscal, Hamilton, 1937; Interim Procurator Fiscal, Airdrie, 1938; Crown Office: Legal Assistant, 1941, Principal Assistant, 1945, Crown Agent for Scotland, 1967-74; since 1974, has served on a number of bodies connected with criminal procedure, police administration, forensic pathology services, the law of human transplants and the care and resettlement of offenders; Chairman, Corstorphine Trust. Recreations: golf; gardening. Address: (h.) Achray, 20 Dovecot Road, Corstorphine, Edinburgh, EH12 7LE; T.-031-334 4096.

Bowey, Professor Angela Marilyn, BA (Econ), PhD, FIPM, FIMS. Professor of Business Administration and Director of Pay and Reward Research Centre, Strathclyde University, since 1976; Commissioner, Equal Opportunities Commission, since 1980; Member, Police Advisory Board for Scotland; b. 20.10.40, Blackpool; 3 s.; 2 d. Educ. Withington Girls' School, Manchester; Manchester University. Worked as Mathematician on design of refuelling cycles for nuclear power stations; Assistant Lecturer in Sociology, Elizabeth Gaskell College of Education, Manchester, 12 months; Research Associate, then Lecturer, Manchester Business School, 1968-76; author of eight books and numerous articles on pay, productivity, manpower planning and organisation theory. Address: (h.) 9 Grosvenor Crescent, Glasgow, G12; T.-041-552 4400.

Bowie, Graham Maitland, MA, LLB. Director of Planning, Lothian Regional Council, since 1975; b. 11.11.31, Alloa; m., Jennifer; 1 s.; 2 d. Educ. Alloa Academy; St. Andrews University; Glasgow University. Glasgow Chamber of Commerce, 1957-59; Ford Motor Co., 1959-64; Edinburgh Corporation Education Department, 1964-69; Inner London Education Authority,

1969-75. Recreations: music; golf; walking. Address: (b.) Lothian Regional Council, Regional Headquarters, George IV Bridge, Edinburgh, EH1 1UQ; T.-031-229 9292.

Bowling, Dudley James Francis, DSc, BSc, PhD, CBiol, MIBiol. Reader in Plant Science, Aberdeen University, since 1981; b. 20.5.37, Kingston upon Hull; m., Sheila Mary Daun; d. Educ. Hull Grammar School; Nottingham University; Aberdeen University. Aberdeen University: Assistant in Botany, 1961; Lecturer in Botany, 1963; Senior Lecturer in Botany, 1974; Visiting Scientist, DSIR, Palmerston North, New Zealand, 1976-77. Publication: Uptake of Ions by Plant Roots, 1976. Recreations: gardening; model railways. Address: (b.) Department of Plant Science, St. Machar Drive, Old Aberdeen, AB9 2UD; T.-Aberdeen 40241, Ext. 5242.

Bowman, Derek Edward, BA, MA, CertEd. Senior Lecturer, Department of German, Edinburgh University; b. 13.1.31, Liverpool; m., Marianne Margarete Recktenwald; 2 d. Educ. Liverpool Institute; Liverpool University; Cambridge University. Sergeant, RAEC, 1953-55; school master: King Edward VI School, Southampton, 1957-62; Haberdashers' Aske's School, Elstree, 1962-64; Lecturer, Edinburgh University, since 1964. Felicia Heman's Prize for Lyric Poetry, 1969. Publications: The Poor Man of Toggenburg (translation of Ulrich Braker), 1970; A Few Words about Shakespeare's Plays (translation of Ulrich Braker), 1979; Life into Autobiography: A Study of Goethe's "Dichtung and Wahrheit", 1971. Recreations: gardening; music. Address: Department of German, Edinburgh University, Edinburgh.

Bowman, Professor William Cameron, BPharm, PhD, DSc, FIBiol, FPS, FRSE, HonFFARCS. Professor and Head of Department of Physiology and Pharmacology, Strathclyde University, since 1966; b. 26.4.30, Carlisle; m., Anne Wylie Stafford; 1 s.; 1 d. Educ. Carlisle Grammar School; London University. RAF (commissioned officer), 1955-57; Lecturer, then Reader in Pharmacology, London University, 1952-66. Dean, School of Pharmaceutical Sciences, Strathclyde University, 1974-77; Member: Nomenclature Committee, BP Commission, 1964-67; Biology Committee, MOD, 1966-75; TCT and SEAR Sub-Committees, CSM, 1972-83; Biomedical Research Committee, SHHD, 1980-85; Chairman, Committee, British Pharmacological Society, 1981-84. Publications: Textbook of Pharmacology, 1968, 1980; Pharmacology of Neuromuscular Function, 1980. Address: Department of Physiology and Pharmacology, Strathclyde University, Glasgow, G1 1XW; T.-041-552 4400.

Bown, Professor Lalage Jean, OBE, MA (Oxon), DrUniv (Open University), FRSA. Professor and Director, Department of Adult and Continuing Education, Glasgow University, since 1981; b. 1.4.27, Croydon. Educ. Wycombe Abbey School, Buckinghamshire; Cheltenham Ladies' College; Somerville College, Oxford. Resident Tutor: University College of the Gold Coast, 1949-55; Makerere University College, Uganda, 1955-59; successively Tutorial Advisor, Assistant Director, Deputy Director, Extra-Mural Department,

Ibadan University, 1960-66 (Associate Professor, 1962-66); Director of Extra-Mural Studies and Professor Ad Personam, University of Zambia, 1966-70; Professor of Adult Education, Ahmadu Bello University, Nigeria, 1971-76; successively Professor of Adult Education and Dean of Education, Lagos University, 1977-80. Member: Scottish Community Education Council; Executive Committee, Scottish Institute of Adult Education; Board of Governors, Newbattle Abbey College; Board of Directors, Network; Management Committee, Scottish Centre for Tuition of the Disabled; Board, The British Council; Governing Body, Institute of Development Studies; President, Development Studies Association; Honorary Vice-President, National Union of Townswomen's Guilds; Honorary Vice-President, WEA. Publications: eight academic books. Recreation: travel. Address: (b.) Department of Adult and Continuing Education, Glasgow University, 57-61 Oakfield Avenue, Glasgow, G12 8LW; T.-041-339 8855, Ext. 392.

Bownes, Thomas Alexander, BSc. Rector, Invergordon Academy, since 1975; b. 20.9.26, Carlisle; m., Ivy Slater Gunn; 1 s. Educ. Dalziel High School, Motherwell; Glasgow University. Teacher of Science and Mathematics: Dalziel High School, Motherwell, 1953-56; Tomintoul Secondary School, 1956-59; Teacher of Science, Alva Academy, 1959-60; Principal Teacher of Science, Grange Secondary School, Alloa, 1960-68; Lornshill Academy, Alloa: Principal Teacher of Chemistry, 1968-70; Principal Teacher of Guidance, 1970-73; Assistant Rector, Perth High School, 1973-75. Recreations: walking; golf; singing. Address: (h.) Hillcrest, Westwood, Invergordon, IV18 OJW; T.-0349 852706.

Bowser of Argaty and the King's Lundies, David Stewart, JP, BA (Agric). Landowner; President, Blackface Sheep Breeders' Association, since 1983; b. 11.3.26; m.; 1 s.; 4 d. Educ. Harrow; Trinity College, Cambridge. Captain, Scots Guards, 1944-47; Forestry Commissioner, 1974-82; President, Highland Cattle Society, 1970-72; Member, Perth County Council, 1954-61. Address: Auchlyne, Killin, Perthshire.

Boyd, Brian, MA, MEd. Head Teacher, Barrhead High School, since 1983; b. 25.4.48, Glasgow; m., Margo Nicol. Educ. St. Mungo's Academy; Glasgow University. Teacher of English, St. Stephen's High School, Port Glasgow, 1970-72; Principal Teacher of English: St. Aelred's High School, Paisley, 1972-73, St. Cuthbert's High School, Johnstone, 1974-79; Assistant Head Teacher, Barrhead High School, 1979-83. Member: Scottish Central Committee on English, 1977-80; SED Task Group on Guidance, since 1983. Recreations: soccer; reading; addressing meetings on mixed-ability teaching. Address: (b.) Barrhead High School, Aurs Road, Barrhead, Renfrewshire; T.-041-881 5757.

Boyd, David Hugh Aird, MB, ChB, MD, FRCPEdin. Consultant Physician, Leith Hospital and Western General Hospital, Edinburgh, since 1975; Honorary Senior Lecturer, Department of Medicine, Edinburgh University, since 1976; b. 8.1.27, Larbert; m., Betty Meldrum

Mutch; 1 s.; 1 d. Educ. Falkirk High School; Edinburgh University. House Officer, Falkirk and District Royal Infirmary; Captain, RAMC, West Africa Command; Senior House Officer, Stirling Royal Infirmary; Registrar, Eastern and Northern General Hospitals, Edinburgh; Senior Registrar, Western General Hospital, Edinburgh; Lecturer, Department of Materia Medica, Glasgow University; Consultant Physician, Caithness and Sutherland Hospitals. Royal College of Physicians, Edinburgh: Past Secretary; Council Member; Editor, College Chronicle. Recreations: ornithology; photography; hill-walking; curling. Address: (h.) 25 Cherry Tree Park, Balerno, Edinburgh, EH15 5AQ; T.-031-449 4200.

Boyd, Edward. Playwright; b. 11.5.16, Stevenston, Ayrshire. Worked with Unity Theatre, Glasgow, 1945-49, as Stage Manager, occasional Actor and finally Producer (Heartbreak House and An Inspector Calls); has written extensively for television, including The Odd Man series (Screen Writer's Guild Award), The Lower Largo Sequence, The View from Daniel Pike; author of the book The Dark Number, 1973; film script, Robbery, 1967.

Boyd, Gavin, CBE (1977), MA (Hons), LLB. Consultant, Boyds, Solicitors, since 1978; Chairman, Scottish Opera Theatre Royal, since 1973; Chairman, J.W. Galloway, since 1983; b. 4.8.28; m., Kathleen Elizabeth Skinner; 1 s. Educ. Glasgow Academy; Glasgow University. Partner, Boyds, Solicitors, 1955-77; Director, Stenhouse Holdings Ltd., 1970-79 (Chairman, 1971-78); Director, Scottish Opera, since 1970; Director, North Sea Assets plc, since 1972; Director, Paterson Jenks plc, 1972-81; Director, Scottish Television plc, since 1973; Director, Ferranti plc, since 1975; Director, British Carpets plc, 1977-81; Director, Merchant House of Glasgow, since 1982. Chairman, Court, Strathclyde University, since 1983; Hon. LLD, Strathclyde, 1982. Recreations: music and the performing arts; yacht racing; cruising. Address: (h.) 4A Prince Albert Road, Glasgow, G12 9JX.

Boyd, Professor Ian Alexander, MD, PhD, DSc, FRCP, FRSE. Buchanan Professor of Physiology, Glasgow University, since 1966; Vice Chairman, Scottish Schoolboys Club, since 1966; b. 23.5.27, Glasgow; m., June Leonore Peiser McCrae; 2 s. Educ. Glasgow Academy; The Leys, Cambridge; Glasgow University; London University. House Officer, Ruchill Fever Hospital and Stobhill Hospital, Glasgow, 1950-51; Research Scholar in Physiology, Glasgow University, 1951-54; Honorary Research Assistant in Biophysics, University College, London, 1954-55; Lecturer in Physiology, Glasgow University, 1955-60; Visiting Research Fellow, Australian National University, Canberra, and Utah University, Salt Lake City, 1961-62; Senior Lecturer in Physiology, then Reader, Glasgow University, 1961-66. Member: Committee, Physiological Society, 1972-76, British National Committee of Physiological Sciences, 1978-85; Bellahouston Gold Medal, 1967; Zworykin Prize for Medical Electronics, 1962; for the film The Muscle Spindle, 1970, won BMA Silver Medal, 1971, Gold Medal, Marburg, 1971, and American

Film Festival Award, 1972. Governor, Rannoch School, Kinloch Rannoch, since 1984. Publication: The Muscle Spindle (Co-author), 1985. Recreations: gardening; angling; youth club leadership. Address: (h.) Bramwell, Bankers Brae, Balfron, G63 OPY; T.-0360 40773.

Boyd, James Ferguson, MD, FRCPEdin, FRCPath, FRCPSGlas. Senior Lecturer in Pathology of Infectious Diseases, Glasgow University, since 1961; Honorary Consultant Pathologist, Greater Glasgow Health Board, since 1961; b. 6.5.25, Kilbirnie, Ayrshire; m., Christina M. MacLeod; 2 s.; 2 d. Educ. Hillhead High School, Glasgow; Carrick Academy, Maybole; Glasgow University. Resident, Hairmyres Hospital, East Kilbride, and Royal Alexandra Infirmary, Paisley, 1948-49; Royal Army Medical Corps, 1949-51; Resident, Western Infirmary, Glasgow, 1951-52; trainee posts in pathology, Western Infirmary, Glasgow, and Area Laboratory, Stirling Royal Infirmary, 1952-57; Lecturer in Pathology, Glasgow University, 1957-61, with secondment to Royal Maternity Hospital and Royal Hospital for Sick Children, Glasgow; Senior Lecturer, Ruchill Hospital, Western Infirmary and Gartnavel General Hospital, Glasgow, since 1961. Recreations: golf; walking. Address: (h.) 44 Woodend Drive, Jordanhill, Glasgow, G13 1TQ; T.-041-959 2708.

Boyd, John Morton, FRSE, BSc, PhD, DSc. Member, Commission on Ecology, since 1976; Director, Scotland, Nature Conservancy Council, 1971-85; b. 31.1.25, Darvel; m.; 4 s. Educ. Kilmarnock Academy; Glasgow University. Member, Council, National Trust for Scotland, 1971-85; Member, Council, Royal Society of Edinburgh, 1978-81; Member, Council, Royal Scottish Zoological Society, since 1980.

Boyd, William Dalziel, MB, ChB, FRCPEdin, FRCPsych, DPM. Commissioner, Mental Welfare Commission for Scotland, since 1984; Consultant Psychiatrist, Lothian Health Board, since 1967; Honorary Senior Lecturer, Edinburgh University, since 1967; b. 9.11.30, Cupar, Fife; m., Betty Ledingham Gordon; 3 s.; 1 d. Educ. Trinity College, Glenalmond; Edinburgh University. National Service, Royal Army Medical Corps; training posts at Rosslynlee Hospital, Midlothian; Edinburgh Royal Infirmary; Royal Edinburgh Hospital; Consultant Psychiatrist: Herdmanflat Hospital, Haddington; Royal Edinburgh Hospital; Physician Superintendent, Royal Edinburgh Hospital. Chairman: Scottish Division, Royal College of Psychiatrists; Edinburgh and Leith Old People's Welfare Council. Recreation: improving old houses and old gardens. Address: (h.) Kirkbrae House, 10 Randolph Cliff, Edinburgh, EH3 7UA; T.-031-225 3289.

Boyes, John, MA (Hons). HM Inspector of Schools, since 1974; b. 20.5.43, Greenock; m., Margaret Anne Peat; 1 s.; 1 d. Educ. Greenock High School; Glasgow University. Taught French and German, Alloa Academy and Denny High School, 1967-74. Recreation: crossing i's and dotting t's. Address: (b.) Scottish Education Department, Empire House, 131 West Nile Street, Glasgow; T.-041-332 0141.

Boyes, John, CA, FBIS. Secretary, Scottish Motor Trade Association, since 1977; b. 1.5.47, Edinburgh; m., Sheila McLeod; 2 s.; 1 d. Educ. Cargilfield School, Edinburgh; Rugby. Formerly Company Secretary, John Goodall & Co. Ltd., Dunfermline. Recreation: almost anything to do with spaceflight or the armed forces. Address: (b.) 3 Palmerston Place, Edinburgh, EH12 5AQ; T.-031-225 3643.

Boyle, Very Rev. Hugh Noonan, PhL, STL. Administrator, Metropolitan Cathedral Church of St. Andrew, Glasgow, since 1983 (Canon, Chapter of Metropolitan Cathedral Church, since 1984); Archivist, Archdiocese of Glasgow, since 1973; b. 14.1.35, Glasgow. Educ. St. Aloysius' College, Glasgow; Glasgow University; Pontifical Scots College and Pontifical Gregorian University, Rome, 1956-63. National Service, RAF, 1954-56; ordained priest, Rome, 1962; Assistant Priest: St. Philomena's, Glasgow, 1963-66, St. Eunan's, Clydebank, 1966-76; Archdiocese of Glasgow: Assistant Archivist, 1967-73; Chancellor, 1976-83. Editor, Catholic Directory for Scotland and Western Catholic Calendar, since issues of 1975; Member: Scottish Catholic Communications Commission, since 1979; Scottish Catholic Heritage Commission, since 1981; Patron, Hutcheson's Hospital, since 1983. Recreations: music (listening); walking. Address: St. Andrew's Cathedral House, 190 Clyde Street, Glasgow, G1 4JY; T.-041-221 3096.

Boyle, Iain Thomson, BSc (Hons), MB, ChB, FRCP, FRCPSGlas. Reader in Medicine, Glasgow University and Glasgow Royal Infirmary, since 1984; Depute Medical Advisor, Strathclyde University, since 1980; b. 7.10.35, Glasgow; m., Elizabeth Johnston Carmichael; 1 s.; 2 d. Educ. Paisley Grammar School; Glasgow University. Lecturer in Medicine, Glasgow University and Glasgow Royal Infirmary, 1964-70; Hartenstein Research Fellow, Wisconsin University, 1970-72; Senior Lecturer in Medicine, Glasgow University and Glasgow Royal Infirmary, 1973-84. Editor, Scottish Medical Journal, 1978-83; Co-Editor, Bone, since 1983; Secretary: Scottish Society for Experimental Medicine, since 1984; Scottish Society of Physicians, since 1984; President, Caledonian Philatelic Society, 1983-84. Fletcher Prize, Royal College of Physicians and Surgeons of Glasgow, 1973. Recreations: philately; Scottish social history; angling; gardening; golf. Address: (h.) 7 Lochbrae Drive, High Burnside, Rutherglen, Glasgow, G73 5QL.

Boyle, James Leo, BSc, PhD, CChem, MRSC. Chairman, Freeport Scotland Ltd., since 1983; Member, Kyle and Carrick District Council, since 1975; b. Glasgow; m., Helen McAuley; 2 s.; 2 d. Educ. St. Aloysius College, Glasgow; Glasgow University. Employed in various branches of industry, 1938-78; Member, and sometime Provost, Girvan Town Council, 1954-75; Provost, Kyle and Carrick, 1980-84. Recreation: gardening. Address: (h.) 13 North Park Avenue, Girvan, Ayrshire; T.-Girvan 3295.

Boyle, Sheriff John Sebastian, BL. Sheriff of South Strathclyde, Dumfries and Galloway, at Airdrie, since 1983. Educ. St. Aloysius College, Glasgow; Glasgow University. Solicitor,

Glasgow, 1955-83; President, Glasgow Bar Association, 1962-63; Member, Scottish Arts Council, 1966-72; Council Member, Law Society of Scotland, 1968-75; Member, Criminal Injuries Compensation Board, 1975-83.

Boyle, John Stirling, MA, DPA, MIPR. Director of Public Affairs, ScotRail, since 1983; b. 17.9.39, Paisley; m., Helen Dickson Wallace; 2 s.; 1 d. Educ. Camphill School, Paisley; Glasgow University. Schoolteacher; Journalist, D.C. Thomson; Technical Writer; Health Education Officer, Stirling County Council; Public Relations Officer, Heriot-Watt University; Director External Relations, Scottish Council (Development and Industry). Council Member, National Youth Orchestra of Scotland. Address: (b.) ScotRail House, 58 Port Dundas Road, Glasgow, G4 OHG; T.-041-332 9811.

Boyle, Sir Lawrence, KB, JP, BCom, PhD, IPFA, CBIM. Financial and Management Consultant; Director: Scottish Mutual Assurance Society; Pension Fund Property Unit Trust; Short Loan & Mortgage Co. Ltd.; Visiting Professor, Strathclyde Business School, since 1980; b. 31.1.20, Balerno, Midlothian; m., Mary McWilliam; 1 s.; 3 d. Educ. Holy Cross Academy, Leith; Edinburgh University. Depute County Treasurer, Midlothian County Council, 1951-62; Glasgow Corporation: Depute City Chamberlain, 1962-70, City Chamberlain, 1970-74; Chief Executive, Strathclyde Regional Council, 1974-80. Member of Court, Strathclyde University, 1980-85 (Chairman, Finance Committee); Chairman, Scottish National Orchestra, 1980-84. Recreation: music. Address: (h.) 24 Broomburn Drive, Newton Mearns, Glasgow, G77 5JF; T.-041-639 3776.

Boys, John, ARSA, DA, FRIBA, FRIAS. Partner, The Boys Jarvis Partnership, architects, since 1958; Commissioner, Royal Fine Arts Commission for Scotland; b. 23.8.28, Kirriemuir, Angus; m., Bridget Jensen; 2 s.; 1 d. Educ. Glasgow School of Art; Dundee School of Art. Royal Army Education Corps, Egypt and Kenya, 1946-48; joined The Boys Jarvis Partnership; finalist (with others), Sydney Opera House Competition; various other prizes with the Boys Jarvis Partnership; Founder Member, New Glasgow Society; case worker, Scottish Georgian Society; former Council Member, RIAS; Member, RIAS Investigation Committee; former Assessor: RIAS; RIBA; New Saltire Society Planning Award; Professional Studies (Part III) Assessor, Universities of Edinburgh, Heriot-Watt and Glasgow. Recreations: painting; rough gardening; curling; sailing. Address: (b.) 19 Woodside Place, Glasgow, G3 7QL; T.-041-332 2228.

Bradley, Professor Paul Frank, BDS, LDSRCS, MB, BS, LRCP, MRCS, FDSRCS(Eng), FDSRCS(Ed). Professor of Oral and Maxillofacial Surgery, Edinburgh University, since 1983; Honorary Consultant in Oral and Maxillofacial Surgery, Lothian Health Board, since 1983; b. 9.8.35, Birmingham; m., Ceinwen Susan; 1 s.; 1 d. Educ. King Edward School, Birmingham; London University; Birmingham University. Senior Registrar in Oral and Maxillofacial Surgery, Westminster Hospital, Queen Mary's, Roehampton and University College Hospital, London, 1968-72; Assistant Professor in Oral Surgery, Washington University, USA, 1970-71; Senior Lecturer in Oral Surgery, Liverpool University, 1972-77; Consultant in Oral and Maxillofacial Surgery, Clwyd Area Health Authority, North Wales, and Research Associate to Liverpool University, 1977-83; former Council Member, British Association of Oral and Maxillofacial Surgeons. Publication: Cryosurgery of the Maxillofacial Region, 1985. Recreations: amateur theatre; painting; fishing. Address: (b.) Department of Oral and Maxillofacial Surgery, Edinburgh University, Old High School, High School Yards, Edinburgh, EH1 1LZ; T.-031-667 1011, Ext. 4335.

Bradley, William Michael, LLB. Secretary, Aberdeen University, since 1984; b. 9.5.40, Portadown, Northern Ireland; m., Patricia Ann Wesson; 1 d. Educ. Rossall School; Queens University, Belfast. Ministry of Agriculture, Northern Ireland, 1962-59; Administrative Service, Hong Kong Government, 1969-79; Secretary, University and Polytechnic Grants Committee, Hong Kong, 1979-84. Recreation: model railway. Address: (b.) Aberdeen University, University Offices, Regent Walk, Aberdeen, AB9 1FX; T.-Aberdeen 40341.

Braid, James, JP. Member: North East Fife District Council, since 1980; Fife Regional Council, since 1981; b. 1.4.12, St. Monans, Fife; m., Alison Cruickshank; 1 s.; 2 d. Educ. Waid Academy, Anstruther. RAF (flying), 1940-52; Provost of St. Monans and Member, Fife County Council, 1952-75; Member, North East Fife District Council and Fife Regional Council, 1975-78; Member: Executive Committee, St. Andrews and North East Fife Area Tourist Board, since 1983; Forth River Purification Board, since 1980; Trustee and Committee Member, Scottish Fisheries Museum, since 1982. Freeman of St. Monans. Recreations: bowling; football. Address: (h.) 16 West Shore, St. Monans, Fife, KY10 2BT; T.-St. Monans 262.

Brand, Professor Charles Peter, MA, PhD. Professor of Italian, Edinburgh University, since 1966 (Vice-Principal, since 1984); b. 7.2.23, Cambridge; m., Gunvor Hellgren; 1 s.; 3 d. Educ. Cambridgeshire High School; Trinity Hall, Cambridge. Lecturer in Italian, Cambridge University, 1952-66; Fellow and Tutor, Trinity Hall, Cambridge, 1958-66. Editor, Modern Language Review, 1970-76. Publications: Italy and the English Romantics, 1957; T. Tasso, 1965; L. Ariosto, 1974; Writers of Italy (Editor). Recreations: sport; gardening. Address: (h.) 21 Succoth Park, Edinburgh, EH12 6BX; T.-031-337 1980.

Brand, Hon. Lord, (David William Robert Brand), QC (Scot). Senator of the College of Justice in Scotland, since 1972; b. 21.10.23; m., 1, Rose Josephine Devlin (deceased); 4 d.; 2, Bridget Veronica Lynch. Educ. Stonyhurst College; Edinburgh University. Commissioned Argyll and Sutherland Highlanders, 1942; Captain, 1945; admitted, Faculty of Advocates, 1948;

Advocate-Depute, 1957-59; Senior Advocate-Depute, 1964; Sheriff of Dumfries and Galloway, 1968; Sheriff of Roxburgh, Berwick and Selkirk, 1970; Solicitor-General for Scotland, 1970-72.

Brand, Janet Mary Valentine, BA (Hons), DipTP, MRTPI. Senior Lecturer, Strathclyde University, since 1973; b. 19.4.44, Bath; m., Robert E. Lamb; 1 d. Educ. County High School for Girls, Brentwood; Exeter University; Mid Essex Technical College. Local authority appointments in Departments of Planning, Essex County Council, London Borough of Barking and City of London, 1965-70; Senior Lecturer, Department of Planning, South Bank Polytechnic, 1970-73. Convener, Education Committee, Scottish Branch, RTPI; Moderator and Reviser, SCOTEC, since 1978. Recreations: skiing; gardening; family pursuits; travelling. Address: (b.) Department of Urban and Regional Planning, Strathclyde University, Livingstone Tower, Richmond Street, Glasgow; T.-041-552 4400, Ext. 3905/6.

Brand, John Arthur. Senior Lecturer in Politics, Strathclyde University; b. 4.8.34, Aberdeen; 1 d. Educ. Aberdeen Grammar School; Aberdeen University; London School of Economics. Assistant in Politics, Glasgow University, 1959-61; Lecturer in Politics, Reading University, 1961-63; Lecturer in the Politics of Education, London University, 1963-64; joined Strathclyde University as Lecturer in Politics, 1964. Chairman: Campaign for a Scottish Assembly, 1979-83; Glasgow Community Relations Committee, 1968-71. Recreations: skiing; tennis; music. Address: (h.) 17 Kew Terrace, Glasgow, G12 OTT; T.-041-339 1675.

Branscombe, Professor Peter John, MA (Oxon), PhD. Professor of Austrian Studies, St. Andrews University, since 1979; b. 7.12.29, Sittingbourne, Kent; m., Marina Riley; 2 s.; 1 d. Educ. Dulwich College; Worcester College, Oxford; Bedford College, London. Joined St. Andrews University, 1959, as Lecturer, then Senior Lecturer, in German. Governor, Royal Scottish Academy of Music and Drama, 1967-73; served on Awarding Panel for Schlegel-Tieck Prize, 1971-79 (Convener, 1974-77); Member: Music Committee, Scottish Arts Council, 1973-80; Scottish Arts Council, 1976-79; Chairman, SAC Working Party investigating the record industry in Scotland, 1976-77; Chairman, Conference of University Teachers of German in Scotland, since 1983. Publications: Heine: Selected Verse, 1967; Austrian Life and Literature 1780-1938; Eight Essays (Editor), 1978; Schubert Studies (Editor), 1982. Recreations: natural history; walking; music; theatre. Address: (b.) Department of German, The University, St. Andrews, Fife, KY16 9PH; T.-St. Andrews 76161, Ext. 331.

Brant, Douglas, IPFA, FRVA, MBIM. Director of Finance, Strathkelvin District Council, since 1974; b. 27.6.42, Motherwell; m., Valerie Margaret; 1 s.; 1 d. Educ. Dalziel High School, Motherwell; Scottish College of Commerce. Trainee and Accountancy Assistant, Burgh of Motherwell and Wishaw, 1959-64; Burgh of Bishopbriggs: Assistant and Depute Town Chamberlain, 1964-68, Town Chamberlain, 1968-75.

Chairman, Scottish Branch, CIPFA. Recreations: golf; curling. Address: (b.) PO Box 4, Tom Johnston House, Civic Way, Kirkintilloch, G66 4TJ.

Braterman, Paul Sydney, MA, DPhil, DSC, CChem, FRSC. Senior Lecturer in Chemistry, Glasgow University, since 1977; b. 28.8.38, London; 2 s. Educ. St. Paul's; Balliol College, Oxford. Postdoctoral Research Fellow, 1962-65; joined Glasgow University, 1965. Publications: Metal Carbonyl Spectra, 1975; Reactions of Coordinated Ligands (Editor/Co-Author), 1986. Recreations: talking and listening; the arts. Address: (b.) Department of Chemistry, Glasgow University, Glasgow, G12 8QQ; T.-041-339 8855.

Bray, Jeremy William, MP, PhD. MP (Labour), Motherwell South, since 1983; Opposition Spokesman on Science and Technology, since 1983; b. 29.6.30, Hong Kong; m., Elizabeth Trowell; 4 d. Educ. Aberystwyth Grammar School; Kingswood School, Bath; Jesus College, Cambridge; Harvard University. Technical Officer, Wilton works, ICI, 1956-62; MP, Middlesbrough West, 1962-70; Member, Select Committee on Nationalised Industries, 1962-64; Chairman, Labour Science and Technology Group, 1964-66; Member, Economic Affairs Estimates Sub-Committee, 1964-66; Parliamentary Secretary, Ministry of Power, 1966-67; Joint Parliamentary Secretary, Ministry of Technology, 1967-69; Director, Mullard Ltd., 1970-73; Chairman, Fabian Society, 1971-72; Co-Director, Programme of Research into Econometric Methods, Imperial College, 1971-74; Consultant, Battelle Research Centre, Geneva, 1973; Senior Research Fellow, Strathclyde University, 1974, and Visiting Professor, 1974-79; Deputy Chairman, Christian Aid, 1972-83; MP, Motherwell and Wishaw, 1979-83; Member, Treasury and Civil Service Select Committee, 1979-83; Chairman, Sub-Committee, Treasury and Civil Service Select Committee, 1981-82. Publications: Decision in Government, 1970; Production Purpose and Structure, 1982. Recreation: sailing. Address: (b.) House of Commons, London, SW1A OAA.

Bremner, James W., FCCA, ARVA, MBIM. Director of Finance, Highland Regional Council, since 1975; b. 29.5.33, Forfar; m., Ethel; 1 s.; 1 d. Educ. Forfar Academy. RAF, 1951-54; Accountant, Angus County Council, 1955-65; Ross and Cromarty County Council: Depute County Treasurer, 1965-70; County Treasurer, 1970-75. Recreation: golf. Address: (b.) Highland Regional Council, Glenurquhart Road, Inverness; T.-0463 234121.

Breslin, William, MA, BSc, DipEd. Director of Administration, Fife Regional Council, since 1983; b. 26.6.37, Edinburgh; m., Nancy Miller Green; 3 s. Educ. Broughton Higher Grade School; Edinburgh University; London University. Teacher, 1960-65; Principal Teacher, 1965-70; Organiser (Secondary Education), 1970-75; Depute Director (Education), 1975-83. Recreations: music; art; travel. Address: (b.) Fife Regional Council, Fife House (01), North Street, Glenrothes, Fife, KY7 5LT; T.-Glenrothes 754411, Ext. 3603.

Brewis, (Henry) John. MA (Oxon). Lord Lieutenant, Wigtown, since 1982; b. 8.4.20, Scarborough; m., Faith MacTaggart Stewart; 3 s.; 1 d. Educ. Eton College; New College, Oxford. Royal Artillery (Major), 1940-46; Barrister-at-law, Middle Temple, 1946-51; Wigtown County Council, 1955-59 (Chairman, Finance Committee); MP (Conservative), Galloway, 1959-74; PPS to Lord Advocate, 1960-61; Chairman, Select Committee on Scottish Affairs, 1971-72; Member, European Parliament, 1973-75. Regional Chairman, Scottish Landowners Federation, 1978-80; Chairman, Scottish Timber Growers, 1980-83; Director, Border Television p.l.c., since 1977. Recreations: forestry; gardening. Address: (h.) Ardwell House, Stranraer, Wigtownshire.

Brian, Paul Vaughan, BSc. Rector, Biggar High School, since 1985 (Rector, Hutchesons' Grammar School, Glasgow, 1984-85); b. 14.6.42, Wokingham; m., Helen Margaret Balneaves; 1 s.; 1 d. Educ. Perth Academy; Edinburgh University; Heriot-Watt College. Assistant Headmaster, Garnock Academy, Kilbirnie, 1974; Depute Rector, Marr College, Troon, 1977; Headteacher, Gryffe High School, Bridge of Weir, 1979. Scientific Officer, Scottish Hindu Kush Expedition, 1968. Recreations: mountaineering; golf; gardening. Address: (b.) Biggar High School, Biggar, Lanarkshire.

Bridges, Roy Charles, BA, PhD, FRGS, FRHistS. Senior Lecturer in History, Aberdeen University, since 1971 (Chairman, African Studies Group, since 1983); b. 26.9.32, Aylesbury; m., Jill Margaret Bridges; 2 s.; 2 d. Educ. Harrow Weald County Grammar School; Keele University; London University. Lecturer in History, Makerere University, Uganda, 1960-64; joined Aberdeen University as Lecturer, 1964; Head, History Department, 1977-82; Secretary, African Studies Group, 1966-83. Member, History Panel, Scottish Examination Board, since 1983; Visiting Professor, Indiana University; President, Aberdeen Branch, Historical Association; Treasurer, Scottish Institute of Missionary Studies. Publications: Nations and Empires (Co-author), 1969; J.A. Grant in Africa, 1982. Recreations: cricket; geology; walking. Address: (b.) Department of History, King's College, Aberdeen, AB9 2UB; T.-Aberdeen 40241, Ext. 6563.

Brock, Professor David John Henry, BA (Oxon), PhD, MRCPath, FRSE. Professor of Human Genetics, Edinburgh University, since 1985; Director, Human Genetics Unit, Edinburgh University, since 1983; b. 5.6.36, London; m., Sheila Abercromby; 4 s. Educ. Diocesan College, Cape Town; Cape Town University; Oxford University. Postdoctoral Fellow: Massachussets Institute of Technology, 1962-63; Harvard University, 1963-66; Oxford University, 1966-67; Senior Scientific Officer, ARC Animal Breeding Research Organisation, 1967-68; joined Edinburgh University as Lecturer in Human Genetics, 1968; appointed Reader, 1978. Address: (b.) Human Genetics Unit, Western General Hospital, Edinburgh; T.-031-332 7917.

Brockie, Rev. Colin Glynn Frederick, BSc (Eng), BD. Minister, Grange Church, Kilmarnock, since 1978; b. 17.7.42, Westcliff-on-Sea,

Essex; m., Barbara Katherine Gordon; 2 s.; 1 d. Educ. Musselburgh Grammar School; Aberdeen Grammar School; Aberdeen University. Probationer Assistant, Mastrick Church, Aberdeen, 1967-68; Minister, St. Martin's Church, Edinburgh, 1968-78. Chaplain, Ayrshire Mission to the Deaf, since 1982; Honorary Secretary and Treasurer, Scottish Church History Society. Recreations: billiards; squash; photography; computing. Address: Grange Manse, 51 Portland Road, Kilmarnock; T.-Kilmarnock 25311.

Brockington, John Leonard, MA, DPhil. Senior Lecturer in Sanskrit, Edinburgh University, since 1982 (Head of Department, since 1975); b. 5.12.40, Oxford; m., Mary Fairweather; 1 s.; 1 d. Educ. Mill Hill School; Corpus Christi College, Oxford. Lecturer in Sanskrit, Edinburgh University, 1965-82. Publications: The Sacred Thread, 1981; Righteous Rama, 1984. Address: (h.) 99 Cluny Gardens, Edinburgh, EH10 6BW; T.-031-447 7580.

Brocklebank, Ted. Head of News and Current Affairs, Grampian Television, since 1977; b. 24.9.42, St. Andrews; 2 s. Educ. Madras College, St. Andrews. D.C. Thomson, Dundee, 1960-63; Freelance Journalist, 1963-65; Scottish TV, 1965-70; Reporter, Grampian TV, 1970-76. Won BAFTA Award for What Price Oil?; Radio Industries Club of Scotland Special Award (Documentary) for Tale of Two Cities. Recreations: rugby; music; reading; living in Scotland. Address: (b.) Grampian TV, Queen's Cross, Aberdeen, AB9 2XJ.

Brocklesby, Professor David William, Dr.Vet.Med. (Zurich), FRCPath, FRCVS. Professor of Tropical Animal Health and Director of the Centre for Tropical Veterinary Medicine, Edinburgh University, since 1978; b. 12.2.29, Grimsby; m., Jennifer Mary Hubble; 1 s.; 3 d. Educ. Sedbergh School, Yorkshire; Royal Veterinary College, London; London School of Hygiene and Tropical Medicine. Veterinary Research Officer, East African Veterinary Research Organisation, Muguga, Kenya (Head, Division of Protozoal Diseases), 1955-66; Head, Department of Animal Health, Fisons Pest Control Ltd., Saffron Walden, 1966-67; Head, Department of Parasitology, ARC Institute for Research on Animal Diseases, Compton, Berkshire, 1967-78. Member, Editorial Board: Research in Veterinary Science; British Veterinary Journal; Tropical Animal Health and Production. Recreations: worrying; reading The Times; watching TV. Address: (b.) Centre for Tropical Veterinary Medicine, Easter Bush, Roslin, Midlothian; T.-031-445 2001.

Brodie, David M., BSc. Chairman, Scottish Parent Teacher Council, since 1982; Personnel Manager, British Steel Corporation, Scottish Steel and Tube Works, since 1984; b. 5.1.44, Bothwell, Lanarkshire; m., Phyllis; 1 s.; 1 d. Educ. Coatbridge High School; Glasgow University. Education and Training Officer, Colvilles Ltd., 1965-69; Personnel Manager, Marinite Ltd., Cape Group, 1969-71; British Steel Corporation: Graduate Recruitment Co-ordinator,

General Steels Division, 1971-74; Senior Industrial Relations Officer, Head Office (London), 1974-77; Industrial Relations Manager, Scottish Division (Heavy Works), 1977-80; Personnel Manager, BSC Plates (Scotland), 1980-84. Scottish Parent Teacher Council: Member, since 1980; Vice-Chairman, 1981-82; Member, Consultative Committee on Curriculum, since 1983. Recreations: play a little golf (badly) and occasionally watch Airdrieonians play soccer (equally badly!). Address: (b.) British Steel Corporation, Clydesdale Works, Bellshill, Lanarkshire, ML4 2RR; T.-0698 749233.

Brodie, Donald Ian Fordyce, BSc. Head of Production Resources and Engineering, BBC Scotland, since 1981; b. 25.9.36, Elgin; m., Christine; 3 s. Educ. Nairn Academy; Aberdeen University. Graduate Apprentice, Associated Electrical Industries, 1961-64; Engineer, Transmission, South of Scotland Electricity Board, 1964-69; Transmission Planning Engineer, Northern Ireland Joint Electricity Authority, 1969-72; Power Station Manager, Northern Ireland Electricity Service, 1972-79; Head of Production Services and Engineering, BBC Northern Ireland, 1979-81. Recreations: climbing; walking; golf. Address: (b.) BBC Scotland, Broadcasting House, Queen Margaret Drive, Glasgow, G12 8DG.

Brodie, James W., JP, CEng, MICE. Secretary: Fife Building Trades Employers Association, since 1984; Kirkcaldy District Chamber of Commerce, since 1984; Member, Kirkcaldy District Council, since 1974; b. 20.5.30, Freuchie, Fife; m., Evelyn. Educ. Bell Baxter School, Cupar; Heriot-Watt College, Edinburgh. Civil engineer, City of Edinburgh, 1963-74; Principal Engineer, Department of Highways, Lothian Region, 1974-82; Member and Chairman, Works Committee, Kirkcaldy Town Council, 1969-74; Member, Fife Water Board; Director, Abbeyfield Society, Kirkcaldy; Member, College Council, Kirkcaldy College of Technology; Chairman, Argos Youth Centre, Kirkcaldy. Recreation: golf. Address: 9A West Fergus Place, Kirkcaldy, Fife.

Brodie of Brodie, (Montagu) Ninian Alexander, DL, JP; b. 12.6.12, Forres; m., Helena Penelope Budgen (deceased); 1 s.; 1 d. Educ. Eton. Trained Webber-Douglas School of Dramatic Art, 1933-35; professional Actor and Director, occasional broadcasts, 1935-40; served with Royal Artillery, including North Africa and Italy, 1940-45; returned to stage, with occasional films and broadcasts, 1945-50; managed estate, market garden, etc., Brodie Castle, from 1950; gave Brodie Castle and part of estate to National Trust for Scotland, 1979; voluntary work as guide etc., since 1980. Life Member, National Trust for Scotland. Recreations: shooting; hill-walking; collecting paintings. Address: (h.) Brodie Castle, Forres, Moray, IV36 OTE; T.-Brodie 202.

Brodie, Very Rev. Peter Philip, MA, BD, LLB, DD. Minister, St. Mungo's, Alloa, since 1947; b. 22.10.16, Airdrie; m., Constance Lindsay Hope; 3 s.; 1 d. Educ. Airdrie Academy; Glasgow University; Trinity College, Glasgow. Minister, St. Mary's, Kirkintilloch, 1942-47; Moderator,

General Assembly of the Church of Scotland, 1978-79; Convener, General Administration Committee, 1976-80; Business Convener, 1976-80; Vice Convener, General Trustees, 1973-85; Chairman, General Trustees; Chairman, Judicial Commission, since 1983; Chairman, Joint Report, Methodist/Church of Scotland Conversation; Moderator, Synod of Forth, 1976. Recreations: gardening; fishing. Address: Manse of St. Mungo's, Claremont, Alloa; T.-Alloa 213872.

Brodie, Robert, MA, LLB. Deputy Solicitor to Secretary of State for Scotland, since 1984; b. 9.4.38, Dundee; m., Jean Margaret McDonald; 2 s.; 2 d. Educ. Morgan Academy, Dundee; St. Andrews University; Queen's College, Dundee. Scottish Office: Legal Assistant, 1965; Senior Legal Assistant, 1970; Deputy Director, Scottish Courts Administration, 1975; Assistant Solicitor, Scottish Office, 1982. Recreations: music; hill-walking. Address: (h.) 45 Stirling Road, Edinburgh; T.-031-552 2028.

Brodie, William, BSc, MIBiol. Rector, Wallace High School, Stirling, since 1984; b. 16.9.37, Hamilton; m., Helen Bland; 1 s.; 1 d. Educ. Hamilton Academy; Glasgow University; Paisley College of Technology. Teacher, Wishaw High School, 1965-67; Principal Teacher of Biology, Hutchesons' Grammar School, Glasgow, 1967-74; Assistant Rector, Graeme High School, Falkirk, 1974-79; Depute Rector, Kirkintilloch High School, 1979-81; Rector, Balfron High School, 1981-84. Council Member, Headteachers Association of Scotland. Recreations: golf; tennis; gardening. Address: (b.) Wallace High School, Dumyat Road, Stirling; T.-0786 62166.

Brodley, John Inglis, DA, RIBA, RIAS. Director of Architectural and Technical Services, Kirkcaldy District Council, since 1980; b. 11.2.24, Dunfermline; m., Isabel. Educ. Dunfermline High School; Edinburgh College of Art. Royal Engineers, 1942-47; Assistant Architect, City of Glasgow, 1951-55; Chief Assistant Architect, Burgh of Hamilton, 1955-61; Depute Burgh Architect, Burgh of Kirkcaldy, 1961-75; Depute Director of Architectural and Technical Services, Kirkcaldy District Council, 1975-80. Recreations: golf; gardening. Address: (b.) Forth House, Abbotshall Road, Kirkcaldy, KY1 1RU; T.-0592 261144.

Brogan, Colm, BA (Cantab). Writer and Columnist, Glasgow Herald, since 1972; b. 18.2.47, Glasgow; m., Kathryn Dalgleish; 2 s. Educ. St. Mungo's Academy, Glasgow; Glasgow University; St. John's College, Cambridge. Contributor, various publications at home and abroad; intermittent broadcaster. Recreation: sleeping. Address: (b.) Glasgow Herald, 195 Albion Street, Glasgow; T.-041-552 6255.

Brooker, William Dixon, BSc. Director, Department of Adult Education and Extra-Mural Studies, Aberdeen University, since 1981; b. 13.12.31, Calcutta; m., Margaret Laura Parkinson; 1 s.; 1 d. Educ. Aberdeen Grammar School; Aberdeen University. Principal Teacher of Geography: Aberlour High School; Keith Grammar School; King Richard School,

Dhekelia, Cyprus; Keith Grammar School; Tutor Organiser in Extra-Mural Studies, Aberdeen University, 1966. President, Scottish Mountaineering Club, 1972-74 (Honorary Editor, SMC Journal, since 1975); Vice-Chairman: Mountaineering Council of Scotland, 1979-81; Scottish Mountain Leader Training Board, 1978-80. Recreations: mountaineering; skiing; travel; photography. Address: (h.) 25 Deeview Road South, Cults, Aberdeen; T.-0224 861055.

Brookes, Brian Sydney, MBE, BSc, MSc, MIBiol. Freelance Naturalist and Ecologist, and Consultant in environmental education and conservation, since 1985; b. 4.5.36, Beckenham, Kent; m., Margaret Mary; 3 s.; 1 d. Educ. Beckenham and Penge Grammar School; King's College, London; Dundee University. Teaching in London schools, seven years; Assistant Warden, field centre in Devon, two years; Warden, Kindrogan Field Centre, Perthshire, 18 years. Sometime Council Member, Botanical Society of the British Isles; various committees, Scottish Wildlife Trust. Recreations: bee-keeping; photography. Address: (h.) Glenshieling, Hatton Road, Blairgowrie, Perthshire, PH10 7HZ; T.-0250 4605.

Brookes, Douglas Whittaker, TD. Secretary, Inverness and District Chamber of Commerce, since 1980; b. 3.1.19, Sheffield; m., May; 1 s.; 1 d. War Service, 1939-46 (Captain, RE); AI Welders Ltd., Inverness, 1946-80: Sales Manager; Sales Director; Managing Director and Chief Executive. Served with local regiment, TA, Lovat Scouts, 1950-66 (latterly Major, Second-in-Command). Recreations: golf; hill-walking; reading. Address: (h.) 13A Island Bank Road, Inverness, IV2 4QN; T.-0463 233570.

Brooks, Professor Charles Joseph William, PhD, DSc, DIC, ARCS, FRSE. Titular Professor of Chemistry, Glasgow University, since 1976; b. 28.9.27, London; m., Gillian M.W. Staniforth; 1 s.; 1 d. Educ. Surbiton County Grammar School; Royal College of Science, London University. Assistant Lecturer, Department of Chemistry and Biochemistry, St. Thomas's Hospital, London, 1954-56; Member, MRC scientific staff, research units, Glasgow, 1956-63; Chemistry Department, Glasgow University: Lecturer, 1963; Senior Lecturer, 1966; Reader, 1973; Visiting Professor: Baylor College of Medicine, Houston, Texas, 1963 and 1965; Japan Society for Promotion of Science, 1977. Editor, Gas Chromatography - Mass Spectrometry Abstracts, since 1974; Member, Editorial Advisory Board: Biomedical Mass Spectrometry; Journal of Chromatography Biomedical Applications; Journal of High Resolution Chromatography and Chromatography Communications. Recreations: travel; music. Address: (b.) Chemistry Department, Glasgow University, Glasgow, G12 8QQ; T.-041-339 8855.

Brooks, Professor David Neil, BA, MSc, PhD. Titular Professor, Department of Psychological Medicine, Glasgow University, since 1984; b. 6.3.44, Huddersfield; m., Christine; 2 s.; 1 d. Educ. William Hulme's Grammar School, Manchester; University of Wales; Leeds University; Glasgow University. Senior Lecturer in Clinical

Psychology, Glasgow University, 1972-84; Head of Postgraduate Training Course in Clinical Psychology, Glasgow University; External Examiner in Clinical Psychology: British Psychological Society; Surrey University; London University; External Examiner in Behavioural Sciences, Edinburgh University. Member, Neuroscience Grants Committee, Medical Research Council, 1979-85; Secretary, MRC Co-ordinating Group on Rehabilitation After Acute Brain Damage. Recreations: shooting; working. Address: (h.) 30 Crawford Road, Milngavie, Glasgow, G62 7LF.

Brooks, Patrick William, BSc, MB, ChB, DPM, MRCPsych. Senior Medical Officer, Scottish Home and Health Department, since 1981; b. 17.5.38, Hereford. Educ. Hereford High School; Bishop Vesey's Grammar School, Sutton Coldfield; Edinburgh University. Royal Edinburgh and associated hospitals, including State Hospital, Carstairs, and Western General Hospital, Edinburgh: Senior House Officer, 1964-66; Registrar, 1966-69; Senior Registrar, 1969-74; Medical Officer, Scottish Home and Health Department, 1974-81. A founder Member, Edinburgh Festival Fringe Society, 1969 (Vice-Chairman, 1964-71); Chairman, Edinburgh Playhouse Society, 1975-81; Secretary, Lothian Playhouse Trust, 1981-83; Secretary and Treasurer, Edinburgh Friends of Scottish Ballet. Recreations: opera; ballet; music; theatre; cinema; modern Scottish art; travel. Address: (h.) 11 Thirlestane Road, Edinburgh, EH9 1AL.

Broster, Rev. David, BA. Minister, Kilbirnie: St. Columba's, since 1983; b. 14.3.44, Liverpool; m., Margaret Ann; 2 d. Educ. Liverpool Institute High School; United Theological College, University of Wales; Open University. Dip., Theology; Cert., Pastoral Studies. Ordained by Presbyterian Church of Wales, 1969; Minister: Park Place, Tredegar, Gwent, 1969-78, Clubmoor Presbyterian Church of Wales, Liverpool, 1978-83; Clerk, Association in East, Presbyterian Church of Wales, 1981-83. Recreations: computers; gardening; advanced driving. Address: St. Columba's Manse, Kilbirnie, Ayrshire, KA25 7JU; T.-0505 683342.

Brotherston, Sir John (Howie Flint), Kt (1972), FRCPEdin, FRCPGlas, FFCM, FRCP, DPH, Hon. FRSH, Hon. LLD (Aberdeen), Hon. MD (Bristol), MA, MB, ChB, MD. Professor of Community Medicine, Edinburgh University, 1977-80; b. 9.3.15, Edinburgh; m.; 2 s.; 2 d. Educ. George Watson's College, Edinburgh; Edinburgh University. RAMC, 1941-46; Professor of Public Health and Social Medicine, Edinburgh University, 1955-64; Chief Medical Officer, Scottish Home and Health Department, 1964-77; Member, MRC, 1974-77; Honorary Physician to The Queen, 1965-68.

Broun, Rev. Canon Claud Michael, BA (Oxon). Rector, St. Mary the Virgin, Hamilton, since 1975; b. 9.2.30, Edinburgh; m., Janice Ann Watson; 2 s.; 1 d. Educ. Edinburgh Academy; Brasenose College, Oxford. Rector, St. Cuthbert's, Cambuslang, 1962-75; Canon, St. Mary's Cathedral, Glasgow, since 1983. Editor,

Truth and Unity newsletter. Recreations: cricket; hill-walking; crosswords. Address: St. Mary's House, Auchingramont Road, Hamilton, ML3 6JP; T.-Hamilton 423725.

Brown, Professor Alan Geoffrey, BSc, MB, ChB, PhD, FRSE. Professor of Veterinary Physiology, Edinburgh University, since 1984; b. 20.4.40, Nottingham; m., Judith Brown; 1 s.; 1 d. Educ. Mundella School, Nottingham; Edinburgh University. Assistant Lecturer, then Lecturer in Veterinary Physiology, Edinburgh University, 1964-68; Beit Memorial Fellow for Medical Research, 1968-71; Research Fellow supported by MRC, 1971-74; Lecturer, then Reader in Veterinary Physiology, Edinburgh University, 1974-84; holder, MRC Research Fellowship for academic staff, 1980-85. Member, Editorial Boards, several scientific journals. Recreations: music; gardening; walking; reading. Address: (b.) Department of Veterinary Physiology, Edinburgh University, Edinburgh, EH9 1QH; T.-031-667 1011.

Brown, Charles, JP. Member, Glasgow District Council, since 1980; full-time official, National Union of Tailor and Garment Workers, since 1956; b. 4.11.21, Stirling; m., Margaret; 2 d. Educ. Pirn Street Advanced School, Glasgow. Governor, Baillies Institution; former Member, Glasgow Northern Hospital Board; Past Chairman, Glasgow Trades Council. Recreations: bowling; swimming; golf. Address: (h.) 211 Onslow Drive, Glasgow, G31; T.-041-554 4633.

Brown, Professor Charles Malcolm, BSc, PhD, DSc, FRSA, FIBiol, FRSE. Professor of Microbiology, Heriot-Watt University, since 1979; Director, Riccarton Laboratory, Fermentech Ltd., since 1984; b. 21.9.41, Gisland; m., Diane Mary Bryant; 3 d. Educ. Houghton-le-Spring Grammar School; Birmingham University. Lecturer in Microbiology, Newcastle-upon-Tyne University, 1966-73; Senior Lecturer, Dundee University, 1973-79. Editor-in-Chief, Microbiological Sciences; Council Member: Scottish Marine Biological Association; Society for General Microbiology; Director, Bioscot Ltd. Recreations: music; walking. Address: (b.) Heriot-Watt University, Chambers Street, Edinburgh, EH1 1HX; T.-031-225 8432.

Brown, Daniel Martin, MA (Hons). Principal, Barmulloch College, since 1977; b. 4.12.28, Clydebank; m., Isabella Montgomery; 1 s.; 1 d. Educ. Clydebank High School; Dumbarton Academy; Glasgow University; Jordanhill College. Education Officer, RAF, 1952-54 (final rank, flying officer); Teacher of English and History: Vale of Leven Academy, 1954-56; Gordon Schools, Huntly, 1956-62; Teacher of English, Dunfermline High School, 1962-64; Senior Lecturer in English, Langside College of Further Education, Glasgow, 1964-70; Cardonald College, Glasgow: Head, Department of Communication Arts, 1970-75; Depute Principal, 1975-77. Chairman, Moderating Committee, SCOTBEC, 1975-78; Further Education Representative, Strathclyde Regional Council, 1980-83; Member, Officer Group on Post-Compulsory Education; Further Education Representative, Strathclyde Regional Council Joint Planning Group for Training in

Community Work; College Organiser, College Public Speaking Annual Competition, Glasgow Junior Chamber of Commerce. Recreations: reading (especially 20th-century novelists); theatre; films; angling; bowling. Address: (h.) 45 Lanton Road, Newlands, Glasgow, G43 2SR; T.-041-637 8169.

Brown, David Blair, MA, LLB. Rector, Dunfermline High School, since 1983; b. 6.5.38, Glasgow; m., Marjory Kathleen Muir; 2 s.; 1 d. Educ. Hutchesons' Boys Grammar School, Glasgow; Glasgow University; Jordanhill College of Education. Teacher, Hutchesons' Boys Grammar School; Principal Teacher of History, Renfrew High School, 1970-74; Assistant Rector, Stonelaw High School, 1974-78; Depute Rector and Acting Head, Dalbeattie High School, 1978-81; Assistant Rector, Musselburgh Grammar School, 1981-83. Member, children's panel, since 1976; Church activities. Recreations: walking; cycling; gardening; motoring; skating; theatre; music. Address: (h.) Damar, 130 Terregles Avenue, Maxwell Park, Glasgow, G41; T.-041-423 0604.

Brown, David Henry. Principal, Scottish Home and Health Department, since 1983; b. 13.5.40, Edinburgh; m., Catherine Agnes Moffat; 1 s.; 3 d. Educ. Broughton Senior Secondary School, Edinburgh. Scottish Tourist Board, 1969-72; Scottish Council (Development and Industry), 1973-77; Scottish Education Department, 1978-83 (Secretary, Scottish Council for Community Education, 1979-82). Recreations: hill-walking; road-running. Address: (h.) 23 Pentland Grove, Edinburgh, EH10 6NR; T.-031-445 1724.

Brown, David Kynd, BSc (Hons), PhD, CEng, FIMechE, MRINA. Senior Lecturer in Mechanical Engineering, Glasgow University, since 1980; Director and Secretary, Fracture Mechanics Consultants Ltd., since 1976; b. 24.10.43, Bearsden; m., Jean Caroline Macdonald; 2 d. Educ. Kelvinside Academy, Glasgow; Glasgow University. Postgraduate apprentice, James Howden & Co. Ltd., Glasgow, 1965-67; Assistant Lecturer, then Lecturer in Mechanical Enginering, Glasgow University, 1967-80; Visiting Professor, Rhode Island University, 1974-75. Publication: Introduction to the Finite Element Method using Basic Programs, 1984. Recreations: Scottish bagpipes; curling; Boys' Brigade. Address: (b.) Department of Mechanical Engineering, Glasgow University, G12 8QQ; T.-041-339 8855.

Brown, Denis, MSc, FCCA. Director of Finance, Edinburgh University, since 1984; b. 27.8.42, Manchester; 4 s.; 1 d. Educ. Manchester Central Grammar School; Bradford University. Audit practice; Accountant, Shell UK; Systems Analyst, British Leyland; Corporate Finance Executive Assistant, Commercial Union, London, 1972-75; Financial Controller, Procon UK, 1975-77; Director of Finance, Open University, 1977-84. Address: (b.) Old College, South Bridge, Edinburgh, EH18 9YL; T.-031-667 1011, Ext. 4246.

Brown, Professor Donald Houston, JP, BSc, PhD, DSc. Professor in Inorganic Chemistry, Strathclyde University, since 1983; b. 26.2.30,

Kilmarnock; widower; 2 s.; 1 d. Educ. Kilmarnock Academy; Glasgow University. Recreations: golf; bridge. Address: (h.) 4 Howard Street, Kilmarnock; T.-Kilmarnock 21632.

Brown, Eric. Professional Golfer; b. 1925, Edinburgh. Won PGA Match-Play, 1960-62, Swiss Open, 1951, Italian Open, 1952, Penfold, 1952, Irish Open, 1953, Portuguese Open, 1953, Dunlop Masters, 1957, Gleneagles-Saxone Am.-Pro. Foursomes, 1957, Stuart C. Goodwin 5000 Guineas, 1956 (jointly), Yorkshire Evening News, 1958, Dunlop, 1960; won Scottish Professional Championship, seven times, joint winner, once; Scottish Amateur Champion, 1946; Leader, PGA Order of Merit, 1957; Ryder Cup player, four times (non-playing Captain, twice); awarded Golf Writers' Trophy, 1957.

Brown, Ewan, MA, LLB, CA. Director: Noble Grossart Ltd., since 1971; Scottish Transport Group; Scottish Development Finance; b. 23.3.42, Perth; m., Christine; 1 s.; 1 d. Educ. Perth Academy; St. Andrews University. Session Clerk, Mayfield Parish Church, Edinburgh. Recreations: family; golf. Address: (b.) 48 Queen Street, Edinburgh; T.-031-226 7011.

Brown, George, BL. Chief Executive Officer, Dunfermline District Council, since 1974; b. 2.1.33, Falkirk; m., Sarah; 2 s.; 1 d. Educ. Falkirk High School; Edinburgh University. Solicitor. Assistant Solicitor: Allan Dawson Simpson & Hampton, WS, 1954-55; Falkirk Burgh, 1955-59; Dunfermline Burgh, 1959-62; Town Clerk and Chamberlain, Linlithgow Burgh, 1962-70; Town Clerk and Chief Executive, Bathgate Burgh, 1970-74. Member, Executive Committee, SOLACE. Recreations: gardening; philosophy. Address: (b.) City Chambers, Dunfermline, Fife; T.-Dunfermline 722711.

Brown, George Mackay, OBE, MA, Hon MA (Open University), Hon LLD (Dundee), Hon DLitt (Glasgow), FRSL. Poet and story-teller; b. 17.10.21, Stromness, Orkney. Educ. Stromness Academy; Newbattle Abbey College; Edinburgh University. Author of: (short stories) A Time to Keep, Hawkfall, The Sun's Net, Andrina; (poetry) Selected Poems, Winterfold, Voyages; (novels) Greenvoe, Magnus, Time in a Red Coat; various plays. Recreation: reading. Address: (h.) 3 Mayburn Court, Stromness, Orkney, KW16 3DH.

Brown, Gordon. MP (Labour), Dunfermline East, since 1983. Educ. Kirkcaldy High School. Second Student Rector, Edinburgh University; Past Chairman, Scottish Labour Party; former Journalist, Scotish Television.

Brown, Hamish Macmillan. Author, Lecturer, Photographer and Mountaineer; b. 13.8.34, Colombo, Sri Lanka. Educ. several schools abroad; Dollar Academy. National Service, RAF, Middle East/East Africa; Assistant, Martyrs' Memorial Church, Paisley; first-ever full-time appointment in outdoor education (Braehead School, Fife); served many years on Scottish Mountain Leadership Board; has led expeditions world-wide for mountaineering, skiing, trekking,

canoeing, etc. Publications: Hamish's Mountain Walk, 1979 (SAC award); Hamish's Groats End Walk, 1981 (Smith's Travel Prize shortlist); Time Gentlemen, Some Collected Poems, 1983; Eye to the Hills, 1982; Five Bird Stories, 1984; Poems of the Scottish Hills (Editor), 1982; Speak to the Hills (Co-Editor), 1985. Recreations: gardening; "bird" philately; books; music. Address: 21 Carlin Craig, Kinghorn, Fife, KY3 9RX; T.-0592 890422.

Brown, Hugh D. MP (Labour), Glasgow Provan, since 1964; b. May, 1919. Educ. Allan Glen's School; Whitehill Secondary School, Glasgow. Former Civil Servant, Ministry of Pensions and National Insurance; Member, Glasgow Corporation, 1954-64; Under Secretary of State for Scotland with responsibilities for housing and agriculture and fisheries, 1974-79; Member, Select Committee on Members' Salaries, 1981-82.

Brown, Iain Shaw Forbes. Managing Director, Galloway Gazette Ltd., since 1982; b. 17.5.38, Newton Stewart; m., Anne; 1 s.; 1 d. Educ. Barnard Castle School, Co. Durham; Heriot-Watt College, Edinburgh. Reporter, Ayr Advertiser, 1956-59; Sub-Editor, Scottish Daily Express, 1959; BBC: News Assistant/Reporter, Glasgow, 1959-60, News Assistant, London, 1962-64; Editor, Galloway Gazette, 1964; Managing Editor, Galloway Gazette, Carrick Gazette, Stornoway Gazette, 1972-82. Recreation: golf. Address: (b.) 71 Victoria Street, Newton Stewart; T.-0671 2503.

Brown, Ian Durno, FICE, FIMunE, MIWPC, FBIM. Director of Water Services, Grampian Regional Council, since 1978; b. 8.9.24, Aberdeen; m., Eveline; 2 s. Educ. Robert Gordon's College; Robert Gordon's Technical College. RAF, 1943-47; Junior Engineer, North of Scotland Hydro-Electric Board, 1947-49; Junior Assistant Engineer, Aberdeen Harbour Board, 1949-53; Graduate Assistant Engineer, Burgh Surveyor's Office, Perth, 1953-54; County Surveyor's Office, Aberdeen: Assistant Engineer, 1954-68; Senior Engineering Assistant, 1968-69; Chief Assistant, 1969-73; Depute County Drainage Engineer, 1973-74; Grampian Regional Council: Depute Director, Water Services Department, 1974-76; Senior Depute Director, 1976-78. Recreations: walking; photography. Address: (b.) Grampian Regional Council, Woodhill House, Ashgrove Road West, Aberdeen; T.-0224 39528.

Brown, Ian Forbes, FIB (Scot). Director and Chief Executive, British Linen Bank, since 1979; Member, British National Oil Corporation, since 1983; Director, Motherwell Bridge Holdings Ltd., since 1983; b. 5.3.29, Glasgow; m., Margaret Catherine; 1 s.; 1 d. Educ. Glasgow High School. Has spent entire career with Bank of Scotland, apart from five years spent in Canada; executive responsibilities in Bank of Scotland International Division. Recreations: golf; travelling; reading. Address: (h.) 22 Cammo Gardens, Edinburgh, EH4 8EQ; T.-031-339 1640.

Brown, Ian Johnston Hilton, MA (Hons). Rector, Strathaven Academy, since 1976; b. 5.10.37, Aberdeen; m., Anne Christina Carson; 2 s. Educ. Royal High School, Edinburgh; Edinburgh

University; Moray House College of Education. Teacher, Kirkcaldy High School, 1961-66; Principal Teacher, Bishopbriggs High School, 1966-71; Assistant Head Teacher, Cathkin High School, 1971-74; Depute Rector, Hunter High School, 1974-76. Recreations: hill-walking; swimming; reading; theatre-going; badminton. Address: (b.) Strathaven Academy, Crawford Street, Strathaven, Lanarkshire, ML10 6AE; T.-Strathaven 20126.

Brown, James Armour, RD, BL. Partner, Kerr, Barrie & Duncan (formerly Kerr, Barrie & Goss), Solicitors, Glasgow, since 1957; b. 20.7.30, Rutherglen; m., Alexina Mary Robertson McArthur; 1 s. Educ. Rutherglen Academy; Glasgow University. Served law apprenticeship with Kerr, Barrie & Goss, 1947-50; subsequently in private practice as a Solicitor; National Service, Royal Navy, 1951-53; commissioned RNVR, 1952; transferred to permanent RNVR, 1953, and served with Clyde Division, 1953-72, as Captain's Secretary, Supply Officer and Executive Officer; Commander, 1967; Captain, 1972; Senior Reserve Supply Officer on staff of Admiral Commanding Reserves, 1973-76; Naval ADC to The Queen, 1975-76; Member, Suite of Lord High Commissioner to General Assembly of Church of Scotland (Earl of Mansfield), 1961-62 and (Duke of Gloucester), 1963; Session Clerk, Stonelaw Parish Church, Rutherglen, 1964-81; Member, Church of Scotland Committee on Chaplains to HM Forces, 1975-82 (Vice-Convener, 1979-82); Clerk, Incorporation of Bakers of Glasgow, since 1964; Deacon, Society of Deacons and Free Preseses of Glasgow, 1978-80; Member, Glasgow Committee, Order of St. John of Jerusalem, since 1961 (Chairman, since 1982); Member, Chapter of the Priory of Scotland of the Order of St. John, since 1970; KStJ, 1975; Preceptor of Torphichen, Priory of Scotland, since 1984. Recreation: historical research, particularly in relation to World War I aviation. Address: (h.) 25 Calderwood Road, Rutherglen, Glasgow, G73 3HD; T.-041-647 2051.

Brown, James Lamont, MA, MEd. Chairman, Board of Governors, Jordanhill College of Education, since 1983; b. 14.8.17, Dunlop, Ayrshire; m., Irene Banks; 3 d. Educ. High School of Glasgow; Glasgow University; Jordanhill College of Education. Army Service, RA and AEC, 1940-46; Teacher, primary and secondary schools, Glasgow, 1946-49; Administrative Assistant, Education Department, Aberdeen City, 1949-52; Lanarkshire: Assistant Director of Education, 1952-58, Depute Director of Education, 1958-61; Director of Education, Dumfriesshire, 1961-75. Elder, Church of Scotland. Recreations: bowls; gardening. Address: (h.) 1 Livilands Gate, Stirling, FK8 2AT; T.-0786 75141.

Brown, Professor John Campbell, BSc, PhD, DSc, FRAS, FRSE. Professor of Astrophysics, Glasgow University, since 1984; b. 4.2.47, Dumbarton; m., Dr. Margaret I. Brown; 1 s.; 1 d. Educ. Hartfield Primary School; Dumbarton High School; Glasgow University. Glasgow University Astronomy Department: Research Assistant, 1968-70, Lecturer, 1970-78, Senior Lecturer, 1978-80, Reader, 1980-84; DAAD Fellow,

Tubingen University, 1971-72; ESRO/GROC Fellow, Space Research Laboratory, Utrecht, 1973-74; Visitor: Australian National University, 1975, High Altitude Observatory, Colorado, 1977; NASA Associate Professor, Maryland University, 1980; NSF Fellow, University of California at San Diego, 1984. SERC Solar System Committee, 1980-83; Council, Royal Astronomical Society, since 1984; Member, International Astronomical Union, since 1976. Recreations: cyling; walking; painting; lapidary; conjuring; photography; woodwork. Address: (b.) Department of Astronomy, Glasgow University, Glasgow, G12 8QW; T.-041-339 8855.

Brown, John Clouston, AIB (Scot). Member, Orkney Islands Council, since 1978; b. 4.10.14, Stromness, Orkney; m., Maria Sinclair Flett; 2 s.; 1 d. Educ. Stromness Academy. Joined Union Bank of Scotland Ltd., Stromness, Orkney, 1931; RAF, Burma and India, 1941-45; Manager, Stromness Branch, Union Bank of Scotland (subsequently Bank of Scotland), 1954-74. Past Chairman, Stromness Golf Club; former Secretary: Stromness Chamber of Commerce, Kirkwall Arts Club; former Treasurer, Orkney Agricultural Society. Recreations: golf; fishing; drama. Address: (h.) Breck, Birsay, Orkney, KW17 2LY; T.-Birsay 349.

Brown, John Keith, MB, ChB, FRCP, DCH. Consultant Paediatric Neurologist; b. 21.5.37; m., Frances; 2 s.; 1 d. Educ. Manchester University. President, British Association of Paediatric Neurology, since 1984 (Treasurer, 1981-84); Editor, Developmental Medicine, Child Neurology; Member, National Panel of Specialists (Medical Paediatrics), Royal College of Physicians, Edinburgh; Member, Vaccine Damage Panel, Department of Health and Social Security; Expert Assessor, Medical Defence Union and Scottish Health Services Central Legal Office; numerous special presentations and overseas lectures; Distinguished Guest, Asian Paediatric Society, 1985; Visiting British Council Professor, McGill University, Cape Town, Manitoba and Malaysia.

Brown, Rev. Joseph, MA. Minister, Yetholm, Linton, Morebattle and Hownam, since 1967; b. 2.10.27, Edinburgh; m., Dolina MacDonald; 1 s.; 1 d. Educ. George Heriot's School; Edinburgh University; New College, Edinburgh. Royal Army Chaplain's Department, 1954-57 (attached, Cameron Highlanders); Minister: Kilbrandon and Kilchattan, Argyll, 1957-63, St. Ninian's Musselburgh, 1963-67. Recreations: working glebe; gardening; playing bagpipes. Address: The Manse, Kirk Yetholm, Kelso, Roxburghshire; T.-Yetholm 308.

Brown, Kenneth Joseph, BSc, PhD. Senior Lecturer, Department of Mathematics, Heriot-Watt University, since 1981; b. 20.12.45, Aberdeen; m., Elizabeth Taylor Lobban; 1 s.; 2 d. Educ. Banchory Academy; Aberdeen University; Dundee University. Lecturer, Department of Mathematics, Heriot-Watt University, 1970-81. Recreations: tennis; bridge. Address: (h.) 3 Highlea Grove, Balerno, Midlothian; T.-031-449 5314.

Brown, Madeline, MB, ChB, MRCPsy, DPsy. Consultant Child Psychiatrist, Royal Aberdeen Children's Hospital, since 1982; b. 30.10.37, Aberdeen; m., Ian R. Brown; 2 s. Educ. Aberdeen Academy: Aberdeen University. Recreations: hill-walking; badminton; drama. Address: (h.) 37 Argyll Place, Aberdeen; T.-0224 633996.

Brown, Neil Dallas, DA, ARSA. Painter; Lecturer, Department of Fine Art Studies (Painting Studios), Glasgow School of Art, since 1979; b. 10.8.38, Elgin; m., Georgina Ballantyne; 2 d. Educ. Bell Baxter High School, Cupar; Duncan of Jordanstone College of Art, Dundee; Royal Academy Schools, London. Visiting Lecturer, School of Design, Duncan of Jordanstone College of Art, since 1968; Visiting Lecturer in Painting, Glasgow School of Art, since 1976; since completing training, 28 one-man exhibitions, in Dundee, Manchester, Edinburgh, London (eight), Glasgow, York, Basle, Paris, Stirling, Belfast, Aberdeen and Kirkcaldy; won 10 awards for painting; has been Guest Artist, Dollar Summer School for the Arts, Croydon College of Art, Strathclyde University, Ulster Polytechnic, Grays School of Art (Aberdeen), Maryland Institute College of Art (Baltimore), Newport College of Art (Wales). Recreations: fishing; running. Address: (h.) Tayside, 55 Cupar Road, Newport-on-Tay, Fife, DD6 8DF; T.-542130.

Brown, Ormond John. Honorary Sheriff of Tayside, Central and Fife, at Stirling, since 1982; b. 30.1.22, Gourock; m., Margaret Eileen Beard; 2 d. Educ. Gourock High School; Greenock High School. Entered Sheriff Clerk service, Scotland, 1939; served Second World War, 1941-45, Outer Hebrides, North Africa, Italy, Greece, Austria; Training Organiser, Scottish Court Service, 1957; Sheriff Clerk of Perthshire, 1970; Principal Clerk of Justiciary, 1971-75; Principal Clerk of Session and Justiciary, 1975-82. Past Chairman, Royal British Legion, Dunblane; Past Captain, Dunblane New Golf Club. Recreations: listening to music; playing indifferent but enthusiastic golf; gardening; remembering the great days of the Clyde steamers; hoping for the revival of Greenock Morton. Address: (h.) Ormar, 29 Atholl Place, Dunblane, Perthshire; T.-0786 822186.

Brown, Professor Peter Evans, PhD, FRSE. Professor of Geology, Aberdeen University, since 1973 (Head, Department of Geology and Mineralogy, since 1981); b. 5.4.30, Kendal; m., Thelma Smith; 2 s. Educ. Kendal School; Manchester University. Mineralogist/Geologist, Geological Survey of Tanganyika; Lecturer/Senior Lecturer in Geology, Sheffield University. Fellow, Geological Society. Recreations: mountaineering; exploration. Address: (b.) Department of Geology and Mineralogy, Aberdeen University, Marischal College, Aberdeen, AB9 1AS; T.-0224 40241, Ext. 273.

Brown, Professor Peter Melville, MA (Oxon), DPhil. Stevenson Professor of Italian, Glasgow University, since 1975; b. 7.7.26, Todmorden; m., Aileen Taylor Tough; 2 s.; 1 d. Educ.

Todmorden Grammar School; Magdalen College, Oxford; Scuola Normale Superiore, Pisa. Aberdeen University: Assistant Lecturer in Italian, 1955-57, Lecturer in Italian, 1957-66, Senior Lecturer in Italian, 1966-72; Professor of Italian, Hull University, 1972-75. Publication: Lionardo Salviati: A Critical Biography, 1975. Recreation: travel. Address: (h.) 18 Cleveden Gardens, Kelvinside, Glasgow, G12 OPT; T.-041-357 1651.

Brown, Peter Robert, MB, BCh, DTM&H, DA, FFARCS. Consultant Anaesthetist, Perth Royal Infirmary, since 1975; b. 19.11.31, Manchester; m., Ann Kathleen; 1 s.; 1 d. Educ. Oswestry, Bradford and Altrincham Grammar Schools; Queen's University, Belfast. Short service commission, RAMC, 1960-64; Consultant, Huddersfield Royal Infirmary, 1967-75. Faculty Tutor, Faculty of Anaesthetists, Royal College of Surgeons, England. Recreations: golf; photography; music; World War I aviation literature; gardening; decorating. Address: (h.) Craig House, by Pitcairngreen, Perth; T.-073 884 268.

Brown, Ralph Alexander Stark, MA, LLB. Procurator Fiscal, Cupar, since 1977; b. 16.6.27, Glasgow; m., Mary Bell; 1 s. Educ. Glasgow Academy; Glasgow University. Solicitor: private practice, 1956-71, local government, 1971-74; Procurator Fiscal service, since 1974. Recreations: music; gardening; travel; photography. Address: (b.) County Buildings, Cupar, Fife, KY15 4LS; T.-Cupar 54991.

Brown, Robert Edward, LLB (Hons), NP. Solicitor; Member, Glasgow District Council, and Leader, Liberal Group, since 1977; b. 25.12.47, Newcastle-upon-Tyne; m., Gwen Morris; 1 s.; 1 d. Educ. Gordon Schools, Huntly; Aberdeen University. Legal apprenticeship, Aberdeen, 1969-71; Procurator Fiscal Depute, Dumbarton, 1972-74; Assistant, then Partner, Ross Harper & Murphy, Rutherglen and Glasgow, since 1974. Parliamentary candidate (Liberal), Rutherglen, October 1974, 1979 and 1983; first Liberal, Glasgow District Council; former Secretary, North Aberdeen Liberals; former Member, Scottish Liberal Party Executive and Local Government Organiser; Debates Convenor, Strathclyde Junior Chamber, 1973; Chairman, Rutherglen Citizens' Advice Bureau, 1980-83; Honorary President, Rutherglen Bowling Club, since 1977. Recreations: politics; reading; history; science fiction. Address: (h.) 3 Douglas Avenue, Rutherglen, Glasgow; T.-041-634 2353.

Brown, Robert Thomson. Member (SNP), Kilmarnock and Loudoun District Council, since 1984; b. 26.12.26, Kilmarnock; m., Isobel Sandford Paton; 2 s.; 1 d. Educ. Dreghorn School. Royal Artillery, 1945-47 (Gunner); Massey-Ferguson, 1949-80; Member (SNP), Kilmarnock and Loudoun District Council, 1977-80; Member, Electricity Consultative Council, 1977-81; Chairman: Crosshouse Community Council, 1980-83, Crosshouse Old People's Welfare Association, since 1980. Recreation: study of life and works of Robert Burns. Address: (h.) Mossgiel, 8 Craigie Place, Crosshouse, Ayrshire, KA2 OJR; T.-Kilmarnock 36327.

Brown, Rev. Robin Graeme, BA, BD. Principal, St. Colm's Education Centre and College, since 1984; b. 27.11.32, Alverstoke, Hampshire; m., Sibyl Enid Clarke; 1 s.; 2 d. Educ. Fettes College, Edinburgh; Cambridge University; Edinburgh University; Heidelberg University. Principal, St. Columba's College, Alice, South Africa, 1971-73; Leader, Iona Community, 1974-81. Address: (h.) 24 Inverleith Terrace, Edinburgh, EH3 5NU; T. 031-332 1156.

Brown, Ronald. MP (Labour), Edinburgh Leith, since 1979; b. June, 1940. Educ. Ainslie Park High School, Edinburgh. Member, Lothian Regional Council, 1974-79.

Brown, William, CBE (1971). Managing Director, Scottish Television, since 1966 (Deputy Chairman, since 1974); b. 24.6.29, Ayr; m., Nancy Jennifer Hunter; 1 s.; 3 d. Educ. Ayr Academy; Edinburgh University. STV: London Sales Manager, 1958-61, Sales Director, 1961-63, Deputy Managing Director, 1963-66. Lord Willis Award for services to TV, 1982; Royal Television Society Gold Medal for outstanding services to TV, 1984; Chairman, Council, ITCA, 1968-69, 1978-80; Director, ITN, 1972-77; Director, ITP, since 1968; Director, Channel 4, 1980-84. Recreation: golf. Address: (b.) STV, Cowcaddens, Glasgow, G2 3PR.

Brown, William, BL, SSC, NP. Solicitor; Senior Partner, Ranken & Reid, SSC; b. 18.3.32, Dunfermline; m., Anne Sword; 2 d. Educ. Dunfermline High School; Edinburgh University. National Service commission, RAOC, 1952; joined Ranken & Reid, 1960. Member, Society of High Constables of Edinburgh. Recreations: golf; music; shooting. Address: (h.) Glenavon, 45 Barnton Avenue, Edinburgh, EH4 6JJ; T.-031-336 4227.

Brown, William Hunter, ERD, MSc, FLA. Keeper, National Library of Scotland, since 1973; b. 18.5.28, Loanhead; m. 1, Janet McKay (deceased); 2, Ruth Crowl; 2 s. Educ. Royal High School, Edinburgh; Edinburgh College of Art; Strathclyde University. Librarian, Royal Botanic Garden, Edinburgh, 1960-67; Deputy Librarian, Heriot-Watt University, 1967-68; Principal Librarian, Moray House College of Education, 1968-72. Honorary Associate, Royal Botanic Garden, Edinburgh. President, Scottish Library Association, 1979; serves on numerous national and international committees; Major, Royal Engineers (AER), ret., 1968. Publication: The Royal Botanic Garden, Edinburgh, 1670-1970 (Co-author), 1970. Recreations: music; gardening; travel. Address: (h.) 15 Palmerston Road, Edinburgh, EH9 1TL; T.-031-667 4769.

Browne, Ronald Grant, DA. Folk Entertainer ("The Corries"), since 1961; Portrait Painter, since 1979; b. 20.8.37, Edinburgh; m., Patricia Isabella Elliot; 2 s.; 1 d. Educ. Boroughmuir School, Edinburgh; Edinburgh College of Art. Teacher of Art and Painting, 1959-63; folk entertaining, 1963-79; folk entertaining and portrait painting, since 1979.

Browning, George Kenneth Spencer, BSc, PhD. Director of Computing Services, Glasgow University, since 1970; Managing Director, Computing Services (University of Glasgow) Ltd., since 1982; b. 3.12.38, Dumfries; m., Dr. Janet Paton Finlayson; 2 d. Educ. Glasgow Academy; Glasgow University. Assistant Lecturer, then Lecturer, Department of Natural Philosophy, Glasgow University, 1963-70. Member: Programme Committee, National Development Programme in Computer Assisted Learning, 1973-77, Standing Committee, Inter-University Committee on Computing, 1978-81; Editor, IUCC Bulletin (now University Computing), 1980-82; Honorary Treasurer, Kilmardinny Music Circle, Bearsden. Recreations: listening to music; computer photo-typesetting. Address: (h.) Arnprior, 48 Mitre Road, Jordanhill, Glasgow, G14 9LE; T.-041-959 5753.

Browning, J. Robin, BA (Hons), FIB (Scot). Divisional General Manager, Bank of Scotland, since 1983; b. 29.7.39, Kirkcaldy; m., Christine Campbell; 1 s.; 1 d. Educ. Morgan Academy, Dundee; Strathclyde University. Bank of Scotland: Assistant Management Accountant, 1971-74, Assistant Manager (Corporate Planning), 1974-77; British Linen Bank Ltd.: Manager, 1977-79, Assistant Director, 1979-81, Director, 1981-82; Assistant General Manager, Bank of Scotland, 1982-83. Chairman, Tax and Accountancy Committee, Equipment Leasing Association, 1980-82. Recreations: curling; gardening; DIY enthusiast. Address: (b.) Management Services Division, Bank of Scotland, 2 Bankhead, Crossway North, Sighthill, Edinburgh, EH11; T.-031-443 4111.

Brownlie, Alistair Rutherford, MA, LLB, SSC. Solicitor; Secretary, Society of Solicitors in the Supreme Courts of Scotland, since 1970; b. 5.4.24, Edinburgh; m., Martha Barron Mounsey. Educ. George Watson's Boys College, Edinburgh; Edinburgh University. Served World War II as radio operator, 658 Air OP Squadron, RAF, in Europe and India; apprenticed to J. & R.A. Robertson, WS; thereafter Solicitor in private practice, Edinburgh; former Member, Council of Law Society of Scotland; Legal Aid Central Committee; founder Member and Past President, Forensic Science Society; Contributor, Criminal Law Review; Member, Government Technical Panel 9 on instrumental breath analysis; Elder, Church of Scotland and Congregational Union of Scotland. Recreations: the pen, the spade and the saw. Address: (h.) 8 Braid Mount, Edinburgh; T.-031-447 4255.

Brownlie, Rev. Gavin Dunipace, MA. Minister, Ladyloan St. Columba's Church, Arbroath, since 1961; b. 9.6.27, Glasgow; m., Frances Duff; 2 s.; 1 d. Educ. Hillhead School; Glasgow High School; Hamilton Academy; Glasgow University. Assistant Minister, St. Bride's, Edinburgh, 1953-55; Minister, Redding and Westquarter Parish Church, 1955-61. Founder Chairman, Arbroath Children's Panel Advisory Committee, 1970-74; Member, Tayside CPAC, 1974-78; Member, Tayside Education Committee, 1982. Recreations: golf; bowling; curling; bridge; swimming. Address: Ladyloan Manse, Dishlandtown Street, Arbroath, DD11 1QU; T.-0241 72356.

Brownlie, James M., MInstWM, MREHinstS. Director of Environmental Health, Motherwell District Council, since 1983. Trained and served with Burgh of Motherwell and Wishaw; Chief Cleansing Officer, Motherwell District Council, 1979. Address: (b.) Civic Centre, Motherwell, ML1 1TW; T.-Motherwell 66166.

Bruce, George, OBE (1984), MA, LittD. Writer/Lecturer; b. 10.3.09, Fraserburgh; m., Elizabeth Duncan; 1 s.; 1 d. Educ. Fraserburgh Academy; Aberdeen University. Teacher, English Department, Dundee High School, 1935-46; BBC Producer, Aberdeen, 1946-56; BBC Talks (Documentary) Producer, Edinburgh, with special responsibility for arts programmes, 1956-70; first Fellow in Creative Writing, Glasgow University, 1971-73; Visiting Professor, Union Theological Seminary, Richmond, Virginia, and Writer in Residence, Prescott College, Arizona, 1974; Visiting Professor of English, College of Wooster, Ohio, 1976-77; Scottish-Australian Writing Fellow, 1982; E. Hervey Evans Distinguished Fellow, St. Andrews Presbyterian College, North Carolina, 1985; Vice-Chairman, Council, Saltire Society; Council Member, Advisory Council of the Arts in Scotland; Extra-Mural Lecturer, Glasgow, St. Andrews and Edinburgh Universities; Editor, The Scottish Review, 1975-76. Publications: verse: Sea Talk, 1944; Selected Poems, 1947; Landscapes and Figures, 1967; Collected Poems, 1970; The Red Sky, 1985; prose: Scottish Sculpture Today (Co-author), 1947; Anne Redpath, 1974; The City of Edinburgh, 1974; Festival in the North, 1975; Some Practical Good, 1975; as Editor: The Scottish Literary Revival, 1962; Scottish Poetry Anthologies 1-6 (Co-Editor), 1966-72. Recreation: visiting friends. Address: 25 Warriston Crescent, Edinburgh, EH3 5LB; T.-031-556 3848.

Bruce, John Wilkinson, AHWC, CChem, MRSC, BSc, BA. Member, Annandale and Eskdale District Council, since 1984; b. 10.2.25, Leith; 2 d. Educ. Broughton Secondary School, Edinburgh; Heriot-Watt College, Edinburgh. Industrial Chemist: Stewart and Lloyds, Corby, 1945-47, SCWS Junction Mills, Leith, 1947-52; Teacher: Earlston, Berwickshire, 1954-58, Duns, 1958-63; Principal Teacher of Science, Langholm, 1963-83 (also Deputy Rector, 1965-83). Educational Institute of Scotland: President, Berwickshire Branch, 1962-62, President, Dumfriesshire Branch, 1968-69; President, Langholm Congregational Church, 1966-70; Member, Langholm Town Council, 1966-72, and 1973-75; President, Honours Graduate Teachers' Association, 1980-84. Recreations: bridge; bowls; amateur operatics; philosophy. Address: (h.) 14 John Street, Langholm, Dumfriesshire, DG13 OAD.

Bruce, Malcolm Gray, MP, MA, MSc. MP (Liberal), Gordon, since 1983; Liberal Parliamentary Spokesman on Scottish Affairs, 1983-85, on Energy, since 1985; Vice-Chairman, Political, Scottish Liberal Party, 1975-84; b. 17.11.44, Birkenhead; m., Jane Wilson; 1 s.; 1 d. Educ. Wrekin College; Strathclyde University; St. Andrews University. Trainee Journalist, Liverpool Daily Post & Echo, 1966-67; Section Buyer, Boots the

Chemist, 1968-69; Fashion Retailing Executive, A. Goldberg & Sons, 1969-70; Press and Information Officer, NESDA, 1971-75; Marketing Director, Noroil Publishing, 1975-81; Director, Aberdeen Petroleum Publishing; Editor/Publisher, Aberdeen Petroleum Report, 1981-83; Co-Editor, Scottish Petroleum Annual, 1st and 2nd editions. Recreations: reading; music; theatre; hill-walking; cycling; travel. Address: (h.) East View, Woodside Road, Torphins, Aberdeenshire, AB3 4JR; T.-033982 386.

Brumfitt, Professor John Henry, MA, DPhil (Oxon). Professor of French, St. Andrews University, since 1969; b. 5.4.21, Shipley; m., 1, Patricia Renee Grand; 2, Margaret Anne Ford; 1 s.; 2 d. Educ. Bradford Grammar School; Queen's College, Oxford. Laming Travelling Fellow, Queen's College, Oxford, 1947-48; Lecturer in French, University College, Oxford, 1948-51; St. Andrews University: Lecturer in French, 1951-59, Senior Lecturer, 1959-69; Member, Editorial Boards, French Studies and Forum for Modern Language Studies. Publications: The French Enlightenment; Voltaire Historian. Address: (b.) Department of French, St. Andrews University, St. Andrews, Fife; T.-0334 76161.

Bryant, David Murray, BSc, PhD, ARCS, DIC. Senior Lecturer in Biology, Stirling University, since 1980; b. 24.9.45, Norwich; m., Dr. Victoria Margaret Turton; 1 s.; 1 d. Educ. Greshams School, Holt, Norfolk; Imperial College, London University. Lecturer in Biology, Stirling University, 1970-80. Council Member, Scottish Ornithologists Club. Recreations: skiing; natural history; books; painting; modern dance; newspapers. Address: (b.) Department of Biological Science, Stirling University, Stirling, FK9 4LA; T.-Stirling 73171.

Bryden, Bill. Head of Drama, BBC Scotland, since 1985; b. 12.4.42, Greenock. Educ. Greenock High School. Assistant Director: Royal Court Theatre, London, 1968, Royal Lyceum Theatre, Edinburgh, 1970-74; Associate Director, National Theatre, since 1974; author of the plays: Willie Rough, 1971, Benny Lynch, 1973; directed a revival of The Thrie Estates, Edinburgh Festival, 1973; former Member, Board of Directors, Scottish Television.

Bryden, John Stephens, MB, ChB, MSC, FFCM, DipSocMed, MBCS. Community Medicine Specialist, Greater Glasgow Health Board, since 1984; Health Information Consultant; b. 20.11.32, Glasgow; m., Dr. Grace Macfarlane; 1 s.; 2 d. Educ. Rothesay Academy; Glasgow University; Strathclyde University. National Service; accident and emergency medicine; general practice, Glasgow; Medical Superintendent, Royal Alexandra Infirmary, Paisley; Chief Administrative Medical Officer, Argyll and Clyde Health Board; Senior Epidemiologist, Scottish Head Injury Management Study; Director, PIMMS (medical manpower database). Chairman, Headway (voluntary body for the care of the head injured). Recreation: sailing. Address: (b.) Southern General Hospital, 1345 Govan Road, Glasgow, G4 5TF; T.-041-445 2466.

Bryden, Sir William (James), Kt (1978), CBE (1970), QC (Scot); b. 2.10.09; m.; 2 s.; 1 d. Educ. Perth Academy; Brasenose College, Oxford; Edinburgh University. Sheriff Principal of Lothians and Borders, 1975-78; Sheriff of Chancery in Scotland, 1973-78.

Bryson, Archibald Gordon Stuart, CA. Chartered Accountant, since 1935; a Director, Scottish Society for the Prevention of Cruelty of Animals, since 1953; a Director, Royal Blind Asylum, since 1950; b. Edinburgh; m., Eleanor; 1 d. Educ. Edinburgh Academy. CA, India, 1935-46; RINVR, 1941-46; CA, Edinburgh, since 1946. Honorary Treasurer, British Ornithologists Union, 1955-75. Address: (h.) 48 Frogston Road West, Edinburgh, EH10 7AJ; T.-031-445 1082.

Buccleuch, 9th Duke of, and Queensberry, 11th Duke of (Walter Francis John Montagu Douglas Scott), KT (1978), VRD, JP. Lt.Comdr., RNR; Captain, Queen's Bodyguard for Scotland (Royal Company of Archers); Lord Lieutenant of Roxburgh, since 1974, and of Ettrick and Lauderdale, since 1975; b. 23.9.23, London; m., Jane McNeill, daughter of John McNeill, QC, Appin, Argyll; 3 s.; 1 d. Educ. Eton; Christ Church, Oxford. Served World War II, RNVR; MP (Conservative), Edinburgh North, 1960-73; PPS to the Scottish Office, 1961-64; Chairman, Conservative Party Forestry Committee, 1967-73; Chairman, Royal Association for Disability and Rehabilitation; President: Royal Highland and Agricultural Society of Scotland, 1969, St. Andrew's Ambulance Association, Royal Scottish Agricultural Benevolent Institution, Scottish National Institution for War Blinded, Royal Blind Asylum and School, Galloway Cattle Society, East of Scotland Agricultural Society, 1976, Commonwealth Forestry Association; Vice-President, Royal Scottish Society for Prevention of Cruelty to Children; Honorary President: Animal Diseases Research Association, Scottish Agricultural Organisation Society; DL: Selkirk, 1955, Midlothian, 1960, Roxburgh, 1962, Dumfries, 1974. Address: Bowhill, Selkirk; T.-Selkirk 20732; and Drumlanrig Castle, Thornhill; T.-Thornhill 30248.

Buchan, Andrew Strachan, FIB (Scot). Local Director, Scotland, Barclays Bank PLC, since 1985; b. 12.1.31, Peterhead; m., Jean Eleanor Gilmore; 2 s. Educ. Peterhead Academy; Manchester Business School; Administrative Staff College, Henley. Various managerial posts, Royal Bank of Scotland plc, Edinburgh, Glasgow and London, 1963-77; General Manager (Central Region), Royal Bank of Scotland plc, 1977-85. Council Member, Institute of Bankers in Scotland (Examiner in Practical Banking, 1968-72); Treasurer for Scotland, Scottish Appeals Committee, Police Dependants' Trust. Recreation: golf. Address: (b.) Barclays Bank PLC, 35 St. Andrew Square, Edinburgh, EH2 2AD; T.-031-557 2464.

Buchan of Auchmacoy, Captain David William Sinclair, JP. Chief of the Name of Buchan; b. 18.9.29; m.; 4 s.; 1 d. Educ. Eton; Royal Military Academy, Sandhurst. Commissioned Gordon Highlanders, 1949; ADC to GOC, Singapore, 1951-53; Member, London Stock Exchange; Member, Queen's Bodyguard for Scotland (Royal Company of Archers). Address: (h.) Auchmacoy House, Ellon, Aberdeenshire.

Buchan, Dennis, DA, ARSA. Painter; Lecturer; Duncan of Jordanstone College of Art, since 1965; b. 25.4.37, Arbroath; 1 s.; 1 d. Educ. Arbroath High School; Dundee College of Art; Hospitalfield College. National Service, 1960-62; Latimer Award, RSA, 1962; elected ARSA, 1975; Member, Scottish Arts Council Panel on Art, 1978-80; travelled extensively; works in private and public collections, UK and USA. Recreations: non-specific. Address: 9 Shore, Arbroath; T.-Arbroath 78757.

Buchan, Gilbert, CBE, RD, MBE. Member, Banff and Buchan District Council, since 1984; Honorary President, Scottish Fishermen's Federation, since 1982; Honorary President, Scottish Pelagic Fishermen's Association, since 1982; b. 25.5.12, Inverallochy; m., Jessie; 3 d. Educ. Inverallochy School (left aged 14). Fishing since 1927; skipper, since 1933, owner, since 1942; Royal Navy, RNR, 1938 (Lt.Cmdr., RNR, ret., 1962); Director, then Vice-Chairman, Scottish Herring Producers; Scottish Fishermen's Federation: Director, 1974, Vice-President, 1977, President, 1978-82; Member: SFIA, 1980-82, Scottish Herring Industry Board, 1965-80; founder Director, Scottish Fishermen's Producer Organisation, 1974-80; Member, Sea Fish Industry Authority, 1980-82; lectures on interaction of fishing and oil. Recreation: golf. Address: (h.) 7 Mid Street, Inverallochy, Aberdeenshire; T.-034 65 2278.

Buchan, Janey. Member, European Parliament, for Glasgow, since 1979; b. 30.4.26; m., Norman Buchan (qv); 1 s. Past Chairman, Scottish Gas Consumers' Council; former Vice-Chairman, Education Committee, Strathclyde Regional Council.

Buchan, Norman, MP, MA. MP (Labour), Paisley South, since 1983; Opposition Spokesman for the Arts; b. 27.10.22, Helmsdale; m., Janey Kent (see Janey Buchan); 1 s. Educ. Kirkwall Grammar School; Hyndland Secondary School; Glasgow University. Royal Tank Regiment (North Africa, Sicily and Italy), 1942-45; Teacher of English and History; MP, Renfrewshire West, 1964-83; Parliamentary Under Secretary, Scottish Office, 1967-70; Opposition Spokesman on Agriculture, Fisheries and Food, 1970-74; Minister of State, MAFF, March 1974 (resigned, October 1974); Opposition Spokesman on: Social Security, 1980-81, Food, Agriculture and Fisheries, 1981. Publications: 101 Scottish Songs (Editor); The Scottish Folksinger (Editor), 1973; The MacDunciad, 1977. Address: (h.) 72 Peel Street, Glasgow, G11 5LR; T.-041-339 2583.

Buchan, Tom, MA (Hons). Writer; b. 19.6.31, Glasgow; 2 s.; 1 d. Educ. Aberdeen Grammar School; Balfron High School; Jordanhill College School; Glasgow University. Professor of English, Madras University; Director, Community House, Glasgow; Senior Lecturer in English, Clydebank

College of Further Education; Artistic Director, Craigmillar Festival; Director, Kalachaitanya Madras Theatre Company; Director, Offshore Theatre Company, Edinburgh; Director, Dumbarton Festival. Publications: Happy Landings; Dolphins at Cochin; Poems 1969-72; Exorcism; Forwords; (plays) Tell Charlie Thanks for the Truss; The Great Northern Welly Boot Show (with Billy Connolly); Knox and Mary; Over The Top; Bunker; God. Address: (h.) Auchenames House, Portencross, West Kilbride, Ayrshire, KA23 2RE; T.-West Kilbride 823594.

Buchan-Hepburn, Sir Ninian (Buchan Archibald John), 6th Bt. Painter; b. 8.10.22. Educ. St. Aubyn's, Rottingdean; Canford School, Wimborne, Dorset. Served Queen's Own Cameron Highlanders, India and Burma, 1939-45; studied painting, Byam Shaw School of Art; exhibited widely.

Buchanan, Daniel Albert Porteous, JP. Member, Lothian Regional Council, since 1982; Magistrate, District Court, since 1974; b. 22.7.28, Edinburgh; m., Cathrine Stewart Murdoch; 1 s.; 2 d.; 1 step-s.; 2 step-d. Sometime company director (ret.); Member, Edinburgh Corporation, 1960-63. Chairman, Edinburgh District Leprosy Mission. Address: (h.) 2 Riversdale Grove, Murrayfield, Edinburgh, EH12 5QS; T.-031-337 8934.

Buchanan, Derek Watson King, MB, ChB, MRCGP. Scottish Secretary, British Medical Association, since 1981; b. 6.9.24, Dundee; m., Sandra; 2 d. Educ. Morgan Academy; Dundee High School; St. Andrews University. House Surgeon, Dundee Royal Infirmary, 1946-47; Captain, RAMC, 1947-49; general practice, 1949-73; Assistant Scottish Secretary, BMA, 1974-81. Secretary, Dundee Local Medical Committee, 1960-73; Member: Dundee Executive Council, NHS, Ninewells Hospital Board of Management; County Director, Dundee Branch, British Red Cross Society; Honorary Surgeon, St. Andrews Ambulance Association. Recreation: golf. Address: (b.) British Medical Association, 7 Drumsheugh Gardens, Edinburgh, EH3 7QP; T.-031-225 7184.

Buchanan, Jane Helen Park, JP. Member, Fife Health Board, since 1979; Travel Consultant, since 1982; b. 24.3.42, Perth; m., James Buchanan; 1 s.; 1 d. Educ. Morrison's Academy, Crieff; Ross's Commercial College. Member, North East Fife District Council, 1976-80 (Chairman, Recreation and Tourism Committee, 1977-80); Vice Chairman, North East Fife Conservative Association, since 1977; Director: Scottish Agritours, since 1982, Scottish Farmhouse Holidays, since 1982. Nuffield Farming Scholarship, 1981. Recreations: bridge; squash; golf; curling. Address: Drumtenant, Ladybank, Fife, KY7 7UG; T.-0337 30451.

Buchanan, Professor John Grant, MA, PhD, ScD, CChem, FRSC, FRSE. Professor of Organic Chemistry, Heriot-Watt University, Edinburgh, since 1969; b. 26.9.26, Dumbarton; m., Sheila Elena Lugg; 3 s. Educ. Dumbarton Academy; Glasgow Academy; Christ's College, Cambridge.

Research Fellow, University of California, Berkeley, 1951-52; Research Assistant, Lister Institute of Preventive Medicine, London, 1952-54; Newcastle-upon-Tyne University: Lecturer in Organic Chemistry, 1955, Senior Lecturer, 1962, Reader, 1965. Council Member, Royal Society of Edinburgh, 1980-83; Member, Editorial Board: Carbohydrate Research, since 1965, Nucleosides and Nucleotides, since 1982; Council Member, Royal Society of Chemistry, 1980-81 and 1982-85. Recreations: golf; listening to music. Add (h.) Evergreen, 61 South Barnton Avenue, Edinburgh, EH4 6AN; T.-031-336 6296.

Buchanan, Percival William, MA (Hons), LLB, FBIM. Director of Administration and Legal Services, Central Regional Council, since 1974; b. 17.9.25, Airdrie; m., Anna Dunlop Barron; 1 s.; 1 d. Educ. Peterhead Academy; Aberdeen University. Legal Assistant, Butchart & Rennet, Advocates, Aberdeen, 1954-56; Senior Legal Assistant, Corporation of the City of Aberdeen, 1957-62; Burgh of Alloa: Depute Town Clerk, 1962-63, Town Clerk, 1963-74. Member, Scottish Arts Council and its Music Committee, 1972-75; Chairman, Society of Directors of Administration in Scotland, 1983-84. Recreations: music; hill-walking; sailing. Address: (b.) Viewforth, Stirling, FK8 2ET; T.-0786 73111.

Buchanan, Richard, JP, Hon. FLA. Member, Board of Directors, Glasgow Citizens' Theatre; Honorary President, Scottish Library Association; b. 3.5.12. Councillor, City of Glasgow, 1949-64; City Treasurer, 1960-63; MP, Springburn, 1964-79.

Buchanan, William Menzies, DA. Head of Fine Art Studies, Glasgow School of Art, since 1977; b. 7.10.32, Caroni Estate, Trinidad, West Indies. Educ. Glasgow School of Art. Art Teacher, Glasgow, 1956-61; Exhibitions Officer, then Art Director, Scottish Arts Council, 1961-77. Publications: Scottish Art Review, 1965, 1967, 1973; Seven Scottish Painters catalogue, IBM New York, 1965; The Glasgow Boys catalogue, 1968; Joan Eardley, 1976; Mr Henry and Mr Hornel Visit Japan catalogue, 1978; Japonisme in Art (Contributor), 1980; A Companion to Scottish Culture (Contributor), 1981; The Stormy Blast catalogue, Stirling University, 1981; The Golden Age of British Photography (Contributor), 1984; The Photographic Collector (Contributor), 1985. Recreations: gardening; cooking. Address: (b.) Glasgow School of Art, 167 Renfrew Street, Glasgow, G3 6RQ; T.-041-332 9797.

Buchanan-Smith, Alick. MP (Conservative), Kincardine and Deeside; Minister of State, Department of Energy, since 1983; b. 8.4.32, Currie, Midlothian; m., Janet Lawrie; 1 s.; 3 d. Educ. Edinburgh Academy; Glenalmond; Cambridge University; Edinburgh University. Parliamentary Under Secretary, Scottish Office, 1970-74; Minister of State, MAFF, 1979-83. Address: (b.) House of Commons, London, SW1A OAA.

Buchanan-Smith, Robin D., BA, ThM. Member, Board of Directors, Scottish Television, since 1982; Chancellor's Assessor, St. Andrews

University; b. 1.2.36, Currie, Midlothian; m., Sheena Mary Edwards; 2 s. Educ. Edinburgh Academy; Glenalmond; Cambridge University; Edinburgh University; Princeton Theological Seminary. Minister, Christ's Church, Dunollie, Oban, 1962-66; Chaplain, St. Andrews University, 1966-73. Chaplain: 8th Argylls, 1962-66, Highland Volunteer, 1967-69; British Council of Churches Preacher to USA, 1968; Commodore, Royal Highland Yacht Club. Recreations: sailing; Scotland. Address: Isle of Eriska, Ledaig, Argyll, PA37 1SD; T.-0631 72 371.

Budd, Stanley Alec. Scottish Representative, Commission of the European Communities, since 1975; b. 22.5.31, Edinburgh; m., Wilma McQueen Cuthbert; 3 s.; 1 d. Educ. George Heriot's School, Edinburgh. Newspaperman, D.C. Thomson & Co., Dundee, 1947-57; National Service, 1949-51; Research Writer, Foreign Office, 1957-60; Diplomatic Service (Lebanon, Malaysia), 1960-69; Assistant, European Integration Department, Foreign and Commonwealth Office, 1969-71; Deputy Head of Information, Scottish Information Office, 1971-72; Press Secretary to Chancellor of the Duchy of Lancaster, 1972-74; Chief Information Officer, Cabinet Office, 1974-75. Recreations: music; oriental antiques; bridge. Address: (b.) 7 Alva Street, Edinburgh; T.-031-225 2058.

Buist, Thomas Alexander Seaton, MB, ChB, FRCR, FRCSEdin, FRCPEdin, DMRD, DObstRCOG. Consultant Radiologist, Edinburgh Royal Infirmary, since 1970; Honorary Senior Lecturer, Edinburgh University, since 1970; b. 1.1.31, Glasgow; m., Margery Allen Oliver; 1 s.; 3 d. Educ. Melville College, Edinburgh; Edinburgh University. Medical Officer, RAF (Mountain Rescue Team); Associate Staff Physician, Grace and St. Clare's Hospitals, Newfoundland; Staff Radiologist, Toronto General Hospital. Chairman, Lothian Area Division of Radiology. Recreations: squash; windsurfing. Address: (b.) Department of Radiology, Royal Infirmary, Edinburgh, EH3 9YW; T.-031-229 2477.

Bullough, Professor Donald Auberon, MA, FSA, FRHistS. Professor of Mediaeval History, St. Andrews University, since 1973 (Dean, Faculty of Arts, since 1984); b. 13.6.28, Stoke; m., Belinda Jane Turland; 2 d. Educ. Newcastle-under-Lyme High School; St. John's College, Oxford. National Service, RA, 1946-48; studied abroad, 1950-52; Fereday Fellow, St. John's College, Oxford, 1952-55; Lecturer, Edinburgh University, 1955-66 (Reader Elect, 1966); Warden, Holland House, Edinburgh University, 1960-63; Visiting Professor, Southern Methodist University, 1965-66; Professor of Mediaeval History, Nottingham University, 1966-73; Director, Paul Elek Ltd., 1968-79; Acting Director, British School at Rome, 1984 (Chairman, Faculty of History, Archaeology and Letters, 1975-79); Ford's Lecturer in English History, Oxford University, 1979-80; Andrew Mellon Lecturer, Catholic University, Washington, 1980; Raleigh Lecturer, British Academy, 1985. Recreations: talk; looking at buildings; postal history. Address: (h.) 23 South Street, St. Andrews, Fife, KY16 9QS; T.-0334 72932.

Bundy, Alan Richard, BSc, PhD. Reader, Department of Artificial Intelligence, Edinburgh University, since 1984; b. 18.5.47, Isleworth; m., D. Josephine A. Maule; 1 d. Educ. Heston Secondary Modern School; Springgrove Grammar School; Leicester University. Tutorial Assistant, Department of Mathematics, Leicester University, 1970-71; Edinburgh University: Research Fellow, Metamathematics Unit, 1971-74, Lecturer, Department of Artificial Intelligence, 1974-84. AISB: Editor, Newsletter, 1973-76, Treasurer, 1977-80; Editorial Board: Artificial Intelligence Journal, Journal of Automated Reasoning. Publications: Artificial Intelligence: An Introductory Course, 1978; The Computer Modelling of Mathematical Reasoning, 1983; The Catalogue of Artificial Intelligence Tools, 1984; Symbolic Computation (Series Editor). Recreations: wine and beer making; walking. Address: (b.) Department of Artificial Intelligence, Edinburgh University, Hope Park Square, Edinburgh, EH8 9NW; T.-031-667 1011, Ext. 6507.

Bunney, Herrick, LVO, BMus, FRCO, ARCM. Organist and Master of the Music, St. Giles' Cathedral, Edinburgh, since 1946; b. London; m., Mary Howarth Cutting; 1 s.; 1 d. Educ. University College School; Royal College of Music. Organist to Edinburgh University, until 1981; former Conductor: Edinburgh Royal Choral Union, Edinburgh University Singers, The Elizabethan Singers (London), St. Cecilia Singers; Council Member, Edinburgh International Festival, Royal College of Organists, National Youth Orchestra of Scotland. Recreations: hill-walking; bird-watching. Address: (h.) 3 Upper Coltbridge Terrace, Edinburgh, EH12 6AD; T.-031-337 6494.

Burdon, Professor Roy Hunter, BSc, PhD, FRSA, FRSE. Professor of Molecular Biology, Strathclyde University, since 1985; b. 27.4.38, Glasgow; 2 s. Educ. Glasgow Academy; St. Andrews University. Assistant Lecturer, Glasgow University, 1959; Research Fellow, New York University, 1963; Glasgow University: Lecturer in Biochemistry, 1964, Senior Lecturer, 1967, Reader, 1974, Professor (Titular), 1977; Guest Professor of Microbiology, Polytechnical University of Denmark, 1977-78. Biochemical Society (UK): Honorary Meeting Secretary, 1981-85, Honorary General Secretary, 1985. Recreations: music; painting; golf. Address: (h.) 144 Mugdock Road, Milngavie, Glasgow, G62 8NP; T.-041-956 1689.

Burgess, John Moncrieff, BSc, MIEDO. Director of Research and Development, Shetland Islands Council, since 1975; b. 8.9.36, Scousburgh; m., Patricia Margaret; 2 s. Educ. Anderson Educational Institute; Aberdeen University. Lecturer, North of Scotland College of Agriculture, 1961-64; Assistant Lands Officer, then Lands Officer, Department of Agriculture and Fisheries for Scotland, 1964-75. Recreations: boating; fishing. Address: (b.) 93 St. Olaf Street, Lerwick, Shetland; T.-0595 3535.

Burley, Lindsay Elizabeth, MB, ChB, FRCPE, MRCGP. Consultant Physician in Geriatric Medicine, East Fortune Hospital, North Berwick, since 1982; b. 2.10.50, Blackpool; m., Robin Burley. Educ. Queen Mary School, Lytham; Edinburgh University. Address: (b.) East Fortune Hospital, North Berwick, East Lothian, EH39 5JX; T.-0620 88244.

Burley, Roger, BSc, PhD, CEng, FIChemE, MIE(Aust), MAIME. Senior Lecturer, Department of Chemical and Process Engineering, Heriot-Watt University, since 1975; Director, Dunedin PED, since 1982; Director, IMOD Ltd., since 1984; b. 25.8.41, Leeds; m., Elayne Mary; 2 s.; 1 d. Educ. Hymers College, Hull; Newport (Essex) Grammar School; Leeds University. Research Fellow, Leeds University, 1964-68; chemical engineer, research and development, CSIRO, Australia, 1968-72; Lecturer, Heriot-Watt University, 1972-75. Member: University Senate, 1975-82, University Court, 1978-82; Member, Editorial Board, Chemical Engineer. Recreations: squash; tennis; badminton; bridge. Address: (b.) Department of Chemical and Process Engineering, Heriot-Watt University, Chambers Street, Edinburgh, EH1 1HX; T.-031-225 8432.

Burness, George Milne, PhC, MPS. Member, Highland Regional Council, since 1978 (Chairman, Finance Committee, since 1982); proprietor pharmacist, since 1972; b. 18.4.43, Glasgow; m., May Buchan Ritchie; 3 s.; 1 d. Educ. Aberdeen Grammar School; Robert Gordon's Institute of Technology. Chief Pharmacist, Anglo American Corporation, Chililabowbwe, Zambia, 1967-72; Member: Cromarty Firth Port Authority, 1980-82, Ross and Cromarty District Council, 1980-84; Chairman, Ross, Cromarty and Skye Area, SDP; Member, Council for Social Democracy; Chairman, Dingwall and District Chamber of Commerce. Recreations: golf; swimming; study of theology. Address: (h.) 9 Churchill Drive, Dingwall, IV15 9RD; T.-0349 63126.

Burnett, Charles John, CStJ, DA, AMA, FSAScot. Head, Design Department, National Museum of Antiquities of Scotland, since 1971; Chairman, Heraldry Society of Scotland, since 1983; Dingwall Pursuivant of Arms, since 1983; b. 6.11.40, Sandhaven, by Fraserburgh; m., Aileen E. McIntyre; 2 s.; 1 d. Educ. Fraserburgh Academy; Gray's School of Art, Aberdeen; Aberdeen College of Education. Advertising Department, House of Fraser, Aberdeen, 1963-64; Exhibitions Division, Central Office of Information, 1964-68 (on team which planned British pavilion for World Fair, Montreal, 1967); Assistant Curator, Letchworth Museum and Art Gallery, 1968-71. Heraldic Adviser, Girl Guide Association in Scotland, since 1978; Limner, Priory of the Order of St. John in Scotland, since 1974; Associate Member, Academie Internationale D'Heraldique, since 1982. Recreations: reading; visiting places of historic interest. Address: (h.) 3 Hermitage Terrace, Morningside, Edinburgh; T.-031-447 5472.

Burnett, John Harrison, FRSE, FIBiol, BA, MA, DPhil. Principal and Vice-Chancellor, Edinburgh University, since 1979; b. 21.1.22; m.; 2 s. Educ. Kingswood School, Bath; Merton College, Oxford. Lt., RNVR, 1942-46

(mentioned in Despatches). Lecturer, Lincoln College, 1948-49; University Lecturer and Demonstrator, Oxford, 1949-53; Lecturer, Liverpool University, 1954-55; Professor of Botany: St. Andrews University, 1955-60, King's College, Newcastle, Durham University, 1961-63, Newcastle University, 1963-68; Regius Professor of Botany, Glasgow Univrsity, 1968-70; Sibthorpian Professor of Rural Economy and Fellow, St. John's College, Oxford, 1970-79. Chairman, Scottish Horticultural Research Institute, 1959-74. Address: (b.) Old College, Edinburgh University, South Bridge, Edinburgh.

Burnett, Michael Rodger, BSc. Farmer, since 1960; Employer Member, Agricultural Training Board, since 1978; Employer Member, Agricultural Wages Board, since 1976; b. 26.7.35, Edinburgh; 1 s.; 2 d. Educ. Morrison's Academy, Crieff; Edinburgh University. Chairman, Highland Region Education Committee, 1973-77; President, National Farmers Union of Scotland, 1977-79; Chairman, BBC Agricultural Advisory Committee for Scotland, since 1980; Parliamentary Liberal candidate: Caithness and Sutherland, 1974, Moray, 1984. Reader, Church of Scotland. Recreations: bridge; golf. Address: (h.) Pulrossie Farm, Dornoch, Sutherland; T.-086 288 206.

Burnett, Robert Gemmill, LLB, SSC, NP. Solicitor, since 1972; b. 18.1.49, Kilmarnock; m., Patricia Margaret Masson; 1 d. Educ. George Heriot's School, Edinburgh; Edinburgh University. Apprentice, then Assistant, then Partner, Drummond & Co. Secretary: Society of Procurators of Midlothian, Lothian Allelon Society. Recreations: cricket; golf; gardening. Address: (b.) 31/32 Moray Place, Edinburgh; T.-031-226 5151.

Burnett, William, BSc. Acting Principal, Kingsway Technical College, since 1984; b. 21.1.26, Bo'ness; m., Lilias Baird Smith; 1 s.; 1 d. Educ. Bo'ness Academy; Heriot-Watt College, Edinburgh. Apprenticeship as colliery electrician, Kinneil Colliery, Bo'ness, 1940-46; colliery electrician, Kinneil Colliery, 1946-49 and 1952-53; management trainee, then Assistant to Area Electrical Engineer, NCB Alloa Area, 1953-57; Assistant Teacher of Mining Electrical Engineering: Falkirk Mining Institute, 1957-62, Falkirk Technical College, 1962-67; Senior Teacher of Mining Electrial Engineering, Falkirk Technical College, 1967-69; Lecturer in Electrical Engineering, School of Further Education, Jordanhill College of Education, 1969-71; Depute Principal, Perth College of Further Education, 1971-84. Session Clerk, St. Andrew's Church of Scotland, Blairgowrie, since 1977. Recreations: golf; stamp collecting; choirs. Address: (h.) Stronvar, 2 Manor Gardens, Blairgowrie, PH10 6JS; T.-Blairgowrie 2729.

Burns, James, JP. Convener, Strathclyde Regional Council, since 1982; b. 8.2.31, Shotts; m., Jean Ward; 2 s. Educ. St. Patrick's School, Shotts; Coatbridge Technical College. Engineer, NCB, 1948-71; Member: Lanark County Council, 1967-75, Lanarkshire Health Board, 1973-77, Strathclyde Regional Council, since 1974; Chairman, General Purposes Committee,

1975-82; Vice-Convener, 1978-82; Chairman, Visiting Committee, HM Prison, Shotts, since 1980; Honorary Vice-President, SNO Chorus, since 1982; Member: Commonwealth Games Council for Scotland, since 1982, Main Organising Committee, 1986 Commonwealth Games, since 1982; Honorary President: Strathclyde Community Relations Council, since 1982, Princess Louise Scottish Hospital, since 1982; Vice-President, Glasgow Western St. Andrew's Youth Club, since 1982; Patron: Strathclyde Youth Club Association, since 1982, YMCA Sports Centre, since 1982; Vice-President, St. Andrew's Ambulance Association, since 1984; Honorary President, Scottish Retirement Council, since 1984; Patron, Scottish Pakistani Assocication, 1984. Recreations: fishing; golf. Address: (h.) 57 Springhill Road, Shotts, ML7 5JA; T.-Shotts 20187.

Burnside, Bryce Miller, BSc, PhD, CEng, MIMechE. Senior Lecturer, Department of Mechanical Engineering, Heriot-Watt University, since 1966; b. 16.7.32, Glasgow; m.; 1 s.; 1 d. Educ. Allan Glen's School, Glasgow; Glasgow University. Sub-section leader, Aerodynamics Department, Armstrong Siddeley Motors Ltd., Coventry, 1955-58; Research Assistant, then Lecturer, Department of Mechanical Engineering, Glasgow University, 1958-66; Visiting Professor, Department of Mechanical and Aero Engineering, Carleton University, Ottawa, 1981. Recreations: Scottish country dancing; golf. Address: (b.) Department of Mechanical Engineering, Heriot-Watt University, Riccarton, Edinburgh, EH14 4AS; T.-031-449 5111.

Burrows, Professor Clifford Robert, BSc, PhD, CEng, FIMechE. Professor of Dynamics and Control, Strathclyde University, since 1982; b. 20.7.37, Shoeburyness; m., Margaret Evelyn; 3 s.; 1 d. Educ. Westcliff Grammar School; University of Wales, Swansea; London University. Industrial training, Thames Board Mills Ltd., 1955-58; undergraduate and Research Assistant, University College, Swansea, 1958-63; Lecturer, then Senior Lecturer, then Principal Lecturer, West Ham College of Technology, 1963-69; Lecturer, then Reader, Sussex University, 1969-82. Non-stipendiary Priest, Church of England, since 1977; won Best Paper Award, American Control Council, 1976; consultant to industry and Government establishments. Recreations: family life and gardening; travel. Address: (b.) Department of Dynamics and Control, Strathclyde University, 75 Montrose Street, Glasgow, G1; T.-041-552 4400.

Burstall, Professor Rodney M., MA, MSc, PhD. Professor of Computer Science, Edinburgh University, since 1979; b. 11.11.34, Liverpool; m., Seija-Leena; 3 d. Educ. George V Grammar School, Southport; King's College, Cambridge; Birmingham University. Operational Research Consultant, Brussels, 1959; Operational Research and Programming, Reed Paper Group, Kent, 1960; Research Fellow, Birmingham University, 1962; Research Fellow, Lecturer, Reader, Professor, Department of Artificial Intelligence, Edinburgh University, 1964-79. Emissary to UK for Venerable Chogyam Trungpa Rinpoche,

Buddhist Meditation Master, 1982. Address: (b.) Department of Computer Science, Edinburgh University, King's Buildings, Mayfield Road, Edinburgh, EH9 3JZ; T.-031-667 1081.

Burton, Lord (Michael Evan Victor Baillie). Landowner and Farmer; Member, Inverness District Council, since 1984; Executive Member, Scottish Landowners Federation, since 1963; District Commissioner, Inverness Branch, Pony Club, since 1963; b. 27.6.27, Burton-on-Trent; m., 1, Elizabeth Ursula Foster Wise (m. diss.); 2, Denise Cliffe; 2 s.; 4 d. Educ. Eton; Army. Scots Guards, 1942 (Lt., 1944); Lovat Scouts, 1948; Member, Inverness County Council, 1948-75; JP, 1961-75; Deputy Lieutenant, Inverness, 1963-65; has served on numerous committees. Recreations: shooting, fishing and hunting (not much time); looking after the estate. Address: Dochfour, Inverness; T.-046 386 252.

Burton, Richard Francis, BA (Cantab), PhD. Senior Lecturer in Physiology, Glasgow University, since 1965; b. 15.6.36, Twickenham; 2 s.; 1 d. Educ. Oundle; Downing College, Cambridge; London University. Assistant Professor, Zoology, Toronto University, 1963-65. Publication: Ringer Solutions and Physiological Salines. Recreations: music; poetry. Address: (b.) Institute of Physiology, Glasgow University, Glasgow, G12 8QQ; T.-041-339 8855.

Bush, Peter William, BA (Hons), PhD, FRGS. Assistant Director, Glasgow College of Technology, since 1984; b. 8.11.45, Liverpool; m., Judith Worthington; 1 s.; 1 d. Educ. St. Mary's College, Liverpool; University College, London; Leeds University. Lecturer, then Senior Lecturer, then Principal Lecturer in Geography, North Staffs Polytechnic, 1970-81; Head, Department of Humanities, Glasgow College of Technology, 1981-84. Recreations: squash; music; running. Address: (b.) Glasgow College of Technology, Cowcaddens Road, Glasgow, G4 0BA; T.-041-332 7090.

Bushe, Frederick, ARSA, DA, DAE. Sculptor, since 1956; Director, Scottish Sculpture Workshop, since 1979; b. 1.3.31, Coatbridge; m., Fiona M.S. Marr; 1 d.; 3 s.; 1 d. by pr. m. Educ. Our Lady's High School, Motherwell; Glasgow School of Art. Lecturer in Sculpture: Liverpool College of Education, 1962-69, Aberdeen College of Education, 1969-79; full-time Artist since 1979; established Scottish Sculpture Workshop and Scottish Sculpture Open Exhibition; one-man exhibitions: 57 Gallery, Edinburgh, 1962, Bluecoat Gallery, Liverpool, 1966, Demarco Gallery, Edinburgh, 1971, Compass Gallery, Glasgow, 1974, Peterloo Gallery, Manchester, 1975, Stirling Gallery, Stirling, 1978, Talbot Rice Arts Centre, Edinburgh, 1982; numerous group exhibitions. Recreation: listening to music. Address: (h.) Rose Cottage, Lumsden, Huntly, Aberdeenshire; T.-046 48 223.

Busuttil, Anthony, MD, MRCPath, DMJ(Path). Consultant Pathologist, Lothian Health Board, since 1978; Senior Lecturer in Pathology, Edinburgh University, since 1978; Police Surgeon, Lothian and Borders Police, since 1980; b.

30.12.45, Rabat, Malta; m., Angela; 3 s. Educ.
St. Aloysius' College, Malta; Royal University
of Malta. Junior posts, Western Infirmary, Glasgow; Lecturer in Pathology, Glasgow University.
Address: (h.) 78 Hillpark Avenue, Edinburgh,
EH4 7AL; T.-031-336 3241.

Bute, 6th Marquess of, (John Crichton-Stuart),
JP. Hereditary Sheriff of Bute; Hereditary
Keeper of Rothesay Castle; b. 27.2.33; m., 1,
Nicola Weld-Forester (m. diss.); 2 s.; 1 d.; 1 d.
(deceased); 2, Jennifer Percy. Educ. Ampleforth
College; Trinity College, Cambridge. Chairman,
Scottish Standing Committee for Voluntary
International Aid, 1964-68; Chairman, Council
and Executive Committee, National Trust for
Scotland, 1969-84 (Vice-President, since 1984);
Chairman, Scottish Committee, National Fund
for Research into Crippling Diseases, since
1966; Chairman, Historic Buildings Council
for Scotland, since 1983; Chairman, Museums
Advisory Board (Scotland), since 1984; Trustee,
National Galleries of Scotland, since 1980; Honorary Sheriff-Substitute, Bute, 1976; Convener,
Buteshire County Council, 1967-70; DL Bute,
1961; Lord Lieutenant, 1967-75; Hon. LLD,
Glasgow, 1970. Address: (h.) Mount Stuart,
Rothesay, Isle of Bute.

Butler, Anthony Robert, BSc, PhD, DSc, AKC.
Reader in Chemistry, St. Andrews University,
since 1965; b. 28.11.36, Croydon, Surrey; m.,
Janet Anderson. Educ. Selhurst; King's
College, London. Consulting Editor, Cartermill
Publishing, 1980; Lecturer, Fleming Centenary
Celebration, Darvel, 1981. Recreations:
hill-walking; music; writing Chinese characters. Address: (b.) Chemistry Department, St.
Andrews University, St. Andrews; T.-0334 76161.

Butler, Rev. John Michael Francis, DipTh,
DipMS, MBIM, AIPM. Minister of Religion
(Congregational), since 1953; General Secretary, Scripture Union - Scotland, since 1965; b.
12.3.28, Petersfield; m., Charlotte Matilda; 2 s.;
1 d. Educ. Churchers College, Petersfield; New
College, London. Minister: Laira and Plympton
Congregational Churches, 1953-59; Helensburgh
Congregational Church, 1959-64. Recreations:
Christian activity; reading and book reviewing;
sailing; bad photography. Address: (b.) 280 St.
Vincent Street, Glasgow, G2 5RT; T.-041-221
0051.

Butler, Vincent Frederick, DA, RSA. Sculptor
since 1950; b. 27.10.33, Manchester; m., Camilla
Meazza; 2 s. Educ. Edinburgh College of Art;
Academy of Fine Art, Milan. Works in bronze
(figurative); numerous one-man exhibitions in
various cities; major retrospective show, City
Art Centre, Edinburgh, 1981; Teacher of Sculpture, Nigeria, 1960-63; now teaching, Edinburgh
College of Art. Address: (h.) 17 Deanpark
Crescent, Edinburgh, EH4 1PH; T.-031-332 5884.

Butter, David Henry, MC. Lord Lieutenant,
Perth and Kinross, since 1975; Landowner and
Company Director; b. 18.3.20, London; m.,
Myra Alice Wernher; 1 s.; 4 d. Educ. Eton
College; Oxford University. Served in World
War II, 2nd Lt., Scots Guards, 1940; served in
Western Desert, North Africa, Sicily and Italy

(ADC to GOC 8th Army, 1944); Temporary
Major, 1946; retired, 1948; Brigadier, Queen's
Bodyguard for Scotland (Royal Company of
Archers); President, Highland TAVR, 1979-84;
Member, Perth County Council, 1955-74; Deputy
Lieutenant, Perthshire, 1956; Vice Lieutenant,
Perthshire, 1960-71; Lord Lieutenant of County
of Perth, 1971-75, of Kinross, 1974-75; Governor:
Gordonstoun School, Aberlour House School,
Butterstone House School; Honorary President,
Perthshire Battalion, Boys Brigade. Recreations:
golf; skiing; travel; shooting. Address: Cluniemore, Pitlochry, Perthshire; T.-0796 2006.

Butter, Professor Peter Herbert. Regius Professor of English Language and Literature, Glasgow
University, since 1965; b. 7.4.21, Coldstream; m.,
Bridget Younger; 1 s.; 2 d. Educ. Charterhouse;
Balliol College, Oxford. Royal Artillery, 1941-46; Lecturer in English, Edinburgh University,
1948-58; Professor of English, Queen's University, Belfast, 1958-65. Secretary/Treasurer,
International Association of University Professors of English, 1965-71. Publications: Shelley's
Idols of the Cave, 1954; Francis Thompson,
1961; Edwin Muir, 1962; Edwin Muir: Man
and Poet, 1966; Shelley's Alastor, Prometheus
Unbound and Other Poems (Editor), 1971;
Selected Letters of Edwin Muir (Editor), 1974;
William Blake: Selected Poems (Editor), 1982.
Recreations: gardening; hill-walking. Address:
(h.) Ashfield, Prieston Road, Bridge of Weir,
Renfrewshire, PA11 3AW; T.-Bridge of Weir
613139.

Butterfield, Alan W., MA, DipEd, JP. Rector, Hamilton Grammar School, since 1971; b.
1.5.33, Dundee; m., Rosemary; 1 s.; 1 d. Educ.
Dundee High School; St. Andrews University.
Teacher of English and History, Harris Academy, Dundee; Special Assistant of English and
History, Dunfermline High School; Principal
Teacher of English: Broxburn Academy, Trinity
Academy, Edinburgh; Depute Rector, Falkirk
High School. President, Headteachers' Association of Scotland, 1984-85. Recreation: Rotary.
Address: (h.) 23 Langside Road, Bothwell,
Lanarkshire; T.-853505.

Butterworth, Neil, MA, HonFLCM. Head of
Music Department, Napier College, Edinburgh,
since 1968; Music Critic, Times Educational
Supplement, since 1983; Broadcaster; b. 4.9.34,
Streatham, London; m., Anna Mary Barnes;
3 d. Educ. Rutlish School, Surrey; Nottingham
University; London University; Guildhall School
of Music, London. Lecturer, Kingston College
of Technology, 1960-68; Conductor: Sutton Symphony Orchestra, 1960-64, Glasgow Orchestral
Society, 1975-83; Chairman, Incorporated Society
of Musicians, Edinburgh Centre, since 1981;
Churchill Fellowship, 1975. Publications: Haydn,
1976; Dvorak, 1980; Dictionary of American
Composers, 1983; Aaron Copland, 1984; Samuel
Barber, 1985. Recreations: autographs; collecting
books and records; giant jigsaw puzzles. Address:
(h.) The White House, Inveresk, Musselburgh,
Midlothian; T.-031-665 3497.

Byers, Rev. Alan James. Minister, Boddam
Parish Church, Peterhead, since 1971; b. 7.4.26,
Girvan; m., Mairi Catriona Laing; 3 s.; 1 d.

Educ. Girvan Secondary School; Edinburgh University; New College. RAF, 1944-48; Chaplain to hydro-electric workers' camps, 1955-56; Assistant Minister, Ardchattan, 1959; Minister, Presbyterian Church of Ghana (Northern Ghana), 1960-71. Officiating Chaplain, RAF Buchan; Member, Boddam and District Community Council. Recreations: photography; DIY. Address: The Manse, Boddam, Peterhead, AB4 7AS; T.-0779 72650.

Byron, Stuart, FCA. Executive Director, Ross Hall Hospital, Glasgow, since 1981; b. 2.7.43, Fareham; m., Linda Dorey; 1 s.; 2 d. Educ. Lysses School, Fareham; Barton-Peveril Grammar School. Recreations: sailing; golf; reading. Address: (b.) 221 Crookston Road, Glasgow, G52 3NQ; T.-041-810 3151.

C

Caddie, James Murdoch, MBIM. Chief Executive Officer, Epilepsy Association of Scotland, since 1977; b. 2.11.27, Glasgow; m., Grace Betty; 2 d. Educ. Whitehill Senior Secondary School, Glasgow. Administrator: South of Scotland Electricity Board, 1948-71, National Health Service, 1971-77. Member: local Health Council, 1978-83; Glasgow Council for Welfare of the Disabled. Recreations: gardening; travel. Address: (b.) 48 Govan Road, Glasgow, G51 1JL; T.-041-427 4911.

Caddy, Brian, BSc, PhD, CChem, MRIC. Senior Lecturer in Forensic Science, Strathclyde University, since 1978; b. 26.3.37, Burslem, Stoke-on-Trent; m., Beryl Ashworth; 1 s.; 1 d. Educ. Middleport Secondary Modern School; Longton High School; Sheffield University. Strathclyde University: MRC Research Fellow, 1963, Lecturer in Forensic Science, 1966. Council Member, Forensic Science Society. Recreations: music; reading; gardening; walking the dog; relaxing. Address: (b.) Forensic Science Unit, Strathclyde University, Glasgow; T.-041-552 4400.

Cadell, Patrick Moubray, BA. Keeper of Manuscripts, National Library of Scotland, since 1983; b. 17.3.41, Linlithgow; m., Sarah King; 2 s.; 1 d. Educ. Merchiston Castle School, Edinburgh; Cambridge University; Toulouse University. Information Officer, British Museum; Assistant Keeper, Department of MSS: British Library, then National Library of Scotland. Clerk, Abbey Court of Holyrood; Chairman, Society of Archivists, Scottish Region; Past President, West Lothian History and Amenity Society. Recreations: walking; music. Address: (b.) National Library of Scotland, George IV Bridge, Edinburgh, EH1 1EW; T.-031-226 4531.

Caird, Professor Francis Irvine, MA, DM, FRCP, FRCPSGlas. David Cargill Professor of Geriatric Medicine, Glasgow University, since 1979; b. 24.8.28, Glastonbury; m., Angela Margaret Alsop (deceased); 1 s.; 2 d. Educ. Winchester College; New College, Oxford. Medical Registrar, General Hospital, Birmingham, and RPGMS, Hammersmith; Senior Registrar and Medical Tutor, Radcliffe Infirmary, Oxford; Senior Lecturer and Reader in Geriatric Medicine, Glasgow University. Recreation: travel. Address: (h.) 4 Colquhoun Drive, Bearsden, Glasgow, G61 4NQ; T.-041-942 7785.

Caird, James Bowman, MA (Hons), DipEd. Council Member (former Vice-President), Association for Scottish Literary Studies; retired HM Inspector of Schools; b. 6.7.13, West Linton; m., Janet H. Kirkwood; 2 d. Educ. Boroughmuir School, Edinburgh; Edinburgh University; The Sorbonne, Paris; Moray House College of Education. Assistant Teacher of English: Wick High School, 1938, Trinity Academy, Edinburgh, 1938-40; Army Service (Royal Artillery, Army Education Corps), 1940-46; Principal Teacher of English, Peebles High School, 1946-47; HM Inspector of Schools in Dumfries, Glasgow, Stirlingshire and the Highlands, 1947-74. Past President, Inverness Field Club; Member, Culloden Committee, National Trust for Scotland. Recreations: reading; continental travel; TV viewing. Address: 1 Drummond Crescent, Inverness; T.-0463 232858.

Caird, Professor James Brown, MA (Edin), D de l'Univ (Rennes). Professor of Geography, Dundee University, since 1975; b. 3.4.28, Perth; m., Isa Macaskill; 1 s.; 3 d. Educ. Perth Academy; Edinburgh University; Rennes University. RAF, Education Branch, 1952-55; Assistant, Lecturer, Senior Lecturer, Glasgow University, 1955-64, 1966-74; Reader and Acting Head of Department, Ife University, Nigeria, 1964-66; Dean, Faculty of Environmental Studies, Dundee University, 1975-78. Member, Dundee University Court, since 1979; Elder, Church of Scotland, since 1960; President, Abertay Historical Society, since 1985. Recreations: angling; gardening. Address: (h.) 3 Hyndford Street, Dundee, DD2 1HQ; T.-0382 67748.

Cairncross, Robert George, MB, ChB, MRCP (UK), MRCGP. Deputy Secretary, Scottish Council for Postgraduate Medical Education, since 1984; Honorary Lecturer, Centre for Medical Education, Dundee University, since 1984; b. 6.7.40, Dundee. Educ. Robert Gordon's College, Aberdeen; Aberdeen University. Registrar, Lothian Health Board, 1972-75; trainee General Practitioner, Edinburgh University, 1975-76; Lecturer in Medical Education, Dundee University, 1976-81; Educational Adviser, College of Medicine, ABHA, Saudi Arabia, 1981-83; Project Director, Dundee University, 1983-84. Address: (b.) Scottish Council for Postgraduate Medical Education, 8 Queen Street, Edinburgh, EH2 1JE; T.-031-225 4365.

Cairney, John, BA. Writer, Actor and Director; Director, Shanter Productions and Theatre Consultants (Scotland), since 1968; Director,

John Cairney & Company Ltd., since 1984; b. 16.2.30, Baillieston, Glasgow; m., 1, Sheila Cowan (m. diss.); 2, Alannah O'Sullivan; 1 s. by pr. m.; 4 d. by pr. m. Educ. St. Mungo's Academy; Royal Scottish Academy of Music and Drama (Diploma in Drama). Stage actor: Glasgow Citizens' Theatre, 1953-54; Bristol Old Vic, 1954-56; film actor: Rank Organisation, 1956-65, ABPC, Columbia Pictures, 1956-65; TV actor, BBC, London, 1965-68; Founder Director, Burns Festival, Ayr, 1975-79; numerous stage appearances playing Robert Burns; wrote and directed, 1970-85: A Mackintosh Experience, The William McGonagall Story, The Private Life of R.L.S., The Ivor Novello Story, The Scotland Story, The Robert Service Story, Oscar Wilde, and Dorothy Parker, for Shanter Productions; played leading role in TV serials and series: This Man Craig, 1965-67, Burns, 1968, Scotch on the Rocks, 1971. Jubilee Medal, 1977. Recreations: theatre biographies; city street walking. Address: 44 St. Vincent Crescent, Glasgow, G3 8NG; T.-041-221 2785.

Cairns, Gordon McLean, MA, LLB, NP. Solicitor; Honorary Sheriff, Stranraer, since 1981; b. 31.7.38, Calcutta; m., Elizabeth (daughter of Professor Sir Robert Grieve); 1 s.; 1 d. Educ. Edinburgh Academy; Edinburgh University. Solicitor in private practice, since 1961. Recreations: all sports; bridge. Address: (h.) Birchgrove, Whitehouse Road, Stranraer; T.-0776 2984.

Cairns, Robert, MA, DipEd. Member, City of Edinburgh District Council, since 1974 (Convenor, Planning Policy Sub-Committee, since 1984); b. 16.7.47, Dundee; m., Pauline Reidy; 2 s. Educ. Morgan Academy; Edinburgh University; Moray House College of Education. Assistant Editor, Scottish National Dictionary, 1969-74; Parliamentary candidate (Labour), North Edinburgh, 1973, February 1974; Teacher, James Gillespie's High School, since 1975; Chairman, Old Town Conservation Advisory Committee, since 1984; Board Member: Royal Lyceum Theatre Company, Edinvar Housing Association, Old Town Community Development Project. Recreations: gardening; theatre. Address: (h.) 223 Ferry Road, Edinburgh; T.-031-552 3027.

Cairns, Robert Alan, BSc, PhD, MInstP. Reader in Applied Mathematics, St. Andrews University, since 1985; b. 12.3.45, Glasgow; m., Ann E. Mackay. Educ. Allan Glen's School, Glasgow; Glasgow University. Lecturer in Applied Mathematics, St. Andrews University, 1970-83; Reader, 1983-85; Consultant, UKAEA Culham Laboratory, since 1984. Committee Member, Plasma Physics Group, Institute of Physics, 1981-84; Member, Editorial Board, Plasma Physics, since 1983. Publication: Plasma Physics, 1985. Recreations: music (listening to and playing recorder and baroque flute); golf; hill-walking. Address: (b.) Department of Applied Mathematics, St. Andrews University, North Haugh, St. Andrews, Fife, KY16 9SS; T.-0334 76161, Ext. 8150.

Calder, Andrew Alexander, MD, FRCOG, MRCPGlas. Senior Lecturer in Obstetrics and Gynaecology, Glasgow University, since 1978; Consultant Gynaecologist, Glasgow Royal Infirmary, since 1978; Consultant Obstetrician, Glasgow Royal Maternity Hospital, since 1978; b. 17.1.45, Aberdeen; m., Valerie Anne; 1 s.; 2 d. Educ. Glasgow Academy; Glasgow University. Clinical training posts in obstetrics and gynaecology, 1969-72: Queen Mother's Hospital, Western Infirmary, Royal Maternity Hospital and Royal Infirmary, (all Glasgow); Research Fellow, Nuffield Department of Obstetrics and Gynaecology, Oxford University, 1972-75; Lecturer in Obstetrics and Gynaecology, Glasgow University, 1975-78. Postgraduate Adviser in Obstetrics and Gynaecology for West of Scotland; Secretary, Munro Kerr Society for the Study of Reproductive Biology; Blair Bell Memorial Lecturer, RCOG, 1977; WHO Travelling Fellow, 1985. Recreations: music; golf; curling. Address: (b.) University Department of Obstetrics and Gynaecology, Glasgow Royal Infirmary, Level 3, University Tower, 10 Alexandra Parade, Glasgow; T.-041-552 8316.

Calder, Angus Lindsay, MA, DPhil. Staff Tutor in Arts, Open University in Scotland, since 1979; Co-Editor, Journal of Commonwealth Literature, since 1980; Convener, Scottish Poetry Library, since 1983; b. 5.2.42, Sutton, Surrey; m., Jennifer Daiches; 1 s.; 2 d. Educ. Wallington County Grammar School; Kings College, Cambridge. Lecturer in Literature, Nairobi University, 1968-71; Visiting Lecturer, Chancellor College, Malawi University, 1978. Member, Board of Directors: Fruitmarket Gallery, Royal Lyceum Theatre Company; Editorial Committee, Cencrastus; Eric Gregory Award for Poetry, 1967. Publications: The People's War: Britain 1939-1945, 1969 (John Llewelyn Rhys Memorial Prize); Revolutionary Empire, 1981 (Scottish Arts Council Book Award). Recreations: curling; cricket. Address: (b.) 60 Melville Street, Edinburgh, EH3 7HF; T.-031-226 3851.

Calder, George D., BA (Hons), LLB. Director for Scotland, Manpower Services Commission, since 1985; b. 20.12.47, Edinburgh; m., Kathleen Bonar; 2 d. Educ. George Watson's College, Edinburgh; Pembroke College, Cambridge; Edinburgh University. Department of Employment, 1971-74; Member, George Thomson's Cabinet, EEC, Brussels, 1974-76; Treasury, 1976-79; MSC Special Programmes Operations Manager (Scotland), 1979-82; Training Division Area Manager, Glasgow City, 1982-83; MSC Regional Director, Northern Region, 1983-85. Recreations: gardening; football; cricket; hill-walking.

Calder, Jenni, BA, MPhil. Freelance Writer; Lecturer, Royal Scottish Museum, Edinburgh, since 1978; b. 3.12.41, Chicago, Illinois; 1 s.; 2 d. Educ. Perse School for Girls, Cambridge; Cambridge University; London University. Freelance writer, 1966-78; taught and lectured in Scotland, England, Kenya and USA; Lecturer in English, Nairobi University, 1968-69. Chairperson, Scottish Branch, Royal Anthropological Institute; Member, Scottish Writers Against the Bomb. Publications: Chronicles of Conscience: a study of George Orwell and Arthur Koestler, 1968; Scott (with Angus Calder), 1969; There Must be a Lone Ranger: the Myth and Reality of the

American West, 1974; Women and Marriage in Victorian Fiction, 1976; Brave New World and Nineteen Eighty Four, 1976; Heroes: from Byron to Guevara, 1977; The Victorian Home, 1977; The Victorian Home from Old Photographs, 1979; RLS, A Life Study, 1980; The Robert Louis Stevenson Companion (Editor), 1980; Robert Louis Stevenson and Victorian Scotland (Editor), 1981; The Strange Case of Dr Jekyll and Mr Hyde (Editor), 1979; Kidnapped (Editor); Catriona (Editor), 1981. Recreations: music; films; walking the dog. Address: (h.) 18 Springfield Road, South Queensferry, West Lothian; T.-031-331 2765.

Calder, John, Honorary Sheriff, Lothians and Peebles; Vice Lieutenant, West Lothian; b. 11.7.14, Dundee; 1 s.; 1 d. Educ. Morgan Academy, Dundee; University College, Dundee; Edinburgh University. Solicitor; Depute Town Clerk, Kirkcaldy; County Clerk, West Lothian; retired. District Governor, Rotary International District 102, 1962; Secretary, West Lothian Twinning Association, since 1972; Verdienstkreuz Am Bande (FDR) awarded by Bundesprasident, 1983. Address: (h.) Woodlands, 8 Dundas Street, Bo'ness, West Lothian; T.-0506 822311.

Calder, John Forbes, MB, ChB, FRCR, DMRD, DObtRCOG. Senior Lecturer in Radiology, Aberdeen University, since 1980; Honorary Consultant Radiologist, Grampian Health Board, since 1980; b. 13.5.42, Glasgow; m., Marion Taylor; 1 s.; 1 d. Educ. Glasgow High School; Glasgow University. House Officer, Southern General Hospital, Glasgow; Government Medical Officer, Malawi; Registrar in Radiology, Glasgow Royal Infirmary; Senior Registrar in Radiology; Victoria Infirmary, Glasgow, then Nairobi University, Kenya. Recreations: hillwalking; photography; swimming; music. Address: (h.) 49 Cairnlee Avenue East, Cults, Aberdeen, AB1 9NU; T.-0224 861672.

Calder, Robert Russell, MA. Critic, Philosophical Writer, Historian of Ideas, Poet, Freelance Journalist, Book Reviewer; b. 22.4.50, Burnbank. Educ. Hamilton Academy; Glasgow University; Edinburgh University. Editor: Chapman, 1974-76, Lines Review, 1976-77; Theatre Critic and Feature Writer, Scot, since 1983; Council Member, Heritage Society of Scotland; various writings on Edwin Muir; poetry: Il Re Giovane, 1976, Ettrick & Annan, 1981. Recreations: music - opera singing; jazz piano. Address: (h.) 23 Glenlee Street, Burnbank, Hamilton, ML3 9JB; T.-0698 824244.

Calderwood, Robert, LLB (Hons). Chief Executive, Strathclyde Regional Council, since 1980; b. 1.3.32; m., Meryl Anne; 3 s.; 1 d. Educ. William Hulme's School, Manchester; Manchester University. Town Clerk: Salford, 1966-69, Bolton, 1969-73, Manchester, 1973-79. Address: Strathclyde Regional Council, Regional HQ, 20 India Street, Glasgow, G2 4PF.

Caldwell, David Cleland, SHNC, MA, BPhil. Secretary, Robert Gordon's Institute of Technology, since 1984; b. 25.2.44, Glasgow; m., Ann Scott Macrae; 1 s.; 1 d. Educ. George Watson's

College, Edinburgh; St. Andrews University; Glasgow University. Warwick University: Lecturer in Politics, 1969-76, Administrative Assistant, 1976-77, Assistant Registrar, 1977-80; Registry Officer, Aberdeen University, 1980-84. Member: Warwick District Council, 1979-80, Grampian Regional Council, 1983-84; Parliamentary candidate (Labour), North East Fife, 1983; Member, Aberdeen Grammar School Council, since 1983. Address: (b.) Robert Gordon's Institute of Technology, Schoolhill, Aberdeen, AB9 1FR; T.-0224 633611.

Caldwell, David Hepburn, MA, PhD, FSAScot. Assistant Keeper in Charge of the Medieval Department, National Museum of Antiquities of Scotland, since 1983; b. 15.12.51, Kilwinning, Ayrshire; m., Margaret Anne McGovern; 2 d. Educ. Ardrossan Academy; Edinburgh University. Joined staff, National Museum of Antiquities, 1973. Publications: The Scottish Armoury, 1979; Scottish Weapons and Fortifications, 1981. Recreation: travelling. Address: (h.) 3 James Park, Burntisland, Fife, KY3 9EW; T.-872175.

Caldwell, Rev. James, MA. Minister of Religion (retired); Member, Tayside Health Board, since 1981; b. 12.5.16, Larkhall, Lanarkshire; m., Marjory Bruce Harvie; 2 s.; 1 d. Educ. Hamilton Academy; St. Andrews University; St. Mary's College, St. Andrews. Ordained by Glasgow Presbytery; Assistant Minister, Govan Old Parish Church, 1943; inducted Rossland Church, Bishopton, 1945; inducted Kirriemuir, 1952; Moderator, Forfar Presbytery, 1955-56; translated to Shawlands Old Parish Church, 1958; became Minister, united charge with Langside Avenue Church, 1963; Chaplain, Victoria Infirmary, Glasgow, 1962-78; translated to Abernethy and Dron Parish Church, Perthshire, 1978; linked with Arngask, Glenfarg, 1979; Member, Advisory Board of Church of Scotland, 1980-81; Moderator, Perth Presbytery, 1983-84; first Chairman, Glasgow (SE) Health Council, 1975-78; Tayside Health Board: Convener, General Medical Practitioners' Committee and Special Leave Committee, 1984-85. Recreations: walking; gardening; travel. Address: (h.) 26 Dalhousie Place, Arbroath, DD11 2BT; T.-Arbroath 70670.

Caldwell, Sheila Marion, BA (Hons). Head, St. Columba's School, Kilmacolm, since 1976; b. England; m., Major Robert Caldwell, TD. Educ. Tunbridge Wells Grammar School; University College, London. Founder/Principal, Yejide Girls' Grammar School, Ibadan, Nigeria; first Principal, Girls' Secondary (Government) School, Lilongwe, Malawi; Depute Head, Mills Grammar School, Framlingham, Suffolk. Treasurer, Secondary Heads' Association, Scotland, since 1984. Recreations: exploring new places and new ideas; reading; walking; music/opera; interior design (theory and practice). Address: (b.) St. Columba's School, Duchal Road, Kilmacolm, Renfrewshire, PA13 4AU; T.-Kilmacolm 2238.

Callen, Rev. John Robertson, MA, BD. Minister, Lochgilphead Parish Church, since 1962; Member, Committee to Elect the Moderator.

Nominee, and Member, Board of World Mission and Unity, General Assembly, Church of Scotland; b. 12.12.35, Glengarnock; m., Isobel Annie Morrison; 2 s. Educ. Spier's School; Glasgow University and Trinity College. Moderator: Inveraray Presbytery, 1966, South Argyll Presbytery, 1983; Chaplain, Lochgilphead Hospitals, 1963-79; Local Secretary, National Bible Society of Scotland, since 1963; Lochgilphead Secretary, Christian Aid, since 1966; first Chairperson, Lochgilphead Community Council, 1977-79; Leader, Holy Land tour, 1983; Lyon Court grant of arms, 1968. Publication: Social Directory of Lochgilphead, 1972. Recreations: football refereeing, 1967-83; hill-walking; golf. Address: Parish Manse, Manse Brae, Lochgilphead, Argyll, PA31 8QZ; T.-0546 2238.

Calman, Professor Kenneth Charles, MD, PhD, MRCP, FRCS, FRSE. Dean of Postgraduate Medicine, Glasgow University, since 1984; b. 25.12.41, Glasgow; m., Ann; 1 s.; 2 d. Educ. Allan Glen's School, Glasgow; Glasgow University. Lecturer in Surgery, Western Infirmary, Glasgow, 1968-72; MRC Clinical Research Fellow, London, 1972-73; Professor of Oncology, Glasgow University, 1974-84. Recreations: golf; jogging; gardening. Address: (h.) 585 Anniesland Road, Glasgow; T.-041-954 9423.

Cameron, Alan Iain, BSc. Rector, Ellon Academy, since 1981; b. 21.9.41, Southend, Argyll; m., Elizabeth Margaret; 2 s.; 1 d. Educ. Campbeltown Grammar School; Glasgow University; Jordanhill College of Education. Science Teacher, Campbeltown Grammar School, 1964-67; Head of Science, Invergordon Academy, 1967-73; Head of Chemistry, Mackie Academy, 1973-77; Depute Rector, Selkirk High School, 1977-81. Elder, Church of Scotland. Recreations: music; drama; art; most sports. Address: (h.) The Neuk, Station Road, Ellon, Aberdeenshire; T.-20130.

Cameron, Allan John, VL, JP. Member, Ross and Cromarty District Council, since 1975; Farmer and Landowner, since 1947; b. 25.3.17, Edinburgh; m., Elizabeth Vaughan-Lee; 2 s.; 2 d. Educ. Harrow; Royal Military College. Regular officer, Queen's Own Cameron Highlanders, 1936-47 (ret. Major); Member, Ross and Cromarty County Council, 1955-75 (Chairman, Education Committee, 1962-75); former Commissioner: Red Deer Commission, Countryside Commission for Scotland; former Member, BBC Council for Scotland; President, Royal Caledonian Curling Club, 1963. Recreations: curling; golf; shooting; fishing; gardening. Address: (h.) Allangrange, Munlochy, Ross and Cromarty; T.-046381 249.

Cameron, Rev. Charles Millar, BA, BD, PhD. Minister, St. Ninian's Parish Church, Dunfermline, since 1980; b. 31.5.51, Glasgow; m., Sharon Elizabeth Tweed. Educ. Woodside Secondary School, Glasgow; Stirling University; Glasgow University. World Alliance of Reformed Churches Scholar, Western Theological Seminary, Michigan, 1978-79. Address: (h.) 1 Pitbauchlie Bank, Dunfermline, KY11 5DP; T.-0383 722256.

Cameron of Lochiel, Colonel Sir Donald (Hamish), KT (1973), CVO, TD, JP; 26th Chief of the Clan Cameron; Lord Lieutenant, County of Inverness, since 1971; Chartered Accountant; b. 12.9.10; m.; 2 s.; 1 d. Educ. Harrow; Balliol College, Oxford. Lt.-Col. commanding 4/5th Bn. (TA), Queen's Own Cameron Highlanders, 1955-57; Colonel, 1957 (TARO); Vice-Chairman, Royal Bank of Scotland, 1969-80; Chairman, Culter Guard Bridge Holdings Ltd., 1970-76; Chairman, Scottish Widows Life Assurance Society, 1964-67; President, Scottish Landowners Federation, since 1979; Past President, Royal Highland and Agricultural Society of Scotland. Address: (h.) Achnacarry, Spean Bridge, Inverness-shire.

Cameron, Dugald, DA, FSIAD. Head of Design, Glasgow School of Art, since 1982; Partner, Squadron Prints, since 1977; Industrial Design Consultant, since 1965; b. 4.10.39, Glasgow; m., Nancy Inglis. Educ. Glasgow High School; Glasgow School of Art. Industrial Designer, Hard Aluminium Surfaces Ltd., 1962-65; Visiting Lecturer, Glasgow School of Art, 1963-70; Head of Product Design, Glasgow School of Art, 1970-82. Member: Engineering Advisory Committee, Scottish Committee, Council of Industrial Design, since 1966, Industrial Design (Engineering) Panel and 3D Design Board, CNAA, since 1978, Scottish Committee of Higher Education, Design Council, since 1984. Recreations: railways; flying (lapsed private pilot). Address: (h.) Achnacraig, Skelmorlie, Ayrshire.

Cameron, Duncan Inglis, JP, BL, CA. Director of Administration and Secretary, Heriot-Watt University, since 1965; b. 26.8.27, Glasgow; m., Elizabeth Pearl Heron; 2 s.; 1 d. Educ. Glasgow High School; Glasgow University. RAF, 1945-48; CA apprentice, Alfred Tongue & Co., 1948-51; Qualified Assistant, Cooper Brothers & Co., 1951-52; Assistant Accountant, Edinburgh University, 1952-65; Commonwealth Universities Administrative Fellow, 1972. President, Edinburgh Junior Chamber of Commerce, 1962-63; Governor, Keil School, Dumbarton, 1967-85; Chairman of Council, Royal Scottish Geographical Society, since 1983 (Trustee, since 1973); Chairman, Bioscot Ltd., 1983-84; Member, Universities Central Council on Admissions, since 1967; Chairman, Edinburgh Society of Glasgow University Graduates, 1984-85; Session Clerk, St. Ninian's Church, Corstorphine, since 1969. Officer of the Royal Norwegian Order of St. Olav, 1979. Recreations: travel; photography. Address: (b.) Heriot-Watt University, Riccarton, Edinburgh, EH14 4AS; T.-031-449 5111.

Cameron, Ewen Cameron, OBE, JP. Sheep and Highland Cattle Breeder; Managing Director: Lochearnhead Hotel, since 1947, Lochearnhead Development Company, since 1955; Member, Perth and Kinross District Council, since 1980 (Convenor, Leisure and Recreation Committee); Member, Tayside Health Board; Member, Scottish Sports Council; b. 23.12.26, Lochearnhead; m., Davina Anne Frew; 1 s.; 1 d. Educ. Glenalmond College. Member: Perth County Council, 1964-75, Stirling District Council, 1974-77 (Environmental Health Convener); Vice-Chairman,

Cumbernauld Development Corporation, 1973-77 (Member, 1963-73); Chairman, British Water Ski Federation, 1965-70; President, Balquhidder, Lochearnhead and Strathyre Highland Games; Chairman, Board of Perth Prison, 1980-84; Vice-President, Royal Highland Agricultural Society, 1981. Highland Games Champion of Scotland (Heavy Events), 1953. Recreations: curling; shooting; golf; dominos. Address: (h.) Ben Ouhr, Lochearnhead, Perthshire; T.-05673 231.

Cameron, Gordon Stewart, RSA, DA. Artist; b. 27.4.16, Aberdeen; m., Ellen Malcolm, RSA. Educ. Robert Gordon's College, Aberdeen; Gray's School of Art, Aberdeen. Part-time Lecturer, Gray's School of Art, 1946-51; Lecturer, Dundee College of Art, 1952; Senior Lecturer, Duncan of Jordanstone College of Art, 1967; elected, ARSA, 1958, Academician, 1971; work in public galleries in Scotland and in private collections in various parts of the world. Address: (h.) 7 Auburn Terrace, Invergowrie, Dundee; T.-Invergowrie 318.

Cameron, Hector, MB, ChB, FRCSG, DO. Consultant Ophthalmic Surgeon, since 1963; Surgical Registrar, Ayr County Council; Member, Ayrshire and Arran Health Board; b. 10.4.24, Glasgow; 1 s.; 1 d. Educ. Glasgow High School; Glasgow University. Past Chairman, Scottish Marriage Guidance Council. Recreations: golf; music. Address: (h.) Meadowland, Southwood Road, Troon, KA10 7EL; T.-0292 313258.

Cameron, Hector MacDonald, OBE, MD, FRCPath. Senior Lecturer in Pathology, Edinburgh University, since 1974; Honorary Consultant, Lothian Health Board, since 1974; Honorary Consultant, Borders Health Board, since 1982; b. 20.12.22, Aberdeen; m., Frances Maude Majury; 2 s.; 2 d. Educ. Methodist College, Belfast; Queen's University, Belfast. Consultant Pathologist: Stobhill Hospital, Glasgow, 1956-64; University Department of Pathology, Glasgow Royal Infirmary, 1964-70; Honorary Lecturer, Glasgow University, 1964-70; Professor of Pathology, Nairobi University, 1967-74. Publication: Liver Cell Cancer (Co-Editor), 1976. Recreations: music; hill-walking. Address: (h.) 25 Gallowhill, Peebles, EH45 9BG; T.-0721 21172.

Cameron, James Alistair, MB, ChB, FRCPEdin. Consultant Physician, Dumfries and Galloway Royal Infirmary; Honorary Senior Lecturer, Aberdeen University; b. 10.3.23, Glasgow; m., Elizabeth Jean Galbraith; 2 s.; 2 d. Educ. Glasgow Academy; Glasgow University. Recreations: fishing (Guinness Book of Records entry as former British freshwater record holder); golf. Address: (h.) Westwood, 103 Edinburgh Road, Dumfries, DG1 1JX; T.-Dumfries 55599.

Cameron, Rev. Professor James Kerr, MA, BD, PhD, FRHistS. Professor of Ecclesiastical History, St. Andrews University; b. 5.3.24, Methven; m., Emma Leslie Birse; 1 s. Educ. Oban High School; St. Andrews University; Hartford Theological Seminary, Hartford, Connecticut. Ordained as Assistant Minister,

Church of the Holy Rude, Stirling, 1952; appointed Lecturer in Church History, Aberdeen University, 1955; Lecturer, then Senior Lecturer in Ecclesiastical History, St. Andrews University; Dean, Faculty of Divinity, 1978-83. President: Ecclesiastical History Society, 1976-77, British Sub-Commission, Commission Internationale d'Histoire Ecclesiastique Comparee, since 1979; Vice-President, International Association for Neo-Latin Studies, 1979-81. Publications: Letters of John Johnstone and Robert Howie, 1963; First Book of Discipline, 1972; contributions to: Acta Conventus Neo-Latini Amstelodamensis, 1973; Advocates of Reform, 1953; The Scottish Tradition, 1974; Renaissance and Renewal in Christian History, 1977; Reform and Reformation: England and the Continent, 1979; Origins and Nature of the Scottish Enlightenment, 1982; A Companion to Scottish Culture. Recreation: gardening. Address: (h.) Priorscroft, 71 Hepburn Gardens, St. Andrews, KY16 9LS; T.-0334 73996.

Cameron, Hon. Lord, (John Cameron), KT (1978), Kt (1954), DSC, LLD (Aberdeen and Edinburgh), DLitt (Heriot-Watt), HRSA, FRSGS. Senator of the College of Justice in Scotland and Lord of Session, 1955-85; b. 1900; m., 1, Eileen Dorothea Burrell (deceased); 1 s.; 2 d.; 2, Iris Shepherd. Educ. Edinburgh Academy; Edinburgh University. Served World War I with RNVR; Advocate, 1924; Advocate-Depute, 1929-36; QC (Scot), 1936; RNVR, 1939-44 (Despatches); Sheriff of Inverness, Elgin and Nairn, 1945; Sheriff of Inverness, Moray, Nairn and Ross and Cromarty, 1946-48; Dean of Faculty of Advocates, 1948-55; DL Edinburgh, 1953-84; Hon. FRSE, 1983; Hon. FBA, 1983; DUniv, Edinburgh, 1983.

Cameron, Professor John Robinson, MA, BPhil. Regius Professor of Logic, Aberdeen University, since 1979; b. 24.6.36, Glasgow; m., Mary Elizabeth Ranson (deceased); 1 s.; 2 d. Educ. Dundee High School; St. Andrews University. Harkness Fellow, USA, 1959-61; Lecturer in Philosophy, Queen's College, Dundee, 1962 (Dundee University from 1967); appointed Senior Lecturer in Philosophy, 1973. Recreation: bricolage. Address: (b.) Department of Philosophy, Aberdeen University, King's College, Aberdeen, AB9 2UB; T.-Aberdeen 40241, Ext. 5280.

Cameron, John Taylor, QC, BA, LLB. Queen's Counsel, since 1973; Keeper of the Advocates Library, since 1977; b. 24.4.34, Dundee; m., Bridget Deirdre Sloan. Educ. Fettes College; Corpus Christi College, Oxford; Edinburgh University. Admitted to Faculty of Advocates, 1960; Lecturer in Public Law, Edinburgh University, 1960-64; Advocate Depute, 1977-80. Address: (h.) 17 Moray Place, Edinburgh.

Cameron, Rev. Dr. John Urquhart, BA, BSc, PhD, BD, ThD. Minister, Parish of Broughty Ferry, since 1974; b. 10.6.43, Dundee; m., Jill Sjoberg; 1 s.; 1 d. Educ. Falkirk High School; St. Andrews University; Edinburgh University; University of Southern California. Marketing Executive, Beechams, London, 1969-73; Assistant Minister, Wellington Church, Glasgow,

1973-74; Chaplain, Royal Naval Reserve, 1976-81; Marketing Consultant, Pergamon Press, Oxford, 1977-81; Religious Education Department, Dundee High School, since 1980; winter sports Journalist, since 1981; Chaplain, Royal Caledonian Curling Club. National and international honours in both summer and winter sports, 1960-83; sports scholarship, University of Southern California, 1962-64. Recreations: golf; skiing; curling. Address: St. Stephen's Manse, 33 Camperdown Street, Broughty Ferry; T.-0382 77403.

Cameron, Provost Kenneth, JP. Provost of Nithsdale District Council, since 1984 (Chairman, Policy and Resources Committee, since 1984); b. 26.2.33, Glasgow; m., Mary McGeorge Coupland; 1 s.; 2 d. Educ. Dumfries High School. Fire brigade employee (retired); Past Chairman: Dumfries District Council, Dumfries Area Education Committee, Locharbriggs Community Council; Member, Nithsdale District Council, since 1975; Member, Electricity Consultative Council for South of Scotland District; Depute Traffic Commissioner; Member, COSLA. Recreation: former SFA referee. Address: (h.) 59 Wallamhill Road, Locharbriggs, Dumfries; T.-0387 710367.

Cameron of Lochbroom, Lord (Kenneth John Cameron), Life Baron (1984), PC (1984), MA (Oxon), LLB, QC. Lord Advocate, since 1984; b. 11.6.31, Edinburgh; m., Jean Pamela Murray; 2 d. Educ. Edinburgh Academy; Corpus Christi College, Oxford; Edinburgh University. Advocate, 1958; Queen's Counsel, 1972; President, Pensions Appeal Tribunal for Scotland, 1976; Chairman, Committee of Investigation Under Agricultural Marketing Act 1958, 1980; Advocate Depute, 1981. Recreations: fishing; sailing. Address: (h.) 10 Belford Terrace, Edinburgh.

Cameron, Rev. Dr. Nigel Malcolm de Segur, MA (Cantab), BD, PhD. Warden, Rutherford House, Edinburgh, since 1982; Associate Minister, Holyrood Abbey Church, Edinburgh, since 1982; b. 5.8.52, Folkestone; m., Shenach Jean McKerracher; 1 s.; 3 d. Educ. Bradford Grammar School; Emmanuel College, Cambridge; New College, Edinburgh. Assistant Minister, Dunblane Cathedral, 1977-78; Secretary, Scottish Evangelical Research Trust, since 1981; General Editor; Evangel, A Quarterly Review of Biblical, Practical and Contemporary Theology, since 1981, Scottish Bulletin of Evangelical Theology, since 1983, Ethics and Medicine: A Quarterly Newsletter, since 1984. Publications: In The Beginning (Editor), 1980; Freedom and the Fundamentals, 1982; Say 'Our Father': a Christian Perspective on the Motherhood of God Debate (Co-author), 1983; Evolution and the Authority of the Bible, 1983; The Kirk's Doctrinal Standards, 1984; Method without Madness?: An Evangelical Approach to 'Doing' Theology, 1984; The Evangelical-Liberal Debate, 1984. Recreations: gardening; writing to The Times. Address: (h.) 7 Durham Road, Edinburgh; T.-031-554 1206.

Cameron, Richard William Grant, DA, RIBA, DipTP, MRTPI. Director of Planning, Highland Regional Council, since 1981; b. 2.5.37, Edinburgh; m., Mary Elizabeth; 2 d. Educ. Royal High School, Edinburgh; Edinburgh College of Art; Heriot-Watt University. Assistant Architect, Richard E. Moira and B.L.C. Moira Architects, 1959-63; Assistant Planning Officer: Livingston Development Corporation, 1963-66, Central Mortgage and Housing Corporation, Canada, 1966-69; Planning Consultant, Department of National Defence, Canada, 1969-70; Depute Planning Officer: Inverness County Council, 1970-75, Highland Regional Council, 1970-81. Member: Culloden Sub-Committee, National Trust for Scotland, Regional Advisory Committee (North of Scotland), Forestry Commission, Highland Area Farming, Forestry and Wildlife Advisory Group; Member, Scottish Advisory Commitee, Nature Conservancy Council. Recreations: bagpipe playing; golf; sailing. Address: (b.) Regional Buildings, Glenurquhart Road, Inverness; T.-0463 234121.

Cameron, William John, MA, BD. Principal Emeritus, Free Church of Scotland College, since 1977; b. 29.11.07, Brora; m., 1, Lilias Rownsfell Brown (deceased); 2, Murdina Macaulay Smith; 1 s.; 2 d. Educ. Nicolson Public Higher Grade School, Stornoway; Edinburgh University; Free Church College, Edinburgh. Minister, Free Church of Scotland: Burghead, Morayshire, 1932-50, Buccleuch-Greyfriars, Edinburgh, 1950-53; Professor of New Testament Language and Theology, Free Church College, 1953-77 (Principal, 1973-77); Principal Clerk, Free Church of Scotland General Assembly, 1963-76 (Moderator, 1977). Publications: contributions to: New Bible Commentary, 1953; Baker's Dictionary of Theology, 1960; The New Testament from 26 Translations, 1967; Zondervan Pictorial Bible Encyclopedia, 1975; Illustrated Bible Dictionary, 1980. Recreation: walking. Address: (h.) 19 Kilmaurs Road, Edinburgh, EH16 5DA; T.-031-667 6121.

Campbell, Ailsa Morag, BSc, PhD, FRSE. Senior Lecturer in Biochemistry, Glasgow University, since 1979; b. 16.3.43, Aberdeen: m., Thomas Campbell (m. diss.); 1 s.; 1 d. Educ. Laurel Bank School, Glasgow; Edinburgh University; Glasgow University. Lecturer in Biochemistry, Glasgow University, 1969-79; Visiting Professor, Vanderbilt University, Tennessee, 1978. Recreations: gardening; music. Address: (b.) Department of Biochemistry, Glasgow University, G12 8QQ; T.-041-339 8855, Ext. 627.

Campbell, Alan Grant, LLB. Director of Law and Administration, Grampian Regional Council, since 1984; b. 4.12.46, Aberdeen; m., Susan Black; 1 s.; 2 d. Educ. Aberdeen Grammar School; Aberdeen University. Aberdeen County Council: Law apprentice/Solicitor, 1968-72, Senior Legal Assistant, 1972-75; Grampian Regional Council: Assistant Director of Law and Administration, 1975-79, Depute Director, 1979-84. Seminar Leader, Diploma in Legal Practice, Aberdeen University. Recreation: cycling. Address: Woodhill House, Ashgrove Road West, Aberdeen, AB9 2LU; T.-0224 682222, Ext. 2111.

Campbell, Professor Alexander George MacPherson, MB, ChB, FRCPEdin, DCH. Professor of Child Health, Aberdeen University, since 1973; Honorary Consultant Paediatrician, Grampian Health Board, since 1973; b. 3.2.31, Glasgow; m., Sheila Mary MacDonald; 1 s.; 2 d. Educ. Dollar Academy; Glasgow University. Paediatric Registrar, Royal Hospital for Sick Children, Edinburgh, 1959-61; Senior House Officer, Hospital for Sick Children, London, 1961-62; Assistant Chief Resident, Children's Hospital of Philadelphia, 1962-63; Fellow in Paediatric Cardiology, Hospital for Sick Children, Toronto, 1963-64; Fellow in Fetal and Neonatal Physiology, Nuffield Institute for Medical Research, Oxford, 1964-66; Lecturer in Child Health, St. Andrews University, 1966-67; Assistant, then Associate Professor of Paediatrics, Yale University School of Medicine, 1967-73. Member, Grampian Health Board; Editorial Committee, Archives of Disease in Childhood. Recreation: golf. Address: (b.) Department of Child Health, Aberdeen University, Aberdeen; T.-0224 681818, Ext. 2471.

Campbell, Alistair Bromley, OBE. Member, Scottish Land Court, since 1981; Chairman, Scottish Conservation Projects Trust, since 1984; Chairman, Scottish Executive Committee, Association of Agriculture, since 1980; b. 23.6.27, Charing, Kent; m., Rosemary Pullar; 1 s.; 2 d. Educ. Tonbridge School. Training in agriculture, 1944-47; self-employed Farmer, 1948-81; Agricultural Consultant, Adviser, Arbiter, Valuer, 1968-81; Agricultural Adviser and Valuer, South of Scotland Electricity Board, 1972-81; Vice-Chairman, Countryside Commission for Scotland, 1972-81; Member, Secretary of State's Panel of Agricultural Arbiters, 1968-81; former Council Member, Scottish Agricultural Arbiters Association; Member, Council of Management, Strathcarron Hospice, Denny; Council Member, British Trust for Conservation Volunteers (Chairman, Scottish Regional Committee, 1975-84); Church Warden, St. Mary's Episcopal Church, Dunblane, since 1960; Honorary Vice-President and a Director, Doune and Dunblane Agricultural Society; Past President, Dunblane Branch, National Farmers Union of Scotland; former Council Member and former Convener, Legal Committee, NFU of Scotland; General Commissioner of Income Tax, since 1971. Recreations: work; shooting; enjoying countryside; farming. Address: (h.) Grainston Farm, Kilbryde, Dunblane, Perthshire, FK15 9NF; T.-0786 823304.

Campbell, Arthur McLure. Principal Clerk of Session and Justiciary, Scotland, since 1982; b. 15.8.32, Glasgow. Educ. Queen's Park School, Glasgow. Admiralty Supplies Directorate, 1953-54; entered Scottish Court Service (Sheriff Clerk Branch), 1954; Departmental Legal Qualification, 1956; Sheriff Clerk Depute, Kilmarnock, 1957-60; Sheriff Clerk of Orkney, 1961-65; seconded HM Treasury (O. & M.), 1965-69 (Secretary, Lord Chancellor's Committee on Resealing of Probates and Confirmations, 1967-68, and Secretary, Scottish Office Committee on Money Transfer Services, 1968-69); Sheriff Clerk, Airdrie, 1969-72; Principal, Scottish Court Service Staff Training Centre, 1973-74; Assistant Sheriff Clerk of Glasgow, 1974-81. Chairman, Sheriff Clerks' Association, 1971-72. Address: (b.) Parliament House, Edinburgh, EH1 1RQ; T.-031-225 2595.

Campbell, Catherine, JP, BSc, BA (Hons), MSc. Member, Scottish Milk Marketing Board, since 1981; Chairman, Cumbernauld "I" Tech, since 1984; b. 10.1.40, Glasgow; m., John Campbell; 2 s.; 1 d. Educ. Notre Dame High School; Glasgow University; Open University; Strathclyde University. Teacher of Mathematics, 1962-68; Member, Cumbernauld and Kilsyth District Council, 1969-78; Member, Cumbernauld Development Corporation, 1975-84. Jubilee Medal, 1977. Recreations: horse riding; homecrafts. Address: (h.) 10 Westray Road, Cumbernauld, G67 1NN; T.-023 67 24834.

Campbell, Rev. Colin, MA, BD, DipTh. Minister, Williamwood Parish Church, since 1949; b. 30.8.16, Greenock; m., Margaret Thomson Paton; 2 s. Educ. Greenock Academy; Hutchesons' Boys Grammar School, Glasgow; Glasgow University; Trinity College. Minister: Erskine Church, Kilwinning, 1940-44, East Church, Johnstone, 1944-49. Recreations: golf; swimming; classical music; reading. Address: Birnam, 4 Golf Road, Clarkston, Glasgow, G76 7LZ; T.-041-638 1215.

Campbell, Colin MacIver, MA (Hons). Head Teacher, Westwood Secondary School, Easterhouse, Glasgow, since 1977; b. 31.8.38, Ralston, Paisley; m., Evelyn J.M.; 3 s. Educ. Paisley Grammar School; Glasgow University; Jordanhill College of Education. Teacher: Hillhead High School, 1961-63, Paisley Grammar School, 1963-67; Principal Teacher, Greenock Academy, 1967-73; Depute Head Teacher, Merksworth High School, Paisley, 1973-77. Elder, Church of Scotland; Chairman, Renfrew West/Inverclyde SNP; Past Chairman, Kilbarchan Civic Society; former Vice-Chairman, Kilbarchan Community Council. Recreations: jogging; military history; DIY; politics. Address: (h.) Braeside, Shuttle Street, Kilbarchan, Renfrewshire; T.-Kilbarchan 2713.

Campbell, Sir Colin Moffat, Bt, MC. Chairman, James Finlay plc, since 1975; b. 4.8.25; m., Mary Anne Chichester Bain; 2 s.; 1 d. (deceased). Educ. Stowe. Scots Guards, 1943-47 (Captain); joined James Finlay & Co. Ltd., 1948. Chairman, Tea Board of Kenya, 1961-71; Chairman, East African Tea Trade Association, 1960-61, 1962-63, 1966-67; Member, Scottish Council, CBI, since 1979; Member, Council, CBI, since 1981; Deputy Chairman, Commonwealth Development Corporation, since 1983. Recreations: gardening; racing; cards. Address: (h.) Kilbryde Castle, Dunblane, Perthshire.

Campbell, David A., MA. Assistant Secretary, Scottish Office, since 1978; b. 5.11.34, Concepcion, Chile; m., Philippa Louise Bunting; 1 s.; 3 d. Educ. Oundle; King's College, Cambridge. King's Own Scottish Borderers, 1956-58; HM Diplomatic Service, 1960-78. Trustee, Rudolf Steiner School of Edinburgh. Recreations: books; the arts; horses. Address: (h.) Old Costerton, Midlothian; T.-Humbie 682.

Campbell, David Ross, FISD, MInstM. Chairman and Chief Executive, Guthrie Newspaper Group, since 1984; Chief Executive, Clyde

Cablevision Ltd., since 1984; b. 27.9.43, Glasgow; m., Moira. Educ. Whitehill School, Glasgow; James Watt Memorial College, Greenock. Previously worked for: international marine radio company; Union Castle SS Company; Sperry Rand; Scottish and Universal Group of companies. Director, Glasgow Chamber of Commerce, since 1981; Liveryman of the City of London. Recreations: golf; walking; swimming. Address: (b.) Herald Street, Ardrossan, KA22 8BX; T.-0294 64321.

Campbell, Donald, MA, FEIS. Rector, Castle Douglas High School, since 1967; b. 21.9.27, Tarbert, Harris; m., Doreen Watson Fergusson; 2 s.; 1 d. Educ. Sir E. Scott School, Tarbert; Portree Secondary School; Edinburgh University. Teacher of Mathematics: Peterhead Academy, Castle Douglas High School; Principal Teacher of Mathematics: Dalbeattie High School, Castle Douglas High School; Deputy Rector, Castle Douglas High School. Chairman, Castle Douglas Cancer Relief Committee; Session Clerk, St. Ringan's Church, Castle Douglas. Recreations: gardening; peat cutting. Address: (h.) Rockville, Ernespie Road, Castle Douglas; T.-0556 2127.

Campbell, Donald. Playwright; b. 25.2.40, Wick. Full-time Writer, since 1974; his play, The Jesuit, first produced, Traverse, Edinburgh, 1976, then Trinity Theatre, Dublin; other plays including Somerville the Soldier, Traverse, 1978, and The Widows of Clyth.

Campbell, Doris Margaret, MD, MRCOG. Senior Lecturer in Obstetrics and Gynaecology and Reproductive Physiology, Aberdeen University, since 1984; b. 24.1.42, Aberdeen; m., Alasdair James Campbell; 1 s.; 1 d. Educ. Aberdeen High School for Girls; Aberdeen University. Resident house officer posts, Aberdeen, 1967-69; Research Fellow, Aberdeen University, 1969-73; Registrar in Obstetrics and Gynaecology, Aberdeen Hospitals, 1973-74; Lecturer in Obstetrics and Gynaecology and Physiology, Aberdeen University, 1974-84. Former Member, Scottish Women's Hockey Council. Recreations: bridge; badminton; guiding. Address: (h.) 77 Blenheim Place, Aberdeen; T.-Aberdeen 639984.

Campbell, Rev. George Houstoun. Minister, John Knox Church, Stewarton, since 1971; b. 29.4.27, Glasgow; m., Elspeth Gibb Campbell Adams; 1 s.; 3 d. Educ. Whitehill Senior Secondary School, Glasgow; Glasgow University; Trinity College. Post Office and civil service, 1941-52; Missionary of Church of Scotland to Church of Central Africa Presbyterian, Malawi, 1957-71. Moderator, Presbytery of Irvine and Kilmarnock, 1980-81; President, Scottish Feed the Minds. Publications: Lonely Warrior; Tikuwababitiziraci Wana? Recreations: reading; gardening; visiting new places. Address: John Knox Manse, 27 Avenue Street, Stewarton, Kilmarnock, KA3 5AP; T.-0560 82418.

Campbell of Croy, Baron, (Gordon Thomas Calthrop Campbell), PC (1970), MC (and Bar); Consultant, oil industry, since 1975; Chairman, Scottish Board, Alliance Building Society, since 1976; Chairman, Stoic Insurance Services, since 1979; Member, Lords' Select Committee on the European Communities, since 1978; b. 8.6.21; m.; 2 s.; 1 d. Educ. Wellington. Commissioned, Regular Army, 1939; RA, 1942 (Major); wounded, 1945; entered HM Foreign Service, 1946; MP (Conservative), Moray and Nairn, 1959-74; Secretary of State for Scotland, 1970-74; Chairman, Scottish Committee, International Year of Disabled, 1981; Trustee, Thomson Foundation, since 1980. Address: (h.) Holme Rose, Cawdor, Nairnshire.

Campbell, Hugh Hall, QC, BA (Hons), MA (Oxon), LLB (Hons). Queen's Counsel, since 1983; b. 18.2.44, Glasgow; m., Eleanor Jane Hare; 3 s. Educ. Glasgow Academy; Trinity College, Glenalmond; Exeter College, Oxford; Edinburgh University. Called to Scottish Bar, 1969; Standing Junior Counsel to Admiralty, 1976. Recreations: music; hill-walking; golf. Address: (h.) 12 Ainslie Place, Edinburgh, EH3 6AS; T.-031-225 2067.

Campbell, Iain, BSc, PhD. Senior Lecturer in Microbiology, Heriot-Watt University, since 1971; b. 24.6.37, North Queensferry; m., Sarah Catherine; 1 s.; 1 d. Educ. Dunfermline High School; Edinburgh University. Lecturer, Heriot-Watt University, 1961-71. Recreations: sailing; photography. Address: (h.) 46 Pentland Terrace, Edinburgh, EH10 6HD; T.-031-447 4492.

Campbell, Ian. MP (Labour), Dumbarton, since 1983 (Dunbartonshire West, 1970-83); b. 26.4.26. Educ. Dumbarton Academy; Royal Technical College. Former Member: Dumbarton Town Council, Dunbarton County Council; Provost of Dumbarton, 1962-70; PPS to Secretary of State for Scotland, 1976-79.

Campbell, Ian, MA, PhD. Reader in English Literature, Edinburgh University; b. 25.8.42, Lausanne, Switzerland. Educ. schools in Lausanne, Rothiemay, Findochty, Buckie and Stonehaven; Aberdeen University; Edinburgh University. Joined Edinburgh University as Assistant Lecturer, then Lecturer in English Literature; visiting appointments in France, Switzerland, Germany, Canada and USA. President, Carlyle Society; Associate Editor, Carlyle Letters; Past President, Scottish Association for the Speaking of Verse. Recreations: music; sport; travel; history. Address: (b.) Department of English, Edinburgh University, George Square, Edinburgh, EH8 9JX; T.-031-667 1011.

Campbell, Ian Gordon, ARIAS, RIBA. Director of Architectural Services, East Lothian District Council, since 1975; b. 5.9.30, Paisley; m., Caryl; 2 s. Educ. Paisley Grammar School; Glasgow School of Architecture. Royal Engineers, 1955-57; Paisley Corporation: Architectural Assistant, 1952-55, Assistant Architect, 1957-61; Chief Architect, Royal Burgh of Rutherglen, 1961-65; Group Architect, Crudens, 1965-71; Burgh Architect, Royal Burgh of Irvine, 1971-75. Secretary, Association of Chief Architects of Scottish Local Authorities, 1978-80 (President, 1980-82); Council Member, RIAS, 1982-85; Area Commissioner, East Lothian Scout Council, since 1981. Recreations: hill-walking; fishing; painting.

Campbell, Ian William, BSc, MB, ChB, MRCP (UK), FRCPEdin. Consultant Physician, Victoria Hospital, Kirkcaldy, since 1978; Honorary Senior Lecturer, Department of Medicine, Edinburgh University, since 1978; Honorary Senior Lecturer, Department of Physiology, St. Andrews University, since 1978; b. 23.11.45, East Wemyss, Fife; m., Catherine McEwan Burges; 1 s.; 2 d. Educ. Buckhaven High School; Edinburgh University. Senior Medical Registrar, Medical Registrar and Registrar, Diabetes and Metabolism, Edinburgh Royal Infirmary; SHO, Eastern General Hospital, Edinburgh. Member, Medical Advisory Council, British Diabetic Association; Council Member, International Study Group of Insulin Treatment with Implantable Devices, Vienna and Minneapolis. Publication: Diagnosis and Management of Endocrine Diseases (Co-author), 1981. Recreations: tennis; squash; golf. Address: (h.) Strathearn, 19 Victoria Road, Lundin Links, Fife, KY8 6AZ; T.-0333 320533.

Campbell, Sir Ilay (Mark), 7th Bt of Succoth; President, Association for Protection of Rural Scotland; b. 29.5.27; m.; 2 d. Educ. Eton; Christ Church, Oxford.

Campbell, James, BL. Town Clerk Depute, Glasgow District Council, since 1974; b. 20.3.37, Glasgow; m., Leslie Jane Mickel Campbell; 1 s.; 1 d. Educ. Glasgow High School; Glasgow University. Glasgow Corporation: Legal Assistant, Planning Committee, 1959, Chief Solicitor, Housing Committee, 1973. Recreations: golf; bridge. Address: (b.) Town Clerk's Office, City Chambers, Glasgow, G2 1DU; T.-041-227 4515.

Campbell, John Craig. Member, Grampian Regional Council, since 1974 (Chairman of Education, since 1981); Director, Langstane Press Ltd., Aberdeen, since 1946; b. 28.3.15, Aberdeen; m., Anna Wilson Harrison; 1 s. Educ. Morgan Academy, Dundee. Past President, Aberdeen Master Printers; Past Chairman, South Aberdeen Conservative Association; former Member: Manpower Services Commission (Scotland), Scottish Master Printers Education Committee, Paper Publishing Industry Training Board; Chairman, Oakbank (List D) School; Member: Grampian/Tayside Area Manpower Board, Convention of Scottish Local Authorities, Scottish Joint Negotiating Committee (Education). Recreation: golf. Address: (h.) 110 Mastrick Drive, Aberdeen; T.-0224 691122.

Campbell, Rev. Keith, BSc, BD. Minister, Broughty Ferry: St. Aidan's, Dundee, since 1968; b. 19.12.32, Gourock; m., Christine Mary Beaton MacFarlane; 1 s. (deceased); 2 d. Educ. Strathallan School; Glasgow University. Minister, Edinkillie, Morayshire, 1963-68. Past Chairman, Dundee Local Health Council; former Depute Chairman, Dundee College of Education. Recreations: swimming; gardening; photography. Address: St. Aidan's Manse, 63 Collingwood Street, Barnhill, Dundee; T.-0382 79253.

Campbell, Kenneth Murray, MA, LLB, WS. Solicitor; Secretary, Royal Scottish Agricultural Benevolent Institution, since 1966; Secretary, Scottish Agricultural Arbiters' Association, since

1966; b. 20.10.30, Dumfries; m., Madeleine Jean Gillie; 1 s.; 1 d. Educ. Dumfries Academy; Edinburgh University. Education Officer, RAF, 1954-56; Solicitor in private practice, Edinburgh, since 1956. Publication: Connell on the Agricultural Holdings (Scotland) Acts (Joint Editor, 6th edition). Recreations: gardening; reading. Address: (b.) 10 Dublin Street, Edinburgh; T.-031 556 2993.

Campbell, Malcolm, MA (Hons), PhD. Reader in Greek, St. Andrews University, since 1984; b. 10.11.43, Shrewsbury; m., Dorothy Helen Fear; 2 s. Educ. Boroughmuir School, Edinburgh; Edinburgh University; Balliol College, Oxford. Lecturer, St. Andrews University, since 1968. Publications: A Commentary on Quintus Smyrnaeus, Posthomerica XII, 1981; Echoes and Imitations of Early Epic in Apollonius Rhodius, 1981; Index verborum in Apollonium Rhodium, 1983; Studies in the Third Book of Apollonius Rhodius' Argonautica, 1983; A Lexicon to Triphiodous, 1985. Recreations: music; philately. Address: (b.) Department of Greek, The University, St. Andrews, Fife.

Campbell, Sir Matthew, KBE (1963), CB (1959), FRSE. Deputy Chairman, White Fish Authority, 1968-78; b. 23.5.07; m.; 2 s. Educ. Hamilton Academy; Glasgow University. Secretary, Department of Agriculture and Fisheries for Scotland, 1958-68.

Campbell, Murdo. Member, Inverness District Council, since 1974; Assessor, Crofters Commission, since 1964; b. 7.4.02, Armadale, Sutherland; m., Christina; 9 s.; 5 d. Educ. Kinbrace School (left aged 15). Sub-postmaster and crofter, Torness, 42 years (retired, 1983); served on former Inverness County and District Councils, 1964-74; former Member, Inverness Local Health Council; former Secretary and Treasurer: Stratherrick Public Hall Committee, Stratherrick Gun Club; former Session Clerk and Clerk, Congregational Board, Dores and Boleskine Church of Scotland. Recreations: deerstalking; clay pigeon shooting; salmon fishing. Address: (h.) The Birches, 1 Dores Road, Inverness; T.-Inverness 238181.

Campbell, Robert Craig, BSc, MInstM. Director, Overseas Projects Unit, Scottish Council (Development and Industry), since 1984; b. 29.4.47, Glasgow; m., Elizabeth Helen C.; 2 d. Educ. Glasgow Academy; St. Andrews University. Scottish Council: Research Executive, 1970-77, Research Director, 1977-84. Recreation: angling. Address: (b.) Scottish Council (Development and Industry), 23 Chester Street, Edinburgh; T.-031-225 7911.

Campbell, Robert Kenneth, BSc (Hons), DipEd, CPhys, MInstP. Rector, Greenock Academy, since 1967; b. 10.2.27, Paisley; m., Patricia Stephenson; 2 d. Educ. George Heriot's School, Edinburgh; Edinburgh University; Moray House College of Education; Heriot-Watt College. Research Physicist, Unilever Ltd., Port Sunlight, 1948-50; teacher training, 1950-51; Teacher of Mathematics and Science, Daniel Stewart's College, 1951-56; Senior Teacher of Science, Government High School, Nassau, 1956-59; Teacher of Mathematics and Science, Daniel Stewart's College, 1959-60; Principal Teacher of Science, Websters Seminary, Kirriemuir, 1960-62; Principal Teacher of Physics, Paisley Grammar School, 1962-67. Past President, Greenock Rotary Club; Elder, Ashton Church of Scotland; Chairman, Fort Matilda Playing Fields Union. Recreations: golf; bridge. Address: (h.) 98 Newark Street, Greenock, PA16 7TG; T.-0475 22727.

Campbell, Rev. Roderick D.M., BD, FSA Scot. Minister, Mearns Parish Church, since 1979; b. 1.8.43, Glasgow; m., Susan Norman; 2 d. Educ. Daniel Stewart's College, Edinburgh; Arbroath High School; Jordanhill College of Education; New College, Edinburgh. Teacher, Technical Subjects, Glasgow, Tanzania and London, 1967-70; Associate Minister, St. Andrew's, Nairobi, 1975-78. Convener, Lodging House Mission, Glasgow Presbytery, since 1981; Chaplain, 1/ 52 Lowland Volunteers, TA. Recreations: swimming; sailing. Address: The Manse of Mearns, Newton Mearns, Glasow, G77 5BU; T.-041-639 1410.

Campbell, Samuel, FIPS. Vice-Convener, Midlothian District Council, since 1984 (Chairman, Housing and Recreation Committees); Chairman, National Committee for Non-Denominational Schools, since 1980; b. 16.9.31, Cambusnethan; m., Elizabeth McMillan; 2 s.; 1 d. Educ. Newmains Secondary School. Former Member, Midlothian County Council; Secretary, COSLA Labour Group. Recreations: works of Robert Burns; supporting Glasgow Rangers. Address: (h.) 6 Kaimes View, Danderhall, Dalkeith, Midlothian; T.-031-663 4213.

Campbell, Thomas. Member, Perth and Kinross District Council, since 1983; Chairman, George Campbell & Son Ltd., Edinburgh and Perth, since 1983; b. 13.8.25, Edinburgh; m., Sheila Margaret; 3 s. Educ. Melville College, Edinburgh; Manchester University. Royal Engineers, 1943-47; worked in family business, 1948-54; Unilever: Ghana and Nigeria, 1954-69, UK, 1969-73. Recreation: golf. Address: Balnabeggan, Bridge of Cally, Perthshire.

Campbell, Professor Thomas Douglas, BA (Oxon), MA, PhD. Professor of Jurisprudence, Glasgow University, since 1979 (Dean, Faculty of Law, since 1983); Mental Welfare Commissioner for Scotland, since 1984; b. 3.3.38, Lenzie; 1 s.; 1 d. Educ. Loretto School; Glasgow University; Oxford University. National Service, 1956-58 (2nd Lt., 1st Regt., Royal Horse Artillery); Glasgow University: Lecturer in Politics, 1964-69, Lecturer in Moral Philosophy, 1969-73; Professor of Philosophy, Stirling University, 1973-79. Chairman, Link: Glasgow Association for Mental Health, since 1984. Publications: Adam Smith's Science and Morals, 1970; Seven Theories of Human Society, 1981; The Left and Rights, 1983. Recreations: golf; dog walking. Address: (h.) 3 Mingarry Street, Glasgow, G20; T.-041-946 5508.

Campbell, Walter Menzies, QC, MA, LLB. Advocate, since 1968; Queen's Counsel, since 1982; part-time Chairman, VAT Tribunal, since 1984; Member, Legal Aid Central Committee, since 1983; Member, Broadcasting Council for Scotland, since 1984; Chairman, Royal Lyceum Theatre, Edinburgh, since 1984; b. 22.5.41, Glasgow; m., Elspeth Mary Urquhart. Educ. Hillhead High School, Glasgow; Glasgow University; Stanford University, California. President, Glasgow University Union, 1964-65; took part in Olympic Games, Tokyo, 1964; AAA 220-yards champion, 1964, 1967; Captain, UK athletics team, Commonwealth Games, Jamaica, 1966; UK 100-metres record holder, 1967-74. Advocate Depute, 1977-80; Standing Junior Counsel to the Army in Scotland, 1980-82. Parliamentary candidate (Liberal): Greenock and Port Glasgow, February, 1974, and October, 1974, East Fife, 1979, North East Fife, 1983; Chairman, Scottish Liberal Party, 1975-77; Member, Scottish Sports Council, 1971-81. Recreations: all sports; music; theatre. Address: (b.) Advocates Library, Parliament House, Edinburgh; T.-031-226 5071.

Campbell, William Henry John, MA, LLB. Solicitor; Honorary Sheriff, South Strathclyde (Dumfries and Galloway), since 1982; Member, Dumfries and Galloway Health Board, since 1981; b. 4.4.30, Newton Mearns; m., Elwin Louise Watson; 2 d. Educ. Dumfries Academy; Fettes College; St. Andrews University; Union College, Schenectady, USA; Glasgow University. Qualified as Solicitor, 1955; National Service, 1955-57 (commissioned 7th Royal Tank Rgt.); Burgh Prosecutor, Moffat, Lochmaben and Dalbeattie, for number of years; Panel of Chairmen, National Insurance Tribunals, 1976-79; former Council Member, Law Society of Scotland. Athletics blue, St. Andrews University, 1952; sometime President and Captain, Dumfries Rugby Club; Secretary and Treasurer, Dumfries and Galloway Golf Club, 1958-63; Captain, Southerness Golf Club, 1975-76. Recreations: golf; garden; wife and family; all forms of sport. Address: (h.) Criffell House, Kirkbean, Dumfries; T.-Kirkbean 243.

Campbell, Rev. William John, MA. Minister, Free Church of Scotland, Portree, since 1983; b. 18.11.33, Garrabost, Lewis; m., Margaret Mary Morrison; 1 s.; 2 d. Educ. Nicolson Institute; Aberdeen University; Free Church College, Edinburgh. National Service, RAMC, 1955-57; Actuarial Clerk, Scottish Mutual Assurance Society, Glasgow; Minister: Detroit, Michigan, 1968-72, Park, Lewis, 1972-83. Address: Free Church Manse, Portree, Isle of Skye; T.-0478 2678.

Campbell, Rev. William Murdoch Maclean, BD, CPS. Minister, Lundie and Muirhead Church, Dundee, since 1978; b. 7.7.42, Inverness; m., Catherine Brown Macleod Laing; 2 d. Educ. Central School, Inverness; Kingussie Senior Secondary School; Edinburgh University; New College, Edinburgh. Bank of Scotland, St. Andrews and Dundee, 1961-65; student attachment, West Kirk of Calder, 1969-70; Associate Minister, Kilmallie linked with Glengarry, 1970-73; Minister, Braes of Rannoch linked with Kinloch Rannoch, 1973-78. Member, Executive Council, Scottish Veterans Residences; Convener, Home Mission Committee, Dundee Presbytery; Chaplain, Tay

Division, Royal Naval Reserve. Recreations: walking; photography; collecting music on record and tape; ornithology and wild flowers; wide reading; bee-keeping; gardening. Address: 149 Coupar Angus Road, Muirhead of Liff, Dundee, DD2 5QN; T.-0382 580210.

Campbell-Gibson, Lt.Comdr. R.N. (Ret.) Hugh Desmond. Member, Executive Committee, Association for Protection of Rural Scotland; County Organiser, Argyll, Scotland's Gardens Scheme; b. 18.8.24; m., Deirdre Wilson; 2 s.; 1 d. Educ. Royal Naval College, Dartmouth. Naval cadet, 1937-41; served Royal Navy, 1941-60; war service convoy duties, Atlantic and Mediterranean; farmed Glenlussa, by Campbeltown, 1960-68; farmed and ran hotel, Dunmor, Seil, Argyll, 1969-83. Chairman, Kilmelford and Kilninver Community Council. Recreations: gardening; skiing. Address: (h.) Tighnamara, Melfort, Kilmelford, Argyll; T.-Kilmelford 224.

Campsie, Alistair Keith, SDA. Author, Journalist and Piper; b. 27.1.29, Inverness; m., Robbie Anderson; 2 s.; 1 d. Educ. West Sussex High School; Lanark Grammar School; West of Scotland College of Agriculture. Inspector of Agriculture, Sudan Government Service, 1949; Cocoa Survey Officer, Nigeria, 1951; experimental staff, National Institute of Agricultural Engineering (Scotland), 1953; Country Editor, Weekly Scotsman, 1954; Sub-Editor, Verse Writer, Scottish Daily Mail, 1955; Founder Editor, East African Farmer and Planter, 1956; Chief Sub-Editor, Weekly Scotsman, 1957; designed and appointed first Editor, Geneva Weekly Tribune, 1958; Chief Feature Writer, Scottish Daily Mail, 1959; Columnist, Science Correspondent and Senior Writer, Scottish Daily Express, 1962-73. Publications: Poems and a Pibroch (with Hugh MacDiarmid), 1972; By Law Protected, 1976; The MacCrimmon Legend or The Madness of Angus Mackay, 1980; We Bought a Country Pub (under pen-name Alan Mackinnon), 1984; Perfect Poison, 1985; Pibroch: the Tangled Web (radio series), 1985; The Clarinda Conspiracy (in press). Recreations: bagpipes (playing and composing); good whisky; self-important people. Address: Piper's Private Hotel, Union Place, Montrose; T.-0674 72298.

Canavan, Dennis, MP, BSc (Hons), DipEd. MP (Labour), Falkirk West, since 1983; b. 8.8.42, Cowdenbeath; m., Elnor Stewart; 3 s.; 1 d. Educ. St. Bride's and St. Columba's School, Cowdenbeath; Edinburgh University. Principal Teacher of Mathematics, St. Modan's High School, Stirling, 1970-74; Assistant Head, Holyrood High School, Edinburgh, 1974; Leader, Labour Group, Stirling District Council, 1974; MP, West Stirlingshire, 1974-83; Chairman, Scottish Parliamentary Labour Group, 1980-81 (Education Convener, since 1975); Vice-Chairman, PLP Foreign Affairs Committee, since 1984, and Northern Ireland Committee, since 1983; Member, Foreign Affairs Select Committee, since 1982; Parliamentary Spokesman for Scottish Committee on Mobility for Disabled, since 1976, and Scottish Spina Bifida Association, since 1976; Honorary President, Milton Amateurs Football Club. Recreations: marathon running;

hill-climbing; fishing; swimming; football (former Scottish Universities football internationalist). Address: (h.) 15 Margaret Road, Bannockburn, Stirling, FK7 OJG; T.-0786 812581.

Candlish, Kenneth Henry, BL, JP, DL, NP. Solicitor, since 1947; Deputy Lieutenant, Berwickshire; Clerk, Berwickshire Lieutenancy; b. 22.8.24, Edinburgh; m., Isobel Robertson-Brown; 2 d. Educ. George Watson's; Edinburgh University. Depute County Clerk, West Lothian, 1951-64; County Clerk, Berwickshire, 1964-75. Recreations: photography; wine-making; music. Address: (b.) 47 Market Square, Duns, Berwickshire; T.-Duns 82752.

Cannon, James Logie, JP. Member, Cumnock and Doon Valley District Council, since 1984 (Chairman, Housing Committee, since 1985); b. 14.11.48, Muirkirk; m., Helen Northcote; 1 d. Educ. Muirkirk Secondary School. Member, Ayrshire Valleys Tourist Board; Member, Muirkirk Community Council. Recreations: reading history; going to the races. Address: (h.) 96 Henderson Drive, Muirkirk, Ayrshire, KA18 3PZ; T.-Muirkirk 61637.

Cannon, Professor Thomas, BSc (Hons), FRSA, FIntFxp, FIPDm. Professor of Business Studies, Stirling University, since 1981; Director, Scottish Enterprise Foundation, since 1982; Chairman, Scottish Association of Small Business Education, since 1983; b. 20.11.46, Liverpool; m., Frances Constable; 1 s.; 1 d. Educ. St. Francis Xaviers School, Liverpool; Borough Polytechnic. Research Assistant, Aske Research; Research Associate, Warwick University; Lecturer, Enfield College of Technology; Brand Manager, Imperial Group; Lecturer, Durham University. Publications: Basic Marketing; Advertising: The Economic Implications. Recreations: soccer fan, especially Everton FC; walking; squash; being with family. Address: (h.) 2 Westerton Drive, Bridge of Allan, Stirling; T.-Stirling 73171.

Cant, Harry Wallace, MA, LLB, WS, NP. Solicitor, since 1954; Clerk and Treasurer, Iona Cathedral Trust, 1965-85; b. 5.7.18, Edinburgh; m., Mary Fleming Hamilton; 3 s.; 1 d. Educ. George Watson's College, Edinburgh; Edinburgh University. War Service, 1939-46 (Capt., Royal Artillery, 51st Highland Division, Western Desert, Sicily, France and Germany); wounded France, 1944; Partner: Menzies & Thomson, WS, 1954, J. & F. Anderson, WS, 1966; Consultant, J. & F. Anderson, WS, since 1984. Secretary, Edinburgh Musical Festival Association, 1958-67; Secretary, Scottish Society of Women Artists, 1960-68. Recreations: golf; reading. Address: (h.) 77 Craiglockhart Road, Edinburgh, EH14 1EL; T.-031-441 3512.

Cant, Rev. Harry William Macphail, MA, BD. Minister, St. Magnus Cathedral, Kirkwall, since 1968; Chaplain to The Queen in Scotland, since 1972; b. 3.4.21; m.; 1 s.; 2 d. Educ. Edinburgh Academy; Edinburgh University; Union Theological Seminary, New York. Minister, Fallin Parish Church, Stirling, 1951-56; Scottish Secretary, Student Christian Movement, 1956-59; Minister, St. Thomas's Parish Church, 1960-68.

Caplan, Sheriff Principal Philip Isaac, MA, LLB, QC. Sheriff Principal of North Strathclyde, since 1983; b. 24.2.29, Glasgow; m., Joyce Stone (2nd m.); 2 s.; 2 d. Educ. Eastwood School; Glasgow University. Solicitor, 1952-56; called to Bar, 1957; Standing Junior Counsel to Accountant of Court, 1964-70; Chairman, Plant Varieties and Seeds Tribunal, Scotland, 1977-79; Sheriff of Lothian and Borders, at Edinburgh, 1979-83; Member, Sheriff Courts Rules Council, 1984. Vice-Chairman, Scottish Association for the Study of Delinquency, since 1982; ARPS (1983), AFIAP (1985). Recreations: photography; sailing; bridge; music; reading. Address: (h.) Auchenlea, Torwood Hill Road, Rhu, Dunbartonshire; T.-0436 820359.

Capperauld, Ian, MB, ChB, DObst, RCOG, FRCSEdin, FRCSGlas. Executive Director, Research and Development, Ethicon Ltd., since 1969; Consultant Surgeon, since 1962; Medical Director, Huntly Nursing Home, since 1981; Member, Lothian Health Board, since 1981; b. 23.10.33, New Cumnock; m., Wilma Hyslop Young; 2 s. Educ. Cumnock Academy; Glasgow University; Edinburgh University. Served as Major, RAMC, 1959-69 (Consultant Surgeon). Recreations: fishing; shooting. Address: (b.) Ethicon Ltd., PO Box 408, Bankhead Avenue, Edinburgh; T.-031-453 5555.

Carbery, Professor Thomas Francis, OBE, MSc, PhD, DPA. Professor of Business Information, Strathclyde University, since 1985; Member, Broadcasting Complaints Commission, since 1981; b. 18.1.25, Glasgow; m., Ellen Donnelly; 1 s.; 2 d. Educ. St. Aloysius' College, Glasgow; Glasgow University; Scottish College of Commerce. Cadet navigator/meteorologist, RAF, 1943-47; civil servant, 1947-61; Lecturer, then Senior Lecturer, Scottish College of Commerce, 1961-64; Strathclyde University: Senior Lecturer in Government-Business Relations, 1964-75, Head, Department of Office Organisation, 1975-79; Professor of Office Organisation, 1979-85. Member: Independent Broadcasting Authority, 1970-79, Royal Commission on Gambling, 1975-77, Transport Users Consultative Committee (Chairman, Scottish TUCC), 1975-81, Scottish Consumer Council (latterly Vice-Chairman), 1976-84; Vice-Chairman, Glasgow Fabian Society; Chairman, Scottish Branch, Public and Co-operative Enterprise; Chairman, Scottish Transport Research Group; Joint Editor, Bulletin of Society for Co-operative Studies; Chairman, Inter-Denominational Chaplaincy Commission, Strathclyde University. Recreations: conversation; watching television; spectating at association football; very bad golf. Address: (h.) 32 Crompton Avenue, Glasgow, G44 5TH; T.-041-637 0514.

Cargill, Kenneth George, MA, LLB. Deputy Editor (former Editor (Output)), News and Current Affairs, Television, BBC Scotland, since 1984; b. 17.2.47, Arbroath. Educ. Arbroath High School; Edinburgh University. Current Affairs, BBC TV, Scotland: Researcher, Current Affairs, 1972-73, Reporter, Current Account, 1973-78, Director, Public Account, 1978-79, Producer, Current Account, 1979-81, Producer, Agenda, 1981-83; Producer, People and Power, London,

1983; Editor of the Day, Scotland 60 Minutes, 1983-84. Address: (b.) BBC, Broadcasting House, Queen Margaret Drive, Glasgow, G12 OPQ.

Carlton, George, OBE, BCom, BL, FCIS, RD. Member, Local Government Boundary Commission for Scotland, since 1980; Deputy Chairman, Local Government Boundary Commission, since 1985; Local Commissioner of Income Tax (Lanarkshire), since 1982; Senior Tutor (part-time), Glasgow University, since 1980; b. 25.6.23, Coatbridge; m., Helen Clark Love; 3 s. Educ. Coatbridge High School; Glasgow University; London University. Lanarkshire County Council: Solicitor, 1954-57, Deputy County Clerk, 1957-74, County Clerk, 1974-75; Director of Administration, Strathclyde Regional Council, 1975-80; Senior Tutor (part-time), Strathclyde University, 1980-84. Past President: Uddingston Cricket Club, Uddingston Cricket and Sports Club; former Captain, Bothwell Castle Golf Club; Elder, Church of Scotland. Recreations: golf; curling; reading; watching cricket. Address: (h.) Kingarth, Fairyknowe Gardens, Bothwell, Glasgow, G71 8RW; T.-Bothwell 853181.

Carlyle, Walter, JP. Member, Dumfries and Galloway Regional Council, since 1975 (Chairman, Roads and Transportation Committee, since 1978); Traffic Commissioner, since 1982; Business Executive; b. 29.4.16, Wamphray, Dumfriesshire; m., Mary Jardine. Educ. Lockerbie Academy. Served 79th armoured division, France and Germany, 1942-45; elected Member, Lockerbie Burgh Council, 1950 (Bailie, 1968); Provost of Lockerbie, 1962-75; Member, Dumfries County Council, 1962-75; Deputy Traffic Commissioner, 1975; Chairman, local Rating Appeals Panel, since 1983. Recreations: golf; curling; Rotary and Church activities. Address: (h.) Pinehurst, 1 Glenannan Avenue, Lockerbie, Dumfriesshire, DG11 2EG; T.-Lockerbie 2529.

Carmichael, Hugh Alisdair, MB, ChB, MRCP. Consultant Physician, Vale of Leven Hospital, Alexandria, since 1979; b. 21.11.45, Dingwall; m., Rosamund Mary Brannan; 1 s.; 3 d. Educ. Ardrossan Academy; Glasgow University. Glasgow Royal Infirmary: Resident House Surgeon, 1970-71, Resident House Physician, 1971, Senior House Officer in Haematology, 1971-72, Senior House Officer in Medicine, 1972-74, Registrar in Medicine and Gastroenterology, 1974-77; Senior Registrar in Medicine, Western Infirmary, Glasgow, and Gartnavel Hospital, 1977-79. Address: (b.) Vale of Leven Hospital, Alexandria, Dunbartonshire; T.-Alexandria 54121.

Carmichael, Sir John, KBE (1955). Director, Adobe Oil and Gas Corporation, Texas, since 1973; b. 22.4.10; m.; 1 s.; 3 d. Educ. Madras College, St. Andrews; St. Andrews University; University of Michigan. Financial and Economic Adviser to Sudan Government, 1955-59; Member, UK Delegation, General Assembly, United Nations, 1959; Member, Scottish Gas Board, 1960-70; Member, Scottish Industrial Development Advisory Board, 1972-79; Deputy Chairman, Independent Television Authority, 1960-64; Chairman, Herring Industry Board,

1962-65; Director, Fisons Ltd., 1961-80; Director, Grampian Television, 1965-72; Director, Jute Industries Ltd. (later Sidlaw Industries Ltd.), 1966-80; Director, Royal Bank of Scotland, 1966-80; Member, Social and Economic Committee, EEC, 1973-74.

Carmichael, Kay. Social Worker; b. 22.11.25; m., Neil George Carmichael (see Baron Carmichael of Kelvingrove); 1 d. Lecturer, then Senior Lecturer, Department of Social Administration and Social Work, Glasgow University, 1962-80; Member, subsequently Deputy Chairman, Supplementary Benefits Commission, 1969-80.

Carmichael, Margaret Mary, BMus, ARCM. Principal, Oxenfoord Castle School, Pathhead, since 1979; b. 1.2.40, Alyth, Perthshire. Educ. Bedford High School; Guildhall School of Music and Drama, London. Head of Music, City of London School for Girls, 1970-74; Lecturer in Music, Goldsmiths' College, London University, 1975-78. Chairman, Music at Oxenfoord (Summer Music School), since 1981. Recreations: theatre; travel. Address: (b.) Oxenfoord Castle School, Pathhead, Midlothian, EH37 5UD; T.-0875 320241.

Carmichael of Kelvingrove, Baron, (Neil George Carmichael). Life Peer; b. 1921; m., Catherine McIntosh Rankin (see Kay Carmichael); 1 d. Educ. Royal College of Science and Technology, Glasgow. Former Member, Glasgow Corporation; MP (Labour), Woodside, 1962-74, Kelvingrove, 1974-83; Joint Parliamentary Secretary, Ministry of Transport, 1967-69; Parliamentary Secretary, Ministry of Technology, 1969-70; Parliamentary Under-Secretary of State, DoE, 1974-75, DoI, 1975-76.

Carmichael, Peter, CBE, DSc. Director, Small Business and Electronics, Scottish Development Agency, since 1982; b. 26.3.33, Dunblane; m., June; 2 s.; 4 d. by pr. m. Educ. McLaren High School, Callander; Glasgow University. Design engineer, Ferranti Ltd., Edinburgh, 1958-65; Hewlett-Packard, South Queensferry: Project Leader, 1965-67, Production Engineering Manager, 1968-73, Engineering Manager, 1973-75, Manufacturing Manager, 1975-76, Division General Manager, 1976-82, Joint Managing Director, 1980-82. Chairman, Wigtown Rural Development Company. Recreations: fishing; antique clock restoration. Address: (h.) 86 Craiglea Drive, Edinburgh, 10; T.-031-447 6334.

Carmichael of Carmichael (Richard John). 26th Baron of Carmichael, since 1980; 30th Chief of Name and Arms of Carmichael, since 1981; Chartered Accountant; Farmer; b. 1.12.48, Stamford; m., Patricia Margaret Branson; 1 s.; 2 d. Educ. Hyton Hill Preparatory School; Kimbolton School; Coventry College of Technology. Audit Senior, Coopers and Lybrand, Tanzania, 1972; Audit Manager, Granger Craig Tunnicliffe, Tauranga, New Zealand, 1974; FCA, 1976, ACA, 1971; Factor/Owner, Carmichael Estate, 1980; claims family titles: Earldom of Hyndford, Viscountcies of Inglisberry and Nemphlar, and Lordship Carmichael of Carmichael. Member, Supreme Council of Scottish Chiefs; Secretary

Carmichael Anstruther District Charitable Association; New Zealand Orienteering Champion, 1977; Grade One Controller, British Orienteering Federation. Recreations: orienteering; skiing; Clan Carmichael Association. Address: Carmichael House, Carmichael, by Biggar, Lanarkshire, ML12 6PG; T.-08993 336.

Carmichael, Rev. William, BSc, DipFor, FLS. Minister, Restalrig Parish Church, since 1972; b. 2.3.18, Moneymore, Co. Londonderry, Northern Ireland; m., Lilian N. Campbell; 1 s.; 1 d. Educ. Rainey Endowed School; Greenmount Agricultural College; Trinity College, Dublin; Aberdeen University; Oxford University; Edinburgh University. Ministry of Supply, Northern Ireland, 1941-44; Colonial Forest Service, Tanganyika, 1948-70. Recreations: rugby; mountaineering; swimming. Address: Restalrig Manse, 43 Moira Terrace, Edinburgh; T.-031-669 7329.

Carmichael, William Fleming, PhD, CEng, MICE, DipAd. Depute Head, Department of Architecture, Edinburgh College of Art and Heriot-Watt University, since 1984; b. 24.2.23, Brechin; m., D.H. Martin; 3 d. Educ. Brechin High School; Heriot-Watt University. Local government engineering posts, Brechin, Kirkcaldy, Dundee, Fife; Army Service, Royal Engineers (Lt.); Lecturer, School of Architecture, Dundee; Consulting Engineer/Partner, R. Cowan & Associates. RIBA Research Fellow, 1957. Recreations: golf; hill-walking; music. Address: (h.) 97 Gardiner Road, Edinburgh; T.-031-332 2818.

Carmichael, William George, BL. Procurator Fiscal, Airdrie, since 1981; b. 26.2.33, Glasgow; m., Elizabeth Gemmell; 1 s.; 2 d. Educ. Eastwood School; Glasgow University. Legal Assistant: Hamilton Town Council, 1958-60, Argyll County Council, 1960-62, Ayr Town Council, 1962-64; joined Procurator Fiscal service, 1965. Recreations: golf; squash; music. Address: (b.) Sheriff Court, Graham Street, Airdrie; T.-Airdrie 511121.

Carnall, Geoffrey Douglas, MA, BLitt. Reader in English Literature, Edinburgh University, since 1969; b. 1.2.27, Croydon, Surrey; m., Elisabeth Seale Murray; 1 s.; 2 d. Educ. Perse School, Cambridge; Magdalen College, Oxford. Lecturer in English, Queen's University, Belfast, 1952-60; Lecturer, then Senior Lecturer in English Literature, Edinburgh University, 1960-69. Chairman, Edinburgh Council for Nuclear Disarmament, 1963-70; Elder, South-East Scotland Monthly Meeting, Society of Friends (Quakers), since 1970; Chairman, Edinburgh Christian Campaign for Nuclear Disarmament, 1982-85. Publications: Robert Southey and His Age, 1960; Robert Southey, 1964; The Mid-Eighteenth Century (Volume 8, Oxford History of English Literature) (Co-author), 1979. Recreation: demonstrating against nuclear weapons. Address: (b.) Department of English Literature, David Hume Tower, George Square, Edinburgh, EH8; T.-031-667 1011.

Carnegie, Leslie Thompson, CBE (1980), BL, JP. Chief Executive, Dumfries and Galloway Regional Council, 1974-85; Honorary Sheriff, since 1960; b. 16.8.20, Aberdeen; m., Isobel Jane McCombie, J.P. Educ. Aberdeen Grammar School; Aberdeen University. Legal Department, Aberdeen Corporation, 1939-48; Depute County Clerk, East Lothian, 1948-54; County Clerk, Dumfries County Council, 1954-75. Past President, Society of County Clerks in Scotland; Clerk, Dumfries Lieutenancy, 1954-85. Recreations: gardening; music appreciation; sporting activities. Address: (h.) Marchhill Park, Dumfries.

Carnegy of Lour, Baroness, (Elizabeth Patricia Carnegy of Lour). Chairman, Scottish Council for Community Education, since 1981; President for Scotland, Girl Guides Association, since 1979; b. 28.4.25. Educ. Downham School, Essex. Member, Tayside Regional Council, 1974-82 (Convener, Education Committee, 1977-81); Member, MSC, 1979-82 (Chairman, Committee for Scotland, 1981-83); Member, Council for Tertiary Education in Scotland, since 1979; Honorary Sheriff, since 1969.

Carr, John Roger, JP, FRICS. Director, Moray Estates Development Co., since 1954; Chairman, Countryside Commission for Scotland, from 1 January, 1986 (Member, since 1979); b. 18.1.27, Ackworth, Yorkshire; m., Cathrine Elise Dickson-Smith; 2 s. Educ. Ackworth & Ayton (Quaker) School. Factor, Walker Scottish Estates Co., Ballater; Factor, subsequently Director and General Manager, Moray Estates Development Co., Forres; former Convenor, Scottish Recreational Land Association; former Council Member, Scottish Landowners Association; former District Councillor, Moray. Recreations: walking; gardening; shooting. Address: (b.) Estates Office, Forres, Moray; T.-03097 2213.

Carr, Rev. Walter Stanley, MA. Minister, St. Columba's Parish Church, Largs, since 1966; b. 3.3.24, Edinburgh; m., Margaret Linton Spittal; 2 d. Educ. George Heriot's School, Edinburgh; Edinburgh University; New College, Edinburgh. Minister: St. Paul's Parish Church, Dunfermline, 1951-64, Avon Street and Brandon Parish Church, Hamilton, 1964-66; former Moderator: Dunfermline and Kinross Presbytery, Ardrossan Presbytery; Vice-Convener, Business Committee, Ardrossan Presbytery; Chairman, Paton Trust; Member, Executive Committee, Abbeyfield Largs Society; Chaplain, Royal British Legion, Largs. Recreations: gardening; swimming; artist. Address: (h.) 17 Beachway, Largs, KA30 8QH; T.-Largs 673107.

Carrol, Charles Gordon, MA, DipEd. Director, Commonwealth Institute, Scotland, since 1971; b. 21.3.35, Edinburgh; 3 s. Educ. Melville College, Edinburgh; Edinburgh University; Moray House College of Education. Education Officer: Government of Nigeria, 1959-65, Commonwealth Institute, Scotland, 1965-71. Lay Member, Press Council, 1978-83. Recreations: walking; angling; reading; cooking. Address: (h.) 11 Dukehaugh, Peebles; T.-0721 21296.

Carroll, Jean A., BSc (Hons). Principal, Dunfermline College of Physical Education, since 1983; President, Scottish Physical Education Association, since 1984; b. 6.10.29, Dewsbury. Educ. Wheelwright Grammar School; St. Mary's College, Cheltenham; I.M. Marsh College, Liverpool; Bristol University. Teacher in Yorkshire and Cumbria; Lecturer, Senior Lecturer and Principal Lecturer, Hereford, London and Birmingham. Recreations: jogging; reading. Address: (b.) Dunfermline College of Physical Education, Cramond Road North, Edinburgh; T.-031-336 6001.

Carroll, Robert Peter, MA, PhD. Senior Lecturer, Department of Biblical Studies, Glasgow University, since 1981; b. 18.1.41, Dublin; m., Mary Anne Alice Stevens; 2 s.; 1 d. Educ. High School, Dublin; Trinity College, Dublin University; Edinburgh University. After postgraduate degree, worked as swimming pool attendant, barman, brickie's mate, secondary school teacher; Glasgow University: Assistant Lecturer in Semitic Languages, 1968, Lecturer in Old Testament Language and Literature, 1969. Publications: When Prophecy Failed, 1979; From Chaos to Covenant, 1981; Jeremiah: A Commentary (in press). Recreations: cinema; cricket; beer-drinking; day-dreaming. Address: (h.) 5 Marchmont Terrace, Glasgow, G12 9LT; T.-041-339 4211.

Carson, Thomas Richard, BSc (Hons), PhD. Reader in Astrophysics, St. Andrews University; b. Enniskillen, Northern Ireland; m., Ursula Margaret Mary Davies; 1 s. Educ. Portora Royal School; Queen's University, Belfast. Assistant Lecturer, Department of Natural Philosophy, Glasgow University; Senior Scientific Officer, UK Atomic Weapons Research Establishment, Aldermaston; Senior Lecturer, Department of Astronomy, St. Andrews University; Visiting Professor, Colorado University; Senior Research Associate, NASA Institute for Space Studies, New York; Visiting Staff Member, Los Alamos National Laboratory, University of California. Publication: Atoms and Molecules in Astrophysics (Editor, with M.J. Roberts), 1972. Recreations: squash; tennis; swimming; skiing. Address: (h.) 7 Cairnsden Gardens, St. Andrews, Fife, KY16 8SQ; T.-0334 73813.

Carter, Christopher John, BA (Hons), PhD, MRTPI, FBIM, FRSA. Vice Principal, Duncan of Jordanstone College of Art, since 1981; b. 5.2.41, Capel, Surrey; m., Ann Fisher Prince; 1 s.; 1 d. Educ. Ottershaw School, Chertsey, Surrey; Birmingham University; Glasgow University. Town Planning Assistant, Cumbernauld Development Corporation, 1963-64 and 1967-68; Visiting Lecturer in Geography, Brock University, St. Catharines, Ontario, 1968-69; Lecturer/Senior Lecturer in Planning, Glasgow School of Art, 1969-76; Principal Lecturer in Planning, Coventry (Lanchester) Polytechnic, 1976-78; Senior Lecturer/Head of Department of Town and Regional Planning, Duncan of Jordanstone College of Art, 1978-81. Winner, RTPI Prize, 1970. Publication: Innovations in Planning Thought and Practice at Cumbernauld New Town 1956-62. Recreations: skiing; running; photography; music. Address: (h.) 39 Haston Crescent, Kinnoull, Perth; T.-0738 36802.

Carter, Professor David Craig, MB, ChB, MD, FRCSEdin, FRCSGlas. Professor of Surgery, Glasgow University, since 1979; Honorary Consultant, Glasgow Royal Infirmary, since 1979; b. 1.9.40, Penrith; m., Ilske; 2 s. Educ. St. Andrews University. Lecturer in Clinical Surgery, Edinburgh University, 1969-74; 12-month secondment as Lecturer in Surgery, Makerere University, Kampala, Uganda, 1972; Senior Lecturer in Surgery, Edinburgh University, 1974-79; 12-month secondment as Associate Professor of Surgery, University of California, 1976. Council Member, Royal College of Surgeons of Edinburgh, 1980. Moynihan Prize, 1973; James IV Association of Surgeons Travelling Fellow, 1975. Recreations: golf; music. Address: (b.) University Department of Surgery, Royal Infirmary, Glasgow, G31 2ER; T.-041-552 3535.

Carter, George Robert, MIPM, MBIM. Personnel Services Controller, Christian Salvesen PLC, since 1974; Director, Christian Salvesen (Food Services) Ltd., since 1977; Member, CBI (Scotland) Council, since 1980 (Chairman, Employment Committee, since 1980); Member, Manpower Services Committee (Scotland), since 1980; b. 26.2.31, Youghal, Ireland; m., Margaret Elizabeth Andrew; 2 s.; 1 d. Educ. Christian Brothers Primary and Secondary School. Merchant Navy, 1949-54; trade union official, 1954-63; various personnel management roles, Chrysler (UK) Ltd., 1963-68; Consultant, Department of Employment, 1968-70; Personnel Director, Beaverbrook Newspaper Group, 1970-74. Member: Administration Committee, Scottish Business Education Council, 1977-79, CBI Industrial Relations Committee (Scotland), 1977-80. Recreations: music; reading; photography. Address: (h.) 12A Ravelston Park, Edinburgh, EH4 3DX; T.-031-332 7914.

Carter, Tom, OBE, ACIS, ACMA, CIPFA. Director of Finance, Grampian Regional Council, since 1975; b. 27.12.23, Carlisle; m., Gill; 2 s. Educ. Birkenhead Park High School. 7th Bn., Royal Tank Rgt., 1942-44; various clerical posts, mainly with former LMS Railway, 1939-47; Birkenhead: Clerk, Parks and Cemeteries Department, 1947-48, Accountancy Assistant, 1948-55; Technical Assistant, rising to Assistant Secretary, former IMTA, 1955-61; Deputy County Treasurer, Holland (Lincolnshire), 1961-68; County Treasurer, Moray and Nairn, 1968-75. Past Chairman, Directors of Finance (Scotland) Section, CPFA; Member, Local Government Finance Working Party; former Commissioner, Public Works Loan Board. Recreations: walking; bridge; gardening; wine-making; reading. Address: (b.) Woodhill House, Ashgrove Road West, Aberdeen, AB9 2LU; T.-0224 682222, Ext. 2200.

Cartwright, Rev. Alan Charles David, BSc, BD. Minister, Parishes of Fogo and Swinton with Leitholm, since 1976, with Ladykirk with Whitsome, since 1978; b. 14.7.47, Glasgow; m., Mary Elizabeth Lawson Bissett; 1 s.; 2 d. Educ. Hutchesons Boys Grammar School; Strathclyde University; Glasgow University. Project Leader, Wiggins Teape Ltd., 1968-72; Assistant Minister, Cameron with Largoward with St. Leonard's, 1975-76. Moderator, Synod of the Borders,

1982-83; Moderator, Duns Presbytery, 1984-85. Recreations: athletics; studying local history; drinking coffee. Address: The Manse, Swinton, Duns, Berwickshire, TD11 3JJ; T.-Swinton 228.

Carty, Matthew John, MB, ChB, FRCSEdin, FRCS, RCPSGlas, FRCOG. Consultant Obstetrician and Gynaecologist, Southern General Hospital, Glasgow, since 1977; b. 8.3.42, Hamilton; m., Caroline Martin; 2 s.; 2 d. Educ. St. Aloysius College, Glasgow; Glasgow University. Lecturer in Midwifery, Nairobi University, Kenya, 1970-71; Lecturer in Midwifery, Glasgow University, 1972-77. Recreations: squash; golf; tennis; jogging. Address: (h.) 31 Monreith Road, Newlands, Glasgow; T.-041-632 1033.

Carus, David Alexander, BSc, CEng, MIMechE, AKC. Member, City of Dundee District Council, since 1984; Biomedical Engineer, Dundee Limb Fitting Centre, since 1980; Honorary Lecturer, Dundee University, since 1981; b. 14.10.51, Accrington; m., Sally Margaret; 2 s. Educ. West Park Grammar School, St. Helens; Kings College, London University. RAF, 1973-80 (Flt.-Lt. Engineer Officer). Trustee: Orchar Art Gallery; City of Dundee Children's Holiday Fund. Recreations: reading politics; carpentry. Address: (h.) Balcairn, 28 Camphill Road, Broughty Ferry, Dundee; T.-75448.

Casey, Gordon. Housing Convenor, Clydebank District Council, since 1984 (Member of Council, since 1982); b. 14.7.54, Johnstone; m., Bridget. Educ. Clydebank High School. Recreations: snooker; football; reading. Address: (h.) 3 Cochno Street, Clydebank; T.-041-952 9710.

Cash, John David, BSc, MB, PhD, MRCPath, FRCPE. National Medical Director, Scottish National Blood Transfusion Service, since 1979; b. 3.4.36, Reading; m., Angela Mary Thomson; 1 s.; 1 d. Educ. Ashville College, Harrogate; Edinburgh University. Edinburgh and South East Scotland Blood Transfusion Service: Deputy Director, 1969, Regional Director, 1974. Adviser in Blood Transfusion, Scottish Home and Health Department; Adviser, WHO. Recreations: fishing; gardening. Address: (b.) Scottish National Blood Transfusion Service, Headquarters Unit, Ellen's Glen Road, Edinburgh, EH17 7QT; T.-031-664 2317.

Caskie, Rev. J. Colin, BA, BD. Minister, Carnoustie Parish, since 1983; b. 17.8.47, Glasgow; m., Alison McDougall; 2 s.; 1 d. Educ. Knightswood Secondary School; Strathclyde University; Glasgow University. Parish Minister, Penilee, Glasgow, 1977-83. Recreations: railways; gardening. Address: 44 Terrace Road, Carnoustie, Angus, DD7 7AR; T.-0241 52289.

Cater, Sir John Robert (Sir Robin), Kt (1984). Chairman, Distillers Co. Ltd., 1976-83; b. 25.4.19; m.; 1 d. Educ. George Watson's College, Edinburgh; Cambridge University. Managing Director, John Haig & Co. Ltd., 1965-70. Played for Britain in Walker Cup Team (golf), 1955.

Catley, Brian John, MA, PhD. Senior Lecturer in Biochemistry, Department of Brewing and Biological Sciences, Heriot-Watt University, since 1978; b. 15.11.36, Salisbury, Wiltshire; m., Elizabeth Ferguson Eyres; 1 s.; 1 d. Educ. Bradford Grammar School; St. Catherine's College, Oxford. Research Chemist, Ilford Ltd., 1961-64; Assistant Lecturer, 1965-67; Guest Investigator, Rockefeller University, New York, 1967-68; Assistant Professor, Miami University, 1968-72; Lecturer, Heriot-Watt University, 1972-78. Convenor, Reserve Management Committee, Balerno, Scottish Wildlife Trust. Recreations: photography; travel. Address: (b.) Department of Brewing and Biological Sciences, Heriot-Watt University, Chambers Street, Edinburgh; T.-031-225 8432, Ext. 170.

Cattanach, John Harkness, VM, JP. Member, Highland Regional Council, since 1982; Member, Nairn District Council, since 1974; b. 19.1.19, Tobermory; m., Williamina Fraser; 1 s. Educ. Kingussie Secondary School; Skerry's College, Glasgow. Army Officer, 1938-46 (Captain); ran own business, 1946-50; accountant, 1950-55; own business, 1956-74. Awarded Order of the Silver Cross of Virtuti Militari by the Polish Government in exile. Address: (h.) Lorne House, Geddes, by Nairn, IV12 5SB; T.-06677 279 and 397.

Catto, Graeme R.D., MB, ChB (Hons), MD (Hons), FRCP, FRCPGlas. Reader in Medicine, Aberdeen University, since 1985; Honorary Consultant Physician/Nephrologist, since 1977; b. 24.4.45, Aberdeen; m., Joan Sievewright; 1 s.; 1 d. Educ. Robert Gordon's College; Aberdeen University. Research Fellow/Lecturer/Senior Lecturer in Medicine, Aberdeen University, 1970-85; Harkness Fellow of Commonwealth Fund of New York, 1975-77 (Fellow in Medicine, Harvard Medical School and Peter Bent Brigham Hospital, Boston). Recreations: fresh air; France. Address: (b.) Department of Medicine, Aberdeen University, Foresterhill, Aberdeen, AB9 2ZB; T.-0224 681818.

Cawdor, 6th Earl, (Hugh John Vaughan Campbell), FSA, FRICS; b. 6.9.32; m., 1, Cathryn Hinde (m. diss.); 2 s.; 3 d.; 2, Countess Angelika Ilona Lazansky von Bukowa. Educ. Eton; Magdalen College, Oxford; Royal Agricultural College, Cirencester. Address: (h.) Cawdor Castle, Nairn.

Cay, David Robert Bellamy, MA, LLB, FSA Scot. Advocate, since 1954; Member, Supreme Court Committee, Law Society of Scotland, since 1975; b. 7.11.29, Aberdeen; m., Elizabeth Lorna Jamieson (see Elizabeth Lorna Cay); 1 s.; 1 d. Educ. Aberdeen Grammar School; Aberdeen University. Standing Counsel, Ministry of Labour (subsequently Department of Employment and Productivity); Standing Counsel, Department of Transport; defended last man to be hanged in Scotland. Recreations: golf; reading; travel. Address: (h.) 12 India Street, Edinburgh, EH3 6EZ; T.-031-225 3640.

Cay, Elizabeth Lorna, MD, FRCPsych, MRCPEdin, DPM. Consultant in Rehabilitation Medicine, since 1975; Honorary Senior Lecturer, Edinburgh University, since 1976; b. 11.1.31, Cawdor, Nairn; m., David Robert Bellamy Cay (qv); 1 s.; 1 d. Educ. Elgin Academy; Peebles

Burgh and County High School; Edinburgh University. President, Scottish Society of Rehabilitation Medicine; Temporary Advisor, WHO; Chairman, Edinburgh Committee for Coordination of Services for the Disabled. Address: (h.) 12 India Street, Edinburgh, EH3 6EZ; T.-031-225 3640.

Chadwick, Professor Charles, MA, DU (Paris). Professor of French, Aberdeen University, since 1968; b. 23.11.24, Widnes; m., Nora O'Brien. Educ. Grammar School, Widnes; Liverpool University; Paris University. Lecturer, Liverpool University, 1951-65; Reader, Manchester University, 1965-68; Dean, Faculty of Arts, Aberdeen, 1982-85. Publications: Etudes Sur Rimbaud, 1959; Mallarme, 1961; Symbolism, 1971; Verlaine, 1973; Rimbaud, 1979. Recreation: gardening. Address: (h.) The Beeches, William Street, Torphins, Aberdeenshire, AB3 4JR; T.-033982 489.

Chalmers, Alaster Hood, JP. Member, East Kilbride District Council, since 1977; b. 8.11.48, Glasgow; m., Margaret Fullerton MacCallum; 2 s. Educ. Kelvinside Academy, Glasgow. Vice Chairman, East Kilbride Constituency Conservative Association. Recreations: bowls; badminton; golf. Address: (h.) 4 Avenel Crescent, Strathaven, Lanarkshire; T.-Strathaven 21979.

Chalmers, Rev. George Angus, MA, BD, MLitt. Minister, Westpark Church, Denny, since 1968; b. 30.7.37, Murroes, near Dundee; m., Helen Burt Taylor; 2 d. Educ. Morgan Academy, Dundee; St. Andrews University; Stirling University. Minister, Greenlaw Church, 1962-68. Treasurer, Scottish Church Theology Society. Recreations: music; Indian religous theology. Address: Westpark Manse, 13 Baxter Crescent, Denny, Stirlingshire, FK6 5EZ; T.-0324 823782.

Chalmers, George Lovie, MB, ChB, FRCPEdin, FRCPGlas. Consultant Physician in administrative charge, Glasgow Eastern District Geriatrics Service, since 1985; Honorary Clinical Lecturer in Geriatric Medicine, Glasgow University, since 1969; b. 12.1.33, Aberdeen; m., Jean Sutherland; 2 s.; 3 d. Educ. Aberdeen Grammar School; Aberdeen University. House Officer posts, Inverness and Victoria Infirmary, Glasgow; Registrar posts in General Medicine, Aberdeen, and Geriatric Medicine, Dundee; Senior Registrar in Geriatrics, Dundee, and Honorary Tutor in Medicine, St. Andrews University, 1965; Consultant Physician in Geriatric Medicine, Western Infirmary and Gartnavel Hospital, Glasgow, 1967-85. Elder, Church of Scotland. Publications: Caring for the Elderly Sick, 1980; Advanced Geriatric Medicine 2 (Contributor), 1982; Medicine and the Christian Mind (Contributor), 1975; WHO Handbook on Heart Disease in the Elderly (Contributor) (in press). Recreations: walking; swimming; boating; fishing; reading; writing. Address: 37 Cleveden Road, Glasgow, G12 0PH; T.-041-339 1757.

Chalmers, Ian Donald, BSc, PhD, CEng, MIEE, MInstP. Senior Lecturer in Electrical Engineering, Strathclyde University, since 1983; b. 4.6.40, London; m., Margaret Campbell; 2

s.; 1 d. Educ. Montrose Academy; Strathclyde University. Senior Research Fellow, CEGB, 1968-73; Lecturer in Electrical Engineering, 1973-83. Chairman, Professional Group S3, IEE (London), 1984-86. Recreation: golf. Address: (h.) 13 Vennel Street, Stewarton, Kilmarnock, KA3 5HL; T.-0560 82903.

Chalmers, Rev. John Pearson, BD, CertPS. Minister, Renton Trinity Parish Church, since 1979; b. 5.6.52, Bothwell; m., Elizabeth Barbara Boning; 1 s.; 1 d. Educ. Marr College, Troon; Strathclyde University; Glasgow University. Probationer Assistant, Netherlee Parish Church, 1978-79. Clerk, Dumbarton Presbytery, since 1982. Recreations: golf; bee-keeping; photography. Address: Trinity Manse, Main Street, Renton, Dumbarton; T.-0389 52017.

Chalmers, Patrick Edward Bruce, NDA, BScA. Controller, BBC Scotland, since 1983; b. 26.10.39, Chapel of Garioch, Aberdeenshire; m., Ailza Catherine Reid; 3 d. Educ. Fettes College, Edinburgh; North of Scotland College of Agriculture; Durham University. Joined BBC as Radio Talks Producer, Scotland, 1963; TV Producer, 1965; Senior Producer, Aberdeen, 1970; Head of Television, Scotland, 1979-82; General Manager, Co-Productions, TV, London, 1982. Member, Grampian Region Children's Panel, 1974-79. Recreations: skiing; gardening. Address: (h.) Corblelack, Logie Coldstone, Aboyne, Aberdeenshire.

Chalmers-Watson, Keith, SDA. Farmer, since 1964; Chairman and Managing Director, D.C. Watson & Sons (Fenton Barns) Ltd.; b. 20.7.45, Edinburgh; m., Kirsteen Henderson; 3 d. Educ. Loretto; East of Scotland Agricultural College. Chairman, Ardtaraig Salmon Ltd.; Director: Fenton Barns (Scotland) Ltd., David Morin (Builders) Ltd. Executive and Council Member, Royal Zoological Society of Scotland; Council Member: World Pheasant Association, British Turkey Federation. Recreations: rare game-bird conservation and aviculture. Address: Fenton Barns, North Berwick, East Lothian; T.-062 085 225.

Chapman, Alan, CA, JP. Director, Aberdeen Construction Group PLC, since 1970; Director, Lyle Offshore Group PLC, since 1983; b. 18.3.27, Aberdeen; m., Vera Margaret; 2 s.; 1 d. Educ. Central School, Aberdeen. Joined Aberdeen Construction Group, 1955. President, Aberdeen Junior Chamber of Commerce, 1963; Governor, Robert Gordon's Institute of Technology, 1983. Recreations: golf; sailing. Address: 38 Rubislaw Park Road, Aberdeen; T.-Aberdeen 37249.

Chapman, Charles Duncan, OBE, MA, LLB. Honorary Sheriff, since 1960; b. 11.2.13, Denny, Stirlingshire; m., Margaret Martin Henry; 1 s.; 1 d. Educ. Morrison's Academy, Crieff; Edinburgh University. Legal apprentice; Royal Artillery, 1939-45 (Major, 1943); Kirkcaldy Town Council, 1945-75: Legal Assistant, Depute Town Clerk, Town Clerk; Chief Executive, Kirkcaldy District Council, 1975-78. Past Chairman, Law Committee, Convention of Burghs; former Member, Central Probation Council; served on a number of Government committees and working parties; former Council Member, Law Society of Scotland; Director, Link Housing Association; Vice Chairman, Kirkcaldy Citizens' Advice Bureau; Committee Member, Kingdom Housing Association. Publication: The Licensing Scotland Act 1976. Recreation: bowling. Address: (h.) 15 Stanley Park, Kirkcaldy; T.-0592 201270.

Chapman, Francis Ian, FRSA, CBIM. Chairman and Chief Executive, William Collins PLC, since 1981; Chairman, Radio Clyde Ltd., since 1972; Chairman, Council, Strathclyde University Business School, since 1985; b. 26.10.25, St. Fergus, Aberdeenshire; m., Marjory Stewart Swinton; 1 s.; 1 d. Educ. Shawlands Academy, Glasgow; Ommer School of Music; Royal Scottish Academy of Music. War Service: RAF air crew cadet, 1943-44; National Service coal mines, 1945-47. William Collins: trainee, 1947, Sales Representative, New York Branch, 1950, General Sales Manager, London, 1955, appointed to main operating Board as Group Sales Director, 1959; appointed to Board, William Collins (Holdings) Ltd. as Joint Managing Director, 1967; Deputy Chairman, William Collins (Holdings) Ltd., 1976; Chairman, William Collins Publishers Ltd., 1979; Chairman, Hatchards Ltd., since 1976; Board Member, Pan Books Ltd., 1962-84; Chairman, Harvill Press Ltd., since 1976; Board Member, Book Tokens Ltd., since 1981; Member, Governing Council, SCOTBIC, since 1983; Board Member, IRN Ltd., 1983-85; President, Publishers Association, 1979; Trustee, Book Trade Benevolent Society, since 1982; Board Member, Scottish Opera Theatre Royal Ltd., 1974-79. Recreations: golf; swimming; skiing; music. Address: (b.) Westerhills Road, Bishopbriggs, Glasgow, G64 2QT.

Chapman, John N., MA, PhD, MInstP. Reader in Natural Philosophy, Glasgow University, since 1974; b. 21.11.47, Sheffield; m., Judith M.; 1 s.; 1 d. Educ. King Edward VII School, Sheffield; St. John's College and Fitzwilliam College, Cambridge. Research Fellow, Fitzwilliam College, Cambridge; Lecturer, Glasgow University. Former officer: British Joint Committee for Electron Microscopy and Institute of Physics. Publication: Quantitative Electron Microscopy (Co-Editor). Recreations: photography; walking; squash. Address: (b.) Department of Natural Philosophy, Glasgow University, Glasgow, G12 8QQ; T.-041-339 8855, Ext. 462.

Chappell, Leslie Harold, BSc (Hons), PhD. Senior Lecturer in Zoology, Aberdeen University, since 1980; b. 2.10.41, London; m., Eileen Helen Garside; 1 s.; 1 d. Educ. St. Dunstan's College, London; Leeds University. Research Fellow, Rice University, Houston, Texas, 1967-70; Lecturer, Queen Mary College, London University, 1970-71; Research Fellow, Molteno Institute, Cambridge University, 1971-73; Lecturer, Aberdeen University, 1973-80. Honorary General Secretary, British Society for Parasitology, since 1983 (Council Member, since 1981). Publication: Physiology of Parasites, 1980. Recreation: squash. Address: (b.) Department of Zoology, Aberdeen University, Tillydrone Avenue, Aberdeen, AB9 2TN; T.-0224 40241, Ext. 6440.

Charlton, Professor Graham, BDS, MDS, FDSRCS. Professor of Conservative Dentistry and Head of Department, Edinburgh University, since 1978; b. 15.10.28, Newbiggin-By-Sea, Northumberland; m., Stella Dobson; 2 s.; 1 d. Educ. Bedlington Grammar School; St. John's, York; Durham University. Teaching Certificate. Teacher in Northumberland, 1948-52 (including period of National Service); Dental School, 1952-58; general dental practice, 1958-64; Lecturer, then Senior Lecturer/Honorary Consultant, Bristol University, 1964-78 (Clinical Dean, Dental School, Bristol, 1975-78). Dean of Dental Studies, Edinburgh University, 1978-83. Address: (b.) Dental School, Chambers Street, Edinburgh, EH1 1JA; T.-031-225 9511.

Chatwin, John Malcolm, BSc (Eng), CEng, MIEE, MInstM. Chief Commercial Officer, North of Scotland Hydro Electric Board, since 1984; b. 19.7.45, Banstead, Surrey; m., Elizabeth Joy; 1 s.; 2 d. Educ. City of London School; University College, London. General Assistant Engineer, London Electricity Board, 1967; First Engineer (Tariffs), South Eastern Electricity Board, 1973; Electricity Council: Senior Engineer (Tariffs), 1977, Head of Pricing Policy, 1979; Deputy Chief Commercial Officer, North of Scotland Hydro Electric Board, 1980. Recreations: Rotary; sailing. Address: (b.) 16 Rothesay Terrace, Edinburgh; T.-031-225 1361.

Cherry, Rev. Alastair Jack, BD. Minister, Scoonie Kirk, Leven, since 1982; b. 13.3.44, Glasgow; m., Fiona Mairi Murchison; 2 s. Educ. Bellahouston Academy, Glasgow; Glasgow University. Staff, Clydesdale Bank Ltd., 1964-76; studied for ministry, 1976-82. Vice Chairman, Leven Social Services Group; Convener, Home Mission Committee, Kirkcaldy Presbytery. Recreations: music; dramatic art; walking; a little golf. Address: Manse of Scoonie Kirk, Links Road, Leven, Fife; T.-Leven 26518.

Chessor, George Clinton, MB, ChB. Hospital Practitioner, Sauchie Hospital, since 1970; b. 4.8.20, Fraserburgh; m., Doris Jean Chessor; 1 s.; 1 d. Educ. Keith Grammar School; Aberdeen University. Chairman, Abbeyfield Society, Alloa; Member, Management Committee, Citizens Advice Bureau, Alloa; Elder, Church of Scotland; Past President, BMA Stirling Division; former Member, Forth Valley Health Board. Recreations: collectors' cars; golf. Address: (h.) 152 Claremont, Alloa; T.-0259 723817.

Chestnut, Rev. Alexander, BA. Minister, St. Mark's Greenbank Church, Greenock, since 1963; b. 2.5.21, Ballymoney, Northern Ireland; m., Elizabeth Elliott; 1 s.; 3 d. Educ. Ballycastle High School; Magee University College; Trinity College, Dublin; Presbyterian College, Belfast. Army (ROAC and REME), 1941-46; Minister, Loughbrickland and Scarva Presbyterian Churches, 1948-63. Recreations: bee-keeping; gardening; crosswords. Address: 131 Finnart Street, Greenock, PA16 8HT; T.-0475 21116.

Cheyne, Rev. Professor Alexander Campbell, MA (Hons), BLitt, BD, HonDLitt (Memorial University, Newfoundland). Professor of Ecclesiastical History, Edinburgh University, since 1964; Principal, New College, Edinburgh, since 1984; b. 1.6.24, Errol, Perthshire. Educ. Kirkcaldy High School; Edinburgh University; Oriel College, Oxford; Basel University, Switzerland. National Service, Black Watch and RAEC (Instructor, Army School of Education), 1946-48; Glasgow University: Assistant Lecturer, 1950-51, Lecturer in History, 1951-53; New College and Basel University, 1953-57; Lecturer in Ecclesiastical History, Edinburgh University, 1958-64. Carnegie Scholar, 1948-50; Aitken Fellow, 1956-57; Visiting Professor, Wooster College, Ohio, 1973; Chalmers Lecturer (Trinity College, Glasgow, and Christ's College, Aberdeen), 1976-80; Visiting Fellow, Wolfson College, Cambridge, 1979; Burns Lecturer, Knox College, Dunedin, New Zealand, 1980. Publications: The Transforming of the Kirk: Victorian Scotland's Religious Revolution, 1983; The Practical and the Pious: Essays on Thomas Chalmers 1780-1847 (Editor), 1985; contributions to: Reformation and Revolution: Essays presented to Hugh Watt, 1967, The Westminster Confession in the Church Today, 1982; introduction to Movements of Religious Thoughts in Britain during the Nineteenth Century, 1971. Recreations: classical music; walking; foreign travel. Address: (b.) New College, Edinburgh; T.-031-225 8400.

Cheyne, Alexander Ian, MB, ChB, DPM, MRCPsych. Consultant Psychiatrist, Gartnavel Royal Hospital, Glasgow, since 1972; Consultant Psychiatrist, Leverndale Hospital, Glasgow, since 1970; Senior Registrar, Gartnavel Royal Hospital, Glasgow, since 1968; b. 29.9.30, Rangoon, Burma; m., Jean MacDonald Edmonds; 3 d. Educ. Aberdeen Grammar School; Aberdeen University. House Officer: Aberdeen Royal Infirmary, 1954-55, Glasgow Royal Infirmary, 1955; Medical Officer, RAMC, 1955-57; Trainee, general practice, Banchory, 1957-58; Principal, general practice, Cambridgeshire, 1958-64; Registrar, Crichton Royal, Dumfries, 1965-67; Psychiatrist, Hillcrest Hospital, Adelaide, 1967-68. Recreations: squash; golf; walking. Address: (h.) 34 Thorn Road, Bearsden, Glasgow; T.-041-942 2439.

Chick, Jonathan Dale, MA (Cantab), MB, ChB, MPhil, MRCP, MRCPsych. Consultant Psychiatrist, Royal Edinburgh Hospital, since 1979; part-time Senior Lecturer, Edinburgh University, since 1979; b. 23.4.45, Wallasey; m., Josephine Anna; 2 s. Educ. Queen Elizabeth Grammar School, Darlington; Corpus Christi College, Cambridge; Edinburgh University. Posts in Edinburgh teaching hospitals, 1971-76; scientific staff, MRC Unit for Epidemiological Studies in Psychiatry, 1976-79. Adviser, WHO; awarded Royal College of Psychiatrists Research Medal and Prize. Publication: Drinking Problems (Co-author), 1984. Recreations: music; literature; visual arts. Address: (h.) 8 Abbotsford Park, Edinburgh; T.-031-447 6027.

Chilton, Rev. Ronald Michael Leeman, BD. Minister, Corgarff and Strathdon linked with Glenbuchat-Towie, since 1981; b. 13.10.44, Belfast; m., Jennifer Katherine Campbell; 2 s.; 2 d. Educ. Sir Joseph Williamson's Mathematical School, Rochester, Kent; Poole Grammar

School; Edinburgh University. Probationer Assistant, St. John's Church, Largs, 1971-72; Minister: Applecross, Wester Ross, 1972-78, Burnbank Parish Church, Hamilton, 1978-81. Publication: Reformed Book of Common Order (Contributor), 1977. Recreations: philately; reading; writing (books); Russian orchestral music 1840-1943. Address: The Manse, Strathdon, Aberdeenshire; T. 097 52 216.

Chisholm, Rev. Archibald Freeland, MA. Minister, Braes of Rannoch with Foss and Rannoch, since 1984; b. 27.10.32, Glasgow; m., Margaret Downer Rice; 4 d. Educ. Perth Academy; St. Andrews University; New College, Edinburgh. Minister, Bantu Presbyterian Church of South Africa, Gordon Memorial, Natal, 1958-67; Tutor, Federal Theological Seminary of Southern Africa, 1964-65; Minister: Stamperland Parish Church, Glasgow, 1968-76, St. Andrew's Parish Church, Leven, 1976-84. Address: The Manse, Kinloch Rannoch, Pitlochry, PH16 5QA; T.-08822 381.

Chisholm, Duncan Douglas, MB, ChB, MRCPsych, DPM. Consultant Child and Adolescent Psychiatrist, Department of Child and Family Psychiatry, Royal Aberdeen Children's Hospital, since 1975; Clinical Senior Lecturer, Department of Mental Health, Aberdeen University, since 1975; b. 8.10.41, Grantown-on-Spey; m., Rosemary Galloway Doyle; 2 d. Educ. Grantown Grammar School; Aberdeen University. Pre-registration House Officer, Aberdeen, 1965-66; post-registration Senior House Officer/Registrar, Royal Cornhill Hospital and Ross Clinic, Aberdeen, 1966-70; Senior Registrar in Child and Adolescent Psychiatry, 1970-75 (including one-year sabbatical, Clarke Institute of Psychiatry, Toronto, 1973-74). Member, Executive Committee, Child and Adolescent Psychiatry Section, Scottish Division, Royal College of Psychiatrists; Committee Member: Aberdeen Family Conciliation Service and Grampian Branch, Association for Family Therapy. Recreations: reading; chess; crosswords; literature, history and culture of Scotland and Scottish Highlands. Address: (h.) Figurettes, 31 Westburn Drive, Aberdeen, AB2 5BY; T.-0224 636549.

Chisholm, Duncan Fraser. Managing Director, Duncan Chisholm & Sons Ltd., Inverness, since 1979; Member, Inverness District Council, since 1984; Member, Board of Governors, Eden Court Theatre, Inverness, since 1984; President, Clan Chisholm Society, since 1978; b. 14.4.41, Inverness; m., Mary Rebecca MacRae; 1 s.; 1 d. Educ. Inverness High School. Council Member, Inverness, Loch Ness and Nairn Tourist Board, since 1979; President, Inverness and Highland Chamber of Commerce, 1983-84 (Vice-President, 1982-83); Elder, Church of Scotland; Past President, Inverness Wine Appreciation Society; Assistant Area Scout Commissioner, 1975-78. Recreations: swimming; badminton. Address: (b.) 47-53 Castle Street, Inverness; T.-0463 234599.

Chisholm, Professor Geoffrey Duncan, ChM, FRCS, FRCSEdin. Professor of Surgery, Edinburgh University, since 1977; Director, Nuffield Transplant Unit, Edinburgh, since 1977; Honorary Senior Lecturer, Institute of Urology, London University, since 1972; b. 30.9.31, Hawera, New Zealand; m., Angela Jane; 2 s. Educ. Malvern College; St. Andrews University. Research Fellow, John Hopkins Hospital, Baltimore, 1961-62; Consultant Urological Surgeon, Hammersmith Hospital, London, 1967-77; Honorary Senior Lecturer, Royal Postgraduate Medical School, 1967-77. Chairman, British Prostate Group, 1975-80; Vice President: British Association of Surgical Oncologists, 1980-81, British Association of Urological Surgeons, since 1984; Chairman, European Society of Urological Oncology and Endocrinology, since 1985; Council Member, Royal College of Surgeons of Edinburgh, since 1984; Managing Editor, Urological Research, 1977-81; Editor, British Journal of Urology, since 1977. Publications: Scientific Foundation of Urology (Joint Editor); Clinical Practice in Urology (Series Editor). Recreations: gardening; wine tasting; squash racquets. Address: (h.) 8 Ettrick Road, Edinburgh, EH10 5BJ; T.-031-229 7173.

Chiswick, Derek, MB, ChB, MPhil, MRCPsych. Senior Lecturer in Forensic Psychiatry, Edinburgh University, since 1980; Honorary Consultant Psychiatrist, State Hospital, Carstairs, since 1980; Honorary Consultant Psychiatrist, Lothian Health Board, since 1980; b. 7.1.45, Hampton, Middlesex; m., Ann Williams; 3 d. Educ. Preston Manor County School, Wembley; Liverpool University. Parole Board for Scotland: Member, 1983, Vice-Chairman, 1984; Chairman, Working Group on Suicide Precautions, Glenochil Young Offenders' Institution and Detention Centre, 1984-85. Recreation: relaxing with family. Address: (h.) 6 St. Catherine's Place, Edinburgh, EH9 1NU; T.-031-667 2444.

Christer, Anthony H., BSc, MSc, PhD, FIMA, FOR. Reader in Operational Research, Strathclyde University, since 1974; b. 21.11.40, Wincanton; m., Frieda Lilian; 3 s.; 1 d. Educ. Grove Park Secondary Modern School, London; London University; Strathclyde University. Lecturer in Mathematics, then Lecturer/Senior Lecturer in Operational Research, Strathclyde University. Mathematics and Operational Research Consultant, Royal Navy; Operations Consultant to industry; Chairman, Operational Research Group of Scotland, 1982-85; Member, Operational Research Council, since 1985. Recreations: canoeing; fishing; walking. Address: (b.) Department of Operational Research, Strathclyde University, Glasgow.

Christian, Professor Reginald Frank, MA (Hons) (Oxon). Professor of Russian and Head of Department, St. Andrews University, since 1966; b. 9.8.24, Liverpool; m., Rosalind Iris Napier; 1 s.; 1 d. Educ. Liverpool Institute High School; Queen's College, Oxford. RAF, 1943-46 (aircrew), flying on 231 Sqdn. and 6 Atlantic Ferry Unit (Pilot Officer, 1944); Foreign Office (British Embassy, Moscow), 1949-50; Lecturer and Head of Russian Department, Liverpool University, 1950-55; Senior Lecturer, then Professor of Russian and Head of Department, Birmingham University, 1955-66; Visiting Professor: McGill

University, Montreal, 1961-62, Institute of Foreign Languages, Moscow, 1964-65; Dean, Faculty of Arts, St. Andrews University, 1975-78; Member, University Court, 1971-73, 1981-85. President, British Universities Association of Slavists, 1967-70; Member, International Committee of Slavists, 1970-75; Honorary Vice-President, Association of Teachers of Russian; Member, UGC Arts Sub-Committee on Russian studies. Publications: Russian Syntax (with F.M. Borras), 1959 and 1971; Korolenko's Siberia, 1954; Tolstoy's War and Peace: A Study, 1962; Russian Prose Composition (with F.M. Borras), 1964 and 1974; Tolstoy: A Critical Introduction, 1969; Tolstoy's Letters, edited, translated and annotated, 1978. Recreations: violin; fell-walking; Russian philately; formerly association football. Address: (h.) The Roundel, St. Andrews, Fife; T.-St. Andrews 73322.

Christie, Rev. Andrew Cormack, LTh. Minister, Ferryhill North Church, Aberdeen, since 1984; b. 25.5.35, Stonehaven; m., Norma Rosemary Scott Watson; 2 s.; 1 d. Educ. Mackie Academy, Stonehaven; Banchory Academy; Aberdeen College of Commerce; Christ's College, Aberdeen; King's College, Aberdeen. Grocer, Northern Co-operative Society Ltd., 18 years; Assistant Minister, St. George's, Tillydrone; Minister, Clatt linked with Rhynie, 1975-84. Former Community Councillor, Rhynie. Recreations: supporting Aberdeen FC; golf. Address: 50 Sycamore Place, Aberdeen, AB1 2SZ; T.-0224 580865.

Christie, Ian Falconer, BSc, PhD, FICE, FIPHE, MIWES, CEng. Senior Lecturer in Civil Engineering, Edinburgh University, since 1965; b. 9.5.24, Glasgow; m., Joyce Forsyth; 1 s.; 2 d. Educ. Hillhead High School; Glasgow University. Hydroballistics research work, Ministry of Aircraft Production, 1944-46; Civil Engineering Assistant, Babtie, Shaw and Morton, 1947-56; Senior Scientific Officer, Road Research Laboratory, DSIR, 1956-57; Lecturer in Civil Engineering, Edinburgh University, 1957-65. Chairman, Edinburgh and East of Scotland Association, Institution of Civil Engineers, 1983-84. Recreations: golf; bridge; art appreciation. Address: (b.) Department of Civil Engineering and Building Science, Edinburgh University, Mayfield Road, Edinburgh, EH9 3JL; T.-031-667 1081, Ext. 3381.

Christie, Very Rev. James, SJ, MA, MSc, CQSW, MInstGA. Director, The Garnethill Centre, Glasgow, since 1980; Superior, The Jesuit Community, Craighead Retreat House, since 1983; b. 3.7.40, Bellshill, Lanarkshire. Educ. Our Lady's High School, Motherwell; St. Aloysius College, Glasgow; Campion Hall, Oxford; Columbia University; Southampton University; London School of Economics. Ordained Priest, Society of Jesus, 1970; parish work and training in Paris, 1970-71; on staff of Fors Vitae Institute, Johannesburg, 1971-72; School Counsellor, Wimbledon College, 1973-75; Depute Director, The Dympna Centre, London, 1977-80. Recreation: hill-walking. Address: Craighead Retreat House, Bothwell, Glasgow, G71 8AU; T.-Hamilton 285300.

Christie, John Belford Wilson, CBE, BA (Cantab), LLB, HonLLD (Dundee, 1977); Advocate; b. 4.5.14, Allanton, Lanarkshire; m., Christine Isobel Syme Arnott; 4 d. Educ. Merchiston Castle School; Cambridge University; Edinburgh University. Admitted to Faculty of Advocates, 1939; on active service, RNVR, 1939-46; Sheriff-Substitute, Western Division, Dumfries and Galloway, 1948-55; Sheriff of Tayside, Central and Fife, at Dundee, 1955-83. Member, Parole Board for Scotland, 1967-73; Member: Queen's College Council, St. Andrews University, 1960-67, University Court, Dundee University, 1967-75; Honorary Lecturer, Department of Private Law, Dundee University. Recreation: golf. Address: (h.) Annsmuir Farm, Ladybank, Fife; T.-0337 30480.

Christie, Robert Alexander, LLB. Chief Executive and Director of Administration, Berwickshire District Council, since 1977; b. 24.1.45, Preston. Educ. Balshaw's Grammar School, Leyland, Lancashire; St. Andrews University. Dumfries County Council: Principal Legal Assistant, 1969-71, Depute County Clerk, 1971-73; Depute County Clerk, Argyll County Council, 1973-75; Depute Director of Administration, Argyll and Bute District Council, 1975-76; Chief Executive, Lochaber District Council, 1976-77. Recreations: cooking; reading; listening to music. Address: (b.) District Council Offices, 8 Newtown Street, Duns, Berwickshire, TD11 3DT; T.-0361 82600.

Christie, Rev. Robert Smillie, MA, BD, ThM. Minister, West High Church, Kilmarnock, since 1973; b. 24.5.35, Glasgow; m., Marilyn Joan Brinsfield; 1 s.; 3 d. Educ. King's Park School, Glasgow; Glasgow University; Edinburgh University; Bonn University; Princeton University. Assistant Minister, St. George's West, Edinburgh, 1963-65; Minister, Liberton-Northfield, Edinbrugh, 1966-73. Executive Member, Ayrshire Council on Alcoholism; Consultant, Ayrshire Cancer Support Group. Recreations: tennis; reading; furniture restoring. Address: 25 Glasgow Road, Kilmarnock, Ayrshire; T.-0563 25302.

Christie, Rev. Ronald Campbell, MA, BD, MTh. Minister, Wick (Martyrs) and Keiss Free Church of Scotland, since 1978; b. 2.5.43, Kilwinning, Ayrshire; m., Morag MacRae; 1 d. Educ. Ardrossan Academy; Edinburgh University; Free Church of Scotland College, Edinburgh; Westminster Seminary, Philadelphia. Former missionary, Free Church of Scotland in Peru; Editor, The Instructor, since 1984; Clerk, Free Church Training of the Ministry Committee, since 1983. Address: Free Church Manse, South Road, Wick, KW1 4NH; T.-0955 2994.

Christie, Terry, BSc (Hons). Head Teacher, Ainslie Park High School, since 1982; Manager, Meadowbank Thistle FC, since 1980; b. 16.12.42, Edinburgh; m., Margaret; 2 s. Educ. Holy Cross Academy, Edinburgh; Edinburgh University. Depute Rector, Trinity Academy, 1978-82. Played football for Dundee, Raith Rovers and Stirling Albion, 1960-74; Coach, Meadowbank Thistle, 1978-80. Recreations: golf; bridge; snooker; reading. Address: (h.) 17/1 Fingzies Place, Edinburgh, EH6 8AW; T.-031-554 6671.

Christie, Sheriff William James, LLB. Sheriff of Tayside, Central and Fife, at Kirkcaldy, since 1979; b. 1.11.32; m.; 3 s. Educ. Holy Cross Academy, Edinburgh; Edinburgh University. Private practice, 1956-79; Member, Council, Law Society of Scotland, 1975-79.

Christie, William W., DSc, PhD. Head, Department of Biological Chemistry, Hannah Research Institute, Ayr, since 1980; b. 18.8.39, Kirkcaldy; m., Norma; 2 s. Educ. Buckhaven High School; St. Andrews University. Joined Hannah Research Institute, 1967. Publications: Lipid Analysis; Lipid Metabolism in Ruminant Animals. Recreation: gardening. Address: (b.) Hannah Research Institute, Ayr; T.-0292 76013.

Christman, Rev. William James, BA, BD. Minister, Ayr St. Columba, since 1981; b. 6.9.38, Joplin, Missouri; m., Georgina Boyle; 2 d. Educ. Joplin High School, Missouri; Grinnell College, Iowa; Edinburgh University; Harvard University. Assistant Lecturer in Ecclesiastical History, Edinburgh University, 1963-65; Minister: Richmond Craigmillar Parish Church, Edinburgh, 1965-69, Lochwood Parish Church, Easterhouse, Glasgow, 1970-76, Lansdowne Parish Church, Glasgow, 1977-81. Honorary President, Scottish Churches' Football Association, since 1980. Publication: The Christman File, 1978. Recreation: music. Address: 2 Hazelwood Road, Ayr, KA7 2PY; T.-Ayr 283125.

Clapham, Christopher R.J., MA, DPhil. Senior Lecturer in Mathematics, Aberdeen University, since 1974; b. 3.10.38, Beckenham, Kent; m., E. Ruth; 2 s.; 2 d. Educ. Dulwich College; Magdalen College, Oxford. Lecturer in Mathematics: Bristol University, 1962-65, Ahmadu Bello University, Zaria, Nigeria, 1965-68, Aberdeen University, 1968-74; Senior Lecturer in Mathematics, National University of Lesotho, 1975-77. Publications: Introduction to Abstract Algebra, 1969; Introduction to Mathematical Analysis, 1973. Recreations: music; choral conductor; church organist. Address: (b.) Department of Mathematics, Aberdeen University, Aberdeen; T.-Aberdeen 40241.

Clark, Alastair Trevor, CBE (1976), LVO (1974), MA (Oxon). Barrister; Member, Secretary of State's Museums Advisory Board, since 1983; Trustee, National Museums of Scotland, since 1985; Member, Lothian Health Board, since 1981; Member, City of Edinburgh District Council, since 1980; b. 10.6.23, Glasgow; m., Hilary Agnes Mackenzie Anderson. Educ. Giffnock Academy; Glasgow Academy; Edinburgh Academy; Magdalen College, Oxford; Middle Temple (Inns of Court). War service, Queen's Own Cameron Highlanders and Royal West African Frontier Force, Nigeria, India and Burma, 1942-46; Administrative Branch, HM Colonial Service (later HMOCS): Nigeria, 1949-59 (Secretary to Cabinet, Northern Region; Senior District Officer); Hong Kong, 1960-72 (Director of Social Welfare; Deputy and Acting Director of Urban Services; Acting Chairman Urban Council; Clerk of Councils; Principal Assistant Colonial Secretary, etc.), Western Pacific, 1972-77 (Chief Secretary Western Pacific High Commission, Deputy and Acting Governor, Solomon Islands); retired, 1977; Vice-President, Hong Kong Scout Association, 1965-72; Joint Founder, HK Outward Bound School; Honorary Secretary, St. John's Cathedral Council, 1963-72; Country Leader Fellowship to USA, 1972; Leverhulme Trust Grant, 1979-81; Member, Scottish Museums Council, since 1980 (Chairman, 1981-84); Vice-Chairman, Committee of Area Museum Councils, 1983-84; Member: Museums Association Council, since 1983, Edinburgh International Festival Council, since 1980; a Governor, Edinburgh Filmhouse, 1980-84; a Director, Royal Lyceum Theatre Company, 1982-84; Member, Court of Directors, Edinburgh Academy, 1979-84. Recreations: music; books; theatre; netsuke; cartophily. Address: (h.) 11 Ramsay Garden, Edinburgh, EH1 2NA; T.-031-225 8070.

Clark, Alistair Campbell, MA, LLB. Partner, Blackadder, Reid, Johnston (formerly Reid, Johnston, Bell & Henderson), Solicitors, Dundee, since 1961; Council Member, Law Society of Scotland, since 1982; b. 4.3.33, Dundee; m., Evelyn M. Clark; 3 s. Educ. Grove Academy, Broughty Ferry; St. Andrews University. Dean, Faculty of Procurators and Solicitors in Dundee, 1979-81; Secretary, Royal Dundee Institution for the Blind, since 1967; Past Chairman, Broughty Ferry Round Table; Past President, Claverhouse Rotary Club, Dundee. Recreations: family; travel; erratic golf. Address: (b.) 34 Reform Street, Dundee; T.-0382 29222.

Clark, David, BA, MA. Director, Scottish Marriage Guidance Council, since 1984; b. 17.7.53, Thornaby-on-Tees; m., Diane; 2 s. Educ. Acklam Hall School, Middlesbrough; Newcastle-upon-Tyne University. Research Assistant, Sheffield City Polytechnic, 1977-79; Lecturer, Newcastle-upon-Tyne University, 1979-80; Research Sociologist, MRC Medical Sociology Unit, Aberdeen, 1980-84. Publications: Between Pulpit and Pew: folk religion in a North Yorkshire fishing village, 1982; Making A Go of It: a study of stepfamilies in Sheffield (with Jacqueline Burgoyne), 1984. Recreations: rock, jazz and folk music; the red wines of Bordeaux; country life and landscape. Address: (b.) 26 Frederick Street, Edinburgh; T.-031-225 5006.

Clark, David Findlay, MA, PhD, FBPsS. Director, Area Clinical Psychology Services, Grampian Health Board, since 1966; Clinical Senior Lecturer, Department of Mental Health, Aberdeen University, since 1966; b. 30.5.30, Aberdeen; m., Janet Ann Stephen; 2 d. Educ. Banff Academy; Aberdeen University. Flying Officer, RAF, 1951-53; Psychologist, Leicester Industrial Rehabilitation Unit, 1953-56; Senior, then Principal Clinical Psychologist, Leicester Area Clinical Psychology Service, and part-time Lecturer, Leicester University and Technical College, 1956-66; WHO short-term Consultant, Sri Lanka, 1977; various lecturing commitments in Canada and USA, since 1968. Honorary Sheriff, Grampian and Highlands; Governor, Aberdeen College of Education; Member, Grampian Children's Panel, 1970-85; Past Chairman, Clinical Division, British Psychological Society.

Publication: Help, Hospitals and the Handicapped, 1984. Recreations: photography; squash; sailing; chess; guitar playing; painting and drawing. Address: (h.) Glendeveron, 8 Deveron Terrace, Banff, AB4 1BB; T.-026 12 2624.

Clark, Frederick Stanley, CBE (1985), TD, DL. Controller for Scotland, Department of Health and Social Security, since 1982; b. 17.11.26, Dumfries; m., Josephine Kathleen; 1 s. Educ. Carlisle Grammar School. Entered Civil Service, 1942; Ministry of National Insurance, 1948; Private Secretary to Parliamentary Under Secretary, DHSS, 1968; Principal, 1969; seconded Hong Kong Government as Assistant Director General, Social Welfare Department, then Deputy Director, 1973-76; Assistant Secretary, DHSS, 1980; Controller, Northern Region. TA, 1948-69 (Commanding 5 South Staffords, 1966, Commanding 5/6 Staffords, 1968, Colonel TAVR, 1969); Deputy Lieutenant, Staffordshire, 1969. Recreations: travel; antiques. Address: (h.) 2 Clayhills Park, Balerno, Midlothian, EH14 7BH; T.-031-449 6171.

Clark, George Logan, MB, ChB, FRCSEdin, FRCSGlas; b. 19.7.19, Brodick, Isle of Arran; m., Bethia Smith Howat; 1 s.; 2 d. Educ. Kelvinside Academy, Glasgow; Glasgow University. House Officer, Stirling Royal Infirmary, 1942-43; RAMC, 1943-46; postgraduate studies, Glasgow, 1946-48; Senior Registrar, Orthopaedics, Chester Royal Infirmary, Glasgow Royal Infirmary, 1952; Bridge of Earn: Consultant Orthopaedic Surgeon, 1965-75, Consultant in charge, Orthopaedic Unit, 1975-84. Fellow, British Orthopaedic Association; High Constable of Perth; Captain, Blairgowrie Golf Club; Scottish curling coach. Recreations: golf; curling. Address: (h.) 4 Charlotte Place, Perth, PH1 5LS; T.-Perth 35945.

Clark, Ian Robertson, CBE, FCCA, IPFA, FRVA. Joint Managing Director, Britoil plc, 1982-85; Member, Scottish Economic Council, since 1978; Member, Glasgow University Court, since 1980; b. 18.1.39; m.; 1 s.; 1 d. Educ. Dalziel High School, Motherwell. Former Chief Executive, Shetland Islands Council; Member, BNOC, 1976-82. Hon. LLD, Glasgow, 1979.

Clark, Rev. John, FPhS. Minister, St. Blane's, Dunblane, since 1980; b. 28.6.23, Kilmarnock; m., Mary Cameron Graham; 2 d. Educ. Kilmarnock Academy; Glasgow University; Trinity College, Glasgow. RAC, 1942-46; Assistant Minister, Riccarton Parish Church, Kilmarnock, 1948-49; Minister, St. Serf's Church, Dysart, 1949-55; first Minister, Drumry: St. Mary's Parish Church, Drumchapel, Glasgow, 1955-60; Minister, Kennoway Parish Church, 1960-80; Moderator, Kirkcaldy Presbytery, 1966-67; Moderator, Stirling Presbytery, 1984-85. Publication: New Ways to Worship (Contributor), 1980. Recreations: driving; swimming; painting; crosswords; listening to music. Address: (h.) 49 Roman Way, Dunblane, FK15 9DJ; T.-0786 822268.

Clark, Kenneth James, JP, MA, LLB. Chief Executive, Borders Regional Council, since 1974; b. 30.4.33, Perth; m., Marion; 3 s. Educ. Dundee High School; St. Andrews University.

National Service, Queen's Own Cameron Highlanders, 1955-57; Legal and Administrative Assistant, Roxburgh County Council, 1962-63; Banff County Council: Legal and Administrative Assistant, 1963-64, Assistant County Clerk, 1964-65, Deputy County Clerk, 1965-66; Deputy County Clerk, Berwick County Council, 1966-71; County Clerk, Ross and Cromarty County Council, 1971-74. Member, Working Group for Scotland on Handling of Complaints against the Police, 1974; Member, Committee of Inquiry into Local Government in Scotland (The Stodart Committee), 1981. Address: (b.) Regional Headquarters, Newton St. Boswells, Melrose, TD6 0SA; T.-0835 23301.

Clark, Leslie, MA, BSc, MEd. HM Chief Inspector of Schools, since 1980; b. 24.6.29, Newcastle-upon-Tyne; m., Anne Mcdonald; 2 d. Educ. Rutherford College for Boys, Newcastle; Kings College, Durham University. Teacher, Bo'ness Academy, 1951-55; Principal Teacher, Kelso High School, 1955-61; Lecturer, Jordanhill College of Education, 1961-65; HM Inspector of Schools, 1965-80. Recreations: walking; swimming; Spanish language. Address: (b.) HM Inspectors of Schools' Office, Empire House, 131 West Nile Street, Glasgow, G1 2RX.

Clark, Robert John Whitten. Head, Home Defence and Emergency Services Co-ordination Division, Scottish Home and Health Department, since 1979; b. 29.9.32, Edinburgh; m., Christine Margaret Reid; 1 s.; 1 d. Educ. George Heriot's School, Edinburgh. Scottish Education Department: various appointments, 1949-69, including Private Secretary to Secretary of Department, 1960-61, Head, Teacher Training Branch, 1967-69, Head, Schools Branch, 1969-73, Head, Children's Hearings Branch, Social Work Services Group, 1973-75, Head, Children's Division, Social Work Services Group, 1975-76, Head, List D (Approved) Schools Division, Social Work Services Group, 1976-79. Former Captain and Past President, Edinburgh and District Civil Service Golfing Society; Captain, Scottish Education Department Golf Club, 1984-85; former Vice-Captain, Scottish Civil Service Golfing Society. Recreations: travel; golf; reading; gardening. Address: (h.) 39 Gordon Road, Edinburgh, EH12 6LZ; T.-031-334 4312.

Clarke, Peter, CBE, BSc, PhD, LLD, CChem, FRSC. Chairman, Scottish Vocational Education Council, since 1985; Chairman, Aberdeen Enterprise Trust Ltd., since 1984; Chairman, Council for National Academic Awards Committee for Scotland, since 1982; Member, Council for Professions Supplementary to Medicine, 1977-85; b. 18.3.22, Mansfield; m., Ethel; 2 s. Educ. Queen Elizabeth's Grammar School, Mansfield; University College, Nottingham. Principal, Robert Gordon's Institute of Technology, Aberdeen, 1970-85. President, Association of Principals of Colleges, 1980-81; Member, Science and Engineering Research Council, 1978-82; President, Aberdeen Welsh Society, 1979-80; President, Aberdeen Business and Professional Club, 1976-77. Recreations: gardening; jogging; swimming. Address: (h.) Tulloch Lodge, 511 North Deeside Road, Cults, Aberdeen, AB1 9ES; T.-0224 867136.

Clarke, Thomas, CBE, MP, JP. MP (Labour), Monklands West, since 1983; b. 10.1.41, Coatbridge. Educ. Columba High School, Coatbridge. Former Assistant Director, Scottish Council for Educational Technology; Provost of Monklands, 1975-82; Past President, Convention of Scottish Local Authorities; MP, Coatbridge and Airdrie, 1982-83. Recreations: films; walking; reading. Address: (h.) 12 Lugar Street, Coatbridge; T.-0236 22550.

Clarkson, Euan Neilson Kerr, MA, PhD, DSc, FRSE. Reader in Geology, Edinburgh University, since 1981; b. 9.5.37, Newcastle-upon-Tyne; m., Cynthia Margaret Cowie; 4 s. Educ. Shrewsbury School; Emmanuel College, Cambridge. Department of Geology, Edinburgh University: Assistant Lecturer, 1963-65, Lecturer, 1965-78, Senior Lecturer, 1978-81; Associate Dean, Science Faculty, 1978-81. Publication: Invertebrate Palaeontology and Evolution, 1979. Recreations: hill-walking; classical music; reading; gardening. Address: (h.) 4 Cluny Place, Edinburgh, EH10 4RL; T.-031-447 2248.

Clayson, Christopher William, CBE (1974), MB, ChB, DPH, MD, FRCPEdin, FRCP, Hon. FACP, Hon. FRACP, Hon. FRCPGlas, Hon. FRCGP. Chairman, Scottish Licensing Law Committee, 1971-73; President, Royal College of Physicians of Edinburgh, 1966-70; b. 11.9.03; m. Educ. George Heriot's School; Edinburgh University. Chairman, Scottish Council for Postgraduate Medical Education, 1970-74.

Clayton, Ruth M. Reader, Department of Genetics, Edinburgh University; b. London; 3 s.; 1 d. Educ. North London Collegiate School; Dr. Williams' School, Dolgelley, Merioneth; Somerville College, Oxford. Edinburgh University: Assistant Lecturer, Lecturer, Senior Lecturer; Visiting Professor, Japan and Canada; Councillor, International Society for Eye Research, since 1984; Chairperson, EURAGE Cataract Group, 1980-82. Publications: 160 scientific publications and others in bio-ethics and related problems. Recreations: enjoying family and friends; reading; art/crafts. Address: (b.) Department of Genetics, Edinburgh University, West Mains Road, Edinburgh, 9; T.-031-667 1081, Ext. 3543.

Clements, John Barklie, BSc, PhD. Reader in Virology, Glasgow University, since 1984; b. 14.3.46, Belfast. Educ. Belfast Royal Academy; Queen's University, Belfast. Research Fellow, California Institute of Technology, 1971-73; joined Institute of Virology, Glasgow University, 1973; Cancer Research Campaign Travelling Fellow, Department of Biochemistry and Molecular Biology, Harvard University, 1983; Council Member, Society for General Microbiology, 1984. Recreations: walking; golf; music. Address: (b.) Department of Virology, Institute of Virology, Glasgow University, Glasgow; T.-041-339 8855.

Clemson, Gareth, BMus (Auckland), BMus (Edinburgh). Teacher of violin and viola, since 1975; Composer, since 1956; b. 1.10.33, Thames, New Zealand; m., Thora Clyne; 2 s.; 1 d. Educ. St. Peter's School, New Zealand; King's College, New Zealand; Auckland University; Edinburgh University. Music teaching, New Zealand, Edinburgh and West Lothian, 1960-65; string Teacher, West Lothian, since 1975; lessons in composition from Thomas Wilson, 1963-65; chamber works including Nexus I and II, Waters of Separation, The Singing Cat, Invocation; broadcasts, New Zealand and Scotland; Founder, Chameleon Ensemble. Michael Joseph Savage Award, New Zealand, 1954-56. Recreations: drawing and painting; photography; philately; cats. Address: (h.) Tillywhally Cottage, Milnathort, Kinross-shire, KY13 7RN; T.-Kinross 64297.

Clerk of Penicuik, Sir John Dutton, 10th Bt, CBE (1966), VRD, FRSE, JP. Lord Lieutenant of Midlothian, since 1972; b. 30.1.17; m.; 2 s.; 2 d. Educ. Stowe. Brigadier, Queen's Bodyguard for Scotland (Royal Company of Archers). Address: (h.) Penicuik House, Penicuik, Midlothian.

Clifford, John Grant, DA, MA, ARSA. Painter, since 1970; Lecturer, Fine Art School, Duncan of Jordanstone College of Art, Dundee, since 1970; b. 14.4.44, Perth; m., Kirsty Kirkwood; 3 s.; 3 d. Educ. Perth High School; Duncan of Jordanstone College of Art, Dundee; Royal College of Art, London. Taught part-time, Dundee Art College, 1970-76, full-time since 1976; exhibited in most major Scottish exhibitions; twice winner, British Institute Award, Royal Academy of Arts; winner, Guthrie Medal for painting, RSA. Recreations: walking; music; reading; conversation. Address: (h.) Woodcliff House, by Newburgh, Cupar, Fife.

Clifford, Timothy Peter Plint, BA, AMA. Director, National Galleries of Scotland, since 1984; b. 26.1.46, England; m., Jane Olivia Paterson; 1 d. Educ. Sherborne; Perugia University; Courtauld Institute, London University. Manchester City Art Galleries: Assistant Keeper, Department of Paintings, 1968-72, Acting Keeper, 1972; Assistant Keeper (First Class): Department of Ceramics, Victoria and Albert Museum, London, 1972-76, Department of Prints and Drawings, British Museum, London, 1976-78; Director, Manchester City Art Galleries, 1978-84. Chairman, International Committee for Museums of Fine Art, ICOM, since 1980; Member, Museums and Galleries Commission, since 1983; Member, Executive Committee, Scottish Museums Council; Vice President, Turner Society, 1984; FRSA. Recreations: shooting; bird-watching; collecting butterflies and moths. Address: (h.) Society House, The Hopetoun Estate, South Queensferry, West Lothian.

Clive, Eric McCredie, MA, LLB, LLM, SJD. Full-time Member, Scottish Law Commission, since 1981; b. 24.7.38, Stranraer; m., Kay McLeman; 2 s.; 3 d. Educ. Stranraer Academy; Stranraer High School; Edinburgh University. Department of Scots Law, Edinburgh University: Lecturer, 1962-69, Senior Lecturer, 1969-75, Reader, 1975-77, Professor, 1977-81. Publications: The Law of Husband and Wife in Scotland, 2nd edition, 1982; Scots Law for Journalists (Co-author), 4th edition, 1984. Recreations: gardening; bee-keeping; hill-walking; skiing; chess. Address: (h.) 14 York Road, Edinburgh, EH5 3EH; T.-031-552 2875.

Cluness, Alexander Jamieson, LLB. Solicitor; Chief Executive, Shetland Fish Processors Association, since 1984; Member, Shetland Islands Council, since 1973 (Chairman, Leisure and Recreation Commitee); b. 1.5.41, Lerwick; m., Elizabeth; 1 s.; 1 d. Educ. Anderson Educational Institute; Aberdeen University. Procurator Fiscal, 1973-75; Solicitor, Shetland Islands Council, 1975-77; Solicitor in private practice, since 1977. Secretary, then Chairman, Shetland Council of Social Service. Recreations: golf; reading. Address: (h.) 5 Twageos Road, Lerwick, Shetland; T.-Lerwick 5612.

Clunie, Henry, DipTech, JP. Honorary Sheriff, since 1967; b. 30.6.07, Leith; m., Harriot Shearer Wilson; 1 s.; 1 d. Educ. Trinity Academy, Leith; Moray House College of Education. Deputy Rector, Dornoch Academy, 1968-72; Town Councillor, Royal Burgh of Dornoch, 1958-74 (Provost, 1965-74); created Freeman of the Burgh, 1973; appointed Commissioner of Income Tax; Member, Sutherland District Council, 1974-78. Recreations: music; amateur drama. Address: (h.) 29 Macdonald Road, Dornoch, Sutherland; T.-0862 810201.

Clunies-Ross, Professor Anthony Ian, BA (Melbourne), MA (Cantab). Professor in Economics, Strathclyde University, since 1978; b. 9.3.32, Sydney, New South Wales; m., Morag McVey; 2 s.; 2 d. Educ. Knox Grammar School, Sydney; Scotch College, Melbourne; Melbourne University; Pembroke College, Cambridge. Tutor in History, Melbourne University, 1958-59; Lecturer, then Senior Lecturer in Economics, Monash University, 1961-67; Senior Lecturer, then Professor in Economics, University of Papua New Guinea, 1967-74; Temporary Lecturer, then Senior Lecturer in Economics, Strathclyde University, 1975-78. Chairman, Australian Student Christian Movement, 1963-66; Member, St. Andrews Diocesan Synod, Scottish Episcopal Church, since 1984. Publications: One Per Cent: The Case for Greater Australian Foreign Aid, 1963 (Co-author); Australia and Nuclear Weapons (Co-author), 1966; Alternative Strategies for Papua New Guinea, (Co-author), 1973; The Taxation of Mineral Rent (Co-author), 1983; Migrants from Fifty Villages, 1984. Recreations: swimming; gardening. Address: (h.) Railway Cottage, Kinbuck, Dunblane, Perthshire, FK15 ONL; T.-Dunblane 822684.

Clyde, Hon. Lord, (James John Clyde), QC (Scot), BA, LLB. Senator of the College of Justice, since 1985; b. 29.1.32; m.; 2 s. Educ. Edinburgh Academy; Corpus Christi College, Oxford; Edinburgh University. Called to Scottish Bar, 1959; Advocate-Depute, 1973-74; Chancellor to Bishop of Argyll and the Isles, since 1972; Member, Scottish Valuation Advisory Council, since 1972; Chairman, Medical Appeal Tribunal, since 1974.

Clydesmuir, Baron, (Ronald John Bilsland Colville), KT (1972), CB (1965), MBE (1944), TD; Lord Lieutenant, Lanarkshire, since 1963; Lieutenant, Queen's Bodyguard for Scotland (Royal Company of Archers); President, Scottish Council (Development and Industry), since 1978; b. 21.5.17; m.; 2 s.; 2 d. Educ. Charterhouse;

Trinity College, Cambridge. The Cameronians (Scottish Rifles), 1939-45; commanded 6/7th Bn., The Cameronians, TA, 1953-56; Director, Colvilles Ltd., 1958-70; Governor, British Linen Bank, 1966-71; Governor, Bank of Scotland, 1972-81; Director, Scottish Provident Institution, since 1954; Director, Barclays Bank, 1972-82; Chairman, North Sea Assets Ltd., since 1972; Chairman, Executive Committee, Scottish Council (Development and Industry), 1966-78; President, Scottish Council of Physical Recreation, 1964-72; Hon. LLD, Strathclyde, 1968; Hon. DSc, Heriot-Watt, 1971. Address: (h.) Langlees House, Biggar, Lanarkshire.

Clyne, Rev. Douglas Roy, BD. Minister, Old Parish Church, Fraserburgh, since 1973; b. 9.11.41, Inverness; m., Annette Taylor; 1 s. Educ. Inverness High School; Aberdeen University. Accountancy (Inverness County Council and Highland Printers Ltd.), 1956-68; studied for the ministry, 1968-72; Assistant Minister, Mastrick Parish Church, Aberdeen, 1972-73. Address: Old Parish Church Manse, 97 Saltoun Place, Fraserburgh, AB4 5RY; T.-0346 28536.

Coates, Leon, MA (Cantab), LRAM, ARCO. Lecturer in Music, Edinburgh University, since 1965; b. 15.6.37, Wolverhampton; m., Heather Patricia Johnston. Educ. Derby School; St. John's College, Cambridge. Composer, pianist, organist, St. Andrew's and St. George's Church, Edinburgh, since 1981; Conductor: Edinburgh Chamber Orchestra, 1965-75, Edinburgh Symphony Orchestra, 1973-85; Harpsichordist, Scottish Baroque Ensemble, 1970-77; broadcasts as pianist and harpsichordist; compositions broadcast on Radio 3, Radio 4 Scotland and Radio Eireann. Recreation: hill-walking. Address: (h.) 31 Scotland Street, Edinburgh, EH3; T.-031-556 2240.

Coats, Sir William David, KB, HonLLD (Strathclyde), 1977. Chairman, Coats Patons PLC, since 1981; Deputy Chairman, Clydesdale Bank PLC, since 1985; b. 25.7.24, Glasgow; m., The Hon. Elizabeth L.G. MacAndrew; 2 s.; 1 d. Educ. Eton College. Joined J. & P. Coats Ltd., 1948, as management trainee; held various appointments and became a Director, 1957; appointed Director, Coats Patons PLC, on its formation, 1960; Deputy Chairman, 1979. Chairman, Glasgow Coordinating Committee, Cancer Research Campaign. Recreations: golf; shooting. Address: (b.) 155 St. Vincent Street, Glasgow, G2 5PA; T.-041-221 8711.

Cochran, Francis Gordon, BA (Oxon), LLB. Solicitor; Partner, Cochran & Macpherson, then Adam, Cochran & Co., since 1963; b. 7.4.34, Aberdeen; m., Ann Jill Reynolds; 3 s.; 1 d. Educ. Loretto; Trinity College, Oxford; Aberdeen University. President, Aberdeenshire Cricket Club; Vice President, Scottish Cricket Union. Recreations: cricket; squash. Address: 290 North Deeside Road, Aberdeen; T.-Aberdeen 588913.

Cochran, Hugh Douglas, BA (Oxon), LLB. Advocate in Aberdeen, since 1958; b. 26.4.32, Aberdeen; m., Sarah Beverly Sissons; 4 s.; 2 d.

Educ. Loretto; Trinity College, Oxford; Edinburgh University. Partner: Cochran & Macpherson, 1958-80, Adam, Cochran & Co., since 1980. Secretary: Blairmore School Educational Trust Ltd., since 1959, Aberdeen Association for the Prevention of Cruelty to Animals, since 1972; Chairman, Castlehill Housing Association Ltd., since 1981; Member, Grampian Health Board, since 1983; Registrar, Diocese of Aberdeen and Orkney, since 1984. Recreations: sailing; collecting stamps. Address: 6 Bon Accord Square, Aberdeen, AB9 1XU; T.-Aberdeen 588913.

Cochran, Matt. Director (Scotland), Advisory, Conciliation and Arbitration Service, since 1981; b. 8.3.29, Glasgow; m., Mary Kathleen; 2 s. Department of Employment, Glasgow, Edinburgh, London; Foreign and Commonwealth Office, USA, Mexico, Central America; Manpower Services Commission, Edinburgh; ACAS, Glasgow. Address: (b.) Advisory, Conciliation and Arbitration Service, 123/157 Bothwell Street, Glasgow; T.-041-204 2677.

Cochran, William, MB, ChB, FRCSEdin, FRCSGlas. Consultant Paediatric and Neonatal Surgeon and Consultant in charge Accident and Emergency Department, Royal Hospital for Sick Children, Glasgow, since 1977; Honorary Clinical Lecturer, Glasgow University, since 1978; b. 4.5.27, Sandhead, Wigtownshire; m., Pamela White; 2 s.; 1 d. Educ. Allan Glen's School, Glasgow; Fraserburgh Academy; Aberdeen University. Demonstrator, Department of Anatomy, Aberdeen University; Paediatric Surgical Registrar, Edinburgh Northern Group Hospitals; Senior Paediatric Surgical Registrar, Royal Hospital for Sick Children, Belfast; Consultant Paediatric Surgeon, Belfast Hospitals and Honorary Clinical Lecturer, Queen's University, Belfast. Secretary, Scottish Surgical Paediatric Society; Member, Special Advisory Committee (A/E) to Committee for Higher Surgical Training. Address: (h.) 8 Seafield Avenue, Bearsden, Dunbartonshire, G61 3LB; T.-041-943 0579.

Cochrane, Alexander John Cameron, MA (Oxon). Headmaster, Fettes College, Edinburgh, since 1979; b. 19.7.33, Edinburgh; m., Rosemary Aline Ogg; 1 s.; 2 d. Educ. The Edinburgh Academy; University College, Oxford. Assistant Master, St. Edward's School, Oxford, 1957-66; Warden, Brathay Hall, Ambleside, Cumbria, 1966-70; Assistant Director of Education, City of Edinburgh, 1970-74; Headmaster, Arnold School, Blackpool, 1974-79. Member, Lancashire Education Committee, 1976-79; Member, Outward Bound Trust Council, since 1979; Member, RA Council for Scotland; Member, Scottish Committee, Duke of Edinburgh's Award; Chairman, Outward Bound Loch Eil; Governor, Clifton Hall School, Aiglon College. Recreations: games; mountains; music. Address: The Lodge, Fettes College, Edinburgh,EH4 1QX; T.-031-332 2281.

Cochrane, William Robertson, MA (Hons). Head Teacher, Greenwood Academy, since 1972; b. 2.6.26, Darvel; m., Sheila E. Currie; 3 s.; 1 d. Educ. Galston Higher Grade School; Kilmarnock Academy; Glasgow University. Assistant Teacher of English and History, Dreghorn Junior Secondary School, 1950-53; Assistant Teacher, then Principal Teacher of English, History and Geography, Newmilns Junior Secondary School, 1953-60; Principal Teacher of History: Carrick Academy, 1960-68, Belmont Academy, 1968-70; Depute Rector, Ravenspark Academy, 1970-72. Recreation: golf. Address: (h.) 33 Ellisland Drive, Kilmarnock; T.-Kilmarnock 24652.

Cockburn, Professor Forrester, MD, FRCPGlas, FRCPEdin, DCH. Samson Gemmell Professor of Child Health, Glasgow University, since 1977; b. 13.10.34, Edinburgh; m., Alison Fisher Grieve; 2 s. Educ. Leith Academy; Edinburgh University. Early medical training, Edinburgh Royal Infirmary, Royal Hospital for Sick Children, Edinburgh, and Simpson Memorial Maternity Pavilion, Edinburgh; Research Fellow in Paediatric Metabolic Disease, Boston University; Visiting Professor, San Juan University, Puerto Rico; Nuffield Fellow, Institute for Medical Research, Oxford University; Wellcome Senior Research Fellow, then Senior Lecturer, Department of Child Life and Health, Edinburgh University. Publications: a number of textbooks on neonatal medicine, nutrition and metabolic diseases. Recreation: sailing. Address: (b.) University Department of Child Health, Royal Hospital for Sick Children, Yorkhill, Glasgow, G3 8SJ; T.-041-339 8888.

Cockburn, John Shearer, MB, ChB, ChM, FRCSEdin. Consultant Cardiothoracic Surgeon, Aberdeen Royal Infirmary, since 1978; Clinical Senior Lecturer in Cardiothoracic Surgery, Aberdeen University, since 1978; b. 25.8.42, Turriff; m., Ethel Mary Mitchell Duncan; 1 s.; 1 d. Educ. Gordon Schools, Huntly; Keith Grammar School; Aberdeen University. Pre-registration Resident Medical Officer, then Senior House Officer in Thoracic Surgery, Aberdeen Royal Infirmary, 1966-68; Senior House Officer in General Surgery, Llandough Hospital, Cardiff, 1968-69; Registrar in Surgery, Aberdeen Royal Infirmary, 1969-73, and Research Fellow, Uppsala, Sweden, 1971-72; Registrar in Cardiac Surgery, Glasgow Royal Infirmary, 1973-74; Senior Registrar in Cardiothoracic Surgery, London and Southampton, 1974-77. Recreations: music (clarinet playing); squash; snooker; soccer; rugby. Address: (h.) Castieton House, 15 The Chanonry, Old Aberdeen, AB2 1RQ; T.-Aberdeen 493957.

Cocker, Douglas, DA, ARSA. Sculptor, since 1968; Lecturer in Sculpture, Grays School of Art, Aberdeen, since 1982; b. 23.3.45, Alyth, Perthshire; m., Elizabeth Filshie; 2 s.; 1 d. Educ. Blairgowrie High School; Duncan of Jordanstone College of Art, Dundee. SED Travelling Scholar, Italy and Greece, 1966; RSA Andrew Carnegie Travelling Scholar, 1967; RSA Benno Schotz Award, 1967; Greenshields Foundation (Montreal) Fellowship, 1968-69 (studies in New York and Greece); RSA Latimer Award, 1970; Arts Council of GB Award, 1977; East Midlands Arts Award, 1979; Visiting Artist: Newcastle Polytechnic, Duncan of Jordanstone College of Art, Edinburgh College of Art and Temple University, Philadelphia. Fourteen one-man exhibitions, 1969-84; numerous group and mixed exhibitions, 1970-85; various commissions. Recreations: reading; travel; sport. Address: (h.) Craigveigh, Gordon Crescent, Aboyne, Aberdeenshire; T.-Aboyne 2011.

Coggins, John Richard, MA, PhD. Senior Lecturer in Biochemistry, Glasgow University, since 1978; b. 15.1.44, Bristol; m., Dr. Lesley F. Watson; 1 s. Educ. Bristol Grammar School; Queen's College, Oxford. Post-doctoral Fellow: Biology Department, Brookhaven National Laboratory, New York, 1970-72, Biochemistry Department, Cambridge University, 1972-74; Lecturer, Biochemistry Department, Glasgow University, 1974-78. Chairman, Molecular Enzymology Group, Biochemical Society, 1982-85; Chairman, Biophysics and Biochemistry Committee, SERC, 1985-88. Recreations: sailing; travelling. Address: (b.) Department of Biochemistry, Glasgow University, Glasgow, G12 8QQ; T.-041-339 8855, Ext. 7267.

Cohen, Cyril, FRCPEdin, FRCPGlas. Director, Scottish Hospital Advisory Service; Consultant Physician in Geriatric Medicine, since 1962; Honorary Senior Lecturer, Dundee University, since 1962; b. 2.11.25, Manchester; m., Sarah E. Nixon; 2 s. Educ. Manchester Central High School; Victoria University, Manchester. Embarked on career in geriatric medicine, 1952. Past Member/Chairman, Angus District and Tayside Area Medical Committees; Secretary/Chairman, Tayside Area Hospital Medical Services Committee; Member, Scottish and UK Central Committee, Hospital Medical Services, and Chairman, Geriatric Medicine Subcommittee; Past Chairman, Scottish Branch, British Geriatric Society (former Council Member); Member, Panel on Nutrition of the Elderly, COMA; Chairman, Advisory Committee on the Elderly, Scottish Health Education Group. Honorary Vice-President, Dundee and District Branch, British Diabetic Association; Life Member, Manchester Medical Society; Past President, Montrose Burns Club; Member, Brechin School Council; Secretary, Aberlemno Community Council. Recreations: photography; short walks; being at home. Address: (h.) Mansefield, Aberlemno, Forfar, DD8 3PD; T.-030-783 259.

Cohen, George Cormack, MA, LLB. Advocate; b. 16.12.09, Glasgow; m., Elizabeth Wallace; 1 s.; 1 d. Educ. Kelvinside Academy, Glasgow; Glasgow University. Admitted to Faculty of Advocates, 1935; Sheriff of Caithness at Wick, 1944-51; Sheriff of Ayrshire at Kilmarnock, 1951-55; Sheriff of Lothians and Peebles at Edinburgh, 1955-66. Recreations: gardening; travel. Address: (h.) 37B Lauder Road, Edinburgh, EH9 1UE; T.-031-668 1689.

Cohen, Professor Philip, BSc, PhD, FRS, FRSE. Royal Society Research Professor, Dundee University, since 1984; b. 22.7.45, London; m., Patricia Townsend Wade; 1 s.; 1 d. Educ. Hendon County Grammar School; University College, London. Science Research Council/NATO postdoctoral Fellow, Department of Biochemistry, University of Washington, 1969-71; Dundee University: Lecturer in Biochemistry, 1971-78,

Reader in Biochemistry, 1978-81, Professor of Enzymology, 1981-84. Federation of European Biochemical Societies Anniversary Prize, 1977; Colworth Medal, British Biochemical Society, 1978. Publication: Control of Enzyme Activity, 1976. Recreations: chess; golf; natural history. Address: (h.) Inverbay, Invergowrie, Dundee, DD2 5DG; T.-08267 328.

Coke, Professor Simon, MA (Oxon). Professor of International Business, Edinburgh University, since 1972; b. 27.6.32, Bicester, Oxfordshire; m., Diana Margaret Evison; 1 s.; 2 d. Educ. Ridley College, Ontario; Pembroke College, Oxford. General Manager, Japan, etc., Johnson & Johnson, 1964-68; Marketing Executive, Beecham Overseas, 1968-72; Head, Department of Business Studies, Edinburgh University, 1984; Dean, Scottish Business School, 1981-83; Director, Japan Asset Trust. Address: (b.) Department of Business Studies, Edinburgh University, 50 George Square, Edinburgh, EH8 9JY; T.-031-667 1011.

Cole, Professor Alfred John, BSc, MSc, PhD, FBCS. Professor of Computational Science, St. Andrews University, since 1969; b. 11.4.25, London; m., Christina Brotherson Carnie; 1 s. Educ. Preston Manor County School; University College, London. Lecturer: Heriot-Watt College, Edinburgh, 1952-55, Queen's College, Dundee, 1955-61; Senior Lecturer and Director, Computing Laboratory, Leicester University, 1961-65; Reader and Director, Computing Laboratory, St. Andrews University, 1965-69 (Head, Department of Computational Science). Publication: Macroprocessors, 1976. Recreations: beer and wine-making; concertina playing; East Fife FC supporter. Address: (h.) Inisheer, Barnyards, Kilconquhar, Fife; T.-033 334 378.

Cole-Hamilton, Arthur Richard, BA, CA, FIB(Scot). Director and Chief General Manager, Clydesdale Bank PLC, since 1982; b. 8.5.35, Kilwinning; m., Prudence Ann; 1 s.; 2 d. Educ. Ardrossan Academy; Loretto School; Cambridge University. Partner, Brechin Cole-Hamilton & Co., CA, 1962-67; various appointments, Clydesdale Bank, 1967-82; appointed Chief General Manager, 1982, Director, 1984. Council Member, Institute of Chartered Accountants of Scotland (Chairman, Finance and General Purposes Committee, 1984); Vice-President, Institute of Bankers in Scotland. Recreation: golf. Address: (b.) 30 St. Vincent Place, Glasgow; T.-041-248 7070.

Cole-Hamilton, Professor David John, BSc, PhD, GRSC. Irvine Professor of Chemistry, St. Andrews University, since 1985; b. 22.5.48, Bovey Tracey; m., Elizabeth Ann Brown; 1 s.; 1 d. Educ. Haileybury and ISC; Hertford; Edinburgh University. Research Assistant, Temporary Lecturer, Imperial College, 1974-78; Lecturer, Senior Lecturer, Liverpool University, 1978-85. Sir Edward Frankland Fellow, Royal Society of Chemistry, 1984-85; Corday Morgan Medallist, 1983. Address: (b.) Department of Chemistry, The Purdie Building, St. Andrews, Fife, KY16 9ST; T.-0334 76161.

Coleman, Eric Norman, MD, FRCPEdin, FRCPGlas. Consultant Physician and Physician-in-Charge, Department of Cardiology, Royal

Hospital for Sick Children, Glasgow, since 1961; Honorary Clinical Lecturer in Child Health, Glasgow University, since 1964; b. 22.6.25, Ayr. Educ. Bearsden Academy; Glasgow University. Captain, RAMC, 1949-51; Senior Registrar, Royal Hospital for Sick Children, Glasgow, 1957-58; Lecturer in Child Health, Glasgow University, 1958-61. Honorary Secretary, Scottish Paediatric Society, 1964-80; President, Society of Cardiological Technicians, 1975-78; regional postgraduate Adviser in paediatrics; Vice-Chairman, MRCP (UK) Part 2 Examining Board; Chairman of Examiners for the Diploma in Chld Health, Glasgow; Medical Adviser, Society of Cardiological Technicians. Recreations: music; theology. Address: (b.) Royal Hospital for Sick Children, Glasgow, G3 8JJ; T.-041-339 8888, Ext. 591.

Collee, Professor John Gerald, MD, FRCPath, FRCPEdin. Professor and Head of Department of Bacteriology, Edinburgh University, since 1979; Chief Bacteriologist, Edinburgh Royal Infirmary, since 1979; b. 10.5.29, Bo'ness; m., Isobel McNay Galbraith; 2 s.; 1 d. Educ. Bo'ness Academy; Edinburgh Academy; Edinburgh University. House Physician, 1951-52; Army medical service, 1952-54 (Captain, RAMC); General Practitioner, 1954-55; Lecturer in Bacteriology, Edinburgh, 1955-63; WHO Visiting Professor of Bacteriology, Baroda, India, 1963-64; Edinburgh University: Senior Lecturer and Honorary Consultant Bacteriologist, 1964-70, Reader in Bacteriology, 1970-74, Personal Professor of Bacteriology, 1974-79; Editor and Chairman, Journal of Medical Microbiology. Recreations: woodwork; mechanics; fishing; music; painting. Address: (b.) Department of Bacteriology, University Medical School, Teviot Place, Edinburgh, EH8 9AG; T.-031-667 1011, Ext. 2207.

Collie, George Francis, CBE (Civil), MBE (Military), JP, BL. Honorary Sheriff, Grampian Region, at Aberdeen, since 1974; retired Advocate in Aberdeen and Notary Public; b. 1.4.09, Aberdeen; m., Margery Constance Fullarton; 2 s. Educ. Aberdeen Grammar School; Aberdeen University. Partner, then Senior Partner, James & George Collie, Advocates in Aberdeen; Deputy Chairman, then Chairman, Board of Management for Aberdeen Special Hospitals, 1952-68. Honorary Colonel, 51st Highland Division, RASC (TA) and later Honorary Colonel, 153 Highland Regiment, RCT (V), 1964-72. Recreation: vintage cars. Address: (h.) Morkeu, Cults, Aberdeen, AB1 9PT; T.-0224 867636.

Collie, Ian, MA, MEd, MBIM, FSA Scot. Director of Education, Central Regional Council, since 1975; b. 20.7.33, Grantown-on-Spey; m., Helen; 1 s.; 1 d. Educ. Kingussie Secondary School; Aberdeen University; Glasgow University. Army, 1956-58; teacher, Renfrewshire, 1958-64; lecturer, Glasgow, 1964-66; Junior Assistant Director of Education, then Senior Assistant Director, Stirlingshire, 1966-69; Depute Director, Dunbartonshire, 1969-73; Sole Depute, Stirlingshire, 1973-75. Chairman, Scottish Committee on Open Learning. Publication: Selections from Modern Writings (Editor). Recreations: hill-walking; squash. Address: (b.) Viewforth, Stirling; T.-Stirling 3111, Ext. 503.

Collins, Emeritus Professor Jeffrey Hamilton, BSc, MSc, FEng, FIEE, FInstP, FIERE, FIEEE, FRSE. Emeritus Professor of Electrical Engineering and University Fellow, Edinburgh University, since 1984; Director, Scottish Electronics Technology Group, Glasgow, since 1984; Director, Burr-Brown Ltd., since 1985; Director, Advent Technology plc, Edinburgh, since 1981; b. 22.4.30, Luton; m., Sally Parfitt; 2 s. Educ. Royal Grammar School, Guildford; London University. Lecturer, then Senior Lecturer, Department of Electrical Engineering, Glasgow University, 1957-66; Research Engineer, Stanford University, California, 1966-70; Director of Physical Sciences, Autonetics Division, Rockwell International, California, 1968-70; Director, MESL (later Racal-MESL), 1970-81; Edinburgh University: Research Professor, then Professor of Industrial Electronics, 1970-77, Professor of Electrical Engineering and Head of Department, 1977-84. Deputy Chairman, Electronics Division, Institution of Electrical Engineers; awarded Hewlett-Packard Europhysics Prize, 1979. Recreations: renovating houses; gardening. Address: (h.) Nether Craigour, Broadgait, Gullane, EH31 2DH.

Collins, Kenneth, BSc (Hons), MSc. Member, European Parliament, for East Strathclyde, since 1979; b. 12.8.39; m.; 1 s.; 1 d. Educ. Hamilton Academy; Glasgow University; Strathclyde University. Tutor-Organiser, WEA, 1966-67; Lecturer: Glasgow College of Building, 1967-69, Paisley College of Technology, 1969-79; former East Kilbride Town and District Councillor; Member, Lanark County Council, 1973-75; Member, East Kilbride Development Corporation, 1976-79; Deputy Leader, Labour Group, European Parliament, since 1979.

Collins, Lyndhurst, BA, DipEd, MA, PhD. Senior Lecturer in Geography, Edinburgh University, since 1970; b. 2.5.41, Maesteg, Wales; m., Valerie Anne; 2 s.; 1 d. Educ. Bridgend Grammar School; Hull University; Fitzwilliam College, Cambridge; Toronto University. Consultant, Statistics Canada, 1969-70; Lecturer, Edinburgh University, 1970-83. Publications: Industrial Migration in Ontario, 1972; Locational Dynamics of Manufacturing Activity (Joint Editor), 1975; The Use of Models in the Social Sciences (Editor), 1976; Industrial Decline and Regeneration (Editor), 1982. Recreation: renovations. Address: (h.) Capielaw Cottage, Capielaw, near Rosewell, Midlothian; T.-031-440 2015.

Colquhoun of Luss, Captain Sir Ivar (Iain), 8th Bt, JP, DL; Honorary Sheriff; Chief of the Clan; b. 4.1.16; m.; 1 s.; 1 d.; 1 s. (deceased). Educ. Eton. Address: (h.) Camstraddan, Luss, Dunbartonshire.

Colraine, James, MA (Hons), FSA Scot. Rector, Dumbarton Academy, since 1970; b. 4.12.30, Clydebank; m., Olive McLean; 1 d. Educ. Dumbarton Academy; Glasgow University; Jordanhill College of Education. Army (National Service), 1954-56; Assistant in Classics, Jordanhill College School, 1957-61; Principal Teacher of Classics: Broxburn Academy, 1961-64, Cumbernauld High School, 1964-68; Depute Rector,

Clydebank High School, 1968-70. Elder, New Kilpatrick Parish Church, Bearsden. Recreations: golf; bowls; walking; music; reading; snooker. Address: (b.) Dumbarton Academy, Dumbarton, G82; T.-Dumbarton 63373.

Coltart, George John Letham, TD, MA, MSc, CEng, MICE. Senior Lecturer, Department of Civil Engineering, Heriot-Watt University, since 1966; b. 2.2.29, Edinburgh; m., Inger Christina Larsson; 1 s.; 1 d. Educ. George Watson's College, Edinburgh; Royal Military Academy, Sandhurst; King's College, Cambridge; Cornell University, New York. Commissioned, Royal Engineers, 1949, serving in regimental and staff appointments including DAA and QMC, 5 Brigade, and OC 51 Field Squadron (Airfields); retired, 1966; commanded University OTC, 1972-74; TA Colonel, 1975-80; Convener, Lothian Area, TAVRA. Recreations: walking; restoration of old buildings. Address: (h.) Napier House, 8 Colinton Road, Edinburgh, EH10 5DS; T.-031-447 6314.

Colvin, David. Chief Social Work Adviser, Scottish Office, since 1980; b. 31.1.31, Glasgow; m., Elma Findlay; 2 s.; 3 d. Educ. Whitehill School, Glasgow; Glasgow University; Edinburgh University. Probation Officer, Glasgow, 1955-60; Psychiatric Social Worker, Scottish Prison and Borstal Service, Scottish Home and Health Department, 1960-61; Senior Psychiatric Social Worker, Crichton Royal Hospital, Child Psychiatric Unit, 1961-65; Director, Family Casework Unit, Paisley, 1965-66; Welfare Officer, SHHD, 1966-68; joined SED as Social Work Adviser, 1968. Senior Associate Research Fellow, Brunel University, 1978; Honorary Adviser, British Red Cross, since 1982. Recreations: collector; swimming; climbing; golf; gardens; social affairs. Address: (h.) Sea Brae, Marine Terrace, Gullane, East Lothian, EH31 2AZ; T.-Gullane 842139.

Common, Michael Stuart, BA, BPhil. Senior Lecturer in Economics, Stirling University, since 1979; b. 30.8.40, Walton on Thames; m., Branwen; 2 d. Educ. Hampton Grammar School; Liverpool University. Assistant Lecturer, Liverpool University, 1967-68; Lecturer, Southampton University, 1968-78. Address: (b.) Department of Economics, Stirling University, Stirling, FK9 4LA; T.-0786 3171.

Condliffe, John, BA (Oxon), MPhil, MInstPet. Director, North East, Scottish Development Agency, since 1984; b. 17.9.46, Portsmouth. Educ. Portsmouth Grammar School; Magdalen College, Oxford; University College, London. Corporate planning, Greater London Council; Industrial Development Executive, London Docklands Development Team; Senior Lecturer in Economics, Polytechnic of Central London; Head of Area Programmes, Scottish Development Agency. Recreations: music; visual arts. Address: (b.) Scottish Development Agency, 10 Queen's Road, Aberdeen; T.-Aberdeen 641791.

Conn, Stewart. Poet and Playwright; Head, Radio Drama Department, BBC Scotland; b. 1936. Author of numerous stage plays, including Breakdown, Glasgow Citizens', 1961; I Didn't Always Live Here, Citizens', 1967; The Burning, Royal Lyceum, Edinburgh, 1971; Thistlewood, Traverse, Edinburgh, 1975; Count Your Blessings, Pitlochry Festival Theatre, 1975; poetry including An Ear to the Ground (Poetry Book Society Choice) and Under the Ice (SAC Book Award); Literary Advisor, Royal Lyceum Theatre, 1973-75; former Member, Drama Panel, Scottish Arts Council.

Connarty, Michael, BA, DipEd, DCE, JP. Member, Stirling District Council, since 1977 (Council Leader); Teacher of learning impaired children, since 1975; b. 3.9.47, Coatbridge; m., Margaret Doran; 1 s.; 1 d. Educ. St. Patrick's High School, Coatbridge; Stirling University; Jordanhill College of Education; Glasgow University. Member, Scottish Executive, Labour Party, 1981, 1984, 1985; Member, Labour Party NEC Local Government Advisory Committee; Member, Convention of Scottish Local Authorities; Vice-Chair, Socialist Educational Association, 1983-85; Council Member, Educational Institute of Scotland, 1984-85; Founding Secretary, Labour Coordinating Committee (Scotland). Address: (h.) 5 Princes Street, Stirling, FK8 2HQ.

Connor, James Michael, MD, BSc (Hons), MB, ChB (Hons), MRCP. Wellcome Trust Senior Lecturer and Honorary Consultant in Medical Genetics, Glasgow University, since 1984; b. 18.6.51, Grappenhall, England; m., Dr. Rachel A.C. Educ. Lymm Grammar School, Cheshire; Liverpool University. House Officer, Liverpool Royal Infirmary; Resident in Internal Medicine, Johns Hopkins Hospital, USA; University Research Fellow, Liverpool University; Instructor in Internal Medicine, Johns Hopkins Hospital, USA; Consultant in Medical Genetics, Duncan Guthrie Institute of Medical Genetics, Yorkhill, Glasgow. Publications: Soft Tissue Ossification, 1983; Essential Medical Genetics (Co-author), 1984; Self-Assessment in Medical Genetics (Co-author), 1985. Recreations: board-sailing; skiing. Address: (h.) Westbank Cottage, 84 Montgomery Street, Eaglesham; T.-Eaglesham 2626.

Conti, Rt. Rev. Mario Joseph, STL, PhL. Bishop of Aberdeen, since 1977; Member, Secretariat for the Promotion of Christian Unity, Rome, since 1984; Member, International Commission for English in the Liturgy, since 1978; b. 20.3.34, Elgin. Educ. St. Marie's Convent; Springfield School, Elgin; Blairs College; Pontifical Gregorian University, Rome. Ordained priest, Rome, 1958; Curate, St. Mary's Cathedral, Aberdeen, 1959-62; Parish Priest, St. Joachim's, Wick and St. Anne's, Thurso, 1962. Member, Order of Merit, Italian Republic; President-Treasurer, SCIAF, 1977-85; President, National Liturgy Commission; Chairman, Scottish Catholic Heritage Commission. Recreations: music; art. Address: Bishop's House, 156 King's Gate, Aberdeen; T.-0224 319154.

Cook, Fraser Murray, OBE, BSc, MIMechE, CEng, FInstPet. Chairman, Cumbernauld Development Corporation, since 1983; Vice Chairman, Forth Ports Authority, since 1985; Member, Highlands and Islands Development Consultative

Council, since 1974; b. 29.12.17, Conon Bridge, Ross-shire; m., Eve Smith Reid. Educ. Inverness Royal Academy; Morgan Academy, Dundee; St. Andrews University. Engineering graduate apprentice, Pumpherston Oil Co. Ltd., 1939-41; REME, South East Asia Command, 1941-46; Assistant to Manager, Pumpherston Oil Co. Ltd., 1946-48; Production Engineer, latterly Oil Construction Engineer, Southern Africa, 1948-53; Engineer, BP Oil Grangemouth Refinery Ltd., 1953-56; Manager, Pumpherston Oil Co. Ltd., 1956-62; Works Manager: BP Oil Grangemouth Refinery Ltd., 1962-66, BP Oil Llandarcy Refinery Ltd., 1966-69; General Manager, then Managing Director and General Manager, BP Oil Grangemouth Refinery Ltd., 1969-77. Member, Conference of Stirling University, since 1978. Recreations: some golf; photography. Address: Littleton Cottage, Cultoquhey, by Crieff, Perthshire, PH7 3NF; T.-Crieff 3537.

Cook, Rev. James Stanley Stephen Ronald Tweedie, BD, DipPSS. Minister, Hamilton West Parish Church, since 1974; b. 18.8.35, Tullibody; m., Jean Douglas McLachlan; 2 s.; 1 d. Educ. Whitehill Senior Secondary School, Glasgow; St. Andrews University. Apprentice quantity surveyor, Glasgow, 1953-54; regular soldier, REME, 1954-57; Assistant Preventive Officer, Waterguard Department, HM Customs and Excise, 1957-61; Officer, HM Customs and Excise, 1961-69; studied for the ministry, 1969-74. Chairman, Cruse (Lanarkshire); former Vice-Chairman, Hamilton/East Kilbride Local Health Council; Provincial Grand Master, Lanarkshire (Middle Ward), 1983-86. Recreations: music; photography. Address: West Manse, 43 Bothwell Road, Hamilton, ML3 OBB; T.-Hamilton 458770.

Cook, John, ChM, FRCSEdin, FRSE. Consultant Surgeon, Eastern General Hospital, Edinburgh, since 1964; b. 9.5.26, Calcutta, India; m., Patricia Mary Bligh; 1 s.; 4 d. Educ. Fettes College; Edinburgh University. First Assistant in Surgery, Makerere University College, Kampala, Uganda; Reader in Surgery, University of East Africa, 1955-64; Consultant Surgeon: Deaconess Hospital, 1965-68, Leith Hospital, 1969-77; Royal College of Surgeons of Edinburgh: Honorary Secretary, 1969-72, Council Member, 1974-84; Wade Professor of Surgical Studies, 1982-85; Representative Member, General Medical Council, since 1982; International Federation of Surgical Colleges: Honorary Secretary, 1974-84, Member, Executive Council, since 1984. Recreations: music; fishing. Address: (h.) 24 Duddingston Park, Edinburgh, EH15 1JX; T.-031-669 2123.

Cook, Rev. John Weir, MA, BD. Minister, Henderson Church, Kilmarnock, since 1970; b. 10.2.37, Greenock; m., Elizabeth Anne Gifford; 1 s.; 2 d. Educ. Greenock Academy; High School of Glasgow; Glasgow University. Peter Marshall Scholar, Princeton, 1962; Minister, St. Andrews Church, Calcutta, 1963-70; Chairman, Clinical Theology Association, since 1984; Convener, Publicity Committee, Church of Scotland, 1984; accredited by British Association for Counselling, 1984. Recreations: reading; sport; after-dinner speaking. Address: 52 London Road, Kilmarnock; T.-0563 23113.

Cook, Rev. Robert, BA, BD. Minister, South Parish Church, Girvan, since 1980; b. 24.12.54, Kilmarnock; m., Janice Shields. Educ. Kilmarnock Academy; Strathclyde University; Glasgow University. National Chaplain, Girls' Brigade, since 1983; Young Adult Advisor, Ayr Presbytery. Address: 30 Henrietta Street, Girvan, KA26 9AL; T.-0465 3370.

Cook, Robin. MP (Labour), Livingston, since 1983 (Edinburgh Central, 1974-83); b. 28.2.46. Educ. Aberdeen Grammar School; Royal High School, Edinburgh; Edinburgh University. Former Tutor and Organiser in Adult Education; contested Edinburgh North, 1970; former Vice-Chairman, PLP Defence Group; Past Chairman, Housing Sub-Committee, Scottish Labour Group; Opposition Spokesman on Treasury and Economic Affairs, since 1980.

Cooke, David John, BSc, MSc, PhD, ABPsS. Principal Clinical Psychologist, Douglas Inch Centre, Glasgow, since 1984; Honorary Lecturer, Glasgow University, since 1984; b. 13.7.52, Glasgow; m., Janet Ruth Salter. Educ. Larbert High School; St. Andrews University; Newcastle-upon-Tyne University; Glasgow University. Clinical Psychologist, Gartnavel Royal Hospital, 1976-83. Recreations: sailing; opera; cooking. Address: (b.) Douglas Inch Centre, 2 Woodside Terrace, Glasgow, G3 7UY; T.-041-332 3844.

Cooke, Nicholas Huxley, MA (Oxon). Director, The Scottish Conservation Projects Trust, since 1984; b. 6.5.44, Godalming, Surrey; m., Anne Landon; 1 s.; 3 d. Educ. Charterhouse School; Worcester College, Oxford. Retail management, London, 1967; chartered accountancy training, London, 1968-71; British International Paper, London, 1972-78; Director (Scotland), British Trust for Conservation Volunteers, 1978-84. Council Member, Ecological Parks Trust, London; Member, Executive Committee, Scottish Environmental Education Council; Member, Environment Resource Centre Trust, Edinburgh. Recreations: fishing; walking; photography; outdoor conservation work. Address: (b.) 70 Main Street, Doune, Perthshire, FK16 6BW; T.-0786 841479.

Cooney, Neil, MA (Hons), DipEd, JP. Member, Aberdeen District Council, since 1983 (Convener, Leisure and Recreation Committee, since 1984); Principal Teacher of History, Cults Academy, since 1971; Member, General Teaching Council for Scotland, since 1983; b. 17.8.43, Aberdeen; m., Aileen Joan Cooney. Educ. Robert Gordon's College, Aberdeen; Aberdeen University; Aberdeen College of Education. Vice-Chairman, Aberdeen City Labour Party, 1983-85; President, Aberdeen Branch, Educational Institute of Scotland, 1981-83. Recreations: cricket; swimming; local history; folk music. Address: (h.) 128 Don Street, Woodside, Aberdeen; T.-Aberdeen 46920.

Cooper, Professor Neil Louis, BA, MA, BPhil. Professor in Moral Philosophy, Dundee University, since 1981 (Head, Department of Philosophy, since 1980); b. 25.4.30, Ilford; m., Beryl Barwell Turner; 1 s.; 1 d. Educ. Westminster City School; City of London School; Balliol

College, Oxford (Domus Exhibitioner); Senior Scholar, New College, Oxford, 1953-55; John Locke Scholar, 1954. RAF, 1948-49; Lecturer in Philosophy, Queen's College 1956-67; Dundee University: Senior Lecturer in Philosophy, 1967-69, Reader in Philosophy, 1969-81, Dean of Students, Faculty of Social Sciences and Letters, 1972-74, Member, Senate, since 1978. Publications: The Definition of Morality (Contributor), 1970; Weakness of Will (Contributor), 1971; The Diversity of Moral Thinking, 1981; Philosophers on Education (Contributor), 1986. Recreations: conversation; reading; listening to music; playing with ideas. Address: (h.) 2 Minto Place, Dundee, DD2 1BR; T.-Dundee 66518.

Cooper, Ronald, CEng, FICE, FIAS. Director of Technical Services, Edinburgh District Council, since 1983; b. 12.11.36, Aberdeen; m., Diane; 3 s.; 1 d. Educ. Aberdeen Academy. Apprentice civil engineer, Aberdeen Harbour Board; National Service, Royal Engineers; Engineer, Aberdeen Corporation; Depute Master of Works, Edinburgh Corporation; Director of Building Control, Edinburgh District Council, 1974-83. Recreations: golf; work. Address: (b.) City Chambers, High Street, Edinburgh; T.-031-225 2424, Ext. 5300.

Cooper, Sheena M.M., MA. Rector, Aboyne Academy and Deeside Community Centre; b. 7.3.39, Bellshill. Educ. Dalziel High School, Motherwell; Glasgow University. Teacher of History, Dalziel High School, Motherwell, 1962-68; Lecturer in History, Elizabeth Gaskell College of Education, Manchester, 1968-70; Woman Adviser, then Assistant Rector, Montrose Academy, 1970-76; Rector, John Neilson High School, Paisley, 1976-83. Member: Council for Teritary Education in Scotland, 1979-83, Scottish Examination Board, since 1984, Scottish Vocational Education Council, since 1985, Religious Advisory Council, BBC, since 1980; President, Education Section, British Association for Advancement of Science, 1978-79. Recreations: golf; singing; walking. Address: (b.) Aboyne Academy and Deeside Community Centre, Aboyne; T.-0339 2222, Ext. 24.

Copeman, George E., MBE. Honorary Sheriff, Banff and Buchan; b. 11.12.03, Hornsey, Middlesex; m., Dorothy Mary Busby; 1 d. Former Director and Manager, Crosse & Blackwell Ltd., Peterhead; war-time Canning Adviser, Ministry of Food, for North of Scotland; former Treasurer, Magistrate and Chairman, Peterhead Public Health and Water Committee; former Member: Aberdeen County Council, North-East Counties Police Board, Herring Industry Advisory Council, Scottish Council (Development and Industry) Manpower Committee, Peterhead Scottish Week Committee. Address: (h.) 2 Lochside Road, Denmore Park, Bridge of Don, Aberdeen, AB2 8AE; T.-0224 704481.

Coppock, Professor John Terence, MA, PhD, FBA, FRSE. Ogilvie Professor of Geography, Edinburgh University, since 1965 (Honorary Director, Tourism and Recreation Research Unit, since 1980); Member, Scottish Sports Council, since 1976; b. 2.6.21, Cardiff; m., Sheila Mary

Burnett; 1 s.; 1 d. Educ. Penarth County School; Queens' College, Cambridge. Civil Servant, 1938-47 (Lord Chancellor's Department, Ministry of Works, Customs and Excise); War Service, Army, 1939-46 (Commissioned, 1941); Departmental Demonstrator, Department of Geography, Cambridge University, 1949-50; University College, London: Assistant Lecturer, 1950-52, Lecturer, 1952-64, Reader, 1964-65. Institute of British Geographers: Vice-President, 1971-73, President, 1973-74; Vice-President, Royal Scottish Geographical Society, since 1975. Recreations: badminton; walking; natural history; listening to music. Address: (b.) Department of Geography, Edinburgh University, Drummond Street, Edinburgh, EH8 9XP; T.-031-667 1011, Ext. 4267.

Corbet, Professor Philip Steven, BSc, PhD, DSc, ScD, FIBiol, FESC. Professor of Zoology, Dundee University, since 1980 (Head, Department of Biological Sciences, since 1983); b. 21.5.29, Kuala Lumpur, Malaysia; 1 d. Educ. Dauntsey's School, Wiltshire; Reading University; Cambridge University. Zoologist, East African Fisheries Research Organisation, Jinja, Uganda, 1954-57; Entomologist: East African Virus Research Organisation, Entebbe, Uganda, 1957-62, Entomology Research Institute, Canada Department of Agriculture, Ottawa, 1962-67; Director, Research Institute, Canada Department of Agriculture, Belleville, Ontario, 1967-71; Professor and Chairman, Department of Biology, Waterloo University, Ontario, 1971-74; Professor and Director, Joint Centre for Environmental Sciences, Canterbury University and Lincoln College, New Zealand, 1974-78; Professor, Department of Zoology, Canterbury University, New Zealand, 1978-80. Entomological Society of Canada: President, 1971, Gold Medal, 1974, Fellow, 1976; Commonwealth Visiting Professor, Cambridge University, 1979-80. Recreations: natural history; music. Address: (b.) Department of Biological Sciences, The University, Dundee, DD1 4HN; T.-0382 23181.

Cordiner, Rev. John. Minister, Portpatrick, since 1981; b. 7.5.24, Glasgow; m., Doris Emily McDowell; 1 s.; 1 d. Educ. North Kelvinside Senior Secondary School, Glasgow; Glasgow University; Trinity College, Glasgow. GPO, 1938; Royal Navy, 1942-45 (Radio Operator); war service candidates course for the ministry, Glasgow University, 1946-49; ordained and inducted, Lundie and Fowlis, 1950; inducted, first minister of Mains of Fintry, Dundee, 1953; inducted Minister, Lincluden, 1961 (linked with Holywood, 1962); sometime Moderator: Dumfries Synod, Dumfries Presbytery. Recreations: short wave radio; photography; art. Address: The Manse, Portpatrick, Stranraer, DG9 8TD; T.-077 681 226.

Cormack, Professor Richard Melville, MA, BSc, DipMathStat, PhD, FRSE. Professor of Statistics, St. Andrews University, since 1972; Member, Natural Environment Research Council, since 1983; Member, Scottish Universities Council on Entrance, since 1982; b. 12.3.35, Glasgow; m., Edith Whittaker. Educ. Glasgow Academy; Cambridge University; London University (External); Aberdeen University. Lecturer in Statistics, Aberdeen University, 1956-66; Assistant

Professor, University of Washington, 1964-65; Senior Lecturer, Edinburgh University, 1966-72. Honorary Secretary, Biometric Society (British Region), 1970-77; President (International), Biometric Society, 1980-81. Publications: The Statistical Argument; Sampling Biological Populations (Editor), Spatial and Temporal Analysis in Ecology (Editor). Recreations: photography; music; hill-walking. Address: (h.) 58 Buchanan Gardens, St. Andrews, Fife; T.-0334 76970.

Cormie, James E.D., BL. Chief Executive, Perth and Kinross District Council, since 1981; b. 30.7.30, Edinburgh; m., Stella Anne Moir; 1 s.; 1 d. Educ. Robert Gordon's College, Aberdeen; Aberdeen University. Depute Town Clerk, Perth, 1966; Director of Administration and Legal Services, Perth and Kinross District, 1975. Clerk to Lieutenancy, Perth and Kinross; Company Secretary: Perth and Kinross Recreational Facilities Ltd., Perth Festival of the Arts Ltd., Bowerswell Memorial Homes (Perth) Ltd.; Member, Society of High Constables of the City of Perth; Member, Secretary of State's Advisory Committee on Scotland's Travelling People. Recreations: cine photography; golf; hill-walking. Address: (b.) Council Building, 2 High Street, Perth, PH1 5PH; T.-0738 39911.

Cornell, Jim Scott, CEng, FICE. Deputy General Manager, British Rail, Scottish Region, since 1984; b. 3.8.39, York; m., Wynne Eileen; 1 s.; 1 d. Educ. Thirsk Grammar School; Bradford Institute of Technology. British Rail: student apprentice civil engineer, 1959; series of civil engineering management posts, 1968-76; Divisional Civil Engineer, King's Cross, 1976-78; Divisional Civil Engineer, Newcastle, 1978-81; Assistant Regional Civil Engineer, York, 1981-83; Regional Civil Engineer Scotland, 1983-84. Recreations: golf; hill-walking; gardening. Address: (b.) ScotRail House, 58 Port Dundas Road, Glasgow.

Cornish, Melvyn David, BSc, PGCE. Assistant Secretary, Edinburgh University, since 1982; b. 29.6.48, Leighton Buzzard; m., Eileen Joyce Easterbrook; 1 s.; 1 d. Educ. Cedars Grammar School, Leighton Buzzard; Leicester University. Chemistry Teacher, Jamaica and Cumbria, 1970-73; Administrator, Leicester Polytechnic, 1973-78; Senior Administrative Officer, Edinburgh University, 1978. Recreations: walking; cinema; travel; family. Address: (b.) Old College, South Bridge, Edinburgh; T.-031-667 1011.

Cornwell, Professor John Francis, PhD, BSc, DIC, ARCS, FRSE. Professor of Theoretical Physics, St. Andrews University, since 1979 (Chairman, Physics Department, 1984-85); b. 28.1.37, London; m., Elizabeth Margaret Burfitt; 2 d. Educ. Ealing Grammar School; Imperial College, London. Lecturer in Applied Mathematics, Leeds University, 1961-67; St. Andrews University: Lecturer in Theoretical Physics, 1967-73, Reader, 1973-79. Publications: Group Theory in Physics, two volumes, 1984; Group Theory and Electronic Energy Bands in Solids, 1969. Recreations: sailing; hill-walking; tennis; badminton; golf. Address: (b.) Department of Physics, St. Andrews University, North Haugh, St. Andrews, Fife, KY16 9SS; T.-0334 76161.

Cornwell, Keith, BSc, PhD, CEng, MIMechE. Senior Lecturer in Mechanical Engineering, Heriot-Watt University, since 1979; Managing Director, KC Products Ltd., North Berwick, since 1982; b. 4.4.42, Abingdon; m., Sheila Joan Mott; 1 s.; 1 d. Educ. City University, London. Research Fellow, then Lecturer, Middlesex Polytechnic; Lecturer, Heriot-Watt University. Publication: The Flow of Heat. Recreations: walking; old cars. Address: (h.) 2 Carperstane, North Berwick, East Lothian, EH39 5PA; T.-0620 2673.

Corrie, John Alexander. MP (Conservative), Bute and North Ayrshire, since 1974; b. 1935; m.; 1 s.; 2 d. Educ. Kirkcudbright Academy; George Watson's College, Edinburgh; Lincoln Agricultural College, New Zealand. Commissioned from the ranks, New Zealand Army, 1957; National Chairman, Scottish Young Conservatives, 1964; Council Member, National Farmers Union of Scotland, 1965; Chairman, Kirkcudbright Conservative Association, 1966; Lecturer, British Wool Marketing Board, 1967-74, and Agricultural Training Board, 1969-74; appointed Scottish Conservative spokesman on education, 1974; Member, European Parliament, 1975 and 1977-79; Vice President, EEC/Turkey Committee; appointed Opposition Whip, 1975 (resigned, 1976); elected to Council, Belted Galloway Cattle Society, 1978; PPS to Secretary of State for Scotland, 1979-81; elected to Council, National Cattle Breeders Association, 1979; introduced private member's Bill on abortion law reform, 1979; Chairman, Scottish Conservative Backbench Committee, 1981; elected Leader, Conservative Group on Scottish Affairs, 1982; farms family farm in Kirkcudbright. Address: (b.) House of Commons, Westminster, London.

Corsar, Charles Herbert Kenneth, OBE, TD, JP, DL, MA. Farmer, since 1953; Secretary for Scotland, Duke of Edinburgh's Award, since 1966; b. 13.5.26, Edinburgh; m., Mary Drummond Buchanan-Smith (see Mary Drummond Corsar); 2 s.; 2 d. Educ. Merchiston Castle; King's College, Cambridge. Commissioned, The Royal Scots TA, 1948; commanded 8/9 Bn.,The Royal Scots TA, 1964-67; Edinburgh and Heriot-Watt Universities OTC, 1967-72; TA Colonel, 1972-75; Hon ADC to The Queen, 1977-81; Honorary Colonel, 1/52 Lowland Volunteers, since 1975; Chairman, Lowland TA and VR Association, since 1984; Zone Commissioner, Home Defence, East of Scotland; County Councillor, Midlothian, 1958-67; Deputy Lieutenant, Midlothian; Vice President and Chairman of Executive, The Boys Brigade, 1970, and President, Edinburgh Bn., Boys Brigade, since 1969; Chairman, Scottish Standing Conference of Voluntary Youth Organisations, 1973-78; Governor, Merchiston Castle School; Chairman of Governors, Clifton Hall School; Chairman, Wellington List D School, 1978-84; Chairman, Earl Haig Fund Scotland, since 1984; Secretary, Royal Jubilee and Princes' Trusts (Lothian and Borders); Member, Scottish Sports Council, 1972-75; Elder, Church of Scotland, since 1956. Recreations: gardening; bee-keeping; shooting. Address: (h.) Burg Torloisk, Ulva Ferry, Isle of Mull; T.-Ulva Ferry 289; 11 Ainslie Place, Edinburgh; T.-031-225 6318.

Corsar, The Hon. Mrs Mary Drummond, MA. Chairman Scotland, Women's Royal Voluntary Service, since 1981; Vice Chairman, Women's Royal Voluntary Service, since 1984; Member, Parole Board for Scotland, since 1982; b. 8.7.27, Edinburgh; m., Colonel Charles H.K. Corsar (qv); 2 s.; 2 d. Educ. Westbourne, Glasgow; St. Denis, Edinburgh; Edinburgh University. Midlothian Girl Guides: Secretary, 1951-66, County Commissioner, 1966-72; Deputy Chief Commissioner, Girl Guides Scotland, 1972-77; Member, Executive Committee, Trefoil Centre, since 1975; Member, Visiting Committee, Glenochil Young Offenders Institution and Detention Centre, since 1976; Member, Management Committee, Church of Scotland Youth Centre, Carberry, 1976-82; Honorary President, Scottish Women's Athletic Association. Recreation: hill-walking. Address: (b.) 19 Grosvenor Crescent, Edinburgh; T.-031-337 2261.

Cottrell, Professor Glen Alfred, BSc, PhD, DSc. Professor of Neuropharmacology, St. Andrews University; b. 19.8.38, London; m., Ann Rainbow; 2 s.; 1 d. Educ. Shene Grammar School; Southampton University. Research Fellow, Harvard; Lecturer, Senior Lecturer, Reader, St. Andrews University. Recreations: sailing; running. Address: (h.) 34 Grange Road, St. Andrews, KY16 8LF; T.-0334 74985.

Coull, Professor Alexander, BSc, PhD, CEng, FRSE, FICE, FIStructE, FASCE. Regius Professor of Civil Engineering, Glasgow University, since 1977; b. 20.6.31, Peterhead; m., Frances Bruce Moir; 1 s.; 2 d. Educ. Peterhead Academy; Aberdeen University. Research Assistant, MIT, USA, 1955; Structural Engineer, English Electric Co. Ltd., 1955-57; Lecturer in Engineering, Aberdeen University, 1957-62; Lecturer in Civil Engineering, Southampton University, 1962-66; Professor of Structural Engineering, Strathclyde University, 1967-76. Chairman, Clyde Estuary Amenity Council, since 1981; awarded Telford Premium, 1973, and Trevithick Premium, 1974, Institution of Civil Engineers. Publications: Tall Buildings, 1967; Fundamentals of Structural Theory, 1972. Recreations: golf; hill-walking. Address: (h.) 11 Blackwood Road, Milngavie, Glasgow, G62 7LB; T.-041-956 1655.

Coull, James Reid, MA, PhD. Senior Lecturer in Geography, Aberdeen University, since 1972; b. 18.2.35, Peterhead. Educ. Peterhead Academy; Aberdeen University. University Assistant, 1959-61; Lecturer, 1961-72. Address: (b.) Department of Geography, Aberdeen University, Aberdeen.

Coull, Rev. Morris Cowper, BD. Minister, Hillington Park Parish Church, Glasgow, since 1983; b. 12.4.41, Largs; m., Ann Duthie; 1 s.; 1 d. Educ. Allan Glen's School; Newbattle Abbey College; Glasgow University; Trinity College. Assistant Minister, Bearsden South Parish Church, 1972-74; Minister, New Cumnock (Old) Parish Church, 1974-83. Address: 61 Ralston Avenue, Glasgow, G52; T.-041-882 7000.

Coull, Samuel. Member, Grampian Regional Council, since 1978; Member, Banff and Buchan District Council, since 1977; b. 21.6.40, Peterhead; m., Ann F.S. Barclay; 1 d. Educ. Peterhead Academy. Member, Peterhead Harbour Trust. Recreations: gardening; reading. Address: (h.) 16 Lendrum Terrace, Stirlinghill, Boddam, Aberdeenshire; T.-Peterhead 76323.

Couper, Robert Jackson, FIH, FBIM, MIIM, MRSH, MSAAT, MHTTA. Director of Housing, Argyll and Bute District Council, since 1974; b. 20.4.27, Paisley; m., Ann Templeton; 2 s.; 1 d. Educ. Camphill Secondary School, Paisley; Glasgow School of Architecture; Royal College of Technology, Glasgow; Glasgow College of Commerce; Glasgow College of Building. Apprentice architect, Abercrombie & Maitland, 1945-53; Royal Navy, 1945-48; Burgh of Milngavie: Architectural Assistant, 1953-68, Interim Burgh Surveyor, 1968, Assistant Burgh Surveyor (Housing), 1968-70; Housing Manager, Burgh of Port Glasgow, 1970-74; part-time Lecturer, Glasgow College of Building, 1970-74. Session Clerk, St. Lukes Church of Scotland, 1964-72; Vice Chairman, Scottish Local Authorities Special Housing Group, since 1976; Chairman, Strathclyde Chief Housing Officers Group, 1980-83; Chairman, Association of Chief Housing Officers (Northern Area), 1984; Secretary, Chief Officers Group, Scottish Branch, Institute of Housing, since 1984. Recreations: sailing; art; heraldry. Address: (b.) Kilmory, Lochgilphead, Argyll, PA31 6RT; T.-0546 2127.

Courtney, James McNiven, BSc, PhD, ARCST, CChem, FRSC, FPRI. Senior Lecturer, Bioengineering Unit, Strathclyde University, since 1981; Visiting Professor, Wilhelm Pieck University, Rostock, GDR, since 1978; b. 25.3.40, Glasgow; m., Ellen Miller Courtney; 2 s.; 1 d. Educ. Whitehill Senior Secondary School; Royal College of Science and Technology; Strathclyde University. Rubber technologist: MacLellan Rubber Ltd., Glasgow, 1962-65, Uniroyal Ltd., Dumfries, 1965-66; Lecturer, Bioengineering Unit, Strathclyde University, 1969-81. Recreation: football supporter (Glasgow Rangers). Address: (b.) Strathclyde University, Bioengineering Unit, 106 Rottenrow, Glasgow; T.-041-552 4400.

Coutts, Captain Ben, MBE. Farmer and Estate Manager; Member, Perth and Kinross District Council, since 1984; b. 26.4.16, Glasgow; m., Sally Hutchinson; 3 s.; 2 d. Educ. Glasgow Academy. Surrey and Sussex Yeomanry, 1938-42; managed Millhills and Benchallum Estates, 1947-51; farmed Gaskbeg Newtonmore, 1951-59, and factored four adjoining estates; bred Smithfield Champion, 1956; founder Member, HFRO, 1952; Council Member, NFU, 1952-59; factored Ardkinglas Estate, 1959-64 and Blackmount Estate, 1961-85; English Speaking Union scholarship, USA, 1959; Nuffield scholarship, Australia, New Zealand and South Africa, 1964; Past Chairman: Strathspey Farmers Club, Glenorchy and Innishail Horticultural and Agricultural Society; Chairman, Ardoch Agricultural Society; Vice-President, Royal Smithfield Club; regular farming broadcaster since 1947; Parliamentary Liberal candidate, Perth and Kinross, 1983; Elder, Church of Scotland. Recreations: a bit of shooting and drinking. Address: Woodburn Farm, Crieff, Perthshire.

Coutts, Findlay Macrury, MA, LLB. Director of Administration, Dunfermline District Council, since 1975; b. 16.3.43, Aberdeen; m., Christine; 1 s.; 1 d. Educ. Aberdeen Grammar School; Aberdeen University. Law apprentice/Legal Assistant, Hamilton Town Council, 1966-69; Town Clerk, Cupar, 1969-75. Recreations: good food; golf; town twinning. Address: (b.) City Chambers, Dunfermline; T.-Dunfermline 722711.

Coutts, Brigadier Francis Henderson, CBE, DL. Chairman, VIP and Hospitality Committee, 1986 Commonwealth Games; Honorary Appeals Organiser, The Seagull Trust; b. 8.7.18, Glasgow; m., Morag Russell Fullerton; 2 d. Educ. Glasgow Academy; Army Staff College, Camberley. Metropolitan Police, 1937-40; in the ranks, London Scottish, 1940-41; commissioned King's Own Scottish Borderers, 1941-73; Colonel, 1970-80; CO Infantry Junior Leaders Bn., 1959-62; GSO 1 Singapore Base District, 1962-64; Commander 155 (Lowland) Brigade TA, 1965-67; Chief of Staff, Scottish Command, 1967-68; Divisional Brigadier, Scottish Division, 1968-70; Commander, Highland Area, 1970-73; General Secretary, Royal British Legion Scotland and Earl Haig Fund Scotland, 1973-83; President, Scottish Rugby Union, 1977-78; Elder, Colinton Parish Church; Chairman, East of Scotland SSAFA; Joint President, Friends of St. Andrew's, Jerusalem; Member, Management Committee, Royal British Legion Housing Association. Recreations: gardening; golf; Grouse; piping. Address: (h.) 5 Gillsland Road, Edinburgh, EH10 5BW; T.-031-337 4920.

Coutts, Rev. Fred, MA, BD. Minister, Mastrick Parish Church, Aberdeen, since 1984; b. 13.1.47, Forfar; m., Mary Lawson Fraser Gill; 2 s.; 1 d. Educ. Brechin High School; Dollar Academy; St. Andrews University; Edinburgh University. Assistant Minister, Linwood Parish Church, 1972-74; Minister, Buckie North, 1974-84. Chairman: Buckie Community Council, 1981-83, Moray Firth Community Radio Association, 1982-83. Recreations: music; photography; home computing. Address: 13 Beechgrove Avenue, Aberdeen, AB2 4EZ; T.-Aberdeen 638011.

Coutts, John R.T., BSc, PhD. Senior Lecturer in Obstetrics and Gynaecology, Glasgow University, since 1972; b. 10.7.41, Dundee; m., Marjory R.B.; 1 s.; 2 d. Educ. Morgan Academy, Dundee; St. Andrews University. Dundee University: Research Fellow in Obstetrics and Gynaecology, 1966-69, Honorary Lecturer in Obstetrics and Gynaecology, 1969-70; Lecturer, Glasgow University, 1970-72. Publication: The Functional Morphology of the Human Ovary (Editor). Recreations: squash; bowling. Address: (b.) Department of Obstetrics and Gynaecology, Glasgow Royal Infirmary, 10 Alexandra Parade, Glasgow; T.-041-552 3535.

Cowan, Brigadier Colin Hunter, CBE, DL, MA, CEng, MICE, FRSA. Chief Executive, Cumbernauld Development Corporation, 1970-85; b. 16.10.20, Edinburgh; m., Elizabeth Williamson (deceased); 2 s.; 1 d. Educ. Wellington College; Trinity College, Cambridge. Commissioned, Royal Engineers, 1940; service in India and Burma, Royal Bombay Sappers and Miners,

1942-46; staff and regimental appointments, UK and Malta, 1951-60; commanded Field Engineer Regiment, Germany, 1960-63; Defence Adviser, UK Mission to UNO, New York, 1964-66; Chief Staff Officer to Engineer-in-Chief (Army), Ministry of Defence, 1966-68; Brigadier, Engineer Plans (Army), Ministry of Defence, 1968-70. Chairman, Services Resettlement Committee, Scotland. Recreations: hill-walking; photography; music. Address: (h.) Hillcroft, Dullatur, by Glasgow, G68 OAW; T.-023-67 23242.

Cowan, David Lockhart, MB, ChB, FRCSEdin. Consultant Otolaryngologist, City Hospital, Royal Hospital for Sick Children and Western General Hospital, Edinburgh, since 1974; Honorary Senior Lecturer, Edinburgh University; b. 30.6.41, Edinburgh; m., Eileen M. Masterton; 3 s.; 1 d. Educ. George Watson's College, Edinburgh; Trinity College, Glenalmond; Edinburgh University. Scottish Representative, Council, British Association of Otolaryngologists. Publications: Logan Turner's Diseases of the Ear, Nose and Throat (Co-author); Paediatric Otolaryngology (Co-author). Recreations: golf; all sport. Address: (h.) 28 Braid Hills Road, Edinburgh, EH10 6HY; T.-031-447 3424.

Cowan, Professor Ian Borthwick, MA, PhD, FRHistS. Professor in Scottish History, Glasgow University, since 1983; b. 16.4.32, Dumfries; m., Anna Little Telford; 3 d. Educ. Dumfries Academy; Edinburgh University. Education Officer, RAF, 1954-56; Assistant Lecturer in Scottish History, Edinburgh University, 1956-59; Lecturer in History, Newbattle Abbey College, 1959-62; Glasgow University: Lecturer in Scottish History, 1962-70, Senior Lecturer, 1970-77, Reader, 1977-83. Treasurer: Scottish History Society, Scottish Historical Trust; Past President, Scottish Church History Society; Vice President, The Historical Association; Member, Irish Manuscripts Advisory Committee on Papal Records. Publications: The Parishes of Medieval Scotland, 1967; Scottish Supplications to Rome 1428-32 (with A.I. Dunlop), 1970; The Enigma of Mary Stewart, 1971; The Scottish Covenanters 1660-1689, 1976; Medieval Religious Houses: Scotland (with D.E. Easson), 1976; Renaissance and Reformation in Scotland (with D. Shaw), 1982; The Scottish Reformation, 1982; Knights of St. John of Jerusalem in Scotland (with P.H.R. Mackay and A. Macquarrie), 1983. Recreation: travel. Address: (h.) 119 Balshagray Avenue, Glasgow, G11 7EG; T.-041-954 8494.

Cowan, James Robertson, CBE, BSc, CEng, FIMinE, CBIM. Deputy Chairman, National Coal Board, since 1982; Chairman, Scottish Brick Corporation, since 1980; Deputy Chairman, British Investment Trust, since 1985; b. 12.9.19, Motherwell; m., Harriet Good Forrest; 2 d. Educ. Dalziel High School, Motherwell; Glasgow University. National Coal Board: Colliery Manager, 1945, Area Production Manager, 1957, Area General Manager, 1965, Director Scottish Area, 1971, full-time Member for Industrial Relations 1980. Visiting Professor, Strathclyde University, 1978; Past President, Mining Institute of Scotland. Recreations: golf; fishing. Address: (h.) Dale House, 31 Muirfield Park, Gullane, EH31 2DY; T.-0620 843398.

Cowan, Professor John, BSc (Hons), MSc, PhD, FIStructE, FICE. Professor of Engineering Education, Heriot-Watt University, since 1982; b. 19.3.32, Glasgow; m., Audrey Walker Cowan; 3 s.; 1 d. Educ. High School of Glasgow; Edinburgh University; Heriot-Watt University. Design engineer, Blyth & Blyth, Edinburgh, 1952-64; joined Heriot-Watt University as Lecturer, 1964; awards, Institution of Structural Engineers and Czech Ministry of Higher Education for work in engineering education research. Secretary, Scottish Schoolboys' Club. Recreations: reading; music; photography. Address: (b.) Civil Engineering Learning Unit, Heriot-Watt University, Riccarton, Currie, Edinburgh, EH14 4AS; T.-031-449 5111.

Cowan, Robert, MA. Chairman, Highlands and Islands Development Board, since 1982; Board Member, Scottish Development Agency; Member, Broadcasting Council for Scotland, since 1984; b. 27.7.32, Edinburgh; m., Margaret Morton Dewar; 2 d. Educ. Edinburgh Academy; Edinburgh University. Fisons Ltd., 1958-62; Wolsey Ltd., 1962-65; PA Management Consultants Ltd., 1965-82. Recreations: gardening; sailing. Address: (h.) The Old Manse, Farr, Inverness-shire; T.-08083 209.

Cowan, Robert L., MA, LLB. Regional Secretary, Lothian Regional Council, since 1982; b. 27.9.36, Edinburgh; m.; 3 children. Educ. Leith Academy, Edinburgh; Edinburgh University. Legal Assistant: Edinburgh Corporation, 1959-62, Perth County Council, 1962-64; Assistant Town Clerk, Burgh of Hawick, 1964-65; Edinburgh Corporation: Principal Legal Assistant, 1965-71, Depute Town Clerk, 1971-75; Deputy Director of Administration, Lothian Regional Council, 1975-82. Honorary Treasurer, Society of Directors of Administration in Scotland. Address: (b.) Regional Headquarters, George IV Bridge, Edinburgh; T.-031-229 9292.

Cowe, Alan Wilson, MA, LLB. Secretary and Clerk, Church of Scotland General Trustees, since 1964; b. 9.8.38, Kelso; m., Agnes Cunningham Dick. Educ. Dunfermline High School; Edinburgh University. Law apprentice, Simpson Kinmont & Maxwell, WS, Edinburgh; Assistant to Secretary, Church of Scotland General Trustees, 1963-64. Recreations: long-distance running; hill-walking. Address: (b.) 121 George Street, Edinburgh; T.-031-225 5722.

Cowie, Rev. James Morton, BD. Minister, Burnfoot Parish Church, Hawick, since 1984; b. 17.7.48, Aberdeen; m., Margaret Adams Davidson; 1 s.; 1 d. Educ. Aberdeen Academy; Aberdeen University; United Theological Seminary, Minnesota; Edinburgh University. Assistant Warden, St. Ninian's Training Centre, Crieff; Minister, Fordyce Parish Church. Chairman, local branch, RSSPCC. Recreations: sailing; computers. Address: 29 Wilton Hill, Hawick, Roxburghshire; T.-0450 73181.

Cowie, Professor John McKenzie Grant, BSc, PhD, CChem, FRSC, FRSE. Professor of Chemistry (and Head of Department), Stirling University, since 1973; b. 31.5.33, Edinburgh;

m., Agnes Neilson Campbell; 1 s.; 1 d. Educ. Royal High School, Edinburgh; Edinburgh University. Research Officer, National Research Council of Canada, Ottawa, 1958-67; Lecturer, Essex University, 1967-69; Senior Lecturer, Stirling University, 1969-73. Vice Chairman, Scottish Paraplegic Association. Recreations: reading; painting; listening to music. Address: (h.) Traquair, 50 Back Road, Dollar, Clackmannanshire; T.-Dollar 2031.

Cowie, Hon. Lord, (William Lorn Kerr Cowie). Senator of the College of Justice in Scotland, since 1977; b. 1.6.26; m.; 2 s.; 2 d. Educ. Fettes College; Clare College, Cambridge; Glasgow University. Sub-Lt., RNVR, 1944-47; Member, Faculty of Advocates, 1952; QC (Scot), 1967.

Cowley, Professor Roger A., MA, PhD, FRS, FRSE, FInstP. Professor of Physics, Edinburgh University, since 1970; b. 24.2.39, Woodford Green; m., Sheila Joyce Wells; 1 d. Educ. Brentwood School, Essex; Cambridge University. Research Fellow, Trinity Hall, Cambridge, 1962-64; Research Officer, Atomic Energy of Canada, 1964-70. Address: (b.) Department of Physics, Edinburgh University, Mayfield Road, Edinburgh; T.-031-667 1081.

Cowley, Sally Margaret. Conservative Group Leader, Banff and Buchan District Council, since 1984; b. 2.2.53, Caversham; m., Richard B.; 2 s.; 1 d. Educ. Monks Walk School, Welwyn Garden City. Recreations: squash; skiing; theatre. Address: (h.) Northcote, North Street, Mintlaw, Aberdeenshire; T.-Mintlaw 2158.

Cowpe, Jonathan George, BDS (Hons), FDSRCS Ed, PhD. Senior Lecturer in Dental Surgery, Dundee University, since 1985; Honorary Consultant in Oral Surgery, since 1985; b. 23.4.52, Manchester; m., Marianne. Educ. Cheltenham College; Manchester University. Resident House Officer in Oral Surgery, Manchester Dental Hospital, 1975-76; Resident Senior House Officer in Oral Surgery, Bolton General Hospital, 1976-78; Dundee Dental Hospital: Registrar in Oral Surgery, 1978-80, Lecturer and Honorary Senior Registrar in Oral Surgery, 1980-84. Toller Research Prize, 1981; Howard Elder Research Prize, 1983; Vice President, Dundee Dental Club. Recreations: golf; squash; hill-walking. Address: (h.) Kinbank, 9 Bay Road, Wormit, Fife; T.-Newport 541767.

Cox, John, BA (Hons). Artistic Director, Scottish Opera, since 1982; b. 12.3.35, Bristol. Educ. Queen Elizabeth's Hospital, Bristol; Oxford University. Freelance Director, plays and opera, since 1959; BBC TV Director, 1963-64; Director of Production, Glyndebourne Festival Opera, 1971-81. Recreations: gardens and gardening.

Coyle, Very Rev. Mgr. Francis Coyle, JCL. Parish Priest, St. Philomena's, Glasgow; b. 2.8.24, Glasgow. Educ. St. Aloysius College, Glasgow; St. Peter's College, Bearsden; Gregorian University, Rome. Assistant Priest, St. Andrew's Cathedral, 1949-52; Secretary, Archdiocese of Glasgow, 1952-68; Personal Secretary,

Archbishop Scanlan, 1968-72; Assistant Priest, St. Charles, 1952-71; Chancellor, Archdiocese of Glasgow, 1971-74; Catholic Representative, Strathclyde Region Education Committee, 1974-83; Vice President, Catholic Education Commission, 1974-83. Chaplain of Honour to the Pope, 1972; JP, Glasgow, 1980. Recreations: golf; photography. Address: St. Philomena's, 1255 Royston Road, Glasgow, G33; T.-041-770 4237.

Cracknell, (William) Martin. Chief Executive, Glenrothes Development Corporation, since 1976; b. 24.6.29, Leicester; m., Gillian Goatcher; 2 s.; 2 d. Educ. St. Edwards School, Oxford; Royal Military Academy, Sandhurst. Army, Royal Green Jackets, 1947-69; British Printing Industries Federation, 1969-76. Address: (b.) Balbirnie House, Glenrothes, Fife; T.-0592 754343.

Cradock, John Whitby, CA. Chairman, Richard Irvin & Sons Ltd., since 1980; Chairman, Aberdeen Harbour Board, since 1984; Trustee and Member of Board, Trustee Savings Bank Scotland, since 1983; b. 28.6.29, Beckenham, Kent; m., Vina McInnes; 3 s. Educ. Aberdeen Grammar School. Recreations: golf; curling. Address: (h.) 100 Kings Gate, Aberdeen; T.-0224 313901.

Craig, Alex. R., BSc. Headmaster, Hillhead High School, Glasgow, since 1976; b. 27.10.28, Cleland; m., Nessie; 2 s.; 1 d. Educ. Wishaw High School; Glasgow University. Secretary, Wishaw Bowling Club. Recreations: bowling; photography; DIY. Address: (b.) Hillhead High School, Oakfield Avenue, Glasgow; T.-041-339 8200.

Craig, Emeritus Professor Gordon Younger, BSc, PhD, MIGeol, FRSE. Emeritus Professor of Geology, Edinburgh University, since 1984; President, International Commission on the History of the Geological Sciences, since 1984; b. 17.1.25, Milngavie; m., Elizabeth Mary; 2 s. Educ. Hillhead High School; Bearsden Academy; Glasgow University; Edinburgh University. Joined Edinburgh University as Lecturer, 1947; James Hutton Professor of Geology, 1967-84. Publications: Geology of Scotland (Editor), 1983; James Hutton: The Lost Drawings (Co-author), 1977; A Geological Miscellany (Co-author), 1982. Recreations: golf; gardening. Address: (h.) 14 Kevock Road, Lasswade, Edinburgh, EH18 1HT; T.-031-663 8275.

Craig, James, OBE, MA, LLB, WS, NP. Retired solicitor; b. 15.9.14, Ardrossan; m., Alice Norris Leith; 1 s.; 1 d. Educ. Aberdeen Grammar School; Aberdeen University. Qualified as Solicitor, 1938; Royal Navy and Fleet Air Arm (Lt. Cmdr., RNVR); former Assistant Registrar of Friendly Societies for Scotland; former Assistant Certification Officer for Trade Unions and Employers Associations; former Treasurer, HM Commissioners Trust Funds for Queen Victoria School, Dunblane; former Secretary and Treasurer, Scottish Naval, Military and Air Force Veterans Residences. Recreation: now only golf. Address: (h.) 12 Royal Circus, Edinburgh; T.-031-226 6432.

Craig, James Leith Johnstone, MA, LLB, WS. Solicitor; Assistant Registrar of Friendly Societies for Scotland, since 1981; Assistant Certification Officer for Trade Unions and Employers Associations for Scotland, since 1980; b. 23.5.44, Aberdeen; m., Susan Mary McDowell; 1 s.; 1 d. Educ. George Watson's College; Edinburgh University. Apprentice, W. & J. Burness, WS, Edinburgh, 1966-68; Assistant, A. & J.L. Innes, Solicitors, Kirkcaldy, 1968-71; Partner, R. Addison Smith & Co., WS, Edinburgh, 1972-82; Partner, Balfour & Manson, Solicitors, Edinburgh, since 1982. Recreations: golf; skiing. Address: (b.) 58 Frederick Street, Edinburgh; T.-031-225 8291.

Craig, John Alexander, BSc, DipTP, MICE, MIHT, MRTPI, FRSA. Head, Department of Town and Country Planning, Edinburgh College of Art/Heriot-Watt University, since 1978; Dean, Faculty of Environmental Studies, Heriot-Watt University, since 1983; b. 18.5.32, Warrington, Lancashire; m., Jessie Crawford Inglis; 1 s.; 2 d. Educ. Invergordon Academy; Glasgow University; Edinburgh College of Art. National Service, RAF, 1955-57; Structural Engineer, P. & W. McLellan Ltd., Glasgow, 1957-59; Assistant Civil Engineer: Cumbernauld Development Corporation, 1959-63, Livingston Development Corporation, 1963-66; Lecturer, Department of Town and Country Planning, Edinburgh College of Art, 1966-78; private practice as Consultant Civil Engineer, 1968-77; part-time Lecturer, Coatbridge Technical College, 1957-63; Examiner, Glasgow and West of Scotland Committee for Technical Education, 1961-63; Member, Executive Committee, Scottish Branch, RTPI, 1979-83. Recreations: gardening; DIY house and car maintenance. Address: (h.) 1 Newland Avenue, Bathgate, West Lothian, EH48 1EE; T.-0506 53824.

Craig, John Warrender, LDS, RCSE, DPD. Chief Administrative Dental Officer, Lothian Health Board, since 1974; Honorary Senior Lecturer, Department of Preventive Dentistry, Edinburgh University, since 1974; b. 21.3.28, South Africa; m., Hazel Campbell Henry; 2 s. Educ. George Heriot's School, Edinburgh; Edinburgh University; St. Andrews University. Chief Dental Officer, Inverness County Council, 1958; Senior Hospital Dental Officer, Eastern Regional Hospital Board, and Clinical Lecturer in Operative Dental Surgery, Department of Orthodontics and Children's Dentistry, St. Andrews University, 1961; Chief Dental Officer, City of Edinburgh, 1965. British Dental Association: former Secretary, Highland and Dundee Sections, President, East of Scotland Branch, 1976-77; British Paedodontic Society: Chairman, East of Scotland Branch, 1970-73, National President, 1972-73; National President, British Association for the Study of Community Dentistry, 1978-79. Publications: The Management of Traumatized Incisor Teeth of Children (Co-author), 1970. Recreations: squash; music; gardening. Address: (h.) 1 Liberton Gardens, Edinburgh, EH16 6JX; T.-031-664 3195.

Craig, Rev. John Wilson, MA, BD. Minister, St. Stephen's Comely Bank Parish Church, since 1963; b. 5.2.25, Paisley; m., Helen McArthur;

3 s. Educ. Camphill Secondary School, Paisley; Glasgow University. Student Assistant: Sherwood Church, Paisley, 1948-50, Cardonald Church, Glasgow, 1950-51; Minister, Radnor Park Church, Clydebank, 1951-63. Industrial Chaplain, Ferranti (Edinburgh). Recreations: stamp collecting; walking; touring. Address: 8 Blinkbonny Crescent, Edinburgh, EH4 3NB; T.-031-332 3364.

Craig, Rev. Maxwell Davidson, MA, BD, ThM. Minister, Wellington Church, Glasgow, since 1973; Convener, Church and Nation Committee, Church of Scotland, since 1984; b. 25.12.31; m., Janet Margaret Macgregor; 3 d. Educ. Bradford Grammar School; Harrow School; Oriel College, Oxford; Edinburgh University. National Service, 1st Bn., Argyll and Sutherland Highlanders (2nd Lt.), 1954-56. Assistant Principal, Ministry of Labour, 1957-61; Private Secretary to Parliamentary Secretary, 1959-61; left London and civil service to train for ministry of Church of Scotland, 1961; ThM, Princeton, 1965; Minister, Grahamston Parish Church, Falkirk, 1966-73; Chairman: Falkirk Children's Panel, 1970-72, Hillhead Housing Association Ltd., since 1975; Member, Strathclyde Children's Panel, since 1973. Recreations: hill-walking; dinghy sailing; squash. Address: 27 Kingsborough Gardens, Glasgow, G12 9NH; T.-041-339 3627.

Craig, Rev. Neil Douglas, MA, BD. Minister, Craignair linked with Urr, since 1980; b. 7.8.22, Waterbeck; m., Florence Grimmond Sproul; 1 s.; 1 d. Educ. Royal High School, Edinburgh; Edinburgh University. Minister: St. Andrews Church, Hawick, 1947-53, Carstairs and Carstairs Junction, 1953-61, Craignair Church, Dalbeattie, 1961-80; former Convener, Youth Committee, Lanark Presbytery; Convener, Maintenance of the Ministry Committee, Dumfries Presbytery; Convener, General Assembly Committee on Probatioers and Transference of Ministers. Chairman: Dalbeattie Nursing Association, Lindsay Trust (Dalbeattie). Recreations: cricket; golf; gardening. Address: (h.) Langdale, Lochanhead, Dumfries; T.-0387 73 222.

Craig, Robert James, MB, ChB, MRCPsych, MPhil. Consultant psychiatrist; Consultant, Rosslynlee Hospital; b. 13.5.47, Newcastle; m., Élaine Catherine May; 1 s. Educ. Daniel Stewart's College; Edinburgh University. House Officer: Head Injuries and Neurosurgery, Edinburgh Royal Infirmary and Western General Hospital, Edinburgh, General Medicine, Eastern General Hospital, Edinburgh; Senior House Officer, General Medicine, Edenhall Hospital, Musselburgh; Registrar, Psychiatry, Rosslynlee Hospital, Roslin; Senior Registrar, Psychiatry, Royal Edinburgh Hospital. Address: (b.) Rosslynlee Hospital, Roslin, Midlothian, EH25 9QE; T.-031-440 2313.

Craig, Rev. William, BA, LTh. Minister, Cambusbarron, since 1974; b. 15.11.32, Lanarkshire; m., Margaret Campbell Gibb; 3 s. Educ. Whitehill Secondary School; Glasgow University; Open University. Recreations: reading; gardening. Address: 22 Douglas Terrace, Stirling, FK7 9LL; T.-Stirling 64108.

Craigen, Jim (James Mark), MP, MLitt, FBIM, JP. MP (Labour and Co-operative), Glasgow Maryhill, since February 1974; Deputy Labour Spokesman on Scottish Affairs, since 1983; b. 2.8.38, Glasgow; m., Sheena Millar. Educ. Shawlands Academy; Strathclyde University; Heriot-Watt University. Compositor, 1954-61; Industrial Relations Assistant, Scottish Gas Board, 1963-64; Assistant Secretary: Scottish TUC, 1964-68, Scottish Business Education Council, 1968-74; PPS to Secretary of State for Scotland, 1974-76; Member: UK Delegation to Council of Europe, 1976-80; Chairman, Scottish Labour Group of MPs, 1978-79; Member, Commons' Employment Select Committee, 1980-83 (Chairman, 1982-83). Glasgow City Councillor, 1965-68, and Magistrate, 1966-68; Member: Scottish Ambulance Board, 1966-71, Scottish Committee, Race Relations Board, 1967-70; Governor, Scottish Police College, 1970-74. Recreations: writing; walking; music; films. Address: House of Commons, London, SW1; T.-01-219 4558.

Craik, Alexander Duncan Davidson, BSc, PhD, FRSE. Reader in Applied Mathematics, St. Andrews University, since 1974; b. 25.8.38, Brechin; m., Elizabeth Mary Farmer; 1 s.; 1 d. Educ. Brechin High School; St. Andrews University; Cambridge University. St. Andrews University: Lecturer in Applied Mathematics, 1963-70, Senior Lecturer, 1970-74. Publication: Wave Interactions and Fluid Flows, 1985. Address: (h.) 92 Hepburn Gardens, St. Andrews, KY16 9LN; T.-0334 72992.

Craik, Sheriff Roger George, QC (Scot), MA, LLB. Sheriff of Lothian and Borders, since 1984; b. 22.11.40; m.; 1 s.; 1 d. Educ. Lockerbie Academy; Breadalbane Academy, Aberfeldy; George Watson's Boys' College; Edinburgh University. Solicitor, 1962; Orr Dignam & Co., Pakistan, 1963-65; called to Scottish Bar, 1966; Advocate Depute, 1980-83.

Craik, Wendy Ann, BA, PhD. Senior Lecturer in English, Aberdeen University, since 1972; b. 7.2.34, London; 1 s. Educ. Tiffin School, Kingston-on-Thames; Leicester University. Part-time Tutor, WEA and University Extension Courses, Vaughan College, Leicester, 1959-63; Principal English Teacher, Oadby Beauchamp Grammar School, Leicester, 1963-65; Lecturer in English, Aberdeen University, 1965-72. Publications: Jane Austen: the Six Novels; Jane Austen in her Time; Elizabeth Gaskell and the 19th Century Novel; The Bronte Novels. Address: (b.) Department of English, Kings College, Aberdeen; T.-0224 40241.

Cramond, Ronald Duncan, MA, FBIM, FSA Scot. Deputy Chairman, Highlands and Islands Development Board, since 1983; Trustee, National Museums of Scotland, since 1985; Member, Scottish Tourist Board, since 1985; b. 22.3.27, Leith; m., Constance MacGregor; 1 s.; 1 d. Educ. George Heriot's School; Edinburgh University. Commissioned Royal Scots, 1950; entered War Office, 1951; Private Secretary to Parliamentary Under Secretary of State, Scottish Office, 1956; Principal, Department of Health for Scotland,

1957; Mactaggart Fellow, Glasgow University, 1962; Haldane Medallist in Public Administration, 1964; Assistant Secretary, Scottish Development Department, 1966; Under Secretary, 1973; Under Secretary, Department of Agriculture and Fisheries for Scotland, 1977. Publication: Housing Policy in Scotland, 1966. Recreations: golf; hill-walking; geriatric rugby refereeing. Address: (b.) Highlands and Islands Development Board, Bridge House, 27 Bank Street, Inverness, IV1 1QR; T.-0463 234171.

Crampin, Stuart, BSc, PhD, ScD, FRAS. SPSO (Individual Merit), British Geological Survey, since 1976; Honorary Fellow, Geophysics Department, Edinburgh University, since 1971; Chairman, IASPEI Commission on Wave Propagation in Real Media, since 1983; b. 22.10.35, Tiptree, Essex; m., Roma Eluned Williams; 2 d. Educ. Maldon Grammar School; King's College, London; Pembroke College, Cambridge. Research Fellow, Uppsala University, 1963-65; Gassiot Fellow in Seismology, NERC, 1966-69; PSO, Institute of Geological Sciences, 1969-76. Recreations: hill-walking; travelling. Address: (b.) British Geological Survey, Murchison House, West Mains Road, Edinburgh, EH9 3LA; T.-031-667 1000.

Crampsey, Robert A. McN., MA (Hons), ARCM. Rector, St. Ambrose High School, Coatbridge, since 1974; freelance Broadcaster; Writer; b. 8.7.30, Glasgow; m., Dr. Veronica R. Carson; 4 d. Educ. Holyrood School, Glasgow; Glasgow University; London University (External). RAF, 1952-55 (demobilised in rank of Flt. Lt.); Head of History Department, St. Aloysius College, Glasgow, 1967-71; Assistant Head Teacher, Holyrood Secondary School, 1971-74. Winner, Brain of Britain, BBC, 1965; Churchill Fellow, 1970; semi-finalist, Mastermind, 1972-73; Radio Clyde Sports Commentator, since 1974. Publications: History of Queen's Park FC; Puerto Rico; The Manager; The Scottish Footballer; The Edinburgh Pirate (Arts Council Award); The Run Out. Recreations: travel; things Hispanic; listening to and playing music; cricket. Address: (h.) 15 Myrtle Park, Glasgow, G42; T.-041-423 2735.

Crawford, Henry Paton Fowler, MBE. Member, Scottish Agricultural Development Council; Member, Scottish Committee, Scottish Institute of Agricultural Engineering; Member, Scottish Agricultural Consultative Panel; b. 14.1.21, Harthill; m., Robina Cessford; 2 s.; 1 d. Educ. Harthill School. Left school aged 14 and worked on farm for 17 years; took up post as District Organiser, Scottish Farm Servants Union (subsequently known as the Scottish Agriculture, Horticulture and Forestry Section, TGWU); appointed Sectional Secretary for Scotland; now retired. Address: (h.) 9 Woodside Park, Kelso, Roxburghshire; T.-Kelso 24328.

Crawford, Iain Padruig. Author, Journalist, Playwright and Broadcaster; b. 21.1.22, Inverness; 3 s.; 1 d. Educ. Inverness Academy; Jordanhill College School, Glasgow. Cadet in Merchant Navy, Officer in Royal Navy, 1939-46; Journalist, 1947-51; BBC, 1951-55; freelance Writer, 1955-59; Journalist in Scotland and London,

1959-64; worked as Film Critic and Travel Editor, Sunday Express; TV programmes and plays for ATV, Harlech, BBC; Publicity Director: Edinburgh International Festival, 1973-80, Scottish Opera, 1980-81; author of plays, Broomstick over Badenoch and Under The Light, and books including The Burning Sea, The Sinclair Exclusive, Scare The Gentle Citizen, The Cafe Royal, The Profumo Affair, London Man, The Havana Cigar, What About Wine, Gateway to Wine, Wine on a Budget, Make Me a Wine Connoisseur, Open Guide to Royal St. George's and Sandwich, Open Guide to Royal Troon and Kyle, Open Guide to the Old Course and St. Andrews; eight-part film series, Held in Trust, STV. Recreations: music; golf; wine; watching rugby; other people's archaeology; French; Italian. Address: (h.) 173 Bruntsfield Place, Edinburgh, EH10 4DG; T.-031-229 2746.

Crawford, Robert Caldwell. Composer; b. 18.4.25, Edinburgh; m., Alison Braedine Orr; 1 s.; 1 d. Educ. Melville College, Edinburgh; Keswick Grammar School; Guildhall School of Music, London. Freelance Composer and Critic until 1970; BBC Music Producer, 1970-85; Chairman, Music Advisory Committee for Sir James Caird's Travelling Scholarships Trust, since 1978. Recreations: carpentry; hill-walking; gardening. Address: (h.) 41 Moray Place, Edinburgh, EH3 6BT; T.-031-225 6120.

Crawford, Professor Robert MacGregor Martyn, BSc, DocSciNat (Liege), FRSE. Professor of Plant Ecology, St. Andrews University, since 1977 (Provost, St. Leonard's College, since 1983); b. 30.5.34, Glasgow; m., Barbara Elizabeth Hall; 1 s. Educ. Glasgow Academy; Glasgow University; Liege University; Munich University; Moscow University. Lecturer, then Reader in Botany, St. Andrews University; Past President, Edinburgh Botanical Society; Editor, Flora. Recreations: European languages; music; photography. Address: (b.) Department of Plant Biology and Ecology, The University, St. Andrews, KY16 9AJ; T.-0334 76161.

Crawford, Stewart. Area Organiser, Union of Shop Distributive and Allied Workers, since 1978; Member, East Kilbride District Council, since 1984; b. 15.4.36, Glasgow; m., Marion Mulhall; 2 s. Educ. St. Gerards Senior Secondary School, Glasgow. Apprentice baker, 1951; baker until 1972; elected Organiser, Scottish Union of Bakers, 1972. Recreations: gardening; all sports as spectator. Address: (b.) 342 Albert Road, Glasgow, G41 5PS.

Crawford, Rev. Victor. Minister, Acharacle linked with Ardnamurchan, since 1980; b. 17.2.29, Dublin; m., Iris Frances Anderson; 1 s.; 3 d. Educ. St. George's National School, Dublin; New College, Edinburgh. Former foreman printer; lay missionary, Church of Scotland, Lovedale, South Africa, 1965-76. Address: The Manse, Acharacle, Argyll, PH36 4JU; T.-096 785 665.

Crean, Gerard Patrick, PhD, FRCPEdin, FRCPGlas. Consultant Physician-in-charge, Gastro-Intestinal Centre, Southern General Hospital, Glasgow, since 1967; Director, Diagnostic

Methodology Research Unit, Southern General Hospital, Glasgow, since 1970; Honorary Lecturer, Glasgow University, since 1970; b. 1.5.27, Courtown Harbour, County Wexford; m., Janice Dodds Mathieson; 1 s.; 2 d. Educ. Rockwell College, Cashel, County Tipperary; University College, Dublin. House appointments, Mater Misericordiae Hospital, Dublin, Western General Hospital, Edinburgh and Edinburgh Royal Infirmary; Registrar, then Senior Registrar, Western General Hospital, Edinburgh; Member, scientific staff, Medical Research Council Clinical Endocrinology Unit, Edinburgh; Honorary Lecturer, Department of Therapeutics, Edinburgh University; Visiting Professor in Physiology, Pennsylvania University. Clarke Prize, Edinburgh Pathological Club; contributed to several textbooks. Honorary Secretary, Scottish Fiddle Orchestra. Recreations: fiddle playing; traditional music; history of Antarctic exploration; golf. Address: (h.) St. Ronan's, Duchal Road, Kilmacolm, PA13 4AY; T.-Kilmacolm 2504.

Cresser, Malcolm Stewart, PhD, DIC, BSc, ARCS, FRSC, CChem. Senior Lecturer, Department of Soil Science, Aberdeen University, since 1982; b. 17.4.46, London; m., Louise Elizabeth Blackburn; 1 s.; 2 d. Educ. St. Ignatius College, Tottenham; Imperial College, London. Lecturer, Department of Soil Science, Aberdeen University, 1970-82; awarded 11th SAC Silver Medal, 1984. Publications: Solvent Extraction in Flame Spectroscopic Analysis; Environmental Chemical Analysis (Co-author). Recreations: painting; drawing; gardening. Address: (b.) Department of Soil Science, Meston Walk, Old Aberdeen, AB9 2UE; T.-0224 40241, Ext. 5675.

Cresswell, Lyell Richard, BMus (Hons), MusM, PhD. Cramb-Hinrichsen Fellow in Composition, Glasgow University, since 1982; b. 13.10.44, Wellington, New Zealand; m., Catherine Mawson. Educ. Victoria University of Wellington; Toronto University; Aberdeen University. Music Organiser, Chapter Arts Centre, Cardiff; Forman Fellow in Composition, Edinburgh University; Canadian Commonwealth scholarship, 1969-70; Dutch Government bursary, 1974-75; Ian Whyte Award, 1978; APRA Silver Scroll, 1979. Address: (h.) 4 Leslie Place, Edinburgh, EH4 1NQ; T.-031-332 9181.

Crichton, Charles Maitland Makgill, of That Ilk. Owner, Monzie and Largo Estates, since 1968; Managing Director, Monzie Joinery Ltd., since 1970; b. 25.7.42, Crieff; m., Isla Susan Gloag; 1 s. Educ. Winchester. Economics Intelligence Department, Bank of England, 1963-68. President, Crieff Branch, NFU; Chairman, Kinross and West Perthshire Conservative Association; Conservative candidate, Greenock and Port Glasgow, 1983, Northumbria (European Election), 1984. Recreation: cross-country skiing. Address: Monzie Castle, Crieff, Perthshire; T.-0764 3110.

Crichton, Rev. James, MA, BD, MTh. Minister, Crosshill linked with Dalrymple, since 1981; b. 1.10.44, Glasgow; m.; 2 s.; 1 d. Educ. Eastbank Academy; Glasgow University. Minister, Crosshill, 1969-81; Chaplain, Ayr County

Hospital, 1982-84; Member, South Ayrshire Health Council, since 1984; Moderator, Ayr Presbytery, 1984-85; Chairman, Scottish Reformation Society, since 1982. Publications: The Story of the Crosshill Churches; The Carrick Covenanters; Ayr Presbytery 1581-1981 (Co-author). Recreation: worrying about Rangers. Address: 30 Garden Street, Dalrymple, Ayrshire; T.-Dalrymple 263.

Crichton, James Peter. Farmer; Member, East Lothian District Council, since 1974; b. 6.3.34, Dunbar; m., Catherine Hazel Woolf; 2 s. Educ. Glenalmond College. Managing Director, grain co-operative; Tax Commissioner. Recreations: golf; attending orchestral concerts and opera. Address: Falsely, Innerwick, Dunbar, EH42 1SQ; T.-036 84 256.

Crichton, Thomas Kennedy, MBIM. Director of Industrial Liaison, Heriot-Watt University, Edinburgh, since 1982; b. 4.8.25, Edinburgh; m., Davida Anne Whiteford; 1 s.; 3 d. Educ. Daniel Stewart's College, Edinburgh; Heriot-Watt College, Edinburgh. Entered Royal Navy, 1943; commissioned, 1944; active service in light coastal forces in Channel, North Sea and Atlantic; Parts and Service Manager, James Ross & Sons (Motors) Ltd., Edinburgh, 1947-62; Divisional Manager, SAAB (Gt. Britain) Ltd., 1962-78; joined Heriot-Watt University, 1979. Director: Edinburgh Petroleum Development Services Ltd., Loch Ness Wellington Association Ltd.; Elder, Cramond Kirk. Recreations: walking and driving; now spectator only of rugby, climbing and motor sport. Address: (b.) Unilink, Heriot-Watt University, Riccarton, Edinburgh, EH14 4AS; T.-031-449 5111.

Croan, Sheriff Thomas Malcolm, MA, LLB. Sheriff of North Strathclyde at Kilmarnock, since 1983; b. 7.8.32, Edinburgh; m., Joan Kilpatrick Law; 1 s.; 3 d. Educ. St. Joseph's College, Dumfries; Edinburgh University. Admitted to Faculty of Advocates, 1956; Standing Junior Counsel, Scottish Development Department, 1964-65 and (for highways work), 1967-69; Advocate Depute, 1965-66; Sheriff of Grampian, Highland and Islands at Banff and Peterhead, 1969-83. Recreation: sailing. Address: (h.) Overdale, 113 Bentinck Drive, Troon.

Croft, Roy John, SRR, DCR. Superintendent Radiographer, Perth Royal Infirmary, since 1959; Chairman, Scottish Branch, College of Radiographers; b. 7.9.21, Newmarket; m., Margaret Erskine; 1 s.; 1 d. Educ. Archbishop Temple's Secondary School, Lambeth. Dark room technician, Brompton Hospital; student radiographer, West London Hospital; Sgt. Radiographer, RAMC, 1941-46; Superintendent Radiographer: Queen Mary's Hospital, Sidcup, Kent, Orpington Hospital, Kent. Secretary and Chairman, Tayside Sub-Branch, College of Radiographers; Scottish Member, Radiographers Board, Council of Professions Supplementary to Medicine; Member, Tayside Health Board, 1981-85; Elder, St. John's Kirk, Perth. Recreations: gardening; photography; wine-making. Address: (h.) 62 Jeanfield Road, Perth, PH1 1NZ; T.-0738 21805.

Crofton, Sir John Wenman, Kt (1977). Professor of Respiratory Diseases and Tuberculosis, Edinburgh University, 1952-77; b. 1912; m.; 2 s.; 3 d. Educ. Tonbridge; Sidney Sussex College, Cambridge; St. Thomas's Hospital. Vice-Principal, Edinburgh University, 1969-70; President, Royal College of Physicians of Edinburgh, 1973-76.

Crofts, Roger Stanley, BA, MLitt, CertEd. Assistant Secretary, Highlands and Tourism Division, Industry Department for Scotland, since 1984; b. 17.1.44, Leicester. Educ. Hinckley Grammar School; Liverpool University; Leicester University. Research Assistant in Geography: Aberdeen University, 1966-72, University College, London, 1972-74; entered Scottish Office, 1974; Senior Research Officer, 1974-78; Principal Research Officer, 1978-84. Recreations: gardening; choral singing; hill-walking. Address: (h.) 19 Manor Place, Edinburgh, EH3 7DX; T.-031-225 1177.

Cromartie, Earl of, (Roderick Grant Francis Mackenzie), MC, TD, JP, DL. Chief of the Clan Mackenzie; b. 24.10.04; m., 1, Dorothy Downing Porter (m. diss.); 2 d.; 2, Olga Mendoza (m. diss.); 1 s.; 3, Lilias Richard MacLeod. Educ. Charterhouse; Sandhurst. Major, Seaforth Highlanders (retired); Convener: Ross and Cromarty County Council, 1971-75, Ross and Cromarty District Council, 1975-77; Honorary Sheriff; Freeman of Ross and Cromarty, 1977. Address: (h.) Castle Leod, Strathpeffer, Ross and Cromarty.

Crombie, John Somerville Brand, BL, WS, NP. Partner, Alex. Morison & Co., WS, Edinburgh, since 1956; Director, Scottish Metropolitan Lands and Investments Ltd., since 1960; Director, Alna Press Ltd., since 1955; Director, Key Housing Association Ltd.; Director, Scotcap Ltd.; b. 10.8.29, Coatbridge; m., Isabella Rankin Cursiter; 3 d. Educ. Royal High School, Edinburgh; Edinburgh University. Formerly Secretary, Edinburgh Branch, Scottish Society for the Mentally Handicapped and Chairman, SSMH and Key Housing Association; Elder, Church of Scotland. Recreations: gardening; golf; curling; music. Address: (b.) 33 Queen Street, Edinburgh, EH2 1LE; T.-031-226 6541.

Crombie, Rev. William Duncan, MA (Hons), BD, HCF. Minister, Calton New Parish Church linked with St. Andrew's Parish Church, Glasgow, since 1976; b. 11.6.22, Milngavie; m., Margaret Harkness Kerr; 2 d. Educ. Bearsden Academy; Glasgow University. Minister, Townhead Church, Dumfries, 1947-51; Army Chaplain, 1951-54; Minister, Calton New Parish Church, 1955-76. Recreations: yachting; shooting. Address: (h.) 26 Circus Drive, Glasgow, G31 2JH; T.-041-554 5695.

Croom, Sir John (Halliday), Kt (1975), TD (1946), FRCP, FRCPEdin. President, Royal College of Physicians of Edinburgh, 1970-73; b. 2.7.09; m.; 1 s.; 1 d. Educ. Trinity College, Glenalmond; Gonville and Caius College, Cambridge; Edinburgh University. Lt.-Col., RAMC, Second World War (mentioned in Despatches); Consultant Physician, Edinburgh Royal Infirmary, 1946-74, Chalmers Hospital, Edinburgh,

1960-66; Chairman, Scottish Committee, Action on Smoking and Health, 1972-77; Chairman, Scottish Health Services Scientific Council, 1972-75; Chairman, Scottish Council for Postgraduate Medical Education, 1974-79.

Crosbie, Ian Martin, FCII. Member, Lothian Regional Council, since 1982; b. 26.5.22, Edinburgh; m., Lily; 1 s. Educ. Daniel Stewart's College, Edinburgh. Joined Scottish Life Assurance Company, 1939; RAF, 1941-46; management, Scottish Life Assurance Company, 1970-84; Council Member, Insurance Society of Edinburgh, 1973-83 (Honorary Treasurer, 1978-83). Secretary, Society of High Constables of Edinburgh. Recreations: golf; tennis; music; gardening; photography. Address: (h.) 4 Braehead Avenue, Edinburgh, EH4 6BA; T.-031-339 6233.

Crosby, William Scott, CBE (1982), BL. Lawyer; President, Society of Advocates in Aberdeen, since 1984; b. 31.7.18, Hawick; m., Margaret Elizabeth Bell; 3 s. Educ. Hawick High School; Edinburgh University. Army Service, 1939-46; Croix de Guerre, 1945; acted as Brigade Major 152 Brigade, 1945; Partner, Storie, Cruden & Simpson, Advocates, Aberdeen, since 1949; Chairman, Grampian Health Board, 1973-82. Former Treasurer, Society of Advocates in Aberdeen. Recreations: golf; swimming; walking; music; language study; gardening. Address: (h.) 82 Beaconsfield Place, Aberdeen; T.-Aberdeen 643067.

Crosfield, Very Rev. George Philip Chorley, MA (Cantab). Provost, St. Mary's Cathedral, Edinburgh, since 1970; b. 9.9.24, London; m., Susan Mary Jullion; 1 s.; 2 d. Educ. George Watson's College, Edinburgh; Selwyn College, Cambridge. Royal Artillery, 1942-46 (Captain); Priest, 1952; Assistant Curate: St. David's, Pilton, Edinburgh, 1951-53, St. Andrew's, St. Andrews, 1953-55; Rector, St. Cuthbert's, Hawick, 1955-60; Chaplain, Gordonstoun School, 1960-68; Canon and Vice-Provost, St. Mary's Cathedral, Edinburgh, 1968-70. Recreations: walking; reading; carpentry. Address: (h.) 8 Lansdowne Crescent, Edinburgh, EH12 5EQ; T.-031-225 2978.

Cross, Rev. Brian Frank, MA. Minister, Coalburn Parish Church, since 1961; b. 17.9.27, Hampstead. Educ. Finchley County School; Edinburgh University. RA, 1947-48 (2nd Lt.); underground labourer, NCB Scotland, 1951-52; General Studies Teacher, NCB Trainees, 1952-54; Assistant, Crown Court Church, London, 1957-60. Recreations: travel; classical music; amateur photography; reading. Address: 7 Schoolhouse Avenue, Coalburn, Lanarkshire, ML11 OLL; T.-055 582 641.

Cross, Ronald John, BSc, PhD, CChem, FRSC. Senior Lecturer in Inorganic Chemistry, Glasgow University, since 1967; b. 1.2.41, Alnwick, Northumberland; m., Janet Wheeler; 1 d. Educ. Duke's School, Alnwick; Blyth Grammar School; Durham University. Research Assistant, MIT, Cambridge, Massachusetts; joined Glasgow University, 1967. Recreation: private pilot. Address: (b.) Chemistry Department, Glasgow University, Glasgow, G12 8QQ; T.-041-339 8855.

Crossling, Frank Turner, MB, ChB, FRCSG, FRCSEng. Consultant General Surgeon, Stobhill General Hospital, Glasgow, since 1962; b. 16.8.27, Aberdeen; m., Margaret Elizabeth Abdy; 1 s. Educ. Robert Gordon's College, Aberdeen; Aberdeen University. Series of surgical posts in Aberdeen, London and Glasgow; seconded to University of East Africa, Nairobi, 1967, to help set up a medical school. Recreations: photography; classical music; gardening; dry fly fishing. Address: (h.) 28 North Grange Road, Bearsden, Glasgow, G61 3AF; T.-041-943 0409.

Cruickshank, Alistair Booth, MA. Lecturer, Glasgow University, since 1965; Member, Forth Valley Health Board, since 1977; b. 3.8.31, Dumfries; m., Sheena Carlin Brown; 2 s.; 1 d. Educ. High School of Stirling; Glasgow University; Georgia University. Flying Officer, Education Branch, RAF, 1956-58; Glasgow University, 1958-61; Nottingham University, 1961-65. Member, Clackmannan District Council, 1974-77; Area Commissioner, Scouts, Clackmannanshire, since 1980. Recreations: fishing; scouting. Address: (b.) Department of Geography, Glasgow University, Glasgow, G12 8QQ; T.-041-339 8855.

Cruickshank, Robert James, SSC. Honorary Sheriff at Ayr; b. 1.8.15, Irvine; b. Isabella Jackson McDougall; 1 d. Educ. Cumnock Academy; Edinburgh University. Depute Procurator Fiscal: Aberdeen, 1943-47, Ayr, 1947-51; Senior Depute Procurator Fiscal, Edinburgh, 1951-54; Procurator Fiscal: Falkirk, 1954-58, Ayr, 1959-76. Address: (h.) Corncairn, 5 Abbot's Way, Doonfoot, Ayr, KA7 4EZ; T.-Ayr 41533.

Culshaw, Professor Brian, BSc, PhD, CEng, MIEE. Professor of Electronics, Strathclyde University, since 1983; b. 24.9.45, Ormskirk; m., Patricia Brigid; 2 d. Educ. Ormskirk Grammar School; University College, London. Research Fellow, Cornell University, 1970; Technical Staff Member, Bell Northern Research, Ottawa, 1970-73; University College, London: Research Fellow, 1974-75, Lecturer, 1975-82, Reader, 1983. Recreations: walking; photography; music and opera; theatre. Address: (h.) Cromdale, Gryffe Road, Kilmacolm, Renfrewshire, PA13 4BD; T.-050587 2460.

Cumming, James William Hunter, RSA, RSW, DA, PPSSA. Painter; b. 24.12.22, Dunfermline; m., Betty Elston; 1 s.; 1 d. Educ. Dunfermline High School; Edinburgh College of Art; Edinburgh University. RAF Volunteer Reserve, 1941-46 (flew SEAAF); Lecturer, Drawing, Painting, History of Art, Edinburgh, 1950-60; Senior Lecturer, Mural Department and School of Drawing and Painting, Edinburgh, 1960-82; President, Society of Scottish Artists, 1958-61; contributor to BBC radio and television arts programmes, 1958-68; elected ARSA and RSW, 1962; wrote outline and script for film, Three Scottish Painters; Member, Broadcasting Council for Scotland, 1969-75; elected Royal Scottish Academician, 1970; Treasurer, RSA, 1973-78; Council Member, National Academic Awards of Great Britain, 1974-79 (Fine Art Board Assessor and Member, Committee for Research Degree Awards); Secretary, RSA, 1978-80;

Royal Scottish Academy Award, 1951; awarded scholarship in the Humanities, International Seminar, Harvard University, 1964; awarded Prize by Royal Scottish Society of Painters in Watercolour, 1977; Lothian Region Award, RSW Centenary Exhibition, Edinburgh, 1980. Recreation: watching the world go by. Address: Studio, Swallow Cottage, Lennel, near Coldstream, Berwickshire; T.-0890 2064.

Cumming, Robert Currie, BL, FIBS, AIB, FRCSEdin (Hon.). Chairman, English Speaking Union - Scotland, since 1984; Non-Executive Director, Adam & Co. PLC, since 1983; b. 21.5.21, Strathaven; m., Mary Jean McDonald Crombie. Educ. Hutchesons' Grammar School, Glasgow; Glasgow University. Former Executive Director, Royal Bank of Scotland Group PLC and Royal Bank of Scotland PLC. Trustee and Council Member, Royal Scottish Geographical Society; Member, Finance Committee, Royal Blind Asylum; Member, Investment Committee and Finance Committee, Royal College of Surgeons, Edinburgh; Member, Investment Committee, Church of Scotland Trust; Representative to University Conference, Stirling University. Recreations: fishing; golf; walking. Address: (h.) 3 Succoth Park, Edinburgh, EH12 6BX; T.-031-337 1910.

Cumming, Ronald Patrick, MB, ChB, FRCSEdin. Consultant Surgeon, Shetland Hospitals, since 1957; Honorary Senior Lecturer in Surgery, Aberdeen University, since 1980; b. 15.8.23, Golspie; m., Norma Gladys Kitson; 2 s. Educ. Golspie Secondary School; Aberdeen University. General practice assistant, Huntly and Rhynie, Aberdeenshire; Assistant Lecturer in Anatomy, Aberdeen University; junior surgical posts in Worcester, Burnley, and Aberdeen; Fellow: British Medical Association, Association of Surgeons of Great Britain and Ireland. JP; Honorary Sheriff; Chairman, Shetland Committee for Employment of Disabled People; former Member, Lerwick Town Council and Shetland County Council; Junior Bailie, Lerwick Town Council, 1972-75; President, Shetland Fiddlers Society. Publication: Aspects of Health and Safety in Oil Development (Co-Editor). Recreations: golf; badminton; gardening; reading; music. Address: (h.) 62 Hammerfield Avenue, Aberdeen; T.-0224 313192.

Cummins, John George, MA, PhD. Reader in Spanish, Aberdeen University, since 1980 (Head of Department of Spanish, since 1979); b. 26.9.37, Hull; m., Elaine S. Rockett; 2 s.; 1 d. Educ. Malet Lambert School, Hull; Manchester University. Assistant in Spanish, St. Andrews University, 1961-63; Lecturer in Spanish, Birmingham University, 1963-64; Aberdeen University: Lecturer in Spanish, 1964-72, Senior Lecturer in Spanish, 1972-80. Recreations: shooting; fishing. Address: (b.) Department of Spanish, King's College, Aberdeen University, Old Aberdeen; T.-Aberdeen 40241.

Cunningham, Professor Ian M.M., CBE, FRSE, FIBiol, Bsc, PhD. Professor of Agriculture, Glasgow University, since 1980; Principal, West of Scotland Agricultural College, since 1980; b. 30.9.25, Kirknewton; m., Agnes Whitelaw

Frew. Educ. Lanark Grammar School; Edinburgh University. Assistant Economist, West of Scotland Agricultural College, 1946-47; Lecturer in Agriculture, Durham School of Agriculture, 1947-50; Lecturer, then Senior Lecturer, Edinburgh University, 1950-68; Director, Hill Farming Research Organisation, 1968-80. Member: Farm Animal Welfare Council, Hill Farming Advisory Committee, Scotland; George Hedley Memorial Award for services to the sheep industry; Massey Ferguson Award for services to British agriculture. Address: (h.) Bruaich, High Corton, by Ayr; T.-0292 41233.

Cunningham, John Wylie Rodger. Director General and Secretary, St. Andrew's Ambulance Association, since 1983; b. 4.4.45, Kilmarnock; m., Agnes Margaret Elizabeth (Margot). Educ. Irvine Royal Academy. Entered journalism with George Outram group, including several years with the Glasgow Herald; moved into administration, 1968, and spent eight years on secretariat of National Farmers' Union of Scotland; joined Charles Barker Scotland as senior Public Relations Executive; Scottish Regional Public Affairs Officer, Royal Scottish Automobile Club. Recreations: cinema and theatre; sport, especially cricket and rugby; eating out; military history; writing; walking; hard work. Address: (h.) Birnam Lodge, Stevenston Road, Kilwinning, Ayrshire; T.-0294 52338.

Curle, Professor Samuel Newby, BSc, MSc, PhD, FRSE. Gregory Professor of Applied Mathematics, St. Andrews University, since 1967 (Dean, Faculty of Science, since 1982); b. 18.6.30, Sunderland; m., Shirley Kingsford Campion; 3 s.; 1 d. Educ. Bede School, Sunderland; Manchester University. Assistant Lecturer, Mathematics Department, Manchester University, 1953-54; Scientific Officer, Aerodynamics Division, National Physical Laboratory, 1954-61; Southampton University: Reader, Department of Aeronautics/Astronautics, 1961-64, Reader, Department of Mathematics, 1964-67. Orville Wright Prize, Royal Aeronautical Society, 1963; Secretary, Methodist International House, Southampton, 1964-67. Recreations: music; cricket; soccer. Address: (b.) Mathematical Institute, North Haugh, St. Andrews, KY16 9SS; T.-0334 76161.

Curran, Ronald. Scottish National Officer, National Union of Public Employees, since 1975; President, Scottish Trades Union Congress, 1986; b. 8.6.27, North Shields; m., Doreen Stoneman; 1 s.; 2 d. Educ. Ralph Gardner Secondary School, North Shields; Newbattle Abbey College. NUPE: full-time Area Officer, 1967, Deputy Divisional Officer, 1970; Scottish TUC: Member, General Council, since 1978, Chairman Health and Social Services Committee, 1979-81, Chairman Local Government Sub-Committee, since 1979, Chairman, General Purposes Committee, since 1984, Chairman, Economic Committee, since 1985. Recreations: painting; drawing; writing. Address: (h.) 90 Newbattle Abbey Crescent, Dalkeith, Midlothian; T.-031-663 1323.

Curran, Professor Sir Samuel Crowe, Kt, DL, MA, BSc, PhD, DSc, FInstP, FInstE, FRSE, FRS, CEng, DEng, FEng. Visiting Professor of Energy Studies, Glasgow University; Scientific Adviser to various organisations; b. 23.5.12, Ballymena, Northern Ireland; m.; 3 s.; 1 d. Educ. Wishaw High School; Glasgow University; Cambridge University; California University. Research, Glasgow University, Cambridge University; war research, MAP and Ministry of Supply in radar and atom bomb (Manhattan project); staff, Physics Department, Glasgow University; Chief Scientist, UKAEA at AWRE (also on board, UKAEA, Harwell); Principal, Royal College of Science and Technology, Glasgow; Principal and Vice-Chancellor, Strathclyde University. Publications: books on nuclear radiation and energy topics. Recreations: golf; horology. Address: (h.) 93 Kelvin Court, Glasgow, G12 OAH; T.-041-334 8329.

Currie, Professor Sir Alastair Robert, Kt, MB, ChB, Hon DSc, FRCP, FRCPEdin, FRCPGlas, FRCSE, FRCPath, FRSE. Professor of Pathology, Edinburgh University, since 1972; Honorary Consultant Pathologist, Lothian Health Board, since 1972; Pathologist, Edinburgh Royal Infirmary, since 1972; b. 8.10.21, Isle of Islay; m., Jeanne Marion Clarke, MB, ChB; 3 s.; 2 d. Educ. High School of Glasgow; Glasgow University. Lecturer and Senior Lecturer in Pathology, Glasgow University and Glasgow Royal Infirmary, 1945-59; Head, Division of Pathology, Imperial Cancer Research Fund, London, 1959-62; Regius Professor of Pathology, Aberdeen University, 1962-72. Deputy Chairman, Council, and Chairman, Executive Committee, Cancer Research Campaign; Member, UK Coordinating Committee on Cancer Research. Recreation: reading. Address: (h.) 42 Murrayfield Avenue, Edinburgh, EH12 6AY; T.-031-337 3100.

Currie, Alexander Monteith, OBE, BA, BLitt. Secretary, Edinburgh University, since 1978; b. 2.5.26, Stevenston; m., Pamela Mary Breeze; 2 s. Educ. Stevenston Higher Grade School; Portmadoc Grammar School; Bangor University; St. Catherine's College, Oxford. Administrative Officer, Manchester University, 1952-61; Academic Secretary, Liverpool University, 1962-65; Registrar and Secretary, Sheffield University, 1965-78. Address: (h.) 13 Moray Place, Edinburgh, EH3 6DT; T.-031-225 7775.

Currie, Rev. David Edward Paxton, BSc, BD. Minister, West Kirk, East Kilbride, since 1983; b. 27.6.50, Glasgow; m., Gwen; 1 s.; 2 d. Educ. Hunter High School, East Kilbride; Duncanrig Senior Secondary School, East Kilbride; Strathclyde University; Glasgow University. Apprentice metallurgist, Rolls Royce, Hillington, 1967-70; studied, Strathclyde University, 1970-74; Rolls Royce: Production Engineer, Hillington, 1974-77, Development Engineer, East Kilbride, 1977-79; studied for the ministry, 1979-82; probationery year, Rutherglen Stonelaw, 1982-83. Recreations: skiing; running. Address: 1 Barr Terrace, West Mains, East Kilbride, G74 1AP; T.-East Kilbride 20753.

Currie, Euan Kinnaird Cockburn, JP. Honorary Sheriff, since 1979; Hotelier, since 1964; b. 4.10.37, Grantown on Spey; m., 1, Rosemary C. Mitchell; 2, Joan C. Bowie; 3 s.; 2 d.

Educ. Gordonstoun School; West of Scotland Agricultural College. Dairy farming, 1958-64; 11th Bn., Seaforth Highlanders, 1963-66 (Lt.); Member, Royal Burgh of Dornoch Town Council, 1968-74 (Dean of Guild and Junior Bailie); Member, Sutherland Education Authority, 1973-74; Founder Member, Royal Burgh of Dornoch Business and Trades Association; winner, Grouse/SCWS Silver Jubilee Community Project. Recreations: curling; golf; reading; bird-watching; Scottish history. Address: (h.) An Cardach, Burghfield, Dornoch; T.-0862 810212.

Currie, Rev. James, MA, BD, JP, FSA Scot. Minister, Dunlop, since 1972; b. 16.1.21, Blackwaterfoot, Arran; m., Margaret Flora Maclean; 3 s. Educ. Shiskine Public School; Keil School; Glasgow University and Trinity College, Glasgow. Minister: Old Kirk of Edinburgh, 1944; Millburn Renton, 1950-55, St. James (Pollok), Glasgow, 1955-72. Honorary President, East Park Home for Infirm Children. Recreations: leading pilgrim parties to Holy Land (44 times), India and Oberammergau. Address: 73 Main Street, Dunlop; T.-0560 84878.

Currie, James W., BSc (Hons), DRTC, FIEE, CEng. Chief Engineer, Generation Design and Construction, South of Scotland Electricity Board; b. 25.7.24, Ayr; m., Mary E. Procter; 1 s.; 1 d. Educ. Irvine Royal Academy; Glasgow University; Royal Technical College. Army Service, 1944-47; Kennedy & Donkin, Consulting Engineers, 1947-52; Montreal Engineering Company, Canada and Venezuela, 1952-55; Associated Industrial Consultants, 1955-56; Kennedy & Donkin, Consulting Engineers, 1956-62; joined SSEB, 1962. Past President: Scottish Ski Club, Scottish National Ski Council; former Vice President, British National Ski Federation. Recreations: skiing; golf; sailing. Address: (b.) SSEB, Cathcart House, Spean Street, Glasgow, G44 4BE; T.-041-637 7177.

Currie, John (Ian) C., CChem, MRSC, FIWPC, FIPHE, MIWES. Director and River Inspector, Tweed River Purification Board, since 1964; b. 19.10.33, Glasgow; m., Margaret A.; 3 s.; 1 d. Educ. Shawlands Academy, Glasgow; Paisley Technical College. Assistant Inspector and Chemist, Tweed River Purification Board, 1955-61; Assistant Inspector, Clyde River Purification Board, 1961-64; Pollution Prevention Officer, Usk River Authority, 1964. Recreation: golf. Address: (b.) Burnbrae, Mossilee Road, Galashiels; T.-0896 2425.

Currie, Rev. Robert, MA. Community Minister, Partick, Glasgow, since 1984; Chaplain, Queen Mother's Hospital, Glasgow, since 1978 and Royal Hospital for Sick Children, Glasgow, since 1984; b. 9.12.24, Aberdeen; m., Sheila Thomson; 1 s.; 2 d. Educ. Robert Gordon's College; Central School, Aberdeen; Aberdeen University; Christ's College, Aberdeen. Minister: Boquhanran, Clydebank, 1955-69, Dowanhill, Glasgow, 1969-84; Member, Publications Committee, Iona Community, since 1972; former Secretary, Scottish Pastoral Association (now defunct). Recreation: listening to choral, organ and orchestral music. Address: 61 Dowanside Road, Glasgow, G12 9DL; T.-041-334 5111.

Currie, Professor Ronald Ian, CBE (1977), FIBiol, FRSE, BSc (Hons). Director and Secretary, Scottish Marine Biological Association, since 1966; b. 10.10.28; m., Cecilia de Garis; 1 s.; 1 d. Educ. Glasgow University; Copenhagen University. Joined Royal Naval Scientific Service, 1949; seconded to National Institute of Oceanography; William Scoresby Expedition, South Africa, 1950; Discovery Expedition, Antarctica, 1951; Chairman, Biological Planning Committee, International Indian Ocean Expedition, 1960; Indian Ocean Expedition, 1963 and 1964; Secretary: International Association for Biological Oceanography, 1964-66 (President, 1966-70), Scientific Committee on Oceanic Research, International Council of Scientific Unions, 1972-78; Honorary Secretary, Challenger Society, since 1956; Honorary Professor, Heriot-Watt University, 1979. Recreations: cooking; hill-walking; shooting; local history. Address: (h.) Kilmore House, Kilmore, by Oban, Argyll; T.-Kilmore 248.

Curtis, Professor Adam Sebastian Genevieve, MA, PhD. Professor of Cell Biology, Glasgow University, since 1967; b. 3.1.34, London; m., Ann Park; 2 d. Educ. Aldenham School; Kings College, Cambridge. University College, London: Honorary Research Assistant, 1957-62, Lecturer in Zoology, 1962-67. Director, Company of Biologists Ltd., since 1961; Governor, Westbourne School, since 1985; Council Member, Royal Society of Edinburgh, since 1983; Editor, Scottish Diver magazine, since 1978; President, Scottish Sub-Aqua Club, 1972-76. Recreations: sports diving; gardening. Address: (h.) 2 Kirklee Circus, Glasgow, G12 OTW; T.-041-339 2152.

Curtis, G. Ronald, BSc, CEng, FICE, FSA Scot. Reservoir Safety Engineer, North of Scotland Hydro-Electric Board, since 1971; Member, British National Committee on Large Dams; Chairman, Historic Roads and Bridges Committee, Association for the Protection of Rural Scotland, since 1983; b. 24.4.25, Edinburgh; m.; 4 s. Educ. George Watson's College, Edinburgh; Edinburgh University. Design of sewage works, J.D. & D.M. Watson, Consulting Civil Engineers, London, 1947-49; design and construction of sewerage and water supply schemes, Babtie Shaw and Morton, Consulting Civil Engineers, Glasgow, 1949-58; joined North of Scotland Hydro-Electric Board, 1958. Elder, Church of Scotland, since 1962; Leader, Scout Movement, 1943-75. Recreations: Scotland; archaeology; historic Highland roads and bridges; megalithic astronomy. Address: (h.) 4 Braid Mount Rise, Edinburgh, EH10 6JW.

Cuschieri, Professor Alfred, MD, ChM, FRCS, FRCSEdin. Professor of Surgery, Dundee University, since 1976; Honorary Senior Consultant Surgeon, Tayside Health Board, since 1976; President, British Association of Surgical Oncology, since 1984; b. 30.9.38, Sliema, Malta; m., Dr. M.P. Holley; 3 d. Educ. St. Aloysius College; Royal University of Malta; Liverpool University. Reader in Surgery, Liverpool University, 1972-76; Secretary, Surgical Research Society, 1976-79; Council Member, Royal College of

Surgeons of Edinburgh, since 1982. Publications: Essential Surgical Practice; Introduction to Research in Medical Sciences; Common Bile Duct Exploration. Recreations: fishing; music. Address: (b.) Ninewells Hospital and Medical School, Dundee, DD1 9SY; T.-Dundee 60111, Ext. 2174.

Cusine, Douglas James, LLB. Senior Lecturer in Conveyancing and Professional Practice of Law, Aberdeen University, since 1982; b. 2.9.46, Glasgow; m., Marilyn Calvert Ramsay; 1 s.; 1 d. Educ. Hutchesons' Boys' Grammar School; Glasgow University. Solicitor, 1971; Lecturer in Private Law: Glasgow University, 1974-76, Aberdeen University, 1977-82. Publication: Marine Pollution: Law and Practice (Co-Editor), 1980. Recreations: swimming; walking; bird-watching. Address: (h.) New Mearns, Downies, Portlethen, Aberdeen; T.-0224 780334.

Cuthbert, James R., MA, MSc, DPhil. Chief Statistician, Scottish Education Department, since 1982; b. 20.7.46, Irvine. Educ. Glasgow University; Sussex University. Lecturer in Statistics, Glasgow University, 1970-74; civil servant (Scottish Office and HM Treasury), since 1974. Address: (b.) Scottish Education Department, 43 Jeffrey Street, Edinburgh.

Cuthbert, William Moncrieff, DL. Chairman of Council and Executive Committee, National Trust for Scotland, since 1984; Managing Director, Clyde Shipping Company Ltd., since 1971; b. 22.6.36; m.; 2 s.; 1 d. Educ. Shrewsbury School. Member, Queen's Bodyguard for Scotland (Royal Company of Archers); DL Stirling and Falkirk, 1984.

Cuthbertson, Sir David Paton, Kt (1965), CBE (1957), MD, DSc, FRSE, FRCPEdin. Honorary Senior Research Fellow in Pathological Biochemistry, Glasgow University; Honorary Consultant, Biochemical Department, Glasgow Royal Infirmary; b. 9.5.00; m.; 2 s.; 1 d. Educ. Glasgow University. Director, Rowett Research Institute, 1945-65.

Cuthbertson, Iain. Actor; b. 4.1.30. Acted, Citizens', Glasgow, 1958-60; made London debut with the Citizens' in Gay Landscape, 1958; played title role in The Wallace, Edinburgh Festival, Edinburgh Festival, 1960; Member, Pitlochry Festival company, 1961; General Manager and Director of Productions, Citizens', 1962-65; there created the role of Armstrong in Armstrong's Last Goodnight; Associate Director, Royal Court Theatre, London, 1965; there played Musgrave in Sergeant Musgrave's Dance; Director, Perth Theatre, 1967-68; played the leading role in Sutherland's Law (TV series).

Cuthbertson, Ian Jardine, LLB, NP. Partner, Dorman, Jeffrey & Co., Solicitors, Glasgow and Edinburgh, since 1979; b. 8.5.51, Glasgow; m., Sally Jane; 1 s.; 2 d. Educ. Jordanhill College School, Glasgow; Glasgow University. Apprenticeship, Messrs Boyds; admitted as Solicitor, 1974; Partner, Messrs Boyds, 1978; jointly founded firm of Dorman Jeffrey & Co., 1979. Honorary Legal Adviser, St. Mungo Group,

Riding for the Disabled Association. Recreations: rugby; swimming; reading; computers. Address: (b.) 140 West George Street, Glasgow, G2 2HH; T.-041-332 7916.

Cuthell, Rev. Thomas Cuthbertson, MA, BD. Senior Minister, St. Cuthbert's Parish Church, Edinburgh, since 1976; b. 18.2.41, Falkirk. Educ. Bo'ness Academy; Edinburgh University. Assistant Minister, St. Giles Cathedral, Edinburgh, 1964-66; Minister, North Kirk, Uphall, 1966-76. Chairman, West End Council of Churches, Edinburgh. Recreations: yacht racing; music; squash. Address: (h.) 22 Learmonth Terrace, Edinburgh, EH4 1PG; T.-031-332 6138.

Cutt, Ronald Torrance, CA. Finance Officer, Heriot-Watt University, since 1977; b. 8.4.33, Edinburgh; m., Sheila; 1 s.; 1 d. Educ. George Heriot's School, Edinburgh. Accountant: Regional Hospital Board, Edinburgh, Northern Hospital Board; Deputy Bursar, Heriot-Watt University. Address: (h.) 10 Loch Road, Edinburgh, EH4 3PW; T.-031-336 3289.

Czerkawska, Catherine Lucy, MA (Hons); MA (postgraduate). Freelance Writer and Dramatist; b. 3.12.50, Leeds; m., Alan Lees. Educ. Queen Margaret's Academy, Ayr; St. Michael's Academy, Kilwinning; Edinburgh University; Leeds University. Began by writing and reading poetry; on leaving university, wrote and published two books of poetry (White Boats and A Book of Men); taught EFL in Finland and Poland for three years; returned to Scotland to work as Community Writer in Fife; thereafter, full-time freelance Writer working on radio and television drama, original plays and adaptations, short stories, features, etc.; author, Fisherfolk of Carrick; Pye Radio Award, Best Play of 1980, for Oh Flower of Scotland; Scottish Radio Industries Club Award, 1983, for Bonnie Blue Hen. Recreations: karate; swimming; travel; local history; cookery; films. Address: c/o A.D. Peters and Co. Ltd., 10 Buckingham Street, London, WC2N 6BU; T.-01-839 2556.

D

Daft, Melvin Francis James, BSc, PhD, DSc, FRSE. Senior Lecturer, Department of Biological Sciences, Dundee University, since 1973; b. 19.1.35, Welwyn, Hertfordshire; m., Margaret Elizabeth Hill; 2 s. Educ. Welwyn Garden City Grammar School; Exeter University. Assistant Lecturer, 1961; Lecturer, 1963. Recreations: golf (badly); gardening. Address: (b.) Department of Biological Sciences, The University, Dundee, DD1 4HN; T.-0382 23181, Ext. 4257.

Dagg, John Hunter, MD (Hons), FRCPGlas, FRCPEdin. Consultant Physician, Western Infirmary, Glasgow, since 1972; Honorary Lecturer in Medicine, Glasgow University, since 1962;

b. 23.3.33, Rutherglen. Educ. High School of Glasgow; Glasgow University. Junior hospital posts, Glasgow and Paisley, 1958-65; Senior US Public Health Service Fellòw, University of Washington Medical School, 1965-67; Senior Wellcome Fellow in Clinical Science, University Department of Medicine, Western Infirmary, Glasgow, 1968-72. Honorary Curator, Art Collection, and other activities, Royal College of Physicians and Surgeons, Glasgow; Member, Medical Advisory Committee, Greater Glasgow Health Board. Recreations: classical music, especially as pianist; hill-walking; gardening. Address: (h.) 26 Westbourne Gardens, Glasgow, G12; T.-041-334 2981.

Daiches, David, MA, DPhil (Oxon), PhD (Cantab), FRSL, FRSE. Director, Institute of Advanced Studies in the Humanities, Edinburgh University, since 1980; b. 2.9.12; m., 1, Isobel J. Mackay (deceased); 1 s.; 2 d.; 2, Hazel Neville. Educ. George Watson's College, Edinburgh; Edinburgh University; Balliol College, Oxford. Professor of English, Sussex University, 1961-77 (Dean, School of English Studies, 1961-68); author of numerous works of criticism and biography.

Daiches, Lionel Henry, QC (Scot), MA, LLB; b. 8.3.11; m., Dorothy Estelle Bernstein (m. diss.); 2 s. Educ. George Watson's College, Edinburgh; Edinburgh University. Admitted, Scottish Bar, 1946; QC, 1956; Sheriff-Substitute of Lanarkshire, at Glasgow, 1962-67.

Dalby, Martin, BMus, ARCM. Head of Music, BBC Scotland, since 1972; b. 25.4.42, Aberdeen; m., Hilary. Educ. Aberdeen Grammar School; Royal College of Music. Music Producer, BBC Radio 3, 1965-71; Cramb Research Fellow in Composition, Glasgow University, 1971-72; freelance Composer. Recreations: railways; bird-watching; hill-walking. Address: (h.) 23 Muirpark Way, Drymen, near Glasgow, G63 ODX.

Dale, Brian Graeme, LLB, WS, NP. Partner, Brooke & Brown, WS, Dunbar, since 1974; Convener, Board of Administration, General Synod, Scottish Episcopal Church, since 1980; b. 20.11.46, London; m., Judith Gail de Beaufort Franklin; 4 s.; 1 d. Educ. Bristol Grammar School; Aberdeen University. Legal apprentice, Shepherd & Wedderburn, WS, Edinburgh, 1968-70; Assistant, then Partner, Stuart & Stuart Cairns & Co., WS, Edinburgh, 1970-85; Treasurer, 1971, Secretary, 1974, Registrar, 1974, Diocese of Edinburgh, Scottish Episcopal Church; Dean, East Lothian Faculty of Procurators, 1984-86. Secretary, St. Mary's Music School Trust Ltd.; Chairman, Dunbar & District Round Table, 1984-85; Honorary Secretary, Abbeyfield Society (Dunbar) Ltd. Recreations: music; badminton and sport in general; singing; family life; organ-playing. Address: (h.) 2 Newhouse Terrace, Dunbar, East Lothian; T.-Dunbar 62059.

Dalgety, Ramsay Robertson, LLB (Hons). Advocate, since 1972; b. 2.7.45, Edinburgh; m., Mary Margaret Bernard; 1 s.; 1 d. Educ. High School of Dundee; St. Andrews University.

Member, City of Edinburgh District Council, 1974-80; a Director, Scottish Opera Ltd., since 1980; Chairman/Director, Venture Shipping Ltd., since 1983; Trustee, Opera Singers Pension Fund (London), since 1983. Address: 196 Craigleith Road, Edinburgh, EH4 2EE; T.-031-332 1417.

Dalgleish, Douglas George, BSc, PhD. Head, Department of Physical Chemistry, Hannah Research Institute, Ayr, since 1972; b. 16.2.43, Edinburgh; m., Janet Margaret Lyall; 1 s.; 1 d. Educ. George Watson's College, Edinburgh; Edinburgh University. Postdoctoral research, Department of Clinical Biochemistry, Oxford University; fellowship to Universitat Erlangen-Nurnburg. Recreations: winter: curling and (perforce) home decorating; summer: pursuit of trout and salmon. Address: (h.) 4 Corsehill Road, Ayr, KA7 2ST; T.-Ayr 262771.

Dalgleish, Robert Goodfellow Dakers, MBE, JP. Member, Edinburgh District Council, since 1980; Chairman, Edinburgh District Licensing Board, since 1984; b. 8.3.30, Edinburgh; m., Margaret Catherine Heron; 3 s.; 1 d. Educ. George Heriot's School; Heriot-Watt College. Apprentice industrial chemist, laboratory technician, draughtsman, spares engineer and engineering designer, Ferranti; worked briefly at Tugela Ferry Mission Hospital, South Africa, 1957; Member, Edinburgh District Council, 1974-77; Member, Lothian Health Board, 1976-80; Chairman, Edinburgh Health Council, 1981-84. Sunday School teacher, 15 years; youth club leader, 17 years; trade union steward, 15 years; Member, Church of Scotland Society, Religion, Technology Project, 14 years; Congregational lay preacher, 12 years; Past Chairman, Leith Labour Party. Recreations: being at home; studying light aircraft design; genealogy; swimming; photography. Address: (h.) 1 Granton Park Avenue, Edinburgh.

Dalhousie, Earl of (Simon Ramsay), KT, GCVO, GBE, MC, LLD. Lord Lieutenant, County of Angus, since 1967; Lord Chamberlain to Queen Elizabeth, the Queen Mother, since 1965; Chancellor, Dundee University, since 1977; b. 17.10.14, London; m., Margaret Elizabeth Mary Stirling; 3 s.; 2 d. Educ. Eton; Christ Church, Oxford. Major, 4/5 Black Watch TA; served overseas, 1939-45 (prisoner); MP, Forfar, 1945-50; Conservative Whip, 1946-48; Governor-General, Federation of Rhodesia and Nyasaland, 1957-63. President: Save the Children Fund, Scotland, Victoria League in Sconland. Address: (h.) Brechin Castle, Brechin, Angus; T.-035-62 2176.

Dallas, Alexander James, FIA (Scot). Honorary Sheriff, Wick, since 1978; Manager/Auctioneer, Wick and Thurso Branches, Aberdeen & Northern Marts Ltd.; b. 30.9.29, Turriff, Aberdeenshire; m., Elizabeth Campbell Ogston; 1 d. Educ. Turriff Academy. Joined Aberdeen & Northern Marts Ltd., 1944; National Service, RAF. Chairman, Caithness Indoor Riding Association, since 1982; Past President, Caithness Agricultural Society. Recreations: gardening; golf. Address: (h.) Deveron, Miller Avenue, Wick; T.-Wick 2436.

Dalrymple, Major The Hon. Colin James, DL, JP, BA. Farmer and Landowner, since 1956; b. 19.2.20, Ford, Midlothian; m., Fiona Jane Edwards; 1 s.; 3 d. Educ. Eton College; Trinity College, Cambridge. Served with Scots Guards, 1939-56; Member, Midlothian County Council, 1967-75; active supporter, Scottish Landowners Federation and National Farmers Union of Scotland. Recreations: shooting; fishing. Address: Oxenfoord Mains, Dalkeith.

Dalrymple, Sir Hew (Fleetwood) Hamilton-, 10th Bt (created 1697), KCVO, 1985 (CVO, 1974). Vice-Lieutenant, East Lothian, since 1973; Vice-Chairman, Scottish & Newcastle Breweries, since 1983 (Director, since 1967); Chairman, Scottish American Investment, since 1985 (Director, since 1967); b. 9.4.26; m., Lady Anne-Louise Mary Keppel; 4 s. Educ. Ampleforth; Staff College, Camberley, 1957. DAAG HQ 3rd Division, 1958-60; Regimental Adjt., Grenadier Guards, 1960-62; retired, 1962; Lieutenant, Queen's Bodyguard for Scotland (Royal Company of Archers), Adjutant, 1964-85; President: East Lothian Scout Council, East Lothian Council for Voluntary Services; DL, East Lothian, 1964. Address: Leuchie, North Berwick, East Lothian; T.-North Berwick 2903.

Dalrymple-Hamilton of Bargany, Captain North Edward Frederick, CVO (1961), MBE (1953), DSC (1943), JP, DL. Brigadier, Queen's Bodyguard for Scotland (Royal Company of Archers); b. 17.2.22; m., 1, Hon. Mary Colville (deceased); 2 s.; 2, Antoinette Beech. Educ. Eton. Royal Navy: Director of Naval Signals, 1965, Director, Weapons Equipment Surface, 1967, retired, 1970. Address: (h.) Lovestone House, Bargany, Girvan, Ayrshire.

Dalyell, Tam. MP (Labour), Linlithgow, since 1983 (West Lothian, 1962-83); b. 9.8.32. Educ. Edinburgh Academy; Eton; King's College, Cambridge. Teacher and Author; Member, European Parliament, 1975-79; Member, Public Accounts Committee, 1963-65; Member, Select Committee on Science and Technology, 1965-68; Vice-Chairman, PLP, 1975-76; Member, Select Committee on European Secondary Legislation, 1974-75; Opposition Spokesman on Science, 1980-82.

Dalziel, Colonel William Alexander, CBE (1980), OStJ, TD, JP, DL, KLJ. Chairman, Transport Users Consultative Committee for Scotland; Chairman, Gas Consumers Council for Scotland; Chairman, Magistrates Committee, Edinburgh; Deputy Lord Lieutenant, Edinburgh, since 1977; b. 6.5.21, Dumbarton; m., Elizabeth Alexander Melville; 1 d. Army Service (Colonel); Deputy Chief Signals Officer, Scottish Command; worked in retail clothing trade, transport industry, fishing industry. Recreations: golf; gardening. Address: (h.) Gowanfield, 6 Orchard Road South, Edinburgh, EH4 3HF.

Daniels, Peter William, MA (Hons). Chief Executive, Clydesdale District Council, since 1983; b. 8.6.49, Wishaw; m., Anne; 2 s.; 1 d. Educ. Brandon High School, Motherwell; Dalziel High School, Motherwell; Glasgow University;

Jordanhill College of Education. Lecturer (A) in Public Administration, Bell College of Technology, Hamilton, 1972-75; Personal Assistant to Chief Executive, Renfrew District Council, 1975-81; Assistant Chief Executive, Leicester CC, 1981-83. Past Chairman, Scottish Symphony Orchestra Trust; former elected Member, East Kilbride District Council; former Vice-Chairman, Manpower Committee, COSLA. Recreations: classical music; chess; cycling; running. Address: (b.) Clydesdale District Council, District Offices, South Vennel, Lanark, ML11 7JT; T.-Lanark 61331.

Darwent, Rt. Rev. Frederick Charles, LTh (Hon). Bishop of Aberdeen and Orkney, since 1978; b. 20.4.27, Liverpool; m., 1, Edna Lilian Waugh (deceased); 2 d.; 2, Roma Evelyn Fraser. Educ. Warbreck School, Liverpool; Ormskirk Grammar School; Wells Theological College, Somerset. Followed a banking career, 1943-61; War Service, Far East, 1945-48; ordained Deacon, 1963, Priest, 1964, Diocese of Liverpool; Curate, Pemberton, Wigan, 1963-65; Rector: Strichen, 1965-71, New Pitsligo, 1965-78, Fraserburgh, 1971-78; Canon, St. Andrew's Cathedral, Aberdeen, 1971; Dean of Aberdeen and Orkney, 1973-78. Recreations: amateur stage (acting and production); calligraphy; music. Address: (b.) Diocesan Office, 16 Crown Terrace, Aberdeen, AB1 2HD; T.-Aberdeen 580172.

Das, Sachinandan, MB, BS, FRCR, DMRT. Consultant Radiotherapist and Oncologist, Ninewells Hospital, Dundee, since 1977; Honorary Senior Lecturer in Radiotherapy and Oncology, Dundee University, since 1977; Visiting Consultant Radiotherapist and Oncologist, Perth Royal Infirmary, since 1977; b. 1.8.44, Cuttack, India; m., Dr. Subhalaxmi; 1 s.; 1 d. Educ. Ravenshaw Collegiate School; SCB Medical College, Cuttack, India; Utkal University. Senior House Officer in Radiotherapy, Plymouth General Hospital, 1969-70; Registrar in Radiotherapy and Oncology, then Senior Registrar, Mersey Regional Centre for Radiotherapy, Liverpool, 1970-77; Member: Standing Scottish Committee, National Medical Consultative Committee, Scottish Paediatric Oncology Group, Joint Radiological Safety Committee, Radiation Hazards Sub-Committee, Area Oncology Committee. Recreations: hill-walking; table tennis; reading. Address: (h.) Grapevine, 42 Menzieshill Road, Dundee, DD2 1PU; T.-Dundee 642915.

Datta, Dipankar, MB, BS, FRCPGlas. Consultant Physician (with special interest in gastroenterology), since 1975; b. 30.1.33, Chittagong, India; m., Dr. J.B. Datta; 1 s.; 1 d. Educ. Calcutta University. Member, Central Executive Committee, Scottish Council, United Nations Association; Member, Lanarkshire Health Board. Recreations: reading - history, economics and international politics. Address: (h.) 9 Kirkvale Crescent, Newton Mearns, Glasgow, G77 5HB; T.-041-639 1515.

Davey, Christopher John, BA (Hons), FSA Scot. Senior Lecturer in History, Dundee University, since 1979 (Member, University Court, since 1981); b. 25.10.38, Epsom; m., Nancy Taylor; 1 s.; 1 d. Educ. Steyning Grammar School; London

School of Economics. Temporary Assistant Lecturer, Sheffield University; Assistant Lecturer, then Lecturer, Queen's College, St. Andrews University; Lecturer, Dundee University, 1967-79; (first) Students' Assessor on Senate, 1968-71; Dean of Students, Faculty of Arts and Social Sciences, 1975-79; elected Member of Senate, 1971-81; Chairman, University External Liaison Committee, since 1979. Chairman, Dundee Area Scout Council; Secretary, Dundee Historical Association (President, 1978-81); Council Member, Abertay Historical Society (President, 1977-79); President, Dundee Association of University Teachers, 1971-73. Recreations: watching birds; writing poetry; collecting goss china. Address: (b.) Department of Modern History, University of Dundee, Dundee; T.-0382 23181.

Davidson, Alan Ingram, ChM, FRCSEdin, DObstRCOG. Consultant Surgeon, Aberdeen Royal Infirmary, since 1974; Honorary Senior Lecturer in Surgery, Aberdeen University, since 1974; b. 25.3.35, Aberdeen; m., Margaret Elizabeth Mackay; 1 s.; 1 d. Educ. Robert Gordon's College, Aberdeen; Aberdeen University. House Officer, Aberdeen Royal Infirmary, 1959-60; National Service, Royal Army Medical Corps, 1960-62; Lecturer, Department of Pathology, Aberdeen, 1963-64; Registrar and Senior Registrar, Aberdeen Royal Infirmary, 1964-74. Recreations: gardening; watching TV; music. Address: (h.) 20 Hillview Road, Cults, Aberdeen; T.-Aberdeen 867347.

Davidson, Alistair Hunter Beattie, MA. HM Inspector of Schools (Higher Grade), since 1981; b. 2.4.31, Glasgow; m., Marion Turner Maxwell; 1 s.; 1 d. Educ. Hillhead High School, Glasgow; Glasgow University. Primary Teacher, Possil School, Glasgow, 1954-55; Education Officer, RAF, 1955-57; English Teacher: Albert Secondary School, Glasgow, 1957-58, Hutchesons' Boys' Grammar School, Glasgow, 1958-63; Principal Teacher of English, Annan Academy, 1963-66; HM Inspector of Schools, Northern Divisional staff, 1966-81. Address: (b.) 43 Jeffrey Street, Edinburgh; T.-031-556 9233.

Davidson, Hon. Lord, (Charles Kemp Davidson), QC (Scot). Senator of the College of Justice in Scotland, since 1983; b. 13.4.29, Edinburgh; m.; 1 s.; 2 d. Educ. Fettes College, Edinburgh; Brasenose College, Oxford; Edinburgh University. Admitted, Faculty of Advocates, 1956; QC, 1969; Faculty of Advocates: Vice-Dean, 1977-79, Dean, 1979-83, Keeper, Advocates' Library, 1972-76; Procurator, General Assembly, Church of Scotland, 1972-83.

Davidson, Donald Allen, BSc, PhD. Senior Lecturer, Department of Geography, Strathclyde University, since 1981; b. 27.4.45, Lumphanan; m., Caroline E. Brown; 2 d. Educ. Robert Gordon's College, Aberdeen; Aberdeen University; Sheffield University. Junior Research Fellow, Sheffield University, 1967-71; Lecturer, St. David's University College, Wales, 1971-76. Publications: Soils and Land Use Planning; Science for Physical Geographers. Recreations: gardening; the countryside; music. Address: (h.) 51 Braehead Avenue, Milngavie, Glasgow; T.-041-956 1829.

Davidson, Douglas, DCR, SRR. Group Superintendent Radiographer, Aberdeen Royal Infirmary, since 1982; Member, Grampian Health Board; Council Member, College and Society of Radiographers, 1982-85; b. 8.2.32, Aberdeen; m., Margaret Farquhar; 1 s.; 1 d. Educ. Robert Gordon's College, Aberdeen; Grampian School of Radiography. National Service, RAMC, 1950-52; Radiographer: Chalmers Hospital, Banff, 1954-55, Aberdeen Royal Infirmary, since 1955. Recreations: golf; swimming; watching sport of all kinds. Address: (h.) 23 Ronaldsay Road, Aberdeen, AB2 6ND; T.-0224 310486.

Davidson, Duncan Lewis Watt, BSc (Hons), MB, ChB, FRCPEdin. Consultant Neurologist, Tayside Health Board, since 1976; Honorary Senior Lecturer in Medicine, Dundee University, since 1976; b. 16.5.40, Kingston, Jamaica; m., Dr. Anne V.M. Maiden; 4 s.; 1 d. Educ. Knox College, Jamaica; Edinburgh University. House Officer, Senior House Officer, Registrar and Senior Registrar posts in medicine and neurology, Edinburgh, 1966-75; Peel Travelling Fellowship, Montreal, 1973-74; MRC clinical scientific staff, MRC Brain Metabolism Unit, Edinburgh, 1975-76. Recreations: gardening; golf. Address: (h.) Brooksby, Queens Terrace, St. Andrews, Fife; T.-0334 76108.

Davidson, James Duncan Gordon, MVO (1947). Chief Executive, Royal Highland and Agricultural Society of Scotland, since 1970; b. 10.1.27. Educ. RN College, Dartmouth; Downing College, Cambridge. Royal Navy, 1944-55; MP, West Aberdeenshire, 1966-70.

Davidson, James Masson, MA, LLB, NP. Assistant Secretary, Edinburgh University, since 1969; b. 28.12.33, St. Cyrus, Montrose; m., Joan Clark Thomson; 2 s. Educ. Fettes College; St. Andrews University; Edinburgh University. Legal apprenticeship, Mackenzie & Kermack, WS, 1955-58; National Service, RAF, 1959-61 (Pilot Officer, Directorate of Legal Services); Edinburgh University: Administrative Assistant, Secretary's Office, 1961-65, Senior Administrative Officer, Secretary's Office, 1965-67; Registrar, Mauritius University, 1967-68. Member, Society of High Constables of Edinburgh. Recreations: Scottish country dancing; golf; bridge; gardening. Address: (h.) 2 Ettrick Grove, Edinburgh, EH10 5AW; T.-031-229 1678.

Davidson, John, MA. Director, CBI Scotland, since 1979; b. 26.7.30, Bearsden, Dunbartonshire; m., Marilyn Menzies Davidson; 2 d. Educ. Glasgow Academy; Trinity College, Glenalmond; St. John's College, Cambridge; Royal College of Science and Technology, Glasgow. North British Locomotive Co. Ltd., Glasgow, 1954-56; Singer Manufacturing Co. Ltd., Clydebank, 1958-65; Scottish Conservative Central Office, 1965-75; Director, Scottish Federation of Housing Associations, 1975-79; Member: Manpower Services Committee for Scotland, since 1979, Scottish Business Education Council, since 1982; Trustee: Bield Retirement Housing Trust, Scottish Housing Association Charitable Trust, Scottish Disability Foundation; Member,

Salvation Army Housing Association (Scotland). Recreations: photography; cattle raising. Address: (h.) Rinnans, Balfron, Stirlingshire; T.-041-332 8661.

Davidson, John F., MB, ChB, FRCPEdin, FRCPath. Consultant Haematologist, Glasgow Royal Infirmary, since 1969; b. 11.1.34, Lumphanan; m., Laura G. Middleton; 1 s.; 1 d. Educ. Robert Gordon's College, Aberdeen; Aberdeen University. Surgeon Lt., RN; Registrar in Medicine, Aberdeen Royal Infirmary; Research Registrar in Medicine, then Senior Registrar in Haematology, Glasgow Royal Infirmary. Secretary, British Society for Haematalogy; Editor, Progress in Fibrinolysis, Volumes I to VII; Chairman, International Committee on Fibrinolysis, 1976-84. Recreation: gardening. Address: (b.) Department of Haematology, Glasgow Royal Infirmary, Glasgow; T.-041-552 3535, Ext. 5125.

Davidson, John Knight, MD, FRCPEdin, FRCPGlas, FRCR, FRACR (Hon). Consultant Radiologist in administrative charge, Western Infirmary/Gartnavel General Hospital, Glasgow, since 1967; Consultant Radiologist, Ross Hall Hospital, since 1984; b. 17.8.25, Edinburgh; m., Edith E. McKelvie; 2 s.; 1 d. Educ. George Watson's Boys College, Edinburgh; Edinburgh University. Royal Army Medical Corps, 1949-51; Senior Registrar, St. Bartholomews Hospital, London, 1956-60; Council Member: Medical and Dental Defence Union for Scotland, since 1971, Royal College of Radiologists, since 1984; Chairman, Standing Scottish Committee, Royal College of Radiologists, since 1985; Member, Bone Necrosis Group, Decompression Sickness Panel, MRC, since 1965; Consultant Adviser, US Navy, on diving medicine, 1974-78; Rohan Williams Travelling Professor, Australasia, 1977; Chairman, Examining Board, FRCR, 1976-79; Member, Scottish Sub-Committee on Distinction and Meritorious Service Awards, 1982-84; Council Member, Royal Glasgow Institute for the Fine Arts; Editor, Aseptic Necrosis of Bone. Recreations: golf; bridge; the arts; opera; meeting people. Address: (h.) 31 Newlands Road, Glasgow, G43 2JG; T.-041-632 3113; (b.) Consulting Rooms, 901 Sauchiehall Street, Glasgow.

Davidson, John Marr, MA, LLB, WS. Partner, W. & J. Burness, WS, since 1954; b. 22.6.23, Lanark; m., Sylvia Russell; 1 s.; 1 d. Educ. Edinburgh Academy; Edinbrgh University. Service in Italy, Middle East, Europe, with Cameronians (Scottish Rifles), attaining rank of Captain, 1942-46; Law Apprentice, then Partner, Auld and Macdonald, WS, 1946-54. High Constable, Holyrood; Director, various limited companies. Recreations: shooting; fishing. Address: (h.) 66 Barnton Park Crescent, Edinburgh, EH4 6EN; T.-031-339 5387.

Davidson, Julie Wilson. Television Critic, Glasgow Herald, since 1981; Freelance Contributor, BBC, Granada TV, The Times, The Observer, etc., since 1981; b. Motherwell; m., Harry Reid (qv); 1 d. Educ. Aberdeen High School for Girls. Trainee Journalist, D.C. Thomson Ltd., Dundee,

1961-64; Feature Writer and Sub-Editor, Aberdeen Press & Journal, 1964-67; The Scotsman: Feature Writer, 1967-77, Columnist, 1977-81. Columnist/Critic of the Year, Scottish Press Awards, 1985. Recreations: reading; walking; travelling; lunching. Address: (h.) 15 Albion Buildings, Ingram Street, Glasgow; T.-041-552 8403.

Davidson, Neil Forbes, BA, LLB, MSc, LLM. Advocate; b. 13.9.50, St. Andrews; m., Regina Sprissler. Educ. Stirling University; Bradford University; Edinburgh University. Analyst, Scrimgeour Kemp-Gee, London, 1972-73; Executive, Noble Grossart Ltd., Edinburgh, 1974; Speechwriter, London, 1975; legal training, 1977-79; practice at Scottish Bar, since 1979. Publication: Scrimgeour's North Sea Oil and Gas Review, 1973. Recreation: taekwondo. Address: (h.) 2 Moray Place, Edinburgh, EH3 6DS; T.-031-225 6177.

Davidson, Neil McDonald, MA, DM, FRCP, FRCPEdin. Consultant Physician, Eastern General Hospital, Edinburgh, since 1978; Senior Lecturer in Medicine, Edinburgh University, since 1978; Assistant Director of Studies (Medicine), Edinburgh Postgraduate Board for Medicine, since 1985; b. 15.5.40, Leamington Spa; m., Jill Ann; 3 s.; 1 d. Educ. Epsom College; Merton College, Oxford; St. Thomas's Hospital, London. House Officer, St. Thomas's Hospital and Hammersmith Hospital, London; Medical Registrar, St. Thomas's Hospital, London; Senior Medical Registrar, Lecturer and Senior Lecturer in Medicine, Ahmadu Bello University, Zaria, Nigeria; Lecturer in Medicine, Edinburgh University. Recreation: collecting antique maps. Address: (h.) 43 Blackford Road, Grange, Edinburgh, EH9 2DT; T.-031-667 3960.

Davidson, Professor Robert, MA, BD, DD. Professor of Old Testament Language and Literature, Glasgow University, since 1972; Principal, Trinity College, Glasgow, since 1981; b. 30.3.27, Markinch, Fife; m., Elizabeth May Robertson; 5 s.; 4 d. Educ. Bell-Baxter School, Cupar; St. Andrews University. Lecturer in Biblical Studies, Aberdeen University, 1953-60; Lecturer in Hebrew and Old Testament Studies, St. Andrews University, 1960-66; Lecturer/Senior Lecturer in Old Testament, Edinburgh University, 1966-72. Publications: The Bible Speaks, 1959; The Old Testament, 1964; Geneses 1 - 11, 1973; Genesis 12 - 50, 1979; The Bible in Religious Education, 1979; The Courage to Doubt, 1983; Jeremiah Volume 1, 1983. Recreations: music; gardening. Address: (h.) 357 Albert Drive, Glasgow, G41 5PH; T.-041-427 5793.

Davidson, William Keith, CBE, JP, FRCGP, DPA. Chairman, Scottish Health Services Planning Council; Vice President (and Fellow), British Medical Association; Member, General Medical Council; General Medical Practitioner, since 1952; b. 20.11.26, Glasgow; m., Dr. Mary W.A. Davidson; 1 s.; 1 d. Educ. Coatbridge Secondary School; Glasgow University. Honorary President, Glagow Eastern Medical Society, 1984-85. Recreation: gardening. Address: (h.) Dunvegan, Hornshill Farm Road, Stepps, Glasgow, G33 6DE; T.-041-779 2103.

Davidson-Lamb, Richard William, MB, ChB, FFARCS, DObstRCOG. Consultant Anaesthetist, Aberdeen Royal Infirmary, since 1978; b. Bedford; m., Nanette Jamieson Flockhart; 2 d. Educ. Crypt School, Gloucester; Aberdeen University. Address: (h.) 21 Cairn Gardens, Cults, Aberdeen; T.-Aberdeen 868835.

Davie, Elspeth, DA. Writer; b. Kilmarnock; m., George Elder Davie; 1 d. Educ. George Watson's College; Edinburgh University; Edinburgh Art College. Taught Art for several years in the Borders, Aberdeen and Northern Ireland; author of three novels: Providings, Creating A Scene, Climbers on a Stair; four collections of short stories: The Spark, The High Tide Talker, The Night of the Funny Hats, A Traveller's Room; two Arts Council Awards; received Katherine Mansfield Prize, 1978. Recreations: reading; walking; films. Address: (h.) 155/17 Orchard Brae Gardens, Edinburgh, EH4; T.-031-332 8297.

Davie, Ivor Turnbull, MB, ChB, FFARCS. Consultant Anaesthetist, Western General Hospital, Edinburgh, since 1971; Honorary Senior Lecturer, Edinburgh University, since 1979; Lecturer, Central Midwives Board (Scotland), since 1974; b. 23.2.35, Edinburgh; m., Jane Elizabeth Fleischmann; 1 s.; 1 d. Educ. Royal High School, Edinburgh; Edinburgh University. Member, Board of Examiners, Faculty of Anaesthetists, Royal College of Surgeons of England (Primary FFARCS, 1978-84, Part II FFARCS, since 1985); Tutor, Faculty of Anaesthetists, since 1979; Member, Editorial Board, British Journal of Obstetrics and Gynaecology, 1980-84; Visiting Medical Officer, Westmead Centre, Sydney, NSW, 1983. Address: (b.) Department of Anaesthesia, Western General Hospital, Edinburgh, EH4 2XU; T.-031-332 2525.

Davie, Robert Alastair, MA, BCom. Secretary/Director, Sea Fish Industry Authority, since 1981; b. 28.10.38, Edinburgh; m., Carol Haig Davie; 2 s. Educ. George Watson's College; Edinburgh University. Recreation: golf. Address: (h.) 4 Riselaw Place, Edinburgh, EH10 6HP; T.-031-447 5168.

Davies, Alan, MA, PhD, DipEd, DipGenLing. Reader in Applied Linguistics, Edinburgh University, since 1984; b. 17.2.31, Neath; m., Anne Margaret; 1 s.; 3 d. Educ. Bishop Newton's School, Leicester; Corpus Christi College, Oxford. Assistant Teacher, 1955-62: Royal Grammar School, High Wycombe, Queen Elizabeth's School, Barnet and Kamusinga Secondary School, Kenya; Senior Research Associate, Birmingham University, 1962-65; Lecturer, then Senior Lecturer, Edinburgh University, 1965-84; Professor and Head of Department of English, Tribhuvan University, Kathmandu, Nepal, 1969-71 (on secondment). Chairman, British Association of Applied Linguistics, 1976-79; Secretary General, International Association of Applied Linguistics, 1978-81; President, TESOL (Scotland), since 1983; Member, British Council English Teaching Advisory Committee, 1979-85; Editor, Applied Linguistics, since 1984. Publications (as Editor): Language Testing Symposium, 1968; Problems of Language and Learning, 1975; Language and Learning in Early Childhood, 1977;

Testing and Experimental Methods, 1977; Language and Learning in Home and School, 1979; Interlanguage, 1984. Recreations: Quakerism; cycling. Address: (b.) Edinburgh University, Department of Applied Linguistics, 14 Buccleuch Place, Edinburgh, EH8 9LN; T.-031-667 1011.

Davies, Christopher Henry, BA (Hons), DipEd, FBIM. Managing Director, Nairn Floors Ltd., Kirkcaldy, since 1983; b. 6.11.39, Wolverhampton; m., Elisabeth; 2 s. Educ. Wolverhampton Grammar School; University College, Durham; Queens College, Cambridge. General Manager: Commercial Plastics GMBH, Austria, Nairn Australia; International Operations Director, Nairn International Ltd., Newcastle; Sales/Marketing Director, Nairn Floors Ltd., Kirkcaldy. Recreations: music; walking; board-sailing. Address: (h.) 7 West Carnethy Avenue, Colinton, Edinburgh; T.-0592 261111.

Davies, David Lloyd, MD, FRCP. Senior Lecturer in Medicine, Glasgow University, since 1973; Honorary Consultant Physician; b. 1.3.38, Swansea; m., Catherine G. Drummond; 1 d. Educ. Llandovery College; St. Mary's Hospital, London. Various hospital appointments: St. Mary's Hospital, London, Colonial Hospital, Gibraltar, Postgraduate Medical School, Hammersmith, Chelmsford and Essex Hospital, Western Infirmary, Glasgow. Recreations: marquetry; music; gardening; sport. Address: (h.) 9 Matilda Road, Pollokshields, Glasgow, G41; T.-041-423 0052.

Davies, David Somerville, FTCL, ARCM. Artistic Director, Paragon Ensemble, since 1980; b. 13.6.54, Dunfermline. Educ. Dunfermline High School; Royal Scottish Academy of Music; Edinburgh University. Assistant Principal Flute, Scottish National Orchestra; Principal Flute, Scottish Opera; Freelance Recitalist and Conductor; awarded Tovey Memorial Prize and Clutterbuck Scholarship. Recreations: reading; photography. Address: (h.) Ostlers Cottage, Corsebar Lane, Paisley, PA2 9LL; T.-041-884 2965.

Davies, Graham Michael, BA, PhD, FBPS. Senior Lecturer, Department of Psychology, Aberdeen University, since 1977; b. 19.2.43, Cirencester; 1 s.; 1 d. Educ. Bodmin Grammar School; Hull University. Assistant Lecturer, then Lecturer, Aberdeen University, 1967-77. Chairman, Scottish Branch, British Psychological Society, since 1984. Publications: Perceiving and Remembering Faces (Co-author), 1981; Identification Parades: A Psychological Evaluation, 1982. Recreations: walking; reading; thinking. Address: (b.) Department of Psychology, Kings College, The University, Old Aberdeen, AB9 2UB; T.-0224 40241, Ext. 6470.

Davies, John Booth, BA, PhD. Senior Lecturer in Psychology, Strathclyde University, since 1982; b. 15.4.44, Manchester; m., Shirley Irving; 1 s.; 1 d. Educ. Chethams School, Manchester; Hyde County Grammar School; University College, Durham. Research Assistant, then Lecturer, Strathclyde University, 1969-82. Member, Royal College of Psychiatrists Committee on Drugs and Addiction. Publications: Teenagers and

Alochol, 1972; The Psychology of Music, 1978. Recreations: music; cycling; smallholding. Address: (h.) Crofthead of Gree Farm, Fenwick, Ayrshire; T.-05606 749.

Davis, Christine A.M., MA, DipEd. Chairman, Electricity Consultative Council for the North of Scotland, since 1980 (Member, since 1974); Member, North of Scotland Hydro-Electric Board, since 1980; Lay Member, Legal Aid Central Committee, since 1980; Member, Scottish Examination Board, since 1982; b. 5.3.44, Salisbury, Wiltshire; m., Robin John Davis; 2 d. Educ. Perth Academy; Ayr Academy; St. Andrews University; Aberdeen University; Aberdeen College of Education. Teacher of History and Modern Studies, Cumbernauld High School and High School of Stirling, 1967-69; joined Dunblane Town Council and Perth and Kinross Joint County Council, 1972; undertook research in Canada on Ontario Hydro and small claims in Ontario courts, 1977-78; Teacher of Modern Studies, HM Institution, Cornton Vale, since 1979. Active Member, Religious Society of Friends (Quakers). Recreations: embroidery; bird-watching; walking. Address: (h.) 24 Newton Crescent, Dunblane, Perthshire, FK15 ODZ; T.-Dunblane 823226.

Davis, Margaret Thomson. Novelist; b. Bathgate; 2 s. Educ. Albert Secondary School. Worked as children's nurse; Red Cross nurse; short story writer; novelist; author of autobiography, The Making of a Novelist; novels include The Breadmakers, A Baby Might Be Crying, A Sort of Peace, The Prisoner, The Prince and the Tobacco Lords, Roots of Bondage, Scorpion in the Fire, The Dark Side of Pleasure, A Very Civilised Man, Light and Dark; Lecturer in Creative Writing. Honorary President, Strathkelvin Writers Club; Trustee, The Phoenix (Scotland) Trust. Recreations: reading; being with friends. Address: 17 Niddrie Square, Queens Park, Glasgow, G42 8QX; T.-041-423 3314.

Davis, Robert Gunn. Member, Mental Welfare Commission for Scotland, since 1984; Social Work Adviser (Mental Health), Strathclyde Region, since 1977; b. 11.5.38, Edinburgh; m., Mildred Bennett; 1 s.; 1 d. Educ. Daniel Stewart's College, Edinburgh. Certificate of Qualification in Probation Work, Jordanhill College, 1968. Probation Officer, City of Glasgow, before 1969; Senior Social Worker, then Social Work Training Officer, Lanark County Council, 1970-75; Recruitment and Training Officer, Strathclyde Region Social Work Department, 1975-77. Founder Member, British Association of Social Workers. Recreations: vintage/elderly motorcycle restoration; pedal cycling (racing and record breaking in 1950s, now touring only). Address: (h.) 5 Braid Green, Livingston, West Lothian, EH54 8PN; T.-Livingston 39148.

Davison, Bryan, RIBA. Director of Design and Technical Services, Shetland Islands Council, since 1975; b. 1.3.29. Address: (b.) 92 St. Olaf Street, Lerwick, Shetland; T.-Lerwick 3535.

Davison, Edward Cowper, MA, DipEd. Assistant Secretary, Scottish Education Department, since 1984; b. 31.10.40, Darlington; m., Anna Fay Henderson; 2 d. Educ. Dame Allan's School, Newcastle-upon-Tyne; Glasgow University; London University Institute of Education. Assistant Master, Tottenham County School, 1964-68; administrative staff, Glasgow University, 1969-75; Principal: Scottish Education Department, 1975-79, Department of Agriculture and Fisheries for Scotland, 1979-82, Scottish Office Central Services, 1982-84. Recreations: the piano; not gardening. Address: (h.) 14 Plewlands Terrace, Edinburgh, EH10 5JZ; T.-031-447 3289.

Davison, Peter Sinclair, BSc, PhD, ARIC, MIInfS. Director of Research, Scientific Documentation Centre Ltd., since 1962; Member, Fife Regional Council, since 1975; b. 21.1.30, Edinburgh; m., Joan Plummer; 1 s.; 1 d. Educ. George Watson's Boys' College, Edinburgh; Edinburgh University. RAF, 1956-58 (Flt. Lt.); Technical Officer (Research), ICI Ltd., Billingham, 1958-59; established Scientific Documentation Centre, 1958; Editor for European Commission: Euroabstracts, 1977-83, European Environmental Science Synopses, 1983; Parliamentary Candidate (Conservative): Hamilton, 1979, Dunfermline West, 1983. Recreations: travel; admiring man's cultural heritage; DIY. Address: (h.) Halbeath House, Dunfermline, Fife, KY12 OTZ; T.-0383 723535.

Dawson, Professor John Alan, BSc, MPhil, PhD, MIPDM. Fraser of Allander Professor of Distributive Studies, Stirling University, since 1983; b. 19.8.44, Hyde; m., Jocelyn Barker; 1 s.; 1 d. Educ. Lady Manners School, Bakewell; University College, London; Nottingham University. Lecturer, Nottingham University; Lecturer, Senior Lecturer, Reader, St. David's University College, Wales; Visiting Lecturer, University of Western Australia; Visiting Research Fellow, Australian National University; Visiting Professor, Florida State University; Member, Distributive Trades Committee, NEDC. Honorary Secretary, Institute of British Geographers. Publications: Evaluating the Human Environment, 1973; Man and His World, 1975; Computing for Geographers, 1976; Small-Scale Retailing in the UK, 1979; Marketing Environment, 1979; Retail Geography, 1980; Commercial Distribution in Europe, 1982; Teach Yourself Geography, 1983; Shopping Centre Development, 1983; Computer Methods for Geographers, 1985. Recreations: sport; writing. Address: (b.) Stirling University, Stirling; T.-0786 73171.

Dawson, Mary, PhD, FPS. Reader in Pharmacy, Strathclyde University; b. West Maryston. Educ. Airdrie Academy; Royal Technical College, Glasgow. Career spent almost entirely in Department of Pharmacy, Strathclyde University. Awarded Felix Wankel International Prize for research; Member of numerous committees concerned with pharmacy, the health service and animal welfare. Recreations: motor sport; photography. Address: (b.) Department of Pharmacy, Strathclyde University, Glasgow, G1 1XW; T.-041-552 4400.

Dawson, Thomas Cameron, SBStJ. Vice Chairman, Rangers Football Club, since 1984; Managing Director, Dawson Motors, Helensburgh, since 1963; b. 12.1.29, Rhu; m., Margaret

McFadzean; 1 s. Educ. Hermitage Academy. Army Service, Royal Military Police, three years. Recreation: flying (private pilot's licence). Address: (h.) Sunnyside House, 34 West King Street, Helensburgh, G84 8EB; T.-0436 3860.

Deans, Rev. Graham Douglas Sutherland, MA, BD (Hons). Minister, Denbeath and Methilhill Parish Churches, since 1978; b. 15.8.53, Aberdeen; m., Marina Punler. Educ. Mackie Academy, Stonehaven; Aberdeen University. Assistant Minister, Craigsbank Parish Church, Corstorphine, 1977-78; Depute Clerk and Treasurer, Kirkcaldy Presbytery, since 1981. Publication: A History of Denbeath Church, 1980. Recreation: music. Address: 9 Chemiss Road, Methilhill, Fife, KY8 2BS; T.-0592 713142.

de Bono, David Paul, MA, MD (Cantab), FRCPEdin. Consultant Physician, Cardiac Department, Edinburgh Royal Infirmary, since 1979; part-time Senior Lecturer, Department of Medicine, Edinburgh University, since 1980; b. 19.1.47, Sliema, Malta; m., Anne Fingleton; 2 s. Educ. St. Edward's College, Malta; Downside School; Trinity Hall, Cambridge; St. George's Hospital, London. Fellow and Director of Medical Studies, Trinity Hall, Cambridge; Lecturer in Cardiovascular Medicine, Oxford University. Recreations: model aeroplanes; sailing. Address: (h.) 8 Lygon Road, Edinburgh, EH16 5QE; T.-031-667 5526.

Deen, Sayyed Misbah, MSc, PhD, DIC, FBCS. Senior Lecturer in Computing Science, Aberdeen University, since 1974; b. 1.2.38, Kishorganj, Bangladesh; m., Rudaina Adil; 2 s. Educ. Dacca University; Imperial College, London. Senior Scientific Officer: Pakistan Atomic Commission, 1965, Science Research Council, UK, 1967; Executive, Scicon, London, 1970; Lecturer in Computing Science, Aberdeen University, 1973. Chairman, several national and international research conferences on computer datbases. Publications: two textbooks on computer databases. Address: (b.) Department of Computing Science, Aberdeen University, Aberdeen; T.-0224 40241.

Deeprose, William Montgomery, MSc, ARCST, FRSA. Chief Executive, Design Council Scotland, since 1984; b. 21.5.42, Glasgow; m., Alexandra Catherine Sutherland; 2 s. Educ. Whitehill Senior Secondary School; Strathclyde University. Principal Scientific Officer, National Engineering Laboratory, 1969-78; Technical Director, Woods of Colchester, 1978-83; Chairman, British Standard Fan and Fan Noise Committee, 1980-84; Member, Engineering Sciences Division, IMechE EHMFF Committee, since 1982, HEVAC Technical Commission, 1982-84. Recreations: squash; tennis; early music. Address: (b.) 72 St. Vincent Street, Glasgow, G2 5TN; T.-041-221 6121.

Dees, Emeritus Professor Norman, BA (Hons). Professor Emeritus, Glasgow University, since 1981; b. 7.4.16, Newcastle-upon-Tyne; m., Dorothy Eunice Welch (deceased); 2 d. Educ. Heaton Grammar School, Newcastle-upon-Tyne; Manchester University. Commissioned, Durham Light Infantry, 1940-45; Senior Tutor,

Hollroyde College, Manchester University, 1945-47; Lecturer/Senior Lecturer, Newcastle University, 1947-56; Senior Cultural Relations Officer, Berlin, 1956-58; Deputy Director Adult Education, Newcastle University, 1958-61; Director (Professor) of Adult Education, Glasgow University, 1961-81; Chairman, Executive, and President, Scottish Institute of Adult Education, 1968-80 (Honorary Fellow); Visiting Professor, Wisconsin University, 1976-77; sometime Governor, Newbattle Abbey; Member, European Bureau of Adult Education. Queen's Medal. Publications: Europe in Revolution; Teachers and Taught; You Live and Learn. Recreations: reading; walking. Address: (h.) 4 Park Crescent, Bearsden, Glasgow, G61 4HL; T.-041-942 3872.

Dehn, Rudolf, MSc, ARCS. Minister, Erskine and Fergushill, Kilwinning, since 1975; b. 14.5.21, Hamburg, Germany; m., Mary Stewart Tyre; 1 s. Educ. "The Johanneum", Hamburg; Imperial College, London; New College, Edinburgh. GEC Research Laboratories, Wembley, 1951-56; Colonial Office/Government of Nigeria, Nigerian College of Technology, 1956-61; Physicist, UKAEA, Dounreay, Caithness, 1962-73; studied for the ministry, 1973-75. Recreations: music; swimming; horology (repairing and collecting old clocks); chess. Address: Ruhamah, 34 Underwood Road, Prestwick, Ayrshire, KA9 2EX; T.-0292 77401.

De La Rue, Richard Michael, BSc, MASc, PhD, CEng, MIEE. Reader, Department of Electronics and Electrical Engineering, Glasgow University, since 1985; b. 15.5.45, Reading; m., Barbara; 1 s.; 1 d. Educ. Forest Grammar School, Berkshire; University College, London; Toronto University. Glasgow University: Lecturer, 1971-82, Senior Lecturer, 1982-85; Consultant, Bell Laboratories, New Jersey, 1978; Visiting Lecturer, Tohoku University, Japan, 1980. Recreations: hill-walking; climbing; skiing; squash; concerts; theatre-going. Address: (b.) Department of Electronics and Electrical Engineering, The University, Glasgow, G12 8QQ; T.-041-339 8855.

Demarco, Richard, RSW, SSA. Director, The Richard Demarco Gallery Ltd., Edinburgh, since 1966; b. 9.7.30; m. Educ. Holy Cross Academy, Edinburgh; Edinburgh College of Art. Art Master, Duns Scotus Academy, Edinburgh, 1956-67; Vice-Chairman and Director, Traverse Art Gallery, 1963-67; Director, Scottish International Education Trust, 1972-74.

Denholm, James Allan, CA. Director, William Grant & Sons Ltd., since 1975; Chairman, East Kilbride Development Corporation, since 1983 (Member, since 1979); b. 27.9.36, Glasgow; m., Elizabeth Avril McLachlan; 1 s.; 1 d. Educ. Hutchesons Boys Grammar School, Glasgow; Institute of Chartered Accountants of Scotland. Apprenticed, McFarlane Hutton & Patrick, CA, Glasgow (Sir William McLintock prizeman); Chief Accountant, A. & W. Smith & Co. Ltd., Glasgow, 1960-66; Secretary, William Grant & Sons Ltd., since 1966; Council Member, Institute of Chartered Accountants of Scotland, 1978-83. Director and Treasurer, Glasgow YMCA,

1966-79; Chairman, Glasgow Junior Chamber of Commerce, 1972-73; Visitor of the Incorporation of Maltmen in Glasgow, 1980-81; President, 49 Wine and Spirit Club of Scotland, 1983-84; Trustee: Scottish Chartered Accountants Trust for Education, The Queen's College, Glasgow Educational Trust. Recreations: shooting; golf; curling. Address: (h.) Greencroft, 19 Colquhoun Drive, Bearsden, Glasgow; T.-041-942 1773.

Denholm, Col. Sir William (Lang), Kt (1965), TD, DL. Chairman, J. & J. Denholm Ltd., 1966-74; b. 23.2.01; m.; 2 s.; 1 d. Educ. Greenock Academy; Greenock Collegiate. Chairman, Shipping Federation, 1962-65; Joint Chairman, National Maritime Board, 1962-65; President, International Shipping Federation, 1962-67.

Dennis, Richard Benson, PhD, BSc, MInstP. Managing Director, Edinburgh Instruments Ltd.; Senior Lecturer, Heriot-Watt University; Founder, Mutek Gmbh, West Germany; b. 15.7.45, Weymouth; m., Beate Stamm; 2 d. Educ. Weymouth Grammar School; Reading University. SRC Postdoctoral Fellow, Reading; Guest Fellow, Freiburg University, 1968-70; Lecturer/ Senior Lecturer, Heriot-Watt University, since 1970; Alexander von Humboldt Fellow, Munich University, 1976-78; Member, Editorial Board, High Temperature Technology; Joint Winner, Department of Industry EPIC Award (Education in Partnership with Industry and Commerce), 1982. Recreations: bridge; sport. Address: (b.) Edinburgh Instruments Ltd., Riccarton, Currie, Edinburgh; T.-031-449 5844.

Denny, Sir Alistair Maurice Archibald, 3rd Bt; b. 11.9.22; m.; 2 s.; 1 s. (deceased). Educ. Marlborough. Fleet Air Arm, 1944-46; William Denny & Bros, 1948-63. Chairman, St. Andrews Links Management Committee, 1980-81.

Deregowski, Jan Bronislaw, BSc, BA, PhD. Reader in Psychology, Aberdeen University, since 1981; b. 1.3.33, Pinsk, Poland; m., Eva Loft Nielsen; 2 s.; 1 d. Educ. London University. Lecturer, then Senior Lecturer, Aberdeen University, 1969-81. Publications: Illusions, Patterns and Pictures: a cross-cultural perspective; Distortion in Art. Address: (b.) Department of Psychology, King's College, Old Aberdeen, AB9 2UB; T.-Aberdeen 40241.

Derwent, Lavinia, MBE. Writer; b. Jedburgh, Roxburghshire. Educ. Jedburgh Grammar School. Creator of Tammy Troot; author of numerous books for children including the Macpherson books and Sula series; author of autobiographical books, including A Breath of Border Air and Lady of the Manse; TV broadcaster; Council Member, Society of Authors; Past President, Scottish PEN; Committee Member, Stars for Spastics. Address: (h.) 1 Great Western Terrace, Glasgow, G12 OUP; T.-041-334 9172.

Desselberger, Ulrich, MD. Senior Lecturer in Virology, Glasgow University, since 1976; Honorary Consultant, Greater Glasgow Health Board; b. 22.7.37, Darmstadt, Germany; m., Elisabeth Wieczorek; 2 s.; 2 d. Educ. Ludwig Georgs-Gymnasium, Darmstadt; Universities of:

Frankfurt/Main, Marburg Lahn, Berlin/ West, Paris. Research Assistant, Institutes of Pathology, RVK and Klinikum Westend, Berlin, 1968-69; Research Assistant then Consultant, Institute of Virology, Hannover Medical School, Hannover, 1970-76; Fulbright Research Fellow, Department of Microbiology, Mount Sinai School of Medicine, New York, 1977-79. Editorial Board, Journal of Medical Virology. Address: (b.) Institute of Virology, Glasgow University, Church Street, Glasgow, G11; T.-041-339 8822.

Devenay, William Thomas, BSc (Eng) (Hons), FICE, FIWES, FBIM. Director of Water, Strathclyde Regional Council, since 1974. Address: (b.) 419 Balmore Road, Glasgow, G22 6NU; T.0041-336 5333.

Devereux, Alan Robert, CBE, DL, CEng, FIProdE, FBIM. Chairman, Scottish Tourist Board, since 1980; Director, Scottish Mutual Assurance Society, since 1976; Director, Walter Alexander PLC, since 1980; Scottish Adviser, Hambros Bank Ltd., since 1984; Director, Hambro Scotland Ltd., since 1984; Member, British Tourist Authority, since 1980; Director, Solsgirth Investment Trust Ltd., since 1981; b. 18.4.33, Frinton-on-Sea; m., Gloria Alma Hair; 1 s. Educ. Colchester School; Clacton County High School; Mid Essex Technical College. Marconi's Wireless Telegraph Company: apprentice, 1950-55, Standards Engineer, 1955-56; Technical Production Manager, Halex Division, British Xylonite Company, 1956-58; Technical Sales Manager, SPA Division, Sanitas Trust, 1958-65; General Manager, Dobar Engineering, 1965-67; various managerial posts, Norcros Ltd., 1967-69; Group Managing Director, Norcros Ltd., 1969-78; Deputy Chairman, Scotcros Ltd., 1978-80. CBI: Chairman, Scotland, 1977-79 (Deputy Chairman, 1975-77), Council Member, 1972-84, Member, President's Advisory Committee, 1979; UK Regional Chairman, 1979; Chairman, Small Industries Council for Rural Areas of Scotland, 1975-77; Member, Scottish Development Agency, 1977-83; Chairman, Scottish Appeals Committee, Police Dependants' Trust; Scottish Free Enterprise Award, 1978; Deputy Lieutenant, Renfrewshire, since 1985. Recreations: work; amateur radio; reading. Address: (h.) 293 Fenwick Road, Giffnock, Glasgow, G46 6UH; T.-041-638 2586.

Devine, Rt. Rev. Joseph. Bishop of Motherwell, since 1983; b. 7.8.37. Educ. Blairs College, Aberdeen; St. Peter's College, Dumbarton; Scots College, Rome. Ordained Priest in Glasgow, 1960; Assistant Priest, Glasgow, 1965-67; Lecturer in Philosophy, St. Peter's College, Dumbarton, 1967-74; a Chaplain to Catholic students, Glasgow University, 1974-77; Titular Bishop of Voli and Auxiliary to Archbishop of Glasgow, 1977-83.

Dewar, Donald Campbell, MP, MA, LLB. MP (Labour), Glasgow Garscadden, since 1978; Opposition Spokesman on Scottish Affairs, since 1983; b. 21.8.37, Glasgow; 1 s.; 1 d. Educ. Glasgow Academy; Glasgow University. Practised as Solicitor in Glasgow; MP, Aberdeen South, 1966-70; PPS to Tony Crosland, 1967; Chairman, Select Committee on Scottish Affairs,

1980-81; Member, Scottish front bench team, since 1981; elected to Shadow Cabinet, 1984. Address: (h.) 23 Cleveden Road, Glasgow, G12; T.-041-334 2374.

Dewar, Hugh, ACIS. Chief Executive and Secretary, Royal Scottish Automobile Club, since 1980; b. 14.11.36, Newmilns; m., Irene Anne; 1 s.; 1 d. Educ. Edinburgh Academy. Farming and accountancy in Zimbabwe, 1959-73; Lithgows (Holdings) Ltd., 1974-80; Member, RAC British Motor Sport Council, since 1981; Joint Secretary, Standing Joint Committee, RAC, AA and RSAC, since 1981. Steward, RAC. Recreations: golf; curling; rugby (watching). Address: (h.) 9 Craignethan Road, Whitecraigs, Glasgow, G46 6SQ; T.-041-639 8597.

Dewar, Ian Kennedy, SDA, NDA, FRAgS. Regional Training Adviser Scotland, Agricultural Training Board, since 1967; b. 16.1.31, Keltneyburn; m., Jane Dickson Mackenzie; 3 s.; 1 d. Educ. Breadalbane Academy, Aberfeldy; East of Scotland College of Agriculture. HM Forces, 1954-56 (Sergeant Instructor); Teacher, Fife, 1956-59; Organiser of Agricultural Education, Berwickshire, 1959-67. Recreations: gardening; reading. Address: (h.) School House, Redgorton, Perth, PH1 3EL; T.-Stanley 828882.

Dewar, Richard Houston, DA, FRIBA, FRIAS. Chairman, Board of Governors, Duncan of Jordanstone College of Art, since 1977; Senior Partner, W.M. Wilson and Partners, Architects, Dundee, since 1971; b. 13.1.21, Ardler, by Meigle; 1 s.; 1 d. Educ. Forfar Academy; Dundee Institute of Art and Technology. Military Service, 1940-46. President, Dundee Institute of Architects, 1975-77; Governor, Dundee Institute of Art and Technology, 1968-72. Address: (b.) W.M. Wilson & Partners, 26 Castle Street, Dundee; T.-0382 22099.

Dick, David, OBE, DIC, CEng, FIEE, FIERE, FRSA. Principal, Stevenson College of Further Education, Edinburgh, since 1969; Chairman, Fire Services Examination Board (Scotland); Member, Construction Industry Training Board, 1976-85; b. 20.3.29, Edinburgh; m., Muriel Elsie Margaret Buchanan; 5 d. Educ. Boroughmuir School, Edinburgh; Heriot-Watt College, Edinburgh; Imperial College, London. Head, Department of Electrical Engineering, Coatbridge Technical College, 1960-64; Depute Principal, Napier College of Science and Technology, Edinburgh, 1964-69. MSC: Chairman, Lothian District Manpower Committee, 1981-82, Member, Lothian and Borders Area Manpower Board, 1982-85; Member, various committees, Scottish Technical Education Council and Scottish Business Education Council; Past Chairman, Scottish Committee, Institution of Electronic and Radio Engineers; Honorary President, Edinburgh and District Spastics Association. Recreations: music (flute); gardening. Address: (h.) Broomhills, Frogston Road East, Edinburgh; T.-031-664 3136.

Dick, Professor David Andrew Thomas, MB, ChB, MA, DPhil, DSc. Cox Professor of Anatomy, Dundee University, since 1968; b. 11.6.27, Glasgow; m., Elizabeth Graham Reid; 3 s.

Educ. Hillhead High School, Glasgow; Glasgow University; Balliol College, Oxford. Demonstrator of Anatomy: Glasgow University, 1953-55, Oxford University, 1955-58; Carlsberg-Wellcome Research Fellow, Copenhagen, 1958-59; University Lecturer in Anatomy, Oxford, 1959-67; US Public Health Service Research Fellow, Duke University, Durham, North Carolina, 1966-67. Publication: Cell Water, 1966. Recreation: hillwalking. Address: (b.) Department of Anatomy, Dundee University, Dundee, DD1 4HN; T.-Dundee 23181.

Dick, Professor Heather M., MD, FRCPGlas, FRCPath. Professor of Medical Microbiology, Dundee University, since 1984; Visiting Professor (Immunology), Strathclyde University, since 1981; b. 14.11.32, London; m., Alex. L. Dick; 1 d. Educ. Harris Academy, Dundee; Queen's College, Dundee (St. Andrews University). Resident House Officer, Dundee Royal Infirmary and Ruchill Hospital, Glasgow, 1957-59; Assistant, Department of Bacteriology, St. Andrews University, 1959-61; Lecturer, Department of Bacteriology, Glasgow University, 1964-71; Consultant in Clinical Immunology, Glasgow Royal Infirmary, 1971-84. Publication: Topley and Wilson's Principles of Bacteriology and Immunity, 7th Edition (Joint Editor, Volume 1). Recreation: music. Address: (b.) Department of Medical Microbiology, Ninewells Hospital, Dundee, DD1 9SY; T.-0382 60111, Ext. 2166.

Dick, Sheriff John Alexander, MC (1944), QC (Scot), MA, LLB. Sheriff Principal of Glasgow and Strathkelvin, since 1980; b. 1.1.20; m. Educ. Waid Academy, Anstruther; Edinburgh University. London Scottish, 1940; commissioned Royal Scots, 1942; called to Scottish Bar, 1949; Lecturer in Public Law, Edinburgh University, 1953-60; Sheriff of Lothians and Borders, at Edinburgh, 1969-78; Sheriff Principal of North Strathclyde, 1978-82.

Dick, Rev. John Hunter Addison, MA (Hons), MSc, BD (Hons). Minister, Ferryhill South, Aberdeen, since 1982; b. 27.12.45, Dunfermline; m., Gillian Averil Ogle-Skan; 3 s. Educ. Dunfermline High School; Edinburgh University. Research Assistant, Air Pollution Survey, Edinburgh University, 1967-70; Senior Tutor in Geography, Queensland University, Australia, 1970-78; student of divinity, 1978-81; Assistant Minister, Fairmilehead Parish Church, Edinburgh, 1981-82. Recreations: music; philately; badminton. Address: The Manse, 54 Polmuir Road, Aberdeen, AB1 2RT; T.-0224 586933.

Dick, Rev. Thomas, MA. Minister of Dunkeld, since 1974; b. 23.8.26, Rutherglen; m., Annie Margaret Muir McBride; 2 s. Educ. Rutherglen Academy; Glasgow University. Irvine (Relief) Church, 1951-61; Scotstoun East Church, 1961-74. Past President, Kelvin Rotary Club; former Moderator, Dunkeld and Meigle Presbytery. Recreations: gardening; hill-walking; music. Address: Cathedral Manse, Dunkeld, Perthshire, PH8 OAW; T.-03502 249.

Dickens, Lewis Miller, ARICS. Director of Technical Services, Cunninghame District Council, since 1982; b. 15.8.27, Glasgow; m., Margaret;

1 s.; 2 d. Educ. Hermitage Academy, Helensburgh. Royal Navy, 1942-46; Assistant Quantity Surveyor, Aberdeen County Council, 1952-56; Ayr County Council: Senior Quantity Surveyor, 1956-71, Depute Chief Quantity Surveyor, 1971-74, Chief Quantity Surveyor, 1974-75; Depute Director of Technical Services, Cunninghame District Council, 1975-82. Recreation: Scout Association. Address: (b.) Cunninghame District Council, Cunninghame House, Friars Croft, Irvine, KA12 8EE; T.-Irvine 74166.

Dickie, Rev. Michael Mure, BSc (Agric). Minister, Ayr: Castlehill, since 1967; b. 7.7.28, Glasgow; m., Marjory Jack Smith; 1 s.; 2 d. Educ. Dundee High School; Melville College, Edinburgh; Edinburgh University. 2nd Bn., Royal Scots; Minister: Rothiemay Parish, 1955-61, St. David's Church, Bathgate, 1961-67; Member, West Lothian Education Committee, 1963-67; first Chairman, Ayr Burgh Children's Panel; Secretary, Steering Committee for Community Councils in Ayr; Member, Forehill and Holmston Community Council, three years; Chaplain, "R" Division, Strathclyde Police. Recreations: hillwalking; drawing. Address: Castlehill Manse, 3 Hillfoot Road, Ayr, KA7 3LF; T.-Ayr 267332.

Dickie, Thomas, JP. Chairman, Garnock Valley Development Executive, since 1984; Member, Cunninghame District Council, since 1975 (Convener, 1980-84); Chairman, Cunninghame District Licensing Board, since 1980; b. 5.12.30, Beith; m., Janette Coulter Brown. Educ. Beith Academy; Speirs' Secondary School; Glasgow and West of Scotland Commercial College. Office boy to Personnel Manager, Redpath Engineering Ltd., 1946-80; Member, Board, Irvine Development Corporation, 1981-84; Chairman, Kilbirnie Labour Party, since 1967; Treasurer, Cunninghame North Constituency Labour Party. Recreations: caravanning; walking; music. Address: (h.) 45 Loadingbank Court, Kilbirnie, Ayrshire, KA25 6JX; T.-0505 682205.

Dickinson, Professor Harry Thomas, BA, DipEd, MA, PhD, FRHistS. Professor of British History, Edinburgh University, since 1980; b. 9.3.39, Gateshead; m., Jennifer Elizabeth Galtry; 1 s.; 1 d. Educ. Gateshead Grammar School; Durham University; Newcastle University. Teacher of History, Washington Grammar School, 1961-64; Earl Grey Fellow, Newcastle University, 1964-66; History Department, Edinburgh University: Assistant Lecturer, 1966-68, Lecturer, 1968-73, Reader, 1973-80; Visiting Professor, Nanjing University, China, 1980 and 1983. Fulbright Scholar, 1973; Huntington Library Fellowship, 1973; Folger Shakespeare Library Fellowship, 1973; Winston Churchill Fellow, 1980. Publications: Bolingbroke; Walpole and the Whig Supremacy; Liberty and Property; British Radicals and the French Revolution; The Correspondence of Sir James Clavering; Politics and Literature in the 18th Century; The Political Works of Thomas Spence; Caricatures and the Constitution 1760-1832. Recreations: reading; swimming. Address: (h.) 44 Viewforth Terrace, Edinburgh, EH10 4LJ; T.-031-229 1379.

Dickinson, Professor John Philip, MA, MSc, PhD, AASA CPA, ACIS, FRSA, FBIM. Professor of Accountancy, Glasgow University,

since 1985; b. 29.4.45, Morecambe; m., Christine Houghton; 1 s.; 2 d. Educ. Morecambe Grammar School; Cambridge University; Leeds University. Lecturer, Department of Management Studies and Associate Lecturer in Operational Research, Leeds University, 1968-71; Lecturer, Department of Accounting and Finance, Lancaster University, 1971-75; Senior Lecturer, Department of Accounting and Finance, University of Western Australia, 1975-80; Senior Lecturer, Department of Accountancy, Dundee University, 1980-81; Professor of Accountancy, Stirling University, 1981-85. Publications: Portfolio Theory, 1974; Risk and Uncertainty in Accounting and Finance, 1974; Statistics for Business Finance and Accounting, 1976; Portfolio Analysis and Capital Markets, 1977. Recreations: photography; wine and beer-making; travel. Address: (b.) Department of Accountancy, School of Financial Studies, 65/69 Southpark Avenue, University of Glasgow, Glasgow, G12 8LE; T.-041-339 8855.

Dickson, Alastair Ronald, LLB, WS. Partner, Dickson Minto, WS, since 1985; b. 16.1.51, Glasgow; m., Josephine D. Conlon; 2 s.; 1 d. Educ. Glasgow Academy; Trinity College, Glenalmond; Edinburgh University. Partner, Dundas & Wilson, 1978-85; Director: Quayle Munro Ltd., since 1983, J.W. Galloway Ltd., since 1984. Address: (b.) 22 Ainslie Place, Edinburgh; T.-031-225 4455.

Dickson, Captain Alexander Forrest, OBE, RD, FRIN. Commissioner of Northern Lighthouses, since 1979; Pilotage Commissioner; b. 23.6.20, Edinburgh; m., Norma Cochrane; 3 s.; 2 d. Educ. George Watson's; Leith Nautical College. Apprentice, P. Henderson and Co., 1936-39; Royal Navy service in destroyers, 1939-45; Lecturer, Leith Nautical College, 1945-49; Shell International Marine Co. Ltd., 1949-79 (Director Operations, 1968-79). Recreations: fishing; gardening; golf. Address: (h.) Birchburn, Kenmore, Perthshire; T.-08873 283.

Dickson, James Holms, BSc, MA, PhD, FLS. Senior Lecturer in Botany, Glasgow University, since 1979; b. 29.4.37, Glasgow; m., Camilla Ada Lambert; 1 s.; 1 d. Educ. Bellahouston Academy; Glasgow University; Cambridge University. Assistant, then Senior Assistant in Research, Botany School, Cambridge University, 1961-70; Member, Royal Society Expedition to Tristan da Cunha, 1962; Resarch Fellow and Official Fellow, Clare College, Cambridge, 1963-70; Lecturer in Botany, Glasgow University, 1970-79. President, Glasgow Natural History Society, 1976-79. Recreation: gardening. Address: (h.) 113 Clober Road, Milngavie, Glasgow, G62 7LS; T.-041-956 4103.

Dickson, Leonard Elliot, CBE, MC, TD, DL, BA (Cantab), LLB. Retired Solicitor; b. 17.3.15, Edinburgh; m., Mary Elisabeth Cuthbertson; 1 s.; 1 d. Educ. Uppingham; Magdalene College, Cambridge; Glasgow University. 1st Bn., Glasgow Highlanders HLI, 1939-46; former Senior Partner, Dickson, Haddow & Co., Solicitors, Glasgow (retired, 1985); Clerk, Clyde Lighthouses Trust, 1953-65; Secretary, Glasgow Society of Sons of Clergy, 1953-83; serving

Officer, TA, 1939-55 (Lt. Col. commanding 1st Bn., Glasgow Highlanders, 1952-55); Chairman, Lowland TAVR, 1968-70; Member, Glasgow Executive Council, NHS, 1956-74 (Vice Chairman, 1970-74). Recreations: travel; gardening. Address: (h.) Bridge End, Gartmore, Stirling, FK8 3RR; T.-087 72 220.

Dillon, J. Shaun H., DRSAM (Comp), FSA Scot. Professional Musician; Composer, Oboist and Teacher of Woodwind; b. 30.12.44, Sutton Coldfield. Educ. Berwickshire High School; Fettes College; Royal Scottish Academy of Music; Guildhall School of Music. Studied composition with Frank Spedding and Edmund Rubbra; awarded prize for composition for Leicestershire Schools Orchestra, 1965; commissions from various bodies, including Scottish Amateur Music Association; Instructor of Woodwind: Edinburgh Corporation, 1967-72, Aberdeen Corporation (latterly Grampian Region), 1972-81; Freelance Musician, since 1981; sometime Director of Music, St. Mary's Cathedral, Aberdeen; two Suites of Airs and Graces for strings published; Secretary, Association of Instrumental and Vocal Specialists, 1975-78. Recreations: reading, especially history, literature; crosswords; playing flute (badly) in ceilidh bands. Address: (b.) 34 Richmond Street, Aberdeen, AB2 4TR; T.-Aberdeen 630954.

Dilworth, Rev. Gerard Mark, OSB, MA, PhD, FRHistS, FSA Scot. Keeper, Scottish Catholic Archives, Edinburgh, since 1979; b. 18.4.24. Educ. St. Andrew's School, Edinburgh; Fort Augustus Abbey School, Invernessshire; Oxford University; Edinburgh University. Fort Augustus Abbey School: Senior Modern Languages Master, 1956-59, Headmaster, 1959-72; Parish Priest, Fort Augustus, 1974-79; Editor, The Innes Review, 1979-84. Publication: The Scots in Franconia. Address: (b.) Columba House, 16 Drummond Place, Edinburgh, EH3 6PL; T.-031-556 3661.

Dingle, Professor Robert Balson, FRSE, BA (Cantab), PhD (Cantab). Professor of Theoretical Physics, St. Andrews University, since 1960; b. 26.3.26, Manchester; m., Helen Glenronnie Munro; 2 d. Educ. Bournemouth Secondary School; Cambridge University. Fellow, St. John's College, Cambridge, 1948-52; Theoretician to Royal Society Mond Laboratory, Cambridge, 1949-52; Chief Assistant in Theoretical Physics, Technical University of Delft, Holland, 1952-53; Fellow, National Research Council, Ottawa, 1953-54; Reader in Theoretical Physics, University of Western Australia, 1954-60. Publication: Asymptotic Expansions: Their Derivation and Interpretation, 1973. Recreations: music; local history; gastronomy. Address: (h.) 6 Lawhead Road East, St. Andrews, Fife, KY16 9ND; T.-0334 74287.

Dinnis, Alan Russel, BSc, PhD, CEng, FIEE. Senior Lecturer in Electrical Engineering, Edinburgh University, since 1979; b. 7.7.36, Edinburgh; 3 d. Educ. Shrewsbury School; Edinburgh Academy; Edinburgh University. Assistant, then Lecturer, Edinburgh University, 1958-79. IEE: Chairman, SE Scotland Sub-Centre, 1974-75,

Chairman, Scottish Centre, Science, Education and Management Section, 1977-79. Address: (h.) 84 Polwarth Terrace, Edinburgh, EH11 1NN; T.-031-337 3966.

Divers, Stuart. Chairman, Policy and Resources Committee, Clydebank District Council, since 1984 (Member of Council, since 1974); b. 22.5.48, Glasgow; 1 s. Educ. St. Columba's High School; Stow College; Clydebank College. Past Chairman, Clydebank District General Purposes, Technical Services, Community Development Committees; former Labour Group Leader. Recreation: athletics. Address: (h.) 395 Kilbowie Road, Clydebank; T.-041-952 3438.

Dix, Neville John, BSc, PhD. Senior Lecturer in Biological Science, Stirling University, since 1969; b. 13.1.34, Norwich; m., Heather Duff; 1 s.; 2 d. Educ. City of Norwich School; Sheffield University. Lecturer in Mycology, Chelsea College, London, 1958-67; Lecturer in Biological Science, Stirling University, 1967-69. Editor, Transactions of the British Mycological Society. Recreation: long-distance walking. Address: (b.) Department of Biological Science, Stirling University, Stirling; T.-Stirling 73171.

Dixon, Charles, BSc, PhD, FIMA, FRMetS, MBCS. Senior Lecturer in Mathematics, Dundee University, since 1976 (Adviser of Studies in Faculty of Science, since 1975); b. 27.2.35, Dundee. Educ. Morgan Academy, Dundee; St. Andrews University. Assistant Lecturer in Mathematics, Queen's College, Dundee, and St. Andrews University, 1957-60; Research Assistant, Department of Meteorology, Imperial College, London, 1960-62; Lecturer in Mathematics, Queen's College, Dundee, then Dundee University, 1962-76; Visiting Senior Lecturer, University of Western Australia, 1969 and 1974; Visiting Professor, New Mexico State University, 1980. President, Dundee YMCA; Vice-President, Dundee Bn., Boys Brigade. Publications: Applied Mathematics of Science and Engineering, 1971; Numerical Analysis, 1974; Advanced Calculus, 1981. Recreations: squash; curling; playing bagpipes. Address: (b.) Department of Mathematical Sciences, Dundee University, Dundee, DD1 4HN; T.-0382 23181, Ext. 4495.

Dobson, Maurice Nils, DipTP, FRTPI. Director of Development, Stirling District Council, since 1984; b. 25.1.32, Northallerton, North Yorkshire; m., Ellen; 2 s. Educ. Northallerton Grammar School; Leeds College of Art. Planning Assistant, North Riding of Yorkshire County Council, 1948; RAF, 1950-52; Planning Assistant, Barnsley Borough Council, 1955; Senior Planning Assistant: City of Hull Borough Council, 1960, Cumberland County Council, 1961; Depute Director of Planning, Stirling County Council, 1965; Director of Planning and Building Control, Stirling District Council, 1974. Past President, Scottish Society of Directors of Planning; Member, Executive Council, Scottish Branch, Town and Country Planning Association; Member, Joint Negotiating Committee for Chief Officers in Scotland; Past President, Stirling and District Camera Club. Recreations: photography; bowls. Address: (b.) Development Directorate, Municipal Buildings, Stirling; T.-Stirling 79000.

Dobson, Ronald Matthew, MA, PhD. Senior Lecturer in Agricultural Zoology, Glasgow University, since 1974; b. 18.12.25, Blackburn, Lancashire; b. Ruth Hilda Nash; 2 s.; 3 d. Educ. Queen Elizabeth's Grammar School, Blackburn; Cambridge University; London University. Insect Infestation Inspector, Ministry of Food, then Department of Agriculture for Scotland, 1945-49; Research Assistant, Wye College, London University, 1950-53; Scientific Officer, then Senior Scientific Officer, Rothamsted Experimental Station, 1953-59; Lecturer, Glasgow University, 1959-74. Fellow, Royal Entomological Society of London; Honorary Editor, Glasgow Naturalist. Publications: Insects and Other Invertebrates in Colour (adaptation); numerous scientific and natural history articles. Recreations: music; house renovation; boating. Address: (h.) 664 Clarkston Road, Glasgow, G44 3YS; T.-041-637 3476.

Dodd, Raymond Henry, MA, BMus, ARAM. Cellist and Composter; Head, Department of Music, Aberdeen University; b. 31.3.29; m., Doreen Joyce; 1 s.; 1 d. Educ. Bryanston School; Royal Academy of Music; Worcester College, Oxford. Music Master, Sedbergh School, 1951-55; Aberdeen University: Lecturer in Music, 1956, Senior Lecturer in Music, 1971; Visiting Professor of Music, Wilson College, USA, 1972-73. Various orchestral and chamber music compositions; a Governor, Royal Scottish Academy of Music and Drama; a Director: North East of Scotland Music School, Scottish Music Information Centre; awarded Szymanowski Medal, Polish Ministry of Art and Culture, 1982. Recreation: Indian music. Address: (h.) 14 The Chanonry, Old Aberdeen, Aberdeen, AB2 1RP; T.-0224 45752.

Dohan, Francis Thomas. Director of Personnel and Management Services, City of Aberdeen District Council, since 1974; b. 18.4.41, Edinburgh; m., Anne; 2 s.; 1 d. Educ. Holy Cross Academy. Depute Establishment Officer: Scottish Special Housing Association, 1968-72, Aberdeen Corporation, 1972-74. Recreation: golf. Address: (b.) St. Nicholas House, Broad Street, Aberdeen; T.-0224 642121.

Doig, Andrew, MB, ChB, FRCPEdin, FRCP. Consultant Physician, Edinburgh Royal Infirmary, since 1963; Senior Lecturer in Medicine, Edinburgh University, since 1963; b. 18.12.24, Edinburgh; m., Anne Bisset Duthie; 1 s.; 1 d. Educ. Boroughmuir School, Edinburgh; Edinburgh University; Illinois University. Junior medical posts, Edinburgh Royal Infirmary and Victoria Hospital, Burnley; Assistant Lecturer in Medicine, Edinburgh University; postdoctoral Research Fellow, United States Public Health Service. Recreations: hill-walking; photography. Address: (h.) 13 Nile Grove, Edinburgh, EH10 4RE; T.-031-447 4160.

Doig, Very Rev. Andrew Beveridge, MA, BD, DD. Moderator, General Assembly of the Church of Scotland, 1981-82; b. 18.9.14, Carluke; m., 1, Nan Carruthers (deceased); 1 d.; 2, Barbara Young; 1 s.; 1 d. Educ. Hyndland Secondary School, Glasgow; Glasgow University; Trinity College, Glasgow; Union Theological Seminary, New York. Missionary, Church of Scotland, to Nyasaland, 1939; Senior Chaplain to the Forces, East Africa Command, 1940-45; Secretary, Blantyre Mission Council, 1946-53; Member: Government Advisory Committee on African Education, 1948-53, Nyasaland Legislative Council, 1946-53; seconded from missionary service to be Nominated Member for African Interests, Central Africa Federal Assembly, 1953-58; General Secretary, Blantyre Synod, Church of Central Africa, Presbyterian, 1958-62; Minister, St. John's and King's Park, Dalkeith, 1962-72; Clerk, Dalkeith Presbytery, 1965-72; Member, Overseas Council, Church of Scotland, and Convener, Christian Aid, 1967-70; General Secretary, National Bible Society of Scotland, 1972-82; Member, Executive Committee for Europe in worldwide United Bible Societies, 1974-82. Recreation: golf. Address: (h.) The Eildons, Moulin Square, Pitlochry, PH16 5EW; T.-0796 2892.

Doig, James Alexander, MB, ChB, FRCSEdin, FRCSGlas. Consultant Surgeon in Otolaryngology, Glasgow Royal Infirmary, since 1960; Consultant in Neuro-otology, Institute of Neurological Sciences, since 1970; Honorary Clinical Lecturer, Glasgow University, since 1960; Consultant Otolaryngologist, Strathclyde University, since 1980; b. 1926, Dundee; m., Pamela Alison Mais; 1 d. Educ. Dundee High School; St. Andrews University. House Surgeon, Aberdeen Royal Infirmary; House Physician, Dundee Royal Infrmary; House Surgeon (Otolaryngology), Dundee Royal Infirmary; Temporary Major, RAMC; Registrar (Otolaryngology), Aberdeen Royal Infirmary; Registrar (General Surgery), Bangour General Hospital; Senior Registrar (Otolaryngology), Aberdeen Royal Infirmary; Consultant Surgeon (Otolaryngology), Law Hospital. Publications: papers in various medical journals and Contributor to Scientific Foundations of Neurology. Recreations: gardening; fishing; music. Address: (b.) 901 Sauchiehall Street, Glasgow, G3 7TD; T.-041-339 5550.

Doig, John Scott. Sheriff Clerk, Districts of Dumbarton and Oban, since 1979; b. 24.11.38, Dundee; m., Margaret; 1 s.; 1 d. Entered Sheriff Clerk Service, 1956; Secretary, Sheriff Court Rules Council, 1973-79. Deputy Session Clerk, Killermont Parish Church, Bearsden. Recreations: bowls; badminton; curling. Address: (h.) 117 Rannoch Drive, Bearsden, Glasgow; T.-041-942 5635.

Dolan, Philip John, DASS. Area Officer, Social Work, Strathclyde, since 1976; Executive Member, Scottish Council on Disability, since 1982; b. 26.4.36, Glasgow; m., Sheila Reid; 1 s. Educ. St. Mungo's Academy, Glasgow; Glasgow University; Hull University. Printing industry, 1951-64; entered social work service, 1968. Member, Hamilton/East Kilbride Health Council, 1975-82 (Chairman, 1978-80); Member, Prison Local Review Committee, since 1976; Executive Member, Haemophilia Society (Scottish Group), since 1976. Recreations: music; reading; travel. Address: (h.) 160 Camphill Avenue, Langside, Glasgow, G41 3DT; T.-041-649 0050.

116   WHO'S WHO IN SCOTLAND

Donachy, John Archibald, MA, FBIM. Director, The Polecon Co. Ltd., since 1970; Governor, British Film Institute, since 1974; Chairman, Scottish Film Council, since 1984; b. Edinburgh; m., Jilly Pollard; 1 s.; 1 d. Educ. George Heriot's School; High School of Glasgow; Glasgow University. Recreations: gardening; golf; cooking; films; music. Address: (b.) 22A Rutland Square, Edinburgh, EH1 2BB; T.-031-228 6391.

Donald, George Malcolm, ARSA, RSW, DA, ATC, MEd. Assistant to Vice-Principal and Lecturer, School of Drawing/Painting, Edinburgh College of Art; Printmaker; b. 12.9.43, Ootacamund, South India; 1 s.; 1 d. Educ. Robert Gordon's College; Aberdeen Academy; Edinburgh College of Art; Hornsey College of Art; Edinburgh University. Joined Edinburgh College of Art as Lecturer, 1969; Visiting Lecturer, five Faculties of Art in India, 1979; Visiting Professor of Art, 1981, and Visiting Professor, Drawing and Anatomy, 1985, University of Central Florida; Latimer Award, RSA, 1970; Guthrie Award, RSA, 1973; Scottish Arts Council Bursary, 1973; RSA Gillies Bequest Travel Award to India, 1978; SAC Travel and Study Award, Indiana, 1981; RSA Gillies Prize, 1982; RSW Mary Marshall Brown Award, 1983; former Council Member: SSA, Printmakers Workshop (Edinburgh); former Member, Scottish Arts Council Awards Committee; one man shows, Florida, 1985, Helsinki, 1985, Edinburgh Festival, 1985. Adress: (b.) Edinburgh College of Art, Lauriston Place, Edinburgh; T.-031-229 9311.

Donald, James Forrest. Director, His Majesty's Theatre, Aberdeen, since 1971; b. 14.3.34, Aberdeen; m., Anne Gerrie; 1 s.; 1 d. Educ. Gordonstoun School. Recreation: golf. Address: (b.) His Majesty's Theatre, Aberdeen; T.-Aberdeen 637788.

Donald, Rev. Thomas Wilson, LTh, CA. Minister, linked charge of Bowden with Lilliesleaf, since 1977; b. 31.12.23, Glasgow; m., Margaret E. Mitchell; 2 s.; 2 d. Educ. Hillhead High School, Glasgow; Glasgow University. Royal Navy, 1942-46; Partner, Wylie & Bisset, CA, Glasgow, 1955-74. Address: Manse of Bowden, Melrose, Roxburghshire, TD6 OSU; T.-0835 22220.

Donaldson, David Abercrombie, RSA, RP, RGI. Painter; Her Majesty's Painter and Limner in Scotland, since 1977; b. 29.6.16; m., 1, Kathleen Boyd Maxwell; 1 s.; 2, Maria Krystyna Mora-Szorc; 2 d. Educ. Coatbridge Secondary School; Glasgow School of Art. Head of Painting School, Glasgow School of Art, 1967-81; Hon. LLD, Strathclyde, 1971.

Donaldson, Professor Gordon Bryce, MA, PhD, MInstP. Professor, Department of Applied Physics, Strathclyde University, since 1985 (Head of Department, since 1984); b. 10.8.41, Edinburgh; m., Christina Martin; 1 s.; 1 d. Educ. Glasgow Academy; Christ's College, Cambridge. Cavendish Laboratory, Cambridge, 1962-65; Lecturer in Physics, Lancaster University, 1966-75; Strathclyde University: Lecturer, 1976, Senior Lecturer, 1978; Visiting Scientist and Fulbright Scholar, University of California,

1975; Visiting Professor, University of Virginia, 1981. Governor, Glasgow Academicals War Memorial Trust. Address: (b.) Department of Applied Physics, Strathclyde University, Glasgow, G4 ONG; T.-041-552 4400.

Donaldson, James Andrew, BDS. General Dental Practitioner; Member, Aberdeen District Council, since 1984; b. 28.2.57, Glasgow; m., Dr. Patricia H. Winter. Educ. Coatbridge High School; Dundee University. Associate in various dental practices, 1979-83; began own practice, 1983. Recreations: skiing; squash; BA studies, Open University. Address: (h.) The Manse, Bridge Street, Cruden Bay, Aberdeenshire; T.-077981 3313.

Donaldson, James T., BA (Hons), MEd. HM Inspector of Schools, since 1982; b. 4.3.45, Ecclefechan; m., Maureen; 1 s.; 2 d. Educ. Wallace Hall Academy; Strathclyde University; Edinburgh University. Lecturer, Edinburgh College of Commerce, 1968-73; Lecturer/Senior Lecturer, Queen Margaret College, Edinburgh, 1973-79; Head, Department of Business Studies, Telford College of Further Education, Edinburgh, 1979-82. Recreations: golf; running. Address: (b.) Room 3/26, New St. Andrew's House, Scottish Education Department, St. James Centre, Edinburgh, EH1; T.-031-556 8400.

Donaldson, Marion Butters. Director, Marion Donaldson Ltd., since 1970; b. 1.10.44, Glasgow; m., David L. Donaldson; 2 s.; 1 d. Educ. Shawlands Academy; Jordanhill College of Education (Teaching Diploma). Teacher, London and Airdrie, 1965-66; with husband, founded fashion design business, 1966; later incorporated into Marion Donaldson Ltd. Recreations: sailing; interior design; restoring French "ruines". Address: (b.) 93 Candleriggs, Glasgow, G1 1NP; T.-041-552 8071.

Donaldson, Robert, MA, PhD. Keeper, Division 2, Department of Printed Books, National Library of Scotland, since 1975; b. 13.12.26, Edinburgh; m., Elizabeth Macpherson; 1 s.; 1 d. Educ. George Heriot's School, Edinburgh; Edinburgh University. Assistant Librarian, Edinburgh University Library, 1949-59; Sub-Librarian (Keeper of Special Collections), Glasgow University Library, 1959-62; National Library of Scotland: Assistant Keeper, Department of Printed Books, 1962-72, Deputy Keeper, Department of Printed Books, 1972-74. Editor, The Bibliotheck, 1959-69; President, Edinburgh Bibliographical Society, 1977-80; Chairman, Scottish Group, University, College and Research Section, Library Association, 1980-82; Chairman, Rare Books Group, since 1983. Recreation: listening to music. Address: (b.) National Library of Scotland, George IV Bridge, Edinburgh, EH1 1EW; T.-031-226 4531.

Donaldson, Professor William Anderson, OBE, MA, BA, DipMathStat. Professor of Operational Research, Strathclyde University, since 1971; b. 20.1.27, Glasgow; m., Constance Mary Taylor Wilson; 1 s.; 1 d. Educ. Queen's Park Secondary School; Glasgow University; St. John's College, Cambridge. Glasgow University: Assistant Lecturer in Mathematics, 1946-48, Lecturer,

1951-55; Data Processing Manager, Rolls-Royce Ltd. (Scottish Group), 1955-62; Strathclyde University: Senior Lecturer, 1962-68, Reader, 1968-71. Member, Scottish Advisory Committee on Computers in the Health Service, 1970-74; Member, then Chairman, Information and Computer Services Advisory Group, 1975-85; Vice-President, Operational Research Society, 1978-80. Recreations: mountaineering; skiing; canoeing; thinking. Address: (h.) 2 Edgehill Road, Bearsden, Glasgow, G61 3AD; T.-041-942 1295.

Donaldson, (William) Blair (MacGregor), MB, ChB, FRCS, DO. Consultant Ophthalmic Surgeon, since 1979; Senior Lecturer in Ophthalmology, Aberdeen University, since 1979; b. 24.12.40, Edinburgh; m., Marjorie Stuart; 1 d. Educ. Edinburgh Academy; Edinburgh University. Junior hospital appointments in Tasmania and Scotland. Recreations: skiing; tennis; golf. Address: (h.) 45 Carlton Place, Aberdeen, AB2 4BR; T.-0224 641166.

Donnelly, Dougie. Radio and Television Broadcaster, since 1976; b. 7.6.53, Glasgow; m., Linda; 1 d. Educ. Hamilton Academy; Strathclyde University. Studied law at University; joined Radio Clyde to present music programmes, 1976, and BBC TV Scotland as Sports Presenter and Commentator, 1978; Presenter, Friday Night With Dougie Donnelly, BBC TV Scotland (two series); Presenter, Dougie Donnelly Mid Morning Show, Radio Clyde (sixth year). Scottish Radio Personality of Year, 1979 and 1982; Scottish TV Personality of Year, 1982; Member: Stars Organisation for Spastics, Lords Taverners. Recreations: golf; reading; socialising; work. Address: (b.) c/o David John Associates, 6 Victoria Crescent Road, Glasgow, G12 9DB; T.-041-357 0532.

Donnelly, James Joseph, FRICS, FCIOB. Chartered Quantity Surveyor; Chairman, Board of Governors, Dundee College of Technology, since 1975 (Member, since 1968); b. 14.3.30, Dundee; m., Catherine; 4 d. Educ. Lawside R.C. Academy, Dundee; Dundee College of Technology. Sole Partner, private practice, since 1979. Office-bearer, Dundee Old People's Welfare Committee. Recreations: golf; curling; gardening. Address: (h.) 6 Castleroy Road, Broughty Ferry, Dundee, DD5 2LQ; T.-0382 76820.

Donnison, Professor David. Professor of Town and Regional Planning, Glasgow University, since 1980; b. 19.1.26. Lecturer: Manchester University, 1950-53, Toronto University, 1953-55; London School of Economics and Political Science: Reader, 1956-61, Professor, 1961-69; Director, Centre for Environmental Studies, London, 1969-75; Supplementary Benefits Commission, 1975-80. Address: (b.) Glasgow University, Glasgow, G12 8RT.

Donovan, Professor Robert John, BSc, PhD, CChem, FRSC, FRSE. Professor of Physical Chemistry, Edinburgh University, since 1979 (Head, Chemistry Department, since 1984); b. 13.7.41, Nantwich; m., Marion Colclough; 1 d.

Educ. Sandbach School; University College of Wales, Aberystwyth; Cambridge University. Research Fellow, Gonville and Caius College, 1966-70; Edinburgh University: Lecturer in Physical Chemistry, 1970-74, Reader in Chemistry, 1974-79. Member, Physical Chemistry Panel, Science & Engineering Research Council, 1977-80; Member, Management Committee, SERC Synchrotron Radiation Source, Daresbury, 1977-80; Member, SERC Synchroton Radiation Facility Committee, 1979-84; awarded Corday-Morgan Medal and Prize, Royal Society of Chemistry, 1975; Member, Faraday Council, Royal Society of Chemistry, 1981-83 (President, Local Area, since 1985). Recreations: hill-walking; skiing; sail-boarding. Address: (b.) Department of Chemistry, Edinburgh University, West Mains Road, Edinburgh, EH9 3JJ; T.-031-667 1081 (Ext. 3408).

Dorman, Arthur Brian, LLB, FBIM. Solicitor, since 1969; Founding Partner, Dorman, Jeffrey & Co., Glasgow and Edinburgh, since 1979; b. 21.6.45, Glasgow; m., Christine Angela; 1 s.; 1 d. Educ. Hillhead High School; Glasgow University. Recreation: occasional golf. Address: (b.) Provincial House, 140 West George Street, Glasgow, G2 2HH; T.-041-332 7916.

Dorward, Adam Paterson, FCFI. Member, Borders Health Board (Convener, Finance Committee), since 1978; a Governor, Scottish College of Textiles; b. 11.6.22, Galashiels; m., Jean MacPherson Ovens; 2 s. Educ. Sedbergh School; St. John's College, Cambridge; Dundee School of Economics; Tailor & Cutter Academy; Stevenson College. RAF, 1942-46 (Flt Lt Pilot, Flying Instructor); J. & J. Dorward Ltd., Gala Forest: joined, 1946, appointed Designer/Production Manager, 1948, appointed Director, 1952, Managing Director, 1972, Chairman, 1978; negotiated amalgamation with Dawson International, remaining Managing Director for 18 months; administration, Youth Opportunities Programme and Youth Training Scheme, Borders Regional Council, 1982-84; Business Consultant, 1984; Production Co-ordinator, clothing manufacturer, since 1985. Town and County Councillor, 1955-60; Member, Board, Galashiels Further Education College, 1955-60; Deacon, Galashiels Manufacturers' Corporation, 1960; a Governor, St. Mary's Preparatory School, Melrose, 1960; Council Member, Clothing Manufacturers' Federation of GB, 1973-81; Chairman, Scottish Clothing Manufacturers' Association, 1975-79; Past Chairman, Border Counties TSB; former Trustee, TSB of South of Scotland; Member, Eildon Housing Association, since 1978; Trustee, R.S. Hayward Trust. Recreations: sports; gardening; wine-making. Address: (h.) Caddon Lynns, Clovenfords, Galashiels, TD1 3LF; T.-0896 85 259.

Dorward, David Campbell, MA, GRSM, LRAM. Composer, since 1944; Music Producer, BBC, since 1962; b. 7.8.33, Dundee; m., Janet Offord; 1 s.; 2 d. Educ. Morgan Academy, Dundee; St. Andrews University; Royal Academy of Music. Teaching, 1960-61; Freelance, 1961-62. Arts Adviser, Lamp of Lothian Collegiate Trust, since 1967; Member, Scottish Arts

Council, 1972-78; Consultant Director, Performing Right Society, since 1985; Patron's Fund Award, 1958; Royal Philharmonic Prizewinner, 1958; compositions include four string quartets, symphony, four concertos, Tonight Mrs Morrison (one-act opera), A Christmas Carol (musical), and incidental music for TV, radio, film and stage. Recreations: photography; computers; walking in the country. Address: (h.) 10 Dean Park Crescent, Edinburgh, EH4 1PH; T.-031-332 3002.

Douglas, Rev. Andrew Morrison, MA. Minister, High Church, Hilton, Aberdeen; b. 23.2.30, Orange, Australia; m., Margaret Rennie; 2 s.; 2 d. Educ. Robert Gordon's College; Aberdeen University. Minister: Lochcraig Church, Fife, 1957-63, Bonaccord St. Paul's, Aberdeen, 1963-72, Southesk, Brechin, 1972-77. Chaplain, Aberdeen Maternity and Sick Children's Hospitals, 1968-71. Recreations: gardening; games. Address: 25 Argyll Place, Aberdeen, AB2 4HU; T.-Aberdeen 636672.

Douglas, Rev. Colin Rutherford, MA, BD, STM. Minister, Airdrie St. Columba's, since 1973; b. 10.4.42, Leven. Educ. George Watson's College; Dundee High School; Loretto School; St. Andrews University; Edinburgh University. Scottish half-mile Schools Champion, 1960. Address: St. Columba's Manse, 22 Arthur Avenue, Airdrie, ML6 9EZ; T.-Airdrie 62029.

Douglas, Very Rev. Hugh Osborne, KCVO, CBE, DD, LLD. Minister of Religion (retired); Moderator, General Assembly of the Church of Scotland, 1970-71; b. 11.9.11, Glasgow; m., Isabel C. Rutherford; 1 s.; 2 d. Educ. Glasgow Academy; Glasgow University; Trinity College, Glasgow. Assistant Minister, Govan Old Parish Church, 1934-39; ordained, 1937; Minister, St. John's, Leven, 1939-42; War Service, Church of Scotland Huts, 1942; Minister, North Leith, Edinburgh, 1942-51; Minister, Dundee Parish Church (St. Mary's), 1951-77; Dean of the Chapel Royal in Scotland, 1974-81; Convener, General Assembly Committee on fourth Centenary of Reformation, 1954-60; Convener, General Assembly Special Committee on Religious Education, 1960-64; Member, Legal Aid Central Committee, Law Society of Scotland, 1955-80; Member: Scottish Religious Advisory Committee, BBC, 1956-58, General Advisory Council, BBC, 1966-69; Centenary Preacher, St. Andrew's Church, Brisbane, 1962; Visiting Lecturer, Christian Council of Ghana, 1967; Honorary Governor, Glasgow Academy, since 1971. Publications: What Is Christian Marriage?, 1946; Coping With Life, 1964. Recreations: golf; reading; writing. Address: (h.) Broomlea, 7a Windmill Road, St. Andrews, KY16 9JJ; T.-0334 73232.

Douglas, Rev. Iain Mackechnie, MA, BD, MPhil, DipEd. Minister, St. Andrew's Parish Church, Montrose, since 1980; b. 25.6.35, Eccles, Berwickshire; m., E.W. Shirley Harris; 1 s. Educ. Eccles Public School; George Watson's Boys' College, Edinburgh; Edinburgh University. Missionary, Church of Scotland, 1960-68; ordained, Madras Diocese, Church of South India,

1960; Lecturer, Tamilnad Theological College, 1963-68; Teacher of Religious Education, Hawick High School, 1969-74; Principal Teacher of Religious Education, Morgan Academy, Dundee, 1974-80. Publications: Famulus Christi (Contributor), 1976; Sacris Erudiri (Contributor), 1974-75. Address: 49 Northesk Road, Montrose, DD10 8TQ; T.-Montrose 72060.

Douglas, Rev. Ian Percy, LTh. Minister, Craigiebuckler Parish Church, Aberdeen, since 1982; b. 2.5.38, Inverurie; m., Celia Gerrard; 2 s. Educ. Inverurie Academy; Aberdeen University. Junior Salesman, Isaac Benzie Ltd., Aberdeen, 1954-56; 1st Bn., Seaforth Highlanders, 1956-59; Departmental Manager, Isaac Benzie Ltd., 1960-65; Training and Personnel Officer, House of Fraser, 1965-67; studied for the ministry, 1967-73; Minister, Viewforth Parish Church, Edinburgh, 1974-82. TA Chaplain, 205 General Hospital Unit, 1979-81; Patron, Aberdeen Trinity Hall; Burgess of Guild of Burgh of Aberdeen. Recreations: music; bowls. Address: Craigiebuckler Manse, Springfield Road, Aberdeen, AB1 8AA.

Douglas, James Hall, MA, LLB. Honorary Sheriff, since 1983; b. 16.9.21, Glasgow; m., Louisa Hemsworth. Educ. Whitehill Senior Secondary School, Glasgow; Glasgow University. RAF, 1940-46; Procurator Fiscal service, 1951-82, at Ayr, Glasgow, Stranraer and Dunfermline; Procurator Fiscal, Dunfermline, 1967-82. Recreations: reading; gardening; music; philately. Address: (h.) 1 Canmore Grove, Dunfermline, KY12 OJT; T.-Dunfermline 725486.

Douglas, James Turner, Honorary Sheriff, since 1971; retired Solicitor; b. 12.9.16, Perth; m., Isobel Barrie Campbell; 1 s.; 1 d. Educ. Perth Academy; Edinburgh University. Qualified as Solicitor, 1939; Army, 1939-45 (POW, Germany, 1940-45); Solicitor in Perth, 1945-83 (Senior Partner, Macnab, Gordon & Douglas, 1962-83). President, Scottish Golf Union, 1972-74; Past Captain, Craigie Hill and Blairgowrie Golf Clubs; Past Captain and President, Perthshire Rugby Club; Past President: Perth Rotary Club, Society of Solicitors of City and County of Perth. Recreations: golf; in younger days, rugby. Address: (h.) 1 Springbank, Isla Road, Perth, PH2 7HB; T.-Perth 21576.

Douglas, John Aitken, DPE, DMS, MBIM, FILAM. Director of Recreation Services, Inverclyde District Council, since 1974; b. 8.4.41, Duns; m., Anne; 1 s.; 1 d. Educ. Berwickshire High School, Duns; Scottish School of Physical Education, Jordanhill College of Education; Glasgow College of Technology. Teacher of Physical Education, Dollar Academy, 1963-65; Assistant Lecturer in Physical Education, Glasgow University, 1965-66; Lecturer in Physical Education, Strathclyde University, 1966-67; Manager, Bellahouston Sports Centre, Glasgow, 1967-71; Recreation Officer, Bishopbriggs Burgh Council, 1971-74. Churchill Fellow, 1970; Past Chairman: British and Irish Basketball Federation, 1972-73, Association of Recreation Managers, 1973-74 and 1979-80; National Executive, Institute of Leisure and Amenity Management, since 1982 (Chairman, Scottish Region, 1984-85). Recreations: hockey; squash; caravanning; skiing; sailboarding. Address: (b.) Municipal Buildings, Greenock; T.-0475 24400.

Douglas, Neil James, MD, FRCP. Senior Lecturer in Respiratory Medicine, Edinburgh University, since 1983; Consultant Physician, since 1983; b. 28.5.49, Edinburgh; m., Dr. Sue Galloway; 1 s.; 1 d. Educ. Dundee High School; Trinity College, Glenalmond; St. Andrews University; Edinburgh University. Lecturer in Medicine, Edinburgh University, 1974-83; MRC Travelling Fellow, University of Colorado, 1980-81. Recreations: fishing; gardening; eating. Address: (b.) Department of Respiratory Medicine, City Hospital, Greenbank Drive, Edinburgh; T.-031-447 1001.

Douglas, Richard. MP (Labour), Dunfermline West, since 1983 (Dunfermline, 1979-83); b. 4.1.32. Educ. Govan High School; Co-operative College; Strathclyde University. MP, Stirlingshire East and Clackmannan, 1970-74; Member, Public Accounts Committee, 1979-83.

Douglas, Sadie Naomi. Administrative Director, Scottish Civic Trust, since 1983; b. Huddersfield; m., Alexander Douglas (deceased); 1 s. Educ. Longley Hall, Huddersfield; Huddersfield Technical College. Worked with Oxfam, 1966-70; Organising Secretary, Facelift Glasgow, 1970-73; Trust Secretary, Scottish Civic Trust, 1973-83. Member, Countrywide Holiday Association (President, Glasgow CHA Club); Member, Scottish Countryside Activities Council. Recreation: hill-walking. Address: (h.) Hillhouse, Ardneil Avenue, West Kilbride, Ayrshire, KA23; T.-0294 822465.

Douglas-Hamilton, Lord James Alexander, MP, MA, LLB. MP (Conservative), Edinburgh West, since 1974; Parliamentary Private Secretary to Malcolm Rifkind, Minister at the Foreign Office; b. 31.7.42, Strathaven; m., Susan Buchan; 4 s. Educ. Eton; Balliol College, Oxford; Edinburgh University. Advocate at Scots Bar, 1968; Member, Edinburgh Town Council, 1972; Scottish Conservative Whip, 1977; a Lord Comr, HM Treasury, and Government Whip for Scottish Conservative Members, 1979-81; Captain, Cameronian Coy, 2nd Bn., Lowland Volunteers (RARO), 1972; Honorary President, Scottish Amateur Boxing Association, since 1975; President, Royal Commonwealth Society in Scotland, since 1979; President, Scottish Council, United Nations Association, since 1981. Oxford Boxing Blue, 1961; President, Oxford Union Society, 1964. Publications: Motive For A Mission: The Story Behind Hess's Flight to Britain, 1971; The Air Battle for Malta: The Diaries of a Fighter Pilot, 1981; Roof of the World, 1983. Recreations: golf; forestry. Address: (h.) 12 Quality Street Lane, Davidsons Mains, Edinburgh; T.-031-336 4213.

Douglas-Home, (Lavinia) Caroline, FSA Scot. Estate Factor, Douglas and Angus Estates, since 1959; Trustee, National Museum of Antiquities of Scotland, 1982-85; Deputy Lieutenant, Berwickshire, since 1983; b. 11.10.37. Educ. privately. Woman of the Bedchamber (Temporary) to Queen Elizabeth the Queen Mother, 1963-65; Lady-In-Waiting (Temporary) to Duchess of Kent, 1966-67. Recreations: hunting; fishing; reading; antiquities. Address: (h.) Dove Cottage, The Hirsel, Coldstream, Berwickshire; T.-0890 2834.

Dourish, James Anthony, MA (Hons). Rector, Trinity High School, Renfrew, since 1979; b. 7.2.37, Glasgow; m., Honor Burns; 3 s.; 1 d. Educ. St. Aloysius' College, Glasgow; Glasgow University. Teacher of Classics, St. Aloysius' College, Glasgow, 1960-67; Principal Teacher of Classics: St. Gregory's, Glasgow, 1967-71, Holyrood, Glasgow, 1972-73; Assistant Head Teacher, St. Margaret Mary's, Glasgow, 1974-77; Depute Head Teacher, Cardinal Newman High School, Bellshill, 1977-79. Choirmaster/Organist, St.Andrew's Cathedral, Glasgow, 1975-82; Past President, Rutherglen Lawn Tennis Club. Recreations: tennis; hill-walking; music. Address: (h.) 46 Viewpark Drive, Burnside, near Glasgow; T.-041-647 1021.

Dow, Lt. Col. Leslie Phillips Graham, OBE. Producer, Edinburgh Military Tattoo, since 1975; b. 13.1.26, Glasgow; m., Joan Robinson; 2 d. Educ. Belhaven Hill, Dunbar; Marlborough College. Commissioned, The Cameronians (Scottish Rifles), 1946; 1st Bn., Gibraltar, Trieste, Hong Kong and Malaya, 1947-51; C-in-C's Staff, Singapore, 1952-54; Adjt., 1st Bn., 1955; Staff College, 1956; Staff (Brigade Major), 1957-59; Company Commander, 1st Bn., Kenya and BAOR, 1959-61; Company Commander, RMA, Sandhurst, 1962-64; MA to GOC Kenya, 1965; with 1st Bn., 1966-68; commanded in Aden until standdown, Douglas, Lanarkshire, May, 1968; voluntary retirement, 1969. Member, The Monks of St. Giles. Recreations: shooting; gardening; French wine; classical music; composing indifferent light verse. Address: (h.) 22A Northumberland Street, Edinburgh, EH3 6LS; T.-031-557 0467.

Dowdalls, Edward Joseph, JP, BSc. Principal, Coatbridge College; b. 6.3.26, Coatbridge. Educ. Our Lady's High School, Motherwell; Glasgow University. Member, Coatbridge Burgh Council, 1958-74 (Provost, 1967-70); Member, Lanarkshire Health Board, 1973-81 (Chairman, 1977-81). Recreations: reading; watching sport. Address: (h.) 72 Drumpellier Avenue, Coatbridge; T.-Coatbridge 23889.

Downie, Rev. Alexander George. Minister, Saline linked with Blairingone, since 1958; b. 15.6.23, Tarland; m., Jean; 1 s.; 2 d. Educ. Morpeth Grammar School; St. Andrews University. Army, 1942-47; commissioned, 1945, attached to 1st Mahratta Light Infantry; with British Occupation Forces, Japan, 1947; promoted Captain, 1947. Assistant Minister, St. Ninian's Parish Church, Stirling, 1951-53; Minister, Saline Parish Church, 1953-58. Moderator, Dunfermline and Kinross Presbytery, 1964-65. Address: The Manse, Saline, Fife; T.-New Oakley 852240.

Downie, Alfred, BA, ACMA, MBIM. Finance Director, Sea Fish Industry Authority, since 1982; b. 9.6.39, Falkirk; m., Margaret Cuthbertson; 1 s.; 1 d. Educ. Falkirk High School; Open University. Management Trainee, oil industry, 1957-63; Cost Accountant, petrochemicals, 1964-66; Chief Accountant, ironfounding, 1967-70; Accountant, public body, 1971-81. Recreation: golf. Address: (b.) 10 Young Street, Edinburgh, EH2 4JQ; T.-031-225 2515.

Downie, Allan Watson, MB, FRCP. Senior Lecturer, Department of Medicine, Aberdeen University, since 1965; Honorary Consultant Neurologist, Grampian Area Health Board, since 1965; b. 9.2.25, Aberdeen; m., Jean Mildred Paine; 4 s.; 2 d. Educ. Robert Gordon's College, Aberdeen; Aberdeen University. Early neurological training, various London hospitals; spent eight years as neurologist and University teacher, University of North Carolina Medical School. Address: (h.) Moorlands, Main Street, Newburgh, Aberdeenshire.

Downie, James Hubert. FRSA. Barrister; Member, Western Isles Health Board; Chairman, Management Committee, Co-Chomunn na Hearadh Ltd. (Harris Community Co-operative); b. 13.5.23, Northwood, Middlesex; m., Joyce Wyllie Milne; 3 d. Educ. Merchant Taylor's School, Northwood. Royal Navy, 1941-58 (retired as Lt.-Comdr); Shell-Mex & BP Ltd.: joined, 1959, Manager, Industrial Relations and Manpower Division, 1966-67, Manager, Trade Relations Division, 1967-75. Recreations: angling; gardening; bird-watching. Address: (h.) Dumarin Strond, Isle of Harris, Western Isles; T.-0859 82 247.

Downie, Professor Robert S., MA, BPhil. Professor of Moral Philosophy, Glasgow University, since 1969 (Stevenson Lecturer in Medical Ethics, since 1984); b. 19.4.33, Glasgow; m., Eileen Dorothea Flynn; 3 d. Educ. High School of Glasgow; Glasgow University; Queen's College, Oxford. Tutor, Worcester College, Oxford, 1958-59; Glasgow University: Lecturer in Moral Philosophy, 1959-68, Senior Lecturer, 1968-69; Visiting Professor: Syracuse University, New York, 1963-64, Dalhousie University, Nova Scotia, 1976. Publications: Government Action and Morality, 1964; Respect for Persons, 1969; Roles and Values, 1971; Education and Personal Relationships, 1974; Caring and Curing, 1980. Recreation: music. Address: (b.) Department of Philosophy, Glasgow University, G12 8QQ; T.-041-339 8855.

Downie, Thomas Cochrane, BSc, PhD, DipFE, CChem, FRSC, FICorrST. Vice-Principal, Paisley College of Technology, since 1974; b. 6.7.24, Glasgow; m., Janet Brown Gillespie; 3 d. Educ. Bellahouston Academy, Glasgow; Glasgow University. Technical Officer, ICI Nobel Division, Ardeer, 1952-54; Lecturer in Chemistry, Dundee College of Technology, 1954-58; Senior/Principal Lecturer, Newcastle Polytechnic (Rutherford College), 1958-70; Head, School of Chemistry, Thames Polytechnic, 1971-74. Council Member: Royal Institute of Chemistry, 1972-74, Chemical Society, 1972-74, Institution

of Corrosion Science and Technology, 1981-83; Council for Applied Science in Scotland, since 1980; Member, CNAA Committee for Scotland, since 1984. Recreations: hill-walking; bridge. Address: (b.) Paisley College of Technology, High Street, Paisley, PA1 2BE; T.-041-887 1241.

Downs, Ian, DipArch, DipTP, RIBA, MRTPI, ARIAS. Chief Architect/Planner and Director of Technical Services, Irvine Development Corporation; b. 21.2.37, Withensea, East Yorkshire; 1 s.; 1 d. Educ. Withensea High School; Hull School of Architecture; Manchester University. Architect, Cumbernauld Development Corporation, 1960-63; Architect/Planner: United States (private practice, working on New Towns), 1964-65, Wilson & Womersely, 1965-66; Group Architect, Livingston Development Corporation, 1966-69; Assistant Chief Architect: Redditch Development Corporation, 1969-76, West Midlands Metropolitan County Council, 1976-79. Recreation: sailing. Address: (b.) Irvine Development Corporation, Perceton House, Irvine; T.-Irvine 214100.

Dowson, Henry Richard, BSc, PhD, FRSE. Reader in Mathematics, Glasgow University, since 1975; Editor-in-Chief, Glasgow Mathematical Journal, since 1975; b. 2.3.39, Newcastle-upon-Tyne. Educ. Royal Grammar School, Newcastle-upon-Tyne; King's College, Newcastle-upon-Tyne; St. John's College, Cambridge. Assistant Lecturer, Department of Pure Mathematics, University College of Swansea, 1963-65; Lecturer, Department of Mathematics, Newcastle-upon-Tyne University, 1965-66; Assistant Professor, Illinois University, 1966-68; Department of Mathematics, Glasgow University: Lecturer, 1968-73, Senior Lecturer, 1973-75. Publication: Spectral Theory of Linear Operators, 1978. Recreation: bridge; numismatics. Address: (b.) Department of Mathematics, University Gardens, Glasgow, G12 8QW; T.-041-339 8855, Ext. 7179.

Doyle, Rev. David Wallace, MA (Hons), BD (Hons). Minister, Tulliallan and Kincardine Parish Church, since 1977; b. 12.4.48, Glasgow; m., Alison Wightman Britton; 1 s.; 1 d. Educ. High School of Glasgow; Glasgow University; Corpus Christi College, Cambridge. Assistant Minister, East Kilbride Old Parish Church, 1973-74; Black Fellowship, awarded by Glasgow University for postgraduate study at Cambridge, 1974-77. Recreations: music; reading. Address: The Manse, Kincardine, Alloa, FK10 4QZ; T.-Kincardine 30538.

Doyle, Rev. Ian Bruce, MA, BD, PhD. Joint Secretary, Department of Ministry and Mission, Church of Scotland, since 1984; b. 11.9.21, Methil, Fife; m., Anne Watt Wallace; 2 s. Educ. Buckhaven High School; St. Andrews University; New College, Edinburgh. Served with Church of Scotland Huts, Germany, 1945-46; Assistant to Rev. D.P. Thomson, Evangelist, 1946; Minister: St. Mary's, Motherwell, 1946-60, Eastwood, Glasgow, 1960-77; Convener: Home Mission Committee, 1970-74, Home Board, 1974-77; Secretary, Department of Home Mission, 1977-84; Secretary, Prison Chaplaincies Board, since

1977; Religious Advisor to Scottish Television, since 1975. Publications: This Jesus; Covenanting Theology; DP, a memoir of Dr. D.P. Thomson. Recreation: reading. Address: (h.) 21 Lygon Road, Edinburgh; T.-031-667 2697.

Drape, Iain Bethune, TD. Member, Wigtown District Council, since 1975 (Chairman, Licensing Board, since 1975); b. 13.3.27, Whithorn; m., Elizabeth Margerie; 1 s.; 1 d. Educ. Whithorn Junior Secondary School; George Watson's College, Edinburgh. Town Councillor, Whithorn, 1953-75 (Provost, 1969-75). Commissioner of Income Tax; Church Elder. Recreation: golf. Address: (h.) Rosscairn, Isle of Whithorn, Newton Stewart; T.-Whithorn 302.

Draper, Ivan Thomas, MB, ChB, FRCPEdin, FRCPGlas. Consultant Neurologist, Institute of Neurological Sciences, Glasgow, since 1965; b. 11.9.32, Derby; m., Muriel May Munro. Educ. Bemrose School; Aberdeen University. Fellow, Department of Medicine, Johns Hopkins Hospital, Baltimore, 1962-63. Past President, Scottish Ornithologists Club. Publication: Lecture Notes on Neurology, 6th Edition. Recreations: birds; books; fish. Address: (b.) Institute of Neurological Sciences, Southern General Hospital, Govan Road, Glasgow.

Draper, Paul Richard, BA, MA, PhD. Esmee Fairbairn Senior Lecturer in Finance, Strathclyde University, since 1978; b. 28.12.46, Hayes; m., Janet Margaret; 1 s.; 1 d. Educ. Hayes County Grammar School; Exeter University; Reading University; Stirling University. Lecturer: St. Andrews University, Edinburgh University. Director MSc in Financial Studies, Strathclyde University, 1980-83. Recreation: home computing. Address: (h.) 19 Upper Gray Street, Newington, Edinburgh; T.-031-667 4087.

Draper, Professor Ronald Philip, BA, PhD. Professor of English, Aberdeen University, since 1973 (Head of Department, since 1984); b. 3.10.28, Nottingham; m., Irene Margaret Aldridge; 3 d. Educ. Nottingham High School; Nottingham University. Tutorial Assistant, Nottingham University, 1951-53; Education Officer, RAF, 1953-55; Lecturer in English, Adelaide University, 1955-56; Leicester University: Assistant Lecturer in English, 1957-58, Lecturer, 1958-68, Senior Lecturer, 1968-73. Publications: D.H. Lawrence, 1964; D.H. Lawrence (Profiles in Literature), 1969; D.H. Lawrence, The Critical Heritage, 1970; Hardy, The Tragic Novels, 1975; George Eliot, The Mill on the Floss and Silas Marner, 1978; Tragedy, Developments in Criticism, 1980; Shakespeare, A Midsummer Night's Dream, 1980; Shakespeare, Cymbeline, 1980; Lyric Tragedy, 1985; Shakespeare, The Winter's Tale, 1985. Recreations: reading; listening to music; walking. Address: (b.) English Department, Taylor Building, King's College, Old Aberdeen, AB9 2UB; T.-0224 40241.

Drever, Harry Sinclair, MBE, JP, AIB (Scot). Consultant, Gerald Eve & Co., Chartered Surveyors, London, since 1974; Chairman, Hjaltland Housing Association Ltd., since 1982; Honorary Sheriff, Grampian, Highlands and Islands at Shetland, since 1961; b. 28.10.05, St. Margaret's, Hope, Orkney; m., Katherine J.C. Moffat. Educ. St. Margaret's Hope Secondary School. Union Bank of Scotland Ltd. and Bank of Scotland, 1921-70 (Manager, Lerwick and Scalloway Branches, 1950-70); Shetland County Councillor, 1958-70 (sometime Chairman, Finance Committee); Member, Board of Management, Shetland Hospitals, 1959-70 (latterly Chairman, Finance Committee); Chairman, Zetland Territorial and Air Forces Association, until 1968; former Honorary Secretary, Shetland Branch, National Savings Committee; former Honorary Treasurer: Shetland Branch, British Red Cross Society, Shetland Tourist Association, Shetland Dog Trials Association, Shetland Swimming Pool Association. Recreations: golf; billiards; restoring antique furniture. Address: (h.) Vogalee, 78 St. Olaf Street, Lerwick; T.-0595 3783.

Drever, James, MA (Hons), MA (Cantab), LLD, FRSE. Principal and Vice-Chancellor, Dundee University, 1967-78; b. 29.1.10; m.; 1 s.; 1 d. Educ. Royal High School, Edinburgh; Edinburgh University; Cambridge University. Royal Navy, 1941-45; Professor of Psychology, Edinburgh University, 1944-66. President, British Psychological Society, 1960-61.

Drey, Professor Charles Nicholas Crawford, PhD, CChem, FRSC. Head, School of Chemistry, Robert Gordon's Institute of Technology, Aberdeen, since 1976; b. 26.12.34, Manchester; m., Lindsay Jane; 2 s. Educ. Liverpool Institute High School for Boys; Liverpool Regional College of Technology; Liverpool University. Chemist, Peter Spence & Son, Widnes, 1959-60; postgraduate student, Liverpool University, 1960-63; Research Associate, Department of Biochemistry, Yale University, 1963-65; Lecturer, Wolverhampton Polytechnic, 1965-66; Senior Lecturer and Principal Lecturer, Department of Polymer Science and Technology, Polytechnic of the South Bank, 1967-75; Royal Society Visiting Scientist, Institute of Organic and Biochemistry, Prague, 1968-69; Visiting Professor: Department of Biochemistry, Wayne State University, 1970, Department of Chemistry, Georgia University, 1982. Former Member, Chemistry Board, CNAA; former Chairman, NE Scotland Section, Royal Society of Chemistry; Chairman, Heads of Chemistry Departments in Polytechnics. Recreations: squash; trout fishing; theatre; reading; gardening; hill-walking. Address: (b.) School of Chemistry, RGIT, St. Andrew Street, Aberdeen, AB1 1HG; T.-0224 633611, Ext. 524.

Dron, Kenneth Walker, MA (Hons), DipEd. Rector, Brechin High School, since 1969; b. 2.6.29, Stonehaven. Educ. Mackie Academy; Aberdeen University; Aberdeen College of Education. Education Officer, RAF, 1952-53; Assistant Teacher of English, Buckhaven High School, 1954-56; Special Assistant Teacher of English, Kirkcaldy High School, 1956-60; Principal Teacher of English, Grove Academy, Dundee, 1960-66; Depute Rector, Falkirk High School, 1966-69. Past President, Tayside Secondary Headteachers' Association; President, Headteachers' Association of Scotland, 1980-81

(Press Secretary, since 1972); Member, Scottish Examination Board, since 1984. Recreations: writing light verse; sports journalism; operatic production; after-dinner speaking. Address: (h.) Grove House, St. Andrew Street, Brechin, DD9 6JJ.

Drucker, Henry M., BA, PhD. Senior Lecturer in Politics, Edinburgh University, since 1978; b. 29.4.42, Paterson, New Jersey; m., Nancy Livia Newman. Educ. London School of Economics. Publications: Breakaway: The Scottish Labour Party, 1977; Doctrine and Ethos in the Labour Party, 1978; Developments in British Politics, 1983; The Yearbook of Scottish Government, 1976-82. Address: (b.) Department of Politics, Edinburgh University, 31 Buccleuch Place, Edinburgh; T.-031-667 1011.

Drummond, George Gordon, BSc, CEng, MInstEnergy, MAIME, CBIM. Board Member, Highlands and Islands Development Board, since 1977; Vice Chairman, Cromarty Firth Port Authority, since 1983; Chairman, Scottish Board, British Institute of Management, since 1983; b. 9.9.26, Dundee; m., Jennie Cook Lowe; 1 s.; 1 d. Educ. High School of Dundee; St. Andrews University; Liverpool College of Technology; Administrative Staff College, Henley. Trainee, Scottish Gas Board; Project Engineer, North Western Gas Board; Senior Project Engineer, British Aluminium Co. Ltd.; BACO: Manager, Kinlochleven, Production Manager, London, Manager, Warrington Factories, Manager, Invergordon; Managing Director, BA Primary Aluminium Ltd., Inverness. Publication: The Invergordon Smelter: A Case Study in Management, 1977. Recreations: mountaineering; music; reading; current affairs. Address: (b.) Highlands and Islands Development Board, Bridge House, Bank Street, Inverness; T.-0463 234171.

Drummond, Rev. Gilbert, DipTh. Minister, Trinity Church, Renfrew, since 1967; b. 16.2.23, Airdrie; m., Elizabeth Forrester; 2 d. Educ. Coatbridge High School; Glasgow University; Trinity College, Glasgow. RAF, 1941-46; worked in local government, until 1958; studied, 1958-63; Minister, St. Luke's and St. John's Church, Montrose, 1963-67. Recreations: bowls; walking; swimming. Address: 25 Paisley Road, Renfrew; T.-041-886 2131.

Drummond, Humphrey, MC. Writer and Farmer; b. 18.9.22, Old Buckenham, Norfolk; m., Hon. Cherry Drummond of Megginch; 3 s.; 3 d. Educ. Eton; Trinity College, Cambridge. Captain, 1st Mountain Regiment; General Secretary, Council for Preservation of Rural Wales; Welsh Representative, National Trust; Chairman, Society of Authors (Scotland), 1976-82. Publications: Our Man in Scotland; The Queen's Man; The King's Enemy; Falconry For You; Falconry. Recreations: falconry; mechanical musical instruments; pre-Raphaelitism. Address: Megginch Castle, Errol, Perthshire; T.-Errol 222.

Drummond, John. Honorary Sheriff, Rothesay, since 1978; Chairman, Rothesay Civic Guild; b. 25.5.11, Glasgow; m., Jean Gordon Watson; 1 d. Educ. Albert Road Academy, Glasgow.

Entered Clydesdale Bank Ltd., 1927; Manager: Chryston Branch, 1960-64, Rothesay Branch, 1964-74. Honorary Treasurer, Clyde Estuary Amenity Council; Secretary, Rothesay Probus Club; Past President, Buteshire Natural History Society. Recreations: photography; motoring; bowling; gardening. Address: (h.) Auchencairn, 30 Crichton Road, Rothesay, Isle of Bute, PA20 9JR; T.-0700 2017.

Drummond, Rev. John Whiteford, MA, BD. Minister, Linwood Parish Church, since 1973; b. 27.6.46, Glasgow; m., Barbara S. Grant; 3 d. Educ. Bearsden Academy; Glasgow University. Probationer Assistant, St. Francis-in-the-East Church, Bridgeton, Glasgow, 1970-71; Ordained Assistant, King's Park Parish Church, Glasgow, 1971-73. Recreations: spending time with family; reading. Address: The Manse, Linwood, Paisley, PA3 3DL; T.-Johnstone 25131.

Drummond, Rev. Norman Walker, MA, BD. Headmaster, Loretto School, since 1984; b. 1.4.52, Greenock; m., Lady Elizabeth Kennedy; 1 s.; 2 d. Educ. Crawfordton House, Dumfriesshire; Merchiston Castle School; Fitzwilliam College, Cambridge; New College, Edinburgh. Chaplain to the Forces, 1976-82; Depot, The Parachute Regiment and Airborne Forces, 1977-78; 1st Bn., The Black Watch (Royal Highland Regiment), 1978-82; Chaplain, Fettes College, 1982-84. Chairman, Musselburgh and District Council of Social Services. Publication: The First Twenty Five Years (the official history of the Black Watch Kirk Session). Recreations: rugby football; cricket; golf; curling; traditional jazz; Isle of Skye. Address: Pinkie House, Loretto School, Musselburgh, East Lothian; T.-031-665 2567.

Drummond, Rev. Robert Hugh. Minister, Pitsligo Parish Church, since 1981; b. 18.11.25, Ajmer, India; m., May Cummings; 4 s. Educ. George Watson's College; St. Andrews University; Edinburgh University. Student Assistant Minister, Liberton Northfield; Assistant Minister: St. Giles' and St. Columba's, Elgin, North Church, Aberdeen; Army Chaplain; Minister: Eskdalemuir Parish Church, Kilmuir-Easter Parish Church, Thornton Parish Church. Recreations: cycling; swimming; tennis; golf; hill-walking; violin. Address: Pitsligo Manse, Rosehearty, Fraserburgh, AB4 4JL; T.-03467 237.

Drummond, William S.G., JP. Member, Lothian Regional Council, since 1978; b. 22.3.29, Whitburn; m., Sarah McInulty; 3 s.; 1 d. Educ. Whitburn Secondary School. Member, West Lothian County Council, 1962-75 (Housing Convener, 1970-75). Chairman, Blackridge Branch, Earl Haig Fund, Scotland. Address: (h.) 9 Bedlormie Drive, Blackridge, EH48 3RT; T.-Harthill 51489.

Dryburgh, (Alexander) Fraser, DipCE, AMIRS. Director for Scotland, Royal Society for the Prevention of Accidents, since 1982; Secretary, Scottish Accident Prevention Council, since 1982; b. 29.4.52, Dunfermline; m., Janice M. Williamson; 1 s.; 1 d. Educ. Glenrothes High School; Moray House College of Education.

Taught in primary schools in Fife, 1972-77; joined RoSPA, 1977, as Professional Assistant to Director of Safety Education; became Road Safety Liaison Officer, West of Scotland, 1979. Actively involved in Edinburgh Hospital Broadcasting Service; Member, Mid Calder Community Council. Recreations: broadcasting; motor sport. Address: (h.) 3 Torphichen Avenue, Mid Calder, West Lothian, EH53 OLA; T.-0506 880218.

Dryden, Professor Myles Muir, BSc (Econ), MBA, PhD. Professor of Management Studies, Glasgow University, since 1972; b. 21.9.31, Dundee; m., Margaret Mary Cargill; 1 s.; 1 d. Educ. Kirkcaldy High School; London School of Economics; Cornell University. National Service, 1st Bn., Black Watch, BAOR, 1950-52; Assistant Professor of Finance, Sloan School of Industrial Management, Massachusetts Institute of Technology, 1960; Lecturer, then Reader in Economics, Edinburgh University, 1963-72; appointed to first Chair of Management Studies, Glasgow University, 1972 (Head of Department, until 1980); Member, Scottish Business School Council, 1975-79; Member, Editorial Board, Journal of Applied Economics; has published in a number of professional journals; research on capital budgeting, share price behaviour and portfolio management. Recreations: pottering about either in boats, in the garden, or with microcomputers. Address: (b.) Department of Management Studies, 25/7 Bute Gardens, Glasgow University, Glasgow, G12 8RT; T.-041-339 8855, Ext. 664.

Drysdale, Thomas Henry, LLB, WS. Solicitor; Partner, Shepherd & Wedderburn, WS, Edinburgh, since 1967; Chairman, Edinburgh Solicitors' Property Centre, since 1981; b. 23.11.42, Buchlyvie; m., Caroline Shaw; 1 s.; 2 d. Educ. Cargilfield; Glenalmond; Edinburgh University. Recreations: skiing; walking. Address: (b.) 16 Charlotte Square, Edinburgh, EH2 4YS; T.-031-225 8585.

Dudley Edwards, Owen, BA, FRHistS. Reader in Commonwealth and American History, Edinburgh University, since 1979; b. 27.3.38, Dublin; m., Barbara Balbirnie Lee; 1 s.; 2 d. Educ. Belvedere College, Dublin; University College, Dublin; Johns Hopkins University, Baltimore. Visiting Lecturer in History, University of Oragon, 1963-65; Assistant Lecturer in History, Aberdeen University, 1966-68; Lecturer in History, Edinburgh University, 1968-79; Visiting Lecturer, California State University of San Francisco, 1972-73; Visiting Associate Professor, University of South Carolina, 1973; Journalist and Broadcaster, notably for Irish Times, since 1959, and BBC, since 1969; contributor to various journals, especially The Scotsman. Life Member: American Historical Association, Organisation of American Historians; External Examiner: Queen's University, Belfast, Bradford University, Manchester University. Publications: Celtic Nationalism (with Gwynfor Evans, Ioan Rhys and Hugh MacDiarmid), 1968; The Sins of Our Fathers - Roots of Conflict in Northern Ireland, 1970; The Mind of an Activist - James Connolly, 1971; P.G. Wodehouse - a Critical and

Historical Essay, 1977; Burke and Hare, 1980; The Quest for Sherlock Holmes: a Biographical Study of Arthur Conan Doyle, 1982; as Editor/ Contributor: 1916 - The Easter Rising (with Fergus Pyle), 1968; Conor Cruise O'Brien Introduces Ireland, 1969; James Connolly: Selected Political Writings (with Bernard C. Ransom), 1973; Scotland, Europe and the American Revolution (with George Shepperson), 1976; Christmas Observed (with Graham Richardson), 1981; Edinburgh (with Graham Richardson), 1983. Recreations: Scottish Nationalism; playing chess badly. Address: (b.) Department of History, Edinburgh University, George Square, Edinburgh; T.-031-664 3526.

Duff, John Hume, MA (Cantab), MA (Edin), DipEd (Oxon). Rector, Kelvinside Academy, since 1980; b. 24.4.40, Edinburgh. Educ. St. Mary's School, Melrose; Edinburgh Academy; Corpus Christi College, Cambridge; Edinburgh University; Brasenose College, Oxford. Housemaster and Head of History Department, Kelly College, Tavistock, Devon, 1967-80. Major, TA. Recreations: squash rackets; skiing; hill-walking; foreign travel. Address: (b.) Kelvinside Academy, 33 Kirklee Road, Glasgow, G12 OSW; T.-041-357 3376.

Duff, Robert Beauchamp (Robin), MA (Cantab). President, The Scottish Ballet, since 1984; Chairman, Air Transport Users Committee, since 1984; b. 27.2.15, London. Educ. Winchester; Trinity College, Cambridge. BBC Announcer and War Correspondent; Bureau Chief, Paris, then New Delhi, for Daily Express; Personal Assistant to HH Maharaja of Bundi; Chairman, Health and Welfare Committee, Aberdeen County Council, 1957-64; former Member: Scottish Housing Advisory Committee, Scottish Hygiene Advisory Committee, Meat and Livestock Commission; Chairman, The Scottish Ballet, 1974-84; Hotelier; Broadcaster; Laird of Meldrum and Byth. Recreations: gardening; travel. Address: (h.) Meldrum House, Aberdeenshire, AB5 OAE; T.-065-12 2294.

Duffield, Brian Snowden. Vice Principal, Dunfermline College of Physical Education, since 1983; b. 27.8.43, Doncaster; m., Irene Mary Scott; 4 s.; 1 d. Educ. Doncaster Grammar School; Hull University. Tourism and Recreation Research Unit, Department of Geography, Edinburgh University, 1967-83: Research Fellow, 1968-72, Research Director, 1972-76, Senior Research Fellow and Deputy Director, 1976-81, Director, 1981-83; part-time Lecturer, Department of Geography, 1980-82; Visiting Research Fellowship, Bergen University, 1981; Corresponding Editor, Leisure Sciences, since 1984; Member, Editorial Board, Applied Geography, 1981-83. Publications: Recreation in the Countryside: a spatial analysis (Co-author), 1975; The Leisure Planning Process (Co-author), 1979; A Digest of Sports Statistics (Co-Editor), 1983; Recreation Site Survey Manual: methods and techniques for conducting visitor surveys (Co-author), 1983. Recreations: politics; conversation; art and literature; gastronomy; squash; work. Address: (h.) Cockle Mill, School Brae, Cramond, Edinburgh, EH4 6JN; T.-031-336 7657.

Duffty, Paul, MB, ChB, MRCP, LMCC. Consultant Paediatrician, since 1982; Senior Lecturer in Child Health, Aberdeen University, since 1982; b. 1.9.46, Leeds; m., Lesley Marjory Macdonald; 2 d. Educ. Leeds Central High School; Aberdeen University. Lecturer in Child Health, Aberdeen University, 1972-75; Trainee in General Practice, Aberdeen, 1975-76; Lecturer in Child Health, Aberdeen University, 1976-78; Fellow in Neonatology, Toronto University, 1978-80; Staff Paediatrician, Hospital for Sick Children, Toronto, and Assistant Professor, Toronto University, 1980-82. Recreations: hill-walking; cross-country skiing; philately. Address: (h.) 13 Louisville Avenue, Aberdeen; T.-0224 317072.

Duffus, Carol Margaret, BSc, MS, PhD, DIC, DSc. Lecturer in Agricultural Biochemistry, Edinburgh School of Agriculture, since 1968 (Acting Head of Department, since 1983). Educ. Victoria College, Belfast; Queen's University, Belfast; Michigan University; Imperial College, London. Lecturer in Biochemistry, Warwick University, 1966-68. Publications: Seeds and Their Uses (Co-author), 1980; Carbohydrate Metabolism in Plants (Co-author), 1984. Recreations: chamber music; gardening. Address: (b.) Department of Agricultural Biochemistry, School of Agriculture, Edinburgh University, West Mains Road, Edinburgh, EH9 3JG; T.-031-667 1041.

Duffus, John Henderson, BSc, PhD, DSc, CBiol, MIBiol, CChem, FRSC. Senior Lecturer in Environmental Toxicology, Heriot-Watt University, since 1980. Educ. Arbroath High School; Edinburgh University; Heriot-Watt University. Research Fellow in Warwick University, 1965-67, Edinburgh University, 1967-70; Lecturer, Heriot-Watt University, 1970-80; WHO Consultant, Manpower Development for Toxicology and Chemical Safety, since 1981. Publications: Environmental Toxicology, 1980; Carbohydrate Metabolism in Plants (Co-author), 1984. Recreation: golf. Address: (b.) Heriot-Watt University, Chambers Street, Edinburgh, EH1 1HX; T.-031-225 8432.

Duffy, David. Housing Chairman, Kirkcaldy District Council; b. 29.7.20, Methil; m., Alice Smith; 1 s.; 3 d. Elected, Buckhaven and Methil Town Council, 1970; Member, Kirkcaldy District Council, since re-organisation; Member, COSLA Housing Committee; Secretary, Local Branch, Labour Party and Vice-Chairman, Kirkcaldy CLP. Recreations: any sports. Address: (h.) 123 Den Walk, Buckhaven, Fife; T.-Buckhaven 2604.

Duffy, Mgr. Francis Canon, VG. Vicar General to RC Bishop of Galloway, since 1975; Parish Priest, Troon, since 1982; b. 15.10.14, Edinburgh. Educ. Holy Cross Academy, Edinburgh; Blairs College, Aberdeen; Pontifical Scots College, Rome; Gregorian University, Rome. Ordained Priest (Rome), 1938; Curate, Ayr, 1939-41; Professor, Blairs College, Aberdeen, 1941-55; parish work in various towns, since 1955; Monsignor, since 1972. RC Religious Adviser, Scottish Television, 1958-78; Member, Dumfries Education Committee, 1963-72; Composer of congregational Church music and hymns. Address: 4 Cessnock Road, Troon, KA8 6NJ; T.-Troon 313541.

Duffy, John Alastair, BSc, PhD, DSc, CChem, FRSC. Senior Lecturer in Chemistry, Aberdeen University, since 1977; b. 24.9.32, Birmingham; m., Muriel F.L. Ramsay; 1 s.; 1 d. Educ. Solihull School, Warwickshire; Sheffield University. Research Chemist, Albright & Wilson, Oldbury, 1958-59; Lecturer in Inorganic Chemistry, Wolverhampton Polytechnic, 1959-61; Senior Lecturer in Inorganic Chemistry, NE Wales Institute, 1961-65; Lecturer in Chemistry, Aberdeen University, 1966-77; Assessor in Inorganic Chemistry for Ordinary and Higher National Certificates and Diplomas in Scotland, 1971-82; Consultant to Schott Glaswerke, Mainz, West Germany, since 1984. Publication: General Inorganic Chemistry, 1966. Recreations: 20th-century opera; music. Address: (h.) 33 Beechgrove Terrace, Aberdeen, AB2 4DR; T.-0224 641752.

Duguid, David Walker, BL, DPA. Chief Executive and Director of Administration, Midlothian District Council, since 1975; b. 27.11.22, Paisley; m., May; 2 s. Educ. Camphill School, Paisley; Glasgow University; London University. Military Service, 1942-46. Depute County Clerk, Midlothian County Council, 1964-75; Clerk of the Peace, Midlothian; Clerk to Lieutenancy, Midlothian. Recreations: golf; music; reading. Address: 1 Eskdaill Court, Dalkeith; T.-031-663 2881.

Dukes, Paul, BA (Cantab), MA, PhD. Reader in History, Aberdeen University, since 1975; b. 5.4.34, Wallington; m., Rosemary Mackay; 1 s.; 1 d. Educ. Wallington County Grammar School; Cambridge University. Advisory Editor, History Today. Publications: several books on aspects of Russian, American and European history. Recreations: hill-walking; travel. Address: (b.) History Department, Aberdeen University, Aberdeen; T.-0224 40241.

Dulverton, 2nd Baron, (Frederick Anthony Hamilton Wills), CBE, TD, MA, DL. Member, The Red Deer Commission; b. 19.12.15, London; m., Ruth Violet Mary; 2 s.; 1 d. Educ. Eton; Magdalen College, Oxford. Commissioned Lovat Scouts, 1935 (Major, 1943); President: Bath and West Agricultural Society, 1973, British Deer Society, 1973, Three Counties Agricultural Society, 1975, Timber Growers United Kingdom, 1983; Chairman, Dulverton Trust; Council Member, WWF (UK) and Wildfowl Trust; awarded Gold Medal, Royal Forestry Society. Recreations: field sports; nature photography. Address: (h.) Fassfern, Kinlocheil, Fort William, Inverness-shire; T.-039783 232.

Dunbar, John Greenwell, MA, FSA, FSA Scot, HonFRIAS. Secretary, Royal Commission on the Ancient and Historical Monuments of Scotland, since 1978; b. 1.3.30, London; m., Elizabeth Mill Blyth. Educ. University College School, London; Balliol College, Oxford. Joined staff, Royal Commission on the Ancient and Historical Monuments of Scotland, 1953; Member,

Ancient Monuments Board for Scotland, since 1978. Publications: The Historic Architecture of Scotland, 1966; Accounts of the Masters of Works, Volume 2 (1616-1649), (Joint Editor), 1982. Address: (h.) Paties Mill, Carlops, by Penicuik, Midlothian, EH26 9NF; T.-West Linton 60250.

Dunbar-Nasmith, Rear Admiral David Arthur, CB, DSC, DL. Chairman, Moray and Nairn Newspaper Company, since 1982; Member, British Waterways Board, since 1980; Director, Cairngorm Chairlift Company, since 1973; b. 21.2.21, Glen of Rothes, Rothes; m., Elizaabeth Bowlby; 2 s.; 2 d. Educ. Lockers Park; Royal Naval College, Dartmouth. To sea, 1939; War service, Atlantic and Mediterranean; Commanding Officer, HM Ships Haydon, 1943-44, Peacock, 1945-46, Moon, 1946, Rowena, 1946-48, Enard Bay, 1951, Alert, 1954-56, Berwick and 5th Frigate Squadron, 1961-63, Commodore Amphibious Forces, 1966-67; Naval Secretary, 1967-70; Flag Officer Scotland and Northern Ireland, 1970-72; Member, Highlands and Islands Development Board, 1973-83 (Chairman, 1981-82, Deputy Chairman, 1972-81); Member: Countryside Commission for Scotland, 1972-76, North of Scotland Hydro Electric Board, 1982-85; Gentleman Usher of the Green Rod to the Order of the Thistle; Vice Lieutenant, County of Moray; Member, Queen's Bodyguard for Scotland (Royal Company of Archers). Recreations: sailing; shooting; skiing. Address: (h.) Glen of Rothes, Rothes, Moray; T.-03403 216.

Dunbar-Nasmith, Professor James Duncan, CBE, BA, DA, RIBA, PPRIAS, FRSA, FRSE. Professor and Head, Department of Architecture, Heriot-Watt University and Edinburgh College of Art, since 1978; Partner, The Law and Dunbar-Nasmith Partnership, Architects, Edinburgh and Forres, since 1957; b. 15.3.27, Dartmouth. Educ. Lockers Park; Winchester College; Trinity College, Cambridge; Edinburgh College of Art. Lt., Scots Guards, 1945-48; ARIBA, 1954; President: Edinburgh Architectural Association, 1967-69, Royal Incorporation of Architects in Scotland, 1971-73; Member, RIBA Council, 1967-73 (Vice-President and Chairman, Board of Architectural Education, 1972-73); Council, ARCUK, 1976-84, Board of Education, since 1976 (Vice Chairman, 1977); Member: Royal Commission on Ancient and Historical Monuments of Scotland, since 1972, Ancient Monuments Board for Scotland, 1969-82 (interim Chairman, 1972-73), Historic Buildings Council for Scotland, since 1966; Trustee: Scottish Civic Trust, Architectural Heritage Fund, Theatres Trust; Member: Edinburgh New Town Conservation Committee, Old Town Conservation Advisory Committee; Council Member, Edinburgh Festival Society, since 1966 (Deputy Chairman, 1981-85). Recreations: music; theatre; skiing; sailing. Address: (b.) 16 Dublin Street, Edinburgh, EH1 3RE; T.-031-556 8631.

Duncan, David Graham Bruce, DipArch, DipTP, RIBA, MRTPI. Director of Physical Planning, East Lothian District Council, since 1975; b. 23.8.36, Derby; m., Helen Teresa; 2 s. Educ. George Heriot's School, Edinburgh; Edinburgh

College of Art. Architect/Planner, R.E. & B.L.C. Moira, Architects and Planning Consultants, Edinburgh, 1960-63; Architect/Planner, Government of State of Singapore, 1963-67; Assistant Planner, then Depute County Planning Officer, East Lothian County Council, 1967-75. Chairman, Scottish Society of Directors of Planning; Planning Adviser, COSLA. Address: (b.) Council Buildings, Haddington, East Lothian; T.-Haddington 4161.

Duncan, Geoffrey Cheyne Calderhead, BL, NP. Partner, Kerr, Barrie & Duncan, since 1970; b. 6.10.29, Whitecraigs, Glasgow; m., Lorna Dowling; 1 s.; 1 d. Educ. Belmont House School; Glasgow Academy; Glasgow University. Partner, Aitken, Hamilton & Duncan, 1951-70; Chairman, Glasgow Junior Chamber of Commerce, 1963-64; Director, The Girls' School Company Ltd., since 1964 (Chairman, since 1977); Chairman, St. Columba's School, 1972-83; Director, The West of Scotland School Company Ltd., 1972-77 and since 1980; Member, Board of Management, Glasgow South Western Hospitals, 1964-69; Member, Clyde River Purification Board, 1969-75; Director, Glasgow Chamber of Commerce, since 1972; Chairman, Glasgow Post Office Advisory Committee, 1974-84; Member, Post Office Users' National Council, since 1974; Chairman, Post Office Users' Council for Scotland, since 1984 (Member, since 1974); Chairman, Advisory Committee on Telecommunications for Scotland, since 1984; Secretary, Clyde Cruising Club, 1964-69; Secretary, International Clyde Regetta, 1967; Council Member, Clyde Yacht Clubs' Association, 1967-73; Member, Scottish Council, Royal Yachting Association, 1967-73; Director, The Merchants' House of Glasgow, since 1982; Member, Glasgow Committee, Royal National Lifeboat Institution, since 1980; Council Member, Royal Faculty of Procurators in Glasgow, 1981-84; Trustee, George Craig Trust Fund, since 1980; Member, Executive Committee, Abbeyfield Quarrier's Society, since 1981; Member, Council of Management, Quarrier's Homes, since 1985; Director, The Scottish Cremation Society Ltd., since 1982. Recreations: sailing; golf; curling; photography. Address: (h.) Westwood, Bridge of Weir, Renfrewshire; T.-Bridge of Weir 612566.

Duncan, Ian Douglas, MB, ChB, FRCOG. Senior Lecturer in Obstetrics and Gynaecology, Dundee University, since 1978; Honorary Consultant in Obstetrics and Gynaecology, Tayside Health Board, since 1978; b. 7.11.43, Edinburgh; m., Jennifer Ross Conacher; 2 s.; 1 d. Educ. Harris Academy, Dundee; St. Andrews University. House Officer, Surgery and Medicine, Maryfield Hospital, Dundee, 1967-68; Senior House Officer, Urology, Ballochmyle Hospital, Mauchline, 1968-69; Registrar in Obstetrics and Gynaecology, Dundee Royal Infirmary, 1969-72; Faculty Fellow in Gynaecologic Oncology, Duke University Medical Center, 1972-74; Senior Registrar/Lecturer in Obstetrics and Gynaecology, Ninewells Hospital, Dundee, 1974-78. John Kynoch Scholarship, 1967; Senior Fulbright Scholarship, 1972; British Society for Colposcopy and Cervical Pathology: Treasurer, 1979-82, Secretary, 1982-85, President, since

1985; Treasurer, British Gynaecological Cancer Society, since 1985. Recreations: golf; gardening. Address: (h.) Invertay, 299 Strathmartine Road, Dundee, DD3 8NS; T.-Dundee 826628.

Duncan, Rev. James, DipTh, MPhS, FSA Scot. Minister, Blair Atholl and Struan, since 1980; b. 28.1.26, Glasgow; m., Christine Margaret Fisher; 2 s. Educ. Eastbank Academy, Glasgow; Glasgow University. War Service, 1943-46; seconded to Colonial Office, London, 1944; seconded to Australian Army in British North Borneo; ADC Chief Civil Affairs Staff Officer, British Borneo; Harrisons and Crosfield, British Borneo, 1946-47; various Sales Representative jobs, until 1956; joined Unilever (Batchelors Catering Supplies) as Special Accounts Manager. Recreations: music; watching TV; wine-making; good food and wine. Address: The Manse, Blair Atholl, Pitlochry, PH18 5SX; T.-079681 213.

Duncan, James Lindsay, BVMS, PhD, MRCVS. Reader in Veterinary Parasitology, Glasgow University, since 1982; b. 26.2.41, Law, Carluke; m., Helen M.; 1 d. Educ. Wishaw High School; Glasgow University. Veterinary Practice, UK, and clinical teaching posts, Kenya, 1964-70; Glasgow University: Research Fellow, Department of Veterinary Parasitology, 1970-76, Lecturer, 1976-79, Senior Lecturer, 1979-82; Consultant, joint FAO/IAEA Animal Health Division, International Atomic Energy Agency, Vienna; Co-author of several textbooks. Recreations: tennis; squash; golf; music. Address: (h.) Woodside Farm, Crossford, Carluke, Lanark, ML8 5QN; T.-0555 86254.

Duncan, James Wann, MBE, JP, MIMFT. Vice-Chairman, Tayside Health Board (Convener, General Purposes Committee); Convener, Personnel and Accommodation Sub-Committee, Management Committee, Common Services Agency; b. 14.7.25, Dundee; m., Hilda Mackenzie Gray; 3 d. Educ. Stobswell Secondary School; Dundee College of Technology. Former Convener, Property Equipment Supplies Committee, General Board of Management, Dundee General Hospitals; former Vice-Convener, General Purposes Committee, General Board of Management, Dundee Northern Hospitals; former Member, Dundee Town Council (Senior Magistrate); former Convener: Dundee Art Galleries and Museums Committee, Further Education Committee, Dundee Police Committee; former Member, Board of Governors, Scottish Police College; Member, Dundee District Council, 1974-77 (Convener, Planning and Development Committee); Chairman, Dundee City Labour Party, 1960-62; Member, Scottish Council, SDP (Chairman, Dundee and Angus Area); Scottish Representative, National Committee for Dental Technicians, USDAW; former Member: STUC Health and Social Services Committee, Dundee University Court. Recreations: golf; gardening; DIY. Address: (h.) 13 Clive Road, Downfield, Dundee, DD3 8LP; T.-0382 825488.

Duncan, John Glenroy, DPA. Employment Manager, Scotland, Manpower Services Commission, since 1982; b. 18.4.29, Coatbridge; m., Jessie Gardner Taylor; 1 s.; 1 d. Educ.

Coatbridge High School; Glasgow University. Various appointments, Ministry of Labour and Department of Employment, 1946-72, latterly as Training Officer for Scotland administering Government Training Centres and other schemes. Recreations: bowling; golf; reading; music. Address: (b.) Manpower Services Commission, Employment Office for Scotland, 9 St. Andrew Square, Edinburgh, EH2 2QX; T.-031-225 8500.

Duncan, John Lindsay, BSc, PhD, DSc. Reader in Chemistry, Aberdeen University, since 1982; Convener, Science Panel, Scottish Universities Council on Entrance, since 1983; b. 3.2.37, Edinburgh; m., Anne Shearer; 2 d. Educ. Melville College, Edinburgh; Edinburgh University. ICI Research Fellow, Reading University, 1961-64; Aberdeen University: Lecturer, 1964-74, Senior Lecturer, 1974-82; Chairman, SEB/CCC Joint Working Party to revise Certificate of Sixth Year Studies, Chemistry Syllabus, 1978-80. Publication: High Resolution Vibration-Rotation Spectroscopy, 1983. Recreations: music; art; gardening. Address: (b.) Department of Chemistry, Aberdeen University, Meston Walk, Old Aberdeen, AB9 2UE; T.-0224 40241.

Duncan, Malcolm McGregor, MA, LLB, WS. Chief Executive, The City of Edinburgh, since 1980; b. 23.1.22, Bedlington, Northumberland; m., Winifred Petrie; 2 s.; 1 d. Educ. George Watson's College, Edinburgh; Edinburgh University. RAF, 1942-46; private legal practice, 1946-51; various appointments, Edinburgh Corporation, 1951-71; Depute Town Clerk, Edinburgh, 1971; Director of Administration, City of Edinburgh Council, 1975-80. Recreations: playing golf; watching other sports; listening to music. Address: (b.) City Chambers, Edinburgh; t.-031-225 2424, Ext. 5050.

Duncan, Thomas, NP. Solicitor, since 1940; Honorary Sheriff at Montrose, since 1981; b. 17.6.17, Glasgow; m., Jean Gardner Skeoch; 2 d. Educ. Glasgow University. Qualified as Solicitor, 1940; Army, 1940-46 (Major, RA, Rhine Army); enrolled as Solicitor, 1946. President, Montrose Branch, Royal British Legion, Scotland; Past President, Montrose Chamber of Commerce; Past Captain, Royal Albert Golf Club. Recreation: golf. Address: 192 High Street, Montrose, Angus; T.-0674 72533.

Duncan Millar, Ian Alastair, CBE, MC, MA, MICE, CEng, DL, JP. Chairman, Consultative Committee on Freshwater Fisheries, since 1981; Member, Queen's Bodyguard for Scotland (Royal Company of Archers); b. 22.11.14, Alloa; m., Louise Reid McCosh; 2 s.; 2 d. Educ. Greshams School, Holt; Trinity College, Cambridge. Civil Engineer, Sir Alexander Gibb & Partners, 1937-51 (except War years); War Service, Corps of Royal Engineers, Western Desert, Europe (with Highland Division); wounded; twice mentioned in Despatches; retired as Major; Resident Engineer i/c Pitlochry Dam and Power Station, 1946-51; Member: Perth and Kinross County Council, 1946-74 (Convener, 1970-74), Tayside Regional Council, 1974-78 (Convener, 1974-78), North of Scotland Hydro Electric Board, 1956-70 (Depute Chairman, 1970-72); Director: Macdonald

Fraser & Co., Perth, 1961-84, United Auctions (Scotland) Ltd., 1963-67 (Chairman, 1967-74); fought Parliamentary elections as Liberal, Banff, 1945, Kinross and West Perth, 1949 and 1963. Chairman, Scottish Branch, Institute of Fisheries Management, 1980-83; Vice President, Royal Highland and Agricultural Society of Scotland, 1972. Recreations: fishing; shooting; knowing about salmon. Address: (h.) Remony, Aberfeldy, Perthshire; T.-Kenmore 209.

Dundas, Charles Robert, TD, MB, ChB, FFARCS, FRCP, RCPSGlas. Senior Lecturer in Anaesthesia, Aberdeen University, since 1976; b. 20.6.34, Glasgow; m., Dr. Valerie Flook. Educ. Grangemouth High School; Edinburgh University. House Surgeon and House Physician, Falkirk and District Royal Infirmary, 1959-60; Aberdeen Royal Infirmary: Senior House Officer in Anaesthesia, 1960-62, Research Fellow, then Senior Registrar in Anaesthesia, 1962-69; Consultant Anaesthetist, Grampian Health Board, 1970-76. Major, RAMC (V), 372 MFST. Recreations: fishing; gardening; sailing. Address: (b.) Department of Surgery, Aberdeen University, Aberdeen.

Dundee, Earl of, (Alexander Henry Scrymgeour). Hereditary Royal Standard-Bearer for Scotland; b. 5.6.49; m., Siobhan Mary Llewellyn; 1 s.; 1 d. Educ. Eton; St. Andrews University. Address: (b.) Farm Office, Birkhill, Cupar, Fife.

Dundonald, 14th Earl of, (Ian Douglas Leonard Cochrane); b. 6.12.18; m., 1, Aphra Farquhar (deceased); 1 s.; 1 d.; 2, Ann Margaret Harkness. Educ. Wellington College; Sandhurst. Joined The Black Watch, 1938; served Second World War (Company Commander, 6th Bn., 1944-45); retired from Army, 1953; Representative Peer for Scotland, 1959-63; Chairman, Anglo-Chilean Society, 1958-65; Company Director. Address: Lochnell Castle, Ledaig, Argyll.

Dunlop, Alastair Barr, FRICS. Member, Lothian Health Board, since 1983; Chairman, Central and South, Scottish Conservative and Unionist Association and Chairman, Conservative Standing Committee, Lothians; b. 27.12.33, Calcutta; m., Catriona C.L.H. MacLaurin; 1 s.; 1 d. Educ. Radley. National Service, 1952-54 (active service, Malaya: 2nd Lt., 1st Bn., RWK); commerce, City of London, 1954-58; agricultural student, 1959-61; Land Agent, Inverness, 1962-71 (Partner, Bingham Hughes & Macpherson); Joint Founding Director, Martin Paterson Associates Ltd., 1971. Chairman, Edinburgh and Borders Branch, RICS, 1977; Life Member, Institute of Directors; Chairman, Edinburgh Branch, World Wildlife Fund; Member, Marchmont Community Council; small farm/woodland interest in Galloway. Recreations: golf; skiing; fine arts. Address: 46 Dick Place, Edinburgh, EH9 2JB; T.-031-667 5343.

Dunlop, Rev. Alexander Ian, TD, MA, BD. Minister, St. Stephen's Parish Church, Edinburgh, since 1949; Chairman of Trustees, Churches and Universities (Scotland) Widows and Orphans Fund, since 1965; Chairman of Directors,

Edinburgh and East of Scotland Society for the Deaf, since 1978; General Trustee, Church of Scotland, since 1972; b. 16.5.16, Paisley; m., Marion Shena Davidson Napier; 2 s. Educ. Paisley Grammar School; Glasgow University; Trinity College, Glasgow. Assistant Minister and Locum, Houston, 1939; Locum Minister, Lochgilphead, 1939-42; Chaplain, 10th HLI, European Campaign, 1942-46 (wounded and mentioned in Despatches); Senior Chaplain, 15th (Scottish) Division and Low Countries, 1946; Assistant Minister, St. Columba's (Pont Street), London, 1946-49; Territorial Chaplain, 7/9th Royal Scots, 1950-57; Senior Chaplain, 52nd Division TA and DACG (TA), Scottish Command, 1957-67; part-time Lecturer in Church History, Edinburgh University, 1957-63; Chalmers Lecturer, 1960-64; Convener: Deaconess Board, 1961-65, Unions and Readjustments Committee, 1965-70; Moderator, Edinburgh Presbytery, 1966; President, Scottish Church Theology Society, 1964-65; Honorary President, Scottish Church History Society, 1968-71; Member, Merchant Company Education Board (Edinburgh), 1968-83; Chairman: Church of Scotland Orphans Trustees, since 1976, Hope Trustees, since 1978; Secretary, Edinburgh Destitute Sick Society, since 1978; Member, Executive, Scottish Association for the Deaf, since 1967. Publications: Campaign in Europe 1944-45 (10th HLI) (Editor), 1945; William Carstares and the Kirk by Law Established, 1967; The Judgement of Burns, 1979. Address: 11 Bellevue Place, Edinburgh, EH7 4BS; T.-031-556 2259.

Dunlop, Alexander Scott, MA (Hons). Rector, Blairgowrie High School, since 1978; b. 24.2.34, Stevenston; m., Elspeth Jean Mitchell; 4 s. Educ. Stevenston Higher Grade School; Ardrossan Academy; Glasgow University; Jordanhill College. Teacher: Irvine Royal Academy, 1957, Ardrossan Academy, 1959; Special Assistant, Ardrossan Academy, 1965; Principal Teacher of English, Stevenston High School, 1968; Assistant Rector, Auchenharvie Academy, 1971; Depute Rector, Garnock Academy, Kilbirnie, 1974. Organist and Choirmaster: St. John's Church of Scotland, Ardrossan, 1958-68, St. Cuthbert South Beach Church, Saltcoats, 1968-78, St. Andrew's, Blairgowrie, since 1984; Member, Royal College of Organists; Fellow, National Chrysanthemum Society. Recreations: music; growing and exhbiting chrysanths, sweet peas, roses; golf. Address: (b.) The High School, Blairgowrie, Perthshire, PH10 6PW; T.-Blairgowrie 3445/6.

Dunlop, Rev. Alistair John, MA, FSA Scot. Minister, Saddell and Carradale, since 1979; b. 18.3.39, Glasgow; m., Elaine Marion Seton Smith; 4 s. Educ. Hutchesons' Boys' Grammar School; Glasgow University; Trinity College, Glasgow. Assistant Minister, Dunblane Cathedral, 1964-65; Minister: Kirriemuir St. Ninian's, 1965-70, Beith: High, 1970-79; Moderator: Ardrossan Presbytery, 1974-75, South Argyll Presbytery, 1982. Scout Leader, 28th Argyll Scout Troop. Recreations: gardening; TV watching; thinking about working. Address: The Manse, Carradale, Campbeltown, Argyll, PA28 6QG; T.-058 33 253.

Dunlop, Frank, CBE (1977), BA (Hons). Director, Edinburgh International Festival, since 1983; b. 15.2.27. Educ. Kibworth Beauchamp Grammar School; University College, London. Administrator and Associate Director, National Theatre of Gt. Britain, 1967-71; Founder, 1969, Director, 1969-78 and 1980-83, The Young Vic. Address: (b.) Edinburgh International Festival, 44 Chandos Place, London, WC2.

Dunlop, James M., CBE, JP, MA, LLB. Chief Executive, Fife Regional Council, since 1974; b. 24.7.22, Glasgow; m., Helen; 2 d. Educ. Glasgow University. Legal Assistant, Aberdeen County Council, 1950-52; Senior Legal Assistant, then Depute County Clerk, Dumfries County Council, 1952-62; County Clerk: Ross and Cromarty County Council, 1962-71, Fife County Council, 1971-74. Clerk to the Lieutenancy, Fife; Elder, Church of Scotland. Recreations: golf; gardening. Address: (b.) Fife House, North Street, Glenrothes, Fife, KY7 5LT; T.-Glenrothes 754411.

Dunlop, Sir Thomas, 3rd Bt. Partner, Thomas Dunlop & Sons, Glasgow, since 1938; b. 11.4.12; m., Adda Mary Alison Smith; 1 s.; 1 d.; 1 d. (deceased). Educ. Shrewsbury; St. John's College, Cambridge. Past Chairman, Savings Bank of Scotland; Vice-President, Royal Alfred Seafarers' Society.

Dunn, Angus Mackay, PhD, MRCVS. Senior Lecturer in Veterinary Parasitology, Glasgow University, since 1960; b. 28.9.21, Clydebank; m., Catriona Blair McCaig Cowan; 2 s. Educ. High School of Glasgow; Glasgow Veterinary College; Edinburgh University. Veterinary Officer, Ministry of Agriculture; Scientific Officer: Moredun Institute, Edinburgh, then Agricultural Research Council, Department of Zoology, Edinburgh University; Senior Scientific Officer, Moredun Institute, Edinburgh; Lecturer in Veterinary Parasitology, Glasgow University. Editor, publication of Veterinary Deer Society; awarded Bronze Medal, Academie Veterinaire de France. Publications: Veterinary Helminthology (two editions); Veterinary Parasitology (Co-author). Recreations: writing; painting; music; gardening. Address: (h.) 28 Gartconnell Road, Bearsden, Glasgow, G61 3BW; T.-041-942 6309.

Dunn, Bill, BA. Managing Director, Garnock Valley Development Executive Ltd., since 1984; b. 26.2.48, Ayr; m., Sheila; 2 s.; 2 d. Educ. Ayr Academy; Strathclyde University. Transport Manager, National Freight Corporation/ British (later Scottish) Road Services, 1970-73; Administrator, Ayrshire Joint Police Committee, 1973; Internal Audit Department, British Steel Corporation, Glasgow, 1973-81; Garnock Valley Task Force: Project Co-ordinator, 1981-83, Business Development Consultant, 1983-84. Recreations: family; golf; football; music; DIY; model railways. Address: (b.) 44 Main Street, Kilbirnie, Ayrshire, KA25 7BY; T.-0505 685455.

Dunn, Douglas Eaglesham, BA, FRSL. Writer, since 1971; b. 23.10.42, Inchinnan. Educ. Renfrew High School; Camphill Senior Secondary School, Paisley; Hull University. Books of poems: Terry Street, 1969, The Happier Life,

1972, Love or Nothing, 1974, Barbarians, 1979, St. Kilda's Parliament, 1981, Elegies, 1985; Secret Villages (short stories), 1985; books edited: A Choice of Lord Byron's Verse, 1974, The Poetry of Scotland, 1979, A Rumoured City: New Poets from Hull, 1982; Two Decades of Irish Writing: a Critical Survey, 1975; author of radio and TV plays, and TV films using commentaries in verse. Gregory Award, 1968; Somerset Maugham Award, 1972; Geoffrey Faber Memorial Prize, 1975; Hawthornden Prize, 1982. Address: (h.) c/o Faber & Faber Ltd., 3 Queen Square, London, WC1N 3AV.

Dunn, Rev. William Stuart, LTh. Minister, Crosshill Parish Church, Motherwell, since 1982; b. 17.4.41, Portlethen, Kincardineshire; m., Elspeth Mairi MacPhail; 1 s.; 3 d. Educ. Mackie Academy, Stonehaven; Christs College and Aberdeen University. Apprentice Chartered Accountant, 1959; began divinity course, Christs College, Aberdeen, 1964; licensed by Aberdeen Presbytery, 1969; Assistant, North and East Church of St. Nicholas, Aberdeen, 1969-70; Minister, Dreghorn and Pearston Old Parish Church, 1970-82. Recreations: music; sport; gardening; motoring; boating. Address: Crosshill Manse, 15 Orchard Street, Motherwell, ML1 3JE; T.-0698 63410.

Dunnet, Professor George Mackenzie, BSc, PhD, DSc, FRSE, FIBiol, FRSA. Regius Professor of Natural History, Aberdeen University, since 1974 (Dean, Faculty of Science, since 1984); Chairman, Shetland Oil Terminal Environmental Advisory Group, since 1977; b. 19.4.28, Dunnet, Caithness; m., Margaret Henderson Thomson; 1 s.; 2 d. Educ. Peterhead Academy; Aberdeen University. Research Fellow, Oxford University, 1952; Research Officer, CSIRO, Australia, 1953-58; Lecturer/Senior Lecturer in Zoology, Aberdeen University, 1958-71; Professor of Zoology, Aberdeen University, 1971-74; Senior Research Fellow, DSIR, New Zealand, 1968-69. Member, Committees: The Nature Conservancy, Nature Conservancy Council, Natural Environment Research Council; Chairman, Advisory Committees for Protection of Birds (Scotland, and England and Wales); Red Deer Commission; Council Member, Scottish Marine Biological Association; President, British Ecological Society, 1979-81. Recreations: walking; croquet. Address: (h.) Whinhill, Inverebrie, Ellon, Aberdeen, AB4 9PT; T.-03587 215.

Dunnett, Alastair MacTavish, HonLLD (Strathclyde). Director, Thomson Scottish Petroleum Ltd., since 1979; b. 26.12.08, Kilmacolm; m., Dorothy Halliday (see Dorothy Dunnett); 2 s. Educ. Overnewton School; Hillhead High School, Glasgow. Entered Commercial Bank of Scotland Ltd., 1925; Co-Founder, The Claymore Press, 1933-34; Glasgow Weekly Herald, 1935-36; The Bulletin, 1936-37; Daily Record, 1937-40; Chief Press Officer, Secretary of State for Scotland, 1940-46; Editor: Daily Record, 1946-55, The Scotsman, 1956-72; Managing Director, Scotsman Publications Ltd., 1962-70 (Chairman, 1970-74); Chairman, Thomson Scottish Petroleum Ltd., Edinburgh, 1971-79; Member, Executive Board, Thomson Organisation Ltd., 1973-78; Director, Scottish Television, 1975-79; a Governor,

Pitlochry Festival Theatre; Member: Press Council, 1959-62, Scottish Tourist Board, 1962-70, Council, National Trust for Scotland, 1962-70, Scottish International Education Trust, Scottish Theatre Ballet Committee, Scottish Opera Committee. Publications: Treasure at Sonnach, 1935; Heard Tell, 1946; Quest by Canoe, 1950; Highlands and Islands of Scotland, 1951; The Duke's Day, No Thanks to the Duke, 1978; Among Friends (autobiography), 1984; author of plays: The Original John Mackay, 1956; Fit to Print, 1962. Recreations: sailing; riding; walking. Address: (h.) 87 Colinton Road, Edinburgh, EH10 5DF; T.-031-337 2107.

Dunnett, Dorothy. Writer, since 1960; Portrait Painter, since 1950; b. 25.8.23, Dunfermline; m., Alastair M. Dunnett (qv); 2 s. Civil Service: Assistant Press Officer, Scottish Government Departments, Edinburgh, 1940-46, Executive Officer, Board of Trade, Glasgow, 1946-55; Trustee for the Secretary of State for Scotland, Scottish National War Memorial, since 1962; Director, Scottish Television p.l.c., since 1979; Member, Scottish Executive Committee, National Book League, since 1984. Publications (novels): The Game of Kings, 1961; Queens' Play, 1964; The Disorderly Knights, 1966; Dolly and the Singing Bird, 1968; Pawn in Frankincense, 1969; Dolly and the Cookie Bird, 1970; The Ringed Castle, 1971; Dolly and the Doctor Bird, 1971; Dolly and the Starry Bird, 1973; Checkmate, 1975; Dolly and the Nanny Bird, 1976; King Hereafter, 1982; Dolly and the Bird of Paradise, 1983; Contributor to Scottish Short Stories, anthology, 1973. Recreations: travel; sailing; opera; orchestral music; ballet. Address (h.) 87 Colinton Road, Edinburgh, EH10 5DF; T.-031-337 2107.

Dunning, Joseph, CBE (1977). Chairman, Lothian Health Board, 1983-84; Principal, Napier College of Commerce and Technology, Edinburgh, 1963-81; b. 9.10.20; m., Edith Mary Barlow (deceased); 1 s.; 1 d. Educ. London University; Durham University; Manchester College of Technology.

Dunpark, Hon. Lord, (Alastair McPherson Johnston), TD, BA, LLB, FSA Scot. Senator of the College of Justice in Scotland and Lord of Session, since 1971; b. 15.12.15; m., 1, Katharine Margaret Mitchell (deceased); 3 s.; 2, Kathleen Macfie. Educ. Merchiston Castle School; Jesus College, Cambridge; Edinburgh University. RA (TA), 1939-46 (mentioned in Despatches); Major, 1943; admitted, Faculty of Advocates, 1946; QC (Scot), 1958; Sheriff of Dumfries and Galloway, 1966-68; Member, Scottish Law Commission, 1968-71; President, Edinburgh Marriage Guidance Council, since 1973; Chairman, The Cockburn Association, 1969-74.

Dunsire, Thomas, MA, LLB, WS. Partner, J. & J. Milligan, WS, Edinburgh (now Morton, Fraser & Milligan, WS), since 1951; b. 16.11.26, Rangoon, Burma; m., Jean Mary. Educ. Morrison's Academy, Crieff; Edinburgh University. Royal Navy; Solicitor and WS, 1950. Chairman, Governors, Morrison's Academy, since 1984. Recreations: formerly rugby, football, golf and cricket. Address: (h.) 40 Liberton Brae, Edinburgh.

Dunsmore, Helen S., BSc, PhD, FRSC, CChem. Senior Lecturer (part-time), Department of Chemistry, Glasgow University, since 1984; President, International Federation of University Women, since 1983; b. 15.11.26, Greenock. Educ. Greenock High School; Glasgow University. Postdoctoral Fellow, National Research Council of Canada, Ottawa, 1953-56; Research Assistant, Royal Technical University, Stockholm, 1956-59; Lecturer, then Senior Lecturer, Glasgow University, 1959-83 (Senior Adviser, Studies in Science, since 1974). Address: (b.) Chemistry Department, Glasgow University, Glasgow, G12 8QQ; T.-041-339 8855, Ext. 401.

Durnin, Professor John V.G.A., MA, MB, ChB, DSc, FRCP, FRSE. Professor of Physiology, Glasgow University, since 1977; b. 23.4.23, Stirling; m., Joan Grimshaw; 4 s.; 2 d. Educ. Robert Gordon's College, Aberdeen; Aberdeen University; Glasgow University. Resident Hospital Officer in Medicine, Surgery and Clinical Pathology, four years; Lecturer/Reader, Institute of Physiology, Glasgow University; WHO and FAO Consultant in Nutrition in several developing countries, including Burma, Ghana, Ethiopia, Mexico, Peru and Chile; Honorary Civilian Consultant to the Army in Physiology and Nutrition. Member, Board of Directors, Scottish Ballet. Recreations: squash; golf; skiing; hill-walking; ballet. Address: (h.) Buchanan Castle, Drymen, Glasgow; T.-Drymen 60677.

Durrand, George, MBE. Director of Technical and Housing Services, Sutherland District Council, since 1974; b. 25.8.29, Wick; m., Janet; 2 s.; 1 d. National Service, 1947-50; Caithness County Council, 1950-66; Sutherland County Council, 1966-74. Address: Council Offices, Meadows, Dornoch, Sutherland; T.-0862 810491.

Dutch, Henry D.M., FIPR. Head of Public Relations, Strathclyde Regional Council, since 1975. Educ. Montrose Academy. Journalist, Glasgow Herald, 1954-67; Public Relations Officer: Scottish Special Housing Association, 1967-72, Corporation of City of Glasgow, 1972-75. Auxiliary Minister, Church of Scotland. Recreations: golf; walking; hill-climbing. Address: (b.) Strathclyde House, 20 India Street, Glasgow, G2 4PF; T.-041-227 3425.

Dutch, Mary Jane, MA. Member, SDP/Liberal Alliance, Dumbarton District Council, since 1984; Teacher, Lomond School, since 1965; b. 11.1.25, Montrose; m., Rev. John Henry Dutch (deceased); 1 s.; 1 d. Educ. Montrose Academy; St. Andrews University. Past President, Helensburgh Inner Wheel. Recreations: bridge; painting. Address: (h.) 5 Lomond Court, Helensburgh; T.-Helensburgh 5429.

Duthie, Professor John Hume, MA, PhD, DipEd. Professor of Education, Stirling University, since 1973; b. 25.10.33, Galashiels; m., Doreen Plummer; 1 s.; 1 d. Educ. Galashiels Academy; Langholm Academy; Dumfries Academy; Hawick High School; Edinburgh University; Durham University. School Teacher; Lecturer, Moray House College of Education; Research Director, Scottish Primary School Survey, SED;

Lecturer, then Senior Lecturer, Stirling University. Publications: The Primary School Survey: A Study of the Teacher's Day; Auxillaries in the Classroom. Recreations: music (jazz); cooking; gardening; photography. Address: (h.) Cairnhill, Doune Road, Dunblane, Perthshire; T.-Dunblane 822213.

Duthie, Norman, LDS, MDS. Senior Principal Dental Surgeon, Norman Duthie and Associates, since 1953; Honorary Senior Lecturer, Dundee University, since 1981, and Hospital Practitioner, Dundee Dental School, since 1978; Regional Adviser in General Dental Practice, North Eastern Regional Postgraduate Medical Education Committee, since 1983; b. 7.11.26, Aberdeen; m., Ethel Audrey Connon; 2 s. Educ. Robert Gordon's College, Aberdeen; St. Andrews University; Dundee University. Army (REME), 1944-48; Assistant Dental Surgeon, General Practice, 1953-54; part-time Assistant Dental Surgeon, Department of Dental Prosthetics, Dundee Dental Hospital, 1968-78; Honorary Lecturer, Dundee University, 1968-81. Served on: Aberdeen Local Dental Committee, Aberdeen NHS Executive Council, General Dental Services Committee, General Dental Services Committee (Scottish Sub-Committee), British Dental Association (Scottish Committee), Board of Management, British Dental Guild, Scottish Standing Dental Advisory Committee. Address: (h.) 1 Gladstone Place, Queen's Cross, Aberdeen; T.-0224 322959.

Duthie, Robert Grieve, CBE (1978), CA, LLD, CBIM, FRSA. Chairman, Scottish Development Agency, since 1979; Director, Insight Group PLC (formerly Black & Edgington (Holdings) PLC); Chairman, Insight International Tours Ltd. and Blacks Travel Agency Ltd., since 1952; Director, Royal Bank of Scotland plc, since 1978; Director, British Assets Trust plc, since 1977; Director, Edinburgh American Asset Trust plc, since 1977; Chairman, Bruntons (Musselburgh) plc, since 1984; b. 2.10.28, Greenock; m., Violetta Noel Maclean; 2 s.; 1 d. Educ. Greenock Academy. Apprentice Chartered Accountant, Thomson Jackson Gourlay and Taylor, CA, 1946-51; joined Blacks of Greenock, 1952; appointed Managing Director, 1962; Chairman, Black & Edgington, 1972-83. Chairman, Inverkip Society, 1966; Director, Greenock Chamber of Commerce, 1966; Member, Clyde Port Authority, 1971-83 (Chairman, 1977-80); Director, Greenock Provident Bank, 1969-75 (Chairman, 1975); Member, Scottish Telecommunications Board, 1972-77; Council Member, Institute of Chartered Accountants of Scotland, 1973-78; Member: East Kilbride Development Corporation, 1976-78, Strathclyde Region Local Valuation Appeal Panel, 1976-83; CBI Tax Liaison Officer for Scotland, 1976-79; Chairman, Made Up Textile Association of Great Britain, 1972; Member: British Institute of Management Scottish Committee, 1976, Glasgow and West of Scotland Committee, Scottish Council (Development and Industry), 1975-79; Captain: Greenock Club, 1972, Greenock Cricket Club, 1960-61; Commissioner, Queen Victoria School, Dunblane, since 1972; Commissioner, Scottish Congregational Ministers Pension Fund, since 1973; Member, Scottish Economic Council, since 1980; President, Twelfth Province Royal

Caledonian Curling Club, since 1983; Treasurer, Nelson Street EU Congregational Church, Greenock, since 1970. Awarded Honorary Degree of Doctor of Laws, Strathclyde University, 1984. Recreations: curling; golf. Address: (h.) Fairhaven, 181 Finnart Street, Greenock, PA16 8JA; T.-Greenock 22642.

Dyer, James A.T., MB, ChB (Hons), MRCPsych. Consultant Psychiatrist, Royal Edinburgh Hospital, since 1981; Honorary Senior Lecturer in Psychiatry, Edinburgh University, since 1981; b. 31.12.46, Arbroath; m., Lorna M.S.; 2 s.; 1 d. Educ. Bo'ness Academy; Robert Gordon's College, Aberdeen; Aberdeen University. House jobs in Aberdeen hospitals, 1970-71; Trainee General Practitioner, Skene, Aberdeenshire, 1971-72; junior clinical appointments, then Senior Registrar in Psychiatry, Royal Edinburgh Hospital, 1972-77; Scientific Officer, MRC Unit for Epidemiological Studies in Psychiatry, Edinburgh, 1977-80. Member, Medical Campaign Against Nuclear Weapons (Press Officer, Edinburgh Branch, and Convener, Scottish Working Group on psychological aspects of nuclear arms race). Recreations: holidays; eating out; home and family. Address: (h.) 86 Morningside Drive, Edinburgh, EH10 5NT; T.-031-447 8148.

Dymond, John Henry, MA, DPhil (Oxon). Senior Lecturer in Chemistry, Glasgow University, since 1984; b. 19.11.39, Beckenham, Kent; m., Joan Rowles; 2 s. Educ. Beckenham and Penge Grammar School; St. Catherine's College, Oxford. NSF Research Chemist, University of California, Berkeley, 1965-67; Glasgow University: ICI Research Fellow, 1968-70, Lecturer in Chemistry, 1970; Visiting Research Fellow, Australian National University, 1979-80 and 1982. Awarded Helsinki University Medal, 1977. Publications: the Virial Coefficients of Gases (with E.B. Smith), 1969; The Virial Coefficients of Pure Gases and Mixtures (with E.B. Smith), 1979. Recreations: Scouting; hill-walking; gardening. Address: (h.) Dunmore Cottage, Balfron, G63; T.-Balfron 40377.

E

Eadie, Alexander. MP (Labour), Midlothian, since 1966; b. 23.6.20. Educ. Buckhaven Senior Secondary School. Former Miners' Agent; contested Ayr, 1959 and 1964; Under Secretary of State for Energy, 1974-79.

Eadie, John, BSc (Hons), FRAgS. Director, Hill Farming Research Organisation, since 1980; b. 6.11.30, Polton, Midlothian; m., Jean Young Dunlevie; 1 s.; 2 d. Educ. Linlithgow Academy; Edinburgh University. National Agricultural Advisory Service, MAFF, 1954-61; Hill Farming Research Organisation: joined, 1961, Head of Animal Production and Nutrition, 1974-80.

Research Medal, Royal Agricultural Society of England, 1978. Address: (b.) Hill Farming Research Organisation, Bush Estate, Penicuik, Midlothian; T.-031-445 3401.

Eady, George E., MA (Econ) (Hons). Senior Depute Principal, Aberdeen College of Commerce, since 1962; b. 22.10.23, Feltham, Middlesex; m., Peggy Mairi Smith; 2 s. Educ. Ashford Grammar School; Aberdeen University. Royal Navy, 1941-49; organisation management, jute industry, 1953-56; Lecturer/Management Consultant, Leicester Polytechnic, 1956-62. Address: (b.) College of Commerce, Holburn Street, Aberdeen; T.-Aberdeen 572811.

Earley, Very Rev. John Canon. Parish Priest, St. Aidan's, Johnstone, since 1960; b. 24.2.15, Bailieboro, Ireland. Educ. St. Anne's Primary, Bailieboro; Blackrock College, Dublin; St. Peter's College, Wexford. Ordained Priest, 1940; St. Mary's, Hamilton, 1940-46; St. Mary's, Greenock, 1946-51; St. Margaret's, Johnstone, 1951-60; Canon, Cathedral Chapter, 1972. Chaplain, Sea-Rescue Forces at Greenock, 1947-49; served on School Council; Member, Management Board: St. Charles Private Hospital, since 1972, St. John's List D School, Glasgow. Address: St. Aidan's Presbytery, Johnstone; T.-Johnstone 20900.

Eason, Professor George, MSc, PhD, FIMA, FRSE. Professor of Mathematics for Applied Scientists, Strathclyde University, since 1970; b. 19.3.30, Chesterfield; m., 1, Olive Holdstock (deceased); 2, Esme Beryl Burgess; 2 d. Educ. Clay Cross Tupton Hall Grammar School; Birmingham University; Keele University. Scientific Officer, RARDE, Ministry of Defence, 1954-56; Lecturer in Applied Mathematics, Newcastle-upon-Tyne University, 1957-61; Senior Lecturer, then Reader, Strathclyde University, 1961-70; Visiting Professor, Wisconsin University, 1968-69. IMA: Chairman, Scottish Branch, 1974-76, Council Member, 1976-79. Publication: Mathematics and Statistics for the Biosciences (Co-author). Recreations: hill-walking; jogging; music. Address: (h.) 1 Greenfield Court, Balfron, Glasgow, G63 OQG; T.-0360 40546.

Eastmond, Clifford John, BSc, MD, FRCP. Consultant Rheumatologist, Grampian Health Board, since 1979; Clinical Senior Lecturer, Aberdeen University, since 1979; b. 19.1.45, Ashton-under-Lyne; m., Margaret Wadsworth; 2 s.; 1 d. Educ. Audenshaw Grammar School; Edinburgh University. House Officer posts, Edinburgh, one year; moved to Liverpool for further training, subsequently to Rheumatism Unit, Leeds. Elder, Church of Scotland. Recreations: golf; skiing; hill-walking; swimming; music. Address: (h.) Whinmoor, 34 Leslie Crescent, Westhill, Skene, Aberdeenshire; T.-0224 741009.

Easton, Rev. David John Courtney, MA, BD. Minister, Burnside Parish Church, Glasgow, since 1977; b. 7.10.40, Bogota, Colombia; m., Edith Stevenson; 2 s.; 1 d. Educ. Arbroath High School; Aberdeen University. Minister, Hamilton-Bardrainney Parish Church, Port

Glasgow, 1967-77. Chairman, Scottish Tear Fund Advisory Committee; Member, Rutherford House Council. Recreation: music. Address: 59 Blairbeth Road, Burnside, Rutherglen, Glasgow, G73 4JD; T.-041-634 1233.

Easton, Robert William Simpson, CBE (1980), CEng, FIMechE, FIMarE, FRINA. Chairman and Managing Director, Yarrow Shipbuilders Ltd., since 1979; Chairman, Clyde Port Authority, since 1983; b. 30.10.22, Glasgow; m., Jean Fraser; 1 s.; 1 d. Educ. Govan High School, Glasgow; Royal Technical College, Glasgow. Apprentice, Marine Engineer, Draughtsman, Estimator, 1939-51; Manager, Yarrow & Co. Ltd., 1951-65; Yarrow Shipbuilders Ltd.: Director, 1965-70, Deputy Managing Director, 1970-77, Managing Director, 1977-79; Main Board Director, Yarrow & Co. Ltd., 1971-77. Vice-President, Clyde Shipbuilders Association, 1972-79; Member, Worshipful Company of Shipwrights, 1982; Freeman, City of London, 1982; Council Member, RINA, 1983; Trustee, Seagull Trust, 1984. Recreations: sailing; golf; walking; family. Address: (h.) Springfield, Stuckenduff Road, Shandon, Dunbartonshire; T.-0436 820 677.

Easton, Robin Gardner, MA, DipEd. Rector, High School of Glasgow, since 1983; b. 6.10.43, Glasgow; m., Eleanor Mary McIlroy; 1 s.; 1 d. Educ. Kelvinside Academy; Sedbergh School; Christ's College, Cambridge; Wadham College, Oxford. Teacher of French and German, Melville College, Edinburgh, 1966-72; Housemaster and Deputy Head, French Department, Daniel Stewart's and Melville College, 1972-78; Head, Modern Languages, George Watson's College, 1979-83. Elder, Church of Scotland; former Council Member, Scripture Union; Member, HMC. Recreations: rugby; tennis; squash; hill-walking; reading; television. Address: (h.) 21 Stirling Drive, Bearsden, Glasgow, G61 4NU; T.-041-943 0368.

Ebsworth, Professor Evelyn A.V., BA, PhD, MA, ScD, FRSE. Crum Brown Professor of Chemistry, Edinburgh University, since 1967; b. 14.2.33, Richmond, Yorkshire; m., Mary Salter; 1 s.; 3 d. Educ. Marlborough School; King's College, Cambridge. Fellow, King's College, Cambridge, 1957-59; Research Associate, Princeton University, 1958-59; Christ's College, Cambridge: Demonstrator, 1959-64, Lecturer, 1964-67. President, Dalton Division, Chemical Society (Vice-President, Society, 1976-79); Fellow, Royal Institute of Chemistry; Chemical Society Award for Main Group Element Chemistry, 1979; Kipping Award, American Chemical Society, 1980; Corresponding Member, Gottingen Academy of Sciences, 1983. Recreation: opera. Address: (b.) Chemistry Department, Edinburgh University, Kings Buildings, West Mains Road, Edinburgh, EH9 3JJ; T.-031-667 1081, Ext. 3417.

Eccles, John Harold, DipEd. Head Teacher, North Walls School, Orkney, since 1980; b. 29.7.46, Darwen, Lancashire; m., Sylvia Howie; 1 s.; 2 d. Educ. Blackburn College of Technology; Alsager College of Education. Teacher in Cheshire; Head Teacher: Eday Primary School,

Dounby Primary School. Member, Scottish Executive Committee, Professional Association of Teachers, since 1983 (Chairman, Professional Services Committee); Member, Joint Consultative Committee, Orkney Islands Council, since 1976. Recreations: all sports; folk music; pony trekking. Address: (h.) Burra House, Hoy, Stromness, Orkney; T.-Hoy 266.

Eddison, James Andrew, MA, FICE, FRSE. Senior Partner, Blyth & Blyth, Consulting Engineers; Chairman, Scottish Life Assurance Company; Director, Merchiston Developments (Edinburgh) Ltd.; Director, Blyth & Blyth Service Co. Ltd.; b. 9.5.21, Aberdeen; m., Mary J. Rayner; 1 d. Educ. Rugby; Trinity College, Cambridge. Recreations: fishing; gardening; grandchildren. Address: (b.) 135 George Street, Edinburgh, EH2 4JX; T.-031-225 6283.

Ede, Donald Albert, BSc, MS, PhD, FRSE, FRSA. Reader in Zoology, Glasgow University, since 1971; b. 4.5.26, Brighton; m., Eleanor Lambert; 2 s. Educ. Varndean School, Brighton; London University; Northwestern University, USA; Edinburgh University. Assistant Lecturer, Edinburgh University, 1953-56; Lecturer, Wye College, London University, 1957-62; Principal Scientific Officer, Poultry Research Centre, Edinburgh, 1962-70; Visiting Lecturer: Iowa University, Massachusetts University, McGill University, Poona University. Recreation: painting. Address: (h.) 5 Learmonth Terrace, Edinburgh, EH4 1PG.

Eden, Tim Osborn Bryan, MB, BS, D(Obst)RCOG, MRCP, FRCPEdin. Consultant Paediatric Haematologist/Oncologist, Royal Hospital for Sick Children, Edinburgh, since 1982; part-time Senior Lecturer, Edinburgh University, since 1982; b. 2.4.47, Birmingham; m., Randi Forsgren; 1 s.; 1 d. Educ. Grimsby Wintringham Grammar School; University College and Hospital, London. House Physician, University College Hospital, London; Senior House Physician (Obstetrics), Isle of Wight; Registrar, Paediatrics, Royal Hospital for Sick Children, Edinburgh; Registrar, Haematology, Edinburgh Hospitals; Postdoctoral Fellow, Stanford University, California; Lecturer in Child Life and Health, Edinburgh University; Consultant Clinical Haematologist, Bristol Children's Hospital. Chairman, Scottish Paediatric Oncology Group; Coordinator, MRC Eighth Childhood Leukaemia Trial; Member, Scottish Committee, Malcolm Sargent Fund. Recreations: family; politics. Address: (b.) Royal Hospital for Sick Children, Edinburgh; T.-031-667 1991.

Edge, David Owen, BA, MA, PhD, FRAS, FRSA. Director, Science Studies Unit, Edinburgh University, since 1966 (Reader in Science Studies, since 1979); b. 4.9.32, High Wycombe; m., Barbara Corsie; 2 s.; 1 d. Educ. Aberdeen Grammar School; Leys School, Cambridge; Gonville and Caius College, Cambridge. Assistant Physics Master, Perse School, Cambridge; Producer, Science Unit, Talks Department, BBC Radio, London, 1959-66; Senior Fellow, Society for the Humanities, and Senior Research Associate, Science, Technology and Society Program,

Cornell University, 1973; Member, Edinburgh University Court, since 1983; Scottish HQ Adviser for Students, Scout Association, since 1966; President (Past Chairman), Scout & Guide Graduate Association; Circuit Steward, Methodist Church, Edinburgh and Forth Circuit, since 1983; Editor, Social Studies of Science, since 1971; Member, various CNAA panels and committees, since 1972. Publications: Astronomy Transformed (Co-author), 1976; Science in Context (Co-Editor), 1982. Recreations: hillwalking; music; watching sport - especially soccer and baseball. Address: (h.) 25 Gilmour Road, Edinburgh, EH16 5NS; T.-031-667 3497.

Edge, Robert Michael, BSc, PhD, MIChemE, CEng. Senior Lecturer, Department of Chemical and Process Engineering, Strathclyde University, since 1974; b. 11.10.33, Birmingham; m., Ursula Elisabeth. Educ. Oldbury Grammar School; Birmingham Univesity. Scientific Officer, Warren Spring Laboratory; Research Fellow, Loughborough University; Lecturer, Strathclyde University. Recreations: fell-walking; rock gardening; music; theatre. Address: (b.) Department of Chemical and Process Engineering, Strathclyde University, George Street, Glasgow; T.-041-552 4400.

Edward, Professor David Alexander Ogilvy, CMG, QC, MA, LLB. Salvesen Professor of European Institutions, Edinburgh University, since 1985; Advocate, since 1962; Trustee, National Library of Scotland, since 1966; Member, Law Advisory Committee, British Council; Chairman, Continental Assets Trust plc; Director, Adam & Company plc; Director, Harris Tweed Association Ltd.; Member, Panel of Arbitrators, International Centre for Settlement of Investment Disputes; b. 14.11.34, Perth; m., Elizabeth Young McSherry; 2 s.; 2 d. Educ. Sedbergh School; University College, Oxford; Edinburgh University. National Service, RNVR, 1956-57 (Sub-Lt.); admitted Advocate, 1962; Clerk, Faculty of Advocates, 1967-70, Treasurer, 1970-77; President, Consultative Committee, Bars and Law Societies of the European Community, 1978-80. Address: (h.) 32 Heriot Row, Edinburgh, EH3 6ES; T.-031-225 7153; (b.) Centre of European Governmental Studies, University of Edinburgh, EH8 9YL; T.-031-667 1011, Ext. 4215.

Edward, Neil, MB, ChB, FRCPEdin. Consultant Physician, Grampian Health Board, since 1973; Clinical Senior Lecturer, Aberdeen University, since 1973; b. 8.1.38, Aberdeen; m., Dr. Vivien E.M. Smith; 1 s.; 1 d. Educ. Aberdeen Grammar School; Aberdeen University. Lecturer in Medicine, Aberdeen University; Instructor in Medicine, Temple University, Philadelphia.

Edwards, Professor Arthur David, BSc, DIC, PhD, MICE, CEng, FRSA. Professor of Civil Engineering, Heriot-Watt University, since 1980; b. 11.11.25, Eastbourne; m., Jean Margaret; 1 s.; 1 d. Educ. Eastbourne Grammar School; Northampton Engineering College; Imperial College of Science and Technology, London. Various appointments in civil engineering industry, 1950-56; Imperial College of Science and

Technology, London: Lecturer in Civil Engineering, 1957-66, Senior Lecturer, 1966-80. Telford Premium, ICE, 1970, 1973, 1983. Recreations: music; sailing; snooker. Address: (b.) Department of Civil Engineering, Heriot-Watt University, Riccarton, Edinburgh, EH14 4AS; T.-031-449 5111.

Edwards, Professor Christopher Richard Watkin, MA, MB, BChir, MD, FRCP, FRCPEdin. Professor of Clinical Medicine, Edinburgh University, since 1980; Honorary Consultant Physician, Lothian Health Board, since 1980; Chairman, Department of Medicine, Western General Hospital, since 1981; b. 12.2.42, Irvinestown, Northern Ireland; m., Dr. Sally Edwards; 2 s.; 1 d. Educ. Marlborough; Cambridge University. Junior House Officer posts, St. Bartholomew's Hospital; Senior House Officer posts, Brompton and Hammersmith Hospitals; Lecturer, St. Bartholomew's Hospital Medical College, 1968-72; Visiting Fellow, Bethesda, USA, 1972-73; Senior Lecturer and Honorary Consultant Physician, St. Bartholomew's Hospital, 1975-80. Recreations: drawing; painting; golf. Address: (b.) Department of Medicine, Western General Hospital, Edinburgh; T.-031-332 2525.

Edwards, Elizabeth Alice, BSc, SRN, SCM. Chief Area Nursing Officer, Dumfries and Galloway Health Board, since 1980; b. Coleraine. Educ. Coleraine High School; Edinburgh University. Ward Sister, Royal Victoria Hospital, Belfast, 1960-64; nursing in North America, 1965-67; Department Sister and Assistant Matron, Royal Victoria Hospital, Belfast, 1967-69; full-time student at University, 1969-72; Principal Nursing Officer, Edinburgh Northern Hospitals Group, 1972-74; District Nursing Officer, North Lothian District, Lothian Health Board, 1974-80. Member, National Board for Nursing, Midwifery and Health Visiting for Scotland, 1983; Member, United Kingdom Central Council for Nursing, Midwifery and Health Visiting, 1984. Address: (b.) Dumfries and Galloway Health Board, Nithbank, Dumfries; T.-0387 53181.

Edwards, Frederick Edward, RD (and Clasp), BA, FBIM, FISW. Director of Social Work, Strathclyde Regional Council, since 1976; b. 9.4.31; m.; 2 s.; 1 d. Educ. St. Edward's College, Liverpool; Glasgow University. Director of Social Work: Moray and Nairn, 1969-74, Grampian, 1974-76.

Edwards, George Lowden, CEng, MIMechE, MIProdE, FBIM, FInstPet. Director, MacDougalls Advertising PLC, since 1985; Trustee, Scottish Civic Trust; Member, Careers Advisory Committee, St. Andrews University; b. 6.2.39, Kirriemuir; m., Sylvia Izatt; 1 d. Educ. Webster's Seminary, Kirriemuir; Dundee Institute of Technology. Production Engineer, Burroughs Machines Ltd., Cumbernauld, 1961-64; Development Division, Scottish Council (Development and Industry), Edinburgh, 1964-67; General Manager, GR Designs Ltd., Perth, 1967-68; London Director, Scottish Council (Development and Industry), 1968-78; Manager, Public Affairs Scotland, Conoco (UK) Ltd., Aberdeen, 1978-83; Manager, Public Affairs, Conoco (UK)

Ltd., 1983-85. Council Member, Institute of Petroleum. Recreations: music; travel; food and wine. Address: (h.) 1 Back Dean, Ravelston Terrace, Edinburgh, EH4 3UA.

Edwards, Paul Geoffrey, MA (Cantab), BA. Reader in English Literature, Edinburgh University; b. 31.7.26, Birmingham; m., Maj Ingbritt Nilsson; 2 d. Educ. St. Philip's School, Birmingham; Hatfield College, Durham; Emmanuel College, Cambridge. Taught English, St. Augustine's College, Cape Coast, Ghana, 1954-57; Lecturer in English, Sierra Leone University, 1957-63; joined Edinburgh University, 1963; Visiting Professor, at various times: University of California, New York State University, Bangkok University, Singapore University. Publications: West African Narrative, 1963; Through African Eyes, 1966; Equiano's Travels, 1967; Legendary Fiction in Medieval Iceland (Co-author), 1970; Black Personalities in the Era of the Slave Trade (Co-author), 1983; Icelandic Sagas (Co-translator). Recreations: teaching; translating sagas. Address: (h.) 82 Kirk Brae, Edinburgh, EH16 6JA.

Edwards, Rev. Peter John Smallman, BD, MTh, FSJ. Priest-in-Charge, St. Ninian's Church, Invergordon, since 1981; Synod Clerk, Diocese of Moray, Ross and Caithness, since 1985; Principal, Moray Ordination Course, since 1981; b. 22.4.48, Hereford; m., Nita Mary. Educ. Haverfordwest Grammar School; University College of North Wales, Bangor; Lincoln Theological College. Curate, Llanelli, 1973-76; Precentor, Inverness Cathedral, 1976-77; Rector, Walton West with Talbenny and Haroldston West, South Wales, 1977-81; Canon, Inverness Cathedral, since 1981; Examining Chaplain to Bishops of Moray, since 1981, and St. David's, since 1982. Recreations: woodwork; communications; goading depressed prelates. Address: St. Ninian's House, 132 High Street, Invergordon; T.-Invergordon 852392.

Egginton, Gay, BSc (Hons), PGCE. Headmistress, Laurel Bank School, Glasgow, since 1984; b. 28.2.44, Woking. Educ. St. George's School, Edinburgh; Harrogate College, Yorkshire; London University. Teacher of Chemistry, Priory Comprehensive School, Lewes, 1965-70; Head of Chemistry, Priory County Grammar School, Shrewsbury, 1970-75; Head of Chemistry and Upper School, St. Margaret's School, Edinburgh, 1975-84. Recreations: travel; socialising; reading; computing. Address: (b.) Laurel Bank School, 4 Lilybank Terrace, Glasgow, G12.

Eilbeck, John Christopher, BA, PhD, FIMA. Head, Department of Mathematics, Heriot-Watt University, since 1984; b. 8.4.45, Whitehaven; m., Lesley; 3 s. Educ. Whitehaven Grammar School; Queen's College, Oxford; Lancaster University. Royal Society European Fellow, ICTP, Trieste, 1969-70; Research Assistant, Department of Mathematics, UMIST, Manchester, 1970-73; Heriot-Watt University: Lecturer, Department of Mathematics, 1973-80, Senior Lecturer, 1980-85, Reader, 1985; Long-term Visiting Fellow, Center for Nonlinear Studies, Los Alamos National Laboratory, New Mexico,

1983-84. Publications: Rock Climbing in the Lake District (Co-author), 1975; Solitons and Nonlinear Wave Equations (Co-author), 1982. Recreation: mountaineering. Address: (b.) Department of Mathematics, Heriot-Watt University, Riccarton, Edinburgh, EH15 4AS; T.-031-449 5111.

Eisner, Professor Edward, BA (Cantab), PhD (Cantab), CPhys, FInstP, FRSE. Professor of Applied Physics, Strathclyde University, since 1968; b. 20.12.29, Sarvar, Hungary; 1 s.; 2 d. Educ. Herbert Strutt School, Belper; Gonville and Caius College, Cambridge. Scientific Officer/Senior Scientific Officer, Safety in Mines Research Establishment, Buxton and Sheffield, 1954-60; Member, Technical Staff, Bell Telephone Laboratories, New Jersey, 1960-68; Head, Department of Applied Physics, Strathclyde University, 1968-84; Professor (part-time) and Consultant (part-time), since 1984. Recreations: walking; photography; architecture and archaeology; French and France. Address: (b.) Department of Applied Physics, Strathclyde University, 107 Rottenrow, Glasgow, G4 ONG; T.-041-552 4400, Ext. 3379.

Elder, Robert Ian, TD, MA (Hons). Rector, Webster's High School, Kirriemuir, since 1968; b. 4.8.23, Edinburgh; m., Edna B.I. Manson; 1 s. Educ. George Watson's Boys' College, Edinburgh; Edinburgh University. Commissioned, Royal Scots, 1942-46, serving in North West Europe and Far East (post-war service, TA); Teacher: Norton Park Secondary School, Edinburgh, 1948-50, George Heriot's School, Edinburgh, 1950-67. Address: (b.) Webster's High School, Kirriemuir, Angus; T.-Kirriemuir 72840.

Elders, Rev. (Iain) Alasdair, MA, BD. Minister, Broughton McDonald Parish Church, Edinburgh, since 1973; b. 17.4.39, Sunderland; m., Hazel Stewart Steven; 1 s.; 1 d. Educ. Daniel Stewart's College, Edinburgh; Edinburgh University. Assistant Minister: Edinburgh: St. Andrew's, 1961-63, Edinburgh: High (St. Giles Cathedral), 1963-65; Minister, Cumbernauld: Abronhill (church extension charge), 1965-73. Secretary, Cumbernauld Council of Churches, 1967-72; Chairman, Council of East End Churches of Edinburgh, 1978-82; Vice Chairman, New Town Community Council, since 1983; Scout Commissioner, since 1966 (Assistant Area Commissioner, since 1983). Address: Broughton McDonald Manse, 103 East Claremont Street, Edinburgh, EH7 4JA; T.-031-556 7313.

Elgin, 11th Earl of, and Kincardine, 15th Earl of, (Andrew Douglas Alexander Thomas Bruce), KT (1981), DL, JP; 37th Chief of the Name of Bruce; Brigadier, Queen's Bodyguard for Scotland (Royal Company of Archers); b. 17.2.24; m., Victoria Usher; 3 s.; 2 d. Educ. Eton; Balliol College, Oxford. President, Scottish Amicable Life Assurance Society, since 1975; Chairman, National Savings Committee for Scotland, 1972-78; Member, Scottish Postal Board, since 1980; Lord High Commissioner, General Assembly, Church of Scotland, 1980-81; Grand Master

Mason of Scotland, 1961-65; President, Royal Caledonian Curling Club, 1968-69; Hon. LLD, Dundee, 1977, Glasgow, 1983. Address: (h.) Broomhall, Dunfermline, KY11 3DU.

Eliott of Stobs, Sir Arthur Francis Augustus Boswell, 11th Bt. Chief of the Clan Elliot; b. 2.1.15; m., Frances Aileen McClean; 1 d. Educ. Harrow; King's College, Cambridge. 2nd Lt., King's Own Scottish Borderers (TA), 1939; Major, 1944; King's African Rifles, 1941-45; Member, Queen's Bodyguard for Scotland (Royal Company of Archers). Address: (h.) Redheugh, Newcastleton, Roxburghshire.

Elliot, Gerald Henry, BA, MA, FRSE. Chairman, Christian Salvesen PLC, since 1981; Chairman, Scottish Provident Institution, since 1983; Chairman, Scottish Arts Council, since 1980; b. 24.12.23, Edinburgh; m., Margaret Ruth Whale; 2 s.; 1 d. Educ. Marlborough College; New College, Oxford. Joined Christian Salvesen, 1948; whaling, fishing and shipping management, 1950-73; appointed Managing Director, 1973; Secretary, National Whaling Board, 1953-62; Chairman, Forth Ports Authority, 1973-79; Chairman, Chambers & Fargus, 1975-79; Member: National Ports Council, 1978-81, Arts Council of Great Britain, since 1980; Chairman, Scottish Unit Managers, since 1984; Consul for Finland in Edinburgh and Leith, since 1957; Member, Edinburgh University Court, since 1984; Council Member, Royal Society of Edinburgh, 1978-81; former Member, Council, National Trust for Scotland; Secretary and Chairman, Scottish Branch, Royal Institute of International Affairs, 1963-77. Order of the White Rose of Finland, Knight of First Class, 1975. Address: (b.) 50 East Fettes Avenue, Edinburgh, EH4 1EQ; T.-031-552 7101.

Elliot, John. Farmer; Member, Scottish Agricultural Development Council; Regional Member, British Wool Marketing Board, for Southern Scotland; b. 29.5.47, Duns, Berwickshire; m., Joan Kathleen Wight; 1 s.; 1 d. Educ. St. Mary School, Melrose; Edinburgh Academy. Nuffield Scholar, US and Canada, 1982; President, Mid and East Berwick, National Farmers Union of Scotland; Chairman, Longformacus and Cranshaws Community Council; Session Clerk, Kirk of Lammermuir. Recreations: spectator sports; reading; writing; agriculture. Address: Rawburn, Duns, Berwickshire, TD11 3PE; T.-036 17 221.

Elliot of Harwood, Baroness, (Katharine Elliot), DBE (1958), JP. Life Peer; b. 15.1.03; m., Rt. Hon. Walter Elliot, PC, CH (deceased). Educ. Abbot's Hill, Hemel Hempstead; Paris. Chairman: National Union of Conservative and Unionist Associations, 1956-67, Carnegie UK Trust, since 1965, Consumer Council, 1963-68; UK Delegate to General Assembly, United Nations, 1954-56-57; Vice-Convener, Roxburgh County Council, 1974; Hon. LLD, Glasgow, 1959. Address: (h.) Harwood, Bonchester Bridge, Hawick, Roxburghshire.

Elliot, Thomas, JP. Farmer; a Director, Royal Highland and Agricultural Society of Scotland; a Director, Animal Diseases Research Association;

Member, Hill Farming Advisory Committee for Scotland; b. 6.4.26, Galashiels; m., Patrena Jennifer Mundell; 1 s.; 2 d. Educ. St. Mary's School; Loretto. President, Border Area, National Farmers Union of Scotland, 1974-76 (Chairman, Selkirk Branch, 1968); President, South Country Cheviot Society, 1971-73; Member, Southern Regional Committee, British Wool Board. Played rugby, Gala RFC, 1945-58; 14 caps for Scotland, 1955-58; Barbarians, 1956; British Lions, South African tour, 1955. "Border Man of the Year", Tweeddale Press, 1979; Elder, Caddonfoot Church. Recreations: watching rugby; reading books; farming. Address: Newhall, Clovenfords, Galashiels; T.-Clovenfords 260.

Elliott, Robert F., BA (Oxon), MA. Senior Lecturer in Political Economy, Aberdeen University, since 1982; b. 15.6.47, Thurlow, Suffolk; m., Susan Elliott Gutteridge; 1 s. Educ. Haverhill Secondary Modern School, Suffolk; Ruskin College and Balliol College, Oxford. Joined Aberdeen University, 1973, as Research Fellow, then Lecturer; acted as Consultant to numerous public and private sector organisations, including McGaw Committee of Inquiry into Civil Service Pay, the EEC Commission and Highlands and Islands Development Board, on issues of pay and employment. Publications: Pay in the Public Sector, 1981; Incomes Policies, Inflation and Relative Pay, 1981; Incomes Policy, 1981. Recreations: music; reading; golf; house decorating (in reverse order of priority). Address: (h.) 11 Richmondhill Place, Aberdeen, AB2 4EN; T.-0224 314901.

Elliott, Hon. Lord (Walter Archibald Elliott), QC, MC, BL. President, Lands Tribunal for Scotland, since 1971; Chairman, Scottish Land Court, since 1978; Brigadier, Queen's Bodyguard for Scotland (Royal Company of Archers), since 1983; b. 6.9.22, London; m., Susan Isobel MacKenzie Ross; 2 s. Educ. Eton College; Edinburgh University. 2nd Bn., Scots Guards, 1943-45 (Staff Captain, 1947); Advocate and at the Inner Temple, Barrister-at-Law, 1950; QC (Scotland), 1963. Publication: Us and Them: a study of group consciousness, 1985. Recreations: gardening; skiing; shooting. Address: (h.) Morton House, 19 Winton Loan, Edinburgh, EH10 7AW; T.-031-445 2548.

Ellis, Hadyn Douglas, BA, PhD. Senior Lecturer in Psychology, Aberdeen University, since 1979; b. 25.10.45, Newport, Gwent; m., Diane Margaret Newton; 3 s. Educ. St. Julians High School, Newport; Reading University. Lecturer in Psychology, Aberdeen University, 1970-79; research work for Home Office on forensic aspects of testimony. Publications: Perceiving and Remembering Faces (Co-author), 1981; Identification Evidence (Co-author), 1982. Recreations: reading; walking; golf; watching soccer; TV. Address: (h.) 43 Fountainhall Road, Aberdeen, AB2 4EW; T.-0224 639161.

Ellis, Jean B.M., OBE, BSc, MB, ChB, JP. Member, Mental Welfare Commission for Scotland, since 1984; Member, Scottish Hospital Endowment Research Trust, since 1978; President, Aberdeen and NE Association for Mental Health; b. 13.9.20, Poona, India; m., Richard T. Ellis (qv); 2 s.; 2 d. Educ. Malvern Girls College; Aberdeen University. Past Chairman: Aberdeen Marriage Guidance Council, Royal Cornhill and Associated Hospitals Board of Management; former Member: NE Regional Hospital Board, Nurses and Midwives Whitley Council (Management Side), Grampian Health Board; President, Aberdeen and NE Association for Mental Health. Address: (h.) 18 Rubislaw Den North, Aberdeen, AB2 4AN; T.-0224 36680.

Ellis, Laurence Edward, MA, AFIMA. Rector, The Edinburgh Academy, since 1977; b. 21.4.32, Great Yarmouth; m., Elizabeth Ogilvie; 2 s.; 1 d. Educ. Winchester College; Trinity College, Cambridge. National Service, Rifle Brigade, 1950-52 (2nd Lt.); Assistant Master and Housemaster, Marlborough College, 1955-77. Council Member, ISCO; Reader, Church of England; Co-author, SMP Mathematics texts; article in Dictionary of National Biography on A.L.F. Smith. Recreations: music; reading; crosswords; woodwork. Address: (h.) 50 Inverleith Place, Edinburgh, 3.

Ellis, Richard Tunstall, OBE, DL, MA, LLB. Chairman, Trustee Savings Bank Scotland, since 1983; Member, TSB Group Central Board, since 1976; Chairman, TSB Group Pension Trust Ltd., since 1976; b. 6.9.18, Liverpool; m., Jean Bruce Maitland Porter (see Jean B.M. Ellis); 2 s.; 2 d. Educ. Merchant Taylors School, Crosby; Silcoates School, Wakefield; Aberdeen University. Captain, Royal Signals, 1939-45 (POW, Germany); Chairman of Governors, Dunfermline College of Physical Education, 1964-67; Governor, Aberdeen College of Education, 1969-75; Member: Scottish Board, Norwich Union Insurance Society, 1973-80, Aberdeen Board, Bank of Scotland, 1972-82; Member, Aberdeen University Court, since 1984, Council, National Trust for Scotland, since 1984; Chairman, Aberdeen Branch, Institute of Directors, since 1983. Recreations: golf; hill-walking; skiing. Address: (h.) 18 Rubislaw Den North, Aberdeen, AB2 4AN; T.-0224 316680.

Elston, Peter Kenneth. Minister, Dalgety Parish Church, since 1971; 4.4.33, Sheffield; m., Jessie Holmes; 2 s. Educ. High Storrs Grammar School, Sheffield; Wesley College, Leeds. Minister: Motherwell Methodist Church, 1961-67, Newcastle-upon-Tyne Methodist Church, 1967-69. Address: 9 St. Colme Drive, Dalgety Bay, Fife.

Elvidge, John William, BA (Oxon). Assistant Secretary, Scottish Office (Finance Officer, Industry Department for Scotland and Scottish Development Department), since 1984; b. 9.2.51, Edmonton, Middlesex. Educ. Sir George Monoux School, Walthamstow; St. Catherine's College, Oxford. Scottish Office: Administration Trainee, 1973-76, HEO(A), 1976-78, Principal, 1978-84 (Housing Division, SDD, 1978-83, Finance Division, 1983-84). Recreations: appreciating other people's creativity; observing other people's politics. Address: (b.) Room 8/21 New St. Andrews House, Edinburgh, EH1; T.-031-556 8400, Ext. 5340.

Embrey, John Derek, FCA. Group Finance Director, Dawson International PLC, since 1982; b. 14.7.45, Shrewsbury. Educ. Bishop Vesey's School, Sutton Coldfield. Recreations: horse riding; skiing; theatre. Address: Dawson International PLC, Lochleven Mills, Kinross; T.-0577 63521.

Emslie, Baron, (George Carlyle Emslie), PC (1972), MBE (1946). Lord Justice-General of Scotland and Lord President of the Court of Session, since 1972; Life Peer; b. 6.12.19; m.; 3 s. Educ. High School of Glasgow; Glasgow University. Commissioned Argyll and Sutherland Highlanders, 1940; Brigade Major (Infantry), 1944-46; Advocate, 1948; QC (Scot), 1957; Sheriff of Perth and Angus, 1963-66; Dean, Faculty of Advocates, 1965-70; Senator of the College of Justice in Scotland and Lord of Session, 1970-72; Chairman, Scottish Agricultural Wages Board, 1969-73; Hon. LLD, Glasgow, 1973.

Emslie, John Frederick. Member, Kincardine and Deeside District Council, since 1980 (Chairman, Planning Committee, since 1984); Chairman, Kincardine and Deeside Tourist Board, since 1985; Electrical Contractor, since 1952; b. 27.6.29, Stonehaven; m., Alice Moira Christie; 2 s.; 2 d. Educ. Mackie Academy, Stonehaven. Served apprenticeship, 1945-50; National Service, 1950-52; began own business, 1952. Chairman, Kincardine and Deeside Recreation Grounds Trustees, since 1981; Deputy Provincial Grand Master, Masonic Order. Recreations: golf; swimming; cycling; walking. Address: 11-13 Ann Street, Stonehaven; T.-Stonehaven 62417.

Emslie-Smith, Donald, MD (Hons), ChB, FRCP, FRCPEdin. Reader in Medicine, Dundee University, since 1971; Honorary Consultant Physician (Cardiologist), Tayside Health Board, since 1961; b. 12.4.22, Aberdeen; m., Ann Elizabeth Milne; 1 s.; 1 d. Educ. Trinity College, Glenalmond; Aberdeen University. House Physician, Aberdeen Royal Infirmary; RAFVR (Medical Branch), UK and Middle East; Registrar in Cardiology, Dundee Royal Infirmary; Edward Wilson Memorial Research Fellow, Baker Institute, Melbourne; Tutor and Senior Registrar in Medicine, Royal Postgraduate Medical School and Hammersmith Hospital, London; Senior Lecturer in Medicine, St. Andrews University. Council Member, Association of Physicians of Great Britain and Ireland, 1977-80. Publications: Textbook of Physiology (Co-author); Accidental Hypothermia, 1977. Recreations: fly-fishing; dinghy sailing; music. Address: (b.) University Department of Medicine, Ninewells Hospital and Medical School, Dundee, DD1 9SY; T.-0382 60111.

Engeset, Jetmund, MB, ChB, FRCS, ChM (Hons). Senior Lecturer, Department of Surgery, Aberdeen University; Consultant Surgeon; Surgeon to the Queen in Scotland, since 1985; b. 22.7.38, Oslo; m., Anne; 2 d. Educ. Slemdal and Ris Skole, Oslo; Aberdeen University. Recreations: angling; gardening; skiing; squash. Address: (h.) Pine Lodge, 315 North Deeside Road, Milltimber, Aberdeen, AB1 ODL; T.-Aberdeen 733753.

English, Peter Roderick, BSc (Hons), NDA (Hons), PhD. Senior Lecturer in Animal Husbandry, Aberdeen University; b. 9.3.37, Glen Urquhart, Inverness-shire; m., Anne Dunlop Mackay; 2 s.; 1 d. Educ. Balnain Public School; Arnisdale School; Glen Urquhart Senior Secondary School; Inverness Royal Academy; Aberdeen University. Farm Manager; Aberdeen University: Assistant Lecturer, Research Fellow, Lecturer. Won David Black Award, 1984, for major contribution to British pig industry. Publications: The Sow - Improving Her Efficiency; Glen Urquhart. Recreations: athletics; shinty (first Editor, Shinty Yearbook); writing; travel; hard labour. Address: (h.) Arnisdale, 13 Fintray Road, Aberdeen, AB1 8HL; T.-Aberdeen 319306.

Entwistle, Professor Noel James, BSc, PGCE, PhD, FBPsS. Bell Professor of Education, Edinburgh University, since 1978; Director, Godfrey Thomson Unit for Educational Research, since 1978; b. 26.12.36, Bolton; m., Dorothy Bocking; 1 d. Educ. King's School, Ely; Sheffield University; Aberdeen University. Teacher, Rossall School, Fleetwood, 1961-64; Research Fellow, Aberdeen University, 1964-68; Department of Educational Research, Lancaster University: Lecturer, 1968, Senior Lecturer, Professor, 1971. Editor, British Journal of Educational Psychology, 1975-79; Governor, St. Margaret's School; Chairman, Innovation, Research and Development Committee, Microelectronics in Education Committee. Recreations: reading; walking; golf. Address: (b.) 10 Buccleuch Place, Edinburgh, EH8 9JT; T.-031-667 1011.

Erickson, Professor John, MA, FRSE, FBA. Director of Defence Studies, Edinburgh University, since 1967; b. 17.4.29, South Shields; m., Ljubica; 1 s.; 1 d. Educ. South Shields High School; St. John's College, Cambridge. Research Fellow, St. Antony's College, Oxford; Lecturer, Department of History, St. Andrews University; Lecturer/Reader, Department of Government, Manchester University; Reader/Professor, Defence Studies, Edinburgh University. President, Association of Civil Defence and Emergency Planning Officers, until 1984. Publications: The Soviet High Command, 1962; The Road to Stalingrad, 1975; The Road to Berlin, 1984. Recreation: model-making. Address: (b.) 31 Buccleuch Place, Edinburgh; T.-031-667 1011.

Erskine, Donald Seymour, DL, FRICS. Factor and Director of Estates, National Trust for Scotland, since 1961; b. 28.5.25, London; m., Catharine Annandale McLelland; 1 s.; 4 d. Educ. Wellington College. RA (Airborne), 1943-47 (Captain); Pupil, Drumlanrig Estate, 1947-49; Factor, Country Gentlemen's Association, Edinburgh, 1950-55; Factor to Mr A.L.P.F. Wallace, 1955-61. Member, Queen's Bodyguard for Scotland (Royal Company of Archers); Deputy Lieutenant, Perth and Kinross; Elder, Church of Scotland. Recreations: shooting; singing. Address: (h.) Cleish House, Cleish, Kinross-shire; T.-057 75 232.

Erskine, Sir (Thomas) David, 5th Bt, JP. Vice Lord-Lieutenant, Fife Region, since 1981; b. 31.7.12; m.; 2 s.; 1 s. (deceased). Educ. Eton;

Magdalene College, Cambridge. Retired Major, Indian Corps of Engineers; Convener, Fife County Council, 1970-73; DL, Fife, 1955-81.

Erskine-Hill, Sir Robert, 2nd Bt. Chairman, Life Association of Scotland, since 1960; b. 6.2.17; m.; 2 s.; 2 d. Educ. Eton; Trinity College, Cambridge. RNVR, 1939-45; Partner, Chiene & Tait, CA, 1946-80; Member, Queen's Bodyguard for Scotland (Royal Company of Archers).

Eunson, David Moyes. Headmaster, Ross High School, Tranent, since 1972; b. 20.3.32, Westray, Orkney; m., Zena Glass; 1 s.; 4 d. Educ. Stromness Academy; Edinburgh University. Teacher, Dollar Academy; Principal Teacher of Mathematics: Campbeltown Grammar School, Hawick High School; Member, Scottish Mathematical Council, 1971-77; Council Member, Headteachers' Association of Scotland, 1980-85. Active in several missionary societies. Recreations: gardening; music; crosswords; family. Address: (b.) Ross High School, Tranent, East Lothian; T.-610 433.

Eunson, Edwin Russell, JP. Convener, Orkney Islands Council, since 1978 (Chairman, Policy and Resources Committee, since 1978); b. 25.12.17, Kirkwall; m., Margaret Rosa Nicolson. Educ. Kirkwall Grammar School. Member, Kirkwall Town Council, 1947-68 (Dean of Guild, 1955, Treasurer, 1955-57, Bailie, 1957-68); Member, Orkney County Council, 1947-55; Member, Orkney Islands Council, since 1974 (Chairman: Development, Planning and Control Committee, 1974-77, Social Work and Environmental Health Committee, 1977-78); Member: Highlands and Islands Development Consultative Council, Scottish Council (Development and Industry) Executive Committee; Chairman, Orkney Committee for Employment of Disabled Persons; Member, Policy Committee, COSLA; Session Clerk, Kirkwall East Church, since 1955; Chairman: Orkney Liberal Association, 1962-78, Orkney Council of Social Service, 1968-74, Kirkwall Chamber of Commerce, 1970-72. Recreations: reading; walking dogs. Address: (h.) Newhallea, Glaitness Road, Kirkwall, Orkney; T.-0856 3367.

Evans, Charles, CEng, MIMechE, MIRTE. Director of Public Transport, Lothian Regional Council, since 1978; b. 30.8.37, Chadderton, Lancashire; m., Cherie; 3 s.; 1 d. Educ. North Chadderton Secondary Modern School; Oldham Technical College. Apprentice Engineer/ Engineer, Oldham Corporation Passenger Transport, 1952-63; Assistant Engineer, Manchester Corporation, 1963-65; Edinburgh Corporation: Assistant Chief Engineer, 1965-71, Chief Engineer, 1971-75; Depute Director, Lothian Regional Council, 1975-78. Vice-President, Bus and Coach Council. Recreations: golf; caravanning. Address: (b.) 14 Queen Street, Edinburgh, EH2 1JL; T.-031-554 4494.

Evans, David Pugh, ARCA, ARSA, RSW. Painter; b. 20.11.42, Abercarn, South Wales. Educ. Newbridge Grammar School; Newport College of Art; Royal College of Art. Taught, Edinburgh College of Art, 1965-68; Granada Arts

Fellow, York University, 1968-69; Edinburgh College of Art, 1969-75; travelled and painted in USA, 1975-76; resumed teaching, Edinbugh College of Art, 1976; one-man exhibitions: Marjorie Parr Gallery, London, 1970, 1972, 1974, Gilbert Parr Gallery, London, 1977, 1980, Fruit Market Gallery, Edinburgh, 1982, Mercury Gallery, London, 1985; Royal College of Art Silver Medal for Painting, 1965. Address: (h.) 6 Fettes Row, Edinburgh, EH3 6SF; T.-031-556 3726.

Evans, Sheriff George James, MA, LLB. Sheriff of Glasgow and Strathkelvin, at Glasgow, since 1983; b. 16.7.44; m.; 2 d. Educ. Ardrossan Academy; Glasgow University; Edinburgh University. Advocate, 1973.

Evans, James, RD, JP, DL, BSc, CEng, FRINA, MIMechE. Managing Director, Eyemouth Boat Building Co. Ltd., since 1968; Chairman, Berwickshire District Council, since 1980; Chairman, Fishing Boat Builders Association, since 1979; b. 9.5.33, South Shields; m., Patricia Alexena Kerr; 1 s.; 2 d. Educ. Merchiston Castle School; Kings College, Durham. Apprenticeship, 1950-56; Royal Navy, 1956-58; YARD, 1958-63; UKAEA, 1963-68; RNR, 1956-80 (retired as Captain (E) RNR); Member, Eyemouth Burgh Council, 1972-75; Berwickshire County Council; Vice-Chairman and Finance Chairman, Berwickshire District Council, 1974-80; Member, Fishing Industry Safety Group; awarded Silver Medal, Nuclear Engineering Society, 1962; Hon ADC, The Queen, 1979-80; Deputy Lieutenant, Berwickshire, since 1978; Chairman, Berwick Freemen's Guild, since 1975. Address: (h.) Makore, Northburn View, Eyemouth, Berwickshire; T.-Eyemouth 50231.

Evans, John, MB, BCh, BSc, MRCP, FRCPsych, DPM. Consultant Adolescent Psychiatrist in charge Young People's Unit, Royal Edinburgh Hospital, since 1967; Honorary Senior Lecturer in Psychiatry, Edinburgh University, since 1972; b. 10.7.26, Wales; m., Dr. Heti Davies; 1 s.; 2 d. Educ. Whitchurch Grammar School; Welsh National School of Medicine. Senior Registrar in Child Psychiatry, Tavistock Clinic, London, 1969-73; Senior Hospital Medical Officer, Cassel Hospital, London, 1973-75; Consultant Child Psychiatrist, Royal Hospital for Sick Children, Edinburgh, 1965-75 (Consultant in Adolescent Psychiatry, since 1966); Founder and Editor, Journal of Adolescence, 1976-84. Publication: Adolescent and Pre-adolescent Psychiatry, 1982. Recreations: gardening; music. Address: (h.) 35 Moray Place, Edinburgh, EH3 6BX; T.-031-225 9506.

Evans, Peter Geoffrey, BMus, ARCM. Freelance Pianist, Teacher and Conductor, since 1974; Member, Scottish Arts Council, since 1984; b. 13.1.50, Redhill, Surrey. Educ. Trinity School, Croydon; Edinburgh University; Hochshule fur Musik, Vienna. Solo piano recitals and performances in various duos and ensembles throughout Britain, as well as in West Germany, Austria, USA and USSR; frequent broadcasts, BBC Radio 3 and Radio Scotland and recordings for BBC TV, Scottish TV, French Radio, Swedish Radio,

Hyperion Records; concert appearances as Soloist with all major professional orchestras in Scotland and National Youth Orchestra of Scotland; Principal Conductor and Co-Founder, Meadows Chamber Orchestra, Edinburgh; close association with the chamber music and masterclasses of Sandor Vegh's International Musicians' Seminar, Cornwall; Member, SAC Music Committee, since 1982. Recreations: theatre; films; tennis; golf. Address: (h.) 114 Comiston Road, Edinburgh, EH10 5QL; T.-031-447 6414.

Evans, Robin Anthony, BSc, MChemA, CChem, FRSC, AIFST. Public Analyst, Tayside Regional Council, since 1975; b. 23.8.39, Penarth, South Glamorganshire; m., Jennifer; 2 s.; 1 d. Educ. Penarth Grammar School; University College of South Wales and Monmouthshire, Cardiff. Assistant Analyst, Glamorgan County Council, 1961-70; Principal Assistant Analyst, Bristol Corporation, 1970-73; Public Analyst and Agricultural Analyst, Dundee Corporation, 1973-75. Honorary Secretary, Association of Public Analysts of Scotland. Recreations: golf and sport in general; hospital radio; media action; gardening. Address: (b.) 24 Mains Loan, Dundee, DD4 7AA; T.-0382 455909.

Eveling, Stanley, BA, BPhil. Playwright; University Fellow, Edinburgh University, since 1984; Television Critic, The Scotsman, since 1970; b. 4.8.25, Newcastle-upon-Tyne; m., Kate Howell; 2 s.; 2 d. Educ. Rutherford College, Newcastle-upon-Tyne; King's College, Newcastle; Lincoln College, Oxford. Usual drab academic life; Senior Lecturer, Department of Philosophy, Edinburgh University, 1961-84; writer of 26 plays for radio, TV and stage, some much travelled and still travelling, many produced for Edinburgh Festival and Traverse Theatre. Recreations: golf; tennis; computer studies. Address: (h.) 30 Comely Bank, Edinburgh, EH4 1AJ; T.-031-332 1905.

Everett, Robert Anthony, BA, BSc, CPhys, MInstP, AFIMA, ASTA. Headteacher, Fort Augustus Secondary School, since 1971; b. 5.6.31, Battle, Sussex; m., Christina Laird Hastings Brown; 3 s.; 2 d. Educ. St. Mary's Academy, Bathgate; Edinburgh University; Moray House College of Education; Open University. National Service, Royal Signals; Teacher of Science, Bathgate Academy; Principal Teacher of Science, Dornoch Academy; Principal Teacher of Physics: Camphill Senior Secondary School, Paisley, Galashiels Academy; Headteacher, Leverhulme Memorial Secondary School, Leverburgh, Isle of Harris. Sometime Secretary, Fort Augustus Village Council; Secretary, Fort Augustus/ Glenmoriston Community Council; Chairman, Fort Augustus Royal British Legion (Scotland); Elder, Fort Augustus Church of Scotland. Recreation: swimming. Address: (h.) The Schoolhouse, Fort Augustus, Inverness-shire, PH32 4DR; T.-0320 6235.

Ewan, Edmund Alan, MA, DipEd, DPhil. Vice-Principal, Moray House College of Education, Edinburgh, since 1984; b. 30.10.31, Bridge of Earn; m., Elizabeth Miller Calder; 2 s. Educ. Perth Academy; St. Andrews University; Oxford

University. Assistant Director of Education, Fife County Council, 1961-66; Head, Department of Educational Management and Administration, Moray House College of Education, 1967-84. Honorary Secretary: Scottish Association for Educational Management and Administration, 1972-81, British Educational Management and Administration Society, 1974-83. Recreation: hill-walking. Address: (b.) Moray House College of Education, Holyrood Road, Edinburgh, EH8 8AQ; T.-031-556 8455.

Ewen, Robert, OBE, TD, MA. Secretary of the University Court, Glasgow University, since 1985; b. 3.3.39, Clydebank; m., Eleanor Irene Grayson; 1 s.; 1 d. Educ. Inverness Royal Academy; Aberdeen University. Aberdeen University: Clerk, Faculty of Arts, 1964-73, Clerk, Senatus Academicus, 1973-79, Deputy Secretary, 1976-85. Lt. Col., Royal Engineers (TA). Recreations: golf; squash; shooting; hill-walking. Address: (b.) University of Glasgow, Glasgow, G12 8QQ; T.-041-339 8855.

Ewing, David John, MA, MD, FRCPEdin. Wellcome Trust Senior Lecturer in Medicine, Edinburgh University, since 1980; Honorary Consultant Physician, Lothian Health Board; b. 27.8.40, London; m., E. Anne Bellamy; 2 d. Educ. Dulwich College; Jesus College, Cambridge; Guy's Hospital, London. Lecturer in Medicine, Edinburgh University. Recreations: reading; walking. Address: (b.) Department of Medicine, Royal Infirmary, Edinburgh, EH3 9YW.

Ewing, Harry. MP (Labour), Falkirk East, since 1983 (Stirling and Falkirk, 1971-74, Stirling, Falkirk and Grangemouth, 1974-83); b. 20.1.31; m.; 1 s.; 1 d. Educ. Beath High School, Cowdenbeath. Under Secretary of State, Scottish Office, 1974-79.

Ewing, Winifred Margaret, MA, LLB. Member (SNP), European Parliament, for Highlands and Islands, since 1979; b. 10.7.29; m.; 2 s.; 1 d. Educ. Queen's Park Senior Secondary School; Glasgow University. Solicitor, 1952; Lecturer in Law, Scottish College of Commerce, 1954-56; private practice, since 1956; Glasgow Bar Association: Secretary, 1961-67, President, 1970-71; MP (SNP), Hamilton, 1967-70, Moray and Nairn, 1974-79; Vice-President, SNP; Member, European Parliament, 1976-79.

F

Fagan, Ken. Leader, City of Dundee District Council, since 1982; Vice-President, COSLA, since 1984; b. 5.5.44, Perth; m., Joan; 2 s.; 2 d. Educ. Perth Academy; Dundee College of Technology (Diploma, Management Studies). Dundee District Council: elected, 1977, City Treasurer, 1980-82. Executive Member, Scottish

Labour Party, 1982-84; Member, Labour Party NEC Local Government Sub-Committee. Address: (b.) City Chambers, Dundee; T.-Dundee 23141.

Fair, James Stuart, MA, LLB, WS, NP. Solicitor; Honorary Sheriff; Lecturer, Dundee University; Clerk, Commissioners of Inland Revenue (Dundee District); Director of various investment trust companies; b. 30.9.30, Perth; m., Anne Lesley Cameron; 2 s.; 1 d. Educ. Perth Academy; St. Andrews University; Edinburgh University. Member: Dundee Port Authority, Dundee University Court, Tayside Health Board; Vice-President, Dundee and Tayside Chamber of Commerce & Industry; Member, Review Committee, Perth Prison; Member, Scottish Solicitors' Discipline Tribunal; Council Member, Society of Writers to Her Majesty's Signet. President, Dundee Choral Union; Secretary and Founder Member, Abbeyfield (Dundee) Society Ltd. Address: (b.) Whitehall Chambers, 11 Whitehall Street, Dundee, DD1 4AE; T.-0382 29111.

Fairbairn of Fordell, Nicholas Hardwick, QC, KLJ, MA, LPB, MP. MP (Conservative), Perth and Kinross, since 1983; Queen's Counsel, since 1972; b. 24.12.33, Edinburgh; m., Suzanne Mary Wheeler; 3 d. Educ. Loretto; Edinburgh University. Called to the Scots Bar, 1957; MP, Kinross and West Perthshire, 1974-83; Solicitor General, 1979-82; Commissioner of Northern Lighthouses, 1979-82. Honorary President and Founder: Society for Preservation of Duddingston, Edinburgh Brook Advisory Centre; Honorary President, Dysart and Dundonald Pipe Band. Publication: Alastair MacLean's Scotland (Contributor). Recreations: painting; broadcasting. Address: (h.) Fordell Castle, by Dunfermline, Fife.

Fairbairn, Sir Robert, Kt (1975), JP. Chairman, Clydesdale Bank plc, 1975-85; b. 25.9.10; m.; 2 s.; 1 d. Educ. Perth Academy. Joined Clydesdale Bank at Perth, 1927; Lt.-Comdr., RNVR, 1939-46; appointed General Manager, Clydesdale Bank, 1958; Director, 1967; Vice-Chairman, 1971; Member, Board of Directors, British National Oil Corporation, 1976-79; President, Institute of Bankers in Scotland, 1961-63; President, Scottish Economic Society, 1966-69; Chairman, Scottish Industrial Development Advisory Board, 1972-81; Vice Chairman, Institute of Fiscal Studies (Scotland), since 1976.

Fairgrieve, James Hanratty, DA, ARSA, RSW. Painter; Lecturer in Drawing and Painting, Edinburgh College of Art, since 1968; b. 17.6.44, Prestonpans; m., Margaret D. Ross; 2 s.; 1 d. Educ. Preston Lodge Senior Secondary School; Edinburgh College of Art. Postgraduate study, 1966-67; Travelling Scholarship, Italy, 1968; President, SSA, 1978-82; exhibited in Britain and Europe, since 1966. Recreation: angling. Address: (h.) Burnbrae, Gordon, Berwickshire; T.-Gordon 357.

Fairgrieve, Sir (Thomas) Russell, CBE, TD, JP. Chairman, Crawford Halls Partnership, Edinburgh; Director, William Baird & Co., PLC, since 1975; Director, Bain Dawes (Scotland) Ltd., Edinburgh, since 1984; b. 3.5.24, Galashiels;

m., Millie Mitchell; 1 s.; 3 d. Educ. St. Mary's School, Melrose; Sedbergh School, Yorkshire. Commissioned, 8th Gurkha Rifles (Indian Army), 1943; Company Commander, 1/8th Gurkha Rifles, 1944-46 (Burma, Malaya and Java); TA, 4th KOSB, 1947-63 (Major). Director, Laidlaw & Fairgrieve Ltd., 1953-68 (Managing Director, 1958-68); Director, Dawson International PLC, 1961-73 (Group Yarn Sales Director, 1965-68); Chairman, Scottish Young Conservatives, 1950-51; President, Scottish Conservative Association, 1965-66; MP, Aberdeenshire West, 1974-83; Chairman, Scottish Conservative Group for Europe, 1974-78; Scottish Conservative Whip, 1975; Chairman, Scottish Conservative Party, 1975-80; Under-Secretary of State for Scotland, 1979-81; Member, Consultative Assembly, Council of Europe and WEU, 1982-83. Address: (h.) Pankalan, Bolside, Galashiels; T.-0896 2278.

Fairrie, Lt. Col. Adam Angus. Regimental Secretary, Queen's Own Highlanders, since 1978; b. 9.12.34, Bromborough; m., Elizabeth Rachel Pryor; 1 s.; 1 d. Educ. Stowe; Royal Military Academy, Sandhurst. Commissioned, Queen's Own Cameron Highlanders, 1955; served Korea, Aden, UK; to Queen's Own Highlanders, 1961; Adjutant 4/5 Camerons TA, 1961-63; seconded to Jamaica Regiment, 1963-65; Staff College, Camberley, 1966; DAA and QMG 12 Infantry Brigade, 1967-68; Company Commander 1st Bn. Queen's Own Highlanders in Sharjah and Edinburgh, 1969-70; Instructor, Junior Div. Staff College, 1970-73; BATT, Sudan, 1973; National Defence College, Latimer, 1973-74; Commanding Officer 1st Bn. Queen's Own Highlanders, 1974-77, in Germany, Belize, UK; retired, 1978; Chairman, Highland Branch, Regimental Association. Publication: Cuidich 'n Righ (a history of the Queen's Own Highlanders). Recreations: enjoying Highland life and music; painting; photography; Highland and regimental history. Address: (b.) RHQ, Queen's Own Highlanders, Cameron Barracks, Inverness; T.-Inverness 224380.

Fairweather, Andrew Burton, TD, MBIM. Director of Office Management, Scottish Office, since 1982; b. 26.2.31, Edinburgh; m., Elizabeth Brown; 3 s. Educ. Royal High School, Edinburgh; Edinburgh University. Clerical Officer, HM Customs and Excise, 1949; Executive Officer: Accountant of Court for Scotland, 1949, Department of Health for Scotland, 1951 (Secretary, Scottish Medical Practices Committee, 1954-58); Higher Executive Officer, Department of Health for Scotland and Scottish Development Department, 1958; Senior Executive Officer, Scottish Development Department, 1965 (Secretary, Rent Assessment Panel for Scotland, 1965-67); Principal: Chief Administrative Officer, Civil Service College, Edinburgh, 1970, Scottish Economic Planning Department, 1972, Scottish Development Department, 1974 (Secretary, Local Government Staff and Property Commissions, 1974-77), Scottish Office Central Services, 1981. Rifle Brigade, RAEC; Royal Scots (TA) and Royal Corps of Transport (TA); Commanding Officer, 495 Liaison Unit (BAOR), Royal Corps of Transport (TA), 1977-81; Colonel, Regular Army Reserve of Officers, 1982. Address: (h.) 127 Silverknowes Gardens, Edinburgh.

Falconer, Allan Leslie. Company Director, Westerfolds Farms Ltd., since 1960; Chairman and Managing Director, Tyock Development Co. Ltd., since 1962; Honorary Sheriff, since 1974; b. 1.6.10, Elgin; m., Margaret Mackenzie Fraser; 3 d. Educ. Elgin Academy; Edinburgh University. Solicitor; Town Clerk, Burgh of Rothes; Major, Seaforth Highlanders; Chairman and Clerk to Salmon District Fishery Boards; Factor to Estates; Clerk, Commissioners of Income Tax, Moray. Recreations: golf; curling; bowling; shooting. Address: (h.) Cromal, Elgin, Morayshire; T.-Elgin 7477.

Falconer, Ian McLeod, BSc, CEng, MICE. Buildings Officer, Dundee University, since 1979; b. 21.7.31, Aberdeen; m., Brenda; 2 s.; 1 d. Educ. Aberdeen Academy; Aberdeen University. Worked in hydro-electric, building and civil engineering contracting throughout Scotland until 1979; commissioned in Royal Engineers during National Service, 1956; appointed Specialist Adviser, House of Commons Committee on Scottish Affairs, 1982, for inquiry into dampness in housing. Recreations: swimming; golf; Rotary; reading. Address: (b.) The University, Dundee; T.-0382 23181.

Fallon, Edward. Member, Lothian Regional Council, since 1982; b. 10.11.47, Edinburgh; m., Jennifer Mary; 1 s.; 1 d. Educ. St. Anthony's RC School, Leith; Edinburgh Building School; Napier College. Member, various school and college Councils; STUC delegate, DHSS Appeal Tribunal. Recreation: golf. Address: (h.) 51 Caiystane Gardens, Edinburgh, EH10 6TD; T.-031-445 1334.

Fallon, Ronald John, BSc, MD, FRCPath, FRCPGlas. Consultant in Laboratory Medicine, Ruchill Hospital, Glasgow, since 1961; Honorary Lecturer in Bacteriology, Immunology and Infectious Diseases, Glasgow University, since 1961; b. 1.2.28, Wallasey; m., Valerie Frances Kirkham; 4 d. Educ. Wallasey Grammar School; Liverpool University. Temporary Assistant Lecturer in Bacteriology, Liverpool University, 1953-55; Junior Bacteriologist, Royal Naval Hospital, Plymouth, 1955-57; Lecturer in Bacteriology, Glasgow University, 1957-61. Member: Advisory Committee on Dangerous Pathogens, Microbiological Advisory Committee DHSS; Member, Microbiology Sub-Committee, Scientific Services Advisory Group, Scottish Health Services Council; Chairman, Scottish Branch, British Society for the Study of Infection; Chairman, Central Sterilising Club. Recreations: singing; country dancing; gardening. Address: (b.) Department of Laboratory Medicine, Ruchill Hospital, Glasgow; T.-041-946 7120.

Farquhar, Charles Don Petrie, JP, DL. Area Manager, Community Industry, since 1972; Member, Dundee District Council, since 1974; b. 4.5.37, Dundee; m., Mary Martin Gardiner; 2 d. Educ. Stobswell Secondary School; Dundee Trades College; NCLC. Time-served engineer; elected Dundee Corporation, 1965; former Magistrate and Chairman of various Committees; served Royal Engineers (TRG NCO); Supervisory Staff, Plant Engineering Division, NCR;

elected Dundee District Council, 1974; Lord Provost and Lord Lieutenant, City of Dundee District, 1975-77; Chairman, District Licensing Board and District Licesning Committee; Chairman, Tayside Committee for Employment of Disabled People. Recreations: fresh-water angling; numismatics; DIY; pool; golf. Address: (h.) 15 Sutherland Crescent, Dundee, DD2 2HP.

Farquhar, Rev. Ronald Middleton, MA, CF, ACF. Minister, Monigaff, since 1957 and Bargrennan, since 1962; Clerk, Wigtown and Stranraer Presbytery, since 1960; b. 26.5.29, London; m., Betty Freda Raybould; 1 s.; 2 d. Educ. Mackie Academy, Stonehaven; East Ham Grammar School for Boys; Edinburgh University. Chaplain, HM Prison, Penninghame, 1971-76 and since 1980; commissioned Chaplain, KOSB Battalion ACF, since 1959; Past Chairman, Wigtownshire Marriage Guidance Council; Past President, Newton Stewart Rotary Club; Chairman, Cree Valley Community Council, since 1983. Recreations: curling; travelling; music appreciation. Address: The Manse of Monigaff, Newton Stewart, Wigtownshire, DG8 6SH; T.-0671 2143.

Farquharson, Captain Alwyne Arthur Compton, MC, JP. Landowner and Farmer; b. 1.05.19, London; m., Frances Strickland Lovell Oldham. Educ. Eton; Oxford University. War Service, 1939-46 (Royal Scots Greys); Member, Aberdeen County Council and Deeside District Council, 1949-75. Address: Invercauld, Braemar, Aberdeenshire; Torloisk, Isle of Mull, Argyll.

Farquharson, Captain Colin Andrew, JP, DL, FRICS. Chartered Surveyor and Land Agent, since 1953; Member, Grampian Health Board, since 1981; Director, MacRobert Farms (Douneside), since 1971; b. 9.8.23; m., Jean Sybil Mary Hamilton (deceased); 2 d.; 1 d. deceased. Educ. Rugby. Grenadier Guards, 1942-48; ADC to Field Marshal Sir Harald Alexander (Earl Alexander of Tunis), 1942-48; Member, Board of Management, Royal Cornhill Hospitals, 1962-74; Chairman, Gordon Local Health Council, 1975-78; DL, Aberdeenshire, 1966; Vice Lord Lieutenant, Aberdeenshire, 1983; Member, Queen's Bodyguard for Scotland (Royal Company of Archers), since 1964. Recreations: shooting; fishing; farming. Address: Whitehouse, Alford, Aberdeenshire.

Farrell, Sheriff James Aloysius, MA, LLB. Sheriff of Glasgow and Strathkelvin, since 1984; b. 14.5.43; m.; 2 d. Educ. St. Aloysius College; Glasgow University; Dundee University. Admitted, Faculty of Advocates, 1974; Advocate-Depute, 1979-83.

Farrington, Brian Francis, BA, MA. Director, Aberdeen University Language Laboratories, since 1972; b. 6.7.25, Dublin; m., Olivia McMahon; 2 s.; 2 d. Educ. St. Columba's College, Co. Dublin; Trinity College, Dublin; Manchester University. Lecturer in English, British Institute in Paris; Charge de Conferences, Institut des Etudes Politiques; ENS de Saint-Cloud; Lecturer in French, Manchester University; Senior

Lecturer in French, Aberdeen University. Publication: Emigrant of a Hundred Townlands (Poems), 1968. Recreation: mountaineering. Address: (b.) 3 Cedar Place, Aberdeen, AB2 3SZ; T.-Aberdeen 636250.

Farrow, Robert Henry, FIHT. Member, Highland Regional Council; Managing Director, Highland Bitumens Ltd.; Director, Road Emulsions Association Ltd.; b. 19.2.23, London; 2 d. Educ. Battersea Polytechnic. War Service, Royal Navy; local poltics, Somerset (sometime Chairman, Somerset County Council SE Area Planning Committee); Mayor of Chard, 1973-74 and 1974-75; Member: CBI Northern Committee, Highlands and Islands Fire Board; Chairman, Nairn District Planning Committee; Chairman, Nairn Local Health Council. Recreations: golf; dramatics; local government service. Address: (h.) 5 Rowan Place, Nairn, 1V12 4TL; T.-Nairn 52809.

Farry, James. Secretary, The Scottish Football League, since 1979; b. 1.7.54, Glasgow; m., Elaine Margaret; 1 s.; 1 d. Educ. Queens Park Secondary School; Hunter High School; Claremont High School. Recreations: occasional fishing; regular spectating football matches. Address: (b.) 188 West Regent Street, Glasgow, G2 4RY; T.-041-248 3844.

Fasken, Robert Alexander, CBE. Governor, Eden Court Theatre, Inverness; Honorary Vice-President, Scottish Youth Hostels Association; b. 5.11.22, Edinburgh; m., Nancy Blanch; 1 s. Educ. George Watson's College. Department of Agriculture and Fisheries for Scotland, 1939-65; Secretary, Advisory Panel on Highlands and Islands, 1961-65; Secretary, Highlands and Islands Development Board, 1965-75; Member, HIDB, 1975-84; Chairman, Highlands and Islands Tourism Council, 1976-84; Member, Scottish Tourist Board, 1975-84. Recreations: reading; chess; gardening. Address: (h.) 79 Stratherrick Road, Inverness, IV4 4LL; T.-0463 233378.

Faulds, Rev. Norman Livingstone, MA, BD. Minister, Granton, Edinburgh, since 1978; b. 17.12.42, Ayr; m., Jennifer Cowan Neil Pennie. Educ. Ayr Academy; Glasgow University; Edinburgh University. Student Assistant, St. Matthew's Church, Edinburgh, 1965-66; Sub Warden, New College Residence, 1966-67; Assistant Minister, Crown Court Church, London, 1967-68; Minister, St. George's-Tillydrone, Aberdeen, 1968-78. Chaplain, Royal Victoria Hospital, Edinburgh, since 1984; Leader, Tell Scotland Student Team, 1964-65; President, Edinburgh University Theological Society, 1966-67. Recreations: travel; photography; Biblical manuscripts. Address: Granton Parish Church, 55 Boswall Parkway, Edinburgh, EH5 2DB; T.-031-552 3033.

Faulkner, Professor Douglas, WhSch, PhD, RCNC, FEng, FRINA, FIStructE, FRSA. Professor and Head, Department of Naval Architecture and Ocean Engineering, Glasgow University; b. 29.12.29, Gibraltar; m., Jenifer Ann Cole-Adams; 3 d. Educ. Sutton High School, Plymouth; HM Dockyard Technical College,

Devonport; Royal Naval College, Greenwich. Aircraft carrier design, 1955-57; production engineering, 1957-59; structural research, NCRE Dunfermline, 1959-63; Assistant Professor of Naval Construction, RNC, Greenwich, 1963-66; Structural Adviser to Ship Department, Bath, 1966-68; Naval Construction Officer attached to British Embassy, Washington DC, 1968-70; Member, Ship Research Committee, National Academy of Sciences, 1968-71; Research Associate and Defence Fellow, MIT, 1970-71; Structural Adviser, Ship Department, Bath, and Merrison Box Girder Bridge Committee, 1971-73; UK Representative, Standing Committee, International Ship Structures Congress, since 1973; Head, Department of Naval Architecture and Ocean Engineering, Glasgow University, since 1973. Recreations: hill-walking; music; chess; GO. Address: (h.) 57 Bellshaugh Place, Glasgow, G12 OPF; T.-041-339 8855.

Faulkner, Geoffrey Edward, MB, ChB, DPM, MRCPsych. Consultant Psychiatrist, since 1957; Medical Administrator, Kingseat Hospital, Aberdeenshire, since 1982; Senior Clinical Lecturer, Department of Mental Health, Aberdeen University; b. 17.6.23, Twickenham; m., Alison Mairi McKenzie (deceased); 2 d. Educ. Priory School, Shrewsbury; Birmingham University. House Officer, Queen Elizabeth Hospital, Birmingham; Senior Registrar, Hollymoor Hospital, Birmingham. Recreations: sailing; fishing; photography; music. Address: (b.) Kingseat Hospital, Newmachar, Aberdeenshire; T.-0224 973 2253.

Fawkes, Rev. George Miller Allan, BA, BSc. Minister, Lonmay linked with Rathen West, since 1979; b. 20.3.35, Glasgow; m., Beatrice B.A. Forbes; 1 s.; 1 d. Educ. Irvine Royal Academy; Glasgow University; Open University; Aberdeen University. FSS, 1961-71; MInstP, 1976-80. Statistician, Pilkington Bros., St. Helens, 1957-58; Education Officer, RAF, 1958-61; Statistician, Stewarts and Lloyds, Clydesdale Works, 1961-64; Lecturer, Inverness Technical College, 1964-77. Recreations: reading; family history; relationship between religion and science. Address: The Manse, Lonmay, Fraserburgh, AB4 4UJ; T.-0346 32227.

Fenton, Alexander, MA, BA, DLitt, FSA, FSA Scot. Director, National Museum of Antiquities of Scotland, since 1978; Research Director, National Museums of Scotland, since 1985; b. 26.6.29, Shotts; m., Evelyn Elizabeth Hunter; 2 d. Educ. Turriff Academy; Aberdeen University; Cambridge University. Senior Assistant Editor, Scottish National Dictionary, 1955-59; part-time Lecturer, English as a Foreign Language, Edinburgh University, 1958-60; National Museum of Antiquities of Scotland: Assistant Keeper, 1959-75, Deputy Keeper, 1975-78; part-time Lecturer, Department of Scottish History, Edinburgh University, since 1974; Honorary Fellow, School of Scottish Studies, since 1969; Foreign Member: Royal Gustav Adolf Academy, Sweden, since 1978, Royal Danish Academy of Sciences and Letters, since 1979; Honorary Member: Volkskundliche Kommission fur Westfalen, since 1980, Hungarian Ethnographical Society, since 1983; Jury Member, Europa Prize for Folk Art, since 1975; President, Permanent International Committee of the International Secretariat for Research on the History of Agricultural Implements; Secretary, Permanently Standing Organising Board, European Ethnological Atlas; President, Scottish Vernacular Buildings Working Group; Secretary, Scottish Country Life Museums Trust; Secretary and Trustee, Friends of the Dictionary of the Older Scottish Tongue; Co-Editor: Tools and Tillage, since 1968, The Review of Scottish Culture, since 1984. Publications: The Various Names of Shetland, 1973, 1977; Scottish Country Life, 1976 (Scottish Arts Council Book Award); The Diary of a Parish Clerk (translation from Danish), 1976; The Island Blackhouse, A Guide to the Blackhouse at 42 Arnol, Lewis, 1978; A Farming Township, A Guide to Auchindrain, the Museum of Argyll Farming Life, 1978; The Northern Isles, Orkney and Shetland, 1978 (Dag Stromback Award); The Rural Architecture of Scotland (Co-author), 1981; The Shape of the Past I, 1985; If All The World Were a Blackbird (translation), 1985. Recreation: languages. Address: (b.) National Museum of Antiquities of Scotland, Queen Street, Edinburgh, EH2 1JD; T.-031-557 3550.

Fenton, Professor George Wallace, MB, FRCPEdin, FRCPsych, MRCP, DPM. Professor of Psychiatry, Dundee University, since 1983; Honorary Consultant Psychiatrist, Tayside Health Board, since 1983; b. 30.7.31, Londonderry; m.; 1 s. Educ. Ballymena Academy; Queen's University, Belfast. Lecturer, Academic Department of Psychiatry, Middlesex Hospital, 1964-66; Maudsley Hospital, London: Consultant Psychiatrist, 1967-75, Consultant in Charge, Epilepsy Unit, 1969-75, Consult Neurophysiologist, 1968-75; Senior Lecturer, Institute of Psychiatry, London University, 1967-75; Professor of Mental Health, Queen's University, Belfast, 1976-83. Publications: Event Related Potentials in Personality and Psychopathology (Co-author), 1982; numerous papers on clinical neurophysiology and neuropsychiatry. Recreations: sailing; history; literature; th Address: (b.) University Department of Psychiatry, Ninewells Hospital, Dundee, DD1 9SY; T.-Dundee 60111, Ext. 2121.

Fenwick, Hubert Walter Wandesford. Writer; b. 17.7.16, Glasgow. Educ. Huntley School, New Zealand; Royal Grammar School, Newcastle-upon-Tyne. Architectural student; qualified, 1950; office of Ian G. Lindsay, then Lorimer & Matthew, Edinburgh; gave up architectural career, 1958; RIBA Examiner for Scotland in History of Architecture, until post abolished; Assistant Secretary and PRO, Scottish Georgian Society, 1960-65; Council Member, Cockburn Association, 1966; Scottish Editor, Church Illustrated, 1959-64; Editor and Manager, Edinburgh Tatler and Glasgow Illustrated, 1966-67; regular contributor to Scots Magazine, 25 years, and other journals. Publications: Architect Royal; Auld Alliance; Scotland's Historic Buildings; Scotland's Castles; Chateaux of France; Scotland's Abbeys and Cathedrals; View of the Lowlands; Scottish Baronial Houses. Recreations: foreign travel; architectural history; sketching and photography (for own books and articles); gardening. Address: 15 Randolph Crescent, Edinburgh, 3; T.-031-225 7982.

Ferguson, Alexander, MA (Hons), LLB. HM Chief Inspector of Schools, since 1982; b. 18.9.28, Coatbridge; m., Margaret Rosalind; 1 s.; 3 d. Educ. Coatbridge Secondary School; Glasgow University. Teacher/Principal Teacher, 1953-67; HM Inspector, 1967-74; HM Inspector (HG), 1974-82. Recreations: gardening; study of city architecture.

Ferguson, Alexander Chapman, OBE. Manager, Aberdeen Football Club, since 1978; b. 31.12.41, Glasgow; m., Catherine; 3 s. Educ. Govan High School. Player: Queens Park, 1958-60, St. Johnstone, 1960-64, Dunfermline, 1964-67, Rangers, 1967-69, Falkirk, 1969-73, Ayr United, 1973-74; Manager: East Stirling, St. Mirren, 1974-78; won two League caps as player (v. England and Northern Ireland, 1967). Honorary Vice-President, Boys Brigade Scotland. Address: (b.) Aberdeen Football Club, Pittodrie Stadium, Aberdeen; T.-Aberdeen 632328.

Ferguson, James Murray, BSc (Econ), MPhil, DipEd, FCIS, FBIM, FRSA, FSA Scot. Principal, Aberdeen College of Commerce, since 1982; b. 21.4.28, Almondbank, Perthshire; m., Moira McDougall; 2 d. Educ. Perth Academy; London University; Edinburgh University; Dundee University; Moray House College of Education. Military Service, 1946-79: full-time, Army Emergency Reserve, Territorials, T&AVR, Regular Army Reserve of Officers (final rank of Major); variety of business appointments, mainly in insurance, investment and finance, 1952-64; lectureships in range of management subjects, various higher educational establishments, 1965-76; Principal, Elmwood College, Fife, 1976-82. Governor: Further Education Staff College, Coombe Lodge, Bristol, Aberdeen College of Education. Recreations: sporting: badminton, tennis, hill-walking; non-sporting: reading, writing, public speaking, local history studies. Address: (h.) 45 Desswood Place, Aberdeen, AB2 4EE; T.-Aberdeen 631480.

Ferguson, Rev. John, Lth. Minister, Portree, since 1980; b. 30.3.37, North Uist; m., Effie MacPhail; 2 s.; 1 d. Educ. Paible School; Glasgow University and Trinity College; Faith Mission Bible College. Evangelism in Ireland and Scotland, 1961-66; Minister, Ness, Isle of Lewis, 1973-80. Publication: Pilgrim's Progress (translated into Gaelic for children). Recreations: fishing; art. Address: Church of Scotland Manse, Portree, Isle of Skye; T.-0478 2019.

Ferguson, John Alexander, BSc, DRCST. Her Majesty's Senior Chief Inspector of Schools, since 1981; b. 16.10.27, Airdrie; m., Jean Stewart; 2 s.; 1 d. Educ. Coatbridge Secondary School; Glasgow University. National Service, 1947-49; Teacher, Airdrie Central School, 1950-51; Coatbridge Technical College: Lecturer, 1951-55, Head, Department of Engineering, 1955-61; HM Inspector of Schools, 1961-72; Assistant Secretary, Scottish Education Department, 1972-75; HM Depute Senior Chief Inspector of Schools, 1975-81. Recreations: tennis; badminton; bridge. Address: (b.) Scottish Education Department, New St. Andrew's House, Edinburgh, EH1 3SY; T.-031-556 8400, Ext. 5459.

Ferguson, John Gordon, MA, BSc. Rector, Linlithgow Academy, since 1972; b. 5.2.27, Edinburgh; m., Rose; 2 d. Educ. George Heriot's School, Edinburgh; Edinburgh University; Heriot-Watt University. Royal Navy, 1946-49; Assistant Teacher of Mathematics: Lasswade Senior Secondary School, 1950-55, Royal High School, Edinburgh, 1955-58; Linlithgow Academy: Principal Teacher of Mathematics, 1959-71, Depute Rector, 1971-72. Member, Modular Mathematics Organisation, since 1972; President, Linlithgow and Bo'ness Rotary Club, 1985-86. Recreation: bowling. Address: (h.) Willowdene, St. Ninian's Road, Linlithgow; T.-0506 844270.

Ferguson, John McNeill, BSc, CChem, FRSC. Rector, Lornshill Academy, Alloa, since 1976; b. 9.5.23, Colintraive, Argyll; m., Margaret Mary Bennett; 1 d. Educ. Dunoon Grammar School; Glasgow University; Jordanhill College of Education. Assistant Chemist, Beatties Bakeries Ltd., Glasgow; Works Chemist, John Laird and Son Ltd., Glasgow; Teacher of Science: Rutherglen Academy, Dunoon Grammar School; Principal Teacher of Science, Rothesay Academy; Principal Teacher of Chemistry, Hutchesons' Girls' Grammar School, Glasgow; Assistant Rector, Johnstone High School; Rector, Sanquhar Academy. Council Member, Headteachers' Association of Scotland; former Governor, Craigie College of Education; Deacon, Alloa Baptist Church. Recreations: gardening; walking; reading. Address: (h.) Colintraive, Cowan Terrace, Dollar, Clackmannanshire, FK14 7AP; T.-02594 2355.

Ferguson, Leonard, MBE (1968), FIH, FRSH. Director of Housing Management, Scottish Special Housing Association, since 1969; b. 30.1.26, Glasgow; m., Valerie A.; 3 s.; 1 d. Educ. Gourock High School. Clerk, British Rail, 1941-43; Ft. Sergeant, RAF, 1943-48; Clerk, Marine Department, British Rail, 1948-50; Clerk, Housing Department, Greenock Corporation, 1950-51; Assistant Housing Manager, Scottish Special Housing Association, 1951-56; Housing Manager, UK Atomic Weapons Establishment, Aldermaston, 1956-57; Housing Manager: Aberdeen County Council, 1957-63, East Kilbride Development Corporation, 1963-69. Member, Management Committee, Ark Housing Association; Past Chairman, Chief Officers Group, Institute of Housing, Scotland; Member, Royal Observer Corps. Recreations: gardening; sailing; hill-walking. Address: (b.) 15/21 Palmerston Place, Edinburgh, EH12 5AJ; T.-031-225 1281.

Ferguson, Patricia Ann Hatrick, BSc, AMICE. Director, Hatrick Bruce Group, since 1977; Member, Fife Health Board, since 1983 (Vice Chairman, since 1985); Member, General Practice Finance Corporation, since 1984; Member, Glenrothes Development Corporation, since 1985; Member, National Insurance Claims and Social Security Tribunals, Department of Health and Social Security, since 1984; b. Dundee; m., Euan Bruce Ferguson. Educ. St. Margaret's, Aberdeen; Dundee High School; St. Andrews University; Royal Military College of Science. Civil Engineer, George Wimpey, 1972-73; Resi-

dent Engineer, Redpath Dorman Long (North Sea), 1973-77. Recreations: dressage; music. Address: (h.) Lydiard House, Milton of Balgonie, Glenrothes, Fife, KY7 6QD; T.-0592 758305.

Ferguson, Robert Greig, MREHIS, MIWM. Director of Environmental Health, Caithness District Council, since 1975; b. 30.7.42, Saltcoats; m., Ruth; 1 s.; 2 d. Educ. Ardrossan Academy; School of Building, Cambuslang; David Dale College, Glasgow; Coatbridge Technical College; Dundee University. Assistant Sanitary Inspector, Clackmannan County Council, 1966-67; District Sanitary Inspector, Angus County Council, 1967-70; Caithness County Council: Depute County Sanitary Inspector, 1970-71, County Sanitary Inspector, 1971-75. Recreations: golf; snooker. Address: (b.) Council Offices, 77 High Street, Wick; T.-Wick 3761, Ext. 231.

Ferguson, William, BSc, CEng, FICE, FIPHE, MIWPC. Assistant Chief Engineer, Scottish Development Department, since 1977; b. Ayr; m., Helen Moir Manson; 1 s.; 1 d. Educ. Ayr Academy; London University; Delft Technological University. Various appointments in civil and public health engineering, including Chief Assistant Engineer, Midlothian County Council, and Engineering Inspector, Scottish Development Department. Chairman, Scottish Centre, Institution of Public Health Engineers, 1969-70. Recreations: family; DIY; skiing. Address: (h.) 13 Barnton Park Drive, Edinburgh, EH4 6HF; T.-031-336 4602.

Ferguson, Rev. William Brown, BA, BD. Minister, Annan Old Parish Church, since 1974; b. 15.12.46, Bonnybridge; m., Marian Isabella Charters; 2 d. Educ. Denny High School; Durham University; Edinburgh University. Assistant Minister, St. Columba's Church of Scotland, London, 1971-74; Moderator, Annandale and Eskdale Presbytery, 1979-80. Recreations: reading; talking. Address: The Manse, 10 Hecklegirth Road, Annan, DG12 6HN; T.-Annan 3438.

Ferguson, William James. Farmer, since 1954; Vice Chairman, Aberdeen and District Milk Marketing Board; Vice Chairman, North of Scotland College of Agriculture, since 1984; b. 3.4.33, Aberdeen; m., Carroll Isobella Milne; 1 s.; 3 d. Educ. Turriff Academy; North of Scotland College of Agriculture. National Service, 1st Bn., Gordon Highlanders, 1952-54; serving in Malaya during the emergency. Member, Scottish Country Life Museums Trust Ltd.; Member, Technical Committee, Crichton Royal Dairy Farm, Dumfries; Member, Council of Scottish Agricultural Colleges; Member, Technical Committee, Macaulay Institute of Soil Research; Chairman, Farm, Forestry, Wildlife Advisory Group, Grampian Region; Member, Technical Committee, Scottish Farm Buildings Investigation Unit. Recreations: golf; field sports. Address: Rothiebrisbane, Fyvie, Turriff, Aberdeenshire, AB5 8LE; T.-06516 213.

Fergusson of Kilkerran, Sir Charles, 9th Bt; b. 10.5.31; m., Hon. Amanda Mary Noel-Paton; 2 s. Educ. Eton; Edinburgh and East of Scotland College of Agriculture.

Fergusson, James A., MB, ChB, MRCGP. Regional Medical Officer, Scottish Home and Health Department, since 1973; b. 17.7.24, Glasgow; m., Christine Irvine; 2 s.; 1 d. Educ. Hillhead High School; Glasgow University. Medical Assistant: Gynaecology Department, Western Infirmary, Glasgow, 1948, Obstetric Department, Stobhill Hospital, Glasgow, 1948-49, Medical Department, Victoria Infirmary, Glasgow, 1949; General Medical Practitioner, Glasgow, 1949-73; Physician, Cowglen Hospital, 1964-73. Session Clerk, Giffnock South Parish Church. Publication: Potassium Studies in Elderly, 1971. Recreations: golf; fishing. Address: (h.) 10 Dorian Drive, Glasgow, G76 7NP; T.-041-638 9847.

Fergusson, Thomas Edgar Syme, MB, ChB, MRCGP, DRCOG. Regional Medical Officer, Scottish Home and Health Department, since 1974; b. 24.10.29, Glasgow; m., Charis Wilson Boyle; 1 s.; 2 d. Educ. Hillhead High School; Glasgow University. General Practitioner, 1954-74; part-time Medical Officer, Duntocher Hospital, 1961-74. Recreations: golf; gardening; music. Address: (h.) 1 Edgehill Road, Bearsden, Glasgow, G61 3AD; T.-041-942 0380.

Fernie, Professor Eric Campbell, BA, FSA, FSA Scot. Watson Gordon Professor of Fine Art, Edinburgh University, since 1984; b. 9.6.39, Edinburgh; m., Margaret Lorraine; 1 s.; 2 d. Educ. Marist Brothers College, Johannesburg; Witwatersrand University; London University. Lecturer, Witwatersrand University, 1964-67; East Anglia University: Lecturer, 1967-74; Senior Lecturer, 1974-84, Dean, School of Fine Art and Music, 1977-81. Treasurer, Association of Art Historians. Publication: The Architecture of the Anglo-Saxons. Address: (b.) 19 George Square, Edinburgh, EH8 9LD; T.-031-667 1011.

Ferrier, Rev. Hugh M., MA. Minister, North Free Church of Scotland, Inverness, since 1975; b. 11.6.25, Greenock; m., Georgina M. Cameron; 3 s.; 1 d. Educ. Greenock Highlanders Academy and High School; Edinburgh University; Free Church College, Edinburgh. Ordained, 1952; Minister: Golspie, 1952-60, Knockbain, Ross-shire, 1960-63, Partick, Glasgow, 1963-75; Vice-Convener, Training of Ministry Committee, Free Church of Scotland; Moderator, General Assembly, 1978. Address: Aden House, 5 Annfield Road, Inverness; T.-0463 231981.

Ferrier, Professor Robert Patton, MA (Cantab), BSc, PhD, FInstP, FRSE. Professor of Natural Philosophy, Glasgow University, since 1973; b. 4.1.34, Dundee; m., Valerie Jane Duncan; 2 s.; 1 d. Educ. Morgan Academy, Dundee; Queen's College, Dundee, St. Andrews University. Scientific Officer, AERE Harwell, 1959-61; Research Associate, Massachusetts Institute of Technology, 1961-62; Senior Research Assistant, Cavendish Laboratory, Cambridge, 1962-65; Fellow, Fitzwilliam College, Cambridge, 1964-73; Assistant Director of Research, Cavendish Laboratory, Cambridge, 1965-71; Lecturer in Physics, Cambridge University, 1971-73; Guest Scientist, IBM Research Division, California,

1972-73. Member, Physics Committee, SERC, 1979-82 (Chairman, Semiconductor and Surface Physics Sub-Committee, 1979-82). Recreations: tennis; reading crime novels; garden and house maintenance. Address: Department of Natural Philosophy, The University, Glasgow, G12 8QQ; T.-041-339 8855, Ext. 7388.

Ferrier, Baron, (Victor Ferrier Noel-Paton), ED, DL. Life Peer; b. 1900; m., Joane Mary (deceased); 1 s.; 3 d. Educ. Cargilfield; Edinburgh Academy. Former Company Director, India and UK; Past Chairman, Federation of Electricity Undertakings of India and Indian Roads and Transport Development Association; Deputy Speaker, House of Lords, 1970-73; Member, Queen's Bodyguard for Scotland (Royal Company of Archers). Address: (h.) Kilkerran, Maybole, Ayrshire.

Ferrier, Rev. Walter McGill, MA (Hons), BD. Minister, St. Andrew's Church, North Berwick, since 1952; b. 20.4.18, Buckhaven, Fife; m., Gillian Mary George; 2 s. Educ. Bathgate Academy; Edinburgh University. Assistant Minister, St. Michael's Church, Dumfries; Minister, High Church, Airdrie, 1946-52. Member, North Berwick Community Council, 1975-79; President, North Berwick Rotary Club, 1973. Publications: The North Berwick Story, 1980; The Last Hundred Years (history of Church), 1983. Recreations: repairing and maintaining talking books for the blind; local history; wine-making. Address: Manse of St. Andrew, 50 St. Baldred's Road, North Berwick, EH39 4PU; T.-0620 2803.

Ferrier, William George, BSc, PhD. Senior Lecturer in Physics, Dundee University, since 1968 (Director, Schools Liaison, since 1974); b. 28.9.30, Dundee; m., Nancy; 2 d. Educ. Morgan Academy; University College, Dundee. Scientific Officer, Aldermaston, 1954-56; Research Scientist, British Rayon Research Association, 1956-57. Past President, Abertay Rotary Club. Recreation: golf. Address: (h.) 15 Castleroy Crescent, Broughty Ferry; T.-0382 77179.

Fewson, Professor Charles Arthur, BSc, PhD, FRSE, FIBiol. Titular Professor, Department of Biochemistry, Glasgow University, since 1982; b. 8.9.37, Selby, Yorkshire; m., Margaret C.R. Moir; 2 d. Educ. Hymers College, Hull; Nottingham University; Bristol University. Research Fellow, Cornell University, New York, 1961-63; Department of Biochemistry, Glasgow University: Assistant Lecturer, 1963-64, Lecturer, 1964-68, Senior Lecturer, 1968-79, Reader, 1979-82. Recreation: watching cricket. Address: (h.) 39 Falkland Street, Glasgow, G12 9QZ; T.-041-339 1304.

Fiddes, Sheriff James Raffan, QC (Scot). Sheriff of South Strathclyde, Dumfries and Galloway, at Hamilton, since 1977; b. 1.2.19. Educ. Aberdeen Grammar School; Glasgow University; Balliol College, Oxford. Advocate, 1948.

Fielding, Mary. Member, Sutherland District Council, since 1984; b. 21.2.30, Cleethorpes; m., Ronald Fielding; 1 s.; 2 d. Secretary, Sutherland Federation, SWRI, 1979-85 (Chairman,

1985); President, Red Cross, Brora, since 1984. Recreation: Producer, Youth Drama Group, annual pantomimes, etc. Address: (h.) Montrose Cottage, 1 High Street, Brora.

Fife, 3rd Duke of, (James George Alexander Bannerman Carnegie). Vice-President, British Olympic Association; Vice-Patron, Braemar Royal Highland Society; b. 23.9.29; m., Hon. Caroline Cicely Dewar (m. diss.); 1 s.; 1 d. Educ. Gordonstoun. Address: (h.) Elsick House, Stonehaven, Kincardineshire, AB3 2NT.

Finch, Professor Ronald George, BA (Hons), MA, PhD. Professor of German Language and Literature, Glasgow University, since 1974; b. 19.10.25, Barmouth, Wales; m., Esther Marian Martin; 1 s.; 1 d. Educ. Ardwyn School, Aberystwyth; University College of Wales, Aberystwyth: University College of Wales, Aberystwyth: Assistant, Department of German, 1948; Assistant Lecturer in German, 1949; Lecturer, 1951; Queen's University, Belfast: Grade A Lecturer in German, 1954, Senior Lecturer, 1962, Reader, 1968, Professor, 1970. Recreations: walking; foreign travel. Address: (b.) Department of German Language and Literature, Modern Languages Building, Glasgow University, Glasgow, G12 8QQ; T.-041-339 8855.

Findlay, Alexander, MBE. Chairman, Lothian Health Board, since 1984 (Member, since 1974); Member, Board of Management, Royal Edinburgh Hospital Group, since 1971; b. 9.5.26, Dundee; m., Margaret Milne; 2 s. Educ. Harris Academy, Dundee. Joined GPO Telephones as apprentice, 1942; worked in various divisions until retiring from Executive Grouping, 1984. Chief Scouts Award for services to Scouting, 1978; Penicuik Town Councillor, 1971-74. Recreations: golf; travel. Address: (h.) 54 Rullion Road, Penicuik, Midlothian; T.-0968 73443.

Findlay, James Gordon, QBE (1979), QJM, JP. Member, Tayside Regional Council, since 1975; Chairman, Angus Justices Committee, since 1968; Farmer, since 1945; Director, Animal Diseases Research Organisation; Member, Hill Farming Advisory Committee, since 1962; b. 31.8.16, Angus; b. Annie Lamond; 1 s.; 3 d. Educ. Morgan Academy. Shepherd, 1931-39; soldier, 1939-45; Farm Manager, 1945; Governor, East of Scotland College of Agriculture, 1954-70; County Councillor, 1951-75; Vice-Convener, County of Angus, 1971-75 (Chairman, Planning Committee, 1968-75); Chairman, District Courts Association of Scotland, 1983-84; President, Blackface Sheep Breeders Association, 1974-76; Life Member, Royal Highland and Agricultural Society; Member, Panel of Agricultural Arbiters. Recreations: dog handling; historical study; dialect preservation. Address: (h.) Linrie Herdhill, Kirriemuir, Angus; T.-Kirriemuir 73427.

Findlay, Richard, DDA. Managing Director, Radio Forth, since 1977; m., Elspeth; 2 s.; 1 d. Educ. Royal Scottish Academy of Music and Drama. Chairman, Association of Independent Radio Contractors; Director: Radio Marketing Bureau Ltd., Fruit Market Gallery Ltd.; Consultant, Scottish Committee, International Youth Year, 1985; Member, Scottish Community Education Council. Address: (b.) Radio Forth Ltd., Forth House, Forth Street, Edinburgh.

Findlay, Richard Martin, LLB, NP. Partner, Ranken & Reid, SSC, Edinburgh, since 1979; b. 18.12.51, Aberdeen. Educ. Gordon Schools, Huntly; Aberdeen University. Trained, Wilsone & Duffus, Advocates, Aberdeen; Legal Assistant, Commercial Department, Maclay Murray & Spens, Glasgow and Edinburgh. Business Manager, Edinburgh Music Theatre Company; Director, Krazy Kat Theatre Company Ltd.; Company Secretary and Business Manager, Performing Arts Ensemble Ltd.; Executive Committee Member, St. John's Association of Scotland (Edinburgh). Recreations: music; theatre; opera; cinema. Address: 7 Albyn Place, Edinburgh, EH2 4NN; T.-031-226 6576.

Findlay, Robert Jones, MA (Hons). Head Teacher, Loudoun Academy, Galston, since 1979; b. 18.12.34, Kilmarnock; m., Ellen Cameron; 1 s.; 1 d. Educ. Kilmarnock Academy; Glasgow University. Teacher of Modern Languages: Carrick Academy, Maybole, Ayr Academy; Principal Teacher of Modern Languages, Cumnock Academy; Assistant Head Teacher, James Hamilton Academy, Kilmarnock; Depute Head Teacher, Greenwood Academy, Irvine. Recreations: curling; fishing; rugby supporter. Address: (h.) 12 Woodend Road, Alloway, Ayr; T.-0292 41275.

Finlay, Ian, CBE, MA, HRSA. Professor of Antiquities, Royal Scottish Academy; Writer and Art Historian; b. 2.12.06, Auckland, New Zealand; m., Mary Scott Pringle; 2 s.; 1 d. Educ. Edinburgh Academy; Edinburgh University. Joined Royal Scottish Museum, 1932; Deputy Regional Information Officer Scotland (Ministry of Information), 1942-45; Secretary, Royal Fine Art Commission for Scotland, 1953-61; Royal Scottish Museum: Keeper, Department of Art and Ethnography, 1955-61, Director, 1961-71. Former Member: International Council of Museums, Counseil de Direction Gazette des Beaux Arts; former Vice-Chairman, Scottish Arts Council; Freeman, City of London; Member, Livery Worshipful Company of Goldsmiths; Guest, State Department, US, 1960. Publications: Scotland, 1945; Scottish Art, 1945; Art in Scotland, 1948; Scottish Crafts, 1948; A History of Scottish Gold and Silver Work, 1956; Scotland (enlarged edition), 1957; The Lothians, 1960; The Highlands, 1963; The Lowlands, 1967; Celtic Art: An Introduction, 1973; Priceless Heritage: The Future of Museums, 1977; Columba, 1979. Recreation: gardening. Address: (h.) Currie Riggs, Balerno, Midlothian, EH14 5AG; T.-031-449 4249.

Finlayson, Geoffrey Beauchamp Alistair Moubray, MA, BLitt, FRHistS. Reader in Modern History, Glasgow University, since 1982; b. 17.7.34, Campsie; m., Elizabeth Frew Dempster; 2 d. Educ. Melville College, Edinburgh; Glasgow Academy; Glasgow University; Balliol College, Oxford. Joined Glasgow University, 1959, as

Assistant Lecturer, then Lecturer, then Senior Lecturer (Head, Department of Modern History, 1979-82); Visiting Professor, Queens College of City University of New York, 1972-73. Session Clerk, Newlands (South) Church, Glasgow, 1977-82; Member, History Panel, Scottish Universities Council on Entrance; Observer, History Panel, Scottish Examination Board; Life Member, Fife, Kinross and Clackmannan Society; Member, Westbourne School for Girls Ltd., Glasgow. Publications: The Seventh Earl of Shaftesbury, 1981 (Scottish Arts Council Book Award); England in the Eighteen Thirties, Decade of Reform, 1969. Recreations: music; cricket. Address: (h.) 11 Burnhead Road, Glasgow, G43 2SU; T.-041-637 2418.

Finlayson, Niall Diarmid Campbell, MB, ChB, PhD, FRCP, FRCPEdin. Consultant Physician, Edinburgh Royal Infirmary, since 1973; Honorary Senior Lecturer, Department of Medicine, Edinburgh University, since 1973; b. 21.4.39, Georgetown, Guyana; m., Dale Kristin Anderson; 1 s.; 1 d. Educ. Loretto School, Musselburgh; Edinburgh University. Lecturer in Therapeutics, Edinburgh University, 1965-69; Assistant Professor of Medicine, New York Hospital-Cornell Medical College, New York, 1970-72. Address: (h.) 10 Queens Crescent, Edinburgh, EH9 2AZ; T.-031-667 9369.

Finnie, James Ross, CA. Chairman, Scottish Liberal Party, since 1982; Member, Inverclyde District Council, since 1977; Director, James Finlay Corporation Ltd., since 1978; b. 11.2.47, Greenock; m., Phyllis Sinclair; 1 s.; 1 d. Educ. Greenock Academy. Member, Executive Committee, Scottish Council (Development and Industry), since 1976; Convener, Planning and Development Committee, Inverclyde District Council, 1977-80; Vice Chairman, Scottish Liberal Party, 1980-82. Address: (h.) 97 Octavia Terrace, Greenock, PA16 7PY; T.-0475 31495.

Fisher, Rev. Ian Riddock, MA. Minister, Fernhill and Cathkin Parish Church, Rutherglen, since 1972; Convener, Buildings and Mission Committee, Glasgow Presbytery, since 1981; b. 12.2.33, Glasgow; m., Mairi Matheson; 2 d. Educ. Kelvinside Academy, Glasgow; Glasgow University; Edinburgh University. Scottish Travelling Secretary, Inter-Varsity Fellowship, 1960-64; Minister, Maybole West Parish Church, 1964-72. Recreations: walking; reading. Address: 82 Blairbeth Road, Rutherglen, Glasgow, G73 4JA; T.-041-634 1508.

Fitzgerald, William Knight, CBE, LLD, JP, DL. Convener, Tayside Regional Council, since 1978; Chairman, Tay Road Bridge Joint Board, since 1975 (and 1970-73); b. 19.3.09, Potchestroom, South Africa; m., 1, Elizabeth Grant (deceased); 2, Margaret Wilkie; 3 s. Educ. Robertson Grammar School, South Africa. Member, Dundee University Court, since 1970; former Lord Provost of Dundee and City Treasurer; Past President, Convention of Scottish Local Authorities; Member, Board of Directors, Dundee High School; former Vice Chairman, Dundee College of Art and Technology; President, Dundee Battalion, Boys' Brigade; Honorary

President: Dundee Business Club, Dundee and District Retirement Council; Chairman, Dundee Prisoners' Aid Society; President, Tayside Community Relations Council. Recreations: gardening; reading. Address: (h.) 1 Roxburgh Terrace, Dundee; T.-Dundee 68475.

FitzPatrick, Ewart Adsil, PhD. Senior Lecturer, Soil Science Department, Aberdeen University, since 1969; b. 17.10.26, Bridgetown, Barbados; m., Morag Sutherland; 1 s.; 1 d. Educ. Harrison College, Barbados; Imperial College of Tropical Agriculture, Trinidad. Aberdeen University: Assistant, 1951-54, Lecturer, 1954-69. Publications: Pedology: A Systematic Approach to Soil Science; An Introduction to Soil Science; Soils, Their Formation, Classification and Distribution; Micromorphology of Soils. Address: (b.) Department of Soil Science, Aberdeen University, Aberdeen; T.-0224 40241, Ext. 5674.

Fitzpatrick, Joseph. Member, Kirkcaldy District Council (Vice-Chairman, Planning Committee); Community Education Worker, Glenrothes; b. 5.8.57, Irvine; m., Rosemary A. Johnston. Educ. St. Michael's Academy, Kilwinning; Moray House College, Edinburgh (Diploma in Community Education). Secretary, Glenrothes South Labour Party. Recreations: reading; swimming; current affairs. Address: (h.) 160 Dunbeath Drive, Pitteuchar, Glenrothes, Fife.

Fleming, Archibald Macdonald, MA, BCom, PhD. Director, Management Development Programmes, Strathclyde Business School, Strathclyde University, since 1984; Lecturer, Department of Information Science, Strathclyde University, since 1968; Consultant on Management Training and Development, since 1970; b. 19.6.36, Glasgow; m., Joan Moore; 1 s.; 1 d. Educ. Langholm Academy; Dumfries Academy; Edinburgh University. W. & T. Avery, 1961-63; IBM (UK) Ltd., 1963-64; Sumlock Comptometer Ltd., 1964-68; Consultancies: Scottish Co-operative Wholesale Society, 1969, Hotel and Catering Industry Training Board, 1971, Scottish Engineering Employers Association, 1973. Member, Strathclyde Children's Panel; Member, Committee on Food Processing Opportunities in Scotland, Scottish Council (Development and Industry). Publication: Scottish Business Dictionary (with B. McKenna). Recreation: reading, observing and talking on Scotland and the Scots. Address: (b.) 130 Rottenrow, Glasgow, G4 0GE; T.-041-552 7141.

Fleming, Ian, RSA, RSW, RWA, DA, LLD (Aberdeen University, 1984). Painter; b. 19.11.06, Glasgow; m., Catherine Margaret Weetch; 1 s.; 2 d. Educ. Hyndland School, Glasgow; Glasgow School of Art; Jordanhill College of Education. Lecturer, Glasgow School of Art, 1931-40; War Service, 1940-43: Glasgow Police (Maryhill F Division), direct commission into Army, 1943-46, service in Normandy, Belgium, Germany; Lecturer, Glasgow School of Art, 1946-48; Warden, Patrick Allen-Fraser Art College, Hospitalfield, 1948-54; Head, Grays School of Art, Robert Gordon's Institute of Technology, 1954-72. Recreations: none, except art. Address: (h.) 15 Fonthill Road, Aberdeen, AB1 2UN; T.-0224 580680.

Fleming, John Baxter, RSW, DA, MSIAD, Hon RGI. Artist; b. 13.9.12, Dumbarton; m., Helen Macfarlane Stewart; 2 s. Educ. Dumbarton Academy; Glasgow School of Art. Interior Designer, 1935-39; produced colour schemes for many Glasgow cinemas; Radio Officer, 1940-45; Senior Lecturer, then Senior Tutor, then Academic Registrar, Glasgow School of Art, 1946-77; illustrated 1,000 articles by Professor Meiklejohn (MFMM) in Glasgow Herald; Honorary Secretary, Royal Glasgow Institute of the Fine Arts, 1964-71; designed Scottish regional 6d stamp, 1959. Publications (as Illustrator): As The Falcon Her Bells; Science in Focus; Science in Action; A Galloway Shepherd; Pioneers of Science; Human Engineering. Recreation: bird watching. Address: (h.) Rockhouse, 23 Shoregate, Crail, Fife, KY10 3SU; T.-Crail 50493.

Fleming, Maurice. Editor, The Scots Magazine, since 1974; b. Blairgowrie; m., Nanette Dalgleish; 2 s.; 1 d. Educ. Blairgowrie High School. Trained in hotel management before entering journalism; worked on various magazines; has had three full-length plays performed professionally, as well as one-act plays by amateurs; regular Drama Critic, Scottish Theatre News; founder Member: Traditional Music and Song Association of Scotland, Scottish Poetry Library; Chairman, Blairgowrie, Rattray and District Civic Trust; Past Chairman, Blair in Bloom. Recreations: theatre; reading; bird-watching; enjoying the countryside; folksong and folklore. Address: (h.) Craigard, Perth Road, Blairgowrie; T.-Blairgowrie 3633.

Fleming, Thomas Bryan, CA. Managing Director, The Metallic Manufacturing Co. Ltd., Ardrossan, since 1981; Council Member, Institute of Chartered Accountants of Scotland; b. 31.7.32, Glasgow; m., Mary Christine St. Clair Reid (deceased); 1 s.; 1 d. Educ. Allan Glen's School. Apprentice Chartered Accountant, 1949-55; RAF, 1956-57; Audit Clerk, Fraser, Lawson & Laing, CAs, 1958-61; Accountant, Blackwood, Morton & Sons Ltd., 1961-70; Financial Director, Metallic Manufacturing Co. Ltd., 1970-81. Recreations: music; mountaineering. Address: (h.) Townend House, Dalry, Ayrshire; T.-029 483 2020.

Fleming, Tom. Artistic Director, Scottish Theatre Company; b. 29.6.27, Edinburgh. Co-Founder, Edinburgh Gateway Company, 1953; directed and acted in numerous productions there; joined Royal Shakespeare Company at Stratford upon Avon, 1962, and played several classical roles, including Brutus in Julius Caesar, the Earl of Kent in King Lear, and the title role in Cymberline; toured with RSC in USSR, USA and Europe, 1964; appointed Director, new Royal Lyceum Theatre Company, 1965; there played title role in Galileo; appeared on television in title role of Jesus of Nazareth; Television Commentator on ceremonial occasions; played Divine Correction, The Thrie Estates, Edinburgh Festival, 1959 and 1973; author of play, Miracle at Midnight.

Fletcher, Alexander. MP (Conservative), Edinburgh Central, since 1983 (Edinburgh North, 1973-83); Chartered Accountant; b. 26.8.29.

Educ. Greenock High School. Member, East Kilbride Development Corporation, 1971-73; Member, Select Committee on Science and Technology, 1974-76; Member, European Parliament, 1976-77; Under Secretary of State for Scotland, 1979-83; Under-Secretary of State for Industry, 1983-85.

Fletcher, Duncan Johnston Brown, MB, ChB, DPH, FFCM, MIMC. Community Medicine Specialist, Greater Glasgow Health Board, since 1974; b. 11.4.22, Glasgow; m., Jessie Olive Johnston; 1 s.; 2 d. Educ. Hutchesons' Grammar School, Glasgow; Glasgow University. Accounts and Statistics Clerk, Clyde Navigation Trust; Royal Navy (Combined Operations), Sub-Lt. (E), RNVR; Medical Officer, Public Health Department, Glasgow Corporation; Surgeon Lt., RNR, Royal Navy; Deputy Medical Superintendent, Glasgow Royal Infirmary; Medical Superintendent, Greenock and District, Dunoon and Rothesay Hospitals. Former Committee Member, Epilepsy Association of Scotland; President, Scottish Conjurers' Association; Secretary, Scottish Association of Magical Societies; Member, Inner Magic Circle. Address: (b.) Western Infirmary, Glasgow; T.-041-339 8822.

Fletcher, Malcolm, MB, ChB, FRCPGlas, DPhysMed. Consultant in Geriatric Medicine, Glasgow Royal Infirmary, since 1965; b. 29.11.20, Giffnock; m., Nancy Dempster Baxter; 2 s.; 1 d. Educ. High School of Glasgow; St. Andrews University. Junior House Surgeon, Victoria Infirmary, Glasgow; Royal Army Medical Corps, 1944-48 (Specialist in Physical Medicine, RAMC, Scottish Command, 1947-48); Senior Registrar, Department of Physical Medicine, St. Helier Hospital, Surrey, 1950-54; Registrar in Medicine, Glasgow Royal Infirmary, 1955-60; Senior Hospital Medical Officer, Gartloch Hospital, Glasgow, 1960-65. Member, Glasgow NE Psychiatric Hospitals Board of Management, 1967-74; President, Glasgow Eastern Medical Society, 1981-82; President, Scottish Society of Rehabilitation Medicine, 1981-83. Recreations: gardening; golf; skiing. Address: (h.) Barbush, 3 Orchard Drive, Giffnock, Glasgow.

Fletcher, Stewart, BSc, MIBiol, MB, ChB, FRCPath. Senior Lecturer in Pathology, Edinburgh University; Honorary Consultant, Lothian Health Board; b. 8.4.32, Glasgow; m., Lorna Campbell Dryburgh; 3 d. Educ. Hillhead High School, Glasgow; Glasgow University. Bacteriologist, Western Infirmary, Glasgow, 1959-61; Pathologist, Glasgow University (Western Infirmary and Royal Hospital for Sick Children), 1961-66. Recreations: reading; thinking and working in the sciences and engineering. Address: (h.) 56 Polwarth Terrace, Edinburgh, EH11 1NJ; T.-031-337 5504.

Flett, James. JP. Chairman, City of Edinburgh Valuation Appeal Committee; Honorary Sheriff, Lothians and Borders; b. 26.1.17, Findochty; m., Jean Walker Ross; 1 s. Educ. Findochty Public School; Heriot-Watt University; Royal Military College, Sandhurst. Commissioned, Seaforth Highlanders; Chief Official, Royal Burgh of

Linlithgow (retired). Governor, West Lothian Educational Trust; Member, JP Advisory Committee. Address: (h.) Craigenroan, Linlithgow, West Lothian; T.-Linlithgow 842344.

Flint, Professor David, TD, MA, BL, CA. Professor of Accountancy, Glasgow University, 1964-85 (Vice-Principal, 1981-85); b. 24.2.19, Glasgow; m., Dorothy Mary Maclachlan Jardine; 2 s.; 1 d. Educ. High School of Glasgow; Glasgow University. Royal Signals, 1939-46 (Major; mentioned in Despatches); Partner, Mann Judd Gordon & Company, Chartered Accountants, Glasgow, 1951-71; Lecturer (part-time), Glasgow University, 1950-60; Dean, Faculty of Law, 1971-73; Council Member, Scottish Business School, 1971-77; Institute of Chartered Accountants of Scotland: President, 1975-76, Vice-President, 1973-75, Convener, Research Advisory Committee, 1974-75 and 1977-84, Convener, Working Party on Future Policy, 1976-79, Convener, Taxation Review and Research Sub-Commitee, 1960-64; Trustee, Scottish Chartered Accountants Trust for Education, since 1981; Member, Management Training and Development Committee, Central Training Council, 1966-70; Member, Management and Industrial Relations Committee, Social Science Research Council, 1970-72 and 1978-80; Member, Social Sciences Panel, Scottish Universities Council on Entrance, 1968-72; Chairman, Association of University Teachers of Accounting, 1969; Member, Company Law Committee, Law Society of Scotland, 1976-85; Scottish Economic Society: Treasurer, 1954-62, Vice-President, since 1977; Member, Commission for Local Authority Accounts in Scotland, 1978-80; President, European Accounting Association, 1983-84. Recreation: golf. Address: (h.) 3 Merrylee Road, Newlands, Glasgow, G43 2SH; T.-041-637 3060.

Flockhart, (David) Ross, BA, BD. Director, Scottish Council for Community and Voluntary Organisations, since 1972; b. 20.3.27, Newcastle, NSW, Australia; m., Pamela Ellison Macartney; 3 s.; 1 d.; 1 d. (deceased). Educ. Knox Grammar School, Sydney; Sydney University; Edinburgh University. Royal Australian Engineers, 1945-46; Chaplain to Overseas Students, Edinburgh, 1955-58; Parish Minister (Church of Scotland), Northfield, Aberdeen, 1958-63; Warden, Carberry Tower, Musselburgh, 1963-66; Lecturer and Senior Lecturer, School of Community Studies, Moray House College of Education, 1966-72; Member, Scottish Arts Council, 1976-82; Trustee, Community Projects Foundation. Recreations: bee-keeping; sailing; jackarooing. Address: (h.) Longwood, Humbie, East Lothian; T.-Humbie 208.

Florence, Professor Alexander Taylor, BSc, PhD, DSc, CChem, FRSC, MPS. James P. Todd Professor of Pharmacy, Strathclyde University, since 1976; b. 9.9.40, London; m., Elizabeth Catherine McRae; 2 s.; 1 d. Educ. Queen's Park School, Glasgow; Glasgow University; Royal College of Science and Technology, Glasgow. Strathclyde University: Medical Research Council Junior Fellow, 1965-66; Lecturer, then Senior Lecturer, in Pharmaceutical Chemistry, 1966-76; Member, Committee on Safety of Medicines, CSM, since 1981; Vice Chairman, Chemistry, Pharmacy and Standards Sub-Committee, CSM (Member, since 1972); Member, Chemistry Committee, SERC, since 1983; Member, Nuffield Inquiry into Pharmacy, 1984-85. British Pharmaceutical Conference Science Award, 1974. Recreations: music; painting. Address: (b.) Strathclyde University, Department of Pharmacy, Royal College, Glasgow, G1 1XW; T.-041-552 4400, Ext. 2135.

Florey, Professor Charles Du Ve, MD, MPH, FFCM. Professor of Community Medicine, Dundee University, since 1983. Instructor, Assistant Professor, Yale University, 1963-69; Member, Scientific Staff, MRC, 1969-71; Senior Lecturer, then Reader, then Professor, St. Thomas's Hospital Medical School, 1971-83; Member, Committee on Data Protection, 1976-78. Publications: Introduction to Community Medicine; Methods for Cohort Studies of Chronic Airflow Limitation. Address: (b.) Department of Community Medicine, Ninewells Hospital and Medical School, Dundee, DD1 9SY; T.-0382 60111.

Fluendy, Malcolm A.D., MA, DPhil, DSc, CChem, FRSC, MInstP, FRSE. Reader in Chemistry, Edinburgh University; b. 28.3.35, London; m., Annette Pidgeon; 2 s. Educ. Westminster City School; Balliol College, Oxford. National Service, 1953-55 (Lt., Royal Signals); Royal Naval Scientific Service, 1955-56; Balliol College, Oxford, 1956-62; Research Fellow: University of California, Berkeley, 1962-63, Harvard University, 1963-64; joined Edinburgh University as Lecturer, 1964. Chairman, Molecular Beam Group, Chemical Society, 1974-79. Publication: Molecular Beams. Recreations: sailing; cruising (yachtmaster). Address: (b.) Department of Chemistry, West Mains Road, Edinburgh, EH9 3JJ; T.-031-667 1081.

Forbes, Charles Douglas, MD, MB, ChB, FRCP, FRCPGlas, FRCPEdin. Reader in Medicine, Glasgow University, since 1985; Honorary Consultant Physician, Glasgow Royal Infirmary; b. 9.10.38, Glasgow; m., Janette MacDonald Robertson; 2 s. Educ. High School of Glasgow; Glasgow University. Assistant Lecturer in Materia Medica, Glasgow University; Lecturer in Medicine, Makerere, Uganda; Registrar in Medicine, Glasgow Royal Infirmary; Fellow, American Heart Association; Fullbright Fellow; Director, Regional Haemophilia Centre, Glasgow. Member, Medical Advisory Committee, Haemophilia Society. Recreations: gardening; stamp collecting. Address: (h.) 93 St. Andrews Drive, Glasgow, G41 4DH; T.-041-423 4414.

Forbes, Very Rev. Graham J.T., MA, BD. Provost, St. Ninian's Cathedral, Perth, since 1982; b. 10.6.51, Edinburgh; m., Jane Miller; 3 s. Educ. George Heriot's School, Edinburgh; Aberdeen University; Edinburgh University. Curate, Old St. Paul's, Edinburgh, 1976-82; Chairman, Canongate Youth Project, 1977-83; Chairman, Lothian Association of Youth Clubs, since 1981; Member, Scottish Community Education Council, since 1982; Chairman, Scottish Intermediate Treatment Resource Centre, since 1982; Member, Edinburgh Area Board, Manpower Services

Commission, 1980-83; Chairman, Youth Affairs Group, Scottish Community Education Council, since 1982. Address: St. Ninian's House, 47 Balhousie Street, Perth; T.-0738 26874/27982.

Forbes, Rev. Iain MacDonald, BSc, BD. Minister, Howe of Fife, since 1983; b. 16.12.39, Johnstone; m., Margaet Ruth Macartney; 3 s.; 3 d. Educ. Thurso Miller Academy; Blairgowrie High School; Edinburgh University; Aberdeen University. Assistant, St. Andrew's, Clermiston, 1964-65; Missionary, Presbyterian Church of East Africa, outreach in Kieni resettlement schemes, Kenya, 1965-69; Home Organisation Secretary, Overseas Council, Church of Scotland, 1970-75; Minister, Benbecula Parish Church, 1975-83. District Commissioner, Uist District Scout Association, 1977-83. Recreations: gardening; general handyman; walking; music; reading. Address: The Manse, 83 Church Street, Ladybank, Cupar, Fife, KY7 7ND; T.-0337 30513.

Forbes, Sheriff John Stuart, MA, LLB. Sheriff of Tayside, Central and Fife, at Dunfermline, since 1980; b. 31.1.36; m.; 1 s.; 2 d. Educ. Glasgow High School; Glasgow University. Solicitor, 1959-61; Advocate, 1962-76; Sheriff of Lothian and Borders, 1976-80.

Forbes, 22nd Lord, (Nigel Ivan Forbes), KBE (1960), JP, DL. Premier Lord of Scotland; Director, Grampian Television Ltd.; Director, Blenheim Travel Ltd.; Chairman, Rolawn Ltd.; President, Scottish Scout Association, since 1970; b. 19.2.18; m., Hon. Rosemary Katharine Hamilton-Russell; 2 s.; 1 d. Educ. Harrow; Sandhurst. Retired Major, Grenadier Guards; Representative Peer of Scotland, 1955-63; Minister of State, Scottish Office, 1958-59; Member, Aberdeen and District Milk Marketing Board, 1962-72; Chairman, River Don District Board, 1962-73; President, Royal Highland and Agricultural Society of Scotland, 1958-59; Member, Sports Council for Scotland, 1966-71; Chairman, Scottish Branch, National Playing Fields Association, 1965-80; Deputy Chairman, Tennant Caledonian Breweries Ltd., 1964-74. Address: (h.) Balforbes, Alford, Aberdeenshire.

Forbes, William, MB, ChB, MD, PhD, FRCSEdin, MFCM. Senior Medical Officer, Scottish Home and Health Department, since 1974; Senior Lecturer, Edinburgh University, since 1978; b. Glasgow; m., Mima Hodge Todd; 3 s. Educ. Govan High School; Glasgow University. Medical and surgical posts, Southern General Hospital, Glasgow, 1959-60; Lecturer in Physiology, Institute of Physiology, Glasgow University, 1960-63; Registrar in General Surgery, Western Infirmary, Glasgow, 1963-66; Lecturer and Senior Registrar in Cardiovascular Surgery, Glasgow Royal Infirmary, 1966-70; Senior Research Fellow, National Heart Hospital, London, 1970-72; Chief Scientist Office, DHSS, London, 1972-74. Recreations: Scottish history and culture; football and sport. Address: (h.) 144 Mayfield Road, Edinburgh, EH9 3AL.

Forbes, Captain William Frederick Eustace. Vice Lord-Lieutenant of Stirling and Falkirk, since 1984; Member, Forestry Commission, since 1982; b. 6.7.31; m.; 2 d. Educ. Eton. Coldstream Guards, 1950-59; Chairman, Scottish Woodland Owners' Association, 1974-77; Chairman, Scottish Branch, National Playing Fields Association, since 1980. Address: (h.) Dinning House, Gargunnock, Stirling, FK8 3BQ.

Ford, Rev. Alan Andrew, BD, AIB (Scot). Minister, Airdrie New Monkland and Greengairs, since 1977; b. 8.6.48, Glasgow; m., Mary Douglas; 2 d. Educ. McGill School, Glasgow; High School of Glasgow; Glasgow University. Bank Officer, Bank of Scotland, 1965-70; student, 1970-75; Assistant Minister, Mains of Fintry Parish Church, Dundee, 1976-77. Treasurer, Mid-Lanark Amateur Radio Society; Member, Monklands Evangelical Council. Recreations: amateur radio; caravanning. Address: Manse of New Monkland, Glenmavis, Airdrie, ML6 ONW; T.-Airdrie 63286.

Ford, James Allan, CB, MC. Author; Trustee, National Library of Scotland, since 1981; b. 10.6.20, Auchtermuchty; m., Isobel Dunnett; 1 s.; 1 d. Educ. Royal High School, Edinburgh; Edinburgh University. Employment Clerk, Ministry of Labour, 1938-39; Executive Officer, Inland Revenue, 1939-40; Captain, The Royal Scots, 1940-46 (POW, Far East, 1941-45); Exective Officer, Inland Revenue, 1946-47; Department of Agriculture for Scotland, 1947-66 (Assistant Secretary, 1958); Registrar General for Scotland, 1966-69; Under Secretary, Scottish Office, 1969-79. Publications (novels): The Brave White Flag, 1961; Season of Escape, 1963; A Statue for a Public Place, 1965; A Judge of Men, 1968; The Mouth of Truth, 1972. Recreations: trout fishing; gardening. Address: (h.) 29 Lady Road, Edinburgh, EH16 5PA; T.-031-667 4489.

Ford, James Angus, MB, ChB, FRCPEdin, FRCPGlas, DCH. Consultant Paediatrician, since 1975; Deputy Chairman, Scottish Council, British Medical Association, since 1984 (Chairman, Scottish Committee of Hospital Medical Services, since 1983); b. 5.11.43, Arbroath; m., Dr. Veronica T. Reid. Educ. Kelvinside Academy; Glasgow University. House appointments: Glasgow Royal, Southern General, Stobhill, Belvidere; Registrar/Senior Registrar, Stobhill; Consultant appointments: Rutherglen Maternity Hospital, Royal Hospital for Sick Children, Glasgow; Territorial Army: six years, 6/7th Bn., Cameronians (Scottish Rifles), Captain; BMA: Chairman, Hospital Junior Staff Committee (Scotland), Deputy Chairman, HJSC (UK), Member of Council (Scottish and UK), Member, Joint Consultants Committee (Scottish and UK). Recreation: gardening. Address: (h.) 27 Ralston Road, Bearsden, Glasgow; T.-041-942 4273.

Forde, Michael Christopher, BEng, MSc, PhD, CEng, MICE, MIHT. Senior Lecturer in Civil Engineering, Edinburgh University, since 1984; Director, Civil Techn NDT Ltd., Galashiels, since 1984; b. 15.2.44, Sale, Cheshire; m., Edna Johnson-Williams; 1 s.; 1 d. Educ. De La Salle College; Liverpool University; Birmingham University. Christiani-Shand, 1966-67; County Surveyor's Department, Cheshire County

Council, 1967-69; Research Student, Birmingham University, 1969-73; Lecturer, Edinburgh University, 1973-84. Recreations: travel; reading. Address: (h.) Tintern House, 46 Cluny Gardens, Edinburgh, EH10 6BN; T.-031-447 4960.

Fordyce, James Alexander Oswald, JP. Vice Convener, Tayside Regional Council, since 1981 (Convener, Roads Committee, since 1982); Seed Potato Merchant and Farmer; b. 25.10.26, Auchterarder; m., May Mitchell Stark; 3 d. Educ. Auchterarder High School; Morrison's Academy, Crieff. Member, Auchterarder Town Council, 1957-74 (Provost, seven years); Member, Tayside Regional Council, since 1974 (former Convener of Education). Member, Board of Governors, Morrison's Academy, Crieff. Recreations: curling; bowling; golf. Address: (h.) Merrion, Western Road, Auchterarder; T.-Auchterarder 2215.

Forwell, Harold Christie. Senior Partner, Carlton Bakeries, Kirkcaldy, since 1955; Member, Fife Health Board; Member, Industrial Tribunals (Scotland); Director, Kirkcaldy District Chamber of Commerce; b. 16.8.25, Kirkcaldy; m., Isobel Russell Stuart; 1 s.; 1 d. Educ. George Watson's College, Edinburgh; Queen's University, Belfast. Past Chairman, National Joint Committee for Scottish Baking Industry; former Member, Retail Wages Council (BFCS Scotland); Past President: Scottish Association of Master Bakers, Kirkcaldy Rotary Club. Queen's Jubilee Medal, 1977. Recreations: sailing; travel. Address: (h.) 4 West Fergus Place, Kirkcaldy, Fife; T.-0592 260474.

Forrest, Andrew. Chairman, The Stock Exchange, Scottish Unit, 1983-85; Senior Partner, Wishart Brodie & Co., since 1982; b. 26.7.26, Dalkeith; m., Michele Paula Renee; 4 s. Educ. Edinburgh Academy. Merchant Navy, 1944-47; entered stockbroking, 1947; elected Member, 1951; original firm, Watson, Forrest & Watt, amalgamated with Wishart Brodie & Co., 1967; served on Edinburgh Stock Exchange Association, 1958-60, 1964-66, 1968-70 (Chairman, 1971-73); served on Scottish Unit, 1975-78; Council Member, The Stock Exchange, London, 1979-81. Recreations: golf; fishing. Address: (h.) 9 Glencairn Crescent, Edinburgh, EH12 5BS; T.-031-225 4873.

Forrest, Professor Andrew Patrick McEwen, BSc, MD, ChM, FRCS, FRCSEdin, FRCSGlas, DSc (Hon), FACS (Hon), FRSE. Regius Professor of Clinical Surgery, Edinburgh University, since 1970; Chief Scientist (part-time), Scottish Home and Health Department, since 1981; b. 25.3.23, Mount Vernon, Lanarkshire; m., Margaret Anne Steward; 1 s.; 2 d. Educ. Dundee High School; St. Andrews University. House Surgeon, Dundee Royal Infirmary; Surgeon Lieutenant, RNVR; Mayo Foundation Fellow; Lecturer and Senior Lecturer, Glasgow University; Professor of Surgery, Welsh National School of Medicine. Member: Medical Sub-Committee of University Grants Committee, Medical Research Council, Scientific Advisory Committee of Cancer Research Campaign; Council Member, Royal College of Surgeons of Edinburgh;

Advisory Board for Research Councils; Civilian Consultant (Surgery), Royal Navy. Secretary and President, Surgical Research Society; Secretary, Scottish Society of Experimental Medicine; Member, Kirk Session, St. Giles Cathedral. Publications: Prognostic Factors in Breast Cancer (Co-author), 1968; Principles and Practice of Surgery (Co-author), 1985. Recreation: sailing. Address: (b.) Edinburgh University, Department of Clinical Surgery, Royal Infirmary, Edinburgh, EH3 9YW; T.-031-228 1783.

Forrest, Walter Hill, MA, DipEd. Headmaster, Stronsay Secondary School, since 1956; b. 4.3.23, Lanark; m., Paula Buchanan; 1 s.; 2 d. Educ. Larkhall Academy; Glasgow University. Commissioned service, Royal Navy; Headmaster, Flotta Primary School, Orkney, 1951-56. Reader, Church of Scotland. Recreation: gardening. Address: (b.) Stronsay Secondary School, Orkney; T.-Stronsay 246.

Forrester, Professor Alexander Robert, BSc, PhD, DSc, FRSC, FRSE. Professor of Chemistry, Aberdeen University, since 1985; b. 14.11.35, Kelty, Fife; m., Myrna Ross; 1 s.; 3 d. Educ. Alloa Academy; Stirling High School; Heriot-Watt University; Aberdeen University. Lecturer, Paisley Technical College, 1959-60; PhD, Aberdeen, 1960-63; Aberdeen University: Assistant Lecturer, 1963-65, Lecturer, 1965-67, Senior Lecturer, 1977-82; Reader, 1982-85. Recreation: golf. Address: (b.) Chemistry Department, Aberdeen University, Aberdeen; T.-Aberdeen 40241, Ext. 5645.

Forrester, Professor Duncan Baillie, MA (Hons), BD, DPhil. Professor of Christian Ethics and Practical Theology, New College, Edinburgh, since 1978; Chairman, Edinburgh Council of Social Service, since 1983; Church of Scotland Minister; b. 10.11.33, Edinburgh; m., Rev. Margaret McDonald; 1 s.; 1 d. Educ. Madras College, St. Andrews; St. Andrews University; Chicago University; Edinburgh University. Part-time Assistant in Politics, Edinburgh University, 1957-58; Assistant Minister, Hillside Church, Edinburgh, and Leader of St. James Mission, 1960-61; as Church of Scotland Missionary, Lecturer and then Professor of Politics, Madras Christian College, Tambaram, South India, 1962-70; ordained Presbyter, Church of South India, 1962; part-time Lecturer in Politics, Edinburgh University, 1966-67; Chaplain and Lecturer in Politics, Sussex University. Publications: Caste & Christianity, 1980; Encounter with God (author), 1983; Studies in the History of Worship in Scotland (Co-Editor), 1984; Christianity and the Future of Welfare, 1985. Recreations: hill-walking; reading; listening to music. Address: (h.) 7 Murrayfield Avenue, Edinburgh, EH12 6AU; T.-031-337 5646.

Forrester, Frederick Lindsay, MA (Hons), DipEd, MBIM, FEIS. Organising Secretary, Educational Institute of Scotland, since 1975; b. 10.2.35, Glasgow; m., Ann V. Garrity; 1 s.; 1 d. Educ. Victoria Drive Senior Secondary School, Glasgow; Glasgow University; Jordanhill College of Education. Teacher of English, Glasgow secondary schools, 1962-64; Teacher of English and General Studies, Coatbridge Technical College, 1964-67; Assistant Secretary, Educational Institute of Scotland, 1967-75. Contributor to Times Educational Supplement Scotland. Recreations: walking; cycling; swimming; foreign travel. Address: (h.) 28 Liberton Drive, Edinburgh, EH16 6NN; T.-031-664 4797.

Forrester, John McColl, MA, BM, BCh, DObstRCOG, MRCGP. Senior Medical Officer, Scottish Home and Health Department, since 1985; b. 15.9.23, Roslin; m., Hilary Margaret; 1 s.; 2 d. Educ. Edinburgh Academy; St. Andrews University; Oxford University. Formerly Senior Lecturer in Physiology, Edinburgh University. Publication: Companion to Medical Studies (Editor). Recreations: travel; photography. Address: (h.) 120 Morningside Drive, Edinburgh, EH10 5NS.

Forrester, Professor John Vincent, MD, FRCSEdin. Cockburn Professor of Ophthalmology, Aberdeen University, since 1984; Honorary Consultant Ophthalmologist; b. 11.9.46, Glasgow; m., Anne Gray; 2 s.; 2 d. Educ. St. Aloysius College, Glasgow; Glasgow University. Ophthalmologist in training, Glasgow Hospitals, 1972-79; MRC Travelling Fellow, Columbia University, New York, 1976-77; Consultant Ophthalmologist, Southern General Hospital, Glasgow, and Honorary Clinical Lecturer, Glasgow University, 1979-84. Recreation: family life. Address: (h.) 12 Urie Crescent, Stonehaven; T.-0569 62303.

Forsyth of That Ilk, Alistair Charles William, JP, FSCA, FSA Scot, FInstPet. Baron of Ethie; Chief of the Name and Clan of Forsyth; b. 7.12.29; m., Ann Hughes; 4 s. Educ. St. Paul's School; Queen Mary College, London. Company Director; Chairman: Caledonian Oil Co. Ltd., Farmers' Supply Association of Scotland Ltd., Melroses Ltd., Hargreaves Reiss and Quinn Ltd., Seatainers Services Ltd., Pentleton and Hare Ltd., Clark Constable Ltd., Miles & Kitson Ltd., Andrew Whyte & Son Ltd.; CStJ. Address: (h.) Ethie Castle, by Arbroath, Angus, DD11 5SP.

Forsyth, Constance Catherine, MB, ChB, MD, FRCPLond, FRCPEdin. Reader, Department of Child Health, Dundee University, since 1975; b. 25.7.23, Edinburgh. Educ. George Watson's Ladies' College, Edinburgh; Edinburgh University. Carnegie Research Scholar, Edinburgh University; Research Fellow, Toronto University; Registrar, then Research Fellow, The Hospital for Sick Children, Great Ormond Street, London; Dundee University: Lecturer, Department of Child Health, 1955-62, Senior Lecturer, 1962-75. Recreations: hill-walking; golf; swimming; bridge; music; travelling; caravanning. Address: (h.) 5A Glamis Drive, Dundee, DD2 1QG; T.-Dundee 66412.

Forsyth, David J.C., MA (Hons). Reader, Department of Economics, Strathclyde University, since 1980; b. 4.6.40, Elgin; m., Gillian A. Dunmore (deceased); 4 s. Educ. Elgin Academy; Aberdeen University. Economics Lecturer: Strathclyde, 1963-64, Aberdeen, 1964; Visiting Professor, Ghana University, 1971-72; Senior Lecturer, Strathclyde University, 1973-80; UNDP Special Advisor on Technology Policy, Fiji, 1982-83; Reader in Economics, Strathclyde University, 1980-81 and since 1984. Publications: books on American investment in Scotland and technology policy. Recreations: cricket; golf; squash; antiquarianism. Address: (b.) Department of Economics, Strathclyde University, Cathedral Street, Glasgow; T.-041-552 4400, Ext. 3840.

Forsyth, Rev. David Stuart, MA. Minister, Belhelvie Church (formerly Belhevie North), since 1948; b. 10.7.20, Glasgow; m., Mary Irvine Summers; 1 d. Educ. Largs Higher Grade School; Ardrossan Academy; Glasgow University and Trinity College. Ordained, 1947. Moderator, Gordon Presbytery, 1976-77. Recreations: walking; football; reading; sailing. Address: Manse of Belhelvie, Balmedie, Aberdeen, AB4 OYB; T.-Balmedie 2227.

Forsyth, Jean Stewart Woodburn, MA, LLB. Advocate; b. 1.9.21, Glasgow; m., Mary Stewart James Forsyth, QC (deceased); 2 s.; 2 d. Educ. Queen's Park Secondary School; Glasgow University. Chairman, SSA Tribunal, Glasgow. Recreations: reading; swimming. Address: (h.) Albany Mansions, 347 Renfrew Street, Glasgow, G3 6UW; T.-041-332 3768.

Forsyth, Michael Bruce, MA. MP (Conservative), Stirling, since 1983; b. 16.10.54, Montrose; m., Susan Jane; 1 s.; 1 d. Educ. Arbroath High School; St. Andrews University. National Chairman, Federation of Conservative Students, 1976; Member, Westminster City Council, 1978-83; Vice Chairman, Conservative Environment back bench Committee; Member, Select Committee on Scottish Affairs; Honorary President, Scottish Federation of Conservative Students; Director: Michael Forsyth Associates, Michael Forsyth Ltd. Publications: Reservicing Britain; Reservicing Health; The Myths of Privatisation; Down with the Rates; Politics on the Rates. Recreations: mountaineering; astronomy. Address: House of Commons, London, SW1.

Fort, Nicholas, DipArch, RIBA, FRIAS, MRTPI. Director of Planning, City of Edinburgh Council, since 1975. Educ. Durham University. Planning Officer, Durham, 1947-48; Chief Planning Officer, Gateshead County Borough, 1948-51; City of Edinburgh: Principal Planning Officer, 1951-60, Depute Town Planning Officer, 1960-73, City Planning Officer, 1973-75. Address: (b.) City Chambers, 18 Market Street, Edinburgh, EH1 1BJ; T.-031-225 2424.

Forteviot, 3rd Baron, (Henry Evelyn Alexander Dewar), MBE (1943), DL; b. 23.2.06; m.; 2 s.; 2 d. Educ. Eton; St. John's College, Oxford. Black Watch (RHR), 1939-45; Deputy Lieutenant, Perth, 1961; Chairman, John Dewar & Sons Ltd., 1954-76. Address: (h.) Dupplin Castle, Perth.

Foster, John, CBE, FRICS, FRTPI, RIBA, ARIAS, FRSA. Director, Countryside Commission for Scotland, 1968-85; b. 13.8.20, Glasgow;

m., Daphne Househam. Educ. Whitehill School, Glasgow; Royal Technical College, Glasgow. Surveyor with private firm in Glasgow, 1937; Air Ministry during War; Assistant Planning Officer: Kirkcudbright County Council, 1945-47, Planning Officer, Holland County Council, 1948-52; Deputy Planning Officer, Peak Park Planning Board, 1952-54; Director, Peak District National Park Board, 1954-68. Honorary Vice-President, Countrywide Holidays Association; Member, Planning and Development Divisional Council, RICS (Penfold Silver Medallist); Life Member, National Trust for Scotland. Recreations: walking; swimming; photography; philately; reading; travel (whenever possible). Address: (h.) Birchover, Ferntower Road, Crieff, PH7 3DH; T.-0764 2336.

Foster, Professor John Odell, MA, PhD. Professor of Applied Social Studies, Paisley College, since 1981; b. 21.10.40, Hertford; m., Renee Prendergast. Educ. Guildford Grammar School; St. Catherine's College, Cambridge. Postdoctoral Research Fellow, St. Catherine's College, Cambridge, 1965-68; Lecturer in Politics, Strathclyde University, 1968-81. Publication: Class Struggle and the Industrial Revolution, 1974. Recreation: hill-walking. Address: (h.) 9 Taransay Street, Glasgow, G51; T.-041-440 0437.

Foster, Professor Roy, MA, DPhil, DSc, FRSC, FRSE. Professor of Physical-Organic Chemistry, Dundee University, since 1969; b. 29.7.28, Leicester; m., Delwen Eluned Rodd; 1 s.; 2 d. Educ. Wyggeston School, Leicester; Wadham College, Oxford. Research Fellow, Department of Pharmacology, Oxford University, 1953-56; Queen's College, Dundee (St. Andrews University): Senior Edward A. Deeds Fellow, 1956-59, Lecturer in Organic Chemistry, 1959-63, Senior Lecturer, 1963-66, Reader, 1966-67 (thence Dundee University, 1967-69). British Association for the Advancement of Science: Member of Council, Member, General Committee, Chairman, Tayside and Fife Branch, 1977-84; Dundee University: sometime Member of Court, Dean, Faculty of Science, Head, Department of Chemistry. Recreation: gardening. Address: (b.) Chemistry Department, Dundee University, Dundee, DD1 4HN; T.-0382 23181.

Fotheringham, John, OBE. Managing Director, North Eastern Farmers Ltd., since 1972; Chairman, Scottish Seed Potato Development Council, since 1981; Chairman, Grampian Tractors Ltd., since 1976; Chairman, Aberdeen University Research and Industrial Services Ltd., since 1985; b. 5.6.23, Kincardine, Fife; m., Isobel Mary Ballantyne; 1 s.; 2 d. Educ. Dunfermline High School. Royal Navy, 1941-47 (Lt., RNVR); National Bank of Scotland Ltd., 1947-49; District Manager, J. Bibby and Sons Ltd., 1949-53; Assistant Manager, Barclay, Ross & Hutchison Ltd., Aberdeen, 1953-55; Managing Director, Northern Agricultural Lime Co., Aberdeen, 1955-64; Unilever Ltd., 1964-72 (latterly Managing Director, United Agricultural Merchants Ltd.). Member, Scottish Agricultural Organisation Society Ltd., since 1972; President, United Kingdom Agricultural Supply Trade Association, 1977-78; Member: Aberdeen Harbour Board, since 1978, Co-operative Development Agency, since 1984;

Convener, Scottish Rotary Youth Leadership Award Scheme, since 1984; Council Member, Aberdeen Chamber of Commerce, since 1984; Member, Aberdeen University Court, since 1984; Grampian Industrialist of the Year, 1983. Recreations: golf; swimming. Address: (h.) East Neuk, Milltimber, Aberdeen, AB1 ODN; T.-Aberdeen 734614.

Foulds, Professor Wallace Stewart, MD, ChM, FRCS, FRCSGlas, DO. Tennent Professor of Ophthalmology, Glasgow University, since 1964; Honorary Consultant Ophthalmologist, Greater Glasgow Health Board, since 1964; b. 26.4.24, London; m., Margaret Holmes Walls; 1 s.; 2 d. Educ. George Watson's Boys College, Edinburgh; Paisley Grammar School; Glasgow University. RAF Medical Branch, 1946-49; training posts, Moorfields Eye Hospital, London, 1952-54; Research Fellow, Institute of Ophthalmology, London University, and Senior Registrar, University College Hospital, London, 1954-58; Consultant Ophthalmologist, Addenbrookes Hospital, Cambridge, 1958-64; Honorary Lecturer, Cambridge University and Research Fellow, London University, 1958-64. Past President: Ophthalmological Society of UK, Faculty of Ophthalmologists; Chairman, European Association for Eye Research. Recreations: sailing; diving. Address: (b.) Tennent Institute of Ophthalmology, Western Infirmary, Glasgow, G11 6NT; T.-041-339 8822, Ext. 4640.

Foulkes, George, MP, JP, BSc. MP (Labour), Carrick, Cumnock and Doon Valley, since 1979; Opposition Spokesman on Foreign Affairs, since 1984; b. 21.1.42, Oswestry; m., Elizabeth Anna; 2 s.; 1 d. Educ. Keith Grammar School; Haberdashers' Aske's School; Edinburgh University. President, Scottish Union of Students, 1964-66; Director: European League for Economic Co-operation, 1967-68, Enterprise Youth, 1968-73, Age Concern Scotland, 1973-79; Chairman: Lothian Region Education Committee, 1974-79, Education Committee, COSLA, 1975-79; Rector's Assessor, Edinburgh University, 1968-71. Recreation: boating. Address: (h.) 8 Southpark Road, Ayr, KA7 2TL; T.-Ayr 265776.

Fowkes, Frederick Jeffery, DLC, ADPHE, DipEd. Chairman, Scottish Congregational Union, since 1984; b. 20.5.34, Belper; m., Lilian Mary; 3 d. Educ. Herbert Strutt Grammar School; Loughborough University; Leeds University; Glasgow University. Head of Physical Education: Ripley Secondary Technical School, Swanwick Hall Grammar School; Lecturer, Hamilton College of Education; Lecturer in Physical Education and Psychology, Jordanhill College. General Secretary, Airdrie YM/YMCA; Past Chairman, Mid Lanark District Council of Congregational Churches; Member, General Council, Congregational Union; Chairman, Scottish Colleges of Education Sports Association. Address: (h.) 20 Hillfoot Drive, Wishaw; T.-Cambusnethan 385407.

Fox, Donald Peter, BSc, PhD, MIBiol. Senior Lecturer in Genetics, Aberdeen University, since 1978; b. 16.5.42, Doncaster; m., Christine Mary Ross; 1 s.; 1 d. Educ. Thorne Grammar

School, Yorkshire; Durham University; Birmingham University. Aberdeen University: Assistant Lecturer in Genetics, 1966-67, Lecturer, 1967-78. Chairman, Aberdeen Young Diabetics, 1979-83; Member, Editorial Board, Heredity, 1978-84; Secretary, Coordinating Committee for Cytology and Genetics, British Association for the Advancement of Science, 1974-77. Recreations: skiing; hill-walking; badminton. Address: (h.) 33 Earlswclls Road, Cults, Aberdeen; T.-0224 868579.

Fox, George Frew, CA. Chairman, Dundee United Football Club; b. 18.11.13, Carnoustie; m., Violet J. Low; 2 d. Educ. Grove Academy, Dundee. Commenced practice as CA, 1938; War Service, 1940-46; resumed practice, 1946; retired, 1978; former Treasurer, Scottish Football Association (Life Member); Life Member: Carnoustie Golf Club, Broughty Golf Club, Forfarshire Football Association, Tayside Athletic Club; Honorary President, Carnoustie Panmure FC; Honorary Vice President, Broughty Operatic Society. Recreation: golf. Address: (h.) 17 Lochty Street, Carnoustie, Angus.

Fox, John Edward, BDSEdin, FDS, RCSEdin. Consultant Oral Surgeon, Tayside Health Board, since 1972; Honorary Senior Lecturer, Dundee University, since 1972; b. 30.6.31, Birmingham; m., Valerie May Anderson; 2 s.; 2 d. Educ. Haverfordwest Grammar School; Edinburgh University. Left school at 16 and followed a business career; entered Edinburgh University to study dentistry, 1957; Lecturer in Periodontology, Edinburgh Dental School; Registrar in Oral Surgery, Edinburgh Royal Infirmary; Senior Registrar in Oral Surgery, St. James Hospital, Leeds. Chairman, Scottish Committee for Hospital Dental Services. Recreations: sailing; hill-walking. Address: (h.) 16 Corsie Avenue, Perth, PH2 7BS; T.-Perth 29145.

Fraile, Professor Medardo, PhD. Writer; Personal Professor in Spanish, Strathclyde University, since 1983; b. 21.3.25, Madrid; m., Janet H. Gallagher; 1 d. Educ. Madrid University. Teacher of Spanish language and literature, Ramiro de Maeztu Secondary School, Madrid, 1956-64; Assistant in Spanish, Southampton University, 1964-67; Strathclyde University: Assistant Lecturer in Spanish, 1967-68, Lecturer, 1968-79, Reader, 1979-83. Travelling Scholarship for authors, 1954; Premio Sesamo for short story writing, 1956; literary grant, Juan March Foundation, 1960; Book of the Year award, 1965; La Estafeta Literaria Prize for short stories, 1970; Hucha de Oro Prize for short stories, 1971; research grant, Carnegie Trust, 1975. Publications: several collections of short stories and books of literary criticism. Recreations: swimming; walking. Address: (h.) 24 Etive Crescent, Bishopbriggs, Glasgow, G64 1ES; T.-041-772 4421.

Frain, Ian Millar, MA, JP. Rector, Mearns Academy, since 1968; b. 29.9.27, Auckland, New Zealand; m., Lorna; 3 d. Educ. Robert Gordon's College, Aberdeen; Aberdeen University. Provost of Laurencekirk, 1978; Kincardine and Deeside District Council: Chairman, 1975-84;

Vice-Convener, since 1984; Chairman, Kincardine and Deeside Area Tourist Board, 1982-84. Convener, Laurencekirk Meals on Wheels Service. Recreations: rugby (Gordonian rugby "cap"); tennis; golf. Address: (h.) The Firs, Laurencekirk; T.-Laurencekirk 458.

Frame, Robert, FRICS. Assessor and Electoral Registration Officer, Dumfries and Galloway Region, since 1975; b. 1.9.25, Glassford, Lanarkshire; m., Margaret Paterson; 1 d. Educ. Hamilton Academy; College of Estate Management (External). Assessor and Electoral Registration Officer: County of Dumfries, 1956-57, Counties of Dumfries, Kirkcudbright and Wigtown, 1967-75. President, Association of Lands Valuation Assessors of Scotland, 1966-68; President, Scottish Assessors' Association, since 1984. Address: (b.) Huntingdon, 27 Moffat Road, Dumfries, DG1 1NB; T.-0387 63711.

France, Professor Peter, MA, PhD. Professor of French, Edinburgh University, since 1980; b. 19.10.35, Londonderry; m., Sian Reynolds; 3 d. Educ. Bradford Grammar School; Magdalen College, Oxford. Fellow, Magdalen College, Oxford, 1960-63; Lecturer, then Reader in French, Sussex University, 1963-80; French Editor, Modern Languages Review, 1979-85. Publications: Racine's Rhetoric, 1965; Rhetoric and Truth in France, 1972; Poets of Modern Russia, 1983; Diderot, 1983. Address: (b.) Department of French, 4 Buccleuch Place, Edinburgh, EH8 9LW; T.-031-667 1011.

Francey, David Maxwell, FRSA, MInstAM, MInstVT. Company Director; Management and Public Relations Consultant; Freelance Broadcaster; b. 22.2.24, Glasgow; m., Sheila Cameron; 1 s. Educ. Hyndland School, Glasgow; Learmonth College, Edinburgh; Stow College. RAF VR (wartime); Ministry of Civil Aviation; Ministry of Transport; Scottish Gas Board; South of Scotland Electricity Board; Freelance Sports Reporter and Commentator, BBC, since 1952; has broadcast major football events from more than 20 countries. Recreations: public speaking; singing; conversation; football at all levels. Address: (h.) 57 Arisdale Crescent, Newton Mearns, Glasgow, G77 6HB; T.-041-639 4638.

Francis, John Michael, BSc, ARCS, PhD, DIC. Director Scotland, Nature Conservancy Council, since 1984; b. 1.5.39, London; m., Eileen; 2 d. Educ. Gowerton Grammar School, near Swansea; Imperial College of Science and Technology, London University. CEGB Berkeley Nuclear Laboratories, 1963-70; Director, Society, Religion and Technology Project, Church of Scotland, 1970-74; Senior Research Fellow, Heriot-Watt University, 1974-76; Principal, Scottish Development Department, 1976-81; Assistant Secretary, Scottish Office, 1981-84. Consultant, World Council of Churches, 1970-83; Chairman, SRT Project, Church of Scotland. Publications: Scotland in Turmoil, 1972; Changing Directions, 1973; Facing Up to Nuclear Power, 1976. Recreations: theatre; hill-walking; ecumenical travels. Address: (h.) 49 Gilmour Road, Newington, Edinburgh, EH16 5NU; T.-031-667 3996.

Franklin, Mark Newman, MA (Oxon), PhD. Senior Lecturer in Political Science, Strathclyde University; Social Research Consultant, since 1971; b. 29.1.42; m., Carole Elizabeth Madelaine; 1 s.; 1 d. Educ. Dauntsey's School; Balliol College, Oxford; Cornell University. Visiting Fellow, St. Anne's College, Oxford, 1968; joined Strathclyde University as Lecturer in Politics, 1969; Visiting Professor, Chicago University, 1974-75, and Senior Study Director, National Opinion Research Center; Senior Visiting Fellow, Edinburgh University, 1977-78; Scientific Study Director, European Science Foundation, 1984-85; Visiting Professor, University of Iowa, 1984-85; sometime Consultant, Equal Opportunities Commission, and other public bodies. Publications: A User's Guide to the SCSS Conversational Statistical System, 1980; The Decline of Class Voting in Britain, 1985. Recreations: sailing (yachtmaster); swimming; music; theatre. Address: (b.) Department of Politics, Strathclyde University, Glasgow, G1 1XQ; T.-041-552 4400.

Fraser, Andrew Robertson. Leader, Midlothian District Council, since 1984; b. 20.5.29, Aberdeen; m., Isabel Churchard Murdoch; 1 s.; 1 d. Educ. Frederick Street Junior Secondary School, Aberdeen; Stevenson College of Further Education, Edinburgh. Post Office employee, since 1943; Vice-Chairman, Midlothian Constituency Labour Party, 1975-81; Chairman, Lothian Region Labour Party, 1976-78; Member, Midlothian District Council, since 1980; Member: YM/YWCA Management Group, CAB Management Committee. Address: (h.) 18 Philip Place, Penicuik, Midlothian; T.-0968 75624.

Fraser, Brian Mitchell, BA (Hons), PhD, DGA. Director of Personnel, Glasgow University, since 1982; b. 31.7.43, Paisley; m., Hannah Orr Weir Burt; 3 s. Educ. Camphill High School, Paisley; London University; Strathclyde University. Civil Servant, 1962-70; Senior Administrator, Paisley College of Technology, 1970-78; Lecturer in History, Glasgow College of Technology, since 1977; Boys' Brigade historian and leader. Publication: Sure and Stedfast - A History of the Boys' Brigade (Co-author), 1983. Recreations: youth work; golf; family. Address: (h.) Glenrona, Holehouse Road, Eaglesham; T.-Eaglesham 2416.

Fraser, Callum George, BSc, PhD, FAACB, FACB. Top Grade Biochemist, Ninewells Hospital and Medical School, since 1983; Honorary Senior Lecturer, Dundee University, since 1983; b. 3.1.45, Dundee; m., Stella Sim; 2 d. Educ. Dunfermline High School; Perth Academy; Aberdeen University. Postdoctoral Fellow, National Research Council of Canada, 1969-70; Lecturer in Chemical Pathology, Aberdeen University, and Honorary Biochemist, Grampian Health Board, 1970-75; Chief Clinical Biochemist, Flinders Medical Centre, South Australia, 1975-83; Honorary Senior Lecturer, then Honorary Associate Professor, Flinders University of South Australia, 1975-83. Member, Education Committee, International Federation of Clinical Chemistry; Member, Commission on Teaching of Clinical Chemistry, International Union of Pure and Applied Chemistry; Member, Editorial Boards, Advances in Clinical Chemistry and Clinical Physiology and Biochemistry. Recreations: gardening; reading; travel. Address: (b.) Department of Biochemical Medicine, Ninewells Hospital, Dundee, DD1 9SY; T.-0382 60111.

Fraser, Sir Campbell, BCom, LLD (Strathclyde), DUniv (Stirling), CBIM, FRSE. Chairman, Scottish Television plc, since 1975; Director, British Petroleum plc, since 1978; Director, BAT Industries plc, since 1979; b. 2.5.23, Dunblane; m., Maria Harvey McLaren; 2 d. Educ. McLaren High School, Callander; Glasgow University; Dundee School of Economics. Many positions in Dunlop company (Sole Managing Director, 1972-78, Chairman, 1978-83); Board Member: Bridgewater Paper, Tandem Computers; President, Confederation of British Industry, 1982-84 (Deputy President, 1981-82); Director, Scottish Opera; Trustee, The Economist; Stirling University; President, Society of Business Economists, 1973-85. Recreations: reading; walking; supporting Dundee Football Club. Address: (b.) Scottish Television plc, 7 Adelaide Street, London, WC2N 4LZ; T.-01-836 1500.

Fraser, Charles Annand, LVO, WS, DL. Partner, W. & J. Burness, WS, since 1956; Purse Bearer to Lord High Commissioner to General Assembly of Church of Scotland, since 1969; Chairman: Japan Assets Trust PLC, Morgan Grenfell (Scotland) Ltd.; Director: Adam Trust Company PLC, Walter Alexander PLC, Anglo Scottish Investment Trust PLC, British Assets Trust PLC, W. & J. Burness Trustees Ltd., Edinburgh American Assets Trust PLC, Edinburgh Venture Enterprise Trust, Grosvenor Developments, The Murrayfield PLC, Scottish Widows' Fund and Life Assurance Society, Scottish Television PLC, Scottish Business in the Community, Signetics (UK) Ltd., Solsgirth Investment Trust Co. Ltd., United Biscuits (Holdings) PLC; b. 16.10.28, Humbie, East Lothian; m., Ann Scott-Kerr; 4 s. Educ. Hamilton Academy; Edinburgh University. Council Member, Institute of Directors, since 1983 (Chairman, Scottish Division, 1978-81); Governor, Fettes College, since 1976; served on Court, Heriot-Watt University; Council Member, Law Society of Scotland, 1966-72; Trustee, Scottish Civic Trust. Recreations: gardening; skiing; squash; piping. Address: (h.) Shepherd House, Inveresk, Midlothian; T.-031-665 2570.

Fraser, David McKee, BSc, MB, ChB, FRCPEdin. Consultant Physician, Milesmark Hospital, Dunfermline, since 1979; Postgraduate Clinical Tutor, West Fife, since 1981; Honorary Senior Lecturer, Department of Medicine, Edinburgh University, since 1979; b. 11.4.47, Dunfermline; m., M. Joan Park; 1 s.; 1 d. Educ. Dunfermline High School; Edinburgh University. Junior hospital posts, South-East Regional Hospital Board, then Lothian Health Board, 1971-79. Address: (h.) Gowan Brae, 120 Garvock Hill, Dunfermline.

Fraser, Douglas Jamieson. Poet; b. 12.1.10, Edinburgh; m., Eva Nisbet Greenshields; 2 s.; 1 d. Educ. George Heriot's School. Spent 44 years with Standard Life Assurance Company, Edinburgh; awarded Queen's Silver Jubilee Medal.

Publications: Landscape of Delight; Rhymes o' Auld Reekie; Where the Dark Branches Part; Treasure for Eyes to Hold. Recreation: painting. Address: (h.) 2 Keith Terrace, Edinburgh, EH4 3NJ; T.-031-332 5176.

Fraser, Elwena D.A. Honorary Sheriff, Tayside, Central and Fife, since 1982; Member, Rateable Valuation Appeal Committee, since 1975; Governor, Dundee College of Technology, since 1969; b. 5.9.31, Lowestoft; m., Dr. Ian Tuke Fraser; 2 s.; 1 d. Educ. Craigholm School, Glasgow; Calder Girls' School, Seascale. Journalist, Scottish Daily Express, 1950-54; Member, Perth Town Council, 1969-72; Member, Education Committee, Perth County Council, 1969-72; Member, Dundee University Adult Education Committee, 1969-72; Member, Executive Committee, Perth Tourist Association, 1969-72; Member, Executive Committee, Perth Festival of the Arts, 1971-81; Board Member, Perth College of Further Education, 1972-78 (Chairman, 1975-78); Honorary Manager, Trustee Savings Bank (Perthshire), 1973-75; Member, Gas Consumers Council for Scotland, since 1973; Member, BBC Broadcasting Council for Scotland, 1977-80. Recreations: swimming; gardening. Address: (h.) 15 Spoutwells Avenue, Scone, Perthshire, PH2 6RP; T.-0738 51310.

Fraser, Sir Hugh. 2nd Bt. Chairman, Sir Hugh and Sir Group; b. 18.12.36. Educ. St. Mary's, Melrose; Kelvinside Academy. Director of various companies.

Fraser, Hugh Donald George, QPM, DipSM, FBIM, MIPM, MIIRSM. Senior Assistant Secretary, Heriot-Watt University, since 1971; Member, Lothian Regional Council, since 1982; Honorary Secretary, Scottish Chamber of Safety, since 1979; b. Edinburgh; m., Margaret Jane Stothard; 1 s.; 2 d. War Service, RAF Aircrew, 1939-45 (Pilot); Edinburgh City Police, 1941-71; Chief Superintendent, Research and Planning Branch, Home Office, London, 1966-68; Deputy Commandant, Scottish Police College, 1968-71. Honorary Secretary, Edinburgh and District Spastic Association, 14 years; Member: Edinburgh Accident Prevention Council, Lothian Retirement Committee. Recreations: Burns' enthusiast; work with senior citizens; jogging; the theatre. Address: (h.) 181 Braid Road, Edinburgh, EH10 6JA; T.-031-447 1270.

Fraser, Ian Ross, MA (Hons), MEd. Rector, Inverness Royal Academy, since 1971; b. 16.4.30, Carmyle, Lanarkshire; m., Trudy C. Marshall; 3 s.; 1 d. Educ. Aberdeen Grammar School; Aberdeen University; Aberdeen College of Education. Principal Teacher of Geography, Elgin Academy, 1960-66; Rector, Waid Academy, Anstruther, 1966-71; Member, Ruthven Committee on Ancillary Staff in Secondary Schools, 1973-76; Honorary Secretary, 1975-77, and President, 1978-79, Headteachers' Association of Scotland; Chairman, Highland Region Curriculum Coordinating Group, 1980-84; Chairman, Scottish Central Committee on Social Subjects, 1981-83; Chairman, Steering Committee, S1/2 Social Subjects Development Programme, since 1983; Member: Consultative Committee on the Curriculum, CCC Executive Committee, Committee

on Secondary Education. Recreations: tennis; badminton; fishing; hill-walking. Address: (h.) Yendor, Dores Road, Inverness, IV2 4XE; T.-0463 232862.

Fraser, Ian Scott, BSc (Econ), LLB, DEc, DPA, FBIM. Barrister-at-Law; Advocate; b. 21.7.18, Dundee; m., Kathleen Mary Fraser; 1 s.; 1 d. Educ. Fort William High School; London University. Civil Service: Admiralty, 1936-46, Ministry of Pensions and National Insurance, 1946-55 and 1961-63, Treasury, 1955-57 (seconded to NATO (Shape) Paris 1956-57); United Nations official, 1957-61 and 1963-76, serving in Ethiopia and other African countries, New York, Middle East; travel and further education, 1976-81; practising Advocate, since 1981; Chairman, Board of Directors, Scottish Rights of Way Society Ltd., since 1983; Life Member, National Trust for Scotland and Royal Scottish Geographical Society. Recreations: travel; photography; motor caravanning; walking. Address: (h.) 1 Mayfield Gardens, Edinburgh, EH9 2AX; T.-031-667 3681.

Fraser, Professor Sir James David, 2nd Bt, FRCSEdin, FRCS, ChM, BA, MB, ChB. Postgraduate Dean, Faculty of Medicine, Edinburgh University, since 1981; b. 19.7.24; m.; 2 s. Educ. Edinburgh Academy; Magdalen College, Oxford. President, Royal College of Surgeons of Edinburgh, since 1982.

Fraser, James Edward, MA (Aberdeen), BA (Cantab). Under Secretary, Scottish Home and Health Department, since 1981; b. 16.12.31, Aberdeen; m., Patricia Louise Stewart; 2 s. Educ. Aberdeen Grammar School; Aberdeen University; Christ's College, Cambridge. Royal Artillery, 1953-55 (Staff Captain, "Q", Tel-El-Kebir, 1954-55); Assistant Principal, Scottish Home Department, 1957-60; Private Secretary to Permanent Under-Secretary of State, Scottish Office, 1960-62; Private Secretary to Parliamentary Under-Secretary of State, Scottish Office, 1962; Principal, 1962-69: SHHD, 1962-64, Cabinet Office, 1964-66, HM Treasury, 1966-68, SHHD, 1968-69; Assistant Secretary: SHHD, 1970-76, Scottish Office Finance Division, 1976; Under Secretary, Local Government Finance Group, Scottish Office, 1976-81. Recreations: reading; music; walking. Address: (h.) 59 Murrayfield Gardens, Edinburgh, EH12 6DH; T.-031-337 2274.

Fraser, John, MA. Rector, Mackie Academy, Stonehaven, since 1975; b. 8.8.36, Inverness; m., Judith Helen Procter; 2 d. Educ. Inverness Royal Academy; Aberdeen University; Aberdeen College of Education. Teacher, Harris Academy, 1960-66; Principal Teacher of History, Buckie High School, 1966-72; Assistant Head Teacher and Depute Rector, Peterhead Academy, 1972-75; Governor, Aberdeen College of Education, since 1984; Member: GTC, 1979-83; Grampian Region Education Committee, 1975-78; Regional Convener, SSTA, since 1975. Conductor: Buckie Choral Union, 1968-72, Peterhead Choral Society, 1972-75; Organist in various churches. Recreations: music; DIY. Address: (b.) Slug Road, Stonehaven; T.-Stonehaven 62071/2.

Fraser, Very Rev. John Annand, MBE (1940), TD, DD. Extra Chaplain to The Queen, in Scotland, since 1964; b. 21.6.94; m.; 1 s.; 1 d. Educ. Robert Gordon's College, Aberdeen; Inverness Royal Academy; Aberdeen University; Edinburgh University. Moderator, General Assembly, Church of Scotland, 1958-59.

Fraser, John A.W., MA, FEIS. Headmaster, Scalloway Junior High School, since 1966; Deputy Lieutenant for Shetland, since 1985; b. 9.11.28, Lerwick; m., Jane Ann Jamieson; 2 s. Educ. Anderson Educational Institute; Edinburgh University; Moray House College of Education. Education Officer, RAF, 1950-52; Teacher, Baltasound Junior Secondary School, 1952-54; Head Teacher: Haroldswick Primary School, 1954-59, Aith Junior High School, 1959-66. Member, National Council, EIS. Recreation: committees! Address: (h.) Broadwinds, Castle Street, Scalloway, Shetland; T.-Scalloway 644.

Fraser, Rev. John Gillies. Minister, Elderpark Macgregor Memorial Parish Church, Glasgow, since 1970; b. 5.7.14, Glasgow; m., Jessie MacKenzie Mayer; 1 s.; 3 d. Educ. Shawlands Academy; Glasgow University and Trinity College. Public Assistance Department (later Social Service Department), Glasgow Corporation, 1931-48; Ministry of National Insurance, 1948; divinity student, 1948-50; Minister/Missionary, Church of Scotland, Northern Rhodesia, 1950-60; Minister, Macgregor Memorial Church, 1960-70. Scottish Assistant Secretary, Crusaders' Union, 1935-47; Secretary, South West Glasgow Sunday School Union, 1942-47. Recreation: gardening. Address: (h.) 2 Drumoyne Avenue, Glasgow, G51 4AP; T.-041-445 3529.

Fraser, Keith James, FILAM, DipLD. Director of Parks and Recreation, City of Glasgow District Council, since 1981; b. 11.11.32, Blackpool; m., Margaret; 1 s.; 1 d. Educ. Blackpool Grammar School. Youth gardener/gardener Class II, Blackpool Parks Department, 1949-50 and 1953-56; probationer, Royal Botanic Gardens, Edinburgh, 1956-59; junior technical assistant, Stoke-on-Trent Parks Department, 1959-62; horticultural assistant, City of Glasgow Parks and Botanic Gardens Department, 1962-65; Deputy Director of Parks and Cemeteries, City of Belfast, 1965-69; Depute Director of Parks and Botanic Gardens, City of Glasgow, 1969-74; Director of Parks, City of Glasgow District Council, 1974-81. Recreations: cricket; swimming; reading; gardening. Address: (b.) 20 Trongate, Glasgow, G1 5ES; T.-041-227 5058.

Fraser, Peter, QC, MP. Solicitor-General for Scotland, since 1982; MP, Angus East, since 1983 (Angus South, 1979-83); b. 29.5.45. Educ. Loretto School; Gonville and Caius College, Cambridge; Edinburgh University. Advocate; Lecturer in Constitutional Law, Heriot-Watt University, 1971-75; Chairman, Scottish Conservative Lawyers Law Reform Group, 1976.

Fraser, Raymond Morris, LLB (Hons). Advocate, since 1971; b. 16.2.47, Edinburgh. Educ. George Heriot's School, Edinburgh; Edinburgh

University. Conservative Parliamentary candidate, Orkney and Shetland, October, 1974; instigator of visit to Angola, 1976, to defend British mercenaries at war crimes trial. Address: (h.) Bonaly Tower, Edinburgh; T.-031-441 3804.

Fraser, Robert W., BSc (Hons), FICE, FIWES, MIPHE. Director, Water and Drainage Services, Borders Regional Council, since 1981; b. 13.5.39, Kirkcaldy; m., Elizabeth; 1 s.; 1 d. Educ. Kirkcaldy High School; Edinburgh University. Address: (b.) West Grove, Waverley Road, Melrose, TD6 9SJ; T.-Melrose 2056.

Fraser, Simon William Hetherington, LLB, NP. Partner, Flowers & Co., Solicitors, Glasgow, since 1976; b. 2.4.51, Carlisle; m., Sheena Janet; 1 d. Educ. Glasgow Academy; Glasgow University. Glasgow Bar Association: Secretary, 1977-79, President, 1981-82. Recreations: cricket; snooker. Address: (b.) 134 Holland Street, Glasgow; T.-041-221 5344.

Fraser, Rt. Hon. Thomas, PC (1964). Chairman, North of Scotland Hydro-Electric Board, 1967-73; Minister of Transport, 1964-65; b. 18.2.11; m.; 1 s.; 1 d. MP (Labour), Hamilton, 1943-67; Joint Parliamentary Under-Secretary of State, Scottish Office, 1945-51.

Fraser of Tullybelton, Baron, (Walter Ian Reid Fraser), PC (1974), QC, BA (Oxon), LLB. Life Peer; Lord of Appeal in Ordinary, since 1975; b. 3.2.11; m.; 1 s. Educ. Repton; Balliol College, Oxford. Advocate, 1936; Lecturer in Constitutional Law, Glasgow University, 1936, Edinburgh University, 1948; Army, 1939-45; QC, 1953; Dean, Faculty of Advocates, 1959-64; Senator of the College of Justice in Scotland, 1964-74; Hon. LLD, Glasgow, 1970, Edinburgh, 1978.

Fraser, William. Director of Cleansing, Inverness District Council, since 1974; b. 4.10.34, Aberdeen. Corporation of City of Aberdeen: Apprentice Sanitary Inspector, 1952-56, Assistant District Sanitary Inspector, 1956-60; Junior Assistant Sanitary Inspector, Kincardine County Council, 1960-61; Assistant Sanitary Inspector/Senior Assistant Sanitary Inspector, Perth and Kinross County Council, 1961-71; Depute County Sanitary Inspector and Depute Master of Works, Ross and Cromarty County Council, 1971-75. Address: (b.) 33 Lotland Street, Inverness; T.-Inverness 230634.

Fraser, William Hamish, MA, DPhil. Senior Lecturer in History, Strathclyde University, since 1977; b. 30.6.41, Keith; m., Helen Tuach; 1 d. Educ. Keith Grammar School; Aberdeen University; Sussex University. Lecturer in History, Strathclyde University, 1976-77; Co-Editor, Scottish Economic and Social History. Publications: Trade Unions and Society 1850-1880, 1973; Workers and Employers, 1981; The Coming of the Mass Market, 1982. Recreations: hill-walking; skiing; cleaning canals. Address: (h.) 112 High Station Road, Falkirk, FK1 5LN; T.-0324 22868.

Fraser, William Irvine, MD, FRCPsych, DPM. Consultant Psychiatrist, since 1969; part-time Senior Lecturer, Edinburgh University, since

1975; Editor, Journal of Mental Deficiency Research, since 1983; b. 3.2.40, Greenock; m., Joyce Gilchrist; 2 s. Educ. Greenock Academy; Glasgow University. Physician Superintendent, Lynebank Hospital, Fife, 1974-78; Council Member, International Association for Scientific Study of Mental Handicap, since 1982; Executive Member, Projects Committee, Mental Health Foundation. Publications: Care and Training of the Mentally Handicapped; Communication with Normal and Retarded Children. Recreation: sailing. Address: (h.) 16 Braehead Drive, Edinburgh; T.-031-339 4041.

Fraser, Sir William Kerr, GCB (1984). Permanent Under Secretary of State, Scottish Office, since 1978; b. 18.3.29; m.; 3 s.; 1 d. Educ. Eastwood School; Glasgow University. Scottish Home Department, 1955; Private Secretary to Parliamentary Under Secretary, 1959, and to Secretary of State for Scotland, 1966-67; Assistant Secretary, Regional Development Division, 1967-71; Under Secretary, Scottish Home and Health Department, 1971-75; Deputy Secretary, Scottish Office, 1975-78. Hon. LLD, Glasgow, 1982.

Freeman, Christopher Paul, BSc, MB, ChB, MPhil, MRCPsych. Consultant Psychiatrist, Royal Edinburgh Hospital, Edinburgh, since 1980; Senior Lecturer, Department of Psychiatry, Edinburgh University, since 1980; Psychiatric Tutor, Royal Edinburgh Hospital, since 1983; b. 21.4.47, York; m., Heather; 2 s. Educ. Nunthorpe School, York; Edinburgh University. Royal College of Psychiatrists Gaskell Gold Medal. Recreations: tennis; squash; growing bonsaii trees. Address: (h.) 62 Morningside Drive, Edinburgh, EH10 5NQ; T.-031-447 5664.

Freer, John Henry, BSc, MSc, PhD. Reader in Microbiology, Glasgow University, since 1982 (Head, Department of Microbiology, since 1984); b. 17.11.36, Kasauli, India; m., Jocelyn Avril Williams; 4 d. Educ. Durham University; Nottingham University; Birmingham University. Lecturer in Microbiology, New South Wales University, Australia, 1962-65; New York University Medical Centre: Associate Research Scientist, then Assistant Professor, Microbiology, 1965-68; Senior Lecturer, Microbiology Department, Glasgow University, 1968-82; Senior Editor, Journal of General Microbiology. Publication: Bacterial Protein Toxins (Joint Editor), 1984. Recreations: sailing; painting. Address: (b.) Department of Microbiology, Glasgow University, 56 Dumbarton Road, Glasgow, G11 6NU; T.-041-339 8855, Ext. 602.

Freshney, Robert Ian, BSc, PhD. Senior Lecturer, Department of Medical Oncology, Glasgow University, since 1984; b. 16.2.38, Paisley; m., Mary Struthers; 1 s.; 1 d. Educ. Ayr Academy; Glasgow University. Research Fellow, Biochemistry Department, Glasgow University, 1963-64; Postdoctoral Research Fellow, Department of Zoology, Wisconsin University, 1964-65; Research Fellow, Biochemistry Department, Glasgow University, 1965-66; Member, Research Staff, Beatson Institute for Cancer Research, Glasgow, 1966-81; Lecturer, Department of

Medical Oncology, Glasgow University, 1981-84. Past President, European Tissue Culture Society; Member, Editorial Board, Anticancer Research. Publication: Culture of Animal Cells. Recreations: photography; DIY activities; painting. Address: (h.) 24 Greenwood Drive, Bearsden, Glasgow, G61 2HA; T.-041-942 4782.

Friedman, Leonard Matthew. Artistic Director, Scottish Ensemble, since 1969; Artistic Director, Friedman Ensemble (and Players), since 1973; Duo Recitalist with Allan Schiller, since 1982; b. 11.12.30, London; 2 s.; 3 d. Educ. Coopers Company School; Guildhall School of Music and Drama. Founder/Co-Founder/Leader/or Director of: Hadyn Orchestra, Kalmar Chamber Orchestra, Tilford Bach, London Bach, Bremen Bach, Northern Sinfonia, Cremona Quartet, International Mozart Ensemble, Friedman Ensemble, Scottish Baroque, Aleph Ensemble, Scottish Ensemble; Guest Leader/Deputy Leader of: Royal Philharmonic, Bremen Philharmonic, Westphalia Symphony, English Opera Group, Glyndebourne, Scottish Opera, Scottish Ballet, Italian Opera Company, Festival Ballet, English Chamber, Scottish Chamber, Royal Ballet, etc.; numerous broadcasts, summer schools, festivals, lectures, records; Gold Medal, Guildhall School of Music and Drama; Citizen of the Year, Edinburgh, 1980, for aiding the development of SBE, SCO and Queen's Hall. Recreations: relative religion; philosophy; cricket; politics (global). Address: (h.) 17a Dublin Street, Edinburgh, EH1 3PG; T.-031-556 2398.

Friend, James, MA, MB, ChB, FRCPEdin. Consultant in Thoracic Medicine, Grampian Health Board, since 1973; Clinical Senior Lecturer in Medicine, Aberdeen University, since 1973; b. 2.6.38, Edinburgh; m., Elizabeth; 1 s.; 2 d. Educ. Edinburgh Academy; Gonville and Caius College, Cambridge; Edinburgh University. Hospital posts in Edinburgh and Oxford; Dorothy Temple Cross Fellowship, Seattle, 1971-72; British Thoracic Society: Secretary, Research Committee, 1980-84, Council Member, since 1983. Recreation: the Scottish hills. Address: (b.) City Hospital, Aberdeen, AB2 1NJ; T.-0224 633333.

Froude, Rev. J. Kenneth, MA, BD (Hons). Minister, St. Brycedale Church, Kirkcaldy, since 1979; b. 8.12.50, Glasgow. Educ. Hillhead High School; Aberdeen University. Trained in personnel management; Assistant Minister, Northfield, Aberdeen, 1978-79. Education Convener, Kirkcaldy Presbytery; Member, local Careers Service Committee. Recreations: running; singing; squash; mountaineering. Address: 6 East Fergus Place, Kirkcaldy; T.-0592 264480.

Fry, Derek John, MA, DPhil, BM, BCh. Senior Lecturer in Anatomy, Dundee University, since 1978; b. 19.8.43, London; m., Carol; 2 d. Educ. Dulwich College; Oxford University; St. Bartholomew's Hospital Medical School. House Physician, Medical Professorial Unit, St. Bartholomew's Hopsital, London, 1970; House Surgeon, Royal Sussex County Hospital, Brighton, 1970-71; Dundee University: Demonstrator in Anatomy, 1971-72, Lecturer in Anatomy, 1972-78. Treasurer, Scottish Churches Action for

World Development; World Development and Lay Social Responsibility Secretary, Scottish District, Methodist Church. Recreations: hill-walking; early music; squash; gardening; amusing children. Address: (h.) 28 Westfield Road, Broughty Ferry, Dundee, DD5 1ED; T.-Dundee 79430.

Fullarton, John Hamilton, ARIBA, ARIAS, DipTP. Director of Technical Services, Scottish Special Housing Association, since 1979; b. 21.2.31, Dalry, Ayrshire; m., Elvera Peebles; 1 s. Educ. Dalry High School; Glasgow School of Art; Royal Technical College, Glasgow; Edinburgh College of Art. Architect with local authorities before joining Scottish Office, 1964; Superintending Architect, Scottish Development Department, 1970-78; Head of New Towns, Construction Industry Division, Scottish Economic Planning Department, 1978-79. Research Fellowship, Urban Planning, Edinburgh College of Art, 1966-67. Publications: Scottish Housing Handbooks: Space Standards, 1969; Housing for the Elderly, 1970. Address: (h.) 7 Queens Crescent, Edinburgh, EH9 2AZ; T.-031-667 5809.

Fulton, Rikki. Actor; b. 15.4.24, Glasgow; m., Kate Matheson. Educ. Whitehill Secondary School. Invalided out of RNVR as Sub-Lt., 1945; began professional career broadcasting with BBC in Glasgow; Presenter, BBC Showband, London, 1951-55; appeared in numerous pantomimes and revues with Howard & Wyndham from 1955, including Five Past Eight shows; television work including Scotch & Wry (creator, Rev. I.M. Jolly) and starring roles in The Miser, A Winter's Tale and an episode of Bergerac; films including The Dollar Bottom, Gorky Park, Local Hero, Comfort and Joy and The Girl in the Picture; played leading role in stage production of Let Wives Tak Tent, 1981. Scottish TV Personality of the Year, 1963 and 1979; Best Light Entertainment Performance of the Year, 1969 and 1983. Recreations: bridge; chess; reading; music (listening and piano); writing; painting. Address: (b.) Richard Stone Management, London, WC2N; T.-01-839 6421.

Fulton, William Francis Monteith, BSc, MD (Hons), MB, ChB, FRCP, FRCPGlas, FRCPEdin. Reader, Department of Materia Medica, Glasgow University, 1977-84; Consultant Physician, Stobhill General Hospital, Glasgow, 1958-84; b. 12.12.19, Aberdeen; m., Dr. Frances I. Melrose; 1 s.; 1 d. Educ. Bryanston School, Dorset; Glasgow University. Resident Physician and Surgeon, Western Infirmary, Glasgow, 1945-46; National Service, Merchant Navy, 1946-48 (Ships Surgeon); joined National Health Service, 1950; Research Assistant, Cardiology, Edinburgh University, 1952-53; Senior Lecturer, Department of Materia Medica, Glasgow University, 1958-77; Senior Fellow, Cardiology, The Johns Hopkins Hospital, Baltimore, 1963-64; Foundation Professor of Medicine, Nairobi University, 1967-72. Publications: The Coronary Arteries, 1965; Modern Trends in Pharmacology and Therapeutics, 1967. Address: (h.) Woodhill, Braemar, AB3 5XX; T.-033 83 239.

Fulton, Sheriff William John, BL. Sheriff of Grampian, Highlands and Islands at Inverness, since 1976; b. 17.12.40, Glasgow; m., Marion Thomson Freeland; 1 s.; 1 d. Educ. Glasgow Boys' High School; Glasgow University. Wright & Crawford, Solicitors, Paisley: Assistant, 1963, Partner, 1968-76. Founder Member, Black Isle Theatre Club. Recreations: amateur drama; golf; military history. Address: (b.) The Castle, Inverness; T.-Inverness 230782.

Furley, Peter Anthony, MA, DPhil. Senior Lecturer, Department of Geography, Edinburgh University, since 1978; b. 5.8.35, Gravesend, Kent; m., Margaret Brenda; 1 s.; 3 d. Educ. Brasenose College, Oxford. Professor of Ecology, Brasilia University, 1976-78. Publication: Geography of the Biosphere, 1983. Address: (h.) Hawthorn Villa, Manor Place, Main Street, Aberlady, East Lothian; T.-08757 318.

Furman, Brian Laurence, BPharm, PhD, MPS. Senior Lecturer in Pharmacology, Strathclyde University, since 1982; b. 6.9.43, Leeds; m., Karen; 2 s. Educ. Roundhay School, Leeds; Bradford University. Lecturer in Pharmacology, Strathclyde University, 1969-82; Visiting Scientist, Mayo Clinic, Rochester, Minnesota, 1980. Recreations: distance running; reading; listening to music. Address: (b.) Department of Physiology and Pharmacology, Strathclyde University, George Street, Glasgow; T.-041-552 4400.

Furnell, James R.G., MA (Hons), DCP, PhD, ABPsS. Principal Clinical Psychologist (Child Health), Forth Valley Health Board, since 1980; b. 20.2.46, London; m., Lesley Anne Ross; 1 s.; 1 d. Educ. Leighton Park Society of Friends School, Reading; Aberdeen University; Glasgow University; Stirling University. Clinical Psychologist, Royal Hospital for Sick Children, Glasgow, 1970-72; Senior Clinical Psychologist, Forth Valley Health Board, 1972-80. Member, National Consultative Committee of Scientists in Professions Allied to Medicine, since 1983 (Secretary, Clinical Psychology Sub-Committee); Member, Forth Valley Health Board, since 1984. Recreations: flying; cross-country skiing. Address: (h.) Glensherup House, Glendevon, by Dollar, Perthshire, FK14 7JY; T.-Glendevon 234.

Furness, Professor Nicholas Arthur, BA, Drphil. Professor of German, Edinburgh University, since 1969; b. 9.12.23, Newcastle-upon-Tyne; m., Sylvia Bone; 1 s.; 3 d. Educ. Royal Grammar School, Newcastle-upon-Tyne; King's College, Newcastle; Innsbruck University. Temporary Lecturer in German, King's College, Newcastle, 1952-53; Assistant Lecturer in German, Manchester University, 1953-54; Lecturer, then Senior Lecturer in German, Edinburgh University, 1954-69. Recreations: travel; theatre; gardening; painting and paperhanging; music. Address: (b.) Department of German, David Hume Tower, George Square, Edinburgh, EH8 9JX; T.-031-667 1011.

Furness, Professor Raymond Stephen, BA, MA, PhD. Professor of German, St. Andrews University, since 1984; b. 25.10.33, Builth Wells; m., Janice Fairey; 1 s.; 2 d. Educ. Welwyn Garden City Grammar School; University College,

Swansea. Modern Languages Department, University of Manchester Institute of Science and Technology; Department of German, Manchester University. Publications: Expressionism; Literary History of Germany 1890-1945; Wagner and Literature. Recreation: astrology. Address: (h.) The Dirdale, Boarhills, St. Andrews, KY16 8PP; T.-033 488 469.

Furniss, James Cyril, MPhil, ARTCS, CTax, FTI, MInstM. Principal, Scottish College of Textiles, since 1976; b. 17.7.31, Sale, Cheshire; m., Jennifer Mary; 1 s. Educ. Sale County Grammar School; Leeds University; Royal Technical College, Salford. Textile Producer, Joshua Hoyle & Sons Ltd., Manchester; Research Technologist, British Rayon Research Association, Manchester; Assistant Lecturer, Lecturer, Senior Lecturer in Textiles, latterly Head of Department of Textiles, Carpet Technology and Associated Subjects, Kidderminster College; Vice-Principal, East Warwickshire College, Rugby. Member and former Secretary, Committee of Principals of Central Institutions, Scotland; Member, Board of Management, Highland Craftpoint Ltd., Inverness; Director, Scottish Textile & Technical Centre Ltd., Galashiels; Chairman, Central Institutions Committee for Educational Technology; Management Committee Adviser, SJNC; Member: Design Council, Scottish Design Council, Council of CNAA. Recreations: hill-walking; gardening; travel; music; theatre. Address: (b.) Scottish College of Textiles, Galashiels; T.-Galashiels 3351.

Fyall, Andrew. Director, Public Relations and Tourism, City of Edinburgh, since 1976; b. 13.11.32, Port Gordon; m., Elizabeth; 1 s.; 2 d. Educ. Kirkcaldy High School. Foreign Correspondent/Feature Writer, Daily Express, 1955-76. Recreation: golf. Address: (b.) 3 Princes Street, Waverley Market, Edinburgh; T.-031-557 2727.

Fyfe, James Eckford, MBE, BL. Solicitor; b. 1.6.20, Glasgow; m., Isobel M. Buchanan; 3 s. Educ. High School of Glasgow; Glasgow University. Chairman, Glasgow Social Security Appeal Tribunal, since 1985; Vice-Chairman, Argyll and Clyde Health Board, 1983-85; Past Preses, The Grand Antiquity Society of Glasgow. Recreations: golf; bridge. Address: (b.) 190 St. Vincent Street, Glasgow; T.-041-221 9005.

Fyfe, Thomas, MD, FRCP. Consultant Physician, Southern General Hospital, Glasgow, since 1978; Honorary Clinical Lecturer, Glasgow University, since 1976; Member, Inverclyde District Council, since 1984; b. 7.1.39, Gourock; m., Katherine Copland; 2 s.; 1 d. Educ. Greenock Academy; Glasgow University. Recreations: golf; bridge. Address: (h.) Drummochy, Kilmacolm; T.-Kilmacolm 2367.

Fyfe, William Morton, MD, FRCP, FRCPGlas, FRCPEdin, DCH. Consultant Paediatrician, Stobhill Hospital and Royal Hospital for Sick Children, Glasgow; b. 27.4.23, Glasgow; m., Elizabeth L. Millar; 2 s.; 2 d. Educ. High School of Glasgow; Glasgow University. House Physician, Stobhill Hospital, Glasgow, 1945; National Service, RAMC, 1946-48; Paediatric Registrar, Stobhill Hospital and Royal Hospital for Sick Children, Glasgow; Consultant Paediatrician, Renfrewshire. Recreations: golf; skiing; gardening. Address: (h.) 77 Drymen Road, Bearsden, Glasgow; T.-041-942 2166.

Fyfe, William Stevenson. Chairman, Ayrshire and Arran Health Board, since 1981; Member, UK Nursing and Midwifery Staffs Negotiating Council, since 1985; Chairman, Coastal Crafts and Printing Ltd., since 1982; b. 10.6.35, Glasgow; m., Ena Cochran; 1 s.; 1 d. Educ. Dollar Academy; Scottish College of Commerce. Town Councillor, Prestwick, 1967-73 (Magistrate, 1970-73, Acting Treasurer, 1971-73); Ayr County Councillor, 1970-73; appointed to Ayrshire and Arran Health Board, 1973 (Financial Convener, 1973-81); Member, Scottish Health Service Planning Council; Chairman, Scottish Chairmen's Gradings Committee; Member, Management Side, Re-organisation Sub-Committee (Scotland), General Whitley Council. Recreation: golf. Address: (h.) Ford House, Pennyglen, Culzean, KA19 8JW.

G

Gal, Hans, OBE, DPhil (Vienna), DMus (Edinburgh). Composer and Writer; b. 5.8.90, Vienna; m., Hanna; 1 d. Educ. School and University, Vienna. Lecturer, Vienna University, 1919-29; Director, Municipal College of Music, Mainz, 1929-33; Lecturer, Edinburgh University, 1945-65; published 109 works of music, including four operas, two oratorios, orchestral music, chamber music, piano music. Address: (h.) 16 Blacket Place, Edinburgh, 9; T.-031-667 1657.

Galbraith, James Donald, MA, MLitt, DipMedStud. Curator of Historical Records, Scottish Record Office, since 1984; b. 26.4.43, Aberdeen; m., Dr. Frances Jennifer Shaw. Educ. Robert Gordon's College, Aberdeen; Aberdeen University. Executive Officer, Ministry of Aviation, 1962; Scottish Record Office: Research Assistant, 1970, Senior Research Assistant, 1974, Assistant Keeper, 1976. Captain, 3/51st Highland Volunteers, 1982. Recreations: hill-walking; skiing; manuscript illumination; early music. Address: (h.) 118 Mayfield Road, Edinburgh; T.-031-667 5723.

Galbraith, Hugh, BSc (Hons), PhD. Senior Lecturer, Department of Agriculture, Aberdeen University, since 1983; b. 29.5.47, Campbeltown; m., Alexandra Jean MacFarlane; 1 d. Educ. Oban High School; Strathclyde University; Aberdeen University. Biochemist, North of Scotland College of Agriculture, 1972-83. Recreations: golf; reading; football spectating. Address: (b.) School of Agriculture, 581 King Street, Aberdeen, AB9 1UD; T.-0224 40291.

Galbraith, Russell. Assistant Controller of Programmes, Scottish Television, since 1983; b. 8.2.35, Glasgow; m., Harriet; 1 s.; 3 d. Educ. Govan High School, Glasgow. Staff Reporter, Glasgow Evening News, 1955-57; Sunday Mail, 1957-58; The Scotsman, 1958-62; STV, since 1962: Reporter, Here and Now, 1962-64, Programme Editor, News and Current Affairs, 1964-66, Producer/Director, 1966-72, Head of News, Current Affairs and Sport, 1972-79, Programme Administration Controller, 1979-83. Won Radio Industries Club of Scotland Award, Best Programme, 1970, for Debate, 1971 for Patterns of Folk; Executive Producer, I Can Hear You Smile, RTS Best Regional Programme Award, 1984. Recreations: cycling; curling; chess. Address: (b.) STV, Cowcaddens, Glasgow, G2 3PR.

Gall, James, LDS, RFPS. Deputy Chief Dental Officer, Scottish Home and Health Department, since 1976; Honorary Visiting Dental Surgeon, Glasgow Dental School and Hospital, since 1964; Senior Dental Adviser, Prisons Division, Scottish Office, and Senior Dental Adviser, Supplies Division and Building Division, Common Services Agency, NHS, since 1977; b. 21.4.24, Wishaw; m., Margaret Law Cran; 1 s.; 2 d. Educ. Bellshill Academy; Glasgow University. General Dental Practitioner, 1948-74; joined SHHD as Dental Officer, 1974; elected to local Dental Committee, Lanarkshire, 1958-74 (Member, Executive Council); Member, Area Dental Committee, Lanarkshire Health Board, 1974-85; Dental Member, Scottish Dental Estimates Board, 1971-74; Chairman, Scottish Branch, British Society of Medical and Dental Hypnosis Society, 1970 (National Chairman, 1977-80, President, 1980-82); Life Founder Fellow, Federation Dentaire International; Provincial Fellow, Royal Society of Medicine; Life Fellow, Royal Zoological Society of Scotland. President, Clyde Toastmasters Club, 1962; served in Boys Brigade as Officer, 1st Bellshill. Publication: Modern Trends in Hypnosis (Contributor), 1983. Recreations: gardening; golf; boating; music; reading; bridge; football. Address: (h.) The Bungalow, Douglas Gardens, Uddingston, Glasgow; T.-Uddingston 812878.

Gallacher, Tom. Writer; b. 16.2.34, Alexandria. Stage plays: Our Kindness to 5 Persons, 1969; Mr Joyce is Leaving Paris, 1971; Revival, 1972; Three to Play, 1972; Schellenbrack, 1973; Bright Scene Fading, 1973; The Only Street, 1973; Personal Effects, 1974; A Laughing Matter, 1975; Hallowe'en, 1975; The Sea Change, 1976; A Presbyterian Wooing (adapted from Pitcairne's The Assembly), 1976; The Evidence of Tiny Tim, 1977; Wha's Like Us - Fortunately!, 1978; Stage Door Canteen, 1978; Deacon Brodie (adapted from Stevenson and Henley), 1978; Jenny, 1979; Natural Causes, 1980; The Parole of Don Juan, 1981; The Treasure Ship (adapted from Brandane), 1982. Publications: (fiction): Hunting Shadows, 1981; Apprentice, 1983; Journeyman, 1984; Survivor, 1985. Address: (b.) Michael Imison Playwrights Ltd., 28 Almeida Street, London, N1 1TD.

Gallagher, Very Rev. Clarence, SJ, MA (Oxon), DCL. Rector, St. Aloysius' College, Glasgow, since 1981; Lecturer in Canon Law, St. Peter's College, since 1981; b. 17.11.29, Detroit. Educ. Blairs College, Aberdeen; Gregorian University, Rome; Oxford University. Lecturer in Canon Law: Heythrop College, London University, Gregorian University, Rome. Publication: Canon Law and the Christian Community. Address: St. Aloysius', 56 Hill Street, Glasgow, G3 6RT; T.-041-332 3039.

Gallagher, Hugh Canon. Parish Priest, St. Mary's, Greenock, since 1972; Diocesan Treasurer, since 1975; b. 30.4.20, Clydebank. Educ. St. Patrick's High School, Dumbarton; St. Peter's College, Bearsden. Assistant Priest, Gourock, 1945-56; Vice Rector, Royal Scots College, Valladolid, Spain, 1956-63; Chaplain, Little Sisters of the Poor, Greenock, 1964-69; Parish Priest, St. Columba's, Renfrew, 1969-72. President, Inverclyde Voluntary Association for Mental Health. Recreations: golf; music. Address: St. Mary's Rectory, 14 Patrick Street, Greenock, PA16 8NA; T.-Greenock 21084.

Gallagher, James Moore, MA, LLB, NP. Director of Administration and Legal Services, East Kilbride District Council, since 1975; b. 2.5.27, Bellshill; m., Margaret Ann; 3 s.; 1 d. Educ. Our Lady's High School, Motherwell; Glasgow University. Successively with East Kilbride Development Corporation, Burgh of East Kilbride and East Kilbride District Council, since 1953. Recreation: bowling. Address: (b.) Civic Centre, East Kilbride; T.-East Kilbride 28777.

Gallagher, Sister Maire T., MA (Hons), DCE. Headteacher, Notre Dame High School, Dumbarton, since 1974; Sister of Notre Dame Religious Congregation, since 1959; Chairman, Committee on Secondary Education, Consultative Committee on the Curriculum, since 1983; b. 27.5.33, Glasgow. Educ. Notre Dame High School, Glasgow; Glasgow University; Notre Dame College of Education. Principal Teacher of History, Notre Dame High School, Glasgow; Lecturer in Secondary Education, Notre Dame College of Education. Member, Consultative Committee on the Curriculum, since 1976; Member, Executive, Secondary Heads Association (Scottish Branch), 1976-83; Coordinator, Christian Life Movement Groups, West of Scotland. Recreations: reading; dress-making; bird-watching. Address: (h.) Convent of Notre Dame, Cardross Road, Dumbarton, G82 4JH; T.-Dumbarton 62361.

Gallivan, Bernard, BSc, MBCS, ALA. Director, Scottish Library Network, since 1976; b. 14.3.38, Cardiff; m., Patricia Ann Jeniffer Haines. Educ. St. Illtyd's College, Cardiff; Reading University. Computer Engineer, Standard Telephones & Cables Ltd., 1960-64; Principal Engineer, International Computers Ltd., 1964-67; Assistant Director, Library Research Unit, Lancaster University, 1970-76. Recreations: shooting; walking. Address: (h.) 12 Forthview Road, Blackhall, Edinburgh; T.-031-226 4531.

Galpern, Baron, (Myer Galpern), Kt (1960), DL, JP. Life Peer; b. 1903. Educ. Glasgow University. Lord Provost of Glasgow, 1958-60; MP (Labour), Glasgow Shettleston, 1959-79; Hon. LLD, Glasgow, 1961.

Garden, Neville Abbot. Presenter, BBC Radio Scotland (Good Morning Scotland, since 1978, and The Musical Garden, since 1979); Writer and Lecturer on musical and media matters; b. 13.2.36, Edinburgh; m., Jane Fowler; 1 d.; 3 d. by pr. m. Educ. George Watson's College, Edinburgh. Reporter, Sub-Editor, Feature Writer, Evening Dispatch, 1953-63; Daily Columnist and Music Critic, Edinburgh Evening News, 1963-64; Senior Feature Writer, Scottish Daily Express, 1964-78; Music Critic and Columnist, Sunday Standard, 1981-83; regular Contributor to magazine programmes and Presenter, Arts in Scotland, Prospect, Twelve Noon, BBC Radio, 1952-78. Child Actor, Children's Hour, etc., 1948-52. Founder Member, Edinburgh Symphony Orchestra, 1965; Conductor: Edinburgh Grand Opera, seven years; Edinburgh Ballet Theatre, nine years; Edinburgh Chamber Orchestra; Producer and Musical Director, Southern Light Opera Company, since 1979. Address: (b.) BBC, 5 Queen Street, Edinburgh.

Gardiner, Alexander Quentin, MB, ChB, PhD, FRCPsych, DPM. Consultant Psychiatrist, Royal Cornhill Hospital, Aberdeen, since 1971; Clinical Senior Lecturer in Mental Health, Aberdeen University, since 1971; b. 5.5.35, Aberdeen; m., Rhoda Margaret Primrose; 2 s.; 1 d. Educ. Strathallan School; Robert Gordon's College, Aberdeen; Aberdeen University. MRC Research Fellow, 1964-67; Research Associate, Yale University School of Medicine, 1969-70. Recreation: salmon fishing. Address: (h.) The Firs, Bieldside, Aberdeen, AB1 9DT; T.-0224 867504.

Gardiner, Austen James Sutherland, MB, ChB, MD, MRCP, FRCPGlas, FRCPEdin. Consultant Physician and Postgraduate Tutor, Monklands Hospital, Lanarkshire, since 1976; b. 27.1.34, Aberdeen; m., Ruth Duncan; 2 s.; 1 d. Educ. Aberdeen Grammar School; Aberdeen University. Research in junior teaching post, University Department of Surgery and Medicine, Aberdeen; Registrar and Senior Registrar (Internal) Medicine, Aberdeen Teaching Hospital; Honorary Elective of Medicine, Department of Medicine; Research Fellow, Department of Medicine, Magill University, Montreal, 1968-70; Senior Registrar, Aberdeen Group of Teaching Hospitals, 1970-76. Recreations: golf; shooting; fishing. Address: (h.) Farringford, St. Margaret's Drive, Dunblane; T.-0786 822124.

Gardiner, Thomas, BL. Solicitor; b. 26.7.30, Cambuslang; m., Aileen June Howden; 2 s.; 1 d. Educ. West Coats School, Cambuslang; High School of Glasgow; Glasgow University. National Service, RAF Legal Services, Middle East; Partner, Anderson & Gardiner, Solicitors, 1956 (amalgamated with McClure Naismith & Co., 1984); Solicitor to Finance Houses Association and CCTA. Chairman, Rutherglen Conservative Association; twice Captain, Cambuslang Golf Club. Recreations: golf; reading. Address (h.) 143 Brownside Road, Cambuslang; T.-041-641 8832.

Gardner, Agnes Jardine, MBE, JP. Vice-Chairman, North East Fife District Council, since 1984 (Vice-Chairman, Housing Committee, since 1976); Vice-Chairman, Scottish National Housing and Town Planning Council, since 1980; m., Thomas Gardner; 1 d. Educ. Blairgowrie High School. Apprenticeship in legal firms; Diploma, Scottish Local Government Law and Finance; Town Clerk, St. Monans, 1972-75; Member, Anstruther Town Council, 1958-75; Honorary Secretary: East Neuk of Fife Branch, Cancer Relief, East Neuk of Fife Merchants and Traders Association. Recreations: reading; gardening. Address: (h.) Westerlea, Anstruther, Fife; T.-0333 310759.

Gardner, David Alistair. Chairman, Alistair Gardner Enterprises Limited, since 1966; Chairman, Moray Firth Radio Limited, since 1980; b. 10.10.30, Glasgow; m., Sheila Maree Stewart; 1 d. Educ. Fettes College, Edinburgh; Ross Hall, Scottish Hotel School, Glasgow. Involved in hotel/licensed trade as Manager/Owner/Director, since 1950; freelance, BBC Radio, 1958-80; own programme, Moray Firth Radio, since 1982; former Senior Bailie, Dornoch Town Council; former Member, Sutherland County Council; Past Chairman, North of Scotland Water Board. Co-Founder, Inverness Hospitals Broadcasting Service. Recreations: broadcasting; travel; golf. Address: (h.) Altyre, 10 Abertarff Road, Inverness, IV2 3NW; T.-0463 230684.

Gardner, John Victor, ARICS. Operations Director (Scotland), The Housing Corporation, since 1982; b. 26.2.40, Edinburgh; m., Helen Margaret; 1 s.; 2 d. Educ. Royal High School, Edinburgh; Heriot-Watt College. Surveyor with Ross and Morton, Edinburgh, 1960-62; with City Architect, Edinburgh Corporation, 1962-69; with Midlothian County Council, 1969-70; with Scottish Special Housing Association, 1970-72; Chief Housing Improvements Officer, Edinburgh Corporation/Edinburgh District Council, 1972-82. Elder, Church of Scotland, 1967-82; Winston Churchill Fellow, 1979; Prison Visitor; Past President, Royal High School FP Club. Recreations: music; religion; photography; cooking; travel. Address: (h.) 104 Comiston Drive, Edinburgh, EH10 5QU; T.-031-447 6859.

Gardner, Raymond Alexander. Features Editor, Glasgow Herald, since 1978 (also "Trencherman", Restaurant and Hotel Critic, since 1982); b. 6.11.44, Glasgow. Educ. High School of Glasgow. Various editorial positions, Fleet Street and Scotland; Columnist, Travel Writer and Author; Contributor to Harpers, Quick Magazine (Munich), Options, The Scotland Book, Motor Boat and Yachting, Radio Clyde, Radio Scotland, RTE. Publications: Land of Time Enough - A Journey Through the Waterways of Ireland; Glasgow - A Celebration (Contributor). Recreation: doing nothing on boats in Ireland. Address: (b.) Glasgow Herald, 195 Albion Street, Glasgow, G1; T.-041-552 6255.

Gardner, Robert George, BSc, PhD, CEng, MIChemE. Senior Lecturer in Chemical Technology, Strathclyde University, since 1972; b. 1.1.28, Paisley; m., Ailsa W. McCrone; 2 d. Educ. Paisley Grammar School; Glasgow University. Scientist, NCB (Central West Area), 1952-54; Lecturer, Royal Technical College, 1954-72;

Titular Professor, Buenos Aires University, 1967; Visiting Professor, University of Nigeria, 1980. Recreations: sailing; hill-walking; archaeology. Address: (h.) 58 Gailes Road, Troon, KA10 6TA; T.-Troon 313032.

Garlick, Peter James, MA (Cantab), PhD. Member, Physiology Division, Rowett Research Institute, since 1983; b. 17.10.45, Halifax; m., Margaret Anita McNurlan; 1 s.; 1 d. Educ. Queen Elizabeth Grammar School, Wakefield; St. John's College, Cambridge. MRC Tropical Metabolism Research Unit, London; Department of Human Nutrition, London School of Hygiene and Tropical Medicine, 1970-73; Department of Nutritional Sciences, Wisconsin University, 1973-74; Royal Society/J. Sainsbury Research Fellow, then External Scientific Staff of MRC, London School of Hygiene and Tropical Medicine, 1974-83. Deputy Chairman, Biochemical Journal. Publication: Protein Turnover in Mammalian Tissues and in the Whole Body. Address: (b.) Rowett Research Institute, Bucksburn, Aberdeen, AB2 9SB; T.-0224 712751, Ext. 319.

Garner-Smith, Brigadier Kenneth James, OBE, DL, MA. Deputy Lieutenant, Inverness-shire, since 1964; Honorary Sheriff, Inverness-shire, since 1967; Member, Queen's Bodyguard for Scotland (Royal Company of Archers), since 1953; b. 30.3.04; m., Mary Macdonald of Aird and Vallay; 1 s.; 2 d. Educ. Charterhouse; Trinity College, Oxford. Commissioned Seaforth Highlanders, 1925; campaigns: Palestine (Despatches, 1936), North Africa, 1942-43; Staff College (various staff appointments); Military Attache: HM Embassy, Oslo, 1945-48, HM Embassy, Ankara, 1954-57; Member, Inverness County Council, 1961-75; Chairman, Inverness CC Education Committee, 1968-75. Address: (h.) Cottage of Aird, Aird House, Inverness, IV1 2AA; T.-0463 231212.

Garnock, Viscount, (David Lindesay-Bethune). Company Director; b. 9.2.26; m., Penelope Crossley; 1 s.; 1 d. by pr. m. Chairman, Air Transport Users Committee, 1983-84; Chairman, British Carpet Manufacturers' Association Export Council, since 1976; Vice-President, Transport Trust, since 1973; Member, Queen's Bodyguard for Scotland (Royal Company of Archers).

Garraway, Professor William Michael, MD, MSc, MRCP, FRCGP, FFCM, DObstRCOG, DCH. Professor of Community Medicine, Edinburgh University, since 1983; b. 26.1.42, Dumfries; m., Alison Mary Haggart; 1 s.; 1 d. Educ. Carlisle Grammar School; Edinburgh University; London University; Mayo Graduate School of Medicine. Lecturer, Department of Community Medicine, Edinburgh University, 1972-77 (Senior Lecturer, 1978-81); Consultant Epidemiologist, Mayo Clinic, Rochester, USA, 1981-83. Recreations: hill-walking; cross-country skiing. Address: (b.) Usher Institute, Warrender Park Road, Edinburgh, EH9 2RA.

Garrett, James Allan, MB, ChB, FRCSEdin, FRCSGlas. Consultant Surgeon, Stobhill Hospital, Glasgow, since 1967; b. 8.3.28, Glasgow; m.,

Margaret Keddie; 1 s.; 1 d. Educ. Hutchesons' Grammar School, Glasgow; Glasgow University. Captain, RAMC, 1952-54; House Officer, Registrar and Senior Registrar, Glasgow Royal Infirmary, 1954-67. Address: (h.) 12 Richmond Drive, Cambuslang, Glasgow, G72 8BH; T.-041-641 2888.

Garrity, Rev. Thomas Alan Whiteway, BSc, BD. Minister, The Auld Kirk of Ayr (St. John The Baptist), since 1982; b. 13.7.43, Glasgow; m., Elizabeth Caroline Whiteford; 2 d. Educ. Allan Glen's School; Glasgow University; Edinburgh University. Assistant Minister, Dundee Parish Church (St. Mary's); Minister, Fraserburgh South. Recreations: photography; golf. Address: The Manse, 58 Monument Road, Ayr; T.-Ayr 262580.

Garrod, Simon Christopher, MA, PhD. Senior Lecturer in Psychology, Glasgow University, since 1984; b. 19.11.47, London; m., Celia Wright Smith; 1 s.; 1 d. Educ. Bradfield College, Berkshire; Oxford University; Princeton University. Lecturer in Psychology, Glasgow University, 1974-84; Visiting Fellow, Max Planck Institute for Psycholinguistics, Nijmegen. Publication: Understanding Written Language, 1981. Recreations: fishing; painting. Address: (h.) 24 Polnoon Street, Eaglesham, Glasgow, G76; T.-Eaglesham 2583.

Gartside, Peter, BEd (Hons). Advisor, Scottish Council for Educational Technology, since 1980; Secretary, Scottish Committee on Open Learning, since 1983; b. 31.10.32, Oldham; m., Kathleen; 1 s. Educ. East Oldham High School; Chester Diocesan Training College; Charlotte Mason College of Education. National Service, Royal Scots Greys, 1951-53; Teacher, Hollinwood County Secondary School, Oldham, 1955-57; Housemaster, The Blue Coat School, Oldham, 1957-68; Head of House, Hattersley County Comprehensive School, 1968-70; Warden, Workington Teachers' Centre, Cumbria, 1970-76; Education Department, Independent Broadcasting Authority, 1977-78; Warden, West Cumbria Teachers' Centre, 1978-79. Former Honorary Secretary, National Committee of Teachers' Audio/Visual Aids Groups; former Member, BBC Radio Carlisle Education Education Advisory Panel. Recreations: walking; travel; music. Address (h.) 74 Victoria Crescent Road, Glasgow, G12 9JN; T.-041-334 9314.

Garvie, Alexander Femister, MA. Senior Lecturer, Department of Greek, Glasgow University, since 1972; b. 29.1.34, Edinburgh; m., Jane Wallace Johnstone; 1 s.; 1 d. Educ. George Watson's College, Edinburgh; Edinburgh University; Cambridge University. Assistant, then Lecturer, Department of Greek, Glasgow University, 1960-72; Visiting Gillespie Professor, College of Wooster, Ohio, 1967-68; Visiting Assistant Professor, Ohio State University, 1968. Publications: Aeschylus' Supplices: Play and Trilogy, 1969; Aeschylus Choephori: Introduction and Commentary, 1986. Recreations: music; hill-walking. Address: (h.) 93 Stirling Drive, Bishopbriggs, Glasgow; T.-041-772 4140.

Garvie, Ian Graham Donaldson, MA (Hons), BLitt, DipEd. Rector, Auchmuty High School, Glenrothes, since 1976; b. 7.6.29, Perth; m., Margaret M.C. McIntosh. Educ. Perth Academy; Edinburgh University; Moray House College of Education; Exeter College, Oxford. RAF Education Branch; Assistant Teacher, Classics, Special Assistant Teacher, High School of Stirling; Principal Teacher, Bellshill Academy; Principal Teacher, Assistant Rector, Dunfermline High School. Secretary, Fife Secondary Headteachers' Association; Assistant Secretary, Headteachers' Association of Scotland; Chairman, Mid-Fife Newstape (talking newspaper for the blind); Member, Chairman's Committee, Fife Society for the Blind. Recreation: hill-walking. Address: (h.) 23 Lakeside Road, Kirkcaldy, KY2 5QJ; T.-0592 756554.

Gaskin, Professor Maxwell, DFC (and bar), MA. Jaffrey Professor of Political Economy, Aberdeen University, 1965-85; b. 18.11.21, Liverpool; m., Brenda Stewart; 1 s.; 3 d. Educ. Quarry Bank School, Liverpool; Liverpool University. War Service, RAF, 1941-46; Lecturer and Senior Lecturer in Economics, Glasgow University, 1951-65; Head, Department of Political Economy, Aberdeen University, 1965-81; Economic Consultant to Secretary of State for Scotland, since 1965; Member, Scottish Agricultural Wages Board, since 1972; Chairman, Foresterhill and Associated Hospitals Board, 1972-74; Chairman, Flax and Hemp and Retail Bespoke Tailoring Wages Councils, since 1978; Member, Civil Engineering EDC, 1978-84; Chairman, Section F, British Association, 1978-79; President, Scottish Economic Society, 1981-84; Fellow, Royal Economic Society. Publications: The Scottish Banks: A Modern Survey, 1965; North East Scotland: A Survey of its Development Potential (Co-author), 1969; Economic Impact of North Sea Oil on Scotland (Co-author), 1978; Employment in Insurance, Banking and Finance in Scotland, 1980; The Political Economy of Tolerable Survival (Editor), 1981. Recreations: music; gardening. Address: (h.) Westfield, Ancrum, Roxburghshire, TD8 6XA; T.-08535 237.

Gaston, Rev. Arthur Raymond, MA, BD. Minister, Dollar with Muckhart with Glendevon, since 1975; Director, National Bible Society of Scotland, since 1980; b. 25.5.36, Atherstone; m., Evelyn Wilson Mather; 1 s.; 2 d. Educ. Gordon Schools, Huntly; Aberdeen University; Scottish Congregational College. Teacher of Mathematics, King's Park School, Glasgow; preparatory study for service with London Missionary Society; Principal, Theological College, Fianarantsoa, Madagascar, 1962-67 (also District Missionary and Head of senior school); entry to Church of Scotland following return to Britain, 1967; Minister, Sauchie Parish Church, 1969-75. Member, Board of Governors, Dollar Academy. Recreations: walking; lepidoptery; water-colour painting. Address: Dollar Manse, 2 Manse Road, Dollar, FK14 7AJ; T.-Dollar 2601.

Gayre of Gayre and Nigg, Lt. Col. Robert, MA, DPhil, DFSc, DSc; Grand Commander, Order of St. Lazarus; b. 6.8.07; m., Mary Nina Terry (deceased); 1 s. Educ. Edinburgh University; Exeter College, Oxford. Commissioned Officer, Supplementary Reserve Royal Artillery, 1931; War Service, 1939; transferred to Regular Army Reserve, 1941; Staff Officer for Education, HQ Airborne Forces, 1941; Major HQ, Oxford District, 1941; Lt. Col., Educational Adviser, Allied Military Government for Italy, 1943; Professor of Anthropology, University of Saugor, India, 1954. Member, Royal Society of Naples. Recreation: sailing. Address: Minard Castle, Argyll; 10 St. Colme Street, Edinburgh.

Geary, Martin Charles, RD, MA, LLB. Advocate, since 1980; b. 25.8.50, Taplow, Berkshire; m., Irene Maud Bailey; 2 s. Educ. Abingdon School; Edinburgh University. Qualified as Solicitor, 1979; commenced Pupillage at Bar, 1979; called to Bar, 1980. Member, Royal Naval Reserve, since 1969 (Lt. Commander). Recreations: walking; skiing; sailing. Address: (b.) Advocates Library, Parliament House, Edinburgh, EH1 1RF; T.-031-226 5071.

Geddes, Eric, OStJ, IPFA, FRVA, MBCS, MBIM. Chief Executive, Central Regional Council, since 1974; b. 5.2.22, Dumfries; m., Nancy; 2 s. Educ. Dumfries Academy. Dumfries Town Council: Apprentice Accountant, 1939-41, Assistant Town Chamberlain and House Factor, 1946-51; Chief Assistant to County Treasurer and Collector, Angus County Council, 1951-54; Depute County Treasurer, Collector and House Factor, Dunbarton County Council, 1954-62; County Treasurer and Collector, Midlothian County Council, 1962-75. Chairman, SOLACE, 1983-84; Chairman, JNC, Chief Officials in Scotland, 1983-84; former Commissioner, Public Works Loan Board. Recreations: farming; golf; shooting; curling. Address: (b.) Viewforth, Stirling; T.-Stirling 73111.

Geddes, James Clarke, MA (Hons), DipEd, FRSA. Director of Adult Education and Extra-Mural Studies, St. Andrews University, since 1967; b. 19.12.22, Inverbervie; m., Muriel Lesley McNab; 2 s.; 2 d. Educ. Mackie Academy, Stonehaven; Aberdeen University. RAF (Radar Mechanic); Civil Service (Ministry of Labour); Teacher of English, Robert Gordon's College. Governor, Newbattle Abbey College; Board Member, Camp America; Council Member, Council for Adult Education and Member, Working Party on Education of the Elderly. Recreation: foreign travel - study tours abroad. Address: (b.) St. Andrews University, 3 St. Mary's Place, St. Andrews, KY16 9UY; T.-0334 73429.

Gellatly, Ian Robert George, CA. President, Scottish Football League; 2nd Vice President, Scottish Football Association (Chairman, International Committee); Chairman, Dundee Football Club PLC, since 1972; b. 5.11.38, Dundee; m., Anne May Horsburgh; 1 s.; 1 d. Educ. Dundee High School; Lathallan Preparatory School; Merchiston Castle. Partner, Miller McIntyre Gellatly, CA, Dundee, since 1964. Recreations: golf; curling. Address: (h.) Mains of Fowlis, Invergowrie, by Dundee; T.-Longforgan 229.

Gemmell, Curtis Glen, BSc, PhD, MIBiol, MRCPath. Senior Lecturer, Department of Bacteriology, Glasgow University, since 1976; Honorary Bacteriologist, Greater Glasgow Health Board, since 1976; b. 26.8.41, Beith, Ayrshire; m., Anne Margaret; 2 d. Educ. Spier's School, Beith; Glasgow University. Glasgow University: Assistant Lecturer, 1966-68, Lecturer, 1968-69; Paisley College of Technology: Lecturer, 1969-71, Senior Lecturer, 1971-76; Visiting Assistant Professor, Minnesota University, Minneapolis, 1979-80. Recreations: gardening; golf. Address: (h.) Sunninghill, 19 Lawmarnock Crescent, Bridge of Weir, PA11 3AS; T.-Bridge of Weir 613350.

Gemmell, Vera. Member, Fife Regional Council; Board Member, Glenrothes Development Corporation; b. 28.6.34, New Elgin, Moray; m., P.J. Gemmell; 5 s.; 5 d. Educ. Milne's School, Fochabers. Recreations: walking; knitting. Address: (h.) 108 Broom Road, Glenrothes, KY6 2BQ; T.-Glenrothes 755688.

Gennard, Professor John, BA (Econ), MA (Econ). Professor of Industrial Relations, Strathclyde University, since 1981; b. 26.4.44, Manchester; m., Florence Anne Russell; 1 s.; 1 d. Educ. Hulme Grammar School for Boys; Sheffield University; Manchester University. Research Officer, Industrial Relations Department, then Lecturer in Industrial Relations, London School of Economics, 1968-81. Publications: The Reluctant Militants (Co-author), 1972; Financing Strikers, 1978; Industrial Relations and Job Security, 1984. Recreations: football; swimming; politics; trade unions; food and drink. Address: (h.) 4 South Avenue, Carluke, Lanarkshire; T.-0555 72095.

George, Albert George. Member, Shetland Health Board, since 1983; Fire Officer, Sullom Voe Terminal, since 1980; b. 23.3.40, London; m., Valerie Constance; 3 s. Educ. St. Mary's School, Hornsey. Flour Confectioner, 1956-61; Fireman, Middlesex Fire Brigade, 1961-65; Leading Fireman, then Sub Officer, Gloucestershire Fire Service, 1967-78. Area Scout Commissioner, Shetland, since 1981. Recreations: gardening; walking. Address: (h.) 7 Vista Vird, Brae, Shetland, ZE2 9QG; T.-Brae 487.

George, Professor William David, MB, BS, FRCS, MS. Professor of Surgery, Glasgow University, since 1981; b. 22.3.43, Reading; m., Helen Marie Moran; 1 s.; 3 d. Educ. Henley Grammar School; London University. Lecturer in Surgery, Manchester University, 1973-77; Senior Lecturer in Surgery, Liverpool University, 1977-81. Member, National Committees, British Association of Surgical Oncology and Surgical Research Society. Recreations: veteran rowing; golf. Address: (b.) University Department of Surgery, Western Infirmary, Glasgow, G11 6NT; T.-041-339 8822.

Gerrard, John Henry Atkinson, DA (Edin), MA (Cantab), ARIAS, FRSA, RIBA. Technical Director, Scottish Civic Trust, since 1984; b. 15.9.34, Leicester; m., Dr. Margaret Mackay.

Educ. Abbotsholme; Corpus Christi College, Cambridge; Edinburgh College of Art. Assistant Architect: Sheffield Corporation, 1961-63, Planning Department, Oxford City Council, 1965-68; Assistant Director, Scottish Civic Trust, 1968-84. Recreation: travelling hopefully. Address: (b.) Scottish Civic Trust, 24 George Square, Glasgow; T.-041-221 1466.

Gerrard, Michael Anthony, MA, AIL. Chief Executive, Shetland Islands Council, since 1983; b. 17.8.35, London; m., Heather Margaret; 1 s.; 3 d. Educ. Finchley Grammar School; Lincoln College, Oxford. John Dale Ltd., London, 1959-63; Coates Bros. & Co. Ltd., London, 1963-74; Secretary, Haringey Community Health Council, 1974-77; Secretary, Association of Community Health Councils for England and Wales, 1977-83. Address: (b.) Town Hall, Lerwick; T.-0595 3535.

Gerson, Jack Barton. Dramatist and Novelist; b. 31.7.28, Glasgow; 1 d. Educ. Hillhead High School, Glasgow. RAF, two years; worked in advertising and cinema distribution, 1949-59; writing full-time since 1959; won BBC Television Play Competition, 1959, for Three Ring Circus; has written more than 100 hours of television drama; created two series, The Regiment and The Omega Factor; 14 radio plays; novels include Whitehall Sanction, Assassination Run, Treachery Game and The Back of the Tiger. Recreations: cinema; reading; swimming; Caribbean Islands; sleeping in front of television set. Address: (b.) c/o Harvey Unna & Stephen Durbridge, 24 Pottery Lane, Holland Park, London, W11 4LZ; T.-01-727 1346.

Gerver, Elisabeth, BA (Hons), MA, PhD. Director, Scottish Institute of Adult Education, since 1983; b. 15.4.41, Winnipeg; m., Dr. David Gerver (deceased); 1 s.; 1 d. Educ. Wolfville High School, Nova Scotia; Dalhousie University, Canada; Toronto University; King's College, London. Lecturer in Communications, Newcastle upon Tyne Polytechnic, 1968-69; part-time Lecturer in English and American Literature, Durham University, 1969-71; part-time staff, Open University, 1971-84; Lecturer in Communication, Queen Margaret College, Edinburgh, 1974-83; part-time Tutor/Organiser of Preparatory Studies, Stirling University, 1976-79; Director (on secondment), Scottish Community Education Microelectronics Project, Glasgow, 1981-82; part-time Lecturer in Information Technology, Strathclyde University, 1983-84. Council Member: Scottish Council for Community Education, 1979-82, Scottish Community Education Council, 1982-83; Member, BBC Continuing Education Advisory Council, since 1983; Member and Member, Chairman's Executive, Scottish Committee on Open Learning, since 1983; Member, Scottish Committee, Open University in Scotland, 1974-79; Member, Admissions Committee, Open University, 1978-79; Executive Member, Scottish Institute of Adult Education, 1979-83 (Chairman, 1980-83); Member, Steering Committee, European Bureau of Adult Education, since 1983; Member, Board of Directors, Network Scotland Ltd., since 1984. Publications: Computers and Adult Learning, 1984; Humanising Technology, 1985. Recreations: spare time spent with children, at the performing arts, in the garden, on the hills, in front of computer! Address: (b.) Scottish Institute of Adult Education, 30 Rutland Square, Edinburgh, EH1 2BW; T.-031-229 0331.

Gettinby, George, BSc, DPhil. Senior Lecturer in Statistics, Strathclyde University, since 1983; b. 23.2.49, Larne, Northern Ireland; m., Ruth Armstrong; 2 s. Educ. Larne Technical College; Queen's University, Belfast; University of Ulster. Lecturer in Mathematics, Strathclyde University, 1974-83. President, Society of Veterinary Epidemiology and Preventive Medicine, 1984-85; Consultant to International Laboratory for Research on Animal Diseases, Nairobi, 1979-85. Address: (b.) Department of Mathematics, Strathclyde University, Glasgow; T.-041-552 4400.

Gibson, Sir Alexander (Drummond), KB (1977), CBE (1967), Hon RAM (1969), Hon FRCM (1973), Hon FRSAM (1973), Hon RSA (1975), O. St. J. (1975), FRSE (1978), FRSA (1980), Hon LLD (Aberdeen), 1968, Hon DMus (Glasgow), 1972, DUniv (Stirling), 1972; Hon Doctor, Open University, 1978, LRAM, ARCM, ARCO. Principal Conductor and Musical Director, Scottish National Orchestra, since 1959; Founder and Artistic Director, Scottish Opera, since 1962; b. 11.2.26, Motherwell; m., Anne Veronica Waggett; 3 s.; 1 d. Educ. Dalziel High School, Motherwell; Glasgow University; Royal College of Music; Mozarteum, Salzburg, Austria; Accademia Chigiano, Siena, Italy. Royal Signals, 1944-48; Repetiteur and Assistant Conductor, Sadler's Wells Opera, 1951-52; Assistant Conductor, BBC Scottish Orchestra, Glasgow, 1952-54; Sadler's Wells Opera: Staff Conductor, 1954-57, Musical Director, 1957-59; Principal Guest Conductor, Houston Symphony Orchestra, 1981-82 and 1982-83. Freeman, Burgh of Motherwell and Wishaw, 1964; St. Mungo Prize, 1970; Arnold Bax Memorial Medal for Conducting, 1959; ISM Musician of the Year Award, 1976; Sibelius Medal, 1978; Musician of the Year, British Music Year Book, 1980.

Gibson, Archibald Turner, FIB (Scot). Joint General Manager, Bank of Scotland, since 1983; b. 6.6.32, Paisley; m., Ellen Campbell McNiven; 1 s.; 2 d. Educ. Paisley Grammar School; Harvard Business School. Bank of Scotland: Assistant General Manager, International Division, 1974-80, Divisional General Manager, Marketing and Development, 1980-83. Recreations: tennis; gardening; theatre; art. Address: (b.) Bank of Scotland, Uberior House, Grassmarket, Edinburgh; T.-031-442 7777.

Gibson, Ernest Douglas, JP, DPE, DCE. Vice-Chairman, Nithsdale District Council, since 1984 (Chairman, Finance Sub-Committee, since 1984); Chairman, Dumfries Constituency Association, SNP, since 1984; b. 30.11.28, Edinburgh; m., Isobel Doreen Gass; 2 s.; 1 d. Educ. Portobello Secondary School; Jordanhill College, Glasgow. Head Teacher: Glenzier School, 1959-67, Duncow School, 1967-74, Noblehill School, 1974-84; elected, Dumfries District Council, 1973; Member, Nithsdale District Council, since 1974; Parliamentary candidate, Dumfries, 1979 and 1983. Recreations: golf; angling. Address: (h.) 29 Ardwall Road, Dumfries, DG1 3AQ; T.-0387 54651.

Gibson, Rev. Henry Montgomerie, MA, BD. Minister, The High Kirk, Dundee, since 1979; b. 11.6.36, Wishaw; m., Dr. Anne Margaret Thomson; 1 s. Educ. Wishaw Academy; Hamilton Academy; Glasgow University. Assistant Minister, Glasgow Cathedral, 1960; Minister: Carmunnock Parish Church, Glasgow, 1961-71, Aberfeldy, 1971-79; Convener, Church of Scotland Working Party on Alcohol and Drugs, 1975-81. Recreations: reading; table tennis (occasionally). Address: High Kirk Manse, 6 Adelaide Place, Dundee, DD3 6LF; T.-Dundee 22955.

Gibson, John Alan, MD, FLS, FSA. Director, Scottish Natural History Library, since 1974; Chairman, Clyde Area Branch, Scottish Wildlife Trust, since 1969; Honorary Secretary, British Medical Association, since 1957; b. 15.5.26, Kilbarchan; m., Dr. Mary M. Baxter; 1 d. Educ. Lindisfarne School; Paisley Grammar School; Glasgow University. Family Doctor, village of Kilbarchan; Editor, The Scottish Naturalist; Scottish Representative, Society for the History of Natural History; Chairman, Scottish Natural History Trust; Honorary Secretary, Scottish Society for the Protection of Birds. Queen's Silver Jubilee Medal, 1977; Fellowship, BMA, 1982. Publications: Mammals of Clyde Area, 1980; Birds of Clyde Area, 1981; Atlas of Clyde Vertebrates, 1985. Recreations: natural history; golf (Royal Troon). Address: (h.) Foremount House, Kilbarchan, Renfrewshire, PA10 2EZ; T.-Kilbarchan 2410.

Gibson, Rev. John Clark Love, MA, BD, DPhil. Head, Department of Hebrew and Old Testament Studies, Edinburgh University, since 1983; b. 28.5.30, Coatbridge; m., Agnes Gilmour Russell; 4 s.; 1 d. Educ. Coatbridge High School; Glasgow University; Magdalen College, Oxford. Licensed as Probationer, Church of Scotland, 1956; Assistant Minister, Bellshill West, 1956; Minister, Newmachar, 1959-62; Edinburgh University: Lecturer in Hebrew and Semitic Languages, 1962-73, Reader, since 1973. Publications: Textbook of Hebrew Inscriptions, 1971; Textbook of Aramaic Inscriptions, 1975; Canaanite Myths and Legends, 1978; Textbook of Phoenician Inscriptions, 1982; Daily Study Bible (Old Testament) (General Editor and author of volumes on Genesis and Job). Recreations: Burns; golf. Address: (h.) 10 South Morton Street, Edinburgh, EH15 2NB; T.-031-669 3635.

Gibson, Rev. Michael, BD (Hons), STM. Minister, The Park Church, Giffnock, since 1974; Member, Eastwood District Council, since 1984; b. 30.3.36, Methlick, Aberdeenshire; m., Margaret Helen Fyffe; 1 s.; 1 d. Educ. Robert Gordon's College, Aberdeen; Aberdeen University; Union Theological Seminary, New York. Chairman, Giffnock and Thornliebank Community Council, 1978-84. Recreations: golf; gardening. Address: 41 Rouken Glen Road, Thornliebank, Glasgow, G46 7JD; T.-041-638 3023.

Gibson, Peter Robert, MA (Hons). Director, Scottish Consumer Council, since 1977; b. 11.9.47, Dunlop, Ayrshire; m., Amanda Kate Britain. Educ. Glasgow Academy; Elk Grove Senior High School, California; St. Andrews University; University of California, Davis. Teaching Assistant, University of California, Davis, 1969-70; Marketing Trainee, Unilever, 1970-71; Regional Organiser, Shelter, Surrey and Hampshire, 1971-73; National Groups Organiser, War on Want, 1973-74; Director, Shelter Scotland, 1974-77. Member, Scottish Housing Advisory Committee, 1977-79; Founder Member, Scottish Homeless Group, 1977; Member, council for Freedom of Information. Recreations: home improvement (involuntary); Italy; eating out; trashy TV and cinema; cats. Address: (h.) Dunluce House, Prospect Road, Dullatur, G68 OAN

Gibson, Robert Myles, ERD, TD, CStJ, MD, MSc, FRCS, FRCSEdin. Vice President, Royal College of Surgeons of Edinburgh, since 1982; Honorary Consultant Neurosurgeon to the Army, since 1960; Consultant Neurosurgeon, Leeds General Infirmary, since 1959; b. 6.5.27, Dunragit, Wigtownshire; m., Ena Millar; 1 s.; 1 d. Educ. Kilmarnock Academy; Glasgow University; McGill University, Montreal. Various surgical appointments, Edinburgh, Oxford, London and Leeds; Senior Lecturer in Neurosurgery, Leeds University; Officer Commanding Field Surgical Units, TA, and Adviser to Ministry of Defence and BAOR; former Deputy Chairman, Central Committee, Hospital Medical Services; Member, Armed Forces Medical Advisory Board; Mitchiner Medallist, Royal College of Surgeons of England. Recreations: golf; Director, York City FC; steam railway preservation.

Gibson, Thomas, MSc, FRIBA, FRICS, FRIAS. Director of Technical Services, East Kilbride Development Corporation, since 1982; b. 23.1.30, Barrhead; m., Sheila Hamilton; 1 s.; 1 d. Educ. Camphill School, Paisley; Glasgow School of Art; Strathclyde University. Various architectural posts in variety of local authority, private practice and industrial offices, 1947-60; Senior Lecturer, Department of Land Economics, Paisley College of Technology, 1960-82. Past President, Paisley Rotary Club; President-Elect: Paisley Bohemian Club, Paisley Burns Club. Recreations: playing golf; watching cricket; after-dinner speaking; writing poetry. Address: (h.) Dunvegan, 19 Southfield Avenue, Paisley, PA2 8BY; T.-041-884 2147.

Gifford, Rev. Professor Douglas John, TD, BLitt, MA (Oxon). Professor of Spanish, St. Andrews University, since 1975; Non-Stipendiary Episcopalian Chaplain to St. Andrews University, since 1981; Director, The Renaissance Group, since 1976; b. 21.7.24, Buenos Aires; m., Hazel Mary Collingwood; 3 s.; 1 d. Educ. Queen's College, Oxford. British Army Intelligence Corps, 1943-47; served in Normandy and Holland with 51st Highland Division; Lecturer, then Senior Lecturer, St. Andrews University, 1950-75; Commanding Officer, University OTC, 1960-67 (retired with rank of Lt. Col.); ordained in Episcopal Church of Scotland, 1981. Publications: Textos Linguistilos Del Medioevo Espanol (Co-author), 1959; Carnival & Coca-Leaf (Co-author); Gods, Spirits and Warriors, Mythology of Central and South America. Recreations: squash; golf; music. Address: 3 Balfour Place, St. Andrews, KY16 9RQ; T.-0334 72742.

Gilbert, Colin, BA (Hons). Comedy Producer, BBC Scotland, since 1983; b. 3.4.52, Glasgow; m., Joanna; 1 s.; 1 d. Educ. St. Paul's School; York University. Script Editor, Not The 9 O'Clock News, 1980-82; Producer: A Kick Up the Eighties, 1983, Naked Radio, 1984. Address: (b.) BBC Scotland, Queen Margaret Drive, Glasgow, G12 8DG.

Gilbert, Robert Henry, BL, WS. Secretary, Legal Aid Scotland and Senior Deputy Secretary, Law Society of Scotland, since 1982; b. 30.10.24, Inverness; m., Margaret I. Garden; 1 s.; 1 d. Educ. Sedbergh School; Edinburgh University. Resident Magistrate, Tanganyika (latterly Tanzania), 1956-66; Secretary, Glasgow and North Argyll Legal Aid Committee, 1966-82. Address: (h.) 47 Buchanan Drive, Bearsden, Glasgow; T.-041-942 4227.

Gilchrist, Sir Andrew Graham, KCMG (1964). Chairman, Highlands and Islands Development Board, 1970-76; former Ambassador; b. 19.4.10; m.; 2 s.; 1 d. Educ. Edinburgh Academy; Exeter College, Oxford. Diplomatic Service, 1933-70; War Service as Major, Force 136, SE Asia (mentioned in Despatches).

Gilchrist, Bernard, MBE, MA (Hons) (Oxon). Chief Executive, Scottish Wildlife Trust, since 1965; b. 20.5.19, Manchester; m., Jean W. Gregory; 2 s.; 1 d. Educ. Manchester Grammar School; Queen's College, Oxford. Tanganyika: Forest Officer, HM Colonial/Overseas Civil Service, 1942-62 (Conservator of Forests, 1960), Conservator of Forests, Tanganyika/Tanzania Government Service, 1962-65. Recreations: countryside; natural history; hill-walking; photography. Address: (h.) 9 Murrayfield Gardens, Edinburgh, EH12 6DG; T.-031-337 3869.

Gilchrist, Douglas Smith, DCE. Member, Cumbernauld and Kilsyth District Council (Convener, Policy and Resources Committee); Member, General Teaching Council, since 1983; President, Dunbartonshire EIS, since 1984; b. 25.2.29, Glasgow; m., Irene Claire Burridge; 2 s.; 2 d. Educ. Jordanhill College School; Jordanhill College of Education. Company Representative, 1951-60; Taxi Owner/Driver, 1960-69; Student Teacher, 1969-71; Schoolteacher, since 1971; Senior Vice President, NUS Scotland, 1970-71; Member, Executive, Dunbartonshire EIS, since 1974; Member, Gas Consumers Council, since 1982; Member, Licensing Board, Cumbernauld and Kilsyth District, since 1984. Recreations: snooker; home computing. Address: (h.) 17A Clouden Road, South Kildrum, Cumbernauld; T.-Cumbernauld 24070.

Gilchrist, James. Chairman, Finance Committee, Lothian Regional Council, since 1984; Vice-Chairman, Napier College, Edinburgh; b.

1.7.43, Edinburgh; m., June Gilchrist; 1 s.; 2 d. Educ. George Heriot's School, Edinburgh. Elected to Lothian Regional Council, 1975; Chairman, Education Committee, 1982-84; Member, Edinburgh University Court, since 1982. Address: (b.) 19 St. Andrew Square, Edinburgh, EH2 1YE; T.-031-225 2211.

Gilchrist, Thomas, BSc, PhD, CChem, FRSC. Managing Director, Ross Fraser Ltd. and Giltech Ltd., since 1984; b. 18.6.36, Ayr; m., Fiona Christina Brown; 2 d. Educ. Ayr Academy; Glasgow University. Assistant Lecturer in Chemistry, Glasgow University, 1961-62; Research Chemist: Canadian Industries Ltd., Quebec, 1962-64, ICI Ltd., Stevenston, Ayrshire, 1964-69; Strathclyde University: Lecturer in Bioengineering, 1969, Head of Division of Artificial Organs, Bioengineering Unit, 1972, Senior Lecturer in Bioengineering, 1975-84. Section Editor, International Journal of Artificial Organs. Recreations: golf; curling. Address: (h.) The Lodge, 67 Midton Road, Ayr, KA7 2TW; T.-Ayr 266088.

Giles, Sir Alexander Falconer, KBE (1965), CMG (1960). Resident Commissioner, Basutoland, 1962-65 (British Government Representative there, 1965-66); General Secretary, Scotland, Royal Over-Seas League, 1976-78; b. 1915; m.; 2 step s.; 1 step d. Educ. Edinburgh Academy; Edinburgh University; Balliol College, Oxford. Colonial Service, 1947-66; Director, Toc H, 1968-74.

Giles, Cecilia Elspeth, CBE, MA. Assistant Secretary, Edinburgh University, since 1972; Committee of Vice-Chancellors and Principals' Administrative Training Officer (seconded part-time), 1983-85; b. Dumfries. Educ. Queen Margaret's School, Yorkshire; Edinburgh University. Administrative staff, Khartoum University, 1956-57; joined Administrative staff, Edinburgh University, 1957; appointed by Secretary of State for Employment, 1982, to consider representations against proposals to refuse or revoke licences to carry on an employment agency or business; Chairman, Conservative Political Centre Committee in Scotland. Publication: Tourism in Scotland (Co-author). Recreations: entertaining friends, family and godchildren; theatre. Address: (b.) Old College, South Bridge, Edinburgh, EH8 9YL.

Giles, George, AMCIT, FBIM. General Manager, Prestwick Airport, since 1983; b. 1.11.30, Bristol; m., Freda Elizabeth; 1 s.; 2 d. Educ. Queen Elizabeth Royal Blackburn Grammar School; Fairfield Grammar School, Bristol. Meteorological Office, 1947-69; Institution of Professional Civil Servants, 1969-76; British Airports Authority: Training Manager, 1976-77, Personnel Manager, Scottish Airports, 1977-83. Member, Executive Council, Ayrshire and Burns Country Tourist Board. Recreations: reading; music; gardening; theatre. Address: (h.) Bamburi, 13 Doonholm Park, Alloway, Ayrshire, KA6 6BH; T.-0292 43660.

Gillanders, Farquhar, MA. Registrar, Glasgow University, since 1982; b. 2.4.23, Applecross, Ross-shire; m., Janet MacConnachie Hyndman; 1

s. Educ. Dingwall Academy; Glasgow University. War Service, 7th Gurkha Rifles. Glasgow University: Lecturer in Economics, 1950-66, Assistant Registrar, 1966-74, Deputy Registrar, 1974-82. Recreation: illegal fishing. Address: (h.) 16 Beaumont Gate, Glasgow, G12 9ED; T.-041-339 3142.

Gilles, Professor Dennis Cyril, BSc, PhD, FRSE, FRSA, FIMA, FBCS. Professor of Computing Science, Glasgow University, since 1966; b. 7.4.25, London; m., Valerie Mary Gardiner; 2 s.; 2 d. Educ. Chislehurst and Sidcup Grammar School; Imperial College, London. Mathematician, Scientific Computing Service Ltd., London, 1949-55; Research Fellow, Computing Machine Laboratory, Manchester University, 1955-57; Director, Computing Laboratory, Glasgow University, 1957-66. Address: (h.) 21 Bruce Road, Glasgow, G41 5EE; T.-041-429 7733.

Gillespie, Professor John Spence, MB, ChB, PhD, FIBiol, FRCPGlas, FRSE. Professor and Head of Department of Pharmacology, Glasgow University, since 1968; b. 5.9.26, Dumbarton; m., Jemima Simpson Ross; 4 s.; 1 d. Educ. Dumbarton Academy; Glasgow University. National Service as RMO, 1950-52; McCunn Research Scholar in Physiology, Glasgow University, 1953-55; Faulds Fellow, then Sharpey Scholar, Physiology Department, University College, London, 1955-57; Lecturer in Physiology, Glasgow University, 1957-59; Sophie Fricke Research Fellow, Royal Society, Rockefeller Institute, 1959-60; Glasgow University: Senior Lecturer in Physiology, 1961-63, Henry Head Research Fellow, Royal Society, 1963-68; Vice-Principal, Glasgow University, since 1983; Honorary Secretary, Physiological Society, 1966-72; Council Member, Research Defence Society, 1974-77; Committee Member, British Pharmacological Society, 1973-76. Recreations: gardening; painting. Address: (b.) Department of Pharmacology, Glasgow University, Glasgow, G12 8QQ; T.-041-339 8855, Ext. 481.

Gillett, Eric, MA. Commissioner (Ombudsman) for Local Administration in Scotland, since 1982; b. 22.7.20. Joined Scottish Office after War service; occupied various posts in fields of planning and other local government services, police matters and fisheries policy, national and international; Chairman, International Commission for North-west Atlantic Fisheries, 1973-76; Head, Scottish Development Department, 1976-80. Chairman, Scottish Association of Citizens Advice Bureaux; Vice-Chairman, Scottish Wildlife Trust. Recreations: playing a variety of instruments and conducting amateur music groups. Address: (b.) 5 Shandwick Place, Edinburgh, EH12 4RG; T.-031-229 4472.

Gillies, Anne Bethea, MA, LLB. Advocate; Honorary Sheriff of South Strathclyde, Dumfries and Galloway, at Lanark, since 1960; Member, Valuation Appeal Panel, Strathclyde, since 1974; b. 12.4.22, Lochgilphead, Argyll; m., Sheriff Principal M.G. Gillies, T.D., Q.C. (qv). Educ. Sherborne School for Girls, Dorset; Edinburgh

University. Served in WAAF, until 1946; called to Scottish Bar, 1951; married, 1954. Recreations: gardening; cats. Address: (h.) Redwalls, Biggar, Lanarkshire, ML12 6HA; T.-Biggar 20281.

Gillies (Maurice) Gordon, TD (and Bar), QC (Scot). Sheriff Principal of South Strathclyde, Dumfries and Galloway, since 1982; b. 17.10.16; m., Anne Bethea McCall-Smith (see Anne Bethea Gillies). Educ. Aberdeen Grammar School; Merchiston Castle; Edinburgh University. Advocate, 1946; Advocate Depute, 1953-58; Sheriff of Lanarkshire (later South Strathclyde, Dumfries and Galloway), 1958-82.

Gillies, Professor William, MA (Edin), MA (Oxon). Professor of Celtic, Edinburgh University, since 1979; b. 15.9.42, Stirling; m., Valerie; 1 s.; 2 d. Educ. Oban High School; Edinburgh University; Corpus Christi College, Oxford; Dublin University. Dublin Institute for Advanced Studies, 1969-70; Lecturer, Edinburgh University, 1970-79. Director, Acair Ltd., Comunn na Gaidhlig. Recreations: walking; gardening; music. Address: (h.) 67 Braid Avenue, Edinburgh, EH10 6ED.

Gillon, Hamish William, FFA, FPMI. Assistant General Manager and Pensions Manager, Scottish Provident Institution, since 1980; Council Member, Royal Zoological Society of Scotland; b. 22.1.40, Edinburgh; m., Sandra; 1 s.; 1 d. Educ. Royal High School, Edinburgh. Various appointments, Scottish Provident Institution, since 1965. Assistant Area Commissioner, The Scout Association. Address: (b.) 6 St. Andrew Square, Edinburgh, EH2 2YA; T.-031-556 9181.

Gilmore, Stan, BA (Hons), MEd (Hons), DipEd, DSD, LTCL. Lecturer in Education, Stirling University, since 1972; Member, Strathclyde Regional Council, since 1982; b. 11.1.29, New York City; m., Anne J.J.; 1 s.; 1 d. Educ. North Kelvinside School, Glasgow; Jordanhill College of Education; University College, London. Various teaching appointments in primary and secondary schools, 1956-62; Lecturer: Central College of Commerce, Glasgow, 1962-66, Hamilton College of Education, 1966-72. Director, New Glasgow Hospice Company. Recreations: theatre-going; travel; reading. Address: (h.) 11 Poplar Drive, Lenzie, Glasgow, G66 4DN; T.-041-776 1409.

Gilmour, Colonel Allan Macdonald, OBE, MC (and Bar), DSC (USA). Lord Lieutenant of Sutherland, since 1972; Member, Highland Regional Council, since 1976; Member, Sutherland District Council, since 1974; b. 23.11.16, Edinburgh; m., Jean Wood; 3 s.; 1 d. Educ. Cargilfield, Edinburgh; Winchester College; Trinity College, Oxford. Commissioned Seaforth Highlanders, 1939; served War in Middle East, Sicily and NW Europe; Regimental and Staff appointments, 1945-69, including Instructor, Staff College, Quetta, and Chief of Staff, Ghana Armed Forces; Member, Sutherland County Council, 1970; Member, Highland Health Board, 1974 (Chairman, 1982-84); DL, Sutherland, 1969; Member: Highland River Purification Board, since 1978, Highlands and Islands Development Consultative Council, since 1980; Chairman, East

Sutherland Council of Social Service, 1972-76; Board Member, Scottish National Orchestra Society, since 1976. Recreation: fishing. Address: (h.) Invernauld, Rosehall, Lairg, Sutherland; T.-054 984 204.

Gilmour, Andrew Parr, BSc (Hons). Rector, Rothesay Academy, since 1983; b. 26.4.46, Glasgow; m., Elizabeth Morrison MacPherson; 1 s.; 2 d. Educ. Allan Glen's School, Glasgow; Glasgow University. Teacher of Chemistry, Allan Glen's School, 1969; Dunoon Grammar School: Principal Teacher of Chemistry, 1972, Assistant Rector, 1975; Depute Head Teacher, Mearns Castle High School, 1981. Recreations: sailing; badminton; rugby (spectating nowadays); swimming. Address: (h.) Millford, 34 Mount Stuart Road, Rothesay, Isle of Bute; T.-Rothesay 3336.

Gilmour, Douglas Graham, BSc (Hons), MB, ChB, MD, FRCS. Consultant Vascular Surgeon, Glasgow Royal Infirmary, since 1983; b. 15.4.47, Glasgow; m., Evelyn Jean; 2 s.; 2 d. Educ. Kelvinside Academy, Glasgow; Glasgow University. House Surgeon/Physician, then Senior House Officer/Registrar in Surgery, Western Infirmary, Glasgow, 1971-77; Glasgow Royal Infirmary: Senior Registrar in Surgery, 1977-80, Senior Lecturer (Honorary Consultant) in Surgery, 1980-83. Recreations: family; golf; skiing. Address: (b.) Vascular Surgery Department, Royal Infirmary, Glasgow; T.-041-552 3535, Ext. 5503.

Gilmour, Hugh Montgomery, MB, ChB, MRCPath. Senior Lecturer in Pathology, Edinburgh University, since 1979; Honorary Consultant, Lothian Health Board, since 1979; b. 17.5.43, Edinburgh; m., Alison Mary Little; 2 s. Educ. George Heriot's School; Edinburgh University. House Officer appointments in medicine and surgery, Bangour General Hospital, 1967-68; Lecturer, Department of Pathology, Edinburgh University, 1968-79. Recreations: golf; gardening. Address: (b.) University Medical School, Teviot Place, Edinburgh, EH8 9AG; T.-031-667 1011.

Gilmour, Sir John Edward, 3rd Bt, DSO, TD, JP, BA. Lord Lieutenant of Fife, since 1980; b. 24.10.12, Edinburgh; m., Ursula Mabyn Wills; 2 s. Educ. Eton College; Trinity Hall, Cambridge; Dundee School of Economics. Served with Fife and Forfar Yeomanry, 1939-45; served on Fife County Council, 1951-61; MP (Conservative), East Fife, 1961-79; Chairman, Conservative Party in Scotland, 1965-67. Recreation: gardening. Address: (h.) Montrave, Leven, Fife, KY8 5NY; T.-Leven 26159.

Gilmour, William, ARIBA, ARIAS, MRTPI. Director of Architecture, Planning and Technical Services, Kyle and Carrick District Council, since 1974; b. 11.4.31, Cumnock, Ayrshire. Educ. Tarbolton Public School. Address: (b.) Burns House, Burns Statue Square, Ayr; T.-Ayr 281511, Ext. 2220.

Gilmour, William McIntosh, OStJ, BL. Honorary Sheriff, Dumbarton; Lawyer; b. 9.3.23, Newcastle-upon-Tyne; m., Elinor Adams. Educ.

Hillhead High School; Cally House, Gatehouse of Fleet; Glasgow University. Early experience with legal firms in Glasgow; became Partner, latterly Senior Partner, in firms in Dunbartonshire; now in practice in Milngavie; former Dean, Faculty of Solicitors in Dunbartonshire; founder Member and Past President, Clydebank Rotary Club; Past Deacon, Society of Deacons and Free Presces; Chairman for Dunbartonshire, Order of St. John. Recreations: eating; dogwalking (formerly, motor sport). Address: (h.) 65 Killermont Road, Bearsden, Glasgow; T.-041-942 0498.

Gilray, George, MB, ChB, DPH, FFCM. Senior Medical Officer, Scottish Home and Health Department, since 1976; b. 6.11.29, Edinburgh; m., Anne Bertram Pringle; 2 s.; 2 d. Educ. George Heriot's School, Edinburgh; Edinburgh University. After pre-registration hospital appointments, served in RAF Medical Branch, 1955-76. Recreations: reading; sailing. Address: (h.) 10 Barntongate Avenue, Edinburgh, EH4 8BB; T.-031-339 1431.

Gilroy, Ian Duncan, MA (Hons), DipEd. Rector, Madras College, St. Andrews, since 1975; b. 16.12.22, Dundee; m., Isobel Keane; 3 d. Educ. Harris Academy, Dundee; St. Andrews University. Teacher of English and History, later Principal Teacher of English, Morgan Academy, Dundee, 1949-64; Lecturer in English, Dundee College of Education, 1964-69; Rector, Mackie Academy, Stonehaven, 1969-75. Member, Education Committee, SSTA, 1972-84; Member, NE Regional Nurse Training Committee, 1972-75; Member, Scottish Examinations Board, 1976-84; Chairman, Scottish Central Committee on Physical Education, 1978-81. Recreations: painting; sailing; golf. Address: (h.) 1 Westview, St. Andrews, Fife; T.-St. Andrews 73067.

Gimingham, Professor Charles Henry, BA, PhD, ScD, FRSE, FIBiol. Regius Professor of Botany, Aberdeen University, since 1981; b. 28.4.23, Leamington; m., Elizabeth Caroline Baird; 3 d. Educ. Gresham's School, Holt, Norfolk; Emmanuel College, Cambridge. Research Assistant, Imperial College, London, 1944-45; Department of Botany, Aberdeen University: Assistant, 1946-48, Lecturer, 1948-61, Senior Lecturer, 1961-64, Reader, 1964-69, Professor, since 1969, Head of Department, since 1981; Member: Scottish Committee of Nature Conservancy, 1966-69, Scottish Advisory Committee, Nature Conservancy Council, 1970-80, Countryside Commission for Scotland, since 1980; President, Botanical Society of Edinburgh, 1982-84; Member, Board of Management, Hill Farming Research Organisation, since 1981; Member, Governing Body, Aberdeen College of Education, since 1981; Member, Council of Management, Macaulay Institute for Soil Research, since 1983; British Ecological Society: Joint Secretary, 1956-61, Vice-President, 1962-64, Joint Editor, Journal of Ecology, 1975-78, President Elect, 1984. Publications: Ecology of Heathlands, 1972; Introduction to Heathland Ecology, 1975. Recreations: hill-walking; photography; history and culture of Japan. Address: (h.) 2 Carden Terrace, Aberdeen.

Gimson, George Stanley, QC (Scot). Chairman, Pensions Appeals Tribunals, Scotland, since 1975; b. 1915. Educ. High School of Glasgow; Glasgow University. Advocate, 1949; Sheriff Principal of Aberdeen, Kincardine and Banff, 1972-74; Sheriff Principal of Grampian, Highland and Islands, 1975-82; Trustee, National Library of Scotland, 1963-76; Chairman, RSSPCC, Edinburgh, 1972-76; Hon. LLD, Aberdeen, 1981. Address: (h.) 11 Royal Circus, Edinburgh, EH3 6TL.

Ginsborg, Professor Bernard Lionel, PhD, DSc, FRSE. Professor of Pharmacology, Edinburgh University, since 1976; b. 22.1.25, London; m., Andrina Taffler; 2 d. Educ. Owen's School, London; Reading University; University College, London. Medical Research Council Scholar, then Stothert Research Fellow of the Royal Society, University College, London, 1951-56; Lecturer in Biophysics, University College, London, 1956-57; Scientific staff, Medical Research Council, 1957-62; Lecturer, then Reader, Department of Pharmacology, Edinburgh University, 1962-76 (Head of Department, 1980-85). Address: (b.) Department of Pharmacology, University Medical School, 1 George Square, Edinburgh, EH8 9JZ; T.-031-667 1011.

Girdwood, Richard Stuart Haxton, LLB, WS. Barrister and Solicitor in the Supreme Court of Victoria, Australia; Director, Legal Practice Unit, Edinburgh University, since 1979; b. 3.5.47, Edinburgh; m., Roberta Anne Egan; 3 s. Educ. George Watson's College; Edinburgh University. Legal practice in Edinburgh firm; Corporate Solicitor, Melbourne, Australia; Lecturer, Department of Scots Law, Edinburgh University. Recreations: horse riding; antiquarian books. Address: (b.) Faculty of Law, Edinburgh University, Old College, South Bridge, Edinburgh; T.-031-667 1011.

Girdwood, Professor Ronald Haxton, CBE, MD, PhD, FRCPEd, FRCP, FRCPI, FRCPath, Hon. FACP, Hon. FRACP, FRSE. President, Royal College of Physicians of Edinburgh, 1982-85; Chairman, Scottish National Blood Transfusion Association, since 1981; b. 19.3.17, Arbroath; m., Mary Elizabeth Williams; 1 s.; 1 d. Educ. Daniel Stewart's College, Edinburgh; Edinburgh University; Michigan University. Directed under EMS Scheme to Astley Ainslie Hospital, Edinburgh, then dealing with Army patients, 1941; Army service, RAMC, UK and India, 1942-46, successively as Lt., Captain, Major and Lt.-Col. (when posted to Burma); Lecturer, then Senior Lecturer, Reader in Medicine, Edinburgh University, 1946-62; Research Fellow, Michigan University, 1948-49; Consultant Physician, Edinburgh Royal Infirmary, 1950-82; Professor of Therapeutics and Clinical Pharmacology, Edinburgh University, 1962-82 (Dean, Faculty of Medicine, 1975-79); Chairman, Scotish Group, Nutrition Society, 1961-62; President, British Society for Haematology, 1963-64; Chairman, Executive Committee, Edinburgh and SE Scotland Blood Transfusion Association, since 1970; Member, UK Committee on Safety of Medicines, 1972-83; Chairman, Medico-Pharmaceutical Forum, 1985; Suniti Panja Gold Medal, Calcutta School of Tropical Medicine, 1980; given the

Freedom of Sirajgunj, Bangladesh, 1984. Recreations: writing; photography; painting in oils. Address: (h.) 2 Hermitage Drive, Edinburgh, EH10 6DD; T.-031-447 5137.

Gladden, Margaret Hay, MB, BS, MRCS, LRCP, DCH, PhD. Senior Lecturer in Physiology, Glasgow University, since 1983; b. 21.12.40, Oswaldtwistle, Lancashire; m., Dr. John Womersley; 2 s.; 2 d. Educ. Accrington Girls High School; Royal Free Hospital Medical School. Houseman, 1965-66; SHO in Paediatrics, 1966-67; Holt Fellow, Liverpool University, then MRC Junior Research Fellow, Liverpool University, 1967-70; Research Fellow, then Lecturer in Physiology, Glasgow University, 1971-83. Publications: The Muscle Spindle, 1985; Feedback and Motor Control (Joint Editor), 1985. Recreations: music; hill-walking; sculling. Address: (b.) Institute of Physiology, Glasgow University, Glasgow, G12 8QQ; T.-041-339 8855.

Glasgow, 10th Earl of, (Patrick Robin Archibald Boyle). Television Director/Producer; b. 30.7.39; m., Isabel Mary James; 1 s.; 1 d. Educ. Eton; Paris University. Sub.-Lt., RNR, 1959-60; Producer/Director, Yorkshire TV, 1968-70; freelance Film Producer, since 1971; formed Kelburn Country Centre, 1977. Address (b.) South Offices, Kelburn Estate, Fairlie, Ayrshire.

Glashan, Alexander James, BSc (Hons). Rector, Elgin Academy, since 1964; b. 8.6.22, Inverness; m., Vera Baillie Ritchie; 3 d. Educ. Inverness Royal Academy; Aberdeen University; Aberdeen College of Education. War Service as Radar Officer, REME, 1942-46 (final rank of Captain); Teacher of Mathematics, Kilmarnock Academy, 1949-50; Principal Teacher of Mathematics, Carrick Academy, Maybole, 1950-56; Headmaster, Muirkirk Junior Secondary School, 1956-61; Rector, Turriff Academy, 1961-64. President, Moray Bn., Boys' Brigade, 1966-77; President, Grampian Headteachers' Association, 1978-80; President, Headteachers' Association of Scotland, 1982-83; President, Elgin Rotary Club, 1974-75. Recreation: golf. Address: (h.) Torbruad, 6 Hamilton Crescent, Elgin, Moray; T.-0343 2916.

Glashan, John Irvine, CA. Director of Finance, Ross and Cromarty District Council, since 1975; b. 23.8.38, Nairn; m., Elizabeth; 2 s.; 1 d. Educ. Aberdeen Grammar School; Forres Academy; Ballater Junior Secondary School. Accountant, City of Aberdeen, 1964-67; Depute County Treasurer, Moray and Nairn Joint County Council, 1968-75. Recreation: bowling. Address: (b.) County Buildings, Dingwall; T.-Dingwall 63381.

Glass, Alexander, MA, DipEd. Rector, Dingwall Academy, since 1977; b. 1.6.32, Dunbar; m., Edith Margaret Duncan Baxter; 3 d. Educ. Dunbar Grammar School; Edinburgh University; Heidelberg University; University of Aix-en-Provence. Teacher of Modern Languages, Montrose Academy, 1958-60; Special Assistant Teacher of Modern Languages, Oban High School, 1960-62; Principal Teacher of Modern Languages, Nairn Academy, 1962-65; Principal Teacher of French and Assistant Rector, Perth

Academy, 1965-72; Rector, Milne's High School, Fochabers, 1972-77. Chairman, COSPEN; Chairman, Highland Region Working Party for Modern Languages; Deputy Regional Chairman, Highland Region Children's Panel, Reader, Church of Scotland; Chairman, Highland Division, Scottish Community Drama Association and Inverness District, SCDA; Secretary, Scottish Secondary Schools' Travel Trust. Recreations: amateur drama; foreign travel; Rotary. Address: (h.) Craigton, Tulloch Avenue, Dingwall, IV15 9LH; T.-0349 63258.

Glasser, Professor Fredrik Paul, BA, BSc, PhD, DSc, FInstCeram, FRSE. Professor of Chemistry, Aberdeen University, since 1983; b. 2.5.29; m., Dr. Lesley Scott Dent; 1 s.; 2 d. Educ. Cambridge University; Aberdeen University. Research Fellow, Pennsylvania State University, 1957-59; Aberdeen University: Research Fellow, 1959-61, Lecturer, Senior Lecturer, Reader. Chairman, Grampian Region Children's Panel, 1981-84. Address: (b.) Department of Chemistry, Aberdeen University, Meston Walk, Old Aberdeen, AB9 2UE; T.-0224 40241, Ext. 5640.

Glen, Alastair Campbell Agnew, MD, BSc. Consultant Clinical Biochemist, Victoria Infirmary, Glasgow, since 1970; Honorary Clinical Lecturer, Glasgow University, since 1982; b. 3.8.36, Glasgow; m., Lesley Gordon; 2 s.; 1 d. Educ. Glasgow Academy; Glasgow University. House Surgeon and House Physician, Glasgow Royal Infirmary and Victoria Infirmary, Glasgow, 1960; MRC Award for Further Studies in the Research Sciences, 1961; Registrar in Biochemistry, Western Infirmary, Glasgow, 1963; Research Associate, Massachusetts Institute of Technology, 1966; Victoria Infirmary, Glasgow: Senior Registrar in Biochemistry, 1967, Consultant Biochemist, 1970. Recreations: almost anything from skiing and angling to Scottish politics. Address: (h.) 276A Nithsdale Road, Glasgow, G41 5LP; T.-041-427 2131.

Glen, Eric Stanger, MB, ChB, FRCSGlas, FRCSEdin. Consultant Urological Surgeon, Walton Urological Teaching and Research Centre, Southern General Hospital, Glasgow; Honorary Clinical Lecturer, Glasgow University; Member, Surgical Examination Panel, Royal College of Physicians and Surgeons of Glasgow; b. 20.10.34, Glasgow; m., Dr. Patricia. Educ. Glasgow University. Pre-Consultant posts, Western and Victoria Infirmaries, Glasgow; Ship Surgeon, Royal Fleet Auxiliary. Member, Steering Group on Incontinence, King's Fund, London; Honorary Secretary, International Continence Society. Recreations: travel; writing; computer applications. Address: (h.) 9 St. John's Road, Pollokshields, Glasgow, G41 5RJ; T.-041-423 0759.

Glen, James Robert, CA. Director, The Scottish Investment Trust PLC, since 1981 (Manager, since 1969); Deputy Chairman, The Scottish Life Assurance Co., since 1984 (Director, since 1971); Director, Pict Petroleum, since 1971; Director, Limehouse Productions, since 1983; Director, News (UK) Ltd., since 1985; b. 27.5.30, Perth; m., Alison Helen Margaret Brown; 3 s. Educ. Merchiston Castle School. 2nd Lt., RA, 1954-56;

Secretary, C.W. Carr, 1956-58; Baillie, Gifford & Co., 1958-62; joined Scottish Investment Trust, 1962. Address: (b.) 6 Albyn Place, Edinburgh; T.-031-225 7781.

Glen, John Alasdair. Secretary, AFRC Animal Breeding Research Organisation, since 1984; b. 16.5.46, Edinburgh; 3 s. Educ. Daniel Stewart's College, Edinburgh. Bank of Scotland, 1964-70; Assistant Secretary: Hill Farming Research Organisation, 1978, Animal Breeding Research Organisation, 1983. Secretary (Scotland) and Member, Committee of Management, Crown Housing Association Ltd. Recreations: squash; reading; climbing; outdoor activities. Address: (h.) St. Swithin's, Ninemileburn, Midlothian, EH26 9LZ; T.-Penicuik 73993.

Glen, Norman MacLeod, CBE, TD, MA, JP. Leader, Conservative Group, Dumbarton District Council, since 1974; b. 22.12.11, Glasgow; m., Dr. Janet M.S. Glen (deceased); 2 s.; 2 d. Educ. Glasgow Academy; Glasgow University. Retail trade as Buyer, Director and Managing Director, John Glen & Co. Ltd., Glasgow, 1932-74; War Service, six years; TA (mostly 474 HAA Regt RA), 1938-56 (Lt. Colonel, 1954-56); Parliamentary candidate (Liberal), 1945, (Conservative), 1951, 1955, 1959, 1964, 1966 and By-Election, Woodside, 1962; elected, Helensburgh Town Council, 1966 (last Provost of Helensburgh, 1970-75); Elder, West Kirk of Helensburgh. Recreation: walking. Address: (h.) Cawdor Lodge, 109 Sinclair Street, Helensburgh, G84 9QD; T.-0436 3497.

Glenarthur, 4th Baron, (Simon Mark Arthur), Bt. Parliamentary Under Secretary of State, Department of Health and Social Security, since 1983; b. 7.10.44; m.; 1 s.; 1 d. Educ. Eton. Retired Major, 10th Royal Hussars (PWO); Helicopter Captain, British Airways, 1976-82; a Lord in Waiting, 1982-83. Address: (h.) Birch Hill, Torphins, Banchory, Kincardineshire.

Glencross, Rev. William McCallum, LTh. Minister, Macdonald Memorial Church, Bellshill, since 1973; b. 29.7.34, Sanquhar; m., Agnes Jane Crate; 3 d. Educ. Sanquhar Academy; Dumfries Academy; Glasgow University. Mining Surveyor, NCB, 1950-63; Parish Minister, Whalsay and Skerries (Shetland Islands), 1968-73. Address: Macdonald Memorial Manse, 346 Main Street, Bellshill, Lanarkshire; T.-Bellshill 842177.

Glennie, Charles Milne, MA, PhD. Registrar General for Scotland, since 1982; b. 29.10.34, Edinburgh; m., Eileen Margaret Mason; 1 d. Educ. Fettes College; Edinburgh University; Cambridge University; Yale University. Address: (b.) New Register House, Edinburgh, EH1 3YT; T.-031-556 3952.

Glidewell, Christopher, MA, PhD, FRSC. Reader in Chemistry, St. Andrews University, since 1982; b. 7.6.44, Bedford; m., Sheila Margaret Hutchison; 2 s.; 1 d. Educ. Bedford School; Clare College, Cambridge. Fellow, Gonville and Caius College, Cambridge, 1969-72; Lecturer, St. Andrews University, 1972-82. Address: (b.) Department of Chemistry, St. Andrews, Fife; T.-0334 76161.

Gloag, Matthew Irving. Director, Matthew Gloag & Son Ltd., since 1971; b. 1.12.47, Perth; m., Dilly Moon; 2 d. Chairman, Scottish Licensed Trade Association, 1984-85. Address: (b.) 33 Kinnoull Street, Perth, PH1 5EU; T.-0738 21101.

Glover, John Hardie, OBE, RSA, FRIBA, FRIAS. Consultant Architect (retired), Sir Basil Spence Glover & Ferguson, since 1980; b. 21.2.13, North Berwick; m., Laura Milicent James; 1 s.; 1 d. Educ. North Berwick High School; Edinburgh College of Art, School of Architecture. When qualified, joined firm of Leslie Graham Thomson, Architect, 1936; served RE, 1940-46, Britain and India; joined Council of Industrial Design as Exhibition Officer; joined Basil Spence, 1947 (Partner, 1948-80). Recreations: fishing; gardening; furniture-making. Address: (h.) The Coach House, Belford Place, Edinburgh, 4; T.-031-332 6107.

Glover, Sue, MA. Writer; b. 1.3.43, Edinburgh; m., John Glover; 2 s. Educ. St. George's School, Edinburgh; Montpellier University; Edinburgh University. Original drama and other scriptwriting for radio, television and theatre; theatre productions include The Seal Wife, Edinburgh Festival, 1980, An Island in Largo, Byre Theatre, 1981, and The Bubble Boy, Glasgow Tron, 1981; televised version of The Bubble Boy won a silver medal, New York Film and Television Festival, and a merit, Chicago International Film Festival, 1983. Recreations: house and garden. Address: Castlefield Cottage, Castlebank Road, Cupar, Fife; T.-Cupar 53664.

Goddard, Kenneth George, BA, IPFA. Director of Finance, Skye and Lochalsh District Council, since 1981; b. 14.1.47, Pembroke Dock; m., Jennifer; 2 s. Educ. Pembroke Grammar School; St. Davids University, Lampeter. Inland Revenue, 1970-72; Pembroke Borough Council, 1972-74; South Pembrokeshire District Council, 1974-78; joined Skye and Lochalsh District Council, 1978. Address: (b.) Park Road, Portree, Isle of Skye, IV51 9EP; T.-0478 2341.

Godden, Tony Richard Hillier, CB, BSc (Econ). Secretary, Scottish Development Department, since 1980; b. 13.11.27, Barnstaple; m., Marjorie Florence Snell; 1 s.; 2 d. Educ. Barnstaple Grammar School; London School of Economics. Commissioned, RAF Education Branch, 1950; entered Civil Service, 1951; first appointed to Colonial Office: Private Secretary to Parliamentary Under Secretary of State, 1954-55; seconded to Cabinet Office, 1957-59; joined Scottish Home Department, 1961; Assistant Secretary, Scottish Development Department, 1964; Under Secretary, 1969; Secretary, Scottish Economic Planning Development, 1973-80. Address: (b.) New St. Andrews House, Edinburgh, EH1 3SZ; T.-031-556 8400.

Godfray, Martin Francis, BSc, CChem, FRSC, MChemA. Public Analyst, Official Agricultural Analyst and Scientific Adviser, Lothian, Borders and Highland Regional Councils and Orkney and Shetland Islands Councils, since 1980; b. 10.5.45, Barry, Glamorgan; m., Heather Jean; 1 s.; 2 d. Educ. Barry Boys Grammar Technical

School; Birmingham University. Deputy Public Analyst and Deputy Agricultural Analyst, London Boroughs of Southwark, Greenwich, Islington and Tower Hamlets, 1973-80. Address: (b.) Regional Laboratory, 2 Cranston Street, Edinburgh, EH8 8BE; T.-031-229 9292, Ext. 3662.

Godman, Norman. MP (Labour), Greenock and Port Glasgow, since 1983; b. 1937. Educ. Hull University. Teacher and former Shipwright.

Godwin, David. General Secretary, Scottish Council for Civil Liberties, since 1979; b. 9.2.44, Shirley; m., Caryl Margaret Annabella Buchanan; 2 d. Educ. Dalziel High School, Motherwell; Glasgow University. Active in civil liberties and issues of local provision, including community-based housing movement, since 1970. Recreations: wild plants and human institutions. Address: (b.) 146 Holland Street, Glasgow; T.-041-332 5960.

Gold, William, CA. Chief Executive, Dundee Port Authority, since 1974; b. 23.2.27, Larbert; m., Elizabeth M.H. McRorie; 2 s.; 1 d. Educ. Falkirk High School. Admitted Institute of Chartered Accountants of Scotland, 1950; Brown Fleming & Murray, CA, 1950-52; Matthew Wylie & Co. Ltd., 1952-72 (Joint Managing Director, 1967-72); Chief Accountant, Dundee Port Authority, 1972-74. Session Clerk, Barry Parish Church; 2nd Deputy Chairman, British Ports Association. Recreations: golf; Rotary. Address: (h.) The Dormers, Barry, Carnoustie; T.-0241 53297.

Goldberg, Professor Sir Abraham, KB, MD, DSc, FRCP, FRCPEdin, FRCPGlas, FRSE. Regius Professor of the Practice of Medicine, Glasgow University, since 1978; Chairman, Committee on Safety of Medicines, since 1980; b. 7.12.23, Edinburgh; m., Clarice Cussin; 2 s.; 1 d. Educ. Sciennes School, Edinburgh; George Heriot's School, Edinburgh; Edinburgh University. House Physician, Royal Hospital for Sick Children, Edinburgh, 1946-47; RAMC, 1947-49 (granted rank of honorary Major on discharge); Nuffield Research Fellow, UCH Medical School, London, 1952-54; Eli Lilly Travelling Fellow in Medicine (MRC), Department of Medicine, Utah University, 1956; Glasgow University: Lecturer in Medicine, 1956-57, Titular Professor of Medicine, 1967-70, Regius Professor of Materia Medica, 1970-78. Chairman, Grants Committee 1, Clinical Research Board, MRC, 1973-77; Member, Chief Scientist's Committee, SHHD, 1977-83; Chairman, Biomedical Research Committee, SHHD, 1977-83; Editor, Scottish Medical Journal, 1962-63. Publications: Diseases of Porphyrin Metabolism (Co-author), 1967; Recent Advances in Haematology (Joint Editor), 1971; Clinics in Haematology "The Porphyrias" (Co-author), 1980. Recreations: medical history; literature; writing; walking; swimming. Address: (b.) Glasgow University, Department of Medicine, Gardiner Institute, Western Infirmary, Glasgow, G11 6NT; T.-041-339 2800.

Goldie, David. Farmer; Member, Scottish Training Committee, Agricultural Training Board, since 1982; Member, Scottish Agricultural Development Council, since 1983; Director, Royal Highland and Agricultural Society, since 1976; b. 30.7.37, Dumfries; m., Ann Irving; 3 s. Educ. Wallace Hall Academy, Closeburn, Thornhill. Chairman, Annandale Young Farmers Club, 1958-59; Elder and Treasurer, Ruthwell Church, since 1968; founder Chairman, local Community Council, 1978-81; Chairman, Dumfries Agricultural Society, 1977-79. Address: (h.) Longbridgemuir, Clarencefield, Dumfries; T.-038 787 210.

Goodall, Alexander, MA (Hons). Principal, Wester Hailes Education Centre, since 1982; b. 25.8.38, Dolphinton, Peebles-shire; 1 s.; 1 d. Educ. Portobello High School; Edinburgh University; Moray House College of Education. Teacher of History, Niddrie Marischal Secondary School, 1961-64; Education Officer, Teso College, Uganda, 1964-69; Preston Lodge High School: Principal Teacher of History, 1969-74, Assistant Head Teacher, 1974-78; Depute Principal, Wester Hailes Education Centre, 1978-82. Editor, Scottish History Teaching Review. Publication: Economics and Development (Co-author). Recreations: trout angling; rubber bridge. Address: (b.) 5 Murrayburn Drive, Edinburgh; T.-031-442 2201.

Goodall, Henry Bushman, MB, ChB, MD, FRCPath. Reader in Haematology, Pathology Department, Dundee University, since 1981; Honorary Consultant Haematologist, since 1960; b. 18.6.21, Dundee; m., Janet McIntosh; 1 s.; 1 d. Educ. Errol Public School; Perth Academy; St. Andrews University. Junior House Officer (Medical and Surgical), 1944-45; Trainee Pathologist, 1944-46; RAMC, 1946-48; Lecturer in Pathology, St. Andrews University, 1948-58; Senior Lecturer, Universities of St. Andrews and Dundee, 1958-81. Former Member, Scientific Services Advisory Group, SHHD (Chairman, Haematology Committee); Past Chairman, Dundee Round Table. Recreations: gardening; golf; photography. Address: (h.) 16 Hazel Avenue, Dundee, DD2 1QD; T.-0382 65247.

Gooday, Professor Graham W., BSc, PhD. Professor of Microbiology, Aberdeen University, since 1984; b. 19.2.42, Colchester; m., Margaret A. Mealing; 1 s.; 2 d. Educ. Hove Grammar School for Boys; Bristol University. VSO, Sierra Leone, 1964; Research Fellowships: Leeds University, 1967, Glasgow and Oxford Universities, 1969; Lecturer, Senior Lecturer, Reader, Aberdeen University, 1972-84; Member, Aquatic Life Sciences Committee, NERC, since 1984; Council Member, British Mycological Society, 1974-77; Council Member, Society for General Microbiology, 1976-80; awarded first Fleming Lectureship, Society for General Microbiology, 1976. Recreation: open countryside. Address: (b.) Department of Microbiology, Marischal College, University, Aberdeen, AB9 1AS; T.-0224 40241.

Goodlad, George Alexander James, BSc, PhD. Reader in Biochemistry, St. Andrews University, since 1980; b. 13.6.30, Lerwick; m., Catherine McGhee Clark; 2 s.; 1 d. Educ. Allan Glen's School, Glasgow; Glasgow University. Carnegie Research Scholar; Civil Service Senior Research Fellow; BEIT Memorial Research Fellow; Lecturer, then Senior Lecturer, then Reader in

Biochemistry, St. Andrews University. Recreations: badminton; walking. Address: (h.) 29 Kilrymont Road, St. Andrews, Fife, KY16 8DE; T.-0334 72212.

Goodman, Anthony Eric, MA (Oxon), BLitt (Oxon), FRHistS. Reader in History, Edinburgh University, since 1983; b. 21.7.36, London; m., Jacqueline; 1 d. Educ. Selhurst Grammar School, Croydon; Magdalen College, Oxford. Joined staff, Edinburgh University, 1961. Secretary, Edinburgh Branch, Historical Association, since 1975. Publications: The Loyal Conspiracy, 1971; A History of England from Edward II to James I, 1977; The Wars of the Roses, 1981. Recreation: getting to know the Borders. Address: (h.) 23 Kirkhill Gardens, Edinburgh, EH16 5DF; T.-031-667 5988.

Goodwin, Matthew Dean, CBE, CA. Chairman, Hewden Stuart Plant PLC; Director, Murray Ventures PLC; Director, Murray Technology PLC; Director, F/S Assurance; Member, Irvine Development Corporation; Honorary Treasurer, Scottish Conservative Party; b. 12.6.29, Dalserf; m., Margaret Eileen Colvil; 2 d. Educ. Glasgow Academy. Recreations: shooting; bridge; farming. Address: (b.) 135 Buchanan Street, Glasgow; T.-041-221 7331.

Goold, Sir James Duncan, KB (1983), CA, FCIOB, FFB. Director, Mactaggart & Mickel Ltd., since 1965; Director, American Trust PLC, since 1984; Director, Morgan Grenfell (Scotland) Ltd., since 1982; Chairman, Scottish Conservative Party, since 1983; b. 28.5.34, Glasgow; m., Sheena Paton; 2 s.; 1 d. Educ. Glasgow Academy. Worked in Australia and New Zealand with Price Waterhouse & Co.; joined Mactaggart & Mickel Ltd. as Company Secretary, 1961; President: Scottish Building Contractors' Association, 1971, Scottish National Federation of Building Trades Employers, 1977-78; Honorary Treasurer, Scottish Building Employers' Federation, 1979-81; Chairman, Conservative Board of Finance Scotland, 1980-83; Honorary Treasurer, Scottish Conservative and Unionist Association, 1980-83; Honorary President, Eastwood Conservative Association, since 1978; Chairman, East Renfrewshire Conservative Association, 1974-77; Chairman, CBI Scotland, 1981-83; Council Member, CBI, since 1979 (Member, Employment Policy Committee, since 1983); Member, Panel, Department of Trade, Insolvency Law Review; Member, Scottish Hospital Endowments Research Trust; Governor: Glasgow Academy, Paisley Technical College; Elder, Mearns Parish Church; Trustee, Ferguson Bequest; Council Member, National Trust for Scotland, 1978-83; Member, Committee of Ten, Tenovus-Scotland; Recreations: golf; tennis; walking. Address: (b.) 107 West Regent Street, Glasgow, G2 2BH; T.-041-332 0001.

Gordon, (Alexander) Esme, RSA, FRIBA, FRIAS; b. 12.9.10, Edinburgh; m., Betsy McCurry; 2 s.; 1 d. Educ. Edinburgh Academy; School of Architecture, Edinburgh College of Art; RIBA. Owen Jones Scholar, 1934; worked for three years in London office of Sir John Burnet; Tait & Lorne, FFRIBA; set up own

practice as Architect in Edinburgh, 1936; War Service, RE, Europe; President, Edinburgh Architectural Association, 1955-57; Member, Scottish Committee, Arts Council of GB, 1959-67; Honorary Secretary, RSA, 1972-77. Publications: A Short History of St. Giles Cathedral, 1954; The Principles of Church Building, Furnishing, Equipment and Decoration, 1963; The Royal Scottish Academy 1826-1976, 1976. Recreations: art; drawing; travel; gardening. Address: (h.) 10a Greenhill Park, Edinburgh, EH10 4DW; T.-031-447 7530.

Gordon, Allan Jan, MA (Cantab), BSc, MB, ChB, MRCOG. Consultant Obstetrician and Gynaecologist, since 1981; b. 23.6.46, Glasgow; m., Elizabeth Margaret Elliott; 1 s.; 1 d. Educ. Hillhead High School, Glasgow; Glasgow University. House Officer, Glasgow Royal Infirmary; Senior House Officer posts in Obstetrics, Gynaecology and Pathology, Western Infirmary, Royal Infirmary, Royal Maternity and Queen Mother's Hospital, Glasgow; Registrar in Obstetrics and Gynaecology, Royal Infirmary and Royal Maternity Hospital, Glasgow; Clinical Lecturer, Cambridge University, 1978-81. Council Member, Lothian Marriage Counselling Service; Member, Iona Community. Recreations: music; reading; jogging; sailing; hill-walking. Address: (h.) 27 Hatton Place, Edinburgh, EH9 1UB.

Gordon, Boyd. Fisheries Secretary, Department of Agriculture and Fisheries for Scotland, since 1982; b. 18.9.26, Musselburgh; m., Elizabeth Mabel Smith; 2 d. Educ. Musselburgh Grammar School. Military Service, Royal Scots; joined Civil Service, initially with Ministry of Labour, then Inland Revenue; joined Department of Agriculture and Fisheries for Scotland, 1953; Principal dealing with Salmon and Freshwater Fisheries Administration and Fisheries Research and Development, 1962-73; Assistant Secretary, Agriculture Economic Policy, EEC Co-ordination and Agriculture Marketing, 1973-82. Recreations: golf; gardening; local Church matters. Address: (h.) 87 Duddingston Road, Edinburgh; T.-031-669 4380.

Gordon, George, MB, ChB, FRCSE, FRCOG. Consultant Obstetrician and Gynaecologist, Dumfries and Galloway, since 1969; b. 4.9.36, Markinch, Fife; m., Rosemary Gould Hutchison; 1 s.; 1 d. Educ. Edinburgh University. Senior Registrar, Western General Hospital, Edinburgh, 1966-69; Member, Scottish Confidential Enquiry Committee, Maternal Mortality; Member, Central Midwives Board for Scotland, 1978-84; External Examiner, Edinburgh University, 1978-82; Examiner, FRCS Edinburgh and DRCOG London; Member, RCOG Scottish Executive; Member, Panel for Higher Professional Training, RCOG; Honorary Secretary, Dumfries and Stewartry Division, BMA, since 1975. Recreations: music; Scottish literature; golf; gardening. Address: (b.) Dumfries and Galloway Royal Infirmary, Bankend Road, Dumfries, DG1 4AP.

Gordon, George, MA (Hons), PhD. Dean, Faculty of Arts and Social Studies, Strathclyde University, since 1984 (Senior Lecturer in Geography, since 1980); Governor, Jordanhill

College of Education, since 1982; b. 14.11.39, Edinburgh; m., Jane Taylor Collins; 2 d. Educ. George Heriot's School; Edinburgh University. Edinburgh University: Vans Dunlop Scholar, 1962-64, Demonstrator, 1964-65; Strathclyde University: Assistant Lecturer, 1965-66, Lecturer, 1966-80; served on SUCE and SCE Geography Panels; Member, SCOVACT; Recorder, Section E, British Association for the Advancement of Science; former Member, General Assembly of Open University; Member, Senate and Court, Strathclyde University. Publications: Perspectives of the Scottish City (Editor), 1985; Scottish Urban History, 1983; The Making of Scottish Geography (Co-author), 1984; Settlement Geography, 1983; Urban Geography, 1981. Recreations: theatre-going; watching sport. Address: (b.) Department of Geography, Strathclyde University, Richmond Street, Glasgow; T.-041-552 4400, Ext. 3334.

Gordon, George Park Douglas, BSc (Hons), CChem, MRSC. Regional HM Inspector of Schools, Strathclyde/District HM Inspector, Glasgow, since 1982; b. 23.10.37, Peterhead; m., Karein L.M.; 1 s.; 1 d. Educ. Peterhead Academy; Aberdeen University; Aberdeen College of Education. Teacher of Science, Peterhead Academy, 1961-64; Principal Teacher of Science, Dornoch Academy, 1964-67; Assistant Adviser in Science, Glasgow, 1967-69; HM Inspector of Schools, 1969-75 (Higher Grade since 1975). Elder, St. Paul's Church, Milngavie. Recreations: golf; squash; gardening; reading; watching Rangers FC; supporting Aberdeen FC. Address: (h.) Suilven, 8 Ewing Walk, Fairways, Milngavie, G62 6EG; T.-041-956 5131.

Gordon, Sheriff Gerald Henry, QC, MA, LLB, PhD, LLD. Sheriff of Glasgow and Strathkelvin, since 1978; b. 17.6.29, Glasgow; m., Marjorie Joseph; 1 s.; 2 d. Educ. Queen's Park Senior Secondary School; Glasgow University. Advocate, 1953; Procurator Fiscal Depute, Edinburgh, 1960-65; Edinburgh University: Head, Department of Criminal Law and Criminology, 1965-72, Personal Professor of Criminal Law, 1969-72, Dean, Faculty of Law, 1970-73, Professor of Scots Law, 1972-76; Sheriff of South Strathclyde, Dumfries and Galloway, at Hamilton, 1976-77; Member, Interdepartmental Committee on Scottish Criminal Procedure, 1970-77. Publications: Criminal Law of Scotland, 1967, 1978; Renton & Brown's Criminal Procedure (Editor), 1972, 1983. Recreations: Jewish studies; coffee conversation; swimming. Address: (h.) 52 Eastwoodmains Road, Giffnock, Glasgow; T.-041-638 8614.

Gordon, Hugh Francis Canon. Parish Priest, St. Michael's RC Church, Linlithgow, since 1980; Director, Laetare Youth Hostel and Christian Conference Centre, since 1980; b. 18.11.10, Inverness. Educ. Stonyhurst College, Lancashire; Heriot-Watt College, Edinburgh; Oscott College, Birmingham. Ordained, 1937; Curate, Inverness, 1937; Army Chaplain, 1940 (Egypt and El Alamain, 51st Highland Division); Osnabruck, 1946, developing civilian parish church and first Catholic school in Germany after the fall of Hitler; Priest: Selkirk, St. Andrews, Edinburgh St. Margaret's and St. John the Evangelist; founded Linlithgow Scripture Centre for Christian Unity; Executive Member, Scottish Catholic Lay Apostolate Council; Member, Order for Christian Unity. Recreations: anything to help restoration of Christian unity; stopped tennis, golf, fishing. Address: St. Michael's, 53 Blackness Road, Linlithgow, West Lothian; T.-0506 842145.

Gordon, James Stuart, CBE, MA (Hons). Managing Director, Radio Clyde, since 1973; Chairman, Scottish Exhibition Centre, since 1983; Member, Scottish Development Agency, since 1981; Member, Glasgow University Court, since 1984; b. 17.5.36, Glasgow; m., Anne Stevenson; 2 s.; 1 d. Educ. St. Aloysius College, Glasgow; Glasgow University. Political Editor, STV, 1965-73. Winner, Observer Mace Debating Tournament, 1957; Sony Special Award for Services to Radio, 1984. Recreations: his children; genealogy; golf. Address: (b.) Radio Clyde, Clydebank Business Park, Clydebank; T.-041-941 1111.

Gordon, Canon Kenneth Davidson, MA. Rector, St. Devenick's Episcopal Church, Bieldside, Aberdeen, since 1971; Examining Chaplain to Bishop of Aberdeen and Orkney, since 1978; Warden of Lay Readers, Diocese of Aberdeen and Orkney, since 1978; b. 27.12.35, Edinburgh; m., Edith Jessica Newing; 2 s. Educ. George Heriot's School, Edinburgh; Edinburgh University; Tyndale Hall, Bristol. Curate, St. Helens Parish Church, Lancashire, 1960-66 (with charge of St. Andrew's Mission Church, 1962-66); Vicar, St. George the Martyr's Parish Church, Bolton, 1966-71; Canon, St. Andrew's Cathedral, Aberdeen, since 1981. Member, Faith and Order Board, and Liturgy Committee, General Synod, Scottish Episcopal Church. Recreations: birdwatching; golf; photography; model railways. Address: The Rectory, Bieldside, Aberdeen, AB1 9AP; T.-0224 861552.

Gordon, Nicholas Hugh, MB, ChB, FFARCS. Consultant Anaesthetist, since 1974; Honorary Senior Lecturer, Edinburgh University; b. 6.5.41, Edinburgh; m., Alison Catherine Gordon; 1 s.; 3 d. Educ. Fort Augustus School; Edinburgh University. Former Lecturer, Edinburgh University; former Secretary, Scottish Society for the History of Medicine; Secretary, Edinburgh and East of Scotland Society of Anaesthetists. Recreation: fishing. Address: (h.) 4 Laverockbank Terrace, Edinburgh, EH5 3BJ; T.-031-552 4783.

Gordon, Professor William Morrison, MA, LLB, PhD. Douglas Professor of Civil Law, Glasgow University, since 1969; Solicitor (non-practising), since 1956; b. 3.3.33, Inverurie; m., Isabella Evelyn Melitta Robertson; 2 s.; 2 d. Educ. Inverurie Academy; Robert Gordon's College, Aberdeen; Aberdeen University. National Service, Royal Navy, 1955-57; Assistant in Jurisprudence, Aberdeen University, 1957-60; Glasgow University: Lecturer in Civil Law, 1960-65, Senior Lecturer in Law, 1965-69 (and Sub-Dean of Faculty); Dean of Faculty, 1974-76. Elder, Jordanhill Parish Church; Literary Director, The Stair Society. Publications: Studies in Transfer of Property by Tradition, 1970; articles. Recreation: golf. Address: (b.) Department of Legal History, Stair Building, University, Glasgow, G12 8QQ; T.-041-339 8855, Ext. 7387.

Gordon-Duff, Lachlan Cecil, TD, DL, JP. Chairman, Water Services, Grampian Regional Council, since 1978; Chairman, North East River Purification Board, since 1980; b. 23.11.14, Co. Cork, Eire; m., Patricia De Chair; 2 s. Educ. Eton College; Royal Military College, Sandhurst. Joined Gordon Highlanders, 1936; served World War II; commanded 8th Argylls, 1956; retired, 1960 (rank of Colonel); joined Banff County Council, 1961; Member, Grampian Regional Council, since 1974. Recreation: gardening. Address: (h.) White House of Park, Cornhill, Banff, AB4 2AX; T.-046 66 269.

Gordon-Duff, Col. Thomas Robert, MC, JP. Lord Lieutenant of Banffshire, since 1964; b. 1911; m., Jean Moir (deceased); 1 s. Educ. Eton; Sandhurst. 2nd Lt., Rifle Brigade, 1932; served World War II; retired, 1947; Lt.-Col., 5/6 Bn., Gordon Highlanders (TA), 1947; Convener, Banff County Council, 1962-70. Address: (h.) Drummuir, Keith, Banffshire.

Gordon Lennox, Lt.-Gen. Sir George (Charles), KBE (1964), CB (1959), CVO (1952), DSO (1943). GOC-in-C Scottish Command and Governor of Edinburgh Castle, 1964-66; b. 29.5.08; m.; 2 s. Educ. Eton; Sandhurst. Commandant, RMA, Sandhurst, 1960-63; Director-General of Military Training, 1963-64. Address: (h.) Gordon Castle, Fochabers, Morayshire.

Gorman, Brian, MA. Director, English-Speaking Union in Scotland, since 1984; b. 31.10.51, Wishaw. Educ. Our Lady's High School, Motherwell; Glasgow University; Jordanhill College of Education. Teacher of Modern Studies, Columba High School, Coatbridge, 1974-76; Principal Teacher of Modern Studies, St. John's High School, Dundee, 1976-78; Group Travel and Transport Manager, Cotters Travel and Leisure Group, 1978-84. Recreations: theatre; debating. Address: (b.) 22 Atholl Crescent, Edinburgh; T.-031-229 1528.

Gorman, Martyn Lee, BSc, PhD. Senior Lecturer in Zoology, Aberdeen University, since 1984; b. 15.11.44, Holmfirth; m., Margaret; 1 s.; 1 d. Educ. Holme Valley Grammar School; Aberdeen University. Lecturer in Biology, University of the South Pacific, Fiji, 1970-73; Lecturer in Zoology, Aberdeen University, 1973-84. Recreations: archery; computer programming. Address: (b.) Culterty Field Station, Newburgh, Aberdeenshire; T.-03586 631.

Gosden, Roger Gordon, BSc, PhD, FZS. Senior Lecturer in Physiology, Medical School, Edinburgh University, since 1976; b. 23.9.48, Ryde, Isle of Wight; m., Carole Ann Walsh; 2 s. Educ. Chislehurst and Sidcup Grammar School; Bristol University; Cambridge University. MRC Research Fellow, Cambridge University, 1973-74 and 1975-76; Population Council Research Fellow, Duke University, USA, 1974-75; Visiting Scientist, University of Southern California, 1979 and 1982. Member, Church and Nation Committee, Church of Scotland. Publication: Biology of Menopause, 1985. Recreations: natural history; painting. Address: (b.) Department of Physiology, University Medical School, Edinburgh, EH8 9AG; T.-031-667 1011.

Goskirk, Rev. John Leslie, LTh. Minister, Lairg Parish Church, since 1968, and Rogart Parish Church, since 1970; b. 16.3.38, Glasgow; m., Myra Hendry Fisher; 2 s.; 2 d. Educ. High School of Glasgow; Glasgow University and Trinity College. Clerk, Sutherland Presbytery; Past Chairman, former Golspie, Rogart and Lairg District Council; Past Chairman, Lairg Community Council. Address: The Manse, Lairg, Sutherland.

Gosling, Allan Gladstone, RIBA, RIAS, DipArch. Director, Scottish Services, Property Services Agency, since 1983; b. 4.7.33, Preston; m., Janet Pamela; 1 d. Educ. Kirkham Grammar School; Birmingham School of Architecture. Private practice, Birmingham, 1957-59; National Service, Royal Artillery, 1959-61 (2nd Lt.); Works Organisation Architect, War Office, 1961-63; Architect, Ministry of Housing, 1963-72; PSA: Regional Works Officer, North West Region, 1972-76, Director, Midland Region, 1976-83. Recreations: DIY; gardening; walking. Address: (h.) 7 Ventnor Terrace, Edinburgh, EH9 2BL; T.-031-667 8511.

Gossip, Michael A.J., BL, NP, FBIM. Chief Executive, Argyll and Bute District Council, since 1974; b. 27.4.33, Edinburgh; m., Margaret; 1 s.; 2 d. Educ. George Watson's Boys' College, Edinburgh; Edinburgh University. Legal Assistant, Midlothian County Council, 1955-57; Dumfries County Council: Senior Legal Assistant, 1957-60, Depute County Clerk, 1960-71; Argyll County Council: Depute County Clerk, 1971-72, County Clerk, 1972-75. Recreations: bowls; gardening. Address: (b.) Kilmory Castle, Lochgilphead, Argyll; T.-0546 2127.

Gotts, Iain McEwan, DipLE, DipTP, ARICS, MRTPI. Director, PEIDA, Planning and Economic Consultants, since 1976; b. 26.2.47, Glasgow; m., Pamela; 1 s.; 2 d. Educ. Jordanhill College, Glasgow; Paisley College of Technology; Heriot-Watt University/Edinburgh College of Art. Trainee Surveyor, British Rail Property Department, Glasgow, 1965-68; further education, 1968-72; Surveyor/Land Economist, Wright & Partners, Edinburgh, 1972-76. Publication: Impact of Oil Pollution on Tourism, 1979. Recreations: piano; golf; rugby refereeing. Address: (b.) 10 Chester Street, Edinburgh, EH3 7RA; T.-031-225 5737.

Goudie, Professor Robert Barclay, MD, FRCPGlas, FRCPath, FRSE. St. Mungo (Notman) Professor of Pathology, Glasgow University, since 1970; b. 13.11.28, Glasgow; m., Lilian Duke Munro; 3 s.; 1 d. Educ. Hutchesons' Grammar School; Glasgow University. Squadron Leader, RAF Medical Branch, Institute of Pathology and Tropical Medicine, Halton, 1954-56; Lecturer, Senior Lecturer, Reader, University Department of Pathology, Western Infirmary, Glasgow, 1956-70; Nuffield Fellow in Medicine, Cambridge University, 1959-60. Recreation: golf. Address: (b.) University Department of Pathology, Royal Infirmary, Glasgow, G4 0SF; T.-041-552 3535, Ext. 5327.

Gough, Robert Kerr Livingstone, JP. Convener, Fife Regional Council, since 1978; Member, Forth Ports Authority, since 1970; Vice Chairman,

Glenrothes Development Corporation, since 1978; b. 1.8.24, Buckhaven; m., Margaret; 2 s.; 1 d. Educ. Buckhaven High School. Member, Buckhaven and Methil Town Council and Fife County Council, 1956; Vice Convener, Fife Regional Council, 1975; Member: Forth Road Bridge Joint Board, 1979, Tay Road Bridge Joint Board, 1979, Forth River Purification Board, 1979. Recreations: gardening; welfare of the young and old and physically handicapped. Address: (h.) 46 Stark Street, Buckhaven, Fife; T.-Buckhaven 713308.

Gourlay, Harry. MP (Labour), Kirkcaldy, since 1959; b. 10.7.16. Educ. Kirkcaldy High School. Member, Kirkcaldy Town Council, 1946-60 and Fife County Council, 1947-60; Chairman, Scottish Parliamentary Labour Group, 1975-77; Deputy Speaker and Deputy Chairman, Ways and Means, 1968-70; Chairman, Scottish Grand and Scottish Standing Committees, 1979-81.

Gourlay, (John) Malcolm, BCom, CA (Ont). Chief Executive, Clyde Petroleum p.l.c., since 1983; b. 19.9.42, Ootacamund, India; m., Avril May Weekes; 1 s.; 2 d. Educ. Merchiston Castle School, Edinburgh; Edinburgh University. Clarkson Gordon & Co., Chartered Accountants, Toronto, 1964-67; Singer & Friedlander, Glasgow, 1968-77 (Local Director, 1971-77); Clyde Petroleum p.l.c.: Director, since 1973, Managing Director, 1977-83. Recreations: golf; skiing; opera. Address: (b.) Coddington Court, Coddington, Ledbury, Herefordshire; T.-0531 86 511.

Gove, Robert Morrison, BSc (Eng), CEng, FIEE. Chief Engineer, Transmission/Distribution, South of Scotland Electricity Board, since 1977; b. 2.7.26, Aberdeen; m., Doris Jean Shorthouse; 1 s.; 1 d. Educ. Robert Gordon's College, Aberdeen; Aberdeen University. Royal Engineers (E/M Officer CRE N. Malaya), 1947-49; Graduate Apprentice, then Staff Engineer, British Thomson Houston Co. Ltd., Rugby, 1949-53; Assistant Engineer, British Electricity Authority, Portobello, 1953-56; Deputy Resident Engineer, Chapelcross, and Design Engineer, Werz and McLellan, Consulting Engineers, Newcastle, 1956-63; Technical Engineer, North of Scotland Hydro Electric Board, 1963-77. Recreations: music; gardening; golf. Address: (h.) 5 Darvel Drive, Newton Mearns, Glasgow; T.-041-639 7401.

Gow, Sheriff Neil, QC (Scot), MA, LLB, FSA Scot. Sheriff of South Strathclyde, at Ayr, since 1976; b. 24.4.32; m., Joanna Sutherland; 1 s. Educ. Merchiston Castle School; Glasgow University; Edinburgh University. Captain, Intelligence Corps (BAOR); Advocate, 1957-76; Member, Regional Council, Scottish Conservative Association; President, Auchinleck Boswell Society.

Gowenlock, Professor Brian Glover, PhD, DSc, CChem, FRSC, FRSE. Professor of Chemistry, Heriot-Watt University, since 1966; Member, University Grants Committee, 1976-85; Assessor Member, Scottish Tertiary Education Advisory Council, since 1984; b. 9.2.26, Oldham; m.,

Margaret Davis; 1 s.; 2 d. Educ. Hulme Grammar School; Manchester University. Assistant Lecturer, then Lecturer in Chemistry, University College of Swansea, 1948-55; Lecturer, then Senior Lecturer in Chemistry, Birmingham University, 1955-66; Visiting Scientist, National Research Council of Canada, Ottawa, 1963; Erskine Memorial Fellow, Canterbury University, Christchurch, 1976. Recreations: genealogy; foreign travel. Address: (h.) 49 Lygon Road, Edinburgh, EH16 5QA; T.-031-667 8506.

Gowland, David Alexander, BA, PhD, PGCE. Senior Lecturer in Modern History, Dundee University, since 1982 (Convener, Committee for Contemporary European Studies, since 1979); b. 1.4.42, Reading; m., Helen Janet Mackinlay; 2 d. Educ. Culford; Manchester University; London University. Dundee University: Assistant Lecturer in Modern History, 1967-69, Lecturer in Modern History, 1970-81, Dean of Students, Faculty of Arts and Social Sciences, 1979-83; Honorary Lecturer, Civil Service College, 1970-76. Publications: Common Market or Community?, 1973; Methodist Secessions, 1979; Scottish Methodism in the Early Victorian Period, 1981. Recreation: golf. Address: (b.) Department of Modern History, Dundee University, Dundee; T.-Dundee 23181.

Grace, Very Rev. Canon Thomas Augustine. Parish Priest, St. Peter's, Glenburn, Paisley, since 1974 (Member, Cathedral Chapter, Diocese of Paisley, since 1979); b. 6.11.19, Glasgow. Educ. St. Mungo's Academy, Glasgow; St. Peter's Theological College, Bearsden. Ordained to priesthood, St. Andrew's Cathedral, Glasgow, 1944; Curate: St. Joseph's, Stepps, 1944-47, St. John's, Barrhead, 1947-68, St. Ninian's, Gourock, 1968-70; Parish Priest, St. Mungo's, Greenock, 1970-74. Recreations: reading; music; gardening. Address: St. Peter's, 154 Braehead Road, Glenburn, Paisley, PA2 8NG; T.-041-884 2435.

Graeme, Malcolm Laurie, VRD, MA, MB, BChir, MFCM, DPH, MRCS, LRCP. Member, Fife Health Board, since 1983; b. 16.9.19, Guernsey; m., Dr. Patricia Doreen Shurly, MRCP; 1 d. Educ. Stowe; Jesus College, Cambridge; St. George's Hospital Medical School (Devitt-Pendlebury Scholarship). Surgeon Lt./Surgeon Lt. Cdr., RNVR/RNR, 1944-64; Public Health Service, London County Council, London Borough of Barnet and London Borough of Enfield, 1957-70; Medical Branch, Civil Service, Department of Education and Science and Department of Health and Social Security, 1970-79; District Councillor, NE Fife, 1980-84; Member, Executive Committee, NE Fife Conservative Association; Member, Fife Committee, King George's Fund for Sailors. Recreations: gardening; politics. Address: (h.) Little Bartilly, Ceres, by Cupar, Fife, KY15 5QG; T.-Ceres 238.

Graesser, Neil Walter, MIFM. Chairman, Highland River Purification Board, since 1976; Chairman of the Council, Association of Scottish District Salmon Fishery Boards, since 1969; Member, Management Committee, Atlantic Salmon Trust, since 1969; Freshwater Fisheries

Consultant, since 1950; Landowner, since 1967; b. 22.10.28, Froncysyllte, North Wales; m., Audrey Jennifer Christianna Tapp; 1 s.; 1 d. Educ. Oundle; Llysfasi Farm Institute. Brief period in RAF; studied farming; managed a farm, 1950-67; made life's study of salmon and salmon fishing; author of books on salmon and salmon fishing. Recreations: shooting; fishing. Address: Rosehall, Lairg, Sutherland, IV27 4BD; T.-Rosehall 202.

Graham, Alex, BSc, CA. Member, Inverness District Council, since 1980; b. 25.7.52, Borve, Isle of Lewis; m., Lesley Anne Ballantyne; 1 s. Educ. Nicolson Institute; Edinburgh University. Member, National Executive Committee, Scottish Liberal Party, 1980-81. Recreations: reading; walking. Address: (h.) 47 Craigard Terrace, Inverness, IV3 6PS; T.-0463 223507.

Graham, Dennis C., DSc, PhD, CChem, FRSC, FInstBiol, FRSA, FRSE. Director, Agricultural Scientific Services, Department of Agriculture and Fisheries for Scotland, since 1981; b. 2.12.29, Carlisle. Educ. Carlisle Grammar School; Durham University; Edinburgh University. Recreation: cultivation of alpine plants. Address: 447 Lanark Road, Edinburgh, EH14 5BA; T.-031-453 3459.

Graham, Major General Frederick Clarence Campbell, CB, DSO; b. 14.12.08, Helensburgh; m., Phyllis MacMahon; 3 s. Educ. Eton College; Royal Military College, Sandhurst. Gazetted to Argyll and Sutherland Highlanders, 1929; served in Hong Kong, Shanghai, Rawalpindi, India; saw active service in Western Desert, Crete, Syria, Palestine, India, Italy; twice mentioned in Despatches; commanded 1st Bn., Argyll and Sutherland Highlanders on active service in Italy, 1944-45; appointed Colonel of the Argylls, 1958-72; GOC, 51st Highland Division, 1958-68; Lord Lieutenant, Central Region, Stirling and Falkirk, 1975-79. Address: (h.) Mackeanston House, Doune, Perthshire.

Graham, James, MB, ChB, FRCSGlas, FRCSEdin. Consultant Orthopaedic Surgeon, Western Infirmary and Gartnavel General Hospital, Glasgow, since 1976; Honorary Clinical Lecturer, Glasgow University, since 1976; b. 2.3.36, Stonehouse; m., Wilma Edith Melville; 1 s.; 1 d. Educ. Hamilton Academy; Glasgow University. House Officer posts, Western Infirmary and Southern General Hospital, Glasgow; basic surgical training, Vale of Leven Hospital, Alexandria, and Western Infirmary, Glasgow; orthopaedic training in Western Infirmary, Royal Hospital for Sick Children and Southern General Hospital, Glasgow and Massachusetts General Hospital; appointed Senior Lecturer in Orthopaedics and Honorary Consultant Orthopaedic Surgeon, Western Infirmary and Gartnavel General Hospital, 1972; research, teaching and clinical fellowship to Harvard University and Massachusetts General Hospital, Boston, 1968-69; British Orthopaedic Association ABC Travelling Felowship to North America, 1974. Recreations: rugby (watching); golf (participating); DIY. Address: (b.) Department of Orthopaedics, Western Infirmary, Glasgow, G11 6NT; T.-041-339 8822.

Graham, Marquis of, (James Graham). Member, Queen's Bodyguard for Scotland (Royal Company of Archers), since 1980; b. 6.4.35; m., Catherine Elizabeth MacDonell; 2 s.; 1 d. Educ. Loretto. Council Member, National Farmers' Union of Scotland, 1982-84. Address: (h.) Auchmar, Drymen, Glasgow.

Graham, John James, OBE, MA, FEIS. Member, Shetland Islands Council (Vice-Chairman, Education Committee), since 1982; Chairman, Shetland Movement, since 1982; Joint Editor, The New Shetlander, since 1956; b. 12.7.21, Lerwick; m., Beryl Smith; 3 s.; 2 d. Educ. Lerwick Central Secondary School; Edinburgh University. RAF Training Command, 1941-44, Bomber Command, 1944-46; Principal Teacher of English, Anderson Educational Institute, Lerwick, 1950-66; Headmaster: Lerwick Central Secondary School, 1966-70, Anderson High School, Lerwick, 1970-82; Member: Consultative Committee on the Curriculum, 1976-80, Broadcasting Council for Scotland, 1981-84; President, Shetland Folk Society. Publications: A Grammar and Usage of the Shetland Dialect (Co-author); Northern Lights (Joint Editor); The Shetland Dictionary. Recreations: local history; golf. Address: (h.) 26 King Harald Street, Lerwick, Shetland; T.-Lerwick 3425.

Graham, John Michael Denning, LLB (Hons), NP. Solicitor and Notary Public, since 1970; Director, Loklat Builders, since 1983; Director, Bollinger Properties, since 1982; Chairman, Rent Assessment Committee, Glasgow, since 1983; b. 7.9.44, Kirkintilloch; m., Christina Jeanne Sinclair; 2 s. Educ. Royal Belfast Academical Institution; Queen's University, Belfast. Joint Senior Partner, Paterson Robertson & Graham, Solicitors, since 1971. Recreations: tennis; golf; Address: (h.) St. Michael's, Garngaber Avenue, Lenzie, G66; T.-041-221 7691.

Graham, Professor Neil Bonnette, BSc, PhD, CChem, FRSC, FPRI. Research Professor in Chemical Technology, Strathclyde University, since 1982; Technical Director, Polysystems Limited, since 1982; b. 23.5.33, Liverpool; 1 s.; 3 d. Educ. Alsop High School, Liverpool; Liverpool University. Research Chemist, Research Scientist, Canadian Industries Ltd., MacMasterville PQ, Canada, 1956-67; Assistant Group Head, then Group Head, Polymer Chemistry, ICI, Runcorn, Cheshire; Young Professor of Chemical Technology, Strathclyde University, 1973-82. Member: Advisory Committee on Dental and Surgical Materials, Society of Chemical Industry Committee for Colloid and Surface Chemistry, International Editorial Board of Biomaterials; Vice-Chairman, West of Scotland Division, Chemical Society, 1975-77; Governor of Keil School, since 1978. Recreations: music; walking. Address: (b.) Strathclyde University, Department of Pure and Applied Chemistry, Thomas Graham Building, 295 Cathedral Street, Glasgow, G1 1XL; T.-041-552 4400, Ext. 2231.

Graham, Nigel John O. Member, Highland Regional Council, since 1983; Chairman, Scottish Advisory Committee, RSPB; b. 28.7.27, Worcestershire; m., Margaret; 2 s.; 2 d. Educ.

Marlborough College. Highland Light Infantry, 1945-53; TA, Queen's Own Cameron Highlanders, 1953-61; farmer, 1953-83; Member, Nairn County Council, 1966-72. Chairman: Highlands and Islands Conservative Council, Inverness Nairn and Lochaber Conservative Association. Recreation: bird-watching. Address: (h.) Househill, Nairn; T.-Nairn 53241.

Graham, Sir Norman William, Kt (1971), CB (1961), FRSE. Secretary, Scottish Education Department, 1964-73; b. 11.10.13; m.; 2 s.; 1 d. Educ. High School of Glasgow; Glasgow University. Hon. DLitt, Heriot-Watt, 1971; DUniv, Stirling, 1974.

Graham, Ronald Cairns, MB, ChB, DipSocMed, FRCP, FFCM. General Manager, Tayside Health Board, since 1985; Honorary Senior Lecturer, Dundee University, since 1969; b. 8.10.31, Airdrie; m., Christine Fraser Osborne; 2 s.; 1 d. Educ. Airdrie Academy; Glasgow University. Deputy Medical Superintendent, Edinburgh Royal Infirmary; Assistant Senior Administrative Medical Officer, South-Eastern Regional Hospital Board; Eastern Regional Hospital Board; Deputy Senior Administrative Medical Officer, Senior Administrative Medical Officer; Chief Administrative Medical Officer, Tayside Health Board, 1973-85. Recreation: fishing. Address: (h.) 34 Dalgleish Road, Dundee; T.-Dundee 43146.

Graham, William, MA. Freelance Writer; b. 27.2.13, Carluke; m., Jean C. Simpson; 1 s.; 1 d. Educ. Wishaw High School; Glasgow University; Jordanhill College of Education. Organist; Teacher; Nurseryman; Airman; Author. Former Secretary and President, Ayr Burns Club; Past Preses, Scots Language Society. Publications: That Ye Inherit; Twa-Three Sangs and Stories; The Talking Scots Quiz Book; The Scots Word Book. Recreations: music; gardening. Address: (h.) 48 Mount Charles Crescent, Alloway, Ayrshire; T.-Ayr 43701.

Grainger, David Shepherd, JP. Provost and Chairman, Clydebank District Council, since 1985; b. 3.8.43, Edinburgh; m., Sarah; 1 d. Educ. Clydebank High School; Lennox Technical College. Recreations: music; reading. Address: (h.) 4 Napier Court, Old Kilpatrick, Glasgow; T.-Duntocher 78867.

Grant, Angus Watt. Member, Central Regional Council, since 1982; b. 15.7.19, Ballater; m., Margaret Grant. Educ. Aldenham School, Hertfordshire; Manchester Business School. Management Trainee, 1936-39; commissioned, Royal Marines, 1939-46; Personnel Officer/Manager, Dunlop Rubber Co., Birmingham and Durban (South Africa), 1946-52; Regional Director, National Development and Management Foundation, South Africa, 1953-54; Manager, Employment and Training, Stanvac Refining Co., Durban, 1954-56; Chairman, Executive Committee, Executive Director, Management Services and PA to Chairman, United Tobacco Co. Ltd., Johannesburg, 1956-74; Manager, Senior Management Studies, BAT Industries Ltd., 1974-80. Past Chairman: Programme Committee,

Institute of Directors (South Africa Branch), Industrial Council for the Tobacco Industry, South Africa; former Member, Executive Committee, Computer Society of South Africa, and National Development and Management Foundation, South Africa. Recreations: rifle and pistol shooting; photography; cooking. Address: (h.) 11 Mid Shore, Pittenweem, Fife, KY10 2NL.

Grant, Colin Drummond, BSc, PhD, CEng, FIChemE. Reader in Chemical and Process Engineering, Strathclyde University, since 1983; b. 3.6.46, Glasgow; m., Maida Elizabeth; 2 s. Educ. Fettes College, Edinburgh; Strathclyde University. Student Apprentice, Babcock and Wilcox Ltd., 1963-67; Strathclyde University: Research Student, 1967-70, Lecturer, 1970-82, Senior Lecturer, 1982-83. Secretary, Scottish Branch, Institution of Chemical Engineers, 1975-83. Recreations: mountaineering; tennis; squash. Address: (h.) 28 Essex Drive, Jordanhill, Glasgow, G14; T.-041-959 7148.

Grant, Donald Blane, TD, CA. Partner, Thomson, McLintock & Co., since 1950; Chairman, Tayside Health Board, since 1984; Director, Dundee and London Investment Trust PLC; Director, HAT Group PLC; Director, Don Brothers, Buist p.l.c.; b. 8.10.21, Dundee; m., Lavinia Margaret Ruth Ritchie; 3 d. Educ. Dundee High School. Royal Artillery, 1939-46 (retired as Major). Chairman: Mathew Trust, Caird Travelling Scholarships Trust. Recreations: golf; fishing; shooting; gardening. Address: (b.) Royal Exchange, Dundee; T.-0382 22763.

Grant, Sheriff Douglas Marr Kelso. Sheriff of South Strathclyde, Dumfries and Galloway (formerly of Ayr and Bute), since 1966; b. 5.4.17; m.; 2 s.; 2 d. Educ. Rugby; Peterhouse, Cambridge. Army, 1940-46; called to Bar, Gray's Inn, 1945; admitted, Faculty of Advocates, 1959.

Grant, Ian David. Farmer; President, National Farmers Union of Scotland, since 1984; b. 28.7.43, Dundee; m., Eileen May Louisa Yule; 3 d. Educ. Strathallan School; East of Scotland College of Agriculture. Farms at Thorn, Alyth; NFU: President, Blairgowrie Branch, 1970-71; President, Perth Area, 1976; National Council Delegate, since 1977; Convener, Cereals Committee, 1980-81-82; Vice-President, 1981-82-83; Chairman, EEC Cereals Working Party, since 1982 and International Federation of Agricultural Producers, Grains Committee, since 1984; Vice Chairman, East of Scotland Farmers Ltd.; Council Member, SAOS Ltd; Council Member, Royal Smithfield Club. Recreations: shooting; swimming; music. Address: (h.) Thorn, Alyth, Blairgowrie, PH11 8NP; T.-082-83 2253.

Grant, Ian Faulconer Heathcoat, JP, DL. Director: Croftinloan (Holdings) Ltd., since 1983, First Charlotte Assets Trust PLC, since 1982, Glenmoriston Estates Limited, since 1964, Glenmoriston Gold & Silversmiths Limited, since 1978, Highland Forest Products PLC, since 1983, Highland Mobiles Limited, since 1978, Japan Assets Trust PLC, since 1981, Lorne Exploration PLC, since 1983, Lorne Petroleum Limited, since 1984, MacDougalls Advertising PLC, since

1985, McKinroy Limited, since 1981, Pacific Assets Trust PLC, since 1985, Royal Bank of Scotland PLC, since 1982, Scottish Woodland Owners Association (Commercial) Limited, since 1985, Thomas Tait & Sons Limited, since 1984; b. 3.6.39, Singapore; m., Sally; 1 s.; 3 d. Educ. Cargilfield; Sedbergh; Liverpool College of Commerce. ICI Ltd., 1957-62; various positions, Jardine Matheson & Co. Ltd., Hong Kong, 1962-73, culminating in directorship on Main Board of parent company, as well as directorships in a number of associate companies. Address: (b.) Glenmoriston Estates Ltd., Glenmoriston, near Inverness; T.-0320 51202.

Grant, Rev. James Gordon, MA, BD. Minister, Portland Church, Troon, since 1965; Vice-Convener, Board of World Mission and Unity, Church of Scotland, since 1984; b. 5.7.32, Glasgow; m., Susan Ann Hewitt; 2 s.; 1 d. Educ. High School of Stirling; St. Andrews University. Ordained, 1957; Probationer Assistant, St. Mungo's Parish Church, Alloa, 1957-59; Minister, Dyce Parish Church, Aberdeen, 1959-65; Convener, Inter-Church Relations Committee, 1983-84. Recreations: golf; climbing; ornithology. Address: (h.) Portland Manse, 89 South Beach, Troon, KA10 6EQ; T.-0292 313285.

Grant, Major James MacAlpine Gregor, TD, NDA, MRAC. Landowner and Farmer, since 1961; b. 18.2.38, Nakuru, Kenya; m., Sara Marjory; 3 d. Educ. Eton; Royal Agricultural College, Cirencester. National Service, Queen's Own Cameron Highlanders, 1957-58; TA with 4/5th Queen's Own Cameron Highlanders; Volunteers with 51st Highland Volunteers. Address: Roskill House, Munlochy, Ross-shire, IV8 8PA; T.-Munlochy 207.

Grant, James Shaw, CBE, LLD, FRSE, FRAgS, MA. Author; b. 22.5.10, Stornoway; m., Catherine Mary Stewart. Educ. Nicolson Institute, Stornoway; Glasgow University. Editor, Stornoway Gazettee, 1932-63; Governor, Pitlochry Festival Theatre, 1954-84 (Chairman, 1971-83); Member, Crofters Commission, 1955-78 (Chairman, 1963-78); Director, Grampian TV, 1969-80; Member: Highlands and Islands Development Board, 1970-82, Scottish Advisory Committee, British Council, since 1972; Chairman, Harris Tweed Association Ltd., 1972-84; Member, Council, National Trust for Scotland, 1979-84; author of plays: Tarravore, The Magic Rowan, Legend is Born, Comrade the King. Publications: Highland Villages, 1977; Their Children Will See, 1979; The Hub of My Universe, 1982; Surprise Island, 1983; The Gaelic Vikings, 1984. Recreation: photography. Address: (h.) Ardgrianach, Inshes, Inverness; T.-Inverness 231476.

Grant, John Paxton, LLB, LLM. Senior Lecturer and Head, Department of Public International Law, Glasgow University, since 1974 (Dean, Faculty of Law and Financial Studies, since 1985); b. 22.2.44, Edinburgh; m., Elaine E. Sutherland. Educ. George Heriot's School, Edinburgh; Edinburgh University; Pennsylvania University. Lecturer, Faculty of Law: Aberdeen University, 1967-71, Dundee University, 1971-74; Visiting Professor: Saint Louis University School of Law, 1981, Northwestern School of Law, Lewis and Clark College, 1984; Member, Children's Panel: Aberdeenshire and Kincardine, 1970-71, Dundee, 1971-74, Strathclyde, 1974-81. Publications: Independence and Devolution (Editor), 1976; The Impact of Marine Pollution: Law and Practice (Joint Editor), 1980; The Encyclopaedic Dictionary of International Law (Joint General Editor), 1985. Recreations: walking; travelling. Address: (h.) 87 Warrender Park Road, Edinburgh, EH9 1EW; T.-031-229 7705.

Grant, Very Rev. Malcolm Etheridge, BSc (Hons), BD (Hons). Provost and Rector, Cathedral Church of S. Mary the Virgin, Glasgow, since 1981; b. 6.8.44, Maidstone; m., Katrina Russell Nuttall. Educ. Dunfermline High School; Edinburgh University; Edinburgh Theological College. Assistant Curate: S. Mary's Cathedral, Glasgow, 1969-72, Grantham Parish Church, in charge of Church of the Epiphany, Earlesfield, 1972; Team Vicar, Earlesfield, Grantham Team Ministry, 1972-78; Priest-in-Charge, S. Ninian's, Invergordon, 1978-81; Examining Chaplain to Bishop of Moray, Ross and Caithness, 1979-81; Member, Highland Region Education Committee, 1979-81. Address: S. Mary's Cathedral Rectory, 45 Rowallan Gardens, Glasgow, G11 7LH; T.-041-339 4956.

Grant, Maurice Alexander, MA. Principal, Industry Department for Scotland, since 1983; b. 1.1.41, Portree; m., Isabel Alison MacDonald; 1 d. Educ. Dunoon Grammar School; Glasgow University. Executive Officer: Department of Health for Scotland, 1961-62, Scottish Development Department, 1962-66; Higher Executive Officer, then Senior Executive Officer, Scottish Development Department, 1966-81; Principal, Scottish Economic Planning Department, 1981-83. Recreation: collecting antiquarian books. Address: (h.) 8 Nantwich Drive, Edinburgh, EH7 6QS; T.-031-669 7347.

Grant, Murdo Macdonald, MA (Hons), DipEd. Rector, Kingussie High School, since 1968; b. 20.3.32, Drumnadrochit; m., Cora Laing Gerrard; 2 s.; 1 d. Educ. Glen Urquhart Secondary School; Aberdeen University. Commissioned Service, RAF, 1955-57; Teacher, Nairn Academy; Principal Teacher of English, Golspie High School, 1964-68. Chairman, Badenoch & Strathspey Music Festival; Chairman, Area Primary Sports Association; Founder Member and Past President, Spey Valley Rotary Club; Member, Scottish Central Committee on Physical Education; Board Member, Cairngorm Recreation Trust; Vice-President, Badenoch Arts Club. Recreations: sailing (cruising); angling; hillwalking; reading. Address: (h.) Tor Na Sith, West Terrace, Kingussie, Inverness-shire; T.-05402 498.

Grant, Professor Nigel Duncan Cameron, MA, Med, PhD. Professor of Education, Glasgow University, since 1978; b. 8.6.32, Glasgow; m., Valerie Keeling Evans; 1 s.; 1 d. Educ. Inverness Royal Academy; Glasgow University. Teacher of English, Glasgow secondary schools, 1957-60; Lecturer in Education, Jordanhill College of Education, 1960-65; Lecturer in Educational Studies, then Reader, Edinburgh University,

1965-78. Past Chairman and President, British Comparative and International Education Society; former Executive Member, Comparative Education Society in Europe; Past Chairman, Scottish Educational Research Association; Educational Consultant, Comann Sgoiltean Da-Chananach Ghlaschu; Member, Executive Committee, Advisory Council for the Arts in Scotland; Member, Editorial Board, Comparative Education; Board of Governors, Jordanhill College of Education. Publications: Soviet Education, 1964; Society, Schools and Progress in Eastern Europe, 1969; Education and Nation-Building in the Third World (Editor and Co-author), 1971; A Mythology of British Education (Co-author), 1974; Scottish Universities: The Case for Devolution (Co-author), 1976; Patterns of Education in the British Isles (Co-author), 1977; The Crisis of Scottish Education, 1982. Recreations: theatre; music; poetry; natural history; languages; art; travel; calligraphy. Address: (b.) Department of Education, Glasgow University, Glasgow, G12 8QQ; T.-041-339 8855.

Grant of Dalvey, Sir Patrick Alexander Benedict, 14th Bt, FSA Scot, LLB. Chieftain of Clan Donnachy; Company Director; b. 5.2.53; m., Dr. Carolyn Elizabeth Highet; 2 s. Educ. St. Conleth's College, Dublin; The Abbey School, Fort Augustus; Glasgow University.

Grant-Wood, John, MA (Hons). Headmaster, Firrhill High School, Edinburgh, since 1975; b. 8.6.31, Ashton-under-Lyne; m., Pamela Irene; 1 s. Educ. Audenshaw Grammar School; Edinburgh University. Bank of Scotland; RAF; Headmaster, Livister Primary School, Shetland; Senior Housemaster, United World College of the Atlantic, South Wales; Depute Headmaster, Firrhill High School; twice elected to Court, Heriot-Watt University; Council Member: Royal Scottish Geographical Society, North Regional Examinations Board Examinations Committee; President, Scottish Area, Secondary Heads Association. Publication: Educating for Tomorrow (Contributor). Recreations: travel; railways; canals; music. Address: (h.) Rossarden, 20 Greenhill Gardens, Edinburgh; T.-031-447 3882.

Grassie, Professor Norman, BSc, PhD, DSc, CChem, FRSC, FRSE. Professor of Chemistry, Glasgow University, since 1971; b. 28.5.24, Aberdeen; m., Catherine Beaton; 1 s.; 2 d. Educ. Nicolson Institute, Stornoway; Aberdeen University. DSIR Senior Research Fellow, Birmingham University, 1948-50; ICI Research Fellow, Glasgow University, 1950-55; Glasgow University: Lecturer, 1955, Senior Lecturer, 1963, Reader, 1967, Titular Professor, 1971; Visiting Professor, Universities of: Mainz, 1967, Delaware, 1969, Malaysia, 1975-77, Merida (Venezuela), 1979. Publications: numerous books, mainly on topics related to polymer stability and degradation. Recreations: bridge; hill-walking; ballroom dancing; grandchildren; Church activities. Address: (h.) 15 Lovat Avenue, Bearsden, Glasgow, G61 3LQ; T.-041-942 8768.

Gratwick, Adrian Stuart, MA (Cantab), DPhil (Oxon). Reader in Humanity, St. Andrews University, since 1983; b. 31.3.43, Stanmore, Middlesex; m., Jennifer Rosemary Clark; 1 s.

Educ. St. Aloysius' College, Glasgow; St. Brendan's College, Bristol; St. John's College, Cambridge; Balliol College, Oxford. St. Andrews University: Assistant Lecturer in Humanity, 1966, Lecturer, 1969. Recreations: walking; gardening; woodwork. Address: (b.) Department of Humanity, St. Salvator's College, St. Andrews, Fife; T.-0334 76161, Ext. 492.

Gray, Adam, NDA, NDD. Farmer; Director, Royal Highland Agricultural Society, since 1976; Director, Scottish Milk Marketing Board, since 1981; Governor, West of Scotland Agricultural College, since 1976; b. 6.8.29, Borgue, Kirkcudbright; 3 s. Educ. George Watson's Boys College; West of Scotland Agricultural College. Nuffield Scholar, 1955; Past President, Stewartry NFU; Member, NFU Council; former Council Member, British Simmental Cattle Society; Past Chairman, SW Scotland Grassland Society; former Chairman, Kirkcudbright District Council; Honorary President, Stewartry Agricultural Society; Council Member: Scottish Agricultural Arbiters Association, Hannah Research Institute; Secretary, Kirkcudbright Burns Club; Past President, Kirkcudbright Rotary Club. Recreations: rugby; local history. Address: (h.) Ingleston, Borgue, Kirkcudbright; T.-05577 208.

Gray, Alasdair. Artist and Writer; b. 28.12.34, Glasgow; m., nobody, now; 1 s. Educ. Whitehill Senior Secondary School; Glasgow Art School. Part-time Art Teacher, 1959-62; Scene Painter, 1963-64; has since lived by drawing, painting, writing; Glasgow People's Palace has a collection of his portraits and cityscapes. Publications: novels: Lanark; 1982 Janine; The Fall of Kelvin Walker; anthologies: Unlikely Stories, Mostly; Lean Tales (this last also containing work by Jim Kelman and Agnes Owens). Recreations: reading; talking to friends; drinking; walking. Address: (h.) 39 Kersland Street, Glasgow, G12.

Gray, Alexander, MA, LLB. Solicitor; Honorary Sheriff, Dumbarton; b. 6.5.12, Glasgow; m., Margaret; 2 s. Educ. Hillhead High School; Glasgow University; Edinburgh University. Recreations: Gaelic; golf. Address: (h.) Kildalton, Cardross, G82 5NS; T.-841234.

Gray, Eric, MA (Hons). Rector, Beath High School, Cowdenbeath, since 1973; b. 4.4.27, Aberdeen; m., Elizabeth M. Davidson; 1 s. Educ. Robert Gordon's College, Aberdeen; Aberdeen University. Teacher/Special Assistant in Modern Languages, Wishaw High School, 1952-60; Principal Teacher of Modern Languages: Lasswade High School, 1960-65, Mary Erskine School, 1965-70; Assistant/Depute Rector, Airdrie Academy, 1970-73. Member, General Convocation, Heriot-Watt University; Past Chairman, Edinburgh Universities and Schools Club; Elder, St. Margaret's Parish Church, Dunfermline. Recreations: music; walking; gardening. Address: (h.) 15 Mulberry Drive, Dunfermline, KY11 5BZ; T.-0383 727079.

Gray, Ethel Marian, CBE, JP, MA, LLD, FEIS. President, Scottish Institute of Adult Education, since 1984; Vice-Chairman, Board of Governors, The Queen's College, Glasgow, since 1980;

Chairman, Education Project for Older People, Age Concern Scotland, since 1982; b. 19.4.23, Glasgow; m., George Deans Gray (qv). Educ. Hutchesons' Girls Grammar School; Paisley Grammar School; Glasgow University. Teacher of English, 1946-52; Lecturer in English and Drama, Jordanhill College, 1952-63; Founding Principal, Craigie College of Education, Ayr, 1963-75; Director, Scottish Adult Literacy Agency, 1976-79; Chairman, National Book League Scotland, 1977-81; Member of Court, Chairman of Staffing Committee and Joint Faculty Staff Review Board, Herot-Watt University, 1979-84; Advisor in Adult Education, IBA, since 1983; Member, Scottish Tertiary Education Advisory Council, since 1984; Member, STV Education Advisory Committee, since 1981; Member, Scottish Community Education Council, 1979-85 (Chairman, Communications and Technology Group and Chairman, Management Committee, Micro-Electronics Project); Member, Crawford Commission on Radio and Television Coverage, 1973-75; Member, Committee of Enquiry on the Police, 1977-79; Member, Consultative Committee on the Curriculum, 1965-71. Recreations: reading; travelling; theatre. Address: (h.) 7 Greenbank Crescent, Edinburgh, EH10 5TE; T.-031-447 5403.

Gray, George Deans, CBE, MA. Member, Board of Education, Church of Scotland, since 1980; b. 23.5.08, Edinburgh; m., Ethel Marian Rennie (see Ethel Marian Gray). Educ. Royal High School, Edinburgh; Edinburgh University. Teacher of Classics: Musselburgh Grammar School, 1931-37, George Watson's College, Edinburgh, 1937-45; Principal Teacher, Royal High School, Edinburgh, 1946-59; Secretary, Scottish Council for the Training of Teachers, 1959-66; Registrar (first), General Teaching Council for Scotland, 1966-72; Honorary General Secretary, Scottish Secondary Teachers Association, 1945-59; Chairman: Classical Association (Edinburgh and SE Centre), 1968-73, Scottish Dyslexia Association, 1980-82. Recreations: choral singing; classical music; piano; gardening. Address: (h.) 7 Greenbank Crescent, Edinburgh, EH10 5TE; T.-031-447 5403.

Gray, Gilbert A., MA (Hons), FRGS. Head Teacher, Uddingston Grammar School, since 1981; b. 13.9.24, Dundee; m., Daphne Foley; 2 s.; 2 d. Educ. Dunfermline High School; Edinburgh University; Moray House College of Education. RAF, 1943-47 (34 operations with 106 Squadron, Bomber Command, service in UK and India); Teacher of Geography: King's Road School, Rosyth, 1952-54, Aberdeen Academy, 1955-58; Lanark Grammar School: Principal Teacher of Geography, 1959-72, Assistant Head Teacher, 1972-73; Lecturer, Jordanhill College of Education, 1973-74; Adviser in Geography, Lanarkshire, 1974-81. Former Secretary, Scottish Association of Geography Teachers (Past President); former Senior Assistant Examiner, Scottish Examination Board. Address: (h.) 19 Millar Street, Glassford, Strathaven, Lanarkshire, ML10 6TD; T.-Strathaven 22241.

Gray, His Eminence Cardinal Gordon Joseph, MA (Hon.), Hon. DD. Archbishop of St. Andrews and Edinburgh, 1951-85; b. 10.8.10.

Educ. Holy Cross Academy, Edinburgh; St. John's Seminary, Wonersh. Assistant-Priest, St. Andrews, 1935-41; Parish Priest, Hawick, 1941-47; Rector, Blairs College, Aberdeen, 1947-51.

Gray, Hugh. Member, North East Fife District Council, since 1984; Member, St. Andrews Links Management Committee, since 1984; b. 10.5.31, Glasgow; m., Jane Henderson Innes; 2 s. Educ. Queen's Park School; Skerry's College, Glasgow. Journalist, 23 years, first 19 years with Beaverbrook Newspapers Ltd., then as Senior Scottish Feature Writer, TV Times; since 1970, Hotelier in St. Andrews. Recreations: golf; bridge; snooker. Address: Beachway House Private Hotel, 4-8 Murray Park, St. Andrews, Fife; T.-0334 73319.

Gray, Iain George Fowler. Finance Officer, Department of Agriculture and Fisheries for Scotland and Scottish Education Department, since 1984; b. 3.5.39, Glasgow. Educ. Albert Road Academy, Glasgow; Roseburn, Edinburgh; Royal High School, Edinburgh. Joined War Office as Executive Officer, 1960; PS/DUS (B), 1964-65; joined Scottish Office as Assistant Principal, 1965, Principal, 1969; SED to 1971; Private Secretary to Minister of State, 1971-72; SDD, 1973; SEPD, 1973-77; DAFS (Assistant Secretary), 1978-84. Recreations: golf; badminton. Address: (b.) New St. Andrews House, Edinburgh; T.-031-556 8400.

Gray, James Allan, MB, ChB, FRCPEdin. Consultant in Communicable Diseases, City Hospital, Edinburgh, since 1969; part-time Senior Lecturer, Department of Medicine, Edinburgh University, since 1969; Assistant Principal Medical Officer, Scottish Widows' Fund, Edinburgh, since 1979; b. 24.3.35, Bristol; m., Jennifer Margaret Newton Hunter; 1 s.; 2 d. Educ. St. Paul's School, London; Edinburgh University. House Surgeon and Physician posts, Edinburgh and Middlesbrough; Short Service Commission, RAF Medical Branch, 1960-63; Senior House Officer, Research Fellow and Registrar posts, Edinburgh, 1965-67; Registrar, Bristol Royal Infirmary, 1967-68; Senior Registrar, Royal Free Hospital (Department of Infectious Diseases), London, 1968-69; Assistant Director of Studies (Medicine), Edinburgh Post-Graduate Board, 1976-84; Fellow, Royal Medical Society (Senior President, 1958-59); Founder Editor, Res Medica, 1957-58; Assistant Editor, Journal of Infection, since 1979. Publications: Antibacterial Drugs Today (Co-author), 1983; Infectious Diseases (Co-author), 1984. Recreations: hillwalking; pottery collecting; photography. Address: (h.) St. Andrews Cottage, 15 Lauder Road, Edinburgh, EH9 2EN; T.-031-667 4124.

Gray of Contin, Baron, (James (Hamish) Hector Northey Gray), PC (1982). Life Peer; Minister of State, Scottish Office, since 1983; b. 28.6.27; m.; 2 s.; 1 d. Educ. Inverness Royal Academy. Queen's Own Cameron Highlanders, 1945-48; Member, Inverness Town Council, 1965-70; MP (Conservative), Ross and Cromarty, 1970-83; Minister of State, Department of Energy, 1979-83.

Gray, James Nicol, LRCP (E), LRCS (E), LRPF & S (Glas), DMJ, AFOM. Medical Adviser, Lothian Regional Council, since 1977; Medical Adviser, Lothians and Borders Police, since 1967; Medical Adviser, Lothians and Borders Fire Brigade; b. 29.3.22, Manchester; m., Pamela Ann Walker; 1 s.; 2 d. Educ. George Watson's College; Edinburgh University and School of Medicine. General Practice, 1965-77. Recreation: golf. Address: (h.) 3 Suffolk Road, Edinburgh, EH16 5NR; T.-031-667 1494.

Gray, Professor James Robertson, BSc, DipActMaths, FFA, FIMA, FSS. Professor and Head, Department of Actuarial Mathematics and Statistics, Heriot-Watt University, since 1971; b. 21.2.26, Dundee; m., Catherine McAulay Towner. Educ. High School of Dundee; Edinburgh University. Actuarial Trainee, Scottish Life Assurance Company, 1947-49; St. Andrews University: Lecturer in Mathematics, 1949-50, Lecturer in Statistics, 1950-62, Senior Lecturer in Statistics (also Head of Department), 1962-71; Heriot-Watt University: established first Department of Actuarial Science in UK; Dean, Faculty of Science, 1978-81; Council Member, Faculty of Actuaries, since 1969 (Vice-President); Vice-Chairman, Scottish Examination Board, since 1984 (Convener of Examinations Committee, since 1982); former Vice-Chairman, Scottish Universities Council on Entrance; Past Chairman: Scottish Branch, Institute of Mathematics and Its Applications, Edinburgh Branch, Royal Statistical Society. Recreations: golf; hill-walking; bridge; music; Rotary. Address: (h.) Green Gables, 9 Cammo Gardens, Edinburgh, EH4 8EJ; T.-031-339 3330.

Gray, John Alexander. Broadcasting Consultant, since 1978; b. 5.7.18, London. GPO Film Unit, 1937-39; BBC, 1940-78, mainly in News and Monitoring, and in programme departments in Scotland. Director: Scottish Ballet, Traverse Theatre; Scottish Chairman, Writers' Guild of Great Britain. Recreation: hill-walking. Address: (h.) 13 Comely Bank Row, Edinburgh, EH4 1EA; T.-031-332 8270.

Gray, Rev. John Anderson. Minister, Ballieston Mure Memorial, Glasgow, since 1972; b. 27.4.21, Glasgow; m., Mary Amelia Richardson; 1 s.; 1 d. Educ. Queen's Park School; Glasgow University and Trinity College. Army, 1941-46 (Lt., RA and Argyll and Sutherland Highlanders); Minister, Port Glasgow Old; Royal Army Chaplain; Minister: Liberton Northfield, Edinburgh, Strone and Ardentinny (and Auxiliary Chaplain to USA Navy, Holy Loch). Recreations: pottering in garden; golf; fishing. Address: The Holyns, Ardentinny, by Dunoon, Argyll.

Gray, Robert, OStJ, JP. Lord Provost of Glasgow; Lord-Lieutenant of Glasgow, since 1984; Chairman, Greater Glasgow Tourist Board, since 1984; b. 3.3.28, Glasgow; m., Mary McCartney; 1 d. Educ. St. Mungo's Academy; Glasgow College of Building. Joiner; Clerk of Works; Lecturer and Senior Lecturer in Building Subjects; elected Member, Glasgow District Council, 1974; Chairman, Licensing Committee, 1975-77; Vice Chairman, JP Committee, 1976-77; City Treasurer, 1980-84; Member, Scottish Confederation of Tourism; President, Prince and Princess of Wales Hospice; Honorary President, Save the Children Fund; Trustee, University of Glasgow Trust; Patron, Glasgow Branch, British Red Cross Society. Recreations: walking; spectator sports; reading; opera; music. Address: (b.) City Chambers, Glasgow, G2 1DU; T.-041-227 4002.

Gray, Robert Stirton. Chairman and Managing Director, Charles Gray Builders (Holdings) Limited; b. 4.12.34, Dundee; m., Mary Rae Thorburn; 2 s.; 3 d. Educ. Gordonstoun. President, Scottish Building Employers Federation. Recreations: squash; golf. Address: (b.) 4 Francis Street, Dundee, DD3 8HJ; T.-0382 817373.

Gray, Professor Sidney John, BEc, PhD, FCCA, AASA, CPA, ACIS, MBIM. Professor of Accountancy, Glasgow University, since 1978 (Head, Department of Accountancy, since 1979, and Chairman, School of Financial Studies, since 1984); b. 3.10.42, Woodford; m., Hilary Fenella Jones; 1 d. Educ. Bedford Modern School; Sydney University. Peirce Leslie and Co. Ltd., UK and India, 1961-67; Burns Philp Pty Ltd., Australia, 1967-68; Tutor in Accounting, Sydney University, 1972; Lecturer in Accounting and Finance, Lancaster University, 1974-78; Secretary General, European Accounting Association, 1982-83; Member, Accounting Standards Committee for UK and Ireland, since 1984. Publications: International Financial Reporting, 1984; Information Disclosure and the Multinational Corporation, 1984; International Accounting and Transnational Decisions, 1983. Recreations: golf; tennis; travel. Address: (h.) 21 Lampson Road, Killearn, Stirlingshire, G63 9PD; T.-0360 50707.

Gray, Thomas G.F., BSc, PhD, CEng, MIMechE, MWeldI. Reader in Mechanical Engineering, Strathclyde University, since 1981; b. 16.12.40, Montego Bay, Jamaica; m., Stella M. Smith; 3 d. Educ. Balfron High School; Glasgow University. Entered industry as Welding Development Engineer; Lecturer, then Senior Lecturer, Strathclyde University. Elder, Lenzie Union Parish Church. Publication: Rational Welding Design. Recreations: music; walking. Address: (h.) 4A Auchinloch Road, Lenzie; T.-041-776 3569.

Gray, Sir William Stevenson, Kt (1974), JP, DL. Solicitor and Notary Public; Chairman, Third Eye Centre, Glasgow, since 1975; Chairman, Glasgow Independent Hospital Ltd. (Ross Hall Hospital), since 1982; Vice-President, Glasgow Citizens' Theatre, since 1975; Vice-President, Scottish Association for Care and Resettlement of Offenders, since 1982; Council Member, Strathclyde University Business School, since 1978; b. 3.5.28; m.; 1 s.; 1 d. Educ. Hillhead High School; Glasgow University. Chairman, Scottish Special Housing Association, 1966-72; Chairman, Irvine New Town Development Corporation, 1974-76; Chairman, Scotland West Industrial Promotion Group, 1972-75; Chairman, Scottish Development Agency, 1975-79; Lord Provost, City of Glasgow, and Lord Lieutenant, County of the City of Glasgow, 1972-75; Hon. LLD. Strathclyde, 1974, Glasgow, 1980.

Grayson, Michael C., MB, ChB, FRCSEdin, DO, FRMS, SDMBCS. Consultant Ophthalmologist, Fife Health Board, since 1974; Honorary Senior Lecturer, Edinburgh University, since 1975; b. 27.9.38, Stamford; m., Olive MacNaughtan; 2 s.; 2 d. Educ. Salford Grammar School; Edinburgh University. Research Associate, Pennsylvania University, 1969-70; Senior Tutor, Ophthalmology, Cardiff Royal Infirmary; Secretary, Fife Division, BMA; Chairman, Ophthalmology Sub-Committee, Scottish Committee for Hospital Medical Services. Secretary, Tayside and Fife Chess Association. Recreation: chess. Address: (h.) 2 Greenmount Drive, Burntisland, Fife, KY3 9JH; T.-Burntisland 872640.

Green, Charles W. Golfer; b. 1932, Dumbarton. Won Scottish Amateur Championship, 1970, 1982, 1983 (Runner-up, 1971, 1980); won Scottish Open Amateur Stroke-Play Championship, 1975; leading amateur, Open Championship, 1962; awarded Frank Moran Trophy, 1974; played for Gt. Britain in Walker Cup, 1963-69-71-73-75 (non-playing Captain, 1983-85).

Green, Christopher Edward Wastie, MA (Oxon), FCIT. General Manager, British Rail, Scotland, since 1984; b. 7.9.43, Winchester; m., Mitzie Petzold; 1 s.; 1 d. Educ. St. Paul's School, London; Oriel College, Oxford. British Rail: joined as Management Trainee, 1965, Area Manager, Hull, 1973, Divisional Operating Manager, Wimbledon, 1977, Chief Operating Manager, Scotland, 1980, Deputy General Manager, Scotland, 1983. Director, Glasgow Chamber of Commerce, since 1984. Recreations: family; architecture; history; walking; swimming; reading. Address: (h.) 2 Queens Crescent, Edinburgh, EH9 2AZ; T.-031-667 6083.

Green, Donald, CEng, MIMechE, MIE, MBIM. Chief Engineer, Generation Operation, South of Scotland Electricity Board, since 1980; b. 26.7.26, Heywood; m., Margaret; 2 d. Educ. Windy Harbour School, Birkdale; Warrington Technical College; St. Helens Technical College. Deputy Manager, Connah's Quay Power Station, CEGB; SSEB: Deputy Manager, Kincardine Power Station, Manager, Longannet Power Station, Generation Engineer (Conventional), Generation Operation, Deputy Chief Engineer, Generation Operation. Recreations: touring; golf; DIY. Address: (b.) SSEB, Cathcart House, Spean Street, Glasgow, G44 4BE; T.-041-637 7177.

Green, Lawrence Love. Senior Secretary (Region 4), National Union of Seamen, Scotland and North East England; Joint Chairman, Scottish District Maritime Board; b. 17.9.23, Glasgow; m., Eileen Egan; 3 s. Educ. Lambhill Street Secondary School. Seafaring from 1940; entered trade union movement in 1955 as full-time officer, National Union of Seamen. Vice-Chairman, Port Welfare Committee; Member, Management Committee, Veteran Seafarers Association. Recreations: spectator sports (soccer, boxing, rugby). Address: (h.) 1425 Paisley Road West, Glasgow; T.-041-882 6954.

Green, Malcolm Eric, ACMA. Director of Finance, Shetland Islands Council, since 1983; b. 14.5.40, Derby; m., Sheila; 2 s. Educ. Bemrose

Grammar School, Derby. Management Accountant, ICI Ltd., 1959-64; Works Accountant, English Electric Ltd., 1964-68; Group Financial Analyst, Guardian and Manchester Evening News Ltd., 1968-74; Sales Development Manager, Manchester Evening News Ltd., 1974-78; Shetland Islands Council: Assistant Director of Finance, 1978-79, Deputy Director of Finance, 1979-83. Recreation: fiddle playing. Address: (b.) 4 Market Street, Lerwick, Shetland; T.-0595 3535.

Green, Malcolm Robert, MA, DPhil. Chairman, Education Committee, Strathclyde Regional Council, since 1982; Chairman, Education Committee, Convention of Scottish Local Authorities, since 1978; Lecturer in Roman History, Glasgow University, since 1967; b. 4.1.43, Leicester; m., Mary Margaret Pratley; 1 s.; 2 d. Educ. Wyggeston Grammar School, Leicester; Magdalen College, Oxford. Commissioner, Manpower Services Commission; Chairman, Management Sides, Scottish Joint Negotiating Committees for Teaching Staff in Schools and Further Education; Chairman, National Committee for the In-Service Training of Teachers. Address: (b.) Strathclyde House, 20 India Street, Glasgow, G2 4PF; T.-041-227 3453.

Green, Peter, BA, MA, PhD. Senior Lecturer, Department of Urban and Regional Planning, Strathclyde University, since 1967; b. 15.11.31, Sheffield; m., Margaret Carol; 4 s. Educ. Keighley Boys' Grammar School; Cockburn High School; Leeds University. HM Forces; Lecturer in Geography; Visiting Professor, University of Nigeria, 1975-76. Publications: History of Planning; Planning in Scotland. Recreations: cricket; hill-walking. Address: (b.) Department of Urban and Regional Planning, Strathclyde University, Glasgow; T.-041-552 4400.

Greene, John Gerald, MA, PhD. Head of Psychological Services, Western District, Greater Glasgow Health Board; Clinical Lecturer, Glasgow University; b. 10.3.38, Glasgow; m., Dr. Elisabeth Rose Hamil; 2 s.; 2 d. Educ. St. Aloysius College, Glasgow; Glasgow University. Trainee Clinical Psychologist, Crichton Royal Hospital, Dumfries, 1962-64; Senior Psychologist, 1965-70; Principal Psychologist, Gartnavel Royal Hospital, Glasgow, 1970-82; Top Grade Psychologist, Greater Glasgow Health Board, since 1982; Chairman, National (Scotland) Scientific Consultative Committee on Clinical Psychological Services, 1985; Secretary (1975-77) and Chairman (1977-79), Consultative Committee on Psychological Services, Greater Glasgow Health Board; Secretary and Treasurer, Scottish Branch Committee, Division of Clinical Psychology, 1977-81. Publications: The Social and Psychological Origins of the Climacteric Syndrome, 1984; Clinical Psychology in the Scottish Health Service (Co-author), 1984. Recreations: music; tennis. Address: (b.) Psychology Department, Gartnavel Royal Hospital, Glasgow, G12 OXH.

Greene, John Henderson, MA, LLB. Partner, MacRoberts, Solicitors, Glasgow, Edinburgh and Paisley; b. 2.6.32, Kilmarnock; m., Catriona McGillivray Scott; 1 s. Educ. Merchiston Castle School, Edinburgh; Edinburgh University.

Assistant, Joseph Kirkland & Son, Solicitors, Saltcoats, 1958-60; Assistant, MacRobert Son & Hutchison, Solicitors, 1960 (appointed Partner, 1961); Law Society of Scotland: Vice-Convener, Company Law Committee, former Member, Bankruptcy and Liquidation Committee; former Council Member, Royal Faculty of Procurators, Glasgow; founder Chairman, Troon Round Table, 1964; Member, Committee, Royal Troon Golf Club, 1978-81; Elder, Portland Church, Troon; Director, Glasgow Ayrshire Society. Recreations: golf; gardening. Address: (h.) Silvertrees, 7 Lady Margaret Drive, Troon, KA10 7AL; T.-Troon 312482.

Greenhalgh, Professor James Francis Derek, MA, MS, PhD. Professor of Animal Production and Health, Aberdeen University, since 1978; b. 4.10.32, Frodsham, Cheshire; m., Isoline Gee; 3 s. Educ. King's School, Chester; Cambridge University; Illinois University; Aberdeen University. Lecturer in Agricultural Chemistry, Edinburgh School of Agriculture, 1959-63; Senior (then Principal) Scientific Officer, Rowett Research Institute, Aberdeen, 1963-78; Editor, Animal Feed Science and Technology. Publication: Animal Nutrition (Co-author). Recreations: hockey; hill-walking. Address: (b.) School of Agriculture, 581 King Street, Aberdeen, AB9 1UD; T.-Aberdeen 40291.

Greening, Professor John Raymond, BSc, PhD, DSc, FInstP, FRSE. Professor of Medical Physics, Edinburgh University, since 1966; Director, Department of Medical Physics and Medical Engineering, Edinburgh University and SE Scotland Health Boards, since 1957; b. 9.2.22, Richmond, Surrey; m., Audrey Winifred King; 2 s. Educ. Richmond County School; London University. Assistant, National Physical Laboratory, Teddington, 1940-46; Assistant Physicist, Westminster Hospital, London, 1946-49; Principal Physicist, St. George's Hospital, London, 1949-57. Publication: Fundamentals of Radiation Dosimetry. Address: (b.) Department of Medical Physics and Medical Enginering, Royal Infirmary, Edinburgh, EH3 9YW; T.-031-229 7883.

Greenock, William, MA. Principal, Clydebank College, since 1984; b. 3.2.37, Glasgow; 2 d. Educ. Allan Glen's School; Glasgow University. Teacher, secondary schools, 1959-65; David Dale College, 1965-68; Langside College, 1968-70; Reid Kerr College, 1970-75; Anniesland College, 1975-82; Ayr College, 1982-84. Session Clerk, Langside Parish Church, Glasgow. Recreation: golf. Address: (b.) Clydebank College, Kilbowie Road, Clydebank, G81 2AA; T.-041-952 7771.

Greenwood, David, MA. Director, Centre for Defence Studies, Aberdeen University, since 1976; b. 6.2.37, Rochdale, Lancashire; m., Helen Ramshaw (separated); 2 s. Educ. Manchester Grammar School; Liverpool University. Education Branch, RAF, 1959-66; Economic Adviser, Ministry of Defence, 1966-67; Aberdeen University: Lecturer in Higher Defence Studies, 1967-70, Senior Lecturer, 1970-74, Reader, since 1974; Member, Honeywell Advisory Council, 1982-85; Director, BDMI Ltd.,

since 1984; Consultant to several organisations in Europe and North America; Member, Foreign and Commonwealth Office Advisory Panel on Arms Control and Disarmament; Member, Editorial Advisory Board, Strategic Studies. Publication: Budgeting for Defence, 1972. Address: (b.) Centre for Defence Studies, Wright Building, Dunbar Street, Aberdeen, AB9 2TY; T.-0224 40241, Ext. 5414.

Gregson, William Derek Hadfield, CBE, DL, DFH, CEng, FIEE, CBIM, FRSA. Director, Ferranti Holdings; Deputy Chairman, British Airports Authority; Commissioner of Northern Lighthouses; b. 27.1.20; m., Rosalind Helen Reeves; 3 s.; 1 d. Educ. UK and Switzerland. Director: Anderson Strathclyde, British Telecoms (Scotland), Brammer, East of Scotland Industrial Investments PLC; Consultant, ICI. Recreations: woodwork; books; automation in the home. Address: (h.) 15 Barnton Avenue, Edinburgh, EH4 6AJ; T.-031-336 3896.

Greig, Rev. James Carruthers Gorrie, BA, MA (Cantab), BD, STM. Minister, St. Matthew's Church, Paisley, since 1979; Freelance Translator, since 1955; b. 23.2.27, Moffat; m., Elsa Clark Carlile; 1 s.; 2 d. Educ. Glasgow Academy; Gonville and Caius College, Cambridge; Glasgow University; Union Theological Seminary, New York. National Service, largely as Sergeant-Instructor, RAEC, 1948-50; Redpath Brown & Co. Ltd., 1950-52; theological training, Glasgow and New York, 1951-54; Minister, Closeburn, 1955-59; Professor of New Testament, Westminster College, Cambridge, 1959-63; Lecturer in Religious Education, Jordanhill College of Education, Glasgow, 1963-79; Moderator, Paisley Presbytery, 1981; Chairman, The John Buchan Society. Publications: The Serpent in the Wilderness, 1961; various theological translations and articles. Recreations: photography; music; walking; some swimming; writing. Address: 17 Hunterhill Road, Paisley, PA2 6SR; T.-041-889 8027.

Greig, Thomas Ogilvie, BA (Hons), MA. Divisional Specialist in Primary Education (Northern), HM Inspectorate of Schools, since 1981; b. 13.8.40, Alexandria; m., Jean Sloan Frater; 1 s.; 1 d. Educ. Vale of Leven Academy; Glasgow University; London University. Teacher, 1964-68: Hartfield School, Hawick High School, Hermitage Academy; Teacher in Further Education, 1964-70; Acting Headteacher, Arrochar Primary, 1968; Assistant Headteacher, Hermitage Primary, Helensburgh, 1968-70; Tutor/Counsellor, Open University, 1974-77; Lecturer in Social Studies/Primary Education, Craigie College of Education, Ayr, 1970; Education Officer (Consultative Committee on the Curriculum), 1977; appointed HM Inspector of Schools, 1979. Sports Correspondent, BBC, 1968-79; Examiner, then Assistant Chief Examiner (English), Scottish Examination Board, 1967-79. Publications: Activity Methods in the Middle Years, 1975; History of Clyde Football Club, 1978. Recreations: golf; public speaking; works of Robert Burns. Address: (h.) Rozelle, 4 Corsie Drive, Perth; T.-Perth 22164.

Grier, Arnold Macfarlane, MB, ChB, FRCSEdin. Consultant Ear, Nose and Throat Surgeon, Highland Health Board, since 1962; Chairman, Scottish Association for the Deaf; b. 5.9.21, Musselburgh; m., Elisabeth J. Kluten; 2 s.; 1 d. Educ. Musselburgh Grmamar School; Edinburgh University. Recreations: gardening; aviculture. Address: (h.) Elmbank, 68 Culduthel Road, Inverness; T.-Inverness 234682.

Grier, Scott, MA, CA. Managing Director, Loganair Limited, since 1983; b. 7.3.41, Kilmacolm; m., Frieda Gardiner; 2 s. Educ. Greenock High School; Glasgow University. Apprenticed, Grahams Rintoul & Co., 1962-66; Accountant, Ardrossan Harbour Company, 1967-76; Loganair: Financial/Commercial Manager and Secretary, 1976, Financial Director, 1977. Recreations: golf; philately. Address: (h.) Lagavulin, 23 Overton Drive, West Kilbride, KA23 9LQ; T.-0294 823138.

Grieve, Professor Andrew Robert, DDS, BDS, FDS RCSEd. Professor of Conservative Dentistry, Dundee University, since 1980 (Senior Adviser of Studies in Dentistry, since 1982); Consultant in Restorative Dentistry, Tayside Health Board, since 1980; b. 23.5.39, Stirling; m., Frances M. Ritchie; 2 d. Educ. Perth Academy; St. Andrews University. Junior hospital appointments and general dental practice; Lecturer in Operative Dental Surgery and Dental Therapeutics, St. Andrews University, 1963-65; Lecturer in Conservative Dentistry, Birmingham University, 1965; appointed Senior Lecturer and Consultant in Restorative Dentistry, Birmingham Area Health Authority (Teaching), 1975. Member, Dental Council, Royal College of Surgeons of Edinburgh; Council Member: British Society for Restorative Dentistry, Royal Odonto-Chirugical Society of Scotland. Recreation: hill-walking. Address: (b.) Department of Conservative Dentistry, Dental School, The University, Dundee, DD1 4HN; T.-0382 26041.

Grieve, John. Actor; b. Glasgow. Trained, Royal Scottish Academy of Music and Drama (James Bridie Gold Medallist); appeared in Tyrone Guthrie's production of The Anatomist, Citizens', Glasgow, 1968; numerous other performances on the Scottish stage, including leading roles in Benny Lynch, The Bevellers and The Flouers o' Edinburgh, Royal Lyceum, Edinburgh; television work includes The Vital Spark; numerous appearances in pantomime; appeared with Scottish Theatre Company in Waiting for Godot, 1985. Address: (b.) c/o David White Associates, 31 Kings Road, London, SW3.

Grieve, Kathleen Zia, MBE, BSc. Organiser, Network Scotland Ltd., since 1975; b. 25.9.20, Aberdeen; m., Rev. G.M. Denny Grieve; 2 s.; 1 d. Educ. St. Margaret's School for Girls, Aberdeen; Aberdeen University. Technical Assistant, BBC, 1941-44; service in Church of Scotland from 1944, including National Vice-Convener, Home Board, four years, National President, Woman's Guild, 1966-69; represented Church of Scotland, World Alliance of Reformed Churches meeting, Nairobi, 1970; Member, Church of Scotland Committee of Forty (Honorary Secretary, 1972-78); appointed Organiser, Scottish Telephone Referral Service for Adult Literacy (which became Network Scotland Ltd.), 1975; founder Member, then Honorary Secretary, Dyslexia Scotwest; founder Member, Trustee and Administrator, Pet Fostering Service Scotland. Recreations: walking dog; reading; sewing; catering; upholstery; chess; motoring. Address: (h.) 11 Mirrlees Drive, Glasgow, G12 OSH; T.-041-339 1605.

Grieve, Professor Sir Robert, Kt (1969), MA, FRSE, FRTPI, MICE. Chairman, Highlands and Islands Development Consultative Council, since 1978; Honorary President: Scottish Rights of Way Society, New Glasgow Society, Inverness Civic Trust, Stewartry Mountaineering Club, RTPI (Scottish Branch), Friends of Loch Lomond, Scottish Countryside Rangers Association; Professor Emeritus, Glasgow University; b. 11.12.10; m.; 2 s.; 2 d. Educ. North Kelvinside School, Glasgow; Royal College of Science and Technology, Glasgow. Local government, 1927-44; Civil Service, 1946-54; Chief Planner, Scottish Office, 1960-64; Professor of Town and Regional Planning, Glasgow University, 1964-74; Chairman, Highlands and Islands Development Board, 1965-70. Gold Medal, RTPI, 1974; Hon. DLitt, Heriot-Watt; Hon. LLD, Strathclyde; Hon. FRIAS.

Grieve, Hon. Lord, (William Robertson Grieve), VRD (1958), QC (Scot), MA, LLB. Senator of the College of Justice in Scotland, since 1972; b. 21.10.17; m.; 1 s.; 1 d. Educ. Glasgow Academy; Sedbergh; Glasgow University. RN, 1939-46; admitted, Faculty of Advocates, 1947; QC (Scot), 1957; Advocate-Depute (Home), 1962-64; Sheriff-Principal of Renfrew and Argyll, 1964-72; Procurator of the Church of Scotland, 1969-72.

Griffin, Thomas Kinnear, LLB. Depute Chief Executive, Ettrick and Lauderdale District Council, since 1983; b. 2.3.48, Hamilton; m., Deirdre. Educ. Lenzie Academy; Glasgow University. Private practice, 1972-75; Kyle and Carrick District Council: Legal Assistant, 1975-79, Senior Legal Assistant, 1979-83. Address: (b.) Council Chambers, Paton Street, Galashiels; T.-Galashiels 4751.

Griffiths, Professor Peter Denham, BSc, MD, LRCP, MRCS, FRCPath, MBCS. Professor of Biochemical Medicine, Dundee University, since 1968 (Vice-Principal, 1979-85, Dean of Medicine and Dentistry, since 1985); Consultant, Tayside Health Board, since 1966; b. 16.6.27, Southampton; m., Joy Burgess; 3 s.; 1 d. Educ. King Edward VI School, Southampton; Guy's Hospital, London University. House appointments, Guy's Hospital, 1956-57; Junior Lecturer in Physiology, Guy's Hospital, 1957-58; Registrar and Senior Registrar, Guy's and Lewisham Hospitals, 1958-64; Consultant Pathologist, Harlow Hospitals Group, 1964-66; Senior Lecturer in Clinical Chemistry/Honorary Consultant, St. Andrews University, then Dundee University, 1966-68. Sometime Chairman of Council, Association of Clinical Biochemists; Director, Drug

Development Scotland; Director, Dundee Repertory Theatre. Recreations: music; theatre; domestic activities. Address: (b.) Department of Biochemical Medicine, Ninewells Hospital and Medical School, Dundee, DD1 9SY; T.-0382 60111, Ext. 2164.

Grigor, Kenneth McNeill, BSc, MB, ChB, MD, MRCPath. Senior Lecturer in Pathology, Edinburgh University, since 1980; Honorary Consultant in Pathology, Edinburgh Royal Infirmary, since 1980; b. 15.5.44, Glasgow; m., Jacqueline Hardie; 3 d. Educ. Kelvinside Academy, Glasgow; Glasgow University. Hospital attachments and pathology training in Glasgow, 1969-71; cancer research and pathology, London, 1971-78; pathology, Edinburgh, since 1979. Recreations: gardening; rugby refereeing. Address: (h.) 6 Barnton Gardens, Edinburgh, EH4 6AF; T.-031-336 2824.

Grimble, Professor Michael John, BSc, BA, PhD, DSc, FIEE, Sen MIEEE, FIMA, CEng. Professor of Industrial Systems and Director, Industrial Control Unit, Strathclyde University, since 1981 (Chairman, Department of Electronic and Electrical Engineering, since 1984); b. 30.10.43, Grimsby; m., Wendy; 1 s.; 1 d. Educ. Grimsby College of Further Education; Birmingham University. Electrical apprentice, CIBA Chemicals, Grimsby; Engineer, Associated Electrical Industries; Research Engineer, Imperial College of Science & Technology; Senior Engineer, GEC Electrical Projects Ltd.; Reader in Control Engineering, Sheffield City Polytechnic. Heaviside Premium, IEE, 1978; Coopers Hill War Memorial Prize and Medal, IEE/IME/ICE, 1979. Recreation: reading. Address: (b.) Department of Electronic and Electrical Engineering, Strathclyde University, Royal College, 204 George Street, Glasgow, G1 1XW; T.-041-552 4400.

Grimmond, Iain William, BAcc (Hons), CA. Treasurer, Erskine Hospital for Disabled Ex-Servicemen, since 1981; b. 8.8.55, Girvan; m., Marjory Anne Gordon Chisholm; 1 s.; 1 d. Educ. Hutchesons' Boys Grammar School; Glasgow University. Trainee CA, Ernst & Whinney, Glasgow, 1976-79; Assistant Treasurer, Erskine Hospital, 1979-81. Elder, Giffnock South Parish Church; Honorary Treasurer, Paisley Art Institute. Recreations: golf; badminton; reading. Address: (h.) 12 Weaver Avenue, Crookfur, Newton Mearns, Glasgow, G77 6AS; T.-041-639 4894.

Grimond, Baron, (Joseph Grimond), TD, PC. Life Peer; Leader, Parliamentary Liberal Party, 1956-67; Chancellor, University of Kent at Canterbury, since 1970; Trustee, Manchester Guardian and Evening News Ltd., since 1967; b. 29.7.13; m., Hon. Laura Miranda (see Lady Laura Miranda Grimond); 2 s.; 1 d.; 1 s. deceased. Educ. Eton; Balliol College, Oxford. Called to the Bar, Middle Temple, 1937; Fife and Forfar Yeomanry and Staff 53 Division (Major), Second World War; Director of Personnel, European Office, UNRRA, 1945-47; Secretary, National Trust for Scotland, 1947-49;

MP (Liberal), Orkney and Shetland, 1950-83; Rector: Edinburgh University, 1960-63, Aberdeen University, 1969-72; Hon. LLD: Edinburgh, 1960, Aberdeen, 1972, Birmingham, 1974, Buckingham, 1983; Hon. DCL, Kent, 1970.

Grimond, Lady Laura Miranda. President, Women's Liberal Federation; Honorary Sheriff, Kirkwall, since 1977; Member, Board of Trustees, National Museum of Antiquities of Scotland, 1972-85; Member, Ancient Monuments Board of Scotland, since 1980; b. 13.10.18, London; m., Rt. Hon Lord Grimond of Firth (qv); 2 s.; 1 s. (deceased); 1 d. Educ. privately; Schwarzwald Gymnasium, Vienna; College Sevigne, Paris. Magistrate, Richmond, Surrey, 1955-59; fought West Aberdeenshire as Liberal, 1970; Member, Orkney Islands Council, 1974-80 (Chairman: Housing Committee, 1974-76, Services Committee, 1978-80); first Chairman, Orkney Heritage Society. Address: (h.) The Old Manse of Firth, Kirkwall, Orkney.

Grimstone, Rev. Alexander Francis, MA. Minister, Calton Parkhead Church, Glasgow, since 1969; b. 9.6.21, Dunragit, Wigtownshire; m., Doreen Minnie Buchanan; 1 s. Educ. Stranraer High School; Glasgow University and Trinity College. RAF, 1942-46. Assistant Minister, Glasgow Cathedral, 1949-50; Minister: Stamperland Parish Church, Glasgow, 1950-56, Holy Trinity Church, Bridge of Allan, 1956-66, Banchory Ternan East Church, 1966-68, Fetlar, 1968-69. Vice-Chairman, Glasgow and West of Scotland Hospital Sunday Fund. Recreations: golf; motoring. Address: 98 Drumover Drive, Glasgow, G31 5RP; T.-041-556 2520.

Grinyer, Professor John Raymond, MSc, FCA. Professor of Accountancy, Dundee University, since 1976 (Head, Department of Accountancy and Business Finance, since 1976, Dean, Faculty of Law, since 1984); b. 3.3.35, London; m., Shirley Florence Marshall; 1 s.; 2 d. Educ. Central Park Secondary Modern School, London; London School of Economics. London Electricity Board, 1950-53; National Service, RAMC, 1953-55; Halifax Building Society, 1955-56; Martin Redhead & Co., Accountants, 1956-60; Hope Agar & Co., Chartered Accountants, 1960-62; Kemp Chatteris & Co., Chartered Accountants, 1962-63; Lecturer, Harlow Technical College, 1963-66; City of London Polytechnic, 1966-71; Cranfield School of Management, 1971-76. Recreations: dinghy sailing; Member, Royal Tay Yacht Club. Address: (b.) The University, Dundee, DD1 4HN; T.-Dundee 23181, Ext. 4192.

Grinyer, Professor Peter Hugh, MA (Oxon), PhD. Esmee Fairbairn Professor of Economics (Finance and Investment) St. Andrews University, since 1979 (Vice-Principal of the University, since 1985); b. 3.3.35, London; m., Sylvia Joyce Boraston; 2 s. Educ. Balliol College, Oxford; London School of Economics. Senior Managerial Trainee, Unilever Ltd., 1957-59; Personal Assistant to Managing Director, E.R. Holloway Ltd., 1959-61; Lecturer and Senior Lecturer, Hendon College of Technology, 1961-64; Lecturer, The City University, London, 1965-69; The City University Business School: Senior Lecturer and Co-ordinator of Research, 1969-72, Reader, 1972-74, Professor of Business Strategy, 1974-79. Member, Sub-Committee on Management and Business Studies, University Grants Committee, 1979-85; Director, Glenrothes Enterprise Trust; Consultant to NEDO on Sharpbenders Project; Non-Executive Director, John Brown plc, since 1984. Recreations: mountain walking; golf; listening to music. Address: (b.) Department of Economics, St. Andrews University, St. Salvator's College, St. Andrews, Fife, KY16 9AL; T.-0334 76161, Ext. 417.

Groat, John Malcolm Freswick, MBE, JP. Postmaster, Longhope, Orkney, since 1964; Company Director: Orkney Islands Shipping Co. Ltd., J.M.F. Groat & Sons Ltd., Orkney Seaport Supplies Ltd.; Secretary, Longhope Lifeboat, since 1962; b. 9.9.23, Longhope, Orkney; m., Edna Mary Yule. War Service, 150 Lancaster Squadron, RAF. Clerk, Hoy and Walls District Council, 1953-74; Agent, Department of Social Security, 1953-74; Clerk, School Management Commitee, Walls and Flotta, 1953-74; Registrar of Births etc., Hoy and Walls, 1953-74; Provincial Grand Master, Orkney and Zetland, 1979-84; Trustee, Longhope Lifeboat Disaster Fund, since 1969; Agent, Shipwrecked Mariners Society; Secretary, Longhope British Legion, 1948-53; Secretary, Longhope Sailing Club, 1950-60. Address: (h.) Moasound, Longhope, Orkney; T.-241.

Groom, Rev. Colin John, MA. Member, Fife Regional Council, since 1982; Associate Minister, Cowdenbeath Cairns Parish Church, since 1982; b. 29.1.34, Harrow; m., Eileen; 1 s.; 1 d. Educ. Harrow County Grammar School; Wesley House, Cambridge University; New College, Edinburgh University. Methodist Minister, Shropshire, 1960-67; Methodist Minister and Industrial Chaplain, Leeds, 1967-70; Minister, Cardenden Parish Church, 1972-82 (resigned charge in favour of Christian involvement in politics); Vice-Chairman, Buildings and Property Committee, Fife Regional Council; Fife Representative, Nuclear Free Zones Scotland Committee; Co-Chairman, Railway Development Society (Scotland), 1983-84. Recreation: doing nothing in middle of nowhere. Address: (h.) 28 Woodend Road, Cardenden, Fife, KY5 ONE; T.-0592 720432.

Grossart, Angus McFarlane McLeod, LLD, MA, CA. Advocate; Merchant Banker; Director: American Trust PLC, since 1973, Cockburn Taylor Holdings Limited, since 1981, Drummond Petroleum Limited (Canada), since 1982, Edinburgh Fund Managers PLC, since 1983 (Chairman), Goldcrest Films & Television Holdings Limited, since 1983, International Caledonian Assets Limited, since 1972, Noble Grossart Limited, since 1969, Noble Grossart Holdings Limited, since 1980, Noble Grossart Investments Limited, since 1969, North Sea Assets PLC, since 1972, Pict Petroleum PLC, since 1970, Phoenician Holdings Limited (Canada), since 1979, Reed Stenhouse Companies Limited (Canada), 1973, The Royal Bank of Scotland plc, since 1982, The Scottish Investment Trust PLC, 1973 (Chairman), Wright Dental Group

Limited, since 1973; b. 14.4.37, Glasgow; m., Gay Kerr Dodd; 1 d. Educ. Glasgow Academy; Glasgow University. CA apprentice, Thomson McLintock, 1958-62; Advocate, Scottish Bar, 1969-72; Managing Director, Noble Grossart Ltd., since 1969. Former Editor, British Tax Encyclopaedia and British Tax Review. Recreations: golf; restoring castle in Fife. Address: (b.) 48 Queen Street, Edinburgh, EH2 3NR; T.-031-226 7011.

Grove-White, Ion Greer, MA (Cantab), MB, BChir, FFA RCS(Eng). Consultant Anaesthetist, Angus Hospitals and Dundee Teaching Hospitals, since 1973; b. 5.7.39, London; m., Patricia Sheila Forbes Annand; 3 s.; 1 d. Educ. Rugby School; St. John's College, Cambridge; London Hospital Medical College. House Officer, The London Hospital, also Aberdeen City Hospitals; Registrar and Senior Registrar, Aberdeen Hospitals. Chairman, Montrose District Scout Association; Member, Scottish American Community Relations Committee; Chairman, Angus Division, BMA; President, North East of Scotland Society of Anaesthetists. Recreation: hillwalking. Address: (h.) White House, Hillside, Montrose, Angus, DD10 9HZ; T.-067483 466.

Guidi, Bruno G.F., MA, MEd, FRSA. Principal, Langside College, Glasgow, since 1977; b. Glasgow; m., Agnes-Therese Curran; 2 s. Educ. St. Aloysius College, Glasgow; Glasgow University. War Service, 1942-47; schools education, 1947-58; further education, since 1958; Depute Principal, Cardonald College, Glasgow, 1971-75; Principal, Barmulloch College, Glasgow, 1975-77; Chairman, Joint Management Committee, West of Scotland Scheme, Certificate in Social Service; Governor, Jordanhill College of Education; Member: Scottish Nursery Nurses' Examination Board, Scottish Retirement Council Executive Committee, Glasgow School of Occupational Therapy Advisory Committee. Recreations: music (opera); travel; reading; sport; swimming. Address: (h.) 32 Madison Avenue, Glasgow, G44 5AQ; T.-041-637 1462.

Guild, Ivor Reginald, CBE, MA, LLB, WS. Partner, Shepherd & Wedderburn, WS, since 1950; Chairman of Trustees, National Museum of Antiquities; Procurator Fiscal to the Lyon Court; b. 2.4.24, Dundee. Educ. Cargilfield; Rugby; New College, Oxford; Edinburgh University. Chairman: First Scottish American Trust PLC, Northern American Trust PLC, Edinburgh Investment Trust PLC; Director, Fleming Universal Trust PLC, Beaufoy (1981) Limited. Editor, Scottish Genealogist; Bailie, Abbey Court of Holyroodhouse; Trustee, Edinburgh University; Secretary and Treasurer, Stair Society; Secretary, Edinburgh Angus Club. Recreations: golf; genealogy. Address: (b.) 16 Charlotte Square, Edinburgh, EH2 4YS; T.-031-225 8585.

Guild, Prue Marcia. A Director, Scottish Society for the Prevention of Cruelty to Animals; b. 25.4.85, Southsea; m., Lt. Col. John Royes Guild, DSO. Educ. Francis Holland Girls School, London; Harcombe House School of Domestic Science, Lyme Regis. Women's Land Army,

1939-40; Home Guard, 1941-45; work for Red Cross, Riding for the Disabled; Member, Local Committee, Save the Children Fund. Recreations: racing; riding; bowls; hill-walking; reading; dress-making; writing poetry; knitting; cooking; gardening. Address: (h.) Athole Cottage, Kirkton, by Hawick, Roxburghshire; T.-0450 73525.

Guild, Stuart Alexander, TD, BL. Writer to the Signet, since 1950; b. 25.1.24, Edinburgh; m., Fiona Catherine MacCulloch; 1 s.; 2 d. Educ. Edinburgh Academy; George Watson's College, Edinburgh; Queen's University, Belfast; Edinburgh University. Royal Artillery, 1942-47; Territorial Army (RA), 1947-67; Honorary Treasurer and Shooting Convenor, Army Cadet Force Association (Scotland); Council Member, Army Cadet Force Association; Member, Royal Artillery Council of Scotland; Council Member, National Smallbore Rifle Association; President, Lothian & Peebles Home Guard Rifle Association;; Council Member, Lothian Smallbore Shooting Association; Governor, Melville Trust; Chairman, Sandilands Memorial Trust. Recreations: golf; target shooting; photography. Address: (b.) 5 Rutland Square, Edinburgh; T.-031-229 5394.

Gunn, Alexander Anton, MB, ChB, CHM, FRCSEdin. Consultant Surgeon, Bangour General Hospital, since 1964; b. 25.2.28, Edinburgh; m., Dorothy Robinson; 1 s.; 3 d. Educ. Edinburgh Academy; Edinburgh University. Council Member: Royal College of Surgeons, Edinburgh, Scottish Council for Postgraduate Medical Education, British Journal of Surgery; Member, Health Service Research Committee (Scotland); National Panel, NHS Scotland; Examiner: Royal College of Surgeons, Edinburgh, Edinburgh University. Recreations: golf; fishing; sketching; gardening. Address: (h.) 4 Corrennie Drive, Edinburgh, EH10 6EQ; T.-031-447 1339.

Gunn, Rev. Alexander MacLean, MA, BD. Minister, St. David's Knightswood Parish Church, since 1973; b. 26.2.43, Inverness; m., Ruth Rankine; 1 s.; 1 d. Educ. Edinburgh Academy; Dingwall Academy; Edinburgh University and New College. Minister, Wick St. Andrews and Thrumster, 1967-73; Member, Education Committee, Caithness County Council, 1968-73. Address: The Manse, 60 Southbrae Drive, Glasgow, G13 1QD; T.-041-959 2904.

Gunn, Bunty Moffat, OBE (1981), JP, DSCHE. Chairman, Lanarkshire Health Board, since 1981; b., 4.9.23, Perth; m., Hugh McVane Houston Gunn; 3 s.; 1 d. Educ. Grange School for Girls; Grangemouth High School. Member: Lanark County Council, 1970-73, Strathclyde Regional Council, 1973-82; Chairman, Scottish Council for Health Education, 1974-80; Member, Lanarkshire Health Board, since 1973; Vice-President, Royal British Legion, CS and W Branch, 1978; Member, CSA Management Committee, since 1985. Recreations: golf; theatre; light classical music; reading. Address: (h.) Kinnoul, 1 Beech Avenue, High Burnside, Rutherglen; T.-041-634 4510.

Gunn, Professor Sir John Currie, Kt (1982), CBE (1976), MA, FRSE, FIMA, FInstP. Cargill Professor of Natural Philosophy, Glasgow University, 1949-82; b. 13.9.16; m.; 1 s. Educ. Glasgow Academy; Glasgow University; St. John's College, Cambridge.

Gunstone, Professor Frank Denby, BSc, PhD, DSc, FRSC, FRSE, CChem. Professor of Chemistry, St. Andrews University, since 1971; b. 27.10.23, Chadderton; m., Eleanor Eineen Hill; 2 s.; 1 d. Educ. Oldham Hulme Grammar School; Holt High School, Liverpool; Liverpool University. Lecturer, Glasgow University, 1946-54; St. Andrews University: Lecturer, 1954-59, Senior Lecturer, 1959-65, Reader, 1965-71. Lipid Award, American Oil Chemists' Society, 1973; Hildith Lecturer, 1975; Kaufmann Lecturer, 1976. Address: (h.) Rumgally House, Cupar, Fife, KY15 5SY; T.-0334 53613.

Guthrie, James King, BSc, CEng, MICE. Director, Aberdeen Construction Group P.L.C., since 1981; Managing Director, Alexander Hall & Son (Builders) Ltd., since 1980; Director, Hall & Robertson Ltd., since 1982; b. 12.29, Glasgow; m., Katherine; 1 s.; 4 d. Educ. Jordanhill College School; Glasgow University. National Service, Royal Engineers, 1955-57 (2nd Lt.); Senior Engineer, G. Wimpey Ltd., 1957-64; Project Manager, A.M. Carmichael Ltd., 1964-70; Area Manager/Director, Tarmac Construction Ltd., 1970-80. Recreations: golf; sailing; music. Address (h.) Eildon House, Banchory, AB3 3XX; T.-03302 2435.

Guthrie, Rev. John Tennyson, JP, FSA Scot, MA (Hons). Minister, Cullen and Deskford, since 1967 (of Cullen, since 1937); Clerk, Synod of Aberdeen, now Grampian, since 1961; b. 18.10.07, Findhorn, Moray; m., 1, Margaret E. Scrimgeour; 2, Betty M. MacArthur; 3 d. Educ. Blairgowrie High School; Robert Gordon's College, Aberdeen; Glasgow University and Trinity College. Licensed by Glasgow Presbytery, 1935; Assistant Minister, Paisley High, 1935-37; ordained and inducted to Cullen Old, 1937; Minister, united charge of Cullen Old and Cullen Seafield as Cullen Parish Church, 1946; Clerk, Presbyteries of: Fordyce, Strathbogie and Fordyce, Moray, at various times since 1945; elected to Cullen Town Council, 1946 (Treasurer, 1948); Member, Education Committee, Banff County Council, 1948-65; Chairman, Cullen Community Council, 1975-80; Patron, Scottish Local History Conference, Newbattle Abbey College, 1983; Member, Church of Scotland General Trustees, 1969-79; Past Chairman: Banffshire Field Club, Banffshire Society; Past President, Banff Rotary Club. Publications: Third Statistical Account - Parish of Cullen, 1961; Cullen Auld Kirk, 1962. Recreations: bowling; golf. Address: The Manse, Cullen, Banffshire, AB5 2UU; T.-0542 40249.

Gwynn, John Michael, MA (Cantab), ARICS. Chief Land Agent, Forestry Commission, since 1980; b. 30.4.26, Malvern; m., Nancy Pollitt; 3 s.; 1 d. Educ. Cambridgeshire High School; Trinity College, Cambridge. Address: (b.) 231 Corstorphine Road, Edinburgh, EH12 7AT; T.-031-334 0303.

H

Haddington, 12th Earl of, (George Baillie-Hamilton), KT (1951), MC, TD, FRSE, FSA Scot, LLD (Glasgow). President, Society of Antiquaries of Scotland; President, Scottish Georgian Society; b. 18.9.94; m., Sarah Cook; 1 s.; 1 d. Educ. Eton; Sandhurst. Royal Scots Greys, 1915-18; served Second World War (Wing Commander, RAFVR, 1941-45); Captain, Queen's Bodyguard for Scotland (Royal Company of Archers), 1953-74; HM Lieutenant, County of Berwick, 1952-69. Address: (h.) Tyninghame, Dunbar, East Lothian.

Haddow, Rev. Angus Halley, BSc. Minister, Garthdee Parish Church, Aberdeen, since 1981; Clerk, Aberdeen Presbytery, since 1981; b. 27.11.32, Wishaw; m., Marjory Walsh; 1 s.; 2 d. Educ. Wishaw High School; Glasgow University and Trinity College. Science Teacher, Greenfield Secondary School, 1957-60; Assistant Minister, Newarthill, 1962-63; Minister: Largo St. David's Parish Church, 1963-71, Trinity Parish Church, Aberdeen, 1971-81. Recreations: reading; parapsychology; hill-walking; music. Address: 27 Ramsay Gardens, Aberdeen, AB1 7AE; T.-Aberdeen 317452.

Haddow, Charlotte Logie, JP. Member, Fife Health Board, since 1983 (and 1970-79); Chairman, Fife Nurse Training Committee; Member, Central and Fife Area Manpower Board; Member, Social Security Appeals Tribunal; Trade Union Officer; b. 23.4.35, Buckhaven; 1 s.; 1 d. Educ. Buckhaven High School. Chairman, Labour Party in Scotland, 1967-77; Parliamentary candidate, Edinburgh South, 1974; former Town Councillor. Address: (h.) 49 Aberdour Road, Burntisland, Fife; T.-0592 872453.

Haddow, Sir (Thomas) Douglas, KCB (1966), FRSE. Permanent Under Secretary of State, Scottish Office, 1965-73; b. 9.2.13. Educ. George Watson's College, Edinburgh; Edinburgh University; Trinity College, Cambridge. Chairman, North of Scotland Hydro-Electric Board, 1973-78; Chairman, Court, Heriot-Watt University, 1978-84; Hon. LLD, Strathclyde, 1967; Hon. DLitt, Heriot-Watt University, 1971.

Haggart, Most Rev. Alastair Iain Macdonald, Lth, BA, MA. Bishop of Edinburgh, since 1975; Primus of the Episcopal Church in Scotland, since 1977; b. 10.10.15; m., 1, Margaret Agnes Trundle (deceased); 2 d.; 2, Mary Elizabeth Scholes (see Mary E. Haggart). Educ. Hatfield College; Durham University; Edinburgh Theological College. Provost, St. Paul's Cathedral, Dundee, 1959-71; Principal and Pantonian Professor, Episcopal Theological College, Edinburgh, 1971-75; Canon, St. Mary's Cathedral, Edinburgh, 1971-75; Hon. LLD, Dundee, 1970.

Haggart, David Ballantine, JP, MA. Head of Careers Service, Aberdeen University, since 1963; b. 15.3.34, Dundee; m., Gwendolen Hall; 3 s. Educ. Aberdeen Grammar School; Aberdeen University. National Service, Band of Royal Corps of Signals, 1956-58; Teacher, Perth and Kinross County Council, 1958-59; Youth Employment Officer, City of Aberdeen, 1959-63; Member, Justices' Committee, Aberdeen, since 1976; Chairman, Ferryhill Community Council, 1976-82; Housing Management Convener, Castlehill Housing Association, since 1984; Chairman, Aberdeen and NE Scotland Music Festival, 1982-84; Writer and Producer, educational television programmes, including The Interview (Royal Television Society award); regular radio broadcasts, mainly on religious programmes; Presenter, Sunday Best, Northsound Radio, since 1981. Recreations: songwriting; motoring; local history. Address: (h.) 24 Polmuir Road, Aberdeen, AB1 2SY; T.-0224 584176.

Haggart, Mary Elizabeth, OBE. Chairman, Scottish Board of Nursing Midwifery and Health Visiting, 1980-83; b. 8.4.24, Leicester; m., Most Rev. A.I.M. Haggart. Educ. Wyggeston Grammar School for Girls, Leicester; Leicester Royal Infirmary and Children's Hospital. Leicester Royal Infirmary: Staff Nurse, 1947-48, Night Sister, 1948-50, Ward Sister, 1950-56, Night Superintendent, 1956-58, Assistant Matron, 1958-61; Assisant Matron, Brook General Hospital, London, 1962-64; Matron, Dundee Royal Infirmary and Matron Designate, Ninewells Hospital, Dundee, 1964-68; Chief Nursing Officer, Board of Managements, Dundee General Hospitals and Ninewells Hospital, 1968-73; Chief Area Nursing Officer, Tayside Health Board, 1974-82; President, Scottish Association of Nurse Administrators, 1972-77; Member, Scottish Board, Royal College of Nursing, 1965-70; Member, General Nursing Council for Scotland, 1965-70 and 1978-82; Member, Standing Nursing and Midwifery Committee, 1971-74 (Vice Chairman, 1973-74); Member, Action on Smoking and Health Scotland, 1978-82 (Chairman, Working Party, Smoking and Nurses); Governor, Dundee College of Technology, 1978-82; Honorary Lecturer, Department of Community Medicine, Dundee University and Medical School, 1980-82; Member, Management Committee, Carstairs State Hospital, 1982; Member, United Kingdom Central Council for Nursing Midwifery and Health Visiting, 1980-82. Recreations: walking; music; travel. Address: (h.) 19 Eglinton Crescent, Edinburgh, EH12 5RY; T.-031-337 8948.

Haggarty, Rev. William Gordon, DipEd, LTh, CPS. Minister, North Church of St. Andrew, Aberdeen, since 1976; b. 27.4.41, Glasgow; m., Wendy H. Nicoll; 1 d. Educ. High School of Glasgow; Glasgow University; Edinburgh University; New College, Edinburgh. Constable, City of Glasgow Police (Gorbals Division and Road Patrol), 1962-65; divinity course, New College, 1966-69; Assistant, Dunblane Cathedral, 1970-71; Minister, Glasgow Chryston, 1971-76. Honorary Vice-President, Aberdeen Bn., Boys Brigade; Chairman, Linksfield Academy School Council; Chaplain: HM Theatre, Aberdeen, and Grampian Police. Recreations: swimming; walking; family. Address: The Manse, 51 Osborne Place, Aberdeen, AB2 4BX; T.-0224 646429.

Haggarty, William McLaughlan, TD, BL. Solicitor, since 1950; Honorary Sheriff, South Strathclyde, Dumfries and Galloway; b. 22.2.26, Glasgow; m., Olive Dorothy Mary Speirs; 1 s.; 1

d. Educ. High School of Glasgow; Glasgow University. War Service, Merchant Navy, 1943-47; Chairman, National Insurance Tribunal, North and South Ayrshire, since 1963; Commanding Officer, 264 (Scottish) Regiment, Royal Corps of Transport (TA), 1966; Dean, Ayr Faculty of Solicitors, 1982; Governor, Craigie College of Education, Ayr, 1983. Recreations: golf; travel; gardening. Address: (b.) 4 Alloway Place, Ayr; T.-0292 263549.

Hague, Clifford Bertram, MA, DipTP, MRTPI. Senior Lecturer, Heriot-Watt University/ Edinburgh College of Art, since 1973; Course Tutor, Open University, since 1974; b. 22.8.44, Manchester; m., Irene; 1 s.; 3 d. Educ. North Manchester Grammar School; Magdalene College, Cambridge; Manchester University. Planning Assistant, Glasgow Corporation Planning Department, 1968-69; Lecturer, Department of Town and Country Planning, Heriot-Watt University/Edinburgh College of Art, 1969-73; Council Member, Royal Town Planning Institute (Past Chairman, Scottish Branch). Publication: The Development of Planning Thought: A Critical Perspective, 1984. Recreation: cricket. Address: (b.) Department of Town and Country Planning, Edinburgh College of Art, Edinburgh, EH3 9DF; T.-031-229 9311.

Haig of Bemersyde, The Earl, (George Alexander Eugene Douglas), OBE, DL, MA, KStJ. Painter; b. 15.3.18, London; 1 s.; 2 d. Educ. Cargilfield; Stowe School; Christ Church, Oxford. 2nd Lt., Royal Scots Greys, 1938; retired on account of disability, 1951 (rank of Captain); attended Camberwell School of Arts and Crafts; paintings in many public and private collections; served Second World War; taken prisoner, 1942; Member, Royal Fine Art Commission for Scotland, 1958-61; Chairman, SE South East Scotland Disablement Advisory Committee, 1960-73; Trustee, Scottish National War Memorial, since 1961 (present Chairman); Trustee, National Galleries of Scotland, 1962-72; Member, Scottish Arts Council, 1968-74; Past Chairman, Royal British Legion Scotland (present President); President, Earl Haig Fund Scotland; Chairman, Scottish Branch, Officers Association; Patron, Seagull Trust; President, Scottish Craft Centre, 1952-73; Vice President, Scottish National Institution for War Blinded and of Royal Blind Asylum, since 1960. Recreations: fishing; shooting. Address: (h.) Bemersyde, Melrose, TD6 9DP; T.-08352 2762.

Hajducki, Andrew Michael, MA. Advocate; Barrister-at-Law; b. 12.11.52, London; m., Gayle Shepherd; 1 s.; 1 d. Educ. Dulwich College; Cambridge University. Address: (b.) Advocates' Library, Parliament House, Edinburgh.

Haksar, Vinit, BA, MA, DPhil. Reader in Philosophy, Edinburgh University, since 1980; b. 4.9.37, Vienna; 2 s.; 1 d. Educ. Doon School; Oxford University. St. Andrews University: Assistant in Philosophy, 1962-64, Lecturer, 1964-69; Lecturer in Philosophy, Edinburgh University, 1969-80. Publication: Equality, Liberty and Perfectionism, 1979. Recreation: tennis. Address: (h.) 63 Findhorn Place, Edinburgh; T.-031-667 3474.

Halcro-Johnston, Hugh, JP, BSc, AMIEE. Member, Orkney Islands Council, since 1981; Chairman, Weyland Farms Ltd., since 1983; Director, Orkney Towage Company Ltd., since 1982; b. 7.11.36, Lahore; m., Erica Browne; 1 s.; 1 d. Educ. Marlborough College; Edinburgh University. Joined Alcan Industries, Banbury, 1961; Division Head, Alcan International, 1966; Group Manager, Electrical and Export, Alcan Booth Extrusions (now British Alcan), 1971; returned to Orkney, 1979, to manage family farm of Gyre, Orphir. Treasurer, Orphir Community Association; Chairman, Orkney Branch, Save the Children. Recreations: country pursuits. Address: Orphir House, Orphir, Orkney, KW17 2RD; T.-Orphir 200.

Haldane, Johnston Douglas, MB, FRCPEdin, FRCPsych, DPM. Psychotherapist and Consultant; Chairman, Scottish Marriage Guidance Council; b. 13.3.26, Annan; m., Kathleen McKirdy; 3 s. Educ. Lockerbie Academy; Dumbarton Academy; Dumfries Academy; Edinburgh University. Consultant Psychiatrist, Department of Child and Family Psychiatry, Stratheden Hospital, Cupar; Senior Lecturer, Department of Mental Health, Aberdeen University. Chairman, Friends of the Crawford Centre for the Arts, St. Andrews. Recreations: gardening; the arts. Address: (h.) Tarlogie, 54 Hepburn Gardens, St. Andrews, Fife, KY16 9DG.

Halford-MacLeod, Ruairidh, FSA Scot, FSTS. Secretary, Rural Forum, since 1984; Community Worker, Scottish Council of Community and Voluntary Organisations, since 1976; Honorary Treasurer, Scottish Tartans Society, since 1983; b. 7.2.44, Alexandria, Egypt; m., Anne S. McDougall; 1 s.; 1 d. Educ. Winchester College; St. Andrews University. Short-service commission, Queen's Own Highlanders (Seaforth and Camerons), 1969-72; Secretary, Harris Craft Guild, 1972-76; Secretary, Harris Council of Social Service, 1973-76; Editor, Clan MacLeod Magazine, 1974-82; Vice President, Clan MacLeod Society of Scotland, since 1984; Associate Professor of Scottish History, Noth Idaho College, Idaho, since 1980. Recreation: curling. Address: (h.) 49 Upper Greens, Auchtermuchty, Fife, KY14 7BX; T.-0337 28631.

Hall, Graham Stanley, BSc, PhD. Senior Lecturer in Mathematics, Aberdeen University, since 1982; b. 5.9.46, Warrington; m., Dr. Elizabeth Helen Rowe; 1 s.; 1 d. Educ. Boteler Grammar School, Warrington; Newcastle-upon-Tyne University. Earl Grey Memorial Fellowship, Newcastle-upon-Tyne University, 1971-73; Lecturer in Mathematics, Aberdeen University, 1973-82; Visiting Senior Lecturer in Mathematics, Monash University, Australia, 1982; numerous other short-term visiting positions at Universities in Europe, USA, Australia, Middle East. Recreations: sport; hill-walking; reading; music. Address: (b.) Department of Mathematics, Aberdeen University, Aberdeen, AB9 2TY; T.-0224 40241.

Hall, John Cecil, MA (Oxon). Senior Lecturer in Moral Philosophy, St. Andrews University, since 1974; b. 12.10.30, Valparai, India; m., Ursula Eunice Ewins; 2 s.; 1 d. Educ. Kingswood

School, Bath; Balliol College, Oxford. National Service, RAF, 1951-53; Assistant Principal, Ministry of Agriculture, Fisheries and Food, 1955-58; Lecturer in Moral Philosophy, St. Andrews University, 1960-74. Publication: Rousseau: An Introduction to his Political Philosophy, 1973. Recreation: choral singing. Address: (h.) 25 Hepburn Gardens, St. Andrews, Fife, KY16 9DG; T.-0334 72214.

Hall, Samuel James, BL, NP, WS. Solicitor, since 1951; Partner, Robson, McLean, Paterson, WS, since 1957; Legal Assessor, Professional Conduct Committee, United Kingdom Central Council for Nursing, Midwifery and Health Visiting; b. 29.5.30, Edinburgh; m., Olive Douglas Kerr; 2 s.; 1 d. Educ. Daniel Stewart's College, Edinburgh; Edinburgh University. Officer, Royal Army Service Corps, until 1953. Recreations: golf; good food. Address: (h.) 22 Denham Green Terrace, Edinburgh; T.-031-552 1836.

Hall, William, DFC, FRICS. Member, Lands Tribunal for Scotland, since 1971; Member, Lands Tribunal for England and Wales, since 1979; Honorary Sheriff, Paisley, since 1974; b. 25.7.19, Paisley; m., Margaret Semple Gibson; 1 s.; 3 d. Educ. Paisley Grammar School. Pilot, RAF, 1939-45 (Despatches); Senior Partner, R. & W. Hall, Chartered Surveyors, Paisley, 1949-79; Chairman, Scottish Branch, Royal Institution of Chartered Surveyors, 1971; Member, Valuation Advisory Council, 1970-80; Executive Member, Erskine Hospital, since 1976. Recreation: golf. Address: (h.) Windyridge, Brediland Road, Paisley, PA2 9HX; T.-Brediland 3614.

Hall, William Andrew McDonald, MA (Hons). Head Teacher, Dalry Secondary School, Kirkcudbrightshire, since 1973; b. 12.2.37, Airdrie; m., Catherine R.; 1 s.; 2 d. Educ. Airdrie Academy; Glasgow University. Teacher of History, Hamilton Academy, 1962-66; Principal Teacher of History, Mackie Academy, Stonehaven, 1966-73. Recreations: reading; golf; Airdrieonians Football Club; cinema. Address: (b.) Dalry Secondary School, St. John's Town of Dalry, Kirkcudbrightshire, DG7 3UU; T.-064 43 259.

Hall, (William) Douglas, OBE (1985), BA, FMA. Keeper, Scottish National Gallery of Modern Art, since 1961; b. 9.10.26, London; m., 1, Helen Elizabeth Ellis (m. diss.); 1 s.; 1 d.; 2, Matilda Mary Mitchell. Educ. University College School, Hampstead; University College and Courtauld Institute of Art, London University, 1948-52. Intelligence Corps, 1945-48 (Middle East); Manchester City Art Galleries: Keeper, Rutherston Collection, 1953-58, Keeper, City Art Gallery, 1958-59, Deputy Director, 1959-61; Member, Scottish Arts Council, c. 1968-78; Member, Fine Arts Advisory Committee, British Council; Governor, Glasgow School of Art. Recreations: music; travel. Address: (h.) 56 India Street, Edinburgh, EH3 6HD; T.-031-226 4959.

Halliday, Clive Benson, MIFireE. Firemaster, Strathclyde Regional Council, since 1984; b. 27.1.35, Prestatyn, North Wales; m., Margaret Morwena; 1 s.; 1 d. Fireman to Divisional Officer, Manchester Fire Brigade, 1960-74; Senior Divisional Officer, Greater Manchester Fire Service, 1974-78; Assistant/Deputy Chief Fire Officer, Staffordshire Fire Brigade, 1978-82; Chief Fire Officer, Northern Ireland Fire Brigade, 1982-84. Recreations: choral singing; fishing. Address: (b.) Fire Brigade Headquarters, Bothwell Road, Hamilton; T.-0698 284200.

Halliday, James, MA, MLitt, JP. Chairman, Scots Independent Newspapers; Member, National Executive, Scottish National Party; Principal Lecturer in History, Dundee College of Education, since 1979; b. 27.2.27, Wemyss Bay; m., Olive Campbell; 2 s. Educ. Greenock High School; Glasgow University. Teacher: Ardeer FE Centre, 1953, Kildonan Secondary School, Coatbridge, 1954-56, Uddingston Grammar School, 1956-58, Dunfermline High School, 1958-67; Lecturer in History, Dundee College of Education, 1967-79. Chairman, Scottish National Party, 1956-60; Parliamentary candidate: Stirling and Falkirk Burghs, 1955 and 1959, West Fife, 1970. Publications: World in Transformation - America; Scotland The Separate; Story of Scotland (Co-author). Recreations: reading; folk music; football spectating. Address: (h.) 10 Argyle Street, Dundee, DD4 7AL; T.-Dunblane 41159.

Halls, Michael, FREHIS. Director of Environmental Services, Ettrick and Lauderdale District Council, since 1975; b. 6.12.39, Galashiels; m., Sheila; 1 s.; 1 d. Educ. Galashiels Academy; Heriot-Watt. Trainee Burgh Surveyor, Galashiels Town Council, 1959-62; Additional Public Health Inspector, Thame Urban District Council, 1963-64; Galashiels Town Council: Assistant Burgh Surveyor and Sanitary Inspector, 1964-68, Depute Burgh Surveyor, 1968-71, Burgh Surveyor, 1971-75. Last Honorary Secretary, Scottish Institute of Environmental Health, 1978-83; first Senior Vice-President, Royal Environmental Health Institute of Scotland. Recreation: golf; philately; wine-making/drinking; music; eating. Address: (B.) PO Box 4, Paton Street, Galashiels, TD1 3AS; T.-0896 4751.

Halstead, Cyril Arthur, AE, BSc. Senior Lecturer in Geography, Glasgow University; b. 19.5.22, London; m., Annette Joan Shade. Educ. Parmiter's Foundation, London; University College, London. RAFVR, 1941-45 (Flt. Lt., Technical Branch); TRE, 1942-44 (now RSRE Malvern); Sqdn. Ldr., Royal Auxiliary Air Force, 1949-82. Lay Reader and Synod Member, Scottish Episcopal Church. Recreation: hill-walking. Address: (h.) The Hill, Dunlop, Ayrshire, KA3 4DH; T.-0560 84646.

Hamblen, Professor David Lawrence, MB, BS, PhD, FRCS, FRCSEdin, FRCSGlas. Professor of Orthopaedic Surgery, Glasgow University, since 1972; Honorary Consultant in Orthopaedic Surgery, Greater Glasgow Health Board, since 1972; Visiting Professor to National Centre for Training and Education in Prosthetics and Orthotics, Strathclyde University, since 1981; b. 31.8.34, London; m., Gillian; 1 s.; 2 d. Educ. Roan School, Greenwich; London University. The London Hospital, 1963-66; Teaching Fellow in Orthopaedics, Harvard Medical School/ Massachusetts General Hospital, 1966-67; Lecturer in Orthopaedics, Nuffield Orthopaedic Centre, Oxford, 1967-68; Senior Lecturer in Orthopaedics/Honorary Consultant, Edinburgh University/South East Regional Hospital Board, 1968-72; Member, Chief Scientist Committee, SHHD, since 1983; Member, Editorial Board, Journal of Bone and Joint Surgery, 1978-82 and since 1985. Recreation: golf. Address: (b.) University Department of Orthopaedic Surgery, Western Infirmary, Glasgow, G11 6NT; T.-041-339 8822.

Hamill, Sir Patrick, QPM, OStJ. Chief Constable of Strathclyde, 1977-85; Member, General Convocation, Strathclyde University; b. 29.4.30, Clydebank; m., Nellie Gillespie; 4 s.; 1 d. Educ. St. Patrick's High School, Dumbarton. Joined Dunbartonshire Constabulary, 1950, and rose through the ranks until promoted Chief Superintendent, 1970; transferred to City of Glasgow Police, 1972; appointed Assistant Chief Constable, 1974; became a member of Strathclyde Police, 1975, and attended the Royal College of Defence Studies, 1976; President, Association of Chief Police Officers (Scotland), 1982-83, Honorary Secretary and Treasurer, 1983-85; Member, Board of Governors, St. Aloysius College, Glasgow. Recreations: walking; gardening; golf.

Hamilton, Andrew. General Manager, Edinburgh Airport, since 1978; b. 1.5.25, Uddingston; m., Betty; 1 s.; 2 d. Educ. Uddingston Grammar School. Royal Navy, 1943-60; Ministry of Civil Aviation, 1960-66; British Airports Authority: Assistant General Manager, Prestwick Airport, 1966-74, General Manager, Aberdeen Airport, 1974-78. Recreation: golf. Address: (b.) Scottish Airports, Edinburgh Airport, Edinburgh, EH12 9DN; T.-031-344 3151.

Hamilton, 15th Duke of, and Brandon, 12th Duke of, (Angus Alan Douglas Douglas-Hamilton). Premier Peer of Scotland; Hereditary Keeper of Palace of Holyroodhouse; b. 13.9.38; m., Sarah Scott; 2 s.; 2 d. Educ. Eton; Balliol College, Oxford. Flt.-Lt., RAF (retired, 1967); flying instructor, 1965; Test Pilot, Scottish Aviation, 1971-72; Member, Queen's Bodyguard for Scotland (Royal Company of Archers), since 1975; KStJ, 1975. Address: (h.) Lennoxlove, Haddington, East Lothian.

Hamilton, Barbara, MB, BCh, MRCPsych, DipPsychoth. Medical Officer, Mental Welfare Commission for Scotland, since 1984; b. 19.2.44, Belfast; m., Dr. David Stewart Hamilton (qv); 2 s.; 3 d. Educ. Methodist College, Belfast; Queen's University, Belfast. Address: (h.) Viewfield, Queens Road, Aberlour, Banffshire, AB3 9PR; T.-03405 489.

Hamilton, Christine Jean (Gordon), JP, BSc (Agr), NDD, CDD. A Director, Royal Highland Agricultural Society of Scotland (Glasgow Region), since 1977; a Director, Royal Scottish Agricultural Benevolent Institution (Lanarkshire); b. 24.6.19, Huntly, Aberdeenshire; m., Matthew Hamilton (deceased); 2 s.; 2 d. Educ. Gordon Schools, Huntly; Aberdeen University;

North of Scotland College of Agriculture; West of Scotland College of Agriculture. Address: Woolfords, Cobbinshaw, West Calder, EH55 8LJ; T.-Auchengray 224.

Hamilton, Rev. David Gentles, MA (Hons), BD (Hons). Curriculum Officer, Church of Scotland Department of Education; b. 31.10.40, Glasgow; m., Elsa Catherine Nicolson; 2 s. Educ. Woodside Senior Secondary School, Glasgow; Glasgow University. Electrical engineering design work, 1956-63; Assistant to Church of Scotland congregations of Barlanark, Merrylea, High Carntyne, 1963-71; ordained, 1971; Minister, Troon St. Meddans, 1971-78; Hastie Memorial Lectureship, Glasgow University, 1975-77; Theologian in Residence, Arkansas College and First Presbyterian Church, USA, 1976; Convener, Division on Children, Church of Scotland Department of Education, 1977-80; Convener, Youth Committee, Church of Scotland, 1978; Minister, Bearsden South Church, 1978-80; Chairman, British Council of Churches Consultative Group on Ministry among Children, since 1982; Author and Editor of Christian education publications, videos. Publication: Children - The Challenge to the Church (Co-author). Recreations: hillwalking; jazz trumpet; Mozart; gardening; spy thrillers. Address: (h.) 79 Finlay Rise, Milngavie, Glasgow.

Hamilton, David Stewart, MB, BCh, BAO, MRCPsych, DRCOG, AssocRCGP. Consultant Psychiatrist; Honorary Senior Lecturer in Mental Health, Aberdeen University, since 1983; b. Belfast; m., Dr. Barbara Hamilton (qv); 2 s.; 3 d. Address: (h.) Viewfield, Queens Road, Aberlour, Banffshire, AB3 9PR; T.-03405 489.

Hamilton, Douglas P., BSc (Hons), DipEd, JP. Member, North East Fife District Council, since 1974; a Director, Byre Theatre, St. Andrews; b. 8.9.26, St. Andrews; m., Pamela J. McKane; 1 s. Educ. Madras College, St. Andrews; St. Andrews University. Management Trainee/Production Manager, Unilever, 1948-51; Teacher, 1952-58; Assistant Training Manager, UKAEA, 1958-60; Lecturer, then Head, Department of Science Mathematics, Kingsway Technical College, Dundee, 1960-84. Depute Traffic Commissioner; Member, St. Andrews Links Management Committee; Member, Endowment Committee, Madras College; Vice-Chairman, Planning Committee, North East Fife District Council. Recreations: golf; music (Church organ); gardening. Address: (h.) Craigston, 36 Craig Road, Tayport, Fife, DD6 9LE.

Hamilton, Frank D. Director (Scotland), Royal Society for the Protection of Birds, since 1972; b. 13.11.32, Edinburgh; m., Kathleen; 1 s.; 1 d. Educ. George Watson's College, Edinburgh. Various posts in industry; joined RSPB, 1958, based first in London, then at HQ, Bedfordshire; developed UK film shows, education, sales and membership; established office in Northern Ireland; returned to Scotland, 1970. Council Member, Scottish Ornithologists Club; Member, Secretary of State for Scotland's Forum on the Environment and previous Advisory Committee on Protection of Birds; Scottish Representative, International Council for the Protection of Birds

(British Section); has sat on Council of Irish Wildbird Conservancy. Recreations: birdwatching and bird surveys; walking; wine-making; tropical fish; model railways. Address: (h.) 23 Campbell Road, Longniddry, East Lothian, EH32 ONP; T.-0875 52387.

Hamilton, James. MP (Labour), Motherwell North, since 1983 (Bothwell, 1964-83); b. 11.3.18. Member, Lanarkshire County Council, 1955-65; Past Chairman, PLP Trade Union Group; Assistant Government Whip, 1969-70; Opposition Whip, 1970-74; Vice-Chamberlain of the Household, 1974-78; Comptroller, 1978-79; Member, Select Committee on Selection; President, Constructional Engineering Union, 1968-70.

Hamilton, James, JP, MREHIS. Director of Environmental Health, Clydesdale District Council, since 1984; b. 16.3.34, Coalburn. Educ. Larkhall Academy; Paisley Technical College. Environmental Health Officer, Lanarkshire County Council, 1951-75; Environmental Health Services Manager, Clydesdale District Council, 1975-84. Address: (b.) District Offices, South Vennel, Lanark; T.-Lanark 61331.

Hamilton, James Millar, OBE, MA. Rector, Harris Academy, Dundee, since 1969; b. 3.12.22, Hamilton; m., Mae; 1 s.; 2 d. Educ. Hamilton Academy; Glasgow University; Jordanhill College. Taught, Larkhall Academy and Hamilton Academy; Principal Teacher of English, then Deputy Rector, Kirkcaldy High School; Past Chairman, Board of Governors, Dundee College of Education; founder Chairman, Hamilton Round Table; Past President, Claverhouse Rotary Club, Dundee; Member, Pack Committee. Recreations: golf; reading; walking; photography. Address: (h.) 33 Dunmore Gardens, Dundee; T.-Dundee 68304.

Hamilton, Lt. Cdr. John, JP. Retired Farmer and Estate Manager, since 1981; almost a Gentleman, since 1922; Honorary Sheriff, Ayr, since 1976; b. 24.2.11, Edinburgh; m., Angela D.; 1 d. (by pr. m.). Educ. Dartmouth; Greenwich. Served, Royal Navy, 1924-46 (invalided); Fleet Air Arm Observer, 1936, AGO, 1940; farmed and ran estate, 1947-81; Freeman, Royal Burgh of Ayr, 1969. Recreation: propagation. Address: (h.) Monkwood, by Ayr, KA7 4TT; T.-0292 41331.

Hamilton, Loudon Pearson, MA (Hons). Secretary, Department of Agriculture and Fisheries for Scotland, since 1984; b. 12.1.32, Glasgow; m., Anna Mackinnon Young; 2 s. Educ. Hutchesons Grammar School, Glasgow; Glasgow University. National Service, RA, 1953-55 (2nd Lt.); Inspector of Taxes, Inland Revenue, 1956-60; Assistant Principal, Department of Agriculture and Fisheries for Scotland, 1960; Private Secretary to Parliamentary Under Secetary of State for Scotland, 1963-64; First Secretary, Agriculture, British Embassy, Copenhagen and The Hague, 1966-70; Assistant Secretary, Department of Agriculture and Fisheries for Scotland, 1973-79; Principal Establishment Officer, Scottish Office, 1979-84. Address: (b.) DAFS, Chesser House, 500 Gorgie Road, Edinburgh, EH11 3AN; T.-031-443 4020.

Hamilton, Martha, MA, DipEd, DipAdEd. Headmistress, St. Leonards School, St. Andrews, since 1970; b. Edinburgh; m., Robert R. Steedman. Educ. Roedean; St. Andrews University; Cambridge University. Principal, Paljor Namgyal Girls High School, Gangtok, Sikkim, 1959-66; awarded Pema Dorji, for services to education. Recreations: photography; skiing. Address: (b.) St. Leonards School, St. Andrews, Fife; T.-0334 72126.

Hamilton, Robert Thomson, LLB. Procurator Fiscal, Dunfermline, since 1982; b. 28.2.41, Glasgow; m., Jean; 1 s.; 1 d. Educ. Hamilton Academy; Edinburgh University. Estate Duty Office, Inland Revenue, Edinburgh, 1963-67; private practice in law, 1967-70; Procurator Fiscal Depute: Glasgow, 1970-72, Hamilton, 1972-77; Principal Legal Assistant, Crown Office, Edinburgh, 1977-79; Assistant Procurator Fiscal, Edinburgh, 1979-82. Recreations: bowling; thinking about taking exercise. Address: (b.) Procurator Fiscal's Office, Sheriff Court House, Dunfermline, Fife; T.-Dunfermline 723688.

Hamilton, Steven Fraser, JP, BL, DPA, DMS. Town Clerk and Chief Executive, City of Glasgow District Council, since 1979; b. 10.10.31, Glasgow; m., Dorothy; 1 s.; 1 d. Educ. Victoria Drive Senior Secondary School, Glasgow; Glasgow University; Glasgow College of Technology. Began as Law Apprentice in Town Clerk's Office, Glasgow, 1948; graduated and qualified as Solicitor; appointed Legal Assistant, 2A, 1953; promoted to IA, 1957; Senior Legal Assistant, 1959; Principal Legal Assistant, 1962; Town Clerk Depute, Glasgow, 1973; Director of Administration and Legal Services, 1974. Recreations: golf; bridge; listening to music; opera; ballet. Address: (b.) City Chambers, Glasgow, G2 1DU; T.-041-227 4501.

Hamilton, William, MB, ChB, MD, FRCPGlas, FRCPEdin, DPH, DCH. Paediatrician and Paediatric Endocrinologist, Department of Child Health, Royal Hospital for Sick Children, Glasgow, since 1961; University Senior Lecturer, since 1962; b. 22.12.22, Holytown, Lanarkshire; m., Elizabeth Janet Beveridge; 2 s. Educ. Holytown Public School; Dalziel High School, Motherwell; Glasgow University. House Physician/House Surgeon posts, Glasgow, 1952-54; general practice, 1954-56; Registrar medical post, Inverness, 1957-61; Senior Registrar in Paediatrics, 1961-62. Advisor on Postgraduate and Undergraduate Education and Training, Fatah Medical School, Tripoli, Libya. Publications: Clinical Paediatric Endocrinology, 1972; Surgical Treatment of Endocrine Disease. Recreations: gardening; vintage car enthusiast. Address: (h.) 81 Woodend Drive, Glasgow, G13 1QF; T.-041-954 9961.

Hamilton, Professor (William) Allan, BSc, PhD, FRSE. Professor of Microbiology, Aberdeen University, since 1980 (Head of Department, since 1975); Chairman, National Collections of Industrial and Marine Bacteria Ltd., since 1983; Chairman, Micran Ltd., since 1984; b. 4.4.36, Glasgow. Educ. Hutchesons' Boys Grammar School; Glasgow University. Postdoctoral Research Fellow: Illinois University, 1961-62, Rio de

Janeiro University, 1962-63; Scientist, Unilever Research, Bedford, 1963-67; Lecturer/Senior Lecturer, Department of Biochemistry, Aberdeen University, 1967-75; Senior Lecturer/Reader, Department of Microbiology, Aberdeen University, 1975-80. Recreations: sailing; wine. Address: (h.) 175 Queen's Road, Aberdeen, AB1 8BS; T.-0224 313434.

Hamilton, William Winter, MP. MP (Labour), Central Fife (formerly West Fife), since 1950; b. 26.6.17, Herrington, Co. Durham; 1 s.; 1 d. Educ. Washington Grammar School; Sheffield University. HM Forces, 1941-46; Teacher, Yorkshire, 1946-50. Publication: My Queen and I, 1975. Recreations: attacking monarchy and establishment; reading; gardening. Address: (b.) House of Commons, Westminster, London; T.-01-219 8000, Ext. 3559.

Hammerton, Desmond, BSc, CBiol, FIBiol, FIWES, FIWPC, FBIM, FRSE. Director, Clyde River Purification Board, since 1975; Consultant, World Health Organisation, since 1977; b. 17.11.29, Wakefield, Yorkshire; m., Jean Taylor; 2 s.; 2 d. Educ. Harrow Weald County School; Birkbeck College, London University. Assistant Biologist, Metropolitan Water Board, 1953-55; Research Biologist, Bristol Waterworks, 1955-58; Principal Assistant, Lothians River Purification Board, 1958-62; Director, Hydrobiological Research Unit, Khartoum University, 1962-71; Deputy Director, Clyde River Purification Board, 1971-74. Member, Aquatic Life Sciences Grants Committee, Natural Environment Research Council, 1975-79; Member, Marine Pollution Monitoring Management Group and its Steering Committee, since 1974; Member, Steering Committee for the Development of Environmental Quality Objectives and Standards, Department of Environment, 1981; Member, Scottish Council, Institute of Biology, 1973-76; elected to Committee of Environment Division, Institute of Biology, 1977 (Chairman, Environment Division, 1980-82); elected to Scottish Branch Committee, Institute of Water Pollution Control, 1980 (Chairman, Scottish Branch, 1983); Representative, Institution of Water Engineers and Scientists, Acid Rain Working Group, Watt Committee on Energy, 1983-84. Recreations: chess; tennis; hill-walking. Address: (h.) 7 Fairfield Place, Bothwell, Glasgow, G7 8RP; T.-Bothwell 852261.

Hammond, John, BSc, BDS, FDS, HDD, DipEd. Senior Lecturer in Prosthodontics, Glasgow University, since 1973; Consultant Dental Surgeon, Greater Glasgow Health Board, since 1973; b. 6.7.28, Airdrie; m., Mary M. Stewart; 1 s.; 1 d. Educ. Airdrie Academy; Glasgow University. Education Officer, RAF, 1951-55; Lecturer in Prosthodontics, Glasgow University, 1961-73; Secretary, Dental Council, Royal College of Physicians and Surgeons (Glasgow), 1976-83; Chairman, Lanarkshire Area Dental Committee, 1977-80. President, Glasgow Dental Students Society, 1958-59; President, Lanarkshire Golf Association, 1967-68. Recreations: golf; photography. Address: (b.) Glasgow Dental Hospital and School, 378 Sauchiehall Street, Glasgow; T.-041-332 7020.

Hammond, John Arthur, PhD, MRCVS, DVSM, DTVM, DAP&E. Senior Lecturer, Faculty of Veterinary Medicine, Edinburgh University, since 1978; b. 21.5.25, Bale, Norfolk; m., Annemarie. Educ. Greshams School; Royal Veterinary College; London University; Edinburgh University. Assistant in general practice, 1949-51; Veterinary Officer/Veterinary Research Officer, Tanganyika/Tanzania, 1951-65; Principal Scientific Officer, East African Veterinary Research Organisation, Kenya, 1967-69. Recreations: travel; cricket; gardening. Address: (b.) Centre for Tropical Veterinary Medicine, Easter Bush, Roslin, Midlothian, EH25 9RG; T.-031-445 2001.

Hamnett, Brian Roger, BA (Hons), MA, PhD (Cantab). Senior Lecturer, Department of History, Strathclyde University, since 1974; b. 29.11.42, Colchester. Educ. Peterhouse, Cambridge. Assistant Professor, Department of History, New York State University, 1968-72; University Research Fellow, Reading University, 1972-74. Publications: Politics and Trade in Southern Mexico 1750-1821, 1971; Revolution and Counter-Revolution in Mexico and Peru 1800-1824: Liberalism, Royalism and Separatism, 1978; Spanish Politics in the Revolutionary Era 1800-1820, in press; Roots of Insurgency: Mexican Regions 1750-1824, in press. Recreations: travel; cinema; music; literature; writing. Address: (b.) Department of History, Strathclyde University, McCance Building, 16 Richmond Street, Glasgow, G1 1XQ.

Hampson, Stephen F., MA, BPhil. Assistant Secretary, Industry Department for Scotland, since 1984; b. 27.10.45, Grimsby; m., Gunilla Brunk; 1 s.; 1 d. Educ. The Leys School, Cambridge; University College, Oxford. Lecturer, Department of Political Economy, Aberdeen University, 1969-71; Economist, National Economic Development Office, 1971-75; Economic Adviser, Scottish Office, 1975-78 and 1982-84; First Secretary, British High Commission, New Delhi, 1978-81. Recreation: modern Indian literature. Address: (h.) Glenelg, Park Road, Kilmacolm, Renfrewshire; T.-Kilmacolm 2615.

Haney, Rev. Hugh Baird. Minister, John Ross Memorial Church for the Deaf, Glasgow, since 1982; b. 3.7.29, Irvine; m., Catherine Murray Campbell; 1 s.; 1 d. Educ. Kilmarnock Academy. Missionary to the Deaf, 1960-66; Minister to the Deaf in Falkirk, 1966-75, in Renfrewshire, 1975-82. Recreations: reading; travel; gardening; DIY. Address: Dungoyne, 132 Sandy Road, Renfrew, PA4 OBX; T.-041-886 3115.

Hanley, Clifford. Writer and Performer; Emeritus Professor, York University, Toronto; b. 28.10.22, Glasgow; m., Anna Clark; 1 s.; 2 d. Educ. Eastbank Academy, Glasgow. Journalist, since 1940; Novelist, since 1957; Songwriter; Broadcaster; Member, Scottish Arts Council, 1965-72; Member, Inland Waterways Advisory Council, 1970-73; Professor of Literature, York University, Toronto, 1979-80. Publications: Dancing in the Streets; Love from Everybody; The Taste of Too Much; Nothing but the Best; The System; The Redhaired Bitch; It's Different

Abroad; The Italian Gadget; The Chosen Instrument; The Scots; Another Street, Another Dance. Recreations: music; talk; golf. Address: (h.) 36 Munro Road, Glasgow, G13 1SF.

Hanley, Very Rev. Hugh Hanley, SCJ, STL. Superior, Smithstone House, Kilwinning, since 1983; b. 8.8.51, Port Glasgow. Educ. Woodcote Hall, Newport, Shropshire; St. Joseph's, Malpas, Cheshire. Member, Sacred Heart Fathers, 1970; ordained Priest, St. John's, Port Glasgow, 1976; Smithstone House, Kilwinning, 1976-77; Holy Rood Church, Market Rasen, 1977-78; St. John Ogilvie's, Bourtreehill, Irvine, 1978-80; Gregorian University, Rome, 1980-82; Dehon House, Little Sutton, South Wirral, 1982-83. Recreations: various sports; reading. Address: Smithstone House, Kilwinning, Ayrshire, KA13 6PL; T.- 0294 52515.

Hanlon, Rt. Rev. John Breslin, STB. Parish Priest, St. Mary's, Dundee, since 1981; b. 27.8.30, Dundee. Educ. Lawside Academy, Dundee; Seminaire St. Sulpice, Paris. National Service, Army, 1948-50; Assistant Priest: St. Andrew's Cathedral, 1957, St. Leonard's, Dundee, 1957-60, Alloa, 1960-64, St. Mary's, Lochee, 1964-66; Parish Priest: Carnoustie/Monifieth, 1966-72, St. Teresa's, Dundee, 1972-76; Administrator, St. Andrew's Cathedral, 1976-81. RC Representative, Education Committee, Tayside Regional Council, 1973-81; Dunkeld Representative, John Ogilvie Committee, 1964-76; Vicar-General, Diocese of Dunkeld, 1975-81. Recreations: Scottish history; coins/medals/stamps; bowls. Address: St. Mary's, 41 High Street, Lochee, Dundee, DD2 3AP; T.-0382 611282.

Hannay of Kirkdale and That Ilk, Ramsay William Rainsford. Landowner, Farmer, Caravan Park Operator, since 1964; Barrister-at-Law, Inner Temple; b. 15.6.11, India; m., Margaret Wiseman; 1 s.; 1 d. Educ. Winchester College; Trinity College, Cambridge (Hons. degree in Law). Called to the Bar and practised in the Bankruptcy Court; called up for service in the Forces, 1939; commissioned, HLI; served throughout the War in Europe, with a short spell in USA and Canada; demobilised with rank of Major; Legal Assistant, then Assistant Solicitor, Board of Trade, 1946-64; Honorary Sheriff, Stewartry of Kirkcudbright; Member, Queen's Bodyguard for Scotland (Royal Company of Archers); President, Dumfries and Galloway Boy Scouts Association; Chief of the Clan Hannay. Recreations: sailing; shooting; fishing. Address: (h.) Cardoness, Gatehouse-of-Fleet, Kirkcudbrightshire; T.-Mossyard 207.

Hardman, Norman, BSc, PhD, CBiol, FIBiol, CChem, FRSC. Senior Lecturer in Biochemistry, Aberdeen University, since 1981; b. 6.9.45, Farnworth, Lancashire. Educ. Smithills School, Bolton; London University; Manchester University. MRC Research Fellow, Manchester University, 1970-71, 1972-73; Research Fellow, Harvard Medical School, Boston, 1971-72; Lecturer in Biochemistry, Aberdeen University, 1973-81. Recreations: painting; skiing; walking. Address: (b.) Department of Biochemistry, Aberdeen University, Marischal College, Aberdeen, AB9 1AS; T.-0224 40241.

Hare Duke, Rt. Rev. Michael Geoffrey, BA, MA. Bishop of St. Andrews, Dunkeld and Dunblane, since 1969; b. 28.11.25; m.; 1 s.; 3 d. Educ. Bradfield College; Trinity College, Oxford. Sub-Lt., RNVR, 1944-46; Deacon, 1952; Priest, 1953. Chairman, Scottish Association for Mental Health, since 1978.

Hargreave, Timothy Bruce, MB, MS, FRCSEdin, FRCS. Senior Lecturer, Department of Surgery, Edinburgh University, since 1978; Honorary Consultant Urological and Transplant Surgeon, Western General Hospital, Edinburgh, since 1978; b. 23.3.44, Lytham; m., Molly; 2 d. Educ. Harrow; University College Hospital, London University. Senior Registrar: Western Infirmary, Glasgow; University College Hospital, London; Medical Officer, Paray Mission Hospital, Lesotho. Secretary, Scottish Urological Association. Publications: Diagnosis and Management of Renal and Urinary Disease; Male Infertility (Editor). Recreation: skiing. Address: (h.) 39 Murrayfield Gardens, Edinburgh; T.-031-337 3879.

Harkes, Rev. George. Minister, Cumbernauld Old, since 1971; b. 2.1.29, Edinburgh; m., Jennifer Rae Edgar; 2 s. Educ. James Gillespie's School; Edinburgh University. Rothiemay Parish Church, 1962-65; RAF Chaplain, 1965-67; Summerfield Parish Church, 1967-71. Recreations: sport; rugby; squash; walking (hill). Address: Baronhill, Cumbernauld, Glasgow; T.-Cumbernauld 21912.

Harkness, William, LLB, CA. Director and Secretary, The Weir Group PLC, since 1982; b. 1.4.43, Glasgow; m., Maura Brogan; 1 s. Educ. Greenock Academy; Glasgow University. Qualified as Chartered Accountant, 1967; admitted as Solicitor, 1970; joined The Weir Group as Legal Assistant, 1971, Group Secretary, 1977. Member, Parliamentary and Law Committee, Institute of Chartered Accountants of Scotland. Recreations: golf; bridge; travel in outer isles and West of Ireland. Address: (h.) 54A Esplanade, Greenock; T.-0475 23000.

Harle, John Tate, BSc (Hons), MS, FRAgS. Managing Director, Cluny Home Farms Ltd., since 1966; Director, Storeylake (Agriculture) Ltd., since 1983; Vice-Chairman, Scottish Agricultural Development Council, since 1983 (Member, since 1977); Member, Governing Body, Grassland Research Institute, 1981-85 (now Member, Governing Body, Animal and Grassland Research Institute); Member, Governing Body, Rowett Research Institute, since 1983; Member, Aberdeen and District Milk Marketing Board, since 1983; b. 3.9.41, Washington, England; m., Margaret Muriel; 2 s. Educ. Bede Grammar School, Sunderland; Durham University; Iowa State University. Part-time Lecturer, Agricultural Economics, Aberdeen University. Recreations: hill-walking; skiing; squash; classical guitar. Address: Little Ley Farmhouse, Tillyfourie, Inverurie, Aberdeenshire, AB3 7SA; T.-033 03 355.

Harley, Roy Macgregor, LLB, NP, SSC. Solicitor; b. 29.10.48, Glasgow; m., Yvonne Mazodier. Educ. Hermitage Academy, Helensburgh;

Aberdeen University. Solicitor in private practice, Edinburgh, since 1972; Council Member, SSC, 1983; Tutor in Criminal Law, Edinburgh University, 1984. Recreations: squash; guitar; Francophile. Address: (h.) 14 Dean Park Crescent, Edinburgh, EH4 1PH.

Harper, Professor Alexander Murray, MB, ChB, MD (Hons). Professor of Surgical Physiology, Glasgow University, since 1981; Honorary Consultant Clinical Physiologist, Greater Glasgow Health Board, since 1970; b. 31.5.33, Glasgow; m., Charlotte Maria Fossleitner; 2 s.; 1 d. Educ. Hutchesons' Grammar School; Glasgow University. House Physician and Surgeon, Southern General Hospital and Glasgow Royal Infirmary, 1957-58; McIntyre Research Scholar in Clinical Surgery, Glasgow Royal Infirmary, 1958-60; Scientific Assistant, Medical Research Council, 1960-63; Wellcome Senior Research Fellow in Clinical Science and Honorary Lecturer in Surgery, Glasgow University, 1963-68; Glasgow University: Senior Lecturer in Surgery and Surgical Physiology, 1968-69, Reader, 1969-81. Editor in Chief, Journal of Cerebral Blood Flow and Metabolism, since 1981; David Patey Prize, Surgical Research Society, 1966; H.G. Wolff Award, American Association for Study of Headache, 1968; Gold Medal, British Migraine Association, 1976; Honorary Fellow, American Heart Association (Stroke Council), 1980. Recreations: fishing; contract bridge; gardening. Address: (b.) Wellcome Surgical Institute, Glasgow University, Garscube Estate, Bearsden Road, Glasgow, G61 1QH; T.-041-942 2248.

Harper, Professor Anthony John, BA, MA, PhD, CertEd. Professor of German Studies, Strathclyde University, since 1979; b. 26.5.38, Bristol; m., Sandra; 1 s.; 2 d. Educ. Clifton College, Bristol; Bristol University; Exeter University. Lecturer, Department of German, Edinburgh University, 1962-79. Publications: German Today (Co-author), 1967; David Schirmer - A Poet of the German Baroque, 1977; Time and Change, Essays on German and European Literature, 1982; Schriften zur Lyrik Leipzigs 1620-1670, 1985. Address: (b.) Department of Modern Languages, Strathclyde University, 26 Richmond Street, Glasgow, G1 1XH; T.-041-552 4400.

Harper, Rev. David Little, BSc, BD (Hons). Minister, St. Meddan's Church, Troon, since 1979; b. 31.10.47, Moffat; m., Janis Mary Clark; 2 s. Educ. Morton Academy, Thornhill; Dumfries Academy; Edinburgh University. Assistant Minister, Cumbernauld St. Mungo's, 1971-72; first Minister, New Erskine Parish Church, 1972-79. Member, Scottish Advisory Committee, Independent Broadcasting Authority, 1974-79; Scottish Member, Religious Advisory Panel, IBA, 1978-79. Recreations: squash; golf; hill-walking. Address: St. Meddan's Manse, 27 Bentinck Drive, Troon, Ayrshire; T.-0292 311784.

Harper, Douglas Ross, BSc, MD, FRCSEdin, FRCSEng. Consultant Surgeon, Forth Valley Health Board, since 1976; Examiner, Royal College of Surgeons of Edinburgh, since 1979;

Honorary Senior Lecturer, Department of Clinical Surgery, Edinburgh University, since 1976; b. 16.2.40, Aberdeen; m., Dorothy Constance Wisely; 1 s.; 3 d. Educ. Aberdeen Grammar School; Aberdeen University. House Officer, Registrar and Fellow in Vascular Surgery, Aberdeen Royal Infirmary, 1967-73; Senior Registrar, Edinburgh Royal Infirmary, 1973-76. Elder, Bridge of Allan Chalmers Church of Scotland. Recreations: hill-walking; geology; woodwork. Address: (h.) Glenallan, 16 Upper Glen Road, Bridge of Allan, Stirlingshire, FK9 4PX; T.-0786 832242.

Harper, Edward James, MA, BMus, ARCM, LRAM. Composer, since 1957; Lecturer in Music, Edinburgh University, since 1964; Director, New Music Group of Scotland, since 1973; b. 17.3.41, Taunton; m., Dorothy Caroline Shanks. Educ. King Edward VI School, Guildford; Royal College of Music, London; Christ Church, Oxford. Main works as a Composer: Piano Concerto, 1971, Bartok Games, 1972, Ricercari in Memoriam Luigi Dallapiccola, 1975, Fanny Robin (chamber opera), Chester Mass, 1979, Clarinet Concerto, 1981, Hedda Gabler (opera, commissioned for Scottish Opera), 1985. Address: (h.) 48 Dudley Gardens, Edinburgh, EH6 4PS.

Harper, John Ross, MA, LLB. Senior Partner, Ross Harper & Murphy, Solicitors, since 1962; b. 20.3.35, Glasgow; m., Ursula; 2 s.; 1 d. Educ. Hutchesons' Boys Grammar School; Glasgow University. Member, Secretary of State's Team on Management Budgeting for the Health Service; Chairman, Services Committee, Finance Committee and Health Promotion Committee, Greater Glasgow Health Board; Temporary Sheriff; Parliamentary Commissioner; Tutor in Criminal Advocacy, Strathclyde University; Past President, Glasgow Bar Association; Council Member, Law Society of Scotland; Chairman, Criminal Law Division, International Bar Association; Chairman, Scottish Society of Conservative Lawyers; former Parliamentary candidate (Conservative), Hamilton and West Renfrewshire. Publications: Glasgow Rape Case; My Client My Lord; A Practitioner's Guide to the Criminal Courts; Fingertip Criminal Law. Recreations: angling; bridge; shooting. Address: (b.) 163 Ingram Street, Glasgow; T.-041-552 6343.

Harris, Elizabeth Bruce Anderson, BA, DCE. Member, Dunfermline District Council, since 1984; Member, Alliance Scottish Education Policy Group; Teacher; b. 29.4.57, Dunfermline. Educ. Beath Senior High School; Dundee College of Education; Open University. Vice-Chairman, Dunfermline Liberal Association, 1982-84. Recreations: aerobic dancing; golf; skiing. Address: (h.) 38 Arthur Street, Dunfermline, Fife; T.-0383 724838.

Harris, Gordon Scott, BSc, PhD, FRSC, CChem. Senior Lecturer, Chemistry Department, St. Andrews University, since 1965; b. 28.9.31, Alexandria; m., Eleanor Mackay; 2 s. Educ. Vale of Leven Academy; Glasgow University; Sidney Sussex College, Cambridge University. Ramsay Memorial Fellowship, Cambridge University, 1956-58; ICI Research Fellowship, Glasgow

University, 1958-59; Lecturer in Chemistry, Glasgow University, 1959-65; Member, Scottish Examination Board, 1979-82. Recreations: gardening; golf; walking. Address: (b.) Chemistry Department, St. Andrews University, St. Andrews, Fife; T.-St. Andrews 76161.

Harris, Rev. John William Forsyth, MA. Minister, St. Mary's Parish Church, Motherwell, since 1977; b. 10.3.42, Hampshire; m., Ellen Lesley Kirkpatrick Lamont; 1 s.; 2 d. Educ. Merchant Taylors' School, London; St. Andrews University; New College, Edinburgh University. Ordained Assistant, St. Mary's, Haddington, 1967-70; Minister, St. Andrew's Parish Church, Irvine, 1970-77; Convener, Home Mission and Church and Industry Committees, Hamilton Presbytery, 1982-85; Member, Home Mission Committee, General Assembly, 1982-85; Member, Church and Nation Committee, General Assembly, since 1983; Convener, Inter-Church Relations Committee, Hamilton Presbytery, since 1984; Convener: Irvine Christian Aid Committee, 1974-77, Motherwell Christian Aid Committee, 1980-85. Fencing Blue, St. Andrews and Edinburgh. Recreation: golf played very badly. Address: 19 Orchard Street, Motherwell; T.-0698 63472.

Harris, Paul Anthony, MA (Hons). Publisher; b. 22.7.48, Barnhurst; m., Carolann. Educ. Bradford Grammar School; Elgin Academy; Aberdeen University. Project Director, Capital Radio, 1970-71; Managing Director, Impulse Publications, 1971-73; Charles Skilton Publishing Ltd., 1973-74; Managing Director, Paul Harris Publishing, 1974-85; General Manager, Waterfront Communications Ltd., since 1985; Past Chairman, Scottish Publishers Association. Publications: When Pirates Ruled The Waves, 1968; The Garvie Trial, 1969; Oil, 1974; To Be A Pirate King, 1972; Broadcasting from the High Seas, 1976; Concise Dictionary of Scottish Painters, 1977; Investing in Scottish Pictures, 1978; Scotland An Anthology, 1984. Recreations: painting; film production; writing. Address: 34 Bernard Street, Edinburgh, EH6 6PR.

Harris, Colonel Wesley. Territorial Commander for Scotland, Salvation Army, since 1982; b. 25.11.28, Cardiff; m., Margaret Sansom; 1 s.; 1 d. Educ. Clark's College, Cardiff. Commissioned as a Salvation Army Officer, 1948; worked in various parts of England, including Margate, Croydon and Exeter, followed by command of Regent Hall Corps, London; General Secretary, Salvation Army in Scotland, 1973-76; Chief Secretary, Salvation Army, Southern Australia, 1978-82; former Editor, The War Cry, and former Editor in Chief, all Salvation Army publications. Address: (b.) Houldsworth Street, Glasgow, G3 8DU; T.-041-221 3378.

Harrison, Anthony Frederick, CEng, FIEE, FIERE, FBIM. Director of Telecommunications, Scottish Office, since 1974; b. 20.2.29, Northampton; m., Doreen Caughlin; 1 s. Educ. Tollington Grammar School, London; Hendon Technical College. Began career in GPO, London and Dollis Hill Research Station; helped introduce first error-correcting radiotelegraph system;

joined MEL Equipment Ltd. as Project Manager, 1962; designed first GPO Data Test Set; joined Marconi Space and Defence as Project Group Manager, 1968; Leader, European Consortium, providing all electronics, communications and guidance for European Space Tug; Head of Telecommunications, Greater London Council, 1972-74. Address: (b.) St. Andrews House, Waterloo Place, Edinburgh, EH1 3DE; T.-031-556 8501.

Harrison, Bryan Desmond, BSc, PhD, FRSE. Head, Virology Division, Scottish Crop Research Institute, since 1984; b. 16.6.31, Purley, Surrey; m., Elizabeth Ann Latham-Warde; 2 s.; 1 d. Educ. Whitgift School, Croydon; Reading University. Agricultural Research Council Postgraduate Research Student, 1952-54; Scientific Officer, Scottish Horticultural Research Institute, 1954-57; Senior and Principal Scientific Officer, Rothamsted Experimental Station, 1957-66; Scottish Horticultural Research Institute/Scottish Crop Research Institute: Principal Scientific Officer, 1966, Senior Principal Scientific Officer (Individual Merit), 1969, Deputy Chief Scientific Officer (Individual Merit), 1981; Past President, Association of Applied Biologists. Recreation: gardening. Address: (b.) Scottish Crop Research Institute, Invergowrie, Dundee, DD2 5DA; T.-082 67731.

Harrison, Cameron, BSc (Hons), MEd. Rector, The Gordon Schools, Huntly, since 1982; b. 27.8.45, Mauchline, Ayrshire; m., Pearl; 1 s.; 1 d. Educ. Cumnock Academy; Strathclyde University; Glasgow University; Stirling University. Teacher, Greenock Academy, 1968-71; Principal Teacher of Physics, Graeme High School, Falkirk, 1971-79; Depute Rector, Kirkcudbright Academy, 1979-82; various involvements with SCEEB (now SEB) as setter etc. and with CCC Sub-Committees (Member, JWP on Higher Physics, 1976-79); Member, several research advisory committees; Chairman, Scottish Central Committee for Physical Education. Recreations: lay preacher; used to play rugby (still pretends to!); music; will admit, under pressure, to singing rather badly. Address: (h.) Kirkside, Cairney, Huntly, AB5 4TR; T.-0466 87207.

Harrison, Derek John, BSc, FICFor. Forestry Consultant and Valuer; Member, Red Deer Commission, since 1965; b. 11.6.26, Stoke Poges; m., Janet Leslie Mennie Kennedy; 2 s.; 1 d. Educ. Eastbourne College; Aberdeen University; Queens College, Cambridge. War Service, Fleet Air Arm; Assistant Superintendent, Somaliland Police; Woodlands Manager, Moray Estates Development Company, 1960-77; Fellow, Institute of Chartered Foresters. Recreations: sailing; shooting; stalking; fishing; prodding bureaucrats. Address: Cornhill, Ardgay, Ross-shire, IV24 3BP; T.-08632 319.

Harrison, Lloyd, BA (Oxon). Rector, Dollar Academy, since 1984; b. 4.8.34, Bradford; m., Moira Middlemas; 2 s.; 1 d. Educ. Bradford Grammar School; Queen's College, Oxford. Head of Classics: Trinity College, Glenalmond, 1960-68, Leeds Grammar School, 1968-70; Deputy Head, Colne Valley High School, 1970-75; Head: Steyning Grammar School, West Sussex,

1975-78, Northallerton Grammar School, 1979-84. Recreations: books; gardens; walking and running in lonely places. Address: (h.) 2 Academy Place, Dollar, Clackmannanshire; T.-025 94 2160.

Harrison, Sydney. Chairman, Gazette Group Newspapers, since 1963; Chairman, James Paton Ltd., Printers, since 1970; Editor, Scot, since 1981; b. 13.4.13, Glasgow; m., Joan Morris. Educ. Whitehill School, Glasgow. Journalist, various newspapers, 1927-37; Sub-Editor, Glasgow Herald, 1938-39; Army, 1939-46 (Lt.-Col., 1944); Editor, Scottish Field, 1946-63; Director, Scottish Counties Newspapers, 1950-63; Councillor, 4th District, Renfrewshire, 1956-67; Member, Council of Industrial Design, Board of Trade, 1955-65; Honorary Member, Scottish PEN; Member, Committee, National Trust Weavers Cottage, since 1960; Chairman, Renfrew District Arts Guild, 1978-81; President, Paisley Burns Club, 1984-85. Recreations: curling; motoring; caravanning. Address: (h.) Aviemore, Brookfield, Renfrewshire, PA5 8UG; T.-Johnstone 20634.

Hart, Dame Judith. MP (Labour), Clydesdale, since 1983 (Lanark, 1959-83); b. 1924. Educ. Royal Grammar School, Clitheroe; London School of Economics and London University. Under Secretary, Scottish Office, 1964-66; Minister of State, Commonwealth Office, 1966-67; Paymaster General, 1968-69; Minister of Overseas Development, 1969-70; Opposition Spokesman on Overseas Development, 1970-74; Minister for Overseas Development, 1974-75 and 1977-79; Opposition Spokesman on Overseas Development, 1979-80; Chairman, Labour Party, 1981-82.

Hart, Maidie (Jenny Marianne), MA (Hons). Founder President, Scottish Convention of Women, since 1981; Executive Member, Scottish Churches Council; Member, Church of Scotland Board of Communications; Member, Church of Scotland Board of World Mission and Unity; b. 15.12.16, Brookfield, Renfrewshire; m., William Douglas Hart; 2 d. Educ. St. Columba's School for Girls, Kilmacolm; St. Andrews University. Church of Scotland: Vice Convener, Home Board, 1967-70, National Vice-President, Woman's Guild, 1967-70, National President, Woman's Guild, 1972-75, Elder, since 1974; Executive Member, Women's National Commission, 1974-76; Member, Coordinating Committee, UK International Woman's Year, 1974-76 (Chairwoman, Scottish Steering Committee); first Chairwoman, Scottish Convention of Women, 1977; Vice President, British Council of Churches, 1978-81; Church of Scotland Delegate to World Council of Churches, 5th Assembly, 1975, WCC European Conference, 1978, WCC Human Rights and Mission Women's Conference, 1980, WCC Sheffield International Conference, 1981. Recreations: travel; walking; family; reading; garden; cooking. Address: (h.) 40 East Barnton Avenue, Edinburgh, EH4 6AQ; T.-031-336 3524.

Hart, Professor Ralph Thomas, BCom, MA, FSS, FBIM. Professor and Head of Business School, Robert Gordon's Institute of Technology, since 1970; Director, Wall Colmonoy Ltd.,

Pontardawe, South Wales, since 1964; Director, Aberdeen and District Milk Marketing Board, since 1979; b. 20.4.30, Newcastle-upon-Tyne; m., Hazel Margaret Norton; 2 s.; 1 d. Educ. Dame Allan's Boys' School; King's College, Durham; Strathclyde University. Industrial appointments, 1950-59, with Electricity Authority, Metal Box Co. Ltd. and National Coal Board; Lecturer, Municipal College of Commerce and Rutherford College of Technology, Newcastle, 1959-62; Senior Lecturer, Scottish Woollen Technical College, 1962-65; Head, Management Studies, Scottish College of Textiles, 1965-70; Dean, Faculty of Arts, Robert Gordon's Institute of Technology, 1974-79; Member: Board for Diploma in Commerce, since 1969; Scottish Business Education Council, 1973-85 (Chairman, Professional Studies Sector Committee); Member, various committees and boards, Council for National Academic Awards, 1973-83; Chairman, Appeals Committee, Aberdeen, Scottish Health Services, 1974; Member, MSC Training of Trainers Advisory Group, 1981-84. Recreations: fly fishing; tennis; Continental touring. Address: (h.) Grefsen House, Findon Village, Aberdeen; T.-Aberdeen 780330.

Harte, Ben, BA, MA, PhD (Cantab). Reader in Geology, Edinburgh University, since 1981; b. 30.5.41, Blackpool; m., Angela Elizabeth Kelly; 1 s.; 2 d. Educ. Salford Grammar School; Trinity College, Cambridge. Geology Department, Edinburgh University: Assistant Lecturer, 1965-67, Lecturer, 1967-81; Guest Investigator, Carnegie Institution of Washington, 1974-75; Visiting Associate Professor, Yale University, 1982. Vice-President, Edinburgh Geological Society, 1981-83; Chairman, Metamorphic Studies Group, Geological Society of London and Mineralogical Society of Great Britain and N. Ireland, 1983-85; Editor, Journal of Petrology, 1978-85. Recreations: sport (squash, tennis); joinery. Address: (b.) Grant Institute of Geology, West Mains Road, Edinburgh, EH9 3JW; T.-031-667 1081.

Hartnoll, Mary C., BA (Hons). Director of Social Work, Grampian Regional Council, since 1978; b. 31.5.39, Bristol. Educ. Colton's Girls School, Bristol; Bedford College, London University. Child Care Officer, Dorset County Council, 1961-63; various posts, Reading County Borough, 1963-74; Berkshire County Council: Assistant Director, 1974-75, Divisional Director, 1975-77. Member, Board of Directors: National Institute of Social Work, Northsound Radio. Recreations: natural history; walking. Address: (b.) Woodhill House, Ashgrove Road West, Aberdeen, AB9 2LU; T.-0224 682222, Ext. 2570.

Harvey, Alan L., BSc, PhD. Senior Lecturer in Physiology and Pharmacology, Strathclyde University, since 1983; b. 23.6.50, Glasgow. Educ. Hutchesons', Glasgow; Strathclyde University. Lecturer in Physiology and Pharmacology, Strathclyde University, 1974-83. British Pharmacological Society Sandoz Prize, 1983; British Pharmaceutical Conference Science Award, 1983. Publiation: The Pharmacology of Nerve and Muscle in Tissue Culture, 1984. Address: (b.) Department of Physiology and Pharmacology, Strathclyde University, Glasgow, G1 1XW; T.-041-552 4400.

Harvey, Jake, DA, ARSA. Sculptor; b. 3.6.48, Kelso; 1 s.; 2 d. Educ. Kelso High Secondary School; Edinburgh College of Art. Travelling Scholarship to Greece, Ægean Islands, Crete, 1971; ARSA, 1977; commissioned to make the Hugh MacDiarmid Memorial Sculpture, 1982; Lecturer in Sculpture; Trustee, Scottish Sculpture Trust. Recreation: fishing. Address: (h.) Maxton Cross, Maxton, St. Boswells, Roxburghshire; T.-0835 22650.

Harvey-Jamieson, Rodger Ridout, TD, LLB, WS, NP. Partner, Murray Beith & Murray, WS, since 1973; b. 30.6.47, Edinburgh; m., Alison Mary Whitworth; 1 s.; 1 d. Educ. Edinburgh Academy; Edinburgh University. Solicitor in private practice, since 1971; Committee Member, SSAFA East of Scotland Region; Trustee, The Seagull Trust; Member, Queen's Bodyguard for Scotland (Royal Company of Archers). Recreation: sailing. Address: (b.) 39 Castle Street, Edinburgh; T.-031-225 1200.

Harvie, John, MA (Hons). Headteacher, Claremont High School, since 1980; b. 17.8.33, Dalry, Ayrshire; m., Jean D.T. Wallace; 1 s.; 1 d. Educ. Dalry Senior Secondary School; Glasgow University. Teacher: Kilbirnie Junior Secondary School, 1959-61, Duncanrig Secondary School, East Kilbride, 1961-70; Claremont High School: Principal Teacher of Modern Languages, 1970-73, Head of Upper School, 1973-75; Headteacher, Rosehall High School, Coatbridge, 1975-80. Former Treasurer, East Kilbride Badminton League; Chairman, East Kilbride Headteachers Association; Committee Member, Torrance House Golf Club. Recreations: badminton; golf; watching football. Address: (h.) Murrayfield, 3 Clamps Grove, East Kilbride, Glasgow, G74 2EZ; T.-East Kilbride 21352.

Harwood, Raymond Jeffrey, BSc, PhD, CChem, FRSC. Vice Principal and Head, Department of Technology, Scottish College of Textiles; b. 14.11.40, Birmingham; m., Cynthia Mary; 3 s. Educ. Central Grammar School; Manchester University. Continuous career in education, since 1966; Joint Secretary, Salaries Committee, Central Institutions Academic Staff, 1976-78; Member, Academic Board, Napier College, since 1979; Director, Scottish Textile and Technical Centre, since 1984. Training Officer, Mountain Rescue Committee of Scotland, 1976-81. Recreations: mountaineering/mountain rescue. Address: (b.) Scottish College of Textiles, Galashiels, Selkirkshire, TD1 3HF; T.-0896 3351.

Haslett, Rev. William Larmour, MA. Minister, Newark Parish Church, Port Glasgow, since 1973; Moderator, Greenock Presbytery, 1984-85; b. 30.10.40, Belfast; m., Doris Isobel O'Neill; 2 s.; 1 d. Educ. Royal Belfast Academical Institution; Magee University College, Londonderry; Trinity College, Dublin; Presbyterian College, Belfast. Assistant Minister, Newtownbreda Presbyterian Church, Belfast, 1966-69; Minister, Downshire Road Presbyterian Church, Newry, Co. Down, 1969-73. Member, Port Glasgow School Council, since 1978; Fellowship in Continuing Education, Virginia Theological Seminary, 1968. Publication:

Newark Parish Church, Port Glasgow, Chronicles of Two Hundred Years 1774-1974, 1975. Recreations: puppetry (Member, Union Internationale de La Marionnette); reading; family. Address: Newark Parish Manse, Alderwood Road, Port Glasgow, PA14 5LE; T.-0475 41178.

Haughey, Douglas Paterson, BE (Hons), ME (Distn), PhD, CEng, FIChemE. Head, Engineering Department, Scottish Institute of Agricultural Engineering, since 1981; b. 5.10.40, Sydney; m., Edwina Anne; 1 s.; 1 d. Educ. Auckland Grammar School, New Zealand; Canterbury University, New Zealand; Edinburgh University. Divisional Head, Engineering, Meat Industry Research Institute of New Zealand, 1967-78; Process Development Manager, Laporte Industries Ltd., General Chemicals Division, 1978-81. Member, Solids Drying Group, Institution of Chemical Engineers. Publication: book on transportation of frozen meat in insulated containers. Recreations: house restoration; scripophily. Address: (b.) Scottish Institute of Agricultural Engineering, Bush Estate, Penicuik, Midlothian, EH26 OPH; T.-031-445 2147.

Havergal, Giles. Director, Citizens' Theatre, Glasgow, since 1969; b. 9.6.38. Artistic Director, Palace Theatre, Watford, 1966-68.

Hawkins, Anthony Donald, BSc, PhD, FSA Scot. Deputy Director of Fisheries Research for Scotland, since 1983; b. 25.3.42, Dorset; m., Susan Mary; 1 s. Educ. Poole Grammar School; Bristol University. Entered Scottish Office as Scientific Officer, Marine Laboratory, Aberdeen, 1965; Senior Scientific Officer, 1969, Principal Scientific Officer, 1972, Senior Principal Scientific Officer, 1978, Deputy Chief Scientific Officer, 1983, responsible to the Director of Fisheries Research for management of Marine Laboratory, Aberdeen, and Freshwater Fisheries Laboratory, Pitlochry; conducts research into behaviour and physiology of fish; awarded A.B. Wood Medal, Institute of Acoustics, 1978; Honorary Lecturer in Marine Biology, St. Andrews University. Publications: books on fish physiology and aquarium systems. Recreations: reading; angling; soccer; breeding whippets. Address: (b.) Marine Laboratory, PO Box 101, Victoria Road, Torry, Aberdeen; T.-0224 876544.

Haworth, John Roger, BA (Hons), RTPI. Director of Planning and Development, Western Isles Council, since 1974; b. 4.2.46, Worsley, Manchester; m., Margaret; 2 s.; 1 d. Educ. Bolton School; Manchester University. Planning Assistant, Stirling County Council, 1968-71; Ross and Cromarty County Council: Assistant Planning Officer, 1971-73, Assistant Planning Officer (Western Isles), 1973-74. Recreations: reading; music; films; history; travel. Address: (b.) Council Offices, Sandwick Road, Stornoway, PA82 2BW; T.-0851 3773, Ext. 490.

Hay, Alan, FSA Scot. Genealogist and Record Agent; Council Member, Royal Celtic Society, since 1984; Council Member, Scottish Tartans Soiety, since 1984 (Honorary Secretary, since 1985); b. 26.9.62, Ellon, Aberdeenshire.

Freelance Genealogist, 1982; Consultant, Burke's Peerage, 1984; Niadh Nask, 1984; Genealogist and Archivist, Clan Hay, 1983. Recreations: climbing; shooting; squash; heraldry. Address: (h.) 6 Scott Terrace, Belhelvie, Aberdeen, AB4 0YT; T.-Balmedie 3424.

Hay, John Crawford, MA, LLB. Solicitor, since 1935; Honorary Sheriff, since 1971; b. 8.5.10, Mauchline, Ayrshire; m., Jean Primrose Wright; 1 s.; 2 d. Educ. Ayr Academy; Glasgow University. War service, Royal Corps of Signals, GHQ India (final rank, Major); former Member, Medical Executive Council of Ayrshire and Southern Ayrshire Hospitals Board; former Vice President, Saltire Society (and former Secretary, Ayr Branch). Recreations: Scottish country dancing; encouraging good standards in maintaining buildings, old and new, street furniture, lamp posts, trees in streets, and general tidy-ness; music; gardening. Address: (h.) Brownhill, 63 Midton Road, Ayr, KA7 2TN; T.-0292 262078.

Hay, John McWhirter. Sheriff Clerk and Auditor of Court, Dunfermline, since 1980; b. 27.4.43, Glasgow; m., Mary Wilkie Munro; 3 d. Educ. Clydebank High School. Clerical Officer: Glasgow Sheriff Court, 1960-63; Dumbarton Sheriff Court, 1963-65; Second Class Depute, Glasgow Sheriff Court, 1965-71; First Class Depute, Ayr Sheriff Court, 1971-80. Captain, Troon St. Meddans Golf Club, 1975; Match Secretary, Dunfermline Golf Club, 1981-83. Recreations: versatile sportsman, first love golf (single figure handicap, since 1972). Address: (b.) Sheriff Clerk's Office, 1/6 Carnegie Drive, Dunfermline, Fife; T.-Dunfermline 724666.

Hay, Professor Robert Walker, BSc, PhD, CChem, FRSC, FRSE. Professor of Chemistry, Stirling University, since 1984; b. 17.9.34, Stirling; m., Alison Laird; 1 s.; 3 d. Educ. Stirling High School; Glasgow University. Assistant Lecturer, Glasgow University, 1959; subsequently worked at Esso Research; Lecturer, Senior Lecturer and Reader, Victoria University, Wellington, New Zealand, 1961; Reader, Stirling University, 1971. Publications: Bioinorganic Chemistry, 1984; numerous scientific papers. Recreations: walking; travel; caravanning; reading. Address: (b.) Chemistry Department, Stirling University, Stirling, FK9 4LA; T.-0786 73171.

Hay, William Flett, MBE. President, Scottish Fishermen's Federation, since 1982; Member, Sea Fish Industry Authority, since 1983; b. 7.10.29, Findochty; m., Sheila Reid; 1 s.; 1 d. Educ. Portsoy School. Took up sea going career in the fishing industry at the age of 14; took command of own vessel, 1954; retired from active sea going career, 1984; Chairman, Scottish White Fish Producers' Association, 1976-82. Recreation: bowling. Address: (h.) Mara Vista, Marine Terrace, Portsoy, Banffshire; T.-0261 42454.

Hayes, Sir John Osler Chattock, KCB, OBE. Lord Lieutenant of Ross and Cromarty, Skye and Lochalsh, since 1977; Deputy Chairman, Gordonstoun School, since 1977; b. 9.5.13; m.,

Hon. Rosalind Mary Finlay; 2 s.; 1 d. Educ. Royal Naval College, Dartmouth. War service, 1939-45, Atlantic/HMS Repulse/Singapore/Russian Convoys/Malta; Real Admiral, Naval Secretary to First Lord of Admiralty, 1962-64; Vice Admiral/Rear Admiral, Flag Officer 2nd in command Western Fleet, 1964-66; Vice Admiral, Flag Officer Scotland and Northern Ireland, 1966-68; Member, Queen's Bodyguard for Scotland (Royal Company of Archers), since 1969; President, King George's Fund for Sailors, Scotland, 1968-79; Vice Patron, Royal National Mission for Deep Sea Fishermen, since 1968. Recreations: music; writing; walking. Address: (h.) Arabella House, by Tain, Ross and Cromarty, IV19 1QJ; T.-Nigg Station 293.

Haynes, Dorothy Kate. Writer; b. 12.10.18, Lanark; m., John S. Gray; 2 s. Educ. Lanark Grammar School; St. Margaret's Episcopal School, Aberlour. Member, Lanark Town Council, 1972-75. Winner, Tom Gallon Award, 1947; Winner, SAWC Constable Trophy; many short stories published and broadcast; regular writer for Scots Magazine. Publications: (novels) Winter's Traces; Robin Ritchie; The Gibsons of Glasgow; (short stories): Thou Shalt not Suffer a Witch; Peacocks and Pagodas; (autobiography): Haste ye Back. Recreations: singing; reading. Address: (h.) 14 Quarryknowe, Lanark, ML11 7AH; T.-0555 3834.

Hayward, Richard Scott, BSc, PhD. Senior Lecturer in Molecular Biology, Edinburgh University, since 1979; b. 30.10.35, Belfast; m., Mary Eileen Byrne; 2 s.; 1 d. Educ. Newtown School, Waterford; Campbell College, Belfast; Queen's University, Belfast. Instructor in Biochemistry, Argonne Cancer Research Hospital, Chicago University, 1962-66; Member, Microbial Genetics (later Molecular Genetics) Research Unit, Medical Research Council, Hammersmith Hospital, London, then Edinburgh University, 1966-74; Edinburgh University: Honorary Research Fellow, 1974-77, Lecturer, Department of Molecular Biology, 1977-79. Former Treasurer and Secretary, Morningside Ward (later Churchill-Braid), Labour Party. Recreations: being in the country; DIY; research; theatregoing. Address: (b.) Department of Molecular Biology, Edinburgh University, Mayfield Road, Edinburgh, EH9 3JR; T.-031-667 1081, Ext. 2884.

Heading, Robert Campbell, BSc, MD, FRCP. Consultant Physician, Edinburgh Royal Infirmary, since 1975; Senior Lecturer in Medicine, Edinburgh University, since 1975; b. 3.7.41, Stepps, Lanarkshire; m., Patricia Mary Goldie; 2 s.; 1 d. Educ. Birkenhead School; King Edward's School, Birmingham; Edinburgh University. Vice Chairman, Medical Staff Committee, Edinburgh Royal Infirmary, since 1983. Address: (h.) 38 Frogston Road West, Edinburgh, EH10 7AJ; T.-031-445 1552.

Healy, Sister Angela Mary, BA (Hons), CertEd, DipTh. Headmistress, Kilgraston Boarding and Day School for Girls, Bridge of Earn, since 1982; b. 28.12.24, Wexford, Ireland. Educ. Convent of the Sacred Heart, Roscrea, Ireland; Open University; London University. Entered

Society of the Sacred Heart, 1943; student, 1945-47; Montessori Teacher, 1947-53; Kilgraston School: Mistress of Discipline, 1953-60, Deputy Headmistress, 1960-68; Assistant Headmistress, Mount Anville School, 1968-71; Dean of Residence, Convent School, Armagh, 1971-74; Open University studies, 1974-75; Senior Mistress (Acting Deputy Head, one year), St. Catherine's College, Armagh, N. Ireland, 1976-81; sabbatical year studying clinical pastoral education, Andover Newton College, Boston, USA, 1981-82. Member, General Teaching Council. Recreations: yoga; walking; reading. Address: Convent of the Sacred Heart, Kilgraston, Bridge of Earn, Perth; T.-0738 812973.

Healy, Raymond Michael, BSc. Rector, Our Lady's High School, Cumbernauld, since 1976; b. 8.7.40, Glasgow; m., Margaret Bradburn; 2 s. Educ. St. Aloysius College, Glasgow; Glasgow University; Jordanhill College of Education. Research Department: Babcock & Wilcox Ltd., Renfrew, 1961-62, Sandeman Bros., Glasow, 1962-63; Teacher: St. Margaret Mary's Secondary School,Glasgow, 1964-65, St. Aloysius College, Glasgow, 1965-69; Principal Teacher of Chemistry, St. Aloysius College, Glasgow, 1969-72; Assistant Headteacher, St. Andrew's High School, Clydebank, 1972-74; Depute Headteacher, St. Patrick's High School, Dumbarton, 1974-76. Member, Scottish Central Committee on Science, 1978-81. Recreation: golf. Address: (b.) Our Lady's High School, Downfield Road, Cumbernauld, G67 1LA.

Heaney, Henry Joseph, MA, FLA. University Librarian and Keeper of the Hunterian Books and MSS, Glasgow University, since 1978; b. 2.1.35, Newry, Northern Ireland; m., Mary Elizabeth Moloney. Educ. Abbey Grammar School, Newry; Queen's University, Belfast. Assistant Librarian, Queen's University, Belfast, 1959-62; Librarian, Magee University College, Londonderry, 1962-67; Deputy Librarian, New University of Ulster, 1967-69; Assistant Secretary, Standing Conference of National and University Libraries, 1969-72; Librarian: Queen's University, Belfast, 1972-74, University College, Dublin, 1975-78. Member, Advisory Committee on Public Library Service, Northern Ireland, 1965; Chairman, NI Branch, Library Association, 1966, 1973; Trustee, National Library of Scotland, since 1980; Chairman, British Library Ad Hoc Working Party on Union Catalogues, 1982; Member, British Library Reference Division Advisory Committee, since 1982; Member, British Library Lending Division Advisory Committee, since 1983; Member, British Eighteenth Century Short Title Catalogue Committee, since 1983. Address: (b.) Glasgow University Library, Hillhead Street, Glasgow, G12 8QE; T.-041-334 2122.

Hearne, John Michael, BMus, MMus. Chairman, Scottish Society of Composers, since 1980; Professional Singer (Bass Baritone); Lecturer, Aberdeen College of Education, since 1970; b. 19.9.37, Reading; m., Margaret Gillespie Jarvie. Educ. Torquay Grammar School; St. Luke's College, Exeter; University College of Wales, Aberystwyth. Teaching, Rugeley, Staffordshire,

1959-60; Warehouseman/Driver, Torquay, 1961-64; Teaching: Tonlistarskoli Borgarfjardar, Iceland, 1968-69, UCW Aberystwyth, 1969-70; Composer, vocal, instrumental and incidental music; Member, John Currie Singers; McEwen Commission, Glasgow University, 1979; President, Garioch Lions Club, 1984-85; Chorus Manager, Aberdeen International Youth Festival, since 1978; won Radio Forth Trophy, 1985, for most outstanding work on Edinburgh Festival Fringe. Recreations: motoring and travel (1954 Daimler Roadster). Address: (h.) Smidskot, Fawells, Keith-Hall, Inverurie, AB5 OLN; T.-065 182 274.

Heasman, Michael Anthony, FRCPEdin, FFCM, DPH. Director, Information Services Division, Scottish Health Service, Common Services Agency, since 1974; Expert in Health Statistics, World Health Organisation, since 1965; Honorary Senior Lecturer, Department of Community Medicine, Edinburgh University, since 1976; b. 9.9.26, Colchester; m., Barbara Nelly Stevens; 1 s.; 1 d. Educ. Felsted School; St. Mary's Hospital, London University. RAF Medical Branch, 1948-53; Research Fellowships, London School of Hygiene, 1954-56; Medical Statistician, General Register Office, London, 1956-61; Senior Medical Officer, Ministry of Health, 1961-65; Principal Medical Officer, Scottish Home and Health Department, 1965-74. Recreations: hill-walking; literature. Address: (h.) 1 Monkrigg Steading, Haddington, East Lothian, EH41 4LB; T.-062 082 3516.

Heatley, George Weir Scott, LLB, NP. Solicitor, since 1974; Director, Thomas J. Walls Limited, since 1980; b. 5.4.48, Glasgow; m., Margaret Elliot Ritchie; 1 s.; 1 d. Educ. Annan Academy; Rickerby House School; Fettes College; Aberdeen University. Address: (b.) 28 Rutland Square, Edinburgh, EH1 2BX; T.-031-229 3535.

Heatly, Peter, CBE, DL, BSc, CEng, FICE. Chairman, Peter Heatly & Co. Ltd., since 1958; Chairman, Scottish Sports Council, since 1975; Chairman, Commonwealth Games Federation, since 1982; b. 9.6.24, Edinburgh; m., Mae Calder Cochrane. Educ. Leith Academy; Edinburgh University. Structural Designer, Redpath Brown & Co. Ltd., 1946; Lecturer in Civil Engineering, Edinburgh University, 1948. Chairman, International Diving Committee. Recreations: swimming; gardening; travel. Address: (h.) Lanrig, Balerno, Edinburgh, EH14 7AJ; T.-031-449 3998.

Hector, Gordon Matthews, CMG (1966), CBE (1961), MA (Oxon). Chairman, Scottish Council, Victoria League; Vice President, The St. Andrew Society; Secretary to Assembly Council, General Assembly of Church of Scotland, 1980-85; b. 9.6.18, Aberdeen; m., Dr. Mary Forrest Gray; 1 s.; 2 d. Educ. St. Mary's School, Melrose; Edinburgh Academy; Lincoln College, Oxford. HM Colonial Administrative Service and Overseas Civil Service, 1946-66: District Commissioner, Kenya, Secretary, Kenya Road Authority, Secretary to Government of Seychelles, 1952-55, Acting Governor, 1953, Deputy Resident Commissioner and Government Secretary, Basutoland (now Lesotho), 1956-64,

Deputy British Government Representative, Lesotho, 1965-66; Aberdeen University: Clerk to University Court, 1967, Deputy Secretary, 1976-80. OBE, 1955. Fellow, Commonwealth Fund, 1939; Burgess of Guild, Aberdeen; elected Member, West End Community Council, Edinburgh; Court of Directors, Edinburgh Academy, 1967-75; Member, Board of Managers, Oakbank List D School. Recreations: town and country walking; railways ancient and modern; grandchildren. Address: (h.) 18 Magdala Crescent, Edinburgh, EH12 5BD; T.-031-346 2317.

Hedley, Professor Anthony Johnson, MB, ChB, MD, DipSocMed, MRCP, MFCM, FRCPEdin, FFCM, HonMD (Khon Kaen, Thailand). Henry Mechan Professor of Public Health, Glasgow University, since 1983; b. 8.4.41, Greenmount, Lancashire; m., Elizabeth-Anne Walsh. Educ. Rydal; Aberdeen University; Edinburgh University. Research Fellow in Materia Medica, Aberdeen University, 1966-69; Honorary Assistant and Registrar in Therapeutics and Pharmacology, Dundee University, 1969-72; Fellow in Community Medicine, Scottish Health Service, 1972-74; Lecturer in Community Medicine, Aberdeen University, 1974-76; Senior Lecturer in Community Health, Nottingham University, 1976-83; Medical Adviser, Faculties of Medicine and Public Health, University of Khon Kaen, Thailand. Recreations: running; target shooting; photography. Address: (b.) Department of Community Medicine, Glasgow University, Glasgow, G12 8QQ; T.-041-339 8855.

Heller, Martin Fuller Vernon. Actor, since 1947; b. 20.2.27, Manchester; m., Joyce Allan; 2 s.; 4 d. Educ. Rondebosch Boys High School, Cape Town; Central School of Speech Training and Dramatic Art, London. Compass Players, 1948-52; repertory seasons and/or individual productions at following Scottish theatres: St. Andrews Byre, Edinburgh Gateway, Glasgow Citizens' (eight seasons), Edinburgh Royal Lyceum, Edinburgh Traverse, Dundee Repertory, Perth Repertory, Pitlochry Festival; appeared in England at Morecambe, Preston, Carlisle, Birmingham, Coventry, Leicester and Hammersmith; extensive television and radio work; directed two plays for Dundee Repertory Theatre and a programme, Edinburgh - The Golden Age, for The Lamp of Lothian, Haddington, and later for the Lyceum Theatre, Edinburgh. Equity: Member, Scottish Committee, 15 years, National Council, three times; Member, Scottish Arts Council, 1975-82 (latterly Chairman, Drama Committee); Board Member, Scottish Youth Theatre; Observer, Board, Royal Lyceum Theatre; Board Member, Pitlochry Festival Theatre; Governor, Royal Scottish Academy of Music and Drama, since 1982. Recreations: politics; history; listening to music. Address: (h.) 54 Hermiston, Currie, Midlothian, EH14 4AQ; T.-031-449 4055.

Hemingway, Professor R. Gordon, MSc, PhD, FIBiol. Professor of Animal Husbandry, Glasgow University Veterinary School, since 1969; b. 6.4.25, Sheffield; m., Dorothy E. Adam; 2 d. Educ. King Edward VII School, Sheffield; Leeds University. Ministry of Agriculture and Fisheries, 1946-48; Royal Agricultural College, Cirencester, 1948-53; joined Glasgow University, 1953. Past Chairman: Agriculture Group, Society of Chemical Industry, Scottish Group, Nutrition Society. Recreations: golf; gardening; grandchildren. Address: (h.) 12 Westbourne Crescent, Bearsden, Glasgow; T.-041-942 8321.

Henderson, Andrew Kerr, MB, ChB, FRCP. Consultant Physician, County Hospital, Oban, since 1977; Postgraduate Tutor in Medicine, since 1980; Honorary Clinical Lecturer, Glasgow University, since 1981; b. 1.3.46, Hawick; m., Doreen Innes Wilkinson; 1 s.; 2 d. Educ. Glasgow Academy; Glasgow University. Medical Registrar, Western Infirmary, Glasgow; Medical Registrar/Senior Registrar, Glasgow Royal Infirmary. Chairman, Counties Branch, Scottish Schoolboys' Club. Recreations: gardening; hill-walking. Address: (h.) Birkmoss, North Connel, Argyll; T.-Connel 379.

Henderson, Douglas John, BA. Organiser, General, Municipal, Boilermakers & Allied Trades Union, since 1977; Member, Executive, Scottish Council of the Labour Party, since 1979 (Chairman, Scottish Council, 1984-85); b. 9.6.49, Edinburgh; m., Janet Margaret Graham. Educ. Waid Academy, Anstruther; Strathclyde University. Employed by Rolls Royce, 1966-67; British Rail, 1968; joined GMWU, 1973 (became GMBATU, 1983); Member, Knitting Economic Development Committee, NEDO; Workers' Leader, Rope, Twine and Net Wages Council. Recreations: mountaineering; cross-country skiing; athletics. Address: (h.) 145 Balshagray Avenue, Glasgow, G11; T.-041-954 4023.

Henderson, Douglas Mackay, FRSE, FLS. Regius Keeper, Royal Botanic Garden, Edinburgh, since 1970; b. 30.8.27; m.; 1 s.; 2 d. Educ. Blairgowrie High School; Edinburgh University. Joined Royal Botanic Garden, Edinburgh, 1951; Honorary Professor, Edinburgh University, since 1983.

Henderson, Elizabeth Kidd, MA (Hons), MEd (Hons). Headmistress, Westbourne School, since 1970; b. 25.5.28, Dunfermline. Educ. Dunfermline High School; Edinburgh University; St. Andrews University. Mathematics Teacher, Morrison's Academy, Crieff; Second Master, Mathematics, Dundee High School; Principal Teacher of Mathematics, Aberdeen High School; former Secretary, Mathematics Panel, Scottish Examination Board; President, Scottish Area, Secondary Heads Association; President, Glasgow Mathematical Association. Vice-Chairman, Community Council. Publication: Modern Mathematics for Schools (Co-author). Recreations: walking; golf. Address: (b.) Westbourne School, 1 Winton Drive, Glasgow, G12 OPY; T.-041-339 6006.

Henderson, Rt. Rev. George Kennedy Buchanan, MBE, BA, JP. Bishop of Argyll and the Isles, since 1977; b. 5.12.21, Oban; m., Isobel Fergusson Bowman. Educ. Oban High School; Durham University. Assistant Curate, Christ Church, Glasgow, 1943-48; Chaplain, Bishop of Argyll and the Isles, 1948-50; Rector,

St. Andrew's, Fort William, 1950-77; Canon, St. John's Cathedral, Oban, 1962; Dean of Argyll, 1974. Honorary Burgess of Fort William, 1972; Honorary Sheriff, 1974. Address: Bishop's House, Fort William, PH33 6HD; T.-Fort William 4230.

Henderson, Rev. Grahame McLaren, BD. Minister, Glengarry linked with Kilmonivaig, since 1974; b. 10.6.43, Aberdeen; m., Kathleen Munro Moir; 1 s.; 1 d. Educ. Robert Gordon's College, Aberdeen; Aberdeen University; Edinburgh University. David Henderson (Jewellers) Ltd., Aberdeen, 1959-66; Probationer Assistant, Kirknewton and East Calder, 1973-74. Chairman, Lochaber High School, 1979-82; Moderator, Lochaber Presbytery, 1979-80; Moderator, Synod of South Highlands, 1980-82. Recreations: ship cruising; caravanning. Address: Kilmonivaig Manse, Spean Bridge, Inverness-shire, PH34 4DX; T.-0397 81 244.

Henderson, Iain, BA, LLB. Procurator Fiscal, Campbeltown; b. 20.12.39, Lochaber; m., Margaret Lydia. Address: (b.) Sheriff Court, Castlehill, Campbeltown, Argyll; T.-0586 53383.

Henderson, (James Stewart) Barry, MBCS. MP (Conservative), North East Fife, since 1983 (East Fife, 1979-83, East Dunbartonshire, February to October, 1974); Management Consultant, since 1976; b. 29.4.36, Kirkcaldy; m., Janet; 2 s. Educ. Lathallan and Stowe Schools. National Service, Scots Guards, 1954-56; employed in electronics and computer industry, 1957-66 and 1970-75; Information Officer, Scottish Conservative Party, 1966-70; Member: Select Committee on Scottish Affairs, since 1980, Parliamentary Information Technology Committee, since 1981, Chairman's Panel, 1981-83; Chairman, Scottish Conservative Members Committee, 1983-84; Parliamentary Private Secretary to Treasury Minister, since 1984. Address: (h.) Old Gillingshill, by Anstruther, Fife.

Henderson, John, RIBA, ARIAS. Director of Architecture, Dumfries and Galloway Regional Council, since 1979; b. 22.12.31. Educ. School of Architecture, Dundee. Architect's Department, Bank of Scotland, 1956-61; Dumfries County Council: Principal Assistant, 1961-70, Depute County Architect, 1971-73; Assistant to Chief Executive, Dumfries and Galloway Regional Council, 1974-79. Address: (b.) Park House, 2 Annan Road, Dumfries; T.-0387 63933.

Henderson, John Harley, JP. Member, City of Dundee District Council, since 1974 (Convener of Housing, since 1984); Teacher of Mathematics, St. John's High School, Dundee, since 1976; b. 17.8.41, Dundee; m., Peggy Henderson; 1 s.; 1 d. Educ. Lawside Academy, Dundee; Dundee College of Technology. Former Divisional Council Secretary, AUEW-TASS; Dundee District Council: former Secretary and Leader, Administration Group, former Convener of Cleansing, former Convener of Planning and Development; Member, Housing Committee, COSLA; Member, Board of Governors, Dundee College of Technology. Address (h.) 24 Burrelton Gardens, Dundee; T.-0382 811982.

Henderson, Admiral Sir Nigel Stuart, GBE (1968), KCB (1962), DL. President, Royal British Legion, Scotland, 1974-80; Deputy Lieutenant, Stewartry of Kirkcudbright, since 1973; b. 1.8.09; m.; 1 s.; 2 d. Educ. Cheltenham College. Director-General of Training, Admiralty, 1960-62; C-in-C Plymouth, 1962-65; Admiral, 1963; Head of British Defence Staffs, Washington and UK Representative, Military Committee, NATO, 1965-68; Chairman, Military Committee, NATO, 1968-71.

Henderson, Rev. Robert John, DSO, MA, BD, FSA Scot. Minister, Cairneyhill and Limekilns, since 1984; b. 5.5.25, Edinburgh; m., 1, Margaret Grace Raddall (deceased); 2, Charlotte McKenzie Clunie; 2 s.; 2 d. Educ. George Heriot's School, Edinburgh; Edinburgh University and New College. Served Black Watch and Parachute Regiment, 1943-47; wounded and decorated as Lt., 1945; Student Assistant to Selby Wright, Canongate; Probationer Assistant to David Orr, Burntisland St. Columba's; Minister: Drumchapel St. Mark's (Church Extension), Elgin St. Giles, Melrose St. Cuthbert's; Past Chairman, Roxburgh Children's Panel Advisory Committee. Publication: Life in Bible Times (Co-author), 1967. Recreations: rugby; hill-walking; malt whisky tasting; country dancing. Address: 10 Church Street, Limekilns, Fife, KY11 3HT; T.-Limekilns 872341.

Henderson, Thomas Wilson. Director, John Turnbull & Sons Ltd., Hawick, since 1983; Member, Ettrick and Lauderdale District Council, since 1974; Honorary Provost of Selkirk, since 1978; b. 28.9.41, Selkirk; m., Catherine Helen Herbert; 2 s. Educ. Selkirk Public School; Selkirk High School; Scottish College of Textiles; Paisley College of Technology. Served apprenticeship as dyer with George Roberts & Co. Ltd., Selkirk, 1957-61; Dyer, 1961-78; Assistant Manager, John Turnbull & Sons Ltd., Hawick, 1978-83; involved in management buy-out, 1983; Member, Selkirk Town Council, 1973-75; Corporate Member, Society of Dyers and Colourists; holder of various offices, Transport and General Workers Union, since 1970; Organiser, Scottish National Party, Ayr Constituency, 1967-70. Recreations: hill-walking; horse-riding; reading; folk music; jazz; football; cricket. Address: (h.) Raehurst, 1 Raeburn Meadow, Selkirk; T.-0750 20821.

Henderson, Sheriff William Crichton, MA, LLB. Sheriff of Tayside, Central and Fife, at Stirling, since 1972; b. 10.6.31; m.; 2 d. Educ. George Watson's Boys' College; Edinburgh University. Solicitor, 1954; called to Scottish Bar, 1957; practised as Advocate, 1957-68; Sheriff of Renfrew and Argyll, at Paisley, 1968-72; Chairman, Supreme Court Legal Aid Committee, 1967-68.

Henderson, William Leonard Edgar, BSc (Hons). Principal, Falkirk College of Technology, since 1984; b. 9.5.39, Kilmarnock; m., Janette Anne; 2 d. Educ. Camphill School, Paisley; London University. Lecturer, Engineering and Associated Subjects, Anniesland College, 1966-68; Lecturer, Engineering Subjects, Stow College/Glasgow College of Technology, 1968-70; Senior Lecturer in Engineering, Anniesland College, 1970-74;

Head, Department of Science and Mathematics, Cardonald College, 1974-77; Depute Principal, Kingsway Technical College, Dundee, 1977-84; Member, Council for Tertiary Education in Scotland, 1979-83; Member/Convener, Mathematics Panel, SCEEB, 1975-81. Recreations: walking; microelectronics. Address: (b.) Falkirk College of Technology, Grangemouth Road, Falkirk, FK2 9AD; T.-0324 24981.

Henderson, William Ross, TD. Director, Scottish Conservative Party, since 1984; b. 15.9.36, Sunderland; m., Valerie Helen Thomas; 1 s.; 1 d. Educ. Argyle House School, Sunderland. National Service, RAMC and RAOC, 1958-60 (Commissioned); Agent and Secretary, Newcastle-upon-Tyne West Conservative and Unionist Association, 1961-68; Deputy Central Office Agent, Greater London Area, 1968-76; Conservative Party Training Officer, 1976-79; Central Office Agent, East of England Area, 1980-84. Recreations: gardening; reading; Territorial Army. Address: (b.) 3 Chester Street, Edinburgh, 3; T.-031-226 4426.

Hendrie, Eric. Deputy Leader, Labour Group, Grampian Regional Council, since 1978 (Education Spokesperson, Labour Group, since 1978); b. 11.9.25, Glasgow; m., Isabel; 1 s.; 1 d. Educ. Lambhill School, Glasgow; Royal Technical College, Glasgow. Councillor: Aberdeen Corporation, 1970-75; Grampian Regional Council, since 1975. Address: (h.) 37 New Park Road, Aberdeen, AB2 6UT; T.-0224 691723.

Hendry, Professor Arnold William, BSc, PhD, DSc, FICE, FIStructE, FRSE. Professor of Civil Engineering, Edinburgh University, since 1964; b. 10.9.21, Buckie; m., Elizabeth Lois Alice Inglis; 1 s.; 1 d. Educ. Buckie High School; Aberdeen University. Assistant Civil Engineer, Sir William Arrol & Co. Ltd., Glasgow, 1941-43; Lecturer in Civil Engineering, Aberdeen University, 1943-49; Reader in Civil Engineering, King's College, London, 1949-51; Professor of Civil Engineering and Dean, Faculty of Engineering, Khartoum University, 1951-57; Professor of Building Science, Liverpool University, 1957-63. Recreations: walking; DIY; bird-watching. Address: (h.) 2 Castlelaw Road, Edinburgh, EH13 ODN; T.-031-441 4141.

Hendry, Joy McLaggan, MA (Hons), DipEd. Editor, Chapman Magazine, since 1972; Writer; b. 3.2.53, Perth. Educ. Perth Academy; Edinburgh University. Former teacher; Co-Editor, Chapman, 1972-76, Sole Editor, since 1976; Deputy Convener, Scottish Poetry Library Association; Member, Committee for the Advancement of Scottish Literature in Schools; writes poetry; gives lectures and talks and performances of poetry and song. Publications: Scots: The Way Forward; The Cart of Gold; Critical Essays on Sorley MacLean (Co-Editor), in press. Recreations: going to theatre; cinema; reading. Address: 35 East Claremont Street, Edinburgh, EH7 4HT; T.-031-556 5863.

Hendry, Leo Brough, MSc, MEd, PhD, FBPS. Senior Lecturer in Education, Aberdeen University, since 1978; b. 12.11.35, Glasgow; m., Philomena Walsh; 2 d. Educ. Hermitage Academy, Helensburgh; Jordanhill College of Education, Glasgow; Bradford University; Leicester University; Aberdeen University. School Teacher in Scottish and English schools, including two posts as Head of Department, 1957-64; Lecturer in Education and Physical Education, College of St. Mark and St. John's, Chelsea, London University Institute, 1964-66; Head of Human Movement Studies, Trinity and All Saints' Colleges, Leeds University Institute, 1966-71; Lecturer in Education, Aberdeen University, 1971-78. Member, Scottish Council for Research in Education. Publications: School, Sport, Leisure: three dimensions of adolescence, 1978; Adolescents and Leisure, 1981; Growing Up and Going Out, 1983; Personality and Performance in Physical Education and Sport (Co-author), 1974; Physical Education in England (Co-author), 1976; Towards Community Education (Co-author), 1980. Recreations: golf; writing; broadcasting; presenting papers at international conferences! Address: (b.) Department of Education, Aberdeen University, Aberdeen, AB9 2UB; T.-0224 40241, Ext. 6588.

Henriksen, Henry Neil, BSc, MEd. Rector, The James Young High School, since 1982; b. 2.9.33, Edinburgh; m., Edith Robb; 2 s. Educ. Royal High School, Edinburgh; Edinburgh University; Strathclyde University. Taught at Portobello, Falkirk High, Forrester; Depute Head, Penicuik High School. Recreations: television; climbing Allermuir. Address: (h.) 16 Redford Loan, Edinburgh, EH13 OAX; T.-031-441 2282.

Henry, Alastair William. Farmer, since 1952; Member, Grampian Regional Council, since 1982; b. 14.5.29, Laurencekirk; m., Olive Margaret Chaplin; 1 d. Educ. Montrose Academy. British Red Cross: Director, Kincardine and Deeside Branch, 1973-82, Council Member, Scotland, since 1974; North Angus & Mearns Conservative Association: Chairman, 1974-77, President, 1977-80; Chairman, NE Scotland Conservative Euro Constituency, 1978-81; Vice President, Scottish Conservative & Unionist Association, 1981-83; Chairman, Kincardine and Deeside Members Centre, National Trust for Scotland, 1980-82; Governor, Royal Aberdeen Workshops for the Blind, since 1982; Director, Haven Products Ltd. (Sheltered Workshops), since 1979; Elder, Church of Scotland, since 1960. Recreations: politics; gardening. Address: Hatton, Laurencekirk, Kincardineshire; T.-067 484 202.

Henry, Elizabeth Hamilton, MA, DipEd, FESB, LRAM, LGSM. Regional Officer for Scotland, English Speaking Board, since 1984; Member, City of Aberdeen District Council, since 1977; Proprietor, Children's Day Care Centre, since 1970; b. 16.3.27, Glasgow. Educ. Hutchesons' Girls' Grammar School; Glasgow University; Aberdeen University. Taught English in Gorbals, 1948-51; peripatetic Teacher of Speech and Drama, Dunbartonshire, 1951-53; Principal Lecturer in Speech and Drama, Aberdeen College of Education, 1954-70; President, Soroptimist International of Aberdeen, 1963-64 and 1977-79;

President-elect, Divisional Union of Scotland North, Soroptimist International of Great Britain and Ireland; Senior Examiner, English Speaking Board, since 1960; Aberdeen Chairman, International Year of the Child, 1979; Member, Aberdeen Committee, United Nations Association. Recreations: reading; music; theatre; walking with dog. Address: (h.) 23 Kingshill Road, Aberdeen, AB2 4JY; T.-0224 314855.

Henry, Gordon Edward, DA, MSIAD. Director of Development and Tourism, Aberdeen City Council, since 1977; b. 23.9.37, Elgin; m., Elizabeth Browne; 2 s. Educ. Elgin Academy; Grays School of Art; Aberdeen College of Education. Art Teacher, Lecturer and Freelance Designer, 1960-63; Aberdeen University Press: Staff Designer, 1963-69, Design Manager, 1969-71, Company Director, 1971-75; City of Aberdeen: Depute Director PR, 1975-77, Director of Information and Tourism, 1977. Director, Aberdeen Tourist Board and Gordon District Tourist Board. Recreations: painting; golf; swimming; reading. Address: (b.) St. Nicholas House, Aberdeen, AB9 1DE; T.-0224 642121.

Henry, Professor Peter (formerly H.P. Zuntz), MA (Oxon), DipEd (Leeds). Professor and Head, Department of Slavonic Languages and Literatures, Glasgow University, since 1975; b. 21.4.26, Marburg, Germany; m., Brenda Grace Lewis (m. diss.); 1 s.; 3 d. Educ. St. Knud's Skole, Copenhagen; Mellemskole, Birkerod, Denmark; St. Edward's School, Oxford; St. John's College, Oxford. Left Germany, 1936; Denmark, 1936-39, then Britain; Royal Tank Regiment, 1943-47; Senior Master, St. John's College Choir School, Cambridge, 1952; Russian Instructor, Joint Services School for Linguists, Coulsdon, 1952-54; Senior German Master, Haverfordwest Grammar School, 1954-57; Lecturer in Russian, Liverpool University, 1957-63; Senior Lecturer in Charge, Department of Russian Studies, Hull University, 1963-74. Editor, Scottish Slavonic Review, since 1983; British Universities Association of Slavists: Member, Executive Committee, 1964-66, 1978-81; Honorary Vice-President, Association of Teachers of Russian. Publications: three-volume course in Russian prose composition, 1964-65; edited texts (Pushkin, Chekhov, Bunin, Paustovsky); two-volume anthology of Soviet satire; Gazeta: Clippings from the Soviet Press (with K. Young); A Hamlet of His Time: Vsevolod Garshin; translations of stories by Paustovsky and Garshin; articles and reviews. Recreations: travel; music; theatre. Address: (b.) Department of Slavonic Languages and Literatures, Hetherington Building, Glasgow University, Glasgow, G12 8QQ; T.-041-339 8855, Ext. 5587.

Hepburn, Gavin Andrew Harley, ACMA, ACIS. Chairman, Fife Indmar PLC, since 1976; Director, Bruntons PLC, since 1983; Director, Robert Taylor (Holdings) Ltd., since 1984; Local Director, TSB Scotland, since 1983; Trustee, Scottish Hospital Trust, since 1984; Executive Council Member, Scottish Council (Development and Industry), since 1983; b. 6.12.37, Kirkcaldy; m., Anne Margaret Mitchell; 2 s.; 1 d. Educ. Loretto School; Dundee Technical College.

Chairman, Forth Port Authority, 1976-84; Council Member, CBI Scotland, 1975-79. Recreations: fishing; squash; golf. Address: (h.) 22 Boglily Road, Kirkcaldy, Fife; T.-0592 260947.

Hepburn, Professor Ronald William, MA, PhD. Professor of Moral Philosophy, Edinburgh University, since 1975; b. 16.3.27, Aberdeen; m., Agnes Forbes Anderson; 2 s.; 1 d. Educ. Aberdeen Grammar School; Aberdeen University. Assistant, then Lecturer, Department of Moral Philosophy, Aberdeen University, 1952-60; Visiting Associate Professor, New York University, 1959-60; Professor of Philosophy and Head of Department, Nottingham University, 1960-64; Professor of Philosophy, Edinburgh University, 1964-75; Stanton Lecturer, Cambridge University, 1965-68; Heslington Lecture, York University, 1970; Margaret Harris Lectures on Religion, Dundee University, 1974. Publications: Christianity and Paradox, 1958; Wonder and Other Essays, 1984. Recreation: hill-walking. Address: (b.) Department of Philosophy, David Hume Tower, George Square, Edinburgh, EH8 9JX; T.-031-667 1011.

Hepworth, James Michael, BA. Senior Lecturer in Sociology, Aberdeen University, since 1981; b. 21.12.38, Wakefield; m., Marian Bywell; 1 s.; 2 d. Educ. Ossett Grammar School; Kibworth Beauchamp Grammar School; Hull University. Assistant Careers Advisory Officer, Sutton Coldfield, 1961-65; Assistant Lecturer in Social Studies, Monkwearmouth College of Further Education, Sunderland, 1965-66; Lecturer in Sociology, Teesside Polytechnic, Middlesbrough, 1967-71; Senior Lecturer in Sociology, Lanchester Polytechnic, Coventry, 1971; Lecturer in Sociology, Aberdeen University, 1972-81. Chairman, Mid Life Centre Development Group, since 1983; Director, Midlifestyle Ltd., since 1984; Review Editor, Theory, Culture and Society; Founder Member, Centre for the Study of Adult Life; Member, Crime Writers Association. Publications: Blackmail, 1975; Confession: Studies in Deviance and Religion (Co-author), 1982; Surviving Middle Age, 1982. Recreations: gardening; literature and art; walking. Address: (h.) Rose Cottage, Whiterashes, Aberdeen, AB5 0QP; T.-Whiterashes 319.

Herbert, Rodney Andrew, BSc, PhD, MIBiol. Senior Lecturer in Microbiology, Dundee University, since 1982; b. 27.6.44, York; m., Helen Joyce Macpherson Millard; 2 s. Educ. Archbishop Holgates Grammar School, York; Bradford University; Aberdeen University. Research Fellow, Edinburgh University, 1970-71; Lecturer in Microbiology, Dundee University, 1971-82. Convener, Scottish Branch, Society of General Microbiology; Senior Visiting Scientist: British Antarctic Survey, 1976-77, Ross Sea, Antarctica, 1982-83. Recreations: music; walking; gardening. Address: (b.) Department of Biological Sciences, Dundee University, Dundee, DD1 4HN; T.-Dundee 23181, Ext. 608.

Herbison, Rt. Hon. Margaret McCrorie, PC (1964). MP (Labour), North Lanark, 1945-70; Lord High Commissioner to the General Assembly of the Church of Scotland, 1970-71; b. 11.3.07.

Educ. Bellshill Academy; Glasgow University. Joint Parliamentary Under Secretary of State, Scottish Office, 1950-51; Minister of Pensions and National Insurance, 1964-66; Minister of Social Security, 1966-67; Chairman, Select Committee on Overseas Aid, 1969; Chairman, Labour Party, 1957; Scotswoman of the Year, 1970; Hon. LLD, Glasgow, 1970.

Herd, James Peter, MBE, WS, NP. Partner, Beveridge, Herd & Sandilands, WS, Kirkcaldy, since 1951; b. 18.5.20, Kirkcaldy; m., Marjory Phimister Mitchell; 3 s.; 2 d. Educ. Edinburgh Academy; St. Andrews University; Edinburgh University. Army Service as Major, Black Watch, UK and South East Asia, 1939-46; Local Director, Royal Insurance Group, since 1951; Trustee, Kirkcaldy and District Trustee Savings Bank, 1952-83; Director, Kirkcaldy Ice Rink Limited, since 1982; Director, Kirkcaldy Abbeyfield Society. Recreations: curling; gardening. Address: (b.) 1 East Fergus Place, Kirkcaldy, Fife, KY1 1XT; T.-0592 261616.

Herdman, John Macmillan, MA (Hons) (Cantab). Writer, since 1963; b. 20.7.41, Edinburgh; m., Dolina Maclennan. Educ. Merchiston Castle School, Edinburgh; Magdalene College, Cambridge. Creative Writing Fellow, Edinburgh University, 1977-79; Scottish Arts Council bursaries, 1976 and 1982; Scottish Arts Council Book Award, 1978. Publications: Descent, 1968; A Truth Lover, 1973; Memoirs of My Aunt Minnie/Clapperton, 1974; Pagan's Pilgrimage, 1978; Stories Short and Tall, 1979; Voice Without Restraint: Bob Dylan's Lyrics and Their Background, 1982. Recreations: reading; walking; listening to music. Address: (h.) Woodlands, St. Andrew's Crescent, Bridge of Tilt, Blair Atholl, Perthshire, PH18 5SX; T.-Blair Atholl 403.

Heriot, Rev. Charles Rattray, BA. Minister, Brightons Parish Church, since 1967; Clerk, Falkirk Presbytery, Church of Scotland, since 1980; b. 9.4.31, Glasgow; m., Audrey J.L. Scott; 1 s.; 1 d. Educ. Hyndland Senior Secondary School; Glasgow University and Trinity College. Minister, Kenmure Parish Church, 1962-67. Member, Brightons Community Council. Recreations: reading; walking. Address: The Manse, Brightons, Falkirk, FK2 OJP; T.-Polmont 712062.

Hern, John E.C., MA, BSc, DM (Oxon), FRCP. Consultant Neurologist, Aberdeen, since 1972; b. 10.12.36, Southsea; m., Avril Drew; 3 s.; 1 d. Educ. Marlborough College; New College, Oxford; Guy's Hospital, London. Training posts in neurology, National Hospitals for Nervous Diseases, Guy's Hospital, London, 1965-72. Recreation: small-scale farming. Address: (h.) Woodside of Horner, Kemnay, Inverurie, Aberdeenshire; T.-Kemnay 42536.

Herries, Sir Michael Alexander Robert Young-, Kt (1975), OBE (1968), MC (1945), DL. Chairman, The Royal Bank of Scotland plc, since 1976; Chairman, The Royal Bank of Scotland Group plc, since 1978; Chairman, Scottish Mortgage and Trust PLC, since 1984; b. 28.2.23; m.; 2 s.;

1 d. Educ. Eton; Trinity College, Cambridge. KOSB, 1942-47; Jardine Matheson & Co. Ltd., 1948-70 (Chairman and Managing Director, 1963-70); Chairman, Scottish Disability Foundation, since 1982; Member, Queen's Bodyguard for Scotland (Royal Company of Archers).

Herriot, Jenny. Member, National Executive, Scottish National Party, since 1983 (Convenor, European Liaison Committee, since 1984); b. 24.1.44, Kirkcaldy; m., James Taggart; 1 s.; 1 d. Educ. Kirkcaldy High School; Glasgow Royal Infirmary. NHS Radiographer, 1964-84; Owner of Picture Framing and Gallery Business, since 1984; Clerk, National Assembly, SNP, 1982-83; Parliamentary candidate, Eastwood, General Election, 1983; Member, National Council, SNP, since 1982; Candidate, Strathclyde West, European Election, 1984. Recreations: painting; walking. Address: (h.) 28 Skibo Avenue, Glenrothes, Fife; T.-0592 773 495.

Herron, Very. Rev. Andrew, ATCL, MA, BD, LLB, DD, LLD. Moderator, General Assembly of Church of Scotland, 1971; b. 29.9.09, Glasgow; m., Joanna Fraser Neill; 4 d. Educ. Strathbungo H.G. School; Albert Road Academy; Glasgow University and Trinity College. Minister: Linwood, 1936-40, Houston and Killellan, 1940-59; Clerk, Glasgow Presbytery, 1959-81. Baird Lecturer, 1985. Publications: Record Apart, 1972; Guide to the General Assembly, 1976; Guide to Congregational Affairs, 1979; Guide to the Presbytery, 1982; contributed article on Houston to Third Statistical Account. Address: (h.) 36 Darnley Road, Glasgow, G41 4NE; T.-041-423 6422.

Herschell, David John, FSA Scot. Trustee and Executive Member, Scottish Tartans Society; b. 26.10.44, London; m., Hazel Joyce Giddins; 1 s.; 1 d. Editor, Tartans (Newsletter, Scottish Tartans Society). Publication: Francis Edward Robinson (1833-1910) - His Background and Early Life. Recreations: Scottish history and culture; campanology. Address: (h.) Braidon, Ancaster Lane, Comrie, Perthshire, PH6 2DT; T.-0764 70666.

Hervey, Sandor Geza Joseph, MA, DPhil (Oxon). Reader in Linguistics, St. Andrews University, since 1980; b. 1.7.42, Rimaszombat, Hungary; m., Mary Diana Holdsworth; 5 d. Educ. Salesian College, Cowley, Oxford; New College, Oxford. Lecturer in Linguistics, St. Andrews University, 1972-80. Member, Comite de Lecture, Journal La Linguistique. Publication: Semiotic Perspectives, 1982. Recreations: miscellaneous sports; music; poetry. Address: (b.) St. Andrews University, St. Andrews, Fife, KY16 9PH; T.-St. Andrews 76161, Ext. 435.

Hesketh, John Barrie, MBE. Artistic Director, Mull Little Theatre, since 1966; b. 11.4.30, Birmingham; m., Marianne (deceased); 3 s. Educ. Buxton College; Sheffield University; Central School of Speech and Drama. Actor and TV Announcer, 1954-60; Adviser, Scottish Community Drama Association, 1960-62; inaugurated Mull Little Theatre, 1966. STV Award for Services to Scottish Theatre, 1970; Fellow Commoner,

Churchill College, Cambridge, 1979-85. Recreation: painting (water colourist). Address: (b.) Mull Little Theatre, Dervaig, Isle of Mull, Argyll, PA75 6QW; T.-06884 267.

Hesketh, Nigel George Francis. Member, Stewartry District Council, since 1984; Founder, Galloway Lodge Preserves, 1970; b. 10.5.45, Simla, India; m., Fiona Mary Wylie; 1 s. Educ. Stowe School; Royal Military Academy, Sandhurst. Served with 4th/7th Royal Dragoon Guards; Member, Inner Temple. Community Councillor, Gatehouse-of-Fleet; Chairman, Gatehouse-of-Fleet Burns Club. Publication: Commercial English for Foreign Correspondents. Recreation: classical modern studies. Address: (h.) Bleachfield, Gatehouse-of-Fleet, Stewartry of Kirkcudbright; T.-Gatehouse 357.

Hetherington, Professor (Hector) Alastair, MA. Research Professor in Media Studies, Stirling University, since 1982; b. 31.10.19, Llanishen, Glamorgan; m., Sheila Cameron; 2 s.; 2 d. Educ. Corpus Christi College, Oxford. Army, 1940-46; Glasgow Herald, 1946-50; The Guardian, 1950-75 (Foreign Editor, 1953-56, Editor, 1956-75); BBC Scotland, 1976-79; Director, Scotquest (film company), since 1982; Chairman, The Scott Trust (owners, The Guardian and Manchester Evening News), since 1984; various films for Channel Four. Publications: Guardian Years, 1981; News, Newspapers and Television, 1985. Recreation: hill-walking. Address: (h.) 38 Chalton Road, Bridge of Allan, Stirling, FK9 4EF; T.-0786 832168.

Hewitt, David S., MA, PhD. Senior Lecturer in English, Aberdeen University, since 1982; b. 22.4.42, Hawick; m., Angela Catherine Williams; 1 s.; 1 d. Educ. Melrose Grammar School; George Watson's College, Edinburgh; Edinburgh University; Aberdeen University. Aberdeen University: Assistant Lecturer in English, 1964, Lecturer, 1968; Treasurer, Association for Scottish Literary Studies, since 1973; Editor-in-Chief, critical edition, Waverley Novels, 1984; Elder and Treasurer, Restoration Appeal, Cathedral Church of St. Machar, Old Aberdeen; Managing Editor, New Writing Scotland, since 1983. Publications: Scott on Himself (Editor), 1982; Literature of the North, 1983; Scott and His Influence, 1984. Address: (b.) Department of English, Aberdeen University, Aberdeen, AB9 2UB; T.-0224 40241.

Heywood, Philip, MA, DPhil, FRSE. Senior Lecturer in Mathematics, Edinburgh University, since 1965; b. 27.9.29, Holmfirth, Yorkshire; m., 1, Ruth Logie; 1 s.; 1 d.; 2, Moira Elizabeth McArthur; 1 s. Educ. Bradford Grammar School; New College, Oxford. Edinburgh University: Assistant, 1952-54, Lecturer, 1954-65. Recreations: music (violin, viola); squash; tennis. Address: (b.) Department of Mathematics, James Clerk Maxwell Building, Mayfield Road, Edinburgh, EH9 3JZ; T.-031-667 1081.

Hider, Calvin Fraser, MB, ChB, FFARCS. Consultant Anaesthetist, Edinburgh Royal Infirmary, since 1964; Honorary Senior Lecturer, Faculty of Medicine, Edinburgh University; b. 29.5.30, Glasgow; m., Jean M.D. Dott; 3 d. Educ. George Watson's Boys College, Edinburgh; Edinburgh University. Medical training, Dumfries and Galloway Royal Infirmary and Edinburgh Royal Infirmary; RNVR, Surgeon (Lt.-Cdr.), 1955-64. Recreations: sailing; sheep-breeding (Jacob). Address: (h.) Marchwell Cottage, Penicuik, Midlothian, EH26 OPX; T.-0968 72680.

Higgs, Malcolm Slade, AADip, PhD, RIBA, ARIAS. Senior Lecturer in Architectural History, Edinburgh University, since 1974; b. 18.10.35, London; 1 s.; 1 d. Educ. University College School, London; Architectural Association School of Architecture, London. Assistant Architect, 1960-62; Architect, Planning and Development Ltd., London, 1962-64; Lecturer in Architectural History, Edinburgh University, 1964-74; American Council of Learned Societies Research Fellow, Columbia and Harvard Universities, 1972-73. Chairman, Architectural Heritage Society of Scotland. Recreation: collecting. Address: (h.) 4 Royal Circus, Edinburgh, EH3 6SR; T.-031-225 5275.

Higgs, Professor Peter Ware, BSc, MSc, PhD, FRS, FRSE. Professor of Theoretical Physics, Edinburgh University, since 1980; b. 29.5.29, Newcastle-upon-Tyne; m., Jo Ann Williamson; 2 s. Educ. Cotham Grammar School, Bristol; King's College, London. Postdoctoral Fellow, Edinburgh University, 1954-56, and London University, 1956-58; Lecturer in Mathematics, University College, London, 1958-60; Lecturer in Mathematical Physics, then Reader, Edinburgh University, 1960-80. Hughes Medal, Royal Society, 1981; Rutherford Medal, Institute of Physics, 1984. Recreations: music; walking; swimming. Address: (h.) 2 Darnaway Street, Edinburgh, EH3 6BG; T.-031-225 7060.

Highgate, James Brown, CBE (1981), MA, LLB, JP. Senior Partner, Brownlie Watson & Beckett, Solicitors, since 1976 (Partner, since 1951); b. 18.6.20, Glasgow. Educ. High School of Glasgow; Glasgow University. Served, Royal Artillery and Royal Indian Artillery, 1941-46 (demobilised as Major); appointed General Commissioner of Income Tax, 1969 (Chairman, Glasgow North Division, 1981); Member, Strathclyde Advisory Board, Salvation Army, since 1970; Joint Honorary Secretary, Scottish Conservative and Unionist Association, since 1973; Honorary President, Hamilton and Motherwell North Conservative Constituencies; Elder, Park Church of Scotland, Uddingston; Governor, High School of Glasgow. Recreation: now restricted to golf. Address: (h.) Broomlands, 121 Kylepark Drive, Uddingston, Glasgow; T.-Uddingston 813377.

Hill, Alexander Reid, BSc, PhD, MIBiol, FRSE. Senior Lecturer in Agricultural Zoology, Glasgow University; b. 17.10.19, Dundee; m., Mary Barbara Watt; 2 s.; 1 d. Educ. Harris Academy, Dundee; University College, St. Andrews University. Carnegie Research Scholar, St. Andrews University, 1941-43; Member, Scientific Civil Service, 1943-46; on Scientific Staff, East Malling Research Station, Maidstone, 1946-49;

joined Zoology Department, Glasgow University, 1949; awarded Carnegie Travelling Fellowship and Kellogg Foundation Fellowship to visit and work in Canada and USA, 1955; Visiting Professor, University of California, 1955. Recreations: sketching; photography; listening to music. Address: (h.) 35 Rowallan Gardens, Broomhill, Glasgow, G11 7LH; T.-041-334 1785.

Hill, Pamela. Writer; b. 26.11.20, Nairobi, Kenya. Educ. Hutchesons' Girls' Grammar School; Glasgow School of Art; Glasgow University. Publications: Flaming Janet; Marjory of Scotland; Forget Not Ariadne; The Malvie Inheritance; The Incumbent; The Green Salamander; The House of Cray; Duchess Cain; Still Blooms The Rose; The Governess; My Lady Glamis, in press. Recreations: pottery; bull terriers. Address: 11 Bank Street, Wigtown, DG8 9HR; T.-Wigtown 2277.

Hill, Richard Inglis, BSc (Hons), FICE, FIHT. Director of Roads and Transportation, Borders Regional Council, since 1974; b. 8.5.33, Callander; m., Margaret; 2 s. Educ. McLaren High School, Callander; Royal College of Science and Technology, Glasgow. Perth and Kinross Joint County Council: student assistant, 1951-53, graduate assistant, 1954-56, Assistant Engineer, 1958-59, Senior Engineer, 1959-61, Senior Supervisory Engineer, 1961-65, Assistant County Surveyor, 1965-72; County Surveyor and Engineer, Selkirk County Council, 1972-75. Chairman, Scottish Branch, County Surveyors' Society. Recreations: golf; music. Address: (b.) Regional HQ, Newtown St. Boswells, Roxburghshire, TD6 OSA; T.-St. Boswells 23301.

Hill, Professor William George, BSc, MS, PhD, DSc, FRSE, FRS. Professor of Animal Genetics, Edinburgh University, since 1983; b. 7.8.40, Hemel Hempstead; m., C. Rosemary Austin; 1 s.; 2 d. Educ. St. Albans School; London University; University of California; Iowa State University; Edinburgh University. Edinburgh University: Assistant Lecturer, 1965-67, Lecturer, 1967-74, Reader, 1974-83; Visiting Research Associate, Iowa State University, 1967-68-69-72; Visiting Professor: University of Minnesota, 1966, Iowa State University, 1978, North Carolina State University, 1979; Consultant Geneticist: Cotswold Pig Development Co., 1965-85, British Friesian Cattle Society, since 1978; sometime Editor, Animal Production and Biometrics. Recreations: farming; bridge. Address: (h.) 4 Gordon Terrace, Edinburgh, EH16 5QH; T.-031-667 3680.

Hillhouse, Muriel Muir Harvey, MA. Solicitor, since 1932; Honorary Sheriff, South Strathclyde, Dumfries and Galloway, at Ayr, since 1983; b. 14.11.07, Ayr. Educ. Ayr Academy; Glasgow University. Address: 16 Carrick Park, Ayr, KA7 2SL; T.-Ayr 263472.

Hillhouse, Robert Russell, MA. Under Secretary, Scottish Education Department, since 1985; b. 23.4.38, Glasgow; m., Alison Fraser; 2 d. Educ. Hutchesons' Grammar School, Glasgow; Glasgow University. Entered Home Civil Service as Assistant Principal, Scottish Education Department, 1962; Principal, 1966; HM Treasury, 1971;

Assistant Secretary, Scottish Office, 1974; Scottish Home and Health Department, 1977; Principal Finance Officer, Scottish Office, 1980-85. Recreation: making music (Scottish Philharmonic Singers). Address: (h.) 48 Dreghorn Loan, Edinburgh, EH13 ODD; T.-031-441 1587.

Hillis, William Stewart, MB, ChB, MRCP, FRCPGlas. Senior Lecturer in Clinical Pharmacology, Glasgow University, since 1979; Honorary Consultant Cardiologist, Glasgow Area Health Board, since 1979; b. 28.9.43, Elderslie, Renfrewshire; m., Anne Marshall Craigie; 3 s.; 1 d. Educ. Clydebank High School; Glasgow University. House Officer in Surgery, Western Infirmary, Glasgow, 1967; House Officer in Medicine, Southern General Hospital, 1968-70; Registrar/Senior Registrar in Cardiology, Glasgow Royal Infirmary, 1970-77 (Research Fellow in Cardiology, Vanderbilt University Hospital, Nashville, Tennessee, 1973-74); Consultant Physician, Stobhill Hospital, 1977-79; Honorary Physician, Scottish Football Association, since 1980. Publication: Treatment of Cardiovascular Disease (Co-author). Recreation: football. Address: (h.) 20 Airthrey Avenue, Jordanhill, Glasgow; T.-041-959 1699.

Hills, Graham John, PhD, DSc, CChem, FRSC, FRSE, Hon DSc (Lodz and Southampton), Hon LLD (Glasgow). Principal and Vice-Chancellor, Strathclyde University, since 1980; b. 9.4.26, Leigh-on-Sea; m., Mary Jane McNaughton; 1 s.; 3 d. Educ. Westcliff High School for Boys; Birkbeck College and Imperial College, London University. Lecturer in Physical Chemistry, Imperial College, 1949-62; Professor of Physical Chemistry, Southampton University, 1962-80; Visiting Professor, University of Western Ontario, 1968; Visiting Professor and National Science Foundation Fellow, Case-Western Reserve University, Ohio, 1968-69; Visiting Professor, Buenos Aires University, 1976; Member, Pay Review Board for Nurses, Midwives and Professions Allied to Medicine, since 1983; Council Member, Royal Society of Chemistry, since 1983; President, International Society of Electrochemistry, 1982-84; Director, Glasgow Chamber of Commerce, since 1981; Commander Insignia, Order of Merit of Polish People's Republic. Publications: Reference Electrodes, 1961; Polarography, 1964. Recreations: music; hill-walking; European politics. Address: (b.) Principal's Office, McCance Building, 16 Richmond Street, Glasgow, G1 1XQ; T.-041-552 4400, Ext. 2000.

Hind, Archie. Novelist and Playwright; b. 1928. Author of The Dear Green Place, 1966; former Writer in Residence to the community in Aberdeen.

Hingston, David Robert, LLB, NP. Procurator Fiscal, Caithness; b. 29.7.48, Assam, India. Educ. Morrison's Academy, Crieff; Edinburgh University. Address: (b.) Procurator Fiscal's Office, Sheriff Court House, Wick, Caithness; T.-Wick 2197/8.

Hingston, Peter, BSc. Trust Director, Inverclyde Enterprise Trust Ltd., since 1984; b. 18.6.50, Assam, India; m., Charlotte. Educ. Morrison's

Academy, Crieff; Daniel Stewart's College, Edinburgh; Glasgow University; Christ Church, Oxford. Engineer Branch, RAF, 1972-78 (Flt.-Lt.); Principal Engineer (Design), Racal Electronics, 1979-81; Proprietor, Intruder Alarms, Barbados, West Indies, 1981-84. Recreations: writing; product design. Address: (b.) Inverclyde Enterprise Trust Ltd., 26 Clyde Square, Greenock; T.-0475 86240.

Hirst, Michael William, MP, LLB, CA. MP (Conservative), Strathkelvin and Bearsden, since 1983; Member, Select Committee on Scottish Affairs, since 1983; Vice Chairman, Backbench Party Organisation Committee; b. 2.1.46, Glasgow; m., Naomi Ferguson Wilson; 1 s.; 2 d. Educ. Glasgow Academy; Glasgow University. Partner, Peat Marwick Mitchell & Co., Chartered Accountants, until 1983 (now Consultant); contested: Central Dunbartonshire, February and October, 1974, East Dunbartonshire, 1979; Chairman, Scottish Conservative Candidates Association, 1978-81; Director, Weavers Society of Anderston; Member, Executive Committee, Princess Louise Scottish Hospital, Erskine; Elder, Kelvinside Hillhead Parish Church. Recreations: golf; hill-walking. Address: (h.) Enderley, Baldernock Road, Milngavie, Glasgow, G62 8DU; T.-041-956 1213.

Hitchman, Professor Michael L., BSc, DPhil, CChem, FRSC. Young Professor of Chemistry, Strathclyde University, since 1984; b. 17.8.41, Woburn, Bedfordshire; m., Pauline J. Thompson; 1 s.; 2 d. Educ. Stratton Grammar School, Biggleswade; Queen Mary College and King's College, London University; University College, Oxford. Assistant Lecturer in Chemistry, Leicester Regional College of Technology, 1963-65; Junior Research Fellow, Wolfson College, Oxford, 1968-70; ICI Postdoctoral Research Fellow, Physical Chemistry Laboratory, Oxford University, 1968-70; Chief Scientist, Orbisphere Corporation, Geneva, 1970-73; Staff Scientist, Laboratories RCA Ltd., Zurich, 1973-79; Lecturer, then Senior Lecturer, Salford University, 1979-84. Royal Society of Chemistry: Vice Chairman, Electroanalytical Group, Treasurer, Electrochemistry Group. Publications: Ring-disk Electrodes (Co-author), 1971; Measurement of Dissolved Oxygen, 1978. Recreations: family; keep fit; walking; DIY; theatre-going. Address: (b.) Department of Pure and Applied Chemistry, Strathclyde University, 295 Cathedral Street, Glasgow, G1 1XL; T.-041-552 4400.

Hoare, Peter, DM, MA, BM, BCH, MRCPsych. Consultant Psychiatrist, Royal Hospital for Sick Children, Edinburgh, since 1980; part-time Senior Lecturer, Edinburgh University, since 1980; b. 30.10.45, Liverpool; m., Barbara Jane; 1 s.; 2 d. Educ. St. Mary's College, Crosby, Liverpool; Oxford University. Former Lecturer, Department of Psychiatry, Oxford University. Recreations: squash; opera. Address: (b.) Department of Child and Family Psychiatry, Royal Hospital for Sick Children, 3 Rillbank Terrace, Edinburgh; T.-031-668 2251.

Hobsbaum, Philip Dennis, MA, PhD, LRAM, LGSM. Reader in English Literature, Glasgow University, since 1979; b. 29.6.32, London; m.,

Rosemary Phillips. Educ. Belle Vue Grammar School, Bradford; Downing College, Cambridge; Sheffield University. Lecturer in English, Queen's University, Belfast, 1962-66; Lecturer, then Senior Lecturer in English Literature, Glasgow University, 1966-79. Publications: The Place's Fault, 1964; In Retreat, 1966; Coming Out Fighting, 1969; A Theory of Communication, 1970; A Reader's Guide to Charles Dickens, 1972; Tradition and Experiment, 1979; A Reader's Guide to D.H. Lawrence, 1981; Essentials of Literary Criticism, 1983. Recreation: walking the dog. Address: (b.) Department of English Literature, Glasgow University, Glasgow; T.-041-339 8855.

Hoey, James Francis, BL, LMRTPI. Chief Executive, City of Dundee District Council, since 1981. Address: (b.) City Chambers, Dundee, DD1 3BY; T.-Dundee 23141.

Holmes, George Dennis, CB (1979), FRSE, BSc (Hons). Director-General and Deputy Chairman, Forestry Commission, since 1977; b. 9.11.26; m.; 3 d. Educ. John Bright's School, Llandudno; University of Wales. Joined Forestry Commission, 1948.

Holmes, Professor Peter Henry, BVMS, PhD, MRCVS. Head, Department of Veterinary Physiology, Glasgow University, since 1978; b. 6.6.42, Beverley; m., Ruth Helen Holmes; 2 d. Educ. Beverley Grammar School; Glasgow University. Lecturer, Senior Lecturer, Reader, Titular Professor in Veterinary Physiology, Glasgow University, since 1969; various overseas projects in East Africa, particularly in Ethiopia. Recreations: sailing; hill-walking. Address: (b.) Department of Veterinary Physiology, Glasgow University Veterinary School, Bearsden Road, Glasgow; T.-041-942 2301.

Home of the Hirsel, Rt. Hon. Lord (Alexander Frederick Douglas-Home), KT; Life Peer; b. 2.7.03, London; m., Elizabeth Alington; 1 s.; 3 d. Educ. Eton College; Christ Church, Oxford. Minister of State, Scottish Office, 1951-55; Secretary of State: Commonwealth Office, 1955-60, Foreign Office, 1960-63; Prime Minister, 1963-64; Secretary of State, Foreign and Commonwealth Office, 1970-74. Publications: The Way The Wind Blows (autobiography), 1976; Border Reflections, 1979; Letters to a Grandson, 1984. Recreations: fishing; shooting; gardening. Address: (h.) The Hirsel, Coldstream, Berwickshire; T.-0890 2345.

Home Robertson, John David, MP. MP (Labour), East Lothian, since 1983 (Berwick & East Lothian, 1978-83); b. 5.12.48, Edinburgh; m., Catherine Brewster; 2 s. Educ. Ampleforth College; West of Scotland Agricultural College. Farmer; Member: Berwickshire District Council, 1974-78, Borders Health Board, 1975-78; Chairman, Eastern Borders Citizens' Advice Bureau, 1976-78; Member, Select Committee on Scottish Affairs, 1979-83; Chairman, Scottish Group of Labour MPs, 1983; Scottish Labour Whip, 1983-84; Opposition Front Bench Spokesman on Agriculture, since 1984. Address: (b.) House of Commons, Westminster, London, SW1A OAA; T.-01-219 4135.

Hood, Rev. (Elizabeth) Lorna, MA, BD. Minister, Renfrew North, since 1979; Member, Scottish Churches Council, since 1982; b. 21.4.53, Irvine; m., Peter Finlay Hood; 1 d. Educ. Kilmarnock Academy; Glasgow University. Delegate, World Alliance of Reformed Churches, Ottawa, 1982. Recreation: reading. Address: (h.) 1 Alexandra Drive, Renfrew; T.-041-886 2074.

Hood, Professor Neil, MA, MLitt. Professor of Business Policy, Department of Marketing, Strathclyde University, since 1979; Associate Dean, Strathclyde Business School, since 1982; Co-Director, Strathclyde International Business Unit, since 1983; b. 10.8.43, Wishaw; m., Anna Watson Clark; 1 s.; 1 d. Educ. Wishaw High School; Glasgow University. Research Fellow, Scottish College of Textiles, 1966-68; Lecturer/Senior Lecturer, Paisley College of Technology, 1968-78; Economic Adviser, Scottish Economic Planning Department, 1979; Visiting Professor of International Business, University of Texas, Dallas, 1981; Visiting Professor, Institute of International Business, Stockholm School of Economics, since 1982; Director, Euroscot Meat Exports Ltd., since 1981; Economic Consultant to Secretary of State for Scotland, since 1980; Director, Scottish Development Finance Ltd., since 1984; Investment Adviser, Castleforth Fund Manages, since 1984; Director, LIFE Ltd., since 1984; Board Member, Irvine Development Corporation, since 1985. President, European International Business Association. Publications: Industrial Marketing - A Study of Textiles (Co-author), 1970; Chrysler UK: A Corporation in Transition (Co-author), 1977; The Economics of Multinational Enterprise (Co-author), 1979; European Development Strategies of US Multinationals Located in Scotland (Co-author), 1980; Multinationals in Retreat: The Scottish Experience (Co-author), 1982; Multinational Investment Strategies in the British Isles (Co-author), 1983; Industry, Policy and the Scottish Economy (Co-Editor), 1984; Transnational Corporations in the Textile Industry (Co-author), 1984; Recreations: swimming; reading. Address: (h.) Teviot, 12 Carlisle Road, Hamilton, ML3 7DB; T.-0698 424870.

Hood, Norman Arthur, MB, ChB, FRCPEdin. Consultant Physician in Geriatric Medicine, since 1977; Honorary Senior Lecturer, Edinburgh University, since 1977; b. 20.3.47, Kilmacolm; m., Margaret; 2 s. Educ. Paisley Grammar School; Glasgow University. House Physician, Western Infirmary, Glasgow; House Surgeon, Glasgow Royal Infirmary; Senior Registrar in Geriatric Medicine, Stobhill Hospital, Glasgow. Address: (h.) Willowbank, Glebe Street, Dalkeith; T.-031-663 1262.

Hook, Professor Andrew Dunnet, MA, PhD. Bradley Professor of English Literature, Glasgow University, since 1979 (Head, Department of English Literature, since 1982); b. 21.12.32, Wick; m., Judith Ann (deceased); 2 s.; 1 d. Educ. Wick High School; Daniel Stewart's College, Edinburgh; Edinburgh University; Manchester University; Princeton University. Edinburgh University: Assistant Lecturer in English Literature, 1961-63, Lecturer in American Literature,

1963-70; Senior Lecturer in English, Aberdeen University, 1970-79; CNAA: Chairman, American Studies Panel, Chairman, English Studies Panel, Member, Combined Studies Humanities Board; Member, Scottish Examination Board, since 1984. Publications: Scotland and America 1750-1835, 1975; American Literature in Context 1865-1900, 1983; Scott's Waverley (Editor), 1971; Charlotte Bronte's Shirley (Editor, with Judith Hook), 1974; Dos Passos: A Collection of Critical Essays (Editor), 1974. Recreations: theatre; opera; catching up on reading. Address: (b.) Department of English Literature, Glasgow University, Glasgow, G12 8QQ; T.-041-339 8855, Ext. 226.

Hooper, Martin Leslie, MA, PhD. Senior Lecturer, Department of Pathology, Edinburgh University, since 1980; b. 1.3.47, Walsall. Educ. Queen Mary's Grammar School, Walsall; Jesus College, Cambridge. MRC Research Scholar, MRC Laboratory of Molecular Biology, Cambridge, 1968-71; EMBO Research Fellow, Centre de Genetique Moleculaire Gif-Sur-Yvette, France, 1972-73; Research Fellow, Cancer Research Campaign Cell Genetics Group, Institute of Genetics, Glasgow, 1973-80. Publication: Mammalian Cell Genetics, 1985. Recreations: squash; opera. Address: (b.) Department of Pathology, Teviot Place, Edinburgh, EH8 9AG; T.-031-667 1011.

Hope, David Terence, MB, ChB, FRCS, ChM. Consultant Neurosurgeon, Aberdeen Royal Infirmary, since 1982; b. 2.4.46, Newcastle-upon-Tyne; m., Vanessa Mary Richardson; 1 s.; 2 d. Educ. Rutherford Grammar School, Newcastle-upon-Tyne; Liverpool University Medical School. MRC Training Fellow, National Hospital for Nervous Disease, London, 1976; Senior Registrar: Frenchay Hospital, Bristol, Baptist Memorial, Memphis, Tennessee. Recreations: field sports; ornithology. Address: (h.) Kushipara, Parkhill, Dyce, Aberdeen; T.-0224 725512.

Hope, John George, JP. Chairman, Planning Committee, Midlothian District Council, since 1980; b. 2.10.22, Auchendinny; m., Thomasina Ruth Porteous; 1 s.; 1 d. Educ. Penicuik Secondary School. Midlothian District Council: Chairman, Planning Committee, 1975-77 (and since 1980), Vice-Convener, 1980-84; Chairman, Loanhead Branch, AUEW, 1958-84; President, Penicuik Silver Band; Chairman, Penicuik Social Facilities Committee; Vice-Chairman, Penicuik YMCA Management Committee; Member, Management Board, Wellington School. Recreations: golf; gardening; walking; dancing. Address: (h.) 39 Windsor Road, Penicuik, Midlothian; T.-Penicuik 72840.

Hope, William, MA. Rector, Elgin High School, since 1978; b. 26.9.43, Scotland; m., Patricia Miller. Educ. Dalbeattie High School; Kirkcudbright Academy; Edinburgh University; Jordanhill College of Education. Alloa Academy: Assistant Teacher, Principal Teacher of Guidance; Assistant Rector, Lochaber High School. Chairman, Moray Branch, UNICEF; Vice Chairman, Elgin and District Branch, Cancer

Relief; Vice Chairman, Edinburgh University Club of Moray. Recreations: umpiring hockey and cricket; fishing. Address: (b.) Elgin High School, High School Drive, Elgin, Moray; T.-0343 45181/2.

Hope-Dunbar, Sir David, 8th Bt; b. 13.7.41; m. Kathleen Kenrick; 1 s.; 2 d. Educ. Eton; Royal Agricultural College, Cirencester. Address: (h.) Banks Farm, Kirkcudbright.

Horlick, Sir John (James Macdonald), 5th Bt. Director, Highland Fish Farmers, since 1978; b. 9.4.22; m.; 1 s.; 2 d. Educ. Eton; Babson Institute of Business Administration, USA. Captain, Coldstream Guards, Second World War; Past Chairman, Horlicks Ltd. Address: (h.) Tournaig, Poolewe, Achnasheen, Ross-shire.

Horn, David Bowes, BSc, PhD, CChem, FRSC, FRCPath, FRSE. Head, Department of Clinical Chemistry, Western General Hospital, Edinburgh, since 1966; Honorary Senior Lecturer in Clinical Chemistry, Edinburgh University, since 1966; b. 18.8.28, Edinburgh; m., Shirley Kay Riddell; 2 d. Educ. Daniel Stewart's College, Edinburgh; Heriot-Watt University, Edinburgh; Edinburgh University. Senior Grade Biochemist: Vale of Leven Hospital, Alexandria, 1956, Queen Elizabeth Hospital, Birmingham, 1959; Biochemist, Royal Victoria Infirmary, Newcastle-upon-Tyne, and Honorary Lecturer, Department of Clinical Biochemistry, Newcastle-upon-Tyne University, 1959. Past Chairman, Scottish Region, Association of Clinical Biochemists (former Member, ACB National Council); Past Chairman, Scientific Services Advisory Group Clinical Chemistry Sub-Committee; Royal Society of Chemistry Representative, Mastership in Clinical Biochemistry Examination Board. Recreations: gardening; walking. Address: (b.) Department of Clinical Chemistry, Western General Hospital, Crewe Road, Edinburgh, EH4 2XU; T.-031-332 2525.

Hornby, John Murgatroyd, FCCA, ATII, FRVA. Director of Finance, Bearsden and Milngavie District Council, since 1975; b. 6.3.32, London; m., Helen Anne; 2 d. Educ. George Watson's Boys' College, Edinburgh. William Bishop & Co., CA, Edinburgh, 1948-56; Wylie & Hutton, CA, Edinburgh, 1956-57; N.C. Campbell & Co., CA, Haddington, 1957-64; Town Chamberlain, Royal Burgh of Haddington, 1964-67; Burgh Chamberlain, Burgh of Milngavie, 1967-75. Address: (b.) Boclair, Bearsden, Glasgow, G61 2TQ; T.-041-942 2262.

Horne, Rev. Archibald Sinclair. Minister, Reformed Presbyterian Church of Scotland, since 1955; Secretary/Lecturer, Scottish Reformation Society, since 1964; b. 9.3.27, Cockenzie, East Lothian; 2 s.; 1 d. Educ. Preston Lodge Secondary School; New College, Edinburgh. Fisherman, 1941-46; Army (Royal Signals), 1946-48; retail fish trade, 1949-54; Student Minister, then Minister, Reformed Presbyterian Church, Loanhead, 1954-63. Editor, Bulwark, magazine of Scottish Reformation Society, since 1981. Publications: Torchbearers of the Truth, Sketches of the Covenanters, 1968; In The Steps of the Covenanters, 1974. Recreations: weight training; golf; photographing and recording locations of historical events. Address: (b.) 17 George IV Bridge, Edinburgh, EH1 1EE; T.-031-225 1836.

Horne, Norman John, MA (Hons). Headteacher, Harlaw Academy, Aberdeen, since 1985; b. 10.12.37, Turriff, Aberdeenshire; m., Ann Gavin; 1 s.; 2 d. Educ. Aberdeen Grammar School; Aberdeen University. Teacher of Classics, Hamilton Academy, 1961-66; Principal Classics Teacher: Nicolson Institute, Stornoway, 1966-71, Inverness Royal Academy, 1971-72; Assistant Rector, Inverness High School, 1972-77; Rector, Milne's High School, Fochabers, 1977-85. Recreations: sport (golf, table tennis); music (jazz). Address: (h.) 18 Oakwood Avenue, Elgin; T.-Elgin 2129.

Horner, Rev. Alan Philip, BA, BD. Chairman, Methodist Synod in Scotland, since 1982; Methodist Minister, since 1958; b. 8.3.34, Northallerton; m., Margaret Adams; 2 d. Educ. Stockton-on-Tees Grammar School; King James I Grammar School, Bishop Auckland; Durham University; Manchester University. Ministry: Kendal, 1958-62, Harlow, 1962-68, Warrington, 1968-77, Chester, 1977-82. Recreations: walking; photography; gardening; swimming; music; poetry. Address: 7 Rowanlea Drive, Giffnock, Glasgow, G46 6BS; T.-041-633 1434.

Horner, Robert Malcolm Wigglesworth, CEng, BSc, PhD, MICE, MBIM. Head, Department of Civil Engineering, Dundee University, since 1985; b. 27.7.42, Bury; m., Beverley Anne Wesley; 1 s.; 1 d. Educ. The Bolton School; University College, London. Civil Engineer, Taylor Woodrow Construction Ltd., 1966-77; Lecturer, Department of Civil Engineering, Dundee University, 1977-83, Senior Lecturer, 1983. Founder Chairman, Dundee Branch, Opening Windows on Engineering; Winner, CIOB Ian Murray Leslie Award, 1980 and 1984. Recreations: squash; gardening. Address: (h.) Westfield Cottage, 11 Westfield Place, Dundee, DD1 4JU; T.-0382 25933.

Hornibrook, John Nevill, BSc, CEng, FIChemE. Works Director, Roche Products Ltd., Dalry, Ayrshire, since 1981; Member, CBI Scottish Regional Council; b. 25.10.28, Gerrards Cross, Buckinghamshire; m., Dr. (Norma) Gillian Newbury; 2 d. Educ. Wellington College; Birmingham University. National Service, Royal Navy, 1949-51 (Sub-Lt., (E) RNVR, later promoted to Lt.-Cdr., RNR); Assistant Production Superintendent, Trinidad Leaseholds, BWI, 1951-55; Senior Chemical Engineer, Power Gas Corporation, 1955-58; Monsanto Chemicals Ltd., 1958-72: Senior Chemical Engineer, London, Technical Manager, Alta Labs, Bombay, Production Superintendent, Ruabon, North Wales; joined Roche Products Ltd., Dalry, 1972 (Works Manager, 1973-81). Vice-President, Institution of Chemical Engineers, 1983-85; Director, Ayrshire Chamber of Industries, since 1975; Member, Scottish Regional Committee, Chemical Industries Association. Recreations: sailing; gardening. Address: (b.) Roche Products Ltd., Dalry, Ayrshire, KA24 5JJ; T.-029 483 2345.

Horobin, John Charles, BSc, PhD. Assistant Director of Adult Education and Extra-Mural Studies, St. Andrews University, since 1974; b. 13.2.45, Long Eaton; m., Jean Margaret; 1 s.; 1 d. Educ. Long Eaton Grammar School; King's College, London University; Durham University. Tutor-Organiser, WEA, Plymouth and West Devon, 1971-74. Honorary International Secretary, Scottish Institute of Adult Education; Chairman, Fife and Kinross Branch, Scottish Wildlife Trust. Recreations: music; gardening; running. Address: (b.) Department of Adult Education and Extra Mural Studies, St. Andrews University, 3 St. Mary's Place, St. Andrews, KY16 9UY; T.-0334 73429.

Horsburgh, Charles Paton, JP, BL. Senior Town Clerk Depute, City of Glasgow District Council, since 1974; Clerk, City of Glasgow Licensing Board, since 1980; b. 19.12.27, Edinburgh; m., Patricia Morris; 2 d. Educ. Queen's Park Secondary School, Glasgow; Glasgow University. Thirty years with Glasgow Corporation, rising from Apprentice Solicitor to Principal Solicitor, specialising in court work. Honorary Treasurer, Sherwood Church of Scotland, Paisley. Recreations: music; photography; motoring. Address: (b.) Town Clerk's Office, City Chambers, Glasgow, G2 1DU; T.-041-227 4504.

Horsman, Graham Joseph Vivian, OBE (1977), JP, MA. Chairman, Forth Valley Health Board, 1977-85; Member, Scottish Health Service Planning Council, since 1977; Extra-Parliamentary Commissioner Under Private Legislation Procedure (Scotland) Act, since 1976; b. 10.11.19, London; m., Ruth Guest; 2 s.; 2 d. Educ. Whitgift School; Trinity College, Oxford. Councillor, County Borough of Reading, 1946-47; Member, Stirling and Clackmannan Hospitals Board of Management, 1966-69; Chairman, Stirling, Falkirk and Alloa Hospitals Board of Management, 1970-74; Member, Forth Valley Health Board, 1973-77; Member, Committee to Review Assessment in the Third and Fourth Years of Secondary Education in Scotland (Dunning Committee), 1975-77. Chairman, Dollar Civic Trust, 1970-78; Vice-Chairman, Scottish Association of Citizens' Advice Bureaux, 1976-78 (Council Member, 1973-78). Recreations: music; reading; walking. Address: (h.) Woodville House, Dollar, Clackmannanshire; T.-Dollar 2575.

Horspool, William McKie, BSc, PhD, DSc, CChem, FRSC, FRSE. Reader in Organic Chemistry, Dundee University, since 1972; b. 12.8.36, Kilmarnock; m., Una Macfarlane Hamill; 1 s.; 1 d. Educ. Kilmarnock Academy; Strathclyde University; Glasgow University. Postdoctoral Associate, Columbia University, New York, 1964-65; Lecturer in Organic Chemistry, Queen's College, St. Andrews, 1965-72; Visiting Professor, Wisconsin University, 1974; Visiting Professor, Complutense University, Madrid, 1985. Publication: Aspects of Organic Photochemistry, 1976; Synthetic Organic Photochemistry (Editor), 1984; numerous papers in scientific journals. Recreations: gardening; DIY construction; choral singing (Treasurer, Dundee Choral Union). Address: (h.) Waulkmill, Liff, by Dundee, DD2 5LR.

Horton, Fred, MBE, JP. Convenor, Policy and Resources Committee, Kyle and Carrick District Council (Member of Council, since 1974); b. 27.6.18, Sheffield; m., Meta McCrorie. Royal Engineers, 1939-45; served in France and Africa (evacuated, Dunkirk); joined Ministry of Civil Aviation (later British Airports Authority), Prestwick Airport, 1945; Personnel Manager, then Traffic and Commercial Manager (retired, 1981). Provost of Prestwick, 1969-72; Member, Ayr Constituency Conservative Association; Elder, Kingcase Parish Church; Past Master, Prestwick Masonic Lodge; Past President, Prestwick Rotary Club. Recreations: golf; indoor bowling. Address: (h.) Barnweil, 25 Monkton Road, Prestwick, KA9 1AP; T.-0292 78954.

Hossack, Roma Leonora, JP. Chairman, Social Work, Grampian Regional Council; Vice Chairman, Housing, Moray District Council; b. 25.9.37, Elgin. Member: Elgin Town Council, 1972-74, Moray District Council, since 1974, Grampian Regional Council, since 1977; Secretary, Elgin Welfare Committee; Member, Visiting Committee, Porterfield Prison, Inverness. Address: (h.) 46 Gordon Street, New Elgin, Moray; T.-Elgin 7776.

Houldsworth, David Henry, LLB, WS. Solicitor, since 1975; b. 19.2.53, Forres; m., Sarah Jane Hogg. Educ. Eton College; Edinburgh University. Member, Queen's Bodyguard for Scotland (Royal Company of Archers), since 1984. Recreations: skiing; fishing; golf; shooting. Address: (h.) 2 Primrose Bank Road, Edinburgh.

Houldsworth, Sir Reginald (Douglas Henry), 4th Bt, OBE, TD, DL. Landowner; b. 9.7.03; m.; 1 s.; 2 d. Educ. Shrewsbury School; Cambridge University. Commanded Ayrshire Yeomanry, 1940-42, 4 Pack Mule Group, 1943-45; Deputy Lieutenant, Ayrshire, since 1970. Address: (h.) Kirkbride, Maybole, Ayrshire.

Houlihan, Dominic Francis Joseph, BSc (Hons), PhD. Senior Lecturer in Zoology, Aberdeen University, since 1984; b. 2.8.45, London; m., Margaret Swanston Catto; 2 s.; 1 d. Educ. St. Bonaventures Grammar School, London; Bristol University. Lecturer in Zoology, Aberdeen University, since 1970; Visiting Lecturer, Malaysia University, 1977; Visiting Researcher, Woods Hole Marine Laboratory, USA, 1982; Giba-Geigy Senior Fellow, 1984; Joint Editor, Gills. Recreations: shooting; French wine. Address: (b.) Department of Zoology, Aberdeen University, Aberdeen; T.-0224 40241.

House, Jack. Journalist and Author; b. 16.5.06, Glasgow. Left school at 15; trained as a CA; became a newspaperman, 1928; worked on all three Glasgow evening newspapers; during the War, served as a Corporal in the Gordon Highlanders, subsequently as Captain (Scenario Editor), Army Kinematograph Service; numerous appearances on TV and radio (former Member, Scottish Round Britain Quiz team); appeared professionally with Charles Macdona Players and Scottish National Players, 1929-32; Editor, Scottish Stage magazine, c. 1930; Critic and Adjudicator, amateur stage; author of numerous books, including Down the Clyde, Scotland for Fun, Square Mile of Murder, The Heart of Glasgow, Pavement in the Sun, Portrait of the Clyde, Glasgow Old and New.

Houslay, Professor Miles Douglas, BSc, PhD. Gardiner Professor of Biochemistry, Glasgow University, since 1984; b. 25.6.50, Wolverhampton; m., Rhian Mair Houslay; 1 s.; 1 d. Educ. Grammar School, Brewood, Stafford; University College, Cardiff; King's College, Cambridge; Cambridge University. ICI Research Fellow and Fellow, Queens College, Cambridge, 1974-76; Lecturer, then Reader in Biochemistry, UMIST, 1976-82; Selby Fellow, Australian Academy of Science, 1984; Colworth Medal, Biochemical Society of Great Britain, 1984; Honorary Research Fellow, California Metabolic Research Foundation, since 1981; Deputy Chairman, Biochemical Journal; Editorial Board, Biochimica Biophysica Alta; Committee Member, Biochemical Society. Publication: Dynamics of Biological Membranes. Address: (b.) Department of Biochemistry, Glasgow University, Glasgow, G12 8QQ; T.-041-339 8855, Ext. 624.

Housley, Edward, MB, ChB, FRCPEdin, FRCP. Consultant Physician, Edinburgh Royal Infirmary, since 1970; part-time Senior Lecturer, Department of Medicine, Edinburgh University, since 1970; b. 10.1.34, Chester, USA; m., Alma Mary; 1 d. Educ. Mundella Grammar School, Nottingham; Birmingham University. Postgraduate training, Department of Medicine, Birmingham University and McGill University, Montreal. Recreation: crossword puzzles. Address: (h.) Duncliffe, 15 Kinellan Road, Edinburgh, EH12 6ES; T.-031-337 4818.

Housley, Richard Sutton, TEng, MCIT, AMIRTE. Head of Internal Transport, Strathclyde Regional Council, since 1975; b. 9.4.26, Airdrie; m., Grace; 2 s. Educ. Airdrie Academy. Depute Transport Manager, Lanark County Council, 1968; Transport Manager, Lanark County Council, 1973. Recreations: bowls; golf; curling. Address: (b.) Strathclyde House, 20 India Street, Glasgow, G2 4PF; T.-041-204 2900.

Houston, Professor George Frederick Barclay, MA, BLitt. Professor, Department of Political Economy, Glasgow University, since 1970; b. 26.10.20, Edinburgh; m., 1, Lilias Adam (deceased); 2, Jean Blackley; 1 s.; 3 d. Educ. George Heriot's School; Edinburgh University; Balliol College, Oxford. Lecturer, 1951, Senior Lecturer, 1966, in Agricultural Economics, Glasgow University; Consultant: FAO, OECD, SOEC, HIDB; Member, British Wool Marketing Board. Publications: Third Statistical Account of Dumfriesshire (Editor); Agrarian Change in the Scottish Highlands (Co-author). Recreations: golf; swimming. Address: (b.) Department of Political Economy, Glasgow University, Glasgow; T.-041-339 8855.

Houston, Stewart Robertson, LLB. Procurator Fiscal, Lanark, since 1981; b. 6.1.48, Hamilton; 3 d. Educ. Lanark Grammar School; Edinburgh University. Law Apprentice, then Solicitor, J. & A. Hastie, SSC, Edinburgh, 1970-73; Depute

City Prosecutor, Edinburgh, 1973-75; Depute Procurator Fiscal, Edinburgh, 1975-76; Legal Assistant, Crown Office, 1976-77; Depute Procurator Fiscal, Edinburgh, 1977-78; Depute Procurator Fiscal, Dumbarton, 1979-81. Member, Board of Management, Loaningdale List D School, Biggar. Recreations: badminton; swimming; walking; modern languages. Address: (h.) Kirkfield, 21 Rowhead Terrace, Biggar, Lanarkshire; T.-0899 20418.

Houston, Thomas, MB, ChB, FFARCS. Consultant in Anaesthetics and Pain Relief, Tayside Health Board, since 1984; Honorary Senior Lecturer in Anaesthetics, since 1984; b. 21.4.49, Kilwinning; m., Anne D. Herd. Educ. Marr College, Troon; Glasgow University. Various House Officer and Senior House Officer posts, until 1976; first anaesthetic post, Victoria Infirmary, Glasgow, 1976; Senior Registrar in Anaesthetics, Manchester, 1981. Recreations: squash; angling; photography; DIY; haute cuisine. Address: (h.) Kinnaird Road, Inchture, Perthshire, PH14 9SE; T.-Inchture 86596.

Houstoun, Andrew Beatty, OBE, MC, DL, JP. Vice President, Scottish Landowners Federation, since 1984; Scottish Member, European Landowners Organisation, since 1976; b. 15.10.22, Cranleigh; m., Mary Elizabeth Spencer-Nairn; 4 s. Educ. Harrow. Regular Army, 1941-56; retired as Major, 1st The Royal Dragoons; farming, Angus and Perthshire, since 1956; commanded Fife and Forfar Yeomanry/Scottish Horse (TA), 1962-65; Angus County Councillor, 1966-75 (Vice Chairman, Education Committee); Convener, Scottish Landowners Federation, 1979-82; Chancellor's Assessor, Dundee University Court, since 1981. Recreations: shooting; skiing. Address: Lintrathen Lodge, Kirriemuir, Angus, DD8 5JJ; T.-057 56 228.

Howard, Very Rev. Donald, BD, AKC. Provost, St. Andrew's Cathedral, Aberdeen, since 1978; Honorary Canon, Christ Church Cathedral, Hartford, Connecticut, since 1979; b. 21.1.27, Hull. Educ. London University. Design Engineer, English Electric Co.; Assistant Priest, Saltburn, North Yorkshire; Rector: Warrenton and Hartswater, N. Cape, South Africa, St. John's, East London, South Africa, Holy Trinity, Haddington. Address: (h.) 15 Morningfield Road, Aberdeen, AB2 4AP; T.-Aberdeen 314765.

Howard-Luck, Clive Andrew, DMA, DCA, FITSA, ACIS. Head of Consumer and Trading Standards, Strathclyde Regional Council, since 1977; b. 27.2.31, Folkestone; m., Babs; 1 s.; 2 d. Educ. Harvey Grammar School, Folkestone. Technical Assistant, Weights and Measures, Folkestone, 1948-55; Provincial Inspector of Weights and Measures, Kenya, 1955-64; Chief Inspector, Weights and Measures, Royal Tunbridge Wells Borough, 1964-74; Chief Trading Standards Officer, City of Westminster Consortium, 1974-77. International and Standards Officer, ITSA, since 1974; Chairman, Factory Enforcement Working Party, LACOTS, 1983-84. Recreations: hill-walking; history of military organisations. Address: (b.) Strathclyde House, 20 India Street, Glasgow, G2 4PF; T.-041-227 3105.

Howat, Robert C.L., MB, ChB, FRCOG. Consultant Obstetrician and Gynaecologist, Royal Maternity Hospital and Royal Infirmary, Glasgow, since 1974; b. 10.7.38, Kilmarnock; m., Janet; 2 s.; 1 d. Educ. Irvine Royal Academy; Glasgow University. House Officer: Glasgow Royal Infirmary, Ayrshire Central Maternity Hospital; General Practitioner: Inverbervie, Glenrothes; Senior House Officer: Ayrshire Central, Stracathro Hospital, Brechin, Kilmarnock Infirmary; Registrar: Falkirk Infirmary, Victoria Infirmary and Royal Maternity Hospital, Glasgow; Senior Registrar, Dundee Teaching Hospitals. Honorary Medical Adviser, Scottish Amateur Swimming Association. Recreations: swimming; golf; gardening. Address: (h.) 1 Coxdale Avenue, Kirkintilloch; T.-041-776 6828.

Howe, Rev. Andrew Youngson, BTh. Minister, Alness, Ross-shire; b. 4.3.28, Dundee; m., Dorothy Alison Thomson; 1 s.; 2 d. Educ. Dundee High School; Queen's College, Dundee; London University. Staff Sergeant, Royal Army Ordinance Corps; Trainee Buyer, then Assistant Buyer, Swan & Edgar, London; Minister, Church of Scotland; commission, RAF VR (T); Assessor, Church of Scotland Schools for Selection of Candidates for the Ministry. Chairman, Alness Academy School Council; Chairman, Easter Ross Save the Children Fund; Honorary Member, Dingwall Rotary Club. Recreations: gardening; model railways. Address: Rosskeen Manse, 15 Perrins Road, Alness, Ross-shire; T.-0349 882265.

Howe, Professor George Melvyn, BSc, MSc, PhD, DSc, FRSE, FRGS. Professor of Geography, Strathclyde University, since 1967; President, Institute of British Geographers, 1985-86; b. 7.4.20, Abercynon, South Wales; m., Patricia Fennell; 3 d. Educ. Caerphilly; University College of Wales, Aberystwyth. RAF, 1940-46; Lecturer/Senior Lecturer/Reader in Geography, University College of Wales, Aberystwyth, 1947-67. Publications: The Soviet Union; The USSR; Wales from the Air; Welsh Landforms and Scenery; National Atlas of Disease Mortality in the United Kingdom; Man, Environment and Disease in Britain; Atlas of Glasgow and West Region of Scotland; Environmental Medicine; Global Geocancerology; A World Geography of Human Diseases. Recreation: travel. Address: (h.) Hendre, 29 Birnam Crescent, Bearsden, Glasgow, G61 2AU; T.-041-942 7223.

Howe, Professor James Alexander Macgregor, MA, PhD. Head, Department of Artificial Intelligence, Edinburgh University, since 1978 (Professor of Artificial Intelligence, since 1985); b. 7.7.37, Glasgow; m., Nan Harvie Bell; 1 s.; 2 d. Educ. Kelvinside Academy, Glasgow; St. Andrews University; Cambridge University. Senior Assistant in Research, Laboratory of Experimental Psychology, Cambridge University, 1964-66; Research Fellow, Lecturer, Senior Lecturer, Reader, Department of Artificial Intelligence, Edinburgh University, 1967-85; Chairman, IKBS Advisory Group, Alvey Directorate; Member, Information Engineering Committee, Science and Engineering Research Council; Chairman, Society for Study of Artificial Intelligence and Simulation of Behaviour. Recreations: skiing; curling; gardening. Address: (h.) 26 Essex Road, Edinburgh, EH4 6LJ; T.-031-339 5390.

Howe, John Murray, ASVA, FSA Scot. Member, Perth and Kinross District Council, since 1978 (Convener, Libraries, Museums and Art Gallery); House Furnisher and Auctioneer, since 1938; b. 25.10.15, Alyth; widower; 2 d. Educ. Alyth Public School; Bruce's Business College, Dundee. Trainee Valuator, Jenners, Edinburgh; Valuator, C. & J. Brown, Edinburgh; Furnisher and Auctioneer, J. & J. Howe, 1940-85; RAF, 1940-46; Vice-Convener, Leisure and Recreation, Perth and Kinross District Council; Chairman, Licensing Board; Past President: East of Scotland House Furnishers Federation, Blairgowrie Rotary Club; former Scout Commissioner. Recreations: motor sport; golf; swimming. Address: (h.) Sidlaw View, Alyth, Perthshire; T.-08283 2595.

Howgego, Joseph, MA (Hons) (Cantab). HM Chief Inspector of Schools, since 1982; b. 4.4.33, Crewe; m., Anne Barbara; 4 s. Educ. Manchester Grammar School; Queens' College, Cambridge. Teaching posts: Birkenhead School, 1955-61; King's School, Chester, 1961-64; King George V School, Southport, 1964-67; HM Inspector of Schools, 1968-82. Chairman, Gullane, Aberlady and Drem Community Council, 1975-77. Recreations: golf; walking; music (choral singing). Address: (h.) Bank House, Main Street, Gullane, East Lothian, EH31 2HD; T.-0620 842348.

Howie, Sir James (William), Kt (1969), MD, FRCP, FRCPGlas, FRCPEdin, FRCPath. Director of the Public Health Laboratory Service, 1963-73; b. 31.12.07; m.; 2 s.; 1 d. Educ. Robert Gordon's College, Aberdeen; Aberdeen University. President, Royal College of Pathologists, 1966-69; President, British Medical Association, 1969-70.

Howie, Professor John Garvie Robertson, MD, PhD, FRCGP. Professor of General Practice, Edinburgh University, since 1980; b. 23.1.37, Glasgow; m., Elizabeth Margaret Donald; 2 s.; 1 d. Educ. High School of Glasgow; Glasgow University. Registrar, Laboratory Medicine, Western Infirmary, Glasgow, 1962-66; General Practitioner, Glasgow, 1966-70; Lecturer/Senior Lecturer in General Practice, Aberdeen University, 1970-80; Member: Biomedical Research Committee, SHHD, 1977-81, Health Services Research Committee, SHHD, since 1982; Chairman, Association of University Teachers of General Practice. Publication: Research in General Practice. Recreations: golf; gardening; music. Address: (h.) 4 Ravelrig Park, Balerno, Midlothian, EH14 7DL; T.-031-449 6305.

Howie, Professor John Mackintosh, MA, DPhil, DSc, FRSE. Regius Professor of Mathematics, St. Andrews University, since 1970; b. 23.5.36, Chryston, Lanarkshire; m., Dorothy Joyce Miller; 2 d. Educ. Robert Gordon's College, Aberdeen; Aberdeen University. Assistant in Mathematics, Aberdeen University, 1958-59; Assistant, then Lecturer in Mathematics, Glasgow

University, 1961-67; Senior Lecturer in Mathematics, Stirling University, 1967-70; visiting appointments: Tulane University, 1964-65, State University of New York at Buffalo, 1969-70, University of Western Australia, 1968, Monash University, 1979; Dean of Science, St. Andrews University, 1976-79. President, Edinburgh Mathematical Society, 1972-73; Vice-President, London Mathematical Society, since 1984; Convener, SCEEB Mathematics Panel, 1970-73; Chairman, Scottish Central Committee on Mathematics, 1975-81; Member, Committee to Review Examinations (Dunning Committee), 1975-77; Chairman, Governors, Dundee College of Education, since 1983; Keith Prize, Royal Society of Edinburgh, 1979-81. Publications: An Introduction to Semigroup Theory, 1976; papers in mathematical journals. Recreations: music; gardening. Address: (b.) Mathematical Institute, St. Andrews University, North Haugh, St. Andrews, KY16 9SS; T.-0334 76161.

Howie, Professor Peter William, MD, FRCOG. Professor of Obstetrics and Gynaecology, Dundee University, since 1981; b. 21.11.39, Aberdeen; m., Anne Jardine Quigg; 1 s.; 1 d. Educ. High School of Glasgow; Glasgow University. Astor Foundation Research Fellow, Royal College of Pathologists, 1970-71; Lecturer, then Senior Lecturer, Department of Obstetrics and Gynaecology, Glasgow University, 1971-78; Clinical Consultant, Medical Research Council Reproductive Biology Unit, Edinburgh, 1978-81. Recreations: golf; watching sport. Address: (h.) 8 Travebank Gardens, Monifieth, Dundee, DD5 4ET; T.-0382 534802.

Howitt, Lewis Finnigan, MB, ChB, DPH, FFCM, MRCP. Senior Medical Officer, Scottish Home and Health Department, since 1974; b. 27.5.28, Aberdeen; m., Sheila Helen Elizabeth Burns; 1 s.; 1 d. Educ. Aberdeen Central School; Aberdeen University. House Officer; Medical Officer, RAF; Medical Officer, Counties of Roxburgh and Selkirk Public Health Department; Medical Officer, then Senior Medical Officer, City of Edinburgh Public Health Department; Deputy Medical Officer of Health, Counties of Midlothian and Peebles Public Health Department; Medical Officer, SHHD. Recreations: gardening; golf. Address: (h.) 27 Cluny Drive, Edinburgh, EH10 6DT; T.-031-447 5849.

Howson, Alexander, ALA. Director of Libraries and Museums, Falkirk District Council, since 1975; b. 22.3.38, Motherwell; m., Nancy. Educ. Dalziel High School; Scottish School of Librarianship. Various posts, Lanark County Library, 1956-66; Students' and Reference Librarian, Stafford County Library, 1966-67; Depute County Librarian, Aberdeenshire, 1967-69; Burgh Librarian, Falkirk, 1969-75. President, Scottish Library Association, 1981; Member, British Library Advisory Committee on Lending Services, 1979-82. Recreation: golf. Address: (b.) Public Library, Hope Street, Falkirk, FK1 5AU; T.-Falkirk 24911, Ext. 2204.

Hoyle, Robert Stansfield, BSc, FBIM. Director of Corporate Services, Building and Works Department, Glasgow District Council, since 1982; b. 23.3.35, Darlington; m., Wenna. Various

positions, UK, USA, Germany, Libya, Univac Division, Sperry Rand, 1963-68; Marketing Manager, IBM, Libya, Lebanon, Kuwait, 1968-73; OECD Consultant, Turkey, visiting Assistant Professor, Middle East Technical University, 1973-76; Management Services Superintendent, CDM, Namibia, 1976-77; Deputy Programme Control Manager, Parsons Corporation, Saudi Arabia, 1979-80.

Hubbuck, Professor John Reginald, MA (Cantab), MA, DPhil (Oxon), FRSE. Professor of Mathematics, Aberdeen University, since 1978 (Head, Department of Mathematics, 1980-85); Vice President, Edinburgh Mathematical Society, since 1984; b. 3.5.41, Girvan; m., Anne Neilson; 1 s.; 1 d. Educ. Manchester Grammar School; Queens' College, Cambridge; Pembroke College, Oxford. Fellow: Gonville and Caius College, Cambridge, 1970-72, Magdalen College, Oxford, 1972-76. Recreation: hill-walking. Address: (h.) 8 Fonthill Terrace, Aberdeen, AB1 2UR; T.-0224 588738.

Huckle, Derek Arthur, CA, FBIM, FIIM, FCCA. Principal, Kirkcaldy College of Technology, since 1984; b. 25.1.30, Newtown St. Boswells; m., Janette; 2 d. Educ. Galashiels Academy. National Service, 1954-56; paper making, 1956-70; further education, since 1970. Chairman, Fife Branch, British Institute of Management. Address: (b.) Kirkcaldy College of Technology, St. Brycedale Avenue, Kirkcaldy, KY1 1EX; T.-0592 268591.

Hudson, Christopher Sydney, DSO (and Bar), FBIM, CPIM. Board Member, Scottish Council of Community and Voluntary Organisations; b. 1.8.16, Tunbridge Wells; m., Ruth Julia Risse; 1 d. Educ. privately, in Switzerland. Army Service, Royal Fusiliers and SOE, 1940-45 (Lt.-Col.); Control Commission for Germany (British and US Sectors), 1946-53; Personnel Manager in overseas companies, Shell International Petroleum Co., Israel, Trinidad, Zaire, Algeria; seconded to International Labour Organisation, Geneva, 1966; Executive in charge of Personnel, Training and Industrial Relations, Bank of Scotland, 1968-80. Croix de Guerre with Palme. Recreations: golf; swimming. Address: (h.) Invereil House, North Berwick, East Lothian, EH39 5DH; T.-0620 3646.

Huggins, Astrid Ilfra, JP, MA, DipSocAdmin. Chairman, Education Committee, Lothian Regional Council, since 1984; b. 19.4.36, Edinburgh; m., Martin Huggins (m. diss.); 2 d. Educ. Harrogate College; Edinburgh University. Former Editor, Focus on Social Work and Service in Scotland; former Member, Broadcasting Council for Scotland; Member: Mental Welfare Commission for Scotland, Scottish Arts Council Community Programmes Committee, General Teaching Council, Scottish Examination Board. Recreations: politics; skiing; travel; art. Address: (h.) 11 Ann Street, Edinburgh, EH4 1PL; T.-031-332 1455.

Hughes, Professor Ian Simpson, BSc, PhD, FInstP, FRSE. Professor, Department of Natural Philosophy, Glasgow University, since 1971; b.

1.11.30, Liverpool; m., Isobel Mary; 1 s.; 1 d. Educ. High School of Glasgow; Glasgow University. Research Fellow, Nuclear and Particle Physics, Glasgow University, 1955-57; Research Associate, Particle Physics, Duke University and Lawrence Radiation Laboratory, Berkeley, USA, 1957-58; Lecturer, Senior Lecturer, Reader, Department of Natural Philosophy, Glasgow University, 1958-71; Member, Nuclear Physics Board, Science and Engineering Research Council, 1969-73 and 1980-83 and of numerous SERC Committees. Recreations: literature - poetry, fiction, travel, history; mountaineering; music. Address: (b.) Department of Natural Philosophy, The University, Glasgow, G12 8QQ; T.-041-339 8855.

Hughes, Professor John, BSc, CEng, FIMechE. Professor and Director, National Centre for Prosthetics and Orthotics, Strathclyde University, since 1972; b. 20.4.34, Renfrew; m., Margaret Scoular Crichton; 2 d. Educ. Camphill School; Strathclyde University. Worked in shipbuilding and engineering, 1950-63; Strathclyde University: Lecturer in Mechanical Engineering Design, 1963-67, Senior Lecturer, Bioengineering Unit, 1967-72; President-Elect, International Society for Prosthetics and Orthotics. Recreations: golf; gardening. Address: (b.) Strathclyde University, Curran Building, 131 St. James' Road, Glasgow, G4 OLS; T.-041-552 4049.

Hughes, Robert. MP (Labour), Aberdeen North, since 1970; b. 3.1.32. Educ. Benoni High School, Transvaal; Pietermaritzburg Technical College, Natal. Member, Aberdeen Town Council, 1962-71; Under Secretary of State for Scotland, 1974-75; Chairman, Select Committee on Scottish Affairs, 1981-82; appointed Opposition Spokesman on Transport, 1981; Chairman, Anti-Apartheid Movement.

Hughes, Professor Sean Patrick Francis, MS, FRCSEdin, FRCSEdin Orth, FRCS, FRCSI. George Harrison Law Professor of Orthopaedic Surgery, Edinburgh University, since 1979; Honorary Consultant Orthopaedic Surgeon, Edinburgh Royal Infirmary, Princess Margaret Rose Orthopaedic Hospital and Royal Hospital for Sick Children, Edinburgh; b. 2.12.41, Farnham; m., Felicity Mary Anderson; 1 s.; 2 d. Educ. Downside School; London University. Senior Registrar, Orthopaedics, Middlesex Hospital and Royal National Orthopaedic Hospital; Research Fellow, Mayo Clinic, USA; Director of Orthopaedic Unit, Royal Postgraduate Medical School, London; Council Member, Royal College of Surgeons of Edinburgh. Publications: The Basis and Practice of Orthopaedics (Co-author), 1980; The Basis and Practice of Traumatology (Editor), 1983. Recreations: golf; sailing; lying in the sun. Address: (h.) 9 Corrennie Gardens, Edinburgh; T.-031-447 1443.

Hughes, Baron, (William Hughes), PC (1970), CBE (1956), DL. Life Peer, since 1961; President, Scottish Federation of Housing Associations, since 1975; President, Scottish Association for Mental Health, since 1975; Member, Council of Europe and Western European Union, since 1976; Company Director; b. 22.1.11; m.; 2 d. Educ. Balfour Street Public School, Dundee;

Dundee Technical College. Commissioned RAOC, 1944 (demobilised as Captain, 1946); City Treasurer, Dundee, 1946-47; Lord Provost of Dundee and HM Lieutenant of County of City of Dundee, 1954-60; Member, North of Scotland Hydro-Electric Board, 1957-64; Chairman: Glenrothes Development Corporation, 1960-64, East Kilbride Development Corporation, 1975-82; Chairman, Royal Commission on Legal Services in Scotland, 1976-80; Joint Parliamentary Under Secretary of State for Scotland, 1964-69; Minister of State for Scotland, 1969-70, 1974-75; Hon. LLD, St. Andrews, 1960.

Hughes, William Young, BSc, MPS. Chief Executive, Grampian Holdings p.l.c., since 1976 (Chairman, since 1985); b. 12.4.40, Milnrow, Lancaster; m., Anne Macdonald Richardson; 2 s.; 1 d. Educ. Firth Park Grammar School, Sheffield; Glasgow University. Member, CBI Council, Scotland (Chairman, CBI Education and Training Committee); Member, Manpower Services Committee, Scotland. Address: (b.) Stag House, Castlebank Street, Glasgow, G11 6DY; T.-041-357 2000.

Hughes Hallett, David John, FRICS. Director, Scottish Landowners' Federation, since 1982; Secretary, Scottish Recreational Land Association, since 1982; b. 19.6.47, Dunfermline; m., Anne Wright; 2 s.; 1 d. Educ. Fettes College. Trained in estate management, Kerse Estates, and with Strutt and Parker, Edinburgh and Ipswich; miscellaneous work in Australia; a Vice-Chairman, Scottish Branch, Royal Institution of Chartered Surveyors (Past Chairman, RICS Land Agency and Agriculture Committee, Scotland, and of RICS Edinburgh Area). Recreations: sailing; shooting. Address: (b.) 18 Abercromby Place, Edinburgh; T.-031-556 4466.

Hume, Sir Alan (Blyth), KT, CB, MA. Chairman, Edinburgh New Town Conservation Committee, since 1975; b. 5.1.13, Broxburn; m., Marion Morton Garrett; 1 s.; 1 d. Educ. George Heriot's School, Edinburgh; Edinburgh University. Scottish Office: entered, 1936, Under Secretary, Scottish Home Department, 1957-59, Assistant Under Secretary of State, 1959-62, Under Secretary, Ministry of Public Building and Works, 1963-64, Secretary, Scottish Development Department, 1965-73; Chairman, Ancient Monuments Board for Scotland, 1973-81. Recreations: golf; fishing. Address: (h.) 12 Oswald Road, Edinburgh, EH9 2HJ; T.-031-667 2440.

Hume, James Douglas Howden, CBE, BSc, CEng, FIMechE. Deputy Chairman and Managing Director, Howden Group PLC, since 1973; b. 4.5.28, Melbourne, Australia; m., June Katharine Spriggs; 1 s.; 2 d. Educ. Loretto; Strathclyde University; Glasgow University. Royal Artillery, 1944-46 (2nd Lt.); engineering training: James Howden & Company Limited, 1948-54, Production Engineering Limited, 1954-55; James Howden & Company Limited: Production Manager, 1955-56, appointed Director, 1957, Joint Managing Director, 1960, Managing Director, 1963; Managing Director, Howden Group PLC, 1968. Recreation: sailing. Address: (b.) 195 Scotland Street, Glasgow, G5 8PJ; T.-041-429 4747.

Humphrey, James Malcolm Marcus, OStJ, MA, FRICS. Depute Chairman of Finance, Grampian Regional Council, since 1978; Grand Master Mason of Scotland, since 1983; b. 1.5.38, Montreal, Canada; m., Sabrina Margaret Pooley; 2 s.; 2 d. Educ. Eton College; Oxford University. Conservative Parliamentary candidate, North Aberdeen, 1966; Council Member, National Farmers Union of Scotland, 1968-73; Member, Aberdeen County Council, 1970-75 (Chairman of Finance, 1973-75); Chairman of Finance, Grampian Regional Council, 1974-78 (Leader, Conservative Group, 1974-78); Chairman, Clinterty Agricultural College Council; Member, Queen's Bodyguard for Scotland (Royal Company of Archers); Chairman, North of Scotland Board, Eagle Star Group. Recreations: shooting; fishing; photography. Address: (h.) Dinnet, Aboyne, Aberdeenshire.

Hunt, Tony, MA, BLitt. Reader in French, St. Andrews University, since 1979; b. 21.3.44, Bebington. Educ. Birkenhead School; Worcester College, Oxford. Lecturer in French, St. Andrews University, 1968-79; Honorary Treasurer, Anglo-Norman Text Society; Chief Bibliographer, British Branch, International Courtly Literature Society; Member, Editorial Board, Rhetorica (University of California). Recreation: playing the double-bass. Address: (b.) Department of French, St. Andrews University, St. Andrews, Fife; T.-0334 76161, Ext. 352.

Hunter, Sheriff Adam Kenneth Fisher, MA (Hons), LLB. Sheriff of North Strathclyde (formerly Renfrew and Argyll), at Paisley, since 1953; b. 1920; m.; 1 s.; 2 d. Educ. Dunfermline High School; St. Andrews University; Edinburgh University. Called to Bar, 1946; Chairman, Supreme Court Legal Aid Committee, 1949-53.

Hunter, Rev. Archibald MacBride, MA, BD, PhD, DPhil, DD. Professor of New Testament, Aberdeen University, 1945-71 and Master of Christ's College, Aberdeen, 1957-71; Author of books on the New Testament; b. 16.1.06, Kilwinning; m., Margaret Wylie Swanson; 1 s.; 1 d. Educ. Hutchesons' Grammar School, Glasgow; Glasgow University; Oxford University; Marburg University. Church of Scotland Minister, Comrie, Perthshire, 1934-37; Yates Professor of New Testament, Mansfield College, Oxford, 1937-42; Minister, Kinnoull, Perth, 1942-45; Hastie Lecturer, 1938; Lee Lecturer, 1950; Sprunt Lecturer, Richmond, Virginia, 1954; author of 30 books. Recreations: walking; fishing. Address: (h.) Dunira, 32 Gartconnell Road, Bearsden, Glasgow; T.-041-942 3406.

Hunter, Edward Anthony, BSc, MPhil. Principal Scientific Officer, AFRC Unit of Statistics, Edinburgh University, since 1967; b. 12.2.43, Newcastle-upon-Tyne; m., Janet M. Bruce; 1 s.; 1 d. Educ. Lasswade Secondary School; Edinburgh University. Recreations: playing bridge; reading. Address: (b.) AFRC Unit of Statistics, Edinburgh University, King's Buildings, Edinburgh; T.-031-667 1081, Ext. 2605.

Hunter, George Alexander, OBE (1980). Secretary, Commonwealth Games Council for Scotland, since 1978; General Secretary, XIII Commonwealth Games Edinburgh 1986, since 1982; Founder Governor, Scottish Sports Aid Foundation, since 1980; b. 24.2.26, Edinburgh; m., Eileen Elizabeth. Educ. George Watson's College, Edinburgh. Served with Cameronians, seconded to 17th Dogara Regiment, Indian Army, 1944-47 (Captain); Lawson Donaldson Seeds Ltd., 1942-82 (Director, 15 years); Secretary, Scottish Amateur Rowing Association, 1948-78 (President, 1978-84); Adviser, Sports Aid Foundation, since 1979; Treasurer, Commonwealth Games Council for Scotland, 1962-78; Member, Scottish Sports Council, 1976-84 (Chairman, Games and Sports Committee, 1976-84); Chairman, Scottish Standing Conference for Sport, 1977-84. Address: (h.) 139 Old Dalkeith Road, Edinburgh; T.-031-664 1070.

Hunter, James Albert, TD, LRCPE, LRCSE, LRFP&SG. Chairman, Social Work Committee, Shetland Islands Council; b. 2.5.14, Eshaness, Shetland; 4 s.; 2 d. Educ. Anderson Educational Institute, Lerwick; School of Medicine, Royal Colleges, Edinburgh. Captain, Royal Army Medical Corps, 1940-46; Medical Officer: Bangour Hospital, Midlothian, 1946, Bridge of Earn Hospital, Perthshire, 1946-47; Junior Assistant Tuberculosis Officer, Edinburgh, 1947; General Practitioner, Bixter and Voe, Shetland, 1947-78. Recreations: photography; fishing. Address: (h.) Kohima, Gott, Shetland, ZE2 9SG; T.-Gott 367.

Hunter, Professor John, MA, PhD, FIMA. Professor of Mathematics, Glasgow University, since 1976; b. 11.8.22, Airdrie; m., Brenda Laval Chesterton; 1 s.; 1 d. Educ. Airdrie Academy; Glasgow University; St. John's College, Cambridge. Lecturer, then Senior Lecturer in Mathematics, Glasgow University, 1951-76; Visiting Professor: Swarthmore College, USA, 1964-65, Auckland University, New Zealand, 1981; Visiting Lecturer, Mathematics in Architecture, Glasgow College of Art, 1965-71. Rayleigh Prize for Mathematical Research, Cambridge, 1951; Chairman, Scottish Mathematical Council. Recreations: golf; hill-walking; art; listening to music. Address: (b.) Department of Mathematics, Glasgow University, Glasgow, G12 8QW; T.-041-339 8855.

Hunter, Professor John Angus Alexander, BA, MD, FRCPEdin. Grant Professor of Dermatology, Edinburgh University, since 1981; b. 16.6.39, Edinburgh; m., Ruth Mary Farrow; 1 s.; 2 d. Educ. Loretto School; Pembroke College, Cambridge; Edinburgh University. Research Fellow, Institute of Dermatology, London, 1967; Registrar, Department of Dermatology, Edinburgh Royal Infirmary, 1968-70; Exchange Research Fellow, Department of Dermatology, Minnesota University, 1968; Lecturer, Department of Dermatology, Edinburgh University, 1970-74; Consultant Dermatologist, Lothian Health Board, 1974-80; Member, Executive Committee of Investigative Group, British Association of Dermatologists, 1974-76; Executive Committee, British Association of Dermatologists, 1977-79; SEC, Scottish Dermatological Society, 1980-82; Member, Specialist Advisory Committee (Dermatology), Joint Committee of Higher Medical Training, 1983; Member, Scottish Committee for Hospital Medical Services, 1983. Publication: Common Diseases of the Skin (Co-Editor). Recreations: music; gardening; tropical fish; golf. Address: (h.) Leewood, Rosslyn Castle, Roslin, Midlothian, EH25 9PZ; T.-031-440 2181.

Hunter, Hon. Lord, (John Oswald Mair Hunter), VRD. Senator of the College of Justice in Scotland, since 1961; b. 21.2.13; m.; 1 s.; 1 d. Educ. Edinburgh Academy; Rugby; New College, Oxford; Edinburgh University. Served Second World War (mentioned in Despatches); Lt.-Comdr., RNVR (retired, 1949); called to Bar, Inner Temple, 1937; admitted, Faculty of Advocates, 1937; QC (Scot), 1951; Advocate Depute (Home), 1954-57; Sheriff of Ayr and Bute, 1957-61; Chairman, Scottish Law Commission, 1971-81; Chairman, Scottish Council on Crime, 1972-75; Deputy Chairman, Boundary Commission for Scotland, 1971-76; Honorary President, Scottish Association for Study of Delinquency, since 1971.

Hunter, Mollie. Writer; b. 30.6.22, Longniddry; m., Thomas McIlwraith; 2 s. Educ. Preston Lodge School. Freelance Journalist, until 1960; Writer of various types of fiction (fantasy, historical novels, "realism") for children of varying age groups; 24 titles published, including Talent Is Not Enough, on the craft of writing for children; travelled extensively (Australia, New Zealand, Canada, USA); Lecturer on writing for children; Writer-in-Residence, Dalhousie University, Halifax, Canada, on several occasions; awarded Arbuthnot Lectureship, 1975, and Carnegie Medal, 1975. Recreations: reading; gardening; music. Address: The Shieling, Milton, by Drumnadrochit, Inverness-shire; T.-04562 267.

Hunter, Robert Dalglish, MBE. Consultant, R.D. Hunter and Company, Solicitors, Cumnock, since 1976; Honorary Sheriff, Ayr, since 1974; b. 4.8.13, Cumnock; m., Mary Reid Park; 2 s.; 2 d. Educ. Cumnock Academy; Glasgow University. Solicitor and Notary Public, R.D. Hunter and Company, Solicitors, 1941-76; Town Clerk, Cumnock, 1941-75 (Depute Town Clerk, 1936-41); JP Procurator Fiscal, 1941-75; District Prosecutor, 1975-76; Clerk, Cumnock Burgh Police Court, 1941-75; Manager, then Joint Manager, Cumnock and New Cumnock Branches, Commercial Bank of Scotland, later National Commercial Bank, ultimately Royal Bank of Scotland, 1941-76; Company Secretary: Cumnock Knitwear Ltd., 1964-65, Holyrood Knitwear Ltd., 1964-66, Falmer Manufacturing Company (Cumnock) Ltd., 1964-66; Chairman: Kyle Knitwear Ltd., 1966-76, Radio Ayrshire Ltd., 1980-83; Member, Scottish Board of Directors, Century Insurance Company Ltd., 1947-76; Member: Committee of Management, Scottish Orchestra, 1941-46, Ayrshire Army Cadet Force League, 1950-77, Scottish Advisory Council, BBC, 1950-52, Scottish Music Advisory Committee, BBC, 1952-55; Chairman: Kilmarnock Theatre Trust, 1958-59, Ayrshire Music Festival, 1959-61 (President, 1962-64); Member, ITA (Scottish Committee), 1959-65; Convention of Royal Burghs of Scotland: Chairman, Committee on Music, the Arts and Broadcasting, 1964-66, Vice-Chairman, Committee on Industry and Transport, 1968-70; Member, Committee of Enquiry on Library Services in Scotland, 1965-66;

Scottish Arts Council: Member, 1966-73, Chairman, Working Party on Touring Arrangements, 1970-71, Chairman, Working Party on Ballet and Dance in Scotland, 1972-73, Member, Regional Development Committee, 1975-77; Chairman, South Ayrshire Constituency Conservative Party, 1967-70; Member, Broadcasting Council for Scotland, 1968-74; Chairman, Scottish Civic Entertainment Association, 1970-80 (Life President, since 1980); Member: MacRobert Advisory Council, Stirling University, since 1970, Scottish Information Service for the Disabled, 1973-78; Medal of Merit from Chief Scout, 1955 (Bar, 1965); Honorary Burgess, Burgh of Cumnock and Holmhead, 1975; Dean, Ayr Faculty of Solicitors, 1976-77; President, Ayr Chamber of Commerce, 1977-79. Address: (h.) The Homestead, Cumnock, Ayrshire, KA18 1AP.

Hunter, Robert Leslie Cockburn, MA, LLB, WS, FCI (Arb). Chairman, Industrial Tribunals (Scotland), 1976-85; Chairman, Social Security Appeal Tribunals, since 1983; Lecturer in Law, Aberdeen University, since 1971; b. 31.12.34, Polmont, Stirlingshire; m., Joan Gwendolen Mappin (m. diss.); 2 s. Educ. Loretto School; St. Andrews University; Edinburgh University. National Service, Royal Signals, 1953-55; Law Apprentice, Gillespie and Paterson, WS, Patrick and James, WS, 1960-63; Assistant Solicitor, Patrick and James, WS, 1963-64; Legal Assistant, Inverness County Council, 1964-66; Lecturer in Jurisprudence, Dundee University, 1966-71; occasional Lecturer, Petroleum Training Institute, Stavanger, Norway, 1982-84; Honorary Secretary, Aberdeen Association of University Teachers, 1974-75; Governor, Robert Gordon's Institute of Technology, since 1982 (Chairman, 1982-85); Elder, Queen's Cross Church of Scotland, Aberdeen, since 1982. Recreations: choral singing; reading (in literature, history and philosophy); cycling. Address: (h.) Primrose Cottage, Place of Tilliefoure, by Monymusk, Inverurie, Aberdeenshire, AB3 7JB; T.-Monymusk 357.

Hunter, Russell. Actor; b. 18.2.25, Glasgow. Former shipyard worker; began acting as an amateur; made professional debut with Glasgow Unity Theatre, 1947; appeared in repertory with Edinburgh Gateway, Edinburgh Traverse and Glasgow Citizens'; acted with the RSC, Bristol Old Vic and at the Old Vic, London; played title role in The Servant o' Twa Maisters, 1965, opening production of Edinburgh Civic Theatre Company; played The Pope in Galileo, also at Royal Lyceum; played The Gravedigger in Hamlet, Assembly Hall, Edinburgh Festival; took title role in Cocky, one-man play, 1969; played Jock, solo play, 1972.

Hunter-Blair, Sir James, 7th Bt; b. 7.5.89; m., 1, Jean McIntyre (deceased); 2 s.; 2, Ethel Norah Collins (deceased). Educ. Wellington; Balliol College, Oxford; Christ's College, Cambridge. Seaforth Highlanders, 1915-19; District Officer, Forestry Commission, 1920-28. Address: (h.) Milton, Maybole, Ayrshire.

Hurford, Professor James Raymond, BA, PhD. Professor of General Linguistics, Edinburgh University, since 1979; b. 16.7.41, Reading; m.,

Sue Ann Davis; 2 d. Educ. Exeter School; St. John's College, Cambridge; University College, London. Research Fellow, System Development Corporation, Santa Monica, California, 1967-68; Assistant Professor, University of California, 1968-71; Lecturer, Senior Lecturer, Lancaster University, 1972-79. Publications: The Linguistic Theory of Numerals, 1975; Semantics: A Coursebook (Co-author), 1983. Recreations: gardening; recorder playing. Address: (h.) 14 East Brighton Crescent, Portobello, Edinburgh.

Hutcheon, Andrew William, MB, ChB, MD, MRCP, FRCP. Consultant Physician to Aberdeen Hospitals, since 1978; Consultant Medical Oncologist, since 1978; Senior Lecturer in Medicine, Aberdeen University, since 1978; b. 21.5.43, Aberdeen; m., Christine Gray Cusiter; 1 s.; 2 d. Educ. Robert Gordon's College, Aberdeen; Aberdeen University. House Physician, Aberdeen Royal Infirmary, 1968; House Surgeon, Balfour Hospital, Orkney, 1969; Western Infirmary, Glasgow: Senior House Physician, 1970, Registrar in General Medicine, 1971; University Department of Medicine, Glasgow: Research Fellow, 1973, Senior Registrar, 1975; Senior Registrar, Royal Marsden Hospital, London, 1977. Recreations: skiing; curling; long distance running. Address: (h.) Moreseat, 159 Midstocket Road, Aberdeen, AB2 4LU; T.-0224 637204.

Hutcheon, James Fox, CEng, MICE, MIHT, MIBCO. Chief Engineer and Master of Works, City of Dundee District Council, since 1983; b. 17.1.39, Dundee; m., Jesma White Dykes; 2 d. Educ. Forfar Academy; Montrose Academy; Dundee College of Art and Technology. Pupil under Agreement to County Engineer, Angus County Council, 1957-62; Assistant Engineer, then Senior Assistant Engineer, Arbroath Town Council, 1962-70; Senior Assistant Engineer, then Principal Assistant Engineer, Dundee Corporation, 1970-75; Depute Chief Engineer, City of Dundee District Council, 1975-83. Recreations: gardening; music; golf. Address: (h.) 75 Collingwood Street, Barnhill, Dundee, DD5 2UF; T.-0382 77371.

Hutcheson, Rev. Norman McKenzie, MA, BD. Minister, Saint Andrew's Parish Church, Kirkcaldy, since 1973; b. 11.10.48, Leven, Fife; m., Elizabeth Gilchrist Anderson; 2 d. Educ. Hillhead High School, Glasgow; Glasgow University; Edinburgh University. Member, General Assembly Committees, since 1975: Finance, Practice and Procedure, Social Responsibility; Moderator, Kirkcaldy Presbytery, 1984. Recreations: walking; photography. Address: 15 Harcourt Road, Kirkcaldy, Fife; T.-0592 260811.

Hutchinson, John Stuart Morley, BSc, PhD, DipAgrSci, MIBiol. Senior Lecturer, School of Agriculture, Aberdeen University, since 1980; b. 6.12.32, Exeter; m., Helen Kenley. Educ. Solihull; Nottingham University; Cambridge University. Junior Research Fellow, Aberdeen University, 1957-59; Lecturer, Senior Lecturer, St. Thomas's Hospital Medical School, London University, 1959-77; Visiting Research Associate, Harvard University, 1965-66; Lecturer, Aberdeen University, 1978-80; Member, Editorial

Boards, Journal of Endocrinology and Animal Reproduction Science. Publications: The Endocrine Hypothalamus (Joint Editor), 1978; The Hypothalamo Pituitary Control of The Ovary, 1979. Recreations: gardening; reading; rugby. Address: (b.) School of Agriculture, Aberdeen University, Aberdeen; T.-0224 40291.

Hutchison, Rev. Alexander Scott, MA, BD, DD. Minister, Rubislaw Parish Church, Aberdeen, since 1968; b. 22.7.26, Uddingston, Glasgow; m., Gillian Alice Curry; 2 s.; 4 d. Educ. Bell-Baxter School, Cupar; St. Andrews University and St. Mary's College. Church of Scotland Chaplain to Overseas Students, 1954-59; Minister, Ceres, Fife, 1959-68; Chairman, International Year of Disabled People (Aberdeen), 1981; Member, Post Office Users Council (Scotland); Disabled Scot of the Year, 1982; Honorary DD, St. Andrews; Burgess (Aberdeen). Recreation: bread and broth making. Address: 45 Rubislaw Den South, Aberdeen, AB2 6BD; T.-0224 314878.

Hutchison, David, MA, MLitt. Senior Lecturer in Communication Studies, Glasgow College of Technology, since 1975; b. 24.9.44, West Kilbride; m., Pauleen Frew; 2 d. Educ. Ardrossan Academy; Glasgow University. Tutor/Organiser, WEA (West of Scotland), 1966-69; Teacher, Reid Kerr College, Paisley, 1969-71; Lecturer in Communication Studies, Glasgow College of Technology, 1971-75; Member, West Kilbride District Council, 1970-75 (Chairman, 1972-75); author of play, Deadline, Pitlochry Festival Theatre, 1980. Publications: The Modern Scottish Theatre, 1977; Headlines: the Media in Scotland (Editor), 1978. Recreations: walking; swimming; the arts. Address: (b.) Department of Humanities, Glasgow College of Technology, Cowcaddens Road, Glasgow, G4 0BA; T.-041-332 7090.

Hutchison, Lt.-Comdr. Sir (George) Ian Clark, Kt (1954). Member, Queen's Bodyguard for Scotland (Royal Company of Archers); b. 4.1.03; m., Sheena Campbell (deceased); 1 d. Educ. Edinburgh Academy; RN Colleges. Joined Navy, 1916; Member, Edinburgh Town Council, 1935-41; rejoined Navy, 1939; MP (Unionist), Edinburgh West, 1941-59; Deputy Lieutenant, County of City of Edinburgh, 1958-84.

Hutchison, Rev. Henry, BD, BEd, MA, MLitt, PhD, DipRE, LLCM. Minister, Carmunnock Parish Church, Glasgow, since 1977; b. 4.5.23, Alloa; m., Ann Sheila Maree Ross; 1 s. Educ. Alloa Academy; Dollar Academy; Edinburgh University; Glasgow University; Jordanhill College of Education; Toronto University. War service, RAF; Minister: Erskine Church, Saltcoats, 1948-53, Crosshill-Victoria Church, Glasgow, 1953-57, St. Paul's Presbyterian Church, Peterborough, Ontario, 1957-60; Principal, Stanstead College, Quebec, 1960-63; Assistant Professor of Education, Brandon University, Manitoba, 1965-67; Lecturer in Education, Glasgow University, 1967-77; Moderator, Peterborough Presbytery, Ontario, 1959. Publications: The Church and Spiritual Healing, 1955; A Faith to Live By, 1959; The Beatitudes and Modern Life, 1960; Scottish Public Educational Documents, 1973; Kirk Life in Old Carmunnock, 1978; Carmunnock Church 1854-1947, 1979; God Believes in You!, 1980; Well I'm Blessed!, 1981, Have a Word with God, 1981; Healing through Worship, 1981; A Faith that Conquers, 1982. Recreations: music; bowls; walking. Address: 161 Waterside Road, Carmunnock, Glasgow, G76 9AJ; T.-041-644 1578.

Hutchison, Ian Somerville, OBE, JP. Chairman, Eastwood District Licensing Board; Member, Eastwood District Council (Chairman of Planning); Vice Chairman, Scottish National Housing & Town Planning Council; Member, Scottish Valuation Advisory Council, since 1982; Member, Historic Buildings Council for Scotland, since 1983; Managing Director, Timbertection Ltd., since 1973; b. 10.4.28, Glasgow; m., Aileen Wallace; 2 s.; 2 d. Educ. Hutchesons' Boys' Grammar School. Elected to First (Eastwood) District Council, 1967, Renfrew County Council, 1970, Eastwood District Council, 1974; Provost, Eastwood, 1974-80; Delegate, COSLA, since 1975 (Vice President, COSLA, 1979-82); Member, Management Committee, Planning Exchange; Member, Renfrewshire Valuation Appeals Committee; Governor, The Queen's College, Glasgow, since 1973 (Chairman of Governors, since 1980). Recreations: gardening; fishing. Address: (h.) 39 Hazelwood Avenue, Newton Mearns, Glasgow, G77 5QT; T.-041-639 2186.

Hutchison, James Kenneth, CA. Chief Executive, Scottish Sports Council, since 1972; b. 3.7.34, Edinburgh. Educ. George Heriot's School; Edinburgh University. CA apprentice and Audit Assistant, 1952-59; RAF Officer, Secretarial Branch, 1959-63; Scottish Council of Physical Recreation: Depute Secretary, 1964-68, General Secretary, 1968-72; Trustee and Honorary Secretary, Scottish Disability Foundation; Trustee, Scottish Physical Recreation Fund; Past Chairman, Edinburgh Sports Club Ltd.; Past President, George Heriot's School (FP) Rugby Club. Recreations: golf; swimming; theatre; good food and wine. Address: (b.) 1 St. Colme Street, Edinburgh, EH3 6AA; T.-031-225 8411.

Hutchison, Sir Peter Craft, Bt, BA. Chairman, Hutchison & Craft Ltd., Insurance Brokers, and associated/subsidiary companies; Director, Stakis plc, since 1979; Board Member, Scottish Tourist Board, since 1981; Chairman, Board of Trustees, Royal Botanic Garden, Edinburgh; b. 5.6.35, London; m., Virginia Colville; 1 s. Educ. Eton; Magdalene College, Cambridge. National Service, Royal Scots Greys (2nd Lt.); Northern Assurance Co. (London); Director of various companies involved in banking, engineering, etc.; Past Chairman, Ailsa Shipbuilding Co. Ltd.; Deacon, Incorporation of Hammermen of Glasgow, 1984-85. Recreations: plant hunting; gardening; calligraphy. Address: (h.) Milton House, Milton, by Dumbarton, G82 2TU; T.-Dumbarton 61609.

Hutton, Alasdair Henry, TD. Member (Conservative), European Parliament, for South Scotland, since 1979; b. 19.5.40; m.; 2 s. Educ. Dollar Academy; Brisbane State High School, Australia. Journalist and Broadcaster.

Hutton, James Thomas, ARCM. Composer; Visiting Teacher of Music, since 1960; b. 12.5.23, Glasgow; m., Anne Jamieson Bowes; 1 s. Educ. Provanside Secondary School; Glasgow University; Royal Scottish Academy of Music. Worked for Renfrewshire Education Authority, 1960-64, Lanarkshire Education Authority, since 1964; entirely self-taught Composer of orchestral music; works include two symphonies, two concert-overtures, piano concerto, chamber music, and works for brass band, solo piano and organ; has also composed and arranged music for jazz orchestras and groups. Recreation: playing jazz piano. Address: (h.) 88 Warwick, East Kilbride; T.-East Kilbride 25895.

Hyslop, Kenneth Alexander, BSc. Rector, Leith Academy, since 1983; b. 7.12.39, Edinburgh; m., Sheena Isabel Hyslop; 1 s.; 1 d. Educ. Boroughmuir Secondary School; Heriot-Watt University. Science Teacher, Currie High School, 1964-69; Newbattle High School: Principal Teacher of Science, 1969-72, Assistant Headteacher, 1972-73; Headteacher, Castlebrae High School, 1977-83. Address: (b.) Leith Academy, Duke Street, Edinburgh; T.-031-554 0606.

I

Idiens, Dale, BA, DipEd. Keeper, Department of Art and Archaeology, Royal Scottish Museum, since 1983; b. 13.5.42, Prestatyn. Educ. Wycombe High School, High Wycombe; Leicester University. Royal Scottish Museum, Department of Art and Archaeology: Assistant Keeper in Charge of Ethnography, 1964, Deputy Keeper, 1979. Address: (b.) Royal Scottish Museum, Edinburgh; T.-031-225 7534.

Illingworth, Sir Charles Frederick William, Kt (1961), CBE (1946). Regius Professor of Surgery, Glasgow University, 1939-64; Honorary Surgeon to The Queen, in Scotland, 1961-65; Extra Surgeon, since 1965; b. 8.5.99; m., Eleanor Mary Bennett (deceased); 4 s. Educ. Heath Grammar School, Halifax; Edinburgh University.

Illsley, William Allen, BA, MA, DipEd, PhD, FRSA. Principal, Dundee College of Education, since 1979; b. 24.9.21, Startforth, near Barnard Castle; m., Doris Gorrey; 2 s. Educ. Barnard Castle School; St. Chad's College, Durham University; St. Andrews University. War service, Grenadier Guards, Reconnaissance Corps and 2nd Royal Lancers (Indian Army); teaching; Senior Education Officer, Northern Nigeria; Dundee College of Education: Lecturer, Senior Lecturer, Assistant Principal. Publications: text books on the teaching of Shakespeare and English; County of Angus volume, Third Statistical Account of Scotland (Editor). Recreations: angling; gardening; walking. Address: (h.) Dromore, Strathern Road, West Ferry, Dundee; T.-0382 79301.

Inch, Sir John Ritchie, Kt (1972), CVO (1969), CBE (1958), QPM (1961). Chief Constable, Edinburgh City Police, 1955-75; b. 14.5.11; m.; 1 s.; 2 d. Educ. Hamilton Academy; Glasgow University.

Inglis, Rev. Donald Bain Carrick, MA, MEd, BD. Minister, St. Andrew's Parish Church, Turriff, since 1983; b. 17.12.41, Aberdeen; m., Yvonne M.S. Cook; 1 s.; 2 d. Educ. Aberdeen Grammar School; Aberdeen University; Aberdeen College of Education; Glasgow University. Teacher of English and History at Aberdeen and Ellon Academy, 1964-68; Educational Psychologist, then Senior Educational Psychologist, Lanarkshire, 1968-72; Assistant Minister, Bathgate High Church, 1975-77; Educational Psychologist, then Senior Educational Psychologist, Fife, 1977-83. Former Member, Executive Committee, Psychologists' Section, Educational Institute of Scotland; Convener, Education Committee, Buchan Presbytery. Recreations: violin playing; swimming; hill-walking; cycling. Address: St. Andrew's Manse, Balmellie Road, Turriff, Aberdeenshire, AB5 7DP; T.-Turriff 63240.

Inglis, Florence R., MBE, JP. Member, Monklands District Council, since 1974; b. Rugby, Warwickshire; m., Francis Moncur Inglis (deceased); 1 d. Educ. Redlands Girls School; Rugby Technical College. Former Member, Coatbridge Town Council; Member, various Committees attached to local Conservative Association; served as Magistrate, JP Court and District Court. Recreations: reading; crosswords; walking; sailing. Address: (h.) 5 Woodlands Drive, Coatbridge; T.-Coatbridge 24739.

Inglis, Professor James Alistair Macfarlane, CBE (1984), MA, LLB. Professor of Conveyancing, Glasgow University, since 1979; Professor of Professional Legal Practice, since 1984 (first holder of Chair); Partner, McClure, Naismith, Anderson & Gardiner, Solicitors, Glasgow, since 1956; b. 24.12.28, Kilmarnock; m., Mary Elizabeth Howie; 2 s.; 3 d. Educ. Kilmarnock Academy; Fettes College; St. Andrews University; Glasgow University. Qualified as Solicitor, 1952; appointed Professor of Conveyancing, Glasgow University, 1979; Member: Board of Management, Victoria and Leverndale Hospitals, 1964-74; Greater Glasgow Health Board, 1975-83; President, Rent Assessment Panel for Scotland, since 1976; Vice Chairman, Glasgow Hospitals Auxiliary Association, since 1975; Convener, Ad Hoc Committee, Church of Scotland, into Legal Services of Church, 1978-79; Session Clerk, Caldwell Parish Church, since 1963. Recreations: golf; curling. Address: (h.) Crioch, Uplawmoor, Glasgow; T.-Uplawmoor 315.

Inglis, William Caldwell, MA (Hons). Rector, Largs Academy, since 1973; b. 22.12.36, Ayr; m., Helga Goldschmidt; 2 s.; 3 d. Educ. Ayr Academy; Glasgow University. Teacher of History, Irvine Royal Academy, 1959-64; Principal Teacher of History, Geography and Modern Studies, Dalmellington High School, 1964-66; Principal Teacher of History and Modern Studies,

Cumnock Academy, 1966-70; Depute Rector, Auchinleck Academy, 1970-72. Founder President, Irvine Royal Academicals Rugby Football Club. Recreation: gardening; swimming. Address: (b.) Largs Academy, Flatt Road, Largs; T.-0475 673205.

Ingram, Hugh Albert Pugh, BA (Cantab), PhD. Lecturer in Botany (Ecology), Dundee University, since 1966; Vice-Chairman (Conservation and Science), Scottish Wildlife Trust, since 1982; b. 29.4.37, Rugby; m., Dr. Ruth Hunter; 1 s.; 1 d. Educ. Lawrence Sheriff School, Rugby; Rugby School; Emmanuel College, Cambridge; Hatfield College, Durham. Demonstrator in Botany, University College of North Wales, Bangor, 1963-64; Staff Tutor in Natural Science, Department of Extra-Mural Studies, Bristol University, 1964-65; Member, UK Committee, International Peat Society. Recreations: music (clarinet, piano); literature; rural history; hill-walking. Address: (h.) Johnstonfield, Newburgh, Cupar, Fife, KY14 6JG.

Ingram, Malcolm David, BSc, PhD, DSc, CChem, FRSC. Senior Lecturer in Chemistry, Aberdeen University, since 1965; b. 18.1.39, Wallasey; m., Lorna Hardman; 1 s.; 1 d. Educ. Oldershaw Grammar School; Liverpool University. Research Associate, Rensselaer Polytechnic Institute, Troy, New York, 1964-65; Lecturer in Chemistry, Aberdeen University, 1965-78; Visiting Professor, College of William and Mary, Williamsburg, Virginia, 1978-79. Recreations: tennis; badminton; church music. Address: (b.) Department of Chemistry, Aberdeen University, Meston Walk, Aberdeen, AB9 2UE; T.-0224 40241.

Ingram-Brown, Leslie, FISMM, MBIM, MRIN. Editor, Nautical Magazine, since 1980; Joint Managing Director, Brown, Son & Ferguson Ltd., since 1980; b. 24.5.47, Glasgow; m., Susanna. Educ. Shawlands Academy; Hutchesons' Boys' Grammar School; Glasgow College of Commerce. Brown, Son & Ferguson Ltd.: Assistant Company Secretary, 1968-72, Company Secretary/Director, 1972-80. Recreations: curling; cricket; golf; reading. Address: (b.) 4/10 Darnley Street, Glasgow, G41 2SD.

Inkson, Robert Henry Ewen, BSc, FSS, FIS. Head, Department of Statistics, Macaulay Institute for Soil Research, since 1968; b. 1.10.24, Aberdeen; m., Jean Davidson McArthur. Educ. Aberdeen Central School; Aberdeen University. Macaulay Institute for Soil Research: Scientific Officer, 1951-54, Senior Scientific Officer, 1954-63, Principal Scientific Officer, since 1963. Chairman and Treasurer, Aberdeen Unitarian Church; Secretary, Scottish Unitarian Association; Associate Member, General Assembly of Unitarian and Free Christian Churches. Recreations: music; gardening. Address: (h.) 39 Woodend Place, Aberdeen, AB2 6AP; T.-0224 35304.

Innes of Edingight, Malcolm Rognvald, CVO, MA, LLB, WS, FSA Scot. Lord Lyon King of Arms, since 1981; Secretary to Order of the Thistle, since 1981; b. 25.5.38, Edinburgh; m.,

Joan Hay; 3 s. Educ. Edinburgh Academy; Edinburgh University. Carrick Pursuivant, 1958; Marchmont Herald, 1971; Lyon Clerk and Keeper of the Record, 1966; Member, Queen's Bodyguard for Scotland (Royal Company of Archers); President, Scottish Heraldry Society. Recreations: archery; shooting; fishing. Address: (b.) Court of the Lord Lyon, HM New Register House, Edinburgh; T.-031-556 7255.

Innes, Norman Lindsay, BSc, PhD, DSc, FIBiol. Head, Plant Breeding Division, Scottish Crop Research Institute, since 1984; b. 3.5.34, Kirriemuir; m., Marjory Niven Farquhar; 1 s.; 1 d. Educ. Websters High School, Kirriemuir; Aberdeen University; Cambridge University. Senior Cotton Breeder: Sudan, 1958-66, Uganda, 1966-71; Head, Cotton Research Unit, Uganda, 1972; National Vegetable Research Station, Wellesbourne: Head, Plant Breeding Section, 1973-84, Deputy Director, 1977-84; Honorary Lecturer, then Honorary Professor, Birmingham University, 1973-84; Governing Board Member, International Crops Research Institute for Semi-Arid Tropics, India, since 1982; Honorary Senior Lecturer, St. Andrews University, since 1984; Chairman, British Association of Plant Breeders, 1982-84; Member, Oxfam Council of Trustees, 1982-85. Recreations: golf; gardening; photography; stamp collecting; travel. Address: (b.) Scottish Crop Research Institute, Invergowrie, Dundee, DD2 5DA; T.-082 67 731.

Innes, Richard Threlfall, BA, LLB. Honorary Sheriff, Fife; retired Solicitor; b. 5.9.00, Kirkcaldy; m., Jean Davidson; 2 s.; 3 d. Educ. Cargilfield; Fettes; Oxford University; Edinburgh University. Former Secretary, Kirkcaldy Chamber of Commerce; former Clerk, Commissioners of Income Tax. Recreations: gardening; golf. Address: (h.) 14 Boglily Road, Kirkcaldy, Fife; T.-0592 263287.

Inness, Peter Henderson, BMus (Hons), PhD. Composer; b. 13.12.46, Falkirk; m., Sheena MacBrayne; 2 d. Educ. Falkirk High School; Edinburgh University; Royal College of Music, London. Lecturer in Music, Aberdeen University, 1969-84; Visiting Professor of Music, Evansville University, Indiana, 1984-85; more than 30 works as Composer; also organist, pianist and conductor; numerous broadcasts of compositions by BBC; publication of choral, organ and piano music; Adjudicator at music festivals in Scotland; numerous commissions for compositions, including several funded by Scottish Arts Council and Arts Council of GB; Member, BBC Music Advisory Panel (Scotland), 1976-79; Member, Scottish Music Archive. Recreations: driving; golf; walking; travelling; squash. Address: (h.) 105 North Deeside Road, Bieldside, Aberdeen, AB1 9DS; T.-0224 867129.

Ireland, James Cecil Hardin. Trustee, Scottish Rugby Union, since 1951 (President, 1950-51); b. 10.12.03, Glasgow; m., Margaret Stewart McLean. Educ. High School of Glasgow. Singer Manufacturing Co. Ltd.; William Younger & Co. Ltd.; War service, RNVR and Royal Marines, 1940-46; Dundee Manager, William Younger & Co. Ltd.; London Manager, Scottish & Newcastle Breweries (retired, 1968); rugby international, 1925-26-27; Scottish Rugby Union Committee, 1936; international Referee, 1938-39; Chairman, four Home Unions Tours Committee, 1946-51; Honorary Vice President, South Africa Rugby Board, 1964; President, Glasgow High School Club, 1964-65; Elder, St. Columba's Church of Scotland, London, 1960-68. Recreations: spectating at all sports; renewing friendships. Address: (h.) 10 Abbots View, Polmont, FK2 0QL; T.-Polmont 713400.

Ireland, Dr. Kenneth, OBE, DUniv, FRSA, FTS, BL. Freelance Arts Fundraising Consultant, since 1984; Consultant, Hanover Fine Arts (Edinburgh), since 1985; b. 17.6.20, Edinburgh; m., Moira Margaret Lamb; 2 s. Educ. Edinburgh Academy; Edinburgh University. Law Apprentice, Steedman Ramage & Co., WS, Edinburgh, 1938-41; War service: Royal Artillery, Gnr/Sgt., 1941-42, Intelligence Corps, Sgt./S. Sgt./WO II, 1942-46; Lt. (TA), 1948-52; General Manager: Park Theatre Club, Glasgow, 1946-49, Pitlochry Festival Theatre, 1951-53; Pitlochry Festival Society Ltd.: General Manager, 1953-57, Festival Director and Secretary, 1957-83 (retired, 1984); Board Member, Scottish Tourist Board, 1966-69; Chairman, Tourist Association of Scotland, 1967-69; Deputy Chairman, Scottish Tourist Consultative Council, 1977-83; Chairman, Federation of Scottish Theatre Ltd., since 1984; Board Member, Scottish Ballet, since 1985; Member, Advisory Council for the Arts in Scotland, since 1984; Member, Scotland's Gardens Scheme, since 1967; Trustee, J.D. Fergusson Art Foundation, since 1970; ESU Scotland Thyne Scholarship, 1970; Bill Heron Trophy, 1981 (first recipient for services to tourism). Recreations: foreign travel; theatre-going; galleries; reading. Address: (h.) 10 Ravelston Rise, Edinburgh, EH4 3LH; T.-031-346 2292.

Ireland, Sheriff Ronald David, QC. Sheriff, Lothian and Borders, at Edinburgh, since 1972; b. 13.3.25, Edinburgh. Educ. George Watson's College, Edinburgh; Balliol College, Oxford (Scholar); Edinburgh University. Advocate, 1952; Clerk, Faculty of Advocates, 1957-58; Professor of Scots Law, Aberdeen University, 1958-71; QC, 1964; Dean, Faculty of Law, Aberdeen University, 1964-67; Chairman, Board of Management, Aberdeen General Hospitals, 1964-71; Director, Scottish Courts Administration, 1975-78. Address: (h.) 6a Greenhill Gardens, Edinburgh, EH10 4BW.

Ireland, Thomas, Extra Master, FRIN. Principal, Glasgow College of Nautical Studies, since 1978; b. 24.3.26, Leslie, Fife; m., Jean Cameron Hepburn; 1 s.; 1 d. Educ. Bell-Baxter High School, Cupar; Leith Nautical College, Edinburgh. Deck Cadet and Deck Officer, Merchant Navy, 1943-55; Lecturer, Leith Nautical College, 1955-66; Master-in-Charge, TS Dolphin, 1967-68; Head, Department of Navigation and Vice Principal, Leith Nautical College, 1969-75; Principal, The Nautical College, Fleetwood, 1975-78. Chairman, SCOTEC Nautical Science Committee, since 1978; Member, Merchant Navy Training Board, since 1983. Address: (h.) 33 Gailes Road, Barassie, Troon, KA10 6TB; T.-0292 313115.

Ironside, Leonard. Member, Grampian Regional Council, since 1982; Commonwealth Professional Wrestling Champion, since 1981; b. 16.2.50, Aberdeen. Educ. Hilton Academy, Aberdeen. Section Manager, Department of Health and Social Security, since 1976. Won Commonwealth Professional Wrestling Championship at Middleweight, 1979; lost Championship, 1981; regained title, 1981; gained European Lightweight title, 1985. Recreations: yoga teacher; also play tennis, squash, badminton, swimming. Address: (h.) 239 North Anderson Drive, Aberdeen; T.-Aberdeen 696005.

Irvine, Andrew Robertson, MBE (1979). Rugby Player; b. 16.9.51, Edinburgh; m., Audrey; 2 d. Educ. George Heriot's School, Edinburgh; Edinburgh University. Captained George Heriot's School, Scottish Schools, Heriots FP, Edinburgh, Scotland; holds records for: most international points scored (273 for Scotland, 28 for British Lions in three tours (nine tests)) and most tries scored by a full back (10); made international debut against All Blacks, 1972; 51 caps for Scotland; works as a Chartered Surveyor.

Irvine, George Bruce, BSc. Head Teacher, Sandwick Junior High School, since 1974; b. 12.2.23, Bressay, Shetland; m., Catherine M.S. Manson; 1 s.; 1 d. Educ. Anderson Educational Institute, Lerwick; Aberdeen University. Royal Navy, 1945-47 (Engineer Officer); Teacher: Cunningsburgh Primary School, 1948-49, Happyhansel Junior Secondary School, 1949-53, Hamnavoe Junior Secondary School, 1953-55, Sandwick Junior High School, since 1955 (Depute Head Teacher, 1971-74). Has served on management committees of numerous local organisations, including Dunrossness District Council and Sandwick Community Council. Recreations: (no longer as active participant): sailing; fishing; drama. Address: (h.) Fairwinds, Sandwick, Shetland; T.-095 05 241.

Irvine, James Williamson, MBE, JP, MA, FEIS. Honorary Sheriff, Lerwick, since 1977; b. 10.3.17, Virkie, Shetland; m., Isabella E. White; 1 s.; 1 d. Educ. Virkie Public School; Anderson Educational Institute; Edinburgh Unversity; Moray House College of Education. Army, 1940-46; Further Education Officer, Shetland, 1946-50; Teacher in Shetland, 1950-77; Headmaster, Lerwick Central School, 1966-77; First Chairman, Shetland Movement. Publications: Footprints, 1980; Up-Helly-Aa, 1982; Lerwick, 1985. Recreation: reading. Address: (h.) Brekkheim, 4 Midgarth Crescent, Lerwick, Shetland Isles.

Irvine, John Rutherford, JP. Chairman, Roxburgh District Council, since 1980; Honorary Provost of Hawick, since 1982; b. 14.6.40, Hawick; m., Eileen Millar; 1 s. Educ. Hawick High School; Henderson Technical College, Hawick. Joined Roxburgh District Council, 1975; Vice-Convener, Housing Committee, 1977-80. Address: (h.) Airenlea, 3 Teviot Crescent, Hawick, Roxburghshire; T.-0450 75959.

Irvine Robertson, Alexander, TD, DL, MA, LLB. Solicitor, since 1936; Honorary Sheriff, Tayside, Central and Fife; b. 12.11.12, Stirling; m., Jean Margaret Fraser; 3 s.; 1 d. Educ. Fettes College, Edinburgh; Edinburgh University. Territorial Army, 1931-53 (retired, Bt. Colonel); Councillor, Royal Burgh of Stirling, 1946-50; Chairman, Stirlingshire T & AF Association, 1965-68; Secretary, Stirlingshire and Clackmannanshire (later Central Region) Valuation Appeal Committee, 1956-85; Chairman, Visiting Committee, Cornton Vale Borstal Institution, 1960-70; Session Clerk, Church of the Holy Rude, Stirling, 1958-85. Publication: Peacetime (History of 7th Bn., Argyll and Sutherland Highlanders, 1908-58). Recreations: reading; golf. Address: (h.) 6 Park Avenue, Stirling; T.-Stirling 74526.

Irving, Rev. George, MA. Parish Minister, Ecclefechan and Brydekirk; b. 23.2.17, parish of Crossmichael; m., Maybell Ellen Allan Swan; 4 d. Educ. Castle Douglas High School; Kirkcudbright Academy; Edinburgh University. Deputy Warden, New College Settlement, Pleasance, Edinburgh; overseas service, HM Forces, in Church of Scotland Huts and Canteens (mentioned in Despatches); Parish Minister: Gallatown, Kirkcaldy, five years, Kirkoswald, Ayrshire, ten years, Kirkliston, West Lothian, five years, St. Paul's, Edinburgh, ten years, Canonbie with Langholm, three years; Convener, Church of Scotland Committee on Huts and Canteens for HM Forces, 1965-67; Convener, Rural Panel, Home Board, six years. Recreations: gardening; travel. Address: Manse of Hoddom, Ecclefechan, Lockerbie, DG11 3BU; T.-Ecclefechan 357.

Irving, Gordon, MA (Hons). Writer, Journalist and Broadcaster; b. 4.12.18, Annan; m., Elizabeth Dickie; 1 s. Educ. Dumfries Academy; Edinburgh University. Staff Journalist, Daily Record, Edinburgh and Glasgow; Reuters' News Agency, London; TV Guide, Scotland; The Viewer, Scotland; Freelance Writer/Journalist, since 1964; Scotland Correspondent, Variety, New York. Publications: Great Scot! (biography of Sir Harry Lauder); The Good Auld Days; The Solway Smugglers; The Wit of the Scots; The Wit of Robert Burns; The Devil on Wheels; Brush Up Your Scotland; Annie Laurie; Take No Notice and Take No More Notice! (World's Funniest Signs); The First 200 Years (Story of Dumfries and Galloway Royal Infirmary). Recreations: video; motoring to Spain; collecting trivia. Address: (h.) 36 Whittingehame Court, Glasgow, G12 OBG; T.-041-357 2265.

Irving, James Wyllie, TD, SSC. Solicitor, since 1937; Partner, Primrose & Gordon, Dumfries; Honorary Sheriff, South Strathclyde, Dumfries and Galloway, at Dumfries, since 1963; Notary Public; b. 21.4.14, Dumfries; m., Henrietta Mary Purcell. Educ. Fettes College; Glasgow University. Cheshire Regiment, 1939-45 (Major); Territorial Army, KOSB, 1948-59 (Major); Civil Defence Depute Group Controller, SW Scotland, 1960-68; Secretary, County of Dumfries Valuation Appeal Committee, 1956-72; Chairman, South West Scotland Local Employment Committee, 1960-74; Member, Board of Management, Dumfries and Galloway Hospitals, 1965-71 (Chairman, 1968-71); Chairman, Board of Management, Dumfries and Galloway and Crichton Royal Hospitals, 1972-74; Chairman, Dumfries and Galloway Health Board, 1973-80; Secretary, Dumfries and Kirkcudbrightshire Ploughing Association, 1955-72; Chairman, Local Board of Directors, Scottish Union and National Insurance Company. Recreation: gardening. Address: (h.) Kirkbrae (the Old Manse), Lochruton, near Dumfries; T.-Lochfoot 301.

Irving, Ronald Eckford Mill, MA, DPhil (Oxon). Reader in Politics, Edinburgh University, since 1981; b. 14.7.39, Glasgow; m., Christine Mary Gaudin; 4 d. Educ. Merchiston Castle School; St. Edmund Hall, Oxford. Schoolmaster, 1961-65; Lecturer in Politics: Bristol University, 1968-69, Edinburgh University, 1969-81. Publications: Christian Democracy in France, 1973; The First Indochina War: French and American Policy in Vietnam 1945-54, 1975; The Christian Democratic Parties of Western Europe, 1979. Recreations: golf; piping. Address: (h.) 76 Murrayfield Gardens, Edinburgh, EH12 6DQ; T.-031-337 3663.

Irwin, Professor David George, MA, PhD, FSA, FRSA. Professor of History of Art and Head of Department, Aberdeen University, since 1970; b. 24.6.33, London; m., Francina Sorabji; 1 s.; 1 d. Educ. Holgate Grammar School, Barnsley; Queen's College, Oxford (Exhibitioner); Courtauld Institute of Art, London University. Lecturer in History of Fine Art, Glasgow University, 1959-70; Past President, British Society for 18th Century Studies; former Council Member, Walpole Society; former Member, Art Panel, Scottish Arts Council; Committee Member, Aberdeen Art Gallery; former Committee Member, Scottish Georgian Society; elected Member, International Association of Art Critics; won Laurence Binyon Prize, Oxford, 1956. Publications: English Neoclassical Art; Paul Klee; Visual Arts, Taste and Criticism; Winckelmann, Writings on Art; John Flaxman, Sculptor, Illustrator, Designer; Scottish Painters, At Home and Abroad, 1700 to 1900 (with Francina Sorabji). Recreations: swimming; walking; travel. Address: (b.) Department of History of Art, King's College, Old Aberdeen, Aberdeen, AB9 2UB; T.-0224 40241.

Irwin, Ian Sutherland, CBE (1982), BL, CA, IPFA, FCIT. Deputy Chairman and Managing Director, Scottish Transport Group, since 1975; b. 20.2.33; m.; 2 s. Educ. Whitehill Senior Secondary School, Glasgow; Glasgow University. President, Bus and Coach Council, 1979-80; Vice-President, International Union of Public Transport, since 1981.

Isaac, David Gilmour Davies, MA (Hons) (Oxon), PhD. Rector, Hutchesons' Grammar School, Glasgow, since 1978; b. 13.7.24, Fochriw, Glamorgan; m., Sheena Reith Steele; 1 s.; 1 d. Educ. Sir Edward Lewis's School, Pengam, Glamorgan; Jesus College, Oxford; Edinburgh University. House Tutor and Scholarship Historian, Edinburgh Academy, 1945-62 (House Master, 1959-62); Headmaster, King Henry VIII School, Abergavenny, 1962-68; Rector, Marr College, Troon, 1968-78; Member, Headmasters'

Conference, 1978-84; Council Member and Editor, Welsh Headmasters' Review; Secretary, Edinburgh Academical Football Club, 1959-62; Governor, Wellington School, Ayr; Elder, Portland Church, Troon. Recreations: golf; music; wine-making. Address: (h.) 1 Polo Gardens, Troon, Ayrshire; T.-0292 313804.

Izod, (Kenneth) John, BA (Hons), PhD. Senior Lecturer in charge, Film and Media Studies, Stirling University, since 1978; b. 4.3.40, Shepperton; m., Irene Chew Geok Keng; 1 s.; 1 d. Educ. Prince Edward School, Harare City, Zimbabwe; Leeds University. Clerk articled to Chartered Accountant, 1958-63; Projectionist, mobile cinema unit, 1963; Lecturer in English, New University of Ulster, 1969-78; Member, Scottish Film Council, since 1978 (and of its Executive, since 1984); Chairman, Stirling Film Theatre, since 1982. Publication: Reading the Screen, 1984. Address: (b.) Film and Media Studies, University, Stirling, FK9 4LA; T.-0786 73171.

J

Jack, James John, MA, LLB, SSC. Solicitor, since 1951; Honorary Sheriff, North Strathclyde, at Paisley, since 1979; Chairman, Paisley Local Legal Aid Committee, since 1979 (Member, since 1970); b. Cambuslang; m., Patricia Evelyn Geater. Educ. Hamilton Academy; Paisley Grammar School; Glasgow University. Partner, T. & W. Walker & Laird, Solicitors, Paisley, since 1954 (Senior Partner, since 1962); Burgh Prosecutor, Paisley, 1962-75; Clerk of the Peace, Renfrewshire, 1963-75; Council Member, Law Society of Scotland, 1977-83. Recreations: DIY; painting; reading; golf. Address: (b.) 7/9 Gilmour Street, Paisley; T.-041-887 5271.

Jack, Professor Robert Barr, MA, LLB. Partner, McGrigor, Donald & Co., (from 1985 called McGrigor Donald & Moncrieffs), Solicitors, Glasgow, since 1957; Professor of Mercantile Law, Glasgow University, since 1978; b. 18.3.28; m., Anna Thorburn Thomson; 2 s. Educ. Kilsyth Academy; High School of Glasgow; Glasgow University. Admitted as Solicitor in Scotland, 1951; Convener, Company Law Committee, Law Society of Scotland, 1978-85 (Member, from 1971); Member, Scottish Law Commission, 1974-77; Scottish Observer, Insolvency Law Review Committee, Department of Trade, 1977-82; Member, DoT Advisory Panel on Company Law, 1980-83; Lay Member, Council for the Securities Industry, and Council of the Stock Exchange, since 1983; Chairman, Brownlee plc, Glasgow, since 1984 (Director, since 1974); Director: Bank of Scotland, since 1985, Scottish Metropolitan Property plc, since 1980, Clyde Football Club Ltd., since 1980, Joseph Dunn (Bottlers) Ltd., since 1983; Chairman, Scottish National Council of YMCAs, 1966-73; President, Scottish National Union of YMCAs, since 1983; Member, Executive Committee, Quarrier's Homes, 1972-84 (Member, Council of Management, 1971-84); Chairman, Hutchesons' Educational Trust, Glasgow, since 1980 (Governor, since 1978). Recreations: golf; hopeful support of one of Glasgow's less fashionable football teams; a dedicated lover of Isle of Arran, which serves as a retreat and restorative. Address: (h.) 39 Mansewood Road, Glasgow, G43 1TN; T.-041-632 1659.

Jack, Ronald Dyce Sadler, MA, PhD. Reader in Medieval and Scottish Literature, Edinburgh University, since 1978; b. 3.4.41, Ayr; m., Christabel Margaret Nicolson; 2 d. Educ. Ayr Academy; Glasgow University; Edinburgh University. Department of English Literature: Assistant Lecturer, 1965, Lecturer, 1968, Associate Dean, Faculty of Arts, 1971-73; Visiting Professor, Virginia University, 1973-74; Member, Universities Central Council on Admissions, 1973-76; Pierpont Morgan Scholar, British Academy, 1976; Advising Editor, Scotia, since 1980; Member, Scottish Universities Council on Entrance, since 1981; Governor, Newbattle Abbey College, since 1984. Publications: Robert MacLellan's Jamie the Saxt (Co-Editor), 1970; Scottish Prose 1550-1700, 1972; The Italian Influence on Scottish Literature, 1972; A Choice of Scottish Verse 1560-1660, 1978; The Art of Robert Burns (Co-author), 1982; Sir Thomas Urquhart, The Jewel (Co-author), 1984; Alexander Montgomerie, 1985. Recreations: golf; zoology; theatre. Address: (b.) Department of English Literature, Edinburgh University, David Hume Tower, George Square, Edinburgh, EH8 9JX.

Jack, William, BSc, PhD. Senior Lecturer in Physics, Glasgow University, and Radiation Protection Adviser, Glasgow University, since 1972; b. 2.2.33, Dundee; m., Elizabeth Maclachlan Reidie; 2 s.; 2 d. Educ. Harris Academy, Dundee; St. Andrews University; Glasgow University. Glasgow University: Assistant Lecturer, 1958, Lecturer, 1960. Address: (h.) 10 Heather Avenue, Bearsden, Glasgow; T.-041-942 6407.

Jackson, Anthony Arthur, MA, MSc, FICDDip. Member, Fife Regional Council, since 1978; Lecturer in Economics, St. Andrews University, since 1973; Member, General Council, Institute of Civil Defence, since 1981; b. 18.6.46, London; m., Alicia; 3 d. Educ. Westminster City School; Gonville and Caius College, Cambridge; Reading University. Agricultural Economist, Malawi Government, 1968-71; St. Andrews University: Stanley Smith Senior Fellow, 1971-73, Assistant Dean of Students, Faculty of Arts, 1983; FAO/FFHC Food and Nutrition Consultant, Malawi Government, 1973-76; Warning Officer, 1975-81, and Sector Scientific Adviser, UKWMO, since 1981; Editor, Journal of Institute of Civil Defence, since 1982; Group Leader, Conservative Group, Fife Regional Council, since 1982; Director, Byre Theatre; Diploma, Institute of Civil Defence and Gerald Drewitt Medal, 1980. Recreations: theatre; cricket; philately. Address: (h.) Creinch, Peat Inn, by Cupar, Fife, KY15 5LH; T.-033-484 275.

Jackson, David Edward Pritchett, MA, PhD (Cantab). Senior Lecturer in Arabic Studies, St. Andrews University, since 1984 (Chairman, Department of Arabic Studies, since 1979); b. 9.12.41, Calcutta, India; m., Margaret Letitia Brown. Educ. Tynemouth School; Rossall School; Pembroke College, Cambridge. Research Fellow, Pembroke College, Cambridge, 1967-70; St. Andrews University: Assistant Lecturer, Arabic Language and Literature, 1967-68, Lecturer in Arabic Studies, 1968-84. Publication: Saladin (Co-author). Recreations: the river; music; food; golf. Address: (h.) 5 River Terrace, Guardbridge, by St. Andrews, Fife, KY16 OXA; T.-Leuchars 8986.

Jackson, Jack, BSc (Hons), PhD, MIBiol. HM Inspector of Schools, since 1983; b. 31.5.44, Ayr; m., Sheilah Margaret Fulton; 1 s.; 3 d. Educ. Ayr Academy; Glasgow University; Jordanhill College of Education. Demonstrator, Zoology Department, Glasgow University, 1966-69; Lecturer in Zoology, West of Scotland Agricultural College, 1969-72; Assistant Teacher of Biology, Cathkin High School, 1972-73; Principal Teacher of Biology, Ayr Academy, 1973-83. Senior Examiner and Setter, Scottish Examination Board, 1978-83; Director, Board, Scottish Youth Theatre, 1979-82; Member, Scottish Council, Institute of Biology, 1980-83. Recreations: family life; gardening; hill-walking; conservation. Address: (b.) Chesser House West, 502 Gorgie Road, Edinburgh; T.-031-443 4020.

Jackson, John. Member, Greater Glasgow Health Board; Shop Steward; b. 10.9.24, Glasgow; m., Isabella Gilligan; 2 s.; 3 d. Educ. Finnieston Street School. Branch Secretary, Communist Party; Executive Member, Trades Council. Recreations: swimming; cycling. Address: 55 Newington Street, Glasgow; T.-041-778 4692.

Jackson, Joseph Michael, BA, PhD. Senior Lecturer in Economics, Dundee University, since 1967; b. 23.2.25, Newport, Gwent; m., Miriam Cecily Andrews; 3 s.; 2 d. Educ. Newport High School; University College of Wales, Aberystwyth; Manchester University. Temporary Clerk, Ministry of War Transport, 1941-43; RAF, 1943-46; Research Assistant, University College of Wales, Aberystwyth, 1949-52; Assistant Lecturer in Economics, Bedford College, London University, 1952-55; Lecturer in Economics, Queen's College, Dundee, 1958-67. Member, Board of Management, Dundee Northern Hospital Group, 1970-74; Member, Scottish Catholic Education Commission. Publications: The Control of Monopoly in the United Kingdom (Co-author), 1960; Family Income, 1963; Human Values and the Economic System, 1966; Wages and Labour Economics, 1970; Little's Economics for Students (revised), 1971; Dundee Volume, Third Statistical Account of Scotland, 1977. Recreations: swimming; music; photography. Address: (b.) Department of Economics, The University, Dundee, DD1 4HN; T.-Dundee 23181, Ext. 4378.

Jackson, Michael Peart, BA, MA. Senior Lecturer, Department of Sociology, Stirling University, since 1970; Chairman, Supplementary Benefit Appeal Tribunal; b. 1.7.47, Oldham;

m., Sylvia; 1 s.; 1 d. Educ. Hulme Grammar School, Oldham; Hull University. Publications: Labour Relations on Docks, 1973; Price of Coal, 1974; Industrial Relations, 1977; Financial Aid Through Social Work, 1979; Work Creation - International Experiences, 1979; Trade Unions, 1982; British Work Creation Programmes, 1982; Youth Unemployment. Address: (b.) Department of Sociology, Stirling University, Stirling; T.-0786 73171.

Jackson, Richard Dodds, MA, DipEd. Deputy Director (Personnel and Supplies), Scottish Prison Service, since 1982; b. 13.9.37, Galashiels; m., Brenda Routledge Jackson; 1 s.; 1 d. Educ. St. Mary's School, Melrose; Royal High School, Edinburgh; St. Andrews University; Moray House College of Education. Teacher of English, Broughton Secondary School, Edinburgh, and Daniel Stewart's College, Edinburgh, 1961-70; HM Inspector of Schools and FE Colleges, 1970-75; Scottish Education Department: Temporary Principal, Arts Branch, 1975-78, Assistant Secretary, Social Work Services Group, 1978-82. Recreation: theatre and opera work. Address: (b.) St. Margaret's House, London Road, Edinburgh; T.-031-661 6181.

Jackson, Robert Penman, MIBM. General Manager, Public Works Department, City of Dundee District Council, since 1984; b. 2.4.47, Dunfermline; m., Helen Paxton; 1 s.; 1 d. Educ. Beath Senior High School, Cowdenbeath; Napier College of Science and Technology, Edinburgh. RSAS Diploma. Burgh Surveyor and Sanitary Inspector, Lochgelly Town Council, 1971-75; Assistant Director of Technical Services, Dunfermline District Council, 1975-84. Honorary Secretary, Lochgelly Old Folks' Reunion Committee. Recreations: golf; squash. Address: (b.) 353 Clepington Road, Dundee; T.-Dundee 23141, Ext. 4729.

Jacobson, Ivan, BSc, MB, ChB, FRCSEdin. Consultant Neurosurgeon, Tayside Health Board, since 1966; Senior Lecturer in Neurosurgery, Dundee University, since 1966; b. 12.8.32, Johannesburg; m., Elizabeth Jean Lamb; 1 s.; 2 d. Educ. Jeppe High School, Johannesburg; Witwatersrand University. Postgraduate neurosurgical training, Royal Infirmary and Western General Hospital, Edinburgh, 1959-66; Scottish Hospital Endowment Research Fellow, Glasgow University, 1960-62. Examiner in Neurosurgery, Royal College of Surgeons, Edinburgh; Citizen of Dundee, 1984. Address: (b.) Department of Neurosurgery, Ward 20, Dundee Royal Infirmary, Dundee, DD1 9ND; T.-Dundee 23125.

Jahoda, Professor Gustav, MSc, PhD, FBPS. Professor of Psychology, Strathclyde University, since 1964; b. 11.10.20, Vienna; m., Jean Catherine Buchanan; 3 s.; 1 d. Educ. London University. Oxford Extra-Mural Delegacy; Manchester University; University of Ghana; Glasgow University. Past President (now Fellow), International Association for Cross-Cultural Psychology. Recreations: fishing; gardening. Address: (b.) Department of Psychology, Strathclyde University, 155 George Street, Glasgow, G1 1RD; T.-041-552 4400.

James, C. Peter, PPIWPC (Dip), FIWES, FIPHE. Director, Solway River Purification Board, since 1954; b. 30.4.27, Manchester; m., Grace Irene; 1 s.; 1 d. Educ. Sale Grammar School; Manchester College of Technology. Trainee Inspector, Lancashire Rivers Board, 1943-51; District Inspector, Yorkshire Ouse River Board, 1951-54. President, Institute of Water Pollution Control, 1980-81 (Honorary Treasurer, since 1981); WHO Consultant on Water Pollution Control Management; holder Arthur Sidney Bedell Award, American Water Pollution Control Federation; President, Dumfries Rotary Club, 1984-85; awarded Queen's Silver Jubilee Medal, 1977. Recreations: haaf-net fishing; photography; gardening; wine making. Address: (h.) Gullsway, Glencaple, Dumfries, DG1 4RF; T.-Glencaple 285.

James, David Sheard, MB, ChB, DipEd, DCH, DPM, MRCPsych. Consultant Child Psychiatrist, Royal Hospital for Sick Children, Glasgow, since 1971; Visiting Psychiatrist, Thorntoun Residential School, near Kilmarnock, since 1971; b. 19.2.39, Harrogate; m., Hilary; 1 s.; 2 d. Educ. Warwick School; Sheffield University. Paediatrics, Sheffield Children's Hospital; Registrar in Psychiatry, Mapperley Hospital, Nottingham; Research Registrar, United Sheffield Hospitals; Senior Registrar, Child Psychiatry, Birmingham Children's Hospital and Charles Burns Clinic. Publication: Families Without Hope (Co-author), 1975. Recreations: motor vehicles; model railway. Address: (h.) Waterside, Lochlibo Road, Uplawmoor, Glasgow, G78 4AA; T.-Uplawmoor 269.

James, Geoffrey Bennett, MB, ChB, FRCOG. Consultant Obstetrician and Gynaecologist, since 1970; Honorary Senior Lecturer, Dundee University, since 1970; b. 21.8.32, Morpeth; m., Ann Barber; 3 d. Educ. Heversham School, Westmorland; St. Andrews University. Postgraduate experience, Dundee Royal Infirmary and Nuffield Institute for Medical Research, Oxford; Wellcome Research Fellow, Department of Obstetrics, Dundee University; Assistant Professor, Florida University; Eden Fellow, Royal College of Obstetricians and Gynaecologists. Recreation: squash - playing, coaching, refereeing. Address: (h.) Dunglass, 284 Arbroath Road, Broughty Ferry, Dundee, DD5 1QN; T.-Dundee 74853.

James, Professor (William) Philip (Trehearne), MA, MD, DSc, FRCP, FRCPEdin. Director, Rowett Research Institute, Aberdeen, since 1982; Research Professor, Aberdeen University, since 1983; b. 27.6.38, Liverpool; m., Jean Hamilton Moorhouse; 1 s.; 1 d. Educ. Bala School, North Wales; Ackworth School, Yorkshire; University College, London. Senior House Physician, Whittington Hospital, London, 1963-65; Clinical Research Scientist, Medical Research Council Tropical Metabolism Research Unit, Kingston, Jamaica, 1965-68; Harvard Research Fellow, Massachusetts General Hospital, 1968-69; Wellcome Trust Research Fellow, MRC Gastroenterology Unit, London, 1969-70; Senior Lecturer, Department of Human Nutrition, London School of Hygiene and Tropical Medicine, and Honorary Consultant, UCH, 1970-74;

Assistant Director, MRC Dunn Nutrition Unit, and Honorary Consultant Physician, Addenbrooke's Hospital, Cambridge, 1974-82. Sir David Cuthbertson Lecturer; Van den Berghs & Jurgens Reporting Award; Amos Memorial Lecturer; Sir Thomas Middleton Memorial Lecturer; Member, Panel on Diet and Heart Disease, Department of Health; Member, Committee on Toxicity and on Irradiated and Novel Foods; Food Advisory Committee, Ministry of Agriculture; Joint Advisory Committee on Nutrition Education; Vice-Chairman, FAO/WHO/UNU Commission on Energy and Protein Requirements; Advisor, WHO Committee on Implementation of Measures for Prevention of Heart Disease. Address: (b.) Rowett Research Institute, Greenburn Road, Bucksburn, Aberdeen, AB2 9SB; T.-0224 712751.

Jameson, John Valentine McCulloch, JP, BSc, FRICS. Convener, Dumfries and Galloway Regional Council, since 1983; Partner, G.M. Thomson & Co., Chartered Surveyors, since 1970; b. 5.10.33, Twynholm, Stewartry of Kirkcudbright; m., Mary Irene Butters; 1 s.; 2 d. Educ. Rugby School; College of Estate Management (External). Commissioned 4/7 Royal Dragoon Guards, 1952-54; Shell Petroleum Co., London, 1954-57; Richard Costain (Canada) Ltd., Toronto, 1958-64. Member and Bailie, Gatehouse-of-Fleet Town Council, 1970-75; Chairman, Finance Committee, Dumfries and Galloway Regional Council, 1975-83; Chairman, Dumfries and Galloway Tourist Association, 1978-82; Chairman, Scottish Branch, Royal Institution of Chartered Surveyors, 1981-82; Council Member, National Trust for Scotland, 1980-84; Treasurer, Anwoth and Girthon Kirk Session. Recreations: gardening; shooting; squash; hill-walking. Address: (h.) Hillfoot, Gatehouse-of-Fleet; T.-05574 389.

Jamieson, David. Honorary Sheriff, South Strathclyde, Dumfries and Galloway, since 1976; Chairman, Rent Tribunals, Lanarkshire; a Chairman, National Insurance and Supplementary Benefit Tribunals, Lanarkshire; b. 10.8.17, Glasgow; m., Pauline Bainbridge; 1 d. Educ. Albert Road Academy, Glasgow; Glasgow University. Six years in HM Forces during Second World War; practising Solicitor in Hamilton; Honorary Secretary, Uddingston Ratepayers and Electors Committee, since 1946. Publications: Uddingston, The Village (parts one to five), 1974-84; Uddingston in Picture Postcards, 1984. Recreations: hill-walking; horticulture. Address: (b.) 22 Clydesdale Street, Hamilton; T.-Hamilton 281767.

Jamieson, Rev. Gordon David, MA, BD. Minister, Elie, Kilconquhar and Colinsburgh, since 1979; b. 1.3.49, Glasgow; m., Annette Sutherland; 1 s.; 1 d. Educ. Hamilton Academy; Edinburgh University. Minister, Schaw Kirk, Drongan, 1974-79. Recreation: golf. Address: The Manse, Kilconquhar, Leven, Fife, KY9 1LF; T.-033-334 584.

Jamieson, Morley. Writer; b. 29.5.17, Newlandrig, Midlothian; m., Flora Macdonald; 1 s.; 1 d. Educ. (left school at early age due to serious illness); Newbattle Abbey College, Dalkeith; Coleg Harlech, Gwynedd. Quarryman, 1932-39; Bookseller, 1942-81; won Scottish Arts Council Award, 1980. Publications: The Old Wife (short stories), 1972; Nine Poems, 1976; Ten Poems, 1978; Notes on the Short Story, 1980. Recreation: conversation. Address: (h.) Viewbank Cottage, Lasswade, Midlothian, EH18 1AL; T.-031-663 8734.

Japp, William Wilson, FCCA. Chief Executive, Nithsdale District Council, since 1984; b. 5.9.29, Dundee; m., Helen; 2 s. Educ. Harris Academy, Dundee. Dundee Corporation: Clerical Assistant, 1947-56, Accountancy Assistant, 1956-61; Assistant Town Chamberlain, Arbroath Town Council, 1961-64; Depute Town Chamberlain, Dumfries Town Council, 1964-75; Director of Finance, Nithsdale District Council, 1975-84. Address: (b.) Municipal Chambers, Buccleuch Street, Dumfries; T.-0387 53166.

Jardine, Sir (Andrew) Rupert (John) Buchanan-, 4th Bt, MC, DL. Landowner; b. 2.2.23; m., Jane Fiona Edmonstone (m. diss.); 1 s.; 1 d. Educ. Harrow; Royal Agricultural College. Retired Major, Royal Horse Guards; Joint Master, Dumfriesshire Foxhounds, 1950; Deputy Lieutenant, Dumfriesshire, 1978. Address: (h.) Dixons, Lockerbie, Dumfriesshire.

Jardine, Sheriff James Christopher Macnaughton, BL. Sheriff of Glasgow and Strathkelvin, since 1979; b. 18.1.30; m.; 1 d. Educ. Glasgow Academy; Gresham House, Ayrshire; Glasgow University. Lt., RASC, 1950-52; Solicitor in practice practice, 1955-69; Sheriff of Stirling, Dunbarton and Clackmannan, later North Strathclyde, at Dumbarton, 1969-79.

Jardine, Robert, MA. Rector, Queen Margaret Academy, Ayr, since 1977; b. 15.6.30, Renton, Dunbartonshire; m., Norah Tiernan; 1 s.; 1 d. Educ. St. Patrick's High School, Dumbarton; Glasgow University. Teacher: St. Augustine's Secondary School, Glasgow, 1956-61, St. Aloysius College, Glasgow, 1961-67; Principal Teacher of Modern Languages, then Assistant Head Teacher, Holyrood Secondary School, Glasgow, 1967-77. Recreations: music; tennis; golf. Address: (h.) 18 Auchendoon Crescent, Ayr, KA6 4AS; T.-0292 265223.

Jardine, Stewart, BSc (Hons). Head Teacher, Carrick Academy, Maybole, since 1982; b. 8.1.42, Crosshill, Ayrshire; m., Kathleen E.A. Passant; 2 s. Educ. Carrick Academy, Maybole; Glasgow University; Jordanhill College of Education. Girvan Academy: Teacher of Science, 1964-68, Principal Teacher of Physics, 1968-74; Assistant Head Teacher, 1974-76, Depute Head Teacher, 1976-82. Past Chairman, Girvan and District Round Table; Member, Golf Committee, Turnberry Golf Club. Recreations: golf; reading; computing. Address: (h.) 8 Connor Court, Girvan; T.-0465 3508.

Jardine of Applegirth, Colonel Sir William Edward, Baronet of Nova Scotia (created, 1672); TD, OBE (1966), JP, DL; Chief, Clan Jardine;

Farmer, 1960-84; Member, Dumfries and Galloway Regional Council, since 1982; Chairman, Solway River Purification Board; b. 15.4.17, Lockerbie; m., Ann Graham Maitland; 2 s. King's Own Scottish Borderers, 1939-67; commanded 4/5 KOSB (TA), 1963-67; Member, Dumfries County Council, 1963-75 (Chairman, Road Committee); Member, Annandale and Eskdale District Council, 1975-82 (Chairman, General Purposes Committee); Member, Queen's Bodyguard for Scotland (Royal Company of Archers); Member, Standing Council of Scottish Chiefs; Chairman, Scottish River Purification Boards Association, 1981-82. Recreation: shooting. Address: (h.) Denbie, Lockerbie, Dumfriesshire, DG11 1DH; T.-Carrutherstown 631.

Jardine, William Graham, BSc, MSc, PhD, ScD, FGS. Reader, Department of Geology, Glasgow University, since 1978; b. 13.3.27, Glasgow; m., Elizabeth Ann Garven; 3 s.; 1 d. Educ. Allan Glen's High School, Glasgow, 1939-44; Glasgow University; McGill University, Canada; Emmanuel College, Cambridge. National Service, 1950-52 (2nd Lt., Royal Signals, GHQ Signals Regiment, Suez Canal Zone); Soil Survey, Scotland: Scientific Officer, 1955-58, Senior Scientific Officer, 1958-59; Glasgow University: Lecturer, Department of Geology, 1959-66, Senior Lecturer, 1966-78. Council Member, Geological Society of Glasgow, 1961-64; Quaternary Research Association (of Britain): Secretary, 1970-74, Vice-President, 1974-76; Secretary-General, Tenth Congress, International Union for Quaternary Research (INQUA), Birmingham, 1977; President, INQUA Sub-Commission on Shorelines of NW Europe, 1977-82; INQUA Sub-Committee, British National Committee for Geology, 1966-82; President, Glasgow Archaeological Society, 1981-84; Editorial Advisory Board, Quaternary Science Reviews, since 1984; E.J. Garwood Fund, Geological Society of London, 1963; Member, Congregational Board, 1961-81, and Kirk Session, since 1978, Westerton (Bearsden) Church of Scotland. Recreation: Westerton Male Voice Choir. Address: (b.) Department of Geology, Glasgow University, Glasgow, G12 8QQ; T.-041-339 8855, Ext. 5443.

Jardine Paterson, Lt.-Col. Arthur James, OBE, TD, JP. Lord Lieutenant, Dumfriesshire, since 1982; b. 14.7.18, Windsor; m., Mary Fearne Balfour-Kinnear; 1 d. Educ. Eton; Cambridge University. Served Second World War, KOSB, NW Europe; commanded 5th Bn, KOSB, 1955-58; Chairman, Dumfries and Galloway T&AFA, 1963; Member: Dumfries County Council, 1960-75 (Vice Convener), Dumfries and Galloway Regional Council, 1975-82 (Vice Convener); Past Chairman, Dumfries and Galloway Water Board; President, Dumfries & Lockerbie Agricultural Society, since 1962. Recreation: shooting. Address: (h.) Skairfield, Lockerbie, DG11 1JL; T.-Lochmaben 201.

Jarvi, Neeme. Musical Director and Principal Conductor, Scottish National Orchestra, since 1984; b. 1937, Estonia. Educ. Tallinn Music School; Leningrad State Conservatory. Director, Estonian Radio and Television Orchestra, 1963; Chief Conductor, Opera Theatre, Estonia,

1963-76; emigrated to North America, 1980, making his debut with New York Philharmonic Orchestra; Principal Conductor, Gothenburg Symphony Orchestra; regularly conducts the San Francisco, Toronto and Montreal Symphony Orchestras.

Jarvis, Professor Paul Gordon, PhD, Fil dr, FRSE. Professor of Forestry and Natural Resources, Edinburgh University, since 1975; b. 23.5.35, Tunbridge Wells; m., Margaret Susan Gostelow; 1 s.; 2 d. Educ. Sir Anthony Brown's School, Brentwood; Oriel College, Oxford. PhD study, Sheffield University, 1957-60; Postdoctoral Fellow, NATO, Institute of Plant Physiology, Uppsala University, 1960-62; Senior Lecturer in Plant Physiology, Royal College of Agriculture, Uppsala; Visiting Research Fellow, Division of Land Research, CSIRO, Australia; Aberdeen University: Lecturer in Botany, 1966-72, Senior Lecturer, 1972-75. Council Member, Society for Experimental Biology, 1977-80; Commissioner, Countryside Commission for Scotland, 1976-78; Member, Governing Body, Scottish Crops Research Institute, since 1977; Co-Founder and Sectional Editor, Plant, Cell and Environment; Co-Founder and Editor, Current Advances in Ecological Sciences; serves on various other editorial or review boards. Address: (h.) Belmont, 47 Eskbank Road, Dalkeith, Midlothian, EH22 3BH; T.-031-663 8676.

Jarvis, Roland John, FBIM. Managing Director and Group Chief Executive, Low and Bonar PLC, since 1984; b. 23.6.32, London; m., Pamela; 2 s.; 2 d. Educ. Royal Liberty School. Ford Motor (Planning and Analysis), 1965; Group Comptroller, AEI/GEC, 1967; Financial Controller, Chrysler, 1970; Financial Director, Crane Fruehauf, 1972; TI Raleigh Industries: Financial Director, 1976-80, Managing Director, 1980-84. Recreations: tennis; golf; music. Address: (b.) Bonar House, Faraday Street, Dundee, DD1 9JA.

Jarvis, William. Solicitor, since 1932; Honorary Sheriff, since 1962; Clerk to Lieutenancy; b. 19.4.11, Dunfermline; m., Helen Dalrymple; 2 s. Educ. Dunfermline High School; Edinburgh University. Partner, Wilson & Jarvis, Solicitors, Alloa, since 1937 (Senior Partner, since 1947); Member, National Health Executive Council, 1963-73; Member, Forth Valley Health Board, 1973-78; Honorary Secretary, Clackmannanshire Boy Scouts Association, 15 years; Honorary Treasurer, Alloa YMCA, 25 years; Elder, West Church, Alloa, since 1947; Founder Member and Past Chairman, Abbeyfield (Alloa and District) Society; President, Alloa Rotary Club, 1961. Recreation: bowling. Address: (h.) Greycraigs, 142 Claremont, Alloa; T.-Alloa 212466.

Jasinski, Alfons B., DA, RSW. Artist; Teacher of Art; b. 14.9.45, Falkirk; m., Ann E.M. Conlan; 1 s.; 2 d. Educ. St. Modan's High School, Stirling; Edinburgh College of Art. Travelling Scholarship to Italy, 1969; began teaching, Balwearie High School, Kirkcaldy, 1969; Latimer Award, RSA, 1975; one-man exhibitions: Loomshop, 1971-72-74-76-80-82, Kirkcaldy Art Gallery, 1974, The Scottish Gallery, 1976, Cornerstone,

Dunblane, 1976, Gallery 22, Cupar, 1984; works in various public and private collections. Address: (h.) 15 Normand Road, Dysart, Fife, KY1 2XN; T.-0592 52505.

Jauncey, Hon. Lord, (Charles Eliot Jauncey), QC (Scot), BA, LLB. Senator of the College of Justice in Scotland, since 1979; b. 8.5.25; m., 1, Jean Cunninghame Graham (m. diss.); 2 s.; 1 d., 2, Elizabeth Ballingal (m. diss.); 3, Camilla Cathcart; 1 d. Educ. Radley; Christ Church, Oxford; Glasgow University. Served Second World War (Sub-Lt., RNVR); Advocate, 1949; QC (Scot), 1963; Sheriff Principal of Fife and Kinross, 1971-74; Honorary Sheriff Substitute of Perthshire, 1962; Member, Queen's Bodyguard for Scotland (Royal Company of Archers), 1951; Member, Historic Buildings Council for Scotland.

Jeeves, Professor Malcolm Alexander, MA, PhD (Cantab), FBPsS, FRSE. Vice-Principal, St. Andrews University, since 1981 (Professor of Psychology, since 1969); b. 16.11.26, Stamford, England; m., Ruth Elisabeth Hartridge; 2 d. Educ. Stamford School; St. John's College, Cambridge University. Lt., 1st Bn., Sherwood Foresters, BAOR, 1945-48; Exhibitioner, St. John's College, Cambridge, 1948-52; research and teaching, Cambridge and Harvard Universities, 1952-56; Lecturer, Leeds University, 1956-59; Professor and Head, Department of Psychology, Adelaide University, 1959-69 (Dean, Faculty of Arts, 1963-64); Committee Member, International Neuropsychological Symposium; Editor, Neuropsychologia. Publications: Analysis of Structural Learning (Co-author); Psychology Survey No. 3 (Editor); Experimental Psychology: An introduction for biologists; The Effects of Structural Relations upon Transfer (Co-author); Thinking in Structures (Co-author); Behavioural Science and Christianity (Editor); Free to be Different (Co-author); Psychology and Christianity: The View Both Ways; The Scientific Enterprise and Christian Faith. Recreations: walking; music; fishing. Address: (b.) Department of Psychology, St. Andrews University, St. Andrews, KY16 9JU; T.-0334 76161.

Jeffares, Professor Alexander Norman, MA, PhD, DPhil, Dde'lU, FAHA, FRSE, FRSL, FRSA. Professor of English Studies, Stirling University, since 1974; Managing Director, Academic Advisory Services Ltd.; Director, Colin Smythe Ltd.; b. 11.8.20, Dublin; m., Jeanne Agnes Calembert; 1 d. Educ. The High School, Dublin; Trinity College, Dublin; Oriel College, Oxford. Lecturer in Classics, Trinity College, Dublin, 1943-45; Lector in English, Groningen University, 1946-48; Lecturer in English Literature, Edinburgh University, 1949-51; Professor of English Language and Literature, Adelaide, 1951-56; Professor of English Literature, Leeds, 1957-74. Secretary, Australian Humanities Research Council, 1954-57; Honorary Fellow, Australian Academy of Humanities; Founding Chairman, Association for Commonwealth Literary and Language Studies, 1966-68 (Honorary Life Fellow); Founding Chairman, International Association for Study of Anglo-Irish Literature, 1968-70 (Honorary Life President, since 1973); Member, Scottish Arts Council (Chairman, Literature Committee, 1977-83, Vice Chairman,

1980-84); Member, Arts Council of GB, 1980-84; Chairman, National Book League Scotland, since 1985; Member, Executive Committee, National Book League; Vice-Chairman, Muckhart Community Council, since 1979. Publications: Yeats: Man and Poet; Seven Centuries of Poetry; The Scientific Background (Co-author); A Commentary on the Poems of Yeats; A Commentary on the Plays of Yeats (Co-author); History of Anglo-Irish Literature; Restoration Drama; New Commentary on Poems of Yeats. Recreations: drawing; painting; restoring old houses. Address: (b.) Department of English Studies, The University, Stirling; T.-0786 973171.

Jeffery, Professor Jonathan, MA, BSc, DPhil, CChem, FRSC, CBiol, FIBiol, FRSA, FRSE. Professor of Biochemistry, Aberdeen University, since 1983; b. 29.7.35, Liverpool; m., Christa Torriano-Williams; 2 d. Educ. Liverpool Institute High School; Jesus College, Oxford University. Research Biochemist, ICI, 1962-66; Aberdeen University: Lecturer in Chemical Pathology, 1966-72, Lecturer in Biochemistry, 1972-74, Senior Lecturer in Biochemistry, 1974-83. Recreations: country walks; some interest in theatre, visual arts and music. Address: (b.) Department of Biochemistry, Aberdeen University, Marischal College, Aberdeen, AB9 1AS; T.-0224 40241.

Jeffrey, Rev. Eric William Sinclair, JP, MA. Minister, Bristo Memorial Church, Craigmillar, Edinburgh, since 1978; b. 12.2.29, Coatbridge; m., Carol Elizabeth Dover Wilson; 4 s.; 2 d. Educ. High School of Glasgow; Glasgow University and Trinity College. Missionary in Malawi, 1954-69; Minister, Dalmeny and Abercorn, 1969-78. Recreations: playing double bass in the Scottish Sinfonia; qualified cricket umpire; golf. Address: 3 Spence Street, Edinburgh, EH16 5AG; T.-031-668 2722.

Jeffrey, Ian William McDonald, PhD, FDS, LDS, RCSEdin. Senior Lecturer in Conservative Dentistry, Dundee University, since 1978; b. 11.1.31, Edinburgh; m., Jean McKenzie; 2 s.; 1 d. Educ. George Heriot's, Edinburgh; John Bright Grammar School, Llandudno; Edinburgh University. National Service, Egypt, 1953-55; Colonial Service, Uganda, 1955-58; Registrar, Eastern Regional Hospital Board, 1959-60; Lecturing Staff, Dundee University, since 1960; Examiner, Royal College of Surgeons, Edinburgh; Visiting Lecturer, Nairobi University. Recreations: mountaineering; travel; house and car maintenance; photography. Address: (h.) Norwood, McKenzie Street, Carnoustie, Angus; T.-Carnoustie 52405.

Jeffrey, John J., BSc (Hons), BA (Ed), DipEd, CEng, MRINA, MIIM, MBIM. Depute Principal, Inverness College of Further and Higher Education, since 1970; Liaison Officer (Inverness), Open University, since 1972; b. 29.7.35, Greenock; m., Norma May McGregor; 1 s.; 2 d. Educ. Greenock High School; Strathclyde University; Open University; Aberdeen University; Paisley College of Technology. Began career as apprentice/design draughtsman, Scott Lithgow (Shipbuilders), 1950-61; Nuclear Power Station Engineer, English Electric, Leicester, 1961-63;

Lecturer in Naval Architecture/Engineering, then Senior Lecturer, Kirkcaldy College of Technology, 1963-67; Second Depute Principal, Aberdeen Technical College, 1967-70. Recreations: golf; tennis; computing. Address: (b.) Inverness College of Further and Higher Education, 3 Longman Road, Longman South, Inverness; T.-0463 236681.

Jeffreys, John Alexander David, MA, DPhil, CChem, FRSC. Senior Lecturer, Department of Pure and Applied Chemistry, Strathclyde University; b. 14.1.27, Camborne. Educ. St. Paul's School, London; Exeter College, Oxford. Staff, Chemistry Department, Glasgow University, 1951-55; ICI Fellow, Leeds University, 1955-57; Lecturer in Chemistry, Royal Veterinary College, London, 1958-59. Recreation: enjoyment of the environment. Address: (b.) Department of Chemistry, Strathclyde University, Glasgow; T.-041-552 4400, Ext. 2259.

Jeffreys-Jones, Rhodri, BA (Wales), PhD (Cantab). Senior Lecturer in History, Edinburgh University, since 1983; b. 28.7.42, Carmarthen; m., Janetta Carolina Minkiewicz; 2 d. Educ. Ysgol Ardudwy; University of Wales; Cambridge University; Michigan University; Harvard University. Tutor: Harvard, 1965-66, Fitzwilliam College, Cambridge, 1966-67; Assistant Lecturer, then Lecturer, Edinburgh University, 1967-83; Fellow, Charles Warren Center for the Study of American History, Harvard, 1971-72. Publications: Violence and Reform in American History; American Espionage: From Secret Service to CIA; Eagle Against Empire: American Opposition to European Imperialism 1914-82 (Editor); The Growth of Federal Power in American History (Joint Editor). Recreations: squash; snooker; vegetable gardening. Address: (b.) Department of History, Edinburgh University, William Robertson Building, George Square, Edinburgh, EH8 9JY; T.-031-667 1011.

Jeffries, Professor David John, OBE, BA, FHCIMA, FTS. Professor and Head, Scottish Hotel School, Strathclyde University, since 1983; b. 19.12.31, Gillingham, Kent; m., Marie-Joelle Thibault; 1 s.; 4 d. Educ. Mansfield School, Durban, South Africa; City of Bath School; Sheffield University; Salamanca University, Spain. Joined British Travel Association as Graduate Trainee, 1955; successively Research Officer, Assistant General Manager, London, and Manager for France; transferred to English Tourist Board on passing of Development of Tourism Act, 1969; Director, English Tourist Board with responsibility for marketing and research, 1969-83; National Chairman, Tourism Society; Governor, The Queen's College,Glasgow. Recreations: being with family; reading P.G. Wodehouse. Address: (b.) Scottish Hotel School, Strathclyde University, Curran Building, 94 Cathedral Street, Glasgow; T.-041-552 4400.

Jenkins, Robin, MA. Novelist; b. 11.9.12; m.; s.; 2 d. Educ. Hamilton Academy; Glasgow University. Author of: Happy for the Child, The Thistle and the Grail, The Cone-Gatherers, Guests of War, The Missionaries, The Changeling, Some Kind of Grace, Dust on the Paw, The Tiger of Gold, A Love of Innocence, The Sardana Dancers, A Very Scotch Affair, The Holy Tree, The Expatriates, A Toast to the Lord, A Far Cry from Bowmore, A Figure of Fun, A Would-be Saint, Fergus Lamont.

Jenkins, Rt. Hon. Roy Harris, PC (1964). MP (SDP), Glasgow Hillhead, since 1982; Leader, Social Democratic Party, 1982-83; b. 11.11.20; m., Jennifer Morris; 2 s.; 1 d. Educ. Abersychan Grammar School; University College, Cardiff; Balliol College, Oxford. RA, 1942-46 (Captain, 1944-46); MP (Labour): Central Southwark, 1948-50, Birmingham Stechford, 1950-76; Minister of Aviation, 1964-65; Home Secretary, 1965-67, 1974-76; Chancellor of the Exchequer, 1967-70; Deputy Leader, Labour Party, 1970-72; President, European Commission, 1977-81.

Jenner, Rev. Albert. Minister, Kingussie, since 1973; Clerk, Abernethy Presbytery, since 1981; b. 7.4.24, Glasgow; m., Isabel MacKenzie MacDonald. Educ. Hillhead High School; Alva Academy; Edinburgh University. War Service, Royal Armoured Corps, 1942-47; Student Assistant, Prestonfield Church, Edinburgh, 1949-50; Minister: Kinnettles, 1951-56, Kelvinside Old, Glasgow, 1956-66, St. Andrew's-Trinity, Johnstone, 1966-73; Moderator: Abernethy Presbytery, 1975-76, Synod of Southern Highlands, 1977-78; Chairman, Kingussie High School Council, since 1975; Chaplain and Past President, Kingussie Branch, Royal British Legion Scotland; Programme Convener, Badenoch and Strathspey Music Festival. Recreations: music; reading; golf. Address: The Manse, West Terrace, Kingussie, Inverness-shire, PH21 1HA; T.-Kingussie 311.

Jennett, Professor Bryan, MD, FRCS. Professor of Neurosurgery, Glasgow University, since 1968 (Dean, Faculty of Medicine, since 1981); Director, MRC Head Injury Programme, since 1979; b. 1.3.26, Twickenham, Middlesex; m., Professor Sheila Jennett (qv); 3 s.; 1 d. Educ. King's College, Wimbledon; King George V School, Southport; Liverpool University. Lecturer in Neurosurgery, Manchester University; Rockefeller Travelling Fellow, University of California; Hunterian Professor, Royal College of Surgeons of England. Member, Medical Research Council; Member, Chief Scientist Committee, Scotland; Rock Carling Fellow. Publications: Epilepsy After Non-Missile Head Injuries; Introduction to Neurosurgery; High Technology Medicine - Benefits and Burdens. Recreations: writing; cruising under sail. Address: (h.) 4 Cleveden Drive, Glasgow, G12 OSE; T.-041-334 5148.

Jennett, Professor Sheila, MD, PhD, FRCPGlas. Titular Professor of Physiology, Glasgow University, since 1985; b. 28.1.26, Liverpool; m., Professor Bryan Jennett (qv); 3 s.; 1 d. Educ. Aigburth Vale High School, Liverpool; Liverpool University. Junior hospital appointments in surgery, spinal injuries, geriatrics and respiratory medicine, 1949-62; Lecturer, then Senior Lecturer, then Reader in Physiology, Glasgow University, 1963-85. Committee Member, Physiological Society, 1981-85. Recreations: sailing; music; walking. Address: (h.) 4 Cleveden Drive, Glasgow, G12 OSE; T.-041-334 5148.

Jennings, Kevin, MB, MRCP. Consultant Cardiologist, Aberdeen Royal Infirmary, since 1983; b. 9.3.47, Charleville, Eire; m., Heather; 2 s. Educ. Downside; St. Bartholomew's Hospital, London. Registrar: King's College Hospital, London, London Chest Hospital; Senior Registrar, Freeman Hospital, Newcastle-upon-Tyne. Recreations: theatre; ballet; golf; windsurfing. Address: (b.) 15 Carlton Place, Aberdeen, AB2 4BR; T.-Aberdeen 645833.

Jillings, Lewis George, MA (Hons), PhD. Senior Lecturer in German, Stirling University, since 1982 (Member, University Court, since 1978); b. 7.1.42, Auckland; m., Margaret Nicholas; 2 d. Educ. Auckland Grammar School; Auckland University; Basel University; London University. Lecturer in German, Stirling University, 1968-82. Vice-Chairman, Stirling Burgh Liberals, since 1983; Assistant Secretary, British Branch, International Arthurian Society, since 1980. Publications: Martin Luther Selections, 1977; Diu Crone of Heinrich von dem Turlein, 1980; Notes on Steppenwolf by Hermann Hesse, 1981. Recreations: reading; politicking. Address: (h.) 2 Royal Gardens, Stirling; T.-Stirling 62225.

Jimack, Professor Peter David, BA, PhD. Professor of French, Stirling University, since 1972; b. 29.9.30, London; m., Christine Mary; 1 s.; 3 d. Educ. Tottenham Grammar School; Southampton University. Assistant Master: Churcher's College, Petersfield, 1954-57, Cotham Grammar School, Bristol, 1957-58; Birmingham University: Assistant Lecturer, 1959-61, Lecturer, 1961-66, Senior Lecturer, 1966-72. Recreations: gardening; swimming; watching films. Address: (h.) 6 Banavie Road, Glasgow, G11 5AN; T.-041-334 5926.

Johnson, Brian Edward, BSc, PhD. Senior Lecturer, Department of Dermatology, Dundee University, since 1976; b. 5.1.36, Croydon; m., Ann; 2 d. Educ. Whitgift; London University. Research Assistant, Institute of Dermatology, London University, 1958-65; Research Associate, Dermatology, then Assistant Professor, Cornell University Medical Center, 1965-69; Lecturer in Dermatology, Dundee University, 1970-76. Recreations: choral singing; pottering. Address: (b.) Department of Dermatology, Dundee University, Ninewells Hospital and Medical School, Dundee; T.-Dundee 60111, Ext. 2239.

Johnson, David (Charles), MA, BA, PhD. Composer; Musical Historian; b. 27.10.42, Edinburgh; 1 s. Educ. Aberdeen University; St. John's College, Cambridge. Part-time teaching jobs, since 1970: Rudolf Steiner School of Edinburgh, Napier College, Edinburgh, Open University; Member, Scottish Music Information Centre Advisory Committee, since 1983; Postdoctoral Fellowship, Music Faculty, Edinburgh University, 1979-80; awarded Scottish Arts Council Writer's Bursary, 1979; Musical Correspondent, Glasgow Herald and Musical Times; compositions include four operas, an orchestral suite, chamber music, songs, etc. Publications: Music and Society in Lowland Scotland, 1972; Scottish Fiddle Music in the 18th Century, 1984; contributions to the New Grove Dictionary of Music, 1981. Address: (h.) 1 Hill Square, Edinburgh, EH8 9DR; T.-031-667 7054.

Johnson, Michael R.W., BSc, PhD, DIC, FRSE. Scientific Officer, British Geological Survey, since 1955; Reader, Edinburgh University, since 1967; b. 12.4.30, Nottingham; 1 s.; 1 d. Educ. Loughborough College School; Nottingham University; Imperial College, London. Lecturer, Edinburgh University, 1957-68. Address: (b.) Grant Institute of Geology, Kings Buildings, West Mains Road, Edinburgh, EH9 3JW; T.-031-667 1081, Ext. 3575.

Johnson, Richard Patrick Craig, BSc, PhD, CIBiol, MIBiol. Senior Lecturer, Department of Plant Science, Aberdeen University, since 1974; b. 3.3.36, London; m., Philippa Mary; 1 s.; 3 d. Educ. St. Albans School; Queen Mary College, London. Research Assistant, Botany Department, Bedford College, London, 1960-62; Botany Department, Aberdeen University: Research Assistant, 1962-64, Assistant Lecturer, 1964-67, Lecturer, 1967-74. Address: (b.) Department of Plant Science, Aberdeen University, Aberdeen, AB9 2UD.

Johnson, Sir Ronald (Ernest Charles), Kt (1970), CB (1962), JP. Secretary of Commissions for Scotland, 1972-78; b. 3.5.13; m.; 2 s.; 1 s. deceased. Educ. Portsmouth Grammar School; St. John's College, Cambridge. Secretary, Scottish Home and Health Department, 1963-72.

Johnson, Roy Arthur, CA. Partner, Coopers & Lybrand, Glasgow, since 1966, and Cork Gully, Glasgow, since 1981; Council Member, Institute of Chartered Accountants of Scotland, since 1984; b. 3.3.37, Wanstead, Essex; m., Heather Campbell; 2 s. Educ. Lancing College. Deacon, Incorporation of Cordiners, Glasgow, 1976-77. Recreations: golf; gardening; photography. Address: (b.) Kintyre House, 209 West George Street, Glasgow; T.-041-248 2644.

Johnson-Ferguson, Sir Neil (Edward), 3rd Bt, TD. Vice-Lieutenant, Dumfriesshire, since 1965; b. 2.5.05; m., Sheila Marion Jervis; 4 s. Educ. Winchester; Trinity College, Cambridge. Lt.-Col., Royal Corps of Signals, 1945.

Johnson-Marshall, Professor Percy Edwin Alan, CMG, DipArch, MA, RIBA, FRTPI, RIBA, DistTP. Professor of Urban Design and Regional Planning, Edinburgh University, since 1964; Partner, Percy Johnson-Marshall and Partners, since 1960; b. 20.1.15, Ajmer, India; m., April Bridger; 3 s.; 4 d. Educ. Queen Elizabeth School, Kirkby Lonsdale; School of Architecture, Liverpool University. Various posts, local government, 1936-38; Senior Planning Architect, Coventry City Council, 1938-41; War Service, Royal Engineers, India and Burma, 1941-46; Advisor to Government of Burma for National Outline Plan, 1945-46; Regional Planning Officer, Ministry of Town and Country Planning, 1946-48; Planner in charge, London's Comprehensive Development Areas, LCC, 1949-59; Senior Lecturer, then Reader, Edinburgh University, 1959-64. Member: RIBA Council, 1951-75, RTPI Council, 1950-75, RIAS Council, 1964-74. Recreations: reading; writing; travel. Address: (h.) Bella Vista, 64 The Causeway, Duddingston, Edinburgh, EH15 3PZ; T.-031-661 2019.

Johnston, Alan Charles Macpherson, BA (Hons) (Cantab), LLB. Queen's Counsel (1980); b. 13.1.42, Stirling; m., Anthea Jean; 3 s. Educ. Edinburgh Academy; Loretto School; Jesus College, Cambridge; Edinburgh University. Advocate, 1967; Standing Junior Counsel, Scottish Home and Health Department, 1972; Treasurer, Faculty of Advocates, since 1977; Advocate Depute, 1978-82. Publication: Introduction to Law of Scotland 7th Edition (Joint Editor). Recreation: general leisure. Address: (h.) 3 Circus Gardens, Edinburgh; T.-031-225 1862.

Johnston, Alastair J.C., BSc, CEng, FIProdE, FBIM. General Manager, Uniroyal Ltd., Dumfries, since 1982; Member, CBI Scottish Council; b. 16.9.28, Dundee; m., Morag Campbell; 2 s. Educ. Harris Academy, Dundee; St. Andrews University. Apprenticeship, Caledon Shipyard, Dundee; Industrial Engineering Manager, North British Rubber Co., Edinburgh; Plant Manager, Armstrong Cork Co., Gateshead; Director and General Manager, William Briggs Ltd., Dundee; Managing Director: Permanite Ltd., Waltham Abbey, Trident Equipment Ltd., Ware. Deputy Chairman, Enterprise Trust, Dumfries. Address: (h.) Benridge, 93 Edinburgh Road, Dumfries, DG1 1JX; T.-0387 52350.

Johnston, Sheriff Alexander Graham, LLB, BA. Sheriff of Grampian, Highland and Islands, since 1982; b. 16.7.44; m.; 2 step d.; 2 s. by pr. m. Educ. Edinburgh Academy; Strathallan School; Edinburgh University; University College, Oxford. Solicitor and WS, 1971; Partner, private practice, 1972-82.

Johnston, Brian Bernard, BMSc, MB, ChB, DPM, MRCPsych. Consultant Psychiatrist, Royal Dundee Liff Hospital, since 1984; Honorary Senior Lecturer, Department of Psychiatry, Dundee University, since 1984; b. 16.5.38, Dundee; m., Mary Delaney; 2 s.; 1 d. Educ. Lawside Academy, Dundee; Queen's College, St. Andrews; Dundee University. Telecommunications engineer, Post Office Engineering Department, 1954-65; National Service, RAF, Singapore, Malaya, 1956-58 (Ground Wireless Technician); medical student, 1965-72; House Officer, Orthopaedic Surgery/General Medicine, Dundee Royal Infirmary, 1972-73; Senior House Officer, Registrar, Senior Registrar in Psychiatry, Royal Dundee Liff Hospital, 1973-79; Consultant Psychiatrist, Stratheden Hospital, Cupar, 1979-84. Recreations: jogging; golf; skating; swimming; hill-walking. Address: (h.) Ad Astra, 127 Kinghorne Road, Lawside, Dundee, DD3 6PW; T.-Dundee 28146.

Johnston, David Scott, BA. Director and General Secretary, National Farmers' Union of Scotland, since 1978; b. 18.12.32, Dundee; m., Sheila Kirkby; 3 s. Educ. Harris Academy, Dundee; Rutherford Grammar School, Newcastle; Hatfield College, Durham University. Economics Researcher, Tube Investments, Birmingham, until 1957; joined NFU of Scotland as Assistant Secretary, 1957 (Deputy General Secretary, 1972-78); UK Representative, General Experts

Committee, COPA, three years. Recreation: mountaineering. Address: (b.) 17 Grosvenor Crescent, Edinburgh, EH12 5EN; T.-031-337 4333.

Johnston, Douglas Bell, BSc, MSc, MRTPI, MIH. Director of Housing, Stirling District Council, since 1983; b. 30.7.49, Motherwell. Educ. Dalziel High School, Motherwell; Strathclyde University. Architectural Assistant: Clydebank Burgh Council, 1973, Greater London Council, 1974; Glasgow District Council: Environmental Revitalisation Officer, 1977-79, Principal Officer Environmental Revitalisation, 1979-81, District Property Controller (East), 1981-82; Depute Director of Housing, Stirling District Council, 1982-83. Recreations: walking; not watching television. Address: (b.) Municipal Buildings, Stirling; T.-Stirling 79000.

Johnston, Hon. Lord, (Douglas Harold Johnston), TD, QC (Scot). Senator of the College of Justice in Scotland, 1961-78; b. 1907; m.; 2 s.; 2 d. Educ. Aberdeen Grammar School; St. John's College, Oxford; Edinburgh University. Called to the Bar, Inner Temple, 1931; Scottish Bar, 1932; Advocate Depute, 1945; Solicitor-General for Scotland, 1947-51; MP (Labour), Paisley, 1948-61.

Johnston, Gary Hugh. Member, Highland Regional Council, since 1982; President, Inverness and Highland Chamber of Commerce; Member, Board of Governors, Eden Court Theatre, since 1982; Building Consultant, since 1978; b. 5.5.57, Inverness; m., Terry S. Educ. Millburn Academy, Inverness; Inverness College. Address: (b.) G.H. Johnston, Building Consultants, 51 Castle Street, Inverness; T.-0463 237229.

Johnston, Professor Ian Alistair, BSc, PhD. Professor of Comparative Physiology (Personal Chair) and Director, Gatty Marine Laboratory, St. Andrews University, since 1985; b. 13.4.49, Barking, Essex; m., Dr. Rhona S. Johnston. Educ. Addey and Stanhope Grammar School, London; Hull University. NERC Postdoctoral Research Fellow, Bristol University, 1973-75; Lecturer in Physiology, St. Andrews University, 1976-84; Reader, 1984-85; Visiting Senior Lecturer, Department of Veterinary Physiology, Nairobi University, 1981; Visiting Scientist, British Antarctic Survey base, Signy Island, South Orkneys, 1983-84; awarded Scientific Medal, Zoological Society of London. Recreations: photography; walking; reading. Address: (b.) Department of Physiology, St. Andrews University, St. Andrews, KY16 9TS; T.-0334 76161, Ext. 7197.

Johnston, James Kenneth Buchanan, TD, BL. Senior Partner, Brown Mair Mackintosh & Co., Solicitors, Glasgow, since 1982 (Partner, since 1950); Vice Chairman, Royal Yachting Association Scotland, since 1985; b. 4.9.15, Stirling; widower; 1 s. (deceased); 1 d. Educ. Stirling High School; Glasgow University. Organist and Choirmaster, 1930-39; Service in Territorial Army, 1936-39; War Service in Middle East and Far East, 1939-44 (rank of Lt.-Col.); graduated a Solicitor, 1945. Commodore, Royal Scottish Motor Yacht Club, 1968-71; Legal Adviser,

Royal Yachting Association Scotland; awarded RYA Award, 1983, for services to yachting. Address: (h.) 40 Lanton Road, Newlands, Glasgow; T.-041-637 2975.

Johnston, John Robert, BSc, PhD, FIBiol. Reader, Department of Bioscience and Biotechnology, Strathclyde University, since 1983; b. 6.10.34, Leven, Fife; m., Janet Ronthrone Reekie; 3 s. Educ. Buckhaven High School; St. Andrews University. Teaching Associate, University of California, Berkeley; Research Scientist, Brewing Research Foundation, Nutfield, Surrey; Lecturer, then Senior Lecturer; Strathclyde University. Council Member, Royal Philosophical Society of Glasgow. Recreations: outdoor activities; theatre and music; community affairs. Address: (b.) Department of Bioscience and Biotechnology, Strathclyde University, Glasgow, G1 1XW; T.-041-552 4400.

Johnston, Robert, BL. Solicitor, since 1951; Notary Public, since 1951; Honorary Sheriff, Dumfries, since 1971; b. 26.3.26, Burnmouth, Berwickshire; m., Mary Ross Wilson. Educ. Kirk High School, Cleveland, Ohio; Eyemouth High School; St.Andrews University; Edinburgh University. Solicitor, Balfour & Manson, SSC, Edinburgh, 1951-55; Partner, Austins, Solicitors, Dalbeattie, since 1955; Town Clerk, Dalbeattie, 1961-71; JP Procurator Fiscal, Kirkcudbrightshire, 1956-71; former Council Member, Law Society of Scotland; Member, Scottish Solicitors Discipline Tribunal, since 1982. Recreations: sailing; angling. Address: (h.) Aldouran, Southwick Road, Dalbeattie, Kirkcudbrightshire; T.-0556 610449.

Johnston, Robert Neilson, MD, FRCP, FRCPEdin. Consultant Physician in Respiratory Medicine; Honorary Senior Lecturer, Dundee University, since 1955; b. 13.12.21, Buluwayo, Southern Rhodesia; m., 1, Muriel Bryan; 2, Elizabeth Semple; 1 s.; 2 d. Educ. Aberdeen Grammar School; Aberdeen University. War Service, RAMC, Gold Coast, West Africa; Medical Registrar, Brompton Hospital, London; Fulbright Scholar and Visiting Fellow, Columbia University Bellevue Hospital, New York; Assistant Physician, Department of Respiratory Medicine, Hammersmith Hospital, London. Member, Research Committee, BTA; Past President, Scottish Thoracic Society; Council Member, Scottish Branch, Chest, Heart and Stroke Association. Recreation: gardening. Address: (h.) 50 Albany Road, West Ferry, Dundee, DD5 1NW; T.-Dundee 78538.

Johnston, Robert S., MA (Hons). HM Chief Inspector of Schools i/c Research Unit and Management of Educational Resource Units, SED, since 1983; b. 24.6.24, Kilsyth; m., Edna Rosaline Hampshire; 2 d. Educ. Lenzie Academy; Glasgow University. War service, Artillery; Teacher of English/Head, English Department, Temple Moor School, Leeds, 1949-61; Lecturer, English Department, Jordanhill College, 1961-63; HM Inspectorate: Eastern Division and secondment to SED administration, 1963-69, District Inspector, Glasgow, 1969-73, Chief Inspector of Schools i/c Northern Division, 1974-83. President, Dundee Branch, Glasgow

University Graduates Association. Recreations: golf; gardening; the modern novel. Address: (h.) 67 Elie Avenue, Barnhill, Dundee; T.-0382 75341.

Johnston, Sir Russell, Kt (1985), MP, MA (Hons). MP (Liberal), Inverness, Nairn and Lochaber (formerly Inverness), since 1964; Member, UK Delegation, Council of Europe, since 1984; b. 28.7.32, Edinburgh; m., Joan Graham Menzies; 3 s. Educ. Carbost Public School; Portree High School; Edinburgh University; Moray House College of Education. National Service: commissioned into Intelligence Corps and 2nd i/c British Intelligence Unit, Berlin, 1958-59; History Teacher, Liberton Secondary School, Edinburgh, 1961-63; Research Assistant, Scottish Liberal Party, 1963-64; Joint Parliamentary Adviser, Educational Institute of Scotland, 1964-70; Member, Royal Commission on Local Government in Scotland, 1966-69; Parliamentary Spokesman for Scottish National Federation for the Welfare of the Blind, since 1967; Parliamentary Representative, Royal National Institute for the Blind, since 1977; Member, Select Committee on Scottish Affairs, 1969; Parliamentary Adviser, Scottish Police Federation, 1971-75; Scottish Liberal Party: elected to Executive, 1961, and Organisation Committee, 1962, Vice Chairman, 1965, Chairman, 1970-74, Leader, since 1974; Liberal Party Spokesman on Education, 1964-66, on Foreign Affairs, 1970-75 and 1979-85, on Scotland, 1970-73, 1975-83, and since 1985, on Devolution, 1975, on Defence, since 1983; Member, European Parliament, 1973-75 and 1976-79; Vice President, European Liberal Group and Group Spokesman on Regional Policy, 1973-75; Vice President of the Parliament's Political Committee, 1976-79; Member, Western European Union Assembly and Representative to Council of Europe, 1984-85. Recreations: reading; photography; shinty. Address: (h.) House of Commons, London, SW1A OAA; T.-01-219 5180.

Johnston, Thomas Lothian, MA, PhD, FRSA, FRSE, CBIM. Principal and Vice-Chancellor, Heriot-Watt University, since 1981; b. 9.3.27, Whitburn; m., Joan Fahmy; 2 s.; 3 d. Educ. Hawick High School; Edinburgh University; Stockholm University. Lecturer in Political Economy, Edinburgh University, 1953-65; Professor of Economics, Heriot-Watt University, 1966-76; Chairman, Manpower Services Committee for Scotland, 1977-80; academic appointments in other countries: Illinois University, 1957, 1962-63, Queen's University, Canada, 1965, Western Australian Institute of Technology, 1979, Visiting Professor, International Institute for Labour Studies, Geneva, 1973; Arbitrator, Chairman of Wages Councils, since 1965. Publications: Collective Bargaining in Sweden, 1962; Economic Expansion and Structural Change, 1963; The Structure and Growth of the Scottish Economy (Co-author), 1971; Introduction to Industrial Relations, 1981. Recreations: gardening; walking. Address: (h.) 14 Mansionhouse Road, Edinburgh, EH9 1TZ; T.-031-667 1439.

Johnston, Thomas Ross, BA (Hons), BEd. Member (SNP), Cumbernauld and Kilsyth District Council, since 1984; Principal Teacher of History, Cumbernauld High School, since 1977; b. 16.1.47, Glasgow; m., Catherine Maclean MacMillan; 1 d. Educ. Bellahouston Academy, Glasgow; Glasgow University; London University; Jordanhill College of Education. Teacher of History: Govan High School, 1970-72, Cumbernauld High School, 1972-77. SNP Parliamentary candidate, Monklands East, 1983. Recreations: reciter and speaker on Robert Burns; sea fishing. Address: (h.) 26 Drumpellier Gardens, Condorrat, Cumbernauld, G67 4NT; T.-Cumbernauld 29437.

Johnston, William, MBE, JP. Member, Tayside Regional Council, since 1978 (Convener, Police and Fire Committee); Chairman, Montrose Football Club; b. 25.10.12, Montrose; m., Jean Stirton Young; 1 s.; 3 d. Educ. Cookney Public School, Kincardineshire. Newsagent; Past Chairman, Montrose Branch, Royal British Legion; former Member, Montrose Town Council (Provost, 12 years); Vice-Chairman, Scottish Accident Prevention Council; Member, Scottish American Relations Committee, RAF Edzell, 22 years; a Trustee, Montrose Harbour Trust; Freeman, Royal Burgh of Montrose; Honorary Sheriff, Angus; Past President, Montrose Rotary Club; Past Chairman, Montrose Branch, British Red Cross. Recreation: amateur entertainer for 40 years. Address: (h.) 8 Wellington Park, Montrose, Angus; T.-Montrose 72847.

Johnston, Very Rev. William Bryce, MA, BD, DD. Minister, Colinton Parish Church, since 1964; Chaplain to The Queen in Scotland, since 1981; b. 16.9.21, Edinburgh; m., Ruth Margaret Cowley; 1 s.; 2 d. Educ. George Watson's College, Edinburgh; Edinburgh University. Chaplain to the Forces, 1945-49; Minister: St. Andrew's Church, Bo'ness, 1949-55, St. George's Church, Greenock, 1955-64; Chaplain, HM Prison, Greenock, 1959-64; Convener, General Assembly Committees: Adult Christian Education, 1970-72, Church and Nation, 1972-76, Inter-Church Relations, 1979-81; Moderator of the General Assembly, 1980; Cunningham Lecturer, New College, 1968-71; Visiting Lecturer in Social Ethics, Heriot-Watt University, since 1966; Member, Broadcasting Council for Scotland, since 1983. Publications: translations of Karl Barth and John Calvin. Recreations: organplaying; bowls. Address: (h.) The Manse of Colinton, Edinburgh, EH13 OJR; T.-031-441 2315.

Johnston, William Greer, MBA, CA. Managing Director, Sutherland Transport and Trading Co. Ltd., since 1969; Member, Highland Health Board, since 1983; b. 10.12.40, Old Kilpatrick; m., Moira Alice Haldane Smith; 3 s.; 1 d. Educ. Clydebank High School; Glasgow University. Qualified Chartered Accountant, 1962; various posts in accounting firms, then in engineering and car retail distribution, 1962-69; Member, Highland Regional Council, 1974-78 (Chairman, Education Committee); District Councillor, 1974-80 (Chairman, Environmental Health and Leisure and Recreation). Chairman, Scripture Union Scotland, 1979-84; Treasurer, Scripture Union International, since 1985. Recreations: photography; stamp collecting; family. Address: (h.) Beannach, Lairg, Sutherland; T.-0549 2113.

Johnstone, Alexander Henry, BSc, PhD, DipREd, CChem, FRSC. Reader in Chemical Education, Glasgow University, since 1984 (Head, Science Education Research Group, since 1972); Secretary, Education Research Group, Royal Society of Chemistry, since 1983; b. 17.10.30, Edinburgh; m., Martha Y. Cuthbertson; 2 s. Educ. Leith Academy; Edinburgh University; Glasgow University; Moray House College of Education. Commissioned, Royal Corps of Signals; Assistant Teacher of Chemistry, George Watson's College, Edinburgh; Head of Chemistry Department, High School of Stirling; Lecturer, then Senior Lecturer in Chemistry, Glasgow University. Vice-President, Royal Society of Chemistry (President, Education Division); Consultant to Consultative Committee on the Curriculum. Recreations: hill-walking; photography; archaeology; lay preaching. Address: (b.) Department of Chemistry, The University, Glasgow, G12 8QQ; T.-041-339 8855, Ext. 5172.

Johnstone, David Alexander, MA, LLB, WS, NP. Writer to the Signet; Partner, Messrs Shepherd & Wedderburn, WS, Edinburgh, since 1985; b. 23.1.38, Penrith; m., Christine Jane Adams Tait; 1 s.; 3 d. Educ. Kirkcudbright Academy; Edinburgh University. Partner, G.W. Tait & Sons, SSC, Edinburgh, 1970-85. Recreations: family life; golf; gardening; story writing. Address: (h.) Cruachan, Gosford Road, Longniddry, East Lothian; T.-0875 52188.

Johnstone, David C.M., MA. Rector, Plockton High School, since 1976; b. 17.3.33, Dumfries; m., Jeanette Lamont; 1 s. Educ. Dumfries Academy; Edinburgh University. Teacher of Russian, High School of Stirling, 1960-70; Careers Adviser, Edinburgh University, 1971-72; Gracemount High School, Edinburgh: Assistant Headteacher, 1972-74, Deputy Headteacher, 1974-76. Recreation: music (Church organist). Address: (b.) Plockton High School, Plockton, Ross-shire, IV52 8TU; T.-059 984 372.

Johnstone, David Kirkpatrick. Director of Programmes, Scottish Television, since 1975; b. 4.7.26, Kilmarnock; m., Kay. Educ. Ayr Academy. Scottish Television, since 1957: News Editor, Programme Director, Producer, Head of News and Current Affairs, Assistant Controller of Programmes, Controller of Programmes. Chairman, Regional Controllers' Committee, ITCA, 1984-85. Recreations: golf; travel. Address: (b.) Scottish Television, Cowcaddens, Glasgow, G2 3PR.

Johnstone, Ian Temple, MA (Cantab), LLB (Edin), WS, NP. Partner, Biggart Baillie & Gifford, WS, formerly Baillie & Gifford WS and Biggart Lumsden & Co., since 1950; b. 25.2.23, Edinburgh; m., Frances Ferenbach; 3 d. Educ. Edinburgh Academy; Corpus Christi College, Cambridge; Edinburgh University. Royal Artillery, 1942-46 (final rank of Staff Captain after transfer to Q Movements Burma Command); qualified, 1949; Director, Friends Provident Life Office, since 1964; Director, Inch Kenneth Kajang Rubber PLC, since 1970; Chairman, Baillie Gifford Shin Nippon PLC, since 1985; General Commissioner of Income Tax; Past

President, Scottish Lawn Tennis Association; Council Member, Lawn Tennis Association, 1969-79; Chairman, St. Margaret's School, Edinburgh Limited. Recreations: following sport - football, tennis, cricket, rugby; listening to music; photography; gentle hill-walking. Address: 3 Glenfinlas Street, Edinburgh, EH3; T.-031-226 5541.

Johnstone, John Raymond, BA, CA. Chairman, Murray Johnstone Ltd., since 1984 (Managing Director, since 1968); Chairman, Scottish Opera, since 1983; Director, Scottish Amicable Life Assurance Society (Chairman, 1983-85); b. 27.10.29, London; m., Susan Sara; 5 step-s.; 2 d. Educ. Eton; Trinity College, Cambridge. Investment Analyst, Robert Fleming & Co. Ltd., London, 1955-60; Partner (CA), Brown, Fleming & Murray (later Whinney Murray & Co.), 1960-68; Chairman: Dominion Insurance Co. Ltd., Dominion Insurance Holdings Ltd., Kemper-Murray Johnstone International Inc.; Landel Insurance Holdings Ltd.; Murray Electronics PLC; Murray Technology Investments PLC; Murray Management Ltd.; various other Directorships. Recreations: fishing; shooting; opera; art. Address: (h.) Wards, Gartocharn, Dunbartonshire.

Johnstone, Professor William, MA (Hons), BD. Professor of Hebrew and Semitic Languages, Aberdeen University, since 1980; Minister, Church of Scotland, since 1963; b. 6.5.36, Glasgow; m., Elizabeth M. Ward; 1 s.; 1 d. Educ. Hamilton Academy; Glasgow University; Marburg University. Aberdeen University: Lecturer in Hebrew and Semitic Languages, Aberdeen University, 1962-72, Senior Lecturer, 1972-80, Dean, Faculty of Divinity, since 1983. Recreation: alternative work. Address: (h.) 37 Rubislaw Den South, Aberdeen, AB2 6BD; T.-Aberdeen 316022.

Jolly, Douglas, BSc (Hons). Rector, Viewforth High School, since 1981; b. 30.6.38, Dundee; m., Elizabeth Smith; 2 d. Educ. Grove Academy, Broughty Ferry; St. Andrews University. Principal Teacher of Physics, Lawside Academy, 1964-72; Assistant Rector, Craigie High School, 1972-75; Depute Rector, Arbroath High School, 1975-81; Member, Central Committee for Science Teaching in Scotland, 1972-75. Committee Member, Balbirnie Park Golf Club; Elder, Markinch Parish Church. Recreations: golf; gardening; travel. Address: (h.) 16 Orchard Drive, Glenrothes, Fife; T.-Glenrothes 757039.

Jolly, Rev. John, BA. Minister, Old Partick Parish Church, Glasgow, since 1966; b. 14.5.23, Angus; m., Elizabeth Walker Cruickshank; 1 s.; 1 d. Educ. Forfar Academy; St. Andrews University. RAF, 1941-45; Assistant Minister, North Church, Aberdeen; Minister: St. Nicholas-Kincorth Church, Aberdeen, 1951-57, Bluevale Parish Church, Glasgow, 1957-66; Glasgow Presbytery: Convener, Education Committee, since 1982 (Moderator, since 1984); Member, Education Committee, General Assembly. Governor, Hutchesons Grammar School; Member, Scottish Prison Chaplains' Board. Recreations: walking; gardening. Address: (h.) 49 Downanside Road, Glasgow, G12 9DW; T.-041-339 2651.

Jones, Arthur Stanley, BSc, PhD, CBiol, MIBiol. Deputy Director, Rowett Research Institute, since 1983 (Head, Department of Applied Nutrition and Chairman, Division of Applied Sciences), since 1973; b. 17.5.32, Belfast; m., Mary Margaret Smith; 3 s.; 1 d. Educ. Gosforth Grammar School; Durham University; Aberdeen University. Farmed, 1960-84; Kirkley Hall Farm Institute and Durham University, 1951-55; Military Service, 1955-57; Agricultural Research Council Scholarship, 1957-58; joined Rowett Research Institute, 1959. Recreations: sailing; gardening; flying. Address: (b.) Rowett Research Institute, Bucksburn, Aberdeen, AB2 9SB; T.-0224 712751.

Jones, Colin Irving, FCA, ATII. Chartered Accountant; Lecturer in Accounting and Taxation, since 1973; Member, Ettrick and Lauderdale District Council, since 1983 (Vice-Convener, Environmental Health); b. 10.3.33, Gateshead; m., Mary June Henrietta; 1 s. Educ. Gateshead Grammar School. National Service, RAF; worked in industry, 1960-73. Parliamentary candidate, Linlithgow, General Election, 1983. Recreation: music. Address: (h.) Rigfoot, Midlem, Selkirk, TD7 4QF; T.-Lilliesleaf 306.

Jones, Professor Douglas Samuel, MBE, MA, DSc, HonDSc, FIMA, FRSE, FRS. Ivory Professor of Mathematics, Dundee University, since 1964; b. 10.1.22, Corby, Northamptonshire; m., Ivy Styles; 1 s.; 1 d. Educ. Wolverhampton Grammar School; Corpus Christi College, Oxford. Flt.-Lt., RAF; Commonwealth Fellow, Massachusetts Institute of Technology; Lecturer, Manchester University; Professor, Keele University; Visiting Professor, New York University; Member, University Grants Committee; Chairman, Mathematics Committee; Computer Board; Member, Open University Visiting Committee; won Van der Pol Gold Medal; Keith Prize, RSE. Recreation: not answering questionnaires. Address: (b.) Department of Mathematical Sciences, The University, Dundee, DD1 4HN; T.-Dundee 23181.

Jones, Rev. Edward Gwynfai, BA (Hons). Minister, St. Rollox Church of Scotland, Glasgow, since 1967; Convener, Unions and Readjustments Committee, Glasgow Presbytery, since 1981; b. 20.5.37, Aberystwyth, Wales; m., Elspeth Mary Margretta; 2 d. Educ. Pontardawe Grammar School, Wales; Durham University. Minister, Tow Law Presbyterian Church, Co. Durham, 1964-67. Address: 42 Melville Gardens, Bishopbriggs, Glasgow, G64 3DE; T.-041-772 2848.

Jones, Huw, MA. Senior Lecturer in Geography, Dundee University, since 1975; b. 22.7.38, Llanidloes; 2 s. Educ. Newtown Boys Grammar School, Powys; University College of Wales, Aberystwyth. Address: (h.) 43 Albert Road, Broughty Ferry, Dundee, DD5 1AY; T.-0382 79684.

Jones, Professor Peter (Howard), MA. Professor of Philosophy, Edinburgh University, since 1984 (Deputy Director, Institute for Advanced Studies in the Humanities, since 1984); b. 18.12.35,

London; m., Elizabeth Jean Roberton; 2 d. Educ. Highgate School; Queens' College, Cambridge. Regional Officer, The British Council, London, 1960-61; Research Scholar, Cambridge University, 1961-63; Assistant Lecturer in Philosophy, Nottingham University, 1963-64; Edinburgh University: Lecturer in Philosophy, 1964-77, Reader, 1977-84; Visiting Professor of Philosophy: Rochester University, New York, 1969-70, Dartmouth College, New Hampshire, 1973, 1983, Carleton College, Minnesota, 1974, Oklahoma University, 1978, Baylor University, 1978; Distinguished Foreign Scholar, Mid-America State Universities, 1978; Visiting Fellow, Humanities Research Centre, Australian National University, 1984. Publications: Philosophy and the Novel, 1975; Hume's Sentiments, 1982. Recreations: opera; chamber music; the arts, including architecture; travel; photography. Address: (b.) Department of Philosophy, David Hume Tower, George Square, Edinburgh, 8; T.-031-667 1011.

Jones, Rodney, BSc (Hons). Head, Fish Team, Marine Laboratory, Aberdeen, since 1985; b. 21.12.27, Cheltenham; m., Sheila Clouston; 1 s.; 2 d. Educ. Cheltenham Grammar School; Liverpool University. Marine Laboratory, Aberdeen: Scientific Officer, 1948-54, Senior Scientific Officer, 1954-63, Principal Scientific Officer, 1963-78, Senior Principal Scientific Officer, since 1978. Address: (b.) Marine Laboratory, Aberdeen; T.-Aberdeen 876544.

Jones, William. Sheriff Clerk, Dumfries, and Joint Auditor, Sheriff Court, Dumfries, since 1983; b. 20.12.42, Dingwall; m., Norma Anne McElnay; 1 s.; 1 d. Educ. Hamilton Academy. Clerk, Sheriff Clerks' Branch, Scottish Court Service, 1961-65; Sheriff Clerk Depute: Perth, 1966-69, Edinburgh, 1969-74; Training Officer, Scottish Court Service Staff Training Centre, Glasgow, 1974-77; Sheriff Clerk Depute, Dunfermline, 1977-79; seconded Scottish Courts Administration, Edinburgh, 1979-83. Recreations: gardening; reading; music. Address: (h.) 8 Craigvale Court, Dumfries, DG1 4QH; T.-0387 65013.

Jordan, Lt. Col. Howard Alfred John, MBE, FCIT. Director, Scottish Engineering Employers' Association, since 1980; b. 26.3.36, Edinburgh; m., Patricia Ann Tomlin; 1 s.; 1 d. Educ. Broughton Secondary School. Army, 1954-80; Lt. Col., Royal Corps of Transport; service in UK (including Northern Ireland), Singapore, BAOR; commanded 154 (Lowland) Transport Regiment RCT(V). Chairman, Carmunnock Community Council, since 1980; Chairman, Strathclyde Group, National Council for Conservation of Plants and Gardens, since 1983; Honorary President, Carmunnock British Legion, since 1980; Member, Lowland TA Council, since 1981; Member, CBI Scotland Employment Committee, since 1981. Address: (b.) 105 West George Street, Glasgow, G2 1QL; T.-041-221 3181.

Joughin, Michael, CBE, JP, FBIM, FRAgS. Chairman, North of Scotland Hydro-Electric Board, since 1983; Member, South of Scotland Electricity Board; Farmer, since 1952; b. 26.4.26,

Devonport; m., 1, Lesley Roy Petrie; 2, Anne S.H. Hutchison; 1 s.; 1 d. Educ. Kelly College, Tavistock, Devon. Royal Marines, 1944-52 (Lt.); seconded, Fleet Air Arm, 1946-49 (ditched off Malta, 1949, invalided, 1952). Chairman, North of Scotland Milk Marketing Board, 1974-83; Past Chairman, Grassland and Forage Committee, JCC; Chairman, Scottish Agricultural Development Council, 1971-80; Chairman, Governors, North of Scotland College of Agriculture, 1969-72; President, National Farmers Union of Scotland, 1964-66; Deputy Lieutenant, County of Moray, 1974-80; Governor: Rowett Research Institute, Aberdeen, 1968-74, Scottish Plant Breeding Station, 1969-74, Animal Diseases Research Association, Edinburgh, 1969-74; Chairman, Governors, Blairmore Preparatory School, near Huntly, 1966-72; Member: Scottish Constitutional Committee (Douglas-Home Committee), 1969-70, Intervention Board for Agricultural Produce, 1972-76, National Economic Development Council for Agriculture, 1967-70; Past Chairman, NEDC Working Party on Livestock; Member: Agricultural Marketing Development Executive Committee, 1965-68, British Farm Produce Council, 1965-66; former Member: Selection Committee, Nuffield Farming Scholarships, Awards Committee, Massey-Ferguson National Award for Services to UK Agriculture; Chairman: North of Scotland Grassland Society, 1970-71, Elgin Market Green Auction Co., 1969-70; Founder Presenter, Country Focus (farming programme), Grampian Television, 1961-64 and 1967-69; Captain, 11th Bn., Seaforth Highlanders (TA), 1952-53. Recreation: sailing. Address: (h.) Elderslie, Findhorn, Moray; T.-03093 2277.

Jung, Roland Tadeusz, BA, MA, MB, BChir, MD, MRCS, LRCP, MRCP, FRCPEdin. Consultant Physician (Specialist in Endocrinology and Diabetes), since 1982; Honorary Senior Lecturer, Dundee University, since 1982; b. 8.2.48, Glasgow; m., Felicity King. Educ. St. Anselm's College, Wirral; Pembroke College, Cambridge; St. Thomas Hospital and Medical School, London. MRC Clinical Scientific Officer, Dunn Nutrition Unit, Cambridge, and Honorary Senior Registrar, Addenbrooke's Hospital, Cambridge, 1977-79; Senior Registrar in Endocrinology and Diabetes, Royal Postgraduate Medical School, Hammersmith Hospital, London, 1980-82. Publication: Endocrine Problems in Oncology (Co-Editor), 1984. Recreation: gardening. Address: (b.) Department of Medicine, Ninewells Hospital and Medical School, Dundee; T.-Dundee 60111.

K

Kane, Jack, OBE, JP, DL, Dr hc (Edin). Chairman, Age Concern Scotland, since 1983; Honorary President: Workers Educational Association (SE Scotland), Craigmillar Festival

Society, Jack Kane Centre; b. 1.4.11, Addiewell, Midlothian; m., Anne Murphy; 1 s.; 2 d. Educ. Bathgate Academy. Librarian, 1937-55; War Service, Royal Artillery, 1940-46; District Secretary, Workers Educational Association (SE Scotland), 1955-76; Chairman, South of Scotland Electricity Consultative Council, 1977-80; Chairman, Board of Trustees, National Galleries of Scotland, 1975-80; Councillor, Edinburgh, 1938-75 (Bailie, 1947-51, Lord Provost, 1972-75). Recreations: reading; walking. Address: (h.) 88 Thirlestane Road, Edinburgh, EH9 1AS; T.-031-447 7757.

Karolyi, Otto Jozsef, BMus, AMusTCL. Senior Lecturer and Head, Department of Music, Stirling University, since 1978; b. 26.3.34, Paris; m., Benedikte Uttenthal; 1 s. Educ. Champagnat French-Hungarian School, Budapest; Werboczy and Berzsenyi Gymnasiums, Budapest; Bela Bartok Conservatoire, Budapest; Akademie fur Musick und danstellende kunst, Wien; Trinity College of Music, London; London University. Freelance writing; WEA Tutor, ILEA and Oxford districts; Tutor, Extra-Mural Department, London University; Director of Music, Hampden House School; Music Therapist, St. John's Hospital, Stone and Napsbury Hospital, St. Albans; Visiting Lecturer, London University, Imperial College of Science and Technology; Tutor and Head, Department of Musicianship, Watford School of Music; part-time Tutor and Counsellor, Open University; Senior Lecturer, City of Leeds College of Music. Publication: Introducing Music. Recreations: languages; literature; the arts. Address: (b.) Stirling University, Stirling; T.-0786 73171.

Kay, Sir Andrew Watt, Kt (1973). Chairman, Scottish Hospital Endowments Research Trust, since 1983; Regius Professor of Surgery, Glasgow University, 1964-81; b. 14.8.16; m.; 2 s.; 2 d. Educ. Ayr Academy; Glasgow University. Part-time Chief Scientist, Scottish Home and Health Department, 1973-81.

Kay, Robin Noel Brunyate, MA, PhD (Cantab), FRSE. Head, Department of Physiology and Veterinary Services, Rowett Research Institute, 1965-85; b. 22.12.28, London; m., Brenda Grace; 1 s.; 2 d. Educ. Leighton Park School, Reading; Caius College, Cambridge. Joined Rowett Research Institute, 1956; now graded Senior Principal Scientific Officer; Visiting Research Worker/Lecturer/Professor: Melbourne University, 1960, Veterinary School of Toulouse, 1970, Nairobi Unversity, 1974, Alberta University, 1984. Recreations: hill-walking; travel; gardening; family. Address: (h.) 386 North Deeside Road, Cults, Aberdeen, AB1 9SS; T.-0224 868221.

Kay, William, MA. Freelance Broadcaster/Writer/Producer; b. 24.9.51, Galston, Ayrshire; m., Maria Joao de Almeida da Cruz Dinis; 1 d. Educ. Galston High School; Kilmarnock Academy; Edinburgh University. After graduation, money earned on oil rig; launched working tour of Thailand, South Korea, Hawaii, Canada, USA, Mexico; worked as researcher; Producer, Odyssey series, Radio Scotland; produced about 40 documentaries on diverse aspects of working-

class oral history. Commandeur d'Honneur, Commanderie du Bontemps de Medoc et des Graves. Publications: Odyssey: Voices from Scotland's Recent Past (Editor); Odyssey: The Second Collection (Editor); Knee Deep in Claret: A Celebration of Wine and Scotland (Co-author); Made in Scotland (poetry); Jute (play for radio). Recreations: the wean; wine; languages; films; Dundee United. Address: (h.) 6b Craigmillar Park, Edinburgh, EH16 5NE.

Kean, Eric Maclean, JP, FRICS. Consultant, Kean, Kennedy and Partners, since 1975; Member, Edinburgh District Council, since 1974; b. 17.10.19, Edinburgh; m., June Patricia Makin. Educ. George Heriot's; Heriot-Watt. Senior Partner, Kean, Kennedy and Partners, 1945-75; Edinburgh Town Council: Member, 1965-75, Chairman, Planning Committee, 1968-71, Bailie/Senior Bailie, 1971-74; Edinburgh District Council: Chairman, Licensing Board, 1978-82, Deputy Chairman of Council, 1982-84. Recreation: golf. Address: (h.) 55 St. Alban's Road, Edinburgh; T.-031-667 2233.

Keane, Professor Simon Michael, MA, LLB, PhD, CA. Professor of Accountancy, Glasgow University, since 1983; b. 8.4.33, Glasgow; m., Mary; 1 d. Educ. St. Aloysius College; Glasgow University. Investigating Accountant, Admiralty, 1965-67; Lecturer, Glasgow College of Commerce, 1967-69; Glasgow University: Lecturer, 1969-81, Reader, 1981-83. Publications: Efficient Market Hypothesis, 1980; Stock Market Efficiency, 1983. Recreations: golf; painting. Address: (b.) 67 Southpark Avenue, Glasgow, G12; T.-041-339 8855.

Kearney, Sheriff Brian, MA, LLB. Sheriff of Glasgow and Strathkelvin, since 1977; b. 25.8.35; m.; 3 s.; 1 d. Educ. Greenock Academy; Glasgow University. Solicitor, 1960; Partner, Biggart, Lumsden & Co., 1965; Sheriff of North Strathclyde, at Dumbarton, 1974-77; Chairman, Glasgow Marriage Guidance Council, since 1977.

Keates, John S., OBE, MA. Reader in Cartography, Glasgow University, since 1980; b. 22.11.25, Wallasey; m., Eve; 1 s.; 1 d. Educ. Wallasey Grammar School; University College, Oxford. Cartographic Editor: Clarendon Press, Oxford, 1949-54, Penguin Books, 1954-56, Esselte Map Service, Stockholm, 1956-60; joined Glasgow University, 1960; Editor, Cartographic Journal, 1963-70; Member, Royal Society National Sub-Committee for Cartography, 1970-79; Member, Course Committee B5, Moderator and Assessor (Cartography), SCOTEC, since 1970; Member, Commission B, International Cartographic Association, since 1972. Publications: Cartographic Design and Production, 1973; Understanding Maps, 1982. Recreations: angling; photography; wood turning. Address: (h.) 11B Winton Drive, Glasgow, G12 OPZ; T.-041-357 2190.

Kee, A. Alistair, MA, BD, STM, PhD. Head, Department of Religious Studies, Glasgow University, since 1976; b. 17.4.37, Alexandria; m., Anne Paterson; 1 s.; 1 d. Educ. Clydebank High School; Glasgow University; Union Theological Seminary, New York. Lecturer: University

College of Rhodesia, 1964-67, Hull University, 1967-76; Senior Lecturer, then Reader, Glasgow University, since 1976; Visiting Professor, Augusta College, Georgia, 1982-83; Director, SCM Press Ltd.; Governor, Merchiston Castle School, Edinburgh. Publications: The Way of Transcendence; A Reader in Political Theology; Constantine Versus Christ. Recreation: golf. Address: (b.) Department of Religious Studies, Glasgow University, Glasgow; T.-041-339 8855.

Keegan, James Douglas, LLB, SSC, NP, ACI (Arb). Solicitor, since 1975; Notary Public, since 1975; Council Member, Law Society of Scotland, since 1982; b. 25.9.51, Uddingston; m., Anne Kirkland; 1 d. Educ. Our Lady's High School, Motherwell; Strathclyde University. Apprentice, John James Teague, 1973-75; joined Constable Farquarson & Co. as Assistant, 1975, Partner, 1976; Partner, Drummond & Co., since 1978; Secretary, Faculty of Procurators of Linlithgowshire, 1981-84. Recreations: nothing abnormal. Address: (b.) 31/32 Moray Place, Edinburgh; T.-031-226 5151.

Keenan, J. Melvin. Aberdeen District Officer, Transport and General Workers Union, since 1977; Member, Sea Fish Industry Authority, since 1981; b. 13.6.49, Falkirk; m., Nancy; 2 s. Educ. St. Modans High School, Stirling; Stow College, Glasgow; Esk Valley Technical College. Inveresk Paper Co., 1964-70; BP Chemicals International Ltd. and BP Oil Ltd., 1970-76. Member, EEC Joint Committee on Social Problems in Sea Fishing, since 1978; Trustee, Scottish Trawler Fishermen's Pension Scheme, since 1981. Publication: Fishing: The Way Forward (Co-author), 1980. Recreations: country life; poetry; judo. Address: (b.) 44 King Street, Aberdeen; T.-0224 645271.

Keenan, Peter. Boxer; b. 1929, Glasgow; m., Cissy; 1 s.; 2 d. Won Scottish Flyweight title, 1948, before turning professional; won two Lonsdale belts outright; British Champion, 1951-53, 1954-59; Empire Champion, 1955-59; European Champion, 1951-52, 1953; failed to beat Vic Toweel, 1952, for World title; promoted boxing in Glasgow for a number of years.

Keir, Professor Hamish Macdonald, BSc, PhD, DSc, CBiol, FIBiol, CChem, FRSC, FRSE. Professor of Biochemistry and Vice-Principal, Aberdeen University, since 1968; Chairman, Council of Management, Macaulay Institute for Soil Research, Aberdeen, since 1983; Vice-Chairman, Board of Governors, Rowett Research Institute, Aberdeen, since 1972; b. 5.9.31, Moffat; m., Eleanor Louise Campbell; 1 s.; 2 d. Educ. Ayr Academy; Glasgow University; Yale University. Honorary Secretary, The Biochemical Society; Member, Cell Board, Medical Research Council; Chairman, IMB, Natural Environment Research Council; Member, Ethical and Research Committees, Grampian Health Board; President of Council, Federation of European Biochemical Societies; serves on Committees, International Union of Biochemistry; Member, Board of Governors, North of Scotland College of Agriculture; Member: Science and Engineering Research Council (Biology), University Grants Committee (Biology); Member, Universities of Scotland Joint Purchasing Consortium; Director: AURIS Ltd., AUMS Ltd., SEQUAL Ltd., NCIMB Ltd.; Chairman, Grampian Region, Tenovus-Scotland. Recreations: piano; golf; travel. Address: (b.) Department of Biochemistry, Aberdeen University, Marischal College, Aberdeen, AB9 1AS; T.-0224 40241, Ext. 249.

Keith of Kinkel, Baron, (Henry Shanks Keith), PC (1976). Life Peer, since 1977; Lord of Appeal in Ordinary, since 1977; b. 7.2.22; m.; 4 s.; 1 d. Educ. Edinburgh Academy; Magdalen College, Oxford; Edinburgh University. Served Second World War (mentioned in Despatches); Advocate, 1950; Barrister, Gray's Inn, 1951; QC (Scot), 1962; Sheriff Principal of Roxburgh, Berwick and Selkirk, 1970-71; Senator of the College of Justice in Scotland, 1971-77; Chairman, Scottish Valuation Advisory Council, 1972-76; Deputy Chairman, Parliamentary Boundary Commission for Scotland, 1976.

Kelbie, Sheriff David, LLB (Hons); Sheriff of North Strathclyde, at Dumbarton, since 1979; b. 28.2.45, Inverurie; m., Helen Mary Smith; 1 s.; 1 d. Educ. Inverurie Academy; Aberdeen University. Passed Advocate, 1968; Associate Lecturer, Heriot-Watt University, 1971-76; Secretary, Scottish Congregational College, 1974-82. Recreations: sailing; hill-walking; reading; learning. Address: (h.) 52 Abercromby Crescent, Helensburgh, Dunbartonshire; T.-Helensburgh 4690.

Kellett, Roger John, MA, MB, BChir, FRCP, FRCPEdin. Consultant Physician, Eastern General Hospital, Edinburgh, and Roodlands General Hospital, Haddington, since 1975; part-time Senior Lecturer in Medicine, Edinburgh University, since 1975; b. 17.6.40, Bradford; m., Anne Margaret Watson Lewis; 2 d. Educ. Bradford Grammar School; Emmanuel College, Cambridge. House Surgeon and House Physician, The London Hospital, 1964-65; Medical Registrar, Chelmsford Group of Hospitals, 1966-69; Lecturer in Medicine, Western Infirmary, Glasgow, 1969-75; Member, Lothian Health Board. Address: (h.) 5 Burgess Terrace, Edinburgh, EH9 2BD; T.-031-667 0300.

Kelly, John R.S., BSc, CEng, MIMechE. Chairman, Lothian and Borders Fire Board, since 1983; Member, Lothian Regional Council, since 1982; b. 28.1.38, Edinburgh; m., Janis E. Leslie; 1 s.; 2 d. Educ. George Watson's College, Edinburgh; Edinburgh University. Engineer, Ferranti Ltd., 1960-63; Managing Director, John Kelly & Son, 1968-70; Assistant to Managing Director, A.V.W. Equipment Ltd., 1971-73; Building Services Engineer: J.E. Greiner Ltd., 1973-75, Sir Robert McAlpine & Sons Ltd., 1976-82; Manager, Plumbing and Heating Department, Miller Construction (Northern) Ltd., since 1982. Recreations: golf; rugby football (spectator). Address: (h.) 9 Dalrymple Crescent, Edinburgh, EH9 2NU; T.-031-667 5912.

Kelly, Michael, CBE (1983), JP, DL, BSc (Econ), PhD. Lord Rector, Glasgow University, since 1983; Journalist and Broadcaster; b. 1.11.40; m.; 1

s.; 2 d. Educ. Strathclyde University. Assistant Lecturer in Economics, Aberdeen University, 1965-67; Lecturer in Economics, Strathclyde University, 1967-84; Lord Provost of Glasgow, 1980-84; Hon. LLD, Glasgow, 1984; Scot of the Year, 1983; OStJ, 1983.

Kelnar, Christopher J.H., MA, MB, BChir, FRCP, DCH. Consultant Paediatrician, Royal Hospital for Sick Children, Edinburgh, since 1983; part-time Senior Lecturer, Department of Child Life and Health, Edinburgh University, since 1983; b. 22.12.47, London; m., Alison; 1 s.; 2 d. Educ. Highgate School, London; Trinity College, Cambridge; St. Bartholomew's Hospital, London. Research Fellow, Paediatric Endocrinology, Middlesex Hospital, London, 1979-81; Senior Registrar, Hospital for Sick Children, Great Ormond Street, London, and Tutor, Institute of Child Health, London, 1981-83. Publication: The Sick Newborn Baby, 1981. Recreations: music; gardening. Address: (b.) Royal Hospital for Sick Children, Sciennes Road, Edinburgh, EH9 1LF; T.-031-667 1991.

Kelso, David Elliot, BSc, MEd, FIPM, FBIM. HM Inspector of Schools, Scottish Education Department, since 1985; b. 25.3.45, Glasgow; m., Dorothy Louise Christie; 1 s.; 2 d. Educ. St. Joseph's College, Dumfries; Edinburgh University; Glasgow University; Dundee University. Personnel Officer, Singer (UK) Ltd., Clydebank, 1968-69; Personnel Manager, Rank Organisation, Kirkcaldy, 1969-71; Lecturer in Management, Glasgow College of Technology, 1971-73; Senior Lecturer, Dundee College of Commerce, 1973-76; Head, Department of Commerce and Business Studies, Falkirk College of Technology, 1976-83; Assistant Principal, 1983-85. Chairman, Central Scotland Branch, British Institute of Management; Chairman, Scottish Humanist Council. Recreations: running; esperanto; hill-walking. Address: (h.) 4 Kilbryde Crescent, Dunblane, Perthshire, FK15 9AZ; T.-0786 822605.

Kelty, William. Chairman, General Purposes Commitee, Grampian Regional Council, since 1978; b. 4.3.16, Keith; m., Margaret Rogers; 1 s.; 1 d. Educ. Keith Grammar School; Newstead School, Perthshire; Royal Technical College, Glasgow. Elected, Keith Town Council, 1946 (Chairman, Water Services; Dean of Guild); Chairman, Keith Football Club; twice Chairman, Keith Rotary Club; Chairman, Keith Swimming Pool Fund. Address: (h.) 43 Moss Street, Keith, AB5 3HH; T.-Keith 2552.

Kemball, Emeritus Professor Charles, MA, ScD, HonDSc, CChem, FRSC, MRIA, FRSE, FRS. Emeritus Professor of Chemistry and University Fellow, Edinburgh University, since 1983; b. 27.3.23, Edinburgh; m., Kathleen Purvis Lynd; 1 s.; 2 d. Educ. Edinburgh Academy; Trinity College, Cambridge. Fellow, Trinity College, 1946-54 (Junior Bursar, 1949-51, Assistant Lecturer, 1951-54); Demonstrator in Physical Chemistry, Cambridge University, 1951-54; Professor of Physical Chemistry, Queen's University, Belfast, 1954-66 (Dean, Faculty of Science, 1957-60, Vice-President, 1962-65); Professor of Chemistry, Edinburgh University, 1966-83 (Dean, Faculty of

Science, 1975-78). President, Royal Institute of Chemistry, 1974-76; Vice-President, Royal Society of Edinburgh, 1971-74, 1982-85; Meldola Medal, RIC, 1951; Corday-Morgan Medal, 1958; Tilden Lecturer, 1960; Surface and Colloid Chemistry Award, Chemical Society, 1972; Ipatieff Prize, American Chemical Society, 1962; Gunning-Victoria Jubilee Prize, Royal Society of Edinburgh, 1976-80. Recreations: hill-walking; card games; wine-making. Address: (h.) 5 Hermitage Drive, Edinburgh, EH10 6DE; T.-031-447 2315.

Kemp, Arnold, MA. Editor, Glasgow Herald, since 1981; b. 15.2.39; m., Sandra Elizabeth; 2 d. Educ. Edinburgh Academy; Edinburgh University. Sub-Editor: The Scotsman, 1959-62, The Guardian, 1962-65; The Scotsman: Production Editor, 1965-70, London Editor, 1970-72, Deputy Editor, 1972-81. Recreations: music; reading; theatre. Address: (b.) 195 Albion Street, Glasgow, G1; T.-041-552 6255.

Kemp, Professor Martin John, MA, FRSA. Professor of Fine Arts, St. Andrews University, since 1981 (Associate Dean, since 1983); b. 5.3.42, Windsor; m., Jill Lightfoot; 1 s.; 1 d. Educ. Windsor Grammar School; Cambridge University; London University. Lecturer: Dalhousie University, Nova Scotia, 1965-66, Glasgow University, 1966-81. Trustee: National Galleries of Scotland, since 1982, Victoria and Albert Museum, London, since 1985; Honorary Professor of History, Royal Scottish Academy, since 1985; Member, Institute for Advanced Study, Princeton, 1984-85. Publication: Leonardo Da Vinci: The Marvellous Works of Nature and Man (1981 Mitchell Prize for Best First Book in Art History). Recreation: sport (especially hockey). Address: (h.) Orillia, 45 Pittenweem Road, Anstruther, Fife; T.-0333 310842.

Kemp, William, BSc, PhD, CChem, FRSC. Senior Lecturer, Heriot-Watt University, since 1960; b. 15.8.32, Glasgow; m., Louisa Jennette McLelland; 2 s.; 1 d. Educ. Govan High School; Glasgow University. Technical Officer, ICI Nobel Division; Lecturer, Paisley College of Technology. Publications: four chemistry text books. Recreations: diverse, often sporting, usually outdoor. Address: (b.) Chemistry Department, Heriot-Watt University, Riccarton, Currie, Edinburgh, EH14 4AS; T.-031-449 5111.

Kendell, Professor Robert Evan, MD, FRCP, FRCPsych. Professor of Psychiatry, Edinburgh University, since 1974; Member, Medical Research Council, since 1984; Member, WHO Expert Advisory Panel on Mental Health, since 1979; b. 28.3.35, Rotherham; m., Ann Whitfield; 2 s.; 2 d. Educ. Mill Hill School; Cambridge University; King's College Hospital Medical School. Visiting Professor, Vermont University College of Medicine, 1969-70; Reader in Psychiatry, Institute of Psychiatry, London University, 1970-74. Publications: The Classification of Depressive Illnesses, 1968; The Role of Diagnosis in Psychiatry, 1975; Companion to Psychiatric Studies (Editor), 1983. Recreations: walking up hills; overeating. Address: (h.) 3 West Castle Road, Edinburgh, EH10 5AT.

Kennedy, Alan Campbell, BL. Chief Executive and Director of Administration and Legal Services, Gordon District Council, since 1974; b. 13.4.26, Aberdeen; m., Margaret; 2 d. Educ. Robert Gordon's College; Aberdeen University. Aberdeen Corporation: Junior Clerk, Senior Clerk, Administrative Assistant, Law Apprentice, Legal Assistant, Senior Legal Assistant, Principal Legal and Administrative Assistant; Burgh Fiscal, Aberdeen, 1964-74; part-time Tutor, Faculty of Law, Aberdeen University. Recreations: hill-walking; cycling; gardening; folk music; reading and studying Doric language of North East Scotland. Address: (b.) Gordon House, Blackhall Road, Inverurie, Aberdeenshire.

Kennedy, Angus Johnston, MA, PhD. Reader in French Language and Literature, Glasgow University; b. 9.8.40, Port Charlotte; m., Marjory McCulloch Shearer; 2 d. Educ. Bearsden Academy; Glasgow University. Glasgow University: Assistant Lecturer in French, 1965, then Lecturer, Senior Lecturer; former Secretary, British Branch, International Arthurian Society. Publications: books on Christine de Pizan. Pizan. Address: (b.) French Department, Glasgow University, Glasgow; T.-041-339 8855, Ext. 584.

Kennedy, Calum. Professional Entertainer and Composer; Hotelier; Property Developer; b. 2.6.28, Orinsay, Stornoway; m., Anne Gillies (deceased); 5 d. Educ. Nicolson Institute, Stornoway; Sir Edward Scott Secondary School, Tarbert, Harris; Glasgow University; Wolsey Hall, Oxford. Army; accountancy and economics; 140 television shows; Proprietor (1964-70), Theatre Royal, Dundee and Tivoli Theatre, Aberdeen; gramophone records manufacturer; show promoter and song writer; former Mod gold medallist; World Festival gold medallist; Grampian TV Personality of the Year, 1964, 1970, 1971; Gold and Silver Disc awards (Pye Records). Recreations: golf; fishing; sailing; gardening. Address: (h.) Leethland House, Leethland, Elderslie, Johnstone.

Kennedy, Charles Peter, MP, MA (Hons). MP (SDP), Ross, Cromarty and Skye, since 1983; an SDP Parliamentary Spokesman on Scottish Affairs, Health, Social Services and Social Security; b. 25.11.59, Inverness. Educ. Lochaber High School, Fort William; Glasgow University; Indiana University. President, Glasgow University Union, 1980-81; Winner, British Observer Mace for Student Debating, 1982; Journalist, BBC Highland, Inverness, 1982; Fulbright Scholar, Indiana University (Bloomington Campus), 1982-83. Honorary President, Young Members' Branch, English Speaking Union. Recreations: reading; writing. Address: (b.) House of Commons, London, SW1A OAA; T.-01-219 5090.

Kennedy, Dermot, MB, ChB, MRCP, DRCOG. Consultant Physician, Department of Infectious Diseases, Ruchill Hospital, Glasgow, since 1978; Honorary Clinical Lecturer, Glasgow University, since 1978; b. 1.1.44, Glasgow; m., Catherine Ann McLaughlin; 1 s. Educ. St. Aloysius College; Holyrood School; Glasgow University. Glasgow University: Lecturer in Infectious Diseases, 1971-75, Epidemiology of Infectious Diseases,

1975-78; Postdoctoral Fellow, Yale University, 1977. Publications: Contributor to three books on atypical pneumonia and legionnaires disease, respiratory infections and extrapulmonary tuberculosis. Recreations: music; history; walking; Scottish affairs; French impressionism. Address: (h.) 81 Randolph Road, Glasgow, G11; T.-041-357 1100.

Kennedy, Frederick John, LLB. Regional Reporter, Strathclyde Regional Council; b. 22.6.40, Grantham; m., Eleanor Mae Watson; 1 s.; 1 d. Educ. High School of Glasgow; Glasgow University. Private, industrial and local government legal practice; former Reporter to the Children's Panel, City of Glasgow; former Director of Administration, Fife Regional Council. Recreations: golf; reading; gardening. Address: (b.) McIver House, 51 Cadogan Street, Glasgow, G2; T.-041-227 6171.

Kennedy, Professor Gavin, BA, MSc, PhD. Professor of Defence Finance, Heriot-Watt University; Chairman, Social Sciences Committee, UK National Commission, UNESCO; Chairman, Social Sciences Advisory Committee, since 1984; b. 20.2.40, Collingham, Yorkshire; m., Patricia Anne; 1 s.; 2 d. Educ. London Nautical School; Strathclyde University. Lecturer: Danbury Management Centre, NE London Polytechnic, 1969-71, Brunel University, 1971-73. Lecturer, National Defence College, Latimer, 1972-74; Senior Lecturer in Economics, Strathclyde University, 1973-85. Publications: Military in the Third World, 1974; Economics of Defence, 1975; Bligh, 1978 (Yorkshire Post Book of the Year, 1979); Death of Captain Cook, 1978; Burden Sharing in NATO, 1979; Mathematics for Innumerate Economists, 1982; Invitation to Statistics, 1983; Everything is Negotiable, 1984; Negotiate Anywhere, 1985; Macro Economics, 1985; Superdeal, 1985. Recreation: reading. Address: (h.) 22 Braid Avenue, Edinburgh; T.-031-447 3000.

Kennedy, Hugh Bryce, MB, ChB, FRCSEdin, FRCSGlas, DO, DTM&H. Consultant Ophthalmologist, Southern General Hospital and Victoria Infirmary, Glasgow, since 1975; b. 10.8.27, Naples, Italy; m., Winifred Elizabeth Geddes; 2 s.; 2 d. Educ. Hutchesons' Grammar School, Glasgow; Glasgow University. Resident House Surgeon, Western Infirmary, Glasgow, and Royal Alexandra Infirmary, Paisley; RAMC, 1952-54 (served, Malaya); Senior House Officer in Medicine, Western Infirmary, Glasgow, 1954-55; Medical Officer in charge of Mission Hospital, Zaire, 1956-70 (including three year leave of absence for training in opthalmology); Ophthalmologist, Stirlingshire area, 1971-72; Senior Registrar in Ophthalmology, Western Infirmary and Gartnavel General Hospital, Glasgow, 1972-74; Consultant Ophthalmologist, Lanarkshire, 1974-75. Recreations: golf; hill-walking. Address: (h.) 53 Marywood Square, Strathbungo, Glasgow, G41 2BN; T.-041-423 3529.

Kennedy, James Henry, MB, ChB, MRCOG. Consultant in Obstetrics and Gynaecology, Royal Maternity Hospital and Royal Infirmary, Glasgow, since 1983; b. 23.4.49, Glasgow; m., Hilary

Lawson Sim; 1 s.; 1 d. Educ. High School of Glasgow; Glasgow University. Recently Lecturer in Obstetrics and Gynaecology, Glasgow University. Scottish Cricket internationalist, 1970-71. Recreations: cricket; curling. Address: (h.) 5 Penrith Avenue, Glasgow, G46.

Kenny, Gavin N.C., BSc (Hons), MD, FFARCS. Senior Lecturer in Anaesthesia, Glasgow University, since 1982; b. 31.1.48, Glasgow; m., Dr. Joan W. Prentice. Educ. Hutchesons' Boys' Grammar School; Glasgow University. Lecturer in Anaesthesia, Glasgow University, 1977-82; Visiting Professor, Duke University, 1981; Visiting Consultant, Groote Schuur Hospital, Capetown, 1983; Guest Visitor, South African Association of Anaesthetists, 1984; has served on variety of committees for anaesthesia and postgraduate medical education in Scotland and England; Editorial Assistant, British Journal of Anaesthesia. Recreations: sailing; skiing; music. Address: (b.) University Department of Anaesthesia, Glasgow Royal Infirmary, Glasgow; T.-041-552 3535, Ext. 5454.

Kerevan, George, JP, MA (Hons). Member, City of Edinburgh District Council, since 1984 (Convener, Theatre and Halls Sub-Committee); Senior Lecturer in Economics, Napier College, Edinburgh, since 1982; b. 28.9.49, Glasgow. Educ. Glasgow University; Edinburgh University. Lecturer in Economics, Napier College, Edinburgh, 1974; Editor: Scottish Socialist, 1976-77; Bulletin of Scottish Politics, 1980-83; broadcasts and writes on Scottish politics and economics; Member: Edinburgh Festival Council, Royal Lyceum Theatre Board, Traverse Theatre Board (former Secretary). Publication: The Case for Scottish Coal (Co-author). Recreations: collecting contemporary Scottish art; cooking; cats. Address: (h.) 14a Dalkeith Street, Edinburgh, EH15; T.-031-669 8234.

Kermack, Sheriff Stuart Ogilvy, BA (Oxon), LLB. Sheriff of Tayside, Central and Fife, at Forfar and Arbroath, since 1971; b. 9.7.34, Edinburgh; m., Barbara Mackenzie; 3 s.; 1 d. Educ. Glasgow Academy; Jesus College, Oxford; Glasgow University. Called to Scottish Bar, 1958; Sheriff, Elgin and Nairn, 1965. Secretary, Scottish Branch, Howard League for Penal Reform. Address: (h.) 7 Littlecauseway, Forfar, Angus; T.-Forfar 64691.

Kernohan, Robert Deans, MA. Editor, Life and Work, The Record of the Church of Scotland, since 1972; Journalist, Writer and occasional Broadcaster; b. 9.1.31, Mount Vernon, Lanarkshire; m., Margaret Buchanan Bannerman; 4 s. Educ. Whitehill School, Glasgow; Glasgow University; Balliol College, Oxford. RAF, 1955-57; Editorial Staff, Glasgow Herald, 1957-67 (Assistant Editor, 1965-66, London Editor, 1966-67); Director-General, Scottish Conservative Central Office, 1967-71; Freelance Journalist and Broadcaster, 1972. Chairman, Federation of Conservative Students, 1954-55; Conservative Parliamentary candidate, 1955, 1959, 1964; Elder, Cramond Kirk, Edinburgh. Publications: Scotland's Life and Work, 1979; William Barclay, The Plain Uncommon Man, 1980; Thoughts through

the Year, 1985; Our Church, 1985. Recreations: rugby-watching; travel; pontification. Address: (b.) 121 George Street, Edinburgh, EH2 4YN; T.-031-225 5722.

Kerr, Alastair Ian Grant, MB, ChB, FRCSGlas, FRCSEdin. Consultant Otolaryngologist, Edinburgh Royal Infirmary, since 1979; Honorary Senior Lecturer, Edinburgh University, since 1979; b. 28.4.45, Elderslie; m., Elizabeth Wilson Carswell; 1 s.; 2 d. Educ. John Neilson Institution, Paisley; Glasgow University. Trainee in Surgery, Western Infirmary, Glasgow, 1969; specialised in otolaryngology, from 1973; Senior Registrar, Edinburgh Royal Infirmary, 1975 (Consultant, 1977). Publications: Clinical Otolaryngology (Contributor); Logan Turners Diseases of Throat, Nose and Ear (Contributor); The New Medicine Otolaryngology (Contributor). Recreations: golf; squash; tennis. Address: (b.) ENT Department, Edinburgh Royal Infirmary, Edinburgh; T.-031-229 2477.

Kerr, Anthony John Crawford, MA (Cantab), DipEd. Author; Conference Interpreter and Translator; b. 9.1.29, Geneva; m., Jacqueline S. Humble; 4 s. (inc. 1 deceased). Educ. Harrow; Trinity College, Cambridge. Schoolmaster, 1952-68; Interpreter, since 1968; Member, Jedburgh Town Council, 1963-65; Member, SNP National Executive, 1963-65; contested Roxburgh, Selkirk and Peebles Parliamentary constituency, 1964 (SNP), 1965 (Independent Scottish Nationalist); several TV appearances in quiz shows including Double Your Money (outright winner), 1959, Mastermind, 1977, and Superscot, 1985; bicycled from London to Capetown, 1951-52; Member, Mensa, since 1961. Publications: Schools of Europe, 1960; Universities of Europe, 1962; Schools of Scotland, 1962; Youth of Europe, 1964; The Crusades, 1966; Time Past and Time Present (5 volumes), 1965-67; The Scottish Opinion Survey, 1967; The Common Market and How it Works, 1977; Ferniehirst Castle, 1985. Recreations: travel; mountain walking; photography; writing letters to newspapers. Address: 52 Castlegate, Jedburgh; T.-0835 63370.

Kerr, Finlay, MB, ChB, DObsRCOG, FRCPEdin, FRCPGlas. Consultant Physician, Raigmore Hospital, Inverness, since 1976; Honorary Senior Lecturer, Aberdeen University, since 1976; b. 8.8.41, Edinburgh; m., Margaret Ann Carnegie Allan; 1 s.; 2 d. Educ. Keil School; Glasgow University. House Physician and Surgeon, Western Infirmary, Glasgow; House Physician, Ruchill Hospital, Glasgow; House Surgeon, Queen Mother's Hospital, Glasgow; Senior House Officer, Western Infirmary, Glasgow; Fellow, University of Southern California; Lecturer in Medicine, then Senior Registrar in Medicine, Edinburgh Royal Infirmary. Recreations: sailing; skiing; walking. Address: (h.) Glendale, 11 Devlin Crescent, Inverness; T.-0463 234779.

Kerr, Isabel Dunlop. Member, Greater Glasgow Health Board, since 1983; Warden, Guild of Aid, Gorbals, Glasgow, since 1974; b. 24.10.21, Glasgow; m., Charles Ferguson Kerr; 1 s.; 1 d. Educ. Bellahouston Academy; Queen's College (as mature student). Assistant Secretary, City of Glasgow Society of Social Service; Paisley Burgh Social Work Department; Guild of Aid. President, Soroptimist International, Glasgow South, 1980-81; Marriage Guidance Counsellor. Recreations: reading; cooking; flower arranging. Address: (h.) 3 Darnley Place, Maxwell Park, Glasgow, G41 4NA; T.-041-424 3997.

Kerr, William John Stanton, BDS, FDS, RCSEdin, MDS, FFD, RCSIrel, DOrthRCS. Senior Lecturer in Orthodontics, Glasgow Dental Hospital and School, since 1977; Honorary Consultant in Orthodontics, since 1978; b. 12.7.41, Belfast; m., Marie-Francoise; 1 d. Educ. Campbell College, Belfast; Queen's University, Belfast. Address: (b.) Glasgow Dental Hospital and School, 378 Sauchiehall Street, Glasgow, G2 3JZ; T.-041-332 7020.

Kerridge, Professor David Frank, BSc, FIS. Professor of Statistics, Aberdeen University, since 1966; b. 27.12.31, Southampton; m., Audrey Heslop (deceased); 2 d. Educ. Barton Peveril School; Southampton University. Statistician, Medical Research Council; Lecturer in Statistics, Sheffield University; Research Fellow, Aberdeen University. Recreations: chess; music. Address: (b.) Statistics Department, King's College, Old Aberdeen, Aberdeen; T.-0224 40241.

Kerrigan, Professor Herbert Aird, MA, LLB (Hons). Advocate, since 1970; b. 2.8.45, Glasgow; 1 s. Educ. Whitehill School, Glasgow; Aberdeen University; Keele University; Hague Academy. Lecturer in Criminal Law and Criminology, Edinburgh University; Lecturer in Scots Law, Edinburgh University; Visiting Professor, University of Southern California, since 1979; Member, Longford Commission, 1972; Church of Scotland: Elder, 1967 (now at Greyfriars Tolbooth and Highland Kirk), Reader, 1969, elected Member, Assembly Council, 1981. Publications: An Introduction to Criminal Procedure in Scotland, 1970; Ministers for the 1980s (Contributor), 1979; The Law of Contempt (Contributing Editor), 1982. Recreation: travel. Address: (h.) 20 Edinburgh Road, Dalkeith, Midlothian, EH22 1JY; T.-031-660 3007.

Kershaw, Peter Whaley, MD, FRCPsych, FRCPEdin, DPM, DObstRCOG. Consultant Psychiatrist, Gartnavel Royal Hospital, Glasgow, since 1970; Honorary Clinical Lecturer, Department of Psychological Medicine, Glasgow University, since 1970; b. 23.2.35, Bradford, Yorkshire; m., Irene Patricia Gibson; 1 s.; 1 d. Educ. Thornton Grammar School, Bradford; Edinburgh University. House Officer posts, Bradford Royal Infirmary, Edinburgh Royal Infirmary, St. Luke's Hospital, Bradford, and Southern General Hospital, Glasgow; Research Fellow, Department of Therapeutics, Edinburgh University; Lecturer, Department of Psychological Medicine, Glasgow University; Consultant Psychiatrist, Ravenscraig Hospital, Greenock. Publication: Rehabilitation in Psychiatric Practice (Contributor). Recreations: running; hill-walking; orienteering; music; art; painting. Address: (h.) Overdale, 2 Carse View Drive, Bearsden, Glasgow, G61 3NJ; T.-041-942 8525.

Khan, Kabir-Ur-Rahman, BA (Hons), LLB, LLM, PhD. Senior Lecturer, Department of Public International Law, Edinburgh University, since 1982 (Lecturer, 1965-82); b. 2.2.25, Firozpur Jhirka, India; m., Isobel Thomson; 1 d. Educ. Raj Rishi College, Alwar; Government College, Ajmere; Agra University; Sind University; London University. Barrister-at-Law, Gray's Inn, 1955; Advocate, High Court of Pakistan, Lahore, 1958-60. Member, Lothian Community Relations Council. Publications: The Law and Organisation of International Commodity Agreements, 1982; International Law of Development and the Law of the GATT, in press. Recreations: walking; inter-faith dialogue; Urdu poetry. Address: (b.) 5 Heriot Row, Edinburgh, EH3 6HU; T.-031-556 2229.

Kibby, Michael Royston, MA, PhD. Senior Lecturer in Biochemistry, Strathclyde University, since 1971; b. 22.4.38, Croydon, Surrey; m., Anne McNicol Fyfe; 1 s.; 3 d. (by pr. m.). Educ. Trinity School of John Whitgift, Croydon; Trinity College, Cambridge; St. Mary's Hospital Medical School, London. Scientific Officer, May & Baker Ltd., Dagenham, Essex, 1961-62; Senior Scientific Officer, Ministry of Defence, 1965-67; Lecturer in Biochemistry, Strathclyde University, 1967-71. Member, Glasgow District Council, 1980-84. Recreations: politics; wildlife photography and conservation. Address: (b.) Biochemistry Division, Department of Bioscience and Biotechnology, Strathclyde University, Glasgow; T.-041-552 4400.

Kidd, Professor Cecil, BSc, PhD. Regius Professor of Physiology, Aberdeen University, since 1984; b. 28.4.33, Shotley Bridge, Co. Durham; m., Margaret Winifred; 3 s. Educ. Queen Elizabeth Grammar School, Darlington; King's College, Newcastle-upon-Tyne; Durham University. Demonstrator in Physiology, King's College, Newcastle-upon-Tyne; Lecturer/Senior Lecturer/Reader in Physiology, Senior Research Associate in Cardiovascular Studies, Leeds University. Recreations: squash; gardening. Address: (b.) Department of Physiology, Marischal College, Aberdeen University, Aberdeen; T.-0224 40241, Ext. 300.

Kidd, David, BSc, PhD. Senior Lecturer, Department of Chemistry, Edinburgh University, since 1973; b. 26.1.30, Livingston. Educ. Bathgate Academy; Edinburgh University. Research Chemist: Albright & Wilson, 1954-56, T. & H. Smith, 1956-64; Chemistry Teacher, George Watson's College, 1964-67; Lecturer, Department of Chemistry, Edinburgh University, 1967-73. Recreations: golf; walking; soccer. Address: (h.) 12 Bloom Place, Livingston Village, Livingston, EH54 7AG; T.-Livingston 411452.

Kidd, David Hamilton, LLB, LLM, WS, NP. Partner, Biggart Baillie & Gifford, WS, since 1978; b. 21.9.49, Edinburgh; m., Geraldine Stephen; 1s. Educ. Edinburgh Academy; Edinburgh University. Research Assistant, Law Faculty, Queen's University, Belfast, 1976-77. Former Secretary, Scottish Legal Computer Research Trust; Society for Computers and Law: Council Member, 1982-84, Secretary, since 1984;

Member, Organisation and Methods Committee, Law Society of Scotland, since 1981. Recreations: cycling; skiing; sailing. Address: (b.) 3 Glenfinlas Street, Edinburgh, EH3 6YY; T.-031-226 5541.

Kidd, Professor Ian Gray, MA (St. Andrews), BA (Oxon). Professor of Greek, St. Andrews University, since 1976; b. 6.3.22, Goretty, Chandernagore, India; m., Sheila Elizabeth Dow; 3 s. Educ. Dundee High School; St. Andrews University; Queen's College, Oxford. St. Andrews University: Lecturer in Greek, 1949, Senior Lecturer, 1965; Visiting Professor, University of Texas at Austin, 1965-66; Member, Institute for Advanced Study, Princeton, 1971-72; St. Andrews University: Personal Professor of Ancient Philosophy, 1973-76, Provost of St. Leonard's College, 1978-83; Member, Institute for Advanced Study, Princeton, 1979-80. Publication: Posidonius, The Fragments, 1972. Recreations: music; reading. Address: (h.) Ladebury, Lade Braes Lane, St. Andrews, Fife, KY16 9EP; T.-0334 74367.

Kidd, Jean Buyers, BA, DipMusEd, LRAM, ARCM. Music Director, Junior and Youth Choruses, Scottish National Orchestra, since 1978; b. Macduff, Banffshire; widow. Educ. Buckie High School; Royal Scottish Academy of Music; Open University. Taught in various Glasgow schools and for many years, Principal Teacher of Music, Bellahouston Academy; former Conductor, Bellahouston Music Society; gave instruction in music and drama to women in Duke Street Prison; former Secretary, Scottish Certificate of Education Examination Board. Recreations: reading; playing chamber music; gardening; craft work. Address: (h.) Carolside, Gowanlea Road, Comrie, Perthshire, PH6 2HD; T.-Comrie 70856.

Kidd, Dame Margaret Henderson, DBE, QC, Hon.LLD (Dundee and Edinburgh); b. 14.3.00, Carriden; m., Donald Somerled Macdonald, WS (deceased); 1 d. Educ. Linlithgow Academy; Edinburgh University. Admitted Advocate, Scottish Bar, 1923; practised as Advocate, 1923-60; Editor, Session Case Reports, Scots Law Times, 1942-76; King's Counsel, 1948; Keeper, Advocates' Library, 1956-71; Sheriff-Principal, Dumfries & Galloway, 1960-66, Perth & Angus, 1966-75; Chairman, East and South of Scotland Society for Welfare of the Blind, 1966-72; Council Chairman, Queen's Nursing Institute (Scotland), 1976-81; Honorary Legal Adviser, Scottish Association of Occupational Therapists, 1958-70. Recreation: walking. Address: (h.) 5 India Street, Edinburgh, EH3 6HA; T.-031-225 3867.

Kiely, John, BSc, MSc. HM Inspector of Schools, 1961-85; b. 27.6.25, Tugby, Leicestershire; m., Mary Macdonald; 3 s.; 1 d. Educ. Bicester County School; Bristol University. Assistant Master, King Edward VII School, Sheffield, 1950-51; Second Mathematics Master, Grimsby Wintringham Grammar School, 1952-55; Senior Lecturer, Royal Naval College, Dartmouth, 1955-58; Head, Mathematics Department, Blundells School, Tiverton, 1958-61. Recreations: reading; gardening. Address: (h.) Suffolkhill House, 28 Dalbeattie Road, Dumfries, DG2 7PL; T.-Dumfries 63429.

Kiernan, Wolfgang E.S., MB, BCG, FRCPsych, FRCPEdin, FRCPGlas, DipPsych(Ed). Physician Superintendent, Gartnavel Royal Hospital, Glasgow, since 1980 (Consultant Psychiatrist, since 1967); Honorary Clinical Lecturer, Department of Psychological Medicine, Glasgow University, since 1967; b. 25.1.32, Lisburn, Northern Ireland; m., Diana; 2 d. Educ. St. Malachy's College, Belfast; Queen's University, Belfast. Lecturer in Psychological Medicine, Edinburgh University, 1960-66; Regional Adviser in Mental Health, SE Asia Region, World Health Organisation, 1975-76; Consultant to WHO on Mental Health matters in SE Asia. Honorary Medical Secretary, Mental Health Foundation (Scotland); Member, Expert Advisory Panel on Mental Health, WHO. Recreations: piano; reading; walking; skiing. Address: (h.) 10 Colquhoun Drive, Bearsden, Glasgow, G61 4NQ; T.-041-942 3197.

Kilbrandon, Lord (Charles James Dalrymple), BA, LLB, LLD, DSc (SocSci); Life Peer; Privy Councillor; b. 15.8.06, Coylton, Ayrshire; m., Ruth Caroline Grant; 2 s.; 3 d. Educ. Charterhouse; Balliol College, Oxford; Edinburgh University. Advocate, 1932; War Service, RA, 1939-45; King's Counsel, 1949; Sheriff of Ayr and Bute, 1954-57, of Perth and Angus, 1957; Dean, Faculty of Advocates, 1957; Senator of the College of Justice, 1959; Lord of Appeal in Ordinary, 1971-77; Honorary Fellow of Balliol, 1970; Honorary Bencher of Gray's Inn, 1971; Visitor of Balliol, 1974; Chairman of a number of Departmental Committees and Royal Commission on the Constitution. Address: (h.) Kilbrandon House, Balvicar, by Oban, Argyll, PA34 4RA; T.-Balvicar 239.

Kilgour, Alistair Crichton, BSc, PhD, FBCS. Senior Lecturer, Computing Science Department, Glasgow University, since 1984; b. 14.8.40, Glasgow; m., Margaret; 3 s. Educ. Allan Glen's School, Glasgow; Glasgow University. Scientific Programmer, English Electric Computers Ltd., 1963-66; Research Associate, Computer-Aided Design Project, Edinburgh University, 1966-74; Lecturer, Computing Science Department, Glasgow University, 1974-84; Consultant on CAD Software, Lattice Logic, Edinburgh, since 1981. Recreations: theatre; films; reading; walking; conservation. Address: (b.) Department of Computing Science, Glasgow University, Glasgow; T.-041-339 8855.

Kilmany, Baron, (William John St. Clair Anstruther-Gray), 1st Bt, PC (1962), MC (1943). Lord Lieutenant of Fife, 1975-80; Chairman of Ways and Means and Deputy Speaker, House of Commons, 1962-64; b. 1905; m.; 2 d. Educ. Eton; Christ Church, Oxford. Retired Major; MP (Unionist), North Lanark, 1931-45, Berwick and East Lothian, 1951-66; Chairman, 1922 Committee, 1964-66; Deputy Lieutenant, Fife, 1953.

Kilmarnock, 7th Baron, (Alastair Ivor Gilbert Boyd). Chief of the Clan Boyd; b. 11.5.27; m., 1, Diana Mary Gibson (deceased); 2, Hilary Ann Bardwell; 1 s. Educ. Bradfield; King's College, Cambridge. Lt., Irish Guards, 1946; Chief SDP Whip, House of Lords, since 1983.

Kimbell, Professor David Rodney Bertram, MA, DPhil, LRAM, FRSA. Professor of Music, St. Andrews University, since 1979; b. 26.6.39, Gillingham, Kent; m., Ingrid Else Emilie Lubbe; 1 s.; 2 d. Educ. Dartford Grammar School; Kent College, Canterbury; Worcester College, Oxford. Lecturer in Music, Edinburgh University, 1965-78. Publication: Verdi in the Age of Italian Romanticism, 1981. Recreations: walking; miscellaneous sports. Address: (h.) 3 Dempster Terrace, St. Andrews, Fife; T.-St. Andrews 72504.

Kincraig, Hon. Lord, (Robert Smith Johnston), QC (Scot), BA (Hons), LLB. Senator of the College of Justice in Scotland, since 1972; b. 10.10.18; m.; 1 s.; 1 d. Educ. Strathallan; St. John's College, Cambridge; Glasgow University. Member, Faculty of Advocates, 1942; Advocate-Depute, 1953-55; QC (Scot), 1955; Home Advocate Depute, 1959-62; Sheriff of Roxburgh, Berwick and Selkirk, 1964-70; Dean, Faculty of Advocates, 1970-72.

King, Alexander, DMS, ACMA, FMS. Convener, Policy and Resources Committee, Angus District Council, since 1984; b. 6.10.44, Dunfermline; 1 d. Educ. Arbroath High School; Dundee College of Technology. William R. Stewart & Sons (Hacklemakers) Ltd.: Management Services Manager, 1973-80, Management Accountant, since 1980. Scottish Region Treasurer, Institute of Management Services, 1967-82; Constituency Treasurer, Angus, Scottish National Party, since 1980. Recreations: gliding; theatre; walking.

King, Derek Gordon, BA. Area Manager, The Housing Corporation, since 1984; Treasurer, Scottish Liberal Party, 1983-85; b. 27.7.49, London. Educ. Harrow County Grammar School; Lancaster University. HM Inspector of Taxes, 1971; Administrator, Loughborough University of Technology, 1972-78; Management Consultant, Universities of Scotland O. & M. Unit, 1978-84. Member, City of Edinburgh District Council, 1980-84 (Liberal Group Leader, 1982-84); Liberal-SDP Alliance candidate, West Edinburgh, General Election, 1983; Scottish Liberal Housing Spokesman, 1982-84. Recreations: travel; cinema; food. Address: (h.) 29 Morton Street, Edinburgh; T.-031-669 2669.

King, Emeritus Professor James Lawrence, MA, PhD. Professor (Emeritus), Edinburgh University, since 1983; Governor, Strathallan School, Perthshire; b. 14.2.22, London; m., Pamela Mary Ward Hitchcock; 1 s.; 1 d. Educ. Latymer Upper School; Jesus College, Cambridge. Navy Department, 1942-68 (Admiralty Research Laboratory, 1942-61); Chief Scientist, Naval Construction Research Establishment, Dunfermline, 1961-68; Regius Professor of Engineering, Edinburgh University, 1968-83. Recreation: walking. Address: (h.) 16 Lyne Park, West Linton, Peeblesshire.

King, John William B., MA, PhD, FIBiol, FRSE. Head, AFRC Animal Breeding Liaison Group, since 1982; Director, AFRC Animal Breeding Research Organisation, since 1974; b. 28.6.27, Stroud; m., Pauline Margaret; 4 s. Educ. Marling School, Oxford; St. Catharine's College,

Cambridge; Edinburgh University. Joined ARC Animal Breeding Research Organisation, 1950; Kellogg Foundation Fellowship to USA, 1954; Advisor, Pig Industry Development Authority, 1959; David Black Award for services to pig industry, 1966; NRC/Nuffield Foundation Fellowship to lecture in Canada, 1970; Visiting Lecturer, Gottingen University, 1973. Recreations: shooting; dog training. Address: (h.) Cottage Farm, West Linton, Peeblesshire; T.-0968 60 448.

Kininmonth, Sir William (Hardie), Kt (1972), PPRSA, FRIBA, FRIAS. Architect; b. 8.11.04. Educ. George Watson's College, Edinburgh; Edinburgh College of Art. President, Royal Scottish Academy, 1969-73; President, Edinburgh Architectural Association, 1951-53; Member, Royal Fine Arts Commission for Scotland, 1952-65; Council Member, RIBA, 1951-53; former Senior Partner, Sir Rowand Anderson, Kininmonth and Paul, Architects, Edinburgh; Hon. LLD, Dundee, 1975.

Kinloch, John, JP, BSc. Farmer; Member, Scottish Agricultural Development Council, since 1979; Member, Consultative Group for Training and Education in Agriculture, since 1983; Member, Scottish Committee, Scottish Institute of Agricultural Engineering, since 1984; Member, Advisory Committee on Birds, since 1977; b. 30.1.41; m., Jeanette Elizabeth MacDonald; 1 s.; 2 d. Educ. Morrison's Academy, Crieff; Edinburgh University. Council Member, National Farmers Union of Scotland, 1974-83 (Convener, Labour and Machinery Committee, 1978-83); Member, Advisory Committee on Birds, 1977-85; Elder, Church of Scotland, since 1966. Recreations: walking; hill-walking. Address: Clathybeg, Gask, Crieff, Perthshire, PH7 3PH; T.-0738 73 213.

Kinninmont, Tom, MA, PhD. Television Drama Producer, BBC Scotland, since 1982; Chairman, Scottish Youth Theatre, since 1981; Playwright; b. 8.6.50, Irvine; m., Kate; 1 d. Educ. Irvine Royal Academy; Glasgow University; Cornell University, New York. Publishing Research Fellow, National Library of Scotland, 1976-78; Radio Drama Producer, BBC, 1978-82. Vice-Chairman, Scottish Society of Playwrights, 1977-81; author of plays: The Provost, 1977, Britannica, 1978, Second Thoughts, 1982, Identical Twins, 1984. Recreations: family life; reading; writing. Address: (b.) BBC, Queen Margaret Drive, Glasgow; T.-041-339 8844.

Kinnis, William Kay Brewster, MA, BL, PhD, DPA. Solicitor and Notary Public; Senior Partner, Miller Jackson, Solicitors, Lenzie, since 1982; Partner, Murdoch Jackson, Solicitors, Glasgow, since 1963; b. 5.1.33, St. Andrews; m., Agnes Inglis Erskine; 2 d. Educ. Hamilton Academy; Glasgow University; London University (External). Partner: MacArthur Stewart & Orr, Solicitors, Oban and Lochgilphead, 1959-62, Town Clerk and Burgh Chamberlain, Lochgilphead, 1960-62; Council Member, Royal Faculty of Procurators, 1980-83; Governor, Baillie's Institution, since 1983. Choral Scholar, Glasgow University, 1954-58; Choirmaster,

Lochgilphead Parish Church, 1959-62; Reader, Church of Scotland, since 1960. Recreations: choral singing; swimming; reading; travel. Address: (b.) 10 Woodside Place, Glasgow, G3 7QJ; T.-041-332 9207.

Kinsella, Mgr. Matthew, VG, PhB, STB. Vicar General, Diocese of Paisley, since 1968; b. 27.7.13, Wishaw. Educ. St. Mary's College, Blairs, Aberdeen; Scots College, Rome; Gregorian University. Ordained Priest, 1938; Curate: St. Peter's, Partick, Glasgow, 1939-45, St. Patrick's, Greenock, 1945-57; Spiritual Director, Scots College, Rome, 1957-61; Parish Priest, St. Andrew's, Greenock, 1961-71; served on numerous educational committees, on Association for Mental Health, and Christian Housing; Administrator, St. Mirin's Cathedral, Paisley, 1971. Member, Children's Panel Advisory Committee, Strathclyde Region. Address: St. Mirin's Cathedral, E. Buchanan Street, Paisley; T.-041-889 2404.

Kintore, 12th Earl of, (James Ian Keith), DL, CEng, AIStructE; b. 25.7.08, Edinburgh; m., Delia Virginia Georgina Loyd; 2 s.; 1 d. Educ. Eton College; Royal School of Mines, London. UK Delegate to Council of Europe and Western European Union, 1954-64; Member, Grampian Regional Council, 1974-78; Commissioner for Income Tax; Past Chairman, Scottish-American Community Relations Committee, RAF, Edzell; Member, Queen's Bodyguard for Scotland (Royal Company of Archers), since 1932. Recreations: shooting; fishing; sailing; travel. Address: (h.) Glenton House, Rickarton, Stonehaven, AB3 2TD; T.-0569 63071.

Kirby, Professor Gordon William, MA, PhD, ScD, CChem, FRSC, FRSE. Regius Professor of Chemistry, Glasgow University, since 1972; b. 20.6.34, Wallasey; 2 s. Educ. Liverpool Institute High School; Liverpool Technical College; Gonville and Caius College, Cambridge. Imperial College, London: 1851 Exhibition Senior Studentship, 1958-60, Assistant Lecturer, 1960-61, Lecturer, 1961-67; Professor of Organic Chemistry, Loughborough University of Technology, 1967-72. Corday-Morgan Medal and Prize, Royal Society of Chemistry, 1969; Tilden Lectureship, Royal Society of Chemistry, 1974-75. Recreation: hill-walking. Address: (b.) Department of Chemistry, Glasgow University, Glasgow, G12 8QQ; T.-041-339 8855, Ext. 416/417.

Kirk, Gordon, MA, MEd. Principal, Moray House College of Education, since 1981; b. 8.5.38, Dunfermline; m., Jane D. Murdoch; 1 s.; 1 d. Educ. Camphill Secondary School, Paisley; Glasgow University. Lecturer in Education, Aberdeen University, 1965-74; Head, Education Department, Jordanhill College of Education, 1974-81; Member, Munn Committee on the Curriculum of the Secondary School, 1974-77; Member: General Teaching Council for Scotland, since 1984, Consultative Committee on the Curriculum, since 1984, Council for National Academic Awards, since 1979; Chairman, Scottish Council for Research in Education, since 1984. Publications: Scottish Education Looks Ahead (Assistant Editor), 1969; Curriculum and Assessment in the Scottish Secondary School,

1982; Moray House and Professional Education (Editor), 1985. Recreations: walking; golf; bridge. Address: (h.) Craigroyston, Broadgait, Gullane, East Lothian; T.-0620 843299.

Kirk, James Foster, BSc. Rector, Tain Royal Academy, since 1979; b. 31.8.41, Bellshill; m., Margo McFarlane; 1 s.; 1 d. Educ. Hamilton Academy; Glasgow University. Entered teaching, 1963; promoted to Principal Teacher of Science, then Principal Teacher of Guidance, then Assistant Rector; moved from Lanarkshire to Highlands, 1975. Recreations: gardening; wine-making; badminton. Address: (h.) The Barn House, Delny, Invergordon, Ross-shire; T.-Kildary 2564.

Kirkbride, George, CEng, FICE, FIHTE, FIBM. Director of Roads, Grampian Regional Council, since 1983; b. 26.5.33, Willington; 1 s.; 2 d. Educ. Aireborough Grammar School; Bradford Technical College. Pupil, Aireborough Urban District Council, 1949-54; Senior Engineer, Bradford Corporation, 1956-59; Senior Engineer, then Chief Assistant, Crewe Borough, 1959-66; Principal Engineer, then Project Coordinator, Wolverhampton Borough, 1966-72; Depute City Engineer, Dundee City, 1972-75; Regional Roads Engineer, Fife Regional Council, 1975-83. Council Member, ASPHE. Recreations: cycling; swimming; musical society. Address: (b.) Woodhill House, Ashgrove Road West, Aberdeen; T.-Aberdeen 682222.

Kirkhill, Baron, (John Farquharson Smith). Life Peer; b. 7.5.30; m.; 1 step-d. Educ. Robert Gordon's College, Aberdeen. Lord Provost, Aberdeen, 1971-75; Minister of State, Scottish Office, 1975-78; Chairman, North of Scotland Hydro-Electric Board, 1979-82; Hon. LLD, Aberdeen, 1974.

Kirkwood, Archy, MP, BSc, NP. MP (Liberal/Alliance), Roxburgh and Berwickshire, since 1983; b. 22.4.46, Glasgow; m., Rosemary; 1 s.; 1 d. Educ. Cranhill School; Heriot-Watt University. Former Personal Assistant to Rt. Hon. David Steel (qv); Solicitor. Recreation: music. Address: (b.) House of Commons, London, SW1A 0AA; T.-01-219 3000.

Kirkwood, Ralph C., BSc, PhD, FRSE. Reader in Biology, Strathclyde University, since 1981; b. 6.7.33, Glasgow; m., Mair Enid; 3 s. Educ. Jordanhill College School, Glasgow; Glasgow University; University of Wales, Aberystwyth. Lecturer, Botany Department, West of Scotland Agricultural College, 1959-64; Strathclyde University: Lecturer, Biology Department, 1964-72, Senior Lecturer, 1972-81; Governor, West of Scotland Agricultural College. Publication: Herbicides and Plant Growth Regulators (Co-author). Recreations: sailing; photography; natural history; walking. Address: (b.) Department of Bioscience and Biotechnology, Biology Division, Todd Centre, Strathclyde University, Glasgow, G1 1XW; T.-041-552 4400.

Kissack, Rev. Captain Albert Westby Grandin, FGSS. Commissioner of Northern Lighthouses; Honorary Chaplain, Missions to Seamen in Scottish Waters; b. 23.3.12, Douglas, Isle of Man; m.,

Phyllis Grace; 2 s. Educ. Douglas High School; Royal Masonic School, Bushey; Liverpool Technical College. Seagoing navigating apprentice, 1928-32; second officer's certificate, 1932, with varied sea service; Master Mariner's foreign-going certificate, 1941; War service, West Africa and the Atlantic, Dunkirk Evacuation and assault on Europe with Allied Forces; joined Isle of Man Steam Packet Company in Irish Sea service, rising to position of Commodore and finally Marine Superintendent, retiring in 1977; took Holy Orders, Church of England, and serves in Auxiliary Ministry.

Kitchen, John Philip, MA, BMus, PhD (Cantab), FRCO, LRAM. Lecturer in Music and University Organist and Choirmaster, St. Andrews University, since 1976; Concert Organist, Harpsichordist, Pianist; b. 27.10.50, Airdrie. Educ. Coatbridge High School; Glasgow University; Cambridge University. Harpsichordist/Organist, Scottish Early Music Consort, Stanesby Recorder Trio, St. Andrews Baroque Trio; BBC and commercial recordings; music reviewer. Recreations: more music; entertaining; doing housework. Address: (b.) Department of Music, St. Andrews University, St. Andrews, KY16 9AL; T.-St. Andrews 76161.

Klein, Bernat, CBE, FSIAD. Chairman and Managing Director, Bernat Klein Ltd., since 1981; b. 6.11.22, Senta, Yugoslavia; m., Margaret Soper; 1 s.; 2 d. Educ. Senta, Yugoslavia; Bezalel School of Arts and Crafts, Jerusalem; Leeds University. Designer: Tootal, Broadhurst, Lee, 1948-49, Munrospun, Edinburgh, 1949-51; Chairman and Managing Director, Colourcraft, 1952-62; Managing Director, Bernat Klein Ltd., 1962-66; Chairman and Managing Director, Bernat Klein Design Ltd., 1966-81. Member, Design Council, 1962-68; Member, Royal Fine Art Commission for Scotland, since 1981. Publications: Eye for Colour, 1965; Design Matters, 1975. Recreations: tennis; reading. Address: High Sunderland, Galashiels; T.-0750 20730.

Kleinpoppen, Professor Hans, DipPhys, Dr re nat & habil. Professor of Experimental Physics, Stirling University, since 1968; b. 30.9.28, Duisburg, Germany. Educ. Giessen University; Heidelberg University; Tubingen University. Visiting Fellow, Colorado University, 1967; Visiting Associate Professor, Columbia University, New York, 1968; Stirling University: Head, Physics Department, 1970-72, Director, Institute of Atomic Physics, 1975-81. Publication: Physics of Atoms and Molecules (Series Editor). Address: (b.) Physics Department, Stirling University, Stirling.

Klopper, Professor Arnold, MB, ChB, MD, PhD, FRCOG. Professor of Reproductive Endocrinology, Aberdeen University, since 1976; Consultant Obstetrician and Gynaecologist, since 1960; b. 8.2.22, Ventersburg, South Africa; m., Mary Katherine Turvey. Educ. Brebner College, Bloemfontein, South Africa; Witwatersrand University, Johannesburg. Hospital residency appointments, Johannesburg and London; Clinical Research Fellow, MRC, Guy's Hospital, and Clinical Endocrinology Research Unit, Edinburgh; appointed to permanent senior scientific staff, MRC, Obstetric Medicine Research Unit, Aberdeen, 1958; Aberdeen University: Senior Lecturer, 1966, Reader, 1972. Honorary Fellow, National Obstetrical Societies, USA, Italy, Finland and Singapore. Publications: Fetus and Placenta; Placental Proteins. Recreations: fishing; shooting; training dogs; watching other people work. Address: (b.) Department of Obstetrics and Gynaecology, Royal Infirmary, Aberdeen; T.-0224 681818, Ext. 3323.

Knight, Alanna, FSA Scot. Novelist; b. Co. Durham; m., Alistair Knight; 2 s. Educ. Jesmond High School. Writing career began, 1965; novels: Legend of the Loch, 1969 (RNA First Novel Award), The October Witch, 1971, This Outward Angel, 1971, Castle Clodha, 1972, Lament for Lost Lovers, 1972, The White Rose, 1974, A Stranger Came By, 1974, The Wicked Wynsleys, 1977; historical novels: The Passionate Kindness, 1974, A Drink for the Bridge, 1976, The Black Duchess, 1980, Castle of Foxes, 1981, Colla's Children, 1982, The Clan, 1985; plays: The Private Life of R.L.S., 1973, Girl on an Empty Swing, 1977; non-fiction: The Robert Louis Stevenson Treasury, 1985; Lecturer in Creative Writing, WEA, 1971-75; Organiser, Meet The Author, Aberdeen, 1973-75; Committee Member: Society of Authors of Scotland, 1972-84; Scottish PEN, 1972-82; Aberdeen Writers' Workshop (Founder and Chairman); Delegate to Scottish Association of Writers. Recreations: walking; reading; creative knitting. Address: (h.) 374 Queen's road, Aberdeen, AB1 8DX; T.-0224 38388.

Knight, Joan, OBE. Artistic Director, Perth Theatre, since 1968; b. 27.9.24, Walton-Le-Dale, Lancashire. Educ. Lark Hill Convent School. Trained, Bristol Old Vic Theatre School; Director and Administrator, Castle Theatre, Farnham, five years; Director, Ludlow Festival, three years; Director of Productions, Pitlochry Festival Theatre, two years; freelance productions for Bristol Old Vic, Birmingham Repertory, Nottingham Playhouse, Royal Lyceum, Edinburgh, Traverse Theatre, Yvonne Arnaud Theatre, Scottish Theatre Company, etc.; directed The Mousetrap, London; Member, Scottish Arts Council (Chairman, Dance and Mime Committee); Governor, Queen Margaret College, Edinburgh. Recreations: cooking; swimming; walking. Address: (h.) Inchbank House, 26 Main Street, Bridgend, Perth.

Knill-Jones, Robin Peter, MA, MB, BChir, MSc, DPH, FRCP, MFCM. Senior Lecturer in Clinical Epidemiology, Glasgow University, since 1979; Honorary Community Medicine Specialist, Greater Glasgow Health Board, since 1984; b. 26.4.40, Freshwater; m., Jennifer Gillian Sykes; 3 d. Educ. Malvern College; Cambridge University; St. Bartholomew's Hospital, London. Research Registrar in Medicine, Liver Unit, King's College Hospital, London; Research Fellow, Department of Medicine, Glasgow University; Honorary Senior Registrar, Department of Medicine, Western Infirmary, Glasgow, 1973-79; Medical Director, Glasgow People's Marathon. Recreations: unmanaged countryside;

microlepidoptera; not smoking; occasional sailing and skiing. Address: (b.) University Department of Community Medicine, 2 Lilybank Gardens, Glasgow, G12 8QQ; T.-041-339 8855.

Knops, Professor Robin John, BSc, PhD, FRSE. Professor of Mathematics, Heriot-Watt University, Edinburgh, since 1971 (Dean of Science, since 1985); b. 30.12.32, London; m., Margaret; 4 s.; 2 d. Educ. Nottingham University. Nottingham University: Assistant Lecturer in Mathematics, 1956-59, Lecturer in Mathematics, 1959-62; Newcastle-upon-Tyne University: Lecturer in Applied Mathematics, 1962-68, Reader in Continuum Mechanics, 1968-71; Head, Department of Mathematics, Heriot-Watt University, 1971-83; Visiting Professor: Cornel University, 1967 and 1968; University of California, Berkeley, 1968; Pisa University, 1974; Ecole Polytechnique Federale Lausanne, Switzerland, 1980; Royal Society of Edinburgh: Council Member, since 1982, Executive Committee Member, since 1982, Meetings Secretary, since 1982, Chief Executive Editor, Proceedings A, since 1982; President, Edinburgh Mathematical Society, 1974-75; Member, Executive Committee, International Society for the Interaction of Mechanics and Mathematics, 1980-84. Publications: Uniqueness Theories in Linear Elasticity (Co-author), 1971; Theory of Elastic Stability (Co-author), 1973. Recreations: walking; reading. Address: (b.) Department of Mathematics, Heriot-Watt University, Edinburgh, EH14 4AS; T.-031-449 5111.

Knowler, John T., PhD. Senior Lecturer in Biochemistry, Glasgow University, since 1983; b. 19.10.42, Whitstable, Kent; m., Susan Penelope; 2 d. Educ. Canterbury Technical School; Glasgow University. Insecticide and pharmaceutical industries, 1962-69 (external degree taken during this period); PhD work, 1969-72; postdoctoral research, Vanderbilt University and Mayo Clinic, USA, 1972-73; Lecturer in Biochemistry, Glasgow University, 1973-83. Recreations: keen amateur naturalist and ornithologist. Address: (b.) Department of Biochemistry, Glasgow University, Glasgow, G12 8QQ; T.-041-339 8855, Ext. 7265.

Knowlton, Richard James, CBE (1983), QFSM, FIFireE, FBIM. HM Chief Inspector of Fire Services, Scotland, since 1984; b. 2.1.28, Southampton; m., Pamela V.; 1 s. Educ. Bishop Wordsworth's School, Salisbury. 42 Commando, Royal Marines, 1945; Fireman, Southampton Fire Brigade, 1948; Station Officer, Worcester City and County, 1959; London Fire Brigade: Assistant Divisional Officer, 1963, Divisional Commander, 1967; Firemaster: South Western Scotland, 1971, Strathclyde, 1975; Chairman, London Branch, Institution of Fire Engineers, 1969; awarded Winston Churchill Fellowship, 1969; National President, Chief and Assistant Chief Fire Officers Association, 1980; National Chairman, Fire Services National Benevolent Fund, 1980; British Representative, Council, European Association of Professional Fire Officers, 1979-85; President, Scottish District Fire Service Sports and Athletics Association, 1985; awarded Queen's Fire Service Medal, 1977. Address: (b.) St. Andrew's House, Edinburgh, EH1 3DE; T.-031-556 8501, Ext. 2833.

Knox, Col. Bryce Muir, MC (and Bar), CStJ, TD, BA (Cantab). Lord Lieutenant, Ayr and Arran, since 1974; b. 4.4.16, Edinburgh; m., Patricia Mary Dunsmuir; 1 s.; 1 d. Educ. Stowe; Trinity College, Cambridge. County of Ayr: Deputy Lieutenant, 1953, Vice Lieutenant, 1970-74; Chairman, W. & J. Knox Ltd., Kilbirnie, 1970-78; Vice-Chairman, Lindustries Ltd., 1979 (Director, 1953-79); served with Ayrshire (ECO) Yeomanry, 1939-45, North Africa and Italy (CO, 1953-56, Hon. Col., 1960-71); Honorary Colonel, Ayrshire Yeomanry Squadron, Queen's Own Yeomanry, 1971-77; President, Lowland TA & VR, 1978-83; Member, Queen's Bodyguard for Scotland (Royal Company of Archers). Publications: brief historical notes of the Ayrshire Yeomanry; History of the Eglinton Hunt. Recreation: country sports. Address: (h.) Martnaham Lodge, by Ayr; T.-Dalrymple 204.

Knox, Graham Ramsay, BSc, PhD, FRSC, CChem. Reader in Chemistry, Strathclyde University, since 1972; b. 10.5.34, Bradford; m., Audrey Storr; 2 s. Educ. Norwich School; Sheffield University; University of California, Los Angeles. Lecturer, 1961, Senior Lecturer, 1969, Department of Pure and Applied Chemistry, Strathclyde University. Recreations: salmon fishing; hill-walking. Address: (b.) Department of Pure and Applied Chemistry, Strathclyde University, Glasgow, G1 1XL; T.-041-552 4400.

Knox, Rev. Ian Swanston Cran, MA (Hons), BD. Minister, St. Mary's Parish Church, Dumfries, since 1957; b. 5.10.21, Bothwell, Lanarkshire; m., Janie Fisher Scott; 2 s.; 1 d. Educ. Glasgow University and Trinity College; Westminster College, Cambridge. Assistant, St. Ninian's, Stirling, 1947-48; Minister: Menstrie, Clackmannshire, 1948-57. Recreations: gardening; music; socialising. Address: 14 Albany Lane, Dumfries; T.-0387 53856.

Knox, John, MB, ChB, FRCP, FRCPGlas, FRCPGlas. Senior Consultant Physician, Highland Health Board, since 1962; Clinical Senior Lecturer, Aberdeen University, since 1962; b. 6.12.26, Whitley Bay; m., Marion K. Aitken (deceased); 2 s. Educ. Hamilton Academy; Glasgow University. Research Fellow, Glasgow University, 1950-52 (Assistant Lecturer, Department of Materia Medica, 1952-55); Senior Medical Registrar, Aberdeen University, 1955-58; Consultant Physician, Grampian Health Board, 1958-62. Past President, Scottish Society of Physicians; Member, National Medical Consultative Committee; Past President, Inverness Rotary Club. Address: (h.) Glentarff, 33 Southside Road, Inverness, IV2 4XA; T.-0463 232189.

Knox, John, RSA, RGI. Head of Painting Studios, Glasgow School of Art, since 1981; b. 16.12.36; m.; 1 s.; 1 d. Educ. Lenzie Academy; Glasgow School of Art. Staff, Duncan of Jordanstone College of Art, Dundee, 1965-81; work in several permanent collections; Member, Scottish Arts Council, 1974-79; Member, Board of Trustees, National Galleries of Scotland, since 1982.

Knox, Professor John Henderson, BSc, PhD, DSc, FRSC, CChem, FRSE, FRS. Director, Wolfson Liquid Chromatography Unit, Edinburgh University, since 1972 (Emeritus Professor of Physical Chemistry, since 1984); b. 21.10.27, Edinburgh; m., Josephine Anne Wissler; 4 s. Educ. George Watson's Boys College, Edinburgh; Edinburgh University; Cambridge University. Edinburgh University: Lecturer, 1953-66, Reader, 1966-74, Professor, 1974-84; Consultant: Bruce Peebles, 1960, du Pont, USA, 1970, Rank Hilger, 1973, Shandon Southern Products, 1975, Kratos, 1981, British Petroleum Company, 1983. Recreations: skiing; hill-walking; sailing. Address: (h.) 67 Morningside Park, Edinburgh; T.-031-447 5057.

Knox, Joseph. Member, Strathclyde Regional Council, since 1978; Member, Clyde River Purification Board, since 1978; b. 3.11.36, Kilwinning, Ayrshire; m., Elizabeth; 1 s.; 3 d. Educ. Camphill School, Paisley. Address: (h.) 2 Hunterhill Avenue, Paisley; T.-041-887 6910.

Knox, Robert, MA, LLB, WS. Senior Partner, Boyd, Jameson & Young WS, Edinburgh, since 1983; Solicitor, since 1959, Partner, since 1962; Solicitor to Ministry of Defence (Army) in Scotland, since 1980; Honorary Consul for Belgium in Edinburgh, since 1982; b. 23.5.35, Paisley; m., Jill Mackness; 2 s.; 1 d. Educ. Paisley Grammar School; Glasgow University; Manchester University; Edinburgh University. Member, Lord Maxwell's Committee on Civil Jurisdiction and Enforcement. Recreations: gardening; photography; foreign travel; music. Address: (b.) 89 Constitution Street, Leith, Edinburgh; T.-031-554 3333.

Knox, Rev. Samuel James, MA, BD, BLitt, PhD, LTCL. Minister, Cockenzie Old Parish Church, Port Seton, 1980-85; b. 23.3.18, Ballymena, Northern Ireland; m., Dr. M.I.R. Apthomas; 2 s.; 2 d. Educ. Ballymena Academy; Belfast University; Edinburgh University; Manchester University; Dublin University. Minister: St. Aidan's Presbyterian Church, Manchester, 1944-49, Abbey Presbyterian Church, Dublin, 1949-61, Holburn Central Parish Church, Aberdeen, 1961-75; overseas missionary service, Nigeria, 1975-80. Chairman, Lifeboat Committee and Christian Aid Committee, Port Seton. Publications: Ireland's Debt to the Huguenots, 1960; Walter Travers: Paragon of Elizabethan Puritanism, 1962. Recreations: swimming; cycling; music.

Knox, William. Author and Journalist; b. 20.2.28, Glasgow; m., Myra Ann McKill; 1 s.; 2 d. Educ. Eastwood School. Deputy News Editor, Evening News, Glasgow, 1957; Scottish Editor, Kemsley Newspapers, Glasgow, 1957-60; News Editor, Scottish Television, 1960-62; Freelance Author and Broadcaster, since 1962; author of about 50 books, including novels of crime, sea and adventure; Presenter, Crime Desk, STV, since 1977; William Knox Collection established Boston University, USA; Past President and Honorary Member, Association of Scottish Motoring Writers; former Member, Scottish Committee, Society of Authors; Past President,

Eastwood Rotary Club; Honorary Editor, Scottish Lifeboat, RNLI. Recreations: motoring; photography; dogs. Address: (h.) 55 Newtonlea Avenue, Newton Mearns, Glasgow, G77 5QF.

Konstam, Peter George, OBE, MD (Frankfurt), FRCSEdin. Honorary Sheriff, Orkney Islands; b. 19.4.08, Frankfurt-on-Main, Germany; m., Dr. Sheila Ritchie; 1 s. Educ. Lessing Gymnasium, Frankfurt; Berlin University; Frankfurt University. Senior Registrar to Professor of Surgery, Aberdeen University; Major, RAMC; Associate Professor of Surgery, Ibadan University; Consultant Surgeon, Orkney Hospitals (retired, 1974). Recreations: piano playing; reading; gardening. Address: (h.) Thule, St. Ola, Orkney Isles; T.-Kirkwall 2821.

Krajewski, Andrew Stephen, BSc, MB, ChB, MRCPath. Senior Lecturer in Pathology, Edinburgh University, since 1983; Honorary Consultant Pathologist, Lothian Health Board, since 1983; b. 28.11.51, Bishops Stortford; m., Dorothy Margaret; 2 s. Educ. Hertford Grammar School; Edinburgh University. Edinburgh University: Lecturer in Pathology, 1975-82, MRC Research Fellow, 1978-81. Address: (h.) 28 Danube Street, Edinburgh, EH4 1NT; T.-031-343 3448.

Kreitman, Norman, FRCPsych, FRCPEdin, MD. Director, MRC Unit for Epidemiological Studies in Psychiatry, since 1971; Honorary Senior Lecturer, Department of Psychiatry, Edinburgh University, since 1971; b. 5.7.27, London; m., Suzanne; 1 s.; 1 d. Educ. King's College, London; Westminster Hospital. Recreations: literature; angling. Address: (h.) 24 Lauder Road, Edinburgh, EH9 2JF; T.-031-667 4346.

Kuenssberg, Nicholas Christopher D., BA (Hons) (Oxon), FCIS, FBIM. Director, J. & P. Coats Ltd., since 1978; Chairman, Dymacast International Ltd., since 1978; Chairman, Textile Mouldings Ltd., since 1982; Non-Executive Director, South of Scotland Electricity Board, since 1984; Member, West of Scotland Board, Bank of Scotland, since 1984; b. 28.10.42, Edinburgh; m., Sally Robertson; 1 s.; 2 d. Educ. Edinburgh Academy; Wadham College, Oxford. Worked overseas, 1964-78; returned to UK as Coats director responsible for finance and precision engineering, latterly responsible for Coats interests in Spanish-speaking Latin America and for materials and logistics. Recreations: squash; languages; opera; travel; printing/publishing. Address: (b.) Coats Patons Ltd., 155 St. Vincent Street, Glasgow, G2 5PA; T.-041-221 8711.

Kyle, James, DSc, MCh, FRCS. Consultant Surgeon, Aberdeen Royal Infirmary, since 1959; Chairman, Representative Body, British Medical Association, since 1984; Chairman, Scottish Joint Consultants Committee, since 1984; b. 26.3.25, Ballymena, Northern Ireland; m., Dorothy Elizabeth Galbraith; 2 d. Educ. Ballymena Academy; Queen's University, Belfast. Scholarship to Mayo Clinic, USA, 1950; Tutor in Surgery, Royal Victoria Hospital, Belfast, 1952; Lecturer in Surgery, Liverpool University, 1957; Senior Lecturer in Surgery, Aberdeen University, since 1959; Member, Grampian Health

Board, 1973-77; Chairman, Scottish Committee for Hospital Medical Services, 1976-79; elected Member, General Medical Council, since 1979. Publications: Peptic Ulcer; Pye's Surgical Handicraft; Crohn's Disease; Scientific Foundations of Surgery. Recreations: Fellow, Royal Philatelic Society, London; licensed radio amateur, GM4 CHX. Address: (h.) Grianan, 74 Rubislaw Den North, Aberdeen, AB2 4AN; T.-Aberdeen 37966.

Kyle, Kenneth Francis, MB, ChB, BAO, MCh (Hons), FRCS, FRCSI. Consultant Urologist, Western Infirmary, Glasgow; b. 19.8.34, Belfast; m., Barbara M. Wilson; 1 s.; 1 d. Educ. Coleraine Academical Institution; Queen's University, Belfast. Previously Urologist, Royal Beatson Memorial Hospital and Stonehouse Hospital; Founder Renal Transplantation Surgeon, Western Infirmary, Glasgow, 1968; first world percutaneous renal transplant pyelolysis, 1984; Honorary Lecturer in Urology, Glasgow University. Publication: Surgery (Contributor). Recreations: golf; hill-walking; travelling; wine-drinking; music; opera. Address: (h.) 13 Campsie View Drive, Blanfield, Glasgow, G63 9JE; T.-Blanefield 70522.

Kyle, Robert, MBE, DL, NP. Honorary Sheriff, Strathclyde, at Airdrie; Deputy Lieutenant, County of Dunbarton; b. 28.3.19, Strathaven; m., Pauline Watson; 3 s.; 1 d. Educ. Strathaven Academy; Hamilton Academy; Glasgow University. War service, six years; Legal Assistant, Kilmarnock Town Council, 1946-48; Depute Town Clerk, Airdrie Town Council, 1948-52; Town Clerk, Kirkintilloch Town Council, 1952-68; Town Clerk and Manager, Cumbernauld Town Council, 1968-74; Chief Executive, Cumbernauld and Kilsyth District Council, 1974-81. Past President, Dumbartonshire Golf Union. Recreations: golf; angling. Address: (h.) 23 Middlemuir Road, Lenzie, Glasgow, G66 4NA; T.-041-776 1861.

Kynoch, Gordon Bryson, CBE, TD, DL, JP. Director, G. & G. Kynoch plc, Keith, since 1922 (former Managing Director and Chairman); Honorary Sheriff, County of Banff, since 1950; b. 8.5.04, Keith; m., Nesta Alicia Janet Thora; 2 s. (inc. 1 deceased); 3 d. Educ. Cargilfield, Edinburgh; Trinity College, Glenalmond. Served Second World War with 14th Army and Gen. HQ India Command; Lt.-Col. (Ret.), Gordon Highlanders (TA); Burgh of Keith: Magistrate, 1947, Provost, 1961; Member, Banffshire County Council, 1946; President, Keith and District Branch, Royal British Legion. Address: (h.) Skara Brae, Broomhill Road, Keith, Banffshire; T.-Keith 2507.

L

Lacey, James Binnie, MA (Hons). Rector, Carnoustie High School, since 1973; b. 16.5.36, Kirkliston, West Lothian; m., Margot Elizabeth

Munro; 2 d. Educ. Royal High School, Edinburgh; Edinburgh University. Principal Teacher of Geography: St. Mary's Academy, Bathgate, 1963-67, Forrester Secondary School, Edinburgh, 1967-71; Assistant Rector, Perth High School, 1971-72. Captain, Carnoustie Mercantile Golf Club, 1974-76; Member, Board of Directors, Dundee Repertory Theatre, 1974-78; Member, Tayside Education Committee, 1975-79; Governor, Dundee College of Education, 1979-83; Member, SCCTE, 1982-84; Honorary President, Carnoustie HSFP Rugby Club, since 1978. Recreations: rugby; golf; curling; reading. Address: (b.) Carnoustie High School, Shanwell Road, Carnoustie, Angus; T.-0241 52601.

Lacome, Myer, MSIAD, MSTD, FRSA, MInstPkg. Principal, College of Art, Dundee, since 1979 (Head of Design School, since 1962); b. 13.11.27, Liverpool; m., Jacci; 1 s.; 2 d. Educ. Liverpool College of Art. National Service, RAF, 1945-47; Design Consultant: New York, 1947-49, London, 1950-59; Senior Lecturer in 3D Design; Consultant Designer to national companies and regional authorities, since 1960; has served on Design Council, SIAD, Crafts Council, Scottish Film Council, CNAA and various education committees. Recreation: self-confessed culture vulture. Address: (b.) College of Art, Perth Road, Dundee; T.-0382 23261.

Lacy, Rev. David William, BA, BD. Minister, Knightswood: St Margaret's, since 1977; b. 26.4.52, Inverness; m., Joan Stewart Robertson; 1 s.; 1 d. Educ. Aberdeen Grammar School; High School of Glasgow; Strathclyde University; Glasgow University. Assistant Minister, St. George's West, Edinburgh, 1975-77. Convener, Glasgow Presbytery Committee on Communications, 1979-84. Recreations: music; golf; swimming. Address: 26 Airthrey Avenue, Glasgow, G14 9LJ; T.-041-959 1094.

Laidlaw, Professor James Cameron, MA, PhD. Vice-Principal, Aberdeen University, since 1984 (Professor of French, since 1975); b. 3.3.37, Ecclefechan; m., Elizabeth Fernie Bosomworth; 1 s.; 2 d. Educ. George Watson's College, Edinburgh; Edinburgh University; Trinity Hall, Cambridge. Research Fellow, Trinity Hall, Cambridge, 1961-63; Lecturer in Medieval French, Queen's University, Belfast, 1963-65; University Assistant Lecturer (from 1969 University Lecturer) in French, and Fellow, Trinity Hall, Cambridge, 1965-74. Member, Arts Sub-Committee, University Grants Committee; Honorary Secretary, Modern Humanities Research Association, 1961-67. Publications: The Future of the Modern Humanities (Editor), 1969; The Poetical Works of Alain Chartier, 1974. Recreations: walking; cycling. Address: (h.) 2 The Chanonry, Old Aberdeen, Aberdeen, AB2 1RP; T.-Aberdeen 42875.

Laing, David Doig. Secretary, Urban/Industrial Mission, Congregational Union of Scotland, since 1971; Member, Strathclyde Regional Council, since 1978 (Chairman, Glasgow Deprivation Group, since 1982); b. 29.11.36, Edinburgh; m., Ruth; 2 s.; 1 d. Educ. Norton Park Junior Secondary School, Edinburgh; Glasgow University;

Scottish Congregational College, Edinburgh. Minister, Govan Congregational Church, 1968-72; Community Minister, Easterhouse, since 1972; Founder Member, Glasgow Industrial Mission Team, 1970; chaired working party on physically handicapped, 1980-82; produced report, The Cost of Living in Hostile Environment; Chaplain, Glasgow Tigers Speedway Team; Member, COSLA Social Work Committee. Recreations: Citizens' Theatre; Scottish Ballet; science fiction; soccer (season ticket holder, Hibernian); speedway racing. Address: 71 Whirlow Road, Glasow, G69 6QE; T.-041-771 1746.

Laing, Professor Ernest William, MA, PhD, FInstP, FRSE. Titular Professor and Head, Department of Natural Philosophy, Glasgow University; b. 12.2.31, Braine-Le-Comte, Belgium; m., Olive Jean Guild Melville; 2 s. Educ. John Neilson School, Paisley; Glasgow University. Senior Scientific Officer, UKAEA Harwell, 1957-60; Glasgow University: Lecturer, 1960-66, Senior Lecturer, 1966-76, Reader, 1976-80, Titular Professor, since 1980. Publication: Plasma Physics, 1979. Recreation: music. Address: (b.) Department of Natural Philosophy, Glasgow University, Glasgow, G12 8QQ; T.-041-339 8855.

Laing, Gerald Ogilvie, NDD. Artist, since 1960; b. 11.2.36, Newcastle-upon-Tyne; 2 s.; 1 d. Educ. Berkhamsted School; Royal Military Academy, Sandhurst; St. Martin's School of Art. Regular Army Officer, 1953-60; has exhibited widely in USA and Europe; has had 30 one-man exhibitions during last 25 years; works included in permanent collections of many museums, including Tate Gallery, Victoria and Albert Museum, Museum of Modern Art, New York, Whitney Museum, Scottish National Gallery of Modern Art, and in the collections of many major universities, including Harvard and Cornell. Address: Kinkell Castle, Ross and Cromarty, IV7 8AT; T.-0349 61485.

Laing, James Findlay, MA (Hons). Under Secretary, Industry Department for Scotland, since 1979; b. 7.11.33, Nairn; m., Christine Joy Canaway; 1 s. Educ. Nairn Academy; Edinburgh University. Assistant Principal and Principal, Scottish Office, 1957-68; Principal, HM Treasury, 1968-71; Assistant Secretary, Scottish Office, 1972-79. Recreations: squash; chess. Address: (b.) New St. Andrew's House, Edinburgh, EH1 3TA; T.-031-556 8400.

Laird, Alexander Fraser, CA. Director of Finance, Glenrothes Development Corporation, since 1975; b. 29.4.26, Edinburgh; m., Dorothy Glen; 3 s. Educ. Leith Academy. Lt., 15th Punjab Regiment, 1944-47; Chief Internal Auditor, Herring Industry Board, 1951-58; Chief Internal Auditor, then Depute Chief Finance Officer, Glenrothes Development Corporation, 1959-75. Recreation: philately. Address: (h.) 2 Braid Drive, Glenrothes, Fife, KY7 4ES; T.-Glenrothes 758059.

Laird, Alexander Peddie, BL, NP. Partner, Laird & Wilson Terris & Co., SCC, Edinburgh, since 1951; b. 14.6.24, Edinburgh; m., Elizabeth Anne Melrose; 2 d. Educ. Daniel Stewart's College,

Edinburgh; Edinburgh University. Joined Army, 1943; commissioned, Royal Artillery; served with 51 (Highland) Division, 1944, and with 6th Airborne Division, 1944-46, in Europe and Palestine; served with Air Observation Post, Royal Artillery, 1946-47, in Palestine; demobilised as Captain, 1947; set up in private practice, 1951. Elder, Cramond Kirk (former Session Clerk). Recreations: golf; walking; gardening. Address: (h.) 68 Barnton Park View, Edinburgh, EH4 6HJ; T.-031-339 2589.

Laird, Endell Johnston. Editor, Sunday Mail; b. 6.10.33, Forfar; m., June Stanners Keenan; 1 s.; 2 d. Educ. Forfar Academy. Worked for Dundee Courier, Daily Express, Evening Times, Daily Record. Recreations: golf; bridge. Address: Sunday Mail, Anderston Quay, Glasgow, G3 8DA.

Laird, James Steel, MA, LLB. Solicitor; Partner, McGrigor Donald & Co. (now McGrigor Donald & Moncrieffs) since 1961; b. 6.9.32, Kilmarnock; 2 d. Educ. Prestwick High School; Ayr Academy; Glasgow University. Served legal apprenticeship, McGrigor Donald & Co., from 1952. Chairman, Pollok School Company (Craigholme School); Member, Giffnock and Thornliebank Community Council. Recreation: golf. Address: (h.) 32 Milverton Road, Whitecraigs, Glasgow.

Lamb, Rev. A. Douglas, MA. Minister, Dalry St. Margaret's, since 1973; b. 9.11.36, Glasgow; m., Jean A. Beattie; 3 s.; 1 d. Educ. Hermitage School, Helensburgh; Glasgow University and Trinity College; Princeton Theological Seminary. Assistant Minister: 1st Presbyterian Church, Philadelphia, 1963, Airdrie West, 1963-65; Minister, Unst, Shetland, 1965-73. Sometime Secretary, Unst Council of Social Service; Editor, Unst Guide Book; sometime President, Garnock Valley Rotary Club; sometime Moderator: Shetland Presbytery, Ardrossan Presbytery. Recreations: hill-walking; history. Address: St. Margaret's Manse, Dalry, Ayrshire; T.-029 483 2234.

Lamb, David, BSc, MB, BS, PhD, FRCPath. Reader in Pathology, Edinburgh University, since 1984; b. 7.7.35, Durham; m., Joan Bishop; 1 s.; 1 d. Educ. Bishop Auckland Grammar School; University College and University College Hospital, London. Senior Lecturer in Pathology, Edinburgh University, 1974-84. Recreations: eating; drinking; fishing; collecting Britannia metal. Address: (b.) Department of Pathology, Edinburgh University, Teviot Place, Edinburgh; T.-031-667 1011, Ext. 2262.

Lamb, Douglas, MB, ChB, FRCSEdin. Consultant Orthopaedic Surgeon, Princess Margaret Rose Orthopaedic Hospital and Royal Infirmary, Edinburgh, since 1954; b. 21.12.21, Edinburgh; b. Joan; 3 s.; 1 d. Educ. Brentwood School; Edinburgh University. Council Member, Royal College of Surgeons, Edinburgh; Editor, The Practice of Hand Surgery. Recreations: gardening; walking. Address: (h.) 16 Corrennie Gardens, Edinburgh, 10; T.-031-447 5866.

Lamb, Professor John, PhD, DSc, FInstP, FAccoustSocAmerica, HonFInstAcoustics, FIEE, FEng, FRSE. James Watt Professor of Electronics and Electrical Engineering, Glasgow University, since 1961; b. 26.9.22, Accrington; m., Margaret May Livesey; 2 s.; 1 d. Educ. Accrington Grammar School; Manchester University. Ministry of Supply, 1943-46; Lecturer, 1946-56, Reader, 1956-61, in Electrical Engineering, Imperial College, London University; Assistant Director, Department of Electrical Engineering, Imperial College, London University, 1958-61; Vice-Principal, Glasgow University, 1977-80; Member, National Electronics Council, UK, 1963-78; Member, Council for National Academic Awards, 1964-70; President, British Society of Rheology, 1970-72; Council Member, Royal Society of Edinburgh, 1980-83; Member, British National Committee for Radio Science, since 1983. Recreations: walking; wine-making; music. Address: (h.) 5 Cleveden Crescent, Glasgow, G12 OPD; T.-041-339 2101.

Lamb, Professor Joseph Fairweather, MB, ChB, BSc, PhD, FRCPEdin, FRSE. Chandos Professor of Physiology, St. Andrews University, since 1969; Senior Secretary, Physiological Society, 1982-85; b. 18.7.28, Brechin; m., Olivia Jane Horne; 4 s.; 1 d. Educ. Brechin High School; Edinburgh University. National Service, 1947-49; House Surgeon, Dumfries Royal Infirmary, 1955-56; House Physician, Eastern General Hospital, Edinburgh, 1956; Research Scholar, then Lecturer, Edinburgh University, 1957-61; Lecturer, then Senior Lecturer, Glasgow University, 1961-69; Editor, Journal of Physiology, 1968-74; Examiner, College of Surgeons of Edinburgh, Glasgow, London; Examiner, Universities of Aberdeen, Dundee, Edinburgh, Bristol, Leeds, Southampton, Lagos, Malaysia, etc. Publication: Essentials of Physiology, 1980. Recreations: boat-building; sailing; amateur radio. Address: (b.) Department of Physiology, St. Salvators College, St. Andrews, Fife, KY16 9TS; T.-St. Andrews 76161.

Lambert, John, FMS, FBIM, FIIM. Director, Scotland and Northern Ireland, British Institute of Management, since 1984; b. 17.4.34, Blyth, Northumberland; m., Constance; 2 d. Educ. Blyth Grammar School; Rutherford College of Technology, Newcastle. Managerial appointments in personnel and management services; Manager, O. & M. Consultancy Services, Co-operative Wholesale Society, 1969-72; Head, Personnel and Management Services, Burgh of Greenock, 1973-75; Director, Personnel and Management Services, Renfrew District Council, 1975-80; General Manager, RTITB, Livingston Motec, 1980-84. Member, Scottish Council (Development and Industry); Conference Member, Stirling University; Member, Scottish Retirement Council; Member: Professional Standards Committee, SCOTBEC, Computer Science Committee, Paisley College of Technology; Captain, Largs Golf Club, 1984-85. Recreations: golf; photography; music. Address: (h.) 72 Greenock Road, Largs, Ayrshire; T.-0475 672402.

Lambert, Professor John Denholm, BSc, PhD, FIMA, FRSE. Professor of Numerical Analysis, Dundee University, since 1977 (Dean, Faculty of Science, since 1984); b. 23.9.32, Aberdeen; m.,

Heather Kirtley; 2 s.; 1 d. Educ. Forfar Academy; St. Andrews University. Royal Naval Scientific Service; Assistant Professor of Mathematics, Memorial University of Newfoundland; Lecturer, Applied Mathematics, St. Andrews University; Senior Lecturer, Mathematics, Aberdeen University; Senior Lecturer in Mathematics, then Reader in Numerical Analysis, Dundee University. Address: (b.) Department of Mathematical Sciences, Dundee University, Dundee, DD1 4HN; T.-Dundee 23181, Ext. 4466.

Lambie, Rev. Andrew Elliot, BD. Minister, linked parishes of Carmichael, Covington, Thankerton and Pettinain, since 1985; b. 10.12.26, Glasgow; m., Elizabeth McCulloch Duncan; 2 s.; 1 d. Educ. Allan Glen's School, Glasgow; Glasgow University and Trinity College. Minister: Linnvale Church, Clydebank, 1957-64, Lerwick and Bressay, Shetland, 1964-80; Clerk, Shetland Presbytery, 1970-78; Associate Minister, Ellon Parish Church, 1980-85. President, Lerwick Choral Society, 1977-80. Recreations: gardening; walking. Address: The Manse, Thankerton, near Biggar, Lanarkshire; T.-Tinto 333.

Lambie, David. MP (Labour), Cunninghame South, since 1983 (Central Ayrshire, 1970-83); b. 13.7.25. Educ. Ardrossan Academy; Glasgow University; Geneva University. Former Teacher; Chairman, Scottish Labour Party, 1964; appointed Chairman, Scottish Parliamentary Labour Group, 1980; Chairman, Select Committee on Scottish Affairs, 1982.

Lambie, Margaret Callander, JP, BSc. Member, Forth Valley Health Board, since 1980; b. Falkirk; m., William Lambie; 2 s.; 1 d. Educ. Falkirk High School; Glasgow University. Member, Central Regional Council, 1978-82; Vice-Chairman, Conservative Women's Scottish Council, 1984-85; Chairman, Falkirk Branch, RNLI. Recreations: bridge; walking. Address: (h.) 5 Gartcows Crescent, Falkirk, FK1 5QH; T.-Falkirk 23283.

Lamond, James Alexander, JP. MP (Labour), Oldham Central and Royton, since 1983 (Oldham East, 1970-83); b. 29.11.28; m., June Rose Wellburn (see June Rose Lamond); 3 d. Lord Provost of Aberdeen, 1970-71; Lord Lieutenant, County of the City of Aberdeen, 1970-71.

Lamond, June Rose. Member, Grampian Regional Council, since 1978; Member, Grampian Health Board, since 1975; Member, Gas Consumers' Council for Scotland, since 1971; b. 12.6.33, Aberdeen; m., James A. Lamond, MP (qv); 3 d. Educ. Aberdeen Demonstration School; Aberdeen College of Commerce. Member, Aberdeen District Council, 1974-77; Member, Aberdeen Women's Aid, 1977. Recreation: tennis. Address: (h.) 15 Belvidere Street, Aberdeen; T.-Aberdeen 638074.

Lamont, Colin C., MA, PhD. Headmaster, Gracemount High School, Edinburgh, since 1983; b. 6.10.44, Glasgow; m.; 2 s. Educ. Robert Gordon's College, Aberdeen; Aberdeen University; Edinburgh University. Teacher, Merchiston

Castle School, Edinburgh; Principal Teacher, Robert Gordon's College, Aberdeen; Adviser in English, Renfrew Division, Strathclyde. Address: (b.) Gracemount High School, Lasswade Road, Edinburgh, EH16 6TZ; T.-031-664 7440.

Lamont, Rev. Stewart Jackson, BSc, BD. Minister, Church of Scotland, since 1972; Freelance Journalist and Broadcaster (Religious Affairs Correspondent, Glasgow Herald), since 1980; b. 8.1.47, Broughty Ferry. Educ. Grove Academy, Broughty Ferry; St. Andrews University. General Council Assessor, St. Andrews University Court, 1970-82; Producer, BBC Religious Department, 1972-80; Freelance Radio and Television Presenter and Producer; part-time Minister, Abernyte, 1980-82. Publications: The Third Angle, 1978; Is Anybody There?, 1980; Religion and the Supernatural (Co-author), 1985; Scientology, in press. Winner, Scottish Schools Debating Competition, 1965; President of the Union, St. Andrews, 1969. Recreations: cooking; classic cars; music; foreign travel. Address: 3 Doune Quadrant, Glasgow, G20 6DN; T.-041-946 3629.

Land, Roger Burton, PhD, BSc, FRSE. Director, AFRC Animal Breeding Research Organisation, since 1982; b. 30.4.40, Shipley; 1 s.; 2 d. Educ. Bradford Grammar School; Nottingham University; Edinburgh University. Hammond Prize, British Society of Animal Production, 1982. Recreations: family activities; gardening. Address: (h.) Eshiels House, Peebles, EH45 8NA; T.-0721 21117.

Lang, Lt.-Gen. Sir Derek, KCB (1967), DSO (1944), MC (1941), DL. GOC-in-C, Scottish Command, and Governor of Edinburgh Castle, 1966-69; President, Army Cadet Force Association (Scotland); b. 7.10.13. Educ. Wellington College; Sandhurst. Director of Army Training, 1964-66.

Lang, Ian Bruce, MP, OStJ, BA. MP (Conservative) Galloway and Upper Nithsdale, since 1983 (Galloway, 1979-83); Lord Commissioner of HM Treasury, since 1983; Scottish Whip, since 1981; Vice-Chairman, Scottish Conservative Party, since 1983; b. 27.6.40, Glasgow; m., Sandra Caroline Montgomerie; 2 d. Educ. Lathallan School; Rugby School; Sidney Sussex College, Cambridge. Member, Select Committee on Scottish Affairs, 1979-81; Honorary President, Scottish Young Conservatives, 1982-84; Trustee, Glasgow Savings Bank and West of Scotland TSB, 1969-82; Member, Queen's Bodyguard for Scotland (Royal Company of Archers), since 1974; Insurance Broker and Company Director, 1962-81. Address (b.) House of Commons, Westminster, London, SW1A OAA.

Langan, John. National Officer, Association of Scientific, Technical and Managerial Staffs, since 1974; Member, Employment Appeal Tribunals; Chairman, Industrial and Social Conditions Committee, Scottish Council (Development and Industry); Member, Scottish Industrial Development Advisory Board; b. 30.12.24, Greenock;

m., Margaret; 1 d. Educ. St. Columba's High School; James Watt Technical College. Active in trade union affairs since 1947; full-time Officer with Coppersmiths' Union, 1956; joined ASSET as a full-time Officer, 1965; Member, General Council, Scottish Trades Union Congress, since 1976 (Chairman of Congress, 1983-84); has chaired a number of STUC Committees and Sub-Committees; Member, Council of Tribunals for Scotland, 1976-82; Member, Board of Governors, Scottish Police College, 1977-81; Chairman, Glasgow District Manpower Services Committee, 1978-82; Member, Scottish Economic Planning Committee, 1979-82; Member: Scottish Anti-Alcohol Unit, Scottish Labour History Society. Recreations: football and cricket (spectating only); golf and bowls (participating). Address: (h.) 8 Margaret Street, Greenock, PA16 8AS; T.-0475 20547.

Langlands, Alistair William. Chairman, Skye and Lochalsh Licensing Board, since 1984; Member, Skye and Lochalsh District Council, since 1978 (Housing Convener, since 1980); b. 15.10.43, Lockerbie; m., Margaret Joyce; 1 s.; 2 d. Educ. Logie Junior Secondary School. Civil Service, five years; diver/fisherman, 14 years. Former Scottish Under-23 Water Polo Representative. Recreations: angling; photography; reading. Address: (h.) 27 Wemyss Place, Kyle of Lochalsh, Ross-shire; T.-0599 4582.

Langton, Professor Norman Harry, BSc, MSc, PhD, CEng, FInstP, FIERE, FRSA. Professor of Physics, Robert Gordon's Institute of Technology, since 1965; b. 15.1.20, Kingston-upon-Hull; m., Janet Sheilah; 1 d. Educ. Malet Lambert School, Hull; Hull University; Nottingham University. Lecturer in Physics, Loughborough College of Technology, 1947-55; Principal Lecturer in Polymer Physics, National College of Rubber Technology, North London Polytechnic, 1955-65. Chairman, Course Committee C2, SCOTEC. Recreations: music; swimming. Address: (b.) Robert Gordon's Institute of Technology, St. Andrew Street, Aberdeen, AB1 1HG; T.-Aberdeen 633611.

Lansdowne, 8th Marquess of, (George John Charles Mercer Nairne Petty-Fitzmaurice), PC (1964); b. 27.11.12; m., 1, Barbara Chase (deceased); 2 s.; 1 d.; 1 d. deceased; 2, Polly Carnegie (m. diss.); 3, Gillian Ann Morgan. Educ. Eton; Christ Church, Oxford. Served Second World War (Major, 1944); Lord-in-Waiting to The Queen, 1957-58; Minister of State for Colonial Affairs, 1962-64, and for Commonwealth Relations, 1963-64; Member, Queen's Bodyguard for Scotland (Royal Company of Archers); Chairman, Victoria League in Scotland, 1952-56. Address: (h.) Meikleour House, Perthshire.

Larkin, Professor Maurice John Milner, MA, PhD. Professor of Modern European History, Edinburgh University, since 1976; b. 12.8.32, Harrow on the Hill; m., Enid Thelma Lowe; 1 s.; 1 d. Educ. St. Philip's Grammar School, Birmingham; Trinity College, Cambridge. Assistant Lecturer, then Lecturer, Glasgow University, 1958-65; Lecturer, then Senior Lecturer, then

Reader, Kent University, 1965-76. Publications: Gathering Pace: Continental Europe 1870-1945, 1969; Church and State after the Dreyfus Affair, 1974; Man and Society in Nineteenth-Century Realism, 1977. Recreations: bird-watching; music; films. Address: (b.) History Department, Edinburgh University, Edinburgh, EH8 9JY; T.-031-667 1011.

Larner, Professor John Patrick, MA, FRHistA. Titular Professor of History, Glasgow University, since 1979; b. 24.3.30, London; m., Christina Ross (deceased); 2 s. Educ. Finchley Grammar School; New College, Oxford. Rome Medieval Scholar, British School of Rome, 1954-57; Lecturer, Glasgow University, 1957-79. Publications: Lords of Romagna, 1965; Culture and Society in Italy, 1971; Florentine Society 1382-1494, 1972; Italy in the Age of Dante, 1980. Recreations: hill-walking; photography. Address: (b.) Department of Medieval History, The University, Glasgow, G12 8QQ; T.-041-339 8855.

Last, Professor Rex William, BA, MA, PhD, FRSA. Professor of Modern Languages, Dundee University, since 1981; b. 30.6.40, Ipswich; m., Oksana S.; 2 s. Educ. Northgate Grammar School, Ipswich; Hull University. Lecturer, Senior Lecturer, Reader in Modern German Literature, Hull University; former Treasurer, Association for Literary and Linguistic Computing; Member: CNAA Languages Board, SCOVACT Council; Director, Lochee Publications. Publications: books on Hans Arp, Erich Kastner, E.M. Remarque, German Dadaist literature, computer applications in language teaching, study skills. Recreation: flying. Address: (h.) 5 Inverary Terrace, Dundee, DD3 6BS; T.-0382 24379.

Latham, Professor John Derek, JP, MA, DPhil, DLitt (Oxon), FRAS, FSA Scot. Iraq Professor of Arabic and Islamic Studies and Head, Muir Institute, Edinburgh University, since 1982; b. 5.4.27, Wigan; m., Jane Elisabeth Coulstock; 1 s.; 1 d. Educ. Wigan Grammar School; Pembroke College, Oxford. HM Treasury Research Fellow, Oxford, 1950-53; Associate Professor and Curator, Middle East Collections, Hoover Institution, Stanford University, California, 1957-58; Lecturer, then Reader in Arabic, Manchester University, 1958-82; Visiting Fellow, St. Cross College, Oxford, 1975. Examiner, Civil Service Commission, since 1968; Member: Middle East Libraries Committee, since 1967 (Chairman, 1971-79), British Society for Middle Eastern Studies, since 1973 (President, 1985-87), Medieval Latin Dictionary Committee (British Academy), since 1970, Fontes Historiae Africanae Committee (British Academy), since 1970 (Chairman, 1971-79); Member, Advisory Committee, Journal of Semitic Studies, 1976-82; General Editor (Joint), Cambridge History of Arabic Literature, since 1982; Editor: Islamic Quarterly, 1970-74; Bulletin of British Society for Middle Eastern Studies, since 1974; Consultant, Supplement to Oxford English Dictionary, since 1984; Trustee, E.J.W. Gibb Memorial, since 1985. Recreations: none (for want of time). Address: (b.) Muir Institute, 7-8 Buccleuch Place, Edinburgh, EH3 9LW; T.-031-667 1011.

Lauderdale, 17th Earl of, (Patrick Francis Maitland), BA (Hons) (Oxon); b. 17.3.11; m., Stanka Lozanitch; 2 s.; 2 d. Educ. Lancing College, Sussex; Brasenose College, Oxford. Journalist, 1933-59; MP (Unionist), Lanark, 1951-59; Company Director.

Laurenson, Robert Andrew, FIB (Scot). Deputy Chief General Manager, Clydesdale Bank PLC, since 1982; Director, Clydesdale Bank Equity Limited, since 1982; Director, Clydesdale Bank Industrial Investments Ltd., since 1982; Director, Scottish Agricultural Securities Corporation plc, since 1984; Director, Clydesdale Bank Finance Corporation Ltd., since 1985; b. 7.7.30, Lerwick; m., Margaret Patterson; 2 s. Educ. Lerwick Central Public School. Clydesdale Bank: Lerwick Branch, 1947, National Service, 1949-50, Lerwick Branch, 1950-56, various branches, 1956-78, Assistant General Manager, Head Office, 1978-82, General Manager, 1982. Member, Scottish Council, Cystic Fibrosis Research Trust. Recreations: golf; bowling; curling; soccer; snooker. Address: (b.) 30 St. Vincent Place, Glasgow, G1 2HL; T.-041-248 7070.

Laver, Professor John David Michael Henry, MA (Hons), DipPh, PhD. Professor of Phonetics, Department of Linguistics, Edinburgh University, since 1985; Director, Centre for Speech Technology Research, Edinburgh University, since 1984; b. 20.1.38, Nowshera, Pakistan; m., Sandy Hutcheson; 3 s.; 1 d. Educ. Churcher's College, Petersfield; Edinburgh University. Assistant Lecturer, then Lecturer in Phonetics, Ibadan University, 1963-66 (Exchange Lecturer, Edinburgh University, 1964-65); Lecturer, then Senior Lecturer in Phonetics, Edinburgh University, 1966-80; Reader and Head of Subject for Phonetics, 1980-84; Visiting Assistant Professor, Department of Linguistics, University of California, 1971; Visiting Research Fellow, Macquarie University, Sydney, 1982; Information Technology Fellowship, Edinburgh, 1983-84. Publications: Communication in Face to Face Interaction (Joint Editor), 1972; Phonetics in Linguistics (Joint Editor), 1973; Voice Quality, 1979; The Phonetic Description of Voice Quality, 1980; The Cognitive Representation of Speech (Joint Editor), 1981. Address: (b.) Centre for Speech Technology Research, Edinburgh University, 80 South Bridge, Edinburgh; T.-031-225 8883.

Laverack, Professor Michael Stuart, BSc, PhD, FIBiol, FRSE. Professor of Marine Biology, St. Andrews University, since 1969; b. 19.3.31, Croydon; m., Maureen Ann; 2 s.; 1 d. Educ. Selhurst Grammar School; Southampton University. Scientific Officer, Nature Conservancy, 1958-60; Lecturer, then Senior Lecturer in Zoology, St. Andrews University, 1960-69. Publications: Lecture Notes in Invertebrate Zoology (Co-author); Physiology of Earthworms. Recreations: photography; walking; gardening; music. Address: (h.) Branxton, Boarhills, St. Andrews, Fife; T.-0334 88241.

Law, Alistair Geekie Robertson, JP, MB, ChB, MRCGP. General Medical Practitioner, since 1950; Member, Tayside Health Board; Chairman, Scottish Council, British Medical Association

(Council Member, UK); b. 26.12.23, Dundee; m., Dr. Marion M.T. Roy; 1 s.; 2 d. Educ. Morgan Academy, Dundee; St. Andrews University. Hospital appointments; RAF. Fellow, BMA; Member, Bonnetmaker Craft. Recreation: golf. Address: (h.) Ianmhor, 21 Thomson Street, Dundee; T.-Dundee 68344.

Law, Elizabeth A., BSc, MB, ChB. Consultant in Mental Deficiency, Ladysbridge Hospital, Banff; Clinical Senior Lecturer in Mental Health, Aberdeen University, since 1975; b. 14.5.26, Inverness; m., George R. Law; 2 d. Educ. Aberdeen University. Assistant Technical Officer, Intelligence Section, ICI, 1948-49; Science Teacher, Aberdeen Academy, 1950-52; Resident Medical Officer, Woodend Hospital, Aberdeen, 1958-59; Assistant Lecturer, Department of Clinical Chemistry, Aberdeen University, 1959-60; Senior House Officer, Skin Department, Woolmanhill, Aberdeen, 1960-61; Research Assistant, Department of Mental Health, Aberdeen University, 1968-72; Registrar, Woodlands Hospital, Aberdeen, 1972-75. Address: (b.) Ladysbridge Hospital, Banff.

Law, Graham Couper, MA (Cantab), ARSA, RIBA, FRIAS. Partner, The Law & Dunbar-Nasmith Partnership, Architects, since 1957; b. 28.9.23, Glasgow; m., Isobel Evelyn Alexander Drysdale; 1 s.; 3 d. Educ. Merchiston Castle School; Kings College, Cambridge. Royal Engineers, 1941-46; ARIBA, 1951; Council Member: Edinburgh Architectural Association, 1964-69, Royal Incorporation of Architects in Scotland, 1965-67; Member: Architects Registration Council, 1967-75, ARCUK Professional Purposes Committee, 1967-73; Chairman, Workshop and Artists Studio Provision (Scotland) Ltd., 1977-81; Member, RIAS Investigation Committee, 1979-85; Associate, Royal Scottish Academy, 1980. Recreations: drawing; skiing; fishing; shooting. Address: (b.) 16 Dublin Street, Edinburgh, EH1 3RE; T.-031-556 8631.

Law, James, QC, MA, LLB. Queen's Counsel, since 1971; b. 7.6.26, Irvine; m., Kathleen Margaret Gibson (see Kathleen Margaret Law); 2 s.; 1 d. Educ. Kilmarnock Academy; Girvan High School; Glasgow University. Admitted to Faculty of Advocates, 1951; Advocate Depute, 1957-64; Member, Criminal Injuries Compensation Board, since 1970. Address: 7 Gloucester Place, Edinburgh, EH3 6EE; T.-031-225 2974.

Law, Kathleen Margaret, MA, LLB. Partner, Balfour & Manson, Solicitors, since 1978; Member, VAT Tribunal, Scotland; b. 11.2.26, Dumbarton; m., James Law, QC (qv); 2 s.; 1 d. Educ. Dumbarton Academy; St. Andrews University; Glasgow University. Admitted as Solicitor, 1952; Tutor in Conveyancing, Edinburgh University, 1978-79. Recreations: family; good holidays; good food; music. Address: (b.) 58 Frederick Street, Edinburgh, EH1 2LS; T.-031-225 8291.

Lawrence, John Henry, FCA. Honorary Sheriff, Kilmarnock; b. 4.5.05, Cardiff; m., Kathleen Clare Craig; 3 s. Educ. Cardiff High School. Senior Clerk, Deloitte & Co., CA, London, 1929-37;

Assistant Secretary, Richardsons Westgarth & Co., Wallsend, 1938-42; Director and Secretary, Glenfield & Kennedy Ltd., Kilmarnock, 1942-70; former Council Member, Glasgow Management Association; Past Chairman, Glasgow Branch, Institute of Office Management; former Director, Kilmarnock Chamber of Industries; former Member, Taxation Committee, CBI; former Committee Member, Athlone Foundation; former Secretary and President, Kilmarnock Rotary Club; former Director, Ayrshire Branch, British Red Cross Society. Recreations: music; golf; bridge. Address: (h.) 10 Wilson Avenue, Troon, KA10 7AF; T.-0292 312776.

Lawrie, Francis James. Principal, General Agricultural Policy and EEC Co-ordination, Department of Agriculture and Fisheries for Scotland, since 1981; Administrative Co-ordinator, Integrated Development Programme for the Western Isles; b. 30.10.45, Edinburgh; m., Ann Macamon Kerr; 2 s.; 1 d. Educ. Royal High School, Edinburgh. Scottish Office: joined, 1964, Executive Officer, Agriculture Labour and Safety, Agricultural Economics, 1964-70, Higher Executive Officer, Local Government Finance, 1970-78, Senior Executive Officer, 1978-81. Recreations: railway modelling; cricket; golf. Address: (b.) Department of Agriculture and Fisheries for Scotland, Chesser House, 500 Gorgie Road, Edinburgh, EH11 3AW; T.-031-443 4020.

Lawson, Alexander Adamson Hutt, MD, FRCPEdin. Consultant Physician, Fife Health Board, since 1969; Honorary Senior Lecturer, Edinburgh University, since 1979; Medical Adviser, War Pensions Appeal Tribunal, Scotland, since 1979; b. 30.7.37, Dunfermline; m., Barbara Helen Donnet; 3 s.; 1 d. Educ. Dunfermline High School; Edinburgh University. Consultant Member, Clinical Teaching Staff, Faculty of Medicine, Edinburgh University, since 1971; Postgraduate Tutor in Medicine, West Fife, 1973-81; Medical Assessor, General Medical Council, since 1982; Member, Fife Health Board, since 1981; President, West Fife Medical Society, 1982-83; Life Trustee, Carnegie Dunfermline Trust and Carnegie United Kingdom Hero Fund, since 1980; Life Trustee, Carnegie United Kingdom Trust, since 1983; Member, Committee of Safety, Efficacy and Adverse Reactions of Drugs (Committee, Safety of Medicines, DHSS, London), 1982-84. Publication: Common Acute Poisonings. Address: (h.) 2 Park Avenue, Dunfermline, Fife, KY12 7HX; T.-Dunfermline 726435.

Lawson, Rev. Alexander Hamilton, THM, THD, FPHS. Minister, Kilbowie Parish Church, Clydebank, since 1955; b. 16.9.21, Toronto, Canada; m., Martha Stevenson MacDonald; 1 s.; 1 d. Educ. Coatbridge Senior Secondary School; Glasgow University; American Bible College, Chicago; Trinity College, Glasgow; Metropolitan College of Law, St. Albans. RAF, 1941-46; Minister, Prestonpans, 1950-55; Moderator, Dumbarton Presbytery, 1970; Member, Education Committee, General Assembly, eight years; served 15 years on Dunbartonshire Education Committee; Joint Chairman, Religious Education/EIS Group, 1963-74; Governor, Hamilton College of Education, 1967-72; Member, British

Atlantic Committee and Representative Speaker, NATO Conference, Wolfheze, 1983; President, Peace Through NATO Committee (Strathclyde), since 1983; frequent writer in Press; occasional TV and radio programme participant. Recreations: (formerly) football, table tennis and snooker. Address: Manse of Kilbowie, Melfort Avenue, Clydebank, G81 2HX; T.-041-952 1381.

Lawson, Rev. Kenneth Charles, MA. National Adult Adviser, Department of Education, Church of Scotland, since 1984; b. 24.12.34, Agadir, Morocco; m., Mary Elizabeth Anderson; 3 s. Educ. Royal High School, Edinburgh; Preston Lodge School; Stranraer High School; Edinburgh University. Assistant Minister, Brechin Cathedral; Sub-Warden, St. Ninian's Training Centre, Crieff; Minister: Paisley South, Cumbernauld St. Mungo. Trainer, Scottish Association for Counselling. Recreations: walking; reading; painting. Address: (b.) Group Relations Office, St. Colm's Education Centre and College, 23 Inverleith Terrace, Edinburgh, EH3 5NX; T.-031-343 2627.

Laybourn, Professor Peter John Robert, MA (Cantab), PhD. Titular Professor in Electronics and Electrical Engineering, Glasgow University, since 1985; b. 30.7.42, London; m., Ann Elizabeth Chandler; 2 d. Educ. William Hulme's Grammar School; Bristol Grammar School; Clare College, Cambridge. Research Assistant, Leeds University, 1963-66; Research Fellow, Southampton University, 1966-71; Lecturer, then Senior Lecturer, then Reader, Glasgow University, 1971-85; Honorary Editor, Part J, IEE Proceedings. Recreations: sailing; boat-building. Address: (h.) Ashgrove, Waterfoot Row, Thorntonhall, Glasgow; T.-041-644 3992.

Laydon, John Patrick, MA, PhD (Cantab). Manager, American Desk, Locate in Scotland, since 1985; b. 3.6.49, London; 2 s.; 1 d. Educ. St. Edmund's College, Ware; Sidney Sussex College, Cambridge. Scottish Office: Finance Division, 1976, Scottish Education Department, 1977, Housing Division, 1977-78, Private Secretary to Minister of State, 1978-79, Private Secretary to Minister for Industry and Education, 1979-80, Industrial Development Division, 1980-84, European Consultant for West Central Scotland (EEC appointment), 1981-84, Director of Marketing, Locate in Scotland, 1984. Recreations: tennis; rugby; hill-walking. Address: (h.) 19 Bellevue Place, Edinburgh; T.-031-556 9905.

Lazarowicz, Mark. Member, Scottish Executive, Labour Party, since 1980; Member, Edinburgh District Council, since 1980 (Chairman, Recreation Committee, since 1984). Address: (h.) 15/1 Weir Court, Edinburgh, EH1 4BD; T.-031-442 4761.

Leach, Donald, BSc, FIMA, MInstP, MBCS. Principal, Queen Margaret College, Edinburgh, since 1985; b. 24.6.31, Croydon; m., June Valentine Reid; 2 s. Educ. John Ruskin Grammar School, Croydon; London University. Pilot Officer, Navigator, RAF, 1951-53; Physicist, British Jute Trade Research Association, Dundee, 1955-65; Technical Director, A.R.

Bolton & Co. Ltd., Edinburgh, 1965-66; Napier College: Lecturer and Senior Lecturer in Mathematics, 1966-68, Head, Department of Mathematics and Computing, 1968-74, Assistant Principal/Dean, Faculty of Science, 1974-85. Member, South-Eastern Regional Hospital Board, 1969-74, and Lothian Health Board, 1977-81; Member: Scottish Health Service Common Services Agency's Advisory Panel on Information Processing, since 1979, Scottish Health Service Planning Council's Information and Computer Systems Advisory Group, since 1981, Computer Steering Committee (Chairman), since 1981; Institute of Mathematics: Council Member, 1978-81, Chairman, Scottish Branch, 1980-83, Member of Joint IMA-Royal Society of London Mathematical Education Committee, 1981-84; Council for National Academic Awards: Member, Combined Studies Science Board, 1975-79, Science Technology and Society Board, 1979-82 (Chairman, 1981-82), Interfaculty Studies Board, 1981-85, Committee for Science and Technology, 1981-84; Chairman, Science Technology and Society Association, 1982-85; Chairman, Mathematics Course Committees, SCOTEC, 1968-80; Chairman, Diploma in Systems Analysis and Design Course Committee, SCOTBEC, since 1981. Liberal candidate, West Edinburgh, 1959, and East Fife, 1961; Labour candidate, West Perthshire, 1970. Recreations: badminton; hill-walking; skiing; cooking. Address: (h.) 8 Ravelston House Park, Edinburgh, EH4 3LU; T.-031-332 3826.

Leach, Howard Frank, BSc, ARCS, PhD, CChem, FRSC. Senior Lecturer in Chemistry, Edinburgh University, since 1980; b. 16.6.35, Holsworthy; m., Kathleen Phyllis Gillard; 1 s.; 1 d. Educ. Okehampton Grammar School; Imperial College, London. Technical Officer, ICI (Alkali) Ltd., 1957-60; ICI Fellow, Exeter University, 1960-66; Lecturer in Chemistry, Edinburgh University, 1966-80. Recreations: hill-walking; bridge; golf. Address: (h.) 65 Lasswade Road, Edinburgh, EH16 6SZ; T.-031-664 2948.

Leask, Lt.-Gen. Sir Henry, KCB (1970), DSO (1945), OBE (1957). GOC Scotland and Governor of Edinburgh Castle, 1969-72; b. 30.6.13; m.; 1 s.; 2 d. Director of Army Training, 1966-69.

Leathar, Douglas Sutherland, MA, PhD. Director, Advertising Research Unit, Department of Marketing, Strathclyde University, since 1979; b. 22.5.47, Dumbarton; m., Christine M.; 1 s. Educ. Robert Gordon's College, Aberdeen; Aberdeen University. Senior Account Manager, Research Bureau Limited, London; Senior Research Fellow, Strathclyde University, 1977-79. Recreation: DIY. Address: (b.) 173 Cathedral Street, Glasgow, G4 ORQ; T.-041-552 4400.

LeComber, Peter George, BSc, PhD, DSc, FInstPhys, FRSE. Reader in Physics, Dundee University; b. 19.2.41, Ilford, Essex; m., Joy Smith; 1 s.; 1 d. Educ. Leicester University. Research Fellow, Purdue University, USA, 1965-67; SERC Research Fellow, Leicester University, 1967-68; Lecturer, Dundee University, 1968. Awarded Maxwell Premium by IEE, 1983; Duddell Medal, I. of P., 1984; Consultant to a number of companies. Recreations: fishing; music; photography. Address: (b.) Carnegie Laboratory of Physics, Dundee University, Dundee, DD1 4HN; T.-Dundee 23181.

Ledger, Philip Stevens, CBE, FRCM, HonRAM. Principal, Royal Scottish Academy of Music and Drama, since 1982; b. 12.12.37, Bexhill-on-Sea; 1 s.; 1 d. Educ. Bexhill Grammar School; King's College, Cambridge. Master of the Music, Chelmsford Cathedral, 1962-65; East Anglia University: Director of Music, 1965-73, Dean, School of Fine Arts and Music, 1968-71; Conductor, Cambridge University Musical Society, 1973-82; Director of Music and Organist, King's College, Cambridge, 1974-82; Editor, Anthems for Choirs 2 and 3; Composer/Editor, Six Carols with Descants. Publication: The Oxford Book of English Madrigals (Editor). Recreations: swimming; theatre. Address: (b.) Royal Scottish Academy of Music and Drama, St. George's Place, Glasgow, G2 1BS; T.-041-332 4101.

Ledingham, Professor Iain McAllan, MB, ChB, MD (Hons), FRCSEdin, FRCPGlas, FRSE. Professor of Intensive Care, Glasgow University, since 1980; Honorary Consultant, Western Infirmary, Glasgow, since 1973; Director, Hyperbaric Unit, Western Infirmary, Glasgow, since 1968; b. 26.2.35, Glasgow; m., Eileen Riste; 3 s. Educ. King's Park Senior Secondary School, Glasgow; Central School, Aberdeen; Glasgow University. Western Infirmary, Glasgow: House Officer appointments, 1958-60, Hall Fellow in Surgery, 1960, Senior Research Fellow (MRC), Lecturer/Senior Lecturer/Reader in Surgery; Chairman, Chairmen of Divisions Committee, Western Infirmary/Gartnavel General Hospital; Member, Greater Glasgow Health Board; author/editor of several books. Recreations: jogging; swimming; sports; hill-walking; music; woodwork; reading. Address: (h.) 37 Hillside Road, Mansewood, Glasgow, G43 1DB; T.-041-649 8709.

Lee, Professor Michael Radcliffe, MA, DM, DPhil (Oxon), FRCP, FRCPE. Professor of Clinical Pharmacology, Edinburgh University, since 1984; b. 21.11.34, Manchester; m., Judith Ann Horrocks; 1 s.; 1 d. Educ. Manchester Grammar School; Brasenose College, Oxford. Beit Memorial Fellow for Medical Research; Lecturer in Medicine, Oxford University; Lecturer in Medicine, St. Thomas's Hospital Medical School; Medical Director, then Managing Director, Weddel Pharmaceuticals Ltd.; Senior Lecturer in Clinical Pharmacology, Leeds University. Publications: books on medicine and hypertension. Recreations: gardening; walking; old trains; old books. Address: (b.) Department of Clinical Pharmacology, Royal Infirmary, Edinburgh; T.-031-229 2477, Ext. 2599.

Lee, Professor Thomas Alexander, MSc, DLitt, CA, ATII, FRSA. Professor of Accountancy and Finance and Head, Department of Accounting, Edinburgh University, since 1974; b. 18.5.41, Edinburgh; m., Ann Margaret Brown; 1 s.; 1 d. Educ. Melville College; Edinburgh University. Peat, Marwick, Mitchell & Co., CA; Lecturer: Strathclyde University, Edinburgh University;

Professor, Liverpool University. Director of Accounting and Auditing Research, Institute of Chartered Accountants of Scotland, 1983-84. Recreations: long distance running; plumbing. Address: (h.) 34 Bramdean Rise, Edinburgh, EH10 6JR.

Lee, Professor William Robert, MD, FRCPath. Professor in Ophthalmic Pathology, Glasgow University, since 1979; b. 14.10.32, Sale, Cheshire; m., Noelle Elisabeth Stinson; 2 d. Educ. William Hulme's Grammar School; Manchester University. House Officer, Manchester Royal Infirmary, 1957-58; Demonstrator in Anatomy, Bristol University, 1958-60; Research Fellow, Institute of Orthopaedics, London, 1960-62; Trainee Pathologist, St. Mary's Hospital, Westminster Hospital, 1962-65; Lecturer, then Senior Lecturer, Glasgow University, 1965-68; MRC Research Fellow, Harvard University, 1969-70; Editor, Current Research In Ophthalmic Electron Microscopy, Volumes 3/4. Recreations: curling; bridge. Address: (h.) High Craigton, Stockiemuir Road, Milngavie, Glasgow, G62 7HA; T.-041-956 3286.

Leechman, Lord (James Graham), MA, BSc, LLB. Senator, College of Justice in Scotland, 1965-76; b. 6.10.06, Glasgow; m., Margaret Helen Edgar; 2 d. Educ. High School of Glasgow; Glasgow University. Admitted Advocate, 1932; Advocate Depute, 1947; Clerk of Justiciary and King's Counsel, 1949; Solicitor General for Scotland, 1964. Recreation: golf. Address: (h.) 626 Queensferry Road, Edinburgh, EH4 6AT; T.-031-339 6513.

Lees, Gordon McArthur, MB, ChB, PhD. Reader, Department of Pharmacology, Aberdeen University, since 1981; Secretary, Editorial Board, British Journal of Pharmacology, since 1984; b. 6.9.38, Dundee; m., Doris Irene Manson; 1 s.; 1 d. Educ. Aberdeen Grammar School; Aberdeen University. House Surgeon, Neurosurgical Unit, and House Physician, Professorial Medical Unit, Aberdeen Royal Infirmary, 1961-62; Aberdeen University: Research Fellow, then Lecturer, Department of Physiology, 1962-68, Lecturer, Department of Pharmacology, 1968-72, Senior Lecturer, 1972-81. Research Associate, Loyola University Stritch School of Medicine, Chicago, 1970 (Visiting Professor, 1974); Visiting Research Scholar, Flinders University of South Australia, 1982-83. Recreations: golf; music; astronomy. Address: (b.) Department of Pharmacology and Editorial Office of British Journal of Pharmacology, Aberdeen University, Aberdeen; T.-0224 40241, Ext. MC 242, and 0224 641559.

Lees, James George Grahame, MA, LLB, NP. Partner, McLean & Stewart, Solicitors, Dunblane, since 1974; Member, Forth Valley Health Board, since 1983 (Chairman, Service Committees, since 1983); Member, Judicial Commission, and Board of Practice and Procedure, General Assembly of the Church of Scotland; b. 22.6.46, Perth; m., Hazel Margaret Raffan; 1 s.; 2 d. Educ. Dundee High School; St. Andrews University; Edinburgh University. Solicitor, J. & F. Anderson, WS, Edinburgh, 1969-72; Solicitor, McLean & Stewart, Solicitors, Dunblane, since

1972. Secretary, Dunblane Sports Club Ltd.; Elder, Dunblane Cathedral Church of Scotland. Recreations: walking; badminton; tennis; photography. Address: (h.) Northbank, St. Margaret's Drive, Dunblane, FK15 ODP; T.-Dunblane 822928.

Lees, Martin McArthur, MD, FRCOG. Consultant Obstetrician and Gynaecologist, Edinburgh Royal Infirmary, since 1969; Senior Lecturer, Edinburgh University, since 1969; b. 24.4.35; m., Maureen Yetton. Educ. Aberdeen Grammar School; Aberdeen University. House Surgeon to Professor Sir Dugald Baird; Research Fellow in Obstetrics and Gynaecology, Edinburgh University; Registrar, then Senior Registrar, to Professor R. J. Kellar, Edinburgh Royal Infirmary; Clinical Tutor, Edinburgh University. Regional Postgraduate Advisor in Obstetrics and Gynaecology; Council Member, Medical and Dental Defence Union of Scotland. Recreations: ornithology; music. Address: (b.) Ward 36, Royal Infirmary, Edinburgh, EH3; T.-031-229 2477.

Lefley, John, MA, ACIS. Director, Scottish Association of Master Bakers, since 1983; Member, Employers' Side, Scottish Bakery Joint Industrial Council, since 1982; b. 23.2.39, Kings Lynn; m., Marjorie K.M. Scott; 1 s.; 1 d. Educ. Culford School; Edinburgh University. Assistant Secretary, NFU of Scotland, 1967-82; Director-Designate, Scottish Association of Master Bakers, 1982-83. Various offices, Scottish Liberal Party, from 1956 (none now held). Recreations: inland waterways; playing bridge (badly); politics (desultory); support of anything Scottish. Address: (h.) 3 Riselaw Road, Edinburgh, EH10 6HR; T.-031-447 1535.

Leggate, Peter James Arthur, JP, FRICS. Chartered Surveyor, since 1967; Farmer, since 1972; a Director, Scottish Society for Prevention of Cruelty to Animals; b. 17.10.43; m., Jenifer Susan Gammell; 1 s.; 1 d. Educ. Wrekin College. Qualified as Chartered Surveyor, 1967; Kenneth Ryden & Partners, 1967-70; P.G. Matineau, Jedburgh, 1970-72; Founder, P.J. Leggate & Co., Edinburgh, 1973-79 (Sole Principal, since 1979). Recreations: horses; sailing; skiing. Address: (h.) Westertoun, Westruther, Gordon, Berwickshire, TD3 6NE; T.-05784 270.

Legge, Joseph Smith, MD, FRCPEdin. Consultant in Thoracic Medicine, Grampian Health Board, since 1977; Honorary Senior Lecturer, Aberdeen University, since 1977; b. 12.11.43, Portessie, Banffshire; m., Sandra Leisk; 1 s.; 1 d. Educ. Buckie High School; Aberdeen University. Recreations: golf; photography. Address: (h.) 76 Fountainhall Road, Aberdeen; T.-0224 639590.

Leighton, Professor Kenneth, MA, DMus, HonDMus, LRAM, HonFRCM. Reid Professor of Music, Edinburgh University; Composer, Pianist, Conductor; b. 2.10.29, Wakefield; m.; 1 s.; 1 d. Educ. Queen Elizabeth Grammar School, Wakefield; Queen's College, Oxford. Gregory Fellow in Music, Leeds University; Lecturer and Reader in Composition, Edinburgh University;

Fellow, Worcester College, Oxford; University Lecturer, Oxford University. More than 100 musical works published, including three symphonies, nine concertos, piano music, chamber music, choral, organ and Church music, one opera. Recreation: walking. Address: (h.) 9 Bright's Crescent, Edinburgh, EH9 2DB; T.-031-667 3113.

Leitch, David Alexander. Under Secretary, Social Work Services Group, Scottish Education Department, since 1983; b. 4.4.31, Bournemouth; m., Marie Tain; 2 s.; 1 d. Ministry of Supply, 1948-58; Department of Agriculture and Fisheries for Scotland: Assistant Principal, 1959, Principal, 1963, Assistant Secretary, 1971; Local Government Finance, Central Services: Assistant Secretary, 1976, Under Secretary, 1981. Recreations: climbing; hill-walking. Address: (h.) 3 The Glebe, Cramond, Edinburgh, EH4 6NW.

Leitch, John Stewart, JP. Member, City of Dundee District Council, since 1974; Member, North of Scotland Hydro Electric Board Consultative Committee, since 1979; b. 14.3.27, Musselburgh; m., Evelyn Stephen Donald. Educ. Harris Academy; Brechin High School. Wholesale Merchant, 1942-45; Royal Navy, 1945-47; Wholesale Merchant, 1947-85. Recreation: gardening. Address: (h.) 16 Shaftesbury Park, Dundee, DD2 1LB; T.-Dundee 644182.

Leithead, Walter Douglas Murray, CA, MCIT. Finance Director, Scottish Road Services Ltd., since 1972, Scottish Parcel Services Ltd., since 1980, and Northern Ireland Carriers Ltd., since 1982; Member, Forth Valley Health Board; b. 29.10.39, Hawick; m., Nancy Ingles; 1 s.; 1 d. Educ. Hawick High School; Glasgow University. Address: (h.) Beechmount, Carronvale Road, Larbert, Stirlingshire; T.-032455 6824.

Lenman, Bruce Philip, MA (Aberdeen), MLitt (Cantab), FRHistSoc. Reader in Modern History, St. Andrews University, since 1983; b. 9.4.38, Aberdeen. Educ. Aberdeen Grammar School; Aberdeen University; St. John's College, Cambridge. Assistant Professor, Victoria University, Canada, 1963; Lecturer in Imperial and Commonwealth History, Queen's College, Dundee (St. Andrews University), 1963-67; Lecturer, Dundee University, 1967-72; United College, St. Andrews: Lecturer, Department of Modern History, 1972-78, Senior Lecturer, 1978-83; British Academy Fellow, Newberry Library, Chicago, 1982; John Carter Brown Library Fellow, Brown University, Providence, RI, 1984. Publications: Esk to Tweed, 1975; An Economic History of Modern Scotland 1660-1976, 1977 (Scottish Arts Council Award); The Jacobite Risings in Britain 1689-1746, 1980 (Scottish Arts Council Award); Scotland 1746-1832, 1981; The Jacobite Clans of the Great Glen 1650-1784, 1984. Recreations: golf; squash; badminton; Scottish country dancing; hill-walking. Address: (b.) Department of Modern History, St. Andrews University, St. Andrews, KY16 9AL; T.-0334 76161.

Lenman, John Andrew Reginald, FRSE, MB, ChB, FRCPEdin. Reader in Neurology, Dundee University, since 1960; Honorary Consultant

Neurologist, Tayside Health Board, since 1960; b. 28.8.24, Shillong, India; m., Muriel Frances Selby-Brown; 1 s.; 3 d. Educ. Michael Hall; Edinburgh University. House Physician, Edinburgh Royal Infirmary and House Surgeon, Neurosurgical Unit, Bangour Hospital, 1948-49; National Service, RAF, 1949-51 (active service, Singapore); Assistant in Physiology, St. Andrews University, 1952-54; Senior House Officer, Edinburgh Royal Infirmary, 1955-56; Research Fellow and Honorary Registrar, Neurology, Northern General Hospital, Edinburgh, 1956-58; First Assistant in Neurology, Kings College, Newcastle-upon-Tyne and Royal Victoria Infirmary, 1958-59. Publications: Clinical Neurophysiology, 1975; Neurological Therapeutics (Co-author), 1981; Clinical Electromyography, 1983 (Co-author). Recreations: hill-walking; reading; music. Address: (h.) 31 Dundee Road West, Broughty Ferry, Dundee, DD5 1NB; T.-0382 77707.

Lennie, Daniel, JP. Chairman, Midlothian District Licensing Board, since 1981; Member, Midlothian District Council, since 1980; b. 6.2.47, Edinburgh; m., Thelma Halliday; 2 s.; 1 d. Educ. St. Margaret's School, Loanhead; St. David's School, Dalkeith. AUEW: Shop Steward, 1973-80, Convener, 1977-80, Bertrams Ltd., Edinburgh; Chairman, Bonnyrigg/Lasswade Community Council, 1978-80; Chairman, Bonnyrigg/Lasswade Labour Party, since 1979; President, Dolphin Club for Mentally Handicapped. Recreations: politics; writing bad doggerel. Address: (h.) 10 Sherwood Walk, Bonnyrigg, Midlothian, EH19 3NL; T.-031-660 3492.

Lennox, Iain MacIntyre, MB, ChB, MRCP, DObstRCOG. Consultant Physician, Geriatric Unit, Victoria Infirmary, since 1980; b. 24.11.48, Glasgow; m., Helen Edith Marshall; 1 s.; 1 d. Educ. Hutchesons' Boys Grammar School, Glasgow; Glasgow University. Secretary, Geriatric Medicine Sub-Committee, Greater Glasgow Area Medical Committee, since 1983; Honorary Medical Adviser, Glasgow Abbeyfield Society. Recreations: golf; squash; badminton. Address: (h.) 29 Langtree Avenue, Whitecraigs, Glasgow, G46; T.-041-638 1480.

Leonard, Robert Charles Frederick, BSc, MD, MB, BS, MRCP, FRCPEdin. Senior Lecturer in Clinical Oncology, Edinburgh University, since 1983; Honorary Consultant Physician, Lothian Health Board, since 1983; b. 11.5.47, Merthyr Tydfil; m., Tania Smith; 3 d. Educ. Merthyr Tydfil County Grammar School; Charing Cross Hospital Medical School, London. House Officer, Charing Cross, West London and Fulham Hospitals, 1971-73; Senior House Officer, Hammersmith Hospital, 1973; Medical Registrar, Oxford Hospitals, 1974-76; Leukaemia Research Fund Fellow, Oxford University, 1976-79; Senior Registrar and University Lecturer, Royal Victoria and General Hospitals, Newcastle-upon-Tyne, 1979-82; Cancer Research Campaign Travelling Fellow, Sidney Farber Cancer Institute and Harvard Medical School, Boston, 1982. Recreations: listening to music; playing soccer. Address: (h.) 59 Woodfield Park, Edinburgh, EH13 ORA; T.-031-441 6131.

Leonard, Wilfred. Member, Western Isles Island Council (Chairman, Planning and Development); Member, Island Policy Committee, Scottish Accident Prevention Council; Member, Highlands and Islands Area Manpower Board, Manpower Services Commission; b. 9.5.12, Humberton, Brafferton, Yorkshire; m., Margaret Ross; 1 s.; 2 d. Educ. Brafferton Church of England School. Staffordshire County Police, 1935-67 (retired in rank of Inspector); Member, Inverness County Council, 1973-74; Past Chairman: Harris District Council, South Harris Agricultural Society, Harris Council of Social Service; former Member, Highlands and Islands Consultative Council. Recreation: gardening. Address: (h.) Cnoc-Na-Ba, Finsbay, Isle of Harris; T.-Manish 232.

Le Roux, Joan Catherine. Member, Argyll and Clyde Health Board, since 1981; b. 23.4.30, Edinburgh; m., Peter Hugo Le Roux; 3 s. Educ. Mary Erskine College. Member, Argyll and Bute Health Council, 1975-80 (Chairman, 1977-79); Chairman, Argyll Conservative Association, 1976-78 (President, 1978-80); Vice-Chairman, Conservative Women's Scottish Council, 1981-82; Chairman, Dunoon and Cowal Cancer Research Committee, since 1970 (Chairman, 1982-85) (National Appeals Committee, 1983). Recreations: reading; sewing; music. Address: (h.) Berryburn, Dunoon, Argyll; T.-0369 2028.

Leslie, Allan Eunson, BSc, FRSH, MREHIS. Director of Environmental Health, Orkney Islands Council, since 1975; b. 15.11.41, Garmouth, Morayshire; m., Vivia Mary Stewart. Educ. Mackie Academy, Stonehaven; Harris Academy, Dundee; Dundee College of Science and Technology; Robert Gordon's College of Further Education; Strathclyde University. Dundee Corporation: Student Sanitary Inspector, 1959-63, Assistant Sanitary Inspector, 1963-64; Assistant Sanitary Inspector, Kincardine County Council, 1964-70; Area Sanitary Inspector, Sutherland County Council, 1970-72. Recreations: gardening; walking; sea fishing; bowls; bridge; reading. Address: (b.) Orkney Islands Council, Environmental Health Department, Council Offices, School Place, Kirkwall, Orkney Isles; T.-0856 3535, Ext. 275.

Leslie, Daniel Coyle, JP. Member, Kirkcaldy District Council, since 1974 (Vice-Chairman, Housing Committee, since 1984); b. 6.2.41, Twechar; m., May Lockhart. Educ. St. Columba RC High School, Cowdenbeath. Member, Kirkcaldy Town Council, 1971-74; Chairman, Kirkcaldy Licensing Board, 1980-84; Past Chairman, Kirkcaldy Justices Committee; former Vice Chairman, Kirkcaldy Constituency Labour Party. Recreation: pottering about in the garden. Address: (h.) 88 Cawdor Crescent, Kirkcaldy, KY2 6LJ; T.-0592 265665.

Leslie, David James, BArch, RIBA, FRIAS. Architect; Partner, Walter Underwood & Partners; President, Glasgow Institute of Architects, 1984-86; Vice-President, Royal Incorporation of Architects in Scotland, since 1984; b. 15.5.32, Glasgow; m., Olive; 2 s.; 1 d. Educ. Hillhead

High School; Glasgow School of Art; Royal College of Science and Technology. Qualified, 1957; Registered Architect, 1959; joined Wylie Shanks & Underwood, 1957, and Walter Underwood & Partners, 1960; Honorary Secretary, Glasgow Institute of Architects, 1979-82 (Vice President, three times). Elder and Property Convener, Netherlee Church, Glasgow; Convener, Festival of Architecture in Scotland, 1984; Convener, Scotstyle Group. Recreations: singing; painting; photography. Address: (b.) 2 La Belle Place, Glasgow, G3 7LH; T.-041-332 7227.

Leslie, Professor Frank Matthews, JP, BSc, PhD, FIMA, FInstP, FRSE. Professor of Mathematics, Strathclyde University, since 1982; b. 8.3.35, Dundee; m., Ellen Leitch Reoch; 1 s.; 1 d. Educ. Harris Academy; Queen's College, Dundee. Assistant Lecturer, Manchester University, 1959-61; Research Associate, MIT, USA, 1961-62; Lecturer, Newcastle University, 1962-68; Visiting Assistant Professor, Johns Hopkins University, USA, 1966-67; Strathclyde University: Senior Lecturer, 1968-71, Reader, 1971-79, Personal Professor, 1979-82; Consultant, RSRE Malvern; Annual Award, British Society of Rheology, 1982. Recreations: golf; hill-walking. Address: (b.) Department of Mathematics, Strathclyde University, Livingstone Tower, 26 Richmond Street, Glasgow, G1 1XH; T.-041-552 4400.

Lessels, Norman, CA. Partner, Chiene & Tait, CA, since 1980; Vice-President, Institute of Chartered Accountants of Scotland; Deputy Chairman, Standard Life Assurance Company; Chairman, Scottish Eastern Investment Trust PLC; Chairman, New Darien Oil Trust plc; Chairman, Heriot Hotels Ltd; Director, Anderson Strathclyde PLC; Director, The Murrayfield plc; Director, James Lindsay & Son plc; b. 2.9.38, Edinburgh; m., Christine Stevenson; 1 s. Educ. Edinburgh Academy. Partner, Ernst & Whinney, until 1980. Recreations: golf; music; bridge. Address: (b.) 3 Albyn Place, Edinburgh; T.-031-225 7515.

Lessnoff, Michael Harry, MA, BPhil. Senior Lecturer in Politics, Glasgow University, since 1976; b. 23.1.40, Glasgow. Educ. High School of Glasgow; Glasgow University; Balliol College, Oxford. Assistant Principal, Department of Education and Science, 1965-66; Lecturer, Department of Politics, Glasgow University, 1966-76; Visiting Associate Professor, College of William and Mary, Williamsburg, USA, 1977-78. Won Snell Exhibition, 1963. Publication: The Structure of Social Science, 1974. Recreations: literature; art; science; travel. Address: (h.) 58 White Street, Glasgow, G11 5EB; T.-041-334 6969.

Letham, David. President, Scottish Football League, 1981-85; Vice President, Scottish Football Association, 1981-85; b. 7.5.22, Glasgow; m., Nessie Balfour; 1 d. Educ. John Street Secondary School, Glasgow; Scottish School of Physical Education, Jordanhill. RAF, 1942-46; Teacher, John Street Secondary School, 1948-82. Member, Queen's Park FC, since 1939. Address: (h.) 15 Beech Avenue, Newton Mearns, Glasgow, G77 5PP; T.-041-639 1216.

Lethbridge, Sir Thomas, 7th Bt; b. 17.7.50; m., Susan Elizabeth Rocke; 4 s.; 1 d. Educ. Milton Abbey; Cirencester Agricultural College. Pedigree Sheep Breeder; Proprietor of game farm. Address: (h.) Mains of Shiels, Sauchen, Aberdeenshire.

Levein, Charles Peter Alexander, MA, PhD. Senior Principal Research Officer, Scottish Office, since 1977; b. 16.5.40, Devonport; 1 s.; 2 d. Educ. Dunfermline High School; Edinburgh University. Demonstrator, Geography Department, Edinburgh University; Research Officer, Central Planning Research Unit, Scottish Development Department; Senior Research Officer, WC Scotland Planning Team; Principal Research Officer, Scottish Office Urban Deprivation Unit. Recreations: squash; golf; bowls; tennis. Address: (h.) 45 The Wynd, Dalgety Bay, Fife; T.-0383 822952.

Leven and Melville, Earl of, (Alexander Robert Melville). Lord Lieutenant, Nairn; Company Director; President, British Ski Federation, since 1981; Honorary President, Scottish National Ski Council; Chairman, Governors, Gordonstoun School, since 1971; b. 13.5.24, London; m., Susan Steuart-Menzies; 2 s.; 1 d. Educ. Eton. Coldstream Guards, 1942-52 (retired as Captain); ADC to Governor General of New Zealand, 1951-52; Convener, Nairn County Council, 1970-74. Recreations: shooting; fishing; skiing. Address: (h.) Glenferness House, Nairn, Scotland, IV12 5UP; T.-03095 202.

Levi, Professor Anthony Herbert Tigar, MA (Oxon), DPhil (Oxon), STL. Buchanan Professor of French Language and Literature, St. Andrews University, since 1971; b. 30.5.29, London; m., Honor Marjorie Riley; 2 d. Educ. Prior Park College; Oxford University; Munich University. Member, Jesuit Order, 1949-71; Lecturer, Reader, Professor, Warwick University, 1965-71; Lecturer, Christ Church, Oxford, and Tutor, Campion Hall, Oxford, 1965-71. Publications: French Moralists: The Theory of the Passions 1585-1649, 1964; Religion in Practice, 1966; Erasmus, The Praise of Folly (Editor), 1971; Humanism in France, 1970. Address: (h.) East Castlemount, North Castle Street, St. Andrews, KY16 9BG; T.-St. Andrews 73926.

Levison, Rev. Christopher Leon, MA, BD (Hons). Minister, Paisley High Church, since 1983; b. 7.4.47, Gorebridge, Midlothian; m., Rosemary Anne Milne Logan; 2 d. Educ. George Watson's College; Kirkcaldy High School; St. Andrews University; Edinburgh University. Assistant Minister, South Leith, 1971-73; Minister, Coltness Memorial Church, Newmains, 1973-78 (also Community Councillor); Associate Chaplain, Aberdeen University, 1978-83. Manager and Trustee, Kibble List D School. Recreations: sailing; hill-walking. Address: 178 Glasgow Road, Paisley, PA1 3LT; T.-041-889 3316.

Lewis, James, JP. Member, Kirkcaldy District Council, since 1984; Area Organiser, Community Education, Fife Regional Council, since 1970; b. 15.7.23, Treorchy, South Wales. Local Chairman, Toc H; Chairman, PHAB, Fife; Chairman,

Glenrothes Community House. Recreations: dogs; music; people. Address: (b.) Youth and Community Office, South Street, Glenrothes, Fife; T.-Glenrothes 743187.

Lewis, John W., BSc, MSc. Senior Lecturer in Management Studies, Glasgow University, since 1983; b. 23.10.40, London; m., Susan; 3 s. Educ. London University and Cranfield. Production Manager and Management Consultant before joining Glasgow University, 1970. Chairman, Scottish Co-operative Development Committee. Address: (h.) 29 Hillside Road, Cardross, Dunbartonshire; T.-Cardross 841592.

Lewis, William Alexander, MBE, FInstWM. General Manager, Cleansing Department, City of Dundee District Council, since 1964; b. 26.8.20, Glasgow; m., Elizabeth Bonar Lewis; 1 s.; 1 d. Educ. Govan Secondary School; Royal Technical College, Glasgow. Manager, Cleansing Department, Greenock, 1959-64. Past President, Institute of Wastes Management. Recreation: golf. Address: (h.) 7 Menteith Street, Dundee; T.-0382 76082.

Liddell, Claire, LRAM, ARCM, DRSAM. Musician/Composer; b. Glasgow. Educ. Royal College of Music, London; Royal Scottish Academy of Music. Compositions mainly for choral ensembles and for voice and piano; arranger of Burns songs and Scots folk songs; other works include song cycles to words by British and American poets; Journalist (music criticism and features on the arts); author of book on improvision and keyboard harmony. Recreations: cricket enthusiast; reading; walking; interest in the arts. T.-North Berwick 3769.

Liddell, Donald John, LLB (Hons). Director of Administration and Legal Services, Clydesdale District Council, since 1984; b. 20.3.50, Hamilton; m., Veronica; 1 s.; 2 d. Educ. Hamilton Academy; Glasgow University. Legal Apprentice/Assistant, Livingston Development Corporation, 1971-75; Legal Assistant/Officer, Clydesdale District Council, 1975-84. Address: (b.) District Offices, South Vennel, Lanark, ML11 7JT; T.-Lanark 61331.

Liddell, Helen Lawrie. Scottish Secretary, Labour Party, since 1977; b. 6.12.50; m.; 1 s. Educ. St. Patrick's High School, Coatbridge; Strathclyde University. STUC, 1971-76; BBC Scotland, 1976-77.

Liddell, John Chalmers, MA, LLB. Depute Chief Executive, Grampian Regional Council, since 1979; b. 25.3.46, Dumfries; m., Laura; 2 s.; 1 d. Educ. High School of Glasgow; St. Andrews University. Depute County Clerk, Berwickshire, 1972; Assistant Director of Administration, Borders Region, 1975; Depute Director of Law and Administration, Grampian Region, 1975. Secretary, Aberdeen Ski Club. Recreations: skiing; golf. Address: (b.) Woodhill House, Ashgrove Road West, Aberdeen, AB9 2LU.

Liddiard, John Kendall, VRD, MA (Oxon), LLB, WS. Writer to the Signet, since 1951; b. 19.2.27, Abbassia, Egypt; m., 1, Sheila Margaret Blyth Cameron; 1 s.; 3 d.; 2, Frances Marion Patricia Rooney or Scollay. Educ. Royal High School, Edinburgh; Queen's College, Oxford; Edinburgh University. Royal Navy, 1944-47; RNVR (subsequently RNR), 1949-73 (Commander); in private practice, since 1951, with Melville & Lindesay, WS, Edinburgh, and Burnett, Walker, Lindesay & Rae, WS, Edinburgh. Recreations: fly fishing; sea angling; railway modelling. Address: (h.) 33 Learmonth Court, Edinburgh, EH4 1PB; T.-031-332 5977.

Liddle, Sir Donald Ross, Kt (1971), JP. Chairman, Cumbernauld Development Corporation, 1972-78; Vice Lord Lieutenant, City of Glasgow, 1978-80; b. 11.10.06; m.; 1 s.; 2 d. Educ. Allan Glen's School, Glasgow. RAOC, 1939-45 (Major, 1944); Lord Provost of Glasgow, 1969-72; Hon. LLD, Strathclyde, 1971.

Lilley, David M.J., BSc, MSc, PhD. Reader in Biochemstry, Dundee University; b. 28.5.48, Colchester; m., Patricia Mary Biddle; 2 d. Educ. Gilberd School, Colchester; Durham University. Research Fellow: Warwick University, 1973-75, Oxford University, 1975-76; Research Investigator, Searle Research Laboratories, 1976-81; Lecturer, Dundee University, 1981. Colworth Medal, Biochemical Society; Committee Member: Nucleotide Group, Biochemical Society (Secretary-Elect), British Biophysical Society. Recreation: tennis. Address: (b.) Biochemistry Department, Dundee University, Dundee, DD1 4HN; T.-0382 23181, Ext. 4243.

Lilwall, Nicholas Brier, BSc, MA, PhD. Head, Agricultural Resource Management Department, Edinburgh School of Agriculture, since 1985; b. 15.8.37, Liverpool; m., Anne; 2 s.; 1 d. Educ. Truro School, Cornwall; Leeds University; Minnesota University. Assistant Lecturer, Leeds University, 1964-66; Research Assistant, Minnesota University, 1967-71; Economist, Edinburgh School of Agriculture, since 1971. Recreation: squash. Address: (b.) Edinburgh School of Agriculture, 6 South Oswald Road, Edinburgh, EH9 2HH; T.-031-668 1921.

Lindop, George Black McMeekin, BSc, MB, ChB, MRCPath. Senior Lecturer in Histopathology, Glasgow University, since 1979; Honorary Consultant in Histopathology, Western Infirmary, Glasgow, since 1979; b. 28.3.45, Glasgow; m., Sharon Ann Cornell; 2 s.; 1 d. Educ. Hillhead High School; Glasgow University. Senior House Officer/Registrar, then Lecturer/Honorary Senior Registrar, Department of Histopathology, Western Infirmary, Glasgow; Consultant Histopathologist, Ayrshire and Arran Health Board; Consulting Editor, Histology/Histopathology. Recreations: sport; the outdoors; music; cinema. Address: (b.) Department of Pathology, Western Infirmary, Glasgow; T.-041-339 8822.

Lindsay, Alistair, MA, LLB, NP, FSA Scot. Editor, Clan Lindsay Society Publications, since 1947; Consultant, Stewarts, Nicol, D. & J. Hill (Partner, 1948-82); b. 5.2.23, Glasgow; m., Agnes Calder Hamilton Neilson; 1 s.; 1 d. Educ. Pollokshields Secondary School; Larkhall Academy; Glasgow University. Governor, Baillies

Institution Free Public Library, six years; Secretary, Old Glasgow Club, 12 years; Secretary, (Glasgow) Ballad Club, 24 years; Life Member, Glasgow Art Gallery and Museums Association; Director: Barloch Proprietors Ltd., Popular Properties Ltd. Publication: The Laird of Barloch 1632-1984, 1985. Recreations: genealogy; local history. Address: (h.) Bruntsfield, 16 Dalziel Drive, Pollokshields, Glasgow, G41; T.-041-423 8440.

Lindsay, Jean Olivia, MA, PhD (Cantab), FRHistS. Chairman, Saltire Society, since 1983; b. 10.12.10, Bangalore, India; m., H.D.R.P. Lindsay; 1 s.; 2 d. Educ. St. Serfs School, Edinburgh; Brympton School, Gibraltar; three schools in Cologne for children of families serving with BAOR; Queen's College, London; Girton College, Cambridge. Research Fellow, Girton College, 1936-39; War Service, Ministry of Information, 1939-41; Research Department, Foreign Office, 1941-43; SOE, 1943-45; Fellow, Girton College, subsequently Director of Studies in History and University Lecturer, 1947-60; Head Mistress, St. George's School for Girls, Edinburgh, 1960-76. Publications: Trade and Peace with Old Spain; various articles; Editor, Cambridge Modern History, Vol. VII. Recreations: history; drawing; entertaining children. Address: (h.) 3 Ann Street, Edinburgh, EH4 1PL; T.-031-332 3979.

Lindsay, John Maurice, CBE, TD, DLitt, HonFRIAS. Consultant, Scottish Civic Trust (Director, 1967-83); Secretary-General, Europa Nostra, since 1983; b. 21.7.18; m., Aileen Joyce Gordon; 1 s.; 3 d. Educ. Glasgow Academy; Scottish National Academy of Music. Drama Critic, Scottish Daily Mail, 1946-47; Music Critic, The Bulletin, 1946-60; Border Television: Programme Controller, 1961-62, Production Controller, 1962-64, Features Executive and Chief Interviewer, 1964-67. Atlantic-Rockefeller Award, 1946; Editor: Scots Review, 1949-50, The Scottish Review, 1975-85; Member, Historic Buildings Council for Scotland, since 1976; Council Member, Association of Scottish Literary Studies, since 1983; Trustee, New Lanark Conservation Trust, since 1985; Vice-Chairman, Formakin Trust, since 1985; Trustee, National Heritage Memorial Fund, 1980-84; HonDLitt, Glasgow, 1982. Publications: poetry: The Advancing Day, 1940; Perhaps To-morrow, 1941; Predicament, 1942; No Crown for Laughter: Poems, 1943; The Enemies of Love: Poems 1941-45, 1946; Selected Poems, 1947; Hurlygush: Poems in Scots, 1948; At the Wood's Edge, 1950; Ode for St. Andrew's Night and Other Poems, 1951; The Exiled Heart: Poems 1941-56, 1957; Snow Warning and Other Poems, 1962; One Later Day and Other Poems, 1964; This Business of Living, 1969; Comings and Goings: Poems, 1971; Selected Poems 1942-72, 1973; The Run from Life, 1975; Walking Without an Overcoat, Poems 1972-76, 1977; Collected Poems, 1979; A Net to Catch the Winds and Other Poems, 1981; The French Mosquitoes' Woman and other diversions and poems; prose: A Pocket Guide to Scottish Culture; The Scottish Renaissance; The Lowlands of Scotland: Glasgow and the North; Robert Burns: The Man, His Work, The Legend; Dunoon: The Gem of the Clyde Coast; The Lowlands of Scotland: Edinburgh and the South; Clyde Waters: Variations and Diversions on a Theme of Pleasure; The Burns Encyclopedia; Killochan Castle; By Yon Bonnie Banks: A Gallimaufry; Environment: A Basic Human Right; Portrait of Glasgow; Robin Philipson; History of Scottish Literature; Lowland Scottish Villages; Francis George Scott and the Scottish Renaissance; The Buildings of Edinburgh (Co-author); Thank You For Having Me: A Personal Memoir; Unknown Scotland (Co-author); The Scottish Castle: A Constable Guide; Count All Men Mortal: The Story of the Scottish Provident Institution; edited various anthologies. Recreations: enjoying and adding to Compact Disc collection; walking. Address: (h.) 7 Milton Hill, Milton, Dumbarton, G82 2TS; T.-Dumbarton 61500.

Lindsay, Nigel Bruce, MA, MLitt. Member, Aberdeen District Council, since 1973; Chairman, Aberdeen and North Committee, Gas Consumers Council for Scotland, since 1984; Regional Organiser, Shelter, North of Scotland, since 1975; b. 27.3.48, Scunthorpe. Educ. Aberdeen University. Member, National Executive, Scottish Liberal Party, 1972-76; Member, Aberdeen University Court, 1976-80. Address: (h.) 18 Lochside Terrace, Bridge of Don, Aberdeen; T.-0224 820575.

Lindsay, 14th Earl of, (William Tucker Lindesay-Bethune); b. 28.4.01; m., Marjory Cross; 2 s.; 2 d. Former Major, Scots Guards; Member, Fife County Council, 1956-64; President, Shipwrecked Fishermen and Mariners Royal Benevolent Society, 1966-76; Deputy Lieutenant, Fife; Member, Queen's Bodyguard for Scotland (Royal Company of Archrs). Address: (h.) Lahill, Upper Largo, Fife, KY8 6JE.

Lingard, Joan Amelia. Author; Chairperson, Society of Authors in Scotland, since 1982; Chairperson, Meet the Author Committee; Board Member, Edinburgh Book Festival; Convenor, Scottish Writers Against the Bomb; b. Edinburgh; 3 d. Educ. Bloomfield Collegiate School, Belfast; Moray House College of Education, Edinburgh. First novel published, 1963; has also written plays for TV, including 18-part series, Maggie, adapted from quartet of teenage books; Council Member, Scottish Arts Council, 1980-84 (Member, Literature Committee, 1980-84); novels: Liam's Daughter, 1963; The Prevailing Wind, 1964; The Tide Comes In, 1966; The Headmaster, 1967; A Sort of Freedom, 1968; The Lord on our Side, 1970; The Second Flowering of Emily Mountjoy, 1979; Greenyards, 1981; Sisters By Rite, 1984; 15 children's books. Recreations: reading; walking; travelling. Address: (b.) David Higham Associates, 5-8 Lower John Street, Golden Square, London, W1R 4HA.

Linkie, William Sinclair. Controller, Inland Revenue, Scotland, since 1983; b. 9.3.31, Edinburgh; m., Primrose; 1 s.; 1 d. Educ. George Heriot's, Edinburgh. Entered Civil Service, 1948; served in Edinburgh, Inverness, Cupar, Dundee and East Kilbride; appointments including District Inspector, Edinburgh 6 District, Principal Inspector i/c Centre 1, Principal Inspector i/c

Edinburgh 5 District. President, Inland Revenue Sports Association, Scotland; Elder, Church of Scotland. Recreations: golf; badminton; choral singing. Address: (b.) 80 Lauriston Place, Edinburgh, EH3 9SL; T.-031-229 9344.

Linklater, John Richard Gordon, BA. Journalist; Education Correspondent, Glasgow Herald, since 1979; b. 29.1.52, Dumfries; m., Gaye Smith; 1 s.; 1 d. Educ. Royal High School, Edinburgh; Stirling University; Glasgow University. Fife Free Press, Kirkcaldy, 1975-76; Evening Express, Aberdeen, 1976-78; joined Glasgow Herald, 1978 (Editor, Education Herald, since 1984). Member, Scottish Committee, National Council for Training of Journalists; Specialist Writer of the Year, Scottish Press Awards, 1985. Recreations: music; reading; Hibernian FC; Burmese cats. Address: (h.) 31 Chester Street, Edinburgh, EH3 7EN; T.-031-225 6862.

Linklater, Marjorie. Member, Board of Directors, St. Magnus Festival, Orkney; Secretary, Stormy Bank Group, Orkney; Vice-Chairman, Orkney Branch, Scottish National Party; b. 19.3.09, Edinburgh; m., Eric Linklater (deceased); 2 s.; 2 d. Educ. St. George's School, Edinburgh; Downe House, Newbury, Berkshire; Royal Academy of Dramatic Art, London. Stage career ended, 1930, after appearing in three plays in West End; returned to Scotland and married Eric Linklater, 1933; SSAFA Representative, 1942-45; Member, Ross and Cromarty County Council, 1953-69; served on Inverness Hospital Board; Member, Scottish Arts Council, 1957-63; former Member, Advisory Council, HIDB; Council Member, European Architectural Heritage Year, 1972-75; joined Scottish National Party, 1979, having progressed from Conservative via Liberal; as Chairman of Orkney Heritage Society, 1977-81, led "No Uranium" campaign to prevent uranium mining in Orkney; at present Secretary, Stormy Bank Group opposed to dumping nuclear waste in seabed off Orkney; founder Chairman, Pier Arts Centre Management Committee; helped to initiate Orkney Folk Festival. Recreations: committees; the arts. Address: (h.) 20 Main Street, Kirkwall, Orkney, KW15 1BU; T.-0856 3619.

Linlithgow, 3rd Marquess of, (Charles William Frederick Hope), MC (1945), TD (1973), MA. Lord Lieutenant of West Lothian, since 1964; Director, Eagle Star Insurance Co. Ltd.; b. 7.4.12; m., 1 Vivien Kenyon Slaney (deceased); 1 s.; 1 d.; 2, Judith Baring. Educ. Eton; Christ Church, Oxford. Served Second World War (POW). Address: (h.) Hopetoun House, South Queensferry, West Lothian, EH30 9SL.

Linn, James, DPA. Assistant Secretary, Scottish Education Department, since 1980; b. 9.1.30, Glasgow; m., Helen Hughes; 4 s.; 3 d. Educ. St. Mungo's Academy, Glasgow; Glasgow University. Department of Health for Scotland, 1950; Scottish Home and Health Department, 1964; Scottish Education Department, 1979. Chairman, Scottish Office Benevolent Society. Recreations: running; golf; choral singing. Address: (b.) 43 Jeffrey Street, Edinburgh; T.-031-556 9233, Ext. 310.

Lisgo, John, BSc (Econ) (Hons), DipEd (Hons). Principal, Lauder Technical College, Dunfermline, since 1983; b. 8.7.40, Seaham, Durham; m., Norma Ranson Peel; 1 s. Educ. Ryhope School, Sunderland; London School of Economics and Political Science; Durham University. Assistant Teacher of History and Mathematics, Boldon Secondary School, 1962-63; Assistant Lecturer in Economics, then Liaison Officer for Adult Education, Monkwearmouth College of Further Education, 1963-72; Stevenson College of Further Education: Senior Lecturer in Social Studies, 1972-75, Head, Department of Language and Social Studies, 1975-80, Assistant Principal, 1980-83. Assistant Convener, Scottish Branch, Association of Principals; Member, NCB Recruitment, Education, Training and Welfare Committee. Recreation: swimming. Address: (b.) Lauder Technical College, Halbeath, Dunfermline, Fife; T.-Dunfermline 726201.

Lister, Rev. Douglas, MA, BD. Minister, Largo Newburn Parish Church, Fife, since 1967; b. 5.7.20, Rothesay; m., Marion Waugh Read (deceased); 1 s.; 3 d. Educ. Rothesay Academy; Glasgow University and Trinity College. Ordained to Royal Army Chaplains' Department, 1945; served, Liverpool Scottish, Gibraltar, 1946, and Royal Scots Greys, Luneburg, 1947-48; Minister, St. Stephen's Church, Carnoustie, 1949-55; Chaplain, Suez Contractors Ltd., Egypt, 1956 (arrested and imprisoned during Suez crisis); Minister, St. Andrews Church, Inverurie, 1957-67. Publication: Largo Kirk, 1968. Recreations: gardening; writing; reading; golf. Address: The Manse, Upper Largo, Fife.

Lister-Kaye, Sir John, 8th Bt. Naturalist; Farmer; b. 8.5.46; m., Sorrel Deirdre; 1 s.; 2 d. Educ. Allhallows School. Founded field studies centre, Highlands, 1970; founder Director, Aigas Trust, 1979. Address: (h.) Aigas House, Beauly, Inverness-shire, IV4 7AD.

Liston, William Alexander, BSc, MB, ChB, FRCOG. Consultant in Obstetrics and Gynaecology, Royal Infirmary and Simpson Memorial Maternity Pavilion, Edinburgh, since 1977; Honorary Senior Lecturer, Edinburgh University, since 1977; b. 24.10.41, Edinburgh; m., Kay Elizabeth Adams; 3 s.; 1 d. Educ. Melville College; St. Andrews University; Edinburgh University. Lecturer, Obstetrics and Gynaecology, Aberdeen University, 1972-75; Senior Lecturer, Obstetrics and Gynaecology, Dar Es Salaam University, 1975-77. Recreations: gardening; ski-mountaineering; hill-walking. Address: (h.) 36A Inverleith Place, Edinburgh; T.-031-552 2994.

Lithgow, Sir William (James), 2nd Bt, DL. Chairman, Lithgows Ltd., since 1959; b. 19.5.34; m., 1, Valerie Helen Scott (deceased); 2, Mary Claire Hill; 2 s.; 1 d. Educ. Winchester College. Chairman, Lithgow Drydocks Ltd., 1967-78; Vice-Chairman, Scott Lithgow Ltd., 1968-78; Chairman, Western Ferries (Argyll) Ltd., since 1972; Chairman, Campbeltown Shipyard Ltd., since 1970; Director, Bank of Scotland, since 1962; Member, Queen's Bodyguard for Scotland (Royal Company of Archers); Past Chairman, Iona Cathedral Trustees Management Board; Hon. LLD, Strathclyde; DL, Renfrewshire, 1970.

Little, Keith, MB, ChB, MD, MRCP, FRCSEdin. Consultant in Accident and Emergency Medicine, Edinburgh Royal Infirmary; b. 26.4.43, Yeadon, Yorkshire; m., Margaret R.; 2 s.; 2 d. Educ. Dalbeattie High School; Dumfries Academy; Edinburgh Medical School. First posts in Edinburgh; moved to Derby as a Registrar in Accident and Emergency Medicine; Consultant, Chester Royal Infirmary, 1974-78. Chairman, Scottish Committee, Medical Commission on Accident Prevention. Publication: Accident and Emergency Resuscitation (Co-author). Recreations: golf; tennis. Address: (b.) Accident and Emergency Department, Royal Infirmary, Edinburgh; T.-031-229 2477.

Little, Teresa Martin, MA. Member, Fife Regional Council (Alliance Group Education Spokesman), since 1982; Vice-President, Dunfermline Liberal Association, since 1984; Member, Alliance Scottish Policy Group on Education, since 1984; b. 15.2.49, Falkirk; 2 s. Educ. St. Joseph's Convent, Girvan; Edinburgh University. Teacher of English/French, St. Andrews High School, Kirkcaldy, 1971-75; Assistant Principal Teacher of English, St. Columba's High School, Dunfermline, 1975-77; Member, Prison Visiting Committee, HM Institution, Cornton Vale, Stirling, since 1982; Liberal/SDP Alliance Parliamentary candidate, Central Fife, 1983. Recreations: tennis; gardening; theatre. Address: (h.) 9 North Roundall, Limekilns, Fife, KY11 3JY; T.-0383 872 189.

Littlejohn, William Hunter, DA, RSA, RSW. Head of Fine Art, Gray's School of Art, Aberdeen, since 1980; b. 16.4.29, Arbroath. Educ. Arbroath High School; Dundee College of Art. Art Teacher: Angus Schools, 1953-56, Arbroath High School, 1956-66; Lecturer, then Head of Painting, Gray's School of Art, 1970-80. Address: (h.) 16 Colvill Place, Arbroath, Angus; T.-Arbroath 74402.

Livingston, David Munro Sheldon, BSc, PhD, FIFST. Dean, Faculty of Science, Robert Gordon's Institute of Technology, since 1982 (Head, School of Nutritional Science, since 1971); b. Montrose; m., Evelyn Irene Soper; 1 s.; 1 d. Educ. Montrose Academy; Aberdeen University. Assistant Lecturer, then Senior Research Fellow, Aberdeen University; Senior Scientific Officer, Rowett Research Institute, Aberdeen; Head of Department, School of Domestic Science, RGIT. Panel Member, SCEEB, 1971-77; Member, Course Committee E4, SCOTEC, since 1972; Member, Dieticians' Board, Education Committee, Liaison Committee, Council for Professions Supplementary to Medicine. Recreations: game and target pistol shooting. Address: (b.) School of Nutritional Science, Robert Gordon's Institute of Technology, Queen's Road, Aberdeen, AB9 2PG; T.-0224 633611.

Livingston, Martin Gerard, MB, ChB, MRCPsych. Senior Lecturer in Psychiatry, Glasgow University, since 1983; Honorary Consulant Psychiatrist, Gartnavel Hospitals, since 1983; b. 19.5.53, Glasgow; m., Hilary Monica; 1 s. Educ. Hillhead High School, Glasgow; Glasgow University. Lecturer in Psychiatry, 1979; Honorary Senior Registrar, 1981; Member, Trainees Committee, Royal College of Psychiatrists, 1982; Secretary, Committee on Community Psychiatry and Rehabilitation, Scottish Division, Royal College of Psychiatrists; Secretary, Psychiatric Sub-Committee, Glasgow Area Medical Committee. Recreations: modern writing; photography; cinema. Address: (b.) Department of Psychological Medicine, 6 Whittingehame Gardens, Glasgow, G12 OAA; T.-041-334 9826.

Livingstone, Hugh, MA. Member, Eastwood District Council, since 1976; Lecturer in Administration, Strathclyde University, since 1966; b. 13.6.40, Greenock; m., Joan Norma Packer; 1 s.; 1 d. Educ. Greenock High School; Glasgow University. Financial Journalist, The Scotsman, 1962-63; Research Assistant/Assistant Lecturer, Royal College of Science and Technology, Glasgow, 1964-66; Member, First Renfrew District Council, 1973-75. Publication: The University: An Organisational Analysis, 1974. Address: (b.) Strathclyde Business School, 130 Rottenrow, Glasgow; T.-041-552 7141.

Livingstone, Jeremy Rae Braithwaite, MB, ChB, FRCSEdin, FRCOG. Consultant Obstetrician and Gynaecologist, Simpson Memorial Maternity Pavilion and Royal Infirmary, Edinburgh, since 1968; b. 24.9.32, Simla, India; m., Diana Marjorie Cox; 4 d. Educ. Clifton Hall School, Newbridge; Clifton College, Bristol; Edinburgh University. House Officer appointments, Bangour General Hospital and Royal Hospital for Sick Children, Edinburgh; National Service, Royal Navy, 1957-59; training posts, Bangour General Hospital, 1960-62, and Edinburgh, 1962-68; Council Member, Royal College of Obstetricians and Gynaecologists, representing Scottish members, 1972-75; seconded as Chairman, Department of Obstetrics and Gynaecology, King Faisal Specialist Hospital and Research Centre, Riyadh, 1975-77; Civil Consultant in Obstetrics and Gynaecology, Royal Navy in Scotland; Honorary Treasurer and Secretary, Edinburgh Obstetrical Society; Chairman, Lothian Division, Obstetrics and Gynaecology, 1981-84. Publication: Farquharson Textbook of Operative Surgery (Contributor). Recreations: golf; reading; music. Address: (h.) 19 Glencairn Crescent, Edinburgh, EH12 5BT; T.-031-337 4472.

Llewelyn, John Edward, BA, MA, BLitt. Senior Lecturer in Philosophy, Edinburgh University, since 1964; b. 1.2.28, Rogerstone, Newport, Gwent; m., Margaret Woolley. Educ. Bassaleg Secondary Grammar School; University College of Wales, Aberystwyth; Edinburgh University; Oxford University. RAF Education Branch; French Air Force College; Liebfrauenschule, Cologne; Department of Philosophy, University of New England, Australia. Publications: Beyond Metaphysics? The Hermeneutic Circle in Contemporary Continental Philosophy, 1985; Derrida on the Threshold of Sense, 1985. Recreation: hill-walking. Address: (b.) Department of Philosophy, David Hume Tower, George Square, Edinburgh, EH8 9JX; T.-031-667 1011.

Lloyd, Douglas Mathon Gent, BSc, DSc, DSc, CChem, FRSC, FRSE. Reader in Chemistry, St. Andrews University, since 1971; b. 19.7.20,

Bristol; m., Lydia. Educ. Colston's School, Bristol; Bristol University. Posts at Sheffield University, Bristol University, St. Andrews University; former Council Member, The Chemical Society; Past Chairman, Tayside Section, Royal Society of Chemistry (now on Perkin Division Council); Provost, St. Leonard's College, St. Andrews, 1972-77; Council Member, Royal Society of Chemistry, since 1985. Recreations: music (organist); travel; wine. Address: (b.) Department of Chemistry, Purdie Building, St. Andrews University, St. Andrews, Fife; T.-St. Andrews 76161.

Lloyd-Jones, Glyn Robin, MA, BA. Author and Novelist; Adviser, Education Department, Dunbartonshire, since 1972; b. 5.10.34, London; m., Sallie Hollocombe; 1 s.; 2 d. Educ. Blundell's School, Tiverton; Selwyn College, Cambridge University; Jordanhill College of Education. Teaching in Scottish secondary schools; Director, Curriculum Development Centre, Clydebank; English-Speaking Union Thyne Travel Scholarship to America, 1974; President, Scottish Association of Writers, since 1981. Publications: children's: Where the Forest and the Garden Meet, 1980; novels: Lord of the Dance (Winner, BBC/Arrow First Novel Competition, 1983); The Dreamhouse, 1985; education books: Assessment: From Principles to Action, 1985; How to Produce Better Worksheets, 1985. Recreations: mountaineering; sea-canoeing; wind-surfing; photography. Address: (h.) 26 East Clyde Street, Helensburgh, G84 7PG; T.-0436 2010.

Lochhead, Liz. Poet and Playwright; b. Motherwell. Educ. Glasgow School of Art. Combined writing and teaching for eight years; first collection of poems published, 1972; former Scottish Arts Council Scottish/Canadian Fellow; volumes of poetry including Memo for Spring, Islands, The Grimm Sisters; plays: Now and Then, True Confessions, Blood and Ice.

Lockhart of the Lee, Angus Hew. Landowner; b. 17.8.46, Dunsyre; m., Susan Elizabeth Normand; 1 s.; 1 d. Educ. Rannoch School, Perthshire; North of Scotland College of Agriculture. Recreations: shooting; water skiing; walking the dog. Address: (b.) Newholm, Dunsyre, Lanark; T.-0968 82254.

Lockhart, Sheriff Brian Alexander, BL. Sheriff, Glasgow and Strathkelvin, since 1981; b. 1.10.42, Ayr; m., Christine Ross Clark; 2 s.; 2 d. Educ. Glasgow Academy; Glasgow University. Partner, Robertson Chalmers and Auld, Solicitors, 1967-79; Sheriff, North Strathclyde, at Paisley, 1979-81. Recreations: fishing; golf; squash; family. Address: (h.) 18 Hamilton Avenue, Glasgow, G41; T.-041-427 1921.

Lockhart, Howard M., MBE, MA. Broadcaster; b. 29.3.12, Ayr. Educ. Ayr Academy; Glasgow High School; Glasgow University. First broadcast, 1923, in Children's Hour as child actor; part-time job as BBC Announcer in Glasgow, 1934; joined BBC staff as Junior Announcer in Edinburgh, 1935; transferred to Aberdeen as General Producer, 1936; served with Royal Artillery in War; returned to BBC in Glasgow as

Variety Producer; produced McFlannels series and supervised all Sir Harry Lauder's broadcasts; loaned to Australian Broadcasting Commission, 1949; resigned BBC, 1950; thereafter presented BBC Housewives' Choice programme; numerous stage productions; lecturing and adjudicating; author of plays, including The Story of Madeleine Smith. Publication: On My Wavelength, 1973. Recreation: loves silent films.

Lockhart, John Heggie, JP. Farmer; Member, Nithsdale District Council, since 1983; b. 15.3.24, Dumfries; m., Isabel Kirkwood; 2 s.; 2 d. Educ. Dumfries Academy. Past Chairman, Annandale Branch, National Farmers Union of Scotland. Address: Bents, Parkgate, Dumfries; T.-Parkgate 636.

Lodge, Adrian Morris, BSc (Hons), MB, ChB, DPM, MRCPsych. Consultant Psychiatrist, Lothian Health Board, since 1978; Honorary Senior Lecturer, Edinburgh University, since 1978; b. 11.5.45, Huddersfield; m., Caroline Lodge; 1 s.; 1 d. Educ. Huddersfield New College; Edinburgh University. Pre-registration year, Western General Hospital, 1969-70; postgraduate training in psychiatry, Royal Edinburgh and Associated Hospitals, 1970-78; now Consultant Psychiatrist (General Psychiatry), Royal Edinburgh Hospital and Hopetoun Unit, Herdmanflat, East Lothian; Chairman, Hopetoun Unit Minibus Project. Recreations: squash (President, Waverley Lawn Tennis and Squash Club); caravanning; gardening. Address: (h.) 39 Braid Road, Edinburgh; T.-031-447 4856.

Logan, Andrew, SDA, NDA. Farmer; Director, Scotfresh Ltd., since 1984; Governor, National Vegetable Research Station, since 1977; Director, Scottish Nuclear Stock Association, since 1983; Member, Scottish Agricultural Development Council, since 1983; b. 24.3.40, Cupar; m., M.L. Fleming; 3 s.; 1 d. Educ. Strathallan School; Edinburgh School of Agriculture. Director: Fifegro, 1973-79, Elba, 1979-84, Central Farmers, 1974-83; Chairman, Soft Fruit and Field Vegetable Committee, Scottish NFU, 1979-83. Recreations: squash; skiing. Address: (h.) Dairsie Mains, Cupar, Fife; T.-Cupar 52808.

Logan, James, CChem, MRIC. Vice-Chairman, Scottish Arts Council, since 1984; Member, Arts Council of Great Britain, since 1984; Director, Scotland the What? comedy revue, since 1970; b. 28.10.27, Haddington; m., Anne Brand; 1 s.; 1 d. Educ. Robert Gordon's Institute. Former Member, Senior Scientific Staff, Macaulay Institute for Soil Research; former Appeal Administrator, Aberdeen Maritime Museum; Founder/Chairman, Friends of Aberdeen Art Gallery and Museums; Committee Member, Aberdeen Art Gallery. Queen's Silver Jubilee Medal. Recreations: theatre; waiting for The Guardian to be delivered. Address: 53 Fountainhall Road, Aberdeen, AB2 4EU; T.-0224 646914.

Logan, Jimmy. Actor/Manager; Comedian; Chairman, Logan Theatres Ltd., since 1964; Chairman, Rita Theatres Ltd., since 1953; Chairman, Dowanhill Productions Ltd., since 1953; b.

4.4.28, Glasgow; m., Pamela de Wilde Donald. Educ. Bellahouston Academy; Gourock High School. One of five children who appeared on stage as The Logan Family; as a youth, toured as an accordionist, juvenile lead and comedian's feed; by the age of 19, was playing star parts at the Metropole, Glasgow; co-starred in the film Floodtide; for many years starred in Five Past Eight (summer revue) and in numerous pantomimes; other stage work includes Rob Roy and A Funny Thing Happened on the Way to the Forum (musicals), The Mating Game and A Bit Between the Teeth (plays); wrote and produced Lauder (one-man show); nine appearances at Royal performances; directed and starred in Jack and the Beanstalk, Eden Court, Inverness, 1984; played Archie Rice in The Entertainer, Byre, St. Andrews, 1984. President, Showbusiness Benevolent Fund; Trustee, Scottish Disability Foundation. Recreations: flying; collecting theatrical memorabilia and old music hall postcards.

Logan, Norman Hunter, MB, ChB, MFCM, DPH, DRCOG, DPA. Unit Medical Officer, Paisley Hospitals, Argyll and Clyde Health Board, since 1984; Secretary, BMA West of Scotland Committee for Community Medicine, since 1983; Member, Scottish Affairs Committee, Faculty of Community Medicine, since 1983; b. 28.8.27, Cleland, Lanarkshire. Educ. High School of Glasgow; Glasgow University. District Medical Officer, Renfrew Health District, 1977-84. President, Clan Maclennan Association; Initiator, Clyde Walkway Project; founder Member and Committee Member, 1975-84, New Lanark Civic Trust; founder Member and Council Member, New Glasgow Society; Honorary President, Cathcart Society; Past President, Glasgow District Council, SNP. Publication: A Clyde Walkway, 1973. Recreations: heraldry and vexillology; phonetics; hill-walking; photography. Address: (h.) 12 Kirkwell Road, Glasgow, G44; T.-041-637 2725.

Logan, Peter, MA. Rector, Lanark Grammar School, 1969-85; b. 20.6.24, Airdrie; m., Jean A. Paterson; 1 s.; 3 d. Educ. Airdrie Academy; Glasgow University. Teacher, Hamilton Academy, 1949-57; Principal Teacher of English: Fraserburgh Academy, 1958-64, Morgan Academy, Dundee, 1964-69. Recreations: reading; music. Address: (h.) 33 Hope Street, Lanark, ML11 7NE; T.-0555 3240.

Logan, Rev. Robert James Victor, MA, BD. Minister, Crown Church, Inverness, since 1970; Clerk, Synod of the Southern Highlands, since 1976; Clerk, Inverness Presbytery, since 1980; b. Kilmarnock. Educ. Dundee High School; St. Andrews University; Edinburgh University. Assistant Minister, Auld Kirk of Ayr, 1962-64; Minister, Newton Parish Church, Dalkeith, 1964-70; Member, Church Boundaries' Commission, 1974-75; Clerk, Synod of Moray, 1972-75; Convener, Nomination Committee, General Assembly, 1979-82; Chairman, successful group applying for franchise to operate Moray Firth Radio, 1979-81. Publication: The Lion, The Pit and the Snowy Day. Recreations: classical music; opera; bridge; reading history. Address: (h.) 39 Southside Road, Inverness, IV2 4XA; T.-0463 231140.

Logan, Rt. Rev. Vincent, DipRE. Roman Catholic Bishop of Dunkeld, since 1981; b. 30.6.41, Bathgate. Educ. Blairs College, Aberdeen; St. Andrew's College, Drygrange. Ordained Priest, 1964; Assistant Priest, St. Margaret's, Edinburgh, 1964-66; Corpus Christi College, London, 1966-67; Chaplain, St. Joseph's Hospital, Rosewell, Midlothian, 1966-67; Adviser in Religious Education, Archdiocese of St. Andrews and Edinburgh, 1967; Parish Priest, St. Mary's, Ratho, 1977-81; Vicar Episcopal for Education, Edinburgh, 1978. Address: Bishop's House, 29 Roseangle, Dundee, DD1 4LS; T.-0382 24327.

Logie, Alexander Wylie, MB, ChB, FRCPEdin, DA, DObstRCOG. Consultant Physician, Borders Health Board, since 1976; b. 5.11.38, Aberdeen; m., Dr. Dorothy E. Caie; 2 s.; 1 d. Educ. Trinity College, Glenalmond; Aberdeen University. Recreations: hill-walking; music. Address: (h.) Cheviot View, Bowden, Melrose, Roxburghshire; T.-0835 22763.

Logie, John Robert Cunningham, MB, ChB, PhD, FRCS, FRCSEdin. Consultant General Surgeon, Inverness Hospitals, since 1981; b. 9.9.46, Aberdeen; m., Sheila C. Will. Educ. Robert Gordon's College, Aberdeen; Trinity College, Glenalmond; Aberdeen University. House Officer, then Senior House Officer, then Lecturer, Department of Surgery, then Senior Registrar, Aberdeen Royal Infirmary. Recreations: rugby refereeing; garden; railways. Address: (h.) 20 Moray Park Avenue, Culloden, Inverness, IV1 2LS; T.-Inverness 792090.

Longair, Professor Malcolm Sim, BSc, MA, PhD, LLD (Hons), FRSE. Astronomer Royal for Scotland, since 1980; Regius Professor of Astronomy, Edinburgh University; Director, Royal Observatory, Edinburgh; b. 18.5.41, Dundee; m., Deborah Howard; 1 s.; 1 d. Educ. Morgan Academy, Dundee; Queen's College, Dundee; Trinity College, Cambridge. Fellow, Clare Hall, Cambridge, 1967-80: Research Fellow, 1967-71, Official Fellow, 1971-80, Praelector of Clare Hall, 1971-77; Visiting Assistant Professor of Radio Astronomy, California Institute of Technology, 1972; Visiting Professor of Astronomy, Institute for Advanced Study, Princeton, 1978; Exchange Visitor to USSR Space Research Institute, Moscow, on six occasions, 1975-79; Holder, Research Fellowship, Royal Commission for the Exhibition of 1851, 1966-68; Holder, James Clerk Maxwell Scholarship, Cavendish Laboratory, Cambridge, 1964-66; Holder, James Caird Scholarship, St. Andrews University, 1963-64. Publications: Observational Cosmology (Co-author), 1978; High Energy Astrophysics, 1981; Theoretical Concepts in Physics, 1984. Recreations: music (especially opera); art and architecture (especially Italian). Address: (h.) 41 Cluny Drive, Edinburgh; T.-031-447 9069.

Loraine, John Alexander, DSc, MB, PhD, FRCPEdin, FRSA, FRSE. Senior Lecturer, Department of Community Medicine, Edinburgh University, since 1979; b. 14.5.24, Edinburgh; m., Alison Blair. Educ. George Watson's Boys' College, Edinburgh; Edinburgh University. Director, MRC Clinical Endocrinology Unit, Edinburgh, 1961-72; Visiting Professor of Endocrinology, Donner Laboratory, University of

California, 1964; MRC External Scientific Staff and Honorary Senior Lecturer, Department of Community Medicine, Edinburgh University, 1972-79; Director, Centre for Human Ecology, Edinburgh University, 1978-84; Chairman, Doctors and Overpopulation Group, since 1972; Vice Chairman, Conservation Society, since 1974. Publications: Hormone Assays and their Clinical Application (Co-author); Recent Research on Gonadotrophic Hormones (Co-author); Fertility and Contraception in the Human Female (Co-author); Sex and the Population Crisis; The Death of Tomorrow; Reproductive Endocrinology and World Population (Editor); Environmental Medicine (Co-Editor); Understanding Homosexuality (Editor); Syndromes of the Seventies; Here Today...(Co-Editor); Global Signposts to the 21st Century; Energy Policies Around the World. Recreations: reading modern history and political biography; music; bridge. Address: (b.) Department of Community Medicine, Edinburgh University, Usher Institute, Warrender Park Road, Edinburgh; T.-031-229 6207.

Lord, Geoffrey, MA, AIB, FRSA. Secretary and Treasurer, Carnegie UK Trust, since 1977; Secretary, The Unemployed Voluntary Action Fund, since 1982; b. 24.2.28, Rochdale; m., Jean; 1 s.; 1 d. Educ. Rochdale Grammar School; Bradford University. Midland Bank Ltd., 1946-58; Greater Manchester Probation and After-Care Service, 1958-76 (Deputy Chief Probation Officer, 1974-76); Vice-President, Selcare Trust; Trustee, Artlink Edinburgh and The Lothians Ltd. Publications: The Arts and Disabilities, 1981; Interpretation of the Environment, 1984. Recreations: the arts; philately; walking; enjoying life. Address: (h.) 9 Craigleith View, Edinburgh.

Lorimer, A. Ross, MD, FRCP, FRCPGlas, FRCPEdin. Consultant Cardiologist, Glasgow Royal Infirmary, since 1970; Honorary Lecturer in Medical Cardiology, since 1970; b. 5.5.37, Bellshill; m., Fiona Marshall; 3 s. Educ. Uddingston Grammar School; High School of Glasgow; Glasgow University. Recreations: reading; walking. Address: (b.) Department of Cardiology, Royal Infirmary, Glasgow.

Lorimer, Hew Martin, HonLLD, RSA. Artist; b. 22.5.07, Scotland; 2 s.; 1 d. Educ. Loretto School; Edinburgh College of Art. Former PRO, The British Council, Scotland; Royal Scottish Academician (retired), now Senior Academician; Fellow, Royal Society of British Sculptors (retired); Past Chairman, St. Andrews Preservation Trust; Representative in Fife, National Trust for Scotland; Custodian, Kellie Castle, Pittenweem. Recreations: music; foreign travel. Address: (h.) Kellie Castle, Pittenweem, Fife, KY10 2RF.

Lothian, Sheriff Andrew, MA, LLB. Sheriff of Glasgow and Strathkelvin, since 1979; b. 6.2.42. Educ. Trinity College, Glenalmond; St. Andrews University; Edinburgh University. Advocate, 1968; Member, Scottish Arts Council Publications Awards Committee, 1970-73.

Lothian, Niall, BA, CA. Senior Lecturer, Department of Accountancy and Finance, Heriot-Watt University, since 1981 (Arthur Young Senior Research Fellow, since 1984); b. 27.2.48, Edinburgh; m., Carol Miller; 1 s.; 1 d. Educ. Daniel Stewart's College, Edinburgh; Heriot-Watt University. Lecturer, Department of Accountancy and Finance, Heriot-Watt University, 1973-81; Visiting Professor: IMEDE, Lausanne, 1979-80, INSEAD, Fontainebleau, 1984; Consultant, United Nations Industrial Development Organisation, Vienna, since 1980. Publications: Accounting for Inflation: Issues and Managerial Practices, 1978; Audit Quality and Value for Money, 1983; How Companies Manage R. & D., 1984. Address: (b.) Department of Accountancy and Finance, Heriot-Watt University, 31-35 Grassmarket, Edinburgh, EH1 2HT; T.-031-225 8432.

Lothian, 12th Marquess of, (Peter Francis Walter Kerr), KCVO, DL. Chairman of Council, Scottish Branch, British Red Cross; b. 8.9.22, Melbourne, near Derby; m., Antonella Newland; 2 s.; 4 d. Educ. Ampleforth College, York; Christ Church, Oxford. Parliamentary Under Secretary, Ministry of Health, 1964; Parliamentary Under Secretary, Foreign and Commonwealth Office, 1970-72; Lord in Waiting, 1972-73; Lord Warden of the Stannaries, 1977-83. Knight of Malta; Brigadier, Queen's Bodyguard for Scotland. Recreations: music; shooting. Address: music; shooting. Address: Monteviot, Jedburgh, Roxburghshire; T.-08353 288.

Louden, Richard Cameron, MA (Hons), DipEd. Depute Director of Education, Strathclyde Regional Council, since 1982. Educ. Dunfermline High School; Edinburgh University; Moray House College of Education. Depute Director of Education, Dunbarton County Council, 1972-75; Senior Education Officer, Renfrew Division, Strathclyde, 1975-82. Member, Consultative Committee on the Curriculum. Address: (b.) Regional Offices, India Street, Glasgow; T.-041-227 2837.

Louden, Rev. Robert Stuart, TD, MA, BD, DD, DLitt. Minister, Church of Scotland, since 1938; b. 11.8.12, Dundee; m., Helen Stewart Wilson; 2 s.; 3 d. Educ. Downfield School; Morgan Academy, Dundee; Edinburgh University; Marburg University; Oxford University. Licensed to preach, 1936; ordained, St. Mary's, Old Aberdeen, 1938; War Service: Chaplain to the Forces, 1939 (Middle East), Prisoner of War, Tobruk, 1942; twice mentioned in Despatches; DACG (TA), Scottish Command, 1958-63; Territorial Decoration (three bars); Minister: Dailly Parish Church, 1945-49, Greyfriars, Edinburgh, 1949-78; Convener, General Assembly Committees: Colonial and Continental, 1957-62, Public Worship, 1965-70; Vice-Convener, Church Hymnary Revision, 1963-73; Vice Chairman and Chairman, Heriot Trust, 1952-75; Vice-President, World Alliance of Reformed Churches, 1964-70; Past President: Scottish Ecclesiological Society, Church Service Society, Scottish Church Society, New College Union, Society for the Relief of the Destitute Sick, Edinburgh Royal Infirmary Samaritan Society; Past Junior and Senior Grand Chaplain, Grand Lodge of Scotland (Masonic); Commandeur de Merite, Order of St. Lazarus of Jerusalem; Order, Cross of St. Mark (second class). Publications: The Church in the World,

1948; The True Face of the Kirk, 1963. Recreations: reading; writing; walking. Address: (h.) 88 Cockburn Crescent, Balerno, Midlothian, EH14 7HU; T.-031-449 4467.

Loudon, John Bruce, MB, ChB, FRCPsych, DPM. Consultant Psychiatrist, Royal Edinburgh Hospital, since 1978 (Deputy Physician Superintendent, since 1980); Honorary Senior Lecturer, Department of Psychiatry, Edinburgh University, since 1978; b. 12.8.43, Edinburgh; m., Susan Mary Lay; 3 s. Educ. Edinburgh Academy; Edinburgh University. Address: (b.) Andrew Duncan Clinic, Morningside, Edinburgh, EH10 5HF; T.-031-447 2011.

Loudon, John Duncan Ott, MB, ChB, FRCSEdin, FRCOG. Consultant Obstetrician and Gynaecologist, Eastern General Hospital, Edinburgh, since 1960; Senior Lecturer, Edinburgh University, since 1961; b. 22.8.24, Edinburgh; m., Nancy Beaton Mann; 2 s. Educ. John Watson's School, Edinburgh; Wyggeston Grammar School, Leicester; Edinburgh University. Senior Registrar in Obstetrics and Gynaecology, Edinburgh Royal Infirmary, 1958-60; Medical Officer, RAF, 1948-50; Adviser in Family Planning, Malta Government, 1976-81; Vice President, Royal College of Obstetricians and Gynaecologists, 1981-84. Recreations: golf; gardening. Address: (h.) 94 Inverleith Place, Edinburgh, EH3 5PA; T.-031-552 1327.

Lovat, Sheriff Leonard Scott, BL. Sheriff of South Strathclyde, Dumfries and Galloway, at Hamilton, since 1978; b. 28.7.26, Gourock; m., Elinor Frances McAlister; 1 s.; 1 d. Educ. St. Aloysius College, Glasgow; Glasgow University. Solicitor, 1948; in partnership, 1955-59; also Assistant to Professor of Civil Law, Glasgow University, 1954-63; Procurator Fiscal Depute, Glasgow, 1960; Cropwood Fellow, Institute of Criminology, Cambridge University, 1971; Senior Assistant Procurator Fiscal, Glasgow and Strathkelvin, 1976. Publication: Climbers' Guide to Glencoe and Ardgour (two volumes), 1959 and 1965. Recreations: music; mountaineering; bird-watching. Address: (h.) 38 Kelvin Court, Glasgow, G12 OAE; T.-041-357 0031.

Lovat, 17th Baron, (Simon Christopher Joseph Fraser), DSO (1942), MC, TD, JP, DL. 24th Chief of Clan Fraser of Lovat; b. 9.7.11; m., Rosamond Broughton; 4 s.; 2 d. Educ. Ampleforth; Magdalen College, Oxford. Served Second World War (Captain, Lovat Scouts, 1939, Lt.-Col., 1942, Brig., Commandos, 1943; wounded); Under Secretary of State for Foreign Affairs, 1945. Address: (h.) Balblair, Beauly, Inverness-shire.

Love, Professor Philip Noel, CBE (1983), MA, LLB. Professor of Conveyancing and Professional Practice of Law, Aberdeen University, since 1974 (Dean, Faculty of Law, 1979-82); b. 25.12.39; m., Isabel Leah; 3 s. Educ. Aberdeen Grammar School; Aberdeen University. Admitted Solicitor in Scotland, 1963; Advocate in Aberdeen, since 1963; Partner, Campbell Connon & Co., Solicitors, Aberdeen, 1963-74 (Consultant, since 1974); Law Society of Scotland: Council Member, since 1975, Examiner, 1975-83, Vice-President, 1980-81, President, 1981-82; Local Chairman, Rent Assessment Panel for Scotland, since 1972; Member, Joint Standing Committee on Legal Education in Scotland, 1976-85 (Chairman, 1976-80); Chairman, Secretary of State for Scotland's Expert Committee on House Purchase and Sale, 1982-84; Vice-President, Scottish Law Agents Society, 1970; Member, Rules Council, Court of Session, since 1968; Council Member, International Bar Association, since 1983; Chairman, Aberdeen Home for Widowers' Children, since 1971; Member, Joint Ethical Committee, Grampian Health Board, since 1984; Honorary Sheriff, Grampian, Highland and Islands, since 1978. Recreations: rugby; squash; golf. Address: (h.) 3A Rubislaw Den North, Aberdeen, AB2 4AL; T.-Aberdeen 313339.

Love, Robert Malcolm, MA (Hons). Head of Drama, Scottish Television, since 1979; b. 9.1.37, Paisley. Educ. Paisley Grammar School; Glasgow University; Washington University. Actor and Director, various repertory companies, including Nottingham Playhouse, 1962-65; Producer, Thames TV, 1966-75, including Public Eye, Van Der Valk; freelance Producer, 1976-79, including Thames TV, LWT, Seacastle Film Productions, Scottish TV. Awards including: Commonwealth Festival, New York TV and Film Festival, Chicago Film Festival, Scottish Radio and Television Industries; nominated for International Emmy, New York, 1982. Recreations: reading; music; theatre; travel. Address: (b.) Scottish Television, Cowcaddens, Glasgow.

Lovelace, 5th Earl of, (Peter Axel William Locke King), b. 26.11.51; m., Kirsteen Kennedy. Address: (h.) Torridon House, Torridon, Ross-shire.

Loveless, Norman Ernest, MA, PhD. Senior Lecturer in Psychology, Dundee University; 1959; b. 9.10.21, London; m., Pamela May Ross; 2 s. Educ. Northern Grammar School, Portsmouth; Edinburgh University. Experimental Assistant, Mine Design Department, Admiralty, 1940-41; Radar Officer, RAF, 1941-47; student, 1947-51; Lecturer in Psychology, St. Andrews University, 1951-52; Lecturer in Industrial Health, Medical School, Newcastle, 1952-59; joined Dundee University as Lecturer, 1959. Recreation: oil painting. Address: (h.) The Limes, Coupar Angus Road, Birkhill, Dundee, DD2 5QE; T.-0382 580425.

Low, Donald Alexander, MA, BPhil, PhD, FRSE, FSA Scot. Reader in English Studies, Stirling University, since 1981; b. 14.5.39, Greenock; m., Sheona Grant MacCorquodale; 1 s.; 1 d. Educ. Greenock Academy; George Heriot's; Hawick High School; St. Andrews University; Cambridge University. Lecturer in English, St. Andrews University, 1966-72; Lecturer in English, Stirling University, 1972-76. Publications: Robert Burns: The Critical Heritage (Editor), 1974; Critical Essays on Robert Burns (Editor), 1975; That Sunny Dome, 1977; Thieves' Kitchen: The Regency Underworld, 1982; Robert Burns: The Kilmarnock Poems (Editor), 1985. Recreations: swimming; music. Address: (h.) 17 Chalton Road, Bridge of Allan, Stirlingshire; T.-0786 832661.

Low, Ian Campbell, BSc, CA. Chairman, Dundee and London Investment Trust PLC, since 1950; Chairman, J.T. Inglis & Sons Ltd., since 1945; b. 15.12.12, Newport, Fife; m., Nora Bolton; 2 d. Educ. Fettes College; St. Andrews University. Deputy Chairman, then Chairman, Low & Bonar PLC, Dundee, 1937-77. Recreations: shooting; fishing; gardening. Address: (h.) Holly Hill, 69 Dundee Road, Broughty Ferry, Dundee, DD5 1NA; T.-0382 79148.

Low, Sir James (Richard) Morrison-, 3rd Bt, DL, DFH, CEng, MIEE. Director, Osborne & Hunter Ltd., Glasgow, since 1956; b. 3.8.25; m., Ann Rawson Gordon; 1 s.; 3 d. Educ. Ardvreck; Harrow; Merchiston. Royal Corps of Signals, 1943-47 (Captain); President, Electrical Contractors Association of Scotland, 1982-84; DL, Fife, 1978. Address: (h.) Kilmaron Castle, Cupar, Fife.

Lowe, Rev. Edwin, MA, BD. Minister, Caldwell, Uplawmoor, since 1971; b. 30.9.23, Port Glasgow; m., Grace Cuthbertson; 2 s.; 1 d. Educ. Port Glasgow High School; Greenock High School; Glasgow University and Trinity College. War Service, RA Signals, BAOR, 1942-46; Student Assistant, Mid Kirk, Greenock, 1948-50; ordained and inducted to Bothwell: Kirkfield and Wooddean, 1950; Minister: Saltcoats North, 1957-63, Aberfeldy, 1963-71. Address: Manse of Caldwell, Uplawmoor, Glasgow, G78 4AL; T.-Uplawmoor 215.

Lowe, John Duncan, MA, LLB. Deputy Crown Agent, since 1984; b. 18.5.48, Alloa; m., Jacqueline M.; 2 s. Educ. Hamilton Academy; Glasgow University. Procurator Fiscal Depute, Kilmarnock, 1974-77; Legal Assistant, Crown Office, 1977-79; Senior Procurator Fiscal Depute, Glasgow, 1979-80; Assistant Procurator Fiscal, Glasgow, 1980-83; Assistant Solicitor, Crown Office, 1983-84. Address: (b.) 5/7 Regent Road, Edinburgh; T.-031-557 3800.

Lowe, Martin John Brodie, BSc, PhD. Secretary and Registrar, St. Andrews University, since 1981; b. 10.4.40, Dorking; m., Janet MacNaughtan; 3 s.; 1 d. Educ. Dunfermline High School; St. Andrews University. British Council Officer, with service in Tanzania and South India, 1965-69; Strathclyde University: Administrative Assistant, 1969-71, Assistant Registrar, 1971-73, Secretary to Senate, 1973-81. National Council, Voluntary Service Overseas, 1976-83; Honorary Secretary, then Chairman, Glasgow and West of Scotland VSO Committee, 1973-81. Recreations: piping; hill-walking; family interests. Address: (b.) College Gate, St. Andrews, Fife, KY16 9AJ; T.-St. Andrews 76161.

Lowson, David Murray, CSS, MA. Member, Parole Board for Scotland, since 1981; b. 24.4.20, Carnoustie; m., Catherine Russell Mitchell; 1 s. Educ. Logie School, Dundee; Liverpool University. Toolmaker (after apprenticeship), until 1947; course in youth and community work, 1947-48; course in social science, 1949-51; Probation Officer, 1951-59; Assistant Governor, Prison Service, England, 1959-62; Lecturer, Liverpool University, 1962-80. Member, Parole Board, England

and Wales, 1973-76; Warden: University Hall, Liverpool, 1970-80, Liverpool University Settlement, 1963-68; Chairman, Peterlee Community Association, 1955; Secretary, Carnoustie Community Council, since 1983; Member, Dundee Children's Panel Advisory Committee, since 1980. Recreations: outdoor activities. Address: (h.) 87 High Street, Carnoustie, Angus, DD7 7EA; T.-Carnoustie 52189.

Lucas, Sir Cyril Edward, Kt (1976), CMG (1956), FRS (1966). Director of Fisheries Research, Scotland, and Director, Marine Laboratory, Aberdeen, 1948-70; b. 30.7.09. Educ. Hull Grammar School; University College, Hull. Hon. LLD, Aberdeen, 1977.

Lucas, Walter Pollock. Company Director; Member, Renfrew District Council, since 1984; b. 17.2.17, Port Glasgow; m., Doreen Ada Bromley; 2 s.; 1 d. Educ. Greenock High School; Herds Commercial College, Greenock; George Commercial College, Greenock. Joined Territorial Army, 1938, as a Gunner, 77th Field Regiment of Artillery; evacuated from Dunkirk, 1940; commissioned, Glasgow Highlanders (9th Bn., HLI), 1941; drafted to India, 1942; seconded to 7/17 DOGRA Regiment, stationed at Fort Salop, North West Frontier; posted to IAOC, 1944, Bombay, as Company Commander, Indian Military Wing; returned to UK, 1945. Vice-Chairman, Paisley Conservative Association, 1980-82; Chairman, Paisley South Conservative Association, 1982; Elder, Paisley Abbey Church, since 1960; Member, Renfrew District Council, 1974-80. Recreations: golf; fresh water fishing. Address: (h.) The Grange, 106 Corsebar Road, Meikleriggs, Paisley, PA2 9PY; T.-041-889 8554.

Ludlam, Christopher A., BSc (Hons), MB, ChB, PhD, FRCP, MRCPath. Consultant Haematologist, Edinburgh Royal Infirmary, since 1980; Director, Edinburgh Haemophilia Reference Centre, since 1980; Senior Lecturer in Medicine, Edinburgh University, since 1980; b. 6.6.46, Edinburgh. Educ. Edinburgh University. MRC Research Fellow, 1972-75; Senior Registrar in Haematology, University Hospital of Wales, Cardiff, 1975-78; Lecturer in Haematology, University of Wales, 1979. Address: (b.) Department of Haematology, Royal Infirmary, Edinburgh; T.-031-229 2473.

Lugton, Rev. George Lockhart, MA, BD. Joint Secretary, Department of Ministry and Mission, Church of Scotland, since 1984; b. 25.9.29, Dunfermline; m., Joan Campsie Leid; 1 s.; 1 d. Educ. Buckhaven High School; Edinburgh University. Assistant Minister, Dysart Barony, 1953-55; Minister, Strathblane, 1955-69; part-time Clerk, Dumbarton Presbytery, 1967-69, then full-time Clerk, 1969-73; Church and Ministry Department: Assistant Secretary, 1973-75, Assistant Secretary and Deputy, 1975-77, Secretary and Deputy, 1977-83. Recreations: music; hill-walking. Address: (b.) 121 George Street, Edinburgh, EH2 4YN; T.-031-225 5722.

Lumsden, George Innes, BSc, FRSE, MIGeol. Deputy Director, British Geological Survey, since 1982; Honorary Fellow, Department of

Geology, Edinburgh University; b. 27.6.26, Peterculter; m., Sheila Thomson; 2 s.; 1 d. Educ. Banchory Academy; Aberdeen University. Geological Survey of GB: Geologist, 1949, Senior Geologist, 1952, Principal Geologist, 1958; District Geologist, Institute of Geological Sciences in charge, South Scotland, 1970; promoted to Assistant Director and Senior Officer for Scotland, 1980. Member, Council of Management, Macaulay Institute for Soil Research; Member, Engineering and Science Advisory Committee, Derby College of Higher Education; Member, Geological Museum Advisory Panel; Member, Editorial Board, Transactions of Royal Society of Edinburgh; Chairman, Directors, Western European Geological Survey's Working Party on Environmental Geology; Fellow, Edinburgh Geological Society. Recreations: music; theatre; sport; gardening.

Lumsden, James Alexander, MBE, TD, BA, LLB, DL. Director, Bank of Scotland, 1958-85; Director, Scottish Provident Institution, 1968-85; b. 24.1.15, Arden, Dunbartonshire; m., Sheila Cross; 3 s. Educ. Cargilfield School, Edinburgh; Rugby School; Corpus Christi College, Cambridge; Glasgow University. Territorial Army, 1937-46; Partner, Maclay Murray & Spens, Solicitors, Glasgow, 1947-82; Director of certain Investment Trust companies managed by Murray Johnstone Ltd., since 1967; Commissioner of Income Tax, County of Dumbarton; Member, Committee on Company Law, 1960-62; Fellow, Law Society of Scotland and Royal Faculty of Procurators, Glasgow. Recreations: shooting; fishing; other country pursuits. Address: (h.) Bannachra, by Helensburgh, Dunbartonshire, G84 9EF; T.-Arden 653.

Lumsden, Professor Keith Grant, MA, PhD. Professor and Director, Esmee Fairbairn Research Centre, Heriot-Watt University, Edinburgh, since 1975; Member, Board of Directors, Hewlett Packard Ltd., since 1982; b. 7.1.35, Bathgate; m., Jean Baillie MacDonald; 1 s. Educ. Bathgate Academy; Edinburgh University; Stanford University, California. Instructor, Department of Economics, then Assistant Professor, Graduate School of Business, Stanford University, 1960-67; Research Associate, Stanford Research Institute, 1965-71; Director, Stanford University Conference: NDTE, 1966, RREE, 1968; Associate Professor, Graduate School of Business, Stanford University, 1968-75; Visiting Professor of Economics, Heriot-Watt University, 1969-70; Director: Economics Education Project, 1969-74, Behavioral Research Laboratories, 1970-72, Capital Preservation Fund Inc., 1971-75, Nielsen Engineering Research Inc., 1972-75; Member, American Economic Association Committee on Economic Education, 1978-81; Academic Director, NSFI Shipping Management Seminar, since 1979; Professor of Economics, Advanced Management College, Stanford University, since 1971; Affiliate Professor of Economics, INSEAD, France; Member, Economics Education 14-16 Project, Manchester University. Publications: The Free Enterprise System, 1963; The Gross National Product, 1964; International Trade, 1965; Microeconomics: A Programmed Book, 1966; Macroeconomics: A Programmed Book, 1966; New Development in the Teaching of Economics (Editor), 1967; Excess Demand and Excess Supply in World Tramp Shipping Markets, 1968; Recent Research in Economics Education (Editor), 1970; Basic Economics: Theory and Cases, 1973; Efficiency in Universities: The La Paz Papers (Editor), 1974; Economics Education in the United Kingdom, 1980. Recreations: tennis; deep sea sports fishing. Address: (h.) 40 Lauder Road, Edinburgh, EH9 1UE.

Lumsden, William Hepburn Russell, DSc, MD, DTM, DTH, FIBiol, FRCPEdin, FRSE. Scientific and Medical Writer; b. 27.3.14, Forfar; m., Pamela Kathleen Bartram; 2 s.; 1 d. Educ. Queen Elizabeth's Grammar School, Darlington; Glasgow University; Liverpool University. MRC Fellow in Tropical Medicine, 1938-41; active service, Malaria Field Laboratories, RAMC, 1941-46; Yellow Fever (subsequently East African Virus) Research Institute, Entebbe, 1947-57; Director, East African Trypanosomiasis Research Organisation, Tororo, 1957-63; Lecturer, Department of Bacteriology, Edinburgh University Medical School, 1963-64; Senior Lecturer, Department of Animal Health, Royal (Dick) School of Veterinary Studies, Edinburgh University, 1964-68; Visiting Professor, Toronto University, 1968; Professor of Medical Protozoology, London School of Hygiene and Tropical Medicine, London University, 1968-79; Senior Editor, Advances in Parasitology, 1978-82; Council Member, Royal Society of Tropical Medicine and Hygiene, 1969-73, 1974-77; Council Member, Royal Zoological Society of Scotland, 1967-68; Member, Expert Advisory Panel on Parasitic Diseases (Trypanosomiasis), WHO, 1962-84; Member, Trypanosomiasis Panel, Ministry of Overseas Development, 1973-79; Member, International Malaria Review Teams, Bangladesh, 1978, Nepal, 1979, Sri Lanka, 1980. Publications: Techniques with Trypanosomes, 1973; Biology of the Kinetoplastida (Editor), 1976 and 1979. Recreations: trout fishing; hill-walking. Address: (h.) 16A Merchiston Crescent, Edinburgh, EH10 5AX; T.-031-229 2702.

Lunan, Duncan Alasdair, MA (Hons), FBIS, DipEd. Author; b. 24.10.45; m., Linda Joyce Donnelly (m. diss.). Educ. Marr College, Troon; Glasgow University. Management Trainee, Christian Salvesen (Managers) Ltd., 1969-70; self-employed (Author), 1970-78; Manager, Astronomy Project, Glasgow Parks Department, 1978-79; SF Critic, Glasgow Herald, 1971-82 and since 1985; regular astronomy column in various papers and magazines; Council Member, Association in Scotland to Research into Astronautics (ASTRA), since 1963 (President, 1966-72 and since 1978). Publications: Man and the Stars, 1974; New Worlds for Old, 1979; Man and the Planets, 1983. Recreation: folk music. Address: c/o 175 Queen Victoria Drive, Scotstounhill, Glasgow, G14 9BP; T.-041-959 1367.

Lundie, Mary Elizabeth, JP, RGN. Matron, The Princess Louise Scottish Hospital, Erskine, since 1977; b. 11.10.36, Barrhead; m., Peter Lundie; 3 s.; 3 d. Educ. St. Margaret's Convent, Paisley. Trained, Western Infirmary, Glasgow, 1954-58; Staff Nurse, Knightwood Hospital, 1962-65, Southern General Hospital, Glasgow, 1965-66; Sister, Gartloch Hospital, Glasgow,

1966-67; Sister and Nursing Officer, Ruchill Hospital, Glasgow, 1967-75; Nursing Officer, The Princess Louise Scottish Hospital, Erskine, 1975-77. Recreations: reading; walking dogs. Address: (h.) Matron's House, Erskine Hospital, Bishopton, Renfrewshire; T.-041-812 5500.

Lunn, George Michael, BSc, DipHWU. Managing Director, Whyte & Mackay Distillers Ltd., since 1983; Director, Whisky Division, Scottish & Universal Investments Ltd., since 1984; Director, Dalmore Distillers Ltd., since 1984; b. 22.7.42, Stirling; m., Jennifer Burgoyne; 3 s.; 1 d. Educ. Kelvinside Academy; Glasgow University; Heriot-Watt University. North of Scotland Distilling Co. Ltd., 1965-68; Distillers Co. (Carbon Dioxide) Ltd., 1968-70; PA Management Consultants, 1970-72; British Carpets Ltd., 1972-78; joined Whyte & Mackay Distillers Ltd., 1978. Member, Glasgow Action Committee, 1985. Recreation: golf. Address: (b.) Whyte & Mackay, Dalmore House, 296-298 St. Vincent Street, Glasgow, G2 5RG; T.-041-248 5771.

Lunt, Dorothy A., DDS, PhD, HDD RFPSG, FSA Scot. Reader in Dental Anatomy and Histology, Glasgow University, since 1981; b. 3.11.31, Stirling. Educ. Alloa Academy; Glasgow University. House Officer, Glasgow Dental Hospital, 1953-55; Assistant Lecturer, Dental Anatomy, Manchester University, 1955-56; Lecturer, Dental Anatomy and Histology, then Senior Lecturer, Glasgow University, 1956-81. Address: (b.) Department of Oral Biology, Glasgow University Dental School, 378 Sauchiehall Street, Glasgow, G2 3JZ; T.-041-332 7020.

Luscombe, Rt. Rev. Lawrence Edward, CA, FSA Scot. Bishop of Brechin, since 1975; b. 10.11.24; m., Dr. Doris Morgan; 1 d. Educ. Kelham College; Kings College, London. Indian Army, 1942-47; Chartered Accountant, 1952; Curate, St. Margaret's, Glasgow, 1963-66; Rector, St. Barnabas', Paisley, 1966-71; Provost, St. Paul's Cathedral, Dundee, 1971-75. Member, Governing Body: Dundee College of Education, Glenalmond College, Lathallan School, Edinburgh Theological College; serving Brother, Order of St. John; Honorary Canon, Trinity Cathedral, Davenport, Iowa, since 1983. Address: 7 Shaftesbury Road, Dundee, DD2 1HF; T.-Dundee 644215.

Lyall, Andrew Finlayson Dunnet, LLB, SSC, NP. Solicitor, since 1970; Notary Public, since 1971; Member, Dundee District Council, since 1984; b. 20.10.47, Nairobi; m., Marguerita Fransen Taylor; 1 s.; 1 d. Educ. Prince of Wales School, Nairobi; Morgan Academy, Dundee; St. Andrews University. Enrolled as a Solicitor in Scotland, 1970; Partner, Simpson Boath Lyall & Co., Dundee. Recreation: fishing. Address: (h.) The Dower House, Liff, by Dundee; T.-Dundee 580716.

Lyall, Michael Hodge, MB, ChB, ChM, FRCSEdin. Consultant Surgeon, Tayside Health Board, since 1975; Honorary Senior Lecturer, Dundee University, since 1975; b. 5.12.41, Methilhill, Fife; m., Catherine B. Jarvie; 3 s.

Educ. Buckhaven High School; St. Andrews University. President, Tayside Division, Ileostomy Association of Great Britain; Member, Scottish Executive Committee, British Digestive Foundation; Chairman, Ninewells Medical Staff Committee. Recreations: Member, North Fife Rotary Club; computing. Address: (h.) 26 Linden Avenue, Newport on Tay, Fife, DD6 8DU.

Lyddon, William Derek Collier, CB, DLitt, BA, RIBA, DipTP, FRTPI. Chief Planner, Scottish Development Department, 1967-85; b. 17.11.25, Loughton, Essex; m., Marian Louise Kaye; 2 d. Educ. Wrekin College; University College, London. Depute Chief Architect Planner, Cumbernauld Development Corporation; Chief Architect Planner, Skelmersdale Development Corporation. President, International Society of City and Regional Planners, 1981-84. Address: (h.) 38 Dick Place, Edinburgh; T.-031-667 2266.

Lyell, 3rd Baron, (Charles Lyell), Bt. Parliamentary Under-Secretary of State, Northern Ireland Office, since 1984; b. 27.3.39. Educ. Eton; Christ Church, Oxford. Scots Guards, 1957-59; CA; Opposition Whip, 1974-79; Government Whip, 1979-84; Member, Queen's Bodyguard for Scotland (Royal Company of Archers). Address: (h.) Kinnordy House, Kirriemuir, Angus.

Lygo, Robert Ernest, BSc. HM Inspector of Schools (Scotland), Higher Grade, since 1972; b. 15.9.29, Warrington; m., Kathleen Mary Newman; 1 s.; 2 d. Educ. Wade Deacon Grammar School; Nottingham University. Station Education Officer, RAF; Teacher of Mathematics, then Head of Department, King Edward VI School, Chelmsford; Deputy Head, Great Baddow Comprehensive School, Chelmsford; HM Inspector of Schools (Scotland). Recreations: walking; gardening. Address: (h.) 25 Charles Crescent, Lenzie, Glasgow, G66 5HH; T.-041-776 4432.

Lyle, Lt.-Col. (Archibald) Michael, JP. Vice Lord Lieutenant, Perth and Kinross, since 1984; b. 1.5.19; m., Hon. Elizabeth Sinclair; 3 d.; 1 d. deceased. Educ. Eton; Trinity College, Oxford. Black Watch, RHR, 1939-45; Chairman, T&AFA, 1959-64; Member, Queen's Bodyguard for Scotland (Royal Company of Archers); Member, Perth and Kinross County Council, 1946-74; Member, Tayside Regional Council, 1974-79.

Lyle, David Angus, MA, LLB, FBIM, FCIS, SSC, NP. Agency Secretary, Scottish Development Agency, and Company Secretary of a number of associated companies, since 1979; b. 7.9.40; m., Dorothy Ann Clark; 1 s.; 3 d. Educ. George Watson's College, Edinburgh; Edinburgh University. Account Executive, advertising agencies, London; indentured, Edinburgh Corporation; Solicitor, Lloyds and Scottish Finance Ltd., Edinburgh; Depute County Clerk, East Lothian County Council; Director of Administration and Law, Dumfries and Galloway Regional Council. Recreations: shooting; golf; bridge. Address: (h.) Ravelston, Glencairn Road, Kilmacolm, Renfrewshire; T.-050587 2321.

Lynch, Andrew Hunter. Member, Dundee District Council (Convener, Special Appeals Committee), since 1980; Chairman, Dundee

Local Health Council; b. 18.3.39, Scunthorpe; m., Elizabeth McConnachie; 1 s. Educ. various schools in Hong Kong, Scotland and England; Dundee Technical College. RAF, 1960-62. Convener, Development Control Committee, Dundee District Council, 1982-84. Recreations: music; crosswords; watching sport. Address: (h.) 13A Pannal Court, Dundee, DD2 3SE; T.-Dundee 816554.

Lyon, Rev. David Henry Scott, MA, BD, STM. Minister, Church of Scotland, since 1952; General Secretary, Board of World Mission and Unity, since 1975; b. 31.7.21, Edinburgh; m., Alison May Haggis; 1 s.; 2 d. Educ. Royal High School, Edinburgh; Edinburgh University; St. Andrews University; Union Theological Seminary, New York. War Service, 2nd Bn., Argyll and Sutherland Highlanders (Captain and Adjutant); mentioned in a Despatch; Scottish Secretary, Student Christian Movement; Church of Scotland Missionary, Nagpur, India; Secretary, National Christian Council of India; Dean, Centre for Training in Christian Mission, Selly Oak, College, Birmingham. Member, Executive Committee, British Council of Churches and Scottish Churches Council; Chairman, Conference for World Mission, BCC. Recreation: gardening. Address: (b.) Church of Scotland, 121 George Street, Edinburgh; T.-031-225 5722.

Lyons, Sheriff Hamilton, BL. Temporary Sheriff, since 1984; b. 3.8.18, Gourock; m., Jean Cathro Blair; 2 s. Educ. Gourock High School; Greenock High School; Glasgow University. Practised as Solicitor in Greenock, 1940-66; Sheriff, Stornoway and Lochmaddy, 1966-68; Sheriff, North Strathclyde (formerly Renfrew and Argyll), 1968-84. Council Member, Law Society of Scotland, 1950-66 (Vice-President, 1962-63); Member: Law Reform Committee for Scotland, 1954-64, Committee of Inquiry on Children and Young Persons, 1961-64, Committee of Enquiry on Sheriff Courts, 1963-67, Sheriff Courts Rules Council, 1952-66, Scottish Probation Advisory and Training Council, 1959-69. Recreation: family. Address: (h.) 14 Cloch Road, Gourock, PA19 1AB; T.-0475 32566.

Lythe, Charlotte Margaret, MA, FSA Scot. Senior Lecturer in Economics, Dundee University, since 1978; b. 15.10.41, Leven, East Yorkshire. Educ. Dundee High School; St. Andrews University. Assistant Lecturer in Political Economy, Aberdeen University; Lecturer in Economics, Queen's College, Dundee, and Dundee University. Member, Social Security Appeals Tribunal, Dundee Area. Recreations: archaeology; local history. Address: (b.) Department of Economics, The University, Dundee, DD1 4HN; T.-0382 23181.

Mac/Mc

McAdam, Robert, MSc, MEd, CEng, MIMechE, MIProdE, AMBIM. Principal, James Watt College, Greenock; b. 7.7.25, Glasgow; m., Elizabeth Campbell Thomsom; 3 s.; 1 d. Educ. Gourock High School; Glasgow University; Strathclyde University; Paisley College. Apprentice Engineer, 1941-45; Engineer, Royal Navy, 1945-47; Design Draughtsman, Scott Shipbuilding & Engineering Company, 1947-49; Shipyard Manager, Smith & Houston, 1949-51; Lecturer, Paisley College, 1952-60, Jordanhill, 1960-75. Address: (h.) 67 Caledonia Crescent, Gourock, Renfrewshire; T.-0475 31592.

MacAllan, Harry Bertram Wedderburn, BL. Writer to the Signet, since 1950; Partner, Maclay, Murray & Spens, Solicitors, Glasgow and Edinburgh, since 1967; b. 14.8.20, St. Andrews; m., Grace Edwards (deceased). Educ. Canford School; Edinburgh University. Intelligence Corps, North Africa, Italy, Greece, India and Malyasia, 1939-45; admitted Solicitor in Scotland, 1950, Advocate in Kenya, 1953 (Partner in legal firm in Kenya, until 1964). Publication: Collected Poems, 1940; Contributor of verse to various journals. Recreations: travel; writing; golf. Address: (b.) 169 West George Street, Glasgow, G2 2LA; T.-041-248 5011.

McAlpine, Ian Archibald McNaughton, OBE (1985), BSc (Hons), NDA, MIM. Managing Director, Scottish Milk Marketing Board, since 1975; Chairman, Company of Scottish Cheesemakers Ltd., since 1972; Chairman, UK Dairy Industry Research Policy Committee, since 1983; b. 27.7.25, Johnstone; m., Garry Helen Bell Greig; 1 s.; 1 d. Educ. Paisley Grammar School; St. Andrews University; Glasgow University; West of Scotland Agricultural Colege. Scottish Milk Marketing Board: joined, 1952, Assistant Marketing Officer, 1954, Marketing Officer, 1958, Marketing Director, 1962, General Manager, 1969; Director, Scottish Milk Publicity Council Ltd., 1967-82, General Manager, 1969; Member, Permanent Committee of Commission C, International Dairy Federation, 1980-84; Member, Council, Hannah Research Institute, since 1983; National President, Society of Dairy Technology, 1980-81. Recreations: golf; curling; gardening; hill-walking. Address: (h.) Knaresby, 6 Newton Avenue, Elderslie, Renfrewshire; T.-0505 22734.

McAlpine, Margaret Helen, JP. Member, City of Edinburgh District Council, since 1977 (Opposition Spokesman on Environmental Health, since 1984); b. 30.12.32, Edinburgh; m., George W. McAlpine; 5 d. Educ. Rudolf Steiner School, Edinburgh. Member, Port of Leith Housing Association, 1975-78; Member, Edinburgh Local Health Council, 1977-80 (Convener, Maternity and Child Care Services, 1978-79); City of Edinburgh District Council: Conservative Group Secretary, 1978-82, 1983-84, Chairman, Environmental Health Committee, 1979-84; Member: Management Committee, Leith Benevolent Association, since 1977, Leith Community Association Executive, since 1977; Chairman, Granton Housing Association, since 1980; Member, Edinburgh Festival Council, since 1982; Vice Chairman, Newhaven and District Community Association, since 1984; Member, Justices Committee, since 1984. Recreations: swimming; reading. Address: (h.) 310 Ferry Road, Goldenacre, Edinburgh, EH5 3NP; T.-031-552 4391.

McAlpine, Stuart Gemmell, MD, FRCP, FRCPGlas. Consultant Physician, Royal Alexandra Infirmary, Paisley, since 1963; Honorary Clinical Lecturer, Glasgow University, since 1968; b. 6.3.27, Glasgow; m., Cynthia Joan McPherson; 2 s.; 1 d. Educ. Glasgow Academy; Glasgow University. Royal Army Medical Corps, 1950-52; medical training, Dumfries and Galloway Royal Infirmary and Glasgow Royal Infirmary; Examiner in Medicine, Glasgow University and Royal College of Physicians and Surgeons of Glasgow; Member, Argyll and Clyde Health Board. Recreations: golf; fishing. Address: (h.) Windyknowe, 168 Southbrae Drive, Glasgow, G13 1TY; T.-041-954 6670.

McAlpine, Thomas, BSc, CEng, MIEE. Managing Director, Chieftain Industries PLC, Livingston, since 1971; b. 23.9.29, Motherwell; m., Isobel Lindsay; 2 s.; 1 d. Educ. Dalziel High School, Motherwell; Strathclyde University. National Service, REME, 1952-54 (2nd Lt.); Chief Engineer, Belmos Co. Ltd., Bellshill, 1954-58; Chief Development Engineer, Mine Safety Appliances, Glasgow, 1958-62; Managing Director, Rowen Engineering Co. Ltd., Glasgow, 1962-71. Executive Vice Chairman Administration, Scottish National Party (former Vice President, SNP); Parliamentary candidate, Clydesdale (Lanark), 1974, 1979, 1983. Recreations: when young, played rugby, swimming and tennis. Address: (h.) Millrig House, Millrig Road, Wiston, by Biggar, Lanarkshire, ML12 6HT; T.-Lamington 683.

McAndrew, Alexander, FIB (Scot), FCIS, NP, Solicitor. General Manager (Administration), The Royal Bank of Scotland plc, since 1978; b. 22.7.26, Thornton, Fife; m., Edith; 1 s.; 1 d. Educ. Buckhaven High School. Joined Commercial Bank of Scotland Ltd., Kirkcaldy, 1941; transferred to Head Office, Edinburgh, 1946; Assistant Law Secretary, 1959; Assistant Secretary and Joint Law Secretary, 1966; Secretary of the Bank, 1971. Honorary Treasurer, Edinburgh and East of Scotland Branch, Institute of Chartered Secretaries and Administrators; Honorary Treasurer, Scottish Disability Foundation. Recreations: curling; golf; gardening. Address: (h.) Whitecrest, 15 Craigs Bank, Edinburgh, EH12 8HD; T.-031-339 4388.

McArdle, Colin S., MD, FRCS, FRCSEdin, FRCSGlas. Consultant Surgeon, University Department of Surgery, Glasgow Royal Infirmary, since 1981; b. 10.10.39, Glasgow; m., June M.C. Merchant; 2 s.; 1 d. Educ. Jordanhill College School; Glasgow University. Senior Registrar in General Surgery, Western Infirmary, Glasgow, 1972-75; Consultant Surgeon: Victoria Infirmary, Glasgow, 1975-78, Glasgow Royal Infirmary, 1978-80. Address: (h.) 4 Collylinn Road, Bearsden, Glasgow.

MacArthur, Allan Ian, BD, JP. Minister, Lochcarron Parish, since 1973; Member, Crofters Commission, since 1984; District Councillor, since 1984; b. 25.5.28, Marvig, Isle of Lewis; m., Effie Macleod; 1 s.; 6 d. Educ. Nicolson Institute, Stornoway; Glasgow University and Trinity College. Meteorologist, Air Ministry and Falkland Islands Dependencies Survey, Antarctica;

teaching; Minister of Religion and Presbytery Clerk. Member, Local Health Council; former Secretary and Vice-Chairman, Community Council. Address: Church of Scotland Manse, Lochcarron, Ross-shire, IV54 8YD; T.-05202 278.

Macarthur, Sheriff Charles Ramsay, QC (Scot). Sheriff of Tayside, Central and Fife, since 1981; m. Educ. Glasgow University. Royal Navy, 1942-46; Solicitor, 1952-59; Scottish Bar, 1960; Sheriff of the Lothians and Borders, 1974-76.

Macarthur, Edith. Actress; b. Ardrossan, Ayrshire. Educ. Ardrossan Academy. Began career, 1948, with Wilson Barrett Company, then Perth Repertory, Gateway Theatre Company, Citizens' Theatre, Glasgow, Bristol Old Vic, Royal Shakespeare Company, Ochtertyre Theatre, Royal Lyceum Theatre Company, West End; television work includes The Borderers, Sunset Song, Weir of Hermiston, Sutherland's Law; plays the "lady laird" in Take the High Road, STV; recent stage appearances in solo-performance play, Marie of Scotland, Jamie the Saxt and The Thrie Estates for the Scottish Theatre Company. Recreations: music; books. Address: (b.) c/o Larry Dalzell Associates Ltd., 126 Kennington Park Road, London, SE11 4DJ.

McArthur, Rev. Farquhar MacDonald, LTh, BD. Minister, Kirk o'Field Pleasance, Edinburgh, since 1974; b. 8.6.39, Glasgow; m., Euphemia MacGilp Lindsay Shaw; 3 d. Educ. St. George's Road Junior Secondary School; Glasgow University; Edinburgh University. Served engineering apprenticeship, Barr & Stroud Ltd., 1955-60; journeyman scientific instrument-maker, 1960-65; relief Teacher of Engineering, 1965-67; Probationer Assistant, then Locum, Renfield. Fieldwork Director, Faculty of Divinity, New College, Edinburgh. Recreations: distance running; swimming; hill-walking; music; reading. Address: (h.) 36a Lauder Road, Edinburgh, EH9 2JF; T.-031-667 7954.

Macartney, W.J. Allan, MA, BLitt, PhD. Staff Tutor, Social Sciences, The Open University in Scotland, since 1975; Honorary Fellow, Edinburgh University, since 1981; Member, National Executive Committee, Scottish National Party, since 1984; b. 1941, Accra, Ghana; m, J.D. Anne Forsyth; 2 s.; 1 d. Educ. Elgin Academy; Tuebingen University; Marburg University; Edinburgh University; Glasgow University. Teacher, Eastern Nigeria, 1963-64; Lecturer in Government and Administration, University of Botswana, Lesotho and Swaziland, 1966-74 (Assistant Dean, 1971-74); Research Fellow, Edinburgh University, 1974-75; Honorary Secretary, Unit for the Study of Government in Scotland, 1980-82; Chairman, Scottish Self-Government College, since 1982; Chairman, Saint Andrew Society, since 1978; Church of Scotland Elder, since 1979; Parliamentary candidate (SNP), 1970, 1979, 1983 (Foreign Affairs Spokesman, since 1984). Publications: Readings in Boleswa Government, 1971; The Referendum Experience: Scotland 1979, 1981; Islands of Europe, 1984. Recreations: music; languages; walking; vexillogy. Address: (b.) The Open University in Scotland, 60 Melville Street, Edinburgh, EH3 7HF; T.-031-226 3851.

Macaskill, Allan Nicolson. Chairman, Lorn, Mid Argyll, Kintyre and Islay Licensing Board, since 1984; Vice Chairman, Tourism, Leisure and Recreation Committee, Argyll and Bute District Council, since 1984; Vice Chairman, Association of Scottish Self Caterers, since 1985; b. 10.2.43, Stirling; m., Elizabeth Dawn; 1 s.; 1 d. Educ. Oban High School; Glasgow High School; Anniesland College of Further Education. Recreations: reading; sport, especially athletics. Address: (h.) Ullinish, Balvicar Farm, by Oban; T.-08523 221.

MacAskill, Norman Alexander, JP. Vice-Chairman, Crofters Commission, since 1966; b. 1.11.24, Lochinver; m., Joan Logan Brown; 2 s. Educ. Lochinver Public School; Golspie High School. Customs and Excise Officer; Social Welfare Officer, North West Sutherland; Secretary, North and West Sutherland Council of Social Service; Chairman: Sutherland Tourist Organisation, Sutherland Valuation Appeals Committee; Member, Highlands and Islands Area Manpower Board, MSC; Member, Scottish Rent Assessment Panel. Recreations: fishing; music; history; archaeology. Address: (h.) 8 Cruamer, Lochinver, Lairg, Sutherland; T.-057 14 291.

Macaulay, Rev. Donald, OBE, JP. Parish Minister, Park, Isle of Lewis, since 1968; Vice Convener, Western Isles Council; Member, HIDB Consultative Council; b. 25.2.26, Great Bernera; m., Catherine Macleod; 3 s.; 3 d. Educ. Great Bernera School; Aberdeen University. Several years a fisherman; Member: Ross and Cromarty County Council, 1969-75, Lewis District Council, 1969-75; Convener, Western Isles Council, 1974-82; Member, COSLA Policy Committee, 1975-82; Member, Comunn na Gaelic. Recreations: fishing; travel; local history; silviculture. Address: Park Manse, Isle of Lewis; T.-0851 88 257.

Macaulay, Donald, MA (Aberdeen), BA (Cantab), DipGenLing. Reader in Celtic, Aberdeen University, since 1980 (Head, Celtic Department, since 1967); b. 21.5.30, Bernerna, Isle of Lewis; m., Ella Murray Sangster; 1 s.; 1 d. Educ. Nicolson Institute, Stornoway; Aberdeen University; Cambridge University. Taught: English Language, Edinburgh University, 1958-60; Irish and Gaelic, Trinity College, Dublin, 1960-63; Applied Linguistics, Edinburgh University, 1963-67; Celtic Studies, Aberdeen University, since 1967. Chairman, Gaelic Committee, CCC; Editor, Scottish Gaelic Studies; Secretary, International Committee for the Study of Celtic Cultures, UNESCO; Gaelic poet: Scobhrach as a' Chlaich, 1967; Editor, Nua-bhardachd Ghaidhlig, 1976. Recreations: beagle walking; TV movies. Address: (h.) North Deeside Road, Peterculter, Aberdeenshire, AB1 OQB; T.-0224 732217.

McAvoy, Thomas McLaughlin. Member, Strathclyde Regional Council, since 1982; b. 14.12.43, Rutherglen; m., Eleanor Kerr; 4 s. Past Chairman, Rutherglen Community Council, Fernhill Tenants Association and Rutherglen Federation of Tenants Associations. Address: (h.) 70 Kingsburn Grove, Rutherglen, Glasgow, G73 2EX; T.-041-643 1954.

MacBain, Gordon Campbell, MB, FRCSGlas, FRCSEdin. Consultant Surgeon, Southern General Hospital, Glasgow, since 1974; b. 29.4.38, Glasgow; m., Margaret Janet Wilson; 1 s.; 1 d. Educ. High School of Glasgow; Glasgow University. Health Service appointments; Leverhulme Research Fellow, Royal College of Surgeons of England; Lecturer in Surgery, Nairobi University; further Health Service posts; Director, Ross Hall Hospital, Glasgow; Trustee, Forum Arts Society. Recreations: golf; squash; skiing; amateur operatics. Address: (h.) 55 Drumlin Drive, Milngavie, Glasgow, G62 6NF; T.-041-956 3388.

Macbeth, Alastair Murdoch, MA, DPhil. Senior Lecturer, Department of Education, Glasgow University, since 1973; b. 26.4.35, Oxford; m., Rosemary; 2 s.; 1 d. Educ. Oundle; Oriel College, Oxford. Pilot, RAF, 1953-55; ICI, 1958-62; Teacher, 1962-67; Headteacher, King George VI Secondary School, Honiara, 1967-72. Educational Adviser: Scottish Parent Teacher Council, European Parents' Association, Scottish Consumer Council, and various other bodies. Publications: Scottish School Councils, 1980; The Child Between, 1984. Recreations: painting; jogging; mountains.

McBride, James. Scottish Regional Secretary, UCATT, since 1983; Operatives' Secretary, Scottish Regional Committee for the Building Industry; b. 15.8.30, Glasgow; m., Aileen Josephine; 3 d. Educ. St. Gerards Secondary School. Scottish Regional Organiser, UCATT, 1978-83. Recreations: gardening; swimming. Address: (b.) 6 Fitzroy Place, Glasgow, G3 7RL; T.-041-221 4893.

MacCabe, Professor Colin Myles Joseph, MA, PhD. Head of Production, British Film Institute, since 1985; Visiting Professor, Strathclyde University, since 1985; Chairman, John Logie Baird Centre for Research in Television and Film, since 1985; b. 9.2.49, London; 1 s.; 1 d. Educ. St. Benedict's School, London; Trinity College, Cambridge. Research Fellow, Emmanuel College, Cambridge, 1974-76; Fellow, King's College, Cambridge, 1976-81; Assistant Lecturer, Faculty of English, 1976-81; Professor of English Studies, Strathclyde University, 1981-85. Publications: James Joyce and the Revolution of the Word, 1979; Godard: Images, Sounds, Politics, 1980; Theatrical Essays: Film, Linguistics, Literature, 1985. Recreations: eating; drinking; talking. Address: (b.) Department of English Studies, Strathclyde University, Glasgow; T.-041-552 4400.

McCabe, Rev. George Elrick, JP, BA. Minister, Dalkeith St. John's and King's Park, since 1973; b. 3.9.25, Berhampore, India; m., Mollie; 1 s.; 1 d. Educ. Woodstock, Mussoorie, India; Boroughmuir School, Edinburgh; London University; New College, Edinburgh; Open University. Left school to take up farming in the Borders, 1940; Farm and Estate Manager, Dr. Graham's Homes, Kalimpong, India, 1949; ordained Baptist Minister, Port Ellen, Islay, 1958; ordained Church of Scotland Minister, Glendevon linked with Muckhart, 1967; elected Member, Perth and Kinross County Council, 1970; Moderator, Lothian Presbytery, 1977-78; Moderator, Lothian Synod, 1979-80. Recreations: gardening; travel. Address: (h.) 51 Eskbank Road, Dalkeith, Midlothian, EH22 3BU; T.-031-663 3114.

MacCaig, Norman, OBE, MA, DLitt (Edinburgh), DUniv (Stirling), FRSL, FRSE, ARSA. Poet; b. 14.11.10, Edinburgh; m., Isabel; 1 s.; 1 d. Educ. Royal High School, Edinburgh; Edinburgh University. Former schoolteacher; former Writer in Residence, Edinburgh University; former Reader in Poetry, Stirling University; publications of poetry: Far Cry, 1943, The Inward Eye, 1946, Riding Lights, 1955, The Sinai Sort, 1957, A Common Grace, 1960, A Round of Applause, 1962, Measures, 1965, Surroundings, 1966, Rings on a Tree, 1968, A Man in my Position, 1969, The White Bird, 1973, The World's Room, 1974, Tree of Strings, 1977, The Equal Skies, 1980, A World of Difference, 1983; Selected Poems, 1971; Penguin Modern Poets 21, 1972; Old Maps and New (selected poems), 1978; Collected Poems, 1985; awards: seven Scottish Arts Council awards, two Society of Author awards; Heinemann Award, Cholmondely Award. Recreations: literature; music; fishing. Address: 7 Leamington Terrace, Edinburgh, EH10 4JW; T.-031-229 1809.

McCall, James, BSc, MEd, PhD, ABPsS. Vice-Principal, Jordanhill College of Education, since 1983; b. 14.7.41, Kilmarnock; m., Mary Elizabeth Stuart Maclean; 3 s. Educ. Kilmarnock Academy; Glasgow University; Aberdeen University; Jordanhill College of Education. Teacher of Science, Hillhead High School, Glasgow; Principal Teacher of Physics, Queen's Park Secondary School, Glasgow; Lecturer in Educational Psychology, Aberdeen College of Education; Head, Psychology Department, Jordanhill College of Education. Publication: Techniques for the Assessment of Practical Skills in Foundation Science, 1983. Recreations: bridge; golf; skiing. Address: (b.) Jordanhill College of Education, Southbrae Drive, Glasgow, G13 1PP; T.-041-959 1232.

McCall, James Robertson, MA (Hons). Proprietor, James McCall Publishing and Public Relations Consultancy, since 1984; b. 3.1.48, Moffat. Educ. Ayr Academy; Glasgow University. Graduate Trainee, Associated Book Publishers, London, 1970-72; Production Controller, Longman Group, 1972-74; Commissioning Editor, Blackie & Son, Glasgow, 1974, Educational Publishing Director, 1980-84. Joint Founder and first Chairman, Scottish Young Publishers Society, 1977; Member, Board, Educational Publishers Council; Vice Chairman, Scottish Council, Social Democratic Party. Recreations: music; gardening; travel; politics. Address: 26 Middlemuir Road, Lenzie, Glasgow, G66 4NA; T.-041-776 4431.

McCallum, Donald Murdo, CBE, DL, BSc, FEng, FIEE, CBIM, FRSE. Director, Ferranti plc, since 1970; Chairman, Ferranti Defence Systems Ltd., since 1984; Chairman, Ferranti Industrial Electronics Ltd., since 1984; General Manager, Ferranti Scottish Group, 1968-85; b.

6.8.22, Edinburgh; m., 1, Barbara Clark (deceased); 1 d.; 2, Margaret Illingworth. Educ. George Watson's Boys' College; Edinburgh University. Admiralty Signal Establishment, 1942-46; Standard Telecommunication Laboratories, 1946; joined Ferranti, 1947; Chairman: Scottish Tertiary Education Advisory Council, since 1984, Scottish Council (Development and Industry), since 1985; Trustee, Scottish Civic Trust. Recreations: fishing; photography. Address: (h.) 46 Heriot Row, Edinburgh, 3; T.-031-225 9331.

McCallum, Forbes, JP, MA, DipPM, AIPM. Member, City of Aberdeen District Council, since 1977; Lecturer, Business School, Robert Gordon's Institute of Technology, Aberdeen, since 1975; b. 10.6.47, Aberdeen. Educ. Aberdeen Grammar School; Aberdeen University; Robert Gordon's Institute of Technology, Aberdeen. Personnel Officer, Glaxo Laboratories Ltd., 1969-73; Personnel Manager, Richards Ltd., 1973-75. Deputy Chairman, Scottish Liberal Party, 1975-79; Parliamentary candidate (Liberal), North Aberdeen, 1970 and 1974 (February and October). Address: (h.) 43D Jute Street, Aberdeen, AB2 3EX; T.-0224 635661.

MacCallum, James Richard, BSc, PhD, DSc, CChem, FRSC. Reader in Chemistry, St. Andrews University; b. 3.5.36, Kilmartin; m., Eleanor Margaret Thomson; 2 s.; 1 d. Educ. Dumfries Academy; Glasgow University. Technical Officer, ICI Fibres Division, 1961-62; ICI Research Fellow, Aberdeen University, 1962-63; Lecturer, St. Andrews University, 1964. Elder, St. Leonards Church, St. Andrews. Recreation: golf. Address: (h.) 9 Cairnsden Gardens, St. Andrews, Fife; T.-0334 73152.

McCallum, John, BA, DPA. Head, Teacher Training Branch, Scottish Education Department, since 1976; b. 12.6.25, Glasgow; m., Hazel Stacey. Educ. Allan Glen's School; Glasgow University; Open University. War Service; various career service appointments, Department of Health for Scotland, Scottish Development Department, Scottish Home and Health Department and Scottish Education Department; Head, Civil Contingencies Branch, SHHD, 1973. Former TA Officer (Major, RASC (TA)); Reader and Elder, Church of Scotland. Recreations: all things Gaelic; dog walking; talking. Address: (h.) 15 The Crescent, Morningside Drive, Edinburgh, EH10 5NX; T.-031-447 8339.

MacCallum, Neil Robb. National Secretary, Scottish National Party, since 1981; b. 15.5.54, Edinburgh. Educ. Firrhill High School, Edinburgh; Napier College, Edinburgh. Parliamentary candidate (SNP), Edinburgh South, 1983; Assistant National Secretary, SNP, 1980-81; Member, Edinburgh District Council, 1977-80. Recreations: reading; folk music. Address: (h.) 18 Redford Avenue, Edinburgh, EH13 0BU; T.-031-441 3724.

Maccallum, Norman Ronald Low, BSc, PhD, CEng, FIMechE. Reader in Mechanical Engineering, Glasgow University, since 1982; b. 18.2.31, Walston, Lanarkshire; m., Mary Bentley Alexander; 1 s.; 2 d. Educ. Allan Glen's

School, Glasgow; Glasgow University. Assistant in Mechanical Engineering, Glasgow University, 1952-55; National Service, Royal Navy, 1955-57 (final rank: Sub-Lt.); Lecturer in Mechanical Engineering, Glasgow University, 1957-61; Performance Engineer, Rolls-Royce Ltd. (Scottish Group), 1961-62; Lecturer in Mechanical Engineering, then Senior Lecturer, Glasgow University, 1962-72. Session Clerk, Trinity Church, Cambuslang. Recreation: singing. Address: (h.) 43 Stewarton Drive, Cambuslang, Glasgow, G72 8DQ.

McCallum, Tom. Member, Dumfries and Galloway Regional Council, since 1978 (Vice-Chairman, Manpower Committee); Member, Nithsdale District Council, since 1977 (Vice-Chairman, General Purposes Committee); b. 2.10.17, Forth, Lanarkshire; m., Elizabeth Napier Young; 1 s.; 1 d. Educ. Forth School. Entered baking trade in family business; served in Black Watch (RHR), 1939-46 (Sergeant); Master Baker, 1946-72. Treasurer, An Comunn Gaidhealach, Dumfries; Secretary, Age Concern, Dumfries. Recreations: singing; country dancing; meeting people. Address: (h.) 7 Barnton Place, Dumfries, DG1 4HH; T.-0387 62021.

McCalman, Donald, BSc, MEd. HM Inspector of Schools, since 1970; b.26.9.27, Glasgow; m., Mary Jane Elizabeth McMath; 2 s.; 1 d. Educ. Glasgow University. Teacher of Chemistry, Glasgow, 1949-55; Education Officer, Kenya, 1955-57; Surveyor/Base Leader, British Antarctic Survey, 1957-60; Education Officer, Kenya, 1960-63; Lecturer/Senior Lecturer, Dundee College of Education, 1963-70. Polar Medal, 1963. Recreations: sailing; mountaineering. Address: (b.) New St. Andrew's House, St. James Centre, Edinburgh, EH1; T.-031-556 8400.

McCance, Neil Anderson Davis, MBIM, DMS. Secretary, Hannah Research Institute, Ayr, since 1975; b. 19.8.29, Kobe, Japan; m., Anne Rosemary McOwan; 1 s.; 1 d. Educ. Edinburgh Academy; Royal Military Academy, Sandhurst. Commissioned, The Royal Scots (The Royal Regiment), 1949; retired, 1974, with rank of Major after service in UK and abroad. Recreations: mostly countryside pursuits; gardening. Address: (h.) Woodside, Bridgend Mains, Sundrum, by Ayr; T.-0292 570394.

McCann, Peter Toland McAree, CBE (1977), JP, DL. Solicitor and Notary Public; b. 2.8.24; m.; 1 s. Educ. St. Mungo's Academy; Glasgow University. Lord Provost and Lord Lieutenant, City of Glasgow, 1975-77.

McCann, William Stephen, CA, CBIM. Chairman and Managing Director, Hiram Walker & Sons (Scotland) PLC; Council Member, Scotch Whisky Association, since 1971; b. 14.11.21, Edinburgh; m., Doreen Kate Hackwood; 1 s.; 1 d. Educ. George Heriot's School; Edinburgh University. RAF, 1941-46 (Flt.-Lt./Bomber Navigator); British Petroleum Co. Ltd., London, 1947-61 (Assistant General Manager); Managing Director, Overseas Activities, British Aluminium Co. Ltd., London, 1961-63; joined Hiram Walker & Sons (Scotland) PLC, 1963; appointed Managing Director, 1969. Member, NEDO Working Groups on Scotch Whisky, 1978 and 1984. Recreations: gardening; reading; travel. Address: (b.) Glasgow Road, Dumbarton, G82 1ND;T.-0389 65111.

McCarthy, James, BSc. Deputy Director (Scotland), Nature Conservancy Council, since 1975; b. 6.5.36, Dundee; m.; 2 s.; 1 d. Educ. Harris Academy, Dundee; Aberdeen University; University of East Africa, Kampala. Military Service, 1954-56 (Royal Marines, commissioned Black Watch, seconded King's African Rifles); Leverhulme Scholar, Makerere College, Kampala, 1959-61; Assistant Conservator of Forests, Tanzania, and Lecturer in Forest Ecology, Forest Training School, 1961-63; Deputy Regional Officer (North England), Nature Conservancy, 1963-69. Churchill Fellow, USA, 1976; Assessor, Scottish Environmental Education Council. Recreation: cross-country skiing. Address: (h.) 6a Ettrick Road, Edinburgh; T.-031-229 1916.

McCartney, Adam Scott, NDD(T). Director of Creameries, Scottish Milk Marketing Board, since 1980; b. 10.3.38, Crieff; m., Kathryn Margaret; 2 d. Educ. Morrison's Academy, Crieff; West of Scotland Agricultural College. Management appointments, Express Dairy Company Ltd., 1961-73; Production Director, Scottish Milk Marketing Board, 1973-80. Recreations: sport; gardening. Address: (h.) 8 Brackendene, Houston, Renfrewshire.

McCartney, Hugh. MP (Labour), Clydebank and Milngavie, since 1983 (Dunbartonshire Central, 1974-83, Dunbartonshire East, 1970-74); b. 3.1.20. Educ. Royal Technical College, Glasgow. Town Councillor, Kirkintilloch, 1955-70; Member, Dunbarton County Council, 1965-70.

McClellan, John Forrest, MA. Under Secretary, Industry Department for Scotland, 1980-85; b. 15.8.32, Glasgow; m., Eva Maria Pressel; 3 s.; 1 d. Educ. Aberdeen Grammar School; Aberdeen University. 2nd Lt., Gordon Highlanders and Nigeria Regiment, Royal West African Frontier Force, 1954-56; entered Civil Service, 1956; Assistant Principal, Scottish Education Department, 1956-59; Private Secretary to Permanent Under Secretary of State, Scottish Office, 1959-60; Principal, Scottish Education Department, 1960-68; Civil Service Fellow, Glasgow University, 1968-69; Scottish Education Department: Assistant Secretary, Schools Division, 1969-71, Assistant Secretary, Higher Education Division, 1971-77; Assistant Under Secretary of State, Scottish Office, 1977-80. Recreations: gardening; walking. Address: (h.) Grangeneuk, West Linton, Peeblesshire; T.-West Linton 60502.

McClelland, David Brian Lorimer, MB, ChB, BSc (Hons), MD, FRCPEdin. Regional Director, Edinburgh and SE Scotland Blood Transfusion Service, since 1979; part-time Senior Lecturer, Department of Clinical Pharmacology, Edinburgh University, since 1979; b. 12.5.44, Dublin; m., Elizabeth Rae; 2 s.; 2 d. Educ. Calday Grange Grammar School, Cheshire; Edinburgh University. Recreations: family; windsurfing. Address: (b.) Regional Transfusion Centre, Royal Infirmary, Edinburgh; T.-031-229 2585.

McClelland, Samuel Edward, BSc, PhD. HM Chief Inspector of Schools, since 1973; b. 8.4.31, Belfast; m., Margaret E. Pike; 3 s. Educ. Methodist College, Belfast; Queen's University, Belfast; Reading University. Research and teaching appointments; HM Inspector of Schools. Recreation: the great outdoors. Address: (b.) Scottish Office, New St. Andrews House, Edinburgh; T.-031-556 8400.

McClelland, Thomas Henry, BAgr, MIBiol. Head, Animal Production Department, West of Scotland Agricultural College, since 1975; Director, Kirton/Auchtertyre Farms, WSAC, since 1975; b. 10.5.34, Belfast; m., Maureen Mardon; 1 s.; 2 d. Educ. Belfast Royal Academy; Queen's University of Belfast. Lecturer, Government Agricultural College, Northern Ireland, 1959-68; Research Scientist, Animal Breeding Research Organisation, 1968-75. Member, Governing Board, Hill Farming Research Organisation, since 1981; Session Clerk, Ardoch Parish Church, Braco. Recreations: reading; gardening; sport. Address: (h.) 15 Grinnan Road, Braco, Perthshire; T.-Braco 308.

McClure, David, RSA, RSW. Head of Drawing and Painting, Duncan of Jordanstone College of Art, Dundee, since 1983; b. 20.2.26; m.; 2 s.; 1 d. Educ. Queen's Park School, Glasgow; Glasgow University; Edinburgh University; Edinburgh College of Art. One man exhibitions, Palermo, Edinburgh, London, Birmingham.

McCluskey, Baron, (John Herbert McCluskey), QC (Scot), MA, LLB. Life Peer; b. 12.6.29; m.; 2 s.; 1 d. Educ. St. Bede's Grammar School, Manchester; Holy Cross Academy, Edinburgh; Edinburgh University. Admitted Faculty of Advocates, 1955; Advocate-Depute, 1964-71; Sheriff Principal of Dumfries and Galloway, 1973-74; Solicitor General for Scotland, 1974-79.

McColl, Ian, CBE (1983). Vice-President, Newspaper Press Fund, since 1981; Chairman, Media Division, Commonwealth Games, Scotland 1986, since 1983; b. 22.2.15; m.; 1 d. Educ. Hillhead High School. RAF, 1940-46 (mentioned in Despatches); Editor, Scottish Daily Express, 1961-71; Editor, Daily Express, 1971-74; Chairman, Scottish Express Newspapers Ltd., 1975-82.

McColl, James Hamilton, NDH, SDH, SHM. Horticulturalist; b. 19.9.35, Kilmarnock; m., Billie; 1 s.; 1 d. Educ. Kilmarnock Academy; West of Scotland Agricultural College. Staff Member, WSAC, Auchincruive, Ayr, 1956-59; Assistant Head Gardener, Reading University Botanic Garden, 1959-61; Horticultural Adviser/Lecturer, Shropshire Education Authority, 1961-67; Horticultural Adviser: MAFF, Leicestershire, Northants and Rutland, 1967-73; North of Scotland College of Agriculture, 1973-78; Project Manager, Waste Heat Recovery, Glengarioch Distillery, Oldmeldrum, since 1981; Co-Presenter, The Beechgrove Garden, BBC TV Scotland, since 1978; Convener, Glasshouse and Nursery Committee, National Farmers Union of Scotland. Recreations: golf; curling; music; rugby; fishing. Address: (b.) Glengarioch Distillery, Oldmeldrum, Aberdeenshire; T.-065 12 2706.

McConnell, Professor Francis Ian, BVMS, MA, PhD, MRCPath, MRCVS. Professor of Veterinary Pathology, Edinburgh University, since 1983; b. 6.11.40, Glasgow; m., Anna; 3 s.; 2 d. Educ. St. Aloysius' College, Glasgow; Glasgow University. Wellcome Trust Postdoctoral Research Fellow, Department of Experimental Pathology, ARC Institute of Animal Physiology, Babrahamm, Cambridge, 1970-72; Research Fellow, Clare Hall, Cambridge, 1970-72; Senior Lecturer in Immunology, Royal Postgraduate Medical School, London University, 1972-75; Senior Scientist, MRC Unit on Mechanisms in Tumour Immunity, The Medical School, Cambridge; Member, Governing Body, Animal Virus Research Institute and Houghton Poultry Research Institute. Recreation: hill-walking. Address: (b.) University of Edinburgh, Royal (Dick) School of Veterinary Studies, Summerhall, Edinburgh, EH1 1QH; T.-031-667 1011, Ext. 5322.

McConnell, Jack Wilson, BSc, DipEd. Member, Stirling District Council, since 1984 (Secretary, Labour Group, since 1984); Teacher, Lornshill Academy, Alloa, since 1983; b. 30.6.60, Irvine. Educ. Arran High School; Stirling University. President, Students Association, Stirling University, 1980-82; Deputy Chairperson, National Union of Students (Scotland), 1982-83; Vice Chairperson, Leisure and Recreation Committee, Stirling District Council, since 1984; Executive Member, Clackmannan, Educational Institute of Scotland; Chairperson, Stirling District Arts Council, since 1984. Recreations: squash; swimming; campaigning against apartheid. Address: (h.) 10 Manse Crescent, Stirling; T.-0786 61391.

McConnell, Walter Scott, PhC, MPS. Community Pharmacist, since 1962; Director, Ayrshire Pharmaceuticals Ltd., since 1964; Chairman, Pharmaceutical General Council (Scotland); Member, Ayrshire and Arran Health Board; Member, Local Review Committee, HM Prison, Dungavel; b. 7.4.36, Kilmarnock; m.; 1 s.; 3 d. Educ. Kilmarnock Academy; Royal Technical College, Glasgow. Recreations: curling; golf. Address: (h.) 27 Mauchline Road, Hurlford, Kilmarnock, KA1 5AB; T.-0563 25393.

McCorkindale, Neil, MA, BSc, FRAS. Rector, Perth Academy, since 1970; b. 28.8.21, Southend, Argyll; m., C. Jean Falconer; 2 d. Educ. Dunoon Grammar School; Glasgow University. Assistant Teacher of Mathematics, 1950-53; Principal Teacher of Mathematics: Nairn Academy, 1953-55, Elgin Academy, 1955-61; Rector: Rothesay Academy, 1961-65, Ayr Academy, 1965-69. President, Perth and District Bn., Boys' Brigade; Chairman, Perth Cancer Research Committee. Recreations: travel; gardening; golf. Address: (h.) 3 Hamilton Place, Perth; T.-0738 22597.

McCormick, David. Chairman, Industrial Development Committee, Dumfries and Galloway Regional Council, since 1982; Director, Wigtown Rural Development Company, since 1983; Trustee Director, Nithsdale, Annan and Eskdale and Stewartry Enterprise Trust, since 1984; b. 5.5.18, Kirkconnel; m., Mary-Ann Edgar Carruthers; 1 s.; 1 d. Educ. Sanquhar Academy.

Started in coal-mining, 1934; Underground Deputy, 1954-65; Training Department, NCB, Barony Colliery, 1965-76; elected to Dumfries and Galloway Regional Council, 1978; Member, Consultative Committee, Scottish Development Agency, 1984; Member, Board of Directors, Dumfries Technical College and Barony Agricultural College, 1982; Commandant, Upper Nithsdale First Aid Section, since 1976; Chairman, Kirkconnel Co-operative Society; Chairman, Management Committee, MSC Schemes, Upper Nithsdale. Recreations: gardening; photography; motoring. Address: (h.) 21 Libry Street, Kelloholm, Kirkconnel, Dumfriesshire, DG4 6RS; T.-Kirkconnel 401.

MacCormick, Professor (Donald) Neil, MA, LLD. Regius Professor of Public Law, Edinburgh University, since 1972; b. 27.5.41, Glasgow; m., Karen (Caroline) Rona Barr; 3 d. Educ. High School of Glasgow; Glasgow University; Balliol College, Oxford. Lecturer in Jurisprudence, Queen's College, Dundee, 1965-67; Fellow, Balliol College, 1967-72; Oxford University: CUF Lecturer, 1968-72, Pro-Proctor, 1970-71; Dean, Faculty of Law, Edinburgh University, 1973-76 and since 1985; Senate Assessor, University Court, 1982-85; Member, Broadcasting Council for Scotland, since 1985. President, Oxford Union, 1965; Executive Member, Scottish National Party, 1978-81, and Council Member, 1978-84. Address: (h.) Dalhousie Chesters, Bonnyrigg, Midlothian; T.-031-660 3354.

McCormick, John, MA, MEd. The Secretary and Head of Information, BBC Scotland, since 1982; b. 24.6.44, Irvine; m., Jean; 1 s.; 1 d. Educ. St. Michael's College, Irvine; Glasgow University. BBC: Education Officer, Glasgow, 1970-75, Senior Education Officer, School Broadcasting Council for Scotland, 1975-82. Address: (h.) Callandale, Gallowhill Road, Lenzie, Glasgow.

MacCorquodale, Andrew Robb, FRICS. Regional Assessor, Central Regional Council, since 1982; b. 8.5.34, Larbert; m., Helen Walls; 1 s.; 1 d. Educ. Montrose Academy; Larbert High School; Heriot-Watt University. Trainee Valuer, Stirling County Council, 1950; Junior Valuer, Stirling and Clackmannan Joint Valuation Authority, 1956; Depute Assessor, Central Regional Council, 1975. Recreations: sailing; gardening; rugby; art; folk music. Address: (b.) Viewforth, Stirling; T.-Stirling 73111.

McCourt, Peter Aloysius, BSc, AdvDipRE. Rector, St. Mary's Academy, Bathgate, since 1982; b. 14.6.35, Kilwinning; m., Veronica Wilkins; 1 s.; 2 d. Educ. St. Joseph's High School, Kilmarnock; Heriot-Watt University. Royal Corps of Signals, 1954-56; industry, 1956-65; student, 1965-69; St. Augustine's High School: Teacher, 1969, Principal Teacher, Physics, 1970; Depute Head, Holy Rood High School, 1978. Recreations: opera; browsing in bookshops; jogging. Address: (h.) 2 Riversdale Road, Edinburgh, EH12 5YN; T.-031-337 4519.

McCreath, Alexander, FInstWM, MRSH, MIEH. Director of Cleansing, City of Edinburgh District Council, since 1977; b. Glasgow; m.,

Anne; 1 s.; 1 d. Educ. Allan Glen's School, Glasgow; St. Andrews University. Glasgow Corporation, 1946-48; Assistant Health Inspector, Arbroath, 1948-50; various posts, Grangemouth Town Council, 1950-74 (finally Director of Environmental Health/Public Cleansing); Depute Director Environmental Health, Falkirk District Council, 1974-77. Recreations: golf; fishing. Address: (b.) King's Stables Road, Edinburgh, EH1 2JZ; T.-031-225 2424.

McCrone, Iain Alistair, SDA. Farmer and Company Director; b. 29.3.34, Glasgow; m., Yvonne Findlay; 4 d. Educ. Glasgow Academy; Trinity College, Glenalmond; West of Scotland Agricultural College. Farming on own account, since 1956; Managing Director, McCrone Farmers Ltd., since 1958; began fish farming, 1968; Director, Highland Trout Co. (now McConnell Salmon Ltd.); Director, Otter Ferry Salmon Ltd., since 1974; Member, Fife Regional Council, 1978-82; Parliamentary candidate (Conservative), Central Fife, 1979; Council Member, National Farmers Union of Scotland, 1977-82; Board Member, Glenrothes Development Corporation, since 1980; Member, Fife Health Board, since 1983; Nuffield Farming Scholar, 1966; President, Scottish Conservative and Unionist Association, since 1985 (Vice President, 1983-85). Recreations: golf; squash; rugby (spectator). Address: (h.) Cardsknolls, Markinch, Fife, KY7 6LP; T.-0337 30267.

McCrone, Robert Gavin Loudon, CB, MA, MSc, PhD, FRSE. Secretary, Industry Department for Scotland, since 1980; Chief Economic Adviser, Scottish Office, since 1972; b. 2.2.33, Ayr; m., Alexandra Bruce Waddell; 2 s.; 1 d. Educ. St. Catharine's College, Cambridge; University of Wales; Glasgow University. Fisons Ltd., 1959-60; Lecturer in Economics, Glasgow University, 1960-65; Fellow, Brasenose College, Oxford, 1965-70; Consultant, UNESCO, 1964; Member, NEDC Working Party on Agricultural Policy, 1967-68; Adviser, House of Commons Select Committee on Scottish Affairs, 1969-70; Senior Economic Adviser, Scottish Office, 1970-72; Under Secretary, 1972-80; Council Member: Royal Economic Society, 1977-82, Scottish Economic Society, since 1982; Visiting Professor, Strathclyde University, since 1983. Publications: The Economics of Subsidising Agriculture, 1962; Scotland's Economic Progress 1951-60, 1963; Regional Policy in Britain, 1969; Scotland's Future, 1969. Recreation: walking. Address: (b.) New St. Andrews House, Edinburgh; T.-031-556 8400.

McCrorie, Ian, BSc. Chorusmaster, Scottish Philharmonic Singers, since 1976; Assistant Rector, Greenock Academy, since 1975; b. 6.5.41, Greenock; m., Olive Simpson Bolton; 2 s. Educ. Greenock Academy; Glasgow University. Founded Toad Choir, Greenock, which appeared in numerous BBC Songs of Praise programmes and won 1975 National Choral Competition, Royal Albert Hall, London; this choir became the nucleus of the Scottish Philharmonic Singers, established in 1976; has prepared the choir to work under several distinguished conductors; Organist and Choirmaster, Mid Kirk of Greenock, since 1964; former Assistant to Arthur

Oldham, Edinburgh Festival Chorus; has been Choral Director, International Festival of Youth Orchestras, Aberdeen; has conducted at Festivals in France and Poland; Past President and Convener of Cruising, Clyde River Steamer Club; author of numerous booklets and articles on Clyde and West Highland steamers. Recreations: as above! Address: (h.) 72 Newton Street, Greenock; T.-0475 26689.

McCue, William, OBE (1982), LRAM. Bass Singer; b. 17.8.34, Allanton, Shotts; m., Patricia Carrick; 1 d. Educ. Calderhead High School; Royal Scottish Academy of Music; Royal Academy of Music. Began professional singing career in 1960; his work has included opera, oratorio, recital, concert, cabaret, pantomime and stage musical, radio and TV; has travelled throughout the world, making numerous visits to USA, Canada, USSR, Iceland, Europe and Israel; has made various recordings of Scots songs and Negro spirituals; Chairman, SALVO; former Member, Scottish Arts Council. Recreations: watching all sport; listening to all kinds of music; gardening; escaping to the Scottish countryside. Address: (h.) Sweethope House, Bothwell, Glasgow, G71 8BT; T.-0698 853241.

McCulloch, Henry, BL. Chief Executive and Director of Administration, Badenoch and Strathspey District Council, since 1974; b. 17.12.35, Bieldside, Aberdeen; m., Freda; 1 s.; 2 d. Educ. George Watson's College; Edinburgh University. Legal Assistant: City of Edinburgh, 1960-64, Burgh of Falkirk, 1964-66; Senior Legal and Administrative Assistant, Roxburgh County Council, 1966-68; Depute County Clerk, Dumfries County Council, 1968-74. Recreations: skiing; sailing; golf. T.-05402 555.

McCulloch, Norman Hamilton. Secretary, Red Deer Commission, since 1978; b. 13.7.30, Longniddry; m., Joyce Ann; 2 s. Educ. Royal High School, Edinburgh. Scottish Education Department, 1947-49; National Service, RAF, 1949-52; rejoined SED, 1952-68; Scottish Economic Planning Department/Scottish Development Department, 1968-78. Recreations: golf; bridge; conservation. Address: (b.) Red Deer Commission, Knowsley, 82 Fairfield Road, Inverness, IV3 5LH; T.-0463 231751.

McCulloch, William Scott, MC, BL. Chief Executive, Angus District Council, since 1974; b. 2.1.22, Dundee. Dundee Corporation, 1937-42 and 1947-56; Town Clerk, Forfar, 1956-68; Depute County Clerk, Angus County Council, 1968-75. Recreations: golf; bridge. Address: (b.) County Buildings, Forfar, DD8 3LG; T.-Forfar 65101.

McCunn, Archibald Eddington, BSc (Hons), CEng, MIMechE, FBIM. Board Member, Highlands and Islands Development Board, since 1985; b. 27.5.27, Motherwell; m., Olive Isobel Johnston; 1 s.; 1 d. Educ. Dalziel High School; Strathclyde University; IMEDE, Lausanne. Development Engineer, Colvilles Ltd., Clyde Iron Works, 1952-54; Assistant to General Manager (Construction), Ravenscraig Steelworks, 1954-57; Chief Engineer (Ironworks), Ravenscraig,

1957-63; Senior Consultant, Inbucon/AIC, 1963-67; Divisional Chairman, Stenhouse Industries, 1967-71; Divisional Chairman/Consultant, Grampian Holdings plc, 1971-85; Elder, Church of Scotland, 35 years; Visiting Lecturer, Strathclyde University. Recreations: curling; tennis; painting; music; walking; gardening. Address: (h.) 2 McIntosh Way, Motherwell, ML1 3BB; T.-0698 53500.

McCurley, Anna Anderson, MP, MA. MP (Conservative), Renfrew West and Inverclyde, since 1983; b. 18.1.43, Glasgow; m., Dr. John McCurley; 1 d. Educ. Glasgow High School for Girls; Glasgow University; Strathclyde University; Jordanhill College of Education. Teacher and Lecturer, 1978-82; Member, Strathclyde Regional Council, 1978-82; Member, Scottish Select Committee, since 1984. Recreations: music; reading; cooking; driving. Address: (h.) 263A Nithsdale Road, Glasgow, G41 5AW; T.-041-427 3330.

McCutcheon, James, MA (Hons). Head Teacher, St. Michael's Academy, Kilwinning, since 1976; b. Kilmarnock; m., Joan Cullinane; 3 s. Educ. St. Joseph's Academy, Kilmarnock; Glasgow University. Principal Teacher of Classics, then Assistant Head Teacher, St. Michael's Academy, Kilwinning; Depute Head Teacher, St. Joseph's Academy, Kilmarnock. President, Kilwinning Rotary Club, 1985-86. Recreations: reading; music; various sports. Address: (h.) 7 Graystones, Kilwinning, Ayrshire.

McDevitt, Professor Denis Gordon, DSc, MD, FRCP, FRCPI. Professor of Clinical Pharmacology, Dundee University Medical School, since 1984; Honorary Consultant Physician, Tayside Health Board, since 1984; b. 17.11.37, Belfast; m., Anne McKee; 2 s.; 1 d. Educ. Campbell College, Belfast; Queen's University, Belfast. Assistant Professor of Medicine and Consultant Physician, Christian Medical College, Ludhiana, North India, 1968-71; Senior Lecturer in Clinical Pharmacology and Consultant Physician, Queen's University Medical School, 1971-76; Merck International Fellow in Clinical Pharmacology, Vanderbilt University, Nashville, Tennessee, 1974-75; Reader in Clinical Pharmacology, Queen's University Medical School, 1976-78; Professor of Clinical Pharmacology, Queen's University of Belfast and Consultant Physician, Belfast Teaching Hospitals, 1978-83. Chairman, Clinical Section, British Pharmacological Society, since 1985 (Secretary, 1978-82). Recreations: golf; classical music. Address: (h.) 1 Godfrey Street, Barnhill, Dundee, DD5 2QZ.

McDiarmid, John Michael. Farmer; Member, Red Deer Commission; Council Member, National Farmers Union of Scotland; Member, Panel of Agricultural Arbiters; b. 21.5.35, Dundee; 3 s. Educ. Merchiston Castle School; North of Scotland College of Agriculture. Lt., KOSB, 1956-58, Malaya; Member: Perth and Kinross County Council, 1964-70, Perth and Kinross District Council, 1970-75. Chairman, Aberfeldy Recreation Centre Ltd. Recreation: curling. Address: Mains of Murthly, Aberfeldy, Perthshire; T.-0887 20427.

McDonald, Alastair. Radio, Television, Stage and Recording Personality; Folk Singer; Programme Presenter and Discussion Guest; Entertainer; b. 28.10.41, Glasgow; m., Anne; 2 s. Educ. Strathbungo Senior Secondary School. Recordings include White Wings, Glencoe and Other Requests, Journey Through Scotland, Heads and Tales, Sing A Song of Scotland, Journey Through Scotland Volume 2. Recreations: inert athlete and hindsight student. Address: (b.) The Entertainment Company, 61 St. Vincent Crescent, Glasgow, G3 8NQ; T.-041-204 2444.

McDonald, Rev. Alexander, BA, CMIWSc. Minister, St. Mark's Church, Oldhall, Paisley, since 1974; b. 5.11.37, Bishopbriggs; m., Essdale Helen McLeod; 2 s.; 1 d. Educ. Bishopbriggs Higher Grade School; Whitehill Senior Secondary School, Glasgow; Glasgow University and Trinity College. Management in timber trade, 1952-54; RAF, 1954-56; management in timber trade, 1956-58, motor trade, 1958-62; student, 1962-68; Minister, St. David's, Bathgate, 1968-74. Trustee, Scottish Television Staff Trust; wide range of involvement with Boys' Brigade in Scotland, Scottish Spastics, Mentally Handicapped Children, ACCORD, Christian Aid and many others; regular broadcaster. Recreations: reading; walking; fishing. Address: St. Mark's Church, Glasgow Road, Paisley; T.-041-889 4279.

MacDonald, Rev. Alexander James, MA, DipTh. Minister, Bon Accord Free Church of Scotland, Aberdeen, since 1983; b. 17.3.49, Kildonan, Sutherland; m., Evelyn; 2 s.; 2 d. Educ. Golspie High School; Edinburgh University; Free Church College. Minister, Bishopbriggs Free Church, 1973-83; Chaplain, Woodilee Mental Hospital, 1974-77; Clerk, Training of the Ministry Committee, Free Church Assembly, 1978-83; Free Church Lecturer/Chaplain, Aberdeen College of Education; Moderator, Free Presbytery of Glasgow, 1979-80; Exhibition Designer, Thomas Chalmers Bicentenary Exhibition, 1980. Recreations: guitar; rock music (especially Bob Dylan); football; reading. Address: (h.) 77 Forest Avenue, Aberdeen; T.-0224 324630.

MacDonald, Alexandrina, BA. Honorary Sheriff, Oban; b. 7.4.23, Edinburgh; m., Rev. Alexander MacDonald (deceased); 1 s.; 2 d. Educ. George Watson's Ladies College; Open University. Nurse training, City Hospital, Edinburgh, 1939-45; Location Counsellor, Open University, 1984. Various appointments, Girl Guide movement. Recreations: reading; countryside; travel. Address (h.) 1 Albany Street, Oban, Argyll; T.-0631 62946.

Macdonald, Alistair. Member, Clydebank District Council, since 1980 (Chairman, Environmental Services, since 1984); Member, South of Scotland Electricity Consultative Board, since 1980; b. 29.5.41, Aird, Uig, Isle of Lewis; m., Elizabeth; 2 s. Educ. Dumbarton Academy. Police service, 10 years; staff, British Leyland (Albion Motors), 14 years; Proprietor, Clydebank Cleaning Services, since 1985; APEX: former Branch Chairman and Secretary, former Member, Scottish Executive Committee, former Vice Chairman, Scottish Area Council; Vice Chairman, Scottish Engineering Advisory Council,

until 1985; former Executive Council Member, Clydebank District Trades Council; Past Chairman and Secretary, Kilbowie Branch, Labour Party; Chairman, Housing Committee, Clydebank District Council, 1980-84; Founder Member, UB40 (Clydebank Unemployed Workers Centre); former Member, Clyde River Purification Board; Member, Greater Glasgow Area Tourist Board; first person to address British Labour Party Conference in Gaelic. Recreations: angling; snooker. Address: (h.) 32 Hawthorn Street, Clydebank, Dunbartonshire; T.-Duntocher 79503.

MacDonald, Sheriff Alistair Archibald, MA, LLB. Sheriff of Grampian, Highland and Islands, at Kirkwall and Lerwick, since 1968; b. 8.5.27, Edinburgh; m., Jill Russell; 1 s.; 1 d. Educ. Broughton School; Edinburgh University. Army Service, Intelligence Corps, 1945-48; called to Scottish Bar, 1954; Sheriff Substitute of Caithness, Sutherland, Orkney and Shetland, at Lerwick, 1961-68. Address: (h.) Westhall, Shetland Isles; T.-Lerwick 2711.

Macdonald, Alister Gordon, BSc, PhD. Reader in Physiology, Aberdeen University, since 1984; b. 25.1.40, London; m., Jennifer; 1 s.; 2 d. Educ. Boys' High School, Trowbridge, Wiltshire; Bristol University. University of East Anglia, 1963-69; joined Aberdeen University as Lecturer in Physiology, 1969. Publications: Physiological Aspects of Deep Sea Biology, 1975; Physiological Aspects of Anaesthetics and Inert Gases, 1978. Recreations: hill-walking; badminton; music. Address: (b.) Physiology Department, Marischal College, Aberdeen, AB9 1AS; T.-Aberdeen 40241.

MacDonald, Angus Lamont MacKinnon, DA, RIBA, FRIAS. Chartered Architect; Partner, James Parr & Partners, Architects, since 1973; President, Dundee Institute of Architects and Vice-President, Royal Incorporation of Architects in Scotland, since 1984; b. 2.9.38, Uig, Isle of Skye; m., Morag A.C. MacLean; 2 s.; 1 d. Educ. Perth Academy; Portree High School; Perth High School; Duncan of Jordanstone College of Art, Dundee. James Parr & Partners, Broughty Ferry: Assistant Architect, 1963, Associate Architect, 1968, Partner, since 1973, Senior Partner responsible for housing etc., 1982; Assessor, Civic Trust Awards, 1983; Chairman, Perthshire and Angus Provincial Mod; Vice Chairman, Dundee Highland Society; Committee Member, St. Aiden's Project for Disabled Youngsters, Dundee. Recreations: painting; singing (Gaelic choir and barber shop quartette); canoeing; travel. Address: (h.) Foxmount East, 8A Reres Road, Broughty Ferry, Dundee; T.-0382 76763.

Macdonald, Angus Stewart, CBE, DL, FRAgS. Chairman, Scottish Agricultural Development Council, since 1980; b. 7.4.35, Edinburgh; m., Janet Ann Somerville; 3 s. Educ. Conon Bridge School; Gordonstoun School. Past Chairman, Royal Highland and Agricultural Society; Director: British Wool Marketing Board and associated companies, Reith & Anderson (Tain and Dingwall) Ltd., Gordonstoun School,

Aberlour School, Hill Farming Research Organisation, Highlands and Islands Development Board, Panel of Agricultural Arbiters, Grampian Television, Scottish English and Welsh Wool Growers Ltd. Recreation: field sports. Address: Torgorm, Conon Bridge, Dingwall, Ross-shire; T.-0349 61365.

MacDonald, Bruce B., BSc, PhD, ARCST, CEng, MIChemE. Senior Lecturer, Department of Pure and Applied Chemistry, Strathclyde University; b. 6.2.31, Glasgow; m., Laura M. Dodds; 2 s. Educ. Govan High School; Glasgow University. Recreations: golf; tennis; bridge. Address: (h.) 107 South Beach, Troon, KA10 6EQ; T.-0292 311403.

Macdonald, David N., BSc (Hons), DipEd. Head Teacher, Langholm Academy, since 1980; b. 4.11.42, Edinburgh; m., Sandra Crerar-Gilbert; 2 d. Educ. Royal High School, Edinburgh; Heriot-Watt College, Edinburgh. Assistant Teacher of Mathematics: Boroughmuir Secondary School, 1965, Liberton Secondary School, 1966-68; Principal Teacher of Mathematics, Annan Academy, 1968-73; Depute Rector, Annan Academy, 1973-80. Secretary, Langholm Rotary Club; Member, Langholm/Ewes/Westerkirk Community Council; Committee Member, Langholm Rugby Club. Address: (h.) Sorbie Cottage, Drove Road, Langholm, DG13 OJW; T.-0541 80531.

MacDonald, Donald, JP. Member, Western Isles Islands Council, since 1976; Assessor, Crofters Commission; Director, Harris Tweed Association; b. 8.12.11, Scarp, Harris; m., Margaret Murray (deceased); 3 d. Educ. Sir E. Scott Secondary School, Harris; Inverness Royal Academy; Skerry's College. Police Constable, Glasgow, 1932-49; District Social Welfare Officer, Isle of Harris, 1949-76; also Clerk and Treasurer, Harris District Council and other local appointments; Elder, Church of Scotland, since 1949 (Sunday School Superintendent, 16 years, and Session Clerk). Address: (h.) 2 Bunauonedra, Isle of Harris; T.-0859 2127.

Macdonald, Donald, MA (Hons). Headmaster, Paible Secondary School, North Uist, since 1973; b. 12.10.39, North Uist; m., Iris E. Fraser; 2 d. Educ. Paible Secondary School; Inverness Royal Academy; Aberdeen University; Jordanhill College of Education. Teacher of Classics, then Principal Teacher, Anderson High School, Lerwick, 1963-73; Teacher Representative, Education Committee, 1975-78 and since 1981; Member, Joint Consultative Committee (Teaching Staff), since 1975; Member, Committee on Gaelic, CCC; Member, Joint Working Party on Gaelic Standard Grade. Recreations: shooting; fishing; part-time farming. Address: (h.) Druimard, Bayhead, North Uist.

Macdonald, Donald Alistair, OBE, DipSoc, AAPSW. Director of Social Work, Borders Regional Council, since 1975; Mental Welfare Commissioner, Scotland, since 1984; b. 18.2.28, Larbert; m., Grace Catherine; 1 s.; 2 d. Educ. Larbert High School; Edinburgh University. Senior Psychiatric Social Worker, Renfrewshire

Mental Hospitals; Senior Case Work Supervisor, then Training Officer, Staffordshire County Council; Deputy County Welfare Officer, Derbyshire County Council; Director of Social Work, Roxburgh County Council. Chairman, Scottish Branch, British Agencies for Adoption and Fostering. Recreations: gardening; golf; running. Address: (h.) Northumbria, Darnick, Melrose, Roxburghshire, TD6 9AJ; T.-089682 2250.

MacDonald, Donald Gordon, RD, BDS, PhD, MRCPath. Reader in Oral Medicine and Pathology, Glasgow University, since 1982; Consultant Oral Pathologist, Glasgow Dental Hospital, since 1974; b. 5.7.42, Glasgow; m., Emma Lindsay Cordiner; 2 s.; 1 d. Educ. Kelvinside Academy, Glasgow; Glasgow University. Assistant, then Lecturer, Glasgow University, 1964-69; Visiting Associate Professor in Oral Pathology, University of Illinois, 1969-70; Lecturer, Senior Lecturer in Oral Medicine and Pathology, Glasgow University, 1970-82; Editor, Glasgow Dental Journal, 1969-75; Honorary Consultant Forensic Odontologist, Strathclyde Police, since 1976; Honorary Secretary, Association of Head and Neck Oncologists of Great Britain. Recreation: Royal Naval Reserve (Commanding Officer, HMS Graham, Clyde Division, since 1982). Address: (h.) 2 Dougalston Gardens South, Milngavie, Glasgow; T.-041-956 2075.

MacDonald, Donald John, BSc. Rector, Thurso High School, since 1980; b. 25.5.39, Glasgow; 1 s.; 2 d. Educ. Lionel School, Lewis; Govan High School, Glasgow; Glasgow University; Jordanhill College of Education. Teacher of Science, Govan High School; Principal Teacher of Physics: Kirkwall Grammar School, Govan High School; Assistant Head, Linwood High School; Depute Rector, Dingwall Academy; Assistant Divisional Education Officer, Highland Region. Address: (h.) 3 Church Street, Halkirk, Caithness.

McDonald, Sir Duncan, Kt (1983), CBE (1976), DSc, BSc, FH-WC, FRSE, FEng, FIEE, CBIM, SMIEEE. Chairman, Northern Engineering Industries plc, since 1980; b. 20.9.21; m.; 3 s.; 1 d. Educ. Dunfermline High School; Edinburgh University.

Macdonald, Rev. Finlay Angus John, MA, BD, PhD. Minister, Jordanhill Parish Church, Glasgow, since 1977; b. 1.7.45, Watford; m., Elizabeth Mary Stuart; 2 s. Educ. Dundee High School; St. Andrews University. Assistant Minister, Bo'ness Old Kirk, 1970-71; Minister, Menstrie Parish Church, 1971-77; Junior Clerk and Treasurer, Stirling and Dunblane Presbytery, 1973-77; Convener, Church of Scotland Working Group on Children and Communion, 1980-82; Convener, Advance Planning Group, Church of Scotland Youth Education Committee, 1982-84; Co-Editor and Contributor, Children at the Table, 1982; Convener, Legal Questions Committee, Board of Practice and Procedure, 1984-85; Vice-Convener, Business Committee, General Assembly, 1985. Recreations: music; angling; reading; gardening. Address: (h.) 96 Southbrae Drive, Glasgow, G13 1TZ; T.-041-959 1310.

McDonald, George Alexander, MD, FRCP, FRCPath. Consultant Haematologist, Glasgow Royal Infirmary, since 1964; b. 21.12.24, Cults, Aberdeen; m., Margaret M. Mackie; 2 s.; 1 d. Educ. Milne's High School, Fochabers; Aberdeen University. House Surgeon, then House Physician, Aberdeen Royal Infirmary; Senior Research Fellow, then Lecturer in Medicine, Aberdeen University; Senior Registrar in Haematology, Glasgow Royal Infirmary; Past President, British Society for Haematology; International Counsellor, International Society of Haematology. Publication: Atlas of Haematology (Co-author). Recreations: golf; gardening; fishing. Address: (h.) 21 Blackwood Road, Milngavie, Glasgow, G62 7LB; T.-041-956 3103.

McDonald, Gerard, MA, BA (Hons), DPE. Head Teacher, St. Leonard's Secondary School, Glasgow, since 1983; b. 26.11.39, Motherwell; m., Eileen Mary Gibson; 2 s. Educ. St. Aloysius' College; Glasgow University; Strathclyde University. Teacher, St. Aloysius' College, 1961-71; Principal Teacher, then Assistant Head Teacher, St. Roch's Secondary School, 1971-80; Depute Head Teacher, St. Ninian's High School, Kirkintilloch, 1980-83. Recreations: rugby football; golf. Address: (b.) 62 Lochend Road, Glasgow, G34 ONY; T.-041-771 4986.

Macdonald, 8th Baron, (Godfrey James Macdonald of Macdonald). Chief of the Name and Arms of Macdonald; b. 28.11.47; m., Claire Catlow; 1 s.; 3 d. Address: (h.) Kinloch Lodge, Isle of Skye.

MacDonald, Gus. Director of Programmes, Scottish Television; Television Journalist; b. 20.8.40, Larkhall; m., Teen; 2 d. Educ. Allan Glen's School, Glasgow. Marine engineer, Stephens, Linthouse, 1955-62; Circulation and Publicity Manager, Tribune, 1963-65; Investigative Journalist, The Scotsman, 1965-67; Editor, Financial Scotsman, 1966-67; Investigative Bureau, World in Action, Granada, 1967-69; Editor/Executive Producer, World in Action, 1969-75; successively Head of Current Affairs, Head of Regional Programmes, Head of Features, Granada; Writer/Presenter, Camera: Early Photography, 1979-80, MacDiarmid: Hammer and Thistle; Presenter, variously, World in Action, What the Papers Say, Devil's Advocate, Union World; Election and Party Conference coverage; Channel Four's "Ombudsman" for viewers' complaints on Right to Reply, since 1982; BAFTA Award, current affairs; National Viewers and Listeners' Association Award, 1985; founder Chairman, Edinburgh International Television Festival, 1976; Visiting Professor, Film and Media Studies, Stirling University, 1985-86. Publications: Grierson: Television and Documentary, 1977; Camera: Victorian Eyewitness, 1979. Recreations: words; pictures; exploring Scotland. Address: (b.) Scottish Television, Cowcaddens, Glasgow, G2 3PR.

Macdonald, Professor Hugh John, MA, PhD, FRSA. Gardiner Professor of Music, Glasgow University, since 1980; b. 31.1.40, Newbury; m., Elizabeth Babb. Educ. Winchester College; Pembroke College, Cambridge. Lecturer in Music: Cambridge University, 1966-71, Oxford University, 1971-80; Visiting Professor in Musicology, Indiana University, 1979; General Editor, New Berlioz Edition. Publications: Skryabin, 1978; Berlioz, 1981. Recreation: bridges. Address: (b.) Department of Music, Glasgow University, Glasgow; T.-041-339 8855, Ext. 571.

MacDonald, Iain Davies, BMus. Composer; Head of Music, Greenfaulds High School, Cumbernauld, since 1975; Music Director, Cumbernauld Music Centre, since 1982; b. 15.2.51, Greenock; m., Nancy; 1 s.; 1 d. Educ. Allan Glen's School, Glasgow; Glasgow University; Moray House College of Education. Music Teacher, Renfrew High School, 1972-75; Co-Founder and Musical Director, Greenfaulds Theatre Group, since 1977; Composer (in collaboration with Iain Fraser): Christmas Story (cantata, 1977), American Suite (wind band/choral, 1979, orchestral/choral, 1980), Indecision (musical, 1981); Sole Composer and Author, Scottish March (wind band, 1980, wind band and brass band, 1982), Sonatina (wind band, 1982), The Chess Game (musical, 1983), Chances (musical, 1984). Recreations: sailing; board sailing. Address: (h.) 8 Main Street, Chryston, Glasgow, G69 9DH; T.-041-779 1595.

Macdonald, Iain Gordon, MA, DipAdEd. Member, Strathclyde Regional Council, since 1982; Scottish Education Officer, Cooperative Movement, since 1979; Vice-Chairman, Scottish Institute of Adult Education, since 1983; b. 20.12.47, Edinburgh; m., Joan Sheila Winter. Educ. Melville College, Edinburgh; Edinburgh University. Inner London Education Authority, 1973-79; Executive Member, Scottish Education and Action for Development; Chairman, Alternative Employment Study Group; Member, Cooperatives Committee, Labour Coordinating Committee. Recreations: skiing; golf; gardening. Address: (h.) Station House, Rhu, Dunbartonshire; T.-820719.

Macdonald, Iain Smith, QHP, MD, FRCPEdin, FFCM, DPH. Chief Medical Officer, Scottish Home and Health Department, since 1985; b. 14.7.27, Greenock; m., Sheila Foster; 1 s.; 1 d. Educ. Glasgow University. Lecturer in Public Health, Glasgow University, 1955-57; Deputy Medical Officer of Health: County Borough of Bury, 1957-59, County Borough of Bolton, 1959-64; joined Scottish Home and Health Department, 1964. Address: (h.) 36 Dumyat Drive, Falkirk, FK1 5PA; T.-Falkirk 25100.

MacDonald, Ian Arthur, JP, BSc. Headmaster, Linksfield Academy, since 1971; Presiding Justice, Aberdeen District Court, since 1979; b. 24.12.27, Aberdeen; m., Doreen Smith; 1 s.; 1 d. Educ. Robert Gordon's College, Aberdeen; Aberdeen University. Gordon Highlanders, 1945-48; Teacher of Science, Hilton Secondary School, 1952-60; Principal Teacher of Science, then Deputy Headteacher, Summerhill Academy, 1960-71. Secretary, Grampian Secondary Head Teachers Association, since 1981; Trustee, Aberdeen Endowments Trust, since 1984. Recreations: gardening; badminton; hill-walking. Address: (b.) Linksfield Academy, 520 King Street, Aberdeen, AB2 1SS; T.-Aberdeen 41343.

Macdonald, Ian Hamish, OBE, AIB (Scot), CBIM. Chief General Manager, TSB Scotland, since 1983; b. 30.12.26, Inverness; m., Patricia; 1 d. Educ. Inverness Royal Academy; Inverness Technical College. RAFVR, 1944; Queen's Own Cameron Highlanders, 1945 (Captain, 1948); Mercantile Bank, 1948-59; Hongkong and Shanghai Banking Corporation: Manager, 1959-72, General Manager, India, 1972-73, General Manager International, 1973-80, Executive Director, 1980-83; Chairman, The Hongkong Bank of Canada, 1982; Director: TSB Trustcard Ltd., since 1983, ScotBIC Governing Council, since 1983, TSB Scotland Nominees Ltd., since 1984, TSB Scotland (Investment) Nominees Ltd., since 1984, TSB Travellers Cheques Ltd., since 1984, Kerarn Ltd., since 1984, Crescent Japan Investment Trust plc, since 1984, New Tokyo Investment Trust plc, since 1984. Recreations: fishing; golf; bridge. Address: (h.) First Floor, 24 Moray Place, Edinburgh, EH3 6DA.

Macdonald, Ian Robert, MA, PhD. Senior Lecturer in Spanish, Aberdeen University, since 1984; b. 4.5.39, The Hague; m., Frances Mary Alexander; 3 s. Educ. Whitgift School; St. Andrews University. United Steel, 1961-64; literary research in Spain, 1964-65; Lecturer in Spanish, Aberdeen University, 1965-84. Publication: Gabriel Miro: His Private Library and His Literary Background, 1975. Recreations: reading; walking; carpentry. Address: (h.) 47 North Deeside Road, Peterculter, Aberdeen, AB1 OQL; T.-0224 732284.

Macdonald of Aird and Vallay, James Garner Smith, MA. Assistant Director, Kleinwort Benson Ltd., Merchant Bankers; b. 4.2.50, Edinburgh; m., Elisabeth Wolff; 1 s.; 1 d. Educ. Eton; The Queen's College, Oxford. Member, Queen's Bodyguard for Scotland (Royal Company of Archers), since 1982. Recreations: golf; skiing. Address: (h.) Aird House, Inverness, IV1 2AA; 5 Campden Hill Court, London, W8.

McDonald, Professor Janet B.I., MA. Professor of Drama, Glasgow University, since 1979; b. 28.7.41, Netherlee, Renfrewshire; m., Ian James McDonald; 1 d. Educ. Hutchesons' Girls' Grammar School; Glasgow University. Member, Governing Body, Royal Scottish Academy of Music and Drama, since 1979; Chairman, Drama and Theatre Board, Council for National Academic Awards, since 1981; Chairman, Standing Committee of University Departments of Drama, 1982-85; Chairman, Drama Committee, Scottish Arts Council, since 1985; Fellow, Royal Society of Arts. Address: (b.) 53 Hillhead Street, Glasgow, G12 8QE; T.-041-334 6831.

Macdonald, Rev. John, MA, AEA. Minister, Lochee Old Parish Church, Dundee, 1949-85; Clerk, Synod of Perth and Angus, Church of Scotland, since 1977; b. 31.3.15, Braenish, Uig, Isle of Lewis; m., Eileen Ivy Sheila O'Flynn; 4 s.; 1 d. Educ. Nicolson Institute, Stornoway; Keil School, Dumbarton; Glasgow University; Aberdeen University. War Service, RAF, 1942-46 (Pilot); Chaplain: RAFVR, 1953-56, RAuxAF, 1956-65, ATC, 1965-85. Address: (h.) 12 Hyndford Street, Dundee, DD2 1HQ; T.-0382 68655.

Macdonald, Joseph Mackay, FIB (Scot). General Manager, UK Banking, The Royal Bank of Scotland plc, since 1985; b. 16.9.34, Halkirk, Caithness; m., Marlene G. Mackay; 1 s.; 1 d. Educ. Miller Academy, Thurso; Administrative Staff College, Henley. Commercial Bank of Scotland Ltd., 1950-59; National Commercial Bank of Scotland Ltd., 1959-69; Royal Bank of Scotland plc: various appointments, 1969-82, General Manager (Northern Region), 1982-85. Recreations: angling, curling, reading. Address (b.) 9 Rubislaw Terrace, Aberdeen, AB9 8YQ; T.-0224 646626.

Macdonald, John, BA, DipTechEd. Headmaster, Brora High School, Sutherland, since 1973; b. 14.6.29, Uig, Isle of Lewis; 1 s.; 1 d. Educ. Nicolson Institute, Stornoway; Aberdeen College of Education. Teacher, Preston Lodge High School, Prestonpans, 1952; Teacher of Technical Subjects, Kinlochleven Secondary School, 1956; Deputy Head, Farr Secondary School, Bettyhill, 1963. Council Member, Association of Head Teachers (Scotland), since 1984. Recreations: hill-walking; sailing; canoeing; fishing. Address: (h.) Thirlmere, Golf Road, Brora, KW9 6QS; T.-0408 21476.

McDonald, John, JP, MA (Hons). Rector, Inverness High School, since 1983; b. 29.8.31, Aberdeen; m., Betty M. Christie; 1 s.; 2 d. Educ. Elgin Academy; Aberdeen University; Aberdeen College of Education. Ft. Lt., RAF, Education Branch, 1955-58; Teacher of Geography, Elgin Academy, 1958-60; Principal Teacher of Geography, Nairn Academy, 1960-63; Principal Teacher of Geography, then Depute Rector, Inverness High School, 1963-83. Chairman, Justices Committee, Nairn District. Recreations: skiing; golf; sailing; hill-walking; lapidary; caravanning. Address: (h.) Kirkgate, 3 Seabank Road, Nairn; T.-Nairn 52199.

Macdonald, Keith, BA. Leader, Labour Group, Kyle and Carrick District Council, since 1984; b. 21.2.53, Edinburgh. Educ. Annan Academy; Stirling University. Teacher, 1974-76; Bookseller, 1976-79; Publisher, 1979-83. Recreations: the arts; reading. Address: (h.) 63 Craigie Avenue, Ayr; T.-Ayr 260933.

MacDonald, Rev. Kenneth Mackinnon, CertTheo. Free Church Minister, Rosskeen (Invergordon and Alness), since 1984; b. 9.1.35, Skinidin, Skye; m., Reta Cromarty; 2 s.; 2 d. Educ. Portree High School; Free Church College. Army, Seaforth Highlanders, Eyypt, Germany, Aden, 1953-55; Uniformed Branch, HM Customs and Excise, Glasgow Docks, London Heathrow, Aberdeen and Stornoway, 1957-80; Free Church College, 1980-84. Member, Western Isles Council, 1973-76; Chairman, Western Isles Branch, Mentally Handicapped Action Committee, 1977-80; Member, Western Isles Children's Panel, 1977-80; capped seven times for Scotland as amateur footballer. Recreations: football; athletics. Address: Rosskeen Free Church Manse, Rosskeen, Invergordon, IV18 OPP; T.-0349 85 2406.

MacDonald, Margo. Broadcaster; b. Hamilton; m., Jim Sillars; 1 step s.; 2 d.; 2 step-d. Educ. Hamilton Academy; Dunfermline College.

Teacher, 1963-65; barmaid and mother, 1965-73; Member of Parliament, 1973-74; Broadcaster/ Writer, 1974-78; Director, Shelter, Scotland, 1978-81; Radio Forth: Broadcaster, 1981-83, Editor, Topical Programmes, 1983-85.

Macdonald, Norman Malcolm. Writer; b. 24.7.27, Thunder Bay, Canada; m., Mairi F. Educ. Nicolson Institute; Newbattle Abbey College. New Zealand Air Force, 1949-57; journalism and administration at various periods; Administrator, Fir Chlis (Gaelic theatre company), 1978-80; Secretary, Sabhal Mor Ostaig Gaelic College, 1982-83. Publications: Calum Tod (novel); Fad (poetry); The Shutter Falls, Anna Chaimbeul, The Catechist (plays); Call Na h'Iolaire (historical). Recreation: walking. Address: 14 Tong, Isle of Lewis.

McDonald, Peter, BSc, MSc, PhD, DSc, CChem, FRSC, FRSE. Fellow, Edinburgh University, 1983-85; b. 20.5.26, Carlisle; m., Agnes Mary Hay; 3 s. Educ. Carlisle Grammar School; Durham University. Lecturer in Agricultural Chemistry: Harper Adams Agricultural College, Newport, Shropshire, 1947-49, University College of Khartoum, Sudan, 1950-52, Edinburgh School of Agriculture, 1952-64; Head of Agricultural Biochemstry Department, Edinburgh School of Agriculture, 1964-83, Reader, Edinburgh University, 1972-83. Publications: The Biochemistry of Silage, 1981; Animal Nutrition (Co-author), 1966. Recreations: music; gardening; genealogy. Address: (h.) 1 Swanston Grove, Edinburgh, EH10 7BN; T.-031-445 1537.

Macdonald, Peter Cameron, SDA. Convener, Scottish Landowners Federation, since 1985; Farmer, since 1961; Director, J. Dickson & Son, Gunmakers, since 1968; b. 14.12.37, Edinburgh; m., Barbara Helen Drimmie Ballantyne; 2 step-s. Educ. Loretto; East of Scotland College of Agriculture. Council Member: Scottish Landowners Federation, since 1970, Blackface Sheepbreeders Association, 1970-74; Member, Forth River Purification Board, since 1979; Director, Royal Highland and Agricultural Society of Scotland, 1985; Council Member, Scottish Salmon Angling Federation. Recreations: fishing; shooting; golf. Address: Colzium Farm, Kirknewton, Midlothian, EH27 8DH; T.-0506 880607.

McDonald, Hon. Lord, (Robert Howat McDonald), MC (1944), QC (Scot), MA, LLB. Senator of the College of Justice in Scotland, since 1973; b. 15.5.16; m. Educ. John Neilson Institution, Paisley. KOSB, 1939-46 (mentioned in Despatches); admitted, Faculty of Advocates, 1946; QC (Scot), 1957; Sheriff Principal of Ayr and Bute, 1966-71; President, Industrial Tribunals for Scotland, 1972-73; Chairman, General Nursing Council for Scotland, 1970-73; Chairman, Mental Welfare Commission for Scotland, 1965-73.

Macdonald, Vice-Admiral Sir Roderick Douglas, KBE (1978). Artist; b. 25.2.21; m., 1, Joan Willis (m. diss.); 2 s.; 1 s. deceased; 2, Pamela Bartosik. Educ. Fettes. Entered Royal Navy,

1939; Captain of the Fleet, 1970; COS to C-in-C, Naval Home Command, 1973-76; ADC to The Queen, 1975; COS to Comdr., Allied Naval Forces Southern Europe, 1976-79. Address: (h.) Ollach, Braes, Skye.

MacDonald, Professor Simon Gavin George, MA, PhD, FInstP, FRSE. Professor of Physics, Dundee University, since 1973 (Head, Department of Physics, since 1979); Deputy Chairman, Universities General Council on Admissions, since 1983; b. 5.9.23, Beauly, Inverness-shire; m., Eva Leonie Austerlitz; 1 s.; 1 d. Educ. George Heriot's, Edinburgh; Edinburgh University. Junior Scientific Officer, Royal Aircraft Establishment, Farnborough, 1943-46; Lecturer in Physics, St. Andrews University, 1948-57; Senior Lecturer in Physics: University College of the West Indies, 1957-62, St. Andrews University, 1962-67; Dundee University: Senior Lecturer in Physics, 1967-73, Dean of Science, 1970-83, Vice-Principal, 1974-79; Member, Scottish Universities Council on Entrance, 1969-82 (Vice-Convener, 1973-77, Convener, 1977-82); Chairman, Technical Committee, UCCA, 1979-83; Chairman, Board of Directors, Dundee Repertory Theatre, since 1975. Publications: Problems and Solutions in General Physics; Physics for Biology and Premedical Students; Physics for the Life and Health Sciences. Recreations: bridge; golf; fiction writing. Address: (b.) Department of Physics, Dundee University, Dundee, DD1 4HN; T.-0382 23181.

Macdonald, William Alexander, JP, AIB. Honorary Sheriff, since 1972; b. 9.1.21, Banffshire; m., Millicent M. Brodie. Educ. Turriff Academy; Banff Academy. Joined Trustee Savings Bank, 1939; RAF, 1941-46; Manager, Trustee Savings Bank: Stornoway, 1949-52, Peterhead, 1952-84. Chairman: Peterhead Scottish Week, Peterhead Community Centre, Banff Buchan Crime Prevention Panel; Treasurer, Peterhead Aged and Infirm Committee; Treasurer, Frank Jack Court (Housing Association); Session Clerk, Peterhead Old Parish Church, since 1954; Past President, Peterhead Rotary Club. Recreation: gardening. Address: (h.) 6 Kinmundy Road, Peterhead, AB4 6AY; T.-0779 72103.

MacDonell of Glengarry, Air Cdre. Aeneas Ranald Donald, CB, DFC. 22nd Chief of Glengarry; Member, Standing Council of Scottish Chiefs; Trustee, Clan Donald Lands Trust; Trustee, Finlaggan Trust; b. 15.11.13, Baku, Russia; m., 1, Diana Dorothy Keane; 2 s.; 1 d.; 2, Lois Eirene Frances Streatfeild; 1 s.; 1 d. Educ. Hurtspierpoint College; Royal Air Force College, Cranwell. RAF Officer, 1931-64; seconded to Fleet Air Arm, 1935-37; Flying Instructor, 1938-39; Air Ministry; Officer Commanding Spitfire Squadron during Battle of Britain; POW, Germany, 1941-45; Chief Flying Instructor, RAF College, Cranwell; Air Attache, Moscow, 1956-58; Director of Management and Work Study, Ministry of Defence, 1960-64; Construction Industry Training Board, 1967-72; Head, Commercial Department, Industrial Society, 1972-76; Partner, John Courtis & Partners, Management Selection Consultants; retired and moved to Scotland, 1981. Honorary President, Ross and Cromarty Branch, Soliders', Sailors' and Airmen's Families Association. Recreation: bird watching. Address: (h.) Elonbank, 23 Castle Street, Fortrose, Ross-shire, IV10 8TH; T.-0381 20121.

MacDougall of MacDougall, Madam, (Coline Helen Elizabeth). 30th Chief of Clan MacDougall; b. 17.8.04; m., Leslie Grahame-Thomson (deceased). Address: (h.) Dunollie Castle, Oban, Argyll.

McDougall, Jack Craig, RIBA, FRIAS, FFB, FBIM. Director of Architectural and Related Services, Strathclyde Regional Council, since 1981; b. 10.4.32, Glasgow; m., Elspeth Liddell Nixon; 1 s.; 1 d. Educ. Allan Glen's School, Glasgow; Glasgow School of Art. Depute County Architect: Lanarkshire County Council, 1966, Renfrewshire County Council, 1967; Senior Depute County Architect, Renfrewshire, 1972; Depute Director of Architectural and Related Services, Strathclyde Regional Council, 1974-81. Council Member: RIBA, since 1980, RIAS, since 1980, GIA (Glasgow Institute of Architects), since 1974; Honorary Treasurer/Registrar, Association of Chief Architects of Scottish Local Authorities; Elder, Church of Scotland, since 1974. Recreations: caravanning; visiting European capital cities; interest in wine. Address: (b.) Department of Architectural and Related Services, Strathclyde House, 20 India Street, Glasgow, G2 4PF; T.-041-227 2100.

Macdougall, Rev. Malcolm McAllister, BD, DChrEd. Minister, St. James' Parish Church, Portobello, Edinburgh, since 1981; b. 20.3.52, Greenock; m., Janet Fiona MacVicar; 1 s. Educ. Greenock Academy; Kelvinside Academy; Edinburgh University. Worked in rope and canvas industry, and in banking, before entering ministry. Recreations: walking in the country; broadcasting; reading; various sports. Address: 63 Durham Terrace, Edinburgh, EH15 1QG; T.-031-669 1767.

MacDougall, Robert Hugh, MB, ChB, DMRT, FRCS, FRCR. Consultant Radiotherapist and Oncologist, Tayside Health Board, since 1982; Honorary Senior Lecturer, Dundee University; b. 9.8.49, Dundee; m., Moira Jean Gray; 1 s.; 1 d. Educ. High School of Dundee; St. Andrews University; Edinburgh University. Demonstrator in Anatomy, St. Andrews University; Registrar in Surgery, Aberdeen Royal Infirmary; Lecturer in Clinical Oncology, Edinburgh University. Recreations: curling; fishing; reading. Address: (b.) Department of Radiotherapy and Oncology, Ninewells Hospital, Dundee; T.-Dundee 60111.

McDowall, Stuart, CBE, MA. Senior Lecturer in Economics, St. Andrews University, since 1967; Deputy Chairman, Central Arbitration Committee, since 1976; Member, Local Government Boundary Commission for Scotland, since 1982; Member, Monopolies and Mergers Commission, since 1985; b. 19.4.26, Liverpool; m., Margaret B.W. Gyle; 3 s. Educ. Liverpool Institute; St. Andrews University. Master, United College of St. Salvator and St. Leonard, 1976-80. Secretary, Scottish Economic Society, 1970-76; Member, Committee of Inquiry into Powers and Functions

of the Islands Councils of Scotland, 1982-84; Arbitrator for ACAS, since 1975. Recreations: golf; hill-walking; gardening; music. Address: (h.) 10 Woodburn Terrace, St. Andrews, Fife, KY16 8BA; T.-0334 73247.

McDowall, William Crocket, BA (Oxon); FRSE. Barrister at Law (Gray's Inn); Member, Board, Irvine Development Corporation, since 1981; Member, Scottish Joint Negotiating Committee for Teaching Staff in Further Education, since 1982; b. 16.10.17, Rangoon, Burma; m., Margery Haswell Wilson; 2 s.; 3 d. Educ. Glasgow Academy; Queen's College, Oxford. Sudan Political Service, 1939 (Assistant District Commissioner); Sudan Auxiliary Defence Force, Bimbashi, 1940-42; District Commissioner, 1942-45; Sudan Legal Department, 1946; Judge of the High Court, Sudan, 1951; joined ICI Nobel Division, 1955; Chief Executive, Nobel's Explosives Co. Ltd., 1976-79. Honorary Governor, Glasgow Academy; Governor, Glasgow School of Art. Recreations: walking; gardening. Address: (h.) Old Mill, Dunlop, Kilmarnock; T.-Stewarton 84877.

MacDowell, Professor Douglas Maurice, MA. Professor of Greek, Glasgow University, since 1971; b. 8.3.31, London. Educ. Highgate School; Balliol College, Oxford. Schoolmaster, 1954-58; Manchester University: Assistant Lecturer, 1958-61, Lecturer, 1961-68, Senior Lecturer, 1968-70, Reader, 1970-71; Visiting Fellow, Merton College, Oxford, 1969; President, Glasgow Centre, Classical Association of Scotland, 1973-75, 1977-79, 1982-84; Chairman, 1973-76, and Vice President, since 1976, Scottish Hellenic Society; Chairman, Council, Classical Association of Scotland, 1976-82. Publications: Andokides: On the Mysteries, 1962; Athenian Homicide Law, 1963; Aristophanes: Wasps, 1971; The Law in Classical Athens, 1978. Address: (b.) Glasgow University, Glasgow, G12 8QQ.

MacEachen, Catherine, RGN, SCM, QIDNS, PWT. Member, Western Isles Health Board, since 1979; District Nursing Sister, since 1951; b. 24.10.25, Sunamul, Benbecula; m., Donald Alex MacEachen; 1 s.; 1 d. Educ. Balivanich School. Member, Local Division, Northern Regional Hospital Board, 1964-74; Member, Local Health Council, 1975-79; Member, Community Council, 1978-80; Local Councillor for Benbecula, 1980-82; Trustee, Benbecula Community Association, since 1982; Treasurer, Benbecula Committee, National Society for Cancer Relief, since 1977. Recreations: music; travel; folklore; Gaelic poetry. Address: (h.) 15 Aird, Benbecula, Western Isles; T.-0870 2124.

McEwan, David, BSc, CEng, MICE, FCIOB. Principal, Glasgow College of Building and Printing, since 1972; Chairman, Scottish Branch, Association of Principals of Colleges, since 1985; Chairman, Scottish Central Committee on Technical Education, since 1982; b. 9.2.27, Beith, Ayrshire; m., Helen Barlow Gebbie; 1 s.; 1 d. Educ. Spiers School, Beith; Glasgow University. Lt., Royal Engineers, during Military Service, 1945-48; Graduate Engineer, Kirkcudbright County Council, 1950-52; Assistant Engineer,

Clydebank Town Council, 1952-54; Lecturer and Senior Lecturer, Paisley College, 1954-65; HM Inspector, Scottish Education Department, 1965-67; Principal, Glasgow College of Building, 1967-71. Member, numerous UK and Scottish Committees on education and training and on church buildings. Recreations: travel; photography; wine; food; clan society. Address: (b.) Glasgow College of Building and Printing, 60 North Hanover Street, Glasgow, G1 2BP; T.-041-332 9969.

McEwan, Helen Purdie, MD, FRCOG, FRCSGlas. Consultant Obstetrician and Gynaecologist, Royal Infirmary and Royal Maternity Hospital, Glasgow, since 1976; Honorary Clinical Lecturer, Glasgow University, since 1972; President, Royal Medico Chirurgical Society, Glasgow, 1984-85; b. 8.8.38, Glasgow. Educ. Jordanhill College School; Glasgow University. House Surgeon, Western Infirmary, to Sir Charles Illingworth; Senior House Officer, Gynaecology, Victoria Infirmary and Western Infirmary; Ure Scholar, Western Infirmary; Registrar, Royal Maternity and Royal Samaritan Hospital; Senior Registrar, Glasgow Teaching Hospitals. Member, Advisory Board, Women's Health Concern. Recreations: visiting Western Highlands and Islands; music. Address: (h.) 47 Westland Drive, Glasgow, G14 9PE.

McEwan, Very Rev. Mgr. Hugh Gerard, DD. Parish Priest, St. Michael's, Dumbarton, since 1973; Vicar Episcopal for Ecumenism, Diocese of Glasgow, since 1975; b. 7.5.25, Glasgow. Educ. Blairs College, Aberdeen; Gregorian University, Rome. Tutor, Pontifical Scots College, Rome, 1951-60 (Vice-Rector, 1960-66); Secretary to Archbishop of Glasgow, 1966-68; Priest, St. Margaret's, Kinning Park, Glasgow, 1968-73; nominated Member, Dunbarton County Council, 1973-75. Publications: The Second Vatican Council; Bishop Grey Graham. Recreation: collecting antiques and Victoriana. Address: St. Michael's, 2 Cardross Road, Dumbarton; T.-Dumbarton 62709.

McEwan, Louis Vincent, BSc, DipAgrEcon. Head, Fisheries III Division (Structural Policy and Enforcement), Department of Agriculture and Fisheries for Scotland, since 1983; b. 23.7.32, Edinburgh; m., Sheila Brigid Myles Connolly; 4 s.; 1 d. Educ. St. Andrew's Priory; Melville College, Edinburgh; Edinburgh University; Reading University; Michigan State University; Glasgow University. Agricultural Economist, DAFS, 1955-72; Kellogg Fellow, Michigan State University, 1961-62; Agricultural Attache, British Embassy, Washington DC, 1972-74; DAFS: Fisheries Economist, 1974-76, Assistant Secretary, 1976; Head, Crops Division, 1976-82, and of Capital Grants and Animal Health Division, 1982-83. Recreations: gardening; golf; music. Address: (b.) Chesser House, Gorgie Road, Edinburgh, EH11 3AW; T.-031-443 4020.

McEwan, Robert Peter, CA. Director of Finance and of Property Management, Scottish Development Agency, since 1977; Director, Scottish Development Finance, since 1982; Director, Scottish Exhibition Centre, since 1983; b.

21.9.23, Glasgow; m., Mary (Mollie) Howden; 1 s. Educ. High School of Glasgow. Binder Hamlyn, CA, London; Chief Accountant, Sentinel (Shrewsbury) Ltd.; Divisional Director, PA Management Consultants Ltd.; Director of Industry Services, SDA. Governor, High School of Glasgow; Council Member, Institute of Chartered Accountants of Scotland; Director, Glasgow Garden Festival 1988 Ltd. Recreations: golf; gardening. Address: (b.) 120 Bothwell Street, Glasgow; T.-041-248 2700.

McEwan, Sheriff Robin Gilmour, QC, LLB, PhD. Sheriff of Lanark, since 1982; b. 12.12.43, Glasgow; m., Sheena McIntyre; 2 d. Educ. Paisley Grammar School; Glasgow University. Faulds Fellow in Law, Glasgow University, 1965-68; admitted to Faculty of Advocates, 1967; Standing Junior Counsel, Department of Energy, 1974-76; Advocate Depute, 1976-79; Chairman, Industrial Tribunals, 1981. Publications: Pleading in Court, 1980; A Casebook on Damages (Co-author), 1983. Recreations: formerly: football, boxing; now: golf, skating. Address: (b.) Sheriff Court, Lanark, ML11 7NQ; T.-Lanark 61531.

MacEwan, Canon Sydney Alfred, MA, DMus. Canon of Argyll and the Isles, since 1956; b. 19.10.08, Glasgow. Educ. St. Aloysius College; Hillhead High School; Glasgow University; Royal Academy of Music, London. International Tenor before becoming Priest (ordained, 1944); Protege of Count John McCormack and Sir Compton Mackenzie; sang in all the great concert halls of the world; recorded for Columbia and Parlophone Companies for 39 years; Member, BBC Advisory Council in Scotland, 1945-50; Member, Education Committee: Argyll, 20 years, Highland Region, until 1976; served in Glasgow, Lochgilphead, Rothesay, Kingussie. Publication: On The High Cs (autobiography), 1974. Recreations: golf; yachting; model Clyde steamers. Address: (h.) Bermuda, 33 Dhailling Road, Dunoon, Argyll.

McEwen, John, MB, ChB, PhD, MRCP. Medical Director, Drug Development (Scotland) Ltd., since 1983; Honorary Senior Lecturer, Dundee University, since 1983; Honorary Consultant, Tayside Health Board, since 1984; b. 11.4.43, Uddingston; m., Veronica Rosemary Iverson; 1 s.; 1 d. Educ. Ecclesfield Grammar School; St. Andrews University. Resident Physician/Surgeon, Dundee Hospitals, 1966-67; Lecturer in Therapeutics, Dundee University, 1969-75; Visiting Fellow in Clinical Pharmacology, Vanderbilt University, Tennessee, 1972-74; Director of Clinical Pharmacology, Hoechst, UK, 1975-82. Recreations: keyboard instruments; hill-walking; choral singing. Address: (h.) 1 Osborne Place, Dundee, DD2 1BE; T.-Dundee 641060.

McFadden, Jean Alexandra, JP, MA. Leader, Glasgow District Council, since 1980; Vice Lord Lieutenant, City of Glasgow, since 1980; b. 26.11.41; m. Educ. Glasgow University.

McFadyen, Thomas, MB, ChB. Senior Medical Officer, Erskine Hospital, since 1978; b. 30.11.39, Glasgow. Educ. Allan Glen's School; Glasgow University. Appointments, Glasgow Royal

Infirmary, Law Hospital, Carluke and Royal Alexandra Infirmary, Paisley. Recreation: golf. Address: (h.) Tigh-Na-Coille, Erskine Hospital, Bishopton, PA7 5PU; T.-041-812 7555.

Macfarlane, Rev. Alwyn James Cecil, BA, MA. Associate Minister, The Scots' Church, Melbourne, Australia, since 1985; b. 14.6.22, Edinburgh; m., Joan Cowell Harris; 1 s.; 1 d. Educ. Cargilfield School, Edinburgh; Rugby School; New College, Oxford; New College, Edinburgh. Captain, 6th Black Watch, North Africa, Italy and Greece, 1940-45; entered Ministry, Church of Scotland, 1951; Minister: Fodderty and Strathpeffer, 1952-59, St. Cuthbert's Church, Edinburgh (Associate), 1959-63, Portobello Old, Edinburgh, 1963-68, Newlands (South), Glasgow, 1968-85. Chaplain to The Queen in Scotland; Member, The Queen's Household in Scotland. Recreations: photography; travel. Address: 4-9 Belhaven Place, Edinburgh; (while in Australia) The Scots Church, 99 Russell Street, Melbourne, Victoria, 3000, Australia.

MacFarlane, Rev. David Cockburn, MA. Minister, Old Parish Church of Peebles, since 1970, with Eddleston Parish Church, since 1977, with Lyne and Manor Parish Church, since 1984; b. 10.6.31, Glasgow; m., Penelope Margaret Broadfoot; 3 s. Educ. High School of Glasgow; Glasgow University and Trinity College. Assistant Minister, Dunblane Cathedral, 1956-58; Minister, Aberlady Parish Church, 1959-70; Moderator: Haddington and Dunbar Presbytery, 1968-69, Melrose and Peebles Presbytery, 1977-78; Warden of Neidpath, 1984; President, Peebles Rotary Club, 1974-75. Publications: Aberlady Parish Church, 1967; The Old Parish Church of Peebles, 1973. Recreations: public speaking; reading; painting. Address: (h.) Old Parish Church Manse, Innerleithen Road, Peebles, EH45 8BD; T.-0721 20568.

Macfarlane, Sir James Wright, Kt (1973), PhD, FRSE, CEng, FIEE, FIMechE, JP, DL. Managing Director, Cathcart Investment Co. Ltd., since 1964; b. 2.10.08; m. Educ. Allan Glen's School; Royal Technical College; Glasgow University; London University. Chairman, Macfarlane Engineering Co. Ltd., Cathcart, 1967-69; Past President, Association of County Councils in Scotland; Member, Royal Commission on the Police, 1960-62; Convener, Renfrew County Council, 1967-73; Chairman of Governors, Paisley College of Technology.

Macfarlane, Sir Norman Somerville, Kt (1983). Chairman and Managing Director, Macfarlane Group (Clansman) PLC, since 1973; b. 5.3.26; m.; 1 s.; 4 d. Educ. High School of Glasgow. Director, Clydesdale Bank, since 1980; Director, General Accident Fire & Life Assurance Corporation plc, since 1984; Chairman, American Trust PLC, since 1984; Member, Board, Scottish Development Agency, since 1979; Vice Chairman, Scottish Ballet, since 1983; President, Royal Glasgow Institute of the Fine Arts, since 1976; Member, Court, Glasgow University, since 1979.

Macfarlane, Peter Wilson, BSc, PhD, FBCS. Reader in Medical Cardiology, Glasgow University, since 1980; b. 8.11.42, Glasgow; m., Irene Grace Muir; 2 s. Educ. Hyndland Senior Secondary School, Glasgow; Glasgow University. Glasgow University: Assistant Lecturer in Medical Cardiology, 1967, Lecturer, 1970, Senior Lecturer, 1974; President, 5th International Congress on Electrocardiology, Glasgow, 1978; Secretary, International Council on Electrocardiology; Author/Editor, seven books. Recreations: playing football; running marathons; playing violin. Address: (h.) 12 Barrcraig Road, Bridge of Weir, PA11 3HG; T.-Bridge of Weir 614443.

Macfarlane, Rev. Thomas Gracie, BSc, PhD, BD. Minister, South Shawlands Parish Church, Glasgow, since 1968; b. 10.6.27, Glasgow; m., Davina Shaw Robertson; 3 s. Educ. Allan Glen's School; Royal Technical College; Glasgow University. Research Metallurgist, 1948-53; ordained, 1956; served under Foreign Mission Committee, Church of Scotland, 1956-61, as Missionary with United Church of Central Africa in Rhodesia; Minister, St. James', Falkirk, 1961-68. Address: 51 Lubnaig Road, Glasgow, G43 2RX; T.-041-637 2331.

MacFarlane, Thomas Wallace, DDS, FRCPath, FDSRCPSGlas. Reader in Oral Medicine and Pathology, Glasgow University, since 1984; Honorary Consultant in Oral Microbiology; b. 12.12.42, Glasgow; m., Nancy McEwan; 1 s. Educ. Hyndland Senior Secondary School; Glasgow University. Assistant Lecturer, Dental Histology and Pathology, 1966-69; trained in Medical Microbiology and Histopathology, Glasgow Royal Infirmary; Lecturer in Oral Medicine and Pathology, 1969-77; organised and ran the diagnostic service in Oral Microbiology, Glasgow Dental Hospital and School; Senior Lecturer in Oral Medicine and Pathology and Consultant in Oral Microbiology, 1977. Recreations: music; reading; painting; walking. Address: (b.) Oral Microbiology Unit, Dental Hospital and School, 378 Sauchiehall Street, Glasgow, G2 3JZ; T.-041-332 7020.

McGarry, Andrew Francis, MA, BA (Hons). Head Teacher, St. Maurice's High School, Cumbernauld, since 1976; b. 21.4.32, Glasgow; m., Mary; 1 s.; 1 d. Educ. St. Mungo's Academy, Glasgow; Blairs College, Aberdeen; Glasgow University; London University (External). RAF, 1954-56; Teacher in Glasgow, Lanarkshire, Stirlingshire, Dunbartonshire, 1963-76. Recreation: golf. Address: (h.) 5 Glamis Gardens, Bishopbriggs, Glasgow, G64 3HP; T.-041-772 2488.

McGarry, James Alexander, MB, FRCOG. Consultant in Obstetrics and Gynaecology; Honorary Clinical Lecturer, Glasgow University; Chairman, Area Sub-Committee in Obstetrics and Gynaecology, Glasgow, since 1982; b. 3.6.30, Mossend, Lanarkshire. Educ. Our Lady's High School, Motherwell; Glasgow University. Surgeon Lt., HMS Bulwark, 1955-56; seconded in charge, Department of Obstetrics and Gynaecology, Kenyatta National Hospital, 1965-67. Address: (h.) 57 Fotheringay Road, Glasgow, G41 4NN; T.-041-423 0938.

McGeough, Professor Joseph Anthony, BSc, PhD, DSc, CEng, FIMechE, FIProdE, MIM. Regius Professor of Engineering and Head, Department of Mechanical Engineering, Edinburgh University, since 1983; b. 29.5.40, Kilwinning; m., Brenda Nicholson; 2 s.; 1 d. Educ. St. Michael's College; Glasgow University; Aberdeen University. Research Demonstrator, Leicester University, 1966; Senior Research Fellow, Queensland University, Australia, 1967; Research Metallurgist, International Research and Development Co. Ltd., Newcastle-upon-Tyne, 1968-69; Senior Research Fellow, Strathclyde University, 1969-72; Lecturer in Engineering, Aberdeen University, 1972-77 (Senior Lecturer, 1977-80, Reader, 1980-83). Chairman, Dyce Academy College Council, 1980-83; Honorary Vice-President, Aberdeen University Athletic Association, since 1981. Publication: Principles of Electrochemical Machining, 1974. Recreations: gardening; golf; athletics. Address: (h.) 39 Dreghorn Loan, Colinton, Edinburgh, EH13 ODF; T.-031-441 1302.

McGettrick, Professor Andrew David, BSc, PhD. Head, Computer Science Department, Strathclyde University, since 1984; b. 15.5.44, Glasgow; m., Sheila Margaret Girot; 4 s.; 1 d. Educ. St. Aloysius College, Glasgow; Glasgow University; Peterhouse College, Cambridge. Strathclyde University: Lecturer, 1969-80, Reader in Computer Science, 1980, Professor, 1983. Editor, Addison Wesley's International Computer Science Series, 1980; Chairman, Computing Panel, Scottish Universities Council on Entrance, 1984. Publications: Algol 68, A First and Second Course; An Introduction to the Definition of Programming Languages; Program Verification Using ADA; Graded Problems in Computer Science. Recreations: squash; running. Address: (b.) Computer Science Department, Strathclyde University, Livingstone Tower, 26 Richmond Street, Glasgow; T.-041-552 4400.

McGettrick, Bartholomew John, BSc (Hons), MEd (Hons). Principal, St. Andrew's College of Education, since 1985; Chairman, Catholic Education Commission for Scotland, since 1981; Member, Council for Educational Technology, since 1982; Governor, Scottish Council for Educational Technology, since 1984; b. 16.8.45, Glasgow; m., Elizabeth Maria McLaughlin; 2 s.; 2 d. Educ. St. Aloysius' College, Glasgow; Glasgow University. Teacher and Head, Department of Geography, St. Aloysius' College, Glasgow, 1968-72; Educational Psychologist, Scottish Centre for Social Subjects, 1972-75; Assistant Principal, then Vice-Principal, Notre Dame College of Education (latterly St. Andrew's College of Education), 1975-85. Member, Council for National Academic Awards, Committee for Education, since 1981; Chairman, Association of Higher Academic Staff in Colleges of Education in Scotland, 1982-84; Member, Board of Governors, St. Aloysius' College, Glasgow. Recreations: sports (squash, rugby). Address: (h.) 174 Carmunnock Road, Glasgow, G44 5AJ; T.-041-637 8112.

McGhee, Rev. Robert, DD. Minister, Falkirk St. Andrew's, since 1972; b. 29.7.29, Port Glasgow; m., Mary Stevenson Cunningham; 1 s.; 2 d.

Educ. Port Glasgow High School; Greenock High School; Glasgow University and Trinity College. Trained as cashier/bookkeeper, 1945-54; RAF, 1947-49; ordained and inducted to Pulteneytown St. Andrew's, Wick, 1959; Minister, Newbattle, Dalkeith, 1966-72; Convener, Board of Social Responsibility, Church of Scotland, since 1985 (Convener, Community Care, Social Responsibility, 1977-85); Chairman, Lord's Day Observance Society, Scotland, 1970-74; President, Scottish Evangelistic Council, 1982-85. Address: St. Andrew's Manse, 1 Maggie Woods Loan, Falkirk, FK1 5SJ; T.-Falkirk 23308.

McGhie, Fergus Dunsmore Scott, LCG. Chef/Caterer; Principal, Duncraig Castle College, Plockton, 1974-85; b. 25.6.21, Hamilton; m., 1, Margaret E.L. Shanks (deceased); 2 s.; 2, Rosemary G. Tulloch. Educ. Hamilton Academy; Woodside School, Hamilton. Chef Instructor (and Lecturer), Scottish Hotel School, 1954-60; Head Chef, J.W. Mackie, Edinburgh, 1960-62; Senior Teacher, Catering Subjects, Castlehill School of Baking and Catering, Edinburgh, 1962-67; Head of Section (Professional Cookery), Telford College of Further Education, Edinburgh, 1967-72. Diplome Cordon Culinaire, 1975. Address: (h.) Yasume, 13 Pilmuir Road West, Forres, Moray.

McGibbon, Alistair, MA, MEd. Rector, Woodlands High School, Falkirk, since 1983; b. 3.10.37, Glasgow; m., Jean Ronald; 2 s.; 1 d. Educ. North Kelvinside School; Glasgow University; Stirling University. Teaching appointments in Glasgow, Guildford, Perth (Western Australia), Papua New Guinea, Central Region. Recreations: golf; Church activities. Address: (b.) Woodlands High School, Rennie Street, Falkirk, FK1 5AL; T.-0324 29615.

McGill, Lewis Sinclair, FIB (Scot), MBA. General Manager, Strategic Planning, Royal Bank of Scotland PLC, since 1985; b. 8.4.39, Dundee; m., Ann Mackintosh Mitchell; 2 s. Educ. Forfar Academy; Strathclyde University. National Bank of Scotland Ltd., 1956-59; National Commercial Bank of Scotland Ltd., 1959-69; Royal Bank of Scotland PLC: joined 1969, Assistant General Manager, then General Manager, Southern Region, 1980-85. Vice President, Royal Highland and Agricultural Society, 1985; Director: Scottish Chamber Orchestra Ltd., Colinton Castle Sports Club Ltd. Recreations: music; tennis; golf; squash. Address: (h.) 10 Fernielaw Avenue, Edinburgh, EH13 OEE; T.-031-441 1052.

McGillivray, Rev. (Alexander) Gordon, MA, BD, STM. Clerk, Edinburgh Presbytery, Church of Scotland, since 1973; Depute Clerk, General Assembly, since 1971; b. 22.9.23, Edinburgh; m., Winifred Jean Porter; 2 s.; 2 d. Educ. George Watson's Boys' College, Edinburgh; Edinburgh University; Union Theological Seminary, New York. Royal Artillery, 1942-45; Assistant Minister, St. Cuthbert's Parish Church, Edinburgh, 1949, 1950-51, Minister: Waterbeck Church, 1951-58, Nairn High Church, 1958-73. Recreation: golf. Address: 7 Greenfield Crescent, Balerno, Midlothian, EH14 7HD; T.-031-449 4747.

McGilvray, Professor James William, MA, MLitt. Professor of Economics, Strathclyde University, since 1975; Director, Fraser of Allander Institute, since 1980; b. 21.2.38, Glasgow; m., Alison Ann; 1 s.; 1 d. Educ. St. Columba's College, Dublin; Edinburgh University. Recreations: gardening; squash; shooting. Address: (b.) 100 Cathedral Street, Glasgow, G4 OLN; T.-041-552 4400.

McGirr, Professor Edward McCombie, CBE, BSc, MD, FRCP, FRCPEdin, FRCPGlas, FFCM, FACP (Hon), FRSE. Chairman, Scottish Council for Postgraduate Medical Education, 1979-85; Member, Council, Royal Society of Edinburgh, since 1982; Emeritus Professor, Glasgow University, since 1981; b. 15.6.16, Hamilton; m., Diane Curzon Woods; 1 s.; 3 d. Educ. Hamilton Academy; Glasgow University. RAMC, 1941-47, including posts as graded physician and specialist in medicine; appointments in University Department of Medicine, Glasgow Royal Infirmary, 1947-78, latterly Muirhead Chair of Medicine, Glasgow University, and Physician in charge of wards, Glasgow Royal Infirmary; Dean, Faculty of Medicine, Glasgow University, 1974-81; Administrative Dean and Professor of Administrative Medicine, Glasgow University, 1978-81. President, Royal College of Physicians and Surgeons of Glasgow, 1970-72; Chairman, Scottish Health Service Planning Council, 1978-84; Honorary Physician to the Army in Scotland, 1975-81; sometime Member: Greater Glasgow Health Board, National Radiological Protection Board, General Nursing Council for Scotland, National Board for Nursing, Midwifery and Health Visiting; Past President, Royal Medico-Chirurgical Society of Glasgow. Recreations: reading; curling. Address: (h.) Anchorage House, Bothwell, by Glasgow, G71 8NF; T.-0698 852194.

McGlynn, Archie Smith, BA (Hons), MPhil, DipComm, MIIM. HM Inspector of Schools, since 1976; b. Tarbert, Argyll; m., Leah Sutherland Ross; 1 s.; 1 d. Educ. Tarbert Secondary School; Campbeltown Grammar School; Strathclyde University; Glasgow University. Industry and commerce, 1962-64; Teacher, Kingsridge Secondary School, Glasgow, 1964-65; Lecturer in Economics, Inverness Technical College, 1965-66; Lecturer in Management Studies, Robert Gordon's Institute of Technology, and Donside Paper Company, 1966-68; Head of Business Studies, Glenrothes College, 1968-69; Depute Principal, Glenrothes and Buckhaven College, 1969-75; Chairman, Fife and NE Scotland Branch, Institute of Industrial Managers, 1973-75; Assessor: SCOTBEC Committees in Administrative Studies and Distribution, 1976-83, CNAA Committee for Arts and Social Studies and CNAA Boards in Economics and Public Administration, 1977-84, College Council, Scottish Police College, 1977-82, Sabhal Mor Ostaig, 1981-85; Chairman, 16 plus Action Plan Development Team, Inter Disciplinary Studies, 1983-84; Regional Inspector FE, 1982-84; management of Educational Resources Unit, since 1985; Editor, Glenrothes Management Studies Series, 1970-75; Elder, Abbotshall Church. Recreations: hedgehogs; poetry; music; wine-making; following

Fife Flyers. Address: (b.) Room 4/47, New St. Andrews House, Edinburgh; T.-031-556 8400.

McGlynn, Rt. Rev. Lord Abbot (James Aloysius) Donald, OCSO, STL, SLJ. Monk, Order of Cistercians of Strict Observance, since 1952; Abbot of Nunraw, since 1969; b. 13.8.34, Glasgow. Educ. Holyrood School, Glasgow; St. Bernardine's School, Buckinghamshire; Gregorian University, Rome. President, Scottish Council of Major Religious Superiors, 1974-77; President, British Isles Regional Council of Cistercian Abbeys, 1980-84; Official Roman Catholic Visitor to the General Assembly, Church of Scotland, 1976 and 1985; Commandeur Ecclesiastique, Military & Hospitaller Order of St. Lazarus of Jerusalem, 1985; Patron, Friends of the Beatitudes, Madras; Patron, Haddington Pilgrimage of St. Mary & the Three Kings. Recreations: iconography; farm work. Address: Sancta Maria Abbey, Nunraw, Garvald, Haddington, EH41 4LW; T.-062 083 223.

McGonigle, Brendan Oliver, BA, PHD. Senior Lecturer in Psychology, Edinburgh University, since 1981; b. 18.5.39, Belfast; m., Rachael Anne; 3 d. Educ. St. Malachy's College, Belfast; Queen's University, Belfast. MRC Research Fellow, Durham University; Lecturer in Psychology, Oxford University, and Tutor, St. Catherine's, St. John's and Trinity Colleges; Assistant Professor, Pennsylvania State University, USA, and Research Associate (National Institute of Health), Institute of Science and Engineering, University Park, Pennsylvania. Publication: Reasoning and Discourse. Recreations: fishing; motor caravanning. Address: (h.) 8 Doune Terrace, Edinburgh, EH3 6DY; T.-031-226 3402.

McGovern, John Gerard, JP, BSc, MRSC. Headteacher, Our Lady's High School, Broxburn, since 1978; b. 16.1.34, Cambuslang; m., Elizabeth Kearney; 2 s.; 3 d. Educ. Our Lady's High School, Motherwell; Glasgow University. National Service, Royal Signals (awarded GSM (Cyprus)); Teacher of Science (Chemistry), Our Lady's High School, Motherwell; Principal Teacher of Science/Chemistry, St. David's High School, Dalkeith; Depute Headteacher: Our Lady's High School, Broxburn, St. David's, Dalkeith. Address: (h.) 85 Ambrose Rise, Dedridge, Livingston, West Lothian; T.-0506 414880.

McGovern, Peter David, BSc (Econ), MSc, PhD, MTPI. Assistant Chief Planner, Scottish Development Department, since 1972; b. 2.1.27, Edinburgh. Educ. London School of Economics. Recreations: mountain sports; tree planting; music.

McGowan, Rev. Andrew T.B., BD, STM. Minister, Mallaig and the Small Isles, since 1980; b. 30.1.54, Glasgow; m., June S. Watson; 2 s. Educ. Uddingston Grammar School; Aberdeen University; Union Theological Seminary, New York. Assistant Minister, St. Cuthbert's, Edinburgh, 1978-80. Member, Council, Rutherford House, Edinburgh; Moderator, Lochaber Presbytery, 1983-84; Secretary, Scottish Evangelical Theology Society, 1980-85. Recreations: hillwalking; chess; guitar. Address: The Manse, Mallaig, PH41 4RG; T.-0687 2256.

McGowan, Daniel, MILAM. Director of Recreation and Leisure, Cumbernauld and Kilsyth District Council, since 1978; b. 23.9.41, Coatbridge; widower; 2 s.; 1 d. Educ. St. Patrick's High School, Coatbridge; Coatbridge Technical College. Chairman, Scottish Swimming Coaches Association, since 1980. Recreations: swimming; golf. Address: (b.) Council Offices, Bron Way, Cumbernauld, G67 1DZ; T.-02367 22131.

McGowan, Professor David Alexander, MDS, PhD, FDSRCS, FFDRCSI, FDSRCPSG. Professor of Oral Surgery, Glasgow University, since 1977; Consultant Oral Surgeon, Greater Glasgow Health Board, since 1977; b. 18.6.39, Portadown, Co. Armagh; m., Margaret Vera Macaulay; 1 s.; 2 d. Educ. Portadown College; Queen's University, Belfast. Oral surgery training, Belfast and Aberdeen, 1961-67; Lecturer in Dental Surgery, Queen's University, Belfast, 1968; Lecturer, then Senior Lecturer and Deputy Head, Oral and Maxillofacial Surgery, London Hospital Medical College, 1968-77. Postgraduate Adviser in Dentistry, Glasgow University, since 1977; Chairman, Dental Committee, Scottish Council for Postgraduate Medical Education; Vice-Chairman, Conference of UK Postgraduate Dental Deans/Advisers; Secretary, Dental Council, Royal College of Physicians and Surgeons of Glasgow; former Council Member, British Association of Oral and Maxillofacial Surgeons. Recreations: sailing; music. Address: (b.) Department of Oral Surgery, Glasgow Dental Hospital and School, 378 Sauchiehall Street, Glasgow, G2 3JZ; T.-041-332 7020, Ext. 259.

McGowan, Edward Lowe. Sheriff Clerk and Auditor of Court, Ayr, 1980-85; Auditor, Faculty of Solicitors, Ayr, since 1980; b. 18.5.25, Glasgow; m., Margaret Schoolar Hunter Blackstock; 3 s.; 1 d. Educ. Strathbungo School. Royal Navy, 1943-46; joined Civil Service, 1950; joined Court Service, 1957; Sheriff Clerk, Berwickshire, 1972-75. Recreations: walking; swimming; ballroom dancing; theatre-going. Address: (h.) 3 Pemberton Valley, Alloway, Ayr; T.-0292 43302.

McGowan, Ian Duncan, BA. Keeper (Catalogues and Automation), National Library of Scotland, since 1978; b. 19.9.45, Liverpool; m., Elizabeth Ann Weir; 2 d. Educ. Liverpool Institute; Exeter College, Oxford. Assistant Keeper, National Library of Scotland, 1971-78. Address: (b.) National Library of Scotland, George IV Bridge, Edinburgh, EH1 1EW; T.-031-226 4531.

McGowan, John, LLB. Solicitor, since 1967; Chairman, Social Security Appeal Tribunal, since 1980; Member, Ayr Legal Aid Committee, since 1983; b. 15.1.44, Kilmarnock; m., Elise Smith; 2 s. Educ. St. Joseph's Academy, Kilmarnock; Glasgow University. Admitted Solicitor, 1967; Council Member, Law Society of Scotland, 1982-85. Recreations: golf; squash; tennis; listening to music. Address: (h.) 15 Monument Road, Ayr; T.-Ayr 260139.

McGowan, Stuart Watson, MB, ChB, FFARCS, DA. Consultant Anaesthetist, Dundee Teaching Hospitals, since 1964; b. 31.7.29, Uddingston;

m., Mabel Wilson; 1 s.; 1 d. Educ. Hutchesons' Boys Grammar School, Glasgow; Glasgow University. President, North-East of Scotland Society of Anaesthetists, 1972; President, Dundee Speakers Club, 1972. Recreations: golf; music; travel. Address: (h.) 41 Whitefauld Road, Dundee, DD2 1RJ; T.-0382 65281.

McGrain, Daniel Fergus, MBE (1983). Footballer; b. 1.5.50, Glasgow; m., Laraine; 3 c. Celtic and Scotland Captain; first club, Maryhill Juniors; signed for Celtic, 1967; first cap against Wales, 1973; played in two World Cups - West Germany, 1974, Spain, 1982; played in seven Scottish Cup Finals; testimonial match, 1980; played more than 600 games for Celtic.

McGrath, John. Artistic Director, 7:84 Theatre Companies, since 1971; Producer/Director, Freeway Films, since 1982; b. 1.6.35, Birkenhead; m., Elizabeth Maclennan; 2 s.; 1 d. Educ. Alun Grammar School, Mold, Clwyd; St. John's College, Oxford. Playwright (more than 35 plays produced professionally in UK and abroad); Writer of film screenplays for feature films and TV plays; Director in theatre and TV; Poet and Songwriter; plays for theatre including Events While Guarding the Bofors Gun and The Cheviot, The Stag and the Black, Black Oil; Visiting Judith E. Wilson Fellow, Cambridge, 1979. Publication: A Good Night Out (lectures). Address: (b.) 7:84 Theatre Co., 31 Albany Street, Edinburgh, EH1 3QN; T.-031-557 2442.

McGrath, Tom. Playwright; b. 23.10.40, Rutherglen. Former Writer in Residence, Traverse Theatre, Edinburgh; plays for the stage include Laurel and Hardy, Traverse, Edinburgh, and Mayfair, London, 1976; The Hardman, Traverse, 1977, UK tour and ICA, London, 1978; Sisters, Theatre Royal, Stratford East, 1978; The Android Circuit, Traverse, 1978.

McGregor, Alistair Gerald Crichton, QC, BA, LLB, WS. Temporary Sheriff, since 1984; Student, New College, Edinburgh, training for Ministry, Church of Scotland, since 1983; b. 15.10.37, Sevenoaks, Kent; m., Margaret Dick Lees or McGregor; 2 s.; 1 d. Educ. Charterhouse; Pembroke College, Oxford; Edinbugh University. Solicitor; Advocate; QC; former Standing Junior Counsel to Queen's and Lord Treasurer's Remembrancer, to Scottish Home and Health Department and to Scottish Development Department; Past Chairman, Discipline Committee, Potato Marketing Board; former Clerk, Rules Council, Court of Session; former Tutor in Scots Law, Edinburgh University; Chairman, Family Care; Elder, Church of Scotland. Publication: Obscenity (Co-author). Recreations: squash; tennis; swimming; travel; cinema. Address: (h.) 25 Gillespie Road, Edinburgh, EH13; T.-031-441 1607.

McGregor, Bobby, MBE (1964). Swimmer; b. 3.4.44, Helensburgh; m., Bernadette. Educ. Falkirk High School; Glasgow College of Architecture. Silver Medal, 4 x 100 m. relay, European Championships, 1962; Gold Medal, 100 m. freestyle, European Championships, 1966;

Silver Medal, 110 yards freestyle, Commonwealth Championships, 1962; Silver Medal, 110 yards freestyle, Commonwealth Championships, 1966; Silver Medal, 100 m. freestyle, Olympic Games, 1964; sometime holder, 110 yards world record; now works as an Architect.

MacGregor, Colin, BL, NP. Honorary Sheriff; Senior Partner, McWhinney MacGregor & Co., Solicitors; Director, James A. Cuthbertson Ltd.; b. 15.3.26, Airdrie; m., Frances Mary Anderson; 1 s.; 1 d. Educ. High School of Glasgow; Glasgow University. Senior Partner, Motherwell & MacGregor, Solicitors, 1951-68; Burgh Prosecutor, Airdrie, 1955-75; Dean, Faculty, Airdrie Society of Solicitors, 1979-81. Chairman, Airdrie Round Table, 1964. Recreations: curling; sailing; hill-walking. Address: (h.) The Cedars, Victoria Place, Airdrie; T.-Airdrie 62795.

McGregor, Rev. Duncan James. Minister, parishes of Channelkirk and Lauder Old, since 1982; b. 17.7.35, Edinburgh; m., Constance Anne Aitchison; 3 s. Educ. Edinburgh Academy; Edinburgh University and New College. Worked in paper trade, then in insurance; Secretary: Scottish Anglers' Association, 1966-82, Anglers' Co-operative Association (Scotland), 1972-78, Scottish Joint Committee for Anglers, 1967-80; called to Ministry, 1982. Life Member, Scottish National Angling Clubs Association and Anglers Co-operative Association (Scotland). Recreations: golf; angling; walking; cycling; reading. Address: The Manse of Lauder, Lauder, Berwickshire; T.-05782 320.

MacGregor of MacGregor, Brigadier Sir Gregor, 6th Bt. 23rd Chief of Clan Gregor; b. 22.12.25; m., Fanny Butler; 2 s. Educ. Eton. Commissioned, Scots Guards, 1944; commanding 1st Bn., Scots Guards, 1966-69; Col. Recruiting, HQ Scotland, 1971; Lt.-Col. commanding Scots Guards, 1971-74; Defence and Military Attache, British Embassy, Athens, 1975-78; Comdr., Lowlands, 1978-80; Member, Queen's Bodyguard for Scotland (Royal Company of Archers). Address: (h.) Bannatyne, Newtyle, Blairgowrie, Perthshire.

McGregor, Ian Alexander, MB, ChB, FRCS, FRPFSG, FRCSGlas, ChM, FRACS, FRCSI. Director, West of Scotland Plastic and Oral Surgery Unit, since 1980; President, Royal College of Physicians and Surgeons of Glasgow, since 1984; b. 6.6.21, Glasgow; m., Frances Mary Vint; 3 s. Educ. North Kelvinside Secondary School; Glasgow University. RAMC, 1945-48; Consultant Surgeon, Glasgow Royal Infirmary, 1957; Consultant Plastic Surgeon, Greater Glasgow Health Board, 1959; Visitor, Royal College of Physicians and Surgeons of Glasgow, 1982. Publications: Fundamental Techniques of Plastic Surgery, 1960; Plastic Surgery for Nurses (Coauthor), 1966. Recreations: music; literature; golf. Address: (h.) 7 Ledcameroch Road, Bearsden, Glasgow, G61 4AB; T.-041-942 3419.

MacGregor, Ian George Stewart, MA, MEd, FBIM. Rector, Bathgate Academy, since 1970; b. 29.12.24, Newcastle-upon-Tyne. Educ. Altrincham Grammar School; Bell-Baxter School,

Cupar; St. Andrews University; Edinburgh University; New York University. Assistant Principal, Ministry of Finance, Government of Northern Ireland, 1947-50; Teacher, Buckhaven High School, 1952-53 and 1954-55 (Teaching Fellowship in Psychology, New York University, 1953-54); Principal Administrative Assistant, Edinburgh Corporation Education Department, 1955-59; Assistant Director of Education, Aberdeenshire, 1959-64; Senior Depute Director of Education, West Lothian, 1964-70. Trustee, Edinburgh University General Council Trust; General Council Assessor, Edinburgh University Court; Member, Executive Committee, UCCA; Scottish HQ Commissioner, Scout Association, and Group Scout Leader, 23rd Edinburgh. Recreations: Scouting; photography; travel. Address: (h.) 20 Stewart Avenue, Bo'ness, EH51 9NL; T.-0506 822462.

Macgregor, James Duncan, OBE, MD, FFCM, DPH, DTM&H. Unit Medical Officer, Perth and Kinross, since 1981; Honorary Senior Clinical Lecturer, Department of Community Medicine, Dundee University, since 1982; b. 21.8.27, Invergowrie, Perthshire; m., Rita Moss; 2 s.; 1 d. Educ. Perth Academy; St. Andrews University. House Officer posts, Perth Royal Infirmary and Royal Northern Infirmary, Inverness, 1950-51; joined HM Colonial Medical Service, 1951; posted to Sierra Leone as General Duty MO; transferred to South Pacific Health Service as Senior Medical Officer, 1956; retired from the Overseas Service, 1974, as Director of Medical Services, Solomon Islands; Chief Administrative Medical Officer, Shetland Health Board, 1975; moved to Tayside Health Board as District MO. Red Cross Voluntary Medical Services Medal. Recreations: gardening; hill-walking. Address: (h.) 74 Glasgow Road, Perth, PH2 OPG; T.-Perth 24493.

Macgregor, Janet Elizabeth, OBE, BSc, MB, ChB, MD, FRCPath. Senior Lecturer and Honorary Consultant, Aberdeen University, since 1973; Specialist, Grampian Health Board, since 1968; Research Fellow, Aberdeen University, since 1960; b. 12.1.20, Glasgow; m., Professor A.G. Macgregor (deceased); 3 s.; 1 d. Educ. Bearsden Academy; Glasgow University. Captain, RAMC, 1943-45; Medical Officer, Maternity and Child Welfare, Glasgow, Sheffield and Edinburgh, 1946-59; Research Fellow, Department of Obstetrics and Gynaecology, Aberdeen University, 1960-66; Medical Assistant, Grampian Health Board, 1966-73. Member, Cytology Sub-Committee, Royal College of Pathologists, 1980-82; Chairman and President, British Society for Clinical Cytology, 1977-83; Member, Medical Advisory Committee, Women's National Cancer Control Campaign, since 1977; Member, IARC (WHO) Study Group on Cervical Cancer, 1978-84; Fellow, International Academy of Cytology, since 1963. Address: (h.) Ardruighe, Clachan, Isle of Seil, Argyll; T.-085-23-427.

McGregor, John Cummack, BSc (Hons), MB, ChB, FRCS, FRCSEdin. Consultant Plastic and Reconstructive Surgeon, Lothian Region, based at Regional Plastic Surgery Unit, Bangour General Hospital, since 1980; Honorary Senior Lecturer in Orthopaedics, Edinburgh University, since 1983; b. 21.4.44, Paisley; m., Moira Imray; 1 s.; 1 d. Educ. Paisley Grammar School; Glasgow University. Initial medical and surgical training, Paisley Royal Alexandra Infirmary, Western Infirmary, Glasgow, Stobhill Hospital, Glasgow, Nottingham City Hospital, Canniesburn Plastic Surgery Unit, Glasgow and Bangour General Hospital. Recreations: tennis; badminton; golf; cacti collecting; budgerigar breeding/showing. Address: (b.) Department of Plastic Surgery, Bangour General Hospital, West Lothian.

McGregor, Margaret McGregor, MB, ChB, MRCGP. Member, Grampian Regional Council, since 1982; Member, Grampian Health Board, since 1983; b. 8.6.27, Aberdeen; m., Archibald M. McGregor; 1 s.; 1 s. deceased; 1 d. Educ. Aberdeen High School for Girls; Aberdeen University. General Medical Practitioner, 1959-81; Grampian Regional Council: Vice Chairman, Manpower Services Committee, Representative on COSLA Manpower Committee; Member, JNC Manual Workers Scotland. Recreation: water colour painting. Address: (h.) Lismore, 24 Westfield Road, Turriff, AB5 7AF; T.-Turriff 62420.

McGrew, William Clement, BS, DPhil. Senior Lecturer, Department of Psychology, Stirling University, since 1981 (Director, Primate Research Unit, since 1983); b. 19.6.44, Fort Smith, Arksansas, USA; m., Muriel McLeod MacKenzie. Educ. University School, Norman, Oklahoma; Arkansas University; Oxford University. Edinburgh University: Population Council Fellow, 1968-69, National Institute of Mental Health Fellow, 1969-70, SSRC Research Fellow, 1970-71; Research Associate, Stanford University, 1972-73; Lecturer, Stirling University, 1973-81; Visiting Professor, University of North Carolina, Charlotte, 1980; Nuffield Foundation Research Fellow, Stirling, 1982; European Editor, Ethology and Sociobiology, since 1984. Publication: An Ethological Study of Children's Behaviour, 1972. Recreations: natural history; softball. Address: (b.) Department of Psychology, Stirling University, Stirling, FK9 4LA; T.-0786 73171.

McGrigor, Captain Sir Charles Edward, 5th Bt. Vice-President, RNLI, and Convenor, Scottish Lifeboat Council; Member, Queen's Bodyguard for Scotland (Royal Company of Archers); b. 5.10.22; m., Mary Bettine; 2 s.; 2 d. Educ. Eton. Joined Army, 1941; Rifle Brigade, North Africa, Italy, Austria (mentioned in Despatches); ADC to Duke of Gloucester, 1945-47. Address: (h.) Upper Sonachan, Dalmally, Argyll.

Macgruer, Michael, RIBA, ARIAS. District Architect, Lochaber District Council, since 1984; b. 26.2.51, Inverness; m., Sheena Robertson; 1 s.; 1 d. Educ. Grantown Grammar School; Lochaber High School; Mackintosh School of Architecture, Glasgow. Glasgow District Council: student architect, 1969-77; Project Architect, 1977-83. Address: (b.) Lochaber House, High Street, Fort William; T.-0397 3881.

McGuinness, James Henry, CB (1964). Chairman, Scottish Philharmonic Trust, since 1976; b. 29.9.12; m.; 1 s.; 2 d. Educ. St. Aloysius College;

Glasgow University. Assistant Under Secretary of State, Scottish Office and Chairman, Scottish Economic Planning Board, 1965-72; Senior Research Fellow in Politics, Glasgow University, 1973-74; Chairman, Scottish Baroque Ensemble, 1973-74; Chairman, Scottish Philharmonic Society Ltd., 1974-78.

McGuire, Edward, ARCM, ARAM. Composer; b. 15.2.48, Glasgow. Educ. Royal Academy of Music, London; State Academy of Music, Stockholm. Won National Young Composers Competition, 1969; Rant selected as test piece for 1978 Carl Flesch International Violin Competition; Proms debut, 1982, when Source performed by BBC SSO; String Quartet chosen for 40th Anniversary Concert, SPNM, Barbican, 1983; frequent commissions and broadcasts including Trilogy: Rebirth-Interregnum-Liberation (New Music Group), Euphoria (EIF/Fires of London), Life Songs (John Currie Singers), Songs of New Beginnings (Paragon Ensemble); plays flute with Whistlebinkies folk group. Address: c/o Scottish Music Information Centre, 7 Lilybank Gardens, Glasgow, G12; T.-041-334 6393.

McGuire, Michael, CQSW. Social Worker; Chairman, Finance and General Purposes Committee, Cunninghame District Council, since 1984; b. 15.11.52, Glasgow; m., Anne McKinnon; 1 s. Educ. St. Michael's Academy, Kilwinning; Jordanhill College of Education, Glasgow. ICI Petrochemical Division, 1974-81; elected to Cunninghame District Council, 1980; JP, 1980-84; Chairman, Saltcoats Labour Party; Secretary, Bute and North Ayrshire and Cunninghame North Constituency Labour Parties. Recreations: reading; football; politics. Address: (h.) 5 Eglinton Place, Saltcoats, Ayrshire; T.-0294 66619.

McGuire, Ralph Joseph, BSc, MA, MEd. Senior Lecturer in Clinical Psychology, Edinburgh University, since 1971; Honorary Clinical Psychologist, Lothian Health Board, since 1971; b. 2.3.26, Glasgow; m., Beryl Redfern; 1 s.; 4 d. Educ. St. Aloysius' College, Glasgow; Glasgow University. Research Physicist, BICC, 1944-47; Teacher of Mathematics, 1950-54; Lecturer in Mathematics, 1954-57; Clinical Psychologist, Southern General Hospital, Glasgow, 1957-64; Senior Lecturer in Clinical Psychology, Leeds University, 1964-71. Member, Research Committee, Mental Health Foundation. Recreation: listening to music. Address: (b.) Department of Psychiatry, Royal Edinburgh Hospital, Edinburgh, EH10 5HF; T.-031-447 2011.

McHarg, Elizabeth Adam, MA, PhD. Senior Lecturer in Mathematics, Glasgow University; b. 22.4.23, Coatbridge. Educ. Glasgow High School for Girls; Glasgow University; Girton College, Cambridge. Joined Glasgow University as Lecturer, 1948. Address: (h.) 29 Winton Drive, Glasgow, G12 OPZ; T.-041-339 5431.

Macharg, John Maitland, MA, FFA. General Manager and Actuary, Scottish Provident Institution, since 1970; b. 22.5.28, Glasgow; m.,

Madeline Yates; 2 s.; 1 d. Educ. Glasgow High School; Strathallan School; Glasgow University. Joined Scottish Provident, 1955, as Assistant Actuary. President, Faculty of Actuaries. Recreations: golf; skiing; gardening. Address: (b.) 6 St. Andrew Square, Edinburgh, EH2 2YA; T.-031-556 9181.

McIlvanney, William. Novelist; b. 1936, Kilmarnock. Educ. Kilmarnock Academy; Glasgow University. Teacher (Assistant Rector (Curriculum), Greenwood Academy, Irvine, until 1975); Creative Writing Fellow, Strathclyde University, 1972-73; author of Remedy is None, 1966 (joint winner, Geoffrey Faber Memorial Award, 1967), A Gift from Nessus, 1968 (Scottish Arts Council Publication Award, 1969), Docherty, 1975 (Whitbread Award for Fiction, 1975), Laidlaw.

McIlwain, Alexander Edward, CBE, MA, LLB, WS, SSC. Senior Partner, Leonards, Solicitors, Hamilton; President, Law Society of Scotland, 1983-84; Honorary Sheriff, South Strathclyde, Dumfries and Galloway, at Hamilton, since 1981; b. 4.7.33, Aberdeen; m., Moira Margaret Kinnaird; 3 d. Educ. Aberdeen Grammar School; Aberdeen University. Commissioned, Royal Corps of Signals, 1957-59; Burgh Prosecutor then District Prosecutor, Hamilton, 1966-76; Dean, Society of Solicitors of Hamilton, 1981-83; Member, Legal Aid Central Committee, 1980-83; Member, Lanarkshire Health Board, since 1980; Honorary Member, American Bar Association; Member, Scottish Lawyers for Nuclear Disarmament; Chairman, Lanarkshire Scout Area, since 1981; Temporary Sheriff, since 1984. Recreations: work; gardening; golf. Address: (h.) 7 Bothwell Road, Uddingston, Glasgow; T.-0698 813368.

McIlwraith, Sheriff Arthur Renwick, MA, LLB. Sheriff of South Strathclyde, Dumfries and Galloway, at Airdrie, since 1972; b. 8.4.14; m.; 1 s.; 1 d. Educ. High School of Glasgow; Glasgow University. Highland Light Infantry, 1939-45; Solicitor, 1945-72.

MacInnes, Hamish. OBE, BEM. Writer and Designer; b. 7.7.30, Gatehouse of Fleet. Educ. Gatehouse of Fleet. Mountaineer with numerous expeditions to Himalayas, Amazon and other parts of the world; Deputy Leader, 1975 Everest SW Face Expedition; film Producer/Advisor/ safety expert, with Zinnemann, Connery, Eastwood, etc.; Advisor, BBC TV live outside broadcasts on climbing; author of 16 books on travel and adventure, including two autobiographies and fiction; designed the first all-metal ice axe, Terodactyl ice climbing tools, the MacInnes stretchers; Founder, Search and Rescue Dog Association; Honorary Member, Scottish Mountaineering Club; former President, Alpine Climbing Group; world authority on mountain rescue; Doctor of Laws (Hons), Glasgow University. Recreations: as above. Address: (h.) Glencoe, Argyll; T.-08552 258.

McInnes, Sheriff John Colin, BA (Hons) (Oxon), LLB. Advocate; Sheriff, Tayside, Central and Fife, at Cupar and Perth, since 1974; b. 21.11.38,

Cupar, Fife; m., Elisabeth Mabel Neilson; 1 s.; 1 d. Educ. New Park School, St. Andrews: Cargilfield School, Edinburgh; Merchiston Castle School, Edinburgh; Brasenose College, Oxford; Edinburgh University. 2nd Lt., 8th Royal Tank Regiment, 1956-58; Lt., Fife and Forfar Yeomanry, Scottish Horse, TA, 1958-64; Advocate, 1963; Director, R. Mackness & Co. Ltd., 1964-72; Chairman, Fios Group Ltd., 1970-72; Parliamentary candidate (Conservative), Aberdeen North, 1964; Tutor, Law Faculty, Edinburgh University, 1965-72; in practice, Scottish Bar, 1963-72; Sheriff of Lothian and Peebles, 1972-74. Member, St. Andrews University Court, since 1984. Recreations: fishing; shooting; gardening; photography. Address: (h.) Parkneuk, Blebocraigs, Cupar, Fife; T.-0334 85 366.

McInnes, Marjorie Mary, OBE, AIMSW. Chairman, Scottish Council on Disability, 1980-85; Vice Chairman, Age Concern Scotland, since 1980; b. 21.7.17, Glasgow. Educ. Hutchesons' Girls' Grammar School, Glasgow; Glasgow University; Institute of Medical Social Work. Lady Almoner, Southport General Infirmary, 1942-43; Head Almoner, Hairmyres Hospital, East Kilbride, 1943-48; Head Medical Social Worker: Victoria Infirmary, Glasgow, 1948-55, Western Infirmary, Glasgow, 1955-58; Department of Health for Scotland: Welfare Officer, 1958-62, Chief Welfare Officer, 1962-68; Deputy Chief Social Work Adviser, Social Work Services Group, Scottish Education Department, 1968-78. Member, Council of Management, Atholl Baptist Centre, Pitlochry; Member, Council and Executive Committee, Baptist Union of Scotland; Committee Member, Scottish Baptist College; Member, Board of Directors, Glasgow City Mission; Member, Council of Management, Quarriers Homes, Bridge of Weir. Recreations: music; reading; out of doors/natural world/walking. Address: (h.) 33 Corrour Road, Glasgow, G43 2DZ; T.-041-632 8959.

McIntosh, Alastair David, MB, ChB, FRCOG. Vice Chairman, Highland Health Board, since 1983; b. 16.7.21, Edinburgh; 2 s.; 1 d. Educ. Royal High School, Edinburgh; Edinburgh University. Surgeon/Lt., RNVR, 1945-47; Senior Registrar to Consultant Obstetrician, Bellshill Maternity Hospital, 1952-65; Consultant Obstetrician and Gynaecologist, Raigmore Hospital, 1965-83. Recreations: golf; fishing. Address: (h.) 14B Drummond Road, Inverness, IV2 4NB; T.-0463 233399.

McIntosh, Rev. Colin George, MA, BD (Hons). Minister, St. John's-Renfield Church, Glasgow, since 1976; b. 5.4.51, Glasgow; m., Linda Mary Henderson; 2 d. Educ. Govan High School; Glasgow University. Assistant Minister, Corstorphine, Edinburgh, 1975-76. Assessor, Church of Scotland Selection School; Stanley Mair Memorial Lecturer, Glasgow University, 1984. Recreations: gardening; music; reading. Address: (h.) 26 Leicester Avenue, Glasgow, G12 OLU; T.-041-339 4637.

Macintosh, Farquhar, CBE, MA, DipEd, DLitt, FEIS. Rector, Royal High School, Edinburgh; Chairman, Scottish Examination Board, since

1977; Chairman, School Broadcasting Council for Scotland, since 1981; Vice-Chairman, School Broadcasting Council for UK, since 1984; b. 27.10.23, Isle of Skye; m., Margaret M. Inglis; 2 s.; 2 d. Educ. Portree High School; Edinburgh University; Glasgow University; Jordanhill College of Education. Taught at Greenfield Junior Secondary School, Hamilton, Glasgow Academy and Inverness Royal Academy; Headmaster: Portree High School, Oban High School; Member, Highlands and Islands Development Consultative Council and Convener, Education Committee, 1965-82; Chairman, Jordanhill Board of Governors, 1970-72; Chairman, BBC Secondary Programme Committee, 1972-80; Member, Court, Edinburgh University; Gaelic Correspondent, Weekly Scotsman, 1953-57. Recreations: hill-walking; sea angling. Address: (b.) Royal High School, East Barnton Avenue, Edinburgh, EH4 6JP; T.-031-336 2261.

McIntosh, Professor Francis George, BSc, MSc, CEng, MIEE. Professor of Electronic and Electrical Engineering, Robert Gordon's Institute of Technology, since 1984 (Dean, Faculty of Technology, since 1984, and Head, School of Electronic and Electrical Engineering, since 1982); b. 19.3.42; 1 d. Previously Senior Lecturer, Deputy Head, RGIT. Member, CNAA Electronic Electrical and Control Board; Consultant, Board Member, Aberdeen I. Tech Ltd.; Member, Advisory Committee, MEDC. Address: (b.) RGIT, Schoolhill, Aberdeen, AB9 1FR; T.-0224 633611.

McIntosh, Rev. Hamish Norman Mackenzie, MA. Minister, Fintry; b. 24.8.22, Glasgow; m., Christina Margaret Macdonald. Educ. Albert Senior Secondary School; Glasgow University and Trinity College. Craigneuk Parish, Wishaw; Lamlash, Arran; St. Ninians, Cumnock; Chaplain, RAF. Honorary Citizen, City of Evergreen, Alabama; Honorary Lt.-Col. Aide-de-Camp, Alabama State Militia. Recreations: music; oil painting; American history. Address: (h.) 1 Forth Crescent, Stirling, FK8 1LE.

McIntosh, Iain Redford, ARSA, ARBS, DA. Sculptor; b. 4.1.45, Peterhead; m., Freida; 2 d. Educ. Peterhead Academy; Gray's School of Art. Recreation: sculpture. Address: (h.) The Willows, Powmouth, by Montrose; T.-Bridge of Dun 346.

Macintosh, Joan, CBE (1978), MA. Lay Observer for Scotland (Solicitors Act), since 1983; Chairman of the Council, Insurance Ombudsman Bureau, since 1981; b. 23.11.19; m.; 1 s.; 2 d.; 1 s. deceased. Educ. Oxford University. CAB Organiser, Glasgow, 1972-75; Member, Royal Commission on Legal Services in Scotland, 1975-80; Chairman, Scottish Consumer Council, 1975-80; Vice-Chairman, National Consumer Council, 1976-84; Vice President, National Federation of Consumer Groups; Hon. LLD, Dundee, 1982.

McIntosh, Neil William David, ACIS, MIAM. Chief Executive, Dumfries and Galloway Regional Council, since 1985; b. 30.1.40, Glasgow; m., Marie Elizabeth Lindsay. Educ. King's Park Senior Secondary School, Glasgow. O. and M. Trainee, Honeywell Controls Ltd., Lanarkshire, 1959-62; O. and M. Assistant, Berkshire, Oxford and Reading Joint Management Services Unit, 1962-64; O. and M. Officer, Stewarts and Lloyds Ltd., Lanarkshire, 1964-66; Senior O. and M. Officer, Lanark County Council, 1966-69; Establishment/O. and M. Officer, Inverness County Council, 1969-75; Personnel Officer, Highland Regional Council, 1975-81; Director of Manpower Services, Highland Regional Council, 1981-85; Clerk, Dumfries Lieutenancy, 1985. Recreations: bowling; hill-walking; antique bottle collecting; local history; youth work. Address: (b.) Regional Council Offices, English Street, Dumfries; T.-0387 53141.

Macintosh, Robert Macfarlan, MA, LLB. Solicitor; Chairman, Rent Assessment Committee, Glasgow, since 1966; Honorary Sheriff Substitute, Dumbarton, since 1975; b. 16.6.17, Dumbarton; m., Ann McLean Kelso; 1 s. Educ. Dumbarton Academy; George Watson's College, Edinburgh; Glasgow University. Qualified as Solicitor, 1949; Local Secretary, Dumbarton Legal Aid Committee, 1950-84; Chairman: Dunbartonshire Rent Tribunal, 1960, Glasgow Rent Tribunal, 1974; Clerk to Commissioners of Income Tax, East and West Dunbartonshire, since 1973; President, Dumbarton Burns Club; Captain, Cardross Golf Club. Recreation: golf. Address: (h.) Ardmoy, Peel Street, Cardross, Dunbartonshire.

McIntyre, Alasdair Duncan, BSc, DSc, FRSE. Director, Fishery Research Services for Scotland, since 1983; b. 17.11.26, Helensburgh; m.,Catherine Helen; 1 d. Educ. Hermitage School, Helensburgh; Glasgow University. Joined Marine Laboratory, Department of Agriculture and Fisheries for Scotland, first as a Development Commission Fisheries Student, then as a Scientific Officer; became Senior Principal Scientific Officer, in charge of the laboratory Environmental Team, 1973; Deputy Director, Fishery Research Services, 1977-83; Past Chairman, GESAMP (UN group of experts on the scientific aspects of marine pollution) and ACMP (Advisory Committee on Marine Pollution, International Council for the Exploration of the Sea). Recreation: golf. Address: (b.) Marine Laboratory, PO Box 101, Victoria Road, Aberdeen; T.-Aberdeen 876544.

McIntyre, Archibald Dewar, MB, ChB, DPH, FFCM, MRCPE, DIH, DTM&H. Principal Medical Officer, Scottish Home and Health Department, since 1977; b. 18.2.28, Dunipace; m., Euphemia Hope Houston; 2 s.; 2 d. Educ. Falkirk High School; Edinburgh University. Senior Medical Officer, Overseas Civil Service, Sierra Leone; Depute Medical Officer of Health, Stirling County Council; Depute Secretary, Scottish Council for Postgraduate Medical Education; Senior Medical Officer, Scottish Home and Health Department. Recreations: gardening; photography. Address: (h.) Southfield, Falkirk Road, Linlithgow, EH49 7BQ; T.-0506 842063.

MacIntyre, David John, MA (Hons). Director of Area Operations, Scottish Tourist Board, since 1982; b. 24.1.45, Fort William; m., Margaret

MacKinnon; 1 d. Educ. Lochaber High School; St. Andrews University. Joined British Rail as Planning and Marketing Assistant, 1958; Highlands and Islands Development Board: Statistician, 1970, transferred to Tourism Division, 1971, latterly in charge of all HIDB tourism research and development; also responsible for co-ordinating local network of Area Tourist Boards, since 1971, now performing that duty on national basis with STB. Secretary, Scottish Confederation of Tourism. Recreations: golf; current affairs; gardening. Address: (h.) 8 Stuart Green, Craigmount, Corstorphine, Edinburgh; T.-031-339 6854.

McIntyre, Professor John, CVO, MA, BD, DLitt, DD, DHL, FRSE. Professor of Divinity, Edinburgh University, since 1956; Honorary Chaplain to The Queen in Scotland, since 1974; Dean of the Order of the Thistle, since 1974; b. 20.5.16, Glasgow; m., Jessie Brown Buick; 2 s.; 1 d. Educ. Bathgate Academy; Edinburgh University. Ordained, 1941; Locum Tenens, Parish of Glenorchy and Inishail, 1941-43; Minister, Fenwick, Ayrshire, 1943-45; Hunter Baillie Professor of Theology, St. Andrew's College, Sydney University, 1946-56; Principal, St. Andrew's College, 1950-56; Principal Warden, Pollock Halls of Residence, Edinburgh University, 1960-71; Acting Principal and Vice-Chancellor, Edinburgh University, 1973-74, 1979; Principal, New College, and Dean, Faculty of Divinity, 1968-74; Moderator, General Assembly of the Church of Scotland, 1982; Convener, Board of Education, Church of Scotland; Council Member and Vice President, Royal Society of Edinburgh. Publications: St. Anselm and his Critics, 1954; The Christian Doctrine of History, 1957; On the Love of God, 1962; The Shape of Christology, 1966. Recreation: travel. Address: (h.) 11 Minto Street, Edinburgh, EH9 1RG; T.-031-667 1203.

McIntyre, Robert Douglas, MB, ChB, DPH, JP. President, Scottish National Party, 1958-80; Consultant Physician; b. 9.12.13; m.; 1 s. Educ. Hamilton Academy; Daniel Stewart's College; Edinburgh University. MP (SNP), Motherwell and Wishaw, April to July, 1945; Chairman, SNP, 1948-56; Provost of Stirling, 1967-75; Chancellor's Assessor, Stirling University Court, since 1979; Freeman, Royal Burgh of Stirling, 1975; DUniv, Stirling, 1976.

Macintyre, Robert Mitchell, BSc, DIC, MSc, PhD. Senior Lecturer, Scottish Universities Research and Reactor Centre, Department of Applied Geology, Strathclyde University, since 1968; b. 6.10.39, Bonhill; m., Audrey Ellson; 1 s.; 2 d. Educ. Vale of Leven Academy; Glasgow University; Imperial College; Toronto University. Overseas Postdoctorate Fellow, Cambridge, 1966-68. Recreation: East Kilbride Sports Club. Address: (h.) 102 Dunedin Drive, Hairmyres, East Kilbride, G75 8QH; T.-03552 29360.

MacIver, Duncan Malcolm. Deputy Director, Scottish Prison Service, since 1978; b. 7.5.22, Meerut, India; m., Jessie D.T. Neilson; 2 s.; 1 d. Educ. McLaren High School, Callander. Served in Black Watch and Royal Scots, 1939-47, in Ceylon, India and Burma (14th Army), rank of Sgt.; joined Scottish Prison Service as a prison officer, 1948; promoted to Governor grade, 1960; Assistant Governor, Polmont and Barlinnie; Deputy Governor, Polmont and Perth; Governor: Castle Huntly Borstal, 1969-70, Aberdeen Prison, 1970-73; Assistant Inspector of Prisons, 1973-75; Governor (HQ), 1975-76; Governor, Edinburgh Prison, 1976-78; Controller of Operations (Deputy Director), Scottish Prison Service, since 1978. Recreations: golf; gardening. Address: (h.) 3 Caiystane Drive, Edinburgh; T.-031-445 1734.

MacIver, Roy, MA, LLB. Chief Executive, Western Isles Islands Council (Comhairle Nan Eilean), since 1974; b. 15.10.42, Stornoway; m., Anne; 3 s. Educ. Nicolson Institute, Stornoway; Edinburgh University; Glasgow University. Legal Assistant, Paisley Corporation; Solicitor/Administrator, Dunfermline Town Council, 1970-72; Assistant County Clerk (Lewis), Ross and Cromarty County Council, 1972-74. Recreation: jazz. Address: (b.) Council Offices, Sandwick Road, Stornoway, Isle of Lewis; T.-0851 3773.

McIvor, Derek Stuart, MA, BA (Cantab). Headteacher, Broxburn Academy, since 1976; Educational Consultant, St. Andrew's Scots School, Buenos Aires, since 1981; b. 24.3.26, Edinburgh; m., Audrey Winifred Gibb; 1 s.; 1 d. Educ. Royal High School; Morrison's Academy, Crieff; Trinity Hall, Cambridge; Moray House College of Education. Teacher, Bo'ness Academy, 1951-54; St. Andrew's Scots School, Buenos Aires: Principal Teacher of History, 1954-61, Depute Headmaster, 1956-61, Acting Headmaster, 1960-61; Teacher of History and Geography, Royal High School, 1961-64; Principal Teacher of History and Modern Studies, Liberton High School, 1964-69; Depute Headteacher, Portobello High School, 1969-76; Member, BBC Council for Scotland, 1970-73, and for the UK, 1973-76. Recreations: golf; snooker; bridge; reading; chess. Address: (h.) 19 Cherry Tree Park, Balerno, EH14 5AQ.

Mackay, Angus Victor Peck, MA, BSc, PhD, MB, ChB, FRCPsych. Physician Superintendent, Argyll and Bute Hospital, and MacKintosh Lecturer in Psychological Medicine, Glasgow University, since 1980; Chairman, Research and Clinical Section, Royal College of Psychiatrists (Scotland), since 1981; Psychiatric Representative, Committee on Safety of Medicines, DHSS, since 1983; b. 4.3.43, Edinburgh; m., Elspeth M.W. Norris; 2 s.; 2 d. Educ. George Heriot's School, Edinburgh; Edinburgh University; Churchill and Trinity Colleges, Cambridge. MRC Research Fellow, Cambridge; Member, senior clinical staff, MRC Neurochemical Pharmacology Unit, Cambridge, with appointment as Lector in Pharmacology, Trinity College (latterly, Deputy Director of Unit). Member, Health Service Research Committee of the Chief Scientist for Scotland; Member, Research Committee, Mental Health Foundation; Chairman, Argyll and Clyde Area Psychiatric Sub-Committee; Member, Scottish Executive, Royal College of Psychiatrists. Recreations: rowing; sailing; rhododendrons. Address: (h.) Tigh an Rudha, Ardrishaig, Argyll; T.-0546 3272.

McKay, Sheriff Archibald Charles, MA, LLB. Sheriff of Glasgow and Strathkelvin, since 1979; b. 18.10.29; m.; 1 s.; 3 d. Educ. St. Aloysius' College, Glasgow; Glasgow University. Solicitor, Glasgow, 1957.

Mackay, Charles, BSc, MSc, FIBiol. Chief Agricultural Officer, Department of Agriculture and Fisheries for Scotland, since 1975; b. 12.1.27, Kinloch, Sutherland; m., Marie A.K. Mitchell; 1 s.; 1 d. Educ. Strathmore School; Lairg Higher Grade Public School; Aberdeen University; Kentucky University. DAFS: Temporary Inspector, 1947-48, Assistant Inspector, 1948-54, Inspector, 1954-64, Senior Inspector, 1964-70, Technical Development Officer, 1970-73, Deputy Chief Agricultural Officer, 1973-75. Recreations: fishing; golf. Address: (h.) 35 Boswall Road, Edinburgh, EH5 3RP; T.-031-552 6063.

MacKay, Colin Hinshelwood, MA (Hons). Political Editor, Scottish Television PLC, since 1973 (Presenter, Ways and Means, since 1973); b. 27.8.44, Glasgow; m., Olive E.B. Brownlie; 1 s. Educ. Kelvinside Academy, Glasgow; Glasgow University; Jordanhill College of Education. Reporter/Presenter: Border Television Ltd., 1967-70, Grampian Television Ltd., 1970-73; Principal Presenter, all political programmes, including elections and by-elections, STV, since 1973; ITV Commentator: Papal Visit to Scotland, 1982, CBI Conference, Glasgow, 1983. Winner, Observer Mace, 1967 (British Universities Debating Championship); Member, two-man British Universities Canadian Debating Tour, 1967; Commonwealth Relations Trust Bursar to Canada, 1981. Publications: Kelvinside Academy: 1878-1978, 1978; The Scottish Dimension in Central and Eastern Canada, 1981. Recreations: music (especially opera); reading; writing. Address: (b.) Scottish Television PLC, Glasgow; T.-041-332 9999.

Mackay, David William, FIBiol, FIWPC, FIWES, MIFM, FBIM. Depute Director, Clyde River Purification Board, since 1975; b. 6.4.36, Stirling; m., Maureen. Educ. High School of Stirling; Glasgow University; Strathclyde University. Experimental Officer, Freshwater Fisheries Laboratory, Pitlochry (Department of Agriculture and Fisheries for Scotland), 1959-66; Clyde River Purification Board: Biologist, 1966-68, Marine Survey Officer, 1968-75, Depute Director, 1975-78 and since 1981; Principal Environmental Protection Officer, Government of Hong Kong, 1978-81. Secretary/Treasurer, Scottish Anglers Association; Consultant, World Health Organization. Recreations: scuba diving; golf; shooting; angling. Address: (b.) Rivers House, Murray Road, East Kilbride, Glasgow, G75 OLA; T.-03552 38181.

Mackay, Donald George, MA. Under Secretary, Department of Agriculture and Fisheries for Scotland, since 1983; b. 25.11.29, Dundee; m., Elizabeth Ailsa Barr; 2 s.; 1 d. Educ. Morgan Academy, Dundee; St. Andrews University. National Service, RA; Assistant Principal, Scottish Home Department, 1953; Assistant Private Secretary to Secretary of State for Scotland, 1959; Assistant Secretary, Royal Commission on the Police, 1962-64; Secretary, Royal Commission on Local Government in Scotland, 1966-69; Assistant Secretary, Scottish Development Department and Department of Agriculture and Fisheries for Scotland, 1969-83. Recreations: hill-walking; photography; music. Address: (h.) 38 Cluny Drive, Edinburgh, EH10 6DX; T.-031-447 1851.

MacKay, Professor Donald Iain, MA. Chairman, PEIDA, since 1976; Professorial Fellow, Heriot-Watt University, since 1982; b. 27.2.37, Kobe, Japan; m., Diana Marjory Raffan; 1 s.; 2 d. Educ. Dollar Academy; Aberdeen University. Professor of Political Economy, Aberdeen University, 1971-76; Professor of Economics, Heriot-Watt University, 1976-82; Director: Edinburgh Financial Trust, City of Edinburgh Life Assurance Company, Ainslie Developments Ltd., Adam and Co.; Board Member, Sea Fish Industry Authority, South of Scotland Electricity Board; Vice President, Scottish Association of Public Transport; Member, Scottish Economic Council; Economic Consultant to Secretary of State for Scotland; Governor, National Institute of Economic and Social Research. Recreations: tennis; bridge. Address: (h.) Newfield, 14 Gamekeepers Road, Edinburgh; T.-031-336 1936.

Mackay, Rev. Canon Douglas Brysson. Rector, Church of the Holy Rood, Carnoustie, since 1972; Synod Clerk, Diocese of Brechin, since 1981; Canon, St. Paul's Cathedral, Dundee, since 1981; b. 20.3.27, Glasgow; m., Catherine Elizabeth; 2 d. Educ. Possil Senior Secondary School; Edinburgh Theological College. Precentor, St. Andrew's Cathedral, Inverness, 1958; Rector, Gordon Chapel, Fochabers, 1961 (also Priest-in-Charge, St. Margaret's Church, Aberlour, 1964); Canon, St. Andrew's Cathedral, Inverness, 1965; Synod Clerk, Diocese of Moray, Ross, Caithness, 1965; Honorary Canon, St. Andrew's Cathedral, Inverness, 1972; Convenor of Youth, Moray Diocese, 1965; Brechin Diocese: Convenor, Social Service Board, 1974, Convenor, Joint Board, 1974, Convenor, Administration Board, 1982. President, British Red Cross, Carnoustie, 1974-82; President, British Legion, Carnoustie, 1981; Vice-Chairman, Carnoustie Community Care, 1981; Chairman, Carnoustie Community Council, 1979-81; President, Carnoustie Rotary Club, 1976. Recreations: golf; snooker; reading; music. Address: Holyrood Rectory, Carnoustie, DD7 6AB; T.-Carnoustie 52202.

Mackay, Eileen Alison, MA. Assistant Secretary, Industry Department for Scotland, since 1983; b. 7.7.43, Helmsdale, Sutherland; m., A. Muir Russell (qv). Educ. Dingwall Academy; Edinburgh University. Research Officer, Department of Employment, 1965-72; Principal: Scottish Office, 1972-78, HM Treasury, 1978-80; Adviser, Central Policy Review Staff, Cabinet Office, 1980-83; Assistant Secretary, Scottish Development Agency and New Towns Division, Industry Department for Scotland, since 1983. Address: (b.) New St. Andrews House, Edinburgh.

Mackay, Eric B., MA. Editor, The Scotsman, 1972-85; b. 31.12.22, Aberdeen; 3 s.; 1 d. Educ. Aberdeen Grammar School; Aberdeen University. Reporter, Aberdeen Bon-Accord,

Elgin Courant; Sub-Editor: The Scotsman, 1950, Daily Telegraph, 1951; The Scotsman: Deputy Chief Sub, 1953, London Editor, 1957, Deputy Editor, 1961. Recreations: travel; golf; theatre. Address: (b.) North Bridge, Edinburgh; T.-031-225 2468.

Mackay, James Alexander, MA. Author, Journalist and Publisher; Numismatic and Philatelic Correspondent, Financial Times, since 1972; Editor, the Burns Chronicle, since 1978; b. 21.11.36, Inverness; m., Joyce May Greaves. Educ. Hillhead High School, Glasgow; Glasgow University. Lt., RA Guided Weapons Range, Hebrides, 1959-61; Assistant Keeper, Department of Printed Books, British Museum, in charge of philatelic collections, 1961-71; returned to Scotland as a full-time Writer, 1972; Editor-in-Chief, IPC Stamp Encyclopedia, 1968-72; Columnist on antiques, Financial Times, 1967-72; Publisher of books on philately and postal history; author of more than 100 books on aspects of the applied and decorative arts, numismatics, philately, postal history; books include Robert Bruce, King of Scots, 1974; Rural Crafts in Scotland, 1976; Scottish Postmarks, 1978; The Burns Federation 1885-1985, 1985. Recreations: travel; languages; music (piano-playing). Address: (h.) 11 Newall Terrace, Dumfries, DG1 1LN; T.-0387 55250.

Mackay, Sir James Mackerron, KBE (1966), CB (1964). Deputy Under Secretary of State, Home Office, 1966-67; b. 9.8.07. Educ. Forres Academy; Hamilton Academy; Glasgow University; Oxford University. Member, Scottish Tourist Board, 1967-72; Member, Highlands and Islands Development Board, 1967-72; Member, Countryside Commission for Scotland, 1967-72; Member, Committee of Enquiry into Future of Broadcasting, 1974-77.

Mackay of Clashfern, Baron, (James Peter Hymers Mackay), PC (1979), QC (Scot), FRSE. Lord of Appeal in Ordinary, House of Lords, since 1985; Life Peer; b. 2.7.27; m.; 1 s.; 2 d. Educ. George Heriot's School, Edinburgh; Edinburgh University; Trinity College, Cambridge. Admitted Faculty of Advocates, 1955; Sheriff Principal, Renfrew and Argyll, 1972-74; Vice-Dean, Faculty of Advocates, 1973-76; Dean, 1976-79; Lord Advocate, 1979-84; Senator of the College of Justice, 1984. Member, Scottish Law Commission, 1976-79; Commissioner of Northern Lighthouses, 1975-84; Hon. LLD, Edinburgh, 1983, Dundee, 1983.

McKay, Sir James Wilson, Kt (1971), JP, DL. Lord Provost of Edinburgh and Lord Lieutenant, County of the City of Edinburgh, 1969-72; b. 12.3.12; m.; 3 d. Educ. Dunfermline High School; Portobello Secondary School. RN, 1941-46; Insurance Broker; Hon. DLitt, Heriot-Watt, 1972.

MacKay, John, OBE, MB, ChB, FRCSP. General Medical Practitioner, Govan Health Centre, Glasgow, since 1951; Member, Greater Glasgow Health Board, since 1973; Chairman, Scottish Medical Practices Committee, since 1984; b. 24.7.26, Glasgow; m., Matilda MacLennan Bain; 2 s.; 2 d. Educ. Govan High School;

Glasgow University. Junior House Doctor, Victoria Infirmary and Southern General Hospital, Glasgow, 1949; Ship's Surgeon, 1950; Assistant in General Practice, Govan, 1951-52 (Principal, since 1953); Member, Board of Management, Glasgow South West Hospitals, prior to 1973; Tutor in University Department of General Practice, Glasgow; part-time Medical Referee, Scottish Home and Health Department; Honorary Life Manager, Govan Weavers' Society; Chairman, Glasgow Local Medical Committee, since 1982; Member, Scottish General Medical Services Committee; Member, Scottish Council for Postgraduate Medical Education. Recreations: angling; golf; gardening. Address: (h.) Moorholm, Barr's Brae, Kilmacolm, Renfrewshire, PA13 4DE; T.-Kilmacolm 3234.

MacKay, John. MP (Conservative), Argyll and Bute, since 1983 (Argyll, 1970-83); b. 15.11.38. Educ. Dunoon Grammar School; Campbeltown Grammar School; Glasgow University; Jordanhill College of Education. Former Principal Teacher of Mathematics, Oban High School; Under Secretary of State for Scotland, since 1982.

McKay, John Henderson, BA (Hons), PhD. Lord Provost of Edinburgh, since 1984; Chairman, Edinburgh International Festival Society, since 1984; b. 12.5.29, Kirknewton; m., Catherine Watson Taylor; 1 s.; 1 d. Educ. West Calder High School; Open University. Labourer and Clerk, Pumpherston Oil Co. Ltd., 1948-50; National Service, Royal Artillery, 1950-52; Customs and Excise, since 1952. Recreations: gardening; reading; listening to music. Address: (h.) 2 Buckstone Way, Edinburgh, EH10 OPN; T.-031-445 2865.

McKay, Rev. Johnston Reid, MA (Glasgow), BA (Cantab). Minister, Paisley Abbey, since 1978; Chairman, Scottish Religious Advisory Committee, BBC, since 1981; b. 2.5.42, Glasgow; m., Heather Ann Ayre; 2 s. Educ. High School of Glasgow; Glasgow University; Cambridge University. Assistant Minister, St. Giles' Cathedral, 1967-71; Church Correspondent, Glasgow Herald, 1968-70; Minister, Bellahouston Steven Parish Church, 1971-78; frequent Broadcaster; Governor, Paisley College; Editor, The Bush (Newspaper of Glasgow Presbytery), 1975-78. Publications: From Sleep and From Damnation (with James Miller), 1970; Essays in Honour of William Barclay (Joint Editor), 1976; Through Wood and Nails, 1982. Recreations: good music and bad golf. Address: (b.) The Abbey, Paisley, PA1 1JG; T.-041-889 7654.

Mackay, Peter, MA. Under Secretary, Department of Employment, since 1985; b. 6.7.40, Arbroath; m., Sarah Holdich; 1 s.; 2 d. Educ. Glasgow High School; St. Andrews University. Teacher, New South Wales, Australia, 1962-63; Assistant Principal, Scottish Development Department, 1963; Private Secretary to Ministers of State, Scottish Office, 1966-68; Principal, Scottish Home and Health Department, 1968-73; Private Secretary to Secretaries of State for Scotland, 1973-75; Assistant Secretary, 1975; Head, Local Government Division, Scottish Development Department, 1979-83; Director for Scotland, Manpower Services Commission, 1983-85; on secondment from Scottish Office to Department of Employment, 1985. Nuffield Travelling Fellowship, 1978-79. Recreations: Scotland; easy mountaineering; sailing; sea canoeing; tennis. Address: (h.) 6 Henderland Road, Edinburgh, EH12 6BB; T.-031-337 2830.

Mackay, Robert Ostler. Solicitor, since 1930; Notary Public, since 1955; b. 25.12.07, Greenock; m., 1, Dorothy Lilian Johnson (deceased); 2, Irene Isobel Ray Anderson; 1 s.; 2 d. Educ. Greenock Academy; Alyth Public School; Blairgowrie High School; Edinburgh University. Partner: J.C. Richards & Morrice, Solicitors, Fraserburgh, 1939-45, Ferguson & Petrie, Solicitors, Duns, 1945; Honorary Sheriff, Lothian and Borders, at Duns, since 1981; Council Member, Law Society of Scotland, 1958-79 (Vice-President, 1967-68); Life Member, Cairngorm Club. Recreations: angling; mountaineering. Address: (h.) Nethercraigs, Tighnabruaich, Argyll; T.-0700 811 368.

MacKay, Sheila Stirling. Member, Inverness District Council, since 1980; b. 5.1.39, Inverness; m., Ian Charles MacKay; 2 d. Educ. Inverness Royal Academy. Vice-Chairman, Inverness Housing Committee, since 1984; Member, Board of Governors, Eden Court Theatre, since 1984; Member, Management Committee, Women's Aid; Member, Local Advisory Committee, IBA; Member, Executive Committee, Inverness Nairn and Lochaber Liberal Association. Recreations: reading; gardening. Address: (h.) 92 Culduthel Road, Inverness, IV2 4HH; T.-0463 235448.

Mackay, William Kenneth, BSc, CE, FICE, FIHT, FASCE, MCIT, MConsE. Partner, JMP Consultants Ltd. (formerly Jamieson Mackay & Partners), since 1965; Commissioner, Royal Fine Arts Commission for Scotland, since 1981; Auxiliary Minister, Church of Scotland, since 1984; b. 6.6.30, Moyobamba, Peru; m., Christina D.G. Langmuir; 1 s.; 3 d. Educ. Hillhead High School, Glasgow; Glasgow University. Engineer, NCB, West Fife Area, 1954-57; Senior Engineer, Fife County Council, 1957-59; Group Engineer, Cumbernauld New Town Development Corporation, 1959-65; Consultant, since 1965; Past Chairman, Scottish Branch, Institution of Highways and Transportation; former Member, Planning and Transport Research Advisory Council to UK Government. Recreations: swimming; walking. Address: (b.) Jamieson Mackay & Partners, 20 Royal Terrace, Glasgow, G3 7NY; T.-041-332 3868.

McKean, Charles Alexander, BA, FRSA, FSA Scot. Secretary, Royal Incorporation of Architects in Scotland, since 1979; b. 16.7.46, Glasgow; m., Margaret Yeo; 2 s. Educ. Fettes College; Bristol University. RIBA: Secretary, London Region, 1968-76, Secretary, Eastern Region, 1972-79, Secretary, Community Architecture, 1976-79; Architectural Correspondent, The Times, 1977-83; Director, Wasps; Trustee, Thirlestane Castle; Secretary, RIAS Services Ltd.; author of architectural guides to Edinburgh, Dundee, Stirling, London, Cambridge. Recreations: books; glasses; gardens; stately homes. Address: (b.) 15 Rutland Square, Edinburgh; T.-031-229 7205.

McKechnie, George. Editor, Glasgow Evening Times, since 1980; b. 28.7.46, Edinburgh; m., Janequin Claire Seymour Morris; 2 s. Educ. Portobello High School, Edinburgh. Reporter: Paisley & Renfrewshire Gazette, 1964-66, Edinburgh Evening News, 1966, Scottish Daily Mail, 1966-68, Daily Record, 1968-74; Deputy News Editor/News Editor, Sunday Mail, 1974-76; Assistant Editor, Evening Times, 1976-80. Recreation: reading. Address: (h.) 2 Eglinton Drive, Giffnock, Glasgow; T.-041-638 4664.

Mackechnie, James William, MA (Hons), ALA. Member, Strathclyde Regional Council, since 1982; Chairperson, Scottish Divisional Council, ASTMS, since 1985; b. 19.6.46, Edinburgh. Educ. University College School; Edinburgh University; Strathclyde University. Address: (h.) 32 Gibson Street, Glasgow, G12 8NX; T.-041-334 0617.

MacKeddie, Rev. Douglas, BA. Minister, Maryburgh Free Church, Ross-shire, since 1982; b. 22.7.44, Edinburgh; m., Kathlyn Barbara Wilson; 1 s.; 1 d. Educ. Fortrose Academy; Balmacara School. Coach painter, 1960-72; agricultural representative, 1972-74. Chairman, Forrester High School Council, 1980-81. Address: Maryburgh Free Church Manse, Back Road, Maryburgh, Ross-shire; T.-0349 61281.

McKee, Angus H., MB, ChB, FFARCS. Consultant Anaesthetist, Stobhill Hospital, Glasgow, since 1977; b. 12.2.46, Aberdeen; m., Ruth F. McBain. Educ. Buckhaven High School; Edinburgh University. Initial career in Kirkcaldy and Edinburgh; anaesthetic training in Edinburgh, then Western Infirmary, Glasgow. Recreation: hill-walking. Address: (h.) 16 Clarence Drive, Glasgow, G12 9QX; T.-041-339 9352.

McKee, A. Sheila, MA. Rector, Camelon High School, since 1974. Educ. Falkirk High School; Mary Erskine School; Edinburgh University. Address: (b.) Camelon High School, Falkirk; T.-Falkirk 21719.

McKeever, Francis Bernard, JP. Labour Group Leader, Falkirk District Council, since 1984 (Housing Chairman, since 1980); Member, Housing Committee, COSLA; b. 8.4.45, Falkirk; m., Elizabeth Liddle; 3 s. Educ. St. Modan's High School, Stirling. Member, Grangemouth Town Council, 1972 (Entertainments Convener, 1973-75, Magistrate, 1974-75); Member: Stirling County Council, 1973-75, Falkirk District Council, since 1974 (Depute Provost, 1980-84). Recreation: fishing. Address: (h.) 57 Thistle Avenue, Grangemouth; T.-Grangemouth 486468.

McKellar, Kenneth, BSc. Singer, Composer, Writer; b. 23.6.27, Paisley; m., Hedy Matisse; 1 s.; 1 d. Educ. John Neilson Grammar School, Paisley; Aberdeen University. Gave first concert in a local hall, aged 13; continued singing while at school, university and during his first two years working in forestry; has made numerous records of classical and popular music; numerous tours, especially in Australia and New Zealand; has appeared a number of times at the London Palladium; made the sound track for the film The Great Waltz; TV work includes Night Music,

The Rolf Harris Show, The Good Old Days, At Home with Kenneth McKellar; a Director, Radio Clyde. Recreations: cooking; reading; motor-cycling.

McKelvey, William. MP (Labour), Kilmarnock and Loudoun, since 1979; b. 1934. Educ. Dundee. Former Labour Group Leader, Dundee District Council; former full-time Labour Party and union official; Member, Select Committee on Scottish Affairs.

MacKelvie, Alexander Kenneth, MBE (Mil), VRD, CA. Chartered Accountant, since 1936; Honorary Sheriff; b. 19.2.10, Edinburgh; m., Janet Fraser Gill. Educ. Merchiston Castle School, Edinburgh. RNVR, 1927-53; mobilised service, 1939-45; mentioned in Despatches; Captain, Forth Division, RNVR, 1946-53; former Council Member, Institute of Chartered Accountants of Scotland. Recreations: gardening; walking. Address: (h.) Fernie, Achnacree, Connel, by Oban, Argyll, PA37 1RE; T.-Connel 263.

McKelvie, Campbell John, BSc (Hons), ARCST, FBIM, MICE, MIBM, CEng. Head of Direct Works, Strathclyde Region, since 1979; b. 1.2.32, Tarbert, Argyll; m., Rhona; 2 s. Educ. Marr College, Troon; Glasgow University; Royal College of Science and Technology. Private sector, 1955-75; Senior Depute Head of Direct Works, Strathclyde Region, 1975-79. Recreations: golf; curling; bridge. Address: (b.) Philip Murray Road, Bellshill, Lanarkshire; T.-Bellshill 749121.

Mackenna, Beverly Robertson, MB, ChB, PhD. Senior Lecturer in Physiology, Glasgow University, since 1966; b. 5.12.29, Glasgow; m., Margaret Colvin; 1 d. Educ. Jordanhill College School; Glasgow University. House Officer, Surgery, Stobhill Hospital, Glasgow, 1956; House Officer, Medicine, Western District Hospital, Glasgow, 1957; appointed Lecturer in Physiology, 1957; awarded Sir Henry Wellcome Travelling Fellowship in Medicine to spend year at Karolinska Institute, Stockholm, 1954. Recreations: skiing; golf. Address: (b.) Department of Physiology, Glasgow University, Glasgow, G12 8QQ; T.-041-339 8855.

Mackenzie, Alastair, AIMLS. Member, City of Glasgow District Council, since 1984; b. 8.11.36, Glasgow; m., Grace Smith; 1 s.; 1 d. Educ. High School of Glasgow. Member, Glasgow District Council, 1977-80 (Vice-Chairman, Licensing Committee); Member, City of Glasgow Licensing Board, since 1984; Secretary, Glasgow District Council Conservative Group, since 1985; Vice Chairman, West of Scotland Conservative Local Government Advisory Committee. Recreations: photography; electronics. Address: (h.) 7 Westfield Drive, Glasgow, G52 2SG; T.-041-882 2449.

Mackenzie, A(lexander) Graham, MA, ALA, Librarian, St. Andrews University, since 1976; b. 4.12.28, Glasgow; m., E. Astrid MacKinven; 1 s.; 1 d. Educ. Hutchesons' Boys' Grammar School; Glasgow University. Keeper of Science Books, Durham University Library, 1952-60; Sub-Librarian, Nottingham University Library, 1960-61; Deputy Librarian, Brotherton Library, Leeds University, 1961-63; Librarian, Lancaster University, 1963-76, and Director, Library Research Unit, 1970-76. Honorary Treasurer, SCONUL, since 1982. Recreations: golf; Scottish country dancing; baroque music. Address: (b.) University Library, North Street, St. Andrews, Fife, KY16 9TR; T.-0334 76161.

MacKenzie, Angus Alexander, CA. Chartered Accountant, since 1955; Member, Highland Health Board; b. 1.3.31, Nairn; m., Catherine; 1 d. Educ. Inverness Royal Academy; Edinburgh University. National Service, RAF, 1955-57; in private practice as CA Assistant in Edinburgh, 1957-59, Inverness, 1959-61; commenced in practice on own account, 1961; Chairman, Highland Group, Riding for the Disabled Association; Chairman, PLM Helicopters Ltd.; Local Director, Eagle Star Insurance Co. Recreations: shooting; stalking; hill-walking; gardening. Address: (h.) Tigh an Allt, Tomatin, Inverness-shire; T.-Tomatin 270.

Mackenzie, Charles Patrick, MRCVS, DVSM. Senior Lecturer, Department of Veterinary Medicine, Royal (Dick) School of Veterinary Medicine, Edinburgh University, since 1969; b. 4.11.23, Edinburgh; widower; 2 s. Educ. Morgan Academy, Dundee; Royal (Dick) Veterinary College, Edinburgh. Assistant Veterinary Surgeon, 1952-53; postgraduate study, 1953-54; Assistant Veterinary Surgeon, 1954-55; Veterinary Education and Research Officer, Nigeria, 1955-59; Assistant Veterinary Surgeon, 1959-62; Lecturer, Edinburgh University, 1962-69. Recreations: gardening; reading; photography. Address: (b.) Department of Veterinary Medicine, Royal (Dick) School of Veterinary Medicine, Summerhall, Edinburgh; T.-031-667 1011, Ext. 5224.

MacKenzie, Rev. Colin Norman, MA. Minister, Carinish, North Uist, since 1982; b. 27.8.17, Glasgow; m., Christina Monk; 2 s.; 3 d. Educ. Taransay Public School, Harris; Kingussie Secondary School; St. Andrews University. Minister: Howmore, South Uist, 1947-55, Erskine, Kilwinning, 1955-75, Kirkhill, 1975-82; Broadcaster with BBC, 1952-82; crowned Bard, Rothesay Mod, 1952. Publications: Frontiers of Time, 1969; As A Tale That Is Told, 1971; The Other Half (novel), 1971; Passing Strange, 1973. Address: Carinish Manse, Clachan, North Uist.

Mackenzie, Colin Scott, DL, BL, NP. Procurator Fiscal, Stornoway, since 1969; Director, Harris Tweed Association Ltd., since 1979; Vice Lord Lieutenant of Islands Area, Western Isles, since 1984; b. 7.7.38, Stornoway; m., Christeen E.D. MacLauchlan. Educ. Nicolson Institute; Fettes College; Edinburgh University. Apprenticeship, Simpson & Marwick, WS, 1960; joined family firm of C. Scott Mackenzie & Co., Solicitors, Stornoway and appointed Depute Fiscal, 1960; Partner, 1965; Procurator Fiscal, Lochmaddy, 1975-82; Burgh Prosecutor, Stornoway, 1971-75; JP Fiscal, 1971-75; Deputy Lieutenant and Clerk to Lieutenancy of the Western Isles, 1975; Founder President, Stornoway Flying Club, 1970; Founding Dean, Western Isles Faculty of Solicitors; President, Stornoway Rotary Club,

1977; Chairman, Lewis Pipe Band, since 1978; Area Representative, Royal Trusts, since 1978; County Co-ordinator, Operation Raleigh; Vice Chairman, IYY Local Committee, 1985. Recreations: flying; fishing; squash. Address: (h.) Park House, Matheson Road, Stornoway, Lewis; T.-Stornoway 2008.

Mackenzie, David Chalmers, BSc (Hons). Headmaster, Falkirk High School, since 1971; b. 1.3.28, Aberdeen; m., E. Finlay; 2 d. Educ. Queen's Park School, Glasgow; Glasgow University. Teacher of Chemistry and Physics, High School of Glasgow, 1952-63; Head of Chemistry and Depute Headmaster, George Heriot's School, Edinburgh, 1963-71; Chairman, Board of Governors, Moray House College of Education, since 1977; Member, Heriot-Watt University Convocation and Stirling University Conference; Trustee, Scottish Secondary Schools Travel Trust; Chairman, Central Region Committee, British Heart Foundation; Chairman, Falkirk Burns Club; Past President, Falkirk Rotary Club. Recreations: gardening; bowling; travel. Address: (b.) Falkirk High School, Blinkbonny Road, Falkirk, FK1 5BZ; T.-0324 29511.

Mackenzie, Donald Morrison. Member, Skye and Lochalsh District Council, since 1984; b. 13.4.48, Plockton; m., Susan Thoroughman Muehlke; 1 s. Educ. Plockton High School. Clerical Officer: HM Treasury, London, 1965-68, National Savings Bank, Glasgow, 1968-73; Executive and Higher Executive Officer, Registers of Scotland, Edinburgh, 1973-80. Address: (h.) 3 Frithard Road, Plockton, Wester Ross; T.-059 984 255.

McKenzie, George C., BSc (Hons). Rector, Buckie High School, since 1966; b. 15.10.27, Lossiemouth; m., Nan Slater; 2 d. Educ. Lossiemouth High School; Elgin Academy; Aberdeen University. Principal Teacher of Mathematics: Grantown Grammar School, 1957-61, Elgin Academy, 1961-66. Recreations: golf; bridge; skiing. Address: (h.) 11 James Street, Buckie; T.-Buckie 31187.

Mackenzie, Rev. Gordon Ross, BSc, BD. Minister, Monikie and Newbigging, since 1985; b. 8.1.48, Nairn; m., Sheila Macrae Davis; 1 d. Educ. Nairn Academy; Aberdeen University; Glasgow University. Assistant Adviser, North of Scotland College of Agriculture (Uist and Barra), 1969-72; divinity student, 1972-75; postgraduate studies, Union Theological Seminary, Virginia, USA, 1975-76; Assistant Minister, Chryston, Glasgow, 1976-77; Minister, Kirkmichael and Tomintoul, 1977-85. Recreations: music; gardening. Address: 59B Broomwell Gardens, Monikie, Dundee, DD5 3QP; T.-Newbigging 200.

MacKenzie, Hugh D., MA (Hons). Headteacher, Craigroyston Community High School, since 1972; Director, Craigroyston Curriculum Project, since 1980; b. 29.5.33, Edinburgh; m., Helen Joyce; 1 s.; 1 d. Educ. Royal High School; Edinburgh University; Moray House College of Education, Edinburgh. Education Officer, RAF, 1956-58; Assistant Teacher, Niddrie Marischal Junior Secondary School and Falkirk High School, 1958-62; Principal Teacher: Broxburn Academy, 1962-64, Liberton High School, 1964-70; Deputy Headteacher, Craigmount High School, 1970-72; Scottish Representative, Northern Regional Examination Board, since 1973; Vice-Chairman, Lothian Regional Consultative Committee, since 1984; President, Royal High School Rugby Club; President and Founder Member, Edinburgh Golden Oldies Rugby Club. Recreations: rugby; squash; golf; ornithology; philately; jazz. Address: (h.) 26 Coltbridge Terrace, Edinburgh.

MacKenzie, Ian Kenneth, JP. Chairman, Red Deer Commission, since 1984; Farmer, since 1948; Landowner, since 1968; b. 1.3.31, Nairn; m., Margaret Vera Matheson; 2 s.; 2 d. Educ. Inverness Royal Academy. Member, Scottish Agricultural Consultative Panel; Member, Secretary of State's Panel of Arbiters; Director, Royal Highland and Agricultural Society of Scotland, 1980-84. Recreation: field sports. Address: Drynachan, 2 Culcabock Road, Inverness, IV2 3XW; T.-Inverness 231894.

Mackenzie, Rev. Ian Murdo. Head of Religious Programmes, BBC Scotland, since 1973; b. 3.8.31, Fraserburgh; m., Elizabeth; 1 s.; 1 d. Educ. Fettes College; Edinburgh University. Assistant Organist, St. Giles Cathedral, 1952-60; Editor, Student, Sooth and Breakthrough; Assistant Minister, St. Giles, 1960-62; Assistant General Secretary, Student Christian Movement, 1963-64; Religious Advisor, ABC Television, 1964-67; Executive Producer, Religious Programmes, ABC TV, 1967-68; Executive Producer: From Inner Space, 1966, Don't Just Sit There and Pilgrim's Progress, 1967, The Lion, the Witch, and the Wardrobe, Question 68, and Looking for an Answer, 1968; Executive Producer, Roundhouse, LWT, 1969; Presenter, For Christ's Sake, Grampian TV, 1972; BBC: Series Producer, City of God, Radio Scotland, 1981, Eighth Day and the Yes, No, Don't Know Show, 1975-77, Voyager and Glory Be, 1982-84, Presenter, Angles, 1981, Writer and Presenter, Gates to Space, 1982, Editor, Coast to Coast, 1977. Chairman, Scottish Religious Panel, IBA, 1970-72; Minister, Peterhead Old Parish Church, 1969-73. Publication: Vision and Belief, 1968. Recreations: improvising on the pipe organ and piano; theology; reading newspapers and other fiction; drawing excruciatingly bad cartoons. Address: (h.) 1 Glenan Gardens, Helensburgh, Dunbartonshire.

MacKenzie, James Alexander Mackintosh, FEng, FICE, FIHT. Chief Road Engineer, Scottish Development Department, since 1976; b. 6.5.28, Inverness; m., Pamela D. Nixon; 1 s.; 1 d. Educ. Inverness Royal Academy. Miscellaneous local government appointments, 1950-63; Chief Resident Engineer, Durham County Council, 1963-67; Deputy Director, North Eastern Road Construction Unit, Department of Transport, 1967-71 (Director, 1971-76). Recreations: golf; fishing. Address: (h.) 2 Dean Park, Longniddry, East Lothian, EH32 OQR; T.-Longniddry 52643.

Mackenzie, Rt. Hon. (James) Gregor, PC, MP, JP. MP (Labour), Rutherglen, since 1964; b. 15.11.27, Glasgow; m., Joan Swan Provan;

1 s.; 1 d. Educ. Queens Park School; Glasgow University; Royal Technical College, Glasgow. Member and Magistrate, Glasgow Corporation, 1952-64; PPS to Rt. Hon. James Callaghan, MP, 1965-70; Shadow Minister for Post and Telecommunications, 1970-74; Under Secretary of State for Industry, 1974-75; Minister of State for Industry, 1975-76; Minister of State for Scotland, 1976-79; Member, Committee of Privileges, House of Commons, since 1984. Address: (b.) House of Commons, London, SW1; T.-01-219 4563.

Mackenzie, Keith Roderick Turing, OBE, MC. President, The Golf Foundation; b. 19.1.21, Lucknow, India; m., Barbara Kershaw; 2 s.; 2 d. Educ. Uppingham School; Royal Military College, Sandhurst. 2nd Bn., 6th Gurhka Rifles, 1940-47 (retired Major, 1947); Burmah-Shell Oil Storage and Distributing Co., India, 1947-65; Shell Rhodesia, 1965-66; Secretary, Royal and Ancient Golf Club of St. Andrews, 1967-83. Recreations: golf; gardening. Address: (h.) Eden Hill, Kennedy Gardens, St. Andrews; T.-0334 73581.

MacKenzie, Kenneth John, MA, AM. Under Secretary and Principal Finance Officer, Scottish Office, since 1985; b. 1.5.43, Glasgow; m., Irene Mary Hogarth; 1 s.; 1 d. Educ. Birkenhead School; Pembroke College, Oxford; Stanford University, California. Assistant Principal, Scottish Home and Health Department; Principal, Scottish Education Department; Principal Private Secretary to Secretary of State for Scotland; Assistant Secretary, Scottish Economic Planning Department and Scottish Office Finance Division. Session Clerk, St. Cuthbert's Parish Church, Edinburgh; Past President, Edinburgh Civil Service Dramatic Society. Address: (h.) 29 Regent Terrace, Edinburgh, EH7 5BS; T.-031-557 4530.

MacKenzie, Malcolm Lackie, MA (Hons), MEd. Senior Lecturer in Education, Glasgow University; b. 5.7.38, Clydebank. Educ. Clydebank High School; Glasgow University. Assistant Teacher of English and History, Bearsden Academy, 1961-64; Lecturer in Education, Jordanhill College of Education, 1964-67; joined Department of Education, Glasgow University, 1967; Member, Council of Management, British Educational Administration Society, 1972-76; Member, Working Party set up by CCC on Communication and Implementation of Aims in Secondary Education, 1972-74; Past Chairman, Scottish Association for Educational Management and Administration; Member of Working Party on Educational Policy-making, Administration and Management, Council for Educational Technology for UK, 1974-77; Member, Scottish Central Committee on English, 1978-80; Co-Director, Scottish Schools Councils Research Project, 1976-80; Member, National Advisory Committee on Education, Conservative Party, 1962-82. Address: (h.) 64 Polwarth Street, Hyndland, Glasgow, G12 9TL; T.-041-357 2038.

MacKenzie, Mary, MBE, TD. Member, Grampian Area Health Board, 1981-85; Member, Industrial Tribunals Panel, since 1974; Member, National Advisory Advisory Council on the Employment of Disabled People, since 1977; Chairman, Grampian Committee for the Employment of Disabled People, since 1981; b. 14.2.18, Rochester, Kent; m., J. Strath MacKenzie; 2 s. Educ. Grammar School for Girls, Rochester; London College of Secretaries. Service in ATS, 1938-46, with rank of Chief commander (Lt.-Col.); service in WRAC/TA, 1957-63, with rank of Major; Chairman, Aberdeen-Kincardine Disablement Committee, 1969-81; Membr, Royal Cornhill and Associate Hospitals Board of Management, 1964-74; President, SSAFA (Aberdeen); Vice-Chairman, Tenovus (Grampian). Address: (h.) Rynie, Bieldside, Aberdeen, AB1 9AA; T.-0224 867423.

McKenzie, Rev. Morris Glyndwr, BA, LLB. Barrister and Solicitor, Supreme Court of New Zealand; Minister, South Ronaldsay and Burray, since 1978; b. 10.2.28, Invercargill, New Zealand; m., Janette Zena Lewis. Educ. John McGlashan College, Dunedin, New Zealand; Victoria University College, Wellington, New Zealand; University of Otago, Dunedin, New Zealand; St. Mary's College, St. Andrews. New Zealand: Ministry of Social Security, 1947-48, Ministry of Labour, 1948-55, Ministry of Works, 1955-65, District Solicitor, Ministry of Works, Dunedin, 1965-71, District Solicitor, Ministry of Works, Auckland, 1971-74; student, 1974-76; Assistant Minister, St. James, Forfar, 1976-77. Moderator, Orkney Presbytery, 1983-84. Recreations: walking; cycling; travel; reading; music. Address: Manse of South Ronaldsay and Burray, St. Margaret's Hope, Orkney; T.-St. Margaret's Hope 288.

MacKenzie, Rev. Ronald, MA. Minister, Glenelg and Arnisdale Free Church, since 1980; b. 19.4.36, Glasgow; m., Christina Beaton; 2 s. Educ. Bellahouston Academy; Glasgow University; Free Church College, Edinburgh. Bank of Scotland, 1955-67; University and Divinity College, 1968-74; Detroit, USA, 1974-75; ordained and inducted, Coigach Free Church, 1976. Clerk, Lochcarron Free Presbytery, since 1976. Recreations: reading; walking; gardening. Address: (h.) Free Church Manse, Glenelg, by Kyle, Ross-shire,. IV40 8LA; T.-Glenelg 206.

Mackenzie, Stuart D., DPE, DYCS, DMS, MBA. Director of Leisure and Recreation, Stirling District Council, since 1982; b. 14.8.46, Glasgow; m., Anita. Educ. Eastbank Academy, Glasgow; Jordanhill College of Education; Glasgow College of Technology; Strathclyde University. Activities Organiser, Scottish Association of Boys Clubs, 1968-70; Area Organiser, Glasgow Education Department, 1970-72; Lecturer, Jordanhill College, 1972-77; Depute Director of Leisure and Recreation, Cunninghame District Council, 1977-82. Executive Committee: Scottish Sports Association for the Disabled, 1975-82, Association of Directors of Leisure, Recreation and Tourism, since 1982. Recreations: squash; video filming; driving. Address: (b.) Beechwood House, St. Ninians Road, Stirling, FK8 2AD; T.-Stirling 79000, Ext. 337.

MacKenzie, William, MD, MRCP, FRCPEdin. Consultant Physician, Geriatric Medicine, Western Isles Health Board, since 1976; b. 4.11.19,

Folkestone; m., Kathleen Beryl. Educ. Epsom College; St. Bartholomew's Medical College, London University. House Physician, St. Bartholomew's Hospital, 1943; Resident Medical Officer, Jenny Lind Hospital for Children, Norwich, 1943-44; RAMC as GDMO and RMO until 1946; Registrar in Clinical Pathology, London Hospital, 1947-48; Medical Registrar, St. Giles' Hospital, Camberwell, 1951-57; Research Fellow, Department of Geriatric Medicine, Sunderland, and SHMO, 1957-64; Consultant Physician, Geriatric Medicine, Sunderland Area, Northern Regional Health Authority, 1964-76. Recreations: languages; art. Address: (h.) 3 Goathill Road, Stornoway, Lewis; T.-Stornoway 2667.

McKenzie, Rev. William Moncur, DA. Minister, Laurieknowe Troqueer Parish Church, Dumfries, since 1977; b. 30.12.28, Glasgow; m., Margaret Semple Scott; 1 s.; 2 d. Educ. King's Park Secondary School, Glasgow; Glasgow School of Art; Jordanhill Teacher Training College; Trinity College, Glasgow; St. Colm's Missionary College, Edinburgh. Art Teacher in Glasgow, 1951-55; ordained Minister, 1958; Assistant, St. Mary's, Govan; District Missionary, Lubwa, Northern Rhodesia, Livingstonia Mission, Church of Scotland, 1959-65; integrated into United Church of Zambia, 1965; transferred to Kashinda, Mporokoso, 1968, for lay training and Bible translation; left Zambia, 1977. Chaplain, HM Prison, Dumfries, since 1983; Secretary/Exegete for Chibemba Bible, Zambia (published, 1983); Committee Member, National Bible Society of Scotland, since 1978. Recreations: walking; camping; gardening. Address: The Manse, Troqueer Road, Dumfries, DG2 7DF; T.-0387 53043.

Mackenzie, William Roderick Simon, ARICS. Member, North East Fife District Council, since 1984; President, Zoological Society of Glasgow and West of Scotland; Chartered Quantity Surveyor; b. 2.3.30, Glasgow; m., Margaret Borland Maclachlan; 2 s.; 1 d. Educ. Pollokshields Senior Secondary School, Glasgow; Royal College of Science and Technology, Glasgow. Assistant Quantity Surveyor, Muirhead, Muir & Webster, Glasgow, 1948-64; Quantity Surveyor, Cumbernauld New Town Development Corporation, 1964-69; Senior Quantity Surveyor, Fife County Council, 1969-74; Buildings Office, Dundee University, since 1974. Recreations: writing plays; amateur dramatics; gardening; visiting zoos. Address: (h.) 3 Tarvit Gardens, Cupar, Fife, KY15 5BT; T.-Cupar 52660.

McKeown, Charles. Chairman, Industrial Development Committee, Central Regional Council; Chairman, Board of Directors, Stirling Enterprise Park; b. 27.3.30, Bannockburn; m., Anna Tortolano; 1 s.; 2 d. Educ. St. Modan's High School, Stirling. Engineering apprenticeship, 1945-50 (interrupted by National Service, 1948-50); Henry Ford Co., Detroit, 1955-57. District Councillor, Fallin, Stirling, 1972-73; County Councillor, Bannockburn, 1973-74; Regional Councillor, since 1974. Vice-Chairman, Stirlingshire Educational Trust. Recreations: reading; snooker; golf. Address: (h.) 1 Gillespie Place, Whins of Milton, Stirling; T.-0786 812776.

McKichan, Duncan James, BL. Solicitor; Partner, Maclay Murray & Spens, since 1952; Dean, Royal Faculty of Procurators in Glasgow, since 1983; b. 28.7.24, Wallington, Surrey; m, Leila Campbell Fraser; 2 d. Educ. George Watson's College, Edinburgh; Solihull School; Downing College, Cambridge; Glasgow University. Royal Navy, 1943-46; qualified as Solicitor, 1950. Recreations: gardening; walking; sailing; skiing. Address: (h.) Invermay, Queen Street, Helensburgh; T.-0436 4778.

MacKie, Professor Rona McLeod, MD, FRCP, FRCPGlas, FRCPath, FRSE. Professor of Dermatology, Glasgow University, since 1973; Honorary Consultant Dermatologist, Greater Glasgow Health Board, since 1978; b. 22.5.40, Dundee; m., Dr. Euan MacKie; 1 s.; 1 d. Educ. Laurelbank School, Glasgow; Glasgow University. Registrar, Department of Dermatology, Western Infirmary, Glasgow, 1970-71; Lecturer in Dermatology, Glasgow University, 1971-72; Consultant Dermatologist, Greater Glasgow Health Board, 1972-78. Recreation: skiing. Address: Department of Dermatology, Anderson College Building, 56 Dumbarton Road, Glasgow, G11 6NU; T.-041-339 8855, Ext. 606.

McKillop, George Armstrong, JP. Provost, East Kilbride District Council, since 1984; Chairman, East Kilbride Sports Council, since 1982; Member, East Kilbride Development Corporation, since 1985; b. 22.3.32, Bellshill; m., Susan; 1 s.; 1 d. Educ. Greenfield Secondary School, Hamilton. Elected to East Kilbride District Council, 1979; Deputy Provost, 1980-84; Chairman, Recreation and Leisure Services Committee, 1980-84. Recreations: reading; local history; bowling. Address: (h.) 30 Laurenstone Terrace, East Kilbride, G74 3BU; T.-East Kilbride 26221.

McKillop, James Hugh, BSc, MB, ChB, PhD, MRCP. Senior Lecturer in Medicine, Glasgow University, since 1982; Honorary Consultant Physician, Glasgow Royal Infirmary, since 1982; b. 20.6.48, Glasgow; m., Caroline Annis Oakley; 2 d. Educ. St. Aloysius' College, Glasgow; Glasgow University. House Officer posts, Glasgow Royal Infirmary, Western Infirmary and Royal Hospital for Sick Children, Glasgow, 1972-74; Hall Fellow in Medicine, then Lecturer in Medicine, Glasgow University, 1974-82; Postdoctoral Fellow, Stanford University Medical Center, California, 1979 and 1980. Watson Prize Lectureship, Royal College of Physicians and Surgeons of Glasgow, 1979; Harkness Fellowship, Commonwealth Fund of New York, 1979-80; Robert Reid Newall Award, Stanford University, 1980; Honorary Treasurer, Scottish Society of Experimental Medicine, since 1982; Honorary Secretary, British Nuclear Cardiology Group, since 1982; Symposium Editor, Scottish Medical Journal, since 1984; Council Member, British Nuclear Medicine Society, since 1985. Recreations: music (especially opera); history. Address: (h.) 10 Kirklee Circus, Glasgow, G12 OTW; T.-041-339 7000.

McKim, William Robert, FIB (Scot), MBCS. Managing Director, Royal Bank Group Services Ltd., since 1982; Director, Royal Bank of

Scotland plc, since 1982; Director, Williams and Glyn's Bank plc, since 1982; b. 14.3.28, Carluke; m., Ruby Forrest; 3 s. Educ. Carluke Higher Grade School; Wishaw High School. Joined National Bank of Scotland, 1945; Chief Programmer, National Commercial Bank of Scotland, 1962; appointed Manager, Systems and Programming, 1967; Royal Bank of Scotland: Controller (Electronic Data Processing), 1971, Assistant General Manager (EDP), 1973, General Manager (EDP), 1977. Elder, Davidsons Mains Parish Church, Edinburgh. Recreations: gardening; golf. Address: (b.) Royal Bank of Scotland plc, 36 St. Andrew Square, Edinburgh, EH2 2YB; T.-031-556 8555.

McKinlay, Professor David Gemmell, BSc, PhD, ARCST, CEng, FICE, FASCE, FGS, FRSE. Professor of Civil Engineering, Strathclyde University, since 1974; part-time Consultant, Crouch and Hogg, Glasgow; b. 23.8.24, Glasgow; m., Muriel Lees Donaldson; 1 s.; 1 d. Educ. Allan Glen's School, Glasgow; Royal Technical College, Glasgow; Glasgow University. War Service, commissioned RNVR; County Engineer's staff, Dumfries County; civil engineering consultancy; teaching and research, Royal College of Science and Technology, then Strathclyde University. Member, Subsidence Compensation Review Committee, 1984; Council Member, Institution of Civil Engineers; Chairman, Ground Engineering Group Board; Vice Chairman, Rotary (RIBI) District 123. Recreations: estate development; freshwater fishing; travel. Address: (h.) Spylawbank, Burn Road, Darvel, KA17 ODB; T.-0560 22552.

McKinlay, J.T., BSc, CEng, MIMechE. Controller, Computer Aided Engineering, National Engineering Laboratory, since 1984; b. 12.11.39, Glasgow; m., Aileen Watson; 1 s.; 1 d. Educ. Allan Glen's School; Glasgow University. Development Engineer, ICI, Wilton, 1961-63; Design Engineer, British Hydrocarbon Chemicals, Grangemouth, 1963-65; R. & D. in Computer-Aided Design, then Computer Manager, NEL, 1965-75; Computing Industry Sponsorship, then Personal Assistant to Chief Scientist, Department of Industry, London, 1975-78; Chief Executive, Textiles and Other Manufactures Requirements Board, DTI, London, 1978-84. Recreations: gardening; rugby; collecting Scotch miniatures. Address: (b.) National Engineering Laboratory, East Kilbride, Glasgow, G75 OQU; T.-035 52 20222.

McKinney, Alan. National Organiser and Headquarters Director, Scottish National Party, since 1982; b. 16.10.41, Glasgow; m., Elma; 1 s.; 1 d. Educ. Brechin High School. Time-served refrigeration engineer before entering politics full-time as National Organiser, SNP, 1977; former Election Agent, Dundee East; former elected Member, NEC. Played football for Brechin City. Recreation: golf. Address: (b.) Scottish National Party, 6 North Charlotte Street, Edinburgh; T.-031-226 3661.

McKinnon, Christopher. Chairman, Environmental Health Committee, Edinburgh District Council, since 1984; b. 22.9.41, Edinburgh; m.,

Joyce Smith; 2 s. Educ. Norton Park Junior Secondary School. Labour Member, Edinburgh District Council, since 1977. Recreation: photography. Address: (h.) 20 Darnell Road, Edinburgh, EH5 3PL; T.-031-552 4878.

MacKinnon, Lachlan, BL, DPA, FBIM. Chief Executive Officer, Dumbarton District Council, since 1975; b. 9.1.28, Glasgow; m., Rhoda; 2 s.; 2 d. Educ. Stirling High School; Glasgow University. Legal Assistant: Midlothian County Council, 1951-52, Hamilton Town Council, 1952-54; Depute Town Clerk: Rutherglen Town Council, 1954-57, Clydebank Town Council, 1957-67; Town Clerk, Dumbarton Town Council, 1967-75. Honorary Secretary: Dumbarton Senior Citizens Committee, Local Committee of Scottish Veterans' Garden City Association, Dumbarton District Posts and Telecommunications Advisory Committee. Recreations: curling; hill-walking; reading. Address: (b.) Crosslet House, Argyll Avenue, Dumbarton; T.-Dumbarton 65100.

MacKinnon, Rev. Roderick MacLean, LTh. Minister, Kilmuir and Logie Easter, since 1981; Clerk, Synod of Ross, Sutherland and Caithness, since 1982; b. 28.3.28, Bunavoneadar, Harris; m., Margaret Smith Robertson; 1 s.; 1 d. Educ. Sir Edward Scott School, Tarbert, Harris; Glasgow University and Trinity College. Lay Missionary, Tiree, 1957-62; Student Assistant, St. Columba, Copland Road, 1962-67; ordained and inducted to Daliburgh, South Uist, 1968; Minister, South Uist, 1978; Member, Committee on Priorities of Mission, General Assembly, 1970-72; Member, Home Board, General Assembly, 1974-81; General Trustee, Church of Scotland, since 1978; Clerk, Uist Presbytery, 1970-81; Chairman, Uist Council of Social Service, 1971-73; Member, Western Isles Islands Council, 1974-81 (Chairman, Social Work Committee, 1978-81); Member, Electricity Consultative Council for North of Scotland, 1977-81; Member, Scottish Religious Advisory Committee, BBC, since 1977. Recreation: gardening. Address: The Manse, Delny, Invergordon, Ross-shire; T.-086 284 2280.

Mackintosh, Rev. Canon Aeneas. Rector, St. Baldred's, North Berwick, and St. Adrian's, Gullane, since 1981; Canon, St. Mary's Cathedral, Edinburgh, since 1975; Senior Tutor, Diocese of Edinburgh, since 1974; b. 1.7.27, Inverness; m., Eileen Mary Barlow; 4 s. Educ. Inverness Royal Academy; Kelham Theological College. Precentor, St. Andrew's Cathedral, Inverness, 1952-55; Curate, St. Augustine's, Wisbech, 1955-57; Rector: St. Matthew, Possilpark, 1957-61, Holy Trinity, Haddington, 1961-65; Town Councillor, Haddington, 1962-65; Diocesan Inspector of Church Schools, 1963; Team Priest, St. John's, Princes Street, Edinburgh, 1965-69, and Rector, St. John's, 1969-81. Address: The Rectory, 2 May Terrace, North Berwick, EH39 4BA; T.-North Berwick 2154.

Mackintosh of Mackintosh, Lachlan Ronald Duncan, OBE, JP. 30th Chief of Clan Mackintosh, since 1957; Lord Lieutenant of Inverness, Lochaber, Badenoch and Strathspey, since 1985; Member, Highland Regional Council, since 1974; b. 27.6.28, Camberley; m., Mabel Cecilia Helen ("Celia") Bruce; 1 s.; 2 d.; 1 d. deceased.

Educ. R.N. College, Dartmouth. Seaman Officer, Specialist in Communications, Royal Navy, retiring as Lt.-Cdr., 1963; Chairman, Highland Exhibitions Ltd., 1964-85; Vice President, Scottish Conservative and Unionist Association, 1969-71; Member, Inverness County Council, 1970-75; Chairman, Inverness Prison Visiting Committee, since 1973. Address: Moy Hall, Tomatin, Inverness-shire, IV13 7YQ; T.-Tomatin 211.

Mackintosh, Peter, MIEDO, FInstP. Director of Development, Highland Regional Council, since 1980; b. 7.6.39, Nairn; m., Una; 2 s. Educ. Roses Academic Institute, Nairn. Architectural Assistant: Inverness County Council, 1958-60, Fife County Council, 1960-62; Ross and Cromarty County Council: Senior Architectural Assistant, 1962-72, Assistant Development Officer, 1972-75; Highland Regional Council: Divisional Development Officer, 1975-78, Assistant Director of Development, 1978-80. Recreations: golf; tennis; photography; walking; gardening; music. Address: (b.) Regional Buildings, Glenurquhart Road, Inverness, IV3 5NX; T.-0463 234121.

Maclachlan, Alistair Andrew Duncan, BA (Hons). Rector, Forres Academy, since 1982; b. 14.3.46, Perth; m., Alison M.S. Love; 2 s. Educ. Perth Academy; Strathclyde University. Teacher in various schools, 1969-71; Principal Teacher of Economics and Business Studies, 1971-74; Assistant Rector, Keith Grammar School, 1974-78; Depute Rector, Elgin High School, 1978-82. Secretary and Treasurer, Keith Agricultural Show, 1972-82; Chairman, Elgin Squash Club, since 1982. Recreations: keeping fit; squash; reading; music. Address: (h.) 82 Duncan Drive, Elgin, Moray, IV30 2NH; T.-Elgin 2193.

Maclachlan, Colin, BSc, DipEd, PhD. Senior Lecturer, Department of Mathematics, Aberdeen University, since 1972; b. 2.3.39, Dundee; m., Dorothy Milne; 1 s.; 2 d. Educ. Morgan Academy, Dundee; St. Andrews University; Birmingham University. Assistant Lecturer, Birmingham University, 1964-66; Assistant Professor, Carleton University, Ottawa, 1966-68; Lecturer, Aberdeen University, 1968-72; Visiting Associate Professor, Maryland University, 1975-76; Visiting Lecturer, Ruhr University, Bochum, West Germany, 1982. Recreations: squash; hill-walking. Address: (h.) 18 Monymusk Terrace, Aberdeen; T.-0224 318730.

Maclaren, Allan, MA, PhD. Senior Lecturer in Sociology, Strathclyde University, since 1978; b. 3.11.37, Brechin; m., Marcia Nott; 2 s. Educ. Robert Gordon's College, Aberdeen; Aberdeen University. Worked in printing and publishing industry; former Lecturer, Department of Political Economy, Aberdeen University. Publications: Religion and Social Class, 1974; Social Class in Scotland (Editor), 1976. Recreations: yachting; photography. Address: (b.) Department of Sociology, Strathclyde University, Glasgow, G1.

McLaren, Bill, MBE (1979). Rugby Union Commentator, BBC; Teacher of Physical Education; b. 16.10.23; m., Bette; 2 d. Educ. Hawick High School; Woolmanhill College of Physical Education, Aberdeen. Played wing forward for Hawick; had trial for Scotland but forced to withdraw because of illness; became reporter on local newspaper; first live radio broadcast, Glasgow v. Edinburgh, 1953; now main Rugby Union Commentator, BBC.

MacLaren, Donald, BSc (Agr), MS, PhD. Senior Lecturer in Agriculture, Aberdeen University, since 1984; b. 1.9.42, Douglas, Lanarkshire; m., Eileen Gordon; 2 s. Educ. George Watson's College; Aberdeen University; Cornell University. Graduate Assistant, Cornell University, 1966-70; Lecturer, Aberdeen University, 1970-84; Visiting Professor: Guelph University, Canada, 1974, Cornell University, USA, 1982. Recreations: swimming; tennis; gardening; music. Address: (h.) 68 Kildrummy Road, Aberdeen, AB1 8HT; T.-0224 310660.

McLaren, Donald Stewart, MD, PhD, DTM&H, FRCP. Reader in Clinical Nutrition, Department of Medicine, Edinburgh University, since 1980; b. 4.2.24, London; m., Olga; 1 s.; 1 d. Educ. Reigate; Edinburgh University. Medical Officer, Moorshead Memorial Hospital, India, 1949-53; Medical Research Officer, East African Institute for Medical Research, Tanzania, 1953-63; Professor of Clinical Nutrition and Director, Nutrition Research Programme, School of Medicine, American University of Beirut, Lebanon, 1962-76; President, Edinburgh Medical Missionary Society. Publications: Nutrition and its Disorders; Nutritional Ophthalmology; Textbook of Paediatric Nutrition; Nutrition in the Community; Colour Atlas of Nutritional Disorders; The Bodytone Maintenance Programme. Recreations: electronic organ; golf; American literature. Address: (b.) Department of Medicine, Royal Infirmary, Edinburgh; T.-031-229 2477, Ext. 2055.

MacLaren, Duncan A.S., BL, NP. Board Secretary, South of Scotland Electricity Board, since 1977; b. 14.5.30, Dunvegan, Isle of Skye; m., Jennifer Jackson; 1 s.; 1 d. Educ. George Watson's Boys' College, Edinburgh; Edinburgh University. Legal and other senior appointments, South of Scotland Electricity Board, 1962-72; Board Secretary, North of Scotland Hydro-Electric Board, 1972-77. Address: (b.) Cathcart House, Spean Street, Glasgow; T.-041-637 7177.

MacLaren, Iain Ferguson, MB, ChB, FRCSEdin, FRCS. Consultant Surgeon, Leith Hospital, Edinburgh, since 1985; Consultant Surgeon, Royal Infirmary, Edinburgh, since 1974; Vice-President, Royal College of Surgeons of Edinburgh, since 1983; b. 28.9.27, Edinburgh; m., Dr. Fiona Barbara Heptonstall; 1 s.; 1 d. Educ. Edinburgh Academy; Fettes College; Edinburgh University. Captain, RAMC, Egypt, 1950-52; Surgical Registrar, Royal Hospital for Sick Children, Edinburgh, 1956-58; Senior Surgical Registrar, Royal Infirmary, 1959-63 and 1964-67; Fellow in Surgical Research, Hannemann Medical College and Hospital, Philadelphia, 1963-64; Consultant Surgeon, Deaconess Hospital, Edinburgh, 1967-85; Honorary Secretary, Royal College of Surgeons of Edinburgh, 1972-77 (Council Member, 1977-83); Fellow, Royal

Medical Society (Honorary Treasurer, 1979-85); Chairman, Royal Medical Society Trust, since 1985; Honorary Pipe-Major, Royal Scottish Pipers' Society, 1959-62; Honorary Secretary: Harveian Society of Edinburgh, since 1968, Aesculapian Club, since 1978. Recreations: music; the study of military history; all aspects of Scottish culture. Address: (h.) 3 Minto Street, Edinburgh, EH9 1RG; T.-031-667 3487.

McLaren, Kathryn M., BSc (Hons), MB, ChB, MRCPath. Senior Lecturer in Pathology, Edinburgh University, since 1983; Honorary Consultant, Lothian Health Board, since 1983; b. 26.7.49, Edinburgh. Educ. George Watson's Ladies' College; Edinburgh University. House Surgeon and Physician, Edinburgh Royal Infirmary, 1975; Lecturer in Pathology, 1976-83; Pathology Representative, Scottish Melanoma Group, since 1983. Recreations: London; reading. Address: (b.) Department of Pathology, Edinburgh University Medical School, Teviot Place, Edinburgh, EH8 4AG; T.-031-667 1011.

McLauchlan, Ian. Freelance Sports Journalist and Broadcaster; b. 14.4.42, Tarbolton; m., Eileen; 3 s. Educ. Ayr Academy; Jordanhill College (Diploma, Physical Education). Won 43 Scottish caps for rugby; two British Lions tours; holds record for captaincy of Scotland. Publications: Mighty Mouse, 1980; Scottish Scrapbook, 1981; Rugby Forward Play, 1983; Grand Slam, 1984. Recreations: marathon running; golf. Address: (h.) 9 Albyn Place, Edinburgh, EH2 4NG; T.-031-226 2277.

McLaughlin, Eleanor Thomson, JP. Deputy Chairman, Edinburgh District Council, since 1984 (Chairman, Housing Committee, since 1984); b. Edinburgh; m., Hugh McLaughlin; 1 s.; 2 d. Educ. (h.) 28 Oxgangs Green, Edinburgh; T.-031-445 4052.

McLay, James Durward, BSc, DipEd. Rector, Douglas-Ewart High School, Newton Stewart, since 1971; b. 8.1.36, Falkirk; m., Catherine May Watson; 1 s. Educ. Denny High School; Glasgow University. Taught in Glasgow, 1958-61; Principal Teacher of Geography, Douglas-Ewart High School, 1960-71. Address: (b.) Douglas-Ewart High School, Newton Stewart, DG8 6JQ; T.-0671 3773.

Maclay, 3rd Baron, (Joseph Paton Maclay), Bt. Director, Denholm Maclay (Offshore) Ltd.; b. 11.4.42; m., Elizabeth Anne Buchanan; 2 s.; 1 d. Educ. Winchester; Sorbonne. Director, Denholm Maclay Co. Ltd., 1970-83; Chairman, Scottish Branch, British Sailors Society, 1979-81; Vice Chairman, Glasgow Shipowners & Shipbrokers Benevolent Association, 1982-83.

McLean, Allan Campbell. Author; b. 18.11.22, Walney Island; m., Margaret Elizabeth White; 2 s.; 1 d. Educ. Barrow-in-Furness Junior Technical School. Former Chairman, Scottish Council, Labour Party. Won Frederick Niven Award for The Islander (Best Scottish Novel). Recreation: football. Address: (h.) 1 Balmoral Place, Stockbridge, Edinburgh, EH3 5JA.

MacLean, Rev. Andrew Thomas, BA, BD. Chaplain, Strathclyde University, since 1985; b. 1.2.50, Abadan, Iran; m., Alison Douglas Blair; 1 s.; 1 d. Educ. Bearsden Academy; Clydebank Technical College; Stirling University; Edinburgh University. Co-operative Insurance Society, 1967-70; Partner, Janus Enterprises, 1970-72; Probationer, Loanhead, 1979-80; Minister, Aberdeen Stockethill, 1980-85. Member, Church of Scotland Board of Social Responsibility, since 1981; Member, Grampian Steering Committee on Solvent Abuse, 1982-85; Member, Grampian Committee on Drug Abuse, 1984-85; Chairman, Aberdeen Community Drug Advice and Counselling Service, 1984-85; Manager, Church of Scotland NW Aberdeen Community Project; represents Church of Scotland on Board of Directors, Albyn House Association Ltd. Recreation: sound recording. Address: Chaplaincy Centre, Strathclyde University, John Street, Glasgow; T.-041-552 4400, Ext. 2442.

Maclean, Baron, (Charles Hector Fitzroy Maclean), Bt, KT (1969), GCVO (1971), KBE (1967), PC (1971), JP. 27th Chief of Clan Maclean; a Permanent Lord in Waiting, since 1984; Lord Lieutenant of Argyll, since 1954; Lieutenant, Queen's Bodyguard for Scotland (Royal Company of Archers); Life Peer; b. 5.5.16; m., Elizabeth Mann; 1 s.; 1 d. Educ. Canford School, Wimborne. Served Second World War (mentioned in Despatches); Chief Commissioner for Scotland, Boy Scouts Association, 1954-59; Chief Scout of the UK and Overseas Branches, 1959-71; Chief Scout of the Commonwealth, 1959-75; Lord Chamberlain of HM Household, 1971-84; Chancellor, Royal Victorian Order, 1971-84; Lord High Commissioner, General Assembly of the Church of Scoland, 1984, 1985; Convenor, Standing Council of Scottish Chiefs; President, Argyll T&AFA. Address: (h.) Duart Castle, Isle of Mull.

MacLean, Colin George, MA. Managing Director, Aberdeen University Press, since 1979; b. 3.6.25, Glasgow; m., Moira Smith; 3 s. Educ. Robert Gordon's College, Aberdeen; Aberdeen University. Journalist, Glasgow Bulletin, Daily Telegraph (London), The Times (London); Editor, Times Educational Supplement Scotland, 1965-77; Vice-Chairman, National Youth Orchestra of Scotland, since 1978; President, Scottish Pre-School Playgroup Association, 1980-84; Member, Scottish Arts Council, 1980-84; Member, General Advisory Council, BBC, since 1985. Publication: The Crown & The Thistle (Editor), 1979. Recreation: television. Address: (h.) 3 Cobden Road, Newington, Edinburgh; T.-031-667 5175.

MacLean, Colin MacPhail, BA, BSc, PhD, MIBiol. Principal, Thurso Technical College, since 1983; b. 13.5.35, Glasgow; m., Jean Cameron Armstrong; 2 s. Educ. Victoria Drive School, Glasgow; Glasgow University; Strathclyde University. Member, Post Office Users Council for Scotland; Member, Scottish Advisory Committee to Office of Telecommunications. Recreations: reading; walking; eating; keeping fit. Address: (b.) Thurso Technical College, Ormlie Road, Thurso; T.-0847 66161.

McLean, Donald, CBE, BSc, CEng, FIMechE, FRAeS, CBIM, FIIM, FRSA. Non-Executive Director, South of Scotland Electricity Board, since 1982; Non-Executive Director, East Kilbride Development Corporation, since 1983; Member, Court, Strathclyde University, since 1983; b. 12.10.18, Paisley; m., Olive Marett; 2 s.; 2 d. Educ. Ayr Academy; Paisley Technical College; London University. Joined Rolls-Royce Ltd., Derby, as Designer, 1941; served as Pilot, RAF Transport Command, 1942-46; returned to Rolls-Royce, latterly as Director of Design Engineering, 1967; Programme Director-Scottish Projects, Rolls-Royce, 1969; Director-Scotland, Rolls-Royce, 1970-82; Member, Scottish Economic Council and Careers Advisory Service Council, 1977-83; Member, Design Council, since 1980; Director, Glasgow Chamber of Commerce, 1976-81; Vice President, Scottish Engineering Employers Association, 1971-82. Recreations: gardening; walking; DIY. Address: (h.) Auchengrange, Lochwinnoch, Renfrewshire, PA12 4JS.

Maclean, Sir Donald O.G., FBCO. Deputy Chairman, Scottish Conservative Party, since 1985; President, Scottish Conservative and Unionist Association, 1983-85; Ophthalmic Optician, since 1952; b. Annan; widower; 1 s.; 1 d. Educ. Morrison's Academy, Crieff; Heriot-Watt, Edinburgh. Ophthalmic Optician in Edinburgh, Newcastle, Perth and now Ayr; Member, Ayrshire Local Optical Committee; former Member, Transport Users Local Consultative Committee; Chairman, Ayr Constituency Conservative Association, 1971-75; Chairman, West of Scotland Area Council, Scottish Conservative Association, 1977-78-79; Member, National Union Executive Committee, since 1979 (Member, GP Committee, since 1983); Elder, Church of Scotland; Past President, West Highland Steamer Club. Recreations: photography; reading. Address: (h.) 22 Woodend Road, Alloway, Ayr.

Maclean, Donnie M., DipTechEd. Director, An Comann Gaidhealach, Western Isles Region, since 1978; b. 5.9.36, Coll, Isle of Lewis; m., Lynn Kemp; 2 s.; 1 d. Educ. Back Public School; Nicolson Institute, Stornoway; Duncan of Jordanstone College of Art, Dundee; Moray House College of Education, Edinburgh. Fisherman; Civil Servant; Teacher; Producer, BBC Scotland; National Organiser, Scottish Civic Entertainment Association. Member of Children's Panel; Councillor representing Coll Division; Playwright. Recreations: drama; photography; the arts; crofting; fishing. Address: (h.) 7A Coll, Back, Isle of Lewis; T.-Back 260.

Maclean of Dunconnel, Sir Fitzroy Hew, 1st Bt, CBE (Mil). 15th Hereditary Keeper and Captain of Dunconnel; b. 11.3.11; m., Hon. Mrs Alan Phipps; 2 s. Educ. Eton; Cambridge. Entered Foreign Office, 1933; served Second World War (Brigadier commanding British Military Mission to Jugoslav partisans, 1943-45); MP (Conservative), Lancaster, 1941-59, Bute and North Ayrshire, 1959-74; Parliamentary Under Secretary of State for War and Financial Secretary, War Office, 1954-57; Member, UK Delegation to North Atlantic Assembly, 1962-74; Member,

Council of Europe and WEU, 1972-74; Hon. LLD, Glasgow, 1969, Dundee, 1984; author of works of military history and other books. Address: (h.) Strachur House, Argyll.

Maclean, Sheriff Hector Ronald. Sheriff of North Strathclyde, since 1968; b. 1931; m.; 3 d. Advocate, 1959.

McLean, Hugh, MBE. Provost of Nairn, since 1975; b. 28.2.09, Nairn; m., Annie Henderson Richardson; 1 s. Educ. Nairn Academy; Army Staff College, Camberley. Regular Army, RASC, 1928-50; Tourist Officer, Highland Area, 1954-77. Recreations: bridge; golf. Address: (h.) 7 Seabank Gardens, Nairn, IV12 4RR; T.-Nairn 52286.

MacLean, Ian Teasdale, MA, LLB. Solicitor; Senior Partner, J.D. Mackie & Dewar, since 1982 (Partner, since 1968); Honorary Treasurer, Aberdeen YMCA, since 1970; b. 3.6.40, Stornoway; m., Lavinia May Symonds; 1 s.; 1 d. Educ. Nicolson Institute, Stornoway; Aberdeen University. Qualified as Solicitor, 1964, after three years' indenture with Morice & Wilson, Advocates in Aberdeen; salaried Solicitor, J.D. Mackie & Dewar, Advocates in Aberdeen, 1965-68. Address: (b.) 18 Bon-Accord Square, Aberdeen; T.-0224 596341.

McLean, Jack, DA, MSIAD. Art Teacher, since 1968; Writer and Broadcaster, since 1974; b. Irvine, Ayrshire. Educ. Allan Glen's School, Glasgow; Edinburgh College of Art. Apprentice Welder, 1962-65; various jobs until 1968; Studio Artist, uncertificated Art Teacher, 1968-70; Edinburgh Art College; Jordanhill College of Education; Teacher of Art in Glasgow schools since; began writing with Times Educational Supplement with regular column; Columnist, The Scotsman, 1967-81; Columnist, Glasgow Herald, since 1981; Scottish Vice-Chairman and National Executive Member, National Union of Students, 1970-74; Member, Scottish Council, Educational Institute of Scotland, 1981-82; Commendation, Scottish Press Awards, 1985. Recreations: drinking in public houses (see A. Hind); flashy dressing; not playing tennis. Address: (h.) 103/5 Birness Drive, Glasgow, G43 1TA; T.-041-649 7200.

McLean, James, BSc (Hons). Director of Education, Borders Regional Council, since 1974; b. 9.10.31, Glasgow; m., Wendy; 3 s.; 1 d. Educ. Hyndland Senior Secondary School; Glasgow University. Industrial Assistant, British Petroleum, 1956; Teacher and Special Assistant Teacher, Dunoon Grammar School, 1960-63; Assistant Director of Education, Dumfriesshire, 1963-66; Depute Director of Education, Stewartry of Kirkcudbright, 1966-72; Director of Education, Peeblesshire, 1972-75. Member, Scottish Sports Council, since 1976; Honorary Treasurer, Association of Directors of Education in Scotland, since 1975. Recreations: Rotary; small-holding; swimming; golf; rugby. Address: (b.) Regional Headquarters, Newtown St. Boswells, Roxburghshire; T.-St. Boswells 23301.

McLean, John David Ruari, CBE, DSC, Croix de Guerre. Typographer and Author; b. 10.6.17, Minnigaff; m., Antonia Maxwell Carlisle; 2 s.;

1 d. Educ. Dragon School, Oxford; Eastbourne College. Royal Navy, 1940-45; Tutor in Typography, Royal College of Art, 1948-51; Typographic Adviser, Hulton Press, 1953-60; The Observer, 1960-62; Art Editor, The Connoisseur, 1962-73; Founder-Partner, Rainbird, McLean Ltd., 1951-58; Founder Editor, Motif, 1958-67; Honorary Typographic Adviser to HM Stationery Office, 1966-80; Senior Partner, Ruari McLean Associates Ltd., 1960-81; Trustee, National Library of Scotland, 1981. Publications: Modern Book Design, 1958; Victorian Book Design and Colour Printing, 1963; Magazine Design, 1969; Jan Tschichold, Typographer, 1975; The Thames & Hudson Manual of Typography, 1980. Recreations: sailing; acquiring books. Address: (h.) Pier Cottage, Carsaig, Isle of Mull; T.-Pennyghall 216.

McLean, Joseph Francis. Vice-Chairman, Education Committee, Strathclyde Regional Council, since 1982; Vice-Chairman, Scottish Business Education Council, since 1980; Member, Education Committee, COSLA; b. 26.1.40, Glasgow; m., Maureen McCaffrey; 5 s. Educ. St. Gerards Senior Secondary School, Glasgow; Stow College, Glasgow. Election Agent for Rt. Hon. Bruce Millan, General Elections, 1979 and 1983. Recreations: reading Council reports; watching Celtic occasionally. Address: (b.) Strathclyde Regional Council, India Street, Glasgow; T.-041-227 2197.

MacLean, Ranald Norman Munro, BA, LLB, LLM. Queen's Counsel, since 1977; b. 18.12.38, Aberdeen; m., Pamela Ross; 2 s.; 1 d. Educ. Inverness Royal Academy; Fettes College, Edinburgh; Cambridge University; Edinburgh University; Yale University. Advocate, 1964; Advocate Depute, 1972-75; Advocate Depute (Home), 1979-82; Chairman, Scottish Committee, Council on Tribunals, 1985; Member, Council on Tribunals, 1985. Governor, Fettes Trust, since 1977. Recreations: hill-walking; running; bird watching. Address: (h.) 12 Chalmers Crescent, Edinburgh, EH9 1TS; T.-031-667 6217.

Maclean, Sir Robert (Alexander), KBE (1973), Kt (1955), DL. Honorary President, Stoddard Holdings Ltd.; Vice-President, Scottish Council (Development and Industry); b. 11.4.08; m.; 2 s.; 2 d. Educ. High School of Glasgow. Regional Controller (Scotland), Board of Trade, 1944-46; Chairman: Council of Scottish Chambers of Commerce, 1960-62, Scotish Industrial Estates Corporation, 1955-72; Vice Chairman, Scottish Board for Industry, 1952-60.

MacLean, Sorley, MA (Hons). Poet; b. 1911, Osgaig, Raasay; m., Renee Cameron; 3 d. Educ. Portree High School; Edinburgh University. Teacher of English, Portree and Tobermory; Head, English Department, Boroughmuir School, Edinburgh; Headmaster, Plockton High School; Writer in Residence, Edinburgh University, 1973-75; Filidh (Resident Poet), Sabhal Mor Ostaig, 1975-76; author of: 17 Poems for 6d (with Robert Garioch), 1940; Dain do Eimhir, 1943; Four Points of a Saltire (Co-author), 1970; Poems to Eimhir (translated from the Gaelic by Iain Crichton Smith), 1971; Reothairt is Contraigh, Spring Tide and Neap Tide, Selected Poems 1932-72, 1977.

McLean, Una. Actress; b. Strathaven. Trained, Royal Scottish Academy of Music and Drama; joined Glasgow Citizens', 1959, where she played the leading role in Jack Ronder's Wedding Day; appeared with Jimmy Logan, Jack Radcliffe and Stanley Baxter in Five Past Eight, Alhambra, Glasgow; acted with Duncan Macrae in a revival of See How They Run; joined civic theatre company at the Royal Lyceum, Edinburgh, on its formation; won STV Light Entertainment Award for her performance in Widows Paradise, Metropole, Glasgow, 1968.

Maclean, William James, DA, ARSA, FSA Scot. Lecturer in Fine Art, Duncan of Jordanstone College of Art, Dundee, since 1982; b. 12.10.41, Inverness; m., Marian Forbes Leven; 2 s.; 1 d. Educ. Inverness Royal Academy; HMS Conway; Grays School of Art, Aberdeen. Postgraduate and Travel Scholarship, Scottish Education Trust Award, Visual Arts Bursary, Scottish Arts Council; Benno Schotz Prize; one-man exhibitions in Rome, Glasgow, Edinburgh and London; group exhibitions in Britain, Europe and North America; represented in private and public collections including Arts Council, Contemporary Art Society, Scottish National Gallery of Modern Art, Fitzwilliam Museum, Cambridge, and several Scottish galleries. Address: (h.) Bellevue, 18 Dougall Street, Tayport, Fife.

McLean Cameron, James, TD, DRTC, FICE, FIWES, FBIM. Director of Water and Sewerage, Dumfries and Galloway Regional Council, since 1975; b. 1.8.26, Glasgow; m., Christina Lilly Jardine Brown; 2 d. Educ. Royal Technical College. Royal Engineers, India, Egypt and Kenya and appointments in the contracting industry, 1945-49; appointments with Kirkcudbright, Inverness and Perth County Councils, 1949-65; County Water and Drainage Engineer, Perth County Council, 1965-68; Engineer to South-West of Scotland Water Board, 1968-75. Past President, Scottish Section, Institution of Water Engineers and Scientists; Past President, Association of Water Officers (Scotland); Past President, Dumfries and Galloway Civil Engineering and Architectural Society; Past Chairman, Joint Negotiating Committee for Chief Officials of Local Authorities (Scotland). Recreations: golf; rugby; Rotary. Address: (h.) 73 Rotchell Road, Dumfries; T.-0387 54441.

MacLeary, Professor Alistair Ronald, MSc, DipTP, FRICS, FRTPI, FRSA. MacRobert Professor of Land Economy, Aberdeen University, since 1976 (Dean, Faculty of Law, 1982-85); President, Planning and Development Division, Royal Institution of Chartered Surveyors, 1984-85; b. 12.1.40, Glasgow; m., Claire Leonard; 1 s.; 1 d. Educ. Inverness Royal Academy; College of Estate Management; Heriot-Watt University; Strathclyde University. Assistant Surveyor, Gerald Eve & Co., Chartered Surveyors, 1962-65; Assistant to Director, Murrayfield Real Estate Co. Ltd., 1965-67; Assistant Surveyor and Town Planner/Partner, Wright & Partners, 1967-76; seconded to Department of the Environment, London, 1971-73; Member, Committee of Inquiry into the Acquisition and Occupancy of Agricultural Land, 1977-79; Member, Home

Grown Timber Advisory Committee, Forestry Commission, since 1981; Chairman, Board of Education, Commonwealth Association of Surveying and Land Economy; Member, Grampian Region Valuation Panel; Director, Aberdeen University Research and Industrial Services Ltd. Recreations: golf; shooting; skiing; hill-walking. Address: (h.) 164 Forest Avenue, Aberdeen, AB1 6UN; T.-0224 322940.

MacLeay, Rev. Canon John Henry James, MA. Rector, St. Andrew's, Fort William, since 1978; Canon, St. John's Cathedral, Oban, since 1980; b. 7.12.31, Inverness; m., Jane Speirs Cuthbert; 1 s.; 1 d. Educ. St. Edmund Hall, Oxford. Ordained Deacon, 1957; Priest, 1958; Curate: St. John's, East Dulwich, 1957-60, St. Michael's, Inverness, 1960-62; Rector, St. Michael's, Inverness, 1962-70; Priest-in-Charge, St. Columba's, Grantown-on-Spey and St. John's, Rothiemurchus, 1970-78. Recreations: fishing; reading; visiting old churches and cathedrals. Address: St. Andrew's Rectory, Parade Road, Fort William, PH33 6BA; T.-0397 2979.

MacLehose of Beoch, Baron, (Crawford Murray MacLehose), KT (1983), GBE (1976), KCMG (1971), KCVO (1975), DL. Director, National Westminster Bank, since 1982; Chairman, Victoria League of Commonwealth Friendship, since 1983; Chairman, Scottish Trust for the Physically Disabled; Life Peer; b. 16.10.17; m.; 2 d. Educ. Rugby; Balliol College, Oxford. Served Second World War (Lt., RNVR); joined Foreign Service, 1947; Governor and C-in-C, Hong Kong, 1971-82. Address: (h.) Beoch, Maybole, Ayrshire.

McLellan, Alexander, MA, MEd, FBIM. Director, Scottish Centre for Education Overseas, since 1981; b. 28.5.21, Greenock; m., Muriel Davies. Educ. Greenock High School; Glasgow University. Teacher of General Subjects, Mossvale School, Paisley, 1949-50; Teacher of English and History, Paisley Grammar School, 1950-57; Assistant/Depute Director of Education, City of Aberdeen, 1957-64; Depute Director of Education, then Director of Education, Angus County Council, 1964-75; Lecturer in Educational Administration, Scottish Centre for Education Overseas, Moray House College of Education, Edinburgh, 1975. Chairman, Royal Overseas League (Scotland), 1978-83. Recreations: golfing; gardening; music. Address: (h.) 17 Cumlodden Avenue, Edinburgh, EH12 6DR; T.-031-337 1651.

McLellan, Rev. Andrew Rankin Cowie, MA (Hons), BD (Hons), STM. Minister, Stirling Viewfield, since 1980; b. 16.6.44, Glasgow; m., Irene L. Meek; 2 s. Educ. Kilmarnock Academy; Madras College, St. Andrews; St. Andrews University; Glasgow University; Union Theological Seminary, New York. Assistant Minister, St. George's West, Edinburgh; Minister: Cartsburn Augustine, Greenock; Member, General Assembly Committees; Tutor, Glasgow University and United Church of Zambia; former Member, Inverclyde District Council. Recreation: golf. Address: 7 Windsor Place, Stirling; T.-0786 74534.

McLellan, Archibald Robertson, BSc, PhD. Lecturer in Agricultural Biochemistry, East of Scotland College of Agriculture; b. 20.6.34, Stirling; m., Sheila A. Hogg; 2 s.; 2 d. Educ. Morrison's Academy, Crieff; St. Andrews University; Edinburgh University. Advisory Officer (Beekeeping), East of Scotland College of Agriculture, 1957. Recreation: history, particularly Scottish history and prehistory. Address: (h.) 17 Mayfield Gardens, Edinburgh, EH9 2AX; T.-031-667 8049.

MacLellan, Sir (George) Robin, Kt (1980), CBE (1969), JP. Chairman, Scottish Industrial and Trade Exhibitions Ltd., since 1981; b. 14.11.15; m.; 1 s. Educ. Ardvreck; Clifton College; Ecole de Commerce, Lausanne. Deputy Chairman, British Airports Authority, 1965-75; President, Glasgow Chamber of Commerce, 1970-71; Director, British Tourist Authority, 1974-80; Chairman, Scottish Tourist Board, 1974-80; Member, Council, National Trust for Scotland, since 1974.

McLellan, James Alexander, LLB. Director of Administration, Argyll and Bute District Council, since 1978; b. 23.12.50, Lochgilphead; m., Alexis; 2 s.; 1 d. Educ. Keil School; Glasgow University. Recreations: fishing; rugby; gardening. Address: (b.) Kilmory, Lochgilphead, Argyll, PA31 8RT; T.-0546 2127.

McLelland, John, BVMS, MVSc, PhD, MRCVS. Reader in Veterinary Anatomy, Edinburgh University, since 1981; b. 11.6.37, Kilmarnock; m., Morar; 1 s.; 2 d. Educ. Kilmarnock Academy; Glasgow Academy; Glasgow University; Liverpool University. Pig Industry Development Authority Scholar, Veterinary Hospital, Glasgow University, 1962-63; Egg Marketing Board Scholar, Department of Veterinary Anatomy, Liverpool University, 1964; Assistant Lecturer, then Lecturer, Department of Veterinary Anatomy, Liverpool University, 1964-72; Lecturer, then Senior Lecturer, Department of Veterinary Anatomy, Edinburgh University, 1972-81; Senior Royal Society/Indian National Academy of Sciences Visiting Research Worker, Department of Zoology, Gujarat University, India, 1976; Visiting Lecturer: Vakgroep Funktionele Morfologie, Fakulteit Der Diergeneeskunde, Rijksuniversiteit Te Utrecht, Netherlands, 1980, Department of Veterinary Anatomy, Dar Es Salaam University, 1981, Department of Anatomy and Cellular Biology, Tufts University, Boston, 1984. Publications: Outlines of Avian Anatomy (Co-author), 1975; Form and Function in Birds (Editor), 1979, 1981, 1985; An Introduction to the Functional Anatomy of the Limbs of the Domestic Animals (Co-author), 1984; Birds: Their Structure and Function (Co-author), 1984. Recreations: music; walking; gardening; travel. Address: (h.) Eastcot, Oldhamstocks, East Lothian; T.-Cockburnspath 416.

MacLennan, Alexander Fraser, BL, SSC, NP. Consultant, Balfour & Manson, Edinburgh, since 1984 (Partner, 1946-84); b. 17.9.10, Leith; m., F.G. Elwyn Manson; 1 s. Educ. Broughton Secondary School; Scottish Educational Institute, Edinburgh; Edinburgh University. Served with RAF; Honorary Secretary, Edinburgh Legal

Dispensary; President, Carrubbers Christian Centre, Edinburgh; Preaching Evangelist, Edinburgh Presbytery, Church of Scotland. Recreations: walking; golf. Address: (h.) 100 Ravelston Dykes, Edinburgh; T.-031-337 4341.

MacLennan, David Neall, BSc, FIOA. Senior Principal Scientific Officer, Marine Laboratory, since 1983; b. 26.9.40, Aberdeen; m., Sheila Cormack; 1 s.; 1 d. Educ. Robert Gordon's College; Aberdeen University. Scientific Officer, AERE Harwell, 1962-67; Marine Laboratory, 1967-73; Head Office, Department of Agriculture and Fisheries for Scotland, 1973-75; returned to Marine Laboratory, 1976. Chairman, ICES Fish Capture Working Group. Recreation: bridge (Secretary, Aberdeen Bridge Club). Address: (h.) 2 Stronsay Avenue, Aberdeen; T.-0224 876544.

Maclennan, Duncan, MA, MPhil. Senior Lecturer in Economics, Glasgow University, since 1982 (Director, Centre for Housing Research, since 1983); Economic Adviser to OECD, Paris, since 1981; b. 12.3.49, Glasgow; m., Ruth Hunter Liddell; 1 s.; 1 d. Educ. Allan Glen's Secondary School; Glasgow University. Lecturer in Applied Economics, Glasgow University, 1974-76; Lecturer in Political Economy, Aberdeen University, 1976-78; Lecturer in Applied Economics, Glasgow University, 1979-82; part-time Consultant to Scottish Development Agency, The Housing Corporation, Scottish Office and Department of the Environment; Member, Glasgow Council for Single Homeless; Past President, Allan Glen's Rugby Club. Recreations: playing rugby (slowly); watching television. Address: (b.) Centre for Housing Research, 53 Southpark Avenue, Glasgow; T.-041-339 8855.

MacLennan, Graeme Andrew Yule, CA. Managing Director, Edinburgh Fund Managers PLC, since 1983; b. 24.8.42, Glasgow; m., Diane; 2 s.; 2 d. Educ. Kelvinside Academy, Glasgow. Joined Edinburgh Fund Managers, 1970; Director: Crescent Japan Investment Trust PLC, EFM Unit Trust Managers Ltd., New Australia Investment Trust PLC, New Tokyo Investment Trust PLC, Sydney Fund Managers Ltd. Recreations: hill-walking; angling. Address: (b.) 4 Melville Crescent, Edinburgh, EH3 7JB; T.-031-226 4931.

Maclennan, Robert. MP (SDP), Caithness and Sutherland, since 1981, (Labour), 1966-81; Barrister-at-Law; b. 26.6.36. Educ. Glasgow Academy; Balliol College, Oxford; Trinity College, Cambridge; Columbia University, New York. Parliamentary Under Secretary of State, Department of Prices and Consumer Protection, 1974-79; Opposition Spokesman on Foreign Affairs, 1980-81.

MacLennan of MacLennan, Ronald George. 34th Chief of Clan MacLennan; b. 7.2.25; m., Margaret MacLennan; 1 s.; 2 d. Educ. Boroughmuir Secondary School, Edinburgh; University of Copenhagen. Teacher and Lecturer in Physical Education, 1949-82; Chairman, Kintail Museum Company, since 1983. Address: (h.) The Old Mill, Dores, Inverness.

MacLennan, William Jardine, MD, FRCP, FRCPEdin, FRCPGlas. Reader in Geriatric Medicine, Dundee University, since 1984; Honorary Consultant Physician in Geriatric Medicine, Tayside Health Board, since 1980; b. 11.2.41, Glasgow; m., Fiona Hannah Campbell; 2 s. Educ. Hutchesons' Boys' Grammar School; Glasgow University. House Physician, Stobhill Hospital, Glasgow, 1964; Hansen Research Scholar, then Assistant Lecturer, then Lecturer, Department of Materia Medica, Glasgow University, 1965-69; Senior Registrar in Geriatric Medicine, Stobhill General Hospital and Glasgow Western Infirmary, 1969-71; Senior Lecturer in Geriatric Medicine: Southampton University, 1971-80, Dundee University, 1980-84. Publications: books on clinical care of the elderly, drugs in the elderly and bone disease in the elderly. Recreations: hill-walking; ship-modelling; playing classical guitar badly. Address: (h.) 18 Strathisla Road, West Ferry, Dundee, DD5 1QA; T.-Dundee 78956.

McLeod, Alistair. Manager, Airdrieonians Football Club; Publican; b. 26.2.31, Glasgow; m., Faye; 2 s.; 1 d. Educ. Queen's Park School. Played football for Queen's Park School, Scottish Schools, Third Lanark, St. Mirren, Blackburn, Hibernian, Ayr United; Manager, Ayr United, Aberdeen, Scotland, Ayr United, Motherwell; led Scotland in World Cup, Argentina.

Macleod, Rev. Allan. Minister, Free Church of Scotland, at Sleat; b. 8.2.22, Brue, Barvas; m., Peggy Mackay; 1 s.; 2 d. Educ. Barvas School, Lewis; Aberdeen University; Free Church College, Edinburgh. War service, RN Fleet Air Arm Branch. Recreations: reading; fishing. Address: Free Church Manse, Sleat, Isle of Skye.

MacLeod, Angus, CBE (1967), MA, LLB. Honorary Sheriff, Edinburgh, since 1972; b. 2.4.06, Glasgow; m., Jane Winifred Walker (deceased); 3 s. Educ. Hutchesons' Boys' Grammar School, Glasgow; Glasgow University. Qualified Assistant in Legal Practice, Glasgow, 1929-34; Procurator Fiscal Service, 1934-71; Depute Fiscal at Dunfermline, Glasgow, Edinburgh; Senior Depute, Edinburgh, 1934-42; Procurator Fiscal: Dumfries, 1942-52, Aberdeen, 1952-55, Edinburgh, 1955-71; Temporary Sheriff, 1973-77; Chairman, VAT Appeals Tribunal, 1974-77; co-opted Member, Council, Law Society of Scotland, 1967-73; Member, Grant Committee on the Sheriff Court, 1963-67. Recreations: reading; walking. Address: (h.) 7 Oxford Terrace, Edinburgh, EH4 1PX; T.-031-332 5466.

MacLeod, Bobby, JP. Musician and Hotelier; b. 8.5.25, Tobermory; m., Jean MacCulloch; 3 s.; 1 d. Educ. Tobermory; Aberdeen. RAF, wartime; Musician and Broadcaster, since 1948; Gold Medal, National Accordeon Organisation, 1957; Honorary Life Member, Glasgow Society of Musicians; Provost of Tobermory, 1963-75; Member, Argyll County Council, 1963-75; Member, Rates Appeal Tribunal, since 1979. Recreations: boating; sailing. Address: (h.) Royal Building, Tobermory; T.-0688 2009.

Macleod, Rev. Professor Donald, MA. Professor of Systematic Theology, Free Church College, since 1978; Editor, The Monthly Record, since

1977; Vagrant Preacher, since 1978; b. 24.11.40, Ness, Isle of Lewis; m., Mary Maclean; 3 s. Educ. Nicolson Institute, Stornoway; Glasgow University; Free Church College. Ordained Guy Fawkes Day, 1964; Minister: Kilmallie Free Church, 1964-70, Partick Highland Free Church, Glasgow, 1970-78. Member, Scottish Religious Advisory Commitee, BBC. Recreations: dreaming about cricket, fishing and gardening; Gaelic music. Address: (h.) 84 Craiglea Drive, Edinburgh; T.-031-447 6269.

MacLeod, Donald Ian Kerr, RD*, MA, LLB, WS. Partner, Shepherd & Wedderburn, WS, since 1964; b. 19.4.37, Edinburgh; m., Mary St. Clair Bridge; 1 s.; 2 d. Educ. Aberdeen Grammar School; Aberdeen University; Edinburgh University. Apprentice, MacPherson & Mackay, WS, 1957-60; Assistant, Shepherd & Wedderburn, 1960-64; Solicitor in Scotland to HM Customs and Excise, Department of Employment and Health and Safety Executive, since 1974. Lt.-Cdr., Royal Naval Reserve; Church Elder. Recreations: hockey (Class 1 international umpire); golf. Address: (b.) 16 Charlotte Square, Edinburgh, EH2 4YS; T.-031-225 8585.

MacLeod, Donald Roderick, LLB. Advocate, since 1978; b. 24.9.48, Inverness; m., Susan Mary Fulton; 2 d. Educ. High School of Stirling; Glasgow University. Admitted Solicitor, 1973; called to Scottish Bar, 1978; Member, Scottish Executive Council, Labour Party, 1976-77-79; Labour candidate, Kinross and West Perthshire, 1979. Recreations: angling; hill-walking; music. Address: (h.) 22 Hermitage Gardens, Edinburgh; T.-031-447 8367.

MacLeod, Duncan James, CA. Partner, Ernst & Whinney, Glasgow, since 1960; b. 1.11.34, Edinburgh; m., Joanna Bibby; 2 s.; 1 d. Educ. Eton College. Qualified CA, 1958; Partner, Brown Fleming & Murray, 1960; Director: Bank of Scotland, since 1973, Scottish Provident Institution, since 1975, Weir Group Plc, since 1979; Member, Scottish Industrial Development Advisory Board, 1980; Member, Scottish Tertiary Education Advisory Council, 1984. Chief, Glasgow Skye Association. Recreations: golf; shooting. Address: (b.) Savoy Tower, 77 Renfrew Street, Glasgow; T.-041-333 9699.

MacLeod of Fuinary, Baron, (Very Rev. George Fielden MacLeod), Bt, MC, BA, DD. Life Peer; Moderator, General Assembly of the Church of Scotland, 1957-58; b. 17.6.95; m., Lorna Helen Janet Macleod (deceased); 2 s.; 1 d. Educ. Winchester; Oriel College, Oxford; Edinburgh University; Union Theological College, New York. Served First World War (Captain, Argyll and Sutherland Highlanders); Collegiate Minister, St. Cuthbert's Parish Church, Edinburgh, 1926-30; Minister, Govan Parish Church, Glasgow, 1930-38; Founder, Iona Community (Leader, 1938-67); Rector, Glasgow University, 1968-71. Address: (h.) 23 Learmonth Terrace, Edinburgh.

MacLeod, Professor Iain Alasdair, BSc, PhD, CEng, FICE, FIStructE. Professor of Structural Engineering, Strathclyde University, since 1981;

b. 4.5.39, Glasgow; m., Barbara Jean Booth; 1 s.; 1 d. Educ. Lenzie Academy; Glasgow University. Design Engineer, Crouch and Hogg, Glasgow, 1960-62; Assistant Lecturer in Civil Engineering, Glasgow University, 1962-66; Design Engineer, H.A. Simons Ltd., Vancouver, 1966-67; Structural Engineer, Portland Cement Association, Illinois, 1968-69; Lecturer in Civil Engineering, Glasgow University, 1969-73; Professor and Head, Department of Civil Engineering, Paisley College of Technology, 1973-81; Chairman, Scottish Branch, Institution of Structural Engineers, 1985-86. Recreations: climbing; sailing. Address: (b.) Department of Civil Engineering, Strathclyde University, George Street, Glasgow; T.-041-552 4400.

McLeod, John, ARAM, FTCL, LRAM, ARCM, LTCL. Composer, Conductor and Lecturer; Visiting Lecturer, Royal Scottish Academy of Music and Drama; b. 8.3.34, Aberdeen; m., Margaret Murray; 1 s.; 1 d. Educ. Aberdeen Grammar School; Royal Academy of Music, London. Director of Music, Merchiston Castle School, 1974-85; Guest Conductor: Scottish National Orchestra, Scottish Chamber Orchestra, BBC Scottish Symphony Orchestra; Associate Composer, Scottish Chamber Orchestra, 1980-82; Guinness Prize for British Composers, 1979; Radio Forth Award for Composition, 1981; UK Music Education Award, 1982. Recreations: reading; films; theatre; art galleries; walking. Address: (h.) 31 East Trinity Road, Edinburgh, EH5 3DL; T.-031-552 5644.

MacLeod of MacLeod, John. 29th Chief of Clan MacLeod; b. 10.8.35; m., Melita Kolin; 1 s.; 1 d. Educ. Eton. Address: (h.) Dunvegan Castle, Isle of Skye.

Macleod, Rev. John, MA. Minister, Free Church of Scotland congregation of Duthil-Dores, since 1983; b. 1.1.39, Shawbost, Isle of Lewis; m., Mary Macarthur. Educ. Nicolson Institute, Stornoway; Aberdeen University; Aberdeen College of Education. Torry Academy, Aberdeen: Assistant Teacher of General Subjects, 1961-66, Principal Teacher of Modern Studies, 1966-80. Recreations: gardening; local history. Address: Free Church Manse, Tomatin, Inverness-shire; T.-08 082 294.

MacLeod, Rev. John, MA, DipTh. Minister, Tarbat Free Church of Scotland, Portmahomack, since 1978; b. 14.5.48, Fearn; m., Veda Joy Morrison; 3 s.; 1 d. Educ. Tain Royal Academy; Aberdeen University; Free Church College, Edinburgh. Standard Life Assurance Co., 1969-71; Free Church Missioner to Students, Aberdeen, 1974-75; Preacher, Highland Church, Vancouver, 1976; Preacher, Free Church of Scotland Western Charge, Prince Edward Island, 1977-78; Convener, Psalmody Committee, Free Church of Scotland, 1982-84; Chairman, Moray Firth Radio Christian Council, since 1983. Recreation: family. Address: Free Church Manse, Portmahomack, Tain, Ross-shire, IV20 1YL; T.-086287 467.

MacLeod, John Alexander. Commissioner of Northern Lighthouses, since 1977; b. 31.10.19, Isle of Skye; m., Agnes Campbell Gillespie; 1 s.;

1 d. Educ. Knockbreck Public School; Glasgow Technical College. Merchant Navy career (through the ranks to command), followed by appointment to Marine Superintendent; retired, since 1976. Recreations: gardening; local history. Address: (h.) Halistra, Waternish, Isle of Skye; T.-047 083 206.

Macleod, John Francis Matheson, MA, LLB, NP. Chairman, Crofters Commission, since 1978; Solicitor in Inverness, since 1959; b. 24.1.32, Inverness; m., Alexandra Catherine; 1 s. Educ. Inverness Royal Academy; George Watson's College; Edinburgh University. Solicitor, Fife County Council, 1957-59; in private practice, since 1959; Parliamentary candidate (Liberal): Moray and Nairn, 1964, Western Isles, 1966; Chairman, Highland Region, Scottish Liberal Party, until 1978; former Vice-Chairman, Broadcasting Council for Scotland. Address: (b.) Castle Wynd, Inverness; T.-0463 237231.

MacLeod, John Harvey Aitken, MA (Hons). Rector, Wick High School, since 1977; b. 4.3.36, Vila, New Hebrides; m., Lydia A.W.C. McFarlane; 2 s.; 2 d. Educ. Hamilton Academy; Glasgow University. Taught History and Geography, Kalonga Secondary School, Zambia; Principal Teacher of Geography, Portree High School, Skye; various teaching posts in Fife, latterly as Assistant Rector, Queen Anne High School, Dunfermline; Depute Rector, Oban High School, 1975. Executive Member, Highland Headteachers Association; Lay Preacher. Recreations: photography; music. Address: (h.) Norlands, Ulbster, by Wick, KW2 6AA; T.-Thrumster 265.

MacLeod, Emeritus Professor Malcolm, MD (Hons), FRCPEdin. Professor, Emeritus, in Renal Medicine, Aberdeen University; b. 9.12.16, Glasgow; m., Elizabeth Shaw Ritchie; 1 s. Educ. Nicolson Institute, Stornoway; Aberdeen University. Military Service, Africa, India, SE Asia, 1940-46 (Medical Specialist, RAMC); Lecturer, Senior Lecturer, Reader in Medicine, 1947-80; Personal Professor in Renal Medicine, Aberdeen University, 1981; Honorary Consultant Physician, Aberdeen Royal Infirmary, 1955-82 and Honorary Consultant in charge, Medical Renal Unit, 1966-82; President, Scottish Society of Physicians, 1980. Recreations: natural history; salmon fishing. Address: (h.) 76 Hamilton Place, Aberdeen, AB2 4BA; T.-0224 635537.

MacLeod, Mary, RGN, SCM. Member, Argyll and Clyde Health Board; Assistant Director of Nursing Services, Dumbarton, since 1984; b. 24.10.29, Detroit. Educ. Carloway Public School, Lewis; Nicolson Institute, Stornoway. RGN training, Glasgow Royal Infirmary; SCM training, Part I, Simpson Memorial Maternity Pavilion, Edinburgh, Part II, Glasgow Royal Maternity Hospital; Queen's Nurse and Health Visitor training, Glasgow; District Nurse, Glasgow; Health Visitor, Glasgow and Renfrew; Nursing Officer, then Senior Nursing Officer, Renfrew District. Chairwoman, Paisley and District Branch, Multiple Sclerosis Society; Chairwoman, Steering Committee, Crossroads (Scotland) Care Attendant Scheme, Renfrew

District; Member, National Council, Scottish Association of Nurse Administrators; Member of Committee, Benevolent Fund for Nurses in Scotland; Member, Nurses League Committee, Glasgow Royal Infirmary. Recreations: reading; gardening; cooking; baking; knitting. Address: (h.) 15 Newmains Road, Renfrew, PA4 8LH; T.-041-886 6197.

Macleod, Rev. Murdo Alexander, MA. Minister, Stornoway Free Church, since 1984; Moderator, Lewis Presbytery, Free Church of Scotland, since 1984; b. 15.10.35, Stornoway; m., Annie Bella Nicolson; 5 s.; 1 d. Educ. Nicolson Institute, Stornoway; Aberdeen University; Free Church College. Minister: Drumchapel Free Church, Glasgow, 1966-72, Dingwall Free Church, 1972-78, Greyfriars, Inverness, 1978-84. Recreations: walking; talking. Address: Free Church Manse, Stornoway, Lewis; T.-Stornoway 2279.

Macleod, Murdoch, JP. General Manager, Secretary and Treasurer, Stornoway Pier and Harbour Commission, since 1975; Honorary Sheriff; b. 11.8.32, Shawbost, Isle of Lewis; m., Crisybil; 1 s.; 1 d. Educ. Nicolson Institute, Stornoway. Ross and Cromarty Council: Highways Department, 1955-57, Education Department, 1957-65; Stornoway Town Council: Town Clerk's Department, 1965-68, Town Clerk, 1968-75. Member, Transport Users Consultative Committee for Scotland; Past Chairman, District Courts Association; Chairman, Western Isles Justices Committee; Member, Western Isles Health Board; British Ports Association: Member, Small Ports Committee, Chairman, Scottish Small Port Members; Chairman: Western Isles Committee for Employment of Disabled Persons, Western Isles Arts Guild, Western Isles District of Scottish Community Drama Association; Vice-Chairman, Lewis Pipe Band; Member, British Airways Consumer Council for Highlands and Islands; Committee Member, League of Friends, County Hospital, Stornoway. Recreations: fair weather golf; reading. Address: (h.) 46 Barony Square, Stornoway, Isle of Lewis; T.-0851 3024.

MacLeod, Murdoch James, JP. Member, Skye and Lochalsh District Council, since 1984; Chairman, Raasay Community Council, since 1977; b. 1.7.18, Isle of Raasay; m., Daphne Pearl Palmer; 1 s.; 1 d. Educ. Portree High School. Wartime Service, Royal Artillery, then in Special Investigation Branch, Royal Military Police (demobilised, 1947, with rank of Company Sergeant Major); served in Inverness-shire Constabulary, 1939-69, retiring with rank of Detective Inspector; worked in industrial security until 1972; returned to Isle of Raasay. Recreation: spectator sports. Address: (h.) 5 Clachan, Raasay, by Kyle, Ross-shire, IV40 8PB; T.-Raasay 242.

MacLeod, Rev. Norman. Minister, Orwell with Portmoak, since 1978; Clerk, Perth Presbytery, since 1984; b. 4.10.28, Prestonpans; m., Margaret Lindores; 1 s.; 1 d. Educ. Musselburgh Grammar School; Royal High School, Edinburgh; New College, Edinburgh. Minister: Armadale East, 1960-65, Glenrothes St. Ninian's, 1965-78. Recreations: trying to maintain a large manse garden; travelling. Address: 3 Perth Road, Milnathort, Kinross, KY13 7XU; T.-Kinross 63461.

Macleod, Sheriff Norman Donald, MA, LLB. Sheriff of Glasgow and Strathkelvin, since 1967; b. 6.3.32; m.; 2 s.; 2 d. Educ. Mill Hill School; George Watson's College; Edinburgh University; Hertford College, Oxford. Advocate, 1956; Colonial Administrative Service, Tanganyika, 1957-64; practised, Scots Bar, 1964-67.

MacLeod, Rev. Roderick, MA (Hons), BD, PhD, JP. Minister, Cumlodden and Lochfyneside, Argyll, since 1985; b. 24.6.41, Lochmaddy. Educ. Paible Secondary School; Portree High School; Edinburgh University. Minister, Bernerary, North Uist, 1966-85; Member: Western Isles Islands Council, 1974-82, Western Isles Health Board, 1975-79; Clerk, Uist Presbytery, since 1981; Mackinnon Memorial Lecturer, Cape Breton College, 1979; Visiting Scholar, Harvard Divinity School, 1981; Editor, Gaelic Supplement, Life and Work, since 1980; Founder, Cruisgean (Gaelic newspaper); author of several Gaelic books; writes and broadcasts on Highland affairs in Gaelic and English. Recreations: walking; reading.

MacLeod, Rev. William, BSc, ThM. Minister, Partick Free Church, since 1976; b. 2.11.51, Stornoway; m., Marion Johnston; 1 s. Educ. Nicolson Institute; Aberdeen University; Free Church College; Westminster Theological Seminary, USA. Chaplain to Free Church Eventide Home, 1976-79; Free Church Lecturer in Religious Studies, Jordanhill College of Education, 1977-83; Exit Examiner in Theology, Free Church College, since 1981; Moderator, Glasgow Presbytery, Free Church, 1983-84; Chairman, Lord's Day Observance Society, Glasgow Branch, since 1979; Convener, Church Extension Committee, Free Church, 1984-85. Recreations: reading; gardening; angling. Address: 64 Woodend Drive, Glasgow; T.-041-959 5648.

McLetchie, David William, LLB (Hons), WS. Solicitor; Partner, Tods Murray & Jamieson, WS, since 1980; b. 6.8.52, Edinburgh; m., Barbara Gemmell Baillie; 1 s. Educ. George Heriot's School; Leith Academy; Edinburgh University. Legal apprenticeship, Shepherd & Wedderburn, WS, 1974-76; Solicitor, Tods Murray & Jamieson, WS, 1976-80. Parliamentary candidate (Conservative), Edinburgh Central, 1979; Chairman, Edinburgh Central Conservative Association, since 1982. Recreations: golf; watching Heart of Midlothian FC. Address: (h.) 21 Queen's Avenue, Edinburgh, EH4 2DG; T.-031-332 4691.

McLoone, John, BSc, CChem, MRSC. Headteacher, St. Cuthbert's High School, Johnstone, since 1972; b. 14.7.33, Greenock; m., Francisca Albert Rico; 2 s.; 2 d. Educ. St. Columba's High School, Greenock; Glasgow University. Teacher of Science, St. Columba's High School, Greenock, 1957-65; St. Aelred's High School, Paisley: Principal Teacher of Science, 1965-70, Assistant Headteacher, 1970-72. Recreations: bridge; bowls; photography; gardening; reading. Address: (h.) Beechwood, 24 Broomberry Drive, Gourock, Renfrewshire; T.-Gourock 34691.

McLusky, Donald S., BSc, PhD. Senior Lecturer in Biology, Stirling University, since 1977 (Head, Department of Biological Science, since 1985); b.

27.6.45, Harrogate; m., Ruth Alicia Donald; 1 s.; 2 d. Educ. Latymer Upper School, London; Aberdeen University; Stirling University. Stirling University: Assistant Lecturer, 1968-70, Lecturer, 1970-77; Council Member, Scottish Marine Biological Association, 1976-82 and since 1985. Publications: Ecology of Estuaries, 1971; Physiology and Behaviour of Marine Organisms, 1977; The Estuarine Ecosystem, 1981. Recreations: walking; enjoying the countryside. Address: (h.) 6 Larch Crescent, Doune, Perthshire; T.-0786 841843.

McMahon, Hugh Robertson, MA (Hons). Member (Labour), European Parliament, Strathclyde West, since 1984; b. 17.6.38. Educ. Glasgow University; Jordanhill College. Former teacher.

McMahon, Rt. Rev. Mgr. James. Parish Priest, St. Paul's, Whiteinch, Glasgow, since 1981; Prelate of Honour to Pope John Paul II, since 1980; b. 8.11.21, Paisley. Educ. St. Mirin's Academy, Paisley; Blairs College, Aberdeen; St. Peter's College, Glasgow. Assistant Priest, St. Saviour's, Govan, 1946-57; Spiritual Director, St. Peter's College, 1957-69; Assistant Priest, St. Andrew's Cathedral, Glasgow, 1969-70; Parish Priest, St. John of the Cross, Twechar, Kilsyth, 1970-72; Rector, St. Peter's College, 1972-81; Member, Liturgical Commission, Archdiocese of Glasgow; Vicar Episcopal for Liturgy, Archdiocese of Glasgow, 1979-82. Recreations: golf; swimming; televised sports; reading. Address: St. Paul's Presbytery, 1213 Dumbarton Road, Glasgow, G14 9UP; T.-041-959 1122.

McMahon, Rev. Robert James, BD. Minister, Crossford with Kirkfieldbank, since 1976; b. 28.1.27, Glasgow; m., Jessie Millar Steele; 3 s.; 3 d. Educ. Strathbungo School; Glasgow University. Journalist, Glasgow, 1943-56; student, 1953-59; ordained by Glasgow Presbytery, 1959; Missionary, Church of Scotland, Seoni, Central India, 1960-76 (Minister, United Church of Northern India and from 1970 of the Church of North India). Moderator, Lanark Presbytery, 1982. Publication: To God Be The Glory (account of the Evangelical Fellowship of India 1951-1971). Address: The Manse, Crossford, Carluke, ML8 5RE; T.-055-586 415.

McManus, John, BSc, ARCS, PhD, DIC, FRSE, FGS, MIGeol, MIEnvSci. Reader in Geology, Dundee University, since 1980; Honorary Director, Tay Estuary Research Centre, since 1979; b. 5.6.38, Harwich; m., J. Barbara Beveridge; 2 s.; 1 d. Educ. Harwich County High School; Imperial College, London University. Assistant, then Lecturer, St. Andrews University, 1964-67; Lecturer, then Senior Lecturer, Dundee University, 1967-80; UNESCO Representative, International Commission on Continental Erosion, 1980-84; Consultant on Coastal Erosion and Protection to four Regional Councils; Associate Editor, Continental Shelf Research. President: Cupar Choral Association, 1968-78, Cupar Amateur Opera, since 1978. Recreations: music; bird watching; swimming; stamp collecting. Address: (b.) Department of Geology, The University, Dundee, DD1 4HN; T.-0382 23181.

McMillan, Alan Austen. Solicitor to the Secretary of State for Scotland, since 1984; b. 19.1.26, Ayr; m., Margaret Forbes Park Moncur; 2 s.; 2 d. Educ. Ayr Grammar School; Ayr Academy; Glasgow University. Army, 1944-47; qualified as Solicitor, 1949; Legal/Administrative Assistant, Ayr Town Council, 1949-55; Scottish Office: Legal Assistant, 1955-62, Senior Legal Assistant, 1962-68, Assistant Solicitor, 1968-82, seconded to Cabinet Office Constitution Unit, 1977-78, Deputy Solicitor, 1982-84. Recreations: reading; music; theatre; hill-walking. Address: (b.) New St. Andrews House, Edinburgh; T.-031-556 8400.

MacMillan, Professor Andrew, MA, FRIAS, RIBA, ARSA. Principal, Gillespie Kidd & Coia, Architects, since 1966; Professor of Architecture and Head, Mackintosh School of Architecture, Glasgow University, since 1973; Vice President (Education), Royal Institute of British Architects; b. 11.12.28, Glasgow; m., Angela Lillian McDowell; 1 s.; 3 d. Educ. North Kelvinside Secondary School; Glasgow School of Architecture. Glasgow Corporation, 1945-52; East Kilbride Development Corporation, 1952-54; joined Gillespie Kidd & Coia, 1954 (Partner, 1966); has served as a Member of: CNAA Architecture Board, ARCUK Board of Architectural Education, Scottish Arts Council, GIA Education Committee; Vice-President for Education, RIBA; Vice-President, Prince and Princess of Wales Hospice, 1981; RIBA Bronze Medal, 1965; RIBA Award for Architecture, four times; RSA Gold Medal, 1975; Concrete Society Award, 1978; Carpenter Award, 1982, 1983; various Saltire Society and Civic Trust awards; Member, Forum, Scottish Churches Architectural Heritage Trust. Recreations: travel; sailing; water colour. Address: (b.) Mackintosh School of Architecture, Glasgow University and Glasgow School of Art, 177 Renfrew Street, Glasgow, G3 6RQ; T.-041-332 9797.

Macmillan, Rev. Gilleasbuig Iain, MA, BD. Minister, St. Giles', The High Kirk of Edinburgh, since 1973; Chaplain to The Queen in Scotland, since 1979; b. 21.12.42; m.; 1 d. Educ. Oban High School; Edinburgh University. Minister, Portree, 1969-73.

MacMillan, General Sir Gordon Holmes Alexander, KCB, KCVO, CBE, DSO, MC (two bars), LLD, DL. Chief of the Clan MacMillan; b. 7.1.97, Nabangalore, British India; m., Marian Blakiston-Houston, OBE; 4 s.; 1 d. Educ. St. Edmund's School, Canterbury, Kent; Royal Military College, Sandhurst. Colonel, Argyll and Sutherland Highlanders, 1945-58; General Officer, C-in-C, Scottish Command, and Governor of Edinburgh Castle, 1949-52; Governor and C-in-C of Gibraltar, 1952-55; Chairman, Cumbernauld Development Corporation, 1956-65; Chairman, Greenock Harbour Trust, 1955-65; Member, Queen's Bodyguard for Scotland (Royal Company of Archers). Address: (h.) Finlaystone, Langbank, Renfrewshire, PA14 6TJ.

MacMillan, Hector. Playwright; b. 1929, Glasgow. Author of: The Rising, Dundee Repertory Theatre, 1973; The Sash, Pool Theatre, Edinburgh, 1973; The Royal Visit, Dundee Repertory, 1974; The Gay Gorbals, Traverse, Edinburgh, 1976; Oh What A Lovely Peace, Scottish Youth Theatre, Edinburgh, 1977; Past Chairman, Scottish Society of Playwrights.

Macmillan, Sheriff Iain Alexander, CBE, LLD, BL. Sheriff of South Strathclyde, Dumfries and Galloway, at Hamilton, since 1981; b. 14.11.23, Oban; m., Edith Janet McAulay; 2 s.; 1 d. Educ. Oban High School; Glasgow University; Scottish Commercial College. RAF (France, Germany, India), 1944-47; Solicitor (Sturrock & Co., Kilmarnock), 1952-81; Council Member, Law Society of Scotland, 1964-79 (President, 1976-77); Member: Scottish Council on Crime, 1972-75, General Teaching Council, 1978-81, Ayrshire and Arran Health Board, 1980-81. President, Kilmarnock Rotary Club, 1979-80. Recreations: golf; hill-walking; photography; music. Address: (h.) 2 Castle Drive, Kilmarnock, Ayrshire; T.-0698 282957.

Macmillan, Ian, BSc (Hons), MEd (Hons), DPA. Rector, Bellahouston Academy, since 1973; b. 6.4.31, Glasgow; 2 d. Educ. Albert Secondary School; Glasgow University; Jordanhill College of Education. Balornock Primary School, 1954; Royal Artillery, 1954-56; Albert Secondary School, 1956-62; Victoria Drive Secondary School, 1962-73. ESU Scholar to USA, 1960. Recreations: skiing; swimming. Address: (h.) 13 Naseby Avenue, Naseby Park, Broomhill, Glasgow, G11 7JQ; T.-041-339 9087.

McMillan, James. Member, Argyll and Bute District Council, since 1977; Member, Strathclyde Regional Council, since 1974; b. 20.10.29, Rothesay; m., Christian E.; 1 s. Educ. Rothesay Academy. Elected to Rothesay Town Council, 1958; Treasurer, 1961; Provost of Rothesay, 1964 (re-elected, 1967); Convener, Bute County Council, 1970-73. Recreations: watching sport; relaxing. Address: (h.) 4 Battery Place, Rothesay, PA20 9DH; T.-0700 2755.

Macmillan, (John) Duncan, MA, PhD. Senior Lecturer, Department of Fine Art, Edinburgh University, since 1981; Curator, Talbot Rice Art Centre, Edinburgh University, since 1979; b. 7.3.39, Beaconsfield; m., Vivien Rosemary Hinkley; 2 d. Educ. Gordonstoun School; St. Andrews University; London University; Edinburgh University. Lecturer, Department of Fine Art, Edinburgh University, 1964-81; Chairman, Scottish Society for Art History; Trustee, Scottish Sculpture Trust. Recreation: making things. Address: (h.) 20 Nelson Street, Edinburgh; T.-031-556 7100.

MacMillan, John MacFarlane Bute, MC. Chairman, Edinburgh Venture Enterprise Trust (EVENT), since 1982; Chairman, Design Plus Interiors Ltd.; Director, The Murrayfield PLC; b. 12.8.17, Rothesay; m., Rosaline Daphne May Spencer; 1 s.; 1 d. Educ. Allan Glen's School, Glasgow; Edinburgh University. Regular Army Officer, Royal Artillery, 1939-57; General Manager, then Managing Director, D.S. Crawford Ltd., 1958-62; Director, United Biscuits (Holdings) Ltd., 1962-82; Chairman, D.S. Crawford

Ltd., 1979-82; Chairman, UB Restaurants Ltd., 1979-82. Recreations: bird-watching; walking; swimming; tennis. Address: (h.) 24 Cammo Gardens, Edinburgh, EH4 8EQ; T.-031-226 5783.

McMillan, Joyce Margaret, MA (Hons), DipEd. Arts Journalist and Theatre Critic; Radio Critic, Glasgow Herald, since 1983; Scottish Theatre Critic, The Guardian, since 1984; b. 29.8.52, Paisley. Educ. Paisley Grammar School; St. Andrews University; Edinburgh University. Theatre Reviewer, BBC Radio Scotland and The Scotsman, 1979-81; Theatre Critic, Sunday Standard, 1981-83. Secretary, NUJ Freelance Branch, Edinburgh. Recreations: food; drink; films; music; talking politics; playing with babies. Address: 8 East London Street, Edinburgh, EH7 4BH; T.-031-557 1726.

Macmillan, Marie Alpine, JP. Chairman, Western Isles Health Board, since 1980; Member, Western Isles Islands Council, since 1978; b. 26.4.24, Stornoway; m., Ian M. Macmillan, LDS, RFPS; 1 s.; 1 d. Educ. Hyndland School, Glasgow; West of Scotland Commercial College, Glasgow. Chairman: Electricity Consultative Committee, North of Scotland District; Member: Supplementary Benefit Appeals Tribunal, National Insurance Appeals Tribunal, Pier and Harbour Commission, Justices Committee, Police Committee, Fire Board. Recreations: reading; sewing; golf. Address: (h.) 22 Matheson Road, Stornoway, Isle of Lewis; T.-0851 2760.

McMillan, Michael Dale, BSc, LLB, NP. Senior Partner, Sergeants, Solicitors, East Kilbride, since 1978 (Partner, since 1971); Partner, Macdonalds, Solicitors, Glasgow, since 1978; b. 15.2.44, Edinburgh; m., Isobel Ross Mackie; 2 s.; 1 d. Educ. Edinburgh Academy; Edinburgh University. Secretary: East Kilbride Chamber of Commerce, since 1971, East Kilbride Chamber of Trade, since 1971; Member, East Kilbride Development Corporation, 1979-84. Captain, East Kilbride Golf Club, 1979. Recreations: golf; sailing. Address: (h.) Bonnanhill House, Sandford, Strathaven, Lanarkshire; T.-Strathaven 21210.

McMillan, Russell Alexander, LDS, RFPS. Dental Practitioner, since 1947; part-time Visiting Surgeon, Glasgow Dental Hospital, 1971-85; b. 20.10.20, Dumbarton; m., Mary MacMaster Walker; 2 d. Educ. Dumbarton Academy; Anderson College of Medicine; St. Mungo's College of Medicine; Glasgow Dental Hospital and School. Surgeon Lt. (D), RNVR, 1943-46; Dental Officer, London County Council, 1946-47. Past President, Glasgow Odontological Society. Recreations: painting; golf; gardening; ornithology. Address: (h.) 13A Kirklee Circus, Glasgow, G12 OTW; T.-041-334 5663.

Macmillan, Rev. William Boyd Robertson, MA, BD. Minister, Dundee Parish Church (St. Mary's), since 1978; Convener, Board of Practice and Procedure, since 1984, and of Business Committee, since 1985, General Assembly, Church of Scotland; b. 3.7.27, Keith; m., Mary Adams Bisset Murray. Educ. Royal High School, Edinburgh; Aberdeen University. Royal Navy, 1946-48; Aberdeen University, 1948-54 (President, SRC, 1953-54); Minister: St. Andrew's Church, Bo'ness, 1955-60, Fyvie Parish Church, 1960-67, Bearsden South Church, 1967-78. President, Church Service Society; Chaplain, City of Dundee District Council. Recreations: golf; reading. Address: Manse of Dundee, 371 Blackness Road, Dundee, DD2 1ST; T.-0382 69406.

McMurray, Donald Brown. Director and Harbour Master, Clyde Port Authority, since 1985; Director, Ardrossan Harbour Company Ltd., since 1984; Director, Pilotage Authority, since 1983; b. 16.12.32, Glasgow; m., Joan Tulloch; 2 s. Educ. Hyndland Senior Secondary School; Royal College of Technology and Science. Career in Merchant Navy to rank of Master, 1949-68; Clyde Port Authority: Port Control Officer, 1968-71, Depute Harbour Master, 1971-83. Member, Marine Committee, British Ports Association; Member, PSEC Committee, International Ports Association. Recreation: sailing. Address: (b.) Clyde Port Authority, 16 Robertson Street, Glasgow, G2 8DS; T.-041-221 88733.

Macnab of Macnab, Hon. Diana Mary. Chairman, Scotland's Gardens Scheme, since 1983; b. 6.6.36, Edinburgh; m., J.C. Macnab of Macnab (qv); 2 s.; 2 d. Address: (h.) Finlarig, Killin, Perthshire, FK21 8TN; T.-Killin 259.

Macnab of Macnab, James Charles, JP. Executive, Hill Samuel Investment Services Ltd., since 1982; 23rd Chief, Clan Macnab; b. 14.4.26, London; m., Hon. Diana Mary Anstruther-Gray (see Hon. Diana Mary Macnab of Macnab); 2 s.; 2 d. Educ. Radley College; Ashbury College, Ottawa. Served RAF, Scots Guards, Seaforth Highlanders, 1944-48; gazetted Officer, Royal Federation of Malaya Police Force, 1948-57; managed family estate and farms, 1957-82; former County Councillor, Perth; Member, Central Regional Council, 1978-82; Member, Queen's Bodyguard for Scotland (Royal Company of Archers). Address: (h.) Finlarig, Killin, Perthshire, FK21 8TN; T.-Killin 259.

McNab, John Robert, FRICS. Regional Assessor, Electoral Registration Officer and Estates Officer, Tayside Regional Council, since 1982; b. 17.3.27, Dundee; m., Margaret Davidson; 1 s.; 1 d. Educ. Grove Academy. RAF, 1945-48; qualified as Surveyor, 1954, after training with Lickley Proctor & Burnett, Dundee; Divisional Surveyor to Edinburgh Assessor, 1954-57; County Assessor: Moray and Nairn, 1957-68, Angus, 1968-75; Depute Assessor, Tayside, 1975. Recreations: climbing; gardening. Address: (b.) Tayside House, Crichton Street, Dundee, DD2 3RH; T.-Dundee 23281.

McNair, James Burt Oliver, BSc (Hons), DipEd. Headteacher, Waverley Secondary School, since 1976; b. 20.7.33, Bargeddie, Lanarkshire; m., Muriel Eadie; 1 s.; 2 d. Educ. Woodside Secondary School, Glasgow; Glasgow University. Taught, Gambia High School; Principal Teacher of Physics and Assistant Head, North Kelvinside Secondary School; Depute Head, John Street Secondary School; Chairman, SED Joint

Working Party on Social and Vocational Skills; Chairman, Drumchapel Citizens' Advice Bureau, 1981-84; Vice Chairman, Scripture Union - Scotland. Publication: Basic Knowledge Physics. Address: (b.) 120 Summerhill Road, Glasgow, G15 7LD; T.-041-944 1171.

Macnair, John Bennett, JP. Member, East Lothian District Council, since 1977; b. 28.6.25, Haltwhistle; m., D. Patricia Eldridge; 2 s.; 1 d. Educ. Edinburgh Academy; North Berwick High School; Trinity Academy; Edinburgh and East of Scotland College of Agriculture. Royal Navy, 1942-46. Member, North Berwick Town Council, 1964-75 (Provost, 1971-75); Member, East Lothian County Council, 1967-75 (Vice-Chairman, Education Committee, 1970-75). Vice Chairman, North Berwick Rugby Club; President, North Berwick British Legion; Chairman, North Berwick Boy Scout Executive; Past President, North Berwick Rotary Club. Recreations: shooting; boating; golf; working sheep dogs. Address: (h.) Gilsland, North Berwick, East Lothian.

McNaught, Peter Cairn, MA, MLitt, FRSA. Principal, Craigie College of Education, Ayr, since 1976; b. 29.5.25, Glasgow; m., Else Kristine Sandvad; 1 s.; 1 d. Educ. Hutchesons' Boys' Grammar School, Glasgow; Glasgow University. Teacher, Queen's Park and Hutchesons' Boys' Grammar Schools, Glasgow, 1952-58; Lecturer in English, Moray House College of Education, Edinburgh, 1958-60; Principal Lecturer in English, Aberdeen College of Education, 1960-61; Moray House College of Education: Principal Lecturer in Educational Methods and Senior Assistant Principal, 1961-70, Vice-Principal, 1970-75. Vice-Chairman, Scottish Council for the Validation of Courses for Teachers; Member, General Teaching Council for Scotland; Vice-Chairman, West Sound; Member, STV Staff Trust; United Kingdom Award, Council for Educational Technology, 1982. Recreations: swimming; walking; travel. Address: (b.) Craigie College of Education, Ayr, KA8 OSR; T.-0292 260321.

McNaughton, Professor Blyth, MSc, BSc (Hons), CEng, MIMechE, FInstPet. Professor and Head, School of Mechanical and Offshore Engineering, Robert Gordon's Institute of Technology, since 1971; b. 28.11.30, Crieff; m., Mary Victoria Johnston; 2 s.; 1 d. Educ. Bell-Baxter High School, Cupar; Strathclyde University; Birmingham University. Apprenticed, British Polar Engines, Glasgow; Research Engineer, British Polar Engines and Associated British Engineering, 1947-59; Lecturer and Senior Lecturer, University of Aston and Sunderland Technical College, 1959-66; joined Robert Gordon's Institute of Technology, 1966; Member, SERC Aeronautical and Mechanical Engineering Committee, 1975-78; Member, Petroleum Industry Training Board, 1976-82; Member, Offshore Petroleum Industry Board, since 1982; President, Aberdeen Mechanical Society, 1977-79; Member, CNAA Engineering Board, 1978-82; Member, Secretary of State for Energy Offshore Safety Inquiry, 1979-80. Recreations: golf; gardening; clock repair. Address: (b.) Schoolhill, Aberdeen, AB9 1FR; T.-0224 633611.

Macnaughton, Rev. Douglas Hogarth Hay, MA, BD, FSA Scot. Minister, Bearsden South Parish Church, since 1981; b. 4.6.30, Kilmacolm; m., Sheila Beatrice Kellie; 3 s. Educ. Glasgow Academy; Glasgow University. Ordained, 1956; Minister: Larbert West, 1956-61, Cadder, Bishopbriggs, 1961-73, Hamilton Old and Auchingramont, 1973-81; Convener, Education for the Ministry Committee, General Assembly, 1980-84; Vice-Convener, Board of Nomination to Church Chairs, since 1985; a Director, Church Selection School. Recreations: history; Scottish folk music. Address: 61 Drymen Road, Bearsden, Glasgow, G61 2SU; T.-041-942 0507.

Macnaughton, Edwin George, OBE, JP, MA (Hons). Honorary Sheriff; b. 9.5.02, Aberfeldy; m., Annie Meffan (deceased); 2 d. Educ. Breadalbane Academy; Glasgow University. Assistant Teacher: Airdrie Academy, 1923-27, Dalziel High School, 1927-30; Principal Teacher of Classics: Uddingston Grammar School, 1930-32, Airdrie Academy, 1932-44; Headmaster, St. John's Grammar School, Hamilton, 1944-50; Rector, Hamilton Academy, 1950-67. Joint Author: Approach to Latin series, 1938-53, A New Approach to Latin, I, 1973, II, 1974. Address: (h.) 1A Dunchattan Grove, Troon, Ayrshire; T.-0292 316877.

Macnaughton, James Douglas, BL. Chief Executive, Grampian Regional Council, since 1977; b. 15.12.31, Edinburgh; m., Inger-Marie; 2 s.; 1 d. Educ. Trinity Academy, Edinburgh; Edinburgh University. Colonial Police Service, 1954-62; Aberdeen County Council, 1962-75; Grampian Regional Council, since 1975. Recreations: varied. Address: (b.) Woodhill House, Ashgrove Road West, Aberdeen, AB9 2LU; T.-0224 682222, Ext. 2100.

Macnaughton, Rev. John Anderson, MA, BD. Minister, Hyndland Parish Church, since 1968; b. 30.4.21, London; m., Elizabeth Black Hamilton; 1 s.; 1 d. Educ. High School of Glasgow; Glasgow University. RAF Intelligence, India and Burma, 1941-45; Minister: St. Bride's Parish Church, Glasgow, 1949-57, Park Parish Church, Uddingston, 1957-68. Moderator, Glasgow Presbytery, 1981-82; President, Partick Burns Club, 1985-86. Recreations: golf; hill-walking; theatre-going. Address: Hyndland Manse, 70 Crown Road North, Glasgow, G12 9HW; T.-041-334 1002.

McNaughton, John Ewen, OBE, JP. Chairman, Scotch Quality Beef & Lamb Association, since 1981; Member, British Wool Marketing Board, since 1975; Member, Panel of Agricultural Arbiters, since 1973; Member, Red Deer Commission, since 1975; b. 28.5.33, Edinburgh; m., Jananne Ogilvie Honeyman; 2 s.; 2 d. Educ. Cargilfield; Loretto. Born and bred a hill sheep farmer; after a short spell in America, began farming at Inverlochlarig with father; served on Council, NFU of Scotland; Chairman, National Sheep Association; Council Member, Scottish Agricultural Arbiters Association. Elder, Church of Scotland. Recreations: yachting; stalking. Address: Inverlochlarig, Balquhidder, Lochearnhead, Perthshire, FK19 8PH; T.-087 74 232.

Macnaughton, Professor Malcolm Campbell, MD, FRCPGlas, FRCOG, FRSE. Professor of Obstetrics and Gynaecology, Glasgow University, since 1970; President, Royal College of Obstetricians and Gynaecologists, London, since 1984; b. 4.4.25, Glasgow; m., Margaret-Ann Galt; 2 s.; 3 d. Educ. Glasgow Academy; Glasgow University. RAMC, 1949-51; Lecturer in Obstetrics and Gynaecology, Aberdeen University, 1957-61; Senior Lecturer, St. Andrews University, 1961-66; Consultant, Eastern Regional, 1966-70. Member, Chief Scientist Committee, SHHD; Member, Biomedical Research Committee and Health Service Research Committee, SHHD; Member, MRC Grant Committee and Cell Systems Board, MRC; Member, Scientific Committee, Hospital Recognition Committee, RCOG; Chairman, Scottish Perinatal Mortality Advisory Group. Recreations: walking; fishing; sailing. Address: (h.) 15 Boclair Road, Bearsden, Glasgow, G61 2AF; T.-041-942 1909.

McNay, Rev. James Thomson. Minister, Maxwell Parish Church, Coatbridge, since 1976; Moderator, Hamilton Presbytery, Church of Scotland, 1984-85; b. 6.5.25, Glasgow; m., Morag Fraser Gray; 2 s. Educ. Shawlands Secondary School, Glasgow; Glasgow University. Minister: Chalmers Parish Church, Larkhall, 1955-62, Croftfoot Parish Church, Glasgow, 1962-72, Bon-Accord St. Paul's Parish Church, Aberdeen, 1972-76. Member, General Council, Guide Dogs for the Blind Association (Chairman, Scottish Committee). Recreations: gardening; travel. Address: 4 Laird Street, Coatbridge, ML5 3LJ; T.-Coatbridge 32740.

McNay, W. Gordon, OBE (1978), OStJ, JP, BL. Chief Executive, East Kilbride District Council, since 1975; b. 11.12.25, Wishaw; m., Margaret. Educ. Wishaw High School; Glasgow University. Deputy Town Clerk, Burgh of Airdrie, 1952-53; Senior Deputy Town Clerk, Burgh of Motherwell and Wishaw, 1953-63; Town Clerk, Burgh of East Kilbride, 1963-75. Recreations: golf; photography; philately. Address: (b.) Civic Centre, East Kilbride, G74 1AB; T.-East Kilbride 28777.

McNee, Sir David Blackstock, KB, QPM, FBIM, FRSA, CStJ. President, National Bible Society of Scotland; Non-Executive Director and Adviser to a number of public limited companies; b. 23.3.25; m., Isabella Clayton Hopkins; 1 d. Educ. Woodside Senior Secondary School, Glasgow. Joined City of Glasgow Police, 1946; Deputy Chief Constable, Dunbartonshire Constabulary, 1968; Chief Constable: City of Glasgow Police, 1971-75, Strathclyde Police, 1975-77; Commissioner, Metropolitan Police, 1977-82. President, Royal Life Saving Society; Honorary Vice-President, Boys' Brigade, since 1980; Vice-President, London Federation of Boys Clubs, since 1982; Patron, Scottish Motor Neurone Association, since 1982; Freeman, City of London, 1977; Chairman, Busoga Trust, since 1982; President, Glasgow Bn., The Boys' Brigade, since 1983. Recreations: fishing; golf; music.

Macneil of Barra, Ian Roderick, BA, LLB, FSA Scot. Wigmore Professor of Law, Northwestern University, Chicago, since 1980; b. 20.6.29, New York City; m., Nancy C. Wilson; 2 s.; 1 d. Educ. Scarborough School; Vermont University; Harvard University. Lt., AUS, 1951-53; Commissioned Officer, USAR, 1950-67; practised law, 1956-59; Member, Cornell Law School Faculty, 1959-72, 1974-80; Visiting Professor, University College, Dar es Salaam, 1965-67, Duke Law School, 1971-72; Professor of Law and Member, Centre for Advanced Studies, Virginia University, 1972-74; Visiting Fellow, Centre for Socio-Legal Studies, Wolfson College, Oxford, 1979, and Edinburgh University Faculty of Law, 1979; Guggenheim Fellow, 1978-79. Member, Standing Council of Scottish Chiefs. Recreations: tennis; reading; historical studies. Address: (h.) Kisimul Castle, Isle of Barra, PA80; T.-Castlebay 300.

MacNeill, Daniel Anthony, BEM, JP. Member, Kyle and Carrick District Council, since 1984; b. 25.6.28, Kirkintilloch; m., Agnes Bethia Morgan; 4 s.; 3 d. Educ. Sacred Heart's Academy, Girvan. Joined British Rail, 1945; Royal Engineers, 1946-48; Signal Engineering Technician, British Rail, Girvan, 1955; elected local Officer, NUR, 1963 and regional trades Officer, 1969; Member, Ayrshire and Arran Health Board, 1975-79; Vice Chairman, Carrick, Cumnock and Doon Valley Constituency Labour Party. Recreations: reading; walking; music. Address: (h.) 8 Motehill Crescent, Girvan; T.-0465 2455.

McNeill, George Andrew, BSc (Hons), MSc, MRTPI. Director of Physical Planning, West Lothian District Council, since 1978; b. 9.6.47, Edinburgh; m., Thuridur; 2 s. Educ. Musselburgh Grammar School; Edinburgh University. Engineer/Planner, East Lothian District Council, 1972; Depute Director of Planning and Building Control, Midlothian District Council, 1975. Address: (b.) County Buildings, High Street, Linlithgow, EH49 7EZ; T.-Linlithgow 843121.

McNeill, Ian Cameron, DSc, PhD, BSc. Reader in Chemistry, Glasgow University, since 1977; b. 29.4.32, Glasgow; m., Jessie Robertson Howard; 2 s.; 1 d. Educ. Allan Glen's School, Glasgow; Glasgow University. Assistant in Chemistry, Glasgow University, 1956; ICI Research Fellow, Londonderry Laboratory for Radiochemistry, Durham University, 1958; Lecturer in Chemistry, then Senior Lecturer, Glasgow University, 1961-77. Member, Editorial Board, Polymer Degradation and Stability; Committee Member, Polymer Degradation Discussion Group; Elder, Church of Scotland. Recreations: hill-walking; photography; classical music. Address: (b.) Department of Chemistry, Glasgow University, Glasgow, G12 8QQ; T.-041-339 8855, Ext. 441.

Macneill, Malcolm Torquil, BL, FSA Scot. Honorary Sheriff, Grampian, Highland and Islands; b. 29.11.19, Bowmore; m., Morag Mackinnon; 2 s.; 1 d. Educ. Dunoon Grammar School; Glasgow University. War Service, The Cameronians (Scottish Rifles), 1939-46 (to Major); Territorial Army, The Cameronians and Parachute Regiment, 1947-52 (to Major); Legal Assistant, Scottish Office, 1950; Procurator Fiscal Depute, 1951; Procurator Fiscal: Moray and Nairn, 1961, Aberdeenshire, 1969; Regional Procurator Fiscal, 1975. Marriage Guidance Counsellor, 1956. Recreations: golf; curling; photography. Address: (h.) 56 Gray Street, Aberdeen; T.-0224 316854.

McNeill, Sheriff Peter Grant Brass, PhD, MA (Hons), LLB. Sheriff of Lothian and Borders, at Edinburgh, since 1982; b. 3.3.29; m.; 1 s.; 3 d. Educ. Hillhead High School; Morrison's Academy, Crieff; Glasgow University. Scottish Bar, 1956; Advocate Depute, 1964; Sheriff of Lanarkshire, then Glasgow and Strathkelvin, at Glasgow, 1965-82; President, Sheriffs' Association, since 1982.

McNeill, William, CEng, MIMechE, MIMarE, MBIM. Principal, Perth College of Further Education, since 1971; b. 30.4.30, Broxburn; m., Jean Shirra Smart; 1 s.; 1 d. Educ. Broxburn High School; Heriot-Watt College. Development Engineer, Scottish Oils Branch, British Petroleum, 1968-71; Engineering Lecturer, Ramsay Technical Institute, 1961-64; Lecturer/Senior Lecturer, Jordanhill College of Education, 1964-67; Head of Engineering, Telford College, 1967-68; Depute Principal, Perth Technical College, 1968-71. Depute Chairman, Perth Voluntary Services Association. Recreations: music; golf. Address: (b.) Perth College of Further Education, Crieff Road, Perth, PH1 2NX; T.-Perth 21171.

McNeillie, Isobel Watt, MA (Hons). Headmistress, Craigholme School, Glasgow, since 1974; b. 15.9.30, Johnstone. Educ. Johnstone High School; Paisley Grammar School; Glasgow University. Assistant Teacher, Paisley Grammar School, 1954-60; Exchange Teacher in West Germany, 1958-59; Principal Teacher of German, then Depute Head, Craigholme School, 1960-75. Elder, Church of Scotland, since 1977; Secretary, Secondary Heads Association (Scottish Area), since 1983. Recreations: music; art; bird-watching. Address: (b.) Craigholme School, 72 St. Andrews Drive, Glasgow, G41 4HS; T.-041-427 0375.

McNicol, Professor George Paul, MD, PhD, FRSE, FRCP, FRCPG, FRCPE, FRCPath, FRSA. Principal and Vice-Chancellor, Aberdeen University, since 1981; b. 24.9.29, Glasgow; m., Susan Moira Ritchie; 1 s.; 2 d. Educ. Hillhead High School, Glasgow; Glasgow University. House Surgeon, Western Infirmary, Glasgow, 1952; House Physician, Stobhill General Hospital, Glasgow, 1953; Regimental MO, RAMC, 1953-55; Assistant, Department of Materia Medica and Therapeutics, and Registrar, University Medical Unit, Stobhill General Hospital, 1955-57; University Department of Medicine, Glasgow Royal Infirmary: Registrar, 1957-59, Honorary Senior Registrar, 1961-65; Lecturer in Medicine, 1963-65; Honorary Consultant Physician, 1966-71; Senior Lecturer in Medicine, 1966-70; Reader in Medicine, 1970-71; Professor of Medicine and Honorary Consultant Physician, Leeds General Infirmary, 1971-81; Chairman, Board, Faculty of Medicine, Leeds University, 1978-81; Harkness Fellow, Commonwealth Fund, Department of Internal Medicine, Washington University, 1959-61; Honorary Clinical Lecturer and Honorary Consultant Physician, Makerere UC Medical School Extension, Kenyatta National Hospital, Nairobi, 1965-66. Former Member, Advisory Council on Misuse of Drugs; Chairman, Part I Examining Board, Royal College of Physicians (UK); Member, CICHE; Chairman

of the Governors, Rowett Research Institute, Aberdeen. Recreations: skiing; sailing. Address: (h.) Chanonry Lodge, 13 The Chanonry, Aberdeen, AB2 1RP.

Macnicol, Malcolm Fraser, MB, ChB, BSc (Hons), FRCS, MChOrth, FRCSEd (Orth). Consultant Orthopaedic Surgeon, Edinburgh, since 1980; part-time Senior Lecturer, Edinburgh University, since 1980; b. 18.3.43, Madras, South India; m., Anne Morag; 2 s.; 1 d. Educ. Royal High School, Edinburgh; Edinburgh University; Liverpool University. Research Fellow, Harvard University; Senior Lecturer and Orthopaedic Specialist, University of Western Australia. Publications: Basic Care of the Injured Hand; Aids to Orthopaedics; The Problem Knee. Address: (h.) 10 Bright's Crescent, Edinburgh, EH3 2DD; T.-031-667 6609.

McNidder, David, DA, DipTP, RIBA, ARIAS, MRTPI. Director of Planning and Technical Services, East Kilbride District Council, since 1974; b. Paisley; m.; 1 s. Educ. John Neilson School, Paisley; School of Architecture, Glasgow. Recreations: golf; drawing and painting; philately; gardening. Address: (b.) Civic Centre, East Kilbride; T.-East Kilbride 28777.

McNie, William Malcolm, MA, PhD. Senior Economic Adviser, Economics and Statistics Unit, Industry Department for Scotland, since 1975; b. 18.5.42, Tobermory; m., Mary Philomena; 1 s.; 1 d. Educ. George Watson's College; Caius College, Cambridge University; Columbia University. Economic Assistant, Scottish Office; Economic Adviser, Treasury; Economic Adviser, Customs and Excise. Recreation: golf. Address: (b.) New St. Andrews House, Edinburgh, EH1 3TA; T.-031-556 8400, Ext. 5009.

McPartlin, Sheriff Noel, MA, LLB. Sheriff of Grampian, Highland and Islands, at Peterhead and Banff, since 1983; b. 25.12.39; m.; 3 s.; 3 d. Educ. Galashiels Academy; Edinburgh University. Solicitor, 1964-76.

McPetrie, Sir James (Carnegie), KCMG (1966), OBE (1953). Honorary Fellow, Department of Public Law, Dundee University, since 1976; b. 29.6.11; m.; 1 d. Educ. Madras College, St. Andrews; St. Andrews University; Jesus College, Oxford. Retired from Diplomatic Service, 1971; Chairman, UNESCO Appeals Board, 1973-79; Member, Court, St. Andrews University, since 1982.

MacPhail, Donald John, BSc. Headmaster, Bayble School, Lewis, since 1979; b. 22.10.28, Stornoway; m., Mary Mitchell; 1 s.; 2 d. Educ. Nicolson Institute; Glasgow University. Assistant Teacher of Mathematics and Science, Nicolson Institute, Stornoway, 1959-66; Lecturer in Science, Hamilton College of Education, 1966-71; Headmaster, Leverhulme Memorial School, Harris, 1971-79. Member, Stornoway Trust. Address: (h.) 9 Laxdale, Stornoway, Isle of Lewis; T.-Stornoway 4823.

Macphail, Sheriff Iain Duncan, MA (Hons), LLB. Sheriff of Lothian and Borders, since 1982; b. 24.1.38; m.; 1 s.; 1 d. Educ. George

Watson's College, Edinburgh; Edinburgh University; Glasgow University. Advocate, 1963; practised, Scottish Bar, 1963-73; Sheriff of Lanarkshire, then Glasgow and Strathkelvin, 1973-81; Sheriff of Tayside, Central and Fife, 1981-82.

Macphail, James Gordon Stewart, MA (Oxon), Order of the Nile Fourth Class, FSA Scot. Honorary Sheriff; b. 19.2.00, Madras, India; m., Fiona McLean; 1 s.; 1 d. Educ. Edinburgh Academy; University College, Oxford. Enlisted in Scots Guards, 1918; gazetted 2nd Lt., 3rd Bn., The Royal Scots, 1919; selected for Sudan Political Service, 1922; Assistant District Commissioner, Bereber Province, 1923-24; Assistant District Commissioner, Red Sea and Bahr-eh-Ghazal Provinces, 1925-29; promoted to District Commissioner, Kordofan Province, 1930-33; District Commissioner, Shilluk-Dinka District and sometimes Acting Governor Upper Nile Province, 1934-39; District Commissioner, Northern Province, 1940-42; Chief Air Warden, Atbara; joined the Army, 1942-43; gazetted Bimbashi (Major) in Camel Corps, Sudan Defence Force; retired from Sudan Political Service, 1947; appointed permanent Principal, Administrative Class, Department of Health for Scotland, later Scottish Development Department, 1948-64; worked in Register of Sasines, listing titles of Edinburgh's historic buildings, 1965-69; Life Member, Association for the Protection of Rural Scotland and Stewart Society; Life Member (former Member of Council), National Trust for Scotland; Life Member and Chairman, Council, Clan Chattan Association, 1969-74; Honorary Sheriff Substitute, later Honorary Sheriff. Recreations (formerly) rugby football; golf; tennis; polo; travel; big game hunting; (now) gardening; architecture; painting; literature; various societies. Address: (h.) 21 West Road, Haddington, East Lothian, EH41 3RE; T.-062 082 3156.

McPhee, Rev. Duncan Cameron, MA, BD. Joint Secretary-Depute, Department of Ministry and Mission, Church of Scotland, since 1978; b. 26.10.28, Glasgow; m., Elizabeth Anderson MacGregor; 1 s.; 3 d. Educ. Borden Grammar School, Sittingbourne; Glasgow University. Assistant Minister, Barony of Glasgow, 1953-55; Minister: Dalrymple, 1955-61, Airdrie Broomknoll, 1961-78. Assistant Clerk, Hamilton Presbytery, 1964-72; Clerk, 1972-78. Recreations: music; walking. Address: (b.) 121 George Street, Edinburgh, EH2 4YN; T.-031-225 5722.

McPhee, George, BMus, FRCO, DipMusEd, RSAM. Senior Lecturer, Royal Scottish Academy of Music and Drama, since 1980; Organist and Master of the Choristers, Paisley Abbey, since 1963; b. 10.11.37, Glasgow; m., Margaret Ann Scotland; 1 s.; 2 d. Educ. Woodside Senior Secondary School, Glasgow; Royal Scottish Academy of Music and Drama; Edinburgh University. Studied organ with Herrick Bunney and Fernando Germany; Assistant Organist, St. Giles' Cathedral, 1959-63; joined staff, RSAMD, 1963; Conductor, Scottish Chamber Choir, 1971-75; Conductor, Kilmarnock and District Choral Union, 1975-84; since 1971, has completed 12 recital tours of the United States and Canada; has

been both Soloist and Conductor with Scottish National Orchestra; numerous recordings and broadcasts; has taken part in numerous music festivals as Soloist; Adjudicator; Examiner, Associated Board, Royal Schools of Music; Special Commissioner, Royal School of Church Music; Silver Medal, Worshipful Company of Musicians. Recreations: golf; walking. Address: (h.) 17 Main Road, Castlehead, Paisley, PA2 6AJ; T.-041-889 3528.

Macpherson, Sheriff Alexander Calderwood, MA, LLB. Sheriff of South Strathclyde, Dumfries and Galloway, at Hamilton, since 1978; b. 14.6.39; m.; 2 s. Educ. Glasgow Academy; Glasgow University. Solicitor, 1962; private practice, 1962-78.

McPherson, Andrew Francis, BA, DPSA. Director, Centre for Educational Sociology, and Reader in Sociology, Edinburgh University; b. 6.7.42, Louth; 1 s.; 1 d. Educ. Ripon Grammar School; Queen's College, Oxford. Lecturer, Glasgow University, 1965-68; Edinburgh University: Research Fellow, 1968-72, Lecturer, 1972-79, Senior Lecturer, 1979-83, Reader, since 1983. Publications: The Scottish Sixth, 1976; Tell Them from Me, 1980; Reconstructions of Secondary Education, 1983. Address: (h.) 11 Dalrymple Crescent, Edinburgh.

MacPherson, Archie, BA. Sports Correspondent, BBC Scotland; Rector, Edinburgh University; b. 10.11.34, Glasgow; m.; 2 s. Educ. Coatbridge High School; Jordanhill College. Schoolteacher, 12 years; former Headmaster, Swinton Primary School, Lanarkshire; gave up teaching for broadcasting, 1962.

McPherson, Duncan James, MA, SDA. Farmer, since 1959; b. 29.10.30, Santos, Brazil; m., Vivian Margaret; 1 s.; 1 d. Educ. Robert Gordon's College, Aberdeen; Aberdeen University. Member, Cromarty Town Council, 1964-75, Ross and Cromarty County Council, 1972-75; Highland Regional Council, since 1974 (Chairman, Development Committee, since 1978); Highland Area Chairman, Scottish Council (Development and Industry), since 1978; Member: SDA Consultative Council, HIDB Consultative Council; President, Rosemarkie Golf Club; Past President, Black Isle Farmers Society. Recreations: golf; curling; formerly rugby (Scottish trialist, 1951-56). Address: Cromarty Mains, Cromarty, Ross-shire; T.-038 17 232.

McPherson, Ewan Allan, MSc, MRCVS. Senior Lecturer in Veterinary Medicine, Edinburgh University, since 1956; b. 12.2.17, Auchterarder; m., Margaret Templeton McLeod; 1 d. Educ. Morrison's Academy, Crieff; Royal (Dick) Veterinary College; Edinburgh University. General Veterinary Practice, 1940-42; Veterinary Inspector, Ministry of Agriculture, Fisheries and Food, 1943-51; Lecturer, Edinburgh University, 1951-56. Awarded Richard Hartley Clinical Prize, 1984; Editor, English Edition, Veterinary Encyclopaedia. Recreations: hill-walking; gardening; bee-keeping. Address: (b.) Royal (Dick) School of Veterinary Studies, Easter Bush, Roslin, Midlothian, EH25 9RG; T.-031-445 2001.

McPherson, Frank Murdoch, MA, PhD, DCP, FBPsS. Director, Tayside Area Clinical Psychology Department, since 1980; b. 2.9.38, Aberdeen; m., Dr. K.M.D. McPherson; 1 s.; 1 d. Educ. Aberdeen Grammar School; Aberdeen University; Edinburgh University. Lecturer in Psychology, Edinburgh University, 1960-66 and 1968-71; Research Fellow, Mental Health Research Fund, 1966-68; Visiting Professor, University of Western Ontario, 1970; Senior Lecturer in Psychology, Dundee University, 1971-80. Deputy Chairman, National Consultative Committee of Scientists in Professions Allied to Medicine, 1975-78; British Psychological Society: Chairman, Division of Clinical Psychology, 1977-80, Chairman, Joint Standing Committee, BPS and Royal College of Nursing, 1977-80, Chairman, Professional Affairs Board, 1981-84; Member, Secretary of State's Advisory Committee on Top Grade Clinical Psychologists Posts, 1980-82; Member, PTA Whitley Council Principal Clinical Psychologist Grading Sub-Committee, 1980-82; President, European Federation of Professional Psychologists Associations, since 1982; Temporary Advisor, WHO Regional Office for Europe, since 1982. Recreations: mountaineering; music; supporting Aberdeen FC. Address: (b.) Royal Dundee Liff Hospital, Dundee, DD2 5NF; T.-0382 580441.

Macpherson, Captain Hugh, JP, KLJ, FSA Scot. Chairman, Hugh Macpherson (Scotland) Ltd.; b. 27.4.07, Lothbeg, Sutherland; m., Janet Laing; 2 d. Educ. Loth, Rogart and Sutherland Technical School, Golspie; Shaw Schools Ltd., Toronto, Canada. Past President, Hugh Macpherson Imports Ltd., Canada; former Chief Accountant, Alliance Paper Mills Ltd., Canaa; former Deputy Royal Chief, Order of Scottish Clans, Ontario; former Pipe-Major, St. Catharines Pipe Band, Ontario; former Captain, Canadian Army; Town Councillor, Edinburgh, 15 years (sometime Senior Bailie); Past President, Scottish Road Passenger Transport Association; Council Member, Royal Celtic Society; Vice-Chairman, Scottish International Gathering Trust; Honorary President: Highland Pipers' Society, Edinburgh Sutherland Association; Honorary Vice-President: Clan Macpherson Association, Royal Scottish Pipe Band Association, Cowal Highland Gathering, Edinburgh Gaelic Choir; Honorary Member, Chamber of Commerce, Dunedin, Florida; Elder, Cramond Kirk, Edinburgh, since 1954. Publication: The Wandering Highlander. Recreations: Scottish music; reading; Scottish history and culture. Address: (b.) 17 West Maitland Street, Haymarket, Edinburgh, EH12 5EA; T.-031-225 4008.

Macpherson, Ian, CA. Director and Deputy Chief Executive, British Linen Bank Ltd., since 1979; b. 25.3.36; m., Margaret; 1 s.; 1 d. Educ. Morrison's Academy, Crieff. Recreation: golf. Address: (b.) British Linen Bank Ltd., 4 Melville Street, Edinburgh, EH3 7NZ; T.-031-243 8304.

Macpherson, Ian Alistair, MBE, CStJ, JP, FIMBM, FCIOB, FFB. Director of Works, East Kilbride Development Corporation, since 1973; b. 25.1.35, Glasgow; m., Rebecca; 2 d. Educ. Govan High School; Glasgow College of Building and Printing. Works Manager, East Kilbride Development Corporation, 1965-73. Freeman Citizen of Glasgow; East Kilbride and Lanarkshire Branch Chairman, Most Venerable Order of St. John; Past President, Institute of Municipal Building Management; Chairman, Chartered Institute of Building (Scotland); Past President, East Kilbride Junior Chamber of Commerce; Member, East Kilbride Committee, British Heart Foundation; Past President, East Kilbride Rotary Club; Past President, Bridgeton Burns Club and East Kilbride Burns Club; Member, Master Court, Incorporation of Masons, Trades House of Glasgow. Recreations: golf; curling; raising money for charity. Address: (b.) East Kilbride Development Corporation, Atholl House, East Kilbride, G74 1LU; T.-East Kilbride 41111, Ext. 394.

Macpherson, Ian George, BSc, DipEd. Rector, Eastwood High School, since 1977; b. 29.4.37, Perth; m., Gillian Brian; 2 s. Educ. Perth Academy; St. Andrews University; Edinburgh University; Moray House College of Education. Assistant Teacher of Physics, George Heriot's School, Edinburgh, 1959-62; Principal Teacher of Science, Dornoch Academy, Sutherland, 1962-64; Principal Teacher of Physics, Liberton High School, Edinburgh, 1964-69; Adviser in Science, Renfrewshire, 1969-73; Headmaster, Barrhead High School, 1973-77. Member, Strathclyde Executive, Headteachers' Association of Scotland. Recreations: yachting; choral singing; Rotary (Past President, Barrhead Rotary Club). Address: (h.) 20A Park Road, Paisley, PA2 6JW; T.-041-884 2807.

McPherson, James Alexander Strachan, CBE, MA, BL, LLB, FSA Scot, DL, JP. Solicitor; Partner, Alexander George & Co., Solicitors, Macduff, since 1955; Member, Grampian Regional Council and Chairman, Public Protection Committee, since 1974; Honorary Sheriff, Grampian, Highland and Islands, at Banff, since 1972; Deputy Lieutenant, Banffshire; b. 20.11.27, Wormit; m., Helen Marjorie Perks; 1 s.; 1 d. Educ. Banff Academy; Aberdeen University. Member, Macduff Town Council and Banff County Council, 1958-75; Provost of Macduff, 1972-75; Convener, Banff County Council, 1970-75; Member, Grampian Health Board, 1974-82. Address: (h.) Dun Alastair, 126 Gellymill Street, Macduff; T.-Macduff 32377.

Macpherson of Drumochter, ((James) Gordon Macpherson), 2nd Baron. Chairman and Managing Director, Macpherson, Train & Co. Ltd., since 1964; Chairman, A.J. Macpherson & Co. Ltd., since 1973; b. 22.1.24; m., 1, Dorothy Ruth Coulter (deceased); 2 d.; 1 s. deceased; 2, Catherine MacCarthy; 1 s.; 2 d. Educ. Loretto; Wells House, Malvern. RAF, 1939-45. Address: (h.) Kyllachy, Tomatin, Inverness-shire.

Macpherson, John Hannah Forbes, CBE, OStJ, CA. Senior Partner, Touche Ross & Co., Scotland, since 1964; Chairman, Scottish Mutual Assurance Society, since 1971; Director, Trustee Savings Bank Scotland, since 1984; b. 23.5.26, Glasgow; m., Margaret Graham Roxburgh; 1 s. Educ. Glasgow Academy; Merchiston Castle School, Edinburgh. Royal Naval Volunteer Reserve, 1943; Apprentice CA, Wilson Stirling

& Co., 1947 (qualified, 1949); Partner, Wilson Stirling & Co. (subsequently Touche Ross & Co.), 1956; Chairman: Glasgow Junior Chamber of Commerce, 1965; Scottish Industrial Estates Corporation, 1972, Irvine Development Corporation, 1976; President, Glasgow Chamber of Commerce, 1980; Director: Associated British Engineering PLC, Brownlee PLC, Standard Property PLC; Member, Charity Appeals Committee for Prince and Princess of Wales Hospice, Scottish Disability Foundation, Institute of Neurological Sciences Research; Director, Merchants House and Glasgow Native Benevolent Society. Recreations: gardening; reading. Address: (h.) 16 Collylinn Road, Bearsden, Glasgow; T.-041-942 0042.

MacPherson, Margaret Hope, MA. Children's Author; Chairman, Keep Skye Beautiful Committee, since 1970; b. 29.6.08, Colinton; m., Duncan MacPherson; 7 s. Educ. St. Denis School, Edinburgh; Edinburgh University. Married, farmed, brought up family; local government, 1945-49; Member, Commission of Inquiry into Crofting, 1951-54 (wrote minority report); Secretary, Skye Labour Party, 1961-84. Publications (children's books): Shinty Boys, 1963; The Rough Road, 1965; Ponies for Hire, 1967; The New Tenants, 1968; Battle of the Braes, 1970; The Boy on the Roof, 1972. Recreations: gardening; watching shinty; football; swimming. Address: (h.) Ardrannach, Torvaig, Portree, Skye; T.-0478 2758.

Macpherson, Rev. Stewart MacColl, MA. Minister, Dunfermline Abbey, Fife, since 1969; b. 5.11.25, Armadale; m., Janet May Marshall Tennant; 1 s.; 1 d. Educ. Greenock Academy; Edinburgh University and New College. Minister: Swinton Parish Church, near Duns, 1953-58, St. Kentigern's Church, Lanark, 1958-65, Queen's Park West Church, Glasgow, 1965-69; last Moderator, Dunfermline and Kinross Presbytery. Recreations: music; water colour painting; writing; reading. Address: Abbey Manse, 116 Halbeath Road, Dunfermline, Fife, KY11 4LA; T.-Dunfermline 721022.

Macpherson, Stuart Gowans, MB, ChB, FRCS. Senior Lecturer in Surgery, Glasgow University, since 1977; Honorary Consultant Surgeon, Western Infirmary, Glasgow, since 1977; b. 11.7.45, Glasgow; m., Norma Elizabeth Carslaw; 2 s.; 1 d. Educ. Allan Glen's School, Glasgow; Glasgow University. Surgical training and experience in West of Scotland, with postgraduate training at Harvard Medical School, Boston. Recreations: golf; travelling; reading; family. Address: (b.) Department of Surgery, Western Infirmary, Glasgow, G11 6NT; T.-041-339 8822, Ext. 4710.

Macpherson of Cluny (and Blairgowrie), Colonel the Honourable Sir William, KB (1983), TD, MA. 27th Hereditary Chief of the Clan Macpherson (Cluny-Macpherson); b. 1.4.26; m., Sheila McDonald Brodie; 2 s.; 1 d. Educ. Summer Fields, Oxford; Wellington College; Trinity College, Oxford. Scots Guards, 1944-47 (Captain); 21st Special Air Service Regiment (TA), 1951-65 (Lt.-Col. Commanding, 1962-65); Honorary Colonel, 21st SAS, since 1983. Called to the Bar,

Inner Temple, 1952; Queen's Counsel, 1971-83; Recorder of the Crown Court, 1972-83; Member, Senate and Bar Council, 1979-83; Bencher, Inner Temple, 1978; Judge of the High Court of Justice (of England and Wales), Queen's Bench Division, 1983; Presiding Judge, Northern Circuit, since 1985. Member, Queen's Bodyguard for Scotland (Royal Company of Archers), since 1976; Member, Board of Management, Royal Scottish Corporation. Recreations: golf; fishing; rugby football. Address: (h.) Newton Castle, Blairgowrie, Perthshire; (b.) Royal Courts of Justice, Strand, London, WC2.

Macphie, Charles Stewart. Chairman and Managing Director, Macphie of Glenbervie Ltd., since 1965; President, Bakery and Allied Trades Association, since 1983; Council Member, CBI Scotland; Non-Executive Director, North of Scotland Hydro-Electric Board; Farmer; b. 22.9.29, Baltimore, Maryland; m., Elizabeth Margaret Jill Pearson; 1 s.; 1 d. Educ. Dalhousie Castle School; Rugby. Chairman of Governors, Oxenfoord Castle School; Trustee, Kincardineshire Royal Jubilee Trust. Address: (h.) Knock Hill House, Glenbervie, Kincardineshire; T.-056-94 257.

McQuaid, John, MA (Hons), MEd, PhD. Composer and Psychologist; b. 14.3.09, Lochgelly; m., Mary Darkin. Educ. St. Mungo's Academy, Glasgow; Glasgow University; Edinburgh University. Taught, 1935-40; War Service, 1941-46 (Intelligence Corps), Africa and SE Asia; taught, 1946-51; Psychologist, 1952-77; studied music under Erik Chisholm; numerous broadcasts and public performances of compositions (piano, chamber music, orchestral, etc.). Address: (h.) St. Anne's, 8 Ardrossan Road, Saltcoats, KA21 5BW; T.-0294 63737.

Macquaker, Donald Francis, MA (Oxon), LLB. Chairman, Greater Glasgow Health Board, since 1983; Partner, T.C. Young & Son, Writers, Glasgow, since 1957; b. 21.9.32, Stair; m., Susan Elizabeth Finlayson; 1 s.; 1 d. Educ. Winchester College; Trinity College, Oxford; Glasgow University. Former Member, Board of Management, Glasgow Royal Maternity Hospital and Associated Women's Hospital (latterly Vice-Chairman); Chairman, Finance and General Purposes Committee, Greater Glasgow Health Board, 1974-83. Recreations: shooting; fishing; gardening. Address: (h.) Blackbyres, by Ayr; T.-0292 41088.

McQuarrie, Albert. MP (Conservative), Banff and Buchan, since 1983 (Aberdeenshire East, 1979-83); b. 1.1.18. Educ. Highlanders Academy, Greenock; Greenock High School; Royal College of Science and Technology. Chairman, A. McQuarrie & Son (Great Britain) Ltd., since 1946; Member, Select Committee on Agriculture; Member, Council, Society of Engineers, since 1978.

MacQueen, Professor Jack (John), MA (Glasgow), MA (Cantab), Hon DLitt. Director, School of Scottish Studies, Edinburgh University, since 1969 (Professor of Scottish Literature and Oral Tradition, since 1972); b. 13.2.29, Springboig; m., Winifred W. Macwalter; 3 s. Educ.

Hutchesons' Boys Grammar School; Glasgow University; Christ's College, Cambridge. RAF, 1954-56 (Pilot Officer, Flying Officer); Assistant Professor of English, Washington University, St. Louis, Missouri, 1956-59; Edinburgh University: Lecturer in Medieval English and Scottish Literature, 1959-63, Masson Professor of Medieval and Renaissance Literature, 1963-72. Publications: St. Nynia, 1961; Robert Henryson, 1967; Ballattis of Luve, 1970; Allegory, 1970; Progress and Poetry, 1982; Numerology, 1985; Oxford Book of Scottish Verse (with T. Scott), 1966; A Choice of Scottish Verse 1470-1570 (with W. MacQueen), 1972. Recreations: walking; occasional archaeology; music. Address: (b.) School of Scottish Studies, 27 George Square, Edinburgh, EH8 9LD; T.-031-667 1011, Ext. 6674.

McQueen, James Donaldson Wright, MA, PhD. Deputy Managing Director, Scottish Milk Marketing Board, since 1985; Member, Scottish Dairy Council, since 1983; Director, Taste of Scotland Ltd., since 1984; b. 14.2.37, Dumfries; m., Jean Evelyn Brown; 2 s.; 1 d. Educ. King's Park School, Glasgow; Glasgow University. Assistant Lecturer, Department of Geography, Glasgow University, 1960-61; Junior Manager, Milk Marketing Board (England and Wales), 1961-62; Scottish Milk Marketing Board: Economist, 1962-70, Marketing Services Manager, 1970-78; Marketing Director, 1978-85. Recreations: golf; curling; gardening; photography. Address: (h.) Ormlie, 53 Kingston Road, Bishopton, Renfrewshire, PA7 5BA; T.-Bishopton 862380.

Macqueen, Julie-Ann, OBE, CQSW, BA, SNNEB. Director, Scottish Council for Single Parents, since 1967; b. 30.4.28, Jerusalem. Educ. Convent of Notre Dame de Sion, Jerusalem, London, Shropshire; Edinburgh University; Open University. Nursery Nurse in Edinburgh, 1946-54; between 1954 and 1967, held the posts of Personnel Officer, Crawfords Biscuit Factory, Leith, School Welfare Officer, Dundee and Senior Social Worker, Scottish Child Care Office, Glasgow. Trustee, Buttle Trust for Children (Chairman, Scottish Distribution Committee); a Vice-President, National Out of School Alliance. Publication: Unmarried Parents and their Children. Recreations: reading; listening to music; cooking; house interiors; antiques; travel; people. Address: (b.) 13 Gayfield Square, Edinburgh, EH1 3NX; T.-031-556 3899.

McQuilken, Rev. John Ernest, MA, BD. Minister, Glenaray and Inveraray, since 1983; b. 14.8.27, Port Glasgow; m., Grace Mary Middleton McKenzie; 1 d. Educ. Port Glasgow High School; Greenock High School; Queen's College and St. Mary's College, St. Andrews University. Newspaper Sub-Editor, 1949-62; student, 1962-69; Minister: Drylaw, Edinburgh, 1969-78, Caddonfoot with Heatherlie, Selkirk, 1978-83. Recreations: looking at paintings; poetry; gardening. Address: The Manse, Inveraray, Argyll, PA32 8XT; T.-Inveraray 2060.

Macrae, Rev. Donald Angus, MA, JP. Minister, Tarbert, Harris, since 1956; b. 2.4.18, Miavaig, Isle of Lewis; m., Annie Macleod; 2 s.; 2 d.

Educ. Nicolson Institute, Stornoway; Glasgow University. Minister: Sleat, 1942-49, Benbecula, 1949-56. Address: The Manse, Tarbert, Isle of Harris, PA85 3DF; T.-Harris 2231.

MacRae, Duncan Keith, MA, LLB, NP. Partner, Jenkins & Jardine, Solicitors, Stirling, since 1963; b. 24.9.30, Glenshiel, Ross-shire; m., Edith Watson; 2 s. Educ. Plockton; Aberdeen University. Flying Officer, RAF; Partner, McCulloch & MacRae, Solicitors, Grantown-on-Spey, 1956-62; Member, Council, Scottish Law Agents' Society, since 1976 (Vice President, 1984); Local Secretary, Macmillan Cancer Relief Society; Director, Stirling Ice Rink Co. Ltd. Recreations: curling; shooting; hill-walking; fishing. Address: (b.) 80 Port Street, Stirling, FK8 2LR; T.-Stirling 73032.

MacRae, John C., BSc, PhD. Head, Physiology Division, Rowett Research Institute, since 1985; b. 10.7.42, Skelmersdale, Lancashire; m., Eileen E.; 2 s. Educ. Ormskirk Grammar School; Newcastle University. Research Scientist, Applied Biochemistry Division, Department of Scientific and Industrial Research, Palmerston North, New Zealand, 1968-71; Research Scientist, Hill Farming Research Organisation, Penicuik, 1972-77; Head, Department of Energy Metabolism, Rowett Research Institute, 1978-85. Member, Editorial Board, British Journal of Nutrition, 1977-83; Committee Member, Scottish Group, Nutrition Society, 1973-75 and since 1983. Recreations: sport (golf, cricket); family life. Address: (b.) Rowett Research Institute, Greenburn Road, Bucksburn, Aberdeen; T.-Aberdeen 712751.

Macrae, Col. Robert Andrew Alexander Scarth, MBE (1953), JP. Lord Lieutenant of Orkney, since 1972; Farmer; b. 14.4.15; m.; 2 s. Educ. Lancing; Sandhurst. Member, Orkney County Council, 1970-74, Orkney Islands Council, 1974-78; Vice Chairman, Orkney Health Board, 1974-79.

Macrae-Gibson, O. Duncan, MA, DPhil. Senior Lecturer in English, Aberdeen University, since 1970; b. 30.1.28; m., Frances; 1 s.; 1 d. Educ. Royal Naval College, Dartmouth; St. Catherine's Society, Oxford. Royal Navy, 1949-51; Teacher of maladjusted children, 1955; printing machine assistant, OUP, 1956; Lecturer: Oriel and University Colleges, Oxford, 1957-59, Leicester University, 1959-65, Aberdeen University, 1965-70. Publications: Learning Old English; (editions) Of Arthour and of Merlin; The Old English Riming Poem. Recreations: hill-walking; skiing; riding; tennis. Address: (b.) Department of English, Aberdeen University, King's College, Old Aberdeen, Aberdeen, AB9 2UB; T.-Aberdeen 40241.

MacRitchie, Professor Farquhar, CBE (1968), MA, LLB, Hon. LLD. Consultant, Burnett & Reid, Advocates, Aberdeen, since 1979; b. 1.11.02, Isle of Lewis; m., Isobel Ross; 1 s. (deceased). Educ. Aberdeen University. Aberdeen University: Assistant Lecturer in Law, 1940-45, Lecturer in Mercantile Law, 1945-46, Professor of Conveyancing, 1946-74. Honorary

Sheriff-Substitute, Aberdeen; Convener, Legal Education Committee, Law Society of Scotland, 1955-70; Vice-President, Law Society of Scotland, 1963; Partner, Morice & Wilson, Advocates, Aberdeen, 1939-79. Recreation: golf. Address: (h.) 60 Rubislaw Den North, Aberdeen; T.-Aberdeen 315458.

MacRobert, John Carmichael Thomas, MA (Cantab), MA, LLB (Glasgow), NP. Solicitor, since 1948; Honorary Sheriff, since 1969; Honorary Secretary and Treasurer, Paisley and District Hospitals Voluntary Service Association, since 1947; b. 26.4.18, Edinburgh; m., Anne Rosemary Millar; 1 s.; 2 d. Educ. Craigflower; Rugby; Queens' College, Cambridge; Glasgow University. Captain, Royal Artillery (Despatches, Burma); Secretary, Local Productivity Committee, 15 years; Member, Council, Law Society of Scotland, 1965-77; former Member, Scottish Office Working Parties on Planning Reform and Planning Exchange; Honorary Solicitor, subsequently Trustee, Scottish Civic Trust; Council Member, Clyde Estuary Amenity Council; Honorary President (Past Chairman), Paisley South Conservatives. Recreations: sailing; shooting; gardening. Address: (h.) The Old House, Castlehead, Paisley; T.-041-889 3425; Failte, Colintraive, Argyll; T.-070 084 239.

McSherry, John Craig Cunningham, LLB (Hons), NP. Solicitor, since 1974; b. 21.10.49, Irvine; 2 s. Educ. Ardrossan Academy; Glasgow University. President, University Law Society, 1971-72; Partner, McSherry Halliday & Co., Solicitors; Chairman, Largs and District Citizens' Advice Bureau, 1976-83; Council Member, Law Society of Scotland, 1982-85. Recreations: the arts; skiing; gardening; languages; golf. Address: (b.) 9 Chapelwell Street, Saltcoats, Ayrshire; T.-0294 64366.

MacSween, Iain MacLean, BA (Econ), MPhil. Chief Executive, Scottish Fishermen's Organisation, since 1982; b. 20.9.49, Glasgow; m., Jean Gemmill Martin; 2 s.; 1 d. Educ. Knightswood Secondary School; Strathclyde University; Glasgow University. Fisheries Economics Research Unit, 1973-75; Department of Agriculture and Fisheries for Scotland, 1975-77; Scottish Fishermen's Organisation, since 1977; President, European Federation of Fishermen's Organisations. Address: (b.) 601 Queensferry Road, Edinburgh, EH2 6EA; T.-031-339 7972.

MacSween, Malcolm D., MA (Hons), BLitt. Head Teacher, Abronhill High School, Cumbernauld, since 1978; b. 10.10.34, Torridon, Ross and Cromarty. Educ. Golspie High School; Glasgow University. Teacher, Glasgow schools, 1959-71; Assistant Head Teacher, Shawlands Academy, 1971-75; Depute Head Teacher, Stanely Green High School, Paisley, 1975-78. Elder, Church of Scotland; former Member, Scottish Certificate of Examination Board. Recreations: bowls; reading; walking; visiting places of interest in UK. Address: (b.) Abronhill High School, Larch Road, Cumbernauld, Glasgow.

MacSween, Professor Roderick Norman McIver, BSc, MD, FRCPGlas, FRCPEdin, FRCPath, FRSE. Proffessor of Pathology, Glasgow University, since 1984; Honorary Consultant Pathologist, Western Infirmary, Glasgow, since 1970; b. 2.2.35, Kinloch, Lewis; m., Marjory Pentland Brown; 1 s.; 1 d. Educ. Inverness Royal Academy; Glasgow University. Successively Lecturer, Senior Lecturer, Reader and Titular Professor in Pathology, Glasgow University, 1965-84; Physician/Research and Education Associate, Colorado University Medical Center, Denver, 1968-69; Honorary Fellow, South African Society of Pathologists, 1982; Otago Savings Bank Visiting Professor, Otago University, 1983. President, Royal Medico-Chirurgical Society of Glasgow, 1978-79; Council Member and Honorary Librarian, Royal College of Physicians and Surgeons, Glasgow; Council Member, Royal College of Pathologists; Editor, Histopathology (Journal). Publications: Pathology of the Liver (Co-Editor); Recent Advances in Histopathology, Nos. 11 and 12; Recent Advances in Hepatology, No. 1. Former Captain, Dunaverty and Machrihanish Golf Clubs. Recreations: golf; gardening; opera; hill-walking; more golf! Address: (b.) University Department of Pathology, Western Infirmary, Glasgow, G11 6NT; T.-041-339 8822, Ext. 4732.

McTaggart, Dick, MBE (1985). Boxer; Coach, Scottish Amateur Boxing Association, since 1983; b. 1935, Dundee. Suffered only 24 defeats in 634 contests; Olympic Gold Medallist, Melbourne, 1956; Olympic Bronze Medallist, Rome, 1960; British Empire Lightweight Champion, 1958; European Lightweight Champion, 1961; British Empire Silver Medallist, 1962; winner of five ABA titles, seven Scottish championships, 32 cups, 57 plaques, 49 medals; Assistant Coach, British Olympic Team, Los Angeles Olympics, 1984; works for Rolls Royce.

McTaggart, Robert. MP (Labour), Glasgow Central, since 1980; b. 2.11.45, Glasgow; m., Elizabeth Jardine; 1 s.; 2 d. Educ. Holyrood Secondary School; Stow College; Glasgow College of Building. Shop Steward, EETPU, Govan Shipbuilders, 1971-77; Member, Glasgow Corporation, 1974-75; Member, Glasgow District Council, 1977-80. Recreations: spectating football, athletics; playing snooker, draughts; reading. Address: (h.) 61 St. Mungo Avenue, Glasgow, G4 OPL; T.-01-219 3450.

MacThomas of Finegand, Andrew, FSA Scot. 19th Chief of Clan MacThomas, since 1970; b. 28.8.42, Edinburgh; m., Anneke Cornelia Susanna Kruyning. Educ. in Scotland, then St. Edward's, Oxford. Worked for bank; credit card company; in public relations. Member, Standing Council of Scottish Chiefs; President, Clan MacThomas Society; Vice-President, Clan Chattan Association. Recreations: travel; horseracing. Address: c/o Clan MacThomas Society, 29 Bennan Gardens, Broughty Ferry, Dundee.

MacVicar, Angus, MA, DUniv. Author; b. 28.10.08, Argyll; m., Jean Smith McKerral; 1 s. Educ. Campbeltown Grammar School; Glasgow University. Reporter, Campbeltown Courier, 1931-33; Freelance Author; Army Service, 1940-45 (Captain, RSF); Freelance Author, Journalist, Radio and TV Scriptwriter; published 75 books, including adult novels, children's novels, adult and children's non-fiction, plays;

Honorary Sheriff-Substitute, Argyll, 1965; Doctorate, Stirling University, 1985. Recreations: golf; gardening; amateur drama. Address: (h.) Achnamara, Southend, Campbeltown, Argyll, PA28 6RW; T.-0586 83 228.

MacVicar, Archy, MA. Minister, Dingwall Castle Street, since 1973; b. 18.2.20, Baleshare, North Uist; m., Isobel Maclennan Budge; 3 s.; 1 d. Educ. Paible Public School; Inverness Royal Academy; Glasgow University and Trinity College. RAF, 1941-46; student, 1946-52; Minister: Kilfinichen and Kilvickeon, Isle of Mull, 1952-56, Strath, Broadford, Skye, 1956-73. Address: 16 Achany Road, Dingwall, Ross-shire; T.-Dingwall 63167.

MacVicar, Rev. Kenneth, MBE (Mil), DFC, MA. Minister, Kenmore and Lawers, since 1950; Chaplain in Ordinary to The Queen in Scotland, since 1974; b. 25.8.21; m.; 3 s.; 1 d. Educ. Campbeltown Grammar School; Edinburgh University; St. Andrews University. RAF, 1941-45 (mentioned in Despatches); Clerk, Dunkeld Presbytery, since 1955.

Macvicar, Sheriff Neil, QC (Scot), MA, LLB. Sheriff of Lothian and Borders, at Edinburgh, since 1968; b. 16.5.20; m.; 1 s.; 2 d. Educ. Loretto; Oriel College, Oxford; Edinburgh University. RA, 1940-45; called to Scottish Bar, 1948.

McVie, John, BL, WS, NP. Senior Partner, Anderson & McVie, WS; Honorary Sheriff-Substitute, Lothian and Borders; b. 7.12.19, Edinburgh; m., Lindsaye Woodburn Mair; 1 s.; 1 d. Educ. Royal High School; Edinburgh University. Captain, 7/9th Bn., The Royal Scots, 1940-46 (Signal Officer, North West Europe); Solicitor in private practice in Haddington, since 1947; Town Clerk, Royal Burgh of Haddington, 1951-75. Recreations: fishing; golf; motoring. Address: (h.) Ivybank, Haddington, East Lothian; T.-062-082 3727.

McWilliam, Colin Edgar, MA, FRSA, Hon FRIBA. Senior Lecturer, Architectural History and Conservation, Heriot-Watt University and Edinburgh College of Art, since 1978; b. 19.2.28, London; m., Helene Christine Jannink; 1 s.; 2 d. Educ. Charterhouse; Caius College, Cambridge. Formerly: Officer in Charge, Scottish National Buildings Record; Assistant Secretary, National Trust for Scotland; Morgan Professor of Architectural Design, Louisville University. Member, Council, The Victorian Society; Member, Historic Buildings Council for Scotland; Vice President, Architectural Heritage Society of Scotland; Vice President, Edinburgh Antique and Fine Art Society; Hon. Order of Kentucky Colonels. Publications: Scottish Townscape; Buildings of Scotland - Lothian; Edinburgh (Co-author). Recreation: discovering towns and churches. Address: (b.) Edinburgh College of Art, Lauriston Place, Edinburgh, EH3 9DF; T.-031-229 9311.

McWilliam, James, MA (Hons), DipEd. Rector, Lochaber High School, since 1970; Chairman, Highland Health Board, since 1983; b. 4.10.27, Portsoy, Banffshire; m., Helen C. Brodie; 3 d.

Educ. Fordyce Academy, Banffshire; Glasgow University. Teacher of English, Calderhead School, Shotts, 1951; National Service (Royal Army Education Corps), 1951-53; Teacher, Coatbridge High School, 1953; Special Assistant, Beath High School, Cowdenbeath, 1958; Principal Teacher of English, Campbeltown Grammar School, 1961-70. Member, Highland Health Board, since 1978 (Chairman, Practitioners' Committee, 1981); Honorary Sheriff, Grampian, Highlands and Islands, since 1978; Chairman: Lochaber Music Club, League of Friends of Belford Hospital; Secretary: local committees of British Heart Foundation, Forces Help Society, SSAFA; Past President: Lochaber Rotary Club, Lochaber EIS, Highland Secondary Headteachers Association. Recreations: music; TV; golf (occasionally). Address: (h.) The Schoolhouse, Camaghael, Fort William; T.-0397 2572.

McWilliam, Robert John, MB, ChB, FRCPG, DO. Consultant Ophthalmic Surgeon; Honorary Lecturer, Glasgow University; Civilian Ophthalmic Specialist for Royal Navy in Scotland; b. Glasgow; m., Louisa R. Denholm; 2 s. Educ. High School of Glasgow; Glasgow University. Recreations: fishing; gardening. Address: (h.) 4 Torridon Avenue, Glasgow, G41; T.-041-427 1204.

McWilliam, Rev. Thomas Mathieson, MA, BD. Minister, Lylesland Parish Church, Paisley, since 1980; b. 12.11.39, Glasgow; m., Patricia Jane Godfrey; 1 s.; 1 d. Educ. Eastwood Secondary School; Glasgow University; New College, Edinburgh. Assistant Minister, Auld Kirk of Ayr, 1964-66; Minister: Dundee St. David's North, 1966-72, East Kilbride Greenhills, 1972-80; Convener, Youth Education Committee, General Assembly, 1980-84; Moderator, Paisley Presbytery, 1985-86. Recreations: sea angling; walking; reading; gardening; bowling. Address: (h.) 28 Southfield Avenue, Paisley, PA2 8BY; T.-041-884 2882.

M

Maan, Bashir Ahmed, JP, DL. Company Director, B.A. Mann & Co. Ltd., since 1981; b. 22.10.26, Maan, Pakistan; 1 s.; 3 d. Educ. D.B. High School, Quila Didar Singh; Punjab University. Involved in the struggle for creation of Pakistan as a student, 1943-47; organised rehabilitation of refugees from India in Maan and surrounding areas, 1947-48; emigrated to UK and settled in Glasgow, 1953; Founder Secretary, Glasgow Pakistan Social and Cultural Society, 1955-65 (President, 1966-69); Member, Executive Committee, Glasgow City Labour Party, 1969-70; Vice-Chairman, Glasgow Community Relations Council, 1970-75; Member, Glasgow Corporation, 1970-75 (Magistrate, City of Glasgow, 1971-74; Vice-Chairman, then Chairman, Police Committee, 1971-75); Member, National Road

Safety Committee, 1971-74 and Scottish Accident Prevention Committee, 1971-75; Member, BBC Immigrant Programmes Advisory Committee, 1972-80; Convenor, Pakistan Bill Action Committee, 1973; contested East Fife Parliamentary seat, February 1974; President, Standing Conference of Pakistani Organisations in UK and Eire, 1974-77; Police Judge, City of Glasgow, 1974-75; Member, City of Glasgow District Council, 1975-84; Deputy Chairman, Commission for Racial Equality, 1977-80; Member, Scottish Gas Consumers Council, 1978-81; Bailie, City of Glasgow, 1980-84; Member, Greater Glasgow Health Board, since 1981; Deputy Lieutenant, Glasgow, since 1982; Founder Chairman, Scottish Pakistani Association, since 1984; Judge, City of Glasgow District Courts. Recreations: golf; reading. Address: (h.) 20 Sherbrooke Avenue, Glasgow, G41 4PE; T.-041-427 4057.

Maas, Peter, BSc, MSc, PhD, FInstP. Senior Lecturer in Applied Physics, Strathclyde University, since 1976; b. 9.4.39, Evanston, Illinois; m., Margot; 2 d. Educ. Abbey School, Canon City, Colorado; MIT, Cambridge, Massachusetts; Stanford University; Colorado University. Scientist, Lockheed Missile & Space Co., 1962-65; Research Fellow, Colorado Medical School, Denver, 1969-70; Lecturer in Applied Physics, Strathclyde University, 1970-76. Address: (b.) Department of Applied Physics, Strathclyde University, 107 Rottenrow, Glasgow, G4 ONG; T.-041-552 4400.

Mabon, Rt. Hon. (Jesse) Dickson, PC (1977), MB, ChB. Deputy Chairman, RGC (Offshore) plc, since 1982; b. 1.11.25; m.; 1 s. Educ. North Kelvinside School; Glasgow University. Coalmining; Army, 1944-48; Physician; MP (Labour and Co-op), Greenock, (later called Greenock and Port Glasgow) 1955-81, (SDP) 1981-83; Joint Parliamentary Under Secretary of State for Scotland, 1964-67; Minister of State, Scottish Office, 1967-70; Minister of State, Department of Energy, 1976-79; Past Chairman, Scottish Parliamentary Labour Party; Member, Council of Europe, 1970-72 and 1974-76; Chairman, European Movement, 1975-76; founder Chairman, Manifesto Group, Parliamentary Labour Party, 1974-76.

Machin, George Ian Thom, MA, DPhil, FRHistS. Reader in Modern History, Dundee University, since 1982; b. 3.7.37, Liverpool; m., Dr. Jane Margaret Pallot; 2 s. Educ. Silcoates School, near Wakefield; Jesus College, Oxford. Research Student and Tutor, Oxford University, 1958-61; Assistant Lecturer, then Lecturer in History, Singapore University, 1961-64; Lecturer in Modern History: St. Andrews University, 1964-67, Dundee University, 1967-75 (Senior Lecturer, 1975-82); Course Tutor, Open University in Scotland, 1971-82. Treasurer, Abertay Historical Society, 1966-73; Treasurer, Dundee Branch, Historical Association, since 1981. Publications: The Catholic Question in English Politics 1820 to 1830; Politics and the Churches in Great Britain 1832 to 1868. Recreations: music; hill-walking; swimming. Address: (h.) 100 Tay Street, Newport-on-Tay, Fife, DD6 8AS; T.-0382 543371.

Mack, Alistair John, MB, ChB, MSc, FRCSGlas, FRCSEdin. Consultant Surgeon, Victoria Infirmary, Glasgow, since 1969; b. 12.1.37, Bolton; m., Dr. Alison Mack; 2 s.; 1 d. Educ. The Bolton School; Paisley Grammar School; Glasgow University.

Mack, Donald William, MA. HM Chief Inspector of Schools, since 1984; b. 9.5.32, Dunfermline; m., Catherine; 1 d. Educ. Allan Glen's School, Glasgow; Glasgow University. History Teacher in Glasgow; Lecturer in History, Jordanhill College of Education; Principal Lecturer in Social Studies, Hamilton College of Education; HMI, since 1974. Recreations: photography; rock gardening; bonsai. Address: (b.) Room 4/108 New St. Andrews House, St. James Place, Edinburgh; T.-031-556 8400.

Mack, Jimmy. Broadcaster and Journalist; Presenter, The Jimmy Mack Show, BBC Radio Scotland, since 1979; Presenter, Scotland Today, Scottish Television, since 1985; b. 26.6.34, Greenock; m., Barbara; 1 s.; 1 d. Educ. Lenzie Academy; Bathgate Academy. Insurance Inspector, Guardian Royal Exchange Assurance Co., 1956-70; Producer and Presenter, various programmes, BBC Radio Medway, Kent, 1970-79; since 1979, in addition to daily programme on BBC Radio Scotland also presents Jimmy Mack's Old Gold; Presenter, various programmes, BBC Radios 1, 2 and 4, since 1970; Presenter, various programmes, Grampian TV, since 1980. Publication: The Jimmy Mack Show Book, 1984. Recreation: photography. Address: (h.) 38 Douglas Park Crescent, Bearsden, Glasgow, G61 3DN; T.-041-942 0524.

Mackie, Allister Andrew, JP. Member, West Lothian District Council, since 1974 (Labour Group Leader, since 1977 and Leader of Council, since 1984); b. 30.10.30, Toronto, Canada; m., Patricia McGinley; 1 s.; 2 d. Educ. Kilmarnock Academy. Served apprenticeship as compositor, Kilmarnock Herald, 1948-55; RAF, 1952-54; Imperial Father, Scottish Daily Express, Glasgow, 1964-74; Chairman, Scottish Daily News, 1975; Labour candidate, Lothians, European Assembly, 1978. Recreations: reading; politics; bowls; Burns clubs. Address: (h.) 54 Mid Street, Bathgate, West Lothian; T.-Bathgate 53931.

Mackie, Professor Andrew George, MA, PhD, FRSE, FIMA. Professor of Applied Mathematics, Edinburgh University, since 1968; b. 7.3.27, Tain; m., Elizabeth Maud Hebblethwaite; 1 s.; 1 d. Educ. Tain Royal Academy; Edinburgh University; Cambridge University; St. Andrews University. Lecturer, Dundee University, 1948-50; Bateman Research Fellow and Instructor, California Institute of Technology, 1953-55; Lecturer: Strathclyde University, 1955-56, St. Andrews University, 1956-62; Professor of Applied Mathematics, Victoria University of Wellington, New Zealand, 1962-65; Research Professor, Maryland University, 1966-68; Visiting Professor, California Institute of Technology, 1984 and University of New South Wales, Australia, 1985; Vice-Principal, Edinburgh University, 1980-85; Chairman, Scottish Mathematical Council, 1980-84; President, Edinburgh Mathematical Society, 1982-83. Publication: Boundary Value

Problems, 1965. Recreation: golf. Address: (b.) Department of Mathematics, King's Buildings, Mayfield Road, Edinburgh, EH9 3JZ; T.-031-667 1081, Ext. 2700.

Mackie, (Clarence Roy) Larry, FBIM, MSc, BSc, DN, RGN, RMN. Chief Area Nursing Officer, Ayrshire and Arran Health Board, since 1984; b. 7.6.43, Melita, Manitoba. Educ. Vincent Massey Collegiate Institute, Winnipeg; Sussex University; London University; Aberdeen University; Winnipeg University. Worked in Winnipeg, Toronto, New York, London, Bradford; Divisional Nursing Officer, Lothian Health Board, 1980-83; District Nursing Officer, Greater Glasgow Health Board, 1983-84. Council Member, Scottish Association of Nurse Administrators; elected Member, National Board for Nusing, Midwifery and Health Visiting for Scotland; former Scottish Chairman, RADNO Group; Secretary, Scottish CANOs Group; Member, Information Computer Services Advisory Group for Scotland; Member, Computer Steering Committee Scotland; Member, Standard Systems Committee Scotland; Past Chairman, Lothian Centre, Royal College of Nursing; Past Chairman, Nursing and Midwifery Advisory Committee, Lothian Health Board; former Member, National Nursing and Midwifery Consultative Committee for Scotland. Recreations: reading; walking; skating. Address: (b.) Ayrshire and Arran Health Board, Hunters Avenue, Ayr; T.-Ayr 281821.

Mackie of Benshie, Baron, (George Yull Mackie), CBE, DSO, DFC, LLD. Farmer; Liberal Spokesman on Agriculture and Scotland, House of Lords, since 1975; President, Scottish Liberal Party, since 1983; Life Peer; b. 10.7.19, Aberdeen; m., Lindsay Lyall Sharp; 1 s. (deceased); 3 d. Educ. Aberdeen Grammar School; Aberdeen University. Contested South Angus, 1959; Vice-Chairman (Organisation), Scottish Liberal Party, 1959-64; MP (Liberal), Caithness and Sutherland, 1964-66; Chairman, Scottish Liberal Party, 1965-70; contested Caithness and Sutherland, 1970; contested NE Scotland, European Parliamentary Election, 1979; Member, EEC Scrutiny Committee (D), House of Lords; Executive of Inter-Parliamentary Union; Chairman, Industrial Appeal Committee, Pitlochry Festival Theatre, 1979; Chairman, Angus Committee, Salvation Army, 1976-84; Rector, Dundee University, 1980-83. Recreations: golf; shooting; social life. Address: Ballinshoe, Kirriemuir, Angus; T.-Kirriemuir 73466.

Mackie, James Shivas, BArch (Hons), RIBA, FFB, AFS, MRSH, RIAS. Director of Planning and Technical Services, Inverclyde District Council, since 1975; b. 30.8.33, Glasgow. Educ. Strathclyde University; Glasgow School of Art. Architect: Scottish Gas Board, 1958-60, South of Scotland Electricity Board, 1960-67; Depute Burgh Architect/Town Planning Officer, Burgh of Airdrie, 1967-75. Recreations: painting; gardening; voluntary work. Address: (b.) 158 Dalrymple Street, Greenock, PA15 1HZ.

Mackie, Jean Hughes, JP. Vice-Chairman, Education Committee, Fife Regional Council, since 1978; b. 18.4.19, Dundee; m., Andrew

M. Mackie; 1 s.; 1 d. Educ. Dunfermline High School. Member, Dunfermline Town Council, 1953 (Bailie, 1955-61, Provost, 1961-64, Treasurer, 1964-67); Governor, Dunfermline College of Physical Education; Governor, Leith Nautical College; Past Chairman, Fife Health Board; Member, Carnegie Trust. Recreations: reading; politics. Address: (h.) Glen Isla, 23 Muir Road, Townhill, Dunfermline, Fife; T.-Dunfermline 721281.

Mackie, Sir Maitland, Kt (1982), CBE (1965), JP. Lord Lieutenant of Aberdeenshire, since 1975; Farmer; b. 16.2.12. Educ. Aberdeen Grammar School; Aberdeen University. Convener, Aberdeen County Council, 1967-75; Chairman, NE Development Authority, 1969-75; Chairman, Aberdeen Milk Marketing Board, 1965-82; Chairman, Hanover Housing Association, since 1981; Chairman, Oil Policy Committee, Scottish Council (Development and Industry), since 1975; Chairman, Aberdeen Cable Services, since 1983; Governor, North of Scotland College of Agriculture, since 1968; KStJ; Hon. LLD, Aberdeen, 1977.

Mackie, Maitland, BSc, MA. Farmer; Director, Farmdata, since 1979; b. 21.9.37, Aberdeen; 1 s.; 2 d. Educ. Aberdeen Grammar School; Aberdeen University. Member, Scottish Agricultural Development Council; Chairman, Food Research Committee, Agricultural and Food Research Council; Council Member, National Farmers Union of Scotland. Recreation: Norway. Address: Westertown, Rothienorman, Aberdeenshire; T.-04675 466.

Macklon, Alan Edward Stephen, BSc, PhD. Head, Department of Plant Physiology, Macaulay Institute for Soil Research, since 1984; b. 2.10.36, Dover; m., Bridget Jessamine Carr; 4 s. Educ. Cambridgeshire High School for Boys; Nottingham University; Aberdeen University. Joined Macaulay Institute for Soil Research, 1962; spent a year as Research Associate, Washington State University, 1966-67. Recreation: gardening. Address: (b.) Macaulay Institute for Soil Research, Craigiebuckler, Aberdeen, AB9 2QJ; T.-Aberdeen 318611.

Magee, James, MBE, OStJ, MCIT, MBIM, MIPM. Member, Employers' Panel, Industrial Tribuals (Scotland), since 1981; Vice-President, St. Andrews Ambulance Association and Vice-Chairman of Council, since 1971; Lay Member, Complaints Committee, Law Society of Scotland, since 1985; b. 8.3.20, Paisley; m., Elizabeth Forbes McKay; 1 s. Educ. Camphill School, Paisley; School of Transport, Derby; British Transport Staff College, Woking. LMS Railway and British Railways, Scotland, 1938-74 (Chief Personnel Officer for Scotland); Chief Staff Officer, British Railways Board, London, 1974-78; Member, CBI Scotland Industrial and Training Committees, 1971-80; Member, Careers Service Advisory Council, Scotland, 1971-74; Member, Central Arbitration Committee, Department of Employment, 1977-80; Council Member, Scottish Action Resource Centre, 1977-82; Trustee, New Templars Halls Trust, Paisley; Chairman, Railway Benevolent Institution (Scottish Committee), since 1980; Member, Paisley Presbytery and Synod of Clydesdale, Church of Scotland, since 1960. Recreations: music (choral); golf; social responsibilities. Address: (h.) 8 Stanely Grove, Paisley; T.-041-884 4370.

Magnusson, Magnus, MA (Oxon), FRSE, FRSA, FSA Scot. Broadcaster; Chairman, Ancient Monuments Board for Scotland, since 1981; Chairman, Scottish Churches Architectural Heritage Trust; b. 12.10.29, Reykjavik, Iceland; m., Mamie; 1 s.; 3 d. Educ. Edinburgh Academy; Jesus College, Oxford. Reporter, Scottish Daily Express; Features Writer, The Scotsman; Co-Presenter, Tonight, BBC TV, 1964-65; Presenter: Chronicle, Cause for Concern, Checkpoint, All Things Considered, Mainly Magnus, BC - The Archaeology of the Bible Lands, Living Legends, Vikings!, Mastermind; Rector, Edinburgh University, 1975-78.

Maher, Michael Alexander Ramsey, JP, ABTI. Member, Tweeddale District Council (Chairman of Housing); b. 14.5.18, Glasgow; m., Ellaretta Eckford Montgomery; 1 s.; 1 d. Educ. St. Mungo's Academy, Glasgow. Served with 157 Field Ambulance (TA), RAMC, seven years; Training Officer in Civil Defence, Peeblesshire County Council; transferred to Borders Regional Council on re-organisation; held post of Registrar of Births, Deaths and Marriages for Peebles and District; Treasurer, H. Ballantyne Memorial Institute, Walkerburn, 26 years; Chairman: Walkerburn Community Council, Walkerburn OAP Association, St. James Church Parish Council, Innerleithen. Recreations: gardening; painting. Address: (h.) 2 Park Avenue, Walkerburn, Peebles-shire; T.-Walkerburn 272.

Maiden, Robert Mitchell, FIB (Scot), FBIM. Executive Director, Royal Bank of Scotland plc, since 1982; Executive Director, Williams & Glyn's Bank plc, since 1984; Director, Travellers Cheque Associates Ltd., since 1983; b. 15.9.33, Montrose; m., Margaret M. Nicolson. Educ. Montrose Academy. Joined Royal Bank of Scotland, 1950; Chairman, Royal Bank Leasing Ltd.; a Director, Royal Bank of Scotland Group Insurance Co. Ltd. and National Commercial & Glyn's Ltd. Recreations: music; golf; hillwalking. Address: (h.) Trinafour, Bonaly Road, Edinburgh; T.-031-441 2858.

Main, James, FRICS. Buildings Officer and Factor, Aberdeen University, since 1979; b. 14.12.30, Aberdeen; m., Norma Scott Miller; 1 s.; 2 d. Educ. Aberdeen Central School; College of Estate Management. Apprentice Assistant, Aberdeen County Architect's Department; Quantity Surveyor, Cumbernauld Development Corporation; Deputy Buildings Officer, Aberdeen University. Trustee, Aberdeen International Youth Festival. Address: (h.) 22 Hosefield Avenue, Aberdeen, AB2 4NN; T.-0224 633884.

Main, Kirkland, ARSA, RSW, DA. Lecturer in Drawing and Painting, Edinburgh College of Art, since 1969; Chairman, Association of Lecturers in Scottish Central Institutions, since 1982; b. 1.7.42, Edinburgh; m., Geraldine Francis; 1 d. Educ. Daniel Stewart's College; Edinburgh College of Art. Assistant to Vice Principal,

Edinburgh College of Art, 1980-83 (Governor, 1979-85); Member, Central Institutions Staffs Salaries Committee, 1977-81; Member, Scottish Joint Negotiating Committee, Further Education, since 1982. Address: (h.) 15 Cramond Village, Edinburgh, EH4 6NU.

Mair, Alexander, MBE (1967). Director and Chief Executive, Grampian Television, since 1970; b. 5.11.22, Echt; m., Margaret Isobel. Educ. Skene Central School; School of Accountancy, Glasgow. Company Secretary, Grampian TV, 1961-70; appointed Director, 1967; Director, ITN, since 1979; Chairman, Junior Chamber, Aberdeen, 1960-61. Recreations: golf; skiing. Address: (h.) Ravenswood, 66 Rubislaw Den South, Aberdeen, AB2 6AA.

Mair, Alistair S.F., BSc, FBIM. Managing Director, Caithness Glass PLC, since 1977; b. 20.7.35, Drumblade; m., 1, Anne Garrow (deceased); 2, Mary Bolton; 4 s.; 1 d. Educ. Robert Gordon's College, Aberdeen; Aberdeen University. Rolls Royce, Glasgow, 1957-71: graduate apprentice, PA to General Manager, Production Control Manager, Product Centre Manager; RAF, 1960-62 (short-service commission, Technical Branch); Managing Director, Caithness Glass Ltd., 1971-75; Marketing Director, Worcester Royal Porcelain Co., 1975-76. Member, Scottish Council, CBI; Member, Scottish Committee, CNAA, since 1981; Member, CBI Council, 1985. Recreations: gardening; walking; current affairs. Address: (h.) Dungora, Heathcote Road, Crieff, Perthshire, PH7 4AG; T.-0764 2191.

Mair, Douglas, MA, PhD. Senior Lecturer, Department of Economics, Heriot-Watt University, since 1975; b. 3.6.39, Arbroath; m., Ishbel Fraser; 2 s.; 1 d. Educ. Arbroath High School; St. Andrews University. Ford Motor Company, 1960-63; Scottish Council (Development and Industry), 1963-67; joined Heriot-Watt University, 1967; Scottish Development Department (part-time), 1976-77; Secretary, Section F, British Association, 1980-84. Publication: Structure and Growth of Scottish Economy (Co-author), 1971. Recreations: golf; restoration of Victorian property. Address: (h.) Eskdale, 43 Abercorn Terrace, Edinburgh, EH15 2DG; T.-031-669 2511.

Mair, John, MA (Oxon), LLB. Leader, Conservative Group, Strathclyde Regional Council, since 1982; Solicitor in private practice; b. 12.5.29, Glasgow; m., Catherine; 3 s. Educ. Glasgow Academy; Trinity College, Glenalmond; Oxford University; Glasgow University. Qualified as Solicitor, 1956; Member, Glasgow Corporation, 1970-75; Member, Strathclyde Regional Council, since 1975. Holder, various offices, Conservative Party. Recreations: reading; golf. Address: (b.) 20 India Street, Glasgow, G2 4PF; T.-041-227 3401.

Mair, William Wallace, MA. Secretary, Faculty of Actuaries in Scotland, since 1974; Deputy Secretary, Associated Scottish Life Offices, since 1974; b. 19.6.49, Bellshill; m., Sandra Cunningham; 1 s.; 1 d. Educ. Uddingston Grammar School;

Glasgow University. Assistant Secretary, Royal Institution of Chartered Surveyors, 1969-72; Secretary, Scottish National Federation of Building Trades Employers, 1972-73. Recreations: badminton; cricket; hill-walking; lay preaching. Address: (b.) 23 St. Andrew Square, Edinburgh, EH2 1AQ; T.-031-557 1575.

Maitland-Titterton, Major David Maitland, TD (1947), MA. Marchmont Herald of Arms to Court of Lord Lyon, since 1982; b. 8.8.04; m.; 2 s. Educ. Queens' College, Cambridge. Commissioned, 1924; Ayrshire Yeomanry, 1926; Assistant District Officer, Political Service, Nigeria, 1927-32; served Second World War (Major, 1942); Liaison Officer with Polish Army, 1944; Staff Officer, 51 Highland Division, 1954-63; Falkland Pursuivant Extraordinary, 1969-71; Ormond Pursuivant, 1971-84. Address: (h.) Moberty, Craigton of Airlie, by Kirriemuir, Angus, DD8 5NW.

Makgill Crichton Maitland, Major John David. Lord Lieutenant of Renfrewshire, since 1980; b. 10.9.25; m.; 1 s.; 1 d. Educ. Eton. Served Second World War, Grenadier Guards, 1944-45; retired, 1957, with rank of Captain; Member, Renfrew County Council, 1961-75; Governor, West of Scotland Agricultural College.

Makin, Professor Brian, BSc, PhD, CEng, FIEE, FInstP. Head, Department of Electrical Engineering and Electronics, Dundee University, since 1974; b. 28.12.35, Sheffield; m., Hazel Phillips; 3 s. Educ. High Storrs Grammar School, Sheffield; Southampton University. Scientific Assistant, Avco-Everett, Massachusetts, 1962-63; Project Engineer, W.G. Pye, Cambridge, UK, 1964-66; Lecturer, then Senior Lecturer, Department of Electrical Engineering, Southampton University, 1966-74. Address: (b.) Department of Electrical Engineering and Electronics, The University, Dundee, DD1 4HN; T.-Dundee 23181, Ext. 4394.

Makins, Rev. Gordon William Garnett, BA (Hons). Minister, Sandbank and Kilmun, since 1968; b. 23.12.19, Cosham, Hampshire; m., Flora Stewart Mackenzie; 2 d. Educ. Chiver's School, Southsea; Royal Dockyard School, Portsmouth; Glasgow University. Royal Navy, 1940-51: service in submarines, 1941-46, in Mediterranean, Atlantic, Far East; student, 1951-54; ordained and inducted to Foss and Tenandry, Perthshire, 1954; Minister, Dunfermline North, 1959-68. Recreation: sailing. Address: St. Munn's Manse, Kilmun, by Dunoon, Argyll, PA23 8SD; T.-036 984 461.

Maksymiuk, Jerzy. Principal Conductor, BBC Scottish Symphony Orchestra, since 1983; b. 9.4.36, Grodno, Poland; m., Irena Kirjacka. Educ. Warsaw Academy of Music. Opera House, Warsaw, 1969, conducting Mozart, Stravinsky and modern works; Director, National Radio Orchestra of Poland, 1972-74; Music Director, Polish Chamber Orchestra, since 1972; Composer of music for Polish films. Winner of Polish Cultural Awards for composition and for forming Polish Chamber Orchestra; Polish Cross. Address: (b.) BBC, Queen Margaret Drive, Glasgow, G12 8DG; T.-041-330 2986.

Malcolm, David, MA, LLB. Honorary Sheriff, since 1976; b. 20.6.15, Cromarty; m., Helen Liddell Menzies; 2 s. Educ. Cromarty Higher Grade Public School; Fortrose Academy; Glasgow University. 2nd Bn., Glasgow Highlanders and 9th Gurkha Rifles, 1939-46 (attained rank of Major); Partner, J.M. & J. Mailer, Solicitors, Stirling, 1949-81, retiring as Senior Partner; Dean, Stirling Society of Solicitors and Procurators, 1973-75. Honorary Vice-President (and Past Chairman), Stirling and District Choral Union, since 1984; Past President: Stirling Rotary Club, Stirling Bowling Club; President, Borestone and Stirling Curling Club, Vice-President, Stirling Probus Club; President, Stirling Burns Club; Elder, St. Columba's Church, Stirling, since 1950. Recreations: bowls; curling; golf; choral singing; music. Address: (h.) 5 Royal Gardens, Stirling, FK8 2RJ; T.-0786 73949.

Malcolm, Douglas C., BSc, PhD. Senior Lecturer, Forestry and Natural Resources, Edinburgh University, since 1978; b. 4.12.30, Calcutta; m., M. Jean Wardrop; 4 d. Educ. George Watson's College, Edinburgh; Edinburgh University. District Forest Officer, Forestry Commission, 1954-61; Lecturer, 1961-78. Editor, Forestry. Recreation: gardening. Address: (b.) Department of Forestry and Natural Resources, West Mains Road, Edinburgh, EH9 3JU; T.-031-667 1081.

Malcolm, Finlay Traill, LLB. Chief Executive, Hamilton District Council, since 1984; b. 27.6.45, Dundee; m., Janet; 1 s.; 1 d. Educ. Morgan Academy, Dundee; St. Andrews University. Legal apprenticeship, private practice, Arbroath, 1966-68; Solicitor, private practice, Edinburgh, 1968-69; Solicitor, then Senior Solicitor, Falkirk Town Council, 1969-71; Depute Town Clerk, then Town Clerk, Grangemouth Town Council, 1971-75; Depute Director of Administration and Legal Services, Falkirk District Council, 1975-82; Director of Housing, Falkirk District Council, 1982-84. Recreations: golf; reading; music. Address: (b.) 102 Cadzow Street, Hamilton, ML3 6HH; T.-Hamilton 282323.

Malcolm, Robin Neill Lochnell, DL, JP. Farmer, since 1963; Member, Argyll and Bute District Council, since 1976; President, Scottish Agricultural Organisation Society Ltd., since 1983; b. 11.2.34, Edinburgh; m., Susan Hilary Freeman; 2 s.; 2 d. Educ. Eton; North of Scotland College of Agriculture. National Service, 1st Argyll and Sutherland Highlanders, 1953-54; TA (Captain, 8th Argyll and Sutherland Highlanders), 1955-63; shipping and shipbuilding in London and Glasgow, 1955-63; farming in Argyll, since 1963; Convener, Highlands and Islands Committee, NFU, 1972-74; Chief, Clan Malcolm. Recreations: shooting; swimming. Address: (h.) Duntrune Castle, Kilmartin, Argyll; T.-054 65 283.

Malloch, Rev. Jack, MBE, BL, MA, BD, DipEd. Minister, Church of Scotland, since 1936; b. 18.12.11, Edinburgh; m., 1, Agnes B. Mitchell (deceased); 2, Margaret H. Arnold; 3 s.; 3 d. Educ. George Watson's College, Edinburgh; Edinburgh University and New College; Moray House College of Education; Aberdeen University. Actuarial Assistant, Edinburgh Life

Assurance, 1929-31; Assistant Evangelist, Church of Scotland Home Board, 1937; Evangelical Campaign in Jamaica, 1937-38; Minister, Speirsbridge Church, Thornliebank, Glasgow, 1938-48; with troops in Europe, 1944-45; seconded to Presbyterian Church of Gold Coast, 1948; Principal of its College for teachers and catechists at Akropong; returned to Scotland, 1957; taught Mathematics and Religious Education, Boroughmuir School, Edinburgh, 1958-62; appointment in Religious Education, Aberdeen College of Education, 1962-65; Schoolmaster, Maths and Religious Education, Aberdeen Academy, 1965-79; pleading his own case before House of Lords, 1971, secured a ruling restoring his position as teacher employed, and changing the status of all qualified teachers in Scotland from that of "common servant at law" to that of "public officer fortified by Statute". Recreations: Aberdeen Bach Choir; composition; gardening (sweet peas); writing. Address: (h.) 71 Cromwell Road, Aberdeen, AB1 6UE; T.-0224 314870.

Malone, Desmond Noel Scott, MB, ChB, FRCPEdin. Consultant Physician, Department of Medicine, Milesmark Hospital, Dunfermline, since 1973; Honorary Senior Lecturer, Edinburgh University, since 1981; b. 12.12.34, Edinburgh; m., Kathleen Helena Murray; 2 s.; 2 d. Educ. Mount St. Mary's College, near Sheffield; Edinburgh University Medical School. House Physician, Peel Hospital, Galashiels; Flight Surgeon, Royal Canadian Airforce, Winnipeg; Research Fellow and Registrar, Northern General Hospital, Edinburgh; Medical Registrar, then Senior Medical Registrar, Western General Hospital, Edinburgh. Chairman, Fife Area Medical Committee; President, West Fife Medical Society. Recreations: fishing; windsurfing. Address: (h.) 2 Dalmeny View, Dalgety Bay, Fife, KY11 5LU; T.-0383 822532.

Malone, Peter Gerald, MP, MA, LLB. MP (Conservative), Aberdeen South, since 1983; PPS to Under Secretaries of State, Department of Energy; Solicitor, since 1974; b. 21.7.50, Glasgow; m., Dr. Anne Blyth. Educ. St. Aloysius College; Glasgow University. Recreations: opera; music. Address: (h.) 32 Albyn Lane, Aberdeen; T.-Aberdeen 571779.

Manlove, Colin Nicholas, MA, BLitt. Reader in English Literature, Edinburgh University, since 1984; b. 4.5.42, Falkirk; m., Evelyn Mary Schuftan; 2 s. Educ. Dollar Academy; Edinburgh University. Lecturer in English Literature, Edinburgh University, 1967-84. Publications: Modern Fantasy: Five Studies, 1975; Literature and Reality 1600-1800, 1978; The Gap in Shakespeare: The Motif of Division from Richard II to The Tempest, 1981; The Impulse of Fantasy Literature, 1983; Science Fiction: Ten Explorations, 1986. Address: (b.) Department of English Literature, Edinburgh University, David Hume Tower, George Square, Edinburgh, EH8 9JX; T.-031-667 1011, Ext. 6272.

Mann, Gordon Laurence, DipTP, MRTPI, MInstPet. Director of Planning, Shetland Islands Council, since 1980; b. 28.4.48, Dundee. Address: (h.) Victoria Buildings, The Esplanade, Lerwick; T.-0595 3515.

Mann, Leonard, JP, BEM. Chairman, Housing and Technical Services, Moray District Council, since 1977; b. 27.8.25, Keith; m., Frances; 2 d. Educ. Keith Grammar School. Past Chairman and Secretary, Keith Branch, National Union of Dyers, Bleachers and Textile Workers; elected, Keith Town Council, 1970-75; elected, Moray District Council, 1974; Member, Moray Valuation Appeals Panel; Life Member, Keith Amateur Swimming Club; Chairman of Trustees, Keith Community Bus. Recreations: swimming; walking. Address: (h.) 30 Cameron Drive, Keith, Banffshire; T.-Keith 2868.

Manners, Professor David John, MA, PhD, ScD, DSc, FRSC, FInstBiol, FRSE. Professor of Biochemistry, Heriot-Watt University, since 1965; b. 31.3.28, Castleford; m., Gweneth Mary Chubbock; 2 s.; 1 d. Educ. Grammar School, Castleford; Fitzwilliam House, Cambridge. Lecturer, then Reader in Chemistry, Edinburgh University, 1952-65; awarded Meldola Medal, Royal Institute of Chemistry, 1957; Alsberg-Schoch Memorial Award, American Association of Cereal Chemists, 1984. Recreations: philately; military history. Address: (h.) Department of Brewing and Biological Sciences, Heriot-Watt University, Chambers Street, Edinburgh, EH1 1HX; T.-031-225 8432.

Manning, Professor Aubrey William George, BSc, DPhil, FInstBiol, Dr (h c), FRSE. Professor of Natural History, Department of Zoology, Edinburgh University, since 1973; b. 24.4.30, London; m.; 2 s. by pr. m. Educ. Strode's School, Egham; University College, London; Merton College, Oxford. Research, 1951-54; National Service, Royal Artillery, 1954-56; Lecturer, then Reader in Zoology, Edinburgh University, 1956-73; Member, Scottish Advisory Committee, Nature Conservancy Council, 1982; Member, Advisory Committee on Science, NCC, 1985. Publication: An Introduction to Animal Behaviour, 1979. Recreations: woodland conservation; walking; architecture. Address: (h.) The Old Hall, Ormiston, East Lothian; T.-Pencaitland 340536.

Mansfield and Mansfield, 8th Earl of, (William David Mungo James Murray), JP, DL. Hereditary Keeper of Bruce's Castle of Lochmaben; b. 7.7.30; m., Pamela Joan Foster; 2 s.; 1 d. Educ. Eton; Christ Church, Oxford. Malaya campaign, 1949-50; called to Bar, Inner Temple, 1958; Barrister, 1958-71; Member, British Delegation to European Parliament, 1973-75; Minister of State, Scottish Office, 1979-83; Minister of State, Northern Ireland Office, 1983-84; Director, General Accident, Fire and Life Assurance Corporation Ltd., 1972-79. Address: (h.) Scone Palace, Perthshire, PH2 6BE.

Manson, Alexander Reid, SDA. Farmer; Chairman, Buchan Meat Producers Ltd., since 1982; Vice President, Scottish Agricultural Organisation Society Ltd., since 1983; Trustee, Plunkett Foundation, Oxford, since 1977; b. 2.9.31, Oldmeldrum; m., Ethel Mary Philip; 1 s.; 2 d. Educ. Robert Gordon's College; North of Scotland College of Agriculture. Member, Oldmeldrum Town Council, 1960-65; founder

Chairman, Aberdeen Beef and Calf Ltd., 1962. Recreations: golf; bird-watching. Address: (h.) Kilblean, Oldmeldrum, Inverurie, AB5 ODN; T.-Old Meldrum 2226.

Manson, Thomas Mortimer Yule, MA, DipEd, LLD. Member, Shetland Islands Council, since 1982; b. 9.2.04, Lerwick. Educ. Anderson Educational Institute; Edinburgh University; Moray House College of Education. Trained and qualified as a teacher; entered family printing and newspaper business, 1929; on father's death in 1941, became Proprietor, T. & J. Manson, Lerwick, and Editor, Shetland News (closed, 1963); Reporter, Radio Shetland, 1979-82; Bandmaster, local Boys' Brigade, seven years; Shetland County Scout Commissioner, 14 years (awarded Silver Acorn by Chief Scout); Conductor, Lerwick Brass Band, five years; Secretary, Lerwick Orchestral Society, 35 years; Chairman, Shetland Civic Society, 12 years. Recreation: music. Address: (h.) 93 Gilbertson Road, Lerwick, Shetland; T.-0595 4632.

Mantle, Richard John. Managing Director, Scottish Opera, since 1985; b. 21.1.47, London; m., June Mountain. Educ. Tiffin School, Kingston. Personnel management, Beecham Group, 1969-72; Personnel Manager, J. Walter Thompson Co., 1973-79; Personnel Director, then Deputy Managing Director, English National Opera, 1980-85. Recreations: music; theatre; wine; Church architecture. Address: (b.) 39 Elmbank Crescent, Glasgow, G2; T.-041-332 3321.

Mar, 13th Earl of, and Kellie, 15th Earl of, (John Francis Hervey Erskine). Premier Viscount of Scotland; Hereditary Keeper of Stirling Castle; Lord Lieutenant of Clackmannan, since 1966; b. 15.2.21; m., Pansy Constance Thorne; 3 s.; 1 d. Educ. Eton; Trinity College, Cambridge. Major, Scots Guards (retired, 1954); Major, Argyll and Sutherland Highlanders (TA) (retired, 1959); Vice-Convener, Clackmannan County Council, 1961-64; Chairman, Forth Conservancy Board, 1957-68; Chairman, Clackmannanshire T&AFA, 1961-68; Member, Queen's Bodyguard for Scotland (Royal Company of Archers). Address: (h.) Claremont House, Alloa, Clackmannanshire.

Marjoribanks, Gerald Brian, BA, LRAM, ALAM. Officer for Scotland, Independent Broadcasting Authority, since 1983; b. 22.7.42, Falkirk; m., Kathleen; 2 s.; 1 d. Educ. Falkirk High School; Edinburgh College of Speech and Drama; Open University. Sports Presenter, Sportsreel, Sportscene, Sportsound, BBC Scotland, 1966-83; Lecturer in Drama, Notre Dame College of Education, 1967-79; Co-ordinator of Learning Resources, Dunfermline College of Physical Education, 1979-80; Head of Public Relations, Cumbernauld Development Corporation, 1980-83. Recreations: drama adjudication; badminton; golf; photography. Address: (h.) Underwood, 33 Maggie Wood's Loan, Falkirk, FK1 5HR.

Marjoribanks, Sir James Alexander Milne, KCMG (1965). Chairman, Scotland in Europe, since 1979; b. 29.5.11. Educ. Merchiston; Edinburgh Academy; Edinburgh University. Joined Foreign Service, 1934; Assistant Under Secretary of State, Foreign Office, 1962-65; Ambassador and Head of UK Delegation to EEC, European Atomic Energy Community and ECSC, 1965-71.

Marjoribanks of That Ilk, William Logan, BSc. Member, Standing Council of Scottish Chiefs; b. 26.2.10, Callander; m., Thelma Williamson; 2 s. Educ. Edinburgh Academy; Edinburgh University. Sudan Civil Service, 1932-55; NE of Scotland Representative, National Trust for Scotland, 1955-75. Recreations: gardening; walking; fly-fishing. Address: Kirklands of Forglen, by Turriff, Banffshire, AB5 7JE.

Marker, Commander John (Iain) Hamilton, VRD (and bar), BA, MLitt, FIL, FRMetS, RNR (Rtd.). Depute Principal, Napier College of Commerce and Technology, since 1974; b. 23.9.24, Greenock; m., Elizabeth Urie Macfarlane. Educ. Ulverston Grammar School; Kings College, Durham University. Assistant Master, Middlesex County Secondary School, 1952-54; Assistant Lecturer in Economics, Kingston College of Advanced Technology, 1954-57; Assistant Lecturer/Lecturer in Economics, Isleworth Polytechnic, 1957-62; Head of Department, West London College, 1962-68; Head of Department, then Depute Principal, Edinburgh College of Commerce, 1968-74. Recreations: golf; reading; gardening. Address: (b.) Napier College, Sighthill Court, Edinburgh, EH11 4BN; T.-031-453 6111.

Marker, William Bennett, MA, MEd. Assistant Principal (In-service Education), Jordanhill College of Education, since 1976; b. 5.2.28, Greenock; m., Anne Margaret Manthorpe; 1 s.; 1 d. Educ. Ulverston Grammar School; Wadham College, Oxford. Assistant Teacher, Purbrook Park High School, 1954-56; Assistant Housemaster, Woodbridge School, 1956-58; Senior History Master, Queen Elizabeth School, Kirkby Lonsdale, 1958-67; Schoolmaster Fellow, Hull University, 1967; Lecturer/Senior Lecturer in History, Jordanhill College of Education, 1967-72 (Principal Lecturer (In-service), 1972-75). Member, National Committee for the In-service Training of Teachers, since 1978; Chairman, Strathkelvin and Bearsden Liberal Association. Recreations: hill-walking; opera-going. Address: (h.) 13 Southview Drive, Bearsden, Glasgow, G61 4HQ; T.-041-942 6756.

Marks, Frederick Charles, OBE, MA, LLB, FBIM. General Manager, Scottish Special Housing Association, since 1984; b. 3.12.34, Bellshill; m., Agnes M. Bruce; 3 s.; 1 d. Educ. Wishaw High School; Glasgow University. Depute Town Clerk, Dunfermline, 1963-68; Town Clerk, Hamilton, 1968-75; Chief Executive, Motherwell, 1974-83. Address: (b.) 9-21 Palmerston Place, Edinburgh, EH12 5AJ; T.-031-225 1281.

Marnoch, Derek George, BSc, ACMA. Chief Executive, Aberdeen Chamber of Commerce, since 1983; b. 30.10.35, Aberdeen; m., Kathleen Howard; 3 s. Educ. Aberdeen Grammar School; Aberdeen University. Recreation: golf. Address: (h.) The Gables, Kirk Road, Stonehaven, AB3 2DX; T.-0569 62709.

Marquis, Mary. Broadcaster. Educ. Dunoon Grammar School; Glasgow University; Royal Scottish Academy of Music and Drama. Presenter, Border TV; joined BBC Scotland as Presenter/Interviewer, Six Ten (nightly news magazine); has presented Today and Nationwide from London; Woman's Hour and Good Morning Scotland from Glasgow; Presenter, Reporting Scotland; has presented own series of profiles (First Person Singular) and classical music programme (Encore) and numerous other arts and current affairs programmes.

Marr, Professor Geoffrey Vickers, BSc, PhD, DSc, CPhys, FInstP. Professor of Natural Philosophy, Aberdeen University, since 1981 (Head, Department of Natural Philosophy); b. 30.1.30, Darlington; m., Jean; 2 s.; 1 d. Educ. Queen Elizabeth Grammar School, Darlington; Manchester University; Reading University. Research Fellow, University of Western Ontario, 1954-57; Lecturer, McGill University, Canada, 1957-59; Physicist, English Electric, Leicester, 1959-61; Lecturer, then Reader, Reading University, 1961-81. Recreations: painting; hill-walking; bee-keeping. Address: (b.) Department of Natural Philosophy, Aberdeen University, Aberdeen, AB9 2UE; T.-0224 40241.

Marr, Norman G., SBStJ, DipArch, ARIBA, ARIAS. Director of Planning and Development, Kincardine and Deeside District Council, since 1975; b. 19.5.37, Aberdeen. Educ. Aberdeen Grammar School; Scott Sutherland School of Architecture, Aberdeen. Architectural Assistant, Aberdeen County Council, 1961-66; Senior Research Assistant, Corporation of the City of Aberdeen, Town Planning Department, 1967-69 (Principal Development Assistant, 1970-75). Organist and Choirmaster, Denburn Parish Church, Aberdeen, since 1956; Secretary, Scottish Federation of Organists. Recreations: organ playing/building; swimming; marathon running; hill-walking. Address: (b.) Carlton House, Arduthie Road, Stonehaven, Kincardineshire; T.-0569 62001.

Marsh, Kenneth James, DPhil (Oxon), ME, BE. Deputy Chief Scientific Officer, National Engineering Laboratory, since 1979; b. 13.2.35, Auckland, New Zealand; m., Margaret Ann Wraight; 1 s.; 1 d. Educ. Auckland Grammar School; Auckland University; St. Catherine's College, Oxford. Spent one year in structural engineering practice; came to UK to undertake research in materials engineering; joined NEL as Senior Scientific Officer, then Principal Scientific Officer; Head, Service Loading Division, 1974. Publication: Metal Fatigue (Co-author), 1974. Recreation: hill-walking. Address: (b.) National Engineering Laboratory, East Kilbride, Glasgow; T.-03552 20222.

Marshall, David. MP (Labour), Glasgow Shettleston, since 1979; b. 1941. Former transport worker; Member, Glasgow Corporation, 1972-75; Member, Strathclyde Regional Council, 1974-79; Secretary, Scottish Group of Labour MPs.

Marshall, Enid Ann, MA, LLB, PhD, FRSA. Solicitor; Reader in Business Law, Stirling University, since 1977; Editor, Scottish Law Gazette, since 1983; Chairman, Soical Security Appeal Tribunal, Stirling and Falkirk, since 1984; b. 10.7.32, Boyndie, Banffshire. Educ. Banff Academy; Bell-Baxter School, Cupar; St. Andrews University. Apprentice Solicitor, 1956-59; Lecturer in Law, Dundee College of Technology, 1959-72; Lecturer, then Senior Lecturer, in Business Law, Stirling University, 1972-77. Departmental Editor, Arbitration Section, Journal of Business Law, since 1976. Publications: General Principles of Scots Law; Scottish Cases on Contract; Scottish Cases on Agency; Scottish Cases on Partnerships and Companies; Scots Mercantile Law; Gill on Arbitration; Charlesworth and Cain Company Law (Scottish Editor); Notes on the Law of Property in Scotland (Editor, 3rd edition). Recreations: veganism; animal welfare. Address: (h.) 24 Easter Cornton Road, Stirling, FK9 5ES; T.-Stirling 78865.

Marshall, Professor Ian Howard, MA, BD, PhD (Aberdeen), BA (Cantab). Professor of New Testament Exegesis, Aberdeen University, since 1979; b. 12.1.34, Carlisle; m., Joyce Elizabeth; 1 s.; 3 d. Educ. Aberdeen Grammar School; Aberdeen University; Cambridge University; Gottingen University. Assistant Tutor, Didsbury College, Bristol; Methodist Minister, Darlington; Lecturer, then Senior Lecturer and Reader in New Testament Exegesis, Aberdeen University. Publications: Kept by the Power of God; Luke: Historian and Theologian; The Origins of New Testament Christology; New Testament Interpretation (Editor); The Gospel of Luke; I Believe in the Historical Jesus; The Epistles of John; Acts; Last Supper and Lord's Supper; Biblical Inspiration; 1 and 2 Thessalonians. Address: (b.) Department of New Testament Exegesis, King's College, Aberdeen, AB9 2UB; T.-0224 40241.

Marshall, Margaret Winton Cowie, RGN, SCM, QN. Member, Moray District Council, since 1980; b. 28.11.19, Peterhead; widow; 1 d. Educ. Peterhead Academy. Nursing training, Western General Hospital, Edinburgh, Raigmore Hospital, Inverness, Craigton, St. Andrews, etc.; various nursing posts in Edinburgh, Forfar, Inverness, St. Andrews and Banffshire. WRVS hospital driver and book collector for the forces; Elder, Inveravon Church; founder Member, Glenlivet and Invcravon Community Association (Convener, Welfare Committee). Recreations: music; art; literature; talking with people. Address: (h.) Craighead Cottage, Benrinnes, Aberlour, Banffshire, AB3 9NL; T.-Aberlour 531.

Marshall, Mary Tara, MA, DSA, DASS. Director, Age Concern Scotland, since 1983; b. 13.6.45, Darjeeling, India. Educ. Mary Erskine School for Girls; Edinburgh University; London School of Economics; Liverpool University. Child Care Officer, London Borough of Lambeth, 1967-69; Social Worker, Personal Service Society, Liverpool, 1970-74; Research Organiser, Age Concern, Liverpool, 1974-75; Lecturer in Social Studies, Liverpool University, 1975-83. Publication: Social Work with Old People, 1983. Recreations: photography; bird-watching. Address: (b.) 33 Castle Street, Edinburgh; T.-031-225 5000/1.

Martin, David Weir, BA (Econ). Member (Labour), European Parliament, for Lothians, since 1984; b. 26.8.54; m.; 1 d. Educ. Liberton High School; Heriot-Watt University. Member, Lothian Regional Council, 1982-84.

Martin, Derek Walker, MA, LLB. Chief Executive and Director of Administration, Sutherland District Council, since 1974; b. 4.2.34, Aberdeen; m., Lydia Ann Watson Howard; 1 s.; 1 d. Educ. Robert Gordon's College, Aberdeen; Aberdeen University. Law apprenticeship, Brander and Cruickshank, Advocates in Aberdeen, 1954-57; National Service, 1957-59; Legal and Administrative Assistant, Inverness County Council, 1960-62; Assistant Solicitor, W. & J.S. Gordon, Solicitors, Forfar, 1962-64 (Partner, 1965-67); Assistant County Clerk, then Depute County Clerk, Sutherland County Council, 1967-74; Clerk, Highland River Purification Board (part-time), since 1976. Officer Adviser to Committees of Convention of Scottish Local Authorities; Elder, Church of Scotland. Address: (h.) Glenaveron, Golf Road, Brora, Sutherland; T.-Brora 21455.

Martin, Graham Dunstan, MA, BLitt (Oxon), GradCertEd. Senior Lecturer, French Department, Edinburgh University, since 1982; b. 21.10.32, Leeds; m., 1, Ryllis E. Daniel; 2 s.; 1 d.; 2, Anne M. Crombie; 2 s. Educ. Leeds Grammar School; Oxford University. Teacher: Robert Clack Technical School, Dagenham, 1956, Great Yarmouth Grammar School, 1959; Assistant, Centre Pedagogique Regional, Montpellier, 1962; Teacher, Colchester Royal Grammar School, 1964; Junior Lecturer, then Lecturer, French Department, Edinburgh University, 1965-82. Publications: Paul Valery's Cimetiere Marin, 1971; Language, Truth and Poetry, 1975; The Architecture of Experience, 1981; novels: Giftwish, 1980; Catchfire, 1981; The Soul Master, 1984; Time-Slip, 1986. Address: (b.) French Department, Edinburgh University, 4 Buccleuch Place, Edinburgh, EH8 9LW; T.-031-667 1011, Ext. 6423.

Martin, Rev. James, MA, BD, DD. Minister, High Carntyne, Glasgow, since 1954; b. 21.1.21, Motherwell; m., Marion Gordon Greig; 2 d. Educ. Dalziel High School, Motherwell; Glasgow University. Minister, Newmilns West Church, 1946-54; Convener, Publications Committee, General Assembly, 1978-83 and Board of Communications, since 1983. Publications: Did Jesus Rise from the Dead?; The Reliability of the Gospels; Letters of Caiaphas to Annas; Suffering Man, Loving God; The Road to the Aisle; People in the Jesus Story; A Plain Man in the Holy Land; Listening to the Bible; William Barclay: A Personal Memoir. Recreations: football; operagoing; conversation. Address: 165 Smithycroft Road, Glasgow; T.-041-770 6464.

Martin, James Davidson, MA, BD, PhD. Senior Lecturer in Hebrew and Old Testament, St. Andrews University, since 1977 (Chairman, Department of Biblical Criticism and Hebrew, since 1983); b. 4.5.35, Stirling; m., Frances Margaret Stewart; 1 s.; 2 d. Educ. High School of Stirling; Glasgow University. Minister, Dunscore (Dumfries), 1962-66; Glasgow University: Assistant in Old Testament Language and

Literature, 1966-68, Lecturer in Hebrew, 1968-69. Publication: The Book of Judges. Recreations: music; hill-walking. Address: (h.) 22 Kilrymont Road, St. Andrews, Fife; T.-0334 77361.

Martin, John S.B., BSc. Assistant Secretary, SDD Housing Division 1, Scottish Office, since 1984; b. 7.7.46, West Kilbride; m., Catriona Meldrum; 1 s.; 1 d. Educ. Bell-Baxter High School, Cupar; St. Andrews University. Assistant Principal, Scottish Education Department, 1968-73; Private Secretary to Parliamentary Under Secretary of State, 1971-73; Principal, Scottish Education Department/Central Services/Scottish Home and Health Department, 1973-79; Rayner Scrutinies, Consultative Committee on the Curriculum/SDD Planning, 1979-80; Assistant Secretary, Highlands and Tourism Division, SEPD/IDS, 1980-84. Recreations: tennis; badminton; philately. Address: (b.) St. Andrews House, Edinburgh; T.-031-556 8501.

Martin, Michael John. MP (Labour), Glasgow Springburn, since 1979; b. 3.7.45. Educ. St. Patrick's Boys' School, Glasgow. Former sheet metal worker and trade union organiser; Member, Glasgow Corporation, 1973-74, and Glasgow District Council, 1974-79; PPS to Rt. Hon. Denis Healey, MP, 1981-83.

Martin, Paul Charles, JP, MA (Hons). Leader, Conservative Group, Edinburgh City Council, since 1984 (Member of Council, since 1980); General Secretary, British Youth Council, Scotland, since 1984; b. 10.5.58, Edinburgh. Educ. Royal High School, Edinburgh; Edinburgh University. Chairman, Arts and Recreation Committee, Edinburgh, 1983-84; Conservative Parliamentary candidate, East Edinburgh, 1983; Member, Executive Committee, XIII Commonwealth Games, Edinburgh; Member, Edinburgh Festival Council; Director, Lowlands Housing Association Ltd. Address: (h.) 106 Findlay Gardens, Edinburgh, EH7 6HQ; T.-031-554 4878.

Martin, Robert, MC, BL. Consultant Solicitor, Wright & Crawford, Paisley, since 1985 (Partner, 1946-85); Honorary Sheriff; b. 5.2.17, Wishaw; m., Dr. Jan J. Martin; 1 s.; 1 d. Educ. Dalziel High School, Motherwell; Glasgow University. War Service, 1940-46: Field Artillery and Parachute Brigade, Singapore, India, Middle East, Italy, Greece, France, Germany (commissioned, 1940). Honorary Vice-President, Paisley Branch, Save the Children Fund; Governor, Imperial Cancer Research Fund. Recreations: golf; swimming. Address: (h.) The Willows, 12 Crosbie Wood, Paisley, PA2 OSG; T.-041-884 2113.

Martin, William Barr, PhD, MRCVS, DVSM, FRSE. Director, Moredun Research Institute, Edinburgh, 1977-85; b. 11.8.24, Glasgow; m., Mary E. Morrison; 2 s.; 2 d. Educ. Hutchesons' Grammar School, Glasgow; Glasgow Veterinary School. Lecturer, Department of Veterinary Medicine, Glasgow Veterinary School, 1949-57; Principal Scientific Officer, Animal Virus Research Institute, Pirbright, Surrey, 1957-61; Research Fellow, Department of Virology, Glasgow University, 1961-63; Senior Lecturer, latterly Head, Department of Pathology, University College, Nairobi, 1963-67; Senior Lecturer,

Department of Veterinary Medicine, Glasgow University Veterinary School, 1967-71 (seconded for two years to WHO, Food and Agricultural Organisation, Turkey); Head, Department of Microbiology, Moredun Research Institute, Edinburgh, 1971-77. Council Member, Royal College of Veterinary Surgeons. Publications: Respiratory Diseases of Cattle (Editor); Diseases of Sheep (Editor). Recreations: gardening; golf; curling; vintage cars. Address: (b.) 39 Neidpath Court, Longniddry, East Lothian, EH32 ONS; T.-0875 52291.

Martyn, Douglas Hamilton, BA. Chief Executive, Ardrossan Saltcoats Stevenston Enterprise Trust (ASSET), since 1981; Chairman, Ardrossan Saltcoats Stevenston Enterprise Properties Trust, since 1984; b. 16.9.44, Lanark; m., Patricia Elizabeth Graham; 1 s.; 1 d. Educ. Strathallan School; Strathclyde University. Assistant Marketing, Satchwell Appliance Controls, East Kilbride; Sales Executive, Rank Xerox, Glasgow; Scottish Regional Manager, Granada Television; Chief Executive, Nationwide TV Services Ltd.; Development Officer, Scottish Development Agency. Recreations: bowling; boating. Address: (h.) 2A Airbles Farm Road, Motherwell, Lanarkshire; T.-Motherwell 68723.

Marwick, Ewan, MA. Secretary, Glasgow Chamber of Commerce, since 1982; Secretary, Association of Scottish Chambers of Commerce, since 1982; b. 23.4.52, Edinburgh; m., Helen Daw; 1 s.; 1 d. Educ. Daniel Stewart's College; Edinburgh University. Postgraduate research and consultancy work; Assistant Secretary, Royal Institution of Chartered Surveyors (Scottish Branch); Depute Secretary, Glasgow Chamber of Commerce, 1980-82. A Director, Glasgow Opportunities; Secretary, Glasgow Posts and Telecommunications Advisory Committee. Recreation: field sports. Address: (b.) Glasgow Chamber of Commerce, 30 George Square, Glasgow, G2 1EQ; T.-041-204 2121.

Marwick, George Robert, SDA, DL, JP. Chairman, Swannay Farms Ltd., since 1972; Chairman, Campbeltown Creamery (Holdings) Ltd., since 1974; Deputy Lieutenant, County of Orkney, since 1976; Member, Countryside Commission for Scotland, since 1978; b. 27.2.32, Edinburgh; m., Hanne Jensen; 3 d. Educ. Port Regis; Bryanston; Edinburgh School of Agriculture. Councillor, local government, 1968-78 (Vice-Convener, Orkney County Council, 1970-74, Convener, Orkney Islands Council, 1974-78); Chairman, North of Scotland Water Board, 1970-73; Member, Scottish Agricultural Consultative Panel, since 1972 (formerly Winter Keep Panel, 1964-72); Director, North Eastern Farmers Ltd., since 1968; Director, Orkney Islands Shipping Co., since 1972; Council Member, National Trust for Scotland, 1979-84. Recreations: shooting; tennis; motor sport. Address: (h.) Swannay House, by Evie, Orkney; T.-085-672 365.

Mascarenhas, Armando Carlos Tomas, BA, DipYCS, DipD&P, DipMS. HM Inspector of Schools, since 1974; b. 29.12.35, Bombay, India; m., Frances Smith Matthews; 2 s. Educ. St.

Xavier's High School, Bombay; Bombay University; Open University; Moray House College of Education. Youth Tutor, Fife Education Authority, 1961-63; Secretary, Edinburgh YMCA, 1963-66; Principal Youth and Community Officer, Dundee Education Authority, 1966-74. Former Member: Standing Consultative Council on Youth and Community Service in Scotland, Scottish Council on Crime, Dundee Children's Panel; Founding Chairman, Institute of Community Education. Recreations: hockey; soccer; swimming; art and craft. Address: (b.) HM Inspectors' of Schools Office, St. Andrews House, 141 West Nile Street, Glasgow; T.-041-332 7297.

Mason, Christopher Michael, MA, PhD. Deputy Chairman, Scottish Liberal Party, since 1985; Member, Strathclyde Regional Council, since 1982; Lecturer in Politics, Glasgow University, since 1966; b. 8.3.41, Hexham; m., Stephanie Maycock; 2 d. Educ. Marlborough College; Magdalene College, Cambridge. Alliance candidate, Glasgow, European Elections, 1984. Publication: Effective Management of Resources: The International Politics of the North Sea, 1979. Recreation: sailing. Address: (h.) 17 Beaumont Gate, Glasgow, G12 9ED; T.-041-339 2840.

Mason, Professor David Kean, BDS, MD, FRCS, FDS, FRCPath. Professor of Oral Medicine, Glasgow University, since 1967; Dean of Dental Education, since 1980; Honorary Consultant Dental Surgeon, since 1965; b. 5.11.28, Paisley; m., Judith Armstrong; 2 s.; 1 d. Educ. Paisley Grammar School; Glasgow Academy; St. Andrews University; Glasgow University. RAF Dental Branch, 1952-54; Registrar in Oral Surgery, Dundee, 1954-56; Senior Lecturer in Dental Surgery and Pathology, Glasgow University, 1964-67; Honorary Consultant Dental Surgeon, Glasgow, 1964-67; Chairman, National Dental Consultative Committee, 1976-80 and since 1983; Member: Medicines Commission, 1967-80, Dental Committee, MRC, since 1973; Physiological Systems Board, MRC, 1976-80; GDC, since 1976; Dental Committee, UGC, since 1977 (Chairman, since 1983), Joint Committee for Higher Training in Dentistry, since 1977, Dental Strategy Review Group, 1980-81, Scientific Programme Committee, FDI, since 1980; Convener, Dental Council, RCPGlas, 1977-80; John Tomes Prize, RCS, 1979. Publications: Salivary Glands in Health and Disease (Co-author); Introduction to Oral Medicine (Co-author); Self Assessment: Manuals I and II (Co-Editor); Oral Manifestations of Systemic Disease. Recreations: golf; tennis; gardening; enjoying the pleasure of the countryside. Address: (h.) Greystones, Houston Road, Kilmacolm, Renfrewshire; T.-Kilmacolm 2001.

Mason, Douglas C., BSc. Member, Glenrothes Development Corporation, since 1985; Member, Kirkcaldy District Council, since 1974; Parliamentary Research Assistant, since 1979; b. 30.9.41, Dunfermline. Educ. Bradford Grammar School; St. Andrews University. Conservative Party Organising Secretary, 1969-77; Freelance Journalist, since 1977; Member, Fife County Council, 1967-70; Member, Scottish Housing Advisory Committee, 1978-80; contested Central Fife, General Election, 1983; Vice-Convener,

General Council Business Committee, St. Andrews University. Domestic Policy Adviser, Adam Smith Institute, since 1984. Publications: Allocation and Transfer of Council Houses (Co-author), 1980; The Qualgo Complex, 1984; Revising the Rating System, 1985; Room for Improvement, 1985. Recreations: books; music. Address: (h.) 84 Barnton Place, Glenrothes, Fife; T.-0592 758766.

Mason, Gavin John Finlay, MA, LLB. Solicitor; Secretary and Legal Adviser, Strathclyde Passenger Transport Executive, since 1984; b. 15.5.31, Bargeddie; m., Patricia Hunter Anderson; 1 s.; 1 d. Educ. Hamilton Academy; Glasgow University. Solicitor in private practice, until 1979, then local government service. Address: (h.) 3 Newark Drive, Glasgow, G41 4QJ; T.-041-423 7496.

Mason, Professor John Kenyon French, CBE, MD, FRCPath, DMJ. Regius Professor of Forensic Medicine, Edinburgh University, 1973-85; b. 19.12.19, Lahore; m., Elizabeth Latham (deceased); 2 s. Educ. Downside School; Cambridge University; St. Bartholomew's Hospital. Regular Officer, Medical Branch, RAF, following War Service; Consultant in charge, RAF Department of Aviation and Forensic Pathology, 1957-73. President, British Association in Forensic Medicine, 1981-83; Swiney Prize in Jurisprudence, 1978. Publication: Forensic Medicine for Lawyers, 2nd Edition; Law and Medical Ethics (Co-author). Address: (h.) 66 Craiglea Drive, Edinburgh, EH10 5PF; T.-031-447 2301.

Mason, John Muir, BL, NP. Solicitor; Partner, Waddell & Mackintosh, Troon; Conductor, Strings of Scotland and Scottish Fiddle Orchestra; b. 21.1.40, Kirkwall; m., Jessica Hilary Miller Groat; 3 s. Educ. Kirkwall Grammar School; Douglas Ewart High School, Newton Stewart; Edinburgh University. Apprenticed to Ketchen and Stevens, WS, Edinburgh; Assistant: A.B. & A. Matthews, Newton Stewart, Waddell & Mackintosh, Troon. Founder Chairman, Newton Stewart Round Table; Past President, DEHS FP Association; Honorary Member, Irvine Burns Club. Recreation: music, composition and arrangement. Address: (h.) 27 Victoria Drive, Troon, Ayrshire; T.-Troon 312796.

Mason, Timothy Ian Godson, MA. Director, Scottish Arts Council, since 1980; b. 11.3.45, Little Chalfont, Buckinghamshire; m., Marilyn Williams; 1 s.; 1 d. Educ. Bradfield College, Berkshire; Christ Church, Oxford. Assistant Manager, Oxford Playhouse, 1966-67; Assistant to Peter Daubeny, World Theatre Season, London, 1967-69; Administrator: Ballet Rambert, 1970-75, Royal Exchange Theatre, Manchester, 1975-77; Director, Western Australian Arts Council, 1977-80. Recreations: arts; family. Address: (b.) 19 Charlotte Square, Edinburgh, EH2 4DF; T.-031-226 6051.

Massie, Allan Johnstone, BA, FRSL. Author and Journalist; b. 16.10.38, Singapore; m., Alison Langlands. Educ. Drumtochty Castle; Trinity College, Glenalmond; Trinity College, Cambridge. Schoolmaster, Drumtochty Castle, 1960-71; taught EFL, 1972-75; Creative Writing

Fellow, Edinburgh University, 1982-84; Editor, New Edinburgh Review, 1982-84; Fiction Reviewer, The Scotsman, since 1975; Television Critic, Sunday Standard, 1981-83 (Fraser of Allander Award, Critic of the Year, 1982); Sports Columnist, Glasgow Herald, since 1985. Publications: (novels): Change and Decay in all around I see; The Last Peacock; The Death of Men (Scottish Arts Council Book Award); One Night in Winter; (non-fiction): Muriel Spark; Ill Met by Gaslight; The Caesars; Portrait of Scottish Rugby; (as Editor): Edinburgh and the Borders in Verse; (radio play): Quintet in October. Recreations: watching rugby; cricket; racing; vegetable gardening; walking the dogs. Address: (h.) Thirladean House, Selkirk, TD7 5LU; T.-Selkirk 20393.

Massie, Leslie Alexander, MA, LLB, CM, PJK (Malaysia). Advocate, since 1953; b. 20.5.10, Aberdeen; m., Margot N. Hesketh; 1 d. Educ. Robert Gordon's College, Aberdeen; Aberdeen University. General Legal Practice as Solicitor in Scotland, 1936-37; Examining Officer's Commission, HM Coal Commssion and HM Sasine Office, Scotland, 1938-39; enlisted as private, Royal Scots, 1939; commissioned 2nd Lt., Royal Scots Fusiliers, 1940-42; Captain and Adjutant, 15th (Scottish) Division Infantry Training Battle School, 1943-44; passed SC Military Staff College, Camberley, 1945; Staff Officer (Major), General Headquarters South East Asia Command, XIV Army, 1945; promoted Lt.-Col., Royal Scots Fusiliers, 1945; President, Superior Court (Military) and State Legal Adviser, Malay States of Kedah and Perlis, 1945-46; Assistant Judge-Advocate General GHQ South East Asia Command, 1946-47; President, War Crimes Court, South East Asia, 1947-48; demobilised Army, 1948; passed entry to HM Colonial Legal Service and gazetted as Federal Counsel to Government of Malaya, 1948; later, Senior Federal Counsel; Member, State Executive Council and State Legislative Council in several Malay States and British Settlements; called to Scottish Bar, 1953; took part in deliberations, in respect of British Settlement of Malacca, HM Reid Constitutional Commission, 1957; Solicitor-General, Federation of Malaysia, 1959-60; returned to UK, 1961. Recreations: golf; bowling; gardening. Address: 9 Whitehouse Terrace, Edinburgh, EH9 2EU; T.-031-667 6462.

Masson, Alastair H.B., BA, MB, ChB, FRCSEdin, FFARCS. Consultant Anaesthetist, Edinburgh Royal Infirmary, since 1956; b. 30.1.25, Bathgate; m., Marjorie Nan Paisley-Whyte; 3 s.; 1 d. Educ. Bathgate Academy; Edinburgh University. Visiting Professor of Anaesthesiology, South Western Medical School, Dallas, Texas, 1962-63. President, Scottish Society of Anaesthetists, 1978-79; Honorary Archivist, Royal College of Surgeons, Edinburgh; President, Scottish Society of the History of Medicine. Recreations: golf; hill-walking; music; travel. Address: (h.) 13 Osborne Terrace, Edinburgh.

Mather, Alexander Smith, BSc, PhD. Senior Lecturer, Department of Geography, Aberdeen University, since 1982; b. 17.9.43, Aberdeenshire; m., Grace MacArthur; 1 s. Educ.

Maud School; Peterhead Academy; Aberdeen Grammar School; Aberdeen University. Department of Geography, Aberdeen University: Assistant Lecturer, 1967, Lecturer, 1970. Recreations: hill-walking; angling. Address: (b.) Department of Geography, Aberdeen University, Aberdeen, AB9 2UF; T.-0224 40241, Ext. 5183.

Mather, William Wilson. Secretary, Hill Farming Research Organisation, since 1984; b. 24.7.35, Coldstream; m., Pauline Valerie. Educ. Fettes College. Student Farmer, 1952-55; National Service, 2nd Lt., York and Lancaster Regiment, KOSB (TA), 1955-57; short-service commission, RAF, 1958-70; various administration posts, 1970-74; Administration Officer, Rothamsted Experimental Station, Hertfordshire, 1974-84. Recreations: fishing; shooting; armchair sports; DIY. Address: (h.) The Old School, 51 Whitehill, by Dalkeith, Midlothian; T.-031-660 5602.

Mathers, John S., BSc, NDA, SDA. Regional Administrative Officer, Scotland, Agricultural Training Board, since 1970; b. 5.3.31, Edinburgh; m., Jenny Johnston; 1 d. Educ. Royal High School, Edinburgh; Edinburgh and East of Scotland College of Agriculture; Aberdeen University. Department of Agriculture for Scotland; Shell Chemical Co. Ltd.; National Farmers' Union of Scotland; Agricultural Training Board. Recreations: golf; gardening; walking. Address: (h.) Inverlogie, 45 Carlogie Road, Carnoustie, Angus, DD7 6EW; T.-Carnoustie 52897.

Matheson, Alexander, JP, MPS. Convener, Western Isles Islands Council, since 1982; Member, Western Isles Health Board, since 1972; Member, Stornoway Trust, since 1967; b. 16.11.41, Stornoway; m., Irene Mary Davidson; 2 s.; 2 d. Educ. Nicolson Institute, Stornoway; Robert Gordon's Institute of Technology, Aberdeen. Member: Stornoway Town Council, 1967-75 (Provost, 1971-75), Ross and Cromarty County Council, 1967-75; Chairman, Stornoway Trust, 1971-81; Member, Stornoway Pier and Harbour Commission, since 1967 (Chairman, 1970-71); Chairman, Development Services, Western Isles Islands Council, 1974-80; Vice-Convener, Western Isles Islands Council, 1980-82; Honorary Sheriff, since 1972; Parliamentary candidate (Labour), 1979; Chairman, Lewis Development Fund (now Western Isles Development Fund), since 1972. Address: (h.) 33 Newton Street, Stornoway, Isle of Lewis; T.-0851 2082.

Matheson, Rev. Calum, MA (Hons), DipTh. Minister, Shawbost Free Church, Isle of Lewis, since 1980; b. 27.8.48, Stornoway; m., Betty Broadfoot; 1 s.; 1 d. Educ. Nicolson Institute, Stornoway; Langside College of Further Education, Glasgow; Glasgow University; Free Church College, Edinburgh. Member, Translation Team, Gaelic New Testament, NBSS; Chairman, Lewis Schools Council, since 1984. Recreation: reading. Address: The Manse, Shawbost, Isle of Lewis; T.-0851 71 216.

Matheson, Donald, CA, FBIM. Head, Business Investment Division, Highlands and Islands Development Board, since 1979; b. 3.2.36, Inverness; m., Elizabeth; 1 s.; 1 d. Educ. Inverness. Apprentice and Qualified Assistant, Howden and Molleson, Chartered Accountants, Edinburgh, 1958-63; Financial and Management Accountant, Ethicon Ltd., Edinburgh, 1963-67; joined HIDB, 1967. Recreations: family; curling; swimming; reading. Address: (b.) Bridge Street, Bank Street, Inverness; T.-0463 234171.

Matheson, Very Rev. James Gunn, MA, BD. Moderator, General Assembly of the Church of Scotland, 1975-76; Minister, Portree, 1973-79; b. 1.3.12; m.; 3 s.; 1 d.; 1 d. (deceased). Educ. Inverness Royal Academy; Edinburgh University. Free Church, Olrig, Caithness, 1936-39; Chaplain to HM Forces, 1939-45 (POW, 1941-43); St. Columba's Church, Edinburgh, 1946-51; Knox Church, Dunedin, New Zealand, 1951-61; Secretary, Stewardship and Budget Committee, Church of Scotland, 1961-73.

Mathewson, Alexander Mackechnie, MB, ChB, MRCGP. General Practitioner, Wishaw, since 1950; Member, Lanarkshire Health Board; b. 13.11.23, Glasgow; m., Dorothy Wightman Reid; 3 s. Educ. Irvine Royal Academy; Glasgow University. Former Captain, RAMC. Past Chairman, Lanarkshire Division, BMA. Recreations: golf; curling. Address: (h.) The Beeches, Wishaw, Lanarkshire, ML2 8LF; T.-0698 384789.

Mathewson, George Ross, CBE, BSc, PHD, MBA, LLD, CEng, MIEE. Chief Executive, Scottish Development Agency, since 1981; Chairman, Scottish Development Finance Ltd., since 1982; Director, Scottish Investment Trust PLC, since 1981; b. 14.5.40, Perth; m., Sheila Alexandra Graham Bennett; 2 s. Educ. Perth Academy; St. Andrews University; Canisius College, Buffalo, New York. Assistant Lecturer, St. Andrews University, 1964-67; Systems Engineer (various positions), Bell Aerospace, Buffalo, New York, 1967-72; ICFC: Executive in Edinburgh Area Office, 1972-74, Area Manager, 1974-79, Director and Assistant General Manager, 1979-81. Recreations: rugby; golf; business. Address: (h.) Larach-beg, Corsee Road, Banchory, Kincardineshire, AB3 3RT; T.-Banchory 3482.

Mathie, Hugh Alexander, MA, MEd. Rector, McLaren High School, Callander, since 1985; b. 30.7.35, Dundee; m., Margaret Black; 2 s.; 1 d. Educ. Morgan Academy, Dundee; St. Andrews University. Teacher of Classics, Kilsyth Academy and Kirkton High School, Dundee; Principal Teacher of Classics, Kilsyth Academy and Cumbernauld High School; Assistant Rector, Depute Rector, Greenfaulds High School; Rector, Kilsyth Academy. Recreations: hill-walking; golf. Address: (h.) Welwyn, Firpark Terrace, Cambusbarron, Stirling; T.-Stirling 72900.

Mathieson, John George, CBE, TD, DL, BL. Solicitor, Thornton Oliver, WS, Arbroath; b. 15.6.32, Argyll; m., Shirley Bidder; 1 s.; 1 d. Educ. George Watson's College, Edinburgh; Glasgow University. Territorial Army, 1951-76: Commanding Officer The Highland Regiment RA (T), 1967-69, TA Colonel for Highlands, 1972-76, Chairman, Highlands TA Association, 1976-82. Commenced practice as Solicitor in Glasgow, 1955-57; joined practice of Clark

Oliver, Arbroath, 1957; now a Senior Partner; Chairman, Scottish Solicitors Discipline Tribunal; Secretary, Angus Housing Association; Chairman, Arbroath Branch, Royal British Legion; Chairman, British Legion Housing Association, Wimberley Court, Broughty Ferry; Deputy Lieutenant, Angus, since 1977; Elder, Inverkeilor Church; Chairman, Angus Committee, Duke of Edinburgh Award Scheme; Chairman, Earl Haig Fund, Arbroath; Deputy Chairman, Royal Artillery Council for Scotland. Recreations: shooting; skiing; golf. Address: (h.) Lawton Mill, Inverkeilor, Arbroath, Angus; T.-02413 246.

Matthew, Rev. Stewart Graham, MA, BD. National Adult Adviser, Department of Education, Church of Scotland, since 1984; b. 14.11.39, Dundee; m., Irene Nicol Green; 1 s.; 1 d. Educ. High School of Dundee; St. Andrews University. Assistant Minister, St. Columba's, Glenrothes, 1965-66; Teacher of Religious Education, Swinton Comprehensive School, 1966-69; Minister, St. Ninian's Bellfield, Kilmarnock, 1969-79; joined Department of Education as Assistant Secretary (Education), 1979-84; Editor, Frontline materials, Church of Scotland; Scottish Representative, International Committee for the German Kirchentag; regular Columnist, Life and Work magazine. Recreations: guitar; table tennis; motion pictures. Address: (h.) 10 Silverknowes Midway, Davidson Mains, Edinburgh; T.-031-336 5990.

Matthews, Baird, BL. Solicitor in private practice, since 1950; Honorary Sheriff, Kirkcudbright and Stranraer; b. 19.1.25, Newton Stewart; m., Mary Thomson Hope; 2 s.; 1 d. Educ. Douglas Ewart High School; Edinburgh University. Commissioned, Royal Scots Fusiliers, 1944; demobilised as Captain, 1st Bn., 1947; Partner, A. B. & A. Matthews, Solicitors, Newton Stewart, since 1950; Clerk to General Commissioners of Income Tax, Stranraer and Newton Stewart Districts, from 1952; Burgh Prosecutor, Newton Stewart, from 1968; Depute Procurator Fiscal for Wigtownshire, 1970; Local Director, General Accident Fire and Life Assurance Corporation, 1970; Dean of Faculty of Stewartry of Kirkcudbright Solicitors, 1979; Dean of Faculty of Solicitors of the District of Wigtown, 1983; Chairman, Appeals Tribunal, 1984. Recreations: golf; shooting; curling; sailing. Address: (b.) Bank of Scotland Buildings, Newton Stewart, Wigtownshire; T.-0671 3013.

Matthews, Edward. Director, Edinburgh Council of Social Service, since 1974; b. 11.9.37, Brentford, Middlesex; m., Ann Patricia; 1 s.; 1 d. Educ. Finchley Grammar School; St. Edmund's College, Ware. Curate and Borstal Chaplain, 1961-66; Assistant Director, then Deputy Director, Richmond Fellowship, 1966-74; Member, Lothian Health Board, since 1983; Winston Churchill Fellowship, 1973; Secretary, Edinburgh Lodginghouse Association; Executive Committee Member: Edinburgh University Settlement, SACRO, Edinburgh Cyrenians, Edinburgh Council for Single Homeless, Grassmarket Area Housing Association. Recreations: woodwork; badminton; gardening. Address: (b.) Edinburgh Council of Social Service, 11 St. Colme Street, Edinburgh, EH3 6AG; T.-031-225 4606.

Matthews, Herbert Eric, MA (Oxon), BPhil (Oxon). Senior Lecturer in Philosophy, Aberdeen University, since 1973; b. 24.10.36, Liverpool; m., Hellen Kilpatrick Murray; 2 s. Educ. Liverpool Institute High School for Boys; St. John's College, Oxford. Lecturer in Logic, Aberdeen University, 1963-73. Ethical Consultant, Association for Family Therapy. Publication: Weber Selections (with W.G. Runciman). Recreations: movies; golf; travel; watching football; skiing. Address: (h.) 62 Stanley Street, Aberdeen; T.-Aberdeen 584078.

Matthews, Hugh, LLB (Hons). Advocate, since 1979; b. 4.12.53, Port Glasgow. Educ. St. Joseph's Academy, Kilmarnock; Glasgow University. Apprenticed to James Campbell & Co., WS, Saltcoats, two years; devilled to E.F. Bowen, 1978-79, when admitted to Faculty of Advocates; Standing Junior Counsel for Scotland to Department of Employment, since 1984. Recreations: playing golf, football, snooker and Santa Claus; theatre; good food and fine wines; watching Celtic. Address: (h.) 8 Portland Road, Kilmarnock, Ayrshire; T.-0563 25218.

Matthews, John Duncan, BA, MB, ChB, FRCPEdin. Consultant Physician, Edinburgh Royal Infirmary, since 1956; Vice President, Royal College of Physicians of Edinburgh, since 1982; b. 19.9.21, Rainhill, Lancashire; m., Constance Margaret Moffat; 2 s. Educ. Shrewsbury; Cambridge University; Edinburgh University. Chairman of Physicians, Edinburgh Royal Infirmary, and other NHS Committees; Colonel, RAMC TA; Honorary Consultant, Army in Scotland; Chief Medical Officer, Scottish Provident Institution; Surgeon, High Constables of Holyroodhouse; Secretary, Edinburgh Medical Angling Club. Recreations: cricket; fishing; gardening. Address: (h.) 3 Succoth Gardens, Edinburgh; T.-031-337 2636.

Matthews, Rev. Laurence John, BA, BD. Minister, Nigg Parish Church, Aberdeen, since 1964; b. 30.4.19, Arnside, Westmortland; m., Rachel MacCrimmon; 2 s.; 1 d. Educ. Hyde Secondary School, Manchester; Manchester University; Lancashire Independent College. Minister: Manchester (Stretford), Darvel, Greenock (George Square), Cairney. Publication: Third Statistical Account of Scotland: Kincardineshire (Contributor). Recreations: music; hill-walking. Address: (h.) 7 Redmoss Avenue, Aberdeen, AB1 4JR; T.-Aberdeen 871168.

Maund, Robert Graham, BSc, DipTP, FRTPI. Director of Physical Planning, Strathclyde Regional Council, since 1984; b. 10.11.38, Cheshire; m., Judith L.; 3 s.; 1 d. Educ. Manchester University. City of Manchester: trainee graduate engineer, various planning posts, Assistant City Planning Officer; Greater Manchester Council: Assistant County Planning Officer, Deputy County Planning Officer. Recreations: walking; cross-country running; photography; listening to music; reading; theatre. Address: (b.) Strathclyde House, 20 India Street, Glasgow, G2 4PF; T.-041-227 3626.

Maver, Professor Thomas Watt, BSc (Hons), PhD, FInstE, FRSA. Head, Department of Architecture and Building Science, Strathclyde

University, since 1983 (Professor of Computer Aided Design, since 1982); b. 10.3.38, Glasgow; m., Avril Elizabeth Cuthbertson; 2 d. Educ. Eastwood Secondary School; Glasgow University. Special Research Fellow, Engineering Faculty, Glasgow University, 1961-67; Strathclyde University: Research Fellow, School of Architecture, 1967-70, Director, Architecture and Building Aids Computer Unit, since 1970; Visiting Professor, Department of Architecture, Technical University, Eindhoven; Past Chairman, Design Research Society. Recreation: family. Address: (h.) 8 Kew Terrace, Glasgow, G12; T.-041-339 7185.

Mavor, Professor John, BSc, PhD, CPhys, FInstP, CEng, FIEE, FIERE. Lothian Chair of Microelectronics, Edinburgh University, since 1980 (Head, Department of Electrical Engineering, since 1984); b. 18.7.42, Kilwinning; m., Susan Christina; 2 d. Educ. Bromley Technical High School; City University; London University. AEI Research Laboratories, London, 1964-65; Texas Instruments Ltd., Bedford, 1968-70; Emihus Microcomponents Ltd., Glenrothes, 1970-71; joined Edinburgh University, 1971. Chairman, EUMOS Ltd. Recreations: gardening; hill-walking. Address: (b.) Department of Electrical Engineering, Edinburgh University, King's Buildings, Edinburgh, EH9 3JL; T.-031-667 1081, Ext. 3591.

Mavor, Michael Barclay, CVO, MA. Headmaster, Gordonstoun School, since 1979; b. 29.1.47, Kuala Lipis, Malaysia; m., Elizabeth Sucksmith; 1 s.; 1 d. Educ. Loretto; St. John's College, Cambridge. Woodrow Wilson Teaching Fellow, Northwestern University, Evanston, Illinois, 1969-72; Assistant Master, Tonbridge School, 1972-78; Course Turor (Drama), Open University, 1977-78. Recreations: theatre; writing; fishing; golf. Address: Gordonstoun School, Elgin, Moray, IV30 2RF; T.-0343 830445.

Maxton, John Alston. MP (Labour), Glasgow Cathcart, since 1979; b. 5.5.36. Educ. Lord Williams' Grammar School, Thame; Oxford University. Former Lecturer in Social Studies, Hamilton College.

Maxwell, Donald, MA. Professional Singer; b. 12.12.48, Perth. Educ. Perth Academy; Edinburgh University. Former Teacher of Geography; since 1976, professional Singer with British opera companies and orchestras; Principal Baritone, Scottish Opera, 1978-82; Principal Baritone, Welsh National Opera, 1982-85; guest appearances in Europe and Canada. Recreations: railways; watching cricket. Address: (b.) c/o 6 Murray Crescent, Perth; T.-0738 25956.

Maxwell, John Lyon, MA (Cantab). Member, Stewartry District Council, since 1975; Member, Electricity Consultative Council for South of Scotland District; Farmer; b. 23.9.31, Llanarth, Monmouthshire; m., Lorna Ann Symington; 1 s.; 3 d. Educ. Trinity College, Glenalmond; Emmanuel College, Cambridge. Agricultural Officer, Overseas Agricultural Service, Nyasaland, 1956-64. Recreations: shooting; reading. Address: (h.) Kenmure House, New Galloway, Kirkcudbrightshire; T.-064-42 262.

Maxwell, Hon. Lord (Peter Maxwell), QC, BA, LLB. Senator, College of Justice, since 1973; Chairman, Scottish Law Commission, since 1981; b. 21.5.19, Edinburgh; m., Alison Susan Readman; 1 s.; 2 d. Educ. Wellington College; Balliol College, Oxford; Edinburgh University. Argyll and Sutherland Highlanders and Royal Artillery, 1939-46; called to Scottish Bar, 1951; QC, 1961; Sheriff Principal, Dumfries and Galloway, 1970-73; Member, Royal Commission on Legal Services in Scotland, 1976-80. Address: (h.) 1c Oswald Road, Edinburgh, EH9 2HE; T.-031-667 7444.

Maxwell, Thomas Jefferson, BSc, PhD. Head, Animal Production Department, Hill Farming Research Organisation, since 1981; b. 7.10.40, Aspatria, Cumbria; m., Christine Patrick Speedie; 1 s.; 1 d. Educ. Silcoates School, Wakefield; Edinburgh University. Specialist Animal Production Adviser, East of Scotland College of Agriculture, 1967-70; Research Scientist, Animal Production Department, Hill Farming Research Organisation, 1970-81. Recreations: reading; squash; hill-walking; choral singing. Address: (b.) Hill Farming Research Organisation, Bush Estate, Penicuik, Midlothian; T.-031-445 2421.

Maxwell, William Paul, BA (Oxon), DipEd. Rector, Turriff Academy, since 1976; b. 7.1.33, Kirkcaldy; m., Ruth Isobel Alexander; 2 s. Educ. Kirkcaldy High School; Edinburgh Academy; St. Edmund Hall, Oxford. Taught, Daniel Stewart's College, Edinburgh, 1957-67; Principal Teacher of History: Dunfermline High School, 1967-69, Robert Gordon's College, Aberdeen, 1969-72; Assistant Rector, Elgin Academy, 1972-76. Recreations: music; hill-walking; angling. Address: (b.) Turriff Academy, Victoria Terrace, Turriff, AB5 7EE; T.-0888 63216.

Maxwell Davies, Peter, CBE, MusB (Hons). Composer; Founder and Artistic Director, St. Magnus Festival, Orkney, since 1977; b. 8.9.34, Manchester. Educ. Leigh Grammar School; Royal Manchester College of Music; Manchester University. Director of Music, Cirencester Grammar School, 1959-62; Harkness Fellowship, Princeton University, 1962-64; Professor of Composition, Royal Northern College of Music, Manchester, until 1980; Founder and Artistic Director, Fires of London, since 1971; Artistic Director, Dartington Summer School of Music, 1979-84; Honorary Doctor of Music, Edinburgh University, 1979, Honorary Doctor of Law, Aberdeen University, 1981. Address: (b.) c/o Mrs Judy Arnold, 50 Hogarth Road, London, SW5; T.-01-370 1477.

Maxwell-Scott, Dame Jean (Mary Monica), DCVO (1984). Lady in Waiting to Princess Alice, Duchess of Gloucester, since 1959; b. 8.6.23. VAD Red Cross Nurse, 1941-46. Address: (h.) Abbotsford, Melrose, Roxburghshire, TD6 9BQ.

May, Douglas James, LLB. Advocate; b. 7.5.46, Edinburgh. Educ. George Heriot's; Edinburgh University. Called to Scottish Bar, 1971; Conservative Parliamentary candidate, Edinburgh

East, February, 1974, Glasgow Cathcart, 1983; Vice-Chairman, Society of Conservative Lawyers. Recreations: golf; music; philately. Address: (b.) Advocates Library, Parliament House, Edinburgh.

May, Malcolm Stuart, BA, BD, STM, CQSW. Director, Dundee Association for Social Service, since 1979; b. 9.9.40, Isle of Shapinsay, Orkney; m., Alison Wood; 1 s.; 1 d. Educ. Kilmarnock Academy; The Gordon Schools, Huntly; Hamilton Academy; Queen's University, Belfast; Glasgow University; Union Theological Seminary, New York. Assistant Minister, The Old Kirk, West Pilton, Edinburgh, 1966-68; staff, Iona Community, Glasgow, 1968-72; social work training, 1972-73; Training Officer, Scottish Council of Social Service, 1973-78. Voluntary Organisations Representative, Grampian and Tayside Area Manpower Board, MSC, since 1983. Recreations: reading; choral singing; running; wine-making. Address: (b.) Castlehill House, 1 High Street, Dundee, DD1 1TD; T.-0382 21545.

May, Ranald Stuart, MA, BComm. Senior Lecturer in Economics, St. Andrews University, since 1978; b. 1.5.32, Dundee; m., Jennifer Alison Shewan. Educ. Grove Academy, Dundee; St. Andrews University; Queen's University, Canada. Ft.-Lt., RAF, 1956-59; Finance Officer and Economic Adviser, Shell International Petroleum Company, London and Shell-BP Petroleum Development Company, Nigeria, 1959-63; St. Andrews University: Shell Fellow in Economic Development, 1963-70, Lecturer in Economics, 1970-78. Treasurer, Scottish Economic Society; Arbitrator to ACAS, since 1975. Recreations: golf; gardening. Address: (h.) 1 Albany Place, North Street, St. Andrews, Fife; T.-St. Andrews 72585.

Mayfield, Hon. Lord, (Ian MacDonald), MC (1945), QC (Scot). Senator of the College of Justice in Scotland, since 1981; b. 26.5.21; m.; 1 s.; 1 d. Educ. Colston's School; Edinburgh University. Served Second World War (Captain, Royal Tank Regiment); called to Bar, 1952; Sheriff Principal of Dumfries and Galloway, 1973; President, Industrial Tribunals for Scotland, 1973-81.

Meadows, Peter Swithin, MA (Nat. Sci.) (Cantab), BA (O.U.). Senior Lecturer in Zoology, Glasgow University; b. 24.3.36, London; 1 s.; 1 d. Educ. Westminster; Pembroke College, Cambridge. Commissioned, RAF, 1954-56; Marine Laboratory, Aberdeen, 1959-61; Marine Science Laboratories, UCNW, Bangor, 1961-63; Lecturer, Glasgow University, 1963-75; Nuffield Foundation Fellow, University of the West Indies, 1970-71; Member, Board of Management, UMBS, Millport, since 1975. Recreations: music; visual arts. Address: (b.) Department of Zoology, Glasgow University, Glasgow, G12 8QQ; T.-041-339 8855.

Mearns, James Michie, MA, DL. Rector, Cumbernauld High School, since 1971; Deputy Lieutenant, County of Dunbarton; b. 22.5.30, Inverurie; m., Elizabeth Findlay; 1 s.; 2 d.

Educ. Inverurie Academy; Aberdeen University; Aberdeen College of Education. Principal Teacher of Modern Languages, latterly also Depute Head, Currie High School, 1963-71; Assistant Principal Examiner, SCE Examination Board, 1967-70. Recreations: gardening; choral singing; badminton. Address: (h.) 8 Victoria Terrace, Dullatur, Glasgow; T.-02367 27455.

Meek, Brian Alexander, OBE, JP. Convener, Lothian Regional Council, since 1982; Rugby Correspondent, Scottish Daily and Sunday Express, since 1970; Director, Stewart, Dudgeon and Claridge (Advertising) Ltd., since 1983; b. 8.2.39, Edinburgh; m., Frances C. Horsburgh; 1 s.; 1 d. Educ. Royal High School, Edinburgh; Edinburgh Secretarial College. Joined Scotsman Publications as trainee, then Sub-Editor, Features Writer; transferred to Express Newspapers as Feature Writer, Leader Writer and Rugby Correspondent; elected, Edinburgh Corporation, 1969; Leader, Conservative Group, 1970-72; elected as Bailie, 1972; elected, Lothian Regional Council and Edinburgh District Council, 1973; Leader, Conservative Group, Lothian, since 1973; Chairman, Lothian and Borders Police Board, 1984; Member, Education Board, Merchant Company; Chairman, Race Relations Council. Recreations: golf; theatre. Address: (b.) Lothian Regional Council, Parliament Square, Edinburgh; T.-031-229 9292.

Megson, Raymond James, LLB, NP, SSC. Solicitor; Senior Partner, Megson & Co., SSC, since 1971; b. 4.9.45, Sheffield; m., Kim Frances McCreadie; 3 s.; 1 d. Educ. South Sydney High School; Douglas Ewart School; Edinburgh University. Apprenticeship, Boyd Jameson & Young, WS, Edinburgh; returned to Sydney (where raised); joined Harris & Co., Solicitors; returned to Edinburgh and established own firm; Committee Member, Faculty of Procurators of Midlothian; Chairman, Edinburgh Rugby Referees Society. Scottish Schools Triple Jump Champion, 1964. Recreations: rugby refereeing; golf; badminton; jogging; tennis. Address: (h.) 22 Cluny Drive, Edinburgh; T.-031-447 2343.

Meikle, Elizabeth Aitken, OBE, BPharm, FPS, MCPP. Chief Administrative Pharmaceutical Officer, Greater Glasgow Health Board, since 1978; Assistant Chief Commissioner, Scottish HQ, Scout Association, since 1980; b. 1.8.28, Lenzie, Kirkintilloch. Educ. Frimley and Camberley Secondary School; London University. Pre-registration, Kingston General Hospital; Pharmacist: Kingston, Southern General Hospital, Glasgow, 1951; Senior Pharmacist, Glasgow Eye Infirmary, 1953; Chief Pharmacist, Vale of Leven District General Hospital, 1955-73; Area Pharmacist, Glasgow (South) and District Pharmaceutical Officer; served on Grossett and Noel Hall Committees on Hospital Pharmaceutical Service; sometime Chairman, National Pharmaceutical Consultative Committee; Chairman, Scottish Executive, Pharmaceutical Society, 1982-84; Chairman, Working Group on Pharmaceutical Supplies in Residential Homes, 1983. Recreations: gardening; golf; photography; philately; but all restricted by Scouting activities! Address: (h.) Alderbrae, Buchanan Castle Estate, Drymen, G63 OHX; T.-Drymen 60379.

Meikle, Robert Baxter, MA, DipEd. Recto[...] Alness Academy, since 1975; b. 8.6.33, Kir[...] liston, West Lothian; m., Adrianne Margar[...] Stewart; 1 s.; 1 d. Educ. Broxburn High Schoo[...] Edinburgh University; Moray House College o[...] Education. Sergeant, RAEC, 1956-58; Teach[...] of Geography and Special Assistant, Bell-Baxt[...] High School, Cupar, 1958-64; Principal Teach[...] of Geography, then Assistant Rector, Montrose Academy, 1964-75. Chairman, Highland Region Computer Working Party, 1980-84; Chairman, Saltburn Community Council. Publication: Windows on the Geography of Scotland, 1972-73. Recreations: golf; fell-walking; music; photography; art; the works of Robert Burns. Address: (b.) Alness Academy, Alness, Ross and Cromarty; T.-0349 883341.

Mein, William Main, MA (Hons). HM Inspector of Schools, since 1972; b. 1.7.38, Nairn; m., Dorothy Robertson Steele; 2 d. Educ. Nairn Academy; Edinburgh University; Moray House College of Education. Teacher of Mathematics, Robert Gordon's College, Aberdeen, 1961-65; Principal Teacher of Mathematics, Invergordon Academy, 1965-68; Principal Teacher of Mathematics, then Assistant Headteacher, Dingwall Academy, 1968-72. Elder, Crown Church, Inverness. Recreations: angling; photography; gardening. Address: (h.) The Linn, 11 Beaufort Road, Inverness; T.-0463 238617.

Meldrum, James, JP. Member, Strathclyde Regional Council, since 1978; b. 17.4.32, Hamilton; 2 s.; 1 d. Educ. St. John's Grammar School, Hamilton. Member, East Kilbride Town Council, 1971-75 (Magistrate, 1972-75, Convener, Parks Committee, 1972-75); Member, East Kilbride District Council, 1974-77; various union branch posts in Boilermakers Society, 1966-73. Recreation: bowls (indoor and outdoor). Address: (h.) 67 Struthers Crescent, Calderwood, East Kilbride; T.-East Kilbride 31156.

Meldrum, James, MA. Principal, Scottish Office Establishments Division, since 1985; b. 9.8.52, Kirkintilloch. Educ. Lenzie Academy; Glasgow University. Joined Scottish Office as Administration Trainee, serving in Scottish Economic Planning Department and Scottish Home and Health Department, 1973-76; Higher Executive Officer (Administration), Scottish Economic Planning Department, 1976-79; Principal: Scottish Economic Planning Department, 1979-82, Scottish Development Department, 1982-85. Recreations: reading; music. Address: (b.) Scottish Office Establishments Division, 16 Waterloo Place, Edinburgh; T.-031-556 8400.

Meldrum, John David Philip, BA, MA, PhD (Cantab). Senior Lecturer in Mathematics, Edinburgh University, since 1982; b. 18.7.40, Rabat, Morocco; m., Patricia Sealey; 1 s.; 1 d. Educ. Lycee Lyautey, Casablanca; Ipswich School; Emmanuel College, Cambridge. Fellow, College Lecturer in Pure Mathematics and Director of Studies in Mathematics, Emmanuel College, Cambridge, 1964-69; Director of Studies in Mathematics, New Hall College College, Cambridge, 1964-69; Lecturer in Mathematics, Edinburgh University, 1969-82; Honorary Secretary, Edinburgh Mathematical Society, 1971-80. Member, General Synod, Scottish Episcopal Church,

FRCPLond. Consultant [...] of Neurological Sciences, Glasgow, since 1965; Honorary Clinical Lecturer, Glasgow University, since 1968; b. 9.11.27, Glasgow; m., Eliza Duffus; 1 s.; 3 d. Educ. Shawlands Academy; Glasgow University. RAF Medical Branch; Medical Registrar, Glasgow Royal Infirmary; Academic Registrar, National Hospital for Nervous Diseases, London; Clinical Research Fellow, Medical Research Council, London; Senior Medical Registrar, Glasgow. Councillor, Royal College of Physicians and Surgeons, Glasgow; Chairman, Research Committee, Epilepsy Association of Scotland. Recreations: golf; photography; chess; motoring. Address: (h.) 9 Mirrlees Drive, Glasgow, G12 OSH; T.-041-339 7085.

Melville, Robert Murray, OBE, MB, ChB, DPH, FFCM. Senior Medical Officer, Scottish Home and Health Department, since 1975; b. 7.1.24, Elgin; m., Elizabeth Mary Munro; 3 s.; 1 d. Educ. Elgin Academy; Edinburgh University. Medical Officer: Colonial Service, Malaya, 1954-57, Colonial Service, Sarawak, 1957-61; Overseas Civil Service, Sarawak: Medical Officer, 1961-65, Senior Medical Officer, 1965-66, Assistant Director of Medical Services (Health), 1967-71; Deputy Medical Superintendent, Bangour General Hospital and Deputy Principal Medical Adviser, Livingston, 1971-74; Medical Officer, Scottish Home and Health Department, 1974-75. Recreations: classical music; history; biography; gardening. Address: (h.) Westfield House, West Calder, West Lothian, EH55 8RB; T.-Livingston 410725.

Melvin, John Middleton, MA, LLB. Solicitor and Estate Agent, Notary Public; Advocate in Aberdeen; b. 2.8.24, Aberdeen; m., Margaret Leslie Robertson; 4 s. Educ. Aberdeen Grammar School; Aberdeen University. Gordon Highlanders, UK, Ireland and Europe, 1944-45, then as Captain, Burma and Far East, until 1948; A.C. Morrison & Richards: joined as Assistant Solicitor, appointed Partner, 1957, Senior Partner, 1978; former Clerk of the Peace, County of Aberdeen. Recreations: golf; swimming; travel. Address: (h.) 18 Moray Place, Aberdeen, AB2 4AG; T.-Aberdeen 573321.

Mendelow, A. David, MB, BCh, FRCSEdin, FRCSEdin (SN), PhD. Senior Lecturer, Department of Neurosurgery, Glasgow University, since 1980; Honorary Consultant Neurosurgeon, Southern General Hospital, since 1981; b. 19.5.46, London; m., Anne Y.; 2 s.; 1 d. Educ. Michaelhouse, Balgowan, Natal; Witwatersrand University. Senior Registrar, Department of Neurosurgery, Western General Hospital, Edinburgh. Recreation: sailing. Address: (b.) Department of Neurosurgery, Institute of Neurological Science, Southern General Hospital, Glasgow; T.-041-445 2466.

...sgow University, 1965-68; Visiting Lecturer: ...rida University, 1973, University of the West ...dies, 1976-77. Publication: Accounting Models, ...80. Recreation: book collecting. Address: ...) Faculty of Economic and Social Studies, ...riot-Watt University, Edinburgh, EH1 1HX; ...031-225 8432.

Educ. ...burgh ...ity, Glenalmond College; Keble College, Oxford. Shipbroker, Cargill Grain Co., London and Geneva, 1966; Executive, Christian Salvesen Ltd., Edinburgh, 1971; Director, North British Steel Group PLC, 1977; Scottish Director IT Campaign (DTI), Strathclyde University, 1983. Chairman, Leith Chamber of Commerce, 1978-80; Director, Edinburgh Chamber of Commerce, 1979-82; Council Member, Edinburgh International Festival, 1980-84; President, The Organ Club, 1979-82; Vice-Convener, George Watson's College, 1982-83. Recreations: music; architectural history; travel. Address: (b.) 9 Manor Place, Edinburgh, H3 7DN; T.-031-225 7078.

Menzies, Gordon, MA (Hons), DipEd. Head of Educational Broadcasting, BBC Scotland; b. 30.7.27, Logierait, Perthshire; m., Charlotte; 2 s.; 1 d. Educ. Breadalbane Academy, Aberfeldy; Edinburgh University. Producer/Director, Who Are the Scots?, 1971, The Chiel Amang Us, 1974, Ballad Folk, 1975, History Is My Witness, 1976, Play Golf with Peter Alliss, 1977, Scotch and Wry, 1978-79, Barbara Dickson in Concert, 1980, The World of Golf, 1982, Two Views of Burns, 1979, Scotch and Wry Hogmanay, 1980-82-83-84-85; Editor, The Afternoon Show, 1981-85. Publications: Who Are the Scots?, 1971; The Scottish Nation, 1972; History Is My Witness, 1976; Play Golf, 1977; The World of Golf, 1982. Recreations: golf; squash; curling; theatre. Address: (b.) BBC Scotland, Broadcasting House, Queen Margaret Drive, Glasgow, G12 8DG.

Menzies, Thomas, MB, ChB, FRCSEdin, FRCS, RCPSGlas. Consultant Surgeon, Glasgow Royal Infirmary, since 1966; b. 28.11.22, Crowborough, Sussex; m., Margaret Ledingham Davidson; 1 s.; 2 d. Educ. Aberdeen Grammar School; Aberdeen University. House Surgeon/House Physician, Aberdeen Royal Infirmary; graded Surgeon, RAMC; Surgical Registrar, Aberdeen Royal Infirmary; Senior Surgical Registrar, Hammersmith Hospital, London, and Tutor in Surgery, Postgraduate Medical School of London. Recreations: gardening; angling; philately. Address: (h.) 62 Manse Road, Bearsden, Glasgow, G61 3PN; T.-041-942 7472.

Mepham, Michael James, BSc (Econ), FCA, FCMA. Dean, Faculty of Economic and Social Studies, Heriot-Watt University, since 1983 (Senior Lecturer in Accounting, since 1969); b. 18.4.32, Newport, Gwent; m., Inez Maureen Baker; 1 s.; 1 d. Educ. Newport (St. Julian's) High School, Newport; London University; Strathclyde University. Professional and industrial accounting posts, 1956-60; Senior Lecturer, Slough College of Technology, 1961-65; Lecturer,

Mercer, Roger James, MA, FSA, FSA Scot, MIFA. Reader in European Archaeology, Edinburgh University, since 1982; b. 12.9.44, London; m., Susan; 1 s.; 1 d. Educ. Harrow County Grammar School; Edinburgh University. Inspector of Ancient Monuments, AM Division, Department of the Environment, London, 1969-74; Lecturer, Department of Archaeology, Edinburgh University, 1974-82. Treasurer, Society of Antiquaries of Scotland. Recreations: music; reading; learning. Address: (b.) Department of Archaeology, Edinburgh University, Edinburgh; T.-031-667 1011, Ext. 2548.

Merchant, Bruce Alastair, LLB. Solicitor; Partner, South, Forrest, Mackintosh & Merchant, Inverness, since 1971; b. 17.5.45, Edinburgh; m., Joan Isobel Sinclair Hamilton; 1 s.; 2 d. Educ. Inverness Royal Academy; Aberdeen University. Council Member, Law Society of Scotland, since 1982; Member: Board of Management for Inverness Hospitals, 1971-74, Inverness Local Health Council, 1975-81, Highland Health Board, since 1981. Address: (h.) 3 Crown Circus, Inverness; T.-0463 239980.

Merrick, Malcolm Vivian, MA, BM, BCh (Oxon), MSc, FRCR, MRCPE. Consultant in Nuclear Medicine, Western General Hospital, Edinburgh, since 1974; Senior Lecturer, Department of Medicine, Edinburgh University, since 1974; b. 13.7.38, London; m., Julia Margaret Stern; 2 d. Educ. Kings College School, Wimbledon; Oxford University; London University. Pre-registration and junior hospital appointments, Oxford, 1964-70; Research Fellow in Nuclear Medicine, Royal Post Graduate Medical School, 1970-74. Publication: Essentials of Nuclear Medicine. Recreations: photography; walking; wine-making. Address: (h.) 10 Sycamore Gardens, Edinburgh, EH12 7JJ; T.-031-334 0242.

Merrylees, Andrew, BArch, DipTP, ARSA, RIBA, FRIAS, FSIAD, FFB. Architect; Principal, Andrew Merrylees Associates, since 1985; b. 13.10.33, Newmains; m., Maie Crawford; 2 s.; 1 d. Educ. Wishaw High School; Strathclyde University. Sir Basil Spence, Glover and Ferguson: joined, 1957, Associate, 1968, Partner, 1972; awards: RIBA Bronze Medal, Saltire Award, Civic Trust Award, Art in Architecture Award, Royal Scottish Academy Gold Medal. Recreations: oil painting; cooking; tennis; walking. Address: (b.) 4 Heriot Row, Edinburgh, EH3 6HU; T.-031-557 3808.

Meston, Professor Michael Charles, MA, LLB, JD. Professor of Scots Law, Aberdeen University, since 1971; Chairman, M&D Technology Ltd., since 1981; b. 13.12.32, Aberdeen; m., Dorothea Munro; 2 s. Educ. Robert Gordon's College, Aberdeen; Aberdeen University; Chicago

University. Lecturer in Private Law, Glasgow University, 1959-64; Aberdeen University: Senior Lecturer in Comparative Law, 1964-68, Professor of Jurisprudence, 1968-71; Honorary Sheriff, Grampian Highland and Islands, since 1972; Vice Principal, Aberdeen University, 1979-82; Trustee, National Museum of Antiquities of Scotland, since 1982; Governor, Robert Gordon's College, Aberdeen. Publications: The Succession (Scotland) Act 1964; The Matrimonial Homes (Family Protection) (Scotland) Act 1981. Recreations: golf; photography. Address: (h.) 4 Hamilton Place, Aberdeen, AB2 4BH; T.-Aberdeen 641554.

Michie, David Alan Redpath, RSA, RGI, DA. Head, School of Drawing and Painting, Edinburgh College of Art, since 1982; b. 30.11.28, St. Raphael, France; m., Eileen Anderson Michie; 2 d. Educ. Hawick High School; Edinburgh College of Art. Travelling Scholarship, Italy, 1954-55; Lecturer, Grays School of Art, Aberdeen, 1957-61; Lecturer, Edinburgh College of Art, 1961 (Vice Principal, 1974-77). President, Society of Scottish Artists, 1961-63; Member, General Teaching Council for Scotland, 1975-80; Member, Court, Heriot-Watt University, 1979-82; Council Member, British School at Rome, since 1980; Guthrie Award, RSA, 1964; David Cargill Prize, RGI, 1977; Lothian Region Award, 1977; Sir William Gillies Award, 1980; one-man exhibitions, Mercury Gallery, London, six times, 1966-83, Lothian Region Chambers, 1977, The Scottish Gallery, 1980, Loomshop Gallery, Lower Largo, 1981. Address: (b.) Edinburgh College of Art, Lauriston Place, Edinburgh; T.-031-229 9311.

Michie, James Alexander Davidson, MA, MEd. Director of Education, Grampian Regional Council, since 1974; b. 1.10.26, Keithhall, Aberdeenshire; m., Lena; 2 s. Educ. Mackie Academy, Stonehaven; Aberdeen University. Assistant Director of Education, Fife County Council, 1959-65; Senior Depute Director of Education: Dundee City Corporation, 1965-67, Aberdeen County Council, 1967-68; Director of Education, Aberdeen County Council, 1968-74. Recreations: golf; curling; gardening; literature; foreign travel. Address: (b.) Woodhill House, Ashgrove Road West, Aberdeen, AB9 2LU; T.-0224 682222, Ext. 2500.

Michie, Robert Cook, BSc, CEng, MICE, ARGTC. Honorary Sheriff, Fort William, since 1972; b. 28.12.17, Aberdeen; m., Margaret Barlow; 3 s. Educ. Robert Gordon's College; Aberdeen University. Agent and Engineer, William Tawse Ltd., Civil Engineering Contractors, 1941-49; Deputy Resident, latterly Resident Engineer, Crouch & Hogg, Consulting Civil Engineers, 1949-52; Managing Director, Highland Lime Co., Quarrymasters, 1952-77; Project Manager for quarry and brickworks, 1977-83. Past President, Lochaber Rotary Club. Recreation: motoring. Address: (h.) Forglen, Banavie, Fort William, PH33 7LX; T.-0397-7-287.

Micklem, Henry Spedding, MA, DPhil (Oxon). Reader in Zoology, Edinburgh University, since 1973; b. 11.10.33, Oxford; m., Lisel Ruth Thomas; 3 s. 1 d. Educ. Rugby School; Oriel College, Oxford. Scientific Staff, Medical Research Council; Research Fellow, Institut Pasteur, Paris; Academic Staff, Department of Zoology, Edinburgh University; Visiting Professor, Department of Genetics, Stanford University. Recreation: music. Address: (b.) Department of Zoology, Edinburgh University, West Mains Road, Edinburgh, EH9 3JT; T.-031-667 1081.

Middleton, Francis, MA, LLB. Chairman, Child and Family Trust; Chairman, Scottish Dowsers Association; b. 21.11.13, Rutherglen; m., Edith Muir; 2 s.; 1 d. Educ. Rutherglen Academy; Glasgow University. Solicitor, 1937; Indian Army, 1939 (11 Sikh Regiment); injured, 1942; Judge Advocate General's Branch, 1942-45; 1st Class Interpreter, Urdu, Examiner for India in Punjabi; Advocate, 1946; Sheriff, 1948-78. Director, YMCA; serves on boards of various charitable bodies. Recreations: reading; walking; gardening; public speaking. Address: (h.) 23 Kirklee Road, Glasgow, G12 ORQ; T.-041-339 5586.

Middleton, Sir George, KCVO (1962), MB, ChB. Surgeon Apothecary to HM Household at Balmoral Castle, 1932-73; b. 26.1.05. Educ. Forres Academy; Aberdeen University. Retired Medical Practitioner.

Middleton, Sheriff Kenneth William Bruce, BA, LLB. Sheriff, Lothian and Borders, since 1950; b. 1.10.05, Strathpeffer; m., 1, Ruth Beverly Hill; 2, Simona Vere Iliff; 1 s.; 1 d. Educ. Rossall School; Oxford University; Edinburgh University. Sheriff-Substitute, Perth and Angus, at Forfar, 1946-50. Address: (b.) Sheriff Court House, Haddington, East Lothian; T.-Haddington 2936.

Middleton, Robert, JP. Leader, Labour Group, Grampian Regional Council, since 1979; Member, Scottish Council, Labour Party, since 1978; b. 28.7.32, Aberdeen; m., Audrey Ewen; 2 s. Educ. Aberdeen Grammar School. Started apprenticeship with Post Office Telephones, 1948; now employed with British Telecom as Band F Engineering Manager; Aberdeen Town Council: elected, 1961, appointed Magistrate, 1963, Chairman of Magistrates, 1965-66, Chairman, Education Committee, 1966-69; contested Banffshire as Labour candidate, 1966; contested Aberdeen South, 1974 (twice) and 1983; elected, Grampian Regional Council, 1975. Publication: North Sea Brose. Recreations: golf; reading; writing not very good poetry; travel. Address: (h.) 9 Stronsay Avenue, Aberdeen, AB2 6HX; T.-0224 313366.

Midgley, Professor John Morton, BSc, MSc, PhD, CChem, MRCS, FPS. Professor of Pharmacy, Strathclyde University, since 1984; b. 14.7.37, York; m., Jean Mary Tillyer; 2 s. Educ. Nunthorpe Grammar School, York; Manchester University; London University. Demonstrator, Manchester University, 1959-61; Assistant Lecturer, School of Pharmacy, London University, 1962-65; Reseach Associate, Massachusetts Institute of Technology, 1965-66; Lecturer, then

Senior Lecturer, School of Pharmacy, London University, 1966-83; Visiting Professor, Florida University. Recreations: fly fishing; fisheries management; training labradors; gardening; music. Address: (b.) Strathclyde University, Department of Pharmacy, Royal College, 204 George Street, Glasgow, G1 1XW; T.-041-552 4400, Ext. 2125.

Miles, Rex Stafford, MB, ChB, MRCPath. Senior Lecturer, Edinburgh University, since 1976; Honorary Consultant, Lothian Health Board, since 1976; b. 16.11.42, Beeston, Nottinghamshire; m., Janice Isabel Martin; 3 s.; 1 d. Educ. Southwell Minster Grammar School; Edinburgh University. House Physician, Edinburgh Royal Infirmary; House Surgeon, Peel Hospital, Galashiels; Registrar in Bacteriology, Edinburgh University; Lecturer and Honorary Senior Registrar in Bacteriology, Dundee University. Recreations: golf; photography; Border history. Address: (b.) Edinburgh University Medical School, Teviot Place, Edinburgh, EH8 9AG; T.-031-229 2477.

Millan, Rt. Hon. Bruce, PC, MP, CA. MP (Labour), Glasgow Govan, since 1983; b. 5.10.27, Dundee; m., Gwendoline May Fairey; 1 s.; 1 d. Educ. Harris Academy, Dundee. MP, Glasgow Craigton, 1959-83; Parliamentary Secretary for the RAF, 1964-66; Parliamentary Secretary, Scottish Office, 1966-70; Minister of State, Scottish Office, 1974-76; Secretary of State for Scotland, 1976-79; Opposition Spokesman on Scottish Affairs, 1979-83. Address: (h.) 10 Beech Avenue, Glasgow, G41; T.-041-427 6483.

Millar, Ainslie, TD, FRSAMD, FRICS, FRVA, JP. Chartered Surveyor, since 1949; Chairman, Board of Governors, Royal Scottish Academy of Music and Drama, since 1975; b. 9.4.20, Glasgow; m., Morag Bruce; 3 s. Educ. Glasgow Academy; Fettes College; Glasgow University. Commissioned, TA, 1938; War Service, 1939-46; qualified as Surveyor, 1949; served on several RICS Committees, particularly in field of education; Member, Board, Sadlers Wells Trust, latterly English National Opera, 1959-75; Progressive Councillor, Kelvinside Ward, 1964-69; Co-Founder, Scottish Opera, and Board Member, 1960-82; joined Board, RSAMD, 1965; responsible for preparation and submission to Secretary of State for Scotland of petition seeking special facilities for education of greatly gifted children in music and dance, 1970-71; Chairman, Board, Mull Little Theatre, 1980-82; Chairman, Board, Glasgow International Competition for Junior Violinists, 1969-74. Recreations: reading; listening to music; gardening; keyboard strumming; singing. Address: (h.) Weaver's Cottage, Auchinloch, by Lenzie, Glasgow, G66 5LG; T.-041-776 2558.

Millar, Alexander David, MA, LLB, NP. Solicitor, since 1975; Partner, Bird Semple and Crawford Herron (incorporating C. Scott Mackenzie and Company), since 1982; b. 11.1.50, Selkirk; m., Deborah Stark Goodwin; 2 s. Educ. High School of Stirling; Edinburgh University. Employed by Berwickshire County Council, 1973-75; joined Roxburgh District

Council; appointed Solicitor, Western Isles Islands Council, 1975-82. Council Member, Law Society of Scotland, 1981-85; Dean, Western Isles Faculty of Solicitors, since 1984. Recreations: photography; fishing. Address: (h.) 8 Stewart Drive, Stornoway, Isle of Lewis; T.-0851 4645.

Millar, David A.R., MA. Chaplain, Glasgow University, and Lecturer in Theology and Church History, Faculty of Divinity, since 1964; b. 18.2.25, Glasgow; m., Jean M. Tindal; 1 s.; 1 d. Educ. Glasgow Academy; Glasgow University; St. Andrews University. RAF, India, Germany, 1943-47; Assistant Minister, Wallacetown, Dundee, 1954-56; Minister, Richmond Craigmillar, Edinburgh, 1956-64. Address: (b.) 11 The University, Glasgow, G12 8QG; T.-041-334 8769.

Millar, Henry Rankin, MB, ChB, BMedBiol (Hons), MRCPsych. Consultant Psychiatrist, Southern General Hospital, Glasgow, since 1980; b. 23.4.47, Aberdeen; m., Frances Morgan; 3 d. Educ. Aberdeen Grammar School; Aberdeen University. House Officer, Aberdeen Royal Infirmary, 1972-73; Junior Fellow in Community Medicine, Aberdeen University and Aberdeen Royal Infirmary, 1973-74; Senior House Officer/Registrar in Psychiatry, Royal Edinburgh Hospital, 1975-77; Senior Registrar and Lecturer, Dundee Psychiatric Services and Dundee University, 1977-80. Recreations: golf; walking. Address: (h.) 237 Fenwick Road, Giffnock, Glasgow; T.-041-638 1178.

Millar, Mary Armour, MB, ChB, FRCPGlas, FRCR. Consultant Radiologist, Victoria Infirmary, Glasgow, since 1972; b. 10.8.39, Glasgow. Educ. Queen's Park Senior Secondary School; Glasgow University. Resident House Officer: Stobhill Hospital, Glasgow Royal Infirmary; Victoria Infirmary: Registrar in Medicine, Registrar in Radiology, Senior Registrar. Medical Advisor, Overseas Missionary Fellowship in Scotland; Member, Congregational Board, Sandyford Henderson Memorial Church. Recreations: reading; gardening; hill-walking. Address: (h.) 1 Rosslea Drive, Giffnock, Glasgow, G46 6JW; T.-041-638 3036.

Millar, Peter Carmichael, OBE, MA, LLB, DKS. Deputy Keeper of Her Majesty's Signet, since 1983; Chairman, Church of Scotland General Trustees, 1973-85; Chairman, Mental Welfare Commission for Scotland, since 1983; b. 19.2.27, Glasgow; m., Kirsteen Lindsay Carnegie; 2 s.; 2 d. Educ. Aberdeen Grammar School; Glasgow University; St. Andrews University; Edinburgh University. Royal Navy, 1944-47; Partner, W. & T.P. Manuel, WS, 1954-62; Partner, Aitken Kinnear & Co., WS, since 1963; Clerk, Society of Writers to HM Signet, 1964-83. Recreations: golf; hill-walking; music. Address: (h.) 25 Cramond Road North, Edinburgh, EH4 6LY.

Millar, Thomas H., MA, BA (Hons). Head Teacher, James Hamilton Academy, Kilmarnock, since 1976; b. 13.3.24, Glasgow. Educ. Kilmarnock Academy; Glasgow University; London University. Teacher of History, Irvine Royal Academy and Kilmarnock Academy; Principal

Teacher of History, Dollar Academy and Auchenharvie Academy; Assistant Head Teacher, Ravenspark Academy; Deputy Head Teacher, Greenwood Academy. Recreations: travelling; reading; sailing. Address: (h.) 18 Charles Drive, Troon, Ayrshire; T.-Troon 312993.

Millar, William McIntosh, OBE, BL. Solicitor; Partner, McClure Naismith Anderson & Gardiner, Solicitors, Glasgow, since 1955; Editor, Journal of the Law Society of Scotland, since 1983; b. 10.9.25, Edinburgh; 3 s.; 2 d. Educ. Glasgow Academy; Fettes College; Glasgow University. Royal Signals, 1943-47 (Captain, 1947); Secretary, Fife Kinross & Clackmannan Charitable Society, since 1955 (President, 1961-62, and Patron, since 1985); Chairman, Strathclyde Housing Society Ltd. and 11 associated housing societies, 1966-75; Member, Scottish Housing Advisory Committee, 1970-75; Founder Member, Scottish Federation of Housing Associations, 1976-78; Trustee, Scottish Housing Associations Charitable Trust, 1980 (Chairman, 1985); Director, Citizens Theatre Ltd. and Chairman, Close Theatre Club, 1969-72; Governor, Royal Scottish Academy of Music and Drama, since 1969; Honorary Treasurer, New Academy Concert Society of Scotland; Chairman, Scottish Early Music Association. Recreations: music; writing; avoiding golf and politics. Address: (h.) 34 Cleveden Drive, Glasgow, G12 ORX; T.-041-339 5633.

Miller, Alan Cameron, MA, LLB, FCIT. Advocate; Past Chairman (Scotland), Institute of Transport; b. 10.1.13, Killin, Perthshire; m., Audrey Main; 1 s.; 1 d. Educ. Fettes College; Edinburgh University. Member, Faculty of Advocates, since 1938; Royal Navy, 1940-45; Sheriff, Fort William, 1946-52; Legal Adviser (Scotland) to: British Transport Commission, 1952-62, British Railways Board, 1962-72. Voluntary Tutor, Fettes College. Recreations: golf; music. Address: (h.) 42 Great King Street, Edinburgh; T.-031-556 3800.

Miller, Alastair Robert John Dunlop, BSc, MAg, NDA, FRAgS. Farmer; Chairman, Scotfresh Ltd., since 1973; Member, Scottish Agricultural Development Council; Governor, East of Scotland College of Agriculture; b. 5.3.37, Tranent; m., Margaret Evelyn Lees-Brown; 3 d. Educ. Edinburgh Academy; Rugby; Edinburgh University; Purdue University, USA. Scottish Horticulture Medal. Recreations: golf; travel. Address: (h.) Ferrygate, North Berwick, East Lothian.

Miller, Alexander Ronald, CBE, FRSA, CBIM. Chairman, Motherwell Bridge Holdings Ltd., since 1958; b. 7.11.15, Bothwell. Educ. Craigflower School; Malvern College; Royal Technical College. Member: Scottish Council, CBI, 1955-82 (Chairman, 1963-65), Design Council, 1965-71 (Chairman, Scottish Committee, 1967), Scottish Economic Planning Council (Chairman, Industrial Committee, 1967-71), British Rail Scottish Board, 1966-70, British Rail Design Panel, 1966-82, General Convocation, Strathclyde University, since 1967, Steering Committee, West

Central Scotland Plan, 1970-75, Lanarkshire Health Board, 1973-85 (Chairman, 1973-77), Oil Development Council for Scotland, 1973-78, British Institute of Management Scottish Board, since 1974, College Council, Bell College of Technology, Hamilton, since 1976, Management Committee, Scottish Health Service Common Services Agency (Chairman), 1977-83, Lloyd's Register of Shipping Scottish Committee, since 1977, Lloyd's Register of Shipping General Committee, since 1982, CBI Council, since 1982; Director, Lloyd's Register Quality Assurance Association Ltd., since 1985. President, Lanarkshire Branch, Forces Help Society and Lord Roberts Workshops. Address: (h.) Lairfad Farm, Auldhouse, East Kilbride, G75 9DP; T.-East Kilbride 63275.

Miller, Professor Andrew, MA, BSc, PhD. Professor of Biochemistry, Edinburgh University, since 1984; b. 15.2.36, Kelty, Fife; m., Rosemary S.H. Fyvie; 1 d. Educ. Beath High School; Edinburgh University. Assistant Lecturer in Chemistry, Edinburgh University, 1960-62; Postdoctoral Fellow, CSIRO, Melbourne, and Tutor in Chemistry, Ormond College, Melbourne University, 1962-65; Staff Scientist, MRC Laboratory of Molecular Biology, Cambridge, 1965-66; Lecturer in Molecular Biophysics, Oxford University and (from 1967) Fellow, Wolfson College, 1966-83; on secondment as first Director, European Molecular Biology Laboratory, Grenoble Antenne, France, 1975-80. Committee Member: British Biophysical Society, 1972-74, SERC Synchrotron Radiation Facility Committee, 1979-82, Biological Sciences Committee, 1982-85, Neutron Beam Research Committee, 1982-85; Council Member, Institut Laue-Langevin, 1981-85; Member, MRC Joint Dental Committee, since 1984. Address: (b.) Biochemistry Department, Edinburgh University Medical School, Hugh Robson Building, George Square, Edinburgh, EH8 9XD; T.-031-667 1011, Ext. 2336.

Miller, David Brown, JP, BL. Chief Executive, East Lothian District Council, since 1974; b. 6.7.22, Perth; m., Wilhelmina; 1 s.; 2 d. Educ. Perth Academy; St. Andrews University. Legal Assistant to, later Partner of, Robertson, Dempster & Co., WS, Perth, 1944-57; Legal Assistant: Inverness County Council, 1957-59, East Lothian County Council, 1959-75; Depute County Clerk, later Senior Depute County Clerk, East Lothian, 1967-75. Honorary Secretary, Scottish Branch, SOLACE, since 1983. Recreations: travel; photography; gardening; sport. Address: (b.) Council Buildings, Court Street, Haddington, East Lothian, EH41 3HA; T.-062 082 4161.

Miller, Donald John, BSc, FEng, FIMechE, FIEE. Chairman, South of Scotland Electricity Board, since 1982; b. 9.2.27, London; m., Fay G. Herriot; 1 s.; 2 d. Educ. Banchory Academy; Aberdeen University. Metropolitan-Vickers, 1947-53; British Electricity Authority, 1953-55; Preece Cardew & Rider (Consulting Engineers), 1955-66; Chief Engineer, North of Scotland Hydro-Electric Board, 1966-74; Director of Engineering, SEEB, 1974; appointed Deputy

Chairman, 1979. Chairman, Power Division, IEE, 1977. Recreations: gardening; walking; sailing. Address: (h.) Puldohran, Gryffe Road, Kilmacolm, Renfrewshire; T.-Kilmacolm 3652.

Miller, Edward, MA, MEd. Director of Education, Strathclyde Regional Council, since 1974; b. 30.3.30, Glasgow; m., Margaret T. McLean; 2 s. Educ. Eastbank Academy; Glasgow University. Junior Depute Director of Education, West Lothian, 1959-63; Senior Assistant Director of Education, Stirlingshire, 1963-66; Depute and Senior Depute Director of Education, Glasgow, 1966-74. Recreations: swimming; sailing; reading. Address: (h.) 58 Heather Avenue, Bearsden, Glasgow, G61 3JG.

Miller, Hugh Craig, BSc, MB, ChB, FRCPEdin. Consultant Cardiologist, Edinburgh Royal Infirmary, since 1975; b. 7.4.42, Edinburgh; m., Isobel Margaret; 1 s.; 1 d. Educ. George Watson's College; Edinburgh University. Registrar, Edinburgh Royal Infirmary, 1969-72; Senior Registrar, Brompton Hospital, London, 1972-75; Research Fellow, Duke University, North Carolina, 1973-74; Fulbright Scholar. Recreations: skiing; sailing. Address: (h.) 12 Dick Place, Edinburgh; T.-031-667 4235.

Miller, Professor Hugh Graham, BSc, PhD, DSc, FICFor, FRSE. Professor and Head, Department of Forestry, Aberdeen University, since 1984; b. 22.11.39, Ndola, Zambia; m., Thelma Martin; 1 s.; 1 d. Educ. Kaptagat School, Kenya; Strathallan School; Sutton High School; Aberdeen University. Joined Department of Peat and Forest Soils, Macaulay Institute for Soil Research, 1983. Awarded Institute of Foresters Silvicultural Prize, 1974; elected for International Union of Forest Research Organization's Scientific Achievement Award, 1981. Recreations: curling; sailing; philosophy. Address: (b.) Department of Forestry, Aberdeen University, St. Machar Drive, Aberdeen, AB9 2UU; T.-0224 40241.

Miller, James, RSA, RSW. Professional Artist; b. 25.10.93, Glasgow; m., Mary MacNeill (deceased). Educ. Woodside Secondary School; Glasgow School of Art. Art Teacher, Glasgow Education Authority, 1918-47. Address: (h.) Tigh-na-bruaich, Dunvegan, Skye.

Miller, James, MA, FCIOB, FCIArb, CBIM. Chairman and Managing Director, James Miller & Partners Ltd., since 1970; Director, Life Association of Scotland Ltd., since 1981; Director, Scottish Exhibition Centre Ltd., since 1983; Director, British Linen Bank Ltd., since 1983; b. 1.9.34, Edinburgh; m., 1, Kathleen Dewar (deceased); 2, Iris Lloyd-Webb; 1 s.; 3 d. Educ. Edinburgh Academy; Harrow School; Balliol College, Oxford. National Service, Royal Engineers. James Miller & Partners Ltd.: joined, 1958, appointed Director, 1960; Scottish Representative, Advisory Committee to the Meterological Services, since 1980; Chairman, Federation of Civil Engineering Contractors, 1985-86; Deacon Convener, Incorporated Trades of Edinburgh, 1974-77; President, Edinburgh Chamber of Commerce, 1981-83; Assistant on Court of Merchant Company of Edinburgh,

1982-85. Recreation: shooting. Address: (b.) James Miller & Partners Ltd., Miller House, 18 South Groathill Avenue, Edinburgh, EH4 2LW; T.-031-332 2585.

Miller, James David Frederick, DUniv (Stirling), MA (Cantab), FBIM. Director, Coats Patons PLC, since 1977; Director, Wolverhampton and Dudley Breweries, since 1984; Director, Bonds Coats Patons Ltd., Australia, since 1984; b. 5.1.35, Wolverhampton; m., Saffrey Blackett Oxley; 3 s.; 1 d. Educ. Edinburgh Academy; Emmanuel College, Cambridge; London School of Economics. National Service, Argyll and Sutherland Highlanders, Cameron Highlanders, commissioned in South Staffords, 1953-55; J. & P. Coats Ltd.: joined, 1958, Training Officer, 1964-66, Personnel Manager, 1969; Personnel Manager, Coats Patons Group, 1970; Director, J. & P. Coats Ltd., 1973; Director, Coats Patons (New Zealand) Ltd.; Council Member, Outward Bound Ltd.; Director, Outward Bound Loch Eil Ltd. (Chairman, 1977-84); Chairman, Needle Industries Group, Studley; Deputy Chairman, Aero Needles Group, Redditch; Member, Court, Stirling University, 1978-84; Director, Scottish National Orchestra, 1984; Director, Edinburgh Academy, 1985; Member, CBI Employee Involvement Panel. Recreations: gardening; tennis; golf. Address: (b.) Coats Patons PLC, 155 St. Vincent Street, Glasgow; T.-041-221 8711.

Miller, Professor James Douglas, MD, PhD, FRCSEdin, FRCSGlas, FACS, FRCPEdin. Professor of Surgical Neurology, Edinburgh University, since 1981; b. 20.7.37, Glasgow; m., Margaret Scott Rainey; 2 s. Educ. Glasgow Academy; Glasgow University. Surgical Senior House Officer and Registrar, Glasgow, 1962; Neurosurgical Registrar, Institute of Neurological Sciences, Glasgow, 1965; Medical Research Council Fellow, Department of Surgery, Glasgow University, 1967; Senior Registrar in Neurosurgery, Institute of Neurological Sciences, Glasgow, 1969; US Public Health Service Fellow in Neurosurgery, University of Pennsylvania, 1970; Senior Lecturer in Neurosurgery, Glasgow University, 1971; Professor of Neurosurgery, Virginia Commonwealth University, USA, 1975. Recreation: hill-walking. Address: (h.) 36 Cluny Drive, Edinburgh, EH10 6DX; T.-031-447 5828.

Miller, Rev. James Fergus, BA, BD, MA. Minister, Dunblane Cathedral, since 1984; b. 10.5.44, Perth; m., Karen Kathleen Emory; 2 s.; 2 d. Educ. Dollar Academy; McGill University; Glasgow University. Senior Assistant, St. John's Kirk, Perth; Minister, Maisonneuve-St. Cuthbert's Presbyterian Church, Montreal; Professor's Assistant, Faculty of Religious Studies, McGill University; Assistant Chaplain, Glasgow University; Minister, Old Parish Church, Peterhead; Minister, Dumbarton Riverside Parish Church. Moderator, Dumbarton Presbytery, 1984; General Assembly Preacher, 1982. Publications: From Sleep and From Damnation (Co-author); Biblical Studies: Essays in Honour of William Barclay (Co-Editor); Old and New Testament Literary Criticism; Christianity Without A Halo? Recreations: golf; family; books; music. Address: (h.) Cathedral Manse, Dunblane, Perthshire; T.-Dunblane 822205.

Miller, James Robert. Honorary Sheriff, Wick; b. 13.2.03, Wick; m., Catherine M. Millar. Educ. Wick High School. Until retirement, in business as Agricultural Merchant. Recreations: gardening; motoring. Address: (h.) Scaraben, George Street, Wick, Caithness, KW1 4DL; T.-0955 2513.

Miller, Joan Isobel, OBE, MA. Member, Parole Board for Scotland, since 1983; b. 10.3.27, Banchory; m., T. Angus Miller, DFC. Educ. Banchory Academy; Aberdeen University. Formerly Deputy Headteacher, Castlebrae High School, Edinburgh. Past Chairman, Children's Panel, Midlothian, East Lothian and Peebles; Past Chairman, Children's Panel, Lothian Region; former Member, Local Review Committee, Edinburgh Prison. Recreations: fishing; gardening. Address: (h.) Maybank, 501 Lanark Road West, Balerno, Midlothian; T.-031-449 3840.

Miller, John Dow Booth, MB, ChB, ChM, FRCSEdin, FIBiol. Consultant Surgeon; Senior Lecturer in Surgery, Aberdeen University; b. 10.7.44, Aberdeen; m., Isobel Stewart Murray; 2 s.; 1 d. Educ. Robert Gordon's College, Aberdeen; Aberdeen University. House Surgeon to Academic Unit, Aberdeen Royal Infirmary, then Senior House Officer, Pathology, Maryfield Hospital, Dundee, 1968-69; Senior House Officer, then Registrar in Surgery, Aberdeen, 1970-75; Research Fellow in Surgery, Harvard University, Boston, 1975-76; Senior Registrar and Lecturer in Surgery, Aberdeen University, from 1976. Address: (h.) 16 Granville Place, Aberdeen, AB1 6NZ; T.-0224 36879.

Miller, Rev. John Stewart Abercromby Smith, MA, BD, STM. Minister, Morningside United Church, Edinburgh, since 1975; b. 3.5.28, Gibraltar; m., Lorna Vivien Fraser; 1 s.; 1 d. Educ. Lanark Grammar School; Edinburgh University; Union Theological Seminary, New York. Assistant Minister, St. Giles' Cathedral, Edinburgh, 1953-54; Minister: St. Andrew's, Hawick, 1954-59, Sandyhills, Glasgow, 1959-64, Mortlach and Cabrach, Banffshire, 1964-75. Recreations: reading; listening to music; exploring Britain. Address: (h.) 1 Midmar Avenue, Edinburgh; T.-031-447 8724.

Miller, Maurice Solomon, MB, ChB. MP (Labour), East Kilbride, since 1974 (Glasgow Kelvingrove, 1964-74); b. 16.8.20. Educ. Shawlands Academy, Glasgow; Glasgow University. Former Member, Glasgow Corporation; Bailie, 1954-57, JP, 1957; Assistant Government Whip, 1968-69.

Miller, Richard Tweedie, BL, WS. Senior Partner, Pairman Miller & Murray, WS; Secretary, Lothian Local Medical Committee (General Practice), since 1956; Secretary, General Practitioner Sub-Committee, Lothian Area Medical Committee, since 1956; b. 11.4.15, Edinburgh. Educ. George Watson's Boys' College; Edinburgh University. WS apprenticeship, Bruce & Kerr, WS, Edinburgh; joined 94th HAA Regiment and served in ADGB throughout World War II; commissioned and latterly served as

Brigade Intelligence Officer on staff of 55 Brigade; after the War, joined family legal practice. Voluntary Leader, Tweedie Memorial Boys Club, Edinburgh. Recreations: voluntary youth work; gardening; motoring; rugby football. Address: (b.) 13 Heriot Row, Edinburgh, EH3 6HP; T.-031-557 1558.

Miller, Roger Ogilvy Stewart, BSc, CEng, FCIOB, FFB. Director, James Miller & Partners Ltd., since 1965; Managing Director, Miller Homes Northern Ltd., since 1970; b. 17.4.36, Edinburgh; m., Jean; 2 s.; 2 d. Educ. Edinburgh Academy; Harrow; Edinburgh University. National Service, 1958-60 (commissioned, Royal Engineers); joined James Miller & Partners Ltd., 1960. President, Scottish Building Employers Federation, 1978-79; Member, Scottish Committee, NHBC, 1968-79; Member, Scottish Committee, CBI, since 1982; President, Scottish Housebuilders Association, 1972-74; President, Edinburgh and District Master Builders Association, 1976-77. Recreations: sailing; golf; badminton. Address: (b.) 18 South Groathill Avenue, Edinburgh, EH4 2LW; T.-031-332 2585.

Miller, Ronald Andrew Baird, CBE (1985), CA, BSc. Chairman and Chief Executive, Dawson International p.l.c., since 1982; b. 13.5.37, Edinburgh. Address: (b.) Dawson International p.l.c., Kinross, KY13 7DH.

Miller, Ronald Murdoch. Scottish Officer, Equal Opportunities Commission, since 1978; b. 16.3.33, Dundee; m., Phyllis; 1 s. Educ. Morgan Academy. War Service, Korea/Japan, 1951-53; Youth and Community Worker, Gloucestershire; Deputy Youth and Community Officer, Suffolk; Community Development Officer, Holland (Lincolnshire); Education Researcher (Curriculum), Lanarkshire. Recreations: gardening; rugby referee; ballet (as a spectator); after-dinner speaker. Address: (b.) 249 West George Street, Glasgow; T.-041-226 4591.

Miller, Stanley Scott, MB, ChB, ChM, FRCS. Consultant General and Paediatric Surgeon, since 1976; Honorary Senior Lecturer in Surgery, Aberdeen University, since 1976; b. 24.12.38, Whitley Bay; 2 s.; 3 d. Educ. Robert Gordon's College; Aberdeen University. Research Fellow, Department of Surgery, Aberdeen University, 1970; Senior Surgical Registrar, Aberdeen Royal Infirmary, 1970-74; Resident Assistant Surgeon, Hospital for Sick Children, Great Ormond Street, London, 1975. Member, Executive, British Association of Paediatric Surgeons, 1983. Recreations: fishing; skiing; golfing. Address: (h.) 8 Forest Road, Aberdeen, AB2 4BT; T.-0224 38795.

Miller, Stewart O. Director, Miller Farms (Balbeggie); Member, Perth Branch Committee, National Farmers' Union of Scotland, since 1950 (Branch Chairman, 1955); Director, East of Scotland Farmers, since 1960; Member, Tayside Regional Council, since 1978; Member, Perth and Kinross District Council, since 1980 (Chairman, Policy and Resources Committee and Leader of Coalition Administration); b. 2.4.18, Errol; m.,

Betty L. Penny; 1 s.; 1 d. Educ. Perth Academy. Started work on farm, 1933; took over farm, 1943; elected, Perth and Kinross County Council, 1958 (Chairman, Housing Committee, 1967-75); elected, Perth Branch Committee, National Farmers' Union of Scotland, 1950 (Branch Chairman, 1955); elected, Council, NFU of Scotland; served on various local committees, local Health Board, Perth Presbytery. Address: (h.) Rosefield, Balbeggie, Perth, PH2 6AT; T.-Kinrossie 236.

Miller, Professor William L., MA, PhD. Edward Caird Professor of Politics, Glasgow University, since 1985; b. 12.8.43, Glasgow; m., Fiona Thomson; 2 s.; 1 d. Educ. Aberdeen Grammar School; Royal High School, Edinburgh; Edinburgh University; Newcastle University. Formerly Lecturer, Senior Lecturer and Professor, Strathclyde University; Visiting Professor, Virginia Tech., Blacksburg, Virginia, 1983-84; also taught at Universities of Essex and Cologne; frequent Contributor to Press and TV; Member, Editorial Boards: Electoral Studies, Political Studies. Publications: Electoral Dynamics, 1977; The End of British Politics?, 1981; The Survey Method in the Social and Political Sciences, 1983. Address: (b.) Department of Politics, Glasgow University, G12 8RT; T.-041-339 8855.

Miller of Pittenweem, William Ronald Crawford, MA (Cantab), LLB, WS. Consultant, Steedman, Ramage & Co., WS, Edinburgh, 1984-85; b. 21.5.19, Edinburgh. Educ. Edinburgh Academy; Emmanuel College, Cambridge; Edinburgh University. Served World War II with 1st Bn., The Duke of Wellington's (West Riding) Regiment, in UK, Tunisia, Pantelleria, Italy (wounded at Anzio, 30 January, 1944) and Middle East; attained rank of Major for short period as Acting DAA and QMG at HQ 3 Infantry Brigade; released from Army with retired rank of Captain while Adjutant of 1st DWR; Solicitor and WS, 1949; sometime Member, WS Council; Partner, Steedman, Ramage & Co., WS, 1960-84. Honorary Treasurer, Edinburgh Diocesan Gazette, 14 years, until 1971; Honorary Treasurer, Royal Martyr Church Union, since 1963. Recreations: foreign travel; gardening; historical research of the Priory. Address: (h.) The Priory, Pittenweem, Fife, KY10 2LJ; T.-0333-311 453.

Milligan, Rev. Rodney, FRGS. Minister, Culsalmond linked with Rothienorman, since 1958; b. 27.12.22, Arbroath; m., Jeannie Duguid. Educ. Arbroath High School; St. Andrews University; St. Mary's College. RAFVR, 1941-45; student, 1946-49; ordained as Assistant Minister, Dunfermline Abbey, 1949; Minister, Culsalmond, 1951; Moderator: Garioch Presbytery, 1958-59, Gordon Presbytery, 1984-85. Recreations: philately; oenology. Address: The Manse of Culsalmond, Insch, Aberdeenshire, AB5 6UH; T.-Colpy 235.

Millington, Philip Francis, BSc, MSc, PhD. Reader in Bioengineering, Strathclyde University, since 1970; b. 14.6.30, Birmingham; m., Patricia Rosemary Cooke; 1 s.; 2 d. Educ. St. Philip's Grammar School, Birmingham. Research

and Senior Research Associate, Birmingham University, 1956-62; Lecturer in Histology and Physiology, Bristol University, 1962-68. Tutor in Counselling; Chairman, CRUSE (Glasgow); Catholic Church Representative, Scottish Churches Council Social Responsibility Group; Tutor and Spokesman, CMAC in Scotland. Publication: Skin, 1983. Address: (h.) 27 North Erskine Park, Bearsden, Glasgow; T.-041-942 0495.

Mills, Colin Frederick, MSc, PhD, CChem, FRSC, FRSE. Head, Division of Biochemistry, and Senior Principal Scientific Officer, Rowett Research Institute, since 1966; b. 8.7.26, Swinton, Lancashire; m., D. Beryl; 1 d. Educ. Altrincham Grammar School; Reading University; London University. ARC Unit for Micronutrient Research, Long Ashton Research Station, Bristol University, 1946-47; Assistant Lecturer in Biochemistry, Wye College, London University, 1947-51; joined Rowett Research Institute, 1951. Member, WHO Experts Committee on Trace Elements in Human Nutrition; Chairman, International Committee for Symposia on Trace Elements in Man and Animals; Royal Society for Chemistry John Jeye Gold Medallist (Environmental Studies). Recreations: music; sailing. Address: (b.) Rowett Research Institute, Bucksburn, Aberdeen, AB2 9SB; T.-0224 712751.

Mills, Derek Henry, BSc, MSc, PhD, FIFM. Senior Lecturer, Department of Forestry and Natural Resources, Edinburgh University, since 1965; b. 19.3.28, Bristol; m., Florence Cameron; 1 s.; 1 d. Educ. Clifton House; Harrogate Grammar School; Queen Mary College, London University. RAF, 1947-49; Scientific Officer, Oceanographic Laboratory, Edinburgh, 1954-56; Assistant Scientist, Fisheries Research Board of Canada, 1956-57; Senior Scientific Officer, Freshwater Fisheries Laboratory, Pitlochry, 1957-65. Consultant Biologist to Salmon and Trout Association and Anglers' Co-operative Association; Editor, Journal of Aquaculture and Fisheries Management; Member, River Tweed Purification Board; Council Member, Committee of Management, and Scientific Advisory Panel, Atlantic Salmon Trust. Publications: Salmon and Trout; Introduction to Freshwater Ecology; Scotland's King of Fish; Salmon Rivers of Scotland (Co-author); Salmon in Iceland (Co-author); The Fishing Here is Great. Recreations: angling; hill-walking; horse riding. Address: (h.) 37 Granby Road, Edinburgh, EH16 5NP; T.-031-667 4931.

Mills, Harold Hernshaw, BSc, PhD. Under Secretary, Scottish Development Department, since 1984; b. 2.3.38, Greenock; m., Marion Elizabeth Beattie. Educ. Greenock High School; Glasgow University. Cancer Research Scientist, Roswell Park Memorial Institute, Buffalo, New York, 1962-64; Lecturer, Chemistry Department, Glasgow University, 1964-69; Principal, Scottish Home and Health Department, 1970-76; Assistant Secretary: Scottish Office, 1976-81, Privy Council Office, 1981-83, Scottish Development Department, 1983-84. Address: (b.) Scottish Development Department, New St. Andrews House, Edinburgh, EH1 3SZ; T.-031-556 8400.

Mills, Kenneth Leslie George, MA, BSc, MB, BChir, FRCS, FRCSEdin, FRCSGlas. Consultant Orthopaedic Surgeon, since 1968; b. 16.8.29, Birmingham; 2 d. Educ. High School of Glasgow; Cambridge University; Westminster Hospital, London. Medical Officer, RAF; Senior Lecturer in Orthopaedic Surgery, Dunde University. Publications: Guide to Orthopaedics (Trauma), 1979; Colour Atlas of Accidents and Emergencies, 1984. Address: (h.) 29 Craigiebuckler Avenue, Aberdeen, AB1 7SL; T.-0224 34077.

Mills, Ronald David, BSc, DIC, PhD. Senior Lecturer in Computing Science, Glasgow University, since 1970; b. 10.11.32, Arbroath; m., Fiona Helen McEwen; 1 s.; 1 d. Educ. Arbroath High School; St. Andrews University; Imperial College. Lecturer in Fluid Mechanics, Strathclyde University, 1958-66; ICI Research Fellow, Engineering Department, Cambridge University, 1966-68; Lecturer in Computing Science, Glasgow University, 1968-70. Recreation: golf. Address: (h.) 5 Blackhouse Avenue, Newton Mearns, Glasgow, G77 5HU; T.-041-639 3822.

Milne, Alastair, MA, MEd, ABPsS. HM Inspector of Schools, since 1970; b. 27.10.29, New Pitsligo; m., Margaret M. McHardy (deceased); 1 s. Educ. Banff Academy; Aberdeen University; Aberdeen College of Education. Teacher, Fyvie School, 1955-57; Educational Psychologist, Aberdeen Child Guidance Service, 1957-60; Lecturer, Senior Lecturer, Principal Lecturer, Dundee College of Education, 1960-70. Recreations: reading; hill-walking. Address: (h.) 52 Kelvin Court, Glasgow, G12 OAE; T.-041-357 3684.

Milne, Archibald Cousland, MB, ChB, FFARCS, DA. Consultant Anaesthetist (with administrative responsibility), City Hospital, Edinburgh, since 1965; Consultant Anaesthetist, Edinburgh Royal Infirmary, since 1965; b. 23.9.23, Hawick; m., Mary Noel Brebner; 1 s.; 3 d. Educ. Robert Gordon's College, Aberdeen; Aberdeen University. House Surgeon, Stracathro Hospital, Brechin, 1946-47; Army Service, Malaya, 1947-49 (mentioned in Despatches); House Physician, Children's Hospital and Royal Infirmary, Aberdeen, 1949; Junior Registrar/Registrar in Anaesthesia, Royal Infirmary, Aberdeen, 1950-53; Senior Registrar in Anaesthesia, Royal Infirmary, Edinburgh; Consultant Anaesthetist, Royal Infirmary and Eastern General Hospital, Edinburgh, 1957-65. Session Clerk, Fairmilehead Parish Church. Recreations: ornithology; photography; hill-walking. Address: (h.) 61 Braid Road, Edinburgh, EH10 6AR; T.-031-447 1302.

Milne, Brian, MB, ChB, FRCOG. Consultant Gynaecologist and Obstetrician, Highland Health Board (based at Raigmore Hospital, Inverness), since 1978; Clinical Senior Lecturer, Aberdeen University, since 1978; b. 9.1.42, Elgin; m., Mary I.B.; 2 s. Educ. Keith Grammar School; Aberdeen University. House Officer and Senior House Officer appointments, Aberdeen Royal Infirmary; Registrar appointments, Raigmore Hospital, Inverness and Southern General Hospital, Glasgow; Senior Registrar, Obstetrics

and Gynaecology, Leicester Royal Infirmary, 1974-78. Recreations: golf; curling; Secretary, Inverness Branch, Aberdeen FC Supporters. Address: (h.) Muirfield House, 28 Muirfield Road, Inverness; T.-0463 222134.

Milne, Charles Buchan, MA (Hons). Head Teacher, Hilton Academy, since 1980; b. 7.7.24, Kennethmont; m., Phyllis Mathieson; 3 d. Educ. Robert Gordon's College, Aberdeen; Aberdeen University. Recreations: golf; music. Address: (h.) 45 Baillieswells Crescent, Bieldside, Aberdeen; T.-Aberdeen 868556.

Milne, James. General Secretary, Scottish Trades Union Congress, since 1975; b. 1921. Secretary, Aberdeen Trades Council, 1948-69; Assistant General Secretary, STUC, 1969-75.

Milne, John Alexander, BA, BSc (Hons), PhD. Head, Animal Nutrition Department, Hill Farming Research Organisation, since 1981; b. 22.11.43, Edinburgh; m., Janet Erskine; 1 s. Educ. Edinburgh Academy; Edinburgh University; London University; Open University. Joined Hill Farming Research Organisation, 1970. Chairman, Programmes Committee, British Society of Animal Production. Address: (b.) Bush Estate, Penicuik, Midlothian; T.-031-445 3401.

Milne, John Duff. Broadcasting Journalist, since 1972; b. 13.5.42, Dundee; m., Jennifer Frances Brown; 2 s. Educ. Harris Academy, Dundee. Newspaper Journalist: D.C. Thomson, Dundee; Scotsman Publications, Edinburgh; Broadcasting Journalist: Swiss Broadcasting Corporation, Bern, BBC. Recreations: sport; music. Address: (b.) BBC Scotland, Queen Margaret Drive, Glasgow; T.-041-339 8844.

Milne, Peter Henry, BSc, PhD, CEng, FICE, FInstCES, FIAP, MASCE. Senior Lecturer, Department of Civil Engineering, Strathclyde University, since 1980; b. 17.11.39, Glasgow; m., Helen Cumming Hunter; 2 s. Educ. Kelvinside Academy, Glasgow; Glasgow University; Strathclyde University. Assistant Engineer, James Williamson & Partners, Consulting Civil Engineers, Glasgow, 1964-70; Lecturer, Department of Civil Engineering, Strathclyde University, 1970-80. Publications: Fish and Shellfish Farming in Coastal Waters, 1972; Underwater Engineering Surveys, 1980; Underwater Acoustic Positioning Systems, 1983; Basic Programs for Land Surveying, 1984. Recreations: hill-walking; golf; tennis; diving. Address: (b.) Department of Civil Engineering, Strathclyde University, John Anderson Building, Glasgow, G4 ONG; T.-041-552 4400.

Milne, Thomas Edwardson, MA, MLitt, CertITP. Senior Lecturer, Management Studies, Glasgow University; b. 14.1.37, Newton Mearns; m., Marion Elder Lind Weir; 2 s. Educ. Rutherglen Academy; Glasgow University; Harvard Business School. Commercial Sub-Editor, Glasgow Herald, 1959-60; Market Analyst, Colvilles Ltd., 1960-65; Lecturer in Business Studies, Edinburgh University, 1965-70; joined Glasgow

University as Lecturer in Management Studies, 1970. Editor, European Management Journal. Recreations: gardening; sailing. Address: (h.) 9 Dunavon Crescent, Strathaven, Lanarkshire; T.-0357 21367.

Milner, A.D., MA, DipPsych, PhD. Reader in Psychology, St. Andrews University, since 1985 (Chairman, Department of Psychology, since 1983); b. 16.7.43, Leeds. Educ. Bradford Grammar School; Lincoln College, Oxford. Research Worker, Institute of Psychiatry, London, 1966-70; Lecturer, then Senior Lecturer, St. Andrews University, 1970-85. Address: (b.) Psychological Laboratory, St. Andrews University, St. Andrews, KY16 9JU; T.-0334 76161.

Milner, Professor Arthur John Robin Gorell, BA (Cantab). Professor of Computation Theory, Edinburgh University, since 1984; b. 13.1.34, Yealmpton; m., Lucy; 2 s.; 1 d. Educ. Eton; King's College, Cambridge. National Service, 2nd Lt., Royal Engineers, 1952-54; student, 1954-58; Mathematics Teacher, Marylebone Grammar School, 1959-60; Ferranti Ltd., 1960-63; Mathematics Lecturer, The City University, 1963-68; Research Fellow, University College, Swansea, 1968-70; Research Associate, Artificial Intelligence Laboratory, Stanford University, 1971-72; joined Edinburgh University as Lecturer, 1973. Publications: Edinburgh LCF (Co-author); A Calculus of Communicating Systems. Recreations: music (oboe and piano); carpentry; walking. Address: (h.) 2 Garscube Terrace, Edinburgh, EH12 6BQ; T.-031-337 4823.

Milton, Professor Anthony Stuart, MA, DPhil (Oxon). Professor of Pharmacology and Head of Department, Aberdeen University, since 1973; b. 15.4.34, London; m., Elizabeth Amaret Freeman; 1 s.; 2 d. Educ. Cranleigh School; St. Catherine's College, Oxford. Lecturer, Dartmouth College Medical School, USA, 1959-60; Research Fellow: Stanford University Medical Center, USA, 1960-61, Edinburgh University, 1961-63; Lecturer, then Senior Lecturer, School of Pharmacy, London University, 1966-73. Recreation: breeding and showing Border Terrier dogs. Address: (h.) Stone Cottage, Baillieswells Road, Bieldside, Aberdeen, AB1 9BQ; T.-0224 868651.

Minto, 6th Earl of, (Gilbert Edward George Lariston Elliot-Murray-Kynynmound), MBE (1955). Brigadier, Queen's Bodyguard for Scotland (Royal Company of Archers); Chairman, Scottish Council on Alcoholism, since 1973; Deputy Lieutenant, Borders Region, Roxburgh, Ettrick and Lauderdale, since 1983; b. 19.6.28; m.; 1, Lady Caroline Child-Villiers (m. diss.); 1 s.; 1 d.; 2, Mary Elizabeth Ballantine (deceased). Educ. Eton; Sandhurst. Former Captain, Scots Guards. Address: (h.) Minto, Hawick.

Minto, James Rutherford, OBE, MA, MEd, PhD. General Director, Quarrier's Homes, Bridge of Weir, since 1974; b. 9.4.26, St. Boswells; m., Rosemary; 1 s.; 2 d. Educ. Kirkcudbright Academy; St. Andrews University. Assistant Teacher: Waid Academy, Anstruther, 1951-59, Abraham Lincoln High School,

Philadelphia, 1956-57; Headmaster, then Principal, Dr. Graham's Homes, Kalimpong, India, 1959-71. Vice-Chairman, Strathclyde Branch, Epilepsy Association Scotland. Publication: Graham of Kalimpong. Recreation: golf. Address: (h.) Braehead, Quarrier's Homes, Bridge of Weir, Renfrewshire; T.-Bridge of Weir 612414.

Miquel, Raymond Clive, CBE (1981). Chairman and Managing Director, Arthur Bell & Sons plc; b. 28.5.31; m.; 1 s.; 2 d. Educ. Allan Glen's School, Glasgow; Glasgow Technical College. Joined Arthur Bell & Sons Ltd., 1956, as works study engineer; Deputy Managing Director, 1965; Managing Director, 1968; Chairman, 1973.

Misra, Prem Chandra, BSc, MBBS, DPM (RCP&S, Edin and Glas), FAGS. Deputy Physician Superintendent, Gartloch Hospital, Glasgow, since 1984; Clinical Lecturer, Glasgow University, since 1976; b. 24.7.41, Lucknow, India; m., Sandhya; 1 s.; 2 d. Educ. KK Degree College and King George's Medical College, Lucknow, India; Lucknow University. Rotating Intern, King George's Medical College Hospital, Lucknow, 1967; Demonstrator, Department of Human Physiology, Lucknow University, 1967; Resident Senior House Officer, General Medicine and Geriatrics, Wigan and Leigh Group of Hospitals, 1968-69; Resident House Surgeon, General Surgery, Wigan Royal Infirmary, 1968-69; Resident House Physician, General Medicine, Whelley Hospital, Wigan, 1969-70; Resident Senior House Officer in Psychiatry, then Resident Registrar in Psychiatry, Bolton District General Hospital, 1970-73; Senior Psychiatric Registrar (Midland Area Consultant Training Scheme), Hollymoor Hospital, Birmingham, 1973-76; Consultant Psychiatrist, Solihull Area Health Authority, 1976; appointed Consultant Psychiatrist, Glasgow Royal Infirmary and Duke Street Hospital, 1976; Consultant in Charge, Acorn Street Day Hospital, 1979. President, Indian Association of Strathclyde, since 1981; Member, Executive Committee: Strathclyde Community Relations Council, since 1981, Scottish Council for Racial Equality, 1982; Member, Social and Welfare Committee, CRC, for Ethnic Groups and Vietnam Refugees, 1982; awarded Ludwika Bierkoskigo Medal by Polish Medical Association for "outstanding contributions in the prevention and treatment of disabilities"; Secretary, Division of Psychiatry, Eastern District of Glasgow, since 1980; Member: Executive Committee, British Society of Research on Sex Education, International Scientific Committee on Sexuality and Handicap, Welfare and Advisory Service for Overseas Doctors in Scotland, International Advisory Board of Israel Society of Clinical and Experimental Hypnosis; Executive Committee Member, European Society of Hypnosis; Member, International Committee of Sexologists. Publication: Modern Trends in Hypnosis, 1985. Address: (b.) Gartloch Hospital, Gartcosh, Glasgow, G69 8EJ; T.-041-771 0771.

Mitchell, Archie Mackenzie, MITSA. Director of Trading Standards, Tayside Regional Council, since 1980; b. 23.3.35, Cupar; m., Kathleen; 2 s.; 1 d. Educ. Bell-Baxter High School, Cupar. Trainee Inspector of Weights and Measures, Fife, 1953-58; Inspector of Weights and Measures,

Glasgow, 1959; Ayr County: District Inspector, 1959-69, Depute Chief Inspector, 1969-75; Chief Inspector Consumer Protection (Ayr Sub-Region), Strathclyde, 1975-77; Depute Director, Grampian, 1977-80. Honorary Secretary, Society of Directors of Trading Standards in Scotland, since 1982. Recreations: curling; cricket; rugby. Address: (b.) 1 Riverside Drive, Dundee, DD1 4DB; T.-Dundee 23281.

Mitchell, Bryan, CA. Head of Finance, BBC Scotland, since 1977; b. 9.6.37, Glasgow; m., Myra; 2 d. Educ. Glasgow Academy; Glasgow University. Thomson McLintock & Co., CAs, Glasgow, 1955-63; BBC Scotland: Assistant Scottish Programme Executive, 1964-71, Scottish Programme Executive, 1971-77. Recreations: golf; skiing. Address: (h.) 19 Henderland Road, Bearsden, Glasgow.

Mitchell, David William, CBE. Director, Mallinson-Denny (Scotland) Ltd., since 1980; b. 4.1.33, Glasgow; m., Lynda Guy; 1 d. Educ. Merchiston Castle School. Member, Western Regional Hospital Board, 1965-73; Member, Glasgow Rating Valuation Appeal Committee, 1970-74; Council Member, CBI Scotland, since 1979; Executive Member, Scottish Council (Development and Industry), since 1979; President, Scottish Timber Trade Association, 1980-82; Executive Member, Institute of Directors in Scotland, since 1983; President, Scottish Conservative and Unionist Association, 1980-82; Board Member, Cumbernauld New Town, since 1984. Recreations: golf; shooting; fishing. Address: (h.) Dunmullen House, Blanefield, Stirlingshire, G63 9AJ; T.-0324 483294.

Mitchell, Douglas Thomas, CA. Director of Finance, Fife Regional Council, since 1982; b. 8.12.37, Glasgow; m., Margaret Maxwell; 4 d. Educ. Lanark Grammar School; Tarbert Junior Secondary School; Hamilton Academy; Glasgow University. Thomas Kelly & Co., CA, Glasgow, 1955-64; Lanark County Council: Loans Accountant, 1965-68, Group Accountant, 1968-71, Management Accountant, 1971-72; Depute County Treasurer, Ross and Cromarty County Council, 1972-75; Depute Director of Finance, Highland Regional Council, 1975-76. Recreations: gardening; bowling; walking. Address: (b.) North Street, Glenrothes, Fife; T.-0592 754411.

Mitchell, Rev. Duncan Ross, BA (Hons), BD (Hons). Minister, St. Andrews Church, West Kilbride, since 1980; b. 5.5.42, Boddam, Aberdeenshire; m., Sandra Brown; 2 s.; 1 d. Educ. Hyndland Senior Secondary School, Glasgow; Strathclyde University; Glasgow University. Worked in insurance industry, four years; Minister, Craigmailen UF Church, Bo'ness, 1972-80; Convener, Assembly Youth Committee, UF Church, 1974-79; Member: Scottish Joint Committee on Religious Education, 1974-79, Multilateral Conversation in Scotland, 1976-79; Board of Social Responsibility, Church of Scotland, since 1983; Convener, World Mission and Unity, Ardrossan Presbytery, since 1984. Address: St. Andrew's Manse, 7 Overton Drive, West Kilbride; T.-0294 823142.

Mitchell, Iain Grant, LLB (Hons), FSA Scot. Advocate, since 1976; b. 16.11.51, Edinburgh. Educ. Perth Academy; Edinburgh University. Called to Scottish Bar, 1976; Partner, Mitchells of Perth (Dyers and Cleaners), since 1973; Advisor in Scots Law to Lawtel (Prestel Legal Database), since 1983; Writer and Broadcaster; Past President, Diagnostic Society of Edinburgh; former Vice-President, Edinburgh University Conservative Association; several times Conservative candidate in local government; Vice-Chairman, Edinburgh West Conservative Association; Conservative candidate, Falkirk West, General Election, 1983; Chairman, Scottish Philharmonic Club; Chairman, Trust for the International Opera Theatre of Scotland; Member, Scottish Committee, Royal Institute of International Affairs; Member, Conservative Group for Europe and the European Movement; Member, Faculty of Advocates Committee on European Affairs; Scottish Correspondent, International Legal Practitioner; Committee Member, Perth Civic Trust. Recreations: music and the arts; photography; history; travel; writing; finding enough hours in the day. Address: (b.) Advocates Library, Parliament House, High Street, Edinburgh; T.-031-226 5071.

Mitchell, James F.O., MD, DLO, FRCSEdin. Senior Consultant Ear, Nose and Throat Surgeon, Tayside Area, since 1984; Consultant Otolaryngologist, Dundee, Angus and Perth NHS, since 1951; b. 7.9.21, Edinburgh; 3 s. Educ. George Heriot's School, Edinburgh; Edinburgh University. Army Service, RAMC, 1945-48, Egypt and Palestine, latterly as Major. Chairman, Area Medical Committee, 1981-83; Chairman, British Medical Association, Angus, 1964, and Dundee, 1978. Dundee Chairman, British Subaqua Club, 1969. Recreations: swimming; skiing; caravanning; ornithology; golf. Address: (h.) 19 Rockfield Crescent, Dundee; T.-0382 66092.

Mitchell, Sheriff (James Lachlan) Martin, RD (1969), MA, LLB. Sheriff of Lothian and Borders, since 1974 (at Edinburgh, since 1978); b. 13.6.29. Educ. Cargilfield; Sedbergh; Edinburgh University. Admitted, Faculty of Advocates, 1957; Comdr., RNR, 1966-74.

Mitchell, John, BSc. Head Teacher, Kilsyth Academy, since 1985; b. 4.1.45, Kirkintilloch; m., Irene; 1 s.; 1 d. Educ. Lenzie Academy; Glasgow University. Taught in Glasgow; Principal Teacher of Physics, Balfron High School and Bishopbriggs High School; Assistant Head Teacher, Kilsyth Academy; Deputy Head Teacher, Knightswood Secondary School. Address: (h.) Kilsyth Academy, Balmalloch, Kilsyth, G65 9NF; T.-0236 822244.

Mitchell, John Logan, LLB (Hons). Advocate, since 1974; Advocate Depute, 1981-85; b. 23.6.47, Dumfries; m., Christine Brownlee Thomson; 1 s.; 1 d. Educ. Royal High School, Edinburgh; Edinburgh University. Called to Bar, 1974; Standing Junior Counsel to Forestry Commission; Standing Junior Counsel, Department of Agriculture and Fisheries. Address: (h.) 17 Braid Farm Road, Edinburgh; T.-031-447 8099.

Mitchell, Joseph R., OBE, JP. Member, Banff and Buchan District Council, since 1975 (Vice-Chairman, Housing Committee); Farmer; Vice-Chairman, North East of Scotland Library Committee, since 1984; b. 15.3.14, Old Deer. Educ. Robert Gordon's College, Aberdeen. Director, Fraserburgh Ltd. and C.E. Heath & Co. (Scotland) Ltd.; Chairman, Buchan Meat Producers, 1954-73; Past Chairman, Buchan Poultry Products; Past Chairman, Aberdeen-Kincardine Area, NFU of Scotland; received Royal Northern Agricultural Society Award, 1984; Chairman, East Aberdeenshire Conservative Association, 1976-78. Recreation: bridge. Address: Coburty Mains, Fraserburgh; T.-Rosehearty 206.

Mitchell, Ross, MA, DSA, FHA, MIPM. Secretary, Lothian Health Board, since 1981; b. Glasgow; m., Marion; 1 s. Educ. Hillhead High School, Glasgow; Glasgow University; Manchester University. Eastern Regional Hospital Board: National Administrative Trainee, 1956-58, Administrative Assistant, 1958-60, Work Study Officer, 1960-61; Hospital Secretary, Bridge of Earn Hospital, 1961-65; Deputy Secretary and Treasurer, East Fife Board of Management, 1965-69; Secretary and Treasurer, West Lothian Board of Management, 1969-73; Secretary, Fife Health Board, 1973-81. Member, Management Committee, Common Services Agency for Scottish Health Service. Recreations: squash; golf. Address: (h.) 43 Braehead Road, Edinburgh; T.-031-339 1279.

Mitchell, Professor Ross Galbraith, MD, FRCPEdin, DCH. Professor of Child Health, Dundee University, 1973-85; Member, General Medical Council, since 1983; b. 18.11.20; m., June Phylis Butcher; 1 s.; 3 d. Educ. Kelvinside Academy, Glasgow; Edinburgh University. Surgeon Lt., Royal Naval Volunteer Reserve, 1944-47; junior medical posts, Edinburgh, Liverpool and London, 1947-52; Rockefeller Research Fellow in Physiology, Mayo Clinic, USA, 1952-53; Lecturer in Child Health, St. Andrews University, 1952-55; Consultant Paediatrician, Dundee Teaching Hospitals, 1955-63; Professor of Child Health, Aberdeen University, 1963-72. Chairman, Editorial Board, Spastics International Medical Publications, since 1980; Chairman, Scottish Advisory Council on Child Care, 1966-68; Dean, Faculty of Medicine and Dentistry, Dundee University, 1978-81; Chairman, Aberdeen Association of Social Service, 1971-72; President, Scottish Paediatric Society, 1982-84; President, Harveian Society of Edinburgh, 1982-83. Recreations: fishing; gardening; languages. Address: (h.) Craigard, Abertay Gardens, Barnhill, Dundee, DD5 2SQ; T.-0382 76983.

Mitchell, Ruthven, BSc (Hons), MB, ChB, MD, FRCPath, FRCPGlas. Regional Director, Glasgow and West of Scotland Blood Transfusion Service, since 1978; b. 28.3.36, Cambuslang; m., Eleanor Forbes Burnside; 1 s.; 1 d. Educ. Hamilton Academy; Glasgow University. Glasgow Royal Infirmary: Medical and Surgical House Officer, 1961-62, Senior House Officer in Pathology, 1962-63, Registrar in Pathology, 1963-65, University Lecturer in Pathology, 1965-68; Consultant Pathologist, Ministry of Health,

Tanzania, 1965-67; Deputy Medical Director, Glasgow and West of Scotland Blood Transfusion Service, 1968-78. Recreations: gardening; fishing. Address: (h.) 2 Byron Court, Sweethope Farm Steading, Bothwell, Lanarkshire; T.-0698 853255.

Mitchell, Thomas. Lord Provost, City of Dundee, since 1984; b. 4.9.41, Dundee; m., Gertrude Brown; 2 s. Educ. St. John's High School, Dundee. Elected, City of Dundee District Council, 1980. Recreations: football; hill-walking. Address: (b.) City Chambers, Dundee, DD1 3BY; T.-Dundee 23141.

Mitchison, Professor John Murdoch, ScD, FRS, FRSE. Professor of Zoology, Edinburgh University, since 1963; b. 11.6.22; m., Rosalind Mary Wrong; 1 s.; 3 d. Educ. Winchester College; Trinity College, Cambridge. Army Operational Research, 1941-46; Research Scholar, then Fellow, Trinity College, Cambridge, 1946-54; Lecturer, then Reader in Zoology, Edinburgh University, 1953-62; Member, Edinburgh University Court, 1971-74; Council Member, Scottish Marine Biological Association, 1961-67; Executive Committee Member, International Society for Cell Biology, 1964-72; Member: Biological Committee, SRC, 1972-75, Royal Commission on Environmental Pollution, 1974-79, Science Board, SRC, 1976-79, Working Group on Biological Manpower, DES, 1968-71, Advisory Committee on Safety of Nuclear Installations, Health and Safety Executive, 1981-84; President, British Society for Cell Biology, 1974-77. Publication: The Biology of the Cell Cycle. Address: (h.) Great Yew, Ormiston, East Lothian, EH35 5NJ; T.-Pencaitland 340530.

Mitchison, Naomi, CBE. Writer; b. 1.11.97, Edinburgh; m., Dick Mitchison; 3 s.; 2 d. Educ. Dragon School, Oxford; St. Anne's College, Oxford. Member: Argyll County Council, 1945-65, Highland Panel, 1945-65, Highland and Island Advisory Council, 1965-75; contested Scottish Universities Parliamentary constituency for Labour; author of about 80 books, including: The Corn King and the Spring Queen; Blood of the Martyrs; The Bull Calves; The Big House; Lobsters on the Agenda; Five Men and a Swan; Cleopatra's People; three volumes of autobiography, The Cleansing of the Knife, Images of Africa, What Do You Think Yourself. Address: (h.) Carradale House, Carradale, Campbeltown, Argyll.

Mitchison, Professor Rosalind Mary, MA. Professor of Social History, Edinburgh University, since 1981; b. 11.4.19, Manchester; m., J.M. Mitchison (qv); 1 s.; 3 d. Educ. Channing School, Highgate; Lady Margaret Hall, Oxford. Assistant Lecturer, Manchester University, 1943-46; Tutor, Lady Margaret Hall, Oxford, 1946-47; Assistant: Edinburgh University, 1954-57, Glasgow University, 1962-63; Lecturer: Glasgow University, 1966-67, Edinburgh, from 1967. President, Scottish History Society, 1981-84. Publications: A History of Scotland, 1970; British Population Change since 1860, 1977; Life in Scotland, 1978; Lordship to Patronage: Scotland 1603-1745, 1983. Recreations: walking; skiing. Address: (h.) Great Yew, Ormiston, East Lothian, EH35 5NJ; T.-Pencaitland 340530.

Mithen, Dallas Alfred, CB, BSc, FICFor. President, Institute of Chartered Foresters, since 1984; Chairman, Forestry Training Council, since 1984; b. 5.11.23; m., 1, Peggy Clarke (deceased); 2, Aurel Tresa Dodd; 1 s.; 1 d. Educ. Maidstone Grammar School; University College of North Wales, Bangor. Fleet Air Arm, 1942-46; joined Forestry Commission as District Officer, 1950; Deputy Surveyor, New Forest, and Conservator, SE (England), 1968-71; Senior Officer, Scotland, 1971-75; Head, Forest Management Division, Edinburgh, 1975-76; Commissioner for Harvesting and Marketing, Forestry Commission, 1977-83. Director, Central Scotland Countryside Trust, since 1985. Recreations: swimming; walking; gardening. Address: (h.) Kings Knot, Bonnington Road, Peebles, EH45 9HF; T.-0721 20738.

Moffat of That Ilk, Francis, MC, JP, DL, BA (Econ) (Hons). Chief of the Name and Arms of Moffat, since 1983; Deputy Lieutenant, County of Dumfries, since 1957; b. 21.3.15, Moffat; m., Margaret Carrington; 2 d. Educ. Shrewsbury School; Trinity College, Cambridge. Farming in Roxburghshire, 1937-40; War Service, 1940-45: Major, King's Own Scottish Borderers, severely wounded in Germany, 1945; Farmer and Landowner, Dumfriesshire, 1946-76; succeeded father as County Councillor for Moffat and Wamphray, 1948; President, Moffat Show Society, 1950-57 (Honorary President, since 1957); Member, Association of County Councils in Scotland, 1961-75; Vice-Convener, Dumfries County Council, 1961-69, Convener, 1969-75; Chairman: SW Scotland Joint Planning Working Party, 1969-72, SW Scotland Industrial Development Authority, 1972-75; Member, Board of Management, Small Industries Council for Rural Areas of Scotland, 1972-75; Member, Committee for European Investment in Scotland, 1972-74; Member, Scottish Consultative Committee, Scottish Council (Development and Industry), 1972-75; Council Member, Galloway Cattle Society, 1961-72; President, Dumfriesshire Conservative Association, 1978-85. Recreations: historical and genealogical research; walking; reading. Address: (h.) Redacres, Moffat, Dumfriesshire, DG10 9JT; T.-0683 20045.

Moffat, John, MB, ChB, FRCPsych, DPM. Physician Superintendent, Ravenscraig Hospital, Greenock, since 1968 (Consultant Psychiatrist, since 1965); b. 20.11.28, Renfrew; m., Jean Forsyth; 1 s.; 1 d. Educ. Camphill Secondary School; Glasgow University. Member, Argyll and Clyde Area Health Board, since 1981. Address: (h.) 41 Denholm Street, Greenock; T.-0475 20975.

Moir, Alexander Thomas Boyd, MB, ChB, BSc, PhD, FRCPEdin, MRCPath, MFOM, FIBiol, FIFST. Principal Medical Officer, Scottish Home and Health Department; b. 1.8.39, Bolton; m., Isabel May Sheehan; 1 s.; 2 d. Educ. George Heriot's School, Edinburgh; Edinburgh University. Intern appointment, New York City Hospitals; MRC Scientific/Clinical Scientific Staff, Honorary Registrar/Senior Registrar, Honorary Fellow, Edinburgh University; Senior/Principal Medical Officer, Scottish Home and Health Department. Recreations: playing games; listening to music; reading. Address: (b.) Scottish Home and Health Department, St. Andrews House, Edinburgh, EH1 3DE; T.-031-556 8501.

Moir, Donald Dundas, MD, FFARCS, DA, DRCOG. Consultant Anaesthetist, Queen Mother's Hospital and Western Infirmary, Glasgow, since 1963; Honorary Clinical Lecturer, Glasgow University, since 1970; b. 11.6.29, Kendal, Cumbria; m., Heather Joy Harvey; 2 s. Educ. Hillhead High School, Glasgow; Glasgow University. Junior posts in various Glasgow hospitals, 1952-63; Captain, RAMC, 1953-55; Assistant Professor, Western Reserve University, Cleveland, Ohio, 1961-62. President, Obstetric Anaesthetists Association, since 1984; President, Glasgow and West of Scotland Society of Anaesthetists, 1978-79; Member, Scottish Standing Committee, Faculty of Anaesthetists, 1981-84; British Council Lecturer, Sri Lanka and Israel. Publications: Pain Relief in Labour; Obstetric Anaesthesia and Analgesia. Recreations: golf; walking; gardening. Address: (h.) 1 Westbourne Crescent, Bearsden, Glasgow, G61 4HB; T.-041-942 3791.

Moir, Dorothy Carnegie, MB, ChB, MD, MFCM. Community Medicine Specialist, since 1979; Honorary Senior Clinical Lecturer in Community Medicine, Aberdeen University, since 1979; b. 27.3.42, Aberdeen; m., Alexander D. Moir; 3 s. Educ. Albyn School for Girls, Aberdeen; Aberdeen University. Research Fellow in Therapeutics and Pharmacology, 1966-69; Lecturer in Community Medicine, 1970-79. Address: (h.) 30 Hilltop Road, Cults, Aberdeen; T.-Aberdeen 861327.

Moir, Rev. Ian Andrew, MA, BD. Minister, Old Kirk of Edinburgh, since 1983; b. 9.4.35, Aberdeen; m., Elizabeth; 3 s. Educ. Aberdeen Grammar School; Aberdeen University. Sub-Warden, St. Ninian's Training Centre, Crieff, 1959-61; Superintendent, Pholela High School, Natal, 1962-73; Assistant Secretary, Church of Scotland Overseas Council, 1974-83. Recreations: walking; golf. Address: 24 Pennywell Road, Edinburgh, EH4 4HD; T.-031-332 4354.

Molloy, Daniel Francis. Member, Midlothian District Council, since 1977 (Chairman, Leisure and Recreation Committee, since 1980); Member, Lothian Health Board, since 1979; b. 16.10.52, Glenties, Eire; m., Mara Watson; 1 s.; 1 d. Educ. St. Connels R.C. School. Chairman, Dalkeith OAPs; Executive Member: Dalkeith Arts Guild, Dalkeith CAB; Management Committee, Dalkeith Unemployment Centre. Recreation: walking in countryside. Address: (h.) 8 Jarnac Court, Dalkeith, Midlothian; T.-031-663 2120.

Monaghan, Captain William. Salvation Army Officer, since 1985; Member, Highland Health Board, since 1975; b. 28.4.36, Dundee; m., Margaret Innes; 2 s.; 1 d. Educ. Rockwell Junior Secondary School, Dundee; Jordanhill College of Education, Glasgow. 1st Bn., Seaforth Highlanders, 1954-57; Salvation Army Officer, 1957-64; social work, 1964-74; Highland Region

Social Work Department, 1974-84. Chairman, Inverness Council on Alcoholism, 1982; Bandmaster, Inverness Salvation Army Band, 1970-83. Recreations: reading; gardening; letterpress printing. Address: (h.) 4 Huntly Place, Inverness, IV3 6HA; T.-Inverness 234123.

Moncreiff, 5th Baron, (Harry Robert Wellwood Moncreiff), Bt; b. 4.2.15; m., Enid Marion Watson Locke; 1 s. Educ. Fettes College, Edinburgh. Lt.-Col. (Hon.), RASC (retired). Address: (h.) Tulliebole Castle, Fossoway, Kinross-shire.

Moncrieff, Charles William Kemley, BSc, MA. Rector, Annan Academy, since 1984; b. 12.7.42, Edinburgh; m., Helen Grantham; 1 s.; 1 d. Educ. Ross High School; Edinburgh University; Heriot-Watt University; Moray House College of Education. Teacher of Mathematics and Science: Daliburgh Secondary School, South Uist, Knox Academy, Haddington; Principal Teacher of Mathematics: David Kilpatrick Secondary School, Edinburgh, Gracemount High School, Edinburgh; Assistant Rector, Banff Academy; Depute Rector, Dumfries Academy. Address: (b.) Annan Academy, St. John's Road, Annan, DG12 6AP; T.-Annan 2954.

Moncrieff, Peter Duncan, BSc (Hons), DipEd. Rector, Blantyre High School, since 1974; b. 22.5.28, Perth; m., Doreen J.B. Langlands; 2 s.; 1 d. Educ. Perth Academy; Edinburgh University; Moray House College of Education. First Assistant, Goodlyburn Primary School, Perth, 1958-60; Head Teacher: Aberuthven Primary School, Perthshire, 1960-61, Mallaig Secondary School, 1961-70; Depute Rector, Stonelaw High School, Rutherglen, 1970-74. Children's Panel Member (Past Chairman, Area 10, Glasgow SE); Governor, National Memorial to David Livingstone. Recreations: golf; badminton; swimming; philately. Address: (h.) 184 Wellhall Road, Hamilton, Lanarkshire; T.-Hamilton 425393.

Monelle, Raymond, MA, BMus, PhD, ARCM. Composer; Music Critic, The Scotsman and Opera; Lecturer in Music, Edinburgh University; b. 19.8.37, Bristol; 2 d. Educ. Bristol Grammar School; Pembroke College, Oxford. Address: (h.) Salisbury Green, 18 Holyrood Park Road, Edinburgh, EH16 5AZ.

Money, Alex., CEng, MIMechE, MIProdE, ALCM, AMEME. Principal, Motherwell College, since 1969; b. 25.2.25, Motherwell; m., Isobel McArthur; 1 s.; 1 d. Educ. Dalziel High School, Motherwell; Royal Technical College, Glasgow. Mechanical/Production Engineer; Lecturer. Convener, Association of Principals (Scottish Branch); Member, Consultative Committee on the Curriculum; Chairman, Scottish Consultative Committee/Council Member, City and Guilds of London Institute; Board Member, EITB; Member, Board of Governors, Jordanhill College of Education. Recreations: music; gardening. Address: (h.) 203 Manse Road, Motherwell, ML1 2PY; T.-Motherwell 64225.

Mongredien, Alan, JP, ACMA. Member, Bearsden and Milngavie District Council, since 1980 (Convenor, Policy and Resources Committee, since 1983); Chairman, Bearsden and Milngavie District Licensing Board, since 1980; b. 10.7.44, Glasgow; m., Alexandra Elizabeth Inglis. Educ. Bearsden Academy; Central College of Commerce. Management Accountant, Kings & Co. Ltd., Quarrymasters and Road Surfacing Contractors, Glasgow, since 1972. Elder, Killermont Parish Church, Bearsden. Recreations: gardening; jogging. Address: (h.) 63 Buchanan Drive, Bearsden, Glasgow, G61 2EP; T.-041-942 8998.

Monro, Sir Hector, AE, DL, JP, MP. MP (Conservative), Dumfries, since 1964; Farmer; Company Director; b. 4.10.22, Edinburgh; m., Lady (Anne) Monro; 2 s. Educ. Canford School; Cambridge University; Dundee School of Economics. RAF, 1941-46; Royal Auxiliary Air Force, 1946-53 (Honorary Air Commodore, since 1981); Member, Dumfries County Council, 1952-67 (Chairman, Planning Committee and Joint Police Committee); Scottish Conservative Whip, 1967-70; Lord Commissioner, HM Treasury, 1970-71; Minister of Health and Education, Scottish Office, 1971-74; Opposition Spokesman on Scottish Affairs, 1974-75, Sport, 1974-79; Minister of Sport, 1979-81; Member, Nature Conservancy Council, since 1982; Member, Area Executive, NFU, since 1964; Member, Council, National Trust for Scotland, since 1983; Vice-President, Scottish Rugby Union, 1975, President, 1976-77; Member, Queen's Bodyguard for Scotland (Royal Company of Archers). Recreations: rugby; golf; flying; vintage cars; country sports. Address: (h.) Williamwood, Kirtlebridge, Lockerbie, Dumfriesshire; T.-04615 213.

Monteith, Lt.-Col. Robert Charles Michael, OBE (1981), MC (1943), TD (1945), JP. Vice Lord-Lieutenant of Lanarkshire, since 1964; b. 25.5.14; m., Mira Elizabeth Fanshawe; 1 s. Educ. Ampleforth. CA, 1939; Lanarkshire Yeomanry, 1939-45; Member, East Kilbride Development Corporation, 1972-76; DL, 1955; Past Chairman, Clydesdale (formerly Lanark) District Council; Member, Queen's Bodyguard for Scotland (Royal Company of Archers).

Montgomery, Sir (Basil Henry) David, 9th Bt, JP, DL. Chairman, Forestry Commission, since 1979; b. 20.3.31; m., Delia Reid; 1 s.; 4 d.; 1 s. (deceased). Educ. Eton. Black Watch, 1949-51; Member, Nature Conservancy Council, 1973-79; Vice-Lieutenant, Kinross-shire, 1966-74; Deputy Lieutenant, Perth and Kinross, since 1975; Hon. LLD, Dundee, 1977. Address: (h.) Kinross House, Kinross.

Montgomery, Daniel David William, BSc. Director, Electrical Contractors' Association of Scotland, since 1975; Director and Secretary, Scottish Joint Industry Board, since 1975; Director, Scottish Electrical Contractors' Insurance Ltd., since 1975; b. 24.9.37, Banton, Stirlingshire; m., Joan Elizabeth Allan; 2 s. Educ. Kilsyth Academy; Glasgow University; Royal College of Science and Technology; Heriot-Watt University. Student apprentice, Fairfield Shipbuilding and Engineering Co. Ltd. and Rolls-Royce Ltd.; graduate training, then Organisation and Methods Officer, Joseph Lucas Ltd., Birmingham, and Uniroyal, Edinburgh; joined Electrical Contractors Association of Scotland, 1965, as

Assistant to the Chief Executive. Territorial Army Commission, Royal Engineers, 1963-67. Recreations: golf; hill-walking; reading. Address: (b.) 23 Heriot Row, Edinburgh, EH3 6EW; T.-031-225 7221.

Montgomery, Lorna Elizabeth, JP. Member, Central Regional Council, since 1975; Member, Falkirk District Council, since 1975; b. 5.9.24, Falkirk; m., William Montgomery; 1 s. Educ. Falkirk High School; Falkirk Technical School; Whitehead's Commercial College, Falkirk. Member, Stirling County Council, 1967-75 (Vice-Chairman, Children's Committee, 1967); Chairman, General Purposes Committee, Falkirk District Council, 1977-80; Vice-Chairman, Land and Buildings Commitee, Central Regional Council, 1978-82. Chairman, Falkirk CAB, 1983-84. Recreations: dancing; knitting; reading. Address: (h.) 25 Ramsay Avenue, Laurieston, Falkirk, Stirlingshire; T.-Falkirk 25303.

Moody, John Henry, BA (Hons). Member, Inverclyde District Council, since 1984; Vice Chairman, Inverclyde Liberal Association; Teacher of Art, Greenock High School; b. 23.3.53, Brighton; m., Mary Fraser Buchanan. Educ. Redby Secondary Modern School, Sunderland; Sunderland Polytechnic. Porter/caretaker, Borders Health Board, 1976-77; Civil Servant, 1977-80. Recreations: painting; drawing; photography. Address: (h.) 27 Glenside Road, Port Glasgow, Renfrewshire; T.-0475 706981.

Moon, Brenda Elizabeth, MA, FLA. Librarian, Edinburgh University, since 1980; b. 11.4.31, Stoke on Trent. Educ. Oxford University. Assistant Librarian, Sheffield University, 1955-62; Sub-Librarian, then Deputy Librarian, Hull University, 1962-79. Recreations: walking; gardening; canal cruising. Address: (b.) Edinburgh University Library, George Square, Edinburgh; T.-031-667 1011.

Moore, Andrew F., BL. Chief Officer, SCOTBEC, since 1980; b. 5.12.39, Leven; m., Anne MacGregor; 2 s.; 1 d. Educ. Buckhaven High School; Edinburgh University. Examiner, Estate Duty Office, Edinburgh, 1958-63; Assistant, then Depute Secretary, Scottish Council for Commercial Education, 1963-73; Depute Chief Officer, Scottish Business Education Council, 1973-80. Governor, Scottish Council for Educational Technology, 1976-84; Director, Filmhouse, Edinburgh, 1980-85; Honorary Treasurer, British Association for Commercial and Industrial Education, 1979-81; Chairman, Pedagogical Committee of International Society for Business Education, 1980-83; Vice-Chairman, Levenmouth Enterprise Trust; Member, National Examination Board for Supervisory Studies; Member, Scottish Committee for Open Learning; Member, Jordanhill School of Further Education Committee; Session Clerk, Scoonie Kirk, Leven; President, Leven YMCA. Recreations: golf; youth work. Address: (h.) Annandale, Linksfield Street, Leven, Fife; T.-Leven 26984.

Moore, Kenneth William, BSc, PhD. Head, Local Government Division, Scottish Development Department, since 1984; b. 31.5.41, Glasgow; m.,

Sheila Blackwood; 2 d. Educ. Allan Glen's School, Glasgow; Glasgow University. Joined Civil Service, 1967; variously responsible for Land Tenure Reform, Health Services, Scottish Development Agency; Finance Officer, Scottish Education Department, 1980-83, and Department of Agriculture and Fisheries for Scotland, 1983-84. Recreations: hill-walking; mathematics and computing; cycling; language and languages; bird-watching; music. Address: (h.) 22 Morningside Park, Edinburgh; T.-031-447 2051.

Moore, Michael Ritchie, BSc, PhD. Senior Lecturer in Medicine, Glasgow University, since 1982; b. 24.1.44, Glasgow; m., Alice Briscoe; 1 s.; 2 d. Educ. Falkirk High School; Glasgow University. Glasgow University: Research Assistant, Department of Medicine, 1967, Department of Materia Medica, 1970, Research Fellow, 1973, Lecturer in Materia Medica, 1975, in Medicine, 1978; Chief Professional Officer, Groote Shuur Hospital, Cape Town, 1982; Senior Research Fellow, MRC/UCT Porphyrias Unit, Cape Town University, 1983. Chairman, Kilsyth Community Council, 1985; Secretary and Director, Clock Theatre, Kilsyth, 1984; Committee Member, Tetrapyrrole Discussion Group, 1975. Publication: Disorders of Porphyrin Metabolism, 1985. Recreations: rock climbing and hill-walking; photography; amateur dramatics; gardening. Address: (b.) Porphyrias Unit, University Department of Medicine, Western Infirmary, Glasgow, G11 6NT; T.-041-339 8822.

Moore, Professor Robert Samuel, BA, PhD. Professor of Sociology, Aberdeen University, since 1976 (Head, Department of Sociology, since 1975); b. 3.6.36, Beckenham, Kent; m., Lindy Ruth Parker; 1 s.; 1 d. Educ. Beckenham and Penge County Grammar School for Boys; Hull University. Royal Navy, 1952-61; Research Associate, Birmingham University, 1964-65; Lecturer, Durham University, 1965-70; Senior Lecturer, then Reader, Aberdeen University, 1971-76. Council Member: Institute of Race Relations, 1972-80, British Association for the Advancement of Science, 1969-76 and 1979-84 (President, Sociology Section, 1984-85); Executive Member, British Sociological Association (former Treasurer, Chairman, 1981-82); Chair, Editorial Board, Sociology, since 1984; Member, CNAA Social Research Sub-Committee, since 1983, and CNAA Sociological Studies Board, since 1984. Publications: Race, Community and Conflict (Co-author), 1967; Pitmen Preachers and Politics, 1974; Slamming The Door: The Administration of Immigration Control (Co-author), 1975; Racism and Black Resistance, 1975; The Social Impact of Oil, 1982. Recreations: gardening; photography. Address: (b.) Department of Sociology, Aberdeen University, Aberdeen, AB9 2TY; T.-0224 40241.

Moorhouse, Professor Robert Gordon, MA, PhD, FRSE. Titular Professor, Department of Natural Philosophy, Glasgow University, since 1968; b. 14.3.26, Huddersfield; m., Peggy Gee; 1 s. Educ. Huddersfield College; Cambridge University. Research Fellow and Lecturer, Natural Philosophy, Glasgow University, 1950-61; Principal Scientific Officer, Rutherford-Appleton Laboratory (Science and Engineering Research

Council), 1961-67; Reader, Glasgow University, 1967-68. Publication: The Pion-Nucleon System (Co-author). Address: (b.) Department of Natural Philosophy, Glasgow University, Glasgow, G12 8QQ; T.-041-339 8855.

Moran, James Edward. Director of Tourism, Leisure and Recreation, Argyll and Bute District Council, since 1974; b. 19.7.42, Bearsden; m., Catherine; 2 d. Educ. St. Aloysius College, Glasgow; Scotus Academy, Edinburgh. Scottish Tourist Board, 1960-67; Highlands and Islands Development Board, 1967-71; Dumfries and Galloway Tourist Association, 1971-74. Recreations: angling; travel; DIY. Address: (b.) Kilmory, Lochgilphead; T.-0546 2127.

More, Ian Aitken Ross, BSc, MB, ChB, PhD, MD, MRCPath. Senior Lecturer, Department of Pathology, Glasgow University, since 1978; Consultant, Greater Glasgow Health Board, since 1978; b. 8.8.41, Motherwell; m., Eleanor Russell Gibson. Educ. Hamilton Academy; Glasgow University. BEIT Medical Research Fellow, 1968-71; Lecturer, Glasgow University, 1972-78. Recreations: photography; gardening; electronics. Address: (b.) Pathology Department, Western Infirmary, Glasgow; T.-041-339 8822, Ext. 522.

More, Magnus, MA, BSc, DipEd. Director of Education, Fife Regional Council, since 1985; b. 2.2.34, Wick; m., Audrey; 3 s. Educ. Wick High School; St. Andrews University/Dundee College of Education. Teacher, Oban High School, 1959-62; Principal Teacher, Queen Anne High School, Dunfermline, 1962-67; Assistant Director of Education, Aberdeen County Council, 1967-69; Fife County Council: Assistant Director of Education, 1969-71, Senior Assistant Director of Education, 1971-75, Senior Depute Director of Education, 1975-84. First Chairman, Committee on Special Educational Needs, Consultative Committee on the Curriculum; Member, Convocation, Heriot-Watt University. Recreations: swimming; golf; gardening. Address: (b.) Fife House, North Street, Glenrothes, Fife, KY7 5LT.

Morgan, Edwin (George), OBE, MA, Hon. DLitt (Loughborough). Freelance Writer (Poet, Critic, Translator), since 1980; Emeritus Professor of English, Glasgow University, since 1980; b. 27.4.20, Glasgow. Educ. Rutherglen Academy; High School of Glasgow; Glasgow University. War Service, Royal Army Medical Corps, 1940-46; Glasgow University: Assistant Lecturer in English, 1947, Lecturer, 1950, Senior Lecturer, 1965, Reader, 1971, Titular Professor, 1975; received Cholmondeley Award for Poets, 1968; Hungarian PEN Memorial Medal, 1972; Scottish Arts Council Book Awards, 1968, 1973, 1977, 1978, 1983; Saltire Society and Royal Bank Scottish Literary Award, 1983. Publications: (poetry): The Vision of Cathkin Braes, 1952, Beowulf, 1952, The Cape of Good Hope, 1955, Poems from Eugenio Montale, 1959, Sovpoems, 1961, Collins Albatross Book of Longer Poems (Editor), 1963, Starryveldt, 1965, Emergent Poems, 1967, Gnomes, 1968, The Second Life, 1968, Proverbfolder, 1969, Twelve Songs, 1970, The Horseman's Word, 1970, Scottish Poetry 1-6 (Co-Editor), 1966-72; Glasgow Sonnets, 1972,

Wi the Haill Voice, 1972, The Whittrick, 1973, From Glasgow to Saturn, 1973, Fifty Renascence Love-Poems, 1975, Rites of Passage, 1976, The New Divan, 1977, Colour Poems, 1978, Platen: Selected Poems, 1978, Star Gate, 1979, Scottish Satirical Verse (Editor), 1980, Poems of Thirty Years, 1982, Grafts/Takes, 1983, Sonnets from Scotland, 1984, Selected Poems, 1985; prose: Essays, 1974, East European Poets, 1976, Hugh MacDiarmid, 1976; plays: The Apple-Tree, 1982, Master Peter Pathelin, 1983. Address: (h.) 19 Whittingehame Court, Glasgow, G12 OBG; T.-041-339 6260.

Morgan, Professor Henry Gemmell, BSc, MB, ChB, FRCPEdin, FRCPGlas, FRCPath, FRSE. Professor of Pathological Biochemistry, Glasgow University, since 1965; Director, Institute of Biochemistry, Glasgow Royal Infirmary, since 1967; President, Association of Clinical Biochemists, UK, since 1985; b. 25.12.22, Dundee; m., Margaret Duncan; 1 d. Educ. Merchiston Castle School, Edinburgh; St. Andrews University. Local Defence Volunteers/Home Guard, 1940-44; Lecturer/Senior Lecture in Pathology, St. Andrews University, 1948-65; Research Fellow, Johns Hopkins Medical School, Baltimore, 1956; Adviser to SHDD, WRHB, GGHB, London University etc.; Chairman, Medical Staff Committee, Glasgow Royal Infirmary, since 1984; former External Examiner, Universities of Dublin, Leeds and Newcastle; Secretary, Forfarshire Medical Association, 1960-65. Recreation: travel abroad. Address: (b.) Institute of Biochemistry, Royal Infirmary, Glasgow, G4 OSF.

Morgan, Robin Milne, MA, BA. Principal, Daniel Stewart's and Melville College, since 1976; and The Mary Erskine School, since 1978; b. 2.10.30, Stonehaven; m., Fiona Bruce McLeod Douglas; 3 s.; 1 d. Educ. Mackie Academy, Stonehaven; Aberdeen University; London University. 2nd Lt., Gordon Highlanders, 1952-54; Assistant Master: Arden House Preparatory School, 1955-60, George Watson's College, 1960-70; Headmaster, Campbell College, Belfast, 1970-76. Schoolmaster Fellow Commoner, Pembroke College, Cambridge, 1985; Member, Executive Committee, Combined Cadet Forces Association. Recreations: shooting; hill-walking; listening to music; visiting France; reading history. Address: 9 Inverleith Row, Edinburgh.

Morison, Hon. Lord (Alastair Malcolm Morison), QC, MA, LLB. Senator of the College of Justice, since 1985; b. 12.2.31, Edinburgh; m., Birgitte Hendil; 1 s., 1 d. by pr. m. Educ. Winchester College; Edinburgh University. Advocate, 1956; Chairman: Horserace Betting Levy Appeal Tribunal (Scotland), Medical Appeal Tribunal, Performing Right Tribunal. Recreation: fishing. Address: (h.) 6 Carlton Terrace, Edinburgh, EH7 5DD; T.-031-556 6766.

Morison, Hugh, MA, DipEd. Under Secretary, Scottish Home and Health Department, since 1984; b. 22.11.43, Bognor Regis; m., Marion H. Smithers; 2 d. Educ. Chichester High School for Boys; St. Catherine's College, Oxford. Assistant Principal, Scottish Home and Health Department, 1966-69; Private Secretary to Minister of State, Scottish Office, 1969-70;

Principal: Scottish Education Department, 1971-73, Scottish Economic Planning Department, 1973-79 (seconded to Offshore Supplies Office, Department of Energy, 1974-75); Assistant Secretary, Scottish Economic Planning Department, 1979-82; Gwilym Gibbon Research Fellow, Nuffield College, Oxford, 1982-83; Assistant Secretary, Scottish Development Department, 1983-84. Member of Vestry, St. John's Episcopal Church, Edinburgh. Recreations: sailing; cycling; hill-walking; archaeology. Address: (h.) 26 Hartington Place, Edinburgh, EH10 4LE; T.-031-229 5206.

Morley, Kenneth Donald, BMedBiol (Hons), MB, FRCPEdin, FRACP. Consultant General Physician and Rheumatologist, since 1982; b. 16.4.49, Ripon; m., Susan Margaret Bell Tawse; 2 s.; 1 d. Educ. Dame Allan's Boys School, Newcastle; Aberdeen University. Formerly General Medical Registrar, Christchurch Hospitals, New Zealand; Arthritis and Rheumatism Council Copeman Research Fellow and Honorary Senior Registrar, Hammersmith Hospital, London. Recreations: family; DIY; gardening; hill-walking. Address: (h.) 9 Burnside Road, Invergowrie, Dundee; T.-Invergowrie 673.

Morley, William Neil, RD*, MB, ChB, FRCPEdin, FRCPGlas. Consultant Dermatologist; Civil Consultant to Royal Navy, since 1976; Consultant, Western Infirmary and Royal Hospital for Sick Children, Glasgow, since 1963; Member, Medical Appeal Tribunal, DHSS, since 1977; b. 16.2.30, Bradford; m., Dr. Patricia Morley; 3 s.; 1 d. Educ. Merchiston Castle School; Edinburgh University. House Surgeon and Physician, Edinburgh Royal Infirmary; Surgeon Lt., RNVR, HMS Falcon, Malta; Assistant, Department of Medicine, Edinburgh University; Registrar and Senior Registrar, Dermatology Department, Edinburgh Royal Infirmary. Past President and Secretary, Royal Medical Society; President, Scottish Dermatological Society, 1985. Publication: Colour Atlas of Paediatric Dermatology. Recreations: golf; gardening. Address: (h.) Parkhall, Balfron, Glasgow, G63; T.-Balfron 40124.

Morrice, Rev. Alastair (Alexander McKenzie), MA, BD (Hons). Minister, Holy Trinity Church, Edinburgh, since 1977; b. 15.8.43, Forfar; m., Mary Katherine Elizabeth Gossip; 3 s.; 1 d. Educ. Blairgowrie High School; Edinburgh University. Assistant Minister, South Dalziel, Motherwell, 1967-68; Minister, St. John's, Galashiels, 1968-77. Member, Ministry and Mission Committee, Church of Scotland; Member, Scottish Council BMMF International. Recreations: gardening; golf. Address: 496 Lanark Road, Edinburgh, EH14 5DH; T.-031-453 4089.

Morrice, J. Kenneth W., MD, FRCPsych, DPM. Honorary Consultant Psychiatrist, Grampian Health Board, and Honorary Fellow, Aberdeen University; in private practice; b. 14.7.24, Aberdeen; m., Norah Thompson; 1 s.; 2 d. Educ. Robert Gordon's College, Aberdeen; Aberdeen University. Served RNVR as Surgeon Lt.; trained in psychiatry, Crichton Royal, Dumfries, and Aberdeen Royal Infirmary; appointed Consultant, Dingleton Hospital, 1956; Honorary

Lecturer in Forensic Psychiatry, Edinburgh University; Visiting Psychiatrist, Edinburgh Prison; Consultant, Fort Logan Mental Health Centre, Denver, 1966-67; Consultant Psychiatrist and Senior Clinical Lecturer, Ross Clinic and Department of Mental Health, Aberdeen. Publications: Crisis Intervention; volumes of poetry. Recreations: golf; TV; reading and writing; walking. Address: (b.) 24 Albyn Place, Aberdeen, AB9 1RJ; T.-Aberdeen 572879.

Morris, Alexander Campbell, CEng, DipTP, MICE, MRTPI, MIMunBM. Director of Technical Services, Cumnock and Doon Valley District Council, since 1974; Chairman, Scottish Branch, RTPI, 1985; b. Greenock. Educ. Greenock High School; Strathclyde University. District Engineer, Ministry of Works, Northern Nigeria, 1958-62; Chief Engineer, Surveyor's Office, Ayr Burgh, 1962-69; Chief Planning Assistant, Ayr County Council, 1969-74. Address: (b.) Council Offices, Lugar, Cumnock, KA18 3JQ.

Morris, Alexander Watt, BSc (Hons), MInstP. Principal, Edinburgh Tutorial College and American School of Edinburgh, since 1976; b. 24.11.46, Dunfermline; m., Moira Joan Watson; 1 s. Educ. Dunfermline High School; Edinburgh University. Began teaching career, Musselburgh Grammar School, 1972; Head of Physics, George Watson's Ladies College, 1973 (and to George Watson's College on merger of the schools); founded Edinburgh Tutorial College and American School of Edinburgh. Recreations: good food; hifi; cricket; skiing. Address: (b.) 29 Chester Street, Edinburgh, EH3 7EN; T.-031-225 9888.

Morris, Arthur McGregor, MA, MB, BChir (Cantab), FRCS, FRCSEdin. Consultant Plastic Surgeon, Tayside Health Board, since 1975; Honorary Senior Lecturer in Surgery, Dundee University, since 1975; b. 6.5.41, Heswall, Wirral; m., Victoria Margaret Whitaker; 1 s.; 1 d. Educ. Dulwich College; Selwyn College, Cambridge; Guy's Hospital. House Officer, Guy's Hospital, 1965-66; Anatomy Demonstrator, Newcastle University, 1966-67; Senior House Officer in Surgery, Bristol, 1967-69; Research Registrar, then Casualty Registrar, Guy's Hospital, 1969-71; Plastic Surgery Registrar, Canniesburn Hospital, Glasgow, 1972; Plastic Surgery Senior Registrar, Bangour General Hospital, 1972 75. Recreations: golf; curling; photography; bee-keeping. Address: (b.) Tayside Plastic Surgery Unit, Dundee Royal Infirmary, Dundee; T.-Dundee 23125.

Morris, Arthur Stephen, BA, MA, PhD. Senior Lecturer, Department of Geography, Glasgow University; b. 26.12.36, Broadway, Worcestershire; m., Estela C.; 1 s.; 1 d. Educ. Chipping Campden; Oxford University; Maryland University; Wisconsin University. Instructor/Assistant Professor, Western Michigan University, 1964-67; joined Glasgow University as Lecturer, 1967. Publications: South America, 1979; Latin America, 1981. Recreations: gardening; sailing. Address: (h.) The Old Manse, Shandon, near Helensburgh; T.-041-339 8855.

Morris, Edwin Norbert, BSc, MSc, FIWSc, MIOA. Reader in Building Science, Strathclyde University, since 1972; b. 14.6.23, Glasgow; m.,

Margaret Isabel Watson. Educ. Glasgow Academy; Royal College of Science and Technology; Strathclyde University. Lecturer, Royal College of Science and Technology, 1954; Senior Lecturer, Strathclyde University, 1967. Publication: Buildings, Climate and Energy (Co-author). Recreations: music; social and postal history. Address: (h.) 76 Switchback Road, Bearsden, Glasgow, G61 1AF; T.-041-942 1229.

Morris, Henry, BSc. HM Inspector of Schools (Primary Education), since 1971 (Director, Primary Education Development Project, since 1984); b. 4.8.25, Motherwell; m., Sarah R. Spence; 2 s.; 1 d. Educ. Dalziel High School, Motherwell; Glasgow University. Assistant Teacher: Skelmorlie Primary School, Newmains Primary School, Knowetop Primary School, Motherwell; Assistant Head Teacher, Berryhill Primary School, Wishaw; Head Teacher: Calderbank Primary School, Airdrie, Glenmanor Primary School, Moodiesburn; Senior Lecturer in Education, Callendar Park College, Falkirk. Recreations: photography; music; caravanning; Scottish studies. Address: (h.) 10 Blackcroft Avenue, Gartness, Airdrie; T.-Airdrie 62987.

Morris, Jean Daveena Ogilvy, MBE, MA, MEd. Consultant Clinical Psychologist, Quarrier's Homes, since 1971; Chairman, Parole Board for Scotland, since 1980; b. 28.1.29, Kilmarnock; m., Rev. William J. Morris (qv); 1 s. Educ. Kilmarnock Academy; St. Andrews University. Clinical Psychologist: Royal Hospital for Sick Children, Edinburgh, St. David's Hospital, Cardiff, and Church Village, Pontypridd; Member, Bailie and Convener of Housing, Peterhead Town Council; Member, Aberdeen County Council; Columnist, Aberdeen Press and Journal; Chairman, Christian Action Housing Association; Member, Scottish Federation of Housing Associations; Chairman, Government Committee on Links Between Housing and Social Work (Morris Committee); Chairman, Local Review Committee, Barlinnie Prison; Member, Parole Board, since 1973; Vice-President, Abbeyfield Society Scotland. Badminton Blue, St. Andrews University. Recreations: swimming; holidays in France. Address: (h.) 94 St. Andrews Drive, Glasgow, G41 4RX; T.-041-427 2757.

Morris, John Howell, BSc, PhD, DSc, CChem, FRSC. Senior Lecturer in Inorganic Chemistry, Strathclyde University, since 1975; b. 21.3.38, Cardiff; m., Bethia Reynolds; 3 d. Educ. Cardiff High School; Nottingham University. Research Fellow, Harvard University, 1961-62; Senior Research Associate, Newcastle-upon-Tyne University, 1962-65; Lecturer, then Senior Lecturer, Kingston-upon-Thames College of Technology, 1965-68; Lecturer in Inorganic Chemistry, Strathclyde University, 1968-75; Visiting Associate Professor, Wisconsin University, 1975. Recreation: sailing. Address: (b.) Department of Pure and Applied Chemistry, 195 Cathedral Street, Glasgow, G1 1XL; T.-041-552 4400.

Morris, Robert John, BA, DPhil. Senior Lecturer in Economic History, Edinburgh University, since 1969; b. 12.10.43, Sheffield; m., Barbara Anne; 1 s.; 1 d. Educ. Acklam Hall Grammar School, Middlesbrough; Keble College and Nuffield College, Oxford. Publications: Cholera 1832; Class and Class Consciousness during the Industrial Revolution. Address: (b.) Department of Economic History, Edinburgh University, Old College, South Bridge, Edinburgh, EH8 9YL.

Morris, Thomas Currie, JP, MIM, FEIS. Member, Cunninghame District Council, since 1980; Senior Lecturer in Metallurgy; b. 8.8.20, Glasgow; m., Louise; 1 s. Educ. Allan Glen's School, Glasgow; Royal Technical College. Vice-Chairman, Finance and General Purposes Committee, Cunninghame District Council, 1980-84; Chairman, Course Committee in Metallurgy, SANCAD/SCOTEC, since 1972; Chairman, Foundry Sub-Committee, SCOTEC, since 1976; Chairman, Glasgow Local Association, EIS, 1972-73; Chairman, Strathclyde Regional Committee, EIS, 1974-75. Recreations: golf; swimming. Address: (h.) 24 Braehead, Dalry, Ayrshire; T.-Dalry 2049.

Morris, William, BA, FIOP. Principal, Anniesland College, since 1981; b. 15.5.24, Aberdare, Wales; m., Pauline; 1 s.; 2 d. Educ. Aberdare Boys' Secondary School; Cardiff School of Art; Garnet College, London; London School of Printing and Graphic Arts; Open University. Compositor/Typographer; Lecturer in Typography; Head, Department of Typography and Related Subjects; Depute Principal, Glasgow College of Building and Printing; Board Member, Printing and Publishing Industry Training Board; Member, City and Guilds of London Institute; Committee Member, SCOTEC, SCOTBEC, CGLI. Secretary of the Vestry, St. Cyprian's Church, Lenzie; Chairman, Vocational Service Committee, Kelvin Rotary Club. Recreations: golf; gardening. Address: (h.) 26 Laurel Avenue, Lenzie, Kirkintilloch, Glasgow, G66 4RU; T.-041-776 2716.

Morris, Rev. William James, JP, BA, BD, PhD, LLD, DD, Hon. FRCP&SGlas. Minister, Glasgow Cathedral, since 1967; Chaplain in Ordinary to The Queen in Scotland, since 1969; Chairman, Iona Cathedral Trust, since 1979; b. 22.8.25, Cardiff; m., Jean Daveena Ogilvy Howie (see Jean Daveena Ogilvy Morris); 1 s. Educ. Cardiff High School; University of Wales (Cardiff and Aberystwyth); Edinburgh University. Ordained, 1951; Assistant, Canongate Kirk, Edinburgh, 1949-51; Minister, Barry Island and Cadoxton Presbyterian Church of Wales, 1951-53; Minister: St. David's, Buckhaven, 1953-57, Peterhead Old Parish Church, 1957-67; Chaplain, Peterhead Prison, 1963-67; Chaplain to Lord High Commissioner, 1975-76; Moderator, Deer Presbytery, 1965-66; now Chaplain: Strathclyde Police, Glasgow Academy, High School of Glasgow, Glasgow District Council, Trades House of Glasgow, Glasgow YMCA, West of Scotland Engineers Association, Royal Scottish Automobile Club; Member, Independent Broadcasting Authority, 1979-84 (Chairman, Scottish Advisory Committee); Member, Council of Management, Quarrier's Homes; Member, Convocation, Strathclyde University; Governor, Jordanhill College of Education; Member, Scottish Committee, British Sailors' Society; Honorary President, Glasgow Society of Social

Service. Recreations: being good, careful, and happy (not always simultaneously). Address: (h.) 94 St. Andrews Drive, Glasgow, G41 4RX; T.-041-427 2757.

Morrison, Rev. Angus Wilson, MA, BD. Minister, Braid Parish Church, Edinburgh, since 1977; b. 14.2.34, Glasgow; m., Isobel M.S. Taylor; 1 s.; 2 d. Educ. Epsom College, Surrey; Trinity College, Oxford; New College, Edinburgh. Minister: Whithorn, 1961-67, Cults West, Aberdeen, 1967-77; various periods of service on General Assembly Committees, including Overseas Council, Inter-Church Relations, Board of Education and Selection Schools; Observer for World Alliance of Reformed Churches, Vatican Council II, 1963. Recreations: travel; family. Address: 2 Cluny Avenue, Edinburgh, EH10 4RN; T.-031-447 1871.

Morrison, David, ALA. Poet; Short Story Writer; Painter; Sculptor; b. 4.8.41, Glasgow; m., Edna; 1 s.; 1 d. Educ. various schools; Strathclyde University. County Librarian (Caithness), 1972-75; Wick Branch Librarian, Highland Regional Council, since 1981; Editor, Scotia Rampant, since 1985; Promoter, Pulteney Press, since 1985; Organiser, poetry/music events in Caithness; Organiser, Wick Festival of Poetry, Folk and Jazz, seven years; Editor, Scotia Review, 10 years; always Scottish patriot. Recreations: working for Scottish literature and Scotland as a nation; painting; sculpture. Address: (h.) 3 Moray Street, Wick, Caithness; T.-Wick 3703.

Morrison, James, ARSA, RSW, DA, RGI. Painter in oil and watercolour; Senior Lecturer, Duncan of Jordanstone College of Art, Dundee; b. 11.4.32, Glasgow; m., Dorothy McCormack; 1 s.; 1 d. Educ. Hillhead High School; Glasgow School of Art. Taught part-time, 1955-58; won Torrance Memorial Prize, RGI, 1958; Visiting Artist, Hospitalfield, 1962-63; Council Member, SSA, 1964-67; joined Staff, Duncan of Jordanstone College of Art, 1965; won Arts Council Travelling Scholarship to Greece, 1968; painting in various regions of France, 1976-82; numerous one-man exhibitions since 1956, in Scotland, London, Italy, West Germany; four works in private collection of Duke of Edinburgh and numerous other works in public and private collections; several group exhibitions since 1980 in UK and Europe. Publication: Aff the Squerr. Recreation: playing in a chamber music group. Address: (h.) Craigview House, Usan, Montrose, Angus; T.-Montrose 72639.

Morrison, Rev. Mary Brown, MA (Hons), BD (Hons), DipEd, DipRelEd. Minister, Townhill Parish Church, Dunfermline, since 1978; b. 10.9.35, Edinburgh; m., Peter Keith Morrison; 1 s.; 3 d. Educ. James Gillespie's High School for Girls; Edinburgh University. Teacher, Dalkeith High School, 1958-63; housewife, 1963-75; mature student, 1975-78. Director, National Bible Society of Scotland, 1981-85; Member, Townhill Community Council, since 1983. Publication: Short History of Townhill Parish Church, 1883-1983. Recreations: family holidays; walking; theatre; gardening. Address: Townhill Manse, Dunfermline, Fife; T.-03837 23835.

Morrison, Peter, MA, LLB. Singer and Solicitor; b. 14.8.40, Greenock; m., Irene; 1 s.; 1 d. Educ. Greenock Academy; Glasgow University. Town Clerk's Department: Paisley, 1965, Clydebank, 1966-68; private legal practice thereafter; established own legal practice, 1977; began professional singing engagements at University; passed BBC audition, 1969, and began solo broadcasts; first television series, Castles in the Air, 1971; numerous radio, television and theatre appearances in UK and abroad. Recreations: golf; tennis; non-participating cricket and rugby supporter. Address: (b.) 65 Bath Street, Glasgow; T.-041-331 1029.

Morrison, Peter Angus. Member, Crofters Commission, since 1984; Director, Lewis Land Services Ltd.; b. 31.12.45, Isle of Lewis; m., Murdina; 2 d. Educ. Shawbost School; Lews Castle College. Mechanical engineering apprenticeship, then draughtsman, William Beardmore & Co., Glasgow; contracts draughtsman, John Brown Engineering, Clydebank; Lecturer in Mechanical Engineering, Springburn College of Engineering; Senior Lecturer, Engineering Department, Lews Castle College. Recreation: travel. Address: (h.) 52 Newmarket, Stornoway, Lewis; T.-0851 5338.

Morrison, Rev. Roderick, MA, BD. Minister, High Church, Stornoway, Lewis, since 1981; b. 3.7.43, Lochmaddy; m., Christina Ann MacDonald; 1 s.; 1 d. Educ. Lochportan Public School; Glasgow University and Trinity College. Assistant Minister, Drumchapel Old Parish Church, Glasgow, 1973-74; Minister, Carinish Parish Church, North Uist, 1974-81. Recreations: sailing; fishing; shooting. Address: High Church Manse, 1 Goathill Road, Stornoway, Isle of Lewis; T.-Stornoway 3106.

Morrison, William Charles Carnegie, CA. UK Managing Partner, KMG Thomson McLintock, Chartered Accountants, since 1980; Visiting Professor in Accountancy, Strathclyde University, since 1983; a Vice-President, Scottish Council (Development and Industry), since 1982; b. 10.2.38, Glasgow; m., Joceline Saint; 2 d. (by pr. m.). Educ. Kelvinside Academy, Lathallan; Merchiston Castle School. Qualifed CA, 1961; Thomson, McLintock & Co.: Partner, 1966, Joint Senior Partner, Glasgow and Edinburgh, 1974-80; Director: Scottish Amicable Life Assurance Society, since 1973, Securities Trust of Scotland plc, 1976-80, Brownlee & Co. plc, 1978-80; President, Institute of Chartered Accountants of Scotland, 1984-85; Member, Scottish Telecommunications Board, 1978-80; Member, Scottish Committee, Design Council, 1978-81; Chairman of Governors, Kelvinside Academy, 1975-80; Honorary Treasurer, Transport Trust, since 1982. Recreations: vintage transport and model railways.

Morrison, William Garth, BA, CEng, MIEE, DL. Farmer; Chief Commissioner of Scotland, The Scout Association, since 1981; b. 8.4.43, Edinburgh; m., Gillian Cheetham; 2 s.; 1 d. Educ. Pangbourne College; Pembroke College, Cambridge. Service, Royal Navy, 1961-73, retiring with rank of Lt.; farming, since 1973; appointed

Director, Scotfresh Ltd., formerly Elba Growers Ltd., 1975; Member, Lothian Region Children's Panel, 1976-83 (Chairman, Midlothian/East Lothian Area Panel, 1978-81); Lamp of Lothian Trustee, 1978; Member, Lothian, Borders and Fife Committee, Prince's Trust, 1979, Lothian and Borders Committee, Prince's and Royal Jubilee Trusts, 1983; Member, Society of High Constables of Holyroodhouse, 1979; Deputy Lieutenant, East Lothian, 1984. Recreations: golf; sailing; Scouting. Address: West Fenton, North Berwick, East Lothian; T.-0620 842154.

Morrison, Professor William Russell, BSc, PhD, DSc, FIFST, FRSE. Professor of Food Science, Strathclyde University; b. 14.1.32, Glasgow; m., Anne Ker; 2 s.; 1 d. Educ. High School of Glasgow; Royal College of Science and Technology. Address: (b.) Food Science Division, Strathclyde University, 131 Albion Street, Glasgow, G1 1SD; T.-041-552 2071, Ext. 38.

Morrocco, Alberto, RSA, RSW, RP, RGI, LLD. Painter, since 1938; b. 14.12.17, Aberdeen; 2 s.; 1 d. Educ. Sunnybank School, Aberdeen; Gray's School of Art, Aberdeen. Former Member, Grants Committee, Scottish Arts Council; Member, Royal Fine Art Commission for Scotland. Carnegie Award and Guthrie Award, Royal Scottish Academy; San Vito Romano Prize. Address: Binrock, 456 Perth Road, Dundee; T.-0382 69319.

Morsbach, Helmut, MSc, PhD. Reader in Social Psychology, Glasgow University, since 1983; b. 2.8.37, Rondebosch, South Africa; m., Gisela Dimigen; 2 d. Educ. Bonn University; Stellenbosch University; Hamburg University; Cape Town University. Lecturer in Psychology, Rhodes University, Grahamstown, South Africa, 1964-67; Assistant Professor in Psychology, International Christian University, Tokyo, 1967-69; Lecturer, then Senior Lecturer in Social Psychology, Glasgow University, since 1969. Visiting Professor, International Christian University, 1972; Volkswagen Foundation Grant for studies on Japan, 1977-80; Snell Visitor, Balliol College, Oxford, 1982. Recreation: gliding. Address: (b.) Department of Psychology, Glasgow University, Glasgow, G12 8RT; T.-041-339 8855, Ext. 698.

Morton, Rev. Alasdair J., MA, BD, DipEd, DipRE. General Secretary, Department of Education, Church of Scotland, since 1977; b. 8.6.34, Inverness; m., Gillian M. Richards; 2 s.; 2 d. Educ. Bell-Baxter School, Cupar; St. Andrews University; Hartford Theological Seminary. District Missionary/Minister, Zambia (Northern Rhodesia), 1960-65; Chaplain and Religious Education Lecturer, Malcolm Moffat Teachers' College, Serenje, Zambia, 1966-67; Principal, David Livingstone Teachers' College, Livingstone, Zambia, 1968-72; Minister, Greyfriars Parish Church, Dumfries, 1973-77. Recreations: choral singing; gardening. Address: (b.) 121 George Street, Edinburgh, EH2 4YN; T.-031-225 5722.

Morton, Hugh Gloag, MB, ChB, DPM, MRCPsych. Consultant Child and Adolescent Psychiatrist, Tayside Health Board, since 1975;

Honorary Senior Lecturer in Psychiatry, Dundee University, since 1975; b. 2.6.43, Perth; m., Isobel Patricia Blair Campbell; 2 s.; 1 d. Educ. Strathallan; St. Andrews University. Training appointments, Dundee Psychiatric Services, 1968-71; Lecturer in Psychiatry, Dundee University, 1971-73; Senior Registrar in Child and Adolescent Psychiatry, St. George's Hospital, London, and Queen Mary's Hospital for Children, Carshalton, 1973-75; Member, Child and Adolescent Mental Health Working Group, Scottish Health Service Planning Council, 1978-83. Publication: Psychiatric Problems in Childhood - A Guide for Nurses (Co-author), 1983. Recreations: classical music; fishing; railways; boating; walking. Address: (h.) 7 Viewmount Road, Wormit, Fife, DD6 8NJ; T.-Newport on Tay 541742.

Morton, James Alexander, MB, ChB, FRCPEdin. Principal Medical Officer, Scottish Home and Health Department and Medical Adviser to Scottish Prison Service; b. 5.5.21, Edinburgh; m., Leila Morag Welch; 1 s.; 2 d. Educ. Edinburgh Academy; Edinburgh University. Resident Medical Officer, Edinburgh Royal Infirmary; Medical Officer, RAFVR; General Medical Practitioner. Recreations: golf; gardening. Address: (h.) 16 Fidra Road, North Berwick, East Lothian, EH39 4NG; T.-0620 3669.

Morton, 22nd Earl of, (John Charles Sholto Douglas), DL; b. 19.3.27; m., Sheila Mary Gibbs; 2 s.; 1 d. Deputy Lieutenant, West Lothian, since 1982. Address: (h.) Dalmahoy, Kirknewton, Midlothian.

Morton, Rev. Thomas, MA, BD, LGSM. Minister, Stonelaw Parish Church, Rutherglen, since 1957; b. 14.12.19, Kilmarnock; m., Janette Nichol Wilson. Educ. Kilmarnock Academy; Glasgow University and Trinity College. Student Assistant Minister, Newlands South Church, Glasgow, 1942-43; War Service, Church of Scotland Huts and Canteens, Scapa Flow, Orkney, 1943-44; Minister: West Port Parish Church, Hawick, 1945-51, St. Nicholas' Cardonald, Glasgow, 1951-57; Moderator, Glasgow Presbytery, 1978 (Convener, Business Committee, 1980-85); Convener, Board of Social Responsibility, Church of Scotland, 1981-85. Recreations: music (solo singing); elocution; gardening; photography; swimming. Address: Stonelaw Manse, 80 Blairbeth Road, Burnside, Rutherglen, Glasgow, G73 4JA; T.-041-634 4366.

Morton, William F., MA (Hons). Rector, Coltness High School, Wishaw, since 1974; b. 28.3.32, Glasgow; m., Ena Nicol; 1 d. Educ. Bishopbriggs Higher Grade School; Albert Secondary School, Glasgow; Glasgow University. Hamilton Academy: Teacher, 1956, Special Assistant, 1961, Principal Teacher of English, 1968; Assistant Head Teacher, Hamilton Grammar School, 1973-74. Secretary, Lanarkshire County English Committee, 1971-74; Examiner for Higher Grade English, Scottish Examination Board, 1972-75; Honorary Vice-President, Hamilton Golf Club, since 1981 (Captain, 1976-78); President, Lanarkshire Golf Association, 1974. Address: (h.) 17 Beech Grove, Wishaw, Lanarkshire; T.-0698 384307.

Moss, John Barry, BA, MMet, DEM, CEng. Principal, Esk Valley College, since 1979; b. 18.11.28, Chesterfield. Educ. Staveley Netherthorpe Grammar School; Sheffield University. Quality Control Technician, 1944-52; Assistant Chief Chemist, 1952-54; Lecturer in Further, then Higher Education, 1954-75; College Vice Principal, 1975-79. Mappin Medallist, Sheffield University. Address: (b.) Esk Valley College, Dalkeith, Midlothian, EH22 3AE; T.-031-663 1951.

Moule, Brian, MB, BCh, DMRD, FRCR. Consultant Radiologist, Glasgow Royal Infirmary, since 1966; Honorary Clinical Lecturer, Glasgow University, since 1966; b. 19.9.34, Briton Ferry, Wales; m., Isabel Claire Moule; 1 s.; 1 d. Educ. Neath Grammar School; Welsh National School of Medicine, Cardiff. House Officer in Medicine, then Surgery, Cardiff, 1957-58; Captain, RAMC, 1959-60; Registrar, Senior Registrar in Radiology, 1961-66. Recreations: golf; cricket; walking; reading; music. Address: (h.) Larachmhor, Drymen, Glasgow; T.-036 060 313.

Moule, Rev. Gerald Christopher, BA, BD. Minister, Moffat linked with Wamphray, since 1975; b. 31.8.45, Guildford; m., Patricia Rosemary Parker; 1 s.; 2 d. Educ. Edinburgh Academy; Kelvinside Academy, Glasgow; St. Andrews University; Newcastle upon Tyne University; New College, Edinburgh. Chartered Accountancy articles with Chalmers, Impey & Co., London; Assistant Minister, West Church of St. Nicholas, Aberdeen, 1973-75. Secretary and Treasurer, Scottish Journal of Theology. Recreations: cricket; swimming; travel; hill-walking; gardening. Address: St. Andrew's Manse, Moffat, Dumfriesshire, DG10 9EJ; T.-Moffat 20128.

Mountain, Peter, FRAM, LRAM. Violinist and Conductor; Head, Strings Department, Royal Scottish Academy of Music and Drama, since 1975; Chief String Coach, National Youth Orchestra of Scotland, since 1979; b. 3.10.23, Shipley; m., Angela Dale; 1 s.; 2 d. Educ. Bingley Grammar School; Royal Academy of Music, London. Wartime Service, Royal Marines; Member, Boyd Neel String Orchestra, 1948-51; Member, Philharmonia Orchestra, 1951-55; Leader, Royal Liverpool Philharmonic Orchestra, 1955-66; Section Leader, London Philharmonic Orchestra, 1966-68; Concert Master, Academy of the BBC, 1968-75; Soloist with most British orchestras; Leader of own string quartet; wide experience as Adjudicator and Orchestral Coach. Recreations: photography; the countryside; walking. Address: (h.) 2 Kew Terrace, Glasgow, G12 OTD; T.-041-339 2204.

Mowat, Alastair, MA (Hons), MBIM, FIWM, MBII. Chairman, Scottish Brewers Ltd., since 1983; Chairman, Scottish & Newcastle (Sales) Ltd., since 1984; Marketing Director, Scottish & Newcastle Breweries Plc, since 1982; b. 12.3.39; m., Alison; 1 s.; 1 d. Educ. Edinburgh Academy; Edinburgh University. Unilever, 1961-64; joined S & N B, 1964 (various functions, including production, selling, personnel and retailing).

Recreations: music (jazz and classical); rugby. Address: (b.) Scottish & Newcastle Breweries Plc, 111 Holyrood Road, Abbey Brewery, Edinburgh; T.-031-556 2591.

Mowat, Bill, MA (Hons), FInstPet. Member, Highland Regional Council, since 1978; Trustee, Wick Harbour, since 1978; b. 13.5.43, Thurso. Educ. Wick High School; Edinburgh University. Vice-President, Scottish Union of Students, 1965-66; Editor, Caithness Courier, 1966-68; Reporter, Daily Record, since 1968; Director, John O'Groats Crafts Ltd., since 1974; Honorary Secretary, Highland Branch, NUJ, 1975-78; Vice-President, Inverness Trades Council, 1977-78. Address: (h.) Balquholly, John O'Groats, Caithness; T.-0955 81360.

Mowat, David McIvor, JP, MA. Chief Executive, Edinburgh Chamber of Commerce, since 1968; b. 12.3.39, Bournemouth; m., Anne Birtwistle; 3 d. Educ. Edinburgh Academy; Edinburgh University. Vice-Chairman, Edinburgh Tourist Group, 1982; Director, Edinburgh Financial and General Holdings Ltd., 1980; Chief Executive, Chamber Developments Ltd. Recreations: swimming; walking. Address: (b.) 3 Randolph Crescent, Edinburgh; T.-031-225 5851.

Mowat, Rev. Gilbert Mollison, MA. Minister, Albany, then Albany-Butterburn Church, Dundee, since 1958; b. 28.4.21, Aberdeen; m., Janet Angus Russell; 1 s.; 1 d. Educ. Harris Academy, Dundee; St. Andrews University; Glasgow University and Trinity College. Assistant Minister, Linthouse Church, Glasgow, 1946-48; Minister, Calderbank Parish Church, Airdrie, 1948-58. Moderator, Dundee Presbytery, 1976-77; Director, Tayside and Western Isles Association for the Deaf, since 1974; Member, Dundee Council of Churches, 1973-77. Recreations: tennis; gardening; football follower (Aberdeen); music; car driving. Address: 7 Dunmore Gardens, Ninewells, Dundee, DD2 1PP; T.-Dundee 66013.

Mowat, James, RD, MB, ChB, DObstRCOG, FRCSGlas, FRCSEdin, FRCOG. Consultant Obstetrician and Gynaecologist, since 1971; b. 3.4.37, Wick; m., Colleen Ann McKeown; 1 s.; 1 d. Educ. Keiss Public School; Wick High School; Edinburgh University. Surgeon Commander, Royal Naval Reserve. Recreation: sailing. Address: (b.) 19 Coylton Road, Glasgow, G43 2TA; T.-041-637 4564.

Mowat, Sheriff John Stuart, MA, LLB. Sheriff of Glasgow and Strathkelvin, since 1974; b. 30.1.23, Manchester; m., Anne Cameron Renfrew; 2 s.; 2 d. Educ. High School of Glasgow; Merchiston Castle School; Glasgow University. Served RAF Transport Command, 1942-46 (Flt.-Lt.); Journalist, 1947-52; Advocate, 1952-60; Sheriff of Fife and Kinross, at Dunfermline, 1960-72; at Cupar and Kinross, 1972-74. Office-Bearer, Scottish Liberal Party, 1954-58; Parliamentary candidate, Caithness and Sutherland, 1955; Secretary, Sheriffs Association, 1968-75 (Vice-President, 1984); Trustee: Carnegie Dunfermline

Trust, 1967-74, Carnegie United Kingdom Trust, 1970-74. Recreations: golf; curling; watching football. Address: (h.) 31 Westbourne Gardens, Glasgow, G12 9PF; T.-041-334 3743.

Mowat, Norman Ashley George, MB, ChB, FRCP. Consultant Physician and Gastroenterologist, Aberdeen Teaching Hospitals, since 1975; Clinical Senior Lecturer in Medicine, Aberdeen University, since 1975; b. 11.4.43, Cullen; m., Kathleen Mary Cowie; 1 s.; 2 d. Educ. Fordyce Academy; Aberdeen University. House Officer, then Senior House Officer, then Registrar, Aberdeen Teaching Hospitals, 1966-72; Lecturer in Medicine, Aberdeen University, 1972-73; Lectrer in Gastroenterology and Research Associate, Medical College of St. Bartholomew's, London, 1973-75. Visiting Physician to Shetland Islands; publications include Integrated Clinical Sciences: Gastroenterology (Co-Editor), 1985. Recreations: sailing; golf; soccer; reading; photography. Address: (h.) Bucholie, 13 Kings Cross Road, Aberdeen, AB2 4BF; T.-0224 319223.

Muckart, Rev. Graeme Watson McKinnon, MTheol, FSA Scot. Minister, Erskine Church, Falkirk, since 1983; b. 11.12.43, Dunfermline; m., Mary Elspeth Small; 1 s.; 1 d. Educ. Royal Naval School, Malta; Willesden County Grammar School; Portsmouth Southern Grammar School; Highbury Technical College, Portsmouth; Leeds College of Art; St. Andrews University. Barclays Bank Trustee Department, 1962-64; Trainee Architect, Hampshire County Council, 1964-69; architectural appointments, 1969-76; Member, Resident Staff, Iona Abbey, 1976-78; Assistant Minister, Carrick Knowe Parish Church, Edinburgh, 1982-83. Recreations: painting; photography; heraldry; reading; walking the dog. Address: Erskine Manse, Burnbrae Road, Falkirk, FK1 5SD; T.-0324 23701.

Muir, Rev. Alexander, MA, BD. Minister, Canisbay with Keiss Church of Scotland, since 1982; b. 26.12.40, Rutherglen; m., Catriona Kinloch Male; 3 s. Educ. Rutherglen Academy; Glasgow University; Jordanhill College of Education. Secondary School Teacher, 1964-65; Teacher of English and Bible subjects at an African Bible College in Ibadan, Western Nigeria, 1966-67; Teacher of English, mainly at Dalziel High School, Motherwell, 1967-77; student, 1977-80; Assistant Minister, St. Columba's Parish Church, Largs, 1980-81; Locum, Isle of Barra, 1981. Recreations: walking; reading; guitar playing; singing. Address: The Manse, Canisbay, Caithness, KW1 4YH; T.-John O'Groats 309.

Muir, David Maxwell, BSc, ARCST, PhD, MIChemE, CEng. Senior Lecturer in Chemical Engineering, Strathclyde University, since 1983; Consultant in Air Pollution Control; b. 29.9.42, Glasgow; m., Kay Nicolsen; 2 d. Educ. Eastwood Senior Secondary School; Glasgow University; Strathclyde University. Lecturer in Chemical Engineering, Strathclyde University, 1964-83; Member, Editorial Board, Proceedings of Filtration Society, since 1983; Tutor in Technology, Open University, since 1972. Publications: Guide to Dust and Fume Control, 1984; papers and reports. Recreations: sailing; swimming; golf; music. Address: (b.) Department of Chemical and Process Engineering, Strathclyde University, Glasgow; T.-041-552 4400, Ext. 2410.

Muir, Rev. Frederick Comery, MA, BD, ThM, ARCM. Minister, Stepps Parish Church, since 1983; b. 26.11.32, Glasgow; m., Christine Elizabeth Dickie; 1 s.; 1 d. Educ. Kelvinside Academy; Glasgow University; Princeton Theological College. Assistant Minister, Cathcart South Church, Glasgow, 1957-58; Teaching Fellow, Princeton Theological College, 1959-60; Minister: St. James' Church, Lossiemouth, 1961-72, Whitehill Parish Church, Stepps, 1972-83. Instructor of Music, Gordonstoun School, 1967-71; Conductor, Strathkelvin Choral Society, 1973-78; Vice-Chairman, Scottish Committee, Royal School of Church Music, since 1978; President, Glasgow Society of Organists, 1983-84. Recreations: music-making; hill-walking. Address: 20 Alexandra Avenue, Stepps, Glasgow, G33 6BP; T.-041-779 2504.

Muir, Ian Fraser Kerr, MBE, VRD, MB, MS, FRCS, FRCSEdin. Clinical Senior Lecturer in Surgery, Aberdeen University, since 1969; Consultant in Plastic Surgery, Grampian Health Board, since 1969; b. 26.8.21, West Hartlepool; m., Marion Beatrice Pinks (deceased); 1 s.; 1 d. Educ. Epsom College; London University. House Surgeon, Middlesex Hospital, 1943; Surgeon Lt., RNVR, 1944-47; Surgical Registrar, Middlesex Hospital and Queen Elizabeth Hospital, Birmingham; Senior Surgical Registrar, then Consultant in Plastic Surgery, Mount Vernon Centre for Plastic Surgery (latterly also West Middlesex Hospital). Past President, British Association of Plastic Surgeons; Hunterian Professor, Royal College of Surgeons of England, 1983. Address: (h.) 14 Westerton Road, Cults, Aberdeen, AB1 9NR; T.-Aberdeen 867287.

Muir, James Fraser, BSc, PhD. Senior Lecturer, Institute of Aquaculture, Stirling University, since 1984; Consultant and Advisor to UK and international aquaculture industry, since 1977; b. 7.3.51, Sleaford, Lincolnshire; m., Susan Clare Purser; 2 d. Educ. Dingwall Academy; Edinburgh University; Strathclyde University. Member, Editorial Board, Journal of Aquaculture and Fisheries Management, and Aquaculture Engineering; Co-Editor, Recent Advances in Aquaculture. Address: (b.) Institute of Aquaculture, Stirling University, Stirling, FK9 4LA; T.-0786 73171.

Muir, Sir John (Harling), 3rd Bt, TD, DL. Director, James Finlay & Co. Ltd., 1946-81; Member, Queen's Bodyguard for Scotland (Royal Company of Archers); b. 7.11.10; m.; 5 s.; 2 d. Educ. Stowe. Served Second World War (demobilised with rank of Major); Deputy Lieutenant, Perthshire, since 1966. Address: (h.) Bankhead, Blair Drummond, by Stirling.

Muir, Kenneth Walter, BSc, PhD. Reader in Chemistry, Glasgow University, since 1985; b. 2.9.41, Edinburgh; m., Ljubica; 1 s.; 1 d. Educ. Hutchesons' Boys' Grammar School; Glasgow

University. Lecturer: Sussex University, Glasgow University. Recreations: foreign travel; reading; walking. Address: (b.) Department of Chemistry, Glasgow University, Glasgow; T.-041-339 8855.

Muir, Thomas Copland, BSc, PhD, MPS. Senior Lecturer, Department of Pharmacology, Glasgow University; b. 24.8.33, Newmains, Wishaw; m., Moira M. Gray; 2 d. Educ. Wishaw High School; Glasgow University. Assistant Lecturer, then Lecturer, Glasgow University; Henry Wellcome Travelling Fellow, 1968-69; Senior Research Associate, Mayo Foundation; Member, Editorial Board, British Journal of Pharmacology, 1977-84. Recreations: reading; walking. Address: (b.) Department of Pharmacology, Glasgow University, Glasgow, G12 8QQ; T.-041-339 8855.

Muir, Trevor, BA, MIH, MISW. Director of Housing, City of Aberdeen District Council, since 1981; b. 10.7.49, Glasgow; m., Christine Ann; 1 s.; 1 d. Educ. High School of Glasgow; Langside College; Strathclyde University. Scottish Special Housing Association, 1973-77; City of Glasgow District Council, 1977-81. Recreations: family indulger; social recluse practitioner. Address: (b.) St. Nicholas House, Broad Street, Aberdeen; T.-Aberdeen 642121, Ext. 360.

Muirhead, Douglas Campbell, OBE, BSc (Hons), CEng, MIProdE, FIMC. Chairman, Ardrossan, Saltcoats and Stevenston Enterprise Trust (ASSET), since 1981; Director, Ardrossan, Saltcoats and Stevenston Enterprise Properties Ltd. (APL); Deputy Chairman, Irvine Development Corporation, since 1983; Director, Robert Wilson & Sons (1849) Ltd., since 1981; Vice-President, Ayrshire Chamber of Industries; Member, Glasgow University Court (General Council Assessor); Chairman, Scottish Allied Investors Ltd.; Past Chairman, PA Management Consultants Ltd. and Director, PA International Management Consultants Ltd.; b. 21.2.21, Glasgow; m., Sheila Grace Fenton; 2 s.; 1 d. Educ. Allan Glen's School, Glasgow; Glasgow University. Recreation: travel. Address: (h.) Camlarg, 64 South Beach, Troon, Ayrshire; T.-0292 314920.

Muirshiel, 1st Viscount, (John Scott Maclay), KT (1973), CH (1962), CMG (1944), PC (1952), DL. Lord Lieutenant of Renfrewshire, 1967-80; Secretary of State for Scotland, 1957-62; b. 26.10.05; m., Betty L'Estrange Astley (deceased). Educ. Winchester; Trinity College, Cambridge. MP, Montrose Burghs, 1940-50, Renfrewshire West, 1950-64; Minister of Transport and Civil Aviation, 1951-52; Minister of State for Colonial Affairs, 1956-57; President, Assembly of WEU, 1955-56; Director, Clydesdale Bank, 1970-82; Hon. LLD: Edinburgh, 1963, Strathclyde, 1966, Glasgow, 1970. Address: (h.) Knapps, Kilmacolm, Renfrewshire.

Mulrine, Stephen, MA (Hons). Poet and Playwright; Senior Lecturer in Historical Studies, Glasgow School of Art, since 1983 (Lecturer, 1969-83); Extra-Mural Lecturer in Creative Writing, Glasgow University, since 1970; b. 13.3.37, Glasgow; m., Elizabeth S.K. Lees; 2 s.; 1 d. Educ. St. Mungo's Academy; Glasgow University; Edinburgh University. Member, Board of

Directors, Glasgow Citizens' Theatre, since 1971; Member, Drama Committee, Scottish Arts Council, since 1983; author of six television plays, including The Silly Season (Play for Today), BBC 1, and The House on Kirov Street, BBC; numerous radio plays including serials Deacon Brodie and Mary, Queen of Scots; theatre and poetry criticism. Recreations: theatre-going; reading. Address: (h.) 132 Kingswood Drive, Glasgow, G44 4RB; T.-041-649 2183.

Mundell, Christeen, RGN, SCM. Director of Nursing, Ross Hall Hospital, Glasgow, since 1983; b. 15.7.48, Dunoon. Educ. Dunoon Grammar School; Glasgow Royal Infirmary and Queen Mother's Hospital, Glasgow. Glasgow Royal Infirmary: Staff Nurse, Surgical Unit, 1971, Sister/Night Duty Surgical Area, 1971-72, Senior Sister in charge of University Department of Surgery Wards, 1972-77, Nursing Officer in charge of University Department of Surgery Wards, Acute Receiving Surgical Wards and Urology Wards, 1977-83. Address: (h.) Donrhona, Sandbank, Dunoon; T.-0369 6277.

Mundell, David Gordon, LLB (Hons), DipLP. Member, Annandale and Eskdale District Council, since 1984; Member, Council for Social Democracy, since 1985; Member, SDP Council for Scotland, since 1982; b. 27.5.62, Dumfries. Educ. Lockerbie Academy; Edinburgh University. Youngest Councillor in Scotland; Member, Annandale and Eskdale Sports Council. Recreations: squash; travel; cuisine. Address: (h.) Clifton, Dryfe Road, Lockerbie, Dumfriesshire, DG11 2AJ; T.-057-62 2155.

Munn, Sir James, OBE, MA, DUniv. Chairman, Consultative Committee on the Curriculum, since 1980; Chairman, Manpower Services Committee for Scotland, since 1984; b. 27.7.20, Bridge of Allan; m., Muriel Jean Millar Moles; 1 d. Educ. Stirling High School; Glasgow University. Indian Civil Service, 1941-48; various teaching appointments, Glasgow, 1949-57; Principal Teacher of Modern Languages, Falkirk High School, 1957-66 (Depute Rector, 1962-66); Principal Examiner in Modern Languages, Scottish Examination Board, 1965-66; Rector: Rutherglen Academy, 1966-70, Cathkin High School, 1970-83; Member, University Grants Committee, 1973-82; Member, Consultative Committee on the Curriculum, since 1968; Chairman, Committee to review the Structure of the Curriculum at S3 and S4, 1975-77; Member of Court, Strathclyde University, since 1983. Address: (h.) 4 Kincath Avenue, High Burnside, Glasgow, G73 4RP; T.-041-634 4654.

Munn, Professor Walter Douglas, MA, PhD, DSc, FRSE. Thomas Muir Professor of Mathematics, Glasgow University, since 1973; b. 24.4.29, Kilbarchan; m., Margaret Clare Barlow. Educ. Marr College, Troon; Glasgow University; St. John's College, Cambridge. Scientific Officer, Royal Naval Scientific Service; Assistant in Mathematics, then Lecturer in Mathematics, Glasgow University; Visiting Assistant Professor, Tulane University; Senior Lecturer in Computing Science, then Senior Lecturer in Mathematics, Glasgow University; Professor of Mathematics,

Stirling University. Recreations: music; gardening; hill-walking. Address: (b.) Department of Mathematics, Glasgow University, Glasgow, G12 8QW; T.-041-339 8855, Ext. 207.

Munro, Alexander, MB, ChB, ChM, FRCS. Consultant General Surgeon, Raigmore Hospital, Inverness, since 1978; Clinical Senior Lecturer in Surgery, Aberdeen University, since 1978; b. 5.6.43, Ross and Cromarty; m., Maureen E. McCreath; 2 s.; 1 d. Educ. Fortrose Academy; Aberdeen University. Training in General Surgery at Registrar and Senior Registrar level, Aberdeen Hospitals, 1971-78; specialist training, St. Mark's Hospital, 1977. Recreation: gardening. Address: (h.) 23 Eriskay Road, Inverness; T.-Inverness 223804.

Munro, Rev. David Peacock, MA, BD, STM. Minister, Bearsden North Church, since 1967; b. 7.9.29, Paisley; m., Jessie Scott McPherson; 3 d. Educ. Paisley Grammar School; Glasgow University; Union Theological Seminary, New York. Minister, Aberluthnott Parish Church, 1953-56, Castlehill Church, Ayr, 1956-67. Chairman, General Assembly Board of Education, 1974-79; Convener, General Assembly Education Committee, 1981-85; Editor, Children of the Way (Sunday School Programme), Year One, 1981. Publication: Preface to Teaching. Recreations: golf; gardening. Address: North Manse, 8 Collylinn Road, Bearsden, Glasgow; T.-041-942 0366.

Munro, Gordon McKie, BSc, DipEd. Head Teacher, Tynecastle High School, Edinburgh, since 1983; b. 4.1.44, Glencraig, Fife; m., Nessy; 4 s. Educ. Beath High School; Edinburgh University; Moray House College of Education. Taught Physics, Beath Senior High School, Cowdenbeath, 1967-69; Tynecastle High School: Principal Teacher of Physics, 1970-72, Assistant Head Teacher, 1972-78, Deputy Head Teacher, 1978-83. Secretary and Precentor, Christian Assembly Meeting, Gospel Hall, Ballingry, Fife. Recreations: preaching; teaching; reading; walking (a dog); gardening; building; looking after a donkey. Address: (h.) The Whins, Nether Milton, Crosshill, Fife, KY5 8AN; T.-0592 860 515.

Munro, Isabel, BEM, SRN, SCM. Member, Highland Health Board, since 1981; b. 12.7.15, Shieldaig, Ross and Cromarty; m., Kenneth Munro; 1 s. Educ. Shieldaig, Strathcarron; Glasgow Eastern District Hospital; Royal Maternity Hospital, Glasgow. District Nursing Sister, Evanton, 1939-45; Welfare Officer, Ross and Cromarty Branch, Red Cross, 1961-83; Executive Member, East Ross and Black Isle Council of Social Service; Committee Member, An Comunn Gaidhealach; Past President, Local Branch, SWRI. Recreations: knitting; tapestry; floral art; Scottish country music. Address: (h.) Kildare, Evanton, Dingwall, Ross and Cromarty, IV16 9YW; T.-Evanton 830285.

Munro, James Robertson, CEng, MIEE, FIElecIE, FBIM. Chairman, Munro Projects Ltd. and M.D. Munro Electric (Dundee) Ltd.; Director, Mathew Trust Investmnts Ltd.; President, Electrical Contractors Association; President, Dundee and Tayside Chamber of Commerce; Deacon Convener, Nine Incorporated Trades of Dundee; b. 26.9.22, Dundee; m., Dr. A.M. Crowder; 2 s. Educ. Dundee College of Technology; British Institute of Engineering Technology, London. Recreation: golf. Address: (h.) 5 Nobel Road, Wester Gourdie, Dundee, DD2 4UH.

Munro, John Farquhar, JP. Chairman, Skye and Lochalsh District Council; Haulage and Civil Engineering Contractor; b. 26.8.34, Glenshiel; m., Cecilia Moffat Brown Robertson; 1 s.; 1 d. Educ. Plockton High School; Sea Training College. Merchant marine, 11 years; Member, Highland Regional Council, 1978-82; Chairman, Gaelic Committee, Highland Region, 1978-82; Assessor to Crofters Commission, since 1977; Member, Shipping Advisory Committee, Caledonian MacBrayne; elected, Skye and Lochalsh District Council, 1974; Trustee, Gaelic Language Promotion Trust; Member, Council on Alcoholism, Alcoholics Anonymous; Treasurer, Kintail Parish Church. Recreations: shooting; sailing; drama. Address: (h.) Glomach House, Glenshiel, Wester Ross; T.-059 981 222.

Munro, John Forbes, MB, ChB (Hons), FRCPEdin. Consultant Physician, Eastern General and Edenhall Hospitals, since 1968; part-time Senior Lecturer, Edinburgh University, since 1984; b. 26.6.33, Edinburgh; m., Elizabeth Jean Durell Caird; 3 d. Educ. Edinburgh Academy; Chigwell School, Essex; Edinburgh University. Registrar and Senior Registrar, Edinburgh Royal Infirmary, 1962-68. Recreations: playing mixed hockey. Address: (h.) Backhill, Carberry, near Musselburgh, East Lothian; T.-031-663 4935.

Munro of Foulis, Captain Patrick, TD (1958), DL (1949). 30th Chief of Clan Munro; Vice Lieutenant of Ross and Cromarty, 1968-77; b. 30.8.12; m., Eleanor Mary French; 3 s.; 1 d. Educ. Imperial Service College, Windsor; Sandhurst. 2nd Lt., Seaforth Highlanders, 1933; Captain, 1939; served Second World War (POW); Farmer and Landowner; Honorary Sheriff of Ross and Cromarty. Address: (h.) Foulis Castle, Evanton, Ross-shire.

Munro, Robert William. Trustee, National Museum of Antiquities of Scotland, 1982-85; b. 3.2.14, Kiltearn, Ross-shire; m., Jean Mary Dunlop. Educ. Edinburgh Academy. War Service, Seaforth Highlanders and Inter-Services Public Relations Directorate (India), 1940-46; Editorial Staff, The Scotsman, 1933-59 and 1963-69; Editor-in-Chief, Highland News Group, 1959-63; Chairman, Edinburgh Press Club, 1955-57 (President, 1969-71); Honorary Editor, Clan Munro Association, 1939-71 (Vice-President, since 1963); former Council Member: Society of Antiquaries of Scotland, Scottish History Society, Scottish Genealogy Society. Publications: Donald Monro's Western Isles of Scotland and Genealogies of the Clans 1549 (Editor), 1961; Tain Through the Centuries (Co-author, with wife), 1966; The Glorious Privilege: The History of The Scotsman (Co-author), 1967; Kinsmen and Clansmen, 1971; The Northern Lighthouses, 1976; Highland Clans and Tartans, 1977; Edinburgh and the Borders, 1977; The Munro Tree 1734, 1978; Scottish Lighthouses, 1979; Taming the Rough Bounds, Knoydart 1745-1784, 1984. Recreations: historical research and writing; walking; visiting islands. Address: (h.) 15A Mansionhouse Road, Edinburgh, EH9 1TZ; T.-031-667 4601.

Murchison, Maurine, OBE, MA (Hons). Chairman, Children's Panel Advisory Committee, Highland Region, 1980-85; Member, Consultative Committee on the Curriculum, since 1980; Member, Highlands and Islands Development Consultative Council, since 1978; Member, Police Advisory Board for Scotland, since 1985; b. 25.11.35, London; m., Dr. Murdoch Murchison (qv); 3 s.; 2 d. Educ. James Allen's Girls School, Dulwich; Edinburgh University. Secondary school teaching, 1958-60; homemaker and mother, since 1960; Member, Inverness County Children's Panel, 1971-75 (Chairman, 1972-75); Chairman, Highland Region Children's Panel, 1975-80; Member, Inverness Prison Visiting Committee, 1984-85; Member, Panel for Appeals Tribunal, set up under Social Work Scotland Act 1968, since 1983; Assessor under Race Relations Act, since 1982; Past Chairman: Lifeline Inverness, YWCA, Inverness. Recreations: embroidery; group Bible study; reading (ethics and theology). Address: (h.) Riverdale, 22 Hillview Road, Cults, Aberdeen, AB1 9HB; T.-0224 868327.

Murchison, Murdoch, MB, ChB, DObstRCOG, DPH, DIH, FFCM. Chief Administrative Medical Officer, Grampian Health Board, since 1984; Honorary Clinical Senior Lecturer, Aberdeen University, since 1984; b. 27.10.33, Aultbea, Ross-shire; m., Maurine Tallach (see Maurine Murchison); 3 s.; 2 d. Educ. Invergordon Academy; Edinburgh University. Medical Officer of Health, Inverness County Council and Inverness Burgh Council; Community Medicine Specialist and District Medical Officer, Highland Health Board; Police Surgeon, Northern Constabulary; Medical Officer, Highland and Islands Fire Brigade. Member, Community Medicine Consultative Committee UK; Past Chairman, Scottish Committee for Community Medicine, BMA; Past President, Scottish Society for Community Medicine. Recreations: hill-walking; gardening. Address: (b.) 1 Albyn Place, Aberdeen, AB9 1RE; T.-Aberdeen 589901.

Murdoch, Brian Oliver, BA, PhD, AMusTCL. Senior Lecturer in German, Stirling University, since 1975 (Head, Department of German, since 1982); b. 26.6.44, London; m., Ursula I. Riffer; 1 s.; 1 d. Educ. Sir George Monoux Grammar School, Walthamstow; Exeter University; Goettingen University; Freiburg University; Jesus College, Cambridge. Lecturer in German, Glasgow University; Assistant/Associate Professor of German, Illinois University; Lecturer in German, Stirling University. Editor, Scottish Papers in Germanic Studies, since 1981. Recreations: jazz; numismatics; books. Address: (b.) German Department, Stirling University, Stirling, FK9 4LA; T.-0786 73171, Ext. 2273.

Murdoch, Eileen, MA. Headmistress, St. Augustine's High School, Edinburgh, since 1977; b. Edinburgh. Educ. Holy Cross Academy; Edinburgh University; Craiglockhart College. Recreation: choral singing. Address: (b.) St. Augustine's High School, Broomhouse Road, Edinburgh; T.-031-334 6801.

Murdoch, John, FCMA, JDipMA, CIPFA. Director of Finance and Administration, Irvine Development Corporation, since 1972; b. 31.12.34, Glassford; m., Ann McTaggart Jack; 3 s.; 1 d. Educ. Hamilton Academy; School of Accountancy (Correspondence Courses). Bank Clerk, Bank of Scotland, Hamilton, 1951-53 and 1955-58; National Service, Cameronians (Scottish Rifles), 1953-55; Trainee Cost Accountant, Colvilles Steel Industry, Motherwell, 1958-63; Budget Controller, East Kilbride Development Corporation, 1963-68; Financial Controller, Irvine Development Corporation, 1968-72. Recreations: lay preaching; writing; marathon running; bird-watching. Address: (b.) Irvine Development Corporation, Perceton House, Girdle Toll, Irvine, Ayrshire; T.-Irvine 214100.

Murdoch, Rev. William McCorkindale, BSc, BD, STM, PhD. Minister, Barthol Chapel and Tarves Parish Churches, since 1980; b. 9.3.51, Edinburgh; m., Dr. Helen Buchan Murdoch. Educ. Ashville College, Harrogate; Aberdeen University; Union Theological Seminary, New York. Research Assistant, Department of Geology and Mineralogy, Aberdeen University, 1972-75; Visiting Fellow, Union Theological Seminary, New York, 1978-79. Member, Church of Scotland Panel on Doctrine, since 1984. Recreations: travel; skiing; cookery; fine wine; glaciology. Address: The Manse, Tarves, Ellon, Aberdeenshire; T.-Tarves 250.

Mure, Kenneth Nisbet, MA, LLB, FTII. Advocate, since 1975; b. 11.4.47, Glasgow. Educ. High School of Glasgow; Glasgow University. Part-time Lecturer in Revenue Law, Glasgow University, 1971-83. Address: (b.) Advocates' Library, Edinburgh.

Murison, James, RMN, RGN, BA. Member, Grampian Health Board, since 1975; Superintendent, Willowbank Adult Training Centre and Hostel, since 1967; Deputy Principal Nursing Officer, Bilbohall Hospital, Elgin, since 1960; b. 25.5.29, Aberdeenshire; m., Agnes Gray; 1 s.; 2 d. Educ. Udny Green, Aberdeenshire; Open University; Royal College of Nursing. President: Peterhead Chess Club, since 1968, Longside Tennis Club. Recreations: chess; tennis. Address: (b.) Willowbank Adult Training Centre, Peterhead, Aberdeenshire; T.-St. Fergus 301.

Murphy, Herbert Edward Harnett, ACIT. Regional Director, Scotland and Northern Ireland, Automobile Association, since 1974; b. 31.8.32, Dublin; m., Susan Gillion Hall; 2 s. Educ. Repton School, Derbyshire; Trinity College, Dublin. Member, Transport Committee, Glasgow Chamber of Commerce; Member, Transport Action Scotland Committee; Member, Traffic Committee, XIII Commonwealth Games 1986. Recreations: sailing; golf; hill-walking. Address: (h.) 20 Donaldfield Road, Bridge of Weir, Renfrewshire, PA11 3JG; T.-0505 613118.

Murphy, James Barrie, MB, ChB, DPM, MRCPsych. Consultant Psychiatrist and Honorary Clinical Lecturer, Gartnavel Royal Hospital, Glasgow; b. 27.7.42, Glasgow; m., Jean Wynn Kirkwood; 1 s.; 1 d. Educ. High School of Glasgow; Glasgow University. Consultant Psychiatrist, Dykebar Hospital, Paisley, 1973-80. Address: (b.) Gartnavel Royal Hospital, 1055 Great Western Road, Glasgow, G12 0XH; T.-041-334 6241.

Murphy, Sheriff James Patrick, BL. Sheriff of North Strathclyde, since 1976; b. 24.1.32; m.; 2 s.; 1 d. Educ. Notre Dame Convent; St. Aloysius College, Glasgow; Glasgow University. Solicitor, 1953; Founder, Ross Harper & Murphy, 1961; President, Glasgow Juridical Society, 1962-63; President, Glasgow Bar Association, 1966-67; Member, Council, Law Society of Scotland, 1974-76.

Murphy, John, MILAM. Combined Arts Director, Scottish Arts Council, since 1977; b. 8.2.39, London; m.; 2 s.; 1 d. Educ. Salesian College, Chertsey; Central London Polytechnic. RAF, 1958-60; Peninsular and Oriental Steam Navigation Co., 1960-63; Amalgamated Asphalte Co. Ltd., 1963-66; Music Director, Arts Council of Northern Ireland, 1967-72; Deputy Director, Southern Arts Association, 1972-74; Director, West Midlands Arts, 1974-77. Chairman, Queensferry Association, 1980-83. Publication: The Traditional and Folk Arts of Scotland (SAC Working Party Report). Recreations: drinking; eating high cholesterol foods. Address: (b.) 19 Charlotte Square, Edinburgh, EH2 4DF; T.-031-226 6051.

Murphy, Peter Alexander, MA, MEd. Rector, Whitfield High School, Dundee, since 1976; b. 5.10.32, Aberdeen; m., Margaret Christie; 3 s.; 1 d. Educ. Aberdeen Grammar School; Aberdeen University. Assistant Principal Teacher of English, Aberdeen Grammar School, 1963-65; Principal Teacher of English, Summerhill Academy, Aberdeen, 1965-71; Head Teacher, Logie Secondary School, Dundee, 1971-76. Chairman, Carnoustie Branch, Labour Party; Elder, Carnoustie Church. Publication: Life and Times of Logie School (Co-author). Recreations: hill-walking; hockey; bee-keeping; gardening. Address: (h.) Ashlea, 44 Burnside Street, Carnoustie, Angus; T.-Carnoustie 52106.

Murray, Alex. T.L., CEng, BSc, FIEE. Chief Engineer, North of Scotland Hydro-Electric Board, since 1974; b. 27.6.25, Edinburgh; m., Mary; 1 s.; 1 d. Educ. George Heriot's; Heriot-Watt University. General Assistant Engineer, Central Electricity Board, 1947-48; Assistant Section Engineer, SE Scotland Division, British Electricity Authority, 1948-51; various posts, North of Scotland Hydro-Electric Board, since 1951. Recreations: early music performance; amateur radio; hill-walking. Address: (b.) 16 Rothesay Terrace, Edinburgh, EH3 7SE.

Murray, Athol Laverick, PhD, MA, LLB, FRHistS, FSA Scot. Keeper of the Records of Scotland, since 1985; b. 8.11.30, Tynemouth; m., Irene Joyce Cairns; 1 s.; 1 d. Educ. Lancaster Royal Grammar School; Jesus College, Cambridge; Edinburgh University. Research Assistant, Foreign Office, 1953; Scottish Record Office: Assistant Keeper, 1953-83, Deputy Keeper, 1983-84. Chairman of Council, Scottish Record Society. Address: (b.) Scottish Record Office, HM General Register House, Edinburgh, EH1 3YY; T.-031-556 6585.

Murray, David Edward. Chairman and Managing Director, Murray International Metals, since 1973; b. 14.10.51, Ayr; m., Mrs L.V. Murray; 2 s. Educ. Fettes College; Broughton High School. Young Scottish Businessman of the Year, 1984. Recreations: sports sponsorship, e.g. basketball, hockey, volleyball, etc.; snooker. Address: (b.) Bonnington House, Kirknewton, EH27 8BB; T.-0506 881111.

Murray, Donald, MA. Head Teacher, Sir Edward Scott School, Tarbert, Isle of Harris, since 1981; b. Port of Ness, Isle of Lewis; 2 d. Educ. Nicolson Institute, Stornoway; Glasgow University. Teacher, Calder Street Secondary School, Glasgow; Teacher, Achnamara Residential School, Argyll; Principal Teacher of Guidance, Victoria Drive Secondary School, Glasgow; Assistant Head Teacher (Curriculum), Kingsridge Secondary School, Glasgow. Recreations: angling; gardening; reading. Address: (h.) Balranald, West Tarbert, Isle of Harris; T.-0859 2339.

Murray, Rev. Douglas Millar, MA, BD, PhD. Minister, Polwarth Parish Church, Edinburgh, since 1981; b. 1946, Edinburgh; m., Dr. Freya M. Smith. Educ. George Watson's College, Edinburgh; Edinburgh University; New College, Edinburgh; Fitzwilliam and Westminster Colleges, Cambridge. Minister: St. Bride's Church, Callander, 1976-80, John Ker Memorial Church in deferred union with Candlish Church, Edinburgh, 1980-81 (became Polwarth Church, 1981). Editor, Liturgical Review, 1979-81; Associate Editor, Scottish Journal of Theology, since 1981; Vice-Convener, Panel on Doctrine, General Assembly, Church of Scotland, since 1984. Publication: Studies in the History of Worship in Scotland (Co-Editor). Recreations: golf; Scottish country dancing; hill-walking; sketching. Address: 9 Merchiston Bank Gardens, Edinburgh, EH10 5EB; T.-031-447 2741.

Murray, Gordon Stewart, JP, ARGTC. Member, Strathclyde Regional Council, since 1974; Member, Cumbernauld and Kilsyth District Council, since 1974; b. 15.7.27, Aberdeen; 1 s.; 1 d. Educ. Aberdeen Grammar School; Aberdeen University; Robert Gordon's College of Technology. First and last Provost of Cumbernauld Burgh, 1968-75; first Provost, Cumbernauld and Kilsyth, 1974-80; Senior Engineer, Cumbernauld Development Corporation, 1964-83; former Vice-Chairman and Vice-President, Scottish National Party; Parliamentary candidate, East Dunbartonshire, 1970, East Kilbride, 1974 and 1979, Cumbernauld and Kilsyth, 1983. Recreation: part-time crofter. Address: (h.) 17 Arran Drive, Cumbernauld, Glasgow.

Murray, Hugh Duncan Blue, CEng, MICE, MIHT, MIPLE. Director of Roads and Transportation, Dumfries and Galloway Regional

Council, since 1977; b. 26.9.29, Glasgow; m., Lilian Lawson; 3 s. Educ. Morrison's Academy, Crieff; Royal Technical College, Glasgow. Apprentice Civil Engineer, Royal Burgh of Rutherglen, 1947-52; Junior Engineer, Lanark County Council, 1954-59; Dumbarton County Council: Senior Engineer, 1959-62, Chief Assistant Engineer, 1962-68, Assistant County Surveyor, 1968-72, Depute County Surveyor, 1972-75; Assistant Divisional Engineer, Strathclyde Regional Council, 1975; Senior Depute Director of Roads, Tayside Regional Council, 1975-77. Recreations: rugby; caravanning; gardening; golf; reading; photography. Address: (b.) Council Offices, English Street, Dumfries, DG1 2DD; T.-0387 53141, Ext. 224.

Murray, Isobel (Mary), MA, PhD. Writer and Book Reviewer; Senior Lecturer in English, Aberdeen University, since 1974; b. 14.2.39, Alloa; m., Bob Tait. Educ. Dollar Academy; Edinburgh University. Assistant Lecturer, then Lecturer, Department of English, Aberdeen University; books include several editions of Oscar Wilde, introductions to new editions of J. MacDougall Hay's Gillespie and Ian MacPherson's Shepherds' Calendar; Ten Modern Scottish Novels (with Bob Tait), 1984; wide range of book reviews, especially for The Scotsman, since 1962, and new fiction for Financial Times, 1968-81. Address: (b.) Department of English, King's College, Old Aberdeen, Aberdeen, AB9 2UB; T.-Aberdeen 40241, Ext. 6562.

Murray, Professor James Lothian, BSc, MSc, MIMechE, CEng. Professor of Computer Aided Engineering, Heriot-Watt University, since 1985 (Director, CAE Centre, since 1982); b. 11.6.38, Loanhead; m., Anne Walton; 1 d. Educ. Lasswade Senior Secondary School; Heriot-Watt University. Student apprentice, then Design Engineer, Ferranti Ltd., 1956-66; Heriot-Watt University: Lecturer in Engineering Design, 1966-78, Senior Lecturer in Design and Manufacture, 1978-85, Head, Department of Mechanical Engineering, since 1984. Member: Engineering Panel, CNAA, Art and Design Panel, SUCE; Board Member, Unilink. Recreation: hill-walking. Address: (b.) Department of Mechanical Engineering, Heriot-Watt University, Edinburgh, EH14 4AS; T.-031-449 5111.

Murray, John, QC (Scot), BA (Oxon), LLB. Chairman, Scottish Council of Law Reporting, since 1978; b. 8.7.35; m.; 3 s. Educ. Corpus Christi College, Oxford; Edinburgh University. Advocate, 1962; Member, Scottish Law Commission, since 1979.

Murray, Rev. John James, DipTh. Minister, Free High Church, Oban, since 1978; b. 11.9.34, Dornoch; m., Cynthia MacPhee; 1 s.; 1 d. Educ. Dornoch Academy; Edinburgh University; Free Church College. Worked with insurance company before joining Banner of Truth Trust, 1960, as Assistant Editor; Secretary, Reformation Translation Fellowship, since 1962; Clerk, Argyll and Lochaber Presbytery, since 1983. Address: Free Church Manse, Rockfield Road, Oban, Argyll, PA34 5DQ; T.-0631 62154.

Murray, Jonathan Aidan Muir, BSc, MB, ChB, FRCS, FRACS, MD. Consultant Ear Nose and Throat Surgeon, Edinburgh, since 1983; part-time Senior Lecturer in Otolaryngology, since 1984; b. 16.8.51, Edinburgh; m., Shiona Aitken; 2 s.; 2 d. Educ. Daniel Stewart's College, Edinburgh; Edinburgh University. Address: (h.) The Old Rectory, Lasswade, Midlothian, EH18 1LR; T.-031-660 2694.

Murray, Professor Kenneth, BSc, PhD, FRS. Professor of Molecular Biology, Edinburgh University, since 1976; b. 30.12.30, East Ardsley; m., Noreen E. Parker. Educ. Henry Mellish Grammar School; Birmingham University. Postdoctoral work, Stanford University, California, 1959-64; MRC Scientific Staff, Cambridge, 1964-67; joined Edinburgh University, 1967; leave of absence at European Molecular Biology Laboratory, Heidelberg, 1979-82. Recreations: musical appreciation; reading. Address: (b.) Department of Molecular Biology, Edinburgh University, Mayfield Road, Edinburgh, EH9 3JR; T.-031-667 1081.

Murray, Noreen Elizabeth, FRS, PhD. Reader, Department of Molecular Biology, Edinburgh University, since 1982; b. 26.2.35, Burnley; m., Kenneth Murray (qv). Educ. Lancaster Girls' Grammar School; King's College, London; Birmingham University. Research Associate, Department of Biological Sciences, Stanford University, 1960-64; Research Fellow, Botany School, Cambridge, 1964-67; Edinburgh University: Member, MRC Molecular Genetics Unit, Department of Molecular Biology, 1968-74, Lecturer, then Senior Lecturer, Department of Molecular Biology, 1974-80; Group Leader, European Molecular Biology Laboratory, Heidelberg, 1980-82. Recreation: gardening. Address: (b.) Department of Molecular Biology, Edinburgh University, Mayfield Road, Edinburgh, EH9 3JR; T.-031-667 1081.

Murray, Patrick, VRD, WS. Landowner; Director, Scottish SPCA, since 1952; b. 13.5.11, Edinburgh; m., Doris Herbert Green; 2 d. Educ. Ardvreck, Crieff; Marlborough College. Royal Naval Volunteer Reserve, 1935-55 (Commander); Partner, Murray, Beith & Murray, WS, Edinburgh, 1937-77. Recreations: gardening; forestry; hunting; carriage driving. Address: (h.) Townhead of Cavers, Hawick, Roxburghshire, TD9 8LJ; T.-0450 73604.

Murray, Rt. Hon. Lord (Ronald King Murray), PC (1974). Senator of the College of Justice in Scotland, since 1979; b. 15.6.22; m.; 1 s.; 1 d. Educ. George Watson's College; Edinburgh University; Jesus College, Oxford. Served HM Forces, 1941-46; called to Scottish Bar, 1953; QC (Scot), 1967; Advocate Depute, 1964-67; Senior Advocate-Depute, 1967-70; MP (Labour), Leith, 1970-79; Lord Advocate, 1974-79.

Murray, Rt. Rev. Mgr. Thomas Canon, STL. Parish Priest, Dumbarton, since 1975; b. Wishaw. Educ. Our Lady's High School, Motherwell; Blair's College; Scots College, Rome. Assistant: St. Luke's, Glasgow, Carfin; on staff, Scots College; Parish Priest, Balornock, 1957-75. Address: St. Patrick's, Strathleven Place, Dumbarton, G82 1BA.

Murray, Walter Watson, FRICS. Director of Estates, Grampian Regional Council, since 1975. Educ. Royal College of Science and Technology, Glasgow. NE Counties Valuation Committee, Aberdeen: Senior Valuer, 1957-61, Depute Assessor, 1961-67, Assessor, 1967-75. Secretary, Association of Local Authority Valuers and Estate Surveyors, Scottish Branch. Recreation: hill-walking. Address: (b.) Woodhill House, Ashgrove Road West, Aberdeen, AB9 2LU; T.-0224 682222, Ext. 2440.

Murray, William, JP. Farmer; Chairman, W. Murray (Farming) Ltd., since 1960; Chairman, Border Sheepskins Ltd., since 1966; b. 16.2.17, Gorebridge; m., Fiona Stevenson; 3 s.; 2 d. Educ. Dalhousie Castle School; Merchiston Castle School. Began farming with father, 1934; went to Southern Rhodesia, 1938, to tobacco farm, becoming Manager; served King's African Rifles Defence Force, 1939-42; joined Rhodesian Royal Airforce (invalided out, 1942); returned to UK and became Farm Manager, Redden, Kelso, 1943 (subsequently Tenant and Farmer); acquired Watherston Farm, 1972, and Mid Housebyres Farm, 1983; Committee Member, NFU of Scotland, and Convener, Local Area, 1957-58; Director, Royal Highland and Agricultural Society of Scotland, 1968-84; Treasurer, Sprouston Church, 1950-85; Director, Scottish Agricultural Organisation Society, 1965-70; Convener, Border Union Agricultural Society, 1959-60. Recreations: shooting; foxhunting. Address: Redden, Kelso, Roxburghshire, TD5 8HS; T.-089 083 276.

Murray, William Hutchison, OBE. Author and Mountaineer; b. 18.3.13, Liverpool; m., Anne Burnet Clark. Educ. Glasgow Academy. Union Bank of Scotland, until 1939; Captain, HLI, Western Desert (Prisoner of War, 1942-45); Leader, Scottish Himalayan Expedition, 1950; Deputy Leader, Everest Expedition, 1951; Leader, NW Nepal Expedition, 1953; Commissioner, Countryside Commission for Scotland, 1968-80; Mungo Park Medal, RSGS, 1950; Literary Award, USA Education Board, 1954; Honorary Doctorate, Stirling University, 1975. Publications: Mountaineering in Scotland, 1947; Rock Climbs, Glencoe and Ardgour, 1949; Undiscovered Scotland, 1951; Scottish Himalayan Expedition, 1951; Story of Everest, 1953; Five Frontiers, 1959; The Spurs of Troodos, 1960; Maelstrom, 1962; Highland Landscape, 1962; The Hebrides, 1966; Companion Guide to West Highlands, 1968; The Real MacKay, 1969; The Islands of Western Scotland, 1973; The Scottish Highlands, 1976; The Curling Companion, 1981; Rob Roy MacGregor, 1982. Recreations: mountaineering; sailing. Address: Lochwood, Loch Goil, Argyll.

Murray-Smith, Professor David James, MSc, PhD, CEng, FIEE, MInstMC. Titular Professor in Electronics and Electrical Engineering, Glasgow University; b. 20.10.41, Aberdeen; m., Effie Smith; 2 s. Educ. Aberdeen Grammar School; Aberdeen University; Glasgow University. Engineer, Inertial Systems Department, Ferranti Ltd., Edinburgh, 1964-65; Glasgow University: Assistant, Department of Electrical Engineering,

1965-67, Lecturer, 1967-77, Senior Lecturer, 1977-83, Reader, 1983-85. Past Chairman, United Kingdom Simulation Council; Member, various committees, Institution of Electrical Engineers; Advisory Director, Scottish Engineering Training Scheme Ltd. Recreations: hill-walking; photography; strong interest in railways. Address: (b.) Department of Electronics and Electrical Engineering, Glasgow University, Glasgow, G12 8QQ; T.-041-339 8855.

Murrie, Sir William Stuart, GCB (1964), KBE (1952). Permanent Under-Secretary of State for Scotland, 1959-64; b. 19.12.03. Educ. Harris Academy, Dundee; Edinburgh University; Balliol College, Oxford. Chairman, Board of Trustees, National Galleries of Scotland, 1972-75.

Musgrave, Oliver Charles, BSc, PhD. Senior Lecturer in Organic Chemistry, Aberdeen University, since 1966; b. 30.9.25, Hull; m., Margaret Alice Lawrie; 3 s.; 1 d. Educ. Hymers College, Hull; London University: King's College, London. Lecturer in Chemistry, Royal Technical College, Glasgow, 1949-52; Technical Officer, ICI Ltd., Nobel Division, Ayrshire, 1952-57; Lecturer in Organic Chemistry, Aberdeen University, 1958-66. Fellow, Chemical Society, 1945-83; Member, College Committee, Robert Gordon's College, 1973-82; Chairman, Grampian Orienteers, 1980-84. Recreations: orienteering; mountaineering; not watching television. Address: (b.) Chemistry Department, The University, Old Aberdeen, Aberdeen, AB9 2UE; T.-0224 40241.

Musson, John Nicholas Whitaker, MA (Oxon). Warden, Glenalmond College, since 1972; b. 2.10.27; m., Ann Priest; 1 s.; 3 d. Educ. Clifton College; Brasenose College, Oxford. Lt., Lancashire Fusiliers, 1946-48; HM Overseas Civil Service, 1951-59 (District Officer, N. Nigeria and Lecturer, Institute of Administration, Nigeria); British Petroleum Co., London, 1969-60; Assistant Master and Housemaster, Canford School, Dorset, 1961-72. Chairman, Headmasters' Conference (Scottish Division), 1981-83; Governor: Ardvreck School, Crieff, 1975-79, Beaconhurst Grange School, Stirling, since 1980, Belhaven Hill, Dunbar, since 1979, Cargilfield School, Edinburgh, since 1984. Recreations: hill-walking; history; fine arts. Address: (h.) The Warden's House, Glenalmond College, Perthshire, PH1 3RY; T.-Glenalmond 205.

Mutch, Alexander Fyvie, CBE, JP. Member, Grampian Regional Council, since 1974 (first Convener, 1974-82); b. 23.3.24, Aberdeen; m., Freda Mutch; 1 d. Educ. Aberdeen Central School. Convener, Aberdeen Corporation Cleansing Committee, 1963; Vice-Chairman, North-East Water Board, 1968-70; Magistrate, Aberdeen, 1967; Senior Magistrate, 1968; Chairman, Aberdeen Licensing Court, 1968; Member, Aberdeen University Court, 1974-82; Chairman, South Aberdeen Conservative Association, 1964-68 (President, 1968-72); Senior Vice-President, Conservative Party in Scotland, 1972-73 (President, 1973-74); Leader, Conservative Group, Aberdeen Town Council, 1974-75; Governor, Robert Gordon's College, Aberdeen,

1968-70 and since 1974; Honorary President, Grampian-Houston Association; Honorary Citizen, Houston, Texas. Address: (h.) 28 Salisbury Terrace, Aberdeen; T.-Aberdeen 591520.

Mutch, Fraser, MB, ChB, MRCPath. Senior Registrar in Histopathology, University Department of Pathology, Glasgow Royal Infirmary, since 1981; Honorary Clinical Teacher, Glasgow University, since 1983; b. 2.6.54, Coatbridge. Educ. Coatbridge High School; Glasgow University. Recreations: running; music; theatre. Address: (b.) Department of Pathology, Glasgow Royal Infirmary, Castle Street, Glasgow; T.-041-552 3535, Ext. 4452.

Mutch, John Renwick, MIQ. Director, Aberdeen Construction Group, since 1969; Director, Granite Supply Association, since 1979; b. 7.1.30, Aberdeen; m., Rhoda Argo; 2 s.; 1 d. Educ. Aberdeen Grammar School. Recreations: golf; curling; shooting; fishing. Address: (b.) Whitemyres Avenue, Mastrick, Aberdeen; T.-0224 691333.

Mutch, Robert Alexander, BSc, MSc, MCIBSE. Senior Lecturer, Department of Building, Heriot-Watt University; b. 14.3.33, Edinburgh; m., Maureen Isabel; 1 s.; 1 d. Educ. Broughton Senior Secondary School; Edinburgh University. Teacher: Niddrie Mill Primary School, 1957-60, Edinburgh School of Building and Crafts, 1961-64; Lecturer/Senior Lecturer in Building Science, Department of Building, Heriot-Watt College/University, since 1964. Recreations: reading; badminton. Address: (h.) 22 Duddingston Park, Edinburgh, EH15 1JX; T.-031-669 6735.

Myers, Terence Frederick, BSc, PhD. Senior Lecturer in Psychology and Cognitive Science, Edinburgh University, since 1985; b. 3.4.38, London; m., Helen. Educ. Shooters Hill, London; University College, London. Lecturer in Psychology, Reading University, 1966-68; Research Officer, MRC Speech and Communication Unit, Edinburgh University, 1968-69; Lecturer in Psychology, Edinburgh University, 1969-85 (Academic Secretary, School of Epistemics, since 1982, and Director of Postgraduate Studies in Cognitive Science, since 1985). Publications: The Development of Conversation and Discourse, 1979; The Cognitive Representation of Speech (Co-author), 1981; Reasoning and Discourse Processes (Co-author), 1985. Recreations: music; hill-walking; sailing; skiing. Address: (h.) 19 Ann Street, Edinburgh, EH4 1PL; T.-031-343 2904.

Myles, David Fairlie. Hill Farmer; Member, North of Scotland Hydro-Electric Board, since 1985; Member, Angus District Council, since 1984; Member, Angus Tourist Board, since 1984; Chairman, Dairy Produce Quota Tribunal for Scotland, since 1984; b. 30.5.25, Cortachy, Kirriemuir; m., Janet I. Gall; 2 s.; 2 d. Educ. Brechin High School. Auctioneer's clerk, 1941-43; Royal Marines, 1943-46; Tenant Hill Farmer, since 1946; Director of auction company, 1963-81; Member, Transport Users Consultative Committee for Scotland, 1973-79; Council

Member, NFU of Scotland, 1970-79 (Convener, Organisation and Publicity Committee, 1976-79); Member, Meat Promotion Executive, MLC, 1975-79; Chairman, North Angus and Mearns Constituency Conservative Party, 1971-74; MP (Conservative), Banff, 1979-83; Joint Secretary, Backbench Conservative Agriculture Committee, 1979-83; Secretary, Backbench Conservative European Committee, 1980-83; Member, Select Committee on Agriculture and Select Committee on European Legislation, 1979-83. Recreations: curling; traditional Scottish fiddle music; works of Robert Burns. Address: (h.) Dalbog, Edzell, Brechin, Angus, DD9 7UU; T.-035 64 265.

Myles, Richard, MA (Hons). Rector, Galashiels Academy, since 1974; b. 12.9.26, Denny; m., Janet Mary Anderson (deceased); 1 s. Educ. Denny High School; Glasgow University. Intelligence Corps, Middle East and East Africa, 1945-48. Assistant Teacher of Modern Languages: Grangemouth High School, 1951-55, High School of Stirling, 1955-60, Denny High School, 1960-62; Principal Teacher of Modern Languages: Bathgate Academy, 1962-66, Falkirk High School, 1966-71; Depute Rector, Falkirk High School, 1971-73. Recreations: golf; curling; gardening. Address: (b.) The Academy, Galashiels; T.-0896 4788.

Myles, Thomas Hope Fenton, NP. Solicitor, since 1938; Honorary Sheriff of Tayside Central and Fife, at Perth, since 1982; b. 4.11.16, Kilspindie; m., Marion Merle Elizabeth Leppard; 1 s.; 2 d. Educ. Perth Academy; Edinburgh University. Legal Assistant, 1938-39; RAF, 1939-45; Partner, Campbell, Brooke & Myles, Solicitors, Perth, 1945-82. Recreation: Shetland pony breeding. Address: (h.) Newfargie House, Gateside, Strathmiglo, Fife; T.-05773 339.

N

Nandy, Kashinath, BSc, MSc (Calcutta), MSc (Edinburgh), PhD, FRSE. Deputy Chief Scientific Officer, Royal Observatory, Edinburgh since 1977; b. 1.12.27, Santipur, West Bengal, India; m., Smritilekha; 1 d. Educ. Calcutta University; Edinburgh University. Observatory Assistant, Presidency College Observatory, Calcutta, 1952-59; received International Astronomical Union Grant for Studies Abroad, 1959-60; held Robert Cormack Bequest Fellowship (Royal Society of Edinburgh), 1960-63; Royal Observatory, Edinburgh: Research Fellow, 1963-68, Principal Scientific Officer, 1968-72, Senior Principal Scientific Officer, 1972-77. Fellow, Royal Astronomical Society; Member, International Astronomical Union; Honorary Fellow, Edinburgh University, since 1973; Honorary Research Fellow, University College, London, since 1979; elected Fellow, Royal Society of Liege, 1980. Recreations: reading; travel; photography; surfing. Address: (h.) 36 West Mains Road, Edinburgh, EH9 3BG; T.-031-667 6131.

Naumann, Laurie M. Director, Scottish Council for Single Homeless, since 1978; b. 1943, Saffron Walden; m., Barbara; 2 s.; 2 d. Educ. Edinburgh, Gloucester and Nuremberg Rudolf Steiner; Leicester University. Furniture maker, Gloucestershire; Probation and After Care Officer, Leeds; Social Worker, Edinburgh. Council of Europe Social Fellowship to Finland to study services for the drunken offender, 1976; jointly won Rosemary Delbridge Memorial Trophy for influencing Parliament to legislate, 1983. Recreations: travel; reading; walking; woodwork. Address: (h.) 22 Pettycur Road, Kinghorn, Fife, KY3 9RL; T.-0592 890346.

Naylor, Graham John, MB, ChB, BSc, DPM, MD, FRCPsych. Reader in Psychiatry, Dundee University, since 1980; Honorary Consultant, Royal Dundee Liff Hospital, since 1970; b. 13.2.40, Sheffield; m., Pamela Hilda Moody. Educ. Firth Park Grammar School, Sheffield; Sheffield University. Consultant Psychiatrist, Royal Dundee Liff Hospital, 1970-72; Senior Lecturer, Department of Psychiatry, Dundee University, 1972-80. Address: (b.) Department of Psychiatry, Ninewells Hospital and Medical School, Dundee; T.-Dundee 60111.

Needham, Ted, PhD, BSc, ARCS, DIC, MIBiol. Fish Farmer; Director, Landcatch Ltd. and Pairc Salmon Ltd. (Lewis); Honorary Research Fellow, Aberdeen University; Member, Secretary of State for Scotland's Fisheries Committee; Member, Kincardine and Deeside District Council; b. 7.7.43, Skipton, Yorkshire; m., Jane; 1 s.; 2 d. Educ. Tonbridge School, Kent; Edinburgh University; Imperial College, London. Kincardine County Councillor, 1973-75; Kincardine and Deeside District Councillor, 1974-77 and since 1979 (Chairman, Environmental Health, Leisure and Recreation Committee); Member, Grampian Region Agriculture and Fisheries Committee; Chairman, Scottish Fish Farmers Association, 1976-77; Convener, Fish Farming Committee, National Farmers Union of Scotland, 1977-79; Consultant to Hayes McCubbin Macfarlane, Aberdeen, Highlands and Islands Development Board, Orkney Islands; Columnist, Fish Farmer Magazine; part-time Lecturer, Stirling University, Inverness Technical College. Recreations: skiing; beef cattle; talking. Address: Home Farm, Maryculter, Aberdeen, AB1 OBA; T.-0224 732310.

Neil, Alex., MA (Hons). Director, Cumnock and Doon Enterprise Trust, since 1984; b. 22.8.51, Irvine; m., Isabella Kerr; 1 s. Educ. Dalmellington High School; Ayr Academy; Dundee University. Scottish Research Officer, Labour Party, 1974-76; General Secretary, Scottish Labour Party, 1976-78; Business Manager, Digital Equipment Corporation, 1978-83; Marketing Manager, Future Technology Systems, 1983-84. Recreations: golf; gardening; reading. Address: (h.) Rowallan, Hillside, Patna, Ayrshire; T.-0292 531480.

Neill, Alistair, MA, MS, FFA, FIA, FCII, FPMI. Assistant General Manager, Scottish Widows Fund, since 1977; Honorary Treasurer, Faculty of Actuaries, since 1984; b. 18.11.32, Edinburgh; m., Mary Margaret; 1 s.; 2 d. Educ. George Watson's College; Edinburgh University; Wisconsin University. Actuary in various posts, Scottish Widows Fund. Publication: Life Contingencies, 1977. Recreations: golf; squash; curling. Address: (h.) 24 Bonaly Crescent, Edinburgh; T.-031-441 2038.

Neill, David Lindsay. Master Mariner; Ship's Captain, since 1973; Captain, P.S. Waverley, since 1975; b. 21.5.44, Glasgow; m., Jean Shaw Thompson McLachlan; 1 s.; 2 d. Educ. various schools; Glasgow School of Nautical Studies. Deck Apprentice, 1960-64; Ship's Navigating Officer, 1964-70; Ferry Manager (Isle of Skye), 1970-71; Ship's Navigating Officer, 1971-73. Life Member, Paddle Steamer Preservation Society. Recreations: out of door. Address: (b.) Waverley Excursions Ltd., Anderston Quay, Glasgow, G3 8HA; T.-041-221 8152.

Neill, Gordon Webster McCash, DSO, SSC, NP, FInstD. Solicitor and Notary Public; Honorary Sheriff, since 1981; b. Arbroath; m., Margaret Mary Lamb; 1 s.; 1 d. Educ. Edinburgh Academy. Legal apprenticeship, 1937-39; Pilot, RAF, 1939-46 (DSO, French Croix de Guerres with silver gilt star and silver star); Partner, Neill & Gibb, SSC, 1947; Chairman, Dundee Area Board, British Law Insurance Co. Ltd., 1954; Principal, Neill & Mackintosh, SSC, 1967; Past Chairman, Scottish Gliding Association and Angus Gliding Clubs Ltd.; Past President, Chamber of Commerce, Arbroath Rotary Club and Society of Solicitors and Procurators in Angus. Recreations: gliding; powered flying; shooting; fishing. Address: (b.) 93 High Street, Arbroath, Angus, DD11 1DS; T.-0241 73314.

Neill, Rev. William George, MA, BD. Minister, North Leith, Edinburgh, since 1980; b. 19.8.45, Edinburgh; m., Marjory Joyce Reid; 2 s.; 2 d. Educ. George Heriot's School; Edinburgh University. Assistant Minister, Crown Court Church, London, 1970-71; Minister: Blackbraes and Shieldhill, Falkirk, 1971-75, Scotstoun East, Glasgow, 1975-80; Editor, The Record (Journal, Church Service Society), 1982-86. Recreations: hill-walking; photography; music; jogging. Address: (h.) The Manse of North Leith, 6 Craighall Gardens, Leith, Edinburgh, EH6 4RJ; T.-031-552 4411.

Neill, William Wilson, MA (Hons). Poet; b. 22.2.22, Prestwick; m., Doris Marie; 2 d. (by pr m.). Educ. Ayr Academy; Edinburgh University. Served, RAF; won Stevenson Verse Prize and Grierson Verse Prize while at Edinburgh University; Teacher; crowned Bard, Aviemore Mod, 1969; former Editor, Catalyst; Editor, Lallans (Scots Language magazine); broadcasts, essays in Scotland's three tongues. Publications: Scotland's Castle, 1969; Poems, 1970; Four Points of a Saltire (Co-author), 1970; Despatches Home, 1972; Buile Shuibhne, 1974; Galloway Landscape: Poems, 1981; Cnu a Mogaill: Poems, 1983; Wild Places: Poems, 1985. Address: (h.) Burnside, Crossmichael, Castle Douglas, DG7 3AP; T.-055-667 265.

Neilson, Douglas Gourlay, BSc, PhD, MRSC. Senior Lecturer in Organic Chemistry, Dundee University, since 1969; b. 4.7.30, Dundee; m.,

Grace Christine Goddard; 1 s.; 1 d. Educ. Morgan Academy, Dundee; University College, Dundee; St. Andrews University. Chemistry Master, Bell-Baxter High School, Cupar, 1956-58; Queen's College, Dundee: Assistant Lecturer in Chemistry, 1958-60, Edward A. Deeds Research Fellow and Honorary Lecturer, 1960-62, Lecturer in Chemistry, 1962-69. Marriage Guidance Cousellor and Tutor, Scottish Marriage Guidance Council. Address: (b.) Department of Chemistry, Dundee University, Dundee, DD1 4HN; T.-Dundee 23181, Ext. 4324.

Neilson, William, MA, LLB. Senior Legal Officer, Scottish Office, since 1976; b. 10.2.42, Airdrie; m., Celia Ward; 1 d. Educ. Airdrie Academy; Glasgow University. Procurator Fiscal Depute, 1969-73; admitted to Faculty of Advocates, 1974. Recreations: photography; model shipbuilding; cycling. Address: (h.) 1 East Clapperfield, Edinburgh, EH16; T.-031-664 0595.

Nelson, David Murray, MA, MSc, ABPsS. Senior Lecturer in Psychology, Edinburgh University, since 1979; Partner, Personnel Research Services, since 1977; b. 26.10.34, London; m., Frances Patricia Hamilton-Meikle; 2 s.; 1 d. Educ. Lower School of John Lyon, Harrow; St. Edmund Hall, Oxford; Birkbeck College, London. Assistant Lecturer, Birmingham College of Advanced Technology, 1960-61; Senior Research Officer, London School of Economics, 1962-68; Lecturer in Psychology, Edinburgh University, 1968-79. Chairman, Cystic Fibrosis Research Trust (Edinburgh and SE Scotland), 1976-82; Chairman, Fife Area Social Democratic Party, 1981-83. Recreations: opera; music; travel. Address: (h.) Stripeside, Crombie Point, Dunfermline, Fife; T.-0383 880292.

Nelson, John, TD, JP, DL. Convener, Stewartry District Council, since 1976; Vice Chairman, Solway River Purification Board, since 1980; b. 26.12.18, Irongray, Dumfries; m., Margaret M.C. Shedden; 4 s. Educ. Castle Douglas High School. Farming, 1934-84, except for War years spent with Royal Artillery and Indian Mountain Artillery in Burma; NFU Committee Member, 40 years (Chairman, Stewartry Area, 1960-61); County Councillor, 1971-74; appointed Deputy Lieutenant, 1983. Recreation: horse riding. Address: (h.) Greentop, 4 Castle View, Castle Douglas; T.-Castle Douglas 3143.

Neumann, Jan, CBE, BSc, FEng, FIMechE, FIMarE, MIES, MASME. Managing Director, YARD Ltd., since 1978; Director, Yarrow PLC, since 1978; b. 26.6.24, Prague; m., Barbara Joyce Gove; 2 s. Educ. Friends' School, Great Ayton; London University. Flight Engineer, RAF; Design Engineer, English Electric Co., Rugby; various engineering design and management positions in Admiralty Research Department, Yarrow; received Denny Gold Medal, IMarE, and Thomas Lowe Gray Prize, IMechE. Recreations: swimming; bowls. Address: (b.) YARD Ltd., Charing Cross Tower, Glasgow, G2 4PP; T.-041-204 2737.

Neville, Professor Adam Matthew, DSc, DSc (Eng), PhD, FICE, FIStructE, FCIArb, FRSE. Principal and Vice-Chancellor, Dundee

University, since 1978; Consultant on structural problems; b. 5.2.23; m., Mary; 1 s.; 1 d. Civil Engineer in design and construction; Academic Engineer at several Universities; Dean of Engineering, Calgary University, 1963-67; Head, Department of Civil Engineering, Leeds University, 1968-78. Publications: seven books on concrete, structural analysis and statistics, and numerous research and technical papers. Address: (b.) University of Dundee, Dundee, DD1 4HN.

Newall, Stephen Park. Chairman, Kanthal Limited, since 1980; Chairman, Bulten Limited, since 1980; Chairman, NSC Cartons Limited since 1982; b. 12.4.31, Bearsden, Dunbartonshire; m., Gay Sommerville Craig; 4 s.; 1 d. Educ. Loretto. Commissioned and served with Parachute Regiment, National Service, 1949-51; Sales Manager, A.P. Newall & Co., 1951-57; Managing Director, Bulten-Kanthal Stephen Newall Co. Ltd., 1957-80. Chairman, Epilepsy Association of Scotland, since 1982; Chairman, Finance Committee, University of Strathclyde, since 1985; Council Member, Quarrier's Homes, since 1983; Council Member, Scottish Business School, since 1983; Member, Industry Committee, Scottish Council (Development and Industry), since 1982; Deacon Convener, Trades of Glasgow, 1983-84. Recreations: hill-walking; sailing; music. Address: (h.) Rowaleyn, Rhu, Dunbartonshire; T.-0436 820 521.

Newbould, Peter, BSc, BAgr, DPhil. Head, Plants and Soils Department, Hill Farming Research Organisation, since 1970; b. 24.9.31, Lincoln; m., Doreen Wilson; 1 s.; 1 d. Educ. Priory School, Shrewsbury; Queen's University, Belfast; Lincoln College, Oxford. Research Assistant, Department of Agriculture, Oxford University; ARC Radiobiological Laboratory (subsequently Letcombe Laboratory): Scientific Officer, Senior Scientific Officer, Principal Scientific Officer, Head of Field Studies Section; Senior Principal Scientific Officer, Plants and Soils Department, Hill Farming Research Organisation; Convener, Plant Microbial Interactions Group, Association of Applied Biologists; Member, Editorial Board, Journal of the Science of Food and Agriculture. Recreations: squash; tennis; gardening; photography; reading; amateur dramatics. Address: (b.) Bush Estate, Penicuik, Midlothian, EH26 0PY; T.-031-445 3401.

Newell, Professor Alan F., BSc, PhD, MIEE, CEng. NCR Professor of Electronics and Microcomputer Systems, Dundee University, since 1980 (Director, Dundee University Microcomputer Centre, since 1980); b. 1.3.41, Birmingham; m., Margaret; 1 s.; 2 d. Educ. St. Philip's Grammar School; Birmingham University. Research Engineer, Standard Telecommunication Laboratories; Lecturer, Department of Electronics, Southampton University. Recreations: family life; horse riding. Address: (b.) Microcomputer Centre, The University, Dundee, DD1 4HN; T.-Dundee 23181.

Newis, Kenneth, CB, CVO, MA. Chairman, Queen's Hall (Edinburgh) Ltd.; Chairman, Edinvar Housing Association; Member, Historic

Buildings Council for Scotland; Council Member, Cockburn Association; Director, Scottish Baroque Ensemble Ltd.; Governor, Royal Scottish Academy of Music and Drama; b. 9.11.16, Crewe; m., Kathleen Barrow; 2 d. Educ. Manchester Grammar School; St. John's College, Cambridge. HM Office of Works, London, 1938-70; Under Secretary, Scottish Development Department, 1970-73 (Secretary, 1973-76). Recreation: music. Address: (h.) 11 Abbotsford Park, Edinburgh, EH10 5DZ; T.-031-447 4138.

Newlands, William Jeffrey, MB, ChB, FRCSEdin. Consultant Ear, Nose and Throat Surgeon, Grampian Health Board, since 1981; Clinical Senior Lecturer in Otolaryngology, Aberdeen University, since 1981; b. 9.9.29, Edinburgh; m., Patricia Kathleen St. Quintin Gee; 2 s.; 2 d. Educ. Daniel Stewart's College, Edinburgh; Edinburgh University. Captain, RAMC, 1953-55; specialist training, 1958-65, Edinburgh Royal Infirmary, Western Infirmary, Glasgow, Royal National Throat, Nose and Ear Hospital, London; Otolaryngologist, Brown Clinic, Calgary, 1966; Consultant ENT Surgeon: Grampian Health Board, 1967-77, County Hospital, Uddevalla, Sweden, 1977-78, Lothian Health Board, 1978-79; Professor of Otolaryngology, King Faisal University College of Medicine, Saudi Arabia, 1979-81. Examiner in Otolaryngology, Part 2 Examination, FRCSEdin. Recreations: travel; music. Address: (h.) 4 Camperdown Road, Aberdeen, AB2 4NU; T.-0224 633784.

Newton, Professor Kenneth, BA, PhD. Professor of Political Science, Dundee University, since 1978; b. 15.4.40, London; m., Diana Smith; 1 s.; 2 d. Educ. Reigate Grammar School; Exeter University; Cambridge University. Lecturer, Birmingham University; Research Fellow, Nuffield College, Oxford; Visiting Professor, Pittsburgh University and Madison University. ACLS Research Fellowship to USA. Publications: various books on political science. Recreations: arguing about almost anything, except cricket and football. Address: (b.) Department of Political Science and Social Policy, The University, Dundee; T.-Dundee 23181.

Newton, Lucy Joy, BA, PhD. Senior Lecturer in French, Glasgow University, since 1981; b. Nottingham. Educ. Mundella Grammar School; Leeds University; University College, London. Instructor in French Language and Literature, Wellesley College, Massachusetts, 1964-66; Assistant Lecturer, Leicester University, 1966-67; Lecturer, Glasgow University, 1967-81. Fulbright Scholar, 1964-66; Research Awards from British Academy, French Government, Mellon Foundation, Leverhulme, British Council and Carnegie Trust for Scotland. Recreations: travelling; yoga; films; cats. Address: (b.) Department of French, Glasgow University, G12 8QL; T.-041-339 8855, Ext. 593.

Nicholson, (Charles) Gordon (Brown), QC, MA, LLB. Commissioner, Scottish Law Commission, since 1982; b. 11.9.35, Edinburgh; m., Hazel Mary Nixon; 2 s. Educ. George Watson's College, Edinburgh; Edinburgh University. Admitted to Faculty of Advocates, 1961; Advocate Depute,

1968-70; Sheriff of Dumfries and Galloway, at Dumfries, 1970-76; Sheriff of Lothian and Borders, at Edinburgh, 1976-82. Honorary Vice President, Scottish Association for the Study of Delinquency. Publication: The Law and Practice of Sentencing in Scotland, 1981. Recreations: music; philately. Address: (h.) 1A Abbotsford Park, Edinburgh, EH10 5DX; T.-031-447 4300.

Nicholson, Rev. William. Minister, Banchory Ternan East and Durris, since 1969; General Trustee, Church of Scotland, since 1973; b. 18.10.19, Edinburgh; m., Isabella Tilley; 3 d. Educ. Broughton Secondary School, Edinburgh; Edinburgh University. Apprentice Motor Engineer, 1934-40; Royal Artillery, 1940-45; divinity course, 1945-49; Minister: Cowdenbeath Cairns, 1949-55, Methven, 1955-59, St. Philip's, Joppa, Edinburgh, 1959-69. Clerk, Kincardine and Deeside Presbytery, 1970-82 (Moderator, 1984); Moderator, Synod of Grampian, 1983-85. Recreations: gardening; swimming; stamp collecting. Address: Maybank, 33 Station Road, Banchory, AB3 3XX; T.-Banchory 2109.

Nickson, David Wigley, CBE (1981), DL, CBIM. Chairman, Scottish and Newcastle Breweries plc, since 1983; Chairman, Countryside Commission for Scotland, since 1983; Director, General Accident Fire and Life Assurance Corporation plc; Director, Clydesdale Bank; Director, Edinburgh Investment Trust; Deputy President, CBI, since 1985; b. 27.11.29, Eton; m., Helen Louise Cockcraft; 3 d. Educ. Eton College; Royal Military Academy, Sandhurst. Commissioned, Coldstream Guards, 1949-54; William Collins: joined, 1954, Director, 1961-85, Joint Managing Director, 1967, Vice-Chairman, 1976-83, Group Managing Director, 1979-82; Director: Scottish United Investors plc, 1970-83, Radio Clyde Ltd., 1982-85; Chairman, Pan Books, 1982-83. Member: Scottish Industrial Development Advisory Board, 1975-80, Scottish Economic Council, since 1980, Scottish Committee, Design Council, 1978-81; Chairman, CBI in Scotland, 1979-81; Vice Chairman, Management Committee, Atlantic Salmon Trust, since 1982; Member, Queen's Bodyguard for Scotland (Royal Company of Archers); Deputy Lieutenant, Stirling and Falkirk, since 1982. Recreations: fishing; bird-watching; the countryside. Address: (h.) Renagour, Aberfoyle, Stirling, FK8 3TF; T.-Aberfoyle 275.

Nicol, Rev. Douglas Alexander Oag, MA, BD (Hons). Minister, St. Columba Church, Kilmacolm, since 1982; b. 5.4.48, Dunfermline; m., Anne Wilson Gillespie; 1 s.; 1 d. Educ. Kirkcaldy High School; Edinburgh University; Glasgow University. Assistant Warden, St. Ninian's Centre, Crieff, 1972-76; Minister, Lochside, Dumfries, 1976-82. Chairman, Board of Directors, National Bible Society of Scotland, since 1983; Convener, Evangelism Committee, Church of Scotland, since 1982. Recreations: hill-walking; marathon running. Address: 6 Churchill Road, Kilmacolm, Renfrewshire; T.-Kilmacolm 3271.

Nicol, Malcolm. Member, Falkirk District Council, since 1983; b. 22.4.56, Great Harwood. Educ. Grangemouth High School; Falkirk College of

Technology. Vice-Chairman, Stirling, Falkirk and Grangemouth Conservative Association, 1978-83; Vice-Chairman, Falkirk East Conservative and Unionist Association, since 1983; Member, Central and Southern Area Executive, Scottish Conservative and Unionist Association. Recreation: collecting 19th century Staffordshire figures. Address: (h.) Killin, 14 Carronflats Road, Grangemouth; T.-Grangemouth 471545.

Nicol, Rev. Thomas James Trail, LVO, MBE, MC, MA, DD. Minister, Church of Scotland; Extra Chaplain to the Queen, since 1979; b. 24.1.17, Skelmorlie, Ayrshire; m., Mary Barnfather Taylor; 2 d. Educ. Edinburgh Academy; Dundee High School; Glasgow Academy; Aberdeen Grammar School; Aberdeen University. OCTU and Commission, Black Watch, 1939-42; ordained as Chaplain to the Forces, 1942; RAChD, 1942-46, attached 51 (H) Division; Minister, St. Luke's, Broughty Ferry, 1946-49; regular commission, RAChD, 1949-72; Assistant Chaplain-General, HQ Scotland, 1967-72; Minister, Crathie, 1972-77; Domestic Chaplain in Scotland to the Queen, 1972-79. Recreations: hill-walking; fishing; golf. Address: (h.) Foxknowe, St. Fillans, Perthshire, PH6 2NG; T.-076 485 210.

Nicol, William, MBE, BSc, FCIOB, FInstR. Chairman and Managing Director, Craig-Nicol Limited; b. 9.9.24, Glasgow; m., Margaret Jean McNeill; 2 s.; 1 d. Educ. High School of Glasgow; Gresham House; Glasgow University. President, Glasgow Master Wrights and Builders' Association, 1953-54; Chairman, Glasgow Local Joint Apprenticeship Committee, 1952-61; Chairman, Scottish Building Apprenticeship Council, 1959-67; Member, Board of Governors, Jordanhill College of Education, 1959-67; Deacon, Incorporation of Wrights in Glasgow, 1963-64; Director, Glasgow Chamber of Commerce, 1965-70 (Chairman, Education Committee); Founder Chairman, Scottish Branch, Chartered Institute of Building, 1963-65 (National President, 1970-71, Honorary Treasurer, 1972-76); Member, Construction Industry Training Board, 1964-85 (Chairman, Building Committee, 1967-72); President, Scottish National Federation of Building Trades' Employers, 1969-70 and 1972-73; Governor, Glasgow College of Building and Printing, 1966-75 (first Chairman, Board of Governors) and Vice-Chairman, then Chairman, new College Council, 1976-82; Vice-Chairman, Scottish Technical Education Council, 1973-78 (Chairman, since 1978); Chairman, British Refrigeration and Air Conditioning Association, 1975-77; Chairman, Commercial Section, CECOMAF, 1974-77 (President, CECOMAF, 1979-83); Committee Member, Scottish Branch, Institute of Refrigeration, 1977-81 (elected Vice-Chairman, 1979); Member, Heating, Ventilating, Air Conditioning and Refrigeration Equipment - Economic Development Committee, NEDO, since 1984. Recreations: gardening; walking; reading; golf. Address: (b.) Craig-Nicol Limited, Rosyth Road, Glasgow, G5 OXZ; T.-041-429 5101.

Nicoll, Albert, FEIS, MA (Hons). Honorary Sheriff, Stornoway; b. 9.10.02, Edinburgh; m., Alexina MacLean; 1 d. Educ. George Heriot's School; Broughton Secondary School; Edinburgh University. Nicolson Institute, Stornoway: Principal Teacher of History and Geography, 1927, Head, Continuation Classes, 1939-59, Deputy and Acting Rector, 1960-68; Economics Lecturer, WEA, 1941; first CO, No. 1731 Squadron, ATC, 1942-45; Captain, Stornoway Boys' Brigade, 1941-45; Senior ARP Warden, 1939-45; elected, Stornoway Town Council, 1952; former Member: Stornoway Trust and Pier and Harbour Commission; Member, Ross and Cromarty County Council, 1968-72; Chairman, Lewis Liberal Party; Past Chairman: Lewis Education Committee, Lewis and Harris Museum Committee; first Chairman: Lewis and Harris Health Council, Lewis Council of Social Service; Member, Western Isles Island Council, until 1978; awarded Queen's Jubilee Medal. Coached successful Nicolson Institute team in Top of the Form, 1954. Recreations: football (both codes); reading; gardening. Address: (h.) Eildon, 9 Jamieson Drive, Stornoway, Isle of Lewis; T.-Stornoway 2026.

Nicoll, Douglas Alexander Smith, JP. Honorary Sheriff, Forfar; b. 24.6.18, Forfar; m., Ella Mary Grant; 1 s.; 2 d. Educ. Forfar Academy. Partner, joinery manufacturing firm, Forfar, from 1936; Managing Director and Chairman upon retirement, 1972; Member, Forfar Town Council, seven years; served on Magistrates' Bench, three years; served on Steering Committee for Community Councils in Angus; Elder, Church of Scotland. Recreations: music; bowling. Address: (h.) Dunvegan, 11 Turfbeg Avenue, Forfar, DD8 3LJ; T.-0307 63232.

Nicoll, Eric Hamilton, CBE, FSA Scot, BSc (Hons), FICE, FInstWPC (Dip.), FIPHE. Deputy Chief Engineer, Scottish Development Department, 1976-85; b. 15.5.25, Edinburgh; m., Helen Elizabeth Barnes; 1 s.; 1 d. Educ. George Heriot's School, Edinburgh; Edinburgh University. Engineering Assistant: Midlothian County Council Roads Department, 1945-46, Edinburgh Corporation Water Department, 1946-51; Chief Assistant County Engineer, Midlothian County Council, 1951-62; Scottish Development Department: Engineering Inspector, 1962-68, Senior Engineering Inspector, 1968-72, Assistant Chief Engineer, 1972-75. Recreations: wood sculpture; music; antiquities. Address: (h.) 35 Wardie Road, Edinburgh, EH5 3LJ.

Nicoll, John Duncan Valentine. Director of Housing and Property, Kincardine and Deeside District Council, since 1979; b. 9.9.38, Dundee; m., Alice; 2 d. Educ. Harris Academy, Dundee. Housing Manager, Carnoustie Town Council, 1969-75; Area Housing Manager, Forfar and Kirriemuir, Angus District Council, 1975; Depute Director of Housing, East Lothian District Council, 1975-79. Recreations: badminton; swimming; curling. Address: (b.) 16/22 Allardice Street, Stonehaven, AB3 2BQ; T.-0569 62001.

Nicoll, William Steele McDiarmid, MA, PhD. Senior Lecturer, Department of Humanity, Edinburgh University, since 1984 (Head, Department of Humanity, since 1982); b. 14.11.36, Edinburgh; m., Alison Beatrice Coombs; 1 s.; 2

d. Educ. Edinburgh Academy; Corpus Christi, Cambridge. National Service, Royal Navy, 1955-57 (Russian interpreter); Research Student, then Research Fellow, Corpus Christi College, Cambridge; Lecturer, Department of Humanity, Edinburgh University, 1963-84. Recreations: walking; angling. Address: (h.) 6 Ainslie Place, Edinburgh; T.-031-225 7467.

Nicolson, Alasdair George, MA (Hons). Assistant Principal, Jordanhill College of Education, since 1976; b. 6.12.26, Stepps, Lanarkshire; m., Sylvia Hall; 1 d. Educ. Coatbridge High School; Glasgow University. Teacher/Principal, Modern Studies and History, Airdrie High School, 1951-61; Lecturer in Modern Studies, then Head, Modern Studies Department, Jordanhill College of Education, 1961-76; Principal Examiner, Modern Studies, SCEEB, 1965-74; Member, BBC Schools Broadcasting Council Advisory Committee, 1968-74; Member, STV Education Advisory Committee, since 1981; Member, Scottish Central Committee Social Subjects, 1974-81; Chairman, Scottish Council, United Nations Association, since 1982; Chairman, Saltire Education Committee, 1970-76; Chairman, Association of Lecturers in Colleges of Education in Scotland, 1969-72; Chairman, Association for Liberal Education, 1969-72; Executive Member, Council for Education in the Commonwealth, since 1979; Founder Member, Scottish Environmental Education Council; Chairman, West of Scotland District, WEA, since 1982. Publications: The Cold War, 1972; World Today (Co-author); Europe Today (Co-author). Recreations: swimming; travel. Address: (h.) 12 Somerford Road, Bearsden, Glasgow, G61 1AS; T.-041-942 4933.

Nimmo, Ian Alister. Editor, Evening News, Edinburgh, since 1976; b. 14.10.34, Lahore, Pakistan; m., Grace; 2 s.; 1 d. Educ. Royal School of Dunkeld; Breadalbane Academy. Commissioned, Royal Scots Fusiliers; Reporter, Sub-Editor, D.C. Thomson, Dundee, 1957; Editor, Weekly Scotsman, Edinburgh, 1961; Features Editor, Press and Journal, Aberdeen, 1966; Editor, Evening Gazette, Middlesbrough, 1970. Vice-President, Newspaper Press Fund. Publications: Robert Burns; Portrait of Edinburgh; The Brave Adventure. Recreations: climbing; fly fishing; gardening; painting. Address: (b.) 20 North Bridge, Edinburgh, EH1 1YT; T.-031-225 2468.

Nisbet, Florence Mary, SRN, HV, NNEB. Community Nursing Officer, since 1974; Member, Borders Health Board, since 1983; b. 29.10.31, Monifieth, Dundee; m., Alexander A. Nisbet; 1 s.; 4 d. Educ. Morgan Academy, Dundee. NNEB, Public Health, Dundee, 1948; SRN, Edinburgh Royal Infirmary, 1950-54; Staff Nurse, Western General Hospital, 1970-72; Obstetrics, Simpson Maternity Hospital, Edinburgh, 1971; Health Visitor: Queen Margaret College, Edinburgh, 1972-73, Midlothian District, 1973-75. Chairman, Scottish Health Visitors Association, Borders, 1983-85; Member, Executive, Age Concern Scotland, 1984-85; Member, Liaison Committee, DHSS Galashiels, 1984-85; Secretary, Age Concern Group, Peebles; Chairman, Muscular

Dystrophy Group, Peebles. Recreations: writing children's stories; reading; walking; Open University. Address: (b.) Hay Lodge Health Centre, Neidpath Road, Peebles; T.-Peebles 22080.

Nisbet, Professor John Donald, OBE, MA, BEd, PHD, FEIS, FRSA. Professor of Education, Aberdeen University, since 1963; b. 17.10.22, Rosyth; 1 s.; 1 d. Educ. Dunfermline High School; Edinburgh University; Aberdeen University. RAF, 1943-46; Teacher, 1946-48; Lecturer, 1949-63; Visiting Professor, San Jose, 1961, 1964, Monash, Australia, 1974, Walkato, New Zealand, 1978. Chairman: Educational Research Board, 1972-75, Scottish Committee on Primary Education, 1974-80, Scottish Council for Research in Education, 1975-78; President, British Educational Research Association, 1975; Editor, British Journal of Educational Psychology, 1967-74; Editor, Studies in Higher Education, 1979-84; Editor, World Yearbook of Education, 1985. Recreations: golf; orienteering. Address: (h.) 5 The Chanonry, Aberdeen, AB2 1RP; T.-0224 44375.

Nisbet, Nanette Hendry, MD, FRCPGlas. Consultant Geriatrician, Highland Health Board, since 1971; b. 21.5.25, Glasgow. Educ. Glasgow High School for Girls; Glasgow University. Address: (h.) 28 Broadstone Park, Inverness.

Niven, David, JP. Leader, Conservative Group, North East Fife District Council, since 1984; b. 28.10.14, St. Andrews; m., Jessie Isabella Miller; 1 s.; 1 d. Educ. Madras College, St. Andrews. Elected to St. Andrews Town Council, 1951; Magistrate, 1959; Provost, 1970; elected to North East Fife District Council, 1974; Chairman, 1980; Chairman, St. Andrews and North East Fife District Tourist Board, since 1983; President, Saint Andrews Society of St. Andrews; Chairman, St. Andrews Harbour Trust. Recreations: golf; photography. Address: (h.) 7 John Street, St. Andrews, Fife, KY16 9DB; T.-St. Andrews 74387.

Niven, Peter Stuart Buchanan, LLB. Deputy Secretary, Law Society of Scotland, since 1984; b. 18.8.57, Edinburgh; m., Lynne Temporal. Educ. George Watson's College, Edinburgh; Edinburgh University. Apprenticed to Robson, McLean & Paterson, WS, 1978-80; Qualified Assistant: Fyfe Ireland & Co., WS, 1980-82, Shepherd & Wedderburn, WS, 1982-84. Member, Vestry, Old St. Paul's Scottish Episcopal Church, since 1983. Recreations: tennis; badminton; choral singing; listening to good music; eating out. Address: (h.) 4 Fountainhall Road, Edinburgh; T.-031-226 7411.

Niven, Stuart Matthew, BSc, DipEd. Director, School of Further Education, Jordanhill College of Education, since 1983; b. 1.3.36, Clydebank; m., Jean K. McPhee; 1 s.; 1 d. Educ. Clydebank High School; Glasgow University. Teacher of Mathematics and Physics: Clydebank High School, 1959, Stow College of Engineering, 1961; Head, Department of Mathematics and Physics, Kilmarnock College, 1964; Jordanhill College of Education: Lecturer in Mathematics, 1967, Senior Lecturer in Further Education, 1968, Principal Lecturer, 1970. Member, CNAA Further

Education Board, 1978-84; Chairman, Editorial Board, Journal for Further and Higher Education in Scotland, 1976-83; Chairman, National Liaison Committee on Training of Teachers of Nursing, Midwifery and Health Visiting, since 1983. Recreation: golf. Address: (b.) Jordanhill College of Education, 76 Southbrae Drive, Glasgow, G13 1PP; T.-041-959 1232.

Nixon, Mary MacKenzie, OBE, MA (Hons), DipEd. Archivist, Scottish Girl Guides Association, since 1979; b. Port Arthur, Canada. Educ. High School of Stirling; St. Andrews University. Assistant English Teacher, Riverside School, Stirling; Responsible Assistant, History, High School of Stirling, Falkirk High School; Responsible Assistant, English, Falkirk High School; Head, English Department, Grangemouth High School. Girl Guides Association: County Camp Adviser and Chairman, Training Committee, Stirlingshire; Scotland: Ranger Adviser, Training Adviser, Deputy Scottish Chief Commissioner; Co-ordinator, Silver Jubilee Scheme for Unemployed; Chairman, Netherurd Committee, Scottish Girl Guides Association Training Centre, since 1981. Recreations: genealogy; archaeology; poetry. Address: (h.) Gartlea, 19 Station Road, Bannockburn, FK7 8LE.

Nobes, Professor Christopher William, BA, PhD, FCCA. Professor of Accounting, Strathclyde University, since 1982; b. 20.3.50, Portsmouth; m., Diana Jane. Educ. Portsmouth Grammar School; Exeter University. Business Analyst, Thorn-EMI, 1971-73; Head of Internal Audit, Hambro Life Assurance, 1973-75; Lecturer in Accountancy, Exeter University, 1975-82. Associate Editor, Accounting and Business Research; Member, Company Law Committees, Institute of Chartered Accountants and Groupe d'Etudes des Experts Comptables, EEC; author of eight books. Address: (b.) Department of Accounting and Finance, Curran Building, Strathclyde University, Glasgow, G1; T.-041-552 4400.

Noble, Sheriff David, MA, LLB, WS, JP. Sheriff at Oban, Campbeltown and Fort William, since 1983; b. 11.2.23, Inverness; m., Marjorie Scott Smith; 2 s.; 1 d. Educ. Inverness Royal Academy; Edinburgh University. RAF Bomber Command, 1942-46; Miller Thomson & Robertson, WS, Edinburgh, 1950-83. Recreation: sailing. Address: (h.) Woodhouselee, North Connel, Argyll; T.-Connel 678.

Noble, David Hillhouse, LLB. Chief Executive, Skye and Lochalsh District Council, since 1974; b. 27.4.48, Paisley; m., Hilary; 1 s.; 2 d. Educ. Greenock Academy; Glasgow University. Legal and Administrative Assistant, Argyll County Council, 1972-73; Senior Legal and Administrative Assistant, Inverness County Council, 1973-74. Recreations: board sailing; music. Address: (b.) Council Offices, Park Road, Portree, IV51 9EP; T.-0478 2341.

Noble, Rev. George Strachan, DipTh. Minister, Newarthill, Motherwell, since 1972; b. 29.9.31, Inverallochy, near Fraserburgh; m., Mary Kinsman Addison; 1 s.; 1 d. Educ. Inverallochy Public School; Fraserburgh Academy; Glasgow University; Aberdeen University. Apprentice Auctioneer, fish trade, Fraserburgh, 1948-50; Royal Artillery, 1950-52; Auctioneer, 1952-59; Manager and Director, fishing boat management/fish-selling firm, Fraserburgh, 1959-66; divinity student, 1966-71; Probationer Assistant Minister, Fraserburgh Old Parish Church, 1971-72. Member, Church and Nation Committee, Church of Scotland; Convener, Church and Nation Committee, Hamilton Presbytery. Recreation: sport. Address: The Manse, Church Street, Newarthill, Motherwell, ML1 5HS; T.-0698 860316.

Noble, Iain Andrew, MA. Proprietor, Fearann Eilean Iarmain; Chairman, Noble and Company Ltd.; b. 8.9.35, Berlin. Educ. in China, Argentina and England; University College, Oxford. Scottish Council (Development and Industry), 1964-69; Noble Grossart Ltd., Edinburgh, 1969-72. Chairman, Seaforth Maritime Ltd., 1972-77; Director, Adam and Company plc, since 1983; Director, Darnaway Venture Capital plc, since 1984; Member, Edinburgh University Court, 1970-72; Governor, College of Sabhal Mor Ostaig, 1974-84. Editor, Sources of Finance, 1967-69. Recreations: music and company. Address: An Lamraig, Eilean Iarmain, An t-Eilean, Sgitheanach, IV43 8QR; T.-047 13-266.

Noble, Sir (Thomas Alexander) Fraser, Kt (1971), MBE (1947). Principal and Vice-Chancellor, Aberdeen University, 1976-81; b. 29.4.18; m., Barbara Sinclair; 1 s.; 1 d. Educ. Nairn Academy; Aberdeen University. Secretary and Treasurer, Carnegie Trust for Universities of Scotland, 1957-62; Vice Chancellor, Leicester University, 1962-76.

Noble, Timothy Peter, MA, MBA. Director, Lyle Shipping PLC, since 1976; Director, Lorne Exploration PLC, since 1980; Director, Noble & Company Ltd., since 1980; b. 21.12.43; m., Elizabeth Mary Aitken; 2 s.; 1 d. Educ. Eton College; University College, Oxford; Gray's Inn, London; INSEAD, Fontainebleau. Recreations: wine; astronomy; spectrology; skiing; tennis; bridge. Address: (h.) Ardnahane, Barnton Avenue, Edinburgh; T.-031-336 3565.

Norris, Derrick S., BSc (Hons), MBCS. Director of Computer Services, City of Glasgow, since 1979; b. 17.3.40, Liverpool; m., Pamela Anne; 1 s.; 1 d. Educ. Liverpool Institute; Liverpool University. Statistician/Programmer, Associated Octel, 1963-67; Senior Computer Assistant, Cheshire County Council, 1967-69; Senior Systems Analyst, Lancashire County Council, 1969-74; Deputy Computer Manager, Devon County Council, 1974-78; Assistant County Treasurer (Computer Services), Northamptonshire County Council, 1978-79. Recreations: squash; jogging; walking; shooting; DIY. Address: (b.) 112 Ingram Street, Glasgow, G1 1ET; T.-041-227 4067.

Norris, Michael John, LRAM. Principal Bassoon, BBC Scottish Symphony Orchestra, since 1970; Proprietor, Sirron Publications, since 1981; b. 28.3.34, Hayes; m., Pauline Chase; 1 s.; 1 d. Educ. Acton County Grammar School; Royal Academy of Music; Trinity College, London.

Principal Bassoon: Coldstream Guards Band, 1954-57, Scottish Variety Orchestra, 1962-66; Contra Bassoon, BBC Scottish Symphony Orchestra, 1966-70. Various compositions published. Recreations: composing; chess; hill-walking; conducting; home DIY. Address: (h.) 31 Hawthorn Avenue, Bearsden, Glasgow.

Norton-Smith, Professor John, BA, MA, BLitt, FRSA. Professor of English, Dundee University, since 1977 (Head, Department of English, since 1977); b. 26.6.31, Philadelphia; m., Marianne Cecil; 1 d. Educ. William Penn Charter School; Magdalen College, Oxford. Lecturer: St. Andrews University, 1960, Hull University, 1961-68; Reader, Reading University, 1968-77. Publications: John Lydgate: Poems, 1966; James I of Scotland: The Kingis Quair, 1971; Geoffrey Chaucer, 1974; The Quare of Jelusy, 1976; M.S. Fairfax 16, 1979; William Langland, 1983. Recreations: music; art history. Address: (h.) Glencairn, Tayview Terrace, Newport-on-Tay, Fife; T.-0382 543102.

Norwell, Peter Smith, OBE, TD, JP. Honorary Sheriff, Perth; b. 14.4.12, Perth; m., Elisabeth May Edwards; 3 d. Educ. Dollar Academy. Lt.-Col., RASC, 1944; Secretary, Perthshire Territorial Army Association, 1960-62; Assistant Secretary, Angus, Perthshire and Fife Territorial Army Association, 1962-67; Managing Director, Norwells Perth Footwear Ltd., 1935-60; Town Councillor, Perth, 1946-52; Chairman, Perth Theatre Company, 1968-72. Address: (h.) Greenknowe, Corsiehill, Perth, PH2 7BN; T.-Perth 25681.

Nutt, Professor Cecil Wilfred, BSc, PhD, DSc, CEng, CChem, FIChemE, FRSC, FRSA, FRSE. Professor and Head, Department of Chemical and Process Engineering, Heriot-Watt University, since 1970; b. 27.12.21, Bristol; m., Betty; 2 s. Educ. Dr. Morgan's Secondary School, Bridgwater; Bristol University. Armament Research Department, Ministry of Supply, 1943-47; Lecturer/Senior Lecturer/Reader, Department of Chemical Engineering, Birmingham University, 1948-70. Dean, Faculty of Engineering, Heriot-Watt University, 1978-81; Past Chairman, Scottish Branch, and Council Member, IChemE; Past President and Member, National Executive Council, AUT. Recreations: badminton; foreign travel; gardening. Address: (b.) Department of Chemical and Process Engineering, Heriot-Watt University, Chambers Street, Edinburgh, EH1 1HX; T.-031-225 8432.

O

Oakes, David Alexander, BA (Hons), DipEd, CertEd. Head Teacher, Arran High School, since 1972; b. 21.1.34, Leeds; m., Maureen Ridyard; 2 s. Educ. Rothwell Grammar School; Liverpool University; Sheffield University. Commissioned Officer, Aircrew, RAF, 1955-57 (Pilot); Assistant Geography Teacher, Wirral Grammar School for Boys, 1958-63; Head, Geography Department, Rothwell Grammar School, near Wakefield, 1963-67; Principal Teacher of Geography, Arran High School, 1967-72. Secretary/Treasurer, Arran Mountain Rescue Team; Treasurer, Isle of Arran Accident Prevention Committee; Trustee, Arran Heritage Museum; Treasurer, Arran Music Society. Recreations: hill-walking; travel; crosswords; amateur operatics; reading; golf. Address: (h.) Island Bank, Lamlash, Isle of Arran, KA27 8LG; T.-077 06 279.

Oakley, Charles A., JP, BSc, MEd, CBIM. Honorary President, Glasgow College of Technology, since 1985; Chairman, Central College of Commerce, Glasgow, since 1966; Honorary President, Scottish Film Council, since 1939; b. 30.9.00, Portsmouth; m., Dr. Agnes Stewart (deceased); 2 d. Educ. Devonport High School; Glasgow University. Apprentice, John Brown's Shipyard, 1919-24; qualified naval architect; Lecturer in Industrial Psychology, Glasgow University, 1930-72 (seconded to Civil Service, 1939-53); Scottish Area Officer, Air Ministry; Scottish Controller, Ministry of Aircraft Production, 1940-45; also Controller, North of Ireland, 1944-45; Scottish Controller, Board of Trade, 1945-53; President, Glasgow Chamber of Commerce, 1963-65; President, Association of Scottish Chambers of Commerce, 1966-68. Publications: Men at Work, 1946; The Second City, 1946. Recreation: leading a social life. Address: (h.) 10 Kirklee Circus, Glasgow, G12; T.-041-339 7000.

O Baoill, Colm J.M., MA, PhD. Senior Lecturer in Celtic, Aberdeen University, since 1980; b. 22.9.38, Armagh; m., Frances G.R. O Boyle; 3 d. Educ. St. Patrick's College, Armagh; Queen's University, Belfast. Assistant Lecturer in Celtic, Queen's University, Belfast, 1962-65; Lecturer in Celtic, Aberdeen University, 1966-80. Publications: Bardachd Shilis Na Ceapaich, 1972; Eachann Bacach and Other Maclean Poets, 1979. Address: (h.) 19 King's Crescent, Old Aberdeen, Aberdeen; T.-Aberdeen 637064.

O'Brien, Francis Aloysius, BL, NP. Honorary Sheriff, Dumfries, since 1971; b. 30.8.07, Dumfries; m., Ellen Drysdale Johnstone; 2 d. Educ. St. Joseph's College, Dumfries; Edinburgh University. Depute Procurator Fiscal, 1941-62; Burgh Prosecutor, 1941-44. Dumfries Guild of Players, since 1924: Secretary, 17 years, Treasurer, 3 years, Master, 1973-78, Honorary Life Member, since 1957; Secretary/Treasurer, Dumfries Property Owners, 1941-57; Governor, St. Joseph's College, Dumfries, 1960-82; Dean of Faculty (Dumfriesshire), 1975-77. Recreations: golf; drama. Address: (h.) Belmont, Whinnyhill, Dumfries, DG2 8HE; T.-New Abbey 354.

O'Brien, Sir Frederick William Fitzgerald, KB, QC, MA, LLB. Sheriff Principal, Lothian and Borders, since 1978; Commissioner, Northern Lighthouse Board, since 1965; Convener of Sheriffs Principal, since 1972; b. 19.7.17, Edinburgh; m., Audrey Muriel Owen; 2 s.; 1 d. Educ. Royal High School, Edinburgh; Edinburgh University. Called to Scottish Bar, 1947; QC, 1960; Commissioner, Mental Welfare Commission, 1962-65;

Senior Advocate Depute, Crown Office, 1964-65; Sheriff Principal, Caithness, Sutherland, Orkney and Shetland, 1965-75; Interim Sheriff Principal, Aberdeen, Kincardine and Banff, 1969-71; Sheriff Principal, North Strathclyde, 1975-78; Interim Sheriff Principal, South Strathclyde, 1981; Member, Scottish Medical Practices Committee, 1973-76; Member, Scottish Records Advisory Council, 1974-83; Chairman, Sheriff Court Rules Council, 1975-81; Convener, General Council Business Committee, Edinburgh University, 1980-84; Past President, Royal High School FP Club (Honorary President, since 1980); Director, Royal Lyceum Theatre. Recreations: music; golf. Address: (h.) 22 Arboretum Road, Edinburgh, EH3 5PN; T.-031-552 1923.

O'Brien, Most Rev. Keith Michael Patrick, BSc, DipEd. Archbishop of St. Andrews and Edinburgh, since 1985; b. 17.3.38, Ballycastle, Northern Ireland. Educ. Saint Patrick's, Dumbarton; Holy Cross Academy, Edinburgh; Edinburgh University; St. Andrew's College, Drygrange; Moray House College of Education. Teacher, St. Columba's High School, Fife; Assistant Priest, Kilsyth, then Bathgate; Spiritual Director, St. Andrew's College, Drygrange; Rector, Blairs College, Aberdeen; ordained Archbishop by Cardinal Gray, 1985. Recreations: music; walking. Address: Saint Bennet's, 42 Greenhill Gardens, Edinburgh, EH10 4BJ.

O'Donnell, Mgr. John. Catholic Priest; b. 18.7.18, Dumbarton. Educ. St. Patrick's High School, Dumbarton; St. Peter's College, Bearsden. Ordained, 1944; Motherwell Diocese: Diocesan Secretary, 1948-56, Diocesan Chancellor and Treasurer, 1956-84; appointed Privy Chamberlain, 1956, Domestic Prelate, 1960. Address: 8 The Clachan, Wishaw, Lanarkshire, ML2 7LR; T.-0698 376866.

O Drisceoil, Sean F., BSc, MBA. Principal, Sabhal Mor Ostaig, since 1983; b. 20.9.46, Callan, Co. Kilkenny. Educ. Callan CBS; St. Joseph's CBS, Dublin; University College, Dublin; Galway University. Education Vice-President, Union of Students in Ireland, 1968-70; Quality Control Chemist, then Q.C. Manager, Armour Pharmaceutical (Ireland) Ltd., 1970-74; Recruitment Manager, Merck Sharp & Dohme (Ireland) Ltd., 1974-77; Training Executive, Udaras Na Gaeltachta, 1977-83. Deputy President, Gaelic League, 1981-82. Recreations: swimming; scuba diving; walking. Address: (h.) 26 Tarskavaig, Sleibhte, Eilean Sgitheanach, IV46 8SA.

Ogden, Professor Raymond William, MA, PhD. George Sinclair Professor of Mathematics, Glasgow University, since 1984; b. 19.9.43, Lytham; m., Susanne; 2 s.; 2 d. Educ. Leamington College; Gonville and Caius College, Cambridge. Science Research Council Research Fellow, East Anglia University, 1970-72; Lecturer, then Reader in Mathematics, Bath University, 1972-80; Professor of Mathematics, Brunel University, 1981-84. Publication: Non-linear Elastic Deformations, 1984. Recreations: playing squash; walking; music; gardening. Address: (b.) Department of Mathematics, Glasgow University, Glasgow, G12 8QW; T.-041-339 8855.

Ogilvy, Sir David (John Wilfrid), 13th Bt, DL. Farmer and Landowner; Deputy Lieutenant, East Lothian, since 1971; b. 3.2.14; m., Penelope Mary Ursula Hills; 1 s. Educ. Eton; Trinity College, Oxford. RNVR, 1939-45. Address: (h.) Winton House, Pencaitland, East Lothian, EH34 5AT.

Ogston, Rev. David Dinnes, MA, BD. Minister, St. John's Kirk of Perth, since 1980; b. 25.3.45, Ellon, Aberdeenshire; m., Margaret Macleod; 2 d. Educ. Inverurie Academy; King's College and Christ's College, Aberdeen. Assistant Minister, St. Giles' Cathedral, Edinburgh, 1969-73; Minister, Balerno, 1973-80; author of booklets of prayers. Recreations: late-night films on TV; listening to the blues. Address: 15 Comely Bank, Perth; T.-Perth 21755.

Ogston, Professor Derek, MA, MD, PhD, DSc, FRCPEdin, FRCP, FRSE. Professor of Medicine, Aberdeen University, since 1983 (Dean, Faculty of Medicine, since 1984); b. 31.5.32, Aberdeen; m., Cecilia Marie; 1 s.; 2 d. Educ. King's College School, Wimbledon; Aberdeen University. Aberdeen University: Lecturer in Medicine, 1962-69, Senior Lecturer in Medicine, 1969-75, MRC Travelling Fellow, 1967-68, Reader in Medicine, 1975-76, Regius Professor of Physiology, 1977-83. Publications: Haemostasis: Biochemistry, Physiology and Pathology (Joint Editor), 1977; The Physiology of Haemostasis, 1983; Antifibrinolytic Drugs: Chemistry, Pharmacology and Clinical Usage, 1984. Recreations: gardening; running. Address: (h.) 64 Rubislaw Den South, Aberdeen, AB2 6AX; T.-Aberdeen 316587.

O'Halloran, Sir Charles Ernest, KB. Chairman, Irvine Development Corporation, 1983-85; b. 26.5.24, Liverpool; m., Annie Rowan; 1 s.; 2 d. Educ. Conway Central School, Birkenhead. Member, Ayr Town Council, 1953-74 (Provost, 1964-67); Member, Strathclyde Regional Council, 1974-82 (Convener, 1978-82). Recreations: golf and walking (can be the same). Address: (h.) 40 Savoy Park, Ayr, KA7 2XA; T.-0292 266234.

O'Hara, Philip James. Sheriff Clerk, Peterhead, since 1978, and Banff, since 1985; b. 15.8.46, Glasgow; m., Heather Mary Wallace; 2 s.; 1 d. Educ. Allan Glen's School, Glasgow. Sheriff Clerk Depute, Stirling, 1974-78. Address: (b.) Sheriff Clerk's Office, Sheriff Court, Queen Street, Peterhead, AB4 6TP; T.-Peterhead 76676.

Oliver, Ian Thomas, QPM, LLB, MPhil. Chief Constable, Central Scotland Police, since 1979; b. 24.1.40, London; m., Elsie; 2 s.; 1 d. Educ. Grammar School, Hampton, Middlesex; Nottingham University. Constable to Superintendent, Metropolitan Police, 1961-77; Northumbria Police: Chief Superintendent, 1977, Assistant Chief Constable (Management Services), 1978. Clerk/Treasurer, Sir James Duncan Medal Trust. Address: (b.) Randolphfield, Stirling, FK8 2HD; T.-0786 73161.

Oliver, Brigadier James Alexander, CB, CBE, DSO (and Bar), TD, DL, LLD. Honorary Sheriff, County of Angus; b. 19.3.06, Arbroath;

m., Margaret W. Scott. Educ. Trinity College, Glenalmond. 2nd Lt., Black Watch (TA), 1926; commanded: 7th Black Watch, 1942, 152 Infantry Brigade (Highland Division), 1943, 154 Infantry Brigade (Highland Division), 1944; served World War II in North Africa, Sicily and NW Europe (mentioned in Despatches); ADC to The Queen, 1953-63; Honorary Colonel, 6/7th Black Watch, 1960-67; Honorary Colonel, 51st Highland Volunteers, 1967-70; Member, Angus and Dundee T&AFA, 1938-59 (Chairman, 1945-59); Past Chairman, The Earl Haig Fund Scotland; Vice-Lieutenant, County of Angus, 1967-81. Address: (h.) West Newton, Arbroath, Angus; T.-Arbroath 72579.

Oliver, James Kenneth Murray. Farmer; Director, Royal Highland and Agricultural Society of Scotland, since 1962; b. 1.2.14, Hawick; m., Rhona Mary Purdom Wilkinson; 1 s.; 1 d. Educ. Merchiston Castle, Edinburgh. Army, 1939-46; Chairman and Managing Director, Andrew Oliver & Son Ltd.; as racehorse trainer, trained almost 1,000 winners under National Hunt Rules; rode winner, Scottish Grand National, 1950; trained five winners, Scottish Grand National; four times runner-up, Grand National; trained winners for the Queen Mother; Joint Managing Director, Doncaster Bloodstock Sales Ltd.; Secretary, Teviotdale Farmers Club; Joint Secretary, Buccleuch and Jedforest Point to Point. Recreations: hunting; racing; golf; tennis; squash. Address: (h.) Hassendean Bank, Hawick; T.-0450 87 216.

Oliver, Professor Michael Francis, CBE, MD, MDhc (Bologna and Stockholm), FRCP, FRCPEdin, FFCM, FACC. Duke of Edinburgh Professor of Cardiology, Edinburgh University, since 1979; Senior Cardiologist and Physician, Edinburgh Royal Infirmary, since 1978; b. 3.7.25, Borth; m., 1, Margaret Y. Abbey; 2 s.; 1 s. (deceased); 1 d.; 2, Helen L. Daniel. Educ. Marlborough College, Wiltshire; Edinburgh University. Consultant Physician, Royal Infirmary, and Senior Lecturer in Medicine, Edinburgh University, 1961; Reader in Medicine, 1973; Personal Professor of Cardiology, 1977; Member, Scientific Board, International Society of Cardiology, 1968-78 (Chairman and Council on Atherosclerosis); Chairman, British Atherosclerosis Group, 1970-75; Member, Cardiovascular Panel, Government Committee on Medical Aspects of Food Policy, 1971-74 and 1982-84; UK Representative, Advisory Panel for Cardiovascular Diseases, World Health Organisation, since 1972; Chairman, BBC-Medical Advisory Group in Scotland, 1975-81; Council Member, British Heart Foundation, since 1976; Convener, Cardiology Committee, Scottish Royal Colleges, 1978-81; Convener, Council Committee for Education and Health, Royal College of Physicians of Edinburgh, since 1980; President, British Cardiac Society, 1981-85; Council Member, Royal College of Physicians of Edinburgh, since 1984; Chairman, Honorary Advisory Panel, Cardiovascular Conditions for Fitness to Drive, since 1985; Purkinje Medal, 1981; Polish Cardiac Society Medal, 1984. Recreations: questioning, studying and thinking. Address: (h.) Barley Mill House, Pencaitland, East Lothian, EH34 5EP.

Oliver, Michael Roger, DipTP, MRTPI. Director of Physical Planning, Argyll and Bute District Council, since 1974; b. 16.11.38, Manchester; m., Janet; 1 s.; 2 d. Educ. Burnage Grammar School; Manchester University. Planning Assistant, Lancashire County Council, 1962-64; Deputy Chief Planning Assistant, Bootle County Borough Council, 1964-69; Senior Planning Assistant, Southport County Borough Council, 1969-70; Principal Planning Officer, Manchester City Council, 1970-73; Depute County Planning Officer, Argyll County Council, 1973-75. Recreations: music; railways; local history. Address: (b.) Kilmory Castle, Lochgilphead, Argyll; T.-0546 2127.

Oliver, William A., BSc (Hons). Rector, Cumnock Academy, since 1978; b. 21.2.36, Hawick; m., Janet M. Fulton; 1 s. Educ. Hawick High School; George Watson's College; Edinburgh University; Moray House College of Education. Teacher, Galashiels Academy, 1960-62; Assistant Chief Chemist, United Biscuits, 1962-64; Teacher, Boroughmuir Secondary School, 1964-66; Principal Teacher of Chemistry, then Depute Rector, Wick High School, 1966-78. Recreations: golf; horse-riding; rugby football. Address: (h.) St. Elmo, 19 Cumnock Road, Mauchline, Ayrshire.

O'Malley, Thomas John, BSc (Hons), DipEd. Headmaster, St. David's High School, Dalkeith, since 1975; Chairman, Lothian Regional Consultative Committee on Secondary Education, since 1983; Chairman, Catholic Headteachers' Association of Scotland, since 1984; b. 7.4.37, Edinburgh; m., Maureen; 1 s.; 2 d. Educ. Holy Cross Academy, Edinburgh; Edinburgh University; Moray House College of Education. Assistant Teacher, Holy Cross Academy, 1960-63; Principal Teacher of Chemistry, St. Mary's Academy, Bathgate, 1963-67; Principal Teacher of Physical Sciences, Lawrence Park Collegiate Institute, Toronto, 1967-69; Principal Teacher of Chemistry, St. Anthony's Secondary School, Edinburgh, 1969-72; Assistant Head Teacher, Holyrood High School, Edinburgh, 1972-75. Member, Munn Committee, 1975-77; Member, Cardinal Gray's Advisory Committee on Education. Recreations: shareholder, Hibernian FC; golf; hill-walking. Address: (b.) Abbey Road, Dalkeith, EH22 3AD; T.-031-663 1961.

O'Neill, Martin (John). MP (Labour), Clackmannan, since 1983 (Stirlingshire East and Clackmannan, 1979-83); b. 6.1.45. Educ. Trinity Academy, Edinburgh; Heriot-Watt University; Moray House College of Education. Teacher of Modern Studies, Boroughmuir High School, Edinburgh, 1974-77.

Orr, Ian, MPS. Pharmacist; Honorary Sheriff, South Strathclyde, Dumfries and Galloway, since 1980; Lord Cornet (Standard Bearer), Lanark, since 1961; b. 14.3.26, Lanark; m., Dora Hickey; 1 s. Educ. Lanark Grammar School; Royal Technical College. National Service, RAMC, Egypt, 1947-49. Convener, Christian Stewardship Campaign, Scottish Episcopal Church, Lanark; Committee Member, Linlithgow and Stirlingshire

Hunt; Past President, Lanark Rotary Club; Vice-President, Dante Alighieri Society (Diploma Di Benemerenza and Bronze Medal). Recreations: fox-hunting; golf; foreign travel. Address: (h.) Sezira, St. Patrick's Road, Lanark; T.-0555 2810.

Orr, Sir John Henry, Kt (1979), OBE (1972), QPM (1977). Chief Constable, Lothian and Borders Police, 1975-83; b. 13.6.18; m.; 1 s.; 1 d. Educ. George Heriot's School, Edinburgh. Chief Constable, Dundee, 1960; Chief Constable, Lothians and Peebles, 1968; Past President, Scottish Rugby Union.

Orr, Joseph Charles, BSc, MSc, PhD, DIC. Senior Lecturer in Chemistry, Dundee University; b. 16.1.30, Belfast; m., Kathleen Mary Fulton; 1 s.; 3 d. Educ. Royal Academy, Belfast; Queen's University, Belfast; Imperial College, London; Gottingen University, Germany. Research and teaching in Universities in Britain, Germany and Ecuador; period of secondment to International Atomic Energy Agency and United Nations Development Programme. Recreation: fly fishing the hill lochs of Scotland. Address: (h.) Mansefield, Meigle, Perthshire; T.-08284 302.

Orr Ewing, Major Sir Ronald Archibald, 5th Bt; b. 14.5.12; m., Marion Hester; 2 s.; 2 d. Educ. Eton; Sandhurst. Scots Guards, 1932-53 (Major); DL, Perthshire, 1963; Grand Master Mason of Scotland, 1965-69. Address: (h.) Cardross, Port of Menteith, Stirling.

Osborne, Eric Alexander, MB, ChB, FRCSEdin, FRCSGlas, D(Obst)RCOG. Consultant Ear, Nose and Throat Surgeon, Victoria Infirmary, Glasgow; b. 9.4.36, Glasgow; m., Sheilagh Sophie Wilson; 3 d. Educ. Merchiston Castle School, Edinburgh; Glasgow University. Director, Neilston Agricultural Society. Recreations: shooting; fishing; stalking. Address: (h.) Thorterburn Farm, Neilston, near Glasgow, G78 3AX; T.-050585 222.

Osler, Douglas Alexander, MA (Hons), FSA Scot, DipRE. HM District Inspector of Schools (Higher Grade), Scottish Education Department, since 1974; b. 11.10.42, Edinburgh; m., Wendy I. Cochrane; 1 s.; 1 d. Educ. Royal High School, Edinburgh; Edinburgh University; Moray House College of Education. Assistant Teacher of History/Careers Master, Liberton Secondary School, Edinburgh, 1965-68; Principal Teacher of History, Dunfermline High School, 1968-74. English Speaking Union Fellowship to USA, 1966; Scout Leader, 1960-68; Past Chairman, Newton Mearns and District Round Table. Publications: Queen Margaret of Scotland; Sources for Modern Studies, Volumes 1 and 2. Recreations: bowling; bridge; gardening; reading; making models; watching TV news programmes. Address: (b.) Scottish Education Department, Government Buildings, 28 Longman Road East, Inverness; T.-0463 234141.

Owen, David Gareth, MA, BD (Hons), PhD, MICE, CEng. Head, Department of Offshore Engineering, Heriot-Watt University, since 1982; b. 6.11.40, Brecon, Wales; m., Ann Valerie Wright; 2 d. Educ. Christ College, Brecon; Downing College, Cambridge. Graduate Engineer, John Laing & Son, London; Aerospace Engineer, Marconi Space and Defence Systems, Portsmouth; Lecturer in Civil Engineering, Heriot-Watt University; Visiting Professor, University of New Hampshire; Senior Lecturer, Department of Offshore Engineering, Heriot-Watt University. Recreations: music; travelling; skiing. Address: (h.) 7 Oak Lane, Edinburgh, EH12 6XH; T.-031-339 1740.

Owen, Professor Douglas David Roy, MA, PhD. Professor of French, St. Andrews, since 1972; b. 17.11.22, Norton, Suffolk; m., Berit Mariann; 2 s. Educ. Cambridge and County High School; Nottingham High Pavement School; Nottingham University; St. Catharine's College, Cambridge. St. Andrews University: Lecturer, 1951-64, Senior Lecturer, 1964-71, Reader, 1971-72; General Editor, Forum for Modern Language Studies. Publications: Fabliaux (Joint Editor), 1957; The Evolution of the Grail Legend, 1968; The Vision of Hell, 1970; Arthurian Romance: Seven Essays (Editor), 1970; Two Old French Gauvain Romances (Joint Editor), 1972; The Legend of Roland, 1973; Noble Lovers, 1975. Recreation: golf. Address: (h.) 7 West Acres, St. Andrews, KY16 9UD; T.-St. Andrews 73329.

Owens, Professor David Howard, BSc, ARCS, PhD, FIMA, CEng, MIEE. Professor of Mathematics, Strathclyde University, since 1985; b. 23.4.48, Belper; m., Rosemary; 1 s.; 1 d. Educ. Dronfield Henry Fanshawe Grammar School; Imperial College, London University. Atomic Energy Establishment, Winfrith, Dorchester, 1969-73; Reader in Control Engineering, Sheffield University, 1973-85. Recreations: cycling; small-bore rifle shooting. Address: (b.) Department of Mathematics, Strathclyde University, Livingstone Tower, 26 Richmond Street, Glasgow, G1 1XH; T.-041-552 4400, Ext. 3804.

P

Pacey, Archibald Charles, MA, FEIS. Head Teacher, Greenhall High School, since 1982; Principal Examiner, Scottish Examination Board, since 1970; b. 29.6.31, Kirkcaldy; m., Joan Marion Margaret Henry; 3 s.; 1 d. Educ. Knox Academy, Haddington; Edinburgh University; Moray House College. Captain, RAEC, in BAOR, 1954-57; Principal Teacher of French, Moray House Demonstration School, 1958-61; Teacher of Modern Languages, Dalkeith High School, 1961-64; Principal Teacher of Modern Languages, then Depute Head Teacher, Lasswade High School, 1964-82. Founder Secretary/Treasurer, Lothian Regional Executive, Educational Institute of Scotland; Honorary Secretary, Haddington Rugby Football Club,

1979-84. Recreations: gardening; DIY; wine-making; Midlothian-Heinsberg Twinning. Address: (h.) Carlowrie Cottage, Barleyknowe Road, Gorebridge, Midlothian; T.-0875 20235.

Pacione, Michael, MA, PhD. Senior Lecturer in Geography, Strathclyde University, since 1983; b. 14.10.47, Dundee; m., Christine Hopper; 1 s.; 1 d. Educ. Lawside Academy, Dundee; Dundee University. Lecturer in Geography: Queens University, Belfast, 1973-75, Strathclyde University, Glasgow, 1975-83. Recreations: travel; sports; photography. Address: (b.) Department of Geography, Strathclyde University, Glasgow; T.-041-552 4400.

Pack, Professor Donald Cecil, CBE, MA, DSc, FIMA, FEIS, FRSE. Honorary Professor, Strathclyde University, since 1982; b. 14.4.20, Higham Ferrers; m., Constance Mary Gillam; 2 s.; 1 d. Educ. Wellingborough School; New College, Oxford. Ordnance Board, Cambridge, 1941-43; Armament Research Department, Ministry of Supply, Fort Halstead, 1943-46; Lecturer in Mathematics, St. Andrews University, 1947-52; Visiting Research Associate, Maryland University, 1951-52; Lecturer in Mathematics, Manchester University, 1952-53; Professor of Mathematics, Strathclyde University, 1953-82 (Vice-Principal, 1968-72). Chairman, Scottish Certificate of Education Examination Board, 1969-77; Chairman, Committee of Inquiry into Truancy and Indiscipline in Scottish Schools, 1974-77 ("Pack Report" published by HMSO, 1977); Chairman, National Youth Orchestra of Scotland, since foundation, 1978; Member, Scottish Arts Council, since 1980; Member: General Teaching Council for Scotland, 1966-73, Dunbartonshire Education Committee, 1960-66; Governor, Hamilton College of Education, 1976-81; Council Member, Royal Society of Edinburgh, 1960-63; Honorary Treasurer and Council Member, Institute of Mathematics and its Applications, 1964-72; Member, International Advisory Committee on Rarefied Gas Dynamics Symposia, since 1976; Member, British National Committee for Theoretical Mechanics, 1973-78; Council Member, Gesellschaft fuer angewandte Mathematik und Mechanik, 1977-83; Past President: Edinburgh Mathematical Society, Glasgow Mathematical Association. Recreations: music; gardening; golf. Address: (h.) 18 Buchanan Drive, Bearsden, Glasgow, G61 2EW; T.-041-942 5764.

Packard, Andrew, MA, DSc (Oxon). Reader, Department of Physiology, Medical School, Edinburgh University, since 1976; b. 8.3.29, Sedbergh; m., Elizabeth Ann Davidson; 2 c. (by pr. m.). Educ. Gordonstoun; Pembroke, Oxford. Universities of Auckland and Otago, New Zealand, 1954-59; Naples Zoological Station, Italy, 1959-69; joined Edinburgh University, 1969. Recreations: painting watercolours; travel. Address: (h.) 5 Dundas Street, Edinburgh, EH3 6QG; T.-031-556 2052.

Packer, John Aidan, OBE, BA, ATI. Woollen Manufacturer; b. 19.7.35, Wakefield; m., Carol Lesley Burdin; 1 s.; 2 d. Educ. Queen Elizabeth Grammar School, Wakefield; Munich University; Leeds University. National Service, 1957-59

(commissioned, 1st Bn., KOYLI); joined Reid & Taylor, Langholm, 1959; appointed Director, 1965, Managing Director, 1967; Director, Allied Textile Companies, 1973; Director, Allied Textile Companies Fine Worsted Division, 1981; first President, The Scottish Woollen Industry, 1983; Director, Scottish Textile and Technical Centre, 1984; Governor, Cumbria College of Art and Design, Carlisle; former Member, Board of Management, British Colour Council; Member, Scottish Committee, Design Council, 1974-79; Member, Design Council, 1976-79; Member, Industrial Design Advisory Committee, 1977-79; Member, Steering Committee on Training of Designers, Confederation of British Wool Textiles; Council Member, National Wool Textile Export Corporation; winner, Scottish Free Enterprise Award, 1979; Patron, Register of Apparel and Textile Designers; Fellow, Society of Antiquaries of Scotland; winner of award by Clothing and Footwear Institute, 1982. Recreations: squash; swimming; collecting antiques. Address: (b.) Reid & Taylor, Langholm Woollen Mills, Langholm, Dumfriesshire; T.-0541 80311.

Pagan, Charles David, OBE, BL, WS. Consultant Solicitor; Honorary Sheriff, Cupar, since 1971; b. 7.6.07, Cupar; m., Mary N. Garnham; 3 s.; 1 d. Educ. Bedford; Edinburgh University. Admitted Solicitor, 1929, WS, 1932; Senior Partner, Pagan, Osborne & Grace, 1935-72; Clerk of the Peace of Fife, 1935-75; Joint Manager, British Linen Bank, Cupar, 1932-71. Publication: Justices of the Peace Handbook, 1955. Address: (h.) Belmore, Westfield Road, Cupar, Fife; T.-0334 52555.

Page, Christopher Nigel, BSc, PhD, FLS. Principal Scientific Officer, Royal Botanic Garden, Edinburgh, since 1971; Honorary Lecturer, Department of Botany, Edinburgh University, since 1983; b. 11.11.42, Gloucester; m., Pauline Ann; 1 s.; 2 d. Educ. Cheltenham Grammar School; Kings College, Durham; Newcastle-upon-Tyne University. NATO Overseas Research Fellow, Queensland University, 1968-70; Department of Rural Economy, Oxford University, 1970-71. Nuffield/Leverhulme Overseas Travel Fellowship, 1976-77; Tutor, Scottish Field Studies Council, since 1973; Editor, British Fern Gazette, since 1974. Publication: The Ferns of Britain and Ireland, 1982. Recreations: photography; walking; writing. Address: (h.) 17 Silverknowes Crescent, Edinburgh, EH4 5JE; T.-031-336 1142.

Page, John Graham, ChM, FRCS, MB, ChB. Consultant Accident and Emergency Surgeon, Grampian Health Board, since 1981; Honorary Senior Lecturer in Surgery, Aberdeen University, since 1981; b. 16.2.43, Liverpool; m., Sandra; 1 s.; 2 d. Educ. Robert Gordon's College; Aberdeen University. Lecturer in Pathology, Aberdeen University, 1969; Surgical Registrar, Grampian Health Board, 1972; Research Fellow, Harvard University, Boston, 1974; Registrar, Accident and Emergency, Grampian Health Board, 1979. Publications: A Colour Atlas of Accidents and Emergencies, 1984; A Colour Atlas of Plaster Techniques, 1985; A Colour Atlas of Resuscitation Techniques, 1985. Recreations: skiing; sailing. Address: (h.) 16 Kingswood Avenue, Kingswells, Aberdeen, AB1 8AE; T.-Aberdeen 742945.

Paling, Edwin. Leader, Scottish National Orchestra, since 1976; b. 1948, Nottingham. Educ. Royal Academy of Music. Bournemouth Symphony Orchestra; City of Birmingham Symphony Orchestra; BBC Midland Light Orchestra; joined SNO as Assistant Leader, 1973; Associate Leader, 1974.

Palmer, Godfrey Henry Oliver, MIBiol, BSc, PhD, DSc, FIBrew. University Teacher, Department of Brewing and Biological Sciences, Heriot-Watt University, since 1977; Research Consultant; b. 9.4.40, St. Elizabeth, Jamaica: m., Margaret Ann Wood; 1 s.; 2 d. Educ. Shelbourne Secondary Modern School; Highbury County School; Leicester University; Edinburgh University; Heriot-Watt University. Technician, 1958-61; Brewing Research Foundation, 1968-77. Recreations: reading; watching cereal fields; education of deprived children; friends; ball games; music. Address: (b.) Heriot-Watt University, Department of Brewing and Biological Sciences, Edinburgh; T.-031-225 8432.

Palmer, Robert Allen, BA (Hons). Drama and Dance Director, Scottish Arts Council, since 1980; Theatre Director, since 1971; b. 3.6.47, Toronto; m., Lynn Susan Winston; 1 s.; 1 d. Educ. Forrest Hill Collegiate; York University; Central London Polytechnic. Teacher of English and Drama, Inner London Education Authority and Surrey County Council, 1970-72; Director, Theatre Centre for Young People, 1971-73; Director, Theatremakers, MacRobert Arts Centre, Stirling, 1973-75; Director, Theatre Workshop, Edinburgh, 1975-80; Member, Advisory Panels for Drama and Dance, British Council, since 1980. Recreations: cooking; walking; music. Address: (h.) 46A Blacket Place, Edinburgh.

Panton, John, MBE. Professional Golfer; b. 9.10.16, Pitlochry. Won PGA Match-Play Championship, 1956 (Runner-up, 1968); PGA British Seniors', 1967-69; World Seniors', 1967 (defeated Sam Snead for title); Silver King, 1950; Daks, 1951; North British-Harrogate, 1952; Goodwin Foursomes, 1952; Yorkshire Evening News, 1954; Gleneagles-Saxone Am.-Pro. Foursomes, 1956; Woodlawn Invitation Open (West Germany), 1958-59-60; leading British player, Open Championship, 1956; Leader, PGA Order of Merit (Vardon Trophy), 1951; won Scottish Professional Championship, seven times (and joint Champion, once); Ryder Cup player, 1951-53-61; awarded Golf Writers' Trophy, 1967.

Parbrook, Geoffrey Donald, MD, FFARCS. Senior Lecturer in Anaesthesia, Glasgow University, since 1967; Consultant Anaesthetist, Glasgow Royal Infirmary, since 1967; b. Ferryhill, Co. Durham; m., Evelyn; 3 s. Educ. Birmingham University. Eastman Dental Hospital, London, 1959; Newcastle Regional Chest Surgery Centre, 1960-62; Aberdeen Royal Infirmary, 1962-67. Publication: Basic Physics and Measurement in Anaesthesia, 1985. Address: (b.) University Department of Anaesthesia, Royal Infirmary, 8-16 Alexandra Parade, Glasgow, G31 2ER; T.-041-552 3535.

Park, Andy. Head of Light Entertainment, BBC Scotland, since 1985; b. 14.8.36, Ayr; m., Nan; 2 s.; 1 d. Educ. Dalmellington High School; Ayr Academy; Glasgow School of Art; Jordanhill College of Education. Producer, BBC Radio 2, 1971-73; Head of Entertainment, Radio Clyde, 1973-78; Controller of Programmes, Radio Forth, 1978; Head of Programmes, Radio Clyde, 1978-81; Commissioning Editor for Music, Channel 4, 1981-84; Composer of pop songs, jazz, more than 20 scores for Scottish-made films, etc; won Billboard Trendsetter Award, New York, 1976; Scotstar Award, 1979; Board Member, Masterconcerts Ltd., since 1980; Council Member, Scottish Society of Composers, since 1980. Recreations: listening to, writing and playing music; watching football; dreaming of the days when he could play it. Address: (h.) 23 Tinto Road, Glasgow, G43.

Park, Ian Michael Scott, CBE, MA, LLB. Partner, Paull & Williamsons, Advocates, Aberdeen, since 1961; Member, Criminal Injuries Compensation Board, since 1983; Council Member, Law Society of Scotland, 1974-85; b. 7.4.38, Aberdeen; m., Elizabeth M.L. Struthers; 2 s. Educ. Aberdeen Grammar School; Aberdeen University. Assistant to, subsequently Partner in, Paull & Williamsons; Member, Society of Advocates in Aberdeen, since 1962; sometime part-time Assistant, Department of Public Law, Aberdeen University; President, Law Society of Scotland, 1980-81; Chairman, Aberdeen Citizens Advice Bureau; Secretary, Aberdeen Granite Association, 1962-84; frequent broadcaster on legal topics (Presenter, What's Your Problem, Grampian TV). Recreations: golf; gardening. Address: (h.) 46 Rubislaw Den South, Aberdeen.

Park, Robert Wilson, JP. Honorary Sheriff, Hamilton, since 1964; b. 29.5.00, Strathaven; m., Barbara Thomson Watt; 3 s. Educ. Strathaven Academy; Glasgow University. Scout, 1911-68 (Scoutmaster until 1934, then Member, Treasurer, and Chairman, local Association); Law Apprentice, 1915-23; Solicitor, 1923-81; HLI, 1918-19; Member and Dean, Hamilton Society of Solicitors, 1929-81; Special Constable, 1937-39; Observer Corps, 1939-45; Council Member, Law Society of Scotland, 1966-72. Various offices in Rotary; awarded Silver Acorn for services in Scouting, 1981. Recreation: bowling. Address: (h.) Marlbank, 5 Hawthorn Road, Strathaven, Lanarkshire, ML10 6HA; T.-0357 20204.

Parker, Denis Michael, BA, PhD. Senior Lecturer in Psychology, Aberdeen University, since 1981; b. 26.6.43, Cork; m., Mannell Ruth; 3 s. Educ. St. Ignatius College, London; Durham University. Department of Psychology, Durham University: Research Assistant, 1967-68, Senior Demonstrator, 1968-69, Wheeler Research Fellow, 1969-72; Lecturer, Department of Psychology, Aberdeen University, 1972-81. Treasurer, Scottish Branch, British Psychological Society. Recreations: reading; squash. Address: (h.) 17 Devanha Gardens South, Ferryhill, Aberdeen, AB1 2UG; T.-Aberdeen 583049.

Parker, Professor Geoffrey Parker, PhD, LittD, FBA. Professor of Early Modern History, St. Andrews University, since 1982; b. 25.12.43. Educ. Nottingham High School; Christ's College, Cambridge. Fellow, Christ's College, Cambridge,

1968-72; Lecturer in Modern History, then Reader, St. Andrews University, 1972-82. Address: (b.) Department of Modern History, St. Andrews University, St. Andrews, KY16 9AL.

Parker, Margaret Gray, MBE, MA, JP. Chairman, Royal Scottish Country Dance Society, since 1982; b. 2.12.08, Ayr; m., Irvine T. Parker, MC, MBE (deceased). Educ. Ayr Academy; Glasgow University. Former Depute Head Teacher, John Galt Primary School; Past President, Ayrshire Branch, Infants Mistresses' Association; Member, Kilmarnock Town Council, 1962-84 (Bailie); Provost, Kilmarnock and Loudoun District Council, 1977-80; Member, Ossington Trust and Bill Adams Award Scheme; Chairman, Kilmarnock Branch, Duke of Edinburgh Award Scheme, since 1979; Chairman, Crime Prevention Committee (Kilmarnock), since 1982; Chairman, Piersland Bentinck Support Group and Ayrshire Hospice Committee; Director of Dance, Ayrshire Musical Festival. Recreations: Scottish country dancing; played hockey, tennis and badminton for Ayrshire; politics. Address: (h.) 27 Charles Street, Kilmarnock, KA1 2DX; T.-Kilmarnock 23365.

Parnell, Brian K., BSc, ACGI, DipTP, FRTPI. Head, Department of Planning, Glasgow School of Art, since 1976; Planning Consultant; b. 18.12.22, Brighton; 2 s.; 1 d. Educ. Varndean School, Brighton; London University; Edinburgh College of Art. Captain, EME, 1943-47; Department of Planning, Midlothian County Council, 1949-57; Depute Planning Officer, Stirling County Council, 1957-64; joined Glasow School of Art, 1964; Commissioner, Countryside Commission for Scotland, 1968-80; part-time Planning Inquiry Reporter, Scottish Office, since 1982. Chairman, Association of Scientific Workers (Scottish Area), 1949-69; Member, Board of Governors, Heriot-Watt College, 1954-56; Chairman, Scottish Branch, Royal Town Planning Institute, 1972-73; Executive Committee Member, National Trust for Scotland, 1973-83; Trustee, Scottish Civic Trust, since 1985. Recreations: sailing; swimming; hill-walking; travel. Address: (h.) The Coach House, Long Row, Menstrie, Clackmannanshire, FK11 7EA; T.-0259 60909.

Parr, John Brian, BSc (Econ), MA, PhD. Reader in Applied Economics, Glasgow University, since 1980 (Secretary, Centre for Urban and Regional Research, since 1978); Chairman, British Section, Regional Science Association, since 1981; b. 18.3.41, Epsom; m., Pamela Jean Harkins; 2 d. Educ. Henry Thornton School; London University; University of Washington. Instructor, University of Washington, 1966; Assistant Professor/Associate Professor, University of Pennsylvania, 1967-75; joined Glasgow University as Lecturer, 1975. Editor, Papers of the Regional Science Association, 1968-75; Associate Editor, Journal of Regional Science, since 1978; Member, Board of Management, Urban Studies, since 1981. Publications: Regional Policy: Past Experience and New Directions (Co-Editor); Analysis of Regional Structure: Essays in Honour of August Losch (Co-Editor). Address: (b.) Department of Social and Economic Research, Glasgow University, Glasgow, G12 8RT; T.-041-339 8855, Ext. 7126.

Parratt, Professor James Roy, BPharm, MSc, PhD, DSc, FPS, FIBiol. Professor of Cardiovascular Pharmacology, Strathclyde University, since 1983; b. 19.8.33, London; m., Pamela Joan Lyndon; 2 s.; 1 d. Educ. St. Clement Danes Holborn Estate Grammar School; London University. Spent nine years in Nigeria as Head of Pharmacology, Nigerian School of Pharmacy, then in Physiology, University Medical School; joined Strathclyde University, 1967; appointed Reader, 1970; Personal Professor, Department of Physiology and Pharmacology, 1975-83. Chairman, Cardiac Muscle Research Group, 1980-83; Gold Medal, Szeged University, 1975; Honorary Member, Hungarian Pharmacological Society, 1983; Chairman, Universities and Colleges Christian Fellowship; former Vice-Chairman, Scripture Union; Past Chairman, SUM Fellowship; Lay Preacher, Baptist Unions of Scotland and Great Britain; Honorary President, Baptist Lay Preachers Association of Scotland. Recreation: music. Address: (h.) 16 Russell Drive, Bearsden, Glasgow, G61 3BD; T.-041-942 7164.

Parry, John Wynne Lloyd, TD, MA, DM, BSc, FFARCS. Consultant Anaesthetist, Aberdeen Hospitals, since 1966; Clinical Senior Lecturer, Aberdeen University, since 1970; b. 24.3.29, Llandudno; m., Priscilla Rachel Tate; 1 s.; 1 d. Educ. Barmouth Grammar School; Oxford University; University College Hospital, London. Short-service commission, RAF Medical Branch, 1957-60; principal junior anaesthetic appointments, University College Hospital and Hospital for Sick Children, Great Ormond Street, London, 1960-66; Staff Member, Massachusetts General Hospital and Harvard Medical School, Boston, 1963-64 and 1967-68. Past President, NE Scotland Society of Anaesthetists; Assistant Medical Officer, RNLI, Aberdeen. Recreations: sailing; skiing; model engineering. Address: (h.) 18 Woodburn Avenue, Aberdeen, AB1 8JQ; T.-0224 319350.

Parry, Kenneth Michael, OBE, MB, ChB, FRCPEdin, FFCM, FRCGP, DCH. Secretary, Scottish Council for Postgraduate Medical Education, since 1970; b. 28.5.29, Manchester; m., Maureen Anne Jones; 2 s.; 1 d. Educ. Bristol Grammar School; Bristol University. Senior Administrative Medical Officer, Eastern Regional Hospital Board, 1967-70; Council of Europe Medical Fellow, 1974; William Pickles Lecturer, Royal College of General Practitioners, 1977; Australian Universities Commonwealth Senior Fellow, 1980; Honorary Secretary, Association for Study of Medical Education, since 1984. Recreations: music; painting. Address: (h.) 9 Moray Place, Edinburgh, EH3 6DS; T.-031-226 3054.

Parsons, Professor Ian, BSc, PhD, FGS, FRSE. Professor of Geology, Aberdeen University, since 1983; b. 5.9.39, Manchester; m., Brenda Mary Reah; 3 s. Educ. Beckenham and Penge Grammar School; Durham University. DSIR Research Fellow, Manchester University, 1963-64; Aberdeen University: Assistant Lecturer, 1964-65, Lecturer, 1965-77, Senior Lecturer, 1977-83. Member, NERC Geological Sciences Research Grants Committee, since 1984 and Geological Sciences Training Awards Committee, since

1983; Vice-President, Mineralogical Society, 1981. Recreations: skiing; hill-walking; music. Address: (b.) Department of Geology and Mineralogy, Marischal College, Aberdeen, AB9 1AS; T.-0224 40241, Ext. 277.

Parsons, Professor John William, BSc, PhD, FIBiol. Professor and Head, Department of Soil Science, Aberdeen University, since 1981; b. 20.7.33, Wallasey; m., Gillian Mary; 3 s. Educ. Oldershaw Grammar School; Reading University. Postdoctoral Fellow, Delaware University, 1958-60; Lecturer and Senior Lecturer, Aberdeen University, 1960-81; Visiting Research Fellow, CSIRO Soils Division, Adelaide, 1972-73. Governor, Strathallan School; Member, Council of Management, Macaulay Institute for Soil Research. Recreations: hill-walking; reading. Address: (b.) Department of Soil Science, Aberdeen University, Aberdeen, AB9 2UE; T.-0224 40241.

Pascoe, Ian Philip, BA, MA (Cantab). HM Inspector of Schools, since 1970; b. 30.9.34, Romford, Essex; m., Fay Avril Yelland; 1 s.; 1 d. Educ. Wellington School; Christs College, Cambridge; Kings College, London; Bradford University. Teacher, Bristol Cathedral School; Teacher, HM Forces, Singapore; Lecturer in Geography, Bingley College of Education. Past Scottish Chairman and Council Member, RSPB. Recreations: hill-walking; bird-watching; gardening; reading science fiction; listening to music. Address: (h.) Carbeth Lodge, Drumtian Road, Killearn, Stirlingshire; T.-0360 50022.

Paternoster, Rev. Canon Michael Cosgrove, MA. Rector, St. James' Episcopal Church, Stonehaven, since 1975; Honorary Canon, St. Paul's Cathedral, Dundee, since 1981; b. 13.5.35, East Molesey, Surrey; m., Careth Osborne. Educ. Kingston Grammar School; Pembroke College, Cambridge; Cuddesdon Theological College. Deacon, 1961; Priest, 1962; Curate, St. Andrew's, Surbiton, 1961-63; Chaplain to Anglican students in Dundee, 1964-68; Secretary, Fellowship of St. Alban and St. Sergius, 1968-71; Rector, St. James', Dollar, 1971-75; Secretary, Inter-Church Relations Committee, Scottish Episcopal Church, 1975-82; Member, Doctrine Committee, Scottish Episcopal Church, since 1980. Publications: Thou art There Also, 1967; Stronger Than Death, 1972. Recreations: reading; sketching; bird-watching; listening to music. Address: 35 Gurney Street, Stonehaven, Kincardineshire, AB3 2EB; T.-Stonehaven 62694.

Paterson, Professor Alan Alexander, LLB (Hons), DPhil (Oxon). Professor of Law, Strathclyde University, since 1984; b. 5.6.47, Edinburgh; m., Alison Jane Ross Lowdon; 1 s. Educ. Edinburgh Academy; Edinburgh University; Pembroke College, Oxford. Research Associate, Oxford Centre for Socio-Legal Studies, 1972-73; Lecturer, Law Faculty, Edinburgh University, 1973-84; Visiting Professor, University of New Mexico Law School, 1982. Chairman, Scottish Legal Action Group; Chairman, Scottish Legal Education Trust; Chairman, Scottish Association of Citizens Advice Bureaux Legal Advisory Group. Publications: The Law Lords, 1982; The

Legal System of Scotland (Co-author), 1983. Address: (b.) Strathclyde University Law School, 173 Cathedral Street, Glasgow, G4 ORQ; T.-041-552 4400, Ext. 3341.

Paterson, Professor Alan Keith Gordon, MA (Aberdeen), PhD (Cantab). Professor of Spanish, St. Andrews University, since 1984; b. 8.5.38, Aberdeen; m., Anna Tora Holm; 1 s. Educ. Aberdeen Grammar School; Aberdeen University; Cambridge University. Assistant Lecturer, Lecturer, Senior Lecturer, Queen Mary College, London University, 1965-83. Recreations: hill-walking; motor-cycling; cooking. Address: (h.) Argyll Lodge, 1 Kennedy Gardens, St. Andrews, Fife; T.-St. Andrews 72033.

Paterson, Alexander Brown, MBE, Hon. MA (St. Andrews). Chairman, Byre Theatre, St. Andrews, since 1970; b. 11.4.07, St. Andrews; m., Millie Manson Bridges (deceased); 1 s.; 1 d. Educ. Burgh School, St. Andrews. Founder, Byre Theatre, St. Andrews, 1933 (Administrator, until 1980); wrote several plays including The Open, Re-Union in St. Andrews, The Last Provost, The Herald's Not for Sale, etc.; wrote several guide books on Fife towns and The History of the Byre Theatre; ran a news agency in St. Andrews for more than 50 years and co-edited East Fife Observer; a Director (Past Chairman), Federation of Scottish Theatre; Trustee, Scottish Fisheries Musuem; Trustee, Hamada Trust; served in RAF during World War II; STV award for outstanding service to Scottish theatre, 1971; awarded Jubilee Medal, 1977. Recreations: golf; gardening. Address: (h.) 90 Bridge Street, St. Andrews; T.-0334 74493.

Paterson, Colin Ralston, MA, DM, BSc, FRCPath. Senior Lecturer in Biochemical Medicine, Dundee University, since 1969; Honorary Consultant, Tayside Area Health Board, since 1971; b. 5.10.36, Manchester; m., Sally Hellier; 1 s.; 2 d. Educ. Shrewsbury School; Brasenose College, Oxford; University College Hospital. House Physician, University College Hospital; House Surgeon, Leeds General Infirmary; Assistant Lecturer, Clinical Investigation Unit, Leeds University; Medical Registrar, York. Van den Berghs and Jurgens Nutrition Award, 1972; Chairman, Brittle Bone Society. Publications: Metabolic Disorders of Bone, 1975; Textbook of Physiology and Biochemistry, 9th edition (Co-author), 1976; Textbook of Physiology, 10th edition (Co-author), 1980; Essentials of Human Biochemistry, 1983; Bone Disease in the Elderly (Co-author), 1984. Address: (b.) Department of Biochemical Medicine, Ninewells Hospital, Dundee, DD1 9SY; T.-0382 60111, Ext. 2517.

Paterson, George Marshall, FBIM, MIPM, MITD. Personnel Director, Central Regional Council, since 1974; b. 29.4.31, Falkirk; m., Pearl Dow; 1 s.; 1 d. Educ. Falkirk Technical School. Entered local government service, 1945. Honorary President, Larbert Amateur Operatic Society; Scottish Area Representative for Region No. 3, National Operatic and Dramatic Association; Elder, Larbert Old Church. Recreation: involvement in the amateur operatic movement. Address: (h.) 3 Dobbie Avenue, Larbert, Stirlingshire, FK5 3EP; T.-Larbert 562752.

Paterson, Lt. Col. Howard Cecil, TD, FSA Scot. International Tourism Consultant; Chairman, Taste of Scotland Ltd.; Chairman, Scottish International Gathering Trust; Executive Chairman, The Scots Connection; b. 16.3.20, Edinburgh; m., Isabelle Mary; 1 s. Educ. Daniel Stewart's College, Edinburgh; Edinburgh College of Art. Army, 1939-49; combat duties during War; personnel selection afterwards; Territorial Army, 1949-70; serves on East Scotland TAVR Committee; Assistant Personnel Manager, Jute Industries Ltd., Dundee, 1949-51; Organising Secretary, Scottish Country Industries Development Trust, 1951-66; Senior Director, Scottish Tourist Board, 1966-81. Vice-Chairman, Scottish Aircraft Collection Trust; Vice-Chairman, John Buchan Society; Member, Executive Committee, Rural Forum; Member, Scottish Committee, British Horse Society; Member, Executive Committee, Scottish Trekking and Riding Association. Publication: Tourism in Scotland. Recreations: fishing; shooting; riding; writing; gardening; natural history; history. Address: (h.) Dovewood, West Linton, Peeblesshire, EH46 7DS; T.-0968 60346.

Paterson, (James Edmund) Neil, MA. Author; b. 31.12.15, Greenock; m., Rosabelle MacKenzie; 2 s.; 1 d. Educ. Banff Academy; Edinburgh University. Lt., RNVR minesweepers, 1940-45; variously Member, Chairman of Production, Director, Consultant, Films of Scotland, 1954-79; Governor, British Film Institute, 1958-60; Chairman, Literature Committee, Scottish Arts Council, 1967-76; Member, Planning Committee, National Film School, 1969; Governor, Pitlochry Festival Theatre, 1966-76; Governor, National Film School, 1970-80; Member, Arts Council of GB, 1974-76; Director, Grampian Television, since 1960; Atlantic Award in Literature, 1946; American Academy Award (Oscar), 1959; author of: The China Run, Behold Thy Daughter, And Delilah, Man on the Tight-Rope, The Kidnappers, A Candle to the Devil; various stories and screenplays. Recreations: golf; fishing; bridge. Address: (h.) St. Ronans, Crieff, Perthshire; T.-0764 2615.

Paterson, Rev. (James) Roy (Herkless), MA. Minister, Cairns Church, Milngavie, since 1964; b. 22.2.28, Brechin; m., Elizabeth Moyra Wright; 3 s. Educ. Merchiston Castle School; Edinburgh University. National Service, Royal Signals, 1945-47; Assistant Minister, West Church of St. Nicholas, Aberdeen, 1953-57; Minister, Craigie Parish Church, Perth, 1957-64. Publications: Meeting the Mormons; A Faith for the 1980s. Recreations: golf; photography. Address: 4 Cairns Drive, Milngavie, Glasgow, G62 8AJ; T.-041-956 1717.

Paterson, Sheriff James Veitch. Sheriff of Lothian and Borders, at Jedburgh, Selkirk and Duns, since 1963; b. 16.4.28; m.; 1 s.; 1 d. Educ. Peebles High School; Edinburgh Academy; Lincoln College, Oxford; Edinburgh University. Admitted, Faculty of Advoates, 1953.

Paterson, John Gordon, MB, ChB, DRCOG, DCM, MFCM. Community Medicine Specialist, Grampian Health Board, since 1977; Honorary Senior Lecturer, Aberdeen University, since 1977; Regional Adviser in Community Medicine - Deputy Faculty Adviser (Scotland), since 1978; b. 19.11.41, Blackburn. Educ. Queen Elizabeth's School, Blackburn; Edinburgh University. Hospital posts in East Lothian and Edinburgh, followed by General Practitioner appointments in North Berwick and Selkirk; transferred to public health duties, 1973, as Assistant Medical Officer of Health, Roxburgh and Selkirk; Scottish Health Service Fellow in Community Medicine, 1974-77. Vice President, City of Aberdeen Branch, British Red Cross Society. Address: (h.) 2H Ashvale Court, Aberdeen; T.-0224 571355.

Paterson, Rev. John Hay, BD. Minister, Flowerhill Parish Church, Airdrie, since 1977; b. 13.6.35, Glasgow; m., Ishbel Marian; 3 d. Educ. Moray School; Glasgow University. RAF, 1953-55; industry, 1952-72; Glasgow University, 1972-76; Probationer, East Kilbride Claremont, 1976-77. Address: Flowerhill Manse, 31 Victoria Place, Airdrie, ML6 9BX; T.-Airdrie 63025.

Paterson, John Lamb, DA, ARIBA, FRIAS, FSIAD. Principal, Edinburgh College of Art, since 1984; Architect/Designer, Paterson Associates, since 1966; b. 17.7.31, Sydney, Australia. Educ. Royal High School, Edinburgh; Edinburgh College of Art. Architect, Robert Matthew & Partners, Edinburgh; Lecturer, School of Architecture, Edinburgh College of Art; began practice, Paterson and Associates, Edinburgh; Director, First Year Studies, then Head, School of Design and Crafts, Edinburgh College of Art. Chairman, Scottish Central Committee of Art, 1982-84; Member, Arts Panel, Edinburgh Festival Society. Recreations: swimming; photography. Address: (h.) 24 Young Street Lane North, Edinburgh; T.-031-225 3725.

Paterson, Rev. John Love, MA, BD, STM, FSA Scot. Minister, St. Michael's Parish Church, Linlithgow, since 1977; b. 6.5.38, Ayr; m., Lorna Begg. Educ. Ayr Academy; Glasgow University; Edinburgh University; Union Theological Seminary, New York. Minister: Presbyterian Church of East Africa, 1964-72, St. Andrew's, Nairobi, 1968-72; Chaplain, Stirling University, 1973-77. Moderator, West Lothian Presbytery, 1985. Recreation: gardening. Address: St. Michael's Manse, Linlithgow, West Lothian; T.-0506 842195.

Paterson, Very Rev. John Munn Kirk, ACII, MA, BD. Minister, St. Paul's Church, Milngavie, since 1970; b. 8.10.22, Leeds; m., Geraldine Lilian Parker; 2 s.; 1 d. Educ. Hillhead High School; Edinburgh University. Pilot, RAF, 1940-46; Insurance official, 1946-58; ordained Minister, Church of Scotland, 1964; Minister, St. John's Church, Bathgate, 1964-70. Moderator, General Assembly, Church of Scotland, 1984-85; Life Member, Chartered Insurance Institute. Recreations: fishing; hill-walking. Address: 8 Buchanan Street, Milngavie, Glasgow; T.-041-956 1043.

Paterson, Joseph Hunter, JP. Member, Dunfermline District Council, since 1974; b. 18.12.33, Maddiston, Stirlingshire; m., Jean Gillies

Halliday; 2 s.; 1 d. Educ. Ballingry Junior Secondary School. Member, Lochgelly District Council, 1973-74; Chairman, Lochore and District Old People's Welfare Council; Chairman, Cowdenbeath and District Volunteer Bureau; Chairman, Cowdenbeath Branch, SCEBTA, NUM, Group 2. Recreations: TV viewing; reading; walking. Address: (h.) 30 Abbotsford Road, Lochore, Fife; T.-Ballingry 860872.

Paterson, Peter John, MB, ChB, FRCS. Consultant Urologist, Glasgow Royal Infirmary, since 1978; Honorary Clinical Lecturer in Urology, Glasgow University; b. 7.6.47, Liverpool; m., Sylvia Dawn; 2 d. Educ. Liverpool College; Liverpool University. General postgraduate surgical experience in Liverpool, Nottingham, Glasgow and Falkirk; higher surgical training in Glasgow. Recreations: chess; snooker; walking; swimming; reading; music. Address: (h.) 4 Buchanan Place, Torrance, G64 4HW.

Paterson, (Thomas) Michael, DA. Assistant Head of Educational Programmes, Scottish Television, since 1980; b. 14.4.38, Kirkcaldy; m., Joan; 1 s.; 2 d. Educ. George Watson's Boys' College; Edinburgh College of Art; Moray House College of Education. Teacher of Art, Waid Academy, Anstruther, 1960-64; Special Assistant, George Heriot's, Edinburgh, 1964-67; Head of Art, Marr College, Troon, 1967-69; Lecturer and Programme Director, College Television Service, Craigie College of Education, 1969-80; ETA: Chairman (Scotland), 1979-80, National Executive, since 1978; RTS Awards Convener and Committee Member, Scottish Centre, since 1981; Member, Publicity Committee, General Assembly, Church of Scotland, since 1983. Publication: A Primary Art Course (Co-author). Recreations: golf; painting; gardening; reading. Address: (h.) 1 Laurelbank Road, Maybole, KA19 8BE.

Paterson, Wilma, DRSAM. Freelance Composer/Writer; b. 23.4.44, Dundee; 1 s.; 1 d. Educ. Harris Academy; Royal Scottish Academy of Music. Composition study with Luigi Dallapiccola in Florence; writes all types of music (chamber, orchestral, incidental); music reviews for Glasgow Herald; broadcasts and writes on food and plants. Publications: A Country Cup; Was Byron Anorexic? Address: 27 Hamilton Drive, Glasgow, G12 8DN; T.-041-339 2711.

Patience, Rev. Donald, MA. Minister, Kilmaurs: St. Maurs-Glencairn, since 1963; b. 28.6.28, Blair Atholl; m., Flora Bell; 1 s.; 1 d. Educ. Kingussie School; St. Andrews University. Assistant, St. Ninian's, Stirling, 1953-54; Chaplain, RAF, 1954-57; Minister, Burns Church, Kilsyth, 1958-63. Moderator, Irvine and Kilmarnock Presbytery, 1981-82; Moderator, Synod of Ayr, 1982-83. Recreations: history (particularly of the clans and tartans); hill-walking; jogging; participated in Glasgow Marathon 1982. Address: The Manse, 9 Standalane, Kilmaurs, Ayrshire; T.-Kilmarnock 38289.

Patience, Donald MacAngus, BSc (Hons). Director Investment, Scottish Development Agency, since 1982; b. 10.3.37, Fearn, Ross and Cromarty; m., Patricia Anne; 3 d. Educ. Tain Royal

Academy; St. Andrews University. Research Scientist, General Electric Co., 1960-64; Production Manager, EMI, Middlesex, 1964-67; Area Manager, Liverpool then London, Investors in Industry PLC, 1967-80; Director and Manager, Finance Corporation for Industry, 1980-82. Recreations: tennis; swimming; reading; Stock Exchange investment. Address: (h.) Fir Tops, 2 Camstradden Drive East, Bearsden, Glasgow, G61 4AH; T.-041-943 1236.

Paton, Rev. Iain Ferguson, BD, FCIS. Minister, Newlands (South), Glasgow, since 1985; b. 28.1.41, Edinburgh; m., Marjorie Vickers Macdonald; 1 s.; 1 d. Educ. George Watson's College, Edinburgh; Edinburgh University. Royal Bank of Scotland Ltd., 1957-66; Assistant Secretary, John Menzies (Holdings) Ltd., 1966-68; Senior Registrar, Charlotte Registrars Ltd., 1968-70; Secretary, Scottish Sports Council, 1970-75; Faculty of Divinity, Edinburgh University, 1975-79; Assistant Minister, St. Ninians Church, Corstorphine, 1979-80; Minister, Banchory-Ternan West Parish Church, 1980-85. Former Vice Chairman, Banchory Community Council; former Member, Kincardine and Deeside Local Health Council. Address: Newlands (South) Manse, 24 Monreith Road, Glasgow, G43 2NY; T.-041-632 2588.

Paton, John. Chairman, Taggarts (Motor Holdings) Ltd., since 1975; Chairman, Rangers Football Club PLC, since 1984; Director, John Lawrence Glasgow, since 1983; b. 18.6.23, Glasgow; m., Agnes Gardiner; 1 s.; 1 d. Educ. Crookston Street School, Glasgow. Recreations: football; golf. Address: (b.) 262 Maryhill Road, Glasgow, G20 7YD; T.-041-332 7777.

Paton, William, BSc (Hons). Controller, Design, Materials and Systems Department, National Engineering Laboratory, since 1985; b. 29.11.41, Kilwinning; m., Elizabeth Anne; 2 s. Educ. Douglas Ewart School, Newton Stewart; Glasgow University. Consulting Geophysicist, Seismograph Services Ltd., 1963; Management Trainee, Colvilles Ltd., Ravenscraig, 1964; Research Scientist in Materials, NEL, 1965-76; Offshore Supplies Office, 1976-77; Divisional Manager, Materials Engineering Division, NEL, 1977-84. Recreation: golf. Address: (b.) National Engineering Laboratory, East Kilbride, Glasgow; T.-East Kilbride 20222.

Patrick, James McIntosh, RSA, LLD, ROI, ARE. Artist and Landscape Painter; b. 4.2.07, Dundee; m., Janet Watterston (deceased); 1 s.; 1 d. Educ. Morgan Academy, Dundee; Glasgow School of Art. Guthrie Award, RSA, 1935; paintings in numerous national and municipal collections; Hon. LLD, Dundee, 1973. Address: (h.) The Shrubbery, Magdalen Yard Road, Dundee.

Patterson, Professor Edward McWilliam, BSc, PhD, FRSE, FIMA. Professor of Mathematics, Aberdeen University, since 1965; b. 30.7.26, Whitby; m., 1, Joan Sibald Maddick (deceased); 2, Elizabeth McAllan Hunter; 1 d. Educ. Northallerton Grammar School; Ripon Grammar School; Whitby County School; Lady Lumley's

Grammar School, Pickering; Leeds University. Research Demonstrator in Mathematics, Sheffield University, 1949-51; Lecturer in Mathematics: St. Andrews University, 1951-56, Leeds University, 1956-59; Aberdeen University: Senior Lecturer in Mathematics, 1960-64, Dean, Faculty of Science, 1981-84; Royal Society Visiting Professor, Malaya University, 1973; awarded MakDougall-Brisbane Prize, Royal Society of Edinburgh, 1962; Vice-President, IMA, 1973-74; President, Edinburgh Mathematical Society, 1964-65; Council Member, London Mathematical Society, 1976-80. Publications: Topology, 1956; Elementary Abstract Algebra (Co-author), 1965; Solving Problems in Vector Algebra, 1968. Address: (b.) Department of Mathematics, Edward Wright Building, Dunbar Street, Aberdeen, AB9 2TY; T.-0224 40241.

Patterson, John Stitt, MB, ChB, FRCGP. Senior Medical Officer, Scottish Home and Health Department, since 1981; b. 23.10.23, Arbroath; m., Margaret Madeline Fraser; 3 s.; 2 d. Educ. Arbroath High School; St. Andrews University; Edinburgh University. Army Service, 1942-46; junior appointments in hospital and general practice, 1951-57; Principal in general practice, Westray (Orkney), 1958, Edinburgh, 1961. Secretary, Scottish Council, Royal College of General Practitioners, 1969-72 and 1973-74. Recreations: photography; music; theatre. Address: (h.) 67 Great King Street, Edinburgh; T.-031-556 7647.

Patterson, Martin Douglass, LLB. Deputy Secretary General, General Synod, Scottish Episcopal Church, since 1982; b. 7.3.53, Tynemouth. Educ. George Watson's College, Edinburgh; Birmingham University. Graduate Trainee, Scottish Gas, 1973-75; Senior Administrative Assistant, Common Services Agency, Scottish Health Service, 1975-81. District Secretary for Scouts, Morningside, Edinburgh. Recreations: cricket; singing; football; travelling; computers. Address: (b.) 21 Grosvenor Crescent, Edinburgh, EH12 5EE; T.-031-225 6357.

Pattison, David Arnold, BSc, PhD. Chief Executive, Scottish Tourist Board, 1981-85; Senior Management Consultant, Arthur Young International, since 1985; b. 9.2.41, Kilmarnock; m., Anne Ross Wilson; 2 s.; 1 d. Educ. Kilmarnock Academy; Glasgow University. Planning Assistant, Ayr County Council, 1963-64; PhD studies, Glasgow University, 1964-66; Planning Assistant, Dunbarton County Council, 1966-67; Lecturer, Strathclyde University, 1967-70; Head of Tourism, Highlands and Islands Development Board, 1970-81. External Examiner for postgraduate tourism courses, Strathclyde University, 1981-84. Recreations: reading; watching soccer and rugby; golf; gardening. Address: (b.) Arthur Young International, 17 Abercromby Place, Edinburgh, EH3; T.-031-556 8641.

Pattison, Rev. Kenneth John, MA, BD, STM. Chaplain, Glasgow Royal Infirmary, since 1984; b. 22.4.41, Glasgow; m., Susan Jennifer Brierley Jenkins; 1 s.; 2 d. Educ. Lenzie Academy; Glasgow University; Union Theological Seminary, New York. Missionary of Church of Scotland/Minister, Church of Central Africa Presbyterian,

Malawi, 1967-77; Principal, Kapeni Theological College, Blantyre, Malawi, 1975-77; Minister, Park Parish Church, Ardrossan, 1977-84. Recreations: gardening; hill-walking. Address: (h.) 46 Berridale Avenue, Cathcart, Glasgow, G44 3AE; T.-041-637 2697.

Pattullo, David Bruce, BA. Treasurer and General Manager (Chief Executive), Bank of Scotland, since 1979; Director (Non-Executive), British Linen Bank, since 1977; Director (Non-Executive), Melville Street Investments (Edinburgh) Ltd., since 1976; Director (Non-Executive), Standard Life, since 1985; b. 2.1.38, Edinburgh; m., Fiona Jane Nicholson; 3 s.; 1 d. Educ. Belhaven Hill School; Rugby; Hertford College, Oxford. National Service commission, Royal Scots (seconded to West Africa); joined Bank of Scotland, 1961; winner, first prize, Institute of Bankers in Scotland, 1964; Manager, Investment Services Department, 1966; Chief Executive, Group Merchant Banking Activities, 1972-78; Deputy Treasurer, Bank of Scotland, 1978; Chairman, Committee of Scottish Clearing Bankers, 1982-83; Honorary Treasurer: Malcolm Sergeant Cancer Fund for Children in Scotland, Benevolent Fund for Nurses in Scotland; Fellow, Institute of Bankers in Scotland. Recreation: tennis. Address: (b.) Bank of Scotland, Head Office, The Mound, Edinburgh, EH1 1YZ; T.-031-243 5555.

Paul, Rev. Iain, BSc, PhD, BD, PhD. Minister, Craigneuk and Belhaven Church, Wishaw, since 1976; b. 15.6.39, Glasgow; m., Elizabeth Henderson Findlay Paul; 1 s.; 1 d. Educ. Govan High School; Strathclyde University; Bristol University; Edinburgh University. Postdoctoral research, Sheffield University, 1967-69; Lecturer in Chemistry, Queen Elizabeth College, London University, 1969-71; Assistant Minister, St. Conal's linked with St. Mark's, Kirkconnel, 1974-75. Publications: Science, Theology and Einstein, 1982; Science and Theology in Einstein's Perspective, 1985. Recreations: writing books; reading; music. Address: 100 Glen Road, Wishaw, ML2 7NP; T.-Wishaw 372495.

Paul, Professor James, DipArch, DipTP, FRIBA, FRIAS, FRTPI, AILA. Professor of Architecture, Duncan of Jordanstone College of Art/Dundee University, since 1983; b. 7.10.29, Toronto; m., Elizabeth; 4 s. Educ. Banff Academy; School of Architecture, Aberdeen; School of Town Planning, Royal Technical College, Glasgow. Architect/Planner, Corporation of City of London, 1954-56; School of Architecture, Dundee: Lecturer, 1956, Senior Lecturer, 1959, Head of School, since 1965; private practice: James Parr and Partners, 1957-59, Johnston and Baxter, 1959-62 (Partner), Baxter, Clark and Paul Architects, 1962-79 (Partner), James Paul Associates, since 1979. Address: (b.) Department of Architecture, Duncan of Jordanstone College of Art/Dundee University, 13 Perth Road, Dundee; T.-0382 23261, Ext. 41.

Paul, Professor John P., BSc, PhD, ARCST, CEng, FIMechE, FISPO, FBOA, FRSA, FRSE. Professor and Chairman, Bioengineering Unit, Strathclyde University, since 1978; b. 26.6.27,

Sunderland; m., Elizabeth R. Graham; 1 s.; 2 d. Educ. Aberdeen Grammar School; Allan Glen's School, Glasgow; Royal College of Science and Technology, Glasgow; Glasgow University. Successively Research Assistant, Lecturer and Senior Lecturer in Mechanics of Materials, Royal College of Science and Technology, subsequently Strathclyde University, 1949-69; Visiting Professor, West Virginia University, 1969-70; Reader, then Personal Professor, Bioengineering Unit, Strathclyde University, 1970-78. Elected Vice President, International Society of Biomechanics, 1985; Council Member, European Society of Biomechanics. Publications: Computing in Medicine (Senior Editor), 1981; Biomaterials in Artificial Organs (Senior Editor), 1984. Recreations: formerly rugby; gardening; home maintenance; light reading. Address: (h.) 25 James Watt Road, Milngavie, Glasgow, G62 7JX; T.-041-956 3221.

Paul, Ronald, MA, DipEd. Headmaster, Currie High School, since 1970; b. 6.8.32, Edinburgh; m., Nancy Crawford Logan; 3 s. Educ. Boroughmuir School, Edinburgh; Edinburgh University; Moray House College of Education. Commissioned, RAF, 1955-58; Teacher of Geography, Edinburgh, 1958-65; Principal Teacher, Boroughmuir, 1965-67; Headmaster, James Clark School, Edinburgh, 1968-70. Church Elder; President, Edinburgh Rotary Club, 1982-83; Past President, Lothian Headteachers and Headteachers Association of Scotland; Member, Scottish Examination Board. Recreations: family; travel; reading; music; oil painting. Address: (b.) Currie High School, Dolphin Avenue, Currie, EH14 5RD; T.-031-449 2165.

Pauson, Professor Peter Ludwig, BSc, PhD, CChem, FRSC, FRSE. Freeland Professor of Chemistry, Strathclyde University, since 1959; b. 30.7.25, Bamberg, Germany; m., Lai-ngau Wong; 1 s.; 1 d. Educ. Glasgow University; Sheffield University. Assistant Professor, Duquesne University, Pittsburgh, 1949-51; postdoctoral fellowships: University of Chicago, 1951-52, Harvard University, 1952-53; Lecturer, then Reader, Sheffield University, 1953-59; Visiting Professor: University of Arizona, 1966-67, La Trobe University, Melbourne and Australian National University, Canberra, 1977. Tilden Lectureship, 1960, and Organometallic Chemistry Award, Chemical Society, 1976. Publication: Organometallic Chemistry, 1967. Recreations: skiing; hill-walking; gardening; badminton; listening to music. Address: (b.) Department of Pure and Applied Chemistry, Strathclyde University, Cathedral Street, Glasgow, G1 1XL; T.-041-552 4400.

Pawley, Professor G. Stuart, MA, PhD, FRSE. Professor of Computational Physics, Edinburgh University, since 1985; b. 22.6.37, Ilford; m., Anthea Jean Miller; 2 s.; 1 d. Educ. Bolton School; Corpus Christi College, Cambridge. Lecturer, Edinburgh University, 1964; Reader, 1970; Personal Chair, 1985; Guest Professor, Aarhus University, Denmark, 1969-70. Recreations: choral singing; mountain walking. Address: (b.) Physics Department, Kings Buildings, Edinburgh University, EH9 3JZ; T.-031-667 1081.

Peacock, Professor Alan Turner, DSC, MA, Hon. DUniv (Stirling), Hon. DEcon (Zurich), FBA. Research Professor in Public Finance, Esmee Fairbairn Centre, Heriot-Watt University, since 1985; Executive Director, David Hume Institute, Edinburgh, since 1985; b. 26.6.22, Ryton-on-Tyne; m., Margaret Martha Astell-Burt; 2 s.; 1 d. Educ. Grove Academy; Dundee High School; St. Andrews University. Royal Navy, 1942-45; Lecturer in Economics, St. Andrews, 1947-48; Lecturer, then Reader in Economics, London School of Economics, 1948-56; Professor of Economic Science, Edinburgh University, 1956-62; Professor of Economics, York University, 1962-78 (Deputy Vice Chancellor, 1963-69); Professor of Economics, University College, Buckingham, 1978-80; Principal, then Vice Chancellor, Buckingham University, 1980-84; Chief Economic Adviser, Department of Trade and Industry (on secondment), 1973-76; Member, Royal Commission on the Constitution, 1970-73; Member, Inquiry into Retirement Provision, 1983-85; SSRC Council, 1972-73; President, International Institute of Public Finance, 1966-69; Chairman, Committee on Financing the BBC, since 1985. Recreations: attempting to write music; jogging; hill-walking. Address: (h.) 8 Gilmour Road, Edinburgh, EH16 5NF; T.-031-667 0544.

Peacock, Peter James. Member, Highland Regional Council, since 1982 (Vice-Chairman, Finance Committee); Area Officer, Highlands, Islands, Grampian, Scottish Association of Citizens Advice Bureaux; b. 27.2.52, Edinburgh; 2 s. Educ. Hawick High School; Jordanhill College of Education, Glasgow. Community Worker, Orkney Islands, 1973-75. Co-author, Vice-Chairman, subsequently Chairman of successful applicant group for Independent Local Radio franchise, Moray Firth. Recreations: ornithology; watching rugby union; challenging conventional thought. Address: (h.) 68 Braeside Park, Balloch, Inverness; T.-0463 790371.

Peaker, Professor Malcolm, PhD, FZS, FIBiol, FRSE. Director, Hannah Research Institute, Ayr, since 1981; Hannah Professor of Dairy Science, Glasgow University, since 1981; b. 21.8.43; m.; 3 s. Educ. Henry Mellish Grammar School, Nottingham; Sheffield University; University of Hong Kong.

Pearson, Brigadier Alastair Stevenson, CB (1958), DSO, OBE, MC, TD. Lord Lieutenant of Dunbartonshire, since 1979; Keeper of Dumbarton Castle, since 1981; b. 1.6.15; m.; 3 d. Educ. Kelvinside Academy; Sedbergh. Served Second World War (Lt.-Col., 1942); ADC to The Queen, 1956-61; Hon. Colonel, 15th (Scottish) Bn., The Parachute Regiment (TA), 1963-77 and since 1983. Address: (h.) Tullochan, Gartocharn, by Alexandria, Dunbartonshire.

Pearson, Colin Keith, BSc, PhD. Senior Lecturer in Biochemistry, Aberdeen University, since 1982; b. 5.4.43, Wednesfield; m., Patricia Kathleen; 2 s.; 1 d. Educ. Bilston Boys' Grammar School; Liverpool University. Postdoctoral Fellow, State University of New York, 1968-69, and Liverpool University, 1969-70; Lecturer in

Biochemistry, Aberdeen University, 1970. Recreations: reading; judo. Address: (b.) Biochemistry Department, Marischal College, Aberdeen University, Aberdeen; T.-0224 40241, Ext. 255.

Pearson, Donald William Macintyre, BSc (Hons), MB, ChB, MRCP. Consultant Physician, Aberdeen Teaching Hospitals, since 1984; Clinical Senior Lecturer, Aberdeen University, since 1984; b. 5.9.50, Kilmarnock; m., Margaret J.K. Harris; 2 s.; 1 d. Educ. Cumnock Academy; Glasgow University. Registrar, University Department of Medicine, Glasgow Royal Infirmary, Lecturer in Medicine with Aberdeen University, Raigmore Hospital, Inverness; Senior Registrar in General Medicine, Diabetes and Endocrinology, Grampian Health Board. President, New Cumnock Burns Club, 1985-86. Recreations: football; computing; music; Scottish poetry. Address: (b.) Diabetic Clinic, Woolmanhill, Aberdeen Royal Infirmary, Aberdeen; T.-0224 681818, Ext. 491.

Peat, Rev. Stanley William, BSc, PhD, BD. Minister, St. Serf's Parish Church, Edinburgh, since 1984; b. 5.5.29, Edinburgh; m., Elizabeth Eleanor Smith; 1 s.; 1 d. Educ. George Heriot's School, Edinburgh; Edinburgh University. Lecturer, then Senior Lecturer in Physics, Heriot-Watt College/University, 1957-73; Minister, St. John's Church, Carluke, 1977-84. Recreation: golf. Address: 1 Denham Green Terrace, Edinburgh, EH5 3PG; T.-031-552 4059.

Peat, William Wood Watson, CBE, JP. Farmer; National Governor for Scotland, BBC, since 1984; b. 14.12.22, Denny; m., Jean McHarrie; 2 s.; 1 d. Educ. Denny Public School. Lt., Royal Signals, NW Europe and India, 1940-46; Broadcaster; National Chairman, subsequently President, Scottish Association of Young Farmers Clubs; Member, Stirling County Council, 1959-75 (Vice Convener, 1967-70); Council Member, NFU of Scotland, 1959-78 (President, 1966-67); Member, Scotish River Purification Advisory Committee, 1960-79; Board of Management, RSNH, 1960-72; General Commissioner of Income Tax, since 1962; Chairman, Scottish Advisory Committee, Association of Agriculture, 1974-79 (Vice-President, since 1979); Council, Hannah Research Institute, 1963-82; Council Member, Scottish Agricultural Organisation Society Ltd., since 1963 (President, 1974-77); Member, British Agricultural Council, 1974-84; Member, Board of Management, Oatridge Agricultural College, 1967-75; Governor, West of Scotland Agricultural College (Chairman, since 1983); Director, FMC plc, 1974-83; Member, Central Council for Agricultural and Horticultural Co-operation, 1967-83; Member, Board of Management, British Farm Produce Council, 1964-83, now BFP Committee, Food from Britain, since 1984; Chairman, BBC Scottish Agricultural Advisory Committee, 1971-76; Chairman, Broadcasting Council for Scotland, since 1984. Recreations: amateur radio; flying. Address: (h.) 61 Stirling Road, Larbert, FK5 4SG.

Peddie, Richard L., MA, MEd, ABPsS. Vice-Principal, Craigie College of Education; b. 11.6.28, Grangemouth; m., Nan K. Bell; 1 s.; 2 d.

Educ. Grangemouth High School; Glasgow University. Royal Signals Officer, Allied Supreme HQ (SHAPE), 1951-53; Teacher, Stirlingshire, 1953-56; Educational Psychologist, Ayrshire, 1956-59; Lecturer, Jordanhill College, 1959-64; Head of Psychology Department, Assistant Principal, Vice-Principal, Craigie College of Education, since 1964; Member, General Teaching Council for Scotland, 1970-78; External Examiner in Education, London University Institute, 1971-76; External Examiner, Hamilton College of Education, 1977-80; Member, Scottish Examination Board, 1980-84; Member, Education Committee, British Psychological Society, 1964-68; Chairman, Glasgow University Educational Colloquium, 1966-67; Chairman, Association of Lecturers in Colleges of Education in Scotland (ALCES), 1967-69; Captain, 51 (H) Infantry Division Signals Regiment (TA), 1953-60; Vice-Chairman, Ayr Children's Panel, 1970-74; Member, Scottish Council for Research in Education, 1962-78; Member, Executive Committee, Scottish Division of Educational and Child Psychology, since 1979; Chairman, Association of Higher Academic Staff in Colleges of Education, since 1984; Church of Scotland Elder. Recreations: reading; Rotary; driving; very occasional golf; tennis. Address: (h.) 14 Glenpark Place, Alloway, Ayr, KA7 4SQ; T.-0292 41996.

Peden, Hugh Andrew Mair, JP, MA, LLB, NP. Senior Partner, Peden and Patrick, Solicitors, Glasgow, since 1968; b. 7.11.20, Glasgow; m., Grace Joyce Parker; 1 s.; 1 d. Educ. High School of Glasgow; Glasgow University. Served in 11 Group Fighter Command, RAF, 1941-46; qualified as a Solicitor and became a Partner in family law firm, 1951. Liberal Party Parliamentary Agent, seven consecutive General Elections since 1959, Eastwood (formerly East Renfrewshire). Recreations: politics; supporting Queens Park FC (of which a member for more than 20 years); reading. Address: (h.) Milrig, Glebe Road, Newton Mearns, Glasgow; T.-041-639 2952.

Peden, James McKenzie, BSc, MEng, PhD, CEng, MIChemE, MAIME. Senior Lecturer, Petroleum Engineering Department, Heriot-Watt University, since 1981; Director, Edinburgh Petroleum Development Services Ltd., since 1983; b. 27.9.47, Edinburgh; m., Jacqueline Watson; 1 s.; 1 d. Educ. Darwen Grammar School; Heriot-Watt University. Process Technologist, Shell UK Oil Ltd., 1970-73; Research Engineer, Henry Balfour Ltd., Leven, 1973-74; Sales Development Officer, Distillers Ltd., 1974-75; postgraduate student, 1975-76; Petroleum Engineer, Shell International Petroleum Co., 1976-78; Lecturer, Heriot-Watt University, since 1978. Director, Aberdeen Section, Society of Petroleum Engineers, AIME; Member, SPE and I CHEME; Member, International Editorial Review Committee, SPE Dallas. Recreations: golf; bridge. Address: (h.) Dunella, Station Road, Kinross, KY13 7TU; T.-0577 62708.

Peebles Brown, David Adair, MB, ChB, FRCSEdin, FRCSGlas. Consultant Surgeon, Gartnavel General/Western Infirmary, Glasgow, since 1963; Honorary Clinical Lecturer, Glasgow University, since 1963; b. 4.1.27, Malton, Yorkshire; m., Mary A.F. Findlay; 3 s.; 1 d. Educ.

Shrewsbury School; Glasgow University. Commission, 1st Royal Tank Regiment; medical student, junior surgical trainee, then Consultant Surgeon. Recreations: gardening; ornithology. Address: (h.) 3 Falcon Terrace Lane, Glasgow, G20 OAB; T.-041-945 0920.

Peggie, Robert Galloway Emslie, FCCA, FBCS. Chief Executive, Lothian Regional Council, since 1974; b. 5.1.29, Bo'ness; m., Christine; 1 s.; 1 d. Educ. Lasswade High School. Trainee Accountant, 1946-52; Accountant in industry, 1952-57; Edinburgh Corporation, 1957-72: O. and M. Officer, Assistant City Chamberlain, Deputy City Chamberlain, Reorganisation Steering Committee. Recreation: golf. Address: (b.) Regional Headquarters, George IV Bridge, Edinburgh, EH1 1UQ; T.-031-229 9292.

Pelham Burn, Angus Maitland, JP. Farmer; Vice Lord Lieutenant, Kincardineshire, since 1978; Member, Grampian Regional Council, since 1974; Member, Queen's Bodyguard for Scotland (Royal Company of Archers), since 1968; Director, Bank of Scotland, since 1977; Company Director; b. 13.12.31; m.; 4 d. Educ. Harrow; North of Scotland College of Agriculture. Vice Convener, Kincardine County Council, 1973-75.

Pelly, Frances Elsie, ARSA, DA. Sculptor; b. 21.7.47, Edinburgh. Educ. Morrison's Academy, Crieff; Duncan of Jordanstone College of Art, Dundee. Secondary and primary school teaching, Dumfriesshire, 1973-74; self-employed as Sculptor and part-time lecturing, Dundee, 1974-79; Lecturer in Sculpture, Grays School of Art, Aberdeen, 1979-83. Recreations: learning dressage riding; gardening. Address: 5 Dolphinstone Cottages, Tranent, East Lothian; T.-Tranent 613961.

Pendreigh, David Mackie, MB, ChB, FRCP, FFCM, DPH. Senior Lecturer, Department of Community Medicine, Edinburgh University, since 1978; Honorary Community Medicine Specialist, Lothian Health Board, since 1978; Chief Investigator, WHO Collaborating Centre, Usher Institute, since 1982; b. 13.1.31, Whitburn, West Lothian; m., Gladys Margaret Pendreigh; 2 s.; 1 d. Educ. Bathgate Academy; Edinburgh University. Variety of clinical posts in hospital and general practice, as well as in public health, and two years as a Surgeon Lieutenant in Royal Navy; various posts, Scottish Home and Health Department, 1966-78, latterly as Principal Medical Officer and Director, Scottish Health Services Planning Unit; serves on various NHS Committees. Recreations: walking; tennis; squash. Address: (h.) 22 Bonaly Avenue, Edinburgh, EH13 OET; T.-031-441 1869.

Penman, Ian Dalgleish, MA. Deputy Secretary, Central Services, Scottish Office, since 1984; b. 1.8.31, Glasgow; m., Elisabeth Stewart Strachan; 3 s. Educ. High School of Glasgow; Glasgow University; Balliol College, Oxford. RAF Education Branch, 1955-57; HM Treasury, 1957-58; joined Scottish Office, 1958; Private Secretary to Parliamentary Under Secretary of State, 1960-62; Principal, Scottish Development Department, 1962-70; Assistant Secretary, Establishment Division, 1970-72, Police Division, 1972-78; Under

Secretary, Scottish Development Department, 1978-84. Recreations: swimming; travel; music. Address: (h.) 4 Wardie Avenue, Edinburgh, EH5 2AB; T.-031-552 2180.

Penn, Ian Devis, CBiol, MIBiol, AIMLS. Depute Principal, Dumfries and Galloway College of Technology, since 1983; b. 20.3.40, Bromley; m., Valerie Jane Rolston; 1 s.; 1 d. Educ. Colfe's Grammar School, London; North East Surrey College of Technology. Laboratory technician; Assistant Lecturer in Biology, Chelmsford, Essex; Lecturer B in Biology, Bristol Technical College; Senior Lecturer in Science, then Head, Department of Science, Stevenson College, Edinburgh. Institute of Biology: Chairman, Education Division, since 1984, Vice Chairman, Scottish Branch, since 1983. Recreation: gardening. Address: (h.) Nithsdale, Edinburgh Road, Dumfries; T.-0387 62269.

Pennington, Christopher Royston, BSc (Hons), MB, ChB, MRCP, MD, FRCPEdin. Consultant Physician (General Medicine), since 1979; Honorary Senior Lecturer in Medicine, Dundee University, since 1979; b. 22.2.46, Chard; m., Marcia Jane Barclay; 1 d. Educ. Shebbear College; Manchester University. House Officer, Manchester Royal Infirmary, 1970-71; Registrar in Medicine, Aberdeen Royal Infirmary, 1971-74; Lecturer in Medicine, Dundee University, 1974-79. External Examiner in Medicine, Aberdeen University, 1983-86. Address: (h.) Balnagowan, Braehead, Invergowrie, Dundee.

Penny, Duncan Thomas Cameron, BSc. Rector, Vale of Leven Academy, since 1980; b. 25.2.36, Glasgow; m., Elizabeth M.T. Dunbar; 2 s.; 1 d. Educ. Eastbank Academy, Glasgow; Glasgow University; Jordanhill College. Assistant Teacher, Uddingston Grammar School, 1958; Lecturer, Langside FE College, Glasgow, 1962; Principal Teacher of Mathematics, Blantyre High School, 1966; Senior Housemaster, Larkhall Academy, 1970; Assistant Headteacher, then Depute Headteacher, Clydebank High School, 1973-80. President, Glasgow Mathematical Association; President, West of Scotland Lawn Tennis Association; Council Member, Scottish LTA; Secretary, Strathclyde Regional Executive, HAS. Recreations: tennis; golf; marathon running; reading. Address: (h.) 6 Ledcameroch Road, Bearsden, Glasgow, G61 4AA; T.-041-943 1302.

Pentland, Brian, BSc, MB, ChB, MRCP. Consultant Neurologist in Rehabilitation Medicine, since 1982; Senior Lecturer in Orthopaedic Surgery and Neurosurgery, Edinburgh University, since 1983; b. 24.6.49, Glasgow; m., Gillian Mary Duggua; 4 s. Educ. Liberton High School, Edinburgh; Edinburgh University. Junior hospital appointments in Edinburgh, Cumbria and Dundee; formerly Lecturer in Neurology in Edinburgh. Recreation: hill-walking. Address: (b.) Astley Ainslie Hospital, Grange Loan, Edinburgh, EH9 2HL; T.-031-447 6271.

Peoples, Robin (Robert John), MA (Hons). Artistic Director, Scottish Youth Theatre, since 1983; b. 9.9.54, Londonderry; m., Lamorna

Hutchison; 1 d. Educ. Foyle College, Derry; St. Andrews University. Youth and community work in Northern Ireland; taught at University of Erlangen-Nuremberg, West Germany; awarded Scottish Arts Council Director's Bursary; worked with various theatre companies throughout Scotland. Member, Board, Scottish Puppet Festival. Recreations: theatre; painting; reading; canoeing. Address: (b.) Scottish Youth Theatre, 48 Albany Street, Edinburgh, EH1 3QR; T.-031-557 2224.

Peploe, Denis Frederic Neil, RSA, DA. Artist; b. 25.3.14, Edinburgh; m., Elizabeth Marion Barr; 1 s.; 1 d. Educ. Edinburgh Academy; Edinburgh College of Art. Fellowship, Edinburgh College of Art, 1939-40; War Service, 1940-46 (RA, Intelligence Corps, SOE); Lecturer, Edinburgh College of Art, 1954-79; elected ARSA, 1956, RSA, 1966; Governor, Edinburgh College of Art, 1982. Recreations: hill-walking; mycology. Address: (h.) 18 Mayfield Gardens, Edinburgh; T.-031-667 6164.

Percy, William Robert Victor, TD, MA, BCom. Chairman, Manpower Committee, Lothian Regional Council, since 1982; Deputy Chairman, Livingston Development Corporation, since 1983; b. 4.5.45, Edinburgh. Educ. Melville College, Edinburgh; Edinburgh University. Councillor, Edinburgh Corporation, 1973; elected to Lothian Regional Council, 1974; Chairman: Craigmillar Sheltered Workshop Advisory Board, Social Work General Services Sub Committee; Member, COSLA Manpower Committee; Member, Whitley Council (New Town Staffs), since 1983; Conservative Parliamentary candidate, Edinburgh Leith, 1974; Vice-Chairman, Leith Conservative Association, since 1983; full-time appointments with Small Industries Council for Rural Areas of Scotland, 1969-76 and Scottish Development Agency, 1976-81; Director, W.R.V. Percy & Co.; commissioned, 8/9th Bn., RS (TA), 1963; OC No. 1 (8/9th Bn.) RS Coy TA, 1971-81; Second in Command, 2nd Bn., 52nd Lowland Volunteers, 1984; Elder, St. George's West Church, Edinburgh. Recreations: hill-walking; swimming. Address: (h.) 59 Dundas Street, Edinburgh, EH3 6RS; T.-031-556 1336.

Percy-Robb, Professor Iain Walter, MB, ChB, PhD, FRCPEdin, FRCPath. Professor in Pathological Biochemistry, Glasgow University, since 1984; b. 8.12.35, Glasgow; m., Margaret E. Cormie; 2 s.; 2 d. Educ. George Watson's College, Edinburgh; Edinburgh University. Various clinical posts, 1959-63; research scholar, 1963-65; Lecturer, then Senior Lecturer, then Reader, Edinburgh University, 1965-84. Recreation: golf. Address: (h.) Rossendale, 7 Upper Glenburn Road, Bearsden, Glasgow.

Perfect, Hugh Epton, BSc, MIBiol. Assistant Principal (In-Service, Research and Development), Moray House College of Education; b. 9.4.41, London; m., Susan; 2 d. Educ. Haberdasher's Askes' School, Hampstead; Imperial College, London. Teacher, Windsor Grammar School; Lecturer, Bulmershe College of Education, Reading; Lecturer/Senior Lecturer, Biology Department, Moray House College of Education.

Member: National Committee for the In-Service Training of Teachers, NCITT Working Party on Staff Development, Scottish Council for the Validation of Courses for Teachers, Scottish Committee on Open Learning; Convener, JCCES Advisory Committee on Multicultural Education. Recreations: badminton; gardening; micro-computers. Address: (b.) Moray House College of Education, Holyrood Road, Edinburgh, EH8 8AQ; T.-031-556 8455.

Perrie, Walter, MA. Poet and Critic; b. 5.6.49, Quarter. Educ. Hamilton Academy; Edinburgh University. Founding Editor, Chapman (literary journal); full-time writer, since 1975; five volumes of poetry, one of which, A Lamentation for the Children, won a Scottish Arts Council Book Award; author of critical writings on Hugh MacDiarmid, Muriel Spark, W.H. Auden and Lord Byron; has given numerous lectures, broadcasts and readings in Britain, Europe and Canada; held Scottish-Canadian Writer's Exchange Fellowship, 1984-85, based in Vancouver; received John Downes Memorial Award for Poetry, Gregory Award for Poetry, and two Scottish Arts Council bursaries. Address: (h.) 118 Brankholm Brae, Hamilton, Lanarkshire, ML3 9QR.

Perth, 17th Earl of, (John David Drummond), PC (1957); b. 13.5.07; m., Nancy Seymour Fincke; 2 s. Educ. Downside; Cambridge University. Lt., Intelligence Corps, 1940; War Cabinet Offices, 1942-43; Ministry of Production, 1944-45; Minister of State for Colonial Affairs, 1957-62; Member, Court, St. Andrews University, since 1967; Trustee, National Library of Scotland, since 1968. Address: (h.) Stobhall, by Perth.

Pertwee, Roger Guy, MA, DPhil (Oxon). Senior Lecturer, Department of Pharmacology, Aberdeen University, since 1978; b. 21.9.42, Wembley; m., Teresa; 1 s. Educ. Eastbourne College; Christ Church, Oxford. Postdoctoral research post, Oxford University, 1969-74; Lecturer, Aberdeen University, 1974-78. Member, Senatus, Aberdeen University, since 1982. Recreation: sailing. Address: (b.) Department of Pharmacology, Marischal College, Aberdeen University, Aberdeen; T.-Aberdeen 40241.

Peterkin, George Sim, RMN, RGN, JP. Member, Grampian Health Board, since 1983; Member, Scottish Committee, Council on Tribunals, since 1983; Member, Industrial Tribunals, since 1972; b. 30.12.21, Elgin; m., Mildred Robertson; 2 d. Educ. West End School, Elgin. Royal Navy, 1941-46; Psychiatric Nurse, Bilbohall Hospital, Elgin, 1946-79. Recreations: photography; DIY; reading; trade union affairs. Address: (h.) 24 Pansport Road, Elgin, Morayshire, IV30 1HD; T.-0343 2335.

Peterkin, Rev. Neilson, MA. Minister, The Church of Broom, Newton Mearns, since 1958; b. 1.2.21, Edinburgh; m., Elsa Stewart Ross; 1 s. Educ. Daniel Stewart's College, Edinburgh; Edinburgh University. Chaplain to the Forces, 1945-48; Minister, St. George's Church, Dumfries, 1948-58. Recreations: golf; gardening. Address: 3 Laigh Road, Newton Mearns, Glasgow, G77 5EX; T.-041-639 2916.

Peters, David Alexander, MA, DSA, AHSM. General Manager, Borders Health Board, since 1985; b. 18.10.38, Glasgow; m., Moira Cullen Macpherson; 2 s.; 1 d. Educ. King's Park School, Glasgow; Glasgow University; Manchester University. Hospital Secretary, Greenock Royal Infirmary, Eye Infirmary, ENT Hospital, 1963-66; Eastern Regional Hospital Board, Dundee: Principal Administrative Assistant, 1966-68, Assistant Secretary, 1968-71, Principal Assistant Secretary, 1971-74; District Administrator, Renfrew District, Argyll and Clyde Health Board, 1974-81; Secretary, Borders Health Board, 1981-85. Recreations: curling; tennis; sailing; golf; gardening. Address: (h.) Wildcroft, Gattonside, Melrose, TD6 9NP.

Peterson, George Sholto, NP. Solicitor and Notary Public, since 1956; Honorary Sheriff, since 1982; b. 18.9.27, Lerwick; m., Dorothy Hilda Spence; 2 s.; 4 d. Educ. Lerwick Central Public School; Edinburgh University. Secretary, The Shetland Trust; Factor for the Marquess of Zetland; Senior Partner, Tait & Peterson, Solicitors and Estate Agents, Lerwick; Dean, Faculty of Solicitors in Shetland; Honorary Pastor, Ebenezer Church, Lerwick. Recreations: studying theology; reading; fishing. Address: (b.) Bank of Scotland Buildings, Lerwick, Shetland; T.-0595 3010.

Petrie, Professor James Colquhoun, MB, ChB, FRCPEdin, FRCP. Professor of Clinical Pharmacology, Department of Therapeutics and Clinical Pharmacology, Aberdeen University, since 1985; Honorary Consultant Physician, Aberdeen Teaching Hospitals, since 1971; b. 18.9.41, Aberdeen; m., Dr. M. Xanthe P.; 2 s.; 2 d. Educ. Anieres, Geneva; Robert Gordon's College, Aberdeen; Aberdeen University. Senior Lecturer, 1971-81, Reader, 1981-85, Aberdeen University. Chairman, Lecht Ski Company, since 1976. Recreations: ski; golf; fishing. Address: (b.) Department of Therapeutics and Clinical Pharmacology, Aberdeen Royal Infirmary, Foresterhill, Aberdeen, AB9 2ZB; T.-0224 681818.

Phanjoo, Andre Ludovic, MB, ChB, FRCPsych, DPM. Consultant Psychiatrist, Royal Edinburgh Hospital, since 1972; Honorary Senior Lecturer, Department of Psychiatry, Edinburgh University, since 1982; b. 29.9.37, Port Louis, Mauritius; m., Barbara Elizabeth Darwell; 1 s.; 2 d. Educ. Royal College, Port Louis; Edinburgh University. Postgraduate training in psychiatry, Royal Edinburgh Hospital, 1967-70; appointed Consultant Psychiatrist to Royal Edinburgh Hospital and Rosslynlee Hospital, 1972; Consultant in Geriatric Psychiatry, 1982; Consultant, Catholic Marriage Advisory Council. Recreations: hill-walking; playing the guitar; music/opera; cooking. Address: (h.) 29 Blacket Place, Edinburgh, EH9 1RJ; T.-031-667 9809.

Philip, Alistair Erskine, MA, PhD, FBPsS. Area Co-ordinator, Clinical Psychology Service, Lothian Health Board, since 1980; Member, State Hospital Management Committee, since 1980; Honorary Senior Lecturer, Edinburgh University, since 1980; b. 10.7.38, Aberdeen; m., Betty J. McKay; 1 s.; 2 d. Educ. Aberdeen Grammar School; Aberdeen University; Edinburgh University. Scientific staff, MRC Unit for Epidemiological Studies in Psychiatry, Edinburgh University, 1963-71; Head, Psychology Department, Bangour Village Hospital, 1971-80; Chairman, Clinical Psychology Sub-Committee, National Consultative Committee of Scientists in Professions Allied to Medicine, 1981-85. Publication: Suicidal Behaviour (Co-author), 1972. Recreations: playing hockey; going to auctions. Address: (h.) 37 Meggetland Terrace, Edinburgh, EH14 1AP; T.-031-443 2447.

Philip, Rev. George M., MA. Minister, Sandyford-Henderson Memorial Church, since 1956; b. 11.11.25, Bucksburn, Aberdeenshire; m., Patricia Joy Morrison; 2 s.; 1 d. Educ. Bucksburn School; Central Secondary School, Aberdeen; Aberdeen University. Able seaman, Royal Navy, 1943-47; qualified as Member, Institute of Bankers in Scotland, 1949; licensed by Aberdeen Presbytery, 1953. Moderator, Glasgow Presbytery, 1979-80. Publications: Fundamentals of the Faith; School of Discipleship; Commentary on Book of Job; Daily Bible Reading Notes. Recreation: gardening. Address: 66 Woodend Drive, Glasgow, G13 1TG; T.-041-954 9013.

Philip, Henry Leslie, MA (Hons), BA (Hons), FEIS. Headmaster, Liberton High School, Edinburgh, 1969-85; b. 25.11.27, Aberdeen; m., Jane F.S.; 1 d. Educ. Robert Gordon's College, Aberdeen; Aberdeen University; Cambridge University. Principal Teacher of Classics: Kirkcudbright Academy, 1953-58, Beath High, Cowdenbeath, 1958-62; HM Inspector of Schools, 1962-69. Member: Scottish Examination Board, SCOTBEC, National Committee for In-Service Training of Teachers; Vice President, EIS, 1983-84; Convener, EIS Education Committee, 1981-83, 1984-85; Chairman, Scottish Classics Group. Recreations: golf; Rotary; stamp collecting.

Philip, Michael Stuart, MBE, MA (Oxon), BSc, FICF. Reader in Forestry, Aberdeen University, since 1982; b. 4.11.26, London; m., Audrey Elizabeth Rae; 1 s.; 1 d. Educ. Bancroft's; Kings College, London; Keble College, Oxford. Assistant Conservator of Forests, Uganda, 1947-60; Forest Ecologist, Uganda, 1960-62; Conservator of Forests (Research), Uganda, 1962-64; Lecturer, then Senior Lecturer in Forestry, Aberdeen University, 1964-82; Associate Professor of Forestry, Dar-es-Salaam University, 1977-79. Trustee, Scottish Forestry Trust. Publication: Measuring Trees and Forests. Recreations: gardening; fishing. Address: (h.) 45 Hillview Road, Cults, Aberdeen, AB1 9HA; T.-0224 867132.

Philipson, Sir Robin, PPRSA, Hon. RA. Painter; b. 1916, Broughton-in-Furness. Educ. Dumfries Academy; Edinburgh College of Art. KOSB, India, RIASC, 1940-46; joined staff, Edinburgh College of Art, 1947; RSA Guthrie Award, 1951; ARSA, 1952; RSW, 1955; Head, School of Drawing and Painting, Edinburgh College of Art, 1960; RSA, 1962; Visiting Professor of Painting, Colorado University, 1963; Leverhulme

Travel Award, 1965; FRSA, 1965; Member, Royal Fine Art Commission for Scotland, 1965; Cargill Award, 1967; Secretary, RSA, 1969; Council Member, Edinburgh Festival Society, 1969; Member, Scottish Advisory Committee, British Council, 1971; President, RSA, 1973-83; elected Honorary Royal Academician, 1974; knighted for service to arts in Scotland, 1976; Honorary Doctorate, Stirling University, 1976; Member, Board of Trustees, National Museum of Antiquities for Scotland, 1976; FRSE, 1978; LLD, Aberdeen University, 1978; elected Member, Royal Academy, 1981; DUniv, Heriot-Watt University; retired as Head, School of Drawing and Painting, Edinburgh College of Art, 1982; RSA William J. Macaulay Award, 1983; numerous one-man exhibitions, since 1954. Address: (h.) 23 Crawfurd Road, Edinburgh; T.-031-667 2373.

Phillips, Professor Calbert Inglis, PhD, MD, DPH, FRCS, FRCSEdin, DO, FBOA (Hon.). Professor of Ophthalmology, Edinburgh University; Honorary Consultant Ophthalmic Surgeon, Edinburgh Royal Infirmary; b. 20.3.25, Glasgow; m., C. Anne Fulton; 1 s. Educ. High School of Glasgow; Robert Gordon's College, Aberdeen; Aberdeen University. House Physician and House Surgeon, Aberdeen Royal Infirmary; Registrar, Moorfields Eye Hospital, London; Senior Registrar, St. Thomas' Hospital, London; Research Assistant, Institute of Ophthalmology, London University; Consultant Surgeon, Bristol Eye Hospital; Professor of Ophthalmology, Manchester University. Publications: Clinical Practice and Economics (Editor), 1977; Basic Clinical Ophthalmology, 1984. Recreation: ophthalmology. Address: (b.) Eye Pavilion, Chalmers Street, Edinburgh, EH3 9HA; T.-031-229 2477, Ext. 2578.

Phillips, Rev. David Morgan, BA. Minister, Tillicoultry and Dunning Congregational Church, since 1979; President, Congregational Union of Scotland, 1984-85; b. 17.12.39, Cardiff. Educ. Bo'ness Academy; Llandovery College, Carmarthenshire; University College of South Wales and Monmouthshire, Cardiff; United Theological College, Aberystwyth; Memorial Theological College, Swansea. Minister: Libanus, Ebbw Vale and Barham Beaufort, 1966-69; EU Congregational Church, Tillicoultry, 1969-79; Secretary, Central District Council, Congregational Union of Scotland, 1971-83 and since 1985; Tutor, Scottish Congregational College, since 1984; Chaplain, Stirling University, since 1971. Honorary Vice-President, Hillfoots RFC. Recreations: rugby; angling. Address: 10 Walker Terrace, Tillicoultry, Clackmannanshire; T.-0259 50394.

Phillips, John Brydon Mills, MA. Director, Scottish Association for the Care and Resettlement of Offenders, since 1980; b. 15.6.32, Cheadle Hulme; m., Anna; 1 s.; 3 d. Educ. Mill Hill School; Worcester College, Oxford. Teacher: The Leys School, Cambridge, 1955-60; Campbell College, Belfast, 1960-68; Royal Belfast Academical Institution, 1968-74; Director, Northern Ireland Marriage Guidance Council, 1974-79. Recreations: hill-walking; (motor) caravanning. Address: (h.) 1 Saxe Coburg Street, Edinburgh; T.-031-556 9726.

Phillips, Rev. Thomas Miller, MA (Hons), BD. Minister, Church of Scotland; b. 31.8.14, Newmains, Wishaw; m., Catherine C. Grigor; 1 s.; 1 d. Educ. Wishaw High School; Glasgow University and Trinity College. Parish Minister: John Knox Church, Stewarton, 1939-45, Mid Kirk of Greenock, 1945-64, West Linton and Carlops, 1964-84. Past Chairman and Lessons Convener, Scottish Sunday School Union; Member, European Committee, former World Council of Christian Education. Recreation: gardening. Address: (h.) 20 Station Road, Biggar, Lanarkshire, ML12 6JN; T.-0899 20197.

Phillips, William Denstone Powell, MB, BCh, MRCOG. Consultant Obstetrician and Gynaecologist, Perth Royal Infirmary, since 1982; Honorary Senior Lecturer, Dundee University; b. 18.2.47, Cardiff; m., Alicia Elizabeth Gregg. Educ. Felsted School; Welsh National School of Medicine. House Surgeon/Physician; Senior House Officer, Obstetrics and Gynaecology, University Hospital of Wales, Cardiff, and John Radcliffe Hospital, Oxford; Registrar, Obstetrics and Gynaecology, UHW, Cardiff; Clinical Fellow, Fetal Intensive Care Unit, University of British Columbia; Lecturer, Aberdeen University. Recreations: shooting; fishing; cricket; golf; gardening. Address: (h.) Greylag House, Forteviot, Perthshire, PH2 9BT; T.-076484 245.

Pickard, Willis Ritchie, MA (Hons). Editor, Times Educational Supplement Scotland, since 1977; b. 21.5.41, Dunfermline; m., Ann; 2 d. Educ. Daniel Stewart's College; St. Andrews University. The Scotsman: Leader Writer, 1967-72, Features Editor, 1972-77. Member, Scottish Arts Council; Liberal candidate, East Fife, 1970 and February, 1974. Address: (b.) 56 Hanover Street, Edinburgh, EH2 2DZ; T.-031-225 6393.

Picken, James, MA, DipEd. HM Inspector of Schools, since 1975; b. 7.11.36, Kilmarnock; m., Helen Craig; 1 s. Educ. Kilmarnock Academy; Glasgow University. Teacher, High School of Glasgow; Principal Teacher, Jordanhill College School, Glasgow; Assistant Principal, George Watson's College, Edinburgh. Publication: Ecce Romani. Recreations: philately; chess; music; beach-combing; dogs. Address: (b.) Scottish Education Department, New St. Andrews House, Edinburgh; T.-031-556 8400, Ext. 4771.

Pickett, Professor James, BSc (Econ), MLitt. Professor and Director, David Livingstone Institute, Strathclyde University, since 1973; b. 7.6.29, Greenock; m., Janet C. Hamilton; 1 s.; 2 d. Educ. Greenock Academy; School of Economics, Dundee; Paris University; Glasgow University. Statistician, Dominion Bureau of Statistics, Canada; Lecturer, Strathclyde University; Visiting Professor, Saskatchewan University; Special Economic Adviser, UN Economic Commission for Africa; Senior Lecturer and Professor, Strathclyde University. Member, Council for Social Democracy; regular Consultant to UN, OECD, and EEC. Recreations: photography; walking; listening to music; long-suffering support of Greenock Morton. Address: (b.) Strathclyde University, 16 Richmond Street, Glasgow, G1 1XQ; T.-041-552 4400.

Pighills, Christopher David, MA (Cantab). Headmaster, Strathallan School, Perth, since 1975; b. 27.11.37, Bradford. Educ. Rydal School, North Wales; Christ's College, Cambridge. Assistant Master/Housemaster, Fettes College, 1960-75. Recreations: shooting; dog training; hill-walking; working. Address: (b.) Strathallan School, Perth, PH2 9EG; T.-0738 812546.

Pilcher, Rosamunde. Author; b. 22.9.24, Lelant, Cornwall; 2 s.; 2 d. Educ. St. Clares, Penzance; Howells School, Llandaff. Began publishing short stories, 1945, in Woman and Home, Woman's Weekly, Woman's Journal, etc.; has written 24 novels and a play, The Dashing White Sergeant. Recreations: no time. Address: (h.) Over Pilmore, Invergowrie, by Dundee; T.-Longforgan 239.

Pinkerton, Ian W., TD, MB, ChB, FRCPGlas, FRCPEdin. Consultant Physician, Department of Infectious Diseases, Ruchill Hospital, Glasgow, since 1964; Honorary Lecturer in Infectious Diseases, Glasgow University, since 1964; b. 8.10.28, Glasgow; m., Christina Graham; 2 s.; 3 d. Educ. Allan Glen's School, Glasgow; Glasgow University. Junior hospital appointments, Glasgow and Paisley; National Service, RAMC, Egypt, 1952-54; Lt.-Col., RAMC TA; World Health Organisation Fellow, 1971. President, British Society for the Study of Infection; President, Paisley Philosophical Institution; Past President, Royal Philosophical Society of Glasgow; Council Member, St. Andrews Ambulance Association. Recreations: skiing; golf; photography. Address: (h.) 73 Gartmore Road, Paisley, PA1 3NG; T.-041-889 5632.

Pinkerton, John Macpherson, QC, BA, LLB, FSA Scot. Advocate, since 1966; Queen's Counsel, since 1984; b. 18.4.41, East Kilbride. Educ. Lathallan School; Rugby School; Oxford University; Edinburgh University. Clerk, Faculty of Advocates, 1971-77; Standing Junior Counsel, Countryside Commission for Scotland; Standing Junior Counsel, HM Commissioners of Customs and Excise. Chairman, Scottish Association for Public Transport; Town Planning Convener, Cockburn Association. Recreation: mezzotint collecting. Address: (h.) Arthur Lodge, 60 Dalkeith Road, Edinburgh, EH16 5AD; T.-031-667 5163.

Pirie, Henry Ward, OStJ, MA, LLB. Crossword Compiler, Glasgow Herald, and various publications; b. 13.2.22, Edinburgh; m., Jean Jardine; 4 s. Educ. George Watson's College; Edinburgh University. Royal Scots; Indian Army (Grenadiers), 1944; Advocate, 1947; Sheriff-Substitute of Lanarkshire, at Airdrie, 1954-55; Sheriff-Substitute (later Sheriff) of Lanarkshire, at Glasgow, 1955-74. Past President: Glasgow and West of Scotland Watsonian Club, The Lenzie Club. Recreations: golf; curling; bridge. Address: (h.) 16 Poplar Drive, Lenzie, Glasgow, G66 4DN.

Pirie, Professor Hugh Munro, BVMS, PhD, MRCVS, FRCPath. Professor, Department of Veterinary Pathology, Glasgow University, since 1982; b. 10.4.36, Glasgow; m., Myrtle Elizabeth Stewart Levack; 1 d. Educ. Coatbridge High School; Glasgow University. Rockefeller Foundation Research Fellow, Kenya, 1965; Scientific Editor, Research in Veterinary Science, since 1981; British Council Adviser, Argentina, 1982; President, Association of Veterinary Teachers and Research Workers, 1984. Recreations: travel; gardening; hill-walking; swimming; gastronomy. Address: (h.) North East Corner, Buchanan Castle Estate, Drymen, G63 OHX; T.-0360 60781.

Pirie, Sheriff Iain Gordon, MA, LLB. Sheriff of Glasgow and Strathkelvin, since 1982; b. 15.1.33; m.; 2 s.; 1 d. Educ. Harris Academy, Dundee; St. Andrews University. Procurator Fiscal, Dumfries, 1971-76, Ayr, 1976-79; Sheriff of South Strathclyde, Dumfries and Galloway, 1979-82.

Pirie, John McDonald Strachan, CA. Finance Director, Scottish Milk Marketing Board, since 1983; b. 17.11.38, Ayr; m., Rosetta; 1 s.; 2 d. Educ. Ayr Academy; Glasgow University. Address: (b.) Underwood Road, Paisley; T.-041-887 1234.

Pitt, Douglas Charles, BA, MA, PhD, MBIM. Senior Lecturer in Public Administration, Management and Organisational Analysis, Strathclyde University, since 1983; b. 13.7.43, Greenock; m., Jean Hamilton Spowart. Educ. Varndean Grammar School, Brighton; Exeter University; Manchester University. Executive Officer, Civil Service, 1961-64; Lecturer, Strathclyde University, 1973-83. Editor, Public Administration Bulletin, since 1982; Member, Strathclyde University Senate; Member, Joint University Council for Social and Public Administration. Publications: The Post Office Telecommunications Function, 1980; Public Administration: An Introduction, 1980; Government Departments: An Organisational Analysis, 1981; The Computer Revolution in Public Administration, 1984. Recreations: German; riding; swimming; fishing; skiing; sailing; traditional jazz; bluegrass; opera. Address: (h.) 19 Waterfoot Road, Newton Mearns, Glasgow, G77 5RU; T.-041-639 5359.

Player, Michael Antony, MA, DPhil (Oxon). Senior Lecturer, Department of Natural Philosophy, Aberdeen University, since 1979; b. 3.3.45, Amersham. Educ. Dover County Grammar School; Balliol College, Oxford. Junior Research Fellow in Science, Balliol College, 1969-71; Lecturer, Department of Natural Philosophy, Aberdeen University, 1971-79. Recreation: walking. Address: (b.) Department of Natural Philosophy, Aberdeen University, Aberdeen, AB9 2UE; T.-0224 40241.

Playfair-Hannay of Kingsmuir, Patrick Armour. Farmer; b. 12.7.29, Banstead; m., Frances Ann Roberton; 1 s.; 1 d. Educ. Oundle. National Service, commissioned into RASC; planting tea and rubber in Ceylon, seven years; took up farming in the Border country, 1956. Vice Chairman, Association for Protection of Rural Scotland. Recreation: shooting. Address: Clifton on Bowmont, Kelso, Roxburghshire; T.-057 382 227.

Plotkin, Gordon David, BSc, PhD. Reader in Computer Science, Edinburgh University, since 1982; b. 9.9.46, Glasgow; m., Lynda Margaret; 1 s. Educ. Glasgow High School for Boys; Glasgow University; Edinburgh University. Lecturer, Edinburgh University, 1975-82; British Petroleum Venture Research Fellow, 1981-88; Editor, Information and Control; Series Editor, Oxford University Press. Recreations: chess; hillwalking. Address: (b.) Department of Computer Science, King's Buildings, Edinburgh University, Edinburgh; T.-031-667 1081, Ext. 2775.

Poggi, Professor Gianfranco, MA, PhD. Professor of Sociology, Edinburgh University, since 1974; b. 28.2.34, Modena, Italy; m., Patricia Lipscomb; 1 d. Educ. Liceo Tito Livio, Padua; Universita di Padova; University of California (Berkeley). Assistente, Faculty of Political Sciences, Florence University, 1962-64; Lecturer, then Reader, Department of Sociology, Edinburgh University, 1964-74. Publications: Catholic Action in Italy, 1967; Images of Society: Essays on the sociological theories of Tocqueville, Marx and Durkheim, 1972; The Development of the Modern State: A Sociological Introduction, 1978; Calvinism and the Capitalist Spirit, 1983. Recreations: reading; walking; Chinese cooking. Address: (h.) 34 Braid Crescent, Edinburgh, EH10 6AU; T.-031-447 5504.

Pollock, Alexander, MP, BA (Oxon), LLB. MP (Conservative), Moray, since 1983 (Moray and Nairn, since 1979); Advocate, since 1973; b. 21.7.44, Glasgow; m., Verena Francesca Gertraud Alice Ursula Critchley; 1 s.; 1 d. Educ. Rutherglen Academy; Glasgow Academy; Brasenose College, Oxford; Edinburgh University; Perugia University. Partner, Bonar Mackenzie & Kermack, WS, 1971-73; called to Scottish Bar, 1973; Conservative candidate: West Lothian, General Election, February 1974, Moray and Nairn, General Election, October 1974; Parliamentary Private Secretary to Secretary of State for Scotland, since 1982. Member, Queen's Bodyguard for Scotland (Royal Company of Archers), since 1984. Recreations: walking; music. Address: (h.) Drumdarrach, Forres, Moray.

Pollock, John Denton, BSc, FEIS. General Secretary, The Educational Institute of Scotland, since 1975; b. 21.4.26, Kilmarnock; m., Joyce Margaret Sharpe; 1 s.; 1 d. Educ. Ayr Academy; Royal Technical College, Glasgow; Glasgow University; Jordanhill College of Education. Commissioned Royal Engineers, 1945-48. Teacher, Mauchline Secondary School, 1951-59; Head Teacher, Kilmaurs Secondary School, 1959-65; Rector, Mainholm Academy, Ayr, 1965-74; General Secretary Designate, EIS, 1974. Forestry Commissioner, since 1978; Chairman, Scottish Labour Party, 1959 and 1971; Chairman, STUC, 1981-82 (Vice-Chairman, 1980-81); Member, General Council, STUC, since 1975; Member, Annan Committee on Future of Broadcasting, 1974-77; Member, Manpower Services Committee Scotland, since 1977; Member, National Broadcasting Council for Scotland, since 1985; Charman, European Committee of World Confederation of Organisations of the Teaching Profession, 1980-82, 1982-84, 1984-86; Honorary Vice-President, South West District, SYHA, since 1985. Address: (b.) 46 Moray Place, Edinburgh; T.-031-225 6244.

Pollok, Thomas William. Vice Convenor, Caithness District Council, since 1984; b. 1.4.13, Cambuslang; m., Margaret Brown; 3 s. Educ. Queens Park School, Glasgow. Member, Thurso Town Council, 1959-75 (Provost, 1970-73); Member, Caithness County Council, 1959-75 (Chairman, Education Committee, 1963-75); Member, Caithness District Council, since 1976 (Chairman, Leisure and Recreation Committee, 1976-84); Chairman, Thurso CAB, since 1981; Vice-Chairman, Caithness District Sports Council, since 1984. Recreations: philately; reading; electronics; photography. Address: (h.) 7 Hoy Terrace, Thurso, Caithness, KW14 7PH; T.-Thurso 62802.

Polwarth, Lord, (Henry Alexander Hepburne-Scott), TD, DL, FRSE, FRSA. Vice-Lord-Lieutenant, Borders Region, since 1975; Member, Queen's Bodyguard for Scotland (Royal Company of Archers); Chartered Accountant; b. 17.11.16; m., 1, Caroline Margaret Hay (m. diss.); 1 s.; 3 d.; 2, Jean Jauncey; 1 step s.; 1 step d. Educ. Eton College; King's College, Cambridge. Served Second World War as Captain, Lothians and Border Yeomanry; former Partner, Chiene and Tait, CA, Edinburgh; Governor, Bank of Scotland, 1966-72, Director, since 1974; Chairman, General Accident, Fire & Life Assurance Corporation, 1968-72; Director, ICI Ltd., 1969-72, 1974-81; Director, Halliburton Co., since 1974; Director, Canadian Pacific Ltd., since 1975; Director, Sun Life Assurance Co. of Canada, 1975-84; Minister of State, Scottish Office, 1972-74; Chairman, later President, Scottish Council (Development and Industry), 1955-72; Member, Franco-British Council, since 1981; Chairman, Scottish National Orchestra Society, 1975-79; Chancellor, Aberdeen University, 1966; Hon. LLD: St. Andrews, Aberdeen; Hon. DLitt, Heriot-Watt; DUniv, Stirling. Address: Harden, Hawick; T.-Hawick 72069.

Poole, Sheriff Isobel Anne, LLB. Sheriff of Lothian and Borders; b. 9.12.41, Oxford. Educ. Oxford High School for Girls; Edinburgh University. Advocate. Recreations: country; arts; gardens; friends. Address: (h.) 5 Randolph Place, Edinburgh; T.-031-225 1931.

Popplestone, Robin John, BSc. Reader in Artificial Intelligence, Edinburgh University, since 1984; b. 9.12.38, Bristol; 1 s.; 2 d. Educ. Royal Belfast Academical Institution; Queen's University, Belfast. Assistant Lecturer in Mathematics, Leeds University, 1964-65; Research Fellow, then Lecturer in Artificial Intelligence, Edinburgh University, 1965-84; Visiting Scientist, Massachusetts Institute of Technology, 1981-82; Consultant, Esprit Programme, EEC, 1983-84; Project Specialist, Sichuan University, China, 1985. Address: (h.) 84 Constitution Street, Edinburgh, EH6 9PP; T.-031-553 5905.

Porte, Andrew Lawrie, BSc, PhD, CChem, FRSC. Reader in Chemistry, Glasgow University, since 1983; b. 24.5.31, Ayr. Educ. Ayr Academy; Glasgow University; Illinois University.

Assistant Lecturer, Glasgow University, 1956-58; Fulbright Scholar, Illinois University, 1958-60; Glasgow University: ICI Research Fellow, 1960-61, Lecturer in Chemistry, 1961-72, Senior Lecturer, 1972-83. Recreations: walking; music; languages. Address: (h.) 36 Weymouth Court, 177 Weymouth Drive, Glasgow, G12 OEP; T.-041-334 5059.

Postlethwaite, Professor Roy, BSc, MD, FRCPath. Professor of Virology, Aberdeen University, since 1980; Honorary Consultant Bacteriologist, Grampian Area Health Board, since 1961; b. 26.4.25, Todmorden; m., Joyce; 2 s.; 1 d. Educ. County Grammar School of King Edward VII, Melton Mowbray; Manchester University. Royal Artillery, 1943-47; junior hospital appointments, Manchester Royal Infirmary, 1954-56; Assistant Lecturer/Lecturer in Bacteriology, Manchester University, 1956-61; Senior Lecturer in Bacteriology, Aberdeen University, 1961-80; Nuffield Foundation Medical Fellow, University of Michigan, 1959-60; Visiting Virologist, National Institute for Medical Research, London, 1971-72. Recreations: walking; reading; travel. Address: (b.) Department of Bacteriology, Medical School, Foresterhill, Aberdeen, AB9 2ZD; T.-Aberdeen 681818.

Pottinger, John Inglis Drever ("Don"), LVO, OStJ, MA, DA. Islay Herald of Arms, Lyon Clerk and Keeper of the Records in the Court of the Lord Lyon, since 1981; b. 25.3.19, Carnoustie; m., Agnes Fay Keeling. Educ. George Watson's, Edinburgh; High School of Glasgow; Dundee High School; Edinburgh College of Art; Edinburgh University. Commissioned, 1939; served as regimental officer, Royal Artillery, Field Branch, throughout North African and Italian campaigns and in Palestine with 6 Airborne Division until 1946; winner, Royal Scottish Academy's Chalmers Prize, 1947; Freelance Artist and Portrait Painter, since 1951; exhibited, Royal Scottish Academy; appointed Falkland Pursuivant Extraordinary, 1953; Linlithgow Pursuivant (permanent), 1958; Unicorn Pursuivant, 1961; awarded MVO, 1982, LVO, 1985. Publications: Simple Heraldry, 1953; Simple Custom, 1954; Blood Royal, 1956; Scotland of Old (clan map), 1961; The Clan Headquarters Flags, 1978; The Official Tartan Map, 1977; The Official Chart of the Tower of London, 1978; Kings and Queens of Great Britain, 1976. Address: (h.) 11 Ainslie Place, Edinburgh, EH3 6AS; T.-031-225 6146.

Power, James Patrick, MA (Hons), BA (Hons). Rector, St. Columba's High School, Gourock, since 1975; b. 2.2.27, Renfrew; m., E. Patricia Currie; 1 s.; 1 d. Educ. St. Mirin's Academy, Paisley; Glasgow University; London University; Jordanhill College of Education. Teacher: St. Columba's High School, Greenock, 1948-52, St. Joseph's Academy, Kilmarnock, 1952-56; Principal Teacher of Science, Sacred Heart High School, Girvan, 1956-60; Principal Teacher of Mathematics, St. Joseph's Academy, Kilmarnock, 1960-63; Head, Department of Mathematics and Science, Ayr Technical College, 1963-74; Mathematics Tutor, Open University, 1971-75; Adviser in Mathematics, County of Lanark, 1974-75. Chairman, Scottish Central Committee

on Mathematics, since 1981; Member: Scottish Education/Industry Committee, since 1984, CNAA Committee in Scotland, since 1983, Scottish Mathematical Council, since 1979, Catholic Education Commission, since 1978; Chairman, Joint Working Party on Standard Grade Mathematics; Honorary Treasurer and Past President, Headteachers' Association of Scotland; President, Gourock Rotary Club, 1984-85; Past President, Greenok and District Catenian Association; Past President, Ayr Amateur Opera Company. Address: (b.) St. Columba's High School, Burnside Road, Gourock, PA19 1XX; T.-0475 33271.

Powrie, John ("Ian"). Musician; b. 26.5.23, Strathardle, Blairgowrie; m., Lillias Robina Mailer; 1 s.; 1 d. Educ. Blairgowrie High School. Began playing violin, aged four; completed graduate examination for London College of Violinists, 1936; made first solo broadcast on BBC, 1936; volunteered for RAF Aircrew, 1943; trained as pilot in Canada; demobbed, 1945; formed band, 1949, and began broadcasting Scottish dance music for BBC; one of original entertainer members, BBC's White Heather Club; completed numerous tours with Andy Stewart; played for the Queen twice at Balmoral; completed 50 years recording with a celebration record with Jimmy Shand, 1983; bought a building company in Perth, Western Australia, 1966 and emigrated there; sold all interests, 1984, and returned to Scotland to retire; honoured by National Association of Accordion and Fiddle Clubs, 1983, and presented with portrait for work in Scottish music. Recreations: flying; farming; fishing; shooting. Address: (h.) Corrieburn, Duchally, Auchterarder, Perth; T.-Auchterarder 2805.

Prag, Thomas Gregory Andrew, MA, FBIM. Managing Director, Moray Firth Radio; b. 2.1.47, London; m., Angela; 3 s. Educ. Westminster School; Brasenose College, Oxford. Joined BBC, 1968, as Studio Manager; Producer, BBC Radio Oxford; Programme Organiser, BBC Radio Highland; first Chief Executive, Moray Firth Radio, 1981. Recreations: family; growing vegetables; chasing deer off vegetables. Address: (b.) Moray Firth Radio, PO Box 271, Inverness, IV1 1UJ.

Prain, Alexander Moncur, CBE (1964). Advocate; b. 19.2.08, Longforgan, Perthshire; m., Florence Margaret Robertson. Educ. Edinburgh Academy; Edinburgh University. Advocate, 1932; Army (Major, Royal Armoured Corps), 1939-46; Sheriff-Substitute, Perthshire, 1946-71; retired. Recreation: reading. Address: (h.) Castellar, Crieff, Perthshire; T.-0764 2270.

Preece, Paul Edward, MD, FRCSEdin, FRCS. Senior Lecturer in Surgery, Dundee University, since 1978; Honorary Consultant Surgeon, Tayside Health Board, since 1978; b. 21.10.40, Great Malvern; m., Heather Margaret Angell; 2 d. Educ. Worcester Cathedral King's School; Welsh National School of Medicine, Cardiff. Pre-registration House Officer, Cardiff and Newport, 1966-67; Senior House Officer posts, Oxford, Bristol and Birmingham, 1968-70; Rotational Surgical Registrar, South Wales, 1971-72;

Tenovus and Medical Research Council Research Fellow, 1973-74; Lecturer in Surgery, Welsh National School of Medicine, 1975-77. Council of Europe Fellowship, Germany, 1975. Recreations: music; vintage cars. Address: (h.) 11 Marchfield Road, Dundee, DD2 1JG; T.-0382 68126.

Preen, Alan Frederick, IPFA, MBIM, FRVA. Treasurer, Orkney Health Board, since 1974; b. 10.11.26, London; m., Elaine. Army, 1944-48; Metropolitan Borough of Battersea: Accountancy/Technical Assistant, 1948-54, Senior Auditor, 1954-60, Senior Accountant, 1960-65; London Borough of Wandsworth: Deputy Chief Accountant, 1965-68, Chief Accountant, 1968-69; Treasurer, Richmond (Yorkshire) Rural District Council, 1969-74 (and Chief Officer, Richmond Public Authorities Joint Computer Committee); Treasurer, Richmondshire District Council, 1973-74. Recreations: travelling; walking; lazing; reading; driving; astronomy. Address: (b.) Orkney Health Board, Kirkwall, Orkney, KW15 1BX; T.-0856 2763.

Prenter, Patrick Robert, JP, MA. Managing Director, MacTaggart, Scott & Co. Ltd., since 1967; President, Scottish Engineering Employers Association; Board Member, Forth Ports Authority; b. 9.9.39, Edinburgh; m., Susan Patrick; 2 s.; 2 d. Educ. Loretto; Trinity Hall, Cambridge. Address: (h.) Linden Lodge, Loanhead, Midlothian, EH20 9RZ; T.-032-440 0672.

Prescott, Professor Laurie F., MA, MB, BChir, MD, FRCPEdin. Honorary Consultant Physician, Edinburgh Royal Infirmary, since 1969; Professor of Clinical Pharmacology, Edinburgh University, since 1985; b. 13.5.34, London; m.; 1 s.; 3 d. Educ. Hitchin Boys Grammar School; Cambridge University; Middlesex Hospital Medical School, London. Research Fellow, Johns Hopkins Hospital, Baltimore, 1963-65; Lecturer in Therapeutics, Aberdeen University, 1965-69; Senior Lecturer in Clinical Pharmacology, Edinburgh University, 1969-74, Reader, 1974-85. British Pharmacological Society Lilly Prize, 1978. Recreations: music; walking; gardening; sailing. Address: (h.) Redfern, 24 Colinton Road, Edinburgh, EH10 5EQ; T.-031-447 2571.

Prescott, Robert George Whitelock, MA, PhD, FSA Scot. Lecturer in Psychology, St. Andrews University, since 1974; Director (Ethnology), Scottish Institute of Maritime Studies, since 1983; Trustee, National Museum of Antiquities of Scotland, since 1979; Trustee, Scottish Fisheries Museum, since 1976; b. 9.12.38, Gillingham. Educ. Latymer Upper School; Peterhouse, Cambridge. NATO Research Fellow, Yale University, 1964-66; Senior Assistant in Research, Zoology Department, Cambridge University, 1966-74. Governor, frigate Unicorn (Uncinorn Preservation Trust), since 1984. Recreations: reading; walking; talking; sailing; visiting museums. Address: (b.) St. Andrews University, St. Andrews, Fife; T.-St. Andrews 76161.

Preston, Ian Mathieson Hamilton, BSc, PhD, FEng, MInstP, FIEE. Deputy Chairman, South of Scotland Electricity Board, since 1983; b.

18.7.32, Bournemouth; m., Sheila Hope Pringle; 2 s. Educ. Kilmarnock Academy; Glasgow University. University Assistant Lecturer, 1957-59; joined SSEB as Assistant Reactor Physicist, 1959; various appointments until Chief Engineer, Generation Design and Construction Division, 1972; Director General, Central Electricity Generating Board, Generation Development and Construction Division, 1977-83. Chairman, British Hydromechanics Research Association, since 1985. Recreations: angling; gardening; curling. Address: (b.) South of Scotland Electricity Board, Cathcart House, Spean Street, Glasgow, G44 4BE; T.-041-637 7177.

Preston, Peter Norman, BSc, PhD. Senior Lecturer in Chemistry, Heriot-Watt University, since 1966; b. 28.10.39, Tyldesley, Manchester; m., Veronica; 3 d. Educ. Leigh Grammar School; Nottingham University; Manchester University. Research Chemist, Courtaulds Ltd.; Research Associate: Toronto University, Southampton University. Address: (b.) Chemistry Department, Heriot-Watt University, Riccarton, Edinburgh.

Preston-Thomas, Rev. Canon Colin Barnabas Rashleigh. Priest, Scottish Episcopal Church, since 1954; b. 11.6.28, Exford, Somerset; m., Barbara Anne Davidson. Educ. Bristol Grammar School; King's College, London; Edinburgh Theological College. Curate, St. David's, Pilton, 1953-54; Precentor, Perth Cathedral, 1954-60; Prison Chaplain, Perth, 1955-60; Rector: Rosyth with Inverkeithing, 1960-72, St. John's Forfar, 1972-82, Holy Trinity, Pitlochry, with Kilmaveonaig, Blair Atholl, since 1982; Synod Clerk, St. Andrews Diocese; Canon, Perth Cathedral, since 1968; Diocesan Secretary, since 1980. Recreations: theatre; music. Address: The Parsonage, Perth Road, Pitlochry, PH16 5DJ; T.-Pitlochry 2176.

Prettyman, James Arthur, CEng, MIProdE. Executive Director, Leith Enterprise Trust, since 1984; President, Motherwell Bridge Projects Ltd. (Canada), since 1982; Director and General Manager, Motherwell Bridge Pipe Ltd., since 1970; b. 19.3.31, Hatfield, Hertfordshire; m., Wendy Bell; 2 d. Educ. North Western Polytechnic, London; Hatfield Polytechnic. Student Apprentice/Production Engineer, de Havilland Aircraft; Sub-Lieutenant, Royal Navy (Fleet Air Arm); Management Trainee/Production Superintendent, Brush Electrical Engineering Co. (now Hawker Siddeley); Unit Engineer, Glacier Metal; Manufacturing Manager, Ampep Products; Director, Motherwell Bridge Group. Member, Citizens Advice Management Group. Recreations: fitness; swimming. Address: (b.) 25 Maritime Street, Leith, Edinburgh; T.-031-553 5566.

Price, John Valdimir, BA, MA, PhD. Senior Lecturer in English Literature, Edinburgh University, since 1979; b. 10.7.37, Lamesa, Texas; 1 s.; 2 d. Educ. Texas University. Instructor, San Fernando Valley State College, California, 1962-63; Assistant Professor, University of California, 1963-65; Lecturer in English Literature, Edinburgh University, 1965-79. Publications: The

Ironic Hume, 1965; David Hume, 1968; Tobias Smollett: The Expedition of Humphry Clinker, 1973; Dialogues Concerning Natural Religion (Editor), 1976. Recreation: trains. Address: (h.) 3/3 Buccleuch Street, Edinburgh, EH8 9JN; T.-031-668 3511.

Price, Nicholas Charles, MA, DPhil. Senior Lecturer in Biochemistry, Stirling University, since 1977; b. 12.8.46, Stafford; m., Margaret Hazel Millen; 1 s.; 2 d. Educ. King Edward VI Grammar School, Stafford; Merton and St. John's Colleges, Oxford. Harkness Fellow, University of Pennsylvania Medical School, Philadelphia, 1971-72; Demonstrator in Biochemstry, Oxford University, 1973-74. Publications: Principles and Problems in Physical Chemistry for Biochemists (Co-author); Fundamentals of Enzymology (Co-author). Recreations: running; fund-raising activities. Address: (h.) 29 Inverallan Drive, Bridge of Allan, Stirlingshire, FK9 4JR; T.-0786 833559.

Price, Robert J., BSc, PhD, DSc. Reader in Geography, Glasgow University; b. 19.7.36, Cardiff; m., Mary Frater; 1 s.; 1 d. Educ. St. Illtyd's College, Cardiff; University of Wales, Aberystwyth; Edinburgh University. Assistant Professor: Oklahoma University, 1961-62, Oregon University, 1962-63; joined Glasgow University as Lecturer, 1963. Publications: Glacial and Fluvioglacial Land Forms; Highland Land Forms; Scotland's Environment - The Last 30,000 Years. Recreations: sailing; golf. Address: (b.) Department of Geography, Glasgow University, Glasgow, G12 8QQ; T.-041-339 8855, Ext. 7405.

Priest, Professor Eric Ronald, BSc, MSc, PhD. Professor of Theoretical Solar Physics, St. Andrews University, since 1983; b. 7.11.43, Birmingham; m., Clare Wilson; 3 s.; 1 d. Educ. King Edward VI School, Birmingham; Nottingham University. St. Andrews University: Lecturer in Applied Mathematics, 1968, Reader, 1977. Recreations: bridge; walking; jogging; swimming; children. Address: (b.) Applied Mathematics Department, St. Andrews University, St. Andrews, KY16 9SS; T.-0334 76161.

Priestley, Graham C., BSc, PhD, MIBiol. Senior Lecturer in Dermatology, Edinburgh University, since 1984; b. 11.4.38, Leeds; m., Marjorie; 2 s. Educ. Leeds Grammar School; Durham University; Leeds University; Harvard University. Research Fellow, Leeds University, 1964-66; Research Fellow in Surgery, Harvard University, 1966-68; Project Manager (Dermatology), Beecham Research Laboratories, 1968-70; Research Fellow, Animal Genetics Unit, Edinburgh, 1970-73; Lecturer in Dermatology, Edinburgh University, 1973-84. High Bailiff of the Water of Leith. Publication: Angling in the Lothians, 1983. Recreations: trout fishing; journalism; cricket. Address: (h.) 22 Cherry Tree Crescent, Balerno, Midlothian, EH14 5AL; T.-031-449 4522.

Primrose, Andrew Hardie, BA (Hons) (Oxon), LLB. Solicitor; Partner, Maclay Murray and Spens, Solicitors, Glasgow and Edinburgh; b. 25.9.39, Glasgow; m., Helen Mary Banks; 1 s.; 1 d. Educ. Belmont House School; Glenalmond; University College, Oxford; Glasgow University. Member, Scottish Industrial Estates Corporation, 1973-75; Trustee, West of Scotland Trustee Savings Bank, 1978-84; Local Advisory Trustee, Trustee Savings Bank, Scotland, since 1984; Governor, Belmont House School, Glasgow, since 1983; Vice-Chairman, Section on General Practice, Division 1, International Bar Association; Chairman, Glasgow Junior Chamber of Commerce, 1971-72; President, West of Scotland Football Club, 1981-83; Deacon, Incorporation of Hammermen of Glasgow, 1985-86. Recreations: curling; golf; skiing; squash; hillwalking; jogging. Address: (b.) 169 West George Street, Glasgow, G2 2LA; T.-041-248 5011.

Pringle, Derek Hair, CBE, PhD, DSc, FInstP, FRSE. Chairman, SEEL Limited, Livingston, since 1980; Director, Amersham International PLC, since 1978; Chairman, Bioscot Limited, Edinburgh, since 1983; b. 8.1.26, Edinburgh; m., Anne Collier Caw; 3 s.; 1 d. Educ. George Heriot's School, Edinburgh; Edinburgh University. Research Physicist, Ferranti Ltd., Edinburgh, 1948-59; Nuclear Enterprises Ltd., Edinburgh: Technical Director, 1960-76, Managing Director, 1976-78, Chairman, 1978-80. Member, National Radiological Protection Board, 1969-81; Member, Court, Heriot-Watt University, 1968-77; President, Edinburgh Chamber of Commerce, 1979-81; Vice President, Royal Society of Edinburgh, since 1985. Recreations: golf; gardening. Address: (h.) 75 Trinity Road, Edinburgh, EH5 3JX; T.-031-552 4549.

Prior, William Barrett. Secretary, Countryside Commission for Scotland, since 1971; b. 10.1.31, Edinburgh; m., Mary Bain; 1 s.; 2 d. Educ. George Heriot's School, Edinburgh. Department of Agriculture and Fisheries for Scotland, 1947-49; National Service, RAF, 1949-51; DAFS, 1951-67; Nature Conservancy, 1967-71. Address: (h.) 16 Spoutwells Drive, Scone, Perthshire.

Pritchard, Kenneth William, BL, WS, SSC. Secretary, The Law Society of Scotland, since 1976; Secretary, Scottish Council of Law Reporting, since 1976; Clerk, Registrar of Examiners, since 1976; b. 14.11.33, London; Honorary Sheriff, Dundee; m., Gretta Murray; 2 s.; 1 d. Educ. Dundee High School; Fettes College; St. Andrews University. National Service, Argyll and Sutherland Highlanders, 1955-57; 2nd Lt., 1956; TA, 1957-62 (Captain); joined J. & J. Scrimgeour, Solicitors, Dundee, 1957; Senior Partner, 1970-76; Member: Sheriff Court Rules Council, 1973-76, Lord Dunpark's Committee considering Reparation upon Criminal Conviction, 1973-77; Governor, Moray House College of Education, since 1982; Member, National Trust for Scotland Jubilee Appeal Committee, 1980-82; President, Dundee High School Old Boys Club, 1975-76. Recreation: golf. Address: (h.) 36 Ravelston Dykes, Edinburgh, EH4 3EB; T.-031-332 8584.

Pritchard, Rev. Stanley, MA, OStJ. Appeals Director, Scotland, Royal National Mission to Deep Sea Fishermen; Author; Broadcaster; Preacher; Charity Consultant; b. 18.7.10, Glasgow. Educ. Bellahouston Academy, Glasgow;

Glasgow University. Ordained, 1937; Minister, Martyrs Church of Scotland, Kilmarnock, 1938-41; YMCA Huts and Canteen Service, 1941-42; Minister, Williamwood, 1942-48; Church of Scotland Canteens in Europe, 1945-47; BBC, 1948-76: Appeals Organiser, Radio and Television Producer; Special Award for Children's Drama, 1956; Minister, Stevenson Memorial Church, Glasgow, 1968-79. Chairman, Hospital Sunday Fund; Chairman, Action for Disaster; Trustee, Barbirolli Trust; author of six plays; Writer and Director of several films. Publications: They Happened to Me, 1980; Fish and Ships, 1981; Variations on a Theme, 1982. Recreations: opera; travel; making documentary films; public speaking. Address: (h.) 3 Queen Margaret Road, Glasgow, G20 6DP; T.-041-946 4263.

Pritty, David Walter, BSc. Senior Lecturer, Department of Computer Science, Strathclyde University, since 1983; b. 2.2.37, Glasgow; m., Agnes McDonald; 2 s. Educ. Hamilton Academy; Glasgow University. Ferranti Ltd., Edinburgh, 1958-69; Manager, Burroughs Corporation, Strathleven, 1970-71; Chief Engineer, Plessey Numerical Controls Ltd., 1971-73; Lecturer, Department of Computer Science, Strathclyde University, 1973-82. Publication: Practical Interfacing to Popular Microprocessors. Recreations: offshore cruising (yachting); bridge; swimming. Address: (h.) Edenbank, 66 Colquhoun Street, Helensburgh, G84 9JP; T.-0436 5481.

Procter, Robert Hendry, MA. Secretary, Scottish Council, The Scout Association, since 1982; b. 22.1.31, Alloa; m., Elizabeth Rosemary; 1 s.; 2 d. Educ. Fettes College; Trinity Hall, Cambridge. Commissioned, Royal Corps of Signals (2nd Lt.), 1950; Patons & Baldwins Ltd., 1954-79 (General Manager, from 1969); Director, John Gladstone & Co. Ltd., Galashiels, 1980-82. General Commissioner of Income Tax, Clackmannan Division, 1976-80; Honorary Sheriff, Tayside Central and Fife, at Alloa, 1975. Recreations: hill-walking; golf. Address: (h.) 2 Braid Avenue, Morningside, Edinburgh, EH10 6DR; T.-031-447 1140.

Proctor, George Rennet, BSc, PhD, DSc, CChem, FRSC. Reader in Organic Chemistry, Strathclyde University, since 1979; b. 3.5.28, Ampthill, Bedfordshire; m., Christina Ann Fraser; 2 s.; 1 d. Educ. Robert Gordon's College, Aberdeen; Aberdeen University. 2nd Lt., Royal Engineers, 1946-48; RE (TA), 1948-53; Research Chemist, ICI Pharmaceuticals, 1956-58; Research Fellow, Zurich University, 1960; Royal Society Research Fellow, Yale University, 1963; Visiting Expert, National Cancer Institute, Bethesda, 1975-76; Lecturer and Senior Lecturer, Strathclyde University, 1958-79. Recreations: fishing; gardening. Address: (b.) Department of Pure and Applied Chemistry, Strathclyde University, Glasgow, G1 1XL; T.-041-552 4400, Ext. 2389.

Proctor, John, MA, DPhil (Oxon). Senior Lecturer in Biological Science, Stirling University; b. 1.2.44, Accrington; m., Susan Christine Fogden; 1 d. Educ. St. Mary's College, Blackburn; St. Edmund Hall, Oxford. Lecturer in Biological Sciences, Lancaster University, 1968-69;

postdoctoral Fellow: Stanford University, 1969-70, Liverpool University, 1970-71; joined Stirling University as Lecturer, 1971. Director, Forest Ecology Group, Royal Geographical Society Mulu Expedition, 1977-78; Chief Scientist, Operation Raleigh, Costa Rica, 1985. Recreations: watching television; reading about Accrington Stanley, T.E. Lawrence, old motor cycles and steam locomotives. Address: (h.) Mid-Cambushinnie Cottage, Kinbuck, by Dunblane, Perthshire; T.-0786 822069.

Prosser, (Leslie) Charles, DFA, DAEd. Secretary, Royal Fine Art Commission for Scotland, since 1976; b. 27.10.39, Harrogate; m., Coral; 1 s.; 2 d. Educ. Bath Academy of Art at Corsham Court; Slade School of Fine Art, London University. Assistant Lecturer in Fine Art, Blackpool School of Art, 1962-64; Fine Art research, Royal Academy, Stockholm, 1964-65; Lecturer in Fine Art, Leeds/Jacob Kramer College of Art, 1965-76; research in Art Education, Leeds University, 1974-75. Member, Awards Committee, Royal Incorporation of Architects in Scotland, since 1979; Leverhulme European Arts Research Award, 1964; exhibited paintings; lectured variously on art and design. Recreations: criticising visual arts: sculpting and drawing; cycling; Scottish dancing and hill-walking; plumbing; being not idle in the sun. Address: (h.) 28 Mayfield Terrace, Edinburgh, EH9 1RZ; T.-031-668 1141.

Prosser, William David, QC, MA (Oxon), LLB. Dean, Faculty of Advocate, since 1983; Queen's Counsel, since 1974; b. 23.11.34, Edinburgh; m., Vanessa Lindsay; 2 s.; 2 d. Educ. Edinburgh Academy; Corpus Christi College, Oxford; Edinburgh University. Advocate, 1962; Vice-Dean, Faculty of Advocates, 1979-83. Address: 7 Randolph Crescent, Edinburgh, EH3 7TH; T.-031-225 2709.

Proudfoot, Thomas A., BSc. Rector, Girvan Academy, since 1982; b. 28.2.33, Irvine; m., V. Audrey Howlett; 1 d. Educ. Carrick Academy, Maybole; Glasgow University; Jordanhill College of Education. National Service, Royal Signals; Mathematics Teacher, Irvine Royal Academy and Ravenspark Academy; Assistant Rector, Kilmarnock Academy; Depute Rector, Carrick Academy, Maybole. Elder, Church of Scotland. Recreations: DIY; gardening; badminton. Address: (h.) 8 Ainslie Road, Girvan, KA26 OAY.

Proudfoot, Professor V. Bruce, BA, PhD, FSA, FRSE, FSA Scot. Professor of Geography, St. Andrews University; b. 24.9.30, Belfast; m., Edwina Valmai Windram Field; 2 s. Educ. Royal Belfast Academical Institution; Queen's University, Belfast. Research Officer, Nuffield Quaternary Research Unit, Queen's University, Belfast, 1954-58; Lecturer in Geography: Queen's University, Belfast, 1958-59, Durham University, 1959-67; Hatfield College, Durham: Tutor, 1960-63, Librarian, 1963-65; Visiting Fellow, University of Auckland and Commonwealth Visiting Fellow, Australia, 1966; Alberta University, Edmonton: Associate Professor, 1967-70, Professor, 1970-74; Co-ordinator, Socio-Economic Opportunity Studies and Staff Consultant, Alberta Human Resources Research

Council, 1971-72. Council Member, Royal Society of Edinburgh, 1982-85 (Convener, Earth Science Committee, 1983-85); Chairman, Society for Landscape Studies, 1979-83; Vice-President, Society of Antiquaries of Scotland; Chairman, Rural Geographical Study Group, Institute of British Geographers, 1980-84. Recreation: gardening. Address: (h.) Westgate, Wardlaw Gardens, St. Andrews, KY16 9DW; T.-0334 73293.

Proudfoot, William, FFA. Chief General Manager and Actuary, Scottish Amicable Life Assurance Society, since 1969; b. 4.4.32, Bellshill; 2 d. Educ. Rutherglen Academy. Joined Scottish Amicable, 1948; appointed Assistant Actuary, 1957, Actuary and Secretary for Australia, 1959, Manager and Actuary for Australia, 1961, Assistant General Manager, 1968, General Manager, 1969 (title altered, 1982), Director, 1977. Director, various subsidiaries, Scottish Amicable; Director, Scottish Opera; Director, Standard Property Investment plc; Council Member, Scottish Business School. Recreations: golf; music. Address: (b.) Scottish Amicable Life Assurance Society, 150 St. Vincent Street, Glasgow; T.-041-248 2323.

Provan, James Lyal Clark. Member (Conservative), European Parliament, NE Scotland, since 1979; b. 19.12.36; m.; 2 s.; 1 d. Educ. Ardvreck School, Crieff; Oundle School, Northants; Royal Agricultural College, Cirencester. Member, Tayside Regional Council, 1978-82; Member, Tay River Purification Board, 1978-82; Chairman, East of Scotland Grassland Society, 1973-75.

Pullar, Robert Alexander. Member, Tayside Regional Council, since 1978 (Chairman, Water Services Committee, since 1982); b. 9.10.49, Perth; m., Nancy; 1 d. Educ. Perth High School. Chairman, Perth Prison Visiting Committee, 1984-85. Recreations: music; politics; bowling; golf. Address: (h.) Glenfinlas, Church Lane, Methven, Perth, PH1 3PQ; T.-073884 200.

Pullen, Ian Michael, MB, BS, MRCPsych. Consultant Psychiatrist, Royal Edinburgh Hospital, since 1980; Honorary Senior Lecturer, Edinburgh University, since 1980; b. 19.9.46, Hampstead; m., Prue Matthews; 2 s. Educ. Hemel Hempstead Grammar School; London Hospital Medical College. General Practitioner turned Psychiatrist. Publication: Psychological Aspects of Genetic Counselling (Co-Editor). Recreations: hill-walking; sailing. Address: (h.) 10 Cluny Avenue, Edinburgh.

Punnett, Robert Malcolm, BA, MA (Econ), PhD. Reader in Politics, Strathclyde University, since 1984; b. 1.5.36, Carlisle; m., Marjory Chalmers; 2 d. Educ. Carlisle Grammar School; Sheffield University. Assistant Lecturer in Politics, Sheffield University, 1963-64; Visiting Professor in Political Science: Carleton University, Ottawa, 1967-68; McGill University, Montreal, 1974; McMaster University, Ontario, 1976-77; Visiting Fellow, Australian National University, 1980; Visiting Fellow, University of Western Australia, 1985; Lecturer, then Senior Lecturer, Strathclyde University, from 1964. Publications:

British Government and Politics, 1980; The Prime Minister in Canadian Government and Politics, 1977; Front-Bench Opposition, 1973. Recreation: hill-walking. Address: (b.) Politics Department, Strathclyde University, Glasgow, G1; T.-041-552 4400.

Purser, John Whitley, MA (Hons). Composer and Lecturer; Poet, Playwright and Broadcaster; Manager, Scottish Music Information Centre; b. 10.2.42, Glasgow; 1 s.; 1 d. Educ. Fettes College; Glasgow University; Royal Scottish Academy of Music and Drama. Part-time Lecturer in English Literature, Glasgow University, 1981-85; compositions include two operas, numerous orchestral and chamber works; three books of poetry, The Counting Stick, A Share of the Wind and Amoretti; three radio plays and a radio series, A Change of Tune. Recreations: numerous. Address: (b.) 7 Lilybank Gardens, Glasgow, G12; T.-041-334 6393.

Q

Quigley, Anthony, BSc. Rector, Trinity High School, Rutherglen, since 1979; b. 6.6.40, Dumbarton; m., Margaret White; 2 s.; 1 d. Educ. St. Patrick's High School, Dumbarton; Glasgow University. Teacher, St. Pius' Secondary School, Glasgow, 1963-68; Lecturer, Glenrothes Technical College, 1968-69; Principal Teacher of Mathematics: St. Bride's Secondary School, 1969-70, St. James's High School, Paisley, 1970-71; Assistant Head Teacher: St. James' High School, Paisley, 1971-75, Trinity High School, Renfrew, 1975-77; Depute Head Teacher, Trinity High School, Renfrew, 1977-79. Scriptwriter/Presenter, Glasgow Educational Television Service, 1965-70. Recreations: reading; music. Address: (h.) Rowanlea, 5 St. Andrews Road, Renfrew, PA4 0NS.

R

Racey, Professor Paul Adrian, MA, PhD, DSc. Professor of Zoology, Aberdeen University, since 1985; b. 7.5.44, Wisbech, Cambridgeshire; m., Anna Priscilla Notcutt; 3 s. Educ. Ratcliffe College, Leicester; Downing College, Cambridge. Rothamsted Experimental Station, Harpenden, 1965-66; Zoological Society of London, 1966-70; Unit of Reproductive Biology, Liverpool University, 1970-73; joined Department of Zoology, Aberdeen University, 1973. Recreations: riding; sailing; shooting; farming sheep. Address: (b.) Department of Zoology, Aberdeen University, Tillydrone Avenue, Aberdeen, AB9 2TN; T.-0224 40241.

Radford, Peter F., DPE, MSc, PhD. Director, Department of Physical Education and Recreation, Glasgow University, since 1976; Member, Scottish Sports Council, since 1983; Chairman, Scottish Consultative Group on Sports Medicine and Sports Science, since 1984; b. 20.9.39, Walsall; m., Margaret M. Beard; 1 d. Educ. Tettenhall College, Wolverhampton; Cardiff University; Purdue University, Indiana; Glasgow University. Assistant Professor, McMaster University, School of Physical Education and Athletics, Hamilton, Ontario, 1967-75. Chairman, Scottish Universities Physical Education Association, 1980-81; Member, Scottish Executive, British Association of Sport and Medicine, 1982-84; Member, Glasgow Sports Promotion Council, 1982-85; holder of world record, 200 metres and 220 yards, 1960; Bronze Medal, 100 metres and 4 x 100 metres Relay, Olympic Games, Rome, 1960; British 100 metres record, set in Paris, 1958, remained unbroken for 20 years. Address: (b.) Department of Physical Education and Recreation, Glasgow University, Glasgow, G12 8LT; T.-041-339 8855.

Rado, Emil Richard, BSc (Econ). Senior Lecturer in Development Studies, Glasgow University, since 1965; b. 18.1.31, Budapest; m., Anne Forrest Taylor; 1 s.; 2 d. Educ. Ackworth School; University College, London. Research Fellow and Lecturer in Economics, Ghana University, 1953-60; Visiting Professor, Williams College, USA, 1960-61; Lecturer in Economics, Makerere University College, 1961-65; Senior Research Fellow, Nairobi University (on secondment), 1967-70. Council Member, Development Studies Association and African Studies Association, at various times; has acted as Consultant to World Bank, International Labour Office, OECD and several Governments. Recreations: running; hillwalking; photography; herb-growing. Address: (h.) 18 Kersland Drive, Milngavie, Glasgow, G62 8DG; T.-041-956 1953.

Rae, Barbara, DA, ARSA, RSW. Painter; Lecturer in Drawing and Painting, Glasgow School of Art, since 1975; b. 10.12.43, Falkirk; m., Frank M. Docherty, RSW; 1 s. Educ. Morrison's Academy, Crieff; Edinburgh College of Art; Moray House College of Education. Travelling Scholarship, France and Spain, 1966; Arts Council Awards, 1968, 1975 and 1981; Guthrie Medal, RSA, 1977; May Marshall Brown Award, RSW, 1979; elected Associate, RSA, 1980; RSA Gillies Award, 1983; Calouste Gulbenkian Printmaking Award, 1983; President, Society of Scottish Artists, 1983-84; exhibited in UK, USA and Australia. Recreation: gardening. Address: Calderbank Cottage, Lochwinnoch, Renfrewshire.

Rae, Henry Edward Grant, JP. Lord Provost, City of Aberdeen, since 1984; Lord Lieutenant, City of Aberdeen, since 1984; b. 17.8.25; m.; 1 d. Educ. Queen's Cross School, Aberdeen; Ruthrieston School, Aberdeen. Member, Aberdeen City Council, since 1974.

Rae, Hugh Crawford. Novelist; b. 22.11.35, Glasgow; m., Elizabeth Dunn; 1 d. Educ. Knightswood School. Prolific popular novelist; author of more than 50 tiles, under a variety of pseudonyms, including Stuart Stern, James Albany and Jessica Stirling; books include (as Hugh C. Rae) Skinner, The Marksman, The Shooting Gallery, Harkfast and Privileged Strangers and (as Jessica Stirling) The Spoiled Earth, The Hiring Fair, The Dark Pasture, Treasures on Earth. Recreation: golf. Address: (h.) Drumore Farm Cottage, Balfron Station, Stirlingshire.

Rae, Rev. Peter Crighton, BSc, BD. Minister, Cowdenbeath North with Kirk of Beath, since 1969; b. 4.10.39, St. Albans; m., Margaret Helen West; 2 d. Educ. Kings College School, Wimbledon; Edinburgh University; New College, Edinburgh. In enginering; Assistant Minister, St. Giles and St. Columba's, Elgin. Founder Member, Cowdenbeath Community Council; former Moderator, Dunfermline Presbytery; has served on various Committees of the General Assembly. Recreations: family; cycling; walking; hymnody. Address: The Manse, Stuart Place, Cowdenbeath, Fife; T.-Cowdenbeath 511033.

Rae, Rita Emilia Anna, LLB (Hons). Advocate; b. 20.6.50, Glasgow. Educ. St. Patrick's High School, Coatbridge; Edinburgh University. Apprentice, Biggart, Lumsden & Co., Glasgow, 1972-74; Assistant Solicitor: Balfour & Manson, Edinburgh, 1974, Biggart, Baillie & Gifford, Glasgow, 1974-76; Solicitor and Partner, Ross Harper & Murphy, Glasgow, 1976-81; Devil, 1981-82; Advocate, 1982. Recreations: theatregoing; driving; cycling; riding. Address: (h.) 73 Fotheringay Road, Glasgow; T.-041-423 0781.

Rae, Thomas Ian, MA, PhD. Keeper of Manuscripts (Cataloguing), National Library of Scotland, since 1972; b. 9.6.26, Norwich; m., Margaret Tickle (m. diss.); 3 s. Educ. Hawick High School; Balliol College, Oxford; St. Andrews University. Royal Navy, 1944-47; Assistant Lecturer in History, Glasgow University, 1951-52; Assistant Lecturer in Medieval History, St. Andrews University, 1952-55; Assistant Keeper, Manuscripts, National Library of Scotland, 1955-72. Secretary, Scottish History Society, 1969-76 (Publication Secretary, since 1976); Chairman, Company of Scottish History, 1978-84; Chairman, Scottish Records Association, 1981-83. Publications: The Administration of the Scottish Frontier 1513-1603, 1966; The Burgh Court Book of Selkirk 1503-1545 (Co-author), 1960, 1969; Scotland in the Time of Shakespeare, 1965. Recreations: reading; music. Address: (h.) 26 Marchmont Crescent, Edinburgh, EH9 1HG.

Raeburn, Rev. Alan Cameron, MA, BD. Minister, Battlefield East Church, Glasgow, since 1977; b. 29.5.45, Glasgow; m., Dorothy Rose Polson; 2 s. Educ. Hutchesons' Boys' Grammar School; Glasgow University; Edinburgh University. Probationary Assistant, Bearsden South Church, 1970-71; Minister, Lybster and Bruan, 1971-77. Local Chairman, Bible Society; Committee appointments in Presbytery and General Assembly. Recreations: reading; gardening; music; family life; walking; hill-walking; cycling; other forms of outdoor/indoor exercise. Address: 110 Mount Annan Drive, Glasgow, G44 4RZ; T.-041-632 1514.

Raeburn, John Alexander, TD, MB, ChB, PHD, FRCPEdin. Senior Lecturer, Human Genetics Unit, Department of Medicine, Edinburgh University, since 1972; Honorary Consultant Physician, Lothian Health Board, since 1972; b. 25.6.41, Adlington, Macclesfield; m., Arlene Rose; 1 s.; 2 d. Educ. Loretto School; Edinburgh University. Worked in clinical medicine; now building up a Medical Genetic Service in SE Scotland, providing genetic counselling; Past Chairman, Scottish Down's Syndrome Association; Chairman, Edinburgh and South East of Scotland Branch, Cystic Fibrosis Research Trust, since 1981; Honorary Medical Adviser to AID for Down's Babies in Edinburgh, since 1977. Recreations: reading; fishing; sketching; cycling to work. Address: (h.) 22 Inverleith Row, Edinburgh, EH3 5QH.

Raeburn, Emeritus Professor John Ross, CBE, FRSE, FIBiol, BSc, MA, PhD. Consultant; b. 20.11.22, Kirkcaldy; m., Mary Roberts; 1 s.; 3 d. Educ. Manchester Grammar School; Edinburgh University; Cornell University. Professor, Agricultural Economics, Nanking University, 1936-37; Research Officer, Oxford University, 1938-39; Statistician, then Head of Agricultural Plans Branch, Ministry of Food, 1939-46; Senior Research Officer, Oxford University, 1946-49; Reader in Agricultural Economics, London University, 1949-59; Professor and Head, Department of Agriculture, Aberdeen University, 1959-78; Principal, North of Scotland College of Agriculture, 1963-78; Consultant to World Bank, since 1978; Vice-President, International Association of Agricultural Economists, 1964-70; President, Agricultural Economics Society, 1964-65. Publication: Agriculture: Foundations, Principles and Development. Recreations: travel; gardening; photography. Address: (h.) 30 Morningfield Road, Aberdeen, AB2 4AQ; T.-0224 314010.

Raine, Wendy J.B., BSc, MB, ChB, MRCPsych. Consultant Child and Adolescent Psychiatrist, since 1978; b. 14.11.46, Edinburgh; m., Peter Raine; 1 d. Educ. James Gillespie's High School for Girls, Edinburgh; Edinburgh University. Medical and early psychiatric training, Edinburgh; specialist training, Glasgow and Melbourne; psychotherapy training, Edinburgh. Recreations: hill-walking; St. Kilda; knitting; Victorian children's books. Address: (h.) 5 Westbourne Drive, Bearsden, Glasgow, G61 4BD; T.-041-942 8881.

Ralph, Alexander Hugh Duncan Cameron. Vice Convener, Ross and Cromarty District Council, since 1984; Vice Chairman, Highland River Purification Board, since 1982; Vice Chairman, Scottish River Purification Boards Association, since 1984; b. 21.7.15, Beauly, Invernss-shire; m., Frances Matheson Anderson; 1 d. Educ. Inverness Royal Academy. RAF and RASC/EFI, 1940-47; elected, Invergordon District Council, 1967; elected, Ross and Cromarty County Council, 1970; elected, Ross and Cromarty District Council, 1974 (Chairman, Environmental Health Committee, 1974-84). Recreations: travel; books; selected television programmes. Address: (h.) 5 Ross Crescent, Milton, Kildary, Ross-shire, IV18 0PS; T.-Kildary 2206.

Ralph, Rev. Isaac. Minister, New Pisligo Parish Church, since 1959; Clerk, Buchan Presbytery, since 1984; b. 30.5.21, Nairn; m., Mary Garden Taylor; 2 d. Educ. Nairn Academy; Aberdeen University and Christ's College, Aberdeen. Volunteered for service with Royal Navy, 1941-46; Assistant Minister, Holborn Central Church, Aberdeen, 1949-51; Minister, Tingwall Parish, Shetland, 1951-59; Moderator, Shetland Presbytery, 1955-56 (Clerk, 1956-59); Moderator, Deer Presbytery, 1967-68. President, New Pitsligo Horticultural Society. Recreations: rambling; photography; horticulture. Address: The Manse, 137 High Street, New Pitsligo, Fraserburgh, AB4 4NH; T.-New Pitsligo 256.

Ralston, Andrew Dunlop, BL, NP. Partner, Macnair Clyde & Ralston, Solicitors, Paisley, since 1949 (Senior Partner, since 1981); Honorary Sheriff of North Strathclyde, at Paisley, since 1976; b. 22.5.23, Glasgow; m., Jane Neilson Burns; 3 s. Educ. Allan Glen's School, Glasgow; Glasgow University. Vice-Dean, Faculty of Procurators in Paisley, 1979-81. Honorary Secretary, Scottish Baptist College, 1966-83; Honorary Treasurer, Dennistoun Baptist Church, Glasgow, 1974-77; Life Governor, Imperial Cancer Research Fund, since 1980; Member, Committee of Management, Scottish Baptist Housing Association Ltd., since 1980. Recreations: gardening; walking. Address: (b.) 43 High Street, Paisley; T.-041-887 5181.

Ramage, John Bradley, ALA, MBIM. Chief Librarian, City of Dundee, since 1982; b. 14.1.42, Airdrie; m., Dorothy Laing Cowan; 1 d. Educ. Airdrie Academy; Scottish School of Librarianship. School Librarian, Broxburn Academy, 1962-63; Chief Assistant Librarian, Burgh of Clydebank, 1963-67; Depute Chief Librarian, Burgh of Coatbridge, 1967-73; City of Dundee: Senior Assistant Chief Librarian, 1973-78, Depute Chief Librarian, 1978-82. Member, Scottish Advisory Committee, Independent Broadcasting Authority; Member, Board of Governors, Duncan of Jordanstone College of Art; Trustee, Meadowplace Trust; Secretary, Dundee Film Theatre Committee; Elder, Church of Scotland. Recreations: golf; gardening; home wine-making; DIY. Address: (b.) Central Library, The Wellgate, Dundee, DD1 1DB; T.-0382 23141, Ext. 4323.

Ramage, Professor Robert, BSc, PhD, DSc, MSc, CChem, FRSC. Forbes Professor of Organic Chemistry, Edinburgh University, since 1984; b. 4.10.35, Glasgow; m., Joan Fraser Paterson; 3 d. Educ. Whitehill Senior Secondary School, Glasgow; Glasgow University. Fellow, Harvard College and Fulbright Scholar, Harvard University, 1961-63; Woodward Research Institute, Basle, 1963-64; Lecturer, then Senior Lecturer, Liverpool University, 1964-77; Professor, then Head, Department of Chemistry, UMIST, 1977-84. Recreations: sports; gardening. Address: (h.) 26 Craigleith View, Ravelston, Edinburgh, EH4 3JZ; T.-031-337 1952.

Ramsay, David High. Member, Lothian Regional Council, since 1977 (Chairman, Urban Regeneration Programme Advisory Committee, since 1982); Chairman, Community Opportunities West Lothian Ltd.; Company Secretary, Stoneyburn Workshops Ltd.; b. 25.6.36, Dundee; m., Rosemary Helen; 2 s. Educ. Harris Academy, Dundee. Recreations: golf; philately. Address: (h.) 15 Hardy Gardens, Bathgate, West Lothian; T.-Bathgate 630236.

Ramsay, Professor Donald MacDonald, BSc, PhD, FGS. Professor of Geology, Dundee University, since 1980; b. 17.8.32, Glasgow; m., Elma; 1 s.; 2 d. Educ. Allan Glen's School; Glasgow University. Assistant in Geology, Glasgow University, 1957-59; Dundee University: Lecturer in Geology, 1959, Senior Lecturer, 1966, Reader, 1977. Secretary, then British Correspondent, Project 27 (Caledonide Orogen), International Geological Correlation Programme (UNESCO). Recreation: curling. Address: (b.) Department of Geology, The University, Dundee, DD1 4HN; T.-Dundee 23181, Ext. 4439.

Ramsay, Hamish, MRTPI. Director of Planning, Tayside Regional Council, since 1975; b. 23.3.30, Windygates, Fife; m., Sheila; 2 d. Educ. Buckhaven High School; College of Estate Management. Fife County Council: planning apprentice, 1947-52, Junior Planning Assistant, 1954-56; Corporation of Dundee: Planning Assistant, 1956-65, Depute Town Planning Officer, 1965-69, Chief Planning Officer, 1969-75. Vice-Chairman, Duncan of Jordanstone College of Art, since 1978. Recreations: Rotary; walking. Address: (b.) Tayside House, Crichton Street, Dundee; T.-0382 23281.

Ramsay, John Neville David, FInstFF. Chairman, John G. Borland & Peat Ltd., Glasgow, since 1980; Board Member, Clyde Port Authority, since 1983; b. 18.5.24, Glasgow; m., Olive Doreen; 1 s. Educ. Hutchesons' Boys Grammar School, Glasgow. Joined Anchor Line Ltd., Glasgow, 1940; War Service, RAF (home, North Africa, Italy), 1942-47; John G. Borland & Peat Ltd., Shipbrokers: joined, 1947, appointed Director, 1959, Managing Director, 1978; President, Glasgow and Clyde Shipping Association, 1983; Director, Glasgow Chamber of Commerce, since 1983; Director, Glasgow Shipowners and Shipbrokers Benevolent Association, since 1984. Recreations: angling; painting; gardening; music. Address: (b.) John G. Borland & Peat Ltd., Anderston House, 389 Argyle Street, Glasgow, G2 8NG; T.-041-204 2788.

Ramsay, Sheriff Norman James Gemmill, MA, LLB. Sheriff of South Strathclyde, Dumfries and Galloway, at Kirkcudbright, Stranraer and Dumfries, since 1971; b. 26.8.16; m.; 2 s. Educ. Merchiston Castle School; Edinburgh University. WS, 1939; Advocate, 1956; Puisne Judge of High Court, Northern Rhodesia (later Zambia), 1964-68.

Ramsay, Stuart Drysdale. Member, Dundee District Council, since 1983; b. 7.5.47, Broughty Ferry; m., Wendy. Educ. Harris Academy; Kingsway and Dundee College of Technology. Executive Member, Dundee West Conservative Association; Vice-President, former Dundee Ratepayers' and Electors' Association; Governor, Dundee School Holiday Fund, since 1984. Recreations: squash; tennis; skiing; home computing; car rallying. Address: (h.) Verndale, No. 2 Westyall Farm Cottage, Duntrune, Kellas, by Dundee, DD5 3PD; T.-082625 587.

Ramsey, Professor Peter Herbert, MA, DPhil. Professor of History, Aberdeen University, since 1966; b. 19.11.25, Barnet; m., Priscilla Telford; 3 d. Educ. Mill Hill School; Worcester College, Oxford. Assistant, Glasgow University, 1951-55; Lecturer, Bristol University, 1955-65. Publications: Tudor Economic Problems, 1963; The Price Revolution in Sixteenth Century England, 1971. Recreations: reading; music. Address: (h.) Goose Croft House, Kintore, Aberdeenshire; T.-Kintore 32337.

Randall, Rev. David James, MA, BD, ThM. Minister, Doune Parish Church, Macduff, since 1971; Convener, Business Committee, Buchan Presbytery; b. 5.6.45, Edinburgh; m., Agnes Wardlaw; 3 s.; 1 d. Educ. George Heriot's School; Edinburgh University; Princeton Theological Seminary. Former Moderator, Turriff Presbytery and Buchan Presbytery. Recreation: jogging. Address: (h.) Doune Manse, Macduff, AB4 3QL.

Rankin, Alick Michael. Chief Executive, Scottish & Newcastle Breweries plc, since 1983; b. 23.1.35, London; m., Suzetta Nelson; 1 s.; 3 d. Educ. Eton College; Oxford University. Scots Guards, 1953-55; investment banking, Toronto, 1956-59; Scottish & Newcastle Breweries plc, since 1960. Recreations: fishing; shooting; golf; tennis. Address: (b.) Abbey Brewery, 111 Holyrood Road, Edinburgh, EH8 8YS; T.-031-556 2591.

Rankin, Andrew Kerr McMillan. Assistant Director of Environmental Health, Glasgow District Council, since 1975; Moderator, General Assembly, United Free Church of Scotland, 1984-85; b. 30.3.23, Glasgow; m., Margaret J.H. Crichton; 1 d. Educ. Bishopbriggs High School; Coatbridge High School. War service with RAF as Pilot/Flight Engineer; entered service of Glasgow Corporation Health Department and qualified as Environmental Health Officer; Chairman, Environmental Health Liaison Committee, Greater Glasgow Health Board, since 1983; Chairman, West of Scotland Medical/Veterinary Liaison Group, since 1982; Convener, various Presbytery and General Assembly Committees, United Free Church of Scotland; Moderator of Presbytery, 1977-78; Convener, Executive Council, General Assembly. Recreations: photography; travel. Address: (h.) 59 Kirkintilloch Road, Bishopbriggs, Glasgow, G64 2AE; T.-041-772 1553.

Rankin, Emeritus Professor Robert Alexander, MA, PhD, ScD, FRSAMD, FRSE. Emeritus Professor of Mathematics, Glasgow University, since 1982; Honorary President, Gaelic Society of Glasgow, since 1969; b. 27.10.15, Garlieston, Wigtownshire; m., Mary Ferrier Llewelyn; 1 s.; 3 d. Educ. Whithorn School; Fettes College; Clare College, Cambridge. Fellow, Clare College, 1939-51; War work on rockets, 1940-45; Lecturer, Cambridge University, 1945-51; Assistant Tutor, Clare College, 1947-51; Mason Professor of Pure Mathematics, Birmingham University, 1951-54; Professor of Mathematics, Glasgow University, 1954-82 (Clerk of Senate, 1971-78). Vice-President, Royal Society of Edinburgh, 1960-63; Keith Prize, RSE, 1961-63; Member, Secretary of State's Advisory Council on Education, 1959-61; Vice-President, London Mathematical Society, 1966-68; President, Edinburgh Mathematical Society, 1957-58 and 1978-79. Recreations: music; hill-walking; Gaelic studies. Address: (h.) 98 Kelvin Court, Glasgow, G12 OAH; T.-041-339 2641.

Rankin, Thomas Boyd, CA, ARINA. Financial Director, Yarrow Shipbuilders Ltd., since 1977 (and Joint Company Secretary, since 1981); b. 7.8.39, Londonderry; m., Elspeth Margaret Murray; 1 s.; 1 d. Educ. Foyle College, Londonderry. Thomson McLintock & Co.: articled, 1957-62, Audit Assistant, 1962-71; Yarrow Shipbuilders Ltd.: Financial Accountant, 1971-73, Chief Accountant, 1973-74, Principal Chief Accountant, 1974-77. Recreations: golf; badminton. Address: (b.) Yarrow Shipbuilders Ltd., South Street, Scotstoun, Glasgow, G14 OXN; T.-041-959 1207.

Rankin, Thomas John, MA, FCollP. Head Teacher, Sgoil Dhalabroig, South Uist, since 1981; b. 29.3.47, Glasgow; m., Jean Helen Adams; 2 d. Educ. Strathbungo Secondary School, Glasgow; Glasgow University. Teacher, Bernard Street Junior Secondary School, Glasgow; Teacher, Chizongwe Secondary School, Chipata, Zambia; Deputy Head, Kabulonga School for Boys, Lusaka, Zambia; Examinations Officer, i/c Cambridge School Certificate and London University External Degree Examinations, Ministry of Education, Lusaka; Acting Headmaster, Libala Secondary School, Lusaka; Teacher: West Derby Comprehensive School, Liverpool, Chryston High School, near Glasgow. Address: (b.) Sgoil Dhalabroig, Dalabrog, Isle of South Uist, PA81 5SS; T.-08784 276.

Ransford, Tessa, MA. Director, Scottish Poetry Library; Poet; b. 8.7.38, Bombay; 1 s.; 3 d. Educ. St. Leonard's School, St. Andrews; Edinburgh University; Craiglockhart College of Education. Publicity Department, Oxford University Press, 1958; in Pakistan as wife of missionary, 1960-68; Assistant to the Director, Scottish Institute of Adult Education, 1982-83; books of poetry: Poetry of Persons, 1975, While It Is Yet Day, 1976, Light of the Mind, 1980, Fools and Angels, 1984; first prize, Jubilee poetry competition, Scottish Association for the Speaking of Verse, 1974; Scottish Arts Council Book Award, 1980; Founder and Organiser, School of Poets (open learning workshops for practising poets). Recreation: hill-walking. Address: (b.) Scottish Poetry Library, Tweeddale Court, 14 High Street, Edinburgh, EH1 1TE; T.-031-557 2876.

Rattray, Charles McNab Iverson, BSc, MSc, FIMA, MBCS. Senior Lecturer, Department of Computing Science, Stirling University, since 1978; b. 3.9.38, Burrelton; m., May Rattray; 2 s. Educ. Adelaide Boys' High School; Adelaide University; UMIST, Manchester. Engineer, Ferranti Ltd., Salisbury, South Australia, and Manchester, England, 1959-64; Lecturer, UMIST, 1964-69; Senior Lecturer, MacQuarie University, Sydney, 1969-72; variety of research posts and commercial positions, 1972-78. Whitworth Exhibitioner, 1973-74. Publication: Programming Language Semantics. Recreation: working. Address: (b.) Department of Computing Science, Stirling University, Stirling, FK9 4LA; T.-0786 73171.

Rattray, Ronald Alexander Spalding, CEng, FICE. Director of Technical Services, Renfrew District Council, since 1974; b. 8.4.27, Carnoustie; m., Sheila; 1 s.; 2 d. Educ. Ardrossan Academy; Arbroath High School; Dundee Technical College. Apprentice engineer and surveyor, Monifieth Burgh, 1944-48; Engineering Assistant: Fife County Council, 1948-49, Kirkcaldy Burgh, 1949-51; Chief Assistant Engineer, Pudsey Borough, 1951-55; Deoute Burgh Surveyor and Planning Officer, Dumfries Burgh, 1955-61; Burgh Surveyor, Planning Officer and Master of Works, Dumfries, 1961-69; Technical Services Manager, Hamilton Burgh, 1969-74. Recreations: swimming; bowling; fishing; curling. Address: (b.) Municipal Buildings, Cotton Street, Paisley; T.-041-889 5400.

Raven, Alan Martin, BSc (Hons), PhD, CChem, FRSC, MIBiol. Scientific Adviser, Department of Agriculture and Fisheries for Scotland, since 1982; b. 24.1.30, Lewisham, London; m., Yvonne Valerie Simpson; 2 s.; 1 d. Educ. Cockermouth Grammar School; King's College, Durham University, Newcastle-upon-Tyne; Chemical and Animal Nutrition Research Division, Ministry of Agriculture, Northern Ireland: Scientific Officer, 1955-59, Senior Scientific Officer, 1959-67, Principal Scientific Officer, 1967-72; Assistant Lecturer to Senior Lecturer, Agricultural Chemistry Department, Queen's University, Belfast, 1955-72; West of Scotland Agricultural College: Assistant Director (Development), 1972-75, Deputy Principal, 1975-82. Recreations: reading; travel; theatre; gardening. Address: (b.) Department of Agriculture and Fisheries for Scotland, Chesser House, Gorgie Road, Edinburgh, EH11 3AW; T.-031-443 4020.

Rawcliffe, Rt. Rev. Derek Alec, OBE, BA. Bishop of Glasgow and Galloway, since 1981; b. 8.7.21, Manchester; m., Susan Kathryn Speight. Educ. Sir Thomas Rich's School, Gloucester; Leeds University; College of the Resurrection, Mirfield. Ordained Deacon, 1944; ordained Priest, Worcester, 1945; Assistant Priest, St. George's, Worcester, 1944-47; Assistant Master, then Headmaster, All Hallows School, Pawa, Solomon Islands, 1947-56; Headmaster, St. Mary's School, Maravovo, Guadalcanar, Solomon Islands, 1956-58; Archdeacon of Southern Melanesia, New Hebrides, 1958-74; Assistant Bishop, Diocese of Melanesia, 1974-75; first Bishop of New Hebrides (now Vanuatu), 1975-80. Recreations: music; numismatics. Address: Bishop's House, 48 Drymen Road, Bearsden, Glasgow, G61 2RH; T.-041-943 0612.

Rawlings, Edwin James, DSR. Member, Lothian Health Board; Superintendent Radiographer, City Hospital Group, Edinburgh, since 1956;

b. 1.12.27, Glasgow; m., Catherine; 1 s.; 1 d. Educ. Paisley Grammar School; School of Radiography, Glasgow Royal Infirmary. Army Service, RAMC; worked in diagnostic radiography, NHS, since 1949. Recreations: motor cycling; sailing. Address: (h.) 13 Broomhall Terrace, Edinburgh, EH12 7PZ; T.-031-334 5188.

Rayner, Colin Robert, MB, BS, MS, FRCS, FRCSEdin. Consultant Plastic Surgeon, Grampian Health Board and Royal Aberdeen Children's Hospital, since 1978; Senior Lecturer in Surgery, Aberdeen University, since 1978; b. 28.10.38, London; m., Margaret Mary; 1 s.; 2 d. Educ. St. George's College, Weybridge; Middlesex Hospital, London. General surgical training and pre-registration posts, Middlesex Hospital, Birmingham Accident Hospital, Kent and Sussex Hospital, 1964-71; SHO Plastic Surgery, East Grinstead Hospital, 1971; Registrar and Senior Registrar in head and neck surgery, Westminster and Royal Marsden Hospital, London, 1972-75; Senior Registrar, South Manchester Teaching Hospital, 1976-78. Recreations: skiing; opera; Russian literature; the works of P.J. Wodehouse. Address: 6 Moray Place, Aberdeen; T.-0224 314216.

Redding, Penelope Jane, MB, BS, MRCS, LRCP, MRCPath. Consultant Bacteriologist, Victoria Infirmary, Glasgow, since 1984; Honorary Clinical Teacher, Glasgow University, since 1983; b. 21.11.50, London; m., Christopher John Vincent; 1 s. Educ. Lycee Francais de Londres; University College, London/Westminster Hospital Medical School. House Surgeon, Gynaecology, Queen Mary's, Roehampton, 1974; House Physician, Medicine, St. Stephen's, Fulham, 1975; Rotating SHO, Pathology, Westminster Hospital, 1975-76; Assistant Lecturer, Microbiology, St. Thomas's Hospital, 1976-77; Registrar, Bacteriology and Immunology, Western Infirmary, 1977-80 (Senior Registrar, 1980-84). Publication: Handbook of Intensive Care (Contributor), 1983. Recreations: skiing; swimming; dress-making; opera; ballet. Address: (b.) Bacteriology Department, Victoria Infirmary, Glasgow, G42 9TY; T.-041-649 4545.

Redman, Timothy, GRSM, ARMCM. Composer and Arranger; Conductor; b. 9.11.43, Newcastle-upon-Tyne. Educ. Rutherford Grammar School, Newcastle-upon-Tyne; Royal Manchester College of Music. Teacher of Music and Deputy Headmaster, Salford, Lancashire; Associate Musical Director, Theatre Royal, Newcastle-upon-Tyne, 1973-74; Organist and Master of the Choristers, St. Mary's Cathedral, Glasgow, 1976-79; Associate Director, BBC Scottish Singers, 1977-80; Member, Music Staff, BBC Scotland, since 1974; Founder Chairman, Glasgow Diocesan Music Association, 1976-79 and 1981-83; compositions include organ and choral music, chamber music, music for brass group and concert band. Recreations: cinema; theatre; reading. Address: (h.) 2 Leven Street, Pollokshields, Glasgow, G41 2JQ; T.-041-423 2547.

Redpath, Jean. Singer; Singer in Residence, Stirling University; b. 28.4.37, Leven. Educ. Leven; Buckhaven; Edinburgh University (left before taking degree). Singer of traditional Scottish music; has sung in every state in the USA, where she tours several times a year; lectures at summer school, Stirling University, each year; numerous radio and TV appearances, UK, USA and Australia. Recreations: singing!; photography. Address: (h.) Sunnyknowe, The Promenade, Leven, Fife; T.-0333 23621.

Rees, Alan Tait, MA (Cantab), CQSW. Assistant Director, Edinburgh Council of Social Service, since 1976; Chairman, Committee on Mobility for Scotland, Scottish Council on Disability, since 1979; Convener, Scottish Community Transport Group, since 1983; b. 4.8.31, Shanghai, China; m., Alison Margaret; 2 s.; 2 d. Educ. Kingswood School, Bath; Gonville and Caius College, Cambridge. Community Development Officer, Tanzania; Lecturer in Youth and Community Studies, Moray House College; Organising Secretary, Board for Information in Youth and Community Service, Scotland; Senior Community Development Officer, Council of Social Service for Wales. Treasurer, Scottish Committee, British Association of Social Workers; Trustee, Seagull Trust; Secretary, Handicabs (Lothian). Recreations: gardening; painting; DIY. Address: (h.) 20 Seaforth Drive, Edinburgh, EH4 2BZ; T.-031-332 7317.

Rees, Professor Elmer Gethin, BA (Cantab), PhD (Warwick), MA (Oxon), FRSE. Professor and Head, Department of Mathematics, Edinburgh University, since 1979; b. 19.11.41, Llandybie, Wales; m., Mary Elene; 2 s. Educ. Llandeilo Grammar School; St. Catharine's College, Cambridge. Lecturer, Department of Pure Mathematics, Hull University, 1967-69; Member, Institute for Advanced Study, Princeton, 1969-70; Lecturer, Department of Pure Mathematics, University College of Swansea, 1970-71; Tutorial Fellow, St. Catherine's College, Oxford and Lecturer in Mathematics, Oxford University, 1971-79. Publication: Notes on Geometry. Address: (h.) 23 Blacket Place, Edinburgh, EH9 1RJ; T.-031-667 2747.

Reeves, Philip Thomas Langford, RSA, RSW, RE, RGI, ARCA. Artist; b. 7.7.31, Cheltenham; m., Christine MacLaren; 1 d. Educ. Naunton Park School, Cheltenham; Cheltenham School of Art; Royal College of Art, London. Lecturer in Graphic Design, Glasgow School of Art, 1954-70 (Head of Printmaking, since 1970). Address: (h.) 13 Hamilton Drive, Glasgow, G12 8DN; T.-041-339 0720.

Regent, Peter. Writer and Sculptor; b. 8.12.29, Bury St. Edmunds; m., Karola Hood Zurndorfer; 1 d. Educ. Thetford Grammar School; Keble College, Oxford. Nigerian Government Service, 1954-56; Head of African Section/Research Director, Hansard Society, 1956-59; Staff Tutor in Government, Police Staff College, Bramshill, 1959-65; Head, Department of Liberal and Complementary Studies, Duncan of Jordanstone College of Art, Dundee, 1965-75. Member, North East Fife District Council, since 1984. Publication: Laughing Pig (short stories), 1984. Recreation: walking abroad. Address: (h.) Windhover House, Woodmuir Crescent, Newport-on-Tay, Fife; T.-0382 543192.

Reiach, Alan, OBE, RIBA, ARSA, RSW. Architect; b. 2.3.10, London; m., Patricia Anne; 1 s.; 1 d. Educ. Edinburgh Academy; Edinburgh College of Art. Apprenticed to Sir Robert Lorimer; Travelling Scholarship to USA, 1935-36; worked in office of Robert Atkinson, London, 1936-37; Architect Planner, Scottish Office, 1940-46; ran own practice, 1949-65; joined Eric Hall & Partners, 1965; retired, 1975; Consultant, 1975-80. Publication: Building Scotland (Co-author), 1940. Recreation: painting. Address: (b.) Messrs Reiach & Hall, 6 Darnaway Street, Edinburgh; T.-031-225 8444.

Reid, Alexander (Alastair) James, FIB (Scot). General Manager, UK Banking, Royal Bank of Scotland plc, since 1985; b. 26.8.35, Edinburgh; m., Sandra Elizabeth Johnston; 1 s.; 1 d. Educ. Kingussie Secondary School. Royal Bank of Scotland: Inspector of Branches, 1972, Assistant Superintendent of Branches (Glasgow), 1972, Manager, Glasgow, Charing Cross West, 1975, Superintendent of Branches (Edinburgh), 1978, Assistant General Manager (Southern Region), 1979, General Manager (Southern Region), 1980, Senior General Manager (Banking), 1981. Vice-President, Institute of Bankers in Scotland; Director, Scottish Agricultural Securities Corporation plc; Elder, Craigsbank Church. Recreations: gardening; sport, particularly golf, angling and curling. Address: (b.) 42 St. Andrew Square, Edinburgh, EH2 2YE; T.-031-556 8555.

Reid, Daniel, MD, FRCPGlas, FFCM, DPH. Consultant, Communicable Diseases (Scotland) Unit, since 1969; Honorary Lecturer, Department of Infectious Diseases, Glasgow University, since 1969; b. 5.2.35, Glasgow; m., Eileen Simpson; 2 d. Educ. Allan Glen's School, Glasgow; Glasgow University. House Surgeon, Victoria Infirmary, Glasgow; House Physician, Southern General Hospital, Glasgow; House Surgeon, Stobhill Hospital, Glasgow; Lt./Captain, Royal Army Medical Corps (attached Royal Northumberland Fusiliers, Hong Kong); Registrar, University Department of Infectious Diseases, Ruchill Hospital, Glasgow; Senior Registrar, Epidemiological Research Laboratory, London. Chairman, Advisory Group on Epidemiological Aspects of Infection, Scottish Planning Council. Address: (b.) Communicable Diseases (Scotland) Unit, Ruchill Hospital, Glasgow, G20; T.-041-946 7120.

Reid, Gavin Clydesdale, MA, MSc, PhD. Senior Lecturer in Economics, Edinburgh University, since 1984; b. 25.8.46, Glasgow; 2 s. Educ. Frimley and Camberley Grammar School; Aberdeen University; Southampton University; Edinburgh University. Lecturer in Economics, Edinburgh University, 1971-84; Visiting Associate Professor: Queen's University, Ontario, 1981-82, Denver University, Colorado, 1984. Review Editor, Scottish Journal of Political Economy. Publication: The Kinked Demand Curve Analysis, 1981. Recreations: music; reading; running; badminton. Address: (b.) Department of Economics, Edinburgh University, George Square, Edinburgh, EH8 9JY; T.-031-667 1011.

Reid, George Hunter, BCom, IPFA. Director of Finance and Commercial Development, South of Scotland Electricity Board, since 1968; b.

3.3.25, Kirkliston; m., Helen Borthwick; 3 s. Educ. Broxburn Academy; Edinburgh University. City Chamberlain's Department, Edinburgh Corporation, 1941-49; Royal Navy, 1943-47; various positions with South East Scotland (from 1955, South of Scotland) Electricity Board, since 1949. Address: (h.) 22 Manse Road, Kirkliston, West Lothian, EH29 9DJ; T.-031-333 3085.

Reid, Very Rev. George Thomson Henderson, MC, MA, BD, DD. Minister, Church of Scotland; b. 31.3.10, Leith; m., Anne Guilland Watt; 3 s.; 1 d. Educ. George Watson's Boys College, Edinburgh; Edinburgh University and New College. Minister: Cockenzie, 1935-38, Juniper Green, Edinburgh, 1938-49; Chaplain to the Forces: 3rd Bn., Scots Guards, 1940-44, Senior Chaplain, 15 (5) Division, 1944-45; awarded MC, 1945; Minister: Claremont Church, Glasgow, 1949-55, West Church of St. Andrew, Aberdeen, 1955-75; awarded Doctorate of Divinity by Aberdeen University, 1971; Chaplain to the Queen, 1972; Moderator, General Assembly, Church of Scotland, 1973-74. Recreations: golf; water-colour painting. Address: (h.) 33 Westgarth Avenue, Edinburgh, EH13 OBB; T.-031-441 1299.

Reid, Harry William, BA (Hons). Deputy Editor, Glasgow Herald, since 1983; b. 23.9.47, Glasgow; m., Julie Davidson (qv); 1 d. Educ. Aberdeen Grammar School; Fettes College; Oxford University. The Scotsman: Education Correspondent, 1973-77, Features Editor, 1977-81; Sports Editor, Sunday Standard, 1981-82; Executive Editor, Glasgow Herald, 1982-83. Recreations: reading; walking; supporting Aberdeen Football Club. Address: (h.) 15 Albion Buildings, Ingram Street, Glasgow; T.-041-552 8403.

Reid, Rev. Ian, OBE, JP, BA. Minister, Abbey Church, Kilwinning, since 1975; b. 28.10.16, Guildford; m., Rosemary Findlay; 2 s.; 2 d. Educ. Fettes College; Queens' College, Cambridge; Edinburgh University. 73 AITK Rgt., RA, 1941-73; Chaplain, 7th Cameronians, 1944; Senior Chaplain, 52nd Division; Minister, Old Kirk of Edinburgh, 1947-67; Past Chairman, Edinburgh Marriage Guidance Council; Past Chairman, Education Committee, Scottish Marriage Guidance Council; former Vice Chairman, Edinburgh Council of Social Service; Leader of Iona Community, 1967; former Moderator, Ardrossan Presbytery; Member, Scottish Housing Advisory Committee, 1968. Recreations: gardening; fishing. Address: Abbey Manse, 54 Dalry Road, Kilwinning, Ayrshire; T.-Kilwinning 52606.

Reid, Jimmy. Journalist and Broadcaster; b. 1932. Former Engineer; prominent in campaign to save Upper Clyde Shipbuilders; former Convener of Shop Stewards, AUEW; former (Communist) Member, Clydebank Town Council; joined Labour Party and contested Dundee East, General Election, 1979; Rector, Glasgow University, 1971-74; Columnist, Daily Record.

Reid, John. MA (Hons) (Cantab). Rector, Queen Anne High School, Dunfermline, since 1974; b. 14.6.34, Kirkcaldy; m., Rachel C.B. Cameron; 1 s.; 1 d. Educ. Wallington County Grammar

School; Selwyn College, Cambridge. Assistant Teacher of Geography, Dunfermline High School 1956-65; Principal Teacher of Geography, Larbert High School 1965-73 (Assistant Rector, 1973-74). Vice-President, Headteachers' Association of Scotland, 1984-85; Chairman, Dunfermline Branch, Royal Scottish Geographical Society. Recreations: opera; bridge; golf. Address: (h.) 98 Pilmuir Street, Dunfermline, KY12 0ND.

Reid, Sir John James Andrew, KCMG, CB, TD, MD, DSc, LLD, FRCP, FRCPEdin, FRCPGlas, FFCM, DPH. Chief Medical Officer, Scottish Home and Health Department, since 1977; Member (and Past Chairman), Executive Board, World Health Organisation, since 1973; Honorary Consultant in Community Medicine to the Army, since 1971; b. 21.1.25, Newport-on-Tay; m., Marjorie Crumpton; 1 s.; 4 d. Educ. Bell-Baxter School, Cupar; St. Andrews University. Hospital, Army (National Service) and junior public health posts, 1947-55; Lecturer in Public Health and Social Medicine, St. Andrews University, 1955-59; Deputy County MOH, Northamptonshire, 1959-62; County MOH, Northamptonshire, 1962-67; Buckinghamshire, 1967-72; Deputy Chief Medical Officer, DHSS, 1972-77; Visiting Professor in Health Services Administration, London School of Hygiene and Tropical Medicine, 1973-78. Address: (b.) St. Andrews House, Edinburgh, EH1 3DE; T.-031-556 8501.

Reid, Rev. John Kelman Sutherland, CBE, TD, MA, DD. Member, Editorial Board, Scottish Journal of Theology, since 1948; Member, Church of Scotland Board of World Mission and Unity, since 1961; b. 31.3.10, Leith; m., Margaret Winifrid Brookes. Educ. George Watson's College, Edinburgh; Edinburgh University; Heidelberg University; Basel University; Marburg University; Strasburg University. Professor of Philosophy, Calcutta University, 1935-37; Minister, Craigmillar Park Parish Church, Edinburgh, 1939-52; Chaplain to the Forces with Parachute Regiment, 1942-46; Professor of Theology, Leeds University, 1952-61; Chaplain, Territorial Army, 1948-62; Professor of Systematic Theology, Aberdeen University, 1961-76. Publications: Calvin's Theological Treatises (Editor and Translator), 1954; The Biblical Doctrine of the Ministry, 1955; The Authority of Scripture, 1957; Calvin's Concerning the Eternal Predestination of God (Editor and Translator), 1961; Our Life in Christ, 1963; Presbyterians and Unity, 1966; Christian Apologetics, 1969. Recreation: golf. Address: (h.) 1 Camus Park, Edinburgh, EH10 6RY; T.-031-445 2936.

Reid, Professor John Low, MA, DM, FRCP. Regius Professor of Materia Medica, Glasgow University, since 1978; Consultant Physician, Stobhill Hospital, since 1978; Visiting Professor, Strathclyde University, since 1983; b. 1.10.43, Glasgow; m., Randa Pharaon; 1 s.; 1 d. Educ. Fettes College; Oxford University. MRC Research Fellow, Royal Post Graduate Medical School, London, 1970-73; Travelling Fellow, US National Institutes of Health, Washington, USA, 1973-75; Senior Wellcome Fellow in Clinical Science and Reader in Clinical Pharmacology, Royal Post Graduate Medical School, London,

1975-78. Publications: Lecture Notes in Clinical Pharmacology (Co-author); Clinical Science, 1982-84 (Editor); Handbook of Hypertension (Editor). Recreation: gardening. Address: (b.) Stobhill Hospital, Glasgow; T.-041-558 0111.

Reid, Kenneth Grant, MB, BS, FRCS. Senior Lecturer in Cardiac Surgery, Edinburgh University, since 1979; Honorary Consultant Paediatric Cardiac Surgeon, Royal Hospital for Sick Children, Edinburgh, since 1979; b. 18.11.38, Glasgow; m., Marie Anne Marsham; 3 s. Educ. Battlefield School, Glasgow; Wallington County Grammar School; St. Mary's Hospital Medical School, London University; Oxford University. House appointments, St. Mary's Hospital Medical School, London; Deputy Medical Superintendent, St. Mary's Hospital, London; Demonstrator in Anatomy, then Lecturer in Surgery, Oxford University; Honorary Senior Registrar, United Oxford Hospitals; Senior Registrar, National Heart and Chest Hospitals, London; Senior Surgical Registrar, Sick Children's Hospital, London; Visiting Professor, Government of Saudi Arabia; Hunterian Professor, Royal College of Surgeons of England; St. Mary's-Pittsburgh Exchange Scholar. Recreations: art; music; education; sailing. Address: (h.) 31 Heriot Row, Edinburgh, EH3; T.-031-225 4169.

Reid, Rev. Martin Robertson Betsworth Coutts. Minister, Falkirk West, since 1968; b. 7.10.28, Dundee; m., Alison Thomson Gordon; 2 s.; 1 d. Educ. Stobswell Central Junior Secondary School, Dundee; Dundee College of Art; St. Andrews University; London University. Piano technician, 1943-55; Minister, Strathy and Halladale, 1960-68. Serves on various voluntary and charitable bodies. Recreations: reading; music; walking; woodwork; gardening; administration. Address: West Manse, 38 Camelon Road, Falkirk, FK1 5JH; T.-0324 32242.

Reid, Patricia Maureen, BL. Scottish Chief Commissioner, The Girl Guides' Association, since 1982; b. 29.8.39, Glasgow; m., Graham Douglas Melville Reid; 1 s.; 1 d. Educ. Laurel Bank School, Glasgow; Glasgow University. Qualified as Solicitor, 1961; employed as an Assistant in private practice (part-time, since 1974). Adult Leader Trainer, Girl Guides Association, since 1962; County Commissioner, City of Glasgow Girl Guides, 1979-82. Recreations: sailing; walking; Scottish country dancing. Address: (h.) 64 Crown Road North, Glasgow, G12 9HW; T.-041-357 1351.

Reid, Robert Barrowman, MA. Headmaster, Musselburgh Grammar School, since 1978; b. 23.12.29, Saltcoats; m., Sheila Mathieson Grant; 2 s.; 1 d. Educ. Ardrossan Academy; Glasgow University; Jordanhill College. RAEC, 1952-54; Ardrossan Academy, 1954-64; Musselburgh Grammar School, 1964-69; Headmaster, Newbattle High School, 1969-78. Member, Saltcoats Town Council, 1958-64 (Dean of Guild, Irvine and District Water Board); Council Member, Lothian Headteachers Association, 1973-83 (President, 1979-81); Council Member,

Headteachers Association of Scotland, 1974-84; Member, Scottish Council for Research in Education, 1978-84; Member, Consultative Committee on the Curriculum, since 1983; Member, Church and Nation Committee, Church of Scotland, since 1983. Recreations: horse-riding; swimming; drama.

Reid, Robert Cameron Birnie, BA, CA. Local Senior Partner, Deloitte Haskins & Sells, Aberdeen, since 1980; Director (Chairman), Aberdeen Trust PLC, 1970-85; Chairman, Aberdeen Fund Managers Ltd., since 1984; b. 23.1.28, Aberdeen; m., Pauline; 2 s.; 3 d. Educ. Loretto School; Clare College, Cambridge. National Service, TA; Captain, Royal Corps of Signals; De Yoete & Gorton, Stock Exchange, 1952-53; Price Waterhouse, Toronto, 1953-54; Partner, Meston & Co., CA, Deloitte Haskins & Sells, since 1955. Member, Queen's Bodyguard for Scotland (Royal Company of Archers); Secretary, Aberdeen Squash Racquets Club. Recreations: tennis; skiing; squash. Address: (b.) 6 Golden Square, Aberdeen, AB9 1JB; T.-0224 636555.

Reid, Thomas Shaw Lindsay, CA. Secretary, Shirlaw Allan & Co. Ltd., since 1970; Member, Lanarkshire Health Board, since 1973; b. 16.11.25, Wishaw; m., Rita Mildred Aldred Acum; 2 s.; 1 d. Educ. Hamilton Academy. Apprentice, Thomson McLintock & Co., CA, 1941-43 and 1947-50; RNVR (Sub-Lt. (A)), 1944-47; Peat Marwick Mitchell & Co., CA, 1951-54; Director, G. Brazil & Co. Ltd., 1954-70. Recreation: Motherwell FC spectator. Address: (h.) 26 Rosefield Gardens, Uddingston, G71 7AW.

Reid, William Kennedy, CB, MA. Secretary, Scottish Home and Health Department, since 1984; b. 1931, Aberdeen; m., Ann Campbell; 2 s.; 1 d. Educ. George Watson's College; Edinburgh University; Trinity College, Cambridge. Ministry of Education, 1956; Cabinet Office, 1964; Department of Education and Science, 1967; Scottish Office, 1978. Address: (b.) St. Andrews House, Edinburgh; T.-031-556 8501.

Reid, Sheriff William Macpherson, MA, LLB. Sheriff of Tayside, Central and Fife, since 1983; b. 6.4.38; m.; 3 d. Educ. Elgin Academy; Aberdeen University; Edinburgh University. Admitted Advocate, 1963; Sheriff of Lothian and Borders, 1978; Sheriff of Glasgow and Strathkelvin, 1978-83.

Reilly, Patrick, MA (Hons), BLitt. Senior Lecturer, Department of English Literature, Glasgow University, since 1964; b. 6.1.32, Glasgow; m., Rose Fitzpatrick; 3 s.; 3 d. Educ. St. Mungo's Academy, Glasgow; Glasgow University. Civil Servant, 1948-50; National Service, RAEC, 1950-52; storeman, labourer, clerk, lamplighter, salesman, 1952-57; Glasgow University, 1957-61; Luke Fellowship, Pembroke College, Oxford, 1961-63; Assistant Lecturer, then Lecturer, Glasgow University, 1964-81. Member, Catholic Education Commission of Scotland, since 1977 (Chairman, Adult Education Committee, since 1983). Publications: Jonathan Swift: The Brave

Desponder, 1982; George Orwell: The Age's Adversary, 1985; Modern Scottish Catholicism (Contributor), 1979; Fielding: A Collection of Essays (Contributor), 1985. Recreation: football. Address: (h.) 7 Arundel Drive, Bishopbriggs, Glasgow, G64 3JF; T.-041-772 2320.

Reith, David Stewart, LLB, NP, WS. Partner, Lindsays WS, Solicitors, Edinburgh, since 1976; b. 15.4.51, Edinburgh; m., Fiona Lennox Munro (see Fiona Lennox Reith). Educ. Fettes College; Aberdeen University. Company Secretary, Lothian Building Preservation Trust, since 1984; Secretary and Treasurer, Ponton House Association, Edinburgh, since 1982; Member, National Committee, Architectural Heritage Society of Scotland. Recreations: curling; running; French language; wine. Address: (h.) 29 Northumberland Street, Edinburgh, EH3 6LR; T.-031-556 1625.

Reith, Fiona Lennox, LLB, WS. Advocate, since 1983; b. 17.7.55, Ipswich; m., David Stewart Reith (qv). Educ. St. Dorothy's Convent, Malta; Perth Academy; Aberdeen University. Solicitor, 1979-82. Recreations: film and theatregoing; eating out; holidays. Address: (h.) 29 Northumberland Street, Edinburgh, EH3 6LR; T.-031-556 1625.

Renfrew, Rt. Rev. Charles McDonald, PhL, STL. Assistant Bishop in Glasgow (Titular See Abula), since 1977; b. 21.6.29, Glasgow. Educ. St. Aloysius College, Glasgow; Scots College, Rome; Gregorian University, Rome. Ordained Priest in Rome, 1953; Assistant Priest, Immaculate Conception, Glasgow, 1953-56; Professor of English and Music, and Bursar, St. Mary's College, Blairs, 1956; first Rector, St. Vincent's College, Langbank, 1961; Chaplain to Sisters of Notre Dame, Glasgow, and Vicar General of Glasgow, 1974; ordained Titular Bishop of Abula, 1977; Head, Commission for Pastoral and Social Care, since 1984; Member, Kidney Research Committee Scotland and Second Chance Committee Scotland. Publications: St. Vincent's Prayer Book; Rambling Through Life; Pageant of Holiness. Recreations: classical music; history of Glasgow. Address: 38 Mansionhouse Road, Glasgow, G41; T.-041-649 2228.

Rennie, Rev. Alistair McRae, MA, BD. Minister, Kincardine, Croick and Edderton, since 1976; b. 2.11.14, Glasgow; m., Ruth Tullis Cochran; 4 s. (inc. 1 deceased); 1 d. Educ. Shawlands Secondary School; Glasgow University. Travelling Secretary, Inter-Varsity Fellowship of Evangelical Unions, 1937-41; Minister: South Church, Montrose, 1941-48, Dalziel North Church, Motherwell, 1948-55; Missionary, Church of Scotland, Malawi (Nyasaland), 1955-75. Recreations: music; walking. Address: The Manse, Ardgay, Ross-shire, IV24 3BG; T.-Ardgay 285.

Rennie, Brenda Louise, LLB, NP. Solicitor; Partner, Balfour & Manson, Edinburgh, since 1976; b. 21.12.47, Aberdeen; m., Donald G. Rennie, WS. Educ. Aberdeen Academy; Aberdeen University. Qualified as Solicitor, 1971; Chairman, Finance Committee, Girl Guides Association (Scotland); Member, UK Finance Committee,

Girl Guides Association. Recreations: travel; architecture; history; literature. Address: (h.) 7 Blinkbonny Crescent, Edinburgh, EH4 3NB; T.-031-332 3046.

Rennie, Rev. Donald Blair, MA. Minister, Cults East Parish Church, since 1974; b. 7.3.31, Dundee; m., Ann Beckett; 2 s.; 1 d. Educ. Harris Academy, Dundee; St. Andrews University. Assistant Minister, Govan Old Parish Church, 1955-57; Minister: Balornock North, Glasgow, 1957-64, St. Ninian's, Larkfield, Greenock, 1964-74. Recreations: music; pipe-organ restoration; playing violin, guitar and double bass. Address: Cults East Manse, Cults, Aberdeen, AB1 9TD; T.-0224 867587.

Rennie, James Alexander Norris, MD, FRCP. Consultant Physician (Rheumatology), since 1979; b. 28.1.47, Dunfermline; m., Margaret; 2 s.; 1 d. Educ. Dunfermline High School; Aberdeen University. Lecturer, Department of Medicine, Aberdeen University, 1973-76; Senior Registrar, General Medicine/Rheumatology, Glasgow, 1976-79. Recreations: DIY; china painting; football. Address: (h.) 13 Belvidere Street, Aberdeen, AB2 4QS; T.-Aberdeen 632172.

Rennie, Rev. James Benjamin, MA. Minister, Leochel, Cushnie and Lynturk linked with Tough, since 1983; b. 27.9.33, Craigellachie, Banffshire; m., Margaret Gordon Pirie; 1 s. Educ. Banff Academy; Aberdeen University and Christ's College. Assistant Minister, St. Andrew's Parish Church, Dundee, 1958-59; Minister: Kinlochleven, 1959-67, Blackford, Perthshire, 1967-83. Address: The Manse, Muir of Fowlis, Alford, Aberdeenshire, AB3 8JU; T.-Muir of Fowlis 239.

Rennie, James Stark, BDS, PhD, FDSRCPS, MRCPath. Consultant Oral Pathologist, since 1983; Senior Lecturer, Glasgow University, since 1984; b. 22.5.49, Glasgow; m., Ann Maris Campbell; 2 s. Educ. Coatbridge High School; Glasgow University. Spent two years as a House Officer, Glasgow Dental Hospital; awarded three year MRC Research Fellowship; Lecturer, Department of Oral Medicine and Pathology, Glasgow University, 1977; Melbourne University Scholarship, 1980; returned to UK, 1982, as Lecturer, Glasgow University; appointed Consultant in Oral Pathology, Glasgow Dental Hospital. Recreations: golf; squash; fishing. Address: (h.) Southview, 12 Station Road, Balfron, G63 OSY.

Rennie, Professor Michael John, BSc, MSc, PhD. Professor and Head, Department of Physiology, Dundee University, since 1983; b. 28.7.46, Wallsend on Tyne; m., Anne MacGregor Gill; 1 s.; 2 d. Educ. Royal Grammar School, Newcastle-upon-Tyne; Hull University; Manchester University; Glasgow University. Research Assistant, Department of Neurology, Glasgow University, 1970-74; MRC Travelling Fellow and Instructor, Washington University, St. Louis, 1974-76; Muscular Dystrophy Association of America Fellow and Instructor, Washington University, 1976-77; Lecturer in Human Metabolism, School of Medicine, University College, London, 1977-79; Wellcome Senior Lecturer, Department of Medicine, University College,

London, 1979-83. Member, Editorial Boards: Clinical Science, Medicine in Science and Sports, European Journal of Applied Physiology. Recreations: reading; outdoor pursuits; working with hands; cooking. Address: (b.) Department of Physiology, The University, Dundee, DD1 4HN; T.-0382 23181, Ext. 4572.

Renton, Rev. Ian Paterson, JP, FSA Scot. Minister, St. Colm's Parish Kirk, Dalry, Edinburgh, since 1966; b. 22.3.26, Kirkcaldy; m., Ann Gordon Mutter Macpherson; 2 s.; 1 d. Educ. Sinclairtown and Viewforth Schools, Kirkcaldy; Newbattle Abbey College; Glasgow University; St. Mary's College, St. Andrews. Shipping Clerk, Robert Wemyss & Co., Kirkcaldy, 1941-44; Sergeant, 3rd Bn., Scots Guards, 1944-47; Ministry of Labour, Kirkcaldy, 1947-48; Newbattle Abbey College, 1948-50; Youth Clubs Organiser, Roxburghshire, 1950-53; divinity studies, 1953-58; Assistant Minister, North Kirk, Aberdeen, 1958-60; Minister, St. Mark's Church, Greenwich, London, 1960-66. Member, Edinburgh City Education Committee, 1970-76; Governor: Moray House College, 1971-79, Donaldson's School, Edinburgh, 1972-75, Newbattle Abbey College, 1973-76; Member, General Assembly Committee on Education, 1973-79; Joint Chairman, Scottish Joint Committee on Religious Education, 1974-79; Member, Lothian Region Education Committee, 1977-78; Member, Edinburgh Children's Panel, 1971-74; Executive Member, Broadcasting Council, Radio Forth, 1976-79; Member, DHSS Social Security Tribunal, 1978-84; Member, Church of Scotland Board of Education, 1983-85; Member, Committee on Medical Ethics, Lothian Health Board, since 1984; regular Contributor, BBC, STV, Radio Forth, since 1973. Recreations: climbing; golfing; gardening; drystane diking; archaeological excavation, Byzantine site, Shelomi, Israel. Address: 1 Merchiston Gardens, Edinburgh, EH10 5DD; T.-031-337 1107.

Renton, Jean Paul, PhD, MRCVS. Senior Lecturer, Department of Veterinary Surgery, Glasgow University; b. 22.2.29, Stirling; 1 s. Educ. Stirling High School; Glasgow Veterinary College. Assistant in veterinary practice, 1952-58; became Partner in veterinary practice, 1958; joined Glasgow University, 1961, as Assistant Lecturer. Recreations: farming; music; art and design. Address: (h.) Burnhouse Cottage, Denny, Stirlingshire; T.-0324 822181.

Renton, John B., MBE. General Secretary, Scottish Prison Officers' Association, since 1971; b. 7.6.32, Coldstream; m., A. Marie; 5 s. Educ. Coldstream and Kelso High School. Police Constable, Edinburgh City Police, 1952-58; Scottish Prison Service: Prison Officer, Saughton, 1959-62, Clerk Officer, Barlinnie, 1962-65, Clerk Officer, Dumfries, 1965-67, Principal Clerk Officer, 1967-71. Address: (b.) 21 Calder Road, Edinburgh; T.-031-443 8105.

Renton, Stuart, MBE, ARSA, DA, FRIBA, ARIAS. Architect; Senior Partner, Reiach and Hall, since 1982; b. 15.9.29, Edinburgh; m., Ethnie; 1 s.; 1 d. Educ. Royal High School, Edinburgh; Edinburgh College of Art. Military Service, RAF and RAFVR; Partner, Alan Reiach and Partners, 1957; Partner, Reiach and Hall, 1965; External Examiner, several universities; Assessor for architectural awards schemes; Governor, Edinburgh College of Art, 1985. Recreations: skiing; game fishing. Address: (b.) 6 Darnaway Street, Edinburgh, EH3 6BG; T.-031-225 8844.

Renwick, Professor John Peter, MA, PhD, DLitt. Professor of French, Edinburgh University, since 1980; b. 25.5.39, Gillingham; m., Claudette Gorse; 1 s.; 1 d. Educ. Gillingham Grammar School; St. Bartholomew's Grammar School, Newbury; St. Catherine's College, Oxford; Sorbonne. Assistant Lecturer, then Lecturer, Glasgow University, 1964-66; Fellow, Churchill College, Cambridge, 1966-72; Maitre de Conferences Associe, Departement de Francais, Universite de Clermont-Ferrand, 1970-71, 1972-74; Professor of French, New University of Ulster, 1974-80 (Pro-Vice-Chancellor, 1978-80). Publications: La destinee posthume de Jean-Francois Marmontel, 1972; Marmontel, Memoires, 1972; Marmontel, Voltaire and the Belisaire affair, 1974; Marmontel, Correspondence, 1974; Catalogue de la bibliotheque de Jean-Baptiste Massillon, 1977; Voltaire et Morangies, ou les Lumieres l'ont echappe belle, 1982. Address: Buccleuch Place, Edinburgh, EH8 2LW; T.-031-667 1011.

Rettie, James Philip, TD. Chairman, Sea Fish Industry Authority, since 1981; Farmer; b. 7.12.26, Dundee; m., 1, Helen Grant; 2, Diana Harvey; 2 s.; 1 d. Educ. Trinity College, Glenalmond. Royal Engineers, 1945-48; William Low & Co. PLC, 1948-85 (Chairman, 1980-85); Honorary Col.: 117 (Highland) Field Support Squadron, RE, TAVR, since 1982, 277 (ADR) Field Squadron, RE, TAVR, since 1984. Recreations: shooting; gardening; hill-walking. Address: (h.) Wester Ballindean, Inchture, Perthshire, PH14 9QS; T.-082 886 337.

Reynolds, Adrian, DipRADA. Artistic Director, Byre Theatre, St. Andrews, since 1981; b. 3.5.43, Leeds; m., Marion Anne; 1 d. Educ. King Edward's School, Birmingham; Royal Academy of Dramatic Art. Ten years an Actor, two of which at the Mermaid Theatre, one in Vivat! Vivat Regina!, London; Assistant Director, Civic Theatre, Chelmsford, 1969-70; Associate Director, Salisbury Playhouse, 1974-77; Theatre Director, Manitou-Wabing Theatre, Ontario, 1977-79; Guest Director: Nuffield Theatre, Southampton, 1978-79, Lyceum, Edinburgh, 1980, Scarborough, 1981-82. Recreations: supporting Manchester United; writing; walking four dogs. Address: (h.) 2 Woodpark Cottages, Ceres, Fife, KY15 5QU; T.-0334 82 445.

Rhind, William, MA (Hons), BSc. Honorary Sheriff, Grampian, Highlands and Islands; b. 11.9.07, Inverurie; m., Georgia L. Ollason; 1 d. Educ. Inverurie Academy; Aberdeen University; Aberdeen Teacher Training College. Anderson High School, Lerwick: Principal Teacher of Mathematics, 1931-47, Deputy Headmaster, 1947-52, Headmaster, 1952-70. Recreations: bridge; music; reading; angling. Address: (h.) Kelda, 6 Lovers Loan, Lerwick, Shetland; T.-0595 2238.

Rhodes, Joseph, MA (Hons). Rector, Dunoon Grammar School, since 1981; b. 9.12.45, Irvine; m., Ann T. Robertson; 3 s.; 2 d. Educ. Ayr Academy; Glasgow University; Jordanhill College. Assistant Teacher (History), Kilmarnock Academy, 1969-71; Principal Teacher of History, Auchenharvie Academy, 1971-74; Assistant Rector, Garnock Academy, 1974-77; Depute Rector, Oban High School, 1977-81. Member, Glenkin Outdoor Centre Trust; Crime Prevention Panel; Strathclyde Regional Executive, Headteachers' Association of Scotland. Recreations: gardening; snooker; other interests largely subsumed by those of the children, e.g. now an authority on the "Star Wars" trilogy. Address: (h.) Firbank, North Campbell Road, Innellan, Argyll; T.-Innellan 387.

Riach, Rev. Donald, BL. Minister, St. Peter's Church, Thurso, since 1965; b. 25.6.36, London; m., Jean Blyth; 3 s.; 1 d. Educ. Newcastle Royal Grammar School; St. Andrews University; Edinburgh University. National Service, 1955-57; Assistant Minister, Newbattle Parish Church, 1963-65. President, Thurso Bible Society. Recreation: walking. Address: 46 Rose Street, Thurso, Caithness, KW14 7HN; T.-Thurso 62456.

Richards, Professor Bryan Edward, BSc, DIC, PhD, CEng, FRAeS, AFAIAA. Mechan Professor of Engineering and Head, Department of Aeronautics and Fluid Mechanics, Glasgow University, since 1980 (Dean of Engineering, since 1984); b. 30.6.38, Hornchurch, Essex; m., Margaret Dorothy Owen; 2 s.; 2 d. Educ. Palmer's School, Grays, Essex; Queen Mary College, London University. Aerodynamicist, Aircraft, Bristol Aeroplane Company, 1960-62; Research Assistant, Hypersonic Aerodynamics, Department of Aeronautics, Imperial College, 1962-66; Assistant Professor, Associate Professor, then Professor, Von Karman Institute for Fluid Dynamics, Rhode-St-Genese, Belgium, 1966-79. Recreations: sailing; walking. Address: (b.) Department of Aeronautics and Fluid Mechanics, James Watt Building, Glasgow University, Glasgow, G12 8QQ; T.-041-339 8855, Ext. 304.

Richards, Glyn, BA, BD, MA, BLitt. Senior Lecturer in Religious Studies, Stirling University, since 1976 (Head, Department of Religious Studies, since 1977); b. 6.8.23, Rhymney; m., Helga; 2 s.; 2 d. Educ. Rhymney Grammar School; University of Wales; McMaster University; Oxford University. Minister of Religion; Extra Mural Lecturer, University of Wales; Tutor, McMaster University, Canada; Lecturer, Carleton University, Ottawa; Lecturer, Stirling University; Visiting Lecturer, International Christian University, Tokyo; Founder and Editor, Scottish Journal of Religious Studies. Publications: The Development of Theological Liberalism, 1957; The Philosophy of Gandhi, 1981; A Sourcebook in Modern Hinduism, 1984. Recreations: travel; golf; reading. Address: (b.) Department of Religious Studies, Stirling University, Stirling; T.-Stirling 73171.

Richards, John Deacon, CBE, AADip, DUniv, ARSA, RIBA, PPRIAS. Partner, Robert Matthew, Johnson-Marshall and Partners, since

1964 (Chairman, since 1983); Chairman, Scottish Committee, Housing Corporation, and Board Member, Housing Corporation, since 1982; b. 7.5.31, Shanghai; m., Margaret Brown; 1 s.; 3 d. Educ. Cranleigh School, Surrey; Architectural Association School of Architecture, London. Works include Stirling University, Royal Commonwealth Pool (Edinburgh), Airport Terminals, Edinburgh and Aberdeen; Member, Royal Fine Art Commission for Scotland, since 1975; Agrement Board, 1980-83; Member, Williams Committee on National Museums and Galleries, 1981; Gold Medallist, RSA, 1972; Past President, Royal Incorporation of Architects in Scotland, 1983-85; Governor, Edinburgh College of Art, since 1982. Recreation: country life. Address: (h.) Lady's Field, Whitekirk, East Lothian; T.-Whitekirk 206.

Richards, Kenneth, BSc (Eng), CEng, FICE, FIWES, FBIM. Director of Water and Drainage, Lothian Regional Council, since 1979; b. 13.5.25, London; m., Patricia; 1 s.; 1 d. Educ. Alleynes School; London University. Various local government posts, 1946-60; Deputy Borough Engineer, Chesterfield, 1960-65; Borough Engineer, High Wycombe, 1965-73; Technical Services Officer, Wycombe District Council, 1973-79. Recreations: hill-walking; music; travel. Address: (b.) 6 Cockburn Street, Edinburgh; T.-031-229 9292.

Richardson, Geoffrey Alan, MA, PhD, CertEd, DipEd (Man). Principal, The Queen's College, Glasgow, since 1976; b. 27.7.36, Preston; m., Jill S.; 2 d. Educ. Hutton Grammar School, Lancashire; Fitzwilliam College, Cambridge; Glasgow University; Exeter University; Sheffield Polytechnic. School teaching, UK/Australia, 1959-66; Lecturer/Senior Lecturer/Warden, Edge Hill College, Lancashire, 1966-72; The Senior Tutor, Ilkley College, Yorkshire, 1972-76. Recreations: music; fishing; walking. Address: (b.) The Queen's College, Glasgow, 1 Park Drive, Glasgow, G3 6LP; T.-041-334 8141.

Richardson, Professor Jeremy John, BA (Hons), MA (Econ), PhD. Professor of Politics, Strathclyde University, since 1982; b. 15.4.42, Bridgnorth; m., Anne; 1 s.; 1 d. Educ. Wenlock Edge School; Keele University; Manchester University. Assistant Lecturer, Lecturer, Senior Lecturer and Reader in Politics, Keele University, 1966-82; Member, Civil Service College Advisory Council and Final Selection Board, Civil Service Commission. Publications: Campaigning for the Environment; The Policy-Making Process; Governing Under Pressure; Pressure Groups in Britain; Policy Styles in Western Europe; Unemployment: Policy Responses of Western Democracies. Recreations: hill-walking; tennis; gardening. Address: (h.) 1 Duchess Park, Helensburgh, Dunbartonshire; T.-Helensburgh 5321.

Richardson, Michael John, BSc, MSc. Assistant Director and Head, Potato and Plant Health Division, Agricultural Scientific Services, Department of Agriculture and Fisheries for Scotland, since 1979; b. 10.7.38, St. Albans; m., Barbara Anne Cooper; 2 s. Educ. St. Albans County Grammar School; Nottingham University. School teacher, Ripley, Derbyshire, 1959-60; Research Associate, Trent Polytechnic, Nottingham, 1961-64; Plant Pathologist, DAFS, since 1964. Editor, Transactions of the British Mycological Society. Recreations: gliding; gardening; mycology. Address: (b.) DAFS, Agricultural Scientific Services, East Craigs, Edinburgh, EH12 8NJ; T.-031-339 2355.

Richman, John Christopher Hugh, MSc, BSc, CEng, FRIAgrE, FBIM. Chief Executive, Sea Fish Industry Authority, since 1983; b. 18.4.29, Goole; m., Joan Potts; 2 s. Educ. Hymer's College, Hull; Friends School, Lancaster; Leeds University; Newcastle University. Managing Director, Ransomes (South Africa) Pty; Director, Ransomes, Sims & Jeffries Ltd.; Group Managing Director, The Gascoigne Group. President, Agricultural Engineers' Association. Recreations: sailing; fishing. Address: (h.) 2A Ainslie Place, Edinburgh, EH3 6AR; T.-031-225 8765.

Richmond, H. Anthony, MA (Oxon), PhL, STL. Headmaster, St. Aloysius' College, Glasgow, since 1977; Member, Society of Jesus (Jesuit), since 1949; Catholic Priest, since 1965; b. 7.6.31, Preston. Educ. Preston Catholic College; Heythrop College; Oxford University. First vows, 1951; Teacher: Beaumont College, Old Windsor, 1960-62 and 1966-67, Stonyhurst College, 1968-77 (Depute Headmaster, 1975-77). Recreations: travel; languages; ornithology; jogging; reading (novels, history, politics, theology); music. Address: (b.) 45 Hill Street, Glasgow, G3 6RJ; T.-041-332 3190.

Rickets, Brigadier Reginald Anthony Scott. Managing Director, Irvine Development Corporation, since 1981; Vice President, Ayrshire Chamber of Industries, since 1984; b. 13.12.29, Weybridge; m., Elizabeth Ann Serjeant; 1 s.; 1 d. Educ. St. George's College, Weybridge; Royal Military Academy, Sandhurst. 2nd Lt., RE, 1949; served with Airborne, armoured and field engineers, UK, Cyrenaica, Egypt, Malaya, Borneo, Hong Kong and BAOR; special employment military forces, Malaya, 1955-59; Staff College, Camberley, 1962; BM Engr. Gp., BAOR, 1963-66; OC 67 Gurkha Independent Field Squadron, 1966-68; DS Staff College, 1968-70; Commander, Gurkha Engineers/CRE Hong Kong, 1970-73; COS British Sector, Berlin, 1973-77; Col. GS RSME, 1977-78; Chief Engr., UKLF, 1978-81. Recreation: sailing (DTI Ocean Skipper and RYA Coach/Examiner). Address: (b.) Irvine Development Corporation, Perceton House, Irvine, KA11 2AL; T.-0294 214100.

Rickman, Professor Geoffrey Edwin, MA, DPhil (Oxon), FSA. Professor of Roman History, St. Andrews University, since 1981; b. 9.10.32, Cherat, India; m., Ann Rosemary Wilson; 1 s.; 1 d. Educ. Peter Symonds' School, Winchester; Brasenose College, Oxford. Junior Research Fellow, Queen's College, Oxford; St. Andrews University: Lecturer in Ancient History, Senior Lecturer, Professor; Visiting Fellow, Brasenose College, Oxford. Council Member, Society for Promotion of Roman Studies; Member, Faculty of Archaeology, History and Letters, British School at Rome (Chairman, since 1984). Publications: Roman Granaries and Storebuildings,

1971; The Corn Supply of Ancient Rome, 1985. Recreations: opera; swimming. Address: (h.) 56 Hepburn Gardens, St. Andrews, Fife; T.-St. Andrews 72063.

Riddell, Frank Gordon, BSc, PhD. Reader in Chemistry, Stirling University, since 1967; Member, Stirling District Council, since 1984; b. 19.4.40, Liverpool; m., Joan Bayley; 2 s.; 2 d. Educ. Merchant Taylors School, Crosby; Liverpool University. Stirling University: Lecturer in Chemistry, 1967, Senior Lecturer, 1979. Recreations: angling; fencing. Address: (h.) 1 Glebe Crescent, Stirling, FK8 2JB; T.-0786 72288.

Riddle, Robert William, OBE. Joint General Secretary, Royal British Legion Scotland/Earl Haig Fund (Scotland), since 1983; b. 19.1.33, Galashiels; m., Ann Mary Munro Millar; 3 d. Educ. Stonyhurst. 2nd Lt., King's Own Scottish Borderers, 1953; Staff College, 1963; Brigade Major, 157 (L) Brigade TA, Glasgow, 1964; Commanding Officer, 1st Bn., King's Own Scottish Borderers, 1971; Military Secretary, CINC BAOR, 1974; Colonel AQ 3rd Armoured Division, 1977; Brigadier Scottish Division, 1980; retired, 1983. Colonel, King's Own Scottish Borderers; Member, Queen's Bodyguard for Scotland (Royal Company of Archers). Recreations: field sports; golf; tennis. Address: (h.) Old Harestanes, Blyth Bridge, West Linton, Peeblesshire, EH46 7AH; T.-07215 2255.

Ridley-Thomas, Roger, FBIM, FInstD, MISM. Managing Director, The Scotsman Publications Ltd., since 1984; b. 14.7.39, Norwich; m., Sandra Grace Macbeth; 2 s.; 2 d. Educ. Greshams; Cardiff Business School. Display Advertisement Manager, Western Mail and Echo Ltd., 1968-70; General Display Manager, Newcastle Chronicle & Journal, 1970-72; The Scotsman Publications Ltd.: Executive Assistant, 1972-74, Assistant Managing Director, 1974-80; Managing Director, Aberdeen Journals Ltd., 1980-84. Past President, Scottish Daily Newspaper Society; Member, CBI Council. Recreations: hill-walking; shooting; golf; tennis; swimming; large houses; travel. Address: (b.) 20 North Bridge, Edinburgh, EH1 1YT; T.-031-225 2468.

Riemersma, Rudolph Arend, BSc, MSc, PhD. Assistant Director, Cardiovascular Research Unit, Edinburgh University, since 1975 (British Heart Foundation Senior Lecturer in Cardiac Biochemistry, since 1979); b. 9.5.43, Hengelo, Netherlands; m., Eva J. Nieuwenhuis; 1 s.; 1 d. Educ. Charlois Lyceum, Rotterdam; Leyden University; Edinburgh University. Biochemist, Department of Cardiology, Academic Hospital, Utrecht; postgraduate research, Royal Medical School, Hammersmith Hospital, London; Research Fellow, Edinburgh University, 1973. Board Member, European Society of Clinical Investigation. Recreations: athletics; skiing; hill-walking; botany. Address: (b.) Cardiovascular Research Unit, Hugh Robson Building, George Square, Edinburgh; T.-031-667 1011.

Rifkind, Malcolm Leslie, MP, QC, LLB, MSc. MP (Conservative), Edinburgh Pentlands, since 1974; Minister of State, Foreign and Commonwealth Office, since 1983; b. 21.6.46, Edinburgh; m., Edith Amalia Steinberg; 1 s.; 1 d. Educ. George Watson's College, Edinburgh; Edinburgh University. Lecturer, University of Rhodesia, 1967-68; called to Scottish Bar, 1970; Opposition Front-Bench Spokesman on Scottish Affairs, 1975-76; Member, Select Committee on European Secondary Legislation, 1975-76; Chairman, Scottish Conservatives' Devolution Committee, 1976; Joint Secretary, Conservative Parliamentary Foreign and Commonwealth Affairs Committee, 1977-79; Member, Select Committee on Overseas Development, 1978-79; Parliamentary Under-Secretary of State, Scottish Office, 1979-82; Parliamentary Under-Secretary of State, Foreign and Commonwealth Office, 1982-83. Address: (b.) House of Commons, London, SW1.

Rigby, Philip, MB, ChB, DPhysMed, DTM&H. Consultant in Rehabilitation Medicine, Highland Health Board, since 1975; Clinical Senior Lecturer (Medicine), Aberdeen University, since 1978; b. 31.12.23, Birmingham; m., Dina Elizabeth; 1 s.; 2 d. Educ. Handsworth Grammar School, Birmingham; Birmingham University; School of Tropical Medicine, Liverpool University. Junior hospital appointments, Infectious Diseases Hospital, Birmingham, Liverpool Chest Hospital, CEFN Mably Hospital, near Cardiff; Medical Missionary Service, Morocco, 1949-63; Medical Officer, Clerkenwell and Islington Medical Mission, London, 1963-68; Assistant Physician in Physical Medicine and Rheumatology, King Edward Memorial Hospital, Ealing and Chase Farm Hospital, Enfield, 1969-75. Honorary Secretary, Scottish Society of Rehabilitation Medicine, 1981-84; Chairman, Inverness Panel, REMAP. Address: (h.) 26 Drumfield Road, Inverness, IV2 4XQ; T.-0463 221601.

Rioch, Charles Turner, MA. Member, Orkney Islands Council, since 1983; b. 9.4.15, Keith; m., Helen Frances Wilson; 1 s.; 2 d. Educ. Mackie Academy, Stonehaven; Aberdeen University. Major, 116 Regiment (Gordon Highlanders), RAC; served at home, India and Burma, 1939-47; Personnel Manager, 1948-50; retail fish, fruit and game manager, 1950-60; Member, Callendar Town Council, 1956-59; Teacher, Stranraer High School, 1960-69; Head Teacher, North Walls School, Orkney, 1969-80. Chairman, Orkney Branch, Burma Star Association, since 1980. Recreations: mountaineering; travel in Middle and Far East. Address: (h.) 34 St. Colm's Quadrant, Longhope, Stromness, Orkney, KW16 3PH; T.-Longhope 327.

Ripley, Professor Brian David, MA, PhD, FSS. Professor of Statistics, Strathclyde University, since 1983; b. 29.4.52, Farnborough, Hampshire; m., Ruth Mary Appleton. Educ. Farnborough Grammar School; Churchill College, Cambridge. Lecturer, then Reader in Statistics, Imperial College, London University, 1976-83. Member, International Statistical Institute; Member, International Council for Bird Preservation. Publication: Spatial Statistics. Recreations: natural history; walking; photography. Address: (b.) Department of Mathematics, Strathclyde University, 26 Richmond Street, Glasgow, G1 1XH; T.-041-552 4400.

Risk, Sheriff Douglas James. Sheriff of Grampian, Highland and Islands, at Aberdeen, since 1979; b. 23.1.41; m.; 3 s.; 1 d. Educ. Glasgow Academy; Gonville and Caius College, Cambridge; Glasgow University. Admitted Advocate, 1966; Sheriff of Lothian and Borders, at Edinburgh, 1977-79.

Risk, Sir Thomas Neilson, BL, LLD Glasgow (1985). Governor, Bank of Scotland, since 1981; Director, Standard Life Assurance Company, since 1965; Director, Shell UK Ltd., since 1982; b. 13.9.22, Glasgow; m., Suzanne Eiloart; 4 s. Educ. Kelvinside Academy, Glasgow; Glasgow University. Flight Lt., RAF, 1941-46; RAFVR, 1946-53; Partner, Maclay, Murray & Spens, Solicitors, 1950-81; Director, MSA (Britain) Ltd., since 1958; Chairman, Standard Life Assurance Company, 1969-77; Director, Howden Group, since 1971; Director, Merchants Trust, since 1973; Director, British Linen Bank Limited (Governor, since 1977); Director, Barclays Bank, 1983-85; Member, Scottish Industrial Development Board, 1972-75; Member, Scottish Economic Planning Council, since 1983. Trustee, Hamilton Bequest. Recreation: golf. Address: (h.) 10 Belford Place, Edinburgh, EH4 3DH; T.-031-332 9425.

Ritchie, Alastair Newton Bethune. Partner, Sheppards and Chase, Stock and Money Brokers, since 1960; Member, Stirling District Council, since 1977; b. 30.4.21, London; m., Isobel Sinclair; 1 s.; 1 d. Educ. Harrow School; Corpus Christi College, Cambridge. Scots Guards, 1940-58; campaign North-West Europe, 1944-45; wounded; mentioned in Despatches; active service, Malaya and Far East, 1947-49; Canadian Army Staff College, 1951; Assistant Military Attache, Canada, 1952-53; active service, Canal Zone, Egypt, 1954; retired as Major, 1958; Argyll and Sutherland Highlanders TA, 1966-68; Partner, Drunkie Farms, Callander, 1967-81. Member, Queen's Bodyguard for Scotland (Royal Company of Archers), since 1966; Deputy Lieutenant, Central Region (Stirling and Falkirk), since 1979. Recreations: gardening; fishing; travel; philately; music; photography. Address: (h.) Avonbeith, Callander, Perthshire, FK17 8BN; T.-0877 30078.

Ritchie, Anthony Elliot, CBE, MA, DSc, MD, FCSP, FRSE, LLD. Secretary and Treasurer, Carnegie Trust for the Universities of Scotland, 1969-86; b. 30.3.15, Edinburgh; m., Elizabeth Lambie Knox; 1 s.; 3 d. Educ. Edinburgh Academy; Aberdeen University; Edinburgh University. Carnegie Scholar, Lecturer and Senior Lecturer in Physiology, Edinburgh University, 1941-48; Professor of Physiology, St. Andrews University, 1948-69; Honorary Consultant, Eastern Regional Hospital Board, 1950-69; Chairman, Scottish Committee on Science Education, 1970-78; Chairman, Scottish University Entrance Board, 1963-69; Member, British Library Board, 1973-80; Member, Houghton Committee on Teachers' Pay; Trustee, National Library of Scotland. Royal Society of Edinburgh: Fellow, 1951, General Secretary, 1966-76; Bicentenary Gold Medal, 1983; Hon. DSc (St. Andrews); Hon. LLD (Strathclyde). Recreations: reading; hill-walking; mechanics; electronics. Address: (h.) 12 Ravelston Park, Edinburgh, EH4 3DX; T.-031-332 6560.

Ritchie, Effie Barclay, JP. Member, Dunfermline District Council (Convener, Housing Committee), since 1980; b. 1.5.27, Kinross; m., Tom Ritchie (deceased); 1 s.; 2 d. Educ. Ballingry Junior High School. Member, West Fife Educational Trust; Member, Carnegie Dunfermline and Hero Fund Trust; Member, SLASH; President, Wellwood Old Folks Association; Vice President, Dunduff Branch, WRI; Chairman, Dunfermline Branch, Arthritis Care. Recreations: classical music; reading; history. Address: (h.) Schoolhouse, Main Road, Wellwood, Dunfermline; T.-0383 723520.

Ritchie, George Fraser, MA, LLB. Solicitor; b. 26.5.42, Dundee; m., Sheila Stewart Anderson; 1 s.; 1 d. Educ. Dundee High School; St. Andrews University; Edinburgh University. Solicitor, private practice, since 1968; Partner, Hendry & Fenton, Solicitors, Dundee, since 1972; Council Member, Law Society of Scotland, since 1979; Convener, Legal Aid, 1982-83; Convener, Professional Remuneration, since 1983. Secretary, High School of Dundee Trust. Recreations: golf; hill-walking; music (non-participant). Address (b.) 21 South Tay Street, Dundee; T.-Dundee 22785.

Ritchie, Ian Charles Stewart, MA (Cantab). General Manager, Scottish Chamber Orchestra, since 1984; b. 19.6.53, London; m., Angela Mary Reid; 2 d. Educ. Stowe School; Royal College of Music; Trinity College, Cambridge; Guildhall School of Music and Drama. Promotion Manager, Universal Edition (Music Publishers), 1976-79; General Manager, City of London Sinfonia, 1979-84; Artistic Director, City of London Festival, 1983-84; Member, Advisory Panel on Music, Arts Council of GB, since 1983; Council Member, National Youth Orchestra of Scotland; Trustee, Scottish Musicians' Benevolent Fund; Council Member, Grosvenor Chamber Group; Director, Association of British Orchestras; Trustee, Edinburgh International Lunchtime Concert Trust. Recreations: watching cricket (MCC member); playing various sports (including golf); crosswords. Address: (h.) 15 Rothesay Place, Edinburgh, EH3 7SQ; T.-031-667 0121.

Ritchie, Rev. Malcolm Alexander. Minister, Kilbrandon and Kilchattan, since 1982; b. 8.6.20, Beckenham, Kent; m., Heather Peebles Brown; 2 s.; 1 d. Educ. Dulwich College; King's College, Wimbledon; Edinburgh University and New College. Commissioned, Royal Regiment of Artillery, 1941; honorary rank of Captain, 1946; licensed to preach, 1950; Children's Evangelist and Staff Worker, Scripture Union, 1950; Minister: Broughty Ferry - St. James's, 1955-69, Strathblane, 1969-82; Chairman, Waldensian Missions Aid Society in Scotland, 1979; preached, centenary service of Scripture Union, Assembly Hall, Edinburgh, 1957. Recreation: boats; music. Address: The Manse, Easdale, Oban, Argyll; T.-Balvicar 240.

Ritchie, Martha Kilpatrick. Member, Forth Valley Health Board; Teacher; b. 21.1.40, Edinburgh. Educ. Bathgate Academy; Bo'ness Academy; Moray House College of Education.

Twenty years' teaching service in Scotland; one year teaching in Canada; three years with British Families Education Service, West Germany. Member, local Schools Council. Address: (h.) Grange Knowe, 58 Grange Terrace, Bo'ness, West Lothian.

Ritchie, Murray. Journalist; Assistant Editor, Glasgow Herald, since 1981; b. 5.9.41, Dumfries; m., Andree Margaret Bryce; 1 s.; 2 d. Educ. High School of Glasgow. Scottish Farmer, 1958-60; Dumfries and Galloway Standard, 1960-65; Scottish Daily Record, 1965-67; East African Standard, 1967-71; joined Glasgow Herald, 1971. Journalist of the Year, Fraser Press Awards, 1980. Recreations: golf; folk music. Address: (h.) 64 Falloch Road, Milngavie, Glasgow; t.-041-956 1129.

Ritchie, William Rennie, BSc (Hons), DipEd. HM Depute Senior Chief Inspector of Schools, since 1984; b. 14.7.28, Kirkcaldy; m., Jan Murrie; 1 s.; 1 d. Educ. Kirkcaldy High School; Edinburgh University. RAF, 1946-48; Physics Teacher, Kirkcaldy High School, 1953-62; Nuffield Foundation, 1962-63; HM Inspector (Science), 1963-73; HM Chief Inspector (Eastern Division, then 16-18 Development), 1973-84. Nuffield Foundation Scholarship, 1962-63; Commonwealth Fellowship (Australia), 1971. Recreations: music; golf. Address: (b.) Scottish Education Department, Room 4/101 New St. Andrews House, Edinburgh; T.-031-556 8400.

Ritson, Bruce, MD, FRCPsych, DipPsych. Consultant Psychiatrist, Royal Edinburgh Hospital, since 1972; Senior Lecturer in Psychiatry, Edinburgh University, since 1972; Consultant, Gogarburn Hospital, Edinburgh, since 1972; b. 20.3.37, Elgin; m., Eileen Carey; 1 s.; 1 d. Educ. Edinburgh Academy; Edinburgh University; Harvard University. Trained in medicine, Edinburgh; postgraduate training in psychiatry, Edinburgh, Harvard and California; Director, Sheffield Region Addiction Unit, 1968-71; at present Consultant with special responsibility for alcohol-related problems; Consultant to World Health Organisation on several occasions. Chairman, Howard League in Scotland; Executive Member, Medical Council on Alcoholism; Council Member, Action Against Alcohol Abuse. Recreations: friends; squash; theatre. Address: (b.) Andrew Duncan Clinic, Royal Edinburgh Hospital, Morningside Park, Edinburgh; T.-031-447 2011.

Roach, Professor Gary Francis, BSc, MSc, PhD. Professor of Mathematics, Strathclyde University, since 1979 (Dean, Faculty of Science, since 1982); b. 8.10.33, Penpedairheol, South Wales; m., Isabella Grace Willins Nicol. Educ. University College, South Wales and Monmouthshire; London University; Manchester University. RAF (Education Branch), Flying Officer, 1955-58; Research Mathematician, British Petroleum Co. Ltd., 1958-61; Lecturer, Manchester University Institute of Science and Technology, 1961-66; Visiting Professor, University of British Columbia, 1966-67; Strathclyde University: Lecturer, 1967-70, Senior Lecturer, 1970-71, Reader, 1971-79. Fellow, Royal Astronomical Society;

Fellow, Institute of Mathematics and its Applications; Fellow, Royal Society of Edinburgh; Past President, Edinburgh Mathematical Society. Recreations: mountaineering; photography; philately; gardening; music. Address: (b.) Department of Mathematics, Strathclyde University, Livingstone Tower, 26 Richmond Street, Glasgow, G1 1XH; T.-041-552 4400, Ext. 3800.

Robb, Alan, DA, MA, RCA. Head, School of Fine Art, Duncan of Jordanstone College of Art, Dundee, since 1978; b. 24.2.46, Glasgow; m., Cynthia J. Neilson; 1 s.; 1 d. Educ. Robert Gordon's College, Aberdeen; Grays School of Art; Royal College of Art. Assistant Art Master, Oundle School, 1972-75; Crawford School of Art: Lecturer in Painting, 1975-78, Head of Painting, 1978-80, Head of Fine Art, 1980-83; Chief External Examiner in Art, NCEA Ireland, 1981-83; one-man exhibitions: New 57 Gallery, 1972, Yarrow Gallery, Oundle, 1973, Cork Arts Society, 1976; touring two-man exhibition, 1978-79; several group exhibitions. Publication: Irish Contemporary Art.

Robb, Colin Denholm, BSc (Econ) (Hons). Member, East Kilbride District Council, since 1979; Board Member, East Kilbride Development Corporation, since 1983; Lecturer in Economics, Bell College, Hamilton, since 1978; b. 14.10.46, Rutherglen; m., Mariet; b. 1 s.; 1 d. Educ. Rutherglen Academy; Glasgow College of Technology; Strathclyde University (postgraduate degree course). Leader, Labour Group, and Chairman, Policy and Resources Committee, East Kilbride District Council, 1980-83. Recreations: reading; hill-walking; photography. Address: (h.) 22 Loch Torridon, East Kilbride, G74 2ET; T.-East Kilbride 24337.

Robb, Graham, DRSAM. Freelance Musician and Composer; Lecturer in Music; Musical Director and Arranger; b. 7.8.50, Aberdeen; m., Erica Gunn; 2 s. Educ. Aberdeen Grammar School; Royal Scottish Academy of Music. Double bass player, BBC Scottish Symphony Orchestra, 1971-76; freelance double bass and bass guitar player, since 1976; founder Member, "Head" (jazz rock band), 1969-78; formed various jazz-rock bands; music for BBC TV and radio, theatre and schools; commissioned by Platform Jazz Society, 1975, to write 50-minute song cycle. Recreations: music; preparation and consumption of food and drink. Address: (h.) Tigh-Na-Beithe, Birnam, Perthshire; T.-Dunkeld 371.

Robb, James Turnbull, JP. Member, Tayside Health Board, since 1979; National Vice-President, Society of St. Vincent de Paul, since 1975; Member, Industrial Tribunal Panel, since 1978; b. 30.9.25, Dundee; m., Winifred Giblin; 3 s.; 4 d. Educ. St. John's Junior Secondary School. Recreations: gardening; voluntary work. Address: (h.) 24 Forebank Road, Dundee; T.-0382 25609.

Robb, Rev. William Clement, LTh. Minister, Tarbert, Argyll; b. 18.9.40, Elderslie. Educ. Dumfries Academy; Glasgow University. Minister, Delting, Shetland; Chaplain, British Sailors

Society, Aberdeen; Senior Chaplain, Scotland, British Sailors Society; Minister, St. Christopher's, Pollok. Chairman, Scottish Branch, Paddle Steamer Preservation Society. Address: The Manse, Tarbert, Argyll; T.-Tarbert 288.

Robbins, Professor Keith Gilbert, MA, DPhil, DLitt. Professor of Modern History, Glasgow University, since 1980; b. 9.4.40, Bristol; m., Janet Carey; 3 s.; 1 d. Educ. Bristol Grammar School; Magdalen and St. Antony's Colleges, Oxford. Lecturer in History, York University, 1963-71; Professor of History, University College of North Wales, 1971-79; Raleigh Lecturer, British Academy, 1984; Editor, History, since 1977; Vice-President, Royal Historical Society. Publications: Munich 1938, 1968; Sir Edward Grey, 1971; The Abolition of War, 1976; John Bright, 1979; The Eclipse of a Great Power: Modern Britain, 1983; The First World War, 1984. Recreations: music; walking; gardening. Address: (b.) Department of Modern History, Glasgow University, Glasgow; T.-041-339 8855, Ext. 522.

Roberton, William Russell, JP. Member, Angus District Council, since 1980 (Housing Convener, since 1984); b. 19.4.44, Glasgow; m., Genevieve Heather; 2 d. Educ. Arbroath High School. Telecommunications Superintendent, British Telecom. Recreation: golf. Address: (h.) 11 Inchgarth Avenue, Forfar, Angus; T.-0307 64040.

Roberts, Edward Frederick Denis, MA, PhD, FRSE, FLA. Librarian, National Library of Scotland, since 1970; b. 16.6.27, Belfast; m., Irene Richardson; 1 s.; 1 d. Educ. Royal Belfast Academical Institution; Queen's University, Belfast. Research Assistant, Department of History, Queen's University, Belfast, 1951-55; National Library of Scotland: Assistant Keeper, Department of Manuscripts, 1955-66, Secretary of the Library, 1966-67; Librarian, Trinity College, Dublin, 1967-70; Honorary Professor, Edinburgh University, 1975. Address: (h.) 6 Oswald Court, Edinburgh, EH9 2HY; T.-031-667 9473.

Roberts, Dame Jean, DBE (1962), JP, DL. Lord Provost of Glasgow and Lord Lieutenant of the County of the City of Glasgow, 1960-63; Chairman, Cumbernauld Development Corporation, 1965-72; Chairman, Scottish National Orchestra Society, 1970-75.

Roberts, Rev. Maurice Jonathon, BA, BD, DipEd. Minister, Ayr Free Church of Scotland, since 1974; b. 8.3.38, Timperley, Cheshire; m., Alexandra Macleod; 1 d. Educ. Lymm Grammar School; Durham University; London University; Free Church College. Schoolteacher, 14 years; Minister, 11 years; former Editor, Free Church youth magazine; former Convener, Public Questions Committee, Free Church. Recreation: reading. Address: (b.) Free Church Manse, 8 Inverkar Road, Ayr, KA7 2JT; T.-0292 266043.

Roberts, M. Maureen, BSc, MB, BCh, MD. Director, Edinburgh Breast Screening Clinic, since 1979; Senior Lecturer, Edinburgh University,

since 1977; b. 15.3.36, Newport, Gwent; m., Robert Ellis; 1 s.; 1 d. Educ. Newport High School for Girls; Welsh National School of Medicine, Cardiff. House Officer appointments, Cardiff and Newport Hospitals; Lecturer, Surgical Unit, Cardiff Royal Infirmary, 1967-71; Lecturer, Department of Clinical Surgery, Edinburgh University, 1971-77 (Senior Lecturer, from 1977). Secretary, British Breast Group. Recreations: countryside (especially Scotland); yoga; reading; theatre. Address: (b.) Department of Clinical Surgery, Royal Infirmary, Edinburgh, EH3; T.-031-346 1824.

Roberts, Ronald John, BVMS, MRCVS, FRCPath, FIBiol, FRSE. Director, Institute of Aquaculture, Stirling University, since 1971; b. 28.3.41; m., Helen Macgregor; 2 s. Educ. Campbeltown Grammar School; Glasgow University. Lecturer, Glasgow University, 1964-71; Consultant: Department of Agriculture and Fisheries for Scotland, 1967-70, Overseas Development Administration, since 1974, United Nations, since 1976; Council Member, Royal Society of Edinburgh; Buckland Professor of Fisheries, Buckland Foundation, 1985; Editor, Journal of Fish Diseases. Recreations: golf at Machrihanish Golf Club; squash. Address: (b.) Institute of Aquaculture, Stirling University, Stirling; T.-Stirling 73171.

Roberts, Stewart Muir, OBE, DL, JP, FEIS, BA, MA. Honorary Sheriff, Ettrick and Lauderdale; Governor, Merchiston Castle School, since 1962; b. 4.2.08, Selkirk; m., Marguerite Hugh Considine; 1 s.; 2 d. Educ. Merchiston Castle School; Clare College, Cambridge; Scottish Woollens' Technical College, Galashiels. Director, George Roberts & Co. Ltd., 1936-62 (Managing Director, 1956-62); Director, Roberts, Thorburn and Noble, 1962-73; Army Service, 1943-46; Standard Bearer, Royal Burgh of Selkirk, 1934; Member, Selkirk Town Council, 1935-75 (Provost, 1955-61); Member, Selkirk County Council, 1937-75 (Chairman, County Education Committee, 1948-75); Member and Chairman, Education Committee, Borders Regional Council, 1974-78; Vice-Convenor, Borders Regional Council, 1974-78; Member, Scottish Council on Alcoholism, 1975-85; Member, Dunning Committee, 1976-79. Recreations: golf; fishing; curling; bee-keeping. Address: (h.) Tweedknowe, Selkirk; T.-0750 20224.

Roberts, Sir William (James Denby), 3rd Bt; b. 10.8.36. Educ. Rugby; Royal Agricultural College, Cirencester. Founded Strathallan Aircraft Collection, 1969. Address: (h.) Strathallan Castle, Auchterarder, Perthshire.

Robertson, Alexander, MA, PhD. Senior Lecturer, Department of Social Policy, Edinburgh University, since 1981; Associate Dean (Postgraduate), Faculty of Social Science, since 1982; b. 13.8.39, Aberdeen; m., Elaine Walden; 2 s.; 1 d. Educ. Robert Gordon's College; Aberdeen University; Edinburgh University. Research Assistant, Leicester University, 1962-64; Research Officer, Essex University, 1965-66; Lecturer in Sociology, Ipswich Civic College, 1966-68; Scientific Officer, MRC Unit for Epidemiological Studies in Psychiatry, Edinburgh University,

1968-72; Lecturer, Edinburgh University, 1972-81; Visiting Professor, McMaster University, Ontario, 1977. Publications: Improving Social Intervention (Editor), 1983; Social Policy and the Quality of Life (Editor), 1985. Recreations: sport; playing violin; languages; music; reading. Address: (h.) 11 Merchiston Park, Edinburgh, EH10 4PW; T.-031-229 1182.

Robertson, Alistair John, BMedBiol (Hons), MB, ChB, MRCPath. Consultant in Administrative Charge, Perth and Kinross Unit Laboratories, since 1982; Consultant Histopathologist, Tayside Health Board, since 1982; Honorary Senior Lecturer in.Pathology, Dundee University, since 1982; b. 29.6.50, Aberdeen; m., Frances Elizabeth Smith. Educ. Aberdeen Grammar School; Aberdeen University. House Physician, Ninewells Hospital, Dundee, 1975; House Surgeon, Aberdeen Royal Infirmary, 1976; Senior House Officer in Pathology, Ninewells Hospital, 1976; Lecturer in Pathology, Ninewells Hospital, 1977. Recreations: golf; curling; caravanning; philately. Address: (b.) The Laboratory, Rose Crescent, Perth Royal Infirmary, Perth; T.-Perth 23311.

Robertson, Allan. Member, Inverclyde District Council, since 1980; Consumer Relations Officer, South of Scotland Electricity Board (Greenock); b. 29.5.54, Port Glasgow. Educ. Port Glasgow High School. Secretary, Port Glasgow Community Council, 1976-80. Address: (h.) 19 Brightside Avenue, Port Glasgow, Renfrewshire; T.-Port Glasgow 45982.

Robertson, Andrew Alexander, CIPFA, MBCS. Computing and Services Controller, North of Scotland Hydro-Electric Board, since 1983; b. 3.1.35, Cowdenbeath; m., Louise Wilson; 1 s.; 1 d. Educ. Dunfermline High School; Glasgow College of Commerce. Internal Auditor, then Systems and Programming Manager, SSEB; NSHEB: Computer Manager, Computing and Accounting Services Manager, Deputy Chief Financial Officer. Founder Chairman, NE Scotland Branch, British Computer Society. Recreations: golf; gardening; travel. Address: (b.) 16 Rothesay Terrace, Edinburgh, EH3 7SE; T.-031-225 1361.

Robertson, Brenda Margaret, JP. Member, Orkney Islands Council, since 1974; Member, Children's Panel Advisory Committee; Member, Highlands and Islands Fire Board; b. 8.9.24, Scarborough; m., John MacDonald Robertson, BL, NP; 1 s.; 1 d. Educ. Scarborough Girls' High School; University College, St. Andrews. Wartime service, WRNS (Naval Intelligence); District Commissioner for Guides, Stromness and West Mainland; Member, Stromness Town Council, 1961-74; County Councillor; Member, Executive Council, NHS; Governor, Aberdeen College of Education. Recreations: reading; arts generally. Address: (h.) Berridale, Stromness, Orkney.

Robertson, Rev. Charles, MA, JP. Minister, Canongate Kirk, since 1978; b. 22.10.40, Glasgow; m., Alison Margaret Malloch; 1 s.; 2 d. Educ. Camphill School, Paisley; Edinburgh University. Assistant Minister, North Morningside Church, Edinburgh, 1964-65; Minister, Kiltearn, Ross and Cromarty, 1965-78. Secretary, Panel on Worship, General Assembly; Vice-Chairman, Board, Queensberry House Hospital. Recreations: books; music. Address: Manse of Canongate, Edinburgh, EH8 8BR; T.-031-556 3515.

Robertson, Rev. Daniel McCallum, MA. Minister, Auchinleck, since 1967; b. 20.4.35, Bathgate; m., Anne Moffat Affleck; 2 s.; 2 d. Educ. Bathgate Academy; Edinburgh University and New College. Student Assistant, Broughton Place, Edinburgh, 1958-59; Probationer Assistant, St. Cuthbert's, Edinburgh, 1959-60; Minister: Camelon Trinity, Falkirk, 1960-67, Auchinleck Barony, 1967-80, linked charge of Auchinleck Barony/Peden, 1980-83, and united charge of Auchinleck, since 1983. Representative, Ayr Presbytery, on Cumnock and District Schools Council. Recreations: crosswords; music; gardening; DIY motor mechanics; walking the dog. Address: 28 Mauchline Road, Auchinleck, Ayrshire, KA18 2BN; T.-Cumnock 21108.

Robertson, Sheriff Daphne Jean Black, WS, MA, LLB. Sheriff of Glasgow and Strathkelvin, since 1979; b. 31.3.37; m., Donald Buchanan Robertson, QC. Educ. Hillhead High School; Greenock Academy; Edinburgh University; Glasgow University. Admitted Solicitor, 1961.

Robertson, David Greig, MA, MEd. Director of Education, Tayside Regional Council, since 1975; b. 29.12.24, Dundee; m., Margaret; 3 s. Educ. Morgan Academy, Dundee; St. Andrews University. Teacher, Dundee and Dollar, 1952-58; Assistant Director of Education: Berwickshire, 1958-61, Dundee, 1961-64; Director of Education: Selkirkshire, 1964-72, Dundee, 1972-75. Honorary President, Scottish Amateur Music Association; former Trustee, Central Bureau for Educational Visits and Exchanges; Member, Consultative Committee on the Curriculum. Recreations: reading; caravanning; music. Address: (b.) Tayside House, 28 Crichton Street, Dundee, DD1 3RJ; T.-0382 23281, Ext. 3654.

Robertson, David Hunter Henderson, MB, ChB, FRCPEdin, DTM&H. Consultant Physician, Genito-Urinary Medicine, since 1964; Head, Department of Genito-Urinary Medicine, Edinburgh University, since 1968; b. 6.11.24, Edinburgh; m., Vera Alison Cameron MacLachlan; 1 s.; 2 d. Educ. Fettes College, Edinburgh; Edinburgh University. Surgeon Lt., RNVR, 1949-51; Medical Officer, Sewa, Haji Hospital, Dar-es-Salaam, Tanganyika, 1952-55; Medical Research Officer, then Senior Medical Research Officer, East African Trypanosomiasis Research Organisation, Uganda, 1955-63; Registrar, Department of Venereology, Edinburgh Royal Infirmary, 1963-64; Consultant Venereologist: Sunderland Area and South Shields District, 1964-65, Edinburgh Royal Infirmary, 1965-68. Publication: Clinical Practice in Sexually Transmissible Diseases (Senior co-author), 1980. Recreation: numismatics. Address: (h.) 92 Lasswade Road, Edinburgh; T.-031-664 1884.

Robertson, David James Alan, MPS. Honorary Sheriff, Ross and Cromarty; Community Pharmacist, since 1966; b. 2.8.41, Tain; m., Ray F.

Waddell; 1 d.; 1 step d. Educ. Tain Royal Academy; Robert Gordon's Technical College. Address: (h.) Graham Villa, Tain, Ross-shire; T.-Tain 2003.

Robertson, Edmund Frederick, BSc, MSc, PhD. Senior Lecturer in Pure Mathematics, St. Andrews University, since 1984; b. 1.6.43, St. Andrews; m., Helena Francesca Slebarski; 2 s. Educ. Madras College, St. Andrews; St. Andrews University; Warwick University. Assistant Lecturer, then Lecturer in Pure Mathematics, St. Andrews University, 1968-84. Recreation: family. Address: (h.) 41 Irvine Crescent, St. Andrews, Fife, KY16 8LG; T.-St. Andrews 73459.

Robertson, Elizabeth Margaret, MB, ChB, FRCR, DMRD. Consultant Radiologist, Aberdeen Royal Infirmary, since 1982; b. 7.10.51, Aberdeen. Educ. St. Margaret's School for Girls, Aberdeen; Aberdeen University. Two years as Senior Registrar, Queen Mary's Hospital, Roehampton, and Westminster Hospital, London. Recreations: antiques; golf. Address: (h.) 7 Queen's Avenue, Aberdeen, AB1 6WA; T.-0224 316552.

Robertson, Elliot Ramsay, BSc, ARCST, CEng, MIMechE, FBIPP, FMPA, FRSA. Consulting Engineer and Photographer; b. 23.5.29, Rutherglen; m., Hazel M. Sweet; 1 s.; 1 d. Educ. Rutherglen Academy; Royal Technical College, Glasgow; Glasgow University. Lecturer, Royal College of Science and Technology, Glasgow, 1956-58; Senior Lecturer, Strathclyde University, 1968-85; former Director of Leader Training, Glasgow County Scout Council. Recreations: sailing; skiing; photography; painting. Address: Tigh Geal, North Connel, Oban, Argyll, PA37 1QZ; T.-Connel 352.

Robertson, Rev. Fergus Alexander, MA, BD. Minister, Dalneigh and Bona Church, Inverness; b. 25.4.45, Malvern; m., A. Valery Macrae; 2 d. Educ. George Heriot's School, Edinburgh; Edinburgh University; St. Andrews University. Assistant Minister, West Pilton, Edinburgh. Moderator, Inverness Presbytery, 1984-85. Recreations: swimming; skiing. Address: The Manse, 9 St. Mungo Road, Inverness; T.-0463 232339.

Robertson, Professor Forbes W., BSc, PhD, DSc, FIBiol, FRSE. Professor and Head, Department of Genetics, Aberdeen University, since 1970; b. 29.1.20, Vancouver, Canada; m., Katherine Louise; 2 s.; 1 d. Educ. Robert Gordon's College, Aberdeen; Aberdeen University. Member, ARC Unit of Animal Genetics, Institute of Animal Genetics, Edinburgh University, 1946-70. Recreations: gardening; hill-walking; photography. Address: (b.) Department of Genetics, Aberdeen University, Aberdeen; T.-0224 40241.

Robertson, George F., FRICS, FCIArb. Partner, Robertson and Dawson, Chartered Surveyors, Edinburgh, since 1970; Chairman, Scottish Building Contract Committee, since 1983; Vice President, Rent Assessment Panel for Scotland, since 1984; b. 14.7.32, Edinburgh; m., Anne McGonigle; 3 d. Educ. George Heriot's School,

Edinburgh; Heriot-Watt College, Edinburgh. Arbiter; Lecturer (part-time), School of Architecture, Edinburgh College of Art/Heriot-Watt University, 1964-84; Chairman, Joint Standing Committee of Architects, Surveyors and Building Contractors in Scotland, 1976-78; Chairman, Board of Governors, Leith Nautical College, 1976-78; Lay Member, Scottish Solicitors Discipline Tribunal, since 1976; Chairman, Scottish Branch, Royal Institution of Chartered Surveyors, 1984-85. Director, Queensberry House Hospital, Edinburgh. Recreations: working; gardening; hill-walking; Greece; researching Scottish market crosses. Address: (h.) Gladsheil, Campbell Court, Longniddry, East Lothian.

Robertson, George Islay Macneill, MP, MA. MP (Labour), Hamilton, since 1978; Deputy Opposition Spokesman on Foreign and Commonwealth Affairs, since 1981; b. 12.4.46, Port Ellen, Islay; m., Sandra Wallace; 2 s.; 1 d. Educ. Dunoon Grammar School; Dundee University; St. Andrews University. Tayside Study Economics Group, 1968-69; Scottish Organiser, General, Municipal, Boilermakers Union, 1969-78; Chairman, Scottish Labour Party, 1977-78; Member, Scottish Executive, Labour Party, 1973-79; PPS to Secretary of State for Social Services, 1979; Opposition Spokesman on Scottish Affairs, 1979-80, on Defence, 1980-81, on Foreign and Commonwealth Affairs, since 1981; Principal Spokesman on Europe, since 1985. Council Member, Royal Institute of International Affairs; Council Member, National Trust for Scotland; Board Member, Great Britain/East Europe Centre; Council Member, British Atlantic Committee. Recreations: family; photography. Address: (h.) 3 Argyle Park, Dunblane, Perthshire.

Robertson, George Slessor, MD, FFARCS. Consultant Anaesthetist, since 1969; Honorary Senior Lecturer in Anaesthesia, Aberdeen University; b. 30.12.33, Peterhead; m., Audrey E. McDonald; 1 s.; 2 d. Educ. Peterhead Academy; Aberdeen University. Early medical training, Aberdeen, London and Winnipeg. Recreations: golf; hill-walking; picture-framing. Address: (b.) Department of Anaesthesia, Royal Infirmary, Foresterhill, Aberdeen, AB9 2ZB; T.-0224 681818.

Robertson, Ian, DipMusEd, BMus (Hons). Head of Music and Chorus Director, Scottish Opera; b. 7.10.47, Dundee; m., Helen Russell; 1 d. Educ. Grove Academy, Dundee; Glasgow University; Royal Scottish Academy of Music and Drama. Career as solo pianist; frequent concert appearances, Wigmore Hall and Edinburgh Festival; has conducted numerous operas for Scottish Opera, including The Barber of Seville, The Pearl Fishers, Il Seraglio, The Magic Flute, The Mastersingers, L'Elisir d'Amore, Rigoletto, and Scottish Television's Susanna's Secret. Recreation: golf. Address: (h.) Sherbrooke House, 17 Sherbrook Avenue, Glasgow; T.-041-427 0017.

Robertson of Brackla, Maj.-Gen. Ian Argyll, CB (1968), MBE (1947), MA, DL. Vice Lord Lieutenant, Highland Region (Nairn), since 1980; b. 17.7.13; m.; 2 d. Educ. Winchester College; Trinbity College, Oxford. Commanding 51st

Highland Division, 1964-66; Director of Army Equipment Policy, Ministry of Defence, 1966-68. Chairman, Royal British Legion, Scotland, 1974-77.

Robertson, Ian Barr, MA, LLB. Solicitor; Advocate in Aberdeen; Member, Grampian Regional Council, since 1974 (Chairman, Transportation and Roads Committee, since 1978); Honorary Sheriff, Grampian, Highland and Islands, at Stonehaven; b. Aberdeen; m., Vi L. Johnston; 2 s.; 1 d. Educ. Mackie Academy; Fettes College; Aberdeen University. King's Regiment and KAR, 1939-46 (Captain); Partner, Cunningham & Robertson, Solicitors, Stonehaven, since 1951; Joint Town Clerk, then Town Clerk, Stonehaven, 1957-75; Council Member, Law Society of Scotland, 1972-75; President, Society of Town Clerks in Scotland, 1973-75; Member, Aberdeen Harbour Board, 1975; Member, Peterhead Bay Authority, 1978; Director, Imperial Cancer Research Fund, 1984; Past President, Stonehaven Rotary Club; Elder, Stonehaven South. Recreations: rough shooting; fishing; theatre; snooker. Address: (h.) 15 Bath Street, Stonehaven; T.-Stonehaven 62879.

Robertson, Ian Macbeth, CB, LVO. Chairman, Board of Governors, Edinburgh College of Art, since 1981; Director, Royal Lyceum Theatre Company, 1978-85; b. 1.2.18, Crookedholm, Ayrshire; m., Anne Stewart Marshall. Educ. Melville College; Edinburgh University. Served, Middle East and Italy, Royal Artillery and London Scottish, 1940-46; entered Scottish Office, 1946; Private Secretary to Minister of State, 1951-52, and to Secretary of State for Scotland, 1952-55; Under Secretary, Scottish Office, Scottish Development Department and Scottish Education Department, 1963-78; Secretary of Commissions for Scotland, 1978-83; JP, Edinburgh, 1978. Member, Williams Committee on National Museums and Galleries in Scotland, 1979-81; Chairman, Scottish United Services Museum Advisory Committee, 1970-85. Address: (h.) 8 Middleby Street, Edinburgh, EH9 1TD; T.-031-667 3999.

Robertson, Hon. Lord, (Ian Macdonald Robertson), TD (1946), QC (Scot), BA, LLB. Senator of the College of Justice in Scotland, since 1966; b. 30.10.12; m.; 1 s.; 2 d. Educ. Merchiston Castle; Balliol College, Oxford; Edinburgh University. Served Second World War, 8th Bn., The Royal Scots (The Royal Regiment) (mentioned in Despatches); Member, Faculty of Advocates, 1939; Advocate-Depute, 1949-51; QC (Scot), 1954; Sheriff of Ayr and Bute, 1961-66; Sheriff of Perth and Angus, 1966; Chairman, Medical Appeals Tribunal, 1957-63; Chairman, Scottish Joint Council for Teachers' Salaries, 1965-81; Chairman, Scottish Valuation Advisory Council, 1977.

Robertson, Ian Sherriff, BSc, PhD, CBiol, MBiol. University Fellow, Department of Animal Health, Edinburgh University, since 1983; b. 16.4.28, Mandalay, Burma; m., Morag Niven; 1 s.; 2 d. Educ. George Watson's College, Edinburgh; Edinburgh University; Cambridge University. Lecturer in Animal Husbandry and Production, Royal (Dick) School of Veterinary

Studies, Edinburgh University, 1953 (Senior Lecturer, 1973). Recreations: golf; gardening. Address: (b.) Veterinary Field Station, Roslin, Midlothian; T.-031-445 2001.

Robertson, Rev. Ian William, MA, BD. Minister, Colvend, Southwick and Kirkbean, since 1974; b. 18.12.25, Glasgow; 5 s. Educ. Hutchesons' Grammar School, Glasgow; Glasgow University; Edinburgh University; Marburg University. Minister: Galston New, 1956-65, Crosshill Queen's Park, Glasgow, 1965-74. Publication: Fides Quaerens Intellectum (Translator), 1960. Address: The Manse, Colvend, by Dalbeattie, DG5 4QN; T.-055 663 255.

Robertson, Sir James (Anderson), Kt (1968), CBE (1963), QPM (1961). Chief Constable of Glasgow, 1960-71; Chairman, Scotland Committee, National Children's Home; Chairman, Glasgow Standing Conference of Voluntary Youth Organisations; Honorary President, Glasgow Bn., Boys' Brigade; b. 8.4.06; m.; 2 s.; 1 d.

Robertson, James Downie, ARSA, RSW, RGI, DA. Painter; Senior Lecturer, Drawing and Painting Department, Glasgow School of Art, since 1975; b. 2.11.31, Cowdenbeath; m., Ursula Orr Crawford; 2 step s.; 1 step d. Educ. Hillhead High School, Glasgow; Glasgow School of Art. Teacher, Keith Grammar School, 1957-58; part-time Lecturer, Glasgow School of Art, 1959; full-time, 1967; Carghill Award, RGI; May Marshall Brown Award, RSW, 1976; Sir William Gillies Award, RSW, 1981; Carghill Award, RGI, 1982; Shell Expro Award, 1985; one-man exhibitions: Douglas & Foulis Gallery, 1961, Forum Gallery, Barcelona, 1963, ESU Gallery, Edinburgh, 1966, Loomshop, Fife, 1972, Art Space Gallery, Aberdeen, 1980, Gallery 10, London, 1982, Christopher Hull Gallery, London, 1984. Recreations: music; snooker; reading. Address: (h.) Sandspoint, Glencairn Road, Kilmacolm, Renfrewshire; T.-Kilmacolm 3110.

Robertson, Rev. James Henry, BSc, BD. Minister, Thornliebank Church, since 1985; b. 24.3.49, Edinburgh; m., Morag Margaret Sinclair; 2 s.; 1 d. Educ. Greenhall High School; Edinburgh University. Assistant Minister, Muirhouse, Edinburgh, 1973-75; Minister: St. Ninian's, Greenock, 1975-85. Member, Research and Publications Committee, Rutherford House. Recreations: squash; singing; gardening; walking. Address: Thornliebank Manse, 73 Rouken Glen Road, Thornliebank, Glasgow, G46 7JD.

Robertson, James Taylor, BSc, FICE, FIWES, MBIM. Director of Water and Drainage, Central Regional Council, since 1974; b. 2.4.26, Edinburgh; m., Margaret Ruth; 2 d. Educ. George Watson's Boys' College, Edinburgh; Edinburgh University. Apprentice and Assistant, J. & A. Leslie & Reid, 1948-52; New Works Assistant, Colchester Corporation Waterworks, 1952-54; Assistant Supplies Engineer, then Assistant Distribution Engineer, Bristol Waterworks Company, 1954-61; Depute City Water Engineer, Dundee Corporation, 1961-68; Depute Engineer, then Engineer, Mid Scotland Water Board, 1968-75. Council Member, Water Research Centre. Recreations: golf; walking. Address: (b.) Woodlands, Stirling, FK8 2HB; T.-0786 62811.

Robertson, John Davie Manson, OBE (1978), BL, FSA Scot. Chairman, Robertson Group of Companies, since 1980; Chairman, Orkney Health Board, since 1983 (Member, since 1974); b. 6.11.29, Golspie; m., Elizabeth Amelia Macpherson; 2 s.; 2 d. Educ. Kirkwall Grammar School; Edinburgh University. Member, Rent Assessment Panel for Scotland; Member, Orkney Valuation Appeal Committee; Honorary Vice Consul for Denmark, 1972; Honorary Consul, Federal Republic of Germany, 1976; Honorary Sheriff, Grampian, Highland and Islands, 1977; Past Chairman, Highlands and Islands Savings Committee; Past Chairman, Children's Panel for Orkney, 1971-76; Past Chairman, Children's Panel, Orkney Advisory Committee, 1977-82; former Member, Board of Management, Orkney Hospitals, 1970-74. Royal Order of Knight of Dannebrog, 1982. Publication: Uppies and Doonies, 1967. Recreations: squash; rough shooting. Address: (h.) Shorelands, Kirkwall, Orkney; T.-Kirkwall 2530.

Robertson, Lewis, CBE, FRSE, FRSA. Chairman, F.H. Lloyd Holdings plc, since 1982; Chairman, Triplex plc, since 1983; Chairman, National Girobank Scotland, since 1984; Chairman, Thomas Borthwick & Sons plc, since 1985; b. 28.11.22, Dundee; m., Elspeth Badenoch; 3 s.; 1 d. Educ. Trinity College, Glenalmond. Apprentice Chartered Accountant, 1939-42; RAF, 1942-46; entered family textile business, 1946; appointed Managing Director, Robertson Industrial Textiles, 1954; first Managing Director, Scott & Robertson, 1965 (Chairman, 1968); resigned, 1970; Chief Executive, Grampian Holdings, Glasgow, 1971-76 (also Deputy Chairman, 1972-76); Non-Executive Director, Scottish & Newcastle Breweries, since 1975; Chairman, Scottish Board (and UK Council Member), British Institute of Management, 1981-83; Chairman, Eastern Regional Hospitals Board, 1960-70; Member, Committee of Enquiry into the Relationship of the Pharmaceutical Industry with the NHS, 1965-67; Member, Monopolies (later Monopolies and Mergers) Commission, 1969-76; Deputy Chairman and first Chief Executive, Scottish Development Agency, 1976-81; Member, Scottish Economic Council, 1977-83; Member, Restrictive Practices Court, since 1983; Member, Scottish Postal Board, since 1984; Trustee, since 1963, and Member, Executive Committee, since 1964, Carnegie Trust for the Universities of Scotland; Member, Court, Dundee University, 1967-70 (first Finance Chairman); Council Member, Scottish Business School, 1978-83; Chairman, Scottish Arts Council, and Member, Arts Council of GB, 1970-71; Chairman, Scottish Advisory Committee, British Council, since 1978; Council Member, Scottish History Society, since 1984; first Chairman, Policy Committee, Scottish Episcopal Church, 1974-76; Trustee, Foundation for the Study of Christianity and Society, since 1980; Honorary Doctorate of Laws, Dundee University, 1971. Recreations: work; foreign travel; computer use; music. Address: 32 Saxe Coburg Place, Edinburgh, EH3 5BP; T.-031-332 5221.

Robertson, Richard Ross, RSA, FRBS, DA. Sculptor; b. 10.9.14, Aberdeen; m., Kathleen May Matts; 2 d. Educ. Paisley Grammar School; Glasgow School of Art; Aberdeen Art School. Work exhibited in Aberdeen public parks and several public buildings in city and county of Aberdeen; also exhibited in several private collections in Britain, America and Holland; retired Lecturer in Sculpture, Gray's School of Art, Aberdeen. Recreations: carving; gardening; walking. Address: (h.) Creaguir, Woodlands Road, Rosemount, Blairgowrie, Perthshire; T.-0250 4970.

Robertson, Robert, CBE, JP, FEIS. Member, Strathclyde Regional Council, since 1974; b. 15.8.09, Shapensay, Orkney; m., Jean Murdoch Moffatt; 1 s.; 1 d. Educ. Forres Academy; Royal Technical College, Glasgow. Local government service since 1952; Convener, former Renfrewshire County Council; Chairman, former Renfrewshire Education Committee, 13 years; Chairman, Standing Committee for the Supply and Training of Teachers in Further Education (Robertson Report); Member, Board of Governors, Jordanhill College of Education; Member, various College Councils. Recreations: fishing; painting. Address: (h.) 24 Broadwood Park, Alloway, Ayrshire; T.-0292 43820; Castlehill, near Maybole, Ayrshire; T.-029 250 337.

Robertson, Robert Allan, BSc (Hons). Head, Department of Peat and Forest Soils, Macaulay Institute for Soil Research, since 1979; b. 15.1.25, Helensburgh; m., Sheena W. Chalmers; 2 d. Educ. Hermitage School, Helensburgh; Glasgow University. Joined Department of Soil Survey, Macaulay Institute, 1951. Member, Scottish Sports Council; Vice-President, International Peat Society. Address: (b.) Macaulay Institute for Soil Research, Craigiebuckler, Aberdeen; T.-Aberdeen 318611.

Robertson, Rev. Robert Campbell. Community Minister, Church of Scotland (Glasgow City Centre), since 1977; b. 28.2.35, Glasgow. Educ. Allan Glen's School, Glasgow; Glasgow University and Trinity College. Leader, Calton Youth Club, 1965-68; Deputy Warden, Carberry Tower, 1968-72; Warden, Community House, Glasgow, 1972-77. Executive Member, Strathclyde Association of Youth Clubs. Recreations: films; theatre; playing music. Address: 12B/30 St. Vincent Terrace, Glasgow, G3 8UT; T.-041-204 1541.

Robertson, Roderick. Managing Director, Robertsons of Tain Ltd.; Honorary Sheriff, Tain and Dingwall, 1976; b. 24.8.35, Tain; m., Elizabeth Martin Steele; 1 s. Educ. Tain Royal Academy. Agricultural engineering apprenticeship, 1951-56; Army, 1956-59; began in business (agricultural engineering), 1959; elected, Tain Town Council, 1965 (Chairman of Development, Dean of Guild and Senior Bailie); JP, 1975; appointed Member, Valuation Appeal Committee, Ross and Cromarty, Skye and Lochalsh, 1980; Chairman, Justices of the Peace Committee, Ross and Cromarty, 1980; Chairman, Local Royal British Legion Housing Association, 1984; Member, Tain Community Council. Recreations: flying; shooting; fishing; judo. Address: (h.) Craigton, Provost Ferguson Drive, Tain, Ross-shire; T.-0862 2151.

Robertson, Ronald Foote, CBE, MD, FRCPEdin, FRCP, FRCPGlas. Physician to The Queen in Scotland, since 1977; Consultant Physician, Edinburgh Royal Infirmary, since 1974; Principal Medical Officer, Scottish Life Assurance Company, since 1968; b. 27.12.20, Aberdeen; m., Dorothy Wilkinson; 2 d. Educ. Perth Academy; Edinburgh University. Consultant Physician: Leith Hospital, 1959-74, Deaconess Hospital, 1958-83; President, Royal College of Physicians of Edinburgh, 1976-79; President, British Medical Association, 1983-84; Member, General Medical Council, since 1979; Honorary Fellow, College of Physicians and Surgeons, Pakistan, 1977; Honorary FACP, 1978; Honorary FRCPI, 1978; Honorary FRACP, 1979. Recreations: curling; gardening; fishing. Address: (h.) 15 Wester Coates Terrace, Edinburgh, EH12 5LR; T.-031-337 6377.

Robertson, Sidney Park, MBE, TD, JP, DL, BCom. Director, S. & J.D. Robertson & Co. Ltd. Group of Companies; Honorary Sheriff, Grampian, Highlands and Islands, since 1969; b. 12.3.14, Kirkwall; m., Elsa Miller Croy; 1 s.; 1 d. Educ. Kirkwall Grammar School; Edinburgh University. Commissioned, Royal Artillery, 1940 (Despatches, NW Europe, 1945); Lt.-Col. Commanding Lovat Scouts, 1962-65; Brigadier, CRA 51st Highland Division, 1966-67; Chairman, Orkney Hospitals Board of Management/Orkney Health Board, 1965-79; Honorary Area Vice-President (Orkney), Royal British Legion, since 1975; Honorary Colonel, 102 (Ulster and Scottish) Light Air Defence Regiment, Royal Artillery, 1975-80; Vice President, National Artillery Association, since 1977; Chairman, Royal Artillery Council of Scotland, 1980-84; Honorary President, Orkney Bn., Boys' Brigade; Vice-President, RNLI, since 1985. Recreations: travel; fishing. Address: (h.) Daisybank, Kirkwall, Orkney; T.-0856 2085.

Robinson, Helen Mairi Johnstone, MA. Editor-in-Chief, Concise Scots Dictionary, since 1973; b. 21.1.45, Glasgow; m., David B. Robinson; 1 s.; 1 d. Educ. George Watson's Ladies' College, Edinburgh; Edinburgh University. Scottish National Dictionary: Junior Assistant Editor, 1966, Assistant Editor, 1967, Senior Assistant Editor, 1972. Address: (b.) 27 George Square, Edinburgh, EH8 9LD.

Robinson, Rev. Keith Simpson Paton, MA. Minister, North Merchiston Church, Edinburgh, since 1966; b. 8.12.22, Troon; m., Christine Walker; 1 s.; 1 d. Educ. Marr College, Troon; Glasgow University; New College, Edinburgh. Served for four years in the Forces, attaining rank of Lt. in Royal Armoured Corps; served in Burma Campaign with 3rd Dragoon Guards; Minister: Harwood Church, West Calder, 1950-56, Walkerburn, 1956-66. Recreations: some golf; a little gardening; much rugby spectating. Address: (h.) 11 Robb's Loan, Edinburgh, EH14 1SD; T.-031-443 1598.

Robson, Professor James Scott, MB, ChB (Hons), MD, FRCPEdin, FRCP. Professor of Medicine, Edinburgh University, since 1977;

Physician in charge, Medical Renal Unit, Edinburgh Royal Infirmary, since 1959; b. 19.5.21, Hawick; m., Mary Kynoch MacDonald; 2 s. Educ. Hawick High School; Edinburgh University; New York University. RAMC (Captain), India, Palestine and Egypt, 1945-48; Rockefeller Research Fellow, Harvard University, 1949-50; Edinburgh University: Senior Lecturer in Therapeutics, 1959, Reader in Therapeutics, 1961, in Medicine, 1968; Honorary Associate Professor of Medicine, Harvard, 1962; Merck Sharpe & Dome Visiting Professor to Australia, 1968. President, Renal Association, London, 1977-80; sometime Member, Editorial Board, and Deputy Chairman, Clinical Science and other medical journals; Member, Biomedical Research Committee, SH&HD; Chairman, Sub-Committee in Medicine, National Medical Consultative Committee. Publication: Companion to Medical Studies (Co-Editor). Recreations: gardening; theatre; reading and writing. Address: (h.) 1 Grant Avenue, Edinburgh, EH13 ODS; T.-031-441 3508.

Robson, Professor William Wallace, MA (Oxon). Masson Professor of English Literature, Edinburgh University, since 1972; b. 20.6.23, Plymouth; m., Anne-Varna Moses; 2 s. Educ. Leeds High School and Modern School; New College, Oxford. Assistant Lecturer, King's College, London, 1944-46; Lecturer, Lincoln and Queen's Colleges, Oxford, 1944-46; Fellow, Lincoln College, Oxford, 1948-70; Professor of English, Sussex University, 1970-72; Visiting Professor: University of Southern California, 1953, Adelaide University, 1956, Delaware University, 1963-64; Elizabeth Drew Professor, Smith College, USA, 1968-69; Visiting Fellow: All Souls College, Oxford, 1981, New College, Oxford, 1985. Publications: Critical Essays, 1966; The Signs Among Us, 1968; Modern English Literature, 1970; The Definition of Literature, 1982. Recreations: non-strenuous games of many kinds. Address: (b.) Department of English Literature, Edinburgh University, David Hume Tower, George Square, Edinburgh, EH8; T.-031-667 1011.

Rochester, Professor Colin Herbert, BSc, PhD, DSc, CChem, FRSC, FRSE. Baxter Professor of Chemistry, Dundee University, since 1980; b. 20.3.37, Coventry; m., Jennifer Mary Orrell; 2 s.; 2 d. Educ. Hymers College, Hull; Royal Liberty School, Romford; King's College, London University. Nottingham University: Assistant Lecturer in Physical Chemistry, 1962-64, Lecturer, 1964-72, Reader, 1972-80. Publication: Acidity Functions, 1970. Recreations: fossil collecting; swimming. Address: (b.) Chemistry Department, The University, Dundee, DD1 4HN; T.-0382 23181.

Rochford, Professor Gerard, BA, BSc. Professor of Social Work Studies, Aberdeen University, since 1978; Psychotherapist; b. 17.12.32, Dorking; m., Anne Prime; 3 s.; 7 d. Educ. Worcester Royal Grammar School; Hull University; Oxford University. Medical Research Council, 1960-63; Lecturer in Psychology: Aberdeen University, 1963-67, Hong Kong University, 1967-70; Lecturer/Senior Lecturer, Aberdeen

University, 1970-78. Honorary Vice-President, SCOPE; Case-Discussion Leader, Marriage Guidance Council. Recreations: family; friends; poetry. Address: (h.) 47 Waverley Place, Aberdeen; T.-Aberdeen 644873.

Rodger, James McPhail, BSc, MEd. Headmaster, Portree High School, since 1971; b. 15.9.33, Cleland, Lanarkshire; m., Jessie Tyre Crawford; 4 d. Educ. Wishaw High School; Glasgow University; Jordanhill College. Flying Officer, RAF, 1956; Teacher of Mathematics, Hamilton Academy, 1959-64; Principal Teacher of Mathematics and latterly Depute Headmaster, Carluke High School, 1964-71. Member, Consultative Committee on the Curriculum, 1980-83. Professional footballer: Glasgow Rangers, 1952-55, St. Mirren, 1955-62, Heart of Midlothian, 1962-65. Recreations: bridge; golf; hill-walking; gardening; reading. Address: (b.) Portree High School, Portree, Isle of Skye; T.-0478 2030.

Rodger, William J., JP. Chairman, Policy and Resources Committee, Kirkcaldy District Council, since 1984; Chairman, Kirkcaldy Licensing Board, since 1984; Chairman, Kirkcaldy Justices Committee, since 1982; b. 14.10.32, Buckhaven; m., Joan; 3 s. Educ. Buckhaven High School. Member, Buckhaven and Methil Town Council, 1971; Member, Kirkcaldy District Council, since 1974. Recreation: golf when time allows. Address: (h.) 70 Kirkland Walk, Methil, Leven, Fife, KY8 2AB; T.-0333 26673.

Rogan, Rev. William Henry, MA, BD, DD, JP. Minister, Church of Scotland; Extra Chaplain to the Queen; b. b. 1.1.08, Logie Coldstone; m., Norah Violet Henderson; 1 s.; 2 d. Educ. Royal High School, Edinburgh; Edinburgh University. Assistant, St. Cuthbert's, Edinburgh; Minister: Whithorn, 1932-37, Helensburgh St. Brides, 1937-50, Paisley Abbey, 1950-69, Humbie, 1969-74; Army Chaplain, 1943-46; President, Scottish Church Society, 1972-74; Convener, Church of Scotland Youth Committee, 1968-72; Chaplain in Ordinary to the Queen, 1963-78. Recreations: music; drama; angling. Address: (h.) Westwood, Lauder, Berwickshire; T.-Lauder 415.

Rogers, Christopher David, BA, MA. Senior Lecturer in Economics, Dundee University, since 1981; Associate Editor, Journal of Energy and Natural Resources Law, since 1983; b. 31.5.44, Leigh; m., Ann Burns; 3 s. Educ. Bolton School; Liverpool University. Assistant Lecturer, then Lecturer, University College of Wales, Aberystwyth, 1967-70; Lecturer, Dundee University, 1970-75; Chief Project Officer, Commonwealth Secretariat, London, 1976; Economic Affairs Officer, United Nations Conference on Trade and Development, 1977-78; Lecturer in Economics, Dundee University, 1979-81. Recreations: hill-walking; cooking; gardening. Address: (b.) Department of Economics, Dundee University, Dundee, DD1 4HN; T.-0382 23181.

Rogers, Rev. James Murdoch, BA (Hons), BD. Minister, Roseangle Ryehill Church, Dundee, since 1980; Convener, Board of World Mission and Unity, Church of Scotland, since 1984; Parish Minister to Dundee University, since 1980; b. 22.11.28, Limavady, Northern Ireland; m., Doris Young; 2 s. Educ. Coleraine Academical Institution; Queen's University, Belfast; Presbyterian College, Belfast. Minister, Second Presbyterian Church, Saintfield, 1955-65; Moderator, Down Presbytery; Secretary, Irish Council of Churches, 1963-65; Minister, Ryehill Church, Dundee, 1965-80; Chairman, Hospital Sub-Committee, Home Board; Vice-Convener, Overseas Council, Church of Scotland, 1977-80; Chairman, Departmental Board of Overseas Missions and Inter-Church Relations, 1977-83; Exchange Preacher, British Council of Churches, National Council of Churches, USA; Member, Board of Directors, Royal Dundee Institution for the Blind, since 1966. Recreations: golf; gardening; photography; travel; Rotarian. Address: (h.) 15 West Park Road, Dundee, DD2 1NU; T.-Dundee 67460.

Rogers, Mary Elizabeth, MA (Oxon), MS, PhD. Lecturer in Zoology, Edinburgh University, since 1973; b. 11.11.41, Bitton, near Bristol. Educ. Gardenhurst School, Burnham-on-Sea; Lady Margaret Hall, Oxford. Teaching Assistant, Biology: Minnesota University, 1962-63, Yale University, 1963-64; Predoctoral Fellow, Yale University, 1964-67; NATO Postdoctoral Fellow, Palermo, Italy, 1967-68; SRC Postdoctoral Fellow, Edinburgh University, 1968-69; University Demonstrator, Edinburgh, 1969-73. Council and Executive Committee Member, Edinburgh Zoo. Recreations: hill-walking; tennis; squash; reading. Address: (h.) 72 Great King Street, Edinburgh, EH3 6QU; T.-031-667 1081.

Rogerson, Robert William Kelly Cupples, BArch, FRIBA, FRIAS, FSA Scot, MRSH. Member, Scottish Council on Disability; Chairman, Committee on Access for Scotland; Council Member, National Trust for Scotland; b. 14.5.17, Glasgow; m., Mary Clark MacNeill; 1 s.; 1 d. Educ. High School of Glasgow; Strathclyde University. Architect in private practice, 1955-56 and 1958-82 (Partner, Watson Salmond & Gray, 1956-58); Lecturer, School of Architecture, Glasgow School of Art; Past Chairman, Glasgow Building Guardian Committee; Past Chairman, RIAS Trustees of The Hill House, Helensburgh; Past Chairman, Committee on Access for Scotland; Founder and Chairman, Glasgow Summer School; Member, Committee on Artistic Matters, Church of Scotland. Publication: A Place at Work (Co-author). Recreations: gardening; travelling abroad. Address: (h.) 49 Roman Court, Roman Road, Bearsden, Glasgow, G61 2NW; T.-041-942 3997.

Rollo, Thomas Landale, OBE, MC, TD, MA, LLB. Solicitor (Senior Partner in family legal firm, since 1951); b. 7.1.08, Cupar; m., Gladys Isobel Ledingham (deceased); 1 s. Educ. Bell-Baxter School, Cupar; St. Andrews University; Glasgow University. Joined family practice, 1934; Territorial Army, 1938-52; served with 7th and 6/7th Black Watch; active service, North Africa, Sicily and NW Europe, 1939-45; Town Clerk, Falkland, 1964-74; Member, Court, St. Andrews University, 1973-78; Member, Council, Law Society of Scotland, 1973-78; Church Elder. Recreations: at one time most games and sailing; now only golf. Address: (h.) Brackland, Cupar, Fife; T.-0334 54081.

Rorke, Professor John, CBE, PhD, BSc, CEng, FIMechE, FRSE. Professor of Mechanical Engineering, Heriot-Watt University, since 1980 (Vice Principal, since 1984); b. 2.9.23, Dumbarton; m., Jane Craig Buchanan; 2 d. Educ. Dumbarton Academy; Royal Technical College, Glasgow. Lecturer, Strathclyde University, 1946-51; Assistant to Engineering Director, Alexander Stephen & Sons Ltd., 1951-56; Technical Manager, then General Manager and Engineering Director, William Denny & Bros. Ltd., 1956-63; Technical Director, then Sales Director, Managing Director and Chairman, Brown Bros. & Co. Ltd. and Chairman, John Hastie of Greenock Ltd., 1963-78; Managing Director, Vickers Offshore Group, 1978 (Director of Planning, Vickers PLC, 1979-80). President, Institution of Engineers and Shipbuilders in Scotland; Council Member, Institution of Mechanical Engineers. Recreations: bridge; golf. Address: (h.) 3 Barnton Park Grove, Edinburgh; T.-031-336 3044.

Rose, David, BA, NDA, CertEd. Principal, Barony Agricultural College, Dumfries, since 1980; Member, Agricultural Training Board, since 1983; b. 6.7.40, Denton, Manchester; m., Pauline Anne Rose; 1 s.; 1 d. Educ. Seale-Hayne College of Agriculture; Open University. Assistant Farm Manager, Wiltshire, 1962-66; Lecturer in Agriculture, Cumbria College of Agriculture and Forestry, 1967-70; Senior Lecturer in Agriculture, Bishop Burton College of Agriculture, 1970-74; Vice-Principal, Oatridge College of Agriculture, 1974-80. Recreation: hill-walking. Address: (b.) Barony Agricultural College, Parkgate, Dumfries; T.-038 786 251.

Rose, Ian Cameron, CBE, TD. Chairman, Toward Civic Trust; b. Scotland; m., Catherine Laura Margaret Neilson. Educ. Glasgow. Managed timber camps and trading posts, Nigeria, 1930-33; Local Government Officer, Glasgow, 1934-39; War Service, 1939-46 (Lt.-Col.); District Commissioner, Sudan Political Service, 1946-55; District Commissioner, Uganda, 1955-60; Permanent Secretary, Ministry of Health, Buganda, 1960-63; Administrator, Rediffusion (Scotland) Ltd., 1964-65; Secretariat, Birmingham Chamber of Commerce and Industry, 1966-68; Government Secretary, St. Helena and its Dependencies, 1968-74. Recreations: golf; swimming. Address: (h.) Laurain, Sandy Beach, Innellan, Argyll; T.-Innellan 367.

Rose, Professor Richard, BA, DPhil. Director and Professor of Public Policy, Centre for the Study of Public Policy, Strathclyde University, since 1976; b. 9.4.33; m.; 2 s.; 1 d. Lecturer in Government, Manchester University, 1961-66; Professor of Politics, Strathclyde University, 1966-82.

Rose, William, BEM, JP, ISM. Member, Grampian Regional Council, since 1974; b. 12.7.11, Aberdeen; m., Isabel Begg Pirie; 1 s. Educ. Robert Gordon's Institute of Technology. External Member, Aberdeen Town Council Education Committee, 1964-68; Town Councillor, Aberdeen, 1968-75; Member, North of Scotland River Purification Board, since 1981; Member, Aberdeen Endowment Trust, 1969-75 and since 1983; Governor, Oakbank School, 1968-75 and since 1983; various offices, including National Executive Member, Post Office Engineering Union; Secretary, Staff Side, Regional Whitley Council, 1965-72; Executive Member, Aberdeen Lads Club, since 1965. Recreation: bowling. Address: (h.) 73 Hazlehead Crescent, Aberdeen, AB1 8EX; T.-Aberdeen 319245.

Rosebery, 7th Earl, (Neil Archibald Primrose), DL; b. 11.2.29; m., Alison Mary Deirdre Reid; 1 s.; 4 d. Educ. Stowe; New College, Oxford. Address: (h.) Dalmeny House, South Queensferry, West Lothian.

Rosie, Professor Aeneas Murdoch, BSc, MSc, PhD, CEng, FIEE, MIEEE. Professor of Telecommunications, Strathclyde University, since 1973; b. 6.6.31, Wick; m., June Foley; 1 s.; 1 d. Educ. Wick High School; Glasgow University; Birmingham University. Electronic Engineer, Pye Radio Company; Research Fellow, Birmingham University; Lecturer, Senior Lecturer and Reader, Queen's University, Belfast. Recreations: sailing; formerly squash. Address: (h.) Mertoun, Rhu Road Higher, Helensburgh, Dunbartonshire.

Rosie, George. Scottish Affairs Correspondent, The Sunday Times, since 1976; b. 27.2.41, Edinburgh; m., Elizabeth Ann; 2 s.; 1 d. Educ. Trinity Academy, Edinburgh; Edinburgh School of Architecture. Editor, Interior Design magazine, 1966-68; freelance magazine writer, 1968-76. Publications: The British in Vietnam, 1970; Cromarty, 1975; The Ludwig Initiative, 1978; Hugh Miller, 1982. Recreation: hill-walking. Address: 70 Comiston Drive, Edinburgh, EH10 5QS; T.-031-447 9660.

Rosin, Leslie, BL. Company Director; Member, Eastwood District Council, since 1984; b. 31.8.31, London; m., Hilary Langman; 1 s.; 2 d. Educ. Hutchesons' Grammar School; Glasgow University. Chairman, Eastwood Conservative Association. Recreation: harpsichord maker. Address: (h.) 23 Greenhill Avenue, Glasgow, G46 6QQ; T.-041-638 3333.

Ross, Alastair Robertson, OStJ, DA, ARSA, FRBS, FSA Scot, FRSA. Artist; Lecturer in Fine Art, Duncan of Jordanstone College of Art, Dundee, since 1966; Scottish Representative and Council Member, Royal Society of British Sculptors, since 1972; b. 8.8.41, Perth; m., Kathryn Margaret Greig Wilson; 1 d. Educ. St. Mary's Episcopal School, Dunblane; McLaren High School, Callander; Duncan of Jordanstone College of Art, Dundee. SED Postgraduate Scholarship, 1965-66; Royal Scottish Academy Carnegie Travelling Scholarship, 1965; Duncan of Drumfork Scholarship, 1965; award winner, Paris Salon, 1967; Medaille de Bronze, Societe des Artistes Francais, 1968; Medaille D'Argent, 1970; Council Member, Society of Scottish Artists, 1972-75; exhibited work widely in UK and abroad. Recreations: genealogy; heraldry; travel. Address: (h.) Ravenscourt, 28 Albany Terrace, Dundee, DD3 6HS; T.-0382 24235.

Ross, Rev. David Sinclair, BSc, MSc, PhD, BD. Minister, Old Parish Church, Peterhead, since 1978; Church of Scotland Representative, Grampian Regional Education Committee, since 1981; b. 24.7.45, Aberdeen; m., Heather Guldmar Watt; 2 s. Educ. Aberdeen Academy; Aberdeen University; Glasgow University. Research Chemist, West Germany, 1971-74. Chairman, Peterhead Disabled Club; President, Peterhead Rugby FC. Recreations: choral singing; rugby. Address: 49 King Street, Peterhead, AB4 6TA; T.-0779 72618.

Ross, Rt. Hon. Lord, (Donald MacArthur Ross), QC (Scot), MA, LLB. Lord Justice Clerk, since 1985 (Senator of the College of Justice in Scotland and Lord of Session, 1977); b. 29.3.27; m.; 2 d. Educ. Dundee High School; Edinburgh University. 2nd Lt., Black Watch, 1947-49; Advocate, 1952; QC (Scot), 1964; Dean, Faculty of Advocates, 1967-73; Sheriff Principal of Ayr and Bute, 1972-73; Deputy Chairman, Boundary Commission for Scotland, since 1977.

Ross, Professor Donald Sutherland, BSc, PhD, ARCST, FEng, FIMechE, FIProdE, FRSA. Professor of Production Engineering and Head, Department of Production Management and Manufacturing Technology, Strathclyde University, since 1966; b. 12.7.23, Glasgow; m., Catherine. Educ. Albert Senior Secondary School, Glasgow; London University; Glasgow University; Strathclyde University. Apprentice and Production Engineer, Rolls Royce Ltd., 1939-45; Production Engineer, Vactric Ltd., Airdrie, 1946-47; Teacher, Marr College, Troon, 1947-50; Lecturer, Royal College, Glasgow, 1951-59; Assistant to Works Director, L. Sterne, Hillington, 1960-61; Lecturer/Senior Lecturer, Strathclyde University, 1961-66. Address: (b.) Strathclyde University, Montrose Street, Glasgow, G1 1XJ; T.-041-552 4400, Ext. 2329.

Ross, Duncan. Principal, Benmore Centre for Outdoor Education, since 1975; Commissioner, Countryside Commission for Scotland, since 1971; Vice Chairman, Scottish Mountain Leader Training Board, since 1983; b. 29.4.33, Sandbank, Argyll; m., Kathryn Dilworth. Educ. Moray House College of Education, Edinburgh. Pilot, RAF, 1951-57; Instructor, National Mountain Training Centre, Glenmore Lodge, 1963-71; Deputy Principal, Benmore Centre for Outdoor Education, 1971-75. Recreations: mountaineering; sailing; skiing; nature study and conservation; reading. Address: (b.) Benmore Centre for Outdoor Education, by Dunoon, Argyll; T.-0369 6337.

Ross, Ernest. MP (Labour), Dundee West, since 1979; b. 27.7.42, Dundee; m., June; 2 s.; 1 d. Educ. St. John's Junior Secondary School. Apprentice Marine Fitter, Caledon Shipyard; Quality Control Inspector/Engineer, Timex. Recreations: football; cricket. Address: (b.) House of Commons, London, SW1A 0AA; T.-01-219 4071.

Ross, Graham Tullis, LVO. Director, Scottish Business in the Community (SCOTBIC), since 1982; b. 5.7.28, Edinburgh; m., Margot; 1 s.; 2 d. Educ. George Watson's College, Edinburgh. Director, Macvitties Guest & Co. Ltd., Edinburgh, 1955-65; Managing Director, Macvitties Guest (Edinburgh), A.F. Reid (Glasgow), 1965-71; Managing Director, A.A. Laing Ltd. and Ross Restaurants Ltd., 1971-76; Managing Director, D.S. Crawford (Catering) Ltd., 1976-82. Chairman, Scottish Hotel and Catering Institute, 1968-72; Chairman, Napier College Advisory Committee, 1970-85; former Scottish rugby internationalist. Recreation: hill-walking. Address: (h.) 81 Craiglockhart Road, Edinburgh; T.-031-556 9761.

Ross, Helen Elizabeth, BA, MA (Oxon), PhD (Cantab). Reader in Psychology, Stirling University, since 1983; b. 2.12.35, London. Educ. South Hampstead High School; Somerville College, Oxford; Newnham College, Cambridge. Assistant Mistress, schools in London and Oxfordshire, 1959-61; Research Assistant and student, Psychological Laboratory, Cambridge University, 1961-65; Lecturer in Psychology: Hull University, 1965-68, Stirling University, 1969-72; Senior Lecturer in Psychology, Stirling University, 1972-83; Research Fellow, DFVLR Institute for Aerospace Medicine, Bonn, 1980-81; Leverhulme Fellowship, 1983-84. Publications: Behaviour and Perception in Strange Environments, 1974; E.H. Weber: The Sense of Touch (Co-translator), 1978. Recreations: skiing; curling; hill-walking; traditional music. Address: (b.) Department of Psychology, Stirling University, Stirling, FK9 4LA; T.-0786 73171.

Ross, Rev. John Durham, BA, DipEd. Industrial Chaplain, Dundee Area; b. 8.6.32, Mansfield, Victoria, Australia; m., Violet Cooper Shearer; 1 s.; 1 d. Educ. Wesley College, Melbourne; Melbourne University and Ormond College. Chaplain, RAN, 1958-60; Assistant Minister, Govan Old, Glasgow, 1960-63; Associate Minister, Double Bay, Sydney, Australia, 1964-66; Leader, World Council of Churches ecumenical teams in Italy, later also Co-ordinator of teams in Greece and Cyprus and liaison for North African teams, 1966-73; Minister, Langside, Glasgow, 1974-84. First Chairman, Battlefield and Langside Community Council; Co-Chairman, Langside and Battlefield Caring Service. Address: (h.) 6 Hill Street, Broughty Ferry, Dundee, DD5 2JL; T.-Dundee 78729.

Ross, John George, PhD, FRCVS, BAgr, DVSM. Director, Veterinary Laboratory, Ministry of Agriculture, Fisheries and Food, since 1970; b. 1.12.25, Glasgow; m., Vera; 1 s.; 3 d. Educ. Allan Glen's School, Glasgow; Lairg Secondary School; Glasgow University; Edinburgh University; Belfast University. Colonial Veterinary Service, until 1960; Northern Ireland Veterinary Laboratory, 1961-70. Recreation: golf. Address: (h.) Tighvadie, Lower Broomieknowe, Lasswade, Midlothian; T.-031-663 6525.

Ross, John Graham, DSO, MBE, TD, DL. Solicitor; Honorary Sheriff, Dundee, since 1971; Deputy Lieutenant, City of Dundee, since 1975; b. 13.4.21, Dundee; m., Kathleen Mary Pain; 3 s.; 1 d. Educ. Dundee High School.

Commissioned, Black Watch (RHR), 1939-41, Parachute Regiment, 1941-46, 15th Bn., Parachute Regiment (TA), 1949-53; Partner, Ross Strachan & Co., Solicitors, Dundee, 1949. Recreation: gardening. Address: (h.) 13 Rockfield Crescent, Dundee; T.-Dundee 67887.

Ross, Rev. Kenneth Rankin, BA, BD (Hons). Minister, Unst, Shetland, since 1982; b. 31.5.58, Glasgow; m., Hester Ferguson Carmichael; 2 s. Educ. Kelvinside Academy, Glasgow; Edinburgh University and New College. Secretary, Life (Shetland); Member, Systematic Theology Group, Rutherford House; Captain, 1st Unst Boys' Brigade. Recreations: hill-walking; gardening; squash; reading. Address: Manse of Unst, Baltasound, Shetland; T.-095 781 335.

Ross, Peter Edward, MSc, PhD. Senior Lecturer, Department of Medicine, Dundee University, since 1983; b. 17.10.45, Perth; m., Joan; 2 d. Educ. County High School, Arnold, Nottinghamshire; Dundee University. Postdoctoral Research Fellow, Department of Medicine, Dundee University, 1974-76; non-clinical Lecturer, Department of Medicine, and Honorary Lecturer, Department of Biochemistry, Dundee, 1976-83; Visiting Lecturer, Basrah University, 1979. President, Dundee and District Squash Rackets Association; Council Member, Scottish Squash Rackets Association. Recreations: squash; travel; reading; music. Address: (b.) Department of Medicine, Ninewells Hospital and Medical School, Dundee, DD1 9SY; T.-Dundee 60111, Ext. 2456.

Ross, Philip Wesley, TD, MB, ChB, MD, MRCPath, MIBiol, FLS. Consultant, Edinburgh Royal Infirmary, and Senior Lecturer in Bacteriology, Edinburgh University, since 1973; b. 6.6.36, Aberdeen; m., Stella Joyce Shand; 2 s.; 1 d. Educ. Turriff Academy; Robert Gordon's College, Aberdeen; Aberdeen University. Senior Warden, Edinburgh University, 1972-83. Lt.-Col., RAMC (TA); Officer commanding Medical Division and Edinburgh Detachment 205 Scottish General Hospital, 1975-80. Recreations: music; walking; tennis. Address: (h.) 18 Old Church Lane, Duddingston, Edinburgh, EH15 3PX; T.-031-661 5415.

Ross, Thomas Alexander, CStJ, BL, PhD. Senior Partner, Russel & Aitken, WS, Falkirk, Edinburgh and Denny; Honorary Sheriff, Tayside, Central and Fife; b. 18.7.06, Selkirk; m., Eleanor Tyson; 1 s. Educ. Selkirk School; Edinburgh University. Director of Administration, Far Eastern Bureau of Political Intelligence, Department of the Foreign Office in Delhi and Chungking, 1944; Governor, Christ's Hospital. Recreations: travelling; shooting. Address: (b.) Russel & Aitken, WS, King's Court, Falkirk; T.-Falkirk 22888.

Ross of Marnock, Baron, (William Ross), PC (1964), MBE (Mil) (1945), MA. Life Peer; b. 7.4.11; m.; 2 d. Educ. Ayr Academy; Glasgow University. Schoolmaster; served Second World War, HLI, R. Signals (Major); MP (Labour), Kilmarnock, 1946-79; Secretary of State for Scotland, 1964-70, 1974-76; Opposition Spokesman

on Scottish Affairs, 1970-74; Hon. LLD: St. Andrews, 1967, Strathclyde, 1969, Glasgow, 1978; Lord High Commissioner, General Assembly of Church of Scotland, 1978-80.

Ross, William, FRICS. Director of Economic Development and Estates, City of Edinburgh District Council, since 1984; b. 2.2.41, Rutherglen; m., Margaret; 2 s.; 1 d. Educ. Rutherglen Academy; Glasgow University. Trainee, London County Council; Negotiator, Hillier Parker May and Rowden; Valuer, Glasgow Corporation; District Surveyor, British Rail Property Board; Group Development Surveyor, Maxwell Property Development Company; self-employed; Principal Surveyor (Development), Grampian Regional Council; Depute Director of Estates, Edinburgh District Council. Recreations: gardening; chess; family. Address: (b.) 375 High Street, Edinburgh; T.-031-225 2424, Ext. 5800.

Ross Stewart, David Andrew, BA (Cantab). Managing Director, John Bartholomew & Son Ltd., since 1968; b. 30.11.30, Edinburgh; m., Susan Olive Routh; 2 s. Educ. Rugby School; Cambridge University. Assistant General Manager, Alex. Cowan & Sons (NZ) Ltd., 1959-62; General Manager, Alex. Cowan & Sons (Stationery) Ltd., 1962-66; General Manager, Spicers (Stationery) Ltd., 1966-68. Director, Scottish Provident Institution; Director, Bruntons (Musselburgh) plc; Chairman, St. Andrew Trust plc; Director, East of Scotland Industrial Investments plc; Member, Scottish Advisory Board, Abbey National Building Society; Chairman, Trade Development Committee, Scottish Council (Development and Industry). Recreations: fishing; gardening; golf. Address: (b.) 12 Duncan Street, Edinburgh, EH9 1TA; T.-031-667 9341.

Round, Professor Nicholas Grenville, MA, DPhil. Stevenson Professor of Hispanic Studies, Glasgow University, since 1972; b. 6.6.38, Looe, Cornwall; m., Ann Le Vin; 1 d. Educ. Launceston College; Pembroke College, Oxford. Lecturer, then Reader in Spanish, Queen's University, Belfast, 1962-72; Warden, Alanbrooke Hall, Queen's University, Belfast, 1970-72. Publications: Unamuno: Abel Sanche: A Critical Guide, 1974; The Greatest Man Uncrowned: A Study of the Fall of Alvaro de Luna, 1985. Recreations: reading; drawing; politics; hill-walking; music; all aspects of Cornwall. Address: (h.) 11 Dougalston Avenue, Milngavie, Glasgow; T.-041-956 2507.

Rowe, Michael, BA (Hons). Benefit Manager, Scotland, Department of Employment, since 1981; b. 30.5.37, Stoke-on-Trent; m., Kathleen Marie; 2 s. Educ. High School, Newcastle-under-Lyme; St. Catherine's College, Oxford University. Department of Employment: various posts, Midlands Region, 1961-70, First Secretary, UK Delegation to European Communities in Brussels, 1970-72, various posts, London, 1972-81. Recreations: family; involvement in youth club activities; enjoying good food and wine. Address: (b.) Department of Employment, Office for Scotland, Robbs Loan, Edinburgh; T.-031-443 8731, Ext. 480.

Rowland, Alan Corbett, BSc, MRCVS. Senior Lecturer in Veterinary Pathology, Edinburgh University, since 1978 (Associate Dean, since 1981); b. 22.2.31, Middlesbrough; 1 s.; 1 d. Educ. Acklam Hall Grammar School; Edinburgh University. General Practitioner, 1956-58; Lecturer, Department of Veterinary Pathology, Edinburgh University, 1958-78. Member, University Senate, 1974-80; Member, Editorial Board, Journal of Veterinary Science Communications; Referee, Journal of Tropical Animal Health and Production; External Examiner for undergraduate pathology, London and Cambridge Veterinary Schools; British Council Adviser, Swine Pathology Institute, Brazil. Address: (b.) Royal (Dick) School of Veterinary Studies, Department of Veterinary Pathology, Easter Bush, Roslin, Midlothian; T.-031-445 2001.

Roxburgh, Stuart T.D., MB, ChB, FRCSEdin. Consultant Ophthalmologist, Perth Royal Infirmary, since 1981; b. 10.5.50, Glasgow; m., Christine; 2 s. Educ. Camphill High School, Paisley; Glasgow University. T.-0738 34347.

Roxburghe, 10th Duke of, (Guy David Innes-Ker), b. 18.11.54; m., Lady Jane Meriel Grosvenor; 2 s.; 1 d. Educ. Eton; Sandhurst; Magdalene College, Cambridge. Address: (h.) Floors Castle, Kelso.

Roy, Rev. Alan John, BSc, BD, MA. Minister, Ogilvie & Stobswell, Dundee, since 1985; b. 27.12.34, Edinburgh; m., Roma Mary Hutchison Finlayson; 2 s.; 1 d. Educ. Daniel Stewart's College, Edinburgh; Edinburgh University; Swedish Theological Institute, Jerusalem. Missionary, Church of Scotland, with the United Church of Zambia, 1961-72, first as District Minister, Serenje, then as Tutor, Ministerial Training College, Mindolo, Kitwe; Minister, Park, Dundee, 1972-76; became Minister, United Congregation of Stobswell, 1976. Vice-President, Scottish Central Committee, Feed the Minds; Chairman, Dundee Auxiliary, Leprosy Mission. Recreations: golf; stamp collecting. Address: (h.) 23 Shamrock Street, Dundee, DD4 7AH; T.-Dundee 41333.

Roy, Rev. Alistair Anderson, MA, BD. Minister, Wick Berea, since 1955; Member, Caithness District Council, since 1978; b. 13.4.27, Oldmeldrum; m., Jean Morrison McIntosh; 2 s. Educ. Elgin Academy; Aberdeen University. Assistant Minister, Brechin Cathedral, 1952-55. Address: (h.) Mansefield, Miller Avenue, Wick; T.-Wick 2822.

Roy, Rev. James Alexander, MA, BD. Minister, Lochee West, Dundee, since 1973; Chairman, Children's Panel for Tayside, since 1983; Clerk, Dundee Presbytery, Church of Scotland, since 1985; b. 21.2.40, Comrie; m., Sheila Munro Fitzgerald; 1 s.; 2 d. Educ. Morrison's Academy, Crieff; St. Andrews University. Minister, Dunnottar Parish Church, Stonehaven, 1966-73. Address: Churchmount, 3 Coupar Angus Road, Dundee, DD2 3HG; T.-0382 611415.

Royle, Trevor Bridge, MA. Author and Broadcaster; Editor, Lines Review; b. 26.1.45, Mysore, India; m., Dr. Hannah Mary Rathbone; 3 s.

Educ. Madras College, St. Andrews; Aberdeen University. Editor, William Blackwood & Sons Ltd.; Literature Director, Scottish Arts Council, 1971-79; Council Member, Scottish National Dictionary Association; Scottish Arts Council Book Award, 1983. Publications: We'll Support You Evermore: The Impertinent Saga of Scottish Fitba' (Co-Editor), 1976; Jock Tamson's Bairns (Editor), 1977; Precipitous City: The Story of Literary Edinburgh, 1980; A Diary of Edinburgh, 1981; Edinburgh, 1982; Death Before Dishonour: The True Story of Fighting Mac, 1982; The Macmillan Companion to Scottish Literature, 1983; James and Jim: The Biography of James Kennaway, 1983; The Kitchener Enigma, 1985; The Best Years of their Lives: The Post-War National Service Experience, 1986; radio plays: Magnificat, 1984; Old Alliances, 1985. Recreations: rugby football; hill-walking; music. Address: (h.) 6 James Street, Edinburgh, EH15 2DS; T.-031-669 2116.

Ruffell, James Gordon, CBE (1966), MA. Director, Coats Patons Plc, since 1971; Managing Director, Linhas Corrente, Sao Paulo, Brazil, since 1976; b. 15.11.23, Southampton; m., Susan; 2 s.; 1 d. Educ. Taunton's, Southampton; Queen's College, Oxford. Pilot, RAF, 1942-45; Manager, J. & P. Coats Ltd., Argentine and Middle East, 1949-57; Managing Director, Cucirini Cantoni Coats SpA, Milan, 1957-67; Director, Patons & Baldwins Ltd. and J. & P. Coats Ltd., 1967-71; Director, Coats Patons Plc, 1971; Managing Director, Coats Patons (UK) Ltd., 1971-76. President, British Chamber of Commerce in Italy, 1960-66; President, Royal British Legion, Sao Paulo, 1978; President, British Chamber of Commerce in Brazil, 1983-85. Recreation: fishing. Address: (b.) 155 St. Vincent Street, Glasgow; T.-041-221 8711.

Runnalls, Graham Arthur, BA, MA, DipGenLing, DLitt. Reader in French, Edinburgh University; b. 21.11.37, Exmouth; m., Anne K.; 2 d. Educ. Exmouth Grammar School; Exeter University. Assistant Lecturer in French, Exeter University, 1962-63; Lecturer in French, North London Polytechnic, 1963-66; joined Edinburgh University as Lecturer, 1966. President, International Society for the Study of Medieval Theatre. Recreations: opera; sport, especially badminton, tennis and running. Address: (h.) 85A Colinton Road, Edinburgh, EH10 5DF; T.-031-337 1737.

Rusby, Sir Cameron, KCB, LVO. Chief Executive, Scottish Society for Prevention of Cruelty to Animals, since 1983; b. 20.2.26, Sliema, Malta; m., Marion Elizabeth Bell; 2 d. Educ. Wootton Court School, near Canterbury; Royal Naval College, Dartmouth. Thirty nine years in Royal Navy, reaching rank of Vice Admiral; retired, 1982. Chairman, Village Committee, 13th Commonwealth Games. Recreations: sailing; skiing; equitation. Address: c/o Bank of Scotland, 70 High Street, Peebles, EH45 8AQ.

Russell, Alexander James, JP. Member, Highland Regional Council, since 1974 (Chairman, Education Committee, since 1978); b. 23.11.19, Newtonmore; m., Edith Henderson Cowan; 1 s.; 2 d. Educ. Kingussie Secondary

School; Edinburgh University (did not complete studies). Badenoch District Councillor, 1954; Inverness County Councillor, 1968-74. Recreations: curling; golf; fishing. Address: (h.) Cairndearg, Newtonmore, PH20 1BL; T.-054 03 262.

Russell, (Alastair) Muir, BSc. Head, Energy Division, Industry Department for Scotland, since 1983; b. 9.1.49, Glasgow; m., Eileen A. Mackay (qv). Educ. High School of Glasgow; Glasgow University. Assistant Principal, Scottish Office, 1970; Principal, Scottish Office, 1974; Secretary, Scottish Development Agency, 1975-76; Assistant Secretary, Scottish Office, 1981; Principal Private Secretary to Secretary of State for Scotland, 1981-83. Recreations: music; food and wine. Address: (b.) New St. Andrews House, Edinburgh, EH1; T.-031-556 8400.

Russell, Sheriff Albert Muir Galloway, QC, BA (Oxon), LLB. Sheriff, Grampian, Highland and Islands, at Aberdeen, since 1971; b. 26.10.25, Edinburgh; m., Margaret Winifred Millar; 2 s.; 2 d. Educ. Edinburgh Academy; Wellington College; Brasenose College, Oxford; Edinburgh University. Lt., Scots Guards, 1944-47; Member, Faculty of Advocates, 1951; Standing Junior Counsel to Board of Trade, Department of Agriculture and Forestry Commission; QC (Scot), 1965; Vice Chairman, Board of Management, Southern Group of Hospitals, Edinburgh, 1966-70; Governor, Moray House College of Education, 1965-70; Member, Sheriff Court Rules Council, since 1978. Recreations: golf; music. Address: (h.) Easter Ord House, Skene, Aberdeenshire, AB3 6SQ; T.-0224 740228.

Russell, Rev. Archibald, MA. Minister, Duror linked with Glencoe, since 1979; Clerk, Lochaber Presbytery, Church of Scotland, since 1982; Moderator, Synod of the Southern Highlands, since 1985; b. 17.11.24, Cleland, Lanarkshire; m., Elma Sandeman Watson; 2 s. Educ. Wishaw High School; Glasgow University. Assistant, South Dalziel Parish Church, Motherwell; Minister: Holyrood Abbey, Edinburgh, St. Mark's Lancefield, Glasgow, Anderston Parish Church, Glasgow; first Community Minister of Church of Scotland (based at Drumchapel, Glasgow). Founder Editor, Drumchapel News. Recreations: gardening; local history. Address: Manse of Duror and Glencoe, Brecklet, Ballachulish, Argyll, PA39 4JG; T.-085 52 209.

Russell, David Cairns, FRICS. Deputy Director of Building and Chief Quantity Surveyor, Scottish Development Department, since 1980; b. 21.8.30, Glasgow; m., Moira Young Whitehill; 3 s. Educ. Hutchesons' Boys Grammar School, Glasgow; Royal Technical College, Glasgow. Apprentice Quantity Surveyor, 1947-54 (including National Service); appointments in private practice, 1954-68; joined Scottish Development Department, 1968. Recreations: hill-walking; swimming; bridge. Address: (h.) 20 Blinkbonny Crescent, Edinburgh, EH4 3NB; T.-031-332 5081.

Russell, Dennis Bertram, BArch, RIBA, RIAS, DipTP, FRTPI. Director of Architectural Services, Falkirk District Council, since 1974; b. 21.3.21, Plymouth; m., Jane; 1 s. Educ. Alloa

Academy; Glasgow School of Architecture. Depute Burgh Architect and Planning Officer, Falkirk Town Council, 1965. Recreations: cine sound photography; dance band musician; DIY; fishing; golf; garden design and layout; owner of ladies' boutique. Address: (b.) Municipal Buildings, Westbank, Falkirk; T.-Falkirk 24911, Ext. 2330.

Russell, George Stuart, BL, CA, WS, OBE. Member, Queen's Bodyguard for Scotland (Royal Company of Archers); Senior Partner, Strathern & Blair, WS, 1972-82 (Partner, 1937-82); b. 21.1.14, Edinburgh; m.; 1 s.; 3 d. Educ. Edinburgh Academy; Belhaven Hill; Harrow; Edinburgh University. CA, 1937; served Second World War, 1939-45 (Lt. Col.); then pursued a legal career; Fiscal, WS Society, 1973-79; closely involved in work of National Trust for Scotland, 1951-82; Treasurer, Iona Community, 1947-65; Vice President, UK, Abbeyfield Society, 1975-83. Recreations: fishing; walking. Address: (h.) 59 Braid Road, Edinburgh, EH10; T.-031-447 6009.

Russell, Rev. John, MA. Minister, Tillicoultry Parish Church, since 1978; b. 29.5.33, Glasgow; m., Sheila Spence; 2 s. Educ. Cathedral School, Bombay; High School of Glasgow; Glasgow University. Licensed by Glasgow Presbytery, 1957; ordained by United Church of Canada, 1959; Assistant Minister: Trinity United Church, Kitchener, Ontario, 1958-60; South Dalziel Church, Motherwell, 1960-62; Minister: Scots Church, Rotterdam, 1963-72; Southend Parish Church, Kintyre, 1972-78; Member of various General Assembly Committees, since 1972. Recreations: travel; reading. Address: The Manse, Dollar Road, Tillicoultry, Clackmannanshire, FK13 6PD; T.-0259 50340.

Russell, Michael William, MA. Executive Director, Network Scotland Ltd., since 1983; b. 9.8.53; m., Cathleen Macaskill. Educ. Marr College, Troon; Edinburgh University. Creative Producer, Church of Scotland, 1974-77; Director, Cinema Sgire, Western Isles, 1977-81; Founder and first Director, Celtic Film and Television Festival, 1980; Secretary General, Association for Film and Television in the Celtic Countries, 1981-83. Prospective Parliamentary candidate (SNP), Clydesdale, since 1985; Sub-Deacon, Episcopal Church in Scotland. Recreation: cookery. Address: (h.) 3 The Terrace, Tillietudlem, by Lesmahagow, Lanarkshire, ML11 9PN; T.-Crossford 276.

Russell, Sheriff Terence Francis, BL. Sheriff, North Strathclyde, at Kilmarnock, since 1983; b. 12.4.31, Glasgow; m., Mary Ann Kennedy; 2 d. Educ. St. Mungo's Academy, Glasgow; Glasgow University. Solicitor: Glasgow, 1955-58, Bombay High Court, 1958-63, Glasgow, 1963-81; Sheriff, North Strathclyde, at Oban and Campbeltown and Grampian, Highland and Islands, at Fort William, 1981-83. Recreations: gardening; painting. Address: (h.) 1 Sutherland Avenue, Glasgow, G41; T.-041-427 1745.

Russell, Terence Melvin, BArch, PhD, ARIBA, ARIAS. Associate Dean, Faculty of Social Sciences, Edinburgh University, since 1984; b. 2.10.39, Sheffield; m., Mary Cecilia; 1 s.; 1

d. Educ. Central Technical School, Sheffield; Sheffield University. Architect: Robert Matthew, Johnson-Marshall & Partners, Edinburgh, 1967-68, Research Unit, Scottish Special Housing Association, 1968-70; Edinburgh University: Lecturer/Senior Lecturer in Architecture, 1970-81, Faculty of Social Sciences (Schools Liaison), 1981-84. Publication: Bibliographical Index (32-volume subject guide to printed books about architecture and related fields) (Editor and Compiler). Recreations: music; photography; houses and gardens. Address: (h.) 13 Kilgraston Road, Edinburgh, EH9 2DX; T.-031-667 1590.

Russell, Professor William C., BSc, PhD. Professor of Biochemistry, St. Andrews University, since 1984; b. 9.8.30; Glasgow; m., 1, Dorothy Ada Brown (deceased); 1 s.; 1 d.; 2, Reta McDougall. Educ. Allan Glen's School, Glasgow; Glasgow University. Locke Research Fellow, Institute of Virology, Glasgow, 1959-63; Eleanor Roosevelt International Cancer Fellow, Toronto University, 1963-64; Member, MRC Scientific Staff, National Institute for Medical Research, London, 1964-84. Editor, Journal of General Virology, 1972-77; Convener, Virus Group, Society for General Microbiology, since 1984. Address: (b.) Department of Biochemistry and Microbiology, St. Andrews University, Irvine Building, North Street, St. Andrews, KY16 9AL; T.-0334 76161.

Rutherford, Jean, MA (Oxon), DipEd. Headmistress, The Park School, Glasgow, since 1974; b. 17.10.32, South Shields. Educ. South Shields High School; St. Anne's College, Oxford. Christ's Hospital, 1955-58; Selly Oak Colleges, 1958-59; Cours Secondaire Protestant Cotonou Dahomey AOF, 1959-63; Church High School, Sunderland, 1963-66; Christ's Hospital, 1966-71 (Head of Modern Languages); Deputy Head, Church High School, Sunderland, 1971-74. Member, Methodist Synod (Scotland) Committees for Education and Ministerial Candidates. Recreations: opera; reading. Address: (b.) 25 Lynedoch Street, Glasgow, G3 6EX; T.-041-332 0426.

Rutherford, Walter Angus, BA, ACP. Chairman, General Purposes Committee, Annandale and Eskdale District Council, since 1984; Chairman, Annan Fishery Board, since 1984; Vice Chairman, Dumfriesshire Education Trust, since 1984; b. 24.9.21, Newcastle-upon-Tyne; m., Phyllis; 1 step s.; 1 d. Educ. Heaton Grammar School; Goldsmiths College, London; Open University. Royal Navy; Teacher, Newcastle and Northumberland, 1945-56; Head Teacher, Roxburghshire and Dumfriesshire, 1956-82; elected, Annandale and Eskdale District Council, 1977; Reader, Church of Scotland; Chairman, Annan Community Education Project; Member, Dumfriesshire EIS Executive, 1968-82; Honorary Life Member, EIS. Recreations: gardening; reading; swimming. Address: (h.) Holmlea, Eaglesfield, Lockerbie, Dumfriesshire.

Rutherford, William Hay, MA, LLB. Advocate in Aberdeen, since 1949; Partner, Raeburn Christie & Co., since 1978; Honorary Sheriff, Grampian, Highland and Islands, since 1974; b. 9.11.16, Forres; m., Dr. Jean Aitken Steel Wilson; 1 s.; 2 d. Educ. Forres Academy;

Aberdeen University. Law Apprentice, James & George Collie, Advocate, Aberdeen, 1936-39; 51st Highland Division, Royal Signals, 1939-46 (taken prisoner, St. Valery, France, 1940; held prisoner, Stalag VIIIB, Upper Silesia, 1940-45); Legal Assistant, John Angus, Advocate, Aberdeen, 1946-61; Partner, Christie, Buthlay & Rutherford, Advocates, Aberdeen, 1962-78; Treasurer, Society of Advocates, Aberdeen, 1984-85; Session Clerk, Kirk of St. Nicholas (City Kirk of Aberdeen), since 1954; President, Royal Northern Agricultural Society, 1980. Recreations: country walking and wildlife study; organisation of equestrian events. Address: (b.) 16 Albyn Place, Aberdeen; T.-0224 640101.

Ruthven, Ian Scott, MB, ChB, FRCPEdin, FRCPGlas, DObstRCOG. Consultant Paediatrician, Ayrshire and Arran Health Board, since 1969; Postgraduate Tutor, South Ayrshire Hospitals, since 1981; b. 9.3.37, Glasgow; m., Louisa Mary Jolly; 1 s.; 2 d. Educ. High School of Glasgow; Glasgow University. Junior hospital appointments, various Glasgow hospitals and in New Jersey, USA. Chairman, Ayrshire Paediatric Division and Chairman, Ayrshire and Arran Committee for Hospital Medical Services; Member, Paediatric Committee, Royal College of Physicians and Surgeons of Glasgow. Recreations: golf; angling; hill-walking. Address: (h.) Westholme, 10 Victoria Drive, Troon, KA10 6EN; T.-0292 313006.

Ryan, James, PhL, BD. Deputy Secretary, Dundee University, since 1980; b. 2.3.31, Denny; m., Winifred Frances O'Donnell; 2 s.; 2 d. Educ. Blairs College, Aberdeen; Gregorian University, Rome. Commissioned, Argyll and Sutherland Highlanders, 1954; seconded Royal West African Frontier Force (1st Bn., Gold Coast Regiment), 1955; Teacher, 1957; HMOCS (Sierra Leone), 1958-64; Chairman, two Commissions of Enquiry, 1963; Assistant Secretary, St. Andrews University, 1964-67; Assistant Secretary, Senior Assistant Secretary, Deputy Secretary, Dundee University, 1967-85. Secretary, Abertay Rotary Club. Recreations: bowling; swimming; reading. Address: (h.) 6 Fontstane Crescent, Monifieth, Dundee, DD5 4JZ; T.-0382 532711.

Ryan, John D., BDS. Dental Surgeon; Chairman, Argyll and Clyde Health Board, since 1979; Chairman, Information and Computer Services Advisory Group, Scottish Health Services Planning Council, since 1985; b. 10.1.43, Glasgow; m., Margaret; 1 s.; 1 d. Educ. St. Ninian's High School, Kirkintilloch; Glasgow University. Member, 4th District Council, Renfrewshire, 1968-70; Member, Greenock Corporation, 1973-75; Member, Inverclyde District Council, 1974-77; joined Argyll and Clyde Health Board, 1974 (Vice Chairman, 1977-79). Recreations: golf; sailing. Address: (h.) 35 Esplanade, Greenock; T.-0475 27649.

S

St. Clair-Ford, Robin Sam. General Organiser, Scotland's Gardens Scheme, since 1982; b. 6.6.41, Fareham; m., Alison Frances; 2 s. Educ.

Nautical College, Pangbourne; Royal Military Academy, Sandhurst. Officer, KOYLI, 1961-71 (last appointment, Adjutant Light Infantry Depot, Shrewsbury); Sales Executive, Ashton Containers Ltd., 1971-76; self-employed retailer, 1976-82. Recreations: travel; golf; running a family. Address: (h.) 21 Claremont Crescent, Edinburgh, EH7 4HX; T.-031-557 3444.

Salmond, Alexander Elliot Anderson, MA (Hons). Economist; Vice-Chairman (Publicity), Scottish National Party, since 1985; b. 31.12.54, Linlithgow; m., Moira McGlashan. Educ. Linlithgow Academy; St. Andrews University. Vice-President: Federation of Student Nationalists, 1974-77, St. Andrews University SRC, 1977-78; Student Representative, St. Andrews University Senate, 1977-78; Founder Member, SNP 79 Group, 1979; Assistant Agricultural and Fisheries Economist, DAFS, 1978-80; SNP National Executive, 1981-82, 1983-85; Committee Member, Scottish Socialist Economic Review, since 1984. Recreations: golf; reading. Address: (h.) Rivaldscreen House, Linlithgow, West Lothian; T.-Linlithgow 845445.

Salmond, David, BSc, MSc. Government Statistician (Vital Statistics, General Register Office); b. 28.7.49, Edinburgh; m., Margaret; 2 s. Educ. Royal High School, Edinburgh; St. Andrews University. Lecturer in Statistics, Heriot-Watt University, 1972-75; Government Statistician: Central Services, 1975, Housing, 1978, Fisheries, 1978, Census, General Register Office, 1982, Vital Statistics, since 1983. Recreations: family; PET; survival. Address: (h.) 17 St. Catherine's Place, Edinburgh, EH9 1NU; T.-031-667 8348.

Salmond, Rev. James Sommerville, BA, BD, MTh. Minister, Holytown Parish Church, since 1979; b. 13.1.51, Broxburn; m., Catherine F. Wildy; 4 d. Educ. West Calder High School; Whitburn Academy; Leeds University; Edinburgh University. Serves on the Committees of Scottish Reformation Society, National Church Association, etc.; regular contributor to radio and TV programmes on evangelical issues. Publication: Evangelicals within the Kirk 1690-1843. Recreations: field sports; riding. Address: The Manse, Holytown, Motherwell; T.-Holytown 832622.

Salter, Bruce Lloyd. Member, Grampian Regional Council, since 1980; Director, Scottish National Orchestra Society, since 1983; Director, Voluntary Service, Aberdeen, since 1983; Member, Aberdeen Harbour Board, since 1984; b. 11.10.58, Aberdeen; m., Linda Westland. Educ. Robert Gordon's College, Aberdeen. Chairman, Aberdeen North Constituency Labour Party, 1979-81. Recreations: drawing; writing; local history; watching sport. Address: (h.) 28 Holburn Road, Aberdeen; T.-Aberdeen 571834.

Saltoun, Lady, (Flora Marjory Fraser). Chief of Clan Fraser; b. 18.10.30; m., Captain Alexander Ramsay of Mar; 3 d. Address: (h.) Cairnbulg Castle, Fraserburgh, Aberdeenshire.

Salzen, Professor Eric Arthur, BSc, PhD. Professor of Psychology, Aberdeen University, since 1973 (Head, Department of Psychology, since 1977); b. 28.4.30, London; m., Heather Ann Fairlie; 2 d. Educ. Wanstead County High School; Edinburgh University. Assistant in Zoology, Edinburgh University, 1954-55; Scientific Officer, HM Overseas Civil Service, 1955-56; Research Assistant and Lecturer in Psychology, Durham University, 1956-60; Lecturer in Zoology, Liverpool University, 1960-64; Associate Professor and Professor of Psychology, Waterloo University, Ontario, 1964-68; Senior Lecturer and Reader in Psychology, Aberdeen University, 1968-73. Recreation: travel. Address: (b.) Psychology Department, King's College, Aberdeen University, Aberdeen; T.-0224 40241.

Sandeman, Mary (Mary Gove Mackinnon). Singer; b. 10.7.47, Edinburgh; m., Dr. Angus J.A. Mackinnon; 2 s. Educ. St. Denis School, Edinburgh. Began to learn Gaelic and singing at aged 10; gained diploma in domestic science and secretarial training; worked in TV Department, Heriot-Watt University, before marrying and going to live in Isle of Harris; lived in Canada for a period; in 1981, had a "No 1" hit record in nine countries with song called Japanese Boy under the stage name of Aneka. Recreations: singing and yet more singing!; travel; walking; being entertained. Address: (h.) Iona, Doune Road, Dunblane, FK15 OAT; T.-0786 824087.

Sandeman, The Hon. Mrs (Sylvia Margaret). Member, Scottish Consumer Council; Member, Scottish Sports Council; Member, Scottish Council on Disability; b. 29.7.49, Irvine; m., Ronald L. Sandeman; 1 d. Educ. Downe House, Newbury. Recreation: sailing. Address: (h.) Oakdene, Armadale Road, Rhu, Dunbartonshire, G84 7UE; T.-0436 820867.

Sanders, Sir Robert Tait, KBE (1980), CMG (1974). Secretary to the Cabinet, Government of Fiji, 1970-79; b. 2.2.25; m.; 3 s. Educ. Dunfermline High School; Fettes College, Edinburgh; Cambridge University; London School of Economics. Served Second World War (Lt., 1st Bn., Royal Scots); joined HM Overseas Civil Service, Fiji, 1950; Fiji Independence Medal, 1970.

Sanders, Samuel Chandrarajan, MBBS, MRCP, DMJ. Consultant Physician, Geriatric Medicine, Glasgow West, since 1976; Honorary Clinical Lecturer, Geriatric Medicine, Glasgow University, since 1977; b. 1.7.32, Jaffna, Sri Lanka; m., Irene Saravanamuttu; 1 s.; 2 d. Educ. Jaffna College, Sri Lanka; Ceylon University. Resident HO, Ceylon, 1957-58; varied experience in medicine, surgery, neurosurgery, public health and forensic medicine, Sri Lanka, 1958-70; postgraduate training, forensic medicine and clinical therapeutics, Glasgow University, Guy's Hospital, London and Edinburgh Royal Infirmary, 1971-72; Registrar, then Senior Registrar, Glasgow Western District, 1973-76. Recreations: sport; reading; fishing. Address: (h.) 28 Hillfoot Drive, Bearsden, Glasgow, G61 3QF; T.-041-942 9388.

Sanderson, Rev. Alastair William Murdoch, LTh, BA. Minister, Shawlands Cross Church, since 1976; b. 27.4.42, Glasgow; m., Elizabeth T.; 3

s.; 1 d. Educ. Clydebank High School; Glasgow University; Open University. Minister, Ervie-Kirkcolm, 1971-76; former Convener, Parish Education Committee, Wigtown and Stranraer Presbytery; serves on various Committees, Glasgow Presbytery. Recreations: swimming; hill-walking. Address: 29 St. Ronans Drive, Shawlands, Glasgow, G41 3SQ; T.-041-632 9046.

Sanderson, Sir (Charles) Russell, Kt (1981). Company Director; President, Scottish Conservative and Unionist Association, 1977-79; b. 30.4.33; m.; 2 s.; 2 d. Educ. St. Mary's School, Melrose; Trinity College, Glenalmond; Scottish College of Textiles; Bradford College.

Sanderson, Eric Fenton, LLB, CA. Director, The British Linen Bank Ltd., since 1984; b. 14.10.51, Dundee; m., Patricia Ann Shaw; 3 d. Educ. Morgan Academy, Dundee; Dundee University. Qualified CA with Touche Ross & Co.; joined British Linen Bank Ltd., 1976. Recreations: gardening; photography. Address: (b.) 4 Melville Street, Edinburgh, EH3 7NZ; T.-031-226 4071.

Sanderson, Professor Jeffrey John, BSc, PhD. Professor of Theoretical Plasma Physics, St. Andrews University, since 1985 (Reader in Applied Mathematics, 1975-85); b. 25.4.37, Birmingham; m., Mirjana Adamovic; 1 s.; 1 d. Educ. George Dixon Grammar School, Birmingham; Birmingham University; Manchester University. Research Associate, Maryland University, 1961-64; Theoretical Physicist, English Electric Co., Whetstone, 1964-66; Lecturer, then Senior Lecturer in Applied Mathematics, St. Andrews University, 1966-75; Visiting Professor, Department of Physics, College of William and Mary, USA, 1976-77. Publications: Plasma Dynamics (Co-author), 1969; Laser Plasma Interactions (Joint Editor), 1979. Recreations: chess; Scottish country dancing; five-a-side football; cricket. Address: (b.) North Haugh, St. Andrews, KY16 9SS; T.-0334 76161, Ext. 8135.

Sanderson, Very Rev. Peter Oliver, BA, DipTh. Provost, St. Paul's Episcopal Cathedral, Dundee, since 1984; b. 26.1.29, South Shields; m., Doreen Gibson; 2 s.; 1 d. Educ. South Shields High School; St. Chad's College, Durham University. Assistant Curate, Houghton-Le-Spring, Durham, 1954-59; Rector, St. Thomas-Ye-Vale, Jamaica, 1959-63; Chaplain, RAF, 1963-67; Vicar, Winksley-cum-Grantley and Aldfield with Studley, Ripon, 1967-74; Vicar, St. Aidan's, Leeds, 1974-84. Address: Cathedral Rectory, 4 Richmond Terrace, Dundee, DD2 1BQ; T.-0382 68548.

Sanderson, William. Farmer; Director, Royal Highland and Agricultural Society of Scotland; Director and Chairman, Aberdeen Angus Producers (South of Scotland) Ltd.; b. 9.3.38, Lanark; m., Netta; 4 d. Educ. Dalkeith High School. Past Chairman, South Midlothian and Lothians and Peeblesshire Young Farmers Clubs; Past Chairman, Dalkeith Agricultural Society; President, Royal Caledonian Curling Club, 1984-85; Past President, Oxenfoord and Edinburgh Curling Clubs; Scottish Curling Champion, 1971

and 1978 (2nd, World Championship, 1971). Recreations: curling; exhibiting livestock. Address: (h.) Blackshiels Farm, Blackshiels, Pathhead, Midlothian; T.-Humbie 288.

Sanderson, Very Rev. William Roy, MA, DD. Minister, Church of Scotland; Extra Chaplain to The Queen in Scotland, since 1977 (Chaplain-in-Ordinary, 1965-77); b. 23.9.07, Leith; m., Muriel Easton; 3 s.; 2 d. Educ. Fettes College; Oriel College, Oxford; New College, Edinburgh. Ordained, 1933; Assistant Minister, St. Giles' Cathedral, 1932-34; Minister: St. Andrew's, Lochgelly, 1935-39, The Barony of Glasgow, 1939-63, Stenton with Whittingehame, 1963-73; Moderator, Glasgow Presbytery, 1958 and Haddington and Dunbar Presbytery, 1972-74; Moderator, General Assembly, 1967; Hon. DD (Glasgow), 1959; Chairman, Scottish Religious Advisory Committee, BBC, 1961-71; Member, Central Religious Advisory Committee, BBC and ITA, 1961-71; Governor, Fettes College, 1967-77; Honorary President, Church Service Society; President, New College Union, 1975. Recreations: reading; walking. Address: (h.) 1A York Road, North Berwick, EH39 4LS; T.-0620 2780.

Sandham, Andrew, BDS, LDSRCS, FDSRCS, DOrth. Senior Lecturer in Orthodontics, Edinburgh University, since 1982; Consultant Orthodontist (Head, Clinical Department of Orthodontics), Edinburgh Dental School, since 1982; b. 22.1.43, Mansfield, Nottinghamshire. Educ. King Edward VI School, Stourbridge; Durham University. Dentist, Norwegian Health Service, 1966-67; House Surgeon, Birmingham Dental and London Hospital, 1967-68; Registrar, Birmingham Dental Hospital, 1968-71; Lecturer in Children's Dentistry and Orthodontics, Dundee University, 1971-74; Lecturer in Orthodontics, Birmingham University, 1974-76; Consultant Orthodontist: Fife Health Board, 1976-78, Birmingham Area Health Authority, 1978-82. Examiner, Royal College of Surgeons, Edinburgh. Recreations: travel; fine art; aviation. Address: (b.) Edinburgh University Dental School, Chambers Street, Edinburgh, EH1 1JA; T.-031-225 9511.

Sandilands, Robert Ian, MA. Deputy Director and General Secretary, National Farmers' Union of Scotland, since 1978 (Assistant General Secretary, 1972-78); b. 23.9.34, Dumfries; m., Frances Margaret Elliot; 1 s.; 2 d. Educ. Langholm Academy; Dumfries Academy; Edinburgh University. Caterpillar Tractor Company Ltd., Tannochside, 1957-60; Secretary, Lanark Area Executive, NFU of Scotland, 1960-72. Recreations: golf; photography; walking. Address: (b.) 17 Grosvenor Crescent, Edinburgh, EH12 5EN; T.-031-337 4333.

Sanford, Professor Anthony John, BSc, PhD, ABPsS. Professor of Psychology, Glasgow University, since 1982 (Head, Department of Psychology, since 1983); b. 5.7.44, Birmingham; m., Valerie Ann; 1 d. Educ. Waverley Grammar School; Leeds University; Cambridge University. MRC Research Scholar, Applied Psychology Unit, Cambridge; Postdoctoral Research Fellow, then Lecturer in Psychology, Dundee University; Senior Lecturer, then Reader in Psychology, Glasgow University. Gifford Lecturer in Natural Theology, Glasgow, 1984. Publications: Understanding Written Language (Co-author); Models, Mind and Man; Cognition and Cognitive Psychology. Recreations: hill-walking; industrial archaeology; music; cooking. Address: (b.) Department of Psychology, Glasgow University, Glasgow; T.-041-339 8855.

Sangster, Rev. Roderick Gordon, BD, CPS. Minister, St. Gerardine's High Church, Lossiemouth, since 1983; b. 2.10.50, Aberdeen; m., Frances Anne Richards; 1 s.; 3 d. Educ. Aberdeen Grammar School; Aberdeen University. Joined Metropolitan Police, 1971; moved to Aberdeen City Police; left police, 1977; Assistant Minister, St. Leonard's with Cameron with Largoward, St. Andrews, 1982-83. Member, Board of World Mission and Unity, Church of Scotland; Organiser, Christian Aid, Lossiemouth. Recreations: all sports; music; reading. Address: St. Gerardine's Manse, Lossiemouth; T.-034381 3146.

Sarson, William C.T., BSc (Hons), MEd. Rector, Mintlaw Academy, since 1981; b. 23.9.38, Edinburgh; m., Lorna E. Black; 3 s. Educ. Lasswade Senior Secondary School; Edinburgh University. Production Engineer, Honeywell Controls, Newhouse; Physics Master, Edinburgh Academy; Principal Teacher of Physics and Assistant Head Teacher, Liberton High School; Depute Rector, Douglas Ewart High School, Newton Stewart. Recreations: swimming; hillwalking; computing. Address: (b.) Station Road, Mintlaw, Peterhead, AB4 8FN; T.-07712 2994.

Saunders, David Stanley, BSc, PhD. Reader in Zoology, Edinburgh University, since 1974; b. 12.3.35, Pinner; m., Jean Margaret Comrie Doughty; 3 s. Educ. Pinner County Grammar School; King's College, London; London School of Hygiene and Tropical Medicine. Joined academic staff, Zoology Department, Edinburgh, 1958; Visiting Professor: Stanford University, California, 1971-72, North Carolina University, 1983. Publications: Insect Clocks; Introduction to Biological Rhythms. Recreations: cycling; gardening; photography. Address: (b.) Department of Zoology, West Mains Road, Edinburgh, EH9 3JT; T.-031-667 1081.

Saunders, Francis William, MBE, ERD, JP, CEng, MICE, MCIOB. Member, Central Regional Council; b. 2.7.06, Liverpool; m., Mary Winifred Service. Educ. Glasgow Academy; Royal Technical College, Glasgow. Civil Engineer, private and public appointments, 1923-39; commissioned, Royal Engineers Regular Army Reserve, 1936; Army service, BEF (France), MEF (Western Desert, Palestine, Transjordan), CMF (Italy, Greece), 1939-47; Regular Army Reserve (rank of Lt.-Col.), 1947-61; Civil Engineer, public service, 1947-49; travelled privately in Antipodes, 1949-50; private practice as Civil Engineer, 1950-85. Former Member, Stirling Town Council; President, Glasgow Branch, Royal Engineers Association. Recreations: travel; domestic life. Address: (h.) 1 Royal Gardens, Stirling, FK8 2RJ; T.-Stirling 73975.

Saunders, James, BSc, FRSC, CChem. Director, International Forum, Scottish Council (Development and Industry), since 1969; b. 12.10.25, Edinburgh; m., Agnes Dorothy Hipkins (deceased); 1 s.; 1 d. Educ. Boroughmuir Secondary School; Edinburgh University. Chief Chemist, W. & M. Duncan Ltd., 1946-58; Research Director, Cerebos Ltd., 1958-69. Member, Food Additives and Contaminants Committee, 1970-76. Recreation: golf. Address: (h.) 68 Pentland View, Edinburgh, EH10 6PS; T.-031-445 1578.

Savage, Rev. Gordon Matthew Alexander, MA, BD. Minister, Maxwelltown West, Dumfries, since 1984; b. 25.8.51, Old Kilpatrick; m., Mairi Janet MacKenzie. Educ. Glasgow Academy; Edinburgh University. Assistant Minister: Dyce Parish Church, 1975-76, Dunblane Cathedral, 1976-77; Minister: Almondbank, Tibbermore and Logiealmond, 1977-84. Junior Chaplain to Moderator, General Assembly, 1982; Junior Clerk, Perth Presbytery, 1980-83. Recreations: railways; model railways; music. Address: Maxwelltown West Manse, 11 Laurieknowe, Dumfries, DG2 7AH; T.-0387 52929.

Savidge, Malcolm Kemp, JP, MA. Vice-Chairman, Labour Group, Aberdeen City Council, since 1980 (Convener of Libraries, since 1984); Teacher of Mathematics, Kincorth Academy, Aberdeen, since 1973; b. 9.5.46, Redhill, Surrey. Educ. Wallington County Grammar School, Surrey; Aberdeen University; Aberdeen College of Education. Computer and Production Control Assistant, Bryans' Electronic Instruments Ltd., Mitcham, 1970-71; Mathematics Teacher: Greenwood Dale School, Nottingham, 1971, Peterhead Academy, 1972-73. Governor, Aberdeen College of Education, since 1980; Governor, Robert Gordon's Institute of Technology, since 1981; Director, Scottish National Orchestra, since 1985; Educational Institute of Scotland: Aberdeen President, 1977-79, Grampian Regional Secretary, 1978-81, Grampian President, 1983-84, Member, National Council, since 1980, Member, National Executive, 1982-84; Treasurer, Aberdeen City Labour Party, 1981-84. Recreations: exploring life; spectator sport; crosswords and puzzles; reading; real ale; the arts. Address: (h.) 13F Belmont Road, Aberdeen, AB2 3SR; T.-0224 632369.

Savin, John Andrew, MA, MD (Cantab), FRCP, FRCPEdin, DIH. Consultant Dermatologist, Edinburgh Royal Infirmary, since 1971; Senior Lecturer, Dermatology Department, Edinburgh University, since 1971; b. 10.1.35, London; m., Patricia Margaret Steel; 2 s.; 2 d. Educ. Epsom College; Trinity Hall, Cambridge; St. Thomas's Hospital, London. Royal Naval Medical Service, 1960-64; Registrar to Skin Department, St. George's Hospital, London; Senior Registrar, St. John's Hospital for Diseases of the Skin, and St. Thomas's Hospital, London; Co-Editor, Recent Advances in Dermatology; Associate Editor, British Journal of Dermatology; former Secretary, Scottish Dermatological Society. Recreations: golf; literature. Address: (h.) 86 Murrayfield Gardens, Edinburgh; T.-031-337 7768.

Scaife, Professor John Graham, PhD. Professor of Molecular Parasitology, Edinburgh University, since 1984; b. 23.9.34, Leeds; 2 d. Educ. Leeds Modern School; University College, London. Scientific staff, MRC Microbial Genetics Unit, 1961-74; Senior Lecturer, then Reader, Edinburgh University, 1974-84. Member, MRC Cell Board, 1981-85 (Chairman, Grants Committee, 1982-85). Recreation: gardening. Address: (b.) Department of Molecular Biology, King's Buildings, Mayfield Road, Edinburgh, EH9 3JR; T.-031-667 1081, Ext. 2889.

Schaffer, Professor Heinz Rudolph, BA, PhD, FBPsS. Professor of Psychology, Strathclyde University, since 1970; b. 21.7.26, Berlin; m., Evelyn Blanche; 1 s.; 1 d. Educ. Ackworth School, Yorkshire; Birkbeck College, London. Research Psychologist, Tavistock Clinic, London, 1951-55; Principal Psychologist, Royal Hospital for Sick Children, Glasgow, 1955-63; Lecturer, then Senior Lecturer and Reader, Strathclyde University, 1964-70; Nuffield Fellowship, North Carolina University, 1971; Van Leer Fellowship, Jerusalem, 1976. Council Member, Social Science Research Council, 1976-78; President, Section J, British Association for the Advancement of Science, 1984-85. Recreations: walking; travelling. Address: (h.) 89 Roman Court, Bearsden, Glasgow, G61 2NW; T.-041-942 0197.

Schuster, Ida. Actress; Member, Drama Committee, Scottish Arts Council, since 1984; b. Glasgow; m., Dr. Allan Berkeley; 2 s. Founder Member, Glasgow Jewish Institute Players; appeared in leading role in Glasgow Unity Theatre's first production (Awake and Sing), 1941; played Leah in The Dybbuk, Jewish Arts Festival, 1951; Member, Pitlochry Festival Theatre Company, 1974; directed and acted for Glasgow University Arts Theatre; has appeared in almost every Scottish theatre; one of the original cast of John Byrne's The Slab Boys; three Edinburgh Festivals; recent appearances at Glasgow Citizens' Theatre. Recreations: gardening; golf; swimming; reading. Address: (h.) 1 Arran Drive, Giffnock, Glasgow, G46 7NL; T.-041-638 6789.

Schwarz, J.C. Peter, MA, BSc, PhD. Vice-Dean, Faculty of Science, Edinburgh University, since 1972 (Senior Lecturer in Chemistry, since 1970); b. 6.5.27, Bremen; m., Catherine Collocott; 3 d. Educ. St. Andrew's College, Dublin; Trinity College, Dublin. Assistant Lecturer in Chemistry, TCD, 1950-53; ICI Fellow, Edinburgh University, 1953-56; Lecturer in Chemistry: TCD, 1956-57, Edinburgh University, 1957-70. Recreations: DIY; computing. Address: (b.) Faculty of Science Office, West Mains Road, Edinburgh, EH9 3JY; T.-031-667 1081.

Scothorne, Professor Raymond John, BSc, MD, FRSE, FRCSG. Regius Professor of Anatomy, Glasgow University, since 1973; b. 13.6.20, Nottingham; m., Audrey Gillott; 1 s.; 2 d. Educ. Royal Grammar School, Newcastle-upon-Tyne; Leeds University; Chicago University. Lecturer in Anatomy, Leeds University, 1944-50; Senior Lecturer, Glasgow University, 1950-60; Professor of Anatomy, Newcastle-upon-Tyne University, 1960-73. Anatomical Society of Gt. Britain and Ireland: Honorary Secretary, 1967-71, President, 1971-73. Recreations: the countryside; labrador dogs. Address: (b.) Department of Anatomy, Glasgow University, Glasgow; T.-041-339 8855.

Scott, Alan Bridgwood, MA. Assistant Secretary, Countryside, Environment and Rural Division, Scottish Development Department, since 1985 (Assistant Secretary, Department of Agriculture and Fisheries for Scotland, 1978-85); b. 18.8.43, Wishaw; m., Frances Elizabeth; 2 d. Educ. Wishaw High School; Glasgow University. Department of Agriculture and Fisheries for Scotland, 1965-68; Private Secretary to Joint Parliamentary Under Secretary of State, 1968-70; DAFS (Fisheries), 1970-72; Diplomatic Service (Office of the UK Permanent Representative to the European Communities, Brussels), 1972-76; DAFS (Livestock Products), since 1976. Address: (b.) New St. Andrew's House, Edinburgh, EH1 3SK.

Scott, Alexander. Writer; b. 1920, Aberdeen; m.; 2 s. Educ. Aberdeen Academy; Aberdeen University. Royal Artillery, 1941-43 (commissioned, 1943); Gordon Highlanders, 1943 (wounded, Normandy, 1944; MC, 1945). Lecturer, then Senior Lecturer in Scottish Literature, Glasgow University; appointed Head, Department of Scottish Literature, 1971; Co-Editor, Scots Review, 1950-51; Editor, Saltire Review, 1954-57; Secretary, Universities Committee on Scottish Literature, 1968; President, Association for Scottish Literary Studies, 1976; author of (verse and drama): Prometheus 48, The Latest in Elegies, Selected Poems, Untrue Thomas, Mouth Music, Cantrips, Greek Fire, Double Agent, Selected Poems 1943-74, A Double Scotch with Edwin Morgan; (prose) Still Life: William Soutar, The MacDiarmid Makars, Modern Scottish Literature 1920-1975; (plays) Right Royal, Citizens', Glasgow, 1954, Tam O'Shanter's Tryst, Citizens', Glasgow, 1955, Truth to Tell, Citizens', Glasgow, 1958.

Scott, Bill, RSA. Sculptor; Senior Lecturer, Edinburgh College of Art, since 1976 (Lecturer, since 1962); b. 16.8.35, Moniaive; m., Phyllis Owen Scott; 1 s.; 2 d. Educ. Dumfries Academy; Edinburgh College of Art. One-man exhibitions: Compass Gallery, 1972, Stirling Gallery, 1974, New 57 Gallery, 1979, Lamp of Lothian, 1980, Art Space Gallery, 1980; numerous group exhibitions. Address: (h.) 61 Main Street, Roslin, Midlothian, EH25 9NF; T.-031-440 2544.

Scott, Donald Bruce, MD, FRCPEdin, FFARCS. Consultant Anaesthetist, Edinburgh Royal Infirmary, since 1959; Member, Board, Faculty of Anaesthetists, Royal College of Surgeons of England, since 1981; President, European Society of Regional Anaesthesians, since 1982; b. 16.12.25, Sydney; m., Joan Isobel; 4 s.; 2 d. Educ. Hove Grammar School; Edinburgh University. Colonial Medical Service, Ghana, four years; training in anaesthesia, Edinburgh, six years; Consultant, NHS, Edinburgh Royal Infirmary, since 1959. Past President, Scottish Society of Anaesthetists; Past President, Obstetric Anaesthetists Association. Publication: Handbook of Epidural Anaesthesia (Co-author). Recreations: golf; food and wine. Address: (h.) 1 Zetland Place, Edinburgh, EH5 3HU; T.-032-552 3317.

Scott, Eoin Flett. Member, Orkney Islands Council (Chairman, Development, Planning & Control Committee, since 1984); Farmer; b. 12.6.42, Orkney. Educ. Stromness Academy. Commissioner of Inland Revenue; Member, Highland TA Volunteer Reserve Association; Governor, Aberdeen College of Education; Member, BBC General Advisory Council; Session Clerk, Firth Church, since 1978. Recreations: archaeology; geology; numismatics. Address: (h.) Redland, Firth, Orkney, KW17 2EU; T.-0856 76 214.

Scott, George Gordon. Solicitor Consultant; Honorary Sheriff, Dumfries, since 1971; b. 29.5.12, Dumfries; m., Constance Elizabeth Offord; 2 d. Educ. Dumfries Academy; Glasgow University. Solicitor in private practice, 1936-80. Has held various Church offices and secretaryships of employers' trade associations. Recreations: gardening; reading. Address: (h.) 166 Annan Road, Dumfries, DG1 3HA; T.-Dumfries 54961.

Scott, Rev. Gideon George, MA, BD, ThM. Minister, St. David's North, Dundee, since 1973; b. 6.8.35, Alexandria; m., Margaret Anne Allan; 2 s. Educ. Dumbarton Academy; Glasgow University; Princeton Theological Seminary. Assistant: St. Stephen's Blythswood, Glasgow, 1961, West Second-Avenue Presbyterian Church, Columbus, Ohio, 1962; Locum Preacher, Rosneath, St. Modan's, 1962; Teacher of Religious Education, Vale of Leven Academy, 1962; Minister, Wester Coates, Edinburgh, 1963-73; Extra-Mural Lecturer in Religion, Dundee University, 1978-79 - 1982-83. Secretary, Scottish Church Theology Society, 1966-71; Regional Tutor in Divinity and Practical Theology to Candidates for the Auxiliary Ministry of the Church of Scotland, since 1983. Recreations: listening to classical music; reading. Address: The Manse of St. David's North, 38 Albany Terrace, Dundee; T.-0382 21394.

Scott, Gordon Ramsay, BSc, MS, PhD, MRCVS. Reader in Tropical Animal Health, Edinburgh University, since 1978; Consultant Virologist, Food and Agricultural Organisation, since 1963; b. 6.7.23, Arbroath; m., Joan Henderson Walker; 1 s.; 2 d. Educ. Arbroath High School; Royal (Dick) Veterinary College, Edinburgh; Wisconsin University. Private practice, 1946-49; Virologist, Veterinary Laboratory, Kabete, Kenya, 1950-52 (Head, Virus Section, 1952-56); Head, Division of Virus Diseases, East African Veterinary Research Organisation, 1956-62; Acting Director, EAVRO, Kenya, 1959, 1962; Lecturer, then Senior Lecturer, Tropical Veterinary Medicine, Edinburgh University, 1963-78. Recreations: biometry; growing vegetables; travel. Address: (h.) 22 Frogston Road West, Edinburgh, EH10 7AR; T.-031-445 1658.

Scott, Rev. Ian Gray, BSc, BD, STM. Minister, Greenbank Parish Church, Edinburgh, since 1983; b. 31.5.41, Kirkcaldy; m., Alexandrina Angus; 1 d. Educ. Kirkcaldy High School; St. Andrews University; Union Theological Seminary, New York. Assistant Minister, St. Mungo's, Alloa, 1965-66; Minister: Holy Trinity Church, Bridge of Allan, 1966-76, Holburn Central, Aberdeen, 1976-83; Convener, Panel

on Doctrine, General Assembly, 1978-82; part-time Lecturer, Faculty of Divinity, Aberdeen University, 1977-79; founder Member, Ministry and Psychotherapy Group; Trustee, Harry Guntrip Memorial Trust. Past President, Stirling Bn., Boys' Brigade. Recreations: reading; photography; caravanning; golf (so called). Address: 112 Greenbank Crescent, Edinburgh, EH10 5SZ; T.-031-447 4032.

Scott, James Archibald, LVO, MA (Hons). Secretary, Scottish Education Department, since 1984; b. 5.3.32, Jaffa, Palestine; m., Dr. Elizabeth A.J. Buchan-Hepburn; 3 s.; 1 d. Educ. Dollar Academy; St. Andrews University; Queen's University, Ontario. RAF Aircrew, 1954-56; joined Commonwealth Relations Office, 1956; First Secretary, UK High Commission, New Delhi, 1958-62 and UK Mission to UN, New York, 1962-65; transferred to Scottish Office, 1965; Private Secretary to Secretary of State for Scotland, 1969-71; Assistant Secretary, Scottish Development Department, 1971; Under-Secretary, Industry Department for Scotland, 1976-84. Recreations: music; golf. Address: (b.) New St. Andrew's House, Edinburgh, EH1 3SY; T.-031-556 8400.

Scott, Rev. James Finlay. Minister, Dyce Parish Church, since 1966; b. 12.11.31, Strachur, Argyll; m., Isobel Macleod Mackie; 1 s.; 1 d. Educ. Keil School, Dumbarton; Aberdeen University; Christ's College, Aberdeen. Assistant Minister, St. Giles, Elgin, 1957-59; Minister, Rhynie with Clatt, 1959-66. Address: 144 Victoria Street, Dyce, Aberdeen, AB2 0BE; T.-0224 722380.

Scott, James Henry Shielswood, MB, ChB, FRCS. Senior Orthopaedic Surgeon, Lothian Health Board, since 1982; b. 13.10.21, Meerut, India; m., Rhoda Margaret Murray; 2 s.; 2 d. Educ. Glasgow Academy; Trinity College, Glenalmond; Edinburgh University. Honorary Consultant Orthopaedic Surgeon, Edinburgh University, 1960-61. Recreations: golf; malt whisky. Address: (h.) 39 Dick Place, Edinburgh, EH9 2JA; T.-031-667 1637.

Scott, John, DL, JP. Member, Orkney Islands Council, since 1962; Director, Orkney Islands Shipping Company, since 1962; b. 3.9.21, Papa Stronsay; m., Margaret Ann Pottinger; 4 d. Educ. Stromness Academy. Home Guard; Auxiliary in Charge, HM Coastguard, Westray; Army Cadet Force (Honorary Captain, retired); President, Local Committee, National Farmers Union; Secretary, Westray Baptist Church, since 1943. Recreations: flying (PPL); sailing; golf; badminton. Address: (h.) Skaill, Westray, Orkney, KW17 2DN; T.-085 77 226.

Scott, John, CEng, MICE. Member, Lothian Regional Council, since 1984; b. 28.6.28, Glasgow; m., Christine Banks McLachlan; 2 s.; 1 d. Educ. Whitehill School, Glasgow; Loughborough College. Commissioned, Royal Engineers, 1949; service in Middle East, Korea, Malaysia, Germany, Norway; retired as Lt.-Col., 1978. Recreations: DIY; photography. Address: (h.) 52 Liberton Drive, Edinburgh, EH16 6NN; T.-031-664 8685.

Scott, Rev. John, LTh. Minister, St. Fillan's Church, Aberdour, since 1975; b. 21.6.31, Edinburgh; m., Catherine McLurg; 2 s.; 1 d. Educ. Royal High School, Edinburgh; Edinburgh University. Printing trade, 1947-63; Assistant Minister, Paisley Abbey, 1968-70; Minister, Viewfield Church, Stirling, 1970-75. Chairman, Aberdour Community Council, since 1984. Recreations: golf; reading. Address: The Manse, Aberdour, Fife; T.-Aberdour 860349.

Scott, John Andrew Ross, JP. Member, Borders Regional Council, since 1985; Journalist; b. 6.5.51, Hawick; m., Christine Evans Collie; 2 s. Educ. Hawick High School. Worked on father's farm, 1966-74; Journalist, Hawick News, 1977-78, Tweeddale Press Group, since 1978; first SDP Member, Roxburgh District Council (1980-85) and Borders Regional Council; Chairman, Roxburgh District Licensing Board, 1984-85; first Chairman, Borders Area Party, SDP, 1981-84; represents Borders on Council for Social Democracy, since 1982. Recreations: broadcasting for Radio Tweed; writing; music; travel; tennis. Address: (h.) 8 Union Street, Hawick, Roxburghshire; T.-0450 76324.

Scott, Joseph McAuley, DPA. Member, Parole Board for Scotland, since 1982; District Social Manager, Social Work Department, Strathclyde Regional Council, 1975-85; b. 3.3.25, Motherwell; m., Margaret Connor; 2 s.; 2 d. Educ. Our Lady's High School, Motherwell; Glasgow University. Royal Navy, 1943-46; Probation Officer, then Senior Probation Officer, then Acting Principal Probation Officer, Lanarkshire, 1953-69; Depute Director of Social Work, Motherwell and Wishaw, 1969; Member, Local Review Committee, Dumfries Young Offenders Institution, 1972-75; Co-Chairman, Strathclyde Region's Officer Member Group on Services for Offender, 1977-78; Member, National Council, Scottish Association for Care and Resettlement of Offenders (Chairman, Strathclyde Workshop-Sub Group, SACRO). Recreations: golf; swimming; choral society; Speakers' Club (Past President). Address: (h.) Holmlea, Cleland Road, Wishaw, Lanarkshire.

Scott, J. Stewart, MB, ChB, FFR, FRCR, DMRT. Director, Tayside Area Radiotherapy and Oncology Service, since 1977; Head, Department of Radiotherapy and Oncology, Dundee University, since 1977; b. 12.2.27, Glasgow; m., Agnes Roberta Dunsmuir; 1 s.; 3 d. Educ. Hillhead High School, Glasgow; Glasgow University. Consultant Radiotherapist and Oncologist, Western Infirmary, Glasgow, 1963-75, Ninewells Hospital, Dundee, 1975-77. President, Scottish Radiological Society, 1983-84; Chairman, East of Scotland and Newcastle Lymphoma Group, since 1983. Recreations: golf; photography. Address: (b.) Department of Radiotherapy and Oncology, Ninewells Hospital, Dundee; T.-0382 60111.

Scott, Paul Henderson, CMG, MA. Convener, Advisory Council for the Arts in Scotland, since 1981; Vice-Chairman, Saltire Society, since 1980; b. 7.11.20, Edinburgh; m., B.C. Sharpe; 1 s.; 1 d. Educ. Royal High School, Edinburgh; Edinburgh University. HM Forces, 1941-47 (Major, RA); HM Diplomatic Service in Foreign Office, Warsaw, La Paz, Havana, Montreal, Vienna, Milan, 1947-80. Publications: 1707, The Union of Scotland and England, 1979; Walter Scott and Scotland, 1981; John Galt, 1985; The Age of MacDiarmid (Co-Editor), 1980; In Bed with an Elephant: The Scottish Experience, 1985. Recreation: skiing. Address: (h.) 33 Drumsheugh Gardens, Edinburgh, EH3 7RN; T.-031-225 1038.

Scott, Sheriff Richard John Dinwoodie, MA, LLB. Sheriff of Grampian, Highland and Islands, at Aberdeen and Stonehaven, since 1977; Honorary Reader, Aberdeen University, since 1980; b. 28.5.39, Manchester; m., Josephine Moretta Blake; 2 d. Educ. Edinburgh Academy; Edinburgh University. Lektor, Folkuniversitet of Sweden, 1960-61; admitted to Faculty of Advocates, 1965; Standing Junior Counsel, Ministry of Defence (Air), 1969; Parliamentary candidate, 1974. Address: (b.) Sheriff's Chambers, Sheriff Court House, Aberdeen, AB9 1AP; T.-Aberdeen 648316.

Scott, Robert Ian, MA, BLitt, MLitt, DipEd. Rector, Banff Academy, since 1965; b. 30.9.25, Inverness; m., Catherine Jane Johnstone Ralston; 1 s.; 2 d. Educ. Inverness Royal Academy; Queen's Park Senior Secondary School, Glasgow; Glasgow University. Teacher of English, Glasgow, 1953-57; Principal Teacher of English, Nicolson Institute, Stornoway, 1957-61; Deputy Rector, Aberdeen Academy, 1962-65. Past President, Banff Rotary Club. Publication: Poetry Anthology From Barbour to Burns (Editor), 1960. Recreations: tennis; badminton; reading. Address: (b.) Banff Academy, Banff, AB4 1BY; T.-Banff 2591.

Scott, Robina Mary, RGN, SCM. Member, Central Regional Council, since 1974; Member, Forth Valley Health Board, since 1983; b. 7.2.28, Braemar; m., John S. Scott. Educ. Ballater Secondary School; College of Nursing, Aberdeen. Member, Alva Town Council and Clackmannan County Council, 1968-74; awarded Silver Jubilee Medal, 1977. Recreations: walking; reading; gardening. Address: (h.) Kinbrae, 4 Myretoungate, Alva, Clackmannanshire; T.-Alva 60343.

Scott, Roy, JP, MB, ChB, MD, FRCSGlas, FRCSEdin. Consultant Urologist, Glasgow Royal Infirmary; Honorary Clinical Lecturer, Glasgow University; b. 17.7.35, Wishaw; m., Janette J.C. Dalgleish; 1 s.; 2 d. Educ. Wishaw High School; Glasgow University. RAMC, Kenya, Aden, UK, 1958-61; Assistant Lecturer, Glasgow University, 1961-62; Stobhill Hospital, Glasgow, 1963-67; Glasgow Royal Infirmary, since 1967; Council Member, British Association of Urological Surgeons, since 1983; Member, Justices Association for Scotland; Council Member, St. Andrew's Ambulance Association. Publications: Urology Illustrated (Co-author); Modern Practical Nursing (Urology) (Co-author); History of Glasgow Kilwinning No. 4. Recreations: fishing; book collecting; history of Glasgow; gardening; lecturing; Robert Burns; music. Address: (h.) Garrion, 27 Forest View, Kildrum, Cumbernauld; T.-Cumbernauld 22683.

Scott, Rev. Thomas Hardy, BPhil, DPS. Administrator, Strathcarron Hospice, Denny, since 1979; Executive Officer for Scotland and Education Secretary for UK, Macmillan Cancer Relief Fund, since 1984; b. 11.5.32, Dundee; m., Dorothy K. Shields; 2 s.; 2 d. Educ. Sedbergh School; Edinburgh University; St. Andrews University. Assistant Minister, St. Giles Cathedral, Edinburgh, 1959-61; Minister, Bonnybridge Parish Church, 1961-66; Chaplain, Heriot-Watt University, 1966-79. Chairman, Edinburgh Council of Social Service, 1974-77; Chairman, Joint Committee on Alcohol Related Problems, Lothian Health Board and Social Work Department, 1978-81. Recreation: fishing. Address: (b.) Strathcarron Hospice, Denny, Stirlingshire; T.-0324 826222.

Scott, Tom, MA, PhD. Writer; b. 6.6.18, Glasgow; m., Margaret Heather Fretwell; 1 s.; 2 d. Educ. Hyndland School, Glasgow; Madras College, St. Andrews; Edinburgh University. Began life in building trade, St. Andrews, 1934; War Service (Nigeria, 1941-43); after few jobs in bookshops in London, freelance Writer until belated University studies via Newbattle Abbey College (under Edwin Muir); first published poem in Poetry London, 1940; first volumes, Seeven Poems O Maister Francis Villon, An Ode Til New Jerusalem, The Ship and Ither Poems; then At the Shrine O The Unkent Sodger, Brand the Builder, The Tree, etc.; edited Oxford Book of Scottish Verse (with John MacQueen), Some Late Medieval Scottish Poets, the Penguin Book of Scottish Verse; for children, Tales of King Robert the Bruce and Tales of Sir William Wallace; criticism: Dunbar, An Exposition of the Poems. Recreations: game fishing; ornithology; music. Address: (h.) 3 Duddingston Park, Edinburgh.

Scott, Walter, CBE, DA, RIBA, FRIAS. Architect, Scott & McIntosh, Edinburgh, since 1964, and Galashiels, since 1975; Member, Borders Health Board, since 1983; b. 26.1.26, Musselburgh; m., Irene Duncan; 1 s.; 2 d. Educ. Musselburgh Grammar School; Edinburgh College of Art; Heriot-Watt University. Royal Engineers, 1944-47 (Captain); joined Architect's Department, South Eastern Regional Hospital Board, 1957; founded Scott & McIntosh, 1964; Member, RIAS Council, 1957-60; President, Scottish Conservation Association, 1970-71; President, Old Musselburgh Club, 1972. Recreations: gardening; curling. Address: (h.) The Glebe, Legerwood, Earlston, Berwickshire; T.-089684 243.

Scott, Professor William, BSc (Hons), CEng, FIMechE, MIProdE, MBIM. Course Supervisor, Manufacturing Sciences and Engineering, Strathclyde University, since 1978 (Manager, Engineering Applications Centre, since 1982); b. 6.11.26, Giffnock; m., Carol Claire Lewin; 1 s.; 1 d. Educ. High School of Glasgow; Glasgow University. Metropolitan Vickers Electrical Co. Ltd., 1947-51; Compressor Division, James Howden & Co. Ltd., 1951-61; Associated Industrial Consultants Ltd., 1961-63; Department of Production Engineering, 1963-78. Recreation:

work. Address: (b.) Room M111, James Weir Building, Strathclyde University, 75 Montrose Street, Glasgow, G1 1XJ; T.-041-552 4400, EXt. 2047.

Scott, Captain William Patrick, OBE, TD, DL. Honorary Sheriff, Grampian, Highland and Islands; Member, Queen's Bodyguard for Scotland (Royal Company of Archers); b. 1.12.10, Lanark; m., Philippa Greig (deceased); 1 s.; 3 d. Educ. Sedbergh. Former Director, Highland Distilleries Co. Ltd.; former Member, Highland TA & VR Association; former County Commissioner, Orkney Boy Scouts; Past Chairman, Orkney LEC; Past Chairman, Orkney RSPB; served with Lanarkshire Yeomanry and on Staff, 206 Infantry Brigade and 184 Infantry Brigade. Recreations: golf; shooting; fishing; gardening. Address: (h.) Kierfiold House, Sandwick, Stromness, Orkney; T.-Sandwick 503.

Scott Brown, Ronald, MA, LLB. Director, Aberdeen Trust PLC, since 1976; Director, Aberdeen Fund Managers Ltd., since 1983; Director, Scottish Unit Managers Ltd., since 1985; b. 14.2.37, Madras; m., Jean Leslie Booth; 3 s. Educ. Aberdeen Grammar School; Aberdeen University. Qualified Solicitor, 1961; Assistant, then Partner, Brander & Cruickshank, Advocates, 1961-83. Member, Board of Governors, Aberdeen College of Education, since 1983. Address: (b.) 9 Queen's Terrace, Aberdeen, AB1 1XL; T.-0224 631999.

Scott-Dempster, Ronald, BL, WS. Writer to the Signet (Consultant), since 1974; Honorary Sheriff, Perthshire, since 1976; b. 8.5.98, Perth; m., Ann Reid; 1 s.; 2 d. Educ. Perth Academy; Edinburgh University. Lt., Royal Field Artillery, 1916-19; wounded, 1917; Partner, Robertson Dempster & Co., WS, 1924-74; Chairman, Court of Referees, 1933-38; Registrar, Diocese of St. Andrews, 1928-74; Treasurer, Perthshire Nursing Federation, 1933-58; Treasurer, Perth Royal Infirmary, 1938-49; Secretary, Territorial Army Association, Perthshire, 1939-49; Lt.-Col., Army Welfare, Perthshire, 1943-50; Director, General Accident Assurance Co., 1948-74, Yorkshire General Life Assurance, 1950-62, English Insurance Co., 1962-77, Grampian Properties Ltd., 1967-77; Consultant, Condie Mackenzie & Co., WS, 1974-85; Deer Consultant, 1977-82; Convener, Executive Council, Scottish Episcopal Church, 1959-67 (Trustee, 1960-85); Vice-Chairman, Perth Branch, Royal British Legion since formation; Life Member, Gaelic Society of Perth and Royal Scottish Pipers Society. Recreations: golf; deer stalking; gardening; piping; hill-walking. Address: (h.) Tayhill, Dunkeld, Perthshire; T.-03502 277.

Scrimgeour, John Beocher, MB, ChB, DObst, RCOG, FRCOG. Consultant Obstetrician and Gynaecologist, since 1972; Honorary Senior Lecturer in Obstetrics and Gynaecology, Edinburgh University, since 1972; b. 22.1.39, Elgin; b. Joyce Morrin; 1 s.; 1 d. Educ. Hawick High School; Edinburgh University. General Practitioner, Edinburgh, 1963-65; Senior House Officer: Stirling Royal Infirmary, 1965, and Registrar, Eastern General Hospital, Edinburgh, 1966-69;

Senior Registrar, Edinburgh Royal Infirmary, 1970-72; Senior Secretary, Edinburgh Obstetrical Society, 1980-85; Chairman, Area Division of Obstetrics and Gynaecology, since 1984. Publication: Towards the Prevention of Fetal Malformation, 1978. Recreations: gardening; golf; tennis. Address: (h.) 4 Kinellan Road, Edinburgh, EH12 6ES; T.-031-337 6027.

Seafield, 13th Earl of, (Ian Derek Francis Ogilvie-Grant), b. 20.3.39; m., 1, Mary Dawn Mackenzie Illingworth (m. diss.); 2 s.; 2, Leila Refaat. Educ. Eton. Address: (h.) Old Cullen, Cullen, Banffshire.

Seagrave, David Robert, LLB (Hons), SSC, NP. Solicitor and Notary Public; Council Member, Law Society of Scotland, since 1981; b. 29.4.43, Berwick-on-Tweed; m., Fiona Lesley Thomson; 1 s.; 1 d. Educ. Newcastle-upon-Tyne; Glasgow University. Banking, insurance, police; Partner, Walker & Sharpe, Solicitors, Dumfries; Secretary, Enterprise Trust for Nithsdale, Annandale/Eskdale and the Stewartry. Recreations: choral singing; shooting; fishing; golf. Address: (h.) Amulree, Islesteps, Dumfries; T.-Dumfries 64523.

Sealey, Barry Edward, BA (Hons) (Cantab), CBIM. Managing Director, Christian Salvesen PLC, since 1981; b. 3.2.36, Bristol; m., Helen Martyn; 1 s.; 1 d. Educ. Dursley Grammar School; St. John's College, Cambridge. Joined Christian Salvesen, 1958, as Trainee; joined Board, 1969; Director, Scottish Equitable Life Assurance Society; Director, Scottish American Investment Trust; Director, Scottish Transport Group; Council Member and Executive Committee, The Industrial Society; Member of the High Constabulary, Port of Leith. Address: (b.) 50 East Fettes Avenue, Edinburgh, EH1 1EQ; T.-031-552 7101.

Searl, John Walter, BSc, PhD. Director, Edinburgh Centre for Mathematical Education, Edinburgh University, since 1984; b. 12.6.37, London; m., Margaret Alison Lewis; 2 s.; 2 d. Educ. Highbury Grove School, London; Southampton University; Edinburgh University. Assistant Lecturer, Northampton College of Advanced Technology, 1958; Lecturer in Mathematics, Edinburgh University, 1963. Publications: An Introduction to the Solution and Application of Differential Equations, 1966; 'O' Mathematics (Co-author), 1983. Recreations: hill-walking; gardening. Address: (h.) 57 Bonaly Crescent, Edinburgh; T.-031-441 5791.

Seaton, Robert, MA, LLB. Secretary of the University, Dundee University, since 1973; b. 2.8.37, Clarkston, Renfrewshire; m., Jennifer Graham Jack; 2 s.; 2 d. Educ. Eastwood Secondary School; Glasgow University; Balliol College, Oxford; Edinburgh University. Administrative Assistant, then Senior Administrative Officer, then Assistant Secretary, Edinburgh University, 1962-73. Director, Dundee Repertory Theatre Ltd., since 1980; Director, TAYTEC Limited, since 1985. Recreations: tennis; squash. Address: (h.) Dunarn, 29 South Street, Newtyle, Angus, PH12 8UQ; T.-Newtyle 330.

Sellar, Allan George, OStJ, JP. Provost of Inverness, since 1980; Chairman, Inverness Harbour Trust, since 1980; Chairman, Governors, Eden Court Theatre, since 1980; Chairman, Culloden Committee, National Trust for Scotland, since 1982; b. 10.10.24, Dufftown; m., Margaret Brenda Fraser; 2 s.; 2 d. Educ. Inverness Royal Academy. RAF, 1943-47; began own business, 1956; Political Organiser, 1962-68; elected, Inverness Town Council, 1972; Member, Highland Regional Council, since 1974; Member, Inverness District Council, since 1974; Member, Executive Committee, National Trust for Scotland. Recreations: golf; caravanning. Address: (h.) 42 Southside Road, Inverness; T.-Inverness 233623.

Selman, Geoffrey George, BSc, PhD. Senior Lecturer in Genetics, Edinburgh University, since 1973; b. 24.4.26, Hampton, Middlesex; m., Elise M.H. Kirk; 2 s. Educ. King Edward VI School, Southampton; King's College, London. Recreations: gardening; music. Address: (b.) Institute of Animal Genetics, King's Buildings, West Mains Road, Edinburgh, EH9 3JN; T.-031-667 1081, Ext. 3696.

Semple, Peter d'Almaine, MD, FRCPGlas. Consultant Physician and Chest Specialist, Inverclyde District, since 1979; b. 30.10.45, Glasgow; m., Judith Mairi Abercromby; 2 d. Educ. Belmont House, Glasgow; Loretto School, Musselburgh; Glasgow University. Various training posts, Glasgow and Dundee teaching hospitals; Consultant General Physician, Inverclyde Royal Hospital and district (including Bute), 1979; Postgraduate Medical Tutor, Inverclyde District, and Honorary Clinical Lecturer, Glasgow University, 1981. Former Council Member, Scottish Thoracic Society; Council Member, Inverclyde and District Faculty of Medicine; Chairman, West of Scotland Branch, British Deer Society, since 1984. Recreations: salmon fishing; shooting; deer stalking; ornithology; golf; curling; sailing. Address: (h.) Allandale, 11 Barrhill Road, Gourock, PA19 1JX; T.-0475 32720.

Semple, Walter George, BL, NP, ACI Arb. Solicitor; Partner, Bird Semple and Crawford Herron, Solicitors, since 1973 (Bird Son & Semple, 1965-73); b. 7.5.42, Glasgow; m., Dr. Lena Ohrstrom; 3 d. Educ. Belmont House, Glasgow; Loretto School; Glasgow University. President, Glasgow Juridical Society, 1968; Tutor and Lecturer (part-time), Glasgow University, 1970-79; Council Member, Law Society of Scotland, 1976-80; Chairman, Scottish Lawyers European Group, 1978-81; Member, Commission Consultative des Barreaux Europeens, 1978-80 and since 1984; President, Association Internationale des Jeunes Avocats, 1983-84; Council Member, Royal Faculty of Procurators in Glasgow, since 1984; Committee Member, Scottish Branch, Institute of Arbitrators, 1985; Convener, International Relations Committee, Law Society of Scoland, since 1984. Recreations: golf; fishing; skiing; music. Address: (h.) 47 Newark Drive, Glasgow, G41 4QA; T.-041-423 7095.

Semple, William David Crowe, BSc (Hons), DipEd, FBIM. Director of Education, Lothian Regional Council, since 1974; b. 11.6.33,

Grangemouth; m., Margaret; 1 s.; 1 d. Educ. Grangemouth High School; Falkirk High School; Glasgow University; Jordanhill College, Glasgow; London University. Education Officer, Northern Rhodesia, 1958-64; Zambia: Deputy Chief Education Officer, 1964-66, Chief Education Officer, 1966-67, Acting Director of Technical Education, 1967-68; Edinburgh Corporation: Assistant Director of Education, 1968-70, Depute Director of Education, 1970-74. Member: University Grants Committee, since 1983, Scottish Council for Tertiary Education, 1979-83, UK National Committee for UNESCO, since 1981; Chairman, Scottish Television Educational Advisory Committee, 1979-85; General Secretary, Association of Directors of Education. Recreation: gardening. Address: (b.) 40 Torphichen Street, Edinburgh; T.-031-229 9166.

Serle, Rev. William, OBE, MB, ChB, DPH, DTM&H. Minister, Church of Scotland, since 1959; Registered Medical Practitioner, since 1935; b. 29.7.12, Edinburgh; m., Sheila Marion Lawrie; 1 s.; 5 d. Educ. George Watson's Boys' College; Edinburgh University. Colonial Medical Service, 1937-57; War Service, 1939-45; Lt.-Col., RAMC, 1st West Africa Field Ambulance; mentioned in Despatches. Publication: Field Guide to the Birds of West Africa (Senior author). Recreation: ornithology. Address: The Manse, Drumoak, near Banchory, AB3 3HA.

Sessford, Rt. Rev. George Minshull. Bishop of Moray, Ross and Caithness, since 1970; b. 7.11.28; m.; 3 d. Educ. St. Andrews University. Curate, St. Mary's Cathedral, Glasgow, 1953; Chaplain, Glasgow University, 1955; Priest-in-Charge, Cumbernauld New Town, 1958; Rector, Forres, 1966.

Sewell, Major Morley Hodkin, MA, PhD, VetMB, MRCVS. Reader in Veterinary Parasitology, Edinburgh University, since 1980; b. 1.9.32, Sheffield; m., Cynthia Margaret-Rose Hanson; 1 s.; 3 d. Educ. King Edward VII School, Sheffield; Cambridge University. Colonial Office Research Scholar, Cambridge, 1957-59; Veterinary Research Officer, Government of Nigeria, 1959-63; Lecturer, then Senior Lecturer, then Reader, Edinburgh University, since 1963. Local Preacher, Methodist Church, since 1958; Vice Chairman, Sum Fellowship, Scottish Committee; Chairman, Midlothian Liberal Association. Recreations: Church; politics; travel. Address: (h.) 14 Craigiebield Crescent, Penicuik, Midlothian.

Shackleton, Rev. William, MA (Hons). Minister, Wellpark West, Greenock, since 1983; b. 19.10.27, Glasgow; m., Margaret Mackenzie Brown; 1 s.; 2 d. Educ. Preston Grammar School; Edinburgh University. Assistant, then Minister, St. Francis-in-the-East, Glasgow. Chairman, Church House Youth Club, Bridgeton; President, Bridgeton Business Club; Patron, Regnal League of Men's Circles. Recreations: writing; golf. Address: 45 Denholm Street, Greenock; T.-0475 21974.

Shand, Jimmy, MBE. Musician and Scottish Country Dance Band Leader; b. 28.1.08, East Wemyss; m., Anne Anderson; 2 s. Educ. East Wemyss School. Has played the accordion and led Scottish danceband at thousands of concert and theatre performances at home and overseas; numerous recordings; several thousand broadcasts. Recreations: motor bikes; sailing.

Shankland, David, JP. Convenor, Cumnock and Doon Valley District Council, since 1984; b. 3.7.43, Mauchline; m., Ellen Park; 1 s.; 2 d. Educ. Cumnock Academy. Member, Cumnock District Council, 1974-75, and Cumnock and Doon Valley District Council, since 1976; Chairman, General Purposes Committee, 1977-80, and Planning Committee, 1980-84; Member, Ayrshire and Arran Health Board, 1978-86; Member, Cumnock and Doon Valley Licensing Court, 1978-86; Chairman, Mauchline Community Association. Recreations: no time. Address: (h.) 38 Welton Road, Mauchline, Ayrshire; T.-0290 50836.

Shanks, Duncan Faichney, ARSA, RGI, DA. Artist; b. 30.8.37, Airdrie; m., Una B. Gordon. Educ. Uddingston Grammar School; Glasgow School of Art. Former part-time Lecturer in Drawing and Painting, Glasgow School of Art; now full-time Painter. Recreation: music.

Shanks, Thomas Henry, MA, LLB. Solicitor and Notary Public, since 1956; Honorary Sheriff, Lanark, since 1982; b. 22.10.30, Lanark; m., Sheila Dales Hunter; 1 s.; 1 d. Educ. Lanark Grammar School; Glasgow University. Intelligence Corps (National Service), 1954-56; Solicitor in general practice, since 1956; Depute Clerk of Peace, County of Lanark, 1961-74; Chairman, Royal Burgh of Lanark Community Council, 1977-80 and since 1983; Member, Hamilton and Lanark Local Legal Aid Committee; Chairman, Lanark Round Table, 1967; Captain, Lanark Golf Club, 1962; Lord Cornet, 1968; Secretary, Lanark Lanimer Committee; Secretary, Clydesdale Upperward Society; Preses, Cairns Church, Lanark; Member, Clydesdale Crime Prevention Panel; Elder, Church of Scotland. Recreation: golf. Address: (h.) Clydesholm Braes, Lanark.

Shannon, David William Francis, BAgr, PhD, DMS. Director, AFRC Poultry Research Centre, since 1978; b. 16.8.41, Lisburn; m., Rosamond Bond; 1 s.; 1 d. Educ. Wallace High School, Lisburn; Queen's University, Belfast. Joined Poultry Research Centre, 1967; Head of Nutrition Department, January to June, 1978. Recreations: golf; bridge. Address: (h.) 60 Liberton Drive, Edinburgh, EH16 6NW.

Sharp, Alexander McLean, JP. Chairman, Fife Regional Planning and Development Committee, since 1974; Chairman, Scottish National Housing and Town Planning Association, since 1982; Chairman, Planning Committee, COSLA, since 1980; b. 13.10.33, Lochgelly; m., Betty Gray; 2 s.; 1 d. Educ. Lochgelly Junior Secondary School. Former Member, Lochgelly Town Council (Provost of Lochgelly, 1973-75); Member, Dunfermline Advisory Board for Justices of the Peace, since 1973; Chairman: Cowdenbeath School Council, Lochgelly Centre Management Committee, Mossmorran/Braefoot Bay Petrochemical Liaison Committee; Vice Chairman, Forth River Bridge Board; Member,

Glenrothes Development Corporation, 1978-84; Deputy Chairman, SDA Consultative Committee; Chairman, Central District, Gas Consumer Council. Recreations: golf; fishing; local interests. Address: (h.) 119 Main Street, Lochgelly, Fife; T.-Lochgelly 780508.

Sharp, Catherine Carmichael, MBE, JP, BCom. Vice-Chairman, Carnegie United Kingdom Trust, since 1982 (Member, since 1960); Vice-Chairman, Fife Valuation Appeal Committee, since 1972; Centre Organiser, British Red Cross Society, since 1975; b. Dunfermline; m., Flt.-Lt. Douglas R. Sharp (deceased); 2 s.; 1 d. Educ. Dunfermline High School; Cranley School for Girls, Edinburgh; Edinburgh University. Chairman, Carnegie Dunfermline and Hero Fund Trusts, 1971-74; Member, Fife Health Board, 1973-85; Member, Social Services Appeal Tribunal, since 1972; Past President, Soroptimist International of Dunfermline. Recreations: travel; music; golf; grandchildren. Address: (h.) 12 Park Place, Dunfermline, Fife, KY12 7QJ; T.-0383 724373.

Sharp, Professor David William Arthur, MA, PhD, CChem, FRSC, FRSE. Ramsay Professor of Chemistry, Glasgow University, since 1968; Convener, Scottish Council for the Validation of Courses for Teachers, since 1983; b. 8.10.31, Folkestone; m., Margaret Cooper; 1 s.; 2 d. Educ. Harvey Grammar School, Folkestone; Sidney Sussex College, Cambridge. Lecturer, Imperial College, London, 1957-61; Strathclyde University, latterly as Professor, 1965-68; Chairman, Scottish Council for Educational Technology, 1975-81; Council Member, Scottish Universities Council on Entrance, 1974-83; Chairman, Committee of Heads of University Chemistry Departments, 1979-81; Governor, Jordanhill College, 1971-79; Member, Scottish Examination Board, 1977-84; Council Member, Royal Society of Chemistry, 1974-77. Publications: A New Dictionary of Chemistry (Editor); Penguin Dictionary of Chemistry (Editor); J. Fluorine Chemistry (Editor). Recreation: walking. Address: (b.) Department of Chemistry, Glasgow University, Glasgow, G12 8QQ; T.-041-339 8855, Ext. 418.

Sharp, Sir George, Kt (1976), OBE, JP, DL. Chairman, Glenrothes Development Corporation, since 1978 (Vice-Chairman, 1973-78); Member, Economic and Social Committee, EEC; b. 8.4.19; m., Elsie May Rodger; 1 s. Educ. Buckhaven High School. Fife County Council: Member, 1954-75, Chairman, Water and Drainage Committee, 1955-61, Chairman, Finance Committee, 1961-72, Convener, 1972-75; Convener, Fife Regional Council, 1974-78; Managing Trustee, Municipal Mutual Insurance Co. Ltd., since 1979; President: Association of County Councils, 1972-74, COSLA, 1975-78; Chairman: Kirkcaldy District Council, 1958-75, Fife and Kinross Water Board, 1967-75, Forth River Purification Board, 1955-67 and 1975-78, Scottish River Purification Advisory Committee, 1967-75, Scottish Tourist Consultative Council, 1979-82; Vice-Chairman, Forth Road Bridge Committee, 1972-78; Member, Scottish Water Advisory Committee, 1962-69, Committee of Enquiry into Salmon and Trout Fishing, 1963, Scottish

Valuation Advisory Committee, 1972, Committee of Enquiry into Local Government Finance, 1974-76, Scottish Development Agency, 1975-80, Royal Commission on Legal Services in Scotland, 1978-80; Director, Grampian Television, since 1975; Member, Scottish Board, National Giro Bank; Director, Municipal Mutual Insurance Ltd. Recreation: golf. Address: (h.) Strathlea, 56 Station Road, Thornton, Fife; T.-Thornton 347.

Sharp, James King, FLA. Director of Libraries, Museums and Art Galleries, Dunfermline District Council, since 1975; b. 27.5.31, Glasgow; m., Elizabeth; 1 s.; 1 d. Educ. Allan Glen's School, Glasgow; Strathclyde University. Library Assistant, Clydebank Public Libraries, 1948-53; Senior Library Assistant, Coatbridge Public Libraries, 1953-56; District Librarian, Lanark County Council, 1956-60; County Librarian, Bute County Council, 1960-65; Librarian and Curator, Dunfermline Town Council, 1965-75. Recreations: golf; motoring; travel. Address: (b.) Library HQ, Abbot Street, Dunfermline, Fife; T.-Dunfermline 723661.

Sharp, James Martin, NDA. Farmer; Convener, Livestock Committee, NFU of Scotland, since 1984; Director, Scotch Quality Beef and Lamb Association, since 1983; Director, Hill Farming Research Organisation, since 1984; b. 19.8.47, Edinburgh; m., Isobel Craig Mackay; 1 s.; 1 d. Educ. Merchiston Castle, Edinburgh; East of Scotland College of Agriculture. Recreation: rugby football. Address: Newbigging Walls, Lauder, Berwickshire; T.-05782 250.

Sharp, John Clarkson Macgregor, MB, ChB, DPH, FFCM, MRCPGlas. Consultant Epidemiologist, Communicable Diseases (Scotland) Unit, Ruchill Hospital, Glasgow, since 1971; b. 20.6.31, New Stevenston, Lanarkshire; m., Elizabeth Anthony Stevenson; 2 d. Educ. Daniel Stewart's College; Edinburgh University. Hospital appointments, Plymouth, Dartford and Bangour; general practice, Edinburgh and Motherwell; Senior Medical Officer, Public Health Department, Edinburgh; Depute County Medical Officer, West Lothian. Honorary Secretary, British Society for the Study of Infection; Honorary Medical Adviser, Scottish Rugby Union. Recreations: golf; squash; tennis; curling. Address: (b.) Communicable Diseases (Scotland) Unit, Ruchill Hospital, Glasgow, G20 9NB; T.-041-946 7120.

Sharp, Nigel Ernest, MA. Assistant Secretary, Scottish Home and Health Department, since 1970; b. 22.5.31, Edinburgh; m., Margaret Martin Taylor; 2 s.; 2 d. Educ. George Watson's College, Edinburgh; St. James School, Maryland, USA; Edinburgh University. National Service, RAEC, 1953-55; Assistant Principal, Scottish Home Department, 1955-60; Principal, 1960-70: Industry and Transport, Housing, Police Administration, Social Work including Children's Hearings; Assistant Secretary, since 1970: NHS General Practitioner Services, Doctors' and Dentists' Remuneration, Trunk Roads, Ancient Monuments, Historic Buildings and Building Control, Law and General. Vice-President, East District, Scottish Hockey Association; Elder, Greenbank

Church. Recreations: hockey; crosswords; jogging; reading; doggerel. Address: (b.) Scottish Home and Health Department, St. Andrew's House, Edinburgh, EH1 3DE; T.-031-556 8501.

Sharples, Peter John, MA (Hons), DipEd. Member, Argyll and Bute District Council, since 1981 (Vice-Chairman, Planning and Building Control Committee, since 1984); Principal Teacher of Modern Languages, Oban High School, since 1972; b. 23.5.36, Preston; m., Moira MacKenzie; 2 s.; 1 d. Educ. Morrison's Academy, Crieff; St. Andrews University; Moray House College; Edinburgh University. Teacher of French, Larbert High School, 1959-62, Oban High School, 1962-72; Secretary, Argyll Liberal Association, 1964-72; joined Conservative Party, 1978; Chairman, North Connel and District Ratepayers Association, since 1978; Member, Argyll and Bute Local Health Council, since 1981. Recreations: fishing; skiing; horse-riding; sailing; computing. Address: (h.) Mortlach, North Connel, Oban, Argyll, PA37 1RD; T.-Connel 387.

Shaw, Rev. Alistair Neil, MA (Hons), BD (Hons). Minister, Relief Parish Church, Bourtreehill, Irvine, since 1982; b. 6.7.53, Kilbarchan; m., Brenda Bruce. Educ. Paisley Grammar School; Glasgow University. Recreations: foreign travel; ancient history; swimming. Address: 68 Dundonald Road, Dreghorn, Irvine, KA11 4AP; T.-Irvine 216939.

Shaw, Andrew Fisher, AFC. Assistant Commandant, Princess Louise Scottish Hospital, since 1948; b. 14.4.23, Glasgow; m., Ina Cameron Simpson; 2 s.; 1 d. Educ. Hutchesons' Boys' Grammar School. Pilot, RAF, 1942-48; Coastal Command, 1955-55; Transport Command, 1955-78; retired as Squadron Leader, 1978. Represented Glasgow, Cheshire and RAF at rugby. Recreations: athletics; tennis; rugby. Address: (h.) Ailsa Lodge, Ferry Road, Bishopton, Renfrewshire; T.-041-812 7603.

Shaw, Professor Donald Leslie, MA, PhD. Professor of Latin American Studies, Edinburgh University, since 1979; b. 11.2.30, Manchester; m., Maria Concetta Cristini; 1 s.; 1 d. Educ. Stand Grammar School; Manchester University. Flying Officer, RAF, 1953-55; Assistant Lecturer, Dublin University, 1955-57; Lecturer, Glasgow University, 1957-64; Edinburgh University: Lecturer, 1964-69, Senior Lecturer, 1969-72, Reader, 1972-79. Recreations: bicycling; gossiping. Address: (h.) 3 Duddingston Road, Edinburgh, EH15 1ND; T.-031-669 3676.

Shaw, Professor Douglas William David, MA, LLB, BD, WS. Professor of Divinity, St. Andrews University, since 1979 (Dean, Faculty of Divinity, since 1983); Minister, Church of Scotland, since 1960; b. 25.6.28, Edinburgh; m., Edinburgh Academy; Loretto; Ashbury College, Ottawa; St. John's College; Cambridge; Edinburgh University. Practised law as WS (Partner, Davidson and Syme, WS, Edinburgh), 1952-57; Assistant Minister, St. George's West Church, Edinburgh, 1960-63; Official Observer, Second Vatican Council, Rome, 1962; Lecturer in Divinity, Edinburgh University, 1963-79; Principal,

New College, and Dean, Faculty of Divinity, Edinburgh, 1973-78; Visiting Fellow, Fitzwilliam College, Cambridge, 1978; Visiting Lecturer, Virginia University, 1979. Publications: Who is God?, 1968; The Dissuaders, 1978. Recreations: squash; golf; hill-walking. Address: (h.) 40 North Bridge, St. Andrews, Fife, KY16 9AQ; T.-0334 77254.

Shaw, Rev. Duncan, BD (Hons), MTh. Minister, St. John's, Bathgate, since 1978; b. 10.4.47, Blantyre. Educ. St. John's Grammar School, Hamilton; Hamilton Academy; Trinity College, Glasgow University. Assistant Minister, Netherlee Parish Church, Glasgow, 1974-77. Clerk, West Lothian Presbytery, since 1982. Address: St. John's Parish Church Manse, Mid Street, Bathgate, EH48 1QD; T.-Bathgate 53146.

Shaw, Jennifer Mary, FSA Scot. Member, Moray District Council, since 1984 (Vice-Chairman, Planning and Development Committee, since 1984); b. 11.4.37, Walkhampton, Devon; m., Edward Nicholas Shaw; 1 s.; 2 d. Educ. Cranborne Chase School; British Institute, Paris; Triangle Secretarial College, London; Clinterty Agricultural College, Aberdeen. Vice-Chairman, State of Penang Family Planning Association, 1965-67; former Member, Executive Committee, Scottish Council of Social Service; Committee Member, Rural Forum Scotland; former Secretary and Chairman, Innes Community Council; Recreations: reading; needlework; cooking; conservation; natural and local history; walking; music; more work. Address: (h.) Sheriffston, Elgin, Moray, IV30 3LA; T.-0343 84 2695.

Shaw, John Fraser, FRCS, FRCSEdin, FRCPEdin. Consultant Neurosurgeon, Department of Surgical Neurology, Western General Hospital and Edinburgh Royal Infirmary, since 1963; part-time Senior Lecturer, Departments of Surgical Neurology and Child Life and Health, Edinburgh University, since 1963; b. 26.2.22, Calcutta; m., Sheila McClelland Wilson; 1 s.; 1 d. Educ. Dulwich College; Guy's Hospital. Past President, European Society of Paediatric Neurosurgery. Address: (h.) 6 Gamekeepers' Park, Edinburgh, EH4 6PA; T.-031-336 2828.

Shaw, Mark Robert, BA, MA, DPhil. Keeper of Natural History, Royal Scottish Museum, since 1983; b. 11.5.45, Sutton Coldfield; m., Francesca Dennis Wilkinson; 2 d. Educ. Dartington Hall School; Oriel College, Oxford. Research Assistant (Entomology), Zoology Department, Manchester University, 1973-77; University Research Fellow, Reading University, 1977-80; Assistant Keeper, Department of Natural History, Royal Scottish Museum, 1980-83. Editorial Advisor, Ecological Entomology. Recreations: field entomology; family life; slash-and-burn gardening. Address: (h.) 48 St. Albans Road, Edinburgh, EH9 2LU; T.-031-667 0577.

Shaw, Thomas Raymond Dunlap, BSc, MD, MRCP. Consultant Cardiologist, Western General Hospital, Edinburgh, since 1983; b. 27.4.43, Dumfries; m., Dr. Paula Shaw; 2 s. Educ. Douglas Ewart High School, Newton Stewart; Glasgow University. Senior House Officer, Western General Hospital, Edinburgh, Edinburgh

Royal Infirmary; Registrar, St. Bartholomew's Hospital, London; Senior Registrar, Edinburgh Teaching Hospitals. Recreations: curling; children; television. Address: (b.) Department of Cardiology, Western General Hospital, Crewe Road, Edinburgh, EH4 2XU; T.-031-332 2525.

Shaw-Stewart, Sir Houston (Mark), 11th Bt, MC (1950), TD. Vice Lord Lieutenant, Strathclyde Region (Eastwood, Renfrew and Inverclyde Districts), since 1980; b. 24.4.31; m., Lucinda Victoria Fletcher. Educ. Eton. Coldstream Guards, 1949; 2nd Lt., Royal Ulster Rifles, Korea, 1950; Ayrshire Yeomanry, 1952; Member, Queen's Bodyguard for Scotland (Royal Company of Archers). Address: (h.) Ardgowan, Inverkip, Renfrewshire.

Shearer, Magnus MacDonald, JP. Lord Lieutenant of Shetland, since 1982; Honorary Consul for Sweden in Shetland and Orkney, since 1958; Honorary Consul for Federal Republic of Germany in Shetland, since 1972; b. 27.2.24; m., Martha Nicolson Henderson; 1 s. Educ. Anderson Educational Institute, Shetland; George Watson's College, Edinburgh. Royal Navy, Atlantic, Mediterranean and Far East, 1942-46; Royal Artillery TA, commissioned 2nd Lt., 1949; TARO, rank Captain, 1959; Honorary Secretary, Lerwick Branch, RNLI, since 1968; Member, Lerwick Town Council, 1963-69; Deputy Lieutenant of Shetland, 1973. Recreations: reading; bird watching; ships. Address: (h.) Birka, Cruester, Bressay, Shetland, ZE2 9EL; T.-0595 82 363.

Shedden, Alexander Denis, BSc, FFA, FSA. President, Faculty of Actuaries in Scotland, 1983-85; Deputy Chief Executive and Secretary, Standard Life Assurance Company, since 1985; b. 7.8.27, Glasgow; m., Catrionia Garland Kerr; 1 s.; 2 d. Educ. Allan Glen's School; Glasgow University. National Service as Education Officer, RAF, 1948-50; Scottish Mutual Assurance Society, Glasgow, 1950-52; Dominion Life Assurance Company, Ontario, Canada, 1952-63; joined Standard Life Assurance Co., 1963. Recreations: bridge; music. Address: (b.) 3 George Street, Edinburgh, EH2 2XZ; T.-031-225 2552.

Sheehan, Sheriff Albert Vincent, MA, LLB. Sheriff of Tayside, Central and Fife, at Falkirk, since 1983; b. 23.8.36, Edinburgh; m., Edna Georgina Scott Hastings; 2 d. Educ. Bo'ness Academy; Edinburgh University. 2nd Lt., 1st Bn., Royal Scots (The Royal Regiment), 1960; Captain, Directorate of Army Legal Services, 1961; Depute Procurator Fiscal, Hamilton, 1961-71; Senior Depute Procurator Fiscal, Glasgow, 1971-74; Deputy Crown Agent for Scotland, 1974-79; Scottish Law Commission, 1979-81; Sheriff of Lothian and Borders, at Edinburgh, 1981-83. Leverhulme Fellow, 1971. Publication: Criminal Procedure in Scotland and France, 1975. Recreations: naval history; travel; sailing. Address: (b.) Sheriff Court House, Falkirk; T.-Falkirk 20822.

Sheehan, Michael John, BSc (Econ), PhD. Member, Aberdeen City Council, since 1984; Lecturer in International Relations, Aberdeen University, since 1979; b. 26.6.54, London. Educ. Cardinal Vaughan School, London; University College of Wales, Aberystwyth. Associate, Aberdeen Centre for Defence Studies, since 1984; Member, Liberal Party Defence Policy Panel, since 1981. Publication: The Arms Race, 1983. Recreations: music; astronomy; Aberdeen and Cardiff City Football Clubs. Address: (b.) Department of Politics, Aberdeen University, Dunbar Street, Aberdeen, AB9 2UB; T.-Aberdeen 40241, Ext. 5201.

Shelton, Richard Graham John, BSc, PhD. Officer-in-Charge, DAFS Freshwater Fisheries Laboratory, Pitlochry, since 1982; b. 3.7.42, Aylesbury; m., Freda Carstairs; 2 s. Educ. Royal Grammar School, High Wycombe; St. Andrews University. Research work, Burnham-on-Crouch Laboratory, MAFF, 1968-72; Assistant to Controller of Fisheries Research and Development, MAFF Fisheries Laboratory, Lowestoft, 1972-76 and (from 1974) DAFS Marine Laboratory, Aberdeen; worked on the population ecology of Crustacea, 1976-82. Recreations: shooting; fishing; steam model railways. Address: (h.) Dalfraoich, Strathtay, Pitlochry, PH9 OPJ; T.-088 74 217.

Shepherd, James, BSc, MB, ChB, PhD, MRCPath. Reader in Pathological Biochemistry, Glasgow University, since 1984; b. 8.4.44, Motherwell; m., Janet Bulloch Kelly; 1 s.; 1 d. Educ. Hamilton Academy; Glasgow University. Lecturer, Glasgow University: Biochemistry, 1968-72, Pathological Biochemistry, 1972-77; Assistant Professor of Medicine, Baylor College of Medicine, Houston, Texas, 1976-77; Senior Lecturer in Pathological Biochemistry, Glasgow University, 1977-84; Visiting Professor of Medicine, Geneva University, 1984. Address: (b.) Department of Biochemistry, Royal Infirmary, Glasgow, G4 OSF; T.-041-552 3535, Ext. 5374.

Shepherd, Thomas William, DipTP, MRTPI. Director of Planning, Dunfermline District Council, since 1974; b. 29.3.33, Kendal, Cumbria; m., Betty Muir; 1 s. Educ. Heversham Grammar School; Edinburgh College of Art. Fife County Council: articled apprentice town planner, 1950-55, Planning Assistant, 1957-60; Planning Officer: Government of Tanganyika, 1960-63, Glenrothes New Town, 1963-66; Senior Planning Assistant, Fife, 1966-74. Recreations: landscape gardening; music. Address: (b.) 3 New Row, Dunfermline, Fife; T.-Dunfermline 736321.

Shepperson, Professor George Albert, MA, CertEd (Cantab). William Robertson Professor of Commonwealth and American History, Edinburgh University, since 1963; b. 7.1.22, Peterborough; m., Joyce Irene Cooper; 1 d. Educ. King's School, Peterborough; St. John's College, Cambridge. Commissioned Northamptonshire Regiment; seconded King's African Rifles; War Service, 1941-46; Lecturer, Senior Lecturer, Reader in History, Edinburgh University, 1948-63; various overseas academic appointments; Dean, Faculty of Arts, Edinburgh, 1974-77; Dean, Scottish Universities Summer School, 1971-76; Chairman, British Association for American Studies, 1971-74; Chairman, Mungo Park Bicentenary Committee, 1971; Chairman,

David Livingstone Documentation Project, since 1973; Chairman, Commonwealth Institute, Scotland, since 1973; founder Member and former Convener, Centre of African Studies and Centre of Canadian Studies, Edinburgh University; President, St. Andrew Society of Edinburgh, 1970-73; Member, Governing Body, Scottish National Memorial to David Livingstone Trust; Joint Editor, Oxford Studies in African Affairs, since 1969. Publications: David Livingstone and the Rovuma; Independent African. Recreations: collecting African and Afro-American documents; theatre. Address: (h.) 23 Ormidale Terrace, Edinburgh; T.-031-337 4424.

Sherrard, Rev. (Henry) Dane, BD. Minister, Buckhaven Parish Church, since 1976; b. 13.3.46, Watford; m., Rachel Joan Hammerton. Educ. Dundee High School; St. Andrews University. President, SRC, St. Andrews, 1965-66; Vice President, Scottish Union of Students, 1966; Assistant, Abronhill Parish Church, 1970; Church of Scotland Minister, Northern Italy (responsible for Seamen's Mission), 1971-76. Area Board Member, MSC, since 1983; Chairman, Aberhill Youth Project, 1979-82; Chairman, Levenmouth Council of Social Service, 1978-82; in 1983, began employment scheme which now employs 500 people. Recreations: theatre and music; a passion for Gilbert and Sullivan and cricket. Address: St. Michael's House, East Lawrence Street, Buckhaven, KY8 1BQ; T.-0592 715577.

Sherratt, Professor David John, BSc, PhD, FRSE. Professor and Head of Genetics, Glasgow University, since 1980; b. 14.6.45, Nuneaton; 1 s.; 2 d. Educ. Loughborough Grammar School; UMIST; Edinburgh University. Research Fellow, California University, 1969-71; Lecturer in Microbial Genetics, Sussex University, 1971-80. Fleming Lecturer, 1982. Recreation: enjoying fresh air. Address: (b.) Department of Genetics, Glasgow University, Church Street, Glasgow, G11 5TS; T.-041-339 8855, Ext. 7113.

Sherriff, Harry. Divisional Organiser, Amalgamated Union of Engineering Workers, since 1973; Member, Greater Glasgow Health Board, since 1977; Member, Industrial Tribunals, since 1983; b. 24.12.20, Glasgow; m., Sarah Dickson (deceased); 1 s.; 3 d. Recreations: football; swimming. Address: (b.) AUEW House, 145 West Regent Street, Glasgow; T.-041-248 7131.

Sherwood, Professor John Neil, DSc, PhD, CChem, FRSC, FRSE. Burmah Professor of Physical Chemistry, Strathclyde University, since 1983; b. 8.11.33, Redruth, Cornwall; m., Margaret Enid Shaw; 2 d. Educ. Aireborough Grammar School; Bede College, Durham University. Research Fellow, Hull University, 1958-60; Lecturer and Reader, Strathclyde University, 1960-83. Recreations: hill-walking; photography; gardening. Address: (b.) Department of Pure and Applied Chemistry, Strathclyde University, Glasgow, G1 1XL; T.-041-552 4400.

Shewan, Rev. Frederick David Fitzgerald, MA, BD. Minister, Muirhouse Parish Church, Edinburgh, since 1980 (Northesk Parish Church, Musselburgh, 1970-80); Convener, Church and Nation Sub-Committee on Mass Media, 1981-85; Convener, Social and Community Interests Committee, Edinburgh Presbytery, since 1983; b. 24.3.42, Whiterashes, Aberdeenshire; m., Iris Patricia Barrack; 2 d. Educ. Inverurie Academy; Kings College and Christ's College, Aberdeen University. Convener, Church and Nation Committee, Lothian Presbytery, 1975; Member, Church and Nation Committee, General Assembly, 1977; President, Scottish Church Theology Society, 1978-81. Publication: The Significance of Modern Israel, 1970. Recreations: reading; hill-walking; classic cars; sport and painting. Address: The Manse, 35 Silverknowes Road, Edinburgh, EH4 5LL; T.-031-336 4546.

Shewan, Henry Alexander, CB (1974), OBE (1946), QC, MA, LLB; b. 7.11.06, Aberdeen; m., Ann Fraser Thomson (deceased); 2 s. Educ. Robert Gordon's College, Aberdeen; Aberdeen University; Emmanuel College, Cambridge. Admitted Scottish Bar, 1933; RAFVR, 1940-45 (Squadron Leader); Standing Junior Counsel to Inland Revenue Scotland, 1947-49; QC, 1949; Referee under Coal Industry Nationalisation Act, 1949-55; Chairman, Medical Appeal Tribunal, 1950-55; National Insurance Commissioner, 1955-80. Chairman, General Nursing Council for Scotland, 1960-62. Address: (h.) 7 Winton Loan, Edinburgh, EH10 7AN; T.-031-445 3239.

Shiach, Sheriff Gordon Iain Wilson, MA, LLB, BA (Hons). Sheriff of Lothian and Borders, at Edinburgh, since 1984; b. 15.10.35, Elgin; m., Margaret Grant Smith; 2 d. Educ. Gordonstoun; Salem; Edinburgh University; Open University. Admitted Advocate, 1960; practised as Advocate, 1960-72; Sheriff of Fife and Kinross, at Dunfermline, 1972-79; Sheriff of Lothian and Borders, at Linlithgow, 1979-84. Recreations: orienteering; swimming; music; the theatre. Address: (b.) Sheriff Court House, Lawnmarket, Edinburgh, EH1; T.-031-226 7181.

Shields, Thomas Gillies, BSc (Hons), PhD, MB, ChB, FRCPGlas, AFOM. Consultant in Hyperbaric Medicine, Grampian Health Board, since 1983; Senior Lecturer in Environmental and Occupational Medicine, Aberdeen University, since 1983; b. 3.1.41, Glasgow; m., Dalys B.R. Fraser; 1 s.; 3 d. Educ. Rothesay Academy; Glasgow University. Medical Officer, Royal Navy, retiring in rank of Surgeon Commander, and Senior Specialist in Underwater Medicine, 1964-82; Senior Medical Officer, Admiralty Marine Technology Establishment Physiological Laboratory, Alverstoke, 1978-82; President, European Undersea Biomedical Society, since 1985; Member, Anglo-Norwegian Diving Medical Advisory Committee; Member, MRC Decompression Sickness and Diving Panel. Recreations: reading; classical music; rebuilding and riding old British motorcycles. Address: (b.) Grampian Health Board, Hyperbaric Medicine Unit, Foresterhill, Aberdeen, AB9 2ZD.

Short, Agnes Jean, BA (Hons), MLitt. Writer; b. Bradford, Yorkshire; m., Anthony Short (qv); 3 s.; 2 d. Educ. Bradford Girls' Grammar School; Exeter University; Aberdeen University. Various secretarial, research and teaching jobs, both in UK and abroad; took up writing, 1966; 11

novels, including several with a Scottish setting; also short stories and radio; Constable Award, 1976. Recreations: dog-walking; whisky-tasting; good food; small hills. Address: (h.) 20 The Chanonry, Aberdeen, AB2 1RQ; T.-0224 42277.

Short, Anthony, BSc (Econ), MA, BLitt. Reader in International Relations, Aberdeen University, since 1977 (Warden, Dunbar Hall, since 1967); b. 26.6.29, Singapore; m., Agnes Russell (see Agnes Jean Short); 3 s.; 2 d. Educ. Hele's School, Exeter; University College, Exeter; London School of Economics; University of Virginia; St. Catherine's, Oxford. National Service, Malaya, 1947-49; Lecturer, Bristol University, 1957-60; Lecturer, University of Malaya 1960-66; Visiting Fellow, Senior Lecturer, Reader, Department of Politics, Aberdeen University. Publication: The Communist Insurrection in Malaya 1948-60. Recreations: malt whisky; wood gathering; temperate hill-walking. Address: (h.) Chaplain's Court, The Chanonry, Aberdeen; T.-0224 42277.

Short, Emeritus Professor David Somerset, MD, PhD, FRCP, FRCPEdin. Honorary Consultant Physician, Grampian Health Board, since 1983; Emeritus Professor in Clinical Medicine, Aberdeen University, since 1983; b. 6.8.18, Weston-super-Mare, Avon; m., Joan Anne McLay; 1 s.; 4 d. Educ. Bristol Grammar School; Cambridge University; Bristol University. RAMC, 1944-47; Senior Registrar in Medicine/Cardiology, Bristol, National Heart Hospital, London Hospital and Middlesex Hospital, London, 1948-59; Consultant Physician, Aberdeen Hospitals and Senior Lecturer, Aberdeen University, 1960-83; former Physician to The Queen in Scotland. Recreation: walking. Address: (h.) 48 Victoria Street, Aberdeen, AB9 2PL; T.-0224 645853.

Short, James, FITSA, DCA. Director of Trading Standards, Lothian Regional Council, since 1974; b. Paisley. Educ. John Neilson High School. Trained in Paisley Weights and Measures Department, 1950-53; Inspector of Weights and Measures, Glasgow Corporation, 1953-58; Inspector in Charge, Weights and Measures Department, Burgh of Clydebank, 1958-59; Chief Inspector, Burgh of Paisley, 1959-74. Recreations: golf; DIY. Address: (b.) 1 Parliament Square, Edinburgh, EH1 1RF; T.-031-229 9292.

Sibbald, Alexander, BSc. Headteacher, Hazlehead Academy, since 1984; b. 8.4.38, Edinburgh; m., Christina W.M. Mallinson; 1 s.; 1 d. Educ. George Heriot's School; Edinburgh University. Assistant Teacher of Science, Lindsay High School, Bathgate, 1961-63; Lecturer, Regent Road Institute, Edinburgh, 1963-66; Principal Teacher of Science, Castlebrae High School, Edinburgh, 1966-75; Assistant Head/Depute Head, Whitburn Academy, West Lothian, 1975-80; Head Teacher, Kemnay Academy, 1981-84. Recreations: wide range of sports; car restoration. Address: (b.) Groat's Road, Aberdeen; T.-Aberdeen 310184.

Sibbald, John Arnold. Librarian, Advocates' Library, Edinburgh, since 1982; b. Glasgow; m., Caroline Mary Paton. Educ. George Watson's

College; Society of the Sacred Mission, Newark; Edinburgh University. Assistant Librarian, Homerton College, Cambridge, 1966-68; Deighton, Bell & Co., Cambridge, 1969-77; Assistant Librarian, Advocates' Library, 1978-82. Address: (h.) 2 Atholl Place, Edinburgh; T.-031-229 1952.

Sillars, Donald Campbell, DA. Convener, Health and General Purposes Committee, Bearsden and Milngavie District Council, since 1984; b. 13.11.28, Purley, Surrey; m. Educ. Purley Grammar School; Bearsden Academy; Glasgow School of Art. Publicity Manager, William Collins Sons & Co. Ltd., Bishopbriggs; Housing Convener, Bearsden and Milngavie District Council, 1977-80; Chairman, Clydebank and Milngavie Conservative and Unionist Association, since 1983. Recreations: walking; fishing; reading. Address: (h.) 16 Tambowie Avenue, Milngavie, Glasgow; T.-041-956 2719.

Sillars, Evelyn Murdoch, MBE, JP, MA. Member, Cunninghame District Council, since 1974; Member, HIDB Consultative Council, since 1975; b. 24.11.23, Ayr; m., Douglas A. Sillars; 4 d. Educ. Ayr Academy; Glasgow University. Intelligence Section, Foreign Office (War Service); Teacher of English and Religious Education; Honorary Secretary, Scottish Committee, War on Want; County Councillor, holding post of County Convener at time of reorganisation (only woman to hold such appointment in Scotland); District Councillor for Arran; Member, Scottish Transport Users Consultative Committee, since 1981; Member, Clyde Shipping Advisory Committee; Executive Member, Arran Council of Social Service; Executive Member, Arran Tourist Association; Centre Organiser for Red Cross; Church Elder. Recreations: music; bridge; bowling. Address: (h.) Mid Mayish House, Brodick, Isle of Arran; T.-0770 2246.

Sillars, James, FBIM. Consultant, since 1980; b. 4.10.37, Ayr; m., Margo MacDonald (qv); 1 s.; 3 d. Educ. Ayr Academy. Member, Ayr Town Council and Ayr County Council Education Committee, 1960s; Member, Western Regional Hospital Board, 1965-70; Head, Organisation Department, Scottish TUC, 1968-70; MP, South Ayrshire, 1970-79. Recreation: reading. Address: (h.) 15 Woodburn Terrace, Edinburgh.

Silver, Kenneth Gordon, MA (Hons), DipEd. Treasurer, Roxburgh and Berwickshire Conservative and Unionist Association, since 1985; b. 1.11.26, Kinross; m., 1, Christina Margaret Brown (m. diss.); 2, Joan Adelaide Wylie; 1 s. (by first m.). Educ. Dollar Academy; United College, St. Andrews. RAF (FO, Education Branch), 1948-50; Assistant Teacher of Classics: North Kelvinside Secondary School, Glasgow, 1952-53, Hyndland Secondary School, Glasgow, 1953-56, Hutchesons' Boys' Grammar School, Glasgow, 1956-59; Principal Teacher of Classics: Biggar High School, 1959-63, Falkirk High School, 1963-71; Rector, Jedburgh Grammar School, 1971-84. Governor, Moray House College of Education, 1975-83; Member, Scottish Examination Board (formerly SCEEB), 1977-84; Member, SCOVACT Validating Panel on Religious Education, since 1983; Chairman,

Jedburgh Branch, Arthritis Rheumatism Council for Research, since 1978; Vice-President, SSTA, 1969-70; Council Member, HAS, 1983-84; President, Jedburgh Rotary Club, 1980-81 and 1984-85; Editor, Rotary District 102 Chronicle, since 1985; Editor, Third Statistical Account of Roxburghshire. Recreations: music; theology; gardening; languages; foreign travel; astrology. Address: (h.) Friarshill, Friarsgate, Jedburgh, TD8 6BN; T.-0835 62485.

Sim, Professor George A., BSc, PhD, CChem, FRSE. Gardiner Professor of Chemistry, Glasgow University, since 1970; b. 26.10.29, Aberdeen; m., Margaret G.T. Gourlay; 1 s.; 1 d. Educ. Ardrossan Academy; Glasgow University. Professor of Chemistry, Illinois University, 1964-66, Sussex University, 1966-70. Corday-Morgan Medal and Prize, The Chemical Society, 1963; Fritzsche Award, American Chemical Society, 1967. Address: (b.) Chemistry Department, Glasgow University, Glasgow, G12 8QQ; T.-041-339 8855, Ext. 419.

Sim, William Jeffrey, BL. Honorary Sheriff, Paisley; b. 14.6.14, Paisley; m., Jean (Sheina) Reid Cullen Cochrane; 1 s. Educ. Paisley Grammar School; Glasgow Academy; Glasgow University. Admitted Solicitor, 1937; joined family firm of Pattison & Sim, Paisley, 1939; War Service, RNVR, 1940-45; returned to practice, 1945 and continued until retirement, 1979; former Dean, Faculty of Procurators in Paisley; Council Member, Law Society of Scotland, 1959-63; closely involved with Savings Bank movement as Trustee, Paisley Trustee Savings Bank, 1948-78 and Chairman of Trustees, 1967-70; also served on Executive Committee, West of Scotland Trustee Savings Bank and TSB Inspection Committee. Address: (h.) Ardyne, Thornly Park Avenue, Paisley; T.-041-884 2344.

Simmers, Brian Maxwell, CA. Partner, S. Easton Simmers & Co., CA, since 1963; Director, Scottish Highland Hotels, since 1963; b. 26.2.40, Glasgow; m., Constance Ann Turner; 3 s. Educ. Glasgow Academy; Larchfield; Loretto. Member, Scottish Sports Council, 1981-84; Deputy Chairman, National Playing Fields Association; Governor, Glasgow Academy; Honorary Secretary, Rugby Internationals' Golfing Society; former Member, Finance Committee, British Red Cross (Glasgow). Played rugby for Scotland (seven caps) and Barbarians. Recreations: rugby; golf; shooting; skiing; windsurfing; squash (retired). Address: (b.) 98 West George Street, Glasgow, G2 1PW; T.-041-332 6538.

Simmers, Graeme Maxwell, OBE, CA. Partner, S. Easton Simmers & Co., CA, since 1961; Chairman, Scottish Highland Hotels Group Ltd., since 1972; Member, Scottish Tourist Board, since 1979; Chairman, Hotel and Catering Benevolent Association (Scotland), since 1984; Vice-Chairman of Governors, Loretto School; Treasurer, Epilepsy Association of Scotland; b. 2.5.35, Glasgow; m., Jennifer M.H. Roxburgh; 2 s.; 2 d. Educ. Glasgow Academy; Loretto School. Qualified CA, 1959; commissioned, Royal Marines, 1959-61; Chairman, Scottish Division, British Hotels, Restaurants and Caterers

Association, 1979-81 (Vice Chairman, Board of Management, 1985). Elder and Treasurer, Killearn Kirk; Member, Championship Committee, Royal and Ancient Golf Club of St. Andrews. Recreations: rugby; golf; skiing; literary society. Address: (h.) Kincaple, Boquhan, Balfron, near Glasgow, G63 ORW; T.-0360 40375.

Simmons, Dennis, CEng, FIEE, FBIM. Chief Commercial Officer, South of Scotland Electricity Board, since 1982; b. 19.9.31, Grimsby. Grimsby Corporation, 1947; Yorkshire Electricity Board, 1954; Eastern Electricity Board, Bedford, 1956; South East Electricity Board, Guildford, 1961; SSEB: Assistant District Engineer, Edinburgh East, 1964, District Engineer, Borders, 1966, District Manager, Ayr, 1967, District Manager, Glasgow South, 1971, Area Manager, Glasgow/Clyde, 1974, Area Manager, Edinburgh, Fife and Borders, 1979; Recreations: golf; tennis; badminton. Address: (b.) Cathcart House, Spean Street, Glasgow; T.-041-637 7177.

Simpson, David Francis, BL, WS. Honorary Sheriff, Cupar, since 1976; b. 6.4.19, Dundee; m., Jessie Ogilvy Steel Dickie (deceased); 1 s. Educ. Edinburgh Academy; Fettes; Edinburgh University. War Service with Cameronians (Scottish Rifles), 1939-46 (Major); wounded, Germany, 1945; practised as Solicitor in Edinburgh, 1948-50 and Cupar, 1950-82. Recreations: golf; walking; reading. Address: (h.) 17 Hallowhill, St. Andrews, Fife; T.-St. Andrews 73677.

Simpson, Hugh David Lorimer, MA, LLB. Solicitor, since 1933; Honorary Sheriff Substitute, Dumfriesshire, since 1972; b. 19.11.08, Moffat; m., 1, Margaret T. Henderson; 2, H. Norah Magill; 1 s.; 2 d. Educ. St. Ninian's, Moffat; Sedbergh; Edinburgh University. Burgh Prosecutor, Moffat, 1934-41; Town Clerk, Moffat, 1941-75; War Service, RAF (Flt.-Lt.); mentioned in Despatches; Dean, Faculty of Procurators of Dumfriesshire, 1967; Secretary, Abbeyfield Moffat and District Society, since 1964; Elder, Church of Scotland, since 1939. Recreation: fishing. Address: (h.) Belmont, Moffat; T.-Moffat 20169.

Simpson, Hugh Walter, MB, ChB, MD, PhD, FRCPath. Reader in Pathology, Glasgow University, since 1978; Head of Pathology, Glasgow Royal Infirmary, since 1984; b. 4.4.31, Ceres, Fife; m., Myrtle Emslie (see Myrtle Simpson); 3 s.; 1 d. Educ. Bryanston; Edinburgh University. Leader of numerous expeditions to polar and tropical regions; awarded Polar Medal and Mungo Park Medal. Recreation: skiing. Address: (h.) 18 Westbourne Gardens, Glasgow, G12; T.-041-339 8331.

Simpson, Ian Christopher, LLB. Advocate, since 1974; Temporary Sheriff, since 1985. Address: (b.) Parliament House, Parliament Square, Edinburgh; T.-031-226 5071.

Simpson, Rev. James Alexander, BSc (Hons), BD, STM. Minister, Dornoch Cathedral, since 1976; b. 9.3.34, Glasgow; m., Helen Gray McCorquodale; 3 s.; 2 d. Educ. Eastwood

Secondary School; Glasgow University; Union Seminary, New York. Minister: Grahamston Church, Falkirk, 1960-66, St. John's Renfield, Glasgow, 1966-76. Publications: There is a time to ....; Marriage Questions Today; Doubts are not Enough. Recreations: golf; photography; writing articles on golf and Highland life. Address: Cathedral Manse, Dornoch, IV25 3HN; T.-086 2810296.

Simpson, James White, BSc, MCIT, MRIN. Port Manager, Grangemouth, since 1982; Director, George Palmer & Son (Stevedores) Ltd., since 1982; b. 30.8.44, St. Andrews; m., Barbara Hutton; 1 s.; 1 d. Educ. Grangemouth High School; Buckhaven High School; Leith Nautical College; Plymouth Polytechnic. Cadet, Furness Prince Lines, 1961-64; Navigating Officer: Shaw Savill Line, 1965-68, Overseas Containers Ltd., 1969-70; Assistant Harbour Master, then Assistant to Port Superintendent, Grangemouth, 1973-77; Port Superintendent, Leith and Granton, 1978-82. Recreation: sailing. Address: (b.) Forth Ports Authority, Dock Office, Grangemouth; T.-0324 482591.

Simpson, Professor John Alexander, MD Hon. (Glasgow), FRCP, FRCPEdin, FRCPGlas, FRSE. Professor of Neurology, Glasgow University, since 1965; Senior Neurologist, Institute of Neurological Sciences, Southern General Hospital, Glasgow, since 1965; Consultant Neurologist, Civil Service Commission, since 1974; b. 30.3.22, Greenock; m., Dr. Elizabeth M.H. Simpson; 2 s.; 1 d. Educ. Greenock Academy; Glasgow University. Surgeon-Lieutenant, RNVR; Registrar in Medicine, Southern General Hospital, Glasgow; Lecturer in Medicine, Glasgow University; MRC Research Fellow, National Hospital for Nervous Diseases, London; Senior Lecturer in Medicine, Glasgow University; Consultant Physician, Western Infirmary, Glasgow; Reader in Neurology, Edinburgh University. President, Association of British Neurologists, 1985-86; Past Chairman, Scottish Epilepsy Association; former Consultant Neurologist to British Army in Scotland; Editor, Journal of Neurology, Neurosurgery and Psychiatry. Recreations: violinist (Glasgow Chamber Orchestra and Scottish Fiddle Orchestra); sailing. Address: (h.) 87 Glencairn Drive, Glasgow, G41 4LL; T.-041-423 2863.

Simpson, John Donald Carmichael, LLB, FRICS, FRVA. Regional Estates Surveyor, Lothian Regional Council, since 1978; b. 14.1.43, Greenock; m., Elizabeth Hastie Fagnen. Educ. Hutchesons Grammar School, Glasgow; London University (External). City Assessor's Office, Glasgow; British Rail Property Board (Scotland); Thomas Binnie & Hendry, Chartered Surveyors, Glasgow; Estates Department, Glasgow Corporation; Depute Head of Estates, Strathclyde Regional Council. Member, Rent Assessment Panel for Scotland. Recreations: golf; music. Address: (b.) Estates Department, Lothian Regional Council, 30/31 Queen Street, Edinburgh, EH2 1LZ; T.-031-225 1399.

Simpson, John Gruer, MB, ChB (Hons), PhD, MRCPath. Senior Lecturer in Pathology, Aberdeen University, since 1978; Honorary Consultant Pathologist, Grampian Health Board,

since 1978; b. 15.5.41, Toronto, Canada. Educ. Fraserburgh Academy; Aberdeen University. Aberdeen Royal Infirmary: Resident Medical Officer, 1965-66, Garden Research Fellow, 1966-67; Aberdeen University: MRC Junior Research Fellow, 1967-68, Lecturer in Pathology, 1968-75; Visiting Professor and NIH Scholar, Michigan University, 1975-77. Treasurer, European Society for Microcirculation; Assistant Editor, Scottish Medical Journal; Regional Representative, Royal College of Pathologists. Recreations: opera; sailing; travel; cooking; red Burgundy. Address: (h.) 37 Thomson Street, Aberdeen, AB2 4QN; T.-0224 637482.

Simpson, John Moir, FRICS, FCIArb. Senior Partner, John M. Simpson & Co., since 1969; Senior Partner, John A. Wilkie, Simpson and Rennie, since 1979; Member, Cumbernauld Development Corporation, since 1983; b. 29.1.28, Glasgow; m., Elizabeth Russell Faulds; 1 s.; 1 d. Educ. Whitehill Secondary School, Glasgow; Royal Technical College, Glasgow. Chief Surveyor, Cumbernauld Development Corporation, 1965-69. Chairman, Advisory Panel, Glasgow College of Building, since 1965; Member, now Vice-Chairman, Valuation Appeals Committee (North Strathclyde), since 1971; Member, now Vice-Chairman, Board of Management, Citizens Advice Board, Cumbernauld, since 1976; Member, Board of Management, Cumbernauld Theatre, since 1979. Recreations: bowling; curling. Address: (h.) 17 Glen View, Cumbernauld, Glasgow, G67 2DA; T.-02367 22933.

Simpson, John Montgomery, MA. Senior Lecturer in Scottish History, Edinburgh University, since 1981; b. 27.10.38, Edinburgh; m., Anne Corstorphine; 1 s.; 2 d. Educ. Daniel Stewart's College; St. Andrews University. Department of History, Sheffield University, 1962-64; Department of Scottish History, Edinburgh University, since 1964. Recreations: music; walking. Address: (b.) Department of Scottish History, Edinburgh University, 50 George Square, Edinburgh, EH8 9JY; T.-031-667 1011, Ext. 6593.

Simpson, Myrtle Lillias. Author and Lecturer; Chairman, Scottish National Ski Council, since 1983; b. 5.7.31, Aldershot; m., Dr. Hugh Simpson (qv); 3 s.; 1 d. Educ. 19 schools (father in Army). Writer/Explorer; author of 12 books, including travel, biography, historical and children's; first woman to ski across Greenland; attempted to ski to North Pole (most northerly point reached by a woman unsupported); numerous journeys in polar regions on ski or canoe; Mungo Park Medal. Recreations: climbing; skiing; canoeing. Address: (h.) Farletter, Kincraig, Inverness-shire; T.-054 04 288.

Simpson, Rae Henderson, FRCSEdin. Director, Rangers Football Club, since 1972 (Chairman, 1975-84); Consultant Orthopaedic Surgeon, North Ayrshire, 1950-80; b. 3.9.15, Glasgow; m., Moira S. Pedersen (deceased); 3 s. Educ. High School of Glasgow; Glassgow University. Senior Resident, Victoria Infirmary, 1940; Orthopaedic Surgeon, RAMC, 1942-46. Recreations: bridge; bowls; golf; soccer. Address: (h.) 55 London Road, Kilmarnock, KA3 7AG; T.-Kilmarnock 24224.

Simpson, Robert Keith, FCCA, IPFA. Controller of Audit, Commission for Local Authority Accounts in Scotland, since 1985; b. 26.7.43, Barrow-in-Furness; m., Brenda Mary Baines; 2 s. Educ. Barrow-in-Furness Grammar School. Accountant, Barrow-in-Furness County Borough Council, 1959-72; Principal Auditor, Bristol City Council, 1972-74; Chief Auditor, Avon County Council, 1974-77; Assistant Director of Finance, South Yorkshire County Council, 1977-82; Depute Controller of Audit, Commission for Local Authority Accounts in Scotland, 1982-85. Former Editor, Audit Bulletin, CIPFA. Publication: Audit in the Public Sector (Co-author). Recreations: archery; hill-walking. Address: (h.) Cerna, 69 Dirleton Avenue, North Berwick; T.-0620 4288.

Sinclair, Allan MacDonald, PhD, FRSE. Reader in Mathematics, Edinburgh University, since 1977; b. 11.7.41, Johannesburg, South Africa; m., Patricia Margaret Bush; 1 s.; 1 d. Educ. Parktown Boys' High School, Johannesburg; Witwatersrand University; Newcastle-upon-Tyne University. Senior Lecturer, 1968-72, and Professor, 1972-73, in Mathematics, Witwatersrand University; Lecturer in Mathematics, Edinburgh University, 1973-77; Visiting Professor, California University, Los Angeles, 1978-79. Recreations: hill-walking; sculpture; Scottish country dancing. Address: (b.) Department of Mathematics, Edinburgh University, James Clark Building, King's Buildings, Mayfield Road, Edinburgh, EH9 3JZ; T.-031-667 1081, Ext. 2812.

Sinclair, Charles Low. Member, Dundee District Council, since 1977; Local Manager, Standard Life Assurance Co., Dundee, since 1971; b. 20.1.29, Edinburgh; m., June Cecily; 1 s.; 2 d. Educ. George Heriot's, Edinburgh; Edinburgh University. National Savings Certificate Division, HM Treasury, London, 1946; Sergeant, RAEC, 1947-49; bartender, 1949-50; University, 1950-51; joined Standard Life Assurance Co., 1951. Recreations: golf; hill-walking; swimming; gardening. Address: (h.) 31 Dawson Road, West Ferry, Dundee; T.-0382 77570.

Sinclair, 17th Lord, (Charles Murray Kennedy St. Clair), MVO (1953). Lord Lieutenant, Dumfries and Galloway Region (District of Stewartry), since 1982; Extra Equerry to the Queen Mother, since 1953; Member, Queen's Bodyguard for Scotland (Royal Company of Archers); b. 21.6.14; m., Anne Lettice Cotterell; 1 s.; 2 d. Educ. Eton; Magdalene College, Cambridge. Served Second World War (mentioned in Despatches); retired Major, Coldstream Guards. Address: (h.) Knocknalling, St. John's Town of Dalry, Castle Douglas, Kirkcudbrightshire.

Sinclair, Rev. Colin Andrew Macalister, BA (Hons), BD (Hons). Minister, Newton-on-Ayr, Ayr, since 1982; b. 16.9.53, Glasgow; m., Ruth Mary Murray; 1 d. Educ. Glasgow Academy; Stirling University; Edinburgh University. Schools Training Officer, Scripture Union, Zambia, 1974-77; Assistant Minister, Palmerston Place, Edinburgh, 1980-82. Publication: Ministers for the 1980s (Contributor). Recreations: family; reading. Address: 5 Montgomerie Terrace, Ayr, KA7 1JL; T.-0292 264251.

Sinclair, George Macdonald, MA, LLB, FBIM. Director of Administration and Law, Dumfries and Galloway Regional Council, since 1979. Educ. High School of Glasgow; Glasgow University. Deputy Town Clerk, Renfrew, 1963-65; Town Clerk, Buckie, 1965-68; Deputy Town Clerk, Ayr, 1968-75; Assistant Director of Administration, Strathclyde Regional Council (Ayr), 1975-79. Recreations: sailing; curling. Address: (b.) Regional Offices, English Street, Dumfries; T.-Dumfries 53141.

Sinclair, John, MB, ChB, FRCSEdin. Consultant Urological Surgeon, Southern General Hospital, Glasgow, since 1975; b. 16.7.41, Kilmarnock; m., Ann Sinclair; 1 s.; 1 d. Educ. Edinburgh Academy; Edinburgh University. Junior hospital appointments, Inverness and Stornoway; Locum, general practice, from Applecross to Auchenshuggle. Recreations: hill-walking; swimming; playing drums; buses and bus operation. Address: (h.) 7 Bridgegait, Milngavie, Glasgow, G62 6NT; T.-041-956 3247.

Sinclair, Sir John (Rollo Norman Blair), 9th Bt; b. 4.11.28. Educ. Wellington College. Lt., Intelligence Corps, 1948-49; Director, The Human Development Trust, since 1970; Director, Natural Health Foundation, since 1982. Address: (h.) Barrock House, Wick, Caithness.

Sinclair, Martin Fraser, MA, CA. Partner, Chiene & Tait, CA, since 1973; Director, Albyn Trust Ltd., since 1973; Director, NESSCO (Aberdeen) Ltd., since 1982; Vice Chairman, English Speaking Union in Scotland (Treasurer, 1973-81); b. 18.7.45, Greenock; m., Patricia Anne Ogilvy Smith; 1 s.; 2 d. Educ. Edinburgh Academy; Edinburgh University. Apprentice, Chiene & Tait, CA; qualified, 1970; Peat Marwick Mitchell & Co., Vancouver, 1970-73. President, Institute of Chartered Accountants Benevolent Association, 1983-84 (Member, Property Committee, since 1979). Athletics Blue, Edinburgh University; Captain, Scottish Universities Athletics Team, 1969. Recreations: skiing; squash; orienteering. Address: (b.) 3 Albyn Place, Edinburgh, EH2 4NQ; T.-031-225 7515.

Sinfield, Professor Robert Adrian, BA, DipSocAdmin. Professor of Social Policy, Edinburgh University, since 1979; b. 3.11.38, Wallington, Surrey; m., Dorothy Anne Palmer; 2 d. Educ. Mercers' School, London; Balliol College, Oxford; London School of Economics. Assistant Lecturer/Lecturer/Senior Lecturer/ Reader in Sociology, Essex University, 1965-79; Visiting Lecturer in Social Work, Bryn Mawr College and Columbia University, 1969-70; consultancies, OECD, 1965-68, 1970, 1983 and UN, 1970-71; Scientific Adviser to DHSS Chief Scientist, since 1980; Convener and Co-Founder, Unemployment Unit, since 1981. Publications: The Long-Term Unemployed, 1968; Which Way for Social Work?, 1969; Industrial Welfare, 1971; The Workless State (Co-Editor), 1981; What Unemployment Means, 1981. Address: (h.) 12 Eden Lane, Edinburgh, EH10 4SD; T.-031-447 2182.

Sircus, Wilfred, MD, PhD, FRCP, FRCPEdin. Consultant Physician in administrative charge, Edinburgh University Gastrointestinal Unit,

Western General Hospital, since 1966; Reader in Medicine, Edinburgh University, since 1969; President, World Organisation for Digestive Endoscopy, since 1983; b. 26.11.19, Liverpool; m., 1, Mill-Luise Kroger; 2, Margaret McNay; 2 s.; 1 d.; 4 step d. Educ. Holt High School; Liverpool University. Medical Officer, 1st Bn., Princess Louise Kensington Regiment, 1943-45; Staff Surgeon and graded Specialist, 46th Division, 1946-47; Registrar, Broadgreen Hospital, Liverpool, 1947-52, Senior Registrar, 1947-49; Lecturer in Applied Physiology, Liverpool University, 1949-51; Clinical Research Fellow, Sheffield, 1951-53; Lecturer in Medicine, Edinburgh University, 1954; part-time Member, External Scientific Staff, MRC, 1959-71; Senior Lecturer in Medicine, Edinburgh University, 1965. Past President, British Society of Digestive Endoscopy; Past President, British Society of Gastroenterology; President, British Digestive Foundation Scottish Appeal. Recreations: painting; golf; visual arts. Address: (h.) 30 Saxe-Coburg Place, Edinburgh, EH3 5BP; T.-031-332 1554.

Sischy, Mark, MA, LLB, SSC, NP. Solicitor in private practice, since 1975; Member, Court of Session Rules Council; Member, Scottish Valuation Advisory Council; Member, Standing Committees, Law Society of Scotland; Member, Executive Committee, Scottish Family Conciliation Service (Lothian); b. 14.7.45, Johannesburg; m., Judith Lewis; 2 d. Educ. George Watson's College, Edinburgh; Edinburgh University. Recreation: armchair sportsman. Address: (b.) Hogarth House, 43 Queen Street, Edinburgh; T.-031-225 2121.

Skene, Hugh Crawford. Composer; b. 24.2.19; m., Barbara Land; 1 d. Educ. Bristol. War Service as Camouflage Officer; graduated, 1949; Director of Orchestra, Buxton College; Founder Member and Musical Director, Buxton Opera Group; Director of Orchestras, City of Norwich School, 1953-73; compositions during this period include Derbyshire Rhapsody, Symphony from East Anglia and the cantata Birthday of Jesus; Musical Director, St. Cecilia Chorus and Orchestra, 13 years; returned to Scotland (Hamilton Grammar School), 1973; Musical Director, Blantyre Choral Society; retired from education service, 1983; later compositions include opera on Dumas' The Black Tulip and Highland symphony; wrote several chamber pieces and solo works, with orchestra, for violin and double bass. Recreation: exploring and photographing remote Scotland. Address: (h.) Crowhills, by Hamilton, Lanarkshire, ML3 7XP; T.-Chapelton 303.

Skinner, Rev. Alistair, BD. Minister, Priestfield Parish Church, Edinburgh, since 1975; b. 22.9.24, Greenock; m., Frances Craigmile; 2 s.; 1 d. Educ. Highlanders' Academy, Greenock; Greenock High School; Hartley-Victoria College, Manchester; Christ's College, Aberdeen. Minister: Dunbar Methodist Church, 1951-54, Lancaster Methodist Circuit, 1954-60, Liverpool Methodist Mission, 1960-63; Assistant Minister, Mastrick Parish Church, Aberdeen, 1963-64; Minister, Douglas and Angus Parish Church, Dundee, 1964-75. Address: 13 Lady Road, Edinburgh, EH16 5PA; T.-031-668 1620.

Skinner, Basil Chisholm, MA, FSA. Director of Extra-Mural Studies, Edinburgh University, since 1975; Chairman, Hopetoun House Preservation Trust, since 1979; Chairman, Conservation Committee, Scottish Development Agency, since 1979; b. 1923, Edinburgh; m., Lydia Mary Mackinnon; 2 s. Educ. Edinburgh Academy; Edinburgh University. Army Service, Yorkshire Yeomanry and Intelligence Corps; Librarian, Glasgow School of Art, 1951-54; Assistant Keeper, Scottish National Portrait Gallery, 1954-66; joined Edinburgh University as Lecturer, 1966; Council Member, National Trust for Scotland, 1970-75; Governor, Edinburgh Academy, 1973-75; Vice-President, Society of Antiquaries of Scotland, 1975-78; Member, Board of Trustees, National Museum of Antiquities, 1975-78; Trustee, Sir Patrick Geddes Memorial Trust, since 1981; Member, Scottish Museum of the Year Award Panel, since 1981; recipient, George Waterston Memorial Award, 1982. Publications: Scottish History in Perspective, 1966; Scots in Italy, 1966; Lime Industry in Lothian, 1970. Recreations: gardening; walking; travel. Address: (b.) Department of Extra-Mural Studies, 11 Buccleuch Place, Edinburgh, 8: T.-031-667 1011.

Skinner, David Neave, BArch, MLArch, RIBA, ALI. Consultant Landscape Architect; Course Director, BA (Hons) Course in Landscape Architecture, Heriot-Watt University/Edinburgh College of Art, since 1974; b. 16.12.28; m., Patricia Mary Coulthwaite; 2 s. Educ. Liverpool University; Pennsylvania University. Private practice in landscape architecture in Edinburgh; Professor of Landscape Architecture, School of Architecture and Planning, New Delhi; Landscape Consultant, Ford Foundation, India; Dean, Faculty of Environmental Sciences, Heriot-Watt University. Publications: The Coast of Scotland, 1974; The Planning and Design of Rural Roads, 1976. Address: (h.) 5 Fingal Place, Edinburgh, EH9 1JX; T.-031-667 1503.

Skinner, Edgar Roy, BSc, PhD, CChem, MRCS. Senior Lecturer in Biochemistry, Aberdeen University, since 1979; b. 17.4.32, Birmingham; m., Sofie Lokke; 1 s.; 1 d. Educ. King Edward VI Grammar School, Birmingham; Birmingham University; University College, London. Assistant Professor of Chemistry, Cornell University, 1958-60; Senior Research Fellow, then Lecturer, Department of Biochemistry, Aberdeen University, 1960-79. Address: (b.) Department of Biochemistry, Aberdeen University, Marischal College, Aberdeen, AB9 1AS; T.-0224 40241.

Slater, Basil Crandles Smith, OBE, MD, MRCP, FRCGP, MFCM, Hon. MCFP (Canada). Director, Scottish Health Services Planning Unit, Scottish Home and Health Department, since 1985; b. 26.7.28, Broxburn; m., Jean Wallace Simpson; 2 s.; 1 d. Educ. Armadale Public School; Bathgate Academy; Edinburgh University. House Physician, Edinburgh Royal Infirmary, 1952; House Surgeon, Bangour General Hospital, 1953; Surgeon Lieutenant, RNVR, 1953-55; General Practitioner, Harrow, Middlesex and Dalkeith, Midlothian, 1955-75; joined Scottish

Home and Health Department, 1975. Former Honorary Secretary and Vice Chairman of Council, Royal College of General Practitioners; former Regional Adviser in General Practice, North West Metropolitan Region; former Vice-President, Section of General Practice, Royal Society of Medicine; first Civilian Consultant in General Practice to Royal Navy. Recreations: bridge (average); bowling (reasonable); fireside sitting (well). Address: (b.) Scottish Home and Health Department, St. Andrews House, Edinburgh; T.-031-556 8501.

Slater, Carolyn Louttit (Buchanan), LLB. Secretary (Legal Education), Law Society of Scotland, since 1978; b. 22.12.47, Glasgow; m., John Cameron Slater. Educ. Hutchesons' Girls' Grammar School, Glasgow; Glasgow University. Apprentice Solicitor and Legal Assistant, Glasgow, 1968-74; Lecturer, Department of Land Economics, Paisley College of Technology, 1974-78. Address: (b.) 26 Drumsheugh Gardens, Edinburgh, EH3 7YR; T.-031-226 7411.

Slater, Peter Anderson, MB, ChB, FRCSEdin. Consultant Orthopaedic Surgeon, Stracathro Hospital and Aberdeen Royal Infirmary, since 1978; b. 6.9.41, Aberdeen; m., Isobel; 1 s.; 2 d. Educ. Prince of Wales School, Nairobi; Aberdeen University. House Officer, Aberdeen Royal Infirmary, 1966-67; Lecturer in Pathology, Aberdeen University, 1967-68; Senior House Officer, General Surgery, Aberdeen Royal Infirmary, 1968-70; Registrar, General Surgery, South Teeside Hospitals, 1970-72; Registrar in Orthopaedics, South Birmingham Hospitals, 1972-75; Senior Registrar in Orthopaedics, Aberdeen Royal Infirmary, 1975-78. Board Member, National Centre for Education and Training in Prosthetics and Orthotics, Strathclyde University. Recreations: DIY; reading science fiction. Address: (h.) 67 Park Road, Brechin, Angus, DD9 7AP; T.-035 62 2554.

Slater, Professor Peter James Bramwell, BSc, PhD, DSc. Kennedy Professor of Natural History, St. Andrews University, since 1984; b. 26.12.42, Edinburgh; m., Elisabeth Vernon Smith; 2 s. Educ. Edinburgh Academy; Glenalmond; Edinburgh University. Demonstrator in Zoology, Edinburgh University, 1966-68; Lecturer in Biology, Sussex University, 1968-84. Secretary, Association for the Study of Animal Behaviour, 1973-78; European Editor, Animal Behaviour, 1979-82; Associate Editor, Advances in the Study of Behavior and of Science Progress. Recreations: walking; ornithology; music; disarmament. Address: (b.) Department of Zoology and Marine Biology, St. Andrews, Fife; T.-0334 76161, Ext. 7218.

Slaven, Professor Anthony, MA, BLitt. Professor of Business History, Glasgow University, since 1979 (Head, Department of Economic History, since 1979); b. 5.10.37, Blantyre; m., Isabelle Dunsheath Cameron; 1 s.; 2 d. Educ. Hamilton Academy; Glasgow University. Assistant Lecturer, Glasgow University, 1960-62; Lecturer in Geography, Queensland University, 1962-64; Glasgow University: Lecturer in Economic History, 1965-70, Colquhoun Lecturer in Business

History, since 1969, Senior Lecturer in Economic History, 1970-79. Council Member, Economic History Society; Member, Editorial Board, Scottish Economic and Social History. Publications: The Development of the West of Scotland; Shipbuilding - A Review of UK Statistics. Recreations: walking; golf; DIY. Address: (b.) Department of Economic History, Adam Smith Building, Glasgow University, Glasgow, G12 8QQ; T.-041-339 8855, Ext. 669.

Slavin, William J., MA, STL. Secretary, RC Justice and Peace Commission, since 1980; b. 17.1.40, Bristol. Educ. Blairs College, Aberdeen; Scots College, Rome; Glasgow University. Assistant Priest, Broomhill, Glasgow, 1965-70; Educational Psychologist, Glasgow Child Guidance Service, 1970-75; Deputy Director, Jessore Training Centre, Bangladesh, 1975-80. Assistant Chaplain, Barlinnie Prison. Recreation: An rud Gaidhealach. Address: (b.) 28 Rose Street, Glasgow, G3 6RE; T.-041-333 0238.

Slawson, Keith Brian, BSc, MB, ChB, FFARCS. Consultant Anaesthetist, Western General Hospital, Edinburgh, since 1966; Honorary Senior Lecturer, Edinburgh University, since 1975; b. 7.9.33, Birmingham; m., Nan; 1 s.; 1 d. Educ. Bradford Grammar School; Edinburgh University. MRC Scientific Assistant, Department of Therapeutics, Edinburgh Royal Infirmary, 1962-63; Lecturer in Anaesthesia, Edinburgh University, 1963-66. Honorary Medical Officer, Scottish Rugby Union. Recreation: refereeing rugby football. Address: (h.) 27 Craigmount View, Edinburgh; T.-031-339 4786.

Sleeman, Professor Brian David, BSc, PhD, DSc, FIMA, FRSE. Professor of Mathematics, Dundee University, since 1976; b. 4.8.39, London; m., Juliet Mary Shea; 2 s.; 1 d. Educ. Tiffin Boys School; Battersea College of Technology; London University. Department of Mathematical Sciences, Dundee University: Assistant Lecturer, 1965-67, Lecturer, 1967-71, Reader, 1971-78. Chairman, Scottish Branch, Institute of Mathematics and its Applications, 1982-84; Member, General Synod and Administration Board, Scottish Episcopal Church. Publications: Multiparameter Spectral Theory in Hilbert Space, 1978; Differential Equations and Mathematical Biology, 1983. Recreations: choral music; hill-walking. Address: (b.) Department of Mathematical Sciences, Dundee University, Dundee, DD1 4HN; T.-0382 23181.

Sleigh, James Douglas, MB, ChB, FRCPath, FRCPGlas. Reader in Bacteriology, Glasgow University, since 1984; Consultant Bacteriologist, Glasgow Royal Infirmary, since 1979; b. 5.7.30, Glasgow; m., Rosemary Margaret Smith; 2 s. Educ. Glasgow Academy; Glasgow University. House appointments, Glasgow Western Infirmary, 1953-54; Pathologist, RAMC, 1954-56; Registrar in Bacteriology, Glasgow Western Infirmary, 1956-58; Lecturer in Bacteriology, Edinburgh University, 1958-65; Consultant Clinical Pathologist, Dunbartonshire Hospitals, 1965-69; Senior Lecturer in Bacteriology, Glasgow University, 1969-84; Consultant Bacteriologist, Glasgow Western Infirmary, 1969-79.

Publication: Notes on Medical Bacteriology (Co-author). Recreations: seeking non-existent bargains; spending time on Arran. Address: (h.) Clynder, 5 Sutherland Avenue, Glasgow, G41 4JJ; T.-041-427 1486.

Sloane, Professor Peter James, BA (Econ), PhD. Professor of Political Economy, Aberdeen University, since 1984; b. 6.8.42, Cheadle Hulme; m., Avril Mary Urquhart; 1 s. Educ. Cheadle Hulme School; Sheffield University; Strathclyde University. Assistant Lecturer and Lecturer, Department of Political Economy, Aberdeen University, 1966-69; Lecturer in Industrial Economics, Nottingham University, 1969-75; Economic Adviser, Department of Employment Unit for Manpower Studies (on secondment), 1973-74; Professor of Economics and Management, Paisley College, 1975-84. Member, Economic and Social Research Council, 1979-85; Council Member, Scottish Economic Society, since 1983. Publications: Sex Discrimination in the Labour Market, 1976; Women and Low Pay, 1980; Sport in the Market?, 1980; Equal Employment Issues, 1981; Tackling Discrimination in the Workplace, 1982. Recreation: sport. Address: (b.) Department of Political Economy, Aberdeen University, Edward Wright Building, Dunbar Street, Old Aberdeen, Aberdeen, AB9 2TY; T.-0224 40241, Ext. 5308.

Small, Christopher. Writer; b. 15.11.19, London. Educ. Dartington; Oxford. Literary Editor and Dramatic Critic, Glasgow Herald, 1955-80; author of Ariel Like A Harpy: Shelley, Mary & Frankenstein; The Road to Miniluv: George Orwell, the State & God; The Printed Word: An Instrument of Popularity.

Small, David William, MA. Managing Director, John Dewar & Sons Ltd., Perth, since 1969; Director, The Distillers Company plc, since 1974; Council Member, Scotch Whisky Association, since 1979; b. 9.6.27, Broughty Ferry; m., Annette Elizabeth Borrie; 2 s.; 1 d. Educ. Glenalmond College; Corpus Christi College, Cambridge. Army, 1945-48 (Lt., Intelligence Corps); The Distillers Co plc, since 1951: Legal and Administration, 1951-60, Director, White Horse Distillers Ltd., 1961-64, President, The Distillers Co. (Canada) Ltd., Toronto, 1964-68. Member, Glenalmond College Council, since 1975; Member, Canada-UK Chamber of Commerce Council, since 1974 (President, 1977). Recreations: gardening; golf; tennis; reading. Address: (b.) Dewar House, Haymarket, London, SW1Y 4DF; T.-01-930 2191.

Small, Professor John Rankin, BSc (Econ), FCCA, FCMA. Professor and Head, Department of Accountancy and Finance, Heriot-Watt University, since 1967; Chairman, Commission for Local Authority Accounts in Scotland, since 1983; b. 28.2.33, Dundee; m., Catherine Wood; 1 s.; 2 d. Educ. Harris Academy; Dundee School of Economics. Industry and commerce; Lecturer, Edinburgh University; Senior Lecturer, Glasgow University. Consultant to various organisations; Council Member, Chartered Association of Certified Accountants (President,

1982-83); Vice-Principal, Heriot-Watt University, 1974-78; Member, Accounts Commission, since 1982. Recreation: golf. Address: (b.) Heriot-Watt University, Grassmarket, Edinburgh; T.-031-225 8432.

Small, Ramsay George, MB, ChB, FFCM, MRCPE, DPH. Community Medicine Specialist, Tayside Health Board, since 1974; Honorary Senior Lecturer in Community Medicine, Dundee University, since 1974; b. 5.2.30, Calcutta; m., Aileen Stiven Masterton; 4 s. Educ. Harris Academy, Dundee; St. Andrews University. Assistant Medical Officer of Health, Ayr County Council, 1958-61; Senior Assistant Medical Officer of Health, then Principal Medical Officer, City of Dundee, 1961-74. Faculty Adviser, Scotland, Faculty of Community Medicine, 1980-83, Convener, Scottish Affairs Committee, since 1983; Member, Scotish Joint Consultants' Committee; Member, Conference of Royal Colleges and Faculties of Scotland; President, Baptist Union of Scotland, 1972-73; Chairman, Eastern Regional Postgraduate Medical Education Committee, 1980-83; Secretary, Broughty Ferry Baptist Church, since 1969. Recreations: bird-watching; music. Address: (h.) 46 Monifieth Road, Broughty Ferry, Dundee, DD5 2RX; T.-Dundee 78408.

Small, Very Rev. Robert Leonard, CBE, MA, DD. Vice Chairman, Age Concern Scotland; Minister of Religion (retired); b. 12.5.05, North Berwick; m., Jane Hay McGregor; 3 s.; 1 d. Educ. North Berwick High School; Edinburgh University and New College. Minister: St. John's, Bathgate, 1931-35, West High, Kilmarnock, 1935-44, Cramond Kirk, Edinburgh, 1944-56, St. Cuthbert's, Edinburgh, 1956-75; Convener, Church of Scotland Committees: Huts and Canteens, Temperance and Morals, Social and Moral Welfare, Stewardship and Budget; Moderator, General Assembly, 1966; Chaplain to the Queen, since 1967; Member, Scottish Advisory Committee on Treatment of Offenders, 1950-66; Chairman, Parole Board for Scotland, 1967-73. Vice-President, Edinburgh Scout Council; Vice-President, Edinburgh Council of Girl Guides; Honorary Vice-President, Boys' Brigade; Regional Chaplain to Air Training Corps, since 1953; OBE, 1957; Chairman, Age Concern Scotland, 1981-83; Chairman, Edinburgh Parkinson's Disease Society. Address: (h.) 5 Craighill Gardens, Edinburgh, EH10 5PY; T.-031-447 4243.

Smart, Alastair, DA, ARSA, ARBS. Sculptor; Lecturer in Sculpture, Duncan of Jordanstone College of Art, Dundee, since 1965; b. 23.2.37, Aberdeen; m., Elizabeth Gowans Ovenstone; 1 s.; 2 d. Educ. Aberdeen Academy; Gray's School of Art, Aberdeen. School Teacher: Banffshire, Gordon Schools, Huntly. RSA Travelling Scholarship; Keith Prize; Benno Schotz Award; Latimer Award; Elizabeth T. Greenshields Award (Canada). Recreations: sculpture; music; theatre. Address: (h.) 242 Coupar Angus Road, Muirhead, by Dundee; T.-0382 580573.

Smart, George Edward, MB, ChB, FRCOG, FRCSEdin. Consultant Obstetrician and Gynaecologist, Simpson Memorial Maternity Pavilion and Royal Infirmary, Edinburgh, since 1976; Honorary Senior Lecturer, Edinburgh University; b. 19.6.35, Shipley, Yorkshire; m., Margaret; 1 s.; 2 d. Educ. Bradford Grammar School; Edinburgh University Medical School. House Physician and Surgeon appointments: Ashford Hospital, Middlesex, 1960, Edinburgh Royal Infirmary, 1961, Bradford Royal Infirmary, St. Lukes Hospital, Bradford, 1962-63; Registrar and Senior Registrar appointments, Simpson Memorial Maternity Pavilion and Royal Infirmary, Edinburgh; Senior Tumor Fellow, State University of New York, 1970-71; Consultant Senior Lecturer, Bristol University, and Honorary Consultant, United Bristol Hospitals, Bristol Maternity Hospital and Southmead Hospital, Bristol, until 1976; Examiner, Royal College of Surgeons, Edinburgh, and Royal College of Obstetricians and Gynaecologists, London. Recreations: swimming; golf; gardening. Address: (h.) Beechcroft, 24 Cramond Road North, Cramond, Edinburgh; T.-031-336 8499.

Smellie, Professor Robert Martin Stuart, BSc, PhD, DSc, FIBiol, FRSE. Cathcart Professor of Biochemistry, Glasgow University, since 1966; Honorary General Secretary, Royal Society of Edinburgh, since 1976; b. 1.4.27, Rothesay; m., Florence Mary Devlin Adams; 2 s. Educ. Dundee High School; Glasgow Academy; St. Andrews University; Glasgow University; New York College of Medicine. Commissioned, Royal Scots Fusiliers, 1947-49; Glasgow University: Assistant Lecturer in Biochemistry, 1949-52, Bite Memorial Fellow, 1952-53, Lecturer, 1953-59; Research Fellow, Department of Biochemistry, New York University College of Medicine, 1955-56; Glasgow University: Senior Lecturer in Biochemistry, 1959-64, Reader in Molecular Biology, 1964-66. Committee Member, Biochemical Society, 1967-71; Symposium Organiser, Biochemical Society, 1970-75; Chairman, Scottish Branch, Institute of Biology, 1967-69. Recreations: fishing; walking; music; foreign travel. Address: (b.) Department of Biochemistry, Glasgow University, Glasgow, G12 8QQ; T.-041-339 8855, Ext. 620.

Smillie, Ian R.D., BL. Chief Executive Officer and Director of Administration, Kyle and Carrick District Council, since 1983; b. 13.9.39, Kilmarnock; m., Margaret; 2 d. Educ. Kilmarnock Academy; Glasgow University. Private practice, 1958-68; Royal Burgh of Ayr, 1968-74 (latterly as Assistant Town Clerk); Director of Administration, Kyle and Carrick District Council, 1974-83. Address: (b.) Burns House, Burns Statue Square, Ayr, KA7 1UP; T.-0292 281511.

Smith, Adam Neil, MD, FRCSE, FRSE. Reader in Surgery, Edinburgh University, since 1963; Consultant Surgeon, Gastro-Intestinal Unit, Edinburgh, since 1962; Adviser in Postgraduate Studies, Royal College of Surgeons, Edinburgh, since 1980; b. 27.6.26, Hamilton; m., Sibyl Mary Veitch Johnstone; 1 s.; 3 d. Educ. Lanark Grammar School; Glasgow University. Academic and Health Service appointments, since 1948; Lecturer in Surgery, Glasgow University; Medical Research Council Fellow; Senior Lecturer,

Edinburgh University and Western General Hospital. Vice-President, Scottish Arts Club; former Surgical Traveller, James IV Surgical Association; former Council Member, Royal College of Surgeons of Edinburgh. Recreation: golf. Address: (h.) 105 Trinity Road, Edinburgh; T.-031-552 3836.

Smith, Sheriff Agnes Lawrie Addie, LLB. Sheriff of Glasgow and Strathkelvin, since 1982; b. 17.6.47. Educ. Hamilton Academy; Glasgow University. Solicitor, 1969; called to the Scottish Bar, 1976; Solicitor, private practice, 1969-71; Procurator Fiscal Depute, 1971-75.

Smith, Sir Alan, Kt (1982), CBE (1976), DFC (1941) and Bar (1942), DL, JP. President, Dawson International plc, Kinross, since 1982; Chairman, Quayle Munro PLC, Edinburgh, since 1982; Director, Global Recovery Investment Trust PLC, London, since 1981; b. 14.3.17, South Shields; m., 1, Margaret Stewart Todd (deceased); 2, Alice Elizabeth Moncur; 3 s.; 2 d. Educ. Bede College, Sunderland. Self-employed, 1931-36; Unilever, 1936-39; RAF, 1939-45; Managing Director, Todd & Duncan Ltd., Kinross, 1946-60; Chairman and Chief Executive, Dawson International, Kinross, 1960-82. Board Member, Scottish Development Agency, since 1982; Board Member, Scottish Tourist Board, since 1983; Kinross Burgh Councillor, 1952-65; Provost of Kinross, 1959-65; Tayside Regional Councillor, since 1979; Financial Convenor, Tayside Region, since 1980. Recreations: work; sailing. Address: (h.) Ardgairney House, Cleish, by Kinross; T.-05775 265.

Smith, Alan Gordon Rae, MA, PhD, FRHistS. Reader in Modern History, Glasgow University, since 1985; b. 22.12.36, Glasgow; m., Isabel Robertson; 1 s.; 1 d. Educ. Glasgow High School; Glasgow University; University College, London. Research Fellow, Institute of Historical Research, London University, 1961-62; Assistant in History, 1962-64, then Lecturer, Glasgow University, 1964-75; Senior Lecturer in Modern History, 1975-85; Review Editor, History (Journal of the Historical Association), since 1984. Publications: The Government of Elizabethan England, 1967; The New Europe, 1969; Science and Society in the Sixteenth and Seventeenth Centuries, 1972; Servant of the Cecils: The Life of Sir Michael Hickes, 1977; The Emergence of a Nation State: The Commonwealth of England 1529-1660, 1984. Recreation: watching sport. Address: (h.) 5 Cargil Avenue, Kilmacolm, Renfrewshire; T.-Kilmacolm 2055.

Smith, Alistair Fairley, MA, MD, FRCPEdin, FRCPath. Senior Lecturer in Clinical Chemistry, Edinburgh University, since 1971; Consultant Clinical Chemist, Edinburgh Royal Infirmary, since 1971; b. 5.10.35, Edinburgh; m., Carol Ann; 1 s.; 1 d. Educ. Bootham School, York; Clare College, Cambridge. House Officer post, London Hospital, 1960-61; House Officer and junior Assistant Pathologist posts, Addenbrookes' Hospital, Cambridge; Lecturer in Clinical Chemistry, Edinburgh University, 1965-71. Publications: Lecture Notes on Clinical Chemistry (Co-author);

Multiple Choice Questions on Clinical Chemistry (Co-author). Recreations: golf; bridge. Address: (b.) Department of Clinical Chemistry, Royal Infirmary, Edinburgh, EH3 9YW; T.-031-229 2477, Ext. 2365.

Smith, Anne, LLB (Hons). Advocate, since 1980; b. 16.3.55, Glasgow; m., David Alexander Smith, WS; 1 s. Educ. Cheadle Girls School; Edinburgh University. Law Apprentice, Shepherd & Wedderburn, WS, Edinburgh, 1977-79; Devilling with J.M. McGhie, then Advocate, now QC, 1979-80. Recreations: music, piano and flute; aerobics. Address: (b.) Advocates Library, Parliament House, Edinburgh; T.-031-226 5071.

Smith, Sheriff Charles, MA, LLB. Sheriff of Glasgow and Strathkelvin, since 1982; b. 15.8.30; m.; 1 s.; 1 d. Educ. Perth Academy; St. Andrews University. Solicitor, private practice, 1956-82; Member, Council, Law Society of Scotland, 1977-82; Member, Perth Town Council, 1966-68.

Smith, Charles, BSc, PhD, DSc. Senior Principal Scientific Officer, AFRC Animal Breeding Research Organisation, Edinburgh, since 1974; b. 28.11.32, Aberdeen; 1 s.; 1 d. Educ. Robert Gordon's College, Aberdeen; Aberdeen University; Iowa State University. Research Scientist, Animal Breeding Research Organisation, Edinburgh, 1958-68; Lecturer in Human Genetics, Edinburgh University, 1968-74. Recreations: squash; gardening; reading. Address: (h.) 4 Alnwickhill Road, Edinburgh; T.-031-664 3301.

Smith, C. Christopher, MB, FRCP. Consultant Physician, General Medicine, Aberdeen Royal Infirmary and Consultant in charge, Regional Infection Unit, City Hospital, Aberdeen, since 1973; Honorary Senior Lecturer, Aberdeen University, since 1973; b. 16.5.39, West Indies; 2 s.; 1 d. Educ. Lodge School, Barbados; Edinburgh University. Registrar, Department of Medicine, Edinburgh Royal Infirmary; Registrar, Thoracic Medicine, then Senior Registrar, Infectious Diseases, City Hospital, Edinburgh; Senior Registrar, Department of Therapeutics, Edinburgh Royal Infirmary; Member, Part I MRCP Examination Board, RCPS; Examiner, MRCP Part II; Editor, Human Health and the Environment. Recreations: cricket; golf; live theatre; jazz music. Address: (b.) Wards 25/26, Aberdeen Royal Infirmary, Foresterhill, Aberdeen, AB2; T.-Aberdeen 681818.

Smith, Sheriff David Buchanan, MA, LLB. Sheriff of North Strathclyde, at Kilmarnock, since 1975; b. 31.10.36; m.,; 2 s.; 1 d. Educ. Paisley Grammar School; Glasgow University; Edinburgh University. Advocate, 1961.

Smith, Rt. Rev. David Macintyre Bell Armour, MA, BD, DUniv, JP. Minister, Logie, since 1965; Moderator, General Assembly of the Church of Scotland, 1985; b. 5.4.23, Perth; m., Mary Kulvear Cumming; 3 s. Educ. Monckton Combe; Peebles High School; St. Andrews University. Minister, Warrender Church, Edinburgh, 1951-61; Exchange Preacher, USA, 1958 and 1961; Minister, Old Partick, Glasgow, 1961-65; Moderator, Stirling and Dunblane Presbytery,

1972-73; Moderator, Perth and Stirling Synod, 1975-76; Vice Convener, Joint Working Party, Church of Scotland, 1980-82; Convener, Church of Scotland Board of Education, 1979-83; Church of Scotland Representative, Stirlingshire Education Committee, 1969-79; Governor, Moray House College of Education, 1983. Recreations: philately; gardening. Address: (h.) 34 Airthrey Road, Stirling, FK9 5JS; T.-Stirling 75085.

Smith, Derek Matthew Hutchison, MA, LLB. Honorary Sheriff, Ayr, since 1971; b. 1.10.10, Glasgow; m., Nora Rawling; 1 s.; 1 d. Educ. Glasgow High School; Glasgow University. Practised as Solicitor in Girvan, 1935-77; appointed Burgh Prosecutor, Maybole, 1969; JP Fiscal, Carrick District, 1970; Tory candidate, South Ayrshire, 1951 and 1955; Council Member, Law Society of Scotland, 1965-76 (first Convener, Society's EEC Committee); Member, Girvan Town Council, 19 years (Provost, 1953-56); Past Chairman, Girvan Invasion Committee; Honorary Treasurer, St. John's Episcopal Church, Girvan. Recreation: walking. Address: (h.) 45 The Loaning, Alloway, Ayr; T.-Alloway 41923.

Smith, Douglas Campbell, MREHIS, MRSH, FInstPet. Director of Environmental Health and Trading Standards, Shetland Islands Council; b. 31.3.28, Lerwick; m., Marguerite May Rosalind; 2 s.; 1 d. Educ. Anderson Educational Institute, Lerwick; Heriot-Watt College, Edinburgh. Zetland County Council, 1949-75 (latterly County Sanitary Inspector/Director of Environmental Health); Director of Environmental Health and Consumer Protection, Shetland Islands Council, 1975-77; Director of Protective Services and Housing, 1977-85. Recreations: brass band; photography. Address: (b.) 3 Commercial Road, Lerwick, ZE1 OLX; T.-0595 3535, Ext. 324.

Smith, Douglas Murray, MA (Hons). Rector, Dumfries Academy, since 1980; b. 2.10.39, Glasgow; m., Patricia Katherine Petrie; 2 d. Educ. Hutchesons' Boys Grammar School; Glasgow University. Co-author of mathematics text books. Recreation: sport. Address: (b.) Dumfries Academy, Dumfries; T.-0387 52846.

Smith, (Edward) Alistair, CBE, MA, PhD. Director, Aberdeen University Development Trust, since 1982; Deputy Chairman, Scottish Conservative Party, since 1981; b. 16.1.39, Aberdeen. Educ. Aberdeen Grammar School; Aberdeen University. Lecturer in Geography, Aberdeen University, since 1963; President, Scottish Conservative and Unionist Association, 1979-81; Member, Grampian Health Board, since 1983. Publications: Europe: A Geographical Survey of the Continent (Co-author), 1979; Scotland's Future Development (Contributor), 1983. Recreations: travel; photography; music. Address: (h.) 68A Beaconsfield Place, Aberdeen, AB2 4AJ; T.-0224 642932.

Smith, Edward Gordon, BA, BSc, DipEd. Head Teacher, Castlebrae High School, Edinburgh, since 1983; b. 10.11.39, Fochabers; m., Ann Smith; 1 s.; 1 d. Educ. Elgin Academy; Aberdeen University. Education Officer, Uganda and Kenya; Teacher, Hyndland Secondary School;

Principal Teacher of Chemistry, North Kelvinside School; Assistant Head Teacher, Firrhill High School; Deputy Head Teacher, Forrester High School. Recreations: sailing; walking; philately. Address: (b.) Castlebrae High School, Greendykes Road, Edinburgh, EH16 4DP; T.-031-661 1282.

Smith, Eric Watson, MIES. Industrial Relations Director, Yarrow Shipbuilders Ltd., since 1977; b. 7.2.31, Glasgow; m., Irene; 2 s. Educ. Whitehill Senior Secondary School; Perth Academy; Royal Technical College, Glasgow. Apprentice Engineer/Draughtsman, A. Stephen & Sons Ltd.; Supervisor, Caterpillar Tractor Ltd.; Superintendent, Engineering Manager, Rootes Motors (Scotland) Ltd.; Plant Engineering Manager, Chrysler UK Ltd.; Works Manager, Yarrow Engineeers (Glasgow) Ltd.; General Manager, Industrial Relations and Personnel, Yarrow Shipbuilders Ltd. Council Member, Institute of Engineers and Shipbuilders, Scotland; Council Member, Anniesland College. Recreations: golf; gardening. Address: (b.) Yarrow Shipbuilders Ltd., Scotstoun, Glasgow, G14 OXN; T.-041-959 1207.

Smith, Francis William, MB, ChB, DMRD, FFRRCS (1). Consultant in Nuclear Medicine, Grampian Health Board, since 1979; Clinical Senior Lecturer in Medicine, Aberdeen University, since 1979; b. 8.1.43, Colchester; m., Pamela Anne Cox; 1 s.; 1 d. Educ. Prince Edward School, Harare; Aberdeen University. Studied nuclear medicine, Hospital for Sick Children, Toronto; in 1980 began first clinical trial of magnetic resonance imaging technique, subsequently applied to medical diagnosis worldwide; Visiting Professor, Cornell University Medical School, British Columbia University and Vanderbilt University, 1981; Visiting Professor, Cornell University Medical School and Ohio State University, 1982; Guest Lecturer, Australia and New Zealand Society of Nuclear Medicine, 1983; Jameson Memorial Lecturer, Royal College of Physicians and Surgeons of Canada, 1984; Past President, Society for Magnetic Resonance Imaging; Co-Editor in Chief, Magnetic Resonance Imaging. Recreations: swimming; fishing; reading. Address: (h.) 7 Primrosehill Road, Cults, Aberdeen, AB1 9ND; T.-Aberdeen 868745.

Smith, George Andrew, MBE, FIH. Director of Housing, City of Dundee District Council, since 1974; b. 6.7.22, Perth; 1 s. Educ. Perth Academy. Housing and Social Development Officer, Cumbernauld Development Corporation, 1960-71; Housing Manager, Liverpool City Council, 1971-74; Visiting Professor of Housing Administration, Stirling University, 1984; President, Institute of Housing, 1984-85; Adviser to Housing Committee, COSLA. Recreations: golf; curling; football; gardening (by necessity). Address: (h.) 6 Dunmore Gardens, Ninewells, Dundee; T.-0382 65563.

Smith, George Ballantyne Pryde, BSc (Hons). Head Teacher, Boclair Academy, since 1976; b. 24.7.31, Glasgow; m., Anne; 3 s. Educ. Albert Secondary School; Strathclyde University; Glasgow University. Teacher: Possil Secondary,

Whitehill Secondary, North Kelvinside Secondary; Principal Teacher of Mathematics, Knightswood Secondary; Head Teacher, Eastbank Academy. Recreations: golf; reading. Address: (b.) Inveroran Drive, Bearsden, Glasgow, G61 2PL; T.-041-943 0717.

Smith, Gordon Matthew, MITSA. Director of Consumer Protection, Dumfries and Galloway Regional Council, since 1982; b. 10.11.44, Ayr; m., Moyra; 1 s.; 1 d. Educ. Ayr Academy. Trainee Trading Standards Officer, Ayr County Council, 1962-66; Trading Standards Officer: Lindsey (Lincolnshire) County Council, 1966-68, Lanark County Council, 1968-72; District Trading Standards Officer, 1972-75; Senior Trading Standards Officer, Strathclyde Regional Council, 1975-79; Assistant Chief Trading Standards Officer, Central Regional Council, 1979-82. Recreations: golf; curling; badminton. Address: (b.) 1 Newall Terrace, Dumfries, DG1 1LN; T.-0387 62217.

Smith, Grahame Francis, MA, PhD. Senior Lecturer, Department of English Studies, Stirling University, since 1970; b. 3.5.33, London; m., Angela Mary; 2 s.; 1 d. Educ. Woodside Senior Secondary School, Glasgow; Aberdeen University; Cambridge University. Taught at California University, Los Angeles, 1963-65; University College, Swansea, 1965-70; secondment to Malawi University, 1982-83. Publications: Dickens, Money and Society, 1968; The Novel and Society: From Defoe to George Elliot, 1984; The Achievement of Graham Greene, 1985. Recreations: cinema; opera; jazz; walking. Address: (b.) Department of English Studies, Stirling University, Stirling, FK9 4LA; T.-078686 3171.

Smith, Hamilton, BSc, PhD, CChem, FRSC, FRCPath. Reader in Forensic Medicine (Toxicology), Glasgow University, since 1984; b. 27.4.34, Stirling; m., Jacqueline Ann Spittal. Educ. Kilsyth Academy; Glasgow University. Glasgow University: MRC Fellow, 1960, Special Research Fellow, 1963, Lecturer in Forensic Medicine Department, 1964, Senior Lecturer, 1973. Publication: Glaister's Medical Jurisprudence and Toxicology, 13th edition. Recreations: golf (New Club, St. Andrews, Crail Golfing Society); gardening. Address: (h.) 1 Park Avenue, Kirkintilloch, Glasgow; T.-041-776 2901.

Smith, Hugh Fleming, MA (Hons), DipEd. HM Depute Senior Chief Inspector of Schools, since 1982; b. 9.6.27, Dunfermline; m., Elizabeth Ross MacGibbon; 2 s.; 1 d. Educ. Waid Academy, Anstruther; St. Andrews University; Heidelberg University; Edinburgh University; Moray House College of Education. RAF, 1944-48; Stevenson Scholar, Scottish Universities, Berlin, 1952-53; Teacher, Morrison's Academy, 1954-55, Lycee Malherbe, Caen, France, 1955-56, Morrison's Academy, 1956-59, Annan Academy, 1959-61; HM Inspector of Schools, 1961-70; HM Inspector of Schools (Higher Grade), 1970-73; HM Chief Inspector of Schools (Higher Education), 1973-80; HM Chief Inspector of Schools (Teacher Education and Supply), 1980-82. Recreations: music; travel; needlework. Address: (b.) Scottish Education Department, New St. Andrews House, Edinburgh; T.-031-556 8400, Ext. 5246.

Smith, Rev. Hugh M.C., LTh. Minister, Cabrach and Mortlach, since 1982; b. 22.2.44, Aberdeen; m., Lily Ann Beaton; 1 s.; 1 d. Educ. Aberdeen Academy; Aberdeen University and Christ's College. Assistant Minister, Cardonald, Glasgow, 1972-73; Minister, Reay, 1973-82. Chairman, Reay Hall Committee, 1974-80; Chairman, Highlands Clubs Council, 1974-76; Member, Church of Scotland Maintenance of the Ministry Committee, 1976-82; Member, Inter Church Relations Committee, 1978-81; Moderator, Caithness Presbytery, 1980-81; Member, Cabrach and Mortlach Community Association, since 1983; Member, Speyside Council of Social Service, since 1983. Address: Mortlach Manse, Dufftown, Banffshire.

Smith, Iain Crichton, OBE, LLD (Dundee), DLitt (Glasgow), MA (Hons). Writer; b. 1.1.28, Glasgow; m., Donalda Gillies Logan; 2 step s. Educ. Nicolson Institute, Stornoway; Aberdeen University. Teacher, Oban High School, 1955-77; full-time Writer, since 1977; Member, Scottish Arts Council (Member, Literature Committee); Fellow, Royal Literary Society; books in English: nine novels, six volumes of short stories, 13 volumes of poetry; books in Gaelic: two novels, five volumes of short stories, four volumes of poetry; translations from Gaelic into English; numerous radio plays in both languages; Poetry Book Society Choice and two recommendations; eight Arts Council awards; awards for Gaelic plays and short stories; award for Gaelic television play; PEN Award, 1970; Scotsman Short Story Award, 1983. Recreation: reading detective stories. Address: Tigh Na Fuaran, Taynuilt, Argyll; T.-Taynuilt 463.

Smith, Iain Graham, LLB, NP. Solicitor; b. 14.4.49; m., Karen; 1 s.; 1 d. Educ. Aberdeen University. Solicitor, Aberdeen County Council; Senior Partner, Iain Smith & Co., Aberdeen, since 1975. President, Junior Chamber. Recreations: soccer; golf; squash. Address: (h.) Orchardhill House, Stonehaven; T.-Stonehaven 62729.

Smith, Iain William, BA (Hons). Member, Fife Regional Council, since 1982; Member, Executive Committees, Scottish Liberal Party and Scottish Young Liberals; b. 1.5.60, Gateside, Fife. Educ. Bell Baxter High School, Cupar; Newcastle-upon-Tyne University. Advice Worker, then Centre Manager, Bonnethill Advice Centre, Dundee, 1982-85; Agent Organiser, North East Fife Liberal Association. Recreations: watching football, cricket, etc.; real ale. Address: (h.) 6 Bankwell Crescent, Strathmiglo, Fife, KY14 7PY; T.-033 76 591.

Smith, Ian Stanley, MB, ChB, FRCSEdin, FRCSGlas, DObstRCOG. Consultant Surgeon, Victoria Infirmary, Glasgow, since 1975; Honorary Clinical Lecturer in Surgery, Glasgow University, since 1975; b. 13.11.39, Glasgow; m., Carole Ann Newby; 1 s.; 1 d. Educ. Glasgow Academy; Glasgow University. Assistant Lecturer in Anatomy, Glasgow University, 1964-65; various junior surgical appointments to hospitals in Western Regional Hospital Board. Examiner in Anatomy and Surgery, Royal College

of Physicians and Surgeons of Glasgow; Examiner in Anatomy, Royal College of Surgeons of Edinburgh. Recreations: golf; mah-jongg; wine-making. Address: (h.) Ashford, 16 Albert Drive, Killermont, Bearsden, Glasgow, G61 2PF; T.-041-942 7452.

Smith, James, OStJ, JP, BSc. Rector, St. Patrick's High School, Coatbridge, since 1972; b. 9.1.24, Glasgow; 2 s.; 3 d. Educ. Holyrood Secondary School, Glasgow; Glasgow University; Strathclyde University. Provost of East Kilbride, 1972-75; Member, East Kilbride Development Corporation, 1972-82; Member, Justice of the Peace Advisory Committee for East Kilbride; Council Member, Headteachers Association of Scotland. Recreations: walking; reading. Address: (h.) 19 Capel Grove, East Kilbride.

Smith, James Aikman, TD, BA, LLB. Advocate; Honorary Sheriff, since 1976; b. 13.6.14, Kilmarnock; m., Katharine Ann Millar; 3 d. Educ. Glasgow Academy; Oxford University; Edinburgh University. Admitted Faculty of Advocates, 1939; served Royal Artillery, 1939-46 (Lt. Col., 1944); North Africa, Italy and Austria; Despatches, Bronze Star US; Sheriff Substitute, Renfrew and Argyll, 1948-52, Roxburgh, Berwick and Selkirk, 1952-57, Aberdeen, Kincardine and Banff, 1967-68; Sheriff of Lothians and Borders, 1968-76; President, Sheriffs' Association, 1969-72; Member, UK Departmental Committee on Probation Service, 1959-62; Member, After Care Council (Scotland), 1962-65; UK Delegate to UN Congress on Crime, Japan, 1970; Chairman, Edinburgh and East of Scotland Branch, English Speaking Union, 1970-74; Vice-President, Cairngorm Club, 1962-65; Chairman, Allelon Society, 1970-76; Elder, Church of Scotland, since 1948; has served on various General Assembly Committees. Recreations: hill-walking; gardening; travel. Address: (h.) 16 Murrayfield Avenue, Edinburgh, EH12 6AX; T.-031-337 8205.

Smith, Rt. Hon. John, QC, MP, MA, LLB. MP (Labour), Monklands East, since 1983 (North Lanarkshire, 1970-83); b. 13.9.38, Dalmally, Argyll; m., Elizabeth Margaret Bennett; 3 d. Educ. Dunoon Grammar School; Glasgow University. Called to Scottish Bar, 1967; QC (Scot), 1983; Parliamentary Under Secretary of State for Energy, 1974-75; Minister of State for Energy, 1975-76; Minister of State, Privy Council Office, 1976-78; Secretary of State for Trade, 1978-79; Member, Shadow Cabinet, since 1979; Principal Opposition Spokesman on Trade and Industry. Recreations: tennis; hill-walking. Address: (h.) 21 Cluny Drive, Edinburgh, EH10 6DW; T.-031-447 3667.

Smith, Rev. John Murdo. Minister, Lochmaddy and Trumisgarry, Uist, since 1963; b. 29.8.27, Shader, Isle of Lewis; m., Mary Margaret Macpherson; 1 s.; 2 d. Educ. Airidhantuim School, Isle of Lewis; Skerry's College, Glasgow; Glasgow University; Aberdeen University. National Service, RAF, 1945-48; Minister, South Uist Howmore, 1956-63; Moderator, Uist Presbytery, 1957, 1973, 1982 (Presbytery Clerk,

1959-71); updated North Uist part, Statistical Account of Scotland; Member, local School Council. Recreations: fishing; hill-walking. Address: (h.) The Manse, Lochmaddy, North Uist.

Smith, Rev. John Raymond, MA, BD. World Mission Secretary, Congregational Union of Scotland, since 1978; b. 12.4.47, Dumfries; m., Isabel Jean McKemmie; 2 d. Educ. Dumfries Academy; Edinburgh University; Geneva University. Minister, School Wynd Congregational Church, Paisley, 1973-82. European Regional Executive Member, Council for World Mission. Recreations: photography; freelance writing. Address: (b.) Congregational Union of Scotland, PO Box 189, Glasgow, G1 2BX; T.-041-332 7667.

Smith, Professor Keith, BA, PhD. Professor of Geography, Strathclyde University, since 1984; b. 9.1.38, Marple; m., Muriel Doris Hyde; 1 s.; 1 d. Educ. Hyde County Grammar School; Hull University. Tutor in Geography, Liverpool University, 1963-65; Lecturer in Geography, Durham University, 1965-70; Strathclyde University: Senior Lecturer, 1971-75, Reader, 1975-82, Personal Professor, 1982-84. Drapers' Company Visiting Lecturer, Adelaide University, 1978. Publications: Water in Britain; Principles of Applied Climatology; Human Adjustment to Flood Hazard. Recreations: hill-walking; badminton. Address: (b.) Department of Geography, Strathclyde University, 26 Richmond Street, Glasgow, G1 1XH; T.-041-552 4400.

Smith, Lawrence D., BSc. Reader in Agricultural Economics, Glasgow University, since 1977; b. 1939, Bedfordshire; m., Evelyn Mavis Stead; 1 s.; 2 d. Educ. Bedford Modern School; Wye College, London University; Linacre College, Oxford. Departmental Lecturer, Agricultural Economics, Research Institute, Oxford University, 1963-66; Lecturer, then Senior Lecturer in Agricultural Economics, Department of Political Economy, Glasgow University. Recreation: gardening. Address: (b.) Department of Political Economy, Glasgow University, Glasgow; T.-041-339 8855.

Smith, Martin, CBE, FRICS. President, Glasgow Chamber of Commerce, since 1984; Senior Partner, Doig & Smith, Chartered Quantity Surveyors, since 1977; Honorary Secretary, Scottish Branch, RICS, since 1979; b. 16.7.22, Glasgow; m., Margaret Emma; 2 s. Educ. Coatbridge High School. Qualified ARICS, 1948; Chairman, Scottish Branch, RICS, 1974-75; Chairman, Scottish Building Contract Committee, 1975-81; Elder, Church of Scotland; Deacon, Incorporation of Gardeners, 1964-65. Recreations: gardening; golf. Address: (b.) 6 Lynedoch Place, Glasgow, G3 6AQ; T.-041-332 8907.

Smith, Murdoch Mackenzie, MPS, MCPP. Chief Administrative Pharmaceutical Officer, Highland Health Board and Western Isles Health Board, since 1975; b. 10.1.37, Inverness; m., Marianne Fergus. Educ. Inverness Royal Academy; Robert Gordon's Institute of Technology, Aberdeen. Pharmacist, T.S. Davidson, Inverness, 1959-63; Pharmacist, Inverness Hospitals, 1963-67 (Deputy Chief Pharmacist, 1967-72); Principal

Pharmacist/Deputy Regional/Area Pharmacist, Northern Regional Hospital Board, 1973-75. Former Member, National Pharmaceutical Consultative Committee; Past Chairman, Northern Scottish Branch, Pharmaceutical Society of GB; Chairman, Cromal Hill Recreation Committee; Past President, Highland Cricket Club and Inverness and District Badminton League; former Member; Ardersier and Petty Community Council, Inverness District Sports Council; former Captain, Highland Cricket Club. Recreations: history; cricket; collecting books and lead soldiers. Address: (h.) Glencoe, Ardersier, Inverness, IV1 2QD; T.-0667 62059.

Smith, Norman William. Deputy Director, Historic Buildings and Monuments, Scottish Development Department, since 1981; b. 25.8.32, Kirkintilloch; m., Dorothy Smith; 2 s. Educ. Lenzie Academy. Clerical Officer and Executive Officer, National Assistance Board, Ministry of Supply and War Department, 1949-62; Higher Executive Officer (1962), Senior Executive Officer (1971), Principal (1974) and Assistant Secretary (1981), Scottish Office. Recreations: Scrabble; photography; choral music; change-ringing. Address: (h.) 5 Carlingnose Point, North Queensferry, Fife; T.-0383 416981.

Smith, Patrick Fleming, MA, MSc, PhD. Senior Lecturer in Mathematics, Glasgow University, since 1984; b. 25.6.43, Perth, Australia; m., Pamela; 1 s.; 2 d. Educ. Lossiemouth High School; Elgin Academy; Aberdeen University; Leeds University. Lecturer in Mathematics, Glasgow University, 1968-84. Recreations: walking; reading; gardening. Address: (b.) Department of Mathematics, Glasgow University, Glasgow, G12 8QW; T.-041-339 8855, Ext. 567.

Smith, Peter Dryburgh. Deputy Director, Scottish Conservative Party, since 1982; b. 15.11.45, Edinburgh. Educ. Lasswade High School. Political Agent, South Edinburgh, 1968-70; National Organiser, Scottish Young Conservatives, 1970-72; Sales Manager, Adam Cramond & Son, 1972-74; Political Agent, East and West Renfrewshire, 1974-82; Euro Agent, Strathclyde West, 1979-82. Recreations: crosswords; reading. Address: (b.) Scottish Conservative Party, 3 Chester Street, Edinburgh, EH3 7RF; T.-031-226 2246.

Smith, Philip Morgans, BSc, PhD, FLS. Senior Lecturer in Botany, Edinburgh University, since 1980; Examiner (Biology), Scottish Examination Board, since 1979; b. 5.2.41, Halesowen; m., Eira Smith; 2 s. Educ. Halesowen Grammar School; Birmingham University. Harkness Fellow, Commonwealth Fund, New York; Lecturer/Senior Lecturer in Botany, Edinburgh University; Moderator/Examiner, Scottish Examination Board; Member, Scottish Central Commitee on Science. Project Director, Botany of the Lothians Floristic Account, Botanical Society of Edinburgh; Vice-President, Botanical Society of Edinburgh; Fellow, Linnean Society. Recreations: cooking; reading; singing; boating; watching trains; botanising; old cars. Address: (h.) 7 Clayhills Park, Balerno, Midlothian, EH14 7BH; T.-031-449 4345.

Smith, Rev. Ralph Colley Philip, MA, STM. Head of Audio Visual Productions, Church of Scotland, since 1985; Minister, Church of Scotland, since 1960; b. 11.3.31, Edinburgh; m., Florence; 2 s. Educ. Edinburgh Academy; St. Andrews University; Edinburgh University; Union Seminary, New York. Minister, Gallatown Church, Kirkcaldy; Religious Broadcasting Assistant, then Producer, Religion, Television, BBC Scotland; Associate Minister, New Kilpatrick Parish Church, Bearsden. Member, Scottish Appeals Advisory Committee (BBC and IBA). Recreations: cello; bowls; golf. Address: (h.) 2 Blackford Hill View, Edinburgh, EH9 3HD.

Smith, Robert Haldane, CA. General Manager, Royal Bank of Scotland PLC, since 1983; Managing Director, National Commercial & Glyns Ltd., since 1983; Joint Managing Director, Charterhouse Development Holdings PLC and Executive Director, Charterhouse Japhet PLC, since 1985; b. 8.8.44, Glasgow; m., Alison Marjorie Bell; 2 d. Educ. Allan Glen's School, Glasgow; Glasgow University. Articled to Robb Ferguson & Co., CA, Glasgow, 1963-68; qualified CA, 1968; ICFC, 1968-82: Area Manager, Brighton, 1973, Business Development Manager, 1978, Assistant General Manager, 1981, Director of several group companies, Investors in Industry, 1981. Director, Castleforth Fund Managers, since 1984. Member, Board of Trustees, National Museums of Scotland. Publication: Managing Your Company's Finances (Co-author). Recreations: amateur drama; running; spectator sports; historic and listed buildings; music. Address: (h.) 4 Lauder Road, Edinburgh; T.-031-667 1400.

Smith, Robert Lupton, OBE, JP, FRICS. Director, Association for the Protection of Rural Scotland, since 1981; Chartered Surveyor in private practice, since 1954; b. 26.4.24, Cheadle Hulme; m.; 3 d. Educ. George Watson's College; College of Estate Management; Heriot-Watt College. Chairman, Scottish Junior Branch, RICS, 1952; Member, Scottish Executive Committee, RICS, 1952-60; elected, Edinburgh Town Council, 1962-74 and Edinburgh District Council, 1974-77; Governor, Edinburgh College of Art, since 1963; fought European Election, 1979, as Liberal; Deputy Traffic Commissioner, 1974-78; Chairman, Good Neighbours Housing Association, since 1984; Scottish Liberal Party: Chairman, Executive Committee, 1971-74, Chairman, 1974, President, 1976-82; Council Member, Royal Scottish Geographical Society, since 1957; Chairman, Scottish Liberal Club, since 1984; Director, Cockburn Conservation Trust Ltd. Recreations: politics; visiting Perthshire and Orkney; reading; looking at fine art. Address: 14A Napier Road, Edinburgh, EH10 5AY; T.-031-229 1898.

Smith, Robin D.P., MA, MCD, MRTPI. Senior Lecturer, Department of Town and Country Planning, Edinburgh College of Art/Heriot-Watt University, since 1975; b. 1.7.30, Cambridge; m., Dorothy; 2 d. Educ. Denstone College; St. Catharine's College, Cambridge; Liverpool University. Junior posts, Cambridgeshire and Huntingdonshire County Councils; Planning Assistant, Northampton County Borough; Research Officer, Bedfordshire County Council; Senior Planning Assistant, Northampton County Borough; Chief Planning Assistant, Borough of Scunthorpe; Technical Officer, East Anglia Consultative Committee; Burgh Planning Officer, Kirkcaldy. Recreations: photography; model railways; music; plays; gardening. Address: (h.) 47 Raith Drive, Kirkcaldy, Fife, KY2 5NS; T.-0592 266510.

Smith, Roger. Editor, The Great Outdoors, since 1977; b. 28.11.38, London; m., Terry; 2 d. Educ. Latymer Upper School, London. Chairman, Scottish Wild Land Group; elected Council Member: National Trust for Scotland, Scottish Conservation Projects Trust; Honorary Vice-President, Habitat Scotland. Publications: Spur Book of Orienteering, 1978; Penguin Book of Orienteering, 1981; The Winding Trail, 1981; Outdoor Scotland, 1981; Weekend Walking, 1982; Visitor's Guide to Scottish Borders, 1983; Jet Guide to Scotland's Countryside, 1985. Recreations: hill-walking; running; orienteering; Scottish history. Address: (h.) 93 Queen Street, Alva, Clackmannan, FK12 5AH; T.-0259 60102.

Smith, Roger Galbraith, MB, ChB, FRCPEdin. Senior Lecturer, Department of Geriatric Medicine, Edinburgh University, since 1976; Honorary Consultant Physician in Geriatric Medicine, Lothian Health Board, since 1976; b. 7.7.42, Edinburgh; m., Margaret Lawson; 1 s.; 1 d. Educ. George Watson's College, Edinburgh; Edinburgh University. Surgeon Lieutenant, Royal Navy, 1967-72; Senior Registrar in Geriatric Medicine, 1973-76. Member, Board of Directors, Queensberry House Hospital, Edinburgh. Recreations: golf; curling. Address: (h.) 56 Alnwickhill Road, Edinburgh; T.-031-664 1745.

Smith, Samuel Gordon, BSc, DipEd. Headteacher, Newbattle High School, since 1978; b. 3.4.43, Bonnyrigg; m., Carol Anne Wallace; 2 s. Educ. Lasswade Secondary School; Edinburgh University. Depute Headteacher, Greenhall High School, 1974-77. Address: (h.) 30 Golf Course Road, Bonnyrigg, Midlothian, EH19 2EZ; T.-031-663 8320.

Smith, Stanley William, MA, PhD (Cantab). Senior Lecturer in English, Dundee University, since 1984 (Students' Assessor on Senate, since 1982); b. 12.1.43, Warrington; 2 s.; 1 d. Educ. Boteler Grammar School, Warrington; Jesus College, Cambridge. Assistant Lecturer in English, Aberdeen University, 1967-68; Lecturer in English, Dundee University, 1968-84. Publications: A Sadly Contracted Hero: The Comic Self in Post-War American Fiction, 1981; Inviolable Voice: History and Twentieth Century Poetry, 1982; 20th Century Poetry, 1983; W.H. Auden, 1985; Edward Thomas, 1986. Recreations: the arts; politics; chess; travel. Address: (b.) English Department, The University, Dundee, DD1 4HN; T.-Dundee 23181, Ext. 4418.

Smith, Thomas James, MBE, MA, JP. Honorary Sheriff; b. 17.6.05, King Edward Parish, Aberdeenshire; m., Alice Mary Mann; 1 s.; 1 d. Educ. Banff Academy; Aberdeen University. Headmaster: Towie School, 1931-43, New

Pitsligo, 1943-48, Peterhead Central School, 1948-70; Member, Peterhead Town Council, 1958-67 and 1970-75; Provost of Peterhead, 1971-75; Chairman, Peterhead Harbour Board and Feuars' Managers, 1971-75; Member, Grampian Regional Council, 1974-78; President, Peterhead Rotary Club and Professional and Business Men's Club; Chairman, Peterhead Burns Club, 1955-76. Recreation: bowls. Address: (h.) 53 Anderson Drive, Aberdeen; T.-Aberdeen 317922.

Smith, W. Cairns S., MB, ChB, MPH, MFCM. Epidemiologist and Leader, Scottish Heart Health Study, since 1983; Honorary Senior Lecturer in Community Medicine, since 1984; Honorary Community Medicine Specialist, Tayside Health Board, since 1984; b. 8.2.51, Aberdeen; m., Christine Morrison; 2 s.; 2 d. Educ. Aberdeen Grammar School; Aberdeen University. Junior medical career, Aberdeen and Glasgow; Superintendent, Leprosy Hospital in India for three years; developed Leprosy Control Programme in India; Member, Leprosy Mission Council and Executive for Scotland (Vice-Chairman). Address: (b.) Cardiovascular Epidemiology Unit, Ninewells Hospital and Medical School, Dundee; T.-0382 641764.

Smith, William Angus, BEM, JP. Chairman, Education Committee, Shetland Islands Council, since 1975 (Vice Chairman, Housing Committee, 1982-85); Chairman, Finance Committee, Lerwick Harbour Trust; b. 20.8.19, Burra Isle, Shetland; m., Daisy Manson; 4 s. Educ. Anderson Educational Institute. Engineer, British Telecomms, 1937-83; Royal Signals, UK, Middle East, Burma, India, Germany, 1940-46; Member, Lerwick Town Council and Zetland County Council, 1967-75; Member, Lerwick Harbour Trust, since 1967 (except for short break); Provost of Lerwick, 1971-74; Member, Shetland Islands Council, since 1975; Member, Shetland Area Health Board, since 1974; Member, Electricity Consultative Council for North of Scotland District, since 1974; Member, Clickimin Recreational Trust. Recreations: crosswords; reading. Address: (h.) 14 Bruce Crescent, Lerwick, Shetland, ZE1 OPB; T.-0595 2121.

Smith, William Anthony. Director, Scottish Office Training Unit, since 1982; b. 14.9.28, Edinburgh; m., Maureen Enid Graham; 2 s.; 2 d. Educ. George Heriot's School, Edinburgh. Various executive posts, Department of Health and Social Security; Senior O. & M. Officer, HM Treasury; Head of O. & M. Unit, Scottish Office; UN Consultant in Management, Costa Rica, and in Organisation Development, Iran; Personnel Manager, Scottish Office. Past Chairman, Edinburgh Oxfam Committee. Recreations: part-time antiquarian and second-hand bookseller; wine-making; reading and writing. Address: (h.) 5 Stirling Road, Edinburgh; T.-031-552 1850.

Smith, William E., CEng, MICE, MIHT. Director of Construction, Shetland Islands Council, since 1975; b. 15.2.31, Lerwick; m., Pamela; 1 s.; 2 d. Educ. Anderson Educational Institute. Zetland County Council: Apprentice Road Surveyor, 1949-53, Assistant Engineer, 1954-55, Depute County Surveyor, 1959-75. Recreations: sailing; golf; music. Address: (b.) Grantfield, Lerwick, Shetland, ZE1 ONT; T.-0595 2024.

Smith, William Ewen, BSc, ARCST, DIC, PhD, DSc. Reader in Chemistry, Strathclyde University, since 1981; b. 21.2.41, Glasgow; m., Frances Helen Williamson; 1 s.; 1 d. Educ. Hutchesons' Boys' Grammar School; Strathclyde University; Imperial College, London. Exchange Visitor, Oak Ridge National Laboratory, Tennessee; SERC and ICI Fellow, University College, London; Lecturer and Senior Lecturer, Strathclyde University. Recreations: golf; sailing; badminton. Address: (b.) Department of Pure and Applied Chemistry, Strathclyde University, Glasgow; T.-041-552 4400, Ext. 2167.

Smith, W. Gordon. Writer; b. 13.12.28, Edinburgh. RAF; Journalist; Radio/TV Producer, BBC, 25 years; author of plays: Vincent, 1971; Jock, 1972; Knox, 1973; Sweeter Than All The Roses, 1974; A North British Working Man's Guide to the Arts, 1975; Wizard, 1976; On the Road to Avizandum, 1977; Marie of Scotland; Xanadu, 1978.

Smout, Professor Thomas Christopher, MA, PhD, FRSE. Professor of Scottish History, St. Andrews University, since 1980; b. 19.12.33, Birmingham; m., Anne-Marie; 1 s.; 1 d. Educ. Leys School, Cambridge; Clare College, Cambridge. Department of Economic History, Edinburgh University, 1959-79. Address: (b.) St. Andrews University, St. Andrews, Fife.

Smylie, Henry Gordon, MB, ChB, MD, FRCPath. Senior Lecturer, Department of Bacteriology, Aberdeen University, and Honorary Consultant, Grampian Health Board, Aberdeen Hospitals, since 1964; b. 31.7.26, Aberdeen; 4 s. Educ. Robert Gordon's College; Aberdeen University. Variously employed in the newspaper, clothing and building industries, farming and forestry; three years' volunteer service, Royal Navy, 1944-47; undergraduate, 1948-54; several months in general practice, then Probationer Lecturer, Bacteriology, Aberdeen University, 1955. Recreations: running; gardening. Address: (h.) Birken Lodge, Bieldside, Aberdeen; T.-Aberdeen 861305.

Smyrl, Joseph Logan, MA, PhD, FIMA. Senior Lecturer, Department of Mathematics, Strathclyde University; b. 4.1.28, Philadelphia; m., Kathleen Harper; 3 s.; 1 d. Educ. Coleraine Academical Institution; Queen's University, Belfast. Assistant Lecturer, Queen's University, Belfast; Lecturer, Royal Technical College, Salford; Lecturer, Royal College of Science and Technology, Glasgow (subsequently Strathclyde University). Publication: Introduction to University Mathematics. Recreation: golf. Address: (b.) Department of Mathematics, Strathclyde University, Livingstone Tower, Richmond Stret, Glasgow, G1 1XQ; T.-041-552 4400, Ext. 3820.

Smyth, James Brian Alan, JP. Secretary, Earl Haig Fund (Scotland), since 1974; Member, Kyle and Carrick District Council, since 1980; b.

30.1.23, Lahore, Pakistan; m., Millicent Doreen; 1 d. Educ. George Watson's College; Fettes College. 2nd Lt./Captain, 13th Frontier Force Rifles, Indian Army, 1941-46; Captain/Major, King's Own Scottish Borderers, 1946-69; mentioned in Despatches; School Bursar, Ashville College, Harrogate, 1969-74. General Secretary, Officers' Association (Scottish Branch), since 1974. Recreations: bridge; golf; gardening. Address: (h.) Naini Tal, 27 Gailes Road, Troon, Ayrshire; T.-Troon 313828.

Smyth, Michael Jessop, MA, PhD, FRAS, FRSE. Senior Lecturer, Department of Astronomy, Edinburgh University, since 1965; b. 12.11.26, Hounslow; m., Mary Florence Isabel Speyer; 2 s. Educ. Hounslow College; Selwyn College, Cambridge. Lecturer in Astronomy, Edinburgh University, 1950-54; Assistant Director and Acting Director, Dunsink Observatory, Dublin, 1954-59; Lecturer in Astronomy, Edinburgh University, 1959-65. Member, British National Committee for Astronomy. Recreations: travel; photography; hill-walking; wine-making. Address: (b.) Royal Observatory, Edinburgh, EH9 3HJ; T.-031-667 3321.

Snaith, David William, MSc, PhD, CEng, MIM, CChem, FRSC. Principal, Stow College, Glasgow, since 1983; b. 30.6.40, Birmingham; m., Susan Willoughby Tucker; 1 s.; 2 d. Educ. Kings Norton Grammar School, Birmingham; Aston University. Research Chemist, Birmingham Small Arms Co. Ltd.; Assistant Lecturer in Chemistry, Matthew Boulton Technical College, Birmingham, 1965; Lecturer in Chemistry, Ipswich Civic College, 1969; Deputy Head, Department of Science and Metallurgy, North Lindsey College of Technology, Scunthorpe, 1974; Head, Department of Science, North East Liverpool Technical College, 1980. Royal Society of Chemistry: Assistant Secretary, East Anglian Section Committee, 1972-74, Chairman, Southumbria Section, 1977-78. Recreations: hill-walking; photography; music; rifle shooting. Address: (b.) Stow College, 43 Shamrock Street, Glasgow, G4 9LD; T.-041-332 1786.

Snedden, Charles, OBE, JP. Deputy Chairman, Scottish Special Housing Association, since 1982; Vice Convener, Central Regional Council, since 1975; b. 28.3.32, Bo'ness; m., Margaret Kidd; 1 s.; 1 d. Educ. Bo'ness Academy. Joined Bo'ness Town Council and West Lothian County Council, 1959; Provost of Bo'ness, 1964-75; Member, Council of Management, Scottish Special Housing Association, since 1978. Honorary President: Bo'ness United FC, Kinneil Colliery Silver Band. Recreations: gardening; reading. Address: (h.) Pennvael, 2 Deanburn Grove, Bo'ness, West Lothian, EH51 ONA; T.-0506 822355.

Snedden, Ian Naismith, OBE (1969), BSc, DSc, BA, MA, FRS, FRSE, FIMA, FRSA. Honorary Research Fellow and Emeritus Professor of Mathematics, Glasgow University; Honorary Visiting Professor of Mathematics, Strathclyde University; Member, Advisory Committee, Scottish Opera; Member, Board of Directors, Citizens' Theatre, Glasgow; b. 8.12.19, Glasgow; m., Mary Campbell Macgregor; 2 s.; 1 d. Educ. Hyndland School, Glasgow; Glasgow

University; Trinity College, Cambridge. Junior Scientific Officer, Ministry of Supply, 1942-45; William Bryce Fellow, Glasgow University, 1945-46; Lecturer in Natural Philosophy, Glasgow University, 1946-50; Professor of Mathematics, University College of North Staffordshire, 1950-56; Simson Professor of Mathematics, Glasgow University, 1956-85. Hon DSc: Warsaw University, Heriot-Watt University, Hull University; Kelvin Medal, Glasgow University; Makdougall-Brisbane Prize, Royal Society of Edinburgh, 1959; Eringen Medal, Society of Engineering Science, 1979; Copernicus Medal, Polish Academy of Sciences; Gold Medal for Culture (Poland), 1983; Member, Order of the Long Leaf Pine (North Carolina), 1964; Commander, Order of Polonia Restituta, 1969; Commander, Order of Merit of Poland, 1979. Recreations: music; painting in oils; photography. Address: (h.) 19 Crown Terrace, Glasgow, G12 9ES; T.-041-339 4114.

Sniper, Woolfred, MB, ChB, DA, FFARCS. Consultant Anaesthetist, Victoria Infirmary, Glasgow, since 1969; b. 20.6.25, Glasgow; m., Doreen Vinestock. Educ. Queens Park School, Glasgow; Glasgow University. Address: (h.) Flat 55, Orchard Court, Thornliebank, Glasgow, G46 7BJ; T.-041-638 6218.

Solomon, John Brian, BSc, PhD, DSc, FIBiol, FRCPath. Senior Lecturer, Immunology Unit, Bacteriology Department, Aberdeen University, since 1968; b. 26.7.24, Cambridge; m., Kathleen Audley Pemberton; 1 s.; 1 d. Educ. Caterham School, Surrey; Nottingham University. Chester Beatty Research Institute, London, 1951-55; Fellow, Professor J. Brachets' Laboratories, Brussels, 1955; Head, Chemical Embryology Unit, Chester Beatty Research Institute, 1955-65; Research Fellow, Hasek's Institute for Experimental Biology and Genetics, Prague, 1963; Senior Research Fellow, Department of Microbiology, Adelaide University, 1965-67. Publication: Foetal and Neonatal Immunology, 1971. Recreations: yachting; cross-country skiing; caravanning. Address: (b.) Immunology Unit, Bacteriology Department, Aberdeen University, Aberdeen, AB9 2ZD; T.-0224 681818, Ext. 2449.

Somerville, Donald Robert, LLB. Director of Legal Services, Inverness District Council, since 1984; b. 19.3.53, Edinburgh; m., Margaret; 3 d. Educ. Scotus Academy, Edinburgh; Edinburgh University. Law Apprentice/Legal Assistant, private practice, 1974-77; Principal Legal Assistant, West Lothian District Council, 1977-84. Recreations: hill-walking; rock/ice climbing. Address: (b.) Town House, Inverness; T.-0463 239111.

Sommerville, John Kenneth, CA. Partner, French & Cowan, CA, Glasgow, since 1970; Council Member, Institute of Chartered Accountants of Scotland, since 1984; b. 1.3.42, Glasgow; m., Iris Alexa Hutchison; 3 d. Educ. Kelvinside Academy; Glasgow University (during CA course). CA apprenticeship, French & Cowan. Member, Board of Governors, Kelvinside Academy, since 1976 (Chairman of Board, since 1985). Recreations: golf; skiing; running. Address: (b.) 144 St. Vincent Street, Glasgow, G2 5LT; T.-041-221 2984.

Sorensen, Rev. Alan Kenneth, BD, DipMin. Minister, Househillwood St. Christopher's Church, Glasgow, since 1983; b. 16.4.57, Dalmuir; m., Elizabeth-Anne; 2 d. Educ. Hutchesons' Boys' Grammar School; Glasgow University. Sometime gravedigger, waiter, van driver, theatre usher; semi-professional musician and comedian; regular religious broadcaster; Departmental Manager, Allied Suppliers, prior to entering parish ministry; recorded LP cassette, Alan Sorensen's Greatest Hit, 1982; former Vice-Chairman, local Branch, Society for Protection of Unborn Children. Recreation: music. Address: 29 Torridon Avenue, Glasgow, G41 5AT; T.-041-427 2596.

Souch, Alec Edward, BSc, PhD, CPhys, FInstP. Chief Engineer, Planning and Services, South of Scotland Electricity Board, since 1979; b. 3.9.25, Canterbury; m., Maisie Levinge; 1 d. Educ. Simon Langton School, Canterbury; London University; Birmingham University. UKAEA, 1955-60; CEGB, 1960-78. Address: (b.) SSEB, Spean Street, Glasgow, G44 4BE; T.-041-637 7177.

Souter, James Gordon, MRCVS, DVSM. Member, Fife Regional Council, since 1976; b. 22.10.06, Stonehaven; m., Grace Elizabeth Geddes, MA (deceased); 1 s.; 2 d. Educ. Aberdeen Grammar School; Royal (Dick) College of Veterinary Studies, Edinburgh University. Assistant in veterinary practice, Ware, Hertfordshire; postgraduate course, Royal (Dick) College of Veterinary Studies; joined staff, MAFF; Veterinary Officer (Assistant), Aberdeen and Aberdeenshire Regional Scheme (later State Veterinary Service); Divisional Veterinary Officer, London; Field Staff, Fife and Kinross. Member, Newport-on-Tay Town Council, 1963-71 (Provost of Newport-on-Tay, 1968-71); Member, Fife County Council, 1968-76. Recreations: rugby football and cricket (now as a spectator). Address: (h.) Dalbradie, Crawford Avenue, Gauldry, Newport-on-Tay, Fife; T.-Gauldry 788.

Souter, William Alexander, MB, ChB (Hons), FRCSEdin. Consultant Orthopaedic Surgeon, Princess Margaret Rose Orthopaedic Hospital and Edinburgh Royal Infirmary, since 1968; Honorary Senior Lecturer, Department of Orthopaedic Surgery, Edinburgh University; b. 11.5.33, Cupar; m., Kathleen Bruce Georgeson Taylor; 1 s.; 2 d. Educ. George Watson's Boys' College, Edinburgh; Edinburgh University. Various House Officer and Registrar appointments, Edinburgh Royal Infirmary and Princess Margaret Rose Orthopaedic Hospital, 1957-61; Registrar in General Surgery, then in Hand Surgery, Derbyshire Royal Infirmary, 1962-64; Senior Registrar in Orthopaedic Surgery, Edinburgh Royal Infirmary and Princess Margaret Rose, 1965-68; Instructor, Department of Orthopaedic Surgery, Washington University, Seattle, 1967; Visiting Professor, Bioengineering Department, Strathclyde University, 1985-88; Examiner, General and Orthopaedic Fellowships, Royal College of Surgeons of Edinburgh; Member, Editorial Board, Journal of Bone and Joint Surgery, 1981-84; first Honorary Secretary,

European Rheumatoid Arthritis Surgical Society, 1979-83; Member, Scientific Co-ordinating Committee, Arthritis and Rheumatism Council, 1977-84; Council Member, British Society for Surgery of the Hand, 1976-78; Council Member (Elect), British Orthopaedic Association, 1986-88; Trustee, International Opera Theatre of Scotland Trust Fund; Elder, St. George's West Church, Edinburgh. Recreations: music; photography; gardening; skiing; golf. Address: (h.) Old Mauricewood Mains, Penicuik, Midlothian, EH26 ONJ; T.-Penicuik 72609.

Southam, Professor John Chambers, MA, MD, FRCPath, FDS. Dean of Dental Studies, Edinburgh University, since 1982 (Professor of Oral Medicine and Oral Pathology, since 1977); b. 3.2.34, Leeds; m., Susan; 2 s. Educ. Leeds Grammar School; Caius College, Cambridge; Leeds University. Lecturer in Oral Pathology, Sheffield University, 1963-69; Lecturer and Senior Lecturer in Dental Surgery, Edinburgh University, 1970-77. Address: (h.) 13 Corstorphine House Avenue, Edinburgh, EH12 7AD; T.-031-334 3013.

Southcott, Barry John, BSc (Econ), ASIA. Managing Director, British Investment Trust, since 1983; Managing Director, Marketable Securities, NCB Pension Fund, now CIN Management Ltd., since 1975; b. 27.3.50, London; m., Lesley Anne Parkinson. Educ. Latymer Upper School; Bradford University. Phillips & Drew, 1971-75; NCB Pension Fund, since 1975. Recreations: tennis; football; music. Address: (b.) 46 Castle Street, Edinburgh.

Southesk, Earl of, (Charles Alexander Carnegie), KCVO, DL; b. 23.9.93, Edinburgh; m., 1, H.H. Princess Maud (deceased); 1 s.; 2, Evelyn Campbell. Educ. Eton; Sandhurst. Scots Guards, 1913; ADC to Viceroy of India, 1917-19. Recreations: shooting; fishing. Address: (h.) Kinnaird Castle, Brechin, Angus; T.-067 481 209.

Spear, Professor Walter Eric, PhD, DSc, FRS, FRSE, FInstP. Professor of Physics, Carnegie Laboratory of Physics, Dundee University, since 1968; b. 20.1.21, Frankfurt/Main, West Germany; m., Hilda Doris King; 2 d. Educ. London University. Lecturer in Physics, Leicester University, 1953; Visiting Professor: Purdue University, 1957-58, Carolina University, 1965-66; Reader in Physics, Leicester University, 1967-68. Max Born Prize, 1977; Europhysics Prize, 1977; Makdougal-Brisbane Medal, Royal Society of Edinburgh, 1981. Recreations: music; languages; literature. Address: (b.) Carnegie Laboratory of Physics, Dundee University, Dundee, DD1 4HN; T.-0382 23181, Ext. 4563.

Spedding, Frank Donald, DMus, ARCM, FRSAMD. Director of Music, Royal Scottish Academy of Music and Drama, since 1981; b. 21.8.29, Liverpool. Educ. Nottingham High School; Royal College of Music, London. Principal Teacher of Music, Quernmore School, Bromley, Kent, 1951-57; joined RSAMD staff, 1958; appointed Head of Academic Studies Department, 1959· many musical compositions, including concertos, chamber music, solo works, scores for numerous documentary films and music for theatre and TV. Prizeman, Royal Philharmonic Society. Recreations: travel; theatre; reading. Address: (b.) Royal Scottish Academy of Music and Drama, Glasgow, G2 1BS; T.-041-332 4101.

Speirs, William MacLeod. Assistant Secretary (Health and Social Services, Education and Training), Scottish TUC, since 1979; Member, Scottish Executive, Labour Party, since 1980; b. 8.3.52, Dumbarton; m., Lynda; 1 s.; 1 d. Educ. John Neilson High School, Paisley; Strathclyde University. Vice-Chairperson, Glasgow Area Manpower Board, MSC; Chairperson, 7:84 Theatre Company (Scotland); Chairperson, West of Scotland Friends of Palestine; Member, Committee of Management, War on Want. Recreations: watching St. Mirren FC; playing football and cricket. Address: (b.) STUC, 16 Woodlands Terrace, Glasgow, G3 6DF; T.-041-332 4946.

Speitel, Hans H., PhD. Senior Lecturer, Department of Scottish Studies, Edinburgh University, since 1979 (Lecturer, since 1963); b. 22.3.37, Erfurt, Germany; m., Inge Jaskulla; 2 d. Educ. Munster University; Kiel University; Frankfurt University; Edinburgh University. Co-Editor, Linguistic Atlas of Scotland, Volumes 1-3; Editor, Scottish Language; Member, Editorial Board, Atlas Linguarum Europae. Recreations: topography of Edinburgh, London; general literature. Address: (h.) 14 Thirlestane Road, Edinburgh, 9; T.-031-447 3946.

Spence, Professor John, ARCST, BSC, MEng, PhD, DSc, CEng, FIMechE. Head, Department of Mechanics of Materials, Strathclyde University, since 1981 (Trades House of Glasgow Professor of Mechanics of Materials, since 1982); b. 5.11.37, Chapelhall; m., Margaret Gray Hudson; 2 s. Educ. Airdrie Academy; Royal College of Science and Technology; Sheffield University. Engineering apprenticeship, Stewarts & Lloyds (now British Steel Corporation); Senior Engineer, then Head of Stress Analysis, Babcock & Wilcox Research Division; Strathclyde University: Lecturer, 1966, Senior Lecturer, Reader. Serves on several national committees, including Institution of Mechanical Engineers and British Standards Institution. Address: (b.) Department of Mechanics of Materials, Strathclyde University, 75 Montrose Street, Glasgow, G1 1XJ; T.-041-552 4400, Ext. 2324.

Spencer, Rt. Rev. Alfred Raymond, OSB. Abbot, Pluscarden Abbey, Elgin, since 1966; b. 28.6.15, Scopwick, Lincoln. Educ. Panton College, Lincoln; Franciscan Friary, Crawley. Joined Capuchin Franciscan Order, 1934; Priest, 1941; pastoral work in England and Wales; Assistant Novice Master, Pantasaph, North Wales, five years; transferred to Benedictine Abbey, Prinknash, 1951; Novice Master, 1953; elected Conventual Prior of Pluscarden, 1966 (Priory given status of Abbey, 1974); confirmed as first Abbot. Address: Pluscarden Abbey, Elgin, Moray, IV30 3UA; T.-034 389 257.

Spiers, Rev. John McLaren, LTh. Minister, Orchardhill Church, Giffnock, since 1977; b. 12.12.43, Edinburgh; m., Janet Diane Watson; 2

d. Educ. George Watson's College, Edinburgh; Glasgow University. Trainee, Scottish Union and National Insurance Company, 1961-65; University, 1966-71; Probationer Assistant, Drumchapel Old Parish Church, Glasgow, 1971-72; Minister, South Church, Barrhead, 1972-77. Recreations: music; art; country pursuits; family life; various sports. Address: 23 Ayr Road, Giffnock, Glasgow, G46 6SB; T.-041-638 4204.

Spilg, Walter Gerson Spence, MB, ChB (Hons), FRCPath. Consultant Pathologist, Victoria Infirmary, Glasgow, since 1972; Honorary Clinical Lecturer, Glasgow University, since 1973; b. 27.10.37, Glasgow; m., Vivien Anne Burns; 1 s.; 2 d. Educ. Hutchesons' Boys' Grammar School, Glasgow; Glasgow University. Registrar in Pathology, Glasgow Royal Infirmary, 1965-68; Senior Registrar in Pathology, Victoria Infirmary, Glasgow, 1968-69; Lecturer in Pathology, Glasgow University (Western Infirmary), 1969-72. Regional Adviser in Postgraduate Education, Royal College of Pathologists; Specialty Adviser in Laboratory Medicine, West of Scotland Committee for Postgraduate Education; Member, Scottish Affairs Committee, Royal College of Pathologists. Recreations: bridge; golf. Address: (h.) 98 Ayr Road, Newton Mearns, Glasgow, G77 6EJ; T.-041-639 3130.

Sprent, Professor Peter, BSc, PhD, FRSE. Statistician and Author; Professor of Statistics, Dundee University, since 1972; b. 28.1.23, Hobart, Australia; m., Janet Irene Findlater. Educ. Hutchins School, Hobart, Tasmania; Tasmania University; London University. Lecturer in Mathematics, Tasmania University, 1948-57; Statistician, East Malling Research Station, 1958-67; Senior Lecturer in Statistics, Dundee University, 1967-72. Sometime Member, Editorial Boards, Journal of Royal Statistical Society, Journal of American Statistical Association, Biometrics. Publications: Models in Regression and Related Topics; Statistics in Action; Quick Statistics. Recreations: aviation; golf; hill-walking. Address: (h.) 32 Birkhill Avenue, Wormit, Newport-on-Tay, DD6 8PW; T.-0382 541706.

Sprigge, Professor Timothy Lauro Squire. Professor of Logic and Metaphysics, Edinburgh University, since 1979; b. 14.1.32, London; m., Giglia Gordon; 1 s.; 2 d. Educ. Gonville and Caius College, Cambridge. Lecturer in Philosophy, University College, London, 1961-63; Lecturer, then Reader in Philosophy, Sussex University, 1963-79. Publications: The Correspondence of Jeremy Bentham, Volumes 1 and 2; Facts, Words and Beliefs; Santayana: An Examination of his Philosophy; The Vindication of Absolute Idealism; Theories of Existence. Recreation: backgammon. Address: (b.) Philosophy Department, David Hume Tower, Edinburgh University, George Square, Edinburgh; T.-031-667 1011.

Sprot of Haystoun, Lt.-Col. Aidan Mark, MC, JP. Lord Lieutenant, Tweeddale, since 1980; Landowner (Haystoun Estate) and Farmer, since 1965; b. 17.6.19, Lilliesleaf. Educ. Belhaven Hill; Stowe. Commissioned, Royal Scots Greys, 1940; served Palestine, 1941-42, Western Desert,

1942-43, Italy, 1943-44, NW Europe, 1944-45; continued serving with Regiment in Germany until 1952, Libya, Egypt and Jordan, 1952-55, UK, 1955-58, Germany, 1958-62; Adjutant, 1944-45; Commanding Officer, 1959-62; retired, 1962. County Councillor, Peeblesshire, 1963-75; DL (Peeblesshire), 1966-80; Member, Queen's Bodyguard for Scotland (Royal Company of Archers), since 1950; County Director, Peeblesshire Branch, Red Cross, 1966-74; County Commissioner, Peeblesshire Scout Association, 1968-73; Honorary Secretary, Royal Caledonian Hunt, 1964-74; Vice-President, Lowlands of Scotland TA&VRA, since 1980. Recreations: country sports; motor cycle touring. Address: (h.) Crookston, by Peebles, EH45 9JQ; T.-Kirkton Manor 209.

Sprott, Gavin Chappell, MA. Head, Scottish Country Life Section, National Museums of Scotland and Curator, Scottish Agricultural Museum, Ingliston; b. 23.7.43, Dundee; m., Maureen Turnbull; 2 s.; 1 d. Educ. Edinburgh University. Research Assistant, Scottish Country Life Department, National Museum of Antiquities of Scotland, 1972-79. Recreations: cycling; walking; restoring and sailing old boats. Address: (b.) National Museums, Queen Street, Edinburgh, EH2; T.-031-557 3550.

Sprott, Trevor Ferguson, RIBA, FRTPI. Director of Physical Planning, Grampian Regional Council, since 1975; b. 22.4.33, Belfast; m., Patricia M.I.; 1 step s.; 1 step d. Educ. Bangor Grammar School; University College, London; Edinburgh University. Assistant Planner, P.E.A. Johnson-Marshall, 1960-61; Group Planner, Cumbernauld Development Corporation, 1961-62; Research Planner, Planning Research Unit, Edinburgh University, 1962-63; Senior Principal Planner, Craigavon Development Commission, Northern Ireland, 1963-72; Regional Planning Adviser, North East of Scotland Joint Planning Advisory Committee, 1972-75. Fellow, Salzburg Seminar in American Studies; Board Member, Centre for Environmental Management and Planning, Aberdeen University; Planning Adviser, COSLA Planning Committee; Vice-Chairman, Scottish Society of Directors of Planning. Recreations: golf; bridge; photography. Address: (b.) Department of Physical Planning, Grampian Regional Council, Woodhill House, Ashgrove Road West, Aberdeen, AB9 2LU; T.-0224 682222, Ext. 2400.

Spurway, Neil Connell, MA, PhD. Senior Lecturer in Physiology, Glasgow University, since 1965; b. 22.8.36, Bradford; m., Alison Katherine; 3 s. Educ. Falmouth Grammar School; Jesus College, Cambridge. National Service, RAF, 1955-57; Assistant, then Lecturer in Physiology, Glasgow University, 1963-65; spent periods abroad, 1964 (Toronto), 1972 (Philadelphia), 1973 (Riyadh). Publication: Authority in Higher Education. Recreations: sailing; boatbuilding; running; philosophy; poetry. Address: (b.) Department of Physiology, Glasgow University, G12 8QQ; T.-041-339 8855, Ext. 499.

Squire, Geoffrey, DFA, ARSA, RSW, RGI. Senior Lecturer, Glasgow School of Art, since 1971; b. 21.2.23, Cleckheaton; m., Jean Marie; 1

s.; 1 d. Educ. Heckmondwike Grammar School; Leeds College of Art; Ruskin School, Oxford; Slade, London. Fleet Air Arm, Europe and Far East, 1942-46. Lecturer, Glasgow School of Art, 1948; elected ARSA, 1977, RGI, 1980, RSW, 1983. Recreation: vintage motoring. Address: (h.) The Studio, Links Place, Elie, Fife.

Stair, 13th Earl of, (John Aymer Dalrymple), KCVO (1978), MBE (1941). Captain General, Queen's Bodyguard for Scotland (Royal Company of Archers), since 1973; b. 9.10.06; m., Davina Bowes-Lyon; 3 s. Educ. Eton; Sandhurst. Colonel (retired), Scots Guards. Address: (h.) Lochinch Castle, Stranraer, Wigtownshire.

Stanforth, Professor Anthony William, BA, MA, Drphil. Professor and Head, Department of Languages, Heriot-Watt University, since 1981; b. 27.7.38, Ipswich; m., Susan Margaret Vale; 2 s. Educ. Ipswich School; King's College, Newcastle (Durham University); Marburg University. Earl Grey Memorial Fellow, Newcastle-upon-Tyne University, 1962-64; Assistant Lecturer, Manchester University, 1964-65; Lecturer, Senior Lecturer, Newcastle-upon-Tyne University, 1965-81; Visiting Assistant Professor, Wisconsin University, 1970-71. Fellow, Royal Society of Arts. Recreation: opera. Address: (b.) Department of Languages, Heriot-Watt University, Chambers Street, Edinburgh, EH1 1HX; T.-031-225 8432.

Stanley-Whyte, Rev. John James, FRGS, FSA Scot. Minister, Church of Scotland, since 1952; Deputy Regional Chaplain, Scotland and Northern Ireland Air Training Corps, since 1983; b. 28.7.23, Liverpool; m., Elinor Mary Barclay; 1 s. Educ. privately; Royal College of Surgeons, Edinburgh; Edinburgh University and New College. Royal Navy, 1942-46; Royal College of Surgeons, Edinburgh, 1946-48; Edinburgh University, 1948-52; Royal Navy Chaplain, 1952, including Fleet Chaplain, Far East Station and Korea, 1952-54; Deputy Editor, Navy News, 1954-55; Director, Sailors' Festival, Loch Fyne, 1958; Moderator, Mid Argyll Presbytery, 1961; Moderator, Argyll and the Isles Synod, 1962; Extra-Chaplain, Moderator of General Assembly, 1959; various parish ministries; Chairman of several voluntary groups and associations. Recreations: cricket and rugby (playing days in past!); golf; painting. Address: (h.) 21 Eglinton Crescent, Edinburgh, EH12 5BY; T.-031-337 7404.

Stanners, Ian Cram, FRICS. Chartered Quantity Surveyor; Vice-Chairman, Scottish Branch, Royal Institution of Chartered Surveyors, since 1984; b. 30.11.38, Glasgow; m., Louise Robertson; 2 d. Educ. Hutchesons' Boys' Grammar School. Chairman, Quantity Surveyors Divisional Committee, Scottish Branch, RICS, 1980-81; Member, Scottish Building Contract Committee, since 1982. Honorary Vice-President, Clyde Amateur Rowing Club. Recreations: rowing; curling. Address: (b.) 21 Woodlands Terrace, Glasgow, G3 6DF; T.-041-332 6032.

Stansfield, David Ashton, BSc, PhD. Senior Lecturer in Biochemistry, Dundee University, since 1974 (Warden, Belmont Hall, since 1974);

b. 28.10.34, Rochdale; m., Elizabeth Glynne Jones; 3 s. Educ. Hulme Grammar School for Boys, Oldham; University College of North Wales, Bangor. Assistant Lecturer in Agricultural Biochemistry, Aberdeen University, 1960-63; Lecturer in Biochemistry, Queen's College, Dundee (latterly Dundee University), 1963-74. Chairman, Dundee Liberal Association; Convenor, Finance and General Purposes Committee, Cleghorn Housing Association; Editorial Adviser, Biochemical Journal. Address: (h.) 7 Hawkhill Place, Dundee; T.-0382 22610.

Stark, Robert, OStJ, NP. Honorary Sheriff, Tayside Central and Fife; Solicitor; b. 28.8.15, Kirkcaldy; m., Mary Elizabeth; 1 s.; 1 d. Educ. Kirkcaldy High School; Edinburgh University. Solicitor, since 1940; Lt., RNVR, 1941-46; Partner, Innes Johnson & Co., 1952-84. Chairman, Rent Assessment Committee; Secretary, Fife Centre, SMTA, 1954-85; Chairman, Fife Branch, St. John Association, 1984-86; Past Chairman, Central and West Fife Conservative Association; former Honorary Secretary, Forces Help Society and Lord Roberts Workshop. Recreations: golf (Captain, Balbirnie Park GC); gardening. Address: (h.) Croft House, Markinch, Fife.

Stavert, Donald James, JP. Member, West Lothian District Council, since 1980 (Chairman, Finance and Manpower Committee, since 1984); National Chairman, Association of Direct Labour Organisations, 1985-86; b. 3.3.48, Edinburgh; m., Sandra McKay; 2 s. Educ. Penicuik High School. Branch Chairman, East of Scotland, Scottish Graphical Division, SOGAT, 1979-81; Member Scottish Executive, Graphical Division, SOGAT, 1976-81; Vice-Chairman, Housing Committee, West Lothian District Council, 1980-84; Community Councillor, 1978-80; Chairman, Livingston Constituency Labour Party, 1983-85; Chairman, West Lothian Labour Party Publications, since 1983; Secretary, West Lothian Centre for Unemployed. Recreations: swimming; walking; reading. Address: (h.) 18 Macfarlane Place, Uphall, West Lothian.

Steedman, Robert Russell, RSA, RIBA, FRIAS, ALI, DA, MLA. Partner, Morris and Steedman, Architects and Landscape Architects; b. 3.1.29, Batu Gajah, Malaysia; m., Martha Hamilton; 1 s.; 2 d. Educ. Loretto School; School of Architecture, Edinburgh College of Art; Pennsylvania University. Governor, Edinburgh College of Art, since 1974; Commissioner, Countryside Commission for Scotland, since 1980; ARSA, 1973, Academician, 1979; Council Member, RSA, 1981 (Deputy President, 1982-83, Secretary, since 1983); Commissioner, Royal Fine Art Commission for Scotland, since 1983; former Member, Council, RIAS; nine Civic Trust Awards, 1963-78; British Steel Award, 1971; RIBA Award for Scotland, 1974; European Heritage Medal, 1975; Association for the Protection of Rural Scotland, 1977; Borders Region Award, 1984. Address: (h.) 11B Belford Mews, Edinburgh; T.-031-225 1697.

Steedman, William, BSc, PhD, CChem, FRSC. Senior Lecturer, Department of Chemistry, Heriot-Watt University, since 1975; b. 30.3.34,

Scarborough; m., Wilma Mary Trail; 1 s.; 2 d. Educ. Allan Glen's School, Glasgow; Glasgow University. Technical Officer, ICI, 1959-60; Lecturer in Applied Organic Chemistry: Heriot-Watt College, 1960-66, Heriot-Watt University, 1966-75. Publication: Chemistry for Engineering and Applied Sciences (Co-author). Recreations: golf; hill-walking. Address: (b.) Department of Chemistry, Heriot-Watt University, Edinburgh; T.-031-449 5111.

Steel, Very Rev. David, MA, BD. Minister, St. Michael's, Linlithgow, 1959-76; Moderator, General Assembly of Church of Scotland, 1974-75; b. 5.10.10; m.; 3 s.; 2 d. Educ. Peterhead Academy; Robert Gordon's College, Aberdeen; Aberdeen University. Minister: Denbeath, 1936-41, Bridgend, Dumbarton, 1941-46; Home Organisation Foreign Mission Secretary, 1946-49; Minister, Parish of East Africa and of St. Andrew's, Nairobi, 1949-57; Associate Minister, St. Cuthbert's, Edinburgh, 1957-59.

Steel, Rt. Hon. David (Martin Scott), PC (1977), MA, LLB. MP (Liberal), Tweeddale, Ettrick and Lauderdale, since 1983 (Roxburgh, Selkirk and Peebles, 1965-83); Leader of the Liberal Party, since 1976; b. 31.3.38; m., Judith Mary MacGregor; 3 s.; 1 d. Educ. Prince of Wales School, Nairobi; George Watson's College, Edinburgh; Edinburgh University. Liberal Chief Whip, 1970-75; Sponsor, Private Member's Bill to reform law on abortion, 1966-67; President, Anti-Apartheid Movement of GB, 1966-69; Chairman, Shelter, Scotland, 1969-73; Rector, Edinburgh University, 1982-85; Journalist and Broadcaster.

Steel, Major Sir (Fiennes) William Strang, 2nd Bt, DL, JP; b. 24.7.12; m., Joan Henderson (deceased); 2 s.; 1 d. (deceased). Educ. Eton; Sandhurst. Retired Major, 17/21st Lancers; Member, Forestry Commission, 1958-73; Convener, Selkirk County Council, 1967-75. Address: (h.) Philiphaugh, Selkirk.

Steel, Rev. George Hutton Bethune, MA, BD. Minister, Alva Parish Church, since 1982; b. 5.11.57, Paisley; m., Lesley Killoch; 2 s. Educ. John Neilson High School, Paisley; Glasgow University. Recreations: classical guitar; photography. Address: The Manse, Ochil Road, Alva, FK12 5JT; T.-Alva 60262.

Steele, Hugh, MRSanA, MRSH, JP. Honorary Sheriff, since 1974; b. 12.8.16; m., Grace Wyllie Lawrie; 2 s. Educ. Strathaven Academy; Hamilton Academy; Royal Technical College, Glasgow. Assistant Sanitary Inspector, Lanarkshire County Council, 15 years; Depute Chief Sanitary Inspector, Sutherland County Council, 1949-60; Chief Sanitary Inspector (then Director of Environmental Health and Master of Works), Sutherland, 1960-74. Elder, Dornoch Cathedral, 26 years (latterly as Session Clerk); Member, Sutherland Presbytery; Life Member, Royal British Legion Scotland; Honorary Grand Junior Deacon, Grand Lodge of Scotland, for services to freemasonry; General Commissioner of Income Tax, since 1976; Chairman, Stafford Court Committee, Royal British Legion Housing Association Ltd. Recreations: golf; bowling; gardening; Scottish country dancing (teacher). Address: (h.) Stra'ven, Rosebery Avenue, Dornoch, Sutherland, IV25 3SZ; T.-0862 810 325.

Steele, Rev. Leslie McMillan, MA, BD (Hons). Minister, Gardner Church, Macduff, since 1973; b. 13.12.47, Edinburgh; m., Lillias Margaret Franks; 4 d. Educ. George Heriot's, Edinburgh; Edinburgh University. Assistant Minister, St. Columba's, Largs, 1972-73; Convener, Overseas Interests Committee, Buchan Presbytery, 1980-84; Moderator, Buchan Presbytery, 1983-84. Recreation: DIY. Address: 15 Ross Street, Macduff, AB4 1NS; T.-0261 32432.

Steele, Thomas Graham. Director of Programmes, Radio Forth, since 1978; b. 11.5.45, Lanark; m., Fiona MacAuslane; 1 s.; 1 d. Educ. Larkhall Academy, Larkhall; Skerry's College, Glasgow. Lobby Correspondent, Scottish Daily Mail; TV and Radio Presenter, BBC Glasgow; Producer, BBC Local Radio; Broadcaster, Radio Clyde; Head of News and Current Affairs, Radio Forth. Member, Programming Committee, Association of Independent Radio Contractors, since 1980; Creator, Festival City Radio. Recreations: sailing; walking; reading; conversation. Address: (b.) Forth House, Forth Street, Edinburgh; T.-031-556 9255.

Stein, Rev. Jock, MA, BD. Minister, Steeple Church, Dundee, since 1976; b. 8.11.41, Edinburgh; m., Margaret E. Munro; 3 d. Educ. Sedbergh School; Cambridge University; Edinburgh University. Work Study Officer, United Steel Companies, Sheffield; Assistant Warden, St. Ninian's Lay Training Centre, Crieff; publishing and lay training, Presbyterian Church of East Africa. Chairman: Dundee Cyrenians, Dundee Liaison Committee on Homelessness, Handsel Trust, Mary Slessor Trust. Publications: Ministers for the '80s (Editor); Our One Baptism; In Christ All Things Hold Together (Co-author). Recreations: music; skiing. Address: 128 Arbroath Road, Dundee; T.-0382 455411.

Stephen, David Smith, MIWM, MITA. Director of Cleansing, City of Aberdeen District Council, since 1981; b. 7.10.32, Tannochside, Lanarkshire; m., Dorothy; 2 s. Educ. Wishaw High School; Paisley Technical College. Apprentice, Burgh of Motherwell and Wishaw, 1950-54; District Inspector: Burgh of Airdrie, 1954-55, Burgh of Coatbridge, 1956-57, Burgh of Motherwell and Wishaw, 1958-60; Area Transport and Cleansing Officer, Midlothian County Council, 1961-64; Depute Director of Cleansing, City of Aberdeen, 1964-81. Recreations: fishing; boating; shooting. Address: (b.) 38 Powis Terrace, Kittybrewster, Aberdeen, AB2 3QE; T.-0224 42221.

Stephen, Rev. Donald Murray, TD, MA, BD, ThM. Minister, Marchmont St. Giles' Parish Church, Edinburgh, since 1974; b. 1.6.36, Dundee; m., Hilda Swan Henriksen; 2 s.; 1 d. Educ. Brechin High School; Richmond Grammar School, Yorkshire; Edinburgh University; Princeton Theological Seminary. Assistant Minister, Westover Hills Presbyterian Church, Arkansas, 1962-64; Minister, Kirkoswald, 1964-74; Chaplain, TA, 1965-85 (attached to 4/5 Bn., RSF, 205 Scottish General Hospital, 2nd Bn., 52nd Lowland Volunteers); Convener, Committee on Chaplains to Her Majesty's Forces, General Assembly. Recreations: golf; curling. Address: 19 Hope Terrace, Edinburgh, EH9 2AP; T.-031-447 2834.

Stephen, Frank H., BA, PhD. Senior Lecturer, Department of Economics, Strathclyde University, since 1979; Managing Editor, Journal of Economic Studies, since 1982; b. 20.11.46, Glasgow; m., Christine Leathard; 2 d. Educ. Queen's Park Secondary School, Glasgow; Strathclyde University. Research Officer, then Head, Economics Department, STUC, 1969-71; Lecturer, Department of Economics, Strathclyde University, 1971-79. Publications: The Performance of Labour-Managed Firms (Editor), 1982; Firms Organisation and Labour (Editor), 1984; The Economic Analysis of Producers' Cooperatives, 1984. Address: (b.) Department of Economics, Strathclyde University, Glasgow; T.-041-552 4400.

Stephen, Professor Kenneth William, BDS, DDSc, HDDRCPS, FDSRCS. Professor of Preventive Dentistry, Glasgow University, since 1984 (Head, Department of Oral Medicine and Pathology, since 1980); Consultant-in-charge, Glasgow School of Dental Hygiene, since 1979; b. 1.10.37, Glasgow; m., Anne Seymour Gardiner; 1 s.; 1 d. Educ. Hillhead High School, Glasgow; Glasgow University. General Dental Practitioner, 1960-64; House Officer, Department of Oral Surgery, Glasgow Dental Hospital, 1964-65; Lecturer, Department of Conservative Dentistry, 1965-68; Lecturer, Department of Oral Medicine and Pathology, Glasgow University, 1968-71; Visiting Lecturer, Department of Oral Physiology, Newcastle-upon-Tyne University, 1969-70; Senior Lecturer, Department of Oral Medicine and Pathology, Glasgow University, 1971-80; Reader, 1980-84. Co-President, European Organisation for Caries Research, 1978-79. Recreations: swimming; hill-walking; skiing; gardening. Address: (b.) Dental School, 378 Sauchiehall Street, Glasgow, G2 3JZ; T.-041-332 7020.

Stephen, Nicol Ross, LLB, DipLP, NP. Solicitor, Milne & Mackinnon, Aberdeen, since 1983; Member, Grampian Regional Council, since 1982; b. 23.3.60, Aberdeen. Educ. Robert Gordon's College, Aberdeen; Aberdeen University; Edinburgh University. Trainee Solicitor, C. & P.H. Chalmers, Aberdeen, 1981-83. Past Chairman, Kincardine and Deeside Liberal Association; Secretary, Liberal Alliance Group, Grampian Regional Council; Member, Aberdeen Local Health Council; Member, Grampian Adult Basic Education Committee; Member, Grampian Society for the Blind Committee. Recreation: golf. Address: (h.) 565 Great Western Road, Aberdeen; T.-Aberdeen 30635.

Stephen, Pamela Judith, BSc (Hons), MB, ChB, MRCP. Consultant in Geriatric Medicine, Perth Royal Infirmary, since 1984; Honorary Senior

Lecturer, Department of Medicine, Dundee University, since 1984; b. 29.1.51, Falkirk. Educ. Mary Erskine School for Girls, Edinburgh; Edinburgh University. Pre-registration House Officer and Senior House Officer, Edinburgh, 1975-77; Medical Registrar, Falkirk, 1977-80; Registrar in Rehabilitation Medicine, Edinburgh, 1980-81; Lecturer, Department of Geriatric Medicine, Edinburgh University, 1982-84. Recreations: classical music; theatre and the arts; gardening; travel. Address: (b.) Geriatric Unit, Perth Royal Infirmary, Perth, PH1 1NX; T.-0738 23311.

Stephen, Stewart Anderson, MB, ChB, FRCPEdin. Consultant Physician in Geriatric Medicine, since 1969; Member, Borders Health Board, since 1982; b. 26.4.23, Dundee; m., Catherine; 2 s.; 1 d. Educ. Grove Academy, Dundee; St. Andrews University. Pilot, RAF, Second World War; spent several years in teaching hospitals to Senior Registrar Grade. Committee Member, Melrose and District Abbeyfield Society. Recreations: golf; gardening. Address: (h.) Friarshall, Gattonside, Melrose, Roxburghshire; T.-Melrose 2610.

Stephenson, Thomas Anthony, BSc, PhD, DIC, DSc, CChem, FRSC. Reader, Department of Chemistry, Edinburgh University, since 1985; b. 12.11.40, Morley; m., Ann Margaret; 1 s.; 1 d. Educ. Batley Grammar School; University College, London; Imperial College, London. Postdoctoral Fellow, Institute of Technology, Cleveland, Ohio, 1965-67; Senior Demonstrator, Department of Chemistry, Newcastle-upon-Tyne University, 1967-69; Lecturer, Department of Chemistry, Edinburgh University, 1969-82, Senior Lecturer, 1982-85. Recreations: all forms of sport; reading. Address: (b.) Department of Chemistry, Edinburgh University, Edinburgh, EH9 3JJ; T.-031-667 1081, Ext. 3442.

Stevely, William Stewart, DPhil, BSc, DipEd. Senior Lecturer in Biochemistry, Glasgow University; b. 6.4.43, West Kilbride; m., Sheila Ann Stalker; 3 s.; 2 d. Educ. Ardrossan Academy; Glasgow University; Oxford University. Glasgow University Representative, College Council, Glasgow College of Technology, 1978-85; Senate Assessor, University Court, Glasgow University, 1984-88. Address: (b.) Department of Biochemistry, Glasgow University, Glasgow, G12 8QQ; T.-041-339 8855, Ext. 7263.

Stevens, Hugh John, WS, LLB, NP. Solicitor; Partner, Brodies WS, Edinburgh, since 1981; Tutor, Diploma in Legal Practice, Edinburgh University Faculty of Law, since 1980; b. 5.11.49, Dunfermline; m., Margaret Elizabeth Macdonald; 2 s.; 1 d. Educ. St. Andrews RC High School, Kirkcaldy; Edinburgh University. Examiner, Capital Taxes Office, Edinburgh, 1971-77; Assistant Solicitor, Brodies WS, 1977-80. Recreations: badminton; football; squash. Address: (b.) 7 Rothesay Terrace, Edinburgh; T.-031-225 8566.

Stevenson, David, BA, PhD. Reader in Scottish History, Aberdeen University, since 1984; Director, Centre for Scottish Studies, Aberdeen University, since 1984; b. 30.4.42, Largs; m.,

Wendy B. McLeod; 2 s. Educ. Gordonstoun; Dublin University; Glasgow University. Aberdeen University: Lecturer in History, 1970-80, Senior Lecturer in History, 1980-84. Honorary Secretary, Scottish History Society, 1976-84; Fellow, Royal Historical Society. Publications: The Scottish Revolution 1637-44, 1973; Revolution and Counter-Revolution in Scotland 1644-51, 1977; Alasdair MacColla and the Highland Problem in the 17th Century, 1980; Scottish Covenanters and Irish Confederates, 1981; The Government of Scotland under the Covenanters 1637-51, 1982. Address: (b.) Department of History, Aberdeen University, Old Aberdeen, AB9 2UB.

Stevenson, David Deas, BCom, CA. Managing Director, Edinburgh Woollen Mill, since 1972; b. 28.11.31, Hawick; m., Alix Jamieson; 2 d. Educ. Langholm Academy; Dumfries Academy; Edinburgh University. British Steel Corporation, 1966-67; Langholm Dyeing Co., 1967-72. Recreations: squash; horses; running. Address: (b.) Waverley Mills, Langholm, Dumfriesshire, DG13 OEB; T.-0541 80611.

Stevenson, James Edward Mackenzie, MA, LLB, NP. Solicitor; Honorary Sheriff Substitute, South Strathclyde, Dumfries and Galloway, at Dumfries; b. 9.11.19, Lockerbie; m., Maureen Mary; 2 s.; 2 d. Educ. Lockerbie Academy; George Watson's Boys College; Edinburgh University. Captain, 131st Field Regiment, RA, Second World War; Partner, McJerrow & Stevenson, Solicitors, Lockerbie; Town Clerk and Chamberlain: Burgh of Lochmaben, 1949-75, Burgh of Lockerbie, 1957-75. Chairman of Directors, South of Scotland Ice Rink, Lockerbie; Clerk, Annan Fishery Board; Clerk, Lockerbie Branch, Earl Haig Fund. Recreations: golf; curling. Address: (h.) Fairfield, St. Brydes Terrace, Lockerbie, Dumfriesshire.

Stevenson, John, MA (Hons). Rector, Moffat Academy, since 1976; b. 13.12.39, Stewarton; m., Jane Dawson Alexander; 2 s.; 1 d. Educ. Stewarton Higher Grade School; Glasgow University; Jordanhill College of Education. Teacher: Stewarton High School, Kilmarnock Academy, Onthank Junior Secondary School, Grange Academy (Kilmarnock), Largs Academy. Address: (h.) Hoppertitty, Beattock, Moffat, Dumfries, DG10 9PJ; T.-06833 337.

Stevenson, John Meikle, BSc, FInstD, FBIM. Farmer; Vice Chairman, Forth River Purification Board, 1982-85; Vice Chairman, Royal Scottish Agricultural Benevolent Institution, since 1982; b. 20.1.31, Aberlady; m., Eileen A.; 2 s.; 1 d. Educ. Trinity College, Glenalmond; Aberdeen University. Councillor, East Lothian County Council, 1961-66; President, East Lothian, National Farmers' Union, 1968-69; Council Member, NFU, 1966-70; Member, Governing Body, British Society for Research in Agricultural Engineering, since 1968; Committee Member, Scottish Institute of Agricultural Engineering, since 1968 (Chairman, since 1984). Recreations: shooting; fishing; gardening; golf. Address: Luffness Mains, Aberlady, East Lothian, EH32 OPZ; T.-Aberlady 212.

Stevenson, John S.K., MB, ChB, FRCGP, D(Obst)RCOG. Senior Lecturer, Department of General Practice, Edinburgh University, since 1968; b. 28.8.29, West Kilbride; m., Helen L. Howes; 3 s.; 1 d. Educ. Ayr Academy; Glasgow University. Principal, general practice, Stevenston, Ayrshire, 1958-68; Member, NHS Executive Council for Ayrshire, 1963-68; Member, Edinburgh and District Council on Alcoholism, 1969-73; Honorary Treasurer, Association of University Teachers of General Practice, 1972-81; Member, BBC Scotland Medical Advisory Group, 1976-84; BBC Scotland Radio Doctor, 1976-78; Member, Biomedical Research Committee, Chief Scientist Organisation, SHHD, 1983-85; Medical Officer, George Heriot's FP Rugby Football Club. Recreations: reading; writing; theatre; travel; holiday golf. Address: (b.) Department of General Practice, Levinson House, 20 West Richmond Street, Edinburgh, EH8 9DX; T.-031-667 1011.

Stevenson, Leslie Forster, MA, BPhil. Reader in Logic and Metaphysics, St. Andrews University, since 1977; b. 15.12.43, Bridgnorth; m., Zinaida Lewczuk. Educ. Friends' School, Lisburn; Campbell College, Belfast; Corpus Christi College, Oxford. Lecturer in Logic and Metaphysics, St. Andrews University, 1968-77. Publications: Seven Theories of Human Nature, 1974; The Metaphysics of Experience, 1982. Recreations: bassoon-playing; hill-walking. Address: (h.) 6 Abbotsford Place, St. Andrews, Fife, KY16 9HQ; T.-0334 74745.

Stevenson, Peter David, MA (Cantab). Director, Noble Grossart Ltd., since 1972; b. 6.3.47, Edinburgh; m., Susan Blades; 1 d. Educ. Edinburgh Academy; Trinity College, Cambridge. Joined Noble Grossart Ltd., 1970, after three years with merchant bank in the City; Non-Executive Chairman, Fios Group; Non-Executive Director: William Low PLC, Macfarlane Group PLC, Laidlaw Group PLC, Murray International Holdings Ltd., Ireland Alloys Holdings Ltd. Address: (h.) 29 Warriston Crescent, Edinburgh, EH3 5LB; T.-031-226 7011.

Stevenson, Robert Orr, BA, FCIS. Secretary, Scottish Special Housing Association, since 1983; b. 27.4.33, Glasgow; m., Anne. Educ. Trinity College, Glenalmond; Christ's College, Cambridge. Beaverbrook Newspapers Ltd.: General Manager, Sunday Express, General Manager, Daily Express, Group General Manager Scotland; Director and General Manager, Felixstowe Dock and Railway Company (Chief Executive, Port of Felixstowe); Managing Director, A.M. Tweedie & Co. Ltd. Recreations: golf; opera. Address: (h.) Muirlea, Gifford, East Lothian; T.-Gifford 586.

Stevenson, Ronald, FRMCM. Composer and Pianist; Broadcaster; Author; b. 6.3.28, Blackburn; m., Marjorie Spedding; 1 s.; 2 d. Educ. Royal Manchester College of Music; Conservatorio Di Santa Cecilia, Rome. Senior Lecturer, Cape Town University, 1963-65; BBC Prom debut in own 2nd Piano Concerto, 1972; Aldeburgh Festival recital with Sir Peter Pears, 1973; Busoni documentary, BBC TV, 1974; BBC Radio Scotland extended series on the bagpipe, clarsach and fiddle music of Scotland, 1980-84; Artist in Residence: Melbourne University, 1980, University of W. Australia, 1982, Conservatory of Shanghai, 1985; published and recorded compositions: Passacaglia for Piano, two Piano Concertos, Violin Concerto (commissioned by Menuhin), Prelude, Fugue and Fantasy for Piano, Prelude and Fugue for Organ. Publication: Western Music. Recreations: hill-walking; reading poetry, biographies and politics. Address: (h.) Townfoot House, West Linton, Peeblesshire; T.-0968 60511.

Stevenson, Ronald Harley, MA, LLB. Chief Executive, Highland Regional Council, since 1981; b. 6.1.34, Dunfermline. Educ. Dunfermline High School; Edinburgh University. County Clerk, Caithness County Council, 1967-75; Joint Director of Law and Administration, Highland Regional Council, 1975-81. Address: (b.) Regional Buildings, Inverness; T.-Inverness 234121.

Stevenson, Sir Simpson, LLD. Provost, Inverclyde District Council, since 1984; Chairman, Scottish Health Services Common Services Agency, since 1983; b. 18.8.21, Greenock; m., Jean Holmes Henry. Educ. Greenock High School. Provost of Greenock, 1962-65; Chairman, Western Regional Hospital Board, 1967-73; Chairman, Greater Glasgow Health Board, 1973-83; knighted, 1976; Hon. LLD, Glasgow University, 1982; Member, Royal Commission on NHS, 1976-79. Address: (h.) The Gables, Reservoir Road, Gourock; T.-0475 31774.

Stevenson, Struan John Stirton, JP. Conservative Group Leader, Kyle and Carrick District Council, since 1983 (Convener, Environmental Services Committee, since 1984); Chairman, Carrick, Cumnock and Doon Valley Conservative Constituency Association, since 1982; Vice Chairman, Conservative Group, COSLA, since 1984; Farmer and Director, J. & R. Stevenson Ltd., Ballantrae; b. 4.4.48, Ballantrae; m., Pat; 2 s. Educ. Strathallan; West of Scotland Agricultural College (Diploma in Agriculture). Elected, Girvan District Council, 1971-75; elected, Kyle and Carrick District Council, 1974; Convener, Leisure and Recreation, 1977-80; Convener, Miscellaneous Services Committee, COSLA, 1977-80; Vice Chairman, South Ayrshire Conservative Constituency Association, 1981-82; Vice Chairman, Ayrshire Justices Committee, since 1984; Member, Kyle and Carrick District Licensing Board, since 1984; Member, Ayrshire and Burns Country Tourist Board; Curator, MacLaurin Trust; Director, Richard Demarco Gallery Ltd., Edinburgh. Recreations: contemporary art fanatic; photography. Address: (h.) Balig House, Ballantrae, Girvan, KA26 0JY; T.-046583 214.

Stevenson, William Trevor, CBE, DL, FCIT. Chairman, Scottish Transport Group, since 1981; Chairman, Hodgson Martin Ventures, since 1982; Chairman, Alex. Wilkie Ltd., since 1977; b. 21.3.21, Peebles; m., Alison Wilson Roy. Educ. Edinburgh Academy. Apprentice Engineer, 1937-41; Engineer, 1941-45; entered family food manufacturing business, Cottage Rusks, 1945;

Managing Director, 1948-54; Chairman, 1954-59; Chief Executive, Cottage Rusks Associates, 1965-69; Regional Director, Ranks Hovis McDougall, 1969-74; Director, various companies in food, engineering, medical, hotel and aviation industries, since 1974; founder Chairman, Gleneagles Hotels, 1981-83; Master, Company of Merchants of City of Edinburgh, 1978-80; Vice President, Edinburgh Chamber of Commerce, since 1983. Recreations: flying; sailing; curling. Address: (h.) 45 Pentland View, Edinburgh, EH10 6PY; T.-031-445 1512.

Stewardson, Raymond Richard, BA (Hons). Rector, John Neilson High School, Paisley, since 1983; b. 26.9.37, Huyton, Merseyside; m., Aileen Agnes Mackie; 1 s.; 1 d. Educ. Prescot Grammar School; Sheffield University; London University (External). Assistant Teacher; Principal Teacher of Geography; Assistant Head Teacher; Depute Rector. Recreations: swimming; gardening. Address: (b.) John Neilson High School, Paisley, PA1 2QZ; T.-041-889 9451/2.

Stewart, A.J. (Ada F. Kay). Playwright and Author; b. 5.3.29, Tottington, Lancashire. Educ. Grammar School, Fleetwood. ATS Scottish Command; first produced play, 1951; repertory actress, 1952-54; BBC TV Staff Writer/Editor/Adaptor, Central Script Section, 1956-59; returned to Scotland, 1959, as stage and TV Writer; winner, BBC New Radio Play competition, 1956; The Man from Thermopylae, presented in Festival of Contemporary Drama, Rheydt, West Germany, 1959, as part of Edinburgh International Festival, 1965, and at Masquers' Theatre, Hollywood, 1972; first recipient, Wendy Wood Memorial Grant, 1982; Polish Gold Cross for achievements in literary field. Publications: Falcon - The Autobiography of His Grace, James the 4, King of Scots, 1970; Died 1513-Born 1929 - The Autobiography of A.J. Stewart, 1978; The Man from Thermopylae, 1981. Recreation: work. Address: 15 Oxford Street, Edinburgh, 8.

Stewart, Alan Aitken. Solicitor; Sole Partner, Curdie & Smith, since 1963; Senior Partner, Curdie Sturrock & Co., since 1983; Clerk, C.K. Marr Educational Trust, since 1970; Honorary Sheriff, Kilmarnock, since 1979; b. 25.1.34, Prestwick; m., Joy; 2 s.; 1 d. Educ. Prestwick High School; Ayr Academy; Glasgow University. Qualified in Law, 1955; Solicitor, 1956; Junior Partner, Curdie & Smith, 1958; Dean, Kilmarnock Faculty of Solicitors, 1978-80; Clerk, Board of Governors, Marr Trust, Troon, since 1970; founder Secretary, Kilmarnock and North Ayrshire Junior Chamber of Commerce (President, 1964); Secretary, Federation of Scottish Junior Chamber of Commerce, 1965 (President, 1966); Vice President, Junior Chamber of Commerce International, 1967; Captain, Kilmarnock (Barassie) Golf Club, 1977. Recreations: golf; swimming; snooker. Address: (b.) 1 Howard Street, Kilmarnock; T.-0563 25118.

Stewart, Alasdair Duncan, CA. Chief Financial Officer, North of Scotland Hydro-Electric Board, since 1975; b. 24.2.33, Perth; m., Audrey Jean Lind Stewart; 3 s. Educ. Perth Academy. J. &

R. Morison & Co., Perth, 1950-59; Stewarts & Lloyds Ltd., Birmingham and Glasgow, 1959-67; P-E Consulting Group, 1967-72; joined North of Scotland Hydro-Electric Board, 1972. Recreation: sailing (West Coast). Address: (b.) 16 Rothesay Terrace, Edinburgh, EH3 7SE; T.-031-225 1361.

Stewart, Sheriff Alastair Lindsay, BA, LLB. Sheriff of Grampian, Highland and Islands, at Aberdeen and Stonehaven, since 1979; Honorary Lecturer, Faculty of Law, Aberdeen University, since 1982; b. 28.11.38, Aberdeen; m., Annabel Claire; 2 s. Educ. Edinburgh Academy; St. Edmund Hall, Oxford; Edinburgh University. Admitted, Faculty of Advocates, 1963; Tutor, Faculty of Law, Edinburgh University, 1963-73; Standing Junior Counsel to the Registrar of Restrictive Trading Agreements, 1968-70; Advocate Depute, 1970-73; Sheriff of Lanarkshire (later South Strathclyde, Dumfries and Galloway), at Airdrie, 1973-79. Governor, Robert Gordon's Institute of Technology, Aberdeen, since 1982; Chairman, Aberdeen Family Conciliation Service, since 1984. Recreations: music; reading. Address: (b.) Sheriff's Chambers, Sheriff Court House, Aberdeen, AB9 1AP; T.-0224 648316.

Stewart, Alexander Donald, BA, LLB, WS. Solicitor in private practice in Glasgow, since 1961; Director, Clyde Cablevision Limited, since 1982; Director, Scottish Amicable Life Assurance Society, since 1985; b. 18.6.33, Edinburgh; m., Virigina Mary Washington; 1 s.; 5 d. Educ. Wellington College, Berkshire; Oxford University; Edinburgh University. Recreations: music; skiing; field sports; curling. Address: (h.) Ardvorlich Cottage, Lochearnhead, Perthshire; T.-05673 212.

Stewart, Alexander Reavell Macdonald, FRICS, FRVA, ACIArb. Chartered Surveyor; Chairman, Scottish Branch, Royal Institution of Chartered Surveyors, 1985-86; b. 14.2.29, Bearsden; m., Keris Duguid Keir; 2 s.; 2 d. Educ. Merchiston Castle School. President: Property Owners and Factors Association Glasgow, 1968-69, National Federation of Property Owners Scotland, 1978-80. Recreations: trout fishing; piping. Address: (b.) 145 North Street, Glasgow; T.-041-221 9191.

Stewart, Andy. Entertainer; Song Writer; b. 30.12.33, Glasgow; m., Sheila Newbigging; 1 s.; 5 d. Educ. Craigie School, Perth; Arbroath High School. Numerous theatre seasons and concert tours in UK and USA, Canada, Australia, New Zealand, South Africa; toured with White Heather Club; Hogmanay shows for BBC TV, Scottish Television and Grampian Television; TV specials including Andy Stewart Show and White Heather Club; 13 Sauchie Street series (radio); wrote the song A Scottish Soldier, and other ballads and monologues. Recreations: golf; reading; watching old films.

Stewart, Clement A., MA, MEd. Head Teacher, Lochgilphead High School, since 1977; b. 9.1.41, Strichen; 3 s. Educ. Aberdeen Grammar School; Aberdeen University. Teacher of Mathematics, Aberdeen Grammar School, 1963-70; Dunoon

Grammar School: Principal Teacher of Mathematics, 1970-72, Assistant Rector, 1972-74, Depute Rector, 1974-77. Session Clerk, Lochgilphead Parish Church. Address: (h.) Dunaverty, Brackley Park, Ardrishaig, Argyll; T.-0546 3027.

Stewart, Rt. Hon. Donald James, PC, MP. MP (Scottish National Party), Western Isles, since 1970; b. 17.10.20, Stornoway; m., Christina MacAulay. Educ. Nicolson Institute, Stornoway. Town and County Councillor, 1951-70; Provost of Stornoway, 1958-64 and 1968-70; Honorary Sheriff. Recreations: photography; fishing; gardening. Address: (h.) Hillcrest, 41 Goathill Road, Stornoway; T.-0851 2672.

Stewart, Douglas Fleming, MA, LLB, WS, NP, FSA Scot. Solicitor (Scotland), Crown Estate Commissioners, since 1970; Partner, J.F. Anderson, WS, since 1961; Secretary, Stewart Society, since 1968; b. 22.5.27, Sydney, Australia; m., Catherine Coleman; 2 d. Educ. George Watson's College, Edinburgh; Edinburgh University. RAF, 1945-48; Session Clerk, Braid Church, Edinburgh, since 1979; Treasurer, Friends of the Royal Scottish Museum, since 1972; Council Member, Royal Celtic Society, since 1981. Recreation: swimming. Address: (b.) 48 Castle Street, Edinburgh, EH2 3LX; T.-031-225 3912.

Stewart of Appin, Sir Dugald Leslie Lorn, KCVO (1972), CMG (1969). British Ambassador to Yugoslavia, 1971-77; b. 10.9.21; m.; 3 s.; 1 d. Educ. Eton; Magdalen College, Oxford. Joined Foreign Office, 1942.

Stewart, Ena Lamont. Playwright; b. 10.2.12, Glasgow; m., Jack Stewart (deceased); 1 s. Educ. Woodside School, Glasgow; Esdaile School, Edinburgh. Assistant, Public Library, Aberdeen, 1930-34; Medical Secretary, Radcliffe, Lancashire, 1934-37; Secretary/Receptionist, Royal Hospital for Sick Children, Glasgow, 1937-41; Baillie's Reference Library, Glasgow: Assistant Librarian, 1953-57, Librarian-in-charge, 1957-66; author of plays: Starched Aprons, Men Should Weep, The Heir to Ardmally, Business in Edinburgh, After Tomorrow (unperformed), Walkies Time, Knocking on the Wall, Towards Evening, High Places. Recreations: reading; listening to music. Address: (h.) 5a Monkton Road, Prestwick, KA9 1AP; T.-0292 76355.

Stewart, Hon. Lord (Ewan George Francis Stewart), MC (1945), QC (Scot). Senator of the College of Justice in Scotland, since 1975; b. 9.5.23; m.; 1 s.; 1 d. Educ. George Watson's College, Edinburgh; Edinburgh University. Served Second World War, 7/9 Bn., The Royal Scots; admitted Faculty of Advocates, 1949; QC (Scot), 1960; Honorary Sheriff-Substitute of the Lothians and Peebles, 1961-64; practised, New Zealand Bar, 1962-64; Solicitor-General for Scotland, 1967-70; Member, Scottish Law Commission, 1971-75; Chairman, Committee on Alternatives to Prosecution, 1977-83; Chairman, Court, Stirling University, 1976-84.

Stewart, Sheriff Ewen, BSc (Agr), MA (Econ), LLB. Sheriff at Wick, since 1962, and at Dornoch and Tain, since 1977; b. 22.4.26; m.; 1 d. Educ. Edinburgh University. Practised, Scottish Bar, 1952-62; Lecturer on Agricultural Law, Edinburgh University, 1957-62.

Stewart, Francis John, MA (Oxon), LLB, TD. Writer to the Signet (retired); Director, American Trust plc; Member, Queen's Bodyguard for Scotland (Royal Company of Archers); b. 11.5.17, Edinburgh; m., Olga Margaret Mounsey; 3 s.; 1 d. Educ. Cargilfield School, Edinburgh; Loretto School; Trinity College, Oxford; Edinburgh University. 1st Bn., Lothians and Borders Yeomanry; Senior Partner, Murray Beith & Murray, WS, Edinburgh (retired); Past Chairman of Governors, Loretto School; Honorary Consul for Principality of Monaco, 1964-85; Chevalier of the Order of St. Charles. Recreation: gardening. Address: (b.) 39 Castle Street, Edinburgh; T.-031-225 1200.

Stewart, Sir Frederick Henry, KB, BSc, PhD, FRSA, DSc Hon. (Aberdeen, Leicester, Heriot-Watt, Durham); FRS, FRSE, FGS. Professor Emeritus, Edinburgh University, since 1982; Trustee, British Museum (Natural History), since 1983; Council Member, Scottish Marine Biological Association, since 1983; b. 16.1.16, Aberdeen; m., Mary Florence Elinor Rainbow. Educ. Fettes College, Edinburgh; Robert Gordon's College, Aberdeen; Aberdeen University; Emmanuel College, Cambridge. Mineralogist, Research Department, Imperial Chemical Industries, 1941-43; Lecturer in Geology, Durham University, 1943-56; Regius Professor of Geology and Mineralogy, Edinburgh University, 1956-82; Member, Council for Scientific Policy, 1967-71 (Assessor, 1971-73); Chairman, Natural Environment Research Council, 1971-73; Chairman, Advisory Board for the Research Councils, 1974-79; Member, Advisory Council for Research and Development, 1976-79. Lyell Fund Award, 1951 and Lyell Medal, 1970, Geological Society of London; Mineralogical Society of America Award, 1952; Clough Medal, Edinburgh Geological Society; Sorby Medal, Yorkshire Geological Society. Publications: The British Caledonides, 1963; Marine Evaporites, 1963. Recreations: fishing; collecting fossil fish. Address: (h.) 79 Morningside Park, Edinburgh, EH10 5EZ; T.-031-447 2620.

Stewart, Professor George, BSc, PhD, CEng, MIChemE, MAIME. Professor of Petroleum Engineering (and Head of Department), Heriot-Watt University, since 1981; Director, Edinburgh Petroleum Development Services, since 1984; b. 4.5.40, Edinburgh; 2 s. Educ. George Heriot's School, Edinburgh; Edinburgh University. Process Engineer, Esso Refinery, Fawley, 1962-63; Assistant Lecturer in Chemical Engineering, Newcastle University, 1963-67; Lecturer in Chemical Engineering, then Senior Lecturer, Heriot-Watt University, 1967-78; Visiting Professor, Texas University, 1976; Senior Reservoir Engineer, Services Techniques Schlumberger, Paris, 1978-81. Recreations: squash; golf; tennis; sailing. Address: (b.) Department of Petroleum Engineering, Heriot-Watt University, Riccarton, Edinburgh, EH14 4AS; T.-031-449 5111, Ext. 2331.

Stewart, George Girdwood, CB, MC, TD, BSc, FICFor, Hon. FLI. Regional Representative for Central and Tayside, National Trust for Scotland, since 1984; Chairman, Scottish Wildlife Trust, since 1981; Member, Countryside Commission for Scotland, since 1981; Member, Environment Panel, British Railways Board, since 1980; b. 12.12.19, Glasgow; m., Shelagh Jean Morven Murray; 1 s.; 1 d. Educ. Kelvinside Academy, Glasgow; Glasgow University; Edinburgh University. Royal Artillery, 1940-46 (mentioned in Despatches); Forestry Commission: District Officer, 1949-60, Assistant Conservator, 1960-67, Conservator (Glasgow), 1967-69, Commissioner, Forest and Estate Management, 1969-79. Commanding Officer, 278 (Lowland) Field Regiment RA (TA), 1956-59; President, Scottish Ski Club, 1971-75; Vice President, National Ski Federation of Great Britain, 1975-78; Fellow, Royal Society of Arts. Recreations: skiing; tennis; studying Scottish painting. Address: (h.) Branklyn House, Dundee Road, Perth, PH2 7BB; T.-0738 25535.

Stewart, George Munro, IPFA, FRVA. Director of Finance, Argyll and Bute District Council, since 1975; b. 9.6.29, Keith; m., Margaret Morag; 1 s.; 1 d. Educ. Dingwall Academy. Senior Finance Assistant, Ross and Cromarty County Council, 1947-60; Assistant County Treasurer, Caithness County Council, 1960-65; Town Chamberlain and Housing Manager:. Wick Town Council, 1965-67, Dunoon Town Council, 1967-75. Recreations: golf; gardening; bridge. Address: (b.) Kilmory, Lochgilphead, Argyll; T.-0546 2127.

Stewart, Henry Anderson. Member, Shetland Islands Council, since 1977; b. 22.8.19, Whalsay; m., Jane Irvine; 6 d. Educ. Anderson Educational Institute. Whalsay and Skerries: District Clerk and Welfare Officer, Clerk to Community Council. War Pensioners' Welfare Representative. Address: (h.) 2 Gardentown, Symbister, Whalsay, Shetland; T.-Symbister 337.

Stewart, Sir Iain (Maxwell), Kt (1968), BSc, FIMechE, FRINA, FIMarE. Company Director; b. 16.6.16. Educ. Loretto School; Glasgow University. Thermotank Ltd.: Director, 1941, Managing Director, 1946, Chairman, 1950-65; Chairman, Fairfields (Glasgow) Ltd., 1966-68; Deputy Chairman, Upper Clyde Shipbuilders Ltd., 1967-68; Member, Board, BEA, 1966-73; Director, Royal Bank of Scotland Ltd.; Director, Radio Clyde; Director, Caledonian Airways; Director, Scottish Television Ltd.; President, Institution of Engineers and Shipbuilders in Scotland, 1961-63; Hon. LLD: Strathclyde, 1975, St. Andrews, 1978.

Stewart, James Blythe, MA, LLB. Advocate; Senior Lecturer in Law, Heriot-Watt University, since 1976; b. 22.4.43, Methil. Educ. Buckhaven High School; Edinburgh University. Research Assistant, Faculty of Law, St. Andrews University, 1966-67; Assistant Lecturer in Law, then Lecturer, Heriot-Watt University, 1967-76. Recreations: bowls; golf; football spectating. Address: (h.) 3 Comely Bank Terrace, Edinburgh, EH4 1AT; T.-031-332 8228.

Stewart, Rev. James Charles, MA, BD, STM. Minister, Kirk of St. Nicholas, Aberdeen, since 1980; b. 29.3.33, Glasgow. Educ. Glasgow Academy; St. Andrews University; Union Theological Seminary, New York. Assistant Minister,

St. John's Kirk of Perth, 1969-74; Minister: St. Andrew's Church, Drumchapel, 1964-74, East Church of St. Nicholas, Aberdeen, 1974-80; Secretary, General Assembly's Committee on Public Worship and Aids to Devotion, 1976-82. Address: (h.) 48 Gray Street, Aberdeen; T.-0224 34056.

Stewart, Very Rev. James Stuart, MA, BD, DD. Minister, Church of Scotland, since 1924; Professor Emeritus, Edinburgh University, since 1966; b. 21.7.96, Dundee; m., Rosamund Anne Barron; 2 s. Educ. Dundee High School; St. Andrews University; University of Bonn on the Rhine. Minister: St. Andrews Church, Auchterarder, 1924-28, Beechgrove Church, Aberdeen, 1928-35, North Morningside Church, Edinburgh, 1935-46; Professor of New Testament, Edinburgh University (New College), 1946-66. Chaplain to the Queen in Scotland; author of ten books on religious themes. Recreation: walking. Address: (h.) 6 Crawford Road, Edinburgh, EH16 5PQ; T.-031-667 1810.

Stewart, Sir James Watson, 4th Bt; b. 8.11.22; m., Avril Veronica Gibb. Educ. Uppingham; Aberdeen University. Served, 1940-47, with Royal Artillery, 1st Special Air Service, Parachute Regiment. Address: (b.) Beach House, Skelmorlie, Ayrshire.

Stewart, John Allan. MP (Conservative), Eastwood, since 1983 (East Renfrewshire, 1979-83); Minister for Industry and Education, Scottish Office, since 1983; b. 1.6.42, St. Andrews; m., Susie Gourlay; 1 s.; 1 d. Educ. Bell Baxter High School, Cupar; St. Andrews University; Harvard University. Lecturer in Political Economy, St. Andrews University, 1965-70; Confederation of British Industry: Head, Regional Development Department, 1971, Deputy Director (Economics), 1973, Scottish Secretary, 1976, Scottish Director, 1978; Under Secretary of State, Scottish Office, 1981-83. Recreations: bridge; reading. Address: (b.) House of Commons, London, SW1A OAA; T.-01-219 5110.

Stewart, John Stanley, MA, LLB. Solicitor in private practice, since 1952; b. 10.11.25, Glasgow; m., 1, Dr. Marianne F. Stewart; 3 s.; 1 d.; 2, Edna W. Smith. Educ. Bellahouston Academy, Glasgow; Glasgow University. Partner: John W. Stewart & Son, until 1962, Thorburn & Paterson, 1962-70, Paterson Holms & Co., Glasgow, since 1970; also part-time Assistant Lecturer in Commercial/Business Law, Glasgow University, 1962-78 (thereafter part-time Lecturer); Member, Panel, Rent Assessment Committee Chairmen, since 1973; Honorary Secretary, Scottish Mountaineering Club, 1958-66; Touring Convener, Scottish Ski Club, 1978-80. Recreations: mountaineering; skiing; sea canoeing; gardening; choral singing. Address: (b.) 113 West Regent Street, Glasgow, G2 2RX; T.-041-248 5341.

Stewart, Kamala Marguerite, MA, DipEd, MLitt, ATCL. Assistant Principal Teacher of English, Wallace High School, Stirling, since 1983; Honorary Sheriff, Stirling, since 1976; b. 1.1.39, Dundee; m., John Macfarlane Stewart; 1 s.; 1 d. Educ. Morgan Academy, Dundee; St.

Andrews University; Dundee College of Education; Stirling University. Teacher, since 1961; Member, Dunblane Town Council, 1971-74; Member, Perth and Kinross County Council, 1971-74; Dean of Guild, Dunblane, 1973-74. Recreations: reading; cooking; theatre and theatrecraft; needlework; lace-making. Address: (h.) Moray Lynn, Kilbryde Grove, Dunblane, FK15 9AY; T.-0786 824247.

Stewart, Kathleen Margaret, MA, LLB, WS, NP. Partner, Balfour & Manson, Solicitors, Edinburgh, since 1983; b. St. Andrews. Educ. Bell Baxter High School, Cupar; St. Andrews University; Sweet Briar College, USA; Edinburgh University. Assistant Lawyer (Corporate Department) in London firm of commercial lawyers, 1975-79, and Scottish firms of commercial lawyers, 1980-83. Tutor (Formation and Management of Companies), Edinburgh University; Guest Lecturer (Company Law), St. Andrews University; Committee Member, Business Committee, St. Andrews University; Member, Edinburgh/Stirling Finance and Investment Seminar; Member, EEC Sub-Committee, Company Law Committee, Law Society of Scotland; Committee Member, Edinburgh New Town Conservative Association. Recreations: horse riding; tennis; squash; bad bridge. Address: (b.) 58 Frederick Street, Edinburgh; T.-031-225 8291.

Stewart, Kenneth Morrison, MPH, MIEH, MREHIS. Director of Environmental Health, Nithsdale District Council, since 1974; b. 11.12.40, Glasgow; m., Margaret; 1 s.; 2 d. Educ. Dumbarton Academy; Harris Academy, Dundee; Dundee Technical College; Dundee University. Dumfries Burgh: Depute EHO, 1969-74, Chief EHO, 1974. Member, Executive Council, Royal Environmental Health Institute of Scotland. Address: (b.) Municipal Chambers, Dumfries, DG1 2AD; T.-0387 53166.

Stewart, Louis K., MBE (1964). Senior Deer Officer, Red Deer Commission, since 1960; b. 26.3.29, Ross-shire; m., Margaret S. McPhee; 2 s.; 2 d. Educ. Dingwall Academy. National Service, Royal Artillery, 1947-48; Stalker: Lochiel Estates, 1948-54, Nature Conservancy, 1954-60. President: Scottish Clay Pigeon Association, 1981-83, Inverness Shinty Club, 1981-83. Recreations: clay pigeon shooting (international); curling; fishing. Address: (h.) 22 Laggan Road, Inverness, IV2 4EH; T.-0463 232478.

Stewart, Rev. Norma Drummond, MA, MEd, DipTh, BD. Minister, Strathbungo Queen's Park Church, Glasgow, since 1979; b. 20.5.36, Glasgow. Educ. Hyndland Secondary School, Glasgow; Glasgow University; Bible Training Institute, Glasgow; Trinity College, Glasgow. Teacher, Garrioch Secondary School, Glasgow, 1958-62; Missionary, Overseas Missionary Fellowship, West Malaysia, 1965-74; ordained to ministry, Church of Scotland, 1977. Selection School Assessor and Regional Tutor for Auxiliary Ministry; Member, Church of Scotland Panel on Doctrine; occasional Lecturer in Old Testament, Glasgow University, since 1977. Recreation: research in Old Testament studies. Address: 5 Newark Drive, Glasgow, G41 4QJ; T.-041-423 4818.

Stewart, Norman MacLeod, BL, SSC. President, Law Society of Scotland, since 1985 (Vice-President, 1984-85); Senior Partner, Allan, Black & McCaskie, Solicitors, Elgin, since 1984; b. 2.12.34, Lossiemouth; m., Mary Slater Campbell; 4 d. Educ. Elgin Academy; Edinburgh University. Training and Legal Assistant, Alex. Morison & Co., WS, Edinburgh, 1954-58; Legal Assistant: McLeod, Solicitor, Portsoy, 1958-59, Allan, Black & McCaskie, Solicitors, Elgin, 1959-61 (Partner, 1961); Council Member, Law Society of Scotland, since 1976 (Convener, Public Relations Committee, 1979-81, and Professional Practice Committee, 1981-84). Past President, Elgin Rotary Club; Past Chairman, Moray Crime Prevention Panel; Member, Committee, Police Dependants' Trust (Grampian). Recreations: walking; golf; music; Spanish culture. Address: (h.) Argyll Lodge, Lossiemouth, Moray; T.-034381 3150.

Stewart, Richard, CBE (1976), JP. Leader, Strathclyde Regional Council, since 1974; b. 27.5.20, Harthill; m., Elizabeth Peat; 1 d. Educ. Harthill School. Member, Lanark County Council, 15 years; full-time Secretary/Organiser, Labour Party, until 1983; Agent for Rt. Hon. Margaret Herbison, MP, 20 years; Agent, Rt. Hon. John Smith, 1970-83; Member, Board of Directors, Scottish Transport Group, since 1975; President, COSLA, 1984; Past Chairman, Scottish Council of Labour Party; Member, Board of Directors, Scottish Exhibition Centre. Recreations: music; chess. Address: (h.) 28 Hawthorn Drive, Harthill, Shotts, Lanarkshire, ML7 5SG; T.-0501 51303.

Stewart, Rev. Robert James, MA, BD, STM. Minister, Bothwell, since 1977; b. 8.7.32, Aberdeen; m., Janette Grier; 1 s.; 1 d. Educ. George Watson's Boys' College, Edinburgh; Edinburgh University; St. Andrews University; Union Theological Seminary, New York. First Minister, new Parish of St. Mark's, Wishaw, 1960-67; Minister, Comrie and Strowan, 1967-77. Recreations: reading; hill-walking; playing the piano. Address: The Manse, Bothwell, Glasgow, G71 8PQ; T.-0698 853189.

Stewart, Robin Reith Wittet, MA, DSA, FHA. General Manager, Highland Health Board, since 1985 (Secretary, 1974-84); Member, Hospital Committee, EEC, since 1980; b. 11.8.35, Cambridge; m., Sara Sutherland; 2 d. Educ. George Watson's College, Edinburgh; Edinburgh University; Cambridge University; Manchester University. Depute Secretary and Treasurer, Glasgow Royal Infirmary, 1963-70; Secretary, Northern Regional Hospital Board, 1970-74. Church of Scotland Elder; President, Inverness and District Choral Society; Past Chairman, Scottish Division, Institute of Health Service Management; former Treasurer, Inverness District Sports Council. Recreations: choral singing; golf; watching rugby. Address: (h.) 20 Crown Avenue, Inverness, IV2 3NF; T.-0463 236493.

Stewart, Ronald Somerville. Head, Food Standards/Welfare Foods Branch, Scottish Home and Health Department, since 1982; b. 6.1.30, Sydney; m., Gwendolene Rita Newton; 2 s. Educ. Harris Academy; Carlisle Grammar School.

Joined Scottish Office, 1950; Head of Branch in following Divisions: Prisons, Housing, Town and Country Planning. Address: (b.) Scottish Home and Health Department, St. Andrews House, Edinburgh.

Stewart, Professor William Duncan Paterson, BSc, PhD, DSc, FRSE, FRS, FIBiol. Boyd-Baxter Professor of Biology, Dundee University, since 1968 (Vice-Principal, since 1985); b. 7.6.35, Glasgow; m., Catherine Macleod; 1 s. Educ. Dunoon Grammar School; Glasgow University. Assistant Lecturer, Nottingham University, 1961-63; Lecturer, Westfield College, London University, 1963-68; Visiting Research Worker, Wisconsin University, 1966 and 1968; Visiting Professor, Kuwait University, 1980 and Otago University, New Zealand, 1984. Chairman: Royal Society Biological Education Committee, 1977-80, Royal Society Study Group on the Nitrogen Cycle, 1979-84; Trustee, Estuarine and Brackish Water Sciences Association, since 1978; Chairman, International Committee on Microbial Ecology, since 1983; Council Member, Royal Society, NERC, AFRC, Scottish Marine Biological Association, Marine Biological Association of UK, Freshwater Biological Association, Lenihan Committee, Royal Society Study Group on Science Education. Address: (h.) 45 Fairfield Road, Broughty Ferry, Dundee; T.-0382 76702.

Stewart-Fitzroy, Captain William Wentworth. Honorary Sheriff, Sutherland; b. 28.9.07, Romford, Essex; m., Patricia Grant (deceased); 3 s.; 1 d. Served, Second World War and in Korea; Captain, Royal Navy (retired); Past President, Stewart Society. Recreations: sailing; hill-walking; collector of rocks and minerals. Address: (h.) Nordhvall, Dornoch, Sutherland, IV25 3QN; T.-Dornoch 810584.

Stewart-Tull, Duncan Eric Stewart, BA, MA, PhD. Senior Lecturer in Microbiology, Glasgow University, since 1976; b. 27.6.37, London; m., Ann Virginia Dumbrell; 1 s.; 1 d. Educ. Tiffin School, Kingston-upon-Thames; Trinity College, Dublin; London Hospital Medical College; Glasgow University. Research Assistant, London Hospital, 1962-63; Assistant Lecturer in Bacteriology, then Lecturer, Glasgow University, 1963-76; Royal Society Visiting Professor, Osaka University Dental School, Japan, 1972-73; Visiting Scientist to Institute Pasteur, Paris, 1981. Vice Chairman, Bishopbriggs and Chryston School Council, 1976-78; Chairman, School Attendance Panel, 1975; Secretary, Strathkelvin Queen's Silver Jubilee Committee, 1977-80; President, Bishopbriggs Ratepayers Association, 1980-82; Convener, Scottish Branch, Society for General Microbiology, 1980-84. Recreations: renovating an old house; simply being alive. Address: (b.) Department of Microbiology, Glasgow University, Alexander Stone Building, Garscube Estate, Bearsden, Glasgow; T.-041-942 2312.

Stiff, John Barry, GradIFireE. Firemaster, Dumfries and Galloway Fire Brigade, since 1984; b. 17.5.43, Sunderland; m., Catherine Ann; 2 s.; 1 d. Educ. Sunderland County Borough Boys' Technical School. Joined Sunderland Fire Brigade, 1964; South Western Area Fire Brigade (Scotland), 1972; Dumfries and Galloway, 1975.

Secretary, No. 7 District (Scotland), Chief and Assistant Chief Fire Officers' Association. Recreations: cars; caravanning; fishing; outdoor pursuits. Address: (b.) Dumfries and Galloway Fire Brigade Headquarters, Brooms Road, Dumfries, DG1 2DZ; T.-0387 52222.

Still, Rev. William. Minister, Gilcomston South Church, Aberdeen, since 1945; Chairman, Trustees, Rutherford House Study Centre, since 1981; b. 8.5.11, Aberdeen. Educ. Aberdeen University and Christ's College. Fish worker in family business; Teacher of music, pianoforte, singing, choral work; Cadet, Salvation Army College, London; Assistant Minister, Springburnhill Parish Church, Glasgow. President, Inter-Varsity Fellowship, 1975-76; President, local University Christian Union, on several occasions. Recreations: walking; music; gardening; art; architecture. Address: 18 Beaconsfield Place, Aberdeen; T.-Aberdeen 644037.

Stimson, Professor William Howard, BSc, PhD, CBiol, FIBiol. Professor of Immunology and Head, Immunology Division, Strathclyde University, since 1981; b. 2.11.43, Liverpool; m., Jean Scott Baird; 1 s.; 1 d. Educ. Prince of Wales School, Nairobi; St. Andrews University. Research Fellow, Department of Obstetrics and Gynaecology, Dundee University, 1970-72; Lecturer, then Senior Lecturer, Biochemistry Department, Strathclyde University, 1973-80. Patron, Scottish Motor Neurone Disease Association; holder, Glasgow Loving Cup, 1982-83; Member, Editorial Boards, three scientific journals. Recreations: mechanical engineering; walking. Address: (b.) Immunology Division, Strathclyde University, 31 Taylor Street, Glasgow, G4 ONR; T.-041-552 4400, Ext. 3729.

Stirling, George Scott, MB, ChB, MRCPGlas, FRCPsych, DPM. Medical Administrator, Crichton Royal Hospital, Dumfries, since 1979 (Consultant Psychiatrist, since 1960); Chairman, Area Medical Committee, Dumfries and Galloway Health Board, since 1983; b. 20.4.26, Aberdeen; m., Yvonne; 1 s.; 1 d. Educ. Robert Gordon's College, Aberdeen; Aberdeen University. House Physician, Royal Cornhill Hospital, Aberdeen; Medical Branch, RAF; House Physician, Woodend General Hospital, Aberdeen; Fellow in Psychiatry, Crichton Royal, Dumfries; Independent Visiting Psychiatrist to Board of Management, State Hospital, Carstairs; Past Chairman, Forensic Section, Scottish Division, Royal College of Psychiatrists (Member, Executive Committee, Scottish Division); Fellow on Council, Royal College of Psychiatrists, London. Member, National Panel of Specialists; Member, Scottish Committee of Hospital Specialists; Member, Parole Board for Scotland; Council of Europe Travelling Fellow; former Vice-Chairman, SASD (Dumfries). Recreations: fishing; shooting; curling; gardening. Address: (h.) Phyllis Park, Murraythwaite, Dalton, Lockerbie, DG11 1DW.

Stirling of Garden, Lt.-Col. James, TD, FRICS. Lord Lieutenant of Stirling and Falkirk, since 1983; b. 8.9.30; m.; 2 s.; 2 d. Educ. Rugby; Trinity College, Cambridge. Partner, K. Ryden & Partners, Chartered Surveyors, since 1962.

Stirling, Kenneth W., MA (Hons). Rector, Dalziel High School, Motherwell, since 1978; b. 19.12.26, Aberdeen. Educ. Robert Gordon's College, Aberdeen; Aberdeen University. Principal Teacher of Modern Languages: Turriff Academy, 1959-62, Beath High School, Cowdenbeath, 1962-72; Assistant Head Teacher, then Depute Rector, Grove Academy, Dundee, 1972-78. Address: (h.) 5 Bonnington Avenue, Lanark, ML11 9AL; T.-0555 2858.

Stirling of Fairburn, Roderick William Kenneth, TD, DL, JP. Landowner and Estate Manager; Vice-Chairman, Red Deer Commission (Member, since 1964); Chairman, Highland Region Valuation Appeal Committee, since 1983; Chairman, Scottish Salmon and White Fish Co. Ltd., since 1980; b. 17.6.32, Muir of Ord; m., Penelope Jane Wright; 4 d. Educ. Wellesley House; Harrow; Aberdeen University. National Service, Scots Guards, 1950-52 (commissioned, 1951); TA service, Seaforth and Queen's Own Highlanders, 1953-69 (retired with rank of Captain); Member, Regional Advisory Committee to Forestry Commission, 1964-85; Local Director, Eagle Star Insurance Co., 1966-85; Director, Moray Firth Salmon Fishing Co. Ltd.; Member, Highland River Purification Board, since 1975; Ross and Cromarty County Councillor, 1970-74 (Chairman of Highways, 1973-74); Member, Ross and Cromarty District Council, 1984; Chairman, Highland Committee, NPFA (appointed to Scottish Council, 1971); Member, Highland Committee, Scottish Landowners Federation (Chairman, 1974-79). Recreations: wild life management; gardening; curling. Address: (h.) Arcan, Muir of Ord, Ross-shire; T.-Urray 207.

Stirling, William Norman, IPFA, DPA, FCIT. Director, Strathclyde Passenger Transport Executive, since 1973; b. 26.2.36, Glasgow; m., Edith; 1 s.; 3 d. Educ. Hamilton Academy; Glasgow College of Commerce; Glasgow University. Lanark County Council, 1953-58; Midlothian County Council, 1958-59; Clydebank Town Council, 1959-61; Motherwell and Wishaw Town Council, 1961-73 (Town Chamberlain and Collector of Rates, Local Taxation Officer and Manager, Municipal Bank, 1970-73). Director, National Transport Tokens Ltd.; Past Chairman, Scottish Branch, CIPFA. Recreations: golf; Robert Burns. Address: (b.) Consort House, 12 West George Street, Glasgow, G2 1HN; T.-041-332 6811.

Stirling-Hamilton, Sir Bruce, 13th Bt; b. 5.8.40; m., Stephanie Campbell; 1 s.; 1 d. Educ. Nautical College, Pangbourne; Sandhurst. Commissioned, Queen's Own Highlanders (Seaforth and Camerons), 1961; Captain, 1967; resigned commission, 1971; Management Consultant. Address: (h.) Afton Lodge, Mossblown, by Ayr.

Stiven, Frederic William Binning, ARSA, MSIAD, DA. Constructivist, Designer and Teacher, since 1954; Head of Design, Grays School of Art, Aberdeen, since 1982; b. 25.4.29, Cowdenbeath; m., Jenny Paton; 2 s.; 2 d. Educ. Beath High School; Edinburgh College of Art. Constructivist work in numerous public and private collections; exhibited in Edinburgh,

Glasgow, Leeds, London, Bergen, Helsinki, Venice and New York; freelance Designer; Royal Scottish Academy Gillies Award, 1985. Address: (h.) 31 Richmondhill Place, Aberdeen, AB2 4EN; T.-0224 324671.

Stobie, Rev. Charles Ian Graham, MA. Minister, Fyvie, since 1975; b. 7.9.16, Bishop Monkton, near Ripon; m., Margaret Johnston Ramsay; 4 d. Educ. Aberdeen Grammar School; Madras College, St. Andrews; St. Andrews University. Assistant Organist to the University and Holy Trinity Parish Church, St. Andrews; Organist, St. James's Church, Broughty Ferry and Bonnygate Church, Cupar; ordained and inducted to parish of Uyeasound, Shetland, 1942; translated to Whalsay, Shetland, 1947, Mossvale, Paisley, 1950, Auchtergaven, Perthshire, 1956, St. Andrews Presbyterian Church, St. John's, Newfoundland, 1960; Lecturer in English, Memorial University, Newfoundland, 1968-69; broadcast Organ Recitalist, CBC; Founder and Conductor, St. John's Bach Singers; President, Newfoundland Branch, Canadian Music Educators' Association. Recreations: music; motoring; golf; writing; Church history. Address: The Manse, Fyvie, Turriff, Aberdeenshire, AB5 8RD; T.-065 16 230.

Stockdale, Elizabeth Joan Noel, MB, ChB, DMRD, FRCR. Consultant Radiologist, Royal Aberdeen Children's Hospital and Aberdeen Royal Infirmary, since 1980; Clinical Senior Lecturer, Aberdeen University, since 1980; b. Chippenham; m., Christopher Leo Stockdale; 2 s.; 1 d. Educ. Aberdeen University. House Surgeon, Aberdeen Royal Infirmary; Senior House Surgeon, Professorial Surgical Unit, Hospital for Sick Children, Great Ormond Street; Registrar, St. George's Hospital; Senior Registrar, Royal National Orthopaedic Hospital, Royal Marsden Hospital, Atkinson Morley's Hospital. Recreations: theatre; classical music; travel. Address: (h.) 1 Grant Road, Banchory, Kincardineshire, AB3 3UW; T.-03302 3096.

Stockwell, Professor Robert, BSc, MB, BS, PhD. Professor of Anatomy, Edinburgh University, since 1981; b. 26.6.33, Hertford; m., Jill Fyfield; 2 s.; 1 d. Educ. Christ's Hospital; London University. Military Service, Royal Corps of Signals, 1951-53; House Surgeon, St. Thomas's Hospital, London, 1960-61; Lecturer in Anatomy, St. Thomas's Hospital Medical School, 1961-67; Senior Lecturer and Reader in Anatomy, Edinburgh University, 1967-81; Editor, Journal of Anatomy, 1983-86. Publication: Biology of Cartilage Cells. Recreations: music; history; carpentry. Address: (b.) Department of Anatomy, University Medical School, Teviot Place, Edinburgh, EH8 9AG; T.-031-667 1011.

Stodart of Leaston, Baron, (James Anthony Stodart), PC (1974). Life Peer; Chairman, Agricultural Credit Corporation Ltd., since 1975; b. 6.6.16; m. Educ. Wellington. MP (Conservative), Edinburgh West, 1959-74; Joint Parliamentary Under Secretary of State, Scottish Office, 1963-64; Minister of State, Ministry of Agriculture, Fisheries and Food, 1972-74; Chairman, Committee of Inquiry into Local Government in Scotland, 1980.

Stokoe, Norman Leslie, MB, ChB, DO, FRCSEdin, FRACS. Consultant Ophthalmic Surgeon, East Fife Hospitals and Princess Alexandra Eye Pavilion, Edinburgh Royal Infirmary, since 1960, and Royal Blind School, Edinburgh, and Scottish National Institution for War Blinded, since 1962; b. 17.5.23, Edinburgh; m., Agnes Wallace Campbell Storrar; 2 c. Educ. George Watson's Boys' College, Edinburgh; Edinburgh University. Senior Registrar and Clinical Tutor, Ophthalmic Department, Edinburgh Royal Infirmary, 1953-55; Senior Registrar, Ophthalmic Department, Leeds General Infirmary, 1955-58; Honorary Assistant Ophthalmic Surgeon, Adelaide Children's Hospital, 1958-59; Lecturer in Ophthalmology, Edinburgh University, 1959-60; Honorary Senior Lecturer, Department of Ophthalmology, Edinburgh University, since 1960; Honorary Lecturer, Department of Physiology, St. Andrews University, since 1979; Examiner in Ophthalmology, final FRCSE Examination, since 1962; President, Scottish Ophthalmological Club, since 1984. Recreations: swimming; choir singing; photography. Address: (h.) 3 Merchiston Park, Edinburgh, EH10 4PW; T.-031-229 8003.

Stone, Professor Frederick Hope, MB, ChB, FRCP, FRCPsych. Professor of Child and Adolescent Psychiatry, Glasgow University, since 1977; Consultant Psychiatrist, Royal Hospital for Sick Children, Glasgow, since 1954; b. 11.9.21, Glasgow; m., Zelda Elston, MA; 2 s.; 1 d. Educ. Hillhead High School, Glasgow; Glasgow University. Acting Director, Lasker Mental Hygiene Clinic, Hadassah, Jerusalem, 1952-54; World Health Organisation Visiting Consultant, 1960, 1964; Member, Kilbrandon Committee, 1963-65; Secretary-General, International Association of Child Psychiatry, 1962-66; Member, Houghton Committee on Adoption, 1968-72; Chairman, Scottish Division, Royal College of Psychiatrists, 1981-84. Publication: Child Psychiatry for Students (Co-author). Address: (h.) 14A Hamilton Avenue, Pollokshields, Glasgow, G41 4JF; T.-041-427 0115.

Stone, Sheriff Marcus, MA, LLB. Sheriff of Lothian and Borders, at Linlithgow, since 1984; b. 22.3.21, Glasgow; m., Jacqueline Barnoin; 3 s.; 2 d. Educ. High School of Glasgow; Glasgow University. Served Second World War; admitted Solicitor, 1949; admitted Faculty of Advocates, 1965; Sheriff of North Strathclyde, at Dumbarton, 1971-76; Sheriff of Glasgow and Strathkelvin, at Glasgow, 1976-84. Publication: Proof of Fact in Criminal Trials, 1984. Recreations: swimming; music. Address: (b.) Sheriff Court House, Court Square, Linlithgow, EH49 7EQ; T.-Linlithgow 684 2922.

Stone, Rev. Walter Vernon, MA, BD. Minister, Langbank Parish Church, 1977-85; b. 2.3.19, Nuremberg; m., Edith Maria Emmy Wolf; 3 s. Educ. Gordonstoun; Edinburgh University. Church of Scotland District Missionary: Malawi, 1949-56, Zambia, 1956-60; Principal of theological college in Zambia, 1960-66; Chief Translator of the Bible into ciBemba, Zambia, 1966-70; Scottish Secretary, United Society for Christian Literature, 1970-77. Marriage Guidance Counsellor, since 1972. Recreations: bridge; Scrabble; hill-walking. Address: (h.) Santis, 10 Finlaystone Road, Kilmacolm, PA13 4RE; T.-050 587 2644.

Storer, James Donald, BSc, ACGI, CEng, MRAeS. Keeper, Department of Science, Technology and Working Life, National Museums of Scotland, since 1985; b. 11.1.28, Hemsworth, Yorkshire; m., Shirley Anne Kent; 1 s.; 1 d. Educ. Hemsworth Grammar School; Imperial College, London. Design Office, Vickers-Armstrongs (Aircraft) Ltd., Weybridge, 1948-66; Assistant Keeper, Department of Technology, Royal Scottish Museum, 1966-78, Keeper, 1978-85. Publications: Steel and Engineering, 1959; Behind the Scenes in an Aircraft Factory, 1965; It's Made Like This: Cars, 1967; The World We Are Making: Aviation, 1968; A Simple History of the Steam Engine, 1969; How to Run an Airport, 1970; How We Find Out About Flight, 1973; Flying Feats, 1977; Book of the Air, 1979; Great Inventions, 1980; Encyclopedia of Transport, 1983; East Fortune: Museum of Flight and History of the Airfield (Co-author), 1983. Recreations: aircraft preservation; travel. Address: (h.) 52 Thomson Road, Currie, Edinburgh; T.-031-449 2843.

Storey, Gerald Francis, BSc, CEng, FICE, FIHT. Assistant Chief Engineer, Scottish Development Department, since 1976; b. 14.5.27, Edinburgh; m., Marjorie Purves; 1 s.; 1 d. Educ. George Heriot's School; Edinburgh University. Argyll County Council; Air Ministry Works Directorate; Macartney Ltd., Contractors; Department of Agriculture and Fisheries; Ministry (now Department) of Transport; seconded to Scottish Office, since 1962. Past Chairman, Scottish Branch, Institution of Highways and Transport; former Member, Road Engineering Board, Institution of Civil Engineers. Recreations: golf; motoring. Address: (h.) 11 Doune Park, Dalgety Bay, Fife; T.-0383 824343.

Stormonth Darling, Sir Jamie, Kt (1983), CBE (1972), MC (1945), TD. Director, National Trust for Scotland, 1971-83; b. 18.7.18; m.; 1 s.; 2 d. Educ. Winchester; Christ Church, Oxford. War Service, 1939-46 (Lt.-Col.); WS, 1949; Member, Queen's Bodyguard for Scotland (Royal Company of Archers), since 1958.

Storrar, George Alexander, MC, BSc, JP. Farmer; Honorary Sheriff; b. 17.9.18, Collessie, Fife; m., Leila Barrie Orchison; 1 s.; 2 d. Educ. Perth Academy; Edinburgh University. Army, 1939-46: Fife and Forfar Yeomanry and Royal Tank Regiment - Major; France, 1940, NW Europe, 1944-46; mentioned in Despatches (2). Trustee, Cupar Savings Bank; Director, Scottish Plant Breeding Station; Member, Fife Valuation Appeal Court. Address: (h.) Halhill, Leckiebank Road, Auchtermuchty, Fife; T.-Auchtermuchty 603.

Stother, Ian G., MA, MB, BChir, FRCSEdin, FRCSGlas. Consultant Orthopaedic Surgeon, Glasgow Royal Infirmary, Stobhill General Hospital and Nuffield McAlpin Clinic, Glasgow, since 1978; b. Lytham; m., Jacqueline;

2 d. Educ. King Edward VII School, Lytham; Kings College, Cambridge; St. George's Hospital Medical School, London. Honorary Clinical Lecturer, Glasgow University; Examiner, Royal College of Physicians and Surgeons of Glasgow; Orthopaedic Adviser, Dance School of Scotland. Recreations: classic cars; golf. Address: (h.) 5 Eastergarngaber Road, Lenzie, Glasgow; T.-041-776 5330.

Stott, Rt. Hon. Lord, (George Gordon Stott), PC (1964), QC (Scot). Senator of the College of Justice in Scotland, 1967-85; b. 22.12.09; m.; 1 s.; 1 d. Educ. Edinburgh Academy; Edinburgh University. Advocate, 1936; QC (Scot), 1950; Advocate Depute, 1947-51; Sheriff of Roxburgh, Berwick and Selkirk, 1961-64; Lord Advocate, 1964-67.

Stout, George Alexander, MA (Hons), ACIS. Joint Manager, The Alliance Trust PLC and The Second Alliance Trust PLC, since 1976 (Director, since 1978); b. 9.11.27, Dundee; m., Dorothy Smith; 1 s.; 3 d. Educ. Morgan Academy, Dundee; Edinburgh University. Adviser, Trustee Savings Banks' International Unit Trust, since 1975; Director: Fleming Claverhouse Investment Trust PLC, since 1977, Advent Technology p.l.c., since 1981, Advent Capital Limited, since 1985. Honorary Lecturer, Dundee University. Recreations: golf; curling; gardening; photography; music; travel. Address: (h.) Uplands, Victoria Street, Monifieth, DD5 4HP.

Stoward, Peter John, MA, MSc, DPhil, DipRMS, FRSE. Reader in Histology, Dundee University, since 1975; b. 27.1.35, Birmingham; m., Barbara Essex Lewis; 1 d. Educ. King Edward's School, Birmingham; Oriel College, Oxford. Assistant Lecturer, University of Aston in Birmingham, 1958-61; Research Assistant, Department of Human Anatomy, Oxford University, 1961-63 and 1965-67; International Research Fellow, National Institutes of Health, Bethesda, Maryland, 1964, 1965; Lecturer, Nuffield Department of Orthopaedic Surgery, Oxford University, 1967-68; Senior Lecturer in Anatomy, Dundee University, 1968-75; Visiting Professor, Pavia University, Italy, since 1980; Editor, Histochemical Journal, since 1967. Diocesan Reader, Scottish Episcopal Church. Publications: Histochemistry: The Widening Horizons (Co-author), 1981; Histochemistry of Secretary Processes (Co-author), 1977. Recreations: sailing; walking; reading. Address: (b.) Department of Anatomy, The University, Dundee, DD1 4HN; T.-0382 23181.

Strachan, Alexander, RIBA, ARIAS. Director of Technical Services, Stewartry District Council, since 1975; b. 8.10.25, Edinburgh; m., Ina; 1 s.; 1 d. Educ. Galashiels Academy. Depute County Architect and Planning Officer, Kirkcudbright County Council, 1962-75. Address: (b.) Council Offices, Kirkcudbright, DG6 4PN; T.-0557 30291.

Strachan, Daniel, OBE, CStJ, KCT, AMM. A Vice-President, St. Andrew's Ambulance Association, and Honorary Corps Commissioner; b. 12.2.17, Greenock; m., Elizabeth Leighton; 1 s.; 1 d. Educ. Greenock High School; Herd's College. Director General; St. Andrew's Ambulance

Association, 1959-83; awarded Certificate and Australian Medal of Merit, 1977, in recognition of service to Association; Member, Joint Revision Committee, First Aid Manual; an Honorary Vice-President, West Lowland Area and Greenock Boys' Brigade Batallions. Address: (h.) Whitehill House, 79 Octavia Terrace, Greenock, PA16 7PX; T.-Gourock 35406.

Strachan, Rev. James Carson, MA, BD. Minister, Hobkirk and Southdean Parish Churches, Hawick, since 1983; b. 11.3.17, Edinburgh; m., Doris Winifred Gardiner; 1 s.; 3 d. Educ. Carrick Academy, Maybole; Edinburgh University. Assistant Minister, Aberdour and Dalgety, Fife, 1941-42; Locum tenens, Pleasance Church, Edinburgh, 1942-43; Minister, Collace Parish Church, 1944-47; Chaplain to the Forces, 1947-63; Minister: Colmonell Parish Church, 1963-67, Lonmay and Rathen West, Aberdeenshire, 1967-78, Mossgreen and Crossgates, Fife, 1978-83. Address: The Manse, Hobkirk, Hawick, TD9 8JU; T.-045-086 636.

Strachan, James Gerrit, BSc, MB, ChB, MPhil, MRCPsych. Consultant Psychiatrist, Royal Edinburgh Hospital, since 1981; Honorary Senior Lecturer, Edinburgh University, since 1981; b. Dublin. Educ. Latymer Upper School, London; Edinburgh University. Registrar and Senior Registrar, Royal Edinburgh and Associated Hospitals; Lecturer, Utrecht University; Forensic Psychiatrist, Pieter Baan Centrum, Utrecht. Address: (b.) Royal Edinburgh Hospital, Morningside Place, Edinburgh, EH10 5HF; T.-031-447 2011.

Strachan, John, JP, MA, LLB. Senior Partner, Davidson & Garden, Advocates, Aberdeen, since 1969; Director, William Wilson Holdings Ltd., since 1979; Director, Osprey Communications P.L.C., since 1982; b. 9.8.29, Fraserburgh; m., Margaret Cheyne; 1 s.; 2 d. Educ. Fraserburgh Academy; Aberdeen University. National Service, 1954-56 (Sub Lt., RNVR); Partner, Davidson & Garden, Advocates, 1958. Recreations: shooting; fishing. Address: (h.) 64 Forest Road, Aberdeen, AB2 4BL; T.-0224 313906.

Strang, Gavin Steel, MP, BSc (Hons), DipAgriSci, PhD. MP (Labour), East Edinburgh, since 1970; Chairman, Parliamentary Labour Party Defence Committee; Member, Parliamentary Select Committee on Agriculture; b. 10.7.43, Dundee; m., Bettina Smith; 1 s. Educ. Morrison's Academy, Crieff; Edinburgh University. Parliamentary Under Secretary of State, Department of Energy, February to October, 1974; Parliamentary Secretary, Ministry of Agriculture, 1974-79. Recreations: golf; swimming; the countryside. Address: (h.) 80 Argyle Crescent, Edinburgh, EH15 2QD; T.-031-669 5999.

Strathmore and Kinghorne, 17th Earl of, (Fergus Michael Claude Bowes Lyon), b. 31.12.28; m., Mary Pamela McCorquodale; 1 s.; 2 d. Educ. Eton; Sandhurst. Commissioned Scots Guards, 1949; transferred to RARO, 1961; Member, Queen's Bodyguard for Scotland (Royal Company of Archers); DL, Angus, 1973. Address: (h.) Glamis Castle, Forfar, Angus.

Street, Margaret Dobson. Vice-Chairman, Saltire Society, since 1984; b. 18.10.20, Hawick; m., Richard Andrew Rutherford Street; 2 s. Educ. Hawick High School; Alva Academy. Civil Servant, 1938-48; Ministry of Labour and National Service, 1938-47; Ministry of National Insurance (Inspectorate), 1947-48; voluntary work since 1948, apart from freelance writing on household and conservation topics; Honorary Secretary (Past Chairman), Leith Civic Trust; Convener, Friends of North Carr Lightship; Member, Edinburgh Health Council, representing Patients Association; Trustee, Robert Hurd Memorial Fund. Recreations: promotion of Scottish cultural activity; conservation; good cooking. Address: (h.) 115 Trinity Road, Edinburgh; T.-031-552 2409.

Stuart, Alastair John, JP, BSc. Member, Perth and Kinross District Council, since 1980 (Convener, Housing and Architectural Services); Schoolteacher; b. 18.10.48, Keith. Educ. Aberlour High School; Keith Grammar School; Aberdeen University; Aberdeen College of Education. Chemistry Teacher: Perth Academy, 1970-78, Menzieshill High, Dundee, 1978-83, Lawside Academy, since 1983; Labour Parliamentary candidate, Perth and Kinross, 1983; Secretary, Perth and Kinross Constituency Labour Party, 1979-81; Chairman, Perth Branch, Musicians' Union, 1980-84; Member, Perth and Kinross Health Council, since 1980. Publication: History of Perth Tramways. Recreations: golf; music; railways and model railways. Address: (h.) Gilloch Hall, Back Street, Bridge of Earn, Perth.

Stuart, Iain Macnaughton, MA (Hons), DipEd. Depute Chief Executive, Strathclyde Regional Council, since 1981; b. 18.6.34, Alexandria; m., Fiona Elizabeth; 2 s.; 1 d. Educ. Morrison's Academy, Crieff; Glasgow University; McGill University. Teacher in Canada, 1957-58; District Officer, N. Rhodesia, 1958-64; Jordanhill College, 1964-65; Teacher, Glasgow Academy, 1965-67; Depute Director of Education, Glasgow Corporation, 1967-73; Education Planner, World Bank, Jamaica, 1973-75; Policy Planning, Strathclyde Regional Council, 1975-81. Recreations: running; climbing; skiing; sailing; golf. Address: (b.) Strathclyde House, India Street, Glasgow; T.-041-227 3367.

Stuart, James Campbell (Hamish), BSc, MSc. Chairman, Policy Resources and Finance, Ross and Cromarty District Council, since 1984; Member, Highlands and Islands Development Board Consultative Council, since 1983; b. 14.9.46, Inverness; m., Mary Madeleine Travers; 3 s.; 1 d. Educ. Dingwall Academy; Aberdeen University; Newcastle-upon-Tyne University. Farmer; Director, Grain Services (Inverness); Member, Ross and Cromarty District Council, since 1974 (Vice Convenor, since 1976); Chairman, Development Committee, 1977-81, 1983-84; Member, Highland Regional Council, 1978-82. Recreations: amateur radio; electronics. Address: (h.) Balavil, Conon Bridge, Ross-shire; T.-0349 61431.

Stuart, William Forbes, BSc, DIC, PhD. Head, Geomagnetism Research Group, British Geological Survey, since 1982 (Chairman, Iaga Division

V, since 1983); b. 10.11.36, Glasgow; m., Margaret Edith; 2 s. Educ. Queen's Park School, Glasgow; Glasgow University; Royal School of Mines. Research Assistant, Imperial College; Senior Research Fellow, Meteorological Office; Research Geophysicist, British Geological Survey. Recreations: boating; fishing; golf; gardening; jogging; the company of young people. Address: (h.) Anston, St. Ninians Avenue, Linlithgow, EH49 7BP; T.-050-684 2009.

Stuart-Smith, Deryk Aubrey, BSc, MD, FRCPGlas, FRCPEdin. Senior Lecturer, Department of Medicine, Glasgow University, since 1970; Consultant Physician, Western Infirmary, Glasgow, since 1970 (Director, Bone Metabolism Research Unit, since 1971); b. 12.4.27, Simla, India; m., Anne Bennoch; 1 s.; 3 d. Educ. Bishop Cotton School; Glasgow University. Publication: Diagnostic Procedures in Disorders of Calcium Metabolism. Recreations: gardening; theatre; science fiction; science fact. Address: (h.) 30 Dolphin Road, Maxwell Park, Glasgow, G41 4DZ; T.-041-423 2430.

Sturgeon, David, BL. Registrar and Deputy Secretary, Heriot-Watt University, since 1967; b. 10.12.35, Kilwinning; m., Nancy McDougall; 2 s.; 1 d. Educ. Dalry High School, Ayrshire; Glasgow University. National Service (RASC - War Office), 1957-59; Trainee Actuary, Scottish Widows Fund, 1959-61; Administrative Assistant, Royal College of Science and Technology (later, Strathclyde University), 1961-67. Secretary and Treasurer, Edinburgh Society of Glasgow University Graduates, since 1971. Recreations: golf; music (particularly Scottish country dance music). Address: (h.) 10 Dalhousie Road, Eskbank, Midlothian, EH22 3AS; T.-031-663 1059.

Sturgeon, Herbert Blain, BA, DipPhil, FRICS. Regional Assessor, Grampian, since 1975; b. 3.11.37, Coylton, Ayrshire; m., Ruth Hamilton; 2 s.; 1 d. Educ. Ayr Academy; Open University; Aberdeen University. County Assessor and Electoral Registration Officer, West Lothian, 1955-65; City Assessor and ERO, Aberdeen, 1965-75. First President, Scottish Assessors' Association, 1974-78; Secretary, Lands Valuation Assessors' Association, 1961-66; Member, Government Committee of Enquiry into Commercial Rating, 1968; Member, Local Government Finance Working Party, until 1984. Session Clerk, Queen's Cross Church, Aberdeen, 1970-82. Recreations: former Scottish Football League referee; Member, Football Grounds Improvement Trust. Address: (h.) Afton, 36 Woodend Place, Aberdeen, AB2 6AN; T.-0224 318948.

Sturrock, Alexander Muir, MBE, TD, Croix de Guere, WS, NP, BA (Oxon). Consultant, Turnbull Simson & Sturrock, WS, Jedburgh, and P. and J. Stormonth Darling, WS, Kelso; b. 21.9.13, Edinburgh; m., Mary Percival Walsh; 1 s.; 2 d. Educ. Edinburgh Academy; Exeter College, Oxford; Edinburgh University. Commissioned, 1939, KOSB posted 6 KOSB; served in Europe until 1945; Adjutant, 6 KOSB, DAA and QMG, 44 (Lowland) Brigade, DAAG 15 (Scottish) Division; rejoined 4 KOSB (TA), 1947; Burgh Prosecutor, Royal Burgh of Jedburgh;

Clerk, Jedburgh District Council; Clerk, River Tweed Commissioners, 1950-82. Recreations: (used to be!) rugby; tennis; golf; shooting; fishing. Address: (h.) Elm Bank, Jedburgh, TD8 6QF; T.-0835 62400.

Sturrock, Norman T., MA (Hons). Manager (Scotland and Northern Ireland), Citibank NA, since 1980; Council Member, CBI Scotland, 1982-85; Director, Edinburgh Chamber of Commerce, since 1984; b. 25.2.48, Glasgow; m., Belinda Mathews; 2 s.; 1 d. Educ. King George V School, Hong Kong; Morrison's Academy, Crieff; St. Andrews University; University of California. ICFC, Scotland and London, 1972-77; joined Citibank NA, 1977. Past Chairman, International Bankers in Scotland; Council Member, Scottish Business in the Community, since 1984. Recreations: golf; reading; current affairs; family. Address: (b.) 4 St. Colme Street, Edinburgh; T.-031-226 6091.

Sturrock, Robert Ralph, MB, ChB, DSc. Reader in Anatomy, Dundee University, since 1981; b. 1.7.43, Dundee; m., Norma Duncan; 1 d. Educ. Dundee High School; St. Andrews University. House Surgeon, Perth Royal Infirmary, 1967-68; House Physician, Stirling Royal Infirmary, 1968; Demonstrator, then Lecturer, Anatomy Department, Dundee University, 1968-77; Visiting Associate Professor of Neuroanatomy, Iowa University, 1976; Senior Lecturer, Dundee, 1977-81. Symington Memorial Prize in Anatomy, 1978. Recreations: reading; running; swimming; hill-walking. Address: (h.) 6 Albany Terrace, Dundee; T.-0382 23578.

Suckling, Professor Colin James, BSc, PhD, CChem, FRSC. Professor of Chemistry, Strathclyde University, since 1984; b. 24.3.47, Birkenhead; m., Catherine Mary Faulkner; 2 s.; 1 d. Educ. Quarry Bank High School, Liverpool; Liverpool University. Lecturer, Department of Pure and Applied Chemistry, Strathclyde University, 1972; Royal Society Smith and Nephew Senior Research Fellow, 1980. Chairman, Strathclyde Branch, National Association for Gifted Children. Publications: Chemistry Through Models (Co-author), 1978; Biological Chemistry (Co-author), 1980; Enzyme Chemistry, Impact and Applications (Co-author), 1984. Recreations: music; horn playing. Address: (b.) Department of Pure and Applied Chemistry, Strathclyde Universtiy, 295 Cathedral Street, Glasgow, G1 1XL; T.-041-552 4400.

Suddaby, John Trevor, BA. Assistant Secretary, Edinburgh University, since 1968; b. 28.3.34, Horbury; m., Margaret Helen Steventon; 1 s.; 1 d. Educ. Bradford Grammar School; Jesus College, Cambridge. National Service (Intelligence Corps), 1955-57; Assistant Research Officer, Ministry of Defence, 1958-62; Administrative Assistant, later Senior Administrative Officer, Edinburgh University, 1962-68. Recreations: music; mountain-walking. Address: (b.) Old College, South Bridge, Edinburgh, EH8 9YL; T.-031-667 1011.

Suess, Nigel M., MA, FIB, FCCA. Director, The British Linen Bank Ltd., since 1979; Director, The Murrayfield p.l.c., since 1982; Director,

Scottish Unit Managers Ltd., since 1983; b. 13.12.45, Chelmsford; m., Maureen Ferguson; 1 d. Educ. Chigwell School; Gonville and Caius College, Cambridge. N.M. Rothschild & Sons Ltd., 1967-77 (Assistant Director, 1974-77); joined The British Linen Bank Ltd., 1978. Recreations: mountaineering; chess; ornithology. Address: (b.) 12 Melville Street, Edinburgh, EH3 7NZ; T.-031-226 4071.

Sullivan, John, MA. Senior Lecturer, Department of Russian, St. Andrews University, since 1983; b. 2.11.37, Sheffield; m., Veronica Margaret Jones; 2 s.; 1 d. Educ. Firth Park Grammar School, Sheffield; Manchester University. Research Assistant, Clarendon Press, Oxford, 1961-64; Lecturer, St. Andrews University, 1964-83 (Admissions Tutor, Faculty of Arts, 1970-73, Assistant Dean, Faculty of Arts, 1980-83). Treasurer, St. Andrews Association of University Teachers, 1974-77. Recreations: cricket; hill-walking. Address: (h.) 1 Hepburn Gardens, St. Andrews, Fife; T.-St. Andrews 72614.

Susskind, Werner, MB, ChB, FRCPGlas, FRCPEdin. Consultant Dermatologist, Victoria Infirmary, Glasgow, since 1965; Honorary Clinical Lecturer in Dermatology, Glasgow University, since 1966; b. 29.4.33, Hamburg; m., Shirley Banks; 2 s. Educ. Hillhead High School, Glasgow; Glasgow University. Recreations: choral singing; photography; golf. Address: (h.) 55 Beech Avenue, Newton Mearns, by Glasgow, G77 5QR; T.-041-639 3265.

Sutcliffe, Roger Graham, BSc, PhD. Senior Lecturer in Genetics, Glasgow University, since 1983; b. 10.11.47, Wokingham, Berkshire. Educ. Oundle School; Manchester University; Edinburgh University. Research Fellow, Department of Genetics, Edinburgh University, 1972-74; Lecturer in Genetics, Glasgow University, since 1974. Honorary Secretary and Treasurer, BSI Materno-Fetal Immunobiology Group. Recreations: trout fishing; cricket. Address: (b.) Institute of Genetics, Church Street, Glasgow, G11 5JS; T.-041-339 8855, Ext. 7108.

Sutherland, Colin John MacLean, LLB (Hons). Advocate, since 1977; b. 20.5.54, Falkirk. Educ. Edinburgh Academy; Edinburgh University. Address: (b.) Advocates' Library, Parliament House, Edinburgh; T.-031-226 5071.

Sutherland, Donald Fraser, CDA, JP. Member, Nithsdale District Council, since 1974 (Chairman, General Purposes Committee, since 1980); Member, Dumfries and Galloway Regional Council, since 1982; b. 12.6.20, Deseado, Argentine; m., Sheila Joan; 2 s.; 1 d. Educ. Leven Higher Grade School; Edinburgh and East of Scotland College of Agriculture. Royal Artillery (H), 1939-45; Agricultural Organiser, Essex Education Committee, 1947-49; Agricultural Representative, BOCM, 1949-50; Agricultural Inspector, DAFS, 1951-76 and Health and Safety Executive, 1976-81. Recreations: reading; travel; television; gardening. Address: (h.) 32 Martinton Road, Heathhall, Dumfries, DG1 3QS; T.-0387 63707.

Sutherland, Elizabeth (Elizabeth Margaret Marshall). Writer; Curator, Groam House Museum, Rosemarkie, since 1982; b. 24.8.26, Kemback, Cupar; m., Rev. John D. Marshall; 2 s.; 1 d. Educ. St. Leonard's Girls' School, St. Andrews; Edinburgh University. Social Worker for Scottish Episcopal Church, 1974-80; author of: Lent Term (Constable Trophy), 1973, The Seer of Kintail, 1974, Hannah Hereafter (Scottish Arts Council Book Award), 1976, The Eye of God, 1977, The Weeping Tree, 1980, Ravens and Black Rain: The Story of Highland Second Sight, 1985. Recreations: Highland history; Gaelic language; gardening; tennis; walking. Address: (h.) 17 Mackenzie Terrace, Rosemarkie, Ross-shire, IV10 8UH; T.-Fortrose 20924.

Sutherland, Countess of, (Elizabeth Millicent Sutherland). Chief of Clan Sutherland; b. 30.3.21; m., Charles Noel Janson; 2 s.; 1 s. (deceased); 1 d. Educ. Queen's College, London; abroad. Land Army, 1939-41; Laboratory Technician, Inverness and London, 1943-45. Address: (h.) Dunrobin Castle, Sutherland.

Sutherland, George Graham Mackay, MA, FEIS. Member, Skye and Lochalsh District Council, since 1984; b. 10.4.24, Creich, Sutherland; m., Effie Maynard. Educ. Portree High School; Aberdeen University. Former Schoolmaster, Morrison's Academy, Crieff; former Member, Council and Executive, Educational Institute of Scotland; former Member, General Teaching Council, Scotland; former Member, Crieff Town Council; Past Chairman, Crieff Co-operative Society. Recreations: work; management of sporting estates. Address: (h.) Glenbrittle, Isle of Skye; T.-047842 223.

Sutherland, George Roberton (Roy), MB, ChB, FRCPEdin, MRCPGlas, FRCR, DMRD. Consultant Radiologist in administrative charge, Stobhill General Hospital and associated Hospitals, since 1977; Honorary Clinical Lecturer, Glasgow University, since 1974; Consultant Radiologist, Nuffield McAlpine Hospital, Glasgow and Bon Secours Nursing Home, Glasgow, since 1981; b. 15.12.31, Glasgow; m., Lorna Hunter Murray; 2 d. Educ. George Heriot's School, Edinburgh; Edinburgh University. Former Honorary Secretary, Dunbartonshire Division, BMA; Treasurer, Scottish Radiological Society; Council Member, Scottish Thoracic Society; Chairman, Hospital Medical Committee, Northern District, Glasgow; Member, Area Medical Committee Executive, Glasgow; Deputy Chairman, Senior Medical Staffing Committee, Glasgow; Chairman, Ethical Committee, Glasgow Northern Hospitals; Member, Sub-Committee in Radiology, National Medical Consultative Committee; Member, Faculty Board, Royal College of Radiologists and Chairman, Computer Advisory Committee; Member, Association of Queen's College, Glasgow; Elder, St. George's Tron, Glasgow. Recreations: electronics; amateur radio, repairing old motor cars, or any other mechanical or electrical device; classical music; photography; gardening; golf. Address: (h.) 22 Montrose Drive, Bearsden, Dunbartonshire; T.-041-942 7802.

Sutherland, Hamish Watson, MB, ChB, FRCOG. Acting Head, Department of Obstetrics and Gynaecology, Aberdeen University, since 1984 (Reader, since 1978); Consultant, Grampian Area Health Board; b. 20.10.33, Kinross; m., Frances Cairns; 2 s. Educ. Dollar Academy; St. Andrews University. Resident appointments, Dundee Royal Infirmary; RAMC, 1959-61; Clinical Officer, British Military Hospital, Munster and Hostert; Senior House Officer/Registrar, Dundee, Falkirk and Glasgow; Lecturer/Honorary Senior Registrar, Department of Obstetrics and Gynaecology, Aberdeen University, 1965 (Senior Lecturer, 1970); Representative, Scottish Medical Schools, Central Midwives Board for Scotland, 1979-83; appointed to UK Central Council for Nursing, Midwifery and Health Visiting, 1983; Member, Scottish Executive Committee, Royal College of Obstetricians and Gynaecologists; Past Chairman, Diabetic Pregnancy Study Group, European Association for the Study of Diabetes. Publication: Carbohydrate Metabolism in Pregnancy and the Newborn (three volumes) (Editor). Recreations: sport; art. Address: (h.) Redstones, 9 Marchbank Road, Aberdeen, AB1 9DJ; T.-Aberdeen 867017.

Sutherland, Professor Hugh Brown, SM, FEng, FICE, FIStructE, FRSE. Professor of Civil Engineering (Head of Department), Glasgow University, since 1964; b. 22.1.20, Glasgow; m., Sheila Doris Oliphant; 1 s.; 1 d. Educ. Allan Glen's School, Glasgow; Royal Technical College; Harvard University. Articled Civil Engineer, 1936-40; Assistant Civil Engineer, Oscar Faber and Partners, 1940-42; Lecturer, Glasgow University, 1942-46; Research Associate, Harvard University, 1947; Research Officer, National Research Council of Canada, 1948; Lecturer, Senior Lecturer, Reader, Glasgow University (Dean, Faculty of Engineering, 1975-78); Vice-President, Institution of Civil Engineers, 1982-84; Member, various Government Advisory Committees. Recreations: golf; sports administration; gardening. Address: (b.) Glasgow University, Glasgow, G12 8QQ; T.-041-339 8855.

Sutherland, James, CBE (1974), MA, LLB, LLD. Partner, McClure Naismith Anderson & Gardiner, Solicitors, Glasgow and Edinburgh, since 1951; b. 15.2.20; m., 1, Elizabeth Kelly Barr; 2 s.; 2, Grace Williamson Dawson. Educ. Queens Park Secondary School, Glasgow; Glasgow University. Royal Signals, 1940-46; Examiner in Scots Law, 1951-55, and Mercantile Law and Industrial Law, 1968-69, Glasgow University; Chairman, Glasgow South National Insurance Tribunal, 1964-66; Member, Board of Management, Glasgow Maternity and Women's Hospitals, 1964-74 (Chairman, 1966-74); Council Member, Law Society of Scotland, 1959-77 (Vice-President, 1969-70, President, 1972-74); Council Member, International Bar Association, since 1972 (Chairman, General Practice Section, 1978-80, Secretary General, 1980-84, President, since 1984); Vice-Chairman, Glasgow Eastern Health Council, 1975-77; Council Member, General Dental Council, since 1975; Deacon, Incorporation of Barbers, Glasgow, 1955-65; Dean, Royal Faculty of Procurators in Glasgow,

1977-80; Member, Court, Strathclyde University, since 1977. Recreation: golf. Address: (h.) Greenacres, 20/1 Easter Belmont Road, Edinburgh, EH12 6EX; T.-031-337 1888.

Sutherland, Margaret, BA (Hons), DipLib. Member, Falkirk District Council; b. 2.10.54, Northallerton; m., Donald Hine. Educ. Middlesbrough High School; Stirling University; Strathclyde University. Trainee Librarian, Falkirk District Council, 1977-80; Information Officer, Scottish Community Education Council, 1980-84; Programme Manager, Scottish Community Education Microelectronics Programme, since 1984; Chairman, Polmont Community Council, 1982-84; Secretary, Falkirk District Labour Group, since 1984. Publication: Computers, Communication and the Community (Co-author), 1985. Recreations: politics; cycling. Address: (h.) 45 Polmont Park, Polmont, FK2 0XT; T.-0324 711069.

Sutherland, Margaret Helen. Head Teacher, Farr Secondary School, Bettyhill; b. 15.11.28. Educ. Wishaw High School; West of Scotland Agricultural College; Jordanhill College of Education. Lecturer, Cumberland/Westmorland Farm School; Assistant Teacher of Science, West Lothian; Depute Head, Beauly Secondary School. Founder President, Soroptimist International of Easter Ross; Past Chairman, Ross and Cromarty Conservative Association. Recreations: golf; gardening; Soroptimists; charity work. Address: (h.) Schoolhouse, Bettyhill, Caithness; T.-064 12 217.

Sutherland, Peter Clark. Member, Caithness District Council, since 1980; b. 31.12.47, Lybster. Educ. Wick High School. Chairman, Lybster Community Association; Secretary, Lybster Portland FC; Secretary, Lybster Playing Fields Association. Recreations: part-time disc jockey; all sports. Address: (h.) 18 Mowat Place, Lybster, Caithness; T.-05932 448.

Sutherland, Hon. Lord (Ranald Iain Sutherland), QC (Scot). Senator of the College of Justice, since 1985; b. 23.1.32; m.; 2 s. Educ. Edinburgh Academy; Edinburgh University. Admitted, Faculty of Advocates, 1956; Advocate Depute, 1962-64, 1971-77; QC (Scot), 1969; Member, Criminal Injuries Compensation Board, since 1977.

Sutherland, Robert, MA, LLB, WS, NP. Senior Lecturer in Private Law, Glasgow University; an Honorary Sheriff, Central, Tayside and Fife, at Stirling; a Chairman, Social Security Appeal Tribunals, Glasgow; Member, Central Region Valuation Appeal Panel; b. 9.9.26, Edinburgh. Educ. George Watson's College; Edinburgh University. Indian Army (Assam Regiment), 1944-47; Partner, Stuart & Stuart, WS, 1955-72. Recreations: Nordic skiing; sailing; baroque music. Address: Glasgow University, Glasgow.

Sutherland, William George MacKenzie, QPM. Chief Constable, Lothian and Borders Police, since 1983; b. 12.11.33, Inverness; m., Jennie Abbott; 2 d. Educ. Inverness Technical High School. Cheshire Police, 1954-73; Surrey Police, 1973-75; Hertfordshire Police, 1975-79; Chief Constable, Bedfordshire Police, 1979-83. Recreations: squash; hill-walking. Address: (b.) Police Headquarters, Fettes Avenue, Edinburgh, EH4 1RB; T.-031-311 3131.

Sutherland, William James, CIPFA, FCMA. Chief Financial Officer, South of Scotland Electricity Board, since 1983; b. 10.6.35, Glasgow; m., Fiona Mackay Begg; 3 s.; 1 d. Educ. Victoria Drive Senior Secondary School, Glasgow; Strathclyde University. Glasgow Corporation, 1952-61; Depute Town Chamberlain, Burgh of Bearsden, 1961-64; Town Chamberlain: Burgh of Bishopbriggs, 1964-68, Burgh of Cumbernauld, 1968-75; Depute Director of Finance, Strathclyde Regional Council, 1975-82. Recreations: golf; table tennis. Address: (b.) South of Scotland Electricity Board, Spean Street, Glasgow, G44 4BE; T.-041-637 7177.

Suttie, James Michael Peter, MRTPI. Director of Planning and Development, Banff and Buchan District Council, since 1980; b. 24.3.48, Arbroath; m., Sylvia; 1 s.; 2 d. Educ. Dundee High School; Duncan of Jordanstone College of Art, Dundee. Principal Planning Officer (Development Control), Dundee Corporation, 1973-75; Principal Planning Assistant (Information), Tayside Regional Council, 1975; Chief Assistant Planning Officer, Fife Regional Council, 1975-80. Honorary Secretary and Treasurer, Executive Committee, Scottish Society of Directors of Planning. Recreations: golf; hill-walking; orienteering; driving. Address: (b.) Town House, Low Street, Banff; T.-02612 2521.

Swan, James Robert Drummond, MA, CBIM. Director, Bass PLC, since 1983 (Chairman, Scottish Division); Chairman and Managing Director, Tennent Caledonian Breweries Ltd., since 1976; Director, Hedges and Butler Ltd., since 1982; Chairman, J.G. Thomon & Co., since 1982; b. 30.6.34, Dundee; m., Rachel; 1 s.; 1 d. Educ. Edinburgh University. Beecham Group; Dorland Advertising Ltd.; Bass PLC. Past President, Brewers Association of Scotland; Past Chairman, Scottish Licensed Trade Association; Late Visitor, Incorporation of Maltmen in Glasgow; Trustee and Member, Management Committee, Scottish Civic Trust; Honorary Consul for Sweden in Glasgow. Recreations: skiing; walking. Address: (b.) 110 Bath Street, Glasgow; T.-041-552 6552.

Swan, Lt. Col. William Bertram, CBE, TD, JP. Lord Lieutenant, Berwickshire, since 1969; Chairman, Rural Forum, Scotland, since 1982; Farmer; b. 19.9.14, Duns; m., Ann Gilroy Hogarth; 4 s. Educ. St. Mary's, Melrose; Edinburgh Academy. Farmer, Blackhouse, Reston, Berwickshire, since 1933; served, 1939-42, with 4th Bn., KOSB (UK and France), 1942-45 with Indian Army; President, National Farmers Union of Scotland, 1961-62; Chairman, Scottish Agricultural Organisation Society, 1966-68; Development Commissioner, 1964-76; President, Scottish Cricket Union, 1972-73; President, Lowlands TA & VRA, since 1983. Recreation: sport. Address: Blackhouse, Eyemouth, Berwickshire; T.-Duns 82842.

Sweeney, Sister Dorothea, MA (Hons), BA (Hons), PhD. Assistant Principal (Inservice and Research), St. Andrew's College of Education, since 1980; b. Glasgow. Educ. Notre Dame High School, Glasgow; Glasgow University; Notre Dame College of Education; Bedford College and LSE, London University; Strathclyde University. Assistant Teacher of English, Our Lady & St. Francis Secondary School, Glasgow, 1960-63; entered Congregation of Sisters of Notre Dame, Sussex, 1963; Assistant Teacher of English, Notre Dame High School, London, 1966-67; Notre Dame College of Education: Lecturer, Department of Psychology, 1970-76, Senior Lecturer, Department of Educational Science, 1976-80. Member, Board of Governors, St. Andrew's College, since 1980; Member, CNAA Inservice Education Board, since 1982; Member, National Inservice Committee, since 1981; Member, National Inter-College Committee for Educational Research, since 1982; Member, Catholic Education Commission (Scotland), 1973-75. Recreations: creative writing; dance; music; art; sport; drama; technology. Address: (b.) St. Andrew's College of Education, 6 Duntocher Road, Bearsden, Glasgow, G61 4QA; T.-041-943 1424.

Sweeney, William John, DRSAM. Composer; b. 5.1.50, Glasgow; m., Susannah Conway; 1 s.; 1 d. Educ. Knightswood Secondary School; Royal Scottish Academy of Music and Drama; Royal Academy of Music. Studied clarinet and composition, 1967-72; principal compositions: Heights of Maccu Piccu, 1978, String Quartet, 1981, Maqam, 1983, Nine Days, 1976; Vice-Chairman, Scottish District Council, Musicians' Union. Recreation: a quiet pint in the Dowanhill Bar. Address: (h.) 37 Lawrence Street, Glasgow, G11 5HD; T.-041-334 9987.

Sweet, Elizabeth Mary, MB, ChB, FRCPEdin, FRCPGlas, FRCR. Consultant Radiologist, Royal Hospital for Sick Children, Glasgow, since 1963, and Queen Mother's Maternity Hospital, Glasgow, since 1964; b. 30.8.28, Bombay. Educ. St. Bride's, Helensburgh; Edinburgh University. President, 22nd Congress, European Society of Paediatric Radiology, Glasgow, 1985. Address: (b.) Royal Hospital for Sick Children, Glasgow, G3 8JJ; T.-041-339 8888.

Swift, Bernard Christopher, BA, MA, PhD. Senior Lecturer in French, Stirling University, since 1973; b. 5.2.37, St. Helens; m., Christine Ramsden; 2 s.; 1 d. Educ. West Park Grammar School, St. Helens; Manchester University; Aberdeen University. Lecturing posts, Geneva University, 1961-63, School of Interpreters, Geneva University, 1962-63, Aberdeen University, 1963-72, Saskatchewan University, 1969-70, McMaster University, Ontario, 1970. Chief Examiner for Certificate of Sixth Year Studies, French, since 1972. Address: (h.) 2 Grant Drive, Dunblane, Perthshire, FK15 9HU; T.-0786 824066.

Swinbank, Peter, BSc, PhD, MInstP. Head, Department of History of Science, Glasgow University, since 1967; b. 4.5.28, Coventry; m., Jean C.M. Hargin; 1 s.; 1 d. Educ. Bablake School, Coventry; Donington Grammar School; Birmingham University. Research Fellow, then Lecturer, Natural Philosophy Department, Glasgow University; Lecturer, Department of Physics, Birmingham University. Recreations: bringing up children; gardening; family history. Address: Glasgow University, Glasgow, G12 8QQ; T.-041-339 8855.

Swinfen, David Berridge, MA, DPhil, FRHistS. Senior Lecturer in Modern History, Dundee University, since 1975 (Head of American Studies, since 1984; Dean of Arts and Social Sciences, since 1985); b. 8.11.36, Kirkcaldy; m., Dr. Ann Pettit; 2 s.; 3 d. Educ. Fettes College, Edinburgh; Hertford College, Oxford. Assistant Lecturer, Queen's College, Dundee, 1963; Lecturer, Queen's College (later Dundee University), 1965. Publications: Imperial Control of Colonial Legislation, 1970; Ruggles' Regiment: the 122nd NY Volunteers, 1982. Recreation: music. Address: (b.) Department of Modern History, Dundee University, Dundee; T.-Dundee 23181, Ext. 4520.

Swinton, Major General Sir John, KCVO, OBE, DL. Deputy Lieutenant, Berwickshire, since 1980; Brigadier, Queen's Bodyguard for Scotland (Royal Company of Archers), since 1977; Honorary Colonel, 2nd Bn., 52nd Lowland Volunteers, since 1983; National Vice-Chairman, Royal British Legion Scotland, since 1984; Council Member, Commonwealth Ex-Servicemen's League, since 1984; Trustee, Scottish National War Memorial, since 1984; Chairman, Thirlestane Castle Trust, since 1984; Trustee, Army Museums Ogilby Trust, since 1978; Chairman, Berwickshire Civic Society, since 1982; Council Member, Berwickshire Naturalists' Club, since 1983; b. 21.4.25, London; m., Judith Balfour Killen; 3 s.; 1 d. Educ. Harrow School. Enlisted Scots Guards, 1943; commissioned, 1944; served NW Europe (twice wounded); Malaya, 1948-51 (Despatches); ADC to Field Marshal Sir William Slim, Governor General of Australia, 1953-54; Regimental Adjutant, Scots Guards, 1960-62; Adjutant, RMA, Sandhurst, 1962-64; comd. 2nd Bn., Scots Guards, 1966-68; Lt.-Col. commanding Scots Guards, 1970-71; Commander, 4th Guards Armoured Brigade, BAOR, 1972-73; Brigadier, Lowlands and Commander, Edinburgh and Glasgow Garrisons, 1975-76; GOC London District and Major General comd. Household Division, 1976-79. Coordinator for Scotland, Duke of Edinburgh's Award 25th Anniversary Appeal, 1980 (Honorary Liaison Officer for the Borders, 1983-85); Chairman, Roxburgh and Berwickshire Conservative Association, 1983-85. Address: (h.) Kimmerghame, Duns, Berwickshire; T.-0361 83277.

Symington, Rev. Alastair Henderson, MA, BD. Minister, New Kilpatrick Parish Church, Bearsden, since 1985; b. 15.4.47, Edinburgh; m., Eileen Margaret Jenkins; 2 d. Educ. Daniel Stewart's College, Edinburgh; Edinburgh University; Tubingen University, West Germany. Assistant Minister, Wellington Church, Glasgow, 1971-72; Chaplain, RAF, 1972-76; Minister, Craiglockhart Parish Church, Edinburgh, 1976-85. Governor, St. Denis and Cranley School

(Past Chairman of Board); Contributor, Scottish Liturgical Review. Publications: Westminster Church Sermons, 1984; Reader's Digest Family Guide to the Bible (Co-author), 1985. Recreations: golf; rugby; music; computing. Address: 51 Manse Road, Bearsden, Glasgow, G61 3PN; T.-041-942 0035.

T

Tait, Eric, MBE, BSc, MPhil. Secretary, Institute of Chartered Accountants of Scotland, since 1984: b. 10.1.45, Edinburgh; m., Jane; 1 s.; 1 d. Educ. George Heriot's School; London University; Royal Military Academy, Sandhurst; Cambridge University. Commissioned, 2nd Lt., Royal Engineers, 1965; mentioned in Despatches; GSO3 HQ 39 Infantry Brigade, 1976; student, Advanced Staff Course, RAF Staff College, Bracknell, 1977; GSO2 SD HQ1 (BR) Corps, 1980; Officer Commanding 7 Field Squadron, RE, 1980-81; Lt. Col., 1982; Directing Staff, Staff College, Camberley, 1982; retired from active list, 1983. Member, Executive, Scottish Council (Development and Industry). Recreations: swimming; hill-walking; reading. Address: (b.) 27 Queen Street, Edinburgh, EH2 1LA; T.-031-225 5673.

Tait, Ivan Ballantyne, TD, KStJ, KLJ, FRCS, FRCSEdin, FRCSGlas. Physician in administrative charge, Genito-Urinary Medical Services in the West of Scotland; b. 14.9.28, Stepps, Lanarkshire; m., Jocelyn Mary Connel Leggatt; 1 s.; 1 d. Educ. Glasgow Academy; Daniel Stewart's College; Edinburgh University. Col., L/RAMC (V); Representative Knight of Justice, Scottish Priory of the Order of St. John; Liveryman, Worshipful Company of Apothecaries; Freeman, City of London; Honorary Surgeon (TA) to the Queen. Recreations: TA; charitable societies. Address: (h.) 6 Lennox Row, Edinburgh, EH5 3HN.

Tasker, George Leith, CA. Senior Partner, Bird, Simpson & Co., CA, Dundee; b. 28.9.30, Dundee; m., Norma Croll; 3 d. Educ. Morgan Academy, Dundee; Cambridge University. CA training, 1947-53; National Service, RAF, 1953-55; Qualified Assistant, Norman J. Bird & Co., CA, 1955-57 (became Partner, 1957, Senior Partner, 1979); Council Member, Institute of Chartered Accountants of Scotland, 1982. Former Council Member, Dundee Civic Trust; Treasurer, Dundee Chamber Music Club; Elder, Church of Scotland. Recreations: music; theatre; travel abroad; art. Address: (h.) 8 Hillcrest Road, Dundee, DD2 1JJ; T.-Dundee 66125.

Taylor, Rev. Alan Hunter Stuart, BA (Hons), MA (Hons), BD. Minister, Holm: Orkney Islands, since 1975; b. 28.3.26, Wick; m., Margaret

Riddell McNay; 2 d. Educ. Morrison's Academy, Crieff; St. Andrews University; London University. Royal Signals and Intelligence Corps, Far East, 1944-48; teaching appointments, John Watson's School, Edinburgh, and Coatbridge High School; Assistant Minister, Auld Kirk of Ayr, 1957-58; Minister: Dryfesdale Parish Church, Lockerbie, 1958-65, Aberlour and Craigellachie, 1965-75. Recreations: music; miscellaneous reading; art; gardening; golf; hillwalking. Address: The Manse, Holm, Kirkwall, Orkney Islands; T.-085 678 218.

Taylor, Rev. Andrew Stark, ThB, FPhS. Minister, Union Church, Greenock, since 1959; b. 3.11.28, Glasgow; m., Mary McEwan; 1 d. Educ. Govan Senior Secondary School; Glasgow University and Trinity College. Staff, Donaldson Brothers and Black Ltd., Shipping Agents, 1944-54; Assistant Minister: Linthouse Church, 1955-57, St. Nicholas Church, Glasgow, 1957-59. Address: 72 Forsyth Street, Greenock; T.-0475 21092.

Taylor, Charles Edwin, CBE, BSc, PhD, FRSE, FIBiol. Director, Scottish Crop Research Institute (formerly Scottish Horticultural Research Institute), since 1972; b. 11.9.23, Oystermouth; m., Dorothy N. Taylor; 1 d. Educ. Cardiff High School; University College, Cardiff. Pilot, RAF, 1943-46; Lecturer in Applied Zoology, Nottingham University School of Agriculture, 1949-56; Senior Entomologist, Federation of Rhodesia and Nyasaland, 1956-59; Head, Zoology Section, Scottish Horticultural Research Institute, 1959-72. President, European Society of Nematologists, 1980-84. Address: (b.) Scottish Crop Research Institute, Invergowrie, Dundee, DD2 5DA; T.-082 67 731.

Taylor, Rev. Howard George, BSc (Hons), BD (Hons). Minister, Innellan, Toward and Inverchaolain, since 1981; b. 6.6.44, Stockport; m., Eleanor Clark; 3 s. Educ. Nottingham University; Edinburgh University. Voluntary Service Overseas, teaching mathematics and physics, Malawi University, 1965-67; Minister in Malawi, 1971-81. Moderator, Dunoon Presbytery, 1984-85. Publications: Faith Seeks Understanding; Pray Today; In Christ All Things Hold Together. Recreation: hill-walking. Address: The Manse, Innellan, Argyll; T.-036 983 276.

Taylor, Rev. Ian, BSc, MA, LTh, DipEd. Minister, Abdie & Dunbog and Newburgh, since 1983; b. 12.10.32, Dundee; m., Joy Coupar, LRAM; 2 s.; 1 d. Educ. Dundee High School; St. Andrews University; Durham University; Sheffield University; Edinburgh University. Teacher, Mathematics Department, Dundee High School; Lecturer in Mathematics, Bretton Hall College of Education; Senior Lecturer in Education, College of Ripon and York St. John; Assistant Minister, St. Giles' Cathedral, Edinburgh. Secretary, History of Education Society, 1968-73; extensive work in adult education (appreciation of music and the arts); Director, Summer Schools in Music, St. Andrews University, 1974-82; numerous courses for Edinburgh and Hull Universities and WEA; has played principal roles in opera and operetta; Producer,

Gilbert and Sullivan Society of Edinburgh, since 1979; compiled Theatre Music Quiz series, Radio Tay; presented own operetta, My Dear Gilbert...My Dear Sullivan, BBC; Writer of revues and documentary plays with music, including Tragic Queen (Mary Queen of Scots), St. Giles' Cathedral, Edinburgh Festival Fringe, 1982, and John Knox (Church of Scotland Video). Publications: How to Produce Concert Versions of Gilbert Sullivan; The Gilbert and Sullivan Quiz Book; The Opera Lover's Quiz Book. Address: The Manse, Cupar Road, Newburgh, Fife, KY14 6HA; T.-0337 40275.

Taylor, John Alistair, MA, DipPsych, PhD, ABPS. Chief Clinical Psychologist, Southern General Hospital, since 1978; Honorary Clinical Lecturer, Department of Psychological Medicine, Glasgow University, since 1978; b. 25.9.43, Dundee. Educ. Edinburgh Academy; St. Andrews University; Edinburgh University.

Taylor, John Henry Bindon, MA (Hons), BD, PGCE, DipEd. Head Teacher, Auchenharvie Academy, Stevenston, since 1980; b. 4.11.26, Swansea; m., Constance Jean Tainsh; 3 s.; 1 d. Educ. Swansea Grammar School; Worcester College, Oxford; Glasgow University. Minister: Lincluden, Dumfries, 1952, St. Mary's Presbyterian, Woolston, Southampton, 1956, Irvine St. Andrews, 1960; Teacher, latterly Assistant Rector, Ravenspark Academy, 1969; Depute Head Teacher, Garnock Academy, Kilbirnie, 1978. Chairman, Joint Working Party, Standard Grade Creative and Aesthetic Studies; Convener, Religious Studies Panel, Scottish Examination Board; Church of Scotland Member, Strathclyde Education Committee; Governor, Craigie College of Education, Ayr. Recreations: walking; writing; numismatics; railway history. Address: (b.) Auchenharvie Academy, Stevenston, Ayrshire.

Taylor, Rev. Canon John Mitchell, MA. Canon, St. Mary's Cathedral, Glasgow, since 1979; b. 23.5.32, Aberdeen; m., Edna Elizabeth Maitland; 1 s.; 1 d. Educ. Banff Academy; Aberdeen University; Theological College, Edinburgh. Curate, St. Margaret's, Aberdeen; Rector: Holy Cross, Knightswood, Glasgow, St. Ninian's, Pollokshields, Glasgow, St. John the Evangelist, Dumfries. Recreations: angling; hill-walking; sketching; music. Address: St. John's Rectory, 8 Newall Terrace, Dumfries; T.-Dumfries 54126.

Taylor, Rt. Rev. Maurice, STD. Bishop of Galloway, since 1981; b. 5.5.26, Hamilton. Educ. St. Aloysius College, Glasgow; Our Lady's High School, Motherwell; Pontifical Gregorian University, Rome. Royal Army Medical Corps, UK, India, Egypt, 1944-47; Assistant Priest: St. Bartholomew's, Coatbridge, 1951-52, St. Bernadette's, Motherwell, 1954-55; Lecturer, St. Peter's College, Cardross, 1955-65; Rector, Royal Scots College, Spain, 1965-74; Parish Priest, Our Lady of Lourdes, East Kilbride, 1974-81. Secretary, Bishop's Conference of Scotland; Vice Chairman, Trustees, Prison-Fellowship, Scotland. Publication: The Scots College in Spain, 1971. Address: 8 Corsehill Road, Ayr, KA7 2ST; T.-Ayr 266750.

Taylor, Michael Alan, BA, MSc, MEd, PhD. Principal, Telford College of Further Education, Edinburgh, since 1985; b. 22.12.45, London; m., Maureen Brown. Educ. Sir George Monoux Grammar School, Walthamstow; Middlesex Polytechnic; Lancaster University; Liverpool University; Keele University. Teacher, London secondary schools, 1968-71; Lecturer, Chorley College of Education, 1971-73; Senior and Principal Lecturer, Ulster Polytechnic, 1973-76; Head, School of Social Sciences and Dean, North East Wales Institute of Higher Education, 1976-82 (Director, Institute of Health Education); Depute Principal, Telford College, 1982-84. Recreations: mountaineering; canoeing; skiing; cycling. Address: (b.) Telford College of Further Education, Crewe Toll, Edinburgh, EH4 2NZ; T.-031-332 2491.

Taylor, Michael Thomas, MA, MEd. Rector, Dyce Academy, Aberdeen, since 1980; b. 17.2.47, Newcastle upon Tyne; m., Sheena Robertson; 1 s.; 2 d. Educ. Rutherford Grammar School, Newcastle upon Tyne; Trinity College, Cambridge; Aberdeen University. Teacher of Chemistry, Cannock Grammar School, 1969-75; Ellon Academy: Principal Teacher of Guidance, 1975-76, Assistant Head Teacher, 1977-78, Depute Rector, 1978-80. Secretary, Newmachar Community Council; Elder, Newmachar Parish Church. Recreations: hill-walking; music. Address: (h.) Loch-An-Eilan, Newmachar, Aberdeen; T.-065 17 2234.

Taylor, Peter Bruce, MB, ChB, FFARCS. Consultant Anaesthetist, since 1979; Honorary Senior Lecturer in Anaesthesia, Dundee University, since 1979; b. 30.6.44, Newcastle-upon-Tyne; m.; 1 s.; 1 d. Educ. Aberdeen Grammar School; Aberdeen University. Short Service commission, RAF, 1968-74; Anaesthetic Registrar, Aberdeen Royal Infirmary, 1974-75; Anaesthetic Senior Registrar, Nottingham AHA, 1976-79; Instructor in Anaesthesia, Michigan University Hospital, 1977-78. Linkman (Tayside), Association of Anaesthetists of GB and Ireland. Recreations: duplicate bridge; reading; philately (specialist in Machin definitives). Address: (b.) Anaesthetic Department, Ninewells Hospital, Dundee, DD1 9SY; T.-Dundee 60111, Ext. 2475.

Taylor, Captain Richard Mitchell, MNI. Port Manager, Fife Ports, Forth Forts Authority, since 1983; b. 19.10.30, Airth, Stirlingshire; m., Aileen Wilson Provan; 2 s. Educ. High School of Stirling; Royal College of Science and Technology, Glasgow. Deck Officer, British India Steam Navigation Company; Senior Marine Officer, Nigerian Ports Authority. Recreations: curling; golf. Address: (h.) Braemar, 87 Pettycur Road, Kinghorn, Fife; T.-0592 890575.

Taylor, Sheriff Robert Richardson, QC (Scot), MA, LLB, PhD. Sheriff Principal of Tayside Central and Fife, since 1975; b. 16.9.19; m.; 2 s.; 1 d. Educ. Glasgow High School; Glasgow University. Called to Scottish Bar, 1944; called to Bar, Middle Temple, 1948; Lecturer in International Private Law, Edinburgh University, 1947-69; Sheriff Principal, Stirling, Dunbarton and Clackmannan, 1971-75.

Taylor, Ross Jenkins, MD, FRCGP, DCH. Senior Lecturer, Department of General Practice, Aberdeen University, since 1978; General Medical Practitioner, Grampian Health Board, since 1980; b. 16.4.43, Glasgow; m., Armida Mary Craig; 2 s.; 2 d. Educ. Thurso High School; Aberdeen University Medical School. RAF Medical Branch, 1965-73; House Officer, Stracathro Hospital, Brechin, 1966-67; Honorary Registrar in Paediatrics, St. George's Hospital, London, 1970; Lecturer, Department of General Practice, Aberdeen University, 1973-78; Academic Member, NHS Prescription Pricing Authority, 1980-83. Butterworth Gold Medal, RCGP, 1977. Recreation: music. Address: (b.) Department of General Practice, Aberdeen University, Foresterhill Health Centre, Westburn Road, Aberdeen, AB9 2AY; T.-0224 697722, Ext. 270.

Taylor, St. Clair S., MA, PhD, DipAnimGen, CBiol, FIBiol. Senior Principal Scientific Officer, AFRC Animal Breeding Research Organisation, Edinburgh, since 1973; Honorary Lecturer in Animal Growth and Development, Edinburgh University, since 1978; b. 26.6.28, Banchory; m., Helen Margaret Gladstone Bain; 2 s.; 2 d. Educ. Robert Gordon's College, Aberdeen; George Watson's College, Edinburgh; Edinburgh University. Joined AFRC Animal Breeding Research Organisation, 1953 (Head, Department of Growth and Efficiency, 1973-83); Member, AFRC Joint Consultative Organisation Cattle Committee on R. & D. Priorities, 1973-77; awarded British Society of Animal Production's Hammond Memorial Prize, 1970; elected Honorary Fellow, Faculty of Science, Edinburgh University, 1983. Recreations: theatre; books; music; wood-carving; clay-modelling; gardening; occasional yoga, tennis, cycling and dancing. Address: (b.) AFRC Animal Breeding Research Organisation, King's Buildings, West Mains Road, Edinburgh, EH9 3JQ; T.-031-667 6901.

Taylor, Professor Samuel Sorby Brittain, BA, PhD. Professor of French, St. Andrews University, since 1977; b. 20.9.30, Dore and Totley, Derbyshire; m., Agnes McCreadie Ewan; 2 d. Educ. High Storrs Grammar School, Sheffield; Birmingham University; Paris University. Royal Navy, 1956-68 (Sub Lt., RNVR); Personnel Research Officer, Dunlop Rubber Co., 1958-60; Institut et Musee Voltaire, Geneva, 1960-63; St. Andrews University: Lecturer, 1963, Reader, 1972, Personal Chair, 1977; Chairman, National Council for Modern Languages, 1981-85; Member, Executive Committee, Complete Works of Voltaire, since 1970; Project Leader, Inter-University French Language Teaching Research and Development Project, since 1980; Chairman, Scottish Joint Working Party for Standard Grade in Modern Languages, 1982-84. Recreations: athletics timekeeping; photography. Address: (b.) Department of French, St. Andrews University, St. Andrews, Fife; T.-0334 76161, Ext. 485.

Taylor, (S.F.) Stan. Head of Radio, BBC Scotland, since 1983; b. 13.4.32, London; m.; 2 s. Educ. Bishopshalt Grammar School. Reporter, 1948-59; joined BBC as Sub-Editor, External Services News, 1959; Editor, Radio News, 1976; Editor, News and Current Affairs, Scotland, 1979.

Taylor of Gryfe, Baron, (Thomas Johnston Taylor), DL, FRSE. Life Peer; b. 27.4.12; m.; 2 d. Educ. Bellahouston Academy. President, Scottish CWS, 1965-70; Chairman, Scottish Railways Board, 1971-80; Chairman, Forestry Commission, 1970-76; Company Director; DL, Renfrewshire; Hon. LLD, Strathclyde, 1974.

Taylor, William Gordon, MA, MRTPI, FBIM. Director, Economic Development and Planning, Fife Regional Council, since 1985; b. 13.2.43, Edinburgh; m., Margaret Frances Carrick McKinnon; 1 s.; 1 d. Educ. George Watson's College; Edinburgh University; Heriot-Watt University. Planning Assistant, Edinburgh Corporation; Area Planning Officer, Fife County Council; Assistant City Planning Officer, Dundee Corporation; Depute Planning Officer, then Director of Physical Planning, Fife Regional Council. Past Chairman, Scottish Society of Directors of Planning; Advisor, EEC Environment Directorate; Advisor on industry and the environment, WHO. Recreations: golf; walking; music; current affairs. Address: (h.) Langdale, 55 Main Street, Dairsie, Fife, KY15 4SR; T.-0334 870503.

Taylor, William Leonard, CBE, BL, JP, DL, Hon. FRTPI. Solicitor; Chairman, Glasgow Citizens' Theatre Ltd., since 1970; Chairman, Planning Exchange, since 1972; Chairman, Scottish Executive, Town and Country Planning Association, since 1953; b. 21.12.16, Glasgow; m., Gladys Carling; 1 s. Educ. Whitehill Secondary School, Glasgow; Glasgow University. Councillor, Glasgow Corporation, 1952-69; Magistrate, City of Glasgow, 1956-60 (Senior Magistrate, 1960-61); Leader, Labour Group, Glasgow Corporation, 1962-69; Leader of Council, 1962-68; Chairman, Livingston Development Corporation, 1965-72 (Member, from 1962); Member, Scottish Advisory Committee on Civil Aviation, 1965-72; Governor, Centre for Environmental Studies, 1966-79; Trustee, Scottish Civic Trust, since 1967; Chairman, Scottish Water Advisory Committee, 1969-72; Member, Extra-Parliamentary Panel under Private Legislation Procedure (Scotland) Act 1936, since 1971; Chairman, Panel of Assessors, River Clyde Planning Study, 1972-74; Chairman, Scottish Advisory Council on Social Work, 1974-81; Vice-Chairman, Commission for Local Authority Accounts in Scotland, 1974-79; Member, Housing Corporation, 1974-80; Member, Scottish Economic Council, 1975-82; Chairman, Scottish Special Housing Association, 1978-81 (Depute Chairman, 1976-78). DL, Glasgow, 1977; Knight, Order of Polonia Restituta (Poland), 1969. Recreations: theatre; reading. Address: (h.) Cruachan, 18 Bruce Road, Glasgow, G41 5EF; T.-041-429 1776.

Teall of Teallach, Dr. D. Gordon, LCP, MEd (Dist.), PhD, FSTS, FSA Scot. Executive Vice-President and Chairman of the Council, Scottish Tartans Society; b. 8.8.24; m., Eleanor Joan; 2 s.; 2 d. Educ. Warwick School; Coopers Hill College; Leicester University. Former Principal, Priory College, Stamford Baron, County of Cambridge and Chairman, RFI Ltd. and PEA Ltd.; Council Member, Independent Schools Association; Honorary Member, Clan Grant;

Honorary Lt.-Col., Militia of the State of Georgia. Publications: A Brief History of the Scottish Tartans Society; The Manx Tartans; The Tradesmen and Corporation of Stamford 1485-1750; The District Tartans of Scotland (Co-author). Recreations: sailing; cross-country skiing; horse riding; wind-surfing; mountain walking; swimming. Address: (h.) Teallach Estate, Fonab, Pitlochry, Perthshire; T.-0796 2345.

Teasdale, Professor Graham Michael, MB, BS, MRCP, FRCSEdin, FRCSGlas. Professor and Head, Department of Neurosurgery, Glasgow University, since 1981; Consultant Neurosurgeon, Institute of Neurological Sciences, Glasgow, since 1975; b. 23.9.40, Spennymoor; m.; 3 s. Educ. Johnston Grammar School, Durham; Durham University. Postgraduate clinical training, Newcastle-upon-Tyne, London and Birmingham, 1963-69; Assistant Lecturer in Anatomy, Glasgow University, 1969-71; specialist training in surgery and neurosurgery, Southern General Hospital, Glasgow, 1971-75; Senior Lecturer, then Reader in Neurosurgery, Glasgow University, 1975-81. Editor, Society of British Neurosurgeons. Publication: The Management of Head Injuries. Recreations: hill-walking; inshore fishing. Address: (b.) University Department of Neurosurgery, Institute of Neurological Sciences, Southern General Hospital, Glasgow; T.-041-445 2466.

Tebbutt, Michael Laurence, MBIM. Administrator, Culzean Castle and Country Park, and National Trust Representative in Ayrshire, since 1982; b. 23.7.31, Stamford; m., Hazel Taylor; 4 d. Educ. Stamford School, Lincolnshire. Royal Navy, 1950-57; Outward Bound Trust, 1957-61; Joint Iron Council, 1961-64; Stevenage Youth Trust, 1964-67; National Federation of Young Farmers Clubs, 1967-69; Comptroller, Knebworth House and Country Park, 1970-72; Administrator, Weston Park, 1972-82. Vice-President, Wrekin Decorative and Fine Art Society; Executive Committee Member, Ayrshire and Burns Country Tourist Board. Recreations: sailing; mountaineering; music; heritage; photography. Address: Culzean Castle, Maybole, Ayrshire; T.-06556 274.

Tedder, Rt. Hon. Lord, (John Michael Tedder), MA, ScD, PhD, DSc, FRSE. Purdie Professor of Chemistry, St. Andrews University, since 1969; b. 4.7.26, London; m., Peggy Eileen Growcott; 2 s.; 1 d. Educ. Dauntsey's School, Wiltshire; Magdalene College, Cambridge; Birmingham University. Research Fellow: Birmingham University, 1950-52, Ohio State University, 1952-53, Edinburgh University, 1953-55; Lecturer, then Reader, Sheffield University, 1955-64; Roscoe Professor of Chemistry, Dundee University, 1964-68. Member, Board of Management, Macaulay Institute of Soil Research, since 1979. Publication: Basic Organic Chemistry, Parts 1-5 (Co-author); Valence Theory (Co-author); The Chemical Bond (Co-author); Radicals (Co-author). Recreation: music. Address: (h.) Little Rathmore, Kennedy Gardens, St. Andrews, Fife; T.-St. Andrews 73546.

Tegner, Ian Nicol, CA. Finance Director, Bowater Industries PLC, since 1971; Council Member, Institute of Chartered Accountants

of Scotland, since 1981; Member, Accounting Standards Committee, since 1984; b. 11.7.33, London; m., Meriel Helen Lush; 1 s.; 1 d. Educ. Rugby School; Harvard Business School. Clarkson Gordon & Co., CA, Toronto, 1958-59; Barton, Mayhew & Co., CA, London, 1959-71 (Partner, 1965-71). Member, Argyllshire Gathering. Recreations: book collecting; walking; travel; choral singing; family life. Address: (h.) Keeper's Cottage, Kilninver, Argyll.

Telfer, Jaye. Sheriff Clerk, Perth, since 1981; b. Gorebridge. Educ. Dalkeith High School. Women's Royal Naval Service, four years; Civil Service (Scottish Courts Service): began as typist, appointed to clerical grades by open competition, intermediate promotions through grades; first woman Sheriff Clerk at Perth. Recreations: Siamese cats; reading; gardening. Address: (h.) 2 Alder Drive, Perth; T.-0738 28709.

Telfer, John, BSc (Hons), NDA, NDD, FRAgS. Principal, Clinterty Agricultural College, Aberdeen, since 1968; b. Langholm; m., Katharine Dent; 1 s.; 2 d. Educ. Lockerbie Academy; Wallace Hall Academy; Durham University; West of Scotland Agricultural College. Farm worker, five years; Lecturer, Cumberland and Westmorland Farm School, five years; Day Release Class Organiser, Aberdeen and Kincardineshire, three years. Young Farmers' and Apprenticeship Committees, SCOTEC; Member, NCA Examination Board; Director, Royal Northern Agricultural Society; Church Elder. Recreation: gardening. Address: (b.) Clinterty Agricultural College, Kinellar, Aberdeen, AB5 0TN; T.-0224 79 393.

Tennant, George, BSc, PhD, CChem, FRSC, FRSE. Reader in Organic Chemistry, Edinburgh University, since 1977; b. 22.2.36, Glasgow; 1 s.; 1 d. Educ. Whitehill Senior Secondary School, Glasgow; Glasgow University. ICI Research Fellow, Aberdeen University, 1961-63; Lecturer: Queen's College, St. Andrews, 1963-65, Edinburgh University, 1965-76; Senior Lecturer, Edinburgh University, 1976-77. Secretary, Heterocyclic Group, Royal Society of Chemistry, 1976-79; Chairman, Edinburgh and SE Scotland Section, Royal Society of Chemistry, 1981-83. Recreations: sport; music; art. Address: (b.) Department of Chemistry, Edinburgh University, West Mains Road, Edinburgh, EH9 3JJ; T.-031-667 1081.

Tennant, Iain Mark. Chairman, Grampian Television PLC, since 1968 (Vice-Chairman, 1960-68); Director, Caledonian Associated Cinemas PLC; Director, Scottish Northern Investment Trust PLC; Director, Clydesdale Bank PLC; Director, Abbey National Building Society (Chairman, Scottish Advisory Board); Director, Moray and Nairn Newspaper Company Ltd.; Crown Estate Commissioner; Honorary Director, Seagram Company Ltd., Montreal; Lord Lieutenant of Morayshire; b. 11.3.19, North Berwick; m., Lady Margaret Ogilvy; 2 s.; 1 d. Educ. Eton College; Magdalene College, Cambridge. Learned about film production, Welwyn Garden City Film Studios; served in Egypt with 2nd Bn., Scots Guards, 1940-42; became Intelligence Officer, 201 Guard's Brigade; captured at the surrender of Tobruk; prisoner of war, Italy and Germany, until 1945; Founder Member, Moray Sea School, 1949; Council Member, Outward Bound Trust, 15 years; joined Board, Gordonstoun School, 1951 (Chairman, 1957-72); Member, Moray and Nairn County Council, 1956-64 (latterly Vice-Chairman, Education Committee); Member, The Times Publishing Co. Ltd., 1962-66; Member, Board, Cairngorm Sports Development Ltd., 1964-76; appointed Chairman, local Disablement Advisory Committee, 1964; Chairman, Glenlivet and Glen Grant Distilleries Ltd., 1964-70 (Chairman, Glenlivet Distillers Ltd., from 1970); Trustee, King George's Jubilee Trust, London, 1967-71; FRSA, 1971; Trustee, Churchill Trust, 1973-76; Member, Board, Courage Ltd., 1974-77; Chairman, Seagram Distillers Ltd. (in London), 1977-82; CBIM, 1983; Elder, Church of Scotland. Recreations: shooting; fishing. Address: (b.) Innes House, Elgin, Moray; T.-Lhanbryde 2410.

Tennant, Professor Neil Wellesley, BA (Hons) (Cantab), PhD (Cantab). Professor and Head, Department of Philosophy, Stirling University, since 1981; b. 1.3.50, Pietermaritzburg, South Africa; m., Sheila Megan Anderson; 2 d. Educ. Maritzburg College, Natal; Cate School, California; Clare College, Cambridge; Wolfson College, Cambridge. Lecturer in Philosophy, Edinburgh, 1974; Visiting Professor, Dartmouth, USA, 1976; British Academy Wolfson Fellow and Alexander von Humboldt Fellow, Munich, 1979; Visiting Fellow, Center for Philosophy of Science, Pittsburgh, and Australian National University, 1985. Publications: Natural Logic, 1978; Philosophy, Evolution and Human Nature (Co-author), 1984. Recreations: cross-country running; swimming; modern dance; barn conversion. Address: (h.) Landrick Stables, Dunblane, Perthshire; T.-0786 824966.

Thaw, David Samson, MBE. Retired Solicitor; Honorary Sheriff, Dunoon, since 1973; b. 19.1.08, Lanark; m., Violet Lightbody; 1 s.; 2 d. Educ. Lanark Grammar School; Lanark Higher Grade School; Glasgow University. Qualified as Solicitor, 1930; private practice, 1930-40; volunteered for RAF; entered Procurator Fiscal Service, 1947; Fiscal, Dunoon District, 1959-73. Recreation: golf (an addict). Address: (h.) Drimvore, Bullwood, Dunoon, Argyll.

Thin, David Ainslie, BSc. Joint Managing Director, James Thin Ltd., since 1962; Chairman, Melven's Bookshops Ltd., since 1972; Director, Book Tokens Ltd., since 1968; b. 9.7.33, Edinburgh; m., Elspeth J.M. Scott; 1 s.; 2 d. Educ. Edinburgh Academy; Loretto School; Edinburgh University. President, Booksellers Association of GB and Ireland, 1976-78. Recreations: golf; travelling; reading. Address: (h.) 60 Fountainhall Road, Edinburgh, EH9 2LP; T.-031-667 2725.

Thom, Arthur David, JP. Member, Falkirk District Council, since 1980; Member, Forth River Purification Board, since 1984; b. 6.1.46, Glasgow; m., Catherine Jeffrey; 1 s. Educ. Grangemouth High School. Member, Electricity Consultative Council for South of Scotland District, 1980-84; Member, Management Committee, Grangemouth CAB. Recreations: golf; photography. Address: (h.) 17 Tweed Street, Grangemouth, FK3 8HA.

Thomas, Professor David Brynmor, MB, BS, BSc, DSc, FRCPEdin, FRCPath, FIBiol, FRSE. Bute Professor and Head, Department of Anatomy and Experimental Pathology, St. Andrews University, since 1973; b. 11.10.30, Cefn Coed y Cymmer, Wales; m., Elizabeth Elma Flanagan; 1 s. Educ. Ysgol-y-Graig and Vaynor & Penderyn Secondary School; University College, London; University College Hopsital Medical School. House Surgeon, University College Hospital and Royal Northern Hospital; Registrar, Neath General Hospital; Lecturer: Bristol University, University of Wales, Oxford University; Senior Lecturer, Birmingham University; Consultant, Biology Division, Oak Ridge National Laboratory, Tennessee; Master, United College of St. Salvator and St. Leonard, St. Andrews University. Recreations: golf; music; photography; walking. Address: (b.) Bute Medical Buildings, St. Salvator's College, St. Andrews, Fife, KY16 9TS; T.-0334 76161, Ext. 7106.

Thomas, David Prys, BSc, PhD, FIMA. Senior Lecturer, Department of Mathematical Sciences, Dundee University, since 1980; b. 4.2.40, Rhyl; m., Joy Beretta; 2 d. Educ. Ruthin School; Holyhead County Secondary School; Liverpool University. Assistant Lecturer, Department of Applied Mathematics, Sheffield University, 1964-65; Lecturer, Department of Mathematics: Queen's College, Dundee, 1965-67; Dundee University, 1967-80; Associate Professor, Department of Mathematical Sciences, New Mexico State University, 1980. Publication: Mathematics Applied to Mechanics, 1977. Recreations: golf; gardening. Address: (b.) Department of Mathematical Sciences, Dundee University, Dundee, DD1 4HN; T.-0382 23181.

Thomas, Professor Michael Frederic, MA, PhD. Professor of Environmental Science, Stirling University, since 1980; b. 15.9.33, London; m., Elizabeth Anne Dadley; 1 s.; 1 d. Educ. Royal Grammar School, Guildford; Reading University. Assistant Lecturer in Geography, Magee University College, Londonderry, 1957-60; Lecturer, Ibadan University, Nigeria, 1960-64; Lecturer, then Senior Lecturer, St. Andrews University, 1964-79; visiting appointments, Universities of Canterbury (New Zealand), New South Wales, Natal, and Fourah Bay College, Sierra Leone. Council Member, Royal Scottish Geographical Society; Past Chairman, British Geomorphological Research Group. Publication: Tropical Geomorphology, 1974. Recreations: listening to music; hill-walking; travel. Address: (b.) Department of Environmental Science, Stirling University, Stirling, FK9 4LA; T.-0786 73171.

Thomas, Phillip Charles, BSc, PhD, FIBiol. Head, Department of Animal Nutrition and Production, Hannah Research Institute, Ayr, since 1979; Honorary Lecturer, Glasgow University, since 1979; b. 17.6.42, Pontypool, Wales; m., Pamela Mary Hirst; 1 s.; 1 d. Educ. Abersychan Grammar School; University College of North

Wales, Bangor. Lecturer, Department of Animal Physiology and Nutrition, Leeds University, 1966-71; Research Scientist, Hannah Research Institute, since 1971. Editor for British Journal of Nutrition. Publications: Nutritional Physiology of Farm Animals, 1983; Silage for Milk Production, 1983. Recreations: watching the garden grow; mini-rugby coaching. Address: (b.) Hannah Research Institute, Ayr, KA6 5HL; T.-0292 76013.

Thomason, Edward, ACII. Vice-Convener, Shetland Islands Council, since 1982 (Chairman, Resources Committee, since 1982); b. 12.8.22, Lerwick; m., Dinah. Educ. Anderson Educational Institute, Lerwick. Councillor, since 1960; Convener, Zetland County Council, 1970-73; Director, Sullom Voe Association Ltd. Recreations: fiddle and accordion music; writing magazine articles. Address: (h.) 6 Mounthooly Place, Lerwick, Shetland; T.-0595 2901.

Thompson, Professor Alan Eric, MA (Hons), PhD. Professor of the Economics of Government, Heriot-Watt University, since 1972; b. 16.9.24; m., Mary Heather Long; 3 s.; 1 d. Educ. Edinburgh University. Edinburgh University: Assistant in Political Economy, 1952-53, Lecturer in Economics, 1953-59 and 1964-71; MP (Labour), Dunfermline, 1959-64; Member, Royal Fine Art Commission for Scotland, 1975-80; Chairman, Northern Offshore Maritime Resources Study, since 1974; Governor, Newbattle Abbey College, since 1975 (Chairman, 1980-83); Member, Local Government Boundaries Commission for Scotland, 1975-80; Member, Scottish Council for Adult Education in HM Forces, since 1973; BBC National Governor for Scotland, 1975-79; Governor, Leith Nautical College, 1981-85; Trustee, Bell's Nautical Trust, since 1981; Parliamentary Adviser, Pharmaceutical General Council (Scotland), since 1984; Chairman, Scottish-Soviet Coordinating Commitee for Trade and Technology, since 1985. Publication: Development of Economic Doctrine (Co-author), 1980. Recreation: writing children's stories and plays. Address: (h.) 11 Upper Gray Street, Edinburgh, EH9 1SN; T.-031-667 2140.

Thompson, Bruce, BA, MA, PhD. Senior Lecturer in German, Stirling University; b. 25.11.41, Kettering; m., Jill; 1 s.; 1 d. Educ. Kettering Grammar School; University College, London. Lecturer in German, Liverpool University, 1964-72; joined Stirling University as Lecturer in German, 1972. Member, Panel of Examiners, GCE A-Level German, Joint Matriculation Board. Recreations: tennis; golf; music. Address: (h.) Fordholm, Cawdor Crescent, Dunblane, Perthshire; T.-Dunblane 823935.

Thompson, Colin, CBE, FRSE, MA, FMA. Chairman, Scottish Museums Council, since 1984; Writer, Lecturer and Broadcaster on art and museums; b. 2.11.19, Berkhamsted; m., Jean A.J. O'Connell; 1 s.; 1 d. Educ. Sedbergh; King's College, Cambridge; Chelsea Polytechnic. War Service, FS Wing (CMP) and GCHQ, 1941-45; Lecturer, Bath Academy of Art, Corsham, 1948-54; joined National Gallery of Scotland as Assistant Keeper, 1954; Director, National Galleries of Scotland, 1977-84. Member, Scottish Arts Council, 1976-83; Member, Edinburgh

Festival Society, since 1979 (Chairman, Fine Art Advisory Panel); founding Chairman, Edinburgh Festival Exhibitions Forum, since 1982; Member, Board of Governors, Edinburgh College of Art; Member, Board of Directors, Fruitmarket Gallery, Edinburgh; Trustee, Buccleuch Heritage Trust. Publications: Pictures for Scotland, 1972; Hugo Van Der Goes and the Trinity Panels in Edinburgh (Co-author), 1974. Address: (h.) Edenkerry, Lasswade, Midlothian, EH18 1LW; T.-031-663 7927.

Thompson, Francis George, FIElecIE, MASEE, TEng, FSA Scot. Author of books on Highland subjects; Senior Lecturer, Lews Castle College, Stornoway; b. 29.3.31, Stornoway; m., Margaret Elaine Pullar; 1 s.; 3 d. Educ. Nicolson Institute, Stornoway. From 1946: supply maintenance electrician, technical writer, assistant publicity manager, lecturer; has held various offices within An Comann Gaidhealach, including editorship of Sruth, bilingual newspaper, 1967-71; books include: Harris and Lewis, 1968; Harris Tweed, 1969; Highlands and Islands, 1974; Portrait of the River Spey, 1979; The National Mod, 1979; Crofting Years, 1985. Recreation: writing! Address: (h.) Am Fasgadh, 5 Rathad na Muilne, Stornoway, Lewis; T.-0851 3812.

Thompson, Professor Ian Bentley, BA, MA, PhD. Professor of Geography, Glasgow University, since 1976; b. 2.1.36, Dewsbury; m., Helene Lamerant; 4 d. Educ. Bourne Grammar School, Lincolnshire; Durham University; Indiana University. Instructor in Geography, Indiana University, 1954-55; Tutor in Geography, Durham University, 1955-56; Assistant Lecturer in Geography, Leeds University, 1956-59; Lecturer, Senior Lecturer, Reader in Geography, Southampton University, 1959-76. Chevalier des Palmes Academiques, 1985. Recreation: ornithology. Address: (h.) 132 Dowanhill Street, Glasgow, G12 9DN; T.-041-339 6298.

Thompson, William Douglas, MB, ChB, PhD, MRCPath. Senior Lecturer in Pathology, Aberdeen University, since 1981; b. 29.10.46, Glasgow; m., Margaret Lilias McNeil Darroch; 3 s. Educ. High School of Glasgow; Glasgow University. Registrar and Lecturer in Pathology, Glasgow Royal Infirmary, 1971-80; Honorary Consultant, Aberdeen Royal Infirmary, since 1981. Recreations: skiing; fishing. Address: (b.) Department of Pathology, Aberdeen Royal Infirmary, Foresterhill, Aberdeen, AB9 2ZD; T.-0224 681818

Thomson, Alan James Reid, FIB (Scot), MIPM, MBIM. Divisional General Manager (Personnel), Bank of Scotland, since 1982; b. 28.10.35, Airdrie; m., Eileen Isobel Millar; 1 s.; 1 d. Educ. Robert Gordon's College, Aberdeen. Bank of Scotland, since 1952; Staff Manager, 1974; Assistant General Manager (Staff), 1978. Member, Scotland Advisory Committee, Understanding British Industry; Member, Council, Institute of Bankers in Scotland (Convenor, Education Committee). Recreations: golf; swimming. Address: (b.) Bank of Scotland, Staff Department, PO Box 133, 62 George Street, Edinburgh, EH2 2RA; T.-031-243 5212.

Thomson, Alexander McEwan, SSC, NP. Solicitor; b. 13.11.17, Dublin; m., Marjorie May Wood; 2 s.; 1 d. Educ. Daniel Stewart's College; George Heriot's School; Edinburgh University. Partner, Drummond & Reid, 1960-69 and Drummond & Co., WS, 1969-83 (Senior Partner, 1970-83); retired, 1983; Solicitor to General Teaching Council for Scotland, 1966-83; Solicitor to Edinburgh (subsequently Lothian Regional) Assessor; President, Society of Solicitors in the Supreme Courts of Scotland, 1979-82. Recreations: gardening; shooting. Address: (h.) Sandyhaugh Cottage, Ashkirk, Selkirk; T.-0750 32257.

Thomson, Alistair MacLachlan. Director, Scottish Prison Service, since 1982; b. 2.7.30, Glasgow; m., Elizabeth McEwan; 2 s.; 1 d. Educ. Allan Glen's School, Glasgow. Entered Civil Service, 1951, as an Executive Officer, Department of Health for Scotland; served in Health Services and Town and Country Planning; Higher Executive Officer, Town and Country Planning, 1959; Assistant Private Secretary to Secretary of State for Scotland, 1964-66; Principal, 1966; Assistant Secretary, Social Work Services, 1975. Recreations: golf; music. Address: (b.) St. Margaret's House, 151 London Road, Edinburgh, EH8 7TQ; T.-031-661 6181, Ext. 399.

Thomson, Rev. Andrew, BA. Minister, Campbeltown Lowland Parish Church, since 1982; b. 12.3.46, Kilwinning, Ayrshire; m., Eleanor Templeton Morrison; 1 s.; 1 d. Educ. Kilwinning High School; Scottish Congregational College. Minister: Stewarton Congregational Church, 1976-79, Coatbridge Congregational Church, 1979-82. Served in Children's Panel system, 1976-80. Recreations: gardening; angling; boating; caravanning; squash; badminton; singing; hill-walking. Address: Lowland Manse, Campbeltown, Argyll, PA28 6AN; T.-0586 52468.

Thomson, Professor Andrew William John, MS, PhD. Professor of Business Policy, Glasgow University, since 1978; Dean, Scottish Business School, since 1983; b. 26.1.36, Stockton; 2 s. Educ. St. Bees School; Oxford University; Cornell University. Brand Manager, Lever Bros., 1961-65; Lecturer, Senior Lecturer, Glasgow University, 1968-78. Director, Scottish Transport Group, 1977-84. Recreations: squash; golf; bridge. Address: (b.) 25 Bute Gardens, Glasgow, G12 8RS; T.-041-339 8855, Ext. 254.

Thomson, Angus William, BSc (Hons), MSc, PhD, MRCPath. Senior Lecturer in Immunopathology, Aberdeen University, since 1982; b. 13.2.48, Inverness; m., Robyn Gai Glover; 1 s.; 1 d. Educ. Inverness Royal Academy; Aberdeen University; Birmingham University. Marr-Walker Research Fellow, Department of Pathology, Aberdeen University, 1974-75; Lecturer in Pathology, Aberdeen University, 1975-82; MRC (UK) Senior Travelling Research Fellow, Kolling Institute of Medical Research, Sydney, Australia, 1981-82. Recreations: badminton; soccer; wine appreciation. Address: (h.) 57 Denview Road, Potterton, Aberdeen, AB4 OZL; T.-03584 3279.

Thomson, Colin, BSc (Hons), PhD, FRSC. Senior Lecturer in Theoretical Chemistry, St. Andrews University, since 1970; Regional Director of Research, National Foundation for Cancer Research, since 1977; Director, Association for International Cancer Research, since 1984; b. 6.7.37, Whitby, Yorkshire; m., Maureen Margaret Green; 2 s.; 2 d. Educ. Whitby Grammar School; Leeds University. Postdoctoral Research Fellow, California University, 1961-63; Postdoctoral (NATO) Research Fellow, Cambridge University, 1963-64; Lecturer in Theoretical Chemistry, St. Andrews University, 1964-70; Committee Member, SERC Computational Chemistry Committee, since 1983; Editor, RSC specialist reports. Recreations: jazz and dance band musician; walking; sailing. Address: (h.) 12 Drumcarrow Road, St. Andrews, KY16 9ST; T.-0334 74820.

Thomson, David Kinnear, CBE, TD, CStJ, JP, DL. Chairman, Perth Festival of the Arts, since 1972; Member, Scottish Opera Advisory Committee, since 1979; Honorary Sheriff, Perth and Kinross, since 1969; b. 26.3.10, Perth. Educ. Perth Academy; Strathallan School. Member, Committee of Management, Trustee Savings Bank, Perth/Tayside, 1959-83; Lord Provost of Perth, 1966-72; Member: Scottish Economic Planning Council, 1968-74, Scottish Council (Development and Industry), 1968-75; Member, IBA, 1969-75; Director, Scottish Opera, 1967-79; Director, Scottish Transport Group, 1972-78; Chairman, Tayside Health Board, 1973-77; Member, Cancer Research Committee (Perth), since 1967. Recreations: walking; golf; listening to music. Address: (h.) Fairhill, Oakbank Road, Perth.

Thomson, David Omond Ronaldshay Stephen, SRN. Member, Lothian Regional Council, since 1982; Company Director, since 1982; b. 16.3.32, Motherwell; m., Mabel Robb Mitchell; 2 s.; 2 d. Educ. Hamilton Academy; Birmingham University. Diploma, Occupational Health Nursing. State Registered General Nurse, 1951-60; Senior Commercial Assistant, ICI Ltd., 1960-80; Community Councillor, Haddington, 1975-77; Member, East Lothian District Council, 1976-83; Scottish Tourist Guide, since 1983; Boys' Brigade Officer. Recreations: piano playing; writing; swimming; studying. Address: (h.) 2 Meadowpark, Haddington, East Lothian; T.-Haddington 3418.

Thomson, Professor Derick S., MA (Aberdeen), BA (Cantab), FRSE. Professor of Celtic, Glasgow University, since 5.8.21, Stornoway; m., Carol Galbraith; 5 s.; 1 d. Educ. Nicolson Institute, Stornoway; Aberdeen University; Cambridge University; University College of North Wales, Bangor. Taught at Edinburgh, Glasgow and Aberdeen Universities before returning to Glasgow as Professor, 1963; Chairman, Gaelic Books Council, since 1968; President, Scottish Gaelic Texts Society; Chairman, Catherine McCaig's Trust; former Member, Scottish Arts Council; first recipient, Ossian Prize, 1974; author of numerous books and articles, including An Introduction to Gaelic Poetry, The Companion to Gaelic Scotland and collections of Gaelic poetry. Address: (h.) 16 Moray Place, Glasgow, G41; T.-041-423 8499.

Thomson, Duncan, MA, PhD. Keeper, Scottish National Portrait Gallery, since 1982; b. 2.10.34, Killearn; m., Julia Jane Macphail; 1 d. Educ. Airdrie Academy; Edinburgh University; Edinburgh College of Art; Moray House College of Education. Teacher of Art; Assistant Keeper, Scottish National Portrait Gallery. Member, Art Committee, and Chairman, Exhibition Panel, Scottish Arts Council; Council Member, Walpole Society. Publication: The Life and Art of George Jamesone, 1974. Recreations: literature; walking; looking. Address: (b.) Scottish National Portrait Gallery, 1 Queen Street, Edinburgh, EH2 1JD; T.-031-556 8921.

Thomson, Rt. Rev. Francis, STL, MA. Parish Priest, St. Isidore's, Biggar, since 1983; President, Theology Commission, Bishops' Conference of Scotland, since 1977; President, Christian Unity Commission, Bishops' Conference of Scotland, since 1977; b. 15.5.17, Edinburgh. Educ. George Watson's College, Edinburgh; Edinburgh University; Christ's College, Cambridge; Pontifical University of St. Thomas, Rome. Ordained Priest, St. Mary's Cathedral, Edinburgh, 1946; Assistant Priest: St. Patrick's, Kilsyth, 1946-48, St. James', St. Andrews, 1949-52, St. Cuthbert's, Edinburgh, 1952-53; Professor of Theology, St. Andrew's College, Drygrange, 1953-60; Rector, St. Mary's College, Blairs, Aberdeen, 1960-65; Bishop of Motherwell, 1965-82. Address: St. Ididore's, 6 Coulter Road, Biggar, Lanarkshire, ML12 6EP; T.-0899 20189.

Thomson, Sir (Frederick Douglas) David, Bt, BA. Deputy Chairman, The Ben Line Steamers Limited, since 1984 (Director, since 1964); Chairman Elect, Britannia Steamship Insurance Association Limited, 1985 (Director, since 1965); Director, Life Association of Scotland Ltd., since 1970; Director, Caledonian Offshore PLC, since 1971; Chairman, Through Transport Marine Mutual Assurance Association (Bermuda) Ltd., since 1984 (Director, since 1973); Director, Danae Investment Trust Ltd., since 1979; Director, Cambrian & General Securities PLC, since 1982; Chairman, Jove Investment Trust PLC, since 1983; Director, Martin Currie Pacific Trust PLC, since 1985; b. 14.2.40, Edinburgh; m.; 2 s.; 1 d. Educ. Eton; University College, London. Recreation: shooting. Address: (h.) Glenbrook House, Balerno, Midlothian; T.-031-449 4116.

Thomson, Rev. Gilbert Little, BA, DipEd. Minister, Stranraer Old Parish Church, since 1985; b. 20.6.35, Airdrie; m., Kathleen M.D. Booth; 3 d. Educ. Airdrie Academy; Aberdeen University; Congregational College; Open University; Alnwick College of Education. Engineer, Lamberton & Co., Coatbridge, 1950-56 and 1958-60; National Service, RE, 1956-58; Minister, Eyemouth Congregational Church, 1965-68; Teacher, Trinity Comprehensive School, Carlisle, 1970-71; Minister, East Kilbride Congregational Church, 1971-75; Teacher, Dalziel High School and Blantyre High School, 1975-76; Minister, Chalmers Church, Wishaw, 1976-85. Recreations: golf; painting; running (marathons); reading. Address: Linden House, Leswalt High Road, Stranraer.

Thomson, Iain Marshall, FIA (Scot). Joint Managing Director, Macdonald, Fraser and Co. Ltd., since 1976; Director, Perth City Auctions, since 1983; b. 28.9.38, Stirling; 2 d. Educ. Lanark Grammar School; George Watson's College, Edinburgh. Joined Macdonald, Fraser & Co. Ltd., 1955; became Auctioneer, 1958; appointed Director, 1970. Council Member, Institute of Auctioneers and Appraisers in Scotland, since 1972; Member, Board, Royal Highland and Agricultural Society of Scotland, since 1981; appointed by Secretary of State for Scotland to Panel of Arbiters, 1983; Past Chairman, Perth and District Junior Agricultural Club. Recreations: golf; fishing. Address: (b.) 17 Caledonian Road, Perth, PH1 5QY; T.-0738 26183.

Thomson, James, BA, FRICS, FRVA. Lands Valuation Assessor and Electoral Registration Officer, Fife Regional Council, since 1973; b. 12.2.31, Glasgow. Chartered Valuation Surveyor, Glasgow Corporation, until 1957; Fife County Council: Chartered Valuation Surveyor, 1957-68, Depute County Assessor and ERO, 1968-73; County Assessor and ERO, 1973-75. Secretary, Scottish Assessors' Association, 1977-82 (Vice-President, since 1984). Address: (b.) Fife House (03), North Street, Glenrothes, Fife, KY7 5LT; T.-0592 757371.

Thomson, James Henry, MA (Hons). HM Chief Inspector of Schools (Basic Education and Special Educational Needs), since 1982; b. 19.4.26, Airdrie; m., Marjorie Gordon Orr; 2 s.; 1 d. Educ. Airdrie Academy; Glasgow University. Teacher of History, Hamilton Academy, 1952; Principal Teacher of History, Airdrie Academy, 1954; HM Inspector of Schools, Aberdeen, 1961; HM District Inspector of Schools, Dundee and Angus, 1966; HM Inspector of Schools, Adviser/Consultant on Building and Curriculum, 1969; HM Chief Inspector of Schools (Primary Education), 1972, (Special Services), 1975. Recreations: golf; walking; music. Address: (b.) SED, Room 4/110 New St. Andrews House, Edinburgh.

Thomson, John, JP, FEIS. Member, Argyll and Bute District Council, since 1975; b. 20.5.10, Bellshill, Lanarkshire; m., Adrienne Sherburn Scott; 1 s.; 1 d. Educ. Bellshill Academy; Jordanhill Training College. Teacher, Lochgilphead School, 1940-43; Royal Observer Corps, 1943-45; served as Staff Officer, HQ and Group Commandant, 281 Group; resumed teaching career, Dunoon Grammar School, 1945; retired as Principal Teacher of Technical Subjects, 1975; 29 years as Headmaster, Dunoon Grammar School FE Centre evening classes; Member, Dunoon Town Council, 1952-58 and 1964-75; last Provost of Dunoon; played cricket for Nairn County and Drumpellier; former Member, Executive Committee, Cowal Highland Gathering. Recreations: watching cricket and rugby; travelling abroad. Address: (h.) Mira Mar, 45 King Street, Dunoon, Argyll, PA23 7PF; T.-0369 3004.

Thomson, John, QFSM, FIFireE. Firemaster, Fife Regional Council, since 1983; b. 2.4.29, Airdrie; m., Janet; 1 s.; 2 d. Educ. Airdrie Academy. Divisional Officer: Grade III, 1968,

Grade II, 1974, Grade I, 1975; Acting Senior Divisional Officer, 1976; Deputy/Assistant Firemaster, 1979. Recreation: golf. Address: (b.) Fire and Rescue Service HQ, Strathore Road, Thornton, Kirkcaldy, KY1 4DF; T.-Glenrothes 774451.

Thomson, John Aidan Francis, MA, DPhil, FRHistS. Reader in Mediaeval History, Glasgow University, since 1983; b. 26.7.34, Edinburgh; m., Katherine J.V. Bell; 1 s.; 1 d. Educ. George Watson's Boys' College, Edinburgh; Edinburgh University; Balliol College, Oxford. Glasgow University: Assistant in Mediaeval History, 1960, Lecturer, 1961, Senior Lecturer, 1974. President, Glasgow Archaeological Society, 1978-81. Publications: The Later Lollards 1414-1520, 1965; Popes and Princes 1417-1517, 1980; The Transformation of Mediaeval England 1370-1529, 1983. Recreations: hill-walking; gardening. Address: (b.) Department of Medieval History, Glasgow University, Glasgow, G12 8QQ; T.-041-339 8855.

Thomson, Rev. John Bruce, MA, BD. Minister, Scone Old Parish Church, since 1983; also Minister, St. David's, Stormontfield, since 1983; Keeper, Benefice Register, Perth Presbytery, since 1984; b. 14.7.44, Edinburgh; m., Margaret Anne Craigen; 1 s.; 1 d. Educ. James Gillespie's Boys' School; George Heriot's School, Edinburgh; Edinburgh University; New College, Edinburgh. Ordained Assistant, Dundee Parish Church (St. Mary's), 1971-74; Minister, Thurso West Church, 1974-83; Moderator, Caithness Presbytery, 1979-80. Contributor, BBC Radio Orkney, Reflections (Grampian TV), Scotspraise (BBC TV); Vice-Chairman, Tay Churches Radio Council, since 1984. Recreations: swimming; golf; Rotary Club of Perth St. John's. Address: The Manse, Burnside, Scone, Perth, PH2 6LP; T.-0738 52030.

Thomson, John C., DDS, LDS, HDD, FDS. Senior Lecturer, Department of Prosthodontics, Glasgow University, since 1968; Consultant, Greater Glasgow Health Board, since 1968; b. 4.2.22, Airdrie; m., Christine M. Rodger; 1 s.; 1 d. Educ. Airdrie Academy; Glasgow Dental Hospital and School. Dental Officer, RAF, 1943-48; General Dental Practitioner, 1948-50; Lecturer, Glasgow University, and Registrar/ Senior Registrar, West Regional Hospital Board, 1950-68. President, Glasgow Odontological Society, 1968; Chairman, Board of Governors, Langside College of Further Education, 1971-74; President, West of Scotland Branch, British Dental Association, 1977. Address: (h.) 10 Mosspark Road, Milngavie, Glasgow, G62 8NJ; T.-041-956 2591.

Thomson, John Coutts, DipArch, DipCD, ARIBA, MRTPI. Head, Department of Urban Design and Regional Planning, Edinburgh University, since 1984; b. 13.6.36, Falkirk; m., Katherine Haig Duncan; 2 s.; 1 d. Educ. Buckie High School; George Heriot's School; Scott Sutherland School of Architecture; Edinburgh University. Architectural Assistant: Boswell Mitchell and Johnson, Glasgow, Cumbernauld Development Corporation; Research Associate, Department of Architecture, Edinburgh University; Visiting Professor, Columbia University;

Research Director, CERTI, Edinburgh University. Broadcaster, Radio Forth; prize-winner, Mound Competition, Edinburgh. Recreations: photography; playing the flute. Address: (b.) Department of Urban Design and Regional Planning, 20 Chambers Street, Edinburgh, EH1 1JZ; T.-031-667 1011.

Thomson, John Robson, BSc. Consultant in Seed Technology, Edinburgh University, since 1984; b. 19.1.10, Kinghorn, Fife; m., Catherine Sheelagh Gallagher; 2 s. Educ. Dalmellington School; Edinburgh University. Assistant Lecturer in Agricultural Botany, Reading University, 1933-38; Khartoum School of Agriculture (latterly as Dean), 1938-46; Senior Inspector of Agriculture, Sudan Government, 1946-50; Scottish Agricultural Scientific Services (latterly as Director), 1950-75; Course Director in Seed Technology, Edinburgh University, 1975-84. President, International Seed Testing Association, 1968-71; Editor, Advances in Research and Technology of Seeds, 1976-84. Publication: An Introduction to Seed Technology, 1979. Address: (h.) 8 Lynedoch Place, Edinburgh, EH3 7PX; T.-031-225 7254.

Thomson, Professor Joseph McGeachy, LLB. Professor of Law, Strathclyde University, since 1984; Deputy General Editor, Stair Memorial Encyclopaedia of the Laws of Scotland, since 1985; b. 6.5.48, Campbeltown. Educ. Keil School, Dumbarton; Edinburgh University. Lecturer in Law, Birmingham University, 1970-74; Lecturer in Laws, King's College, London, 1974-84. Recreations: opera; ballet; food and wine. Address: (h.) 140 Hyndland Road, Glasgow; T.-041-334 6682.

Thomson, Margaret Wallace, RGN, RSCN, SCM, RNT. Chief Executive Officer, National Board for Nurses, Midwives and Health Visitors for Scotland, since 1981; b. 8.6.27, Edinburgh. Educ. Mary Erksine School for Girls; Edinburgh University. Registrar, General Nursing Council for Scotland; Education Officer, General Nursing Council for Scotland; Principal Tutor/Tutor, Belfast, Aberdeen, Nigeria, Edinburgh; Ward Sister/Staff Nurse, Edinburgh. Elder, Church of Scotland. Address: (h.) 28 Blinkbonny Gardens, Edinburgh; T.-031-332 3628.

Thomson, Margery Jean, JP. Non-Executive Member, South of Scotland Electricity Board, since 1980; b. 24.2.27, Bearsden; m., John Alexander Thomson; 2 s.; 2 d. Educ. Beacon School, Bridge of Allan; Glasgow College of Domestic Science. Past Chairman, Dumfriesshire Conservative Association; former Vice-Chairman, South of Scotland Euro Constituency; Centre Organiser, Annan Red Cross. Recreation: curling. Address: (h.) Summerhill House, Annan, Dumfriesshire.

Thomson, Sheriff Nigel Ernest Drummond, MA, LLB. Sheriff of Lothian and Borders, at Edinburgh, since 1976, and at Peebles, since 1983; b. 19.6.26, Aberdeen; m., Snjolaug Magnusson; 1 s.; 1 d. Educ. George Watson's Boys' College; St. Andrews University; Edinburgh University. Called to Scottish Bar, 1953; appointed Sheriff at

Hamilton, 1966; Member, Scottish Arts Council, 1978 (Chairman, Music Committee, 1979-84). Honorary President, Strathaven Arts Guild; Honorary Vice-President, Tenovus-Scotland; Honorary Vice-President, Scottish Association for Counselling. Recreations: music; woodwork; golf. Address: (h.) 50 Grange Road, Edinburgh; T.-031-667 2166.

Thomson, Rev. Peter David, MA, BD. Minister, Comrie and Strowan with Dundurn, since 1978; b. 4.11.41, St. Andrews; m., Margaret Celia Murray; 1 s.; 1 d. Educ. Dundee High School; Edinburgh University; Glasgow University; Tubingen University. Minister, Balmaclellan with Kells, 1968-78; Moderator, Kirkcudbright Presbytery, 1974-75; Convener, Nomination Committee, General Assembly, 1982-85. Chairman, New Galloway and Kells Community Council, 1976-78. Recreations: haphazardly pursued interests in photography, wildlife, music, theology, current affairs. Address: The Manse, Comrie, Perthshire, Ph6 2HE; T.-0764 70269.

Thomson, Rev. Peter George, MA, BD (Hons). Minister, Fullarton Parish Church, Irvine, since 1953; b. 18.5.20, Campsie Glen; m., Pamela I.M. Thorne; 3 s.; 1 d. Educ. Dunbar Grammar School; Edinburgh University and New College. Warden, New College Settlement, Pleasance, Edinburgh; Chaplain with YMCA, Germany; ordained and inducted, St. David's Church, Buckhaven, 1947; Moderator, Irvine and Kilmarnock Presbytery, 1966-67; Moderator, Synod of Ayr; Convener, National Church Extension, Church of Scotland, since 1983. Honorary Chaplain, British Sailors' Society; Honorary Burgess, Royal Burgh of Irvine, 1967. Recreations: gardening; golf. Address: Fullarton Parish Manse, Irvine, Ayrshire; T.-Irvine 79909.

Thomson, Robert Scott, BSc, CChem, MRCS. Rector, Larkhall Academy, since 1974; b. 9.6.33, Newtongrange; m., Helen Mary McIntosh; 1 d. Educ. Newbattle Secondary School; Dalkeith High School; Heriot-Watt University. Scientific Technical Officer, NCB, 1950-59; Chemistry Teacher, George Watson's College, 1963-67; Principal Teacher of Chemistry: Dalkeith High School, 1967-70, George Watson's College, 1970-74. Member, Consultative Committee on the Curriculum; Member, Committee on Secondary Education; Chairman, Committee on Technology; Chairman, Scottish Education Industry Committee. Recreations: reading; gardening; bowling. Address: (b.) Larkhall Academy, Cherryhill, Larkhall, ML9 1QN; T.-Larkhall 881570.

Thomson, Roy Hendry, CStJ, MA (Hons). Chairman, The Scottish Ballet Ltd., since 1983; Leader, Liberal Group, City of Aberdeen District Council, since 1974; Chairman/Director, family motor business, since 1960; b. 27.8.32, Aberdeen; m., Nancy; 3 d. Educ. Aberdeen Grammar School; Aberdeen University. National Service, Gordon Highlanders, 1955-57; personnel and market research, Rowntree & Co. Ltd., 1957-60; Member, General Advisory Council, BBC (former Vice Chairman, Broadcasting Council for Scotland); Member, Priory

Council, Priory of Scotland, Order of St. John; Past President, Rotary Club of Aberdeen; Past President, Mountain Rescue Association, Aberdeen. Recreations: skiing; hill-walking; bee-keeping. Address: (h.) Baillieswells House, Baillieswells Road, Bieldside, Aberdeen, AB1 9BQ; T.-Aberdeen 867960.

Thomson, Rev. Thomas, MA. Minister, Wardie Parish Church, Edinburgh, since 1961; b. 16.3.20, Edinburgh; m., Mary Euphemia McTavish; 1 s. Educ. George Heriot's School, Edinburgh; Edinburgh University; New College, Edinburgh. War Service, 1940-46 (Captain, Gordon Highlanders); Assistant Minister, North Morningside Church, Edinburgh, 1952-54; Minister, Christ's Church, Dunollie, Oban, 1954-61. Governor, George Heriot's Trust, since 1979; Convener, Department of Home Mission, 1980-83; Joint Convener, Department of Ministry and Mission, 1983-84; Moderator, Edinburgh Presbytery, 1982. Recreation: music. Address: Wardie Parish Church Manse, 35 Lomond Road, Edinburgh, EH5 3JN; T.-031-552 3328.

Thomson, Walter, MBE. Editor, Selkirk Advertiser, since 1932; Rugby Writer, Sunday Post, since 1931; b. 20.3.13, Selkirk; m., Gerda; 2 d. Educ. Selkirk High School; Heriot-Watt. Army (Captain), 1940-46. Recreation: photography. Address: (h.) Cruachan, Murrayfield, Selkirk; T.-Selkirk 20261.

Thomson, William Andrew Charles. Director, Ben Line Steamers Ltd., since 1978; Chairman, Forth Ports Authority, since 1984; b. 20.1.48, Edinburgh; m., Cecilia Bernadette Gill; 2 s.; 1 d. Educ. Gordonstoun. Short Service commission, 17/21st Lancers. Chairman, River Tweed Commissioners. Recreations: shooting; fishing; golf. Address: (b.) 33 St. Mary's Street, Edinburgh; T.-031-557 2323.

Thomson, William P.L., MA. Rector, Kirkwall Grammar School, since 1971; b. 9.5.33, Newmilns. Educ. Dundee High School; St. Andrews University. Principal Teacher of History and Geography, then Deputy Headteacher, Anderson High School, Lerwick. Publications: The Little General and the Rousay Crofters; Kelp-Making in Orkney. Address: (b.) Kirkwall Grammar School, Kirkwall, Orkney; T.-0856 2102.

Thores, Orison Alistair, MB, ChB, DObst, DCH, DPH, FRCP, FFCM. Senior Medical Officer, Scottish Home and Health Department, since 1983; b. 2.1.37, Peterhead; m., Barbara Sinclair McLean; 1 s.; 1 d. Educ. Peterhead Academy; Aberdeen University. Junior hospital posts and general practice, NHS Scotland; Flight-Surgeon, Royal Canadian Air Force; Research Fellow, University of British Columbia; Director, Coast and Skeena Health Areas, Government of British Columbia; Senior Medical Consultant and PR Programme Advisor, Ministry of Health, Government of Ontario; Community Medicine Specialist, Fife Health Board. Recreations: sailing; photography; radio. Address: (b.) St. Andrews House, Edinburgh; T.-031-556 8501.

Thorne, Professor James Peter, MA, BLitt (Oxon). Forbes Professor of English Language, Edinburgh University, since 1979; b. 29.1.33, Penarth; m., Edith Mary Forbes; 2 s. Educ. Penarth Grammar School; Jesus College, Oxford. Assistant Lecturer in English Language, Edinburgh University, 1959-61; Assistant Director, USAF Mechanical Analysis of Language Project, Indiana University, 1961-62; Lecturer in English Language, Edinburgh University, 1962-70; Visiting Associate Professor, California University, Berkeley, 1967; Reader in English Language, Edinburgh University, 1970-79; Visiting Professor, Nouvelle Sorbonne, Paris University, 1978-79. Recreations: squash; looking at paintings. Address: (b.) Department of English Language, Edinburgh University, David Hume Tower, George Square, Edinburgh, EH8 9JX; T.-031-667 1011, Ext. 1011.

Thornton, David Dillon, BSc, MSc, DipAg, MS. Senior Principal Scientific Officer, Scientific Adviser's Unit, Department of Agriculture and Fisheries for Scotland, since 1978; b. 16.7.30, Kenton, Wealdstone; m., Mary Edith Thomas; 2 s.; 1 d. Educ. Dulwich College; London University; Reading University; California University. Pasture Agronomist, Department of Veterinary Services, Uganda, 1955-65; Chief Research Officer, Animal Health Research Centre, Uganda, 1965-67; Senior Nutritionist, Department of Veterinary Services, Uganda, 1967-69; FAO Agricultural Officer, Tanzania, 1969-72; FAO Agricultural Officer/Acting Project Manager, Somalia, 1972-73; Development Officer, Scottish Agricultural Development Council, 1974-77; East of Scotland College of Agriculture, seconded to DAFS, Edinburgh, 1977-78. Recreations: archaeology and history; railway modelling; walking. Address: (h.) Flowerfield, Fountain Place, Loanhead, Midlothian, EH20 9DU; T.-031-440 0487.

Thornton-Kemsley, Nigel Scott, OStJ, DL. Managing Director, Thornton Farms Ltd., since 1956; Chairman, North of Scotland College of Agriculture, since 1982; Director, Royal Highland and Agricultural Society of Scotland, since 1971; b. 14.8.33, Chigwell, Essex; m., Judith Gay Sanders; 1 s.; 2 d. Educ. Fettes College; East of Scotland College of Agriculture. National Service: Royal Signals, 1954-56, TA 51st Highland Signal Regiment, 1957-63, 3rd Bn., Gordon Highlanders, 1963-71, OC TAVR Company; Major on retiral; Deputy Lieutenant, Kincardineshire, 1978; President, Aberdeen-Angus Cattle Society, 1981-82; Member, Scottish American Community Relations Council, 1971-80; Chairman, Council, Scottish Agricultural Colleges, 1982-84; Life Governor, Imperial Cancer Research Council, since 1978; Past President, Royal Northern Agricultural Society; Past President, Fettercairn Farmers' Club. Recreation: shooting. Address: Thornton Castle, Laurencekirk, Kincardineshire; T.-056 17 301.

Thorpe, John Elton, BA, PhD. Senior Principal Scientific Officer, Freshwater Fisheries Laboratory, Pitlochry, since 1981; b. 24.1.35, Wolverhampton; m., Judith Anne Johnson; 2 s. Educ. Kingswood School, Bath; Jesus College,

Cambridge. Cambridge Expedition to British Honduras, 1959-60 (Leader); Shell International Chemical Co. Ltd., London, 1960-62; joined DAFS Freshwater Fisheries Laboratory, Pitlochry, 1963. Council Member, Fisheries Society of British Isles, 1974-77, 1978-81, since 1985; Editorial Board, Fisheries Management, 1978-84 and Aquaculture and Fisheries Management, since 1985; Chairman, Killiecrankie and Fincastle Community Council, 1976-78. Publications: four books; 70 scientific papers. Recreations: travelling; Baroque music. Address: (b.) Freshwater Fisheries Laboratory, Pitlochry, Perthshire, PH16 5LW; T.-0796 2060.

Thrower, James Arthur, MA (Dunelm), BLitt (Oxon), PhD. Senior Lecturer in History of Religions, Aberdeen University, since 1970 (Acting Head, Department of Religious Studies, since 1984); b. 5.10.36, Guisborough; m., Judith Elizabeth Gauss; 3 d. Educ. Guisborough Grammar School; Durham University; St. Edmund Hall, Oxford University. Staff Tutor, Eastern District, WEA, 1962-64; Lecturer in Philosophy of Religion, Ghana University, 1964-68; Lecturer in Religious Studies, Bede College, Durham University, 1968-70; Visiting Professor: Helsinki University, 1974, Polish Academy of Sciences, 1976; British Council Exchange Scholar, Leningrad University, 1976 and 1978; Visiting Scholar, Gdansk University, 1981 and 1982; Warden, Balgownie Lodge, Aberdeen University, 1971-82. Publications: A Short History of Western Atheism, 1971; The Alternative Tradition, 1981; Marxist-Leninist "Scientific Atheism", 1983. Recreations: listening to music; photography; travelling; horses. Address: (h.) 233 Clifton Road, Aberdeen; T.-Aberdeen 45641.

Thurso, Viscount, (Robin Macdonald Sinclair), 2nd Viscount, Bt, JP. Lord Lieutenant of Caithness, since 1973; Baron of Thurso; Chairman, Sinclair Family Trust Ltd; Chairman, Lochdhu Hotels Ltd.; Chairman, Thurso Fisheries Ltd.; Chairman, Stephens (Plastics) Ltd.; b. 24.12.22, Kingston Vale; m., Margaret Beaumont Brokensha; 2 s.; 1 d. Educ. Eton; New College, Oxford; Edinburgh University. RAF, 1941-46; Flt.-Lt., 684 Squadron, 540 Squadron; commanded Edinburgh University Air Squadron, 1946; Member, Caithness County Council, 1949, 1952, 1955, 1958; Member, Thurso Town Council, 1957, 1960 (resigned, 1961), 1965, 1968, 1971; President, North Country Cheviot Sheep Society, 1951-54; Chairman, Caithness and Sutherland Youth Employment Committee, 1957-75; Member, Red Deer Commission, 1965-74; President, Highland Society of London, 1980-82; Council Member, Royal National Mission to Deep Sea Fishermen, 1983-85; President, Boys' Brigade, 1985; Vice Lieutenant, Caithness, 1964-73. Recreations: fishing; shooting; amateur drama. Address: Thurso East Mains, Thurso, Caithness, KW14 8HW; T.-0847 62600.

Tilmouth, Professor Michael, MA, PhD. Tovey Professor of Music, Edinburgh University, since 1971; Chairman, The Purcell Society, since 1983; General Editor, Musica Britannica, since 1983; b. 30.11.30, Grimsby; m., Mary Jelliman; 2 s.; 1 d. Educ. Wintringham Grammar School, Grimsby; Christ's College, Cambridge. Lecturer, Glasgow

University, 1959-71. Council Member, Royal Musical Association, 1970-76; Editor, Research Chronicle, 1968-77; Editor, Purcell Society, Volumes 5, 7, 31; Editor, Musica Britannica, Volumes 31, 32, 51; Member, Management Committee, St. Mary's Music School, Edinburgh, since 1975 (Chairman, 1977-80); Council Member, St. George's School for Girls, Edinburgh, since 1981; Director, Scottish Opera, since 1975; Governor, Royal Scottish Academy of Music and Drama, since 1980. Recreations: gardening; reading; eating and drinking. Address: (h.) 62 Northumberland Street, Edinburgh, EH3 6JE; T.-031-556 3293.

Timbury, Professor Morag Crichton, MD, PhD, FRCPath, FRCPGlas, FRSE. Professor in Bacteriology, Glasgow University, since 1978; b. 29.9.30, Bearsden; m., Gerald C. Timbury; 1 d. Educ. St. Bride's School, Helensburgh; Glasgow University. Trained in medical bacteriology; Maurice Bloch Research Fellow in Virology; Senior Lecturer, then Reader in Virology, Glasgow University, 1966-78. Publications: Notes on Medical Virology; Notes on Medical Bacteriology (Co-author). Recreations: reading; mediaeval fortified houses. Address: (b.) Department of Bacteriology, Glasgow Royal Infirmary, Glasgow, G4 OSF; T.-041-552 3535, Ext. 5270.

Timms, Professor Duncan William Graham, BA, PhD (Cantab). Professor, Stirling University, since 1972; b. 11.10.38, Cheltenham; m., Elizabeth Anne Barnes; 1 s.; 1 d. Educ. Pate's Grammar School, Cheltenham; St. Catharine's College, Cambridge. Lecturer, Senior Lecturer, Queensland University, 1962-67; Professor, Auckland University, 1968-72; Deputy Principal, Stirling University, 1978-80 and 1981-84 (Acting Principal and Vice-Chancellor, 1980-81); Visiting Professor, Stockholm University, 1984-85; Chairman, MacRobert Arts Centre. Recreations: map collecting; philately of the South Pacific. Address: (h.) 23 Claremont, Alloa, FK10 2DF; T.-0259 214092.

Tinsley, Emeritus Professor Joseph, BSc, PhD, FRSE, FRSC, CChem. Emeritus Professor of Soil Science, Aberdeen University, since 1981; Chairman, DAFS Residual Manurial Values Committee, since 1976; President, Aberdeen YMCA, since 1984; b. 24.7.16, Wootton Bassett; m., Mary Joan Swain; 4 d. Educ. Reading University. Assistant Agricultural Advisory Chemist, MAFF, SE Counties of England, 1938-43; Lecturer in Agricultural Chemistry, Reading University, 1943-58; Reader in Soil Science and Head of Department, Aberdeen University, 1958-71; first Professor of Soil Science, Aberdeen University, 1971-81. President, British Society of Soil Science, 1970-72. Recreations: exploring landscapes in the UK and overseas; support for Christian organisations and aid to third world countries; photography, mainly to illustrate lectures on scientific and travel topics; family interests. Address: (h.) 52 Victoria Street, Aberdeen, AB1 1XA; T.-0224 646552.

Titterington, Professor (Donald) Michael, BSc, PhD, DipMathStat. Titular Professor of Statistics, Glasgow University, since 1982; b. 20.11.45,

Marple, Cheshire; m., Mary Hourie Philp. Educ. High School of Stirling; Edinburgh University; Cambridge University. Lecturer, then Senior Lecturer, Department of Statistics, Glasgow University, 1972-82; visiting appointments: Princeton University, 1978, State University of New York, 1980, Wisconsin University, 1982, Australian National University, 1982; Associate Editor, Biometrika and Annals of Statistics. Recreations: sailing; hill-walking. Address: (b.) Department of Statistics, Glasgow University, Glasgow, G12 8QQ; T.-041-339 8855.

Titterington, Eric Johnston, BA (Hons), DipSocW. Convenor of Housing, North East Fife District Council, since 1984 (Member, since 1980); Social Worker, Tayside Regional Council, since 1976; b. 2.10.53, Inverness; m., Shirley Ruth Marshall. Educ. Bell Baxter High School, Cupar; Stirling University; Dundee College of Education. Founder Member and first Chairman, East Fife Young Liberals. Recreations: bowls; squash; gardening; hill-walking. Address: (h.) An Treas, Mid Bank Street, Strathmiglo, Fife.

Tivy, Professor Joy, BA, BSc, PhD, FRSE, FRSGS. Professor (Titular), Department of Geography, Glasgow University, since 1976; Chairman, Scottish Field Studies Association, since 1984; b. 24.8.24, Glasgow. Educ. Masonic Girls School and Alexandra College, Dublin; Trinity College, Dublin University; Edinburgh University. Assistant Mistress, Leeds Girls High School; Research Assistant, Department of Planning, Wakefield; Assistant Lecturer and Lecturer, Department of Geography, Edinburgh University; Lecturer, Senior Lecturer, Reader, Department of Geography, Glasgow University; Visiting Research Fellow, Universite de Strasbourg, 1956, Syracuse University, 1963-64, Cornell University, 1971, Lund University, Arhus University, and Australian National University, 1981-83; Editor, Scottish Geographical Magazine, 1955-65; Secretary and Editor, Scottish Field Studies Association, 1960-75; Member, Scottish Advisory Committee to the Nature Conservancy (Scotland), 1974-80. Publications: The Organic Resources of Scotland - their Nature and Evaluation, 1973; Human Impact on the Ecosystem, 1981; Biogeography: The Role of Plants in the Ecosphere, 1982. Recreations: painting; gardening; tapestry. Address: (h.) 51 Hyndland Road, Glasgow; T.-041-339 3801.

Tocher, Gordon James MacLaren, BMus (Hons). Composer and Piano Teacher; b. 30.12.57, Inverness. Educ. Inverness Royal Academy; Aberdeen University. Taught at several schools in Inverness, 1981-84; freelance, since 1984; Conductor, The Inverness Singers; Honorary Assistant Organist, Inverness Cathedral; compositions include piano, chamber and choral works, also choral arrangements of Scottish and other folk songs. Address: (h.) 54 Glenburn Drive, Inverness, IV2 4NE; T.-0463 232345.

Tod, Stewart, DiplArch, FSA Scot. Senior Partner, David Carr Architects, Edinburgh, since 1977 (Stewart Tod & Sons, Kirkcaldy, since 1966); b. 30.4.27, West Wemyss; m., A.

Vivienne J. Nixon; 2 s.; 2 d. Educ. Buckhaven High School; Edinburgh College of Art. RAF, 1945-49; Stratton Davis & Yates, 1952-55; Falkirk District Council, 1955-57; Carr and Matthew, 1957-60; David Carr Architects, 1960-77. Committee Member, Association for the Preservation of Rural Scotland; General Trustee, Church of Scotland; Member, Church of Scotland Board of Practice and Procedure. Recreation: beekeeping. Address: (h.) 12 Greenhill Terrace, Edinburgh; T.-031-447 4625.

Todd, Rev. Andrew Stewart, MA, BD, DD. Minister, St. Machar's Cathedral, Old Aberdeen, since 1967; b. 26.5.26, Alloa; m., Janet Agnes Brown Smith; 2 s.; 2 d. Educ. High School of Stirling; Edinburgh University; Basel University. Assistant Minister, St. Cuthbert's, Edinburgh, 1951-52; Minister: Symington, Lanarkshire, 1952; North Leith, 1960; Member, Church Hymnary Revision Comittee, 1963-73; Convener, General Assembly's Committee on Public Worship and Aids to Devotion, 1974-78; Moderator, Aberdeen Presbytery, 1980-81; Member, Church Hymnary Trust; awarded Honorary Doctorate, Aberdeen University, 1982; translator of three theological books from German into English; Honorary President, Church Service Society; President-Elect, Scottish Church Society. Recreations: music; gardening. Address: 18 The Chanonry, Old Aberdeen, Aberdeen; T.-0224 43688.

Tolley, David Anthony, MB, BS (Lond), FRCS, FRCSEdin. Consultant Urological Surgeon, Edinburgh Royal Infirmary, since 1980; Honorary Senior Lecturer, Department of Surgery/Urology, Edinburgh University, since 1980; b. 29.11.47, Warrington; m., Judith Anne Finn; 3 s.; 1 d. Educ. Manchester Grammar School; Kings College Hospital Medical School, London University. House Surgeon and Physician, Kings College Hospital; Lecturer in Human Morphology, Southampton University; Lecturer in Anatomy and Fulbright Fellow, University of Texas at Houston; Surgical Registrar, Hammersmith and Ealing Hospitals, London; Senior Surgical Registrar (Urology), Kings College Hospital, London; Senior Urological Registrar, Yorkshire Regional Training Scheme. Member, MRC Working Party on Urological Cancer; Chairman, Scottish Urological Oncology Group. Recreations: opera; cross-country; skiing; motor racing. Address: (b.) Murrayfield Hospital, Corstorphine Road, Edinburgh; T.-031-334 0363.

Tong, Peter Stanley, BSc (Agr), NDAgrE. Chairman and Managing Director, Aberdeen Tractors Ltd., Buncksburn, since 1970; (Liberal) Member, Grampian Regional Council, since 1982; b. 23.11.32, Spain; m., Robertina Ritchie; 2 s.; 1 d. Educ. Wrekin College; Wye College, Kent (London University); Harper Adams College. 2nd Lt., Royal Artillery, Cyprus and Germany, 1955-57; worked in industry, England, Scotland and Africa. President (Scottish Region), British Agricultural and Garden Machinery Association, 1980-81; Director, Royal Highland and Agricultural Society of Scotland, 1981-82-83. Recreations: DIY; gardening; curling. Address: Fairley House, Kingswells, Aberdeen, AB1 8SB; T.-0224 740641.

Toothill, Sir John (Norman), Kt (1964), CBE (1955), FRSE. Company Director; b. 11.11.08; m. Educ. Beaminster Grammar School. Retired as Director, Ferranti Ltd., Edinburgh, 1975; author of Toothill Report on the Scottish Economy, 1961; Hon. LLD, Aberdeen, 1966; Hon. DSc, Heriot-Watt, 1968.

Torbet, Thomas Edgar, MB, ChB, FRCSEdin, FRCOG. Consultant Obstetrician and Gynaecologist, since 1967; Honorary Clinical Lecturer, Glasgow University, since 1967; b. 15.3.30, Bearsden; m., Helen Fiona; 1 s. Educ. Morrison's Academy, Crieff; Glasgow University. JP, East Kilbride. Recreations: sailing; skiing. Address: (h.) 10 Easter Road, Busby, Clarkston, Glasgow; T.-041-644 1099.

Torrance, Rev. Iain Richard, MA, BD, DPhil. Minister, Northmavine, Shetland, since 1982; b. 13.1.49, Aberdeen; m., Morag Ann MacHugh; 1 s.; 1 d. Educ. Edinburgh Academy; Monkton Combe School, Bath; Edinburgh University; St. Andrews University; Oriel College, Oxford University. Member, various Church committees; involved in prison visiting and teaching, Edinburgh, 1978-80; Convener, Church of Scotland Committee on the Moonie Cult, 1978-80; Chaplain (TA) to 2/51 Highland, since 1982; Joint Editor, Scottish Journal of Theology, since 1982; author of articles, reviews and translations in various journals. Recreations: walking; travel. Address: Northmavine Manse, Hillswick, Shetland, ZE2 9RW; T.-Hillswick 223.

Torrance, Rev. Professor James Bruce, MA (Hons), BD. Professor of Systematic Theology, Aberdeen University and Christ's College, since 1977 (Dean, Faculty of Divinity, 1978-81); Minister, Church of Scotland, since 1950; b. 3.2.23, Chengtu, Szechwan, West China; m., Mary Heather Aitken; 1 s.; 2 d. Educ. Royal High School, Edinburgh; Edinburgh University and New College; Marburg University; Basle University; Oxford University. RAF, 1943-45; ordained, Invergowrie, Dundee, 1954; Lecturer in Divinity and Dogmatics in History of Christian Thought, 1961, and Senior Lecturer in Christian Dogmatics, 1972, New College, Edinburgh; Visiting Professor of New Testament, Union Theological Seminary, 1960, of Theology, Columbia Theological Seminary, 1965, and Vancouver School of Theology, 1974-75. Convenor, Panel on Doctrine, General Assembly, 1982-86; Convenor, British Council of Churches Commission on Doctrine of Trinity, since 1983; Theological Adviser, World Alliance of Reformed Churches. Recreations: bee-keeping; fishing; swimming; gardening. Address: (h.) Don House, 46 Don Street, Old Aberdeen, Aberdeen, AB2 1UU; T.-0224 41526.

Torrance, Very Rev. Thomas Forsyth, MBE, MA, BD, DrTheol, DLitt, DD, DrTeol, DTheol, DSc, FBA, FRSE. Emeritus Professor, Edinburgh University, since 1979; b. 30.8.13, Chengdu, Sichuan, China; m., Margaret Edith Spear; 2 s.; 1 d. Educ. Canadian School, Chengdu, China; Bellshill Academy, Lanarkshire; Edinburgh University; Basel University; Oriel College, Oxford. Minister: Alyth Barony

Parish Church, 1940-47; served as Church of Scotland Chaplain, 1943-45; Minister, Beechgrove Parish Church, Aberdeen, 1947-50; Edinburgh University: Professor of Church History, 1950-52, Professor of Christian Dogmatics, 1952-79; Moderator, General Assembly of the Church of Scotland, 1976-77. Cross of St. Mark, First Class, 1970; Protoprebyter of Greek Orthodox Church (Hon.), 1973; President, Academie Internationale des Sciences Religieuses, 1972-81. Recreations: formerly golf, squash, fishing; now walking. Address: (h.) 37 Braid Farm Road, Edinburgh, EH10 6LE; T.-031-447 3050.

Torrance, Professor Victor Brownlie, BSc, MSc, PhD, FCIOB, FBIM, FRSA. William Watson Professor and Head, Department of Building, Heriot-Watt University, since 1972; b. 24.2.37, Shotts, Lanarkshire; m., Inez Marjorie Ann Jack; 1 s.; 2 d.; 1 step s.; 1 step d. Educ. Wishaw High School; Heriot-Watt College; Heriot-Watt University; Edinburgh University. Associate Professor and Head, Department of Building and Estate Management, Singapore University, 1966-72; Member, Civil Engineering and Transport Committee and Building Sub-Committee, Science Research Council, 1975-78; Member, Building Board, Council for National Academic Awards, 1976-80; Member, Building Standards Advisory Committee, Research Sub-Committee, since 1982; Member, Panel of Visitors, Building Research Establishment, since 1983; Chairman, RIAS Research Steering Committee; Vice-President, Chartered Institute of Building; Member, Technology Research Sub-Committee, Council for National Academic Awards; Past Chairman, Council of Professors of Building; Partner, Building and Design Consultants, Edinburgh, since 1976; Director, UNITECH, Edinburgh, since 1982. Recreations: music; building; committees; travel; family. Address: (h.) Kerry, 3 Craiginnan Gardens, Dollar, FK14 7JA; T.-02594 2240.

Torrance, William Nisbet, MB, ChB, DipSocMed. Community Medicine Specialist, Manpower Planning and Primary Care, Tayside Health Board, since 1983; b. 28.11.38, Stonehaven, Kincardineshire; m., Anne Helena Imrie; 1 s.; 1 d. Educ. Creighton School and Carlisle Grammar School; Queen's College, St. Andrews. Research Fellow, Community Medicine, 1969-71; Scottish Health Services Fellow in Community Medicine, 1971-74; Community Medicine Specialist, Commissioning then Medical Administrator, Ninewells Hospital/Medical School, 1974-83; Honorary Senior Lecturer, Dundee University, since 1974. Former Secretary and Vice-President, North Fife Rotary Club; Community Councillor; Church Elder. Recreations: epicurean gardening; travelling; people watching. Address: (h.) Spearshill, Tayport, Fife, DD6 9HT; T.-0382 552248.

Toth, Professor Akos George, Dr. Jur., PhD. Professor of Law, Strathclyde University, since 1984; b. 9.2.36, Mezotur, Hungary; m., Sarah Kurucz. Educ. Budapest University; Szeged University; Exeter University. Strathclyde University: Lecturer in Law, 1971-76, Senior Lecturer, 1976-82, Reader, 1982-84. Publication:

Legal Protection of Individuals in the European Communities, 1978. Recreations: travel; music; opera; theatre; swimming; walking. Address: (b.) Strathclyde University, Law School, 173 Cathedral Street, Glasgow, G4 ORQ; T.-041-552 4400.

Toulmin, David. Writer; b. 1.7.13, Rathen, Aberdeenshire; m., Margaret Jane Willox; 3 s. Educ. five public/parish schools. From the age of 14 to 65, earned living by manual labour (farm worker); his first article was published by Farmer and Stock Breeder, 1947; wrote short stories in dialect for local newspapers and the Scots Magazine; five stories broadcast on radio by the BBC; a collection was published as Hard Shining Corn, 1972; has published a further five books; awarded grant by the Scottish Arts Council, 1983; real name, John Reid. Recreations: writing; reading; popular music; cinema; video; television; antiquarian research. Address: (h.) 7 Pittodrie Place, Aberdeen; T.-Aberdeen 634058.

Towart, Rev. Wilfrid James, MA, BD. Minister, Priesthill Parish Church, Glasgow, since 1982; b. 1.3.17, Glasgow; m., Mary Anderson Robertson. Educ. High School of Glasgow; Glasgow University and Trinity College. Assistant Minister, Maxwell Parish Church, 1941-42; Assistant Leader, Church of Scotland Hut, Burrowhead, 1942-43; ordained, 1944; Chaplain to the Forces, 1st Bn., Royal Scots Fusiliers, 1944-47; Minister, Giffnock South Parish Church, Glasgow, 1949-82; Moderator, Glasgow Presbytery, 1983-84. Recreations: cats; reading; walking; listening to music. Address: 498 Clarkston Road, Muirend, Glasgow, G44 3QE; T.-041-637 1630.

Townend, Neil, BA, FCIT, MBIM. Director of Public Transport, Tayside Regional Council, since 1979; b. 27.11.40, Huddersfield; m., Christine; 1 s.; 1 d. Educ. Holme Valley Grammar School; University College of Wales, Aberystwyth. Joined transport industry, 1962; Lothian Region Transport: Traffic Manager, 1973-75, Assistant Director, 1975-77; Director of Operations, Greater Glasgow PTE, 1977-79. Council Member, CIT; Council and Executive Member, Bus and Coach Council. Recreations: family; gardening; music; model railways. Address: (b.) Barrack Street, Dundee; T.-0382 23281.

Trabichoff, Geoffrey Colin, AGSM, LGSM. Leader, BBC Scottish Symphony Orchestra, since 1982; b. 15.4.46, London; m., Judith Orbach; 1 step s.; 1 d. Leader, Gulbenkian Orchestra, Lisbon, 1974-76; Leader, Mannheim Chamber Orchestra, 1976-78; Leader, Hannover State Orchestra, 1978-81. Address: (h.) 40 Woodend Drive, Jordanhill, Glasgow, G13; T.-041-959 3496.

Trainer, Professor James, MA, PhD. Professor of German, Stirling University, since 1969 (Deputy Principal, 1973-78 and since 1982); b. 2.3.32; m., Barbara Herta Reinhard (deceased); 2 s.; 1 d. Educ. St. Andrews University; Free University of Berlin. Lecturer in German, St.

Andrews University, 1958-67; Visiting Professor, Yale University, 1964-65; Convener, SUCE Modern Languages Panel, since 1981; Member, Inter University and Polytechnic Council, since 1983; Member, Scottish Examination Board, 1975-82; Member, SED Postgraduate Awards Committee, since 1978; Member, UK/US Educational Commission, 1985. Recreations: music; cricket; translating. Address: (b.) Stirling University, Stirling; T.-0786 73171.

Tramschek, Anthony Brice, BSc, PhD, CEng, MIMechE, FInstR. Senior Lecturer in Mechanical Engineering, Strathclyde University, since 1981; b. 16.1.38, London; m., Alison Mary Cook; 2 d. Educ. Southend-on-Sea High School for Boys; Nottingham University. Technical Engineer, Rolls-Royce and Associates, Derby, 1963-67; Lecturer, Department of Thermodynamics and Fluid Mechanics, Strathclyde University, 1967-81. Chairman, Scottish Hockey Association, since 1984. Recreations: hockey umpiring; hockey administration; gardening. Address: (h.) 54 Viewpark Drive, Burnside, Rutherglen, Glasgow; T.-041-647 6782.

Tranter, Nigel, OBE, KCLJ, MA (Hon.). Author and Novelist, since 1935; b. 23.11.09, Glasgow; m., May Jean Campbell Grieve (deceased); 1 s. (deceased); 1 d. Educ. St. James' Episcopal School; George Heriot's, Edinburgh. Professional Writer, since 1946; published more than 100 books, including 70 novels; Vice-Convener, Scottish Covenant Association, 1951-55; President, East Lothian Liberal Association, 1960-70; Chairman, National Forth Road Bridge Committee, 1953-57; Chairman, St. Andrew Society of East Lothian, since 1966; President, Scottish PEN, 1962-66 (now Honorary President); Chairman, Society of Authors, Scotland, 1966-70; Chairman, National Book League, Scotland, 1971-73. Vice-Chancellor, Order of St. Lazarus of Jerusalem, since 1982; Honorary Freeman of Blackstone, Virginia, USA, 1980. Recreations: walking; climbing; genealogy; castle architecture. Address: (h.) Quarry House, Aberlady, East Lothian; T.-Aberlady 258.

Traynor, William. Member, Lanarkshire Health Board, since 1983; Member, Supplementary Appeals Tribunals, since 1982; Secretary, Motherwell and Wishaw District Trades Council, since 1982; Organiser, East Kilbride Unemployed Workers Centre; b. 9.7.25, Motherwell; m., Jessie; 2 d. Educ. Motherwell Central School. Former Councillor and Magistrate; former Member, Children's Panel; Past Chairman, Motherwell District Committee, RSSPCC; Member, Motherwell College Council. Recreations: community work; music; writing poetry. Address: (h.) 117 Milton Street, Motherwell, Lanarkshire; T.-Motherwell 63347.

Tremayne, Sydney Durward. Poet and Journalist; b. 15.3.12, Ayr; m., 1, Lily Harrison; 2 s.; 2, Constance Lipop. Educ. Ayr Academy. Principal journalistic appointments: Chief Sub-Editor, then Leader Writer, Daily Mirror, London; Leader Writer, Daily Herald, London. Publications: (poetry): Time and the Wind, 1948; The Hardest Freedom, 1951; The Rock and the Bird, 1955;

The Swans of Berwick, 1962; The Turning Sky, 1969; Selected and New Poems, 1973. Recreations: hills and music. Address: (h.) Minch View, Peterburn, Gairloch, Ross; T.-044 585 221.

Tremlett, Walter Edward, BSc, PhD, FGS. Senior Lecturer in Geology, Glasgow University, since 1965; b. 9.3.26, Winchester; m., Sheila Davison; 1 d. Educ. Peter Symonds' School, Winchester; Southampton University. Army Service, Britain, India and Malaya, 1944-47 (Lt., Royal Indian Engineers); Assistant Lecturer, Southampton University, 1951-54; Lecturer, Glasgow University, 1954-65. Editor, Transactions Geological Society of Glasgow, 1961-63 (President of Society, 1982-85); Editor, Scottish Journal of Geology, 1963-68; Vice-President, Section C, British Association, 1985. Address: (h.) 50 Thomson Drive, Bearsden, Glasgow, G61 3PB; T.-041-942 1557.

Trevarthen, Professor Colwyn Boyd, BSc, MSc, PhD. Professor of Child Psychology and Psychobiology, Edinburgh University, since 1984; b. 2.3.31, Auckland; m., Elizabeth Lee Simmons; 3 s. Educ. Auckland Grammar School; Auckland University. Research Fellow, California Institute of Technology, 1962; USPHS Postdoctoral Fellow (CNRS), Marseille, 1963-66; MRC Research Fellow, Psychological Laboratory, Cambridge University, 1966; Research Fellow in Cognitive Studies, Lecturer in Psychology, Harvard University, 1966-68; Senior Research Fellow, California Institute of Technology, 1969-70; Edinburgh University: Lecturer, 1971-72, Reader, 1973-84, Associate Dean, Social Sciences, 1974-75; Visiting Reader or Professor, La Trobe University, Auckland University, California Institute of Technology, Lagos University, Universite Libre de Bruxelles, Natal University. Recreations: walking; travelling; reading; playing flute. Address: (b.) Department of Psychology, Edinburgh University, 7 George Square, Edinburgh, EH8 9JZ; T.-031-667 1011, Ext. 4441.

Trewin, Nigel Harvey, BSc, PhD, FGS. Senior Lecturer in Geology, Aberdeen University, since 1984; Consultant Sedimentologist, since 1974; b. 9.6.44, Cowes, Isle of Wight; m., Margaret C. Evan Hopkins; 1 s.; 1 d. Educ. Woking County Grammar School; Bristol University; Keele University. Demonstrator in Geology, Keele University, 1965-68; Lecturer in Geology, Aberdeen University, 1968-84. Editor, Scottish Journal of Geology. Recreations: fishing; skiing; natural history; postal history. Address: (b.) Department of Geology, Marischal College, Broad Street, Aberdeen, AB9 1AS; T.-0224 40241.

Trotter, Alexander Richard. Convener, Scottish Landowners Federation, 1982-85; Member, Nature Conservancy Council, since 1985 (Chairman, Scottish Advisory Committee, since 1985); b. 20.2.39, London; m., Julia Henrietta Greenwell; 3 s. Educ. Eton College. Royal Scots Greys, 1958-68; Member, Berwickshire County Council, 1968-74 (Chairman, Roads Committee, 1972-74); Local Director, Eagle Star Insurance Group, since 1971; Chairman, Mortonhall Park Ltd., since 1973; Vice-Chairman, Border Grain Ltd., since 1984. Member, Queen's Bodyguard for

Scotland (Royal Company of Archers). Recreations: skiing; tennis; riding; shooting. Address: Charterhall, Duns, Berwickshire, TD11 3RE; T.-089 084 301.

Trotter, William, MA. Headteacher, Craigmount High School, Edinburgh, since 1969; b. 7.5.28, Greenock; m., Sylvia Rosemary Hall; 1 s.; 1 d. Educ. Hamilton Academy; Glasgow University; Jordanhill College of Education. Teacher of Modern Languages: Airdrie Academy, 1955-58, Forest Hill School, London, 1958-61; Head of Languages Department, Sedgehill School, London, 1961-65; Lecturer in Modern Languages, High Wycombe College of Technology, 1965-67; Deputy Head, Joseph Leckie School, Walsall, 1967-69. Recreations: reading; music; swimming; light-hearted bridge. Address: (h.) 26 Ormidale Terrace, Edinburgh, EH12 6EQ; T.-031-337 6492.

Troup, D. Malcolm, BSc, MSc, CEng, MIMechE, FIProdE, FBIM, FIIM. Chief Executive, Ayr Locality Enterprise Resource Trust, since 1984; b. 2.7.39, Ayr; m., Margaret McQueen; 1 s.; 3 d. Educ. Ayr Academy; Strathclyde University. Senior Liaison Engineer, 1969-72; Factory Manager and Member, Board of Directors, Tanania Diamond Cutting Company, 1973-76; Factory Manager, Diamond Cutting (Malaysia), 1976-80; Industrial and Production Management Expert, United Nations, ILO, 1980-83; Management Consultant, 1983-84. Assistant Treasurer, Scottish Regional Board, Institution of Industrial Managers. Recreations: Rotarian; golf; snooker; bridge; music. Address: (b.) 88 Green Street, Ayr, KA8 8BG; T.-0292 264181.

Troup, Ian McCrae, MB, ChB, DMedRehab. Consultant, Rehabilitation Medicine (Prosthetics/Orthotics), since 1970; Honorary Research Fellow, Department of Orthopaedic and Traumatic Surgery, Dundee University, since 1984; b. 28.1.21, Monifieth; m., Trudie K. Roy; 3 s.; 1 d. Educ. Dundee High School; University College, Dundee. House Surgeon/Casualty Officer, Dundee Royal Infirmary; RAMC: 16th Light Field Ambulance, 79th Armoured Division (Europe) and 5th Field Ambulance, 5th Infantry Brigade (Far East); mentioned in Despatches, 1946; Paediatric Assistant, Dundee Royal Infirmary; General Medical Practitioner; Standing Chairman, Medical Boards, Ministry of Pensions; Member, General Medical Services Committee; Senior Lecturer, Department of Orthopaedic and Traumatic Surgery, Dundee University. Fellow, World Health Organisation; Fellow, Internatonal Society for Prosthetics. Recreations: woodcrafts; natural history; golf; music. Address: (h.) 3 Bonspiel Gardens, Broughty Ferry, Dundee, DD5 2LN; T.-Dundee 74907.

Truman, Donald Ernest Samuel, BA, PhD, MIBiol. Senior Lecturer, Department of Genetics, Edinburgh University, since 1978 (Head, Department of Genetics, since 1984, Director of Biology Teaching Unit, since 1985); b. 23.10.36, Leicester; m., Kathleen Ramsay; 1 s.; 1 d. Educ. Wyggeston School, Leicester; Clare College, Cambridge. NATO Research Fellow, Wenner-Grenn Institute, Stockholm, 1962-63; MRC Epigenetics Research Group, Edinburgh, 1963-72; Lecturer, Department of Genetics, Edinburgh University, 1972-78; Aneurin Bevan Memorial Fellow, Government of India, 1978. Publications: The Biochemistry of Ctyodifferentiation, 1974; Differentiation in Vitro (Joint Editor), 1982; Stability and Switching in Cellular Differentiation, 1982. Recreation: gardening. Address: (b.) Department of Genetics, West Mains Road, Edinburgh, EH9 3JN; T.-031-667 1081.

Truscott, Professor Terence George, BSc, PhD, DSc, CChem, FRSC. Professor of Chemistry, Paisley College, since 1974 (Head, Department of Chemistry, since 1974, Dean, School of Science); b. 8.5.39, Bargoed; m., Marylin; 1 d. Educ. Bargoed Grammar School; University of Wales. Postdoctoral Research Fellow, Minnesota University, 1964-65; Lecturer in Physical Chemistry, Bradford University, 1966-71; Research Group Section Leader, INCO Ltd., Canada, 1971-73. Associate Editor, Journal of Photochemistry and Photobiology; Member, Science Board, SERC. Recreation: bridge. Address: (b.) Paisley College, Department of Chemistry, High Street, Paisley, PA1 2BE; T.-041-887 1241, Ext. 242.

Tucker, John Barry, BA, MA, PhD. Reader in Zoology, St. Andrews University, since 1979; b. 17.3.41, Arundel; m., Janet Stephen Murray; 1 s. Educ. Queen Elizabeth Grammar School, Atherstone; Peterhouse, Cambridge. Fulbright Travel Scholar and Research Associate, Department of Zoology, Indiana University, 1966-68; SERC Research Fellow, Department of Zoology, Cambridge, 1968-69; Lecturer in Zoology, St. Andrews University, 1969-79 (Chairman, Zoology Department, 1982-84). Member, SERC Advisory Group II, 1977-80. Recreations: cycling; hill-walking; tennis; reluctant gardener. Address: (b.) Department of Zoology and Marine Biology, Bute Building, St. Andrews University, St. Andrews, Fife, KY16 9TS; T.-0334 76161.

Tudhope, George Ranken, BSc, MD, FRCP, FRCPEdin. Reader in Therapeutics, Dundee University, since 1964; Consultant Physician, Dundee Teaching Hospitals, since 1964; b. 28.1.24, Newport, Fife; m., Jessie Crookston Stewart; 2 s. Educ. Bell-Baxter School, Cupar; St. Andrews University. House Physician, Dundee Royal Infirmary, 1947; Assistant, Department of Therapeutics, Maryfield Hospital, Dundee, 1950-54; Lecturer, then Senior Lecturer in Therapeutics, Sheffield University, 1954-64 (Consultant Physician, United Sheffield Hospitals, 1960-64); Haematology Research Fellow, Utah University, 1959-60. Address: (h.) 7 Dawson Place, West Ferry, Dundee, DD5 1PS; T.-Dundee 78887.

Tullis, John Ivor, LDS. Chief Administrative Dental Officer, Highland Health Board, since 1974; b. 26.8.24, Dundee; m., Margaret May McAlpine; 2 s.; 1 d. Educ. High School of Dundee; University College, Dundee. Dental Officer, RADC, 1946-52; retired with rank of Major; Assistant in general practice, 1953; Principal in partnership in general practice, Dundee, 1953; Lecturer in Restorative Dentistry, Edinburgh University, 1969. Past President, North of

Scotland Branch, BDA; Past President, Dundee Dental Club. Recreations: cricket; hockey; golf; angling; music. Address: (h.) 4 Cradlehall Park, Westhill, Inverness; T.-0463 791182.

Tullis, Major Ramsey, BA. Vice Lord-Lieutenant of Clackmannanshire, since 1974; Farmer; b. 16.6.16; m., Daphne Mabon; 3 s. Educ. Trinity College, Glenalmond; Worcester College, Oxford. 2nd Lt., Cameronians, 1936; served Second World War (Major, 1943); County Commissioner for Scouts, Clackmannanshire, 1958-73; Income Tax Commissioner, since 1964. Recreations: golf; gardening. Address: (h.) Woodacre, Pool of Muckhart, by Dollar, Clackmannanshire, FK14 7JW.

Tulloch, John Alexander, MC, MD, FRCP, FRCPEdin. Consultant Physician, Stracathro Hospital, since 1966; Honorary Senior Lecturer, Department of Therapeutics, Dundee University, since 1966; b. 23.4.21, Forres; m., Sheena Robin Paisley Whyte; 3 s.; 2 d. Educ. Forres Academy; Edinburgh University. RAMC, 1943-46; Research Scholar, Grocer's Company of London, 1947-49; Registrar in Cardiology, Edinburgh Royal Infirmary, 1949-51; Research Fellow, American Heart Association, New York Hospital, 1951-52; Senior Registrar in Medicine, Edinburgh Royal Infirmary, 1952-55; Senior Lecturer in Medicine, University College of West Indies, Jamaica, 1955-61; Professor of Medicine, Makerere University College, University of East Africa, Uganda, 1961-66 (Dean, Medical Faculty, 1962-63, Member of College Council, 1964-66); Editor, West Indian Medical Journal, 1955-61; Member, Board of Management, Sunnyside Royal Hospital and the Angus Hospitals, 1967-72. Publication: Diabetes Mellitus in the Tropics. Recreations: gardening; golf; reading. Address: (h.) Parklands, Edzell, Angus, DD9 7TF; T.-Edzell 234.

Tumelty, Michael, MA (Hons). Music Critic, Glasgow Herald, since 1983; b. 31.5.46, Hexham; m., Frances; 2 s.; 1 d. Educ. St. Aloysius College, Glasgow; Aberdeen University. Postgraduate research into the music of Debussy, 1974-75; entered teaching, St. Columba's High School, Clydebank (Principal Teacher, 1980-83); served on a variety of working groups on curriculum development; freelance Music Critic, Jewish Echo, 1979-82, and Daily Telegraph, 1982-83. Member, Scottish Central Committee on Music, 1982-83. Recreations: family; avid collector of records; endless fascination with synthesisers and technological musical equipment; photography. Address: (h.) 31 Burlington Avenue, Glasgow, G12 OLJ; T.-041-334 4430.

Tunnell, John, FRAM. Leader, Scottish Chamber Orchestra, since 1974; Professor, Royal Scottish Academy of Music and Drama, since 1974; b. 12.5.36, Stockton-on-Tees; m., Wendy Packard; 2 s.; 1 d. Educ. Bradford Grammar School; Royal Academy of Music (London); Vienna Academy. Member, London String Quartet, 1958-67; founder Member, English Chamber Orchestra and Principal; Leader, Tunnell Piano Trio and Piano Quartet, Thames Chamber

Orchestra, 1969-74, and Vesuvius Ensemble of London; frequent solo appearances, recordings. Recreations: hill-walking; gardening; tennis. Address: (h.) Crawhill Manor, by Bathgate, West Lothian; T.-0506 52991.

Tunstall, David P., BSc (Hons), PhD. Reader in Physics, St. Andrews University, since 1978 (Admissions Officer, University, since 1980); b. 15.7.39, Wellington, England; m., Rosemarie; 2 s.; 1 d. Educ. Whitchurch Grammar School; University College of North Wales. Research Fellow, St. Andrews, 1966-75; Visiting Professor, Cornell, 1973, UCLA, 1979; Senior Lecturer, St. Andrews, 1975-78. Recreations: skiing; hill-walking. Address: (h.) 4 West Acres, St. Andrews, Fife; T.-St. Andrews 73507.

Tunstall-Pedoe, Professor Hugh David, MA, MD, FRCP, FFCM. Professor and Director, Cardiovascular Epidemiology Unit, Ninewells Hospital and Medical School, Dundee, since 1981; Honorary Consultant Cardiologist, since 1981; Honorary Specialist in Community Medicine, since 1981; b. 30.12.39, Southampton; m., Jacqueline Helen; 2 s.; 1 d. Educ. Haberdashers' Aske's School; Dulwich College; King's College, Cambridge; Guy's Hospital Medical School. Junior hospital posts, Guy's, Brompton, National Queen Square and London Hospitals; MRC Social Medicine Unit, 1969-71; Lecturer in Medicine, The London Hospital, 1971-74; Senior Lecturer in Epidemiology and Honorary Physician, and Honorary Community Physician, St. Mary's Hospital and Medical School, London, 1974-81. Chairman, European Society of Cardiology Working Group on Epidemiology and Prevention, since 1983. Recreations: hill-walking; bee-keeping; golf. Address: (b.) Cardiovascular Epidemiology Unit, Ninewells Hospital and Medical School, Dundee, DD1 9SY; T.-0382 644255.

Turley, Alfred, JP, DCM, CPM. Member, Dumfries and Galloway Regional Council, since 1975; b. 30.3.13, Dudley; m., Margaret Linn; 1 s. 7th Hussars, 1932-38; Palestine Police, 1938-48; Malayan Police, 1948-50; Colonial Police Medal for Gallantry; Distinguished Conduct Medal awarded by Sultan of Frengganu, Malaya; Member, Dumfries Town Council, 1964-75. Address: (h.) 109 Annan Road, Dumfries, DG1 3EW; T.-0387 55194.

Turmeau, William Arthur, PhD, CEng, FIMechE. Principal, Napier College, Edinburgh, since 1982; b. 19.9.29, London; m., Margaret Moar Burnett; 1 d. Educ. Stromness Academy, Orkney; Edinburgh University; Moray House College of Education; Heriot-Watt University. Royal Signals, 1947-49; Research Engineer, Northern Electric Co. Ltd., Montreal, 1952-54; Mechanical Engineer, USAF, Goose Bay, Labrador, 1954-56; Contracts Manager, Godfrey Engineering Co. Ltd., Montreal, 1956-61; Lecturer, Bristo Technical Institute, Edinburgh, 1962-64; Napier College: Lecturer and Senior Lecturer, 1964-68, Head, Department of Mechanical Engineering, 1968-75, Assistant Principal and Dean, Faculty of Technology, 1975-82.

Member, Council, CNAA, since 1982 (and Scotland Committee, since 1983); Member, Council, IMechE, since 1983; Member, Council, Society Europeenne de Formation des Ingenieurs, since 1983; Member, British Council CICHE, since 1982. Recreations: modern jazz; Leonardo da Vinci. Address: (h.) 71 Morningside Park, Edinburgh, EH10 5EZ; T.-031-447 4639.

Turnbull, George Ellson, MITSA, FInstPet. Director of Consumer Protection, Highland Regional Council, since 1977; b. 7.11.28, Rosyth; 2 d. Educ. George Heriot's School, Edinburgh. District Inspector of Weights and Measures, Edinburgh Corporation, 1956-65; Inspector of Weights and Measures, Ross and Cromarty County Council, 1965-67; Edinburgh Corporation: Principal Assistant, 1967, Depute Chief Inspector, 1967-70, Depute Director of Trading Standards, 1970-75; Principal Consumer Protection Officer, Lothian Regional Council, 1975-77. Recreations: golf; languages; ballroom and Latin American dancing; philately. Address: (b.) Glenurquhart Road, Inverness, IV3 5NX; T.-0463 234121, Ext. 501.

Turnbull, Robert McIntyre, BSc, PhD. Senior Lecturer in Natural Philosophy, Glasgow University, since 1973; b. 9.3.36, Thornton, Fife; m., Aileen Simpson; 3 s. Educ. Buckhaven High School; St. Andrews University; Glasgow University. Sir James Caird Travelling Scholarship, 1957-60; ICI Research Fellow, 1961-62; Lecturer in Natural Philosophy, Glasgow University, 1962-73. Member, SERC Nuclear Physics Board Particle Physics Committee; Member, Department of Education and Science UK Committee on CERN; Visiting Scientist, European Organisation for Nuclear Research, CERN, since 1961; Director, Scottish Universities Summer School in Physics, 1984. Publications include The Structure of Matter. Recreation: golf. Address: (b.) Department of Natural Philosophy, The University, Glasgow, G12 8QQ; T.-041-339 8855.

Turner, Allan Roderick, MB, ChBEd, FRCSEdin, FRCS. Consultant Surgeon, Dunfermline and West Fife Hospital, since 1979; Honorary Senior Lecturer, Department of Surgery, Edinburgh University, since 1979; b. 18.11.41, Lochmaddy; m., Jean J.C. Macrae; 3 s.; 3 d. Educ. Portree High School; Edinburgh University. Surgical training, Edinburgh, Aberdeen, Liverpool, London; Surgeon to Christian Mission Hospital, Kurdistan, 1973-75; Associate Professor, Department of Surgery, Shiraz University, Iran, 1976. Recreations: gardening; squash; children's hobbies; Celtic languages. Address: (h.) 34 Couston Street, Dunfermline, Fife; T.-Dunfermline 729689.

Turner, Colin William, BSc, AKC. Rector, Glasgow Academy, since 1983; b. 10.12.33, Torquay; m., Priscilla Mary Trickett; 2 s.; 2 d. Educ. Torquay Grammar School; King's College, London University; Exeter University. Edinburgh Academy: Assistant Master, 1958, CCF Contingent Commander, 1960-74, Housemaster, 1975-82. Recreations: mountaineering; caravanning. Address: (h.) 11 Kirklee Terrace, Glasgow, G12 OTH; T.-041-357 1776.

Turner, John R., MA, MusB, FRCO. Organist and Director of Music, Glasgow Cathedral, since 1965; Lecturer, Royal Scottish Academy of Music, since 1965; Organist, Strathclyde University, since 1965; b. Halifax. Educ. Rugby; Jesus College, Cambridge. Recreations: gardening; travel. Address: (h.) 2 Cathkin Cottage, Burnside Road, Glasgow, G73 5RD; T.-041-634 3083.

Turner, Captain John Russell, MCIT, MIMH, MNI. General Manager, Aberdeen Harbour Board, since 1978; b. 17.6.30, Cheadle Hulme; m., Jean Catherine Baker; 1 s.; 2 d. Educ. Kings School, Macclesfield; Thames Nautical Training College, HMS Worcester; UMIST; Cranfield Institute of Technology. Cadet, Royal Naval Reserve; Navigating Officer: Clan Line, P. & O., Cunard Line; Port of Manchester: Assistant Chief Superintending Stevedore, Dock Traffic Superintendent, Assistant Docks Manager; Deputy General Manager, Aberdeen Harbour Board, 1973-78. Liveryman, Honourable Company of Master Mariners; Council Member, British Ports Association; Council Member, Association of Pilotage Authorities, 1978-84; Vice Chairman and Co-Founder, Scottish Advisory Committee, Netherlands British Chamber of Commerce; Council Member, Aberdeen Chamber of Commerce; Vice Chairman, North of Scotland Export Club, 1982-84; Member, Aberdeen Committee, Royal National Lifeboat Institution; Chairman, Grampian-Houston Association; received Freedom of the City of London, 1972. Recreations: golf; travel; historical research; sailing. Address: (b.) Harbour Office, 16 Regent Quay, Aberdeen, AB9 1SS; T.-0224 592571.

Turner, Malcolm, OBE, JP. Chairman, Central Scotland Water Development Board, since 1978; Member, Strathclyde Regional Council, since 1974; b. 13.12.21, Clydebank; m., Margaret Balfour; 1 s. Educ. Clydebank High School. Member: Clydebank Town Council, 1957-75 (Provost, 1966-69), Dunbarton County Council, 1957-75; Member, Cumbernauld Development Corporation, 1975-83. Recreations: angling; caravanning; bowling; golf. Address: (h.) 10A Duncombe View, Clydebank, Dunbartonshire; T.-041-952 3992.

Turner, Lt.-Gen. Sir William (Francis Robert), KBE (1962), CB (1959), DSO (1945). Lord Lieutenant of Dumfries, 1972-82; Ensign, Queen's Bodyguard for Scotland (Royal Company of Archers); b. 12.12.07; m.; 1 s. Educ. Winchester College; Sandhurst. GOC-in-C, Scottish Command, and Governor, Edinburgh Castle, 1961-64.

Turner Thomson, Ann Denise. Interior Designer; Member, Scottish Arts Council; b. 23.5.29, Molesey; m., Gordon Turner Thomson; 1 s.; 3 d. Educ. Sherborne School for Girls, Dorset; St. James's Secretarial College, London. Member, Merchandising Committee, National Trust; Council Member: Cockburn Association, Saltire Society; Member, Saltire Society Housing Awards Panel. Recreations: theatre; opera; reading; sailing; swimming; tennis. Address: 1 South Lauder Road, Edinburgh, EH9 2LL; T.-031-667 3997.

Tweedsmuir, 2nd Baron, (John Norman Stuart Buchan), CBE (1964), CD (1964), FRSE; b. 25.11.11; m., 1, Priscilla Jean Fortescue (deceased); 1 d.; 2, Jean Margherita Grant. Educ. Eton; Brasenose College, Oxford. Lt.-Col., Canadian Infantry Corps, retired; Rector, Aberdeen University, 1948-51; UK Delegate, UN Assembly, 1951-52; Chairman, Advertising Standards Authority, 1971-74; Chairman, Council on Tribunals, 1973-80; Hon. LLD, Aberdeen, 1949. Address: (h.) Potterton House, Balmedie, Aberdeenshire.

Tweedy, Brigadier Oliver Robert. Commandant, Queen Victoria School, Dunblane, since 1985; b. 4.2.30, Newbury; m., Dawn Berrange; 2 s.; 1 d. Educ. Sedbergh School; RMA, Sandhurst. Commissioned, The Black Watch, 1949; commanded 1st Bn., The Black Watch, Scotland, Northern Ireland and Hong Kong, 1971-73; Commander, British Army Advisory Team, Nigeria, 1980-82; Commander, 51 Highland Brigade, 1982-84; ADC to The Queen, 1983; retired, 1985. Recreations: golf; country pursuits. Address: (h.) Inverbraan, Little Dunkeld, Perthshire, PH8 OAD.

Twidell, John W., MA, DPhil. Head, Energy Studies Unit, Strathclyde University, since 1984; b. 4.4.39, Windsor; m., Mary; 2 s.; 1 d. Educ. Maidenhead Grammar School; Lincoln College, Oxford. Lecturer in Physics, Khartoum University, Sudan, 1964-68; Research Fellow, Essex University, 1968-70; Lecturer and Senior Lecturer, Department of Applied Physics, Strathclyde University, 1970-84. Council Member, British Wind Energy Association. Publications include: four-volume Proceedings of Energy for Rural and Island Communities; Dictionary of Energy (Co-author); Renewable Energy Resources (textbook). Recreations: visiting islands; hockey; cataloguing books. Address: (h.) 21 Lynn Drive, Milngavie, Glasgow.

U

Upton, Professor Anthony Frederick, MA (Oxon), AM, FRHistS. Professor of Nordic History, St. Andrews University, since 1984; b. 13.10.29, Stockton Heath, Cheshire; m., Sirkka R.; 3 s. Educ. County Boys' School, Windsor; Queen's College, Oxford. Assistant Lecturer in Modern History, Leeds University, 1952-56; St. Andrews University: Lecturer in Modern History, 1956, Senior Lecturer, 1966, Reader, 1974. Sundry offices, Labour Party in Fife and in educational bodies, e.g. St. Andrews School Council. Recreations: music; literature; politics. Address: (h.) 5 West Acres, St. Andrews, Fife.

Upton, Professor Brian Geoffrey Johnson, BA, MA, DPhil, FRSE. Professor of Petrology, Edinburgh University, since 1982 (Head, Department of Geology, since 1984); Executive Editor, Journal of Petrology, since 1984; b. 2.3.33, London; m., Bodil Aalbaek; 2 s.; 1 d. Educ. Reading School; St. John's College, Oxford. Geological survey of Greenland, 1958-60; Postdoctoral Fellow, California Institute of Technology, 1961-62; Lecturer, then Reader in Geology, Edinburgh University, 1962-82. Recreations: painting; gardening. Address: (h.) 59 Belwood Road, Milton Bridge, Midlothian, EH26 OQN; T.-0968 73500.

Ure, William, BL. Solicitor; b. 17.12.17, Bishopbriggs; m., Jessie Shanks King Duff. Educ. Glasgow Academy; Glasgow University. University and legal training, 1935-39; The Cameronians (Scottish Rifles), 1939-46; legal practice, since 1946. Deacon, Incorporation of Gardeners of Glasgow, 1972-73; Chairman, West Stirlingshire Conservative Association, 1980-83. Recreation: golf. Address: (h.) Belmont, Bardowie, Milngavie, Glasgow; T.-Balmore 20310.

U'ren, William Graham, BSc (Hons), DipTP, FRTPI. Director of Planning and Technical Services, Clydesdale District Council, since 1982; b. 28.12.46, Glasgow; m., Wendy; 2 d. Educ. Aberdeen Grammar School; Aberdeen University; Strathclyde University. Planning Assistant, Clackmannan County Council, 1970-72, Lanark County Council, 1972-75; Principal and Chief Planning Officer, Clydesdale District Council, 1975-82. Past Chairman, Scottish Society of Directors of Planning. Recreations: sport; bird watching; philately. Address: (b.) District Offices, South Vennel, Lanark, ML11 7JT; T.-Lanark 61331.

Urquhart, Alistair P., OBE, MA. Headmaster, Kincorth Academy, Aberdeen; b. 27.7.21, Paisley; m., May Brown (deceased). Educ. John Neilson Institute, Paisley; Glasgow University. War Service, 1941-46 (Captain, Royal Artillery); Teacher of English, then Principal Teacher, Powis Junior Secondary School, Aberdeen, 1947-61; Deputy Headmaster, Summerhill Secondary School, Aberdeen, 1962-66; Headmaster, Old Aberdeen Secondary School, 1966-71. Chairman, Scottish Central Committee on Music, since 1979; President, Scottish Badminton Union, 1970-72. Recreations: golf; badminton; music. Address: (h.) 15 Kingshill Road, Aberdeen; T.-Aberdeen 36100.

Urquhart, Daniel, FCCA. Director of Finance, Banff and Buchan District Council, since 1974; b. 27.4.32, Banff; m., Molly; 1 s.; 1 d. Educ. Banff Academy. Trainee Accountant, Banff County Council, 1955-59; Aberdeen Corporation: Audit Assistant, 1959-61, Accountancy Assistant, 1961-63, Senior Accountancy Assistant, 1963-67; Town Chamberlain, Fraserburgh Town Council, 1967-74. Recreations: golf; bridge; gardening. Address: (b.) St. Leonard's, Sandyhill Road, Banff; T.-Banff 2521.

Urquhart, George, JP. Member, Aberdeen District Council, since 1982 (Convener, Licensing Committee, since 1984); b. 19.4.38, Aberdeen; m., Alice Elizabeth Bush; 3 s. Educ. Frederick Street Junior Secondary School. Member, Grampian Regional Council, 1978-82; Member, Post

Office Users Council, since 1984. Recreations: supporting Aberdeen Football Club; playing table tennis in league. Address: (h.) 10 Arbroath Way, Aberdeen, AB1 5DA; T.-0224 873944.

Urquhart, James Macconnell, MB, ChB, FFCM, DPH. Chairman, Management Committee, Margaret Blackwood Housing for Adult Handicapped, Dundee; Chairman, REMAP, Tayside; Vice-President, Red Cross, Dundee; Deputy Commissioner, Clan Urquhart Association; b. 1.10.18, Wishaw; m., 1, May Harrison (m. diss.); 2, Nora Hanna; 1 s.; 2 d. Educ. Dumfries Academy; High School of Glasgow; Glasgow University. RAF Medical Branch, 1942-68 (retired with rank of Group Captain); War Service, India, Burma; Safety Office, Atomic Trials, Australia, 1956; OC, RAF Hospitals; Community Medicine, Northern Ireland Hospital Authority, 1968-72; Medical Superintendent, Dundee General Hospitals, 1972-75; District Medical Officer, Dundee District, 1975-83. Member, Executive Committee, St. Aidans Project, Dundee; Vice Chairman, Preparation for Retiral Council, Dundee; Trustee, Scottish Trust for Physically Disabled; Trustee, Dundee Trust for Education of Deaf; Member, Diocesan Synod, Brechin. Recreations: reading; photography. Address: (h.) 35 Albany Terrace, Dundee, DD3 6HS; T.-0382 22928.

Urquhart, John Munro, CBE, MA, MEd, FEIS, FSA Scot. Vice Chairman, Board of Trustees, National Museum of Antiquities; Member, Board of Communications, Church of Scotland; b. 16.9.10, Gairloch; m., Adela Margaret Sutherland; 1 s.; 1 d. Educ. Lochgilphead Secondary School; Oban High School; Glasgow University. Schoolmaster, Hutchesons' Boys' Grammar School; Assistant Director of Education, Banffshire; Depute Director of Education, Glasgow; Director of Education, Selkirkshire; Director, Scottish Certificate of Education Examination Board, 1965-75; Consultant Registrar, Caribbean Examinations Council, 1977-78; President, Association of Directors of Education, 1963-64. Boy Scouts County Commissioner, Selkirkshire; edited Statistical Account of Selkirkshire, 1964; District Governor, Rotary District 102, 1980. Recreations: angling; walking; reading; gardening. Address: (h.) 29 Craiglockhart Drive South, Edinburgh, EH14; T.-031-443 3085.

Urquhart, Rev. Thomas Chalmers, MA, DA. Minister, Arisaig and Moidart, since 1964; b. 14.4.15, Anstruther; m., Janet Mora Vicar Craig (Sheena); 1 s. Educ. Greenock Academy; Glasgow University; Glasgow School of Art. Spent some time teaching before entering upon theological course at New College, Edinburgh, 1949-51; ordained, Aberdeen, 1953; Minister, Carlisle (Church of Scotland), 1957-63. Recreations: painting; music; gardening; hill-walking. Address: The Manse, Arisaig, Inverness-shire, PH39; T.-06875 227.

Usher, John Richard, BSc (Hons), MSc, PhD, FIMA. Head, School of Mathematical Sciences and Computer Studies, Robert Gordon's Institute of Technology, since 1983; Chairman, Scottish Branch, Institute of Mathematics and its Applications, since 1985; b. 12.5.44, London; m.,

Sheila Mary; 1 d. Educ. St. Nicholas Grammar School; Hull University; St. Andrews University. Lecturer I, then Lecturer II, Teesside Polytechnic, 1970-74; Senior Lecturer, Glasgow College of Technology, 1974-82. Recreations: squash; bridge; hill-walking; philately. Address: (b.) School of Mathematical Sciences and Computer Studies, Robert Gordon's Institute of Technology, St. Andrew Street, Aberdeen; T.-0224 633611, Ext. 450.

V

Valentine, Ian Balfour, CA. Managing Partner, Binder Hamlyn, Chartered Accountants, Ayr, since 1965 (Scottish Managing Partner, since 1985); Finance Convener, Ayrshire and Arran Health Board, since 1982 (Member, since 1981); b. 17.10.40, Glasgow; m., Elaine; 1 s.; 1 d. Educ. Hutchesons' Boys' Grammar School. Partner, J. Wyllie Guild & Ballantine, 1965 (subsequently Binder Hamlyn). Member, Discipline Committee, Institute of Chartered Accountants of Scotland; Chairman, Ayrshire Association of Chartered Accountants of Scotland, 1976-78; President, Junior Chamber Ayr, 1972-73; Member, Ayr Schools Council, 1976-78; Director, Federation of Scottish Junior Chambers of Commerce, 1973-74; Honorary Secretary and Treasurer, Ayr Rugby Football Club, 1979-84. Recreations: golf; rugby (as spectator); bridge; curling. Address: (b.) 64 Dalblair Road, Ayr; T.-0292 263277.

Valentine, John Young, JP. Member, Falkirk District Council, since 1984; b. 7.3.24, Leven; m., Henrietta Nan Lawson Murdoch. Educ. Leven Junior Secondary School. Member, Stirling County Council, 1967-70, and 1973-74; Member, Falkirk District Council, 1974-80 (Convenor, Amenity and Recreation Committee); Member, Reddingmuirhead Old People's Committee; Secretary, Falkirk East Constituency Association, SNP. Recreations: golf; music; home movies. Address: (h.) 8 Maranatha Crescent, Brightons, Falkirk, FK2 ODF; T.-0324 715715.

Valentine, Keith, MA, LLB. Procurator Fiscal, Stirling, since 1976; b. 10.12.32, Perth; m., Anne Florence Ritchie; 1 s.; 2 d. Educ. Perth Academy; Edinburgh University. RAF Education Branch, 1956-59 (Flt.-Lt.); Procurator Fiscal Service, since 1961, Ayr, Glasgow, Edinburgh and Crown Office; other legal experience in private practice and with General Accident Fire and Life Assurance Corporation Ltd. Chairman, Scottish Branch, British Association for the Study and Prevention of Child Abuse and Neglect, since 1982. Recreations: golf; gardening. Address: (h.) Muircroft, Chalton Road, Bridge of Allan, FK9 4EF.

Vallance, Ramsay, MB, ChB, FRCSGlas, FRCR, DMRD. Consultant Radiologist, Western Infirmary/Gartnavel General Hospital, Glasgow, since

1977; Honorary Clinical Lecturer in Radiology, Glasgow University, since 1979; b. 9.3.45, Port Glasgow; m., Dr. Norma Bryan Stewart; 3 d. Educ. Eastwood Senior Secondary School; Glasgow University. Registrar in Surgery, Western Infirmary/Killearn Hospital, 1970-73; Registrar in Diagnostic Radiology, Southern General Hospital, Glasgow, 1973-75; Senior Registrar in Radiology, Western Infirmary/Gartnavel General Hospital, 1975-77. Church of Scotland Elder. Recreations: photography; classical music; golf. Address: (h.) 56 Russell Drive, Bearsden, Glasgow, G61 3BB; T.-041-942 2931.

Vance, John Peden, MB, ChB, MD, FFARCS, MRCPGlas, DObstRCOG. Consultant Anaesthetist, Glasgow Royal Infirmary, since 1968; Honorary Clinical Lecturer in Anaesthesia, Glasgow University, since 1974; b. 7.6.36, Harthill, Lanarkshire; m., Janet Steele; 2 d. Educ. Airdrie Academy; Glasgow University. Pre-registration appointments, Falkirk Royal Infirmary, Bellshill Maternity Hospital; trained in anaesthesia, Western Infirmary, Glasgow; Educational Fellow, Mount Sinai Hospital, New York, 1966. Recreation: golf. Address: (h.) Traquair, Holmwood Avenue, Uddingston, Glasgow, G71 7AJ; T.-Uddingston 813134.

Vardy, Professor Alan Edward, BSc, PhD, CEng, MICE, MASCE. Professor of Civil Engineering, Dundee University, since 1979 (Deputy Principal, since 1985); Director, Wolfson Bridge Research Unit, since 1980; b. 6.11.45, Sheffield; m., Mary Rosalind; 1 s.; 1 d. Educ. High Storrs Grammar School, Sheffield; Leeds University. Lecturer in Civil Engineering, Leeds University, 1972-75; Royal Society Warren Research Fellow, Cambridge University, 1975-79. Recreations: flying; wind-surfing; skiing; music. Address: (h.) Dunholm, 512 Perth Road, Dundee, DD2 1LW; T.-Dundee 66123.

Varley, William Raymond, BSc, DipTP, FICE, MIHT. Deputy Chief Engineer (Bridges), Scottish Development Department, since 1982; b. 7.7.28, Slaithwaite; m., Margaret Elizabeth Jessop; 2 s.; 1 d. Educ. King James Grammar School, Almondbury; Manchester University. National Service, Royal Engineers, 1951-53; Highway Engineering Department, West Riding County Council, 1954-68; Superintending Engineer (Bridges), NERCU, Department of Transport, 1969-81. Recreation: painting. Address: (b.) Room 3/102 New St. Andrews House, Edinburgh, EH1 1SZ; T.-031-556 8400.

Varty, Professor E. Kenneth C., BA, PhD, FSA. Stevenson Professor of French, Glasgow University, since 1967; b. 18.8.27, Calke, Derbyshire; m., Hety Benninghoff; 2 d. Educ. Bemrose Grammar School, Derby; Nottingham University. Assistant Lecturer, then Lecturer, Keele University, 1953-61; Lecturer, then Senior Lecturer, Leicester University, 1961-67. Dean, Faculty of Arts, Glasgow, 1980-82; Visiting Lecturer, Warwick University, 1967; Visiting Professor, Jerusalem University, 1977; Visiting Research Fellow, Merton College, Oxford, 1974, and Clare Hall, Cambridge, 1983. Address: (b.) French Department, Glasgow University, Glasgow; T.-041-339 8855.

Vaughan, Henry William Campbell, DL, JP, MIPS. Member, Dundee District Council (Lord Provost of Dundee, 1977-80); Deputy Lieutenant, since 1980; b. 15.3.19, Dundee; m., Margaret Cowie Flett; 1 s.; 1 d. Educ. Dundee Training College; Logie and Stobswell Secondary Schools. Stationer, Burns and Harris Ltd., Dundee, 1934-39; RAF (Volunteer Reserve), 1939-46; Chief Buyer, Valentine & Sons, Art Publishers, 1946-64; elected Councillor, 1958; Group Purchasing Officer, Scott & Robertson (Tay Textiles), 1964-75; Stationery Manager, Burns and Harris Ltd., Dundee, 1975-79; Chairman, Tayside Area Council on Alcoholism, 1980-82; Honorary Vice President, Strathspey and Fiddle Society; Lord Lieutenant, 1977-80; awarded Silver Jubilee Medal, 1977. Recreations: cine photography; politics; water colour painting. Address: (h.) 15 Fraser Street, Dundee, DD3 6RE; T.-Dundee 826175.

Veitch, Andrew, JP. Life Underwriter, Imperial Life of Canada, since 1971; Member, Clydebank District Council, since 1975; b. 9.10.40, Hardgate, Dunbartonshre; m., Moira Buchanan; 2 s. Educ. Glasgow Academy. Member, Dunbarton County Council, 1970-75. Recreations: gardening; rough shooting. Address: (h.) 18 Romanhill Road, Hardgate, Clydebank, Dunbartonshire; T.-Duntocher 74092.

Vernon, Kenneth Robert, CBE, BSc, FEng, FIEE, FIMechE. Deputy Chairman and Chief Executive, North of Scotland Hydro-Electric Board, since 1973; b. 15.3.23, Dumfries; m., Pamela Hands; 1 s.; 3 d.; 1 d. deceased. Educ. Dumfries Academy; Glasgow University. BTH Co., Edinburgh Corporation, British Electricity Authority, 1948-55; South of Scotland Electricity Board, 1955-56; North of Scotland Hydro Electric Board: Chief Electrical and Mechanical Engineer, 1964, General Manager, 1966, Board Member, 1970; Director, British Electricity International Ltd., since 1976; Board Member, Northern Ireland Electricity Service, 1979-85. Recreation: fishing. Address: (h.) 10 Keith Crescent, Edinburgh, EH4 3NH; T.-031-332 4610.

Vernon, Richard Geoffrey, BSc, PhD. Head, Department of Lactational Physiology and Biochemistry, Hannah Research Institute, since 1981; Honorary Lecturer, Glasgow University, since 1981; b. 19.2.43, Maidstone; m., Mary Christine Cunliffe; 1 s.; 1 d. Educ. Newcastle High School; Birmingham University. Research Fellow, Toronto University, 1969-72; Senior/Principal Scientific Officer, Hannah Research Institute, 1972-81. Member, Editorial Board, British Journal of Nutrition; Past President, Birmingham University Mountaineering Club; first ascent of Mount Mazinaw, first British ascent, Mount Nautilus. Publication: Physiological Strategies in Lactation (Joint Editor). Recreations: walking; ornithology; mountaineering; bridge; photography. Address: (h.) 29 Knoll Park, Ayr; T.-0292 42195.

Vettese, J.W., MA (Hons), DipEd. Headteacher, Liberton High School, since 1985; b. 31.5.37, Brechin; m., M.L. McLean; 1 s.; 1 d.

Educ. Bathgate Academy; Edinburgh University. Assistant Teacher, Wishaw High School; Housemaster, Stratford Academy, New Jersey; Principal Teacher of Geography: Hunter High School, East Kilbride, Garrion Academy, Wishaw; Assistant Head Teacher, Upper School, Coltness High School, Wishaw; Rector, Calderhead High School, 1979-85. Address: (h.) Marchwood House, Kirk Road, Bathgate, West Lothian; T.-Bathgate 633698.

Vickerman, Professor Keith, BSc, PhD, DSc, FRSE, FRS. Regius Professor of Zoology, Glasgow University, since 1984; Consultant Expert on Parasitic Diseases, World Health Organisation, since 1973; b. 21.3.33, Huddersfield; m., Moira Dutton; 1 d. Educ. King James Grammar School, Almondbury; University College, London. Wellcome Lecturer in Protozoology, University College, London, 1958-63; Tropical Research Fellow, Royal Society, 1963-68; Glasgow University: Reader in Zoology, 1968-74; Professor of Zoology, 1974-84, Head, Department of Zoology, 1979-85. Publication: The Protozoa (Co-author), 1967. Recreations: drawing and painting; gardening. Address: (h.) 16 Mirrlees Drive, Glasgow, G12 OSH; T.-041-334 2794.

W

Waddell, Professor David Alan Gilmour, MA, DPhil, FRHistS. Professor of Modern History, Stirling University, since 1968; b. 22.10.27, Edinburgh; m., Barbara Box; 2 s. Educ. Royal High School, Edinburgh; St. Andrews University; Oxford University. Lecturer, University College of the West Indies, Jamaica, 1954-59; Lecturer and Senior Lecturer, Edinburgh University, 1959-68; visiting appointments, Trinidad, Colombia and California. Member, Scottish Examination Board, since 1982; Vice-President, Scottish Society of the History of Medicine, since 1984. Address: (b.) Department of History, Stirling University, Stirling, FK9 4LA; T.-0786 73171, Ext. 2154.

Wade, Nicholas James, BSc, PhD. Reader in Psychology, Dundee University, since 1978; b. 27.3.42, Retford, Nottinghamshire; m., Christine Whetton; 2 d. Educ. Queen Elizabeth's Grammar School, Mansfield; Edinburgh University; Monash University. Postdoctoral Research Fellow, Max-Planck Institute for Behavioural Physiology, Germany, 1969-70; Lecturer in Psychology, Dundee University, 1970-78. Publications: The Art and Science of Visual Illusions, 1982; Brewster and Wheatstone on Vision, 1983. Recreations: golf; cycling. Address: (h.) 36 Norwood, Newport-on-Tay, Fife, DD6 8DW; T.-0382 543136.

Wade, Terence Leslie Brian, BA, PhD. Reader in Russian, Strathclyde University; b. 19.5.30, Southend-on-Sea; m., Mary Isobel McEwan;

2 d. Educ. Southend-on-Sea High School for Boys; Durham University. National Service, Intelligence Corps, 1953-55; War Office Language Instructor, 1955-63; Lecturer, Scottish College of Commerce, Glasgow, 1963-64; Lecturer, then Senior Lecturer, Strathclyde University, from 1964. Convener, West of Scotland, Association of Teachers of Russian; Editor, Journal of Russian Studies, 1980-86. Publications: Russian Exercises for Language Laboratories (Co-author); The Russian Preposition 'do' and the Concept of Extent; Russia Today (Co-Editor). Address: 1 Cleveden Crescent, Glasgow, G12 OPD; T.-041-339 3947.

Wakeford, Air Marshal Sir Richard (Gordon), KCB (1976), MVO (1961), OBE (1958), AFC (1952). Secretary, RAF Benevolent Fund, Scotland, since 1978; b. 20.4.22; m.; 2 s.; 1 d.; 1 d. (deceased). Educ. Montpelier School, Paignton; Kelly College, Tavistock. Joined RAF, 1941; Commander, N. Maritime Air Region and Air Officer Scotland and N. Ireland, 1970-72; Deputy Chief of Defence Staff, 1975-78.

Walkden, Gordon Mark, BSc, PhD. Member, Kincardine and Deeside District Council, since 1984; Lecturer and Research Scientist, Department of Geology, Aberdeen University, since 1970; Geological Consultant to industry; b. 8.6.44, Edinburgh; m., K. Mary M. Begg; 3 c. Educ. Quintin School, London; Manchester University. Past Chairman, Banchory Community Council. Recreations: building restoration; palaeontology. Address: (h.) Banchory, Kincardineshire.

Walker, Alexander William, JP. Honorary Sheriff, since 1971; Chairman, Finance and General Purposes Committee, Tweeddale District Council, since 1977 (Member of Council, since 1974); Chairman, Tweeddale Licensing Board, since 1975; b. 10.5.24, Peebles; m., Dorothy Margaret. Educ. Kingsland School; Scottish Woollen and Worsted Technical College. D.B. Ballantyne Bros., 1939-70; Air Training Corps, 1941-43, RAF, 1943-46 (Sergeant); Director, Sonido International Ltd. (formerly Fidelitone International Ltd.); elected, Peebles Town Council, 1960-75; Provost, 1967-70; Burgh Treasurer, 1971-75; held every office, Peebles Town Council; Member, Peeblesshire County Council, 1960-70 (Vice Chairman, Finance Committee); Vice Chairman, Tweeddale District Council, 1974-77; Warden, Neidpath Castle, 1971; former Dean, Guildry Corporation of Peebles; former Secretary, Peebles Callants Club. Recreations: football in younger days; now enjoys reading political biographies and drinking whisky and, of course, local government, which unfortunately is no longer local or indeed democratic. Address: (h.) Gadeni, 59 High Street, Peebles; T.-Peebles 21011.

Walker, Sir Allan Grierson, KB, QC, MA, LLB, LLD. Sheriff Principal of Lanarkshire, 1963-74; b. 1.5.07, Dumfries; 1 s. Educ. Whitgift School; Edinburgh University. Practised at Scottish Bar, 1931-39; Sheriff Substitute, Selkirk and Peebles, 1942-45; Sheriff Substitute, Dumbarton, 1945-50;

Sheriff Substitute, Glasgow, 1950-63; Member, Law Reform Committee for Scotland, 1964-70; Chairman, Sheriff Court Rules Council, 1972-74. Publications: The Law of Evidence in Scotland (Co-author); Purves' Scottish Licensing Laws, 7th and 8th editions. Recreations: gardening; walking. Address: (h.) 24 Moffat Road, Dumfries, DG1 1NJ; T.-0387 53583.

Walker, Colin Herriot Macdonald, MD, FRCPEdin, FACC, DCH. Consultant Paediatrician, Tayside Health Board, since 1964; Honorary Reader, Department of Child Health, Dundee University, since 1980 (Honorary Senior Lecturer, 1964-80); b. 15.5.23, Edinburgh; m., Anne E. Gillieson; 1 s.; 1 d. Educ. Melville College, Edinburgh; Edinburgh University. Junior hospital appointments, Edinburgh; Registrar and Senior Registrar, Great Ormond Street Hospital for Sick Children; one year in Australia and six years in America; Chairman, Child Health Computing Committee, London, and Health Statistics Committee, British Paediatric Association; Visiting Lecturer to Belgium, Doha, Kuwait, Korea. Recreations: curling; golf; gardening; swimming. Address: (b.) Department of Child Health, Ninewells Hospital and Medical School, Dundee, DD1 9SY; T.-0382 60111, Ext. 2544.

Walker, Professor David Maxwell, QC, MA, PhD, LLD, Hon. LLD, FBA, FRSE. Regius Professor of Law, Glasgow University, since 1958; b. 9.4.20, Glasgow; m., Margaret Knox. Educ. High School of Glasgow; Glasgow University; Edinburgh University; London University. HLI and Indian Army, 1939-46; Advocate, 1948; in practice, Scottish Bar, 1948-54; Professor of Jurisprudence, Glasgow University, 1954-58; Barrister (Middle Temple),1957; QC (Scot), 1958; Dean, Faculty of Law, Glasgow University, 1956-59; Convener, School of Law, since 1984. Chairman, High School of Glasgow Trust (School Governor). Publications: Law of Damages in Scotland; The Scottish Legal System; Law of Delict in Scotland; Law of Civil Remedies in Scotland; Law of Prescription in Scotland; Law of Contracts in Scotland; Oxford Companion to Law; Principles of Scottish Private Law (four volumes); The Scottish Jurists; Stair's Institutions (Editor); Stair Tercentenary Studies (Editor). Recreations: book collecting; Scottish history; motoring. Address: (b.) Department of Private Law, Glasgow University, Glasgow, G12 8QQ; T.-041-339 8855, Ext. 556.

Walker, David Morrison, DA, FSA Scot, HFRIAS. Principal Inspector of Historic Buildings, Scottish Development Department, since 1978; b. 31.1.33, Dundee; m., Averil Mary Stewart McIlwraith; 1 s. Educ. Morgan Academy, Dundee; Dundee College of Art. Voluntary work for National Buildings Record, Edinburgh, 1952-56; National Service, Royal Engineers, 1956-58; Glasgow Education Authority, 1958-59; Dundee Education Authority, 1959-61; Historic Buildings Branch, Scottish Office: Senior Investigator of Historic Buildings, 1961-76, Principal Investigator of Historic Buildings, 1976-78. Alice David Hitchcock Medallion, 1970. Publications: Architecture of Glasgow (Co-author), 1968;

Buildings of Scotland: Edinburgh (Co-author), 1984; Dundee: An Illustrated Introduction (Co-author), 1984; Dundee Nineteenth Century Mansions, 1958. Address: (b.) 25 Drumsheugh Gardens, Edinburgh, EH3 7RN; T.-031-226 3611.

Walker, Ernest John Munro. Secretary, The Scottish Football Association Ltd., since 1977; b. 20.7.28, Glasgow; m., Anne; 1 s.; 2 d. Educ. Queen's Park Secondary School. Army (Royal Horse Artillery), 1946-48; Assistant Secretary, industrial textile company, 1948-58; Assistant Secretary, Scottish Football Association, 1958-77. Director, Scottish Football Development Association; Director, Scotball Travel and Leisure Ltd.; Member, Main Organising Committee, XIII Commonwealth Games Scotland, 1986. Recreations: golf; fishing; music; travel. Address: (b.) 6 Park Gardens, Glasgow, G3 7YF; T.-041-332 6372.

Walker, Esme, MA, LLB, WS, NP. Vice-Chairman, National Consumer Council, since 1984; Chairman, Scottish Consumer Council, since 1980; b. 7.1.32, Edinburgh; m., Ian Macfarlane Walker; 1 s. Educ. St. George's School for Girls, Edinburgh; Edinburgh University. Lawyer; Member, Lord Chancellor's Committee on Conveyancing. Address: (h.) Clinton House, Whitehouse Loan, Edinburgh; T.-031-447 5191.

Walker, Frank Arneil, BArch, PhD, RIBA, ARIAS, FSA Scot. Senior Lecturer in Architecture, Strathclyde University, since 1982; b. 3.6.38, Paisley; m., M.L. Jasna Havranek; 1 s.; 1 d. Educ. Paisley Grammar School; Glasgow School of Architecture. Private architectural practice, 1960-72 (Partner, Walker and Cunningham, 1967-72); teaching, Strathclyde University, since 1969; has taught and lectured in Poland, Czechoslovakia, Yugoslavia and Turkey. Recreations: walking; watching St. Mirren FC. Address: (h.) Janefield, Gillburn Road, Kilmacolm, Renfrewshire.

Walker, George P. Principal, Pharmaceutical Services Division, Scottish Home and Health Department, since 1982; b. 30.3.44, Dunfermline; m., Isobel H. Anderson; 2 d. Educ. Dunfermline High School. Executive Officer, Government Actuary's Department and SDD, 1962-67; Higher Executive Officer, SDD, 1967-73; Senior Executive Officer, Scottish Office and SHHD, 1973-82. Recreations: hill-walking; other sporting activities. Address: (h.) 5 Transy Grove, Dunfermline, KY12 7QP; T.-0383 720637.

Walker, Ian. Member, Gordon District Council, since 1984; Head Teacher, Westhill Primary School, since 1973; Member, Gordon Local Health Council; b. 1.6.40, Inverurie; m., Mildred Agnes; 1 s.; 1 d. Educ. Daviot School; Inverurie Academy; Aberdeen College of Education. Assistant Teacher, Insch School, 1963-67; Head Teacher: Finzean School, 1967-69, Kinellar School, 1969-73; Member, Aberdeen Advisory Committee, IBA; Member, Joint Library Committee, North East of Scotland Library Service; Member, Working Party on Mathematics in the

Primary School, Grampian Regional Council; Recreations: curling; golf; cricket (Blue, Aberdeen College of Education); reading; listening to all kinds of music; theatre; films. Address: (h.) 11A Arnhall Drive, Westhill, Skene, Aberdeenshire, AB3 6TZ; T.-0224 741783.

Walker, James, CA. Senior Partner, James Rosie & Co., CA, Galashiels and Peebles, since 1968; Chairman, Board of Governors, Scottish College of Textiles; b. 14.6.27, Airdrie; 1 s.; 1 d. Educ. Airdrie Academy. Recreations: golf; bridge. Address: (h.) Broombank, Gattonside, Melrose, Roxburghshire; T.-0896 82 2362.

Walker, Rev. Dr. James Bernard, MA, BD, DPhil. Minister, Galashiels Old Parish and St. Paul's, since 1978; b. 7.5.46, Livingstonia, Malawi; m., Sheila Mary Easton; 3 s. Educ. Hamilton Academy; Edinburgh University; Merton College, Oxford. Ordained, 1975; Associate Minister, Mid Craigie and Wallacetown, Dundee, 1975-78. Recreations: football; hockey; squash; hill-climbing. Address: Old Parish Manse, Barr Road, Galashiels, TD1 3HX; T.-0896 2320.

Walker, Rev. Kenneth Donald Fraser, MA, BD. Minister, Athelstaneford linked with Whitekirk and Tyninghame, since 1976; b. 4.9.42, Tarbert, Argyll; m., Veronica McClay Fraser; 2 s.; 3 d. Educ. Girvan Academy; Edinburgh University. Entered banking profession,1961; licensed to the Ministry, 1974; Assistant Minister, Bearsden South, 1974; ordained, 1976; a Chaplain to Moderator, General Assembly, 1981. Recreations: gardening; hill-walking; squash. Address: The Manse, Athelstaneford, North Berwick, EH39 5BE; T.-062088 378.

Walker, Leslie James, BSc, CEng, FICE, MIHE. Director of Technical Services, Dunfermline District Council, since 1974; b. 10.12.31, Ferryhill, Co. Durham; m., Beatrice; 2 s. Educ. Acklam Hall Grammar School, Middlesbrough; Edinburgh University. Assistant Resident Engineer, Partridge Earp & Partners, Edinburgh, 1953-60; Dunfermline Town Council: Assistant Engineer, 1960-63, Principal Engineer, 1963-70, Depute Burgh Engineer, 1970-75. Recreation: rugby football. Address: (b.) 7 Abbot Street, Dunfermline; T.-Dunfermline 731751.

Walker, Margaret Mary, MB, ChB, MRCPsych, DObstRCOG. Consultant Psychiatrist in Adult Psychiatry, Duke Street Hospital, Glasgow, since 1977; Honorary Clinical Lecturer, Glasgow University, since 1978; b. 11.6.42, Hammersmith; m., Norman G. Niblock. Educ. Greenhead High School, Huddersfield; Glasgow University. House Officer appointments; medical rotation, Glasgow Royal Infirmary; began psychiatric training in Glasgow, 1972. President, Psychosomatic Society (Glasgow), 1982-84. Recreations: hill-walking; geology; archaeology; photography; foreign travel. Address: (b.) Duke Street Hospital, Glasgow; T.-041-556 5222.

Walker, Michael Giles Neish, CBE, MA (Cantab). Chief Executive, Sidlaw Group plc, since 1976; b. 28.8.33, Fife; m., Margaret R. Hills; 2 s.; 1 d. Educ. Shrewsbury School; St.

John's College, Cambridge. National Service, Royal Dragoons, 1952-54 (2nd Lt.); TA, Fife and Forfar Yeomanry, 1954-72 (Major); joined Jute Industries Ltd., 1958 (subsequently name changed to Sidlaw Group); Director, Dundee and London Investment Trust plc, since 1982; Member, North of Scotland Hydro-Electric Board, since 1982; Director, Pict Petroleum PLC. Address: (b.) Sidlaw Group plc, Nethergate Centre, Dundee, DD1 4BR; T.-0382 23161.

Walker, Thomas Wallace, CBE, BL, FIB (Scot). Deputy Governor, British Linen Bank Ltd., since 1975; Chairman, Capital Leasing Ltd., since 1975; Chairman, Macdonald Orr Ltd., since 1982; b. 20.7.13, Paisley. Educ. John Neilson Institution, Paisley; Glasgow University. General Manager, British Linen Bank, 1963-71; Treasurer and General Manager, Bank of Scotland, 1970-74 (Director, 1974-84); founding Chairman, International Energy Bank Ltd., 1973-78; President, Institute of Bankers in Scotland, 1965-67; Director, Life Association of Scotland Ltd., 1978-84; Trustee, Bield Housing Trust; Past Chairman, Abbeyfield Society for Scotland Ltd.; Committee Member (former Treasurer), Malcolm Sargent Cancer Fund for Children (Scotland). Recreation: reading. Address: (h.) Kinfauns, 6 Frogston Terrace, Edinburgh, EH10 7AD; T.-031-445 1164.

Walker, William Buchanan Cowan, MA, LLB. Solicitor; Secretary, Royal Scottish Forestry Society; Farmer and Landowner; b. 27.6.27, Callander; m., Rita Bate; 2 s.; 1 d. Educ. Dollar Academy; Edinburgh Academy; Edinburgh University. Assistant, Robert Stewart & Scott, SSC, Edinburgh; Partner, Henderson and Jackson, WS, Edinburgh; Consultant, Lindsays, WS, Edinburgh; Director, Jamaica Street Ltd.; Director, Glenbervie Estate Co. Ltd.; Director, Garvald School Ltd. Recreations: repairing old buildings; travelling; people watching. Address: (h.) Stoneyknowe, West Linton, Peeblesshire.

Walker, William Connell, MP, FIPM, FBIM, FRSA. MP (Conservative), Tayside North, since 1979; Chairman, British Emerald Airways, since 1985; Defence Spokesman, Scottish Conservative Party, since 1981; b. Dundee; m., Mavis Evelyn; 3 d. Educ. Logie School. Message boy; RAF (commissioned); Training and Education Officer; Director of Personnel; Managing Director. Recreations: gliding; caravanning. Address: (h.) Candletrees, Golf Course Road, Rosemount, Blairgowrie, Perthshire; T.-0250 2660.

Walkingshaw, Francis, NP. Solicitor; Procurator Fiscal, District of Wigtown, since 1983; b. 9.12.42, Edinburgh; m., Penelope Marion Theodosia Brooks McKissock; 2 s. Educ. George Watson's College, Edinburgh. Private practice; joined Procurator Fiscal service, 1975. Recreations: shooting; food and wine. Address: (b.) Sheriff Court House, Lewis Street, Stranraer; T.-0776 4321.

Wall, Ernest Stanley, OBE. Member of Council, International Hockey Federation; Member, Hockey Rules Board; Honorary Secretary, Indoor Hockey Committee, International Hockey

Federation; b. 26.12.24, Edinburgh; m., Maureen Clark; 2 d. Educ. George Heriot's School, Edinburgh. RAF, 1942-47 (Air Gunner); Scottish Office (Scottish Home and Health Department), 1947-84 (retiring as Principal). Former international Umpire, men's hockey; former Honorary Secretary, President and Chairman, Scottish Hockey Association; former Member, Great Britain (Olympic) Men's Hockey Board. Recreations: men's hockey administration; gramophone records. Address: (h.) 69 Montpelier Park, Edinburgh, EH10 4ND; T.-031-229 2713.

Wallace, Professor David Alexander Ross, BSc, PhD, FRSA, FRSE. Professor of Mathematics, Stirling University, since 1973; b. 24.11.33, Cupar. Educ. Stranraer High School; St. Andrews University; Manchester University. Instructor: Princeton University, 1958-59, Harvard University, 1959-60; Research Fellow, then Lecturer, Glasgow University, 1960-65; Senior Lecturer, Aberdeen University, 1965-73. Recreations: tennis; swimming; skiing; badminton. Address: (b.) Department of Mathematics, Stirling University, Stirling, FK9 4LA; T.-0786 73171.

Wallace, Professor David James, BSc, PhD, FRSE. Tait Professor of Mathematical Physics, Edinburgh University, since 1979 (Head, Department of Physics, since 1984); b. 7.10.45, Hawick; m., Elizabeth Anne Yeats; 1 d. Educ. Hawick High School; Edinburgh University. Harkness Fellow, Princeton University, 1970-72; Lecturer in Physics, 1971-78, Reader, 1978-79, Southampton University; Visiting Scientist, Europe, Israel, North and South America. Maxwell Medal, Institute of Physics, 1980. Recreations: running; eating at La Potiniere. Address: (b.) Physics Department, The University, Mayfield Road, Edinburgh, EH9 3JZ; T.-031-667 1081.

Wallace, Rev. Douglas Woodburn, MA (Hons), BD (Hons). Minister, Kilmodan and Colintraive, since 1982; b. 23.9.55, Greenock; m., Janet Rosalind Lee; 2 s. Educ. Greenock Academy; New College, Edinburgh. Member, Church of Scotland Youth Education Committee; Education Convener, Dunoon Presbytery, since 1983. Recreations: long-distance running; music; reading; board games; worship. Address: Kilmodan Manse, Glendaruel, Colintraive, Argyll, PA22 3AA.

Wallace of Campsie, Baron, (George Wallace), JP, DL. Life President, Wallace, Cameron (Holdings) Ltd., since 1981; Life Peer; b. 13.2.15; m. Educ. Queen's Park Secondary School, Glasgow; Glasgow University. Solicitor, since 1950; Honorary Sheriff, Hamilton, since 1971; Chairman, East Kilbride and Stonehouse Development Corporation, 1969-75; Member, South of Scotland Electricity Board, 1966-68; founder Member, Board, Scottish Development Agency, 1975-78; President, Glasgow Chamber of Commerce, 1974-76; Honorary President, Scottish Section, Town and Country Planning Association, since 1969; Chairman, Scottish Executive Committee, British Heart Foundation, 1973-76; Vice-Chairman, Scottish Retirement Council, since 1975.

Wallace, James Moore, CA, FCMA, JdipMA. Financial Director, Scottish Tourist Board, since 1977; b. 9.2.24, Glasgow; m., Janet Elizabeth Niven; 1 s.; 2 d. Educ. High School of Glasgow; Glasgow University. Pilot, RAF, 1943-47; Secretary, Sandeman Bros. Ltd., 1950-62; Chief Accountant, British Relay Ltd., 1962-65; Financial Controller, Philip Morris Inc., 1966-73; General Manager, James Robertson (Preserves) Ltd., 1973-75; Development Director, Scottish Tourist Board, 1975-77. Recreations: golf; sailing; swimming; hill-walking. Address: (h.) 10 Thorn Road, Bearsden, Glasgow, G61 4PP; T.-041-942 4041.

Wallace, James Robert, MP, MA (Cantab), LLB (Edinburgh). MP (Liberal/Alliance), Orkney and Shetland, since 1983; Liberal Parliamentary Spokesman on Energy and Fisheries, 1983-85, on Defence and Fisheries, since 1985; Deputy Whip, since 1985; Advocate, since 1979; b. 25.8.54, Annan; m., Rosemary Janet Fraser; 1 d. Educ. Annan Academy; Downing College, Cambridge; Edinburgh University. Called to Scottish Bar, 1979; contested Dumfries, 1979, and South of Scotland Euro Constituency, 1979; Member, Scottish Liberal Party Executive, 1976-85 (Vice-Chairman, Policy, 1982-85); Honorary President, Scottish Young Liberals, 1984-85. Publication: New Deal for Rural Scotland (Co-Editor), 1983. Recreations: golf; reading; travelling (especially between London and the Northern Isles). Address: (h.) Northwood House, Tankerness, Orkney, KW17 2QS; T.-0856 86 383.

Wallace, John Anderson. Chief Executive, Tayside Regional Council, since 1982; b. 10.7.29, Perth; m., Mary; 1 s.; 1 d. Educ. Perth Academy; Edinburgh University. Solicitor, private practice, 1951-54; Solicitor: Dundee Corporation, 1954-60, Cumbernauld Development Corporation, 1960-66; Deputy Town Clerk, Dundee Corporation, 1966-75; Depute Chief Executive, Tayside, 1975-82. Recreations: golf; bowls; winemaking; music. Address: (b.) Tayside House, 28 Crichton Street, Dundee; T.-Dundee 23281.

Wallace, John David, MA, DipEd, FSA Scot. International Arbiter, Federation Internationale des Echecs; Vice President, Scottish Junior Chess Association; Council Member, Scottish Chess Association; b. 21.11.21, Bulford; m., Jenefer M.H. Bell (deceased); 1 s.; 1 d. Educ. Tonbridge School; St. Andrews University. Army Service, 1940-46 (Captain, Royal Artillery); teaching appointments in Orkney and Fife, 1954-73; Assistant Rector, Madras College, St. Andrews, 1971-73; founding Headmaster, Abbotsgrange Middle School, Grangemouth, 1974-84. Recreations: bridge; chess; curling; hill-walking. Address: (h.) Kirkheugh Cottage, The Shorehead, St. Andrews, Fife, KY16 9RG.

Wallace of That Ilk, Lt.-Col. Malcolm Robert. 34th Chief (1970); Member, Queen's Bodyguard for Scotland (Royal Company of Archers); b. 14.12.21, Perth. Educ. Stowe. Commissioned, The Black Watch, 1941; served 1941-45 (mentioned in Despatches); served Korean War, 1950-51 (Argyll and Sutherland Highlanders) and 1952 (Black Watch); Australian Staff College,

1955; commanded Argyll and Sutherland Highlanders, 1964-67; Regimental Secretary, The Black Watch, 1967-78. Recreations: shooting; fishing. Address: (h.) Hilton of Gask, Auchterarder, Perthshire; T.-Gask 278.

Wallace, Robert Gamble, CEng, FRINA. GRP Production Director, Yarrow Shipbuilders Ltd., Glasgow, since 1981; b. 22.9.20, Gourock; m., Edith; 1 s. Educ. Gourock High School. Lithgows Ltd., 1936-43; James Lamont & Co. Ltd.: Manager, 1943-54, Director, 1954-69, Managing Director, 1969-81. Recreations: golf; snooker. Address: (h.) Avon, 30 Clyde Road, Gourock; T.-0475 31925.

Wallace, Rev. William Fitch, BDS, BD. Minister, Wick St. Andrew's and Thrumster Church, since 1974; Executive Member, Church of Scotland Board of Social Responsibility, since 1985; b. 6.10.39, Falkirk; m., Jean Wyness Hill; 1 s.; 3 d. Educ. Allan Glen's School; Glasgow University; Edinburgh University. Ordained Assistant, St. George's Tron, Glasgow, 1968-71; Missionary Dentist, Addis Ababa, Ethiopia, 1971-73. Chairman, Caithness Local Health Council, 1975-83; Member, Church of Scotland Social Responsibility Committee, 1975-83; Organising Secretary, Wick Primary Schools Action Group, since 1984. Recreations: golf; gardening. Address: St. Andrew's Manse, Coronation Street, Wick, KW1 5LS; T.-Wick 3166.

Wallace, William Villiers, MA, FRHistS. Director, Institute of Soviet and East European Studies, Glasgow University, since 1979; b. 15.12.26, Glasgow; m., Gulli Fyfe; 2 s.; 1 d. Educ. Hutchesons' Boys' Grammar School; Glasgow University; London University. RNVR, 1944-47; appointments in History, Pittsburgh University, London University, Aberdeen University, Durham University, 1953-67; Professor of History, New University of Ulster, 1967-79. Chairman, Scottish Branch, Royal Institute of International Affairs; Vice-Chairman, Association of University Teachers (Scotland). Address: (b.) Institute of Soviet and East European Studies, Glasgow University, 29 Bute Gardens, Glasgow, G12 8RS; T.-041-339 8855.

Walls, Professor Andrew Finlay, MA, BLitt, FSA Scot. Director, Centre for the Study of Christianity in the Non-Western World, since 1983; Professor of Religious Studies, Aberdeen University, since 1979; b. 21.4.28; m., Doreen Mary Harden; 1 s.; 1 d. Librarian, Tyndale House, Cambridge, 1952-57; Lecturer in Theology, Fourah Bay College, Sierra Leone, 1957-62; Head, Department of Religion, Nigeria University, 1962-65; Aberdeen University: Lecturer in Church History, 1966-69, Senior Lecturer, 1969, first Head, Department of Religious Studies, and Riddoch Lecturer in Comparative Religion, 1970, Reader, 1975. Co-opted Member, Aberdeen Education Committee, 1971-74; Aberdeen City Councillor, 1974-80; Convener, Arts and Recreation, COSLA, 1978-80; Chairman, Council for Museums and Galleries in Scotland, 1978-81; Vice-Chairman, Committee of Area Museums Councils, 1980-81; Member, Williams Committee on the future of the national museums, 1979-82; Member, Advisory Committee on Religious Education, General Teaching Council; Trustee, National Museum of Antiquities of Scotland, since 1982; Member, Museums Advisory Board for Scotland, since 1984; Methodist Preacher; Past Chairman, Disablement Income Group, Scotland; President, British Association for the History of Religions, 1977-80; Secretary, Scottish Institute of Missionary Studies; Editor, Journal of Religion in Africa; Member, Scottish Working Party on Religions of the World. Address: (b.) Centre for the Study of Christianity in the Non-Western World, Aberdeen University, Aberdeen, AB9 2UB; T.-0224 40241.

Walsh, David Brian, MB, ChB, MRCPath. Consultant in Clinical Chemistry, Tayside Health Board, since 1973; Honorary Senior Lecturer in Biochemical Medicine, Dundee University, since 1973; b. 3.7.41, Douglas, Isle of Man; m., Maureen; 2 d. Educ. William Hulme's Grammar School, Manchester; Victoria University of Manchester. House Officer posts, St. Woolos Hospital, Newport; Senior House Officer posts in Clinical Pathology, London Hospital and Llandough Hospital, Cardiff; Lecturer in Pathology, Manchester University; Senior Registrar in Chemical Pathology, United Manchester Hospitals. Editor, UTEC Database. Recreations: photography; family. Address: (b.) Department of Biochemical Medicine, Ninewells Hospital, Dundee, DD2 9SY.

Walsh, Ewart Geoffrey, MA, BSc, BM, BCh (Oxon), MD, FRSE, FRCP, FRCPEdin. Reader, Department of Physiology, Edinburgh University; b. 25.11.22, Cheltenham; m., E.P.Y. Watson; 4 d. Educ. Cheltenham Grammar School; Oxford University; Harvard University. Academic career, Edinburgh University, since 1951; WHO Visiting Professor, Baroda Medical School, India, 1963-64. Recreation: playing the flute. Address: (b.) Physiology Department, Teviot Place, Edinburgh, EH8 9AG; T.-031-667 1011.

Walsh, Professor Patrick Gerard, MA, PhD, FRSE. Professor of Humanity, Glasgow University, since 1972; b. 16.8.23, Accrington; m., Eileen Benson Quin; 4 s.; 1 d. Educ. Preston Catholic College; Liverpool University. Lecturer in Ancient Classics, University College, Dublin, 1952-59; Lecturer, Reader, Professor, Department of Humanity, Edinburgh University, 1959-72. Recreations: tennis; travel. Address: (h.) 17 Broom Road, Glasgow, G43 2TP; T.-041-637 4977.

Walsh, Sadie Delores, MB, ChB, MRCPEdin, FRCPEdin. Consultant Physician, Royal Victoria Hospital and Corstorphine Hospital, Edinburgh, since 1980; b. 14.10.32, Kingston, Jamaica; m., John Nuttall; 2 d. Educ. Edinburgh University. House Physician, Roodland General Hospital; House Surgeon, Dumfries and Galloway Royal Infirmary; House Physician, Royal Hospital for Sick Children, Edinburgh; Registrar posts, Respiratory Unit, City Hospital, Edinburgh; general medicine, Western General Hospital, Edinburgh; Registrar, Haematology, Edinburgh Royal Infirmary; Registrar, Geriatric Medicine, Royal Victoria Hospital, Edinburgh; Consultant

Physician, Geriatric Medicine, Fife Health Board, 1975-80. Recreations: hill-walking; skiing; swimming. Address: (h.) 13 Lansdowne Crescent, Edinburgh, EH12 5EH; T.-031-337 2966.

Walton, Professor Ewart Kendall, BSc, PhD, FRSE. Professor of Geology, St. Andrews University, since 1968; b. 28.11.24, Ashington, Northumberland; m., 1, Margaret; 1 s.; 1 d.; 2, Susan Clare; 2 s.; 1 d. Educ. Bedlington Secondary School, Northumberland; King's College, Durham. Assistant, Glasgow University, 1951-54; Lecturer, then Reader, Edinburgh University, 1954-68. President, Association of Teachers of Geology, 1978-80; Member, Scottish Advisory Committee, NCC, 1982-85; Member, Geology Panel, Scottish Examination Board, 1982-85. Address: (b.) Department of Geology, Purdie Building, St. Andrews, Fife, KY16 9ST; T.-0334 76161.

Walton, John Christopher, BSc, PhD, DSc. Senior Lecturer in Chemistry, St. Andrews University, since 1980; b. 4.12.41, St. Albans; m., Jane Lehman; 1 s.; 1 d. Educ. Watford Grammar School for Boys; Sheffield University. Assistant Lecturer: Queen's College, St. Andrews, 1966-67, Dundee University, 1967-69; Lecturer in Chemistry, United College, St. Andrews, 1969-80. Director, Good Health Association (Scotland) Ltd.; Elder, seventh-day Adventist Church. Recreations: music; philosophy. Address: (b.) Department of Chemistry, St. Andrews University, St. Andrews, Fife, KY16 9ST; T.-0334 76161.

Walton, Kenneth D., BMus, GMusRNCM, ARCO. Scottish Music Critic, Daily Telegraph, since 1983; Music Journalist: Classical Music magazine, Sunday Times, Glasgow Herald; b. 20.2.58, Paisley; m., Janis H. Goodfellow; 1 d. Educ. Paisley Grammar School; Glasgow University; Royal Northern College of Music, Manchester. Tutor in Music, Glasgow University, 1982-83; President, Glasgow Society of Organists; Organist and Choirmaster, Lylesland Parish Church, Paisley, since 1982; Conductor, Bridge of Weir Choral Society, 1981-85. Recreation: golf. Address: (h.) 38 Lancaster Avenue, Beith, Ayrshire, KA15 1AR; T.-Beith 3511.

Wannop, Professor Urlan Alistair, MA, MCD, MRTPI. Professor of Urban and Regional Planning, Strathclyde University, since 1981; b. 16.4.31, Newtown St. Boswells; m., Jean; 1 s.; 1 d. Educ. Aberdeen Grammar School; Edinburgh University; Liverpool University. Appointments in public and private practice, 1956-68; Team Leader, Coventry-Solihull-Warwickshire Sub-Regional Planning Study, 1968-71; Director, West Central Scotland Plan, 1972-74; Senior Deputy Director of Planning, Strathclyde Regional Council, 1975-81; Vice-Chairman, Planning Committee, Social Science Research Council, 1978-82; Member, Parliamentary Boundary Commission for Scotland, since 1983. Address: (h.) 43 Lomond Street, Helensburgh, G84 7ES; T.-0436 4622.

Ward, Rev. Alan Henry, MA (Hons), BD (Hons). Minister, Greyfriars' Church, Dumfries, since 1978; b. 2.6.48, Glasgow; m., Alison Lindsay Stead; 2 s. Educ. Hillhead High School, Glasgow; Glasgow University; Edinburgh University; Jordanhill College. Teacher of English, Kingsridge School, Glasgow, 1971-73; Assistant Minister, St. Leonard's Church, St. Andrews, 1976-78. Member, Working Group on Special Educational Needs, Church of Scotland Education Department. Recreations: gardening; early music; photography; reading. Address: Greyfriars' Manse, 4 Georgetown Crescent, Dumfries, DG1 4EQ; T.-0387 62783.

Ward, Brian W., FCCA, IPFA. Director of Finance and Depute Chief Executive, Wigtown District Council, since 1983; b. 29.10.52, Chatham, Kent; m., Margaret E.; 1 s.; 1 d. Address: (b.) District Offices, Sun Street, Stranraer, DG9 7JJ; T.-0776 2151.

Ward, Emeritus Professor Dennis, MA (Cantab). Chairman, Scottish Slavonic Review; Emeritus Professor of Russian, Edinburgh University, since 1984; b. 1.2.24, Rotherham; m., Doreen Mary Robinson; 2 s.; 1 d. Educ. Rotherham Grammar School; Christ's College, Cambridge. Military service, 1943-47: Queen's Royal Regiment, commissioned into York and Lancaster, 1944, Captain, 1946, Russian Interpreter, Allied Control Commission, Berlin, Liaison Officer to Soviet C-in-C's military mission to British Zone, 1946-47; Edinburgh University: Lecturer in Russian, 1949, Senior Lecturer, 1959, Reader, 1961, Professor, 1963; Acting Director, Russian Language Research Project, Essex University, 1967; President, British Universities Association of Slavists; Heath Visiting Professor, Grinnell College, Iowa, 1982; founded (with P. Henry) Scottish Slavonic Review, 1983; Member, Commission on Research and Development in Modern Languages; Member, Editorial Board, Russian Linguistics. Recreations: looking at pictures; painting pictures; visiting prehistoric settlements. Address: (h.) 21B Clermiston Road, Edinburgh, EH12 6XG; T.-031-334 1184.

Wardell, Gareth. Producer-Director, Jam Jar Films, since 1985; Freelance Producer and Presenter, BBC, since 1985; Founder/Director, Arts Education Trust; b. 26.10.46, Edinburgh. Educ. Royal Scottish Academy of Music and Drama; Glasgow University; Jordanhill College of Education. Trainee Actor and Director, various repertory companies; Teacher of Speech and Drama, John Street Secondary School, Glasgow; Lecturer in Speech and Drama, Moray House College of Education, Edinburgh; Founder/Artistic Director, Scottish Youth Theatre/Young Playwrights Festival/Scottish Youth Festival; Head of Youth Programmes, BBC TV and Radio. Recreations: friends; landscape gardening; interior design. Address: 521 Lanark Road West, Balerno, Edinburgh, EH14 7DH; T.-031-449 7227.

Wardell, James Lewis, BSc, PhD. Senior Lecturer in Chemistry, Aberdeen University, since 1984; b. 9.9.39, Eastbourne; m., Sharon Caroleen Munro; 2 d. Educ. Roan School, Greenwich; King's College, London University. Aberdeen University: Assistant Lecturer in Chemistry,

1964-67, Lecturer in Chemistry, 1967-84. Recreations: golf; Aberdeen FC. Address: (b.) Department of Chemistry, Aberdeen University, Aberdeen, AB9 2UE; T.-Aberdeen 40241.

Wardlaw, Professor Alastair Connell, MSc, PhD, DSc, FRSE. Professor of Microbiology, Glasgow University, since 1970; b. 20.1.30, Port of Spain; m., Jacqueline Shirley Jones; 1 s.; 2 d. Educ. Manchester Grammar School; Manchester University. Research Fellow, Western Reserve University, Cleveland, Ohio, 1953-55; Sir Alexander Fleming Research Fellow, St. Mary's Hospital, London, 1955-58; Research Fellow and Research Member, Connaught Laboratories, Toronto, 1958-66; Professor of Microbiology, Toronto University, 1966-70. Member, Marshall Aid Commemoration Commssion. Publication: Sourcebook of Experiments for the Teaching of Microbiology. Recreations: ceramics; gardening; cycle-camping. Address: (h.) 92 Drymen Road, Bearsden, Glasgow, G61 2SY; T.-041-942 2461.

Wardman, Charles Terry, JP. Honorary Sheriff; b. 11.9.13, London; m., Jean Marie Woolveridge; 2 s.; 3 d. Educ. Brighton College. RAF Wing Commander (retired); former Managing Director, A.I.D. Ltd., Shenstone; former Argyll County Councillor; former Member, Argyll and Bute District Council; Past Chairman, Dunoon and Cowal Housing Association. Recreations: sailing; skiing; golf; gardening. Address: (h.) Glendaruel, by Colintraive, Argyll, PA22 3AF.

Warner, Rev. Kenneth, DA (Hons), DipTP, RIBA, MRTPI, ARIAS, BD. Minister, Halkirk linked with Westerdale and Halsary, since 1981; b. 10.12.38, Glasgow; m., Ann Harriet Sangster Maule-Brown; 2 s. Educ. George Watson's Boys' College; Edinburgh College of Art; St. Andrews University. Architect in private practice, Henry Wylie and Partners, Edinburgh, 1963-66; Sir William Holford and Partners, Glasgow, 1966-69; Town Planning: Glasgow Corporation, 1969-72, Motherwell Town Council, 1972-75; Area Planning Officer, Hamilton District Council, 1975, Orkney Islands Council, 1975-78. Moderator, Caithness Presbytery, 1984-85. Recreations: painting; gardening. Address: Abbey Manse, Halkirk, Caithness; T.-Halkirk 227.

Warren, Alastair Kennedy, TD, MA. Editor, Dumfries and Galloway Standard, since 1976; Trustee, The Enterprise Trust for Nithsdale, Annandale/Eskdale and the Stewartry, since 1984; b. 17.7.22, Glasgow; m., Ann Lindsay Maclean; 2 s. Educ. Laurelbank School; Glasgow Academy; Loretto School; Glasgow University. Served at home and overseas, HLI, 1940-46 (from private to Major); Management Trainee, Stewarts and Lloyds, 1950-53; Glasgow Herald: joined, 1954, Business Editor, 1961-63, City Editor, 1964-65, Editor, 1965-74; Regional Editor, Scottish and Universal Newspapers Ltd., Southern Region, 1974-76. Served with 5/6th Bn., HLI (TA), 1976-78; first Chairman, Stewartry Mountaineering Club, 1976-78; Provost, Royal Burgh of New Galloway and Kells Parish, 1978-81. Recreations: hill-walking; running; swimming; poetry; conversation. Address: (h.) Rathan, High Street, New Galloway, Castle Douglas, DG7 3RN; T.-New Galloway 257.

Waterman, Peter George, BPharm (Hons), PhD, FLS. Reader in Phytochemistry, Department of Pharmacy, Strathclyde University, since 1984; b. 28.4.46, Langley, Kent; m., Margaret Humble. Educ. Judd School, Tonbridge; London University. Postgraduate Research Assistant, London University, 1968-69; Lecturer, then Senior Lecturer, Department of Pharmacy, Strathclyde University, 1969-84. Pharmaceutical Society Young Scientist of the Year Award, 1979; Phytochemical Society of Europe Tate & Lyle Award for contribution to Phytochemistry, 1984. Recreations: travel; walking. Address: (b.) Phytochemistry Research Laboratories, Department of Pharmacy, Strathclyde University, Glasgow, G1 1XW; T.-041-552 4400.

Waters, Rev. Robert, MA. General Secretary, Congregational Union of Scotland, since 1971; b. 8.7.30, Edinburgh; m., Magdalene Forrest; 1 s.; 1 d. Educ. Boroughmuir School, Edinburgh; Edinburgh University; Scottish Congregational College; Chicago University. Recreation: trout fishing. Address: (b.) 340 Cathedral Street, Glasgow, G1 2BQ; T.-041-332 7667.

Waterton, John Brian. Group Marketing Director, Dawson International plc, since 1978; b. 10.3.34, Bradford; m., Jane; 2 s.; 2 d. Educ. Giggleswick College. National Service (commissioned, Royal Artillery), 1952-54; wool textile industry, West Yorkshire, 1954-70, latterly as Joint Managing Director of company within Coats Patons Group; branded consumer durables industry, 1970-77, latterly as Deputy Managing Director of German subsidiaries, British-owned group. Member, Council, CBI Scotland, 1978-80. Recreation: golf. Address: (h.) 23 Danube Street, Edinburgh, EH4 1NN; T.-031-332 5505.

Watker, Rev. E. Raymond. Secretary, Methodist Synod in Scotland, since 1976; b. 18.3.28, Rotherham; m., Shirley H. Millns; 2 d. Educ. Handsworth College, Birmingham. Entered Methodist ministry, 1954; Minister, Tranent and Cockenzie, 1954-61; Peterhead, 1961-66, Clydebank and Drumchapel, 1966-73; Superintendent, Greenock Circuit, 1973-85, Kilsyth Circuit, 1985. Recreations: walking; music; photography. Address: (h.) Dormarky, Glasgow Road, Kilsyth, Glasgow, G65 9AE; T.-0236 823135.

Watkins, Trevor Francis, BA, PhD, FSA, FSA Scot. Senior Lecturer, Department of Archaeology, Edinburgh University, since 1979; Secretary, Society of Antiquaries of Scotland, since 1977; b. 20.2.38, Epsom, Surrey; m., Antoinette Marie; 1 s.; 2 d. Educ. Kingston Grammar School; Birmingham University. Research Fellow, Birmingham University; Lecturer, Edinburgh University. Honorary Secretary, British Institute of Archaeology at Ankara; Council Member, British School of Archaeology in Iraq. Recreations: walking; bird-watching; music. Address: (b.) Department of Archaeology, Edinburgh University, 19 George Square, Edinburgh, EH8 9JZ; T.-031-667 1011.

Watkinson, Geoffrey, MD, BS (Lond), FRCP (Lond), FRCPGlas. Consultant Physician and Gastroenterologist, Western Infirmary, Garnavel

General Hospital and Southern General Hospital, Glasgow, since 1969; b. 12.5.21, Bolton; m., Marie Christine; 1 s.; 1 d. Educ. Southgate County School; St. Bartholomew's Hospital, London. House Physician and Senior Registrar, Medical Professorial Unit, St. Bartholomew's Hospital; Medical Branch, RAF (Wing Commander); Leeds University, 1948-60, latterly as Senior Lecturer in Medicine and Honorary Consultant; Physician, Leeds General Infirmary and St. James Hospital, Leeds; Rockefeller Travelling Fellowship in Medicine, 1953-54 (Mayo Clinic, Minnesota); Consultant, York Group of Hospitals, 1961-68, latterly as Senior Physician and Chairman, Medical Division. Council Member, Association of Physicians of Great Britain and Ireland; Member, National Committee of the Review of Medicines, 1979-83; Member, Awards Committee for Scotland, since 1982; Senior Examiner, Membership Examination, Royal College of Physicians of Glasgow and London; Phillip Bushell Lectureship in Australian Gastroenterology, 1969; Council Member and Past President, British Society of Gastroenterology; Secretary General, President and latterly Honorary President, World Organisation of Gastroenterology. Recreations: music; photography; gardening. Address: (h.) 14 Southview Road, Blanefield, Glasgow, G63 9JG; T.-0360 70689.

Watson, Antony Charles Harington, MB, ChB, FRCSEdin. Consultant Plastic Surgeon, Lothian Health Board, since 1972; part-time Senior Lecturer, Department of Clinical Surgery, Edinburgh University, since 1972; Editor, British Journal of Plastic Surgery, since 1985; b. 14.10.36, London; m., Anne Henderson Spence; 1 s.; 3 d. Educ. Barnard Castle School; Edinburgh University. Surgical training, Edinburgh and Florida. Council Member, British Association of Plastic Surgeons, since 1984; Member, Scottish Committee, Medical Commission for Accident Prevention; Examiner for Fellowship, Royal College of Surgeons of Edinburgh; Secretary, Scottish Melanoma Group, 1980-84. Recreations: playing and listening to music; painting and sculpture; spending time with the family. Address: (h.) 6 Duncan Street, Edinburgh, EH9 1SZ; T.-031-667 4022.

Watson, Brian John, MIH. Director of Housing and Property, Banff and Buchan District Council, since 1984; b. 11.8.52, Aberdeen; m., Elaine; 1 s.; 2 d. Educ. Northfield Academy, Aberdeen; Aberdeen College of Commerce. Housing Assistant: Aberdeen Corporation, 1973-76, Moray District Council, 1976-80; Housing Manager, Annandale and Eskdale District Council, 1980-83; Depute Director of Housing Services, Dumbarton District Council, 1983-84. Recreations: badminton; golf; football; music. Address: (b.) 1 Church Street, Macduff; T.-Banff 2521.

Watson, George Alistair, BSc, MSc, PhD, FIMA. Reader, Mathematical Sciences Department, Dundee University, since 1984; b. 30.9.42, Aberfeldy; m., Hilary Mackay. Educ. Breadalbane Academy; Edinburgh University; Australian National University. Demonstrator, Computer Unit, Edinburgh University, 1964-66; Dundee University: Research Fellow, then

Lecturer, Mathematics Department, 1969-82; Senior Lecturer, Mathematical Sciences Department, 1982-84. Recreations: squash; gardening. Address: (h.) 5A Albany Road, West Ferry, Dundee, DD5 1PN; T.-Dundee 79473.

Watson, Gordon Sword, OBE, DL, JP, SSC, FBIM. Member, Tayside Regional Council, since 1982; b. 7.12.16, Dundee; m., Catherine Bower Millar (deceased). Educ. Morgan Academy, Dundee; University College, Dundee. Law apprentice, 1933-40; War Service, RA, 1940-45; Dundee Corporation: Junior Legal Assistant, 1945, Senior Legal Assistant, 1945, Junior Town Clerk Depute, 1948-50, Senior Town Clerk Depute, 1950-66, Town Clerk, 1966-75; Town Clerk and Chief Executive, Dundee District Council, 1975-81. Director, Dundee Industrial Association. Recreations: golf; angling. Address: (h.) 65 Strathern Road, West Ferry, Dundee; T.-Dundee 78181.

Watson, Hamish, MFH, TD, MD, FRCPEdin, FRCP, FAAC. Consultant Cardiologist, Tayside Area, since 1964; Chairman, Section of Cardiology, Department of Medicine, Dundee University, since 1964; Postgraduate Dean and Director of Postgraduate Medical Education, since 1970; b. 26.6.23, Edinburgh; m., Lesley Leigh Dick Wood; 1 s. (deceased); 2 d. Educ. George Watson's College; Edinburgh University. President, Association of European Paediatric Cardiologists, 1963-70; Assistant Editor, British Heart Journal, 1964-68; Member, Scientific Board, International Society of Cardiology and Chairman, Council of Paediatric Cardiology, 1966-72; Convenor, Cardiology Committee, Royal College of Physicians of Edinburgh, 1969-75; Member, Specialist Advisory Committee on Cardiovascular Diseases, 1970-74; Member, Scottish Council for Postgraduate Medical Education, 1970-85; Trustee, Royal College of Physicians of Edinburgh, since 1973; Chairman, Standing Committee, Conference of Postgraduate Deans and Directors of Postgraduate Medical Education of Universities of UK, 1975-79. Recreations: fox-hunting; polo; fishing; horticulture; farming. Address: (h.) Nethermains of Kinnaird, Inchture, Perthshire, PH14 9QX; T.-0828 86303.

Watson, Ian, MA, MEd. Rector, Woodmill High School, Dunfermline, since 1983; b. 13.10.44, Dundee. Educ. Harris Academy, Dundee; St. Andrews University; Dundee University; Aberdeen University. Teacher, Harris Academy, Dundee, 1970-72; Principal Teacher of Geography, Berwickshire High School, Duns, 1972-77; Assistant Rector, Inverurie Academy, 1977-80; Depute Rector, Dyce Academy, Aberdeen, 1980-83. Recreations: skiing; squash; gardening. Address: (b.) Woodmill High School, Shields Road, Dunfermline, Fife; T.-0383 725106.

Watson, (John) Steven, MA (Oxon), FRSE, FRHS, Hon. DLitt, DHL. Principal and Vice Chancellor, St. Andrews University, since 1966; Chairman, Scottish Academic Press, since 1968; Historian and Writer; b. 20.3.16, Hebburn-on-Tyne; m., Heba Sylvia De Cordova; 2 s. Educ. Merchant Taylors School, London; St. John's College, Oxford; Merton College, Oxford. Civil Servant (Secretary to Minister of Fuel and

Power), 1942-45; Tutor, Christ Church, Oxford, 1945-66 (Censor, 1955-61); Visiting Professor, University of South Carolina, 1962-63; Chairman, Board of Modern History, Oxford University. Member: Committee of Enquiry into Oxford University, Home Office Committee on Official Secrets Act. Publications: Law and Working of Constitution; Reign of George III; History of Salters Company of London. Address: (b.) Principal's Office, College Gate, North Street, St. Andrews, Fife; T.-0334 76161.

Watson, Kenneth Charles, MD, FRCPEdin, FRCPath. Consultant Microbiologist, Lothian Health Board, since 1969; Honorary Senior Lecturer, Edinburgh University, since 1969; b. 6.5.25, Aberdeen; m., Alys Margaret Gardener; 1 s.; 1 d. Educ. Robert Gordon's College, Aberdeen; Aberdeen University. House Surgeon and House Physician, Aberdeen Royal Infirmary, 1947-48; RAMC, 1948-50; Assistant, Department of Bacteriology, Aberdeen University, 1950; Bacteriologist, Natal Provincial Government, 1951-56; Natal University: Senior Lecturer, Bacteriology, 1956-64, Professor of Microbiology, 1964-69. Singapore Gold Medal, Aberdeen University, 1959. Recreations: tennis; skiing. Address: (b.) Central Microbiological Laboratories, Western General Hospital, Edinburgh; T.-031-332 2525.

Watson, Peter. Editor, The Press and Journal, since 1975; Director, Aberdeen Journals Ltd., since 1984; b. 2.11.26, Buckie; m., Moira Forbes Reid; 2 d. Recreations: golf; hill-walking. Address: (b.) Lang Stracht, Mastrick, Aberdeen; T.-Aberdeen 690222.

Watson, Roderick, MA, PhD. Poet; Literary Critic and Writer; Lecturer in English, Stirling University, since 1971; b. 12.5.43, Aberdeen; m., Celia Hall Mackie; 1 s.; 1 d. Educ. Aberdeen Grammar School; Aberdeen University; Peterhouse, Cambridge. Lecturer in English, Victoria University, British Columbia, 1965-66; collections of poetry include Trio and True History on the Walls; other books include The Penguin Book of the Bicycle, The Literature of Scotland, and MacDiarmid. Recreation: cycling. Address: (h.) 19 Millar Place, Stirling; T.-Stirling 75971.

Watson, Thomas Anderson, MA, DipEd. Rector, The Waid Academy, since 1982; b. 22.2.35, Pittenweem; m., Joyce Paterson; 1 s.; 1 d. Educ. Waid Academy; Edinburgh University. Bank Clerk, 1951-52; Travelling Teacher, Falkland Islands, 1952-56; Teacher, Oakfield Secondary School, 1956-59; student, 1959-64; Principal Teacher of History, Campbeltown Grammar School, 1964-67; Waid Academy: Principal Teacher, 1967-73, Assistant Rector, 1973-79, Depute Rector, 1979-81. Recreations: tennis; walking; photography; music; local history. Address: (h.) 8 Melville Terrace, Anstruther, Fife; T.-0333 310453.

Watt, Archibald, JP, MA, MEd, FEIS, FSA Scot. Honorary Sheriff, Grampian, Highlands and Islands, since 1979; b. 20.5.14, Aberdeen; m., 1, Anne D.M. Ashton (deceased); 2, Elizabeth

P. White; 1 d. Educ. Robert Gordon's College, Aberdeen; Aberdeen University; Aberdeen College of Education. Teacher of English, Elgin Academy, 1938; Flt.-Lt., RAF Administrative and Special Duties Branch and RAF Regiment, 1941-46; Mackie Academy: Principal Teacher of English, 1949, Deputy Rector, 1962, retired, 1977; Organist, HM Prison, Aberdeen, 1930-38; WEA Organiser for Adult Education, Elgin, 1946-49; WEA Tutor in Psychology, 1946-51; Founder and Organising Secretary, Stonehaven Music Club, since 1949; Member, National Council, and Chairman, Regional and District Committees, Scottish Community Drama Association, 1949-67; Member, National Executive and District Chairman, School Library Association in Scotland, 1952-73; Elder, Church of Scotland, since 1954; Chairman and/or Member, Kincardine District Committee, EIS, 1956-77; Member, Joint Consultative Committee, Kincardine County Council, 1965-77; Queen's Jubilee Medal, 1977; Organist and Clerk, Congregational Board, South Church, Stonehaven, since 1976; Director, Kinneff Old Church Preservation Trust Ltd., since 1979; Founder Member and President, Stonehaven Probus Club, 1981-82; Committee Member, National Trust for Scotland (Kincardine and Deeside Centre), since 1984; author of Reading Lists for the Secondary School, 1966; Highways and Byways Round Stonehaven, 1976; Highways and Byways Round Kincardine, 1985. Recreations: concert and theatre-going; travel; antiquities and archaeology; brass bands; research; golf; choral singing; hill-walking. Address: (h.) Rutlands, Arduthie Road, Stonehaven; T.-Stonehaven 62712.

Watt, Archibald Scott, LCH, SRCH. Member, Borders Regional Council, since 1974; Member, Lothian and Borders Police Board, since 1974; Member, Borders Health Board, since 1978; b. 21.8.29, Loanhead, Midlothian; m., Mary Corbett McNairn Brown; 1 d. RAF, 1947-49; Chiropodist, in private practice, since 1957; elected, Peebles Town Council and Peeblesshire County Council, 1972; TA, 1960-62; Past President, Peebles Rotary Club. Recreation: photography. Address: East Rectory, Tweed Brae, Peebles; T.-Peebles 20803.

Watt, Brian, MD, FRCPath, MIBiol. Consultant Bacteriologist, City Hospital, Edinburgh, since 1982; Honorary Senior Lecturer, Department of Bacteriology, Edinburgh University, since 1974; b. 6.12.41, Edinburgh; m., Hilary Watt; 2 d. Educ. Rudolf Steiner School; Edinburgh University. Lecturer, Department of Bacteriology, Edinburgh University, 1968-73; Consultant Microbiologist, Western General Hospital, 1973-82. Recreations: fishing; gardening; golf; tennis; singing. Address: (h.) Silverburn House, by Penicuik, Midlothian; T.-Penicuik 72085.

Watt, David Edwin, BSc, PhD, DSc, FInstP. Member, British Committee for Radiation Units, since 1983; Member, Sub-Committee, International Committee for Radiation Units, since 1983; Member, Physics and Dosimetry Committee, Medical Research Council, since 1984; b. 16.8.30, Glasgow; m., Dorothea Murphy; 1 s. Educ. Shawlands Academy; Glasgow University. Atomic Weapons Research Establishment,

UKAEA, 1956-61; UKAEA Production Group, Chapelcross, 1961-69; Department of Medical Biophysics, Dundee University, 1969-84; Department of Physics, St. Andrews University, since 1984; recipient of Founder's Medal, Society for Radiological Protection. Publication: High Sensitivity Counting Techniques, 1964. Recreations: gardening; travel; squash; tennis. Address: (b.) Department of Physics, St. Andrews University, St. Andrews, KY16 9SS; T.-0334 76161.

Watt, Hamish, JP. Member, Moray District Council, since 1984; Member, Grampian Regional Council, since 1984; Rector, Aberdeen University, since 1985; b. 27.12.25, Keith; m., Mary N. Grant; 1 s.; 2 d. Educ. Keith Grammar School; St. Andrews University. MP, Banffshire, 1974-79. Recreation: travel. Address: (h.) Mill of Buckie, Buckie; T.-Buckie 32591.

Watt, Iain Alasdair, BSc (Econ), AIB (Scot), ASIA. Director: British Linen Bank, European Assets Trust, New Tokyo Investment Trust, Crescent Japan Investment Trust, New Australia Investment Trust; b. 30.3.45, Edinburgh; m., Lynne Neilson Watt; 3 s. Educ. Edinburgh Academy; Hull University. Manager, Bank of Scotland Investment Services, 1976; Managing Director, British Linen Pension Fund Managers Ltd., 1983. Recreations: rugby; football; swimming. Address: (h.) Sycamore Bank, North Queensferry, Fife; T.-0383 413645.

Watt, Ian Macdonald. Principal, Scottish Education Department, since 1981; Secretary, National Committee for the In-Service Training of Teachers, since 1982; b. 12.4.30, Edinburgh; m., Sheila Macdonald Turner; 2 s. Educ. George Heriot's School, Edinburgh. Served continuously in Scottish Education Department, since 1948 (except for National Service, Royal Army Educational Corps). Captain, Royal Burgess Golfing Society, 1983-85. Recreations: golf; bridge; greenhouse cultivation. Address: (h.) 37 Clerwood Gardens, Edinburgh, EH12 8PX; T.-031-334 5336.

Watt, James Affleck Gilroy, MB, ChB, MD, FRCPEdin, FRCPsych, DPM. Consultant Psychiatrist, Gartnavel Royal Hospital, since 1971; b. 14.7.34, near Edinburgh; m., Shirley Camilla Wilson; 2 s.; 1 d. Educ. Lasswade Senior Secondary School; Edinburgh University. House Officer in Neurosurgery, Medicine and Neurology, 1958-60; Junior Medical Specialist, RAMC, 1960-64 (BAOR); Registrar in Psychiatry, Bangour, 1964-66; Research Fellow in Psychiatry, Edinburgh, 1966-69; Lecturer in Psychiatry, Dundee, 1969-71. Recreations: skiing; chess; glass engraving. Address: (b.) Gartnavel Royal Hospital, 1055 Great Western Road, Glasgow, G12; T.-041-334 6241.

Watt, Jim, MBE (1980). Boxer; b. 18.7.48, Glasgow; m., Margaret; 2 s.; 1 d. Turned professional, 1968; British Lightweight Champion, 1972-73, 1975-77; European Lightweight Champion, 1977-79; World Lightweight Champion, 1979-81; four successful defences of World title; Freedom of Glasgow, 1981. Recreations: golf; playing blues guitar.

Watt, Robert Strachan, MA, FBCS. Chairman, Livingston Development Corporation, since 1982; Chairman, Scotbyte Computers Ltd., since 1979; b. 13.10.32, Aberdeen; m., Lorna Beattie; 1 s.; 2 d. Educ. Robert Gordon's College; Aberdeen University. Member, Glenrothes Development Corporation, 1971-78 (Deputy Chairman, 1978-81); Chairman, Management Committee, Scottish New Towns Computer Service, 1977-81; Member, Whitley Council, 1975-81; Council Member, British Computer Society, 1968-69; Elder, Cramond Kirk; Honorary President, Livingston Voluntary Organisations Council; Member of Court, Heriot-Watt University. Recreations: golf; tennis. Address: (b.) 226 Queensferry Road, Edinburgh, EH4 2DQ; T.-031-343 1005.

Watt, William Percy, JP, NCIA. Dairy Farmer; Chairman, Planning Committee, Moray District Council, since 1984 (Member, since 1978); Scottish Member, United Kingdom Seeds Executive, since 1978; b. 29.4.29, Keith; m., Elizabeth Shand; 4 d. Educ. Keith Grammar School; North of Scotland College of Agriculture. President, National Farmers Union of Scotland, 1976-77; Member, Intervention Board for Agricultural Produce. Address: (h.) Auchoynanie, Keith, Moray; T.-05422 2566.

Watters, Ann Margaret, BSc (Hons). Member, Kirkcaldy District Council, since 1984; Assistant Organiser of Science, Fife Regional Council, since 1972; b. Wallington, Surrey; m., A. Norman Watters; 1 s.; 1 d. Educ. St. Leonard's School, St. Andrews; London University. Research Chemist and Lecturer, 1947-52; Hospital Biochemist, 1953; Science Teacher and Lecturer (FE), 1954-72. Member, Fife and Tayside Executive Committee, British Association for the Advancement of Science; Chairman, Kirkcaldy Civic Society, 1984; Director, Abbeyfield, until 1980; established Wemyss Environmental Education Centre, East Wemyss; author of 17 booklets on Fife coastal walks. Recreations: swimming; walking; jogging; local history. Address: (h.) 17 Townsend Crescent, Kirkcaldy, Fife; T.-0592 266361.

Weatherhead, Alexander Stewart, OBE, TD, MA, LLB. Solicitor; Partner, Tindal Oatts Buchanan and McIlwraith, since 1960; b. 3.8.31, Edinburgh; m., Harriett Foye; 2 d. Educ. Glasgow Academy; Glasgow University. Royal Artillery, 1950-52; TA, 1952; Lt. Col. Commanding 277 (A&SH) Field Regiment, RA (TA), 1965-67, The Lowland Regiment, RA (T), 1967 and Glasgow and Strathclyde Universities OTC, 1970-73; Colonel, 1974; TAVR Colonel, Lowlands (West), 1974-76; ADC (TAVR) to the Queen, 1977-81; Honorary Colonel, Glasgow and Strathclyde Universities OTC, since 1982; Council Member, Law Society of Scotland, 1971-84 (Honorary Vice-President, 1983-84); Member, Royal Commission on Legal Services in Scotland, 1976-80; Council Member, Society for Computers and Law, since 1973 (Chairman, 1981-84); Temporary Sheriff, since 1985. Recreations: sailing; reading; music. Address: (h.) 52 Partickhill Road, Glasgow, G11 5AB; T.-041-334 6277.

Weatherston, William Alastair Paterson, MA (Hons). Director, Scottish Courts Administration, since 1982; b. 20.11.35, Peebles; m., Margaret Jardine; 2 s.; 1 d. Educ. Peebles High School; Edinburgh University. Assistant Principal, Department of Health for Scotland and Scottish Education Department, 1959-63; Private Secretary to Permanent Under Secretary of State, Scottish Office, 1963-64; Principal, Scottish Education Department, 1964-72; Cabinet Office, 1972-74; Assistant Secretary, Scottish Home and Health Department, 1974-77; Scottish Education Department, 1977-79; Central Services, Scottish Office, 1979-82. Recreations: reading; music. Address: (h.) 1 Coltbridge Terrace, Edinburgh, EH12 6AB; T.-031-337 3339.

Weatherstone, Robert Bruce, CA, TD. Member, Lothian Health Board; Member, Scottish Committee, Council on Tribunals; Chairman, Leith Enterprise Trust; Director, Glenrothes Enterprise Trust; Member, Executive Council, Scottish Business in the Community; b. 14.5.26, Bangor; m., Elaine Fisher; 1 s.; 1 d. Educ. Edinburgh Academy; Dollar Academy; Edinburgh University. Director/Secretary, J.T. Salvesen Ltd., Grangemouth, 1954-62; Director and Member, Management Committee, Christian Salvesen Ltd., 1962-83; served in TA, latterly as Colonel, for more than 20 years. Recreations: hill-walking; ornithology. Address: (h.) 27 Ravelston Garden, Edinburgh, EH4 3LE; T.-031-337 4035.

Weaver, John Patrick Acton, MA, BA (Hons), BSc, BM Bch, DM, MCh, FRCSEdin, FRCS. Consultant Urologist, Dundee Royal Infirmary; Honorary Senior Lecturer in Surgery, Dundee University; b. 17.11.27, Oxford; m., Mary Catherine Bainbridge Robinson; 2 s.; 1 d. Educ. Ampleforth; Trinity College, Oxford; Guy's Hospital. Demonstrator in Biochemistry, Oxford University; House Surgeon, Guy's Hospital; Senior Surgical Registrar, Royal Victoria Infirmary, Newcastle-upon-Tyne; Lecturer in Surgery, Newcastle-upon-Tyne University. Recreation: gardening. Address: (b.) 229 Strathmartine Road, Dundee; T.-Dundee 89383.

Webb, Jeffrey R.L., BSc, DPhil, FRSE. Reader in Mathematics, Glasgow University, since 1982; b. 19.12.45, Stourport-on-Severn; m., Angela Millard; 1 s.; 1 d. Educ. King Charles I School, Kidderminster; Sussex University. Royal Society European Programme Fellowship, 1970-71; Science Research Council Fellowship, Sussex University, 1971-73; Lecturer in Mathematics, Glasgow University, 1973-78 and 1979-82; Visiting Associate Professor, Indiana University, 1978-79; Visiting Professor, Tulane University, New Orleans, 1982. Member, Editorial Board, Proceedings of the Royal Society of Edinburgh. Recreations: chess; squash; listening to music. Address: (b.) Mathematics Department, Glasgow University, Glasgow, G12 8QW; T.-041-339 8855, Ext. 7181.

Webb, John Neville, MA, MD (Cantab), FRCPEdin. Consultant Pathologist, Western General Hospital, Edinburgh, since 1969; Honorary Senior Lecturer, Edinburgh University (Chairman and Head, Department of Pathology, Western General Hospital, since 1979);

b. 14.1.35, Carmarthen; m., Pauline Wickham Edmondson; 2 s.; 1 d. Educ. Shrewsbury; Peterhouse, Cambridge; St. Thomas's Hospital Medical School. Recreations:, book collecting; opera; bird-watching· fast cars. Address: (h.) 56 St. Albans Road, Edinburgh; T.-031-667 2637.

Webb, William Grierson, MA (Oxon). Administrator, National Youth Orchestra of Scotland, since 1978; Musical Director, Glasgow Chamber Orchestra, 1981-85; Freelance Conductor; b. 16.10.47, Cardiff; m., Jean Shannon. Educ. Rugby School; Merton College, Oxford. Conductor, Trier Opera House, West Germany, 1973-76; Assistant to General Administrator, Scottish National Orchestra, 1976-78. Member, Executive Committee, National Association of Youth Orchestras. Address: (b.) 3 La Belle Place, Glasgow, G3 7LH; T.-041-332 8311.

Webster, David, FInstD, FBIM. Producer/Director, This Is Scotland (stage and screen promotions), since 1962; Member, Strathclyde Regional Council, since 1974; b. 25.11.24; m., Margaret; 3 s.; 1 d. Convener of Publicity, Oban Town Council, 1970-75; Chairman, Area Tourist Board, 1971-80; Member, Argyll and Bute District Council, 1980-84; Member, Electricity Consultative Council for the North of Scotland District. Recreations: photography; music. Address: (h.) Corriebeg, Oban, Argyll, PA34 5DU; T.-0631 63794.

Webster, David Pirie, DPE, LCSP. Director of Leisure, Recreation and Tourism, Cunninghame District Council, since 1975; b. 18.9.28, Aberdeen; 4 s.; 2 d. Educ. Crowlees Boys School; Aberdeen Training College; Woolmanhill College. Senior Technical Representative, Scottish Council of Physical Recreation, 1954-72; Head of Facilities Planning Division, Scottish Sports Council, 1972-74; Director/Administrator, Magnum Leisure Centre, 1974-75. Director of Weightlifting, Commonwealth Games; Secretary General, World Federation of Heavy Events Athletes. Recreations: writing (28 books); Highland Games; fitness and weight training. Address: (b.) Cunninghame House, Friarscroft, Irvine, KA12 8RG; T.-0294 74166.

Webster, Derek Adrian, CBE (1979). Chairman and Editorial Director, Scottish Daily Record and Sunday Mail Ltd., since 1974; Director, Mirror Group Newspapers, since 1974; Director, Clyde CableVision Ltd., since 1982; b. 24.3.27; m., Dorothy Frances Johnson; 2 s.; 1 d. Educ. St. Peter's, Bournemouth. Royal Navy, 1944-48; Reporter, Western Morning News, 1943; Staff Journalist, Daily Mail, 1949-51; joined Mirror Group, 1952; Northern Editor, Daily Mirror, 1964-67; Editor, Daily Record, 1967-72. Vice Chairman, Age Concern Scotland, 1977-83; Member, Press Council, 1981-84 (Joint Vice Chairman, 1982-84); Honorary Vice President, Newspaper Press Fund. Recreations: boating; gardening. Address: (h.) Gateside, Blanefield, by Glasgow; T.-Blanefield 70252.

Webster, Janice Helen, LLB, CPLF. Deputy Secretary, Law Society of Scotland and Secretary, Scottish Lawyers' European Group; b. 2.4.44, Falkirk; m., R.M. Webster, RD, BA (Cantab);

2 d. Educ. Surbiton Girls High School; Larbert High School; Edinburgh University. Apprenticeship, Cochran Sayers and Cook, Glasgow, 1964-67; admitted Solicitor, 1967; NP, 1972; Legal Assistant, then Senior Solicitor, Falkirk Town Council, 1967-71; Alston Nairn & Hogg, Solicitors, Edinburgh, 1971-74; Deputy Secretary, Law Society of Scotland, 1974-80; State Counsel, then Magistrate, Seychelles, 1980-82; rejoined Law Society of Scotland, 1982. Manager, Palmerston Place Church, Edinburgh; Governor, International School, Seychelles, 1980-82. Publication: Professional Ethics and Practice for Scottish Solicitors (Co-author). Recreations: singing; occasional riding and tennis; frequent dog walking! Address: (h.) 35 Queen's Crescent, Edinburgh, EH9 LBA; T.-031-667 8062.

Webster, Rev. William Thoms, MA. Minister, Dean Parish Church, Edinburgh, since 1974; b. 24.5.18, Bathgate; m., Mary Fowler Godfrey; 1 s.; 1 d. Educ. Bathgate Academy; Glasgow University. Ordained, Pleasance Church, Edinburgh, 1944; Minister: Torryburn and Newmills, 1946-53, College Church, Edinburgh, 1953-61, Muirhouse Parish Church, Edinburgh, 1961-74. President, New College Union, 1980-81. Recreation: gardening. Address: 1 Ravelston Terrace, Edinburgh; T.-031-332 5736.

Wedgwood, Robert Amery. Deputy Lieutenant, Dunbartonshire, since 1964; Honorary Sheriff, since 1955; b. 24.3.04, Dumbarton; m., Jean Hope Henderson; 3 s. Educ. Shrewsbury. Marine Engineer; TA, 9th Bn., Argyll and Sutherland Highlanders, 1928; 54th Light AA Regiment, 1939; served as Major during Second World War. Recreations: tennis; golf. Address: (h.) Dalnair House, Croftamie, by Glasgow, G63; T.-Drymen 60962.

Weeks, David Courtenay, BSc, MA, PhD. Senior Lecturer in Plant Physiology, St. Andrews University; b. 29.4.27, Ceylon (Sri Lanka); m., Mary Lightbourne. Educ. Scotch College, Melbourne; Melbourne University; Cambridge University. University Demonstrator, Cambridge University, 1953-56; joined St. Andrews University as Lecturer, 1957. Address: (b.) Department of Plant Biology and Ecology, St. Andrews University, St. Andrews, Fife, KY16 9AL.

Weeple, Edward John, MA. Assistant Secretary, Scottish Home and Health Department, 1980-85, Department of Agriculture and Fisheries for Scotland, since 1985; b. 15.5.45, Glasgow; 3 s.; 1 d. Educ. St. Aloysius' College, Glasgow; Glasgow University. Entered DHSS, London, 1968; Assistant Principal, 1968-73 (Private Secretary to Minister of Health, 1971-73); Principal, 1973-78; transferred to Scottish Office, 1978; Principal (Industrial Development Division, SEPD), 1978-80. Address: (h.) 19 Lauder Road, Edinburgh; T.-031-668 1150.

Weipers, Professor Sir William (Lee), Kt (1966). Director of Veterinary Education, Glasgow University, 1949-68; b. 21.1.04. Educ. Whitehill School; Glasgow Veterinary College. Dean, Faculty of Veterinary Medicine, Glasgow University, 1968-74.

Weir, Alan David, MBA, CA. Finance Officer, Glasgow University, since 1982; b. 25.11.37, Edinburgh; m., Alys Taylor Macdonald; 2 s. Educ. Mill Hill; Strathclyde University. National Service (commissioned), Black Watch (RHR) and 4th QONR; served Articles with Touche Ross, London; commercial and industrial experience at Board level. Recreations: golf; hill-walking. Address: (h.) 3 Dumgoyne Drive, Bearsden, Glasgow, G61 3AP; T.-041-942 7936.

Weir, Hon. Lord, (David Bruce Weir), QC (Scot), MA, LLB. Senator of the College of Justice in Scotland, since 1985; b. 19.12.31; m.; 3 s. Educ. Kelvinside Academy; Glasgow Academy; The Leys School, Cambridge; Glasgow University. RNR, 1955-64; admitted, Faculty of Advocates, 1959; Advocate Depute for Sheriff Court, 1964; Advocate Depute, 1979-82; Chairman, Medical Appeal Tribunal, 1972-77; Chairman, Pensions Appeals Tribunal for Scotland, 1978-84; Member, Criminal Injuries Compensation Board, 1974-79.

Weir, Professor David Thomas Henderson, MA (Oxon), DPSA, FBIM. Head, Department of Management Studies, Glasgow University, since 1980 (Professor of Organisational Behaviour, since 1974); Head, Glasgow Division, Scottish Business School, since 1980; b. 10.4.39, Chalfont St. Peter; m., Mary; 2 s.; 1 d. Educ. Bradford Grammar School; Queen's College, Oxford. University posts, Universities of Aberdeen, Leeds, Hull and Manchester, 1961-70; Manchester Business School, 1970-74; Dean, Scottish Business School, 1977-79; Member, Committee of Inquiry into the Engineering Profession, 1977-80; Arbitrator, Milk Industry (Scotland), 1983-85; Director, Gulliver Foods, 1980-82. Publications: Sociology of Modern Britain; Social Problems of Modern Britain; Men and Work in Modern Britain; Cities in Modern Britain; Computerguide III; Key Variables in Social Research; New Sociology of Modern Britain. Recreations: fellwalking; music; sport; cooking. Address: (h.) Smorthwaite Hill, Garsdale, Sedbergh, Cumbria; T.-0857 20194.

Weir, Professor Donald Mackay, MB, ChB, FRCPEdin, MD (Hons). Professor of Microbial Immunology, Edinburgh University, since 1983; Honorary Consultant, Lothian Health Board, since 1967; b. 16.9.28, Edinburgh; m., Dr. Cecelia Caroline Blackwell; 3 s. Educ. Edinburgh Academy; Edinburgh University. Research Fellow, Medical Research Council, Rheumatism Research Unit, 1957-61; Edinburgh University: Lecturer, Department of Bacteriology, 1961-67; Senior Lecturer, 1967-78, Reader, 1978-83. Publications: Immunology, An Outline for Students of Medicine and Biology; Handbook of Experimental Immunology (Editor); Principles of Infection and Immunity in Patient Care (Co-author, with wife). Recreation: sailing. Address: (h.) 36 Drummond Place, Edinburgh; T.-031-556 7656.

Weir, Jamie, MB, BS, FRCPEdin, DMRD, FRCR. Consultant Radiologist, Aberdeen Royal Infirmary, since 1976; Senior Lecturer, Aberdeen University, since 1976; b. 22.9.45, Woking; m., Dr. Margaret Jean Weir. Educ. King's College

School, Wimbledon; Middlesex Hospital Medical School. House Physician, then House Surgeon, Middlesex Hospital, 1969; Senior House Officer, Ipswich Hospital, 1970-71; Registrar, then Senior Registrar, Radiology, Middlesex Hospital (latterly also Harefield Hospital), 1971-75. Publications: Atlas of Radiological Anatomy (Co-author); Atlas of Clinical Echocardiography (Co-author). Recreation: golf. Address: (b.) Radiology Department, Aberdeen Royal Infirmary, Foresterhill, Aberdeen; T.-0224 681818.

Weir, John Alexander Campbell. Honorary Sheriff, Cupar, since 1981; Member, Fife Valuation Appeal Committee, since 1981; b. 1.4.21, Glasgow; m., Isabel Mary Sharp; 2 s. Educ. Queen's Park Secondary School, Glasgow. Sheriff Clerk Depute, Argyll, 1949-55; Sheriff Clerk of Galloway, 1955-61; Sheriff Clerk Depute, Aberdeen, 1961-66; Sheriff Clerk of Fife, 1966-74; Sheriff Clerk, Dundee, 1974-81. President, Cupar Rotary Club, 1985. Recreations: bridge; golf; bowls. Address: (h.) 16 Tarvit Avenue, Cupar, Fife; T.-Cupar 53451.

Weir, Michael Eckford Lind, MA, LLB, WS, NP, FCIArb. Solicitor, Weir & Company, WS, since 1960; b. 5.5.38, Edinburgh; m., Hazel Dobson Cunningham; 3 s. Educ. George Watson's College, Edinburgh; Edinburgh University. Part-time Member, Secretary of State for Scotland's Panel for Public Enquiries; Chairman, Rent Assessment Committees; former General Commissioner of Income Tax; President, Edinburgh General Chamber of Commerce, 1966-67; Treasurer, Edinburgh University Sports Union, 1965-80; Honorary Secretary, Scottish Paraplegic Association, since 1984; Honorary Legal Advisor, Scottish Seagull Trust Appeal; Member, General Committee, Amateur Athletics Association, 1961-64; Chairman, Outward Bound Association for Edinburgh and SE Scotland, 1967-71; Member, Council, National Playing Fields Association for Scotland, 1968-71; Secretary, Legal/Concessions Committee, 1970 Commonwealth Games in Edinburgh, 1968-70; Secretary, Scottish Branch, Institute of Arbitrators, 1967-70; Secretary, Blackface Sheepbreeders Association, 1966-71; Member, Independent Examinations Board, Institute of Valuers and Auctioneers, 1979-83. Publication: Law and Practice of Arbitration in Scotland. Recreations: occasional golf, squash and walking. Address: (h.) 1 Pentland Avenue, Edinburgh; T.-031-441 1977.

Weir, Michael Fraser, LLB, NP. Solicitor; Member, Angus District Council, since 1984; b. 24.3.57, Arbroath. Educ. Arbroath High School; Aberdeen University. Legal Apprentice, Myers & Wills, Montrose, 1979-81; Solicitor: Charles Wood & Son, Kirkcaldy, 1981-83, Myers & Wills, Montrose, 1983-84, J. & D.G. Shiell, Brechin, since 1984. Address: (h.) Tigh na Geal, Main Road, Hillside, by Montrose; T.-Hillside 417.

Weir, Tom. Journalist and Photographer; Honorary Vice-President, Scottish Rights of Way Society. Former Ordnance Surveyor; climbed in the Himalayas and began professional photography; author of several books on climbing and Scotland; Presenter, Weir's Way, Scottish Television; Columnist, Glasgow Herald.

Weir, William. Director, Ross & Weir, Dairy and Livestock Farmers; Vice-Chairman, Scottish Milk Marketing Board, since 1982; Chairman, Scottish Dairy Council, since 1983; Council Member, National Farmers Union of Scotland; Director, Royal Association of British Dairy Farmers, since 1982; b. 9.8.24, Lugar, Ayrshire; m., Margaret Ross; 1 s.; 2 d. Educ. Patna and Dalmellington Schools. Past President: World Federation of Ayrshire Cattle Societies, Ayrshire Cattle Society of Great Britain and Ireland; former Director, Cattle Services, Ayr Ltd. Recreations: occasional game of curling; watching football and athletics. Address: Wheatrig, Kilmaurs, Kilmarnock, Ayrshire; T.-0563 38231.

Weir, Viscount, (William Kenneth James Weir), BA. Chairman, The Weir Group PLC, since 1966; Vice-Chairman, J. Rothschild Holdings PLC, since 1985; Director, BICC plc, since 1977; b. 9.11.33, Glasgow; m., 1, Diana MacDougall (m. diss.); 2, Jacqueline Mary Marr; 1 s.; 1 d. Educ. Eton; Trinity College, Cambridge. Member, London Advisory Committee, Hongkong and Shanghai Banking Corporation, since 1980; Director, Transcontinental Services Group NV, since 1982; Deputy Chairman, Charterhouse J. Rothschild PLC, 1983-85; Member, Court, Bank of England, 1972-84; Co-Chairman, RIT and Northern PLC, 1982-83; Director, 1970, Chairman, 1975-82, Great Northern Investment Trust Ltd.; Member, Scottish Economic Council, 1972-85; Director, British Steel Corporation, 1972-76. Recreations: shooting; golf; fishing. Address: (h.) Rodinghead, Mauchline, Ayrshire; T.-Fiveways 233.

Welsby, Philip Douglas, MB, BS, FRCPEdin. Consultant Physician, since 1980; b. 8.11.46, Warrington; m., Dr. Jennifer B. Thorn; 4 d. Educ. Altrincham Grammar School; Royal Free Hospital School of Medicine. Training posts, Surrey, Aberdeen and London. Publication: Infectious Diseases. Recreations: clarinet playing and swimming (not at the same time). Address: (h.) 1 Burnbrae, Maybury Drive, Edinburgh, EH12 8UB.

Welsh, Andrew Paton, MA (Hons), DipEd. Provost of Angus, since 1984; Senior Lecturer in Business Studies and Public Administration, Angus Technical College, since 1983; b. 19.4.44, Glasgow; m., Sheena Margaret Cannon (see Sheena Margaret Welsh); 1 d. Educ. Govan High School; Glasgow University. Member, Stirling District Council, 1974; MP (SNP), South Angus, 1974-79; SNP Parliamentary Spokesman on Housing, 1974-78, Self-Employed and Small Businesses, 1975-79, Agriculture, 1975-79; Parliamentary Chief Whip, 1977-79; SNP Executive Vice Chairman for Administration, 1979-83; Member, National Executive Committee, SNP, since 1983; Parliamentary candidate, East Angus, 1983; Member, Church and Nation Committee, Church of Scotland, 1984-85; Member, Dundee University Court, since 1984; Member, Angus District Health Council; Member, SCOTVEC Public Administration and Moderating Committees. Recreations: music; horse riding. Address: (h.) 22 Monymusk Road, Arbroath, Angus; T.-0241 76291.

Welsh, John Renton. Secretary, Northern Lighthouse Board, since 1977; b. 13.1.27, Peebles; m., Joan Mary Horsburgh; 1 s.; 1 d. Educ. Boroughmuir High School. Northern Lighthouse Board: joined 1950, Personnel Officer, 1971-73, Deputy Secretary, 1973-77. President, Boroughmuir Cricket Club; Vice President, Boroughmuir Rugby Club. Recreations: interested in all sports; gardening; chess; crosswords; travel. Address: (h.) 1 Forthview Terrace, Edinburgh, EH4 2AD; T.-031-332 6804.

Welsh, Sheena Margaret, MA (Hons), DipEd. Member, Angus District Council, since 1980 (Vice Convener, Housing, since 1984); Teacher of children with learning difficulties, Arbroath Academy, since 1977; b. 22.12.48, Dunoon; m., Andrew Paton Welsh (qv); 1 d. Educ. Dunoon Grammar School; Glasgow University. Teacher: Fallin Primary School, 1972-74, Chapelpark Primary School, Forfar, 1974-77; Treasurer, Aldbar WRI, since 1981; elected Member, National Council, SNP, 1984; Chairman, Arbroath Branch, SNP, 1979-81; Member, Independent Local Radio Advisory Committee, Dundee/Perth, since 1980; Member, Electricity Consumers Consultative Committee, Dundee Area, since 1982; Vice Chairman, Angus Local Association, EIS, 1976-77. Recreations: horse riding; cookery; music. Address: (h.) 22 Monymusk Road, Arbroath, Angus; T.-0241 76291.

Welsh Wright, Frederick, JP. Chairman, Public Works and Building Control Committee, Dundee District Council, since 1980; b. Dundee; m., Margaret; 3 s. Educ. Rockwell Secondary School, Dundee. Member, Dundee Corporation, 1973-75 (Convener, Public Libraries, Museums and Art Galleries, 1973-75); Member, Tayside Regional Council, 1974-77 (Labour Group Chief Whip and Further Education Opposition Spokesman, 1974-77); Member, Dundee District Council, since 1977; Member, Central Committee, Gas Consumers Council for Scotland; Member, Perth Prison Visiting Committee; Member, Management Committee, Dundee Resources Centre for Unemployed; Member, Scottish Council, ADLO; Member, Fire Services Scoland Examination Board, 1973-75. Recreations: gardening; DIY; watching all sports; walking. Address: (h.) 2 McKinnon Street, Dundee, DD3 6JN; T.-0382 27669.

Wemyss and March, Earl of, (Francis David Charteris), KT (1966), Hon. LLD (St. Andrews), Hon. DUniv (Edinburgh), JP, BA. Lord Lieutenant, East Lothian, since 1967; b. 19.1.12, London; m., Mavis Gordon Lynette Murray; 1 s.; 1 d. 1 s. (deceased); 1 d. (deceased). Educ. Eton; Balliol College, Oxford. Commissioned, Lovat Scouts (TA), 1932-44; Basutoland Administrative Service, 1937-44; War Service, African Auxiliary Pioneer Corps, Middle East, 1941-44; Chairman, Council, National Trust for Scotland, 1947-67 (President, since 1967); Chairman, Scottish Churches Council, 1964-71; Chairman, Royal Commission on Ancient and Historical Monuments of Scotland, 1949-84; Vice-Chairman, Marie Curie Memorial Foundation (Chairman, Scottish Committee); President, Royal Scottish Geographical Society, 1958-62; Presiuent, National Bible Society of Scotland, 1960-83; Lieutenant, Queen's Bodyguard for Scotland (Royal Company of Archers). Recreations: countryside and conservation. Address: (h.) Gosford House, Longniddry, East Lothian; T.-Aberlady 200/389.

West, Professor Thomas Summers, BSc, PhD, DSc, FRSC, FRSE. Director, Macaulay Institute for Soil Research, Aberdeen, since 1975; b. 18.11.27, Peterhead; m., Margaret O. Lawson; 1 s.; 2 d. Educ. Tarbat School, Portmahomack; Tain Royal Academy; Aberdeen University; Birmingham University. Lecturer in Chemistry, Birmingham University, 1955-63; Imperial College of Science and Technology, London: Reader in Chemistry, 1963-65, Professor of Chemistry, 1965-75. Meldola Medal, Royal Institute of Chemistry; Gold Medal, Society of Analytical Chemistry; President, Society for Analytical Chemistry, 1969-71; Honorary Secretary, Royal Society of Chemistry, 1972-75; President, Analytical Division, International Union of Pure and Applied Chemistry, 1979-81; Secretary General, IUPAC, since 1983; Honorary Research Professor, Aberdeen University, since 1983. Recreations: gardening; motoring; reading; music; fishing. Address: (h.) 31 Baillieswells Drive, Bieldside, Aberdeen, AB1 9AT; T.-0224 868294.

Westcott, Clifford Henry, LRAM, LTCL (GM), ARCM, JP. Chairman, Employment Committee, Kyle and Carrick District Council, since 1984 (Vice Chairman, Finance Committee); Director, Freeport Scotland Ltd., since 1984; b. 30.11.17, Plymouth; m., Christine Mary Blackstock; 1 s. Educ. Devonport High School; London University; Trinity College. RAF, 1940-46; Teacher, 1947-81; Prestwick Town Councillor, 1966-74; Member, Kyle and Carrick District Council, since 1974; Founder, Producer, Musical Director, Prestwick Amateur Operatic Society, 1964-78; Chairman and Treasurer, Prestwick Oxfam Group, since 1970; Chairman, 1977, Treasurer, since 1980, Prestwick Conservative Association; Chairman, Leisure and Recreation Committee, Kyle and Carrick District Council, 1974-79; Committee Member, Ayr and Prestwick RAFA, since 1984; Organiser and Committee Chairman, Prestwick Millennium Celebrations, 1983. Recreations: music; entertaining. Address: (h.) 24 Allanvale Road, Prestwick; T.-Prestwick 78230.

Westcott, Michael John Herbert, BSc (Hons). Assistant Secretary, Edinburgh University; b. 16.4.19, Plymouth. Educ. Hillhead High School; Glasgow University. Ministry of Home Grown Timber Production, 1940-43; Army (Royal Signals), 1943-48 (retired as Major); Colonial Service, Sierra Leone (Administrative Officer), 1948-61. Vice-Chairman, Edinburgh Festival Fringe Society; Honorary President, Edinburgh and SE Scotland VSO Group; Honorary Vice-President, Scottish Branch, Royal Commonwealth Society. Recreation: walking. Address: (h.) 2 Kilgraston Court, Kilgraston Road, Edinburgh, EH9 2ES; T.-031-447 8282.

Westwell, Alan Reynolds, MSc, ACT (Hons), CEng, MIMechE, MIProdE, FCIT. Director General, Strathclyde Passenger Transport

Executive, since 1979; b. 11.4.40, Liverpool; m., Elizabeth Aileen Birrell; 2 s.; 1 d. Educ. Old Swan Technical College; Liverpool Polytechnic; Salford University. Liverpool City Transport, 1956-67; Chief Engineer: Southport Corporation Transport, 1967-69, Coventry Corporation Transport, 1969-72, Glasgow Corporation Transport Department, 1972-74; Director of Public Transport, Tayside Regional Council, 1974-79. President, Scottish Council, Confederation of British Road Passenger Transport, 1983; Chairman, Institution of Mechanical Engineers, Automobile Division, 1982-83; Chairman, Scottish Section, Chartered Institute of Transport, 1983-84. Recreations: golf; swimming; tennis; music; reading. Address: (h.) 12 Glen Drive, Helensburgh, Dunbartonshire, G84 9BJ; T.-0436 71709.

Westwood, Alan, BSc, MSc, PhD, CChem, MRSC, MRCPath. Top Grade Scientist and Head, Department of Paediatric Biochemistry, Royal Hospital for Sick Children, Edinburgh, since 1979; Honorary Research Fellow, Edinburgh University, since 1979; b. 2.3.48, Luton; m., Jennifer Anne; 1 s.; 1 d. Educ. Luton Technical School; Liverpool University; Birmingham University. Clinical Biochemist: Broadgreen Hospital, Liverpool, 1969, Birmingham Children's Hospital, 1970, Liverpool Royal Infirmary, 1976, Edinburgh Royal Hospital for Sick Children, 1979. Chairman, Scottish Region, Association of Clinical Biochemists, since 1984 (Member of Association Council, 1982-85). Recreations: squash; curling; microcomputing. Address: (h.) Fawnspark, Loanstone, by Penicuik, Midlothian, EH26 8PH; T.-Penicuik 78407.

Whaley, Professor Keith, MB, BS, MD, PhD, FRCP, MRCPath. Professor, Department of Pathology, Glasgow University, since 1984; Honorary Consultant in Immunopathology, since 1977; b. 2.9.42, Redcar; m., Mairearad Campbell Whyte; 2 s. Educ. Middlesbrough High School; Newcastle-upon-Tyne University. SHO/Registrar, Medicine/Rheumatology, Centre for Rheumatic Diseases, Glasgow, 1967-69; MRC Research Fellow, then Lecturer, Immunopathology, Glasgow University, 1969-74; Assistant Professor of Medicine, Medical College, Virginia, 1974-76; Lecturer, then Senior Lecturer, then Reader, Glasgow University, 1976-84. Publication: Methods in Complement for Clinical Immunologists. Recreations: sailing; jogging. Address: (b.) Pathology Department, Western Infirmary, Glasgow; T.-041-339 8822, Ext. 4210.

Whaling, Frank, BA, MA, ThD, FRAS, FWLA. Senior Lecturer, Religious Studies, Edinburgh University, since 1984; b. 5.2.34; m., Patricia Hill; 1 s.; 1 d. Educ. Christ's College, Cambridge; Wesley House, Cambridge; Harvard University. Minister: Methodist Church, Birmingham, 1960-62; Methodist Church, India, 1962-66; Methodist Church, Eastbourne, 1966-69; Teaching Fellow, Harvard University, 1971-73; Special Teacher in Religious Studies, Edinburgh University, 1973-84; Director: Edinburgh-Farmington Project, Edinburgh and Oxford, 1971-81; Edinburgh-Cook Project, Edinburgh and Gloucester,

1981-83; Council Member, Shap Working Party, London, since 1973; Chairman/President, Scottish Working Party on Religion in Education, since 1975; Council Member, Christian Education Movement in Scotland, since 1979. Publications: An Approach to Dialogue: Hinduism and Christianity, 1966; The Rise of the Religious Significance of Rama, 1980; John and Charles Wesley: Selected Writings, 1981; The World's Religious Traditions: Current Perspectives in Religious Studies, 1984; Contemporary Approaches to the Study of Religion: The Humanities, 1984, and The Social Sciences, 1985; Religions of the World, 1985. Address: (h.) 29 Ormidale Terrace, Murrayfield, Edinburgh, EH12 6EA.

Wheater, Roger John. Director, Royal Zoological Society of Scotland, since 1972; b. 24.11.33, Brighton; m., Jean Ord Troup; 1 s.; 1 d. Educ. Brighton, Hove and Sussex Grammar School; Brighton Technical College. Commissioned, Royal Sussex Regiment, 1953; 3rd Bn., Gold Coast Regiment, 1953-54; 4/5th Bn., Royal Sussex Regiment (TA), Intelligence Officer, 1954-56; Colonial Police, Uganda, 1956-61; joined Uganda National Parks, 1961, as Warden, Murchison Falls National Park; Director, Uganda National Parks, 1970-72; Council Member, Scottish Wildlife Trust; Vice Chairman, National Federation of Zoological Gardens of Great Britain and Ireland; First Secretary, International Union of Directors of Zoological Gardens; Member, Executive Committee, National Trust for Scotland; President, Association of British Wild Animal Keepers; Chairman, Anthropoid Ape Advisory Panel; Fellow, Royal Society of Edinburgh; Chairman, Monitoring Committee, Zoo Licensing Act; Chairman, Cammo Estate Advisory Committee; President, Edinburgh Mechanised Angling Club. Recreations: shooting; painting; fishing; piping; photography; bird-watching; gardening. Address: (b.) Scottish National Zoological Park, Edinburgh, EH12 6TS; T.-031-336 9171.

Wheatley, Denys Neville, BSc, PhD, DSc, MRCPath, CBiol, FIBiol. Reader in Cell Pathology, Aberdeen University, since 1981; b. 18.3.40, Ascot; m., Pamela Snare; 2 d. Educ. Windsor Grammar School; London University. Research Fellow, Aberdeen University, 1964; MRC Travelling Fellow, Wisconsin University, 1968-69; US Public Health Service supported Fellowship, 1969-70; Research Fellow, then Lecturer in Pathology, then Senior Lecturer, Aberdeen University, 1970-81. Recreations: music; hill-walking; rowing. Address: (b.) Department of Pathology, University Medical Buildings, Foresterhill, Aberdeen, AB9 2ZD; T.-0224 681818.

Wheatley, Baron, (John Wheatley), PC (1947), MA, LLB. Life Peer; Senator of the College of Justice in Scotland, 1954-85; Lord Justice-Clerk, 1972-85; b. 17.1.08; m.; 4 s.; 1 d. Educ. St. Aloysius College, Glasgow; Mount St. Mary's College, Sheffield; Glasgow University. Called to Scottish Bar, 1932; Advocate Depute, 1945-47; MP (Labour), East Edinburgh, 1947-54; Solicitor-General, 1947; QC (Scot), 1947; Lord Advocate, 1947-51; Chairman, Executive Committee, RSSPCC, 1956-79; Chairman, Royal

Commission on Local Government in Scotland, 1966-69; Honorary President, Age Concern (Scotland); Hon. LLD, Glasgow, 1963; DUniv, Stirling, 1976; Hon. FEIS.

Wheatley, Sheriff John Francis, BL. Sheriff, Perthshire and Kinross-shire, at Perth, since 1980; b. 9.5.41, Edinburgh; m., Bronwen Catherine Fraser; 2 s. Educ. Mount St. Mary's College, Derbyshire; Edinburgh University. Called to Scottish Bar, 1966; Standing Counsel to Scottish Development Department, 1968-74; Advocate Depute, 1974-78. Recreations: music; gardening. Address: Braefoot Farmhouse, Fossoway, Kinross-shire; T.-Fossoway 212.

Wheeler, (Harry) Anthony, OBE, PRSA, Hon. RA, Hon. RBS, PPRIAS, FRIBA, BArch, MRTPI, DipTP. Senior Partner, Wheeler & Sproson, Architects and Town Planners, Edinburgh and Kirkcaldy, since 1954; b. 7.11.19, Stranraer; m., Dorothy Jean Campbell; 1 d. Educ. Stranraer High School; Glasgow School of Architecture; Strathclyde University. War Service, Royal Artillery, 1939-46; John Keppie Scholar and Sir Rowand Anderson Studentship, RIBA Grissell Medallist, Neale Bursar; Assistant to City Architect, Oxford, to Sir Herbert Baker & Scott, London; Senior Architect, Glenrothes Development Corporation; began private practice in Fife; Senior Lecturer, Dundee School of Architecture, 1952-58; Saltire Awards and Commendations (19), Civic Trust Awards and Commendations (12), Trustee, Scottish Civic Trust, 1970-83; Member, Royal Fine Art Commission for Scotland; President, Royal Scottish Academy, since 1983. Recreations: sketching and water colours; fishing; music; drama; gardens. Address: (h.) Hawthornbank House, Dean Village, Edinburgh, EH4 3BH.

Wherrett, Brian Spencer, BSc, PhD. Reader, Department of Physics, Heriot-Watt University, since 1983; b. 8.5.46, Bromley; m., Shirley Ruth; 1 s.; 1 d. Educ. Westcliff High School; Reading University. Research Associate, Reading University, 1969-70; Heriot-Watt University: Research Associate, 1970-71, Lecturer, 1971-79, Senior Lecturer, 1979-83; Visiting Professor, North Texas State University, 1981-82. Recreation: squash. Address: (h.) 9 Bryce Road, Currie, Midlothian; T.-031-449 2675.

Whitby, Professor Lionel Gordon, MA, PhD, MD, BChir, FRCP, FRCPEdin, FRCPath, FRSE. Professor of Clinical Chemistry, Edinburgh University, since 1963; Honorary Consultant in Clinical Chemistry, Lothian Health Board, since 1974; Dean, Faculty of Medicine, Edinburgh University, since 1983; b. 18.7.26, London; m., Joan Hunter Sanderson; 1 s.; 2 d. Educ. Eton College; King's College, Cambridge. MRC Scholar for Training in Research, Biochemistry Department, Cambridge University, 1948-51; Fellow, King's College, Cambridge, 1951-55; junior hospital appointments, Middlesex Hospital, London, etc., 1956-58; Registrar in Chemical Pathology, then Lecturer, Royal Postgraduate Medical School, London, 1958-60; Rockefeller Travelling Fellowship, National

Institutes of Health, Bethesda, 1959-60; University Biochemist, Addenbrooke's Hospital, Cambridge, 1960-63; Fellow, Peterhouse, Cambridge, 1961-62; Dean, Faculty of Medicine, Edinburgh University, 1969-72. Visiting Professor of Chemical Pathology, Royal Postgraduate Medical School, 1974; Vice-Principal, Edinburgh University, 1979-83. Recreations: gardening; photography. Address: (b.) Department of Clinical Chemistry, Royal Infirmary, Edinburgh, EH3 9YW; T.-031-229 2477.

White, David J., BSc (Hons), PhD, JP. Rector, Garnock Academy, since 1974; b. 13.12.32, New York; m., Cecilia Wilson; 1 s.; 3 d. Educ. Strathclyde University; Glasgow University. Address: (h.) 30 Mulgrew Avenue, Saltcoats, Ayrshire, KA21 6HP; T.-0294 62568.

White, David Nathaniel James, BSc, DPhil. Reader in Physical Chemistry, Glasgow University, since 1984; b. 12.2.46, Edinburgh; m., Valerie Joyce; 3 s.; 1 d. Educ. West Hatch Technical High School, Chigwell; University of Wales Institute of Science and Technology; Sussex University. Lecturer in Physical Chemistry, Glasgow University, 1974-84. Former Treasurer, Molecular Graphics Society; former holder, Royal Society European and Ramsay Memorial Fellowships. Recreations: skiing; reading; home computers. Address: (b.) Chemistry Department, Glasgow University, Glasgow, G12 8QQ; T.-041-339 8855.

White, Duncan Bryce. Sheriff Clerk, Edinburgh, since 1981; Commissary Clerk, Edinburgh, since 1981; Sheriff Clerk of Chancery, since 1981; b. 3.2.32, Airdrie; m., Ivie White Neill; 2 d. Educ. Coatbridge High School. HM Treasury, 1953; HM Exchequer, 1954; Sheriff Court, Aberdeen, 1955; Sheriff Court, Glasgow, 1961; Sheriff Court, Dunblane, 1964; Principal Training Officer, Scottish Court Service, 1974. Recreations: golf; hill-walking. Address: (h.) Mylnhurst, Old Doune Road, Dunblane, Perthshire; T.-0786 822582.

White, James. MP (Labour), Glasgow Pollok, since 1970; b. 10.4.22. Educ. Knightswood Senior Secondary School. Sponsored Abortion (Amendment) Bill, 1975.

White, Sir Thomas Astley Woollaston, Bt. Honorary Sheriff, Wigtownshire, since 1963; b. 13.5.04; m.; 1 d. Educ. Wellington College. JP, Wigtownshire, 1952.

Whitecross, John Andrew, LLB, BSc (Econ), DPA, FBIM, FInstAM (Dip.). Chief Executive and Director of Administration, Annandale and Eskdale District Council, since 1981; b. 13.4.44, Glasgow; m., Janet Lomax MacNicol; 2 s. Educ. Hillhead High School, Glasgow; Glasgow University; London University. Town Clerk's Office, Glasgow, 1967-74; Depute Chief Executive, Annandale and Eskdale District Council, 1974-77; Director of Administration and Deputy Chief Executive, Inverness District Council, 1977-81. Recreations: philately; rugby refereeing; mini-rugby coaching. Address: (b.) District Council Chambers, High Street, Annan; T.-Annan 3311.

Whiteford, James Barrie, JP. Honorary Sheriff; b. 22.1.06, Glasgow; m., Jessie McK. Bowie; 2 d. Educ. Onslow Drive School, Glasgow. Glasgow Bute Benevolent Society: Director, since 1964, President, 1975-78; President, Rothesay Business Club, 1968-69; Chairman, Bute Savings Bank, 1972-76; President, Rothesay Rotary Club, 1975-76; Trustee, James John Wilkie Almshouses Trust; former Council Member, Baptist Union of Scotland. Address: (h.) 34 Crichton Road, Rothesay, Isle of Bute; T.-0700 3434.

Whitelaw, Ian Macleod. Assistant Secretary, Department of Agriculture and Fisheries for Scotland, since 1984; b. 20.9.42, Edinburgh; m., Rhoda Margaret Thomson; 1 s.; 1 d. Educ. Royal High School, Edinburgh. Scottish Education Department, 1961-71; Secretary, Scottish Agricultural Development Council, 1971-74; DAFS, since 1974. Recreations: sport; history (Scottish/military). Address: (b.) Department of Agriculture and Fisheries for Scotland, Chesser House, 500 Gorgie Road, Edinburgh, EH11 3AW; T.-031-443 4020, Ext. 2176.

Whitelaw, Robert George, MA, MD, FRCOG, DL. Deputy Lieutenant, Fife, since 1969; Honorary Sheriff, since 1978; b. 29.4.13, Motherwell; m., Cicely Mary Ballard; 1 s. Educ. Wishaw High School; Glasgow University. Consultant Obstetrician and Gynaecologist, West Fife Group of Hospitals, 1956-78; External Examiner, Edinburgh University, 1967-71; Examiner; Central Midwives Board for Scotland, General Nursing Council for Scotland, Royal College of Surgeons of Edinburgh, PLAB. Past President, Fife Branch, BMA; Past President, Dunfermline Rotary Club. Recreations: golf; photography; travel. Address: (h.) 64 Garvock Hill, Dunfermline, Fife, KY12 7UU; T.-0383 721209.

Whiteman, Professor Arthur John, BSc, PhD, FInstPet. Professor of Petroleum Geology, Aberdeen University, since 1974; b. 1.1.28, Ormskirk; m., Barbara Ann Chidzey; 2 s.; 2 d. Educ. University College, London; Stanford University; Columbia University. Geologist, Humble Oil and Refining Co. Research Fellowship, Columbia University, 1949-51; Geologist, HM Geologist Survey, Great Britain, 1951-56; Exploration Geologist, Compagnie Des Petroles D'Algerie, Royal Dutch Shell, 1956-60; Consultant Petroleum Geologist, since 1960; Professor of Geology, Khartoum, Sudan, 1960-68; Professor of Petroleum Geology, Ibadan University, Nigeria, 1968-72; Professor of Petroleum Geology, Bergen University, Norway, 1972-74. Publication: Geology of Sudan Republic, 1971; Nigeria: Its Petroleum Geology, Resources and Potential, 1982. Recreation: gardening. Address: (h.) Heugh Head, Aboyne, AB3 5JE; T.-0339 2155.

Whitfield, Ann, MB, BS, MRCS, LRCP, FFARCS, DA. Consultant Anaesthetist, Edinburgh Royal Infirmary; Chairman, Division of Anaesthesia (Lothian); b. 28.7.35, Lindfield, Sussex; m., Professor R.E. Kendell; 2 s.; 2 d. Educ. Sherborne School for Girls, Dorset; Kings College Hospital, London. Pre-registration appointments, Kings College Hospital, Queen Victoria Hospital, East Grinstead; anaesthetic training, St. Giles Hospital, London, Kings College Hospital, Vermont University; Consultant appointments, Lewisham Hospital, Edinburgh Royal Infirmary. Recreations: walking; cooking; reading; flower arranging. Address: (h.) 3 West Castle Road, Edinbrgh, EH10 5AT; T.-031-229 4966.

Whitfield, Professor Charles Richard, MD, FRCOG, FRCPGlas. Regius Professor of Midwifery, Glasgow University, since 1976; Consultant Obstetrician, Queen Mother's Hospital, Glasgow, and Consultant Gynaecologist, Western Infirmary, Glasgow, since 1976; b. 21.10.27, India; m., Marion Douglas; 1 s.; 2 d. Educ. Campbell College, Belfast; Queen's University, Belfast. Resident appointments, Belfast Teaching Hospitals, 1951-53; RAMC, 1953-64 (Senior Specialist in Obstetrics and Gynaecology, 1959-64); Consultant Obstetrician and Gynaecologist, Belfast Teaching Hospitals, 1968-74; Professor of Obstetrics and Gynaecology, Manchester University, 1974-76. Publication: Dewhurst's Postgraduate Textbook of Obstetrics and Gynaecology (Editor). Recreations: trying to remember what they were. Address: (h.) 23 Thorn Road, Bearsden, Glasgow, G61.

Whiting, Brian, MD, FRCPGlas. Consultant Physician (Clinical Pharmacology), since 1977; Reader in Clinical Pharmacology, Glasgow University, since 1982; Secretary, Glasgow Clinical Pharmacology Group, since 1984; b. 6.1.39, Manchester; 2 d. Educ. Stockport Grammar School; Glasgow University. Research and hospital posts, Stobhill General Hospital, Department of Materia Medica, 1965-77; Visiting Professor of Clinical Pharmacology, University of California, San Francisco, 1978-79; returned to Glasgow, 1979; Director, Clinical Pharmacokinetics Laboratory, Department of Materia Medica, Stobhill General Hospital, Glasgow, since 1980; Member, Clinical Section Committee, British Pharmacological Society. Publication: Lecture Notes on Clinical Pharmacology (Co-author). Recreation: electronic and computer music composition. Address: (h.) 2 Milner Road, Glasgow, G13 1QL; T.-041-959 2324.

Whitley, Rev. Laurence Arthur Brown, MA, BD. Minister, Montrose Old Parish, since 1985 (Busby East and West, 1975-85); b. 19.9.49, Port Glasgow; m., Catherine MacLean MacFadyen. Educ. Edinburgh Academy; Edinburgh University; St. Andrews University. Assistant Minister, St. Andrews, Dundee, 1974-75. Parliamentary candidate (SNP), Dumfriesshire, February and October, 1974. Recreation: hockey. Address: 2 Rosehill Road, Montrose, Angus, DD10 8RY; T.-Montrose 72447.

Whitson, Angus Grigor Macbeath, LLB. Vice Chairman, Council, Scottish Tartans Society, since 1984; Honorary Secretary, Angus Branch, British Red Cross Society, since 1969; Company Director; b. 11.3.42, Dundee; m., Elizabeth Marjorie Greville; 2 s.; 1 d. Educ. Loretto School; Edinburgh University. Solicitor, 1966-77; Clerk to the Justices of the Peace for Angus, 1970-76. Recreations: fishing; shooting; sailing; curling; drinking fine spirits and wines. Address: (h.) The Kirklands, by Montrose, Angus.

Whitson, Harold A., CBE, BA. Director, Scottish Mutual Assurance Company, since 1982; Director, Ailsa Investment Trust PLC, since 1972; b. 20.9.16, Esher; m., Rowena Pitt; 1 s.; 2 d. Educ. Rugby School; Trinity College, Cambridge. Royal Engineers, 1940-46; Melville, Dundas and Whitson Ltd., 1946-82; East Kilbride Development Corporation, 1962-79; President, Glasgow Chamber of Commerce, 1967-68; Chairman, Irvine Development Corporation, 1979-82; Director, Scottish National Orchestra; Fellow, Royal Society of Arts. Recreations: gardening; shooting. Address: (h.) Edmonston House, Biggar, ML12 6QY; T.-0899 20063.

Whittemore, Professor Colin Trengove, BSc, PhD, NDA. Professor of Animal Production, Edinburgh University, since 1984; Head, Animal Division, Edinburgh School of Agriculture, since 1984; b. 16.7.42, Chester; m., Chris; 1 s.; 2 d. Educ. Rydal School; Newcastle-upon-Tyne University. Lecturer in Agriculture, Edinburgh University and Head, Animal Production, Advisory and Development, Edinburgh School of Agriculture; Sir John Hammond Memorial Prize for scientific contribution to an understanding of nutrition and growth; Oxford University Blackman Lecture, 1984; Royal Agricultural Society of England Gold Medal for research; Member, Governing Body, HFRO. Recreations: skiing; riding. Address: (b.) Edinburgh University, School of Agriculture, West Mains Road, Edinburgh, EH9 3JG; T.-031-667 1041.

Whittington, Graeme Walter, BA, PhD. Reader in Geography, St. Andrews University, since 1982; b. 25.7.31, Cranleigh. Educ. King Edward VI Royal Grammar School, Guildford; Reading University. St. Andrews University: Assistant, 1959, Lecturer, 1962, Senior Lecturer, 1972; Visiting Lecturer, Natal University, 1971; Member, British Association Committee on Ancient Fields, 1958-73. Publications: Environment and Land Use in Africa (Co-Editor); An Historical Geography of Scotland (Co-Editor). Recreations: gardening; classical music. Address: (h.) 3 Leonard Gardens, St. Andrews, Fife, KY16 8RD; T.-0334 76807.

Whittle, Martin John, MB, ChB, MD, MRCOG. Consultant Obstetrician/Gynaecologist, Queen Mother's Hospital, Glasgow, since 1982; b. 6.7.44, London; m., Lindsay Hall; 1 s. Educ. William Grimshaw Secondary Modern School, London; Manchester University. Left school to work in medical laboratory, 1962; student, 1965-72. Recreations: swimming; music; languages; wine. Address: (h.) 67 Fotheringay Road, Pollokshields, Glasgow.

Whyte, David James, MA. Rector, Golspie High School, since 1983; b. 21.2.40, Cupar; m., Judith; 4 s. Educ. Bell Baxter High School; St. Andrews University; Oxford University. Teacher of English, Strathallan School, 1964-67; Special Assistant, Kirkcaldy High School, 1967-69; Principal Teacher of English, Brechin High School, 1969-74; Assistant Head Teacher, Arbroath Academy, 1974-79; Depute Rector, Peterhead Academy, 1979-83. British athletics international, 1958-60; AAA Long Jump Champion, 1959; Oxford rugby blue, 1963; Scottish rugby international, 1964-67 (13 caps); Chairman, NE Aberdeenshire Members' Centre, National Trust for Scotland. Recreation: bridge. Address: (h.) Tigh Geal, Backies, Golspie, Sutherland; T.-Golspie 3572.

Whyte, George B., CEng, MIMechE. Chairman, Electricity Consultative Council, since 1981; Non-Executive Board Member, South of Scotland Electricity Board, since 1981; b. 18.3.26, Kirkcaldy; m., Joan Walden; 1 s.; 2 d. Educ. Kirkcaldy High School; Heriot-Watt College, Edinburgh. Various appointments, Scottish Agricultural Industries P.L.C., Edinburgh, 1949-84 (latterly Chief Engineer); Member, Electricity Consultative Council, since 1971 (Deputy Chairman, 1979-81). Past President, Fertiliser Society. Recreations: golf; gardening; walking. Address: (b.) 249 West George Street, Glasgow; T.-041-248 5588.

Whyte, Rev. James, BD, DipCE. Minister, Coupar Angus Abbey, Perthshire, since 1981; b. 26.4.46, Glasgow; m., Norma Isabella West; 1 s.; 2 d. Educ. Penilee Secondary School; Jordanhill College, Glasgow; Trinity College, Glasgow. Trained as planning engineer; after graduation, joined staff, Lamp of Lothian Collegiate Trust, Haddington; Organiser of Community Education, Dumbarton, 1971-74; Assistant Principal Community Education Officer, Renfrew Division, Strathclyde Region, 1974-77; entered ministry, Church of Scotland, 1977. Recreations: reading; gardening; family. Address: The Manse of the Abbey, Coupar Angus, Perthshire, PH13 9EF; T.-Coupar Angus 27331.

Whyte, Rev. Professor James Aitken, MA, LLD. Professor of Practical Theology and Christian Ethics, St. Andrews University, since 1958; b. 28.1.20, Leith; m., Elisabeth Wilson Mill; 2 s.; 1 d. Educ. Daniel Stewart's College, Edinburgh; Edinburgh University. Ordained and commissioned as Chaplain to the Forces, 1945; Minister: Dunollie Road Church, Oban, 1948-54, Mayfield North Church, Edinburgh, 1954-58; Dean of Divinity, St. Andrews University, 1968-72; Principal, St. Mary's College, 1978-82; Kerr Lecturer, Glasgow University, 1969-72; Croall Lecturer, Edinburgh University, 1972-73; Hon. LLD, Dundee University, 1981; President, Society for the Study of Theology, 1983-84. Address: (h.) 13 Hope Street, St. Andrews, Fife; T.-St. Andrews 72323.

Whyte, Robert, MB, ChB, FRCPsych, DPM. Consultant Psychotherapist, Duke Street Hospital, Glasgow, since 1979; b. 1.6.41, Edinburgh; m., Susan Frances Milburn; 1 s.; 1 d. Educ. George Heriot's, Edinburgh; St. Andrews University. House Officer in Surgery, Arbroath Infirmary, 1966; House Officer in Medicine, Falkirk and District Royal Infirmary, 1967; Trainee in Psychiatry, Dundee Psychiatric Services, 1967-73; Consultant Psychiatrist, Duke Street Hospital, Glasgow, 1973. Chairman, Scottish Association of Analytical Psychotherapists, since 1983; Member, Scottish Institute of Human Relations. Recreation: running. Address: (h.) Waverley, 70 East Kilbride Road, Busby, Glasgow, G76 8HU; T.-041-644 1659.

Wiener, Gerald, BSc, PhD, DSc, FRSE, FIBiol. Deputy Director, AFRC Animal Breeding Research Organisation, since 1983; b. 25.4.26; 1 s.; 1 d. Educ. City of Oxford High School for Boys; Edinburgh University. AFRC Animal Breeding Research Organisation: Research Scientist, 1947, Head, Department of Physiological Genetics, 1974; Honorary Member, British Society of Animal Production, since 1976; Senior Editor, Animal Production, 1962-75; Chairman, Holy Corner Church Centre Ltd. (community centre development). Recreation: hill-walking. Address: (h.) 7 Viewpark Road, Biggar, Lanarkshire, ML12 6BG; T.-0899 20452.

Wiggins, Ian Stewart. Chief Fatstock Officer for Scotland, Meat and Livestock Commission, since 1979; b. 19.5.32, Glasgow; m., Jean Hopkirk; 1 d. Educ. Hutchesons Grammar School, Glasgow. Wholesale Meat Supply Association, 1948; joined Ministry of Food, 1954; Department of Agriculture, 1956; appointed District Fatstock Officer, Edinburgh District, 1966; Regional Fatstock Officer, 1968. President, Scottish Lawn Tennis Association, 1979-80; Member, Lawn Tennis Council, 1977-81; Honorary Vice-President, SLTA. Recreations: tennis; squash. Address: (h.) Hilltop, Cults, Aberdeen, AB1 9RN; T.-0224 86 8615.

Wight, John James. Farmer; Director, Royal Highland and Agricultural Society of Scotland, since 1981; Council Member, British Charolais Cattle Society, since 1984; b. 3.5.38, Crawford; m., Netta S.S. Struthers; 2 s.; 1 d. Educ. Biggar High School. Member, NFU Committee, Biggar; Member, Biggar Show Committee; former Member, NFU Council; former Council Member, North British Hereford Herd Book Society; Past President, Coulter Curling Club. Recreations: curling; golf. Address: Midlock, Crawford, Biggar, Lanarkshire, ML12 6UA; T.-08642 230.

Wild, John Robin, BDS, DPD, JP. Chief Administrative Dental Officer, Borders Health Board, since 1974; Regional Dental Postgraduate Adviser, SE Regional Committee for Postgraduate Medical Education, since 1982; b. 12.9.41, Scarborough; m., Eleanor Daphne Kerr; 1 s.; 2 d. Educ. Sedbergh School; Edinburgh University; Dundee University. General Dental Practitioner, Scarborough, 1965-71; School Dental Officer, East Lothian, 1971-74; Honorary Member, clinical teaching staff, Edinburgh Dental School, since 1975; Fellow, Edinburgh University, since 1984; Chairman, Scottish Council, British Dental Association; Secretary and Treasurer, Borders Section, British Dental Association; Vice-Chairman, Tweeddale, Ettrick and Lauderdale Conservative and Unionist Association. Recreations: vintage cars (restoration and driving); music; gardening; photography. Address: (h.) Braeheads House, St. Boswells, Roxburghshire; T.-0835 23203.

Wilken, Charles Beaton, MBE, TD. Solicitor; Honorary Sheriff, Grampian, Highlands and Islands, Elgin, since 1970; Consultant, Allan Black & McCaskie, Solicitors, Elgin; b. 29.3.14, Elgin; m., Mary Ethel Vipond; 4 s. Educ.

Elgin Academy; Edinburgh University. Seaforth Highlanders, 1939-46. Recreation: golf. Address: (h.) Kilmorie, 6 Institution Road, Elgin, Moray; T.-Elgin 2707.

Wilkie, Emeritus Professor John Ritchie, MA. Emeritus Professor of German, Aberdeen University, since 1982; b. 24.5.21, Rathen, Aberdeenshire; m., Sheila Ruth Napier; 1 d. Educ. Banff Academy; Aberdeen University; St. John's College, Cambridge; Zurich University. Assistant in German, Aberdeen University, 1945-50; Lecturer, Senior Lecturer, Professor, German Language and Literature, Leeds University, 1950-77; Professor of German, Aberdeen University, 1978-82. Member of Conference of University Teachers of German in Great Britain and Ireland. Publication: A Short History of the German Language (Co-author), 1970. Recreations: music; history (including local history); language and literature; theology. Address: (h.) 90 Desswood Place, Aberdeen, AB2 4DQ; T.-0224 645991.

Wilkie, Neil Keith, MA (Hons). Headteacher, Gairloch High School, (formerly Achtercairn Secondary School), since 1978; b. 5.4.39, Perth; m., Margaret Rawlinson; 1 s. Educ. Perth Academy; Dundee University; Dundee College of Education; East of Scotland College of Agriculture. Sugar planter, Trinidad, six years; resumed academic studies, 1966; Teacher of History and Modern Studies, then Principal Teacher of History, Golspie High School, 1972-78. Treasurer, Gairloch and Dundonnell Parish Church; Member, Gairloch Community Council. Recreations: sport; fishing; gardening. Address: (h.) Rohallion, Achtercairn, Gairloch, Ross-shire; T.-0445 2221.

Wilkins, Professor Malcolm Barrett, BSc, PhD, DSc, AKC, FRSE. Regius Professor of Botany, Glasgow University, since 1970 (Dean, Faculty of Science, since 1985); b. 2.2.33, Cardiff; m., Mary Patricia Maltby; 1 s.; 1 d. (deceased). Educ. Monkton House School, Cardiff; King's College, London University. Lecturer in Botany, King's College, London, 1958-64; Lecturer in Biology, then Professor of Biology, East Anglia University, 1964-67; Professor of Plant Physiology, Nottingham University, 1967-70. Rockefeller Foundation Fellow, Yale University, 1961-62; Corporation Research Fellow, Harvard University, 1962-63; Darwin Lecturer, British Association for the Advancement of Science, 1967; elected Corresponding (Honorary) Member, American Society of Plant Physiologists, 1984; Member, Life Science Working Group, European Space Agency. Recreations: sailing; fishing. Address: (b.) Botany Department, Glasgow University, Glasgow, G12 8QQ; T.-041-339 8855.

Wilkinson, Professor Alexander Birrell, MA, LLB. Professor of Private Law, Dundee University, since 1972; b. 2.2.32, Perth; m., Wendy Imogen Barrett; 1 s.; 1 d. Educ. Perth Academy; St. Andrews University; Edinburgh University. Advocate, 1959; practised at Scottish Bar, 1959-69; Lecturer in Scots Law, Edinburgh University, 1965-69; Sheriff of Stirling, Dunbarton and Clackmannan, at Stirling and Alloa, 1969-72;

Dean, Faculty of Law, Dundee University, 1974-76; a Chairman, Industrial Tribunals (Scotland); Chancellor, Diocese of Brechin, Scottish Episcopal Church; Chairman, Scottish Marriage Guidance Council, 1976-77; Member, Services Group, Scottish Association of CAB, 1979-83. Publication: Gloag and Henderson's Introduction to the Law of Scotland, 8th edition (Co-Editor). Recreations: collecting books and pictures; reading; travel. Address: (h.) 267 Perth Road, Dundee, DD2 1JP; T.-0382 68939.

Wilkinson, Professor Chris D.W., MA, PhD. Titular Professor, Department of Electronics and Electrical Engineering, Glasgow University, since 1982; b. 1.9.40, Blackburn; m., Judith Anne Hughes; 1 s.; 2 d. Educ. Queen Elizabeth's Grammar School, Blackburn; Balliol College, Oxford; Stanford University, California. Engineer, English Electric Valve Company, Chelmsford, 1967-69; Department of Electronics and Electrical Engineering, Glasgow University: Lecturer, 1969, Senior Lecturer, 1975, Reader, 1978. Member, SERC Committees. Recreation: hill-walking. Address: (b.) Department of Electronics and Electrical Engineering, Glasgow University, Glasgow, G12 8QQ; T.-041-339 8855.

Wilkinson, Professor Paul, MA. Professor of International Relations, Aberdeen University, since 1979; Head, Department of Politics and International Relations, since 1985; Writer on conflict and terrorism; b. 9.5.37, Harrow, Middlesex; m., Susan; 2 s.; 1 d. Educ. John Lyon School; University College, Swansea; University of Wales. RAF, 1959-65; Assistant Lecturer in Politics, University College, Cardiff, 1966-68; University of Wales: Lecturer, 1968-75, Senior Lecturer, 1975-77, Reader in Politics, 1978-79; Editorial Adviser, Contemporary Review; Associate Editor, Terrorism: An International Journal; Member, Editorial Board, Conflict Quarterly; Editor, Key Concepts in International Relations; Scottish Free Enterprise Award, 1982. Publications: Social Movement, 1971; Political Terrorism, 1974; Terrorism and the Liberal State, 1977; The New Fascists, 1983; Terrorism: Theory and Practice (Co-author), 1979; British Perspectives on Terrorism (Editor), 1981. Recreations: modern art; poetry; walking. Address: (b.) Department of Politics and International Relations, Aberdeen University, Aberdeen, AB9 2UB; T.-0224 40241.

Wilkinson, Professor Peter Charles, MD, FRSE. Titular Professor in Bacteriology and Immunology, Glasgow University, since 1982; Honorary Consultant in Bacteriology and Immunology, Western Infirmary, Glasgow, since 1970; b. 10.7.32, London; m., Eileen Mary Baron; 2 s.; 1 d. Educ. London Hospital Medical College; London University. House appointments, London Hospital, 1956-58; Flt.-Lt., RAF (Medical Officer), 1958-60; Lecturer in Bacteriology, London Hospital Medical College, 1960-63; Lecturer and Senior Lecturer in Bacteriology and Immunology, Glasgow University, 1964-77; MRC Travelling Fellow, Swiss Research Institute, 1967-69; Reader, Glasgow University, 1977-82; Visiting Professor, Rockefeller University, New York, 1979. Publications: Chemotaxis

and Inflammation; A Dictionary of Immunology (Co-author). Recreations: various interests in the arts. Address: (h.) 26 Randolph Road, Glasgow, G11 7LG.

Wilkinson, Richard Matthew, MInstPS, AHSM. Assistant Director, Supplies Division, Common Services Agency for the Scottish Health Service, since 1983; Member, Strathclyde Regional Council, since 1978; b. 7.9.47, Kilwinning; m., Anne R.R. Hair; 1 s.; 1 d. Educ. Irvine Royal Academy. Civil Servant, 1965-71; Health Service Work Study Officer, 1971-73; Hospital and Health Board Administrator, 1973-80; Supplies Officer, Common Services Agency, 1980-83. Executive Member, Strathclyde Conservative Group; Council Member, Stow College, Glasgow; COSLA Representative, Council, Scottish Association of Young Farmers Clubs; Chairman, Largs and District Crime Prevention Panel; Member, Isle of Arran Tourist Board; Chairman, West Kilbride Committee, Action Research for the Crippled Child; Chairman, Ayrshire Sportsmen's Dinner for Action Research for the Crippled Child; Executive Member, North Cunninghame Conservative and Unionist Association. Recreations: family; theatre; gardening; charity fund-raising. Address: (h.) The Fort, Ardrossan Road, Seamill, West Kilbride; T.-0294 822755.

Wilkinson, Rev. William Brian, MA (Hons), BD (Hons). Minister, Kilmore and Oban Parish Church (Senior Colleague), since 1984; b. 14.4.42, Edinburgh; m., Janet Cameron Inglis. Educ. Peterhead Academy; High School of Stirling; Edinburgh University. Assistant Minister, Gilmerton Parish Church, Edinburgh, 1967-69; Minister: Carnock Parish Church, Fife, 1969-74, Christ's Church, Dunollie, Oban, 1974-83. Council Member, Royal National Mission to Deep Sea Fishermen, since 1980. Recreations: Gaelic choral singing; book (Highland) collecting; walking; swimming. Address: The Manse, Kilmore and Oban Parish Church, Dalriach Road, Oban; T.-Oban 62464.

Willetts, Professor Brian Benjamin, MA, PhD, CEng, MICE. Professor of Engineering, Aberdeen University, since 1985; b. 12.6.36, Old Hill; m., Patricia Margaret Jones; 1 s.; 1 d. Educ. King Edward VI Grammar School, Stourbridge; Emmanuel College, Cambridge. Assistant Engineer, Birmingham Public Works Department; Executive Engineer, Government of Northern Nigeria; lecturing posts, Lanchester Polytechnic and Aberdeen University. President, Aberdeen Association of Civil Engineers, 1984-86. Recreations: gardening; pottering. Address: (h.) Mosscroft, Upper Lochton, Banchory, Kincardineshire; T.-Banchory 2674.

Williams, Professor Sir Alwyn, Kt, DSc, PhD, FRS, FRSE, MRIA, FGS, Hon. FRCPS, Hon. LLD. Principal and Vice-Chancellor, Glasgow University, since 1976; Non-Executive Director, Scottish Daily Record and Sunday Mail Ltd., since 1984; b. 8.6.21, Aberdare, Wales; m., Edith Joan Bevan; 1 s.; 1 d. Educ. Aberdare Boys' Grammar School; University College of Wales, Aberystwyth. Commonwealth Fund Fellow, US

National Museum, 1948-50; Lecturer in Geology, Glasgow University, 1950-54; Professor of Geology, Queen's University, Belfast, 1954-74; Lapworth Professor of Geology, Birmingham University, 1974-76; Member, Scottish Tertiary Education Advisory Council, since 1984; President, Palaeontological Association, 1968-70; Trustee and Chairman, Board of British Museum (Natural History), 1971-79; Chairman of Committee on National Museums and Galleries Scotland, 1979-81; Honorary Fellow, Geological Society of America, since 1970; Foreign Member, Polish Academies of Science, since 1981; Hon. DSc, Universities of Wales, Queen's (Belfast) and Edinburgh; Hon. LLD, Strathclyde. Address: (h.) Principal's Lodging, 12 The Square, Glasgow University, Glasgow, G12 8QG; T.-041-339 0383.

Williams, Arthur, MPS. Chief Administrative Pharmaceutical Officer, Grampian, Orkney and Shetland Health Boards, since 1981; b. 5.11.32, Tarleton, near Preston; m., Barbara; 1 s.; 1 d. Educ. Hutton Grammar School, near Preston; School of Pharmacy, Leicester. Senior Pharmacist, United Manchester Hospitals, 1957-59; Chief Pharmacist: Jewish Hospital, 1959-62, Macclesfield Hospital, 1962-66; Group Chief Pharmacist to Area Pharmaceutical Officer, 1966-81. Merck, Sharp and Dohme Award, 1979. Recreations: gardening; fell-walking; natural history. Address: (b.) Department of Pharmacy, Aberdeen Royal Infirmary, Foresterhill, Aberdeen, AB9 2XJ; T.-0224 681818, Ext. 2399.

Williams, Brian Owen, MD, MRCP, FRCPGlas. Consultant Physician in administrative charge, Geriatric Medical Service, Gartnavel General Hospital, Glasgow, since 1982; b. 27.2.47, Glasgow; m., Martha MacDonald Carmichael; 2 d. Educ. Kings Park Senior Secondary School, Glasgow; Glasgow University Medical School. Senior Lecturer, Geriatric Medicine, Glasgow University, 1979-82; Consultant Physician in Geriatric Medicine, Victoria Infirmary, Glasgow, 1976-79; Councillor, Royal College of Physicians and Surgeons of Glasgow, 1976-83. Recreations: swimming; running; gardening. Address: (h.) 15 Thorn Drive, High Burnside, Glasgow, G73 4RH; T.-041-634 4480.

Williamson, Rev. Colin Raymond, LLB, BD. Minister, Aberdalgie and Dupplin with Forteviot, since 1984; Convener, Panel on Worship, General Assembly, since 1982; b. 20.1.42, Belfast; m., Arlene Elizabeth Geddes; 1 s.; 2 d. Educ. Dumbarton Academy; Glasgow University; New College, Edinburgh. Licensed, 1971; Assistant, Ayr Auld Kirk, 1971-72; ordained, 1972; Minister: Auchencairn with Rerrick, 1972-78, Leith St. Paul's, 1978-84. Secretary, Church Service Society. Recreations: country life; music. Address: Manse of Aberdalgie, Perth, PH2 OQD; T.-0738 25854.

Williamson, Douglas Guthrie, BSc, PhD. Senior Lecturer in Chemistry, Aberdeen University, since 1980 (Assistant Dean, Faculty of Science, since 1979); Member, Scottish Consumer Council, since 1981; b. 2.6.37, Edinburgh; m., Alison J. Donaldson. Educ. Paisley Grammar School;

Glasgow University. Research Fellow (DSIR), Glasgow and Cambridge Universities, 1963-65; Lecturer in Chemistry, Aberdeen University, 1965-80. Secretary, Aberdeen Consumer Group, 1978-83. Recreations: hill-walking; gardens. Address: (h.) 150 Broomhill Road, Aberdeen, AB1 6HY; T.-0224 586847.

Williamson, Professor James, CBE, MB, ChB, FRCPEdin. Professor of Geriatric Medicine, Edinburgh University, since 1976; Honorary Consultant in Geriatric Medicine, Lothian Health Board, since 1976; b. 22.11.20, Wishaw; m., Sheila Mary Blair; 3 s.; 2 d. Educ. Wishaw High School; Glasgow University. General medical training in Glasgow hospitals up to rank of Registrar; general practice, two years; training in respiratory medicine, becoming Consultant in Edinburgh, 1954; converted to geriatric medicine, 1959; Consultant, Edinburgh, until 1973; first holder, Chair of Geriatric Medicine, Liverpool University; first holder, Chair of Geriatric Medicine, Edinburgh University, 1976; Member, General Medical Council; Member, Lothian Health Board; President-Elect, British Geriatrics Society. Recreations: reading; walking. Address: (h.) 14 Ann Street, Edinburgh, EH4 1PJ; T.-031-332 3568.

Williamson, John H.K., BSc (Hons), CEng, MICE. Engineer-in-Chief, Northern Lighthouse Board, since 1978; b. 13.3.26, Edinburgh; 1 s. Educ. George Watson's Boys' College; Edinburgh University. Northern Lighthouse Board: Junior Civil Engineer, 1949, Deputy Engineer-in-Chief, 1972. Recreations: walking; photography; extra-mural classes. Address: (b.) 84 George Street, Edinburgh, EH2 3DA; T.-031-226 7051.

Williamson, Rev. Magnus James Cameron. Minister, Fetlar linked with Yell, since 1982; b. 9.9.34, Nesting, Shetland; m., Eunice Winifred Mary Williamson; 3 s.; 1 d. Educ. Lerwick; Aberdeen. Lay Missionary: Eday, Orkney, 1965-73, Yell and Fetlar, 1973-82. Chairman, Yell and Fetlar School Council; Member, Yell Community Council and Old Haa Trust. Recreation: gardening. Address: The Manse, Mid Yell, Shetland, ZE2 9BN; T.-0957 2283.

Williamson, Roy M.B., DA. Musician (The Corries); Commercial Fisherman. Author, Flower of Scotland. Recreation: painting.

Willocks, James, MD, FRCOG, FRCPGlas. Consultant Obstetrician and Gynaecologist, Queen Mother's Hospital and Western Infirmary, Glasgow, since 1966; Lecturer in Midwifery, Glasgow University, since 1964; Examiner to the Universities of Glasgow and London, Royal College of Obstetricians and Gynaecologists and Royal College of Physicians and Surgeons of Glasgow; b. 29.7.28, East Kilbride; m., Elizabeth M. Cant; 3 d. Educ. Hutchesons' Grammar School; Glasgow University. Regimental Medical Officer, 2nd Gurkha Rifles, 1952-54; Hall Tutorial Fellow, Glasgow University, 1957; Registrar and Senior Registrar, Glasgow Royal Maternity Hospital, 1958-64; Royal College of Obstetricians and Gynaecologists' Specialist

Adviser for the West of Scotland, 1976-81; Chairman, Division of Obstetrics, Queen Mother's Hospital, since 1981; Chairman, Postgraduate Committee in Obstetrics and Gynaecology, Glasgow University, since 1981; President, Glasgow Obstetrical and Gynaecological Society, 1982-84; former Member: Central Midwives Board for Scotland, Scottish Council for Postgraduate Medical Education; Regional Assessor, Enquiry into Maternal Deaths in Scotland; Member, Advisory Committee on Medical Establishments, SHHD. Publication: Essentials of Obstetrics and Gynaecology, 1982. Recreations: literature; music; walking. Address: (h.) 16 Sutherland Avenue, Glasgow, G41 4JH; T.-041-427 6113.

Wills, Jonathan W.G., MA (Hons), PhD. Writer and Broadcaster; Illustrator and Painter; b. 17.6.47, Oxford; m., Lesley M. Roberts; 2 s. Educ. Warwick School; Anderson Educational Institute, Lerwick; Edinburgh University. Reporter, Shetland Times, 1969; Warden and boatman, Noss National Nature Reserve, 1970; Rector, Edinburgh University (first student Rector), 1971; Scottish and NI Organiser, Third World First (Oxfam), 1972; boatman, Muckle Flugga Lighthouse, Unst, 1974; Reporter, Shetland Times, 1976; Senior Producer/Presenter, BBC Radio Scotland, 1977; News Editor, Shetland Times, 1981; Scottish Correspondent, The Times, 1982; Producer, BBC Radio Scotland, 1983; Freelance and Research Assistant to Alex. Falconer, MEP, 1984; Tutor, Media Studies, STUC and individual trade unions, 1984; Senior Reporter, Shetland Times, 1985; Fraser Press Award, 1981-82, for work on Shetland Times; Labour candidate, Orkney and Shetland, 1974 (twice). Publications: (children's books) Magnus Pole, 1975; Linda and the Lighthouse, 1976. Recreations: sailing other people's boats; ornithology; painting; gardening. Address: (h.) Sundside, Bressay, Shetland, ZE2 9ER.

Wills, Leslie Charles, MB, ChB, FRCSEdin. Consultant ENT Surgeon, since 1975; Clinical Senior Lecturer in ENT, Aberdeen University, since 1975; b. 21.2.40, Aberdeen; m., Frances Cumming Gove; 3 d. Educ. Robert Gordon's College; Aberdeen University. Aberdeen University: Lecturer in Anatomy, Clinical Lecturer in ENT; Clinical Lecturer/Senior Registrar in ENT, Royal National Throat, Nose and Ear Hospital, London. Vice Chairman, Board, NE Society for the Deaf; Council Member, British Association of Otolaryngologists; Governor, Albyn School. Address: (h.) Bogjoran, Pitfodels, Cults, Aberdeen; T.-Aberdeen 868149.

Wilson, Alexander McArthur, CA, FACCA, ATII. Honorary Sheriff Substitute, Alloa, since 1975; b. 27.9.08, Charlestown, Fife; m., Helen Comrie Scott; 1 s.; 1 d. Educ. Dunfermline High School. Accountancy practice, Dunfermline, 1926-45 (Partner, 1935-45); carried on accountancy practice, Alloa, 1945-78. Elder, Clackmannan Church, since 1949 (Clerk to Board, 16 years, Treasurer, 14 years); former Treasurer, now Honorary Life Member, Alloa Amateur Operatic Society; Past President, Alloa Rotary Club. Recreations: gardening; bowling; Scottish country dancing; bee-keeping. Address: (h.) 7 The Glebe, Clackmannan; T.-0259 213645.

Wilson, Andrew John, DPA, CIPFA, ACMA. Director of Finance, Gordon District Council, since 1981; b. 4.3.43, Banff. Educ. Banff Academy; London University (External). Accountancy Assistant, Banff County Council, 1969-75; Depute Director of Finance, Banff and Buchan District Council, 1975-81. Address: (b.) Gordon House, Blackhall Road, Inverurie, AB5 9WA; T.-0467 20981, Ext. 209.

Wilson, Catherine Julia. Freelance Opera Singer; Tutor, Royal Northern College of Music, since 1980; b. Glasgow; m., Leonard Hancock. Educ. The Bar Convent, York; Royal Manchester College of Music. Seasons with Glyndebourne Opera Chorus and Arts Council Opera for All, 1958-60; principal role, Glyndebourne Opera, 1960; Principal, Sadlers Wells Opera, 1960-68; freelance work with Scottish Opera, English National Opera, Opera North, English Opera Group, Welsh Opera, and abroad, since 1968; has toured Russia and America. Address: (h.) 34 Glasgow Street, Glasgow, G12; T.-041-334 7771.

Wilson, Sir Charles Haynes, Kt (1965), MA. Principal and Vice-Chancellor, Glasgow University, 1971-76; b. 16.5.09; m.; 1 s.; 2 d. Educ. Hillhead High School; Glasgow University; Oxford University. Principal, University College of Leicester, 1952-57; Vice-Chancellor, Leicester University, 1957-61.

Wilson, Conrad. Music Critic, The Scotsman, since 1963 (also Wine and Food Correspondent, since 1981); b. 7.11.32, Edinburgh; m., Ruth; 1 s.; 1 d. Educ. Daniel Stewart's College, Edinburgh. Music Critic, Evening Dispatch, Edinburgh, 1954-58; Music Editor, Philips Records, Holland, 1958-61; Cultural Correspondent, The Scotsman, London Office, 1961-63. Programme Editor, Edinburgh Festival, 1966-82; freelance Music Lecturer, since 1964; Chairman, Critics' Committee, European Music Year, Arts Council of GB, 1985. Publications: A Critic's Choice, 1966; Scottish Opera, the First Ten Years, 1972; Collins Encyclopedia of Music (revised), 1976. Recreations: music; wine; food; reading; chess; travel; festivals. Address: (h.) 19 Queen Street, Edinburgh; T.-031-226 2859.

Wilson, Forrest. Children's Author and Crossword Compiler; b. 6.12.34, Renfrew; m., Jean Anderson; 1 d. Educ. Renfrew High School; Stow College of Engineering; School of Accountancy. Apprentice watchmaker, 1950; RAF, 1955; storeman/clerk, Skefco Ball Bearing Co., 1957; clerical supervisor, British Oil & Cake Mills, 1959; Scottish Milk Marketing Board: transport accounts, 1968, Creamery Office Manager (Mauchline), 1972; author of: Super Gran, Super Gran Rules OK!, Super Gran Superstar, Super Gran is Magic, Super Gran - The Picture Book, The Television Adventures of Super Gran, More Television Adventures of Super Gran, Super Gran in Orbit, The Adventures of the ABC Mob, Brain Benders. Recreation: composing music. Address: (b.) c/o A.P. Watt, 26/28 Bedford Row, London.

Wilson, Gerald, MA. Under Secretary, Industry Department for Scotland, since 1984; b. 7.9.39, Edinburgh; m., Margaret; 1 s.; 1 d. Educ. Holy

Cross Academy; Edinburgh University. Assistant Principal, Scottish Home and Health Department, 1961-65; Private Secretary, Minister of State for Scotland, 1965-66; Principal, Scottish Home and Health Department, 1966-72; Private Secretary to Lord Privy Seal, 1972-74, to Minister of State, Civil Service Department, 1974; Assistant Secretary, Scottish Economic Planning Department, 1974-77; Counsellor, Office of the UK Permanent Representative to the Economic Communities, Brussels, 1977-82; Assistant Secretary, Scottish Office, 1982-84. Recreation: music. Address: (b.) Alhambra House, 45 Waterloo Street, Glasgow; T.-041-248 2855.

Wilson, Gordon, MA (Hons), DipEd. Head Teacher, Shawlands Academy, Glasgow, since 1983; b. 9.6.33, Glasgow; m., Sybil Scott Ewing; 2 d. Educ. Allan Glen's School, Glasgow; Glasgow University; Jordanhill College of Education. Teacher of Geography: Shawlands Academy, 1960-64, Langside College, 1964-66; Hyndland Secondary School: Principal Teacher of Geography, 1966-71, Assistant Head Teacher, 1971-74, Depute Head Teacher, 1974-75; Head Teacher, John Street Secondary School, 1975-83. Conference Secretary, Headteachers' Association of Scotland. Recreations: badminton; golf. Address: (b.) Shawlands Academy, 31 Moss-side Road, Glasgow, G41 3TR; T.-041-632 1154.

Wilson, Hamish Robert McHattie, MA (Aberdeen), MA, PhD (Cantab), AHSM. Secretary, Grampian Health Board, since 1983; b. 19.1.46, Aberdeen. Educ. Robert Gordon's College, Aberdeen; Aberdeen University; Emmanuel College, Cambridge. Entered Health Service administration, 1972; held posts with Grampian Health Board in planning and primary care. Council Member, Scottish Society of the History of Medicine; Chairman, East of Scotland Branch, Institute of Health Services Management. Recreations: music; reading; theatre; cinema; good food and wine. Address: (b.) 1 Albyn Place, Aberdeen; T.-Aberdeen 589901.

Wilson of Langside, Baron, (Henry Stephen Wilson), PC, QC, LLB. Advocate, since 1946; House of Lords Spokesman for SDP on Scottish Legal Affairs; b. 21.3.16, Glasgow; m., Jessie Forrester Waters. Educ. High School of Glasgow; Glasgow University. Army, 1939-46 (Regimental Officer, HLI and RAC); called to Scottish Bar, 1946; Labour candidate, Dumfries, 1950, 1955, West Edinburgh, 1951; Sheriff, Greenock, 1955-56, Glasgow, 1956-65; Solicitor-General for Scotland, 1965-69; Lord Advocate, 1968-70; Sheriff, Glasgow, 1971-75, Sheriff Principal, Glasgow and Strathkelvin, 1975-77. Recreations: gardening; hill-walking. Address: (h.) Dunallan, Kippen, Stirlingshire, FK8 3HL; T.-Kippen 210.

Wilson, Professor Herbert Rees, BSc, PhD, FInstP, FRSE. Professor and Head, Physics Department, Stirling University, since 1983; b. 28.1.29, Nefyn, Wales; m., Elizabeth Turner; 1 s.; 2 d. Educ. Pwllheli Grammar School; University College of North Wales, Bangor. Research Scientist, Wheatstone Physics Laboratory, King's College, London, 1952-57; Lecturer in Physics,

Queen's College, Dundee, 1957-64; Research Associate, Children's Cancer Research Foundation, Boston, 1962; Senior Lecturer and Reader in Physics, Dundee University, 1964-83. Publication: Diffraction of X-Rays By Proteins, Nucleic Acids and Viruses. Recreations: travel; theatre; art. Address: (h.) Lower Bryanston, St. Margaret's Drive, Dunblane, FK15 ODP; T.-0786 823105.

Wilson, Ian Crawford, BCom, CIPFA. Chief Executive, Inverclyde District Council, since 1974; b. 10.4.36, Glasgow. Educ. Dalziel High School; Edinburgh University. Depute County Treasurer, Berwickshire County Council, 1968-71; Town Chamberlain, Greenock Corporation, 1971-74. Recreations: sailing; hill-walking. Address: (b.) Municipal Buildings, Greenock; T.-0475 24400.

Wilson, Very Rev. Ian George MacQueen, Hon. LTh. Dean, Diocese of Argyll and the Isles, since 1979; b. 6.3.20, Glasgow; m., Janet Todd Kyle. Educ. Albert Road Academy; Edinburgh Theological College. Diocese of Glasgow and Galloway: Deacon, 1950, ordained Priest, 1951, Curate, St. Margaret's Newlands, 1950-52, Priest in charge, St. Gabriel's Govan, 1952-57, Rector, Christ Church, Dalbeattie, 1957-61, Rector, St. John's Baillieston, 1961-64; Diocese of Argyll and the Isles: Rector, St. Paul's Rothesay, 1964-75, Canon, St. John's Cathedral, Oban, 1973-79, Priest in charge, St. Peter's Stornoway, 1975-78, Synod Clerk, Diocese of Argyll and the Isles, 1977-79, Rector, St. John's Ballachulish and St. Mary's Glencoe, 1978-85. Address: The Parsonage, Ardchattan, Bonawe, Oban, Argyll; T.-Bonawe 228.

Wilson, Ian Matthew, CB, MA. Under Secretary, Scottish Education Department, since 1977; b. 12.12.26, Edinburgh; m., Anne Chalmers; 3 s. Educ. George Watson's College; Edinburgh University. Assistant Principal, Scottish Home Department, 1950; Private Secretary to Permanent Under Secretary of State, Scottish Office, 1953-55; Principal, Scottish Home Department, 1955; Assistant Secretary: Scottish Education Department, 1963, Scottish Home and Health Department, 1971; Assistant Under Secretary of State, Scottish Office, 1974-77. Address: (h.) 1 Bonaly Drive, Edinburgh, EH13 OEJ; T.-031-441 2541.

Wilson, James, FBIM. Chief Executive, Livingston Development Corporation, since 1977; b. 12.3.22, Irvine; m., Audrie Veronica Haines; 3 d. Educ. Irvine Royal Academy; Edinburgh Academy. Chairman, Soldiers, Sailors and Airmen's Families Association, West Lothian; Member, Edinburgh University Careers and Advisory Committee; Member, National Affairs Committee, Edinburgh Chamber of Commerce; Member, Scottish Executive, Town and Country Planning Association; Member, Royal Artillery Council for Scotland; Member, Lothian Area Committee, Lowland Territorial Auxiliary and Volunteer Reserve Association; Member, Scottish Committee, Institute of Directors. Recreations: golf; bridge; sailing. Address: (h.) 10 Merchiston Avenue, Edinburgh.

Wilson, James, MB, ChB, FFARCS, DORCOG. Consultant in charge of Obstetric Anaesthestics and Analgesia, Simpson Memorial Maternity Pavilion, Edinburgh Royal Infirmary, since 1972; Honorary Senior Lecturer, Department of Anaesthetics, Edinburgh University, since 1976; b. 11.12.29, Edinburgh; m., Helen C.A. Dawson; 2 s.; 1 d. Educ. Boroughmuir Senior Secondary School, Edinburgh; Edinburgh University. RAMC, 1953-56; Assistant, then Principal, general practice, 1956-65; Senior House Officer, then Registrar in Anaesthetics, 1965-67; Senior Registrar in Anaesthetics, then Lecturer in Anaesthesia, Edinburgh University, 1967-69; Consultant Anaesthetist, Leeds Maternity Hospital and Honorary Clinical Tutor, Leeds University, 1969-72; President and former Secretary, Edinburgh and East of Scotland Society of Anaesthetists. Recreations: curling; gardening; walking; DIY. Address: (h.) 15 Campbell Road, Edinburgh, EH12 6DT; T.-031-357 6763.

Wilson, James W., BSc, MSc. Principal, Angus Technical College, Arbroath, since 1967; b. 12.5.30, Alva; m., Catherine; 1 s.; 2 d. Educ. Dollar Academy; Edinburgh University. Atomic energy industry, 1956-60; operational research, Courtaulds Ltd., 1960-63; Industrial Liaison Officer, Dundee College of Technology, 1963-67. Recreations: gardening; bridge; driving. Address: (b.) Angus Technical College, Keptie Road, Arbroath, Angus; T.-0241 72056.

Wilson, John. Member, Argyll and Bute District Council; b. 19.10.30, Glasgow; m., Geraldine MacLean; 1 s.; 1 d. Educ. Balmore School. Town Councillor and Magistrate, Troon Town Council. Recreations: golf; music. Address: (h.) Tigh Grianach, Lochdon, Isle of Mull, Argyll.

Wilson, John Beattie, BSc (Hons), MD, FRCPEdin. General Medical Practitioner, since 1952; Member, Dumfries and Galloway Health Board, since 1977; b. 5.5.21, Edinburgh; m., Margaret E. Freestone (see Margaret Elizabeth Wilson); 1 s.; 2 d. Educ. George Watson's Boys' College; Edinburgh University. Chairman, Lochmaben and District Community Council, since 1982. Recreations: golf; dog walking. Address: (h.) The Whins, Kinnel Banks, Lochmaben, Lockerbie, DG11 1TD; T.-Lochmaben 215.

Wilson, John McIntyre, BL. Town Clerk and Chief Executive, City of Aberdeen District Council, since 1977; b. 26.5.23, Aberdeen; m., Lena; 1 s. Educ. Robert Gordon's College, Aberdeen; Aberdeen University. Solicitor, private practice, Aberdeen, 1968-60; Corporation of the City of Aberdeen: Solicitor, 1960-69, Second Town Clerk Depute, 1969-71, Senior Town Clerk Depute, 1972-75; Depute Town Clerk and Chief Executive, City of Aberdeen District Council, 1975-77. Address: (b.) Town House, Aberdeen, AB9 1AQ; T.-0224 642121, Ext. 500.

Wilson, John Melville, RIBA, DipTP, MRTPI, MIH. Director of Housing, City of Edinburgh District Council, since 1983; b. 11.9.31, Uphall; m., Mary H.; 2 d. Educ. Lenzie Academy; Clydebank High School; Glasgow School of Architecture; Strathclyde University. Senior Architect, SSHA, 1968-72; Assistant Director of Housing, Edinburgh Corporation, 1972-75; Depute Director of Housing, City of Edinburgh, 1975-83. Recreations: sport; reading. Address: (b.) 23 Waterloo Place, Edinburgh, EH1 3BH; T.-031-225 2424.

Wilson, John Thomas ("Jocky"). Professional Darts Player; b. 22.3.50, St. Andrews; m., Malvina; 2 s.; 1 d. Educ. Waid Academy, Anstruther. British Professional Champion, 1981, 1983; World Professional Champion, 1982; British Open Champion, 1982; British Matchplay Champion, 1980, 1981; BBC2 Bullseye Champion, 1980, 1981; Scottish Masters Champion, 1980, 1983, 1984; BDO Personality of the Year, 1981.

Wilson, Professor Leslie Blakett, BSc, DSc, FBCS. Professor and Head, Computing Science Department, Stirling University, since 1979 (Chairman, Board of Studies for Science, since 1984); b. 1.11.30, Newcastle-upon-Tyne; m., Patricia Kinair; 2 d. Educ. Newcastle Royal Grammar School; Durham University. Scientific Officer/Senior Scientific Officer, Naval Construction Research Establishment, Dunfermline, 1951-64; Lecturer/Senior Lecturer in Computing Science, Newcastle-upon-Tyne University, 1964-79; Visiting Associate Professor, Waterloo University, Canada, 1974. Publications: Information Representation and Manipulation Using Pascal; Computational Combinatorics. Recreations: bridge; cinema; fell-walking; golf. Address: (b.) Computing Science Department, Stirling University, Stirling, FK9 4LA; T.-Stirling 73171, Ext. 2577.

Wilson, Margaret Elizabeth, BA, SRN, JP. Member, Annandale and Eskdale District Council (Vice-Chairman, Housing Committee); Social Worker; b. 14.9.26, Lincoln; m., John Beattie Wilson (qv); 1 s.; 2 d. Educ. Southpark High School, Lincoln; Open University. Theatre sister, Stirling Royal Infirmary; Welfare Officer, Dunfriesshire Branch, BRCS; Coordinator/Training Officer, Dumfries Women's Aid. Recreations: bridge; curling; golf; historical dance society. Address: (h.) The Whins, Kimmelbanks, Lochmaben, DG11 1TD; T.-Lochmaben 679.

Wilson, Michael Jeffrey, BSc, PhD, DSc. Research Soil Scientist; Head, Department of Mineral Soils, Macaulay Institute for Soil Research, since 1983; b. 22.2.37, Liverpool; m., Ann; 2 d. Educ. Merthyr Tydfil County Grammar School; University College of Swansea, Wales. Research Demonstrator in Geology, University College of Cardiff, 1961-64. Secretary, Clay Minerals Group, Mineralogical Society of Gt. Britain, 1978-84. Recreation: cricket. Address: (b.) Department of Mineral Soils, Macaulay Institute for Soil Research, Aberdeen, AB9 2QJ; T.-0224 38611.

Wilson, Norman, OBE. Director, Ramsay Head Press, since 1970; Editor, Books in Scotland, since 1980; 1 s. Ministry of Information, 1940-46; Director, John Menzies, 1950-70; Chairman,

Edinburgh Film Guild; Chairman, Edinburgh Film Festival, 1947-59; Governor, British Film Institute; Chairman, Scottish Publishers Association, 1980-83; President, Scottish Arts Club, 1980-82. Address: (b.) 15 Gloucester Place, Edinburgh, EH3 6EE; T.-031-225 5646.

Wilson, Professor Peter Northcote, BSc, MSc, PhD, FIBiol. Professor of Agriculture and Rural Economy, Edinburgh University, since 1983; Principal, Edinburgh School of Agriculture, since 1983; b. 4.4.28, Beckenham, Kent; m., Maud Ethel Bunn; 2 s.; 1 d. Educ. Whitgift School, Croydon; Wye College, London University; Edinburgh University. Lecturer in Agriculture, Makerere College, East Africa; Senior Lecturer in Agriculture, Imperial College of Tropical Agriculture, Trinidad; Professor of Tropical Agriculture, University of West Indies; Head of Biometrics, Unilever Research Laboratory, Bedford; Agricultural Development Director, SLF Ltd., Liverpool; Chief Agricultural Adviser, BOCM Silcock Ltd., Basingstoke. Past President, British Society of Animal Production; Chairman, Frank Parkinson Agricultural Trust, since 1978. Publications: Agriculture in the Tropics (Co-author); Improved Feeding of Cattle and Sheep (Co-author). Recreations: walking; photography; natural history. Address: (b.) School of Agriculture, Kings Buildings, West Mains Road, Edinburgh, EH9 3JG; T.-031-667 1041.

Wilson, Robert Gordon, MP, BL. MP (Scottish National Party), Dundee East, since 1974; b. 16.4.38, Glasgow; m., Edith M. Hassall; 2 d. Educ. Burnside School; Douglas High School; Edinburgh University. SNP: Assistant National Secretary, 1963-64, National Secretary, 1964-71, Executive Vice Chairman, 1972-73, Senior Vice Chairman, 1973-74, Chairman, since 1979; Rector, Dundee University, since 1983. Recreation: photography. Address: (b.) House of Commons, London, SW1A OAA; T.-01-219 4474.

Wilson, Roy. General Manager, Pitlochry Festival Theatre, since 1961; b. St. Andrews. Educ. Madras College, St. Andrews. Proprietor, grocer's business, St. Andrews, 1953-59; Assistant Manager, Pitlochry Festival Theatre, 1959-61. Recreations: plays and theatre in general; most forms of classical music, with particular interest in choral singing; listening to records; reading. Address: (h.) Kilrymont, Bruach Lane, Pitlochry, Perthshire, PH16 5DG; T.-Pitlochry 2897.

Wilson, Sheriff Roy Alexander, BA (Oxon), LLB, WS. Sheriff of Grampian, Highland and Islands, at Elgin, since 1975; b. 22.10.27, Aberdeen; m., Alison Mary Craig; 1 s.; 1 d. Educ. Aberdeen Grammar School; Merchiston Castle School; Lincoln College, Oxford; Edinburgh University. Solicitor; Partner, then Senior Partner, Allan McNeil & Son, WS, Edinburgh, 1957-75; Chairman, Industrial Relations Tribunals, 1971-75. Past President: Moray Rugby Club, Moray Caring Association; President, Edinburgh University Club of Moray; Treasurer, Fochabers Curling Club. Recreations: curling; golf; spectator sports. Address: (h.) Deansford, Bishopmill, Elgin, Moray, IV30 2EJ; T.-Elgin 7339.

Wilson, Sue, LLB (Hons), DipEd, ADB. Theatre Director and Writer; Artistic Director, Pitlochry Festival Theatre, since 1983; b. 11.3.47, Cheadle Hulme. Educ. St. Hilary's School, Cheshire; London School of Economics; Mather College, Manchester. Associate Director, Liverpool Playhouse, 1973-75; Artistic Director: Mirror Theatre, 1976, Nuffield Theatre, Southampton, 1976-79, Chester Gateway Theatre, 1980-83. Recreations: astrology; alternative medicine. Address: (h.) 12 Dicksons Drive, Newton Park, Chester, Cheshire; T.-0244 40797.

Wilson, Sydney Gordon Forbes, MD, FRCPEdin. Consultant Paediatrician, Tayside Health Board, since 1964; b. 6.5.24, Inverkeilor; m., Eileen Margaret Beattie; 3 s.; 1 d. Educ. Arbroath High School; Trinity College, Glenalmond; Edinburgh University. House Physician, Hospital for Sick Children, Great Ormond Street, London, and Neonatal Department, Hammersmith Hospital, London; Fellow, Paediatric Renal Research, Western Reserve University, Cleveland, Ohio; Paediatric Senior Registrar, Dundee Royal Infirmary; First Assistant, Department of Child Health, Newcastle University; Consultant Paediatrician, Sunderland. Recreations: squash; walking; reading. Address: (h.) 11 Rockfield Crescent, Dundee, DD2 1JE; T.-0382 67411.

Wilson, Emeritus Professor Thomas Brendan, MA, BMus, ARCM. Composer; b. 10.10.27, Trinidad, Colorado; m., Margaret Rayner; 3 s. Educ. St. Mary's College, Aberdeen; Glasgow University; Royal College of Music. RAF, 1945-48; Glasgow University: Lecturer in Music, Extra-Mural Studies, 1957, Reader in Music, Extra-Mural Studies, 1972, Professor, 1977; Member, Scottish Arts Council, 1966-72; Chairman Elect, Executive Committee, Composers Guild; Member, Advisory Commitee, Scottish Music Archive; elected Member, Royal Society of Musicians; compositions include orchestral, choral-orchestral, chamber-orchestral, opera (including The Confessions of a Justified Sinner), ballet, brass band, vocal music of different kinds, and works for a wide variety of chamber ensembles and solo instruments; numerous commissions. Recreations: golf; talking shop. Address: (h.) 120 Downhill Street, Glasgow, G12 9DN; T.-041-339 1699.

Wilson, Thomas Muir, OBE, OStJ, JP. Honorary Sheriff, Ayr, since 1966, Kilmarnock, since 1945; retired Solicitor; b. 11.11.96, Mauchline; m., Inez Hay. Educ. Kilmarnock Academy; Glasgow University. Served in Army and War Office, 1915-18; Solicitor, Glasgow, 1920-40; Superintendent, Special Constabulary, Glasgow Police, 1939-40; Company Commander (Major), Home Guard, 1940-41; Ministry of Supply, London, 1941 (appointed a Deputy Director General of Supply Services, 1942); Director of various companies, 1940-73; first post-War Chairman, Federation of British Industry (Scottish Council), 1946; first President, Kilmarnock and District Chamber of Industries, 1946-47; Member, Scottish Board for Industry, 11 years (Vice-Chairman, two years); Member, Western Regional Hospital Board, three years; Deacon, Incorporation of

Bonnetmakers and Dyers, Trades House of Glasgow, 1946. Recreations: outdoor pursuits, especially fishing. Address: (h.) 35 Monument Road, Ayr, KA7 2QR; T.-Ayr 266254.

Wilson, Thomas Scott, MD, FRCPGlas, FFCM. Community Medicine Specialist, Greater Glasgow Health Board, since 1974; b. 9.10.21, Glasgow; m., Dr. C.I. Maclean; 1 s.; 2 d. Educ. High School of Glasgow; Glasgow University. Assistant Divisional Medical Officer, Glasgow; Divisional Medical Officer, Glasgow; Principal Medical Officer, School Health Service, Glasgow; Depute Medical Officer of Health, then Medical Officer of Health, Glasgow. President, Royal Environmental Health Institute of Scotland, 1984-85; Past President, Royal Sanitary Association of Scotland, 1976-77; Member, Scottish Affairs Committee, Faculty of Community Medicine. Recreations: golf; bowling; reading; gardening. Address: (h.) 75 Stewarton Drive, Cambuslang, Glasgow, G72 8DQ.

Wilson, Professor William Adam, MA, LLB. Lord President Reid Professor of Law, Edinburgh University, since 1972; b. 28.7.28, Glasgow. Educ. Hillhead High School; Glasgow University. Solicitor, 1951-60; Lecturer in Scots Law, Edinburgh University, 1960-72. Recreation: walking. Address: (h.) 2 Great Stuart Street, Edinburgh; T.-031-225 4958.

Wilson, William Murray, MB, ChB, MRCGP. General Medical Practitioner, Dalry, Ayrshire, since 1949; Medical Advisor, Roche Products, Dalry, Ayrshire, since 1965; Medical Referee, Cunninghame District Council, since 1972; Member, Ayrshire and Arran Health Board; b. 19.1.25, Glasgow; m., Elizabeth Carbine; 3 s. Educ. Eastwood Secondary School; Glasgow University. Past Chairman, Local Medical Committee/GP Committee, Area Medical Committee, BMA Ayrshire Division; former Member, General Medical Services Committee, London and Edinburgh; Elder, St. Margaret's Church, Dalry; Member, Education for the Ministry Committee, Church of Scotland; Honorary Lecturer, British Red Cross Society, St. Andrew's Ambulance Association. Recreations: travel; photography. Address: (h.) 22 Courthill Street, Dalry, Ayrshire, KA24 5AN; T.-Dalry 2165.

Wilson, William Ogilvie, MA, AHA, JP. Member, Perth and Kinross District Council, since 1980 (Alliance Group Leader, since 1984); Unit Administrator, Tayside Health Board, since 1984; b. 22.11.47, Broughty Ferry, Dundee; m., Margaret; 2 s. Educ. Perth High School; Dundee University. Assistant Hospital Secretary, then Sector Administrator, Perth Royal Infirmary, 1972-84. Chairman, Management Committee, Oakbank Church and Sunday School; Committee Member, Perth Council of Churches; Press Officer, Perth and Kinross Liberal Association. Recreations: running; swimming; gardening. Address: (h.) 3 Fairhill Avenue, Perth, PH1 1RP; T.-Perth 26270.

Wilson, Rev. William Stewart, DA. Minister, Kirkcudbright, since 1980; b. 8.3.34, Stromness; m., Sheila Stevens; 1 s.; 1 d. Educ. Stromness

Academy; Gray's School of Art; Aberdeen University. Soldier (Instructor, RAEC), two years; Schoolteacher, five years; islander (Fair Isle), nine years; Schoolteacher, four years. Member, Advisory Committee on Artistic Matters, Church of Scotland. Publication: Shipwrecks of Fair Isle, 1970. Recreations: painting; drama; ornithology. Address: 6 Bourtree Avenue, Kirkcudbright; T.-0557 30489.

Wilson, William Walker, BSc, CEng, MIMechE, FBIM. Management Services Controller, South of Scotland Electricity Board, since 1975; b. 9.9.26, Stirling; m., Anne Livingston Ross; 1 s.; 1 d. Educ. Hyndland School, Glasgow; Glasgow University. National Service (commission, RA), 1947-49; engineering posts, SW Scotland Division, BEA, 1949-55; senior engineering posts, CEGB, 1955-62; SSEB: Manager, Braehead Power Station, 1962-67, Manager, Generation Management Services, 1967-72, Group Manager Generation, 1972-75. Recreations: music; golf. Address: (h.) 2 Crosbie Woods, Paisley, PA2 OSG; T.-041-884 8472.

Wilson Smith, Lt. Col. John Logan, OBE. Regimental Secretary, The Royal Scots, since 1983; b. 4.7.27, Harrow; m., Ann Winifred Lyon Corsar; 3 d. Educ. Wellington College. Commissioned, 1946; Lt. Col., 1972; retired, 1977; Chairman, The Royal Scots Association; Director, The Royal Scots Regimental Shop Ltd.; President, SSAFA, Edinburgh and Midlothian. Recreations: forestry; shooting; fishing. Address: (h.) Cumledge, Duns, Berwickshire, TD11 3TB.

Wiltshire, James Phillip, BA, PhD. Chairman, Ayrshire Area Manpower Board, since 1983; Member, Ayrshire and Arran Health Board, since 1982; Member, Scottish Technical Education Council, since 1980; b. 9.5.24, Sheffield; m., Janet Eleanor; 1 s.; 1 d. Educ. Maltby Grammar School; Queens' College, Cambridge. Joined ICI as Research Chemist, Paints Division, Slough, 1947; seconded to Canadian Industries Ltd., Toronto, 1960-62; Research Manager, Nobel Division, ICI, Stevenston, 1969; Policy Group Member, Corporate Laboratory, ICI, Runcorn, 1971; Research and Personnel Director, Nobel's Explosives Co. Ltd., Stevenston, 1973; a CBI Representative, Manpower Services Committee for Scotland, 1980-82; retired from ICI, 1982; Chairman, Ayrshire Marriage Guidance Council, since 1982; Treasurer, Ayrshire Council on Alcoholism, since 1983; Representative, CBI Scotland, on Community Business Scotland, since 1982. Recreations: sailing; hill-walking; a little music and opera. Address: (h.) 19 Park Circus, Ayr, KA7 2DJ; T.-Ayr 263872.

Winney, Robin John, MB, ChB, FRCPEdin. Consultant Renal Physician, Edinburgh Royal Infirmary, since 1978; b. 8.5.44, Dunfermline. Educ. Dunfermline High School; Edinburgh University. Recreations: badminton; curling. Address: (h.) 597 Lanark Road, Juniper Green, Edinburgh, EH14.

Winning, Most Rev. Thomas Joseph, STL, DCL, DD. Archbishop of Glasgow and Metropolitan, since 1974; President, Bishops' Conference of

Scotland, since 1985; b. 3.6.25, Wishaw. Educ. Our Lady's High School, Motherwell; St. Mary's College, Blairs; St. Peter's College; Scots College; Gregorian University, Rome. Ordained Priest, Rome, 1948; Assistant Priest, Chapelhall, 1949-50; Rome (DCL, "Cum Laude"), 1953; Assistant Priest, St. Mary's Hamilton, 1953-57; Cathedral, Motherwell, 1957-58; Chaplain, Franciscans of the Immaculate Conception, Bothwell, 1958-61; Diocesan Secretary, Motherwell, 1956-61; Spiritual Director, Scots College, Rome, 1961-66; Advocate of the Sacred Roman Rota, 1965; Parish Priest, St. Luke's Motherwell, 1966-70; Officialis and Vicar Episcopal, Motherwell Diocese, 1966-70; first President, Scottish Catholic Marriage Tribunal, 1970; nominated Titular Bishop of Louth and Bishop Auxiliary, 1971, and ordained by James Donald Scanlan, Archbishop of Glasgow, November, 1971; Parish Priest, Our Holy Redeemer's Clydebank, 1972-74; translated to Glasgow as Archbishop, 1974; Honorary DD (Glasgow), 1983; awarded Glasgow Loving Cup, 1983. Recreations: watching football; listening to music. Address: (h.) 40 Newlands Road, Glasgow, G43 2JD; T.-041-332 9473.

Winter, Charles M., FIB (Scot). Group Chief Executive, Royal Bank of Scotland p.l.c., since 1985; b. 21.7.33, Dundee; m., Audrey Hynd; 1 s.; 1 d. Educ. Harris Academy, Dundee. Joined Royal Bank of Scotland, 1949; Director, 1981; Director, Royal Bank of Scotland Group, 1981; President, Institute of Bankers in Scotland, 1981-83; Director, Lloyds & Scottish PLC, 1983-84; Chairman, Committee of Scottish Clearing Bankers, 1983-85; Member, Board of Governors, Leith Nautical College, 1979-82; Treasurer, Commonwealth Games, Scotland, 1986. Recreations: golf; choral music. Address: (b.) Royal Bank of Scotland p.l.c., 42 St. Andrew Square, Edinburgh; T.-031-556 8555.

Winton, Alexander, MIFireE. Firemaster, Tayside Fire Brigade, since 1985; b. 13.7.32, Perth; m., Jean; 2 s. Perth and Kinross Fire Brigade, 1958; Instructor, Scottish Fire Service Training School, 1962; Lancashire County Fire Brigade, 1967; East Riding of Yorkshire Fire Brigade, 1970; Angus Area Fire Brigade, 1973; Tayside Fire Brigade, 1975; Deputy Firemaster, Tayside Fire Brigade, 1981. Recreations: golf; curling. Address: (h.) 5 Ferndale Drive, Broughty Ferry, Dundee, DD5 3DB; T.-Dundee 78156.

Wishart, David, BSc, PhD. Assistant Secretary, Scottish Education Department, since 1984; b. 5.7.43, London; m., Doreen Pamela Craig Wishart; 3 s. Educ. Kilburn Grammar School; Truro College; St. Andrews University. Statistician, Civil Service Department, London, 1970-75; Principal, Scottish Office, 1975-77; Chief Statistician, Scottish Office, 1977-81; Director of Statistics, Scottish Office, 1981-84. Fellow: British Computer Society, Royal Statistical Society (elected to Council, 1985). Recreations: cricket; skiing; opera. Address: (h.) 16 Kingsburgh Road, Edinburgh, 12; T.-031-337 1448.

Withers, John Alexander (Jack), FCIL. Librarian and Writer-in-Residence, Scottish-German Centre/Goethe Institut, since 1974; Writer; b.

Glasgow; m., Beate (Bea) Haertel. Educ. North Kelvinside School; Jordanhill College of Education (Youth and Community Diploma). Left school at 14; worked in garage, electrical industry, labouring, National Service, unemployment, razor-blade salesman; long periods abroad, wandering, wondering, working: France, FRG, Italy, Scandinavia, Spain, North Africa; youth worker; freelance writer; ski instructor; librarian; Scottish republican and radical; plays for radio, TV, theatre; James Kennoway Screenplay Award (shared); Scottish Arts Council Awards; short stories published in numerous journals in UK, Denmark and West Germany. Address: (h.) 16 Belmont Crescent, Glasgow; T.-041-339 9492.

Wolfe, William Cuthbertson, CA. President, Scottish National Party, 1980-82; b. 22.2.24; m.; 2 s.; 2 d. Educ. Bathgate Academy; George Watson's College, Edinburgh. Army, 1942-47; Honorary President (Rector), Students' Association, Heriot-Watt University, 1966-69; contested West Lothian for SNP, 1962, 1964, 1966, 1970, 1974 (twice), 1979; Chairman, SNP, 1969-79.

Wolfe Murray, Stephanie. Managing Director, Canongate Publishing Ltd.; b. 27.4.41, Blandford, Dorset; m., Angus; 4 s. Educ. Overstone, Northamptonshire; Florence; Paris. Odd jobs till marriage, 1961; publisher's reader, early 1970s; Past Chairman, Scottish Publishers Association; Council Member, National Book League, Scotland; Member, Publishers Advisory Committee, British Council; Director, Edinburgh Book Festival. Recreation: being in lonely wild places, especially Scotland's West Coast islands. Address: (h.) 20 Leonard's Bank, Edinburgh; T.-031-556 1954.

Wolrige Gordon, Captain Robert. Member, Grampian Regional Council, since 1978 (Deputy Chairman, Planning, since 1982); b. 20.9.28, Esslemont; m., Rosemary Jane Abel Smith; 1 s.; 1 d. (deceased). Educ. Eton College; Royal Military Academy, Sandhurst. Enlisted Grenadier Guards, 1947; commissioned, 1948; Captain, 1953; retired, 1959; Member, Aberdeenshire County Council, 1961-74 (Chairman, Accident Prevention and Civil Defence Committee); farming at Esslemont, since 1959; Grand Master Mason of Scotland, 1974-79; Member, Representative Church Council, 1959-82; Member, Diocesan and Provincial Synod, Scottish Episcopal Church. Recreations: shooting; fishing; history. Address: (h.) Esslemont, Ellon, Aberdeenshire; T.-Ellon 20234.

Wong, Henry H.Y., BSc, PhD, DIC, CEng. Reader, Department of Aeronautics and Fluid Mechanics, Glasgow University, since 1960; b. 23.5.22, Hong Kong; m., Joan Anstey; 2 s.; 1 d. Educ. St. Stephen College, Hong Kong; Jiao-Tong University, Shanghai; Imperial College, London; Glasgow University. Assistant Lecturer, Jiao-Tong University, 1947-48; Engineer, Armstrong Siddeley, 1949; Structural Engineer, Hunting Percival Aircraft, 1949-51; Senior Structural Engineer, de Havilland Aircraft, 1952-57; Senior Lecturer, Heriot-Watt Polytechnic, 1957-59; Lecturer, then Senior Lecturer in Aeronautics and Fluid Mechanics, Glasgow University, from 1960. Former Treasurer and Vice-Chairman,

Kilmardinny Music Circle; Chairman, Glasgow Summer School, since 1979. Recreations: reading; music; painting; swimming. Address: (h.) 77 Antonine Road, Bearsden, Glasgow; T.-041-942 8346.

Wood, Alexander, BA (Hons), MLitt, DipEd. Labour Group Leader and Chairperson, Policy and Resources Committee, Edinburgh District Council; Schoolteacher (on leave of absence); b. 17.11.50, Dundee. Educ. Paisley Grammar School; New University of Ulster; Stirling University; Moray House College; Edinburgh University. Teacher of English, Craigroyston High School, Edinburgh, 1973-75; Community Worker, Pilton Central Association, 1975-77; Teacher of Remedial Education (latterly Principal Teacher), 1977-84; Labour Parliamentary candidate, Dumfriesshire, 1979, West Edinburgh, 1983; Member, Edinburgh District Council, since 1980. Recreations: Brechin City FC; roadrunning; reading; music. Address: (b.) Edinburgh District Council, City Chambers, High Street, Edinburgh; T.-031-225 2424.

Wood, Arthur Murdoch MacTaggart, OBE, MA, LLB. General Secretary, RSSPCC, since 1968; b. 15.12.37, Kilbarchan; 2 s.; 2 d. Educ. George Watson's College, Edinburgh; Edinburgh University. Standard Life Assurance Company, 1960-61; Assistant Secretary, RSSPCC, 1961-68. Address: (b.) RSSPCC, Melville House, 41 Polwarth Terrace, Edinburgh, EH11 1NU; T.-031-337 8539.

Wood, Brian James Barry, PhD, BSc, CChem, FRSC. Reader, Division of Applied Microbiology, Strathclyde University, since 1981; b. 11.7.34, Birmingham. Educ. Kings Norton Grammar School, Birmingham; Birmingham University. Research Biochemist, University of California at Davis, 1959-62; Scientist, Unilever Ltd., Bedford, 1962-68; Strathclyde University: Lecturer, 1968-75, Senior Lecturer, 1975-81; Technical Director, Bean Products Ltd., 1981-84. Representative, Forth and Clyde Canal Society on Glasgow Urban Wildlife Group. Recreations: gardening; Lenzie Rugby FC; work. Address: (b.) Division of Applied Microbiology, Strathclyde University, Glasgow, G1 1XW; T.-041-552 4400.

Wood, George Alexander McDougall, BA. Senior Lecturer in English Studies, Stirling University, since 1975; b. 9.8.38, Hyde. Educ. William Hulme's Grammar School, Manchester; University College, London. Research Assistant, English Department, University College, London, 1962; Librarian, Osborn Collection, Yale University, 1962-66; Fellow, Silliman College, Yale University, 1965-66; Assistant Professor of English, University of California, Santa Barbara, 1966-68; Lecturer, Stirling University, 1968-75. Recreation: railways. Address: (h.) Burn O'Vat, Haining, Dunblane, Perthshire; T.-Dunblane 4878.

Wood, Professor Hamish Christopher Swan, BSc, PhD, CChem, FRSC, FRSE. Vice-Principal, Strathclyde University, since 1984 (Professor of Organic Chemistry, since 1969); b. 8.5.26, Hawick; m., Jean Dumbreck Mitchell; 1 s.; 1 d. Educ. Hawick High School; St. Andrews

University. Lecturer in Chemistry, St. Andrews University, 1950-51; Research Fellow, Australian National University, 1951-53; Lecturer, Senior Lecturer and Reader, Strathclyde University, 1953-69. Address: (b.) Thomas Graham Building, Strathclyde University, 295 Cathedral Street, Glasgow, G1 1XL; T.-041-552 4400.

Wood, Sir Henry (Peart), Kt (1967), CBE (1960). Principal, Jordanhill College of Education, Glasgow, 1949-71; b. 30.11.08; m.; 1 s.; 2 d. Educ. Morpeth Grammar School; Durham University.

Wood, Ian Clark, CBE (1984), LLD, BSc, CBIM. Chairman and Managing Director, John Wood Group PLC, since 1967; Chairman, J.W. Holdings, since 1982; b. 21.7.42, Aberdeen; m., Helen Macrae; 3 s. Educ. Robert Gordon's College, Aberdeen; Aberdeen University. Joined family business, John Wood & Sons, 1964; Board Member, Scottish Development Agency; Member, Sea Fish Industry Authority; Member, CBI Scottish Council (North of Scotland Industry Spokesman); Member, Aberdeen Harbour Board; Fellow, Royal Society of Arts; Member, Offshore Energy Technology Board; Grampian Industrialist of the Year, 1978; Young Scottish Businessman of the Year, 1979; Hon. LLD, 1984. Recreations: squash; family. Address: (b.) John Wood Group PLC, John Wood House, Greenwell Road, East Tullos, Aberdeen; T.-0224 875464.

Wood, Jack Williamson, FRICS, ARVA. Regional Assessor and Electoral Registration Officer, Strathclyde Regional Council, since 1981; b. 15.3.33, Rutherglen; m., Wilma; 2 d. Educ. Rutherglen Academy; Royal College of Science and Technology. Assistant Chief Surveyor, Glasgow, 1964-75; Strathclyde Region: Depute Assessor, 1975-79, Senior Depute Assessor, 1979-81. Recreations: sport (golf); music; literature. Address: (b.) Strathclyde House II, 20 India Street, Glasgow; T.-041-227 3822.

Wood, James Tweedie. Farmer; Chairman, Royal Highland and Agricultural Society; b. 7.9.40, South Queensferry; m., Christine Margaret; 1 s.; 1 d. Educ. Daniel Stewart's College; Edinburgh School of Agriculture. Past President, Edinburgh Curling Club; Past Chairman, East Area, Young Farmers' Clubs; former Governor, East of Scotland College of Agriculture. Recreations: curling; golfing. Address: (h.) Easter Dalmeny, South Queensferry, EH30 9TS; T.-031-331 1347.

Wood, J. Fergus M., TD. Director, The Scottish Woollen Industry, since 1982; b. 10.9.42, Glasgow; m., Francesca Maria Coli; 2 s.; 1 d. Educ. Trinity College, Glenalmond; Oslo University. Sub-Editor, Glasgow Herald, 1960-62; scholarship to Oslo, 1962-64; Features Sub-Editor, Evening Times, Glasgow, 1964-69; Deputy PR Manager, Philips Phonographic Industries, The Netherlands, 1969-73; Information Officer, Stirling University, 1973-82. Major TA. Publication: Three Nights in Perthshire, 1983. Recreations: farming; country sports. Address: (h.) Ledard Farm, Kinlochard, by Stirling, FK8 3TL; T.-08777 219.

Wood, Michael, BSc (Hons), DipCarto, FRGS. Senior Lecturer in Geography (Cartography), Aberdeen University, since 1983; b. 25.6.41. Insch; m., Margaret Russell Lochhead Barr; 2 d. Educ. Aberdeen Grammar School; Aberdeen University; Glasgow University. Research Assistant, then Assistant Lecturer, Department of Geography, Glasgow University, 1964-69; Lecturer, Department of Geography, Aberdeen University, 1969-83; External Examiner for National Certificates in Cartography, Surveying and Planning in Britain, 1971-78; Council Member, British Cartographic Society, since 1971 (President, 1982-84). Publications: Mapping for Field Scientists (Co-author), 1977; numerous maps. Recreations: hill-walking; skiing. Address: (b.) Department of Geography, St. Mary's, High Street, Aberdeen, AB9 2UF; T.-0224 40241, Ext. 5185.

Wood, Robert Anderson, BSc, MB, ChB, FRCPEdin. Consultant Physician, Perth Royal Infirmary, since 1972; Senior Lecturer in Pharmacology and Therapeutics, Dundee University, since 1972; b. 26.5.39, Edinburgh. Educ. Edinburgh Academy; Edinburgh University. Address: (h.) Ballomill House, Abernethy, Perthshire; T.-Abernethy 201.

Wood, Robert Anthony Bowness, MB, ChB, MRCP, FRCSEdin, FRCS. Senior Lecturer in Surgery, Dundee University, and Honorary Consultant Surgeon; b. 12.4.43, Leeds; m., Dr. Elizabeth Spiers; 2 s.; 2 d. Educ. St. Peter's School, York; Leeds University. House Physician/House Surgeon, Leeds, Glasgow, York, London, 1966-69; Registrar/Lecturer, Leeds, Birmingham, Norwich, Cardiff, 1969-74; Senior Registrar, Cardiff, 1974-75; Research Associate/Instructor, Chicago University, 1975-76; Lecturer in Surgery, Cardiff, 1976. Recreations: hill-walking; classical music. Address: (b.) Department of Surgery, Ninewells Hospital and Medical School, Dundee, DD1 9SY; T.-0382 60111.

Wood, William Ferrie, DipArch, DipTP, RIBA, MRTPI. Vice Principal, Edinburgh College of Art, since 1978; b. 23.9.32, Edinburgh. Educ. Daniel Stewart's College, Edinburgh; Edinburgh College of Art. National Service, business, student, 1949-65; Architect/Planner, Robert Matthew, Johnson-Marshall & Partners, Welwyn Garden City, 1965-69; Lecturer, then Senior Lecturer, Department of Town and Country Planning, Heriot-Watt University/Edinburgh College of Art, 1969-78. Recreations: painting; reading; squash. Address: (h.) 26a Dalrymple Crescent, Edinburgh, EH9 2NX; T.-031-667 4370.

Wood-Gush, Professor David Grainger Marcus, PhD, BSc, DipAnimGen, FRSA, FRSE. Honorary Professor, School of Agriculture, Edinburgh University, since 1978; b. 20.11.22, Dordrecht, South Africa; m., Eola Langham Godden; 1 s.; 1 d. Educ. St. Andrews College, Grahamstown, South Africa; Witwatersrand University, Johannesburg; Edinburgh University. Senior Principal Scientific Officer (Special Merit), AFRC, and Head, Ethology Department, AFRC Poultry Research Centre, Edinburgh, 1952-78. Chairman, Association for the Study of Animal Behaviour; President, Society for Veterinary Ethology. Publications: The Behaviour of the Domestic Fowl; Elements of Ethology. Recreations: reading; swimming; hill-walking; historic building preservation. Address: (h.) 26 Nelson Street, Edinburgh, EH3 6LJ; T.-031-556 6488.

Woodruff, Professor Sir Michael, Kt (1969), FRS (1968), FRCS, DSc, MS (Melbourne). Professor of Surgery, Edinburgh University and Surgeon, Edinburgh Royal Infirmary, 1957-76; Director, Nuffield Transplantation Surgery Unit, Edinburgh, 1968-76; b. 3.4.11; m.; 2 s.; 1 d. Educ. Wesley College, Melbourne; University of Melbourne. President, Transplantation Society, 1972-74; Vice-President, Royal Society, 1979.

Woodward, Professor John Frank, BSc, CEng, FICE, FIStructE, FBIM. Professor of Civil Engineering, Paisley College of Technology, since 1982; Visiting Professor, Scottish Business School, since 1970; b. 23.6.33, London; m., Marjorie Isobel; 4 d. Educ. City of Leicester Boys School; Glasgow University. Engineer, latterly Director, associate company, Taylor Woodrow Group, 1956-67; Reader in Management Science, Stirling University, 1968-81. Council Member: British Institute of Management, Association of Project Managers. Recreations: field sports; skiing. Address: (b.) Paisley College of Technology, High Street, Paisley, PA1 2BE; T.-041-887 1241.

Woodward-Nutt, Peter James, BSc, CEng, MIEE, MIERE. Member, Aberdeen City Council, 1980-85; Member, Executive, National Federation of Consumer Groups, since 1977; b. 22.3.35, London; m., Anne Dorothy; 1 s.; 3 d. Educ. Bedales School; Southampton University. Chartered Television Engineer; Member, Scottish Consumer Council, 1977-80; Council Member, Electoral Reform Society, since 1971. Publications: Handbook of Consumer Law (Joint Editor), 1981; Electing the Scottish Assembly (Co-author), 1974. Recreations: computers; home wine-making; assisting with personal problems. Address: (h.) 11 Summerhill Road, Aberdeen; T.-0224 35057.

Wooldridge, Ian, BA (Hons). Artistic Director, Royal Lyceum Theatre Company, Edinburgh, since 1984; b. 11.8.46, Swansea. Educ. King Henry VIII School, Coventry; Cardiff University; Bristol University. Stage Manager and Teacher of Drama, 1968-72; Associate Director, Dark and Light Theatre Company, Brixton, 1972-75; freelance Theatre Director and Drama Consultant, Lothian Region Education Authority, 1975-78; Artistic Director, TAG Theatre Company, Glasgow, 1978-84. Address: (b.) Royal Lyceum Theatre, Grindlay Street, Edinburgh, EH3 9AX; T.-031-229 7404.

Woolrich, David, JP, BSc, ARSM. Chairman, General Purposes Committee, Kirkcaldy District Council, since 1984 (Member of Council, since 1982); b. 22.10.48, Bolton; m., Susan Mary Markland; 2 d. Educ. Bolton School; Imperial College of Science and Technology, London.

Member, Kirkcaldy District Licensing Board, since 1982; Member, General Committee, Scottish Museums Council, since 1984. Address: (b.) Town House, Wemyssfield, Kirkcaldy; T.-Kirkcaldy 261144.

Wordsworth, William Brocklesby. Composer; Honorary President, Scottish Society of Composers, since 1981; Managing Director, Speyside Music Publications Ltd., since 1984; b. 17.12.08, London; m., Frieda Nellie Robson (deceased); 1 s.; 1 s. (deceased); 2 d. Educ. at home; studied music with George Oldroyd in Croydon, later with Sir Donald Tovey in Edinburgh. Has composed 116 numbered works and several unnumbered pieces; orchestral works, including eight symphonies and three concertos, chamber music, including six string quartets, works for one and two instruments, songs, choral works, and one oratorio; first published work, Three Hymn-tune Preludes, Opus 1 (for Organ), 1930-32; recent work includes Eighth Symphony and Agape, Opus 116 (choral work), 1984; won first prize, Clements Memorial Competition, 1941; first prize, Edinburgh International Festival, 1950; Past Chairman, Composers' Guild of Great Britain. Recreations: gardening; golf; carpentry. Address: Ard Insh, Kincraig, Inverness-shire, PH21 1NA; T.-Kincraig 241.

Worrall, Ernest Paterson, MB, ChB, MRCPsych, DPM. Consultant Psychiatrist: Southern General Hospital, Glasgow, since 1980, Ross Hall Hospital, Glasgow, since 1984, Queen's Drive Clinic, Glasgow, since 1982; b. 28.10.42, Hamilton; m., Jean Price; 1 s.; 1 d. Educ. Hamilton Academy; Glasgow University. Lecturer in Psychiatry, Dundee University, 1973-75; Senior Lecturer in Psychological Medicine, Glasgow University, 1975-80. Recreation: triathlons (as active participant). Address: (b.) Department of Psychiatry, Southern General Hospital, Glasgow, G51 1TF; T.-041-445 2466.

Worthington, Tony, BA, MEd. Chairman, Community Development Committee, Strathclyde Regional Council, since 1978; Lecturer, Jordanhill College of Education, since 1971; b. 11.10.41, Hertfordshire; m., Angela; 1 s.; 1 d. Educ. City School, Lincoln; London School of Economics; York University; Glasgow University. Chairman, Strathclyde Community Business Ltd.; Member, Scottish Community Education Council. Recreations: running; fishing; gardening. Address: (h.) 24 Cleddans Crescent, Hardgate, Clydebank; T.-0389 73195.

Wray, David, MD, BDS, MB, ChB, FDS, RCPSGlas. Senior Lecturer, Department of Oral Medicine and Oral Pathology, Edinburgh University, since 1983; Honorary Consultant, Lothian Health Board, since 1983; b. 3.1.51, Carshalton; m., Alison; 2 s. Educ. Uddingston Grammar School; Glasgow University. Temporary Lcturer, Department of Oral Medicine, Glasgow University, 1977-79; Fogarty Visiting Associate, National Institutes of Health, Bethesda, 1979-81; Research Fellow, Royal Dental School, London University, 1982. Honorary Secretary and Treasurer, British Society of Oral Medicine. Recreation: fly fishing. Address: (h.) 6 Randolph Cliff, Edinburgh, EH3 7TZ; T.-031-225 6948.

Wright, Allen. Arts Editor and Drama Critic, The Scotsman, since 1965; b. 22.2.32, Edinburgh; m., Eleanor Wallace; 3 d. Educ. George Watson's College, Edinburgh. Publication: J.M. Barrie: Glamour of Twilight, 1976. Recreation: golf. Address: (h.) Inglewood, 286 Gilmerton Road, Edinburgh, EH17 7PR; T.-031-664 1554.

Wright, David Frederick, MA (Cantab). Senior Lecturer in Ecclesiastical History, Edinburgh University, since 1973; b. 2.10.37, Hayes, Kent; m., Anne-Marie; 1 s.; 1 d. Educ. Christ's College, Cambridge; Lincoln College, Oxford. Edinburgh University: Lecturer, 1964-73, Associate Dean, Faculty of Divinity, 1972-76, Convener, General Assembly of Academic Staff, 1972-74, Member, University Court, since 1984; External Examiner, Universities of Sussex, Liverpool, Durham, Cambridge, etc.; Member, Council of Management, Keston College. Publications: Common Places of Martin Bucer, 1972; Essays in Evangelical Social Ethics (Editor), 1979; Lion Handbook 'History of Christianity (Consultant Editor), 1977. Recreations: walking; gardening; DIY. Address: (h.) 5 Lockharton Gardens, Edinburgh, EH14 1AU; T.-031-443 1001.

Wright, Douglas Stewart. Director, Keep Scotland Tidy, since 1973; Chairman, Beautiful Scotland in Bloom, since 1983; b. 22.7.32, Glasgow; m., May Carswell; 1 s.; 2 d. Educ. Albert Road Academy, Pollokshields. Representative, Scottish Field, 1947-58; National Service, 1st Bn., Cameronians Scottish Rifles (Malaya), 1950-52; General Manager, The Scottish Farmer, 1959-66; Appeals Director, Scottish Council for the Care of Spastics, 1966-73. Committee Member, Stars Organisation for Spastics (Scotland); Honorary Director, Camphill Blair Drummond Appeals Committee. Recreations: hill-walking; specialist in China Tea Clippers. Address: (b.) County Chambers, Cathedral Square, Dunblane, Perthshire, FK15 OAQ.

Wright, Edward, JP. Member, Clydesdale District Council, since 1980 (Leader, Labour Group, since 1984); b. 15.5.52, Motherwell; m., Rita McCutcheon. Educ. Dalziel High School, Motherwell; Bell College of Technology, Hamilton. Engineer, Anderson Strathclyde, Motherwell, since 1968; Shop Steward and Deputy Convener, AUEW (ES), 1975-83; Chairman, Industrial Development, Clydesdale District Council, 1981-84; Director, Lanarkshire Industrial Field Executive, 1982-84; Member, Youth Advisory Committee, STUC, 1975-78; Chairman, Clydesdale Constituency Labour Party, since 1984; Officer, then Officer in charge, 4th Carluke Company, Boys' Brigade, since 1977. Recreations: golf; bowls. Address: (h.) 27 Cartland Avenue, Carluke, ML8 STQ.

Wright, Sir Edward (Maitland), Kt (1977), MA, DPhil, LLD, DSc, FRSE. Research Fellow, Aberdeen University, since 1976; b. 1906; m.; 1 s. Educ. Jesus College and Christ Church, Oxford; University of Gottingen. Aberdeen University: Professor of Mathematics, 1935-62, Vice-Principal, 1961-62, Principal and Vice-Chancellor, 1962-76.

Wright, (Glydon) Bernard, TC, ADPE, MA, FPEA. Director, Scottish School of Physical Education, since 1974; b. 15.3.28, Cwmbran, Gwent; m., Zena; 2 s. Educ. Abersychan Grammar School; Gwent and Cardiff Colleges of Education; Leeds University. Began teaching career, Beckenham and Cray Valley Technical High Schools; Department Head, Forest Hill Comprehensive School, London, 1958; joined Borough Road College, 1962, as Lecturer (later Senior, Principal Lecturer); Conference Director, VIII Commonwealth and International Conference on Sport, Physical Education, Dance, Recreation and Health; has served on numerous national committees, including CNAA Physical Education and Recreation Sports Studies Board, Scottish Central Committee on Physical Education, Physical Education Association (Treasurer), Scottish Council for Physical Education; Visiting Professor, Canada; Consultant in Portugal and Qatar. Recreations: all sporting activities. Address: (b.) Scottish School of Physical Education, Jordanhill College of Education, Southbrae Drive, Glasgow, G13 1PP; T.-041-959 1232, Ext. 242.

Wright, Rev. Kenyon Edward, MA, BA, BSc, MTh. General Secretary, Scottish Churches Council, since 1981; Director, Scottish Churches House, since 1981; b. 31.8.32, Paisley; m., Betty Robinson; 3 d. Educ. Paisley Grammar School; Glasgow University; Cambridge University. Missionary in India, 1955-70; Director, Ecumenical Social and Industrial Institute, Durgapur, India, 1963-70; Director, Urban Ministry, Coventry Cathedral, 1970-74; Canon Residentiary and Director of International Ministry, Coventry Cathedral, 1974-81. Companion of the Order of the Cross of Nails, Coventry Cathedral; Executive Committee Member, Ecumenical Association of Academies and Laity Centres in Europe; Executive Committee Member, Christian Peace Conference. Recreations: reading; walking; travel; living life to the full. Address: (b.) Scottish Churches House, Kirk Street, Dunblane, FK15 0AJ; T.-0786 823588.

Wright, Michael, LLB, LLM, FBIM. Assistant Principal, Napier College, Edinburgh, since 1983; b. 24.5.49, Newcastle-upon-Tyne; m., Pamela Stothart; 2 s.; 1 d. Educ. Durham Johnson Grammar School; Bearsden Academy; Birmingham University. Lecturer, Bristol Polytechnic, 1970-79; Head of Department, Glasgow College of Technology, 1980-83; Member, Public and Social Administration Board, CNAA; Member, Children's Panel. Recreation: sport. Address: (b.) Napier College, Sighthill Court, Edinburgh, EH11 4BN; T.-031-453 6111.

Wright, Professor Norman Gray, BVMS, MRCVS, PhD, DVM, FRCPath, FRSE. Professor of Veterinary Anatomy, Glasgow University, since 1975; b. 19.8.39, Kilmarnock; m., Irene Anne Wright; 2 s. Educ. Kilmarnock Academy; Glasgow University. General veterinary practice, Kilmarnock, 1962-63; Assistant Lecturer/Lecturer/Senior Lecturer, Department of Veterinary Pathology, Glasgow University, 1963-75; awarded G. Norman Hall Gold Medal, Royal College of Veterinary Surgeons, 1975. Recreations: fishing; boating. Address: (h.) 50 Kilmardinny Crescent, Bearsden, Glasgow; T.-041-942 3944.

Wright, Patrick George, MA, PhD, DSc. Reader in Chemistry, Dundee University, since 1977; b. 3.10.32, Henstead, near Beccles, Suffolk; m., Margaret Robson; 2 s.; 1 d. Educ. Lowestoft Grammar School; Cambridge University. Research Fellow, Leeds University, 1956-59; various posts, Queen's College, Dundee (subsequently Dundee University), since 1959. Address: (h.) 16 Duntrune Terrace, West Ferry, Dundee.

Wright, Very Rev. Ronald (William Vernon) Selby, CVO, ChStJ, TD, MA, DD, FRSE, JP. Chaplain, Edinburgh Castle and to the Governor, since 1959; Chaplain, Queen's Bodyguard for Scotland (Royal Company of Archers), since 1973; Extra Chaplain to the Queen, since 1978 (Chaplain, 1961-78); b., 12.6.08, Glasgow. Educ. Edinburgh Academy; Melville College, Edinburgh; Edinburgh University and New College. Minister, The Canongate, 1937-77; Chaplain, 7/9 Royal Scots, 1938-42, 1946-48; Senior Chaplain, 52 Lowland Division, 1942-43; 10 Indian Division, 1944-45; Honorary Senior Chaplain to the Forces, since 1945; Founder Warden, St. Giles (later Canongate) Boys' Club, 1927-78; Moderator: Edinburgh Presbytery, 1963, General Assembly, 1972-73; Radio Padre, BBC, 1942-47; Extra-Ordinary Director, Edinburgh Academy, since 1973. Publications: Asking them Questions; Take Up God's Armour; Another Home. Address: (h.) The Queen's House, 36 Moray Place, Edinburgh, EH3 6BX; T.-031-226 5566.

Wright, Tom, BA (Hons). Writer; b. 8.3.23, Glasgow. Educ. Coatbridge High School; Strathclyde University. Served apprenticeship in embossing and stained glass; Army, 1943-47; served in Europe and Far East, including Japan; began to publish poems and short stories after demobilisation; had first play performed, Edinburgh Festival, 1960; author of There Was A Man; began to write radio and television drama, 1963; former Creative Writing Fellow; former Script Editor, BBC Scotland Drama Department; has also been Script Editor and Story Line Editor, Take The High Road, STV; won Festival Fringe Award, 1984, for Talk of the Devil; Past Chairman, Scottish Committee, Writers' Guild, and Scottish Society of Playwrights. Recreation: listening to music. Address: 318 Churchill Drive, Glasgow, G11.

Wylie, Rt. Hon. Lord, (Norman Russell Wylie), PC (1970), VRD (1961). Senator of the College of Justice in Scotland, since 1974; b. 26.10.23; m.; 3 s. Educ. Paisley Grammar School; St. Edmund Hall, Oxford; Glasgow University; Edinburgh University. Admitted Faculty of Advocates, 1952; QC (Scot), 1964; Advocate Depute, 1959; Solicitor-General for Scotland, 1964; MP (Conservative), Pentlands, Edinburgh, 1964-74; Lord Advocate, 1970-74.

Wylie, Ronald James, OBE, CA, JDipMA. Consultant; b. 31.8.30, Edinburgh; m., Brenda Margaret Wright; 2 s. Apprentice, John M. Geoghegan & Co. Ltd., 1947-52; National Service, 1953-55; Tullis Russell & Co. Ltd.: Cost Accountant, 1955-59, Accountant, 1959-62, Secretary, 1962-72, joined Board, 1971, Joint Managing Director, 1973-81, Chief Executive,

1981-85. Elder, Dysart Kirk; former Council Member, British Paper and Board Industry Federation. Recreation: sailing. Address: 123 Dysart Road, Kirkcaldy, KY1 2BB.

Wylie, Rev. William Andrew, MA. Chaplain, Inverclyde Industrial Mission, since 1985; b. 17.5.27, London; 4 d. Educ. Glasgow Academy; Glasgow University and Trinity College. Minister: Stepps, 1953-59, Scots Kirk, Lausanne, 1959-67; General Secretary, Scottish Churches Council, 1967-71; Minister, St. Andrew's and St. George's, Edinburgh, 1972-85. Chairman of Governors, Aiglon College, Switzerland. Recreations: hill-walking; golf; broadcasting; music. Address: (h.) 29 Denholm Street, Greenock, PA16 8RH; T.-0475 22271.

Wyllie, Gordon Malcolm, LLB, FSA Scot, NP, WS. Partner, Biggart Baillie & Gifford; Clerk to Grand Antiquity Society of Glasgow; Depute Clerk to General Commissioners of Inland Revenue, Glasgow North Division; b. Newton Mearns. Educ. Dunoon Grammar School; Glasgow University. Honorary Treasurer, Edinburgh Summer School in Ancient Greek. Recreations: music; history and the arts generally; country walks; foreign travel. Address: (b.) 105 West George Street, Glasgow; T.-041-221 7020.

Wyllie, Rev. Hugh Rutherford, MA. Minister, Hamilton Old Parish Church, since 1981; Convener, Board of Stewardship and Finance, General Assembly, since 1983; b. 11.10.34, Glasgow; m., Eileen E. Cameron, MA; 2 d. Educ. Hutchesons' Grammar School; Glasgow University. Bank of Scotland, 1951-53 (AIBS); RAF, 1953-55; student, 1956-62; Assistant, Glasgow Cathedral, 1962; Minister: Coatbridge Dunbeth, 1965, Cathcart South, 1972; Convener, Stewardship and Budget Committee, General Assembly, 1978-83. Recreations: gardening; DIY. Address: Mansewood, Union Street, Hamilton, ML3 6NA; T.-0698 420002.

Wyllie, T.W., BSc, CChem, MRSC, CEng, MInstE. Rector, Bannockburn High School, since 1971; b. 8.1.28, Stirling; m., Jessie M. Gordon; 3 s.; 1 d. Educ. Riverside School, Stirling; Falkirk High School; Heriot-Watt University. Scientific Officer, National Coal Board, 1949-59; Teacher of Chemistry, Physics, Mathematics, Graeme High School, Falkirk, 1960-64; Principal Teacher of Science, then Depute Rector, Denny High School, 1964-71. Chairman, Central Region Music Festival Association. Recreations: music; photography; computing; books. Address: (h.) 7 Queen's Drive, Falkirk, FK1 5JJ; T.-0324 23138.

Wynn, Douglas, BSc, MSc (Econ). Member, Central Regional Council, since 1982; Lecturer in Politics, Stirling University, since 1980; b. 6.9.47, Bridgewater, Somerset; 1 s.; 1 d. Educ. Fairfield Grammar School; London University (LSE). Summer School Tutor, Open University; Extra Mural Lecturer, Dundee University; Lecturer in Sociology, Stirling University. Vice-Chairman, Central Region Manpower Committee; Chairman, Central Region Labour Party, 1979-82. Recreations: fishing; mountains; photography. Address: (h.) 8 Arnswell, Sauchie, Clackmannanshire; T.-Alloa 213518.

Wyper, John Irvine, CA. Partner, John Wyper Associates, since 1978; Director, Berkeley Computer Services Ltd., since 1978; Director, Collins Halden (Scotland) Ltd., since 1984; Council Member, Institute of Chartered Accountants of Scotland; b. 25.8.28, Old Kilpatrick; m., Marilyn; 1 s.; 3 d. Educ. Victoria Drive Senior Secondary School. Fleming & Black, CA, 1945-52; David Strathie & Co., CA, 1952-54; Reed Stenhouse Group, 1954-77. Former Captain, Whitecraigs Golf Club. Recreation: golf. Address: (h.) 4 Cavendish Drive, Newton Mearns, Glasgow; T.-041-639 2651.

Y

Yang, Eric Shih-Jung, BSc, MSc, PhD, CEng, MIEE, FIOA. Reader, Department of Electrical and Electronic Engineering, Heriot-Watt University, since 1985; m., Fei Jeannette; 1 d. Educ. Hong Kong University; Queen Mary College, London University. Senior Scientific Officer, British Rail, 1970-72; Lecturer, then Senior Lecturer, Heriot-Watt University, 1972-85. Publications: Low-Noise Electrical Motors, 1981; Machinery Noise Measurement (Co-author), 1985. Address: (b.) Department of Electrical and Electronic Engineering, 31-35 Grassmarket, Edinburgh, EH1 2HT; T.-031-225 8432.

Yarrow, Sir Eric Grant, MBE, DL, CEng, MRINA, FRSE. Chairman, Clydesdale Bank PLC, since 1985 (Director, since 1962); President, Yarrow PLC, since 1985; b. 23.4.20, Glasgow; m., 1, Rosemary Ann Young (deceased); 1 s.; 2, Annette Elizabeth Francoise Steven (m. diss.); 3 s.; 3, Joan Botting; 3 step d. Educ. Marlborough College; Glasgow University. Served engineering apprenticeship, G. & J. Weir, 1938-39; Royal Engineers, 1939-45; served Burma, 1942-45 (Major, RE, 1945); Yarrow & Co. Ltd.: Assistant Manager, 1946, Director, 1948, Managing Director, 1958, Chairman, 1962; Director, Standard Life Assurance Company; Chairman, Executive Committee, Princess Louise Scottish Hospital, Erskine; Council Member, Royal Institution of Naval Architects, since 1957 (Vice President, 1965, Honorary Vice President, 1972); Member, General Committee, Lloyd's Register of Shipping, since 1960; Deacon, Incorporation of Hammermen in Glasgow, 1961-62; Chairman, Yarrow (Shipbuilders) Ltd., 1962-79; Officer (Brother), Order of St. John, since 1965; Deputy Lieutenant, County of Renfrewshire, since 1970; Prime Warden, Worshipful Company of Shipwrights, 1970-71; Council Member, Institute of Directors, since 1983; President, Smeatonican Society of Civil Engineers, 1983-84; President, The Marlburian Club, 1984. Recreations: golf; shooting. Address: (h.) Cloak, Kilmacolm, Renfrewshire, PA13 4SD; T.-Kilmacolm 2067.

Yellowlees, David. Dairy and Arable Farmer; Member, Scottish Milk Marketing Board, since 1964; Member, Scottish Dairy Council, since

1964; b. 23.4.21, Elderslie; m., Robyn Jane Mills Tilley; 2 s.; 1 d. Educ. Merchiston Castle School, Edinburgh. Royal Navy, 1940-46 (Lt., RNVR); began farming, 1947; former Convenor, Press and Publicity Committee, National Farmers' Union of Scotland; Past Chairman, Board of Management, Murthly and Murray Royal Mental Hospitals; former Member, Tayside Area Health Board; Chairman, United Kingdom Milk Promotion Council; Past Chairman, Perth and Kinross Local Health Council; Chairman, Associates of Roxburghe House, Dundee; Trustee, Scottish International Education Trust. Recreations: golf; fishing; reading. Address: Muirhall Farm, Perth, PH2 7BL; T.-Perth 25875.

Yemm, Professor Robert, BDS, BSc, PhD. Professor and Head, Department of Dental Prosthetics and Gerontology, Dundee University, since 1984; b. 31.1.39, Bristol; m., Glenys Margaret; 1 s.; 1 d. Educ. Bristol Grammar School; Bristol University. Lecturer in Dental Prosthetics, Bristol University; Associate Professor, Department of Oral Biology, Alberta University; Lecturer in Dental Medicine (Oral Biology), then Dental Prosthetics, Bristol University; Senior Lecturer (Honorary Consultant), Dental Prosthetics, Dundee University. Recreation: sailing. Address: (h.) 10 Birkhill Avenue, Wormit, Newport-on-Tay, Fife, DD6 8PX; T.-0382 541819.

Yeoman, Joseph Alexander, BL. Director, Scottish Northern Investment Trust PLC, since 1960 (Chairman, since 1984); b. 8.8.20, Forglen, Banffshire; m., Ann Waters; 1 s.; 1 d. Educ. Central Secondary School, Aberdeen; Aberdeen University. Apprentice, Paull & Williamsons, Advocates, 1938-41; 9th Gordon Highlanders, 1941-46; Staff Captain, War Crimes Branch, War Office, 1946; Legal Assistant, Paull & Williamsons, 1946-55 (Partner, since 1955); President, Aberdeen Junior Chamber of Commerce, 1955; President, Federation of Scottish Junior Chambers of Commerce, 1956; Director: Balgownie Properties, Finsbury Data Services and subsidiary, Noble Grossart Investments, The Retirement Properties Consortium, Third Triton Petroleum, Triton Petroleum. Address: (b.) Investment House, 6 Union Row, Aberdeen, AB9 8DQ; T.-0224 631414.

Young, David Paterson, MA. Rector, Kilwinning Academy, since 1977; b. 30.11.37, Rutherglen; m., Jean; 2 s. Educ. Kilmarnock Academy; Aberdeen University. Teaching career in local authority schools: Cumnock Academy, 1961-70, Grange Academy, 1970-77; part-time staff, Open University (Scotland), since 1970; Scottish Liberal Party involvement, 30 years, including national offices and Parliamentary candidate. Recreations: travel; Scottish schools history; tauromachy. Address: (h.) 8 Howard Street, Kilmarnock, KA1 2BP.

Young, Lt.-Gen. Sir David (Tod), KBE (1980), CB (1977), DFC (1952). GOC Scotland and Governor, Edinburgh Castle, 1980-82; b. 17.5.26; m.; 2 s. Educ. George Watson's College, Edinburgh. Commissioned The Royal Scots (The Royal Regiment), 1945 (Colonel, 1975-80).

Young, Edward, MA (Hons). Rector, The Nicolson Institute, since 1968; b. 30.11.25, Motherwell; m., Sheila Hewison; 2 d. Educ. Dalziel High School; Glasgow University. Teacher of English, Hamilton Academy, 1952-61; Principal Teacher of English: Blairgowrie High School, 1961-64, Bell-Baxter High School, 1964-68. Member, Working Party, Transition from School to University, SED, 1970-72; Chairman, Working Party on Drama, SED, 1973-75; Member, Committee on Secondary Education, CCC, 1976-78; Member, Highlands and Islands Development Consultative Council, since 1979; Member, Post Office Users Council for Scotland, since 1984. Recreations: fly fishing; fly dressing; rugby refereeing; reading; gardening. Address: (h.) 1 Goathill Crescent, Stornoway, Isle of Lewis; T.-0851 2204.

Young, George Bell, CBE, MIEx, FInstM, FBIM, FRSA. Managing Director, East Kilbride Development Corporation, since 1973; b. 17.6.24; m., 1, Margaret Wylie Boyd (deceased); 1 s.; 2, Joyce Marguerite McAteer. Educ. Queens Park School, Glasgow. RNVR, 1942-45 (Lt., destroyers and mine-sweepers); Journalist and Feature Writer, Glasgow Herald, 1945-48; North of Scotland Hydro-Electric Board, 1948-52; Chief Executive (London), Scottish Council (Development and Industry), 1952-68; General Manager, East Kilbride Development Corporation, 1968-73. Council Member, National Trust for Scotland, 1974-79; Director, Royal Caledonian Schools, since 1957; Chairman, East Kilbride and District National Savings Committee, 1968-78; Trustee, Strathclyde Scanner Campaign; Scottish Chairman, British Heart Foundation, 1975-79; Chairman, East Kilbride Committee, Order of St. John; Honorary Secretary, Saints and Sinners Club of Scotland, since 1982. Recreations: golf; fishing. Address: (b.) East Kilbride Development Corporation, Atholl House, East Kilbride, G74 1LU; T.-East Kilbride 41111.

Young, Howard Anthony, MB, BS, FRCS. Consultant Otolaryngologist, Grampian Health Board, since 1978; Clinical Senior Lecturer in Otolaryngology, Aberdeen University, since 1978; b. 3.9.45, Swinton, Manchester. Educ. Manchester Grammar School; Newcastle-upon-Tyne University. House Surgeon and Physician, Royal Victoria Infirmary, Newcastle-upon-Tyne, 1968-69; Demonstrator in Pathology, Newcastle-upon-Tyne University, 1969-70; Resident in Neurosurgery and Plastic Surgery, Newcastle General Hospital, 1970-71; Resident in Otolaryngology, Royal National Throat, Nose and Ear Hospital, London, 1971-72; Registrar, Otolaryngology, Royal Victoria Infirmary, Newcastle-upon-Tyne, 1972-74; Senior Registrar and Honorary Lecturer in Otolaryngology, Ninewells Hospital and Medical School, Dundee, 1974-78; TWJ Foundation Travelling Fellowship, 1976. Recreations: golf; natural history. Address: (h.) 18 Edgehill Road, Aberdeen; T.-0224 324554.

Young, Hugh Kenneth, CA, AIB (Scot). Secretary, Bank of Scotland, since 1984; Director, Pentland Oil Exploration Ltd., since 1980; b. 6.5.36, Galashiels; m., Marjory Bruce Wilson; 2 s.; 1 d. Educ. Edinburgh Academy. National Service, 1959-61; commissioned as 2nd Lt., Royal

Scots, subsequently Captain (1966), 1st Bn., 52nd Lowland Volunteers, TAVR; Assistant to Edinburgh Manager, ICFC Ltd., 1962-67; with Schroders Ltd. group, 1967-73, latterly as Manager, J. Henry Schroder Wagg & Co. Ltd.; Local Director in Edinburgh, Edward Bates & Sons Ltd., 1973-75; joined Bank of Scotland, 1975; Head of Corporate Finance, Bank of Scotland Finance Company Ltd., 1976; Director, British Linen Bank Ltd., 1978 (Deputy Chief Executive, 1982). Chairman, Edinburgh Sports Club Ltd. Recreations: squash; tennis; hill-walking. Address: (b.) The Mound, Edinburgh, EH1 1YZ; T.-031-243 5562.

Young, Ian Macrae, BSc, CertEd, MIBiol. Educational Adviser, Scottish Health Education Group, since 1983; b. 20.7.46, Glasgow; m., Anne Crawford; 2 s. Educ. Rutherglen Academy; Paisley College of Technology. Teacher of Science, Camphill High School, Paisley, 1969; Principal Teacher of Biology, Renfrew High School, 1972; Adviser in Science, Renfrew and Argyll and Bute Divisions, Strathclyde Region, 1978. Publications: The Science of Life (series of biology texts). Recreations: folk song; photography; running. Address: (b.) Scottish Health Education Group, Woodburn House, Canaan Lane, Edinburgh, EH10 4SG; T.-031-447 8044.

Young, James. Honorary Sheriff, Alloa; b. 1.2.13, Alloa; m., Constance Alice Nelson Leishman; 1 s.; 1 d. Educ. Alloa Academy; Royal Technical College, Glasgow. Plumbing and Heating and Sheet Metal Contractor until retirement; former Provost of Alloa. Recreations: golf; fishing; caravanning. Address: (b.) San Michele, 68 Claremont, Alloa; T.-Alloa 214225.

Young, James McMicken, FIB, MIBS, MBIM. Joint General Manager, Bank of Scotland, since 1973 (Member, Management Board, since 1981); b. 4.10.25, Stranraer; m., Lillian Frances Judith; 1 s.; 1 d. Educ. Stranraer Academy; Stranraer High School. Bank of Scotland: Assistant Manager, London Chief Office, 1965, Assistant Secretary, 1968, Assistant General Manager, Bank of Scotland, and Manager, Bank of Scotland Finance Co. Ltd. (now British Linen Bank Ltd.), 1972, Director, Bank of Scotland Finance Co. Ltd., 1973; Director: Capital Leasing Ltd., British Linen Bank Ltd., British Linen Leasing Ltd., British Linen Shipping Ltd., Uberior Oil Ltd., Capital Export Services Ltd., Scotland International Finance BV, Capital Leasing (Edinburgh) Ltd., Uberior International Finance Ltd. Recreations: tennis; chess. Address: (h.) 23 Succoth Park, Edinburgh, EH12 6BX; T.-031-337 5479.

Young, John Henderson, OBE (1980), JP, MBIM, MIEx, DL. Member, Glasgow District Council, since 1974; Deputy Lieutenant, Glasgow, since 1981; b. 21.12.30, Glasgow; m., Doris Paterson; 1 s. Educ. Hillhead High School, Glasgow; Scottish College of Commerce. Councillor, Glasgow Corporation, 1964-73, Glasgow District Council, since 1974; Leader, Glasgow City Council, 1977-79; Parliamentary candidate (Conservative), Rutherglen, 1966; Chairman, Cathcart Conservatives, 1964-65, 1968-71;

Vice-Chairman, Glasgow Conservatives, 1969-72; Export Manager, Scotch whisky industry; Vice-Chairman, Scottish Pakistani Association; Kentucky Colonel, 1984; Member, Glasgow Sports Promotion Council; Member, Post Office Advisory Committee. Recreations: tennis; reading; history; animal welfare; meeting people. Address: (h.) 10 Carna Drive, Glasgow, G44 5BB; T.-041-637 9535.

Young, John Maclennan, JP. Convener, Caithness District Council, since 1974; Member, Highland Regional Council, since 1974 (Chairman, Roads and Transport Committee, since 1978); b. 6.6.33, Thurso. Educ. Thurso Miller Academy. Farmer; Member, Caithness County Council, 1961-75; Member, Caithness Western District Council, 1961-75; Chairman, Housing Committee, 1968-73, and Planning Commitee, 1973-75, Caithness County Council; Conservative candidate, Caithness and Sutherland, 1970. Address: (h.) Carsgoe, Halkirk, Caithness; T.-Halkirk 228.

Young, Nicholas John, MA, DPhil (Oxon). Senior Lecturer in Mathematics, Glasgow University, since 1968; b. 20.12.43, Ilkley, Yorkshire; m., Jekaterina Young; 2 d. Educ. Douai School, Berkshire; Queen's College, Oxford. Recreations: chess; sailing; walking. Address: (b.) Department of Mathematics, Glasgow University, Glasgow, G12 8QW; T.-041-339 8855.

Young, Raymond Kennedy, BArch, ARIAS. Chief Officer, Scotland, The Housing Corporation, since 1978; b. 23.1.46, Newcastle-upon-Tyne; m., Jean; 3 s. Educ. High School of Glasgow; Strathclyde University. Strathclyde University Research Group, 1971-74; Housing Corporation, Glasgow Office, 1974-78. Chairman, Govan Festival. Recreations: music; theatre; railway modelling; no sports. Address: (b.) Rosebery House, 9 Haymarket Terrace, Edinburgh, EH12 5YA; T.-031-337 0044.

Young, Robert W.J., BSc (Hons), PhD, CEng, MICE. HM Inspector of Schools, since 1970; b. 14.3.36, Falkirk; m., Cynthia; 2 d. Educ. Melville College, Edinburgh; Edinburgh University. Civil Engineer, British Rail, 1958-61; Edinburgh University, 1961-70, with period of secondment to Khartoum University, Sudan. Recreations: wind-surfing; sailing; skiing; squash. Address: (b.) Room 3/19, Scottish Education Department, New St. Andrews House, St. James Centre, Edinburgh; T.-031-556 8400, Ext. 4781.

Young, Roger, BSc, MBA. Chief Executive, Electronics and Electrical Division, Low & Bonar p.l.c.; b. 14.1.44, Edinburgh; m., Susan; 1 s.; 2 d. Educ. Gordonstoun School; Edinburgh University. Address: (b.) Low & Bonar p.l.c., Bonar House, Faraday Street, Dundee, DD1 9JA; T.-0382 818171.

Young, Sir Roger William, Kt, MA, STh, LHD, FRSE. Principal, George Watson's College, Edinburgh, since 1958; b. 15.11.23, Delhi, India; m., Caroline Mary Christie; 2 s.; 2 d. Educ. Dragon School, Oxford; Westminster School; Christ Church, Oxford. Sub. Lt., RNVR (Navigator), 1942-45; Resident Tutor, St. Catharine's,

Cumberland Lodge, 1949-51; Assistant Master, Manchester Grammar School, 1951-58. Participant, US State Department Foreign Leader Program, 1964; Member, Public Schools' Commission, 1968-70 (Vice Chairman, Scottish Sub-Committee); Secretary and President, Headteachers' Association of Scotland, 1968-74; conducted Enquiry on Stirling University, 1973; Chairman, Headmasters' Conference, 1976; Scottish National Governor, BBC, 1979-84; Member, Edinburgh Marriage Guidance Council, 1960-75; Member, Scottish Council, Christian Education Movement, 1960-81 (Chairman, 1961-67); Member, Edinburgh University Court, 1967-76; Member, Edinburgh Festival Council, 1970-76; Member, Consultative Committee on the Curriculum, 1972-75; Member, Royal Observatory Trust, Edinburgh, since 1981. Recreations: gardening; photography; climbing; golf; knitting. Address: (b.) George Watson's College, Colinton Road, Edinburgh, EH10 5EG; T.-031-447 7931.

Young, Ronald George, MA (Hons), MSc. Secretary, Strathclyde Labour Group, since 1974; Chairman, Policy Sub-Committee on Social Strategy, Strathclyde Region, since 1981; Lecturer, Paisley College, since 1974 (Director, Local Government Unit); b. 3.8.42, Greenock; m., Anna; 2 d. Educ. Greenock High School; Glasgow University. Councillor, since 1968; Chairman, Greenock and Port Glasgow Social Work Committee, 1971-74; Member, COSLA Policy Committee, since 1974. Publication: The Search for Democracy, 1977. Recreations: hillwalking; racquet games; jogging. Address: (h.) 37 Newton Street, Greenock; T.-0475 21890.

Young, Sheriff Sir Stephen Stewart Templeton, 3rd Bt. Sheriff of North Strathclyde, since 1984; b. 24.5.47; m.; 2 s. Educ. Rugby; Trinity College, Oxford; Edinburgh University. Sheriff, Glasgow and Strathkelvin, 1984.

Young, Rev. William Galbraith, MA (Hons), BD, PhD. Retired Bishop, Church of Pakistan; retired Minister, Church of Scotland; b. 10.10.17, Greenock; m., Elizabeth Crawford Wiseman; 1 s.; 2 d. Educ. Greenock Academy; Oban High School; Glasgow University. Private, RAMC, 1940-45 (War service overseas, India, Iraq, Persia, Cyprus); Missionary, Church of Scotland, Punjab, Pakistan, 1947-77; Principal, Murree Language School, 1954-55; Vice-President, West Pakistan Christian Council, 1963-64; Editor, Urdu Textbook Project, Theological Education Fund, 1963-77; Professor of Church History, Gujranwala Theological Seminary, 1966-70; Church of Pakistan: Bishop, 1970-77, Chairman, Liturgical Commission, 1970-77, Deputy Moderator, 1974-77; Minister, Resolis and Urquhart Parish Church, 1977-85; Moderator, Chanonry and Dingwall Presbytery, 1979-80; Moderator, Synod of Ross, Sutherland and Caithness, 1981-82; Chairman, Sialkot Inter-Aid Committee (Flood and Refugee Relief), 1973-77; Vice-Chairman, East Ross and Black Isle Council of Social Service, 1980-82. Publications: Handbook of Source-Materials for Students of Church History up to 650 AD, 1969; Patriarch, Shah and Caliph, 1974; Church of Pakistan - Experimental Services, 1974; The Parish of Urquhart and Logie Wester, 1984; various publications in Urdu.

Recreations: (when young) tennis; (now) choral singing; walking; reading; listening to music. Address: (h.) 29 Ferry Brae, North Kessock, Inverness, IV1 1YH; T.-046 373 581.

Younger of Leckie, 3rd Viscount, (Edward George Younger), OBE (1940); b. 21.11.06; m., Evelyn Margaret McClure (deceased); 3 s.; 1 d. Educ. Winchester; New College, Oxford. Served Second World War; Colonel, Argyll and Sutherland Highlanders (TA); Lord Lieutenant, Stirling and Falkirk, 1964-79. Address: (h.) Leckie, Gargunnock, Stirling.

Younger, Rt. Hon. George (Kenneth Hotson), TD (1964), PC (1979), DL. MP (Conservative), Ayr, since 1964; Secretary of State for Scotland, since 1979; b. 22.9.31; m., Diana Rhona Tuck; 3 s.; 1 d. Educ. Cargilfield School; Winchester College; New College, Oxford. Argyll and Sutherland Highlanders, 1950-51; 7th Bn., Argyll and Sutherland Highlanders (TA), 1951-65; Director, Tennant Caledonian Breweries Ltd., since 1977; Parliamentary Under Secretary of State, Scottish Office, 1970-74; Minister of State for Defence, 1974; Chairman, Conservative Party in Scotland, 1974-75; Member, Queen's Bodyguard for Scotland (Royal Company of Archers); DL, Stirlingshire.

Younger, Sheriff Robert Edward Gilmour, MA, LLB. Sheriff of Tayside, Central and Fife, at Stirling and Falkirk, since 1982; b. 25.9.40, Stirling; m., Helen Jane Hayes; 1 s.; 1 d. Educ. Winchester; New College, Oxford; Edinburgh University; Glasgow University. Advocate, 1968-79; Sheriff of Glasgow and Strathkelvin, at Glasgow, 1979-82. Recreations: out of doors. Address: (h.) Old Leckie, Gargunnock, Stirling; T.-Gargunnock 213.

Younger, Sir William McEwan, 1st Bt, DSO (1942), DL. Chairman, Scottish & Newcastle Breweries Ltd., 1960-69; b. 6.9.05. Educ. Winchester; Balliol College, Oxford. Served Second World War (mentioned in Despatches); Chairman, Conservative Party in Scotland, 1971-74; Member, Queen's Bodyguard for Scotland; Director, British Linen Bank, 1955-71; Director, Scottish Television, 1964-71; Chairman, Highland Tourist (Cairngorm Development) Ltd., 1966-78.

Yule, Professor George Shaw Sandison, BA, MA. Professor of Church History, Aberdeen University, since 1979; b. 21.10.19, Melbourne; m., Valerie Constance East; 1 s.; 2 d. Educ. Scotch College, Melbourne; Melbourne University. Lecturer in History, Melbourne University, 1954-58; Professor of Church History, Ormond College, Melbourne, 1958-78; Minister, Uniting Church in Australia, and since 1979, Church of Scotland. Publications: The Independents in the English Civil War; Puritans in Politics; Luther: Theologian for Catholics and Protestants. Recreations: tennis; surfing; exploring the British countryside. Address: (h.) 7 The Chanonry, Aberdeen, AB2 1RN.

Yule, William. Honorary Sheriff, Tayside, Central and Fife, since 1976; b. 16.2.08, Kirkcaldy; m., Joan Kininmonth; 1 s. Educ. Kirkcaldy

High School; George Watson's Boys' College, Edinburgh. President: Wholesale Grocers Association of Scotland, 1955-56, Kirkcaldy Rotary Club, 1957-58; Chairman, East Fife Hospitals Board of Management, 1963-68; Commissioner of Income Tax, 1964-78. Address: (h.) 16 Victoria Gardens, Kirkcaldy, KY1 1DJ; T.-Kirkcaldy 263356.

Z

Zaman, Syed Aftabuz, MB, BS, FRCS. Consultant Surgeon, Gilbert Bain Hospital, Lerwick, and Clinical Senior Lecturer, Aberdeen University, since 1980; b. 2.1.39, Gaya, India; m., Joan Valerie; 1 d. Educ. Dacca University; Sheffield University. Training posts as House Officer and Registrar, various hospitals in England, 1962-70; Senior Registrar (General Surgery and Urology), Trent Area Health Authority, 1971-74; Chief Surgeon, National Iranian Oil Co., Iran, 1974-79. Chairman, Shetland Area Medical Committee, 1981-82; Member, Shetland Health Board, since 1983; Member, North Eastern Regional Postgraduate Medical Education Committee. Recreations: horse riding; squash; photography. Address: (h.) Kruksi, Upper Sound, Lerwick; T.-0595 4317.